Cyndi's List

A Comprehensive List of
70,000 Genealogy Sites on the Internet

Cyndi's List

A Comprehensive List of
70,000 Genealogy Sites on the Internet

Second Edition

Cyndi Howells

Volume 1

First edition © 1999
Second edition © 2001
Cynthia L. Howells
All rights reserved. No part of this publication
may be reproduced, in any form or by any means,
including electronic reproduction or reproduction
via the Internet, except by permission of the publisher.
Published by Genealogical Publishing Co., Inc.
1001 N. Calvert St., Baltimore, MD 21202
Library of Congress Catalogue Card Number 2001-131454
International Standard Book Number, Volume 1: 0-8063-1681-0
ISBN Set Number: 0-8063-1678-0
Made in the United States of America

Cover artwork designed by Mark Brill

Table of Contents – Volume One

Alphabetical Category Index vii
Topical Category Index xi
Acknowledgments xv
Foreword to the Second Edition xvii
Foreword to the First Edition xix
Introduction xxi
    The History of *Cyndi's List* xxi
    How to Use *Cyndi's List* – The Book xxi
    How to Use *Cyndi's List* – The Web Site xxii
Acadian, Cajun & Creole 1
Adoption 4
African-American 8
America Online ~ AOL 15
    The Genealogy Forum on America Online
Asia & The Pacific 17
Australia & New Zealand 24
Austria / Österreich 39
The Baltic States ~ Estonia, Latvia & Lithuania 43
Baptist 48
Beginners 51
Belgium / Belgique / België 56
Biographies 59
Births & Baptisms 63
Books 66
Calendars & Dates 75
Canada Index 78
    General Canada Sites 79
    Alberta 88
    British Columbia 92
    Canada – Military 97
    Manitoba 101
    New Brunswick 104
    Newfoundland & Labrador 108
    Northwest Territories, Nunavut & the Yukon 112
    Nova Scotia 116
    Ontario 125
    Prince Edward Island 134
    Quebec 138
    Saskatchewan 144
Canals, Rivers & Waterways 148
Catholic 150
Cemeteries & Funeral Homes 153
Census Related Sites Worldwide 174
    International Census Resources
Chat & IRC 177
Citing Sources 180
City Directories 182
Clothing & Costumes 184
Correspondence 185
    Postage, Payments & Letter Writing
Cousins & Kinship 187

The Czech Republic & Slovakia 188
    Including Bohemia, Moravia, Carpatho-Rusyn & the
    Sudetenlands
Databases, Search Sites, Surname Lists 195
    Personal databases & GEDCOM files will be found below
    under "Personal Home Pages" or under "Surnames, Family
    Associations & Family Newsletters"
Death Records 204
Diaries & Letters 207
Dictionaries & Glossaries 211
Eastern Europe 214
Education 222
Events & Activities 224
Family Bibles 226
Famous People 229
Female Ancestors 233
Finding People 236
    Phone Numbers, E-Mail Addresses, Mailing Addresses,
    Places, Etc.
France 239
Genealogy in the Media 249
    News, Radio, Television, Video & Audio
Genealogy Standards & Guidelines 251
    Emphasizing Quality Research Practices
Germans from Russia 253
Germany / Deutschland 260
Greece 274
Handwriting & Script 277
Handy Online Starting Points 279
Heraldry 283
Hispanic, Central & South America, & the West Indies 286
    Including Mexico, Latin America & the Caribbean
Historical Events & People Worldwide 295
Hit a Brick Wall? 298
House & Building Histories 300
How To 302
How To ~ Tutorials & Guides 304
Huguenot 309
Humor & Prose 312
Immigration & Naturalization 314
Italy / Italia 323
Jewish 328
Kids & Teens 336
Land Records, Deeds, Homesteads, Etc. 338
Languages & Translations 342
LDS & Family History Centers 346
    The Church of Jesus Christ of Latter-day Saints
Libraries, Archives & Museums – General Library Sites.......354
Lookups & Free Searches by Volunteers 356
Lost & Found 357
Loyalists 358

Lutheran 360
Magazines, Journals, Columns & Newsletters 362
    Print & Electronic Publications for Genealogy
Mailing Lists 367
Maps, Gazetteers & Geographical Information 376
Marriages 384
Medical, Medicine, Genetics 390
Medieval 396
Mennonite 398
Methodist 401
Microfilm & Microfiche 403
The Middle East 405
Military Resources Worldwide 408
Money 411
Myths, Hoaxes & Scams 412
Names 416
Native American 418
Netherlands / Nederland 425
Newsgroups 430
Newspapers 435
Novelties 442
Obituaries 444
Occupations 450
Odds & Ends 456
    *Interesting & Unusual Genealogy Sites That Don't Fit in
    Other Categories: Genealogy Web Site Awards, Lost &
    Found and much more...*
Oral History & Interviews 458
Organizing Your Research 461
Personal Home Pages
    *This category is not included in this book. However, an
    ever-growing list of Personal Home Pages can be found on
    the* Cyndi's List *web site at* http://www.CyndisList.com/
    personal.htm
Photographs & Memories 463
    *Preserving Your Family's Heirlooms, Treasures &
    Genealogical Research*
Poland / Polska 470
Poorhouses & Poverty 476
Presbyterian 478
Primary Sources 480
Prisons, Prisoners & Outlaws 483
Professional Researchers, Volunteers & Other Research
    Services 487
Quaker 506
Queries & Message Boards 509
Railroads 512
Recipes, Cookbooks & Family Traditions 518
Religion & Churches 519
Reunions 524
ROOTS-L & RootsWeb 526
Royalty & Nobility 528

Scandinavia & the Nordic Countries 532
    General Scandinavia & Nordic Sites 533
    Denmark / Danmark 534
    Finland / Suomi...538
    Iceland / Ísland...542
    Norway / Norge 545
    Sweden / Sverige 550
Schools 555
Ships & Passenger Lists 558
Societies & Groups
    *Family associations and societies can be found under the
    "Surnames, Family Associations & Family Newsletters"
    category*
    General Societies & Groups.........................571
    Fraternal Organizations..............................576
Software & Computers 580
South Africa / Suid-Afrika 599
Spain, Portugal & the Basque Country / España, Portugal y
    El País Vasco 603
Supplies, Charts, Forms, Etc. 608
Surnames, Family Associations & Family Newsletters
    *Sites or resources dedicated to SPECIFIC, individual family
    surnames. Listed alphabetically by SURNAME.*
    General Surname Sites 613
    Alphabetical Listing by Surname
        A 617
        B 624
        C 644
        D 659
        E 669
        F 675
        G 683
        H 694
        I 710
        J 712
        K 716
        L 724
        M 734
        N 752
        O 756
        P 760
        Q 771
        R 773
        S 782
        T 801
        U 809
        V 811
        W 816
        X 829
        Y 830
        Z 832

Alphabetical Category Index

Acadian, Cajun & Creole 1
Adoption 4
African-American 8
Alabama 1087
Alaska 1098
Albania -- *See: Eastern Europe* 214
Alberta 88
American Samoa -- *See: Territories & Possessions (U.S.)* ..1014
America Online ~ AOL 15
Andorra -- *See: Western Europe* 1608
Arizona 1105
Arkansas 1113
Armenia -- *See: Eastern Europe* 214
Asia & The Pacific 17
Australia & New Zealand 24
Austria / Österreich 39
The Baltic States ~ Estonia, Latvia & Lithuania 43
Banat -- *See: Eastern Europe* 214
Baptist 48
Basque -- *See: Spain, Portugal & the Basque Country / España,
   Portugal y El País Vasco* 603
Beginners 51
Belarus -- *See: Eastern Europe* 214
Belgium / Belgique / België 56
Biographies 59
Births & Baptisms 63
Black Dutch -- *See: Unique Peoples* 845
Bohemia -- *See: The Czech Republic & Slovakia* 188
Books 66
Bosnia Herzegovina -- *See: Eastern Europe* 214
Britain -- *See: United Kingdom* 849
British Columbia 92
Bulgaria -- *See: Eastern Europe* 214
Calendars & Dates 75
California 1123
Canada Index 78
Canada – Military 97
Canals, Rivers & Waterways 148
Canal Zone -- *See: Territories & Possessions (U.S.)* 1014
Carpatho-Rusyn -- *See: The Czech Republic & Slovakia* 188
Catholic 150
Cemeteries & Funeral Homes 153
Census Related Sites Worldwide 174
Channel Islands 869
Chat & IRC 177
Citing Sources 180
City Directories 182
Clothing & Costumes 184
Colorado 1139
Connecticut 1148
Correspondence 185

Cousins & Kinship 187
Croatia -- *See: Eastern Europe* 214
The Czech Republic & Slovakia 188
Databases, Search Sites, Surname Lists 195
Death Records 204
Delaware 1158
Denmark / Danmark 534
Diaries & Letters 207
Dictionaries & Glossaries 211
District of Columbia 1165
Doukhobors -- *See: Unique Peoples* 845
Eastern Europe 214
Education 222
England 879
Estonia -- *See: The Baltic States* 43
Events & Activities 224
Family Bibles 226
Famous People 229
Female Ancestors 233
Finding People 236
Finland / Suomi 538
Florida 1171
France 239
Genealogy in the Media 249
Genealogy Standards & Guidelines 251
General Canada Sites 79
General Library Sites 354
General Scandinavia & Nordic Sites 533
General Societies & Groups 571
General Surname Sites 613
General U.K. Sites 850
General U.S. Sites 998
Georgia 1180
Germans from Russia 253
Germany / Deutschland 260
Great Britain -- *See: United Kingdom* 849
Greece 274
Guam -- *See: Territories & Possessions (U.S.)* 1014
Gypsy -- *See: Unique Peoples* 845
Handwriting & Script 277
Handy Online Starting Points 279
Hawaii 1191
Heraldry 283
Hispanic, Central & South America, & the West Indies 286
Historical Events & People Worldwide 295
Hit a Brick Wall? 298
House & Building Histories 300
How To 302
How To ~ Tutorials & Guides 304
Huguenot 309
Humor & Prose 312

Hungary -- *See: Eastern Europe* 214
Iceland / Ísland 542
Idaho 1197
Illinois 1203
Immigration & Naturalization 314
Indiana 1217
Iowa 1231
Ireland & Northern Ireland 915
Isle of Man 938
Italy / Italia 323
Jewish 328
Kansas 1240
Kentucky 1249
Kids & Teens 336
Land Records, Deeds, Homesteads, Etc. 338
Languages & Translations 342
Latvia -- *See: The Baltic States* 43
LDS & Family History Centers 346
Libraries, Archives & Museums – General Library Sites 354
Library of Congress 1004
Liechtenstein -- *See: Western Europe* 1608
Lithuania -- *See: The Baltic States* 43
Lookups & Free Searches by Volunteers 356
Lost & Found 357
Louisiana 1262
Loyalists 358
Lutheran 360
Luxembourg -- *See: Western Europe* 1608
Macedonia -- *See: Eastern Europe* 214
Magazines, Journals, Columns & Newsletters 362
Mailing Lists 367
Maine 1271
Malta -- *See: Western Europe* 1608
Manitoba 101
Maps, Gazetteers & Geographical Information 376
Marriages 384
Maryland 1281
Massachusetts 1293
Medical, Medicine, Genetics 390
Medieval 396
Melungeons -- *See: Unique Peoples* 845
Mennonite 398
Methodist 401
Metis -- *See: Unique Peoples* 845
Michigan 1307
Microfilm & Microfiche 403
The Middle East 405
Military Resources Worldwide 408
Minnesota 1319
Mississippi 1328
Missouri 1336
Moldova -- *See: Eastern Europe* 214
Molokan -- *See: Unique Peoples* 845
Monaco -- *See: Western Europe* 1608
Money 411
Montana 1348

Moravia -- *See: The Czech Republic & Slovakia* 188
Myths, Hoaxes & Scams 412
Names 416
Native American 418
Nebraska 1354
Netherlands / Nederland 425
Nevada 1361
New Brunswick 104
Newfoundland & Labrador 108
New Hampshire 1367
New Jersey 1375
New Mexico 1384
Newsgroups 430
Newspapers 435
New York 1390
North Carolina 1407
North Dakota 1419
Northern Mariana Islands -- *See: Territories & Possessions (U.S.)* ...1014
Northwest Territories, Nunavut & the Yukon 112
Norway / Norge 545
Nova Scotia 116
Novelties 442
Obituaries 444
Occupations 450
Odds & Ends 456
Ohio 1425
Oklahoma 1439
Ontario 125
Oral History & Interviews 458
Oregon 1447
Organizing Your Research 461
Pennsylvania 1455
Personal Home Pages
This category is not included in this book. However, an ever-growing list of Personal Home Pages can be found on the Cyndi's List *web site at* http://www.CyndisList.com/personal.htm
Photographs & Memories 463
Poland / Polska 470
Poorhouses & Poverty 476
Portugal -- *See: Spain, Portugal & the Basque Country / España, Portugal y El País Vasco* ...603
Presbyterian 478
Primary Sources 480
Prince Edward Island 134
Prisons, Prisoners & Outlaws 483
Professional Researchers, Volunteers & Other Research Services ...487
Prussia -- *See: Germany* 260
Puerto Rico -- *See: Territories & Possessions (U.S.)* 1014
Quaker 506
Quebec 138
Queries & Message Boards 509
Railroads 512
Recipes, Cookbooks & Family Traditions 518

Religion & Churches 519
Reunions 524
Rhode Island 1475
Romania -- *See: Eastern Europe* 214
Romani/Romany -- *See: Unique Peoples* 845
ROOTS-L & RootsWeb 526
Royalty & Nobility 528
Rusin/Rusyn -- *See: The Czech Republic & Slovakia* 188
Russia -- *See: Eastern Europe* 214
Ruthenia -- *See: The Czech Republic & Slovakia* 188
Saami -- *See: Unique Peoples* 845
Saskatchewan 144
San Marino -- *See: Western Europe* 1608
Scandinavia & the Nordic Countries Index 532
Schools 555
Scotland 946
Serbia -- *See: Eastern Europe* 214
Ships & Passenger Lists 558
Slovakia -- *See: The Czech Republic & Slovakia* 188
Slovenia -- *See: Eastern Europe* 214
Social Security 1012
Societies & Groups
    Family associations and societies can be found under the
    "Surnames, Family Associations & Family Newsletters"
    category
    General Societies & Groups 571
    Fraternal Organizations 576
Software & Computers 580
Sorbs -- *See: Unique Peoples* 845
South Africa / Suid-Afrika 599
South Carolina 1482
South Dakota 1492
Soviet Union -- *See: Eastern Europe* 214
Spain, Portugal & the Basque Country / España, Portugal y
    El País Vasco 603
The Sudetenlands -- *See: The Czech Republic & Slovakia* 188
Supplies, Charts, Forms, Etc. 608
Surnames, Family Associations & Family Newsletters
    General Surname Sites 613
    Alphabetical Listing by Surname 617
Sweden / Sverige 550

Switzerland / Suisse / Schweiz 834
Taxes 838
Tennessee 1499
Territories & Possessions (U.S.) 1014
Texas 1511
Timelines 840
Travel & Research 842
Turkey -- *See: Eastern Europe* 214
U.K. – Military 970
Ukraine -- *See: Eastern Europe* 214
Unique Peoples & Cultures 845
United Kingdom & Ireland Index 849
United States Index 997
U.S. – Census 1018
U.S. – Civil War ~ War for Southern Independence 1028
U.S. – History 1056
U.S. – Military 1063
U.S. – National Archives 1008
U.S. Virgin Islands -- *See: Territories &*
    Possessions (U.S.) 1014
U.S. – Vital Records 1074
U.S.S.R. -- *See: Eastern Europe* 214
Utah 1527
Vatican City -- *See: Western Europe* 1608
Vermont 1536
Virginia 1544
Volunteer Online Regional Projects 1595
Wales / Cymru 980
Washington 1557
Washington, D.C. 1165
Web Rings for Genealogy 1603
Weights & Measures 1606
Wends -- *See: Unique Peoples* 845
Western Europe 1608
West Virginia 1569
Wills & Probate 1611
Wisconsin 1589
Writing Your Family's History 1614
Wyoming 1589
Yugoslavia -- *See: Eastern Europe* 214

Topical Category Index

Localities

Albania -- *See: Eastern Europe* 214
American Samoa -- *See: Territories & Possessions (U.S.)* ..1014
Andorra -- *See: Western Europe* 1608
Armenia -- *See: Eastern Europe* 214
Asia & The Pacific 17
Australia & New Zealand 24
Austria / Österreich 39
The Baltic States ~ Estonia, Latvia & Lithuania 43
Belarus -- *See: Eastern Europe* 214
Belgium / Belgique / België 56
Bohemia -- *See: The Czech Republic & Slovakia* 188
Bosnia Herzegovina -- *See: Eastern Europe* 214
Britain -- *See: United Kingdom* 849
Bulgaria -- *See: Eastern Europe* 214
Canada Index 78
    General Canada Sites 79
    Alberta 88
    British Columbia 92
    Canada – Military 97
    Manitoba 101
    New Brunswick 104
    Newfoundland & Labrador 108
    Northwest Territories, Nunavut & the Yukon ..112
    Nova Scotia 116
    Ontario 125
    Prince Edward Island 134
    Quebec 138
    Saskatchewan 144
Canal Zone -- *See: Territories & Possessions (U.S.)* ..1014
Croatia -- *See: Eastern Europe* 214
The Czech Republic & Slovakia 188
Denmark / Danmark 534
Eastern Europe 214
England 879
Estonia -- *See: The Baltic States* 43
Finland / Suomi 538
France 239
Germans from Russia 253
Germany / Deutschland 260
Great Britain -- *See: United Kingdom* 849
Greece 274
Guam -- *See: Territories & Possessions (U.S.)* 1014
Hispanic, Central & South America, & the West Indies ..286
Hungary -- *See: Eastern Europe* 214
Iceland / Ísland 542
Ireland & Northern Ireland 915
Italy / Italia 323
Latvia -- *See: The Baltic States* 43
Liechtenstein -- *See: Western Europe* 1608

Lithuania -- *See: The Baltic States* 43
Luxembourg -- *See: Western Europe* 1608
Macedonia -- *See: Eastern Europe* 214
Malta -- *See: Western Europe* 1608
The Middle East 405
Moldova -- *See: Eastern Europe* 214
Monaco -- *See: Western Europe* 1608
Moravia -- *See: The Czech Republic & Slovakia* 188
Netherlands / Nederland 425
North America --
    See: Canada Index 78
    See: United States Index 997
Northern Mariana Islands -- *See: Territories &*
    Possessions (U.S.) 1014
Norway / Norge 545
Poland / Polska 470
Portugal -- *See: Spain, Portugal & the Basque Country /*
    España, Portugal y El País Vasco 603
Prussia -- *See: Germany* 260
Puerto Rico -- *See: Territories & Possessions (U.S.)* ..1014
Romania -- *See: Eastern Europe* 214
Russia -- *See: Eastern Europe* 214
Ruthenia -- *See: The Czech Republic & Slovakia* ..188
San Marino -- *See: Western Europe* 1608
Scandinavia & the Nordic Countries Index 532
    General Scandinavia & Nordic Sites 533
    Denmark / Danmark 534
    Finland / Suomi 538
    Iceland / Ísland 542
    Norway / Norge 545
    Sweden / Sverige 550
Scotland 946
Serbia -- *See: Eastern Europe* 214
Slovakia -- *See: The Czech Republic & Slovakia* 188
Slovenia -- *See: Eastern Europe* 214
South Africa / Suid-Afrika 599
Soviet Union -- *See: Eastern Europe* 214
Spain, Portugal & the Basque Country / España, Portugal y
    El País Vasco 603
The Sudetenlands -- *See: The Czech Republic & Slovakia* ..188
Sweden / Sverige 550
Switzerland / Suisse / Schweiz 834
Turkey -- *See: Eastern Europe* 214
Ukraine -- *See: Eastern Europe* 214
United Kingdom & Ireland Index 849
    General U.K. Sites 850
    Channel Islands 869
    England 879
    Ireland & Northern Ireland 915
    Isle of Man 938

Scotland 946
    U.K. – Military 970
    Wales / Cymru 980
United States Index 997
    General U.S. Sites 998
    Library of Congress 1004
    National Archives 1008
    Social Security 1012
    Territories & Possessions (U.S.) 1014
    U.S. – Census 1018
    U.S. – Civil War ~ War for Southern Independence 1028
    U.S. – History 1056
    U.S. – Military 1063
    U.S. – Vital Records 1074
    Alabama 1087
    Alaska 1098
    Arizona 1105
    Arkansas 1113
    California 1123
    Colorado 1139
    Connecticut 1148
    Delaware 1158
    District of Columbia 1165
    Florida 1171
    Georgia 1180
    Hawaii 1191
    Idaho 1197
    Illinois 1203
    Indiana 1217
    Iowa 1231
    Kansas 1240
    Kentucky 1249
    Louisiana 1262
    Maine 1271
    Maryland 1281
    Massachusetts 1293
    Michigan 1307
    Minnesota 1319
    Mississippi 1328
    Missouri 1336
    Montana 1348
    Nebraska 1354
    Nevada 1361
    New Hampshire 1367
    New Jersey 1375
    New Mexico 1384
    New York 1390
    North Carolina 1407
    North Dakota 1419
    Ohio 1425
    Oklahoma 1439
    Oregon 1447
    Pennsylvania 1455
    Rhode Island 1475
    South Carolina 1482
    South Dakota 1492

    Tennessee 1499
    Texas 1511
    Utah 1527
    Vermont 1536
    Virginia 1544
    Washington 1557
    West Virginia 1569
    Wisconsin 1579
    Wyoming 1589
U.S.S.R. -- *See: Eastern Europe* 214
U.S. Virgin Islands -- *See: Territories & Possessions (U.S.)* 1014
Vatican City -- *See: Western Europe* 1608
Volunteer Online Regional Projects 1595
Wales / Cymru 980
Western Europe 1608
Yugoslavia -- *See: Eastern Europe* 214

Help from Others

Beginners 51
Correspondence 185
Finding People 236
How To 302
How To ~ Tutorials & Guides 304
LDS & Family History Centers 346
Lookups & Free Searches by Volunteers 356
Mailing Lists 367
Newsgroups 430
Oral History & Interviews 458
Personal Home Pages
    This category is not included in this book. However, an ever-growing list of Personal Home Pages can be found on the Cyndi's List web site at http://www.CyndisList.com/personal.htm
Professional Researchers, Volunteers & Other Research Services 487
Queries & Message Boards 509
Reunions 524
Societies & Groups
    General Societies & Groups 571
    Fraternal Organizations 576
Surnames, Family Associations & Family Newsletters
    General Surname Sites 613
    Alphabetical Listing by Surname............617
Volunteer Online Regional Projects 1595

History

Biographies 59
Clothing & Costumes 184
Heraldry 283
Historical Events & People Worldwide 295
House & Building Histories 300
Medieval 396
Oral History & Interviews 458
Poorhouses & Poverty 476
Timelines 840
U.S. – History 1056

Foreword to the Second Edition

It was "love at first site" for me when I stumbled across *Cyndi's List of Genealogy Sites on the Internet*. *Cyndi's List* was only a few months old then, but I was a mere beginner on the Internet, so it wasn't like I was robbing the cradle. *Cyndi's List* is now five years old and, alas, I am still a beginner. That's OK, though. No one has to be a pro when you have the kind of tool that Cyndi Howells has created for us.

It so happened that not too long after I was site smitten with Cyndi, I was asked to talk about genealogy on the Internet to the computer group at the Cosmos Club. Now, at your house the words "Cosmos Club" may not set off any alarms, but if you live or work near Washington, D.C., they ring real loud. The exclusive Cosmos Club is where the Movers and Shakers go in the evening to decide what's going to happen to the rest of us. It is *the* club.

It seemed to me that an appearance in the hallowed Cosmos halls deserved a greater effort than I had recently given at the Fairfax Circle Golden Years Club, so I set about creating a special handout: "Sites I Use on the Internet." Not the greatest of titles, but it got better fast. It began with the address for *Cyndi's List* and this comment:

> "All searches for genealogy information begin at this remarkably comprehensive and well-organized list of links to many thousand different sites that are useful to genealogists. Almost all other genealogy Internet addresses can be found by starting here. Highly useful and highly recommended."

Later, thanks to Cyndi's help, I started my own web site, and those words are still at the top of the page where I keep my own list of favorite links.

For me, spending time on the Internet almost always means checking in with Cyndi right after logging on. It's almost second nature. That's why I giggled and snorted, "Huh?" when I saw the notice about the book version of *Cyndi's List*. Why on God's Green Earth, I huffed, would anyone want *Cyndi's List* in book form when it's right there in front of you on the computer screen, in its most up-to-date form?

Before long, though, I began to realize that a book version wasn't such a dumb idea after all. For one thing, I found myself reaching for one of my favorite reference books—even though I have the entire book on an easily searchable CD and the same information is available free online. Sometimes it's just easier to grab a book than it is to work your way through the online lists. And if grabbing a book is what you are used to doing, then you need a book like *Cyndi's List* to grab! Besides, a book is bit more portable than even a notebook computer. You can read it on the subway—while standing—or take it out fishing. Even if a list of URLs is not your favorite reading, you might learn where you can find your own site to love.

Then there's that "spatial thing." I'm trying to overcome it, but you just can't visualize what you are dealing with when you look at one screen at a time. With a book you can flip a few pages ahead or back and get a feel for what you are dealing with. In spite of all the effort, virtual reality still isn't the same as reality.

My guess is that whichever way you prefer *Cyndi's List*—on the screen or in the book—you can't go wrong. Those "in the know" will tell you so. I ran into one of them the other day, one of those Cosmos computerists, a Mover and Shaker. He's retired now, and not just because of the recent election. He was kind enough to say that he remembered my presentation at "the Club." I responded by saying that I hoped he had learned something useful. "Indeed," he replied, "Two words: *Cyndi's List*."

That really doesn't do justice to all the other important things I had to say, but it does pretty much sum it up. *Cyndi's List* is indeed the place where genealogy begins on the Internet. It's also the place we keep coming back to for guidance in our research. And now that it also comes to us as a book, you can even curl up in bed with it. Try doing that with your computer and monitor.

Richard A. Pence
February 2001

"No-Frills" Category Index

http://www.CyndisList.com/nofrills.htm

This is an alphabetical list of the category pages found on *Cyndi's List*. This index doesn't contain update dates, descriptions or cross-referencing between categories; it is just a simple list of the category pages, shown alphabetically by title. For a more detailed version see the main index page at http://www.CyndisList.com

Alphabetical Category Index

http://www.CyndisList.com/alpha.htm

This is a straight, alphabetical list of *all* of the category pages found on *Cyndi's List*. This index doesn't contain update dates, descriptions or cross-referencing between categories; it is simply a list of the category pages, shown alphabetically by title. For a more detailed version see the main index page at http://www.CyndisList.com

Topical Category Index

http://www.CyndisList.com/topical.htm

This is a topical list of the category pages found on *Cyndi's List*. This index doesn't contain update dates, descriptions or cross-referencing between categories; it is simply a subject-oriented list of the category pages, shown alphabetically by title in each section. For a more detailed version see the main index page at http://www.CyndisList.com

Search It!

http://www.CyndisList.com/searchit.htm

This page describes the methods by which you can search *Cyndi's List*. Additionally, each category page has a search box to use for keyword searches.

Make *Cyndi's List* Your Homepage!

http://www.CyndisList.com/yourhome.htm

Make *Cyndi's List* the first page you see when you start your web browser. The site is here for you to use as a jumping-off point in your daily online research. Think of *Cyndi's List* as a card catalog to the genealogy section in the massive research library that is the Internet.

The CyndisList Mailing List

http://www.CyndisList.com/maillist.htm

A. The CyndisList Mailing List is a free e-mail announcement list. It was created to keep users of the *Cyndi's List* web site (http://www.CyndisList.com) regularly updated regarding the activities on *Cyndi's List*. It is also a means for Cyndi to communicate information that she finds of interest to the genealogical community. Cyndi's messages to the mailing list may include any or all of the following:

1. Frequent updates to the site.
2. New links submitted by visitors to *Cyndi's List*.

3. Activity audit for each category page on *Cyndi's List*:
   - Number of new links.
   - Number of updated/corrected links.
   - Number of deleted links.
4. Names of categories that have been updated.
5. Descriptions of new features or improvements to the site.
6. Answers to frequently asked questions.
7. Announcements and/or news regarding online or offline resources for genealogy.
8. Details on what Cyndi is up to.
9. Anything else that Cyndi wants to announce!

B. This mailing list is for announcements only and is not set up for posts, replies or participatory conversations.

C. Messages regarding updates to the *Cyndi's List* web site are usually sent out daily. In general, there are at least two types of frequent messages sent to subscribers of this mailing list:

1. An automated message that includes a breakdown of the number of links added, updated or deleted on each category page for the previous day.
2. An automated message listing new links that have been submitted to the What's New on *Cyndi's List*? web pages for the previous day.

To subscribe, send an e-mail message to: CyndisList-request@rootsweb.com
In the body include only one word: subscribe

What's New on *Cyndi's List*
http://www.CyndisList.com/whatsnew.htm

This is an index to each of the monthly, temporary, uncategorized pages of new links on *Cyndi's List*. As new links are submitted to me via the "Submit a New Link" form on each category page, they will *temporarily* be added to a page of uncategorized links for that month. Once I place these links in their permanent home on various category pages on *Cyndi's List*, I will remove them from these temporary, uncategorized pages. New links are added to the individual category pages on *Cyndi's List* as I have time to visit, verify and examine each web site. You can identify new links and updated links on *Cyndi's List* by looking for a NEW or UPDATED graphic next to the links.

Submit a New Link to *Cyndi's List*
http://www.CyndisList.com/newlink.htm

Do you have a new web site for genealogy? Do you know of a web site that isn't yet linked on *Cyndi's List*? I intend to add categorized links for all genealogical resources that I find on the Internet. I currently add more than 2,500 new links every month and do my best to keep up with all requests that I receive. Send me any new web sites you know about and I'll try to add them to the list as soon as possible. Please don't send me repetitive requests for the same link. Once I receive the new link requests:

- I will visit each site to verify that the address is correct.
- I will use the title exactly as it is shown on the web site.
- I will determine the categories under which the links will be set up.
- I will set up the link as soon as possible, but I cannot guarantee a specific time frame.

◆ I have automated processes that temporarily add new links to a set of uncategorized pages titled "What's New on *Cyndi's List*?"

*Please note that this form is for links to web sites only. Please do not submit queries with e-mail addresses.

Create a Link to *Cyndi's List*
http://www.CyndisList.com/linkto.htm

If you have a web site of your own, use this page to set up a link to *Cyndi's List*. The page supplies the graphics and the HTML code you need to create the link.

FAQ (Frequently Asked Questions)—About Cyndi and *Cyndi's List*
http://www.CyndisList.com/faq.htm

I receive hundreds of e-mail messages each day, and many of them are filled with questions about me, my list, the time I spend working on the list, etc. I hope that this list of FAQs will solve some of the misconceptions and satisfy everyone's curiosity.

About Sending E-mail to Cyndi
http://www.CyndisList.com/e-mail.htm

Please read this page before sending me e-mail. Many of the questions you may have about the book or the web site are addressed on this page and also on the FAQ page.

Cyndi's Genealogy Home Page Construction Kit
http://www.CyndisList.com/construc.htm

This comprehensive web page has tips, hints, links and more to help you create your personal genealogy home page. The Table of Contents for the Construction Kit is as follows:

1. Find Space on a Web Server to Store Your Web Pages
2. Plan the Layout, Format and Content for Your Web Site
3. Create the Web Pages: HTML Editors and Tutorials
4. Tools for Enhancing Your Web Pages
5. Proofread, Inspect and Validate the Text and HTML Code on the Pages for Accuracy and Usability
6. Upload the Pages to the Web Server
7. Check All Pages for Accessibility
8. Advertise Your New Web Site
9. Common Web Site Problems That I See Every Day
10. Other Web Sites for Genealogy Home Page Creation
11. Books That Cyndi Owns
12. Create a Link to Cyndi's Genealogy Home Page Construction Kit

Internet Stuff You Need to Know
http://www.CyndisList.com/internet.htm

I created this page in order to point fellow genealogists to responsible, helpful resources online that will aid them in understanding some of the mysteries of the Internet. There are a lot of misconceptions, rumors, hoaxes and other bits of misinformation floating about. Hopefully, this page will help to dismiss some of the worries and clear up any confusion. This page includes links for the following topics:

- Computer Viruses
- Cookies
- Copyright Resources on the Web
- E-mail Chain-Letters, Folklore, Hoaxes, Misunderstandings and Scams
- Internet and Computer Terminology
- Netiquette
- Newbies
- Privacy Issues
- Search Engines: Helpful Sites, Articles and Tips
- Software Features and Utilities
- Spam

Disclaimers

http://www.CyndisList.com/disclaim.htm

1. The content on *Cyndi's List* is subject to the owner's discretion.
2. Links will be added to *Cyndi's List* at the owner's discretion.
3. There is no guarantee that all links will be included on *Cyndi's List*.
4. There is no guarantee that links will be added to *Cyndi's List* within a specific time frame.
5. All new resources submitted for inclusion on *Cyndi's List* will be reviewed by the owner prior to categorization.
   - Each URL will be verified for accuracy.
   - Each web site title will be reviewed for correct categorization and alphabetization.
   - Categorization of each link will be at the discretion of the owner.
6. The purpose of *Cyndi's List* is to provide a categorized and cross-referenced index to genealogical resources found online. The intent is for the site to be all-inclusive; however, the owner reserves the right to add and remove links at any time and at her discretion.
7. Links will be added and/or removed without any prior notification at the discretion of the owner.
8. The owner is not responsible for the content found on other web sites that are found linked on *Cyndi's List*.
9. Links to commercial enterprises found on *Cyndi's List* are included as a courtesy. Unless otherwise stated, the existence of these links on *Cyndi's List* does not imply endorsement of the services or products provided by those commercial enterprises.
10. The owner will not knowingly link to sites that derive from or participate in fraudulent or illegal behavior.
11. The owner is not responsible for problems that arise from sites found on the index that derive from or participate in fraudulent or illegal behavior.

ACADIAN, CAJUN & CREOLE

http://www.cyndislist.com/acadian.htm

Category Index

- General Resource Sites
- Libraries, Archives & Museums
- Mailing Lists, Newsgroups & Chat
- People & Families
- Publications, Software & Supplies
- Societies & Groups

◆ General Resource Sites

- **Acadian-Cajun Genealogy & History**
  http://www.genweb.net/acadian-cajun/

- **Acadian/French-Canadian SURNAME Researchers**
  http://www.acadian.org/resrch.html
  From the Acadian Genealogy Homepage.

- **Acadian Genealogy Exchange**
  http://www.acadiangenexch.com/
  A semi-annual newsletter dedicated to Acadians, Cajuns, & French-Canadians. Numerous publications can be found at this web site. Queries are free.

- **Acadian Genealogy Homepage**
  http://www.acadian.org/

- **Acadian Genealogy Links**
  http://www.globalserve.net/~gcrose/acadianl.html

- **Acadian GenWeb**
  http://www.geocities.com/Heartland/Acres/2162/

- **Acadian History and Genealogy**
  http://ourworld.compuserve.com/homepages/lwjones/acadianh.htm
  From Linda Jones' Genealogy - Acadian and French-Canadian Style web site.

- **Les Acadiens auxîles Saint-Pierre et Miquelon**
  http://www.cancom.net/~encyspm/acadie/EAcadien.html
  Islands off the coast of Canada, under the sovereignty of France.

- **The Acadians of Nova Scotia**
  http://www.grassroots.ns.ca/comgrp/acad.htm

- **Avoyelleans: French Creoles**
  http://www.geocities.com/BourbonStreet/1781/

- **Canada**
  http://www.CyndisList.com/canada.htm
  See this category on Cyndi's List for related links.

- **Canadian Genealogy and History Links – Acadian**
  http://www.islandnet.com/~jveinot/cghl/acadian.html

- **Cape Breton Pictorial Cookbook – Acadian**
  http://www.taisbean.com/CBcookbook/acadian.html

- **Centre de recherches généalogiques du Québec**
  http://www.cam.org/~cdrgduq/
  Parchment certificates for sale with more than 4000 names from French-Canadian and Acadian origins.

- **Congrés Mondial Acadien - Louisiane 1999**
  http://www.cma-la99.com/

- **The Early Acadian Period in Nova Scotia 1605 – 1755**
  http://www.ednet.ns.ca/educ/museum/arch/acadia.htm
  From Archaeology in Nova Scotia.

- **Encyclopedia of Cajun Culture**
  http://www.cajunculture.com/

- **Genealogy of Acadia**
  http://www.cam.org/~beaur/gen/acadie-e.html
  From Denis Beauregard.

- **Genetics of the Acadian People**
  http://www.genweb.net/acadian-cajun/genetics.htm
  Describes a conference held regarding the unique genetic history of the Acadian people.

- **The Gumbo Pages**
  http://www.gumbopages.com/
  Culture, history, etc. Previously titled Guide to Acadiana - Acadiana: Les Paroisses Acadiennes.

- **History & Genealogy of Acadians on the Acadian Coast and Bayou Lafourche Basin of Louisiana**
  http://www.geocities.com/Heartland/Pointe/3829/lafourche.html
  History and genealogy of the parishes along the Bayou Lafourche Basin & the "Acadian Coast" including Assumption, Ascension, East Baton Rouge, Iberville, Lafourche, St. James, St. Martin.

- **La Nouvelle-France - Resources Française**
  http://www.culture.fr/culture/nllefce/fr/

- **Our Acadian and French Canadian Ancestral Home**
  http://www.geocities.com/Heartland/Pointe/6106

- **Université de Moncton - Centre d'études acadiennes**
  http://www.umoncton.ca/etudeacadiennes/centre/cea.html
  New Brunswick, Canada.

◆ Libraries, Archives & Museums

- **Acadian Archives – UMFK**
  http://www.umfk.maine.edu/infoserv/archives/welcome.htm

- **The Acadian Odyssey - L'odyssée Acadienne**
  http://collections.ic.gc.ca/acadian/intro/

- Acadia University - Vaughan Memorial Library
  http://www.acadiau.ca/vaughan/
  Wolfville, Nova Scotia, Canada.

- Archives départementales de la Seine-Maritime ~
  France
  http://www.culture.fr/culture/nllefce/fr/rep_ress/ad_76101.htm

◆ Mailing Lists, Newsgroups & Chat

- ACADIAN-CAJUN Mailing List
  http://www.rootsweb.com/~jfuller/gen_mail_country-can.html#ACADIAN-CAJUN

- Acadian-Cajun Mailing List
  http://www.rootsweb.com/~jfuller/gen_mail_country-can.html#Acadian1

- The "Cajun/Acadian" Chat Room
  http://www.acadian.org/chat.html
  From the Acadian Genealogy Homepage.

- FCAGS-RING Mailing List
  http://www.rootsweb.com/~jfuller/gen_mail_country-can.html#FCAGS-RING
  For the members of the French Canadian and Acadian Genealogical Societies (FCAGS) WebRing to discuss the continued development of American, French Canadian, and Acadian Genealogical and Historical Societies and how they can better serve the Genealogical and Historical community.

◆ People & Families

- The Acadian JOHNSON Association / Association
  Des JOHNSON D'acadie
  http://www.geocities.com/BourbonStreet/5102/index.html

- The ARSENAULT / ARSENEAU / ARSENEAULT
  / ARCENEAUX Genealogy Web Site
  http://personal.nbnet.nb.ca/djsavard/Arseno/arseno.htm

- Cyndie BROUSSARD's Genealogy Website
  http://www.eatel.net/~knfmaker/cajunpcr/
  BEARD, BLANCHARD, BROUSSARD, COOPER, DAVIS, DUHON, HENRY, INGRAM, LUCKY, MORELAND, NICKS, THIBODEAUX, TRAHAN, VANCE.

- Genealogy - Acadian and French-Canadian Style
  http://ourworld.compuserve.com/homepages/lwjones/homepage.htm
  General resources and information for surnames: BABIN, BARD, BOUCHER, BOURDAGES, FOURNIER, GAGNON, PLOURDE, POIRIER, and VAILLANCOURT.

- The Habitant's Home Page - Acadian and French
  Canadian Genealogy
  http://habitant.org/

- HEBERT Family Genealogy
  http://www.genweb.net/acadian-cajun//hebert.htm

- Histoire et généalogie - THIBAUDEAU -
  THIBODEAU - History and Genealogy
  http://www.qouest.net/~jljmt/index.htm
  Pierre THIBEAUDEAU, le pionnier Acadien. THIBODAUX, THIBEAUDEAU. THIBAUDEAUX. THIBODEAUX. TEBEDORE.

TIBEDORE, THIBODEAULT, THIBAUDEAULT, THYBAUDEAU, THIBEDEAU, TIBIDO, THIBIDAUX, THIBAUDAU, THIBODOT, BODEAU, BODO, THIBADEAU, THEBADO, TIBBEDEAUX, TIBADO, TOLADO.

- The MELANSON / MELANCON / MALONSON /
  MALANSON Family Project
  http://www.geocities.com/Heartland/Meadows/7961/

- SAMSON Family Home Page
  http://www.familytreemaker.com/users/s/a/m/Charles-A-Samson/
  The Samson Family Homepage traces the descendants of the first Samson immigrants to New France (Quebec) in 1665. Also: BOUDROT, MARTEL, FOUGERE, LANDRY, FOREST, and MARCHAND.

- The SAULNIER Genealogy HomePage
  http://www.geocities.com/Heartland/Acres/6946/
  Descendants of Louis Saulnier and Louise Bastinaud dit Pelletier, who arrived in Acadia (now Nova Scotia) c.1685.

- Steve's Ancestry - German-Acadian Coast Genealogy
  http://users.erols.com/someday/Steve.html
  Altofer, Arsenault, Babin, Benich, Bergeron, Blanchard, Blouin, Bourgeois, Bradley, Broussard, Brou, Doucet, Dugas, Engler, Fannaly, Fleming, Fontenot , Forest, Gaudet, Gauterot, Geisser, Haydel, Hebert, Huber, LeJeune, LeRoux, Mayer, Melanson, Michael, Mire, Mount, Petitpas, Poche, Pusey, Richard, Rome, Roussel, Schexnayder, Schneider, Schaaf , Steeger, Theriot, Trahan, Weilder.

- WALKER - VAUGHN - Acadian Genealogy
  http://pw2.netcom.com/~daglo/gloria.html
  WALKER, VAUGHN, and MORASSE.

◆ Publications, Software & Supplies

- Amazon.com Genealogy Bookstore – Acadian
  http://www.amazon.com/exec/obidos/external-search/?keyword=acadian+genealogy&tag=markcyndisgenealA/

- AudioTapes.com - Genealogical Lectures on Cassette
  Tapes
  - Acadian
    http://www.audiotapes.com/search2.asp?Search=Acadian
  - French Canadian
    http://www.audiotapes.com/search2.asp?Search=French

- Frontier Press Bookstore - Acadian/Cajun Studies
  http://www.frontierpress.com/frontier.cgi?category=acadian

- Portage Technologies - L'Acadie CD-ROM
  http://www.portageinc.com/

- Quintin Publications - Acadian Descendants
  http://www.quintinpublications.com/acadiandescendants.html

- Quintin Publications - Acadian Genealogy and
  Reference
  http://www.quintinpublications.com/acadianreference.html

- Quintin Publications - Acadian History
  http://www.quintinpublications.com/acadianhistory.html

- Quintin Publications - Acadians Outside the Maritimes
  http://www.quintinpublications.com/acadianoutside.html

◆ Societies & Groups

- Acadian Cultural Society Page de la Maison
  http://www.angelfire.com/ma/1755/index.html
- Cajun Clickers Genealogy SIG -Baton Rouge, Louisiana
  http://www.clickers.org/genealogy/
- French Canadian/Acadian Genealogists of Wisconsin
  http://www.fcgw.org/
  The society's objective is to foster and encourage interest and research in French Canadian and Acadian genealogy, heritage, and culture.

- The German-Acadian Coast Historical & Genealogical Society ~ Destrehan, Louisiana
  http://www.rootsweb.com/~lastjohn/geracadn.htm
- St. Augustine Historical Society - Creole Heritage Preservation ~ Isle Brevelle, Louisiana
  http://www.cp-tel.net/creole/
- Société Des Acadiens Et Acadiennes Du Nouveau-Brunswick
  http://www.rbmulti.nb.ca/saanb/saanb.htm
- Society of Acadian Descendants
  http://www.acadian.org/sad.html

ADOPTION
http://www.cyndislist.com/adoption.htm

Category Index:

◆ General Resource Sites

◆ Home Children

◆ Locality Specific

◆ Mailing Lists, Newsgroups & Chat

◆ Orphan Trains

◆ Professional Researchers, Volunteers & Other Research Services

◆ Publications, Software & Supplies

◆ General Resource Sites

- Adoption.com
  http://www.adoption.com/

- Adoption Information, Laws and Reforms
  http://www.webcom.com/kmc/
  From Kevin McCarty.

- The Adoption Registration Coalition
  http://www.regday.org/
  Official Sponsors of International Registration Day.

- Adoption Search
  http://www.adoptionsearch.com/
  The world's first adoption focused search engine.

- Adoption Search and Reunion
  http://www.nmia.com/~rema2/index.html

- AdoptioNetwork
  http://www.adoption.org/

- Adoptee Birthfamily Connections
  http://www.birthfamily.com/

- An Adoptee's Right to Know
  http://www.plumsite.com/shea/

- Adoptee Searcher's Handbook~ Canada
  http://www.ouareau.com/adoptee/

- Becky West's Adoption Page
  http://www.geocities.com/Heartland/Prairie/8066/
  adoption.htm

- Birthmoms Support List
  http://www.geocities.com/Heartland/6436/

- BirthQuest
  http://www.birthquest.org/
  Online searchable database for searching adoptees, birth parents, adoptive parents and siblings.

- Carrie's Adoptee & Genealogy Page
  http://www.mtjeff.com/~bodenst/page3.html

- Dawn's Birthmother/Adoption Resource Page
  http://members.tripod.com/~HevensDawn/adoption.html

- Family Workings Adoption Query Index
  http://www.familyworkings.com/adoption/adqueries.htm

- Footprints From Heaven
  http://www.footprintsfromheaven.com/
  Bimonthly searchable newsletter by state of birth.

- Forget Me Not Family Society
  http://www.portal.ca/~adoption/

- Jewish Orphanages in the United States
  http://www.scruz.net/~elias/hnoh/

- Lia's Links: Adoption Reunion Registries
  http://www.geocities.com/Heartland/Pointe/5729/
  Over 190 online adoption reunion registries listed and over 130 other adoption search links! Plus support links.

- Looking for someone? Find them here!
  http://home.inreach.com/diak3/

- Luanne Pruesner's Internet Adoption Page
  http://users.aol.com/luannep/adoption.htm

- Mari's Place - Adoption Links
  http://www.netreach.net/~steed/

- Missing Birth Children - from Genealogical Journeys in Time
  http://ourworld.compuserve.com/homepages/Strawn/
  missingc.htm

- Missing Birth Parents - from Genealogical Journeys in Time
  http://ourworld.compuserve.com/homepages/Strawn/
  missingb.htm

- Missing Persons - from Genealogical Journeys in Time
  http://ourworld.compuserve.com/homepages/Strawn/
  missingp.htm

- Office for National Statistics - Adoption Certificates ~ U.K.
  http://www.ons.gov.uk/register/frcadopt.htm

- Reunion Registry.com
  http://www.reunionregistry.com/

- RUOut There
  http://adoption.virtualave.net/
  Adoption search bulletin board and information site.

- Searching For People
  http://ddi.digital.net/~islander/

- T.I.E.S Homepage
  http://www.tiessearch.org/
  "Terminal Illness Emergency Search." Program provides free search and support to terminally ill adoptees searching for their birthfamilies.

- The Volunteer Search Network (VSN) Information Page
  http://www.vsn.org/

- World Wide Web Library of Adoptee Related Sites
  http://www.bastards.org/web.htm

- Yahoo!...Adoption
  http://dir.yahoo.com/Society_and_Culture/Families/Parenting/Adoption/

- Yellow Rose Reunions
  http://home.texoma.net/~wfbonner/

- Yourfamily.com - Long Lost Family Bulletin Board
  http://www.yourfamily.com/lost_family.shtml

◆ Home Children

- British Home Children
  http://freepages.genealogy.rootsweb.com/~britishhome
  children
  A site for listing the names of the individual British Home Children.

- British Home Children Mailing List
  http://members.aol.com/gfsjohnf/gen_mail_countrycan.html
  #BRITISHHOMECHILDREN
  A mailing list for those interested in researching the 100,000 British Home Children who were emigrated to Canada by 50 child care organizations to work as indentured farm labourers (18701940).

- Home Children
  http://www.archives.ca/exec/naweb.dll?fs&020110&e&top&0
  From the National Archives of Canada.Between 1869 and the early 1930s, over 100,000 children were sent to Canada from Great Britain during the child emigration movement. Members of the British Isles Family History Society of Greater Ottawa are locating and indexing the names of these Home Children found in passenger lists in the custody of the National Archives of Canada.

  o Home Children Search
    http://www.archives.ca/exec/naweb.dll?fs&02011002&e&
    top&0
    A searchable online index for the years 1865 to 1919 is available online.

- Young Immigrants to Canada
  http://www.dcs.uwaterloo.ca/~marj/genealogy/homeadd.html
  When the topic of child immigrants to Canada is raised many people first think of Barnardo's. Some may know about Annie Macpherson, Maria Rye, Fegan Homes, Dr. Stephenson and the National Children's Home or even some of the Roman Catholic organizations. This web site represents research into all of the organizations which brought children and young women to Canada between 1833 and 1935.

◆ Locality Specific

- The CanadaWide National Registry & Family Finders
  http://www.adopting.org/ffcwnr.html
  Adoption resources & registry.

- The IrelandBornAdoptees Bulletin Board
  http://www.bulletinboards.com/view.cfm?comcode=IRISH

- New Mexico Adoption Registry
  http://www.geocities.com/Heartland/Woods/8681/index.html

- Oregon Adoptive Rights Association
  http://www.oara.org/

- Research Guide - Good British Stock - Child & Youth Migration to Australia
  http://www.naa.gov.au/PUBLICAT/GUIDES/childmig/
  guide.htm
  From the National Archives of Australia.

- Searching In Florida
  http://www.angelfire.com/fl/flsearch/index.html
  Links for adoptees and birthparents searching information mainly in Florida.

- Searching in Ireland - Resources for IrishBorn Adoptees
  http://www.netreach.net/~steed/search.html

- S.E.A.S.Y.P. Greek Adoptees Reunion Registry
  http://www.seasyp.gr

- Tina's Illinois Adoption Registry
  http://www.geocities.com/Heartland/Flats/7366/
  Free adoption registry for those searching in Illinois.

- WARMWashington Adoption Reunion Movement
  http://www.wolfenet.com/~warm/
  Our mission is to provide support, search, reunion, education and training in the life long issues surrounding adoption.

◆ Mailing Lists, Newsgroups & Chat

- Genealogy Resources on the Internet - Adoption Mailing Lists
  http://www.rootsweb.com/~jfuller/gen_mail_adoption.html
  Most of the mailing list links below point to this site, wonderfully maintained by John Fuller

- Adoptees Internet Mailing List
  http://24.8.18.174/AIML/

- ADOPTEES Mailing List
  http://www.rootsweb.com/~jfuller/gen_mail_adoption.html
  #ADOPTEES
  For legal adoptees and "adopteelites" (people who were raised without one or both birth parents, but who were never legally adopted) to seek advice in conducting a search.

- The Adoptees Newsgroup Home Page - soc.adoption.adoptees
  http://www.geocities.com/Heartland/Acres/8126/

- ADOPTFR Mailing List
  http://www.rootsweb.com/~jfuller/gen_mail_adoption.html
  #ADOPTFR

- adoptgene Mailing List
  http://www.rootsweb.com/~jfuller/gen_mail_adoption.html
  #adoptgene
  For the discussion of problems related to adoption.

- ADOPTING Mailing List
  http://www.rootsweb.com/~jfuller/gen_mail_adoption.html
  #ADOPTING
  For anyone touched by adoption. This list offers search help, support, and tips on research related to adoption.

- ADOPTION Mailing List
  http://www.rootsweb.com/~jfuller/gen_mail_adoption.html
  #ADOPTION
  Discussions of anything and everything connected with adoption.

- AdoptionSearchAssist Mailing List
  http://www.rootsweb.com/~jfuller/gen_mail_adoption.html
  #AdoptionSearchAssist
  For adoptees, birth parents, adoptive parents, birth families, and siblings who are searching for one another.

- adoptlivingsearch Mailing List
  http://www.rootsweb.com/~jfuller/gen_mail_adoption.html
  #adoptlivingsearch
  For anyone who is searching for their adopted relatives.

- blackadoptiontriad Mailing List
  http://www.rootsweb.com/~jfuller/gen_mail_adoption.html
  #blackadoptiontriad
  For all AfricanAmericans affected by the adoption experience (e.g., adoptees, adoptive parents, birth parents, siblings) to help others in their search for family members and to share searching stores and reunion experiences.

- FamAdopt Mailing List
  http://www.rootsweb.com/~jfuller/gen_mail_general.html
  #FamAdop
  And the associated web page
  http://public.surfree.com/mfuller/famadopt.htm
  For anyone personally touched by adoption and wishing to trace/share their heritage, genealogists seeking biological/adoptive family information to include an adoptee on their family tree, other interested parties, and those helping others to seek information; and for the sharing of guidelines for searching public records.

- FINDINGINFLORIDA Mailing List
  http://www.rootsweb.com/~jfuller/gen_mail_statesfl.html
  #FINDINGINFLORIDA
  For those conducting adoption searches in Florida.

- IRISHADOPTEESSEARCH Mailing List
  http://www.rootsweb.com/~jfuller/gen_mail_country
  unk.html#IRISHADOPTEESSEARCH

- ITALIADOPTION Mailing List
  http://www.rootsweb.com/~jfuller/gen_mail_adoption.html
  #ITALIADOPTION
  For individuals who were born in Italy and adopted by families in the United States or Canada to seek help in locating birthparents, siblings, or other family members.

- MichiganSearching Mailing List
  http://www.rootsweb.com/~jfuller/gen_mail_adoption.html
  #MichiganSearching
  For adoptees and birth families conducting adoption searches in Michigan.

- PAFind Mailing List
  http://www.rootsweb.com/~jfuller/gen_mail_adoption.html
  #PAFind
  For people who have lost touch with family members due to adoption in Pennsylvania.

- Usenet Newsgroup alt.adoption
  news:alt.adoption
  For adoptees, birthparents, adoptive parents.

- Usenet Newsgroup soc.adoption.adoptees
  news:soc.adoption.adoptees
  The Adoptees Newsgroup.

- Webchat Broadcasting System: Adult Adoptees Chat
  http://chat19.go.com/webchat3.so?cmd=cmd_doorway:
  Adult_Adoptees_Chat

◆ Orphan Trains

- Iowa Orphan Train Project
  http://www.maquoketa.k12.ia.us/orphan_train.html

- Orphans to Iowa
  ftp://ftp.rootsweb.com/pub/usgenweb/ia/various/orphans.txt

- Orphan Train Heritage Society of America, Inc.
  http://pda.republic.net/othsa/

- Orphan Train Resources
  http://www.maquoketa.k12.ia.us/ot%20resource.html

- Orphan Train Riders History
  http://www.hamilton.net/subscribers/hurd/index.html

- Orphan Trains
  http://www.outfitters.com/~melissa/ot/ot.html

- The Orphan Trains
  http://www.pbs.org/wgbh/amex/orphan/index.html
  A PBS American Experience television show regarding this unusual immigrant experience.

- Orphan Trains of Kansas
  http://kuhttp.cc.ukans.edu/carrie/kancoll/articles/orphans/
  index.html

  o A History of the Orphan Trains
    http://raven.cc.ukans.edu/carrie/kancoll/articles/orphans/
    or_hist.htm

  o Index of Children Who Rode the Orphan Trains to Kansas
    http://raven.cc.ukans.edu/carrie/kancoll/articles/orphans/
    or_child.htm

  o Kansas Orphan Train "TimeLine"
    http://raven.cc.ukans.edu/carrie/kancoll/articles/orphans/
    or_timel.htm

  o Orphan Train Bibliographies
    http://www.ukans.edu/carrie/kancoll/articles/orphans/or_
    bibli.htm

- o Other Orphan Train Links
  http://www.hamilton.net/subscribers/hurd/orphan.htm
  Basically a page for links to other Orphan Train pages. My great grandma was a rider and hope this helps. I found her name before she was adopted Angela IVERS, and the year she was "adopted" and who and where she was adopted.

- o A Partial List of Institutions That Orphan Train Children Came From
  http://raven.cc.ukans.edu/carrie/kancoll/articles/orphans/or_homes.htm

- o A Partial List of Kansas Orphan Train Arrivals
  http://raven.cc.ukans.edu/carrie/kancoll/articles/orphans/or_arriv.htm

- o Riders on an Orphan Train to Kansas - 1911
  http://raven.cc.ukans.edu/carrie/kancoll/articles/orphan_train_1911.html

- Orphan Trains of Nebraska
  http://www.rootsweb.com/~neadoptn/Orphan.htm

- The Orphan Trains: Placing Out in America
  http://shop.myfamily.com/ancestrycatalog/product.asp?pf%5Fid=17646&dept%5Fid=10103002
  A book by Marilyn Irvin Holt, for sale from Ancestry.

- Orphan Trains to Missouri
  http://www.system.missouri.edu/upress/spring1997/patrick.htm
  Information about a book from the University of Missouri Press.

- They Rode the Orphan Trains
  http://www.rootsweb.com/~mogrundy/orphans.html

- Yahoo!...U.S. History...19th Century...Orphan Trains
  http://dir.yahoo.com/Arts/Humanities/History/U_S__History/19th_Century/Orphan_Trains/

◆ Professional Researchers, Volunteers & Other Research Services

- Adopted We Search - Assets and Family Research Consultants~ Toronto, Ontario, Canada
  http://www.adoptedwesearch.com/
  Researcher with 15 years experience, specializing in adoption related searches.

- Adoptees Miracle Search Network
  http://www.miraclesearch.com
  Professional who finds adoptees and their birth parents

- Adoption Searches & Investigations~ London, Ontario, Canada
  http://www3.sympatico.ca/searches/
  Licensed, bonded, adoptee search agency. Adoption articles & links. Searches in Canada only. Contact Anne Patterson.

- genealogyPro - Adoption Researchers
  http://genealogyPro.com/directories/adoption.html

- Searchline - Reuniting Adoptees and Birth Parents
  http://www.searchline.co.uk/
  A UKbased professional researcher, specialising in finding and reuniting adoptees and their birth families.

◆ Publications, Software & Supplies

- Amazon.com Genealogy Bookstore - Adoption
  http://www.amazon.com/exec/obidos/externalsearch/?keyword=adoption+genealogy&tag=markcyndisgenealA/

- Ancestor's Attic Discount Genealogy Books - Adoption Books
  http://members.tripod.com/~ancestorsattic/index.html#ADOPT

- AudioTapes.com - Genealogical Lectures on Cassette Tapes - Adoption
  http://www.audiotapes.com/search2.asp?Search=Adoption

- The Seeker Magazine
  http://www.theseeker.com/

AFRICAN-AMERICAN
http://www.cyndislist.com/african.htm

Category Index:

- ◆ General Resource Sites
- ◆ History & Culture
- ◆ Libraries, Archives & Museums
- ◆ Locality Specific
- ◆ Mailing Lists, Newsgroups & Chat
- ◆ Military
- ◆ People & Families

- ◆ Professional Researchers, Volunteers & Other Research Services
- ◆ Publications, Software & Supplies
- ◆ Records: Census, Cemeteries, Land, Obituaries, Personal, Taxes and Vital
- ◆ Slavery
- ◆ Societies & Groups

◆ General Resource Sites

- African American Family Histories and Related Works in the Library of Congress
http://lcweb.loc.gov/rr/genealogy/bib_guid/aframer/
Bibliography listed in order of surname.

- African American Genealogy
http://www.familytreemaker.com/issue12.html
From Family Tree Maker Online.

- African-American Genealogy Ring
http://afamgenealogy.ourfamily.com/

- African-American How-To Guide From Family Tree Maker
http://www.familytreemaker.com/00000360.html

- African Immigration to Maryland
http://www.clis.umd.edu/~mddlmddl/791/communities/html/index.html#african
A scholarly review of immigration into Maryland from the very first colonists to modern immigrants..

- African American Lifelines
http://pages.prodigy.net/cliffmurr/aa_life.htm
How-to for beginners.

- African-American Sources ~ Indiana
http://www.comsource.net/~tnolcox/africanamerican.htm

- The African - Native Genealogy Homepage
http://hometown.aol.com/angelaw859/index.html
Celebrating the Estelusti ~ The Freedmen Oklahoma's Black Indians of the Cherokee, Chickasaw, Choctaw, Creek, and Seminole Nations.

- African Studies WWW (U. Penn)
http://www.sas.upenn.edu/African_Studies/AS.html

- AfriGeneas ~ African Ancestored Genealogy
http://www.afrigeneas.com/

- Afro-American Genealogical Research
http://lcweb.loc.gov/rr/genealogy/bib_guid/afro.html
A "How To" guide from the Library of Congress.

- ALGenWeb: Ethnic Groups: African-American Genealogy and History Sites
http://members.aol.com/blountal/Afmain.html

- Black/African Related Resources
http://www.sas.upenn.edu/African_Studies/Home_Page/mcgee.html

- Blacks in Alaska History Project Inc.
http://www.yukonalaska.com/akblkhist/

- Christine's Genealogy Website
http://www.ccharity.com/
A wealth of African-American resources for genealogy as well as Christine's personal research: The RUSSELLs & COBBs of Jackson, Tennessee; the CHARITYs of Surry and Charles City County, Virginia; the ANDERSONs and PERKINS of Shuqualak, Mississippi; and the SIMMONS of Detroit, Michigan.

- Immigration: The Africans
http://library.thinkquest.org/20619/African.html
A brief history of African immigration to the United States.

- Internet Resources for Students of Afro-American History
http://www.libraries.rutgers.edu/rulib/socsci/hist/afrores.htm

- People of Color in Old Tennessee
http://www.tngenweb.org/tncolor/

- Scientific American: Feature Article: The Puzzle of Hypertension in African-Americans: February 1999
http://www.sciam.com/1999/0299issue/0299cooper.html
Genes are often invoked to account for why high blood pressure is so common among African-Americans. Yet the rates are low in Africans. This discrepancy demonstrates how genes and the environment interact.

- Tracing Your African-American Roots
http://www.sierra.com/sierrahome/familytree/hqarticles/tracingroots/
An online article by Shirley Hogan explaining how to get started.

- Yahoo!...African American...Genealogy
  http://dir.yahoo.com/Society_and_Culture/Cultures_and_
  Groups/Cultures/American__United_States_/African_
  American/History/Genealogy/

◆ History & Culture

- African American History
  http://www.msstate.edu/Archives/History/USA/Afro-
  Amer/afro.html
  *Links from the Historical Text Archive at Mississippi State
  University.*

- African American History
  http://www.ukans.edu/~usa/africanam.html
  Set of links.

- African American History Bookmarks
  http://www.mcps.k12.md.us/curriculum/socialstd/African_Am_
  bookmarks.html
  From Montgomery County Public Schools in Maryland.

- Boston African-American National Historic Site
  http://www.nps.gov/boaf/

- Lest We Forget
  http://www.coax.net/people/LWF/default.htm
  *Documents with focus on the history and culture of African-
  Americans*

  o Genealogy
    http://www.coax.net/people/lwf/genes.htm
    Index page from the LEST WE FORGET Web Site

- The North Star: Tracing The Underground Railroad
  http://www.ugrr.org/

- A Selection of Underground Railroad Resources
  http://www.ugrr.org/web.htm

- Underground Railroad - Taking the Train to
  Freedom
  http://www.nps.gov/undergroundrr/contents.htm

- The Universal Black Pages - History Links
  http://www.ubp.com/History/

- The Walk to Canada - Tracing the Underground
  Railroad
  http://www.ugrr.org/walk.htm

◆ Libraries, Archives & Museums

- A. Philip Randolph/Pullman Porter Museum Gallery
  http://www.wimall.com/pullportermu/
  *Chicago, Illinois museum celebrating this leader in the African
  American labor movement and the African American Railroad
  Attendant.*

- African-American Genealogy Sources in the
  Louisiana Division of the New Orleans Public
  Library
  http://home.gnofn.org/~nopl/guides/black.htm

- African American Monuments, Museums and
  Memorials
  http://www.geocities.com/Athens/Troy/1228/index.html
  Links to African American museums, monuments and cultural sites.

- African American Perspectives: Pamphlets from the
  Daniel A.P. Murray Collection, 1818-1907
  http://lcweb2.loc.gov/ammem/aap/aaphome.html

- Afro-American Sources in Virginia - A Guide To
  Manuscripts
  http://www.upress.virginia.edu/plunkett/mfp.html

- Amistad Research Center
  http://www.arc.tulane.edu/

- Carnegie Library of Pittsburgh - Pennsylvania
  Department: African-American Genealogy
  http://www.clpgh.org/CLP/Pennsylvania/oak_penna32.html

- Connecticut State Library
  http://www.cslnet.ctstateu.edu/index.htm

  o History and Genealogy Unit
    http://www.cslnet.ctstateu.edu/handg.htm

  o Finding Aid to African-American Genealogical
    Resources at the Connecticut State Library
    http://www.cslnet.ctstateu.edu/blagen.htm

- Kentucky's African-American Genealogical Sources
  at the Kentucky Department for Libraries and
  Archives
  http://www.kdla.state.ky.us/arch/blkhist.htm

- Merseyside Maritime Museum ~ Liverpool, England
  http://www.nmgm.org.uk/maritime/index.html

  o Transatlantic Slavery - Against Human Dignity
    http://www.nmgm.org.uk/maritime/slavery.html

  o The Trade Triangle
    http://www.nmgm.org.uk/maritime/slavery/
    maritimeframeset2.html

- Moorland-Spingarn Research Center ~ Washington,
  D.C.
  http://www.founders.howard.edu/moorland-spingarn/
  default.htm
  *One of the world's largest and most comprehensive repositories for
  the documentation of the history and culture of people of African
  descent in Africa, the Americas, and other parts of the world. As one
  of Howard University's major research facilities, the MSRC collects,
  preserves, and makes available for research a wide range of
  resources chronicling the Black experience.*

- Museum of African-American History ~ Detroit,
  Michigan
  http://www.maah-detroit.org/

- The Museum of African Slavery
  http://jhunix.hcf.jhu.edu/~plarson/smuseum/welcome.htm

- The Museum of Afro-American History Boston ~
  Massachusetts
  http://www.afroammuseum.org/

- New Orleans Public Library
  http://www.gnofn.org/~nopl/info/info.htm

  o African American Resource Center
    http://www.gnofn.org/~nopl/info/aarcinfo/aarcinfo.htm

  o A Guide to African American Genealogical
    Research in New Orleans and Louisiana
    http://www.gnofn.org/~nopl/info/aarcinfo/guide.htm

- Rare Book, Manuscript, and Special Collections
  Library, Duke University ~ Durham, North Carolina
  http://scriptorium.lib.duke.edu/

  o African-American Women - On-line Archival
    Exhibits
    http://scriptorium.lib.duke.edu/collections/african-
    american-women.html

  o John Hope Franklin Research Center for African
    and African American Documentation
    http://scriptorium.lib.duke.edu/franklin/

  o Third Person, First Person: Slave Voices from the
    Special Collections Library
    http://scriptorium.lib.duke.edu/slavery/
    *Broadside Collection, Special Collections Library, Duke
    University.*

- Researching African-American History
  http://www.statelib.lib.in.us/www/ihb/aabib.html
  *Researching African-American History in the Indiana State Library
  and Historical Building.*

- Selections from The African-American Mosaic: A
  Library of Congress Exhibit
  http://lcweb.loc.gov/exhibits/african/intro.html

- The Walker African-American Museum & Research
  Center ~ Nevada
  http://members.aol.com/Bigbrwnsis/index.html

◆ Locality Specific

- A Community Remembers - African-American Life
  in Princeton ~ New Jersey
  http://www.princetonol.com/groups/histsoc/aalife/

- African-Americans in Southeastern Ohio
  http://www.seorf.ohiou.edu/~xx057/

- African Americans in Missouri
  http://www.rootsweb.com/~moafram/
  *Resources for African Americans seeking enslaved ancestors in
  Missouri. The site offers slave schedules, marriage records, black
  cemetery listing and a slave database of Missouri slave owners.
  Volunteers transcribe data for a variety of much needed resources.*

- Florida African American Roots
  http://www.rootsweb.com/~flafram/home.html

- Free African Americans of Virginia, North Carolina,
  South Carolina, Maryland and Delaware
  http://www.freeafricanamericans.com/
  *History of over 500 African American families who were free in the
  colonial period through 1820.*

- Freedmen of the Frontier
  http://www.angelfire.com/ar/freedmen
  *African American genealogy and historical reference site for
  western Arkansas and eastern Oklahoma.*

- Profiles of African Americans in Tennessee
  http://picard.tnstate.edu/~library/digital/digitizing.html

- Thomasville's Black History
  http://www.rose.net/blckhist.htm
  Thomasville and Thomas County, Georgia.

- To Know My Name - A Chronological History of
  African Americans in Santa Cruz County ~
  California
  http://www.santacruzpl.org/history/culdiv/know1.html

◆ Mailing Lists, Newsgroups & Chat

- Genealogy Resources on the Internet - African-
  Ancestored Mailing Lists
  http://www.rootsweb.com/~jfuller/gen_mail_african.html
  *Most of the mailing list links below point to this site, wonderfully
  maintained by John Fuller*

- Afrigeneas Chat
  http://www.afrigeneas.com/chat/

- Afrigeneas Mailing list
  http://www.rootsweb.com/~jfuller/gen_mail_african.html
  #AFRIGENEAS

- AL-AfricaAmer Mailing List
  http://www.rootsweb.com/~jfuller/gen_mail_african.html
  #AL-AfricaAmer
  *For anyone with an interest in African American genealogy in
  Alabama.*

- blackadoptiontriad Mailing List
  http://www.rootsweb.com/~jfuller/gen_mail_adoption.html
  #blackadoptiontriad
  *For all African-Americans affected by the adoption experience (e.g.
  adoptees, adoptive parents, birth parents, siblings) to help others in
  their search for family members and to share searching stores and
  reunion experiences.*

- BLACKWARHEROS Mailing List
  http://www.rootsweb.com/~jfuller/gen_mail_wars.html
  #BLACKWARHEROS
  *For anyone with a genealogical or historical interest in Black
  Americans who were "heroes" during any war.*

- Christine's Genealogy Forum
  http://ccharity.com/discus/messages/board-topics.html
  African American genealogy forum.

- GEN-AFRICAN Mailing List
  http://www.rootsweb.com/~jfuller/gen_mail_african.html
  #GEN-AFRICAN
  Gatewayed with the soc.genealogy.african
  newsgroup for the discussion of African genealogy.
  news:soc.genealogy.african

- MSAFRICANAMER Mailing List
  http://www.rootsweb.com/~jfuller/gen_mail_states-ms.html
  #MSAFRICANAMER
  For the discussion and sharing of information regarding all aspects of African-American genealogy in Mississippi.

- OH-AfricaAmer Mailing List
  http://www.rootsweb.com/~jfuller/gen_mail_african.html
  #OH-AfricaAmer
  For anyone with an interest in African American genealogy in Ohio.

- OH-CW-AfricaAmer Mailing List
  http://www.rootsweb.com/~jfuller/gen_mail_african.html
  #OH-CW-AfricaAmer
  For anyone with a genealogical interest in African Americans from Ohio who fought in the Civil War.

- POCSOUTH Mailing List
  http://www.rootsweb.com/~jfuller/gen_mail_african.html
  #POCSOUTH
  "People of Color, South" to open a dialogue with African American genealogists doing research in the thirteen southern United States.

- SLAVEINFO Mailing List
  http://www.rootsweb.com/~jfuller/gen_mail_african.html
  #SLAVEINFO
  For the sharing of genealogical data about slaves in the United States including wills/deeds that show sales and transfer of ownership, vital records (e.g., birth, marriage, death), and information/queries on specific slaves that may be part of your ancestry.

- Usenet Newsgroup soc.genealogy.african
  news:soc.genealogy.african

◆ Military

- 19th Century African Americans in the US Military
  http://members.nbci.com/uscwct/main.html
  Links and and history.

- 34th United States Colored Troops and 2nd South Carolina Volunteers
  http://www.marple.com/34thusct.html

- African-American Civil War Memorial
  http://www.afroamcivilwar.org
  Made possible by AT&T, the Web site provides information for anyone interested in freedom and historical truth or in the valor of the African-American soldiers who fought during the war. An interactive feature allows visitors to find information on the soldiers who served in the war and provides a resource that helps the descendants of these soldiers to keep this history alive. The Web site also features an online store which allows visitors to purchase souvenirs and show their support for the Foundation and it's programs.

- African Americans in the Civil War
  http://www.hist.unt.edu/09w-acwd.htm
  Links to more sites.

- African American Warriors
  http://www.abest.com/~cklose/aawar.htm

- The Buffalo Soldiers on the Western Frontier
  http://www.imh.org/imh/buf/buftoc.html
  From the International Museum of the Horse.

- The Civil War
  http://www.coax.net/people/lwf/data.htm
  Several links and articles from "Lest We Forget".

- The Civil War Soldiers and Sailors System (CWSS)
  http://www.itd.nps.gov/cwss/
  The current version of the CWSS is a new presentation of the names and regimental histories of the African American units in the Union Army.

- Eighth United States Colored Troops
  http://extlab1.entnem.ufl.edu/Olustee/8th_USCI.html

- Fifty-fourth Massachusetts Infantry
  http://extlab1.entnem.ufl.edu/olustee/54th_MS_inf.html

- Guide to Tracing Your African American Civil War Ancestor
  http://www.coax.net/people/lwf/cwguide.htm

- The Revolution's Black Soldiers
  http://home.earthlink.net/~patriot1/blk.html

- Tennessee Colored Pension Applications for C. S. A. Service
  http://www.angelfire.com/wi/Carver/csaaa.html
  This page contains name of African-Americans with Tennessee connections who applied for pensions claiming service with the Confederate States of America during the Civil War.

- United States Colored Troops Resident in Baltimore at the time of the 1890 Census
  http://www.mdarchives.state.md.us/msa/speccol/3096/html/00010001.html

- United States Colored Troops: The Civil War
  http://www.coax.net/people/lwf/usct.htm

◆ People & Families

- The Black Seminoles
  http://www.ccny.cuny.edu/library/News/seminoles2.html

- Eyes of Glory - 200 Years of an Ethnic American Family
  http://www.eyesofglory.com
  Early African and Jewish American history information.

- Heart of Two Nations: African Native Americans
  http://hometown.aol.com/homalosa/index.html
  Overview of the shared history of Native Americans and African Americans that includes bibliography of research and genealogical resources.

- The Life of the Pullman Porter
  http://www.scsra.org/library/porter.html
  Online article by Stewart H. Holbrook.

◆ Professional Researchers, Volunteers & Other Research Services

- Board for Certification of Genealogists - Roster of Those Certified - Specializing in African American Genealogy
  http://www.bcgcertification.org/rosts_@a.html

● Bright and Harris Family Tree
http://home.earthlink.net/~dhsankofa/genealogy92.html
A site specializing in African American genealogy research services, BRIGHT and HARRIS surnames.

◆ Publications, Software & Supplies

● African American Genealogy 1850 - 1880
http://www.gencd.com/sx010001.htm
A CD for sale. Birth and death information extracted from Federal Census records. Names, ages, causes of death and location of death. Cities, Town, Counties. Shows paths traveled by slaves from birth to final destination. For Alabama, Arkansas, Arizona, California, Colorado, Connecticut, District of Columbia, Dakota Territory, Delaware, Florida, Georgia, Idaho, Illinois, Indiana, Iowa, Kansas, Kentucky, Louisiana, Michigan, Minnesota, Mississippi, Montana, Nebraska, Nevada, New Hampshire, North Dakota, Ohio, Oregon, Pennsylvania, South Dakota, Tennessee, Texas, Utah, Vermont, Washington, West Virginia and Wyoming.

● Amazon.com Genealogy Bookstore - African American
http://www.amazon.com/exec/obidos/external-search/
?keyword=african+american+genealogy&tag=
markcyndisgenealA/

● AudioTapes.com - Genealogical Lectures on Cassette Tapes - African-American
http://www.audiotapes.com/search2.asp?Search=African+
American

● African-American Ancestors Among the Five Civilized Tribes
http://www.coax.net/people/lwf/blkind.htm
Description of book for sale.

● African-American Archaeology Newsletter
http://www.newsouthassoc.com/AfAmNewsletter.html
From the New South Associates.

● African American Genealogy: A Bibliography for Beginners
http://www.kdla.state.ky.us/arch/biblforb.htm

● Ancestor's Attic Discount Genealogy Books - African American Genealogy Books
http://members.tripod.com/~ancestorsattic/index.html#secAA

● Databases for the Study of Afro-Louisiana History and Genealogy, 1699-1860
http://lsumvs.sncc.lsu.edu/lsupress/catalog/Backlist/fall99/
99fall_book/hall.html
CD-ROM containing over 100,000 records of African-Americans in Louisiana. Includes Louisiana Slave Database 1719-1820, Louisiana Free Database 1720-1820, a compilation of Louisiana censuses from 1699 through 1860, and various New Orleans, Pensacola, and Mobile censuses from 1784 to 1850.

● Frontier Press Bookstore - African American History / Research
http://www.frontierpress.com/frontier.cgi?category=afr

● GenealogyBookShop.com - African American
http://www.genealogybookshop.com/genealogybookshop/
files/General,African_American/index.html
The online store of Genealogical Publishing Co., Inc. & Clearfield Company.

● Heritage Books - African American
http://www.heritagebooks.com/afr-am.htm

● Missing Pages
http://www.hometown.aol.com/flu234
Book for sale, detailing more than 200 African American pioneer communities. America's Black Towns and Settlements by Morris Turner III.

● Slave Manumissions & Sales in Harford County Maryland 1774-1865
http://www.members.home.net/wsadams/book.html
A book by Carolyn Greenfield Adams. It was once widely held that records did not exist for African American families before 1865. This is not true for Harford County Maryland. This book contains manumission and sales records from 1774-1865 giving information on individuals or families, dates of birth, ages and occupations based on data from over five hundred documents representing a total of about two thousand names which are indexed manumissions.

● The Trans-Atlantic Slave Trade - A Database on CD-ROM
http://www.cup.org/ObjectBuilder/ObjectBuilder.iwx?Process
Name=ProductPage&Merchant_Id=1&product_id=0-521-
62910-1&origin=search&searchField=TITLE&searchString=
slave%20trade
Contains the records of 27,233 transatlantic slave ship voyages made between 1595 and 1866 from all over Europe.

● Willow Bend Bookstore - African-American
http://www.willowbend.net/default.asp

◆ Records: Census, Cemeteries, Land, Obituaries, Personal, Taxes and Vital (Born, Married, Died & Buried)

● African American Cemeteries Online
http://www.prairiebluff.com/millenium/aacemetery/

● African American Census Schedules Online
http://www.prairiebluff.com/aacensus/

● African Americans listed in the 1850 & 1860 Madison County, Tennessee Free Census Schedule
http://www.ccharity.com/tennessee/freetenn.htm

● Black Studies - A select catalog of National Archives microfilm
http://www.nara.gov/publications/microfilm/blackstudies/
blackstd.html

● Federal Records and African-American History
http://www.nara.gov/publications/prologue/aframpro.html

● Freedmen of the Frontier
http://www.angelfire.com/ar/freedmen/
African-American Historical and Genealogical Resource Page of the city of Ft. Smith Arkansas.

- Freedmen's Bureau Online
  http://www.freedmensbureau.com/
  - o Freedman's Bureau, Marriages in Arkansas 1861-1869
    http://www.freedmensbureau.com/arkansas/arkansas
    marriages.htm
  - o Freedman's Bureau, Marriages in Jacksonville, Florida 1861-1869
    http://www.freedmensbureau.com/florida/florida.htm
  - o Freedman's Bureau, Marriages in Mississippi 1863-1865
    http://www.freedmensbureau.com/mississippi/mississippi
    marriages.htm
  - o Freedman's Bureau, Marriages in Tennessee 1865-1869
    http://www.freedmensbureau.com/tennessee/marriages/
    tennesseemarriages.htm
  - o Freedman's Bureau, Marriages in Washington, D.C. 1861-1869, Part 1
    http://www.freedmensbureau.com/washingtondc/
    dcmarriages2.htm
    And Part 2
    http://www.freedmensbureau.com/washingtondc/
    dcmarriages1.htm
  - o Freedmen's Bureau Register of Marriages in Gloucester, Virginia 1861-1869
    http://www.freedmensbureau.com/virginia/gloucester.htm
- Freedmen's Bureau Records
  http://www.rootsweb.com/~flafram/Fmen.html
  Selected Florida records.
- Freedman's Savings and Trust Company and African American Genealogical Research
  http://www.nara.gov/publications/prologue/freedman.html
- Funeral Programs, USA sponsored by LFC of Maryland
  http://www.angelfire.com/md/FUNERALPROGRAMSUSA
  LFC of MARYLAND in it's ongoing attempt to assist, aid and abet the African American Researcher/Historian in their never ending quest for information and documentation, has created and maintains this page of Funeral Programs from across the country.
- Illinois Database of Servitude and Emancipation Records 1722-1863
  http://www.sos.state.il.us/depts/archives/servant.html
  This database includes more than 2000 transactions found in governmental records involving the servitude and emancipation of Africans and, occasionally,Indians in the French and English eras of colonial Illinois (1722-1790) and African-Americans in the American period of Illinois (1790-1863).
- Noxubee County, Mississippi Slave Schedule - 1860 Census
  http://www.ccharity.com/mississippi/1860noxumortpt1.htm
- Records of the Brotherhood of Sleeping Car Porters
  http://www.lexis-nexis.com/cispubs/guides/african_american/
  bscp/bscp3.htm

Description of the microfilmed holdings of the Chicago Historical Society and the Newberry Library.

- Register of Free Blacks Augusta County, Virginia
  http://jefferson.village.virginia.edu/vshadow2/govdoc/
  fblack.html
- Register of Free Negroes and Mulattoes in The Corporation of Staunton
  http://jefferson.village.virginia.edu/vshadow2/govdoc/
  fblack2.html
- Slave Entries in Wills, Deeds, Etc.
  http://home.netcom.com/~jog1/slavedocs.html
  Kentucky, South Carolina, Tennessee, Virginia.
- Slave Information from Various Loudoun Co., VA Documents, 13 Dec 1809 to 30 June 1861
  http://www.rootsweb.com/~valoudou/slaves.html

◆ Slavery

- African American Genealogy Resources: Slavery
  http://ccharity.com/genlinks/Slavery/
  Links from Christine's Genealogy Website.
- AfriGeneas - Slave Data Collection
  http://www.afrigeneas.com/slavedata/
- American Slave Narratives: An Online Anthology
  http://xroads.virginia.edu/~HYPER/wpa/wpahome.html
- Amistad America, Inc. - Building the Freedom Schooner
  http://www.amistadamerica.org/main/welcome.html
- Amistad - "Give Us Free"
  http://news.courant.com/special/amistad/
- Documenting the American South - North American Slave Narratives, Beginnings to 1920
  http://metalab.unc.edu/docsouth/neh/neh.html
- Excerpts from Slave Narratives
  http://vi.uh.edu/pages/mintz/primary.htm
- Exploring Amistad: Race and the Boundaries of Freedom in Antebellum Maritime America
  http://amistad.mysticseaport.org/
- Index to Parish Court Slave Emancipation Petitions, 1814-1843, Orleans Parish, Louisiana
  http://home.gnofn.org/~nopl/inv/vcp/emancip.htm
- Merseyside Maritime Museum ~ Liverpool, England
  http://www.nmgm.org.uk/maritime/index.html
  - o Transatlantic Slavery - Against Human Dignity
    http://www.nmgm.org.uk/maritime/slavery.html
  - o The Trade Triangle
    http://www.nmgm.org.uk/maritime/slavery/maritimeframe
    7set2.html
- North American Slave Narratives
  http://metalab.unc.edu/docsouth/neh/neh.html
  From Documenting the American South.

- The North Star: Tracing The Underground Railroad
  http://www.ugrr.org/

- A Selection of Underground Railroad Resources
  http://www.ugrr.org/web.htm

- Slave Entries in Wills, Deeds, Etc.
  http://home.netcom.com/~jog1/slavedocs.html
  Kentucky, South Carolina, Tennessee, Virginia.

- Slave Information from Various Loudoun Co., VA Documents, 13 Dec 1809 to 30 June 1861
  http://www.rootsweb.com/~valoudou/slaves.htm

- Slave Names from Records - Noxubee County, Mississippi
  http://members.tripod.com/~earphoto/SlaveNames.html
  Names, ages, and other information taken from Probate records books A providing some insight into origin or surnames.

- Slaveowners and Slaves In and Around Dauphin County, Pennsylvania
  http://www.geocities.com/Athens/Parthenon/6329/index.html

- Slavery and Abolition - A Journal of Slave and Post-Slave Studies
  http://www.frankcass.com/jnls/sa.htm

- Slavery in Dauphin County, Pennsylvania
  http://www.geocities.com/Athens/Parthenon/6329/

- Testimony of the Canadian Fugitives
  http://history.cc.ukans.edu/carrie/docs/texts/canadian_slaves.html

- Texas Slavery Project at the University of Houston
  http://www.texasslaveryproject.uh.edu/
  Seeks to recover the names and biographical information for every slave who ever lived in Texas.

- Third Person, First Person: Slave Voices from the Special Collections Library
  http://scriptorium.lib.duke.edu/slavery/
  Broadside Collection, Special Collections Library, Duke University.

- The Trans-Atlantic Slave Trade - A Database on CD-ROM
  http://www.cup.org/ObjectBuilder/ObjectBuilder.iwx?ProcessName=ProductPage&Merchant_Id=1&product_id=0-521-62910-1&origin=search&searchField=TITLE&searchString=slave%20trade
  Contains the records of 27,233 transatlantic slave ship voyages made between 1595 and 1866 from all over Europe.

- Underground Railroad - Taking the Train to Freedom
  http://www.nps.gov/undergroundrr/contents.htm

- United States History Index - WWW-VL: History: US: Slavery
  http://www.ukans.edu/history/VL/USA/slavery.html

- The Walk to Canada - Tracing the Underground Railroad
  http://www.npca.org/walk.html

- Women and Slavery
  http://weber.u.washington.edu/~sunstar/ws200/slavery.htm

- Yahoo!...US History...Slavery
  http://dir.yahoo.com/Arts/Humanities/History/U_S__History/Slavery/

◆ Societies & Groups

- African American Genealogical Group of the Miami Valley ~ Yellow Spring, Ohio
  http://www.coax.net/people/lwf/aaggmv.htm

- African-American Genealogical Society of Cleveland, Ohio
  http://www.familyhistory.com/societyhall/viewmember.asp?societyid=359

- African American Genealogical Society of Northern California ~ Oakland, California
  http://www.aagsnc.org/
  Preserve and promote the study of records of a genealogical and historical nature relating to African American ancestry.

- African-American Genealogy Group (AAGG) ~ Philadelphia, Pennsylvania
  http://www.libertynet.org/aagg/

- African American Heritage Preservation Foundation, Inc.
  http://www.preservenet.cornell.edu/aahpf/homepage.htm
  Dedicated to the preservation of endangered and little known African American historical sites and its history. The foundation acts as a resource center for historical societies, community groups, preservation groups, African American groups, government entities and for individuals needing information pertaining to the preservation of African American historical sites and history.

- African Atlantic Genealogical Society ~ New York
  http://www.africantic.com
  A resource for people whose ancestors have had an African and/or Atlantic-crossing experience.

- African American Heritage Suite
  http://users.erols.com/trirose/index.html

- Afro-American Historical and Genealogical Society ~ Washington, D.C.
  http://www.rootsweb.com/~mdaahgs/

- Afro-American Historical and Genealogical Society - Jean Sampson Scott Greater New York Chapter
  http://www.aahgsny.org/

- California African-American Genealogical Society ~ Los Angeles, California
  http://lam.mus.ca.us/africa/america/caags/

- East Coast African American Genealogists
  http://www.eGroups.com/group/ecaagen/

- The Rhode Island Black Heritage Society
  http://www.providenceri.com/ri_blackheritage/

AMERICA ONLINE ~ AOL

The Genealogy Forum on America Online
http://www.cyndislist.com/aol.htm

Category Index:

◆ The Genealogy Forum on America Online
◆ Genealogy Forum Volunteers

◆ Miscellaneous Help for AOL Users

◆ The Genealogy Forum on America Online Keyword: ROOTS

● The Genealogy Forum on America Online: The Official User's Guide
http://members.aol.com/alonglines/book.html

● The Genealogy Forum on AOL
http://www.genealogyforum.com/
The official web site about this popular forum on America Online.

  ○ Genealogy Forum Home
  http://www.genealogyforum.com/gfaol/home.html

   ● Beginners Center
   http://www.genealogyforum.com/gfaol/beginners.html

   ● Chat Center
   http://www.genealogyforum.com/gfaol/chats.html

   ● File Libraries Center
   http://www.genealogyforum.com/gfaol/files.html

   ● Genealogy Forum News Archives
   http://www.genealogyforum.com/gfnews/gfnews.html

   ● Internet Center
   http://www.genealogyforum.com/gfaol/internet.html

   ● Message Center
   http://www.genealogyforum.com/gfaol/messages.html

   ● Resource Center
   http://www.genealogyforum.com/gfaol/resource.html

   ● Reunion Center
   http://www.genealogyforum.com/gfaol/reunions.html

   ● Surname Center
   http://www.genealogyforum.com/gfaol/surnames.html

   ● What's New!
   http://www.genealogyforum.com/gfaol/whatsnew.html

● Search The Genealogy Forum
http://members.aol.com/gflgeorge/mbsrch1.html

◆ Genealogy Forum Volunteers

● Genealogy Forum Host Pages
http://www.genealogyforum.com/gfnews/july99/hosts.htm
The official list on the Genealogy Forum web site.

  ○ GFSAngela: The African - Native Genealogy Homepage
  http://member.aol.com/angelaw859/index.html

  ○ GFSBrenda: Brenda Bova's Surname Page
  http://members.aol.com/gfsbrenda/index.html

  ○ GFSBubba: The Frank C. MOFFETT Genealogy Home Page
  http://moffett.freeyellow.com/./

  ○ GFSBud: RHOADES/RHODES/RHOADS Family Researchers
  http://members.AOL.com/BUDI/Rhoades.htm

  ○ GFSCarol: Welcome to My Site!
  http://members.aol.com/BACAZ/carol.htm

  ○ GFSDash: GFSDash's Home Page
  http://members.aol.com/GFSDash/index.html

  ○ GFSDiana: Ship Samuel
  http://member.aol.com/ShipSamuel/

  ○ GFSDrew: Drew Smith
  http://home.tampabay.rr.com/drewsmith/

  ○ GFSEagle: Home of the Eaglerangr
  http://www.geocities.com/Heartland/Prairie/2844/

  ○ GFSEddie: The ALBERT Family Tree
  http://AlbertTree.genealogy.org

  ○ GFSGordon: Gordon's Website
  http://members.aol.com/gandr22/index.htm

  ○ GFSHeather: LANE Descendants
  http://homepages.rootsweb.com/~bowers/lane/

  ○ GFS Jill:

   ● Ancestors of Stephen James CLARK
   http://members.aol.com/Jilliemae/txclark.htm

   ● Earra-Ghaidheal na Sìnnsirean (Argyll Ancestors)
   http://members.aol.com/gfsjill/argyll.htm

   ● East Lothian Ancestry
   http://members.aol.com/gfsjill/elothian.htm

   ● Great Lake State Origins
   http://members.aol.com/gfsjill/jmich.html

   ● SYERS Seeker's Nest
   http://members.aol.com/SyerSeeker/index.html

  ○ GFSJohn: Smoky Mountain Ancestral Quest
  http://www.smokykin.com/

o GFSJohnF: John Fuller's Home Page
http://www.rootsweb.com/~jfuller/index.html
Includes his joint project with Chris Gaunt, Genealogy Resources on the Internet and a section on Channel Islands Genealogy.

o GFSJolene: MOE Homepage
http://members.hometown.aol.com/GFSJolene/index.htm

o GFSKKate:
  • Effingham County, Illinois Genealogy - Illinois GenWeb
    http://www.rootsweb.com/~ileffing/
  • Jasper County, Illinois Genealogy - Illinois GenWeb
    http://www.rootsweb.com/~iljasper/

o GFSLadyJay: Julie's Place
http://members.aol.com/the6jays/JuliesPlace.html

o GFSGFSmiltB: Milt Botwinick Professional Genealogist
http://members.aol.com/botwinick/index.htm

o GFSMorgan: George G. Morgan - Genealogist, Author, Columnist and Speaker
http://members.aol.com/alonglines/index.html

o GFSNance:
  • Fishingene's Home Page
    http://members.aol.com/fishingene/index.html
  • Nance's Genealogy & History of NW Ohio
    http://www.geocities.com/Heartland/Pines/4091/index.html

o GFS Pilgrim: Amos & Mary Pilgrims' Family
http://members.aol.com/CKenter838/family.html

o GFSRip: Pam's Patchwork Place
http://members.aol.com/AAtwins94/index.htm

o GFSSam:
  • Notable Women Ancestors
    http://www.rootsweb.com/~nwa/
  • Sam's Genealogy
    http://homepages.rootsweb.com/~sam/

o GFSSearch & GFSLynnB: MARSHALL Genealogy Page
http://homepages.rootsweb.com/~marshall/gene.htm

o GFSSuzanne: Suzanne's French Canadian Genealogy Page
http://members.aol.com/genleves/english/index.html

o GFSTomS: Tom's Genealogy Web Site
http://members.aol.com/tomsluder/index.htm

o GFSVicki:
  • SHERMANs of Yaxley Family History Society
    http://member.aol.com/macpinhead/sherman.html
  • Vicki's Sampler Web Page
    http://member.aol.com/macpinhead/sampler.html

o GFSWaffle:
  • The HOCUTT Family of Celeste Texas
    http://www.angelfire.com/tx2/UncleHiram/index.html
  • Adventures in Genealogy
    http://www.angelfire.com/tx2/UncleHiram/UncleHiram.html

o GFSWillM:
  • Nicholas County WV USGenWeb
    http://www.rootsweb.com/~wvnichol/index.html
  • Appalachian Mountain Families
    http://members.xoom.com/Appalachian/

◆ Miscellaneous Help for AOL Users

• Amazon.com Genealogy Bookstore - America Online
http://www.amazon.com/exec/obidos/external-search/?keyword=america+online+genealogy&tag=markcyndisgenealA/
And AOL
http://www.amazon.com/exec/obidos/external-search/?keyword=aol+genealogy&tag=markcyndisgenealA/

• AOL Hometown
http://hometown.aol.com/
A directory of AOL user home pages.

• AOL Instant Messenger
http://www.aol.com/aim/home.html
A free "buddy list" program for non- AOL users.
  o AOL Instant Messenger Remote
    http://www.aol.com/aim/remote/home.adp
  o AOL Quick Buddy
    http://www.aol.com/aim/quickbuddy/about.html

• AOL NetHelp - Finding Help on AOL
http://www.aol.com/nethelp/findinghelponaol.html

• AOL Netmail
http://www.aol.com/aolmail/
Send and receive your AOL e-mail directly from the Web without using your AOL software.

ASIA & THE PACIFIC
http://www.cyndislist.com/asia.htm

Category Index:

- Angel Island - California
- General Resource Sites
- History & Culture
- Language
- Libraries, Archives & Museums
- Mailing Lists, Newsgroups & Chat
- Maps, Gazetteers & Geographical Information
- Military

- People & Families
- Publications, Software & Supplies
- Queries, Message Boards & Surname Lists
- Records: Census, Cemeteries, Land, Obituaries, Personal, Taxes and Vital
- Societies & Groups
- World GenWeb

◆ Angel Island - California

- **Angel Island - California's "Immigration Station"**
  http://www.fortunecity.com/littleitaly/amalfi/100/angel.htm
  A book published by The Women's American Baptist Home Missionary Society, Chicago, in 1917.

- **Angel Island: Immigrant Journeys of Chinese-Americans**
  http://www.angel-island.com/
  An oral history of Chinese immigrant detainees.

- **Angel Island Immigration Station**
  http://www.angelisland.org/immigr02.html
  The "Ellis Island of the West" in San Francisco is now a National Historic Landmark

- **The Angel Island Immigration Station Foundation**
  http://www.a-better.com/Angel/island.htm
  The Foundation's purpose is to preservation, renovation, and development efforts of Angel Island Immigration Station, a National Historic Landmark, as an interpretive site for Pacific Rim immigration.

- **Angel Island - The Pacific Gateway**
  http://www.immigrationstation.com/
  Angel Island Immigration Station, San Francisco Bay, 1910 to 1940.

- **HoustonChronicle.com - Angel Island: Journeys Remembered by Chinese Houstonians**
  http://www.chron.com/content/chronicle/special/angelisland/intro.html
  Interviews online.

- **Images From the History of the Public Health Service**
  http://www.nlm.nih.gov/exhibition/phs_history/contents.html
  o **Angel Island Arrivals**
    http://www.nlm.nih.gov/exhibition/phs_history/22.html
  o **Angel Island Disinfection of Clothing**
    http://www.nlm.nih.gov/exhibition/phs_history/23.html

  o **Angel Island Testing**
    http://www.nlm.nih.gov/exhibition/phs_history/24.html

- **A Panoramic View of the Angel Island Immigration Station - 1915**
  http://memory.loc.gov/cgi-bin/query/r?ammem/pan:@FIELD(SUBJ+@band(+Angel+Island++San+Francisco+Bay,+Calif.++))

- **Prologue: Angel Island: "Guardian of the Western Gate"**
  http://www.nara.gov/publications/prologue/angel1.html
  Online article from the NARA's Quarterly magazine "Prologue". A history of the Angel Island Immigration Station in San Francisco Bay.

- **San Francisco, California - Immigrant & Passenger Arrivals - Records of the Immigration and Naturalization Service**
  http://www.nara.gov/publications/microfilm/immigrant/rg85.html#sfr
  Lists of microfilm roll numbers from the National Archives and Records Administration.

◆ General Resource Sites

- **Asian Immigration to Maryland**
  http://www.clis.umd.edu/~mddlmddl/791/communities/html/index.html#asian
  A scholarly review of immigration into Maryland from the very first colonists to modern immigrants.

- **British Ancestors in India**
  http://www.ozemail.com.au/~clday/

- **CET -- Discover your ancestors: Asian American genealogy resources**
  http://www.cetel.org/discover.html

- **Chinese Calendar**
  http://www.new-year.co.uk/chinese/calendar.htm

- Chinese Genealogical Resources.
  http://fuzzo.com/genealogy/Asia/chinagen.htm

- Chineseroots.com
  http://www.chineseroots.com/

- Family Tree Maker's Genealogy Site: Chinese Research
  http://www.familytreemaker.com/00000364.html

- Family Tree Maker's Genealogy Site: Filipino Research
  http://www.familytreemaker.com/00000369.html

- Family Tree Maker's Genealogy Site: Japanese Research
  http://www.familytreemaker.com/00000376.html

- Family Tree Maker's Genealogy Site: Korean Research
  http://www.familytreemaker.com/00000377.html

- Family Tree Maker's Genealogy Site: Vietnamese Research
  http://www.familytreemaker.com/00000387.html

- Filipino Americans - Frequently Asked Questions
  http://personal.anderson.ucla.edu/eloisa.borah/filfaqs.htm

- Immigration: The Chinese
  http://library.thinkquest.org/20619/Chinese.html
  A brief history of Chinese immigration to the United States.

- Immigration: The Japanese
  http://library.thinkquest.org/20619/Japanese.html
  A brief history of Japanese immigration to the United States.

- Jamal's Yellow Pages of Pakistan
  http://www.jamals.com/

- Lareau Web Parlour
  http://www.lareau.org/

  - Lareau Web Parlour Genealogy Site
    http://www.lareau.org/geneal.html

  - Pitcairn Island Web Site
    http://www.lareau.org/pitc.html

- Nikkei Homepage
  http://www.kent.wednet.edu/KSD/SJ/Nikkei/Nikkei_home Page.html

- Family History SourceGuide - Research Outline - Philippines
  http://www.familysearch.org/sg/Philippines.html
  From the LDS' FamilySearch.org web site. This outline introduces records and strategies that can help you learn more about your Philippine ancestors. It explains terms associated with Philippine genealogy and describes the content, use, and availability of major genealogical records.

- Passages to India - Genealogy Resources In British India
  http://www.synflux.com.au/~sylcec/index.htm

Includes information on shipping history, extracted vital records from specific newspapers for specific years, and notes on the author's family.

- Pioneer Sikh Asian East Indian Immigration to the Pacific Coast from Punjab
  http://www.lib.ucdavis.edu/punjab/index.html
  Includes a chronology, historical photos, and a list of research specialists.

- Tanikalang Ginto - The Phillipines' Most Comprehensive Web Directory - Family
  http://www.filipinolinks.com/home/genealogy.html

- Western-Chinese Calendar Converter
  http://www.mandarintools.com/calconv.html

◆ History & Culture

- Chinese American History Timeline
  http://www.itp.berkeley.edu/~asam121/timeline.html

- Japanese Canadian Historical Timeline
  http://www.shinnova.com/part/86-jcma/jcma40-e.htm

- A Short Chronology of Japanese American History
  http://www.janet.org/janet_history/niiya_chron.html

- StudyWeb: History: Asian
  http://www.studyweb.com/History/tocasia.htm

- StudyWeb: History: Oceania
  http://www.studyweb.com/History/tococean.htm

- Tanikalang Ginto - The Phillipines' Most Comprehensive Web Directory - History
  http://www.filipinolinks.com/arts/kasaysayan.html

- Yahoo!...China...History
  http://dir.yahoo.com/Regional/Countries/China/Arts_and_Humanities/Humanities/History/

- Yahoo!...India...History
  http://dir.yahoo.com/Regional/Countries/India/Arts_and_Humanities/Humanities/History/

- Yahoo!...Indonesia...Humanities/History
  http://dir.yahoo.com/Regional/Countries/Indonesia/Arts_and_Humanities/Humanities/

- Yahoo!...Japan...History
  http://dir.yahoo.com/Regional/Countries/Japan/Arts_and_Humanities/Humanities/History/

- Yahoo!...Korea,South...Humanities/History
  http://dir.yahoo.com/Regional/Countries/Korea__South/Arts_and_Humanities/Humanities/

◆ Language

- Shodouka
  http://www.shodouka.com/
  Converts unreadable Japanese WWW pages into readable Japanese text. Simply paste the URL of the page you wish converted, hit the "go" button and it will redisplay the page in katakan, hiragana and kangi! You still have to translate the page to English. The page is by Mediator Technologies.

◆ Libraries, Archives & Museums

- ANU - Asian Studies: Online Chinese Libraries
  http://online.anu.edu.au/Asia/Chi/ChiLib.html

- Chinese Cultural Center of San Francisco Home Page
  http://www.c-c-c.org/

- Family History Library Catalog
  http://www.familysearch.org/Search/searchcatalog.asp
  From the FamilySearch web site, an online catalog to the holdings of the LDS Church in Salt Lake City, Utah. Also search for other localities by place name.
  http://www.familysearch.org/fhlc/supermainframeset.asp?display=localitysearch&columns=*,180,0

  o Afghanistan
    http://www.familysearch.org/fhlc/supermainframeset.asp?display=localitydetails&subject=204&subject_disp=Afghanistan&columns=*,180,0

  o American Samoa
    http://www.familysearch.org/fhlc/supermainframeset.asp?display=localitydetails&subject=423&subject_disp=American_Samoa&columns=*,180,0

  o Bangladesh
    http://www.familysearch.org/fhlc/supermainframeset.asp?display=localitydetails&subject=189&subject_disp=Bangladesh&columns=*,180,0

  o Bhutan
    http://www.familysearch.org/fhlc/supermainframeset.asp?display=localitydetails&subject=193&subject_disp=Bhutan&columns=*,180,0

  o Brunei
    http://www.familysearch.org/fhlc/supermainframeset.asp?display=localitydetails&subject=214&subject_disp=Brunei&columns=*,180,0

  o China
    http://www.familysearch.org/fhlc/supermainframeset.asp?display=localitydetails&subject=171&subject_disp=China&columns=*,180,0

    - China, Taiwan
      http://www.familysearch.org/fhlc/supermainframeset.asp?display=localitydetails&subject=165890&subject_disp=China,_Taiwan&columns=*,180,0

    - China, Tibet
      http://www.familysearch.org/fhlc/supermainframeset.asp?display=localitydetails&subject=165984&subject_disp=China,_Tibet&columns=*,180,0

  o Fiji
    http://www.familysearch.org/fhlc/supermainframeset.asp?display=localitydetails&subject=421&subject_disp=Fiji&columns=*,180,0

  o French Polynesia
    http://www.familysearch.org/fhlc/supermainframeset.asp?display=localitydetails&subject=430&subject_disp=French_Polynesia&columns=*,180,0

  o Guam
    http://www.familysearch.org/fhlc/supermainframeset.asp?display=localitydetails&subject=437&subject_disp=Guam&columns=*,180,0

  o India
    http://www.familysearch.org/fhlc/supermainframeset.asp?display=localitydetails&subject=187&subject_disp=India&columns=*,180,0

  o Indonesia
    http://www.familysearch.org/fhlc/supermainframeset.asp?display=localitydetails&subject=217&subject_disp=Indonesia&columns=*,180,0

  o Japan
    http://www.familysearch.org/fhlc/supermainframeset.asp?display=localitydetails&subject=177&subject_disp=Japan&columns=*,180,0

  o Kampuchea
    http://www.familysearch.org/fhlc/supermainframeset.asp?display=localitydetails&subject=215&subject_disp=Kampuchea&columns=*,180,0

  o Kazakstan
    http://www.familysearch.org/fhlc/supermainframeset.asp?display=localitydetails&subject=125&subject_disp=Kazakstan&columns=*,180,0

  o Kiribati
    http://www.familysearch.org/fhlc/supermainframeset.asp?display=localitydetails&subject=438&subject_disp=Kiribati&columns=*,180,0

  o Korea
    http://www.familysearch.org/fhlc/supermainframeset.asp?display=localitydetails&subject=176&subject_disp=Korea&columns=*,180,0

  o Kyrgyzstan
    http://www.familysearch.org/fhlc/supermainframeset.asp?display=localitydetails&subject=124&subject_disp=Kyrgyzstan&columns=*,180,0

  o Laos
    http://www.familysearch.org/fhlc/supermainframeset.asp?display=localitydetails&subject=208&subject_disp=Laos&columns=*,180,0

  o Malaysia
    http://www.familysearch.org/fhlc/supermainframeset.asp?display=localitydetails&subject=209&subject_disp=Malaysia&columns=*,180,0

  o Maldives (Republic)
    http://www.familysearch.org/fhlc/supermainframeset.asp?display=localitydetails&subject=191&subject_disp=Maldives_(Republic)&columns=*,180,0

  o Mariana Islands
    http://www.familysearch.org/fhlc/supermainframeset.asp?display=localitydetails&subject=436&subject_disp=Mariana_Islands&columns=*,180,0

  o Marshall Islands
    http://www.familysearch.org/fhlc/supermainframeset.asp?display=localitydetails&subject=440&subject_disp=Marshall_Islands&columns=*,180,0

  o Melanesia
    http://www.familysearch.org/fhlc/supermainframeset.asp?display=localitydetails&subject=410&subject_disp=Melanesia&columns=*,180,0

  o Micronesia
    http://www.familysearch.org/fhlc/supermainframeset.asp?display=localitydetails&subject=433&subject_disp=Micronesia&columns=*.180.0

o Mongolia
http://www.familysearch.org/fhlc/supermainframeset.asp?
display=localitydetails&subject=175&subject_disp=
Mongolia&columns=*,180,0

o Nauru
http://www.familysearch.org/fhlc/supermainframeset.asp?
display=localitydetails&subject=441&subject_disp=
Nauru&columns=*,180,0

o Nepal
http://www.familysearch.org/fhlc/supermainframeset.asp?
display=localitydetails&subject=192&subject_disp=
Nepal&columns=*,180,0

o New Caledonia
http://www.familysearch.org/fhlc/supermainframeset.asp?
display=localitydetails&subject=412&subject_disp=
New_Caledonia&columns=*,180,0

o Pakistan
http://www.familysearch.org/fhlc/supermainframeset.asp?
display=localitydetails&subject=188&subject_disp=
Pakistan&columns=*,180,0

o Palau
http://www.familysearch.org/fhlc/supermainframeset.asp?
display=localitydetails&subject=435&subject_disp=
Palau&columns=*,180,0

o Papua New Guinea
http://www.familysearch.org/fhlc/supermainframeset.asp?
display=localitydetails&subject=419&subject_disp=
Papua_New_Guinea&columns=*,180,0

o Philippines
http://www.familysearch.org/fhlc/supermainframeset.asp?
display=localitydetails&subject=218&subject_disp=
Philippines&columns=*,180,0

o Polynesia
http://www.familysearch.org/fhlc/supermainframeset.asp?
display=localitydetails&subject=420&subject_disp=
Polynesia&columns=*,180,0

o Singapore
http://www.familysearch.org/fhlc/supermainframeset.asp?
display=localitydetails&subject=211&subject_disp=
Singapore&columns=*,180,0

o Sri Lanka
http://www.familysearch.org/fhlc/supermainframeset.asp?
display=localitydetails&subject=190&subject_disp=
Sri_Lanka&columns=*,180,0

o Tajikistan
http://www.familysearch.org/fhlc/supermainframeset.asp?
display=localitydetails&subject=127&subject_disp=
Tajikistan&columns=*,180,0

o Thailand
http://www.familysearch.org/fhlc/supermainframeset.asp?
display=localitydetails&subject=207&subject_disp=
Thailand&columns=*,180,0

o Tonga
http://www.familysearch.org/fhlc/supermainframeset.asp?
display=localitydetails&subject=422&subject_disp=
Tonga&columns=*,180,0

o Turkmenistan
http://www.familysearch.org/fhlc/supermainframeset.asp?
display=localitydetails&subject=126&subject_disp=
Turkmenistan&columns=*,180,0

o Tuvalu
http://www.familysearch.org/fhlc/supermainframeset.asp?
display=localitydetails&subject=439&subject_disp=
Tuvalu&columns=*,180,0

o Uzbekistan
http://www.familysearch.org/fhlc/supermainframeset.asp?
display=localitydetails&subject=128&subject_disp=
Uzbekistan&columns=*,180,0

o Vanuatu
http://www.familysearch.org/fhlc/supermainframeset.asp?
display=localitydetails&subject=416&subject_disp=
Vanuatu&columns=*,180,0

o Vietnam
http://www.familysearch.org/fhlc/supermainframeset.asp?
display=localitydetails&subject=216&subject_disp=
Vietnam&columns=*,180,0

o Western Samoa
http://www.familysearch.org/fhlc/supermainframeset.asp?
display=localitydetails&subject=424&subject_disp=
Western_Samoa&columns=*,180,0

- Hong Kong Saints Web site - Hong Kong Family History Center
http://www.mosiah.net/hkfhc/

- Hong Kong Special Administrative Region Public Record Office
http://www.info.gov.hk/pro/

- Museum of Chinese American History in Los Angeles
http://www.mcah.org/

- The National Archives ~ Japan
http://www.sorifu.go.jp/english/e1-10.html

- National Archives of Malaysia
http://arkib.gov.my/

- National Archives of Singapore
http://www.museum.org.sg/nas/nas.html

- Repositories of Primary Sources - Asia & the Pacific
http://www.uidaho.edu/special-collections/asia.html
A list of links to online resources from the Univ. of Idaho Library, Special Collections and Archives.

◆ Mailing Lists, Newsgroups & Chat

- ARMENIA Mailing List
http://www.rootsweb.com/~jfuller/gen_mail_country-arm.html#ARMENIA

- CHINA Mailing List
http://www.rootsweb.com/~jfuller/gen_mail_country-chi.html#CHINA

- INDIA Mailing List
http://www.rootsweb.com/~jfuller/gen_mail_country-ind.html#INDIA1
For anyone who is interested in tracing their British and European Ancestors in British India.

- KOREA Mailing List
  http://www.rootsweb.com/~jfuller/gen_mail_country-
  kor.html#KOREA
  For anyone with genealogical interest in Korea.

- NEPAL Mailing List
  http://www.rootsweb.com/~jfuller/gen_mail_country-nep.html
  For anyone with a genealogical interest in Nepal.

- Pacific_Islands Mailing List
  http://www.rootsweb.com/~jfuller/gen_mail_country-
  gen.html#Pacific_Islands
  And the associated web page.
  http://www.rootsweb.com/~nzlwgw/pacific.html
  *For the discussion and collaboration on genealogy and family
  history of indigenous peoples from the Pacific.*

- PAPUA-NEW GUINEA Mailing List
  http://www.rootsweb.com/~jfuller/gen_mail_country-pap.html
  *For anyone with a genealogical interest in Papua New Guinea, and
  the surrounding islands including New Britain (capital city Rabaul)
  and the Solomon Islands.*

- PHILIPPINES Mailing List
  http://www.rootsweb.com/~jfuller/gen_mail_country-phi.html
  *For anyone with a genealogical interest in the Philippines and
  people of Filipino descent around the world.*

- SRILANKA Mailing List
  http://www.rootsweb.com/~jfuller/gen_mail_country-
  sri.html#SRILANKA

◆ Maps, Gazetteers & Geographical Information

- Family History SourceGuide: Map of the Philippines
  http://www.familysearch.org/sg/MPhilippines.html

- Historical Maps of Australia and the Pacific - The
  Perry-Castañeda Library Map Collection
  http://www.lib.utexas.edu:80/Libs/PCL/Map_collection/
  historical/history_austral_pacific.html
  From the University of Texas at Austin.

- India-L Maps & Archives
  http://homepages.rootsweb.com/~poyntz/India/India-La.html

- Map of Palau
  http://www.lib.utexas.edu/Libs/PCL/Map_collection/islands_
  oceans_poles/Palau.jpg
  From the Perry-Castañeda Library at the Univ. of Texas at Austin.

- Maps of Asia - The Perry-Castañeda Library Map
  Collection
  http://www.lib.utexas.edu:80/Libs/PCL/Map_collection/
  asia.html
  From the University of Texas at Austin.

- Maps of Australia and the Pacific - The Perry-
  Castañeda Library Map Collection
  http://www.lib.utexas.edu:80/Libs/PCL/Map_collection/
  australia.html
  From the University of Texas at Austin.

◆ Military

- Civilian Internees of the Japanese in Singapore
  during WWII
  http://user.itl.net/~glen/CivilianInternees.html
  As well as messages regarding that site.
  http://user.itl.net/~glen/CivilianInternees2.html
  From Alex Glendinning's Asian Pages.

- Commonwealth War Graves Commission
  http://www.cwgc.org/
  *They can provide invaluable information to genealogists on the
  location, condition, and other information regarding the
  Commonwealth soldiers' graves in their care. Please include
  International Reply Coupons when writing to them from outside
  Britain.*

- Soldiers Whom the World Have Forgotten
  http://www.geocities.com/Athens/Acropolis/9460/index.html
  *Dedicated to the memory of soldiers & their families who died in
  and around Bangalore, India.*

◆ People & Families

- Ancestors from the former Dutch East Indies
  http://ourworld.compuserve.com/homepages/paulvanV/
  eastindi.htm

- The British in Singapore and Malaya
  http://user.itl.net/~glen/BritishinSingapore%26Malaya.html

- Cambodian Royal Family Tree
  http://www.cambodia.org/facts/kroygene.gif

- Chinese Genealogy: The SING (SIM, SIMS) Family
  http://www.geocities.com/Athens/Styx/7255/tree.html

- ChouOnline 1997
  http://www.idis.com/ChouOnline/
  *Sponsored by The Chou Clansmen Association of America. Covers
  various clan names including: Chow, Chang, Lum, Ching, Goo,
  Woo, Ing, Sun, Chiang, Ho, Kee, Kwock, Lau, Loui, Mao, Wong,
  Yap, Lai, and Choy. Also: Dang, Young, Chock, and Tom.*

- Clanning Around
  http://www.ceres.dti.ne.jp/~pyms/index.htm
  *Mostly genealogy of my family in Ireland, Australia, Japan, New
  Zealand and America*

- The CLAVERIA Heritage
  http://members.tripod.com/~buhiclaveria
  *The geneaological research web-site of the CLAVERIA Family of
  Buhi, Camarines Sur, Philippines.*

- Dutch East-Indies Informationpoint
  http://home.wxs.nl/~vdbroeke/
  *A "guide" for everybody who is interested in Eurasian culture in the
  Netherlands.*

- Family History in India
  http://www.ozemail.com.au/~clday/
  *For British, European and Anglo-Indian family history in India,
  Burma, Pakistan and Bangladesh.*

  o Church Records in Colonial India
    http://www.ozemail.com.au/~clday/churches.htm

o European Cemeteries in India
http://www.ozemail.com.au/~clday/cem.htm

- Burials in Sirajganj, Bangladesh
http://www.ozemail.com.au/~clday/sirajganj.htm

- Register of Burials Cinnamara, Assam
http://www.ozemail.com.au/~clday/assam.htm

o Names of Europeans in Colonial India
http://www.ozemail.com.au/~clday/misc.htm
Links to over 20,000 names.

o Occupations in Colonial India
http://www.ozemail.com.au/~clday/occupations.htm

- Jute in India
http://www.ozemail.com.au/~clday/jute.htm

- Genealogical Gleanings - Royal & Noble Lineages of Tonga, Fiji, Hawaii, Burma and Cambodia
http://www.uq.net.au/~zzhsoszy/index.html

- Hakka Chinese Homepage
http://www.asiawind.com/hakka/

- The Imperial Family of Japan
http://www.geocities.com/Tokyo/Temple/3953/
Biographies and information for the emperors and their families since 1850.

- The LEE Family
http://members.xoom.com/wunble/
The LEE Clan from Taishan originated from Nan Hung via Wunbo.

- OGASAWARA Clan Genealogy
http://members.aol.com/uchuujin/oga.html
Genealogical information of the descendants of OGASAWARA Jiro Nagakiyo (b.1163-d.1242) who descended from the 56th Japanese emperor, Emperor Seiwa (b.849-d.880).

- PANICKER Family History, Kerala, India
http://web2.airmail.net/panicker/
Based on The Panicker Kudumba Charithram Handbook.

- The POYNTZ Family in India
http://www.hal-pc.org/~poyntz/india.html
Selected Extracts from the India Presidencies of Bengal, Bombay and Madras Ecclesiastical Returns of Baptisms, Marriages and Burials 1713-1948.

- Siamese Royalty
http://www.geocities.com/three-b.geo/
Profiles of members of the Thai Royal Family, past and present.

- Stuart TERASHITA's Japanese-American Genealogy Home Page
http://www.geocities.com/SiliconValley/Garage/4464/Home.html
Includes helpful "how-to" information on Japanese genealogical research.

- THIEN Genealogy Home Page
http://www.geocities.com/Tokyo/3998/index.html
The genealogy of Francis THIEN Chung Kong, a Malaysian Chinese Hakka. DENG. TENG. TANG. THIEN. THEAN. THIAN.

- VERGARA Family of the Philippines
http://www.geocities.com/Heartland/Farm/1821/
A collection of not yet connected VERGARA branches in the Philippines, some of whom have immigrated to different countries. It also includes CARASIG, AGUSTIN, MAG-ISA, CRUZ, etc.

◆ Publications, Software & Supplies

- Amazon.com Genealogy Bookstore - Asian
http://www.amazon.com/exec/obidos/external-search/?keyword=asian+genealogy&tag=markcyndisgenealA/

- Ancestor's Attic Discount Genealogy Books - Asian Genealogy Books
http://members.tripod.com/~ancestorsattic/index.html#secAS

- AudioTapes.com - Genealogical Lectures on Cassette Tapes – Chinese
http://www.audiotapes.com/search2.asp?Search=chinese
And Japan
http://www.audiotapes.com/search2.asp?Search=japan

- Books We Own
http://www.rootsweb.com/~bwo/
Find a book from which you would like a lookup and click on the submitter's code at the end of the entry. Once you find the contact information for the submitter, write them a polite request for a lookup.

o India
http://www.rootsweb.com/~bwo/india.html

o Oceania
http://www.rootsweb.com/~bwo/oceania.html

- The Indiaman Magazine
http://www.indiaman.freeserve.co.uk/index.html
Genealogical magazine dedicated to people researching their ancestry of British and European origin in India and southern Asia from 1600 to the 20th century.

◆ Queries, Message Boards & Surname Lists

- Chinese Surnames
http://www.geocities.com/Tokyo/3919/

- Chinese Surname Queries
http://www.ziplink.net/~rey/ch/queries/

- Hikada Family Emblems
http://www.st.rim.or.jp/%7Ezhidaka/index.html
A company which sells Japanese family emblems historically associated with Japanese surnames.

- Hindu Names
http://www.rajiv.org/iu/hindunam.txt

- Indian Last Names
http://www.nssl.noaa.gov/~lakshman/Desh/nms.html

◆ Records: Census, Cemeteries, Land, Obituaries, Personal, Taxes and Vital (Born, Married, Died & Buried)

- India Office Records: Sources for Family History Research
  http://www.bl.uk/collections/oriental/records/iorfamhi.html
  The British Library Oriental and India Office Collections (OIOC).

- Burials in Sirajganj, Bangladesh
  http://www.ozemail.com.au/~clday/sirajganj.htm

- The Cochin Churchbook
  http://www.telebyte.nl/~dessa/cochin.htm
  Baptism & marriages from the Dutch Church in Cochin, India (1754-1804).

- English East India Company Ships
  http://www.ships.clara.net/
  Includes shipping Losses in the Mercantile Service 1600-1834 (includes Shipwrecks, Captures & Missing Vessels).

- Hong Kong Births and Deaths Registries
  http://www.info.gov.hk/immd/english/topical/g/6.htm
  From the Hong Kong Immigration Department. Includes contact information and hours of operation.

- Hong Kong Marriage Registries
  http://www.info.gov.hk/immd/english/topical/g/7.htm
  From the Hong Kong Immigration Department. Includes contact information and hours of operation.

- Register of Burials Cinnamara, Assam
  http://www.ozemail.com.au/~clday/assam.htm

- Research Guide - Chinese Immigrants and Chinese-Australians in New South Wales
  http://www.naa.gov.au/PUBLICAT/GUIDES/chinese/guide.htm
  From the National Archives of Australia.

- Research Guide - Papua New Guinea Records 1883-1942
  http://www.naa.gov.au/PUBLICAT/GUIDES/png/guide.htm
  From the National Archives of Australia.

- Le recensement anglais de Pondichéry en 1796
  http://www.pondichery.com/1796/
  English Pondicherry census in 1796 and deportation of French citizens from Pondicherry by the British in 1799.

- Singapore Birth Extract Application
  http://www.sir.gov.sg/citizen_sc/birthextract-01.html
  From Singapore Immigration & Registration. Online application available.

- Singapore Death Extract Application
  http://www.sir.gov.sg/citizen_sc/deathextract-01.html
  From Singapore Immigration & Registration. Online application available.

- U.S. Immigration and Naturalization Service - Chinese Immigrant Files
  http://www.ins.usdoj.gov/graphics/aboutins/history/CHINESE.html

◆ Societies & Groups

- Association to Commemorate the Chinese Serving in the American Civil War
  http://hometown.aol.com/gordonkwok/accsacw.html

- The British Ancestors in India Society
  http://www.indiaman.freeserve.co.uk/bais.html
  Founded to help family history researchers to trace their ancestors of British and European origin in India and Southern Asia.

- Chinese Historical Society of America
  http://www.chsa.org/

- Chinese Historical Society of Southern California
  http://www.chssc.org/

- The Families in British India Society
  http://www.Links.org/FIBIS/
  For people researching families and their social history in India from 1600 until the present day. Includes any area covered by the East India Company or was ruled by the India Department: the Republic of India, Pakistan, Bangladesh, Burma, Persia and the Persian Gulf, Afghanistan, the Philippines, Malaya, etc.

- Indian Military Historical Society ~ England
  http://www.ozemail.com.au/~clday/imhs.htm

- Indische Genealogische Vereniging [Dutch Indies Genealogical Association]
  http://www.igv.nl/

- The Japanese Canadian National Museum & Archives Society ~ Vancouver, British Columbia, Canada
  http://www.multinova.com/jcnmas/
  Established to collect, preserve, study, exhibit, and interpret historical artifacts and archival material covering the history of Japanese Canadian Society from the 1870's through World War II to the present day.

- Korean American Historical Society (KAHS)
  http://www.kahs.org/

- National Japanese American Historical Society
  http://www.nikkeiheritage.org/

- Sosen of Sasebo - The Sasebo Chapter, NSDAR
  http://www.geocities.com/Heartland/Plains/1789/
  National Daughters of the American Revolution, Sasebo, Japan.

◆ World GenWeb

- Asia GenWeb
  http://www.rootsweb.com/~asiagw/

- PacificGenWeb Project
  http://www.rootsweb.com/~pacifgw/
  Genealogy from the Pacific & Oceania.

AUSTRALIA & NEW ZEALAND

http://www.cyndislist.com/austnz.htm

Category Index:

- ◆ General Resource Sites
- ◆ Government & Cities
- ◆ History & Culture
- ◆ How To
- ◆ Libraries, Archives & Museums
- ◆ Mailing Lists, Newsgroups & Chat
- ◆ Maps, Gazetteers & Geographical Information
- ◆ Military
- ◆ Newspapers
- ◆ People & Families

- ◆ Professional Researchers, Volunteers & Other Research Services
- ◆ Publications, Software & Supplies
- ◆ Queries, Message Boards & Surname Lists
- ◆ Records: Census, Cemeteries, Land, Obituaries, Personal, Taxes and Vital
- ◆ Ships: Convict Lists, Passenger Lists, Etc.
- ◆ Societies & Groups
- ◆ World GenWeb

◆ General Resource Sites

- Aboriginal and Torres Strait Islander Genealogy in Queensland
  http://rosella.apana.org.au/~jgk/aborigene/menu.html
  This site is being developed to encourage those with Aboriginal and Torres Strait Islander ancestry to research their family history, based on contemporaneous documentation and the scientific method, rather than family stories and populist history.

- AGWeb - The Australasian Genealogy Web
  http://home.vicnet.net.au/~AGWeb/agweb.htm

- AustraliaGenWeb
  http://www.rootsweb.com/~auswgw/

- Australian Family History Compendium
  http://www.cohsoft.com.au/afhc/
  - o Genealogy Addresses for the Australian Capital Territory
    http://www.cohsoft.com.au/afhc/act.html
  - o Genealogy Addresses for the State of New South Wales
    http://www.cohsoft.com.au/afhc/nsw.html
  - o Genealogy Addresses for Northern Territory
    http://www.cohsoft.com.au/afhc/nt.html
  - o Genealogy Addresses for the State of Queensland
    http://www.cohsoft.com.au/afhc/qld.html
  - o Genealogy Addresses for the State of South Australia
    http://www.cohsoft.com.au/afhc/sa.html
  - o Genealogy Addresses for the State of Tasmania
    http://www.cohsoft.com.au/afhc/tas.html
  - o Genealogy Addresses for the State of Victoria
    http://www.cohsoft.com.au/afhc/vic.html

- o Genealogy Addresses for the State of Western Australia
  http://www.cohsoft.com.au/afhc/wa.html

- Australian Institute of Genealogical Studies Inc.
  http://www.alphalink.com.au/~aigs/

- BROWNE Tasmanian Genealogy
  http://www.vision.net.au/~jbrowne/
  Convicts, family files, cemetery records, Tasmanian Webring, Tasmanian Forum.

- The Central Register of Indexing Projects in Australia
  http://www.judywebster.gil.com.au/register.html

- David Scott's List of Australian (and NZ) Ged2html Sites
  http://www1.tpgi.com.au/users/dscott/aust_gen.htm

- Emigration Guide ~ Australia
  http://www.standard.net.au/%7ejwilliams/migrate.htm

- Family History Events - Australian Family History Compendium
  http://www.cohsoft.com.au/afhc/announce.html

- Genealogy in Australia
  http://www.pcug.org.au/~mpahlow/welcome.html

- Genealogy in Australia
  http://www2.hunterlink.net.au/~ddrge/genealogy/contents.html
  Bobs Internet Guide to Genealogy in Australia. Terminology, Resources and Descendant lists for ELDRIDGE, GEARY, MEEHAN with more coming.

- Genealogy from Gerringong
  http://www.ozemail.com.au/~johngrah/
  Information for Illawarra area of New South Wales, especially for

the town of Gerringong and its surrounds. Also for the Westernport Settlement of 1826-28 in what is now the state of Victoria. Also the VIDLER surname.

- The Genealogy Resource Page of the Hunter Valley
  http://www.iniaccess.net.au/~patmay/

- Genealogy Sources for Native Australians
  http://www.standard.net.au/~jwilliams/native.htm

- Gum Tree Genealogy Ring
  http://members.tripod.com/~Jules_in_oz/gumtree/

- Judy WEBSTER's Genealogy Info-Page ~ Australia
  http://www.judywebster.gil.com.au/index.html
  Several helpful articles online.

- KiwiGen Web Ring
  http://www.directenergy.com.au/FamilyTrees/KiwiGen/

- Moggill Local History
  http://192.148.225.23/bruce/mogg.html
  ANSTEAD, BIRD, BOYLE, CURRIE, BAINBRIDGE, CAMPBELL, DOYLE, FINLAY, HALLETT, LATHER, MAKEPEACE, OWENS, SEXTON, SHIELD, SUGARS, TWINE and WESTCOTT Families.

- New Zealand Genealogy Search Engine
  http://downtown.co.nz/genealogy/
  Search all the on-line New Zealand passenger lists, family trees, surname interest and other genealogical resource pages.

- New ZealandGenWeb
  http://www.rootsweb.com/~nzlwgw/

- New Zealand White Pages
  http://www.whitepages.co.nz/

- South Australian Family History & Genealogy
  http://www.adelaide.net.au/~bazle/

- Southern Cross Genealogy
  http://www.southernx.com.au/
  Australia's national ISP for Genealogists and Historians.

- Tasmanian Family History Services
  http://www.vision.net.au/~tashistory
  On-line book shop, notice board, church photographs, links, Tasmanian families, immigration, research information and convicts.

- Tasmanian Genealogy Webring
  http://www.vision.net.au/~jbrowne/newpage1.htm

- Telecom New Zealand White Pages
  http://www.whitepages.co.nz/

- Telstra - Australian White & Yellow Pages
  http://www.telstra.com.au/

- White Pages Phone Directory for Australia
  http://www.whitepages.com.au/

- Yahoo!...Australia...Genealogy
  http://dir.yahoo.com/Regional/Countries/Australia/Arts_and_Humanities/Humanities/History/Genealogy/

- Yahoo!...New Zealand...Genealogy
  http://dir.yahoo.com/Regional/Countries/Australia/Arts_and_Humanities/Humanities/History/Genealogy/

◆ Government & Cities

- Australian Commonwealth Government
  http://www.fed.gov.au/

- Parliament of New South Wales
  http://www.parliament.nsw.gov.au/

◆ History & Culture

- Going Abroad
  http://www.actrix.gen.nz/users/ngaiopress/
  Web companion to John MacGibbon's book of the same name, which looks at the motivations and pioneer experiences of early Scots settlers in New Zealand. Also takes a detailed look at the 1840s Glasgow conditions the emigrants escaped from, and the nature of the voyage to NZ.

- GOLD 150 - Celebrating 150 Years of Australian Gold-Rush History
  http://www.ballarat.edu.au/sovhill/gold150//sovhill.htm

- Milton Ulladulla History Site
  http://www.shoalhaven.net.au/~cathyd/

- The New Zealand Historic Places Trust
  http://www.historic.org.nz/

- Strahan, Sarah Island Convict Site, South West Tasmania
  http://www.ozemail.com.au/~kemoon/Strahan.html

- StudyWeb: History: Country History Index: Australia/Oceania Index: Australia
  http://www.studyweb.com/links/804.html

- StudyWeb: History: Country History Index: Australia/Oceania Index: New Zealand
  http://www.studyweb.com/links/805.html

◆ How To

- Australian Genealogy How To Guide
  http://www.familytreemaker.com/00000362.html
  From Family Tree Maker.

- Research Tips for Queensland
  http://www.judywebster.gil.com.au/tips-qld.html

◆ Libraries, Archives & Museums

- Anglican Church of Australia - Diocese of Brisbane Archives
  http://www.anglicanbrisbane.gil.com.au/archives.htm
  The archives holds the records of the Episcopal Office, Registry Office, Accounts Department, Schools Commission, Anglicare; Records of Parishes, Schools, Colleges and Institutions (including Minutes, registers, correspondence, accounting books, plans, photographs, glass slides, Church papers, histories and private clergy papers).

- Archives Office of Tasmania
  http://www.tased.edu.au/archives/

  o Reference Services
    http://www.tased.edu.au/archives/1refsrvs.htm

o Resources for Genealogical Research
http://www.tased.edu.au/archives/1genrcds.html

o Tasmanian Family Link
http://pioneers.tased.edu.au/
A database made up of records of births, deaths, and marriages, as well as other events, that is designed to connect families with ancestors who lived in Tasmania in the 19th century.

- Auckland City Libraries ~ New Zealand
http://akcity.govt.nz/library/

  o Family History
  http://akcity.govt.nz/library/family/family.html

- The Australian National University: Noel Butlin Archives Centre
http://anulib.anu.edu.au/nbac/
Collection of primary source material relating to business and labour. The NBAC holds archives of industrial organisations, businesses, professional associations, industry bodies and the labour movement.

- Australia - New Zealand Family History Centers
http://www.familysearch.org/sg/Australia_and_NZ_FHC.html

- Australia Family History Centers
http://www.genhomepage.com/FHC/Australia.html
A list of addresses, phone numbers and hours of operation from the Genealogy Home Page.

- Australian Capital Territory & National Institution Libraries
http://sunsite.anu.edu.au/search/lib/

- Australian Libraries Gateway (ALG)
http://www.nla.gov.au/libraries/

- Canterbury Public Library ~ New Zealand.
http://www.ccc.govt.nz/library/

- Directory of Archives in Australia - Australian Society of Archivists
http://www.asap.unimelb.edu.au/asa/directory/asa_dir.htm

- Family History Library Catalog
http://www.familysearch.org/Search/searchcatalog.asp
From the FamilySearch web site, an online catalog to the holdings of the LDS Church in Salt Lake City, Utah. Also search for other localities by place name.
http://www.familysearch.org/fhlc/supermainframeset.asp?display=localitysearch&columns=*,180,0

  o Australia
  http://www.familysearch.org/fhlc/supermainframeset.asp?display=localitydetails&subject=418&subject_disp=Australia&columns=*,180,0

    - Australia, Australian Capital Territory
    http://www.familysearch.org/fhlc/supermainframeset.asp?display=localitydetails&subject=216889&subject_disp=Australia,_Australian_Capital_Territory&columns=*,180,0

    - Australia, New South Wales
    http://www.familysearch.org/fhlc/supermainframeset.asp?display=localitydetails&subject=216898&subject_disp=Australia,_New_South_Wales&columns=*,18 0,0

    - Australia, Norfolk Island
    http://www.familysearch.org/fhlc/supermainframeset.asp?display=localitydetails&subject=217675&subject_disp=Australia,_Norfolk_Island&columns=*,180 ,0

    - Australia, Northern Territory
    http://www.familysearch.org/fhlc/supermainframeset.asp?display=localitydetails&subject=217676&subject_disp=Australia,_Northern_Territory&columns=* ,180,0

    - Australia, South Australia
    http://www.familysearch.org/fhlc/supermainframeset.asp?display=localitydetails&subject=219091&subject_disp=Australia,_South_Australia&columns=*,18 0,0

    - Australia, Queensland
    http://www.familysearch.org/fhlc/supermainframeset.asp?display=localitydetails&subject=217687&subject_disp=Australia,_Queensland&columns=*,180,0

    - Australia, Tasmania
    http://www.familysearch.org/fhlc/supermainframeset.asp?display=localitydetails&subject=219316&subject_disp=Australia,_Tasmania&columns=*,180,0

    - Australia, Victoria
    http://www.familysearch.org/fhlc/supermainframeset.asp?display=localitydetails&subject=219510&subject_disp=Australia,_Victoria&columns=*,180,0

    - Australia, Western Australia
    http://www.familysearch.org/fhlc/supermainframeset.asp?display=localitydetails&subject=219856&subject_disp=Australia,_Western_Australia&columns=*, 180,0

  o New Zealand
  http://www.familysearch.org/fhlc/supermainframeset.asp?display=localitydetails&subject=411&subject_disp=New_Zealand&columns=*,180,0

- Family History SourceGuide - Family History Centers - Australia and New Zealand
http://www.familysearch.org/sg/Australia_and_NZ_FHC.html

- Geelong Historical Records Centre
http://www.zades.com.au/geelong/ghrc.html

- Genealogy Library: Flinders University
http://pcm.pcmedia.com.au/tags/docs/flinders.html

- Hamilton History Centre, Inc. ~ Australia
http://www.freenet.com.au/hamilton/HamHisCentre/default.htm
Genealogy and local history research library in the Western District of Victoria.

- Hamilton Public Libraries ~ New Zealand
http://www.hpl.govt.nz/

- High Country Heritage Centre - Information and Research
http://www4.tpgi.com.au/users/omeo/page2.html
Voluntary research service, genealogy and history with a genealogy data base of over 20,000 entries.

- LISWA's Window on the World of Information
http://www.liswa.wa.gov.au/
The Library and Information Service of Western Australia

  o Western Australian Collections
  http://web.liswa.wa.gov.au/westaust.html

- o Western Australian Family History
  http://web.liswa.wa.gov.au/wageneo.html
- o Western Australian Government Records
  http://web.liswa.wa.gov.au/wagovtrec.html
- o Western Australian Maps and Plans
  http://web.liswa.wa.gov.au/wamaps.html
- o Western Australian Newspapers
  http://web.liswa.wa.gov.au/wanews.html
- o Western Australian Oral History
  http://web.liswa.wa.gov.au/waoralhist.html
- o Western Australian Private Archives
  http://web.liswa.wa.gov.au/waprivarch.html

- • Maryborough Family Heritage Institute Inc.
  http://www.satcom.net.au/mfhi/
  Situated in Wharf Street Precinct, the Maryborough Family Heritage Institute is one of the largest research facilities in Queensland. Records on the heritage, history and genealogy are complemented by locally compiled books and a souvenir range.

- • National Archives of Australia
  http://www.naa.gov.au/index.htm
  - o Fact Sheets Subject Index
    http://www.naa.gov.au/research/factshet/factshet.htm#gene
    See the Genealogy section on this page.
    http://www.naa.gov.au/research/factshet/factshet.htm#gene
  - o Finding Families - The Guide to the National Archives of Australia for Genealogists
    http://www.naa.gov.au/PUBLICAT/GUIDES/HTML/family.htm
    A book for sale.
  - o Services to Researchers
    http://www.naa.gov.au/research/index.htm
    - • Getting Started
      http://www.naa.gov.au/research/start/start.htm

- • National Archives of New Zealand / Te Whare Tohu Tuhituhinga O Aotearoa
  http://www.archives.govt.nz/index.html
  - o National Archives of New Zealand: Holdings: Immigration & Shipping Lists
    http://www.archives.govt.nz/holdings/immigration.html

- • National Library of Australia
  http://www.nla.gov.au/

- • National Library of New Zealand
  http://www.natlib.govt.nz/

- • The New South Wales Parliamentary Archives
  http://www.parliament.nsw.gov.au/gi/archives/default.html

- • North Shore Libraries ~ New Zealand
  http://pollux.dslak.co.nz:8001/nsl/nsl.htm

- • Northern Territory Library
  http://www.ntlib.nt.gov.au/

- • Queensland Government State Archives
  http://www.archives.qld.gov.au/welcome.html

- • Repositories of Primary Sources - Asia & the Pacific - Australia
  http://www.uidaho.edu/special-collections/asia.html#au
  A list of links to online resources from the Univ. of Idaho Library, Special Collections and Archives.

- • Repositories of Primary Sources - Asia & the Pacific - New Zealand
  http://www.uidaho.edu/special-collections/asia.html#nz
  A list of links to online resources from the Univ. of Idaho Library, Special Collections and Archives.

- • State Library of New South Wales
  http://www.slnsw.gov.au/
  - o Family History Service
    http://www.slnsw.gov.au/grl/family/family.htm
  - o Mitchell and Dixson Libraries -Australian Research Collections
    http://www.slnsw.gov.au/ml/mitchell.htm

- • State Library of Queensland
  http://www.slq.qld.gov.au/
  - o Family History Information & Research Service
    http://www.slq.qld.gov.au/scd/famhist/index.htm
  - o John Oxley Library of Queensland History
    http://www.slq.qld.gov.au/jol/index.htm
  - o Maps Information & Research Service
    http://www.slq.qld.gov.au/scd/maps/index.htm

- • State Library of South Australia
  http://www.slsa.sa.gov.au/
  - o Family History Source Sheets
    http://www.slsa.sa.gov.au/lib_guide/fh/fh.htm

- • State Library of Tasmania Home Page
  http://www.tased.edu.au/library/
  - o Heritage Collections
    http://www.tased.edu.au/library/heritage/

- • State Library of Victoria
  http://www.slv.vic.gov.au/
  - o Australiana Collections
    http://www.slv.vic.gov.au/slv/latrobe/
  - o Genealogy and Family History Homepage
    http://www.slv.vic.gov.au/slv/genealogy/
  - o Map Collection - An Introduction
    http://www.slv.vic.gov.au/slv/maps/
  - o Newspaper Collection
    http://www.slv.vic.gov.au/slv/newspapers/

- • State Records New South Wales
  http://www.records.nsw.gov.au/

- • Sydney City Council Archives
  http://www.naa.gov.au/research/fedguide/making/nsw/nsw35%2B.htm

- • Ulverstone Local History Museum ~ Tasmania
  http://www.tassie.net.au/~cbroadfi/LocalHistoryMuseum.htm

- The University of New England and Regional
  Archives ~ Armidale
  http://www.une.edu.au/archives/

- The University of Queensland Library
  http://www.library.uq.edu.au/

- University of Sydney Archives
  http://www.usyd.edu.au/su/archives/

◆ Mailing Lists, Newsgroups & Chat

- Genealogy Resources on the Internet - Australia
  Mailing Lists
  http://www.rootsweb.com/~jfuller/gen_mail_country-aus.html
  *Most of the mailing list links below point to this site, wonderfully
  maintained by John Fuller*

- Genealogy Resources on the Internet - New Zealand
  Mailing Lists
  http://www.rootsweb.com/~jfuller/gen_mail_country-nez.html
  *Most of the mailing list links below point to this site, wonderfully
  maintained by John Fuller*

- ARIA Mailing List
  http://www.rootsweb.com/~jfuller/gen_mail_country-aus.html#ARIA-L
  *For Australians and New Zealanders who are researching their
  Italian Heritage, Culture and Ancestry.*

- AUS-NQ Mailing List
  http://www.rootsweb.com/~jfuller/gen_mail_country-aus.html#AUS-NQ
  *For anyone with genealogical or historical interests in North
  Queensland, north from the Tropic of Capricorn to Cape York and
  west to the Northern Territory border.*

- AUS-NSW-Hunter-Valley Mailing List
  http://www.rootsweb.com/~jfuller/gen_mail_country-aus.html#AUS-NSW-Hunter-Valley
  *For anyone with a genealogical interest in Hunter Valley, New
  South Wales, which encompasses the cities of Newcastle, Maitland,
  Cessnock, and Singleton.*

- AUS-NSW-SE Mailing List
  http://www.rootsweb.com/~jfuller/gen_mail_country-aus.html#AUS-NSW-SE
  And the associated web page.
  http://www.zip.com.au/~viv/aus-nsw-se.htm
  For anyone with a genealogical interest in New South Wales (NSW).

- AUS-QLD-SE-Germans Mailing List
  http://www.rootsweb.com/~jfuller/gen_mail_country-aus.html#AUS-QLD-SE-Germans
  *For anyone with a genealogical interest in the descendants of the
  Germans who migrated to South East Queensland.*

- AUS-Tasmania Mailing List
  http://www.rootsweb.com/~jfuller/gen_mail_country-aus.html#AUS-Tasmania

- AUSTRALIA Mailing List
  http://www.rootsweb.com/~jfuller/gen_mail_country-aus.html#AUSTRALIA
  "The Conference of Australian History." For anyone with an interest

*in Australian History - not exclusively genealogy - including the
history of events involving Australians or their ancestors elsewhere
in the world.*

- DPS-SYDNEY Mailing List
  http://www.rootsweb.com/~jfuller/gen_mail_general.html#DPS-SYDNEY
  For the Sydney Dead Persons Society (DPS).

- EMIGRATION-SHIPS-REQUEST Mailing List
  http://www.rootsweb.com/~jfuller/gen_mail_general.html#EMIGRATION-SHIPS
  *A mailing list for anyone who wants to discuss the ships their
  ancestors arrived on or post passenger lists for any ships.*

- FHANQ Mailing List
  http://www.rootsweb.com/~jfuller/gen_mail_country-aus.html#FHANQ
  *For the members of the Family History Association of North
  Queensland to discuss Association activities and to share genealogy
  information on the ancestors and descendants of North Queensland
  families.*

- GENANZ Mailing list
  http://www.rootsweb.com/~jfuller/gen_mail_country-aus.html#GENANZ-L
  Gatewayed with the soc.genealogy.australia+nz
  newsgroup
  news:soc.genealogy.australia+nz
  See also the GENANZ Home Page
  http://www.rootsweb.com/~billingh/
  And the FAQ
  http://www.rootsweb.com/~billingh/genanz-l.htm
  For the discussion of Australia and New Zealand genealogy.

- IFHAA Genealogy Chat - #Australia
  http://www.historyaustralia.org.au/ifhaa/chat.htm
  *A weekly chat session for Australian researchers by the Internet
  Family History Association of Australia (IFHAA).*

◆ Maps, Gazetteers & Geographical Information

- AUSLIG On the Web - Australian Surveying & Land
  Information Group
  http://www.auslig.gov.au/

- Australian Gazetteer
  http://www.ke.com.au/cgi-bin/texhtml?form=AustGaz

- Australian Geographic Place Names (Gazetteer)
  http://www.erin.gov.au/database/gaze_ack.html

- Australian Places - A Gazetteer of Australian Cities,
  Towns and Suburbs
  http://www.arts.monash.edu.au/ncas/multimedia/gazetteer/index.html

- Australia Towns Index
  http://www.atn.com.au/contents.htm

- Geographical Names Board of New South Wales
  http://www.lic.gov.au/gnb/

- Historical Maps of Australia and the Pacific
  http://www.lib.utexas.edu:80/Libs/PCL/Map_collection/
  historical/history_austral_pacific.html
  From the Perry-Castañeda Library Map Collection, The University of Texas at Austin.

- History of Australian Places Index
  http://www.zades.com.au/ozindex/ozindex.html

- LINZ - The New Zealand Geographic Place-Names Database
  http://www.linz.govt.nz/databases/geographic/geoname.html

- Map of New Zealand - Guide to Cities & Towns
  http://www.atonz.com/genealogy/nza2.gif

- MapWorks
  http://www.mapworks.com.au/
  Map shop in Melbourne, Australia specializing in old and current editions of large scale maps for the United Kingdom, Ireland, Germany and more.

- National Library of Australia Map Collection
  http://www.nla.gov.au/map/mapcoll.html

◆ Military

- 460 Squadron RAAF
  http://home.st.net.au/~dunn/460sqdn.htm
  Australians serving in WWII.

- Australian Genealogy Researching Armed Services Personnel
  http://www.pcug.org.au/~mjsparke/mj_page1.html

- Australians in the Boer War - Australians in the Boer War - Oz-Boer Database Project
  http://www.pcug.org.au/~croe/oz_boer0.htm
  This project is dedicated to the memory of the around 20,000 Australians who, a century ago, risked all to serve their Queen, Empire and Country in the Second Anglo-Boer War (1899-1902). Includes a searchable database of Australian soldiers.

- Australian War Medals
  http://www.ozemail.com.au/~qphoto/index.html
  Provides background information on campaign & gallantry awards given to Australian forces. Includes some medal rolls listing individual recipients of medals. Also has a research resource page for researching Australian servicemen.

- Australian War Memorial
  http://www.awm.gov.au/default.htm

  o AWM Collection Databases
    http://www.awm.gov.au/database/default.asp

    • Australian War Memorial Boer War Nominal Roll Database
      http://www.awm.gov.au/database/boer.asp

    • Australian War Memorial Commemorative Roll Database
      http://www.awm.gov.au/database/croll.asp

    • Australian War Memorial Roll of Honour Database
      http://www.awm.gov.au/database/roh.asp

  o First World War Nominal Roll Database
    http://www.awm.gov.au/database/133.asp

  o "G" for George
    http://home.st.net.au/~dunn/g4george.htm
    The Avro Lancaster B1 on display in the Aeroplane Hall at the Australian War Memorial in Canberra, ACT.

- HAGSOC: Australian War Graves in South Africa 1899-1902
  http://www.hagsoc.org.au/sagraves/index.html
  This project, by the Heraldry & Genealogy Society of Canberra, aims to publish the database of burial and memorial locations of Australians who died during the second South African Anglo-Boer War of 1899 - 1902. Also included are biographies, researched by the Society, of selected soldiers from each of the Australian States.

- It's An Honour - The Australian Honours System
  http://www.itsanhonour.gov.au/

  o Search It's An Honour
    http://203.37.24.196/fs_search_start.html
    Searchable awards database from 1901 to 1998.

- New Zealand and the Great War
  http://www.ake.quik.co.nz/phoar/

- New Zealand Defence Forces, 1860 - 1883
  http://www.atonz.com/genealogy/nzdefence.html

- The New Zealand Wars
  http://www.northland.ac.nz/nzwars/index.html

- The Queensland Defence Force
  http://www.ozemail.com.au/~adjutant/moreton/qdf.html

- Research Guide - The Boer War - Australians and the War in South Africa 1899-1902
  http://www.naa.gov.au/PUBLICAT/GUIDES/boerwar/
  guide.htm
  From the National Archives of Australia.

- U.K. - Military
  http://www.CyndisList.com/miluk.htm
  See this category on Cyndi's List for related links.

- Victorian Nurses in the Boer War
  http://users.netconnect.com.au/~ianmac/nurses.html

◆ Newspapers

- Newspaper Collection
  http://www.slv.vic.gov.au/slv/newspapers/
  At the State Library of Victoria.

- Australian Newspapers on the Internet
  http://www.nla.gov.au/oz/npapers.html
  A list from the National Library of Australia

◆ People & Families

- Descendants of Convicts Group Inc.
  http://home.vicnet.net.au/~dcginc/welcome.htm
  A special interest group formed by members of the Genealogical Society of Victoria.

- First Families 2001
  http://home.vicnet.net.au/~family/
  A database and collection of stories about the people of Australia, past and present.

- Jewish Genealogy in Australia
  http://www.zeta.org.au/~feraltek/genealogy/index.html

- The Home Page of Lesley UEBEL
  http://users.bigpond.net.au/convicts
  Complete list of convicts transported between 1793 and April 1800, details place & date of trial, ship, and age of convict. Also lists 1st generation of some Hawkesbury Pioneer Settlers.

- Whakapapa Maori Genealogy
  http://ourworld.compuserve.com/homepages/rhimona/whakapap.htm

◆ Professional Researchers, Volunteers & Other Research Services

- A.A. Genealogy
  http://www.lisp.com.au/~coffey/index.htm
  Family Tree research in Australia and overseas.

- Adelaide proformat
  http://www.users.on.net/proformat/jaunay.html

- Armidale Family & Local History Research ~ New South Wales, Australia
  http://www.angelfire.com/ct/Armidale/index.html

- The Australasian Association of Genealogists and Record Agents
  http://www.aagra.asn.au/

- Australian Emigrant Ship Service
  http://freespace.virgin.net/donald.hazeldine/austral.htm
  A site aimed at genealogists in Australia and New Zealand, providing the history and a photograph of emigrant ships 1875-2000.

- Blanche McMillan and Associates
  http://web.one.net.au/~rowell/
  A professional service specialising in the location of missing persons with regard to adoption, lost relatives, friends, loved ones, school and family reunions, missing heirs with regard to deceased estates, providing an Australian information service for researchers to contact living relatives in Australia by using our data bases, researching genealogy, a certificate service to obtain Birth, Death and Marriage certificates from New Zealand.

- Cemetery Searches, Sydney
  http://homepages.tig.com.au/~tezz/netscape.htm
  This service will locate your ancestors' graves and take photos if required.

- Garrison Communications - Family History Research Services
  http://www.garrisonau.com/
  Specialising in Queensland, with expertise in English, Scottish, Welsh and Irish records.

- GenBritz Down Under
  http://ourworld.compuserve.com/homepages/vivparker/genbritz.htm

A Genealogical Research Service for those living outside the UK but researching in England, Wales, Scotland, Ireland and the Channel Islands. Research within New Zealand also undertaken.

- Genealogy Helplist - Australia
  http://helplist.org/aus/index.shtml

- Genealogy Helplist - New Zealand
  http://helplist.org/nzl/index.shtml

- genealogyPro - Professional Genealogists for Australia
  http://genealogyPro.com/directories/Australia.html

- genealogyPro - Professional Genealogists for New Zealand
  http://genealogyPro.com/directories/NewZealand.html

- Guthrigg Genealogy - Faye Guthrie's Home Page
  http://web.solutions.net.au/~guthrigg/index.htm
  Professional research services and genealogical information on Australian shipping resources, Australian Wills and Inquests, Convict ships.

- Janet Reakes Family History Services
  http://www.familytreeresearch.net/

- Kennedy Research - Australian Family History Research Service
  http://www.marque.com.au/kenres/

- Lynne Fiddick's Family History Research Home Page ~ New South Wales
  http://www.users.bigpond.com/Lynnette_Fiddick/

- Marbract Services - NSW Birth, Death & Marriage Certificate Transcription Service ~ Australia
  http://www.marbract.com.au/
  NSW Births 1788-1905, NSW Marriages 1788-1918 & NSW Deaths 1788-1945.

- NZEF Research Service
  http://www.medal.net/nzef/
  Research Service covering New Zealanders who served in the New Zealand Expeditionary Forces (NZEF) during World War 1 (1914-18).

- Professional Genealogical Research in Queensland
  http://www.judywebster.gil.com.au/prof.html
  Judy Webster.

- Professional Genealogist - Elizabeth K. Parkes - New Zealand
  http://genealogynz.co.nz/

- Professional Genealogist in New Zealand for the UK and Ireland - Tony Fitzgerald
  http://genealogypro.com/tfitzgerald.html

- Sharyn's Secretarial Services - Brisbane Cemetery Photographs
  http://www.ozemail.com.au/~sharynmark/page6.html
  5x7 photos or digital camera photos.

- TimeTrackers
  http://www.timetrackers.com.au/
  *Professional research and practical guidance for 'do-it-yourself'
  family history. Based in Perth, Western Australia. Specialises in UK
  and Australian family history.*

◆ Publications, Software & Supplies

- Adelaide proformat Bookshop
  http://www.users.on.net/proformat/books.html

- Amazon.com Genealogy Bookstore – Australia
  http://www.amazon.com/exec/obidos/external-search/?
  keyword=australia+genealogy&tag=markcyndisgenealA/
  And New Zealand
  http://www.amazon.com/exec/obidos/external-search/?
  keyword=new+zealand+genealogy&tag=markcyndis
  genealA/

- AudioTapes.com - Genealogical Lectures on Cassette
  Tapes – Australia
  http://www.audiotapes.com/search2.asp?Search=Australia
  And New Zealand
  http://www.audiotapes.com/search2.asp?Search=New+
  Zealand

- Australian Family Tree Connections Bookshop
  http://www.aftc.com.au/bookshop.html
  Features publications of AFTC Subscribers.

- Australian Family Tree Connections Magazine
  http://www.aftc.com.au/

- Australian Vital Records Index
  http://www.ldscatalog.com/cgi-bin/ncommerce3/Product
  Display?prrfnbr=2482&prmenbr=1402&CGRY_NUM=
  1440461&RowStart=1&LocCode=FH
  *A CD-ROM for sale from the LDS Church. Contains an indexed
  collection of references to 4.8 million birth, christening, marriage,
  and death records. Covers New South Wales (1788-1888), Tasmania
  (1803-1899), Victoria (1837-1888), and Western Australia (1841-
  1905).*

- Books We Own - Australia
  http://www.rootsweb.com/~bwo/australia.html
  *Find a book from which you would like a lookup and click on the
  submitter's code at the end of the entry. Once you find the contact
  information for the submitter, write them a polite request for a
  lookup.*

- Books We Own - New Zealand
  http://www.rootsweb.com/~bwo/nz.html
  *Find a book from which you would like a lookup and click on the
  submitter's code at the end of the entry. Once you find the contact
  information for the submitter, write them a polite request for a
  lookup.*

- Evagean Genealogy Publishing ~ New Zealand
  http://webnz.com/evagean/

- EZITREE Family History Program
  http://www.ram.net.au/users/ezitree/
  DOS program.

- Fast Books
  http://www.fastbooks.com.au/
  Perfect Bound Paperback Books, Glebe NSW.

- Finding Families - The Guide to the National
  Archives of Australia for Genealogists
  http://www.naa.gov.au/publicat/GUIDES/HTML/family.htm
  Book for sale from the National Archives of Australia.

- Genius Family Tree ~ Windows
  http://www.gensol.com.au/
  "The easy genealogy program".

- Gould Books - Family & Local History Specialist
  http://www.gould.com.au/
  Books, maps, charts, computing, microfiche, video & audio.

- Janet Reakes Books
  http://www.homestead.com/janetreakesbooks/index~ns4.html

- Long Journey for Sevenpence - Assisted Immigration
  to New Zealand from the United Kingdom 1947-
  1975
  http://www.nzhistory.net.nz/Gallery/immigration/Index.htm
  A book available from the Victoria University Press.

- Macbeth Genealogical Services
  http://www.macbeth.com.au/
  Books, fiche, maps, and CD-ROMs.

- My Family History
  http://www.ozemail.com.au/~pkortge/MFH.html
  For Windows WFW & Windows 95, from Australia.

- New Zealand Society of Genealogists - Hardcopy
  Publications
  http://homepages.ihug.co.nz/~nzsg/Publications/hardcopy_
  main.html

- New Zealand Society of Genealogists - Microfiche
  Publications
  http://homepages.ihug.co.nz/~nzsg/Publications/fiche_
  main.html

- RMIT Publishing Genealogy
  http://www.rmitpublishing.com.au/
  Australian databases on CD.

- White Room Genealogical Services
  http://www.whiteroom.com.au/geneal.htm
  *Specialist CD-ROM publishers and distributors. Titles include the
  Australian Chronicles: an index to sources of Australian biography.*

- Yesteryear Links ~ Queensland
  http://www.uq.net.au/yesteryearlinks/

◆ Queries, Message Boards & Surname Lists

- Australia Convicts Message Board
  http://www.InsideTheWeb.com/messageboard/mbs.cgi/
  mb80720

- Australian Family Tree Connections Missing
  Ancestors
  http://www.aftc.com.au/missanc.html

- Australian Family Tree Connections Surname Register
  http://www.aftc.com.au/surname.html

- Australian Genealogy Bulletin Board
  http://www.InsideTheWeb.com/messageboard/mbs.cgi/mb5856

- CANSW - Cornish Surname Interests & Family Queries
  http://www.ozemail.com.au/~jlsymo/cornsurn.htm

- Online Australasian Names Research Directory
  http://www.users.on.net/proformat/ausnames.html

- RootsWeb Surname List - RSL Australia
  http://rsl.rootsweb.com/cgi-bin/rslsql.cgi
  The RSL and this form concept & design are courtesy of Karen Isaacson.

- RootsWeb Surname List - RSL New Zealand
  http://rsl.rootsweb.com/cgi-bin/rslsql.cgi
  The RSL and this form concept & design are courtesy of Karen Isaacson

◆ Records: Census, Cemeteries, Land, Obituaries, Personal, Taxes and Vital (Born, Married, Died & Buried)

- 1880-1920 Otago Daily Times Births Deaths Marriages, Anniversaries Index, Dunedin, New Zealand
  http://www.es.co.nz/~treeves/geneal.htm
  See the details near the end of this page.

- Anne's UK Certificates for Australians
  http://freespace.virgin.net/mark.wainwright6/uk_certificates/
  An Australian living in London who can obtain copies of English, Scottish & Welsh Birth, Marriage and Death Certificates in exchange for payment in Australian dollars.

- Australasia Births, Deaths and Marriages Exchange
  http://www.geocities.com/Athens/Forum/3709/exchange/
  The aim of the Australasia Births, Deaths and Marriages Exchange is to provide to genealogists a free resource, to share information about details contained on birth, death and marriage registrations registered in Australia, New Zealand and Papua New Guinea.

- Australian Registrars of Births, Deaths & Marriages
  http://www.users.on.net/proformat/regs.html

- Australian Vital Records Index
  http://www.familysearch.org/OtherResources/Australian_vital.asp
  CD-ROM available from the Church of Jesus Christ of Latter-day Saints.

- Canterbury Association Passenger Manifests ~ Arrivals in Canterbury, New Zealand
  http://www2.symet.net/whitehouse/nzbound/cbyassoc.htm

- Cemeteries In and Around Gunning Shire, New South Wales
  http://www.pcug.org.au/~gchallin/cemeteries/top.htm

- Censuses in Australian Colonies
  http://www.users.on.net/proformat/census.html
  Provides information on date of census, condition, and where deposited.

- Civil Registration - Australian BDM Criteria
  http://www.users.on.net/proformat/bdm.html

- Commonwealth War Graves Commission
  http://www.cwgc.org/
  Details of 1.7 million members of UK and Commonwealth forces who died in the 1st and 2nd World Wars and other wars, and 60,000 civilian casualties of WWII. Gives details of grave site, date of death, age, usually parents/widow's address.

- Current Cost of Australian Certificates
  http://members.tripod.com/Sally_Hammon/cert_aus.htm
  From Sally Hammon's home page.

- Deaths In the Melbourne Hospital, 1867-1880
  http://home.coffeeonline.com.au/~tfoen/meldeath.html
  An index of foreign born residents of Melbourne who passed away at the Melbourne Hospital between 1867 and 1880.

- Deaths and Memoriams Extracted from the `New Zealand Herald' 1993
  http://www.geocities.com/Heartland/6123/dth_names.html
  From New Zealand. Find a surname of interest then e-mail the owner of the page for details.

- Department of Veterans' Affairs - Office of Australian War Graves
  http://www.dva.gov.au/commem/oawg/wargr.htm
  The Office of Australian War Graves is responsible for making available and for maintaining official commemoration either in a cemetery, crematorium or in an OAWG Garden of Remembrance, to a standard signifying the enduring respect of the nation, for those service personnel who have given their lives either in war or as a result of their war service.

- District Registrars in South Australia
  http://www.users.on.net/proformat/dregs.html

- Family Search Online Distribution Center - Australian Vital Records Index
  http://www.ldscatalog.com/cgi-bin/ncommerce3/ProductDisplay?prrfnbr=2482&prmenbr=1402&CGRY_NUM=1804&RowStart=1&LocCode=FH
  An indexed collection of references to 4.8 million birth, christening, marriage, and death records. This index covers only New South Wales (1788--1888), Tasmania (1803--1899), Victoria (1837--1888), and Western Australia (1841--1905).

- HAGSOC: Australian War Graves in South Africa 1899-1902
  http://www.hagsoc.org.au/sagraves/index.html
  This project, by the Heraldry & Genealogy Society of Canberra, aims to publish the database of burial and memorial locations of Australians who died during the second South African Anglo-Boer War of 1899 - 1902. Also included are biographies, researched by the Society, of selected soldiers from each of the Australian States.

- Immigrants Recruited by the Launceston Aid Immigration Society ~ Tasmania, Australia
  http://www.vision.net.au/~tashistory/immig/title.htm

- Index Projects at the Public Record Office, Victoria's Archives
  http://www.prov.vic.gov.au/6-1.htm

- Italian Australian Records Project
  http://www.vu.edu.au/iarp/

- Location of South Australian Records
  http://www.users.on.net/proformat/research.html
  Including some research guidelines.

- Lonely Graves in South Australia
  http://www.users.on.net/proformat/graves.html

- Marriage Witness Indexes for United Kingdom, and New Zealand
  http://www.genuki.org.uk/mwi/

- Moggill Cemetery
  http://192.148.225.23/bruce/cemetery.html
  A suburb of Brisbane, Queensland.

- New South Wales Family History Document Service
  http://www.ihr.com.au/
  A service which provides you with image files of historical documents used for researching people in New South Wales between 1850 and 1920.

- New South Wales Registry of Births, Deaths and Marriages
  http://www.bdm.nsw.gov.au/

  o Search the Registry Indexes
    http://www.bdm.nsw.gov.au/Services/IndexSrch.html
    Searchable database for Births 1788-1905, Marriages 1788-1945 & Deaths 1788-1945.

- New Zealand Birth and Death Entries
  http://www.geocities.com/Heartland/Forest/2925/nzbdentries.htm
  Shows the format of these civil registration records and what information they record.

- New Zealand Births, Deaths & Marriages Office
  http://www.bdm.govt.nz/diawebsite.nsf/c3649e22547ea840cc25681e0008b39b/c26afa900922c388cc25683e007b9a3f?OpenDocument

- Omeo Cemetery Trust
  http://www4.tpgi.com.au/users/omeo/page3.html
  Access to Omeo Pioneer Cemetery records, including monumental inscriptions. Also Buckland Cemetery.

- Public Record Office - Victoria's Archives
  http://www.prov.vic.gov.au/welcome.htm

  o Holdings and Finding Aids
    http://www.prov.vic.gov.au/hold-aid.htm

- Research Guide - Chinese Immigrants and Chinese-Australians in New South Wales
  http://www.naa.gov.au/PUBLICAT/GUIDES/chinese/guide.htm
  From the National Archives of Australia.

- Research Guide - Good British Stock - Child & Youth Migration to Australia
  http://www.naa.gov.au/PUBLICAT/GUIDES/childmig/guide.htm
  From the National Archives of Australia.

- Research Guide - Safe Haven - Records of the Jewish Experience in Australia
  http://www.naa.gov.au/PUBLICAT/GUIDES/haven/guide.htm
  From the National Archives of Australia.

- South Australian Cemeteries
  http://www.users.on.net/proformat/cems.html

- Spencer Holy Trinity Cemetery
  http://www.terrigal.net.au/~history/spencer.htm
  Cemetery Index for sale.

- Trunkey Creek Cemetery
  http://www.angelfire.com/bc/Cubitt/wizzn.html
  List of headstones in cemetery near Bathurst in New South Wales.

- Victorian Cemeteries
  http://home.primus.com.au/bonzaideas/MelbCems.htm
  This site contains contact info, history, links, source holdings, cemetery diagrams & other relevant information on cemeteries in Melbourne Metro & Regional Victoria.

◆ Ships: Convict Lists, Passenger Lists, Etc.

- AUSNZ Passenger Lists
  http://www.users.on.net/proformat/auspass.html

- Australian Shipping, 1788-1899
  http://www.blaxland.com/ozships/
  Shipping arrivals in Australia, listing passenger ships mainly for NSW, Queensland and some entries for Victoria and Tasmania.

- Australian Shipping Arrivals and Departures 1788 to 1967 - Convictions
  http://www.blaxland.com/ozships/

- Australia's First Fleet
  http://www.pcug.org.au/~pdownes/dps/1stflt.htm
  Convicts transported from England in 1788.

- Australia's Second Fleet
  http://www.pcug.org.au/~pdownes/dps/2ndflt.htm
  Convicts transported from England in 1790.

- Australia's Third Fleet
  http://www.pcug.org.au/~pdownes/dps/3rdflt.txt
  Convicts transported from England in 1791.

- Convict Gangs in 1821
  http://carmen.murdoch.edu.au/community/dps/convicts/victlist.htm
  Alphabetical list of names for 3,217 men, women and children who were issued with rations in Sydney on Saturday September 8, 1821.

- Convicts to Australia - A Guide To Researching Your Convict Ancestors
  http://carmen.murdoch.edu.au/community/dps/convicts/index.html
  In depth information and lists of convicts, ships, a timeline and convict's stories.

- Fifty Years in Queensland: - Living Pioneer Colonists
  http://192.148.225.23/bruce/qldpio.html
  A supplement article to "The Queenslander" Jubilee Issue:- 7 August 1909, which lists names, ages and year of arrival and the ship's name.

- Geelong Maritime Museum
  http://www.zades.com.au/geelong/maritime.html

- Immigrant Ships to New Zealand
  http://www.geocities.com/Heartland/Forest/2925/shipstonz.htm
  The ships in this index were mostly used to transport immigrants to New Zealand during the period 1835 to 1910.

- Immigration to Victoria. British Ports 1852-1879
  http://www.cohsoft.com.au/cgi-bin/db/ship.pl
  Public Record Office of Victoria has indexed the Arrivals to Victorian Ports from British Ports 1852 - 1879.

- Index to Inward Overseas Passengers from Foreign Ports 1852 - 1859
  http://home.vicnet.net.au/~provic/185259/5259indx.htm
  From the PRO Victoria.

- Lincolnshire Archives Index of Convict Records 1787 - 1840
  http://www.demon.co.uk/lincs-archives/convicts.htm

- Mariners and Ships in Australian Waters
  http://sites.archivenet.gov.au/Mariners/
  Indexes transcribed from the Australian Archive Office Reels of the Shipping Master's Office, Inwards Passengers Lists commencing in January, 1873. The lists include crew, passengers, deserters, births/deaths, stowaways, etc.

- National Archives of Ireland: Transportation Records
  http://www.nationalarchives.ie/search01.html
  Convicts from Ireland to Australia, 1788 to 1868.

- On-line Sourcing of Australasian Passenger Lists
  http://www.users.on.net/proformat/auspass2.html
  Queries submitted for ships of interest.

- "Parsee" - Passenger List - Moreton Bay - 11 January 1853
  http://192.148.225.23/bruce/plink.html

- Passenger arrivals at Port Chalmers, New Zealand, March 1848 - January 1851
  http://www.actrix.gen.nz/users/ngaiopress/drhocken.htm

- Passenger List for "Daylight" 1875
  http://homepage.mac.com/warrenj/OtherGenealogy/DaylightPassengers1875.html

The emigrant ship Daylight departed London, England on Thursday 27 May 1875 and arrived in Fremantle, Western Australia on 28 August 1875.

- Passenger List of the Palestine
  http://www.benet.net.au/~brandis/gendata/palestine.html
  From Plymouth, England, 29 November 1852 to Perth, Western Australia, 28 April 1853.

- Passenger Ships at Bluff Before 1900
  http://www.angelfire.com/ok2/cbluff/passengerships.html
  Passenger lists for ships that arrived at the Port of Bluff, New Zealand before the year 1900.

- Passengers on the Emigrant Ship "Emigrant"
  http://www.swinhope.demon.co.uk/genuki/Transcriptions/Emigrant.html
  Sailed from Sunderland 10 September 1852; arrived Melbourne 3 January 1853.

- Passengers on the Emigrant Ship "Lizzie Webber"
  http://www.swinhope.demon.co.uk/genuki/Transcriptions/LizzieWebber.html
  Sailed from Sunderland 31 July 1852; arrived Melbourne 4 December 1852.

- Passengers on the Emigrant Ship "Lord Delaval"
  http://www.swinhope.demon.co.uk/genuki/Transcriptions/LordDelaval.html
  Sailed from Berwick-upon-Tweed on September 13th 1852 for London and on to Port St Philip, Victoria.

- Passengers on the Emigrant Ship "Saldanha"
  http://www.swinhope.demon.co.uk/genuki/Transcriptions/Saldanha.html
  Sailed from Liverpool in the summer of 1856 for Victoria.

- Peter HODGE's Home Page
  http://www.pcug.org.au/~phodge/
  Information regarding the brig "Indian" from Falmouth in mid-1843 bound for Launceston, Tasmania; the "Emigrant" sailed from Plymouth on 9 August 1850 bound for Moreton Bay; and more on emigration, etc.

- Sailing Ship the INDIA Lost at Sea 1841
  http://www.home.gil.com.au/~bbiggar/india.htm
  Sailed from Greenock Scotland on 4 June 1841 bound for the Australian colony of Port Phillip.

- Ships & Passenger Lists
  http://www.CyndisList.com/ships.htm
  Immigration & Naturalization
  http://www.CyndisList.com/immigrat.htm
  See these categories on Cyndi's List for related links.

- Ships to Western Australia 1829 - 1849
  http://www.benet.net.au/~brandis/gendata/1829_49.html

- Ships to Western Australia 1899
  http://www.benet.net.au/~brandis/gendata/1899ship.html

- Ships to Western Australia 1900
  http://www.benet.net.au/~brandis/gendata/1900ship.html

- Ships to Western Australia January and February 1901
  http://www.benet.net.au/~brandis/gendata/1901ship.html

- South Australian Passenger Lists 1836-1840
  http://www.users.on.net/proformat/ships36.html

- South Australian Passenger Lists 1841-1846
  http://www.users.on.net/proformat/ships41.html

- South Australian Passenger Lists 1847-1886
  http://www.users.on.net/proformat/ships47.html

- South Australian Transported Convicts
  http://www.users.on.net/proformat/convicts.html

- System of Transportation
  http://www.nationalarchives.ie/transportation.html
  From the National Archives of Ireland. Very brief outline of transportation of convicts from Ireland to Australia in the 19th century.

- Tantivy! - Homestead of Mindful Works - Fireside Hypothesis
  http://www.angelfire.com/on2/tantivy/
  A complete listing of assisted immigrants arriving in Sydney aboard the Tantivy in 1853 and a list of persons with the surname Ford whom arrived in Australia aboard individual ships.

- Transportation of Irish convicts to Australia (1791-1853)
  http://www.nationalarchives.ie/transp1.html
  From the National Archives of Ireland. Detailed review of the sources available for convict research held at the Archives. Includes links to specific descriptions of record types and their reference class numbers.

- Van Diemens Land Company's Indentured Servants Home Page
  http://www.tassie.net.au/~aduniam/Index.html
  Servants engaged to establish a land grant in Tasmania from 1826. Departure and arrival dates of the ships Tranmere, Caroline, Thomas Lawrie, Emu, Forth and others, and passenger list of those aboard.

- The Wellington Valley Convicts, 1823-31
  http://www.newcastle.edu.au/department/hi/roberts/convicts.htm
  A database of more than 1,000 convicts.

- Women and Female children of the Royal Admiral 1792
  http://www.shoalhaven.net.au/~cathyd/raladies.html

◆ Societies & Groups

- ARHS/nsw - Australian Railway Historical Society, New South Wales Division
  http://www.accsoft.com.au/~arhsnsw/

- Armidale Family History Group ~ New South Wales
  http://www.geocities.com/Heartland/Pointe/5525/

- Australasian Federation of Family History Organisations Inc.
  http://carmen.murdoch.edu.au/~affho/

- Australian Croatian Genealogical and Historical Society
  http://www.geocities.com/Heartland/Hollow/6442/society/

- Australian Institute of Genealogical Studies Inc. ~ Blackburn, Victoria
  http://www.alphalink.com.au/~aigs/

- Australian Jewish Genealogical Society (Victoria) Inc.
  http://www.melbourne.net/csaky/Mainpage%20AJGS.htm

- Australian Jewish Historical Society
  http://www.zeta.org.au/~feraltek/genealogy/ajhs/index.html

- The Australian Light Horse Association
  http://www.lighthorse.org.au/default.htm
  The ALHA's aim is to preserve the history and tradition of the Australian Light Horse and its predecessors.

- Australian Local Family History Societies
  http://www.ihr.com.au/societies.html

- Australian Railway Historical Society (ARHS) - (Victorian Division Inc.)
  http://home.vicnet.net.au/~arhsvic/

- Australia Railway Historical Society - Queensland Division
  http://www.arhs-qld.org.au/

- Australian Society of Archivists
  http://www.archivists.org.au/

- Avoca and District Historical Society Inc, Victoria
  http://home.vicnet.net.au/~adhs/ADHSMain.htm
  The site has links to various indexes of names of those who lived in the Avoca district, including inhabitants of Lamplough and Homebush, thriving towns in the 19C and now no longer existing, also inquests of the district and the Society's members' interests (both surname and subject).

- Ballarat & District Genealogical Society ~ Victoria
  http://www.ballaratgenealogy.org.au/

- Bellarine Historical Society Inc.
  http://www.zades.com.au/bellhs/bellhs.html
  Covering the Bellarine Peninsula in Victoria.

- Benalla Family History Group Inc.
  http://sparky.hypermart.net/bhistory/
  A non profit group formed to promote and encourage the study of family history, and to preserve records pertaining to the North East of Victoria.

- Bendigo Regional Genealogical Society Inc. ~ Victoria
  http://home.vicnet.net.au/~brgs/

- Blue Mountains Family History Society ~ New South Wales, Australia
  http://www.pnc.com.au/~niglehil/bmfhs/bmfhs.htm

- Botany Bay Family History Society
  http://mypage.southernx.com.au/~bbfhs/

- Bothwell Historical Society ~ Tasmania
  http://www.tased.edu.au/tasonline/bothwell/

- Brisbane Dead Persons Society
  http://home.st.net.au/~dps/

- Brisbane Water Historical Society & Henry Kendall Cottage Museum
  http://www.terrigal.net.au/~bwhs/

- Bundaberg Genealogical Association, Inc.
  http://www.geocities.com/Heartland/Ranch/8859/BGA/BGA.htm

- Cairns Historical Society ~ Queensland
  http://www.cairnsmuseum.org.au/histsoc.html

- Calliope & District Heritage Group, Inc.
  http://members.xoom.com/_XMCM/mibbot/Calherinc/frameset2.htm

- Camden Area Family History Society Inc. ~ New South Wales
  http://www.zipworld.com.au/~scrob/cafhs.html

- Cape Banks Family History Society
  http://www.ozemail.com.au/~hazelb/capebank/index.html

- Castlemaine Historical Society, Inc. ~ Victoria
  http://www.castlemaine.net.au/historicalsociety/index.html

- Central Coast Family History Group Inc. ~ Gosford, New South Wales, Australia
  http://www.terrigal.net.au/~ccfhg/

- Central Queensland Family History Association
  http://sites.archivenet.gov.au/cqfha/

- Cessnock District Historical & Family History Society
  http://users.hunterlink.net.au/~ddlc/cessnock.htm

- Chelsea & District Historical Society, Inc.
  http://home.vicnet.net.au/~chelhist/

- Clare Regional History Group
  http://www.ozemail.com.au/~jlsymo/#crhg

- Cohuna & District Historical Society ~ Victoria, Australia
  http://www.cybatech.com.au/~cdhs/

- Colonel Light Gardens Historical Society Inc. ~ Adelaide, South Australia
  http://www.cobweb.com.au/~pknight/clghs/

- Cornish Association of Bendigo and District Inc.
  http://www.bendigo.net.au/users/ellisg/

- Cornish Association of New South Wales
  http://www.ozemail.com.au/~jlsymo/cansw.htm

- Cornish Association of Victoria Inc
  http://home.vicnet.net.au/~caov/index.htm

- Cornish Association of Western Australia Inc.
  http://www.ozemail.com.au/~kevrenor/afca-wa.htm

- Cowra Family History ~ New South Wales
  http://lisp.com.au/~fordhen/famhispage.html

- Dead Persons Society
  http://pcm.pcmedia.com.au/tags/docs/dps.html

- Dead Persons Society (DPS) Canberra ACT Australia - Home Page
  http://www.pcug.org.au/~chowell/dpshome.htm

- Dead Persons Society, Melbourne, Victoria
  http://home.vicnet.net.au/~dpsoc/welcome.htm

- Dead Persons Society, Newcastle, NSW
  http://bhss.inia.net.au/patmay/dps/

- Descendants of Convicts Group Inc.
  http://home.vicnet.net.au/~dcginc/welcome.htm
  A special interest group formed by members of the Genealogical Society of Victoria.

- Dimboola & District Historical Society
  http://home.vicnet.net.au/~dimhist/

- Dromana and District Historical Society Inc.
  http://home.vicnet.net.au/~dromana/

- Dubbo and District Family History Society, Inc.
  http://www.ozemail.com.au/~plantale/ddfhs/

- Echuca / Moama Family History Group, Inc.
  http://avoca.vicnet.net.au/~emfhistory/

- Essendon Historical Society, Inc.
  http://www.alphalink.com.au/~lfrost/Homepage/EHS.html

- Family History Group of Bathurst Inc.
  http://www.lisp.com.au/~bfhg/

- First Fleet Fellowship
  http://home.vicnet.net.au/~firstff/
  A historical society for people who have ancestors who arrived in Australia in 1788 aboard one of the ships of the First Fleet.

- Fleurieu Peninsula Family History Group, Inc.
  http://www.rootsweb.com/~safpfhg/
  Small friendly family history group with an on-line Members Interest Directory. The group will also carry out local research.

- The Geelong Family History Group Inc. (GFHG)
  http://home.vicnet.net.au/~gfamhist/index.htm

- Geelong Historical Society
  http://www.zades.com.au/geelong/ghs.html

- Genealogical Society of Queensland Inc.
  http://home.st.net.au/~dunn/gsq.htm

- Genealogical Society of Tasmania Inc.
  http://www.clients.tas.webnet.com.au/geneal/

- Genealogical Society of the Northern Territory, Inc.
  http://sites.archivenet.gov.au/gsnt/

- Genealogical Society of Victoria Inc.
  http://www.alphalink.com.au/~gsv/

- Geraldton Family History Society
  http://www.wn.com.au/gfhs/
  Western Australian Society. Includes a listing of members surname interests.

- Gerringong and District Historical Society
  http://www.ozemail.com.au/~johngrah/gdhs.html

- Gold Coast & Albert Genealogical Society
  http://www.onthenet.com.au/~annmorse/nerang.html

- Gosford District Local History Study Group ~
  Niagara Park, New South Wales, Australia
  http://www.terrigal.net.au/~history/

- The Heraldry and Genealogy Society of Canberra
  Inc.
  http://www.hagsoc.org.au/

- Heraldry Australia Inc.
  http://expage.com/page/heraldryaustralia
  A Society of Australians promoting the study and use of heraldry.

- IFHAA - Internet Family History Association of
  Australia
  http://www.historyaustralia.org.au/ifhaa/
  *A repository for family history material - includes cemetery
  transcripts, biographies, family stories, local histories and much
  more.*

- Illawarra Family History Group
  http://www.zip.com.au/~viv/ifhg.htm

- Illawarra Historical Society Inc.
  http://www.zip.com.au/~viv/ihs.htm

- Lithgow and District Family History Society Inc. ~
  New South Wales
  http://www.lisp.com.au/~ldfhs/

- Manning Valley Historical Society ~ New South
  Wales
  http://www1.tpgi.com.au/users/lgow/mvhs.html

- Maryborough District Family History Society
  http://www.satcom.net.au/mdfhs/
  *Family history society in Heritage City, Maryborough Qld
  Australia, site of 220,000 immigrants from UK and Germany from
  1860-1900, descendants of families still here plus scattered to other
  places in Australia. Also BigM project, Sydney Mail World War 1
  Photographic Index and info on resources and publications for sale,
  as well as how to research local families via the Net.*

- Melbourne PAF Users Group
  http://www.cohsoft.com.au/afhc/melbpaf.html

- Mid-Gippsland Family History Society, Inc. ~
  Victoria
  http://members.net-tech.com.au/shine/mgfhs.htm

- Mildura & District Genealogical Society Inc.
  http://users.mildura.net.au/users/genealogy/

- The Military Historical Society of Australia
  http://www.pcug.org.au/~astaunto/mhsa.htm

- Milton Ulladulla History Groups
  http://www.shoalhaven.net.au/~cathyd/groups.html

- Moruya & District Historical Society
  http://www.sci.net.au/mgrogan/mhs/

- Nepean District Historical Society ~ New South
  Wales
  http://www.penrithcity.nsw.gov.au/Lib/LocalStudies/ndhs.htm

- Nepean Family History Society, Inc. ~ New South
  Wales
  http://www.penrithcity.nsw.gov.au/NFHS/nfhshome.htm

- New Zealand Society of Genealogists, Inc.
  http://www.genealogy.org.nz/

- The New Zealand Wars Historical Society
  http://www.medal.net/nzwhs.htm
  *The Society was formed to provide a support network for collectors
  interested in the New Zealand War Medal.*

- Omeo Historical Society & Museum
  http://www4.tpgi.com.au/users/omeo/page8.html
  *Unique collection of original records dating back to 1850, many
  indexed.*

- Perth Dead Person's Society
  http://carmen.murdoch.edu.au/community/dps/default.html

- Port Stephens Historical Society
  http://users.hunterlink.net.au/~derea/

- Qld Association of Local and Family History
  Societies ~ Queensland
  http://www.judywebster.gil.com.au/qalfhs.html

- Queensland Family History Society Inc.
  http://www.qfhs.org.au/
  *Large reference library with most major research resources
  (focusing on Australasia, British Isles, and Germany). Largest
  genealogical CD-ROM collection in Australia. Currently compiling
  1.3 million Queensland Genealogical Master Index to sources.
  1,400 members. New members always welcome.*

- Redcliffe & District Family History Group Inc.
  http://www.geocities.com/Heartland/Valley/1899/
  research.html

- Royal Historical Society of Victoria
  http://home.vicnet.net.au/~rhsvic/

- Singleton Family History Society ~ New South
  Wales
  http://www.users.bigpond.com/LRANDREW/singleton/
  sfhspage.htm

- Society of Australian Genealogists
  http://www.sag.org.au/

- South Australian Genealogy & Heraldry Society Inc.
  http://saghs.mtx.net/

- Swan Hill Genealogical & Historical Society Inc.
  http://home.vicnet.net.au/~shghs/
  Located in Swan Hill, Northern Victoria, on the Murray River.

- The Sydney Dead Persons Society
  http://www.ozemail.com.au/~johngrah/dps.html

- Tamworth & District Family History Group Inc. ~
  New South Wales
  http://www.genweb.net/~tdfhgi/index.html

- TILLI-iNFO - Tilligerry & Districts Family History Society ~ New South Wales
  http://www.infoserv.net.au/tilli-info/content/history.html

- The Townsville and District Dead Persons' Society ~ North Queensland
  http://www.ozemail.com.au/~dpsnq/

- Traralgon & District Historical Society ~ Victoria
  http://www.gardencentre.com.au/traralgonhistory/index.htm

- Victorian GUM (Genealogists Using Microcomputers) Inc.
  http://www.vicgum.asn.au/

- Wagga Wagga & District Family History Society (Inc)
  http://members.xoom.com/FHS/
  Contains Members' Interest Register and general information about the situation and facilities of the society.

- Wentworth Historical Society ~ New South Wales
  http://www.wentworth.nsw.gov.au/library/libhist.html

- Werribee Family History Group Home Page ~ Victoria
  http://home.vicnet.net.au/~wfhg/

- Western Australian Genealogical Society Inc.
  http://cleo.murdoch.edu.au/~wags/

- Woodend and District Heritage Society
  http://www.asap.unimelb.edu.au/asa/directory/data/399.htm
  Local & Family History Resource Centre, Woodend, Victoria.

- Woy Woy Local History Research Group ~ New South Wales, Australia
  http://www.terrigal.net.au/~joanf/Wwhg.htm

◆ WorldGenWeb

- AustraliaGenWeb
  http://www.rootsweb.com/~auswgw/

- MelanesiaGenWeb
  http://www.rootsweb.com/~melwgw/

- MicronesiaGenWeb
  http://www.rootsweb.com/~fsmwgw/

- PacificGenWeb
  http://www.rootsweb.com/~pacifgw/

- PolynesiaGenWeb
  http://www.rootsweb.com/~pyfwgw/

AUSTRIA / ÖSTERREICH
http://www.cyndislist.com/austria.htm

Category Index:

- General Resource Sites
- Government & Cities
- History & Culture
- Language, Handwriting & Script
- Libraries, Archives & Museums
- Mailing Lists, Newsgroups & Chat
- Maps, Gazetteers & Geographical Information
- People & Families

- Professional Researchers, Volunteers & Other Research Services
- Publications, Software & Supplies
- Queries, Message Boards & Surname Lists
- Records: Census, Cemeteries, Land, Obituaries, Personal, Taxes and Vital
- Religion & Churches
- Societies & Groups
- WorldGenWeb

◆ General Resource Sites

- The Austrian Genealogy Web Ring
  http://www.yesic.com/~hrafra/atgen.html

- Austro-Hungarian Empire: Cross Index
  http://feefhs.org/ah/indexah.html
  From FEEFHS.

- Family History / Genealogy from the Unofficial Homepage for Austria of The Church of Jesus Christ of Latter-day Saints
  http://www.ettl.co.at/mormon/english/gen_gy.htm

- Genealogical Research in Austria
  http://www.genealogy.net/gene/reg/AUT/austria-en.html

- Genealogy and Heraldry in Slovenia
  http://genealogy.ijp.si/

- Institute for Historical Family Research
  http://ihff.nwy.at/index.htm/
  Genealogical research in the lands of the former Austro-Hungarian Monarchy. Includes: Austria, Czech & Slovak Republics, Hungary, Slovenian Republic, Croatia, Galicia & Bukovina.

- Post & Telekom Austria - Elektronisches Telefonbuch
  http://www.etb.at/

◆ Government & Cities

- Genealogy: Tour Halbturn, Austria
  http://www.HeritageQuest.com/genealogy/europe/html/halbturn.html
  Photos and information about Halbturn from a genealogical perspective, from Heritage Quest Magazine and European Focus.

- Republik Österreich
  http://www.austria.gv.at/

- Wien Online - das Webservice der Stadt Wien
  http://www.magwien.gv.at/

◆ History & Culture

- Austrian History
  http://www.emulateme.com/history/austhist.htm

- StudyWeb: History: Country History Index: Europe Index: Austria
  http://www.studyweb.com/links/4023.html

- Yahoo!...Austria...History
  http://dir.yahoo.com/Regional/Countries/Austria/Arts_and_Humanities/Humanities/History/

◆ Language, Handwriting & Script

- AltaVista Translation Service
  http://babelfish.altavista.digital.com/cgi-bin/translate?
  Input a URL for a web site or a block of plain text and this site will translate for you from German to English or English to German.

- Deciphering Gothic Records
  http://www.futureone.com/~fdearden/page2.htm
  Pamphlet for sale.

- Deutsch Englisches Wörterbuch
  http://www.tu-chemnitz.de/urz/netz/forms/dict.html

- German Letter Writing Guide
  http://www.familysearch.org/rg/guide/LGGerman.ASP
  For genealogical inqueries from FamilySearch.org.

- Form Letters for German Genealogy
  http://www.genealogy.net/gene/misc/letters/

- Fraktur and German Script
  http://www.asherwin.com/fraktur%26script.html

- German-English Letter Translation Specialists
  http://www.win.bright.net/~deichsa/welcome.html

- German-English On-line Dictionary
  http://dictionaries.travlang.com/GermanEnglish/

- German Genealogical Word List
  http://www.familysearch.org/rg/guide/WLGerman.ASP

- German Genealogy: Translation Service
  http://www2.genealogy.net/gene/www/abt/translation.html

- German Illness Translations
  http://pixel.cs.vt.edu/library/articles/link/illness.txt

- German Study Group / German Words
  http://205.216.138.19/~websites/lynnd/vuword.html

- German Translation Service
  http://www.asherwin.com/
  Specializations: German genealogy, Fraktur and German script, legal documents.

- German Translation Service
  http://www.win.bright.net/~jakeschu/welcome.html
  Old Script

- A Glossary of German Words Used in Official Documents
  gopher://Gopher.UToledo.edu:70/00GOPHER_ROOT%3A%5BRESEARCH-RESOURCES.GENEALOGY.GERMAN-GENEALOGY%5DA-GLOSSARY-OF-GERMAN-WORDS.USED-IN-OFFICIAL-DOCUMENTS

- Handwriting Guide: German Gothic
  http://www.familysearch.org/rg/guide/German_Gothic99-36316.ASP

- Moravians - German Script Tutorial
  http://www.mun.ca/rels/morav/script.html
  With Moravian Archival examples

  - German Script Alphabet
    http://www.mun.ca/rels/morav/pics/tutor/mscript2.html

- Old German Handwritten Scripts
  http://www2.genealogy.net/gene/misc/scripts.html

- Old German Professions and Occupations
  http://worldroots.clicktron.com/brigitte/occupat.htm

- Old Spelling Patterns
  http://www.asherwin.com/spelling.html

- Sample Letters in German to Obtain Genealogical Information
  gopher://Gopher.UToledo.edu:70/00GOPHER_ROOT%3A%5BRESEARCH-RESOURCES.GENEALOGY.GERMAN-GENEALOGY%5DGERMAN-SAMPLE-LETTER.FOR-INFORMATION-REQUESTS

- Translation Service only for genealogy related material
  http://www.genealogy.net/gene/misc/translation.html
  Volunteer translators can provide you with translations between Czech, English, Dutch, French, German, & Polish. This service is provided via e-mail. Exact request syntax and length rules must be followed in order to expedite processing.

- Tutorials for Reading Old German, French and English Handwriting, Naming Systems
  http://www.disknet.com/indiana_biolab/eg502.htm

- Walden Font
  http://www.waldenfont.com/
  Several different fonts for sale, including: The Gutenberg Press German Fraktur Fonts and German Script.

◆ Libraries, Archives & Museums

- Archiv der Stadt Linz
  http://www.linz.at/verwaltu/magistra/aemter/arch.htm
  City Archives of Linz.

- Archives in Austria
  http://www.bawue.de/~hanacek/info/aarchive.htm
  Addresses and descriptions in German.

- Family History Centers in Germany, Austria and Switzerland
  http://www.genealogy.net/gene/faqs/LDS.de

- Family History Library Catalog
  http://www.familysearch.org/Search/searchcatalog.asp
  From the FamilySearch web site, an online catalog to the holdings of the LDS Church in Salt Lake City, Utah. Also search for other localities by place name.
  http://www.familysearch.org/fhlc/supermainframeset.asp?display=localitysearch&columns=*,180,0

  - Austria
    http://www.familysearch.org/fhlc/supermainframeset.asp?display=localitydetails&subject=83&subject_disp=Austria&columns=*,180,0

- Family History SourceGuide - Family History Centers - Europe and Scandinavia
  http://www.familysearch.org/sg/Europe_and_Scandinavia_FHC.html
  Austria, Belgium, Denmark, Finland, France, Germany, Hungary, Iceland, Italy, Netherlands, Norway, Portugal, Spain, Sweden, and Switzerland.

- Land Salzburg - Das Landarchiv
  http://www.land-sbg.gv.at/archiv/
  Province of Salzburg Archives.

- Oberösterreichisches Landesarchiv
  http://www.ooe.gv.at/einrichtung/kultur/larchiv.htm
  Province of Upper Austria Archives.

- Oesterreichische Archive / Archives in Austria
  http://www.oesta.gv.at/deudiv/arch_oe.htm
  With telephone numbers, postal addresses, and some links.

- Österreichische Nationalbibliothek / National Library of Austria
  http://www.onb.ac.at/

- Österreichisches Staatsarchiv / Austrian State Archives
  http://www.oesta.gv.at/
  Their introductory page in English.

  - Genealogy/Family History Research
    http://www.oesta.gv.at/engdiv/geneal.htm
    The "customs" of archives and the structure of archival holdings, the peculiarities of Using archives and the administrative organization of archives in Austria are the reason why genealogical research in archives is a time consuming purpose,

considering both the variety of archival holdings of the Austrian State Archives and difficulties to find the relevant information. It is necessary to prepare a solid research strategy.

- Kärntner Landesarchiv
  http://www.buk.ktn.gv.at/landesarchiv/
- Niederösterreichisches Landesarchiv
  http://www.noel.gv.at/service/k/k2/index.htm
  Province of Lower Austria Archives.
- Repositories of Primary Sources - Europe - Austria
  http://www.uidaho.edu/special-collections/euro1.html#at
  A list of links to online resources from the Univ. of Idaho Library, Special Collections and Archives.
- Steiermärkisches Landesarchiv ~ Graz, Austria
  http://www.stmk.gv.at/verwaltung/stla/
- Südtiroler Landesarchiv / South Tyrol Archive
  http://www.provinz.bz.it/sla/d/index_d.htm
  Former Austrian possession now part of Italy.
- Das Vorarlberger Landesarchiv
  http://www.vorarlberg.at/Landesregierung/iib/larchiv.htm
- Wiener Stadt-und Landesarchiv / Viennese City & National Archives
  http://www.magwien.gv.at/ma08/m08_leit.htm

◆ Mailing Lists, Newsgroups & Chat

- Genealogy Resources on the Internet - Austria Mailing Lists
  http://www.rootsweb.com/~jfuller/gen_mail_country-aut.html
  Most of the mailing list links below point to this site, wonderfully maintained by John Fuller
- atgevol@eGroups.com - Austrian Genealogy
  http://www.egroups.com/group/atgevol/info.html
- AUSTRIA Mailing List
  http://www.rootsweb.com/~jfuller/gen_mail_country-aut.html#AUSTRIA
- BURGENLAND-NEWSLETTER Mailing List
  http://www.rootsweb.com/~jfuller/gen_mail_country-aut.html#BURGENLAND-NEWSLETTER
  A read-only mailing list for the distribution of the bi-weekly Burgenland Bunch Newsletter which addresses the Province of Burgenland, Austria and nearby areas of Hungary.
- EXULANTEN Mailing List
  http://www.rootsweb.com/~jfuller/gen_mail_country-aut.html#EXULANTEN
  For anyone with a genealogical interest in the "Exulanten" who are the Protestants that were forced to leave Austria in the 16th-18th centuries.
  - Austrian Genealogy - Exulanten-L Mailing List
    http://www.rootsweb.com/~autwgw/agsfrx.htm
    Exulanten is the name given to the Protestants that were forced out Austria (estimated as many as 100,000) during 16th to 18th century. The largest wave of about 22,000 left the Salzburg area in 1731/32. Most went to East Prussia (Germany - Poland, Lithuania and Latvia) but some went to Siebenbürgen and Banat (today's Romania), Hungary and to parts of today's Slovakia.

- GALICIA Mailing List
  http://www.rootsweb.com/~jfuller/gen_mail_country-aut.html#GALICIA
  A regional special interest group (SIG) mailing list for those interested in researching their Jewish roots in the former Austrian province of Galacia.
- GERSIG Mailing List
  http://www.rootsweb.com/~jfuller/gen_mail_country-aut.html#GERSIG
  A regional special interest group (SIG) mailing list that focuses on Jewish genealogy in German-speaking regions (e.g., Germany, Austria, parts of Switzerland, Alsace, Lorraine, Bohemia, Moravia).
- GOTTSCHEE Mailing List
  http://www.rootsweb.com/~jfuller/gen_mail_country-aut.html#GOTTSCHEE
  For anyone with a genealogical interest in Gottschee, Austria (now known as Kocevje, Slovenia).

◆ Maps, Gazetteers & Geographical Information

- 1858 Map of Vienna
  http://www.lib.utexas.edu/Libs/PCL/Map_collection/historical/Vienna_1858.jpg
- 1882 Map - Austria, including Austria, Styria and Tyrol
  http://feefhs.org/maps/ah/ah-austr.html
  From FEEFHS.
- Austro-Hungarian Empire Map Index
  http://feefhs.org/maps/ah/mapiah.html
  From FEEFHS.
- Map of Austria
  http://www.lib.utexas.edu/Libs/PCL/Map_collection/europe/Austria.GIF
  From the Perry-Castañeda Library at the Univ. of Texas at Austin.

◆ People & Families

- Austria/Hungary Empire
  http://www.worldroots.com/brigitte/royal/royal10.htm
  Historic and genealogical information about royal and nobility family lines.
- Researching the People From 'No Man's Land' - The Carpatho-Rusyns of Austria Hungary
  http://www.carpatho-rusyn.org/peters.htm
  Online article on Carpatho-Rusyn research by by Thomas A. Peters, C.G.R.S.

◆ Professional Researchers, Volunteers & Other Research Services

- Arno Schmitt, Journalist from San Diego, California
  mailto:reporter@adnc.com
  He can help to find relatives, links or sources regarding ancestors by placing articles in German, Austrian and/or Swiss newspapers. For details, e-mail Arno at: reporter@adnc.com.

- European Focus
  http://www.eurofocus.com/
  Photographic portfolios of ancestral towns in Europe created for Genealogy enthusiasts in Germany, Italy, Poland, Scandinavia, Great Britain and more.

- Family Tree Genealogical and Probate Research Bureau Ltd.
  http://www.familytree.hu/
  Professional research service covering the area of what was formerly the Austro - Hungarian Empire, including: Hungary, Slovakia, Czech Republic, Austria, Italy, Transylvania, Croatia, Slovenia, former Yugoslavia (Banat), and the Ukraine (Sub-Carpathian).

- Institute for Historical Family Research
  http://ihff.nwy.at/index.htm/
  Austria, Czech & Slovak Republics, Hungary, Slovenian Republic, Croatia, Galicia & Bukovina.

◆ Publications, Software & Supplies

- Amazon.com Genealogy Bookstore - Austria
  http://www.amazon.com/exec/obidos/external-search/?keyword=austria+genealogy&tag=markcyndisgenealA/

- AudioTapes.com - Genealogical Lectures on Cassette Tapes - Austria
  http://www.audiotapes.com/search2.asp?Search=Austria

- Frontier Press Bookstore - Austria
  http://www.frontierpress.com/frontier.cgi?category=aus

◆ Queries, Message Boards & Surname Lists

- GenConnect at RootsWeb - Austria Visitor Center
  http://cgi.rootsweb.com/~genbbs/index/Austria.html

- Lineages' Free On-line Queries - Austria
  http://www.lineages.com/queries/Search.asp?Country=&Place=

- RootsWeb Surname List - RSL Austria
  http://rsl.rootsweb.com/cgi-bin/rslsql.cgi
  The RSL and this form concept & design are courtesy of Karen Isaacson.

◆ Records: Census, Cemeteries, Land, Obituaries, Personal, Taxes and Vital (Born, Married, Died & Buried)

- Jüdische Matriken Wien/Jewish Records of Vienna
  http://ihff.nwy.at/wj.htm
  From the Institute for Historical Family Research.

◆ Religion & Churches

- Orthodox Parishes in Austria
  http://www.orthodox.net/directry/austria.htm
  Russian Orthodox Church.

- RCNet Catholic Pages of Austria
  http://www.rc.net/austria/

- Ukrainian Greek Catholic Church in Western Austria
  http://members.eunet.at/grcath/

◆ Societies & Groups

- Austrian Genealogy - Societies and Researchers
  http://www.rootsweb.com/~autwgw/agsfr2.htm

- The Burgenland Bunch Genealogy Group
  http://www.spacestar.com/users/hapander/burgen.html
  Genealogists researching the State of Burgenland, Austria and nearby areas of Hungary.

- Gottscheer Heritage and Genealogy Association
  http://www.gottschee.org/~ghga/
  Gottschee, Austria, now known as Kocevje, Slovenia.

◆ WorldGenWeb

- EastEurope GenWeb
  http://www.rootsweb.com/~easeurgw/index.htm

  o Austrian Genealogy - AustriaGenWeb
    http://www.rootsweb.com/~autwgw/
    Genealogical research in Austria. Information, links and posting of queries.

THE BALTIC STATES ~ ESTONIA, LATVIA & LITHUANIA

http://www.cyndislist.com/baltic.htm

Category Index:

- ◆ FEEFHS ~ Federation of East European Family History Societies
- ◆ General Resource Sites
- ◆ History & Culture
- ◆ How To
- ◆ Language, Handwriting, & Script
- ◆ Libraries, Archives & Museums
- ◆ Mailing Lists, Newsgroups & Chat

- ◆ Maps, Gazetteers & Geographical Information
- ◆ Professional Researchers, Volunteers & Other Research Services
- ◆ Publications, Software & Supplies
- ◆ Records: Census, Cemeteries, Land, Obituaries, Personal, Taxes and Vital
- ◆ Religion & Churches
- ◆ Societies & Groups

◆ FEEFHS ~ Federation of East European Family History Societies

- FEEFHS - Federation of East European Family History Societies
  http://feefhs.org/
  - o Ethnic, Religious and National Index of HomePages and FEEFHS Resource Guide Listings
    http://feefhs.org/ethnic.html
    of organizations associated with FEEFHS from 14 countries
  - o FEEFHS Ethnic, Religious and National Cross-Indexes:
    - Baltic Countries: Estonia, Latvia and Lithuania
      http://feefhs.org/baltic/indexblt.html
  - o FEEFHS Full Text Web Site Index Search Engine
    http://feefhs.org/search/
  - o FEEFHS Location (Address) Index of FEEFHS Member Organizations
    http://feefhs.org/location.html
    and other East European Genealogy Organizations.
  - o FEEFHS Significant Additions Index
    http://feefhs.org/webm/sigad96.html
  - o FEEFHS Web Site Master Index
    http://feefhs.org/masteri.html

◆ General Resource Sites

- Dags' Latvian Genealogy Page
  http://feefhs.org/baltic/lv/frg-dag.html
- European Focus
  http://www.eurofocus.com/

Photographic portfolios of ancestral towns in Europe created for Genealogy enthusiasts in Germany, Italy, Poland, Scandinavia, Great Britain and more.

- Institute Country Index
  http://www.columbia.edu/cu/sipa/REGIONAL/ECE/country.html
  Links to online resources for several countries from the Institute on East Central Europe at Columbia University.
- JewishGen Shtetlinks Web Page for Krakes Lithuania - Created by Trevor Tucker and Ada Greenblatt
  http://www.jewishgen.org/litvak/krakes/
- Lithuanian Ancestor Search Bulletin Board
  http://www.fgi.net/~zemaitis/search.html
- Lithuanian Genealogy
  http://www.angelfire.com/ut/Luthuanian/indexn11.html
  - o Lithuanian First Names
    http://www.angelfire.com/ut/Luthuanian/names1.html
- PolishRoots: The Polish Genealogy Source
  http://www.polishroots.org/
- Resources for Sepharadic Genealogy
  http://www.geocities.com/Heartland/Valley/2177/resource.htm
  Sephardic genealogical research begins with the search for your ancestor's country of origin. It could be almost any country where Sephardim lived - Bulgaria, Curacao, Gibraltar, Morocco, Greece, Romania, Tunisia, Turkey, Yugoslavia, any Middle Eastern country, even Germany, Holland, Italy or Malta. Small numbers of Sephardim even lived in Poland and Russia and had names like Levine, Rangel and Calahora.
- The Titled Families of the Polish-Lithuanian Commonwealth
  http://www.pgsa.org/polelith.htm

- The WWW Virtual Library: Russian and East
  European Studies (REESWeb)
  http://www.ucis.pitt.edu/reesweb/
  *Directory of Internet resources for the Balkans, the Baltic states, the
  Caucusus, Central Asia, Central Europe, the CIS, Eastern Europe,
  the NIS, the Russian Federation, and the former Soviet Union.*

- The WorldGenWeb Project
  http://www.worldgenweb.org/
  - o CenEuropeGenWeb
    http://www.rootsweb.com/~ceneurgw/
    - Latvia
      http://www.rootsweb.com/~lvawgw/
    - Rigas
      http://www.rootsweb.com/~lvariga/
    - Talsu
      http://www.rootsweb.com/~lvariga/
    - Lithuania
      http://w3.arobas.net/~simunye/lietuva.html
  - o EastEuropeGenWeb
    http://www.rootsweb.com/~easeurgw/
    - Estonia
      http://www.fortunecity.com/meltingpot/estonia/200/
      genweb.html

◆ History & Culture

- Dates from the history of Estonia
  http://www.ibs.ee/ibs/history/dates.html

- Global Resources for Lithuania
  http://www.angelfire.com/ut/Luthuanian/index.html

- History of Europe, Slavic States
  http://www.worldroots.com/brigitte/royal/royal4.htm
  *Historic and genealogical information about royal and nobility
  family lines.*

- StudyWeb: History: Europe
  http://www.studyweb.com/History/toceurop.htm

◆ How To

- How to find relatives in Lithuania?
  http://neris.mii.lt/heritage/lfcc/howfind.html

- How to Research Your Lithuanian Genealogy
  http://www.angelfire.com/ut/Luthuanian/faq.html

◆ Language, Handwriting, & Script

- FEEFHS Database of Professional Translators
  Specializing in East European Genealogy
  http://feefhs.org/frg/frg-pt.html

- Genealogy: Terms for Document Translation (Lith)
  ~ Lithuania
  http://lark.cc.ukans.edu/~raistlin/genealogy/terms.html

- The History of Written Estonian
  http://www.ibs.ee/ibs/estonian/history.html

- Languages & Translations
  http://www.CyndisList.com/language.htm
  See this category on Cyndi's List for related links.

◆ Libraries, Archives & Museums

- Centre For Estonian Diaspora Studies
  http://www.ut.ee/VEUK/centre.index.html
  *Studies the migration of Estonians, as well as the history, identity,
  language and literature of Estonians abroad.*

- Eesti Ajalooarhiiv - Estonian Historical Archives
  http://www.eha.ee/

- Eesti Rahvusraamatukogu / The National Library of
  Estonia
  http://www.nlib.ee/

- Eesti Riigiarhiiv / The Estonian State Archives
  http://www.ra.gov.ee/riigiarhiiv/

- Family History Library Catalog
  http://www.familysearch.org/Search/searchcatalog.asp
  *From the FamilySearch web site, an online catalog to the holdings
  of the LDS Church in Salt Lake City, Utah. Also search for other
  localities by place name.*
  http://www.familysearch.org/fhlc/supermainframeset.asp?
  display=localitysearch&columns=*,180,0
  - o Estonia
    http://www.familysearch.org/fhlc/supermainframeset.asp?
    display=localitydetails&subject=114&subject_disp=Estonia
    &columns=*,180,0
  - o Latvia
    http://www.familysearch.org/fhlc/supermainframeset.asp?
    display=localitydetails&subject=116&subject_disp=Latvia&
    columns=*,180,0
  - o Lithuania
    http://www.familysearch.org/fhlc/supermainframeset.asp?
    display=localitydetails&subject=118&subject_disp=
    Lithuania&columns=*,180,0
  - o Russia (Empire)
    http://www.familysearch.org/fhlc/supermainframeset.asp?
    display=localitydetails&subject=113&subject_disp=Russia_
    (Empire)&columns=*,180,0

- HELKA - The Helsinki University Libraries OPAC
  http://renki.helsinki.fi/gabriel/en/countries/finland-opac-
  en.html
  *Catalog of the Helsinki University Library system. It has a large
  collection of official publications of the former Russian Empire.*

- Herder-Institut Marberg: About the Institute
  http://www.uni-marburg.de/herder-institut/english/allgemein/
  info.html
  *According to its statutes, the Herder-Institute supports "with its
  collections and as a forum for academic discussion the research on
  the countries and peoples of East Central Europe in their European
  context, with special regard to the history of the historical German
  territories and areas of settlement in East Central Europe. In order
  to fulfill these tasks, the institute conducts its own research." The
  core subject of its work is the area of the present-day states of
  Poland, the Czech Republic, Slovakia, Estonia, Latvia and
  Lithuania.*

- Latvijas Nacionâlâ Bibliotçka / The National Library of Latvia
  http://vip.latnet.lv/LNB/

- Latvijas Valsts Arhîvs / The State Archives of Latvia
  http://www.datapro.lv/lva/index.html

- The Lithuanian Archives in Vilnius
  http://www.angelfire.com/ut/Luthuanian/vilnius.html
  Information on how to use the Archives by post.

- Martynas Mazvydas National Library of Lithuania / Lietuvos Nacionaline Martyno Mazvydo Biblioteka
  http://www.lnb.lt/

- Public Libraries of Europe
  http://dspace.dial.pipex.com/town/square/ac940/eurolib.html

- Repositories of Primary Sources - Europe A-M
  http://www.uidaho.edu/special-collections/euro1.html
  And Europe N-Z
  http://www.uidaho.edu/special-collections/euro2.html
  A list of links to online resources from the Univ. of Idaho Library, Special Collections and Archives

  o Estonia
    http://www.uidaho.edu/special-collections/euro1.html#ee
  o Latvia
    http://www.uidaho.edu/special-collections/euro1.html#lv
  o Lithuania
    http://www.uidaho.edu/special-collections/euro1.html#lt

◆ Mailing Lists, Newsgroups & Chat

- Genealogy Resources on the Internet - Estonia Mailing Lists
  http://www.rootsweb.com/~jfuller/gen_mail_country-est.html

- Genealogy Resources on the Internet - Latvia Mailing Lists
  http://www.rootsweb.com/~jfuller/gen_mail_country-lat.html

- Genealogy Resources on the Internet - Lithuania Mailing Lists
  http://www.rootsweb.com/~jfuller/gen_mail_country-lit.html
  Most of the mailing list links below point to this site, wonderfully maintained by John Fuller

- BALT-L Mailing List
  http://www.rootsweb.com/~jfuller/gen_mail_country-lit.html#BALT-L
  Online forum devoted to communications to and about the Baltic Republics of Lithuania, Latvia and Estonia. Subscription to this list is welcomed from anyone with skills or interests relevant to the Baltics, or who just wants to know what's going on. Short requests to help locate families or villages are carried in general-interest digest messages.

- E-LIST Mailing List
  http://www.rootsweb.com/~jfuller/gen_mail_country-est.html#E-LIST
  A moderated news and discussion list for Estonia-related matters. Primary readership is Estonians abroad and home. Estonian and English languages are used.

- EURO-JEWISH Mailing List
  http://www.rootsweb.com/~jfuller/gen_mail_general.html#EURO-JEWISH
  For anyone with a genealogical interest in the Migration, History, Culture, Heritage and Surname search of the Jewish people from Europe to the United States and their descendants in the United States.

- Exulanten-L Mailing List
  http://www.rootsweb.com/~autwgw/agsfrx.htm
  Exulanten is the name given to the Protestants that were forced out Austria (estimated as many as100,000) during 16th to 18th century. The largest wave of about 22,000 left the Salzburg area in1731/32. Most went to East Prussia (Germany - Poland, Lithuania and Latvia) but some went to Siebenbürgen and Banat (today's Romania), Hungary and to parts of today's Slovakia.

- GEN-SLAVIC Mailing List
  http://www.rootsweb.com/~jfuller/gen_mail_country-pol.html#GEN-SLAVIC
  Gatewayed with the soc.genealogy.slavic newsgroup
  news:soc.genealogy.slavic

- HERBARZ Mailing List
  http://www.rootsweb.com/~jfuller/gen_mail_country-lit.html#HERBARZ
  For the discussion of Polish and Lithuanian heraldry, the history of the armorial clans, and the genealogy of noble families.

- KEIDAN Mailing List
  http://www.rootsweb.com/~jfuller/gen_mail_country-lit.html#KEIDAN
  A mailing list for anyone with roots or interest in Keidan and its history as a Jewish community to share information and discuss its past and present and the region that surrounds it in Lithuania.

- LITHUANIA Mailing List
  http://www.rootsweb.com/~jfuller/gen_mail_country-lit.html#LITHUANIA

- LithuanianGenealogy Mailing List
  http://www.rootsweb.com/~jfuller/gen_mail_country-lit.html#LithuanianGenealogy
  A mailing list for anyone with a genealogical interest in Lithuania.

- LITVAKSIG Mailing List
  http://www.rootsweb.com/~jfuller/gen_mail_country-lit.html#LITVAKSIG
  A regional special interest group (SIG) mailing list for those who are interested in the preservation and computerization of primary sources of genealogical data for the descendants of the Lithuanian Jewish community.

- PolandBorderSurnames Mailing List
  http://www.rootsweb.com/~jfuller/gen_mail_country-pol.html#PolandBorderSurnames
  For anyone researching genealogy in the former historical borders of Poland including Estonia, Latvia, Lithuania, Belarus, Ukraine, Moldova, Slovakia, Czech Republic, Moravia, Hungary, Russia, the Balkans, and East Prussia.

- SUGUSELTS Mailing List
  http://www.rootsweb.com/~jfuller/gen_mail_country-est.html#SUGUSELTS
  An Estonian-language Genealogy list.

◆ Maps, Gazetteers & Geographical Information

- FEEFHS East European Map Room - Map Index
  http://feefhs.org/maps/indexmap.html

- Genealogy Unlimited - Maps and Atlases from Europe
  http://www.genealogyunlimited.com/
  Maps and atlases from Poland, Prussia, and Germany.

- Historical Maps of Russia and the Former Soviet Republics
  http://www.lib.utexas.edu/Libs/PCL/Map_collection/historical/
  history_commonwealth.html

  From the Perry-Castañeda Library Map Collection, The University of Texas at Austin.

- Lithuanian Place Name Changes
  http://www.rootsweb.com/~ilwinneb/placelit.htm
  Lithuanian, Russian & Polish.

- Maps of Europe - The Perry-Castañeda Library Map Collection
  http://www.lib.utexas.edu/Libs/PCL/Map_collection/
  europe.html
  From the University of Texas at Austin.

  o Map of Estonia
    http://www.lib.utexas.edu/Libs/PCL/Map_collection/europe/
    Estonia.gif

  o Map of Ethnic Groups of Eastern Europe
    http://www.lib.utexas.edu/Libs/PCL/Map_collection/europe/
    EEurope_Ethnic_95.jpg

  o Map of Latvia
    http://www.lib.utexas.edu/Libs/PCL/Map_collection/europe/
    Latvia.gif

  o Map of Lithuania
    http://www.lib.utexas.edu/Libs/PCL/Map_collection/europe/
    Lithuania.gif

◆ Professional Researchers, Volunteers & Other Research Services

- Board for Certification of Genealogists - Roster of Those Certified - Specializing in Europe/USSR
  http://www.bcgcertification.org/rosts_@e.html

- European Focus
  http://www.eurofocus.com/
  Photographic portfolios of ancestral towns in Europe created for Genealogy enthusiasts in Belgium, Denmark, Eastern Europe, England, France, Germany, Great Britain, Italy, Netherlands, Norway, Poland, Sweden, Switzerland and more.

- FEEFHS Database of Professional Genealogists Specializing in East European Genealogy
  http://feefhs.org/frg/frg-pg.html

- Gary Mokotoff, Genealogical Lecturer
  http://www.avotaynu.com/gmokotoff.html
  One of the foremost lecturers and authors on Jewish and Eastern European genealogical research.

- genealogyPro - Professional Genealogists for Central and Eastern Europe
  http://genealogyPro.com/directories/Europe.html

- The Snoop Sisters Family History Researchers ~ Nanaimo, B.C. Canada
  http://www.snoopsisters.net/
  England & Wales, Scotland, Ireland & N., Ireland, Eastern Europe, Canada & U.S.

◆ Publications, Software & Supplies

- Amazon.com Genealogy Bookstore - Eastern Europe
  http://www.amazon.com/exec/obidos/external-search/?
  keyword=eastern+europe+genealogy&tag=markcyndis
  genealA/
  And Lithuania
  http://www.amazon.com/exec/obidos/external-search/?
  keyword=lithuania+genealogy&tag=markcyndisgenealA/

- AudioTapes.com - Genealogical Lectures on Cassette Tapes – Baltic
  http://www.audiotapes.com/search2.asp?Search=Baltic
  Estonia
  http://www.audiotapes.com/search2.asp?Search=Estonia
  Latvia
  http://www.audiotapes.com/search2.asp?Search=Latvia
  Lithuania
  http://www.audiotapes.com/search2.asp?Search=Lithuania

- Frontier Press Bookstore - European Research
  http://www.frontierpress.com/frontier.cgi?category=europe

- Genealogy Unlimited - Home Page
  http://www.itsnet.com:80/home/genun/public_html/
  Maps, books & supplies for sale.

- MIPP International, Inc.
  http://www.mipp.msk.ru/books/
  Books for sale from Estonia, Latvia, Lithuania and elsewhere.

◆ Records: Census, Cemeteries, Land, Obituaries, Personal, Taxes and Vital (Born, Married, Died & Buried)

- Museum of Occupations of Estonia - Lists
  http://www.okupatsioon.ee/english/lists/index.html
  Includes lists of political detainees and war dead.

  o Estonian Casualties of the Second World War
    http://www.okupatsioon.ee/propatria/index.html
    Online database of over 6,000 casualties providing surname, given name, rank, unit, decorations, date & place of birth, date & place of death, and burial place.

- Kelmovitz Certificates from Krakes
  http://ds.dial.pipex.com/ttucker/kelmcert.htm
  Family examples of Lithuanian vital records certificates from the 1860s to the early 1900s. Includes scanned images of the certificates.

- Lithuanian Cemeteries in America
  http://www.angelfire.com/ut/Luthuanian/markers.html

- Tocker Certificates from Krakes
  http://ds.dial.pipex.com/ttucker/tockcert.htm
  Family examples of Lithuanian vital records certificates from the 1890s and early 1900s. Includes scanned images of the certificates.

◆ Religion & Churches

- Index to: Religious Personnel in Russia 1853-1854
  http://www.memo.com/jgsr/database/deych.cgi

- Jewish
  http://www.CyndisList.com/jewish.htm
  See this category on Cyndi's List for related links.

- Lithuanian Parishes of the Roman Catholic Diocese in America
  http://www.angelfire.com/ut/Luthuanian/church.html
  Provides contact information.

- Synagogues
  http://www.mznet.org/chamber/pics/synagog.htm
  Pictures of Polish synagogues and former Polish territories now part of Ukraine, Belarus, Lithuania.

◆ Societies & Groups

- Association of the Belarusian Nobility - Zhurtavannie Belaruskaj Sliachty
  http://feefhs.org/by/frg-zbs.html
  Belarus, nobility, Grand Duchy of Lithuanian, genealogy of Belarus, heraldry of Belarus, history of Belarus, Polish-Lithuanian Commonwealth.

- Eesti Genealoogia Selts
  http://www.genealoogia.ee/
  The homepage of the Estonian Genealogical Society.

- FEEFHS - Federation of East European Family History Societies
  http://feefhs.org/

- FEEFHS Location (Address) Index of FEEFHS Member Organizations
  http://feefhs.org/location.html
  And other East European Genealogy Organizations.

- Lithuanian American Genealogy Society (LAGS)
  http://feefhs.org/baltic/lt/frg-lags.html

- Lithuanian Global Genealogical Society
  http://www.lithuaniangenealogy.org/
  Includes a database of over 25,000 names from cemeteries, church directories, etc.

- LitvakSIG (Lithuanian Special Interest Group)
  http://www.jewishgen.org/litvak/
  For researchers of Lithuanian-Jewish genealogy worldwide.

BAPTIST

http://www.cyndislist.com/baptist.htm

Category Index:

◆ General Resource Sites

◆ Libraries, Archives & Museums

◆ Locality Specific

◆ Mailing Lists, Newsgroups & Chat

◆ Publications, Software & Supplies

◆ Societies & Groups

◆ General Resource Sites

● Baptist Church History and Genealogy
http://homepages.rootsweb.com/~baptist/index.html

● Baptist.org - Home Page for All Baptists
http://www.baptist.org/

● Global Baptist Church Directory - All Baptist Churches
http://www.baptistuniverse.com/churches.html

● The Hall of Church History - The Baptists
http://www.gty.org/~phil/baptist.htm
An interesting site with definitions, descriptions and links to a variety of resources for each religious group it highlights.

● Primitive Baptists Online
http://www.primitivebaptist.org/default.asp

● World List of Baptist Churches Online
http://worldlist.baptist.org/

◆ Libraries, Archives & Museums

● The American Baptist - Samuel Colgate Historical Library ~ Rochester, New York
http://www.crds.edu/abhs/default.htm
Purpose is to document the history and thought of the Baptist movement in all of its forms. The Library is believed to hold the largest collection of Baptist related research materials in the world. It holds approximately 80,000 volumes, including over 500 volumes of original church records. More than 400 manuscript collections of Baptist ministers, missionaries, and scholars are kept here.

  ○ Genealogical Services
  http://www.crds.edu/abhs/genealogy.htm

● The Baptist General Convention of Oklahoma Baptist Archives
http://www.bgco.org/SST/gaskin.htm

● Baptist Records in the National Library of Wales
http://www.llgc.org.uk/lc/lcs0054.htm

● Canadian Baptist Archives
http://www.mcmaster.ca/divinity/archives.html
In addition to the records of Canadian Baptist churches, the archives house the records of The Canadian Baptist Ministries (and its predecessor); the Baptist Convention of Ontario & Quebec, the Baptist Union of Western Canada, the Grande Ligne Mission, the

Union d'Églises Baptistes Françaises au Canada, Baptist Women of Canada, McMaster University to 1957, and McMaster Divinity College.

● Freewill Baptist Materials
http://abacus.bates.edu/Library/aboutladd/departments/special/baptist.shtml
From the Ladd Library at Bates College.

● Furman University Libraries
http://library.furman.edu/depts/speccoll/speccoll.htm
The official archives for both the South Carolina Baptist Convention and for Furman University. It also relates to the South Carolina Baptist Historical Society.

● Georgia Baptist History Depository
http://cdsearch.mercer.edu/mainlib/special_collections/GBHD.htm
From Mercer University, Macon, Georgia. Mercer University has collected and preserved Baptist history materials with conscious intent since the late 1870s, following the University's move from Penfield to Macon. At a number of points during the ensuing years, the Georgia Baptist Convention has named the University as the official depository of state Baptist records.

● Hunt Library and Archives of the Woman's Missionary Union
http://www.wmu.com/wmu/resources/library/hla.html

● Kentucky Baptist Archives
http://www.kybaptist.org/archives.htm

● Louisiana Baptist Convention Media Library and Archives
http://www.lbc.org/departments_programs_media.html

● The National Guide to Australian Baptist Historical Resources and Services
http://home.pacific.net.au/~dparker/ng-ndx.htm

● North Carolina Baptist Historical Collection
http://www.wfu.edu/Library/baptist/
From Wake Forest University. Includes searchable online databases.

● Partee Center for Baptist Historical Studies
http://www.jewell.edu/academia/currylibrary/partee/partee.html
From William Jewell College in Liberty, Missouri. Jointly sponsored by the College and the Missouri Baptist Convention, the

Center gives an organized approach to the historical needs of Missouri Baptist churches and fosters an interest in Baptist history of the American Midwest.

- Primitive Baptist Library ~ Carthage, Illinois
  http://www.carthage.lib.il.us/community/churches/primbap/pbl.html

- Riley-Hickingbotham Library Special Collections
  http://www.obu.edu/library/specialcollections.htm
  From Ouachita Baptist University. The archives of the Arkansas Baptist State Convention.

- Samford University Library ~ Birmingham, Alabama
  http://library.samford.edu/
  o Special Collections
    http://library.samford.edu/about/special.shtml
    ▪ The Alabama Baptist Index
      http://library.samford.edu/gateway02/english/

- Southern Baptist Historical Library & Archive ~ Tennessee
  http://www.sbhla.org/
  A world center for the study of Baptist history. Operated by the Council of Seminary Presidents, the SBHLA is one of the major denominational collections in the nation and serves by assignment of the Southern Baptist Convention as the central depository and archives of SBC records.

- Texas Baptist Historical Collection
  http://www.bgct.org/tbhc/
  Purpose is to collect, preserve, and communicate the history of Baptists in Texas.
  o Guide for Church History Writers
    http://www.bgct.org/tbhc/guidhist.htm
  o How to Prepare an Oral History
    http://www.bgct.org/tbhc/oralhist.htm
  o How to Write a Church History
    http://www.bgct.org/tbhc/chhist.htm

◆ Locality Specific

- The Baptist Union of Great Britain
  http://www.baptist.org.uk/

- Beaumont Baptist Church - Church Records ~ Suffolk, England
  http://www.btinternet.com/~beaumontbaptist/Records/index.htm
  Transcribed church records of births, marriages, deaths, membership, and monumental inscriptions from the 1790s to the 1890s.

- Brush Creek Primitive Baptist Church Records (1802-1920)
  http://homepages.rootsweb.com/~mpsmith/
  Brush Creek Primitive Baptist Church of Brush Creek, Smith County, Tennessee was established in May 1802. Continuous Records available from 1828 to 1920.

- Early Members of the First Baptist Church, Holyoke, Massachusetts 1803-1828
  http://www.rootsweb.com/~mahampde/baptist.htm

- First Baptist Church of Ladonia, Texas
  http://www.geocities.com/Heartland/Estates/9755/
  History and information on this church which was established circa 1860.

- History of Baptists in Georgia, 1733-Present
  http://cdsearch.mercer.edu/mainlib/special_collections/GA_Baptists.htm

- LEWIS - LOFTON Family Cemetery
  http://www.geocities.com/wb5hqh/
  Ramah Baptist Church in McCall Creek, Franklin County, Mississippi.

- Northamptonshire Nonconformists
  http://www.geocities.com/grahamsward/noncon.html
  Details of nonconformists or Dissenters in Northamptonshire, England. Includes a directory of chapels of Baptist, Independent & Methodist.

- Rev. Noah Barrell's Record of marriages 1823-1874
  http://www.rootsweb.com/~nycayuga/church/barrell.htm
  Baptist marriages (253) performed by Rev. Barrell between 1823-1874, in New York, Ohio and Wisconsin, including witnesses.

- Victorian London Churches Baptist Union
  http://www.gendocs.demon.co.uk/bapt.html

◆ Mailing Lists, Newsgroups & Chat

- Genealogy Resources on the Internet - Religions / Churches Mailing Lists
  http://www.rootsweb.com/~jfuller/gen_mail_religions.html
  Most of the mailing list links below point to this site, wonderfully maintained by John Fuller

- BAPTIST-ROOTS Mailing List
  http://www.rootsweb.com/~jfuller/gen_mail_religions.html#BAPTIST-ROOTS

- BIBLICAL-GENEALOGY Mailing List
  http://www.rootsweb.com/~jfuller/gen_mail_religions.html#BIBLICAL-GENEALOGY
  For the discussion and sharing of information regarding genealogy in biblical times.

◆ Publications, Software & Supplies

- Amazon.com Genealogy Bookstore - Baptist
  http://www.amazon.com/exec/obidos/external-search/?keyword=baptist+genealogy&tag=markcyndisgenealA/

- AudioTapes.com - Genealogical Lectures on Cassette Tapes - Baptist
  http://www.audiotapes.com/search2.asp?Search=Baptist

- Heritage Books - Seventh Day Baptists
  http://www.heritagebooks.com/baptist.htm

- My Ancestors Were Baptists: How Can I Find Out More About Them?
  http://www.sog.org.uk/acatalog/SoG_Bookshop_Online_My_Ancestors_Series_135.html#a1020s
  Publication for sale from the UK's Society of Genealogists.

◆ Societies & Groups

- American Baptist Historical Society
  http://www.abc-usa.org/abhs/index.html

- Baptist Historical Society ~ United Kingdom
  http://www.baptisthistory.org.uk/index.htm

- Baptist Historical Society of Queensland ~ Australia
  http://thehub.com.au/~dparker/bhsq.htm

- Baptist World Alliance Heritage and Identity Commission
  http://www.congress.baptist-vic.org.au/

- Canadian Baptist Historical Society
  http://www.mcmaster.ca/divinity/historical.html

- Florida Baptist Historical Society
  http://www.fbtc.edu/fbhs/

- The Strict Baptist Historical Society
  http://www.strictbaptisthistory.org.uk/
  For the history of Particular and Strict Baptists in the United Kingdom.

BEGINNERS

http://www.cyndislist.com/beginner.htm

Category Index:

- Beginners Guides, Hints & Tips
- Mailing Lists, Newsgroups & Chat
- Publications, Software & Supplies
- Researching: Birth, Marriage and Death Records
- Researching: Census Records

- Researching: Land Records
- Researching: Localities & Ethnic Groups
- Researching: Military Records
- Researching: Ships, Passenger Lists & Immigration
- Researching: Specialty Records or Topics

◆ Beginners Guides, Hints & Tips

- 26 Genealogy Tips to Get You Started
  http://www.A1WebDesign.com/rebick/26tips.htm
  From Robert Bickham Family Genealogy.

- Beginner's Guide to Family History Research
  http://www.arkansasresearch.com/guide.html
  And an alternate site
  http://www.dhc.net/~jw/guide.html
  By Desmond Walls Allen and Carolyn Earle Billingsley.

- A Crash Course In Genealogy
  http://www.grl.com/grl/start.shtml
  From the Genealogical Research Library.

- Everton Publishers - Getting Started
  http://www.everton.com/intro1.htm

- Family Chronicle - In the VERY Beginning
  http://www.familychronicle.com/begin.htm

- Family History - How Do I Begin?
  http://www.lds.org/fam_his/how_do_i_beg/0-How_Do_I_Begin.html
  From the official LDS Church web site.

- Family History SourceGuide - Discovering Your Family Tree
  http://www.familysearch.org/sg/DisTree.html
  This outline will teach you the five steps of research. 1) Identify what you know about your family. 2) Decide what you want to learn about your family. 3) Select records to search. 4) Obtain and search the record. 5) Use the information.

- Family History SourceGuide - A Guide to Research
  http://www.familysearch.org/sg/Guide_to_Research.html
  This guide teaches you how to find out more about your ancestors using the records available in the Family History Library or one of the Family History Centers throughout the world. It will help you learn to identify what you know about your family, decide what you want to learn about your family, select records to search, obtain and search the records, and use the information.

- First Steps in Genealogy
  http://www.gcpl.lib.oh.us/services/gcr/gen_resources/1ststeps.htm
  From the Greene County Public Library, Ohio.

- Genealogy 101
  http://homepages.rootsweb.com/~bridgett/101a.htm

- Genealogy for the Beginner: A Work in Progress
  http://www.virtualtexan.com/writers/kellow/genbeg.htm
  By Brenda Kellow, C.G.

- A Genealogy Primer
  http://www.sky.net/~mreed/primer.htm

- GEN-NEWBIE-L Home Page
  http://www.rootsweb.com/~newbie/

- Getting Started in Genealogy and Family History
  http://www.genuki.org.uk/gs/

- Getting Started With Genealogical Research
  http://httpsrv.ocs.drexel.edu/grad/sg94e3fd/WEDNESDA.HTM

- Helpful Hints for Successful Searching
  http://www.rootsweb.com/~irlwat/instruct.htm

- How To......
  http://www.cohsoft.com.au/afhc/faq.html
  From the Australian Family History Compendium.

- How-to Get Started on Your Family History
  http://www.firstct.com/fv/pedigree.html

- How To Trace One's Ancestors
  http://www.annie.ne.jp/~dhicks/HowTo.htm

- How To Trace Your Family Tree - Notes For Beginners
  http://website.lineone.net/~glamfhsoc/notes.htm
  From the Glamorgan Family History Society.

- Introduction to Genealogy: An Online Course
  http://www.ngsgenealogy.org/education/content/online/welcome.html
  The National Genealogical Society's online course for beginners.

- National Genealogical Society - Suggestions for Beginners
  http://www.ngsgenealogy.org/getstart/content/suggest.html

- Research Aids for the Family Historian
  http://www.rootsweb.com/~genepool/ogsaids.htm

- ROOTS-L Resources: Info and Tips for Beginning Genealogy
  http://www.rootsweb.com/roots-l/starting.html

- Suggestions for Beginners in Genealogy
  http://pcm.pcmedia.com.au/tags/docs/ngstips1.html

- Suggestions for Tracing Your Family Tree
  http://www.system.missouri.edu/shs/familytr.html
  From the State Historical Society of Missouri.

- Things I Hate and Love About Genealogy and Family History
  http://www.chiprowe.com/articles/genealogy.html

- Tracing Your Family History
  http://www.geocities.com/Heartland/Meadows/9029/

- Tracing Your Family Tree
  http://www.calcna.ab.ca/afhs/bhbegin.html
  By Brian W. Hutchison for the Alberta Family Histories Society.

- Ultimate Family Tree: Get Started with Setting Out
  http://www.uftree.com/UFT/Nav/howtossetting.html

- What Are Archives?
  http://americanhistory.si.edu/archives/a-1.htm
  From the Archives Center of the National Museum of American History.

- Your Great Ancestral Hunt - A Basic Course in American Genealogy
  http://www.graonline.com/lessons/hunt/lessons/lessons.asp
  By Karen Clifford, A.G. Over 60 pages of step-by-step instructions and tips for first time family history hunters. Includes self-tests.

◆ Mailing Lists, Newsgroups & Chat

- Cyndi's List - Chat & IRC
  http://www.CyndisList.com/chat.htm

- Cyndi's List - Mailing Lists
  http://www.CyndisList.com/mailing.htm

- Cyndi's List - Newsgroups
  http://www.CyndisList.com/newsgrps.htm

- Family Tree Finders
  http://www.sodamail.com/site/ftf.shtml
  A Monday through Friday newsletter that provides interesting and useful information for tracing your family tree. It's geared to beginners and experienced family tree trackers of any age! Written by well known genealogist, Rhonda R. McClure.

- GEN-NEWBIE-L Mailing List
  http://www.rootsweb.com/~jfuller/gen_mail_info.html
  #GEN-NEWBIE-L
  A mailing list where people who are new to computers and genealogy may interact using a computer's e-mail program.

- GENTEEN Mailing List
  http://www.rootsweb.com/~jfuller/gen_mail_info.html
  #GENTEEN-L
  For teenagers and young adults who are interested in genealogical research or others who have suggestions or ideas for young genealogists.

- GenTips-L Mailing List
  http://www.rootsweb.com/~jfuller/gen_mail_general.html
  #GenTips-L
  For anyone who has an interest in genealogy. This list hopes to provide tips about obtaining genealogy records and is useful for both beginning genealogists and experts.

- Lost_Newbies Mailing List
  http://www.rootsweb.com/~jfuller/gen_mail_info.html
  #Lost_Newbies
  For people who are new to genealogy and/or the use of the Internet in genealogical research.

- NEWGEN Mailing List
  http://www.rootsweb.com/~jfuller/gen_mail_info.html
  #NEWGEN
  Created to assist those who are quite new to genealogy.

◆ Publications, Software & Supplies

- Amazon.com Genealogy Bookstore - Beginner
  http://www.amazon.com/exec/obidos/external-search/?
  keyword=beginner+genealogy&tag=markcyndisgenealA/

- AudioTapes.com - Genealogical Lectures on Cassette Tapes - Beginner
  http://www.audiotapes.com/search2.asp?Search=beginner

- Cyndi's List - Books
  http://www.CyndisList.com/books.htm

- Cyndi's List - Software & Computers
  http://www.CyndisList.com/software.htm

- Cyndi's List - Supplies, Charts, Forms, Etc.
  http://www.CyndisList.com/supplies.htm

- Frontier Press Bookstore - Beginning Genealogy
  http://www.frontierpress.com/frontier.cgi?category=begin

- GenealogyBookShop.com - Guides and Manuals
  http://www.genealogybookshop.com/genealogybookshop/
  files/General,Guides_and_Manuals/index.html
  The online store of Genealogical Publishing Co., Inc. & Clearfield Company.

- Global Genealogy - General Genealogy Topics & How - To Books
  http://www.globalgenealogy.com/howto.htm

- Heritage Books - Research Aids
  http://www.heritagebooks.com/resaids.htm

- National Genealogical Society - NGS Beginner's Kit
  http://www.ngsgenealogy.org/education/content/beginkit.html

- Repeat Performance - Audio/Video Recording Services
  http://www.repeatperformance.com/
  Tapes of classes and presentations at several genealogy conferences and seminars for the last 18 years.

- The Source: A Guidebook of American Genealogy
  http://www.ancestry.com/home/source/srcindex.htm
  A full, online version of this book, published by Ancestry, edited by Loretto Dennis Szucs and Sandra Hargreaves Luebking.

- Willow Bend Bookstore - How To Genealogy
  http://www.willowbend.net/default.asp

◆ Researching: Birth, Marriage and Death Records

- Cyndi's List - U.S. - Vital Records
  http://www.CyndisList.com/usvital.htm

- Family History SourceGuide - Where to Write for Vital Records
  http://www.cdc.gov/nchs/howto/w2w/w2welcom.htm

- Finding a Marriage Date
  http://www.familytreemaker.com/11_mrgdt.html
  by Karen Clifford, A.G.

- Genealogy Bulletin - Where to Find Birth, Death, Marriage and Divorce Records
  http://www.genealogybulletin.com/archives/HTML/current2.html
  By William Dollarhide.

- Ordering Birth Registration Certificates from the United Kingdom
  http://www.oz.net/~markhow/ukbirths.htm
  Using the LDS Family History Center Resources.

- Researching Your Family's Marriages
  http://www.familytreemaker.com/issue11.html

- RootsWeb's Guide to Tracing Family Trees - Lesson 4: Vital Records: Death, Tombstones and Cemeteries
  http://www.rootsweb.com/~rwguide/lesson4.htm

- RootsWeb's Guide to Tracing Family Trees - Lesson 5: Vital Records: Marriage Records and Evidence
  http://www.rootsweb.com/~rwguide/lesson5.htm

- RootsWeb's Guide to Tracing Family Trees - Lesson 6: Vital Records: Birth Records
  http://www.rootsweb.com/~rwguide/lesson6.htm

- Shaking Your Family Tree: Finding Vital Records The Easy Way
  http://www.uftree.com/bin/fg_auth?/GenealogyNewsstand/ShakingTree/Books/981210.html
  By Myra Vanderpool Gormley, C.G.

- Shaking Your Family Tree: Vital Records
  http://www.uftree.com/bin/fg_auth?/GenealogyNewsstand/ShakingTree/Vital/Vital.html
  By Myra Vanderpool Gormley, C.G.

- Vital Records Information - State Index
  http://vitalrec.com/index.html
  Information about where to obtain vital records (such as birth, death & marriage certificates and divorce decrees) from each state, territory and county of the United States.

- Where to Write for Vital Records
  http://www.cdc.gov/nchswww/howto/w2w/w2welcom.htm
  From the National Center for Health Statistics, United States

◆ Researching: Census Records

- Cyndi's List - Census Related Sites Worldwide
  http://www.CyndisList.com/census2.htm

- Cyndi's List - U.S. - Census
  http://www.CyndisList.com/census.htm

- Guide to the Soundex System
  http://www.lib.auburn.edu/madd/docs/soundexhs.html

- How to Use Soundex for United States Census Records
  http://www.hpl.lib.tx.us/clayton/soundex.html

- Researching with Census Records
  http://www.familytreemaker.com/issue13.html

- Using Census Records
  http://www.micronet.net/users/~searcy/records.htm

- Using the Soundex System
  http://www.ancestry.com/columns/george/03-20-98.htm
  From "Along Those Lines..." by George G. Morgan

◆ Researching: Land Records

- Cyndi's List - Land Records, Deeds, Homesteads, Etc.
  http://www.CyndisList.com/land.htm

- How to Search Deeds
  http://www.dohistory.org/on_your_own/toolkit/deeds.html
  From DoHistory.

  o Form for Deed Research Notes
    http://www.dohistory.org/on_your_own/toolkit/deeds_form.html

- Land Record Reference
  http://www.ultranet.com/~deeds/landref.htm

- Land Records: History of and How to Use Them
  http://homepages.rootsweb.com/~haas/learningcenter/landinfo.html

- Retracing the Trails of Your Ancestors Using Deed Records
  http://www.ultranet.com/~deeds/deeds.htm
  By William Dollarhide, from the Genealogy Bulletin, Issue No. 25, Jan-Feb 1995.

- US Land & Property Research
  http://users.arn.net/~billco/uslpr.htm
  By Bill Utterback for the IIGS University.

◆ Researching: Localities & Ethnic Groups

- African American Genealogy
  http://www.familytreemaker.com/issue12.html

- African American Lifelines
  http://pages.prodigy.net/cliffmurr/aa_life.htm
  How-to for beginners.

- Ancestors from Norway - Getting Started
  http://homepages.rootsweb.com/~norway/na15.html

- Beginning Genealogical Research for England &
  Wales
  http://www.oz.net/~markhow/ukbegin.htm
  By Mark Howells.

- Finding Where Your Ancestors Came From in
  Germany
  http://www.angelfire.com/biz/origins1/ancestors.html

- Finding Your New England Ancestors
  http://www.familytreemaker.com/issue25.html

- Genealogy Research in Stuttgart Libraries and
  Archives
  http://www.kinquest.com/genealogy/resources/stuttgart.html
  Tips and hints by Lisa Petersen.

- German Genealogical Research Before The Church
  Records Begin
  http://www.kinquest.com/genealogy/resources/
  researching.html
  Tips and hints by Lisa Petersen.

- German Research at Libraries and Archives in
  Baden-Wuerttemberg
  http://www.kinquest.com/genealogy/resources/badwue.html
  Tips and hints by Lisa Petersen.

- How To Guide for Native Americans
  http://members.aol.com/bbbenge/page12.html

- Have You Found a Swedish Ancestor?
  http://www.geocities.com/Heartland/Meadows/7095/
  swede.html

- Hvordan Finner Jeg Etterkommere Av De Som
  Utvandret Til USA? / How Do I Find Descendants of
  a Norwegian Immigrant to the USA?
  http://homepages.rootsweb.com/~norway/na14.html
  *In Norwegian; for Norwegians who are tracing descendants of a
  Norwegian immigrant to the USA.*

- An Introduction to Jewish Genealogy in Manitoba
  http://www.concentric.net/~Lkessler/genbegin.shtml

- Irish Research Resources
  http://www.familytreemaker.com/issue30.html

- Native American Genealogy
  http://www.system.missouri.edu/shs/nativeam.html
  A guide from the State Historical Society Of Missouri.

- Researching Ancestors from the United Kingdom
  http://www.oz.net/~markhow/uksearch.htm
  Using the LDS Family History Center Resources.

- Researching Irish Roots
  http://www.familytreemaker.com/issue4.html

- Swedish Information Service - Internet Resources for
  Tracing Your Swedish Roots
  http://www.webcom.com/sis/tracing.html

- Tim's Tips on Pennsylvania German Research
  http://www.geocities.com/Heartland/Plains/3816/how2.html

◆ Researching: Military Records

- Cyndi's List - Canada - Military
  http://www.CyndisList.com/milcan.htm

- Cyndi's List - U.K. - Military
  http://www.CyndisList.com/miluk.htm

- Cyndi's List - U.S. - Civil War ~ War for Southern
  Independence
  http://www.CyndisList.com/cw.htm

- Cyndi's List - U.S. - Military
  http://www.CyndisList.com/military.htm

- How To Obtain A Revolutionary War Pension File
  http://www.teleport.com/~carolynk/howtofil.htm

- How to Order Military & Pension Records for Union
  Civil War Veterans
  http://www.oz.net/~cyndihow/pensions.htm
  From the National Archives.

- Obtaining Military Pension Files from the VA
  http://www.kinquest.com/genealogy/resources/va.html

- Researching Civil War Soldiers
  http://www.familytreemaker.com/issue7.html

- Researching Revolutionary War Veterans
  http://www.familytreemaker.com/issue24.html

- War of 1812 Records: Where and How do I get
  them?
  http://www.rootsweb.com/~kyharris/1812how.htm

◆ Researching: Ships, Passenger Lists & Immigration

- Cyndi's List - Immigration & Naturalization
  http://www.CyndisList.com/immigrat.htm

- Cyndi's List - Ships & Passenger Lists
  http://www.CyndisList.com/ships.htm

- How To Find Your Immigrant Ancestor - Passenger
  and Immigration Lists Index
  http://www.rader.org/how_to.htm

- How to Get Your Ancestor's Papers from the
  Immigration and Naturalization Service
  http://www.italgen.com/immigrat.htm

- LDS Passenger Manifests - A Guide to Using the
  Passenger Lists at Your Local Family History Center
  http://homepage.interaccess.com/~arduinif/tools/ldsmanif.htm

- Passport Application Record Information From the
  National Archives
  http://homepages.rootsweb.com/~godwin/reference/
  passport.html

- Requesting Your Ancestor's Naturalization Records from the INS
  http://yin.interaccess.com/~arduinif/tools/insreque.htm
  A guide by Dennis Piccirillo

◆ Researching: Specialty Records or Topics

- How to do Genealogical Research using FBI Files?
  http://members.aol.com/rechtman/fbi.html

- John's Genealogy Junction - Masonic Records
  http://www.wf.net/~jyates/research.htm
  Information about genealogical information obtainable from records of Masonic lodges.

- Locating Published Genealogies
  http://www.familytreemaker.com/15_genes.html
  By Donna Przecha.

- Local Histories: Finding and Evaluating
  http://www.genealogy.com/genealogy/15_local.html
  By Myra Vanderpool Gormley, C.G.

- Passport Application Record Information From the National Archives
  http://homepages.rootsweb.com/~godwin/reference/passport.html

- Using Federal Documents In Genealogical Research - U.S.
  http://www.history.rochester.edu/jssn/page1.htm

BELGIUM / BELGIQUE / BELGIË
http://www.cyndislist.com/belgium.htm

Category Index:

◆ General Resource Sites

◆ History & Culture

◆ Libraries, Archives & Museums

◆ Mailing Lists, Newsgroups & Chat

◆ Maps, Gazetteers & Geographical Information

◆ People & Families

◆ Professional Researchers, Volunteers & Other Research Services

◆ Publications, Software & Supplies

◆ Queries, Message Boards & Surname Lists

◆ Records: Census, Cemeteries, Land, Obituaries, Personal, Taxes and Vital

◆ Societies & Groups

◆ General Resource Sites

• Belgium - Immigrants in America
http://www.ping.be/picavet/
A complete guide for descendants of Belgian immigrants looking for their roots in Belgium.

• The BELGIUM-ROOTS Project
http://belgium.rootsweb.com/

• Digital Resources Netherlands and Belgium
http://home.wxs.nl/~hjdewit/links_en.html
A list of resources for the Internet, bulletin board systems (bbs) and diskette/CD-Rom.

• The Emigration from the Waasland to the United States and Canada 1830 – 1950
http://www.geocities.com/Heartland/Plains/5666/Picavet.html
Or an alternate site
http://www.concentric.net/~Mikerice/hl/more/gpicavet.shtml
A project by Georges Picavet.

• Genealogie in Limburg
http://home.wxs.nl/~eugdub/

• Genealogy Benelux Home Page
http://www.ufsia.ac.be/genealogy/

• Genealogy Benelux Web Ring
http://www.geocities.com/Heartland/Plains/5521/benelux.htm
Belgium Genealogy, Netherlands & Dutch Genealogy, Luxembourg Genealogy.

• Genealogy in Belgium
http://win-www.uia.ac.be/u/pavp/sdv/index.html

• Genealogy in Belgium
http://win-www.uia.ac.be/u/pavp/sdv/index.html
From Denis Beauregard. Mostly in French until English translation is complete.

• Genealogy in Flanders
http://members.xoom.com/ivodb/flanders/

• Infobel - Find Business & Residential Addresses in Belgium
http://www.infobel.be/infobel/

• STORME's Genealogy Page
http://www.ufsia.ac.be/~estorme/genealogy.html
Many great Benelux resource links. STORME, van WAESBERGHE de LAUSNAY, BLOCK, SCHEERDERS, van SCHOUBROEK, de SCHRYVER, BOSTEELS.

• "Wallonia" - Genealogy Database from French-speaking Belgium
http://www.ufsia.ac.be/genealogy/wallonia/wallonia.htm
Brussels and Wallonia.

◆ History & Culture

• StudyWeb: History: Country History Index: Europe Index: Belgium
http://www.studyweb.com/links/4024.html

◆ Libraries, Archives & Museums

• Archives in Belgium
http://members.xoom.com/janssen_BE/genealogy/BEL-archives/arch.html
Overview of Municipal, Provincial and State Archives, Special Interest and Museum Archives, Regional History Societies and Genealogical Societies in Belgium.

• Archives de l'Etat en Belgique
http://arch.arch.be/MENU_FR.HTML
The state archives in Belgium.

• Archives of Mechelen, Belgium Sources for Genealogy
http://www.mechelen.be/archief/archiefe.htm

• Les Centres Généalogiques SDJ / LDS Family History Centers
http://www.ldsmissions.net/fpm/genealogie.html
France, Belgique, Suisse, Canada.

- Family History Library Catalog
  http://www.familysearch.org/Search/searchcatalog.asp
  From the FamilySearch web site, an online catalog to the holdings of the LDS Church in Salt Lake City, Utah. Also search for other localities by place name.
  http://www.familysearch.org/fhlc/supermainframeset.asp?
  display=localitysearch&columns=*,180,0
  - Belgium
    http://www.familysearch.org/fhlc/supermainframeset.asp?
    display=localitydetails&subject=145&subject_disp=Belgium
    &columns=*,180,0

- Family History SourceGuide - Family History Centers - Europe and Scandinavia
  http://www.familysearch.org/sg/Europe_and_Scandinavia_
  FHC.html
  Austria, Belgium, Denmark, Finland, France, Germany, Hungary, Iceland, Italy, Netherlands, Norway, Portugal, Spain, Sweden, and Switzerland.

- Repositories of Primary Sources - Europe - Belgium
  http://www.uidaho.edu/special-collections/euro1.html#be
  A list of links to online resources from the Univ. of Idaho Library, Special Collections and Archives.

- Royal Museum of the Army and Military History / Koninklijk Museum van het Leger en de krijgsgeschiedenis / Musée royal de l'armée et d'histoire militaire ~ Belgium
  http://www.klm-mra.be/

◆ Mailing Lists, Newsgroups & Chat

- Genealogy Resources on the Internet - Belgium Mailing Lists
  http://www.rootsweb.com/~jfuller/gen_mail_country-blg.html
  Most of the mailing list links below point to this site, wonderfully maintained by John Fuller

- BELGIUM-ROOTS Mailing List
  http://www.rootsweb.com/~jfuller/gen_mail_country-
  blg.html#BELGIUM-ROOTS
  For the descendants of Belgian emigrants/immigrants who are interested in researching their roots in Belgium.

- GEN-BENELUX Mailing List
  http://www.rootsweb.com/~jfuller/gen_mail_country-
  blg.html#GEN-BENELUX
  Gatewayed with the news:soc.genealogy.benelux
  news:soc.genealogy.benelux
  For research in the Benelux region (Belgium, the Netherlands, and Luxembourg).

- GENBNL-L Mailing List
  http://www.rootsweb.com/~jfuller/gen_mail_country-
  blg.html#DUTCH
  Gatewayed with the soc.genealogy.benelux newsgroup
  news:soc.genealogy.benelux
  For research in the Benelux region (Belgium, the Netherlands, and Luxembourg).

◆ Maps, Gazetteers & Geographical Information

- Belgium Place Names
  http://www.ping.be/picavet/Waas_America_Research21.shtml

- Map of Belgium
  http://www.lib.utexas.edu/Libs/PCL/Map_collection/europe/
  BELGIUM.GIF
  From the Perry-Castañeda Library at the Univ. of Texas at Austin.

◆ People & Families

- Ahnentafel/Kwartierstaat Nada Kimberley Klaps
  http://gallery.uunet.be/PRO-GEN.GG.LIMBURG/Klaps.html
  KLAPS, PHETSUWAN, HERMANS, NINSUWAN, GOOSSENS, VERNELEN, JAME, CRAEGHS, MARTENS, SMEYERS.

- Belgium's Royal Family
  http://www.geocities.com/Heartland/Plains/5209/

- BLONDIA and family
  http://members.aol.com/rblondia/genealogy/index.htm

- Familiearchief - Panis, Geusens, Houben, Lindmans en vele andere families
  http://www.falcon.be/familiearchief/

- Genealogiepagina van Luc SILLIS
  http://gallery.uunet.be/luxil/genealogie.htm

- Genealogy of DUBOIS-HAVERMANS
  http://members.xoom.com/Dubke/dub-hav.htm
  Genealogy of Family Dubois-Havermans (Belgium).

- Index of Persons - Famille ADAMS et apparentees
  http://users.skynet.be/sky39882/geneal/persons.htm
  ADAMS, KLEPPER, VAN ACHTER, De KIMPE, VANDERHAEGEN.

- Kings of Belgium
  http://members.xoom.com/ivodb/kings/index.htm

- Male Descendants of Gerardus VAN WIJCK
  http://www.ping.be/~ping2855/

- Marc VERMEIRSSEN's Homepage
  http://bewoner.dma.be/mvermeir/
  Vermeirssen, Vermeerssen, Vermeirsschen, Vermeirssch, Vermeerren.

- The ORBAN's
  http://www.geocities.com/CapeCanaveral/7473/orban.html
  Belgium, Hungary.

- La Page Genealogique De Gilbert MINETTE
  http://users.skynet.be/sky40172/index.htm

- Pascal JANSSENs Genealogy Page
  http://pucky.uia.ac.be/~janssen/genealogy/
  HEBBINCKHUYS, CEULEMANS, SCHAUWERS.

- Piet WOLLAERT
  http://bewoner.dma.be/PietWoll/
  Afstamming van Joannes Wollaert in Oost-Vlaanderen, Belgium.

- VAN BEESEN: Ma Généalogie et autres liens
  http://users.swing.be/patrick.vanbeesen/

◆ Professional Researchers, Volunteers & Other Research Services

- European Focus
  http://www.eurofocus.com/
  Photographic portfolios of ancestral towns in Europe created for Genealogy enthusiasts in Belgium, Denmark, Eastern Europe, England, France, Germany, Great Britain, Italy, Netherlands, Norway, Poland, Sweden, Switzerland and more.

- Genealogy Helplist - Belgium
  http://helplist.org/bel/index.shtml

- Mark Windover's Web Page - Quality Professional Genealogical Research ~ Williamstown, Massachusetts
  http://www.windover.com/
  United States, Canada (including French), England, Scotland, Ireland, Wales, Iceland, Germany, Switzerland, Norway, Sweden, Denmark, France, Belgium, and The Netherlands.

◆ Publications, Software & Supplies

- Amazon.com Genealogy Bookstore - Belgium
  http://www.amazon.com/exec/obidos/external-search/?keyword=belgium+genealogy&tag=markcyndisgenealA/

- Books We Own - Belgium
  http://www.rootsweb.com/~bwo/belgium.html
  Find a book from which you would like a lookup and click on the submitter's code at the end of the entry. Once you find the contact information for the submitter, write them a polite request for a lookup.

- Index: Old Ordnance Survey Maps - The Godfrey Edition
  http://www.alangodfreymaps.co.uk/
  List of UK and Belgium maps available at large scale in the period of about 1890 to 1915.

- PRO-GEN Genealogie àla Carte
  http://www.pro-gen.nl/
  Dutch genealogy program capable of outputs in Dutch, English, French, Frisian and German.

◆ Queries, Message Boards & Surname Lists

- Lineages' Free On-line Queries - Belgium
  http://www.lineages.com/queries/Search.asp?Country=Belgium

- Project Ahnentafels in Limburg / Project Limburgse Kwartierstaten
  http://gallery.uunet.be/PRO-GEN.GG.LIMBURG/Ahnen.html

◆ Records: Census, Cemeteries, Land, Obituaries, Personal, Taxes and Vital (Born, Married, Died & Buried)

- Digital Resources Netherlands and Belgium
  http://home.wxs.nl/~hjdewit/links_en.html
  Digital resources available on the internet, bulletin board systems and on diskette/CD-ROM.

- Stadsarchief van Mechelen. Aanbod voor Genealogen
  http://www.mechelen.be/archief/archief.html
  Archives of Mechelen. Main sources for genealogy

  - Criminaliteit te Mechelen van 1773 tot 1795
    http://www.mechelen.be/archief/Vonnissn.htm
    Criminal records between 1773 and 1795.

  - Mechelen: Register Van De Belastingen Op De Huizen Anno 1722: Sint Katelijneparochie
    http://www.mechelen.be/archief/katelijn.htm
    House Tax Registry anno 1722: Sint Katelijne .

  - Mechelse conscrits of (kandidaat-)soldaten voor het Franse leger (1798-1814)
    http://www.mechelen.be/archief/ConscritIndex2.html
    Conscrits for the French army (1798-1814)

◆ Societies & Groups

- Club De Genealogie De Sambreville (Belgique)
  http://www.multimania.com/bcollard/

- Fédération Généalogique et Héraldique de Belgique / Belgische Federatie voor Genealogie en Heraldiek
  http://www.karolus.org/org/assoc/as-euro/as-be-2a.htm

- Genealogical Society of Flemish Americans
  http://members.xoom.com/GSFA
  GSFA publishes a newsletter and helps people trace their Flemish and Belgian heritage.

- GENSESEM - Cercle de généalogie de Chimay
  http://users.skynet.be/sky38740/

- Histoire des Familles ^ Tournai
  http://users.skynet.be/sky67508/
  Home page de la Section Histoire des Familles de la Société Royale d'Histoire et d'Archéologie de Tournai.

- PRO-GEN gebruikersgroep LIMBURG / PRO-GEN users' group LIMBURG
  http://gallery.uunet.be/PRO-GEN.GG.LIMBURG/index.html

- Sällskapet Vallonättlingar - Society The Descendents of the Walloons of Sweden
  http://www.vallon.a.se/
  A society for the descendents of Belgian emigrants to Sweden in the early seventeenth century. Genealogical research in Sweden, Finland, USA and Belgium.

- Vlaamse Vereniging voor Familiekunde - V.V.F. - Flemish Society of Genealogists
  http://win-www.uia.ac.be/u/pavp/sdv/vvf.htm

BIOGRAPHIES
http://www.cyndislist.com/biograph.htm

Category Index:
- General Resource Sites
- Locality Specific
- People & Families
- Publications, Software & Supplies
- Volunteer Projects

◆ General Resource Sites

- **American Life Histories: Manuscripts from the Federal Writers' Project, 1936-1940**
  http://lcweb2.loc.gov/ammem/wpaintro/wpahome.html
  "These life histories were written by the staff of the Folklore Project of the Federal Writers' Project for the U.S. Works Progress (later Work Projects) Administration (WPA) from 1936-1940. The Library of Congress collection includes 2,900 documents representing the work of over 300 writers from 24 states."

- **Biographical Dictionary**
  http://www.s9.com/biography/
  Covers more than 19,000 notable men and women.

- **biographie-center.com**
  http://www.biography-center.com/

- **Biographies and Histories from Around the World**
  http://vader.castles.com/ftprints/8-000000.html

- **Biography.com**
  http://www.biography.com/
  A biographical database from the makers of the A&E "Biography" series.

- **Bio-Legacy**
  http://www.biolegacy.net
  We create personal biographies for yourself and/or a loved one for all generations to cherish.

- **Celebrate A Life.com**
  http://www.celebratealife.com/biographies/index.asp
  Dedicated to capturing and preserving the stories of people's lives.

- **Colonial Hall: Biographies of America's Founding Fathers**
  http://www.colonialhall.com/

- **Congressional Biographical Directory**
  http://bioguide.congress.gov/biosearch/biosearch.asp
  Biographical directory of the United States Congress 1774 to present.

- **Distinguished Women of Past and Present**
  http://www.DistinguishedWomen.com/

- **Journeyings: Life Stories and Corporate Histories**
  http://www.hotlinkswd.com/journeyings/

- **The LifeStory Institute**
  http://www.kansas.net/~lifestor/

- **North American Slave Narratives**
  http://metalab.unc.edu/docsouth/neh/neh.html
  From Documenting the American South.

- **Universitätsbibliothek TU BS, WBI Recherche**
  http://www.biblio.tu-bs.de/acwww25u/wbi_en/
  World Biographical Index. From K. G. Saur Publishing and Braunschweig University Library. This database is based on the fifth edition of the World Biographical Index containing about 2.4 million short biographical entries for eminent individuals who lived in North and South America, Western and Central Europe, Australia, New Zealand, and Oceania. This edition is also a compiled index to many biographical archives.

◆ Locality Specific

- **Amherst College Biographical Record (1821-1921)**
  http://www.amherst.edu/~rjyanco/genealogy/acbiorecord/
  Biographies of 9,110 graduates and non-graduates of Amherst (Massachusetts) College, from its first hundred years.

- **Beers Biographical Record Online - Washington County, Pennsylvania**
  http://www.chartiers.com/beers-project/beers.html
  Biographical Sketches of Prominent and Representative Citizens and of many of the Early Settled Families.

- **Biographical Sketches Relating to Sussex County ~ New Jersey**
  http://www.gate.net/~pascalfl/bioindex.html

- **Biographies from the Memorial and Biographical Record ~ South Dakota**
  http://www.rootsweb.com/~usgenweb/sd/biography/memor.htm

- **California County Biographies and Histories**
  http://www.compuology.com/cpl/cpl_bio.htm

- **Cowlitz County Biographies ~ Washington**
  http://www.halcyon.com/jennyrt/wacowlitz/bios.html

- **A Centennial Tribute: Creators of the Legacy ~ Palo Alto, California**
  http://www.commerce.digital.com/palo-alto/historical-assoc/centennial-bios/home.html

- **Crawford County, Indiana - Biographies**
  http://cgi.rootsweb.com/~genbbs/genbbs.cgi/USA/In/CrawfordBios

- Decatur County, Iowa Genealogy - Pioneer Biographies
  http://www.rootsweb.com/~iadecat2/bios.htm

- First Person Narratives of the American South
  http://metalab.unc.edu/docsouth/fpn/fpn.html
  From Documenting the American South.

- Florida Biography Index - State Library of Florida
  http://dlis.dos.state.fl.us/stlib/flbioindex.htm

- Goodspeed's Biographies
  http://hometown.aol.com/gengl16616/index.htm
  Transcribed biographies from the "History of Southeast Missouri - Embracing an Historical Account of the counties of Ste. Genevieve, St. Francois, Perry, Cape Girardeau, Bollinger, Madison, New Madrid, Pemiscot, Dunklin, Scott, Mississippi, Stoddard, Butler, Wayne and Iron" published by Goodspeed Publishing Company of Chicago, Illinois in 1888.

- Harrison County Iowa Biographies
  http://www.rootsweb.com/~iaharris/bio/genealog.htm

- Hayden Arizona Pioneer Biographies Collection
  http://www.asu.edu/lib/archives/azbio/
  Collected and written by Senator Carl Hayden of Arizona.

- History of Oklahoma Volume III published 1916 by Joseph B. Thoburn
  http://cgi.rootsweb.com/~genbbs/genbbs.cgi/USA/Ok/OkBios
  Message board with biographies transcribed from the above publication.

- Illinois Biographies
  http://www.lis.uiuc.edu/~sorensen/BIOS.HTM
  Links to biographical sketches of people who have had a relationship with Illinois.

- Indiana Biographies Database
  http://199.8.200.90:591/ibioverview.html
  From the Indiana State Library.

- Indiana Biography
  http://www.ipfw.edu/ipfwhist/indiana/biog.htm
  From the Department of History, Indiana University-Purdue University Fort Wayne.

- Kentuckiana Konnections - Biographies ~ Kentucky & Indiana
  http://www.kentuckianagenealogy.org/boards/messages/13/13.html

- Lewis County Biographies ~ Washington
  http://www.halcyon.com/jennyrt/bios/bios.html

- The Life and Times of South Dakota Pioneers
  http://www.rootsweb.com/~sdpotter/Letters/home.htm

- Biographical Record of Linn County, Iowa ~ Iowa
  http://www.genhist.com/IABios/linn/b1901/b1901.htm

- Louisa County Genealogical Society Biographies ~ Iowa
  http://www.rootsweb.com/~ialcgs/lbios.htm

- Marion County Indiana Biographies
  http://www.ameritech.net/users/iratgregg/marion.html

- Maryville Tennessee Biographies
  http://www.ci.maryville.tn.us/cityhist/biogrphy.htm

- Muscatine County Iowa - Pioneers Page
  http://www.rootsweb.com/~iamusca2/people.htm

- Notable Women Ancestors
  http://www.rootsweb.com/~nwa/

- Ohio Historical Society - Biographies of Ohio Governors
  http://www.ohiohistory.org/onlinedoc/ohgovernment/governors/index.html

- San Francisco Biographies ~ California
  http://www.sfmuseum.org/hist1/index1.html

- SD Biographies ~ South Dakota
  http://www.rootsweb.com/~usgenweb/sd/biography/bios.htm

- Southern Illinois Biographies
  http://members.xoom.com/annable/bioindex.html

- Webster County Biographies ~ Kentucky
  http://www.rootsweb.com/~kywebste/biogs/biogs.htm

- Yukon / Alaska Pioneer Biographies
  http://arcticculture.about.com/culture/arcticculture/library/ya/msub15y.htm?pid=2744&cob=home

◆ People & Families

- Augustine GODWIN of Wyoming Township, Kent County, Michigan
  http://homepages.rootsweb.com/~godwin/family/augustine.html

- Autobiography of the Rev. William GILL
  http://www.genuki.org.uk/big/eng/Indexes/REVWGILL.txt
  A list of names indexed from the book.

- Biography of Jeptha THORNTON
  http://www.rootsweb.com/~ordougla/jeptha.htm
  An Oregon pioneer.

- Biography of Joanna QUAID
  http://www.pclink.com/kg0ay/quaid.htm
  She was born in Ireland and made the trek to the United States in 1836.

- Brave BENBOW
  http://www.islandnet.com/~b.benbow/
  Biography of Admiral John BENBOW 1653 - 1702; British Admiral involved in the Benbow Mutiny; includes genealogies. Published book for sale.

- Francis Marion GAY, Co. F 65th Reg. Georgia Infantry
  http://www.izzy.net/~michaelg/fm-gay.htm

- Genealogical Investigation into Charles J. ARIS
  http://www.oz.net/~markhow/chasaris.htm
  World War I veteran, 16th Queen's Own Lancers, a cavalry unit of the British Army.

- Henry Hudson - The life and times of Henry Hudson, explorer and adventurer
  http://www.georgian.net/rally/hudson/

- Heritage Gateway - Pioneer Journals
  http://heritage.uen.org/cgi-bin/websql/pioneer.hts?type=1
  Members of the LDS church.

- The History of Will STRODE
  http://www.rootsweb.com/~cokitcar/willhist.htm
  Of Kit Carson County, Colorado.

- Isaac Spears SANDERLIN, Private, Co. I, 100th Ohio Volunteer Infantry in the Civil War
  http://www.oz.net/~cyndihow/isaac.htm
  Cyndi's 3rd great-grandfather.

- Journals of Early Members of the Church of Jesus Christ of Latter-day Saints
  http://www.math.byu.edu/~smithw/Lds/LDS/Early-Saints/
  Journals, diaries, biographies and autobiographies of some early Mormons and others who knew Joseph Smith, Jr.

- Letters and Stories - A Pioneer's Story - By Joe PLETCHER, told August 5, 1905
  http://www.geocities.com/Heartland/Hills/5807/story.html

- Letters from an Iowa Soldier in the Civil War
  http://www.civilwarletters.com/home.html
  Part of a collection written by Newton Robert SCOTT, Private, Company A, of the 36th Infantry, Iowa Volunteers to Hannah CONE, his friend and later his wife.

- Life of Polly HART LANE
  http://www.genweb.net/~bowers/lane/pollyp.htm
  Polly Pierce (Pierre) Hart LANE born in 1802 in Kentucky.

- The Life of "Racket" JOHNSON
  http://homepages.rootsweb.com/~godwin/family/racket.html
  As told by his grandson, George Thomas Johnson. About 1794-95 in Sussex.

- MA RYAN, Co B 14th Miss Vol Inf CSA
  http://www.izzy.net/~michaelg/ma-ryan.htm
  Experience of a Confederate Soldier in Camp and Prison in The Civil War 1861-1865.

- MercerGirls.com ~ Washington
  http://www.mercergirls.com/
  They Called Them the "Mercer Girls." Washington Territory's Cargo of Brides.

- My Virtual Reference Desk - Biography / Who's Who
  http://www.refdesk.com/factbiog.html

- Sabbath Keepers in History
  http://www.ozemail.com.au/~sdbbris/books/new/index2.htm
  From the Time of Christ to the 19th Century. Reprints from "Seventh Day Baptists in Europe and America" Volume 1 (pp 11 - 115), American Sabbath Tract Society, Plainfield, New Jersey, 1910.

- The Saga of Bad John HALL
  http://www.geocities.com/Heartland/Bluffs/2784/
  The true story of the legendary Bad John HALL, with family info and pictures.

- This One is on Me
  http://www.iwaynet.net/~lsci/Panhandle/Home.html
  By Dr. James Lee Fisher (1895-1987). The life-story of an old doctor who saw many changes in medicine, in industry, in social customs, and the world in general.

- Time Line for Charles Ransom DeLAP 1828-1945
  http://www.rootsweb.com/~orklamat/delap.html
  An Oregon pioneer.

- Titanic, Alma PAULSON, Genealogi, Släktforskning
  http://w1.426.telia.com/~u42602097/
  Alma BERGLUND (married PAULSON) was one of 3000 people who traveled with Titanic. Read all about her destiny and take a look at my genealogy.

- A Twist Of Fate Over Austria
  http://www.greeceny.com/ol/herb2.htm
  My Uncle Was Killed in a B-24 bomber in WW2 and I interviewed the surviving crew members about what happened that day.

- La Vie De DUPLEIX
  http://members.aol.com/MDruez/dupleix.htm
  Francois Joseph Dupleix, governor of Pondicherry for Louis XV of France in India (mid 18th century).

- Xerxes KNOX, Private, Co. G, 3rd Iowa Cavalry in the Civil War
  http://www.oz.net/~cyndihow/xerxes.htm
  Cyndi's 3rd great-grandfather and a prisoner at Camp Ford in Tyler, Texas.

- A Yankee Prisoner In Texas --- William Ryan
  http://www.greeceny.com/ol/herb.htm
  My great grandfather was in Camp Ford, and this is his story.

◆ Publications, Software & Supplies

- Amazon.com Genealogy Bookstore - Biography
  http://www.amazon.com/exec/obidos/external-search/?keyword=writing+biography+genealogy&tag=markcyndisgenealA/

- AudioTapes.com - Genealogical Lectures on Cassette Tapes - Biography
  http://www.audiotapes.com/search2.asp?Search=biograph

- Family Stories Video Family History
  http://members.aol.com/quickbyte/familystories.html
  Professionally produced, PBS-style documentary of a parent, grandparent, or other family member telling their life story and communicating with generations across time and space, visually and orally, in their own words.

- Frontier Press Bookstore - Biography
  http://www.frontierpress.com/frontier.cgi?category=biog

- Life.com - My Life Software
  http://www.life.com/
  Personal history software that lets you tell your life's story in text, family photos, audio and video.

- MyStory - The Complete Autobiography Writing System!
  http://www.mystorywriter.com/

◆ Volunteer Projects

- **KYBIOGRAPHIES Mailing List**
  http://www.rootsweb.com/~jfuller/gen_mail_states-ky.html#KYBIOGRAPHIES
  A read-only mailing list (no queries or submissions) transmitting biographies on all the Kentucky people cited in the old histories (e.g., Perrins, Collins, church histories).

- **U.S. Biographies Project**
  http://members.tripod.com/~debmurray/usbios/usbiog.html
  A project by Jeff Murphy. Adopt a state and put biographies online!

  - **Alabama Biographies Project**
    http://www.jolts.com/albios/

  - **California County Biographies and Histories**
    http://www.compuology.com/cpl/cpl_bio.htm

  - **Connecticut Biographies Project**
    http://www.jolts.com/ctbios

  - **Delaware Biographies Project**
    http://www.rootsweb.com/~debiog/

  - **District of Columbia Biographies Project**
    http://www.rootsweb.com/~usgenweb/dc/dcfbiopg.htm

  - **Florida Biographies Project**
    http://members.tripod.com/~debmurray/usbios/florida.html

  - **Georgia Biographies Project**
    http://www.jolts.com/gabios/

  - **Idaho Biographies Project**
    http://members.tripod.com/~James_Combs/Idaho.html

  - **Illinois Biographies Project**
    http://www.rootsweb.com/~ilbiog/

  - **Indiana Biographies**
    http://members.tripod.com/~debmurray/indybios/indiana1.htm

  - **Iowa Biographies Project**
    http://www.genhist.com/IABios/

  - **Kansas Biographies**
    http://www.rootsweb.com/~usgenweb/ks/biospage.htm

  - **Kentucky Biographies Project**
    http://www.starbase21.com/kybiog/

  - **KYBIOG-L - Kentucky Biographies Project**
    http://www.rootsweb.com/~jfuller/gen_mail_states-ky.html#KYBIOG-L
    Established to gather biographies of Kentucky citizens as well as those who have moved from Kentucky to other states and whose biographies in that state make reference to their Kentucky backgrounds.

  - **Louisiana Biographies**
    http://www.geocities.com/BourbonStreet/6934/

  - **Michigan Biographies Project**
    http://homepages.rootsweb.com/~usbios/Michigan/mimnpg.html

  - **Minnesota Biographies Project**
    http://homepages.rootsweb.com/~usbios/Minnesota/mn_mnpg.html

  - **Missouri Biographies**
    http://www.rootsweb.com/~usgenweb/mo/biospage.htm

  - **New York Biographies Project**
    http://homepages.rootsweb.com/~usbios/New_York/mnpg.html

  - **Ohio Biographies Project**
    http://homepages.rootsweb.com/~usbios/Ohio/mnpg.html

  - **Oregon Biographies Project**
    http://www.fortunecity.com/millenium/rollingacres/570

  - **Pennsylvania Biographies Project**
    http://homepages.rootsweb.com/~usbios/Pennsylvania/pamnpg.html

  - **Tennessee Biographies Project**
    http://www.hickmanonline.com/tnbio/

  - **Texas Biographies Project**
    http://members.tripod.com/cindyradway/texas.html

  - **USBIOG Mailing List**
    http://www.rootsweb.com/~jfuller/gen_mail_states-gen.html#USBIOG
    For people who are interested in helping coordinate a collection of biographies within their state as part of the US Biographies project.

  - **Virginia Biographies Project**
    http://members.tripod.com/~Yvonne_in_VA/usbios/home.htm

  - **WA Biographies Project**
    http://www.halcyon.com/jennyrt/WABios/index.html

  - **West Virginia Biographies Project**
    http://homepages.rootsweb.com/~usbios/West_Virginia/wvmnpg.html

  - **Wisconsin Biographies Project**
    http://homepages.rootsweb.com/~usbios/Wisconsin/mnpg.html

BIRTHS & BAPTISMS
http://www.cyndislist.com/births.htm

Category Index:
◆ General Resource Sites
◆ Locality Specific

◆ U.S. Vital Records by State

◆ General Resource Sites

- **Family History SourceGuide - Where to Write for Vital Records**
  http://www.familysearch.org/sg/WheToWri.html

- **Genealogy Bulletin - Where to Find Birth, Death, Marriage and Divorce Records**
  http://www.genealogybulletin.com/archives/HTML/current2.html
  By William Dollarhide.

- **Obtaining Vital Records**
  http://www.ancestry.com/columns/george/12-04-98.htm
  From "Along Those Lines..." by George Morgan.

- **Parish and Vital Records List**
  http://www.familysearch.org/sg/PARISH.html
  A list of indexed church and vital records available from the LDS Family History Library.

- **RootsWeb's Guide to Tracing Family Trees - Lesson 6: Vital Records: Birth Records**
  http://www.rootsweb.com/~rwguide/lesson6.htm

- **Shaking Your Family Tree: Finding Vital Records The Easy Way**
  http://www.uftree.com/bin/fg_auth?/GenealogyNewsstand/ShakingTree/Books/981210.html
  By Myra Vanderpool Gormley, C.G.

- **Shaking Your Family Tree: Vital Records**
  http://www.uftree.com/bin/fg_auth?/GenealogyNewsstand/ShakingTree/Vital/Vital.html
  By Myra Vanderpool Gormley, C.G.

- **VitalChek**
  http://www.vitalchek.com
  Certified copies of birth certificates, death certificates, marriage certificates and other vital records.

- **Vital Records for U.S. Research -- The Records Room**
  http://daddezio.com/records/

- **Vital Records Information - State Index**
  http://vitalrec.com/index.html
  Information about where to obtain vital records (such as birth, death & marriage certificates and divorce decrees) from each state, territory and county of the United States.

- **Where to Write for Vital Records**
  http://www.cdc.gov/nchs/howto/w2w/w2welcom.htm
  From the National Center for Health Statistics, United States

◆ Locality Specific

- **Australia & New Zealand**
  See also: Cyndi's List - Australia & New Zealand
  http://www.CyndisList.com/austnz.htm

  - o **1880-1920 Otago Daily Times Births Deaths Marriages, Anniversaries Index, Dunedin, New Zealand**
    http://www.es.co.nz/~treeves/geneal.htm
    See the details near the end of this page.

  - o **Australasia Births, Deaths and Marriages Exchange**
    http://www.geocities.com/Athens/Forum/3709/exchange/
    The aim of the Australasia Births, Deaths and Marriages Exchange is to provide to genealogists a free resource, to share information about details contained on birth, death and marriage registrations registered in Australia, New Zealand and Papua New Guinea.

  - o **Australian Registrars of Births, Deaths & Marriages**
    http://www.users.on.net/proformat/regs.html

  - o **Australian Vital Records Index**
    http://www.ldscatalog.com/cgi-bin/ncommerce3/ProductDisplay?prrfnbr=2482&prmenbr=1402&CGRY_NUM=1440461&RowStart=1&LocCode=FH
    A CD-ROM for sale from the LDS Church. Contains an indexed collection of references to 4.8 million birth, christening, marriage, and death records. Covers New South Wales (1788-1888), Tasmania (1803-1899), Victoria (1837-1888), and Western Australia (1841-1905).

  - o **New South Wales Registry of Births, Deaths and Marriages**
    http://www.bdm.nsw.gov.au/

    - • **Search the Registry Indexes**
      http://www.bdm.nsw.gov.au/Services/IndexSrch.html
      Searchable database for Births 1788-1905, Marriages 1788-1945 & Deaths 1788-1945.

  - o **New Zealand Birth and Death Entries**
    http://www.geocities.com/Heartland/Forest/2925/nzbdentries.htm
    Shows the format of these civil registration records and what information they record.

o New Zealand Births, Deaths & Marriages Office
http://www.bdm.govt.nz/diawebsite.nsf/c3649e22547ea840
cc25681e0008b39b/c26afa900922c388cc25683e007b9a3f
?OpenDocument

● Canada
See also: Cyndi's List - Canada Index
http://www.CyndisList.com/canada.htm

o Alberta Family Histories Society (AFHS)
Genealogical Projects Registry ~ Canada
http://www.afhs.ab.ca/registry/index.html
A central registry which provides a bibliography of genealogical projects, both online and offline, in Canada. The registry is categorized by province/territory, then by record type: births, marriage, census, deaths, and other.

● Alberta - Births
http://www.afhs.ab.ca/registry/regab_birth.html

● British Columbia - Births
http://www.afhs.ab.ca/registry/regbc_birth.html

● Canada - Birth
http://www.afhs.ab.ca/registry/regcan_birth.html

● Manitoba - Births
http://www.afhs.ab.ca/registry/regmb_birth.html

● New Brunswick - Births
http://www.afhs.ab.ca/registry/regnb_birth.html

● Newfoundland & Labrador - Births
http://www.afhs.ab.ca/registry/regnf_birth.html

● Northwest Territories - Births
http://www.afhs.ab.ca/registry/regnt_birth.html

● Nova Scotia - Births
http://www.afhs.ab.ca/registry/regns_birth.html

● Ontario - Births
http://www.afhs.ab.ca/registry/regon_birth.html

● Prince Edward Island - Births
http://www.afhs.ab.ca/registry/regpe_birth.html

● Quebec - Births
http://www.afhs.ab.ca/registry/regqc_birth.html

● Saskatchewan - Births
http://www.afhs.ab.ca/registry/regsk_birth.html

● Yukon - Births
http://www.afhs.ab.ca/registry/regyk_birth.html

o Baptisms in Pictou County by Rev. James
MacGregor, D.D ~ Nova Scotia, Canada
http://www.rootsweb.com/~pictou/bapt1.htm

o Bill Martin's Genealogy Page
http://www.tbaytel.net/bmartin/
Has several articles for Ontario genealogical research, including lists of microfilm numbers for ordering from the archives or an FHC

● Birth, Marriage, Death Indexes for Ontario,
Canada
http://www.tbaytel.net/bmartin/bmd.htm

● Birth, Marriage and Death Application Form
Instructions
http://www.tbaytel.net/bmartin/registry.htm

● LDS Film Numbers for Ontario Birth
Registrations
http://www.tbaytel.net/bmartin/lds-b.htm

o Births and Baptisms at Barney's River ~ Pictou
County, Nova Scotia, Canada
http://www.rootsweb.com/~pictou/birbp.htm

o Births, Deaths and Marriages Reported in Calgary,
Alberta Newspapers, 1883-1899 ~ Canada
http://www.calcna.ab.ca/afhs/news.html

o Northwest Territories, Canada, Birth, Death, and
Marriage Records, 1925 to the Present
http://www.familysearch.org/rg/guide/NT_BMDT3_
Northwest_Territories_Vital_Records.ASP
How to access and utilize these records from FamilySearch.org.

o The Olive Tree Genealogy - Canada - Births
Deaths & Marriages Exchange
http://www.rootsweb.com/~ote/bdm/canada/bdm.htm

o On-Line Database Search
http://gov.nb.ca/archives/ols/ols.htm
From the Provincial Archives of New Brunswick.

● County Birth Registers Index 1801 - 1899
http://gov.nb.ca/archives/ols/gr/rssd/141A2-2/index.htm

● Late Registration of Births: Documentation
Index 1801 - 1904
http://gov.nb.ca/archives/ols/gr/rssd/141A1b/index.htm

● Miscellaneous

o The Cochin Churchbook
http://www.telebyte.nl/~dessa/cochin.htm
Baptism & marriages from the Dutch Church in Cochin, India (1754-1804).

o Hong Kong Births and Deaths Registries
http://www.info.gov.hk/immd/english/topical/g/6.htm
From the Hong Kong Immigration Department. Includes contact information and hours of operation.

o Mexican Parish Records, 1751-1880
http://www.ancestry.com/search/rectype/inddbs/3947.htm
Pay-for-use database of marriage, baptism, and death records from nine Mexican parishes: Matamoros, Agualequas, Mier, Sabinas Hidalgo, Vallecillo, Cadereyta, Camargo, Cerralvo, & Guerrero with over 100,000 records including 400,000 names.

● United Kingdom & Ireland
See also: Cyndi's List - United Kingdom & Ireland Index
http://www.CyndisList.com/uksites.htm

o British Vital Records Index
http://www.ldscatalog.com/cgi-bin/ncommerce3/
ProductDisplay?prrfnbr=11905&prmenbr=1402&CGRY_
NUM=1440461&RowStart=1&LocCode=FH
CD-ROM for sale from the LDS Church. Contains more than 4.7 million christenings, births, and marriages that occurred in England, Wales, Scotland, and Ireland from 1500 to 1888.

o Current Lists of Church of Ireland Parish Registers
and Vestry Minutes at the RCBL, Dublin
http://www.ihaonline.com/rcbl.htm
List by county showing the Church of Ireland (Protestant) parish registers of baptism, marriage, and burial and the vestry minutes

deposited at the Representative Church Body Library in Dublin. Hosted by The Irish At Home and Abroad with permission of the RCBL.

o FreeBMD Project
http://FreeBMD.rootsweb.com/
"FreeBMD stands for Free Births, Marriages, and Deaths. The FreeBMD Project's objective is to provide free Internet access to the Civil Registration index information for England and Wales."

o Holy Trinity Church Baptism, Marriage and Burial Register Index 1840-1899 ~ Tansley, Derbyshire, England
http://freespace.virgin.net/denys.gaskell/tansley.html

o Irish Ancestors - The Records
http://scripts.ireland.com/ancestor/browse/records/index.htm

 • State Registration of Births, Marriages & Deaths
http://scripts.ireland.com/ancestor/browse/records/state/index.htm

o National Archives of Ireland
http://www.nationalarchives.ie/index.html

 • Births, marriages and deaths
http://www.nationalarchives.ie/birthsmarrdeaths.html

o Office for National Statistics - Registration of Births, Adoptions, Marriages and Deaths ~ England and Wales
http://www.statistics.gov.uk/registration/default.asp

o Ordering Birth Registration Certificates from England & Wales
http://www.oz.net/~markhow/ukbirths.htm
Using the LDS Family History Center Resources.

o Public Record Office - Finding Aids - A-Z Index of All Leaflets ~ U.K.
http://www.pro.gov.uk/leaflets/riindex.htm

 • Births, Marriages and Deaths
http://www.pro.gov.uk/leaflets/ri2118.htm

o Registrar of Births, Deaths and Marriages, Dundee ~ Scotland
http://www.dundeecity.gov.uk/dcchtml/sservices/rbdm.html

o Scots Origins
http://www.origins.net/GRO/
Scots Origins is an online "pay-per-view" database of indexes from the genealogical records of the General Register Office for Scotland - the GRO(S). The Scots Origins database contains fully searchable indexes of the Old Parish Registers of births/baptisms and banns/marriages dating from 1553 to 1854, indexes to the Statutory Registers of births, deaths and marriages from 1855 to 1898, and the index to census records for 1891. Extracts of the original entries in the GRO(S) records can be ordered directly from the database. Extract orders are processed by GRO(S) and sent via ordinary mail as paper documents.

 • About Scots Origins
http://www.origins.net/GRO/about.html

 • Information for Family History Searching on the Scots Origins web site of the General Register Office for Scotland
http://www.gro-scotland.gov.uk/grosweb/grosweb.nsf/pages/searchin
From the FAQ on the web site for the General Register Office for Scotland.

 • Scots Origins FAQ
http://www.origins.net/GRO/faq.html

o The UK BDM Exchange
http://web.ukonline.co.uk/graham.pitt/bdm/
A volunteer project to share birth, death and marriage certificates that you have stored in your own research files.

◆ U.S. Vital Records by State
Please See: United States Index - U.S. - Vital Records
http://www.cyndislist.com/usvital.htm

BOOKS
http://www.cyndislist.com/books.htm

Category Index:

◆ General Sources
◆ Family History Publishers
◆ Locality & Topic Specific

◆ Mailing Lists, Newsgroups & Chat
◆ Microfilm & Microfiche
◆ Used Books, Rare Books & Book Search Services

◆ General Sources

- A1Books
  http://www.a1books.com/
  Do a search on a keyword such as "genealogy".

- Advance Genealogy Books
  http://www.advanceplus.com/genealogy/books/index.htm

- Amazon.com Books - Books / Reference / Genealogy
  http://www.amazon.com/exec/obidos/redirect?tag=markcyndisgeneal&path=ts/browse-books/11880

- Ancestor Trails
  http://www.ancestor.com/

- Ancestors Attic - Discount Genealogy Bookshop
  http://members.tripod.com/~ancestorsattic/index.html

- AudioTapes.com - Genealogical Lectures on Cassette Tapes - Books
  http://www.audiotapes.com/search2.asp?Search=books

- Ancestry.com Online Store
  http://shop.ancestry.com/ancestrycatalog/default.asp

◆ Books, Computers, Maps, Miscellaneous, Services.

- Appleton's Fine Used Bookseller and Genealogy ~ Charlotte, North Carolina
  http://www.appletons.com/genealogy/homepage.html
  Genealogy books, software, CD-ROMs, and more. Free genealogy catalog and e-mail list.

- Back Tracks Genealogy Books
  http://www.naxs.com/abingdon/backtrak/catalog.htm

- Barnette's Family Tree Book Company
  http://www.barnettesbooks.com/

- Berlin, Pennsylvania History & Genealogy Page
  http://www.berlinpa.com
  We offer books for sale, Civil War information on the 142nd Pennsylvania, the Whiskey Rebellion & genealogical research.

- Blairs' Book Service
  http://www.glbco.com/
  With a searchable database.

- The Book Craftsman
  http://www.bookcraftsman.com/
  Restoration of books, custom binding.

- Books We Own List
  http://www.rootsweb.com/~bwo/index.html
  A list of resources owned by others who are willing to do lookups in them.

- Boyd Publishing Company Catalog
  http://www.hom.net/~gac/

- Broken Arrow Publishing
  http://clanhuston.com/
  Genealogical and historical publications.

- Closson Press Home Page - Genealogical & Historical Publications
  http://www.clossonpress.com/
  Catalog of books published and available at Closson Press.

- Continuity Press
  http://www.ContinuityPress.com
  Specializing in Melungeon, Tennessee, and Civil War genealogy and history publications.

- Ericson Books ~ Nacogdoches, Texas
  http://www.ericsonbooks.com/

- Essex Books ~ Massachusetts
  http://www.essexbooks.com/
  Tools for the New England researcher, specializing in Massachusetts.

- Everton's Genealogy Supply Store
  http://www.everton.com/webcart/ep-store.htm
  Store with CD-ROM, books, archival quality sheets, binders, magazines and software.

- Family History Bookshop - The Institute of Heraldic and Genealogical Studies
  http://www.ihgs.ac.uk/institute/bookshop.html

- Family Saplings
  http://www.familysaplings.com/
  A mail-order bookstore specializing in quality books, games, journals and charts for young, budding genealogists and for the adults who nurture and educate them.

- FamilyStoreHouse.com
  http://www.familystorehouse.com/fshstore/index.htm
  *The store has a complete line of products from all genealogical
  vendors. In addition to genealogy, FSH offers a wide range products
  for today's family with ready-to-ship food storage, healthy living*

  *nutritionals, educational material, books, computer hardware and
  software as well as unique gifts from around the world. In addition,
  FSH offers a lucrative affiliate program for web site owners to
  receive commission on customers orginating from their site.*

- Family Tree Bookshop ~ Easton, Maryland
  http://www.familytreebookshop.com/

- FamilyTree Genealogy Book Store
  http://genealogy.theshoppe.com/index.htm

- Federation of Family History Societies Publications
  ~ U.K.
  http://www.ffhs.org.uk/pubs/index.htm

- Frontier Press Bookstore - Genealogical and
  Historical Books
  http://www.frontierpress.com/frontier.cgi

- GEN-BOOKS Mailing List
  http://www.rootsweb.com/~jfuller/gen_mail_material.html
  #GEN-BOOKS
  *For anyone with an interest in the buying or selling of new or used
  genealogy books and CDs made from these books.*

- GenByte BookStore
  http://www.rootsweb.com/~pictou/genbyte.htm

- Genealogical Gleanings ~ by Laura Lee Scott
  http://www.pcola.gulf.net/~llscott/tableofc.htm

- Genealogical Journeys In Time - Books for Sale
  http://ourworld.compuserve.com/homepages/Strawn/
  booksfor.htm

- Genealogical Services & The Genealogy Store
  http://www.genservices.com/

- Genealogy Books & Accessories by Janet Reakes
  http://www.mpx.com.au/~frasertravel/hervey/family/books.htm
  From Australia's Immigration and Family History Centre.

- GenealogyBookShop.com
  http://www.genealogybookshop.com/genealogybookshop/
  index.html
  *The online store of Genealogical Publishing Co., Inc. & Clearfield
  Company.*

- Genealogy Bookstore.com
  http://www.genealogybookstore.com/

- Genealogy Research Source
  http://Perry-family.org/books
  *Genealogy books, software, trip planning, sale or exchange of
  genealogy books and more.*

- Genealogystore
  http://go.to/genealogystore
  Genealogy software and books.

- Genealogy Unlimited - Home Page
  http://www.itsnet.com/~genun/

- GEN-MAT Mailing List
  http://www.rootsweb.com/~jfuller/gen_mail_material.html
  #GEN-MAT
  *For anyone who has an interest in the buying or selling of new or
  used genealogical materials (e.g., books, newsletters, CDs,
  magazines).*

- GEN-MAT-15 Mailing List
  http://www.rootsweb.com/~jfuller/gen_mail_material.html
  #GEN-MAT-15
  *For anyone who desires to post the availability of new or used
  genealogical materials (e.g., books, newsletters, CDs, magazines) or
  services for sale at a price of $15 or less.*

- GLOBAL Genealogical Supply
  http://www.globalgenealogy.com/

- Golden West Marketing
  http://www.greenheart.com/rdietz/
  *Surname exchange, limited free searches of database, book list,
  professional researchers.*

- The Handy Book for Genealogists - 9th Edition
  http://www.everton.com/evertonpublishersinc-67/mck-
  htdocs/order-handybook.html
  From Everton Publishers.

- Hearthstone Bookshop ~ Alexandria, Virginia
  http://www.hearthstonebooks.com/

- Heraldry Today
  http://www.heraldrytoday.co.uk/
  Books for heraldry and genealogy.

- Heritage Books, Inc.
  http://www.heritagebooks.com/
  *Books and CD-ROMs with over 1,000 titles in print. Weekly
  drawings for free books and databases.*

- Heritage Books On-line Library
  http://www.heritagebooks.com/library/
  *An on-line library of books of interest to genealogists. The cardfile
  search engine can be used to locate books by surnames, localities,
  and topics of interest.*

- Higginson Book Company
  http://www.higginsonbooks.com/
  In Salem, Massachusetts. Specializing in genealogy and history.

- The Internet Bookshop
  http://www.bookshop.co.uk/hme/hmepge.asp
  Online bookshop in the U.K.

- Lineages, Inc.: Bookstore
  http://www.lineages.com/store/Books.asp

- Lost In Time
  http://www.lostintime.com/
  Books, CDs, software, maps, and accessories.

- Mark and Cyndi's Library
  http://www.oz.net/~markhow/library.htm
  *A list of the genealogy books in our collection, with authors,
  addresses, ISBN numbers and ordering information via
  Amazon.com.*

- The Memorabilia Corner
  http://members.aol.com/TMCorner/index.html
  Forms, flags, maps, software, CDs, tapes, microfilm & microfiche, books, periodicals, photographic conservation & archival materials.

- Mountain Press
  http://www.mountainpress.com
  Books for the southeastern section of the United States from Pennsylvania to Texas, with the emphasis on Tennessee and Virginia.

- National Archives Book Store
  http://www.nara.gov/nara/bookstore/books.html

- National Historical Publishing Co. - Introduction
  http://smtp.tbox.com/natlhist/

- Origins - A Genealogy Book Store ~ Wisconsin
  http://www.angelfire.com/biz/origins1/

- Picton Press
  http://www.pictonpress.com/catalog/index.htm
  Specialize in 17th, 18th, and 19th century material: genealogies of Mayflower passengers; books on New England towns and settlers; and books on German-speaking immigrants from Germany and Switzerland to all of North America.

- Provincial Press
  http://www.provincialpress.com/
  Reference Books by Winston De Ville, Fellow, American Society of Genealogists.

- RootsBooks: A Genealogy and Local History Bookstore!
  http://www.readthemovie.com/rootsbooks/index.html
  An online genealogy bookstore featuring books on local and family histories, how-tos and techniques, ethnic and military research, immigration, software and more.

- SK Publications
  http://www.skpub.com/genie/
  Genealogy research consultants & census books for sale.

- S & N Genealogy Supplies
  http://ourworld.compuserve.com/homepages/Genealogy_Supplies/

- Storbeck's Genealogy Books Maps CD-ROM
  http://www.storbecks.com/

- Sunnydaze Genealogical Research Material & Antiques
  http://www.sunnydaze.com/

- Tattered Cover Book Store
  http://www.tatteredcover.com/cgi-bin/tcpages.pl

- Willow Bend Books
  http://www.willowbend.net/

- Windmill Publications, Inc.
  http://www.comsource.net/~windmill/

- Yahoo!...Genealogy...Publications
  http://dir.yahoo.com/Business_and_Economy/Companies/Information/Genealogy/Publications/

- Ye Olde Genealogie Shoppe ©
  http://www.yogs.com/

- Your Family Legacy
  http://www.webyfl.com/
  Everything for the family history researcher. Genealogy supplies, books, forms, software, and archival supplies. Special items for beginners.

◆ Family History Publishers

- Baronage Press Homepage
  http://www.baronage.co.uk/index.html
  Publishers of electronic newsletters, genealogical and heraldic data and of general information on the history of the British Isles.

- Custom Computer Creation - Genealogy Book Publishing
  http://www.dlcwest.com/~mgwood/book.html

- Evagean Genealogy Publishing ~ New Zealand
  http://webnz.com/evagean/

- Fast Books
  http://www.fastbooks.com.au/
  Perfect Bound Paperback Books, Glebe NSW, Australia.

- Gateway Press
  http://www.gatewaypress.com/
  Helps people self-publish well-designed, quality books at a reasonable cost.

- Genealogy Publishing Service
  http://www.genealogybookstore.com/publishing/

- The Gregath Publishing Company ~ Wyandotte, Oklahoma
  http://www.gregathcompany.com/

- Heritage Books, Inc.
  http://www.heritagebooks.com/authinfo.htm
  Author information - So You Want to Publish a Book?.

- Hollyhock Press
  http://www.hollyhockpress.com/index.html
  Publisher of genealogical books covering the region of Bath, Highland, Augusta and Pocahontas Counties, Virginia and West Virginia.

- Newberry Street Press
  http://www.nehgs.org/NewburySt/press-02.htm
  The special publications division of the New England Historic Genealogical Society.

- Yahoo!...Genealogy...Family History Publishers
  http://dir.yahoo.com/Business_and_Economy/Companies/Information/Genealogy/Family_History_Publishers/

- Storytellers
  http://www.storytellers.net/
  Publishers of books & CDs to preserve your family stories.

◆ Locality & Topic Specific

- **1850 Census Records**
  http://www.angelfire.com/tx/1850censusrecords/
  My books are transcribed from the original records in soft-book form. Each book is indexed.

- **Advance Genealogy Systems ~ Canada**
  http://www.quantumlynx.com/advance/
  Software & books.

- **American Genealogical Research at the DAR, Washington, D.C.**
  http://www.dar.org/library/libpub.html
  A terrific book for sale from the DAR.

- **American Historical Society of Germans from Russia Order Form**
  http://www.ahsgr.org/ahsgrord.html
  AHSGR Books, Maps, Publications, Books on Diskette, Videos, Census Reports.

- **Ancient Pedigrees**
  http://www.infowest.com/ancient/index.html
  A collection of published works called "The World Book of Generations".

- **Antigonish Books of Genealogical and Historical Interest**
  http://www.rootsweb.com/~pictou/biblio.htm
  Nova Scotia, Canada.

- **The Archive CD Books Project**
  http://www.fweb.org.uk/pub/books/index.htm
  Makes CD-ROMs of old and rare books from the United Kingdom available to genealogists and historians at a reasonable price. It is a user-supported project.

- **Arkansas Ancestors - Arkansas and Alabama Genealogy Resource Books**
  http://www.genrecords.com/arkansasancestors/index.htm

- **Arkansas Research ~ Desmond Walls Allen**
  http://www.arkansasresearch.com/
  Arkansas genealogy books for sale including: Death Records, 1850 Census Indexes, Land Patent Series, County Records, Ozark Folk Tales, Military Records, and more.

- **Australian Family Tree Connections Bookshop**
  http://www.aftc.com.au/bookshop.html
  Features publications of AFTC Subscribers.

- **Avotaynu, Inc. Home Page**
  http://www.avotaynu.com/
  Products and information for Jewish genealogy.

- **Bare Roots Publishing Company**
  http://members.aol.com/bareroot/index.html
  Publications for Philadelphia and Philadelphia County.

- **Bergen Historic Books, Inc.**
  http://www.bergenhistoricbooks.com/
  History and genealogy of the early residents of Northern New Jersey and Southern New York.

- **The Best Books on German Passenger Liners**
  http://worldroots.clicktron.com/brigitte/ships.htm

- **Beyond Bartholomew - The Portland Area History ~ Arkansas**
  http://www.seark.net/~history/
  A book for sale by the author. The book's table of contents and a family name list are online here also.

- **The Board for Certification of Genealogists' Genealogical Standards Manual**
  http://www.amazon.com/exec/obidos/ISBN=0916489922/markcyndisgenealA/
  A book by the BCG.

- **Books for Sale : Douglas County, Missouri**
  http://members.aol.com/LaineBelle/HomePage.html
  Cemetery Survey of the Eastern District of Douglas County, Missouri; Death Notices Abstracted from The Douglas County Herald, 1887-1910.

- **Books Related to Irish Migration**
  http://www3.sympatico.ca/kleonard/Irish.html
  A list by Karen Leonard.

- **Borderlands Bookstore**
  http://www.borderlandsbooks.com/
  Historical and genealogical books about Texas, Mexico, Spain, and Portugal.

- **Bridges Genealogy Books and Services**
  http://pw2.netcom.com/~huskyfan/genealogy.html
  Pictou County, Nova Scotia, North Carolina and Virginia.

- **Broadfoot Publishing Company**
  http://broadfoot.wilmington.net
  Publishes Civil War books, genealogy and CD references. Provides compiled service records and pension records research.

- **Broad View Books**
  http://broadviewbooks.com/
  Used Genealogy Books, Local History of Massachusetts, Connecticut, Rhode Island, Vermont and New England.

- **Byron Sistler and Associates, Inc.**
  http://www.mindspring.com/~sistler/
  Over 900 books covering records from Tennessee, Virginia, North Carolina, and Kentucky.

- **Camp Pope Bookshop**
  http://members.aol.com/ckenyoncpb/index.htm
  Specializing in out-of-print books on the American Civil War, Iowa & the Trans-Mississippi Theater.

- **Chapman Record Cameos ~ U.K.**
  http://www.genuki.org.uk/big/Chapman.html
  A series of books by Colin R. Chapman, noted British genealogist.

- **Cherokee Proud: A Guide for Tracing and Honoring Your Cherokee Ancestors**
  http://www.powersource.com/gallery/tonymack/

- **County Heritage, Inc.**
  http://www.countyheritagebooks.com/
  More than 300 county and local histories in the Southeastern United States.

- The Directory of North American Railroads, Associations, Societies, Archives, Libraries, Museums and Their Collections
  http://www.ancestryresearch.com/BookLook/HotPress.htm
  A book by Holly T. Hansen, B.A.

- Edmonston Publishing, Inc.
  http://www.edmonstonpublishing.com/
  Edmonston Publishing publishes books on the Civil War based on original letters and journals. EP also buys and sells antiquarian/used books on the Civil War.

- Family Genealogy on CD-ROMs
  http://www.altpubs.com/
  GATES, WHITE, ADAMS, KIMBALL and COX family histories republished on CD-ROM.

- Fly Leaf Press
  http://www.flyleaf.ie/
  Publishers of Irish family history books.

- A Genealogist's Guide to Discovering Your Italian Ancestors
  http://users.erols.com/lynnn/dyia/main.html
  A book for sale, with excerpts and its table of contents online.

- Genealogy for Armenians
  http://www.itsnet.com/home/gfa/
  This site has excerpts from a book for sale of the same title.

- Genealogy Research Aids
  http://www.nonawilliams.com/
  Abstractions of historical genealogical records, surname newsletters for Braswell, Cunningham, Moreland and Simpson.

- Genealogy Titles from the Vermont Historical Society Book List
  http://www.state.vt.us/vhs/shop/genebks.htm

- GENfair - The Online Family History Fair
  http://www.genfair.com/
  Online sales for the publications from over 15 local Family History Societies in the United Kingdom. Books, microfiche, and more.

- GenLaw Resources, publisher of Western Maryland Genealogy
  http://www.genlawresources.com/WMG.html

- Gibson Guides - Location Guides for Family and Local Historians ~ U.K.
  http://www.genuki.org.uk/big/Gibson.html
  A set of guides to the whereabouts of records, available from the Federation of Family History Societies.

- Gorin Genealogical Publishing - Book List
  http://members.aol.com/kygen/gorin.htm
  Publications cover mostly Kentucky, also has some for Logan County, Illinois and Fentress & Overton Counties, Tennessee.

- Gould Books - Family & Local History Specialist ~ Australia
  http://www.gould.com.au/

- GRD - Genealogical Research Directory
  http://www.ozemail.com.au/~grdxxx
  Worldwide surname queries published in a book and on CD-ROM.

- Guidon Books
  http://www.guidon.com/index.html
  Has an extensive collection of new and out of print books on the American Civil War and Western Americana.

- Hope Farm Press & Bookshop
  http://www.hopefarm.com/
  New York State Regional History, Folklore, Nature, Military, Native American and Genealogy -- Covering Western New York, Adirondacks, Hudson Valley, Catskill Mts & Finger Lakes.

- Iberian Publishing Company's Online Catalog
  http://www.iberian.com/
  Specializing in reference works for genealogists and historians researching the Virginias and other Southeastern U.S. States circa. 1650 - 1850.

- Index: Old Ordnance Survey Maps - The Godfrey Edition
  http://www.alangodfreymaps.co.uk/
  List of UK and Belgium maps available at large scale in the period of about 1890 to 1915.

- Interlink Bookshop Genealogical Services ~ Victoria, B.C. Canada
  http://www.interlinkbookshop.com/

- Iowa Counties - Iowa Internet Book Store
  http://iowa-counties.com/bookstore/

- J & W Enterprises
  http://www.dhc.net/~jw/
  One stop book source on the Internet, specializing in southern states source material.

- Jewish Roots in Poland - Pages from the Past and Archival Inventories
  http://www.rtrfoundation.org/
  A new book by Miriam Weiner.

- John's Genealogy Junction - Masonic Records
  http://www.wf.net/~jyates/research.htm
  Information about genealogical information obtainable from records of Masonic lodges.

- John Townsend - Second-hand Books
  http://business.virgin.net/john.townsend2/
  Out-of-print books, genealogy, topography, local history, antiquarian heraldry books.

- Kegley Books
  http://www.dnai.com/~skegley/KegleyBooks/index.html
  Books by Mary B. Kegley with hundreds of sketches of families of Southwest Virginia.

- Kinseeker Publications
  http://www.angelfire.com/biz/Kinseeker/index.html
  Michigan and Wisconsin.

- Kinship - "Genealogy Resources for Kith and Kin"
  http://www.kinshipny.com/
  Publishers of New York State Research Material.

- La Croix et le lys ~ France
  http://pages.infinit.net/croixlys/

- LDS Booksellers Association
  http://www.ldsba.com/

- Lunenburg County / Nova Scotia Genealogy Book List
  http://www.rootsweb.com/~canns/lunenburg/booklist.htm

- Macbeth Genealogical Services ~ Australia
  http://www.macbeth.com.au/
  Books, fiche, maps, and CD-ROMs.

- March Nineteen Dot Com: Quality Books
  http://www.march19.com
  Books on the final months of the Civil War in North Carolina: Fort Fisher, Wilmington, and Bentonville.

- Martin Genealogy Publications
  http://www.angelfire.com/biz/martingenpub/
  Alabama and Florida.

- Mechling Associates, Inc.
  http://mechlingbooks.com/
  Western Pennsylvania genealogy and history Books.

- Military Publications International Directory
  http://www.islandnet.com/~duke/idmp.htm
  Book for sale from Canada.

- Mines Road Books ~ Fremont, California
  http://cmug.com/~minesroad/
  Specialize in researching and publishing California history and genealogy.

- Mobile Genealogy Society - The MGS Store ~ Alabama
  http://www.siteone.com/clubs/mgs/store.htm

- Monroe DAVIS' Family Book Shelf
  http://members.aol.com/monroegd/index.html
  DAVIS, VAUGHN, WATKINS.

- Mountain Heritage Books
  http://www.wirefire.com/mhb/
  New and used historical and genealogical books for West Virginia and some surrounding states.

- National Historical Publishing Company
  http://www.tbox.com/natlhist/default.html
  Books regarding pension files and service records for the Revolutionary War, War of 1812, Mexican War and Civil War. Indexes to Old Wars and Indian Wars.

- The Naval & Military Press Web Page
  http://www.naval-military-press.co.uk/
  A large selection of military books, many with of interest to the genealogist.

- Native American Genealogical Research & Publishing Company - Civil War
  http://www.nagrpubco.com/Civil%20War.htm

- Native Press
  http://www.ndnscout.com/
  Specialize in American Indian genealogical source material, how-to books for American Indian genealogy, and American Indian Language renewal materials.

- Netting Your Ancestors - Genealogical Research on the Internet
  http://www.CyndisList.com/netting.htm
  My new book from Genealogical Publishing Co.

- New Zealand Society of Genealogists - Hardcopy Publications
  http://homepages.ihug.co.nz/~nzsg/Publications/hardcopy_main.html

- Nova Scotia Book Dealers - Used & Rare
  http://nsgna.ednet.ns.ca/nbst.html

- Nova Scotia / New Brunswick Bookstores - Used & Rare
  http://www.rootsweb.com/~canns/lunenburg/bookstores.htm

- Old Times Not Forgotten: A History of Drew County ~ Arkansas
  http://www.seark.net/~rdea/
  A book for sale by the author. The book's table of contents and a family name list are online here also.

- OLochlainns Irish Families
  http://www.irishroots.com/
  The home page of the Irish Genealogical Foundation and OLochlainns Irish Family Journal.

- The Ontario Genealogical Society's Publications List
  http://www.ogs.on.ca/publications/pub_soc.htm
  Books for sale from the OGS.

- Oregon-California Trails Association (OCTA) Bookstore
  http://calcite.rocky.edu/octa/bookstor.htm

- Ovilla, Texas History Book
  http://home.flash.net/~cmiracle/

- Ozark Books
  http://home.att.net/~rdfortner/
  Supplier of books about the Missouri and Arkansas Ozarks, including Branson.

- Park Genealogical Books
  http://www.parkbooks.com/
  Specialists in genealogy and local history for Minnesota, Wisconsin, North and South Dakota and the surrounding area.

- Pictou Books of Genealogical and Historical Interest
  http://www.rootsweb.com/~pictou/libpic1.htm
  Nova Scotia, Canada.

- Prima's Official Companion to Family Tree Maker Version 5
  http://www.amazon.com/exec/obidos/ISBN%3D0761516778/markcyndisgenealA/103-7528721-1079801
  By Myra Vanderpool Gormley, C.G.

- Public Record Office Bookshop ~ U.K.
  http://www.pro.gov.uk/bookshop/default.htm

- Publications on Rowan County, North Carolina by Jo White Linn
  http://homepages.rootsweb.com/~gormleym/rowan.htm

- Quintin Publications
  http://www.quintinpublications.com/
  Materials relating to Canada.

- Read Ireland Bookstore
  http://www.readireland.ie/

- Regi Magyarorszag "Old Hungary" Bookstore
  http://www.dholmes.com/rm-book.html
  Specializing in Hungarian & Slovak Genealogy.

- Rhode Island Families Association - Genealogical
  Publications and Research
  http://users.erols.com/rigr/
  *Indexed articles from the Rhode Island Genealogical Register, as
  well as publications from a variety of records: probate, wills, vital,
  cemeteries, etc.*

- The Rural Citizen Online Bookstore
  http://www.ruralcitizen.com/
  *Specializes in Southern and Confederate history, culture and
  heritage.*

- Selected Bibliography, Book List Channel Islands
  http://Fox.nstn.ca:80/~nstn1528/booklist.htm

- The Sleeper Co.: Genealogy Books on Washington
  Co., NY
  http://www.sleeperco.com/

- Society of Genealogists Bookshop Online ~ U.K.
  http://www.sog.org.uk/acatalog/welcome.html

- A Student's Guide to African American Genealogy.
  http://www.oryxpress.com/scripts/book.idc?acro=FTAFR
  Also:
  - British American
    http://www.oryxpress.com/scripts/book.idc?acro=FTBRIT
  - Chinese American
    http://www.oryxpress.com/scripts/book.idc?acro=FTCHN
  - German American
    http://www.oryxpress.com/scripts/book.idc?acro=FTGER
  - Irish American
    http://www.oryxpress.com/scripts/book.idc?acro=FTIRI
  - Italian American
    http://www.oryxpress.com/scripts/book.idc?acro=FTITA
  - Japanese American
    http://www.oryxpress.com/scripts/book.idc?acro=FTJAP
  - Jewish American
    http://www.oryxpress.com/scripts/book.idc?acro=FTJEW
  - Mexican American
    http://www.oryxpress.com/scripts/book.idc?acro=FTMEX
  - Native American
    http://www.oryxpress.com/scripts/book.idc?acro=FTNA
  - Polish American
    http://www.oryxpress.com/scripts/book.idc?acro=FTPOL
  - Scandinavian American
    http://www.oryxpress.com/scripts/book.idc?acro=FTSCAN

- Tacoma-Pierce County Genealogical Society -
  Publications for Sale ~ Washington
  http://www.rootsweb.com/~watpcgs/pubs.htm

- TCI Genealogical Resources
  http://www.tcigenealogy.com/
  *Books for research in the Caribbean, Cuba, Central & South
  America.*

- TLC Genealogy Books
  http://www.tlc-gen.com/

- UK Genealogy Books On Line
  http://www.jodenoy.clara.net/genbooks/main.htm
  *Jodenoy Books. Genealogy specialists. Suppliers of any UK
  published genealogy book in print.*

- Victoria History of the Counties of England
  http://ihr.sas.ac.uk/vch/vchnew.asc.html

- West Virginia Book Company
  http://www.wvbookco.com/

- West Virginia Histories Homepage
  http://www.clearlight.com/~wvhh/
  *A listing of history books that have been published relating to West
  Virginia.*

- Western North Carolina Genealogy Page
  http://www.geocities.com/Heartland/Bluffs/9595/
  *Various books on divorce, estates, guardian and wills available for
  the following counties: Ashe, Buncombe, Burke, Caldwell,
  Cherokee, Clay, Cleveland, Graham, Haywood, Henderson, Macon,
  Madison, McDowell, Mitchell, Polk, Rutherford, Transylvania,
  Watauga, Wilkes, Yadkin, and Yancey.*

- Westland Publications Genealogy - Find Immigrant
  Ancestors
  http://www.theriver.com/westlandpubn/
  *Monographic publications of translated documents from Germany,
  Great Britain, France, Switzerland, and Central Europe.*

- White Room Genealogical Services
  http://www.whiteroom.com.au/geneal.htm
  *Specialist CD-ROM publishers and distributors. Titles include the
  Australian Chronicles: an index to sources of Australian biography.*

- Winfield Publishing - Setting Standards in Genealogy
  Publishing
  http://members.aol.com/Winfieldpb/
  *Publisher of genealogy reference books pertaining to the people of
  Ontario.*

- Yesteryear Links ~ Queensland, Australia
  http://www.uq.net.au/~zzmgrinl/

◆ Mailing Lists, Newsgroups & Chat

- Appleton's Mailing List
  http://www.rootsweb.com/~jfuller/gen_mail_material.html
  #Appleton
  *A read-only list with information on new genealogy software, CD-
  ROMs, books, and more from Appleton's Books and Genealogy.*

- **GENAUTHOR** Mailing List
  http://www.rootsweb.com/~jfuller/gen_mail_general.html
  #GENAUTHOR
  For anyone who is planning on preparing and publishing a Family Genealogy book to discuss of all aspects of the effort including organizing your data, choosing a format, selecting a publisher, etc.

- **GEN-BOOKS** Mailing List
  http://www.rootsweb.com/~jfuller/gen_mail_material.html
  #GEN-BOOKS
  For anyone with an interest in the buying or selling of new or used genealogy books and CDs made from these books.

- **GEN-BOOKS** Mailing List
  http://www.rootsweb.com/~jfuller/gen_mail_material.html
  #GEN-BOOKS1
  For announcements of genealogy or history books, maps, post cards, etc. which are available for sale, trade or on-line auction, as well as "want lists" of books or items.

- **GEN-MARKET** Mailing List
  http://www.rootsweb.com/~jfuller/gen_mail_material.html
  #GEN-MARKET
  Gatewayed with the soc.genealogy.marketplace newsgroup for commercial postings of unique interest to genealogists.

- **GEN-MAT** Mailing List
  http://www.rootsweb.com/~jfuller/gen_mail_material.html
  #GEN-MAT
  This is a mailing list for anyone who has an interest in the buying or selling of new or used genealogical materials (e.g., books, newsletters, CDs, magazines).

- **GEN-MAT-15** Mailing List
  http://www.rootsweb.com/~jfuller/gen_mail_material.html
  #GEN-MAT-15
  For anyone who desires to post the availability of new or used genealogical materials (e.g., books, newsletters, CDs, magazines) or services for sale at a price of $15 or less.

- **GEN-MAT-HX** Mailing List
  http://www.rootsweb.com/~jfuller/gen_mail_material.html
  #GEN-MAT-HX
  For anyone who has an interest in the buying or selling of new or used biographies and history books. Publishers of such books are welcome, as are resellers (businesses or individuals cleaning bookshelves).

- **GenSwap** Mailing List
  http://www.rootsweb.com/~jfuller/gen_mail_general.html
  #GenSwap
  For exchanging research time and swapping records for records with others (e.g., researching in your area for someone else in exchange for like efforts on their part).

- **ukbooks-announce** Mailing List
  http://www.rootsweb.com/~jfuller/gen_mail_material.html
  #ukbooks-announce
  A read only mailing list maintained by Jodenoy Books, Genealogy Specialists, in association with Amazon.co.uk. Postings by the owners will include news of web site changes and additions, up and coming publications, and other news.

- **ukbooks-gen** Mailing List
  http://www.rootsweb.com/~jfuller/gen_mail_material.html
  #ukbooks-gen

For the general discussion of genealogy books. Suitable topics include book reviews; recommendations; and queries regarding hard to find, new, or second-hand books.

◆ Used Books, Rare Books & Book Search Services

- **84 Charing Cross, EH? - Good Used/Rare Books ~ Michigan**
  http://www.84cc.com/

- **The Advanced Book Exchange**
  http://www.abebooks.com/

- **Alibris - Books you thought you'd never find.**
  http://www.alibris.com/cgi-bin/texis/searcher

- **alt.bookstore Used Book Exchange**
  http://www.altbookstore.com/usedexchange.html

- **Amazon.com: Auctions / Books**
  http://s1.amazon.com/exec/varzea/ts/browse-auctions/68293/103-3850342-1988612

- **Amazon.com: zShops / Books**
  http://s1.amazon.com/exec/varzea/ts/browse-zshops/68293/103-3850342-1988612

- **Ambra Books & Lesley Aitchison**
  http://www.cornwall-online.co.uk/ambrabooks/
  Buying and selling antiquarian and secondhand books, manuscripts, documents, maps, plans, photographs, albums, and ephemera relating to Cornwall and the West Country - Devon, Dorset, Gloucestershire, Somerset & Wiltshire in the United Kingdom.

- **The Avid Reader Used and Rare Books**
  http://www.avidreader.com/
  Chapel Hill, North Carolina.

- **Barbara Green's Used Genealogy Books**
  http://home.earthlink.net/~genbooks/

- **Bibliofind**
  http://www.bibliofind.com/
  Booksearch, antiquarian books, old books, used books, rare books.

- **Biblioseek.com -- The Book Search Specialists**
  http://www.biblioseek.com

- **bn.com - Rare, Secondhand and Out of Print Book Search**
  http://shop.barnesandnoble.com/oopbooks/oopsearch.asp?userid=2I1ZPQ5T6N&srefer=

- **BookFinder.com: Search for Out of Print and Used Books**
  http://www.bookfinder.com/

- **Book Look**
  http://www.booklook.com/
  America's largest out-of-print book search service.

- **A Bookman's Indiana | A Guide to the State's Used Bookshops & Bibliophilic Resources**
  http://www2.inetdirect.net/~charta/Ind_bks.html

- **Books Out-of-Print**
  http://www.bowker.com/bop/home/index.html
  More than 900,000 out-of-print or out-of-stock-indefinitely titles from 1979 to the present.

- **Broad View Books**
  http://broadviewbooks.com/
  Used Genealogy Books, Local History of Massachusetts, Connecticut, Rhode Island, Vermont and New England.

- **eBay Listings: Books**
  http://listings.ebay.com/aw/listings/list/category267/index.html

- **FLI Antiques & Genealogy**
  http://www.wwd.net/user/tklaiber/index.htm
  Publications for Ohio and Kentucky.

- **Genealogical Journeys In Time - Used Reference Books for Sale**
  http://ourworld.compuserve.com/homepages/Strawn/booklist.htm

- **Iguana Publishing Books and Maps - Genealogy & History**
  http://mav.net/genealogy/
  Old, new and used.

- **Interloc, Inc.**
  http://www.interloc.com/
  A large collection of out-of-print books.

- **Internet Used Book Store**
  http://www.rede.com/books/
  See their genealogy section.

- **Janet's Used Genealogy & History Books**
  http://home.earthlink.net/~janetm1/

- **Jen's Used Book Den**
  http://www.abebooks.com/home/JENSDEN/
  Over 20,000 used books in all categories. Specializing in history, genealogy and historical fiction.

- **John Townsend - Second-hand Books**
  http://business.virgin.net/john.townsend2/
  Out-of-print books, genealogy, topography, local history, antiquarian heraldry books.

- **The McGowan Book Company**
  http://www.mcgowanbooks.com/
  Specializing in locating, buying and selling rare books, Civil War memorabilia, photographs and documents. Also, materials for Americana, African-American history, Church history and Military history.

- **Madigan's Books - Buy & Sell Books of Genealogical Interest**
  http://www.madigansbooks.com/

- **Nova Scotia / New Brunswick Bookstores - Used & Rare**
  http://www.rootsweb.com/~canns/lunenburg/bookstores.htm

- **Pacific Book Auctions Galleries**
  http://www.pacificbook.com/

- **Powell's Books ~ Portland, Oregon**
  http://www.powells.com/
  Used, new and out of print books.

- **Rare Book Reprints**
  http://members.aol.com/rarebk
  Old, "lost," scarce, and rare Carter family books and genealogies.

- **Roots and Branches**
  http://members.aol.com/RebelSher1/index.html
  Used books, forms, maps and the Civil War info.

- **Shorey's Bookstore Inc. ~ Seattle, Washington**
  http://www.serv.net/shorey/
  Used & rare books, out-of-print book searches.

- **Stacey's Book Search Page**
  http://www.highfiber.com/~rmcclend/Index.html
  Genealogy and American/Local History and Miscellaneous Other Items.

- **Tudor Rose Book Shop**
  http://www.abebooks.com/home/Tudor_Rose/
  Rare, used and and out-of-print books, with two locations in Florida and Illinois.

- **Tuttle Antiquarian Books ~ Rutland, Vermont**
  http://www.tuttlebooks.com
  Bookseller of genealogy, regional americana, miscellaneous reference titles and more.

- **UMI's Books on Demand Program**
  http://www.umi.com/hp/Support/BOD/
  A collection of more than 140,000 out-of-print books that can be xerographically reproduced on demand.

- **Yahoo!...Books...Antique, Rare and Used**
  http://dir.yahoo.com/Business_and_Economy/Shopping_and_Services/Books/Booksellers/Antique__Rare__and_Used/

- **Yahoo!...Books...Book Search Services**
  http://dir.yahoo.com/Business_and_Economy/Shopping_and_Services/Books/Book_Search_Services/

- **Yahoo! Auctions: Books**
  http://auctions.yahoo.com/21600-category.html

- **Ye Olde Genealogie Shoppe © - Flea Market**
  http://www.yogs.com/fleamkt.htm

CALENDARS & DATES

http://www.cyndislist.com/calendar.htm

Category Index:

- Birthdate Calendars and Calculators
- General Resource Sites
- Old Style & New Style

- Perpetual Calendars
- Religious Calendars
- Roman Numerals

◆ Birthdate Calendars and Calculators

- Birthdate Calculator
  http://www.angelfire.com/va/ValsGenealogyPage/Calculator.html

- Birthdate CalculatorJavaScript Birthdate Calculator
  http://web2.airmail.net/bhende19/b-date.htm

- Birthdate CalculatorJavaScript Birthdate Calculator
  http://www.geocities.com/Heartland/Lane/4030/birthdate.html

- Birthdate CalculatorJavaScript Birthdate Calculator
  http://fastservers.net/~bgwilliams/jv_birth.htm

- Buckner's Birthdate Calculator
  http://tor-pw1.attcanada.ca/~bgh/bircalc.html
  Calculates birthdate from death date and age of death in day/month/year format.

- Calculating Birth Year Based on Census Information
  http://www.wdbj.net/~wdbj/gen/birthyear/cenindx.html

- Determining Date of Birth - "Formula 8870"
  http://www.rootsweb.com/~hcpd/formula.htm

- JavaScript Birthdate Calculator
  http://www.fia.net/doit/BirthdayCalc.html

- VGS Birthdate Calculator
  http://www.islandnet.com/~vgs/tools/birthdate.html
  From the Victoria Genealogical Society in British Columbia, Canada.

◆ General Resource Sites

- 10,000-Year Calendar
  http://www.calendarhome.com/tyc/
  Choose menu options and view a month or year calendar for any year 1 to 10000 A.D.

- AudioTapes.com - Genealogical Lectures on Cassette Tapes – Calendar
  http://www.audiotapes.com/search2.asp?Search=Calendar

- Calendar
  http://www-nmbe.unibe.ch/cgi-bin/calendar
  Type in a month and year and this form will display the calendar.

- Calendar Form
  http://www.earth.com/calendar
  Type in a month and year - future or past - and it returns a calendar of that month.

- Calendar Conversions
  http://www.genealogy.org/~scottlee/calconvert.cgi
  Scott Lee's free on-line service for converting to/from dates in Gregorian, Julian, French republican and Jewish calendars.

- Calendar : Humanity's Epic Struggle to Determine a True and Accurate Year
  http://www.amazon.com/exec/obidos/ISBN=0380793245/markcyndisgenealA/
  A book by David Ewing Duncan. An excellent general history of how we order the days as we do. Great background reading for genealogists struggling with the changes to our calendar in history.

- Calendars and Their History
  http://astro.nmsu.edu/~lhuber/leaphist.html

- Calendar Conversions
  http://win-www.uia.ac.be/u/pavp/sdv/auxcalendars.htm
  From the Genealogy in Belgium Home Page.

- Calendar Studies
  http://www.magnet.ch/serendipity/cal_stud.html

- Calendar Zone
  http://www.calendarzone.com/

- Census Dates for Countries and Areas of the World: 1946 to 2004
  http://www.census.gov/ipc/www/cendates/
  Shows the dates of census enumerations over the past half century, as well as projected or scheduled enumerations in the near future. for countries around the world.

- Chinese Calendar
  http://www.new-year.co.uk/chinese/calendar.htm

- Chronology and Dating
  http://www.cgp100.dabsol.co.uk/gui/chron.htm

- Day of Week Calculator
  http://www.albion.edu/fac/engl/calendar/weekday.htm

- DAYS Calendar Program for Genealogists
  http://octhygesen.homepage.dk/
  Designed to assist genealogists in finding dates of named days and generally navigate in and between the Julian and Gregorian calendars. The original program was in Danish and intended for Danish/Norwegian genealogists.

- English Calendar
  http://spider.albion.edu/fac/engl/calendar/
  Interactive calendar helps you calculate: Ecclesiastical Calendar, Old and New Style Dating, Day of the Week, Regnal Years.

- Family History SourceGuide - Research Outline - French Republican Calendar
  http://www.familysearch.org/sg/FrRepCal.html

- The French Republican Calendar
  http://www.gefrance.com/calrep/calen.htm
  History of the French republican calendar and conversions to the Gregorian calendar. Official texts. Great dates. In French and English.

- Genealogical dates: A user-friendly guide
  http://www.amazon.com/exec/obidos/ISBN=0897251334/markcyndisgenealA/
  A book by Kenneth L. Smith.

- Genealogy in France: Republican Calendar
  http://www.genealogie.com/rech-fr/calrep-e.html
  Also known as " French Revolutionary Calendar ", this calendar was in used in France from 1793 to 1805, and 1871 (only in Paris).

- Gregorian Calendar
  http://es.rice.edu/ES/humsoc/Galileo/Things/gregorian_calendar.html

- Hermetic Systems: Calendar Studies
  http://www.new-year.co.uk/chinese/calendar.htm

- History of the Western Calendar
  http://ourworld.compuserve.com/homepages/khagen/CalHist.html
    - The Gregorian Calendar Conversion
      http://ourworld.compuserve.com/homepages/khagen/GregConv.html

- Leap Year, 1582-1752 (a query)
  http://www.bearhaven.com/family/leapyear.html

- Leap Years and Our Calendar
  http://www.ips.oz.au/papers/richard/leap.html

- Marking Time - A History of the Months and the Meanings of their Names
  http://www.crowl.org/Lawrence/time/months.html

- Michigan Electronic Library – Calendars
  http://mel.lib.mi.us/reference/REF-calendars.html

- Period Approximation Chart
  http://www.myroots.net/extras/tidbits3.htm
  Helps you to determine time periods to search in with limited data to begin the search.

- Persian Calendar
  http://tehran.stanford.edu/Calendar/calendar.html

- Ready Reference Internet Resources - Date & Time
  http://www.wcsu.ctstateu.edu/library/rr_date_time.html

- Regnal Chronologies
  http://web.raex.com/~obsidian/regindex.html
  A calendar of worldwide royal reigns, arranged geographically.

- Regnal Year Calculator
  http://www.albion.edu/fac/engl/calendar/regnal.htm

- A Summary of the International Standard Date and Time Notation
  http://www.cl.cam.ac.uk/~mgk25/iso-time.html
  International Standard ISO 8601 specifies numeric representations of date and time. This standard notation helps to avoid confusion in international communication caused by the many different national notation.

- 3 Charts for Date to Day of the Week Conversions
  ftp://ftp.rootsweb.com/pub/roots-l/genealog/genealog.dateday
  From the ROOTS-L Library: Dates and Calendars.

- Tom Nunamaker's Census Age Calculator
  http://www.toshop.com/censuscalc.cfm
  For UK census years.

- Universal Calendar Calculator
  http://www.cf-software.com/ucc.htm
  *The Universal Calendar Calculator can display and convert between 10 different calendars: Julian Day Number, Gregorian (New Style), Julian (Old Style), Roman-Julian, French Revolution, Hebrew, Islamic, Chinese, Chinese/Gregorian, and Thai Suriyakati Calendar. The Universal Calendar Calculator also contains: * Dates of holidays for the United States, Christian (Nicean Rule and Modern), Islamic, Jewish, and Chinese. * Regional date of conversion from the Old Style (Julian) to the New Style (Gregorian) for more than 100 localities. * Almost 100 Medieval European Regional Day Name Calendars. These calendars allow you to easily identify the specific Julian Calendar day of many Latin day names given in Medieval documents.*

- Western-Chinese Calendar Converter
  http://www.mandarintools.com/calconv.html

- Yahoo!...Reference...Calendars
  http://dir.yahoo.com/reference/calendars/

◆ Old Style & New Style

- American Plantations and Colonies - Genealogy - Calendar Confusion
  http://www.primenet.com/~langford/sidebars/calendar.htm

- Old Style and New Style Dates - A Summary for Genealogists
  http://www.genuki.org.uk/big/dates.html

- Old Style & New Style Dates for the Quaker Calendar
  http://www.everton.com/usa/GENEALOG/GENEALOG.QUAKERC1

- Old & New Style Dates for the Quaker Calendar
  ftp://ftp.rootsweb.com/pub/roots-l/genealog/genealog.quakerc1
  From the ROOTS-L Library: Dates and Calendars.

- Old and New Style Dating
  http://www.albion.edu/fac/engl/calendar/style.htm

- Universal Calendar Calculator
  http://www.cf-software.com/ucc.htm
  *The Universal Calendar Calculator can display and convert between 10 different calendars: Julian Day Number, Gregorian (New Style), Julian (Old Style), Roman-Julian, French Revolution, Hebrew, Islamic, Chinese, Chinese/Gregorian, and Thai Suriyakati Calendar. The Universal Calendar Calculator also contains: * Dates of holidays for the United States, Christian (Nicean Rule and Modern), Islamic, Jewish, and Chinese. * Regional date of conversion from the Old Style (Julian) to the New Style (Gregorian) for more than 100 localities. * Almost 100 Medieval European Regional Day Name Calendars. These calendars allow you to easily identify the specific Julian Calendar day of many Latin day names given in Medieval documents.*

◆ Perpetual Calendars

- Another Perpetual Calendar
  ftp://ftp.rootsweb.com/pub/roots-l/genealog/genealog.perpcal2
  From the ROOTS-L Library: Dates and Calendars.

- Dates of Easter Sunday and Perpetual Calendar, 1550-2049 (for Great Britain and the Colonies)
  http://www.swinhope.demon.co.uk/genuki/easter/

- A Perpetual Calendar
  ftp://ftp.rootsweb.com/pub/roots-l/genealog/genealog.perpcal
  From the ROOTS-L Library: Dates and Calendars.

- Perpetual Calendar
  http://www.tngenweb.org/sullivan/pcalendar.htm

◆ Religious Calendars

- Calculation of the Ecclesiastical Calendar
  http://www.smart.net/~mmontes/ec-cal.html

- Catholic Calendar Page
  http://www.easterbrooks.com/personal/calendar/index.html

- The Date of Easter
  http://www.ely.anglican.org/cgi-bin/easter

- The Date of Easter
  http://www.rog.nmm.ac.uk/leaflets/easter/easter.html
  Information Leaflet No. 57 from the Royal Greenwich Observatory.

- Dates of Easter, Rosh Hashanah and Passover
  http://quasar.as.utexas.edu/BillInfo/ReligiousCalendars.html

- Dates of Easter Sunday and Perpetual Calendar, 1550-2049 (for Great Britain and the Colonies)
  http://www.swinhope.demon.co.uk/genuki/easter/

- Determining the Date of Easter
  http://www.ips.oz.au/papers/richard/easter.html

- Easter Calculator
  http://www.albion.edu/fac/engl/calendar/easter.htm

- Easter Dates
  http://chariot.net.au/~gmarts/eastcalc.htm

- Easter Dating Method
  http://www.assa.org.au/edm.html

- English Calendar
  http://spider.albion.edu/fac/engl/calendar/
  Interactive calendar helps you calculate: Ecclesiastical Calendar, Old and New Style Dating, Day of the Week, Regnal Years.

- Judaism 101: Jewish Calendar
  http://www.jewfaq.org/calendar.htm

- Old Style & New Style Dates for the Quaker Calendar
  http://www.everton.com/usa/GENEALOG/GENEALOG.QUAKERC1

- Old Style & New Style Dates for the Quaker Calendar
  ftp://ftp.rootsweb.com/pub/roots-l/genealog/genealog.quakerc1
  From the ROOTS-L Library: Dates and Calendars.

- Quaker Dates
  http://www.illuminatrix.com/andria/quaker.html

- A Simplified Easter Dating Method
  http://www.assa.org.au/edm.html

- Yahrzeit Calendar
  http://www.jfda.org/news.html
  Converts Gregorian to Hebrew dates and vice versa. Gives Yizkor dates through 2012.

◆ Roman Numerals

- InnoVision Technologies - Roman Numeral Conversion
  http://www.ivtech.com/roman/

- Roman Digits
  http://utopia.knoware.nl/users/eprebel/Numbers/RomanDigits/index.html

- Roman Numeral Conversion
  http://www.damtp.cam.ac.uk/user/bp10004/cgi_roman.html
  A site that will convert dates for you, following a strict set of rules for the dates.

- Roman Numeral Date Conversion Table
  http://www2.inetdirect.net/~charta/Roman_numerals.html

- Roman Numerals
  http://www.deadline.demon.co.uk/roman/front.htm
  A list of dates converted Arabic numerals to Roman numerals for the years 1450 to 2100.

- Roman Numerals
  http://www.morgan.net.au/pages/roman.htm

- Roman Numerals (Numbers)
  http://www.lib.auburn.edu/serials/docs/training/manual/roman.html

CANADA INDEX

- General Canada Sites
- Alberta
- British Columbia
- Canada – Military
- Manitoba
- New Brunswick
- Newfoundland & Labrador
- Northwest Territories, Nunavut & the Yukon
- Nova Scotia
- Ontario
- Prince Edward Island
- Quebec
- Saskatchewan

CANADA – GENERAL CANADA SITES

http://www.cyndislist.com/gencan.htm

Category Index:

- Canada GenWeb Project
- General Resource Sites
- Government & Cities
- History & Culture
- Home Children
- Libraries, Archives & Museums
- Mailing Lists, Newsgroups & Chat
- Maps, Gazetteers & Geographical Information
- Military
- Newspapers

- People & Families
- Professional Researchers, Volunteers & Other Research Services
- Publications, Software & Supplies
- Queries, Message Boards & Surname Lists
- Records: Census, Cemeteries, Land, Obituaries, Personal, Taxes and Vital
- Religion & Churches
- Societies & Groups

◆ Canada GenWeb Project

- Canada Genealogy / Généalogie du Canada - GenWeb Project Home Page
  http://www.rootsweb.com/~canwgw/

◆ General Resource Sites

- Bob's your Uncle, eh!
  http://indexes.tpl.toronto.on.ca/genealogy/index.asp
  A search engine for genealogy in Canada.

- Canada 411 White Pages
  http://canada411.sympatico.ca/

- Canada Post Corporation / Société canadienne des postes
  http://www.canadapost.ca/
  Postal rates & codes, etc.

- The Canada-Wide National Registry & Family Finders
  http://www.adopting.org/ffcwnr.html
  Adoption resources & registry.

- Canada / Ulster Heritage Site
  http://members.tripod.com/~Ulster_01/index.htm

- Canadian Conference of Mennonite Brethren Churches
  http://www.mbconf.ca/

- Canadian Genealogy and History Links
  http://www.islandnet.com/~jveinot/cghl/cghl.html
  From OCFA and BCCFA.

- Canadian Genealogy Gopher Sites
  gopher://Alpha.CC.UToledo.edu/11GOPHER_ROOT%3a%5b
  000000.RESEARCH-RESOURCES.GENEALOGY.canadian-
  genealogy%5d

- Canadian Genealogy Links
  http://www.50megs.com/genealogy/canada.html

- Canadian Genealogy Made Easy!!
  http://www.geocities.com/Heartland/4051/

- Canadian Heraldry/L'Heraldique
  http://collections.ic.gc.ca/governor/heraldry/

- Genealogy Resources on the Internet: Canada/Canadian
  http://www-personal.umich.edu/~cgaunt/canada.html

- Pension / Employment Records of Employees of the Canadian Nation Railway
  http://globalgenealogy.com/list25.htm

- ROOTS-L Resources: Canada
  http://www.rootsweb.com/roots-l/canada.html

- Sources for Genealogical Research in Canada
  http://www.king.igs.net/~bdmlhm/cangenealogy.html
  Print, Electronic & Other Resources organized by province/ territory.

- Westminster - Canadian Postal Code Lookup Service
  http://www.westminster.ca/cdnlook.htm
  Also has U.S. Zip codes.

- Yahoo!...Canada...Genealogy
  http://dir.yahoo.com/Regional/Countries/Canada/Arts_and_
  Humanities/Humanities/History/Genealogy/

◆ Government & Cities

- Canadian Parliament
  http://www.parl.gc.ca/index.html

- Premiers Ministres du / Prime Ministers of Canada 1867-1996
  http://collections.ic.gc.ca/discourspm/

- Prime Ministers of Canada
  http://cnet.unb.ca/achn/pme/

- Yahoo! Canada....Cities
  http://ca.yahoo.com/regional/countries/canada/cities/

◆ History & Culture

- Canadian Confederation
  http://www.nlc-bnc.ca/confed/e-1867.htm

- Canadian Heritage Information Network
  http://www.chin.gc.ca/

- Canadian History - 20th Century
  http://www.ualberta.ca/~slis/guides/canada/cansub.htm

- Canadian History on the Web
  http://www.interchange.ubc.ca/sneylan/cdnhist.htm

- Canadian Institute for Historical Microreproductions
  http://www.nlc-bnc.ca/cihm/cihm.htm

- Canadian Journal of History - Annales canadiennes d'histoire
  http://www.usask.ca/history/cjh/

- Canadian Maritime Commerce & Canadian Maritime Heritage
  http://www.marmus.ca/

- Canada Orange Heritage Site
  http://members.tripod.com/~firstlight_2/canorange.htm

- Celebrating Women's Achievements: 21 Pioneers
  http://www.nlc-bnc.ca/digiproj/women/ewomen.htm

- CultureNet
  http://www.culturenet.ucalgary.ca/indexen.html

- Department of Canadian Heritage
  http://www.pch.gc.ca/english.htm

- Early Canadiana Online / Notre memoire en ligne
  http://www.canadiana.org/

- Empire of the Bay
  http://www.pbs.org/empireofthebay/
  Companion site to the PBS television program on the Hudson's Bay Company.

- The Great Canadian History Page
  http://www3.sk.sympatico.ca/vavrr/

- Irish Immigration to Grosse Île, Quebec, Canada
  o Grosse Île: The Canadian Ellis Island
    http://www.audiotapes.com/product.asp?ProductCode='GL-33'
    Presentation by Marianna O'Gallagher, available for sale on audio tape.

  o 1847, Grosse Île: A Record of Daily Events
    http://www.amazon.com/exec/obidos/ISBN=0660168782/markcyndisgenealA/
    A book by Andre Charbonneau.

  o Grosse Île Gateway to Canada
    http://www.amazon.com/exec/obidos/ISBN=0969080530/markcyndisgenealA/
    A book by Carraig Books.

  o Grosse Île and the Irish Memorial
    http://parcscanada.risq.qc.ca/grosse_ile/
    From Parks Canada.

    - 1847: A Tragic Year at Grosse Île
      http://parcscanada.risq.qc.ca/grosse_ile/history2_e.html

    - The Changing Role of Grosse Île
      http://parcscanada.risq.qc.ca/grosse_ile/history1_e.html

    - Statistics and more statistics
      http://parcscanada.risq.qc.ca/grosse_ile/history3_e.html

  o Canada's Irish National Monument - Grosse Île in Quebec
    http://homepage.eircom.net/~mcmullins/grosse-ile.htm

  o Irish Visions Documentaries: Grosse Île: Gateway & Graveyard
    http://www.stpatrick.com/mall/visions/documentaries/grosse.htm
    Video for sale.

  o A Register of Deceased Persons at Sea and on Grosse Île
    http://www.amazon.com/exec/obidos/ISBN=0660168774/markcyndisgenealA/
    A book by Andre Charbonneau.

- Parks Canada - National Historic Sites Page
  http://parkscanada.pch.gc.ca/nhs/nhs_e.htm

- Significant Dates in Canadian Railway History
  http://infoweb.magi.com/~churcher/candate/candate.htm

- StudyWeb: History: Canada
  http://www.studyweb.com/History/toccanada.htm

- The Territorial Evolution of Canada
  http://www.nlc-bnc.ca/confed/maps.htm

- Women in Canadian History
  http://chardonnay.niagara.com/~merrwill/

◆ Home Children

- British Home Children
  http://freepages.genealogy.rootsweb.com/~britishhomechildren
  A site for listing the names of the individual British Home Children.

- British Home Children Mailing List
  http://members.aol.com/gfsjohnf/gen_mail_country-can.html#BRITISHHOMECHILDREN
  A mailing list for those interested in researching the 100,000 British Home Children who were emigrated to Canada by 50 child care organizations to work as indentured farm labourers (1870-1940).

- Home Children
  http://www.archives.ca/exec/naweb.dll?fs&020110&e&top&0
  From the National Archives of Canada. Between 1869 and the early 1930s, over 100,000 children were sent to Canada from Great Britain during the child emigration movement. Members of the

British Isles Family History Society of Greater Ottawa are locating and indexing the names of these Home Children found in passenger lists in the custody of the National Archives of Canada.

  o Home Children Search
    http://www.archives.ca/exec/naweb.dll?fs&02011002&e&top&0
    A searchable online index for the years 1865 to 1919 is available online.

- Young Immigrants to Canada
  http://www.dcs.uwaterloo.ca/~marj/genealogy/homeadd.html
  When the topic of child immigrants to Canada is raised many people first think of Barnardo's. Some may know about Annie Macpherson, Maria Rye, Fegan Homes, Dr. Stephenson and the National Children's Home or even some of the Roman Catholic organizations. This web site represents research into all of the organizations which brought children and young women to Canada between 1833 and 1935.

◆ Libraries, Archives & Museums

- Canadian Archival Resources on the Internet
  http://www.usask.ca/archives/menu.html

- Canadian Archive Addresses
  gopher://Gopher.UToledo.edu:70/00GOPHER_ROOT%3A%5B000000.RESEARCH-RESOURCES.GENEALOGY.CANADIAN-GENEALOGY%5DCANADIAN-ARCHIVE-ADDRESSES.

- Canadian Genealogy and History Links - Archives - Libraries - Museums
  http://www.islandnet.com/~jveinot/cghl/archives.html

- Canadian Institute for Historical Microreproductions
  http://www.nlc-bnc.ca/cihm/cihm.htm
  Established to preserve early printed materials (books, annuals, and periodicals) on microfilm for availability to libraries and archives.

- Canadian Library Association
  http://www.cla.amlibs.ca/

- The Canadian Library Index
  http://www.lights.com/canlib/

- CCA Directory of Archival Resources
  http://www.cdncouncilarchives.ca/dir.html
  From the Canadian Council of Archives.

- Les Centres Généalogiques SDJ / LDS Family History Centers
  http://www.ldsmissions.net/fpm/genealogie.html
  France, Belgique, Suisse, Canada.

- Family History Centres in Canada
  http://www.shelburne.nscc.ns.ca/nsgna/fhc/cdnfhc.htm

- Family History Library Catalog
  http://www.familysearch.org/Search/searchcatalog.asp
  From the FamilySearch web site, an online catalog to the holdings of the LDS Church in Salt Lake City, Utah. Also search for other localities by place name.
  http://www.familysearch.org/fhlc/supermainframeset.asp?display=localitysearch&columns=*,180,0

  o Canada
    http://www.familysearch.org/fhlc/supermainframeset.asp?display=localitydetails&subject=299&subject_disp=Canada&columns=*,180,0

- Family History SourceGuide - Family History Centers - Canada
  http://www.familysearch.org/sg/Canada_FHC.html

- FamilySearch - Family History Centers in Canada
  http://www.familysearch.org/Browse/Places/FHC_RESULTS.ASP?FHCCountry=Canada&FHCStateProv=&FHCCounty=&FHCCity=&Submit=Search
  A list of local LDS Family History Centers along with addresses and hours of operation.

- The Genealogical Institute of the Maritimes
  http://www.shelburne.nscc.ns.ca/nsgna/gim/index.html

- Historical Documents from the National Library of Canada
  http://www.nlc-bnc.ca/confed/historic.htm

- HYTELNET Library Catalogs: Canada
  http://www.lights.com/hytelnet/ca0/ca000.html
  Before you use any of the Telnet links, make note of the user name, password and any other logon information.

- LDS Family History Center Address Submission Form
  http://www.genhomepage.com/FHC/submit_fhc_form.html
  "In order to provide an up to date listing of FHC locations, the Genealogy Home Page is sponsoring a volunteer created listing of FHC's. If you know of a Family History Center near you, you are invited to fill in the form..."

- List of Canadian Archives Addresses
  http://www.byu.edu/rel1/jsblab/genealog/programs/text/can-arch.txt

- Maritime History Archive at Memorial University of Newfoundland
  http://www.mun.ca/mha/

- The National Archives of Canada / Archives Nationales du Canada
  http://www.archives.ca/

  o Genealogy Research
    http://www.archives.ca/exec/naweb.dll?fs&020202&e&top&0

  o Immigration Records
    http://www.archives.ca/exec/naweb.dll?fs&02020204&e&top&0

    - Immigration Records (1925-1935)
      http://www.archives.ca/exec/naweb.dll?fs&020118&e&top&0
      Searchable online database provides the volumes and page numbers on which the names of Canadian immigrants appear in the passenger lists.

- National Library of Canada / Bibliothèque nationale du Canada
  http://www.nlc-bnc.ca/

  o National Library Catalogue
    http://www.nlc-bnc.ca/amicus/ecatalog.htm

o Services to Genealogists and Family Historians at the National Library of Canada
http://www.nlc-bnc.ca/services/egnlogy.htm

● Pier 21
http://www.pier21.ns.ca/
Between 1928-1971, at Pier 21 on the Halifax waterfront, 1.5 million immigrants first set foot on Canadian soil. During World War II, 3,000 British evacuee children, 50,000 war brides and their 22,000 children, over 100,000 refugees and 368,000 Canadian troops bound for Europe passed through Pier 21.

o Parks Canada Backgrounder - Pier 21 Halifax
http://parkscanada.pch.gc.ca/library/background/51_e.htm

o Parks Canada News Release - Pier 21 Recognized as a National Historic Site
http://parkscanada.pch.gc.ca/library/newsreleases/english/nr38%5Fe.htm

● Queen's University Libraries ~ Kingston
http://stauffer.queensu.ca/

o Genealogy
http://stauffer.queensu.ca/inforef/guides/genealogy.htm

o Genealogy Resources in Government Documents
http://stauffer.queensu.ca/webdoc/genealogy/

● Special Collections Spécialisées
http://www.nlc-bnc.ca/collectionsp/spcol_e.htm
Directory of special collections of research value in Canadian libraries.

● United Church of Canada Archives Network
http://www.uccan.org/archives/home.htm

● webCATS: Library Catalogues on the World Wide Web - Canada
http://www.lights.com/webcats/countries/CA.html

◆ Mailing Lists, Newsgroups & Chat

● ACADIAN-CAJUN Mailing List
http://www.rootsweb.com/~jfuller/gen_mail_country-can.html#ACADIAN-CAJUN
For anyone with Acadian-Cajun ancestry worldwide.

● Acadian-Cajun Mailing List
http://www.rootsweb.com/~jfuller/gen_mail_country-can.html#Acadian1
For anyone with a genealogical, historical, or general interest in the Acadian and Cajun people of Canada and Louisiana.

● British Home Children Mailing List
http://members.aol.com/gfsjohnf/gen_mail_country-can.html#BRITISHHOMECHILDREN
A mailing list for those interested in researching the 100,000 British Home Children who were emigrated to Canada by 50 child care organizations to work as indentured farm labourers (1870-1940).

● CanadaGenWeb Chat Forum
http://www.geneofun.on.ca/ongenweb/chat.html

● canadaulsterscots Mailing List
http://www.rootsweb.com/~jfuller/gen_mail_country-unk.html#canadaulsterscots
For the exchange and discussion of the genealogy, culture and

history of Canada's Ulster Scots, those persons who came to Canada from the North of Ireland whose ancestors were from Scotland.

● CANADIAN-ROOTS-L Mailing List
http://www.rootsweb.com/~jfuller/gen_mail_country-can.html#CANADIAN-ROOTS

● CAN-ORANGE Mailing List
http://www.rootsweb.com/~jfuller/gen_mail_country-can.html#CAN-ORANGE
And the associated web page
http://members.tripod.com/~firstlight_2/canorange.htm
For persons interested in the genealogy, culture, and history of persons who came to Canada as members of the Orange Association and their descendants and followers.

● GERMAN-CANADIAN Mailing List
http://www.rootsweb.com/~jfuller/gen_mail_country-can.html#GERMAN-CANADIAN
For the discussion of issues concerning the settlement of German speaking immigrants coming from anywhere to Canada.

● Irish-Canadian Mailing List
http://www.rootsweb.com/~jfuller/gen_mail_country-ire.html#Irish-Canadian
For anyone interested in the genealogy, culture, and historical contribution of people who immigrated from Ireland to Canada.

● loyalists-in-canada Mailing List
http://www.rootsweb.com/~jfuller/gen_mail_country-can.html#LOYALIST
For those with loyalist ancestors to help one another research their loyalist history and to post any facts on the subject that they desire. Loyalists are defined as those who left the United States for Canada after the American Revolution for a number of reasons.

● METISGEN Mailing List
http://www.rootsweb.com/~jfuller/gen_mail_general.html#METISGEN
For the discussion and sharing of information regarding the Metis and their descendants. The Metis are North America's Fur Trading Children ... the new nation of individuals born within North America from the first unions of natives and whites.

● SCHAKEL-NL Mailing List
http://www.rootsweb.com/~jfuller/gen_mail_country-net.html#SCHAKEL-NL
For discussions of news events and issues of interest to Canadians and Americans of Dutch origin; Dutch heritage, customs and traditions; immigrant experiences; questions about Dutch legislation, laws, regulations, history etc.; living the Dutch way (e.g., travel, food, drinks); and the ties that bind us. Queries from genealogists related to their Dutch ancestry are welcome.

● SURNAMES-CANADA Mailing List
http://www.rootsweb.com/~jfuller/gen_mail_country-can.html#SURNAMES-CANADA
Gatewayed with the soc.genealogy.surnames.canada newsgroup
news:soc.genealogy.surnames.canada
For surname queries related to Canada.

● UPPER-CANADA Mailing List
http://www.rootsweb.com/~jfuller/gen_mail_country-can.html#UPPER-CANADA
For anyone with a genealogical interest in Upper Canada, the region split from the Province of Quebec after the American

Revolution, including its history and settlement by Loyalists and British and German soldiers, up to and including the year 1841.

◆ Maps, Gazetteers & Geographical Information

- Association of Canadian Map Libraries and Archives / Association des Cartotheques et Archives
  http://www.sscl.uwo.ca/assoc/acml/acmla.html
  ACMLA actively serves as the representative professional group for Canadian map librarians, cartographic archivists and others interested in geographic information in all formats. The site includes a page with books about Canadian maps.

- Canada National Atlas Information Service
  http://www-nais.ccm.emr.ca/

- Canadian Geographical Names / Les noms géographiques du Canada
  http://GeoNames.NRCan.gc.ca/
  - Canadian Geographical Names - Publications
    http://GeoNames.NRCan.gc.ca/english/publications.html
    List of available publications on geographical names including policy documents and manuals, gazetteers, glossaries, newsletters and brochures.
  - Origins of Canada's Geographical Names
    http://GeoNames.NRCan.gc.ca/english/schoolnet/origin.html
  - Places and Names of Canada
    http://www.placesandnames.on.ca/index.html
    How places in Canada received their names.
  - Querying Canadian Geographical Names:
    - Query by Geographical Name
      http://GeoNames.NRCan.gc.ca/english/cgndb.html
      Or Current Names Selected by Coordinates
      http://GeoNames.NRCan.gc.ca/english/cgndb_coord.html
      Search this database of over 500,000 geographical names by name, feature type, region and by province

- Excite Travel: Canada Maps
  http://maps.excite.com/view/?mapurl=/countries/canada

- Geographical Names, Natural Resources Canada - Sources of Local History
  http://geonames.nrcan.gc.ca/english/schoolnet/local_hist.html

- Historical Atlas of Canada Data Dissemination Project
  http://geog.utoronto.ca/hacddp/hacpage.html

- In Search of Your Canadian Past: The Canadian County Atlas Digital Project
  http://imago.library.mcgill.ca/countyatlas/default.asp
  From McGill University's Rare Books and Special Collections Division. A searchable database derived from published county atlases between 1874 & 1881. Searchable by property owners' names or by location. Township maps, portraits and properties have been scanned, with links from the property owners' names in the database.

- K.B. Slocum Books and Maps - Canada
  http://www.treasurenet.com/cgi-bin/treasure/kbslocum/scan/se=Louisiana/sf=mapstate

◆ Military

- The Black Watch (Royal Highland Regiment) of Canada
  http://www.blackwatchcanada.com/

- Books of Remembrance
  http://collections.ic.gc.ca/books/remember.htm
  Contain the names of Canadians who fought in wars and died either during or after them.

- Canadian Air Aces and Heroes - WWI, WWII and Korea
  http://www.accessweb.com/users/mconstab/

- Canadian Genealogy and History Links - Military
  http://www.islandnet.com/~jveinot/cghl/military.html

- The Canadian Great War Homepage
  http://www.rootsweb.com/~ww1can/
  Canada's Role in World War I, 1914 ~ 1918.

- Canadian Military Genealogical FAQ
  http://www.igs.net/~donpark/canmilfaq.htm

- Canadian POW/MIA Information Centre
  http://www.ipsystems.com/powmia/

- Canadian Vietnam Casualties
  http://www.ipsystems.com/powmia/names/names.html

- Canadian War Museum
  http://www.cmcc.muse.digital.ca/cwm/cwmeng/cwmeng.html

- Fatal Casualties in Canadian Contingents of the Boer War
  http://www.islandnet.com/~duke/boercas.htm

- The Lincoln and Welland Regiment
  http://www.iaw.on.ca:80/~awoolley/lincweld.html
  A reserve infantry battalion of the Canadian Forces.

- Military of Old Canada
  http://inforamp.net/~griffish/gene/mil/mil1.html

- Museum of the Regiments
  http://www.nucleus.com/~regiments/

- The Queen's York Rangers (1st American Regiment)
  http://www.inforamp.net/~ihooker/ranger.htm

- RCAF Personnel - Honours and Awards - 1939-1949
  http://www.airforce.ca/citations/wwii/
  An index of 9,200 awards to approx. 8,300 RCAF personnel, announced between 1940 and 1949, for services during the Second World War.

- RCMP History
  http://www.rcmp-grc.gc.ca/html/history.htm

- Soldiers of the First World War - Canadian Expeditionary Force
  http://www.archives.ca/exec/naweb.dll?fs&020106&e&top&0
  An index to the personnel files of over 600,000 soldiers that enlisted during the First World War. Copies of over 50,000 pages of Attestation papers have been scanned and are available online here.

- World War I Canadian Infantry & Cavalry Index
  http://www.bookkeeping.com/rings/genealogy/ww1.html

◆ Newspapers

- AJR NewsLink - Canadian Newspapers
  http://ajr.newslink.org/nonusn.html

- E&P Media Links - Newspaper Sites in Canada
  http://emedia1.mediainfo.com/emedia/results.htm?region=&abbreviation=canada&category=newspaper

- Kidon Media-Link - News Sources from Canada
  http://www.kidon.com/media-link/canada.shtml

- NAA Hotlinks to Newspapers Online - Canadian Newspapers
  http://www.naa.org/hotlinks/searchResult.asp?category=4&country=Canada&name=Canadian+Newspapers&City=1

- NewsDirectory.com: Newspapers: North America: Canada
  http://www.newsdirectory.com/news/press/na/ca/

- Newspapers at the National Library of Canada
  http://www.nlc-bnc.ca/services/enews.htm

◆ People & Families

- Aboriginal Peoples Guide to the Records of the Government of Canada
  http://www.archives.ca/exec/naweb.dll?fs&02020101&e&top&0

- Canadian Adoptees Registry and Classifieds
  http://www.bconnex.net/~rickm/

- Canadian Genealogy and History Links - Personal
  http://www.islandnet.com/~jveinot/cghl/personal.html

- First Nations in Canada
  http://www.inac.gc.ca/pubs/fnic/index.html

- Genealogy - Acadian and French Canadian
  http://ourworld.compuserve.com/homepages/lwjones/

- Geographical Index to the Tribes of the United States and Canada
  http://www.hanksville.org/sand/contacts/tribal/US.html

- Henry Hudson - The life and times of Henry Hudson, explorer and adventurer
  http://www.georgian.net/rally/hudson/

- Internment of Ukrainians in Canada 1914-1920
  http://www.infoukes.com/history/internment/

- Irish-Canadian List
  http://cyndi.bess.tcd.ie/roots/irishcan.htm

- Loyalists
  http://www.CyndisList.com/loyalist.htm
  See this category on Cyndi's List for related links.

- Metis Families
  http://www.televar.com/~gmorin/

- Paul Bunnell will search your Loyalist ancestors - Send e-mail to Paul for details
  mailto:benjamin@capecod.net

- Prussian-Russian-Canadian Mennonite Genealogical Resources
  http://www.mmhs.org/mmhsgen.htm

- Testimony of the Canadian Fugitives
  http://history.cc.ukans.edu/carrie/docs/texts/canadian_slaves.html

- The Walk to Canada - Tracing the Underground Railroad
  http://www.npca.org/walk.html

- Women in Canadian History
  http://www.niagara.com/~merrwill/

◆ Professional Researchers, Volunteers & Other Research Services

- Board for Certification of Genealogists - Roster of Those Certified - Specializing in Canada
  http://www.bcgcertification.org/rosts_@c.html

- Bowers Genealogy Services
  http://www.interlog.com/~kbowers/bgs2.htm
  England, Scotland, Canada

- Canadian Metis Genealogy
  http://genweb.net/~pbg/metis.htm

- The Genealogical Research Library, Toronto, Canada
  http://www.grl.com/grl/index.shtml
  Professional research services & publications.

- Genealogy Helplist - Canada
  http://www.geocities.com/Heartland/Hills/1285/hlCan.html

- genealogyPro - Professional Genealogists for Canada
  http://genealogyPro.com/directories/Canada.html

- inGeneas Canadian Genealogical Research Services ~ Ottawa, Ontario, Canada
  http://www.ingeneas.com/
  Searchable databases containing 50,000+ Canadian passenger and immigration records (c1750 to 1900) including the only electronic version of the free National Archives of Canada Miscellaneous Immigration Index.

- Kenneth G. Aitken & Associates FHS
  http://familyhistory.cjb.net/
  Professional local and family history services, specializing in Western Canadian and English research. Available for seminars, lectures, or private research work.

- Mark Windover's Web Page - Quality Professional Genealogical Research ~ Williamstown, Massachusetts
  http://www.windover.com/
  United States, Canada (including French), England, Scotland, Ireland, Wales, Iceland, Germany, Switzerland, Norway, Sweden, Denmark, France, Belgium, and The Netherlands.

- The Official Iowa Counties Professional Genealogist and Researcher's Registry for Canada
  http://www.iowa-counties.com/gene/canada.htm

- The Snoop Sisters Family History Researchers ~ Nanaimo, B.C. Canada
  http://www.snoopsisters.net/
  England & Wales, Scotland, Ireland & N., Ireland, Eastern Europe, Canada & U.S.

- Traces From Your Past
  http://www.cadvision.com/traces/
  Genealogical Publications, Services and Resources to assist the Family Historian researching in Canada and the United Kingdom .

◆ Publications, Software & Supplies

- Amazon.com Genealogy Bookstore – Canada
  http://www.amazon.com/exec/obidos/external-search/
  ?keyword=canada+genealogy&tag=markcyndisgenealA/
  And Canadian
  http://www.amazon.com/exec/obidos/external-search/
  ?keyword=canadian+genealogy&tag=markcyndisgenealA/

- Ancestor's Attic Discount Genealogy Books - Canadian Genealogy Books
  http://members.tripod.com/~ancestorsattic/index.html#secCA

- AudioTapes.com - Genealogical Lectures on Cassette Tapes - Canada
  http://www.audiotapes.com/search2.asp?Search=Canada
  And Canadian
  http://www.audiotapes.com/search2.asp?Search=Canadian

- Books We Own - Canada
  http://www.rootsweb.com/~bwo/can_gr.html
  Find a book from which you would like a lookup and click on the submitter's code at the end of the entry. Once you find the contact information for the submitter, write them a polite request for a lookup.

- Family History News
  http://www.globalserve.net/~parrspub/
  Canadian genealogical publication.

- Frontier Press Bookstore - Canada
  http://www.frontierpress.com/frontier.cgi?category=can

- GenealogyBookShop.com - Canada
  http://www.genealogybookshop.com/genealogybookshop/
  files/The_World,Canada/index.html
  The online store of Genealogical Publishing Co., Inc. & Clearfield Company.

- Heritage Books - Canadian
  http://www.heritagebooks.com/indian.htm

- Global Genealogical Supply - Misc. Canadian Genealogy & Local History Books
  http://www.globalgenealogy.com/cdamisc.htm

- Quintin Publications - Canada
  http://www.quintinpublications.com/canada.html

- Quintin Publications - Métis and First Nations
  http://www.quintinpublications.com/metis.html

- Willow Bend Bookstore - Canada and Canadians
  http://www.willowbend.net/default.asp

◆ Queries, Message Boards & Surname Lists

- RootsWeb Surname List - RSL Canada
  http://rsl.rootsweb.com/cgi-bin/rslsql.cgi
  The RSL and this form concept & design are courtesy of Karen Isaacson

◆ Records: Census, Cemeteries, Land, Obituaries, Personal, Taxes and Vital (Born, Married, Died & Buried)

- 1901 Census of Canada - Film Numbers
  http://www.tbaytel.net/bmartin/census.htm

- Alberta Family Histories Society (AFHS) Genealogical Projects Registry
  http://www.afhs.ab.ca/registry/index.html
  A central registry, which provides a bibliography of genealogical projects, both online and offline, in Canada. The registry is categorized by province/territory, then by record type: births, marriage, census, deaths, and other.
  - o Canada - Birth
    http://www.afhs.ab.ca/registry/regcan_birth.html
  - o Canada - Census
    http://www.afhs.ab.ca/registry/regcan_census.html
  - o Canada - Deaths
    http://www.afhs.ab.ca/registry/regcan_death.html
  - o Canada - Marriage
    http://www.afhs.ab.ca/registry/regcan_marr.html
  - o Canada - Other
    http://www.afhs.ab.ca/registry/regcan_other.html

- Canadian Genealogy and History Links - Cemetery - Obituary
  http://www.islandnet.com/~jveinot/cghl/cemetery.html

- Canadian Vital Statistics Addresses
  gopher://Gopher.UToledo.edu:70/00GOPHER_ROOT%3A%
  5B000000.RESEARCH-RESOURCES.GENEALOGY.
  CANADIAN-GENEALOGY%5DCANADIAN-VITAL-
  STATISTICS-ADDRESSES.

- Commonwealth War Graves Commission
  http://www.cwgc.org/
  Details of 1.7 million members of UK and Commonwealth forces who died in the 1st and 2nd World Wars and other wars, and 60,000 civilian casualties of WWII. Gives details of grave site, date of death, age, usually parents/widow's address.

- Home Children
  http://www.archives.ca/exec/naweb.dll?fs&020110&e&top&0
  From the National Archives of Canada. Between 1869 and the early 1930s, over 100,000 children were sent to Canada from Great Britain during the child emigration movement. Members of the British Isles Family History Society of Greater Ottawa are locating and indexing the names of these Home Children found in passenger lists in the custody of the National Archives of Canada.

  o Home Children Search
    http://www.archives.ca/exec/naweb.dll?fs&02011002&e&top&0
    A searchable online index for the years 1865 to 1919 is available online.

- Immigrants to Canada in Nineteenth Century - Ships - Emigration Reports - Emigration Handbooks
  http://www.ist.uwaterloo.ca/~marj/genealogy/thevoyage.html

- Immigration to Canada in the Nineteenth Century - Ships - Emigration Reports - Emigration Handbooks
  http://www.ist.uwaterloo.ca/~marj/genealogy/thevoyage.html
  Contains pointers to many other ships lists and sources.

- Irish Famine Migration To New Brunswick, 1845 – 1852
  http://gov.nb.ca/archives/ols/pr/if/index.htm
  Searchable database from the Provincial Archives of New Brunswick.

- The National Registration File of 1940
  http://www.tbaytel.net/bmartin/natreg.htm
  Canada registered everyone at least 16 years old in 1940. These records can provide real help to the genealogist. Full information on these records and how to access them.

- The Olive Tree Genealogy - Canada - Births Deaths & Marriages Exchange
  http://www.rootsweb.com/~ote/bdm/canada/bdm.htm

- Post 1901 Census Project
  http://www.globalgenealogy.com/census/index.htm
  From the Global Gazette. Many concerned Canadians believe that the legislation which enforces permanent concealment of post-1901 census from the public eye, must be changed. If new legislation is not passed by Canada's Parliament, those records may never be available for future generations or us. Worse yet, our detailed census records may be destroyed.

- Sessional Papers of the Government of Canada and British Parliamentary Papers - Names extracted from Government of Canada Reports
  http://www.ist.uwaterloo.ca/~marj/genealogy/sessional papers.html
  Annual reports from various government departments covering such things as names of lighthouse keepers, holders of tavern licenses, cadets at military college, shareholders in banks, etc.

- Sources for Genealogical Research in Canada - Print, Electronic & Other Resources
  http://www.king.igs.net/~bdmlhm/cangenealogy.html
  Links, books, maps, events, contact information, etc. for research in Canada, for Canadian roots, organized into general and regional categories.

◆ Religion & Churches

- Christianity Online Church Locator - Churches in Canada
  http://www.christianity.net/churchlocator/location.php?country=Canada

- Churches dot Net - Global Church Web Pages - Canada
  http://churches.net/churches/internat.html#can

◆ Societies & Groups

- The American-Canadian Genealogical Society
  http://ourworld.compuserve.com:80/homepages/ACGS/homepage.htm
  Leaders in French-Canadian Genealogical Research.

- Association of Canadian Archivists
  http://aca.archives.ca/index.htm

- Canada's National History Society
  http://www.historysociety.ca/

- The Canadian Canal Society / Société des Canaux du Canada
  http://people.becon.org/~ccs/

- Canadian Council of Archives / Conseil canadien des archives
  http://www.cdncouncilarchives.ca/

- Canadian Federation of Genealogical and Family History Societies (CanFed)
  http://www.geocities.com/Athens/Troy/2274/index.html

- Canadian Friends Historical Association
  http://home.interhop.net/~aschrauwe/

- Canadian Genealogical Societies
  gopher://Gopher.UToledo.edu:70/00GOPHER_ROOT%3A%5B000000.RESEARCH-RESOURCES.GENEALOGY.CANADIAN-GENEALOGY%5DCANADIAN-GENEALOGICAL-GROUPS.

- Canadian Genealogy and History Links - Organizations and Societies
  http://www.islandnet.com/~jveinot/cghl/organization.html

- Canadian Oral History Association
  http://www.ncf.carleton.ca/oral-history/

- Canadian Peacekeeping Veterans Association
  http://www.islandnet.com/~duke/cpva.htm

- Canadian Railroad Historical Association - Association canadienne d'histoire ferroviaire
  http://www.exporail.org/association/
  The CRHA aims are the preservation and dissemination of information concerning railway heritage in Canada.

- Grand Orange Lodge of Canada
  http://www.orange.ca/
  Web site for the Loyal Orange Association of Canada, a national fraternal organization.

- IOOF Lodge Website Directory - Canada
  http://norm28.hsc.usc.edu/IOOF/International/Canada.html
  Independent Order of Odd Fellows and Rebekahs.

- Labrador Métis Nation ~ Labrador, Canada
  http://www.labmetis.org/

- Mennonites in Canada
  http://www.mhsc.ca/
  The web site for the Mennonite Historical Society of Canada.

- The United Empire Loyalists' Association of Canada
  ~ Toronto, Ontario, Canada
  http://people.becon.org/~uela/uela1.htm

CANADA – ALBERTA

http://www.cyndislist.com/alberta.htm

Category Index:

- ◆ Canada GenWeb Project
- ◆ Events & Activities
- ◆ General Resource Sites
- ◆ Government & Cities
- ◆ Libraries, Archives & Museums
- ◆ Mailing Lists, Newsgroups & Chat
- ◆ Maps, Gazetteers & Geographical Information
- ◆ Military
- ◆ Newspapers

- ◆ People & Families
- ◆ Professional Researchers, Volunteers & Other Research Services
- ◆ Publications, Software & Supplies
- ◆ Queries, Message Boards & Surname Lists
- ◆ Records: Census, Cemeteries, Land, Obituaries, Personal, Taxes and Vital
- ◆ Religion & Churches
- ◆ Societies & Groups

◆ Canada GenWeb Project

- Alberta GenWeb
  http://users.rootsweb.com/~canab/index.html

◆ Events & Activities

- Alberta Family Histories Society - Gensoft
  http://www.calcna.ab.ca/afhs/gensoft.html

- Alberta Family Histories Society - Wild Rose Seminar
  http://www.calcna.ab.ca/afhs/seminar.html

◆ General Resource Sites

- Canadian Genealogy and History Links - Alberta
  http://www.islandnet.com/~jveinot/cghl/alberta.html

- Genealogy Resources on the Internet: Alberta
  http://www-personal.umich.edu/~cgaunt/canada.html
  #ALBERTA

- Traces: Genealogy Alberta
  http://www.cadvision.com/traces/alta/alberta.html
  New site providing on-line indexes to a variety of material. Small look up fee applies in SOME instances. Main interest area is Calgary & southwestern Alberta.

◆ Government & Cities

- Government of Alberta
  http://www.gov.ab.ca/

- Yahoo! Canada....Alberta: Cities
  http://ca.yahoo.com/regional/countries/canada/provinces_
  and_territories/alberta/cities/

◆ Libraries, Archives & Museums

- Alberta Provincial Government Libraries
  http://www.gov.ab.ca/library/aglchome.html

- Calgary Public Library
  http://www.public-library.calgary.ab.ca/

- Canadian Archival Resources on the Internet - Alberta
  http://www.usask.ca/archives/car/abmenu.html

- The Canadian Library Index - Alberta
  http://www.lights.com/canlib/canlibab.html

- CCA Directory of Archives for Alberta
  http://www.cdncouncilarchives.ca/cca_dir/alberta.html

- City of Edmonton Archives
  http://www.gov.edmonton.ab.ca/comm_services/city_op_
  attractions/archives.html
  In the Prince of Wales Armouries, Heritage Centre.

- Edmonton Public Library
  http://www.publib.edmonton.ab.ca/

  o Genealogy at the Edmonton Public Library
    http://libris.publib.edmonton.ab.ca/genealogy/genealogy_
    at_epl.htm

- Family History Library Catalog
  http://www.familysearch.org/Search/searchcatalog.asp
  From the FamilySearch web site, an online catalog to the holdings of the LDS Church in Salt Lake City, Utah. Also search for other localities by place name.
  http://www.familysearch.org/fhlc/supermainframeset.asp?
  display=localitysearch&columns=*,180,0

  o Canada
    http://www.familysearch.org/fhlc/supermainframeset.asp?
    display=localitydetails&subject=299&subject_disp=Canada
    &columns=*,180,0

    • Alberta
      http://www.familysearch.org/fhlc/supermainframeset.asp
      ?display=localitydetails&subject=301&subject_disp=
      Alberta&columns=*,180,0

- Family History SourceGuide - Family History Centers - Canada
  http://www.familysearch.org/sg/Canada_FHC.html

- FamilySearch - Family History Centers in Alberta
  http://www.familysearch.org/Browse/Places/FHC_
  RESULTS.ASP?FHCCountry=&FHCStateProv=Alberta&
  FHCCounty=&FHCCity=&Submit=Search
  A list of local LDS Family History Centers along with addresses and hours of operation.

- Geographic Index to Archival Institutions
  http://www.glenbow.org/asa/maplist.htm
  From the Archives Society of Alberta.

- Glenbow Archives
  http://www.glenbow.org/archives.htm

- Glenbow Library
  http://www.glenbow.org/library.htm

- HYTELNET - Library Catalogs: Canada: Alberta
  http://www.lights.com/hytelnet/ca0/AB.html
  Before you use any of the Telnet links, make note of the user name, password and any other logon information.

- The Hudson's Bay Company Archives
  http://www.gov.mb.ca/chc/archives/hbca/index.html
  From the Provincial Archives of Manitoba, Canada.

- Lethbridge Family History Center
  http://www.leth.net/fhc/index.htm

- The National Archives of Canada / Archives Nationales du Canada
  http://www.archives.ca/
  o Genealogy Research
    http://www.archives.ca/exec/naweb.dll?fs&020202&e
    &top&0

- National Library of Canada / Bibliothèque nationale du Canada
  http://www.nlc-bnc.ca/
  o Genealogy and Family History at the National Library of Canada
    http://www.nlc-bnc.ca/services/genealogy/gnlogy-e.htm
  o National Library Catalogue
    http://www.nlc-bnc.ca/amicus/ecatalog.htm

- Okotoks Family History Center
  http://www.cadvision.com/Home_Pages/accounts/okfhc/

- United Church of Canada Archives Network: Alberta and Northwest Conference Archives
  http://www.uccan.org/archives/alberta.htm
  A summary of their holdings and contact information.

- Whyte Museum of the Canadian Rockies
  http://www.whyte.org/
  Has an archives research library.

◆ Mailing Lists, Newsgroups & Chat

- ALBERTA Mailing List
  http://www.rootsweb.com/~jfuller/gen_mail_country-
  can.html#ALBERTA

- alberta Mailing List
  http://www.rootsweb.com/~jfuller/gen_mail_country-
  can.html#ALBERTA-CANADA

- CANADIAN ROOTS Mailing List
  http://www.rootsweb.com/~jfuller/gen_mail_country-
  can.html#CANADIAN-ROOTS

- SURNAMES-CANADA Mailing List
  http://www.rootsweb.com/~jfuller/gen_mail_country-
  can.html#SURNAMES-CANADA
  Gatewayed with the soc.genealogy.surnames.canada newsgroup
  news:soc.genealogy.surnames.canada
  For surname queries related to Canada.

◆ Maps, Gazetteers & Geographical Information

- Canadian Geographical Names / Les noms géographiques du Canada
  http://GeoNames.NRCan.gc.ca/
  o Canadian Geographical Names - Publications
    http://GeoNames.NRCan.gc.ca/english/publications.html
    List of available publications on geographical names including policy documents and manuals, gazetteers, glossaries, newsletters and brochures.
  o Origins of Canada's Geographical Names
    http://GeoNames.NRCan.gc.ca/english/schoolnet/
    origin.html
  o Querying Canadian Geographical Names:
    - Query by Geographical Name
      http://Geonames.NRCan.gc.ca/english/cgndb.html
    Current Name Selected by Coordinates
    http://Geonames.NRCan.gc.ca/english/cgndb_
    coord.html
    Search this database of over 500,000 geographical names by name, feature type, region and by province

- Excite Maps: Alberta
  http://maps.excite.com/view/?mapurl=/countries/canada/
  alberta

◆ Military

- Alberta's War Memorials
  http://www.stemnet.nf.ca/monuments/ab.htm
  A project to preserve information about War Memorials throughout Canada on the World Wide Web. The descriptions of these individual cenotaphs often includes names and other information on the dead which can be of interest to the genealogist. .

- Canada - Military
  http://www.CyndisList.com/milcan.htm
  See this category on Cyndi's List for related links.

- The South Alberta Regiment
  http://www.steelchariots.net/29armd.htm
  History of the South Alberta Regiment.

◆ Newspapers

- AJR NewsLink - Alberta Newspapers
  http://ajr.newslink.org/nonusnalb.html

- E&P Media Links - Newspaper Sites in Alberta
  http://emedia1.mediainfo.com/emedia/results.htm?region=
  canada&abbreviation=alberta++++++++++++++++++++++
  +++++++++++&category=newspaper

- NewsDirectory.com: Newspapers: North America:
  Canada: Alberta
  http://www.newsdirectory.com/news/press/na/ca/ab/

◆ People & Families

- Germans from Russia
  http://www.CyndisList.com/germruss.htm
  See this category on Cyndi's List for related links.

- Hutterite Genealogy Cross-Index
  http://feefhs.org/hut/indexhut.html

- Tribes and Bands of Alberta
  http://www.hanksville.org/sand/contacts/tribal/AB.html

◆ Professional Researchers, Volunteers & Other Research Services

- Family Ivy Research
  http://freepages.genealogy.rootsweb.com/~mumford/
  familyivy.html
  Professional genealogy research offering a comprehensive range of genealogical research services, but specializing in Metis genealogy and genealogy in Clay County, Minnesota and Alberta, Canada.

- Gen-Find Research Associates
  http://www.gen-find.com/
  Specialists in Genealogy Research for Ontario & Western Canada, Scotland, Ireland. Also the rest of Canada and Forensic & Probate/Heir Research and 20th Century Research.

◆ Publications, Software & Supplies

- Amazon.com Genealogy Bookstore - Alberta
  http://www.amazon.com/exec/obidos/external-search/?
  keyword=alberta+genealogy&tag=markcyndisgenealA/

- Global Genealogical Supply - Western Canada
  Genealogical & Local History Books
  http://www.globalgenealogy.com/cdawest.htm

- The Greeks in Alberta 1903-1995
  http://www.firstwest.com/greekbook/
  A book by Nina Kolias.

- Interlink Bookshop Genealogical Services ~
  Victoria, B.C., Canada
  http://www.interlinkbookshop.com/

- Quintin Publications - Alberta
  http://www.quintinpublications.com/ab.html

◆ Queries, Message Boards & Surname Lists

- RootsWeb Surname List - RSL Alberta
  http://rsl.rootsweb.com/cgi-bin/rslsql.cgi
  The RSL and this form concept & design are courtesy of Karen Isaacson

◆ Records: Census, Cemeteries, Land, Obituaries, Personal, Taxes and Vital (Born, Married, Died & Buried)

- Alberta Family Histories Society (AFHS)
  Genealogical Projects Registry
  http://www.afhs.ab.ca/registry/index.html
  A central registry, which provides a bibliography of genealogical projects, both online and offline, in Canada. The registry is categorized by province/territory, then by record type: births, marriage, census, deaths, and other.
  - Alberta - Births
    http://www.afhs.ab.ca/registry/regab_birth.html
  - Alberta - Census
    http://www.afhs.ab.ca/registry/regab_census.html
  - Alberta - Death
    http://www.afhs.ab.ca/registry/regab_death.html
  - Alberta - Marriage
    http://www.afhs.ab.ca/registry/regab_marr.html
  - Alberta - Other
    http://www.afhs.ab.ca/registry/regab_other.html

- Alberta Genealogical Society, Edmonton Branch -
  1901 Census Alberta District (No. 202)
  http://www.agsedm.edmonton.ab.ca/1901_census_202_
  online.html

- Alberta Genealogical Society Master Name Index
  http://www.compusmart.ab.ca/abgensoc/nameindex.html
  A database of about 400,000 names, including mostly cemetery records and tombstone inscriptions. They can search the database for a small fee.

- Births, Deaths and Marriages Reported in Calgary,
  Alberta Newspapers, 1883-1899
  http://www.calcna.ab.ca/afhs/news.html

- Camrose County GenWeb - The Cemetery List
  http://www.rootsweb.com/~abcamros/toppage2.htm
  #THE CEMETERY LIST

- Cemetery Register of Youngstown, Alberta, Canada
  http://www.telusplanet.net/public/cfdun/cemnav.htm
  Index for 1913-1990.

- City of Edmonton's Department of Cemeteries - Send
  e-mail to: cemetery@wnet.gov.edmonton.ab.ca to
  find out about your ancestors buried in Edmonton,
  Alberta, Canada
  mailto:cemetery@wnet.gov.edmonton.ab.ca

- Edmonton Community Services - Can we help you find a relative? ~ Alberta
  http://www.gov.edmonton.ab.ca/comm_services/rec_facilities/cemeteries/search.html
  Database of people interred more than 25 years ago (close to 60,000 people) that are in Edmonton Municipal Cemeteries.

- Hilda Baptist Cemetery, Hilda, Alberta, Canada
  http://pixel.cs.vt.edu/library/cemeteries/canada/link/hilda1.txt

- Index to the 1891 Dominion Census Lethbridge Sub-District, Alberta, Northwest Territories
  http://mypage.direct.ca/d/dobee/lethmain.html

- National Archives of Canada - Dominion Land Grants
  http://www.archives.ca/exec/naweb.dll?fs&020111&e&top&0
  Database of grants issued in Manitoba, Saskatchewan, Alberta and the railway belt of British Columbia, c. 1870-1930.

◆ Religion & Churches

- Christianity Online Church Locator - Churches in Alberta
  http://www.christianity.net/churchlocator/location.php?country=Canada&state=Alberta

- Churches of the World - Alberta
  http://www.churchsurf.com/churches/Canada/Alberta
  From the ChurchSurf Christian Directory.

◆ Societies & Groups

- The Alberta Chapter, Germans from Russia Heritage Society
  http://www.grhs.com/chapters/alberta.html

- Alberta Family Histories Society
  http://www.calcna.ab.ca/afhs/

- Alberta Genealogical Society
  http://www.compusmart.ab.ca/abgensoc/

  o Brooks & District Branch of the Alberta Genealogical Society
    http://www.eidnet.org/local/bburrows/bbags/

  o Fort McMurray Branch of the Alberta Genealogical Society
    http://www.compusmart.ab.ca/abgensoc/branches.html#Ft.

  o Grande Prairie & District Branch - Alberta Genealogical Society
    http://www.rootsweb.com/~abgpags/

  o Lethbridge & District Branch of the Alberta Genealogical Society
    http://www.compusmart.ab.ca/abgensoc/branches.html#Lethbridge

- American Historical Society of Germans from Russia - Calgary Canada Chapter
  http://www.ahsgr.org/calgary.html

- Archives Society of Alberta
  http://www.glenbow.org/asa/home.htm

- IOOF Lodge Website Directory - Alberta
  http://norm28.hsc.usc.edu/IOOF/International/Alberta.html
  Independent Order of Odd Fellows and Rebekahs.

- Jewish Genealogical Society (S. Alberta)
  http://www.geocities.com/Heartland/Village/9200/

- The Legal Archives Society of Alberta
  http://www.legalarchivessociety.ab.ca/

- Mennonite Historical Society of Alberta
  http://members.home.net/rempel/mhsa/
  The MHSA is a new society developed to support those who are interested in basic Mennonite history, those doing Mennonite genealogy/family history research, and those who are interested in the preservation and display of Mennonite historical documents and cultural artifacts.

- La Societe Genealogique du Nord-Ouest ~ Edmonton
  http://genweb.net/~pbg/sgno.htm

- Societe Historique et Genealogique de Smoky River
  http://www.telusplanet.net/public/genealfa/English.html
  The "largest French-Canadian genealogical resource library in Western Canada" located in Donnelly, Alberta, Canada in the centre of the Smoky River area in the Peace River region of Northern Alberta.

- Society Hill: Alberta Societies
  http://www.daddezio.com/society/hill.ca/SH-AB-01.html
  A list of addresses for genealogical and historical societies in the province.

CANADA – BRITISH COLUMBIA

http://www.cyndislist.com/bc.htm

Category Index:

- Canada GenWeb Project
- General Resource Sites
- Government & Cities
- History & Culture
- Libraries, Archives & Museums
- Mailing Lists, Newsgroups & Chat
- Maps, Gazetteers & Geographical Information
- Military
- Newspapers

- People & Families
- Professional Researchers, Volunteers & Other Research Services
- Publications, Software & Supplies
- Queries, Message Boards & Surname Lists
- Records: Census, Cemeteries, Land, Obituaries, Personal, Taxes and Vital
- Religion & Churches
- Societies & Groups

◆ Canada GenWeb Project

- British Columbia GenWeb Project
  http://www.rootsweb.com/~canbc/

◆ General Resource Sites

- Canadian Genealogy and History Links - British Columbia
  http://www.islandnet.com/~jveinot/cghl/british-columbia.html

- Genealogy Resources on the Internet: British Columbia
  http://www-personal.umich.edu/~cgaunt/canada.html#BC

◆ Government & Cities

- City Directories Available at the City of Victoria Archives
  http://www.city.victoria.bc.ca/archives/citydir/citydir_list.htm

- City of Vancouver, B.C., Municipal Government
  http://www.city.vancouver.bc.ca/

- City of Victoria
  http://www.city.victoria.bc.ca/

- Government of British Columbia
  http://www.gov.bc.ca/

- Yahoo! Canada....British Columbia: Cities
  http://ca.yahoo.com/regional/countries/canada/provinces_and_territories/british_columbia/cities/

◆ History & Culture

- The British Columbia History Internet/World-Wide Web Page
  http://victoria.tc.ca/Resources/bchistory.html

- British Columbia Museums Association
  http://www.islandnet.com/~bcma/

- Fort St. James National Historic Site
  http://www.harbour.com/parkscan/fsj/

- The Great Depression
  http://trinculo.educ.sfu.ca/pgm/depress/greatdepress.html
  Focusing on the city of Vancouver.

- A History of the Northwest Coast
  http://www.hallman.org/indian/.www.html

◆ Libraries, Archives & Museums

- Archives Association of British Columbia
  http://aabc.bc.ca/aabc/

- British Columbia Archival Resources
  http://aabc.bc.ca/aabc/bcarch.html

- British Columbia Archives & Records Service
  http://www.bcarchives.gov.bc.ca/index.htm

- British Columbia Museums Association
  http://www.MuseumsAssn.bc.ca/

- Canadian Archival Resources on the Internet - British Columbia
  http://www.usask.ca/archives/car/bcmenu.html

- Canadian Directory of Special Collections - Doukhobor Collection
  http://www.nlc-bnc.ca/collectionsp-bin/colldisp/l=0/c=48
  University of British Columbia, Special Collections and University Archives Division.

- The Canadian Library Index - British Columbia
  http://www.lights.com/canlib/canlibbc.html

- CCA Directory of Archives for British Columbia
  http://www.cdncouncilarchives.ca/cca_dir/bc.html

- City of Richmond Archives
  http://www.city.richmond.bc.ca/archives/default.htm

- City of Vancouver Archives
  http://www.city.vancouver.bc.ca/ctyclerk/archives/index.htm
  Comprehensive online searching, including scanned photographs.

- City of Victoria Archives and Records Division
  http://www.city.victoria.bc.ca/archives/index.htm

  o Genealogical Research
    http://www.city.victoria.bc.ca/depts/archives/genogy.htm

- Courtenay & District Museum - Genealogy ~ British Columbia
  http://www.courtenaymuseum.bc.ca/genealogy/index.html
  A web-based guide, tutorial and set of resource links for genealogical researchers.

- Family History Library Catalog
  http://www.familysearch.org/Search/searchcatalog.asp
  From the FamilySearch web site, an online catalog to the holdings of the LDS Church in Salt Lake City, Utah. Also search for other localities by place name.
  http://www.familysearch.org/fhlc/supermainframeset.asp?
  display=localitysearch&columns=*,180,0

  o Canada
    http://www.familysearch.org/fhlc/supermainframeset.asp?
    display=localitydetails&subject=299&subject_disp=Canada
    &columns=*,180,0

    - British Columbia
      http://www.familysearch.org/fhlc/supermainframeset.asp
      ?display=localitydetails&subject=300&subject_disp=Briti
      sh_Columbia&columns=*,180,0

- Family History SourceGuide - Family History Centers - Canada
  http://www.familysearch.org/sg/Canada_FHC.html

- FamilySearch - Family History Centers in British Columbia
  http://www.familysearch.org/Browse/Places/FHC_
  RESULTS.ASP?FHCCountry=&FHCStateProv=British+
  Columbia&FHCCounty=&FHCCity=&Submit=Search
  A list of local LDS Family History Centers along with addresses and hours of operation.

- Guide to Archival Repositories in B.C.
  http://aabc.bc.ca/aabc/bcguide.html

- The Hudson's Bay Company Archives
  http://www.gov.mb.ca/chc/archives/hbca/index.html
  From the Provincial Archives of Manitoba, Canada.

- HYTELNET - Library Catalogs: Canada: British Columbia
  http://www.lights.com/hytelnet/caC/BC.html
  Before you use any of the Telnet links, make note of the user name, password and any other logon information.

- Nanaimo Community Archives
  http://bbs.sd68.nanaimo.bc.ca/nol/community/nca.htm

- The National Archives of Canada / Archives Nationales du Canada
  http://www.archives.ca/

  o Genealogy Research
    http://www.archives.ca/exec/naweb.dll?fs&020202&e
    &top&0

- National Library of Canada / Bibliothèque nationale du Canada
  http://www.nlc-bnc.ca/

  o Genealogy and Family History at the National Library of Canada
    http://www.nlc-bnc.ca/services/genealogy/gnlogy-e.htm

  o National Library Catalogue
    http://www.nlc-bnc.ca/amicus/ecatalog.htm

- Simon Fraser University Archives
  http://www.sfu.ca/archives/

- Surrey Public Library
  http://www.spl.surrey.bc.ca/

- UBC Library Special Collections and University Archives
  http://www.library.ubc.ca/spcoll/

- United Church of Canada Archives Network: British Columbia Conference Archives
  http://www.uccan.org/archives/britishcolumbia.htm
  A summary of their holdings and contact information.

- Vancouver Public Library Central Branch - Special Collections
  http://www.vpl.vancouver.bc.ca/branches/LibrarySquare/spe/
  home.html

◆ Mailing Lists, Newsgroups & Chat

- british-columbia Mailing List
  http://www.rootsweb.com/~jfuller/gen_mail_country-
  can.html#BRITISH-COLUMBIA-CANADA

- CANADIAN ROOTS Mailing List
  http://www.rootsweb.com/~jfuller/gen_mail_country-
  can.html#CANADIAN-ROOTS

- SURNAMES-CANADA Mailing List
  http://www.rootsweb.com/~jfuller/gen_mail_country-
  can.html#SURNAMES-CANADA
  Gatewayed with the soc.genealogy.surnames.canada newsgroup
  news:soc.genealogy.surnames.canada
  For surname queries related to Canada.

◆ Maps, Gazetteers & Geographical Information

- BC Geographical Names Information System
  http://www.gdbc.gov.bc.ca/bcnames/
  Searchable database.

- Canadian Geographical Names / Les noms géographiques du Canada
  http://GeoNames.NRCan.gc.ca/

  o Canadian Geographical Names - Publications
    http://GeoNames.NRCan.gc.ca/english/publications.html
    List of available publications on geographical names including policy documents and manuals, gazetteers, glossaries, newsletters and brochures.

o Origins of Canada's Geographical Names
http://GeoNames.NRCan.gc.ca/english/schoolnet/
origin.html

o Querying Canadian Geographical Names:

- Query by Geographical Name
http://Geonames.NRCan.gc.ca/english/cgndb.html

Current Names Selected by Coordinates
http://Geonames.NRCan.gc.ca/english/cgndb_
coord.html
*Search this database of over 500,000 geographical names by
name, feature type, region and by province*

- Cartographic Records
http://www.bcarchives.gov.bc.ca/cartogr/general/maps.htm

- Excite Maps: British Columbia
http://maps.excite.com/view/?mapurl=/countries/canada/
british_columbia

◆ Military

- British Columbia's War Memorials
http://www.stemnet.nf.ca/monuments/bc.htm
*A project to preserve information about War Memorials throughout
Canada on the World Wide Web. The descriptions of these
individual cenotaphs often includes names and other information on
the dead which can be of interest to the genealogist.*

- Canada - Military
http://www.CyndisList.com/milcan.htm
See this category on Cyndi's List for related links.

◆ Newspapers

- AJR NewsLink - British Columbia Newspapers
http://ajr.newslink.org/nonusnbri.html

- E&P Media Links - Newspaper Sites in British
Columbia
http://emedia1.mediainfo.com/emedia/results.htm?region=
canada&abbreviation=britishcolumbia+++++++++++++++++
++++++++++++++++&category=newspaper

- The First Newspapers on Canada's West Coast: 1858-
1863
http://members.tripod.com/~Hughdoherty/index.htm

- NewsDirectory.com: Newspapers: North America:
Canada: British Columbia
http://www.newsdirectory.com/news/press/na/ca/bc/

◆ People & Families

- Doukhobor Home Page
http://www.dlcwest.com/~r.androsoff/index.htm
*A group of Russian peasants that split from the Russian Orthodox
Church. Large groups of Doukhobors emigrated to Canada and
homesteaded in Saskatchewan and British Columbia.*

- Tribes and Bands of British Columbia
http://www.hanksville.org/sand/contacts/tribal/BC.html

◆ Professional Researchers, Volunteers & Other Research Services

- British Columbia Genealogy Copy Service
http://members.home.net:80/crawf/
*A service for those needing information and certificates from British
Columbia, Canada.*

- Gen-Find Research Associates
http://www.gen-find.com/
*Specialists in Genealogy Research for Ontario & Western Canada,
Scotland, Ireland. Also the rest of Canada and Forensic &
Probate/Heir Research and 20th Century Research.*

- The Snoop Sisters Family History Researchers ~
Nanaimo, B.C. Canada
http://www.snoopsisters.net/
*England & Wales, Scotland, Ireland & N., Ireland, Eastern Europe,
Canada & U.S.*

◆ Publications, Software & Supplies

- Amazon.com Genealogy Bookstore - British
Columbia
http://www.amazon.com/exec/obidos/external-search/
?keyword=british+columbia+genealogy&tag=mark
cyndisgenealA/

- Global Genealogical Supply - Western Canada
Genealogical & Local History Books
http://www.globalgenealogy.com/cdawest.htm

- Interlink Bookshop & Genealogical Services ~
Victoria, B.C. Canada
http://www.interlinkbookshop.com/

- Quintin Publications - British Columbia
http://www.quintinpublications.com/bc.html

◆ Queries, Message Boards & Surname Lists

- RootsWeb Surname List - RSL British Columbia
http://rsl.rootsweb.com/cgi-bin/rslsql.cgi
*The RSL and this form concept & design are courtesy of Karen
Isaacson*

◆ Records: Census, Cemeteries, Land, Obituaries, Personal, Taxes and Vital (Born, Married, Died & Buried)

- Alberta Family Histories Society (AFHS)
Genealogical Projects Registry
http://www.afhs.ab.ca/registry/index.html
*A central registry, which provides a bibliography of genealogical
projects, both online and offline, in Canada. The registry is
categorized by province/territory, then by record type: births,
marriage, census, deaths, and other.*

o British Columbia - Births
http://www.afhs.ab.ca/registry/regbc_birth.html

o British Columbia - Census
http://www.afhs.ab.ca/registry/regbc_census.html

- o British Columbia - Death
  http://www.afhs.ab.ca/registry/regbc_death.html
- o British Columbia - Marriage
  http://www.afhs.ab.ca/registry/regbc_marr.html
- o British Columbia - Other
  http://www.afhs.ab.ca/registry/regbc_other.html
- British Columbia Cemetery Finding Aid
  http://www.islandnet.com/bccfa/homepage.html
- British Columbia Vital Statistics Agency
  http://www.hlth.gov.bc.ca/vs/
  - o British Columbia Vital Statistics Agency - New Adoption Act
    http://www.hlth.gov.bc.ca/vs/adoption/
  - o British Columbia Birth Event
    http://www.hlth.gov.bc.ca/vs/births/
  - o British Columbia Marriage Event
    http://www.hlth.gov.bc.ca/vs/marriage/
  - o British Columbia Death Event
    http://www.hlth.gov.bc.ca/vs/death/
  - o British Columbia Wills Registry
    http://www.hlth.gov.bc.ca/vs/wills/
  - o British Columbia Genealogy
    http://www.hlth.gov.bc.ca/vs/genealogy/
- Campbell River Genealogy Club - 1901 Census - District #3 Vancouver; Sub-district B
  http://www.connected.bc.ca/~genealogy/
- National Archives of Canada - Dominion Land Grants
  http://www.archives.ca/exec/naweb.dll?fs&020111&e&top&0
  Database of grants issued in Manitoba, Saskatchewan, Alberta and the railway belt of British Columbia, c. 1870-1930.
- Nominal Census Homepage
  http://royal.okanagan.bc.ca/census/index.html
  Data for the southern interior of the Province of British Columbia, Canada
  - o Canada Census, 1881 - Yale District
    http://royal.okanagan.bc.ca/census/yale1881.html
  - o Canada Census, 1891 - Yale District
    http://royal.okanagan.bc.ca/census/yale1891.html
  - o The IRC Census, 1877
    http://royal.okanagan.bc.ca/census/ind1877.html
    Indian Reserve Commission.
  - o The OMI Census, 1877
    http://royal.okanagan.bc.ca/census/omi1877.html
    A nominal census of Native peoples taken by the Catholic missionary order, Oblates of Mary Immaculate (OMI)
- Parksville Qualicum Marriages, 1948-1994 ~ Mid-Vancouver Island, BC, Canada
  http://macn.bc.ca/~d69hist/marriage.html
- Vernon and District Family History Society - Cemetery Monument Inscriptions ~ B.C., Canada
  http://www.junction.net/vernhist/V4.html

Vital Events Indexes - BC Archives
http://www.bcarchives.gov.bc.ca/textual/governmt/vstats/v_events.htm
- o Birth Registration Index Search Gateway, 1872 to 1898
  http://www2.bcarchives.gov.bc.ca/cgi-bin/www2vsb
- o Marriage Registration Index Search Gateway, 1872 to 1923
  http://www2.bcarchives.gov.bc.ca/cgi-bin/www2vsm
- o Death Registration Index, 1872 to 1978
  http://www2.bcarchives.gov.bc.ca/cgi-bin/www2vsd

◆ Religion & Churches

- Christianity Online Church Locator - Churches in British Columbia
  http://www.christianity.net/churchlocator/location.php?country=Canada&state=British+Columbia
- Churches of the World - British Columbia
  http://www.churchsurf.com/churches/Canada/British_Columbia/index.htm
  From the ChurchSurf Christian Directory.

◆ Societies & Groups

- Abbotsford Genealogical Society
  http://www3.bc.sympatico.ca/abbotsfordgengroup/AGG.HTML
- Archives Association of British Columbia
  http://www.aabc.bc.ca/aabc/
- Brewery Creek Historical Society ~ Vancouver, B.C., Canada
  http://www.lesliefield.com/bchs/
- The British Columbia Folklore Society
  http://www.folklore.bc.ca/
- British Columbia Genealogical Society
  http://www.npsnet.com/bcgs/
- British Columbia Historical Federation
  http://www.selkirk.bc.ca/bchf/main1.htm
- British Columbia Military Heritage Society
  http://www.clearcf.uvic.ca/bcmhs/
- Campbell River Genealogy Club
  http://www.connected.bc.ca/~genealogy/
- District 69 Historical Society
  http://www.macn.bc.ca/~d69hist/
- Family Footprints Genealogical Society ~ Chetwynd, B.C., Canada
  http://pages.ivillage.com/misc/familyfootprints/index.html
- Germans from Russia Heritage Society, British Columbia Chapter
  http://feefhs.org/grhs/grhs-bc.html
- Heritage Society of British Columbia
  http://www.islandnet.com/~hsbc/

- Heritage Vancouver Society
  http://home.istar.ca/~glenchan/hvsintro.shtml

- IOOF Lodge Website Directory - British Columbia
  http://norm28.hsc.usc.edu/IOOF/International/British
  Columbia.html
  Independent Order of Odd Fellows and Rebekahs.

- The Japanese Canadian National Museum &
  Archives Society ~ Vancouver, British Columbia,
  Canada
  http://www.multinova.com/jcnmas/
  *Established to collect, preserve, study, exhibit, and interpret
  historical artifacts and archival material covering the history of
  Japanese Canadian Society from the 1870's through World War II to
  the present day.*

- Kamloops Family History Society
  http://www.ocis.net/kfhs/

- Kelowna & District Genealogical Society
  http://www.rootsweb.com/~bckdgs/

- Kootenay Lake Historical Society ~ Kaslo, British
  Columbia, Canada
  http://www.kin.bc.ca/Archives/Klhs/klhs.HTML

- Mennonite Historical Society of British Columbia
  http://www.rapidnet.bc.ca/~mennohis/

- Nanaimo Family History Society
  http://www.island.net/~tghayes/

- Nanaimo Historical Society
  http://www.sd68.nanaimo.bc.ca/nol/community/nhistsoc.htm

- The Old Cemeteries Society - Victoria Tombstone
  Tales of Ross Bay Cemetery
  http://www.oldcem.bc.ca/
  *Victoria's Ross Bay Cemetery opened in 1873 to serve the burial
  needs of the growing city of Victoria, British Columbia, Canada.
  Overlooking Ross Bay, it is 11 hectares in size (27.5 acres) and has
  almost 28,000 interments. Not just a burial ground, it serves as a
  park and restful get-away for many people. Come inside and take a
  virtual tour, meet some of the more famous residents, learn about
  issues that concern twentieth-century cemeteries or just enjoy some
  of the stories of this great cemetery.*

- The Slovak Heritage and Cultural Society of British
  Columbia
  http://www.iarelative.com/slovakbc.htm

- Society Hill: British Columbia Societies
  http://www.daddezio.com/society/hill.ca/SH-BC-NDX.html
  *A list of addresses for genealogical and historical societies in the
  province.*

- South Cariboo Genealogy Group
  http://www.welcome.to/southcariboo

- South Okanagan Genealogical Society ~ Penticton,
  British Columbia
  http://www.vip.net/sogs/

- The Vancouver Historical Society
  http://www.vcn.bc.ca/vhs/

- Vernon and District Family History Society
  http://www.junction.net/vernhist/

- Victoria Genealogical Society
  http://www.islandnet.com/~vgs/homepage.html

CANADA – MILITARY

http://www.cyndislist.com/milcan.htm

Category Index:

- ◆ General Resource Sites
- ◆ Historical Military Conflicts, Events or Wars
- ◆ Libraries, Archives & Museums
- ◆ Mailing Lists, Newsgroups & Chat
- ◆ Medals, Awards & Tributes

- ◆ Publications, Software & Supplies
- ◆ Records: Military, Pension, Burial
- ◆ Regimental Rosters, Histories and Home Pages
- ◆ Societies & Groups

◆ General Resource Sites

- Alex Chirnside's Military History Page
  http://www.geocities.com/Broadway/Alley/5443/

- Canadian Air Aces and Heroes – WWI, WWII and Korea
  http://www.accessweb.com/users/mconstab/

- Canadian Genealogy and History Links - Military
  http://www.islandnet.com/~jveinot/cghl/military.html

- Canadian Military Genealogical FAQ
  http://www.ott.igs.net/~donpark/canmilfaq.htm

- The Canadian Military Heritage Project
  http://www.rootsweb.com/~canmil/index.html

- Canadian POW/MIA Information Centre
  http://www.ipsystems.com/powmia/

- Documents in Military History
  http://www.hillsdale.edu/academics/history/Documents/War/
  From Hillsdale College's collection of primary sources for military history.

- Links to the Canadian Armed Forces
  http://www.pinette.net/chris/flags/canada/military/cflinks.html

- RCMP History
  http://www.rcmp-grc.gc.ca/html/history.htm

- The Unofficial Canadian Army Home Page
  http://army.cipherlogic.on.ca/

- Veterans Affairs / Anciens Combattants Canada
  http://www.vac-acc.gc.ca/

◆ Historical Military Conflicts, Events or Wars

- 18th & 19th Century Conflicts
  - o 1755 - The French and Indian War Home Page
    http://web.syr.edu/~laroux/
  - o The French and Indian War - Montcalm and Wolfe
    http://www.digitalhistory.org/wolfe.html

  - o The Hessians
    http://www.cgo.wave.ca/~hessian/
    The loyal German auxiliary soldiers, of King George III, who settled in Canada, after the American Revolution 1776-1783.
  - o Loyalists
    http://www.CyndisList.com/loyalist.htm
    See this category on Cyndi's List for related links

- The Boer War
  - o The Anglo Boer War Discussion Page
    http://www.icon.co.za/~dup42/talk.htm
    This mailing list is for the discussion of the Anglo Boer War and other military related topics pre-1900.
  - o The Book of Remembrance - South African War (1899-1902) and the Nile Expedition (1884-1885)
    http://collections.ic.gc.ca/books/safrica/samain.htm
  - o Fatal Casualties In Canadian Contingents of the Boer War
    http://www.islandnet.com/~duke/boercas.htm
  - o FOB-LIST - Friends of the Boers - E-mail List
    http://www.webcom.com/perspekt/eng/mlist/fob.html
    The primary topic of this mailing list is the centenary commemoration of the 2nd Anglo Boer War (1899-1902).
  - o League of Researchers of South African Historical Battlefields
    http://www.icon.co.za/~dup42/Welcome.html
  - o The South African War Virtual Library
    http://www.uq.net.au/~zzrwotto/

- World War I ~ The Great War
  - o The Book of Remembrance - First World War
    http://collections.ic.gc.ca/books/ww1/ww1main.htm
  - o Canadian Air Aces and Heroes - WWI, WWII and Korea
    http://www2.awinc.com/users/mconstab/
  - o Canadians in Korea - Valour Remembered
    http://www.vac-acc.gc.ca/general/sub.cfm?source=history/KoreaWar/valour
  - o The Canadian Great War Homepage
    http://www.rootsweb.com/~ww1can/
    Canada's Role in World War I, 1914 ~ 1918.

o Catholics of Nova Scotia in World War 1
http://members.tripod.com/~enlist_1/enlist.htm

o The Great War : A Guide to the Service Records of All the World's Fighting Men and Volunteers
http://www.amazon.com/exec/obidos/ISBN=0806315547/markcyndisgenealA/
A book by Christina K. Schaefer.

o Soldiers of the First World War — Canadian Expeditionary Force
http://www.archives.ca/exec/naweb.dll?fs&020106&e&top&0
An index to the personnel files of over 600,000 soldiers that enlisted during the First World War. Copies of over 50,000 pages of Attestation papers have been scanned and are available online here.

o The World War I Document Archive
http://www.lib.byu.edu/~rdh/wwi/
Assembled by volunteers of the World War I Military History List (WWI-L).

o The Western Front Association - Remembering 1914-1918
http://www.westernfront.co.uk/

o World War I, Links to Other Resources
http://raven.cc.ukans.edu/~kansite/ww_one/links.html

o World War I - Trenches on the Web
http://www.worldwar1.com/

● World War II

o The Book of Remembrance - Second World War
http://collections.ic.gc.ca/books/ww2/ww2main.htm

o Canadian Air Aces and Heroes - WWI, WWII and Korea
http://www.accessweb.com/users/mconstab/

o World War II on the Web
http://www.geocities.com/Athens/Oracle/2691/welcome.htm

● The Korean War

o The Book of Remembrance - Korean War
http://collections.ic.gc.ca/books/korea/kamain.htm

o Canadian Air Aces and Heroes - WWI, WWII and Korea
http://www2.awinc.com/users/mconstab/

o Korean War Project
http://www.koreanwar.org/

o The Korean War Project Searchable Database
http://www.netpath.com/~korea/cgi-bin/kccf_search.cgi
Over 33,000 individuals listed as KIA/MIA

o The Korean War - Veterans Affairs Canada
http://www.vac-acc.gc.ca/general/sub.cfm?source=history/koreawar

● Vietnam

o Canadian Vietnam Casualties
http://www.ipsystems.com/powmia/names/names.html

o Military history: Vietnam War (1961-1975)
http://www.cfcsc.dnd.ca/links/milhist/viet.html

o The Vietnam Veterans' Memorial Wall
http://thewall-usa.com/
With a searchable database.

o The Wall on the Web
http://www.vietvet.org/thewall/thewallm.html
Over 58,000 names in this list

◆ Libraries, Archives & Museums

● Canadian War Museum
http://www.cmcc.muse.digital.ca/cwm/cwmeng/cwmeng.html

● Department of National Defence and the Canadian Forces - Directorate of History and Heritage
http://www.dnd.ca/hr/dhh/engraph/about_e.asp

● Museum of the Regiments
http://www.nucleus.com/~regiments/

● Pier 21
http://www.pier21.ns.ca/
Between 1928-1971, at Pier 21 on the Halifax waterfront, 1.5 million immigrants first set foot on Canadian soil. During World War II, 3,000 British evacuee children, 50,000 war brides and their 22,000 children, over 100,000 refugees and 368,000 Canadian troops bound for Europe passed through Pier 21.

● University of Calgary Library - Canadian Military History
http://www.ucalgary.ca/library/subjects/HIST/canmil.html
A bibliography of regimental histories in the University of Calgary Library.

◆ Mailing Lists, Newsgroups & Chat

● Genealogy Resources on the Internet - Wars/Military Mailing Lists
http://www.rootsweb.com/~jfuller/gen_mail_wars.html
Most of the mailing list links below point to this site, wonderfully maintained by John Fuller

● AMERICAN-REVOLUTION Mailing List
http://www.rootsweb.com/~jfuller/gen_mail_wars.html#AMERICAN-REVOLUTION
For the discussion of events during the American Revolution and genealogical matters related to the American Revolution. The French-Indian Wars and the War of 1812 are also suitable topics for discussion.

● FOB-LIST - Friends of the Boers - E-mail List
http://www.webcom.com/perspekt/eng/mlist/fob.html
The primary topic of this mailing list is the centenary commemoration of the 2nd Anglo Boer War (1899-1902).

● LOYALIST-IN-CANADA Mailing List
http://www.rootsweb.com/~jfuller/gen_mail_country-can.html#LOYALIST
For those with loyalist ancestors to help one another research their loyalist history and to post any facts on the subject that they desire. Loyalists are defined as those who left the United States for Canada after the American Revolution for a number of reasons.

● soc.history.war.us-revolution Newsgroup
news:soc.history.war.us-revolution

- soc.history.war.vietnam Newsgroup
  news:soc.history.war.vietnam

- soc.history.war.world-war-ii Newsgroup
  news:soc.history.war.world-war-ii

- WARof1812 Mailing List
  http://www.rootsweb.com/~jfuller/gen_mail_wars.html
  #WARof1812

- WW20-ROOTS-L Mailing List
  http://www.rootsweb.com/~jfuller/gen_mail_wars.html
  #WW20-ROOTS-L
  For the discussion of genealogy in all 20th century wars.

◆ Medals, Awards & Tributes

- Canadian Military Medals and Decorations
  http://www.vac-acc.gc.ca/general/sub.cfm?source=
  collections/cmdp/mainmenu

- Projet Canadien De Memorials De Guerre / Canadian
  War Memorials Project
  http://msnhomepages.talkcity.com/terminus/cdnwm/index.htm

- The Vietnam Veterans' Memorial Wall
  http://thewall-usa.com/
  With a searchable database.

- The Wall on the Web
  http://www.vietvet.org/thewall/thewallm.html
  Over 58,000 names in this list

◆ Publications, Software & Supplies

- Amazon.com Genealogy Bookstore - Canadian
  Military
  http://www.amazon.com/exec/obidos/external-search/
  ?keyword=canada+military&tag=markcyndisgenealA/

- Books of Remembrance
  http://collections.ic.gc.ca/books/
  *Contain the names of Canadians who fought in wars and died either
  during or after them.*

- Boyd Publishing Company - Misc. Military
  http://www.hom.net/~gac/miscmil.htm

- Global Genealogy - Canadian Genealogy & History
  Books: The Loyalists
  http://www.globalgenealogy.com/loyalist.htm

- Hearthstone Bookshop - Military Records
  http://www.hearthstonebooks.com/cgi-bin/webc.cgi/
  st_main.html?catid=19&sid=15fkDVa

- Heritage Books - Loyalists
  http://www.heritagebooks.com/loyal.htm

- Heritage Books - Revolutionary War
  http://www.heritagebooks.com/revwar.htm

- Heritage Books - War of 1812
  http://www.heritagebooks.com/war1812.htm

- Military Publications International Directory
  http://www.islandnet.com/~duke/idmp.htm
  Book for sale from Canada.

- Willow Bend Bookstore
  http://www.willowbend.net/default.asp

◆ Records: Military, Pension, Burial

- Canadian Vietnam Casualties
  http://www.ipsystems.com/powmia/names.html

- Commonwealth War Graves Commission
  http://www.cwgc.org/
  *Details of 1.7 million members of UK and Commonwealth forces
  who died in the 1st and 2nd World Wars and other wars, and 60,000
  civilian casualties of WWII. Gives details of grave site, date of
  death, age, usually parents/widow's address.*

- Death Registration of Soldiers, 1941-1947
  http://gov.nb.ca/archives/ols/gr/rssd/141C6/index.htm
  Searchable database from the New Brunswick Provincial Archives.

- Fatal Casualties In Canadian Contingents of the Boer
  War
  http://www.islandnet.com/~duke/boercas.htm

- Soldiers of the First World War — Canadian
  Expeditionary Force
  http://www.archives.ca/exec/naweb.dll?fs&020106&e&top&0
  *An index to the personnel files of over 600,000 soldiers that enlisted
  during the First World War. Copies of over 50,000 pages of
  Attestation papers have been scanned and are available online here.*

◆ Regimental Rosters, Histories and Home Pages

- 2nd Michigan Volunteer Infantry - A Civil War Re-
  enacting and Information Page
  http://www.geocities.com/Pentagon/Quarters/8558/
  *Canadians involvement in the American Civil War. Why they fought,
  soldiers' bios, Canadian women in the ranks and much more info.*

- The Black Watch (Royal Highland Regiment) of
  Canada
  http://www.blackwatchcanada.com/

- The Cameron Highlanders of Ottawa (CHofO)
  http://infobase.ic.gc.ca/chofo/cameron.htm

- The Canadian Air Force / la Force Aérienne
  Canadienne
  http://www.achq.dnd.ca/

- Captain Samuel Hayden's Company of the King's
  Rangers
  http://users.erols.com/candidus/kings.htm

- King's Rangers
  http://www.cam.org/~dmonk/

- The Lincoln and Welland Regiment
  http://www.iaw.on.ca:80/~awoolley/lincweld.html
  A reserve infantry battalion of the Canadian Forces.

- PPCLI - The Princess Patricias Canadian Light
  Infantry
  http://www.ppcli.com/

- The Queen's York Rangers (1st American Regiment)
  http://www.connection.com/~qyrang/
  An armoured reconnaissance regiment of the Canadian Forces Militia.

- The Rifleman Online - The Queen's Own Rifles of Canada
  http://www.qor.com/

- The Royal Newfoundland Regiment
  http://www3.nf.sympatico.ca/dmarche/

- The (Unofficial) Canadian Army Home Page
  http://www.cyberus.ca/~army/army/

◆ Societies & Groups

- 48th Highlanders of Canada, Old Comrades Association
  http://www.members.home.net/kierstead95/

- British Columbia Military Heritage Society
  http://www.clearcf.uvic.ca/bcmhs/

- Canadian Peacekeeping Veterans Association
  http://www.islandnet.com/~duke/cpva.htm

- General Society of the War of 1812
  http://LanClio.org/1812.htm

- The Royal Canadian Regiment Association
  http://www.execulink.com/~thercran/

- The Western Front Association - Remembering 1914-1918
  http://ourworld.compuserve.com/homepages/cf_baker/

- The Jewish Genealogical Exploration Guide for Manitoba and Saskatchewan (J-GEMS)
  http://www.concentric.net/~Lkessler/jgems.shtml

- Tribes and Bands of Manitoba
  http://www.hanksville.org/sand/contacts/tribal/Man.html

◆ Professional Researchers, Volunteers & Other Research Services

- Gen-Find Research Associates
  http://www.gen-find.com/
  Specialists in Genealogy Research for Ontario & Western Canada, Scotland, Ireland. Also the rest of Canada and Forensic & Probate/Heir Research and 20th Century Research.

◆ Publications, Software & Supplies

- Amazon.com Genealogy Bookstore - Manitoba
  http://www.amazon.com/exec/obidos/external-search/?keyword=manitoba+genealogy&tag=markcyndisgenealA/

- Global Genealogical Supply - Western Canada Genealogical & Local History Books
  http://www.globalgenealogy.com/cdawest.htm

- Interlink Bookshop Genealogical Services ~ Victoria, B.C., Canada
  http://www.interlinkbookshop.com/

- Quintin Publications - Manitoba
  http://www.quintinpublications.com/mb.html

◆ Queries, Message Boards & Surname Lists

- RootsWeb Surname List - RSL Manitoba
  http://rsl.rootsweb.com/cgi-bin/rslsql.cgi
  The RSL and this form concept & design are courtesy of Karen Isaacson

◆ Records: Census, Cemeteries, Land, Obituaries, Personal, Taxes and Vital (Born, Married, Died & Buried)

- Alberta Family Histories Society (AFHS) Genealogical Projects Registry
  http://www.afhs.ab.ca/registry/index.html
  A central registry, which provides a bibliography of genealogical projects, both online and offline, in Canada. The registry is categorized by province/territory, then by record type: births, marriage, census, deaths, and other.
  - Manitoba - Births
    http://www.afhs.ab.ca/registry/regmb_birth.html
  - Manitoba - Census
    http://www.afhs.ab.ca/registry/regmb_census.html
  - Manitoba - Deaths
    http://www.afhs.ab.ca/registry/regmb_death.html
  - Manitoba - Marriage
    http://www.afhs.ab.ca/registry/regmb_marr.html

  - Manitoba - Other
    http://www.afhs.ab.ca/registry/regmb_other.html

- Composite Index of Early Manitoba Mennonite Church Registers
  http://www.mmhs.org/canada/super/super.htm
  Bergthaler (Russia) 1843, Chortitzer (Manitoba) 1878, Chortitzer (Manitoba) 1887, Chortitzer (Manitoba) 1907.

- Manitoba Homestead Records
  http://www.geocities.com/Yosemite/7431/homestead.htm
  Details on how to order these records.

- National Archives of Canada - Dominion Land Grants
  http://www.archives.ca/exec/naweb.dll?fs&020111&e&top&0
  Database of grants issued in Manitoba, Saskatchewan, Alberta and the railway belt of British Columbia, c. 1870-1930.

◆ Religion & Churches

- Centre for Mennonite Brethren Studies ~ Winnipeg, Manitoba
  http://www.mbconf.ca/mbstudies/

- Christianity Online Church Locator - Churches in Manitoba
  http://www.christianity.net/churchlocator/location.php?country=Canada&state=Manitoba

◆ Societies & Groups

- Association for Manitoba Archives
  http://www.pangea.ca/~ama/index.html

- East European Genealogical Society, Inc. (EEGS)
  http://feefhs.org/ca/frg-eegs.html
  Formerly known as the East European Branch of the Manitoba Genealogical Society, Canada.

- The Genealogical Institute of the Jewish Historical Society of Western Canada
  http://www.concentric.net/~lkessler/geninst.shtml

- IOOF Lodge Website Directory - Manitoba
  http://norm28.hsc.usc.edu/IOOF/International/Manitoba.html
  Independent Order of Odd Fellows and Rebekahs.

- Manitoba Genealogical Society
  http://www.mbnet.mb.ca/~mgs/

- Manitoba Living History Society
  http://www.mts.net/~zorniak/
  Re-enacting the Life and Times of the Red River Settlement.

- Manitoba Mennonite Historical Society
  http://www.mmhs.org/

- La Société Historique de Saint-Boniface
  http://www.escape.ca/~shsb/englishindex.htm

- Society Hill: Manitoba Societies
  http://www.daddezio.com/society/hill.ca/SH-MB-NDX.html
  A list of addresses for genealogical and historical societies in the province.

CANADA – NEW BRUNSWICK

http://www.cyndislist.com/newbruns.htm

Category Index:

- ◆ Canada GenWeb Project
- ◆ General Resource Sites
- ◆ Government & Cities
- ◆ History & Culture
- ◆ Libraries, Archives & Museums
- ◆ Mailing Lists, Newsgroups & Chat
- ◆ Maps, Gazetteers & Geographical Information
- ◆ Military
- ◆ Newspapers

- ◆ People & Families
- ◆ Professional Researchers, Volunteers & Other Research Services
- ◆ Publications, Software & Supplies
- ◆ Queries, Message Boards & Surname Lists
- ◆ Records: Census, Cemeteries, Land, Obituaries, Personal, Taxes and Vital
- ◆ Religion & Churches
- ◆ Societies & Groups

◆ Canada GenWeb Project

- NB Gen Links - Researching NB... start here!
  http://www.genweb.net/NBGenLinks
  Online directory dedicated to New Brunswick genealogy.

- New Brunswick / Nouveau-Brunswick GenWeb
  http://www.rootsweb.com/~cannb/

◆ General Resource Sites

- Canadian Genealogy and History Links - New Brunswick
  http://www.islandnet.com/~jveinot/cghl/new-brunswick.html

- Free Queries for New Brunswick, Canada
  mailto:devlin7@attglobal.net
  Rooters searching in Gloucester, Westmorland, Albert, Kings, Kent and Northumberland counties of New Brunswick, Canada can post a free query to Missing Links, a weekly genealogy newspaper column written and managed by Sandra Devlin. Queries should be to a maximum of 35 words PLUS forwarding address. Don't forget your snail mail (mandatory), and optional fax or voice mail, e-mail addresses. Send queries to: devlin7@attglobal.net.

- Genealogy in Queens County, New Brunswick
  http://home.earthlink.net/~jkthompson/genealogy/qc_gene.htm

- Genealogy Resources on the Internet: New Brunswick
  http://www-personal.umich.edu/~cgaunt/canada.html#NB

- Université de Moncton - Centre d'études acadiennes
  http://www.umoncton.ca/etudeacadiennes/centre/cea.html

◆ Government & Cities

- Province of New Brunswick / Province du Nouveau-Brunswick
  http://www.gov.nb.ca/

- Yahoo! Canada....New Brunswick: Cities
  http://ca.yahoo.com/regional/countries/canada/provinces_and_territories/new_brunswick/cities/

◆ History & Culture

- History of the Miramichi
  http://www.mibc.nb.ca/history/default.htm

- Researching Saint John's Building Histories ~ New Brunswick, Canada
  http://www.saintjohn.nbcc.nb.ca/~Heritage/classics/Research.htm
  Information for a variety of buildings in Saint John. The level of documentation differs for all properties. In some cases it may be nothing more than a list of previous property owners and building residents. In others, it could include information on the building designer and/or builder. It might include architectural drawings, or photographs. It is rare to research a property in Saint John where one would find architectural drawings, information on the builder and construction details, historic photographs and information on the property owners.

◆ Libraries, Archives & Museums

- Canadian Archival Resources on the Internet - New Brunswick
  http://www.usask.ca/archives/car/nbmenu.html

- The Canadian Library Index - New Brunswick
  http://www.lights.com/canlib/canlibnb.html

- CCA Directory of Archives for New Brunswick
  http://www.cdncouncilarchives.ca/cca_dir/newbruns.html

- Family History Library Catalog
  http://www.familysearch.org/Search/searchcatalog.asp
  From the FamilySearch web site, an online catalog to the holdings of the LDS Church in Salt Lake City, Utah. Also search for other localities by place name.
  http://www.familysearch.org/fhlc/supermainframeset.asp?display=localitysearch&columns=*,180,0

o Canada
http://www.familysearch.org/fhlc/supermainframeset.asp?display=localitydetails&subject=299&subject_disp=Canada&columns=*,180,0

- New Brunswick
http://www.familysearch.org/fhlc/supermainframeset.asp?display=localitydetails&subject=307&subject_disp=New_Brunswick&columns=*,180,0

- Family History SourceGuide - Family History Centers - Canada
http://www.familysearch.org/sg/Canada_FHC.html

- FamilySearch - Family History Centers in New Brunswick
http://www.familysearch.org/Browse/Places/FHC_RESULTS.ASP?FHCCountry=&FHCStateProv=New+Brunswick&FHCCounty=&FHCCity=&Submit=Search
A list of local LDS Family History Centers along with addresses and hours of operation.

- HYTELNET Library Catalogs: Canada: New Brunswick
http://www.lights.com/hytelnet/ca0/NB.html
Before you use any of the Telnet links, make note of the user name, password and any other logon information.

- The National Archives of Canada / Archives Nationales du Canada
http://www.archives.ca/

o Genealogy Research
http://www.archives.ca/exec/naweb.dll?fs&020202&e&top&0

- National Library of Canada / Bibliothèque nationale du Canada
http://www.nlc-bnc.ca/

o Genealogy and Family History at the National Library of Canada
http://www.nlc-bnc.ca/services/genealogy/gnlogy-e.htm

o National Library Catalogue
http://www.nlc-bnc.ca/amicus/ecatalog.htm

- Planter Studies Centre
http://ace.acadiau.ca/history/PLSTCNTR.HTM

- Provincial Archives of New Brunswick
http://gov.nb.ca/archives/

o Climbing Your Family Tree
http://gov.nb.ca/archives/e/tree/index.htm

o County Guides for the Province of New Brunswick
http://gov.nb.ca/archives/e/county/index.htm
The guides that were previously found linked from this page are now available for download as Word documents via this link.

o On-Line Database Search
http://gov.nb.ca/archives/ols/ols.htm
Includes searchable databases of both public and private records.

- University of New Brunswick Libraries
http://www.lib.unb.ca/

o Archives and Special Collections
http://degaulle.hil.unb.ca/library/archives/

o Genealogical Resources, Harriet Irving Library
http://degaulle.hil.unb.ca/library/subject_guides/Genealogy.html

o Loyalist Collection - Harriet Irving Library
http://www.lib.unb.ca/Collections/Loyalist/

o Reference Department
http://www.lib.unb.ca/Research/Department/

- United Church of Canada Archives Network: Maritime Conference Archives
http://www.uccan.org/archives/maritime.htm
A summary of their holdings and contact information.

◆ Mailing Lists, Newsgroups & Chat

- CANADIAN ROOTS Mailing List
http://www.rootsweb.com/~jfuller/gen_mail_country-can.html#CANADIAN-ROOTS

- new-brunswick Mailing List
http://www.rootsweb.com/~jfuller/gen_mail_country-can.html#NEW-BRUNSWICK-CANADA

- NewBrunswick Mailing List
http://www.rootsweb.com/~jfuller/gen_mail_country-can.html#NewBrunswick

- SURNAMES-CANADA Mailing List
http://www.rootsweb.com/~jfuller/gen_mail_country-can.html#SURNAMES-CANADA
Gatewayed with the soc.genealogy.surnames.canada newsgroup
news:soc.genealogy.surnames.canada
For surname queries related to Canada.

◆ Maps, Gazetteers & Geographical Information

- Canadian Geographical Names / Les noms géographiques du Canada
http://GeoNames.NRCan.gc.ca/

o Canadian Geographical Names - Publications
http://GeoNames.NRCan.gc.ca/english/publications.html
List of available publications on geographical names including policy documents and manuals, gazetteers, glossaries, newsletters and brochures.

o Origins of Canada's Geographical Names
http://GeoNames.NRCan.gc.ca/english/schoolnet/origin.html

o Querying Canadian Geographical Names:

- Query by Geographical Name
http://Geonames.NRCan.gc.ca/english/cgndb.html

Current Names Selected by Coordinates
http://Geonames.NRCan.gc.ca/english/cgndb_coord.html
Search this database of over 500,000 geographical names by name, feature type, region and by province

- Excite Maps: New Brunswick
  http://maps.excite.com/view/?mapurl=/countries/canada/
  new_brunswick

◆ Military

- 1st Battalion, The Royal New Brunswick Regiment
  (Carleton and York)
  http://www.brunswickmicro.nb.ca/242/rnbr.htm

- The Aroostook War (1839)
  http://homepages.rootsweb.com/~godwin/reference/
  aroostook.html
  *Bloodless border conflict between Maine and New Brunswick.
  10,000 Maine militiamen marched to the "war zone," but no shots
  were fired.*

- Canada - Military
  http://www.CyndisList.com/milcan.htm
  See this category on Cyndi's List for related links.

- New Brunswick's War Memorials
  http://www.stemnet.nf.ca/monuments/nb.htm
  *A project to preserve information about War Memorials throughout
  Canada on the World Wide Web. The descriptions of these
  individual cenotaphs often includes names and other information on
  the dead which can be of interest to the genealogist.*

◆ Newspapers

- AJR NewsLink - New Brunswick Newspapers
  http://ajr.newslink.org/nonusnnew.html

- E&P Media Links - Newspaper Sites in New
  Brunswick
  http://emedia1.mediainfo.com/emedia/results.htm?region=
  canada&abbreviation=newbrunswisk++++++++++++++++
  +++++++++++++++++&category=newspaper

- NewsDirectory.com: Newspapers: North America:
  Canada: New Brunswick
  http://www.newsdirectory.com/news/press/na/ca/nb/

- Saint John Times Globe
  http://www.timesglobe.com/main.htm
  Contact information and history regarding this newspaper.

- Telegraph Journal Online
  http://www.telegraphjournal.com/main.htm

◆ People & Families

- The McKINNEYs of Summer Hill And Their
  Neighbors
  http://personal.nbnet.nb.ca/davmc/frames.htm
  *Dedicated to James Alexander McKinney and his wife, Mary Ann
  (Murphy) McKinney who immigrated from County Tyrone, Northern
  Ireland in 1825 and their neighbors, pioneers, who cleared the
  forest land and established the communities of Summer Hill, Dunns
  Corner and Headline.*

- SWEET Family of New Brunswick, Canada
  http://personal.nbnet.nb.ca/bobsweet/home.htm
  *Bannister, Daly, Downie, Driden, Harkan, Hopper, Lachye,
  Leeman, McLaughlin, McLeod, Power, White, Melanson.*

- Tribes and Bands of New Brunswick
  http://www.hanksville.org/sand/contacts/tribal/NB.html

- The VIENNEAU Genealogy
  http://www3.nbnet.nb.ca/davienn/Testpage2ang.htm
  *Vienneau, Cormier, Thériault, Richard, Huard, Lagacé, Couture,
  Pitre.*

◆ Professional Researchers, Volunteers & Other Research Services

- LIFELINES Genealogical Research
  http://www.webspawner.com/users/DonDixonGRSC/
  *Don Dixon, GRS(C), LIFELINES Genealogical Research/
  Genealogical and family history research for New Brunswick,
  Canada.*

◆ Publications, Software & Supplies

- Amazon.com Genealogy Bookstore - New
  Brunswick
  http://www.amazon.com/exec/obidos/external-search/
  ?keyword=new+brunswick+genealogy&tag=mark
  cyndisgenealA/

- AudioTapes.com - Genealogical Lectures on Cassette
  Tapes - New Brunswick
  http://www.audiotapes.com/search2.asp?Search=new+
  brunswick

- Books We Own - New Brunswick
  http://www.rootsweb.com/~bwo/can_nb.html
  *Find a book from which you would like a lookup and click on the
  submitter's code at the end of the entry. Once you find the contact
  information for the submitter, write them a polite request for a
  lookup.*

- Global Genealogical Supply - Atlantic Provinces
  Genealogical & Local History Books
  http://www.globalgenealogy.com/cdaatlan.htm

- Nova Scotia / New Brunswick Bookstores - Used &
  Rare
  http://www.rootsweb.com/~canns/lunenburg/bookstores.htm

- Quintin Publications - New Brunswick
  http://www.quintinpublications.com/nb.html

- W.K.R.P. (Washington/Charlotte Kounty Records
  Preservation) Newsletter
  mailto:shwkrp@aol.com
  *A quarterly newsletter concerning research being done in
  Washington Co., Maine and Charlotte County, New Brunswick. For
  details e-mail Sharon at: shwkrp@aol.com.*

◆ Queries, Message Boards & Surname Lists

- New Brunswick Queries ~ Canada
  http://cgi.rootsweb.com/~genbbs/genbbs.cgi/Canada/
  NewBrunswick/General

- RootsWeb Surname List - RSL New Brunswick
  http://rsl.rootsweb.com/cgi-bin/rslsql.cgi
  The RSL and this form concept & design are courtesy of Karen Isaacson

◆ Records: Census, Cemeteries, Land, Obituaries, Personal, Taxes and Vital ((Born, Married, Died & Buried)

- Alberta Family Histories Society (AFHS) Genealogical Projects Registry
  http://www.afhs.ab.ca/registry/index.html
  A central registry, which provides a bibliography of genealogical projects, both online and offline, in Canada. The registry is categorized by province/territory, then by record type: births, marriage, census, deaths, and other.

  o New Brunswick - Births
    http://www.afhs.ab.ca/registry/regnb_birth.html

  o New Brunswick - Census
    http://www.afhs.ab.ca/registry/regnb_census.html

  o New Brunswick - Deaths
    http://www.afhs.ab.ca/registry/regnb_death.html

  o New Brunswick - Marriage
    http://www.afhs.ab.ca/registry/regnb_marr.html

  o New Brunswick - Other
    http://www.afhs.ab.ca/registry/regnb_other.html

- On-Line Database Search
  http://gov.nb.ca/archives/ols/ols.htm
  From the Provincial Archives.

  o County Birth Registers Index 1801 - 1899
    http://gov.nb.ca/archives/ols/gr/rssd/141A2-2/index.htm

  o Death Certificates: 1920 - 1949
    http://gov.nb.ca/archives/ols/gr/rssd/141C5/index.htm

  o Death Registration of Soldiers, 1941-1947
    http://gov.nb.ca/archives/ols/gr/rssd/141C6/index.htm

  o Index to New Brunswick Marriages 1887 - 1919
    http://gov.nb.ca/archives/ols/gr/rssd/141B7/index.htm

  o Irish Famine Migration to New Brunswick, 1845 – 1852
    http://gov.nb.ca/archives/ols/pr/if/index.htm

  o Late Registration of Births: Documentation Index 1801 - 1904
    http://gov.nb.ca/archives/ols/gr/rssd/141A1b/index.htm

  o Saint John Burial Permits, 1889 - 1919
    http://gov.nb.ca/archives/ols/gr/rssd/315A/index.htm

- PANB/UNB Cadastral Database - Searching the Grantbook Database
  http://degaulle.hil.unb.ca/library/data/panb/panbweb.html
  Records of land settlement in New Brunswick,1765-1800.

◆ Religion & Churches

- Christianity Online Church Locator - Churches in New Brunswick
  http://www.christianity.net/churchlocator/location.php?country=Canada&state=New+Brunswick

◆ Societies & Groups

- Genealogical Society of New Brunswick, Saint John Branch
  http://www.sjfn.nb.ca/community_hall/G/gene1900.html

- IOOF Lodge Website Directory - Atlantic Provinces
  http://norm28.hsc.usc.edu/IOOF/International/Atlantic Provinces.html
  Independent Order of Odd Fellows and Rebekahs.

- New Brunswick Genealogical Society
  http://www.bitheads.com/nbgs/

- Société Des Acadiens Et Acadiennes Du Nouveau-Brunswick
  http://www.rbmulti.nb.ca/saanb/saanb.htm

- Society Hill: New Brunswick Societies
  http://www.daddezio.com/society/hill.ca/SH-NB-NDX.html
  A list of addresses for genealogical and historical societies in the province.

CANADA – NEWFOUNDLAND & LABRADOR

http://www.cyndislist.com/newf-lab.htm

Category Index:

- ◆ Canada GenWeb Project
- ◆ General Resource Sites
- ◆ Government & Cities
- ◆ History & Culture
- ◆ Libraries, Archives & Museums
- ◆ Locality Specific
- ◆ Mailing Lists, Newsgroups & Chat
- ◆ Maps, Gazetteers & Geographical Information
- ◆ Military
- ◆ Newspapers

- ◆ People & Families
- ◆ Professional Researchers, Volunteers & Other Research Services
- ◆ Publications, Software & Supplies
- ◆ Queries, Message Boards & Surname Lists
- ◆ Records: Census, Cemeteries, Land, Obituaries, Personal, Taxes and Vital
- ◆ Religion & Churches
- ◆ Societies & Groups

◆ Canada GenWeb Project

- Newfoundland & Labrador GenWeb Project
  http://www.huronweb.com/genweb/nf.htm

◆ General Resource Sites

- Al Beagan's "Genealogy Notes" of Newfoundland
  http://www.capecod.net/~abeagan/nfld.htm

- Canadian Genealogy and History Links - Newfoundland
  http://www.islandnet.com/~jveinot/cghl/newfoundland.html

- Genealogy Resources on the Internet: Newfoundland and Labrador
  http://www-personal.umich.edu/~cgaunt/canada.html#NFL

- Newfoundland's Grand Banks Genealogy Research Interests Forum
  http://www.chebucto.ns.ca/Heritage/NGB/
  Contains the 1921 census, 1871 thru 1904 business directory, mailing list, church and cemetery records, etc.

◆ Government & Cities

- Government of Newfoundland & Labrador
  http://www.gov.nf.ca/

- Yahoo! Canada....Newfoundland: Cities
  http://ca.yahoo.com/regional/countries/canada/provinces_and_territories/newfoundland/cities/

◆ History & Culture

- The Colony of Avalon ~ Ferryland
  http://www.mediatouch.com/avalon/

- History of the Northern Cod Fishery
  http://www.stemnet.nf.ca./cod/home1.htm

- Newfoundland and Labrador Heritage/Patrimoine de Terre-Neuve et du Labrador
  http://www.heritage.nf.ca/

- Newfoundland, Its Origin, Its Rise and Fall, Also an Epitome of the Jersey Crisis in January 1886. An Episode of the History of Jersey
  http://Fox.nstn.ca:80/~nstn1528/sullivan.htm

- Prowse's History of Newfoundland
  http://www.cuff.com/prowse/

- Religion, Society and Culture In Newfoundland and Labrador
  http://www.ucs.mun.ca/~hrollman/

◆ Libraries, Archives & Museums

- Association of Newfoundland and Labrador Archives
  http://www.infonet.st-johns.nf.ca/providers/anla/anlahome.html

- Canadian Archival Resources on the Internet - Newfoundland and Labrador
  http://www.usask.ca/archives/car/nfmenu.html

- The Canadian Library Index - Newfoundland
  http://www.lights.com/canlib/canlibnf.html

- CCA Directory of Archives for Newfoundland and Labrador
  http://www.cdncouncilarchives.ca/cca_dir/nfld.html

- Family History Library Catalog
  http://www.familysearch.org/Search/searchcatalog.asp
  From the FamilySearch web site, an online catalog to the holdings
  of the LDS Church in Salt Lake City, Utah. Also search for other
  localities by place name.
  http://www.familysearch.org/fhlc/supermainframeset.asp?
  display=localitysearch&columns=*,180,0

  o Canada
    http://www.familysearch.org/fhlc/supermainframeset.asp?
    display=localitydetails&subject=299&subject_disp=Canada
    &columns=*,180,0

    • Newfoundland
      http://www.familysearch.org/fhlc/supermainframeset.asp
      ?display=localitydetails&subject=310&subject_disp=
      Newfoundland&columns=*,180,0

- Family History SourceGuide - Family History
  Centers - Canada
  http://www.familysearch.org/sg/Canada_FHC.html

- FamilySearch - Family History Centers in
  Newfoundland
  http://www.familysearch.org/Browse/Places/FHC_
  RESULTS.ASP?FHCCountry=&FHCStateProv=
  Newfoundland&FHCCounty=&FHCCity=&Submit=Search
  A list of local LDS Family History Centers along with addresses and
  hours of operation.

- HYTELNET Library Catalogs: Canada:
  Newfoundland
  http://www.lights.com/hytelnet/ca0/NF.html
  Before you use any of the Telnet links, make note of the user name,
  password and any other logon information.

- Maritime History Archive at Memorial University of
  Newfoundland
  http://www.mun.ca/mha/

- The National Archives of Canada / Archives
  Nationales du Canada
  http://www.archives.ca/

  o Genealogy Research
    http://www.archives.ca/exec/naweb.dll?fs&020202&e
    &top&0

- National Library of Canada / Bibliothèque nationale
  du Canada
  http://www.nlc-bnc.ca/

  o Genealogy and Family History at the National
    Library of Canada
    http://www.nlc-bnc.ca/services/genealogy/gnlogy-e.htm

  o National Library Catalogue
    http://www.nlc-bnc.ca/amicus/ecatalog.htm

- Newfoundland and Labrador Public Libraries
  http://www.publib.nf.ca/
  Guide to Genealogical Material in the Newfoundland Collection
  http://www.publib.nf.ca/genealogy/

- Provincial Archives of Newfoundland and Labrador
  http://www.gov.nf.ca/panl/

- United Church of Canada Archives Network:
  Newfoundland and Labrador Conference Archives
  http://www.uccan.org/archives/newfoundland.htm
  A summary of their holdings and contact information.

◆ Locality Specific

- Canada Newfoundland Genweb Independent Site
  http://www.rootsweb.com/~nfsjohnw/nfsjohnw.htm
  St. Mary's Bay - Southern Shore

◆ Mailing Lists, Newsgroups & Chat

- atlantic-province Mailing List
  http://www.rootsweb.com/~jfuller/gen_mail_country-
  can.html#ATLANTIC-PROVINCES-CANADA
  For the Atlantic Provinces of Canada - Nova Scotia, Newfoundland,
  Labrador, and Prince Edward Island.

- CANADIAN ROOTS Mailing List
  http://www.rootsweb.com/~jfuller/gen_mail_country-
  can.html#CANADIAN-ROOTS

- Newfoundland and Labrador Genealogical Society
  Mailing List
  http://www3.nf.sympatico.ca/nlgs/nlgsml.htm

- NFLD-LAB Mailing List
  http://www.rootsweb.com/~jfuller/gen_mail_country-
  can.html#NFLD-LAB

- NFLD-ROOTS Mailing List
  http://www.rootsweb.com/~jfuller/gen_mail_country-
  can.html#NFLD-ROOTS

- NLGS-L Mailing List
  http://www.rootsweb.com/~jfuller/gen_mail_country-
  can.html#NLGS-L
  Maintained by the Newfoundland and Labrador Genealogical
  Society (NLGS), for anyone with a genealogical interest in this
  Canadian province.

- SURNAMES-CANADA Mailing List
  http://www.rootsweb.com/~jfuller/gen_mail_country-
  can.html#SURNAMES-CANADA
  Gatewayed with the soc.genealogy.surnames.canada
  newsgroup
  news:soc.genealogy.surnames.canada
  For surname queries related to Canada.

◆ Maps, Gazetteers & Geographical Information

- Canadian Geographical Names / Les noms
  géographiques du Canada
  http://GeoNames.NRCan.gc.ca/

  o Canadian Geographical Names - Publications
    http://GeoNames.NRCan.gc.ca/english/publications.html
    List of available publications on geographical names including
    policy documents and manuals, gazetteers, glossaries,
    newsletters and brochures.

  o Origins of Canada's Geographical Names
    http://GeoNames.NRCan.gc.ca/english/schoolnet/
    origin.html

o Querying Canadian Geographical Names:

- Query by Geographical Name
http://Geonames.NRCan.gc.ca/english/cgndb.html

Current Names Selected by Coordinates
http://Geonames.NRCan.gc.ca/english/cgndb_
coord.html
Search this database of over 500,000 geographical names by name, feature type, region and by province

- Excite Maps: Newfoundland
http://maps.excite.com/view/?mapurl=/countries/canada/
newfoundland

◆ Military

- Canada - Military
http://www.CyndisList.com/milcan.htm
See this category on Cyndi's List for related links.

- Newfoundland's War Memorials
http://www.stemnet.nf.ca/monuments/nf.htm
A project to preserve information about War Memorials throughout Canada on the World Wide Web. The descriptions of these individual cenotaphs often includes names and other information on the dead which can be of interest to the genealogist.

- The Royal Newfoundland Regiment
http://www3.nf.sympatico.ca/dmarche/

◆ Newspapers

- AJR NewsLink - Newfoundland Newspapers
http://ajr.newslink.org/nonusnnewf.html

- E&P Media Links - Newspaper Sites in Newfoundland
http://emedia1.mediainfo.com/emedia/results.htm?region=
canada&abbreviation=newfoundland++++++++++++++++
+++++++++++++&category=newspaper

- Historical Directory of Newfoundland and Labrador Newspapers, 1806-1996
http://www.mun.ca/library/cat/newspapers/papers.htm

- NewsDirectory.com: Newspapers: North America: Canada: Newfoundland
http://www.newsdirectory.com/news/press/na/ca/nf/

◆ People & Families

- Tribes and Bands of Newfoundland
http://www.hanksville.org/sand/contacts/tribal/NF.html

◆ Professional Researchers, Volunteers & Other Research Services

- Gen-Find Research Associates
http://www.gen-find.com/
Specialists in Genealogy Research for Ontario & Western Canada, Scotland, Ireland. Also the rest of Canada and Forensic & Probate/Heir Research and 20th Century Research.

- Professional Genealogist Services for Newfoundland and Labrador - Barbara A. McGrath
http://genealogyPro.com/bmcgrath.html

◆ Publications, Software & Supplies

- Amazon.com Genealogy Bookstore - Newfoundland
http://www.amazon.com/exec/obidos/external-search/?
keyword=newfoundland+genealogy&tag=markcyndisgenealA/

- Quintin Publications - Newfoundland
http://www.quintinpublications.com/nf.html

- R.P.N. Publishing
http://www3.nf.sympatico.ca/gazebo.hill/rpn.html
THE SCHOOL CAR, by Randy P. Noseworthy, recalls the days when a traveling schoolhouse brought the Three R's to Newfoundland's remote railway settlements, 1936-42.

◆ Queries, Message Boards & Surname Lists

- RootsWeb Surname List - RSL Newfoundland
http://rsl.rootsweb.com/cgi-bin/rslsql.cgi
The RSL and this form concept & design are courtesy of Karen Isaacson

◆ Records: Census, Cemeteries, Land, Obituaries, Personal, Taxes and Vital (Born, Married, Died & Buried)

- Alberta Family Histories Society (AFHS) Genealogical Projects Registry
http://www.afhs.ab.ca/registry/index.html
A central registry, which provides a bibliography of genealogical projects, both online and offline, in Canada. The registry is categorized by province/territory, then by record type: births, marriage, census, deaths, and other.

o Newfoundland & Labrador - Births
http://www.afhs.ab.ca/registry/regnf_birth.html

o Newfoundland & Labrador - Census
http://www.afhs.ab.ca/registry/regnf_census.html

o Newfoundland & Labrador - Deaths
http://www.afhs.ab.ca/registry/regnf_death.html

o Newfoundland & Labrador - Marriage
http://www.afhs.ab.ca/registry/regnf_marr.html

o Newfoundland & Labrador - Other
http://www.afhs.ab.ca/registry/regnf_other.html

- David's Family History Stuff
http://www.dms.auburn.edu/~pikedav/family_history/
Including many census resources for Newfoundland.

- Newfoundland's Grand Banks Genealogy Research Interests Forum
http://www.chebucto.ns.ca/Heritage/NGB/

o Newfoundland and Labrador Cemeteries
http://www.chebucto.ns.ca/Heritage/NGB/Cemetery/
index.html

o Newfoundland's Grand Banks Census Material
http://www.chebucto.ns.ca/Heritage/NGB/census.htm
Parts of transcribed censuses from the 1600s to 1945.

- Project 21
http://www.chebucto.ns.ca/Heritage/NGB/C1921/
index.html
*Online transcription of the entire 1921 census for
Newfoundland excepting St. John's.*

o Newfoundland's Grand Banks Directory Material
http://www.chebucto.ns.ca/Heritage/NGB/directory.htm
Transcribed directories from the 1860s to the 1930s.

o Newfoundland and Labrador Parish Records
http://www.chebucto.ns.ca/Heritage/NGB/Parish/index.html

o Newfoundland Wills Index
http://www.chebucto.ns.ca/Heritage/NGB/Wills/index.html
*Indexed by surname for 13,457 entries from 1830 to 1962.
Includes microfilm numbers of their sources and information on
how to obtain the actual wills.*

- Scanned image of one index page
http://www.chebucto.ns.ca/Heritage/NGB/Wills/
willindex.htm

- Scanned image of a will from 1844
http://www.chebucto.ns.ca/Heritage/NGB/Wills/
v1f447.htm

- Newfoundland and Labrador Genealogical Society -
Parish Records and Cemetery Headstone Database
http://www3.nf.sympatico.ca/nlgs/nlgsprcd.htm

◆ Religion & Churches

- Religion, Society and Culture in Newfoundland and
Labrador
http://www.ucs.mun.ca/~hrollman/

◆ Societies & Groups

- IOOF Lodge Website Directory - Atlantic Provinces
http://norm28.hsc.usc.edu/IOOF/International/Atlantic
Provinces.html
Independent Order of Odd Fellows and Rebekahs.

- Newfoundland and Labrador Genealogical Society
Home Page
http://www3.nf.sympatico.ca/nlgs/

- Newfoundland Historical Society
http://www.infonet.st-johns.nf.ca/providers/nfldhist/nhs.html

- Society Hill: Newfoundland Societies
http://www.daddezio.com/society/hill.ca/SH-NF-NDX.html
*A list of addresses for genealogical and historical societies in the
province.*

CANADA – NORTHWEST TERRITORIES, NUNAVUT & THE YUKON

http://www.cyndislist.com/nw-yukon.htm

Category Index:

- ◆ Canada GenWeb Project
- ◆ General Resource Sites
- ◆ Government & Cities
- ◆ History & Culture
- ◆ Libraries, Archives & Museums
- ◆ Mailing Lists, Newsgroups & Chat
- ◆ Maps, Gazetteers & Geographical Information
- ◆ Military
- ◆ Newspapers

- ◆ People & Families
- ◆ Professional Researchers, Volunteers & Other Research Services
- ◆ Publications, Software & Supplies
- ◆ Queries, Message Boards & Surname Lists
- ◆ Records: Census, Cemeteries, Land, Obituaries, Personal, Taxes and Vital
- ◆ Religion & Churches
- ◆ Societies & Groups

◆ Canada GenWeb Project

- Northwest Territories GenWeb
  http://www.polarnet.ca/~taloyoak/genweb/nwt.htm

- Nunavut GenWeb
  http://www.polarnet.ca/~taloyoak/genweb/nunavut.htm
  target=

- Yukon GenWeb
  http://www.rootsweb.com/~canyk/index.html

◆ General Resource Sites

- Canadian Genealogy and History Links - Northwest Territories
  http://www.islandnet.com/~jveinot/cghl/northwest-territories.html

- Canadian Genealogy and History Links - Nunavut
  http://www.islandnet.com/~jveinot/cghl/nunavut.html

- Canadian Genealogy and History Links - Yukon
  http://www.islandnet.com/~jveinot/cghl/yukon.html

- Genealogy Resources on the Internet: Northwest Territories
  http://www-personal.umich.edu/~cgaunt/canada.html#NWT

- Genealogy Resources on the Internet: Yukon Territory
  http://www-personal.umich.edu/~cgaunt/canada.html#YT

- Northwest Territories, Canada, Birth, Death, and Marriage Records, 1925 to the Present
  http://www.familysearch.org/rg/guide/NT_BMDT3_Northwest_Territories_Vital_Records.ASP
  How to access and utilize these records from FamilySearch.org.

- Nunavut, Canada, Explanation of Records and Their History
  http://www.familysearch.org/rg/guide/NN_BMDT3_Explanation_of_Records_for_Nunavat.ASP
  From FamilySearch.org.

- Northwest Territories, Canada Events and Time Periods
  http://www.familysearch.org/rg/events/events1.asp?Locality=Northwest+Territories,+Canada&Id=314
  From FamilySearch.org.

- U.S. - Alaska
  http://www.CyndisList.com/ak.htm
  See this category on Cyndi's List for related links.

- Yukon & Alaska Genealogy Centre
  http://yukonalaska.com/pathfinder/gen/index.html

- Yukon, Canada Events and Time Periods
  http://www.familysearch.org/rg/events/events1.asp?Locality=Yukon,+Canada&Id=313
  From FamilySearch.org.

- Yukon Territory, Canada, Vital Records, 1896 to the Present
  http://www.familysearch.org/rg/guide/YT_BMDT3_Yukon_Territory_Vital_Records.ASP
  How to access and utilize these records from FamilySearch.org .

- Yukon White Pages
  http://whitepages.yknet.yk.ca/
  A listing of holders of Internet e-mail accounts in the Yukon.

◆ Government & Cities

- City of Yellowknife - Virtual City Hall
  http://city.yellowknife.nt.ca/index2.htm

- Government of the Northwest Territories
  http://www.gov.nt.ca/

- Government of Yukon
  http://www.gov.yk.ca/

- Indian and Northern Affairs Canada - Nunavut
  http://www.inac.gc.ca/nunavut/index1.html

- Yahoo! Canada....Northwest Territories: Cities
  http://ca.yahoo.com/regional/countries/canada/provinces_and
  _territories/northwest_territories/cities/

- Yahoo! Canada....Yukon: Cities
  http://ca.yahoo.com/regional/countries/canada/provinces_and
  _territories/yukon/cities/

◆ History & Culture

- Inuktitut
  http://www.isuma.ca/language.html
  The native language of Nunavut

- Northwest Territories, Canada, Historical
  Background
  http://www.familysearch.org/rg/guide/NT_T3_Historical
  Back.ASP
  From FamilySearch.org.

- Nunavut, Canada, Historical Background
  http://www.familysearch.org/rg/guide/NN_T3_Historical
  Back.ASP
  From FamilySearch.org.

- Prince of Wales Northern Heritage Centre,
  Yellowknife, Northwest Territories, Canada
  http://pwnhc.learnnet.nt.ca/

- Yukon and Alaska History - About.com Guide
  http://arcticculture.about.com/culture/arcticculture/library/
  blYAindex.htm?pid=2744&cob=home

- Yukon Territory, Canada, Historical Background
  http://www.familysearch.org/rg/guide/YT_T3_Historical
  Back.ASP
  From FamilySearch.org.

◆ Libraries, Archives & Museums

- Canadian Archival Resources on the Internet -
  Northwest Territories
  http://www.usask.ca/archives/car/ntmenu.html

- Canadian Archival Resources on the Internet - Yukon
  Territory
  http://www.usask.ca/archives/car/ykmenu.html

- The Canadian Library Index - Northwest Territories
  http://www.lights.com/canlib/canlibnw.html

- The Canadian Library Index - Yukon
  http://www.lights.com/canlib/canlibyk.html

- CCA Directory of Archives for Northwest
  Territories
  http://www.cdncouncilarchives.ca/cca_dir/nwt.html

- CCA Directory of Archives for Yukon
  http://www.cdncouncilarchives.ca/cca_dir/yukon.html

- City of Yellowknife: Public Library
  http://city.yellowknife.nt.ca/ResidentInfo/CityHall/Depts/
  Library/library.htm

- Family History Library Catalog
  http://www.familysearch.org/Search/searchcatalog.asp
  *From the FamilySearch web site, an online catalog to the holdings
  of the LDS Church in Salt Lake City, Utah. Also search for other
  localities by place name.*
  http://www.familysearch.org/fhlc/supermainframeset.asp?
  display=localitysearch&columns=*,180,0

  o Canada
    http://www.familysearch.org/fhlc/supermainframeset.asp?
    display=localitydetails&subject=299&subject_disp=Canada
    &columns=*,180,0

    • Northwest Territories
      http://www.familysearch.org/fhlc/supermainframeset.asp
      ?display=localitydetails&subject=314&subject_disp=
      Northwest_Territories&columns=*,180,0

    • Yukon
      http://www.familysearch.org/fhlc/supermainframeset.asp
      ?display=localitydetails&subject=313&subject_disp=
      Yukon&columns=*,180,0

- The Hudson's Bay Company Archives
  http://www.gov.mb.ca/chc/archives/hbca/index.html
  From the Provincial Archives of Manitoba, Canada.

- The National Archives of Canada / Archives
  Nationales du Canada
  http://www.archives.ca/

  o Genealogy Research
    http://www.archives.ca/exec/naweb.dll?fs&020202&e
    &top&0

- National Library of Canada / Bibliothèque nationale
  du Canada
  http://www.nlc-bnc.ca/

  o Genealogy and Family History at the National
    Library of Canada
    http://www.nlc-bnc.ca/services/genealogy/gnlogy-e.htm

  o National Library Catalogue
    http://www.nlc-bnc.ca/amicus/ecatalog.htm

- Northwest Territories Archives
  http://pwnhc.learnnet.nt.ca/programs/archive.htm

- NWT Archives Photographic Database
  http://pwnhc.learnnet.nt.ca/programs/search.htm
  *250,000 photographs preserved at the NWT Archives, Yellowknife,
  Northwest Territories.*

- United Church of Canada Archives Network: Alberta
  and Northwest Conference Archives
  http://www.uccan.org/archives/alberta.htm
  A summary of their holdings and contact information.

- Whitehorse Services: Museums
  http://www.yukonweb.com/community/whitehorse/services/museums.html
- Yukon Archives
  http://yukoncollege.yk.ca/archives/yukarch.html
- Yukon Public Libraries
  http://www.yukoncollege.yk.ca/archives/yuklibrs.html

◆ Mailing Lists, Newsgroups & Chat

- CANADIAN ROOTS Mailing List
  http://www.rootsweb.com/~jfuller/gen_mail_country-can.html#CANADIAN-ROOTS
- northern-canada Mailing List
  http://www.rootsweb.com/~jfuller/gen_mail_country-can.html#NORTHERN-CANADA
- SURNAMES-CANADA Mailing List
  http://www.rootsweb.com/~jfuller/gen_mail_country-can.html#SURNAMES-CANADA
  Gatewayed with the soc.genealogy.surnames.canada newsgroup
  news:soc.genealogy.surnames.canada

◆ Maps, Gazetteers & Geographical Information

- Canadian Geographical Names / Les noms géographiques du Canada
  http://GeoNames.NRCan.gc.ca/
  - Canadian Geographical Names - Publications
    http://GeoNames.NRCan.gc.ca/english/publications.html
    List of available publications on geographical names including policy documents and manuals, gazetteers, glossaries, newsletters and brochures.
  - Origins of Canada's Geographical Names
    http://GeoNames.NRCan.gc.ca/english/schoolnet/origin.html
  - Querying Canadian Geographical Names:
    - Query by Geographical Name
      http://Geonames.NRCan.gc.ca/english/cgndb.html

      Current Names Selected by Coordinates
      http://Geonames.NRCan.gc.ca/english/cgndb_coord.html
      Search this database of over 500,000 geographical names by name, feature type, region and by province
- Excite Maps: Yukon Territory
  http://maps.excite.com/view/?mapurl=/countries/canada/yukon_territory

◆ Military

- Canada - Military
  http://www.CyndisList.com/milcan.htm
  See this category on Cyndi's List for related links.
- Yukon's War Memorials
  http://www.stemnet.nf.ca/monuments/yk.htm

A project to preserve information about War Memorials throughout Canada on the World Wide Web. The descriptions of these individual cenotaphs often includes names and other information on the dead which can be of interest to the genealogist.

◆ Newspapers

- AJR NewsLink - Northwest Territories Newspapers
  http://ajr.newslink.org/nonusnnor.html
- AJR NewsLink - Yukon Newspapers
  http://ajr.newslink.org/nonusnyuk.html
- E&P Media Links - Newspaper Sites in Northwest Territories
  http://emedia1.mediainfo.com/emedia/results.htm?region=canada&abbreviation=northwestterritories++++++++++++++++++++++++++++++++&category=newspaper
- E&P Media Links - Newspaper Sites in Yukon Territory
  http://emedia1.mediainfo.com/emedia/results.htm?region=canada&abbreviation=yukonterritory++++++++++++++++++++++++++++++&category=newspaper
- NewsDirectory.com: Newspapers: North America: Canada: Northwest Territories
  http://www.newsdirectory.com/news/press/na/ca/nt/
- NewsDirectory.com: Newspapers: North America: Canada: Nunavut
  http://www.newsdirectory.com/news/press/na/ca/nu/
- NewsDirectory.com: Newspapers: North America: Canada: Yukon
  http://www.newsdirectory.com/news/press/na/ca/yt/
- Northern News Services Limited ~ Yellowknife
  http://www.nnsl.com/
  Serving communities in Canada's Arctic Northwest Territories and Nunavut.
- Nunatsiaq News
  http://www.nunanet.com/~nunat/
- Slave River Journal Interactive
  http://www.srji.com/homepage.ASP
- Whitehorse Star Daily
  http://www.whitehorsestar.com/
- Yukon News Online
  http://www.yukon-news.com/

◆ People & Families

- Tribes and Bands of Northwest Territories
  http://www.hanksville.org/sand/contacts/tribal/NWT.html
- Tribes and Bands of Yukon
  http://www.hanksville.org/sand/contacts/tribal/YK.html
- Yukon / Alaska Pioneer Biographies
  http://arcticculture.about.com/culture/arcticculture/library/ya/msub15y.htm?pid=2744&cob=home

◆ Professional Researchers, Volunteers & Other Research Services

● Gen-Find Research Associates
http://www.gen-find.com/
Specialists in Genealogy Research for Ontario & Western Canada, Scotland, Ireland. Also the rest of Canada and Forensic & Probate/Heir Research and 20th Century Research.

● Yukon Historic Research
http://www.yukonweb.com/business/yhr/

◆ Publications, Software & Supplies

● Amazon.com Genealogy Bookstore - Yukon
http://www.amazon.com/exec/obidos/external-search/
?keyword=yukon+genealogy&tag=markcyndisgenealA/

● Global Genealogical Supply - Western Canada Genealogical & Local History Books
http://www.globalgenealogy.com/cdawest.htm

● Quintin Publications - Yukon & Northwest Territories
http://www.quintinpublications.com/yk.html

◆ Queries, Message Boards & Surname Lists

● RootsWeb Surname List - RSL Northwest Territories
http://rsl.rootsweb.com/cgi-bin/rslsql.cgi
The RSL and this form concept & design are courtesy of Karen Isaacson

● RootsWeb Surname List - RSL Yukon Territory
http://rsl.rootsweb.com/cgi-bin/rslsql.cgi
The RSL and this form concept & design are courtesy of Karen Isaacson

◆ Records: Census, Cemeteries, Land, Obituaries, Personal, Taxes and Vital (Born, Married, Died & Buried)

● Alberta Family Histories Society (AFHS) Genealogical Projects Registry
http://www.afhs.ab.ca/registry/index.html
A central registry, which provides a bibliography of genealogical projects, both online and offline, in Canada. The registry is categorized by province/territory, then by record type: births, marriage, census, deaths, and other.

  o Northwest Territories - Births
  http://www.afhs.ab.ca/registry/regnt_birth.html

  o Northwest Territories - Census
  http://www.afhs.ab.ca/registry/regnt_census.html

  o Northwest Territories - Deaths
  http://www.afhs.ab.ca/registry/regnt_death.html

  o Northwest Territories - Marriage
  http://www.afhs.ab.ca/registry/regnt_marr.html

  o Northwest Territories - Other
  http://www.afhs.ab.ca/registry/regnt_other.html

  o Yukon - Births
  http://www.afhs.ab.ca/registry/regyk_birth.html

  o Yukon - Census
  http://www.afhs.ab.ca/registry/regyk_census.html

  o Yukon - Deaths
  http://www.afhs.ab.ca/registry/regyk_death.html

  o Yukon - Marriage
  http://www.afhs.ab.ca/registry/regyk_marr.html

  o Yukon - Other
  http://www.afhs.ab.ca/registry/regyk_other.html

● Family Chronicle - Alaska-Yukon Goldrush Participants
http://www.familychronicle.com/klond_d.htm

● Ghosts of the Klondike Gold Rush
http://Gold-Rush.org/
Check out the "Pan for Gold Database".

● Yukon Archival Union List
http://www.whitehorse.microage.ca/yca/sections/yaul/
yaul.html
Searchable database with descriptions of archival material held at publicly-accessible archival repositories in the Yukon Territory.

◆ Religion & Churches

● Christianity Online Church Locator - Churches in Northwest Territories
http://www.christianity.net/churchlocator/location.php?country
=Canada&state=Northwest+Territories

◆ Societies & Groups

● Dawson City Museum and Historical Society
http://users.yknet.yk.ca/dcpages/Museum.html
Has the largest historical collection in the Yukon Territory.

● The N.W.T. Genealogical Society
http://www.ssimicro.com/nonprofit/nwtgs/

● Society Hill: Northwest Territories Societies
http://www.daddezio.com/society/hill.ca/SH-NT-NDX.html
A list of addresses for genealogical and historical societies in the territories.

● Society Hill: Yukon Territory Societies
http://www.daddezio.com/society/hill.ca/SH-YT-NDX.html
A list of addresses for genealogical and historical societies in the territory.

● Yukon Council of Archives.
http://www.whitehorse.microage.ca/yca/

CANADA – NOVA SCOTIA
http://www.cyndislist.com/novascot.htm

Category Index:

- Canada GenWeb Project
- General Resource Sites
- Government & Cities
- History & Culture
- Libraries, Archives & Museums
- Locality Specific
- Mailing Lists, Newsgroups & Chat
- Maps, Gazetteers & Geographical Information
- Military
- Newspapers

- People & Families
- Professional Researchers, Volunteers & Other Research Services
- Publications, Software & Supplies
- Queries, Message Boards & Surname Lists
- Records: Census, Cemeteries, Land, Obituaries, Personal, Taxes and Vital
- Religion & Churches
- Societies & Groups

◆ Canada GenWeb Project

- Nova Scotia GenWeb Project
  http://www.rootsweb.com/~canns/index.html

◆ General Resource Sites

- Canadian Genealogy and History Links - Nova Scotia
  http://www.islandnet.com/~jveinot/cghl/nova-scotia.html

- Family Roots of Pictou and Antigonish Counties, Nova Scotia
  http://www.rootsweb.com/~pictou/index.htm
  Robertson, Oulton, Cunningham, Logan, Pushee, Williams.

- The Genealogical Institute of the Maritimes
  http://www.shelburne.nscc.ns.ca/nsgna/gim/index.html

- Genealogical Record of Colchester Co.
  http://www.shelburne.nscc.ns.ca/nsgna/miller/surnames.htm

- Genealogy Resources on the Internet: Nova Scotia
  http://www-personal.umich.edu/~cgaunt/canada.html#NS

- The Halifax Explosion
  http://www.halifaxinfo.com/B/B4.html

- The Nova Scotia Genealogy Resources Page
  http://www.chebucto.ns.ca/~ab443/genealog.html

◆ Government & Cities

- Government of Nova Scotia Canada
  http://www.gov.ns.ca/index.htm

- Yahoo! Canada....Nova Scotia: Cities
  http://ca.yahoo.com/regional/countries/canada/provinces_and territories/nova scotia/cities/

◆ History & Culture

- The Black Cultural Centre for Nova Scotia
  http://home.istar.ca/~bccns/index.shtml

- Cape Breton Pictorial Cookbook
  http://www.taisbean.com/CBcookbook/home.html

- The Early Acadian Period in Nova Scotia 1605 - 1755
  http://www.ednet.ns.ca/educ/museum/arch/acadia.htm
  From Archaeology in Nova Scotia.

- Highland Village -A Living History Museum & Cultural Centre
  http://www.highlandvillage.ns.ca/

- History of Coal Mining in Nova Scotia - The Louis Frost Notes 1685 to 1962
  http://eagle.uccb.ns.ca/mining/

- History of the Scots in New Scotland (Nova Scotia)
  http://www.chebucto.ns.ca/Humanities/FSCNS/Scots_NS/About_Clans/HtySctNS.html

- Nova Scotia's Electronic Attic
  http://www.alts.net/ns1625/index.html
  Specializing in on-line information about Nova Scotia.

- The Pier 21 Society
  http://www.pier21.ns.ca/
  On the Halifax waterfront, this is the site where over 1.5 million immigrants entered the country between 1928 and 1971.

- Titanic ~ The Unsinkable Ship and Halifax
  http://titanic.gov.ns.ca/
  A site from Halifax, Nova Scotia, Canada, including a list of those buried in cemeteries in Halifax.

◆ Libraries, Archives & Museums

- Acadia University - Vaughan Memorial Library ~ Wolfville
  http://www.acadiau.ca/vaughan/

- Archaeology in Nova Scotia - Nova Scotia Museum
  http://www.ednet.ns.ca/educ/museum/arch/index.htm

- Argyle Township Court House & Archives
  http://ycn.library.ns.ca/~ipatcha/
  Oldest standing courthouse in Canada. Archives for the Municipality of Argyle. Genealogical research center focusing on the families of Yarmouth County, Nova Scotia. This is a region consisting primarily of Acadian, New England Planter, and United Empire Loyalist families.

- Beaton Institute Archive, Cape Breton, Nova Scotia
  http://www.uccb.ns.ca/beaton/

- Canadian Archival Resources on the Internet - Nova Scotia
  http://www.usask.ca/archives/car/nsmenu.html

- The Canadian Library Index - Nova Scotia
  http://www.lights.com/canlib/canlibns.html

- CCA Directory of Archives for Nova Scotia
  http://www.cdncouncilarchives.ca/cca_dir/n_scotia.html

- Colchester Historical Museum And Archives ~ Truro
  http://www.genealogynet.com/Colchester/

- The Council of Nova Scotia Archives (CNSA)
  http://fox.nstn.ca/~cnsa/index.html

- Dartmouth N.S. Family History Centre
  http://nsgna.ednet.ns.ca/fhc/index.html

- Dartmouth Regional Library
  http://www.chebucto.ns.ca/Libraries/DartLibrary/drl.html

- Family History Library Catalog
  http://www.familysearch.org/Search/searchcatalog.asp
  From the FamilySearch web site, an online catalog to the holdings of the LDS Church in Salt Lake City, Utah. Also search for other localities by place name.
  http://www.familysearch.org/fhlc/supermainframeset.asp?display=localitysearch&columns=*,180,0

  o Canada
    http://www.familysearch.org/fhlc/supermainframeset.asp?display=localitydetails&subject=299&subject_disp=Canada&columns=*,180,0

    - Nova Scotia
      http://www.familysearch.org/fhlc/supermainframeset.asp?display=localitydetails&subject=308&subject_disp=Nova_Scotia&columns=*,180,0

- Family History SourceGuide - Family History Centers - Canada
  http://www.familysearch.org/sg/Canada_FHC.html

- FamilySearch - Family History Centers in Nova Scotia
  http://www.familysearch.org/Browse/Places/FHC_RESULTS.ASP?FHCCountry=&FHCStateProv=Nova+Scotia&FHCCounty=&FHCCity=&Submit=Search
  A list of local LDS Family History Centers along with addresses and hours of operation.

- HYTELNET Library Catalogs: Canada: Nova Scotia
  http://www.lights.com/hytelnet/ca0/NS.html
  Before you use any of the Telnet links, make note of the user name, password and any other logon information.

- The National Archives of Canada / Archives Nationales du Canada
  http://www.archives.ca/

  o Genealogy Research
    http://www.archives.ca/exec/naweb.dll?fs&020202&e&top&0

- National Library of Canada / Bibliothèque nationale du Canada
  http://www.nlc-bnc.ca/

  o Genealogy and Family History at the National Library of Canada
    http://www.nlc-bnc.ca/services/genealogy/gnlogy-e.htm

  o National Library Catalogue
    http://www.nlc-bnc.ca/amicus/ecatalog.htm

- Nova Scotia Library Homepages
  http://www.stmarys.ca/administration/library/apla/aplalib2.html

- Nova Scotia Provincial Library
  http://www.nshpl.library.ns.ca/

  o Nova Scotia Regional Libraries
    http://www.nshpl.library.ns.ca/regionals/

    - Annapolis Valley Regional Library
      http://www.nshpl.library.ns.ca/regionals/avr/

    - Cape Breton Regional Library
      http://www.nshpl.library.ns.ca/regionals/cbr/

    - Colchester-East Hants Regional Library
      http://www.nshpl.library.ns.ca/regionals/ceh/

    - Cumberland Regional Library
      http://www.nshpl.library.ns.ca/regionals/cur/

    - Eastern Counties Regional Library
      http://www.nshpl.library.ns.ca/regionals/ecr/

    - Halifax Regional Library
      http://www.chebucto.ns.ca/Libraries/HCRL/HalifaxLibraryHome.html

    - Pictou-Antigonish Regional Library
      http://www.nshpl.library.ns.ca/regionals/par/

    - South Shore Regional Library
      http://www.nshpl.library.ns.ca/regionals/ssr/
      Lunenburg and Queens counties.

    - Western Counties Regional Library
      http://www.nshpl.library.ns.ca/regionals/wcr/

o Online Catalogue on NcompasS
  http://ncompass.library.ns.ca/
  Instructions for using Telnet to access this catalog

- Pier 21
  http://www.pier21.ns.ca/
  Between 1928-1971, at Pier 21 on the Halifax waterfront, 1.5 million immigrants first set foot on Canadian soil. During World War II, 3,000 British evacuee children, 50,000 war brides and their 22,000 children, over 100,000 refugees and 368,000 Canadian troops bound for Europe passed through Pier 21.

  o Parks Canada Backgrounder - Pier 21 Halifax
    http://parkscanada.pch.gc.ca/library/background/51_e.htm

  o Parks Canada News Release - Pier 21 Recognized as a National Historic Site
    http://parkscanada.pch.gc.ca/library/newsreleases/english/nr38%5Fe.htm

  o Pier 21: The Gateway That Changed Canada
    http://www.amazon.com/exec/obidos/ISBN=0889994064/markcyndisgenealA/
    A book by J.P. Leblanc.

- Planter Studies Centre
  http://ace.acadiau.ca/history/PLSTCNTR.HTM

- Queens County Museum
  http://www.geocities.com/Paris/2669/
  Home of the Thomas H. Raddall Research Centre.

- United Church of Canada Archives Network: Maritime Conference Archives
  http://www.uccan.org/archives/maritime.htm
  A summary of their holdings and contact information.

- Yarmouth County Museum and Archives
  http://ycn.library.ns.ca/museum/yarcomus.htm

◆ Locality Specific

- Tancook Island Homepage
  http://freepages.history.rootsweb.com/~tancook/
  General and historical information for Tancook Island, NS including cemetery listings and GEDCOMs for Baker, Crooks, Cross, Hirtle, Heisler, Hutt, Stevens, Langille, Rodenhiser, Wilson.

◆ Mailing Lists, Newsgroups & Chat

- atlantic-province Mailing List
  http://www.rootsweb.com/~jfuller/gen_mail_country-can.html#ATLANTIC-PROVINCES-CANADA
  For the Atlantic Provinces of Canada - Nova Scotia, Newfoundland, Labrador, and Prince Edward Island.

- CANADIAN ROOTS Mailing List
  http://www.rootsweb.com/~jfuller/gen_mail_country-can.html#CANADIAN-ROOTS

- ILMADAME Mailing List
  http://www.rootsweb.com/~jfuller/gen_mail_country-can.html#ILMADAME

- LUNEN-LINKS Mailing List
  http://www.rootsweb.com/~jfuller/gen_mail_country-can.html#LUNEN-LINKS
  For Lunenberg County.

- NOVA-SCOTIA Mailing List
  http://www.rootsweb.com/~jfuller/gen_mail_country-can.html#NOVA-SCOTIA
  And the accompanying FAQ page
  http://www.rootsweb.com/~canns/nsfaq.html

- NSROOTS Mailing List
  http://www.rootsweb.com/~jfuller/gen_mail_country-can.html#NSROOTS
  A "moderated" mailing list, sponsored by the Nova Scotia Genealogy Network Association.

- Pictouroots Mailing List
  http://www.rootsweb.com/~jfuller/gen_mail_country-can.html#Pictouroots
  And the associated web page
  http://www.onelist.com/subscribe.cgi/pictouroots

- SURNAMES-CANADA Mailing List
  http://www.rootsweb.com/~jfuller/gen_mail_country-can.html#SURNAMES-CANADA
  Gatewayed with the soc.genealogy.surnames.canada newsgroup
  news:soc.genealogy.surnames.canada
  For surname queries related to Canada.

◆ Maps, Gazetteers & Geographical Information

- Canadian Geographical Names / Les noms géographiques du Canada
  http://GeoNames.NRCan.gc.ca/

  o Canadian Geographical Names - Publications
    http://GeoNames.NRCan.gc.ca/english/publications.html
    List of available publications on geographical names including policy documents and manuals, gazetteers, glossaries, newsletters and brochures.

  o Origins of Canada's Geographical Names
    http://GeoNames.NRCan.gc.ca/english/schoolnet/origin.html

  o Querying Canadian Geographical Names:

    - Query by Geographical Name
      http://Geonames.NRCan.gc.ca/english/cgndb.html

      Current Names Selected by Coordinates
      http://Geonames.NRCan.gc.ca/english/cgndb_coord.html
      Search this database of over 500,000 geographical names by name, feature type, region and by province

- Excite Maps: Nova Scotia
  http://maps.excite.com/view/?mapurl=/countries/canada/nova_scotia

- Nova Scotia Highway Map
  http://destination-ns.com/map/roadmap.htm

◆ Military

- Canada - Military
  http://www.CyndisList.com/milcan.htm
  See this category on Cyndi's List for related links.

- Catholics of Nova Scotia in World War 1
  http://members.tripod.com/~enlist_1/enlist.htm

- Muster Roll at Gulliver's Hole, St. Mary's Bay and
  Sissiboo ~ Digby, Nova Scotia, Canada
  http://www.rootsweb.com/~canwgw/ns/digby/perm2/
  muster1.htm

- Nova Scotia's War Memorials
  http://www.stemnet.nf.ca/monuments/ns.htm
  *A project to preserve information about War Memorials throughout
  Canada on the World Wide Web. The descriptions of these
  individual cenotaphs often includes names and other information on
  the dead which can be of interest to the genealogist.*

◆ Newspapers

- AJR NewsLink - Nova Scotia Newspapers
  http://ajr.newslink.org/nonusnnov.html

- The Daily News Worldwide ~ Halifax, Nova Scotia
  http://www.hfxnews.southam.ca/

- E&P Media Links - Newspaper Sites in Nova Scotia
  http://emedia1.mediainfo.com/emedia/results.htm?region=
  canada&abbreviation=novascotia+++++++++++++++++++
  ++++++++++&category=newspaper

- The Halifax Herald
  http://www.herald.ns.ca/

- NewsDirectory.com: Newspapers: North America:
  Canada: Nova Scotia
  http://www.newsdirectory.com/news/press/na/ca/ns/

- Nova Scotian Newspapers
  http://nsgna.ednet.ns.ca/nnewsp.html

◆ People & Families

- Acadian, Cajun & Creole
  http://www.CyndisList.com/acadian.htm
  See this category on Cyndi's List for related links.

- The Acadians of Nova Scotia
  http://www.grassroots.ns.ca/comgrp/acad.htm

- Bill NORIN's Web Page
  http://www.geocities.com/Heartland/Pointe/9632
  *A Maritime province site featuring McDONALD, GILLIS,
  McADAMS, MacISAAC and other Gaels on PEI and Cape Breton,
  Nova Scotia.*

- Bissett-Conrod Family
  http://www.mindspring.com/~giammo/Bissett/
  *Descendants of Jacques BISSETT & Anne Catherine METTHEY,
  who emigrated to Nova Scotia in 1752.*

- Christopher GORMAN's Genealogy Page
  http://www.lookup.com/Homepages/70616/home.html
  GORMAN, DALRYMPLE, HENNIGAR.

- The DALRYMPLEs of Nova Scotia
  http://home.mem.net/~dalrympl/

- The DUNN Family of Castle Bay and Dominion,
  Cape Breton Island
  http://www.geocities.com/~dunnfamily/

- Fishing? - It was "A WAY OF LIFE" and Lost At
  Sea
  http://www.geocities.com/Heartland/Prairie/7527/
  *Dedicated to Atlantic Canada fishermen and mariners lost at sea,
  their families and survivors. And to all those from other countries
  who were lost at sea.*

- Four Nova Scotia Families
  http://www.widomaker.com/~gwk/
  *Information about descendants of four families who settled in Nova
  Scotia in the mid 1700s - three Rice families who settled in the
  Annapolis Valley in 1760 and the Graham family who arrived at
  Halifax about 1749.*

- A Internet home for George Rose, and Atlantic
  Canada Genealogy
  http://www.chebucto.ns.ca/~ab936/Profile.html

- Lloyd MAC DONALD Genealogy Page
  http://members.tripod.com/~lemac2/index.html
  Roy, Henderson, Mac Donald, Urquhart, Mac Leod.

- Montbeliard Protestant Settlers to Nova Scotia
  Genealogy
  http://www.montbeliard.org/
  *A starting point for anyone researching the families that emigrated
  from the Principality of Montbeliard to Nova Scotia in 1752.*

- Randall's Genealogy Page
  http://www.interlog.com/~prandall/intro.html
  *Special focus on Bayfield, Antigonish County. Atwater,
  Cunningham, Hulbert, Irish, Kinney, Nichols, Randall, Strople,
  Wambach, Williams, etc.*

- Scots in New Scotland (Nova Scotia)
  http://www.chebucto.ns.ca/Heritage/FSCNS/ScotsHome.html

- Tom ROGERS Family History
  http://www.geocities.com/Heartland/Prairie/8062/
  genealogy.html
  Busby, Cook, Garron, Knowles, Lacey, Nickerson, Rogers, Wilson.

- Tribes and Bands of Nova Scotia
  http://www.hanksville.org/sand/contacts/tribal/NS.html

- Yorkshire 2000
  http://www.tap.nb.ca/tht/york2000.html
  *The Tantramar Heritage Trust is pleased to be the host for
  Yorkshire 2000, a gathering of the descendants of Yorkshire settlers
  who emigrated from northern England, going to Nova Scotia during
  the period 1772-1775.*

◆ Professional Researchers, Volunteers & Other Research Services

- Gen-Find Research Associates
  http://www.gen-find.com/
  *Specialists in Genealogy Research for Ontario & Western Canada,
  Scotland, Ireland. Also the rest of Canada and Forensic &
  Probate/Heir Research and 20th Century Research*

- Roots Cape Breton Genealogy & Family History Centre
  http://eagle.uccb.ns.ca/mining/iona/roots.html
  A computer-assisted research service.

◆ Publications, Software & Supplies

- Amazon.com Genealogy Bookstore - Nova Scotia
  http://www.amazon.com/exec/obidos/external-search/?
  keyword=nova+soctia+genealogy&tag=markcyndisgenealA/

- Antigonish Books of Genealogical and Historical Interest
  http://www.rootsweb.com/~pictou/biblio.htm

- AudioTapes.com - Genealogical Lectures on Cassette Tapes – Nova Scotia
  http://www.audiotapes.com/search2.asp?Search=Nova+Scotia

- Books We Own - Nova Scotia
  http://www.rootsweb.com/~bwo/can_ns.html
  Find a book from which you would like a lookup and click on the submitter's code at the end of the entry. Once you find the contact information for the submitter, write them a polite request for a lookup.

- Bridges Genealogy Books and Services
  http://pw2.netcom.com/~huskyfan/genealogy.html
  Pictou County, Nova Scotia Death Records.

- Global Genealogical Supply - Atlantic Provinces Genealogical & Local History Books
  http://www.globalgenealogy.com/cdaatlan.htm

- Louisa's World - A Genealogy in Context
  http://www3.ns.sympatico.ca/dmcclare/TITLE.HTM
  From the 1815 Diary of a Nova Scotia Farm Girl, Louisa Collins, of Colin Grove, Dartmouth.

- Lunenburg County / Nova Scotia Genealogy Book List
  http://www.rootsweb.com/~canns/lunenburg/booklist.htm

- Nova Scotia Book Dealers - Used & Rare
  http://nsgna.ednet.ns.ca/nbst.html

- Nova Scotia / New Brunswick Bookstores - Used & Rare
  http://www.rootsweb.com/~canns/lunenburg/bookstores.htm

- Pictou Books of Genealogical and Historical Interest
  http://www.rootsweb.com/~pictou/libpic1.htm

- Quintin Publications - Nova Scotia
  http://www.quintinpublications.com/ns.html

◆ Queries, Message Boards & Surname Lists

- Nova Scotians searching surnames
  http://www.chebucto.ns.ca/~ab936/search.html

- RootsWeb Surname List - RSL Nova Scotia
  http://rsl.rootsweb.com/cgi-bin/rslsql.cgi
  The RSL and this form concept & design are courtesy of Karen Isaacson

◆ Records: Census, Cemeteries, Land, Obituaries, Personal, Taxes and Vital (Born, Married, Died & Buried)

- Cemeteries, Funeral Homes & Obituaries
  - Abstracts from the Court of Probate Records for Annapolis County, Nova Scotia
    http://www.widomaker.com/~gwk/abstract.htm
    We are indebted to Wayne W. Walker for making a copy of his Abstracts from the Court of Probate Records for Annapolis County, Nova Scotia available to us on the Internet. The Abstracts are available for download as a ZIP (compressed) file. The text is in ASCII text format which can be read by all word processors.
  - Beaton Cemetery, Millbrook, Pictou County
    http://www.rootsweb.com/~pictou/beaton.htm
  - Black River Cemetery, Pictou County
    http://www.rootsweb.com/~pictou/blackriv.htm
  - Blanchard Road Cemetery, Pictou County
    http://www.rootsweb.com/~pictou/blanch.htm
  - Brookville Cemetery, Pictou County
    http://www.rootsweb.com/~pictou/brookvll.htm
  - Burial Point Cemetery, Merigomish
    http://www.rootsweb.com/~pictou/bpoint.htm
  - Cemeteries of Pictou County
    http://www.rootsweb.com/~pictou/oldest.htm
    Excerpted from "The Stone Book of Pictou County" by Donald Nicholson. The statistics are listed by cemetery, including the oldest birth year, oldest death year, oldest age at death.
  - Chester New Baptist Cemetery, Lunenburg
    http://www.rootsweb.com/~canns/lunenburg/chnbaptist.html
  - Chester Basin Old Baptist Cemetery, Lunenburg
    http://www.rootsweb.com/~canns/lunenburg/cbobaptist.html
  - Church of Holy Spirit Cemetery ~ Hants County
    http://www.rootsweb.com/~nshants/HolySpirit.html
  - Death Notices of Some Early Pictou County Settlers
    http://www.rootsweb.com/~pictou/obits.htm
  - East River St. Mary's Cemetery, Pictou County
    http://www.rootsweb.com/~pictou/eastriv.htm
  - Eden Lake Cemetery, Pictou County
    http://www.rootsweb.com/~pictou/edenlake.htm
  - Five Mile River Cemetery ~ Hants County, Nova Scotia, Canada
    http://www.rootsweb.com/~nshants/FiveMile.html
  - Fox Brook Private Cemetery
    http://www.rootsweb.com/~pictou/foxpriv.htm

o Fraser Cemetery, Blanchard Road, Pictou County
http://www.rootsweb.com/~pictou/fraserb.htm

o Glen Bard Cemetery, James River, Antigonish County
http://www.rootsweb.com/~pictou/antiglb.htm

o Gunn Cemetery, Eden Lake, Pictou County
http://www.rootsweb.com/~pictou/gunn.htm

o Guysborough County Cemetery Listings ~ Nova Scotia, Canada
http://www.angelfire.com/ca4/Patsy/cemindex.html
Cemetery transcriptions, photographs of cemetery gateposts and many obituaries.

o Halifax County - Cemetery Listings
http://www.geocities.com/Heartland/Meadows/3515/Cemetery.htm

o Hattie Cemetery, Avondale, Pictou County
http://www.rootsweb.com/~pictou/hattie.htm

o Heatherton Cemetery, Old Section, Antigonish County
http://www.rootsweb.com/~pictou/hethold.htm

o Hillside Cemetery, Trenton, Pictou County
http://www.rootsweb.com/~pictou/hillside.htm

o Hodson Cemetery, Pictou County
http://www.rootsweb.com/~pictou/hodson.htm

o Holy Trinity Anglican Church Cemetery ~ Hants County
http://www.rootsweb.com/~nshants/holytrinity.html

o Kenzieville Cemetery, Pictou 7ounty
http://www.rootsweb.com/~pictou/nkbr.htm

o Listings for Hillcrest Cemetery est.1830 ~ Upper Musquodoboit, Halifax, Nova Scotia, Canada
http://members.tripod.com/velvet_b/

o The Little Rushton Cemetery
http://msnhomepages.talkcity.com/deckdr/scottyscottage/lilrushtoncem.html
Kolbec, Cumberland County Nova Scotia. A small family cemetery with surnames of RUSHTON, MILLER, ROSS, RODGERS & PIPES.

o Lyons Cemetery Castle Frederick Hants County Nova Scotia
http://www.rootsweb.com/~nshants/LYONS.html

o McKenzie Cemetery, Salt Springs, Pictou County
http://www.rootsweb.com/~pictou/mckenzie.htm

o McLean Cemetery, Hopewell, Pictou County
http://www.rootsweb.com/~pictou/mclhope.htm

o Meiklefield Cemetery, Meiklefield, Pictou County
http://www.rootsweb.com/~pictou/mekfd.htm

o Murray Point Cemetery, Pictou County
http://www.rootsweb.com/~pictou/murpt.htm

o Oak Island Cemetery, Maitland, Hants Co. Nova Scotia
http://www.rootsweb.com/~nshants/Oak.html

o Old Cemetery, Salt Springs, Pictou County
http://www.rootsweb.com/~pictou/oldcem.htm

o Old Mines Road Cemetery, Upper Falmouth, Hants County, Nova Scotia
http://www.rootsweb.com/~nshants/Mines.html

o Pictou Island Pioneer Cemetery
http://www.rootsweb.com/~pictou/pioneer.htm

o Pictou Island Presbyterian Church Cemetery
http://www.rootsweb.com/~pictou/prezz.htm

o Redden Cemetery, Rte 14, Windsor Forks, Hants County N.S.
http://www.rootsweb.com/~nshants/REDDEN2.html

o Rocky Mountain Cemetery, Pictou County
http://www.rootsweb.com/~pictou/rocky.htm

o Roman Catholic Cemetery, Merigomish
http://www.rootsweb.com/~pictou/rcmeri.htm

o Saint Andrew's Cemetery, Old Section, Antigonish County
http://www.rootsweb.com/~pictou/stanold.htm

o Saint Francis Xavier Cemetery est. 1840, Roman Catholic Cemetery, Maitland, Hants Co., Nova Scotia
http://www.rootsweb.com/~nshants/Chapel.html

o Salt Springs Cemetery, Pictou County
http://www.rootsweb.com/~pictou/ssprings.htm

o Sangsters Bridge Cemetery Hants Co. Nova Scotia
http://www.rootsweb.com/~nshants/Sangsters.html

o Stewart's Cemetery, Antigonish County
http://www.rootsweb.com/~pictou/stewart.htm

o St George's Anglican Church Cemetery, Upper Falmouth, Hants County, Nova Scotia
http://www.rootsweb.com/~nshants/georges.html

o St. John The Baptist Anglican Church Cemetery, Latties Brook ~ Hants County
http://www.rootsweb.com/~nshants/Latties.html

o St. Michael's Anglican Church Cemetery ~ Hants County
http://www.rootsweb.com/~nshants/StMich.html

o Vaughan Community Cemetery ~ Hants County
http://www.rootsweb.com/~nshants/vaughan.html

o Vaughan United Church Cemetery ~ Hants County
http://www.rootsweb.com/~nshants/VUnited.html

o Victoria County Cemetery Transcriptions
http://members.tripod.com/~lemac2/index-16.html

o Windsor Forks Cemetery ~ Hants County
http://www.rootsweb.com/~nshants/windsor.html

● Census Indexes & Census Records

o 1901 Census - Lunenburg County, Nova Scotia
http://www.rootsweb.com/~canns/lunenburg/1901census.html

- o Alberta Family Histories Society (AFHS) Genealogical Projects Registry
  http://www.afhs.ab.ca/registry/index.html
  A central registry, which provides a bibliography of genealogical projects, both online and offline, in Canada. The registry is categorized by province/territory, then by record type: births, marriage, census, deaths, and other.
  - • Nova Scotia - Census
    http://www.afhs.ab.ca/registry/regns_census.html
- o Halifax Census (1752)
  - • A-E
    http://www.rootsweb.com/~nshalifa/Hfxcensus2.htm
  - • F-K
    http://www.rootsweb.com/~nshalifa/Hfxcensus1.htm
  - • L-Q
    http://www.rootsweb.com/~nshalifa/Hfxcensus3.htm
  - • R-Z
    http://www.rootsweb.com/~nshalifa/Hfxcensus4.htm
- o Nova Scotia Census Data
  http://www.rootsweb.com/~casoccgs/census.html
- o Nova Scotia Census on Microfilm
  http://nsgna.ednet.ns.ca/ncensus.html
- • Land Records & Tax Rolls
  - o Registry of Deeds - Nova Scotia
    http://nsgna.ednet.ns.ca/ndeed.html
- • Miscellaneous
  - o Alberta Family Histories Society (AFHS) Genealogical Projects Registry
    http://www.afhs.ab.ca/registry/index.html
    A central registry which provides a bibliography of genealogical projects, both online and offline, in Canada. The registry is categorized by province/territory, then by record type: births, marriage, census, deaths, and other.
    - • Nova Scotia - Other
      http://www.afhs.ab.ca/registry/regns_other.html
- • Ships, Passenger Lists & Immigration
  - o Dove Passenger List - 1801
    http://www.rootsweb.com/~pictou/dove1.htm
    Arriving in Pictou County, Nova Scotia, Canada.
  - o Hector Passenger List
    http://www.rootsweb.com/~pictou/hector1.htm
    Voyage to Pictou, Nova Scotia in 1773.
  - o Humphreys Passenger List --- 1806
    http://www.rootsweb.com/~pictou/hmphreys.htm
  - o Lunenburg County, NSGenWeb- Passenger Lists
    http://www.rootsweb.com/~canns/lunenburg/shiplists.html
    - • Cornwallis Ships to Halifax - 1749
      http://www.rootsweb.com/~canns/cornwallis.html
    - • Passenger Lists for Ships Carrying the "Foreign Protestants" to Nova Scotia
      http://www.rootsweb.com/~canns/lunenburg/shiplist2.html
      59 Families 16 May 1752 "SPEEDWELL".

- • Passenger Lists for Ships Carrying the "Foreign Protestants" to Nova Scotia
  http://www.rootsweb.com/~canns/lunenburg/shiplist3.html
  59 Families 30 May 1752 "BETTY".
- • Passenger Lists for Ships Carrying the "Foreign Protestants" to Nova Scotia
  http://www.rootsweb.com/~canns/lunenburg/shiplist11.html
  73 Families 18 May 1751 "SPEEDWELL".
- • Passenger Lists for Ships Carrying the "Foreign Protestants" to Nova Scotia
  http://www.rootsweb.com/~canns/lunenburg/shiplist4.html
  85 Families 2 Jul 1751 "PEARL".
- • Passenger Lists for Ships Carrying the "Foreign Protestants" to Nova Scotia
  http://www.rootsweb.com/~canns/lunenburg/shiplist5.html
  85 Families 5 Jun 1752 "GALE".
- • Passenger Lists for Ships Carrying the "Foreign Protestants" to Nova Scotia
  http://www.rootsweb.com/~canns/lunenburg/shiplist6.html
  85 Families 6 Jun 1752 "PEARL".
- • Passenger Lists for Ships Carrying the "Foreign Protestants" to Nova Scotia
  http://www.rootsweb.com/~canns/lunenburg/shiplist9.html
  99 Families 29 Jun 1750 "ANN".
- • Passenger Lists for Ships Carrying the "Foreign Protestants" to Nova Scotia
  http://www.rootsweb.com/~canns/lunenburg/shiplist1.html
  100 Families of German Protestants 25 Jun 1751 "MURDOCH".
- • Passenger Lists for Ships Carrying the "Foreign Protestants" to Nova Scotia
  http://www.rootsweb.com/~canns/lunenburg/shiplist7.html
  119 Families 30 May 1752 "SALLY".
- • Passenger Lists for Ships Carrying the "Foreign Protestants" to Nova Scotia
  http://www.rootsweb.com/~canns/lunenburg/shiplist8.html
  Foreign Names of Those Arriving with Cornwallis, 1749 and Others of Interest Arriving in 1749.
- • Passenger Lists for Ships Carrying the "Foreign Protestants" to Nova Scotia
  http://www.rootsweb.com/~canns/lunenburg/shiplist12.html
  Settlers Who Are Presumed to Have Arrived on the "ALDERNEY" or the "NANCY" in August and September 1750
- o Nova Scotia Bound
  http://www.geocities.com/Heartland/Meadows/8429/index.html
  A partial list of ships bound for Nova Scotia between 1750 and 1862.

- The Albion Ship List, Surnames A-L
  http://www.geocities.com/Heartland/Meadows/8429/albal.html

  Surnames M-Z
  http://www.geocities.com/Heartland/Meadows/8429/albmz.html
  Arrived in Halifax, Nova Scotia, Canada on May 6, 1774 from Hull, Yorkshire, England.

- The British Queen Passenger List
  http://www.geocities.com/Heartland/Meadows/8429/britqn.html
  Sailed for Nova Scotia from Liverpool, England on April 1st, 1862.

- The Duke of York Passenger List
  http://www.geocities.com/Heartland/Meadows/8429/dyork.html
  Arrived in Halifax, Nova Scotia from Liverpool, England on May 1, 1772.

- Elisabeth and Ann Passenger List
  http://www.geocities.com/Heartland/Meadows/8429/elisann.html
  Sailed for Nova Scotia from Thurso, North Britain on November 8th, 1806.

- The Frank Flint Passenger List
  http://www.geocities.com/Heartland/Meadows/8429/flint.html
  Sailed for Halifax, Nova Scotia from Liverpool, England on May 28th, 1862.

- The Humphreys Passenger List
  http://www.geocities.com/Heartland/Meadows/8429/hmphry.html
  Sailed for Nova Scotia from Tobermory, North Britain on July 14th, 1806.

- The Jenny Ship List
  http://www.geocities.com/Heartland/Meadows/8429/jenny.html
  To Halifax, Nova Scotia, Canada from Hull, Yorkshire, England in April of 1775.

- The Providence Passenger List
  http://www.geocities.com/Heartland/Meadows/8429/prvdnc.html
  Arrived in Halifax on June 1, 1774 from Newcastle Northumberland.

- The Rambler Passenger List
  http://www.geocities.com/Heartland/Meadows/8429/rambler.html
  Sailed for Nova Scotia from Thurso, North Britain on November 8th, 1806.

- The Thomas and William or the Prince George Passenger List
  http://www.geocities.com/Heartland/Meadows/8429/tmwlad.html
  Arrived at Halifax from Scarborough, Yorkshire on May 14/16, 1774.

- The Two Friends Ship List
  http://www.geocities.com/Heartland/Meadows/8429/2friends.html
  Arrived in Halifax, Nova Scotia on May 9, 1774 from Hull, Yorkshire

- Nova Scotia Passenger Lists - The Speedwell and The Ann
  http://www.rootsweb.com/~ote/nsship.htm
- Oughton Passenger List --- 1804
  http://www.rootsweb.com/~pictou/oughton.htm
- The Sarah -- 1801
  http://www.rootsweb.com/~pictou/sarah1.htm
  To Pictou, Nova Scotia.
- Spencer Passenger List--- 1806
  http://www.rootsweb.com/~pictou/spencer.htm

- Vital Records ~ Birth, Marriage & Death
  - Alberta Family Histories Society (AFHS) Genealogical Projects Registry
    http://www.afhs.ab.ca/registry/index.html
    A central registry which provides a bibliography of genealogical projects, both online and offline, in Canada. The registry is categorized by province/territory, then by record type: births, marriage, census, deaths, and other.
    - Nova Scotia - Births
      http://www.afhs.ab.ca/registry/regns_birth.html
    - Nova Scotia - Deaths
      http://www.afhs.ab.ca/registry/regns_death.html
    - Nova Scotia - Marriage
      http://www.afhs.ab.ca/registry/regns_marr.html
  - Baptisms in Pictou County by Rev. James MacGregor, D.D
    http://www.rootsweb.com/~pictou/bapt1.htm
  - Births and Baptisms at Barney's River ~ Pictou County
    http://www.rootsweb.com/~pictou/birbp.htm
  - Candlish Church, Free Presbyterian, Barney's River, Pictou County, Nova Scotia Marriages - 1812-1883
    http://www.rootsweb.com/~pictou/marchr.htm
  - Fortress of Louisbourg Parish Records (1713 - 1758)
    http://collections.ic.gc.ca/louisbourg/genealogy/
  - Lunenburg, Nova Scotia Will Extracts
    http://www.geocities.com/Heartland/Meadows/5699/willtab.html
  - Marriages in Pictou County by Rev. James McGregor
    http://www.rootsweb.com/~pictou/hitches.htm
  - Nova Scotia Vital Statistics Division of Business and Consumer Services
    http://www.gov.ns.ca/bacs/vstat/
  - Nova Scotia Vital Statistics Information from NSGNA
    http://nsgna.ednet.ns.ca/nvitals.html
  - Registrars of Probate
    http://nsgna.ednet.ns.ca/npro.html
    Contact information by county. Provided by the Nova Scotia Genealogy Network Association.

o Surnames of Barney's River, Nova Scotia
http://www.rootsweb.com/~pictou/names.htm
From Pictou County Death Records for the period of 1864--1877

◆ Religion & Churches

- The Anglican Diocese of Nova Scotia
http://fox.nstn.ca/~diocese/

- Christianity Online Church Locator - Churches in Nova Scotia
http://www.christianity.net/churchlocator/location.php?country=Canada&state=Nova+Scotia

- United Church Congregations and Pastoral Charges in Halifax Presbytery
http://www.chebucto.ns.ca/Religion/UCCPresbytery/_Charges.html

◆ Societies & Groups

- Cape Sable Historical Society
http://www.bmhs.ednet.ns.ca/cshs.htm

- Genealogical Association of Nova Scotia
http://www.chebucto.ns.ca/Recreation/GANS/

- Genealogical Institute of the Maritimes
http://nsgna.ednet.ns.ca/gim/

- Hantsport & Area Historical Society
http://nsgna.ednet.ns.ca/hantsport/index.html

- IOOF Lodge Website Directory - Atlantic Provinces
http://norm28.hsc.usc.edu/IOOF/International/Atlantic Provinces.html
Independent Order of Odd Fellows and Rebekahs.

- The Kings Historical Society and Old Kings Courthouse Museum
http://www.go.ednet.ns.ca/~ip96003/

- North Queens Heritage Society
http://www.rootsweb.com/~canns/queens/qcnorth.html

- The Nova Scotia Genealogy Network Association
http://nsgna.ednet.ns.ca/index.html
Dozens of great resources here!.

- Nova Scotia Highland Village Society
http://www.highlandvillage.ns.ca/MainS.html

- Pictou County Genealogy & Heritage Society and McCulloch House Museum
http://www.geocities.com/Colosseum/7374/

- Queens County Historical Society
http://www.rootsweb.com/~canns/queens/qchist.html

- The Royal Nova Scotia Historical Society ~ Dartmouth
http://nsgna.ednet.ns.ca/rnshs/index.html

- Shelburne County Genealogical Society
http://nsgna.ednet.ns.ca/shelburne/index.html

- Society Hill: Nova Scotia Societies
http://www.daddezio.com/society/hill.ca/SH-NS-NDX.html
A list of addresses for genealogical and historical societies in the province.

- South Shore Genealogical Society ~ Lunenburg and Queens Counties
http://www.rootsweb.com/~nslssgs/

- West Hants Historical Society
http://www.glinx.com/~whhs/

CANADA – ONTARIO
http://www.cyndislist.com/ontario.htm

Category Index:

- Canada GenWeb Project
- General Resource Sites
- Government & Cities
- History & Culture
- Libraries, Archives & Museums
- Mailing Lists, Newsgroups & Chat
- Maps, Gazetteers & Geographical Information
- Military
- Newspapers

- People & Families
- Professional Researchers, Volunteers & Other Research Services
- Publications, Software & Supplies
- Queries, Message Boards & Surname Lists
- Records: Census, Cemeteries, Land, Obituaries, Personal, Taxes and Vital
- Religion & Churches
- Societies & Groups

◆ Canada GenWeb Project

- Ontario GenWeb
  http://www.geneofun.on.ca/ongenweb/

◆ General Resource Sites

- Canadian Genealogy and History Links - Ontario
  http://www.islandnet.com/~jveinot/cghl/ontario.html

- Genealogy Research in Ontario
  http://www.xcelco.on.ca/~genealog/#Ontario

- Genealogy Resources on the Internet: Ontario
  http://www-personal.umich.edu/~cgaunt/canada.html
  #ONTARIO

- Glengarry County Ontario and Area
  http://members.tripod.com/~GLENGARRY/index.html

- Norfolk Genealogy
  http://www.norfolkgenealogy.com/

- Ontario Genealogy Resource Page
  http://wwnet.com/~treesrch/ontario.html

◆ Government & Cities

- Government of Ontario, Canada
  http://www.gov.on.ca/

- Yahoo! Canada....Ontario: Cities
  http://ca.yahoo.com/regional/countries/canada/provinces_and
  _territories/ontario/cities/

◆ History & Culture

- Historic Plaques of Ontario
  http://www.waynecook.com/historiclist.html

- A Look at Ontario - History
  http://www.gov.on.ca/MBS/english/look/ont-hist/index.html

◆ Libraries, Archives & Museums

- Archives - Anglican Diocese of Ottawa
  http://ottawa.anglican.ca/archives.html

- Archives Association of Ontario
  http://www.fis.utoronto.ca/people/affiliated/aao/index.htm

- Archives of Ontario
  http://www.archives.gov.on.ca/

  o Genealogical Research
    http://www.archives.gov.on.ca/english/geneal/index.html

- At Port Bruce - Local History and Genealogy
  http://www.ptbruce.kanservu.ca/Genealogy/

- Canadian Archival Resources on the Internet - Ontario
  http://www.usask.ca/archives/car/onmenu.html

- The Canadian Library Index - Ontario
  http://www.lights.com/canlib/canlibon.html

- Canadian Library Websites and Catalogues by Region Ontario
  http://www.nlc-bnc.ca/canlib/eontario.htm

- CCA Directory of Archives for Ontario
  http://www.cdncouncilarchives.ca/cca_dir/ontario.html

- Chatham Public Library
  http://www.wincom.net/CHATHAM/library.htm

- Conrad Grebel College Genealogical Resources
  http://grebel.uwaterloo.ca/mao/gen.html
  Lists genealogical resources held in Conrad Grebel College and the Mennonite Archives of Ontario.

- Directory of Ontario Public Libraries / Répertoire des bibliothèques publiques de l'Ontario
  http://www.library.on.ca/director/dpublib.html

- Doon Heritage Crossroads - Waterloo Regional Curatorial Centre
  http://www.region.waterloo.on.ca/doon/

- Essex County Library
  http://www.essex.county.library.on.ca/

  o Digital Archive and Image Network
    http://www.essex.county.library.on.ca/adi_default.htm
    Indexing of various records including: census; birth, marriages, and death (bmd); newspapers; archived images.

- Family History Centres in Ontario
  http://www.archives.gov.on.ca/english/geneal/fmlyhist.htm

- Family History Library Catalog
  http://www.familysearch.org/Search/searchcatalog.asp
  From the FamilySearch web site, an online catalog to the holdings of the LDS Church in Salt Lake City, Utah. Also search for other localities by place name.
  http://www.familysearch.org/fhlc/supermainframeset.asp?display=localitysearch&columns=*,180,0

  o Canada
    http://www.familysearch.org/fhlc/supermainframeset.asp?display=localitydetails&subject=299&subject_disp=Canada&columns=*,180,0

    • Ontario
      http://www.familysearch.org/fhlc/supermainframeset.asp?display=localitydetails&subject=304&subject_disp=Ontario&columns=*,180,0

- Family History SourceGuide - Family History Centers - Canada
  http://www.familysearch.org/sg/Canada_FHC.html

- HALINET Home Page - The Public Libraries of Halton
  http://www.hhpl.on.ca/

- FamilySearch - Family History Centers in Ontario
  http://www.familysearch.org/Browse/Places/FHC_RESULTS.ASP?FHCCountry=&FHCStateProv=Ontario&FHCCounty=&FHCCity=&Submit=Search
  A list of local LDS Family History Centers along with addresses and hours of operation.

- Hamilton Public Library
  http://www.hpl.hamilton.on.ca/DEFAULT.HTM

  o Special Collections
    http://www.hpl.hamilton.on.ca/LOCAL/SPCOLL/Speccol.htm

    • Canadiana
      http://www.hpl.hamilton.on.ca/LOCAL/SPCOLL/CANA.HTM

    • Genealogy
      http://www.hpl.hamilton.on.ca/LOCAL/SPCOLL/GENEA.HTM

    • Local History
      http://www.hpl.hamilton.on.ca/LOCAL/SPCOLL/LOCAL.HTM

- HYTELNET Library Catalogs: Canada: Ontario
  http://www.lights.com/hytelnet/ca0/ON.html
  Before you use any of the Telnet links, make note of the user name, password and any other logon information.

- London Public Library
  http://discover.lpl.london.on.ca/

- Marine Museum of the Great Lakes at Kingston
  http://www.marmus.ca/

- Mennonite Archives of Ontario
  http://grebel.uwaterloo.ca/mao/

- Mississauga Library System
  http://www.city.mississauga.on.ca/library/default.htm

- The National Archives of Canada / Archives Nationales du Canada
  http://www.archives.ca/

  o Genealogy Research
    http://www.archives.ca/exec/naweb.dll?fs&020202&e&top&0

- National Library of Canada / Bibliothèque nationale du Canada
  http://www.nlc-bnc.ca/

  o Genealogy and Family History at the National Library of Canada
    http://www.nlc-bnc.ca/services/genealogy/gnlogy-e.htm

  o National Library Catalogue
    http://www.nlc-bnc.ca/amicus/ecatalog.htm

- The Niagara Historical Resource Centre
  http://vaxxine.com/fa/notlpl/nhrc.htm

- Ottawa Public Library / Bibliothèque publique d'Ottawa
  http://www.opl.ottawa.on.ca/

- Pickering Public Library
  http://www.picnet.org/

  o Local History
    http://picnet.org/local.htm

- Queen's University Archives ~ Kingston
  http://stauffer.queensu.ca/webarch/

- Queen's University Libraries ~ Kingston
  http://stauffer.queensu.ca/

  o Genealogy
    http://stauffer.queensu.ca/inforef/guides/genealogy.htm

  o Genealogy Resources in Government Documents
    http://stauffer.queensu.ca/webdoc/genealogy/

- Region of Peel Archives
  http://www.region.peel.on.ca/heritage/archives.htm

- The St. Thomas Public Library
  http://www.elgin.net/stpl/public_library.html

- Toronto Public Library
  http://www.mtrl.toronto.on.ca/

  o Special Collections, Genealogy & Maps Centre
    http://www.tpl.toronto.on.ca/TRL/centres/spcoll/index.htm

- Baldwin Room
  http://www.tpl.toronto.on.ca/TRL/centres/spcoll/
  baldwin.htm
  *Broadsides & printed ephemera, books, pamphlets,
  periodicals, manuscripts, historical pictures, newspapers.*

  - Genealogy & Local History
    http://www.tpl.toronto.on.ca/TRL/centres/spcoll/
    resource.htm

  - Maps
    http://www.tpl.toronto.on.ca/TRL/centres/spcoll/
    maps.htm

- Trent University Library ~ Peterborough, Ontario,
  Canada
  http://www.trentu.ca/library/

  o Trent University Archives
    http://www.trentu.ca/library/archives/archives.htm

    - Genealogical Records
      http://www.trentu.ca/library/archives/genealogy.htm

- Trent Valley Archives, Kawartha Ancestral KARA
  http://www.kara.on.ca

- United Church of Canada Archives Network:
  Manitoba and Northwestern Ontario Conference
  Archives
  http://www.uccan.org/archives/manitoba.htm
  A summary of their holdings and contact information.

- United Church of Canada / Victoria University
  Archives
  http://vicu.utoronto.ca/archives/archives.htm
  *Located in Ontario, the holdings in the archives include records for
  the Presbyterian Church in Canada; the Methodist Church
  (Canada); the Congregational Union of Canada; Local Union
  Churches; and the Evangelical United Brethren Church. There are
  also personal papers, biographical files and photographs.*

- The University of Waterloo Electronic Library
  http://www.lib.uwaterloo.ca/

- Uxbridge Public Library
  http://www.uxlib.com/

- The Uxbridge-Scott Museum
  http://www.uxbridge.com/museum/mhome.html
  Including Quaker heritage.

◆ Mailing Lists, Newsgroups & Chat

- Genealogy Resources on the Internet - Canada
  Mailing Lists
  http://www.rootsweb.com/~jfuller/gen_mail_country-can.html
  *Most of the mailing list links below point to this site, wonderfully
  maintained by John Fuller*

- CANADIAN ROOTS Mailing List
  http://www.rootsweb.com/~jfuller/gen_mail_country-
  can.html#CANADIAN-ROOTS

- CAN-ONT-ALGOMA Mailing List
  http://www.rootsweb.com/~jfuller/gen_mail_country-
  can.html#CAN-ONT-ALGOMA

- CAN-ONT-BRANT Mailing List
  http://www.rootsweb.com/~jfuller/gen_mail_country-
  can.html#CAN-ONT-BRANT

- CAN-ONT-ESSEX Mailing List
  http://www.rootsweb.com/~jfuller/gen_mail_country-
  can.html#CAN-ONT-ESSEX

- CAN-ONT-GREY Mailing List
  http://www.rootsweb.com/~jfuller/gen_mail_country-
  can.html#CAN-ONT-GREY

- CAN-ONT-HALDIMAND Mailing List
  http://www.rootsweb.com/~jfuller/gen_mail_country-
  can.html#CAN-ONT-HALDIMAND

- CAN-ONT-HALTON Mailing List
  http://www.rootsweb.com/~jfuller/gen_mail_country-
  can.html#CAN-ONT-HALTON

- CAN-ONT-HURON Mailing List
  http://www.rootsweb.com/~jfuller/gen_mail_country-
  can.html#CAN-ONT-HURON

- CAN-ONT-KENT Mailing List
  http://www.rootsweb.com/~jfuller/gen_mail_country-
  can.html#CAN-ONT-KENT

- CAN-ONT-LAMBTON Mailing List
  http://www.rootsweb.com/~jfuller/gen_mail_country-
  can.html#CAN-ONT-LAMBTON

- CAN-ONT-MIDDLESEX Mailing List
  http://www.rootsweb.com/~jfuller/gen_mail_country-
  can.html#CAN-ONT-MIDDLESEX

- CAN-ONT-NORFOLK Mailing List
  http://www.rootsweb.com/~jfuller/gen_mail_country-
  can.html#CAN-ONT-NORFOLK

- CAN-ONT-NORTHUMBERLAND Mailing List
  http://www.rootsweb.com/~jfuller/gen_mail_country-
  can.html#CAN-ONT-NORTHUMBERLAND

- CAN-ONT-NORTHUMBERLAND-MURRAY
  Mailing List
  http://www.rootsweb.com/~jfuller/gen_mail_country-
  can.html#CAN-ONT-NORTHUMBERLAND-MURRAY

- CAN-ONT-OBITS Mailing List
  http://www.rootsweb.com/~jfuller/gen_mail_country-
  can.html#CAN-ONT-OBITS
  For posting of daily obituaries for the province of Ontario, Canada.

- CAN-ONT-PERTH Mailing List
  http://www.rootsweb.com/~jfuller/gen_mail_country-
  can.html#CAN-ONT-PERTH

- CAN-ONT-SIMCOE Mailing List
  http://www.rootsweb.com/~jfuller/gen_mail_country-
  can.html#CAN-ONT-SIMCOE

- CAN-ONT-WATERLOO Mailing List
  http://www.rootsweb.com/~jfuller/gen_mail_country-
  can.html#CAN-ONT-WATERLOO

- CAN-ONT-WELLINGTON Mailing List
  http://www.rootsweb.com/~jfuller/gen_mail_country-
  can.html#CAN-ONT-WELLINGTON

- CAN-ONT-WENTWORTH Mailing List
  http://www.rootsweb.com/~jfuller/gen_mail_country-
  can.html#CAN-ONT-WENTWORTH

- CAN-ONT-YORK Mailing List
  http://www.rootsweb.com/~jfuller/gen_mail_country-
  can.html#CAN-ONT-YORK

- DUFFERIN Mailing List
  http://www.rootsweb.com/~jfuller/gen_mail_country-
  can.html#DUFFERIN

- Elgin-on Mailing List
  http://www.rootsweb.com/~jfuller/gen_mail_country-
  can.html#Elgin-on

- EONTGEN-L Mailing List
  http://www.rootsweb.com/~jfuller/gen_mail_country-
  can.html#EONTGEN-L
  *For discussions of history, geography and genealogy related to
  Eastern Ontario, Canada: Prince Edward; Hastings; Lennox &
  Addington; Frontenac; Leeds & Grenville; Lanark; Stormont,
  Glengarry & Dundas; Prescott & Russell; and Carleton Counties.*

- loyalists-in-canada Mailing List
  http://www.rootsweb.com/~jfuller/gen_mail_country-
  can.html#LOYALIST
  *For those with loyalist ancestors to help one another research their
  loyalist history and to post any facts on the subject that they desire.
  Loyalists are defined as those who left the United States for Canada
  after the American Revolution for a number of reasons.*

- NIAGARA-ONT Surname Mailing List
  http://www.rootsweb.com/~jfuller/gen_mail_country-
  can.html#NIAGARA-ONT
  *For anyone with a genealogical interest in the Niagara Region of
  Ontario, Canada.*

- ONDURHAM Mailing List ~ Durham County
  http://www.rootsweb.com/~jfuller/gen_mail_country-
  can.html#ONDURHAM

- ontario-daily-obituaries Mailing List
  http://www.rootsweb.com/~jfuller/gen_mail_country-
  can.html#ontario-daily-obituaries
  *For volunteers to post their daily obituaries, for look-up requests of
  obituaries new and old, and for general questions pertaining to
  obituaries in the Province of Ontario, Canada.*

- OntarioGen Mailing List
  http://www.rootsweb.com/~jfuller/gen_mail_country-
  can.html#OntarioGen

- ontario Mailing List
  http://www.rootsweb.com/~jfuller/gen_mail_country-
  can.html#ONTARIO-CANADA

- ONTARIO Mailing List
  http://www.rootsweb.com/~jfuller/gen_mail_country-
  can.html#ONTARIO

- ONT-LEEDS-GRENVILLE Mailing List
  http://www.rootsweb.com/~jfuller/gen_mail_country-
  can.html#ONT-LEEDS-GRENVILLE
  *For anyone with a genealogical interest in the "united counties" of
  Leeds and Grenville, Ontario, Canada.*

- ONT-STORMONT-DUNDAS-GLENGARRY
  Mailing List
  http://www.rootsweb.com/~jfuller/gen_mail_country-
  can.html#ONT-STORMONT-DUNDAS-GLENGARRY
  *For anyone with a genealogical or historical interest in the "united
  counties" of Stormont, Dundas, and Glengarry in eastern Ontario,
  Canada.*

- Oxford-on Mailing List
  http://www.rootsweb.com/~jfuller/gen_mail_country-
  can.html#Oxford-on

- Simcoe-Ont Mailing List
  http://www.rootsweb.com/~jfuller/gen_mail_country-
  can.html#Simcoe-Ont

- SURNAMES-CANADA Mailing List
  http://www.rootsweb.com/~jfuller/gen_mail_country-
  can.html#SURNAMES-CANADA
  Gatewayed with the soc.genealogy.surnames.canada
  newsgroup.
  news:soc.genealogy.surnames.canada
  For surname queries related to Canada.

- UOVGEN - The Upper Ottawa Valley Genealogy
  Mailing List
  http://www.rootsweb.com/~jfuller/gen_mail_country-
  can.html#UOVGEN
  And the corresponding web page
  http://www.valleynet.on.ca/~aa127/uovgen/uovgen.html
  *For Renfrew and Pontiac Counties of the Upper Ottawa Valley
  region of Ontario and Quebec.*

- UPPER-CANADA Mailing List
  http://www.rootsweb.com/~jfuller/gen_mail_country-
  can.html#UPPER-CANADA
  And the corresponding web page
  http://www.rootsweb.com/~ote/lists/uppercanada.htm
  *For anyone with a genealogical interest in Upper Canada, the
  region split from the Province of Quebec after the American
  Revolution, including its history and settlement by Loyalists and
  British and German soldiers, up to and including the year 1867.
  Upper Canada is now the Province of Ontario.*

◆ Maps, Gazetteers & Geographical Information

- Canadian Geographical Names / Les noms
  géographiques du Canada
  http://GeoNames.NRCan.gc.ca/

  o Canadian Geographical Names - Publications
    http://GeoNames.NRCan.gc.ca/english/publications.html
    *List of available publications on geographical names including
    policy documents and manuals, gazetteers, glossaries,
    newsletters and brochures.*

  o Origins of Canada's Geographical Names
    http://GeoNames.NRCan.gc.ca/english/schoolnet/
    origin.html

  o Querying Canadian Geographical Names:
    - Query by Geographical Name
      http://Geonames.NRCan.gc.ca/english/cgndb.html

Current Names Selected by Coordinates
http://Geonames.NRCan.gc.ca/english/cgndb_
coord.html
*Search this database of over 500,000 geographical names by
name, feature type, region and by province*

- Excite Maps: Ontario
http://maps.excite.com/view/?mapurl=/countries/canada/
ontario

- Fire Insurance Plans held by the University of
Waterloo Library
http://www.lib.uwaterloo.ca/locations/umd/cart/fire
insurance.html

- Fire Insurance Plans in York Libraries
http://www.info.library.yorku.ca/depts/map/guidesgoads1.htm
*Canadian fire insurance plans housed in the libraries at York
University, Toronto, Ontario, Canada.*

- In Search of Your Canadian Past: The Canadian
County Atlas Digital Project
http://imago.library.mcgill.ca/countyatlas/default.asp
*From McGill University's Rare Books and Special Collections
Division. A searchable database derived from published county
atlases between 1874 & 1881. Searchable by property owners'
names or by location. Township maps, portraits and properties have
been scanned, with links from the property owners' names in the
database.*

- Ontario Locator
http://www.rootsweb.com/~canon/locator/

- Present Day Ontario
http://www.rootsweb.com/~canon/locator/pdontmap.html

◆ Military

- The Cameron Highlanders of Ottawa (CHofO)
http://infobase.ic.gc.ca/chofo/cameron.htm

- Canada - Military
http://www.CyndisList.com/milcan.htm
See this category on Cyndi's List for related links.

- Ontario's War Memorials
http://www.stemnet.nf.ca/monuments/on.htm
*A project to preserve information about War Memorials throughout
Canada on the World Wide Web. The descriptions of these
individual cenotaphs often includes names and other information on
the dead which can be of interest to the genealogist.*

- Roll of the 1st Regiment, Hastings County, Midland
District, Upper Canada Militia
http://www.iwaynet.net/~bobphillips/muster.htm

◆ Newspapers

- AJR NewsLink - Ontario Newspapers
http://ajr.newslink.org/nonusnont.html

- E&P Media Links - Newspaper Sites in Ontario
http://emedia1.mediainfo.com/emedia/results.htm?region=
canada&abbreviation=ontario++++++++++++++++++++++
++++++++&category=newspaper

- The Hamilton Spectator
http://www.hamiltonspectator.com/

- The Kingston Whig-Standard
http://www.kingstonwhigstandard.com/

- Kitchener Waterloo Record Online
http://www.therecord.com/

- NewsDirectory.com: Newspapers: North America:
Canada: Ontario
http://www.newsdirectory.com/news/press/na/ca/on/

- Ottawa Citizen Online
http://www.ottawacitizen.com/

- The Windsor Star ~ Ontario, Canada
http://www.southam.com/windsorstar/

◆ People & Families

- Loyalists
http://www.CyndisList.com/loyalist.htm
See this category on Cyndi's List for related links.

- The Metis Nation of Ontario
http://www.metisnation.org/

- Tribes and Bands of Ontario
http://www.hanksville.org/sand/contacts/tribal/ON.html

- Young Immigrants to Canada
http://www.dcs.uwaterloo.ca/~marj/genealogy/homeadd.html

◆ Professional Researchers, Volunteers & Other Research Services

- Adopted We Search - Assets and Family Research
Consultants ~ Toronto, Ontario, Canada
http://www.adopted-we-search.com/
*Researcher with 15 years experience, specializing in adoption-
related searches.*

- Adoption Searches & Investigations ~ London,
Ontario
http://www3.sympatico.ca/searches/
*Licensed, bonded, adoptee search agency. Adoption articles & links.
Searches in Canada only. Contact Anne Patterson.*

- Bruce Murduck - Historical, Geographical and
Genealogical Research Services
http://www.ikweb.com/murduck/genealogy/research/
Researcher in Ontario, Canada.

- Diane's Michigan Genealogy Page
http://members.aol.com/DJOslund/index.html
*Professional Genealogist serving Southeastern Michigan,
Southwestern Ontario, Northwestern Ohio.*

- Ed's Ancestral Research Services
http://www3.sympatico.ca/patpamed/
*Specializing in research for Ontario, Canada, but capable of global
research.*

- Forebears Research & Associates ~ London, Ontario
http://www3.sympatico.ca/bill.forebears/

- Forebears Research U.K.
  http://nt.odyssey.on.ca/ewerry/
  Genealogical research for England, Wales and Scotland undertaken in Canada by 25 year veteran of genealogy.

- The Genealogical Research Library ~ Toronto, Ontario
  http://www.grl.com/grl/index.shtml

- Genealogical Research Services in Ontario Canada - Suzanne Schaller
  http://www.cyberus.ca/~suzannes/research.html
  Professional researcher based in Ottawa, Ontario, Canada.

- Gen-Find Research Associates
  http://www.gen-find.com/
  Specialists in Genealogy Research for Ontario & Western Canada, Scotland, Ireland, Forensic Genealogy & 20th Century Research.

- Glenn King - Genealogy Research, Canadian and U.K. records
  mailto:kingdav@limestone.kosone.com
  For details send e-mail to Glenn at: e-mail kingdav@limestone.kosone.com.

- inGeneas Canadian Genealogical Research Services ~ Ottawa
  http://www.ingeneas.com/
  Searchable databases containing 50,000+ Canadian passenger and immigration records (c1750 to 1900) including the only electronic version of the free National Archives of Canada Miscellaneous Immigration Index.

- Jeff Stewart Genealogical Services -- Specializing in Ontario Research
  http://members.aol.com/OntarioGen/
  Based in Toronto, the home of Ontario's major repositories.

- Larry S. Mitchell - Professional Genealogy Research & Services
  http://www.rootsdog.com/
  Professional genealogical research for Michigan, Ontario, Eastern U.S. Resources include internet, census, vital stats, libraries, etc. Able to produce professional looking family history books and albums.

- The Official Iowa Counties Professional Genealogist and Researcher's Registry for Ontario
  http://www.iowa-counties.com/gene/oc.htm

- Susan Burton - Historical and Genealogical Research ~ Toronto
  http://home.ISTAR.CA/~sburton/index.html

◆ Publications, Software & Supplies

- Amazon.com Genealogy Bookstore - Ontario
  http://www.amazon.com/exec/obidos/external-search/?keyword=ontario+genealogy&tag=markcyndisgenealA/

- AudioTapes.com - Genealogical Lectures on Cassette Tapes - Ontario
  http://www.audiotapes.com/search2.asp?Search=Ontario

- Books We Own - Ontario
  http://www.rootsweb.com/~bwo/can_o.html
  Find a book from which you would like a lookup and click on the submitter's code at the end of the entry. Once you find the contact information for the submitter, write them a polite request for a lookup.

- Global Genealogical Supply - Ontario Genealogical & Local History Books
  http://www.globalgenealogy.com/cdaont.htm

- Interlink Bookshop Genealogical Services ~ Victoria, B.C., Canada
  http://www.interlinkbookshop.com/

- The Ontario Genealogical Society's Publications List
  http://www.ogs.on.ca/publications/pub_soc.htm
  Books for sale from the OGS.

- Quintin Publications - Ontario
  http://www.quintinpublications.com/on.html

- Winfield Publishing - Setting Standards in Genealogy Publishing
  http://members.aol.com/Winfieldpb/
  Publisher of genealogy reference books pertaining to the people of Ontario.

◆ Queries, Message Boards & Surname Lists

- Lanark County Genealogical Society Members' Queries
  http://www.globalgenealogy.com/LCGS/LCGSQURY.HTM

- Muskoka Area Genealogy and History Bulletin Board
  http://www.bala.net/bbs/

- Queries - OntarioGenWeb
  http://www.rootsweb.com/~canon/ontquery.html

- RootsWeb Surname List - RSL Ontario
  http://rsl.rootsweb.com/cgi-bin/rslsql.cgi
  The RSL and this form concept & design are courtesy of Karen Isaacson

- Surnames - OntarioGenWeb
  http://www.geocities.com/SoHo/Nook/5996/firstsurnamepage.html

- Waterloo Genealogy Co-operative
  http://members.aol.com/ernm/roots/waterloo.html
  Colleagues Researching Waterloo, Ontario, Canada.

◆ Records: Census, Cemeteries, Land, Obituaries, Personal, Taxes and Vital (Born, Married, Died & Buried)

- 1837 Toronto and Home District Directory
  http://www.rootsweb.com/~onyork/1837.html

- 1842 Malahide Township Elgin County, Ontario Census Index
  http://www.ptbruce.kanservu.ca/Genealogy/census1842.htm

- Alberta Family Histories Society (AFHS) Genealogical Projects Registry
  http://www.afhs.ab.ca/registry/index.html
  A central registry, which provides a bibliography of genealogical projects, both online and offline, in Canada. The registry is categorized by province/territory, then by record type: births, marriage, census, deaths, and other.

  o Ontario - Births
    http://www.afhs.ab.ca/registry/regon_birth.html

  o Ontario - Census
    http://www.afhs.ab.ca/registry/regon_census.html

  o Ontario - Deaths
    http://www.afhs.ab.ca/registry/regon_death.html

  o Ontario - Marriage
    http://www.afhs.ab.ca/registry/regon_marr.html

  o Ontario - Other
    http://www.afhs.ab.ca/registry/regon_other.html

- Bill Martin's Genealogy Page
  http://www.tbaytel.net/bmartin/
  Has several articles for Ontario genealogical research, including lists of microfilm numbers for ordering from the archives or an FHC

  o The Archives of Ontario Microfilm InterLoan Catalog
    http://www.tbaytel.net/bmartin/archives.htm

  o Birth, Marriage, Death Indexes for Ontario, Canada
    http://www.tbaytel.net/bmartin/bmd.htm

  o Birth, Marriage and Death Application Form Instructions
    http://www.tbaytel.net/bmartin/registry.htm

  o LDS Film Numbers for Ontario Birth Registrations
    http://www.tbaytel.net/bmartin/lds-b.htm

  o LDS Film Numbers for Ontario Death Registrations
    http://www.tbaytel.net/bmartin/lds-d.htm

  o LDS Film Numbers for Ontario Marriage Registrations
    http://www.tbaytel.net/bmartin/lds-m.htm

- Erin Township, Wellington Co., Ontario Records
  http://people.ne.mediaone.net/priestner/Erin/Wellington.htm

- Fraktur
  http://www.region.waterloo.on.ca/Jsh2/Fraktur/Frakframeset.htm
  From the Joseph Schneider Haus Collections. Waterloo, Ontario.

  o Fraktur History
    http://www.region.waterloo.on.ca/Jsh2/Fraktur/FHistory.htm

- Lambton County Cemetery Index
  http://www.sarnia.com/groups/ogs/logs1.html

- Land Records in Ontario
  http://wwnet.com/~treesrch/ontland.html

- National Archives of Canada - Index to the 1871 Census of Ontario
  http://www.archives.ca/exec/naweb.dll?fs&020108&e&top&0

- OCFA - The Ontario Cemetery Finding Aid
  http://www.islandnet.com/ocfa/homepage.html

- OCFA: What it is and how to use it
  http://www.rootsweb.com/~onperth/ocfa.html
  An article written by a Perth County OGS member in response to requests for OCFA information.

- Ontario 1871 Census
  http://xcat.stauffer.queensu.ca/census/

- Ontario Vital Statistics Bulletin
  http://www.archives.gov.on.ca/english/virtualrr/info9.htm
  Researching Birth, Death and Marriage Records in Ontario from the Archives of Ontario.

- Preserving Cemeteries
  http://www.gov.on.ca/MCZCR/english/culdiv/heritage/cemetery.htm
  From the Ontario Ministry of Citizenship, Culture, and Recreation. Includes a description of the issues, discussion of applicable laws, and offers a technical manual for sale on how to repair tombstones.

◆ Religion & Churches

- Christianity Online Church Locator - Churches in Ontario
  http://www.christianity.net/churchlocator/location.php?country=Canada&state=Ontario

- Churches in Elgin County
  http://www.eversweb.on.ca/Churches-Elgin/

- A Historical Sketch of the Brethren in Christ Church
  http://www.easynet.ca/~johnb/tunkers/index.html
  "Known as Tunkers in Canada," by George Cober, Gormley, Ontario.

◆ Societies & Groups

- The British Isles Family History Society of Greater Ottawa
  http://www.cyberus.ca/~bifhsgo/

- Bruce County Genealogical Society
  http://www.compunik.com/vmall/bcgs/index.htm

- Cumberland Township Historical Society ~ Cumberland, Ontario, Canada
  http://www.storm.ca/~jeanf/

- East Durham Historical Society ~ Port Hope
  http://www.nhb.com/edhs.htm

- The Glencoe & District Historical Society
  http://www.multiboard.com/~bhurdle/gdhs.html
  Dedicated to the preservation and promotion of family and physical history for Ekfrid, Metcalf, Mosa Tp; and the communities of Appin, Glencoe, Melbourne, Newbury, Wardsville, and the about to be formed S.W. Middlesex; all in the Province of Ontario, Canada.

- Harrow Early Immigrant Research Society
  (H.E.I.R.S.)
  http://www.rootsweb.com/~onheirs/
  *Local historical and genealogical studies of the Township of
  Colchester South and the Town of Harrow, Ontario, as well as
  Essex County references.*

- IOOF Lodge Website Directory - Ontario
  http://norm28.hsc.usc.edu/IOOF/International/Ontario.html
  Independent Order of Odd Fellows and Rebekahs.

- Lanark County Genealogical Society
  http://www.globalgenealogy.com/LCGS/

- Lennox and Addington County Historical Society ~
  Napanee, Ontario, Canada
  http://www.rootsweb.com/~onlennox/

- The London & Middlesex Historical Society
  http://www.londonhistory.org/

- Millbrook & Cavan Historical Society
  http://www.kawartha.net/~mchs/mchs.htm

- Norfolk Historical Society ~ Simcoe
  http://www.norfolklore.com/

- Ontario Chapter of the Association of Professional
  Genealogists
  http://members.aol.com/OntarioAPG/

- Ontario Genealogical Society
  http://www.ogs.on.ca/
  - OGS Branches
    http://www.ogs.on.ca/branches.htm
    - Brant County Branch, Ontario Genealogical
      Society
      http://www.wchat.on.ca:80/public/dwinn/dwinn1/
      ogsbrant.htm
    - Bruce and Grey Branch of the Ontario
      Genealogical Society
      http://www.bmts.com/~bgogs/
    - Elgin County Branch, Ontario Genealogical
      Society
      http://home.ican.net/~bedmonds/ElginOGS/
    - Essex County Branch
      http://www.rootsweb.com/%7Eonsxogs/ogs1.htm
    - Halton-Peel Branch, Ontario Genealogical
      Society
      http://www.hhpl.on.ca/sigs/ogshp/ogshp.htm
    - Hamilton Branch, Ontario Genealogical Society
      http://www.hwcn.org/link/HBOGS/
    - Kent County Branch of the Ontario Genealogical
      Society
      http://www.angelfire.com/on/kentogs/
    - Kingston Branch, Ontario Genealogical Society
      http://post.queensu.ca/~murduckb/kgbrogs.htm
    - Lambton County Branch, Ontario Genealogical
      Society
      http://www.sarnia.com/groups/ogs/lambton_page.html

- Leeds & Grenville Genealogical Society
  http://www.cybertap.com/genealogy/

- London & Middlesex County Branch of the
  Ontario Genealogical Society
  http://www.mirror.org/groups/genealogy/index.html

- Niagara Peninsula Branch
  http://people.becon.org/~nbogs/

- Nipissing District Branch, Ontario Genealogical
  Society
  http://www.onlink.net/~twc/nipogs.htm

- The Norfolk County Branch of the Ontario
  Genealogical Society
  http://www.oxford.net/~mihaley/ogsnb/main.htm

- Ottawa Branch, Ontario Genealogical Society
  http://www.cyberus.ca/~ogsottawa/ogsottawa.htm

- Quinte Branch, Ontario Genealogical Society
  http://www.pec.on.ca/history/geneol.html

- Sault Ste. Marie & District of Algoma, Branch
  of Ontario Genealogical Society
  http://www.soonet.ca/sdbogs-genealogy/

- Simcoe County Branch, Ontario Genealogical
  Society
  http://www.genweb.net/~simcoe/

- Sudbury Branch, Ontario Genealogical Society
  http://www.sudbury.com/Family_Services/Family_
  History/OGS/

- Toronto Branch
  http://www.rootsweb.com/%7Eonttbogs/torbranch.html

- Waterloo-Wellington Branch, Ontario
  Genealogical Society
  http://www.dcs.uwaterloo.ca/~marj/genealogy/ww.html

- La Société Franco-Ontarienne d'Histoire et de
  Généalogie
  http://alumni.laurentian.ca/www/physplant/sfohg/societe.htm

- St. Catharines Historical Society
  http://www.niagara.com/~dmdorey/hssc/hssc.html

- Société Franco-Ontarienne d'histoire et de
  Généalogie
  http://alumni.laurentian.ca/www/physplant/sfohg/societe.htm

- Society Hill: Ontario Societies
  http://www.daddezio.com/society/hill.ca/SH-ON-NDX.html
  *A list of addresses for genealogical and historical societies in the
  province.*

- The Stormont, Dundas and Glengarry Historical
  Society ~ Cornwall, Ontario, Canada
  http://www.cnwl.igs.net/~slm/

- Temiskaming Genealogy Group
  http://www.nt.net/~timetrav/

- The United Empire Loyalists' Association of Canada
  ~ Toronto, Ontario, Canada
  http://people.becon.org/~uela/uela1.htm

- Upper Ottawa Valley Genealogical Group
  http://www.valleynet.on.ca/Culture/Genealogy/UOVGG/index.html

- Waterloo Historical Society
  http://www.dcs.uwaterloo.ca/~marj/history/whs.html

- Wellington County Historical Society
  http://www.dcs.uwaterloo.ca/~marj/history/wellington.html

- West Nissouri Historical Society
  http://www.geocities.com/nissouri_west/
  The society is researching and writing a book about the history of the township, dating from the earliest settlement following the War of 1812 to the present. Family profile submissions are welcome.

CANADA – PRINCE EDWARD ISLAND

http://www.cyndislist.com/pei.htm

Category Index:

- ◆ Canada GenWeb Project
- ◆ General Resource Sites
- ◆ Government & Cities
- ◆ History & Culture
- ◆ Libraries, Archives & Museums
- ◆ Mailing Lists, Newsgroups & Chat
- ◆ Maps, Gazetteers & Geographical Information
- ◆ Military
- ◆ Newspapers

- ◆ People & Families
- ◆ Professional Researchers, Volunteers & Other Research Services
- ◆ Publications, Software & Supplies
- ◆ Queries, Message Boards & Surname Lists
- ◆ Records: Census, Cemeteries, Land, Obituaries, Personal, Taxes and Vital
- ◆ Religion & Churches
- ◆ Societies & Groups

◆ Canada GenWeb Project

- PEGenWeb - P.E.I. GenWeb Project
  http://www.islandregister.com/pegenweb.html

◆ General Resource Sites

- Canadian Genealogy and History Links - Prince Edward Island
  http://www.islandnet.com/~jveinot/cghl/prince-edward-island.html

- Genealogy Resources on the Internet: Prince Edward Island
  http://www-personal.umich.edu/~cgaunt/canada.html#PEI

- The Island Register
  http://www.islandregister.com/
  Prince Edward Island's First Genealogy Home Page.

- Robertson Library Research Guide for Genealogy
  http://www.upei.ca/~library/info/guides/geneal.html

◆ Government & Cities

- The Prince Edward Island Information Centre
  http://www.gov.pe.ca/

- Yahoo! Canada....Prince Edward Island: Cities
  http://ca.yahoo.com/regional/countries/canada/provinces_and_territories/prince_edward_island/cities/

◆ History & Culture

- Heritage Highlights
  http://www.islandregister.com/heritage.html

- Pioneer Life on P.E.I.
  http://www.islandregister.com/life.html

- Prince Edward Island Information Centre
  http://www.gov.pe.ca/

◆ Libraries, Archives & Museums

- Canadian Archival Resources on the Internet - Prince Edward Island
  http://www.usask.ca/archives/car/pemenu.html

- The Canadian Library Index - Prince Edward Island
  http://www.lights.com/canlib/canlibpe.html

- CCA Directory of Archives for Prince Edward Island
  http://www.cdncouncilarchives.ca/cca_dir/pei.html

- Family History Library Catalog
  http://www.familysearch.org/Search/searchcatalog.asp
  From the FamilySearch web site, an online catalog to the holdings of the LDS Church in Salt Lake City, Utah. Also search for other localities by place name.
  http://www.familysearch.org/fhlc/supermainframeset.asp?display=localitysearch&columns=*,180,0

  o Canada
    http://www.familysearch.org/fhlc/supermainframeset.asp?display=localitydetails&subject=299&subject_disp=Canada&columns=*,180,0

    - Prince Edward Island
      http://www.familysearch.org/fhlc/supermainframeset.asp?display=localitydetails&subject=309&subject_disp=Prince_Edward_Island&columns=*,180,0

- FamilySearch - Family History Centers in Prince Edward Island
  http://www.familysearch.org/Browse/Places/FHC_RESULTS.ASP?FHCCountry=&FHCStateProv=Prince+Edward+Island&FHCCounty=&FHCCity=&Submit=Search
  A list of local LDS Family History Centers along with addresses and hours of operation.

- HYTELNET Library Catalogs: Canada: Prince Edward Island
  http://www.lights.com/hytelnet/ca0/PEI.html
  Before you use any of the Telnet links, make note of the user name, password and any other logon information.

- The National Archives of Canada / Archives Nationales du Canada
  http://www.archives.ca/

  o Genealogy Research
    http://www.archives.ca/exec/naweb.dll?fs&020202&e&top&0

- National Library of Canada / Bibliothèque nationale du Canada
  http://www.nlc-bnc.ca/

  o Genealogy and Family History at the National Library of Canada
    http://www.nlc-bnc.ca/services/genealogy/gnlogy-e.htm

  o National Library Catalogue
    http://www.nlc-bnc.ca/amicus/ecatalog.htm

- Prince Edward Island Museum and Heritage Foundation
  http://www.islandregister.com/peimhf.html
  And a description from the Island Register site.
  http://www.metamedia.pe.ca/peimuseum/

- Prince Edward Island Provincial Library Service
  http://www.library.pe.ca/

- Prince Edward Island Public Archives and Records Office
  http://www2.gov.pe.ca/educ/archives/archives_index.asp

  o Genealogical Research
    http://www2.gov.pe.ca/educ/archives/research/research.asp

- Robertson Library Homepage - University of Prince Edward Island
  http://www.upei.ca/~library/

- United Church of Canada Archives Network: Maritime Conference Archives
  http://www.uccan.org/archives/maritime.htm
  A summary of their holdings and contact information.

◆ Mailing Lists, Newsgroups & Chat

- Genealogy Resources on the Internet - Canada Mailing Lists
  http://www.rootsweb.com/~jfuller/gen_mail_country-can.html
  Most of the mailing list links below point to this site, wonderfully maintained by John Fuller

- atlantic-province Mailing List
  http://www.rootsweb.com/~jfuller/gen_mail_country-can.html#ATLANTIC-PROVINCES-CANADA
  For the Atlantic Provinces of Canada - Nova Scotia, Newfoundland, Labrador, and Prince Edward Island.

- CANADIAN ROOTS Mailing List
  http://www.rootsweb.com/~jfuller/gen_mail_country-can.html#CANADIAN-ROOTS

- PEI-GREENWICH Mailing List
  http://www.rootsweb.com/~jfuller/gen_mail_country-can.html#PEI-GREENWICH
  For anyone with a genealogical interest in and around the neighborhood villages of Greenwich, Cablehead, Morell and St Peter's, Prince Edward Island, Canada.

- PEI-ROOTS Mailing List
  http://www.rootsweb.com/~jfuller/gen_mail_country-can.html#PEI-ROOTS

- SURNAMES-CANADA Mailing List
  http://www.rootsweb.com/~jfuller/gen_mail_country-can.html#SURNAMES-CANADA
  Gatewayed with the soc.genealogy.surnames.canada newsgroup.
  news:soc.genealogy.surnames.canada
  For surname queries related to Canada.

◆ Maps, Gazetteers & Geographical Information

- Canadian Geographical Names / Les noms géographiques du Canada
  http://GeoNames.NRCan.gc.ca/

  o Canadian Geographical Names - Publications
    http://GeoNames.NRCan.gc.ca/english/publications.html
    List of available publications on geographical names including policy documents and manuals, gazetteers, glossaries, newsletters and brochures.

  o Origins of Canada's Geographical Names
    http://GeoNames.NRCan.gc.ca/english/schoolnet/origin.html

  o Querying Canadian Geographical Names:

    • Query by Geographical Name
      http://Geonames.NRCan.gc.ca/english/cgndb.html

      Current Names Selected by Coordinates
      http://Geonames.NRCan.gc.ca/english/cgndb_coord.html
      Search this database of over 500,000 geographical names by name, feature type, region and by province

- Excite Maps: Prince Edward Island
  http://maps.excite.com/view/?mapurl=/countries/canada/prince_edward_island

◆ Military

- Canada - Military
  http://www.CyndisList.com/milcan.htm
  See this category on Cyndi's List for related links.

- Prince Edward Island's War Memorials
  http://www.stemnet.nf.ca/monuments/pei.htm
  A project to preserve information about War Memorials throughout Canada on the World Wide Web. The descriptions of these individual cenotaphs often includes names and other information on the dead which can be of interest to the genealogist.

◆ Newspapers

- AJR NewsLink - Prince Edward Island Newspapers
  http://ajr.newslink.org/nonusnpri.html

- E&P Media Links - Newspaper Sites in Prince
  Edward Island
  http://emedia1.mediainfo.com/emedia/results.htm?region=
  canada&abbreviation=princeedwardisland++++++++++++++
  ++++++++++++++++++++&category=newspaper

- NewsDirectory.com: Newspapers: North America:
  Canada: Prince Edward Island
  http://www.newsdirectory.com/news/press/na/ca/pe/

◆ People & Families

- The DYMENT Genealogy - Prince Edward Island
  http://www.sentex.net/~dyment/pei-gen/index.html
  *DYMENT, LADNER, ENMAN, NISBET, and FOLLAND. Also some
  MOORE and RAMSAY from P.E.I.*

- Marge Reid's Irish-Canadian Heritage
  http://homepages.rootsweb.com/~mvreid/mvrgen/irish.html
  Databases, transcriptions, indexes and more.

- Prince Edward Island Surnames
  http://www.islandregister.com/gindex.html

- Tribes and Bands of Prince Edward Island
  http://www.hanksville.org/sand/contacts/tribal/PEI.html

- TROWSDALE / McKAY / MacQUARRIE PEI
  Family Research
  http://members.aol.com/seilg/genea/PEI.htm
  *Trowsdale, Maxfield, MacQuarrie, MacKay and MacLeod, families
  of Queens County, PEI.*

◆ Professional Researchers, Volunteers & Other Research Services

- Gen-Find Research Associates
  http://www.gen-find.com/
  *Specialists in Genealogy Research for Ontario & Western Canada,
  Scotland, Ireland. Also the rest of Canada and Forensic &
  Probate/Heir Research and 20th Century Research.*

◆ Publications, Software & Supplies

- Amazon.com Genealogy Bookstore - Prince Edward
  Island
  http://www.amazon.com/exec/obidos/external-search/
  ?keyword=prince+edward+island+genealogy&tag=
  markcyndisgenealA/

- Books We Own - Prince Edward Island
  http://www.rootsweb.com/~bwo/can_pei.html
  *Find a book from which you would like a lookup and click on the
  submitter's code at the end of the entry. Once you find the contact
  information for the submitter, write them a polite request for a
  lookup.*

- Global Genealogical Supply - Atlantic Provinces
  Genealogical & Local History Books
  http://www.globalgenealogy.com/cdaatlan.htm

- Quintin Publications - Prince Edward Island
  http://www.quintinpublications.com/pei.html

◆ Queries, Message Boards & Surname Lists

- Prince Edward Island Surname List
  http://homepages.rootsweb.com/~canada/pei.htm

- RootsWeb Surname List - RSL Prince Edward Island
  http://rsl.rootsweb.com/cgi-bin/rslsql.cgi
  *The RSL and this form concept & design are courtesy of Karen
  Isaacson*

◆ Records: Census, Cemeteries, Land, Obituaries, Personal, Taxes and Vital (Born, Married, Died & Buried)

- 1768 St. John's Island Heads of Household Census
  http://www.islandregister.com/1768.html

- Alberta Family Histories Society (AFHS)
  Genealogical Projects Registry
  http://www.afhs.ab.ca/registry/index.html
  *A central registry, which provides a bibliography of genealogical
  projects, both online and offline, in Canada. The registry is
  categorized by province/territory, then by record type: births,
  marriage, census, deaths, and other.*

  - Prince Edward Island - Births
    http://www.afhs.ab.ca/registry/regpe_birth.html
  - Prince Edward Island - Census
    http://www.afhs.ab.ca/registry/regpe_census.html
  - Prince Edward Island - Deaths
    http://www.afhs.ab.ca/registry/regpe_death.html
  - Prince Edward Island - Marriage
    http://www.afhs.ab.ca/registry/regpe_marr.html
  - Prince Edward Island - Other
    http://www.afhs.ab.ca/registry/regpe_other.html

- Central United Cemetery -- Dunstaffnage
  http://www.rootsweb.com/~pictou/cucdun.htm

- Covehead Tracadie Marriages 1887-1900
  http://homepages.rootsweb.com/~mvreid/pei/34mar.html
  For Covehead, Corran Ban, Tracadie in Queens County.

- Prince Edward Island Data Pages - Index to PEI
  Database Reports
  http://homepages.rootsweb.com/~mvreid/pei/peidbidx.html
  *A wonderful collection of resources from Marge Reid, including
  probate records, surname indexes for marriage and burial records
  and much more.*

- Index to the 1891 Census of Prince Edward Island
  http://www.edu.pe.ca/paro/1891/index.asp

- Little Sands Cemetery
  http://www.rootsweb.com/~pictou/lilsands.htm

- Long Creek Baptist Church Cemetery
  http://www.rootsweb.com/~pictou/longcree.htm

- Lovely Nelly Passenger Lists, 1774 & 1775
  http://www.rootsweb.com/~pictou/lnell1.htm
  From Galloway, Scotland to Prince Edward Island.

- The Passenger List of the "Alexander," and the Glenaladale Settlers
  http://www.islandregister.com/alexandr.html
  May 1772 from Greenock, Scotland to Prince Edward Island, Canada.

- Passenger List of the "Jane"
  http://www.islandregister.com/jane.html
  From Drimindarach, Scotland, July 12, 1790.

- Passenger List of the "Lucy" 1790
  http://www.islandregister.com/lucy.html
  In the company of the "Jane," from Scotland to Prince Edward Island, Canada.

- PEI Burial Records - 1892-1900
  http://homepages.rootsweb.com/~mvreid/pei/34burabs.html
  St. Eugene's (CoveHead), St. Michael's (Corran Ban), St. Bonaventure's (Tracadie).

- Prince Edward Island Cemeteries Page
  http://www.islandregister.com/cem.html
  Includes "Extract from the Death Registers, St. Patrick's Roman Catholic Church in Ft. Augustus, P.E.I.

- Wood Island Cemetery (established 1882)
  http://www.rootsweb.com/~pictou/wdi.htm

- Wood Islands Pioneer Cemetery 1807--1910
  http://www.rootsweb.com/~pictou/wdislan.htm

◆ Religion & Churches

- The Anglican Diocese of Nova Scotia
  http://fox.nstn.ca/~diocese/

- Christianity Online Church Locator - Churches in Prince Edward Island
  http://www.christianity.net/churchlocator/location.php?country=Canada&state=Prince+Edward+Island

◆ Societies & Groups

- Archives Council of Prince Edward Island
  http://moondog.usask.ca/cca/pei.html

- IOOF Lodge Website Directory - Atlantic Provinces
  http://norm28.hsc.usc.edu/IOOF/International/Atlantic Provinces.html
  Independent Order of Odd Fellows and Rebekahs.

- The Prince Edward Island Genealogical Society
  http://www.islandregister.com/peigs.html

- The Prince Edward Island Museum and Heritage Foundation
  mailto:peimuse@cycor.ca
  E-mail them at: peimuse@cycor.ca and they will accept general queries, as well as queries about books that are available on PEI genealogy and history.

- Prince Edward Island Museum and Heritage Foundation
  http://www.islandregister.com/peimhf.html
  And a description from the Island Register site.
  http://metamedia.pe.ca/peimuseum/

- Society Hill: Prince Edward Island Societies
  http://www.daddezio.com/society/hill.ca/SH-PE-NDX.html
  A list of addresses for genealogical and historical societies in the province.

CANADA – QUEBEC
http://www.cyndislist.com/quebec.htm

Category Index:

- Canada GenWeb Project
- General Resource Sites
- Government & Cities
- History & Culture
- Language, Handwriting & Script
- Libraries, Archives & Museums
- Mailing Lists, Newsgroups & Chat
- Maps, Gazetteers & Geographical Information
- Military
- Newspapers

- People & Families
- Professional Researchers, Volunteers & Other Research Services
- Publications, Software & Supplies
- Queries, Message Boards & Surname Lists
- Records: Census, Cemeteries, Land, Obituaries, Personal, Taxes and Vital
- Religion & Churches
- Societies & Groups

◆ Canada GenWeb Project

- Projet GenWeb du Québec
  http://www.rootsweb.com/~canqc/index.htm

◆ General Resource Sites

- Canadian Genealogy and History Links - Quebec
  http://www.islandnet.com/~jveinot/cghl/quebec.html

- Le Centre de généalogie francophone d'Amérique
  http://www.genealogie.org/

- Denis Beauregard Genealogy Page
  http://www.cam.org/~beaur/gen/welcome.html

- FrancoGène: Votre porte d'entrée vers la généalogie francophone dans Internet
  http://www.genealogie.com/index.html

- FRANCOGENE: Your gateway to the Franco-American and Franco-Canadian Genealogy on the Internet
  http://www.francogene.com/

- Genealogy of Quebec's Native People and francophone Metis
  http://www.cam.org/~beaur/gen/amerin-e.html

- Genealogy Resources on the Internet: Quebec
  http://www-personal.umich.edu/~cgaunt/canada.html#QUEBEC

- L'Anneau Généalogie Québec Genealogy Web Ring
  http://www.aidus-hemond.com/quebecgen.html

- Pontiac County, Quebec Genealogical Resources
  http://www.valleynet.on.ca/~aa127/uovgen/pontiac.html

- Quebec, Canada Events and Time Periods
  http://www.familysearch.org/rg/events/events1.asp?Locality=Quebec,+Canada&Id=305
  From FamilySearch.org.

- Quebec Genealogy Page
  http://www.cam.org/~beaur/gen/quebec-e.html

- Québec Research Outline
  http://www.familysearch.org/rg/guide/Quebec.ASP
  Excellent "How To" from FamilySearch.org.

◆ Government & Cities

- Gouvernement du Québec / Government of Québec
  http://www.gouv.qc.ca/XmlDev/Site/Dhtml/Francais/Index.html#GrandsDossiers

- Yahoo! Canada....Quebec: Cities
  http://ca.yahoo.com/regional/countries/canada/provinces_and_territories/quebec/cities/

◆ History & Culture

- Irish Immigration to Grosse Île, Quebec, Canada
  o 1847, Grosse Île: A Record of Daily Events
    http://www.amazon.com/exec/obidos/ISBN=0660168782/markcyndisgenealA/
    A book by Andre Charbonneau.

  o Grosse Île Gateway to Canada
    http://www.amazon.com/exec/obidos/ISBN=0969080530/markcyndisgenealA/
    A book by Carraig Books.

  o Grosse Île and the Irish Memorial
    http://parcscanada.risq.qc.ca/grosse_ile/
    From Parks Canada.

    • 1847: A Tragic Year at Grosse Île
      http://parcscanada.risq.qc.ca/grosse_ile/history2_e.html

- The Changing Role of Grosse Île
  http://parcscanada.risq.qc.ca/grosse_ile/history1_e.html
  - Statistics and more statistics
    http://parcscanada.risq.qc.ca/grosse_ile/history3_e.html
  o Canada's Irish National Monument - Grosse Île in Quebec
    http://homepage.eircom.net/~mcmullins/grosse-ile.htm
  o Irish Visions Documentaries: Grosse Île: Gateway & Graveyard
    http://www.stpatrick.com/mall/visions/documentaries/grosse.htm
    Video for sale.
  o A Register of Deceased Persons at Sea and on Grosse Île
    http://www.amazon.com/exec/obidos/ISBN=0660168774/markcyndisgenealA/
    A book by Andre Charbonneau.

- La Nouvelle-France - Resources Française
  http://www.culture.fr/culture/nllefce/fr/

- La Ville de Rivière-du-Loup
  http://www.icrdl.net/mlagace/rdl.htm
  Also the City of Rivière-du-Loup by Mireille LAGACÉ
  http://www.icrdl.net/mlagace/rdla.htm

- Quebec, Canada, Historical Background
  http://www.familysearch.org/rg/guide/QC_T3_Historical Back.ASP
  From FamilySearch.org.

◆ Language, Handwriting & Script

- AltaVista Translation Service
  http://babelfish.altavista.digital.com/cgi-bin/translate?
  Input a URL for a web site or a block of plain text and this site will translate for you from French to English or English to French.

- French Letter-Writing Guide
  http://www.familysearch.org/rg/guide/LGFrench.ASP
  For genealogical inqueries from FamilySearch.org.

- French Genealogical Word List
  http://www.familysearch.org/rg/guide/WLFrench.ASP

- Translation Service only for genealogy related material
  http://www.genealogy.net/gene/misc/translation.html
  Volunteer translators can provide you with translations between Czech, English, Dutch, French, German, & Polish. This service is provided via e-mail. Exact request syntax and length rules must be followed in order to expedite processing.

- Tutorials for Reading Old German, French and English Handwriting, Naming Systems
  http://www.disknet.com/indiana_biolab/eg502.htm

◆ Libraries, Archives & Museums

- Archives - Anglican Diocese of Ottawa
  http://ottawa.anglican.ca/archives.html

- Archives départementales de la Seine-Maritime ~ France
  http://www.culture.fr/culture/nllefce/fr/rep_ress/ad_76101.htm

- Archives Nationales du Québec
  http://www.anq.gouv.qc.ca/

- Canadian Archival Resources on the Internet - Québec
  http://www.usask.ca/archives/car/qcmenu.html

- The Canadian Library Index - Quebec
  http://www.lights.com/canlib/canlibpq.html

- CCA Directory of Archives for Quebec
  http://www.cdncouncilarchives.ca/cca_dir/quebec.html

- Les Centres Généalogiques SDJ / LDS Family History Centers
  http://www.et.byu.edu/~harmanc/paris/genealogie.html
  France, Belgique, Suisse, Canada.

- Family History Library Catalog
  http://www.familysearch.org/Search/searchcatalog.asp
  From the FamilySearch web site, an online catalog to the holdings of the LDS Church in Salt Lake City, Utah. Also search for other localities by place name.
  http://www.familysearch.org/fhlc/supermainframeset.asp?display=localitysearch&columns=*,180,0
  o Canada
    http://www.familysearch.org/fhlc/supermainframeset.asp?display=localitydetails&subject=299&subject_disp=Canada&columns=*,180,0
    - Quebec
      http://www.familysearch.org/fhlc/supermainframeset.asp?display=localitydetails&subject=305&subject_disp=Quebec&columns=*,180,0

- Family History SourceGuide - Family History Centers - Canada
  http://www.familysearch.org/sg/Canada_FHC.html

- FamilySearch - Family History Centers in Quebec
  http://www.familysearch.org/Browse/Places/FHC_RESULTS.ASP?FHCCountry=&FHCStateProv=Quebec&FHCCounty=&FHCCity=&Submit=Search
  A list of local LDS Family History Centers along with addresses and hours of operation.

- HYTELNET Library Catalogs: Canada: Quebec
  http://www.lights.com/hytelnet/ca0/PQ.html
  Before you use any of the Telnet links, make note of the user name, password and any other logon information.

- The National Archives of Canada / Archives Nationales du Canada
  http://www.archives.ca/
  o Genealogy Research
    http://www.archives.ca/exec/naweb.dll?fs&020202&e&top&0

- National Library of Canada / Bibliothèque nationale du Canada
  http://www.nlc-bnc.ca/

o Genealogy and Family History at the National Library of Canada
http://www.nlc-bnc.ca/services/genealogy/gnlogy-e.htm

o National Library Catalogue
http://www.nlc-bnc.ca/amicus/ecatalog.htm

- United Church of Canada Archives Network: Montreal and Ottawa Conference Archives
http://www.uccan.org/archives/montreal.htm
A summary of their holdings and contact information.

◆ Mailing Lists, Newsgroups & Chat

- CANADIAN ROOTS Mailing List
http://www.rootsweb.com/~jfuller/gen_mail_country-can.html#CANADIAN-ROOTS

- GEN-FF Mailing List
http://www.rootsweb.com/~jfuller/gen_mail_country-fra.html#GEN-FF-L
Discussion of Francophone genealogy. Gatewayed with fr.rec.genealogie. Mainly in French.

- GEN-FR Mailing List
http://www.rootsweb.com/~jfuller/gen_mail_country-fra.html#GEN-FR-L
Discussion of Francophone genealogy. Gatewayed with soc.genealogy.french. Mainly in English.

- QC-ETANGLO Mailing List
http://www.rootsweb.com/~jfuller/gen_mail_country-can.html#QC-ETANGLO
For anyone researching Anglo-Protestant roots within any of the 11 Quebec, Canada counties that make up the Eastern Townships (i.e., Arthabaska, Brome, Compton, Drummond, Megantic, Missisquoi, Richmond, Shefford, Sherbrooke, Stanstead, Wolfe).

- quebec Mailing List
http://www.rootsweb.com/~jfuller/gen_mail_country-can.html#QUEBEC-CANADA

- SURNAMES-CANADA Mailing List
http://www.rootsweb.com/~jfuller/gen_mail_country-can.html#SURNAMES-CANADA
Gatewayed with the soc.genealogy.surnames.canada newsgroup
news:soc.genealogy.surnames.canada
For surname queries related to Canada.

- UOVGEN - The Upper Ottawa Valley Genealogy Mailing List
http://www.rootsweb.com/~jfuller/gen_mail_country-can.html#UOVGEN
And the corresponding web page
http://www.valleynet.on.ca/~aa127/uovgen/uovgen.html
For Renfrew and Pontiac Counties of the Upper Ottawa Valley region of Ontario and Quebec.

- UPPER-CANADA Mailing List
http://www.rootsweb.com/~jfuller/gen_mail_country-can.html#UPPER-CANADA
For anyone with a genealogical interest in Upper Canada, the region split from the Province of Quebec after the American Revolution, including its history and settlement by Loyalists and British and German soldiers, up to and including the year 1841.

◆ Maps, Gazetteers & Geographical Information

- Canadian Geographical Names / Les noms géographiques du Canada
http://GeoNames.NRCan.gc.ca/

o Canadian Geographical Names - Publications
http://GeoNames.NRCan.gc.ca/english/publications.html
List of available publications on geographical names including policy documents and manuals, gazetteers, glossaries, newsletters and brochures.

o Origins of Canada's Geographical Names
http://GeoNames.NRCan.gc.ca/english/schoolnet/origin.html

o Querying Canadian Geographical Names:

- Query by Geographical Name
http://Geonames.NRCan.gc.ca/english/cgndb.html

Current Names Selected by Coordinates
http://Geonames.NRCan.gc.ca/english/cgndb_coord.html
Search this database of over 500,000 geographical names by name, feature type, region and by province

- Excite Maps: Quebec
http://maps.excite.com/view/?mapurl=/countries/canada/quebec

- Québec, Canada, Boundary Changes and Maps
http://www.familysearch.org/rg/guide/QC_BMDT3_Quebec_Boundary_Changes.ASP
From FamilySearch.org.

◆ Military

- 1755 - The French and Indian War Home Page
http://web.syr.edu/~laroux/

- Canada - Military
http://www.CyndisList.com/milcan.htm
See this category on Cyndi's List for related links.

- Quebec's War Memorials
http://www.stemnet.nf.ca/monuments/pq.htm
A project to preserve information about War Memorials throughout Canada on the World Wide Web. The descriptions of these individual cenotaphs often includes names and other information on the dead which can be of interest to the genealogist.

◆ Newspapers

- AJR NewsLink - Quebec Newspapers
http://ajr.newslink.org/nonusnque.html

- E&P Media Links - Newspaper Sites in Quebec
http://emedia1.mediainfo.com/emedia/results.htm?region=canada&abbreviation=quebec+++++++++++++++++++++++++++++++&category=newspaper

- NewsDirectory.com: Newspapers: North America: Canada: Quebec
http://www.newsdirectory.com/news/press/na/ca/pq/

◆ People & Families

- Acadian, Cajun & Creole
  http://www.CyndisList.com/acadian.htm
  See this category on Cyndi's List for related links.

- Aline's French-Canadian Ancestors
  http://members.tripod.com/~AlineB/index.html
  *CHARTRAND, DESJARDINS, ROIREAU DIT LALIBERTY,
  LIBERTY.*

- Association des Familles MORISSETTE Inc.
  http://www.genealogie.org/famille/morissette/morissette.htm

- Bienvenue chez Mireille LAGACÉ
  http://icrdl.net/~mlagace/
  LAGACÉ, DICKNER, ROY, DUMONT.

- Les Descendants des FRÉCHETTE, Inc.
  http://www.angelfire.com/ca/frechette/

- Descendants of Andre MORIN and Marguerite
  MOREAU
  http://www.newnorth.net/~kind/morin.html
  Settled in Quebec around 1665 and married in 1670.

- Donna's Genealogy Homepage
  http://members.aol.com/donnawalt/donnas.htm
  *ANTAYA, BOULAY, BOEMIER, BERGERON, BOURDEAU,
  DROUILLARD, CLERMONT, DEMERS, MONTMINY, PELLITIER
  and many more.*

- Don's Home Page of Genealogy of the DUBE's
  http://dondube.excelland.com/castle.html
  *ST-LAURENT, DEVINE, BRODEUR, DUBE, LANDRY,
  BONENFANT, BRETON, CHAMPION, LONDON, ARCENEAULT,
  LYONS and McEWIN (McKEONE).*

- Généalogie TELLIER / LAFORTUNE
  http://www3.sympatico.ca/mlafortu/
  LETELLIER, TELLIER, LAFORTUNE.

- Genealogy Home Page of Jacques L'HEUREUX
  http://www.happyones.com/genealogy/index-e.html
  *L'HEUREUX, LEUREAU, BARIL, DUMONT, MUELLER, MERLE
  AND ST-ARNAULT, ST-ARNAUD.*

- Genealogy of Quebec's Native People and
  francophone Metis
  http://www.genealogie.com/quebec/amerin-e.html

- Hebridean Scots of the Province of Quebec
  http://www.geocities.com/~hebridscots/
  *BOHLMAN, BRUMBAUGH, CLAPPER, FELDHAHN, FELDHAN,
  FELDTON, FELTON, FRANT, FRIEND, WALDRON.*

- Le HOUYMET Internet - Home on the Internet of
  Les Descendants de Jean OUIMET, Inc.
  http://www.geocities.com/~couimet/lehouymet.html
  *Ouimet, Houymet, Vilmet, Wemet, Wemett, Wuillemette, Wilmot and
  numerous other spelling variations.*

- Hugi's Homepage
  http://www.connect.ab.ca/~hjobin/
  *Researching French Quebec names. DESHETRES, DESHAIES,
  DESHAYES. PAGE. PROU. PROULX. JOBIN.*

- Karen FARMER's Kinfolk - Genealogy in Nova
  Scotia, Ontario and Quebec
  http://www.geocities.com/Heartland/Plains/7525/
  *BEZANSON, CLEROUX, CROCKETT, FARMER, LANGILLE,
  STEVENS & TATTRIE.*

- La page de la famille PAYER
  http://ww.total.net/~jlpayer/
  BAYER, PAYER, PAYEUR.

- Le Grand-Livre Des Familles LAROCQUE Family
  History Book
  http://www.easynet.ca/~larocque/
  *Descendants of Philibert Couillaud de La Roque de Roquebrune
  who came to Canada in 1665 with the regiment of Carignan, from
  France. Larocque, LaRocque, LaRoque, Roquebrune, Rocbrune,
  LaRock, Rock, Rochbrune, Rockburn, Roburn.*

- The PICHE, PICHETTE and DUPRE Families
  http://www.abacom.com/~dgdupre/

- Régis CORBIN
  http://www.letanu.on.ca/
  CORBIN and BELZILE (Gagnon dit).

- The RODRIGUE Families
  http://www.er.uqam.ca/nobel/g17176/rodrigue/engindex.html
  *Quebec and Ontario in Canada, Louisiana and New England in the
  U.S.*

- Les ROUSSEL en Amérique du Nord / ROUSSEL
  Families in North America
  http://www.cam.org/~mauricel

- Tribes and Bands of Quebec
  http://www.hanksville.org/sand/contacts/tribal/QU.html

◆ Professional Researchers, Volunteers & Other Research Services

- Eastern Townships of Quebec Genealogy
  http://www.virtuel.qc.ca/simmons/
  *Marlene Simmons has indexed over 515,000 church, census,
  newspaper, cemetery, some Vermont vital records, and other
  miscellaneous records. Her site now includes a searchable
  database.*

- The Official Iowa Counties Professional Genealogist
  and Researcher's Registry for Quebec
  http://www.iowa-counties.com/gene/qc.htm

◆ Publications, Software & Supplies

- Amazon.com Genealogy Bookstore - Quebec
  http://www.amazon.com/exec/obidos/external-search/?
  keyword=quebec+genealogy&tag=markcyndisgenealA/

- AudioTapes.com - Genealogical Lectures on Cassette
  Tapes – Quebec
  http://www.audiotapes.com/search2.asp?Search=Quebec
  And French Canadian
  http://www.audiotapes.com/search2.asp?Search=French

- Books We Own - Quebec
  http://www.rootsweb.com/~bwo/can_q.html
  Find a book from which you would like a lookup and click on the submitter's code at the end of the entry. Once you find the contact information for the submitter, write them a polite request for a lookup.

- Centre de recherches généalogiques du Québec
  http://www.cam.org/~cdrgduq/
  Parchment certificates for sale with more than 4,000 names from French-Canadian and Acadian origins.

- Global Genealogical Supply - Quebec (Lower Canada) Genealogical & Local History Books
  http://www.globalgenealogy.com/cdaque.htm

- Quintin Publications - Quebec
  http://www.quintinpublications.com/catalog.html
  The many topics include: General & How-To, History & Geography, Jetté, Drouin, & Tanguay, PRDH Series, Other Reference, Vital Records, Church Census Records, Civil Census Records, Notarial Records, Protestant Records, Origins of Settlers, Family & Regional, Genealogies, French-Canadian/Acadian, Genealogical Review.

◆ Queries, Message Boards & Surname Lists

- RootsWeb Surname List - RSL Quebec
  http://rsl.rootsweb.com/cgi-bin/rslsql.cgi
  The RSL and this form concept & design are courtesy of Karen Isaacson

◆ Records: Census, Cemeteries, Land, Obituaries, Personal, Taxes and Vital (Born, Married, Died & Buried)

- Alberta Family Histories Society (AFHS) Genealogical Projects Registry
  http://www.afhs.ab.ca/registry/index.html
  A central registry, which provides a bibliography of genealogical projects, both online and offline, in Canada. The registry is categorized by province/territory, then by record type: births, marriage, census, deaths, and other.

  o Quebec - Births
    http://www.afhs.ab.ca/registry/regqc_birth.html

  o Quebec - Census
    http://www.afhs.ab.ca/registry/regqc_census.html

  o Quebec - Deaths
    http://www.afhs.ab.ca/registry/regqc_death.html

  o Quebec - Marriage
    http://www.afhs.ab.ca/registry/regqc_marr.html

  o Quebec - Other
    http://www.afhs.ab.ca/registry/regqc_other.html

- French Canadian Heads-of-Households in the Province of Quebec in 1871

  o Cities Beginning with A-C
    http://www.oz.net/~johnbang/genealogy/quebecac.txt

  o D-L
    http://www.oz.net/~johnbang/genealogy/quebecdl.txt

  o L-M
    http://www.oz.net/~johnbang/genealogy/quebeclm.txt

- Index to the 1744 Quebec City Census
  http://www.oz.net/~johnbang/genealogy/1744indx.txt

- Hemmingford Cemetery Records ~ Hemmingford, Quebec, Canada
  http://members.xoom.com/dlmark/cemetery.htm
  6,000 records from 16 Hemmingford, Quebec area cemeteries.

- Mount Royal Cemetery Company ~ Montréal, Québec, Canada
  http://www.mountroyalcem.com/

- Québec, Canada, Catholic Church Records, 1621 to the Present
  http://www.familysearch.org/rg/guide/QC_BMDT3_Quebec_Catholic_Church_Records.ASP
  Information on how and where to use these records from FamilySearch.org.

- Québec, Canada, Church Records
  http://www.familysearch.org/rg/guide/QC_BMDT3_Quebec_Church_Records.ASP
  Information on how and where to use these records from FamilySearch.org.

- Québec, Canada, National Censuses, 1871 to 1901
  http://www.familysearch.org/rg/guide/QC_BMDT3_Census 1871-1901.ASP
  Information on how and where to use these records from FamilySearch.org.

- Québec, Canada, Protestant Church Records, 1766 to the Present
  http://www.familysearch.org/rg/guide/QC_BMDT3_Quebec_Protestant_Church_Records.ASP
  Information on how and where to use these records from FamilySearch.org.

◆ Religion & Churches

- Christianity Online Church Locator - Churches in Quebec
  http://www.christianity.net/churchlocator/location.php?country=Canada&state=Quebec

◆ Societies & Groups

- Association des archivistes du Québec
  http://www.archivistes.qc.ca/

- Club De Généalogie De Longueuil
  http://www.club-genealogie-longueuil.qc.ca/

- Le Club de généalogie d'Hydro-Québec ~ Varennes, Quebec, Canada
  http://rtsq.grics.qc.ca/genealogie/hydroqc.htm

- Fédération des Familles-Souches Québécoises Inc.
  http://www.mediom.qc.ca/~ffsq/

- Fédération québécoise des sociétés de généalogie
  http://www.federationgenealogie.qc.ca/

- FRANCETRES: Genealogie du Quebec - Sociétés de généalogie/Genealogical Societies
  http://www.cam.org/~beaur/gen/qc-bib-f.html#societes

- Genealogy Society of Bay Chaleur ~ New Richmond, Quebec, Canada
  http://gaspe-roots.com/gsbc/index.htm

- IOOF Lodge Website Directory - Quebec
  http://norm28.hsc.usc.edu/IOOF/International/Quebec.html
  Independent Order of Odd Fellows and Rebekahs.

- Jewish Genealogical Society of Montreal
  http://www.gtrdata.com/jgs-montreal/

- Quebec Family History Society
  http://www.cam.org/~qfhs/index.html

- Réseau des archives du Québec
  http://www.raq.qc.ca/raq/index.html

- Parent Finders Montreal
  http://www.PFMTL.org/
  A non-profit organization of volunteers to help and support adoptees, birth parents, siblings and fostered adults seeking their biological roots.

- La Société du patrimoine et d'histoire de la Côte-de-Beaupré
  http://www.genealogie.org/club/sphcb/sphcb.htm

- Société de Généalogie de la Mauricie et des Bois-Francs ~ Trois-Rivières, Quebec, Canada
  http://www.genealogie.org/club/sgmbf/sgmbf.htm

- Société de Généalogie de Lanaudière ~ Joliette, Quebec, Canada
  http://www.genealogie.org/club/sgl/sgl.htm
  Berthier, Joliette, Montcalm, L'Assomption in Quebec.

- Société de généalogie de Québec
  http://www.genealogie.org/club/sgq/sgq.htm

- Société de Généalogie des Cantons de l'Est ~ Sherbrooke, Quebec, Canada
  http://www.genealogie.org/club/sgce/sgce.htm

- Société de généalogie du Saguenay ~ Chicoutimi, Québec, Canada
  http://cybernaute.com/sgs/

- Société d'Histoire et de Généalogie de Rivière-du-Loup
  http://icrdl.net/~mlagace/shgrdla.htm

- Société d'Histoite et de Généalogie de Saint-Casimir (SHGSC)
  http://www.genealogie.org/club/shgsc/

- La Société Généalogie de l'Outaouais ~ Quebec, Canada
  http://www3.sympatico.ca/sgo/

- Société Généalogique Canadienne-Française ~ Montreal
  http://www.sgcf.com/

- Société généalogique d'Argenteuil - Argenteuil County Genealogical Society
  http://rtsq.grics.qc.ca/genealogie/argenteu.htm

- Société Généalogique De L'est Du Québec (SGEQ)
  http://www.genealogie.org/club/sgeq/sgeq.htm

- Society Hill: Quebec Societies
  http://www.daddezio.com/society/hill.ca/SH-QC-NDX.html
  A list of addresses for genealogical and historical societies in the province.

CANADA – SASKATCHEWAN

http://www.cyndislist.com/sask.htm

Category Index:

- Canada GenWeb Project
- General Resource Sites
- Government & Cities
- Libraries, Archives & Museums
- Mailing Lists, Newsgroups & Chat
- Maps, Gazetteers & Geographical Information
- Military
- Newspapers
- People & Families

- Professional Researchers, Volunteers & Other Research Services
- Publications, Software & Supplies
- Queries, Message Boards & Surname Lists
- Records: Census, Cemeteries, Land, Obituaries, Personal, Taxes and Vital
- Religion & Churches
- Societies & Groups

◆ Canada GenWeb Project

- Saskatchewan GenWeb
  http://www.rootsweb.com/~cansk/Saskatchewan/

◆ General Resource Sites

- Canadian Genealogy and History Links - Saskatchewan
  http://www.islandnet.com/~jveinot/cghl/saskatchewan.html

- Genealogy Resources on the Internet: Saskatchewan
  http://www-personal.umich.edu/~cgaunt/canada.html#SASK

- J-GEMS - The Jewish Genealogical Exploration Guide for Manitoba and Saskatchewan
  http://www.concentric.net/~lkessler/jgems.shtml

- St. Joseph's Colony
  http://www.rootsweb.com/~skstjose/stjoseph.html

- Saskatchewan Genealogical Tips
  http://homepages.rootsweb.com/~canada/sask.htm

- Saskatchewan Yellow Pages
  http://www.saskyellowpages.com/
  - Residential Search
    http://www2.saskyellowpages.com/
  - Business Search
    http://www.saskyellowpages.com/search/main.cgi

◆ Government & Cities

- City of Regina - Regina's Heritage Index
  http://www.cityregina.com/info/heritage/index.shtml

- Government of Saskatchewan
  http://www.gov.sk.ca/default.htm

- Yahoo! Canada....Saskatchewan: Cities
  http://ca.yahoo.com/regional/countries/canada/provinces_and_territories/saskatchewan/cities/

◆ Libraries, Archives & Museums

- Canadian Archival Resources on the Internet - Saskatchewan
  http://www.usask.ca/archives/car/skmenu.html

- The Canadian Library Index - Saskatchewan
  http://www.lights.com/canlib/canlibsk.html

- CCA Directory of Archives for Saskatchewan
  http://www.cdncouncilarchives.ca/cca_dir/sask.html

- City of Saskatoon Archives
  http://www.city.saskatoon.sk.ca/cityhall/clerk/archives/archives.htm

- Family History Library Catalog
  http://www.familysearch.org/Search/searchcatalog.asp
  From the FamilySearch web site, an online catalog to the holdings of the LDS Church in Salt Lake City, Utah. Also search for other localities by place name.
  http://www.familysearch.org/fhlc/supermainframeset.asp?display=localitysearch&columns=*,180,0
  - Canada
    http://www.familysearch.org/fhlc/supermainframeset.asp?display=localitydetails&subject=299&subject_disp=Canada&columns=*,180,0
    - Saskatchewan
      http://www.familysearch.org/fhlc/supermainframeset.asp?display=localitydetails&subject=302&subject_disp=Saskatchewan&columns=*,180,0

- Family History SourceGuide - Family History Centers - Canada
  http://www.familysearch.org/sg/Canada_FHC.html

- FamilySearch - Family History Centers in Saskatchewan
  http://www.familysearch.org/Browse/Places/FHC_RESULTS.ASP?FHCCountry=&FHCStateProv=Saskatchewan&FHCCounty=&FHCCity=&Submit=Search
  A list of local LDS Family History Centers along with addresses and hours of operation.

- The Hudson's Bay Company Archives
  http://www.gov.mb.ca/chc/archives/hbca/index.html
  From the Provincial Archives of Manitoba, Canada.

- HYTELNET Library Catalogs: Canada: Saskatchewan
  http://www.lights.com/hytelnet/ca0/SK.html
  Before you use any of the Telnet links, make note of the user name, password and any other logon information.

- The National Archives of Canada / Archives Nationales du Canada
  http://www.archives.ca/
  o Genealogy Research
    http://www.archives.ca/exec/naweb.dll?fs&020202&e&top&0

- National Library of Canada / Bibliothèque nationale du Canada
  http://www.nlc-bnc.ca/
  o Genealogy and Family History at the National Library of Canada
    http://www.nlc-bnc.ca/services/genealogy/gnlogy-e.htm
  o National Library Catalogue
    http://www.nlc-bnc.ca/amicus/ecatalog.htm

- Regina Public Library
  http://rpl.regina.sk.ca/

- Saskatchewan Archives Board
  http://www.gov.sk.ca/govt/archives/
  The Saskatchewan Archives Board serves as the official repository of provincial and municipal governments. The Archives acquires and preserves non-current records having historical value from all government institutions including departments, boards, committees, crown corporations, court houses, and royal commissions. Dating back to the Territorial Period, these records contain a wealth of information on the evolution and administration of government policies. Of special interest are the Saskatchewan homestead records, a source frequently consulted by local and family historians. In addition, the Archives acquires historical records of municipal offices, school districts (except student attendance records), and conservation areas.

- Saskatchewan Provincial Library
  http://www.lib.sk.ca/provlib/provlib.htm

- Saskatoon Public Library
  http://www.publib.saskatoon.sk.ca/

- United Church of Canada Archives Network: Saskatchewan Conference Archives
  http://www.uccan.org/archives/saskatchewan.htm
  A summary of their holdings and contact information.

- University of Saskatchewan - Department of History
  http://www.usask.ca/history/

◆ Mailing Lists, Newsgroups & Chat

- CANADIAN ROOTS Mailing List
  http://www.rootsweb.com/~jfuller/gen_mail_country-can.html#CANADIAN-ROOTS

- CAN-SASKATCHEWAN Mailing List
  http://www.rootsweb.com/~jfuller/gen_mail_country-can.html#CAN-SASKATCHEWAN

- saskatchewan Mailing List
  http://www.rootsweb.com/~jfuller/gen_mail_country-can.html#SASKATCHEWAN-CANADA

- St. Joseph's Colony Mailing List
  http://www.onelist.com/subscribe.cgi/stjosephs
  For the area of St. Joseph's Colony near Unity/Wilkie Saskatchewan.

- SURNAMES-CANADA Mailing List
  http://www.rootsweb.com/~jfuller/gen_mail_country-can.html#SURNAMES-CANADA
  Gatewayed with the soc.genealogy.surnames.Canada newsgroup.
  news:soc.genealogy.surnames.canada
  For surname queries related to Canada.

◆ Maps, Gazetteers & Geographical Information

- Canadian Geographical Names / Les noms géographiques du Canada
  http://GeoNames.NRCan.gc.ca/
  o Canadian Geographical Names - Publications
    http://GeoNames.NRCan.gc.ca/english/publications.html
    List of available publications on geographical names including policy documents and manuals, gazetteers, glossaries, newsletters and brochures.
  o Origins of Canada's Geographical Names
    http://GeoNames.NRCan.gc.ca/english/schoolnet/origin.html
  o Querying Canadian Geographical Names:
    • Query by Geographical Name
      http://Geonames.NRCan.gc.ca/english/cgndb.html
      Current Names Selected by Coordinates
      http://Geonames.NRCan.gc.ca/english/cgndb_coord.html
      Search this database of over 500,000 geographical names by name, feature type, region and by province

- Excite Maps: Saskatchewan
  http://maps.excite.com/view/?mapurl=/countries/canada/saskatchewan

◆ Military

- Canada - Military
  http://www.CyndisList.com/milcan.htm
  See this category on Cyndi's List for related links.

- Saskatchewan's War Memorials
  http://www.stemnet.nf.ca/monuments/sk.htm
  A project to preserve information about War Memorials throughout Canada on the World Wide Web. The descriptions of these individual cenotaphs often includes names and other information on the dead which can be of interest to the genealogist.

◆ Newspapers

- AJR NewsLink - Saskatchewan Newspapers
  http://ajr.newslink.org/nonusnsas.html

- E&P Media Links - Newspaper Sites in Saskatchewan
  http://emedia1.mediainfo.com/emedia/results.htm?region=canada&abbreviation=saskatchewan++++++++++++++++++++++++++++&category=newspaper

- Leader-Post Online ~ Regina
  http://207.195.66.66/cgi-bin/Livelque.acgi$sch=frontpage?frontpage

- NewsDirectory.com: Newspapers: North America: Canada: Saskatchewan
  http://www.newsdirectory.com/news/press/na/ca/sk/

- Prince Albert Daily Herald Online Edition
  http://www.paherald.sk.ca/home.html

- The StarPhoenix Online ~ Saskatoon
  http://www.saskstar.sk.ca/

◆ People & Families

- Doukhobor Home Page
  http://www.dlcwest.com/~r.androsoff/index.htm
  A group of Russian peasants that split from the Russian Orthodox Church. Large groups of Doukhobors emigrated to Canada and homesteaded in Saskatchewan and British Columbia.

- The Doukhobors in Canada: a select bibliography
  http://library.usask.ca/SPCOL/doukhobor.html

- Germans from Russia
  http://www.CyndisList.com/germruss.htm
  See this category on Cyndi's List for related links.

- Hutterite Genealogy HomePage and Cross-Index
  http://feefhs.org/hut/indexhut.html

- The Jewish Genealogical Exploration Guide for Manitoba and Saskatchewan (J-GEMS)
  http://www.concentric.net/~Lkessler/jgems.shtml

- Tribes and Bands of Saskatchewan
  http://www.hanksville.org/sand/contacts/tribal/SK.html

◆ Professional Researchers, Volunteers & Other Research Services

- Gen-Find Research Associates
  http://www.gen-find.com/

Specialists in Genealogy Research for Ontario & Western Canada, Scotland, Ireland. Also the rest of Canada and Forensic & Probate/Heir Research and 20th Century Research.

◆ Publications, Software & Supplies

- Amazon.com Genealogy Bookstore - Saskatchewan
  http://www.amazon.com/exec/obidos/external-search/?keyword=Saskatchewan+genealogy&tag=markcyndis genealA/

- Books We Own - Saskatchewan
  http://www.rootsweb.com/~bwo/can_sas.html
  Find a book from which you would like a lookup and click on the submitter's code at the end of the entry. Once you find the contact information for the submitter, write them a polite request for a lookup.

- Canadian Plains Studies (CPS)
  http://www.cprc.uregina.ca/studies/studies.html
  Monographs, biographies and edited proceedings and documents.

- Global Genealogical Supply - Western Canada Genealogical & Local History Books
  http://www.globalgenealogy.com/cdawest.htm

- Interlink Bookshop Genealogical Services ~ Victoria, B.C., Canada
  http://www.interlinkbookshop.com/

- Quintin Publications - Saskatchewan
  http://www.quintinpublications.com/sk.html

◆ Queries, Message Boards & Surname Lists

- RootsWeb Surname List - RSL Saskatchewan
  http://rsl.rootsweb.com/cgi-bin/rslsql.cgi
  The RSL and this form concept & design are courtesy of Karen Isaacson

◆ Records: Census, Cemeteries, Land, Obituaries, Personal, Taxes and Vital (Born, Married, Died & Buried)

- Alberta Family Histories Society (AFHS) Genealogical Projects Registry
  http://www.afhs.ab.ca/registry/index.html
  A central registry, which provides a bibliography of genealogical projects, both online and offline, in Canada. The registry is categorized by province/territory, then by record type: births, marriage, census, deaths, and other.

  o Saskatchewan - Births
    http://www.afhs.ab.ca/registry/regsk_birth.html

  o Saskatchewan - Census
    http://www.afhs.ab.ca/registry/regsk_census.html

  o Saskatchewan - Death
    http://www.afhs.ab.ca/registry/regsk_death.html

- o Saskatchewan - Marriage
  http://www.afhs.ab.ca/registry/regsk_marr.html
- o Saskatchewan - Other
  http://www.afhs.ab.ca/registry/regsk_other.html
- City of Saskatoon: Woodlawn Cemetery
  http://www.city.saskatoon.sk.ca/departments/public_works/
  cemetery/default.htm
  - o The Nutana Cemetery - Saskatoon's Pioneer
    Cemetery
    http://www.city.saskatoon.sk.ca/departments/public_
    works/cemetery/nutana/nutana1.htm
- Kamsack GenWeb Project - Rural Municipality of
  Hazel Dell No.335 Cemetery Locations, Names and
  Contact Persons ~ Saskatchewan, Canada
  http://www.rootsweb.com/~skkamsac/RMHazelDell.html
- Mennonite Historical Society of Saskatchewan Inc.
  - Saskatchewan Mennonite Cemetery Finding Aid
  http://freepages.genealogy.rootsweb.com/~skmhss/
- National Archives of Canada - Dominion Land
  Grants
  http://www.archives.ca/exec/naweb.dll?fs&020111&e
  &top&0
  *Database of grants issued in Manitoba, Saskatchewan, Alberta
  and the railway belt of British Columbia, c. 1870-1930.*
- Prairie Epitaph - Catholic Cemetery in Salvador,
  Saskatchewan
  http://mars.ark.com/~rbell/html/history/epitaph.html
  Many German Russian families.
- Saskatchewan Cemetery Index
  http://www.saskgenealogy.com/cemetery/cemetery.htm

- Saskatchewan's Transcribed Cemeteries on the
  Internet
  http://homepages.rootsweb.com/~canada/sask/
  cemetery.htm
- Southeast Saskatchewan Cemetery Records
  http://cap.estevan.sk.ca/cemetery.records/
  *This has listing of the burials in several cemeteries in and around
  Estevan, Saskatchewan.*

◆ Religion & Churches

- Christianity Online Church Locator - Churches in
  Saskatchewan
  http://www.christianity.net/churchlocator/location.php?
  country=Canada&state=Ontario

◆ Societies & Groups

- IOOF Lodge Website Directory - Saskatchewan
  http://norm28.hsc.usc.edu/IOOF/International/
  Saskatchewan.html
  Independent Order of Odd Fellows and Rebekahs.
- Saskatchewan Council of Archives
  http://www.usask.ca/archives/sca/sca.html
- Saskatchewan Genealogical Society
  http://www.saskgenealogy.com/
- Saskatoon Branch SGS
  http://www.rootsweb.com/~sksgs/
  Branch of the Saskatchewan Genealogical Society.
- Society Hill: Saskatchewan Societies
  http://www.daddezio.com/society/hill.ca/SH-SK-NDX.html
  *A list of addresses for genealogical and historical societies in the
  province.*

CANALS, RIVERS & WATERWAYS

http://www.cyndislist.com/canals.htm

Category Index:

◆ General Resource Sites
◆ Libraries, Archives & Museums
◆ Locality Specific
◆ Societies & Groups

◆ General Resource Sites

- An American Rivers Bibliography
  http://www.coe.wvu.edu/~venable/asa/miss-bib.htm

- AudioTapes.com - Genealogical Lectures on Cassette Tapes
  - Canal
    http://www.audiotapes.com/search2.asp?Search=canal
  - River
    http://www.audiotapes.com/search2.asp?Search=river
  - Waterway
    http://www.audiotapes.com/search2.asp?Search=waterway

- CANAL-PEOPLE Mailing List
  http://www.rootsweb.com/~jfuller/gen_mail_general.html
  #CANAL-PEOPLE
  For anyone with a genealogical interest in canal workers and barge owners.

- Canals and Inland Waterways of the United States
  http://www.coe.wvu.edu/~venable/asa/am-rivr.htm

- Historic Canals Policy
  http://Parkscanada.pch.gc.ca/library/PC_Guiding_Principles/
  Park108_e.htm
  From Parks Canada Guiding Principles and Operational Policies.

◆ Libraries, Archives & Museums

- Center for Columbia River History ~ Washington state
  http://www.ccrh.org/content.htm

- Guide to New York State Canal Records
  http://www.sara.nysed.gov/holding/aids/canal/content.htm
  The NYS Archives maintains this site which describes 360 series of records documenting New York's canals from the earliest Erie Canal surveys to the completion and operation of the Barge Canal.

- London Canal Museum ~ England
  http://www.charitynet.org/~LCanalMus/

- National Canal Museum ~ Easton, Pennsylvania
  http://www.canals.org/

- The National Waterways Museum at Gloucester ~ England
  http://www.nwm.org.uk/

◆ Locality Specific

- The Black & White - A Short History of the Lancaster Canal 1772-1997
  http://stop.at/canalcaholic
  History of the Lancaster Canal, England, from its beginnings in 1772 to the present day.

- The Chesapeake & Ohio Canal
  http://www.fred.net/kathy/canal.html

- Chesapeake and Ohio Canal National Historical Park
  http://www.nps.gov/choh/co_visit.htm

- A Comprehensive Listing of Ohio Canals and Their Feeders
  http://www.geocities.com/Heartland/Prairie/6687/list.htm

- Delaware and Hudson Canal within Upper Delaware Scenic and Recreational River
  http://www.nps.gov/upde/d&hcanal.htm

- Erie Canal Online ~ Syracuse, New York
  http://www.syracuse.com/features/eriecanal/

- From the Coalfields to the Hudson : A History of the Delaware & Hudson Canal
  http://www.amazon.com/exec/obidos/ISBN=0935796851/
  markcyndisgenealA/
  A book by Larry Lowenthal.

- History of the Erie Canal
  http://www.history.rochester.edu/canal/index.htm

- The History of the New York State Canal System
  http://www.canals.state.ny.us/history/index.html
  A short history of the NYS Canal System. This site is exclusively for information on the current-day canal system has no other historical information, and NO information about canal workers, passengers or boaters.

- The Little Falls Canal ~ New York
  http://www.nysm.nysed.gov/hislittlefallscanal.html

- New York's Oldest Canal
  http://www.nysm.nysed.gov/history/neck/index.html

- Ohio and Erie Canal National Heritage Corridor
  http://www.uakron.edu:80/bustech/canal/mainmenu.html

- Ohio Canal Corridor
  http://www.ohiocanal.org/

- Ohio's Historic Canals
  http://my.ohio.voyager.net/~lstevens/canal/

- Rideau Canal Waterway
  http://www.rideau-info.com/canal/

- Save Buffalo's Canal District ~ New York
  http://members.tripod.com/~wnyroots/index-canal.html
  Support the reestablishment of the Commercial Slip and the historic street network of Buffalo's Canal District. We also support designation of the area as a National Historic Landmark.

- Wabash & Erie Canal through Huntington County, Indiana
  http://user.ctlnet.com/jjosh/

◆ Societies & Groups

- American Canal Society
  http://www.canals.com/ACS/acs.html

- Arkansas River Historical Society Museum ~ Catoosa, Oklahoma
  http://www.tulsaweb.com/port/
  The Society seeks to preserve the history and increase public awareness of the Arkansas River and the development of its basin.

- The Canadian Canal Society / Société des Canaux du Canada
  http://people.becon.org/~ccs/

- Canal Corridor Association
  http://www.canalcor.org/
  The Illinois & Michigan Canal Corridor.

- Canal Society of New Jersey
  http://www.canalsocietynj.org/

- Canal Society of Ohio
  http://my.ohio.voyager.net/~lstevens/canal/csoo/

- Cotswold Canals Trust
  http://www.cotswoldcanals.mcmail.com/
  Restoring the Stroudwater Navigation and Thames & Severn Canal in England.

- Friends of the Delaware Canal ~ Pennsylvania
  http://www.fodc.org/

- Friends of the Trent-Severn Waterway
  http://www.ptbo.igs.net/~ftsw/

- The Railway & Canal Historical Society ~ England
  http://www.bodley.ox.ac.uk/external/rchs/index.html

- Virginia Canals & Navigations Society
  http://organizations.rockbridge.net/canal/

CATHOLIC
http://www.cyndislist.com/catholic.htm

Category Index:
- General Resource Sites
- Libraries, Archives & Museums
- Locality Specific
- Publications, Software & Supplies
- Societies & Groups

◆ General Resource Sites

- Catholic Calendar Page
  http://www.easterbrooks.com/personal/calendar/index.html

- The Hall of Church History - The Catholics
  http://www.gty.org/~phil/catholic.htm
  An interesting site with definitions, descriptions and links to a variety of resources for each religious group it highlights

- Local Catholic Church History and Genealogy Research Guide and Worldwide Directory
  http://home.att.net/~Local_Catholic/
  Research Guide to Local Catholic Church Archdiocese, Diocese and Parishes, History, Biographies and Genealogy information and links Worldwide for both Roman and Eastern Rite.

◆ Libraries, Archives & Museums

- Archdiocese of Atlanta - Archives and History
  http://www.archatl.com/archives.htm
  The Archives of the Archdiocese of Atlanta is the repository for official records of the archdiocese which are to be retained permanently for historical or legal purposes or because they are vital records. Included are records of administration and of curial, parochial, institutional, and confraternity groups in existence currently as well as those which have ceased to exist or which may be created in the future.

- The Archdiocese of Baltimore, Maryland
  http://www.archbalt.org/index.html

  o Archdiocesan Archives - Archdiocese of Baltimore
    http://www.archbalt.org/archdiocese/archives.html
    Provides contact information.

  o Archdiocese of Baltimore - Our Historic Legacy
    http://www.archbalt.org/history/index.html

  o Parishes of the Archdiocese of Baltimore
    http://www.archbalt.org/parishes/parish_list.htm
    Includes information on defunct parishes and where their records are now held.

- The Archdiocese of Chicago's Joseph Cardinal Bernardin Archives & Records Center
  http://www.uschs.com/uscatholic/archives/chicago/home.htm
  The Archdiocese of Chicago's Joseph Cardinal Bernardin Archives & Records Center, with more than 8,000 cubic feet of archival materials, constitutes one of the world's largest repositories of Archdiocesan Archives.

- Archdiocese of Cincinnati - Archives
  http://www.archdiocese-cinti.org/admin/archives.htm
  The Historical Archives of the Chancery maintains a master set of Catholic sacramental records, on microfiche, for the nineteen (19) county area of Southwestern Ohio over which the Archdiocese of Cincinnati currently presides. However, these records are not opened to the general public, and may only be handled by authorized personnel.

- Archidiecezja Pozna–ska
  http://www.archpoznan.org.pl/default.htm
  The Catholic Archdiocese of Poznan Poland has significant information for genealogists. Although most of it is in Polish, it is easy to make out some parts of it. Under "Archiwum Archidiecezjalno" find the address, phone and email for the Archdiocesan Archives which lists all the Catholic churches for which it has baptism, marriage and death records with years included. At bottom of the Archives Homepage find a British map for an English version. Under "Dekanatow i parafii A.P." find a map of the Archdiocese divided into deaconates with the names of all the present Catholic churches listed by the towns where they are located.

- Archives and Records - Diocese of San Jose ~ California
  http://www.dsj.org/records/recordsdsj.htm
  Contact information only.

- Archives of the University of Notre Dame ~ Indiana
  http://www.nd.edu:80/~archives/

  o Catholic Newspapers in Microform: A Directory of Works at Notre Dame
    http://www.nd.edu/~archives/cathnews/

  o Notre Dame Parish Histories
    http://archives1.archives.nd.edu/PARISHES.HTM

  o University Libraries of Notre Dame
    http://www.nd.edu/~ndlibs/

  o University of Notre Dame Archives Guide
    http://archives1.archives.nd.edu/guidecon.htm

- Catholic Diocese of St. Augustine - Archives
  http://diocesestaug.org/
  The archives offers protection for the permanent records of diocesan offices and ministries, parishes, organizations, schools and other institutions. Collected in a central information repository they are available (with restrictions) for reference and research. Here also are maintained the Episcopal archives of the diocese (1857-1967)

and original Cathedral-Basilica Parish registers of St. Augustine (1594-1881). The archives also handles requests for genealogical research and history of Catholicism in Florida.

- **The Catholic Diocese of Syracuse, New York - Diocesan Archives**
  http://www.syrdio.org/Pages/archives.htm
  Maintains archival collections of information and materials of historical value for the diocese and parishes.

- **Catholic Diocese of Wilmington (Dioecesis Vilmingtoniensis)**
  http://www.cdow.org/
  o **Diocese of Wilmington (Roman Catholic) Archives**
  http://www.archives.lib.de.us/research/dehisrec.htm#dowrc
  A description from the Delaware Public Archives web site.

- **Diocesan Archives - Fargo, North Dakota**
  http://www.fargodiocese.org/archives.htm

- **Diocese of Charleston Archives ~ Charleston, South Carolina**
  http://www.catholic-doc.org/archives/archives.html
  Holdings date from 1789 and continue to the present. The Archives include the papers of bishops, the administrative records of diocesan offices, chancery correspondence, and records of various agencies, religious orders, programs, and individuals reflecting the work and goals of the Church. In addition, we have the annual reports of parishes, parish histories, property records, deed and construction files, some architectural drawings, cemetery records, newspapers and photographs. Because individual parishes are required by Canon 535 to maintain their own archives, original registers containing sacramental records are not held in the Diocesan Archives. However, the archives often have microfilm copies of parish registers and these are available to search for sacramental records prior to 1930.

- **Diocese of Pittsburgh Archives and Records Center**
  http://www.diopitt.org/admserv/archives.htm
  The Archives collects and preserves those records of historical significance that document the history of the diocese and of Catholicism in Western Pennsylvania.

- **Genealogical Information Guide**
  http://www.uschs.com/uscatholic/archives/chicago/genealog.htm
  From the Archdiocese of Chicago's Joseph Cardinal Bernardin Archives & Records Center.

- **Leeds Diocesan Archives**
  http://www.leeds-diocese.org.uk/archives1.html
  The archives holds the papers of the Roman Catholic Church in Yorkshire, (1688-; some papers for other parts of the North of England before 1840. Hogarth MSS: 19th-century transcripts of the papers of the secular clergy in Yorkshire, 1660-).

- **Philadelphia Archdiocesan Historical Research Center (PAHRC)**
  http://www.rc.net/philadelphia/pahrc/index.html
  The PAHRC contains marriage and baptismal registers before the year 1900 for parishes presently within the Archdiocese of Philadelphia (Bucks, Chester, Delaware, Montgomery and Philadelphia Counties).

- **Searching for your Catholic Ancestors**
  http://www.diopitt.org/admserv/archiv1.htm
  From the Diocese of Pittsburgh's Archives and Records Center.

- **Seattle Archdiocesan Archives ~ Washington**
  http://www.seattlearch.org/archives/index.htm
  The archives collect, organize, preserve and make available for research records of enduring value which reflect the life and work of the Catholic Church in the Pacific Northwest.

- **U.S. Catholic Documentary Heritage Project**
  http://cf.catholic.org/uschs/index.cfm
  From the U.S. Catholic Historical Society, an online guide to repositories and collections of primary sources documenting the history of Catholicism in the United States.

◆ Locality Specific

- **Associated Catholic Cemeteries - Archdiocese of Seattle**
  http://www.acc-seattle.com/
  An official on-line database of all four Catholic cemeteries in Seattle. You search the database by surname. All names are listed by date of burial; from approx. late 1880's-today.

- **Catholic Church in England & Wales**
  http://www.tasc.ac.uk/cc/

- **Catholic Churches of Maine**
  http://members.mint.net/frenchcx/mecath1.htm

- **Catholic Diocese of Hexham and Newcastle - Map**
  http://www.christusrex.org/www1/CDHN/map.html
  Map of the Catholic provinces and dioceses of England and Wales.

- **Catholic History**
  http://www.catholic-history.org.uk/
  Links of interest for the history of Roman Catholicism in the UK.

- **Catholics of Nova Scotia in World War 1**
  http://members.tripod.com/~enlist_1/enlist.htm

- **Catholic Parish Histories**
  http://www.slcl.lib.mo.us/slcl/sc/sc-j-par.htm
  Jubilee histories in the St. Louis County Library.

- **Cincinnati Catholic Genealogy and History**
  http://www2.eos.net/dajend/catholic.html
  Historical and Genealogical Research: Roman Catholic Resources in Cincinnati and Hamilton County, Ohio. Catholic Church Resources for those researching in Hamilton County and Cincinnati, Ohio including historical information, a bibliography, and profiles of Catholic cemeteries and parishes.

- **Diocesan Sites and Webmasters - U.S. Catholic Dioceses on the Web**
  http://www.catholic-church.org/cid/usa.html

- **DioceseNet - Catholic Information Services**
  http://www.catholic.net/RCC/Diocese/dioceses.html
  Searchable directory of US Catholic dioceses.

- **Guide to Quebec Catholic Parishes and Published Parish Marriage Records**
  http://www.amazon.com/exec/obidos/ISBN=0806345705/markcyndisgenealA/
  A book by Jeanne Sauve White.

- Holy Trinity Church, Boston, Massachusetts
  http://homepages.rootsweb.com/~mvreid/bgrc/htc.html
  This site by Marge Reid has a multitude of resources for the church including the 1895 HTC Parish Directory and an HTC researchers directory, as well as many others.

- Local Catholic Church History and Genealogy Research Guide and Worldwide Directory
  http://home.att.net/~Local_Catholic/
  Research Guide to Local Catholic Church Archdiocese, Diocese and Parishes, History, Biographies and Genealogy information and links Worldwide for both Roman and Eastern Rite.

  o Africa
    http://home.att.net/~Local_Catholic/Catholic-Africa.htm

  o Australia and Oceania
    http://home.att.net/~Local_Catholic/Catholic-Australia-Oceania.htm

  o Canada
    http://home.att.net/~Local_Catholic/Catholic-Canada.htm

  o Central America
    http://home.att.net/~Local_Catholic/Catholic-CAmerica.htm

  o Europe and Asia
    http://home.att.net/~Local_Catholic/Catholic-International.htm

  o Mexico
    http://home.att.net/~Local_Catholic/Catholic-Mexico.htm

  o South America
    http://home.att.net/~Local_Catholic/Catholic-SAmerica.htm

  o United States
    http://home.att.net/~Local_Catholic/usastates.htm

- MCF-ROOTS Mailing List
  http://www.rootsweb.com/~jfuller/gen_mail_states-gen.html#MCF-ROOTS
  A mailing list (Maryland Catholics on the Frontier) for the discussion of descendants of Maryland Catholics who migrated first to Kentucky and then to other parts of the frontier.

- National Conference of Catholic Bishops/United States Catholic Conference
  http://www.nccbuscc.org/dioceses.htm

- PACATHOLICS Mailing List
  http://www.rootsweb.com/~jfuller/gen_mail_states-pa.html#PACATHOLICS
  For messages, queries, and tips for finding your Catholic ancestors that lived in Pennsylvania.

- POLHOME - Polish Catholic Parishes in USA
  http://www.polhome.com/church-p.html

- Roman Catholic Church in Poland
  http://www.ipipan.waw.pl/~klopotek/church/rcc_in_p.htm

- The Roman Catholic Diocese of Providence - Cemeteries ~ Rhode Island
  http://www.providiocese.com/info/cemeteries.html

- Society of Genealogists Bookshop - Catholic
  http://www.sog.org.uk/acatalog/SoG_Bookshop_Online_Catholics_299.html
  A source for books of interest to the family historian researching UK ancestors who were Catholic.

- St. Anthony of Padua Catholic Cemetery, Minneapolis, Minnesota, 1851-1995
  http://www.amazon.com/exec/obidos/ISBN=091570966X/markcyndisgenealA/
  A book by Mary Hawker Bakeman.

- US Catholic Dioceses Addresses
  http://www.mindspring.com/~gchung/catholic.htm
  Addresses and some websites for Catholic dioceses located in US.

- US Dioceses - Diocese Web Sites
  http://www.catholic.org/colweb/dioceses.html
  A directory from the Catholic Online web site.

- Wilmington Diocese Catholic Parish Registers ~ DE
  http://delgensoc.org/dioceswm.html
  A list of microfilm numbers for parish registers available through the LDS Family History Library and Family History Centers. Records included on the microfilm begin in 1790 for baptisms through 1920, marriage and other registers through 1960 (35 Rolls).

◆ Publications, Software & Supplies

- Amazon.com Genealogy Bookstore - Catholic
  http://www.amazon.com/exec/obidos/external-search/?keyword=catholic+genealogy&tag=markcyndisgenealA/

- AudioTapes.com - Genealogical Lectures on Cassette Tapes - Catholic
  http://www.audiotapes.com/search2.asp?Search=Catholic

◆ Societies & Groups

- Catholic Archives Society ~ UK & Ireland
  http://www.catholic-history.org.uk/catharch/

- Catholic Family History Society ~ United Kingdom
  http://www.catholic-history.org.uk/cfhs/index.htm

- Catholic Family History Society of London, England
  http://feefhs.org/uk/frg-cfhs.html

- Catholic Record Society ~ UK & Ireland
  http://www.catholic-history.org.uk/crs/index.htm

- Knights of Columbus
  http://www.kofc.org/

  o Knights of Columbus - History of the Knights
    http://www.kofc.org/kofc/knights/history/history.cfm

- Texas Catholic Historical Society
  http://www.history.swt.edu/Catholic_Southwest.htm

- United States Catholic Historical Society
  http://www.catholic.org/uschs/

CEMETERIES & FUNERAL HOMES
http://www.cyndislist.com/cemetery.htm

Category Index:

◆ General Resource Sites

◆ How To

◆ Locality Specific

◆ Mailing Lists, Newsgroups & Chat

◆ Monuments & Memorials

◆ Professional Researchers, Volunteers & Other Research Services

◆ Publications, Software & Supplies

◆ Societies & Groups

◆ General Resource Sites

● Adventures in Genealogy - Cemeteries
http://www.stategensites.com/unclehiram/cemetery.asp
A weekly genealogy column filled with tips, suggestions and hints from a humorous point of view. This column is about the loss of cemeteries.

● African American Cemeteries Online
http://www.prairiebluff.com/millenium/aacemetery/

● Cemetery Interment Lists on the Internet
http://www.interment.net/

● Cemetery Junction - The Internet Directory of Active and Retired Cemeteries
http://www.daddezio.com/cemetery/index.html

● City of the Silent
http://www.best.com/~gazissax/city.html

● Find A Grave: Noteworthy Gravesites
http://www.findagrave.com/
A listing of celebrity's gravesites.

● Funeral Homes on the Internet
http://www.funeral.net/funeral_homes_on_the_net.htm

● Funeral Net
http://www.funeralnet.com/
Funeral home directory for the U.S.

● A Guide to Cemetery Resources -- Including Databases
http://www.geneasearch.com/cemeteries.htm
Links to cemeteries information on the internet.

● Internet Cemetery / Crematoria Directory
http://www.itcanada.com/~bruce/info/ceminetdir.html

● Memorial Links
http://www.kiva.net/~markh/memorial.html

● The National Museum of Funeral History ~ Houston, Texas
http://www.nmfh.org/
Preserves historical funeral artifacts from the 19th and 20th centuries, and encourages public education about the proud heritage of funeral service.

● The Political Graveyard
http://politicalgraveyard.com/
"The Web Site That Tells Where the Dead Politicians are Buried".

● Preserving Cemeteries
http://www.gov.on.ca/MCZCR/english/culdiv/heritage/cemetery.htm
From the Ontario Ministry of Citizenship, Culture, and Recreation. Includes a description of the issues, discussion of applicable laws, and offers a technical manual for sale on how to repair tombstones.

● Records Room: Cemetery Records Online
http://daddezio.com/records/vital/interment.html

● World Wide Cemetery
http://www.cemetery.org/
A place for Internet users to erect permanent monuments to the dead.

● Yahoo!...Cemeteries
http://dir.yahoo.com/Society_and_Culture/Death_and_Dying/End_of_Life_Issues/Funeral_Services/Cemeteries/

● Yahoo!...Funeral Homes
http://dir.yahoo.com/Business_and_Economy/Companies/Funerals/Funeral_Homes/

◆ How To

● All About Cemeteries and Funeral Homes
http://www.familytreemaker.com/00000049.html

● The Case of the Unreadable Tombstone
http://www.sierra.com/sierrahome/familytree/hqarticles/tombstone/
An online article by Brian E. Michaels describing his quest to decipher odd words found on an ancestor's headstone.

● The Cemetery Column - A Tombstone in Your Palm
http://www.interment.net/column/records/palmpilot/index.htm
An article by Steve Paul Johnson about using your Palm Pilot to record tombstone details in a database.

● Cemetery Research and Gravestone Rubbings...a How To, Site
http://www.angelfire.com/ut/gmachoocho/cemetery411.html
How to research cemeteries, care for tombstones and photograph the stones.

- Cemetery Studies
  http://www.angelfire.com/ky2/cemetery
  Pictures of Spring Grove Cemetery in Cincinnati Ohio and lesson plans for students.

- CGN Cemetery Do's & Don'ts
  http://members.aol.com/ctgravenet/dosdonts.htm
  Includes: Cleaning Basics, Graveyard Maintenance, Gravestone Rubbings, Reading Inscriptions, Should You Seal or Waterproof Gravestones?

- Everything you wanted to know about Gravestone Studies and Rubbing
  http://www.justcallbob.com/grave.html

- Finding a Burial Place in Cemeteries or Cemetery Records
  http://www.familytreemaker.com/00000480.html

- Finding a Death Date in Cemeteries or Cemetery Records
  http://www.familytreemaker.com/00000442.html

- Finding the Hidden Treasures in Tombstone Rubbings
  http://www.firstct.com/fv/t_examp.html

- Frontier Press Bookstore - Cemetery Research / Preservation
  http://www.frontierpress.com/frontier.cgi?category=ceme

- Graven Images
  http://olivetreegenealogy.com/misc/grave.htm
  Describes the symbolism of motifs on gravestones - from The Olive Tree.

- The Gravestone Gallery: Cemetery Curiosities and Tombstone Tributes -- Then, Today and Tomorrow
  http://members.aol.com/fmosconi/article.html
  An article for new and experienced roots-seekers, accompanied by a photo tour that is being expanded regularly, on the role of cemeteries in genealogical research and in our culture.

- A Gravestone Rubbing Primer
  http://www.savinggraves.com/rubbings.htm
  A primer on the art of gravestone rubbings.

- How to Read A Graveyard
  http://www.dohistory.org/on_your_own/toolkit/graveyards.html
  From DoHistory.

- How to do Tombstone Rubbings
  http://www.amberskyline.com/treasuremaps/t_stone.htm

- International Black Sheep Society / Grave Marker Acronyms
  http://homepages.rootsweb.com/~blksheep/acronym.html

- The Joy of Cemeteries
  http://www.sierra.com/sierrahome/familytree/hqarticles/cemeteries/
  Online article by Cathy Wood Osborn introducing cemetery research.

- Locating Cemeteries and Cemetery Records
  http://www.familytreemaker.com/00000050.html

- Planning & Architectural Services - Cemetery Protection
  http://www.preserveala.org/cemetery.html
  Cleaning Gravestones: Use the Gentlest Means Possible, by Camille Bowman.

- Recording Cemeteries with Digital Photography
  http://www.interment.net/column/records/digital/digital.htm
  From the Cemetery Column.

- Researching and Recording Civil War Veterans Burials in Michigan Cemeteries
  http://www.centuryinter.net/suvcw.mi/gr-recgv.html

- Standards for Transcribing Cemetery Headstones
  ftp://ftp.rootsweb.com/pub/roots-l/genealog/genealog.headston

- Tips for Photographing Gravestones
  http://www.genealogy.com/64_gravestones.html

- Tombstone Meanings
  http://homepages.rootsweb.com/~maggieoh/tomb.html

- Tombstone Rubbings
  http://www.firstct.com/fv/t_stone.html

◆ Locality Specific

"A"

- Abel's Hill Cemetery, Chilmark, MA - Photos and Transcripts ~ Massachusetts
  http://www.vineyard.net/vineyard/history/cemetery/ah/index.html
  Photographs, transcripts, and biographical information on 18th century gravestones at Abel's Hill Cemetery in Chilmark, Dukes Co. Mass. on the island of Martha's Vineyard.

- Abney Park Cemetery Trust ~ London, England
  http://www.abney-park.org.uk/

- Addison Township Cemetery Index ~ Du Page County, Illinois
  http://www.dcgs.org/addison/

- Alberta Genealogical Society Master Name Index ~ Canada
  http://www.compusmart.ab.ca/abgensoc/nameindex.html
  A database of about 400,000 names, including mostly cemetery records and tombstone inscriptions. They can search the database for a small fee.

- Alexandra's Family Tree House - Western North Carolina Cemeteries
  http://www.rootsquest.com/~alextree/cemetery/

- Alhambra Cemetery ~ Martinez, California
  http://www.katpher.com/conscty/conscalhcem.html

- Allen County, Ohio Cemetery Page
  http://www.geocities.com/Heartland/Plains/5409/cem.html
  From The GIERHART Family Inn.

- Allendale / Bamberg / Barnwell County Cemeteries ~ *South Carolina*
  http://www.rootsweb.com/~scbarnwe/Cemeteries.htm

- Amador County's Pioneer Cemeteries ~ California
  http://www.maui.net/~mauifun/amador.htm

- Anhart Cemetery, Purdy, MO, Barry Co ~ Missouri
  http://www.geocities.com/Heartland/Farm/3150/
  arnhart2.htm

- The Apache Cemetery, at Apache, Cochise County, Arizona
  http://www.amug.org/~mzwhiz/cemetery.html

- Aquia Church Page - Aquia Cemetery Graveyard Listing
  http://www.aquiachurch.com/GraveYard.html
  Cemetery listing of Aquia Episcopal Church, Stafford, Virginia (Stafford County). Includes cemetery locations and map.

- Arlington National Cemetery
  http://www.arlingtoncemetery.com/

- Arlington National Cemetery
  http://www.mdw.army.mil/cemetery.htm
  General information and a map.

- Associated Catholic Cemeteries - Archdiocese of Seattle ~ Washington
  http://www.acc-seattle.com/
  An official on-line database of all four Catholic cemeteries in Seattle. You search the database by surname. All names are listed by date of burial; from approx. late 1880's-today.

- Autauga County, Alabama Cemetery Listings
  http://searches.rootsweb.com/cgi-bin/autauga/auta-cem.pl

"B"

- Bachman Funeral Home
  http://www.bachmanfuneral.com/
  In Strasburg, Pennsylvania, established 1769, this is the oldest family-owned funeral home in America.

- Barber Corners Quaker Cemetery
  http://www.rootsweb.com/~nycayuga/cem/cem86.htm
  Town of Ledyard, New York.

- Beauregard Parish Cemeteries
  http://www.beaulib.dtx.net/~cemetery/CEMETERY.HTM
  From the Lady Cemetery Hoppers of Louisiana.

- Beaton Cemetery, Millbrook, Pictou County ~ Nova Scotia, Canada
  http://www.rootsweb.com/~pictou/beaton.htm

- Becker County, Minnesota, Cemeteries
  http://www.rootsweb.com/~mnbecker/cemeteries.htm
  List of cemeteries in Becker County, Minnesota with links to GNIS which gives location and online map.

- Black River Cemetery, Pictou County ~ Nova Scotia, Canada
  http://www.rootsweb.com/~pictou/blackriv.htm

- Blanchard Road Cemetery, Pictou County ~ Nova Scotia, Canada
  http://www.rootsweb.com/~pictou/blanch.htm

- Books for Sale : Douglas County, Missouri
  http://members.aol.com/LaineBelle/HomePage.html
  Cemetery Survey of the Eastern District of Douglas County, Missouri; Death Notices Abstracted from The Douglas County Herald, 1887-1910.

- Boren-Reagor Springs Cemetery ~ Texas
  http://www.geocities.com/Heartland/Prairie/1746/
  boren.html
  The Boren-Reagor Springs Cemetery page has biographical information on individuals buried in the cemetery with a completed listing of all who are buried there. Links included to Civil War History of those buried in the cemetery and of other Boren descendants. Also included in the history of the Lee-Peacock Feud.

- Boston Area Cemeteries
  http://www.mindspring.com/~gchung/cemetery.htm
  Addresses of cemeteries located in Suffolk County, Massachusetts.

- British Columbia Cemetery Finding Aid ~ Canada
  http://www.islandnet.com/bccfa/homepage.html

- Brookville Cemetery, Pictou County ~ Nova Scotia, Canada
  http://www.rootsweb.com/~pictou/brookvll.htm

- Brown Co. IL Bell-Perry Cemeteries
  http://www.geocities.com/Heartland/Valley/7991/
  b_p_cems.html

- Bunker Cemetery at Morenci, Arizona
  http://www.rootsweb.com/~azgreenl/grbunker.html

- Burial Point Cemetery, Merigomish ~ Nova Scotia, Canada
  http://www.rootsweb.com/~pictou/bpoint.htm

- Burials of Easton, Plainfield, Mount Bethel, Forks and Dryland ~ Pennsylvania
  http://www.geocities.com/Heartland/6508/#Burials of
  Easton,Plainfield,Mount Bethel,Forks and Dryland

- Burials in Sirajganj, Bangladesh
  http://www.ozemail.com.au/~clday/sirajganj.htm

"C"

- California's Calaveras County Cemeteries
  http://www.angelfire.com/ca2/cemeterykid/
  Includes a partial list of persons buried in the San Andreas, Calaveras County, California, Saint Andrews Catholic Cemetery from 1857 to present.

- Calvary Cemetery St. Louis, Mo KASSEL Surnames ~ Missouri
  http://www.alltel.net/~ps53630/kassellcalvary.html
  Interments: CASSELL / KASSEL / KASSELL surnames.

- Camden and Charlton County Cemetery Records Online ~ Georgia
  http://www.camdencounty.org/gene/cemetery/

- Camp Moore Confederate Cemetery and Museum
  http://home.gulfsouth.verio.net/~harper1/

- Camrose County GenWeb - The Cemetery List ~ Alberta, Canada
  http://www.rootsweb.com/~abcamros/toppage2.htm
  #THE CEMETERY LIST

- Canadian Funeral Home Directory
  http://www.generations.on.ca/funeral.htm

- Canadian Genealogy and History Links - Cemetery - Obituary
  http://www.islandnet.com/~jveinot/cghl/cemetery.html

- Carroll County Arkansas Cemetery Listings
  http://www.rootsweb.com/~arcchs/hscemlst.html
  Tombscriptions of over 50 cemeteries, along with a surname index to these cemeteries hosted by the Carroll County Historical Society.

- Carter County Missouri Cemeteries
  http://www.rootsweb.com/~mocarter/cemetry.htm

  o Aldrich Valley Cemetery
    http://www.rootsweb.com/~mocarter/aldrich.htm

  o Brame Cemetery
    http://www.rootsweb.com/~mocarter/brame.htm

  o Bristol Cemetery
    http://www.rootsweb.com/~mocarter/bristol.htm

  o Eastwood Cemetery
    http://www.rootsweb.com/~mocarter/eastwood.htm

  o Midco Cemtery
    http://www.rootsweb.com/~mocarter/midco.htm

  o Seats Family Cemetery
    http://www.rootsweb.com/~mocarter/seatscmt.htm

- Cascade County Montana Cemetery Index ~ Cascade County
  http://www.rootsweb.com/~mtcascad/Cemetery/cemet.html

- Cave Creek Cemetery
  http://personal.riverusers.com/~keyserroll/cavecreek cem.html
  A partial tombstone listing with photographs of tombstones, located in Fredericksburg, Gillespie County, Texas.

- Cayuga County, NYGenWeb Project Cemetery List
  http://www.rootsweb.com/~nycayuga/cemetery.htm

- Cemeteries
  http://www.totentanz.de/cemetery.htm
  Formerly titled World Wide Index of Cemeteries on the Net

  o Cemeteries in Africa
    http://www.totentanz.de/africa.htm

  o Cemeteries in Asia
    http://www.totentanz.de/asia.htm

  o Cemeteries in Australia
    http://www.totentanz.de/australi.htm

  o Cemeteries in America
    http://www.totentanz.de/america.htm

  o Cemeteries in Europe
    http://www.totentanz.de/europe.htm

  o US Cemeteries
    http://www.totentanz.de/usa.htm

- Cemeteries
  http://www.geocities.com/Heartland/Acres/4348/cemeteries.html
  Two abandoned cemeteries in Cabell County and Wayne County, West Virginia.

- Cemeteries, Graveyards, Burying Grounds
  http://www.potifos.com/cemeteries.html
  Links to resources on cemetery history and preservation.

- Cemeteries in and around Gunning Shire, New South Wales ~ Australia
  http://www.pcug.org.au/~gchallin/cemeteries/top.htm

- Cemeteries in Onondaga County, New York
  http://www.rootsweb.com/~nyononda/CEMETERY.HTM

- Cemeteries: LaPorte County - Michigan City Public Library
  http://www.mclib.org/cemlpco.htm
  Cemetery list with location information.

- Cemeteries Listed on the U.S. Civil War Center Web Page
  http://www.cwc.lsu.edu/cwc/links/hist.htm#Cemeteries

- The Cemeteries of Chautauqua County, NY
  http://www.rootsweb.com/~nychauta/CEMETERY/TOWN_CEM.HTM

- Cemeteries of Delaware County, NY ~ Delaware County, New York
  http://www.rootsweb.com/~nydelawa/cemeter2.html

- Cemeteries of Florida
  http://users.quadra.net/cemetery/

- Cemeteries of Logan Co., Kentucky
  http://geocities.com/scarred40/logancem.html
  Includes individual tombstone pictures.

- Cemeteries of Martha's Vineyard ~ Massachusetts
  http://www.vineyard.net/vineyard/history/cemetery/cemlist.htm
  Links to photographs, transcripts, and notes on gravestones at Company Place Cemetery, West Chop Cemetery, Christiantown, and other sites on Martha's Vineyard.

- Cemeteries of Monroe Co., MI ~ Michigan
  http://206.42.132.11/havekost/cemetery.htm

- Cemeteries of Orleans County, New York
  http://www.rootsweb.com/~nyorlean/cemetery.htm

- Cemeteries of Pictou County ~ Nova Scotia, Canada
  http://www.rootsweb.com/~pictou/oldest.htm
  Excerpted from "The Stone Book of Pictou County" by Donald Nicholson. The statistics are listed by cemetery, including the oldest birth year, oldest death year, oldest age at death.

- Cemeteries of Pleasanton and Dublin, California ~ California
  http://www.l-ags.org/cemtitle.html

- Cemeteries of Republic County, Kansas
  http://skyways.lib.ks.us/genweb/republic/Swedish/CemList.html

Names of those buried at Maple Grove Cemetery in Albion Township; Rose Hill Cemetery (Swedish Cemetery) and Union Cemetery in Grant Township; all in Republic County, KS.

- The Cemeteries of Rutherford County, NC
  http://rfci.net/wdfloyd/

- Cemeteries of Tallahatchie County Mississippi
  http://www.rootsweb.com/~mstallah/cemeteries/index.html

- Cemeteries of the United States
  http://www.gac.edu/~kengelha/usframe.html
  List of cemeteries state by state, county by county.

- Cemeteries of Warren County, Kentucky Page
  http://geocities.com/scarred40/warrencem.html

- Cemeteries Online!
  http://martin.simplenet.com/Cemeteries/
  Database of cemeteries in south-eastern and south-central Pennsylvania.

- Cemetery Headstone Transcriptions
  http://www.icubed.com/~ldill/cemeteries/index.html
  Several cemeteries in Clarion, Forest, Venango, Westmoreland counties in Pennsylvania.

- Cemetery Home Page - Cemeteries Across the Country
  http://home.flash.net/~gtracy01/cemetery/default.htm
  Cemetery indexes for cemeteries in Colorado and Kansas. Includes index, tombstone data, and the ability go order digital copies of tombstones.

- Cemetery Index - Alexandra's Family Tree House
  http://www.rootsquest.com/~alextree/cemetery/
  Western North Carolina cemeteries and more.

- Cemetery Indexes for Washington County, Utah (1852-1996)
  http://www.lofthouse.com/USA/Utah/washington/cemetery/master.html

- Cemetery Index for Tioga and Bradford Counties in PA and Chemung County in NY
  http://www.rootsweb.com/~pabradfo/cemindex.htm

- Cemetery Inscriptions In Little Compton, Newport County, Rhode Island
  ftp://ftp.rootsweb.com/pub/usgenweb/ri/newport/cemetery/cemetery.txt

- Cemetery Pictures from DeWitt County, Illinois
  http://members.xoom.com/Earliene/pages/cemetery.htm

- Cemetery Records of Hampton, New Hampshire
  http://www.hampton.lib.nh.us/hampton/graves/graves.htm

- Cemetery Register of Youngstown, Alberta, Canada
  http://www.telusplanet.net/public/cfdun/cemnav.htm
  Index for 1913-1990.

- Cemetery Searches, Sydney, Australia
  http://homepages.tig.com.au/~tezz/netscape.htm
  This service will locate your ancestors' graves and take photos if required.

- Cemetery Transcription of Converse, Texas, Hermann Son's Cemetery
  http://members.xoom.com/ConverseTx/

- Central Illinois Funeral Homes
  http://www.herald-review.com/1220/homes.html

- Central United Cemetery -- Dunstaffnage ~ Prince Edward Island, Canada
  http://www.rootsweb.com/~pictou/cucdun.htm

- Chalmette National Cemetery ~ Louisiana
  http://www.cwc.lsu.edu/cwc/projects/dbases/chalmla.htm

- Charleston Race Course Prison Dead, SC
  http://members.aol.com/edboots/charlestondead.html
  Union Civil War Prisoners of War originally buried at the Charleston Race Course Cemetery and later reinterred at the Beaufort National Cemetery.

- Chester Basin Old Baptist Cemetery
  http://www.rootsweb.com/~canns/lunenburg/cbobaptist.html
  Chester Basin, Lunenburg, Nova Scotia, Canada.

- Chester Cemeteries Online ~ Pennsylvania
  http://www.rootsweb.com/~pacheste/chetgrav.htm

- Chester New Baptist Cemetery
  http://www.rootsweb.com/~canns/lunenburg/chnbaptist.html
  Chester, Lunenburg, Nova Scotia, Canada.

- Chilton Cemeteries ~ Alabama
  http://members.aol.com/DBGlenn/cemetery.htm
  Includes: Bethany Missionary Baptist Church, Bethel Primitive Baptist Church, Bethsalem Baptist Church, Chestnut Creek Baptist Church, Maple Springs Baptist Church, Mount Pisgah Methodist Church, Poplar Springs Baptist Church, Samaria Baptist Church, Verbena Cemetery.

- Churches and Cemetery Records of Anson County, NC
  http://www.rootsweb.com/~ncanson/cemet.htm

- Church of Holy Spirit Cemetery ~ Hants County, Nova Scotia, Canada
  http://www.rootsweb.com/~nshants/HolySpirit.html

- City of Edmonton's Department of Cemeteries
  mailto:cemetery@wnet.gov.edmonton.ab.ca
  Send e-mail to: cemetery@wnet.gov.edmonton.ab.ca to find out about your ancestors buried in Edmonton, Alberta, Canada.

- City of Redwood City - Union Cemetery ~ California
  http://www.ci.redwood-city.ca.us/parks/union.html

- City of Saskatoon: Woodlawn Cemetery
  http://www.city.saskatoon.sk.ca/departments/public_works/cemetery/default.htm

  o The Nutana Cemetery - Saskatoon's Pioneer Cemetery
    http://www.city.saskatoon.sk.ca/departments/public_works/cemetery/nutana/nutana1.htm

- City of the Silent - Tales from Colma ~ San Francisco, California
  http://www.notfrisco.com/colmatales/index.html

  o Tales from Colma - Notes for Genealogists
    http://www.notfrisco.com/colmatales/sfgen.html

- Civil War Veterans Buried in Stephens Co., OK
  http://homestead.juno.com/sccwvets/index.html
  Collecting, listing & researching the Civil War Veterans (USA & CSA) buried in the county.

- Clark County Cemeteries ~ Indiana
  http://www.geocities.com/Heartland/Plains/5881/index.html

- Clark County, Ohio Cemetery Listings
  http://www.geocities.com/Heartland/Garden/3458

- Clifton Cemetery at Clifton, Arizona
  http://www.rootsweb.com/~azgreenl/clifton.html
  Also known as the Ward's Canyon Cemetery.

- Clinton County, Ohio Cemeteries
  http://www.rootsweb.com/~ohclinto/clincem.html

- Cloverdale Cemetery ~ Hidalgo County, New Mexico
  http://www.rootsweb.com/~nmhidalg/cloverdale.html

- Coloma Cemetery - Carroll County Missouri
  http://millennium.fortunecity.com/postoffice/79/carroll/coloma.html

- Confederate Burials in Mound City National Cemetery ~ Illinois
  http://www.illinoiscivilwar.org/cwmoundcitycem.html

- The Confederate Cemetery
  http://www.angelfire.com/sc/barrito/cemetery.html
  A photographic and written description of the Confederate Cemetery in the old village of Mt. Pleasant, South Carolina. The BSA Eagle Scout project of Barry Floore of BSA Troop 20.

- The Confederate Cemetery List
  http://www.geocities.com/CollegePark/Grounds/7235/
  Lists the final resting places of Confederate Soldiers.

- Confederate Dead at Canton, Mississippi
  http://www.rootsweb.com/~msmadiso/Canton/
  History of Canton during the Civil War, and how hundreds of soldiers came to buried in the Canton Cemetery. New efforts in finding the identification of the 97 unknown soldiers buried there.

- Confederate Soldiers Buried in Our Soldiers Cemetery
  http://members.wbs.net/homepages/n/c/l/nclifton/index.html
  Mount Jackson, Shenandoah County, Virginia.

- Confederate Soldiers Rest, Elmwood Cemetery, Memphis, Tennessee
  http://www.people.memphis.edu/~jcothern/soldrest.htm

- Congregation Mikveh Israel Cemetery ~ Philadelphia, Pennsylvania
  http://www.ushistory.org/tour/_mikvehc.html

- Conneaut Valley Area Soldiers' Graves ~ Pennsylvania
  http://www.toolcity.net/~cvahs/cem/sold/index.html

- The Connecticut Gravestone Network
  http://members.aol.com/ctgravenet/index.htm

- Corinth National Cemetery ~ Mississippi
  http://www2.tsixroads.com/Corinth_MLSANDY/cnc.html

- Cotton City Cemetery ~ New Mexico
  http://www.rootsweb.com/~nmhidalg/cottoncity.html
  This cemetery is located next to the Community Church on Hwy 338, north of Cotton City, NM about 5 miles.

- Cotton City LDS Cemetery ~ New Mexico
  http://www.rootsweb.com/~nmhidalg/cottoncitylds.html
  This cemetery is located next to the LDS Church on Hwy 338, on the north edge of Cotton City, NM.

- Crane Memorial Cemetery 1927-2000
  http://www.rootsweb.com/~txcrane/cranecem.htm
  Complete listing for this cemetery in Crane County, Texas. Listed alphabetically, by block and lot #.

- Crown Hill Cemetery Burial Locator ~ Indiana
  http://www.crownhill.org/cgi-local/db_search.cgi

- Cultural Resource Analysts' Cemetery Database
  http://www.crai-ky.com/cemetery/
  This database represents cemetery data collected over the past 15 or more years from 40 counties in seven states.

"D"

- Dana Rae Pelletier's Cemetery Listings ~ Maine
  http://members.tripod.com/DanaRaePelletier/Cemetery listings.html
  Towns of Burlington, Chester, Enfield, Howland, Lincoln, Lowell, Springfield and Winn.

- Danbury Gravestone Project ~ Connecticut
  http://home.att.net/~gravestones/
  Transcripts of cemetery headstones in 22 cemeteries located in Danbury, CT. Also provided is historical information on the cemeteries, locations, and a query service.

- Daviess Co. Cemeteries
  http://freepages.genealogy.rootsweb.com/~sareid/
  Daviess County, Missouri cemetery information hub: map, driving directions, photos, transcription information, more.

- DC Cemeteries
  http://www.geocities.com/araxnoullis/DC_Cemeteries/DC_Cemeteries.htm

- Decatur County, Tennessee Cemeteries
  http://web.utk.edu/~ddonahue/decatur/decatur.htm

- Delmarva Cemeteries ~ Maryland
  http://www.shoreweb.com/cindy/cemetery.htm

- Denton Co., TX., Pilot Point Cemetery Burials

  o A – G
    ftp://ftp.rootsweb.com/pub/usgenweb/tx/denton/cemeteries/ppcemag.txt

- H – O
  ftp://ftp.rootsweb.com/pub/usgenweb/tx/denton/cemeteries/ppcemho.txt
- P – Z
  ftp://ftp.rootsweb.com/pub/usgenweb/tx/denton/cemeteries/ppcempz.txt

- Department of Veterans' Affairs - Office of Australian War Graves
  http://www.dva.gov.au/commem/oawg/wargr.htm
  The Office of Australian War Graves is responsible for making available and for maintaining official commemoration either in a cemetery, crematorium or in an OAWG Garden of Remembrance, to a standard signifying the enduring respect of the nation, for those service personnel who have given their lives either in war or as a result of their war service.

- Dermott City Cemetery, Chicot County, Arkansas
  - "A - L"
    http://www.seark.net/~sabra/dercemty.txt
  - "M - Z"
    http://www.seark.net/~sabra/dercem2.txt

- Downers Grove and Lisle Township Cemetery Index ~ Du Page County, Illinois
  http://www.dcgs.org/downers/

- Dunstable, Massachusetts Burying Grounds
  http://www.geocities.com/danruth/DunstableCemGrf.html
  A list of many of the persons buried in the Blood Cemetery, Central Cemetery, Little's Station Cemetery, Meeting House Hill Cemetery, Rideout Cemetery and Swallow Cemetery.

"E"

- Eakins Cemetery Records ~ Ponder, Denton County, Texas
  http://www.geocities.com/SoHo/Lofts/6448/EakinsCem.html

- East River St. Mary's, Pictou County ~ Nova Scotia, Canada
  http://www.rootsweb.com/~pictou/eastriv.htm

- Eden Lake Cemetery, Pictou County ~ Nova Scotia, Canada
  http://www.rootsweb.com/~pictou/edenlake.htm

- Edmonton Community Services - Can we help you find a relative? ~ Alberta, Canada
  http://www.gov.edmonton.ab.ca/comm_services/rec_facilities/cemeteries/search.html
  Database of people interred more than 25 years ago (close to 60,000 people) that are in Edmonton Municipal Cemeteries.

- Edmunds County, South Dakota, Cemetery Census -- Interactive Search
  http://www.rootsweb.com/cgi-bin/sdedmunds/cemetery.pl

- The Electric Cemetery
  http://www.ionet.net/~cousin/

- Enid Cemetery Records, Enid, Garfield County, Oklahoma
  http://www.harvestcomm.net/org/garfield_genealogy/ceme-enid.htm

- Erie County, New York Cemeteries Past and Present
  http://members.tripod.com/~wnyroots/
  This site is updated weekly.

- European Cemeteries in India
  http://www.ozemail.com.au/~clday/cem.htm

- Evans Cemetery
  http://welcome.to/evanscemetery
  Located near Sulligent in Lamar County, Alabama.

- Evergreen Cemetery, New Haven, Connecticut
  http://www.geocities.com/TheTropics/1127/evergren.html

"F"

- Fairfax County Cemetery Survey
  http://www.co.fairfax.va.us/library/virginia/varoom/cemsurv.htm
  List of the known burial sites in Fairfax County with links for further information.

- Farnam Cemetery ~ Nebraska
  http://home.4w.com/pages/hoppe/cemetery/

- Fayette County, Alabama Cemetery Records
  http://www.rootsweb.com/~alfayett/FayetteCem.htm

- Fenton Cemetery ~ Fenton, Louisiana
  http://www.geocities.com/fentoncemetery/

- A Few Cemeteries in Maine
  http://www.rootsweb.com/~mefrankl/cem.htm

- First Presbyterian Church Graveyard, Knoxville TN
  http://www.korrnet.org/1stpres/graveyard.htm
  Contains an alphabetical list of those buried in the historic graveyard at First Presbyterian Church of Knoxville, Tennessee. he list includes tombstone inscriptions, some photos, and links to the Congressional Biographies of the three members of Congress buried in the cemetery. This is the oldest cemetery in Knoxville, and it contains the graves of many Tennessee pioneers.

- Five Mile River Cemetery ~ Hants County, Nova Scotia, Canada
  http://www.rootsweb.com/~nshants/FiveMile.html

- Flint Genealogical Society Cemetery Index ~ Michigan
  http://www.rootsweb.com/~mifgs/cemindex/cemindex.html
  While the society's cemetery books are primarily for Genesee County, some also cover a few cemeteries in the surrounding counties of Lapeer, Livingston, Oakland, Saginaw, Shiawassee & Tuscola.

- Forest Lawn Cemetery and Garden Mausoleums ~ Buffalo, New York
  http://www.forest-lawn.com/

- Forest Lawn Cemetery Association, Omaha, Nebraska
  http://www.forestlawnomaha.com/

- Forestville Cemetery ~ Chautauqua County, New York
  http://www.geocities.com/Heartland/Forest/5593/
  forestvilleam.html

- Forks Church Yard - Lutheran Reformed
  http://www.geocities.com/Heartland/6508/FORKS.HTM

- Fort Lawton Cemetery Index
  http://www.geocities.com/Eureka/4458/ftlawcem.html
  Complete index of this federal cemetery in Seattle, Washington.

- Fort Lewis Cemetery ~ Washington
  http://www.geocities.com/Eureka/4458/ftlewcem.html

- Fort Sam Houston National Cemetery ~ San Antonio, Texas
  http://www.rootsweb.com/~txbexar/fshnc00.htm
  All dates of interment are after 1900 through December 31, 1997. The date of interment may not be the first time the individual was interred, so it is not necessarily close to the death date of the individual.

- Fort Stevens Cemetery Index
  http://www.geocities.com/Eureka/4458/ftsteve.html
  Located near Astoria, Oregon.

- Fort Worden Cemetery ~ Port Townsend, Washington
  http://www.geocities.com/Eureka/4458/ftword.html
  An index for this federal cemetery for the military post that is now Fort Worden State Park.

- Four Cemeteries in Livermore, California
  http://www.l-ags.org/livintro.html

- Fox Brook Private Cemetery ~ Nova Scotia, Canada
  http://www.rootsweb.com/~pictou/foxpriv.htm

- Franklin Cemetery
  http://www.rootsweb.com/~azgreenl/grfranklin.html
  An old cemetery in Franklin, Arizona with 356 residents.

- Franklin County, Indiana Cemetery Listing
  http://www.geocities.com/Heartland/Meadows/6863/
  cemetery1.html
  Links to information about individuals buried in cemeteries throughout Franklin County, Indiana.

- Franklin County, Indiana, Comprehensive Cemetery Index
  http://members.aol.com/elasabe/fccem.htm
  Indexes for 137 unduplicated cemeteries in Franklin County, Indiana and links to the 94 cemeteries which have been transcribed.

- Fraser Cemetery, Blanchard Road, Pictou County ~ Nova Scotia, Canada
  http://www.rootsweb.com/~pictou/fraserb.htm

- Fredericksburg Confederate Cemetery ~ Virginia
  http://www.nps.gov/frsp/rebcem.htm

- Fredericksburg National Cemetery ~ Virginia
  http://www.nps.gov/frsp/natcem.htm

- Fred Hatfield's Lafayette #1 Cemetery Inventory ~ New Orleans, Louisiana
  http://geocities.com/hatfield2.geo/
  Search cemetery information by family surname, date of death (1821-1999), by lot sequence or by military reference on plaques.

- Friedensgemeinde Cemetery, Froid, Montana
  http://pixel.cs.vt.edu/library/cemeteries/montana/link/
  damm.txt

"G"

- Gallup Cemetery, Voluntown, Connecticut
  http://www.geocities.com/Vienna/1516/gallup1.html

- Genealogical Research at Oak Woods Cemetery ~ Chicago, Illinois
  http://homepages.rootsweb.com/~godwin/reference/
  oakwoods.html

- The Genealogy Resource Page & Cemetery Database of the Hunter Valley NSW Australia
  http://bhss.inia.net.au/patmay/

- The General Cemetery ~ Sharrow, Sheffield, England
  http://www.shu.ac.uk/web-admin/cemetery/

- Glen Bard Cemetery, James River, Antigonish County ~ Nova Scotia, Canada
  http://www.rootsweb.com/~pictou/antiglb.htm

- Globe Cemetery ~ Gila County, Arizona
  http://www.rootsweb.com/~azgila/globecem.htm

- Grace Lutheran Church & Cemetery, Ohiowa, Fillmore Co., NE
  http://rowbee.inebraska.com/~ksrowe/buch/
  ohgracecem.html
  Church and photos.

- A Grave Situation
  http://www.mindspring.com/~awillcut/graves/
  Some transcriptions of Tuscaloosa County cemeteries.

- Graveyards of Chicago ~ Illinois
  http://www.graveyards.com/

- The Graveyards of Omaha
  http://members.nbci.com/martadawes/
  Graveyards, history and genealogy of the eastern Nebraska and western Iowa areas.

- Graveyards of the Fort Worth/Tarrant County Area ~ Texas
  http://web2.airmail.net/hdbtdw/grvyrds.htm

- Grays Harbor County Washington Cemeteries
  http://www.geocities.com/Heartland/Hills/6201/
  cemeteries.html
  A list of cemeteries and their addresses, plus information on a book in the works from the Grays Harbor Genealogical Society.

- Greensboro Cemetery, Tomnolan, Mississippi
  ftp://ftp.rootsweb.com/pub/usgenweb/ms/webster/
  cemeteries/greensboro.txt

- Greenway Cemetery, Greenway, South Dakota
  http://pixel.cs.vt.edu/library/cemeteries/sodak/link/
  grnway.txt

- Greenwood Cemetery: History ~ Tallahassee,
  Florida
  http://www.ci.tallahassee.fl.us/citytlh/public_works/
  gwhistory.html

- Guernsey Genealogy - The Bailiwick of Guernsey -
  The Stranger Cemetery - Guernsey ~ Channel
  Islands
  http://www.genealogy.guernsey.net/Stranger.html

- A Guide to Mount Hope Cemetery, Rochester, New
  York
  http://204.97.3.30:8080/apps/CITYSITE.NSF/a024191c67aca
  3e28525656c006594d4/18307ab882f4301e85256571000a382
  c?OpenDocument

- Gunn Cemetery, Eden Lake, Pictou County ~ Nova
  Scotia, Canada
  http://www.rootsweb.com/~pictou/gunn.htm

- Guysborough County Cemetery Listings ~ Nova
  Scotia, Canada
  http://www.angelfire.com/ca4/Patsy/cemindex.html
  *Cemetery transcriptions, photographs of cemetery gateposts and
  many obituaries.*

"H"

- Halde Cemetery, Waterville, ME
  http://members.mint.net/frenchcx/haldecm1.htm
  *Oldest Catholic cemetery in the area: 1872-1945; including
  gravestone, genealogical, funeral home and church death records
  with map and index; 56-page equivalent document.*

- Hale Center Cemetery ~ Texas
  http://www.geocities.com/hccem
  A complete listing of all burials since 1888 with history.

- Halifax County - Cemetery Listings ~ Nova Scotia,
  Canada
  http://www.geocities.com/Heartland/Meadows/3515/
  Cemetery.htm

- Harper County Cemeteries ~ Kansas
  http://www.rootsweb.com/~usgenweb/ks/harper/harper.htm

- Hattie Cemetery, Avondale, Pictou County ~ Nova
  Scotia, Canada
  http://www.rootsweb.com/~pictou/hattie.htm

- Heatherton Cemetery, Old Section, Antigonish
  County ~ Nova Scotia, Canada
  http://www.rootsweb.com/~pictou/hethold.htm

- Hemmingford Cemetery Records ~ Hemmingford,
  Quebec, Canada
  http://members.xoom.com/dlmark/cemetery.htm
  6,000 records from 16 Hemmingford, Quebec area cemeteries.

- Henderson County, Tennessee Cemeteries
  http://web.utk.edu/~ddonahue/henderson/hender.htm

- Henry County, AL Cemetery Listings
  http://www.rootsweb.com/~alhenry/cem.htm

- Herkimer/Montgomery Counties Cemetery
  Resources ~ New York
  http://www.rootsweb.com/~nyherkim/cemeteries.html
  *Lists of cemeteries, private cemeteries, funeral homes and microfilm
  resources at the LDS Family History Centers.*

- Hilda Baptist Cemetery, Hilda, Alberta, Canada
  http://pixel.cs.vt.edu/library/cemeteries/canada/link/hilda1.txt

- Hillside Cemetery, Trenton, Pictou County ~ Nova
  Scotia, Canada
  http://www.rootsweb.com/~pictou/hillside.htm

- Historic Cemeteries of Los Angeles ~ California
  http://www.usc.edu/isd/archives/la/cemeteries/

- Historic Cemeteries of Nevada County, California
  http://freepages.genealogy.rootsweb.com/~historic/
  *Thousands of gravestone photographs from historic cemeteries in
  Nevada County, California. The heart of the gold country buried
  many a seeker of gold. Many names include men and women from
  Cornwall, England.*

- Historic Congressional Cemetery ~ Washington,
  D.C.
  http://www.geocities.com/Heartland/Meadows/4633/
  index.html

- Historic Elmwood Cemetery, Memphis, TN
  http://www.elmwoodcemetery.org/main.htm

- Historic Graveyards of The Berkshires ~
  Massachusetts
  http://www.berkshireweb.com/plexus/graveyards/grave
  yards.html

- Historical Landmarks: The Allen Cemetery ~ Texas
  http://aisd2.allen.k12.tx.us/story.nsf/Files/3BB32471BAE69F
  BA86256448005C642B/$FILE/sehome.htm

- Historical Notes - Calvary Cemetery ~ Seattle,
  Washington
  http://www.acc-seattle.com/cchistry.html

- Historische Friedhàfe in Berlin / Historic Cemeteries
  in Berlin ~ Germany
  http://www.zlb.de/projekte/friedhof/index.html

- The History of the Gilliland Cemetery ~ Crowell,
  Texas
  http://www.wfconnection.com/gilliland/cemetery.htm
  A short history and a listing of those buried in the cemetery.

- History of the Seminole Indian Scout Cemetery ~
  Brackettville, Texas
  http://www.coax.net/people/lwf/his_sisc.htm

- Hodson Cemetery, Pictou County ~ Nova Scotia,
  Canada
  http://www.rootsweb.com/~pictou/hodson.htm

- Hollywood Underground
  http://www.hollywood-underground.com/
  The burial sites of Hollywood's most famous stars, moguls and eccentrics.

- Holmes Funeral Co. Book - Saratoga Springs, New York
  http://freenet.buffalo.edu/~ae487/holmes.html
  Aug. 1854 to Dec. 1856.

- Holy Trinity Anglican Church Cemetery ~ Hants County, Nova Scotia, Canada
  http://www.rootsweb.com/~nshants/holytrinity.html

- Honley Cemetery Monumental Inscriptions ~ England
  http://website.lineone.net/~gburhouse/

- Hope Congregational Cemetery, Bethune, Colorado
  http://pixel.cs.vt.edu/library/cemeteries/colorado/link/bethune1.txt

- Howard Cemetery Armsby Road Sutton, Massachusetts
  http://www.geocities.com/Heartland/Pines/4289/cem/howard.html

- Howard County Indiana Selected Cemetery Indexes
  http://www.kokomo.lib.in.us/genealogy/altoindx.html

- Huguenot Cemetery ~ St. John's County, Florida
  http://www.geocities.com/Heartland/Hills/8299/cemetery/hug_cem.htm

"I"

- Idaho Cemetery Index
  http://www2.state.id.us/ishs/Cemetery.html
  From the Idaho State Historical Society.

- Immanuel Lutheran Church Cemetery, Bethune, Colorado
  http://pixel.cs.vt.edu/library/cemeteries/colorado/link/bethune2.txt

- Inactive Cemeteries of Lewis County as transcribed by Lowville Grange #71 in 1965 ~ New York
  http://www.rootsweb.com/~nylewis/inactive.htm

- Indexed burials in Midway Green Cemetery, Aberdeen, New Jersey
  http://www.netlabs.net/hp/gjoynson/midwaygreen.htm
  Indexed list of African American burials in Midway Green Cemetery, Aberdeen (formerly Matawan), Monmouth County, NJ.

- Index for Michigan Cemetery Listings by County
  http://www.rootsweb.com/~migenweb/cemetery1.htm

- Index of Graves at Liberty Hill Primitive Baptist Cemetery ~ Alabama
  http://www.mindspring.com/~awillcut/graves/xlibhill.htm

- Indian Graves and Cemeteries
  http://history.cc.ukans.edu/heritage/werner/indigrav.html

- The Indiana Pioneer Cemeteries Restoration Project
  http://www.rootsweb.com/~inpcrp/

- Indiana State Library Genealogy Division Cemetery Database
  http://www.statelib.lib.in.us/tango3/marriage/cemetery.taf?function=form

- International Jewish Cemetery Project
  http://www.jewishgen.org/cemetery/index.htm

"J"

- Jackson County, Iowa Cemeteries
  http://www.rootsweb.com/~iajackso/Cemetery.html

- Jefferson County, Texas Cemeteries
  http://www.rootsweb.com/~txjeffer/burials/cemeteri.htm

- Jerauld County Cemetery Index
  http://pixel.cs.vt.edu/library/cemeteries/sodak/link/jerauld.txt

- Jewish Cemeteries ~ Hamburg, Germany
  http://www.rrz.uni-hamburg.de/rz3a035/jew_cem.html

- Jewish Cemeteries in Hungary
  http://www.geocities.com/winter_peter_4
  Information about Jewish cemeteries in Hungary. Cemetery surveys, descriptions, addresses of local interests, photo database of gravestones, transcription, translation.

- Jewish Cemetery in Košice / Old Jewish Cemetery at Kosice, Slovakia
  http://www.kosice.sk/history/zidovsky/jevish0.htm
  History of the cemetery, database of 5,517 names of buried persons.

- Jewish Cemetery of Rhodes
  http://www.rhodesjewishmuseum.org/cemetery.htm
  A listing of the 1,167 tombstones in the Jewish cemetery of Rhodes. Includes some photographs and translations of inscriptions.

- JewishGen Hotline: Jewish Cemeteries in New York City
  http://www.jewishgen.org/mentprog/m_nycem.htm

- John F. Denny Collection
  http://www.ubalt.edu/archives/denny/denny.htm
  From the Archives of the University of Baltimore. Holdings of the Denny Funeral Home which operated in Baltimore from the same location for 122 years.

"K"

- Kamsack GenWeb Project - Rural Municipality of Hazel Dell No.335 Cemetery Locations, Names and Contact Persons ~ Saskatchewan, Canada
  http://www.rootsweb.com/~skkamsac/RMHazelDell.html

- Kent County Michigan Master Cemetery List
  http://www.rootsweb.com/~mikent/cemeteries/
  Complete transcription, records availability and location information for all known Kent County Michigan cemeteries.

- Kenzieville Cemetery, Pictou County ~ Nova Scotia Canada
  http://www.rootsweb.com/~pictou/nkbr.htm

- Kewaunee County Cemeteries ~ Wisconsin
  http://www.rootsweb.com/~wikewaun/cemetery.htm

- Kinder McRill Memorial Cemetery ~ Kinder, Louisiana
  http://fp1.centuryinter.net/KinderCemetery/

- KITTERMAN Cemetery ~ Dahlonega Township, Wapello County, Iowa
  http://soli.inav.net/~shepherd/kitt/kit_cem/kit_cem.html

- Kootenai County Cemetery ~ Idaho
  http://www.ior.com/~jmakovec/genealogy/kc_cem.htm

"L"

- Lambton County Cemetery Index ~ Ontario, Canada
  http://www.sarnia.com/groups/ogs/logs1.html

- Lawrence County, PA, Cemetery Readings
  http://members.aol.com/lawcemeteries
  Data for four cemeteries: Shenango U. P., Rich Hill U. P., King's Chapel M. E., Volant.

- Lehigh County Cemetery Locations ~ Pennsylvania
  http://www.geocities.com/Heartland/6508/#Lehigh County

- Letcher County Cemetery Records ~ Kentucky
  http://home.mpinet.net/bcaudill/kygenweb/cem_recs.htm

- Lewisburg Cemetery ~ Pennsylvannia
  http://www.lewisburgcemetery.org/

- Linwood Cemetery, Columbus, Georgia
  http://members.aol.com/CGAutry/linwood.html

- Listings for Hillcrest Cemetery est.1830 ~ Upper Musquodoboit, Halifax, Nova Scotia, Canada
  http://members.tripod.com/velvet_b/

- Lithuanian Cemeteries in America
  http://www.angelfire.com/ut/Luthuanian/markers.html

- The Little Rushton Cemetery
  http://msnhomepages.talkcity.com/deckdr/scottyscottage/lilrushtoncem.html
  Kolbec, Cumberland County Nova Scotia. A small family cemetery with surnames of RUSHTON, MILLER, ROSS, RODGERS & PIPES.

- Little Sands Cemetery ~ Prince Edward Island, Canada
  http://www.rootsweb.com/~pictou/lilsands.htm

- The Liverpool Cemetery
  http://www.geocities.com/Heartland/Cabin/8792/liverpool_cemetery.index.htm
  A listing of the people buried at the Liverpool Cemetery in Liverpool, Brazoria County, Texas.

- Lone Oak Cemetery - Geronimo, Texas
  http://personal.riverusers.com/~keyserroll/loneoak1.html

- Long Creek Baptist Church Cemetery ~ Prince Edward Island, Canada
  http://www.rootsweb.com/~pictou/longcree.htm

- Lookups from the "Galveston, Indiana Cemetery Index, from the Platbooks and Files"
  mailto:dbeheler@indy.net

For Cass, Howard or Miami Counties in Indiana. Send e-mail to Debra Beheler at dbeheler@indy.net.

- Lyona Cemetery...List of Burials ~ Dickinson County, Kansas
  http://skyways.lib.ks.us/genweb/dickinso/lyoncrec.html

- Lyons Cemetery Castle Frederick Hants County Nova Scotia
  http://www.rootsweb.com/~nshants/LYONS.html

"M"

- Mammoth Cave Area Cemeteries
  http://geocities.com/scarred40/MammothCave.html
  Mammoth Cave National Park, in Kentucky, is home to many beautiful cemeteries.

- Maple Grove Cemetery, Granville, OH, Burials from 1864 to Present
  http://www.kinfinder.com/cemeteries/MapleGroveIntro.htm

- Maple Grove Cemetery, Munising, Wetmore, Alger County, Michigan
  http://www.genealogia.fi/emi/emi52i1e.htm

- Maple Grove Cemetery - Wichita, Kansas
  http://www.maplegrovecemetery.org/
  Information regarding Wichita's earliest cemeteries.

- May They Rest in Peace: Kith and Kin at the Highland Cemetery, Dakota County, Minnesota
  http://member.aol.com/baggerjane/highland/

- McKenney Cemetery, Harrison County, Kentucky
  http://www.mindspring.com/~jogt/kygen/mckcem.htm

- McKenzie Cemetery, Salt Springs, Pictou County ~ Nova Scotia, Canada
  http://www.rootsweb.com/~pictou/mckenzie.htm

- McLean Cemetery, Hopewell, Pictou County ~ Nova Scotia, Canada
  http://www.rootsweb.com/~pictou/mclhope.htm

- Meiklefield Cemetery, Meiklefield, Pictou County ~ Nova Scotia, Canada
  http://www.rootsweb.com/~pictou/mekfd.htm

- Memento Mori
  http://www.home.sk/www/dudy/m_index.htm
  Alphabetical list of WWI soldiers buried at Kosice Municipal Cemetery, Kosice, Slovaka.

- Mennonite Historical Society of Saskatchewan Inc. - Saskatchewan Mennonite Cemetery Finding Aid
  http://freepages.genealogy.rootsweb.com/~skmhss/

- Metcalf Cemetery ~ Arizona
  http://www.rootsweb.com/~azgreenl/grmetcalf.html

- The Middle Animas Cemetery ~ Animas, Hidalgo County, New Mexico
  http://www.rootsweb.com/~nmhidalg/manimas.html

- Mills Cemetery, Garland, Texas
  http://www.geocities.com/TheTropics/1127/mills.html

- Moggill Cemetery
  http://192.148.225.23/bruce/cemetery.html
  A suburb of Brisbane, Queensland, Australia.

- Montgomery County Cemetery Project ~
  Pennsylvania
  http://members.aol.com/tmyers8644/mccem.html

- Montgomery County Tennessee Index to Cemeteries
  http://www.clarksville.org/MTCEMS.txt

- Monumental Inscriptions for Genealogists
  http://www.neep.demon.co.uk/mis/index.htm

- Morgan County Cemeteries Lookups - Missouri
  mailto:wmwwms@laurie.net
  Send e-mail to William & Dorothy Williams at wmwwms@laurie.net for lookups to be done in their personal catalog of Morgan County Cemeteries in Missouri. They have visited each of these gravesites and recorded all necessary details for each grave, including the parents of children and maiden name of wives if known. Their database has over 22,000 burials in over 150 cemeteries. Records cover only Morgan County's present boundaries for 1830 through 1996. Copies of these records can also be found in the State Archives, State Historical Library, and the Morgan County Library. Make sure to send a reasonable request and don't forget to thank William & Dorothy for their tremendous generosity!

- Moss Cemetery, Marble, Cherokee County, North Carolina
  http://main.nc.us/OBCGS/mosscem.htm

- Mountain View Cemetery
  http://www.rootsweb.com/~nmhidalg/mtviewcem.html
  Large cemetery North of Lordsburg, New Mexico West of Hwy 70, about 1 mile North of town.

- Mountain View Cemetery
  http://beaverutah.net/cemtry.htm
  Mountain View Cemetery, Beaver, Utah cemetery data.

- Mount Hope Cemetery ~ Bangor, Maine
  http://www.mthopebgr.com/

- Mount Royal Cemetery Company ~ Montréal, Québec, Canada
  http://www.mountroyalcem.com/

- Mt. Adams Cemetery, Glenwood, Klickitat County, Washington
  ftp://ftp.rootsweb.com/pub/usgenweb/wa/klickitat/cemetery/mtadams.txt

- Mt. View Research Cemeteries ~ Page County, Virginia
  http://www.rootsweb.com/~vapage/pagecemeteries/1cemeteries.htm

- Murray Point Cemetery, Pictou County ~ Nova Scotia, Canada
  http://www.rootsweb.com/~pictou/murpt.htm

"N"

- Names of Men Buried In the Confederate Cemeteries of Fredericksburg and Spotsylvania Courthouse
  http://freepages.genealogy.rootsweb.com/~helmsnc/FredCWCEM/
  Listed in state ordered and also alphabetically by surname.

- Native American Cemetery Readers - Genealogy Database
  http://www.nacr.net/
  Subscription-based database of cemetery and other records from Benton County Arkansas and Delaware County Oklahoma.

- National Cemetery System - Department of Veteran Affairs ~ U.S.
  http://www.cem.va.gov/

- National Program for the Grave Sites of Canadian Prime Ministers
  http://parkscanada.pch.gc.ca/pm/english/gravesites_e.htm
  From Parks Canada.

- Nevada County, Arkansas Cemetery Records
  http://www.pcfa.org/depot_museum/cemetery/

- New Bethlehem Community Cemetery ~ Simpson County, Mississippi
  http://genweb.net/~memawh/new_bethlehem_community_cemetery.html

- New York Marble Cemetery, Inc.
  http://www.marblecemetery.org/
  A cemetery of underground marble vaults on lower Manhattan with most burials between 1830 and 1870. The full interment list, a history, and some biographies are posted for 156 underground family vaults containing over 2,000 burials.

- Niagara County, NY Cemeteries
  http://hometown.aol.com/Moecow/

- North Dakota Morticians
  http://www.rootsweb.com/~ndpembin/funeral.txt
  Lists over 100 morticians and funeral homes in North Dakota.

- North East Florida & Some South East George Counties - Listing of Over 610 Cemeteries.
  mailto:cmobley@cfl.rr.com
  Georgia counties include: Charlton, Brantley & Pierce and (one in Echols Co). Send e-mail to Carl Mobley at cmobley@cfl.rr.com, with SPECIFIC given names & surnames and he will do a lookup for you.

- Northampton County Cemetery Locations ~ Pennsylvania
  http://www.geocities.com/Heartland/6508/#Cemeteries

"O"

- Oak Island Cemetery, Maitland, Hants Co. Nova Scotia ~ Canada
  http://www.rootsweb.com/~nshants/Oak.html

- OCFA - The Ontario Cemetery Finding Aid
  http://www.islandnet.com/ocfa/homepage.html

- Old American Cemetery - Kodiak, Alaska
  http://www.ptialaska.net/~vccarmi/OldAmerican.htm
  An inventory, done 22 May 1999, in order of the markers.

- Old Bethel or Presbyterian Cemetery in Bethel NY
  http://www.geocities.com/televisioncity/7783/OldB.html

- Old Blandford Church and Cemetery ~ Petersburg, Virginia
  http://www.rootsweb.com/~vacpeter/cemetery/
  blandfd1.htm

- Old Burial Ground of Middle Fork of Raven Creek - Harrison County, Kentucky
  http://members.aol.com/kygenweb/raven.htm

- The Old Cemeteries Society - Victoria Tombstone Tales of Ross Bay Cemetery ~ British Columbia, Canada
  http://www.oldcem.bc.ca/
  Victoria's Ross Bay Cemetery opened in 1873 to serve the burial needs of the growing city of Victoria, British Columbia, Canada. Overlooking Ross Bay, it is 11 hectares in size (27.5 acres) and has almost 28,000 interments. Not just a burial ground, it serves as a park and restful get-away for many people. Come inside and take a virtual tour, meet some of the more famous residents, learn about issues that concern twentieth-century cemeteries or just enjoy some of the stories of this great cemetery.

- Old Cemetery, Salt Springs, Pictou County ~ Nova Scotia, Canada
  http://www.rootsweb.com/~pictou/oldcem.htm

- Old City Cemetery ~ Lynchburg, Virginia
  http://www.lynchburgbiz.com/occ/index.html

- Old City Cemetery: History ~ Tallahassee, Florida
  http://www.state.fl.us/citytlh/public_works/occhist.html

- Old Colony Burying Ground ~ Granville, Ohio
  http://www.kinfinder.com/cemeteries/OldColonyBurying
  Groun.htm

- Old Huntsville Magazine: Cemetery Records of Madison County ~ Alabama
  http://www.oldhuntsville.com/ceme_records.htm

- Old Kinne Cemetery, Voluntown, Connecticut
  http://www.geocities.com/Vienna/1516/kinne4.html

- Old Liberty Cemetery ~ Tipton, Missouri
  http://www.geocities.com/Heartland/Pointe/5250/
  cemetary.htm

- Old Methodist Church Cemetery, Venus, Pennsylvania
  http://members.aol.com/jadolby/index.htm

- Old Mines Road Cemetery, Upper Falmouth, Hants County, Nova Scotia
  http://www.rootsweb.com/~nshants/Mines.html

- The Old Shaw Baptist Church Cemetery ~ West Chester County, South Carolina
  http://guenthertindlegenealogy.ourfamily.com/shaw.html
  Complete cemetery listing with photos.

- Old Spanish Cemetery ~ St. John's County, Florida
  http://www.geocities.com/Heartland/Hills/8299/cemetery/
  spa_cem.htm

- Old St Joseph's Cemetery, Morganza, St. Mary's Co., Maryland
  ftp://ftp.rootsweb.com/pub/usgenweb/md/stmary/
  cemeteries/oldstjoe.txt
  Several hundred names of burials between the late 1700s and the early 1900s.

- Omeo Cemetery Trust ~ Australia
  http://www4.tpgi.com.au/users/omeo/page3.html
  Access to Omeo Pioneer Cemetery records, including monumental inscriptions. Also Buckland Cemetery.

- Otsego County Cemeteries, Otsego County, NY
  http://www.rootsweb.com/~nyotsego/cemetery.htm

- Our Lady of Good Counsel Church Cemetery ~ St. John's County, Florida
  http://www.geocities.com/Heartland/Hills/8299/cemetery/
  cons_cem.htm

"P"

- Parnell Cemetery, Adair County, Kentucky
  http://angelfire.com/ky/johnparnell/page4.html

- Patoka Presbyterian Church Cemetery ~ Patoka, Gibson County, Indiana
  http://www.angelfire.com/hi/luciefield/oldpatoka.html

- Pauls Valley, Cemetery Mount Olive
  http://www.angelfire.com/ok3/genealogypaulsvalley/
  index.html
  Names, birth dates, death dates, for Mount Olive Cemetery, Pauls Valley, Garvin County, Oklahoma.

- PCFA.ORG Nevada County Arkansas Cemetery Records
  http://www.pcfa.org/depot_museum/cemetery/

- PEI Burial Records - 1892-1900 ~ Canada
  http://homepages.rootsweb.com/~mvreid/pei/
  34burabs.html
  St Eugene's (CoveHead), St Michael's (Corran Ban), St Bonaventure's (Tracadie).

- Petersburg National Battlefield - Poplar Grove National Cemetery ~ Virginia
  http://www.nps.gov/pete/mahan/eduhistpg.html

- Petroleum County Cemetery Index ~ Montana
  http://www.rootsweb.com/~mtpetrol/cemeteryindex.htm
  Links to Petroleum County, Montana cemeteries pages include names and other info in these cemeteries.

- Philipps Cemetery ~ Granville, Ohio
  http://www.kinfinder.com/cemeteries/PhilippsCem.htm

- Pictou Island Pioneer Cemetery ~ Nova Scotia, Canada
  http://www.rootsweb.com/~pictou/pioneer.htm

- Pictou Island Presbyterian Church Cemetery ~ Nova Scotia, Canada
  http://www.rootsweb.com/~pictou/prezz.htm

- Pin Oak Cemetery ~ Milam County, Texas
  http://www.alpha1.net/~unc/j/poc.htm

- Pioneer Cemeteries located on the Fort Lewis Reservation ~ Washington
  http://www.geocities.com/Eureka/4458/pion.html

- Pioneer Cemetery - Horseshoe Bend, Boise County, Idaho
  http://www.rootsquest.com/~idaho/boise/cemhsb.html

- Placerville Cemetery - Boise County, Idaho
  http://www.rootsquest.com/~idaho/boise/cemplacer.html

- Pleasant Grove Methodist Cemetery
  http://home.att.net/~dpdklong/PleasantGrove.html
  Chilton County, Alabama, 1848-1978.

- Plumas County Adventures ~ California
  http://www.csuchico.edu/chem/rcooke/pca.html
  Includes three cemetery databases.

- Portage County (Wisconsin) Cemetery Locator
  http://library.uwsp.edu/cemetery/
  Over 43,000 names located in 67 Portage County cemeteries.

- Portland,OR - Vancouver,WA Cemeteries
  http://members.aol.com/gninnah/cemetery.html
  Portland, Oregon & Vancouver, Washington cemetery, funeral home, & gene contact information.

- PPL Cemetery Index ~ Indiana
  http://www.plainfield.lib.in.us/history/Cemeteries/
  CemeIndex.html-ssi
  Plainfield Public Library, Local and Indiana Information Services, Hendricks County Cemeteries Index.

- Prairie Epitaph - Catholic Cemetery in Salvador, Saskatchewan
  http://mars.ark.com/~rbell/html/history/epitaph.html
  Many German Russian families.

- Preserving Cemetery Data: The North Carolina Cemetery Survey and Protective Legislation
  http://www.arch.dcr.state.nc.us/cemetery.htm

- Prince Edward Island Cemeteries Page
  http://www.islandregister.com/cem.html
  Includes "Extract from the Death Registers, St. Patrick's Roman Catholic Church in Ft. Augustus, P.E.I.

"Q"

- Quaker Burying Ground Morris, New York

  o Surnames A-M
    http://www.rootsweb.com/~nyotsego/cemetery/
    morbga.htm

  o Surnames N-Z
    http://www.rootsweb.com/~nyotsego/cemetery/
    morbgb.htm

- Quaker Cemetery, Knoxville,Tioga County PA
  http://www.rootsweb.com/~patioga/cemetery/quaker.htm

"R"

- Raven Creek Cemetery, Harrison County, Kentucky
  http://pw1.netcom.com/~jog1/ravencreek.html

- Redden Cemetery, Rte 14, Windsor Forks, Hants County N.S. ~ Nova Scotia, Canada
  http://www.rootsweb.com/~nshants/REDDEN2.html

- Register of Burials Cinnamara, Assam
  http://www.ozemail.com.au/~clday/assam.htm

- Rhode Island Cemeteries Database Home Page
  http://members.tripod.com/~debyns/cemetery.html

- Rhode Island Historical Cemeteries Transcription Project
  http://www.rootsweb.com/~rigenweb/cemetery/

- Robeson County, NC Indian Cemetery Page ~ NC
  http://members.aol.com/bjbarnhill/Cemeteries/index.htm
  Partial list of Robeson County Lumbee Indian Cemeteries with surnames Bell, Thomas, Locklear, Blanks, Lowery, Oxendine, Carter, Chavis and many others.

- Rock Island County Cemeteries ~ Illinois
  http://www.rootsweb.com/~ilrockis/cemetery/cemetery.htm

- Rocky Mountain Cemetery, Pictou County ~ Nova Scotia, Canada
  http://www.rootsweb.com/~pictou/rocky.htm

- The Rodeo Cemetery ~ Rodeo, Hidalgo County, NM
  http://www.rootsweb.com/~nmhidalg/rodeocem.html

- Roman Catholic Cemetery, Merigomish ~ Nova Scotia, Canada
  http://www.rootsweb.com/~pictou/rcmeri.htm

- The Roman Catholic Diocese of Providence - Cemeteries ~ Rhode Island
  http://www.providiocese.com/info/cemeteries.html

"S"

- Saint Andrew's Cemetery, Old Section, Antigonish County ~ Nova Scotia, Canada
  http://www.rootsweb.com/~pictou/stanold.htm

- Saint Francis Xavier Cemetery est. 1840, Roman Catholic Cemetery, Maitland, Hants Co., Nova Scotia
  http://www.rootsweb.com/~nshants/Chapel.html

- Salt Springs Cemetery, Pictou County ~ Nova Scotia, Canada
  http://www.rootsweb.com/~pictou/ssprings.htm

- San Francisco Cemeteries ~ California
  http://www.sirius.com/~jblcktt/sfgraves/

- Sangsters Bridge Cemetery Hants Co. Nova Scotia ~ Canada
  http://www.rootsweb.com/~nshants/Sangsters.html

- Saskatchewan Cemetery Index ~ Canada
  http://www.saskgenealogy.com/cemetery/cemetery.htm

- Saskatchewan's Transcribed Cemeteries on the Internet
  http://homepages.rootsweb.com/~canada/sask/cemetery.htm

- SETTLE Cemetery, Rogers County, Oklahoma
  http://www.writeinstyle.com/genealogy/cemeteries/settle cemetery/
  A complete listing of the Settle Family Cemetery in rural Rogers County, Oklahoma. All stones are photographed and transcribed.

- Shelby County Alabama Cemetery Census Index
  http://www.rootsweb.com/~alshelby/cemIndex.html

- Shiloh Cemetery, Delta County, Texas
  http://www.geocities.com/Vienna/1516/shiloh.html

- Sheridan Municipal Cemetery ~ Wyoming
  http://www.rootsweb.com/~wysherid/cem-index.htm

- Silverton, Colorado Hillside Cemetery San Juan County
  http://members.xoom.com/hillsidecem/
  There are many of foreign birth buried there. The index includes genealogical information such as related persons, some places of birth, some descriptions of cause of death.

- Simpson County Cemeteries, Pre-1920 ~ Mississippi
  http://www.littleco.net/Genealogy/cbook.htm

- Simpson Kentucky Cemeteries Page
  http://geocities.com/scarred40/tombsimpson.html
  Pictures of cemeteries in Simpson County, Kentucky.

- Skinnersville Cemetery Amherst NY
  http://www.geocities.com/Heartland/Acres/4218/skinnersville.html

- A Small Town's Civil War History and the Hillside Cemetery Civil War Graves Project
  http://home.sprynet.com/sprynet/nonfarby
  Research done in Middletown New York's historic Hillside Cemetery for the location of and survey of it's Civil War Union Veterans.

- Some Burials at St. Columbkill's Catholic Church Cemetery
  http://www.rootsweb.com/~irish/igsi_published/cemetery/mngobell.htm
  Burials in Belle Creek, Minnesota. Also includes birth date, location, marriage date and location.

- Some South Carolina Cemetery Transcriptions
  http://www.geocities.com/Heartland/Acres/4730/cemetery.html

- South Australian Cemeteries
  http://www.users.on.net/proformat/cems.html

- Southeast Saskatchewan Cemetery Records
  http://cap.estevan.sk.ca/cemetery.records/
  This has listing of the burials in several cemeteries in and around Estevan, Saskatchewan.

- Spencer Holy Trinity Cemetery ~ Australia
  http://www.terrigal.net.au/~history/spencer.htm
  Cemetery Index for sale.

- St. Augustine National Cemetery ~ St. John's County, Florida
  http://www.geocities.com/Heartland/Hills/8299/cemetery/nat_cem.htm

- Stephens County Cemeteries ~ Oklahoma
  http://www.rootsweb.com/~okstephe/cemetery.htm

- Stevensburg Baptist Church Cemetery, Stevensburg, Culpeper County, Virginia
  http://www.rootsweb.com/~takelley/stevebap.htm
  Lists resources for the history of the Stevensburg Baptist Church, Stevensburg, VA, as well as tombstone transcriptions.

- Stewart's Cemetery, Antigonish County ~ Nova Scotia, Canada
  http://www.rootsweb.com/~pictou/stewart.htm

- St. George's Anglican Church Cemetery, Upper Falmouth, Hants County, Nova Scotia ~ Canada
  http://www.rootsweb.com/~nshants/georges.html

- St. John Memorial Gardens ~ Louisiana
  ftp://ftp.rootsweb.com/pub/usgenweb/la/stjohn/cemeteries/stjohn.txt

- St. John The Baptist Anglican Church Cemetery, Latties Brook ~ Hants County, Nova Scotia, Canada
  http://www.rootsweb.com/~nshants/Latties.html

- St. Michael's Anglican Church Cemetery ~ Hants County, Nova Scotia, Canada
  http://www.rootsweb.com/~nshants/StMich.html

- Stony Cemetery ~ Denton County, Texas
  http://www.geocities.com/SoHo/Lofts/6448/StonyCem.html

- Sussex County, NJ Cemetery Indexes ~ New Jersey
  http://www.gate.net/~pascalfl/cemidx.html

"T"

- Texas Roots - Limestone County Cemetery Surveys
  http://www.glade.net/~hcox/cemeteries/cemeteryintro.html

- Texas State Cemetery
  http://www.cemetery.state.tx.us/

- Thurston County, Washington Cemeteries
  http://www.rootsweb.com/~wathurst/thur-cem.htm
  Cemetery records and tombstone inscriptions, along with description and location of each cemetery.

- Toledo's Attic Woodlawn Cemetery Biographies ~ Ohio
  http://www.history.utoledo.edu/att/wood/woodindex.html

- Tombstone Inscriptions of Maryland and Delaware Index to Cemeteries
  http://www.geocities.com/Heartland/8074/stone contents.html

- Tombstone Records from Monroe Co., New York and a Few Church Records
  http://home.eznet.net/~halsey/cem.html

- Tombstone Transcription Project
  http://www.angelfire.com/va/dullesgirl/index.html
  Ozora Baptist Church Cemetery, Grayson, Gwinnett County, GA.

- Tompkins County, NYGenWeb Cemetery Page
  http://www.rootsweb.com/~nytompki/tcem.htm

- Tower Hill Cemetery, Edgartown, MA, Photos and Transcripts ~ Massachusetts
  http://www.vineyard.net/vineyard/history/cemetery/th/index.html
  Photographs, transcripts, and biographical notes on all of the pre-1750 gravestones located at Tower Hill Cemetery (aka "Old Burying Ground").

- T Point Cemetery, Clayhole, Kentucky
  http://genweb.net/~gen-cds/tpoint.html

- Trunkey Creek Cemetery ~ Australia
  http://www.angelfire.com/bc/Cubitt/wizzn.html
  List of headstones in cemetery near Bathurst in New South Wales.

- Tulsa Cemetery Inscriptions No. 1: Rose Hill ~ OK
  http://angelfire.com/oh2/fountainofyouth/cemetery.html

- Tulsa Cemetery Inscriptions No. 5: Oaklawn ~ OK
  http://angelfire.com/oh2/fountainofyouth/oaklawn.html

"U"

- The Ultimate Tour of Highgate Cemetery - The Sexton's Tales ~ London, England
  http://www.tales.ndirect.co.uk/SEXTON_TALE.HTML

- Union Baptist Church Inscriptions ~ Lipscomb, AL
  http://www.geocities.com/Heartland/Meadows/3011/un.htm

- Union Grove Cemetery of Cross County Arkansas Information Page
  http://www.geocities.com/union_grove/index.html
  Burial index, history, and general information.

- Union Prospect Cemetery, Aberdeen, NJ
  http://www.netlabs.net/hp/gjoynson/unionprospect.htm
  Indexed list of African American burials in Union Prospect Cemetery, Aberdeen (formerly Matawan), Monmouth County, New Jersey.

- University of Oxford, Ashmolean Museum, The Department of Antiquities Monumental Brasses ~ England
  http://antiqs-iii.ashmol.ox.ac.uk/ash/departments/antiquities/brass/

- Upsala, Minnesota Cemetery Index
  http://upstel.net/~johns/CemIndex/CemIndex.html

- USCWC Cemetery Listings
  http://www.cwc.lsu.edu/cwc/projects/cemindex.htm
  From the U.S. Civil War Center.

- USGenWeb Tombstone Transcription Project
  http://www.rootsweb.com/~cemetery/

- USGS Mapping Information: GNIS Data Base Query Form
  http://www-nmd.usgs.gov/www/gnis/gnisform.html
  Type in your County & State name and in the Feature box type in the word Cemetery.

- USMA: The West Point Cemetery
  http://www.usma.army.mil/Cemetery/
  Features a map of the West Point Cemetery with links to the famous people buried there.

- Utah Cemetery Inventory - Burials Database
  http://www.dced.state.ut.us/history/Services/lcburials.html
  From the Utah State Historical Society. Lists over 315,000 burials in 208 cemeteries.
  - Burials Search
    http://utstcess.dced.state.ut.us:8080/NEWBURIALS/SilverStream/Pages/pgStandardSearch.html
  - Cemetery Search
    http://utstcess.dced.state.ut.us:8080/NEWBURIALS/SilverStream/Pages/pgCemeterySearch.html
  - List of Cemeteries
    http://www.dced.state.ut.us/history/Services/lccemeteries.html

- The Utica Cemetery ~ Michigan
  http://www.concentric.net/~Ekkm/Utica.html

- Uttoxeter Road Cemetery, Derby, Derbyshire, England, UK
  http://www.derbycity.com/derby/tombs.html

"V"

- Vancouver Barracks Cemetery Index
  http://www.geocities.com/Eureka/4458/vanbar.html
  A federal cemetery near Vancouver, Washington.

- Van Wert County, Ohio Cemeteries
  http://www.rootsweb.com/~ohvanwer/cemetery.htm
  A list of all known cemeteries, compiled by the Van Wert County Genealogical Society.

- Vaughan Community Cemetery ~ Hants County, Nova Scotia, Canada
  http://www.rootsweb.com/~nshants/vaughan.html

- Vaughan United Church Cemetery ~ Hants County, Nova Scotia, Canada
  http://www.rootsweb.com/~nshants/VUnited.html

- Vera Cemetery- History of the Cemetery
  http://wfconnection.com/vera/cemetery.htm
  A history of this rural cemetery in Vera, Knox County, Texas. Listing of those buried there with dates of birth and death.

- Vernon and District Family History Society - Cemetery Monument Inscriptions ~ B.C., Canada
  http://www.junction.net/vernhist/V4.html

- Victoria County Cemetery Transcriptions ~ Nova Scotia, Canada
  http://members.tripod.com/~lemac2/index-16.html

- Victorian Cemeteries ~ Australia
  http://home.primus.com.au/bonzaideas/MelbCems.htm
  This site contains contact info, history, links, source holdings, cemetery diagrams & other relevant information on cemeteries in Melbourne Metro & Regional Victoria.

- Victorian London Cemeteries ~ England
  http://www.gendocs.demon.co.uk/cem.html
  The public cemetery, as distinct from the churchyard, as a proper place for burial, originated in the Victorian period.

"W"

- Ward's Cemetery ~ Arizona
  http://www.rootsweb.com/~azgreenl/wards.html
  A small private cemetery, perched on the side of a hill in Clifton. There are at least six unmarked graves and three that you can no longer read.

- War of 1812 Cemetery, Town of Cheektowaga, Erie County, New York
  http://members.tripod.com/~wnyroots/index-1812.html
  List off burials including soldiers from 12 states and Great Britian.

- Washington Cemetery Project
  http://www.rootsweb.com/~usgenweb/wa/wacem.htm
  From the US GenWeb Archives

  o Eden Valley Cemetery
    ftp://ftp.rootsweb.com/pub/usgenweb/wa/wahkiakum/cemetery/edenvall.txt
    Also known as Buskala Family Cemetery.

  o Elma Catholic Cemetery
    ftp://ftp.rootsweb.com/pub/usgenweb/wa/graysharbor/cemetery/elmacath.txt
    Also known as St. Joseph's Cemetery.

  o Fern Hill Cemetery, Wahkiakum County
    ftp://ftp.rootsweb.com/pub/usgenweb/wa/wahkiakum/cemetery/fernhill.txt

  o Grays River Grange Cemetery, Wahkiakum County
    ftp://ftp.rootsweb.com/pub/usgenweb/wa/wahkiakum/cemetery/graysriv.txt

  o Greenwood Cemetery, Cathlamet, Wahkiakum County
    ftp://ftp.rootsweb.com/pub/usgenweb/wa/wahkiakum/cemetery/greenwd.txt

  o Johns River Cemetery, Markham, Washington
    ftp://ftp.rootsweb.com/pub/usgenweb/wa/graysharbor/cemetery/jriver.txt

  o Mt. Adams Cemetery, Glenwood, Klickitat County, Washington
    ftp://ftp.rootsweb.com/pub/usgenweb/wa/klickita/cemetery/mtadams.txt

  o Old Schafer Homestead Cemetery
    ftp://ftp.rootsweb.com/pub/usgenweb/wa/graysharbor/cemetery/schafer.txt
    Also known as Schafer Valley Cemetery and Satsop Valley Cemetery. Some of the graves here were moved to Shafer Cemetery and to Fern Hill Cemetery.

  o Pioneer Cemetery in Cathlamet, Wahkiakum County
    ftp://ftp.rootsweb.com/pub/usgenweb/wa/wahkiakum/cemetery/pioneer.txt

  o Rosburg Cemetery, Wahkiakum County
    ftp://ftp.rootsweb.com/pub/usgenweb/wa/wahkiakum/cemetery/rosburg.txt

  o Seal River Cemetery, Wahkiakum County
    ftp://ftp.rootsweb.com/pub/usgenweb/wa/wahkiakum/cemetery/sealriv.txt

- Washington County Cemetery Project ~ Indiana
  http://vax1.vigo.lib.in.us/~jmounts/cem.htm

- Washington County, MO Cemeteries ~ Missouri
  http://www.rootsweb.com/~mowashin/cemetery/wccem.html
  23,000+ burials in dozens of cemeteries.

- Waterford Rural Cemetery Records ~ New York
  http://www.rootsweb.com/~nysarato/cembeg.htm

- Waveney District Council - Cemeteries Index
  http://www.waveney.gov.uk/cemetery/cemeteries.html
  From Waveney in Suffolk, England. Includes indexes for cemeteries in Beccles, Bungay, Halesworth, Kirkley, Lowestoft, Southwold, & Wrentham.

- Wells Cemetery ~ Douglas, Arizona
  http://www.amug.org/~mzwhiz/wells.html
  Small family cemetery northeast of Douglas approx 8 miles, near milepost # 374 on Highway 80.

- Werkheiser Cemetery-Forks Township
  http://www.geocities.com/Heartland/6508/#Werkheiser Cemetery

- West Tisbury Village Cemetery Photos and Transcripts ~ Massachusetts
  http://www.vineyard.net/vineyard/history/cemetery/wt/index.html
  Selected 17th and 18th century gravestones of some of the early settlers of Tisbury and West Tisbury, MA. Includes early families of ALLEN, ATHEARN, EDDY, HANCOCK, MANTER, MAYHEW, TORREY, WEST, and others.

- Willoughby Cemetery, Great Valley, Cattaraugus County, New York
  ftp://ftp.rootsweb.com/pub/usgenweb/ny/cattaraugus/greatvalley/ceme0001.txt

- Windsor Forks Cemetery ~ Hants County, Nova Scotia, Canada
  http://www.rootsweb.com/~nshants/windsor.html

- Wood Island Cemetery (established 1882) ~ Prince Edward Island, Canada
  http://www.rootsweb.com/~pictou/wdi.htm

- Wood Islands Pioneer Cemetery 1807--1910 ~ Prince Edward Island, Canada
  http://www.rootsweb.com/~pictou/wdislan.htm

- WSGS--Published Cemetery Inscriptions
  http://www.rootsweb.com/~wsgs/cemetery.htm
  A cemetery name and location index (i.e. Monroe Co., Mt. Hope cem. Sparta, 18 pgs.) to the cemetery inscriptions published in the Wisconsin State Genealogical Society Newsletter. 1,060+ cemeteries are included. Copies of the inscriptions are available for a nominal fee.

"Y"

- Yale Peabody Museum: Geographic Names Information System (GNIS)
  http://www.peabody.yale.edu/other/gnis/
  Search the USGS Geographic Names Database. You can limit the search to a specific county in this state and search for any of the following features: airport arch area arroyo bar basin bay beach bench bend bridge building canal cape cemetery channel church cliff crater crossing dam falls flat forest gap geyser glacier gut harbor hospital island isthmus lake lava levee locale mine oilfield other park pillar plain ppl range rapids reserve reservoir ridge school sea slope spring stream summit swamp tower trail tunnel valley well woods.

- York Township Cemetery Index ~ Du Page County, Illinois
  http://www.dcgs.org/york/

- The Zion Lutheran Church of Helotes - Cemetery Transcriptions ~ San Antonio, Bexar, Texas
  http://lonestar.texas.net/~gdalum/cemetery.html

◆ Mailing Lists, Newsgroups & Chat

- Genealogy Resources on the Internet - Cemeteries / Monuments / Obituaries Mailing Lists
  http://www.rootsweb.com/~jfuller/gen_mail_cemetery.html

- ALEXTREE Mailing List
  http://www.rootsweb.com/~jfuller/gen_mail_cemetery.html #ALEXTREE
  For anyone with an interest in the cemeteries of Western North Carolina. Areas of discussion will include page updates, local cemetery news and announcements, and preservation strategies.

- AR-CEMETERIES Mailing List
  http://www.rootsweb.com/~jfuller/gen_mail_states-ar.html #AR-CEMETERIES
  For anyone interested in locating and preserving historical information about Arkansas cemeteries.

- AZ-CEMETERIES Mailing List
  http://www.rootsweb.com/~jfuller/gen_mail_states-az.html #AZ-CEMETERIES
  For anyone searching for their ancestors in Arizona cemeteries and anyone interested in preserving historical information about Arizona cemeteries.

- CA-DEATH-INDEX Mailing List
  http://www.rootsweb.com/~jfuller/gen_mail_states-ca.html #CA-DEATH-INDEX

For anyone who desires lookups in the California Death Index (July 1905 to 1995) or who has access to the index and can do lookups for other subscribers.

- CEMETERY Mailing List
  http://www.rootsweb.com/~jfuller/gen_mail_cemetery.html #CEMETERY
  For people interested in the many aspects of family graves from caring for the grave of one ancestor to the restoration and preservation of the family cemetery.

- CEMETERY-PHOTOS Mailing List
  http://www.rootsweb.com/~jfuller/gen_mail_cemetery.html #CEMETERY-PHOTOS
  And the Cemetery-Photos-L Website
  http://www.geocities.com/Heartland/Grove/2076/welcome_page.html
  For anyone who is interested in preserving their family's monuments (e.g., gravestones, monuments, war memorials) on film.

- CO-CEMETERIES Mailing List
  http://www.rootsweb.com/~jfuller/gen_mail_states-co.html #CO-CEMETERIES
  For anyone searching for their ancestors in Colorado cemeteries and anyone interested in preserving historical information about Colorado cemeteries.

- DE-CEMETERIES Mailing List
  http://www.rootsweb.com/~jfuller/gen_mail_states-de.html #DE-CEMETERIES
  For anyone interested in locating and preserving historical information about Delaware cemeteries.

- FL-NE-CEMETERY Mailing List
  http://www.rootsweb.com/~jfuller/gen_mail_states-fl.html #FL-NE-CEMETERY
  Main focus is locating human burial sites in the northeast Florida area.

- GRAVE-L Mailing List
  http://www.alsirat.com/silence/mlist.html
  "Grave-L is a new mailing list explicitly for taphophiles -- lovers of cemeteries and funerals. It will be of particular interest to historians, genealogists, funeral directors, cemetery workers, and others concerned with the preservation, folklore, and history of graveyards".

- IA-CEMETERIES Mailing List
  http://www.rootsweb.com/~jfuller/gen_mail_states-ia.html #IA-CEMETERIES
  For anyone searching for their ancestors in Iowa cemeteries and anyone interested in preserving historical information about Iowa cemeteries.

- IL-CEMETERIES Mailing List
  http://www.rootsweb.com/~jfuller/gen_mail_states-il.html #IL-CEMETERIES
  For anyone searching for their ancestors in Illinois cemeteries and anyone interested in preserving historical information about Illinois cemeteries.

- INPCRP Mailing List
  http://www.rootsweb.com/~jfuller/gen_mail_states-in.html #INPCRP
  For anyone interested in the Indiana Pioneer Cemeteries Restoration Project.
  http://www.rootsweb.com/~inpcrp/

- INSCRIPTIONS-L Mailing List
  http://www.rootsweb.com/~jfuller/gen_mail_cemetery.html
  #INSCRIPTIONS
  For anyone who has an interest in genealogy and local history related to Monumental Inscriptions including gravestones, monuments, and war memorials.

- KS-CEMETERIES Mailing List
  http://www.rootsweb.com/~jfuller/gen_mail_states-ks.html
  #KS-CEMETERIES
  For anyone interested in locating and preserving historical information about Kansas cemeteries.

- KY-CEMETERIES Mailing List
  http://www.rootsweb.com/~jfuller/gen_mail_states-ky.html
  #KY-CEMETERIES
  For anyone interested in locating and preserving historical information about Kentucky cemeteries.

- MI-ENGLAND Mailing List
  http://www.rootsweb.com/~jfuller/gen_mail_cemetery.html
  #MI-ENGLAND
  For those interested in Monumental Inscriptions on gravestones, etc. in England.

- MO-CEMETERIES Mailing List
  http://www.rootsweb.com/~jfuller/gen_mail_states-mo.html
  #MO-CEMETERIES
  For anyone interested in locating and preserving historical information about Missouri cemeteries.

- OH-CEMETERIES Mailing List
  http://www.rootsweb.com/~jfuller/gen_mail_states-oh.html
  #OH-CEMETERIES
  For anyone searching for their ancestors in Ohio cemeteries or interested in preserving and sharing historical information about Ohio cemeteries.

- OK-CEMETERIES Mailing List
  http://www.rootsweb.com/~jfuller/gen_mail_states-ok.html
  #OK-CEMETERIES
  For anyone interested in locating and preserving historical information about Oklahoma cemeteries.

- PA-BUCKS-CEMETERIES Mailing List
  http://www.rootsweb.com/~jfuller/gen_mail_states-pa.html
  #PA-BUCKS-CEMETERIES
  For anyone searching for their ancestors in Bucks County, Pennsylvania cemeteries, or interested in preserving historical information about Bucks County cemeteries.

- PA-CARBON-CEMETERIES Mailing List
  http://www.rootsweb.com/~jfuller/gen_mail_states-pa.html
  #PA-CARBON-CEMETERIES
  For anyone searching for their ancestors in Carbon County, Pennsylvania cemeteries, or interested in preserving historical information about Carbon County cemeteries.

- PA-CEMETERIES Mailing List
  http://www.rootsweb.com/~jfuller/gen_mail_states-pa.html
  #PA-CEMETERIES
  For anyone searching for their ancestors in Pennsylvania cemeteries, or interested in preserving historical information about Pennsylvania cemeteries.

- PA-DEL-CEMETERIES Mailing List
  http://www.rootsweb.com/~jfuller/gen_mail_states-pa.html
  #PA-DEL-CEMETERIES
  For anyone searching for their ancestors in Delaware County, Pennsylvania cemeteries, or interested in preserving historical information about Delaware County cemeteries.

- PA-MONTGOMERY-CEMETERIES Mailing List
  http://www.rootsweb.com/~jfuller/gen_mail_states-pa.html
  #PA-MONTGOMERY-CEMETERIES
  For anyone searching for their ancestors in Montgomery County, Pennsylvania cemeteries or interested in preserving historical information about Montgomery County cemeteries.

- PA-PHILA-CEMETERIES Mailing List
  http://www.rootsweb.com/~jfuller/gen_mail_states-pa.html
  #PA-PHILA-CEMETERIES
  For anyone searching for their ancestors in cemeteries in the City and County of Philadelphia, Pennsylvania, or interested in preserving historical information about these cemeteries.

- PerryKyCemeteries Mailing List
  http://www.rootsweb.com/~jfuller/gen_mail_cemetery.html
  #PerryKyCemeteries
  For anyone who is looking for information on the cemeteries of Perry County, Kentucky.

- SC-CEMETERY Mailing List
  http://www.rootsweb.com/~jfuller/gen_mail_cemetery.html
  #SC-CEMETERY
  To discuss the formation of a cemetery preservation society for South Carolina.

- WI-CEMETERIES Mailing List
  http://www.rootsweb.com/~jfuller/gen_mail_states-wi.html
  #WI-CEMETERIES
  For anyone interested in locating and preserving historical information about Wisconsin cemeteries.

◆ Monuments & Memorials

- Affordable Grave Markers
  http://www.affordablegravemarkers.com/
  This site offers new products to help genealogists preserve their family history by making it affordable to mark those unmarked graves with affordable grave markers and cemetery signs.

- Cemetery Research and Gravestone Rubbings...a How To, Site
  http://www.angelfire.com/ut/gmachoocho/cemetery411.html
  How to research cemeteries, care for tombstones and photograph the stones.

- CGN Cemetery Do's & Don'ts
  http://members.aol.com/ctgravenet/dosdonts.htm
  Includes: Cleaning Basics, Graveyard Maintenance, Gravestone Rubbings, Reading Inscriptions, Should You Seal or Waterproof Gravestones?

- Everything you wanted to know about Gravestone Studies and Rubbing
  http://www.justcallbob.com/grave.html

- Finding the Hidden Treasures in Tombstone Rubbings
  http://www.firstct.com/fv/t_examp.html

- Graven Images
  http://www.rootsweb.com/~ote/grave.htm
  Describes the symbolism of motifs on gravestones - from The Olive Tree.

- Gravestone Rubbing Kit
  http://gravestoneartwear.com/rubbingkit.html
  From Gravestone Artwear.

- A Gravestone Rubbing Primer
  http://www.savinggraves.com/rubbings.htm
  A primer on the art of gravestone rubbings.

- How to do Tombstone Rubbings
  http://www.mindspring.com/~mooregen/tombstone.htm

- International Black Sheep Society / Grave Marker Acronyms
  http://homepages.rootsweb.com/~blksheep/acronym.html

- Memorial Family Finder from HobbsHouse
  http://www.hobbshouse.com/
  Find extended family members with Memorial Family Finder, a product that transforms a cemetery headstone or grave marker into a communication tool. Memorial Family Finder is an attractive, unobtrusive container that affixes to a headstone or marker. The unit comes with pre-printed cards on which you can write your contact information, alerting others that you are searching for family information.

- Planning & Architectural Services - Cemetery Protection
  http://www.preserveala.org/cemetery.html
  Cleaning Gravestones: Use the Gentlest Means Possible, by Camille Bowman.

- Sculpture Preservation Co.
  http://indigo.ie/~sculpres/
  Offers maintenance and repair of contemporary sculpture, monuments and cemetery sculpture. Located in Fergus, Dripsey, County Cork, Ireland

- Tips for Photographing Gravestones
  http://www.genealogy.com/64_gravestones.html

- Tombstone Meanings
  http://homepages.rootsweb.com/~maggieoh/tomb.html

- Tombstone Rubbings
  http://www.firstct.com/fv/t_stone.html

◆ Professional Researchers, Volunteers & Other Research Services

- Headstone Hunter
  http://www.headstonehunter.com/
  A network of volunteers who will visit graveyards in their area.

- Headstones in Yorkshire
  http://www.honey23.freeserve.co.uk/Headstones/index.html
  Professional service for finding and recording headstones in Yorkshire, England.

- P&A's Stark County, Ohio Cemetery Picture Service, Obituary, Tombstone Rubbings & County Research
  http://www.rootsweb.com/~ohstark/cemetery.htm

- Sharyn's Secretarial Services - Brisbane Cemetery Photographs ~ Australia
  http://www.ozemail.com.au/~sharynmark/page6.html
  5x7 photos or digital camera photos.

- Southern York County Cemetery Photo Services ~ Pennsylvania
  http://members.aol.com/Lynn4604/prof/index.htm
  35 mm or digital photos of your ancestors' headstones.

◆ Publications, Software & Supplies

- Amazon.com Genealogy Bookstore – Cemetery
  http://www.amazon.com/exec/obidos/external-search/?keyword=cemetery+genealogy&tag=markcyndisgenealA/
  And Funeral Home
  http://www.amazon.com/exec/obidos/external-search/?keyword=funeral+home+genealogy&tag=markcyndisgenealA/

- Aspen 2000 Windows (Cemetery, Funeral Home & Obituary Records
  http://www.dhc.net/~design/aspen.htm
  For indexing, publishing or storing these all important records. Complete publishing features including .rtf, .doc and more. Picture or image attachments are also a feature of this genealogy package.

- AudioTapes.com - Genealogical Lectures on Cassette Tapes - Cemetery
  http://www.audiotapes.com/search2.asp?Search=cemetery

- The Cemetery Column - Cemeteries & Genealogy
  http://www.interment.net/column/index.htm
  An electronic journal on everything associated with cemeteries, including news about cemeteries worldwide, reviews of other websites & books, the art of cemetery sculptures & architecture, and genealogical research.

- Kleerub Paper Company
  http://www.kleerub.com
  Vendor of quality rubbing paper for taking duplicate rubbings. Kleerub Paper Company is a family owned business that has served many monument companies, cemeteries and genealogical associations since 1949.

- Tomb With A View
  http://members.aol.com/TombView/twav.html
  A newsletter devoted to the appreciation, study and preservation of historic U.S. cemeteries. It includes articles, book reviews and an extensive listing of special events in or about cemeteries, such as tours, lectures and special celebrations.

- View•logy - Memorials That Tell A Story
  http://www.leif.com/
  An electronic display unit that installs into traditional grave markers, which includes a visual eulogy.

◆ Societies & Groups

- American Battle Monuments Commission
  http://www.usabmc.com/index.shtml
  Details about cemeteries, memorials and US war dead since WWI.

- Association for Gravestone Studies Home Page
  http://www.gravestonestudies.org/

- Berks County Association for Graveyard Preservation ~ Pennsylvania
  http://www.geocities.com/Heartland/Ranch/3005/graves.html

- Coalition To Protect Maryland Burial Sites, Inc.
  http://www.rootsweb.com/~mdcpmbs/coalition01.htm
  Includes a description of their "Distressed Cemetery Response Kit."

- Commission for the Preservation of Pioneer Jewish Cemeteries and Landmarks
  http://www.jfed.org/magnes/cemecom.htm
  Northern California.

- Commonwealth War Graves Commission
  http://www.cwgc.org/
  Details of 1.7 million members of UK and Commonwealth forces who died in the 1st and 2nd World Wars and other wars, and 60,000 civilian casualties of WWII. Gives details of grave site, date of death, age, usually parents/widow's address.

- Connecticut Gravestone Network
  http://members.aol.com/ctgravenet/index.htm
  Organized in 1995, CGN's purpose is to educate the public on how important old graveyards & cemeteries are to history, and that gravestone carving is a valuable art form.

- Friends of Mt. Moriah
  http://members.xoom.com/FOMM/home.htm
  An organization to assist in the maintenance and help preserve the history of the Mount Moriah Cemetery in Philadelphia, Pennsylvania.

- Headstone Hunter
  http://www.headstonehunter.com/
  A network of volunteers who will visit graveyards in their area.

- Iowa Funeral Directors Association Members
  http://www2.istatinc.com/ifda_members.html

- Jewish Cemetery Association of Massachusetts, Inc.
  http://www.jcam.org/

- Maine Old Cemetery Association
  http://www.rootsweb.com/~memoca/moca.htm

- New Hampshire Old Graveyard Association
  http://www.tiac.net/users/nhsog/nhoga.htm

- Ohio Cemetery Preservation Society
  http://www.rootsweb.com/~ohcps/
  An association dedicated to preserve and protect Ohio's most precious and endangered heritage resources -- our historic cemeteries and burying grounds. A primary goal of OCPS will be to increase the awareness and inestimable value of our cemeteries as sources of community and state pride and encourage groups and individuals to help preserve them as landmarks for future generations to learn from and appreciate.

- The Old Cemeteries Society - Victoria Tombstone Tales of Ross Bay Cemetery
  http://www.oldcem.bc.ca/
  Victoria's Ross Bay Cemetery opened in 1873 to serve the burial needs of the growing city of Victoria, British Columbia, Canada. Overlooking Ross Bay, it is 11 hectares in size (27.5 acres) and has almost 28,000 interments. Not just a burial ground, it serves as a park and restful get-away for many people. Come inside and take a virtual tour, meet some of the more famous residents, learn about issues that concern twentieth-century cemeteries or just enjoy some of the stories of this great cemetery.

- The Slovak Heritage and Cultural Society of British Columbia
  http://www.iarelative.com/slovakbc.htm

- Oregon Historic Cemeteries Association ~ Boring, Oregon
  http://www.familyhistory.com/societyhall/viewmember.asp?societyid=40897

- Save Our Cemeteries, Inc.
  http://home.gnofn.org/~soc/
  Dedicated to the preservation and restoration of the historic cemeteries of Louisiana.

- Save Texas Cemeteries, Inc.
  http://www.rootsweb.com/~txstc/index.html
  Provides information on membership, activities, "Cemetery 911", and a system for cataloging cemeteries in Texas.

- Saving Graves
  http://www.savinggraves.com/index.htm
  Supports and encourages the protection, restoration, & preservation of endangered American cemeteries.

- Saving Southern Cemeteries
  http://www.angelfire.com/ga2/cemetery/
  Organization dedicated to encouraging transcriptions, preserving cemeteries in the South, primarily Georgia, and to educating the public on the dangers facing cemeteries.

- State Association for the Preservation of Iowa Cemeteries
  http://www.sapic.org/
  Provides a list of Iowa funeral homes and materials on preserving monuments - including a video for sale.

- Texas Historical Commission - Coordinator Breathes New Life Into Neglected Historic Cemeteries
  http://www.thc.state.tx.us/Gerron.html
  Describes the work of the Texas Historical Commission in preserving historical cemeteries. Provides information on how to get a cemetery designated as an "Official Historic Texas Cemetery".

- The Vermont Old Cemetery Association
  http://homepages.together.net/~btrutor/voca/vocahome.htm

- Washington State Cemetery Association
  http://www.rootsweb.com/~wapsgs/
  Dedicated to the preservation of old/abandoned cemeteries in Washington state.

- Volksbund Deutsche Kriegsgräberfürsorge e.V.
  http://www.volksbund.de/homepage.htm
  The German Military Grave Registration Service. Maintains 2 million war graves in over 640 cemeteries. Assists in grave identification and restoration. Provides assistance in determining the fate of German war dead.

  o Vermissten und Toten Datenbank
    http://www.volksbund.de/VuTDB/vut_suche.asp
    The Missing and Dead Database. Online searchable database of over 2 million interments.

CENSUS RELATED SITES WORLDWIDE

http://www.cyndislist.com/census2.htm

Category Index:

◆ Census Tools & Information

◆ International Census Indexes & Records

◆ Census Tools & Information

- Amazon.com Genealogy Bookstore - Census
  http://www.amazon.com/exec/obidos/external-search/?
  keyword=census+genealogy&tag=markcyndisgenealA/

- AudioTapes.com - Genealogical Lectures on Cassette
  Tapes - Census
  http://www.audiotapes.com/search2.asp?Search=census

- Calculating Birth Year Based on Census Information
  http://www.wdbj.net/~wdbj/gen/birthyear/cenindx.html

- Census Dates for Countries and Areas of the World:
  1946 to 2004
  http://www.census.gov/ipc/www/cendates/
  *Shows the dates of census enumerations over the past half century,
  as well as projected or scheduled enumerations in the near future
  for countries around the world.*

- Census Information from GENUKI
  http://www.genuki.org.uk/big/eng/census.html
  For England, Scotland & Wales.

- Censuses In Australian Colonies
  http://www.users.on.net/proformat/census.html
  *Provides information on date of census, condition, and where
  deposited.*

- Clooz
  http://www.ancestordetective.com/clooz.htm
  *An electronic filing cabinet and database for systematically storing
  all of the clues to your ancestry that you have been collecting.
  Requires Microsoft Windows 95. Clooz contains templates for all
  U.S. federal censuses, 1841-1891 U.K. censuses, 1852-1901
  Canadian censuses, and 1901 and 1911 Irish censuses, as well as
  generic templates for censuses not included, such as state censuses.*

- Family Census Research
  http://www.dhc.net/~design/fcr30.htm
  Software program for organizing census records.

- Family History SourceGuide
  http://www.familysearch.org/sg/index_s.html
  *Free forms to print from the FamilySearch Internet Genealogy
  Service of the LDS Church.*
  - Canada Census
    - 1851
      http://www.familysearch.org/sg/FCan1851.html
    - 1861
      http://www.familysearch.org/sg/FCan1861.html

- 1871
  http://www.familysearch.org/sg/FCan1871.html
- 1891
  http://www.familysearch.org/sg/FCan1891.html
- 1901
  http://www.familysearch.org/sg/FCan1901.html
  - Other Forms
    - British Census Worksheet
      http://www.familysearch.org/sg/FBritish.html
    - Ireland 1901/1911
      http://www.familysearch.org/sg/FIreland.html

- Finding an Address in the Transcription of the 1881
  Census of England and Wales
  http://people.enternet.com.au/~tmj/c81-adrs.htm

- GENUKI: Devon 1891 Census Project
  http://www.cs.ncl.ac.uk/genuki/DEV/censusproject.html
  *This project aims to provide a free online searchable transcription
  of the 1891 Census for Devon. It is intended as a pilot project,
  testing out organizational procedures and specially-designed
  software which is hoped will prove suitable for, and encourage the
  undertaking of, a planned much larger project, the FreeCEN
  Project, that would encompass other UK counties and census years.*

- Getting into the Norwegian Census
  http://www.rhd.uit.no/nhdc/michael02.htm

- National Archives of Canada - Census Records
  http://www.archives.ca/exec/naweb.dll?fs&02020205&e
  &top&0

- Overview of Soundex
  http://www.bradandkathy.com/genealogy/overviewof
  soundex.html

- Reading Census Handwriting
  http://www.sierra.com/sierrahome/familytree/hqarticles/
  censusreading/
  *Online article by Leland K. Meitzler provides tips & tricks for
  deciphering the enumerator's chicken scratchings.*

- Researching with Census Records
  http://www.familytreemaker.com/issue13.html
  From Family Tree Maker Online.

- Soundex Conversion Program from Genealogy
  Online
  http://www.genealogy.org/soundex.shtml

- Soundex Conversion Program - Surname to Soundex Code
  http://searches.rootsweb.com/cgi-bin/Genea/soundex.sh

- The Soundex Machine
  http://www.nara.gov/genealogy/soundex/soundex.html
  A form to convert surnames to soundex codes; from the National Archives.

- Tom Nunamaker's Census Age Calculator
  http://toshop.com/censuscalc.cfm

- Using the Soundex System
  http://www.ancestry.com/columns/george/03-20-98.htm
  From "Along Those Lines..." by George G. Morgan.

- Victorian Census Project
  http://www.staffs.ac.uk/schools/humanities_and_soc_sciences/census/vichome.htm
  From Staffordshire University. Aims to computerize a number of source documents and related materials relating to Great Britain in the mid-nineteenth century.

  o The Census Enumerators' Books
    http://www.staffs.ac.uk/schools/humanities_and_soc_sciences/census/cebs.htm
    Brief introduction to the Census Enumerators' Books (CEBs) and of their values to sociologists and others with an interest in studying nineteenth-century censuses.

- Yet Another Soundex Converter (YASC)
  http://www.bradandkathy.com/genealogy/yasc.html

◆ International Census Indexes & Records

- 1768 St. John's Island Heads of Household Census ~ Prince Edward Island, Canada
  http://www.islandregister.com/1768.html

- 1842 Census Index - Malahide Township, Elgin County, Canada West / Ontario
  http://www.ptbruce.kanservu.ca/Genealogy/census1842.htm

- 1891 Census of East Hamlet, Ludlow, Shropshire ~ England
  ftp://ftp.rootsweb.com/pub/wggenweb/england/ludlow/easthamlet/shropshire/census/eastha91.txt

- 1901 Census - Lunenburg County, Nova Scotia
  http://www.rootsweb.com/~canns/lunenburg/1901census.html

- 1901 Census of Canada - Film Numbers
  http://www.tbaytel.net/bmartin/census.htm

- Alberta Genealogical Society, Edmonton Branch - 1901 Census Alberta District (No. 202) ~ Canada
  http://www.agsedm.edmonton.ab.ca/1901_census_202_online.html

- Campbell River Genealogy Club - 1901 Census - District #3 Vancouver; Sub-district B ~ British Columbia, Canada
  http://www.connected.bc.ca/~genealogy/

- Censuses of Gloucestershire and Southern Warwickshire
  http://www.silk.net/personal/gordonb/cotswold.htm
  Complete 1851+ Census for Gloucestershire, 552,000 entries - also available on CD.

- General Don's Militia Survey of 1815 ~ Channel Islands
  http://www.societe-jersiaise.org/alexgle/Don.html

- A Guide to the 1851 Census of Canada West: Renfrew County
  http://www.amazon.com/exec/obidos/ISBN=0969176651/markcyndisgenealA/
  A book by Norman Crowder.

- Halifax Census (1752)

  o A-E
    http://www.rootsweb.com/~nshalifa/Hfxcensus1.htm

  o F-K
    http://www.rootsweb.com/~nshalifa/Hfxcensus2.htm

  o L-Q
    http://www.rootsweb.com/~nshalifa/Hfxcensus3.htm

  o R-Z
    http://www.rootsweb.com/~nshalifa/Hfxcensus4.htm

- Index to the 1744 Quebec City Census ~ Quebec, Canada
  http://www.oz.net/~johnbang/genealogy/1744indx.txt

- About the 1891 Census of Prince Edward Island ~ Canada
  http://www.edu.pe.ca/paro/census/info1891.asp

- Index to the 1891 Dominion Census Lethbridge Sub-District, Alberta, Northwest Territories
  http://mypage.direct.ca/d/dobee/lethmain.html

- Leitrim-Roscommon 1901 Census Home Page
  http://www.leitrim-roscommon.com/1901census/
  Searchable database.

- Lokalhistorisk Samling i Århus, Danmark
  http://www.aakb.bib.dk/lokhist/
  Features local history for that area.

  o Folketællinger for Århus området
    http://www.aakb.bib.dk/springbraet/GodeLinks/Aarhus_Kultur.htm
    This site features Århus census for years 1787, 1801, 1834 and 1845

- Mecklenburg-Schwerin Census Records
  http://pages.prodigy.net/jhbowen/census.htm

- National Archives of Canada - Index to the 1871 Census of Ontario
  http://www.archives.ca/exec/naweb.dll?fs&020108&e&top&0

- NFHS Internet Branch - The 1851 British Census Index on CD-ROM - Its availability & usage
  http://www.rootsweb.com/~nfhs/ib/1851cd.htm
  Describes the contents and use of this census index for the English

counties of Devon, Norfolk, and Warwickshire which includes over 1.5 million individuals. Ordering information for this low cost CD-ROM is provided for 5 different countries.

- Nominal Census Homepage
  http://royal.okanagan.bc.ca/census/index.html
  Data for the southern interior of the Province of British Columbia, Canada

  o Canada Census, 1881 - Yale District
    http://royal.okanagan.bc.ca/census/yale1881.html

  o Canada Census, 1891 - Yale District
    http://royal.okanagan.bc.ca/census/yale1891.html

  o The IRC Census, 1877
    http://royal.okanagan.bc.ca/census/ind1877.html
    Indian Reserve Commission.

  o The OMI Census, 1877
    http://royal.okanagan.bc.ca/census/omi1877.html
    A nominal census of Native peoples taken by the Catholic missionary order, Oblates of Mary Immaculate (OMI)

- Norway - 1801 Census
  http://www.uib.no/hi/1801page.html

- Nova Scotia Census Data
  http://www.rootsweb.com/~casoccgs/census.html

- Ontario 1871 Census
  http://xcat.stauffer.queensu.ca/census/

- Post 1901 Census Project
  http://www.tbaytel.net/bmartin/natreg.htm
  From the Global Gazette. Many concerned Canadians believe that the legislation which enforces permanent concealment of post-1901 census from the public eye, must be changed. If new legislation is not passed by Canada's Parliament, those records may never be available for future generations or us. Worse yet, our detailed census records may be destroyed.

- Ron Taylor's UK Census Finding Aids and Indexes
  http://rontay.digiweb.com/
  Mainly from the 1851 Census

  o Born in France and Germany Census Indexes
    http://rontay.digiweb.com/france/

  o Institutionalized Census Indexes
    http://rontay.digiweb.com/institute/
    Including Paupers, Inmates, Convicts, Prisoners and Prostitutes.

  o Occupations Census Indexes
    http://rontay.digiweb.com/visit/occupy/

  o Scots and Irish Strays Census Indexes
    http://rontay.digiweb.com/scot/

  o Strays by County Census Indexes
    http://rontay.digiweb.com/county/

  o Visitors Census Indexes
    http://rontay.digiweb.com/visit/

- Unruh's South Russian Mennonite Census, 1795-1814
  http://pixel.cs.vt.edu/library/census/link/bhu.txt

CHAT & IRC
(IRC = Internet Relay Chat)
http://www.cyndislist.com/chat.htm

Category Index:
◆ Genealogy Chat & IRC Channels Listed by Networks / Server
◆ Genealogy Chat & IRC Home Pages

◆ General IRC Software & How To Guides

◆ Genealogy Chat & IRC Channels Listed by Networks / Server

- AfterNET
  Irc.afternet.org:6667
  - #GenealogyForum
    http://home.flash.net/~gen4m/
  - #Genealogy-n-UK

- AnotherNet
  irc.another.net:6667
  - #genealogy

- DALnet
  http://www.dalnet.com/
  Irc.dal.net:7000
  - #Canadian Gen
  - #Fianna
    (Irish research)
  - #genealogy-events
  - #genealogy-help
    http://www.geocities.com/Heartland/Ranch/4656/
  - #Genealogy_IRC
    http://genweb.net/~genirc/
  - #Gen_Family_Tree
  - #Gentrace
  - #lunie-links
    Lunenburg County, Nova Scotia, Canada

- EFnet
  http://www.efnet.net
  Irc.chat.org:6667
  - #FTMCC
  - #genealogies
  - #genealogy
    http://www.voicenet.com/~bparker1/CHANNEL/index.htm

- IIGS
  http://www.iigs.org/irc/index.htm.en
  Irc.IIGS.org:6667 or 7000

  - #Australia
    http://www.historyaustralia.org.au/ifhaa/chat.htm
  - #Benelux
    http://www.iigs.org/cgi/ircthemes/ircthemes#Belgium, Netherlands, Luxemburg
  - #Canadian-Gen
    http://www.iigs.org/cgi/ircthemes/ircthemes#Canadian Genealogy
  - #cert
    http://www.iigs.org/cgi/ircthemes/ircthemes#Genealogical Research
  - #Cogenweb
    http://www.iigs.org/cgi/ircthemes/ircthemes#Colorado Genealogy
  - #CZER-Group
    http://www.iigs.org/cgi/ircthemes/ircthemes#Bukovina Genealogy
  - #DEUGen
    http://www.iigs.org/cgi/ircthemes/ircthemes#German Genealogy
  - #genealogie.fr
    http://www.iigs.org/cgi/ircthemes/ircthemes#French Genealogy
  - #Ger-Rus
    http://www.geocities.com/Heartland/Acres/4123/irc.htm
  - #htmlhelp
    http://www.iigs.org/cgi/ircthemes/ircthemes#HTML Discussion
  - #IIGS-Ontario
    http://www.iigs.org/cgi/ircthemes/ircthemes#Ontario Genealogy Chat
  - #IIGS-UKgen
    http://www.iigs.org/cgi/ircthemes/ircthemes#UK Genealogy
  - #IIGS-UK-IRE
    http://www.iigs.org/cgi/ircthemes/ircthemes#UK and Ireland Genealogy
  - #IIGS-UnivHelp
    http://www.iigs.org/cgi/ircthemes/ircthemes#IIGS University Chat
  - #Ireland-gen
  - #KY-Estill
    http://www.iigs.org/cgi/ircthemes/ircthemes#Estill County, Kentucky Research

- o #NewEngland
  http://www.iigs.org/cgi/ircthemes/ircthemes#New England
  Genealogy
- o #SE-USA
  http://www.iigs.org/cgi/ircthemes/ircthemes#South-Eastern
  USA Chat
- o #SHANNON
  http://www.iigs.org/cgi/ircthemes/ircthemes#Southern
  SHANNON Genealogies
- NewNet
  Irc.newnet.net:6667
  - o #family_history
  - o #genealogy
    http://www.eskimo.com/~mevers/rogue.htm
  - o #genealogy101
- RootsWeb
  Irc.rootsweb.com:6667 or 7000
  - o #MSGenWeb
    http://www.rootsweb.com/~msgenweb/chat.shtml
- SCS Net
  irc.scscorp.net:6667
  - o #genealogy
- Superchat
  http://www.superchat.org/
  Irc.superchat.org:6660-6668
  - o #Genealogy
    http://nctc.com/~cheyanne/index.html

◆ Genealogy Chat & IRC Home Pages

- CanadaGenWeb Chat Forum
  http://www.geneofun.on.ca/ongenweb/chat.html
- The "Cajun/Acadian" Chat Room
  http://www.acadian.org/chat.html
  From the Acadian Genealogy Homepage.
- The DALnet Genealogy Channels
  http://members.tripod.com/~GenealogyChat/
- Folks Online - FolksChat
  http://www.folksonline.com/folks/commun/folkschat/folkschat.
  htm#chatnow
- Genealogy - About.com - Genealogy Chat
  http://genealogy.about.com/hobbies/genealogy/mpchat.htm
- #Genealogy Forum
  http://www.flash.net/~gen4m/
  Genealogy Channel on Internet Relay Chat (IRC).
- #Genealogy-Help Chat Page on DALnet
  http://www.geocities.com/Heartland/Ranch/4656/
- Genealogy Online - Chat Room
  http://www.genealogy.org/~genchat/
- Genealogy_IRC = International Researcher's Club
  Page
  http://genweb.net/~genirc/

- Genealogy-Native
  http://nctc.com/~cheyanne/
  #Genealogy Channel on Superchat.
- Genealogy-Net - Gene-Net "One on One"
  http://www.geocities.com/Heartland/Meadows/6820/
  genenet.htm
- Generations - Find Your Roots
  http://www.talkspot.com/shows/Generations/
  *A new, interactive multimedia Internet program for genealogy.
  Hosted by Elon Gasper, on Talkspot.com each Wednesday from 5pm
  to 6pm Pacific Time Zone.*
- GEN-IRC Mailing List
  http://www.rootsweb.com/~jfuller/gen_mail_general.html
  #GEN-IRC
- GMW Chat Page
  http://www.citynet.net/mostwanted/prechat.htm
  From Genealogy's Most Wanted.
- Home Page for Genealogy on IRC
  http://www.genealogy.org/~jkatcmi/genealogy-irc/
  welcome.html
  - o Channels and NetWorks
    http://www.genealogy.org/~jkatcmi/genealogy-irc/
    geneycha.htm
    A guide for beginners.
  - o IRC info to deal with channel and Geney01
    http://www.genealogy.org/~jkatcmi/genealogy-irc/
    geneyirc.htm
  - o Regarding the Use of IRC in Genealogy Research
    http://www.genealogy.org/~jkatcmi/genealogy-irc/
    geneyfaq.htm
- IFHAA Genealogy Chat - #Australia
  http://www.historyaustralia.org.au/ifhaa/chat.htm
  *A weekly chat session for Australian researchers by the Internet
  Family History Association of Australia (IFHAA).*
- IIGS - International Internet Genealogical Society,
  I.R.C. Internet Relay Chat
  http://www.iigs.org/irc/index.htm.en
- IRC Channels Events Home Page
  http://www.geocities.com/Heartland/Meadows/6820/
- IRC Chat Line - #Ger-Rus
  http://www.geocities.com/Heartland/Acres/4123/irc.htm
  For researching Germans from Russia.
- Lincoln Co. WV Genealogy Chat Room
  http://www.geocities.com/Tokyo/5303/lincoln.htm
- Mississippi Genealogy IRC Chats
  http://www.rootsweb.com/~msgenweb/chat.shtml
- Montana State Genealogical Society - Montana Chat
  Room
  http://www.geocities.com/Heartland/Fields/6175/
- NewNet #Genealogy's Rogues Gallery
  http://www.eskimo.com/~mevers/rogue.htm

- Northeast Pennsylvania IRC Chat -
  #Luzerne_Co_Genealogy
  http://www.rootsweb.com/~paluzern/chat.htm
- Talk City Genealogy Chat
  http://www.talkcity.com/communities/chat/family.html?room=
  Genealogy
- The Unofficial EFnet #genealogy Channel Home
  Page
  http://www.voicenet.com/~bparker1/CHANNEL/index.htm
  - o The EFnet Genealogy Channel Beginners' Guide to
    Online Genealogy
    http://www.voicenet.com/~bparker1/CHANNEL/
    beginner.htm
- Webchat Broadcasting System: Adult Adoptees Chat
  http://chat19.go.com/webchat3.so?cmd=cmd_doorway:Adult_
  Adoptees_Chat
- Webchat Broadcasting System: Genealogy
  http://chat20.go.com/webchat3.so?cmd=cmd_doorway:
  Genealogy
- Wilibrord's Genealogy Chat Sites
  http://members.tripod.com/~Erala/genealogychat.html

◆ General IRC Software & How To Guides

- Amazon.com Genealogy Bookstore - IRC
  http://www.amazon.com/exec/obidos/external-search/?
  keyword=IRC&tag=markcyndisgenealA/
- Çëñt®ä|ïzë® §ç®ïÞt
  http://members.tripod.com/nicksg/Centralizer/
  A script that improves mIRC, which is an IRC client.
- Chatter's Jargon Dictionary
  http://www.stevegrossman.com/jargpge.htm
- Common Abbreviations
  http://www.talkcity.com/help/abbreviate.html
- The Comprehensive IRC Network List
  http://www.irchelp.org/irchelp/networks/
- DALnet IRC - FAQ
  http://www.dal.net/howto/FAQ.default.html
- EFnet #IRChelp Help Archive
  http://www.irchelp.org/
- Getting the Most from mIRC
  http://home.flash.net/~gen4m/MIRCing.htm
- ichat
  http://www.ichat.com/
  Plug-in software for your browser.

- ICQ
  http://web.icq.com/
- I.I.G.S. - Instructions, FAQs and Links for IRC
  http://www.iigs.org/irc/irclinks.htm.en
- IRC Intro File for Newbies using Windows
  http://www.geocities.com/SiliconValley/Park/6000/
  ircintro.html
- The MacIRC Home Page
  http://www.macirc.com/
  Software for Macintosh.
- mIRC: Homepage of the IRC Chat Client mIRC
  http://www.geocities.com/SiliconValley/Park/6000/index.html
  Software for Windows.
- NewIRCusers.com
  http://www.newircusers.com/
- The Official Ircle Home Page
  http://www.ircle.houseit.com/
  Software for Macintosh.
- OrbitIRC
  http://www.orbitirc.com/
  Software for Windows.
- ParaChat - Wweb-based 100% Java chat software
  http://www.paralogic.com/
- The PIRCH Page
  http://www.pirchat.com/
  *IRC client software for the Windows 3.x, Windows 95 and Windows
  NT.*
- A Quick Guide to Basic mIRC Commands
  http://www.voicenet.com/~bparker1/CHANNEL/mircguide.htm
- The Scripters Guild
  http://www.geocities.com/SiliconValley/Heights/1246/
- Shareware.com - IRC Downloads
  http://search.shareware.com/code/engine/Find?frame=none&
  logop=and&cfrom=quick&orfile=True&hits=25&search=IRC&
  category=All-Categories
- Straight Talk About IRC
  http://home.flash.net/~gen4m/TalkIRC.htm
- Stroud's IRC App Reviews
  http://cws.internet.com/reviews/irc-reviews.html
- Using mIRC with AOL
  http://www.irchelp.org/irchelp/mirc/aol.html
- XiRCON
  http://www.xircon.com/
  IRC Client for Windows 95/NT.
- Yahoo!...Computers and Internet...Chat
  http://dir.yahoo.com/Computers_and_Internet/Internet/Chat/

CITING SOURCES

http://www.cyndislist.com/citing.htm

Category Index:

◆ Citations in Genealogy

◆ Citing Electronic Sources

◆ Forms

◆ Citations in Genealogy

● AudioTapes.com - Genealogical Lectures on Cassette
Tapes – Citing
http://www.audiotapes.com/search2.asp?Search=Citing
Cite
http://www.audiotapes.com/search2.asp?Search=Cite
Citation
http://www.audiotapes.com/search2.asp?Search=Citation

● The Board for Certification of Genealogists'
Genealogical Standards Manual
http://www.amazon.com/exec/obidos/ISBN=0916489922/
markcyndisgenealA/
A book by the BCG.

● Carla's Tips for Sources
http://www.familytreemaker.com/19_carla.html
By Carla Ridenour.

● A Cite For Sore Eyes - Quality Citations for
Electronic Genealogy Sources
http://www.oz.net/~markhow/writing/cite.htm
*Written by Mark Howells for one of several different genealogical
publications.*

● Cite Your Sources : A Manual for Documenting
Family Histories and Genealogical Records
http://www.amazon.com/exec/obidos/ISBN=0878052860/
markcyndisgenealA/
A book by Richard S. Lackey.

● Citing Your Sources
http://www.bcgcertification.org/skbld959.html
*From the Board for Certification of Genealogists - Skill Building -
September 1995.*

● Evidence!: Citation & Analysis for the Family
Historian
http://www.amazon.com/exec/obidos/ISBN=0806315431/
markcyndisgenealA/
A book by Elizabeth Shown Mills.

● Genealogical Evidence: A Guide to the Standard of
Proof Relating to Pedigrees, Ancestry, Heirship and
Family History
http://www.amazon.com/exec/obidos/ISBN=0894121596/
markcyndisgenealA/
A book by Noel C. Stevenson.

● How To Cite Sources
http://www.genealogy.com/genealogy/19_wylie.html
By John Wylie.

● A Note about Sources
http://www.martygrant.com/gen/refs/sources.htm
*Descriptions, opinions and helpful insight into source
documentation, primary evidence and more, from the personal web
site of Marty Grant.*

● Producing Quality Research Notes
http://www.bcgcertification.org/skbld971.html
*From the Board for Certification of Genealogists - Skill Building -
January 1997.*

● RootsWeb's Guide to Tracing Family Trees - Lesson
12: Creating Worthwhile Genealogies: Evidence,
Sources, Documentation, and Citation
http://www.rootsweb.com/~rwguide/lesson12.htm

● Serious Citations
http://www.ancestry.com/columns/george/02-27-98.htm
From "Along Those Lines..." by George G. Morgan.

● Standards for Sound Genealogical Research
http://www.ngsgenealogy.org/about/content/committees/
gene_stan.html
Recommended by the National Genealogical Society.

● Standards for Use of Technology in Genealogical
Research
http://www.ngsgenealogy.org/about/content/committees/
gene_stan.html
Recommended by the National Genealogical Society.

● Standards for Using Records Repositories and
Libraries
http://www.ngsgenealogy.org/about/content/committees/
gene_stan.html
Recommended by the National Genealogical Society.

● SV-PAF-UG Homepage ~ San Jose, California
http://www.svpafug.org/
*Silicon Valley PAF Users Group. Site contains information about
the newly revised Family History Documentation Guidelines.*

● Understanding Sources, Citations, Documentation
and Evaluating Evidence in Genealogy
http://www.pipeline.com/~richardpence/classdoc.htm
By Richard Pence.

- Why Bother? The Value of Documentation in Family History Research
  http://www.genealogy.com/genealogy/19_kory.html
  By Kory Meyerink, MLS, AG.

◆ Citing Electronic Sources

- Beyond the MLA Handbook: Documenting Electronic Sources on the Internet
  http://english.ttu.edu/kairos/1.2/inbox/old_mla.html

- Bibliographic Formats for Citing Electronic Information
  http://www.uvm.edu/~ncrane/estyles/
  o Electronic Sources: APA Style of Citation
    http://www.uvm.edu/~ncrane/estyles/apa.html
  o Electronic Sources: MLA Style of Citation
    http://www.uvm.edu/~ncrane/estyles/mla.html

- A Brief Citation Guide for Internet Sources in History and the Humanities
  http://www2.h-net.msu.edu/~africa/citation.html

- Citation Guides for Electronic Documents
  http://www.ifla.org/I/training/citation/citing.htm
  A good list of links to citation resources.

- Citation Style Guides for Internet and Electronic Sources
  http://www.library.ualberta.ca/library_html/help/pathfinders/style/

- A Cite For Sore Eyes - Quality Citations for Electronic Genealogy Sources
  http://www.oz.net/~markhow/writing/cite.htm
  By Mark Howells.

- Citing Electronic Information in History Papers
  http://www.people.memphis.edu/~mcrouse/elcite.html

- Citing Electronic Sources
  http://library.ups.edu/research/guides/citing.htm
  Collins Memorial Library, University of Puget Sound.

- Citing Electronic Sources - APA and MLA Style
  http://sherrod.etsu.edu/internet/citeweb.html

- Citing Internet - APA Style
  http://www.nhmccd.cc.tx.us/contracts/lrc/kc/CitingElecSources-apa.html

- Citing Internet Resources
  http://www.connectedteacher.com/newsletter/citeintres.asp
  How students should reference online sources in their bibliographies. From Classroom Connect's.

- Citing Online Sources
  http://www.clever.net/quinion/words/articles/citation.htm
  From World Wide Words, Advice Note by Michael B Quinion.

- Citing Online Sources - MLA Style
  http://www.nhmccd.cc.tx.us/contracts/lrc/kc/mla-internet.html

- Columbia Guide to Online Style
  http://www.columbia.edu/cu/cup/cgos/

- Documenting Sources
  http://www.familytreemaker.com/issue19.html
  From Family Tree Maker Online.

- Electronic Sources: APA Style of Citation
  http://www.uvm.edu/~xli/reference/apa.html

- Electronic Sources: MLA Style of Citation
  http://www.uvm.edu/~xli/reference/mla.html

- Electronic Style...the Final Frontier
  http://funnelweb.utcc.utk.edu/~hoemann/style.html

- Guide for Citing Electronic Information
  http://www.wilpaterson.edu/wpcpages/library/citing.htm
  From the Sarah Byrd Askew Library, William Patterson University of New Jersey.

- How do you cite URL's in a bibliography?
  http://www.nrlssc.navy.mil/meta/bibliography.html

- MLA Style
  http://www.mla.org/style/style_index.htm

- Online! Citation Styles
  http://www.bedfordstmartins.com/online/citex.html

- Style Sheets for Citing Internet Resources: MLA, APA, Turabian
  http://www.lib.berkeley.edu/TeachingLib/Guides/Internet/MLAStyleSheet.html

- World Wide Words - Citing Online Sources
  http://www.quinion.com/words/articles/citation.htm

◆ Forms

- Ancestry.com - Source Summary
  http://www.ancestry.com/save/charts/sourcesum.htm

- Genealogy Research Log
  http://www.genrecords.com/forms/genealogyresearchlog.pdf
  Form to print and use from the Genealogy Records Service. Requires the Adobe Acrobat Reader Plugin in order to print the form.
  http://www.adobe.com/products/acrobat/readstep.html

- Research Log
  http://www.lds.org/images/howdoibeg/Research_Log.html
  From the LDS church.

- Research Log
  http://www.pbs.org/kbyu/ancestors/firstseries/teachersguide/tg-images/resrchlg.gif
  With an alternate form in .pdf format
  http://www.pbs.org/kbyu/ancestors/firstseries/teachersguide/pdf/researchlog.pdf
  From the Ancestors television program. The .pdf format requires the Adobe Acrobat Reader Plugin in order to print the form.
  http://www.adobe.com/products/acrobat/readstep.html

CITY DIRECTORIES
http://www.cyndislist.com/citydir.htm

Category Index:

◆ General Resource Sites

◆ Locality Specific

◆ General Resource Sites

- Analyzing City Directories
  http://www.bcgcertification.org/skbld965.html
  From the Board for Certification of Genealogists - Skill Building - May 1996.

- AudioTapes.com - Genealogical Lectures on Cassette Tapes - Directories
  http://www.audiotapes.com/search2.asp?Search=Director

- City Directories
  http://www.ancestry.com/columns/george/03-06-98.htm
  From "Along Those Lines..." by George Morgan.

- City Directories: A Forest of Family Trees
  http://www.citydirectories.psmedia.com/city/essay_main1.html

- City Directories at the Library of Congress
  http://www.kinquest.com/genealogy/resources/citydir.html

- City Directories: Windows on the Past
  http://www.ancestry.com/columns/myra/Shaking_Family_Tree03-19-98.htm
  From Shaking Your Family Tree, by Myra Vanderpool Gormley, C.G.

- Primary Source Media: City Directories Online
  http://www.citydirectories.psmedia.com/
  A pay for use searchable directory of over ninety-nine U.S. city directories from specific years.

- RootsWeb's Guide to Tracing Family Trees - Lesson 20: City Directories and Newspapers
  http://www.rootsweb.com/~rwguide/lesson20.htm

- Telephone and City Directories in the Library of Congress: A Finding Guide
  http://lcweb.loc.gov/rr/genealogy/bib_guid/telephon.html
  By Barbara B. Walsh, Reference Specialist, November 1994.

◆ Locality Specific

- 1828 Buffalo City Directory ~ New York
  http://www.rootsweb.com/~nyerie/buffalo/dir1828.txt

- 1837 Toronto and Home District Directory ~ Ontario
  http://www.rootsweb.com/~onyork/1837.html

- 1890 Cincinnati City Directory Online ~ Ohio
  http://members.aol.com/cintigenealogy/1890citydirectory/

- Alabama Archives: Alabama City Directories
  http://www.archives.state.al.us/referenc/micro.html

- Baltimore City Directories 1796-1964 ~ Maryland
  http://www.pratt.lib.md.us/slrc/md/citydir.html

- California City Directories - Volumes Held
  http://www.calhist.org/Support_Info/Collections/Library-Misc/CalifCityDir.html
  From the California Historical Society.

- Catalog of the Augusta (Georgia) City Directories, 1841-1939
  http://www.amazon.com/exec/obidos/ISBN=0941877051/markcyndisgenealA/
  A book by Alice O. Walker.

- Chataigne's Fredericksburg and Falmouth City Directories 1888-1889 ~ Virginia
  http://departments.mwc.edu/hipr/www/fredericksburg/1889directory.htm

- City Directories for 1816-1829 (Directories for the City of Charleston, South Carolina)
  http://www.amazon.com/exec/obidos/ISBN=0806346655/markcyndisgenealA/
  A book by James W. Hagy.

- City Directories for 1849, 1852 & 1855 (Directories for the City of Charleston, South Carolina)
  http://www.amazon.com/exec/obidos/ISBN=0806348224/markcyndisgenealA/
  A book by James W. Hagy.

- City Directories & Selected Telephone Directories on Microfilm and Microfiche
  http://unix2.nysed.gov/genealogy/citydir.htm
  At the New York State Library.

- City Directories Available at the City of Victoria Archives ~ British Columbia, Canada
  http://www.city.victoria.bc.ca/depts/archives/citydir.htm

- City Directories of the United States
  http://www.lib.umd.edu/UMCP/MICROFORMS/city_directories.html
  Microform Collections from the University of Maryland Libraries.

- Directories for the City of Charleston South Carolina: For the Years 1830-31, 1835-36, 1836, 1837-38, and 1840-41
  http://www.amazon.com/exec/obidos/ISBN=0806346787/markcyndisgenealA/
  A book by James W. Hagy.

- Directory of the Province of Ontario 1857
  http://www.amazon.com/exec/obidos/ISBN=0912606304/
  markcyndisgenealA/
  A book by Thomas B. Wilson.

- Glendale City Directories ~ California
  http://www.library.ci.glendale.ca.us/city_dir.html

- Fredericksburg, Virginia City Directory, 1892
  http://departments.mwc.edu/hipr/www/fredericksburg/
  1892directory.htm

- Highlights of the 1866 City of Denver Business
  Directory
  http://www.archives.state.co.us/dcd/dcdhome.htm
  *Including advertisements, business directory and residential
  directory.*

- The Historian's Craft: Consulting City Directories
  http://www.citydirectories.psmedia.com/city/essay_
  main2.html

- Index to City Directories, A-L, Kansas State
  Historical Society
  http://www.kshs.org/library/cdira-l.htm

- Index to City Directories, M-Z, Kansas State
  Historical Society
  http://www.kshs.org/library/cdirm-z.htm

- Long Island Directories ~ New York
  http://www.rootsweb.com/~nygglshp/Long-Island-
  Directories.html

- Nevada County California Business and Residential
  Directory - 1856
  http://www.compuology.com/cagenweb/nvcd1856.htm

- Newfoundland's Grand Banks Directory Material
  http://www.chebucto.ns.ca/Heritage/NGB/directory.htm
  Transcribed directories from the 1860s to the 1930s.

- Old Huntsville Magazine: Huntsville City Directory
  1859-1860 ~ Alabama
  http://www.rootsweb.com/~almadiso/citydir.htm

- San Francisco City Directories ~ California
  http://www.sfo.com/~timandpamwolf/sfdirect.htm

- San Francisco City Directory (1846)
  http://www.rootsweb.com/~casanfra/1846.htm

- San Francisco History - 1850 City Directory
  http://www.sf50.com/sf/hd850a.htm

- Schenectady City Directories ~ New York
  http://www.scpl.org/citydirectories/index.html
  *Found at the Schenectady County Public Library. Includes an online
  version of the Schenectady Directory and City Register for the years
  1841-2.*

- Shaw's Dublin City Directory 1850 ~ Ireland
  http://www.loughman.dna.ie/dublin1850/index.html
  *Surnames extracted from the Directory plus links to some
  transcriptions of the original entries.*

- South Dakota County and City Directories
  ftp://ftp.rootsweb.com/pub/usgenweb/sd/directory/citydir.txt
  *A list of the directories found in the South Dakota State Archives in
  Pierre.*

- TSLAC City Directories Available in the State
  Archives
  http://www.tsl.state.tx.us/lobby/citydirs.htm
  Texas State Library and Archives Commission.

- YELLOWSTONE MTGenExchange Directories
  Search (City/County Directories) ~ Montana
  http://www.genexchange.org/dirreg.cfm?state=mt&county=
  yellowstone

CLOTHING & COSTUMES
http://www.cyndislist.com/clothing.htm

Category Index:
- ◆ General Resource Sites
- ◆ Jewelry & Accessories
- ◆ Locality Specific
- ◆ Preservation
- ◆ Vendors

◆ General Resource Sites

- Amazon.com Genealogy Bookstore - Clothing
  http://www.amazon.com/exec/obidos/external-search/
  ?keyword=clothing+history&tag=markcyndisgenealA/

- Clothing of the 1830s
  http://www.connerprairie.org/clothing.html

- Costume History
  http://www.costumes.org/pages/costhistpage.htm
  Links to many sites by period which are useful for dating old photographs based on the clothes worn by the subjects.

  o The History of Fashion and Dress
    http://www.costumes.org/pages/fashiondress/thr355
    main.htm

  o Timeline of Costume History
    http://www.costumes.org/pages/timelinepages/timeline.htm

- Dating Portraits - Clothing Styles
  http://www.genealogy.org/~ajmorris/photo/datep18.htm

- Historical Boys Clothing
  http://members.tripod.com/~histclo/

- Notes and Illustrations on Regency Clothing Styles
  http://www.pemberley.com/janeinfo/ppbrokil.html
  With 1895 Charles E. Brock illustrations for Pride and Prejudice.

- Victoriana.com, "Harper's Bazar" - Mourning and Funeral Usages
  http://www.victoriana.com/library/harpers/funeral.html

- Victoriana.com, "Harper's Bazar" - Victorian Bridal Gowns
  http://www.victoriana.com/library/harpers/bride1.html

- Victorian Fashion Pages
  http://www.teasociety.com/victorian/

◆ Jewelry & Accessories

- Clues Among the Family Jewels
  http://www.ancestry.com/library/view/columns/george/
  1517.asp
  From "Along Those Lines..." by George Morgan.

- Mens Collars in History
  http://www.uaf.edu/theatre/students/resumes/res/collars/
  collars.html

- Remembering A Loved One With Mourning Jewelry
  http://www.hairwork.com/remember.htm
  Explains the Victorian custom of creating jewelry, pictures, and other mementos of a loved one from their hair.

- Turn-of-the-Century Hard Collars and Cuffs
  http://www.costumes.org/pages/collars.htm

◆ Locality Specific

- Dressmakers in Brooklyn 1895
  http://www.rootsweb.com/~nygglshp/Brooklyn-
  Dressmakers.html
  Lain's Brooklyn & LI Business Directory of 1895.

- London College of Fashion: College Archive
  http://vads.ahds.ac.uk/search_lcf.html
  A digital record of the London College of Fashion archive.

- Scottish Tartans
  http://www.scottartans.com/

- Tartans of Scotland
  http://www.tartans.scotland.net/

◆ Preservation

- The Care and Preservation of Antique Textiles and Costumes
  http://208.240.92.151/histories/cis/textile.html

- Encyclopedia Smithsonian: Storing Antique Textiles
  http://www.si.edu/resource/faq/nmah/antqtext.htm

- Preserving Precious Textiles
  http://www.ancestry.com/columns/George/05-01-98.htm
  From "Along Those Lines ..." by George Morgan.

◆ Vendors

- Ancestore: Apparel
  http://www.ancestordetective.com/Merchant2/merchant.mv
  ?Screen=CTGY&Store_Code=A&Category_Code=Apparel
  T-Shirts, Sweatshirts, Tote Bags from Ancestor Detective.

- Hattie's Clothesline
  http://www.hattiesclothesline.com/
  "Creative clothing for Family Historians".

- Petersen Reproductions
  http://www.PetersenPrints.com/
  T-shirts, mugs, family tree charts, family register and much more.

CORRESPONDENCE

Postage, Payments & Letter Writing
http://www.cyndislist.com/correspd.htm

Category Index:

◆ Forms & Form Letters

◆ General Resource Sites

◆ Postage & Payments

◆ Postal Services Worldwide

◆ Forms & Form Letters

- Ancestry.com - Correspondence Record
  http://www.ancestry.com/save/charts/correcord.htm

- FamilySearch Internet Genealogy Service - Research Helps
  http://www.familysearch.org/Eng/Search/rg/frameset_rhelps.asp

  o Finnish Letter-Writing Guide
    http://www.familysearch.org/Eng/Search/rg/frameset_rg.asp?Dest=G1&Aid=&Gid=&Lid=&Sid=&Did=&Juris1=&Event=&Year=&Gloss=&Sub=&Tab=&Entry=&Guide=LWGFinland.ASP

  o French Letter-Writing Guide
    http://www.familysearch.org/Eng/Search/rg/frameset_rg.asp?Dest=G1&Aid=&Gid=&Lid=&Sid=&Did=&Juris1=&Event=&Year=&Gloss=&Sub=&Tab=&Entry=&Guide=LGFrench.ASP

  o German Letter-Writing Guide
    http://www.familysearch.org/Eng/Search/rg/frameset_rg.asp?Dest=G1&Aid=&Gid=&Lid=&Sid=&Did=&Juris1=&Event=&Year=&Gloss=&Sub=&Tab=&Entry=&Guide=LGGerman.ASP

  o Italian Letter-Writing Guide
    http://www.familysearch.org/Eng/Search/rg/frameset_rg.asp?Dest=G1&Aid=&Gid=&Lid=&Sid=&Did=&Juris1=&Event=&Year=&Gloss=&Sub=&Tab=&Entry=&Guide=LGItalian.ASP

  o Polish Letter-Writing Guide
    http://www.familysearch.org/Eng/Search/rg/frameset_rg.asp?Dest=G1&Aid=&Gid=&Lid=&Sid=&Did=&Juris1=&Event=&Year=&Gloss=&Sub=&Tab=&Entry=&Guide=LWGPolish.ASP

  o Portuguese Letter-Writing Guide
    http://www.familysearch.org/Eng/Search/rg/frameset_rg.asp?Dest=G1&Aid=&Gid=&Lid=&Sid=&Did=&Juris1=&Event=&Year=&Gloss=&Sub=&Tab=&Entry=&Guide=LWGPortuguese.ASP

  o Spanish Letter-Writing Guide
    http://www.familysearch.org/Eng/Search/rg/frameset_rg.asp?Dest=G1&Aid=&Gid=&Lid=&Sid=&Did=&Juris1=&Event=&Year=&Gloss=&Sub=&Tab=&Entry=&Guide=LWGSpanish.ASP

- Family Tree Maker Online Genealogy How-To - Form Letters and Other Aids
  http://www.familytreemaker.com/00000023.html

  o Correspondence Table
    http://www.familytreemaker.com/00000007.html

  o Form Letters in English
    http://www.familytreemaker.com/ltr_english.html

  o Form Letters in French
    http://www.familytreemaker.com/ltr_french.html

  o Form Letters in German
    http://www.familytreemaker.com/ltr_german.html

  o Form Letters in Italian
    http://www.familytreemaker.com/ltr_italian.html

  o Form Letters in Spanish
    http://www.familytreemaker.com/ltr_spanish.html

- Form Letters for German Genealogy
  http://www2.genealogy.net/gene/www/ghlp/muster.html

- A Letter Used by Family Historians Who Want to Inspect the 1901 and/or 1911 Census ~ England & Wales
  http://members.aol.com/dmccre8728/censusuk.htm

- Sample Letters
  http://home.vicnet.net.au/~dpsoc/sample.htm
  From the Dead Persons Society, Melbourne, Australia

- Sample Letters in German to Obtain Genealogical Information
  gopher://Gopher.UToledo.edu:70/00GOPHER_ROOT%3A%5BRESEARCH-RESOURCES.GENEALOGY.GERMAN-GENEALOGY%5DGERMAN-SAMPLE-LETTER.FOR-INFORMATION-REQUESTS

- Supplies, Charts, Forms, Etc.
  http://www.CyndisList.com/supplies.htm
  See this category on Cyndi's List for related links.

- Universal Family Group Sheet
  http://www.geocities.com/Heartland/Meadows/7970/vfgs.html
  An online form which allows you to enter your data and e-mail it to another researcher.

◆ General Resource Sites

- Essentials of a Genealogical Letter
  http://www.rootscomputing.com/howto/checkl/checkl.htm
  Scroll to the bottom of this web page to read the article.

- The Forms Needed to Order Records from the National Archives
  http://www.ancestry.com/columns/george/05-15-98.htm
  From "Along Those Lines..." by George G. Morgan.

- Genealogy Correspondence: The Writing Rite Done Right
  http://www.ancestry.com/columns/george/09-11-98.htm
  From "Along Those Lines..." by George G. Morgan.

- Let's KISS Our Correspondence: Checking Our Letter Writing Skills
  http://www.audiotapes.com/product.asp?ProductCode='DEN98W3'
  Presentation by Mary McCampbell Bell, available for sale on audiotape.

- Lineages' First Steps - Write Successful Genealogy Queries
  http://www.lineages.com/FirstSteps/WriteQueries.asp

- Queries and Enquiries: There's More to Letter Writing Than Licking the Stamp
  http://www.audiotapes.com/product.asp?ProductCode='AZ-31'
  Presentation by Dorothy L. Martin, available for sale on audio tape.

- Researching From Abroad
  http://www.genuki.org.uk/ab/
  From the GENUKI web site.

- 6 Steps to Writing a Successful Genealogy Query
  http://www.firstct.com/fv/query.html

- What is the proper format for addressing a "snail mail" letter to a foreign country?
  http://www.oz.net/~markhow/genuki/NFK/norffaq.htm#address
  From the Norfolk-L Genealogy Mailing List Frequently Asked Questions web pages.

◆ Postage & Payments

- Britain in the USA - British Currency and Postage Stamps
  http://www.britain-info.org/bis/fsheets/5.stm

- Currency Calculator
  http://www.x-rates.com/calculator.html

- International Reply Coupon Affair
  http://www.ancestry.com/columns/myra/Shaking_Family_Tree08-20-98.htm
  By Myra Vanderpool Gormley, C.G.

- International Reply Coupons
  http://www.iinet.net.au/~davwat/wfhs/irc.html
  A brief description from the Watkins Family History Society.

- Research UK - Reply Paid Postal Service
  http://members.tripod.co.uk/TopNames/research1.html

- Ruesch International, Inc. - Global Payments Services
  http://www.ruesch.com/
  Affordable payment options for sending money to other countries.

- The Universal Currency Converter
  http://www.xe.net/ucc/classic.shtml
  And the Interactive Currency Table
  http://www.xe.net/ict/

- What is the best way to send payments to the United Kingdom from abroad?
  http://www.oz.net/~markhow/genuki/NFK/norffaq.htm#Payments
  From the Norfolk-L Genealogy Mailing List Frequently Asked Questions web pages.

◆ Postal Services Worldwide

- Australia Post - Correct Addressing
  http://www.auspost.com.au/index.asp?link_id=2.241

- Canada Post - How to Format the Postal Code and the Address
  http://www.canadapost.ca/CPC2/addrm/pclookup/pcinfo.html#how

- Postal Authorities
  http://www.execpc.com/~joeluft/postauth.html
  Listed by country.

- Royal Mail - Postal Services Guide ~ U.K.
  http://www.royalmail.com/guide/contents.htm

- United States Postal Service - Addressing and Packaging Your Mail
  http://www.usps.gov/csmrguid/addrpack.htm
  A portion of the "Consumer's Guide to Postal Services and Products".

COUSINS & KINSHIP

http://www.cyndislist.com/cousins.htm

- Amazon.com Genealogy Bookstore - Cousins
  http://www.amazon.com/exec/obidos/external-search/?
  keyword=cousins+genealogy&tag=markcyndisgenealA/

- A Chart for Figuring Relationships
  http://www.rootscomputing.com/howto/cousin/cousin.htm

- A Chart for Figuring Relationships
  http://www.rootsweb.com/~genepool/cousins.htm

- A Chart of Consanguinity
  http://www.geocities.com/BourbonStreet/1769/consangu.html

- Chart to Understanding Cousin Relationships:
  Genealogy by Lotus Dale
  http://www.butterfly.net/lotus/genealogy/cousin1.html

- Consanguinity Chart
  http://www.heirsearch.com/table.htm
  Showing degrees of relationship by blood.

- Cousin Calculator
  http://www.prenticenet.com/roots/tools/cusncalc/cusncalc.htm

- Cousin Chart, How Are Your Related?
  http://members.aol.com/anolelady/cuztable.htm

- Cousin-Finder
  http://www.ionet.net/~cousin/dale23.html

- Cousin Number Counter- Relationship Chart
  http://www.geocities.com/Heartland/Prairie/1956/cousin.html

- Cousin Relationships
  http://home.interpath.net/zanetti/chart2.html

- Cousins - A Chart for Determining Relationships
  http://www.cswnet.com/~sbooks/genealogy/cousins/
  cousins.htm

- Cousins & Cousinhood - It's all Strictly Relative
  http://homepage.interaccess.com/~arduinif/tools/cousins.htm

- Cousins Explained
  http://www.obliquity.com/family/misc/cousin.html

- Everton's -On-Line - Relationship Chart
  http://www.everton.com/relation/relation.htm

- Family Derivative - Cousins, How Far Removed
  http://www.cswnet.com/~mgoad/cousins.htm

- Family Relationship Chart
  http://www.isn.net/~dhunter/cousin.html
  From The Island Register.

- Family Relationships Chart
  http://www.tic.net/~lewis/cousin.html

- Genealogy - Cousins: How Far Removed?
  http://www.cswnet.com/~mgoad/cousins.htm

- The Gene Pool: A Chart for Figuring Relationships
  http://www.rootsweb.com/~genepool/cousins.htm

- GRL Relationship Chart
  http://www.grl.com/grl/relationship.shtml

- The Handy-Dandy Cousin Chart
  http://www3.sympatico.ca/kleonard/chart.html

- Kinship
  http://www.geocities.com/Heartland/Ridge/2072/kinship.htm
  *This explains the relationship of cousins and how they are moved
  from you: 1st, 2nd, 3rd, 4th; once removed, twice removed, etc.*

- Kinship Degree Systems - Systems of Measuring
  Kinship Degree
  http://www.umanitoba.ca/anthropology/tutor/descent/
  cognatic/degree.html
  *Several different systems of counting degrees of bilateral kinship
  relatedness employed by jurists, geneticists, and anthropologists.
  Systems include: Civil Degree, Canon Degree, Collateral Degree,
  Murdock's System, Parentalia.*

- Kissin Cousin Chart
  http://www.teleport.com/~willyw/kissin.html

- Relationship Chart
  http://www.eng.uci.edu/students/mpontius/pontius/7-7.html

- Relationship Chart
  http://members.aol.com/GenTutor/chart.html

- Relationship Chart
  http://members.mint.net/dws/geneal/dl01.htm
  Download from David's Home Page.

- Relationship Chart - How are we related?
  http://www.jewishgen.org/infofiles/related.txt
  A JewishGen InfoFile.

- What Is a First Cousin, Twice Removed?
  http://www.genealogy.com/genealogy/16_cousn.html

THE CZECH REPUBLIC & SLOVAKIA

Including Bohemia, Moravia, Carpatho-Rusyn & the Sudetenlands
http://www.cyndislist.com/czech.htm

Category Index:

- ◆ FEEFHS ~ Federation of East European Family History Societies
- ◆ General Resource Sites
- ◆ History & Culture
- ◆ How To
- ◆ Language, Handwriting, & Script
- ◆ Libraries, Archives & Museums
- ◆ Locality Specific
- ◆ Mailing Lists, Newsgroups & Chat
- ◆ Maps, Gazetteers & Geographical Information
- ◆ Newspapers
- ◆ People & Families
- ◆ Professional Researchers, Volunteers & Other Research Services
- ◆ Publications, Software & Supplies
- ◆ Records: Census, Cemeteries, Land, Obituaries, Personal, Taxes and Vital
- ◆ Religion & Churches
- ◆ Societies & Groups

◆ FEEFHS ~ Federation of East European Family History Societies

- FEEFHS - Federation of East European Family History Societies
  http://feefhs.org/
  - o Ethnic, Religious and National Index of Home Pages and FEEFHS Resource Guide Listings
    http://feefhs.org/ethnic.html
    Of organizations associated with FEEFHS from 14 countries
  - o FEEFHS Ethnic, Religious and National Cross-Indexes:
    - • Austro-Hungarian Empire
      http://feefhs.org/ah/indexah.html
    - • Carpatho-Rusyn, Rusin, Ruthenia
      http://feefhs.org/rusyn/indexcru.html
    - • Czech Republic
      http://feefhs.org/indexcz.html
    - • Slovak Republic
      http://feefhs.org/indexsk.html
  - o FEEFHS Full Text Web Site Index Search Engine
    http://feefhs.org/search/
  - o FEEFHS Location (Address) Index of FEEFHS Member Organizations
    http://feefhs.org/location.html
    And other East European Genealogy Organizations.
  - o FEEFHS Significant Additions Index
    http://feefhs.org/webm/sigad96.html
  - o FEEFHS Web Site Master Index
    http://feefhs.org/masteri.html

◆ General Resource Sites

- The Carpathian Connection
  http://www.tccweb.org/
- Carpathian German Homepage
  http://ourworld-top.cs.com/ycrtmr/index.htm
- Carpatho-Rusyn Genealogy
  http://www.rusyn.com/
- Carpatho-Rusyn Knowledge Base
  http://www.carpatho-rusyn.org/
- The Carpatho-Rusyn Surname Project
  http://www.carpatho-rusyn.org/surnames.htm
- Czech Genealogy
  http://freepages.genealogy.rootsweb.com/~elainetmaddox/czgenealogy.htm
- Czech Genealogy
  http://www.geocities.com/Heartland/Plains/2064/czechgen.htm
- Czechoslovak Genealogy Sites on the Internet
  http://www.genea.cz/zdroje/svet.htm
- The Czechs in America
  http://lcweb.loc.gov/rr/european/imcz/ndl.html
  From the Library of Congress.
- Czech Republic, Bohemia and Moravia Genealogical Research
  http://www.iarelative.com/czech/
- Czech & Slovak Genealogy, Travel Index
  http://members.aol.com/jzel/index.htm
  An index of pages of helpful information for Czech and Slovak genealogy researchers.

- Eastern Slovakia, Slovak and Carpatho-Rusyn Genealogy Research
  http://www.iarelative.com/slovakia.htm

- Finding Your Roots in the Old County of Saris (Saros)
  http://members.aol.com/SLOVMJD/saris.html
  Genealogy in northeastern Slovakia.

- Help in searching for ancestors from the Sudetenland
  http://www.genealogy.net/gene/reg/SUD/sudet_en.html
  German settlement area in Bohemia/Moravia/Austrian Silesia -> Czechoslovakia -> Czech Republic.

- Homepage of Karel Kysilka
  http://members.tripod.com/~zlimpkk/
  Outstanding source of genealogical articles & information regarding the Czech Republic.

  o Czech Surnames
    http://members.tripod.com/~zlimpkk/Genealogy/czech surnames.html

  o Description of Records and Collections of the Moravian Provincial Archives in Brno
    http://members.tripod.com/~zlimpkk/Genealogy/ brnoarchives.html

  o The Development of Parochial Vital Registers in the Bohemian Lands with Special Emphasis on the East Bohemian Areas
    http://members.tripod.com/~zlimpkk/Genealogy/vital reg.html

  o Economical and Social Diversification of the Czech Rural Population during Feudalism
    http://members.tripod.com/~zlimpkk/Genealogy/rural population.html

  o Emigration to the USA from the Policka region in 1850 - 1890
    http://www.fortunecity.com/victorian/durer/23/emigration/ emigration.htm
    Excellent article complete with scanned original documents regarding Czech emigration.

- Nebraska Czech Genealogy
  http://www.radiks.net/~journlst/page2.html

- Our-Slovakia
  http://www.our-slovakia.com/
  Dictionary, recipes, genealogy.

- Patrick Janis' Czech Genealogy Page
  http://www.genealogy.org/~czech/index.html

- PolishRoots: The Polish Genealogy Source
  http://www.polishroots.org/

- Slovak Genealogy
  http://www.slovakia.org/society-geneology.htm
  From Slovakia.org.

- The WorldGenWeb Project
  http://www.worldgenweb.org/

  o EastEuropeGenWeb
    http://www.rootsweb.com/~easeurgw/

- Czech Republic
  http://www.rootsweb.com/~czewgw/
- Slovakia
  http://www.rootsweb.com/~svkwgw/

◆ History & Culture

- History of Europe, Slavic States
  http://www.worldroots.com/brigitte/royal/royal4.htm
  Historic and genealogical information about royal and nobility family lines.

- Slovak.org
  http://www.slovakia.org
  Guide to the Slovak Republic.

- Slovak Republic - Culture and History
  http://slovakemb.com/culture.shtml
  From the Embassy of the Slovak Republic in Washington D.C.

- StudyWeb: History: Europe
  http://www.studyweb.com/History/toceurop.htm

◆ How To

- Genealogical Research in the Czech Republic
  http://www.czech.cz/washington/cons/genealogy.htm
  From the Czech Republic's embassy in Washington, DC.

- How to Find Your Roots
  http://www.carpatho-rusyn.org/cra/petercra.htm
  Online article on Carpatho-Rusyn research. A interview with Mr. Thomas A. Peters - a certified professional genealogist who specializes in, among other things, Carpatho-Rusyn ancestry and the history of Carpatho-Rusyns in northern New Jersey.

- Preparing for Old Country Research - Czechs & Slovaks
  http://www.rootsweb.com/~rwguide/lesson27.htm#Czechs
  From RootsWeb's guide to tracing family trees.

- Slovak and Rusyn Roots; Getting Started
  http://feefhs.org/socslav/hudick1.html

- Tips For Researching Ancestors From the Slovakian Area of the Former Austro-Hungarian Empire
  http://www.carpatho-rusyn.org/slov1.htm
  Online article by John A. Hudick.

◆ Language, Handwriting, & Script

- Basic genealogy vocabulary German-English-Czech
  http://www2.genealogy.net/gene/reg/SUD/dictionary.html

- Czech Fonts for WWW
  http://www.muselik.com/czech/fonts.html

- English - Czech Dictionary
  http://ww2.fce.vutbr.cz/bin/ecd

- FEEFHS Database of Professional Translators Specializing in East European Genealogy
  http://feefhs.org/frg/frg-pt.html

- Languages & Translations
  http://www.CyndisList.com/language.htm
  See this category on Cyndi's List for related links.

- Moravians - German Script Tutorial
  http://www.mun.ca/rels/morav/script.html
  With Moravian Archival examples

  o German Script Alphabet
    http://www.mun.ca/rels/morav/pics/tutor/mscript2.html

- Slovak Language
  http://www.slovak.com/language/index.html
  General site about the Slovak language, including examples of greetings, key phrases and background information. Has actual sound bites. Includes information about a Slovak language CD-ROM for learning this language.

- Slovak Translation Services by Jana Cupková Holmes
  http://www.dholmes.com/janatran.html

◆ Libraries, Archives & Museums

- Archives in Czech Republic
  http://www.genealogy.net/gene/reg/SUD/sudet_crarch_en.html

- Family History Library Catalog
  http://www.familysearch.org/Search/searchcatalog.asp
  From the FamilySearch web site, an online catalog to the holdings of the LDS Church in Salt Lake City, Utah. Also search for other localities by place name.
  http://www.familysearch.org/fhlc/supermainframeset.asp?display=localitysearch&columns=*,180,0

  o Czech Republic
    http://www.familysearch.org/fhlc/supermainframeset.asp?display=localitydetails&subject=86&subject_disp=Czech_Republic&columns=*,180,0

  o Slovakia
    http://www.familysearch.org/fhlc/supermainframeset.asp?display=localitydetails&subject=90&subject_disp=Slovakia&columns=*,180,0

- Family History SourceGuide - Family History Centers - Europe and Scandinavia
  http://www.familysearch.org/sg/Europe_and_Scandinavia_FHC.html
  Austria, Belgium, Denmark, Finland, France, Germany, Hungary, Iceland, Italy, Netherlands, Norway, Portugal, Spain, Sweden, and Switzerland.

- Herder-Institut Marberg: About the Institute
  http://www.uni-marburg.de/herder-institut/english/allgemein/info.html
  According to its statutes, the Herder-Institute supports "with its collections and as a forum for academic discussion the research on the countries and peoples of East Central Europe in their European context, with special regard to the history of the historical German territories and areas of settlement in East Central Europe. In order to fulfill these tasks, the institute conducts its own research." The core subject of its work is the area of the present-day states of Poland, the Czech Republic, Slovakia, Estonia, Latvia and Lithuania.

- Mestska knihovna v Praze / Municipal Library of Prague
  http://www.mlp.cz/

- Odkazy na jiné servery: archivnictví
  http://www.mvcr.cz/archivy/sua/weby.htm
  Archives of the Czech Republic.

  o Adresáø archivù Èeské republiky
    http://www.mvcr.cz/archivy/sua/adresy.htm
    Contact information for archives in the Czech Republic.

- Public Libraries of Europe
  http://dspace.dial.pipex.com/town/square/ac940/eurolib.html

- Repositories of Primary Sources - Europe A-M
  http://www.uidaho.edu/special-collections/euro1.html
  Europe N-Z
  http://www.uidaho.edu/special-collections/euro2.html
  A list of links to online resources from the Univ. of Idaho Library, Special Collections and Archives

  o Czech Republic
    http://www.uidaho.edu/special-collections/euro1.html#cz

- Slovak and Czech Archives
  http://feefhs.org/frl/czs/dg-arch.html

◆ Locality Specific

- Humenne, Slovakia Shtetlinks Website
  http://www.jewishgen.org/shtetlinks/humenne/humenne.htm

- Metzenseifen (Medzev) Homepage
  http://www.metzenseifen.de/
  Historical and genealogical data from Unter- and Ober-Metzenseifen & to preserve Metzenseifen heritage.

- North Moravia Genealogical Sources/Starting Points/Literature
  http://my.bawue.de/~hanacek/egene/enrefov.htm

- Welcome to Stary Maletin, Czech Republic
  http://www.heritagequest.com/genealogy/europe/html/stary_maletin.html
  Photos and information about Berstett, France from a genealogical perspective, from Heritage Quest Magazine and European Focus.

◆ Mailing Lists, Newsgroups & Chat

- Genealogy Resources on the Internet - Czech Republic Mailing Lists
  http://www.rootsweb.com/~jfuller/gen_mail_country-cze.html

- Genealogy Resources on the Internet - Slovak Republic Mailing Lists
  http://www.rootsweb.com/~jfuller/gen_mail_country-slo.html
  Most of the mailing list links below point to this site, wonderfully maintained by John Fuller

- BOHEMIA Mailing List
  http://www.rootsweb.com/~jfuller/gen_mail_country-cze.html#BOHEMIA
  For anyone with a genealogical interest in Bohemia, now part of the Czech Republic.

- CZECH Mailing List
  http://www.rootsweb.com/~jfuller/gen_mail_country-cze.html#CZECH
  For those interested in researching Czech ancestors in the Czech crown lands of Bohemia, Moravia, and Silesia.

- Czech Mail List on RootsWeb
  http://freepages.genealogy.rootsweb.com/~elainetmaddox/

- EURO-JEWISH Mailing List
  http://www.rootsweb.com/jfuller/gen_mail_general.html
  #EURO-JEWISH
  *For anyone with a genealogical interest in the Migration, History,
  Culture, Heritage and Surname search of the Jewish people from
  Europe to the United States and their descendants in the United
  States.*

- Exulanten-L Mailing List
  http://www.rootsweb.com/~autwgw/agsfrx.htm
  *Exulanten is the name given to the Protestants that were forced out
  Austria (estimated as many as 100,000) during 16th to 18th century.
  The largest wave of about 22,000 left the Salzburg area in 1731/32.
  Most went to East Prussia (Germany - Poland, Lithuania and
  Latvia) but some went to Siebenbürgen and Banat (today's
  Romania), Hungary and to parts of today's Slovakia.*

- genea-cz Mailing List
  http://www.rootsweb.com/~jfuller/gen_mail_country-cze.html
  #genea-cz
  *For anyone with a genealogical interest in the Czech Republic. The
  language for the list is Czech, but messages in English are also
  welcome.*

- GEN-SLAVIC Mailing List
  http://www.rootsweb.com/~jfuller/gen_mail_country-cze.html
  #GEN-SLAVIC
  Gatewayed with the soc.genealogy.slavic newsgroup.
  news:soc.genealogy.slavic

- GERMAN-BOHEMIAN-L Mailing List
  http://www.rootsweb.com/~jfuller/gen_mail_country-cze.html
  #GERMAN-BOHEMIAN-L
  *About the culture, genealogy and heritage of the German-speaking
  people of Bohemia and Moravia, now the Czech Republic.*

- GERSIG Mailing List
  http://www.rootsweb.com/~jfuller/gen_mail_country-cze.html
  #GERSIG
  *Focuses on Jewish genealogy in German-speaking regions (e.g.,
  Germany, Austria, parts of Switzerland, Alsace, Lorraine, Bohemia,
  Moravia).*

- MORAVIA Mailing List
  http://www.rootsweb.com/~jfuller/gen_mail_country-cze.html
  #MORAVIA
  *For anyone with a genealogical interest in Moravia, now part of the
  Czech Republic.*

- PolandBorderSurnames Mailing List
  http://www.rootsweb.com/~jfuller/gen_mail_country-cze.html
  #PolandBorderSurnames
  *For anyone researching genealogy in the former historical borders
  of Poland including Estonia, Latvia, Lithuania, Belarus, Ukraine,
  Moldova, Slovakia, Czech Republic, Moravia, Hungary, Russia, the
  Balkans, and East Prussia.*

- Rusyn Genealogy Mailing List
  http://www.topica.com/lists/rusyns

- SLOVAKIA Mailing List
  http://www.rootsweb.com/~jfuller/gen_mail_country-slo.html
  #SLOVAKIA
  For anyone with a genealogical interest in the Slovak Republic.

- SLOVAK-L Mailing List
  http://www.rootsweb.com/jfuller/gen_mail_country-slo.html
  #SLOVAK-L

- SLOVAK-ROOTS Mailing List
  http://www.egroups.com/subscribe/SLOVAK-ROOTS
  *For genealogy inquiries on ancestors who came from the former
  Austria-Hungary, which are generally the modern day countries of
  Hungary, Czech Republic and Slovak Republic.*

- SLOVAK-WORLD Mailing List
  http://www.rootsweb.com/~jfuller/gen_mail_country-slo.html
  #SLOVAK-W
  *An unmoderated mailing list which can be used to contact Slovaks
  around the world to help find lost contacts, join relatives, meet new
  friends, etc.*

- TX-CZECH Mailing List
  http://www.rootsweb.com/~jfuller/gen_mail_country-cze.html
  #TX-CZECH
  *For anyone with a genealogical interest in the immigrants from
  Czechoslovakia to Texas in the 1840-1930 timeframe.*

◆ Maps, Gazetteers & Geographical Information

- Administrativni rozdeleni dnesni Ceske republiky v
  letech 1850 - 1949 / Administrative Division of
  Bohemia, Moravia and Silesia 1850 - 1949
  http://members.tripod.com/~zlimpkk/Topography/cechy_1.htm

- Austro-Hungarian Empire Map Index
  http://feefhs.org/maps/ah/mapiah.html
  From FEEFHS.

- FEEFHS East European Map Room - Map Index
  http://feefhs.org/maps/indexmap.html

- Kraje Moravy - Moravian Regions
  http://members.tripod.com/~zlimpkk/morava/kraje.html

- The List of Internet Sources of Czech Towns and
  Cities - A to P
  http://members.tripod.com/~zlimpkk/Topography/mesta1.html

- The List of Internet Sources of Czech Towns and
  Cities - R to Z
  http://members.tripod.com/~zlimpkk/Topography/mesta2.html

- Maps of South Eastern Europe 900 A.D. - 1881 A.D.
  http://www.lib.utexas.edu/Libs/PCL/Map_collection/historical/
  se_euro1.html
  *From the Perry-Castañeda Library Map Collection, The University
  of Texas at Austin.*

- Maps of Europe - The Perry-Castañeda Library Map
  Collection
  http://www.lib.utexas.edu/Libs/PCL/Map_collection/
  europe.html
  From the University of Texas at Austin.

  o Map of Czech Republic
    http://www.lib.utexas.edu/Libs/PCL/Map_collection/europe/
    CzechRepublic.jpg

o Map of Ethnic Groups of Eastern Europe
http://www.lib.utexas.edu/Libs/PCL/Map_collection/europe/
EEurope_Ethnic_95.jpg

o Map of Slovakia
http://www.lib.utexas.edu/Libs/PCL/Map_collection/europe/
Slovakia_map.jpg

- Political subdivision of Bohemia, Moravia and Silesia
http://members.tripod.com/~zlimpkk/Genealogy/admin.html

◆ Newspapers

- The Prague Post Online
http://www.praguepost.cz/
Online edition of the English-language paper.

◆ People & Families

- Genealogie èeské šlechty
http://www.geocities.com/Heartland/Bluffs/2868/Panstvo.htm
Czech nobility.

◆ Professional Researchers, Volunteers & Other Research Services

- Board for Certification of Genealogists - Roster of Those Certified - Specializing in Europe/USSR
http://www.bcgcertification.org/rosts_@e.html

- CZECH Info Center: Find A Czech Ancestor / Mate Pribuzne v Zamori?
http://www.muselik.com/cac/
14-day free trial, then you subscribe.

- Czechoslovak Genealogical Society Int'l - Professional Genealogical Researchers for Czech and Slovak Republics
http://members.aol.com/cgsi/research.htm

- Czech Service
http://sshaw.freeyellow.com/index.html
Professional research services.

- Czech & Slovak Heritage Tours
http://www.czechheritage.com/
Genealogical tours to the Czech & Slovak Republics plus folk heritage & genealogical information.

- Czech Slovak Travel
http://members.aol.com/jzel/travel.htm

- European Focus
http://www.eurofocus.com/
Photographic portfolios of ancestral towns in Europe created for Genealogy enthusiasts in Belgium, Denmark, Eastern Europe, England, France, Germany, Great Britain, Italy, Netherlands, Norway, Poland, Sweden, Switzerland and more.

- Family Tree Genealogical and Probate Research Bureau Ltd.
http://www.familytree.hu/
Professional research service covering the area of what was formerly the Austro - Hungarian Empire, including: Hungary,
Slovakia, Czech Republic, Austria, Italy, Transylvania, Croatia, Slovenia, former Yugoslavia (Banat), and the Ukraine (Sub-Carpathian).

- FEEFHS Database of Professional Genealogists Specializing in East European Genealogy
http://feefhs.org/frg/frg-pg.html

- Gary Mokotoff, Genealogical Lecturer
http://www.avotaynu.com/gmokotoff.html
One of the foremost lecturers and authors on Jewish and Eastern European genealogical research.

- genealogyPro - Professional Genealogists for Central and Eastern Europe
http://genealogyPro.com/directories/Euro1.html

- genealogyPro - Professional Genealogists for Czech Republic
http://genealogyPro.com/directories/CzechRepublic.html

- HungaroGens Genealogisches Büro / HungaroGens Genealogical Bureau
http://www.genealogy.net/hungarogens/
Genealogical research in Hungary, Austria, Slovakia, Rumania, Slovenia, Jugoslavia.

- Institute for Historical Family Research
http://ihff.nwy.at/index.htm/
Austria, Czech & Slovak Republics, Hungary, Slovenian Republic, Croatia, Galicia & Bukovina.

    o Czech Republic
    http://ihff.nwy.at/b.htm

    o Republic of Slovakia
    http://ihff.nwy.at/c.htm

- P.A.T.H. Finders - Personal Ancestral Tours & History
http://www.abilnet.com/pathfinders/
Specializing in Family History and Travel in the Czech and Slovak Republics.

- Slovakia Research Assistance
http://www.geocities.com/familysk/research.html
Professional genealogist specializing in eastern Slovakia.

- The Snoop Sisters Family History Researchers ~ Nanaimo, B.C. Canada
http://www.snoopsisters.net/
England & Wales, Scotland, Ireland & N., Ireland, Eastern Europe, Canada & U.S.

- T & P Research
http://www.tpresearch.cz/
Genealogy research in the Czech & Slovak Republics plus folk heritage & genealogical information.

◆ Publications, Software & Supplies

- Amazon.com Genealogy Bookstore – Czech
http://www.amazon.com/exec/obidos/external-search/?
keyword=czech+genealogy&tag=markcyndisgenealA/
Slovak
http://www.amazon.com/exec/obidos/external-search/?
keyword=slovak+genealogy&tag=markcyndisgenealA/

Carpatho-Rusyn
http://www.amazon.com/exec/obidos/external-search/?
keyword=carpatho-rusyn&tag=markcyndisgenealA/

- AudioTapes.com - Genealogical Lectures on Cassette Tapes - Czech Republic
http://www.audiotapes.com/search2.asp?Search=Czech Slovak
http://www.audiotapes.com/search2.asp?Search=Slovak

- Bohemian Genealogy Bibliography
http://192.231.205.235/ISC102.HTM

- Books from the Institute for Historical Family Research
http://ihff.nwy.at/werbe.html

- Books We Own - Czech Republic
http://www.rootsweb.com/~bwo/czech.html
Find a book from which you would like a lookup and click on the submitter's code at the end of the entry. Once you find the contact information for the submitter, write them a polite request for a lookup.

- Books We Own - The Republic of Slovakia
http://www.rootsweb.com/~bwo/slovakia.html
Find a book from which you would like a lookup and click on the submitter's code at the end of the entry. Once you find the contact information for the submitter, write them a polite request for a lookup.

- Brother's Keeper Software
http://ourworld.compuserve.com/homepages/Brothers_Keeper/
Downloadable shareware program for Windows. The latest version contains English, French, Norwegian, Danish, Swedish, German, Dutch, Polish, Icelandic, Russian, Slovak, Afrikaans, Czech.

- Frontier Press Bookstore - Czechoslovakia
http://www.frontierpress.com/frontier.cgi?category=cze

- Frontier Press Bookstore - European Research
http://www.frontierpress.com/frontier.cgi?category=europe

- Genealogy Unlimited - Home Page
http://www.itsnet.com:80/home/genun/public_html/
Maps, books & supplies for sale.

- Regi Magyarorszag "Old Hungary" Bookstore
http://www.dholmes.com/rm-book.html
Specializing in Hungarian & Slovak Genealogy.

◆ Records: Census, Cemeteries, Land, Obituaries, Personal, Taxes and Vital (Born, Married, Died & Buried)

- Jewish Cemetery in Košice / Old Jewish Cemetery at Kosice, Slovakia
http://www.kosice.sk/history/zidovsky/jevish0.htm
History of the cemetery, database of 5,517 names of buried persons.

- Memento Mori
http://www.home.sk/www/dudy/m_index.htm
Alphabetical list of WWI soldiers buried at Kosice Municipal Cemetery, Kosice, Slovakia.

◆ Religion & Churches

- Jewish
http://www.CyndisList.com/jewish.htm
See this category on Cyndi's List for related links.

- Saint John the Baptist Carpatho-Russian Orthodox Greek Catholic Church
http://www.tccweb.org/bridgeport.htm#Saint John the Baptist
History of the Church in Bridgeport, Connecticut.

◆ Societies & Groups

- Carpatho-Rusyn Research Center
http://www.carpatho-rusyn.org/crrc/
The Carpatho-Rusyn Research Center is a non-profit cultural research organization whose purpose is to promote knowledge about all aspects of Carpatho-Rusyn culture through the publication and distribution of scholarly and educational material about the Carpatho-Rusyn heritage in Europe and America.

- Carpatho-Rusyn Society Page
http://www.carpatho-rusyn.org/crs/
Slovakia / Carpathian Mts.

- Czech & Slovak American Genealogy Society of Illinois
http://www.csagsi.org/

- Czech & Slovak Genealogical Society of Arizona
http://www.rootsweb.com/~azcsgsa/index.htm

- Czechoslovak Genealogical Society, International
http://www.cgsi.org/

- Czech Heritage Society of Texas
http://www.genealogy.org/~czech/

- FEEFHS - Federation of East European Family History Societies
http://feefhs.org/

- FEEFHS Location (Address) Index of FEEFHS Member Organizations
http://feefhs.org/location.html
And other East European Genealogy Organizations.

- The German-Bohemian Heritage Society
http://www.rootsweb.com/~gbhs/

- Hungarian/American Friendship Society (HAFS)
http://www.dholmes.com/hafs.html
Specializing in Hungarian & Slovak Genealogy.

- The Rusin Association of Minnesota
http://www.carpatho-rusyn.org/rusin/
Preserving the distinct nationality, history, language and heritage of the Rusin people.

- The Slovak Heritage and Cultural Society of British Columbia
http://www.iarelative.com/slovakbc.htm

- Slovenská Genealogicko - Heraldická Spoloènost /
  Slovak Genealogical - Heraldic Society at the Matica
  Slovenská
  http://www.genealogy-heraldry.sk/
  *From the leading Slovak genealogical organization, the most
  comprehensive site on Slovakia related genealogical research and
  activities.*

- The Texas Czech Genealogy Publishing Group
  http://freepages.genealogy.rootsweb.com/~czech/
  *A non-profit group of volunteers dedicated to the free distribution of
  genealogical material for those researching Texas Czechs.*

DATABASES, SEARCH SITES, SURNAME LISTS

http://www.cyndislist.com/database.htm

Category Index:

- ◆ Commercial
- ◆ General
- ◆ Locality Specific
- ◆ Military
- ◆ People & Families

- ◆ Records: Census, Cemeteries, Land, Obituaries, Personal, Taxes and Vital
- ◆ ROOTS-L and RootsWeb
- ◆ Societies & Groups

◆ Commercial

- Ancestry.com Search
  http://www.ancestry.com/search/main.htm
  Search by locality or record type, including Social Security Death Index (SSDI), PERSI, Ancestry World Tree and 10-day free trial databases.

- Everton Publishers
  http://www.everton.com/
  Databases include "Roots" Cellar, Family File, Pedigree Library and GEDSEARCH. Also databases for England, some census and death records.

- Family Tree Maker Online
  http://www.familytreemaker.com/
  Search the Family Finder Index online.

- Design Software
  http://www.dhc.net/~design/search.htm
  Misc. searches and other useful utilities.

- Golden West Marketing
  http://www.greenheart.com/rdietz/
  Surname exchange, limited free searches of database, book list, professional researchers.

- inGeneas Canadian Genealogical Research Services ~ Ottawa, Ontario, Canada
  http://www.ingeneas.com/
  Searchable databases containing 50,000+ Canadian passenger and immigration records (c1750 to 1900) including the only electronic version of the free National Archives of Canada Miscellaneous Immigration Index.

- Legends and Legacies Family Tree Collection
  http://interchange.idc.uvic.ca:80/~legends/library/trees/famtree.html

- Next of Kin™
  http://www.lineages.com/NextOfKin/default.asp
  From Lineages, Inc.

- The Ultimate Family Tree Data Library
  http://www.familyinfo.com/
  From Palladium Interactive. This site is now part of GenealogyLibrary.com. See this link for details on how to update your subscription.

- Westland Publications Genealogy - Find Immigrant Ancestors
  http://www.theriver.com/westlandpubn/
  Search from Thousands of Surnames and Hundreds of Place Names in Germany, Great Britain, France, Switzerland, and Central Europe.

- World Family Tree Submitter List
  http://www.inlink.com/~nomi/wftlist/index.html

- Yahoo! Business and Economy: Companies: Information: Genealogy: Databases
  http://dir.yahoo.com/Business_and_Economy/Companies/Information/Genealogy/Databases/

◆ General

- BirthQuest
  http://www.birthquest.org/
  Online searchable database for searching adoptees, birth parents, adoptive parents and siblings.

- Common Threads
  http://www.gensource.com/common/
  A searchable database with e-mail addresses for submitters.

- Design Software - Genealogy Databases on the World Wide Web, A-M
  http://www.dhc.net/~design/datainda.htm
  Or N-Z
  http://www.dhc.net/~design/dataindx.htm

- FamilySearch Internet Genealogy Service
  http://www.familysearch.org/
  THE genealogy web site of the LDS Church. Includes the ability to search the IGI, the Ancestral File, the Family History Library Catalog, and web site submissions. Also has user mailing lists, online ordering of FHL research materials and allows you to preserve your own research online.

- FEEFHS Cross Index of 27 Surname databases
  http://feefhs.org/index/indexsur.html

- GEDDEX - GEDCOM Index from A.J. Morris
  http://www.genealogy.org/~ajmorris/geddex/geddex.htm

- GENDEX Database
  http://www.gendex.com/
  A searchable index of over 7.7 million names in 2,259 databases, each actively maintained and updated by the database owner.

- GeneaNet Genealogical Database Network
  http://www.geneanet.org/
  Database indexing surnames from before 1850 & corresponding contact information - online or offline.

- Genealogists Index to the World Wide Web
  http://members.aol.com/Genwebindx/index.htm

- GenServ - Family History
  http://www.genserv.com/
  Over 16,500,000 names in 12,500+ GEDCOM databases.

- Growth of Linked Pedigree Databases
  http://www.bearhaven.com/family/growth.html
  A month-by-month list of the growth of some large genealogy databases.

- Indexes Unlimited
  http://www.indexesunlimited.com/index.htm
  Book indexes online.

- my-ged.com - the best little gedcom server on the WWW
  http://www.my-ged.com/

- Online Genealogical Database Index
  http://www.gentree.com/
  From Tim Doyle.

- Personal Home Pages
  http://www.CyndisList.com/personal.htm
  See this category on Cyndi's List for related links.

- Queries & Message Boards
  http://www.CyndisList.com/queries.htm
  See this category on Cyndi's List for related links.

- Scott McGee's GenWeb Page
  http://www.genealogy.org/~smcgee/genweb/genweb.html

- Searchable Genealogy Links [Lauren Knoblauch]
  http://www.bc1.com/users/sgl/
  A large selection of world-wide searchable genealogy links. Sorted geographically and alphabetically.

- Surname Springboard
  http://www.geocities.com/~alacy/spring.htm
  Dedicated to internet researchers who have indexed their GEDCOM data & converted it to HTML pages.

- Surnames, Family Associations & Family Newsletters
  http://www.CyndisList.com/surnames.htm
  See this category on Cyndi's List for related links.

- The SurnameWeb
  http://www.surnameweb.org/
  The Surname Genealogy Web Project.

- What's Your Line?
  http://www.uvol.com/www1st/redeem/surnames.html
  List of surnames being researched from the WWW 1st Ward LDS site.

- World Wide Cemetery
  http://www.interlog.com/~cemetery/

- WWW genealogy databases
  http://www.genhomepage.com/genwww.html

- Yates Publishing - The Computerized Ancestor
  http://www.montana.com/yates/index.html

◆ Locality Specific

- Anglesey, Wales Surname List
  http://www.genuki.org.uk/big/wal/Surnames/agy.htm

- Angus Scotland Surnames List
  http://www.geocities.com/Athens/Parthenon/5020/Angus/

- Argyllshire, Scotland Surname List
  http://members.aol.com/sloinne/Argyll/Surnames.htm

- Australian Family Tree Connections Surname Register
  http://www.aftc.com.au/surname.html

- Ayrshire Surname Database ~ Scotland
  http://home.clara.net/iainkerr/genuki/AYR/SID/indexsid.htm

- Banffshire Surname List ~ Scotland
  http://www.rootsweb.com/~sctban/

- Bedfordshire Surnames List ~ England
  http://homepages.ihug.co.nz/~hughw/bedf.html

- Berkshire Surnames List
  http://www.geocities.com/Heartland/Ranch/5973/berksurname.htm

- Berwickshire Surnames List ~ Scotland
  http://www.vivdunstan.clara.net/genuki/BEW/Surnames/

- Breconshire, Wales Surnames List
  http://www.genuki.org.uk/big/wal/Surnames/bre.htm

- Brule County, SD, History Index -- Interactive Search
  http://www.rootsweb.com/cgi-bin/sdbrulehist/sdbrule.pl
  From the South Dakota Historical Collections, Vol. XXIII, pages 1 184 (1947).

- Buckinghamshire Surnames List ~ England
  http://www.csranet.com/~dcarlsen/genuki/BKM/bucksurname.html

- Caernarfonshire, Wales Surnames List
  http://www.genuki.org.uk/big/wal/Surnames/cae.htm

- Caithness Surnames Research List ~ Scotland
  http://www.frayston.demon.co.uk/genuki/cai/surnames.htm

- Cambridgeshire Surnames List ~ England
  http://www.draytons.free-online.co.uk/cam/surnameslist.html

- Cardiganshire, Wales Surnames List
  http://www.genuki.org.uk/big/wal/Surnames/cgn.htm

- Carmarthenshire, Wales Surnames List
  http://www.genuki.org.uk/big/wal/Surnames/cmn.htm

- Channel Islands Genealogy - Surname Interests List
  http://www.rootsweb.com/~jfuller/ci/surnames.html
- Cheshire Surnames Directory ~ England
  http://www.fhsc.org.uk/surnames/
- Chinese Surnames
  http://www.geocities.com/Tokyo/3919/
- Clackmannanshire Surname List ~ Scotland
  http://www.dgnscrn.demon.co.uk/genuki/CLK/misc/surnames/
- Co. Tyrone, N. Ireland Fellow Genealogists
  http://www.teesee.com/CoTyrone/tyrone.html
- Cornwall, England - Surnames List ~ England
  http://www.cs.ncl.ac.uk/genuki/SurnamesList/Cornwall/
- County Antrim Surname Interest List ~ Ireland
  http://website.lineone.net/~british_isles/ANTRIM/antrimsr.htm
- County Down Surname List ~ Northern Ireland
  http://surhelp-bin.rootsweb.com/surindx.pl?gc=/Ireland/DownObits
- County Galway Surname List ~ Ireland
  http://www.labyrinth.net.au/~quibellg/galway.htm
- County Kerry Surname Interest List ~ Ireland
  http://cgi.rootsweb.com/~genbbs/genbbs.cgi/Ireland/Kerry
- County Kilkenny Ireland Genealogy "Surnames of Kilkenny"
  http://www.rootsweb.com/~irlkik/ksurname.htm
- County Limerick, Ireland Surnames and Queries
  http://www.geocities.com/Athens/Parthenon/6108/limerick.htm
- The County Mayo Surname Interest List ~ Ireland
  http://www.cs.ncl.ac.uk/genuki/SurnamesList/MAY.html
- County of Stirlingshire Surname List
  http://www.jeack.com.au/~treaclbk/surnames/stirling.htm
- County Sutherland, Scotland Surname List
  http://members.aol.com/sloinne/Sutherland/Surnames.htm
- County Westmeath Surname List ~ Ireland
  http://surhelp-bin.rootsweb.com/surindx.pl?gc=/Ireland/Westmeath
- Crown Hill Cemetery Burial Locator
  http://www.crownhill.org/cgi-local/db_search.cgi
  Searchable database for this cemetery in Indiana.
- Cumbria Surnames List ~ England
  http://cumbria-surnames.worldward.com/index.mv
- Danish Emigration Archives
  http://users.cybercity.dk/~ccc13656/
  Searchable database for 1869 to 1904, working on records thru 1940.
- DDD Danish Demographic Database / Dansk Demografisk Database
  http://ddd.sa.dk/
  Search a partial census database for 1787-1850 and the Danish emigrant database for 1868-1900.
- Database Direct Macomb County, Michigan
  http://macomb.mcntv.com/deathrecords/
  Searchable database of Macomb County, Michigan death records from the 1940's to present.
- Denbighshire, Wales Surnames List
  http://www.genuki.org.uk/big/wal/Surnames/den.htm
- Derbyshire Surnames List ~ England
  http://homepage.ihug.co.nz/~hughw/dby.htm
- Devon, England - Surnames List
  http://www.gendex.com/users/branscombe/genuki/devindex.htm
- East and North Riding Surname Interest List ~ England
  http://www.jodenoy.clara.net/erynry/erynry.htm
- East Lothian Surnames List ~ Scotland
  http://www.vivdunstan.clara.net/genuki/ELN/Surnames/
- East of London Surname Overview
  http://ourworld.compuserve.com/homepages/jordan/eolsur01.htm
  Includes the Boroughs of: Hackney, Tower Hamlets within Middlesex County, and Newham, Redbridge, Barking and Dagenham, and Havering within Essex County.
- Essex Surnames List ~ England
  http://wrathall.org/essex/
- Flintshire, Wales Surnames List
  http://www.genuki.org.uk/big/wal/Surnames/fln.htm
- Fylkesarkivet i Sogn og Fjordane - Databases
  http://www.sffarkiv.no/sffbasar/default.asp
- GENUKI Surname Lists
  http://www.genuki.org.uk/indexes/SurnamesLists.html
  Lists for each county in the United Kingdom and Ireland.
- German-Bohemian Immigrant Surname Database
  http://www.rootsweb.com/~gbhs/database/database.html
- Ghosts of the Klondike Gold Rush
  http://www.gold-rush.org/
  Check out the "Pan for Gold Database".
- Glamorganshire, Wales Surnames List
  http://www.genuki.org.uk/big/wal/Surnames/gla.htm
- Gloucestershire Surnames List ~ England
  http://www2.tpg.com.au/users/dsteel/glsnames.htm
- Hamburg Link To Your Roots
  http://www.hamburg.de/LinkToYourRoots/english/start.htm
  Searchable database extracted from the Hamburg Passenger Lists for selected years.
- HampshireSurnames List ~ England
  http://dspace.dial.pipex.com/c.broomfield/ham.htm
- Herefordshire Surnames List ~ England
  http://freespace.virgin.net/isabel.easter/mem.html

- HERRICK Library's Listing of SURNAMES in Ottawa County Michigan
  http://www.macatawa.org/~brianter/herrick.htm

- The Hertfordshire Surnames List ~ England
  http://homepages.ihug.co.nz/~hughw/hertford.html

- Hispanic Surnames Database
  http://users.aol.com/mrosado007/surnames.htm

- Hospital Records Database
  http://hospitalrecords.pro.gov.uk/
  Provides information on the existence and location of the records of the hospitals in the U.K. Currently over 2,800 entries can be found by searching the database using the following simple enquiry screen.

- Huntingdonshire Surnames List ~ England
  http://www.genuki.org.uk/big/eng/HUN/Surnames.html

- In Search of Your Canadian Past: The Canadian County Atlas Digital Project
  http://imago.library.mcgill.ca/countyatlas/default.asp
  From McGill University's Rare Books and Special Collections Division. A searchable database derived from published county atlases between 1874 & 1881. Searchable by property owners' names or by location. Township maps, portraits and properties have been scanned, with links from the property owners' names in the database.

- Jasper County, Indiana Deaths, 1921-77
  http://www.ancestry.com/search/rectype/inddbs/3939.htm
  Searchable database from Ancestry.com.

- Jasper County, Indiana Marriage Index, 1850-1920
  http://www.ancestry.com/search/rectype/inddbs/3745.htm
  Searchable database from Ancestry.com.

- Kent England Surname Interests
  http://www.rootsweb.com/~engken/kentname.htm

- Kingdom of Fife Surnames List ~ Scotland
  http://www.genuki.org.uk/big/scot/Fife/fife.surnames.html

- Kinross-shire Surname List ~ Scotland
  http://www.dgnscrn.demon.co.uk/genuki/KRS/misc/surnames/index.html

- Lanarkshire Surnames List ~ Scotland
  http://freepages.genealogy.rootsweb.com/~slund/lanark.htm

- Leicestershire Surnames List ~ England
  http://www.lodp.demon.co.uk/LEI.html

- Leitrim-Roscommon 1901 Census Home Page
  http://www.leitrim-roscommon.com/1901census/
  Searchable database.

- Leitrim-Roscommon Surname Search ~ Ireland
  http://www.leitrim-roscommon.com/surname_intro.html

- Lincolnshire Surnames ~ England
  http://www.excel.net/~nclark/sur1.htm

- The Liverpool (& area) Surnames List ~ England
  http://www.cgo.wave.ca/~scouse1/list.htm

- London Jews Database
  http://www.jewishgen.org/databases/londweb.htm

- Louisiana Land Records -- Interactive Search
  http://searches.rootsweb.com/cgi-bin/laland/laland.pl
  Pre-1908 Homestead and Cash Entry Patents from the Bureau of Land Management's General Land Office (GLO) Automated Records Project.

- Mecklenburg-Vorpommern Query System
  http://pages.prodigy.net/jhbowen/c3.htm

- Merionethshire, Wales Surnames List
  http://www.genuki.org.uk/big/wal/Surnames/mer.htm

- The Midlothian, Scotland Surnames List
  http://www.geocities.com/~ausjan/midlothian/midlothian.htm

- Missouri Surname Researchers List
  http://www.geocities.com/Heartland/Plains/7113/surnames.htm

- Mobile Genealogy Surname Search Engine ~ Alabama
  http://www.siteone.localweb.com/geneology/surname.asp

- Monmouthshire, Wales Surnames List
  http://www.genuki.org.uk/big/wal/Surnames/mon.htm

- Montgomeryshire, Wales Surnames List
  http://www.genuki.org.uk/big/wal/Surnames/mgy.htm

- Nairnshire Surnames List ~ Scotland
  http://www.geocities.com/~brooms/genuki/surnames/index.html

- Names of Mecklenburg-Schwerin Emigrants 1844-1915
  http://pages.prodigy.net/jhbowen/emig.htm

- New South Wales Registry of Births, Deaths and Marriages
  http://www.bdm.nsw.gov.au/
  o Search the Registry Indexes
    http://www.bdm.nsw.gov.au/Services/IndexSrch.html
    Searchable database for Births 1788-1905, Marriages 1788-1945 & Deaths 1788-1945.

- New York Emigrant Savings Bank Project
  http://www.genexchange.org/esb/index.cfm
  Searchable database of the records for the Emigrant Savings Bank in New York City. Opened in 1850 and run by Irish immigrants for Irish immigrants, the ESB records for emigrants from various countries settling in many states.
  o Emigrant Savings Bank Records
    http://www.nycgenweb.com/emigrant%20savings%20bank%20records.htm
    The first 500 account numbers with account owner names and dates.
  o The New York Emigrant Savings Bank
    http://www.everton.com/FHN/27may99.htm
    Brief article from Everton's regarding the genealogical value of these Bank records.

- A User's Guide to the Emigrant Bank Records
  http://www.nypl.org/research/chss/spe/rbk/faids/
  emigrant.html
  Opened in 1850 and run by Irish immigrants for Irish immigrants, the Emigrant Savings Bank records for immigrants from various countries settling in many states. This is a finding aid and description of these records from the New York Public Library's Manuscripts & Archives Division.

- Niedersachsen Germany Queries
  http://cgi.rootsweb.com/~genbbs/genbbs.cgi/Germany/
  Niedersachsen

- NORDGUIDE
  http://otatrip.hut.fi/nordinfo/nordguide/
  A directory of databases in the Nordic Countries.

- Nordrhein-Westfalen GermanyGenWeb - Index to Surnames, Queries, Researchers and Databases
  http://www.rootsweb.com/~deunrhwf/cc/qryindex.htm

- Norfolk Surnames List ~ England
  http://freespace.virgin.net/isabel.easter/Norfolk/
  Surnames.htm

- North East Lancashire Surname List ~ England
  http://ourworld.compuserve.com/homepages/GAFOSTER/
  n-e-lanc.htm

- Northamptonshire Surnames List ~ England
  http://www.skynet.co.uk/genuki/big/eng/NTH/Surnames/

- Northumberland and Durham, England - Surnames List
  http://gendex.com/users/branscombe/genuki/nblindex.htm

- Northwest History Databases from the Tacoma Public Library
  http://www.tpl.lib.wa.us/nwr/nwdata.htm

- Nottinghamshire Surnames List ~ England
  http://homepages.ihug.co.nz/~hughw/notts.html

- Oklahoma Surnames
  http://www.rootsweb.com/~oknames/

- Online Australasian Names Research Directory
  http://www.users.on.net/proformat/ausnames.html

- On-Line Database Search
  http://gov.nb.ca/archives/ols/ols.htm
  From the New Brunswick Provincial Archives.

  o County Birth Registers Index 1801 - 1899
    http://gov.nb.ca/archives/ols/gr/rssd/141A2-2/index.htm

  o Death Certificates: 1920 - 1949
    http://gov.nb.ca/archives/ols/gr/rssd/141C5/index.htm

  o Death Registration of Soldiers, 1941-1947
    http://gov.nb.ca/archives/ols/gr/rssd/141C6/index.htm

  o Index to New Brunswick Marriages 1887 - 1919
    http://gov.nb.ca/archives/ols/gr/rssd/141B7/index.htm

  o Irish Famine Migration To New Brunswick, 1845 – 1852
    http://gov.nb.ca/archives/ols/pr/if/index.htm

  o Late Registration of Births: Documentation Index 1801 - 1904
    http://gov.nb.ca/archives/ols/gr/rssd/141A1b/index.htm

  o Saint John Burial Permits, 1889 - 1919
    http://gov.nb.ca/archives/ols/gr/rssd/315A/index.htm

- On-line Dorset Names Research Directory
  http://www.users.on.net/proformat/dornames.html

- On-line Irish Names Research Directory
  http://www.users.on.net/proformat/irlnames.html

- On-line Search for Maiden Names of Women in South Holland
  http://users.itsnet.com/~pauld/ksh/
  Searchable database to be used in conjunction with the "Klappers of Zuid Holland" ("Indexes of South Holland"). Approx. 250,000 maiden names, from between 1695 and 1811.

- The Orkney Surnames List
  http://www.tiac.net/users/teschek/genuki/OKI/surnames.htm

- Oxfordshire Surname Interest List (OXSIL) ~ England
  http://www.rootsweb.com/~oxsil/

- Peeblesshire Surnames List ~ Scotland
  http://www.rootsweb.com/~sctpbs/PSL.htm

- Pembrokeshire, Wales Surnames List
  http://www.genuki.org.uk/big/wal/Surnames/pem.htm

- Pennsylvania Dutch (Queries Posted Immediately and Surnames Indexed Every Tuesday)
  http://cgi.rootsweb.com/~genbbs/genbbs.cgi/USA/Pa/Dutch

- Perthshire, Scotland Surnames List
  http://www.geocities.com/Heartland/Plains/3176/perthlist/
  index.html

- Portuguese Genealogist Master Database
  http://www.lusaweb.com/mstrlst.html-ssi

- Prince Edward Island Surname List
  http://homepages.rootsweb.com/~canada/pei.htm

- Radnorshire, Wales Surnames List
  http://www.genuki.org.uk/big/wal/Surnames/rad.htm

- Rafal T. Prinke - Surname List (English)
  http://hum.amu.edu.pl/~rafalp/GEN/wykaz-eng.html

- Rafal T. Prinke - Surname List / Lista Nazwisk (Polish)
  http://hum.amu.edu.pl/~rafalp/GEN/wykaz.html

- Renfrewshire Surnames List ~ Scotland
  http://www.madasafish.com/~andream/

- Roxburghshire Surnames List ~ Scotland
  http://www.vivdunstan.clara.net/genuki/ROX/Surnames/

- The Rutland Surnames List ~ England
  http://www.lodp.demon.co.uk/RUT.html

- Search the USGenWeb Archives Digital Library
  http://www.rootsweb.com/~usgenweb/ussearch.htm

- Selkirkshire Surnames List ~ Scotland
  http://www.vivdunstan.clara.net/genuki/SEL/Surnames/

- Shropshire Surname Interest List ~ England
  http://www.genuki.org.uk/big/eng/Surnames/sal.htm

- Siciliani in the World
  http://diemme.diemme.it/italiani/sicilia/
  E-mail addresses for people researching Sicilian surnames.

- Somerset & Dorset Surnames Index
  http://www.bakery.co.uk/sandd/

- Somerset Surnames Interest List ~ England
  http://www.genuki.org.uk/big/eng/Surnames/som.htm

- Staffordshire Surname Interest List ~ England
  http://www.genuki.org.uk/big/eng/Surnames/sts.htm

- Suffolk Surname List (& More!) ~ England
  http://www.dbitstech.com/leeann/suffolk/

- Surname Helper - Kentuckiana Genealogy ~ Kentucky & Indiana
  http://surhelp-bin.rootsweb.com/surindx.pl?site=kyiana

- Surname List: Dumfriesshire, Kirkcudbrightshire & Wigtownshire ~ Scotland
  http://www.nevisuk.net/dgfhs/surnames/index.html

- Surrey Surname Interest List ~ England
  http://www.genuki.org.uk/big/eng/Surnames/sry.htm

- Sussex Surnames List ~ England
  http://www.c.broomfield.dial.pipex.com/surnames/ssx/ssxname.htm

- The Texas Genealogy Register
  http://www.lsjunction.com/gen.htm

- Texas Physicians Historical Database
  http://www.swmed.edu/library/doctors/doctors.htm
  Searchable database of citations to biographical information related to early Texas physicians from the Texas State Journal of Medicine for 1905-1966 and additional sources.

- Texas Surnames
  http://www.rootsweb.com/~txrusk/txsurnames.html

- Tipperary Surname Interest List ~ Ireland
  http://homepages.ihug.co.nz/~hughw/tip.html

- Tisbury History: On-Line Historical Archives ~ Massachusetts
  http://www.vineyard.net/vineyard/history/

- USGenWeb Archives
  http://www.rootsweb.com/~usgenweb/

- Utah Cemetery Inventory - Burials Database
  http://www.dced.state.ut.us/history/Services/lcburials.html
  From the Utah State Historical Society. Lists over 315,000 burials in 208 cemeteries.

  o Burials Search
    http://utstcess.dced.state.ut.us:8080/NEWBURIALS/Silver Stream/Pages/pgStandardSearch.html

  o Cemetery Search
    http://utstcess.dced.state.ut.us:8080/NEWBURIALS/Silver Stream/Pages/pgCemeterySearch.html

  o List of Cemeteries
    http://www.dced.state.ut.us/history/Services/lccemeteries.html

- Valdez Museum & Historical Archive - Rush Participants Database ~ Alaska
  http://www.alaska.net/~vldzmuse/valdez.htm
  Valdez Gold Rush 1898-1899, Names Database.

- The Warwickshire Surnames List ~ England
  http://homepages.ihug.co.nz/~hughw/warwick.html

- Wayne County Indiana Marriage License Database
  http://www.co.wayne.in.us/marriage/retrieve.cgi
  Searchable database for marriage licenses from 1811 to 1903.

- The Wellington Valley Convicts, 1823-31
  http://www.newcastle.edu.au/department/hi/roberts/convicts.htm
  A database of over 1,000 convicts.

- West Indies Surname Interests List
  http://ourworld.compuserve.com/homepages/vroyal/

- West Lothian Surname List ~ Scotland
  http://www.rootsweb.com/~sctwln/

- West Riding Yorkshire Surname Interests ~ England
  http://members.aol.com/wrylist/wry.htm

- Wexford Surname Interest List ~ Ireland
  http://homepages.ihug.co.nz/~hughw/wexford.html

- Wiltshire Surname Interests List ~ England.
  http://www.genuki.org.uk/big/eng/WIL/interests/surnames.html

- Wisconsin Land Records -- Interactive Search
  http://searches.rootsweb.com/cgi-bin/wisconsin/wisconsin.pl
  Pre-1908 Homestead and Cash Entry Patents from the BLM.

- Worcestershire Surname Interest List ~ England
  http://www.jump.net/~salter/WORSIL.html

◆ Military

- Canada - Military
  http://www.CyndisList.com/milcan.htm
  See this category on Cyndi's List for related links.

- Confederate Pension Records
  http://isadore.tsl.state.tx.us/c/compt/index.html
  From the Texas State Electronic Library. Searchable database of Confederate pensions filed in the state of Texas.

- Military Resources Worldwide
  http://www.CyndisList.com/milres.htm
  See this category on Cyndi's List for related links.

- Roster of Wisconsin Volunteers, War of the Rebellion, 1861-1865
  http://www.shsw.wisc.edu/roster/
  All soldiers known to have participated in Wisconsin's Civil War

regiments. Searchable by surname or regiment. Gives basic data: when enlisted, residence at enlistment, if died, wounded or prisoner, when mustered out.

- Selective Service System | Obtaining Records
  http://www.sss.gov/records.htm
  The Selective Service System is able to provide information from records kept on men currently registered with Selective Service, as well as on men who were registrants as far back as World War I. Includes instructions on how to obtain Selective Service records.

  o Selective Service - Verification
    https://www4.sss.gov/regver/verification_nc.asp
    This online search service allows you to look up a man's Selective Service number, as well as the date he registered. Only registrations of men born on or after January 1, 1960, can be verified through this system.

- U.S. - Civil War ~ War for Southern Independence
  http://www.CyndisList.com/cw.htm
  See this category on Cyndi's List for related links.

- U.S. - Military
  http://www.CyndisList.com/military.htm
  See this category on Cyndi's List for related links.

- Volksbund Deutsche Kriegsgräberfürsorge e.V.
  http://www.volksbund.de/homepage.htm
  The German Military Grave Registration Service. Maintains 2 million war graves in over 640 cemeteries. Assists in grave identification and restoration. Provides assistance in determining the fate of German war dead.

  o Vermissten und Toten Datenbank
    http://www.volksbund.de/VuTDB/vut_suche.asp
    The Missing and Dead Database. Online searchable database of over 2 million interments.

- World War I History Questionnaires
  http://eagle.vsla.edu/wwi/
  From the Library of Virginia.

  o About the World War I History Commission Questionnaires Database
    http://image.vtls.com:8000/bibdatabases/wwiqabout.html
    The Virginia War History Commission was established in 1919 to collect, assemble, edit and publish information and material concerning Virginia's participation in World War I. The Commission conducted a survey of World War I veterans in Virginia through the use of a printed questionnaire. The World War I History Commission Questionnaires Database is a fully-searchable database of over 14,900 records, one for each questionnaire respondent, accessible by name, city/county, and race.

◆ People & Families

- HMS Bounty Genealogies
  http://wavefront.wavefront.com/~pjlareau/bounty6.html

- Huguenot Surnames Index - from Australian Family Tree Connections Magazine
  http://www.aftc.com.au/huguenot.html

- Index to: Religious Personnel in Russia 1853-1854
  http://www.memo.com/jgsr/database/deych.cgi

- The JewishGen Family Finder (JGFF)
  http://www.jewishgen.org/jgff/

- Master Index to President's Genealogical Data
  http://www.dcs.hull.ac.uk/public/genealogy/presidents/gedx.html

- O.M.I.I. Genealogical Project
  http://www.wgbc.org/hindex.htm
  A Swiss Mennonite & German Amish genealogy project.

- Pennsylvania Dutch (Queries Posted Immediately and Surnames Indexed Every Tuesday)
  http://cgi.rootsweb.com/~genbbs/genbbs.cgi/USA/Pa/Dutch

- Surname Helper - Search for a Surname
  http://surhelp.rootsweb.com/srchall.html
  A searchable database of queries and surname registrations posted on various genealogy sites, including USGenWeb and WorldGenWeb.

◆ Records: Census, Cemeteries, Land, Obituaries, Personal, Taxes and Vital (Born, Married, Died & Buried)

- 1872 Foreign-Born Voters of California
  http://feefhs.org/fbvca/fbvcagri.html

- Ancestry.com - Social Security Death Index (SSDI)
  http://www.ancestry.com/search/rectype/vital/ssdi/main.htm

- Arkansas Land Records -- Interactive Search
  http://searches.rootsweb.com/cgi-bin/arkland/arkland.pl

- Census Related Sites Worldwide
  http://www.CyndisList.com/census2.htm
  See this category on Cyndi's List for related links.

- Censuses of the Cotswolds and Southern Warwickshire
  http://www.silk.net/personal/gordonb/cotswold.htm
  Dozens of census extracts for this area in England.

- Database to an Index of Indiana Marriages Through 1850
  http://www.statelib.lib.in.us/www/indiana/genealogy/mirr.html
  Indiana State Library, Genealogy Division.

- Faculty Office Marriage License Index
  http://ourworld.compuserve.com/homepages/David_Squire/faculty.htm
  Index of marriage licenses issued by the Master of Faculties of the Archbishop of Canterbury for the period 1714 to 1850, England.

- Genealogical Death Indexing System, Michigan
  http://www.mdch.state.mi.us/PHA/OSR/gendis/index.htm
  The current system contains information on 150,000 Michigan death records from 1867-1882. Additional records for 1881 and 1882 have been newly added to the system during the week of July 12, 1999.

- Genealogy Online's Event's Database
  http://events.genealogy.org/main.html
  Add to this database and/or search this database of events such as birth, marriage or death, by surname.

- Illinois Statewide Marriage Index 1763-1900
  http://www.sos.state.il.us/depts/archives/marriage.html
  An ongoing project of the Illinois State Archives and the Illinois State Genealogical Society. Not all counties are complete. The sources for this index include original county clerk's marriage records such as marriage registers and licenses as well as publications of county genealogical societies and private individuals.

- Index of Marriages and Deaths in New York Weekly Museum, 1788-1817
  http://users.itsnet.com/~pauld/newyork/

- The Joiner Marriage Index
  http://website.lineone.net/~pjoiner/mindex/mindex.html
  A Marriage Database for County Durham, and the North Riding of Yorkshire in England.

- Kentucky Vital Records Index
  http://ukcc.uky.edu/~vitalrec/
  Marriage / Divorce / Death.

- Lincoln County, Tennessee, Marriages -- Interactive Search
  http://www.rootsweb.com/cgi-bin/tnlincoln/tnlincoln.pl

- Madison County, Iowa Marriages 1850 - 1880
  http://searches.rootsweb.com/cgi-bin/Genea/iowa

- Marriage History Search Form
  http://thor.ddp.state.me.us/archives/plsql/archdev.Marriage_Archive.search_form
  Index to Maine Marriages 1892-1966.

- Marriages from the Sherburn Hospital Registers (1695-1837)
  http://www.cs.ncl.ac.uk/genuki/Transcriptions/DUR/SHO.html
  Northumberland and Durham, England.

- Marriages in Rankin County, Mississippi
  http://www.vanished.com/pages/free_lib/rankin_co.html

- Miami Valley Genealogical Index
  http://www.pcdl.lib.oh.us/miami/miami.htm
  Surname index of census, tax, marriage & wills records for these counties: Butler, Champaign, Clark, Darke, Greene, Hamilton, Mercer, Miami, Montgomery, Preble, Shelby, Warren ~ Ohio.

- National Archives of Canada - Index to the 1871 Census of Ontario
  http://www.archives.ca/exec/naweb.dll?fs&020108&e&top&0

- Norway - 1801 Census
  http://www.uib.no/hi/1801page.html

- Nova Scotia Census Data 1891 Antigonish County
  http://www.rootsweb.com/~casoccgs/census.html

- Obituary Daily Times
  http://www.rootsweb.com/~obituary/

- Ohio Online Death Certificate Index, 1913-1927, and 1933-1937
  http://www.ohiohistory.org/dindex/search.cfm
  Searchable database from the Ohio Historical Society, Archives/Library.

- The Old 300 Genealogical Database ~ Texas
  http://www.bchm.org/Gene/gene.html
  "The 'Old 300' database actually includes a core listing of all settlers who had received land grants in Austin's Colony by the eve of the war for independence from Mexico".

- SAMPUBCO
  http://www.sampubco.com/
  Will Testators Indexes, Naturalization Records Indexes and Census Indexes online. You can order copies of the original source documents for a small fee.

- The San Francisco Call (Newspaper) Database 1875 - 1905
  http://feefhs.org/fdb2/sfcall0.html

- Scots Origins
  http://www.origins.net/GRO/
  An online pay-per-view database of searchable indexes of the GRO(S) index to births/baptisms and banns/marriages from the Old Parish Registers dating from 1553 to 1854, plus the indexes to births, deaths and marriages from 1855 to 1897. The 1881 census data is expected later this year and an index to the 1891 census records is coming soon.

- Seventh-day Adventist Periodical Index
  http://143.207.5.3:82/search/
  Has a searchable obituary index and more.

- Släktdata - Föreningen
  http://www.slaktdata.org/
  Searchable parish registers in Sweden.

- Tacoma Obituary Database ~ Washington
  http://www.tpl.lib.wa.us/v2/nwroom/obit.htm

- U.S. Census
  http://www.CyndisList.com/census.htm
  See this category on Cyndi's List for related links.

- U.S. Census Bureau Name Search
  http://www.census.gov/ftp/pub/genealogy/www/namesearch.html
  This provides name frequency in America from the 1990 census.

- Virginia Quit Rent Rolls, 1704
  http://www.lineages.com/vault/rents_1704_results.asp

- Vital Events Indexes - BC Archives ~ Canada
  http://www.bcarchives.gov.bc.ca/textual/governmt/vstats/v_events.htm

  o Marriage Registration Index Search Gateway, 1872 to 1921
    http://www2.bcarchives.gov.bc.ca/cgi-bin/www2vsm

  o Death Registration Index, 1872 to 1976
    http://www2.bcarchives.gov.bc.ca/cgi-bin/www2vsd

- York County, South Carolina, Census Index - Interactive Search
  http://www.rootsweb.com/cgi-bin/scyork/scyork.pl
  1790 to 1850 heads of household.

◆ ROOTS-L and RootsWeb

- RootsWeb Surname List - Interactive Data Edit/Submission Form
  http://rsl.rootsweb.com/cgi-bin/rsledit.cgi
  Then search the existing entries in the RSL database here:

- RootsWeb Surname List -- Interactive Search
  http://rsl.rootsweb.com/cgi-bin/rslsql.cgi

- Alternate site: RSL Search Program
  http://gen.roc.wayne.edu/fsl.html

- Related list: Roots Location List Name Finder
  http://searches.rootsweb.com/cgi-bin/Genea/rll

- RootsWeb Surname List or RSL Readme File
  http://www.rootsweb.com/roots-l/family.readme.html

- ROOTS-L Library
  http://www.rootsweb.com/roots-l/filelist.html
  Dozens of reference files full of hidden goodies.

- RootsWeb Genealogical Data Cooperative - Search Engines
  http://www.rootsweb.com/rootsweb/searches/
  Several searchable databases on this site, with more coming online each day!

- Search the Archive of ROOTS-L Messages from 1987 through present
  http://searches.rootsweb.com/roots-l.search.html

◆ Societies & Groups

- Bedfordshire Family History Society - Member's Interests
  http://www.kbnet.co.uk/brianp/interests.html
  A list of surnames being researched by the members.

- The Genealogical Society of Broward County Surname List ~ Florida.
  http://www.rootsweb.com/~flgsbc/surmenu.html

- Index of Names Being Researched by Arizona State Genealogical Society Members
  http://www.rootsweb.com/~asgs/nindex.html

- Livermore-Amador Genealogical Society Surname Index
  http://www.l-ags.org/surname.html
  With over 10,000 surname-locality entries.

- MLFHS Internet Group Members Interests
  http://www.onthenet.com.au/~tonylang/Mainpage.html
  Surnames from members of the Manchester and Lancashire Family History Society in England.

- South Carolina Historical Society - Surname Guide
  http://www.schistory.org/library/catalogs/gbrowse.html

- The Skaneateles Historical Society
  http://www.skaneateles.com/historical/
  New York. They have vital statistics records online, including marriage records and death records. A database of over 15,000 records compiled from the old newspaper records from 1831 through 1899.

- South Dakota Genealogical Society Quarterly Index -- Interactive Search
  http://www.rootsweb.com/cgi-bin/sdgsqart/sdgsqart.pl

- Tacoma-Pierce County Genealogical Society - Ancestor Exchange Index ~ Washington
  http://www.rootsweb.com/~watpcgs/ancexch.htm

DEATH RECORDS

http://www.cyndislist.com/deaths.htm

Category Index:

◆ General Resource Sites
◆ Locality Specific

◆ U.S. Vital Records by State

◆ General Resource Sites

- AudioTapes.com - Genealogical Lectures on Cassette Tapes - Death
  http://www.audiotapes.com/search2.asp?Search=death

- Death Records
  http://www.carolyar.com/Deathrecords.htm
  Visitors contribute death record information to this site.

- FamilySearch.org - Where to Write for Vital Records
  http://www.familysearch.org/Eng/Search/rg/frameset_rg.asp?Dest=G1&Aid=&Gid=&Lid=&Sid=&Did=&Juris1=&Event=&Year=&Gloss=&Sub=&Tab=&Entry=&Guide=WheToWri.ASP

- Genealogy Bulletin - Where to Find Birth, Death, Marriage and Divorce Records
  http://www.genealogybulletin.com/archives/HTML/current2.html
  By William Dollarhide.

- Obtaining Vital Records
  http://www.ancestry.com/columns/george/12-04-98.htm
  From "Along Those Lines..." by George Morgan.

- Parish and Vital Records List
  http://www.familysearch.org/Eng/Search/rg/frameset_rg.asp?Dest=G1&Aid=&Gid=&Lid=&Sid=&Did=&Juris1=&Event=&Year=&Gloss=&Sub=&Tab=&Entry=&Guide=PARISH.ASP
  A list of indexed church and vital records available from the LDS Family History Library.

- RootsWeb's Guide to Tracing Family Trees - Lesson 4: Vital Records: Death, Tombstones and Cemeteries
  http://www.rootsweb.com/~rwguide/lesson4.htm

- Shaking Your Family Tree: Finding Vital Records The Easy Way
  http://www.uftree.com/bin/fg_auth?/GenealogyNewsstand/ShakingTree/Books/981210.html
  By Myra Vanderpool Gormley, C.G.

- Shaking Your Family Tree: Vital Records
  http://www.uftree.com/bin/fg_auth?/GenealogyNewsstand/ShakingTree/Vital/Vital.html
  By Myra Vanderpool Gormley, C.G.

- VitalChek
  http://www.vitalchek.com
  Certified copies of birth certificates, death certificates, marriage certificates and other vital records.

- Vital Records for U.S. Research – The Records Room
  http://daddezio.com/records/

- Vital Records Information - State Index
  http://vitalrec.com/index.html
  Information about where to obtain vital records (such as birth, death & marriage certificates and divorce decrees) from each state, territory and county of the United States.

- Where to Write for Vital Records
  http://www.cdc.gov/nchs/howto/w2w/w2welcom.htm
  From the National Center for Health Statistics, United States

◆ Locality Specific

- Australia & New Zealand
  See also: Cyndi's List - Australia & New Zealand
  http://www.CyndisList.com/austnz.htm

  o 1880-1920 Otago Daily Times Births Deaths Marriages, Anniversaries Index, Dunedin, New Zealand
    http://www.kirksoc.co.uk/churches/dunedin.htm
    See the details near the end of this page.

  o Australasia Births, Deaths and Marriages Exchange
    http://www.geocities.com/hutton_l/exchange/
    The aim of the Australasia Births, Deaths and Marriages Exchange is to provide genealogists with a free resource, to share information about details contained on civil and parish registrations registered in Australia, New Zealand and Papua New Guinea.

  o Australian Registrars of Births, Deaths & Marriages
    http://www.users.on.net/proformat/regs.html

  o Australian Vital Records Index
    http://www.ldscatalog.com/cgi-bin/ncommerce3/ProductDisplay?prrfnbr=2482&prmenbr=1402&CGRY_NUM=1440461&RowStart=1&LocCode=FH
    A CD-ROM for sale from the LDS Church. Contains an indexed collection of references to 4.8 million birth, christening, marriage, and death records. Covers New South Wales (1788-1888), Tasmania (1803-1899), Victoria (1837-1888), and Western Australia (1841-1905).

  o Deaths In the Melbourne Hospital, 1867-1880
    http://home.coffeeonline.com.au/~tfoen/meldeath.html
    An index of foreign born residents of Melbourne who passed away at the Melbourne Hospital between 1867 and 1880.

o Deaths and Memoriams Extracted from the `New Zealand Herald' 1993
http://www.geocities.com/Heartland/6123/dth_names.html
From New Zealand. Find a surname of interest then e-mail the owner of the page for details.

o New South Wales Registry of Births, Deaths and Marriages
http://www.bdm.nsw.gov.au/

• Search the Registry Indexes
http://www.bdm.nsw.gov.au/Services/IndexSrch.html
Searchable database for Births 1788-1905, Marriages 1788-1945 & Deaths 1788-1945.

o New Zealand Birth and Death Entries
http://www.geocities.com/Heartland/Forest/2925/nzbdentries.htm
Shows the format of these civil registration records and what information they record.

o New Zealand Births, Deaths & Marriages Office
http://www.bdm.govt.nz/diawebsite.nsf/c3649e22547ea840cc25681e0008b39b/c26afa900922c388cc25683e007b9a3f?OpenDocument

o Tasmanian Family Link
http://pioneers.tased.edu.au/
A database made up of records of births, deaths, and marriages, as well as other events, that is designed to connect families with ancestors who lived in Tasmania in the 19th century.

• Canada
See also: Cyndi's List - Canada Index
http://www.CyndisList.com/canada.htm

o Alberta Family Histories Society (AFHS) Genealogical Projects Registry ~ Canada
http://www.afhs.ab.ca/registry/index.html
A central registry which provides a bibliography of genealogical projects, both online and offline, in Canada. The registry is categorized by province/territory, then by record type: births, marriage, census, deaths, and other.

• Alberta - Death
http://www.afhs.ab.ca/registry/regab_death.html

• British Columbia - Death
http://www.afhs.ab.ca/registry/regbc_death.html

• Canada - Death
http://www.afhs.ab.ca/registry/regcan_death.html

• Manitoba - Death
http://www.afhs.ab.ca/registry/regmb_death.html

• New Brunswick - Death
http://www.afhs.ab.ca/registry/regnb_death.html

• Newfoundland & Labrador - Death
http://www.afhs.ab.ca/registry/regnf_death.html

• Northwest Territories - Death
http://www.afhs.ab.ca/registry/regnt_death.html

• Nova Scotia - Death
http://www.afhs.ab.ca/registry/regns_death.html

• Ontario - Death
http://www.afhs.ab.ca/registry/regon_death.html

• Prince Edward Island - Death
http://www.afhs.ab.ca/registry/regpe_death.html

• Quebec - Death
http://www.afhs.ab.ca/registry/regqc_death.html

• Saskatchewan - Death
http://www.afhs.ab.ca/registry/regsk_death.html

• Yukon - Death
http://www.afhs.ab.ca/registry/regyk_death.html

o Bill Martin's Genealogy Page
http://www.tbaytel.net/bmartin/
Has several articles for Ontario genealogical research, including lists of microfilm numbers for ordering from the archives or an FHC

• Birth, Marriage, Death Indexes for Ontario, Canada
http://www.tbaytel.net/bmartin/bmd.htm

• Birth, Marriage and Death Application Form Instructions
http://www.tbaytel.net/bmartin/registry.htm

o Births, Deaths and Marriages Reported in Calgary, Alberta Newspapers, 1883-1899 ~ Canada
http://www.calcna.ab.ca/afhs/news.html

o Burials at Niagara 1792 to 1829 ~ Ontario, Canada
http://www.tbaytel.net/bmartin/niag-bur.htm

o Northwest Territories, Canada, Birth, Death, and Marriage Records, 1925 to the Present
http://www.familysearch.org/Eng/Search/rg/frameset_rg.asp?Dest=G1&Aid=&Gid=&Lid=&Sid=&Did=&Juris1=&Event=&Year=&Gloss=&Sub=&Tab=&Entry=&Guide=NT_BMDT3_Northwest_Territories_Vital_Records.ASP
How to access and utilize these records from FamilySearch.org.

o The Olive Tree Genealogy - Canada - Births Deaths & Marriages Exchange
http://www.rootsweb.com/~ote/bdm/canada/bdm.htm

o Vital Statistics
http://www.gov.mb.ca/cca/vital.html
From the Manitoba Consumer and Corporate Affairs, information on how to obtain birth, marriage and death certificates from Manitoba, Canada.

• Miscellaneous

o Hong Kong Births and Deaths Registries
http://www.info.gov.hk/immd/english/topical/g/6.htm
From the Hong Kong Immigration Department. Includes contact information and hours of operation.

o Mexican Parish Records, 1751-1880
http://www.ancestry.com/search/rectype/inddbs/3947.htm
Pay-for-use database of marriage, baptism, and death records from nine Mexican parishes: Matamoros, Agualequas, Mier, Sabinas Hidalgo, Vallecillo, Cadereyta, Camargo, Cerralvo, & Guerrero with over 100,000 records including 400,000 names.

• United Kingdom & Ireland
See also: Cyndi's List - United Kingdom & Ireland Index
http://www.CyndisList.com/uksites.htm

o Births, Deaths, and Marriages
http://www.familyrecords.gov.uk/BMDmain.htm
From the United Kingdom's familyrecords.gov consortium.

o British Vital Records Index
http://www.ldscatalog.com/cgi-bin/ncommerce3/Product
Display?prrfnbr=11905&prmenbr=1402&CGRY_NUM=1440
461&RowStart=1&LocCode=FH
CD-ROM for sale from the LDS Church. Contains more than 4.7 million christenings, births, and marriages that occurred in England, Wales, Scotland, and Ireland from 1500 to 1888.

o Cheshire BMD - Cheshire Births, Marriages and Deaths on the Internet
http://www.CheshireBMD.org.uk/
Searchable online index to over 276,000 birth and 125,000 marriages registrations from the county of Cheshire.

o Current Lists of Church of Ireland Parish Registers and Vestry Minutes at the RCBL, Dublin
http://www.ihaonline.com/rcbl.htm
List by county showing the Church of Ireland (Protestant) parish registers of baptism, marriage, and burial and the vestry minutes deposited at the Representative Church Body Library in Dublin. Hosted by The Irish At Home and Abroad with permission of the RCBL.

o FreeBMD Project
http://FreeBMD.rootsweb.com/
"FreeBMD stands for Free Births, Marriages, and Deaths. The FreeBMD Project's objective is to provide free Internet access to the Civil Registration index information for England and Wales."

o Holy Trinity Church Baptism, Marriage and Burial Register Index 1840-1899 ~ Tansley, Derbyshire, England
http://freespace.virgin.net/denys.gaskell/tansley.html

o Irish Ancestors - The Records
http://scripts.ireland.com/ancestor/browse/records/
index.htm

• State Registration of Births, Marriages & Deaths
http://scripts.ireland.com/ancestor/browse/records/
state/index.htm

o National Archives of Ireland
http://www.nationalarchives.ie/index.html

• Births, marriages and deaths
http://www.nationalarchives.ie/birthsmarrdeaths.html

o Office for National Statistics - Registration of Births, Adoptions, Marriages and Deaths ~ England and Wales
http://www.statistics.gov.uk/registration/default.asp

o Ordering Birth Registration Certificates from England & Wales
http://www.oz.net/~markhow/ukbirths.htm
Using the LDS Family History Center Resources.

o Public Record Office - Finding Aids - A-Z Index of All Leaflets ~ U.K.
http://www.pro.gov.uk/leaflets/riindex.htm

• Births, Marriages and Deaths
http://www.pro.gov.uk/leaflets/ri2118.htm

o Registrar of Births, Deaths and Marriages, Dundee ~ Scotland
http://www.dundeecity.gov.uk/dcchtml/sservices/rbdm.html

o Scots Origins
http://www.origins.net/GRO/
Scots Origins is an online "pay-per-view" database of indexes from the genealogical records of the General Register Office for Scotland - the GRO(S). The Scots Origins database contains fully searchable indexes of the Old Parish Registers of births/baptisms and banns/marriages dating from 1553 to 1854, indexes to the Statutory Registers of births, deaths and marriages from 1855 to 1898, and the index to census records for 1891. Extracts of the original entries in the GRO(S) records can be ordered directly from the database. Extract orders are processed by GRO(S) and sent via ordinary mail as paper documents.

• About Scots Origins
http://www.origins.net/GRO/about.html

• Information for Family History Searching on the Scots Origins web site of the General Register Office for Scotland
http://www.gro-scotland.gov.uk/grosweb/grosweb.nsf/
pages/searchin
From the FAQ on the web site for the General Register Office for Scotland.

• Scots Origins FAQ
http://www.origins.net/GRO/faq.html

o The UK BDM Exchange
http://web.ukonline.co.uk/graham.pitt/bdm/
A volunteer project to share birth, death and marriage certificates that you have stored in your own research files.

◆ U.S. Vital Records by State
Please See: United States Index - U.S. - Vital Records
http://www.cyndislist.com/usvital.htm

DIARIES & LETTERS
http://www.cyndislist.com/diaries.htm

Category Index:
- ◆ General Resource Sites
- ◆ Libraries, Archives & Museums
- ◆ Locality Specific
- ◆ Military
- ◆ People & Families

◆ General Resource Sites

- AudioTapes.com - Genealogical Lectures on Cassette Tapes - Diaries
  http://www.audiotapes.com/search2.asp?Search=Diaries

- The Personal Life Diary
  http://www.personallifediary.com
  A 70-year diary that can become a family heirloom.

- What to Do with a Diary You Have Found
  http://www.dohistory.org/on_your_own/toolkit/foundDiary.html
  From DoHistory. If you are lucky enough to find an old diary, here are some tips for what you could do next.

◆ Libraries, Archives & Museums

- Augustana College Library - Special Collections
  http://www.augustana.edu/library/special/index2.html

  o Civil War Diaries
    http://search.augustana.edu/augieweb/library/civil1.html

- Documenting the American South: First Person Narratives of the American South
  http://www.ibiblio.org/docsouth/fpn/fpn.html
  From the Academic Affairs Library of the University of North Carolina at Chapel Hill. Text from diaries, autobiographies, memoirs, travel accounts, and ex-slave narratives of relatively inaccessible populations: women, African Americans, enlisted men, laborers, and Native Americans.

- SCETI: Women's Studies
  http://www.library.upenn.edu/etext/diaries/
  From the University of Pennsylvania Library / Schoenberg Center for Electronic Text & Image

  o Manuscript Diaries of Grace Gilchrist Frend, 1907-1941
    http://www.library.upenn.edu/etext/diaries/gilchrist/

  o Manuscript Diary of Elizabeth Cowperthwaite, 1857-1858
    http://www.library.upenn.edu/etext/diaries/cowper1857/

  o Manuscript Diary of Fanny Ruschenberger, 1858-1881
    http://www.library.upenn.edu/etext/diaries/fanny/

  o Manuscript Diary of Margaret A. Eadie, 1901-1909
    http://www.library.upenn.edu/etext/diaries/eadie/

  o Manuscript Diary of Margaret T. Spaulding, 1870
    http://www.library.upenn.edu/etext/diaries/spaulding1870/

  o Manuscript Diary of Susan Sherman, 1850-1851
    http://www.library.upenn.edu/etext/diaries/sherman1850/

- Valley of the Shadow - Letters & Diaries
  http://jefferson.village.virginia.edu/vshadow2/letters.html
  Features people who lived in Augusta County, Virginia and Franklin County, Pennsylvania before, during and after the U.S. Civil War.

◆ Locality Specific

- Letters from Forgotten Ancestors
  http://www.tngenweb.org/tnletters/
  A Tennessee Genealogy History Project.

- The Life and Times of South Dakota Pioneers
  http://www.rootsweb.com/~sdpotter/Letters/home.htm
  Letters written in the 19th and early 20th centuries.

- Maine Diaries
  http://www.rootsweb.com/~meandrhs/mediary.html
  Maine Diary Directory and letters from a Maine man in the 1849 CA Gold Rush.

◆ Military

- Aquilla Standifird's Civil War Diary
  http://www.carolyar.com/aquillastandifird.htm
  Company D, 23rd Iowa.

- Augustana College Library - Special Collections
  http://www.augustana.edu/library/special/index2.html

  o Civil War Diaries
    http://www.augustana.edu/library/SpecialCollections/civil1.html

- Civil War Diary of Bingham Findley JUNKIN, 100th Pennsylvania Volunteer Infantry ("Roundheads")
  http://www.iwaynet.net/~lsci/junkin/

- The Civil War Diary of E.B. ROOT
  http://www.netrom.com/~merklee/Diary.html

- Civil War Diary of Elias D. MOORE 114th Ohio Volunteer Infantry, Co. A
  http://www.fortunecity.com/westwood/makeover/347/index.htm

- The Civil War Diary of Walter Scott HUFF
  http://www.geocities.com/Heartland/Pointe/3497/
  Co. F 89th Illinois infantry (The Railroad Regiment).

- Civil War Letter Collection of First Lieutenant Rufus Ricksecker, 126th OVI, Part I
  http://www.iwaynet.net/~lsci/Rickpt1.htm
  A collection of 30 letters written between October 12, 1862 and September 18, 1864. Rufus Ricksecker was killed on September 19, 1864 at the Battle of Opequan (Third Winchester).

- Civil War letters of the "Blountsville Boys", Henry, County, Indiana
  http://www.rootsweb.com/~inhenry/civilwar.html
  Many were written by Allen Wesley Galyean.

- Civil War: Iowa Volunteers
  http://www.alaska.net/~design/civilwar/
  Including excerpts from a Civil War diary and letters.

- Diaries and Letters
  http://www.twingroves.district96.k12.il.us/CivilWar/Diaries
  Letters.html
  Links to Civil War diaries and letters online.

- Diary of Mexican-American War: Elias F. HINEY
  http://homepages.rootsweb.com/~sam/elias.html
  Elias Hiney served in Company B, First Regiment of Pennsylvania Volunteers from December 15, 1846 through July 27, 1848 and kept a diary through his entire term of service.

- The Diary of 2nd Lieut. Robert Peyton HAMILTON - 1915
  http://members.tripod.co.uk/PatHamilton/diary/Diary.htm
  The diary of Robert Peyton HAMILTON written from 1st January 1915 until his death in September the same year. Details of training and trench warfare.

- The Emily Project
  http://www.marblehead.net/emily/
  A 1932 diary found in a Vermont flea market led it's new owner on a search for the identity of the writer. Read the diary and learn how the mystery was solved.

- Evacuation- The Diary of One Man's Experience
  http://website.lineone.net/~heathq/index.htm
  The diary of Edwin Richard George QUITTENTON in Northern France during 1940.

- The FREEMAN Diary
  http://www.public.usit.net/mruddy/freeman.htm
  Civil War diary of John Henderson Freeman of Company I of the 34th Mississippi Volunteers, Walthall's Brigade, Gen'l Bragg's Army, CSA.

- Illinois Greyhounds
  http://www.ketzle.com/diary/
  Diary of Henry KETZLE of Company A in the 37th Illinois Infantry from July 1861 through May 1866.

- Letter from Sergeant Joseph Fisher, Company A, 126th Ohio Volunteer Infantry
  http://www.iwaynet.net/~lsci/jfletter.htm
  This letter was written on November 3, 1862 from Camp McCook,

Cumberland, Maryland. It describes the wonder a rural Ohio farmboy feels on his first trip into the mountains with his Regiment. Joseph Fisher was eventually lost at the Wilderness, May 6, 1864.

- Letters, Diaries, Reminiscences, and Manuscripts of New York Soldiers and Nurses
  http://www.snymor.edu/pages/library/local_history/sites/
  letters/

- Letters from an Iowa Soldier in the Civil War
  http://www.civilwarletters.com/home.html
  Part of a collection written by Newton Robert SCOTT, Private, Company A, of the 36th Infantry, Iowa Volunteers to Hannah CONE, his friend and later his wife.

- Letters of the Civil War
  http://www.geocities.com/Pentagon/7914/
  A compilation of letters from the soldiers, sailors, nurses, politicians, ministers and journalists from the newspapers of the cities and towns of Massachusetts, April 1861-December 1865.

- Letters written by Private Justus G. MATTESON during the Civil War
  http://www.ggw.org/10nycav/justus.htm
  MATTESON & HATCH surnames. Cortland County, New York.

- The Memoirs, Diary, and Life of Private Jefferson Moses,Company G, 93rd Illinois Volunteers
  http://www.ioweb.com/civilwar/

- A Michigan Civil War Physician's Diary
  http://www.sos.state.mi.us/history/museum/techstuf/civilwar/
  diarybac.html
  Excerpts from Dr. Cyrus Bacon's diary.

- A Narrative of the Experiences of Robert Pierce While a Soldier in the Civil War
  http://cpcug.org/user/jlacombe/rpierce.html

- Samuel J. BRADLEE'S Civil War Letters
  http://www.bee.net/dmann/
  This site is a collection of letters from a Massachusetts artillery officer to his wife in Boston.

- Valley of the Shadow - Letters & Diaries
  http://jefferson.village.virginia.edu/vshadow2/letters.html
  Features people who lived in Augusta County, Virginia and Franklin County, Pennsylvania before, during and after the U.S. Civil War.

- The Wartime Diary of John WEATHERED
  http://www.nashville.com/~jack.masters/9tncav.htm
  Civil War Diary of John Weathered who served in the 9th Tennessee Confederate Cavalry.

- Women's Civil War Diaries and Papers - Locations
  http://homepages.rootsweb.com/~haas/lotsofnames/
  cwdiaries.html

- Yahoo!...Civil War: Documents: Personal Accounts
  http://dir.yahoo.com/Arts/Humanities/History/U_S__History/
  19th_Century/Civil_War__1861_1865_/Documents/Personal_
  Accounts/
  Diaries and letters.

◆ People & Families

- **1862 Diary of Isaac HURLBURT**
  http://www.doit.com/tdoyle/diaryih.htm
  Fully transcribed 1862 diary of Isaac Hurlburt of Broome County, New York.

- **Absecon Diary of Margie ROTH, 1933-37**
  http://www.absecondiary.com
  Margie Roth wrote her diary during the Great Depression of the 1930s.

- **Aunt Mae's Diary**
  http://www.kcnet.com/~sdjones/auntmae/index.html
  From 1914 to 1919 Mae Youker kept a diary. Surnames included are: YOUKER, ROCKWELL, WOOLEVER.

- **Clarissa Stoddart GOOCH's Diary 1831-32**
  http://genweb.net/~dsinclair/diaryintro.htm
  Clarissa Gooch's diary is an account of her removal with her sister's family from London to Cincinatti, OH, in 1831-32. They traveled by ship to New York City, across New York State on sleighs, and down the Allegheny and Ohio Rivers to Cincinatti on a flat-boat.

- **Cordelia Susan BEIDLER Diary**
  http://www.genweb.net/~wilcox/CSBPage.html

- **Diary of Archibald Little HAGER from 1844-1887**
  http://micosaur.granitecity.com/diary/diary000.htm
  Recorded daily events in Perry County, Missouri, including births, marriages, and deaths from 1844-1887.

- **The Diary of Celia L.E.C. PEEBLES BAILEY**
  http://www.rootsweb.com/~mschocta/celiapeeblesdiary.html
  The Diary of Celia L.E.C. Peebles Bailey, wife of William R. Bailey. Diary Entries from 16 February 1851 to 14 July 1851, with Trading Post Journal Entries from 21 January 1835 to 2 May 1844. William R. and Celia L. E. C. Peebles Bailey were one of the first families to settle in Old Choctaw County, Mississippi, in the 1830's.

- **The Diary of Clinton Harrison MOORE**
  http://www.pcfa.org/genealogy/ClintonHarrisonMoore.html
  Diary of travel from McNairy County, Tennessee to the Republic of Texas in 1839. MOORE, ROBINSON, MARTIN, BARTON, KIZER.

- **Diary of Emily TOWELL**
  http://www.cybernet1.com/homestyle/emily.htm
  A diary written by Emily Towell in 1881. The true story of a group of noble pioneers whose courage and determination gave them the desire to leave their homes in Mercer County, Missouri and crossed the plains in covered wagons to seek new land in the promising west.

- **Diary of Hannah Walton SANDERS, Feb. 5, 1806 - Nov. 28, 1876**
  http://www.alltel.net/~cjwalker/
  Among surnames mentioned are: CURRAN, FLOYD, FOSTER, FULTON, GRAHAM, JACKSON, KINCANNON, NEWELL, SANDERS, TRIGG.

- **The Diary of "Honest" John MARTIN**
  http://www.theballards.net/Harshaw/Martin/Diary/index.html
  Transcribed portions of John Martin's Diary, comprising six volumes. Includes accounts of his exile to Tasmania as well as his later service as MP.

- **Diary of Raymond ALLEN**
  http://www.rootsweb.com/~pabradfo/allendia.htm
  My great grandfathers Diary of a cattle drive from Windham Twp, Bradford County, PA to Connecticut, 1864.

- **Diary of Rev. Clay MacCauley**
  http://jefferson.village.virginia.edu/vshadow2/personal/mccauley.html

- **Diary of William S. PURGITT, 1865 - of New Creek (Keyser), West Virginia**
  http://www.rootsweb.com/~wvminera/purgitt.html

- **Enchanted Mountains Genealogy Society - Diary of Joseph Beaman OVIATT**
  http://www.enchantedmountains.com/diary.html
  Winter of 1847-1848, Keating Township, McKean County, PA.

- **Evacuation- The Diary of One Man's Experience**
  http://website.lineone.net/~heathq/index.htm
  The diary of Edwin Richard George QUITTENTON in Northern France during 1940.

- **The Immigration Diary of Michael Friedrich RADKE, 1848**
  http://members.aol.com/lhchristen/1848.htm
  "This diary is presented to help us understand why families wished to leave Prussia / Germany, to emigrate to America or Australia, in the 1840's."

- **Ingeborg Brigitte Gastel - Diaries**
  http://worldroots.com/brigitte/diaries.htm

- **The James HARSHAW Diary Site**
  http://www.theballards.net/Harshaw/
  A description of the James HARSHAW Diaries and of people of Counties Down and Armagh in the mid-1800s. Also includes an account of John MARTIN, Young Irelander.

- **John Stoner BEIDLER Diaries**
  http://www.genweb.net/~wilcox/JSBPage.html

- **The Journal and Medical Ledgers of Dr. John GREEN - First registered Dr. in Mineral County WV**
  http://users.erols.com/mstaggs/

- **Letter from Adeline WINN of Concord, Massachusetts**
  http://www.rootsweb.com/~valoudou/letters/awinltr.htm
  Written to Mary Dulin (Jenners) Braden of Clinton Co., Indiana March 2, 1831.

- **Letter from Mrs. Elizabeth Braden of Waterford, VA**
  http://www.rootsweb.com/~valoudou/letters/bradene.htm
  To Burr & Mary Braden of Lafayette, IN 21 June 1830.

- **Letters to Sarah Elizabeth (OVERDORF) SMITH**
  http://www.genweb.net/~lorriev/sarahletters.htm

- **Martha BALLARD's Diary Online**
  http://www.dohistory.org/diary/index.html
  The source for the book and film "A Midwife's Tale", Martha Ballard wrote in her diary nearly every day from January 1, 1785 to May 12, 1812 (27 years) for a total of almost 10,000 entries. Her diary is an unparalleled document in early American history.

- Memoirs of the NOHL Family Trip Diary of Friedrich Nohl
  http://www.crossmyt.com/hc/gen/nohlmigd.html

- The Partial* Diary of "Honest" John Martin Young Irelander 1812-1875 Co. Down, Ireland
  http://burgoyne.com/pages/ballark/John/JMIndex.html
  Portions of the diary of John Martin, who was sentenced to Van Diemen's land charged with treason for fighting for home rule in the 1800's. Accounts of his voyage, conversations with John Mitchel, etc.

- Samuel Hervey LAUGHLIN Diary
  http://home.att.net/~jlp1/reports/shlaughlindiary.htm
  Account of his LAUGHLIN and DUNCAN or DUNKIN ancestors. Written in 1845.

- A Vanished Way of Life...
  http://home.fuse.net/wands/
  The diary for 1898 of Sarah Adelia APPLEGATE of Meridian, NY. The diary contains numerous footnotes and information about family relationships for genealogists. APPLEGATE, VAN DOREN, WANDS, HULL, SITTSER, FERRIs.

- WARD Diary 1862
  http://members.aol.com/warddiary/index.html
  Diary of Lucy Parker WARD from 1862 in Ashtabula and Trumbull County Ohio. Surnames: COLEMAN, PERKINS, FOBES, GIDDINGS, PERKINS, GILLET, HART, BABCOCK, LILLIE, SIMPKINS, BROCKWAY, MORSE, MINER, JONES, KEE, WING.

DICTIONARIES & GLOSSARIES
http://www.cyndislist.com/diction.htm

Category Index:

◆ Abbreviations
◆ Genealogy Dictionaries & Glossaries
◆ Miscellaneous
◆ Other Online Dictionaries, Glossaries, Etc.

◆ Abbreviations

- Abbreviations and Acronyms: A Guide for Family Historians
  http://www.amazon.com/exec/obidos/ISBN=0916489949/markcyndisgenealA/
  A book by by Kip Sperry.

- Abbreviations Found in Genealogy
  http://www.rootsweb.com/~rigenweb/abbrev.html

- Abbreviations Used in Genealogy
  http://www.uq.net.au/~zzmgrinl/abbrev.html

- Alphabet Soup: Understanding the Genealogical Community
  http://www.familytreemaker.com/33_kathy.html

- Genealogical Abbreviations
  http://www.pcola.gulf.net/~llscott/abbrevia.htm

- The Genealogists' Handbook - Common (and Not So Common) Abbreviations
  http://www.kentuckianagenealogy.org/guide/help/abbreviations.html
  From Kentuckiana Genealogy.

- Genealogy Abbreviation List
  http://www.niagara.com/~hanam/abbreviations/abbreviations.txt

- Genealogy Abbreviations
  http://homepages.rootsweb.com/~sam/abbr.html

- Making Sense of the Alphabet Soup
  http://www.ancestry.com/library/view/columns/george/1163.asp
  From "Along Those Lines..." by George Morgan.

- ROOTS-L Resources: Abbreviations Used in Genealogy
  http://www.rootsweb.com/roots-l/abbrevs.html

- UK Genealogy - Common Acronyms & Jargon
  http://www.oz.net/~markhow/acronym-uk.htm

◆ Genealogy Dictionaries & Glossaries

- Ancestry's Concise Genealogical Dictionary
  http://www.amazon.com/exec/obidos/ISBN=091648906X/markcyndisgenealA/
  A book by Maurine Harris and Glen Harris.

- Charlotte's Web Genealogical Dictionary
  http://www.charweb.org/gen/gendict.html

- Charts for Reference in Genealogy Research
  http://members.tripod.com/~Silvie/charts.html
  Glossary Chart, Occupation Chart, War Chart, Disease Chart.

- The Correct Spelling of the Word GENEALOGY
  http://www.oz.net/~markhow/writing/spelling.htm
  A little memory aid by Mark Howells.

- Danish-English Genealogy Dictionary
  http://ourworld.compuserve.com/homepages/NormanMadsen/danish.htm

- The Dictionary of Genealogy
  http://www.amazon.com/exec/obidos/ISBN=0713648597/markcyndisgenealA/
  A book by Terrick H. Fitzhugh. An outstanding reference explaining terms and concepts used in UK genealogy.

- Family History SourceGuide
  http://www.familysearch.org/sg/index_s.html
  Genealogical word lists from the FamilySearch Internet Genealogy Service of the LDS Church.
  - o Danish
    http://www.familysearch.org/sg/WLDanish.html
  - o Dutch
    http://www.familysearch.org/sg/WLDutch.html
  - o Finnish
    http://www.familysearch.org/sg/WLFinnis.html
  - o French
    http://www.familysearch.org/sg/WLFrench.html
  - o German
    http://www.familysearch.org/sg/WLGerman.html
  - o Italian
    http://www.familysearch.org/sg/WLItalia.html
  - o Latin
    http://www.familysearch.org/sg/WLLatin.html
  - o Norwegian
    http://www.familysearch.org/sg/WLNorway.html
  - o Polish
    http://www.familysearch.org/sg/WLPolish.html
  - o Danish
    http://www.familysearch.org/sg/WLDanish.html
  - o Portuguese
    http://www.familysearch.org/sg/WLPortug.html

- o Spanish
  http://www.familysearch.org/sg/WLSpanis.html
- o Swedish
  http://www.familysearch.org/sg/WLSweden.html
- Frontier Press Bookstore - Dictionaries
  http://www.frontierpress.com/frontier.cgi?category=dict
- Gareth's Help Page (Technical Words)
  http://www.johngareth.freeserve.co.uk/tech.html
  Excellent resource for UK genealogical terminology.
- Genealogy Definitions
  http://home.earthlink.net/~howardorjeff/i8.htm
- Genealogy Dictionary
  http://home.att.net/~dottsr/diction.html
- Genealogy Dictionary from Dick Eastman
  http://w3g.med.uni-giessen.de/CGB/genetxt/buzzwo.rds
- Genealogy Dictionary from Family Tree Maker
  http://www.familytreemaker.com/00000736.html
- genealogyPro Glossary of Genealogy Terms
  http://genealogyPro.com/details/glossary.html
- Genealogy Terms
  http://homepages.rootsweb.com/~sam/terms.html
- Genealogy: Terms for Document Translation (Lith)
  ~ Lithuania
  http://lark.cc.ukans.edu/~raistlin/genealogy/terms.html
- German-English Genealogical Dictionary
  http://www.amazon.com/exec/obidos/ISBN=0806313420/
  markcyndisgenealA/
  A book by Ernest Thode.
- German Study Group / German Words
  http://205.216.138.19/~websites/lynnd/vuword.html
- Glossary of Genealogical Terms
  http://www.rootsweb.com/~canwgw/ns/digby/perm2/
  glossary.htm
- Glossary of Unusual Words Found in Wills etc.
  http://ourworld.compuserve.com/homepages/dave_tylcoat/
  gloss.htm
- Hearthstone Bookshop - Genealogical Dictionaries
  http://www.hearthstonebooks.com/cgi-bin/webc.cgi/st_
  main.html?catid=10&sid=2Qp5fy81a
- Kentuckiana Genealogy - Genealogy Glossary
  http://www.kentuckianagenealogy.org/guide/help/
  glossary1.html
- Latin Genealogical Word List
  http://www.familysearch.org/sg/WLLatin.html
  From the Family History SourceGuide.
- The Lost Husbands Guide to On-Line Genealogy -
  Glossary of Genealogical Terms
  http://members.aye.net/~dee1234/lost/glossary.html

- OLD-WORDS Mailing List
  http://www.rootsweb.com/~jfuller/gen_mail_general.html
  #OLD-WORDS
  For the discussion of old words, phrases, names, abbreviations, and antique jargon useful to genealogy.
- A Partial List of Latin Genealogy Terms and Their
  English Equivalents
  http://www.arduini.net/tools/latin.htm
- ROOTS-L Resources: Genealogical Terms and
  Definitions
  http://www.rootsweb.com/roots-l/definitions.html
- Swedish Language Basics for Genealogists
  http://genweb.net/~turner/dict.html
  Links to dictionaries and other language resources. The Swedish spelling reform of 1906 and other spelling changes.
- UK Genealogy - Common Acronyms & Jargon
  http://www.oz.net/~markhow/acronym-uk.htm
- Ultimate Family Tree - Glossary of Genealogical
  Terms and Abbreviations
  http://www.uftree.com/UFT/Nav/glossary.html
- The USGenWeb Project Information for Researchers
  - Genealogy Vocabulary
  http://www.usgenweb.org/researchers/vocab.html
- What Did They Mean by That : A Dictionary of
  Historical Terms for Genealogists
  http://www.amazon.com/exec/obidos/ISBN=1556139446/
  markcyndisgenealA/
  A book by Paul Drake.

◆ Miscellaneous

- Amazon.com Genealogy Bookstore - Dictionaries
  http://www.amazon.com/exec/obidos/external-search/?
  keyword=dictionary+genealogy&tag=markcyndisgenealA/
- AmeriSpeak: Expressions of Our Ancestors
  http://www.rootsweb.com/~genepool/amerispeak.htm
- Civil War Soldier Vocabulary
  http://cee.indiana.edu/gopher/Turner_Adventure_Learning/
  Gettysburg_Archive/Other_Resources/Soldier_Vocabulary.txt
- Glossary of Unusual Words Found in Wills etc.
  http://ourworld.compuserve.com/homepages/dave_tylcoat/
  gloss.htm
- Graven Images
  http://olivetreegenealogy.com/misc/grave.shtml
  Describes the symbolism of motifs on gravestones - from The Olive Tree.
- Latin for the Illiterati : Exorcizing the Ghosts of a
  Dead Language
  http://www.amazon.com/exec/obidos/ISBN=0415917751/
  markcyndisgenealA/
  A book by Jon R. Stone.

- More Latin for the Illiterati: A Guide to Everyday Medical, Legal, and Religious Latin
  http://www.amazon.com/exec/obidos/ISBN=0415922119/markcyndisgenealA/
  A book by Jon R. Stone.

- Nicknames List
  http://www.tngenweb.org/franklin/frannick.htm

- Nicknames: Past & Present
  http://www.amazon.com/exec/obidos/ISBN=0929626109/markcyndisgenealA/
  A book by Christine Rose CG, CGL, FASG.

- Our Ancestors' Nicknames
  http://www.uftree.com/UFT/HowTos/SettingOut/nickname1.html

- Shipping Terminology
  http://www.isn.net/~dhunter/terms.html
  With a Prince Edward Island Slant.

- Society of Genealogists Bookshop: Glossaries, Handwriting & Latin ~ U.K.
  http://www.sog.org.uk/acatalog/SoG_Bookshop_Online_Handwriting___Latin_231.html

- Terms of Confusement: Dowry and Dower
  http://www.ancestry.com/columns/myra/Shaking_Family_Tree10-02-97.htm
  From Shaking Your Family Tree by Myra Vanderpool Gormley, C.G.

- WORDS Mailing List
  http://www.rootsweb.com/~jfuller/gen_mail_general.html#WORDS
  And the associated web page
  http://www.rootsweb.com/~genepool/amerispeak.htm
  A lighthearted discussion of English-English/American-English phrases and how they might have originated.

- Ye Olde English Sayings
  http://www.rootsweb.com/~genepool/sayings.htm

◆ Other Online Dictionaries, Glossaries, Etc.

- Hypertext Webster's Interface - from Various Webster's Dictionary Services on the Internet
  http://c.gp.cs.cmu.edu:5103/prog/webster

- A Web of On-Line Dictionaries
  http://www.facstaff.bucknell.edu/rbeard/diction.html
  A huge index of a variety of available dictionaries, including foreign translation sites.

- Online Dictionaries, Glossaries and Encyclopedias
  http://stommel.tamu.edu/~baum/hyperref.html

EASTERN EUROPE
http://www.cyndislist.com/easteuro.htm

Category Index:

- FEEFHS ~ Federation of East European Family History Societies
- General Resource Sites
- History & Culture
- Language, Handwriting, & Script
- Libraries, Archives & Museums
- How To
- Mailing Lists, Newsgroups & Chat
- Maps, Gazetteers & Geographical Information

- People & Families
- Professional Researchers, Volunteers & Other Research Services
- Publications, Software & Supplies
- Records: Census, Cemeteries, Land, Obituaries, Personal, Taxes and Vital
- Religion & Churches
- Societies & Groups
- World GenWeb

◆ FEEFHS ~ Federation of East European Family History Societies

- FEEFHS - Federation of East European Family History Societies
  http://feefhs.org/
  - o Ethnic, Religious and National Index of Home Pages and FEEFHS Resource Guide Listings
    http://feefhs.org/ethnic.html
    Of organizations associated with FEEFHS from 14 countries
  - o FEEFHS Ethnic, Religious and National Cross-Indexes:
    - Austro-Hungarian Empire
      http://feefhs.org/ah/indexah.html
    - Banat
      http://feefhs.org/banat/indexban.html
    - Canadian
      http://feefhs.org/ca/indexcan.html
    - Croatia Genealogy
      http://feefhs.org/cro/indexcro.html
    - Galicia - (Galizien)
      http://feefhs.org/gal/indexgal.html
    - Germans from Russia Historical Collection
      http://feefhs.org/grhc/indexgrc.html
    - Germans from Russia Heritage Society
      http://feefhs.org/grhs/indexgrh.html
    - Hutterite Genealogy
      http://feefhs.org/hut/indexhut.html
    - Jewish Genealogy
      http://feefhs.org/indexjew.html
    - Mennonite
      http://feefhs.org/men/indexmen.html

    - Slovenia Genealogy
      http://feefhs.org/slovenia/indexsi.html
    - Swiss
      http://feefhs.org/ch/indexch.html
  - o FEEFHS Full Text Web Site Index Search Engine
    http://feefhs.org/search/
  - o FEEFHS Location (Address) Index of FEEFHS Member Organizations
    http://feefhs.org/location.html
    And other East European Genealogy Organizations.
  - o FEEFHS Significant Additions Index
    http://feefhs.org/webm/sigad96.html
  - o FEEFHS Web Site Master Index
    http://feefhs.org/masteri.html

◆ General Resource Sites

- AEGEE's former Yugoslavia Information
  http://www.aegee.tue.nl/hrwg/exyu/index.html
- Alex Glendinning's Hungarian Pages
  http://user.itl.net/~glen/Hungarianintro.html
- Armenian Genealogical Web Page
  http://members.aol.com/Gaghjayan/homepage.htm
  Welcome to the first Web Page devoted totally to the genealogical research of Armenians. This project is a natural progression in the evolution of Armenian genealogy.
- Belarus SIG
  http://www.jewishgen.org/belarus/
  Provides research data for Jewish genealogist with roots in the country known as Belarus, formerly Byelorussia or White Russia.
- European Focus
  http://www.eurofocus.com/
  Photographic portfolios of ancestral towns in Europe created for Genealogy enthusiasts in Germany, Italy, Poland, Scandinavia, Great Britain and more.

- FHW Projects: Genealogy Project
  http://www.fhw.gr/fhw/en/projects/genealogy.html
  From the Foundation of the Hellenic World. The Genealogy Project aims at reconstructing the family trees of the Asia Minor refugees, Greek-Orthodox inhabitants of Asia Minor and Pontos (the Black Sea region) who were expelled from their homeland after the Asia Minor disaster in 1922, and took refuge in Greece. The family data to be collected will begin with the grandparents of each Asia Minor refugee, and follow into their posterity.

- The Genealogist - Hungarian Genealogy
  http://www.xcelco.on.ca/~genealog/hungary1.htm

- Genealogy and Heraldry in Slovenia
  http://genealogy.ijp.si/

- Genealogy for Armenians
  http://www.itsnet.com/home/gfa/
  This site has excerpts from a book for sale of the same title.

- German Genealogy: Donauschwaben / Danube-Swabians
  http://www.genealogy.net/gene/reg/ESE/dschwaben.html

- German-Prussian Genealogy Links
  http://www.geocities.com/SiliconValley/Haven/1538/germanpg.html

- Home Page of the Unofficial Dvinsk Genealogy SIG
  http://www.geocities.com/Heartland/Valley/4100/

- Institute Country Index
  http://www.columbia.edu/cu/sipa/REGIONAL/ECE/country.html
  Links to online resources for several countries from the Institute on East Central Europe at Columbia University.

- The Italo-Albanian Heritage Pages
  http://members.aol.com/itaalb1/web/arberesh.htm

- Jewish Records Indexing - Poland
  http://www.jewishgen.org/JRI-PL/

- The Pomeranian Page
  http://www.execpc.com/~kap/pommern1.html

- Prussian Genealogy Links
  http://www.geocities.com/SiliconValley/Haven/1538/prussia.html

- Prussian-Russian-Canadian Mennonite Genealogical Resources
  http://www.mmhs.org/mmhsgen.htm

- Resources for Sepharadic Genealogy
  http://www.geocities.com/Heartland/Valley/2177/resource.htm
  Sepharadic genealogical research begins with the search for your ancestor's country of origin. It could be almost any country where Sephardim lived - Bulgaria, Curacao, Gibraltar, Morocco, Greece, Romania, Tunisia, Turkey, Yugoslavia, any Middle Eastern country, even Germany, Holland, Italy or Malta. Small numbers of Sephardim even lived in Poland and Russia and had names like Levine, Rangel and Calahora.

- Telefonski imenik Slovenije - Slovenian Telephone Directory
  http://tis.telekom.si/

- Ukrainian Genealogy
  http://www.infoukes.com/genealogy/

- Virtual Guide to Belarus - Belarusian Genealogy
  http://www.belarusguide.com/genealogy1/Genelgy.html

- The WWW Virtual Library: Russian and East European Studies (REESWeb)
  http://www.ucis.pitt.edu/reesweb/
  Directory of Internet resources for the Balkans, the Baltic states, the Caucusus, Central Asia, Central Europe, the CIS, Eastern Europe, the NIS, the Russian Federation, and the former Soviet Union.

- Yahoo!...Armenia...Genealogy
  http://dir.yahoo.com/Regional/Countries/Armenia/Arts_and_Humanities/Humanities/History/Genealogy/

- Yahoo!...Ukraine...Genealogy
  http://dir.yahoo.com/Regional/Countries/Ukraine/Arts_and_Humanities/Humanities/History/Genealogy/

◆ History & Culture

- Coats of Arms of the 64 Counties of the Kingdom of Hungary
  http://www.msstate.edu/Archives/History/hungary/counties/counties.html

- History of Europe, Slavic States
  http://www.worldroots.com/brigitte/royal/royal4.htm
  Historic and genealogical information about royal and nobility family lines.

- History of German Settlements in Southern Hungary
  http://feefhs.org/banat/bhistory.html

- The Imperial House of Russia, House of Romanoff
  http://www.romanovfamilyandfund.org/decendants.html

- The Russian Post-Emancipation Household Two Villages in the Moscow Area
  http://www.uib.no/hi/herdis/HerdisKolle.html
  By Herdis Kolle. A description of Russian peasant family life.

- StudyWeb: History: Europe
  http://www.studyweb.com/History/toceurop.htm

◆ How To

- How to Do Croatian Genealogy
  http://www.durham.net/facts/crogen/

◆ Language, Handwriting, & Script

- Alta Vista Translations
  http://www.babelfish.altavista.com/translate.dyn
  Online site which will translate text or web sites from Russian to English.

- The Cyrillic Alphabet
  http://www.friends-partners.org/oldfriends/language/russian-alphabet.html
  A written & audio guide to pronouncing the letters of the Russian alphabet.

- English-Hungarian Dictionary
  http://www.sztaki.hu/services/engdict/index.jhtml

- FEEFHS Database of Professional Translators Specializing in East European Genealogy
  http://feefhs.org/frg/frg-pt.html

- Genealogy: Terms for Document Translation (Lith) ~ Lithuania
  http://lark.cc.ukans.edu/~raistlin/genealogy/terms.html

- Languages & Translations
  http://www.CyndisList.com/language.htm
  See this category on Cyndi's List for related links.

- Translation Service only for genealogy related material
  http://www.genealogy.net/gene/misc/translation.html
  Volunteer translators can provide you with translations between Czech, English, Dutch, French, German, & Polish. This service is provided via e-mail. Exact request syntax and length rules must be followed in order to expedite processing.

◆ Libraries, Archives & Museums

- The Archive of Macedonia
  http://www.unet.com.mk/arhiv/

- Arhiv Jugoslavije / The Archives of Yugoslavia
  http://www.gov.yu/arhiv/a1000001.htm

- Arhiv Republike Slovenije / Archives of the Republic of Slovenia
  http://www.sigov.si/ars/index.html

- Budapest Fõváros Levéltára / Budapest City Archives ~ Hungary
  http://www.fph.hu/bphome/leveltar/INDEXE.HTM

- Family History Library Catalog
  http://www.familysearch.org/Search/searchcatalog.asp
  From the FamilySearch web site, an online catalog to the holdings of the LDS Church in Salt Lake City, Utah. Also search for other localities by place name.
  http://www.familysearch.org/fhlc/supermainframeset.asp?display=localitysearch&columns=*,180,0

  o Albania
  http://www.familysearch.org/fhlc/supermainframeset.asp?display=localitydetails&subject=151&subject_disp=Albania&columns=*,180,0

  o Belarus
  http://www.familysearch.org/fhlc/supermainframeset.asp?display=localitydetails&subject=120&subject_disp=Belarus&columns=*,180,0

  o Bosnia and Herzegovina
  http://www.familysearch.org/fhlc/supermainframeset.asp?display=localitydetails&subject=161&subject_disp=Bosnia_and_Herzegovina&columns=*,180,0

  o Bulgaria
  http://www.familysearch.org/fhlc/supermainframeset.asp?display=localitydetails&subject=167&subject_disp=Bulgaria&columns=*,180,0

  o Croatia
  http://www.familysearch.org/fhlc/supermainframeset.asp?display=localitydetails&subject=157&subject_disp=Croatia&columns=*.180.0

  o Hungary
  http://www.familysearch.org/fhlc/supermainframeset.asp?display=localitydetails&subject=94&subject_disp=Hungary&columns=*,180,0

  o Macedonia
  http://www.familysearch.org/fhlc/supermainframeset.asp?display=localitydetails&subject=165&subject_disp=Macedonia&columns=*,180,0

  o Moldova
  http://www.familysearch.org/fhlc/supermainframeset.asp?display=localitydetails&subject=123&subject_disp=Moldova&columns=*,180,0

  o Montenegro
  http://www.familysearch.org/fhlc/supermainframeset.asp?display=localitydetails&subject=163&subject_disp=Montenegro&columns=*,180,0

  o Romania
  http://www.familysearch.org/fhlc/supermainframeset.asp?display=localitydetails&subject=168&subject_disp=Romania&columns=*,180,0

  o Russia (Empire)
  http://www.familysearch.org/fhlc/supermainframeset.asp?display=localitydetails&subject=113&subject_disp=Russia_(Empire)&columns=*,180,0

  o Serbia
  http://www.familysearch.org/fhlc/supermainframeset.asp?display=localitydetails&subject=155&subject_disp=Serbia&columns=*,180,0

  o Slovenia
  http://www.familysearch.org/fhlc/supermainframeset.asp?display=localitydetails&subject=159&subject_disp=Slovenia&columns=*,180,0

  o Turkey
  http://www.familysearch.org/fhlc/supermainframeset.asp?display=localitydetails&subject=196&subject_disp=Turkey&columns=*,180,0

  o Ukraine
  http://www.familysearch.org/fhlc/supermainframeset.asp?display=localitydetails&subject=121&subject_disp=Ukraine&columns=*,180,0

  o Germany, Preußen (Prussia)
  http://www.familysearch.org/fhlc/supermainframeset.asp?display=localitydetails&subject=37854&subject_disp=Germany,_Preußen&columns=*,180,0

    • Brandenburg
    http://www.familysearch.org/fhlc/supermainframeset.asp?display=localitydetails&subject=37855&subject_disp=Germany,_Preußen,_Brandenburg&columns=*,180,0

    • Hannover
    http://www.familysearch.org/fhlc/supermainframeset.asp?display=localitydetails&subject=38802&subject_disp=Germany,_Preußen,_Hannover&columns=*,180,0

    • Hessen-Nassau
    http://www.familysearch.org/fhlc/supermainframeset.asp?display=localitydetails&subject=40119&subject_disp=Germany,_Preußen,_Hessen-Nassau&columns=*,180,0

    • Hohenzollern
    http://www.familysearch.org/fhlc/supermainframeset.asp?display=localitydetails&subject=41859&subject_disp=Germany,_Preußen,_Hohenzollern&columns=*,180,0

- Ostpreußen (East Prussia)
  http://www.familysearch.org/fhlc/supermainframeset.asp
  ?display=localitydetails&subject=41939&subject_disp=
  Germany,_Preußen,_Ostpreußen&columns=*,180,0

  See also Russia (Empire), Kaliningrad
  http://www.familysearch.org/fhlc/supermainframeset.asp
  ?display=localitydetails&subject=135562&subject_disp=
  Russia_(Empire),_Kaliningrad&columns=*,180,0

- Pommern
  http://www.familysearch.org/fhlc/supermainframeset.asp
  ?display=localitydetails&subject=42731&subject_disp=
  Germany,_Preußen,_Pommern&columns=*,180,0

- Posen
  http://www.familysearch.org/fhlc/supermainframeset.asp
  ?display=localitydetails&subject=43484&subject_disp=
  Germany,_Preußen,_Posen&columns=*,180,0

- Rheinland
  http://www.familysearch.org/fhlc/supermainframeset.asp
  ?display=localitydetails&subject=44415&subject_disp=
  Germany,_Preußen,_Rheinland&columns=*,180,0

- Sachsen (Saxony)
  http://www.familysearch.org/fhlc/supermainframeset.asp
  ?display=localitydetails&subject=46664&subject_disp=
  Germany,_Preußen,_Sachsen&columns=*,180,0

- Schlesien (Silesia)
  http://www.familysearch.org/fhlc/supermainframeset.asp
  ?display=localitydetails&subject=48237&subject_disp=
  Germany,_Preußen,_Schlesien&columns=*,180,0

- Schelswig-Holstein
  http://www.familysearch.org/fhlc/supermainframeset.asp
  ?display=localitydetails&subject=50160&subject_disp=
  Germany,_Preußen,_Schleswig-Holstein&columns=
  *,180,0

- Westfalen (Westphalia)
  http://www.familysearch.org/fhlc/supermainframeset.asp
  ?display=localitydetails&subject=50659&subject_disp=
  Germany,_Preußen,_Westfalen&columns=*,180,0

- Westpreußen (West Prussia)
  http://www.familysearch.org/fhlc/supermainframeset.asp
  ?display=localitydetails&subject=51662&subject_disp=
  Germany,_Preußen,_Westpreußen&columns=*,180,0

- Family History SourceGuide - Family History
  Centers - Europe and Scandinavia
  http://www.familysearch.org/sg/Europe_and_Scandinavia_
  FHC.html
  *Austria, Belgium, Denmark, Finland, France, Germany, Hungary,
  Iceland, Italy, Netherlands, Norway, Portugal, Spain, Sweden, and
  Switzerland.*

- HELKA - The Helsinki University Libraries OPAC
  http://renki.helsinki.fi/gabriel/en/countries/finland-opac-
  en.html
  *Catalog of the Helsinki University Library system. It has a large
  collection of official publications of the former Russian Empire.*

- Herder-Institut Marberg: About the Institute
  http://www.uni-marburg.de/herder-institut/english/allgemein/
  info.html
  *According to its statutes, the Herder-Institute supports "with its
  collections and as a forum for academic discussion the research on
  the countries and peoples of East Central Europe in their European
  context, with special regard to the history of the historical German
  territories and areas of settlement in East Central Europe. In order*

*to fulfill these tasks, the institute conducts its own research." The
core subject of its work is the area of the present-day states of
Poland, the Czech Republic, Slovakia, Estonia, Latvia and
Lithuania.*

- Milli Kütüphane / National Library of Turkey
  http://www.mkutup.gov.tr/index.shtml
  *The TNL collection consists of 1,414,108 works including books,
  periodicals and non-book materials. There are 943,964 books and
  356.340 volumes of periodicals containing newspapers, magazines,
  bulletins and annuals.*

- Nacionalna i sveucilišna knjiznica / National and
  University Library ~ Zagreb, Croatia
  http://www.nsk.hr/index.htm

- Narodna in Univerzitetna Knjiznica / National and
  University Library ~ Ljubljana, Slovenia
  http://nuk.uni-lj.si/

- National and University Library, Ljubljana,
  Slovenija
  http://www.nuk.uni-lj.si/

- Országos Széchényi Könyvtár / National Széchényi
  Library
  http://www.oszk.hu/
  The National Library of Hungary.

- Public Libraries of Europe
  http://dspace.dial.pipex.com/town/square/ac940/eurolib.html

- Repositories of Primary Sources - Europe A-M
  http://www.uidaho.edu/special-collections/euro1.html
  And Europe N-Z
  http://www.uidaho.edu/special-collections/euro2.html
  *A list of links to online resources from the Univ. of Idaho Library,
  Special Collections and Archives*

  o Hungary
     http://www.uidaho.edu/special-collections/euro1.html#hu

  o Russia
     http://www.uidaho.edu/special-collections/euro2.html#ru

  o Slovenia
     http://www.uidaho.edu/special-collections/euro2.html#si

  o Yugoslavia
     http://www.uidaho.edu/special-collections/euro2.html#yu

- Slovene Archives
  http://www.pokarh-mb.si/home.html

◆ Mailing Lists, Newsgroups & Chat

- Banat Genealogy Mailing List Home Page
  http://feefhs.org/banat/frgbanat.html

- BANAT Mailing List
  http://www.rootsweb.com/~jfuller/gen_mail_country-hun.html
  #BANAT
  *For those doing research in the Banat region of what was formerly
  Hungary.*

- BDO Mailing List
  http://www.rootsweb.com/~jfuller/gen_mail_country-rus.html
  #BDO

The Beresan District Odessa (BDO) mailing list is for anyone with a genealogical interest in the Beresan Colonies which were made up of Germans who immigrated to Russia, beginning in the first decade of the 19th century, at the request of Alexander I, Tsar of Russia. The Colonies were located Northeast of the city of Odessa on the Black Sea.

- BERDICHEV Mailing List
  http://www.rootsweb.com/~jfuller/gen_mail_country-rus.html
  #BERDICHEV
  For anyone with a genealogical interest in Berdichev, Ukraine, Russia with a focus on Jewish genealogy.

- Boslovlist Mailing List
  http://www.rootsweb.com/~jfuller/gen_mail_country-ukr.html
  #Boslovlist
  A mailing list for anyone with a genealogical interest in the town of Boslov (Boguslav) in the Ukraine.

- BUKOVINA-GEN Mailing List
  http://www.rootsweb.com/~jfuller/gen_mail_country-rom.html
  #BUKOVINA-GEN
  For those researching their genealogy and family history in Bukovina, a former crownland of the Austrian Empire (a.k.a. Bucovina, Bukowina, Bukovyna, or Buchenland), now divided between Romania and Ukraine.

- EURO-JEWISH Mailing List
  http://www.rootsweb.com/~jfuller/gen_mail_general.html
  #EURO-JEWISH
  For anyone with a genealogical interest in the Migration, History, Culture, Heritage and Surname search of the Jewish people from Europe to the United States and their descendants in the United States.

- Exulanten-L Mailing List
  http://www.rootsweb.com/~autwgw/agsfrx.htm
  Exulanten is the name given to the Protestants that were forced out Austria (estimated as many as100,000) during 16th to 18th century. The largest wave of about 22,000 left the Salzburg area in1731/32. Most went to East Prussia (Germany - Poland, Lithuania and Latvia) but some went to Siebenbürgen and Banat (today's Romania), Hungary and to parts of today's Slovakia.

- Family Tree -- Hungarian Roots Mailing List
  http://www.familytree.hu/hunroots.html

- GEN-SLAVIC Mailing List
  http://www.rootsweb.com/~jfuller/gen_mail_country-pol.html
  #GEN-SLAVIC
  Gatewayed with the soc.genealogy.slavic newsgroup
  news:soc.genealogy.slavic

- GOTTSCHEE Mailing List
  http://www.rootsweb.com/~jfuller/gen_mail_country-slv.html
  #GOTTSCHEE
  For anyone with a genealogical interest in Gottschee, Austria (now known as Kocevje, Slovenia).

- Hungarian American List (HAL)
  http://www.rootsweb.com/~jfuller/gen_mail_country-hun.html
  #HUNGARIAN
  A mailing list for those interested in expressing, sharing, and exchanging their views, ideas, and feelings about Hungary, Hungarians, Hungarian-Americans, and Hungarian culture and genealogy.

- HUNGARY Mailing List
  http://www.rootsweb.com/~jfuller/gen_mail_country-hun.html
  #HUNGARY1

- med-gene Mailing List
  http://www.rootsweb.com/~jfuller/gen_mail_country-gen.html
  #med-gene
  For anyone with a genealogical interest in the Mediterranean area.

- OW-PREUSSEN-L Mailing List
  http://www.rootsweb.com/~jfuller/gen_mail_country-ger.html
  #OW-PREUSSEN-L
  For those interested in sharing and exchanging information on genealogy and history which has a connection to the former East and West Prussia.

- PolandBorderSurnames Mailing List
  http://www.rootsweb.com/~jfuller/gen_mail_country-pol.html
  #PolandBorderSurnames
  For anyone researching genealogy in the former historical borders of Poland including Estonia, Latvia, Lithuania, Belarus, Ukraine, Moldova, Slovakia, Czech Republic, Moravia, Hungary, Russia, the Balkans, and East Prussia.

- POMMERN-L Mailing List
  http://www.rootsweb.com/~jfuller/gen_mail_country-ger.html
  #POMMERN-L
  Genealogy and history which has a connection to Pommerania, both the current Polish part and remaining German parts of the former Prussian province.

- PreussenAmericans Mailing List
  http://www.rootsweb.com/~jfuller/gen_mail_country-ger.html
  #PreussenAmericans
  For anyone with a genealogical interest in Prussian immigrants to America.

- PRUSSIA-ROOTS Mailing List
  http://www.rootsweb.com/~jfuller/gen_mail_country-ger.html
  #PRUSSIA-ROOTS
  For anyone with a genealogical interest in Brandenburg, Hannover (or Hanover), Ostpreussen (East Prussia), Pommern (Pomerania), Posen, Provinz Sachsen (Province of Saxony - northern Saxony), Schleswig-Holstein, Schlesien (Silesia), Westpreussen (West Prussia), Lubeck, Hamburg, and Bremen.

- Radoshkovichlist Mailing List
  http://www.rootsweb.com/~jfuller/gen_mail_country-lit.html
  #Radoshkovichlist
  A mailing list for anyone with a genealogical interest in the town of Radoshkovich (a town on the road from Vilna to Minsk in Eastern Europe).

- Turkish_Jews Mailing List
  http://www.rootsweb.com/~jfuller/gen_mail_country-ser.html
  #Turkish_Jews
  For Sephardic Jewish genealogists with roots in the former Turkish Ottoman Empire including Turkey, Serbia, Greece, and Yugoslavia.

- WorldGenWeb-Preussen Mailing List
  http://www.rootsweb.com/~jfuller/gen_mail_country-ger.html
  #WorldGenWeb-Preussen

◆ Maps, Gazetteers & Geographical Information

- Austro-Hungarian Empire Map Index
  http://feefhs.org/maps/ah/mapiah.html
  From FEEFHS.

- FEEFHS East European Map Room - Map Index
  http://feefhs.org/maps/indexmap.html

- Genealogy Unlimited - Maps and Atlases from Europe
  http://www.genealogyunlimited.com/
  Maps and atlases from Poland, Prussia, and Germany.

- Historical Maps of Russia and the Former Soviet Republics
  http://www.lib.utexas.edu/Libs/PCL/Map_collection/historical/history_commonwealth.html
  From the Perry-Castañeda Library Map Collection, The University of Texas at Austin.

- Maps of South Eastern Europe 900 A.D. - 1881 A.D.
  http://www.lib.utexas.edu/Libs/PCL/Map_collection/historical/se_euro1.html
  From the Perry-Castañeda Library Map Collection, The University of Texas at Austin.

- Maps of Europe - The Perry-Castañeda Library Map Collection
  http://www.lib.utexas.edu/Libs/PCL/Map_collection/europe.html
  From the University of Texas at Austin.

  - Map of Albania
    http://www.lib.utexas.edu/Libs/PCL/Map_collection/europe/Albania.gif
  - Map of Bosnia Herzegovina
    http://www.lib.utexas.edu/Libs/PCL/Map_collection/europe/BosniaHerzegovina.jpg
  - Map of Bulgaria
    http://www.lib.utexas.edu/Libs/PCL/Map_collection/europe/Bulgaria.jpg
  - Map of Chechnya
    http://www.lib.utexas.edu/Libs/PCL/Map_collection/commonwealth/Chechnya.jpg
  - Map of Croatia
    http://www.lib.utexas.edu/Libs/PCL/Map_collection/europe/Croatia.jpg
  - Map of Cyprus
    http://www.lib.utexas.edu/Libs/PCL/Map_collection/europe/Cyprus.gif
  - Map of Ethnic Groups of Eastern Europe
    http://www.lib.utexas.edu/Libs/PCL/Map_collection/europe/EEurope_Ethnic_95.jpg
  - Map of Hungary
    http://www.lib.utexas.edu/Libs/PCL/Map_collection/europe/Hungary.jpg
  - Map of Macedonia
    http://www.lib.utexas.edu/Libs/PCL/Map_collection/europe/MACEDONIA.gif
  - Map of Romania
    http://www.lib.utexas.edu/Libs/PCL/Map_collection/europe/Romania.gif
  - Map of Serbia
    http://www.lib.utexas.edu/Libs/PCL/Map_collection/europe/Serbia.GIF
  - Map of Slovenia
    http://www.lib.utexas.edu/Libs/PCL/Map_collection/europe/Slovenia.jpg

- Map of Odessa
  http://members.aol.com/tgostin/graphics/odessa2.jpg

- Maps of Croatia and Bosnia-Herzegovina
  http://www.applicom.com/maps/

- Home Page of Hungarian Cartography
  http://lazarus.elte.hu/gb/hunkarta/kezdo.htm

◆ People & Families

Individual personal home pages previously listed here can now be found alphabetically under the Personal Home Pages category:
http://www.CyndisList.com/personal.htm
Or under the Surnames category:
http://www.CyndisList.com/surnames.htm

- Bulgarian Royal Family
  http://www.b-info.com/places/Bulgaria/Royal/

- Carpathian German Homepage
  http://ourworld.cs.com/ycrtmr/
  History, culture and news of Carpathian Germans (Germans from Slovakia), with links to genealogical sites, museums, archives etc.

- A Genealogy of the Rulers of the Ancient Hellenic Kingdom and Allied Families
  http://www.pipeline.com.au/users/edpa/geneanc/geneanc.htm

- JewishGen Hungarian Special Interest Group (H-SIG)
  http://www.jewishgen.org/Hungary/
  Information for people with Jewish roots in the area known as "greater Hungary" or pre-Trianon Hungary.

- Romanov Genealogy
  http://www.icon.fi/~timhaapa/

- Russian Royal Links
  http://www.worldroots.com/brigitte/royal/royal2.htm

- Titled Nobility of Russia - Genealogy
  http://www.geocities.com/~tfboettger/russian/

◆ Professional Researchers, Volunteers & Other Research Services

- Board for Certification of Genealogists - Roster of Those Certified - Specializing in Europe/USSR
  http://www.bcgcertification.org/rosts_@e.html

- European Focus
  http://www.eurofocus.com/
  Photographic portfolios of ancestral towns in Europe created for

Genealogy enthusiasts in Belgium, Denmark, Eastern Europe, England, France, Germany, Great Britain, Italy, Netherlands, Norway, Poland, Sweden, Switzerland and more.

- **Family Tree Genealogical and Probate Research Bureau Ltd.**
http://www.familytree.hu/
Professional research service covering the area of what was formerly the Austro - Hungarian Empire, including: Hungary, Slovakia, Czech Republic, Austria, Italy, Transylvania, Croatia, Slovenia, former Yugoslavia (Banat), and the Ukraine (Sub-Carpathian).

- **FEEFHS Database of Professional Genealogists Specializing in East European Genealogy**
http://feefhs.org/frg/frg-pg.html

- **Gary Mokotoff, Genealogical Lecturer**
http://www.avotaynu.com/gmokotoff.html
One of the foremost lecturers and authors on Jewish and Eastern European genealogical research.

- **Genealogy Helplist - Russia**
http://helplist.org/rus/index.shtml

- **genealogyPro - Professional Genealogists for Central and Eastern Europe**
http://genealogyPro.com/directories/Europe.html

- **HungaroGens Genealogisches Büro / HungaroGens Genealogical Bureau**
http://www.genealogy.net/hungarogens/
Genealogical research in Hungary, Austria, Slovakia, Rumania, Slovenia, Jugoslavia.

- **Institute for Historical Family Research**
http://ihff.nwy.at/index.htm/
Austria, Czech & Slovak Republics, Hungary, Slovenian Republic, Croatia, Galicia & Bukovina.
  - o Croatia
  http://ihff.nwy.at/f.htm
  - o Galacia & Bukovian
  http://ihff.nwy.at/g.htm
  - o Hungary
  http://ihff.nwy.at/d.htm
  - o Republic of Slovenia
  http://ihff.nwy.at/e.htm

- **Radix / Services**
http://www.bogardi.com/gen/gx001.htm
Research services in Hungary.

- **The Snoop Sisters Family History Researchers ~ Nanaimo, B.C. Canada**
http://www.snoopsisters.net/
England & Wales, Scotland, Ireland & N., Ireland, Eastern Europe, Canada & U.S.

- **Routes to Roots**
http://www.routestoroots.com/
Tracing Jewish Roots in Poland, Ukraine, Moldova and Belarus.

◆ Publications, Software & Supplies

- **Amazon.com Genealogy Bookstore - Eastern Europe**
http://www.amazon.com/exec/obidos/external-search/?keyword=eastern+europe+genealogy&tag=markcyndisgenealA/
And Amazon.com Genealogy Bookstore - Russia
http://www.amazon.com/exec/obidos/external-search/?keyword=russia+genealogy&tag=markcyndisgenealA/

- **AudioTapes.com - Genealogical Lectures on Cassette Tapes – Russia**
http://www.audiotapes.com/search2.asp?Search=Russia
Ukraine
http://www.audiotapes.com/search2.asp?Search=Ukraine
Hungary
http://www.audiotapes.com/search2.asp?Search=Hungar

- **Books from the Institute for Historical Family Research**
http://ihff.nwy.at/werbe.html

- **Brother's Keeper Software**
http://ourworld.compuserve.com/homepages/Brothers_Keeper/
Downloadable shareware program for Windows. The latest version contains English, French, Norwegian, Danish, Swedish, German, Dutch, Polish, Icelandic, Russian, Slovak, Afrikaans, Czech.

- **A Dictionary of Period Russian Names**
http://www.sca.org/heraldry/paul/index.html

- **Frontier Press Bookstore - European Research**
http://www.frontierpress.com/frontier.cgi?category=europe

- **Frontier Press Bookstore - Hungary**
http://www.frontierpress.com/frontier.cgi?category=hung

- **GenealogyBookShop.com - Hungary/Hungarian**
http://www.genealogybookshop.com/genealogybookshop/files/The_World,Hungary_Hungarian/index.html
The online store of Genealogical Publishing Co., Inc. & Clearfield Company.

- **GenealogyBookShop.com - Russia/Russian**
http://www.genealogybookshop.com/genealogybookshop/files/The_World,Russia_Russian/index.html
The online store of Genealogical Publishing Co., Inc. & Clearfield Company.

- **Genealogy for Armenians**
http://www.itsnet.com/home/gfa/
A book by Nephi K. Kezerian.

- **Genealogy Unlimited - Home Page**
http://www.itsnet.com:80/home/genun/public_html/
Maps, books & supplies for sale.

- **Marriages in Plauschwarren, East Prussia 1778-1802**
http://www.mmhs.org/prussia/plauschm.htm

- **Regi Magyarorszag "Old Hungary" Bookstore**
http://www.dholmes.com/rm-book.html
Specializing in Hungarian & Slovak Genealogy.

- **Wandering Volhynians**
http://pixel.cs.vt.edu/pub/sources/wv.txt

Or Wandering Volhynians - German-Volhynian Newsletter
http://feefhs.org/ca/frg-wv.html
A Magazine for the Descendants of Germans From Volhynia and Poland.

◆ Records: Census, Cemeteries, Land, Obituaries, Personal, Taxes and Vital (Born, Married, Died & Buried)

- Jewish Cemeteries in Hungary
http://www.geocities.com/winter_peter_4
Information about Jewish cemeteries in Hungary. Cemetery surveys, descriptions, addresses of local interests, photo database of gravestones, transcription, translation.

◆ Religion & Churches

- German Baptists in Volhynia ~ Ukraine
http://mypage.direct.ca/d/dobee/volhynia.html

- The Hungarian Reformed Church in Paris 1938
http://user.itl.net/~glen/HungariansinParis.html
A Parisi Magyar Reformatus Egyhaz Presbiteriuma.

- Index to: Religious Personnel in Russia 1853-1854
http://www.memo.com/jgsr/database/deych.cgi

- Jewish
http://www.CyndisList.com/jewish.htm
See this category on Cyndi's List for related links.

- Mennonite
http://www.CyndisList.com/menno.htm
See this category on Cyndi's List for related links.

- Synagogues
http://www.mznet.org/chamber/pics/synagog.htm
Pictures of Polish synagogues and former Polish territories now part of Ukraine, Belarus, Lithuania.

◆ Societies & Groups

- Armenian Genealogical Society
http://feefhs.org/am/frg-amgs.html
This is a small group of dedicated Armenian-Americans who are actively engaged in seeking out Armenian records for preservation through microfilming and in assisting the formation of the first Armenian Family History Center (in-country) at Yeravan.

- Association of the Belarusian Nobility - Zhurtavannie Belaruskaj Sliachty
http://feefhs.org/by/frg-zbs.html
Belarus, nobility, Grand Duchy of Lithuanian, genealogy of Belarus, heraldry of Belarus, history of Belarus, Polish-Lithuanian Commonwealth.

- The Burgenland Bunch Genealogy Group
http://www.spacestar.com/users/hapander/burgen.html
Genealogists researching the State of Burgenland, Austria and nearby areas of Hungary.

- Bukovina Society of the Americas
http://members.aol.com/LJensen/bukovina.html

- FEEFHS - Federation of East European Family History Societies
http://feefhs.org/

- FEEFHS Location (Address) Index of FEEFHS Member Organizations
http://feefhs.org/location.html

- Gottscheer Heritage and Genealogy Association
http://www.gottschee.org/~ghga/
Gottschee, Austria, now known as Kocevje, Slovenia.

- Hungarian/American Friendship Society (HAFS)
http://www.dholmes.com/hafs.html
Specializing in Hungarian & Slovak Genealogy.

- Kielce-Radom SIG
http://www.jewishgen.org/krsig/
Jewish genealogy special interest group researching the southern Russian Polish regions of the Kielce and Radom gubernias.

- Slovenian Genealogical Society / Slovensko Rodoslovno Dru[Tvo
http://genealogy.ijp.si/slovrd/rd.htm

- Slovenian Genealogical Society
mailto:janez.toplisek@fov.uni-mb.si

- Slovenian Genealogy Society (International Headquarters)
http://feefhs.org/slovenia/frg-sgsi.html

- Slovenian Genealogy Society, Ohio Chapter
http://feefhs.org/slovenia/frgsgsoh.html

- Society for German Genealogy in Eastern Europe
http://www.sggee.org/
Devoted to the study of those people with German ancestry (generally of the Lutheran, Baptist, or Catholic faiths) who lived in present-day Poland (including those lands known previously as West and East Prussia, Posen, Silesia, and Pomerania), and also those people who lived in the western part of present-day Ukraine, in the old pre-World War II province of Volhynia (generally from the city of Kiev on the east to the present-day Polish border on the west, and from the city of Zhitomir on the south to the city of Kowel on the north).

- Transylvania Saxon Genealogy and Heritage Society, Inc. ~ Ohio
http://feefhs.org/ah/hu/tsghs/frgtsghs.html

- Unoffical Dvinsk Genealogy SIG
http://www.geocities.com/Heartland/Valley/4100

◆ WorldGenWeb

- The WorldGenWeb Project
http://www.worldgenweb.org/

  o ArmeniaGenWeb
  http://www.rootsweb.com/~armwgw/

  o EastEuropeGenWeb
  http://www.rootsweb.com/~easeurgw/
  Includes: Austria, Albania, Belarus Bosnia-Herzegovina, Bulgaria Croatia, Hungary, Macedonia, Moldova Montenegro, Romania. Russia Serbia. Slovania. Ukraine.

EDUCATION
http://www.cyndislist.com/educate.htm

- Anton's Genealogical Institute
  http://members.aol.com/classfun/roots.html
  Genealogy school.

- Bellevue Community College Continuing Education Online Courses
  http://www.conted.bcc.ctc.edu/users/online/
  - Introduction to Genealogy Online
    http://www.conted.bcc.ctc.edu/users/marends/
    Instructor Marthe Arends.
  - Intermediate Genealogy Online
    http://www.conted.bcc.ctc.edu/users/marends/geneal2/gen2home.htm
  - Focus on U.S. Genealogy: Advancing Your Skills
    http://www.conted.bcc.ctc.edu/users/genusa/

- Board for Certification of Genealogists - Education Suggestions
  http://www.bcgcertification.org/educ.html

- BYU Genealogy and Family History Conference
  http://coned.byu.edu/cw/cwgen/

- BYU Independent Study - Family History Courses
  http://coned.byu.edu/is/

- Cyndi's List - Professional Researchers...Speakers & Authors
  http://www.cyndislist.com/profess.htm#Speakers

- Digital University: Genealogy - So, You Want To Search For Your Roots!
  http://www.digitaledu.com/courses/genealogy.html
  Online course by Virginia Marin.

- Eat, Drink, & Sleep Genealogy: Attend a National Conference
  http://www.genealogy.com/genealogy/28_hinck.html
  By Kathleen W. Hinckley, CGRS.
  - Federation of Genealogical Societies - FGS Conferences
    http://www.fgs.org/fgs-conference.htm
  - GENTECH, Inc.
    http://www.gentech.org/
    A non-profit organization designed to educate genealogists in the use of technology for gathering, storing, sharing and evaluating their research.
  - National Genealogical Society
    http://www.ngsgenealogy.org/

- The Elderhostel Home Page
  http://www.elderhostel.org/

- Family History Education Associates
  http://www.execpc.com/~fhea/
  Specializing in methods and materials for the teaching of family history at all grade levels.

- Family History in the Classroom
  http://www.genealogy.com/74_taylor.html
  Online Article by Maureen Taylor.

- Family Tree Maker's Genealogy Site: Online Genealogy Classes
  http://www.familytreemaker.com/university.html
  From Karen Clifford, Genealogy Research Associates and Marthe Arends, Online Pioneers.

- Genealogical Conferences
  http://www.ancestry.com/dailynews/04_28_99.htm#3
  By Michael John Neill for Ancestry.com Daily News.

- Genealogical Education - Part I - Online and Home Study Courses
  http://www.genealogy.com/genealogy/57_kathy.html
  By Kathleen W. Hinckley, CGRS.

- Genealogical Education - Part II - National Conferences & Institutes
  http://www.genealogy.com/genealogy/59_kathy.html
  By Kathleen W. Hinckley, CGRS.

- Genealogical Education ÷ Part III - Magazines and Journals
  http://www.genealogy.com/genealogy/63_kathy.html
  By Kathleen W. Hinckley, CGRS.

- The Genealogical Institute of Mid-America (GIMA)
  http://www.rootdig.com/gima.html
  A 4-day program co-sponsored by the Illinois State Genealogical Society & the University of Illinois Springfield.

- Genealogy Classes offered through Madison Area Technical College ~ Wisconsin
  http://www.rootsweb.com/~widane/class.htm

- Genealogy Lectures, Seminars, and Workshops
  http://www.rootdig.com/lectures.html
  By Michael John Neill, M.S.

- Genealogy Lesson Plans
  http://members.aol.com/rechtman/genclass.html

- Genealogy - Part of the History/Social Studies Web Site for K-12 Teachers
  http://www.execpc.com/~dboals/geneo.html

- Genealogy Quiz
  http://www.witsend.org/gen/gentest.htm
  A quiz -- with answers -- to see how much you know about family history research.

- In the Classroom
  http://www.myhistory.org/teaching/index.html
  From My History is America's History. Use these activities and lesson plans to make family history part of every child's learning experience.
  - o All Grades
    http://www.myhistory.org/teaching/allgrades.html
  - o Preschool
    http://www.myhistory.org/teaching/preschool.html
  - o Elementary School
    http://www.myhistory.org/teaching/elementary.html
  - o Middle School
    http://www.myhistory.org/teaching/middleschool.html
  - o High School
    http://www.myhistory.org/teaching/highschool.html
- The Institute of Heraldic and Genealogical Studies
  http://www.cs.ncl.ac.uk/genuki/IHGS/
  In Northgate, Canterbury, Kent, England. Offers a correspondence course in genealogy.
- International Internet Genealogical Society University
  http://www.iigs.org/university/index.htm.en
- Mobile Genealogy Society - The Classroom
  http://www.siteone.com/clubs/mgs/classrm.htm
  Information on genealogy classes and workshops offered in the Mobile, Alabama area.
- National Genealogical Society Home Study Course
  http://www.ngsgenealogy.org/education/content/basic/intro.html
  "American Genealogy: A Basic Course".
- National Institute for Genealogical Studies ~ Toronto, Ontario, Canada
  http://www.GenealogicalStudies.com/
  Receive a Certificate in Genealogical Studies jointly from the University of Toronto and the National Institute for Genealogical Studies. Online courses on a variety of genealogical topics from the very basic to the much more advanced; from general topics to quite specific research.

- National Institute on Genealogical Research
  http://www.rootsweb.com/~natgenin/
  The National Institute on Genealogical Research is a one week program that focuses on Federal records at the National Archives. The 2000 program will be held the 10th to 15th of July at the National Archives, Washington, DC. The Institute is for experienced researchers, it is NOT a beginning course in genealogy.
- NEHGS Education Department
  http://www.nehgs.org/Education/EDhome.htm
  Classes, seminar and events calendar from the New England Historic Genealogical Society.
- Repeat Performance - Audio/Video Recording Services
  http://www.repeatperformance.com/
  Tapes of classes and presentations at several genealogy conferences and seminars for the last 18 years.
- Rookie's Guide to Genealogy Research
  http://www.acceleratedgenealogy.com/rookie/rookie.htm
  An outline to a 31-lesson online course.
- Salt Lake Institute of Genealogy
  http://www.infouga.org/institut.htm
  A week-long seminar sponsored by the Utah Genealogical Association.
- Samford University Institute of Genealogy and Historical Research ~ Alabama
  http://www.samford.edu/schools/ighr/ighr.html
- UW Genealogy and Family History Certificate Program
  http://www.outreach.washington.edu/extinfo/certprog/gfh/gfh_main.asp
  From the University of Washington in Seattle.

EVENTS & ACTIVITIES
http://www.cyndislist.com/events.htm

Category Index:

◆ Events Calendars

◆ Reunions

◆ Seminars & Classes

◆ Events Calendars

- Afrigeneas Events Calendar
  http://www.afrigeneas.com/cgi-bin/calendar/calendar.pl?config=calendar.cfg
  For African-American genealogy.

- Australian Family History Events
  http://www.cohsoft.com.au/afhc/announce.html

- Calendar of Events in NY State
  http://www.rootsweb.com/~nygenweb/gencal.htm

- Calendar of Upcoming Events
  http://www.rootsweb.com/~myhf/upevents.htm
  From the Mining Your History Foundation web site, West Virginia.

- Cyndi's Speaking Schedule & Calendar
  http://www.CyndisList.com/speaking.htm

- Eastern Washington Genealogical Society, 1999 Calendar
  http://www.onlinepub.net/ewgs/1999cal.html

- Federation of Genealogical Societies - Calendar
  http://www.fgs.org/fgs-calendar.htm

- GenCon - The Genealogy Events Site
  http://www.rootsweb.com/~autwgw/gencon/

- GenCon - The Genealogy Events Web Ring
  http://www.rootsweb.com/~autwgw/gencon/ring.htm

- Genealogical Events Across North America
  http://familyhistory.flash.net/events.html
  From The Family History Show in Texas.

- Genealogical Forum of Oregon, Inc. Special Events
  http://www.gfo.org/special.htm

- Genealogy - About.com - Genealogy Events Calendar
  http://genealogy.about.com/hobbies/genealogy/gi/pages/mevents.htm

- Genealogy Upcoming Events, Classes, Opportunities - San Diego County Area
  http://www.cgssd.org/events.html

- GENEVA - The GENUKI diary of GENealogical EVents and Activities ~ U.K.
  http://users.ox.ac.uk/~malcolm/genuki/geneva/

- GEN-EVENTS Mailing List
  http://www.rootsweb.com/~jfuller/gen_mail_general.html#GEN-EVENTS
  For the discussion and sharing of information regarding schedules, topics and speakers for genealogy events worldwide including conferences, meetings, conventions, seminars, etc.

- GenieSpeak - Genealogy Speakers Bureau
  http://www.geniespeak.com
  Created to promote and increase contacts between societies and speakers (at all levels), and to list upcoming events and workshop resources.

- German Genealogy: Genealogical Events
  http://www.genealogy.net/gene/ghlp/events.html

- Heritage Quest Events Center
  http://www.HeritageQuest.com/cgi-bin/page.exe?catalog=EventsCenter&file=Sort.htm&@sort@comp.EVcomp=EventPlace:a
  A calendar of events, seminars and conferences held by societies and organizations. Sort the calendar by name, place or date.

- Heritage Quest Genealogy Road Show
  http://www.HeritageQuest.com/genealogy/magazine/html/hq_roadshow.html

- Heritage Quest Research Library - Current Events ~ Sumner, Washington
  http://members.aol.com/hqlibrary/pages/Curevent.html

- NARA Calendar of Events Homepage: Washington, DC
  http://www.nara.gov/nara/events/events.html
  For the National Archives facilities in and around Washington, DC.

- N.E.H.G.S. Calendar of Events - New England Historic Genealogical Society
  http://www.nehgs.org/calendarsection/index.asp

- NGS Calendar
  http://www.ngsgenealogy.org/news/content/calendar.html
  National Genealogical Society.

- OGS Sponsored Events
  http://www.ogs.on.ca/events.htm
  Ontario Genealogical Society.

- Ohio Genealogical Society - OGS Upcoming Events
  http://www.ogs.org/events.htm

- SHHAR Calendar
  http://members.aol.com/shhar/calendar.html
  The Society of Hispanic Historical and Ancestral Research.

- Society of Genealogists: Lectures, Visits and Courses ~ U.K.
  http://www.sog.org.uk/events/

- Tacoma-Pierce County Genealogical Society - Activity Calendar ~ Washington
  http://www.rootsweb.com/~watpcgs/activity.htm

- Tacoma-Pierce County Genealogical Society - Monthly Meetings ~ Washington
  http://www.rootsweb.com/~watpcgs/meetings.htm

- This Week in Genealogy
  http://members.aol.com/genwebindx/twig.htm

- TNGenWeb Project's Calendar of Events for TN
  http://www.tngenweb.org/events/

- Upcoming Events - from Family Tree Maker Online
  http://www.familytreemaker.com/othrevnt.html

- Upcoming Genealogical Events - Genealogy Calendar
  http://www.compuology.com/events.htm
  Maintained by Richard Wilson and sponsored by Compuology.

- Utah Genealogical Events Calendar
  http://www.lib.byu.edu/dept/uvrfhc/utahgenevents.htm
  Lists genealogy/family history events in Utah and southern Idaho. Includes UGA meetings, stake family history fairs, conferences and open houses; genealogy-related user group meetings, and other known classes/workshops.

- Virginia Genealogical Society Events
  http://www.vgs.org/events.htm

- Washington State Genealogical Society - Genealogical Events Calendar
  http://www.rootsweb.com/~wasgs/wsgscal.htm

- Wisconsin Calendar of Lineage Events
  http://www.execpc.com/~drg/drgllcal.html

◆ Reunions

The links in this section have been moved to a new page of their own:

- Cyndi's List - Reunions
  http://www.CyndisList.com/reunions.htm

◆ Seminars & Classes

- 2000 NGS Research Trip to Dublin, Ireland
  http://www.ancestordetective.com/ireland/ngsdublin.htm
  Sponsored by National Genealogical Society, 23-29 September 2000.

- Alberta Family Histories Society - Gensoft ~ Canada
  http://www.calcna.ab.ca/afhs/gensoft.html

- Alberta Family Histories Society - Wild Rose Seminar ~ Canada
  http://www.calcna.ab.ca/afhs/seminar.html

- Congrés Mondial Acadien - LA, 1999
  http://www.genweb.net/acadian-cajun/cmala99.htm

- DGS Fall Conference
  http://www.dallasgenealogy.org/events/fall_conference.htm
  28 October 2000, Dallas Convention Center, Dallas, Texas from the Dallas Genealogical Society.

- Federation of Genealogical Societies - FGS Conferences
  http://www.fgs.org/fgs-conference.htm
  Contact: fgs-office@fgs.org or 1-888-FGS-1500.
  mailto:fgs-office@fgs.org

- Fifth New England Regional Genealogical Conference
  http://www.rootsweb.com/~maplymou/conf/confmain.htm

- Genealogical Conferences & Workshops
  http://www.globalgenealogy.com/confmain.htm
  List from GLOBAL Genealogical Supply.

- The Genealogical Institute of Mid-America (GIMA)
  http://www.rootdig.com/gima.html
  The 7th Annual Genealogical Institute of Mid America will be held in Springfield, Illinois. The event co-sponsored by the University of Illinois and the Illinois State Gene. Soc. will feature Lloyd Bockstruck, Sandra Luebking, and Michael Neill.

- GENTECH 2001
  http://www.gentech.org/2001home.htm
  Dallas, Texas, 2-3 February 2001.

- Germans from Russia Heritage Collection - Conventions, Seminars, and Symposium
  http://www.lib.ndsu.nodak.edu/gerrus/schedule.html

- National Genealogical Society - NGS Conference in the States
  http://www.ngsgenealogy.org/conference/conf_states.html
  31 May—3 June 2000 in Providence, Rhode Island.

- North Carolina Genealogical Society Workshops Schedule
  http://www.ncgenealogy.org/workshops/

- Québec Family History Society - Facilities and Activities
  http://www.cam.org/~qfhs/Facili.html

- Salt Lake Institute of Genealogy
  http://www.infouga.org/institut.htm
  17-21 January 2000.

- Samford University Institute of Genealogy and Historical Research ~ Alabama
  http://www.Samford.Edu/schools/ighr/ighr.html

- Southern California Genealogical Society - SCGS Jamboree ~ Pasadena, California
  http://www.scgsgenealogy.com/jamboree.html

- Utah Genealogical Association Annual Conference
  http://www.infouga.org/confrnce.htm

- Wisconsin State Genealogical Society Seminars
  http://www.rootsweb.com/~wsgs/seminar.htm
  Program and registration forms for the spring and fall seminars.

FAMILY BIBLES
http://www.cyndislist.com/bibles.htm

- A.l. HAMLETT and Mary M. EATON Family Bible
  http://www.dallas.net/~dadhaml/ambible/
  Pictures of the actual Bible pages with text transcriptions.

- Antiquarian Books & Bindery ~ Atlanta, Georgia
  http://www.abebooks.com/home/KAOLINK/
  Specializing in Bible restoration. Also a selection of rare books for sale.

- Bible and Family Records Index
  http://www.cslnet.ctstateu.edu/bible.htm
  At the History and Genealogy Unit, Connecticut State Library.

- The Bible Archives (TBA)
  http://www.geocities.com/Heartland/Fields/2403/
  This is a collection of records transcribed from family Bibles, baptism booklets, death books, etc.

- Bible Records
  http://www.rootsweb.com/~sccalhou/bible1.htm
  From the Calhoun County, South Carolina USGenWeb site.

- Bible Records of Orange County, Indiana
  http://www.usgennet.org/usa/in/county/orange/prebible.htm

- Bible Records Online - Pittsylvania County, Virginia
  http://www.rootsweb.com/~vapittsy/bible.htm

- Bible Records Project
  http://www.genlawresources.com/Bible.html
  The Genealogical Council of Maryland has a form to complete to contribute to Volume Two of their Inventory of Maryland Bible Records.

- Bible Records - Taylor County, Georgia
  http://www.rootsweb.com/~gataylor/taybib.htm

- Bibles - Giles County ~ Tennessee
  http://www.rootsweb.com/~tngiles/bible/bible.htm

- BLOUNT Family Bible
  http://www.genealogy.org/~ajmorris/misc/bible02.htm

- The Book Craftsman - Restoration of Family Bibles
  http://www.bookcraftsman.com/

- Computer Jeannie - Harrison TOTTY Bible
  http://www.jcrogers.com/totty.htm

- Cornelius HICKEY Bible
  http://user.icx.net/~dcruey/CornHBible.html
  Cornelius HICKEY family, son of John HICKEY of Virginia. This family lived in Knox County, Tennessee from 1800.

- The CORNELL and GROOT Family from the GROOT Family Bible Record
  http://vader.castles.com/ftprints/5-010023.html

- Craighead Co. Bible Records ~ Arkansas
  http://www.couchgenweb.com/craighead/bible.htm

- David and Abigail PATTON Bible
  http://www.geocities.com/Heartland/Hills/6538/Patton1.htm

- DAY Family Bible, 1835-1946
  http://www.geocities.com/Heartland/Meadows/1759/bible.html
  The family Bible of Spencer Eliphalet Day and Wealthy A. Nichols of Monroe Co., NY.

- DUNCAN Bible Record (Lee Co.) ~ Alabama
  ftp://ftp.rootsweb.com/pub/usgenweb/al/lee/bible/duncan.txt

- Excerpts from the BURGAN Family Bible
  http://www.geocities.com/Heartland/Acres/3183/bible.html

- Family_Bible Mailing List
  http://www.rootsweb.com/~jfuller/gen_mail_general.html #Family_Bibles
  For the entry ONLY of information on any and all family bibles.

- Family Bible Records in Onondaga County, New York
  http://www.rootsweb.com/~nyononda/BIBLE.HTM

- Family Bibles
  http://ww1.rarebooks.to/webpages2/riverow/riv_coll/bibles/biblfram.htm
  A collection of old family bibles for sale.

- Family Bibles
  http://users.erinet.com/31363/family.htm
  "Rescued" family Bibles for sale.

- Family Bibles ~ Michigan
  http://www.usgennet.org/~minewayg/fmbible.html
  LARABEE, TITUS, DICKINSON, WARREN, HUNTER, WANTZ, AMES, DARLING, FOOT, JOHNSON, STRATTON HESS, COLLINS, BURT, JUDD, KINSEY.

- GARRETT Bible Records - James Madison Garrett, Sr.
  ftp://ftp.rootsweb.com/pub/usgenweb/al/lowndes/bibles/garrett.txt

- Georgia Bible Records
  http://www.rootsweb.com/~gagenweb/records/bible.htm

- ghotes of Virginia - Family Bible Pages
  http://www.esva.net/ghotes/fbrindex.htm

- Greene Co. TNGenWeb Bible Records
  http://cgi.rootsweb.com/~genbbs/genbbs.cgi/USA/Tn/GreeneBibl
  Provides transcriptions of family Bible records for genealogists with ties to Greene Co., TN surnames.

- HART and REYNOLDS Family Bible
  http://www.genealogy.org/~ajmorris/misc/bible01.htm

- Hopkins County Genealogical Society Bibles
  http://www.rootsweb.com/~usgenweb/ky/bibles/hcgs/toc.html

- Ira J. TUCKER Bible Record
  ftp://ftp.rootsweb.com/pub/usgenweb/al/pike/bible/tucker.txt

- Iroquois Co. Genealogical Society - Bible Records Collection ~ Illinois
  http://www.rootsweb.com/~ilicgs/bible/bibindex.htm

- Jeannie Rogers - Harrison TOTTY Bible Record
  http://www.jcrogers.com/totty.htm

- Joseph Henry PATTON Bible
  http://www.geocities.com/Heartland/Hills/6538/Patton2.htm

- Kentucky Bible Records Collection Project
  http://www.geocities.com/Heartland/7578/index.html

- KYGenWeb - Bible Sources
  http://www.rootsweb.com/~kygenweb/sources/bibles.html

- KYNERD (also spelled KINARD later) Bible Record
  ftp://ftp.rootsweb.com/pub/usgenweb/al/perry/bible/kynerd.txt

- Lafleur Archives
  http://www.lafleur.org/
  Provides birth, death and marriage records from authentic Bible records. There are scanned images of Bibles when possible.

- Lenawee Co. Mi Bible Records Forum
  http://cgi.rootsweb.com/~genbbs/genbbs.cgi/USA/Mi/LenaweeBibl

- Library of Virginia Archives and Manuscripts Catalog (Bible Records)
  http://eagle.vsla.edu/bible/

- Library of Virginia, Bible Records and Genealogical Notes
  http://www.lva.lib.va.us/collect/archman/bible.htm

- Morgan County, Indiana, Bible Records
  http://www.geocities.com/Heartland/Meadows/8056/inmorgan/biblerec.html

- NEGenWeb Ancestors' Lost & Found
  http://www.rootsweb.com/~neresour/ancestors/index.html
  Dedicated to reuniting families with the Nebraska memorabilia their ancestors left behind: photos, family Bibles, etc.

- Pennsylvania Family Bibles
  http://www.geocities.com/Heartland/3955/bibles.htm

- Philemon HAWKINS Bible
  http://www.lofthouse.com/warren/bibles/query001.htm#44

- Questioning the Bible
  http://www.ancestry.com/columns/george/08-14-98.htm
  From "Along Those Lines..." by George Morgan.

- Revolutionary War Period Bible, Family & Marriage Records
  http://www.dhc.net/~revwar/
  Index to microfilm volumes of abstracts from pension files.

- Robert L. Taylor's Maine Family Bible Archives
  http://www.rootsweb.com/~meandrhs/taylor/bible/maine.html

- ROBERTSON Family Bible
  http://www.geocities.com/Heartland/Plains/4880/bible.html
  Belonging to James Wiley Robertson (1849-1925) and Millie Ann Jones Robertson (1850-1935).

- STRAW/BURNS Bible Records
  http://www.middlebury.edu/~swilson/bible.html
  NH and Vermont surnames mentioned in this bible that dates from 1790's to 1921: BURNS, STRAW, GRIFFIN, CORBET, ATKINS, DAVIS, STREETER.

- Sumner County, Tennessee Bible Records Project
  http://www.rootsweb.com/~tnsumner/sumnbibl.htm

- Thomas Lee's Bible
  http://www.geocities.com/Heartland/7590/Bible_ThosLee_pg1.htm
  MD>IN>IA with wives Margaret TURNER and Lydia WILSON. Includes HYDE, BOMGARDNER, REMINGTON, CLARK, FARRAR, FISHER, TUCKER, FUQUA and others.

- A Very Old Family Bible
  http://www.swcp.com/~dhickman/articles/hbible.html
  Family Bible of John WOOD of Virginia, West Virginia, and Indiana.

- Warren Co Bibles North Carolina Index to Surnames, Queries, and Researchers
  http://www.lofthouse.com/warren/bibles/qryindex.htm

- The WARREN Family Bible
  http://www.angelfire.com/ny/earthstar/warrenbible.html

- Wayne County Tennessee Bible Records
  http://www.netease.net/wayne/bible.htm

- WPA Reports for Culpeper Co., VA - Bibles
  http://www.rootsweb.com/~takelley/cbibles.htm

◆ Family Tree Maker Online - "How To" Guide

- Finding Birthplace with Bible Records
  http://www.familytreemaker.com/00000419.html

- Finding Marriage Places with Bible Records
  http://www.familytreemaker.com/00000506.html

- Finding Death Dates with Bible Records
  http://www.familytreemaker.com/00000434.html

- Finding a Place of Death with Bible Records
  http://www.familytreemaker.com/00000455.html

- Finding a Burial Place with Bible Records
  http://www.familytreemaker.com/00000472.html

- Finding the Minimum Information for Bible Records - Birth Date
  http://www.familytreemaker.com/00000403.html

- Finding the Minimum Information for Bible Records - Birthplace
  http://www.familytreemaker.com/00000420.html

- Finding the Minimum Information for Bible Records - Spouse's Name
  http://www.familytreemaker.com/00000561.html

- Finding the Minimum Information for Bible Records - Marriage Dates
  http://www.familytreemaker.com/00000490.html

- Finding the Minimum Information for Bible Records - Divorce or Subsequent Marriage
  http://www.familytreemaker.com/00000576.html

- Finding the Minimum Information for Bible Records - Death Date
  http://www.familytreemaker.com/00000435.html

- Finding the Minimum Information for Bible Records - Place of Death
  http://www.familytreemaker.com/00000456.html

- Finding the Minimum Information for Bible Records - Burial Place
  http://www.familytreemaker.com/00000473.html

FAMOUS PEOPLE
http://www.cyndislist.com/famous.htm

Category Index:

◆ Artists & Scientists

◆ Explorers & Adventurers

◆ Entertainers

◆ General Resource Sites

◆ The Mayflower

◆ Miscellaneous

◆ Outlaws & Criminals

◆ Pioneers & Native Americans

◆ Politicians

◆ Religious Figures

◆ Artists & Scientists

● Relatives, Friends and Associates of Isaac Newton
http://www.newton.org.uk/glossary/Gbio.html

● Robert BURNS Family History
http://fox.nstn.ca/~jburness/burns.html
Family history of the Scottish poet Robert Burns including 130 descendants and over 800 other relatives.

● A Shakespeare Genealogy
http://daphne.palomar.edu/shakespeare/timeline/genealogy.htm

◆ Entertainers

● Celine Dion's Family Tree
http://members.spree.com/sip/bons_achats/cdiongen-a.htm

● Deed Poll showing Sir Elton John's change of name
http://learningcurve.pro.gov.uk/virtualmuseum/gallery2/elton/elton.htm
One of the many records held in the UK's Public Record Office.

● Elvis' Genealogy
http://www.people.virginia.edu/~acs5d/bio/geneal.html

● Hollywood Underground
http://www.hollywood-underground.com/
The burial sites of Hollywood's most famous stars, moguls and eccentrics.

● Screamin' Jay Hawkins Jayskids.com
http://www.jayskids.com/
A massive search is underway to locate the children of recently deceased legendary Rhythm & Blues singer Screamin' Jay Hawkins who, by his own estimation, fathered 57 children.

● Notable Kin: Elvis Presley RootsWeb Authors/Compilers 000105
http://www.rootsweb.com/~rwguide/notable/elvis.htm

◆ Explorers & Adventurers

● Henry Hudson - The life and times of Henry Hudson, explorer and adventurer
http://www.georgian.net/rally/hudson/

● HMS Bounty Genealogies
http://www.lareau.org/bounty6.html

● The Lewis & Clark Corps of Discovery Descendant Project
http://home.pacifier.com/~karenl/lewis&.htm
To honor all the participants of the Lewis & Clark Corps of Discovery, The Clatsop County Oregon and The Pacific County Washington Genealogical Societies are offering a "Corps of Discovery Descendant Certificate" to any person that can document they are a descendant to any member of the 1804 - 1806 Lewis & Clark Corps of Discovery.

● Lewis & Clark - The Journey of the Corps of Discovery
http://www.pbs.org/lewisandclark/
The companion web site for the PBS series by Ken Burns.

● List of Officers and Sailors in the First Voyage of Columbus in 1492
http://www.rootsweb.com/~ote/colship.htm
Nina, Pinta, Santa Maria.

● Magellan's Voyages from The Discovery of America by John Fiske published in 1892
http://www.rootsweb.com/~ote/magship.htm
The Victoria and the Trinidad.

● A Roster of the Lewis & Clark Expedition
http://www.rootsweb.com/~genepool/lewiclar.htm

● Yahoo!...History: Exploration: Cook, James (1728-1779)
http://dir.yahoo.com/Arts/Humanities/History/Exploration/Cook__James__1728_1779_/
Dozens of links about this famous explorer.

◆ General Resource Sites

● Amazon.com Genealogy Bookstore - Famous
http://www.amazon.com/exec/obidos/external-search/?keyword=famous+genealogy&tag=markcyndisgenealA/

● Biographical Dictionary
http://www.s9.com/biography/
Covers more than 19,000 notable men and women.

- Celebrity Birth Certificates
  http://www.online-homesales.co.uk/index.htm
  Birth and marriage certificates for celebrities born in the United Kingdom.

- Descendants of Royalty, Historical Figures
  http://www.worldroots.com/brigitte/royal/royal11.htm

- Genealogies of the Famous (and Infamous)
  http://www.idreamof.com/famous.html
  Genealogies for Lizzie Borden, Amelia Earhart and Princess Diana.

- Notable Women Ancestors
  http://www.rootsweb.com/~nwa/

- ROOTS-L Resources: Historical Groups
  http://www.rootsweb.com/roots-l/hist_groups.html
  Links to several articles and sites regarding various groups, such as the Lewis & Clark expedition and many more.

◆ The Mayflower and the Pilgrims

- The ALDEN House Museum
  http://www.alden.org/
  The home of John & Priscilla Alden in Duxbury, Massachusetts.

- The General Society of Mayflower Descendants
  http://www.mayflower.org/

- A Mayflower & New England Study
  http://www.mayflowerfamilies.com/

- MAYFLOWER Mailing List
  http://www.rootsweb.com/~jfuller/gen_mail_states-gen.html
  #MAYFLOWER
  A mailing list for the discussion and sharing of information regarding the descendants of the Mayflower passengers in any place and at any time.

- Mayflower Web Page
  http://members.aol.com/calebj/mayflower.html

- Search & ReSearch Publishing Corp.
  http://www.searchresearchpub.com/
  Supplier of historical databases on CD-ROM including "Mayflower Descendant Legacy".

◆ Miscellaneous

- Ancestry of Clara BARTON
  http://www.genealogy.com/famousfolks/clarab/index.htm

- APPLESEED Alley
  http://www.geocities.com/Heartland/Fields/9587/
  A site devoted to Johnny Appleseed and his family, through his half-brother Nathaniel. Surnames: CHAPMAN, BELL, KELLY, FRAZEE.

- Encyclopedia Mythica: Genealogy tables
  http://www.pantheon.org/mythica/genealogy/

◆ Outlaws & Criminals

- Ancestors of Jesse JAMES
  http://www.genealogy.com/famousfolks/James/

- Ancestry of Lizzie BORDEN
  http://www.uftree.com/UFT/FamousFamilyTrees/Borden/index.htm

- Billy the Kid Outlaw Gang
  http://www.nmia.com/~btkog/index.html

- Chronology of Jesse JAMES
  http://www.sptddog.com/sotp/jesse.html
  Detailed information on activities of the James gang, including several excellent images of Jesse and Frank James.

- Descendants of Wild Bill HICKOCK
  http://www.genealogy.com/famousfolks/Hickok/

- Genealogies of the Famous (and Infamous)
  http://www.idreamof.com/famous.html
  Genealogies for Lizzie Borden, Amelia Earhart and Princess Diana.

- JESSE-JAMES Mailing List
  http://www.rootsweb.com/~jfuller/gen_mail_general.html
  #JESSE-JAMES
  For the discussion and sharing of information regarding the friends and family of the outlaw Jesse James.

- Scribe's Tribute to Billy the Kid
  http://www.geocities.com/SouthBeach/Marina/2057/Billy_the_Kid.html

- Scribe's Tribute to Jesse James
  http://www.geocities.com/SouthBeach/Marina/2057/Jesse_James.html

- Your FBI - History - Famous Cases
  http://www.fbi.gov/yourfbi/history/famcases/famcases.htm

- Wild West Personalities Produce Bang-Up Pedigree
  http://www.genealogy.com/famousfolks/Earp/
  Online article by Myra Vanderpool Gormley, CG.

◆ Pioneers & Native Americans

- Ancestry of Laura Ingalls WILDER
  http://www.genealogy.com/famousfolks/LAURA/

- BOONE Ancestors and Descendants
  http://booneinfo.com/
  Including information on the famous Daniel BOONE.

- The BOONE Family
  http://www.rootsweb.com/~kygenweb/sources/fam/boone.html

- The BOONE-LINCOLN Genealogical Connection
  http://www.everton.com/usa/GENEALOG/GENEALOG.BOON LINC

- DONNER Party
  http://www.tahoenet.com/tdhs/tpdonner.html

- The DONNER Party
  http://members.aol.com/danmrosen/donner/index.htm

- Pocahontas Descendants
  http://www.rootscomputing.com/howto/pocahn/pocahn.htm
  Descendants of Powhatan (Father of Pocahontas).

- POCAHONTAS Mailing List
  http://www.rootsweb.com/~jfuller/gen_mail_natam.html
  #POCAHONTAS
  A mailing list dedicated to the genealogy and history of Pocahontas (c1595-1617), daughter of Powhatan.

◆ Politicians

- Abraham Lincoln and His Ancestors
  http://www.amazon.com/exec/obidos/ISBN=0803294301/
  markcyndisgenealA/
  A book by Ida M. Tarbell, Kenneth J. Winkle.

- Ahnentafels of U.S. Presidents
  http://www.rootsweb.com/~rwguide/presidents/
  U.S. Presidential Ancestor Tables from RootsWeb, compiled by and used with the kind permission of Gary Boyd Roberts of the New England Historic Genealogical Society.

- American Presidential Families
  http://www.amazon.com/exec/obidos/ISBN=0028973054/
  markcyndisgenealA/
  A book by Hugh Brogan, Charles Mosley, David Prebenna.

- Ancestry of Abraham LINCOLN
  http://www.genealogy.com/famousfolks/LINCOLN/

- Ancestry of Dolley MADISON
  http://www.genealogy.com/famousfolks/Madison/

- Ancestry of George WASHINGTON
  http://www.genealogy.com/famousfolks/WASH/

- Ancestry of John Quincy ADAMS
  http://www.uftree.com/UFT/FamousFamilyTrees/Adams/
  index.htm

- Ancestry of Thomas JEFFERSON
  http://www.uftree.com/UFT/FamousFamilyTrees/Jefferson/
  index.htm

- Ancestors of American Presidents: First Definitive
  http://www.amazon.com/exec/obidos/ISBN=0936124199/
  markcyndisgenealA/
  A book by Gary B Roberts.

- BOONE Ancestors and Descendants
  http://booneinfo.com/
  Including information on the famous Daniel BOONE.

- The BOONE Family
  http://www.rootsweb.com/~kygenweb/sources/fam/boone.html

- The BOONE-LINCOLN Genealogical Connection
  http://www.everton.com/usa/GENEALOG/GENEALOG.BOON
  LINC

- Colonial Hall: Biographies of America's Founding Fathers
  http://www.colonialhall.com/

- Congressional Biographical Directory
  http://bioguide.congress.gov/biosearch/biosearch.asp
  Biographical directory of the United States Congress 1774 to present.

- Dead Presidents
  http://starship.python.net/crew/manus/Presidents/index.html

- Gen. James Robertson of TN: History & Genealogy
  http://www.shelby.net/jr/robertsn/genjames.htm
  Gen. James Randolph Robertson is a significant historical personality. Andrew Jackson called him the "Father of Tennessee" for leading the perilous settlement, far beyond the then frontier, into the middle TN area.

- Genealogy of the DAVIS Family
  http://www.ruf.rice.edu/~pjdavis/gene.htm
  Jefferson Davis, President of C.S.A.

- Genealogy of the House of Bonaparte
  http://www.napoleon.org/us/us_mu/dossiers/genealogie/
  genea-principal.html

- Governor John WEBSTER of Hartford, Connecticut and Hadley, Massachusetts
  http://www.rootsweb.com/~genepool/websjohn.htm

- Historic Dynasties
  http://www.afsa.org/fsj/may/mayfocus.html
  Many famous envoys groomed for careers by 'connected' kin. Ambassadors,Cabinet members.

- History Buff's Presidential Library
  http://www.historybuff.com/presidents/index.html

- The Jefferson Scandals: A Rebuttal
  http://www.amazon.com/exec/obidos/ISBN=0819178217/
  markcyndisgenealA/
  A book by Virginius Dabney.

- Master Index to Presidents' Genealogical Data
  http://www.dcs.hull.ac.uk/public/genealogy/presidents/
  gedx.html

- National First Ladies Library
  http://www.firstladies.org/

- National Program for the Grave Sites of Canadian Prime Ministers
  http://parkscanada.pch.gc.ca/pm/english/gravesites_e.htm
  From Parks Canada.

- The National Society of the WASHINGTON Family Descendants
  http://members.tripod.com/~NSWFD/
  Members are descendants of any of the ancestors of George Washington who lived in Colonial America between 1607 and 1732

- The Political Graveyard
  http://politicalgraveyard.com/index.html
  "The Web Site That Tells Where the Dead Politicians are Buried".

- Presidential Ancestral Charts
  http://www.megabits.net/~lthurman/prsdnt/prsdnt.html
  For Washington, Adams, Jefferson, Pierce, Lincoln, Harrison, Bush

- The Presidential Families: From George Washington to Ronald Reagan
  http://www.amazon.com/exec/obidos/ISBN=0870525905/
  markcyndisgenealA/
  A book by E.H. Gwynne-Thomas.

- Presidential Genealogies on the Web
  http://homepages.rootsweb.com/~godwin/reference/prez.html
  A comprehensive list of links.

- Presidential Useless Facts
  http://members.xoom.com/_XMCM/uselessfacts/potus
  useless.html

- Sally Hemings
  http://www.amazon.com/exec/obidos/ISBN=0312247044/
  markcyndisgenealA/
  A book by Barbara Chase-Riboud.

- Sally Hemings and Thomas Jefferson: History,
  Memory, and Civic Culture
  http://www.amazon.com/exec/obidos/ISBN=0813919193/
  markcyndisgenealA/
  A book by Jan Lewis.

- Slave Children of Thomas Jefferson
  http://www.amazon.com/exec/obidos/ISBN=4906574009/
  markcyndisgenealA/
  A book by Samuel H. Sloan.

- Thomas Jefferson and Sally Hemings: An American
  Controversy
  http://www.amazon.com/exec/obidos/ISBN=0813918332/
  markcyndisgenealA/
  A book by Annette Gordon-Reed .

- Ulysses S. Grant Home Page
  http://www.mscomm.com/~ulysses/
  The Internet's largest website on General U.S. Grant.

- U.S. Presidents Genealogies
  http://www.jrac.com/genweb/genweb.html#pres

- Who's Buried in Grant's Tomb? A Tour of
  Presidential Gravesites
  http://www.amazon.com/exec/obidos/ISBN=1881846075/
  markcyndisgenealA/
  A book by Brian Lamb.

◆ Religious Figures

- Chronicle of the Old Testament Kings: The Reign-
  By-Reign Record of the Rulers of Ancient Israel
  http://www.amazon.com/exec/obidos/ISBN=0500050953/
  markcyndisgenealA/
  A book by J.W. Rogerson.

- Chronicle of the Popes: The Reign-by-Reign Record
  of the Papacy over 2000 Years
  http://www.amazon.com/exec/obidos/ISBN=0500017980/
  markcyndisgenealA/
  A book by P. G. Maxwell-Stuart.

- Descendants of * of the Ark NOAH
  http://www.parsonstech.com/genealogy/trees/dmalec/
  burkhamm.htm

- The Genealogies of the Bible: A Neglected Subject
  http://www.custance.org/geneal.html

- Genealogy of Christ According to Matthew
  http://php.indiana.edu/~sanford/christ.html

- Genealogy of Mankind from Adam to Japheth, Shem
  and Ham
  http://www.geocities.com/Tokyo/4241/geneadm2.html

- Papal Genealogy: The Families and Descendants of
  the Popes
  http://www.amazon.com/exec/obidos/ISBN=0786403152/
  markcyndisgenealA/
  A book by George L. Williams.

- Rebecca NURSE Ancestry
  http://www.genealogy.com/famousfolks/Nurse/

- Tracing lineage back to Adam not realistic goal
  http://www.tri-cityherald.com/genealogy/DAY/day6.html
  From The Family Tree by Terence L. Day.

FEMALE ANCESTORS

http://www.cyndislist.com/female.htm

Category Index:

- ◆ General Resource Sites
- ◆ Military
- ◆ Our Foremothers
- ◆ Societies & Groups
- ◆ Women's History Resources

◆ General Resource Sites

- Amazon.com Genealogy Bookstore - Female Ancestors
  http://www.amazon.com/exec/obidos/external-search/?
  keyword=genealogy+women&tag=markcyndisgenealA/

- AudioTapes.com - Genealogical Lectures on Cassette Tapes - Female
  http://www.audiotapes.com/search2.asp?Search=Female

- AUS-HIST-WOMEN Mailing List
  http://www.rootsweb.com/~jfuller/gen_mail_country-aus.html
  #AUS-HIST-WOMEN
  For anyone interested in the genealogy and history of women in Australia.

- Discovering Your Female Ancestors
  http://www.ancestry.com/columns/myra/Shaking_Family_Tree
  03-26-98.htm
  From Shaking Your Family Tree by Myra Vanderpool Gormley, C.G.

- Equipped! Searching for a Female Ancestor Made Easy
  http://jktbw.com/equipped2.htm

- Finding the Elusive Women
  http://www.geocities.com/Heartland/Hills/6354/Women.html
  Gives step-by-step research strategies for tracing your female ancestors.

- First Name Basis
  http://www.hypervigilance.com/genlog/firstname.html
  To aid you in researching when all you know is the first name of a person. Focuses on unusual first names and women's first names when maiden names are unknown.

- The First Woman Who...
  http://main.nc.us/OBCGS/firstwomen.htm

- Genealogy.com: Finding Female Ancestors
  http://www.genealogy.com/genealogy/50_donna.html
  By Donna Przecha.

- A Guide to Materials on Women in The United Methodist Church Archives
  http://www.gcah.org/women.htm
  From The General Commission on Archives and History for The United Methodist Church.

- Jewish Women's Archive
  http://www.jwa.org/
  The mission of the Jewish Women's Archive is to uncover, chronicle and transmit the rich legacy of Jewish women and their contributions to our families and communities, to our people and our world.

- Notable Women Ancestors
  http://www.rootsweb.com/~nwa/
  Collection of biographies submitted primarily by genealogists, often including genealogy information and photos; all with e-mail contacts of the submitter. Includes many of the most researched women: Anne Hutchinson, Sacajawea, Rebecca Nurse, Anne Bradstreet, Mary Dyer, Deborah Sampson, Nancy Hart, and more. NWA categories include: Adventurers, African Americans, Artists, Authors, Educators, Entertainers, Feisty Women, Firsts, Great Mothers, Aunts, Sisters & Grandmas, Health Care/Humanitarian, Heroines, Humorous, Native Americans, Notorious, Pioneers & Emigrants, Politicians, Political Wives & Suffragists, Religious Leaders, Royalty, Survivors, and Witches.

- NOTABLE-WOMEN-ANCESTORS Mailing List
  http://www.rootsweb.com/~jfuller/gen_mail_general.html
  #NOTABLE-WOMEN-ANCESTORS
  For the discussion of female ancestors (famous and not-so-famous) and methods of researching women in conjunction with the NWA web site and the NWA Newsletter "Notable Women Ancestors: The Journal of Women's Genealogy and History".

- Remember the Ladies
  http://pw1.netcom.com/~rilydia/chase/kate.html
  And an alternate address
  http://www.geocities.com/Heartland/4678/kate.html

- Schoolmarms on the Frontier
  http://www.ancestry.com/columns/myra/Shaking_Family_Tree
  06-04-98.htm
  From Shaking Your Family Tree by Myra Vanderpool Gormley, C.G.

- Women and Naturalization Records
  http://www.nara.gov/publications/prologue/natural1.html

◆ Military

- American Women in Uniform, Veterans Too!
  http://userpages.aug.com/captbarb/

- CIVIL-WAR-WOMEN Mailing List
  http://www.rootsweb.com/~jfuller/gen_mail_states-gen.html
  #CIVIL-WAR-WOMEN
  For those who are researching women that served or assisted in the American Civil War.

- Civil War Women - Primary Sources on the Internet
  http://scriptorium.lib.duke.edu/women/cwdocs.html

- Conference on Women and the Civil War
  http://womenandthecivilwar.org/
  The Conference focuses on the service of women to their country during the War Between the States. Participants include academics, independent scholars, reenactors, living history presenters, genealogists, military and government personnel and others who have an interest in women's history.

- The Florence Nightingale Nurses
  http://www.melcombe.freeserve.co.uk/source/nurselist.htm
  An alphabetical list of nurses sent to military hospitals in the east.

- Sabers and Soapsuds: Dragoon Women on the Frontier, 1833-1861
  ftp://history.cc.ukans.edu/pub/history/general/articles/prater1.art

- Victorian Nurses in the Boer War
  http://users.netconnect.com.au/~ianmac/nurses.html

- Women and the Civil War
  http://odyssey.lib.duke.edu/women/civilwar.html
  Manuscript sources in the Special Collections Library at Duke University.

- Women in Military Service for America Memorial Foundation, Inc.
  http://www.womensmemorial.org/

- Women Soldiers of the Civil War
  http://www.nara.gov/publications/prologue/women1.html

- Women's Civil War Diaries and Papers - Locations
  http://homepages.rootsweb.com/~haas/lotsofnames/cwdiaries.html

◆ Our Foremothers

- Anne MARBURY HUTCHINSON
  http://www.rootsweb.com/~nwa/ah.html
  Born in 1591 in Alford, Lincolnshire, England, died 1643 in East Chester, New York.

- Biographies of Historical Women
  http://www.inform.umd.edu:8080/EdRes/Topic/Womens Studies/ReadingRoom/History/Biographies/

- Biography of Joanna QUAID
  http://www.pclink.com/kg0ay/quaid.htm
  She was born in Ireland and made the trek to the United States in 1836.

- Distinguished Women of Past and Present
  http://www.netsrq.com/~dbois/

- Early Illinois Women & Other Unsung Heroes
  http://www.rsa.lib.il.us/~ilwomen/

- Life of Polly Hart LANE
  http://www.genweb.net/~bowers/lane/pollyp.htm
  Polly Pierce (Pierre) Hart LANE born in 1802 in Kentucky.

- Martha Ballard's Diary Online
  http://www.dohistory.org/diary/index.html
  The source for the book and film "A Midwife's Tale", Martha Ballard wrote in her diary nearly every day from January 1, 1785 to May 12, 1812 (27 years) for a total of almost 10,000 entries. Her diary is an unparalleled document in early American history.

- MercerGirls.com ~ Washington
  http://www.mercergirls.com/
  They Called Them the "Mercer Girls." Washington Territory's Cargo of Brides.

- National First Ladies Library
  http://www.firstladies.org/

- Notable Women Ancestors
  http://www.rootsweb.com/~nwa/

- "The Petticoat Invasion": Women at the College of William and Mary 1918-1945
  http://www.swem.wm.edu/SPCOL/women/mainwom.html

- Pocahontas Descendants
  http://www.rootscomputing.com/howto/pocahn/pocahn.htm
  Descendants of Powhatan (Father of Pocahontas).

- 75 Suffragists
  http://www.inform.umd.edu/EdRes/Topic/WomensStudies/ReadingRoom/History/Vote/75-suffragists.html

- While the Women Only Wept : Loyalist Refugee Women
  http://www.amazon.com/exec/obidos/ISBN=0773513175/mark cyndisgenealA/
  A book by Janice Potter-MacKinnon.

- Women and Female children of the Royal Admiral 1792
  http://www.shoalhaven.net.au/~cathyd/raladies.html

- Women in the Gold Rush
  http://goldrush.com/~joann/

◆ Societies & Groups

- Associated Daughters of Early American Witches
  http://www.adeaw.org/
  National society for daughters with proven descent from someone who was accused, tried or executed for witchcraft in American colonies prior to 31 December 1699.

- Dames of the Loyal Legion of the United States of America
  http://www.usmo.com/~momollus/DOLLUS.HTM

- Daughters of Union Veterans of the Civil War
  http://www.starweb2000.com/duvcw/index.html

- National Society of the Daughters of the American Revolution, General Samuel Hopkins Chapter ~ Henderson County, Kentucky
  http://www.rootsweb.com/~kyhender/Henderson/DAR/dar.htm

- National Society of the Daughters of the American Revolution Home Page
  http://www.dar.org/index.html

- United Daughters of the Confederacy
  http://www.hqudc.org/

◆ Women's History Resources

- American Railroad Women Research Project
  http://railroad-women-historysite.org/
  Historic and biographical information about women in the US rail industry.

- American Women's History: A Research Guide
  http://frank.mtsu.edu/~kmiddlet/history/women.html

- American Women in Uniform, Veterans Too!
  http://userpages.aug.com/captbarb/index.html

- Audacious Women: Early British Mormon Immigrants
  http://www.amazon.com/exec/obidos/ISBN=1560850663/markcyndisgenealA/
  A book by Rebecca Bartholomew.

- Convict Maids: The Forced Migration of Women to Australia
  http://www.amazon.com/exec/obidos/ISBN=0521446775/markcyndisgenealA/
  A book by Deborah Oxley.

- Distinguished Women of Past and Present
  http://www.fordham.edu/halsall/women/womensbook.html

- The employments of women; a cyclopaedia of woman's work
  http://moa.umdl.umich.edu/cgi/sgml/moa-idx?notisid=AEB1163
  Scanned online copy of the 1863 book by Virginia Penny.

- Frontier Press Bookstore - Women's History
  http://www.frontierpress.com/frontier.cgi?category=women

- A Guide to Uncovering Women's History in Archival Collections
  http://www.lib.utsa.edu/Archives/links.htm
  This website offers a guide to web pages of archives, libraries, and other repositories that have primary source materials by or about women.

- Guide to Women's History Materials in Manuscript Collections at the Indiana Historical Society
  http://www.indianahistory.org/wombib.htm

- Internet Women's History Sourcebook
  http://www.DistinguishedWomen.com/

- Iowa Women's Archives
  http://www.lib.uiowa.edu/iwa/iwa_page1.htm
  The University of Iowa's collection, much of which has active links which give precise details of the document and its location. Includes letters, diaries, magazine and newspaper articles, government papers, scrapbooks and much more. Includes material on African-American women and rural farm women.

- Irish Women and Irish Migration
  http://www.amazon.com/exec/obidos/ISBN=0718501152/markcyndisgenealA/
  A book by Patrick O'Sullivan.

- Living the Legacy: The Women's Rights Movement 1848 - 1998
  http://www.legacy98.org/

- National Museum of Women's History
  http://www.nmwh.org/

- The National Women's History Project
  http://www.nwhp.org/welcome.html

- Nevada Women's History Project
  http://www.unr.edu/wrc/nwhp/

- Pathfinder for Women's History in the National Archives and Records Administration Library
  http://www.NARA.gov/nara/naralibrary/alic/wmenbib.html

- Social Studies School Service - Women's History Links
  http://www.socialstudies.com/c/@dUbwOpzaMWbxM/Pages/search.html?&Record_Type=Related%20Web%20Sites&Keyword=Women's%20History

- Railway Women in Wartime
  http://business.virgin.net/artemis.agency/railway/
  The history of women railway workers in the United Kingdom.

- The Telegrapher Web Page
  http://www.mindspring.com/~tjepsen/Teleg.html
  Research resources for the history of telegraphy and the work of women in the telegraph industry.

- Women and Slavery
  http://weber.u.washington.edu/~sunstar/ws200/slavery.htm

- Women in Canadian History
  http://www.niagara.com/~merrwill/

- Women in History
  http://www.clements.umich.edu/Gurls/Gurl.html
  A new guide to manuscripts of the Clements Library, University of Michigan, Ann Arbor, Michigan.

- Women in Tennessee History: A Bibliography
  http://www.mtsu.edu/~library/wtn/wtn-home.html

- Women of the West Museum ~ Boulder, Colorado
  http://www.wowmuseum.org/

- Women's Studies - A Research Guide
  http://www.nypl.org/research/chss/grd/resguides/women/index.html
  From the New York Public Library, Humanities and Social Sciences Library.

- Yahoo!...Women's History
  http://dir.yahoo.com/Arts/Humanities/History/Women_s_History/

FINDING PEOPLE

Phone Numbers, E-Mail Addresses, Mailing Addresses, Places, Etc.
http://www.cyndislist.com/finding.htm

Category Index:

◆ E-Mail Addresses and Web Sites

◆ People Searching

◆ Snail Mail Addresses

◆ Telephone Directories

◆ E-Mail Addresses and Web Sites

● 555-1212.com
http://www.555-1212.com/
Look up telephone numbers, e-mail addresses, web sites, and area code lookups also.

● Bigfoot
http://www.bigfoot.com/
Global e-mail directory.

● E-Search - Ireland's E-Mail Directory
http://www.esearch.ie/e-search/Email/Default.asp
13,000-plus voluntary registrants and growing faster every month. Special feature: Sleeper Search - will mail you when the person(s) you name registers with E-Search.

● Find mE-Mail
http://www.findmemail.com/index.htm

● Finding People on the Internet
http://alabanza.com/kabacoff/Inter-Links/phone.html

● Gibraltar E-Mail Directory
http://www.gibraltar.gi/localinfo/gibdirectory.html

● InfoSpace
http://www.infospace.com/

● Internet Address Finder
http://www.iaf.net/

● MESA, your Meta E-mail Search Agent
http://mesa.rrzn.uni-hannover.de/
Parallel searches of six e-mail directories.

● Searching For People
http://ddi.digital.net/~islander/

● Semaphore's National Address Browser & Where Did They Go? Databases
http://www.semaphorecorp.com/default.html

● Sharkey's Search Engine Index: People and Businesses
http://www2.hawaii.edu/~sharkey/links/search/people/people.htm

● Sunny's CyberConnexion...
http://www.geocities.com/TheTropics/3233/

● Unofficial Air Force E-mail Locator
http://www.usaf-locator.com/
Past, present, and retired United States Air Force personnel submit their e-mail address at this site. Folks having home pages are noted.

● WorldPages
http://www.worldpages.com/
Your one-stop directory for telephone, e-mail and web site connections.

● WhoWhere? People Finder
http://www.whowhere.lycos.com/
Find e-mail addresses and people on the Internet.

● Yahoo! People Search
http://people.yahoo.com/

● Yukon White Pages
http://whitepages.yknet.yk.ca/
A listing of holders of Internet e-mail accounts in the Yukon.

◆ People Searching

● Amazon.com Genealogy Bookstore - Finding People
http://www.amazon.com/exec/obidos/external-search/?keyword=find+anyone&tag=markcyndisgenealA/

● ClassMates Online
http://www.classmates.com/index.tf
Helps high school alumni friends find each other.

● CyberPages International - Lost and Missing Relatives
http://www.cyberpages.com/lostprsn.htm

● FamilyBuzz.com
http://www.familybuzz.com
A free online meeting place for family and friends.

● Find People Fast
http://www.fpf.com/

● Military.com
http://www.military.com/
Community center and portal for members of the military and associated individuals.

● Military - Buddies, Pals, Shipmates, Families, and Friends
http://www.shipmates.com/shipmates/

● Military Search Bulletin Board
http://www.geocities.com/Pentagon/Bunker/3965/search.html

- MyFamily.com
  http://www.myfamily.com/front.asp
  Create your own family meeting place on this web site.

- New Zealand White Pages
  http://www.whitepages.co.nz/

- People Finder
  http://www.peoplesite.com/

- Reunion Hall
  http://www.nowandthen.com/lasso.acgi?-response=/reunion/
  index.lasso&-nothing

- Searching For People
  http://ddi.digital.net/~islander/

- The Seeker Magazine
  http://www.the-seeker.com/

- Seekers of the Lost International Reunion Registry
  http://www.seeklost.com/

- Semaphore's National Address Browser & Where
  Did They Go? Databases
  http://www.semaphorecorp.com/default.html

- USTRACE
  http://www.ustrace.com/
  Missing persons, background checks, etc.

- Yahoo! Clubs...Families
  http://clubs.yahoo.com/Family___Home/Families/

◆ Snail Mail Addresses

- 411 Locate
  http://www.411Locate.com/

- Big Book Directory
  http://www.bigbook.com/
  Business yellow pages.

- Canada 411 White Pages
  http://canada411.sympatico.ca/

- Canada Post Corporation / Société canadienne des
  postes
  http://www.canadapost.ca/
  Postal rates & codes, etc.

- Les codes postaux des villes françaises / Postal Codes
  for Towns in France
  http://www.unice.fr/html/French/codePostal.html

- Deutsche Post AG
  http://www.postag.de/
  Postal codes, etc.

- Finding People on the Internet
  http://alabanza.com/kabacoff/Inter-Links/phone.html

- Infobel - Find Business & Residential Addresses in
  Belgium
  http://www.infobel.be/infobel/

- InfoSpace
  http://www.infospace.com/

- infoUSA.com - American Directory Assistance -
  Find A Person
  http://adp.infousa.com/cgi-bin/abicgi/abicgi.pl?BAS_session
  ={bas_session}&BAS_vendor=402&BAS_type=ADP&BAS_
  page=1&BAS_action=search

- National Address and ZIP+4 Browser
  http://www.semaphorecorp.com/

- POSTINFO : World-Address postal information
  service
  http://postinfo.net/postfrho.htm

- RootsWeb Surname List Country Abbreviations ~
  Listed by Country
  http://www.rootsweb.com/roots-l/cabbrev1.html

  o Abbreviations from the RootsWeb Surname List ~
    Listed by Abbreviation
    http://www.rootsweb.com/roots-l/cabbrev2.html

- Searching For People
  http://ddi.digital.net/~islander/

- Semaphore's National Address Browser & Where
  Did They Go? Databases
  http://www.semaphorecorp.com/default.html

- Sharkey's Search Engine Index: People and
  Businesses
  http://www2.hawaii.edu/~sharkey/links/search/people/
  people.htm

- Sunny's CyberConnexion...
  http://www.geocities.com/TheTropics/3233/

- USPS Address and ZIP Code Information
  http://www.usps.gov/ncsc/

- Westminster - Canadian Postal Code Lookup Service
  http://www.westminster.ca/cdnlook.htm
  Also has U.S. Zip codes.

- Yahoo! People Search
  http://people.yahoo.com/

- Zip Codes and Phone Numbers
  http://www.microserve.com/~john/pages/numbers.html

◆ Telephone Directories

- 555-1212.com
  http://www.555-1212.com/
  *Look up telephone numbers, e-mail addresses, web sites, and area
  code lookups also.*

- Advanced Use of Telephone Directories
  http://www.genealogy.com/genealogy/55_kathy.html
  By Kathleen W. Hinckley CGRS.

- AnyWho: Find People - Find E-mail - Toll-Free
  Directory Search
  http://www.anywho.com/

- BigYellow: Your Yellow Pages on the Web
  http://www.bigyellow.com/

- BT PhoneNetUK - UK online phone directory
  http://www.bt.com/phonenetuk/

- Canada 411 White Pages
  http://canada411.sympatico.ca/

- Database America People Finder
  http://www.databaseamerica.com/html/gpfind.htm

- Denmark Telephone & Address Listings
  http://www.ancestry.com/search/rectype/inddbs/4062.htm

- Finding People on the Internet
  http://alabanza.com/kabacoff/Inter-Links/phone.html

- Germany Telephone & Address Listings
  http://www.ancestry.com/search/rectype/inddbs/4064.htm

- Golden Pages Online ~ Ireland
  http://www.goldenpages.ie/dthtml/index.html

- Greek Telephone Directories
  http://www.hellasyellow.gr/

- InfoSpace
  http://www.infospace.com/

- Jamal's Yellow Pages of Pakistan
  http://www.jamals.com/

- New Zealand White Pages
  http://www.whitepages.co.nz/

- On-Line Phone Directories of the World by Bob Coret
  http://www.coret.demon.nl/phone/

- P & T Luxembourg OnLine!
  http://www.editus.lu/
  Online telephone directory.

- LES PAGES BLANCHES - les annuaires de France Telecom, Pages jaunes, Pages Blanches, Les marques, Les rues commercantes, Les pages pro, Adresses E-mail, Voila, assistance de cartographie
  http://www.pagesjaunes.fr/wbpm_pages_blanches.cgi?

- Phonenumbers.net
  http://www.phonenumbers.net/

- Post & Telekom Austria - Elektronisches Telefonbuch
  http://www.etb.at/

- Saskatchewan Yellow Pages
  http://www.saskyellowpages.com/
  Residential Search
  http://www2.saskyellowpages.com/
  Business Search
  http://www.saskyellowpages.com/search/main.cgi

- Searching For People
  http://ddi.digital.net/~islander/

- Semaphore's National Address Browser & Where Did They Go? Databases
  http://www.semaphorecorp.com/default.html

- Sharkey's Search Engine Index: People and Businesses
  http://www2.hawaii.edu/~sharkey/links/search/people/people.htm

- Spanish Yellow Pages - Páginas Amarillas Multimedia
  http://www.paginas-amarillas.es/

- Sunny's CyberConnexion...
  http://www.geocities.com/TheTropics/3233/

- Switchboard
  http://www.switchboard.com/
  If you don't have access to a phone CD try this site for addresses and phone numbers.

- tel.search.ch - Swiss Telephone Directory / Das kostenlose Telefonbuch der Schweiz
  http://tel.search.ch/

- Telecom New Zealand White Pages
  http://www.whitepages.co.nz/

- Telefonski imenik Slovenije - Slovenian Telephone Directory
  http://tis.telekom.si/

- Telephone and City Directories in the Library of Congress: A Finding Guide
  gopher://marvel.loc.gov/00/research/reading.rooms/genealogy/bibs.guides/telephon
  By Barbara B. Walsh, Reference Specialist, November 1994.

- Telephone Directories on the Web, Phone Books, White Pages, Yellow Pages
  http://www.teldir.com/eng/

- Telstra - Australian White & Yellow Pages
  http://www.telstra.com.au/

- The Ultimate White Pages
  http://www.theultimates.com/white/

- White Pages Phone Directory for Australia
  http://www.whitepages.com.au/

- WorldPages
  http://www.worldpages.com/
  Your one-stop directory for telephone, e-mail and web site connections.

- Yahoo! People Search
  http://people.yahoo.com/

FRANCE

http://www.cyndislist.com/france.htm

Category Index:

- ◆ Colonies & Possessions
- ◆ General Resource Sites
- ◆ History & Culture
- ◆ Language, Handwriting & Script
- ◆ Libraries, Archives & Museums
- ◆ Locality Specific
- ◆ Mailing Lists, Newsgroups & Chat
- ◆ Maps, Gazetteers & Geographical Information
- ◆ Military

- ◆ People & Families
- ◆ Professional Researchers, Volunteers & Other Research Services
- ◆ Publications, Software & Supplies
- ◆ Queries, Message Boards & Surname Lists
- ◆ Records: Census, Cemeteries, Land, Obituaries, Personal, Taxes and Vital
- ◆ Societies & Groups
- ◆ WorldGenWeb

◆ Colonies & Possessions

- Asia & The Pacific
  http://www.CyndisList.com/asia.htm
  See this category on Cyndi's List for related links.

- Canada - Quebec
  http://www.CyndisList.com/quebec.htm
  See this category on Cyndi's List for related links.

- FranceGenWeb - Guadeloupe, Martinique et Guyane Française
  http://user.mc.net/~orphans1/fgw/dom-tom/caraibe/

- French PolynesiaGenWeb
  http://www.rootsweb.com/~pyfwgw/frenchp/
  French Polynesia consists of five island groups: The Society Islands; The Marquesas Archipelago ("Hiva"); The Tuamotu Archipelago; The Austral Islands; and Mangareva (also known as the Gambier Islands).

  o Wallis and FutunaGenWeb
    http://www.rootsweb.com/~pyfwgw/wfutuna/index.htm
    In the French territory of Wallis and Futuna Islands existed three kingdoms: Uvea (in the main island) and Alo and Sigave (in Futuna, in the Horn Group that include Futuna, Alofi and minor reefs).

  o TahitiGenWeb
    http://www.rootsweb.com/~pyfwgw/tahiti/index.htm
    The islands of Tahiti lie in the Pacific Ocean west of Hawaii. It is probably the best known of all the Polynesian Islands. Tahiti is part of what is now known as French Polynesia.

- Généalogie d'Haïti et de Saint-Domingue
  http://www.rootsweb.com/~htiwgw/

- Généalogie et Histoire aux Mascareignes
  http://members.aol.com/Reunet/

- Généalogie et Histoire de St-Pierre et Miquelon
  http://209.205.50.254/boblang/

- Hispanic, Central & South America, & the West Indies
  http://www.CyndisList.com/hispanic.htm
  See this category on Cyndi's List for related links.

- L'outre-mer
  http://www.archivesnationales.culture.gouv.fr/caom/fr/caomom.html
  Overseas possessions of France and the date they were lost.

- New CaledoniaGenWeb
  http://www.rootsweb.com/~melwgw/newcal/ncfrench.htm

- ReunionGenWeb
  http://www.ifrance.com/ReunionWeb/Reuniongenweb/default.htm
  Pages consacrées à la généalogie sur l'île de La Réunion.

- SAINT-DOMINGUE Mailing List
  http://www.rootsweb.com/~jfuller/gen_mail_country-gen.html#SAINT-DOMINGUE
  For anyone with a genealogical interest in the former French colony of Saint Domingue (now Haiti).

- Saint-Pierre et Miquelon
  http://209.205.50.254/encyspmweb/english.html
  Saint-Pierre and Miquelon is France's oldest overseas territory. It's also the last fragment of a great North American Empire that stretched from Isle Royal (Cape Breton) to Louisiana.

- U.S. - Louisiana
  http://www.CyndisList.com/la.htm
  See this category on Cyndi's List for related links.

◆ General Resource Sites

- Calendar Conversions
  http://www.genealogy.org/~scottlee/calconvert.cgi
  Scott Lee's free on-line service for converting to/from dates in Gregorian, Julian, French republican and Jewish calendars.

- France Research Outline
  http://www.familysearch.org/rg/guide/France.ASP
  *Excellent "How To" guide for French research from
  FamilySearch.org.*

- FRANCOGENE: Your gateway to Franco-American
  and French-Canadian Genealogy on the Internet
  http://www.francogene.com/
  From Denis Beauregard.

- The French Republican Calendar
  http://www.gefrance.com/calrep/calen.htm
  *History of the French republican calendar and conversions to the
  Gregorian calendar. Official texts. Great dates. In French and
  English.*

- The French Revolution and Genealogy
  http://www.sfhg.org.uk/History4.html

- GENEAL / GENE2000 - Généalogie en Europe /
  Genealogy in Europe
  http://www.gene2000.com/

- Genealogy in France: Republican Calendar
  http://www.genealogie.com/rech-fr/calrep-e.html
  *Also known as " French Revolutionary Calendar ", this calendar
  was in used in France from 1793 to 1805, and 1871 (only in Paris).*

- KAROLUS
  http://www.karolus.org/
  *An Internet database dedicated to genealogy, heraldic, archiving of
  related documentation. There are many helpful articles & lists on
  this site to help you with French genealogical research.*

- LES PAGES BLANCHES - les annuaires de France
  Telecom, Pages jaunes, Pages Blanches, Les
  marques, Les rues commercantes, Les pages pro,
  Adresses E-mail, Voila, assistance de cartographie
  http://www.pagesjaunes.fr/wbpm_pages_blanches.cgi?

- World-Address postal information service: France
  http://postinfo.net/postfrho.htm

- Yahoo!...France...Genealogy
  http://dir.yahoo.com/Regional/Countries/France/Arts_and_
  Humanities/Humanities/History/Genealogy/

◆ History & Culture

- Images de la France d'Autrefois / Old French Picture
  Postcards
  http://france.mediasys.fr:8060/Pages/Sommaire.html
  Searchable by locality.

- La Nouvelle-France - Resources Française
  http://www.culture.fr/culture/nllefce/fr/

- StudyWeb: History: Country History Index: Europe
  Index: France
  http://www.studyweb.com/links/138.html

- Yahoo!...France...History
  http://dir.yahoo.com/Regional/Countries/France/Arts_and_
  Humanities/Humanities/History/

◆ Language, Handwriting & Script

- AltaVista Translation Service
  http://babelfish.altavista.digital.com/cgi-bin/translate?
  *Input a URL for a web site or a block of plain text and this site will
  translate for you from French to English or English to French.*

- French Letter-Writing Guide
  http://www.familysearch.org/rg/guide/LGFrench.ASP
  For genealogical queries from FamilySearch.org.

- French Genealogical Word List
  http://www.familysearch.org/rg/guide/WLFrench.ASP

- Translation Service only for genealogy related
  material
  http://www.genealogy.net/gene/misc/translation.html
  *Volunteer translators can provide you with translations between
  Czech, English, Dutch, French, German, & Polish. This service is
  provided via e-mail. Exact request syntax and length rules must be
  followed in order to expedite processing.*

- Tutorials for Reading Old German, French and
  English Handwriting, Naming Systems
  http://www.disknet.com/indiana_biolab/eg502.htm

◆ Libraries, Archives & Museums

- Archives départementales de la Seine-Maritime
  http://www.culture.fr/culture/nllefce/fr/rep_ress/ad_76101.htm

- Archives diplomatiques
  http://www.france.diplomatie.fr/archives/index.html

- Archives nationale
  http://www.archivesnationales.culture.gouv.fr/
  The French national archives.

  o Centre des archives contemporaines
    http://www.archivesnationales.culture.gouv.fr/cac/fr/
    CACmain.html

  o Centre des archives d'outre-mer
    http://www.archivesnationales.culture.gouv.fr/caom/fr/
    index.html

  o Centre des archives du monde du travail
    http://www.archivesnationales.culture.gouv.fr/camt/

  o Centre historique des archives nationales
    http://www.archivesnationales.culture.gouv.fr/CHAN/
    CHANmain.htm

  o Centre national des microfilms
    http://www.archivesnationales.culture.gouv.fr/cnm/fr/
    index.html

- Bibliothéque Généalogique ~ Paris
  http://www.geocities.com/Eureka/1568/

- Bibliotheque Genealogique D'orleans
  http://perso.cybercable.fr/bgorlean/

- Bibliothéque Nationale de France / National Library
  of France
  http://www.bnf.fr/

- Centre d'accueil et de recherche des Archives nationales (CARAN)
  http://www.culture.fr/culture/sedocum/caran.htm

- Les centres de généalogie
  http://www.alternative.cci-brest.fr/SDJ/centres.htm
  Provides contact information for 54 LDS Family History Centers in France.

- Les Centres Généalogiques SDJ / LDS Family History Centers
  http://www.ldsmissions.net/fpm/genealogie.html
  France, Belgique, Suisse, Canada.

- Les dépôts d'archives en France
  http://webhome.infonie.fr/jomave/archives.html

- Family History Library Catalog
  http://www.familysearch.org/Search/searchcatalog.asp
  From the FamilySearch web site, an online catalog to the holdings of the LDS Church in Salt Lake City, Utah. Also search for other localities by place name.
  http://www.familysearch.org/fhlc/supermainframeset.asp?display=localitysearch&columns=*,180,0

  o France
    http://www.familysearch.org/fhlc/supermainframeset.asp?display=localitydetails&subject=96&subject_disp=France&columns=*,180,0

- Family History SourceGuide - Family History Centers - Europe and Scandinavia
  http://www.familysearch.org/sg/Europe_and_Scandinavia_FHC.html
  Austria, Belgium, Denmark, Finland, France, Germany, Hungary, Iceland, Italy, Netherlands, Norway, Portugal, Spain, Sweden, and Switzerland.

- Repositories of Primary Sources - Europe - France
  http://www.uidaho.edu/special-collections/euro1.html#fr
  A list of links to online resources from the Univ. of Idaho Library, Special Collections and Archives.

◆ Locality Specific

- Atelier de Généalogie de l'Arrondissement de Wissembourg et Environs ~ North Alsace, France
  http://www.multimania.com/agawe/

- Bienvenue en Alsace! / Welcome to Alsace!
  http://members.aol.com/jaw5623/private/alsace/

- The Communities of Alsace A-Z
  http://members.aol.com/RobtBehra/AlsaceA-Z/GenInfo.htm

- Encyclopédie de Saint-Pierre et Miquelon - La France en Amérique du Nord
  http://209.205.50.254/encyspmweb/
  France in North America.

- From Alsace to Lorraine.....through Saarland - Robert WEINLAND's Home Page
  http://perso.club-internet.fr/rweinl/
  Many French resources listed here.

- Généalogy in Alsace
  http://www.chez.com/cgalsace/

- GENEALOR : Généalogie en Lorraine (France) / Genealogy in Lorraine (France)
  http://genealor.net/

- German Genealogy: Elsass / Alsace
  http://www2.genealogy.net/gene/reg/ELS-LOT/alsace.html

◆ Mailing Lists, Newsgroups & Chat

- Genealogy Resources on the Internet - France Mailing Lists
  http://www.rootsweb.com/~jfuller/gen_mail_country-fra.html
  Most of the mailing list links below point to this site, wonderfully maintained by John Fuller

- AFG - Association Française de Généalogie is the sponsor for 96 monitored mailing lists detailed below:
  http://www.afg-2000.org/

  o afg-01 (Ain district)
    http://www.rootsweb.com/~jfuller/gen_mail_country-fra.html#afg-01

  o afg-02 (Aisne district)
    http://www.rootsweb.com/~jfuller/gen_mail_country-fra.html#afg-02

  o afg-03 (Allier district)
    http://www.rootsweb.com/~jfuller/gen_mail_country-fra.html#afg-03

  o afg-04 (Alpes de Haute-Provence district)
    http://www.rootsweb.com/~jfuller/gen_mail_country-fra.html#afg-04

  o afg-05 (Hautes-Alpes district)
    http://www.rootsweb.com/~jfuller/gen_mail_country-fra.html#afg-05

  o afg-06 (Alpes-Maritimes district)
    http://www.rootsweb.com/~jfuller/gen_mail_country-fra.html#afg-06

  o afg-07 (Ardèche district)
    http://www.rootsweb.com/~jfuller/gen_mail_country-fra.html#afg-07

  o afg-08 (Ardennes district)
    http://www.rootsweb.com/~jfuller/gen_mail_country-fra.html#afg-08

  o afg-09 (Ariége district)
    http://www.rootsweb.com/~jfuller/gen_mail_country-fra.html#afg-09

  o afg-10 (Aube district)
    http://www.rootsweb.com/~jfuller/gen_mail_country-fra.html#afg-10

  o afg-11 (Aude district)
    http://www.rootsweb.com/~jfuller/gen_mail_country-fra.html#afg-11

  o afg-12 (Aveyron district)
    http://www.rootsweb.com/~jfuller/gen_mail_country-fra.html#afg-12

  o afg-13 (Bouches-du-Rhône district)
    http://www.rootsweb.com/~jfuller/gen_mail_country-fra.html#afg-13

o afg-14 (Calvados district)
http://www.rootsweb.com/~jfuller/gen_mail_country-fra.html#afg-14

o afg-15 (Cantal district)
http://www.rootsweb.com/~jfuller/gen_mail_country-fra.html#afg-15

o afg-16 (Charente district)
http://www.rootsweb.com/~jfuller/gen_mail_country-fra.html#afg-16

o afg-17 (Charente-Maritime district)
http://www.rootsweb.com/~jfuller/gen_mail_country-fra.html#afg-17

o afg-18 (Cher district)
http://www.rootsweb.com/~jfuller/gen_mail_country-fra.html#afg-18

o afg-19 (Corrèze district)
http://www.rootsweb.com/~jfuller/gen_mail_country-fra.html#afg-19

o afg-20 (Corse district)
http://www.rootsweb.com/~jfuller/gen_mail_country-fra.html#afg-20

o afg-21 (Côte-d'Or district)
http://www.rootsweb.com/~jfuller/gen_mail_country-fra.html#afg-21

o afg-22 (Côtes d'Armor district)
http://www.rootsweb.com/~jfuller/gen_mail_country-fra.html#afg-22

o afg-23 (Creuse district)
http://www.rootsweb.com/~jfuller/gen_mail_country-fra.html#afg-23

o afg-24 (Dordogne district)
http://www.rootsweb.com/~jfuller/gen_mail_country-fra.html#afg-24

o afg-25 (Doubs district)
http://www.rootsweb.com/~jfuller/gen_mail_country-fra.html#afg-25

o afg-26 (Drôme district)
http://www.rootsweb.com/~jfuller/gen_mail_country-fra.html#afg-26

o afg-27 (Eure district)
http://www.rootsweb.com/~jfuller/gen_mail_country-fra.html#afg-27

o afg-28 (Eure-et-Loir district)
http://www.rootsweb.com/~jfuller/gen_mail_country-fra.html#afg-28

o afg-29 (Finistère district)
http://www.rootsweb.com/~jfuller/gen_mail_country-fra.html#afg-29

o afg-30 (Gard district)
http://www.rootsweb.com/~jfuller/gen_mail_country-fra.html#afg-30

o afg-31 (Haute-Garonne district)
http://www.rootsweb.com/~jfuller/gen_mail_country-fra.html#afg-31

o afg-32 (Gers district)
http://www.rootsweb.com/~jfuller/gen_mail_country-fra.html#afg-32

o afg-33 (Gironde district)
http://www.rootsweb.com/~jfuller/gen_mail_country-fra.html#afg-33

o afg-34 (Hérault district)
http://www.rootsweb.com/~jfuller/gen_mail_country-fra.html#afg-34

o afg-35 (Ile-et-Vilaine district)
http://www.rootsweb.com/~jfuller/gen_mail_country-fra.html#afg-35

o afg-36 (Indre district)
http://www.rootsweb.com/~jfuller/gen_mail_country-fra.html#afg-36

o afg-37 (Indre-et-Loire district)
http://www.rootsweb.com/~jfuller/gen_mail_country-fra.html#afg-37

o afg-38 (Isère district)
http://www.rootsweb.com/~jfuller/gen_mail_country-fra.html#afg-38

o afg-39 (Jura district)
http://www.rootsweb.com/~jfuller/gen_mail_country-fra.html#afg-39

o afg-40 (Landes district)
http://www.rootsweb.com/~jfuller/gen_mail_country-fra.html#afg-40

o afg-41 (Loir-et-Cher district)
http://www.rootsweb.com/~jfuller/gen_mail_country-fra.html#afg-41

o afg-42 (Loire district)
http://www.rootsweb.com/~jfuller/gen_mail_country-fra.html#afg-42

o afg-43 (Haute-Loire district)
http://www.rootsweb.com/~jfuller/gen_mail_country-fra.html#afg-43

o afg-44 (Loire-Atlantique district)
http://www.rootsweb.com/~jfuller/gen_mail_country-fra.html#afg-44

o afg-45 (Loiret district)
http://www.rootsweb.com/~jfuller/gen_mail_country-fra.html#afg-45

o afg-46 (Lot district)
http://www.rootsweb.com/~jfuller/gen_mail_country-fra.html#afg-46

o afg-47 (Lot-et-Garonne district)
http://www.rootsweb.com/~jfuller/gen_mail_country-fra.html#afg-47

o afg-48 (Lozère district)
http://www.rootsweb.com/~jfuller/gen_mail_country-fra.html#afg-48

o afg-49 (Maine-et-Loire district)
http://www.rootsweb.com/~jfuller/gen_mail_country-fra.html#afg-49

o afg-50 (Manche district)
http://www.rootsweb.com/~jfuller/gen_mail_country-fra.html#afg-50

o afg-51 (Marne district)
http://www.rootsweb.com/~jfuller/gen_mail_country-fra.html#afg-51

o afg-52 (Haute-Marne district)
http://www.rootsweb.com/~jfuller/gen_mail_country-fra.html#afg-52

o afg-53 (Mayenne district)
http://www.rootsweb.com/~jfuller/gen_mail_country-fra.html#afg-53

o afg-54 (Meurthe-et-Moselle district)
http://www.rootsweb.com/~jfuller/gen_mail_country-fra.html#afg-54

o afg-55 (Meuse district)
http://www.rootsweb.com/~jfuller/gen_mail_country-fra.html#afg-55

o afg-56 (Morbihan district)
http://www.rootsweb.com/~jfuller/gen_mail_country-fra.html#afg-56

o afg-57 (Moselle district)
http://www.rootsweb.com/~jfuller/gen_mail_country-fra.html#afg-57

o afg-58 (Nièvre district)
http://www.rootsweb.com/~jfuller/gen_mail_country-fra.html#afg-58

o afg-59 (Nord district)
http://www.rootsweb.com/~jfuller/gen_mail_country-fra.html#afg-59

o afg-60 (Oise district)
http://www.rootsweb.com/~jfuller/gen_mail_country-fra.html#afg-60

o afg-61 (Orne district)
http://www.rootsweb.com/~jfuller/gen_mail_country-fra.html#afg-61

o afg-62 (Pas-de-Calais district)
http://www.rootsweb.com/~jfuller/gen_mail_country-fra.html#afg-62

o afg-63 (Puy-de-Dôme district)
http://www.rootsweb.com/~jfuller/gen_mail_country-fra.html#afg-63

o afg-64 (Pyrénées-Atlantiques district)
http://www.rootsweb.com/~jfuller/gen_mail_country-fra.html#afg-64

o afg-65 (Haute-Pyrénées district)
http://www.rootsweb.com/~jfuller/gen_mail_country-fra.html#afg-65

o afg-66 (Pyrénées-Orientales district)
http://www.rootsweb.com/~jfuller/gen_mail_country-fra.html#afg-66

o afg-67 (Bas-Rhin district)
http://www.rootsweb.com/~jfuller/gen_mail_country-fra.html#afg-67

o afg-68 (Haut-Rhin district)
http://www.rootsweb.com/~jfuller/gen_mail_country-fra.html#afg-68

o afg-69 (Rhône district)
http://www.rootsweb.com/~jfuller/gen_mail_country-fra.html#afg-69

o afg-70 (Haute-Saône district)
http://www.rootsweb.com/~jfuller/gen_mail_country-fra.html#afg-70

o afg-71 (Saône-et-Loire district)
http://www.rootsweb.com/~jfuller/gen_mail_country-fra.html#afg-71

o afg-72 (Sarthe district)
http://www.rootsweb.com/~jfuller/gen_mail_country-fra.html#afg-72

o afg-73 (Savoie district)
http://www.rootsweb.com/~jfuller/gen_mail_country-fra.html#afg-73

o afg-74 (Haute-Savoie district)
http://www.rootsweb.com/~jfuller/gen_mail_country-fra.html#afg-74

o afg-75 (Ville de Paris district)
http://www.rootsweb.com/~jfuller/gen_mail_country-fra.html#afg-75

o afg-76 (Seine-Maritime district)
http://www.rootsweb.com/~jfuller/gen_mail_country-fra.html#afg-76

o afg-77 (Seine-et-Marne district)
http://www.rootsweb.com/~jfuller/gen_mail_country-fra.html#afg-77

o afg-78 (Yvelines district)
http://www.rootsweb.com/~jfuller/gen_mail_country-fra.html#afg-78

o afg-79 (Deux-Sèvres district)
http://www.rootsweb.com/~jfuller/gen_mail_country-fra.html#afg-79

o afg-80 (Somme district)
http://www.rootsweb.com/~jfuller/gen_mail_country-fra.html#afg-80

o afg-81 (Tarn district)
http://www.rootsweb.com/~jfuller/gen_mail_country-fra.html#afg-81

o afg-82 (Tarn-et-Garonne district)
http://www.rootsweb.com/~jfuller/gen_mail_country-fra.html#afg-82

o afg-83 (Var district)
http://www.rootsweb.com/~jfuller/gen_mail_country-fra.html#afg-83

o afg-84 (Vaucluse district)
http://www.rootsweb.com/~jfuller/gen_mail_country-fra.html#afg-84

o afg-85 (Vendée district)
http://www.rootsweb.com/~jfuller/gen_mail_country-fra.html#afg-85

o afg-86 (Vienne district)
http://www.rootsweb.com/~jfuller/gen_mail_country-fra.html#afg-86

o afg-87 (Haute-Vienne district)
http://www.rootsweb.com/~jfuller/gen_mail_country-fra.html#afg-87

o afg-88 (Vosges district)
http://www.rootsweb.com/~jfuller/gen_mail_country-fra.html#afg-88

o afg-89 (Yonne district)
http://www.rootsweb.com/~jfuller/gen_mail_country-fra.html#afg-89

- o afg-90 (Territoire de Belfort district)
  http://www.rootsweb.com/~jfuller/gen_mail_country-fra.html#afg-90

- o afg-91 (Essonne district)
  http://www.rootsweb.com/~jfuller/gen_mail_country-fra.html#afg-91

- o afg-92 (Hauts-de-Seine district)
  http://www.rootsweb.com/~jfuller/gen_mail_country-fra.html#afg-92

- o afg-93 (Seine-Saint-Denis district)
  http://www.rootsweb.com/~jfuller/gen_mail_country-fra.html#afg-93

- o afg-94 (Val-de-Marne district)
  http://www.rootsweb.com/~jfuller/gen_mail_country-fra.html#afg-94

- o afg-95 (Val-d'Oise district)
  http://www.rootsweb.com/~jfuller/gen_mail_country-fra.html#afg-95

- o afg-dom-tom (Dom-Tom district)
  http://www.rootsweb.com/~jfuller/gen_mail_country-fra.html#afg-dom-tom

- ALSACE-GENEALOGY Mailing List
  http://www.rootsweb.com/~jfuller/gen_mail_country-fra.html#ALSACE-L
  And the corresponding web page
  http://members.aol.com/jaw5623/private/alsace/listes.html
  For anyone interested in Alsace, a border region of France and Germany.

- ALSACE-LORRAINE Mailing List
  http://www.rootsweb.com/~jfuller/gen_mail_country-fra.html#ALSACE-LORRAINE

- Annuaire des Listes Généalogiques sur le Net / Directory of the Genealogical Lists on the Net
  http://ngoret.free.fr/lg_dep.htm
  A map that displays which departments in France have mailing lists available for genealogy.

- BASQUE Mailing List
  http://www.rootsweb.com/~jfuller/gen_mail_country-fra.html#BASQUE
  A "moderated" mailing list, gatewayed with the soc.culture.basque "moderated" newsgroup, that provides Basques the world over with a virtual place to discuss social, political, cultural or any other issues related to Basques, or to request information and discuss matters related to the Basque people and/or their culture. Genealogy queries are an acceptable topic for the list.

- BASQUE-L Mailing List
  http://www.rootsweb.com/~jfuller/gen_mail_country-fra.html#BASQUE-L
  A forum for the dissemination and exchange of information on Basque culture. Genealogy-related issues are often discussed on the list though the main topics of discussion are socio-political current affairs, gastronomy, Basque music, poetry, anthropology (e.g., origin of Basques), etc.

- CHARLEMAGNE Mailing List
  http://www.rootsweb.com/~jfuller/gen_mail_country-ger.html#CHARLEMAGNE
  For anyone researching the genealogy of Charlemagne, also called Charles the Great (742-814), and the history of that time period.

- FCAGS-RING Mailing List
  http://www.rootsweb.com/~jfuller/gen_mail_country-can.html#FCAGS-RING
  For the members of the French Canadian and Acadian Genealogical Societies (FCAGS) WebRing to discuss the continued development of American, French Canadian, and Acadian Genealogical and Historical Societies.

- FRANCO-AMERICAN Mailing List
  http://www.rootsweb.com/~jfuller/gen_mail_country-can.html#FRANCO-AMERICAN
  To facilitate the communication between Americans who are descendants of French-Canadians in order to further their genealogical research efforts.

- fr.comp.applications.genealogie Newsgroup
  news:fr.comp.applications.genealogie
  Gatewayed with the GEN-FF-LOG mailing list for the discussion of genealogy software used by French genealogists.

- GENEA64 Mailing List
  http://www.rootsweb.com/~jfuller/gen_mail_country-fra.html#GENEA64
  For anyone with a genealogical interest in the French Regions of Bearn and Pays Basque.

- GENEALOR Mailing List
  http://www.rootsweb.com/~jfuller/gen_mail_country-fra.html#GENEALOR
  For anyone with a genealogical interest in the French region of Lorraine.

- GEN-FF Mailing List
  http://www.rootsweb.com/~jfuller/gen_mail_country-fra.html#GEN-FF-L
  Discussion of Francophone genealogy. Gatewayed with fr.rec.genealogie. Mainly in French.

- GEN-FR Mailing List
  http://www.rootsweb.com/~jfuller/gen_mail_country-fra.html#GEN-FR-L
  Discussion of Francophone genealogy. Gatewayed with soc.genealogy.french. Mainly in English.

- GERSIG Mailing List
  http://www.rootsweb.com/~jfuller/gen_mail_country-fra.html#GERSIG
  A regional special interest group (SIG) mailing list that focuses on Jewish genealogy in German-speaking regions (e.g., Germany, Austria, parts of Switzerland, Alsace, Lorraine, Bohemia, Moravia).

- Huguenot Mailing List
  http://www.rootsweb.com/~jfuller/gen_mail_religions.html#Huguenot

- HUGUENOTS-WALLOONS-EUROPE Mailing List
  http://www.rootsweb.com/~jfuller/gen_mail_country-fra.html#HUGUENOTS-WALLOONS-EUROPE
  For anyone with a genealogical interest in the research of Huguenots and/or Walloons in Europe.

- KESKASTEL-ALSACE-BOSSUE Mailing List
  http://www.rootsweb.com/~jfuller/gen_mail_country-fra.html#KESKASTEL-ALSACE-BOSSUE
  For anyone with a genealogical interest in the Keskastel, Bas-Rhin region of France and its inhabitants since the 1600s.

- SAINT-DOMINGUE Mailing List
  http://www.rootsweb.com/~jfuller/gen_mail_country-gen.html#SAINT-DOMINGUE
  For anyone with a genealogical interest in the former French colony of Saint Domingue (now Haiti).

- Usenet Newsgroup fr.rec.genealogie
  news:fr.rec.genealogie
  In French, mostly. Gatewayed with Mailing List GEN-FF.

- Usenet Newsgroup soc.genealogy.french
  news:soc.genealogy.french
  Gatewayed with Mailing List GEN-FR.

◆ Maps, Gazetteers & Geographical Information

- Les codes postaux des villes françaises / Postal Codes for Towns in France
  http://www.unice.fr/html/French/codePostal.html

- Le Dictionnaire des communes
  http://www.es-conseil.fr/pramona/p1gen.htm#dico
  If you are searching for a place name in France, or Algeria, Philippe RAMONA will do a lookup for you in this book: "Dictionnaire des Communes de la France, de l'Algérie et des autres colonies Françaises" (Paris 1866).

- Family History SourceGuide - Maps - France
  http://www.familysearch.org/sg/index_s.html

- France Maps - The Perry-Castañeda Library Map Collection
  http://www.lib.utexas.edu/Libs/PCL/Map_collection/france.html
  From the University of Texas at Austin.

◆ Military

- Association des médaillés de Sainte Hélène - 1857
  http://stehelene.geneactes.org/
  A database of more than 80,000 soldiers of Napoleon who received the Ste. Hélène's medal in 1857. French, English, Italian and Dutch versions available.

◆ People & Families

Individual personal home pages previously listed here can now be found alphabetically under the Personal Home Pages category:
http://www.CyndisList.com/personal.htm
or under the Surnames category:
http://www.CyndisList.com/surnames.htm

- Acadian, Cajun & Creole
  http://www.CyndisList.com/acadian.htm
  See this category on Cyndi's List for related links.

- Généalogie des rois de France / Genealogy of the kings of France
  http://ourworld.compuserve.com/homepages/egosuum/

- Genealogy of the House of Bonaparte
  http://www.napoleon.org/us/us_mu/dossiers/genealogie/genea-principal.html

- History of Europe in Medieval Times, France
  http://www.worldroots.com/brigitte/royal/royal6.htm
  Historic and genealogical information about royal and nobility family lines.

- Huguenot
  http://www.CyndisList.com/huguenot.htm
  See this category on Cyndi's List for related links.

- Nomade - Sciences humaines et sociales...Histoire: Généalogie
  http://www.nomade.fr/sciences_sociales/sciences_humaines/histoire_geographie/histoire/genealogie/
  French web directory with many links to personal home pages for genealogy.

◆ Professional Researchers, Volunteers & Other Research Services

- Catherine NOTH - Genealogical Consulting & Research in Alsace and Palatinate
  http://perso.club-internet.fr/noth/
  Conseil et recherches généalogiques en Alsace et au Palatinat - Genealogical Consulting & Researches in Alsace and Palatinate - Paris (F) - Strasbourg (F) - Speyer (D).

- European Focus
  http://www.eurofocus.com/
  Photographic portfolios of ancestral towns in Europe created for Genealogy enthusiasts in Belgium, Denmark, Eastern Europe, England, France, Germany, Great Britain, Italy, Netherlands, Norway, Poland, Sweden, Switzerland and more.

- Genealogy and History in France
  http://www.gefrance.com/

- genealogyPro - Professional Genealogists for France
  http://www.genealogypro.com/directories/France.html

- Mark Windover's Web Page - Quality Professional Genealogical Research ~ Williamstown, Massachusetts
  http://www.windover.com/
  United States, Canada (including French), England, Scotland, Ireland, Wales, Iceland, Germany, Switzerland, Norway, Sweden, Denmark, France, Belgium, and The Netherlands.

- Marsaudon Office of Historical Research & Genealogical Study ~ Avignon, France
  http://perso.wanadoo.fr/cabinet.marsaudon/
  Olivier Marsaudon, professional genealogist in Avignon, is a member of the APG and France's CGP.

◆ Publications, Software & Supplies

- Amazon.com Genealogy Bookstore - France
  http://www.amazon.com/exec/obidos/external-search/?keyword=france+genealogy&tag=markcyndisgenealA/

- ANCESTRA - Logiciel de généalogie
  http://ancestra.virtualave.net/
  From France, for Windows 3.1 & 95.

- AudioTapes.com - Genealogical Lectures on Cassette Tapes - France
  http://www.audiotapes.com/search2.asp?Search=France
  And French
  http://www.audiotapes.com/search2.asp?Search=French

- Books We Own - France
  http://www.rootsweb.com/~bwo/france.html
  Find a book from which you would like a lookup and click on the submitter's code at the end of the entry. Once you find the contact information for the submitter, write them a polite request for a lookup.

- Brother's Keeper Software
  http://ourworld.compuserve.com/homepages/Brothers_Keeper/
  Downloadable shareware program for Windows. The latest version contains English, French, Norwegian, Danish, Swedish, German, Dutch, Polish, Icelandic, Russian, Slovak, Afrikaans, Czech.

- La Croix et le lys
  http://pages.infinit.net/croixlys/
  Publisher of books in genealogy and heraldry.

- Frontier Press Bookstore - France
  http://www.frontierpress.com/frontier.cgi?category=french

- GENEAL
  http://www.geneal.com
  French genealogy software for Windows 98/NT.

- GenealogyBookShop.com - France/French
  http://www.genealogybookshop.com/genealogybookshop/files/The_World,France_French/index.html
  The online store of Genealogical Publishing Co., Inc. & Clearfield Company.

- Généatique pour windows / Geneatique for Windows
  http://www.cdip.com/

- GeneWeb ~ Unix and Windows 95/98/NT
  http://pauillac.inria.fr/~ddr/GeneWeb/
  In French, Dutch, Swedish and English versions.

- GEN-FF-LOG Mailing List
  http://www.rootsweb.com/~jfuller/gen_mail_software.html #GEN-FF-LOG
  Gatewayed with the fr.comp.applications.genealogie newsgroup, for the discussion of genealogy software used by French genealogists.

- Genius Family Tree Program
  http://www.gensol.com.au/info.htm
  An easy to use Windows based Family Tree record keeper.

- GENTREE 99
  http://perso.wanadoo.fr/gentree/
  Genealogy shareware for Windows9x. French, English, German, Italian, Catalan versions.

- Heredis
  http://www.heredis.com/
  French genealogy software program for Macintosh or Windows.

- PRO-GEN Genealogie à la Carte
  http://www.pro-gen.nl/
  Dutch genealogy program capable of outputs in Dutch, English, French, Frisian and German.

- Visual Généalogie
  http://visugene.free.fr/
  French genealogy software program for Windows.

- WinFamily - Anvend Winfamily fra Jamodat til din slektsgransking
  http://www.winfamily.com/
  Genealogy software available in Danish, Swedish, Norwegian, French, German and English.

◆ Queries, Message Boards & Surname Lists

- GeneaNet - Genealogical Database Network
  http://www.geneanet.org/
  A surname database with web site or e-mail references for more than 10 million surnames. French or English versions available.

- GenConnect at RootsWeb - France Visitor Center
  http://cgi.rootsweb.com/~genbbs/index/France.html

- Lineages' Free On-line Queries - France
  http://www.lineages.com/queries/Search.asp?Country=France&Surname=

- RootsWeb Surname List - RSL France
  http://rsl.rootsweb.com/cgi-bin/rslsql.cgi
  The RSL and this form concept & design are courtesy of Karen Isaacson

◆ Records: Census, Cemeteries, Land, Obituaries, Personal, Taxes and Vital (Born, Married, Died & Buried)

- Le recensement anglais de Pondichéry en 1796
  http://www.pondichery.com/1796/
  English Pondicherry census in 1796 and deportation of French citizens from Pondicherry by the British in 1799.

- Geneactes
  http://www.geneactes.org/
  A search engine of all French civil-status records available for free on the Internet.

- Migranet
  http://migranet.geneactes.org/
  A database of 45,000 French marriages in which one of the a people is a "migrant" (married in another department or country other than that of their birth).

- Recherche d'un acte antérieur 1898
  http://www.genealogy.tm.fr/acte.htm
  This is a search engine for the marriage list and some birth records on the French Minitel service.

◆ Societies & Groups

- AFG - Association Française de Généalogie
  http://www.afg-2000.org/

- The American-French Genealogical Society ~ Rhode Island
  http://www.afgs.org/

- The Anglo-French Family History Society ~ Andover, Hampshire, Great Britain
  http://www.karolus.org/org/assoc/as-euro/as-affhs.htm

- Association Catalane de Généalogie
  http://www.multimania.com/numa/ACG.html

- Association de Recherches Généalogiques et Historiques d'Auvergne
  http://web.nat.fr/argha/default.asp

- Association Genealogie Algerie Maroc Tunisie
  http://www.aix-asso.org/gamt/gamt.html

- Association Généalogique de l'Oise
  http://webhome.infonie.fr/jomave/ago/agoindex.html

- Association Généalogique de Relevés et de Recherches
  http://www.multimania.com/agrr/

- Association Genealogique des Alpes-Maritimes et de Monaco
  http://www.multimania.com/numa/Aghamm.html
  Présentation de l'association généalogique des Alpes-Maritimes et de Monaco - Nice - cote d azur.

- Association Généalogique du Pays de Bray
  http://site.voila.fr/agpb7660/

- Association Parisienne de Généalogie Normande
  http://www.chez.com/apgn/

- Associations généalogiques des Provinces du Nord
  http://www.genenord.tm.fr/

- Associations Généalogiques sur le Net
  http://www.multimania.com/numa/assgensurnet.html
  Les associations, cercles et unions généalogiques sur internet. Classement par départements.

- Centre d'Entraide Généalogique de Franche Comté
  http://www.geocities.com/Paris/Rue/3002/cegfc.html

- Centre Departemental D'histoire Des Familles
  http://cdhf.telmat-net.fr/

- Centre Généalogique de l'Ouest ~ Nantes, France
  http://assoc.wanadoo.fr/cgo/

- Centre généalogique de la Haute Marne
  http://www.genealogy.tm.fr/cercle/haute-marne/index.htm

- Centre Genealogique des Landes
  http://www.ifrance.com/cdelmars/

- Centre Généalogique des Pyrénées-Atlantiques (Béarn et Pays Basque)
  http://cgpa.org/

- Centre Généalogique de Touraine
  http://www.karolus.org/membres/cgtouraine.htm

- Centre Genealogique De Touraine
  http://members.aol.com/cgdt/

- Centre Généalogique des Côtes d'Armor
  http://www.genealogy.tm.fr/cercle/cg22/index.htm

- Le Centre Généalogique du Dauphiné
  http://perso.wanadoo.fr/cgd/indexcgd.htm

- Centre Généalogique du Finistère
  http://www.infini.fr/~geneal29/index.html

- Centre Généalogique du Midi-Provence
  http://www.multimania.com/numa/CGMP.html

- Centre Généalogique du Perche
  http://www.multimania.com/cgperche/

- Centre Généalogique et Héraldique de la Marne
  http://www.genealogy.tm.fr/cercle/marne/index.htm

- Centre Généalogique Savoyard ö Paris et Région Parisienne
  http://www.chez.com/savoieparis/

- Cercle Généalogie du Pays de Bitche
  http://www.multimania.com/cgbitche/Francais/index.html

- Cercle de Recherches Généalogiques du Perche-Gou't
  http://www.perche-gouet.net/

- Cercle d'Etudes Généalogiques et Héraldiques de l'Ile-de-France
  http://www.chez.com/ceghif/index.htm

- Cercle Généalogique de Fosses-Marly
  http://cgfm.julius.free.fr/

- Cercle Généalogique de l'Aisne ~ Chateau-Thierry, France
  http://www.multimania.com/mmeresse/annexes/cg.htm

- Cercle Généalogique de la Manche
  http://www.citeweb.net/cg50/

- Cercle Généalogique de Languedoc ~ Toulouse
  http://www.multimania.com/numa/cgl.html

- Le Cercle Généalogique de Moselle-Est
  http://www.geneamosellest.org/

- Cercle Généalogique de Saône et Loire
  http://perso.wanadoo.fr/cgsl/

- Cercle Généalogique de Versailles et des Yvelines
  http://w3.teaser.fr/~bdebreil/cgvy.html

- Cercle genealogique de Villeneuve-le-Garenne et des Hauts-de-Seine
  http://www.karolus.org/membres/cgvlg-92.htm

- Cercle Généalogique du Calvados
  http://www.multimania.com/cegecal/

- Cercle Généalogique du Haut-Berry
  http://www.genea18.org/

- Cercle genealogique du pays de Caux Seine-Maritime
  http://www.genealogy.tm.fr/cercle/cgpc/index.htm

- Le Cercle Généalogique du Sud-Aveyron ~ Millau, France
  http://www.geocities.com/Heartland/8308/

- Cercle Généalogique et Historique Du Pays De Charmes
  http://cghpc.hypermart.net/

- Le Cercle Généalogique et Héraldique de L'Auvergne et du Velay
  http://www.genealogy.tm.fr/cercle/cghav/

- Le Cercle Genealogique Norvillois
  http://www.multimania.com/sourdaine/page04.htm

- Cercle Genealogique Poitevin
  http://members.xoom.com/_XMCM/JeanMi/cgp.htm

- Cercle Généalogique Rouen Seine-Maritime
  http://www.genealogy.tm.fr/cercle/cgrsm/

- Les cercles généalogiques d'Alsace, de Lorraine et de Sarre / Genealogical societies in Alsace, in Lorraine and in Saar
  http://perso.club-internet.fr/rweinl/cercl_en.htm

- Entraide Généalogique du Midi Toulousain
  http://www.chez.com/egmt/

- Etudes Généalogiques Drôme Ardèche
  http://www.es-conseil.fr/pramona/egda.htm

- Fédération des Associations Généalogiques de la Corrèze
  http://www.genealogy.tm.fr/cercle/correze/index.htm

- Fédération Française de Généalogie
  http://www.genefede.org/
  Site officiel de la Fédération française de généalogie / Official site of the French federation of genealogy.

- GENENORD - Le Web Des Associations Généalogiques Des Provinces du Nord
  http://www.genenord.tm.fr/

- L'association Généalogie Gasconne Gersoise
  http://www.multimania.com/geneagg/

- L'Association Généalogique du Pas-de-Calais
  http://www.multimania.com/germinal/agp/agp62.html

- L'Entraide Généalogique Bretagne - Maine - Normandie
  http://www.multimania.com/egbmn/default.htm

- Le Loiret Généalogique
  http://www.karolus.org/membres/loiretgen.htm

- SGBB : Société Généalogique du Bas-Berry
  http://www.genindre.org/sgbb/

- Société d'Etudes des Sept Vallées
  http://www.multimania.com/ugmp/SESV.htm

- Societe des Amateurs de Genealogie de l'Ardeche
  http://www.multimania.com/saga/

- Société Généalogique de l'Yonne
  http://www.multimania.com/sgy/

- Société Généalogique du Lyonnais
  http://sgl.est-ici.org/

- Union Des Cercles Genealogiques et Heraldiques de Normandie
  http://members.aol.com/ucghn/index.htm

- Union des Cercles Généalogiques Lorrains
  http://genealor.net/ucgl/

- Union Généalogique de Bretagne-Pays de la Loire
  http://www.karolus.org/membres/ugbl.htm

- Union Généalogiques Midi & Pyrénées
  http://www.multimania.com/ugmp/

◆ WorldGenWeb

- The WorldGenWeb Project
  http://www.worldgenweb.org/

  o MediterraneanGenWeb
    http://mediterraneangenweb.org/

    - FranceGenWeb
      http://francegenweb.org/
      Porte d'entrée de la généalogie sur internet, en France et Monde entier / Your site for the genealogical researches in France. Part of the WorldGenWeb project.

GENEALOGY IN THE MEDIA

News, Radio, Television, Video & Audio
http://www.cyndislist.com/media.htm

Category Index:

◆ News

◆ Radio

◆ Television

◆ Video & Audio Tapes

◆ News

● FamilySearch Internet Genealogy Service - What's New
http://www.familysearch.org/whats_new.asp
The latest news from the LDS web site.

● Genealogy.com: Press Room
http://www.genealogy.com/pressmain.html

● Genealogy In the News...
http://www.cswnet.com/~sbooks/genealogy/InTheNews/inthenews.htm
Links to news articles on the Internet regarding genealogy.

● GenealogyNews.com - Covering the News Important to Your Research
http://www.genealogynews.com/

● Magazines, Journals, Columns & Newsletters
http://www.CyndisList.com/magazine.htm
See this page on Cyndi's List for related links. Includes sections for: Columns & Columnists; E-mail Newsletters; E-zines ~ Electronic Magazines & Newsletters; Print Magazines, Journals & Newsletters.

● MyFamily.com & Ancestry.com Press Releases
http://www.myfamilyinc.com/pressroom/releases.htm

○ MyFamily.com, Inc. Acquires Number Two Genealogy Site, RootsWeb.com (June 21, 2000)
http://www.myfamilyinc.com/pressroom/rootsweb.htm

● NARA Current Press Release Home Page
http://www.nara.gov/nara/pressrelease/current.html
From the National Archive and Records Administration.

● Paper Roots, A Weekly Round-Up of Genealogy in the News
http://people.ne.mediaone.net/ehwoodward/paperroots.html
By Hobson Woodward.

● RootsWeb - Press & Press Releases
http://www.rootsweb.com/rootsweb/press/

○ RootsWeb Merges with Ancestry.com
http://www.rootsweb.com/rootsweb/merge.html

◆ Radio

● Ancestral Search - Laura M. Bradley
mailto:AncestralSearch@aol.com
"Culture, Genealogy & History on the Radio." The Ancestral Search radio program airs Thursdays at 10 a.m., WBLQ 88.1 FM in Westerly, Rhode Island. For details, send e-mail to Laura: AncestralSearch@aol.com.

● Genealogy on the Air in Rhode Island
http://www.ancestry.com/columns/eastman/eastaug31-99.htm#8
From Eastman's Online Genealogy Newsletter--31 August, 1999.

● Generations - Find Your Roots
http://www.sierra.com/sierrahome/familytree/webcast/
A new, interactive multimedia Internet radio-like chat program for genealogy.

◆ Television

● ABC News - Finding Roots on the Internet
http://abcnews.go.com/onair/DailyNews/wnt990614_genealogy.html

● Ancestors
http://www.pbs.org/kbyu/ancestors/
The second series, airing in June 2000 on PBS television.

○ Ancestors: Find Your Local Airdate
http://www.kbyu.org/ancestorsbroadcast/

○ Ancestors: Video/Audio
http://www.pbs.org/kbyu/ancestors/video/
Online clips from the show on PBS television.

● Ancestors: The First Series
http://www.pbs.org/kbyu/ancestors/firstseries/
Ten episodes that originally aired beginning in January 1997 on PBS television.

○ Ancestors: Searching for Roots
http://www.amazon.com/exec/obidos/ASIN/B00000FELB/
Set of four videotapes for sale.

● Lifetime Television - Genealogy Online
http://www.lifetimetv.com/onair/shows/na/frameset.shtml/techno1106_2856.html

◆ Video & Audio Tapes

- 123Genealogy
  http://www.123genealogy.com/store/index.htm
  Genealogy training videos for sale.

- Ancestors: Product Information
  http://www.pbs.org/kbyu/ancestors/products/
  Home video and instructional video from the new PBS television series.

- Ancestors: Searching for Roots
  http://www.amazon.com/exec/obidos/ASIN/B00000FELB/
  Set of four videotapes for sale.

- Ancestors: Video/Audio
  http://www.pbs.org/kbyu/ancestors/video/
  Online clips from the show on PBS television.

- AudioTapes.com
  http://www.audiotapes.com/
  Genealogy lectures from conferences on tape.

- Genealogy Training Video
  http://123genealogy.com/store/paf/
  For using PAF 4 (Personal Ancestral File) software.

- Irish Visions Documentaries: Grosse Ile: Gateway & Graveyard
  http://www.stpatrick.com/mall/visions/documentaries/grosse.htm
  About the Irish that emigrated to Canada during the famine.

GENEALOGY STANDARDS & GUIDELINES

Emphasizing Quality Research Practices
http://www.cyndislist.com/standard.htm

Category Index:

◆ General Resource Sites
◆ National Genealogical Society

◆ Societies & Groups

◆ General Resource Sites

- The Board for Certification of Genealogists' Genealogical Standards Manual
  http://www.amazon.com/exec/obidos/ISBN=0916489922/
  markcyndisgenealA/
  A book by the BCG.

- Board for Certification of Genealogists - Skill Building Index
  http://www.bcgcertification.org/skbldidx.html
  Columns from OnBoard, the BCG newsletter.

- Certification: Measuring Yourself Against Standards
  http://www.audiotapes.com/product.asp?ProductCode='00NG S-W54'
  Presentation by Kathleen W. Hinckley, available for sale on audio tape.

- Evidence!: Citation & Analysis for the Family Historian
  http://www.amazon.com/exec/obidos/ISBN=0806315431/
  markcyndisgenealA/
  A book by Elizabeth Shown Mills.

- Genealogical Evidence: A Guide to the Standard of Proof Relating to Pedigrees, Ancestry, Heirship and Family History
  http://www.amazon.com/exec/obidos/ISBN=0894121596/
  markcyndisgenealA/
  A book by Noel C. Stevenson.

- Producing Quality Research Notes
  http://www.bcgcertification.org/skbld971.html
  From the Board for Certification of Genealogists - Skill Building - January 1997.

- RootsWeb's Guide to Tracing Family Trees - Lesson 12: Creating Worthwhile Genealogies: Evidence, Sources, Documentation, and Citation
  http://www.rootsweb.com/~rwguide/lesson12.htm

- Understanding Sources, Citations, Documentation and Evaluating Evidence in Genealogy
  http://www.pipeline.com/~richardpence/classdoc.htm
  By Richard Pence.

- Why Bother? The Value of Documentation in Family History Research
  http://www.genealogy.com/genealogy/19_kory.html
  By Kory Meyerink, MLS, AG.

◆ National Genealogical Society

- Cybercousins Seeking Succor - Toward Standards for Genealogy Web Sites
  http://www.audiotapes.com/product.asp?ProductCode='00NG S-S226'
  Presentation by Mark Howells, available for sale on audio tape.

- National Genealogical Society
  http://www.ngsgenealogy.org/
  Arlington, Virginia, United States.
  - Genealogical Standards Committee
    http://www.ngsgenealogy.org/about/content/committees/
    gene_stan.html
    - Standards for Sound Genealogical Research
      http://www.ngsgenealogy.org/about/content/committees/
      gene1_stan.html
    - Standards for Using Records Repositories and Libraries
      http://www.ngsgenealogy.org/about/content/committees/
      gene2_stan.html
    - Standards for Use of Technology in Genealogical Research
      http://www.ngsgenealogy.org/about/content/committees/
      gene3_stan.html
    - Standards for Sharing Information With Others
      http://www.ngsgenealogy.org/about/content/committees/
      gene4_stan.html
    - Guidelines for Publishing Web Pages on the Internet
      http://www.ngsgenealogy.org/about/content/committees/
      gene5_stan.html

◆ Societies & Groups

- Association of Genealogists and Record Agents
  http://www.agra.org.uk
  Professional researchers available in the United Kingdom. Membership of AGRA is limited to those who have demonstrated a high level of competence and expertise. A Code of Practice and a Complaints Procedure are in place.

- Association of Professional Genealogists ~ Denver, Colorado
  http://www.apgen.org/

- Board for Certification of Genealogists ~ Washington, D.C.
  http://www.bcgcertification.org/
  - The Board for Certification of Genealogists' Genealogical Standards Manual
    http://www.amazon.com/exec/obidos/ISBN=0916489922/markcyndisgenealA/
    A book by the BCG.

- Board for Certification of Genealogists - Roster of Those Certified - State/Country Index
  http://www.bcgcertification.org/rost_ix.html

- ISFHWE - International Society of Family History Writers and Editors
  http://www.rootsweb.com/~cgc/index.htm
  Formerly the Council of Genealogy Columnists.

GERMANS FROM RUSSIA

http://www.cyndislist.com/germruss.htm

Category Index:

- General Resource Sites
- History & Culture
- Language, Handwriting & Script
- Mailing Lists, Newsgroups & Chat
- Maps, Gazetteers & Geographical Information
- Medical

- People & Families
- Publications
- Records: Census, Cemeteries, Land, Obituaries, Personal, Taxes and Vital
- Societies & Groups
- Villages & Colonies

◆ General Resource Sites

- **German-Russian Genealogy Links**
  http://www.geocities.com/SiliconValley/Haven/1538/germ_rus.html

- **Germans from Russia Heritage Collection**
  http://www.lib.ndsu.nodak.edu/gerrus/index.html
  From North Dakota State University & Michael Miller.

- **Germans from Russia Heritage Society - GRHS - Cross-Index**
  http://feefhs.org/grhs/indexgrh.html

- **Germans from Russia Historical Collection - GRHC - Cross Index - from FEEFHS**
  http://feefhs.org/grhc/indexgrc.html

- **German / Russian Roots**
  http://www.geocities.com/Heartland/Acres/4123/ger-rus.htm

- **Internet Genealogy - VU University Project Page**
  http://www.geocities.com/SiliconValley/Haven/1538/index2.html
  Many helpful sites for Polish, Irish, German, German-Prussian, German-Russian, & Prussian backgrounds.

- **Janet's Germans from Russia Research**
  http://www.angelfire.com/ks/gerrus/index.html

- **Manisfesto of the Empress Catherine II, issued July 22, 1763**
  http://members.aol.com/jktsn/manifest.htm

- **ODESSA ... a German-Russian Genealogical Library**
  http://pixel.cs.vt.edu/library/odessa.html

- **St. Joseph's Colony ~ Saskatchewan, Canada**
  http://www.rootsweb.com/~skstjose/stjoseph.html

- **Who Are the Germans from Russia?**
  http://www.feefhs.org/frgcdcwt.html

◆ History & Culture

- **Germans from Russia in Portland, Oregon**
  http://www.germans-russia-pdx.com/

- **The History of the Volga-Germans**
  http://www.lhm.org/LID/lidhist.htm

◆ Language, Handwriting & Script

- **AltaVista Translation Service**
  http://babelfish.altavista.digital.com/cgi-bin/translate?
  Input a URL for a web site or a block of plain text and this site will translate for you from German to English or English to German.

- **Deciphering Gothic Records**
  http://www.futureone.com/~fdearden/page2.htm
  Pamphlet for sale.

- **Deutsch Englisches Wörterbuch**
  http://www.tu-chemnitz.de/urz/netz/forms/dict.html

- **German Letter Writing Guide**
  http://www.familysearch.org/rg/guide/LGGerman.ASP
  For genealogical inqueries from FamilySearch.org.

- **Form Letters for German Genealogy**
  http://www.genealogy.net/gene/misc/letters/

- **Fraktur and German Script**
  http://www.asherwin.com/fraktur%26script.html

- **German-English Genealogical Dictionary**
  http://www.amazon.com/exec/obidos/ISBN=0806313420/markcyndisgenealA/
  A book by Ernest Thode.

- **German-English Letter Translation Specialists**
  http://www.win.bright.net/~deichsa/welcome.html

- **German-English On-line Dictionary**
  http://dictionaries.travlang.com/GermanEnglish/

- **German Genealogical Word List**
  http://www.familysearch.org/rg/guide/WLGerman.ASP

- **German Genealogy: Translation Service**
  http://www2.genealogy.net/gene/www/abt/translation.html

- **German Illness Translations**
  http://pixel.cs.vt.edu/library/articles/link/illness.txt

- **German Study Group / German Words**
  http://205.216.138.19/~websites/lynnd/vuword.html

- German Translation Service
  http://www.asherwin.com/
  Specializations: German genealogy, Fraktur and German script, legal documents.

- German Translation Service
  http://www.win.bright.net/~jakeschu/welcome.html
  Old Script

- A Glossary of German Words Used in Official Documents
  gopher://Gopher.UToledo.edu:70/00GOPHER_ROOT%3A%5BRESEARCH-RESOURCES.GENEALOGY.GERMAN-GENEALOGY%5DA-GLOSSARY-OF-GERMAN-WORDS.USED-IN-OFFICIAL-DOCUMENTS

- Handwriting Guide: German Gothic
  http://www.familysearch.org/rg/guide/German_Gothic99-36316.ASP

- If I Can Decipher Germanic Records, So Can You
  http://www.amazon.com/exec/obidos/ISBN=0961542004/markcyndisgenealA/
  A book by Edna Bentz.

- Moravians - German Script Tutorial
  http://www.mun.ca/rels/morav/script.html
  With Moravian Archival examples

  o German Script Alphabet
    http://www.mun.ca/rels/morav/pics/tutor/mscript2.html

- Old German Handwritten Scripts
  http://www2.genealogy.net/gene/misc/scripts.html

- Old German Professions and Occupations
  http://worldroots.clicktron.com/brigitte/occupat.htm

- Old Spelling Patterns
  http://www.asherwin.com/spelling.html

- Sample Letters in German to Obtain Genealogical Information
  gopher://Gopher.UToledo.edu:70/00GOPHER_ROOT%3A%5BRESEARCH-RESOURCES.GENEALOGY.GERMAN-GENEALOGY%5DGERMAN-SAMPLE-LETTER.FOR-INFORMATION-REQUESTS

- Translation Service only for genealogy related material
  http://www.genealogy.net/gene/misc/translation.html
  Volunteer translators can provide you with translations between Czech, English, Dutch, French, German, & Polish. This service is provided via e-mail. Exact request syntax and length rules must be followed in order to expedite processing.

- Tutorials for Reading Old German, French and English Handwriting, Naming Systems
  http://www.disknet.com/indiana_biolab/eg502.htm

- Walden Font
  http://www.waldenfont.com/
  Several different fonts for sale, including: The Gutenberg Press German Fraktur Fonts and German Script.

◆ Mailing Lists, Newsgroups & Chat

- BDO Mailing List
  http://www.rootsweb.com/~jfuller/gen_mail_country-rus.html#BDO
  The Beresan District Odessa (BDO) mailing list is for anyone with a genealogical interest in the Beresan Colonies which were made up of Germans who immigrated to Russia, beginning in the first decade of the 19th century, at the request of Alexander I, Tsar of Russia. The Colonies were located Northeast of the city of Odessa on the Black Sea.

- BESS-GR: Bessarabian Germans From Russia Electronic Discussion Group
  http://www.lib.ndsu.nodak.edu/gerrus/listbessgr.html

- GCRA Mailing List
  http://www.lib.ndsu.nodak.edu/gerrus/listgcra.html
  For those interested in Germans from Russia research and family research oriented specifically to the Glueckstal Colonies of Bergdorf, Glueckstal, Kassel, and Neudorf and their daughter colonies.

- GermanRussian Mailing List
  http://www.rootsweb.com/~jfuller/gen_mail_country-ger.html#GermanRussian
  For individuals who are researching the Black Sea Germans.

- GER-RUS-ARG Mailing List
  http://www.rootsweb.com/~jfuller/gen_mail_country-arg.html#GER-RUS-ARG
  For anyone with a genealogical interest in the Germans who migrated from Russia to Argentina.

- GER-VOLGA Mailing List
  http://www.rootsweb.com/~jfuller/gen_mail_country-rus.html#GER-VOLGA
  For those who are researching Germans from the Volga Valley area of Russia.

- GRDB Mailing List
  http://www.rootsweb.com/~jfuller/gen_mail_country-rus.html#GRDB
  For the discussion of genealogy databases containing German-Russians and their descendants, being developed by the American Historical Society of Germans from Russian (AHSGR).

- GR-GENEALOGY Mailing List
  http://www.rootsweb.com/~jfuller/gen_mail_country-rus.html#GR-GENEALOGY
  For discussions of Germans from Russia genealogy and family research.

- GR-HERITAGE Mailing List
  http://www.rootsweb.com/~jfuller/gen_mail_country-rus.html#GR-HERITAGE
  For general discussions of Germans from Russia history, culture, and folklore.

- IRC Chat Line - #Ger-Rus
  http://www.geocities.com/Heartland/Acres/4123/irc.htm
  For researching Germans from Russia.

- Kutschurgan Mailing List
  http://www.rootsweb.com/~jfuller/gen_mail_country-rus.html#Kutschurgan

For anyone with a genealogical interest in the Kutschurgan Colonies which were made up of Germans who immigrated to Russia, beginning in the first decade of the 19th century, at the request of Alexander I, Tsar of Russia. The Colonies were located Northwest of the city of Odessa on the Black Sea.

- Master E-mail Listing for Germans From Russia
  http://pixel.cs.vt.edu/library/boxes/stahl/mastlist.html

- SURNAMES-GERMAN Mailing List
  http://www.rootsweb.com/~jfuller/gen_mail_country-ger.html
  #SURNAMES-GERMAN
  Gatewayed with the soc.genealogy.surnames.german newsgroup
  news:soc.genealogy.surnames.german
  For surname queries related to German speaking countries.

◆ Maps, Gazetteers & Geographical Information

- Map of Odessa (1892)
  http://www.generationspress.com/samples/odessa2.jpg

- Volga Map Bergseite
  http://www.webbitt.com/volga/map-berg.htm

- Volga Map Wiesenseite
  http://www.webbitt.com/volga/map-wies.htm

◆ Medical

Of particular interest to those of Volga German descent due to the genetics of early onset Familial Alzheimer's Disease.

- Alzheimer's Disease: New Complexities and Some Insight from Molecular Genetic Investigations
  http://www.asri.edu/genetics/brochure/agh/news/jan96/alz.html

- Can You Inherit Alzheimer's Disease?
  http://www.alznsw.asn.au/library/inherit.htm

- New Alzheimer's Candidate Gene
  http://www.accessexcellence.org/WN/SUA06/alz895.html

- New Alzheimer's Gene Discovered On Chromosome 1
  http://www.chiroscience.com/group/news/pressrel/old/pr950818.html

- The Presenilin Genes and Their Role in Early-Onset Familial Alzheimer's Disease
  http://www.coa.uky.edu/ADReview/Tanzi/Tanzi.htm

- Presenilins: a new gene family involved in Alzheimer´s Disease Pathology
  http://www2.hu-berlin.de/strahlenklinik/english/editor.htm

◆ People & Families

- Alemanes del Volga en la Argentina / Germans from Russia in Argentina
  http://comunidad.ciudad.com.ar/ciudadanos/herman/

- AVANT Genealogy Page
  http://www.avalon.net/~avant/Page.htm
  Village of Dreispitz, Volga, Russia and Village of Tarutino, Bessarabia, Russia. Boettcher, Dick, Doering, Heid, Heinitz, Herbel, Hulscher, Kosch/Koth?, Krause, Manske, Roloff, Uttke, Warnke, Wendland.

- Dennis and Patricia Evans' Family History
  http://www.cadvision.com/evansdg/INDEX-1.HTM
  Evans, Harray, Griffiths, Reed, Steinert, Borth, Stregger, Schmidt.

- ELL Family Heritage Page
  http://mars.ark.com/~rbell/html/ellfam.htm
  Ell, Fleck, Jung, Wolfe, Schaan/Schan, Hegel/Hagel, Himmilspach.

- Famous Germans from Russia
  http://www-personal.umich.edu/~steeles/gerrus/

- FEHR's Famous Family
  http://www3.bc.sympatico.ca/donfehr/fehr.htm
  The family of Benjamin Fehr and his wife, Elisabeth, in Manitoba and Saskatchewan, Canada.

- Germans from Russia in Portland, Oregon
  http://www.germans-russia-pdx.com/

- The GEYER Family: Germans from Russia
  http://www.angelfire.com/ny/earthstar/geyer.html
  Descendants of Frederick W. C. Geyer, born about 1808 and his wife Margaret, born about 1813.

- GUENTHER Genealogy - Passionate Possessions of Faith
  http://home1.gte.net/kanetani/guenther/index.htm
  A book for sale about The Jacob Guenther Family 1725-present, including Goertzen, Duerksen, Peters, Warkentin, Adrian, Loewen, Petkau, Isaac, Fadenrecht, Thiessen and others.

- Harold EHRMAN's Web Page
  http://www.ehrman.net/
  EHRMANN, DOCKTER, HAUCK, KNOERTZER.

- HOCHHALTER's WWW Page
  http://www.srv.net/~kata9b/eehpg.html
  Hochhalter, Rudolph, Stolz, Zimbelmann.

- HOHNSTEIN / HOHENSTEIN Surname Project
  http://members.xoom.com/tsterkel/surname_projects/hohnstei.htm

- Hutterite Genealogy Cross-Index
  http://feefhs.org/hut/indexhut.html

- John WALL's Family Tree
  http://www.oz.net/~compass/family/fam_tree.htm
  Baird, Burgess / Easterling, Clark / Whorton or Horton, Gieswein, Johnson, Peanecker or Pinnecker or Penager or Pinager, Wall. Gnadenfeld, Russia; Puschen, Germany.

- LANGMACHER Surname Project
  http://members.xoom.com/tsterkel/surname_projects/langmach.htm

- REMMICK Home Site
  http://members.aol.com/remmick1/
  Remmick.Home.Site.index.html/

German-Russian heritage connected to Edenkoben, Palatinate migration to Worms/Odessa, S. Russia then Streeter, ND, USA. Remmick, Roemmich, Remick, Remich, Roemigius, Roemig.

- SCHUMAN SCHUMANN Surname Project
  http://members.xoom.com/tsterkel/surname_projects/schuman.htm

- STAERKEL, STOERKEL, STÄRKEL, STÖRKEL, STARKEL, STERKEL Surname Project
  http://members.xoom.com/tsterkel/surname_projects/sterkel.htm

- WEITZ, Germans from Russia
  http://www.webbitt.com/weitz/
  This comprehensive site traces the Weitz family from Germany, to Yagodnaya Polayana in the Volga Valley of Russia and onto America. Included are a Weitz descendant tree, ship passenger lists, photos, obituaries and scanned documents.

◆ Publications

- Amazon.com Genealogy Bookstore - Germans From Russia
  http://www.amazon.com/exec/obidos/external-search/?keyword=germans+from+russia+genealogy&tag=markcyndisgenealA/

- AudioTapes.com - Genealogical Lectures on Cassette Tapes - Germans from Russia
  http://www.audiotapes.com/search2.asp?Search=Germans+from+Russia

- The Folks - Books Listing
  http://pixel.cs.vt.edu/pub/sources/booklist.txt

- The "German-Russian Books" list
  http://pixel.cs.vt.edu/pub/sources/grbooks.txt

- Interlink Bookshop Genealogical Services ~ Victoria, B.C., Canada
  http://www.interlinkbookshop.com/

- Wandering Volhynians
  http://pixel.cs.vt.edu/pub/sources/wv.txt
  Or Wandering Volhynians - German-Volhynian Newsletter
  http://feefhs.org/ca/frg-wv.html
  A Magazine for the Descendants of Germans From Volhynia and Poland.

◆ Records: Census, Cemeteries, Land, Obituaries, Personal, Taxes and Vital (Born, Married, Died & Buried)

- The Bessarabian Collection
  http://pixel.cs.vt.edu/library/bess/
  Includes the Bessarabian Index, the Christian Fiess Indices, The Koblenz Exodus Questionnaires/Forms Index and much more.

- Cemeteries
  http://pixel.cs.vt.edu/library/cemeteries/

- Census Records
  http://pixel.cs.vt.edu/library/census/
  - Barnes County, North Dakota 1900 Census of Germans from Russia
    http://pixel.cs.vt.edu/library/census/link/barnes00.txt
  - Barnes County, North Dakota 1910 Census of Germans from Russia
    http://pixel.cs.vt.edu/library/census/link/barnes10.txt
  - Barnes County, North Dakota 1920 Census of Germans from Russia
    http://pixel.cs.vt.edu/library/census/link/barnes20.txt
  - Campbell County, South Dakota 1910 Census of German Russians
    http://pixel.cs.vt.edu/library/census/link/camp10.txt
  - Charles Mix County, South Dakota 1910 Census of German Russians
    http://pixel.cs.vt.edu/library/census/link/cmix10.txt
  - Clark County, South Dakota 1910 Census of German Russians
    http://pixel.cs.vt.edu/library/census/link/clark10.txt
  - Grimes County, Texas 1900 Census, Germans from Russia
    http://pixel.cs.vt.edu/library/census/link/grimes00.txt
  - Grimes County, Texas 1910 Census, Germans from Russia
    http://pixel.cs.vt.edu/library/census/link/grimes10.txt
  - Grimes County, Texas 1920 Census, Germans from Russia
    http://pixel.cs.vt.edu/library/census/link/grimes20.txt
  - McPherson County, South Dakota 1900 Census of German Russians
    http://pixel.cs.vt.edu/library/census/link/mcpher00.txt
  - McPherson County, South Dakota 1910 Census of German Russians
    http://pixel.cs.vt.edu/library/census/link/mcpher10.txt
  - Unruh's South Russian Mennonite Census, 1795-1814
    http://pixel.cs.vt.edu/library/census/link/bhu.txt
  - Walworth County, South Dakota 1900 Census of German Russians
    http://pixel.cs.vt.edu/library/census/link/wal00.txt
  - Walworth County, South Dakota 1910 Census of German Russians
    http://pixel.cs.vt.edu/library/census/link/wal10.txt

- Friedensgemeinde Cemetery, Froid, Montana
  http://pixel.cs.vt.edu/library/cemeteries/montana/link/damm.txt

- The Gluecksthal Reformed Church, Odessa Township, McPherson Co., South Dakota
  http://pixel.cs.vt.edu/library/churches/link/glueck.txt
  Birth records, now in the possession of the Eureka Reformed Church.

- Greenway Cemetery, Greenway, South Dakota
  http://pixel.cs.vt.edu/library/cemeteries/sodak/link/grnway.txt

- Hilda Baptist Cemetery, Hilda, Alberta, Canada
  http://pixel.cs.vt.edu/library/cemeteries/canada/link/hilda1.txt

- Hope Congregational Cemetery, Bethune, Colorado
  http://pixel.cs.vt.edu/library/cemeteries/colorado/link/bethune1.txt

- Immanuel Lutheran Church Cemetery, Bethune, CO
  http://pixel.cs.vt.edu/library/cemeteries/colorado/link/bethune2.txt

- Jerauld County Cemetery Index
  http://pixel.cs.vt.edu/library/cemeteries/sodak/link/jerauld.txt

- Prairie Epitaph - Catholic Cemetery in Salvador, Saskatchewan
  http://mars.ark.com/~rbell/html/history/epitaph.html
  Many German Russian families.

- Settlement Family Registry
  http://www.nathankramer.com/settle/
  A record of the immigrant families of the German-Russian Settlement near Bethune (Burlington), Colorado.

- St. Petersburg Records Database for Glueckstal Colonies
  http://pixel.cs.vt.edu/library/boxes/ehrman/index.html

◆ Societies & Groups

- American Historical Society of Germans from Russia ~ Lincoln, Nebraska
  http://www.ahsgr.org/
  - Arizona Sun Chapter
    http://www.ahsgr.org/azsun.html
  - Calgary Canada Chapter
    http://www.ahsgr.org/calgary.html
  - Central California Chapter
    http://www.ahsgr.org/cacentra.html
  - Central Oklahoma Chapter
    http://www.ahsgr.org/okcentra.html
  - Central Washington Chapter
    http://www.ahsgr.org/wacentra.html
  - Denver Metro Chapter
    http://www.ahsgr.org/codenver.html
  - Florida Suncoast Chapter
    http://www.ahsgr.org/flsuncst.html
  - Golden Wheat Chapter
    http://www.ahsgr.org/ksgolden.html
  - Greater Seattle Chapter
    http://www.ahsgr.org/waseattl.html
  - Kansas Sunflower Chapter
    http://www.ahsgr.org/kssunflo.html
  - Lincoln Nebraska Chapter
    http://www.ahsgr.org/nelincol.html
  - Nation's Capital Area Chapter
    http://www.ahsgr.org/dcapitol.html

- North Star Chapter -- Minnesota
  http://www.ahsgr.org/mnnostar.html
- Northeast Nebraska Chapter
  http://www.ahsgr.org/nenorthe.html
- Northeastern Kansas Chapter
  http://www.ahsgr.org/ksnorthe.html
- Northern Colorado Chapter
  http://www.ahsgr.org/conorthe.html
- Northern Illinois Chapter
  http://www.ahsgr.org/ilnorthe.html
- Olympic Peninsula Chapter - Washington
  http://www.ahsgr.org/waolypen.html
- Oregon Chapter
  http://www.ahsgr.org/orportla.html
- Southeastern Wisconsin Chapter
  http://www.ahsgr.org/wisouthe.html
- Southern California Chapter
  http://www.ehrman.net/ahsgr/casocal.html
- Southwest Michigan Chapter
  http://www.ahsgr.org/misouthw.html
- Ventura Chapter
  http://www.ehrman.net/ahsgr/cavent.html
- Washington Rainier Chapter of Tacoma
  http://www.ahsgr.org/warainer.html

- Bukovina Society of the Americas
  http://members.aol.com/LJensen/bukovina.html

- German-Russian Genealogical Societies
  http://pixel.cs.vt.edu/library/societies.html

- Germans From Russia Heritage Society ~ Bismarck, North Dakota
  http://www.grhs.com/
  - Alberta Chapter
    http://www.grhs.com/alberta.html
  - British Columbia Chapter
    http://feefhs.org/grhs/grhs-bc.html
  - Puget Sound Chapter
    http://www.grhs.com/pugetsnd.html

- Glückstal Colonies Research Association (GCRA)
  http://www.feefhs.org/FRGGCRA/gcra.html

◆ Villages & Colonies

- AHSGR Village Research Coordinators
  http://www.ahsgr.org/ahsgrvcs.html
  American Historical Society of Germans From Russia.

- Alt-Danzig & Neu-Danzig, Russia
  http://members.aol.com/fisherjoy/danzig.html

- German Villages in the Volga Valley of Russia
  http://www.webbitt.com/volga/
  Over 300 German Russian Volga villages are identified in this comprehensive site with links to village web sites. Volga maps, history and other resources are also included.

- Glückstal Surnames Found in the St. Petersburg Records Database
  http://feefhs.org/FRGGCRA/gcra3.html

- Gnadenfeld Molotschna, South Russia, 1835 through 1943
  http://www.primenet.com/~rempel/gnadenfeld/gndntoc.htm
  Memories of Good Times and of Hard Times, Collected by J. C. Krause, Yarrow, British Columbia, 1954.

- GRHS Village Coordinators
  http://www.grhs.com/grhsvcs.html
  Germans From Russia Heritage Society.

- Herzog, Russia Homepage
  http://www.geocities.com/Heartland/Estates/5138/

- History of the Glückstal Colonies
  http://feefhs.org/FRGGCRA/gcra1.html

- Home Page for Village of Novo Nikolaevka
  http://www.best.com/~heli/genealogy/nn.html

- The Hussenbach Villages of Russia
  http://www.teleport.com/~stahl/hussenba.html

- Kamenka - A German Russian Village in the Volga Valley
  http://www.webbitt.com/volga/kamenka/

- Kleinliebental Homepage
  http://www.rootsweb.com/~ukrklieb/
  A village that was founded by German settlers in 1804 near the city of Odessa in Ukraine.

- Kutschurgan Villages Web Site
  http://www.kutschurgan.com/
  Catholic Villages of the Kutschurgan Colony just NW of Odessa.

- Leichtling Home Page
  http://www.geocities.com/Heartland/Flats/5505/
  Leichtling, Saratov, Volga, Russia.

- Lower Jeruslan River Colonies Research Project
  http://members.home.net/jeruslanvillages/

- Messer (aka ust Solicha) Village Database
  http://members.xoom.com/tsterkel/village_projects/messer.htm

- Norka (aka Weigand) Village Database
  http://members.xoom.com/tsterkel/village_projects/norka.htm

- Norka Village
  http://www.jps.net/wulfie/norka.htm

- Obermunjor, Russia Home Page
  http://www.geocities.com/Heartland/Flats/2799/

- Paulskoye, Russia - A Volga German Village
  http://members.aol.com/TCWeeder/index.paulskoye.html

- RemMick's Borodino Bessarabia Home Site
  http://members.aol.com/RemMick/Borodino Bessarabia.index.html/

- St. Petersburg Records Database for Glueckstal Colonies
  http://pixel.cs.vt.edu/library/boxes/ehrman/index.html

- Saratov, Volga, Russia Villages
  http://www.webbitt.com/volga/lower/villages.html
  - Villages of Dreispitz
    http://www.webbitt.com/volga/lower/dreispitz.html
  - Village of Dobrinka
    http://www.webbitt.com/volga/lower/dobrinka.html
  - Village of Galka
    http://www.buckeyenet.net/users/jdye/VillageGalka.html
  - Village of Holstein
    http://www.webbitt.com/volga/holstein/
  - Village of Kraft
    http://www.webbitt.com/volga/lower/kraft.html
  - Village of Mueller
    http://www.webbitt.com/volga/lower/mueller.html
  - Village of Shcherbakovka
    http://www.webbitt.com/volga/lower/shcherbakovka.html
  - Village of Schwab
    http://www.webbitt.com/volga/lower/schwab.html
  - Village of Stephan
    http://www.webbitt.com/volga/lower/stephan.html

- Stahl am Tarlyk (a.k.a. Stepnoje) Village Database
  http://members.xoom.com/tsterkel/village_projects/stahl_t.htm

- Village Compilations - Genealogies
  http://pixel.cs.vt.edu/library/villages/

- Village Coordinators, by Village
  http://pixel.cs.vt.edu/library/vc.html
  Or Village Coordinators, by Surname
  http://pixel.cs.vt.edu/library/village.html

- Village Genealogy Research - Germans from Volga Russia
  http://members.xoom.com/tsterkel/village_projects/villages.htm
  Dedicated to Family History Research for the Russia Volga Colonies: Stahl am Tarlyk, Norka and Messer.

- The Village History Project
  http://pixel.cs.vt.edu/library/history/

- Village of Balzer
  http://www.teleport.com/~herbf/balzer.htm
  Volga Russian Germans.

- The Village of Brunnental, Russia
  http://pixel.cs.vt.edu/library/boxes/stahl/index.html

- The Village of Grimm, Russia
  http://www.angelfire.com/ca/GRIMM/index.html

- Village of Kolb, Russia
  http://pixel.cs.vt.edu/library/kolb.html

- Village of Kratzke, Russia / Zum Dorf von Kratzke, Russland
  http://www.thegrid.net/kratzke/

- Village of Schilling, Russia
  http://home.earthlink.net/~garymartens/schilling.html

- Village Records and Compilations
  http://pixel.cs.vt.edu/library/villages/
  From the Odessa German-Russian Genealogical Library.

- The Volga Deutsch Home Page for Fischer
  http://members.aol.com/RAToepfer/index.htm

- Walter, Russia or (Grechinaya Luka) which means...... Buckwheat Bend
  http://securitydoors.com/walter/

- Yagodnaya Polyana, Russia
  http://pta6000.pld.com:80/skmug1/

GERMANY / DEUTSCHLAND

http://www.cyndislist.com/germany.htm

Category Index:

- General Resource Sites
- History & Culture
- How To
- Language, Handwriting & Script
- Libraries, Archives & Museums
- Locality Specific & Migration
- Mailing Lists, Newsgroups & Chat
- Maps, Gazetteers & Geographical Information
- People & Families

- Professional Researchers, Volunteers & Other Research Services
- Publications, Software & Supplies
- Queries, Message Boards & Surname Lists
- Records: Census, Cemeteries, Land, Obituaries, Personal, Taxes and Vital
- Religion
- Societies & Groups
- WorldGenWeb

◆ General Resource Sites

- Deutsche Post AG
  http://www.postag.de/
  Postal codes, etc.

- Genealogie Im Sudetenland / Böhmen
  http://www.pingweb.de/Kummer/

- German American Cultural Heritage
  http://userweb.piasanet.com/wigger/default.htm

- German Genealogy Cross-Index - from FEEFHS
  http://feefhs.org/indexger.html

- Genealogy.net Home Page
  http://www.genealogy.net/gene/index.html

  o Genealogy.net Home Page
    http://www2.genealogy.net/gene/
    Mirror site in Giessen, Germany.

  o Genealogy.net Home Page
    http://www.genealogy.net/gene/
    Mirror site in Kerpen, Germany.

  o Index to States, Provinces, and Regions
    http://www2.genealogy.net/gene/reg/rindex.htm

- German Genealogy: Genealogical Events
  http://www.genealogy.net/gene/ghlp/events.html

- German Genealogy Links
  http://www.geocities.com/SiliconValley/Haven/1538/german.html

- German Genealogy: Old Units
  http://www.genealogy.net/gene/misc/units/
  Translation table of old to contemporary units of measurement. Includes area, length, volume, weights, counts, speed, coins, & worldwide measurements.

- German Genealogy Sites and Organizations
  http://www.execpc.com/~kap/gene-de.html
  From Kent's Genealogy Trading Post.

- German Genealogy? Start Here!
  http://www.daddezio.com/germgen.html
  From D'ADDEZIO.com.

- German Immigration to Maryland
  http://www.clis.umd.edu/~mddlmddl/791/communities/html/index.html#german
  A scholarly review of immigration into Maryland from the very first colonists to modern immigrants.

- German Migration Resource Center
  http://www.germanmigration.com/default.asp
  Featuring over 14,000 Queries about German Emigrants and Immigrants. Genealogists can submit queries about individuals migrating from Germany in any time period, destination worldwide. Search queries by surname, ship name, immigration year, places of origin or destination. Also see extensive Links and order books about German migration and genealogy.

- German-Prussian Genealogy Links
  http://www.geocities.com/SiliconValley/Haven/1538/germanpg.html

- German Roots: German Genealogy Resources
  http://home.att.net/~wee-monster/

  o German Roots: Emigration and Immigration
    http://home.att.net/~wee-monster/ei.html

    • Finding Passenger Lists 1820 to the 1940s - arrivals at US ports from Europe
      http://home.att.net/~wee-monster/passengers.html

    • Finding Passenger Lists Before 1820
      http://home.att.net/~wee-monster/1820.html

    • Finding Passenger Arrival Records at the Port of Galveston, Texas
      http://home.att.net/~wee-monster/galveston.html

    • Finding Passenger Arrival Records at the Port of Boston, Massachusetts 1820-1943
      http://home.att.net/~wee-monster/boston.html

- Germany Genealogy - WorldGenWeb
  http://www.rootsweb.com/~wggerman/

- Germany Telephone & Address Listings
  http://www.ancestry.com/search/rectype/inddbs/4064.htm

- Immigration: The Germans
  http://library.thinkquest.org/20619/German.html
  A brief history of German immigration to the United States.

- Internet Genealogy - VU University Project Page
  http://www.geocities.com/SiliconValley/Haven/1538/
  index2.html
  Many helpful sites for Polish, Irish, German, German-Prussian, German-Russian, & Prussian backgrounds.

- Internet Sources of German Genealogy
  http://www.bawue.de/~hanacek/info/edatbase.htm

- Misc. German Genealogy Information
  http://worldroots.clicktron.com/brigitte/b4_index.html
  And Germany Information
  http://worldroots.clicktron.com/brigitte/germinfo.htm
  From Brigitte Gastel Lloyd.

- O.M.I.I. Genealogical Project
  http://www.wgbc.org/hindex.htm
  A Swiss Mennonite & German Amish genealogy project.

- Prussian Genealogy Links
  http://www.geocities.com/SiliconValley/Haven/1538/
  prussia.html

- The SGGS "German Card"
  http://feefhs.org/sggs/sggs-gc.html

- Yahoo!...Germany...Genealogy
  http://dir.yahoo.com/Regional/Countries/Germany/Arts_and_
  Humanities/Humanities/History/Genealogy/

◆ History & Culture

- The Forty Eighters
  http://www.tsha.utexas.edu/handbook/online/articles/view/FF/
  pnf1.html
  From the Handbook of Texas Online. Oriented towards Texas Germans but interesting general information on this immigrant group.

- Home Erenfried
  http://sites.netscape.net/erenfried/homepage
  Information relating to the German and imperial aristocracy of the tenth and eleventh centuries.

- StudyWeb: History: Country History Index: Europe Index: Germany
  http://www.studyweb.com/links/140.html

- The Turnverein Movement
  http://www.tsha.utexas.edu/handbook/online/articles/view/TT/
  vnt2.html
  From the Handbook of Texas Online. Oriented towards Texas Germans but interesting general information on these German social clubs.

- Yahoo!...Germany...History
  http://dir.yahoo.com/Regional/Countries/Germany/Arts_and_
  Humanities/Humanities/History/

◆ How To

- Basic Research Outline for German Genealogy
  http://home.att.net/~wee-monster/outline.html
  From the German Roots website.

- Finding Passenger Lists 1820-c.1940
  http://home.att.net/~wee-monster/passengers.html
  A basic tutorial for German Americans by Joe Beine, German Roots Webmaster.

- Finding Where Your Ancestors Came From in Germany
  http://www.angelfire.com/biz/origins1/ancestors.html

- Genealogy Research in Stuttgart Libraries and Archives
  http://www.kinquest.com/genealogy/resources/stuttgart.html
  Tips and hints by Lisa Petersen.

- A Genealogical Handbook of German Research
  http://www.familysearch.org/rg/guide/Ger_BMD_RefDoc_
  HandbookGermanResearch.ASP
  Excellent "How To" guide from FamilySearch.org.

- German Genealogical Research Before The Church Records Begin
  http://www.kinquest.com/genealogy/resources/
  researching.html
  Tips and hints by Lisa Petersen.

- German Research at Libraries and Archives in Baden-Wuerttemberg
  http://www.kinquest.com/genealogy/resources/badwue.html
  Tips and hints by Lisa Petersen.

- Germany Research Outline
  http://www.familysearch.org/sg/Germany.html
  From the Family History SourceGuide.

- Hints for researchers outside Germany
  http://www.bawue.de/~hanacek/info/darchi99.htm#english

◆ Language, Handwriting & Script

- AltaVista Translation Service
  http://babelfish.altavista.digital.com/cgi-bin/translate?
  Input a URL for a web site or a block of plain text and this site will translate for you from German to English or English to German.

- Deciphering Gothic Records
  http://www.futureone.com/~fdearden/page2.htm
  Pamphlet for sale.

- Deutsch Englisches Wörterbuch
  http://www.tu-chemnitz.de/urz/netz/forms/dict.html

- German Letter Writing Guide
  http://www.familysearch.org/rg/guide/LGGerman.ASP
  For genealogical inqueries from FamilySearch.org.

- Form Letters for German Genealogy
  http://www.genealogy.net/gene/misc/letters/

- Fraktur and German Script
  http://www.asherwin.com/fraktur%26script.html

- German-English Genealogical Dictionary
  http://www.amazon.com/exec/obidos/ISBN=0806313420/
  markcyndisgenealA/
  A book by Ernest Thode.

- German-English Letter Translation Specialists
  http://www.win.bright.net/~deichsa/welcome.html

- German-English On-line Dictionary
  http://dictionaries.travlang.com/GermanEnglish/

- German Genealogical Word List
  http://www.familysearch.org/rg/guide/WLGerman.ASP

- German Genealogy: Translation Service
  http://www2.genealogy.net/gene/www/abt/translation.html

- German Illness Translations
  http://pixel.cs.vt.edu/library/articles/link/illness.txt

- German Study Group / German Words
  http://thorin.adnc.com/~lynnd/vuword.html
  Includes time keeping, occupations, illnesses, common genealogical words, and words used in official documents.

- German Translation Service
  http://www.asherwin.com/
  Specializations: German genealogy, Fraktur and German script, legal documents.

- German Translation Service
  http://www.win.bright.net/~jakeschu/welcome.html
  Old Script

- A Glossary of German Words Used in Official Documents
  gopher://Gopher.UToledo.edu:70/00GOPHER_ROOT%3A
  %5BRESEARCH-RESOURCES.GENEALOGY.GERMAN-
  GENEALOGY%5DA-GLOSSARY-OF-GERMAN-WORDS.
  USED-IN-OFFICIAL-DOCUMENTS

- Handwriting Guide: German Gothic
  http://www.familysearch.org/rg/guide/German_Gothic99-
  36316.ASP

- If I Can Decipher Germanic Records, So Can You
  http://www.amazon.com/exec/obidos/ISBN=0961542004/
  markcyndisgenealA/
  A book by Edna Bentz.

- Moravians - German Script Tutorial
  http://www.mun.ca/rels/morav/script.html
  With Moravian Archival examples
  - German Script Alphabet
    http://www.mun.ca/rels/morav/pics/tutor/mscript2.html

- Old German Handwritten Scripts
  http://www2.genealogy.net/gene/misc/scripts.html

- Old German Professions and Occupations
  http://worldroots.clicktron.com/brigitte/occupat.htm

- Old Spelling Patterns
  http://www.asherwin.com/spelling.html

- Patronymics - Ostfriesland-Patronymics
  http://www.asc.csc.cc.il.us/~mneill/html/patronymics.html
  By Michael John Neill.

- Sample Letters in German to Obtain Genealogical Information
  gopher://Gopher.UToledo.edu:70/00GOPHER_ROOT%3A
  %5BRESEARCH-RESOURCES.GENEALOGY.GERMAN-
  GENEALOGY%5DGERMAN-SAMPLE-LETTER.FOR-
  INFORMATION-REQUESTS

- Translation Service only for genealogy related material
  http://www.genealogy.net/gene/misc/translation.html
  Volunteer translators can provide you with translations between Czech, English, Dutch, French, German, & Polish. This service is provided via e-mail. Exact request syntax and length rules must be followed in order to expedite processing.

- Tutorials for Reading Old German, French and English Handwriting, Naming Systems
  http://www.disknet.com/indiana_biolab/eg502.htm

- Walden Font
  http://www.waldenfont.com/
  Several different fonts for sale, including: The Gutenberg Press German Fraktur Fonts and German Script.

◆ Libraries, Archives & Museums

- Archive in Hessen
  http://www.archive.hessen.de/homepage.htm

- Archive in Nordrhein-Westfalen
  http://www.archive.nrw.de/

- Archives in Germany
  http://www.bawue.de/~hanacek/info/earchive.htm

- Archivschule Marburg
  http://www.uni-marburg.de/archivschule/welcome.html
  - Archive im Internet
    http://www.uni-marburg.de/archivschule/fv6.html
    - Archive in Deutschland
      http://www.uni-marburg.de/archivschule/deuarch.html
    - Staatliche Archive im Internet
      http://www.uni-marburg.de/archivschule/deuarch1.html
    - Kommunalarchive im Internet
      http://www.uni-marburg.de/archivschule/deuarch2.html
    - Kirchliche Archive im Internet
      http://www.uni-marburg.de/archivschule/deuarch3.html
    - Literaturachive im Internet
      http://www.uni-marburg.de/archivschule/deuarch4.html
    - Wirtschaftsarchive im Internet
      http://www.uni-marburg.de/archivschule/deuarch5.html
    - Parlamentsarchive und Archive politischer Parteien und Verbände im Internet
      http://www.uni-marburg.de/archivschule/deuarch6.html
    - Universitätsarchive und Archive sonstiger Institutionen im Internet
      http://www.uni-marburg.de/archivschule/deuarch7.html
    - Medienarchive im Internet
      http://www.uni-marburg.de/archivschule/deuarch8.html

- Bavarian State Libraries and the Bavarian Library Network / Bayerischen Staatlichen Bibliotheken und dem Bibliotheksverbund Bayern
  http://www.bib-bvb.de/

- Berlin Central and State Library / Zentral- und Landesbibliothek Berlin (ZLB)
  http://www.zlb.de/

- Bundesarchiv Online
  http://www.bundesarchiv.de/index.html
  The National Archives of Germany.

- Der Bundesbeauftragte für die Unterlagen des Staatssicherheitsdienstes der ehemaligen DDR
  http://www.bstu.de/home.htm
  Federal commission which holds the records of the former East German secret police - the Stasi. Includes a description of their holdings and instructions on who may access these records and the process for doing so.

  o Das Archiv
    http://www.bstu.de/archiv/index.htm

  o The Archives
    http://www.bstu.de/englisch/04.htm

- Civil Archives Libraries and Museums of Saxony
  http://rosella.apana.org.au/~jgk/saxony/civil.html

- Cologne Public Library / StadtBibliothek Köln ~ Germany
  http://www.stbib-koeln.de/

- Die Deutsche Bibliothek
  http://www.ddb.de/

- Evangelisches Zentral-Archiv in Berlin
  http://www.ezab.de/
  Archiv der Evangelischen Kirche in Deutschland und der Evangelischen Kirche der Union.

  o Practical Information and Addresses for Genealogical Research
    http://www.ezab.de/eza10e.html

- Family History Centers in Germany, Austria and Switzerland
  http://www.genealogy.net/gene/faqs/LDS.de

- Family History Library Catalog
  http://www.familysearch.org/Search/searchcatalog.asp
  From the FamilySearch web site, an online catalog to the holdings of the LDS Church in Salt Lake City, Utah. Also search for other localities by place name.
  http://www.familysearch.org/fhlc/supermainframeset.asp?display=localitysearch&columns=*,180,0

  o Germany
    http://www.familysearch.org/fhlc/supermainframeset.asp?display=localitydetails&subject=81&subject_disp=Germany&columns=*,180,0

    - Anhalt
      http://www.familysearch.org/fhlc/supermainframeset.asp?display=localitydetails&subject=29343&subject_disp=Germany,_Anhalt&columns=*,180,0

- Baden
  http://www.familysearch.org/fhlc/supermainframeset.asp?display=localitydetails&subject=29395&subject_disp=Germany,_Baden&columns=*,180,0

- Bayern (Bavaria)
  http://www.familysearch.org/fhlc/supermainframeset.asp?display=localitydetails&subject=31003&subject_disp=Germany,_Bayern&columns=*,180,0

- Braunschweig
  http://www.familysearch.org/fhlc/supermainframeset.asp?display=localitydetails&subject=33707&subject_disp=Germany,_Braunschweig&columns=*,180,0

- Bremen
  http://www.familysearch.org/fhlc/supermainframeset.asp?display=localitydetails&subject=33991&subject_disp=Germany,_Bremen&columns=*,180,0

- Elsaß-Lothringen (Alsace-Lorraine)
  http://www.familysearch.org/fhlc/supermainframeset.asp?display=localitydetails&subject=34028&subject_disp=Germany,_Elsaß-Lothringen&columns=*,180,0

  See also France, Alsace-Lorraine (région)
  http://www.familysearch.org/fhlc/supermainframeset.asp?display=localitydetails&subject=80287&subject_disp=France,_Alsace-Lorraine_(région)&columns=*,180,0

- Hamburg
  http://www.familysearch.org/fhlc/supermainframeset.asp?display=localitydetails&subject=36172&subject_disp=Germany,_Hamburg&columns=*,180,0

- Hessen
  http://www.familysearch.org/fhlc/supermainframeset.asp?display=localitydetails&subject=36194&subject_disp=Germany,_Hessen&columns=*,180,0

- Lippe
  http://www.familysearch.org/fhlc/supermainframeset.asp?display=localitydetails&subject=37058&subject_disp=Germany,_Lippe&columns=*,180,0

- Mecklenburg
  http://www.familysearch.org/fhlc/supermainframeset.asp?display=localitydetails&subject=37156&subject_disp=Germany,_Mecklenburg&columns=*,180,0

- Oldenburg
  http://www.familysearch.org/fhlc/supermainframeset.asp?display=localitydetails&subject=37740&subject_disp=Germany,_Oldenburg&columns=*,180,0

- Preußen (Prussia)
  http://www.familysearch.org/fhlc/supermainframeset.asp?display=localitydetails&subject=37854&subject_disp=Germany,_Preußen&columns=*,180,0

- Sachsen (Saxony)
  http://www.familysearch.org/fhlc/supermainframeset.asp?display=localitydetails&subject=46664&subject_disp=Germany,_Preußen,_Sachsen&columns=*,180,0

  See also Germany, Sachsen
  http://www.familysearch.org/fhlc/supermainframeset.asp?display=localitydetails&subject=52658&subject_disp=Germany,_Sachsen&columns=*,180,0

- Schleswig-Holstein
  http://www.familysearch.org/fhlc/supermainframeset.asp?display=localitydetails&subject=50160&subject_disp=Germany,_Preußen,_Schleswig-Holstein&columns=*,180,0

- Sachsen (Saxony)
  http://www.familysearch.org/fhlc/supermainframeset.asp
  ?display=localitydetails&subject=52658&subject_disp=
  Germany,_Sachsen&columns=*,180,0

  See also Germany, Preußen, Sachsen
  http://www.familysearch.org/fhlc/supermainframeset.asp
  ?display=localitydetails&subject=46664&subject_disp=
  Germany,_Preußen,_Sachsen&columns=*,180,0

- Schaumburg-Lippe
  http://www.familysearch.org/fhlc/supermainframeset.asp
  ?display=localitydetails&subject=55453&subject_disp=
  Germany,_Schaumburg-Lippe&columns=*,180,0

- Thüringen (Thuringia)
  http://www.familysearch.org/fhlc/supermainframeset.asp
  ?display=localitydetails&subject=55577&subject_disp=
  Germany,_Thüringen&columns=*,180,0

- Waldeck
  http://www.familysearch.org/fhlc/supermainframeset.asp
  ?display=localitydetails&subject=56297&subject_disp=
  Germany,_Waldeck&columns=*,180,0

- Württemberg
  http://www.familysearch.org/fhlc/supermainframeset.asp
  ?display=localitydetails&subject=56392&subject_disp=
  Germany,_Württemberg&columns=*,180,0

- Family History SourceGuide - Family History
  Centers - Europe and Scandinavia
  http://www.familysearch.org/sg/Europe_and_Scandinavia_
  FHC.html
  *Austria, Belgium, Denmark, Finland, France, Germany, Hungary,
  Iceland, Italy, Netherlands, Norway, Portugal, Spain, Sweden, and
  Switzerland.*

- Genealogie Forschungsstelle Dortmund
  http://home.t-online.de/home/GFS.Dortmund
  *Genealogie Forschungsstelle der Kirche Jesu Christi der HLT
  (Mormonen) Kostenlose Online-Beratung! Family History Center of
  the LDS Online consultation!*

- HBZ Hochschulbibliothekszentrum Des Landes
  Nordrhein-Westfalen
  http://www.hbz-nrw.de/
  *HBZ - The online utility and service center for academic libraries in
  North Rhine-Westphalia.*

- Landesarchiv Berlin
  http://www.landesarchiv-berlin.de/
  o Landesarchiv Berlin User Information
    http://www.landesarchiv-berlin.de/benutzung-e.htm
  o The Loss of records
    http://www.landesarchiv-berlin.de/archivgut-e.htm

- Landesarchiv Schleswig-Holstein
  http://www.schleswig-holstein.de/archive/lash/index.html

- Landeshauptarchiv Koblenz
  http://www.landeshauptarchiv.de/

- Palatine Heritage Centre ~ Rathkeale, Ireland
  http://www.rathkealehousehotel.com/localsites.htm#Palatine
  Heritage Centre

- Repositories of Primary Sources - Europe - Germany
  http://www.uidaho.edu/special-collections/euro1.html#de
  *A list of links to online resources from the Univ. of Idaho Library,
  Special Collections and Archives.*

- Research Center for German Emigrants in the USA
  http://www.uni-oldenburg.de/nausa/nausae.htm

- Staatliche Archivverwaltung Baden-Württemberg
  http://www.lad-bw.de/

- Die staatlichen Archive Bayerns
  http://www.gda.bayern.de/

- Staatsarchiv Bremen - Bestände-übersicht
  http://www.bremen.de/info/staatsarchiv/bestand/ubersich/
  starter.htm

- Staatsarchiv Hamburg
  http://www.hamburg.de/Behoerden/Staatsarchiv/

- Staatsarchive in Niedersachsen
  http://www.staatsarchive.niedersachsen.de/
  o Quellen zur Auswanderung in den
    niedersächsischen Staatsarchiven
    http://www.staatsarchive.niedersachsen.de/Auswanderer/
    Auswanderer.htm
  o Sources about emigration in the State Archives of
    Lower-Saxony
    http://www.staatsarchive.niedersachsen.de/Auswanderer/
    englisch.htm
    Describes the contents and use of a searchable online database.
  o Online-Findbuch
    http://www.staatsarchive.niedersachsen.de/findbuch/
    Searchable online database.

- Stadtarchiv Koblenz
  http://www.koblenz.de/bildung/stadtarchiv/
  o Emigration from Koblenz
    http://www.koblenz.de/bildung/stadtarchiv/emigrat.html
  o Tracing Family Roots
    http://www.koblenz.de/bildung/stadtarchiv/f-roots.html

- Die thüringischen Staatsarchive
  http://www.thueringen.de/Staatsarchive/

- Württembergische Landesbibliothek Stuttgart /
  Wuerttemberg State Library
  http://www.wlb-stuttgart.de/~www/wlbinfo-home.html
  *Regional library for Baden-Wuerttemberg, for the administrative
  districts of Stuttgart and Tuebingen.*

◆ Locality Specific & Migration

- Bibliser in Amerika
  http://www.geocities.com/Heartland/Meadows/4221/
  *More than 800 emigrants from the small German town of Biblis.
  Beckerle, Bender, Freihaut, Gansmann, Kärcher, Kissel, Reis, Seib
  Seibert.*

- Black Forest Genealogy
  http://www.websters.net/blackforest/

- Bühlertal, Baden Home Page
  http://www.geocities.com/Heartland/Prairie/3974/index.html

- The Communities of Alsace A-Z
  http://members.aol.com/RobtBehra/AlsaceA-Z/GenInfo.htm

- Eastern Europe
  http://www.CyndisList.com/easteuro.htm
  See this category on Cyndi's List for related links.

- Emigrants from Nattheim to USA / Nattheimer Auswanderer nach Amerika
  http://www.mailaender-web.de/ahnen.htm

- Emigrants from Oggenhausen to USA / Oggenhausener Auswanderer nach Amerika
  http://www.mailaender-web.de/ahnen.htm

- Emigrants from Kreis Meschede (Westfalen) to the United States in America
  http://www.westphalia-emigration.de/

- The Emsland Heritage Society
  http://www.geocities.com/Heartland/4018/
  For those seeking histories and genealogies of the peoples and towns making up the region of upper northwest of Germany known as "The Emsland."

- Familienforschung in Pommern
  http://hinterpommern.de/Genealogie/

- From Alsace to Lorraine... ... across Saar
  http://perso.club-internet.fr/rweinl/
  Many French resources listed here.

- Genealogical Research in Bavaria
  http://worldroots.clicktron.com/misc/bg_misc/bavausw.html

- German-Bohemian Immigrant Surname Database
  http://www.rootsweb.com/~gbhs/database/database.html

- German Genealogy: Donauschwaben / Danube-Swabians
  http://www.genealogy.net/gene/reg/ESE/dschwaben.html

- German Genealogy: Elsass / Alsace
  http://www.genealogy.net/gene/reg/ELS-LOT/alsace.html

- Germans from Russia
  http://www.CyndisList.com/germruss.htm
  See this category on Cyndi's List for related links.

- The Great Palatine Migration
  http://www.zekes.com/~dspidell/famresearch/palatine.html

- Help in searching for ancestors from the Sudetenland
  http://www2.genealogy.net/gene/reg/SUD/sudet_en.html
  German settlement area in Bohemia/Moravia/Austrian Silesia -> Czechoslovakia -> Czech Republik.

- History of German Settlements in Southern Hungary
  http://feefhs.org/banat/bhistory.html

- Joseph BROOM's German Heritage Pages
  http://www.geocities.com/~brooms/german.html
  Baden, Bavarian/Franconian, Ostfriesland.

- Kraig Ruckel's Palatine & Pennsylvania Dutch Genealogy Home Page
  http://www.geocities.com/Heartland/3955/

- The Ostfriesen Pages
  http://www.summitsoftware.com/ostfriesen/

- Ostfriesian Genealogical Research by MJ Neill
  http://www.asc.csc.cc.il.us/~mneill/html/ostfriesland.html
  By Michael Neill.

- Ostfriesland Ancestors
  http://www.alaska.net/~dsewell/

- Palatine History
  http://www.rootsweb.com/~ote/palatine.htm
  From The Olive Tree.

- Palatines to America Homepage
  http://palam.org

- The Pomeranian Page
  http://www.execpc.com/~kap/pommern1.html

- Pommern Genealogy Webring Home
  http://www.geocities.com/Heartland/Flats/3528/

- Prussian-Russian-Canadian Mennonite Genealogical Resources
  http://www.mmhs.org/mmhsgen.htm

- Saxon Genealogy
  http://rosella.apana.org.au/~jgk/saxony/menu.html
  Specialising in the Kingdom of Saxony.

- Stemwede Genealogy Home Page
  http://members.tripod.com/~Stemweder/index.html
  Genealogy information for Stemwede, Germany, in North Rhine-Westephalia.

- Villingendorf Site
  http://www.geocities.com/Heartland/Valley/7707/
  Family histories of people of Villingendorf, Rottweil, Germany, especially emigrants to America.

- Vörstetten, Baden, Germany
  http://www.genealogy.org/~smoore/vorstetten.html

- Western Europe
  http://www.CyndisList.com/westeuro.htm
  See this category on Cyndi's List for related links.

- The Wind-Mill
  http://www.geocities.com/Heartland/6166/index.html
  Devoted to exploring Frisian/Ostfriesen/North German heritage and history.

- Wittgenstein History and Genealogy
  http://www.action-research.com/gene/wittpage.htm
  The former counties of Wittgenstein-Berleburg and Wittgenstein-Wittgenstein in the south of the Sauerland.

◆ Mailing Lists, Newsgroups & Chat

- Genealogy Resources on the Internet - Germany/Prussia Mailing Lists
  http://www.rootsweb.com/~jfuller/gen_mail_country-ger.html
  Most of the mailing list links below point to this site, wonderfully maintained by John Fuller

- ALSACE-GENEALOGY Mailing List
  http://www.rootsweb.com/~jfuller/gen_mail_country-
  ger.html#ALSACE-L
  And the corresponding web page
  http://members.aol.com/jaw5623/private/alsace/
  *For anyone interested in Alsace, a border region of France and
  Germany.*

- ALSACE-LORRAINE Mailing List
  http://www.rootsweb.com/~jfuller/gen_mail_country-
  ger.html#ALSACE-LORRAINE

- AUS-QLD-SE-Germans Mailing List
  http://www.rootsweb.com/~jfuller/gen_mail_country-
  ger.html#AUS-QLD-SE-Germans
  *For anyone with a genealogical interest in the descendants of the
  Germans who migrated to South East Queensland, Australia.*

- BADEN-WURTTEMBERG Mailing List
  http://www.rootsweb.com/~jfuller/gen_mail_country-
  ger.html#BADEN-WURTTEMBERG
  For Baden, Hohenzollern, and Wurttemberg.

- BAVARIA Mailing List
  http://www.rootsweb.com/~jfuller/gen_mail_country-
  ger.html#GER-BAVARIA
  *For the kingdom, province and state of Bavaria including the city of
  Munich.*

- BAVARIAN-ANCESTORS Mailing List
  http://www.rootsweb.com/~jfuller/gen_mail_country-
  ger.html#BAVARIAN-ANCESTORS
  *For anyone with a genealogical interest in the state of Bavaria,
  Germany.*

- BRANDENBURG-L Mailing List
  http://www.rootsweb.com/~jfuller/gen_mail_country-
  ger.html#BRANDENBURG-L
  *For those interested in sharing and exchanging information on
  genealogy and history which has a connection to the general area of
  Brandenburg.*

- BUNDESLAND Mailing List
  http://www.rootsweb.com/~jfuller/gen_mail_country-
  ger.html#BUNDESLAND
  *For those trying to find their German roots and interested in
  German history.*

- CHARLEMAGNE Mailing List
  http://www.rootsweb.com/~jfuller/gen_mail_country-
  ger.html#CHARLEMAGNE
  *For anyone researching the genealogy of Charlemagne, also called
  Charles the Great (742-814), and the history of that time period.*

- DEU-BALTISCHE Mailing List
  http://www.rootsweb.com/~jfuller/gen_mail_country-
  ger.html#DEU-BALTISCHE
  *For anyone who is interested in Deutsch-Baltische (Baltic German)
  genealogy.*

- DEU-BAYERN Mailing List
  http://www.rootsweb.com/~jfuller/gen_mail_country-
  ger.html#DEU-BAYERN
  *Focused on helping Bavarian researchers in determining the
  geographic locations of their ancestors.*

- DEU-BERLIN Mailing List
  http://www.rootsweb.com/~jfuller/gen_mail_country-
  ger.html#DEU-BERLIN
  *For anyone with a genealogical interest in the City of Berlin,
  Germany.*

- DEU-CATHOLICFRANCONIA Mailing List
  http://www.rootsweb.com/~jfuller/gen_mail_country-
  ger.html#DEU-CATHOLICFRANCONIA
  *For anyone with a genealogical interest in the catholic parts of
  Franconia, Germany.*

- deu-gene Mailing List
  http://www.rootsweb.com/~jfuller/gen_mail_country-
  ger.html#deu-gene

- DEU-LADBERGEN Mailing List
  http://www.rootsweb.com/~jfuller/gen_mail_country-
  ger.html#DEU-LADBERGEN
  *For anyone conducting genealogical research centered in the town
  of Ladbergen, Kreis Steinfurt, Westphalia, Germany.*

- DEU-NAHAUSEN Mailing List
  http://www.rootsweb.com/~jfuller/gen_mail_country-
  ger.html#DEU-NAHAUSEN
  *For the discussion and sharing of information regarding the
  ancestors and descendants of the residents of Nahausen,
  Brandenburg, Germany.*

- DEU-POMMERN-GREIFENHAGEN Mailing List
  http://www.rootsweb.com/~jfuller/gen_mail_country-
  ger.html#DEU-POMMERN-GREIFENHAGEN
  *For anyone with a genealogical interest in the area of Kreis
  Greifenhagen, Pommern, Germany.*

- DEU-SAUERLAND Mailing List
  http://www.rootsweb.com/~jfuller/gen_mail_country-
  ger.html#DEU-SAUERLAND
  *For anyone with a genealogical interest in the Sauerland area of
  Germany, especially the former "Herzogtum Westfalen".*

- DEU-SCHONAU Mailing List
  http://www.rootsweb.com/~jfuller/gen_mail_country-
  ger.html#DEU-SCHONAU
  *For anyone with a genealogical interest in families from the town of
  Schönau, Germany.*

- DEU-THUERINGEN Mailing List
  http://www.rootsweb.com/~jfuller/gen_mail_country-
  ger.html#DEU-THUERINGEN
  For anyone with a genealogical interest in Thueringen, Germany.

- DEUTSCHLAND Mailing List
  http://www.rootsweb.com/~jfuller/gen_mail_country-
  ger.html#DEUTSCHLAND
  *For anyone with a genealogical interest in Germany and other
  German-speaking areas. The language for the list is strictly
  German.*

- ELBING Mailing List
  http://www.rootsweb.com/~jfuller/gen_mail_country-
  ger.html#ELBING
  *For the discussion of history and genealogy concerning the former
  German and West Prussian city of Elbing, today's Elblag in Poland.*

- **Exulanten-L Mailing List**
  http://www.rootsweb.com/~autwgw/agsfrx.htm
  Exulanten is the name given to the Protestants that were forced out Austria (estimated as many as 100,000) during 16th to 18th century. The largest wave of about 22,000 left the Salzburg area in 1731/32. Most went to East Prussia (Germany - Poland, Lithuania and Latvia) but some went to Siebenbürgen and Banat (today's Romania), Hungary and to parts of today's Slovakia.

- **FamNord Mailing List**
  http://www.rootsweb.com/~jfuller/gen_mail_country-ger.html#FamNord
  For those genealogists who have ancestors in Northern Germany.

- **FRANKEN-L Mailing List**
  http://www.rootsweb.com/~jfuller/gen_mail_country-ger.html#FRANKEN-L
  For those interested in sharing and exchanging information on genealogy and history which has a connection to the area of the three sections of northern Bavaria called Oberfranken, Mittelfranken and Unterfranken.

- **fido.ger.genealogy Newsgroup**
  news:fido.ger.genealogy

- **GEN-DE Mailing List**
  http://www.rootsweb.com/~jfuller/gen_mail_country-ger.html#GEN-DE-L
  Gatewayed with the soc.genealogy.german newsgroup
  news:soc.genealogy.german

- **GERMAN-AMERICAN Mailing List**
  http://www.rootsweb.com/~jfuller/gen_mail_states-gen.html#GERMAN-AMERICAN
  For genealogy related to German immigrants and their families AFTER their arrival in America.

- **GERMAN-BOHEMIAN-L Mailing List**
  http://www.rootsweb.com/~jfuller/gen_mail_country-ger.html#GERMAN-BOHEMIAN-L
  About the culture, genealogy and heritage of the German-speaking people of Bohemia and Moravia, now the Czech Republic.

- **GermanGen Mailing List**
  http://www.rootsweb.com/~jfuller/gen_mail_country-ger.html#GermanGen
  For anyone who is researching their German ancestry.

- **GERMANNA_COLONIES Mailing List**
  http://www.rootsweb.com/~jfuller/gen_mail_states-va.html#GERMAN_COLONIES
  For descendants of the Germanna Colonies (i.e., the original German settlements in Virginia under Governor Spotswood; there were three colonies established, the first being in 1714).

- **GERMAN-KINGDOMS Mailing List**
  http://www.rootsweb.com/~jfuller/gen_mail_country-ger.html#GERMAN-KINGDOMS
  For anyone with a genealogical interest in the Duchies of Thuringen (Thuringia) including Reuss altere Linie, Reuss jungere Linie, Saxe-Altenburg (Sachsen-Altenburg), Saxe-Coburg-Gotha (Sachsen-Koburg-Cotha), Saxe-Meiningen (Sachsen-Meiningen), Saxe-Weimar-Eisenach (Sachsen-Weimar-Eisenach), Schwarzburg-Rudolstadt, Schwarzburg-Sondershausen, Anhalt, and Schaumberg-

Lippe; Braunschweig (Brunswick); Lippe (aka: Lippe-Detmold); Oldenburg; Waldeck; Mecklenburg-Schwerin; and Mecklenburg-Strelitz.

- **GERMAN-TEXAN Mailing List**
  http://www.rootsweb.com/~jfuller/gen_mail_states-tx.html#GERMAN-TEXAN
  For anyone with a genealogical interest in German and Central European immigrants to Texas, especially Germans in the 19th century.

- **GERSIG Mailing List**
  http://www.rootsweb.com/~jfuller/gen_mail_country-ger.html#GERSIG
  A regional special interest group (SIG) mailing list that focuses on Jewish genealogy in German-speaking regions (e.g., Germany, Austria, parts of Switzerland, Alsace, Lorraine, Bohemia, Moravia).

- **HANNOVER-L Mailing List**
  http://www.rootsweb.com/~jfuller/gen_mail_country-ger.html#HANNOVER-L
  Genealogy and history which has a connection to the former Kingdom of Hannover.

- **HESSE Mailing List**
  http://www.rootsweb.com/~jfuller/gen_mail_country-ger.html#GER-HESSEN
  For the kingdoms, principalities, provinces, and state of Hessen (Hesse-Darmstadt, Hesse-Starkenburg, Hesse-Nassau, Waldeck, Rheinhessen) including the city of Frankfurt-A/Main.

- **HESSENLAND Mailing List**
  http://www.rootsweb.com/~jfuller/gen_mail_country-ger.html#HESSENLAND
  Eine Mail Liste fuer deutschsprechende Familienforscher und Historiker fuer die Gegend die man heute mit Hessen bezeichnet. A mailing list for anyone with a genealogical or historical interest in the area known as Hessen in central Germany. The language for the list is German.

- **IRL-PALATINE Mailing List**
  http://www.rootsweb.com/~jfuller/gen_mail_country-ire.html#IRL-PALATINE
  For anyone with a genealogical interest in the German Palatine immigrants to Ireland.

- **KRUMMHORN Mailing List**
  http://www.rootsweb.com/~jfuller/gen_mail_country-ger.html#KRUMMHORN
  For anyone with a genealogical interest in the Krummhorn area of Ostfriesland, Germany.

- **MECKLENBURG-L Mailing List**
  http://www.rootsweb.com/~jfuller/gen_mail_country-ger.html#MECKLENBURG-L
  Genealogy and history which has a connection to the general area of Mecklenburg.

- **MORAVIA Mailing List**
  http://www.rootsweb.com/~jfuller/gen_mail_country-ger.html#MORAVIA
  For anyone with a genealogical interest in Moravia, now part of the Czech Republic.

- **NIEDERSACHSEN Mailing List**
  http://www.rootsweb.com/~jfuller/gen_mail_country-ger.html#NIEDERSACHSEN

- NORDRHEIN-WESTFALEN Mailing List
  http://www.rootsweb.com/~jfuller/gen_mail_country-
  ger.html#NORDRHEIN-WESTFALEN
  *For anyone with a genealogical interest in the state of Nordrhein-
  Westfalen, Germany.*

- OLDENBURG-L Mailing List
  http://www.rootsweb.com/~jfuller/gen_mail_country-
  ger.html#OLDENBURG-L
  *For those interested in sharing and exchanging information on
  genealogy and history which has a connection to the former Grand
  Duchy of Oldenburg.*

- OSTFRIESEN Mailing List
  http://www.rootsweb.com/~jfuller/gen_mail_country-
  ger.html#OSTFRIESEN
  And the Ostfriesen E-Mail Discussion List Web Page
  http://www.summitsoftware.com/pwa/ostfries2.htm
  *For anyone with a genealogical, cultural or historical interest in
  Ostfriesland (East Friesia), Germany.*

- OW-PREUSSEN-L Mailing List
  http://www.rootsweb.com/~jfuller/gen_mail_country-
  ger.html#OW-PREUSSEN-L
  *Genealogy and history which has a connection to the former East
  and West Prussia.*

- PFALZ Mailing List
  http://www.rootsweb.com/~jfuller/gen_mail_country-
  ger.html#PFALZ
  *For anyone with a genealogical interest in the Palatine of Germany
  (area now divided between Saarland, Rheinland-Pfalz and Hessen,
  formerly Bavaria's Rhenish Pfalz).*

- PolandBorderSurnames Mailing List
  http://www.rootsweb.com/~jfuller/gen_mail_country-
  ger.html#PolandBorderSurnames
  *A mailing list of surnames for anyone researching genealogy in the
  former historical borders of Poland including Estonia, Latvia,
  Lithuania, Belarus, Ukraine, Moldova, Slovakia, Czech Republic,
  Moravia, Hungary, Russia, the Balkans, and East Prussia.*

- POMMERN-L Mailing List
  http://www.rootsweb.com/~jfuller/gen_mail_country-
  ger.html#POMMERN-L
  *Genealogy and history which has a connection to Pommerania, both
  the current Polish part and remaining German parts of the former
  Prussian province.*

- POSEN Mailing List
  http://www.rootsweb.com/~jfuller/gen_mail_country-
  ger.html#POSEN
  *For anyone with a genealogical interest in the former Prussian
  province of Posen/Poznan and its adjoining areas (especially
  Silesia), Germany.*

- PreussenAmericans Mailing List
  http://www.rootsweb.com/~jfuller/gen_mail_country-
  ger.html#PreussenAmericans
  *For anyone with a genealogical interest in Prussian immigrants to
  America.*

- PRUSSIA-ROOTS Mailing List
  http://www.rootsweb.com/~jfuller/gen_mail_country-
  ger.html#PRUSSIA-ROOTS
  *For anyone with a genealogical interest in Brandenburg, Hannover
  (or Hanover), Ostpreussen (East Prussia), Pommern (Pomerania),*

Posen, *Provinz Sachsen (Province of Saxony - northern Saxony),
Schleswig-Holstein, Schlesien (Silesia), Westpreussen (West
Prussia), Lubeck, Hamburg, and Bremen.*

- SACHSEN-ANHALT-L Mailing List
  http://www.rootsweb.com/~jfuller/gen_mail_country-
  ger.html#SACHSEN-ANHALT-L
  *Genealogy and history which has a connection to the present area of
  the state of Sachsen-Anhalt.*

- SCHLESIEN-L Mailing List
  http://www.rootsweb.com/~jfuller/gen_mail_country-
  pol.html#SCHLESIEN-L
  *For those with a genealogical interest in the former Prussian
  province of Schlesien (Silesia), which is now mostly in Poland.*

- SCHLESWIG-HOLSTEIN-ROOTS Mailing List
  http://www.rootsweb.com/~jfuller/gen_mail_country-
  ger.html#SCHLESWIG-HOLSTEIN-ROOTS
  *For anyone with a genealogical interest in the German
  province/state of Schleswig-Holstein.*

- SURNAMES-GERMAN Mailing List
  http://www.rootsweb.com/~jfuller/gen_mail_country-
  ger.html#SURNAMES-GERMAN
  Gatewayed with the soc.genealogy.surnames.german
  newsgroup
  news:soc.genealogy.surnames.german
  For surname queries related to German speaking countries.

- TRIER-ROOTS Mailing List
  http://www.rootsweb.com/~jfuller/gen_mail_country-
  ger.html#GER-TRIER-ROOTS
  *For anyone with a genealogical interest in Luxembourg, the
  Saarland, the Rheinland, Westfalen (Westphalia), and the Pfalz
  (used to be between Rheinland and Baden, belonged to Bavaria but
  is now part of Rheinpfalz).*

- Usenet Newsgroup soc.genealogy.german
  news:soc.genealogy.german
  Gatewayed with GEN-DE Mailing List
  http://www.rootsweb.com/~jfuller/gen_mail_country-
  ger.html#GEN-DE-L

- WESTFALEN-L Mailing List
  http://www.rootsweb.com/~jfuller/gen_mail_country-
  ger.html#WESTFALEN-L
  *Genealogy and history which has a connection to the general area
  of Westphalia.*

◆ Maps, Gazetteers & Geographical Information

- Atlas des Deutschen Reichs
  http://www.library.wisc.edu/etext/ravenstein/
  *This 1883 atlas of the German empire includes maps of the
  bordering portions of present-day Austria, Belgium, the Czech
  Republic, Denmark, France, Hungary, Lithuania, Luxembourg, the
  Netherlands, Poland, the Russian Federation, Slovakia, and
  Switzerland. Maps are large scale (1:850,000). Includes a thorough
  gazetteer of place-names. Requires the free Adobe Acrobat reader
  for viewing.*

- Deutschland um 1378 / Germany in 1378
  http://www8.informatik.uni-erlangen.de/html/wwp/
  deutschland1378.html

- Deutschland um 1547 / Germany in 1547
  http://www8.informatik.uni-erlangen.de/html/wwp/deutschland1547.html

- Deutschland um 1648 / Germany in 1648
  http://www8.informatik.uni-erlangen.de/html/wwp/deutschland1648.html

- Falk Online
  http://www.falk-online.de/
  Online maps of major German cities, trip planning, and atlas.

- Genealogy Unlimited - Maps and Atlases from Europe
  http://www.genealogyunlimited.com/
  Maps and atlases from Poland, Prussia, and Germany.

- GEOserv - a German town locator
  http://www2.genealogy.net/gene/www/abt/geoserv.html

- Germany Maps - The Perry-Castañeda Library Map Collection
  http://www.lib.utexas.edu/Libs/PCL/Map_collection/germany.html
  From the University of Texas at Austin.

  o Ancient Germania
    http://www.lib.utexas.edu/Libs/PCL/Map_collection/historical/Ancient_Germania.jpg

  o Germany
    http://www.lib.utexas.edu/Libs/PCL/Map_collection/europe/Germany.jpg

  o Munich 1858
    http://www.lib.utexas.edu/Libs/PCL/Map_collection/historical/Munich_1858.jpg

  o Nuremberg 1858
    http://www.lib.utexas.edu/Libs/PCL/Map_collection/historical/Nuremberg_1858.jpg

- Map List
  http://www.rootsweb.com/~wggerman/map/index.htm
  For Germany from WorldGenWeb.

  o The German Confederation 1815-1871
    http://www.rootsweb.com/~wggerman/map/germanconf.htm

- How to Use the Meyers Gazetteer
  http://www.familysearch.org/rg/guide/GER_T4_-_HowtoUsetheMeyersGazetteer.ASP

- Map of Baden
  http://www.generationspress.com/samples/baden.jpg

- Meyers Orts- und Verkehrs-Lexikon des Deutschen Reichs
  http://www.amazon.com/exec/obidos/ISBN=0806316314/markcyndisgenealA/
  A book by Raymond Wright III.

◆ People & Families

Individual personal home pages previously listed here can now be found alphabetically under the Personal Home Pages category:
http://www.CyndisList.com/personal.htm
Or under the Surnames category:
http://www.CyndisList.com/surnames.htm

- Carpathian German Homepage
  http://ourworld.cs.com/ycrtmr/
  History, culture and news of Carpathian Germans (Germans from Slovakia), with links to genealogical sites, museums, archives etc.

- Emigrants from Reimsbach to America, 1849-1889
  http://home.t-online.de/home/0683291349-0001/auswande.htm
  In the years 1846 to 1889, 106 people emigrated from Reimsbach village in the southwest of Germany, which at that time had about 600 inhabitants.

- German Ancestors up to the Middle Ages
  http://www.worldroots.com/ged/max/
  11,000 individuals, 3,400 surnames from all over Germany. Some lines reaching far into the Middle Ages and beyond. Main families: Amburger, Bartholomé, Bertheau, Boehtlingk, Brückner, Disselhoff, Fliedner, Gschneidinger, Jeiter, Krauße, Krönlein, Müller, Palmer, Schiele, Wagner.

- Links to Germany Royal & Nobility Genealogy Data
  http://worldroots.clicktron.com/brigitte/royal/royal.htm

- Mennonites
  http://www.CyndisList.com/menno.htm
  See This Category On Cyndi's List For Related Links.

- Pommerscher Verein Freistadt
  http://www.execpc.com/~pommern/
  This Site Features Descendants Of Immigrants From The State Of Pommern, Prussia Prior To 1945. It Also Includes A Database Of About 70,000 Names.

- WW-Person
  http://www8.informatik.uni-erlangen.de/html/ww-person.html
  A Database Of Persons Of German Nobility.

◆ Professional Researchers, Volunteers & Other Research Services

- Arno Schmitt, Journalist from San Diego, California
  mailto:reporter@adnc.com
  He can help to find relatives, links or sources regarding ancestors by placing articles in German, Austrian and/or Swiss newspapers. For details, e-mail Arno at: reporter@adnc.com.

- Busia's Roots - Professional Genealogy for Poland and Germany
  http://www.genealogypro.com/busias-roots.html
  Professional genealogy research, specializing in U.S. urban, Polish and German research.

- Catherine NOTH - Genealogical Consulting & Research in Alsace and Palatinate
  http://perso.club-internet.fr/noth/
  Conseil et recherches généalogiques en Alsace et au Palatinat - Genealogical Consulting & Researches in Alsace and Palatinate - Paris (F) - Strasbourg (F) - Speyer (D).

- European Focus
  http://www.eurofocus.com/
  Photographic portfolios of ancestral towns in Europe created for Genealogy enthusiasts in Belgium, Denmark, Eastern Europe, England, France, Germany, Great Britain, Italy, Netherlands, Norway, Poland, Sweden, Switzerland and more.

- Genealogy Helplist - Germany
  http://helplist.org/deu/index.shtml

- genealogyPro - Professional Genealogists for Germany
  http://genealogyPro.com/directories/Germany.html

- German Genealogical Research Service
  http://www.ggrs.com/
  Professional genealogical research in Germany, especially in South Germany (Bayern, Baden, Württemberg, Hessen). Emigration and surname databases that will be built up regularly.

- German Translation Service Old Script
  http://www.win.bright.net/~jakeschu/welcome.html

- IHFF Genealogie Gesellschaft mbH
  http://www.netway.at/ihff/index.htm
  Professional Researcher specializing in: Austria, Czech & Slovak Republics, Hungary, Slovenian Republic, Croatia, Galicia, others.

- Mark Windover's Web Page - Quality Professional Genealogical Research ~ Williamstown, Massachusetts
  http://www.windover.com/
  United States, Canada (including French), England, Scotland, Ireland, Wales, Iceland, Germany, Switzerland, Norway, Sweden, Denmark, France, Belgium, and The Netherlands.

- The Ortenburger and Hackstock Family Home Page
  http://home.earthlink.net/~rortenburger/index.htm
  German and United States family history research performed by Rick Ortenburger.

- Ostpreussen, Ermland Family Roots
  http://www.nex.net.au/users/carlnpat/Ermland.html
  A genealogy site devoted to Ermland, East Prussian descendants, primarily the search for the ancestors from the area around Heilsberg and surrounding areas within Ermland. Site includes links and e-mail address's to other Ermland researchers.

- Richard M. Pope, Certified Genealogist
  http://w3.nai.net/~absuax/
  Specializing in Connecticut, Massachusetts, New York City, Germany.

- Schröeder & Fülling GbR, German Genealogy Research Firm
  http://ourworld.compuserve.com/homepages/German_Genealogy/homepage.htm

◆ Publications, Software & Supplies

- Amazon.com Genealogy Bookstore - Germany
  http://www.amazon.com/exec/obidos/external-search/?keyword=german+genealogy&tag=markcyndisgenealA/

- AudioTapes.com - Genealogical Lectures on Cassette Tapes - German
  http://www.audiotapes.com/search2.asp?Search=German

- Books We Own - Germany
  http://www.rootsweb.com/~bwo/germany.html
  Find a book from which you would like a lookup and click on the

submitter's code at the end of the entry. Once you find the contact information for the submitter, write them a polite request for a lookup.

- Brother's Keeper Software
  http://ourworld.compuserve.com/homepages/Brothers_Keeper/
  Downloadable shareware program for Windows. The latest version contains English, French, Norwegian, Danish, Swedish, German, Dutch, Polish, Icelandic, Russian, Slovak, Afrikaans, Czech.

- DYNAS-TREE ~ Win95 or NT
  http://www.dynas-tree.de/
  German or English.

- Frontier Press Bookstore - Germany
  http://www.frontierpress.com/frontier.cgi?category=ger

- GenealogyBookShop.com - Germany/German
  http://www.genealogybookshop.com/genealogybookshop/files/The_World,Germany_German/index.html
  The online store of Genealogical Publishing Co., Inc. & Clearfield Company.

- Genealogy Unlimited - Home Page
  http://www.itsnet.com:80/home/genun/public_html/
  Maps, books & supplies for sale.

- Genius Family Tree Program
  http://www.mediabase.fi/suku/genupgb.htm
  An easy to use Windows based Family Tree record keeper.

- GENTREE 99
  http://perso.wanadoo.fr/gentree/
  Genealogy shareware for Windows9x. French, English, German, Italian, Catalan versions.

- Heritage Books - German
  http://www.heritagebooks.com/german.htm

- Interlink Bookshop Genealogical Services ~ Victoria, B.C., Canada
  http://www.interlinkbookshop.com/

- Picton Press - German-Speaking
  http://www.pictonpress.com/cgi-bin/oc/picton/index?M4gzEpF4;parent_id=9;14

- PRO-GEN Genealogie àla Carte
  http://www.pro-gen.nl/
  Dutch genealogy program capable of outputs in Dutch, English, French, Frisian and German.

- Stammbaum 4.0 in Stichworten
  http://www3.pair.com/hblanken/stb.htm
  Genealogy software for Windows.

- STAMMBAUM: The Journal of German-Jewish Genealogical Research
  http://www.jewishgen.org/stammbaum/

- Wandering Volhynians
  http://pixel.cs.vt.edu/pub/sources/wv.txt
  A Magazine for the Descendants of Germans From Volhynia and Poland.

- Willow Bend Bookstore - Germans and Germany
  http://www.willowbend.net/default.asp

- The Wind-Mill: A Periodical of Frisian/Germanic Heritage
http://members.aol.com/gowindmill/index.html

- WinFamily - Anvend Winfamily fra Jamodat til din slektsgransking
http://www.winfamily.com/
Genealogy software available in Danish, Swedish, Norwegian, French, German and English.

◆ Queries, Message Boards & Surname Lists

- Mecklenburg-Vorpommern Query System
http://pages.prodigy.net/jhbowen/c3.htm

- Niedersachsen Germany Queries
http://cgi.rootsweb.com/~genbbs/genbbs.cgi/Germany/Niedersachsen

- Nordrhein-Westfalen GermanyGenWeb - Index to Surnames, Queries, Researchers and Databases
http://www.rootsweb.com/~deunrhwf/cc/qryindex.htm

- Schleswig-Holstein Bundeslander Germany Queries
http://cgi.rootsweb.com/~genbbs/genbbs.cgi/Germany/Schleswig-Holstein

- Search Genealogy Queries at German Migration Resource Center
http://www.germanmigration.com/queries/searchgerman.asp
Search more than 42,000 names, which refer to German migration throughout the world, any time period. Search Queries by surname, ship name, immigration year, places of origin or destination.

◆ Records: Census, Cemeteries, Land, Obituaries, Personal, Taxes and Vital (Born, Married, Died & Buried)

- Ahnenpässe und Archive
http://www.s-direktnet.de/homepages/pgleichmar/aua.html

- Baden, Germany Emigration Index, 1866-1911
http://www.ancestry.com/search/rectype/inddbs/4610.htm
Pay-for-use database containing the names of over 28,000 persons who left Baden between 1866 and 1911. Each entry includes the emigrant's name, residence or place of birth, and the year of departure.

- Brandenburg, Prussia Emigration Records
http://www.ancestry.com/search/rectype/inddbs/4121.htm
Pay-for-use database containing 17,500 names of emigrants leaving Brandenburg. Each record provides the emigrant's name, age, occupation, residence, destination and year of emigration.

- Deutsche Auswanderer-Datenbank / German Immigration Database
http://www.deutsche-auswanderer-datenbank.de/enframeset.htm
From the Historisches Museum Bremerhaven. Intends to provide a searchable database of all European emigrants who emigrated to North America from German ports between 1820 and 1939. Sources are passenger lists. Current database may be searched at the museum in Bremerhaven or by mail for a fee.

- Fraktur, Geburts, and Taufscheins
Decorative writings used to commemorate events such as births by the Pennsylvania Dutch. For genealogists, these examples of folk art can be used as alternatives to official birth records. Fraktur is the writing style, Geburts are birthday certificates, and Taufscheins are baptism certificates. They are generically referred to as fraktur.

  o 19th Century Fraktur In Lancaster
http://www-060.connix.com/aweb/archive/fraklead.htm
Article about an exhibit of Fraktur at the Heritage Center Museum of Lancaster County, Pennsylvania.

  o Dietrich Taufschein 1839
http://home.att.net/~long.hair/gallery/dietrich1839.html

  o Fraktur
http://www.mhsc.ca/encyclopedia/contents/F6741ME.html
From the Canadian Mennonite Encyclopedia Online.

  o Fraktur
http://www.region.waterloo.on.ca/Jsh2/Fraktur/Frakframeset.htm
From the Joseph Schneider Haus Collections. Waterloo, Ontario.

    • Fraktur History
http://www.region.waterloo.on.ca/Jsh2/Fraktur/FHistory.htm

  o Fraktur Fanatic
http://www.geocities.com/Paris/2137/folkart.html
Web site dedicated to Fraktur.

  o Fraktur: Folk Art and Family
http://www.thebee.com/aweb/archive/frak.htm
Article on the history of Fraktur.

  o Fraktur: Folk Art and Family
http://www.amazon.com/exec/obidos/ISBN=076430920X/markcyndisgenealA/
A book by Corinne P. Earnest.

  o Fraktur: Folk Art and Family
http://www.amazon.com/exec/obidos/ISBN=076430920X/markcyndisgenealA/
A book by Corinne P. Earnest.

  o Frakturschriften (1762 - 1878) of the German-American Imprint Collection
http://www.library.fandm.edu/archives/fraktur/fraktur.html
From the Franklin & Marshall College Archives and Special Collections.

  o Frakturs sent to the Federal Government as support for Pension and Bounty-Land Applications
http://www.nara.gov/cgi-bin/starfinder/0?path=images.txt&id=demo&pass=&OK=OK
Enter "NWCTB-15-NM22E19" in the first keyword box From the National Archives and Records Administration's NAIL Digital Copies database, there are 166 documents from the case files of Pension and Bounty-Land Warrants based on Revolutionary War Service. These frakturs are they are beautifully scanned examples and show that our ancestors also appreciated their genealogical value.

  o German-American Family Records in the Fraktur Tradition : Unpublished Birth and Baptism Certificates and Bible Records Volume 1
http://www.amazon.com/exec/obidos/ISBN=1879311038/markcyndisgenealA/
A book by Beverly R. Hoch.

o German-American Family Records in the Fraktur Tradition Volume 2
http://www.amazon.com/exec/obidos/ISBN=1879311062/markcyndisgenealA/
A book by Corinne P. Earnest.

o German American Family Records in the Fraktur Tradition Volume 3
http://www.amazon.com/exec/obidos/ISBN=1879311070/markcyndisgenealA/
A book by Russell D. Earnest.

o Genealogist Guide to Fraktur for Genealogical Research
http://www.amazon.com/exec/obidos/ISBN=1879311003/markcyndisgenealA/
A book by Russell D. Earnest.

o German-American Fraktur Birth and Baptism Certificates: Often Overlooked Primary Sources for Genealogists
http://www.audiotapes.com/product.asp?ProductCode='BM-72'
Presentation by Corrine Pattie Earnest, available for sale on audio tape.

o The Gift Is Small the Love Is Great: Pennsylvania German Small Presentation Fraktur
http://www.midcoast.com/~picton/public_html.BASK/catalog/books/1620.htm
A book from Picton Press.

o Gottschall Fraktur Sells for $101,000
http://www.maineantiquedigest.com/articles/gott0796.htm
News item regarding the collectability of Fraktur.

o Major Fraktur Discovery
http://www.maineantiquedigest.com/articles/fra1097.htm
From the Maine Antique Digest.

o Nagel Taufschein 1807
http://home.att.net/~long.hair/gallery/nagel1807.html

o Ontario Fraktur
http://www.amazon.com/exec/obidos/ISBN=0919880088/markcyndisgenealA/

o Pennsylvania Dutch Fraktur Gallery
http://home.att.net/~fraktur/
Exquisite fraktur images. These historic images clearly show the artistic and genealogical value of fraktur..

o Pennsylvania Dutch Frequently Asked Questions (FAQs) - Fraktur
http://midatlantic.rootsweb.com/padutch/faqs/fraktur.html

o The Pennsylvania Historical and Museum Commission - Publications Catalog for Arts & Decorative Arts
http://www.state.pa.us/PA_Exec/Historical_Museum/DPS/pub/catalog/Arts.htm
Several books on Fraktur available from the PHMC.

o A Taufschein (baptismal certificate) from 1807
http://lcweb.loc.gov/exhibits/religion/00261us.jpg
From the Library of Congress.

• "Friedrich der Grosse" Ship Passenger List, Germany to America
http://pw2.netcom.com/~steventw/passlist.html
An original ship passenger list of the March 19, 1898 sailing of the Friedrich der Grosse from Bremen, Germany, to New York.

• Hamburg Link To Your Roots
http://www.hamburg.de/LinkToYourRoots/english/start.htm
Searchable database extracted from the Hamburg Passenger Lists for selected years.

o Emigration Port Hamburg
http://www.hamburg.de/Behoerden/Pressestelle/emigration/englisch/welcome.htm
Excellent online presentation of why Hamburg was a major port of departure for immigrants, how the were treated, what they faced, and how the process of departure worked.

• Historische Friedhöfe in Berlin / Historic Cemeteries in Berlin
http://www.zlb.de/projekte/friedhof/index.html

• Index To Palatine Passenger Lists
http://www.rootsweb.com/~ote/palalist.htm

• Jewish Cemeteries ~ Hamburg, Germany
http://www.rrz.uni-hamburg.de/rz3a035/jew_cem.html

• Marriages in Plauschwarren, East Prussia 1778-1802
http://www.mmhs.org/prussia/plauschm.htm

• Mecklenburg-Schwerin Census Records
http://pages.prodigy.net/jhbowen/census.htm

• Names of Mecklenburg-Schwerin Emigrants 1844-1915
http://pages.prodigy.net/jhbowen/emig.htm

• Search Weil im Schoenbuch Marriages ~ Württemberg, Germany
http://www.kinquest.com/genealogy/databases/marriages.html

• Suchdienste in Deutschland / Tracing Services in Germany
http://www.com-de.pair.com/wast/suchsite.htm
Information and links to tracing services for locating German war dead.

• Volksbund Deutsche Kriegsgräberfürsorge e.V.
http://www.volksbund.de/homepage.htm
The German Military Grave Registration Service. Maintains 2 million war graves in over 640 cemeteries. Assists in grave identification and restoration. Provides assistance in determining the fate of German war dead.

o Vermissten und Toten Datenbank
http://www.volksbund.de/VuTDB/vut_suche.asp
The Missing and Dead Database. Online searchable database of over 2 million interments.

• Wuerttemberg Emigration Index
http://www.ancestry.com/search/rectype/inddbs/3141a.htm
Pay-for-use database contains the names of approximately 60,000 persons who made application to emigrate at Wuerttemberg from

the late eighteenth century to 1900. The information supplied on each person includes: name, date and place of birth, residence at time of application and application date, and microfilm number.

◆ Religion

- Evangelische Kirche in Deutschland
  http://www.ekd.de/ekd/welcome.html

- Evangelisches Zentral-Archiv in Berlin
  http://www.ezab.de/
  Archiv der Evangelischen Kirche in Deutschland und der Evangelischen Kirche der Union.

  o Practical Information and Addresses for Genealogical Research
  http://www.ezab.de/eza10e.html

- Kirchliche Archive im Internet / Church Archives on the Internet
  http://www.uni-marburg.de/archivschule/deuarch3.html

◆ Societies & Groups

- American/Schleswig-Holstein Heritage Society
  http://www.trail.com/~biehl/

- Anglo-German Family History Society - AG-FHS ~ United Kingdom
  http://feefhs.org/uk/frgagfhs.html

- Arbeitsgemeinschaft für mitteldeutsche Familienforschung e.V.
  http://www2.genealogy.net/gene/vereine/AMF/AMF.html

- Arbeitsgemeinschaft ostdeutscher Familienforscher e. V.
  http://www2.genealogy.net/gene/vereine/AGoFF/AGoFF-d.html

- Die Maus e. V. - Gesellschaft fuer Familienforschung in Bremen
  http://www.genealogy.net/vereine/maus
  Die Maus e. V. - Family History and genealogical society of Bremen.

- Düsseldorfer Verein für Familienkunde e.V. / Duesseldorf Society for Family History
  http://members.aol.com/dvffgenea/
  Aktuelles aus dem Duesseldorfer Verein, Veranstaltungen, Ahnenlisten, Software, FOKO-Datenbank usw.; Activities of the society, ancestor-lists, software, FOKO-database etc.

- Emsland Heritage Society
  http://www.geocities.com/Heartland/4018/
  For ALL those interested in the genealogies and histories of the people and towns of the area of Germany-bordering Netherlands>upper north west>North sea>Ems Canal. Towns include: Papenburg, Sögel, Werlte, Hüven, Stavern, Lähn, Spelle and others.

- Genealogical Societies for Saxony - Regional and Local
  http://rosella.apana.org.au/~jgk/saxony/society.html

- Genealogische Vereine
  http://www2.genealogy.net/gene/vereine/
  Genealogy society home pages hosted by Genealogy.net.

- German-Bohemian Heritage Society ~ New Ulm, Minnesota
  http://www.rootsweb.com/~gbhs/

- German Society of Pennsylvania
  http://www.libertynet.org/gsp/
  And a description from GENCAP
  http://www.libertynet.org/gencap/

- Germanic Genealogy Society ~ Saint Paul, Minnesota
  http://www.mtn.org/mgs/branches/german.html

- The Irish Palatine Association
  http://www.local.ie/content/28303.shtml
  Online article from Irish Roots Magazine.

- Ostfriesen Genealogical Society of Minnesota - Genealogy for Ostfriesland, Germany
  http://www.rootsweb.com/~mnogsm/index.htm

- Pommerscher Verein Freistadt / Pomeranian Society of Freistadt ~ Germantown, Wisconsin
  http://www.execpc.com/%7Epommern/

- Sacramento German Genealogy Society ~ California
  http://www.sacgergensoc.org/

- Society for German Genealogy in Eastern Europe
  http://www.sggee.org/
  Devoted to the study of those people with German ancestry (generally of the Lutheran, Baptist, or Catholic faiths) who lived in present-day Poland (including those lands known previously as West and East Prussia, Posen, Silesia, and Pomerania), and also those people who lived in the western part of present-day Ukraine, in the old pre-World War II province of Volhynia (generally from the city of Kiev on the east to the present-day Polish border on the west, and from the city of Zhitomir on the south to the city of Kowel on the north).

- Verein für Familienforschung in Ost- und Westpreußen
  http://www.genealogy.net/gene/vereine/VFFOW/vffow.htm

- Verein für Familien- und Wappenkunde in Württemberg und Baden e.V.
  http://www2.genealogy.net/gene/vereine/VFWKWB/index.html

◆ WorldGenWeb

- Germany Genealogy
  http://www.rootsweb.com/~wggerman/

GREECE
http://www.cyndislist.com/greece.htm

Category Index:

- General Resource Sites
- History & Culture
- Libraries, Archives & Museums
- Mailing Lists, Newsgroups & Chat
- Maps, Gazetteers & Geographical Information
- Military
- People & Families

- Publications, Software & Supplies
- Queries, Message Boards & Surname Lists
- Records: Census, Cemeteries, Land, Obituaries, Personal, Taxes and Vital
- Religion & Churches
- Societies & Groups
- World GenWeb

◆ General Resource Sites

- FHW Projects: Genealogy Project
  http://www.fhw.org/fhw/en/projects/genealogy.html
  From the Foundation of the Hellenic World. The Genealogy Project aims at reconstructing the family trees of the Asia Minor refugees, Greek-Orthodox inhabitants of Asia Minor and Pontos (the Black Sea region) who were expelled from their homeland after the Asia Minor disaster in 1922, and took refuge in Greece. The family data to be collected will begin with the grandparents of each Asia Minor refugee, and follow into their posterity.

- GreekFamilies.com
  http://www.greekfamilies.com/
  Resource for Greek genealogy sites on the Internet.

- Greek Genealogy Articles and Online Tools for Family Research
  http://www.daddezio.com/grekgen.html
  From D'Addezio.com.

- Greek Legacy, Inc.
  http://www.greeklegacy.com/

- Greek Telephone Directories
  http://www.hellasyellow.gr/

- Hellenes-Diaspora Greek Genealogy
  http://hellenes-diaspora.nostos.gr/

- Hellenes-Diaspora Greek Genealogy Web Ring
  http://hellenes-diaspora.nostos.gr/webring.html

- Kypros - Lexicon: Greek-English-Greek Dictionary
  http://www.kypros.org/cgi-bin/lexicon

◆ History & Culture

- Encyclopedia Mythica: Genealogy tables
  http://www.pantheon.org/mythica/genealogy/

- Family Tree of Greek Mythology
  http://chaos1.hypermart.net/myth/ftgm.html

- GoGreece.com - Historical Settings
  http://www.gogreece.com/learn/history/

- GreekForum.com
  http://www.greekforum.com/

- Hellenic Electronic Center
  http://www.greece.org/

- History of the Greek Royal Family
  http://www.xs4all.nl/~ckersten/royal/greece/history.html

- StudyWeb: History: Country History Index: Europe Index: Greece
  http://www.studyweb.com/links/141.html

- Yahoo!...Greece...History
  http://dir.yahoo.com/Regional/Countries/Greece/Arts_and_Humanities/Humanities/History/

◆ Libraries, Archives & Museums

- Archives Department of The Greek Orthodox Archdiocese of America
  http://www.goarch.org/goa/departments/archives/
  The archives document the history, progress, and growth of the Church and its institutions, of the Greek-American community, and of numerous fraternal, social, cultural, and educational organizations.

- Family History Library Catalog
  http://www.familysearch.org/Search/searchcatalog.asp
  From the FamilySearch web site, an online catalog to the holdings of the LDS Church in Salt Lake City, Utah. Also search for other localities by place name.
  http://www.familysearch.org/fhlc/supermainframeset.asp?display=localitysearch&columns=*,180,0

  o Greece
    http://www.familysearch.org/fhlc/supermainframeset.asp?display=localitydetails&subject=150&subject_disp=Greece&columns=*,180,0

- HYTELNET - Library Catalogs: Greece
  http://www.lights.com/hytelnet/gr0/gr000.html
  Before you use any of the Telnet links, make note of the user name, password and any other logon information.

- The Library of N.H.R.F.
  http://www.eie.gr/Activities/library.htm
  National Hellenic Research Foundation.

- Repositories of Primary Sources - Europe
  http://www.uidaho.edu/special-collections/europe.html
  A list of links to online resources from the Univ. of Idaho Library, Special Collections and Archives

  o Greece
    http://www.uidaho.edu/special-collections/euro1.html#gr

- webCATS: Library Catalogues on the World Wide Web - Greece
  http://www.lights.com/webcats/countries/GR.html

◆ Mailing Lists, Newsgroups & Chat

- Genealogy Resources on the Internet - Greece Mailing Lists
  http://www.rootsweb.com/~jfuller/gen_mail_country-gre.html
  Most of the mailing list links below point to this site, wonderfully maintained by John Fuller

- Greek Mailing List Subscribe - Greek Adoptees, Greek Genealogy, Greek Culture
  http://hellenes-diaspora.nostos.gr/listsub.html

- GreekAdoptees Mailing List
  http://www.rootsweb.com/~jfuller/gen_mail_adoption.html#GreekAdoptees
  For all adoptees and birthparents of Hellenic heritage that would like help in searching for one another.

- GreekGen Mailing List
  http://www.rootsweb.com/~jfuller/gen_mail_country-gre.html#GreekGen
  A mailing list dedicated to discussions of Greek genealogy including Greek family heritage, customs, ancestral research, and culture.

- Hellenes-Diaspora Mailing List
  http://www.rootsweb.com/~jfuller/gen_mail_country-gre.html#Hellenes-Diaspora
  For anyone with an interest in Hellenes in the Diaspora. The list will address concerns regarding Hellenes finding long lost friends, family, or connections in Greece or elsewhere around the world and for research concerning their Hellenic family trees.

- KRIEKOUKIOTES-VILIOTES-DIASPORA Mailing List
  http://www.rootsweb.com/~jfuller/gen_mail_country-gre.html#KRIEKOUKIOTES-VILIOTES-DIASPORA
  For anyone with a genealogical or historical interest in Kriekouki (Erithres) and Vilia, Attica, Greece.

- Turkish_Jews Mailing List
  http://www.rootsweb.com/~jfuller/gen_mail_country-ser.html#Turkish_Jews
  For Sephardic Jewish genealogists with roots in the former Turkish Ottoman Empire including Turkey, Serbia, Greece, and Yugoslavia.

◆ Maps, Gazetteers & Geographical Information

- FEEFHS Map Room: The Balkans & SE Europe (1882): North Greece, Macedonia & Albania
  http://feefhs.org/maps/balk/ba-ngre.html

- FEEFHS Map Room: The Balkans and SE Europe (1882): South Greece excluding Crete
  http://feefhs.org/maps/balk/ba-sgre.html

- Greek Maps
  http://users.med.auth.gr/~tsikaras/maps/maps.htm
  Road maps from the Tsikaras Weather Page - Imia isles - Macedonia - Alexander - Makedonia - kardak.

- Lonely Planet - Greece Map
  http://www.lonelyplanet.com.au/dest/eur/graphics/map-gre.htm

- Perry-Castañeda Library Map Collection
  http://www.lib.utexas.edu/Libs/PCL/Map_collection/Map_collection.html
  At the University of Texas at Austin

  o Greece Maps
    http://www.lib.utexas.edu/Libs/PCL/Map_collection/greece.html

- Yahoo!...Greece...Geography
  http://dir.yahoo.com/Regional/Countries/Greece/Science/Geography/

◆ Military

- Ministry of National Defence, Greece
  http://www.mod.gr/
  Official web page of the Greek military.

◆ People & Families

- Dimitri's Greek Heritage Page
  http://www.dimitri.8m.com/greek.html

- Greek Born Adoptees Support
  http://hellenes-diaspora.nostos.gr/GreekAdoptees.html
  Search/Find, Registry, Translation and Cultural Support for Greek Family Reunions Worldwide.

- The Greek Royal Page
  http://www.xs4all.nl/~ckersten/royal/greece.html

- KOUKLAKIS / ANGAVANAKIS Family History
  http://members.aol.com/ctk99/kouklakis.html

- S.E.A.S.Y.P. Greek Adoptees Reunion Registry
  http://www.seasyp.gr

◆ Publications, Software & Supplies

- AudioTapes.com - Genealogical Lectures on Cassette Tapes – Greece
  http://www.audiotapes.com/search2.asp?Search=greece
  And Greek
  http://www.audiotapes.com/search2.asp?Search=greek

- Carved in Stone: The Greek Heritage
  http://www.amazon.com/exec/obidos/ISBN=0967059313/markcyndisgenealA/
  A book by Basil S. Douros.

- The Greek Americans (Immigrant Experience)
  http://www.amazon.com/exec/obidos/ISBN=0791033562/
  markcyndisgenealA/
  A book by Dimitris Monos.

- Greek Genealogy Publications
  http://feefhs.org/gr/pub-lhc.html
  From FEEFHS. Suggested publications for Greek research.

- The Greeks in Alberta 1903-1995
  http://www.firstwest.com/greekbook/
  A book by Nina Kolias.

- The Greeks in America
  http://www.amazon.com/exec/obidos/ISBN=0822510103/
  markcyndisgenealA/
  A book by Jayne Clark Jones.

- A History of the Greeks in the Americas 1453-1938
  http://www.amazon.com/exec/obidos/ISBN=1882792157/
  markcyndisgenealA/
  A book by Paul Koken.

◆ Queries, Message Boards & Surname Lists

- Dimitri's Surname Database
  http://www.dimitri.8m.com/surnames.html
  A database of Greek surnames and their ancestral origins.

- General Greece Queries Message Index
  http://cgi.rootsweb.com/~genbbs/genbbs.cgi/Greece/General
  From GreeceGenWeb and GenConnect at RootsWeb.

- Greece Research List -- GRRL on the FEEFHS Website
  http://feefhs.org/gr/grrl/grrl.html
  For ethnic Greeks and those researchers with ancestors that once lived in Greece.

- Greek Genealogy Surnames Database
  http://hellenes-diaspora.nostos.gr/greeksurnames.html
  From Hellenes-Diaspora Greek Genealogy.

◆ Records: Census, Cemeteries, Land, Obituaries, Personal, Taxes and Vital (Born, Married, Died & Buried)

- Jewish Cemetery of Rhodes
  http://www.rhodesjewishmuseum.org/cemetery.htm
  A listing of the 1,167 tombstones in the Jewish cemetery of Rhodes. Includes some photographs and translations of inscriptions.

◆ Religion & Churches

- Ecumenical Patriarchate of Constantinople
  http://www.patriarchate.org/
  The Ecumenical Patriarchate of Constantinople is the Mother Church of all the local autocephalous or autonomous Orthodox Churches who follow Orthodox faith and canonical order.

- Greek Orthodox Archdiocese of America
  http://www.goarch.org/

- The Jews of Greece
  http://www.bsz.org/agreekjew.htm
  Jews have left their imprint in Greece in many cities and towns over the 2,000 years of the community's history. The current centers of Greek Jewry are Athens (3,000) and Salonika (1,000), although the latter is only a remnant of the huge community that thrived in the city for some 500 years. Jews are also present in Corfu, Chalkis, Joannina, Larissa, Rhodes, Trikala, and Volos.

◆ Societies & Groups

- Council of Hellenes Abroad (SAE) - North & South America
  http://www.saeamerica.org/index.html

- Greek-American Folklore Society ~ Astoria, New York
  http://www.hri.org/GAFS/

- National Hellenic Research Foundation
  http://www.eie.gr/English.htm

- SIPEO - Greek Association of Family History and Tradition
  http://www.sipeo.org/

◆ World GenWeb

- WorldGenWeb
  http://www.worldgenweb.org/
  o MediterraneanGenWeb
    http://www.mediterraneangenweb.org/
    - GreeceGenWeb
      http://mediterraneangenweb.org/greece/

HANDWRITING & SCRIPT
http://www.cyndislist.com/handwrit.htm

Category Index:

◆ General Resource Sites

◆ Locality Specific

◆ Publications, Software & Supplies

◆ General Resource Sites

- Deciphering Old Handwriting
  http://www.firstct.com/fv/oldhand.html

- Examples of Letters of the 17th Century Found in Parish Registers
  http://www.rootsweb.com/~genepool/oldalpha.htm

- Handwriting. 16th and 17th Century English
  http://ourworld.compuserve.com/homepages/dave_tylcoat/handwrit.htm

- Historical Writing
  http://iwhome.com/spectrum/historicl.htm
  Specialized research on the interpretation of historical writing.

- Martha Ballard's Diary Online
  http://www.dohistory.org/diary/index.html
  The source for the book and film "A Midwife's Tale", Martha Ballard wrote in her diary nearly every day from January 1, 1785 to May 12, 1812 (27 years) for a total of almost 10,000 entries. Her diary is an unparalleled document in early American history. This online display of her diary provides some excellent interactive examples of the challenges of deciphering old handwriting.

  o Decoding the Diary
  http://www.dohistory.org/diary/exercises/decoding.html
  To decode Martha Ballard's diary, you will need to understand how she structured her pages, how she recorded the date, and how she used abbreviations and marginalia.

  o How to Read 18th Century British-American Writing
  http://www.dohistory.org/on_your_own/toolkit/writing.html
  Excellent online tutorial on the subject which includes images of primary sources as examples.

  o Magic Lens
  http://www.dohistory.org/diary/exercises/lens/index.html
  The interactive Java applet on this page shows you the original handwriting in Martha's diary and the correct translation of the same.

  o Reading Help for Documents at this Site
  http://www.dohistory.org/about/readinghelp.html
  Hints and tips for reading 18th Century documents.

  o Try Transcribing
  http://www.dohistory.org/diary/exercises/try Transcribing.html
  Practice at transcribing the handwritten words and sentences from Martha Ballard's diary. This interactive page gives you results of how well you did transcribing the handwriting.

- Medieval Paleography
  http://orb.rhodes.edu/textbooks/palindex.html
  An introductory online course to medieval handwriting.

- Methods of Abbreviation in English documents employing Latin
  http://www.bibliographics.com/PALAEOG-lite/HECTOR.htm

- Name and Word Spellings
  http://www.familytreemaker.com/00000015.html
  Includes a brief explanation of errors caused by handwriting.

- OLD-ENGLISH Mailing List
  http://www.rootsweb.com/~jfuller/gen_mail_general.html#OLD-ENGLISH
  For anyone who is deciphering old English documents to discuss interpretations of handwriting and word meanings.

- Old Handwriting Samples
  http://www.rootsweb.com/~ote/writing.htm

- Reading Census Handwriting
  http://www.sierra.com/sierrahome/familytree/hqarticles/censusreading/
  Online article by Leland K. Meitzler provides tips & tricks for deciphering the enumerator's chicken scratchings.

- Searching Old Records--Reading Old Handwriting and Looking for Names
  http://members.aol.com/AdamCo9991/genealogytips9.html

- Some Tips on Reading Old Handwriting
  http://www.sierra.com/sierrahome/familytree/hqarticles/handwriting/
  Online article by Robert Davis providing hints on how to decipher the poor penmanship of the past.

- Tutorials for Reading Old German, French and English Handwriting, Naming Systems
  http://www.disknet.com/indiana_biolab/eg502.htm

- The Written Cyrillic
  http://www.dnaco.net/~ivanjs/written.html
  Image of what the Cyrillic Alphabet looks like written compared to printed Cyrillic.

◆ Locality Specific

- Fraktur Deciphered
  http://www3.shore.net/~anderson/Fraktur.html

- Fraktur and German Script
  http://www.asherwin.com/fraktur%26script.html

- German Translation Service
  http://www.win.bright.net/~jakeschu/welcome.html
  Old Script

- Gotisk Skrift -- The Gothic Script
  http://www.netutah.com/akre/gothalf.htm
  Two alphabets of gothic script handwriting from Norway about 1875.

- Moravians - German Script Tutorial
  http://www.mun.ca/rels/morav/script.html
  With Moravian Archival examples

  o German Script Alphabet
    http://www.mun.ca/rels/morav/pics/tutor/mscript2.html

- Old German Handwritten Scripts
  http://www2.genealogy.net/gene/misc/scripts.html

◆ Publications, Software & Supplies

- Amazon.com Genealogy Bookstore - Handwriting
  http://www.amazon.com/exec/obidos/external-search/?
  keyword=handwriting+genealogy&tag=markcyndisgenealA/

- AudioTapes.com - Genealogical Lectures on Cassette Tapes - Handwriting
  http://www.audiotapes.com/search2.asp?Search=handwriting

- Deciphering Gothic Records
  http://www.futureone.com/~fdearden/page2.htm
  Pamphlet for sale.

- Scottish Handwriting 1500-1700
  http://www.nas.gov.uk/bookshop.htm#Scottish Handwriting 1500-1700:
  A book for sale from the National Archives of Scotland.

- Society of Genealogists Bookshop: Handwriting ~ U.K.
  http://www.sog.org.uk/acatalog/SoG_Bookshop_Online_Handwriting_42.html
  Publications for sale.

- Walden Font
  http://www.waldenfont.com/
  Several different fonts for sale, including: The Gutenberg Press German Fraktur Fonts and German Script.

HANDY ONLINE STARTING POINTS

http://www.cyndislist.com/handy.htm

Category Index:

◆ Genealogy Search Engines
◆ General Lists of Links

◆ Getting Started
◆ Locality & Ethnic Specific

◆ Genealogy Search Engines

● Cyndi's List - Search It!
http://www.CyndisList.com/searchit.htm
Enter a keyword: surname, place name, type of record, etc., then click the Find button.

● Amazon.com Genealogy Bookstore - Genealogy
http://www.amazon.com/exec/obidos/external-search/
?keyword=genealogy&tag=markcyndisgenealA/
This search is preset for the word "genealogy."

● Ancestor Search
http://SearchforAncestors.com
Enter a surname once, search over 30 genealogy search engines.

● Ancestry.com - Search
http://www.ancestry.com/search/main.htm

● FamilySearch Internet Genealogy Service
http://www.familysearch.org/
The largest genealogy resource on the Internet, from the LDS church.

● genealogy: I Found It!
http://www.gensource.com/ifoundit/index.htm

● Genealogy Pages
http://www.genealogypages.com/

● GenealogyPortal.com
http://www.genealogyportal.com
A joint venture of the Genealogy Home Page and the Genealogy Toolbox.

● The Genealogy Register
http://www.genealogyregister.com/
Search engine and genealogy directory, message boards and free home pages.

● Genealogy Search Engines / Genealogie Zoekmachines
http://www.genealogy.2y.net/

● Genealogy Searching Center
http://genealogysearch.org/

● Genealogy Surnames - Genealogy Search Engine - Add Your URL On Genlink Genealogy Index
http://www.genlink.org/
Genlink is a genealogy search engine, capable of indexing all the surnames on your genealogy surnames page in one go if you are using Ged2www, Gedpage, Ged2HTML, Gedbrowser or Ged4Web.

● GenSearcher, All-in-One Genealogy Search Page
http://www.geocities.com/Heartland/Acres/8310/
gensearcher.html

● Google Search: genealogy
http://www.google.com/search?q=genealogy

● HistorySeek! History Search Engine and Historical Information
http://www.historyseek.com
HistorySeek! is a directory search engine specifically made for historians, genealogists, scholars and history enthusiasts.

● NedGen Genealogy Search Engine
http://www.nedgen.nl/
Indexes online family trees of European ancestors.

● New Zealand Genealogy Search Engine
http://downtown.co.nz/genealogy/
Search all the on-line New Zealand passenger lists, family trees, surname interest and other genealogical resource pages.

● Search for Ancestors
http://www.geocities.com/thereids.geo//search/
All the major genealogy surname search engines.

● Surname Finder - Genealogy Specific Search Engine
http://www.surnamefinder.com/

● Yahoo!...Humanities...Genealogy
http://dir.yahoo.com/Arts/Humanities/History/Genealogy/

◆ General Lists of Links

● Access Genealogy - The Genealogy Web Portal
http://www.accessgenealogy.com/

● A.G.I. - Internet Genealogical Directory
http://www.chez.com/agi/intro2.htm

● Ancestor Search
http://www.geocities.com/thereids.geo//search/

● AOL Members' Genealogy Related Web Pages
http://members.aol.com/AHowe1/genwebpgs.html

● A Barrel of Links
http://cpcug.org/user/jlacombe/mark.html

● Cook Memorial Public Library District - Genealogy Referral Page
http://www.cooklib.org/genrefer.htm

- The CyberTree Genealogy Database
  http://home.sprynet.com/~lgk71/

- Discovering Family Histories Resources
  http://freepages.genealogy.rootsweb.com/~northing/
  Genealogy, Ireland, Missing Persons, Resources, USA, USAEthnic, USAMilitary, USARecords, USAVirginia.

- Everton's -On-Line - International Genealogical Resources
  http://www.everton.com/resources/world-resource.html

- Everton's -On-Line - US Genealogical Resources
  http://www.everton.com/resources/usa-resource.html

- Family Genealogy Online: Your Family History Research Guide
  http://www.familygenealogyonline.com/

- Family Tree Maker Online User Home Pages
  http://www.familytreemaker.com/users/

- Family Workings
  http://www.familyworkings.com/
  A free genealogy site for all. Ancestor queries, adoption queries, obituaries, cemeteries, GEDCOMs, researchers, and more.

- Ford Genealogy Club Home Page
  http://www.wwnet.net/~krugman1/fgc/

- Genealogical Journeys In Time
  http://ourworld.compuserve.com/homepages/Strawn/

- Genealogical WWW pages
  http://www.tic.com/gen.html

- Genealogy - About.com
  http://genealogy.about.com/

- Genealogy and Roots ... The Genealogy Beat
  http://www.search-beat.com/roots.htm

- Genealogy.com's Genealogy SiteFinder
  http://www.genealogy.com/links/index.html

- GenealogyDirectory
  http://www.genealogydirectory.com/HomePage/index.asp

- Genealogy Directory Tree
  http://www.listensoftware.com/gdt_app.cgi?Resource_Id=1

- Genealogy Exchange & Surname Registry
  http://www.genexchange.com/
  The GenExchange is a comprehensive "raw" genealogy web site with over 160MB of searchable data

- Genealogy Forum on CompuServe¨
  http://ourworld.compuserve.com/homepages/roots/

- Genealogy Help Network
  http://ghn.genealogy.org/

- Genealogy Home Page
  http://www.genhomepage.com/full.html

- Genealogy Links
  http://members.tripod.com/~FeFiFoFum/index.html

- GenealogyLinks.net
  http://www.genealogylinks.net/
  For USA, UK, England, Scotland, Wales, Ireland, Europe, Canada, Australia & New Zealand.

- Genealogy on the Internet
  http://www.geocities.com/Heartland/6266/genealogy.htm
  From Alan Mann, A.G.

- Genealogy Online
  http://www.genealogy.org/

- GenealogyOutfitters.com
  http://www.genealogyoutfitters.com/
  Genealogy software, message base, web links, news and more.

- Genealogy Pages
  http://www.genealogypages.com/

- Genealogy Personal Home Pages
  http://members.aol.com/Indianbrav/surnames.html

- Genealogy Resources on the Internet
  http://www.rootsweb.com/~jfuller/internet.html
  From John Fuller and Chris Gaunt.

- GenealogySearch.org
  http://genealogysearch.org/

- Genealogy's Most Wanted - Links To Other Sites
  http://www.citynet.net/mostwanted/links.html

- Genealogy Today
  http://www.genealogytoday.com/

- GeneaSearch.com
  http://www.geneasearch.com/

- GenLinks
  http://genlinks.hypermart.net/

- GenLinx
  http://www.genlinx.org/

- GenRoots
  http://www.genroots.org/

- GenSearcher - The All-in-One Genealogy Search Page
  http://www.geocities.com/Heartland/Acres/8310/gensearcher.html

- GEN-SITE-SWAP Mailing List
  http://www.rootsweb.com/~jfuller/gen_mail_computing.html
  #GEN-SITE-SWAP
  For the swapping of good genealogy URLs.

- GenWeb.Net
  http://www.genweb.net/
  A site for genealogy and history research. Free web space and over 10,000 mailing lists.

- GO Network: Genealogy
  http://www.go.com/WebDir/Family/Genealogy?lk=noframes&svx=related

- The Grannies' Genealogy Helper Menu
  http://www.toolcity.net/~vadkins/gen/index.html
  Links to home pages; contacts for newspaper & newsletter queries; other genealogy services.

- Helm's Genealogy Toolbox
  http://genealogy.tbox.com/

- Horus' H-GIG - Genealogy Links for Historians
  http://www.ucr.edu/h-gig/hist-preservation/genea.html

- Internet Genealogical Directory / Annuaire Généalogique Internet
  http://www.chez.com/agi/intro.htm

- Juliana's Links
  http://www.ancestry.com/search/rectype/UserSub/links/main.htm
  A searchable list of genealogy links from Ancestry.com.

- Nerd World: Genealogy
  http://www.nerdworld.com/nw192.html

- Nerd World: Personal Pages - Genealogy
  http://www.nerdworld.com/cgi-bin/subjects.cgi?usr=582&cat=1124

- Olive Tree Genealogy
  http://olivetreegenealogy.com/index.shtml
  Huguenots & Walloons, Ontario Loyalists, Mohawk, Mennonite, Palatines and Dutch Research.

- Questor's Genealogy Jump Start
  http://www.witsend.org/gen/questor.htm
  "Sites that are the most useful in getting started and most likely to give quick results."

- Parsons Genealogy Registry
  http://www.parsonstech.com/genealogy/registry.html

- Personal Views of Genealogy on the Internet
  http://www.everton.com/resources/personal.html

- RAND Genealogy Club Home Page
  http://www.rand.org/personal/Genea/

- Reunion Users with Home Pages
  http://www.leisterpro.com/doc/Users.html

- Richard Wilson's Other Genealogy Web Sites
  http://www.compuology.com/otherweb.htm
  Alphabetical Listing of Genealogy Related Internet Sites Sorted by Topic.

- RootsComputing
  http://www.rootscomputing.com/index.htm

- ROOTS-L Home Page
  http://www.rootsweb.com/roots-l/roots-l.html

- RootsWeb.com
  http://www.rootsweb.com/

- Searchable Genealogy Links [Lauren KNOBLAUCH]
  http://www.bc1.com/users/sgl/

- Sharing Family History on the Internet
  http://www.geocities.com/~wallyg/internet.htm

- Sharkey's Links to Genealogical Links
  http://www2.hawaii.edu/~sharkey/links/genealog/genealog.htm

- Tripod - Interact - Genealogy Pod Publishers
  http://www.tripod.lycos.com/pod_central/

- Ultimate Family Tree: Family Web Pages
  http://www.uftree.com/UFT/Nav/familywebpagesview.html

- WebCrawler: Genealogy
  http://www.webcrawler.com/kids_and_family/hobbies_interests/genealogy/

- What's New With the Genealogy Home Page
  http://www.genhomepage.com/whats_new.html

- WhoWhere? Personal Home Pages - Home Pages:Personal Interests:Genealogy
  http://homepages.whowhere.com/Personal_Interests/Genealogy/

- Yahoo!...Arts:Humanities:History:Genealogy
  http://dir.yahoo.com/Arts/Humanities/History/Genealogy/

- Yahoo!...Arts: Humanities: History: Genealogy: Beginners' Guides
  http://dir.yahoo.com/Arts/Humanities/History/Genealogy/Beginners__Guides/

- Yahoo!...Arts: Humanities: History: Genealogy: Lineages & Surnames
  http://dir.yahoo.com/Arts/Humanities/History/Genealogy/Lineages_and_Surnames/

- Yahoo!...Arts: Humanities: History: Genealogy: Lookups
  http://dir.yahoo.com/Arts/Humanities/History/Genealogy/Lookups/

- Yahoo!...Arts: Humanities: History: Genealogy: Organizations
  http://dir.yahoo.com/Arts/Humanities/History/Genealogy/Organizations/

- Yahoo!...Arts: Humanities: History: Genealogy: Regional and Ethnic Resources
  http://dir.yahoo.com/Arts/Humanities/History/Genealogy/Regional_and_Ethnic_Resources/

- Yahoo!...Arts: Humanities: History: Genealogy: Usenet
  http://dir.yahoo.com/Arts/Humanities/History/Genealogy/Usenet/

- Yourfamily.com Family Home Pages
  http://yourfamily.com/family.cgi

◆ Getting Started

- Ancestry Search
  http://www.ancestry.com/
  Social Security Death Index (SSDI) and other searchable databases.

- Family Tree Maker's Genealogy "How To" Guide
  http://www.familytreemaker.com/mainmenu.html

- GEN-NEWBIE-L Home Page
  http://www.rootsweb.com/~newbie/

- GEN-NEWBIE-L Mailing List
  http://www.rootsweb.com/~jfuller/gen_mail_general.html
  #GEN-NEWBIE-L
  A mailing list where people who are new to computers and genealogy may interact using a computer's e-mail program.

- How To
  http://www.CyndisList.com/howto.htm
  See this category on Cyndi's List for dozens of links to helpful sites and articles.

- ROOTS-L Mailing List
  http://www.rootsweb.com/~jfuller/gen_mail_general.html
  #ROOTS-L
  THE list to start with online! Broad-based genealogy topics and over 10,000 subscribers.

- RootsWeb Surname List Search Engine on Rootsweb
  http://rsl.rootsweb.com/cgi-bin/rslsql.cgi

◆ Locality & Ethnic Specific

- AfriGeneas ~ African Ancestored Genealogy
  http://www.afrigeneas.com/

- Belgium - Immigrants in America
  http://www.ping.be/picavet/
  A complete guide for descendants of Belgian immigrants looking for their roots in Belgium.

- Canadian Genealogy & History Links
  http://www.islandnet.com/~jveinot/cghl/cghl.html

- Federation of East European Family History Societies - FEEFHS
  http://feefhs.org/

- Genealogy Benelux Home Page
  http://www.ufsia.ac.be/genealogy/

- Genealogy.net (Formerly the German Genealogy Home Page)
  http://www.genealogy.net/gene/index.html

- Hispanic Genealogy Crossroads
  http://members.aol.com/mrosado007/crossroads.htm
  Categorized resources from the AOL Hispanic Genealogy Group.

- Irish Ancestors
  http://www.ireland.com/ancestor/

- The Italian Genealogy Home Page
  http://www.italgen.com/

- JewishGen: The Official Home of Jewish Genealogy
  http://www.jewishgen.org/

- Native American Genealogy
  http://hometown.aol.com/bbbenge/front.html

- ROOTS-L Resources: United States Resources
  http://www.rootsweb.com/roots-l/usa.html

- The UK & Ireland Genealogical Information Service (GENUKI)
  http://www.genuki.org.uk/

- The USGenWeb Project
  http://www.usgenweb.org/

HERALDRY

http://www.cyndislist.com/heraldry.htm

- About Achievement of Arms (tm)
  http://members.aol.com/grammarman/grammarstuff/about achieve.html
  Software for designing shields, crests, etc.

- Amazon.com Genealogy Bookstore - Heraldry
  http://www.amazon.com/exec/obidos/external-search/?keyword=heraldry&tag=markcyndisgenealA/

- Armorial de Châlons-en-Champagne
  http://perso.libertysurf.fr/heraldique_europeenne/Chalons/
  An armorial of the most important families in the history of the town of Châlons-en-Champagne (ex-Châlosn-sur-Marne).

- Armorial de Gelre
  http://perso.libertysurf.fr/Armorial_Gelre/
  An edition of one of the most important medieval roll of arms.

- Armorial Lalaing
  http://perso.libertysurf.fr/heraldique_europeenne/Lalaing/
  An edition of this famous medieval roll of arms.

- ars heraldica - Moderne Heraldik mit Tradition - Wappen - und Familiennamenforschung - heraldry
  http://members.magnet.at/ars.heraldica/
  ars heraldica professionally search for the history of your family name, the history of the origin since the time of the crusades and we make handpaintings of the oldest dokumented heraldic symbol. ars heraldica sucht in den Archiven und Bibliotheken die Entstehungsgeschichte Ihres Familiennamens, urkundliche Erwähnungen, berühmte Träger des Familiennamens, urkundlich erwähnte Wappen und belegt die Arbeit.

- The Augustan Society, Inc.
  http://www.augustansociety.org
  An International Genealogical, Historical, Heraldic and Chivalric Society.

- The American College of Heraldry
  http://users.aol.com/ballywoodn/acheraldry.html

- An Anachronist's Encyclopaedia - Heraldry
  http://www.acc.umu.se/~lkj/uma/her.html

- AudioTapes.com - Genealogical Lectures on Cassette Tapes - Heraldry
  http://www.audiotapes.com/search2.asp?Search=heraldry

- Baronage Press
  http://www.baronage.co.uk
  The magazine of The Baronage Press covers many aspects of history and constitutional politics, but is primarily about heraldry and medieval genealogy with an emphasis on Scotland.

- Blasón Virtual, Heráldica en la Red
  http://www.ctv.es/blason/

- Blazon and Blazon95 Software
  http://www.platypus.clara.co.uk/blazon.htm

- The British Heraldic Archive
  http://www.kwtelecom.com/heraldry/

- Caltrap's*Corner
  http://caltrap.bbsnet.com/

- Catholic Encyclopedia: Ecclesiastical Heraldry
  http://www.knight.org/advent/cathen/07243a.htm

- Center For Genealogical Research / Cabinet d'Etudes Généalogiques ~ U.S. & Switzerland
  http://genrsch.com/
  Genealogical research, heraldry and other products throughout Europe.

- Centro De Estudios Heraldicos
  http://www.net64.es/heraldica/

- Chivalric Research 2000
  http://www.geocities.com/Paris/Cathedral/4800/link.html
  A site for all things heraldic, chivalric, genealogical, noble, royal or pertaining to knightly orders.

- Coats of Arms from Ireland and around the World
  http://homepage.eircom.net/~donnaweb/
  Over 800 coats of arms for Irish Families / Clans.

- The College of Arms
  http://www.college-of-arms.gov.uk/

- Crests and Coats of Arms
  http://www.britainUSA.com/bis/fsheets/3.stm#crests
  A paragraph from Britain in the USA: Genealogical Research.

- Dudley Bateman - Heraldic Artist
  http://www.patriot-web.co.uk/batemanheraldry/
  We can supply most forms of heraldic artwork to individual order. Library paintings and wall plaques reproduced by hand from original grant or warrant.

- English Heraldic Dictionary
  http://jagor.srce.hr/~zheimer/heraldry/h.htm

- Estudio Batres Franzese - Genealogía y Heráldica en Argentina
  http://www.estudiobatres.com.ar/

- Family Tree Genealogical and Probate Research Bureau Ltd.
  http://www.familytree.hu/
  Professional research service covering the area of what was formerly the Austro - Hungarian Empire, including: Hungary, Slovakia, Czech Republic, Austria, Italy, Transylvania, Croatia, Slovenia, former Yugoslavia (Banat), and the Ukraine (Sub-Carpathian).

- Frontier Press Bookstore - Heraldry
  http://www.frontierpress.com/frontier.cgi?category=heraldry

- Genealogia e Heráldica Portuguesa - Portuguese Genealogy and Heraldry
  http://www.geocities.com/Heartland/Hills/1008/
  álvaro HOLSTEIN Home Page.

- Genealogy and Heraldry in Slovenia
  http://genealogy.ijp.si/

- GenealogyBookShop.com - Heraldry
  http://www.genealogybookshop.com/genealogybookshop/
  files/General,Heraldry/index.html
  The online store of Genealogical Publishing Co., Inc. & Clearfield Company.

- genealogyPro - Professional Researchers Specializing in Heraldry
  http://genealogyPro.com/directories/heraldry.html

- The Great Hall of the Clans
  http://www.tartans.com/hall.html

- Heraldic Primer: Table of Contents
  http://www.sca.org/heraldry/primer/

- Heráldica Española, Heraldry for Surnames of Spanish Origin
  http://www.ctv.es/artes/
  Heráldica y escudos de armas de apellidos españoles, genealogía, escudos de armas - Heraldry for surnames of Spanish origin, coats of arms, genealogy.

- Heráldica Española
  http://members.xoom.com/chema/
  Heráldica de apellidos de origen español. Heráldica oficial de localidades de España.

- Heraldica - François Velde's Heraldry Site
  http://www.heraldica.org/intro.htm

- Héraldique Européenne
  http://perso.libertysurf.fr/heraldique_europeenne/
  Heraldry of European kingdoms, principalities, duchies, and various others people and families.

- Heraldiska Samfundet
  http://www.users.wineasy.se/elias/hersamf.htm
  A Swedish association for heraldry and related subjects, based in Stockholm, Sweden.

- The Heraldry and Coat of Arms Web Ring
  http://www.geocities.com/Athens/Olympus/4369//Bookplate/
  heraldring/admring.htm

- Heraldry and Vexillology
  http://www.du.edu/~tomills/flags.html

- Heraldry Australia Inc.
  http://expage.com/page/heraldryaustralia
  A Society of Australians promoting the study and use of heraldry.

- Heraldry Contains the DNA of Genealogy, etc.
  http://on.to/genealogy
  Several articles about heraldry, hosted by Allen Foote.

- Heraldry Cross Stitch
  http://www.hometown.aol.com/mcknit1775/paint/arms.htm
  Cross stitch pattern of your family coat of arms.

- Heraldry - Jerry's Heraldry
  http://www.geocities.com/RainForest/Andes/8719/
  Shields, coat of arms and blazons for surnames from A to Z.

- Heraldry/L'Heraldique
  http://collections.ic.gc.ca/governor/heraldry/
  Canadian coat of arms.

- Heraldry Links Page
  http://freepages.genealogy.rootsweb.com/~ruthann/heraldry/
  heraldry.htm

- Heraldry on the Internet
  http://digiserve.com/heraldry/

- Heraldry Page by M.N. Razumkin
  http://sunsite.cs.msu.su/heraldry/
  The Crown of Russian Empire - The Unofficial Home Page.

- Heraldry: a Selected List of References
  http://lcweb.loc.gov/rr/genealogy/bib_guid/herald.html
  Bibliography from the Library of Congress.

- The Heraldry Society
  http://www.kwtelecom.com/heraldry/hersoc/

- Heraldry Software
  http://digiserve.com/heraldry/hersoft.htm

- Heraldry - Thorwulf's Basic Heraldic Primer
  http://www.geocities.com/Area51/Vault/5656/heraldry.html
  An introduction to Finnish armory covering the basic concepts and terminology.

- Heraldry Today
  http://www.heraldrytoday.co.uk/
  Books for heraldry and genealogy.

- HERBARZ Mailing List
  http://www.rootsweb.com/~jfuller/gen_mail_country-lit.html
  #HERBARZ
  For the discussion of Polish and Lithuanian heraldry, the history of the armorial clans, and the genealogy of noble families.

- The Institute of Heraldic and Genealogical Studies ~ U.K.
  http://www.cs.ncl.ac.uk/genuki/IHGS/

- The Institute of Heraldry
  http://www-perscom.army.mil/tagd/tioh/tioh.htm

- International Civic Arms
  http://www.bng.nl/ngw/indexgb.htm
  Over 9,500 arms of towns, states and countries.

- International School of Genealogy, Heraldry and Documentary Sciences
  http://www.geocities.com/chivalric2/ASGHDS/index.html
  Located in Mississippi, it is for beginner and advanced research in family history, genealogy, archival studies, diplomacy, nobiliary law, chivalry, heraldry, and the history of uniforms, decorations, & coins.

- Italian Heraldry, Nobility and Genealogy
  http://www.italgen.com/heraldry.htm

- How Professional Genealogists Determine Ancestral Nobility in Italy
  http://www.italgen.com/nobilit.htm

- Jeff Alvey Genealogy History Heraldry
  http://www.fred.net/jefalvey/jeffhera.html

- John Townsend - Second-hand Books
  http://business.virgin.net/john.townsend2/
  Out-of-print books, genealogy, topography, local history, antiquarian heraldry books.

- Jürgen Maus, Grabador De Escudos, Iniciales Y Emblemas * Lapidarios
  http://www.net64.es/jmaus/
  He is an engraver of coat of arms, initials and emblems in semi and precious stones.

- KAJMORIAL - Kaj Malachowski's Polish Web Armorial
  http://www.geocities.com/Heartland/Plains/2739/herbarz.html
  Links to other web pages that contain Polish heraldry and coats-of-arms for Polish families.

- Kleine Einführung in die Wappenkunde / Introduction in Heraldry ~ in German
  http://www.geocities.com/Colosseum/1959/wappen.html

- Knightly Orders and International Nobility
  http://www.knightlyorders.org/
  Royal and noble heraldry and genealogy, dynastic history, houses of Savoy, Grimaldi, Two Sicilies.

- Pimbley's Dictionary of Heraldry
  http://www.digiserve.com/heraldry/pimbley.htm

- The Points of Heraldry - The Basics of Heraldic Design and Terminology
  http://www2.okstate.edu/people/wcross/Heraldry.html

- Reynolds Hunter Y Puebla Heráldica Y Blasones - Heraldries
  http://www.audinex.es/~hunter/

- RootsWeb's Guide to Tracing Family Trees - Lesson 19: Heraldry for Genealogists
  http://www.rootsweb.com/~rwguide/lesson19.htm

- Society of Genealogists Information Leaflet No. 15 - The Right to Arms
  http://www.sog.org.uk/leaflets/arms.html

- Steven B. Madewell's Coats of Arms Index
  http://freepages.family.rootsweb.com/~heraldry/page_coa.html
  The Coats of Arms Index contains entries and graphic renderings of arms listed in Burke's "General Armory", Rietstap's "Armorial General", and like compendiums.

- Usenet Newsgroup rec.heraldry
  news:rec.heraldry

- Yahoo!...Genealogy:Heraldry & Name Histories
  http://dir.yahoo.com/Business_and_Economy/Shopping_and_Services/History/Genealogy/Heraldry___Name_Histories/

HISPANIC, CENTRAL & SOUTH AMERICA, & THE WEST INDIES

Including Mexico, Latin America & the Caribbean
http://www.cyndislist.com/hispanic.htm

Category Index:

- ◆ General Resource Sites
- ◆ History & Culture
- ◆ Language, Handwriting & Script
- ◆ Libraries, Archives & Museums
- ◆ Mailing Lists, Newsgroups & Chat
- ◆ People & Families
- ◆ Professional Researchers, Volunteers & Other Research Services

- ◆ Publications, Software & Supplies
- ◆ Queries, Message Boards & Surname Lists
- ◆ Records: Census, Cemeteries, Land, Obituaries, Personal, Taxes and Vital
- ◆ Societies & Groups
- ◆ WorldGenWeb Project

◆ General Resource Sites

- Anillo de Genealogía Hispana (Hispanic Genealogy Ring)
  http://www.elanillo.com/
  Paginas de Genealogía Hispana en Español. Hispanic Genealogy pages in Spanish. Lots of great resources for those searching their roots in Spain or Latin American countries.

- AOL Hispanic Genealogy Group's Home Page
  http://users.aol.com/mrosado007/index.htm

- Bibliography for Researchers of Jamaican Genealogy and History
  http://www6.pair.com/silvera/jamgen/jgbibliography.html

- CLNET Genealogy Sources
  http://latino.sscnet.ucla.edu/Test/genealogy.ref.html
  List of Hispanic published resources.

- Cuban Genealogy How To Guide
  http://www.familytreemaker.com/00000365.html

- Dutch Antilles
  http://ourworld.compuserve.com/homepages/paulvanV/nedantil.htm

- Estudio Batres Franzese - Genealogía y Heráldica en Argentina
  http://www.estudiobatres.com.ar/

- Extraordinary Ancestors
  http://www.channel4.com/nextstep/geno/main.html
  Companion web site to the Channel 4 television series.
  - o A Caribbean case study
    http://www.channel4.com/nextstep/geno/geno6.html
  - o Tracing an ancestor who was an immigrant
    http://www.channel4.com/nextstep/geno/geno3.html

- • African-Americans
  http://www.channel4.com/nextstep/geno/geno3b.html
- • Africans
  http://www.channel4.com/nextstep/geno/geno3d.html
- • West Indians
  http://www.channel4.com/nextstep/geno/geno3c.html

- Family History of Jamaica, West Indies
  http://users.pullman.com/mitchelm/jamaica.htm
  From Madeleine Mitchell. ARSCOTT, COVER, MURRAY, LEVY.

- Family Tree Maker's How-To Guide - Institute of Genealogy and History for Latin America
  http://www.familytreemaker.com/00000140.html

- genealogia.com
  http://www.genealogia.com/
  A Comprehensive Hispanic Genealogy Research Web Site Covering all Hispanics Countries Including Spain and Brazil.

- Genealogical Research in South America
  http://www.saqnet.co.uk/users/hrhenly/latinam1.html
  With an emphasis on British settlement.

- Généalogie et Histoire de la Caraïbe
  http://members.aol.com/GHCaraibe/index.html

- Genealogy in Costa Rica
  http://www.decostarica.co.cr/genealogias/index.html

- The Genealogy of Mexico
  http://members.tripod.com/~GaryFelix/index1.htm
  Over 500 surnames of Mexico and research references. List of the Conquistadors that served the King under Cortes. Biographies of the conquistadors. Surnames origins.

- German Genealogy: BRAZIL
  http://www.genealogy.net/gene/reg/WELT/brasil.html
  German migration to Brasil.

- Hispanic Genealogical Research Center of New Mexico
  http://www.hgrc-nm.org/
- Hispanic Genealogy Address Book by Country
  http://members.aol.com/mrosado007/crossroads.htm#HGAB
- Hispanic Genealogy Crossroads
  http://members.aol.com/mrosado007/crossroads.htm
  Categorized resources from the AOL Hispanic Genealogy Group.
- Hispanic Genealogy - The Institute of Genealogy and History for Latin America
  http://www.infowest.com/personal/l/lplatt/
- Hispanic Immigration to Maryland
  http://www.clis.umd.edu/~mddlmddl/791/communities/html/index.html#hispanic
  A scholarly review of immigration into Maryland from the very first colonists to modern immigrants.
- Index to "Historia de Familias Cubanas, Vols 1-9" - (Histories of Cuban Families)
  http://www.cubagenweb.org/jaruco.htm
- Jamaican Family Search
  http://www.jamaicanfamilysearch.com/
- Jamaican Jewish Genealogy
  http://www6.pair.com/silvera/jamgen/index.html
- LatinoLinks - History, Geography, Genealogy, & Culture in Latin America and Iberia
  http://www.latinolinks.net/
  Categorized links for Argentina, Bolivia, Brasil / Brazil, Colombia, Costa Rica, Cuba, Chile, Ecuador, El Salvador, Estados Unidos de América / The United States of America, Guatemala, Honduras, México, Nicaragua, Panamá, Paraguay, Perú, Puerto Rico, República Dominicana / Dominican Republic, Uruguay, Venezuela, España / Spain, Francia / France, Gran Bretaña / Great Britain, Italia / Italy, Portugal .
- Lower Rio Grande Valley / Northeast Mexico Genealogical Research
  http://www.lib.panam.edu/~sc/guides/lrgvgen.html
  Bibliography of materials which are useful to those doing Hispanic genealogical research on families connected with South Texas and Northeast Mexico. Many materials are avaiable through interlibrary loan.
- Mexican Genealogy How To Guide
  http://www.familytreemaker.com/00000379.html
- Spain, Portugal & the Basque Country / España, Portugal y El País Vasco
  http://www.CyndisList.com/spain.htm
  See this category on Cyndi's List for related links.
- The Taino Genealogy Project
  http://www.hartford-hwp.com/taino/docs/proj-6.html
- The Taino Inter-Tribal Council
  http://www.hartford-hwp.com/taino/index.html
- The Tom & Dollie Genealogy Page
  http://spot.Colorado.EDU/~madridt/Home.html

- United States Index
  http://www.CyndisList.com/usa.htm
  Arizona
  http://www.cyndislist.com/az.htm
  California
  http://www.cyndislist.com/ca.htm
  New Mexico
  http://www.cyndislist.com/nm.htm
  Texas
  http://www.cyndislist.com/tx.htm
  See these category pages on Cyndi's List for more links.
- Venezuelan Genealogy / Genealogía de Venezuela
  http://www.geocities.com/Heartland/Ranch/2443/
  List genealogy resources by state including Catholic Church directory and Family History Center records on microfilm.
- West Indian Genealogy Links
  http://ourworld.compuserve.com/homepages/vroyal/links.htm
- Where to Find Jamaican Genealogical Information
  http://www6.pair.com/silvera/jamgen/jgwhere.html
- Yahoo! Clubs Genealogía Hispana
  http://clubs.yahoo.com/clubs/genealogiahispana
- Yahoo! Clubs - Hispanic Genealogy
  http://clubs.yahoo.com/clubs/hispanicgenealogy
- Yahoo!...Hispanic...Genealogy
  http://dir.yahoo.com/Arts/Humanities/History/Genealogy/Regional_and_Ethnic_Resources/Hispanic/
- Yahoo!...Mexico...Genealogy
  http://dir.yahoo.com/Regional/Countries/Mexico/Arts_and_Humanities/Humanities/History/Genealogy/

◆ History & Culture

- The Latin American Alliance
  http://www.latinsynergy.org/
- StudyWeb: History: Caribbean Islands
  http://www.studyweb.com/History/toccarib.htm
- StudyWeb: History: Central America
  http://www.studyweb.com/History/toccenam.htm
- StudyWeb: History: South America
  http://www.studyweb.com/History/tocsoame.htm

◆ Language, Handwriting & Script

- AltaVista Translation Service
  http://babelfish.altavista.digital.com/cgi-bin/translate?
  Input a URL for a web site or a block of plain text and this site will translate for you from Spanish or Portuguese or French to English or from English to Spanish or Portuguese or French.
- Portuguese Genealogical Word List
  http://www.familysearch.org/rg/guide/WLPortug.ASP
- Portuguese Letter Writing Guide
  http://www.familysearch.org/rg/guide/LWGPortuguese.ASP
  For genealogical inquiries from FamilySearch.org.

- Spanish Genealogical Word List
  http://www.familysearch.org/rg/guide/WLSpanis.ASP

- Spanish Letter Writing Guide
  http://www.familysearch.org/rg/guide/LWGSpanish.ASP
  For genealogical inquiries from FamilySearch.org.

◆ Libraries, Archives & Museums

- Archivo Nacional ~ Chile
  http://www.dibam.renib.cl/isc145.html

- Arquivo Nacional ~ Rio de Janeiro - RJ - Brasil
  http://www.mj.gov.br/an/home.html

- Arquivo Público do Distrito Federal ~ Brazil
  http://www.arpdf.df.gov.br/

- Biblioteca Nacional de la República Argentina
  http://www.bibnal.edu.ar/

- Biblioteca Nacional de Maestros República
  Argentina
  http://webbib.mcye.gov.ar/home.htm

- Biblioteca Nacional de Venezuela
  http://www.bnv.bib.ve/

- Family History Library Catalog
  http://www.familysearch.org/Search/searchcatalog.asp
  *From the FamilySearch web site, an online catalog to the holdings
  of the LDS Church in Salt Lake City, Utah. Also search for other
  localities by place name.*
  http://www.familysearch.org/fhlc/supermainframeset.asp?
  display=localitysearch&columns=*,180,0

  o Anguilla
    http://www.familysearch.org/fhlc/supermainframeset.asp?
    display=localitydetails&subject=459&subject_disp=
    Anguilla&columns=*,180,0

  o Antigua and Barbuda
    http://www.familysearch.org/fhlc/supermainframeset.asp?
    display=localitydetails&subject=456&subject_disp=
    Antigua_and_Barbuda&columns=*,180,0

  o Argentina
    http://www.familysearch.org/fhlc/supermainframeset.asp?
    display=localitydetails&subject=393&subject_disp=
    Argentina&columns=*,180,0

  o Aruba
    http://www.familysearch.org/fhlc/supermainframeset.asp?
    display=localitydetails&subject=471&subject_disp=
    Aruba&columns=*,180,0

  o Bahamas
    http://www.familysearch.org/fhlc/supermainframeset.asp?
    display=localitydetails&subject=333&subject_disp=
    Bahamas&columns=*,180,0

  o Barbados
    http://www.familysearch.org/fhlc/supermainframeset.asp?
    display=localitydetails&subject=461&subject_disp=
    Barbados&columns=*,180,0

  o Belize
    http://www.familysearch.org/fhlc/supermainframeset.asp?
    display=localitydetails&subject=320&subject_disp=
    Belize&columns=*,180,0

  o Bermuda
    http://www.familysearch.org/fhlc/supermainframeset.asp?
    display=localitydetails&subject=336&subject_disp=
    Bermuda&columns=*,180,0

  o Bolivia
    http://www.familysearch.org/fhlc/supermainframeset.asp?
    display=localitydetails&subject=395&subject_disp=
    Bolivia&columns=*,180,0

  o Brazil
    http://www.familysearch.org/fhlc/supermainframeset.asp?
    display=localitydetails&subject=391&subject_disp=
    Brazil&columns=*,180,0

  o Chile
    http://www.familysearch.org/fhlc/supermainframeset.asp?
    display=localitydetails&subject=394&subject_disp=
    Chile&columns=*,180,0

  o Colombia
    http://www.familysearch.org/fhlc/supermainframeset.asp?
    display=localitydetails&subject=398&subject_disp=
    Colombia&columns=*,180,0

  o Costa Rica
    http://www.familysearch.org/fhlc/supermainframeset.asp?
    display=localitydetails&subject=324&subject_disp=
    Costa_Rica&columns=*,180,0

  o Cuba
    http://www.familysearch.org/fhlc/supermainframeset.asp?
    display=localitydetails&subject=326&subject_disp=
    Cuba&columns=*,180,0

  o Dominica
    http://www.familysearch.org/fhlc/supermainframeset.asp?
    display=localitydetails&subject=464&subject_disp=
    Dominica&columns=*,180,0

  o Dominican Republic
    http://www.familysearch.org/fhlc/supermainframeset.asp?
    display=localitydetails&subject=328&subject_disp=
    Dominican_Republic&columns=*,180,0

  o El Salvador
    http://www.familysearch.org/fhlc/supermainframeset.asp?
    display=localitydetails&subject=322&subject_disp=
    El_Salvador&columns=*,180,0

  o Grenada
    http://www.familysearch.org/fhlc/supermainframeset.asp?
    display=localitydetails&subject=468&subject_disp=
    Grenada&columns=*,180,0

  o Guadeloupe
    http://www.familysearch.org/fhlc/supermainframeset.asp?
    display=localitydetails&subject=458&subject_disp=
    Guadeloupe&columns=*,180,0

  o Guatemala
    http://www.familysearch.org/fhlc/supermainframeset.asp?
    display=localitydetails&subject=319&subject_disp=
    Guatemala&columns=*,180,0

  o Guiana
    http://www.familysearch.org/fhlc/supermainframeset.asp?
    display=localitydetails&subject=404&subject_disp=
    Guiana&columns=*,180,0

  o Guyana
    http://www.familysearch.org/fhlc/supermainframeset.asp?d
    isplay=localitydetails&subject=403&subject_disp=
    Guyana&columns=*,180,0

o Haiti
http://www.familysearch.org/fhlc/supermainframeset.asp?
display=localitydetails&subject=330&subject_disp=
Haiti&columns=*,180,0

o Honduras
http://www.familysearch.org/fhlc/supermainframeset.asp?
display=localitydetails&subject=321&subject_disp=
Honduras&columns=*,180,0

o Jamaica
http://www.familysearch.org/fhlc/supermainframeset.asp?
display=localitydetails&subject=327&subject_disp=
Jamaica&columns=*,180,0

o Martinique
http://www.familysearch.org/fhlc/supermainframeset.asp?
display=localitydetails&subject=462&subject_disp=
Martinique&columns=*,180,0

o Mexico
http://www.familysearch.org/fhlc/supermainframeset.asp?
display=localitydetails&subject=315&subject_disp=
Mexico&columns=*,180,0

o Montserrat
http://www.familysearch.org/fhlc/supermainframeset.asp?
display=localitydetails&subject=457&subject_disp=
Montserrat&columns=*,180,0

o Netherlands Antilles
http://www.familysearch.org/fhlc/supermainframeset.asp?
display=localitydetails&subject=469&subject_disp=
Netherlands_Antilles&columns=*,180,0

o Nicaragua
http://www.familysearch.org/fhlc/supermainframeset.asp?
display=localitydetails&subject=323&subject_disp=
Nicaragua&columns=*,180,0

o Panama
http://www.familysearch.org/fhlc/supermainframeset.asp?
display=localitydetails&subject=399&subject_disp=
Panama&columns=*,180,0

o Paraguay
http://www.familysearch.org/fhlc/supermainframeset.asp?
display=localitydetails&subject=407&subject_disp=
Paraguay&columns=*,180,0

o Peru
http://www.familysearch.org/fhlc/supermainframeset.asp?
display=localitydetails&subject=396&subject_disp=
Peru&columns=*,180,0

o Puerto Rico
http://www.familysearch.org/fhlc/supermainframeset.asp?
display=localitydetails&subject=332&subject_disp=
Puerto_Rico&columns=*,180,0

o Saint Lucia
http://www.familysearch.org/fhlc/supermainframeset.asp?
display=localitydetails&subject=466&subject_disp=
Saint_Lucia&columns=*,180,0

o Saint Vincent
http://www.familysearch.org/fhlc/supermainframeset.asp?
display=localitydetails&subject=465&subject_disp=
Saint_Vincent&columns=*,180,0

o Suriname
http://www.familysearch.org/fhlc/supermainframeset.asp?
display=localitydetails&subject=406&subject_disp=
Suriname&columns=*,180,0

o Trinidad and Tobago
http://www.familysearch.org/fhlc/supermainframeset.asp?
display=localitydetails&subject=463&subject_disp=
Trinidad_and_Tobago&columns=*,180,0

o Turks and Caicos Islands
http://www.familysearch.org/fhlc/supermainframeset.asp?
display=localitydetails&subject=334&subject_disp=
Turks_and_Caicos_Islands&columns=*,180,0

o Uruguay
http://www.familysearch.org/fhlc/supermainframeset.asp?
display=localitydetails&subject=408&subject_disp=
Uruguay&columns=*,180,0

o Venezuela
http://www.familysearch.org/fhlc/supermainframeset.asp?
display=localitydetails&subject=402&subject_disp=
Venezuela&columns=*,180,0

o Virgin Islands (British)
http://www.familysearch.org/fhlc/supermainframeset.asp?
display=localitydetails&subject=454&subject_disp=
Virgin_Islands_(British)&columns=*,180,0

o Virgin Islands (U.S.)
http://www.familysearch.org/fhlc/supermainframeset.asp?
display=localitydetails&subject=453&subject_disp=
Virgin_Islands_(U.S.)&columns=*,180,0

- Hispanic Genealogy Address Book: Mexican State Archives
http://members.aol.com/mrosado007/mxstarc.htm

- H-Latam Archives
http://h-net2.msu.edu/~latam/archives/
A list of information about Latin American archives, submitted by visitors to the H-Net web site.

- Libraries & Archives in Latin America LANIC
http://www.lanic.utexas.edu/la/region/library/

- National Library of Jamaica
http://www.nlj.org.jm/

- Repositories of Primary Sources: Latin America and the Caribbean
http://www.uidaho.edu/special-collections/mexico.html
A list of links to online resources from the Univ. of Idaho Library, Special Collections and Archives.

- Rio Grande Valley Library System - Special Collections Branch
http://www.cabq.gov/rgvls/specol.html
Albuquerque. Strong in the areas of New Mexico and Hispanic genealogy.

◆ Mailing Lists, Newsgroups & Chat

- Genealogy Resources on the Internet - Mailing Lists
http://www.rootsweb.com/~jfuller/gen_mail.html
Most of the mailing list links below point to this site, wonderfully maintained by John Fuller

- Argentina Mailing Lists
http://www.rootsweb.com/~jfuller/gen_mail_country-arg.html

- Bahamas Mailing Lists
http://www.rootsweb.com/~jfuller/gen_mail_country-bah.html

- Belize Mailing Lists
  http://www.rootsweb.com/~jfuller/gen_mail_country-blz.html
- Brazil Mailing Lists
  http://www.rootsweb.com/~jfuller/gen_mail_country-bra.html
- Cayman Islands Mailing Lists
  http://www.rootsweb.com/~jfuller/gen_mail_country-cay.html
- Chile Mailing Lists
  http://www.rootsweb.com/~jfuller/gen_mail_country-che.html
- Colombia Mailing Lists
  http://www.rootsweb.com/~jfuller/gen_mail_country-col.html
- Costa Rica Mailing Lists
  http://www.rootsweb.com/~jfuller/gen_mail_country-cos.html
- Cuba Mailing Lists
  http://www.rootsweb.com/~jfuller/gen_mail_country-cub.html
- Dominican Republic Mailing Lists
  http://www.rootsweb.com/~jfuller/gen_mail_country-dom.html
- Ecuador Mailing Lists
  http://www.rootsweb.com/~jfuller/gen_mail_country-ecu.html
- El Salvador Mailing Lists
  http://www.rootsweb.com/~jfuller/gen_mail_country-els.html
- Guatemala Mailing Lists
  http://www.rootsweb.com/~jfuller/gen_mail_country-gua.html
- Honduras Mailing Lists
  http://www.rootsweb.com/~jfuller/gen_mail_country-hon.html
- Mexico Mailing Lists
  http://www.rootsweb.com/~jfuller/gen_mail_country-mex.html
- Nicaragua Mailing Lists
  http://www.rootsweb.com/~jfuller/gen_mail_country-nic.html
- Panama Mailing Lists
  http://www.rootsweb.com/~jfuller/gen_mail_country-pan.html
- Peru Mailing Lists
  http://www.rootsweb.com/~jfuller/gen_mail_country-per.html
- West Indies Mailing Lists
  http://www.rootsweb.com/~jfuller/gen_mail_country-wes.html
  - Argentina-L Mailing List
    http://www.rootsweb.com/~jfuller/gen_mail_country-arg.html#Argentina-L
    For anyone with a genealogical interest in Argentina.
  - BAHAMAS Mailing List
    http://www.rootsweb.com/~jfuller/gen_mail_country-bah.html#BAHAMAS
    For anyone with a genealogical interest in the country of the Bahamas.
  - Bahamians Mailing List
    http://www.rootsweb.com/~jfuller/gen_mail_country-bah.html#Bahamians
    For anyone with a genealogical interest in the Bahamas including the sharing of surname interests and the exchange of genealogical and historical information.

- bay-island-genealogy Mailing List
  http://www.rootsweb.com/~jfuller/gen_mail_country-hon.html#bay-island-genealogy
  For anyone with a genealogical interest in the Bay Islands (e.g., Roatan, Utila, Guanaja, Cayos Cochinos) off the northern coast of Spanish Honduras.
- BRAZIL Mailing List
  http://www.rootsweb.com/~jfuller/gen_mail_country-bra.html#BRAZIL
  For anyone with genealogical interest in Brazil.
- Caribbean-AfriGeneas
  http://www.rootsweb.com/~jfuller/gen_mail_african.html#Caribbean-AfriGeneas
  To coordinate, network and strengthen the efforts of those researching African ancestry in the Caribbean region.
- Caribbean Historical & Genealogical Journal
  http://www.tcigenealogy.com/
  From TCI Genealogical Resources.
- CARIBBEAN Mailing List
  http://www.rootsweb.com/~jfuller/gen_mail_country-gen.html#CARIBBEAN
  For anyone with a genealogical or historical interest in the West Indies and the Caribbean.
- cayman-connections Mailing List
  http://www.rootsweb.com/~jfuller/gen_mail_country-cay.html#cayman-connections
  For anyone with a genealogical or historical interest in the Cayman Islands.
- CENSO-LATIN-AMERICA Mailing List
  http://www.rootsweb.com/~jfuller/gen_mail_country-gen.html#CENSO-LATIN-AMERICA
  For the discussion of censuses in Latin America and the documentation of Latin American immigrants in U.S. censuses.
- Chile-genealogy Mailing List
  http://www.rootsweb.com/~jfuller/gen_mail_country-che.html#Chile-genealogy
  For anyone with a genealogical interest in Chile.
- CUBA Mailing List
  http://www.rootsweb.com/~jfuller/gen_mail_country-cub.html#CUBA
- Genealogia Mailing List
  http://www.rootsweb.com/~jfuller/gen_mail_country-bra.html#Genealogia
  For those interested in genealogy in Brazil. The list is dedicated to the search for information on the origins of families, registers in Brazil and abroad, histories of immigrants, meanings of surnames, etc.
- GEN-HISPANIC Mailing List
  http://www.rootsweb.com/~jfuller/gen_mail_country-gen.html#GEN-HISPANIC
  Gatewayed with the soc.genealogy.hispanic newsgroup for the discussion of Hispanic genealogy.
  news:soc.genealogy.hispanic
- GER-RUS-ARG Mailing List
  http://www.rootsweb.com/~jfuller/gen_mail_country-arg.html#GER-RUS-ARG
  For anyone with a genealogical interest in the Germans who migrated from Russia to Argentina.

o **GUATEMALA Mailing List**
http://www.rootsweb.com/~jfuller/gen_mail_country-gua.html#GUATEMALA
For anyone with a genealogical interest in Guatemala.

o **HONDURAS Mailing List**
http://www.rootsweb.com/~jfuller/gen_mail_country-hon.html#HONDURAS
For anyone with a genealogical interest in Honduras.

o **LATAMSIG Mailing List**
http://www.rootsweb.com/~jfuller/gen_mail_country-gen.html#LATAMSIG
A regional special interest group (SIG) mailing list for researchers with Jewish family roots in all countries of Latin America.

o **MadeiraExiles Mailing List**
http://www.rootsweb.com/~jfuller/gen_mail_country-wes.html#MadeiraExiles
Devoted to the research of Dr. Robert Reid Kalley's Portuguese Presbyterian exiles from Madeira, Portugal who emigrated to Trinidad and then to Illinois (ca 1846-1854). Postings regarding research of related exiles who settled in Trinidad, Antigua, St Kitts, Jamaica, Demerara, etc. are also welcome.

o **MEX-AGUASCALIENTES Mailing List**
http://www.rootsweb.com/~jfuller/gen_mail_country-mex.html#MEX-AGUASCALIENTES
For anyone with a genealogical interest in the State of Aguascalientes, Mexico.

o **MEX-BAJA-CALIFORNIA Mailing List**
http://www.rootsweb.com/~jfuller/gen_mail_country-mex.html#MEX-BAJA-CALIFORNIA
For anyone with a genealogical interest in the State of Baja California, Mexico.

o **MEX-BAJA-CALIFORNIA-SUR Mailing List**
http://www.rootsweb.com/~jfuller/gen_mail_country-mex.html#MEX-BAJA-CALIFORNIA-SUR
For anyone with a genealogical interest in the State of Baja California Sur, Mexico.

o **MEX-CAMPECHE Mailing List**
http://www.rootsweb.com/~jfuller/gen_mail_country-mex.html#MEX-CAMPECHE
For anyone with a genealogical interest in the State of Campeche, Mexico.

o **MEX-CHIAPAS Mailing List**
http://www.rootsweb.com/~jfuller/gen_mail_country-mex.html#MEX-CHIAPAS
For anyone with a genealogical interest in the State of Chiapas, Mexico.

o **MEX-CHIHUAHUA Mailing List**
http://www.rootsweb.com/~jfuller/gen_mail_country-mex.html#MEX-CHIHUAHUA
For anyone with a genealogical interest in the State of Chihuahua, Mexico.

o **MEX-COAHUILA**
http://www.rootsweb.com/~jfuller/gen_mail_country-mex.html#MEX-COAHUILA
For anyone with a genealogical interest in the State of Coahuila, Mexico.

o **MEX-COLIMA Mailing List**
http://www.rootsweb.com/~jfuller/gen_mail_country-mex.html#MEX-COLIMA
For anyone with a genealogical interest in the State of Colima, Mexico.

o **MEX-DISTRITO-FEDERAL Mailing List**
http://www.rootsweb.com/~jfuller/gen_mail_country-mex.html#MEX-DISTRITO-FEDERAL
For anyone with a genealogical interest in the Distrito-Federal, Mexico.

o **MEX-DURANGO Mailing List**
http://www.rootsweb.com/~jfuller/gen_mail_country-mex.html#MEX-DURANGO
For anyone with a genealogical interest in the State of Durango, Mexico.

o **MEX-GUANAJUATO Mailing List**
http://www.rootsweb.com/~jfuller/gen_mail_country-mex.html#MEX-GUANAJUATO
For anyone with a genealogical interest in the State of Guanajuato, Mexico.

o **MEX-GUERRERO Mailing List**
http://www.rootsweb.com/~jfuller/gen_mail_country-mex.html#MEX-GUERRERO
For anyone with a genealogical interest in the State of Guerrero, Mexico.

o **MEX-HIDALGO Mailing List**
http://www.rootsweb.com/~jfuller/gen_mail_country-mex.html#MEX-HIDALGO
For anyone with a genealogical interest in the State of Hidalgo, Mexico.

o **MEXICAN-INDIANS**
http://www.rootsweb.com/~jfuller/gen_mail_country-mex.html#MEXICAN-INDIANS
For anyone with a genealogical, historical, or cultural interest in the native peoples of Mexico.

o **MEXICO Mailing List**
http://www.rootsweb.com/~jfuller/gen_mail_country-mex.html#MEXICO

o **MEX-JALISCO Mailing List**
http://www.rootsweb.com/~jfuller/gen_mail_country-mex.html#MEX-JALISCO
For anyone with a genealogical interest in the State of Jalisco, Mexico.

o **MEX-MEXICO Mailing List**
http://www.rootsweb.com/~jfuller/gen_mail_country-mex.html#MEX-MEXICO
For anyone with a genealogical interest in the State of Mexico, Mexico.

o **MEX-MICHOACAN Mailing List**
http://www.rootsweb.com/~jfuller/gen_mail_country-mex.html#MEX-MICHOACAN
For anyone with a genealogical interest in the State of Michoacan, Mexico.

o **MEX-MORELOS Mailing List**
http://www.rootsweb.com/~jfuller/gen_mail_country-mex.html#MEX-MORELOS
For anyone with a genealogical interest in the State of Morelos, Mexico.

o MEX-NAYARIT Mailing List
http://www.rootsweb.com/~jfuller/gen_mail_country-mex.html#MEX-NAYARIT
For anyone with a genealogical interest in the State of Nayarit, Mexico.

o MEX-NUEVO-LEON Mailing List
http://www.rootsweb.com/~jfuller/gen_mail_country-mex.html#MEX-NUEVO-LEON
For anyone with a genealogical interest in the State of Nuevo Leon, Mexico.

o MEX-OAXACA Mailing List
http://www.rootsweb.com/~jfuller/gen_mail_country-mex.html#MEX-OAXACA
For anyone with a genealogical interest in the State of Oaxaca, Mexico.

o MEX-PUEBLA Mailing List
http://www.rootsweb.com/~jfuller/gen_mail_country-mex.html#MEX-PUEBLA
For anyone with a genealogical interest in the State of Puebla, Mexico.

o MEX-QUERETARO Mailing List
http://www.rootsweb.com/~jfuller/gen_mail_country-mex.html#MEX-QUERETARO
For anyone with a genealogical interest in the State of Queretaro, Mexic.

o MEX-QUINTANA-ROO Mailing List
http://www.rootsweb.com/~jfuller/gen_mail_country-mex.html#MEX-QUINTANA-ROO
For anyone with a genealogical interest in the State of Quintana Roo, Mexico.

o MEX-SAN-LUIS-POTOSI Mailing List
http://www.rootsweb.com/~jfuller/gen_mail_country-mex.html#MEX-SAN-LUIS-POTOSI
For anyone with a genealogical interest in the State of San Luis Potosi, Mexico.

o MEX-SINALOA Mailing List
http://www.rootsweb.com/~jfuller/gen_mail_country-mex.html#MEX-SINALOA
For anyone with a genealogical interest in the State of Sinaloa, Mexico.

o MEX-SONORA Mailing List
http://www.rootsweb.com/~jfuller/gen_mail_country-mex.html#MEX-SONORA
For anyone with a genealogical interest in the State of Sonora, Mexico.

o MEX-TABASCO Mailing List
http://www.rootsweb.com/~jfuller/gen_mail_country-mex.html#MEX-TABASCO
For anyone with a genealogical interest in the State of Tabasco, Mexico.

o MEX-TAMAULIPAS Mailing List
http://www.rootsweb.com/~jfuller/gen_mail_country-mex.html#MEX-TAMAULIPAS
For anyone with a genealogical interest in the State of Tamaulipas, Mexico.

o MEX-TLAXCALA Mailing List
http://www.rootsweb.com/~jfuller/gen_mail_country-mex.html#MEX-TLAXCALA
For anyone with a genealogical interest in the State of Tlaxcala, Mexico.

o MEX-VERACRUZ Mailing List
http://www.rootsweb.com/~jfuller/gen_mail_country-mex.html#MEX-VERACRUZ
For anyone with a genealogical interest in the State of Veracruz, Mexico.

o MEX-YUCATAN Mailing List
http://www.rootsweb.com/~jfuller/gen_mail_country-mex.html#MEX-YUCATAN
For anyone with a genealogical interest in the State of Yucatan, Mexico.

o MEX-ZACATECAS Mailing List
http://www.rootsweb.com/~jfuller/gen_mail_country-mex.html#MEX-ZACATECAS
For anyone with a genealogical interest in the State of Zacatecas, Mexico.

o PORTUGUESE-WESTINDIES Mailing List
http://www.rootsweb.com/~jfuller/gen_mail_country-wes.html#PORTUGUESE-WESTINDIES
For anyone with a genealogical interest in the Portuguese immigrants to the West Indies.

o REPUBLICA-DOMINICANA Mailing List
http://www.rootsweb.com/~jfuller/gen_mail_country-dom.html#REPUBLICA-DOMINICANA

o SAINT-DOMINGUE Mailing List
http://www.rootsweb.com/~jfuller/gen_mail_country-gen.html#SAINT-DOMINGUE
For anyone with a genealogical interest in the former French colony of Saint Domingue (now Haiti).

o Search Soc.genealogy.west-indies Posts
http://searches.rootsweb.com/sgwest-indies.html

o SOUTH-AM-EMI Mailing List
http://www.rootsweb.com/~jfuller/gen_mail_country-unk.html#SOUTH-AM-EMI
A mailing list for the discussion and sharing of information regarding emigrants from the United Kingdom to South America during the eighteenth and nineteenth centuries.

o TX-MEX Mailing List
http://www.rootsweb.com/~jfuller/gen_mail_states-tx.html#TX-MEX
For anyone with ancestors who immigrated to Texas from Mexico.

o Usenet Newsgroup soc.genealogy.hispanic
news:soc.genealogy.hispanic

o Usenet Newsgroup soc.genealogy.west-indies
news:soc.genealogy.west-indies

◆ People & Families

- David SILVERA's Home Page
http://www6.pair.com/silvera/
Primarily focused on the Spanish and Portuguese Jewish community in Jamaica, West Indies.

- De Windt's Family Home Page (1810-1996)
http://users.aksi.net/~wilfredo/dewindt.html
Curaçao and Dominican Republic.

- Lucy's Page
http://www.geocities.com/Heartland/Meadows/4296/family.html
MÁLAGA y BERNEDO.

- Michael ROSADO's Genealogy Home Page
  http://users.aol.com/mrosado007/personal/index.htm
  ROSADO PAGÁN, COLÓN CAPÓ, ROSADO DECLET, PAGÁN DECLET, COLÓN LEBRÓN, CAPÓ NAVARRO.

- A Page For My Family
  http://members.tripod.com/~blueflower/index.htm

- La Página de Genealogía de José Rivera Nieves
  http://www.geocities.com/Heartland/Prairie/9311/

- Valerio F. LAUBE - Home Page Genealogia ~ Brazil
  http://users.netuno.com.br/vflaube/vfl_05.htm
  LAUBE, ZOZ, WELTER, MARQUARDT.

- Viola's Web Home
  http://members.aol.com/vrsadler/index.html
  CÁRDENAS, CASTAÑEDA, ELIZONDO, LAZCANO, MARTÍNEZ, RODRÍGUEZ, VILLA.

◆ Professional Researchers, Volunteers & Other Research Services

- Board for Certification of Genealogists - Roster of Those Certified - Specializing in Mexico
  http://www.bcgcertification.org/rosts_@m.html

- Genealogy Helplist - Brazil
  http://helplist.org/bra/index.shtml

◆ Publications, Software & Supplies

- Amazon.com Genealogy Bookstore - Hispanic
  http://www.amazon.com/exec/obidos/external-search/?keyword=hispanic+genealogy&tag=markcyndisgenealA/

- AudioTapes.com - Genealogical Lectures on Cassette Tapes - Hispanic
  http://www.audiotapes.com/search2.asp?Search=hispanic

- Books We Own - Caribbean
  http://www.rootsweb.com/~bwo/caribbean.html
  Find a book from which you would like a lookup and click on the submitter's code at the end of the entry. Once you find the contact information for the submitter, write them a polite request for a lookup.

- Borderlands Bookstore
  http://www.borderlandsbooks.com/
  Historical and genealogical books about Texas, Mexico, Spain, and Portugal.

- Frontier Press Bookstore - Hispanic Research
  http://www.frontierpress.com/frontier.cgi?category=hisp

- GenealogyBookShop.com - Bahamas/Bahamian
  http://www.genealogybookshop.com/genealogybookshop/files/The_World,Bahamas_Bahamian/index.html
  Barbados
  http://www.genealogybookshop.com/genealogybookshop/files/The_World,Barbados/index.html
  Bermuda
  http://www.genealogybookshop.com/genealogybookshop/files/The_World,Bermuda/index.html

Jamaica/Jamaican
  http://www.genealogybookshop.com/genealogybookshop/files/The_World,Jamaica_Jamaican/index.html
  Spain/Spanish/Hispanic
  http://www.genealogybookshop.com/genealogybookshop/files/The_World,Spain_Spanish_Hispanic/index.html
  The online store of Genealogical Publishing Co., Inc. & Clearfield Company.

◆ Queries, Message Boards & Surname Lists

- HGSNY'S Query Boards
  http://www.hispanicgenealogy.com/queries/messageboards.htm
  Hispanic Query Boards from the Hispanic Genealogical Society of New York.

- Hispanic Surnames Database
  http://users.aol.com/mrosado007/surnames.htm

- West Indies Surname Interests List
  http://ourworld.compuserve.com/homepages/vroyal/

◆ Records: Census, Cemeteries, Land, Obituaries, Personal, Taxes and Vital (Born, Married, Died & Buried)

- Mexican Parish Records, 1751-1880
  http://www.ancestry.com/search/rectype/inddbs/3947.htm
  Pay-for-use database of marriage, baptism, and death records from nine Mexican parishes: Matamoros, Agualequas, Mier, Sabinas Hidalgo, Vallecillo, Cadereyta, Camargo, Cerralvo, & Guerrero with over 100,000 records including 400,000 names.

- PRHGS Obituary Index - Cuba
  http://www.rootsweb.com/~prhgs/obits_cuba_01.htm#Cuba
  Obituary Index of Hispanic people born in the Cuba from the Puerto Rican Hispanic Genealogical Society.

- PRHGS Obituary Index - Mexico
  http://www.rootsweb.com/~prhgs/obits_mexico_01.htm
  Obituary Index of Hispanic people born in Mexico from the Puerto Rican Hispanic Genealogical Society.

- PRHGS Obituary Index - USA
  http://www.rootsweb.com/~prhgs/obits_usa_01.htm
  Obituary Index of Hispanic people born in the United States from the Puerto Rican Hispanic Genealogical Society.

- Texas General Land Office - Finding Aids: Spanish and Mexican Land Resources
  http://www.glo.state.tx.us/archives/find_spanmex.html

◆ Societies & Groups

- Asociación de Genealogía Judía de Argentina
  http://www.marben.com.ar/toldot/
  Página Oficial de la Asociacion de Genealogia Judia de Argentina. Jewish Genealogical Society of Argentina (Official Site).

- Hispanic Genealogical Society ~ Houston, Texas
  http://www.brokersys.com/~joguerra/

- Hispanic Genealogical Society of New York
  http://www.hispanicgenealogy.com/

- Instituto Dominicano De Genealogia, Inc.
  http://members.tripod.com/~vmpv/idg

- Jewish Genealogical Society of Argentina
  http://www.jewishgen.org/infofiles/ar-jgs.txt

- National Society of Hispanic Genealogy ~ Denver, Colorado
  http://www.hispanicgen.org/
  Promote an interest and foster expertise, knowledge and further study of the history, ancestry, culture and traditions of the peoples who emigrated, settled, founded, and established communities in the areas of the United States of America formerly known as New Spain and Mexico.

- The Puerto Rican / Hispanic Genealogical Society
  http://www.rootsweb.com/~prhgs/

- Sociedad Puertorriqueña de Genealogía ~ San Juan, Puerto Rico
  http://www.usc.clu.edu/spg/

- The Society of Hispanic Historical and Ancestral Research (SHHAR)
  http://members.aol.com/shhar/index.html
  SHHAR (pronounced "share"), based in Orange County, California, has the specific goal of helping all Hispanics research their family history, regardless of the location of research interest. Commenced in 1986, formalized in 1987, the group has quickly grown to national and international networking status. A networking database is maintained. Registration is open and free.

- Spanish American Genealogical Association (SAGA) ~ Corpus Christi, Texas
  http://members.aol.com/sagacorpus/saga.htm
  Hispanic genealogical association with emphasis on families in northern Mexico and Texas.

- Victoria Hispanic Genealogical & Historical Society of Texas
  http://www.tisd.net/~dcano/vhghost.htm

◆ WorldGenWeb Project

- WorldGenWeb Project
  http://www.worldgenweb.org/
  - CaribbeanGenWeb
    http://www.rootsweb.com/~caribgw/
  - CentralAmGenWeb
    http://www.rootsweb.com/~centamgw/
  - FranceGenWeb - Guadeloupe, Martinique et Guyane Française
    http://user.mc.net/~orphans1/fgw/dom-tom/caraibe/
  - MexicoGenWeb Project
    http://www.rootsweb.com/~mexwgw/
  - SouthAmGenWeb
    http://www.rootsweb.com/~sthamgw/

HISTORICAL EVENTS & PEOPLE WORLDWIDE
http://www.cyndislist.com/historic.htm

Category Index:

- Ellis Island, New York
- General History Resources
- Heading West
- The Mayflower

- People & Families
- Societies & Groups
- The Titanic
- War & The Military

◆ Ellis Island, New York

- The American Immigrant Wall of Honor
  http://www.wallofhonor.com/

- The Ellis Island Home Page
  http://www.ellisisland.org/

- Ellis Island (I-Channel)
  http://www.i-channel.com/features/ellis/

- New York, NY, Ellis Island -- Immigration: 1900-1920
  http://cmp1.ucr.edu/exhibitions/immigration_id.html
  University of California, Riverside, Keystone-Mast Collection, California Museum of Photography. Photographs of immigrants, ships & Ellis Island.

◆ General History Resources

- Amazon.com Genealogy Bookstore - History
  http://www.amazon.com/exec/obidos/redirect?tag=markcyndisgeneal&path=ts/browse-books/9

- DoHistory
  http://www.dohistory.org/
  Explore the process of piecing together the lives of ordinary people in the past. It is an experimental, interactive case study based on the research that went into the book and film "A Midwife's Tale", which were both based upon the remarkable 200 year old diary of midwife/healer Martha Ballard. Learn basic skills and techniques for interpreting fragments that survive from any period in history.

- Historical Documents
  gopher://ucsbuxa.ucsb.edu:3001/11/.stacks/.historical
  Text files of documents such as the Declaration of Independence, the Magna Carta, the Mayflower Compact and more.

- The Historical Text Archive (HTA)
  http://www.msstate.edu/Archives/History/
  Housed at Mississippi State University.

- History Buff's Home Page
  http://www.historybuff.com/index.html
  Created by the Newspaper Collectors Society of America.

- History Channel
  http://www.historychannel.com/

- History Magazine
  http://www.history-magazine.com/
  From the publishers of Family Chronicle Magazine.

- The History Net
  http://www.thehistorynet.com/home.htm
  Where History Lives on the Web.

- The History Place
  http://www.historyplace.com/index.html

- History Today
  http://www.historytoday.com/index.cfm
  The World's Leading History Magazine.

- Horus' Web Links to History Resources
  http://www.ucr.edu/h-gig/horuslinks.html

- HyperHistory Online
  http://www.hyperhistory.com/online_n2/History_n2/a.html

- Index of Resources for Historians
  http://kuhttp.cc.ukans.edu/history/index.html

- Irish History on the Web
  http://wwwvms.utexas.edu/~jdana/irehist.html

- U.S. - History
  http://www.CyndisList.com/hist-us.htm
  See this category on Cyndi's List for related links.

- WWW Sites for Historians
  http://www.hist.unt.edu/09-www.htm

- Yahoo!...History
  http://dir.yahoo.com/Arts/Humanities/History/

◆ Heading West

- Explorers of the West
  http://upanet.uleth.ca/~Haig/

- The Hudson's Bay Company Archives
  http://www.gov.mb.ca/chc/archives/hbca/index.html
  From the Provincial Archives of Manitoba, Canada.

- Mountain Men and the Fur Trade
  http://www.xmission.com/~drudy/amm.html
  Sources of the History of the Fur Trade in the Rocky Mountain West.

- trails west Mailing List
http://www.rootsweb.com/~jfuller/gen_mail_states-gen.html
#trails-west
For those who want to research their family history and post facts on their move west in North America. The trails addressed by the list started at the very beginning of the settlement of North America and are not just the ones in western North America.

◆ The Mayflower

- The ALDEN House Museum
http://www.alden.org/
The home of John & Priscilla Alden in Duxbury, Massachusetts.

- The General Society of Mayflower Descendants
http://www.mayflower.org/

- A Mayflower & New England Study
http://www.mayflowerfamilies.com/

- MAYFLOWER Mailing List
http://www.rootsweb.com/~jfuller/gen_mail_states-gen.html
#MAYFLOWER
A mailing list for the discussion and sharing of information regarding the descendants of the Mayflower passengers in any place and at any time.

- Mayflower Web Page
http://members.aol.com/calebj/mayflower.html

◆ People & Families

- Association for the Preservation of Virginia Antiquities - Jamestown Rediscovery
http://www.apva.org/
  o A Brief History of Jamestown
  http://www.apva.org/history/index.html

- Biographical Dictionary
http://www.s9.com/biography/
Covers more than 19,000 notable men and women.

- Descendants of * of the Ark NOAH
http://www.parsonstech.com/genealogy/trees/dmalec/burkhamm.htm

- Descendants of Royalty, Historical Figures
http://www.worldroots.com/brigitte/royal/royal11.htm

- Genealogy of Mankind from Adam to Japheth, Shem, and Ham
http://www.geocities.com/Tokyo/4241/geneadm2.html

- Henry Hudson - The life and times of Henry Hudson, explorer and adventurer
http://www.georgian.net/rally/hudson/

- HMS Bounty Genealogies
http://www.lareau.org/bounty6.html

- Interpreting The Irish Famine, 1846-1850
http://www.people.virginia.edu/~eas5e/Irish/Famine.html

- Lewis & Clark - The Journey of the Corps of Discovery
http://www.pbs.org/lewisandclark/
The companion web site for the PBS series by Ken Burns.

- List of Officers and Sailors in the First Voyage of Columbus in 1492
http://www.rootsweb.com/~ote/colship.htm
Nina, Pinta, Santa Maria.

- Magellan's Voyages from The Discovery of America by John Fiske published in 1892
http://www.rootsweb.com/~ote/magship.htm
The Victoria and the Trinidad.

- METISGEN Mailing List
http://www.rootsweb.com/~jfuller/gen_mail_general.html
#METISGEN
For the discussion and sharing of information regarding the Metis and their descendants. The Metis are North America's Fur Trading Children ... the new nation of individuals born within North America from the first unions of natives and whites.

- Notable Women Ancestors
http://www.rootsweb.com/~nwa/

- Palatine Emigrants by Kraig Ruckel
http://www.geocities.com/Heartland/3955/palatine.htm

- Palatines to America Homepage
http://www.genealogy.org:80/~palam/

- Pocahontas Descendants
http://www.rootscomputing.com/howto/pocahn/pocahn.htm
Descendants of Powhatan (Father of Pocahontas).

- The Political Graveyard
http://politicalgraveyard.com/
"The Web Site That Tells Where the Dead Politicians are Buried".

- Relatives, Friends and Associates of Isaac Newton
http://www.newtonia.freeserve.co.uk/G/Gbio.html

- Robert BURNS Family History
http://fox.nstn.ca/~jburness/burns.html
Family history of the Scottish poet Robert Burns including 130 descendants and over 800 other relatives.

- Roman Emperors - The Imperial Index
http://www.salve.edu/~dimaiom/impindex.html
An Online Encyclopedia of Roman Emperors.

- ROOTS-L Resources: Historical Groups
http://www.rootsweb.com/roots-l/hist_groups.html
Links to several articles and sites regarding various groups, such as the Lewis & Clark expedition and many more.

- A Roster of the Lewis & Clark Expedition
http://www.rootsweb.com/~genepool/lewiclar.htm

- Royalty & Nobility
http://www.CyndisList.com/royalty.htm
See this category on Cyndi's List for related links.

- A Shakespeare Genealogy
http://daphne.palomar.edu/shakespeare/timeline/genealogy.htm

◆ Societies & Groups

- The Historical Association ~ U.K.
  http://www.history.org.uk/

- National Society Magna Charta Dames and Barons
  http://www.magnacharta.org
  The page provides information about the Society, a national organization with over 16,000 members, meeting throughout the United States. Meetings normally feature talks by historians, legislators, judges concerning the Magna Charta. The site also includes detailed information about the 25 Surety Barons as well as initial information about 56 immigrant ancestors descended from one or more of the Barons. Additional immigrant ancestors will be added in the future.

- Railroad Historical Societies
  http://tucson.com/concor/histsoc.html

◆ The Titanic

- Encyclopedia Titanica
  http://www.encyclopedia-titanica.org/

- In Memoriam: RMS Titanic
  http://miso.wwa.com/~dsp//titanic/

- The Original Titanic Home Page
  http://www.home.gil.com.au/~dalgarry/

- Titanic and Other White Star Ships
  http://members.aol.com/MNichol/Titanic.index.html

- Titanic Passenger List
  http://www.lva.lib.va.us/pubserv/vnp/titanic/p2.htm

- Titanic ~ The Unsinkable Ship and Halifax
  http://titanic.gov.ns.ca/
  A site from Halifax, Nova Scotia, Canada, including a list of those buried in cemeteries in Halifax.

◆ War & The Military

- The Alamo
  http://numedia.tddc.net/sa/alamo/

- AMERICAN-REVOLUTION Mailing List
  http://www.rootsweb.com/~jfuller/gen_mail_states-gen.html
  #AMERICAN-REVOLUTION
  For the discussion of events during the American Revolution and genealogical matters related to the American Revolution. The French-Indian Wars and the War of 1812 are also suitable topics for discussion.

- Canada - Military
  http://www.CyndisList.com/milcan.htm
  See this category on Cyndi's List for related links.

- Dad's War: Finding and Telling Your Father's World War II Story
  http://members.aol.com/dadswar/

- Descendants of Mexican War Veterans
  http://www.dmwv.org/

- The French and Indian Raid on Deerfield, Massachusetts, 1704
  http://www.crossmyt.com/hc/gen/deerfild.html

- Korean War Project
  http://www.koreanwar.org/

- The Mexican-American War Memorial Homepage
  http://sunsite.unam.mx/revistas/1847/

- Michael Meals Presents: www.revwar.com
  http://www.revwar.com/

- Military Resources Worldwide
  http://www.CyndisList.com/milres.htm
  See this category on Cyndi's List for related links.

- Secrets of the Norman Invasion
  http://www.cablenet.net/pages/book/index.htm
  With plates of the Bayeux Tapestry.

- A Selection of Underground Railroad Resources
  http://www.ugrr.org/web.htm

- United States Holocaust Memorial Museum
  http://www.ushmm.org/

- U.S. Civil War ~ The War for Southern Independence
  http://www.CyndisList.com/cw.htm
  See this category on Cyndi's List for related links.

- U.S. Military
  http://www.CyndisList.com/military.htm
  See this category on Cyndi's List for related links.

- Vietnam Era POW/MIA Database
  http://lcweb2.loc.gov/pow/powhome.html
  At the Library of Congress.

- The Wars of Religion
  http://www.lepg.org/wars.htm

HIT A BRICK WALL?

http://www.cyndislist.com/hitbrick.htm

- Books We Own
  http://www.rootsweb.com/~bwo/index.html
  Sometimes it is best to set aside your research problem and put your thoughts elsewhere for a while. Whenever I've done this I can always come back to the problem with a fresh set of eyes. Try volunteering to help others for a while instead. The Books We Own site is a great way to begin!

- Breaking Down Brick Walls
  http://www.audiotapes.com/product.asp?ProductCode= 'BTBKN01'
  Presentation by John Philip Colletta, available for sale on audio tape.

- Breaking Down Immigrant Brick Walls
  http://www.audiotapes.com/product.asp?ProductCode= 'ASJG-49'
  Presentation by Eileen Polakoff, available for sale on audio tape.

- Breaking Through a Brick Wall
  http://www.audiotapes.com/product.asp?ProductCode= 'ASJGCA70'
  Presentation by Boris Feldblyum, available for sale on audio tape.

- Circumventing Blocked Lines
  http://www.audiotapes.com/product.asp?ProductCode= 'FGS00-T-75'
  Presentation by Sandra Hargreaves Luebking, available for sale on audio tape.

- Cyndi's Genealogy Home Page Construction Kit
  http://www.CyndisList.com/construc.htm
  Create your own web page in order to put up a list of your surnames and your research questions, problems & mysteries!

- Finding People
  http://www.CyndisList.com/finding.htm
  Phone Numbers, E-Mail Addresses, Mailing Addresses, Places, Etc.

- First Name Basis
  http://www.hypervigilance.com/genlog/firstname.html
  To aid you in researching when all you know is the first name of a person. Focuses on unusual first names and women's first names when maiden names are unknown.

- Finding "Unfindable" People in the U.S. Census
  http://www.audiotapes.com/product.asp?ProductCode= 'FGS00-S-143'
  Presentation by Larry L. Piatt, available for sale on audio tape.

- Genealogy.com: Discrepancy Charts - Organizing the Inconclusive
  http://www.genealogy.com/genealogy/37_neill.html
  By Michael John Neill.

- Genealogy's Most Wanted
  http://www.citynet.net/mostwanted/
  One of the first sites online to help us get past this brick wall!

- GEN-UNSOLVED-MYSTERIES Mailing List
  http://www.rootsweb.com/~jfuller/gen_mail_general.html
  #GEN-UNSOLVED-MYSTERIES
  For people whose family genealogies include "unsolved mysteries." Postings should include only mysterious disappearances or appearances, unsolved murders, questionable incarcerations, and other mysterious or unsolved events in an ancestor's life. Postings should not include "brick walls" since these would be repetitive of the content of other lists.

- How To
  http://www.CyndisList.com/howto.htm
  Stop by the "How To" category on this site and read through multiple helpful articles on all sorts of research topics. Perhaps the answer is hidden in one of these online resources!

- How-to get past the "Stone Wall Syndrome"
  http://www.firstct.com/fv/stone.html
  A terrific article from Robert Ragan's Treasure Maps site.

- Library of Congress
  http://lcweb.loc.gov/homepage/lchp.html
  One visitor to my site suggested checking the Library of Congress to see if your ancestor had a biography or an autobiography written about him or her. Another visitor pointed out that you should specifically check with the genealogy section "which contains genealogies sent to the the LC, some of them merely typed, many not published."

- Mailing Lists
  http://www.CyndisList.com/mailing.htm
  Join a mailing list for your specific surname or your research locality. Communicate regularly with others who are researching the same names or in the same areas and share ideas, hints, tips and advice.

- Newsgroups
  http://www.CyndisList.com/newsgrps.htm
  Read messages posted on genealogy newsgroups for your specific surname or your research locality. Communicate regularly with others who are researching the same names or in the same areas and share ideas, hints, tips and advice.

- Problem Solving for Genealogists
  http://www.ancestry.com/dailynews/06_24_99.htm#3
  By Michael John Neill for Ancestry.com Daily News.

- Professional Researchers, Volunteers & Other Research Services
  http://www.CyndisList.com/profess.htm
  If all else fails you might consider hiring a professional researcher to do some of the work for you. I can't personally endorse any of the researchers on this page, so you must use your best judgment in obtaining their services. You might also try to "swap" volunteer services with others who need help in your areas of expertise or resources.

- Queries & Message Boards
  http://www.CyndisList.com/queries.htm
  Search through thousands of online queries by other researchers. Make up your own basic/generic query for each person you are working on and post it in as many spots as you can as you sift through other's queries. Stop by each of the USGenWeb pages for the counties you are researching in and look through their queries also.

- Search Engines
  http://www.CyndisList.com/search.htm
  Use any of the search engines on this page to do a search on a specific surname, place name or keyword that you are interested in. Read the help files and the FAQ for each search engine and learn how they each work. Try different combinations of words & phrases to maximize your search results.

- Solve Brickwall Research Problems: Find Living Cousins
  http://www.audiotapes.com/product.asp?ProductCode= 'NGS223'
  Presentation by Kathleen W. Hinckley, available for sale on audio tape.

- Sources of Genealogical Information
  http://www.rootsweb.com/~genepool/sources.htm
  "Have you reached a dead-end in your research? Have you looked in these records yet?!" A checklist of resources you shouldn't overlook in your research. From Joanne Rabun and the Gene Pool.

- UFO-ROOTS Mailing List
  http://www.rootsweb.com/~jfuller/gen_mail_general.html #UFO-ROOTS
  For those whose ancestors arrived from outer space to make connections with others sharing this problem, discuss their ancestry, and provide advice on possible avenues for further research

- Web Rings for Genealogy
  http://www.CyndisList.com/webrings.htm
  Web rings are popping up on genealogy web sites all over the net. A "web ring" is a series of web sites connected to one another via a special link table set up for sites that fit a specific topic. There are several web rings for genealogy, covering everything from general genealogical web sites to the Civil War, Jewish genealogy and Reunion software users. When you see a web ring table on a site you can choose to follow the link to the next site on that ring, or you can skip ahead 5 links or you can choose a random link on the ring. Doesn't this sound like the type of thing you should do when you hit that brick wall in your research? It reminds me of randomly stopping your arm as you rewind a roll of microfilm and you spot your long-lost ancestor on the page in front of you!

- When Your Family History Research Hits the Wall
  http://www.parkbooks.com/Html/res_guid.html
  A research guide from Park Genealogical Books.

- When Your Ox Is in the Ditch : Genealogical How-To Letters
  http://www.amazon.com/exec/obidos/ISBN=0806314842/ markcyndisgenealA/
  A book by Vera McDowell.

HOUSE & BUILDING HISTORIES

http://www.cyndislist.com/houses.htm

- AudioTapes.com - Genealogical Lectures on Cassette Tapes - Houses
  http://www.audiotapes.com/search.asp?Search=House

- Building and House History
  http://www.mnhs.org/library/tips/bldghistory/bldghistory.html
  Minnesota Historical Society.

- County Record Office: Researching Your House
  http://www.warwickshire.gov.uk/general/crohouse.htm
  Warwickshire Libraries & Heritage, England.

- A Field Guide to American Houses
  http://www.amazon.com/exec/obidos/ISBN=0394739698/markcyndisgenealA/
  A book by Virginia & Lee McAlester.

- Fire Insurance Maps
  http://www.CyndisList.com/maps.htm#Fire
  See this category on the Maps page of Cyndi's List for related links.

- Fort Collins Public Library Local History Archive - Researching the History of Your Home
  http://library.ci.fort-collins.co.us/local_history/hist1a.htm

- Greene County Public Library - Dating a Structure
  http://www.gcpl.lib.oh.us/services/gcr/hist_res/dating.htm

- Guernsey Datestones ~ Channel Islands, U.K.
  http://user.itl.net/~glen/stonegsy.html

- Historic Preservation Consulting Services ~ MA
  http://www.tiac.net/users/amland/cnsltg.htm

- House Histories : A Guide to Tracing the Genealogy of Your Home
  http://www.amazon.com/exec/obidos/ISBN=0961487615/markcyndisgenealA/
  A book by Sally Light.

- House History
  http://dialspace.dial.pipex.com/achievements/house.html

- House Stories - The Timothy Kimball Farm c. 1764 ~ New Hampshire
  http://www.conknet.com/~rwoods/house_stories.html

- How to Research the History of Real Estate
  http://www.cmhpf.org/resources/researching.html

- How to Research the History of Your House (or Other Building) in New Orleans ~ Louisiana
  http://www.gnofn.org/~nopl/guides/house/title.htm

- The Jersey Datestones Project ~ Channel Islands, U.K.
  http://www.societe-jersiaise.org/alexgle/stonejsy.html

- Local Monmouth and Monmouthshire House and Family Histories - Genealogy ~ U.K.
  http://www.mresources.co.uk/clarke/

- Looking Back: Researching the History of Your Home
  http://chicagotribune.com/marketplaces/yourplace/print edition/article/0,2669,SAV-9911050085,FF.html
  From the Chicago Tribune.

- Merry Meet and Welcome
  http://www.geocities.com/Athens/Acropolis/5261/bio.html
  Professional house history "detective" in England.

- Norfolk Record Office Leaflets - Sources and Brief Notes on Tracing the History of a House in Norfolk ~ England
  http://www.norfolk.gov.uk/council/departments/nro/nrohouses.htm

- Ottawa Historical Researcher Available
  http://www.freeyellow.com/members5/househistory1/index.html

- Pennsylvania Department: House Histories: A Pathfinder
  http://www.clpgh.org/clp/Pennsylvania/houses.html
  How to Trace the Genealogy of Your Home.

- Researching a Building's History
  http://interoz.com/lubbock/ar02.htm

- Researching Old Houses
  http://www.shentel.net/handley-library/RESHOUSE.htm
  The Archives Room, Handley Regional Library, Winchester - Frederick County Historical Society, Virginia.

- Researching Saint John's Building Histories ~ New Brunswick, Canada
  http://www.saintjohn.nbcc.nb.ca/~Heritage/classics/Research.htm
  Information for a variety of buildings in Saint John. The level of documentation differs for all properties. In some cases it may be nothing more than a list of previous property owners and building residents. In others, it could include information on the building designer and/or builder. It might include architectural drawings, or photographs. It is rare to research a property in Saint John where one would find architectural drawings, information on the builder and construction details, historic photographs and information on the property owners.

- Researching the History of a House at the Local History Department of the Grand Rapids Public Library ~ Michigan
  http://www.grpl.org/coll/lhhousehis.html

- Researching the History of Your House
  http://www2.lib.udel.edu/ref/docs/house-bib.htm
  A Bibliography Prepared by David L. Langenberg, Local History Committee, History Section, R. U. S. A.

- Researching Your Home
  http://www.pastheritage.org/research.html

- Researching Your Older Tacoma Home ~ Washington
  http://www.tpl.lib.wa.us/v2/NWRoom/Build.htm
  Written by Brian Kamens, Northwest Room & Special Collections, Tacoma Public Library.

- Researching Your Old House - California Room - San José Public Library
  http://www.sjpl.lib.ca.us/Adults/CaliforniaRoom/oldhouse.htm

- Research Services - Home History
  http://www.co.dupage.il.us/museum/research.html#history
  From the Dupage County Illinois Historical Museum.

- Society of Genealogists Bookshop - History of Houses ~ U.K.
  http://www.sog.org.uk/acatalog/SoG_Bookshop_Online_History_of_Houses_46.html

- Sources for Building History: A Guide to Researching Historic Buildings in the British Isles
  http://www.jams.swinternet.co.uk/

- Tracing the History of Buildings
  http://www.nas.gov.uk/tracing_the_history_of_buildings.htm
  From the National Archives of Scotland.

- Tracing the History of Your House ~ Michigan
  http://www.macomb.lib.mi.us/mountclemens/tracing.htm
  A Guide to Local Resources Prepared by Mount Clemens Public Library.

- Tracing the History of Your House, UWEC McIntyre Library
  http://www.uwec.edu/Admin/library/Guides/Houshist.html

- Tracing Your Home's History
  http://www.ccpl.lib.oh.us/tracing.htm

- Uncovering Your Home's History
  http://www.paweekly.com/PAW/morgue/real_estate/1997_Jul_25.HOME25.html
  Online article from the Palo Alto Weekly Online Edition.

- The Urban Genealogist
  http://www.pipeline.com/~trob/urban.htm
  Professional house historian and researcher.

  o Notes from The Genealogy of a Tenement
    http://www.pipeline.com/~trob/jgs.htm
    By Tony Robins.

- Websteader: Pioneer Dugouts, 1830-1999
  http://websteader.com/wbstdsd2.htm
  Pictures and descriptions of how dugouts are constructed.

- Websteader: Pioneer Sod Houses, c. 1880-1999
  http://websteader.com/wbstdsd1.htm
  Pictures and descriptions of how sod houses are constructed.

- Writing House History - This Old House
  http://www.imcpl.lib.in.us/ss_hshis.htm

HOW TO

http://www.cyndislist.com/howto.htm

Category Index:

◆ Electronic Genealogical Research
◆ General Genealogical Guides, Hints & Tips

◆ Mailing Lists, Newsgroups & Chat
◆ Publications, Software & Supplies

◆ Electronic Genealogical Research

● Genealogy Web Page Tutorial
http://www.geocities.com/Heartland/Acres/7002/
How to create your own genealogy web page.

● The Internet & Webbing Your Family History
http://www.pe.net/~lucindaw/internet/internet.htm
From the Harper County Genealogical Society.

● Online Research Techniques from Everton's:
Part 1
http://www.everton.com/oe2-5/ort1.htm
Part 2
http://www.everton.com/oe2-6/ort2.htm
Part 3
http://www.everton.com/oe2-7/ort3.htm
Part 4
http://www.everton.com/oe2-8/ort4.htm

● Practical Genealogy Research - Making the Internet Work for You
http://www.zen.co.uk/home/page/joe.houghton/
RESEARCH.HTM

◆ General Genealogical Guides, Hints & Tips

● 20 Ways to Avoid Genealogical Grief
http://www.rootsweb.com/roots-l/20ways.html

● Backward Footprints
http://www.geocities.com/CapitolHill/1025/faq.html

● Board for Certification of Genealogists - Skillbuilding, Index of Available Columns
http://www.bcgcertification.org/skbldidx.html

● Checklist of Home Sources
http://www.rootscomputing.com/howto/checkl/checkl.htm

● The Genealogist's Guide - from Heritage Associates
http://www.granniesworld.com/heritage/guide.htm

● The GenTutor Approach to Climbing Your Family Tree
http://members.aol.com/GenTutor/tutor.html

● Professional Researchers, Volunteers & Other Research Services
http://www.CyndisList.com/profess.htm
See this category on Cyndi's List for related links.

● Repeat Performance - Audio/Video Recording Services
http://www.repeatperformance.com/
Tapes of classes and presentations at several genealogy conferences and seminars for the last 18 years.

● Research Tips on Gathering Your Family Information
http://ourworld.compuserve.com/homepages/Strawn/tips.htm

● Standards for Sound Genealogical Research
http://www.ngsgenealogy.org/about/content/committees/
gene_stan.html
Recommended by the National Genealogical Society.

● Standards for Using Records Repositories and Libraries
http://www.ngsgenealogy.org/about/content/committees/
gene_stan.html
Recommended by the National Genealogical Society.

● Treasure Maps: The "How-To" Genealogy Site
http://www.firstct.com/fv/tmaps.html

● Wanda's Genealogy Tips
http://wlake.com/wandas/genepage.html

● What You Should Know Before Hiring A Professional Genealogist
http://www.genservices.com/documents/HiringAPro.html

◆ Mailing Lists, Newsgroups & Chat

● Family Tree Finders
http://www.sodamail.com/site/ftf.shtml
A Monday through Friday newsletter that provides interesting and useful information for tracing your family tree. It's geared to beginners and experienced family tree trackers of any age! Written by well known genealogist, Rhonda R. McClure.

● GENMTD Mailing List
http://www.rootsweb.com/~jfuller/gen_mail_info.html
#GENMTD-L
Gatewayed with the soc.genealogy.methods newsgroup for the discussion of genealogy research techniques and resources.

- GEN-ROOTERS Mailing List
  http://www.rootsweb.com/~jfuller/gen_mail_religions.html
  #GEN-ROOTERS
  For members of the Church of Jesus Christ of Latter-day Saints to share ideas and helpful hints on the "how-to's" of genealogy.

- GEN-SHARE Mailing List
  http://www.rootsweb.com/~jfuller/gen_mail_info.html
  #GEN-SHARE
  For "seasoned" genealogy researchers to share sources and get help with tough problems. This list is not for the posting of queries addressing searches for specific ancestors and is not recommended for those new to genealogy.

- GenTips-L Mailing List
  http://www.rootsweb.com/~jfuller/gen_mail_general.html
  #GenTips-L
  For anyone who has an interest in genealogy. This list hopes to provide tips about obtaining genealogy records and is useful for both beginning genealogists and experts.

- RESEARCH-HOWTO Mailing List
  http://www.rootsweb.com/~jfuller/gen_mail_general.html
  #RESEARCH-HOWTO
  For those who are just getting started in genealogy research and those who are not novices but need information on where to go when "dead ends" are encountered.

◆ Publications, Software & Supplies

- Amazon.com Genealogy Bookstore - How To
  http://www.amazon.com/exec/obidos/external-search/?
  keyword=how+to+genealogy&tag=markcyndisgenealA/

- American Genealogical Research at the DAR, Washington, D.C.
  http://www.dar.org/library/libpub.html

- Books We Own - Genealogy, General Reference
  http://www.rootsweb.com/~bwo/gen_ref.html
  Find a book from which you would like a lookup and click on the submitter's code at the end of the entry. Once you find the contact information for the submitter, write them a polite request for a lookup.

- Computer Genealogist - New Technology for Genealogy - PERiodical Source Index
  http://www.credible.com/genealg7.html
  An article from Computer Credible Magazine by Alan E. Mann.

- Frontier Press Bookstore - Beginning Genealogy
  http://www.frontierpress.com/frontier.cgi?category=begin

- GenealogyBookShop.com - Guides and Manuals
  http://www.genealogybookshop.com/genealogybookshop/
  files/General,Guides_and_Manuals/index.html
  The online store of Genealogical Publishing Co., Inc. & Clearfield Company.

- Global Genealogy - General Genealogy Topics & How - To Books
  http://www.globalgenealogy.com/howto.htm

- Heritage Books - Research Aids
  http://www.heritagebooks.com/resaids.htm

- Repeat Performance - Audio/Video Recording Services
  http://www.repeatperformance.com/
  Tapes of classes and presentations at several genealogy conferences and seminars for the last 18 years.

- The Source: A Guidebook of American Genealogy
  http://www.ancestry.com/home/source/srcindex.htm
  A full, online version of this book, published by Ancestry, edited by Loretto Dennis Szucs and Sandra Hargreaves Luebking.

- Willow Bend Bookstore - How To Genealogy
  http://www.willowbend.net/default.asp

- Willow Bend Bookstore - Research Aids
  http://www.willowbend.net/default.asp

HOW TO ~ TUTORIALS & GUIDES

http://www.cyndislist.com/howtotut.htm

Category Index:

- ◆ Ancestors: The First Television Series
- ◆ Ancestry.com
- ◆ FamilySearch - Research Helps
- ◆ Genealogy.com

- ◆ Genealogy Research Associates
- ◆ Heritage Quest - Genealogy: Help Guide for Beginners
- ◆ RootsWeb's Guide to Tracing Family Trees

◆ Ancestors: The First Television Series

- ● Ancestors : A Beginner's Guide to Family History and Genealogy
  http://www.amazon.com/exec/obidos/ISBN=0395854105/markcyndisgenealA/
  A book by Jim & Terry Willard and Jane Wilson.

- ● Ancestors: The First Series
  http://www.pbs.org/kbyu/ancestors/firstseries/

- ● Ancestors: The First Series - Charts & Records
  http://www.pbs.org/kbyu/ancestors/firstseries/teachersguide/charts-records.html

- ● Ancestors: The First Series - Teacher's Guide
  http://www.pbs.org/kbyu/ancestors/firstseries/teachersguide/
  From the first television series on PBS, a teacher's guide for starting a family history project
  - o Getting Started
    http://www.pbs.org/kbyu/ancestors/firstseries/teachersguide/episode-one.html
  - o Looking At Home
    http://www.pbs.org/kbyu/ancestors/firstseries/teachersguide/episode-two.html
  - o Gathering Family Stories
    http://www.pbs.org/kbyu/ancestors/firstseries/teachersguide/episode-three.html
  - o The Paper Trail
    http://www.pbs.org/kbyu/ancestors/firstseries/teachersguide/episode-four.html
  - o Libraries And Archives
    http://www.pbs.org/kbyu/ancestors/firstseries/teachersguide/episode-five.html
  - o Military And Census Records
    http://www.pbs.org/kbyu/ancestors/firstseries/teachersguide/episode-six.html
  - o African American Research
    http://www.pbs.org/kbyu/ancestors/firstseries/teachersguide/episode-seven.html
  - o Your Medical Heritage
    http://www.pbs.org/kbyu/ancestors/firstseries/teachersguide/episode-eight.html

- o High Tech Help
  http://www.pbs.org/kbyu/ancestors/firstseries/teachersguide/episode-nine.html
- o Leaving A Legacy
  http://www.pbs.org/kbyu/ancestors/firstseries/teachersguide/episode-ten.html

- ● Ancestors: The First Series - Viewer's Guide To Getting Started
  http://www.pbs.org/kbyu/ancestors/firstseries/viewersguide/
  - o Getting Started
    http://www.pbs.org/kbyu/ancestors/firstseries/viewersguide/episode-one.html
  - o Looking At Home
    http://www.pbs.org/kbyu/ancestors/firstseries/viewersguide/episode-two.html
  - o Gathering Family Stories
    http://www.pbs.org/kbyu/ancestors/firstseries/viewersguide/episode-three.html
  - o The Paper Trail
    http://www.pbs.org/kbyu/ancestors/firstseries/viewersguide/episode-four.html
  - o Libraries And Archives
    http://www.pbs.org/kbyu/ancestors/firstseries/viewersguide/episode-five.html
  - o Military and Census Records
    http://www.pbs.org/kbyu/ancestors/firstseries/viewersguide/episode-six.html
  - o African American Research
    http://www.pbs.org/kbyu/ancestors/firstseries/viewersguide/episode-seven.html
  - o Your Medical Heritage
    http://www.pbs.org/kbyu/ancestors/firstseries/viewersguide/episode-eight.html
  - o High Tech Help
    http://www.pbs.org/kbyu/ancestors/firstseries/viewersguide/episode-nine.html
  - o Leaving A Legacy
    http://www.pbs.org/kbyu/ancestors/firstseries/viewersguide/episode-ten.html

◆ Ancestry.com

- ● Ancestry.com - Learn
  http://www.ancestry.com/learn/main.htm

o Getting Started
  http://www.ancestry.com/learn/start/main.htm
  - First Steps
    http://www.ancestry.com/learn/start/memories.htm
  - Organizing Data
    http://www.ancestry.com/learn/start/surveying.htm
  - Computers & Genealogy
    http://www.ancestry.com/learn/start/traditional.htm
  - Legal Considerations
    http://www.ancestry.com/learn/start/freedom.htm
  - Etiquette
    http://www.ancestry.com/learn/start/etiquette.htm
  - Ethics
    http://www.ancestry.com/learn/start/ethics.htm

o Learning Center
  http://www.ancestry.com/learn/learning/main.htm
  - Expert Help
    http://www.ancestry.com/learn/learning/expert.htm
  - Learn Family History Online
    http://www.ancestry.com/learn/learning/online.htm
  - Genealogy Network
    http://www.ancestry.com/learn/learning/societies.htm
  - Geographic Elements
    http://www.ancestry.com/learn/learning/maps.htm
  - Historical Elements
    http://www.ancestry.com/learn/learning/historic.htm
  - Computer Genealogy
    http://www.ancestry.com/learn/learning/gedcoms.htm

◆ FamilySearch - Family History SourceGuide

- FamilySearch - Research Guidance
  http://www.familysearch.org/Eng/Search/RG/frameset_rg.asp

  o Discovering Your Family Tree
    http://www.familysearch.org/Eng/Search/rg/frameset_
    rg.asp?Dest=G1&Aid=&Gid=&Lid=&Sid=&Did=&Juris1=
    &Event=&Year=&Gloss=&Sub=&Tab=&Entry=&Guide=
    DisTree.ASP

  o A Guide to Research
    http://www.familysearch.org/Eng/Search/rg/frameset_
    rg.asp?Dest=G1&Aid=&Gid=&Lid=&Sid=&Did=&Juris1=
    &Event=&Year=&Gloss=&Sub=&Tab=&Entry=&Guide=
    Guide_to_Research.ASP

  o How Do I Begin?
    http://www.familysearch.org/Eng/Search/RG/guide/all_t3_
    resmeth_-_how_do_i_begin.asp

  o Tips on How to Search the Ancestral File
    http://www.familysearch.org/Eng/Search/af/searchaf_
    hints.asp

  o Tips on How to Search the International
    Genealogical Index
    http://www.familysearch.org/Eng/Search/igi/searchigi_
    hintsasp

o Tracing Immigrant Origins Research Outline
  http://www.familysearch.org/Eng/Search/RG/guide/tracing_
  immigrant_origins.asp

- FamilySearch - Research Helps
  http://www.familysearch.org/Eng/Search/RG/frameset_
  rhelps.asp

◆ Genealogy.com

- Genealogy.com's Genealogy "How-To" Guide
  http://www.genealogy.com/mainmenu.html

  o How-To Articles
    http://www.genealogy.com/backissu.html
    - African American Genealogy
      http://www.familytreemaker.com/issue12.html
    - Aspects of Internet Genealogy
      http://www.familytreemaker.com/issue29.html
    - Caring for Your Family Photos
      http://www.familytreemaker.com/issue10.html
    - Celebrating Kinship Connections -- and Mom!
      http://www.familytreemaker.com/issue16.html
    - Documenting Sources
      http://www.familytreemaker.com/issue19.html
    - Family Archive CD Spotlight
      http://www.familytreemaker.com/issue22.html
    - Family Associations
      http://www.familytreemaker.com/issue26.html
    - Family History Books
      http://www.familytreemaker.com/issue21.html
    - Family Reunions
      http://www.familytreemaker.com/issue1.html
    - Family Traditions
      http://www.familytreemaker.com/issue9.html
    - Finding and Using Previous Research
      http://www.familytreemaker.com/issue15.html
    - Finding Your New England Ancestors
      http://www.familytreemaker.com/issue25.html
    - Genealogical Journeys -- Vacationing with Your
      Ancestors
      http://www.familytreemaker.com/issue17.html
    - Irish Research Resources
      http://www.familytreemaker.com/issue30.html
    - Learning About Your Immigrant Ancestors
      http://www.familytreemaker.com/issue8.html
    - Making Your Overseas Connection
      http://www.familytreemaker.com/issue31.html
    - The National Archives
      http://www.familytreemaker.com/issue3.html
    - Oral Histories
      http://www.familytreemaker.com/issue2.html
    - Organizing for the New Year
      http://www.familytreemaker.com/issue27.html
    - Professional Research
      http://www.familytreemaker.com/issue20.html

- Researching Civil War Soldiers
  http://www.familytreemaker.com/issue7.html
- Researching Irish Roots
  http://www.familytreemaker.com/issue4.html
- Researching Revolutionary War Veterans
  http://www.familytreemaker.com/issue24.html
- Researching with Census Records
  http://www.familytreemaker.com/issue13.html
- Researching with Church Records
  http://www.familytreemaker.com/issue5.html
- Researching Your Family's Marriages
  http://www.familytreemaker.com/issue11.html
- Trees, Trees, Trees!
  http://www.familytreemaker.com/issue23.html
- What's in a Surname?
  http://www.familytreemaker.com/issue18.html
- Why Genealogy Conferences?
  http://www.familytreemaker.com/issue28.html
- World Family Tree Spotlight
  http://www.familytreemaker.com/issue14.html
- Your Family's Health History
  http://www.familytreemaker.com/issue6.html

- Family Tree Maker's Genealogy Site: Online Genealogy Classes
  http://www.familytreemaker.com/university.html
  From Karen Clifford, Genealogy Research Associates and Marthe Arends, Online Pioneers.

◆ Genealogy Research Associates

- Genealogy Research Associates - Free On-line Lessons - The Great Ancestral Hunt
  http://www.graonline.com/cgi-bin/gra/getlesson?-1+0+English+education+graheader+gratrailer

  o A Brief Overview of Family History Research Procedures
    http://www.graonline.com/cgi-bin/gra/getlesson?-1+0+English+education0+graheader+gratrailer

  - Lesson 1: Mapping the Course and Equipment for the Hunt
    http://www.graonline.com/cgi-bin/gra/getlesson?-1+0+English+C0L1P1+graheader+gratrailer

  - Lesson 2: Vital Records
    http://www.graonline.com/cgi-bin/gra/getlesson?-1+0+English+C0L2P1+graheader+gratrailer

  - Lesson 3: Vital Records Substitutes
    http://www.graonline.com/cgi-bin/gra/getlesson?-1+0+English+C0L3P1+graheader+gratrailer

  - Lesson 4: Trail Guides for Ancestral Hunters
    http://www.graonline.com/cgi-bin/gra/getlesson?-1+0+English+C0L4P1+graheader+gratrailer

  - Lesson 5: Shedding Light on Your Clues
    http://www.graonline.com/cgi-bin/gra/getlesson?-1+0+English+C0L5P1+graheader+gratrailer

  - Lesson 6: Your Best Ally in the Hunt - The U.S. Federal Census
    http://www.graonline.com/cgi-bin/gra/getlesson?-1+0+English+C0L6P1+graheader+gratrailer

  o Tracing Immigrant Origins - Course 1: Basic Research Strategies Used to Find Any Ancestor
    http://www.graonline.com/cgi-bin/gra/getlesson?-1+0+English+education1+graheader+gratrailer

  - Lesson 1: Introduction to Immigrant Investigations
    http://www.graonline.com/cgi-bin/gra/getlesson?-1+0+English+C1L1P1+graheader+gratrailer

  - Lesson 2: Identifying the Immigrant
    http://www.graonline.com/cgi-bin/gra/getlesson?-1+0+English+C1L2P1+graheader+gratrailer

  - Lesson 3: Identifying the Immigrant (continued)
    http://www.graonline.com/cgi-bin/gra/getlesson?-1+0+English+C1L3P1+graheader+gratrailer

  - Lesson 4: Identifying the Immigrant (part 3)
    http://www.graonline.com/cgi-bin/gra/getlesson?-1+0+English+C1L4P1+graheader+gratrailer

  - Lesson 5: Discovering the Most About Your Immigrant
    http://www.graonline.com/cgi-bin/gra/getlesson?-1+0+English+C1L5P1+graheader+gratrailer

  - Lesson 6: Reading the Place Name, Part 1
    http://www.graonline.com/cgi-bin/gra/getlesson?-1+0+English+C1L6P1+graheader+gratrailer

  - Lesson 7: Reading the Place Name, Part 2
    http://www.graonline.com/cgi-bin/gra/getlesson?-1+0+English+C1L7P1+graheader+gratrailer

  - Lesson 8: Overview of Immigrant Origins Research Strategies
    http://www.graonline.com/cgi-bin/gra/getlesson?-1+0+English+C1L8P1+graheader+gratrailer

  o Tracing Immigrant Origins - Course 2: Sources and Techniques for Finding 20th Century Immigrants
    http://www.graonline.com/cgi-bin/gra/getlesson?-1+0+English+education2+graheader+gratrailer

  - Lesson 1: 20th Century Immigrants - Home Sources and Vital Records
    http://www.graonline.com/cgi-bin/gra/getlesson?-1+0+English+C2L1P1+graheader+gratrailer

  - Lesson 2: Immigration Passenger Lists
    http://www.graonline.com/cgi-bin/gra/getlesson?-1+0+English+C2L2P1+graheader+gratrailer

  - Lesson 3: Modern Naturalization Records
    http://www.graonline.com/cgi-bin/gra/getlesson?-1+0+English+C2L3P1+graheader+gratrailer

  - Lesson 4: Other Federal Records
    http://www.graonline.com/cgi-bin/gra/getlesson?-1+0+English+C2L4P1+graheader+gratrailer

  o Tracing Immigrant Origins - Course 3: Post-Civil War Immigrant Sources (1865-1890s)
    http://www.graonline.com/cgi-bin/gra/getlesson?-1+0+English+education3+graheader+gratrailer

- Lesson 1: Clues from the Census Records
  http://www.graonline.com/cgi-bin/gra/getlesson?-
  1+0+English+C3L1P1+graheader+gratrailer
- Lesson 2: Church Records
  http://www.graonline.com/cgi-bin/gra/getlesson?-
  1+0+English+C3L2P1+graheader+gratrailer
- Lesson 3: Immigrant Obituaries
  http://www.graonline.com/cgi-bin/gra/getlesson?-
  1+0+English+C3L3P1+graheader+gratrailer
- Lesson 4: Cemeteries
  http://www.graonline.com/cgi-bin/gra/getlesson?-
  1+0+English+C3L4P1+graheader+gratrailer
- Lesson 5: Local Histories and Biographies
  http://www.graonline.com/cgi-bin/gra/getlesson?-
  1+0+English+C3L5P1+graheader+gratrailer
- Lesson 6: Enlisting the Help of Others
  http://www.graonline.com/cgi-bin/gra/getlesson?-
  1+0+English+C3L6P1+graheader+gratrailer

o Tracing Immigrant Origins - Course 4: Immigrant Sources Between 1820 and the Civil War (1865)
  http://www.graonline.com/cgi-bin/gra/getlesson?-
  1+0+English+education4+graheader+gratrailer

- Lesson 1: Enlisting the Military's Help
  http://www.graonline.com/cgi-bin/gra/getlesson?-
  1+0+English+C4L1P1+graheader+gratrailer
- Lesson 2: Compiled Records via Your Computer
  http://www.graonline.com/cgi-bin/gra/getlesson?-
  1+0+English+C4L2P1+graheader+gratrailer
- Lesson 3: Listing the Immigrants: U.S. Customs Passenger Lists
  http://www.graonline.com/cgi-bin/gra/getlesson?-
  1+0+English+C4L3P1+graheader+gratrailer
- Lesson 4: Becoming an American: Early Naturalization Records
  http://www.graonline.com/cgi-bin/gra/getlesson?-
  1+0+English+C4L4P1+graheader+gratrailer
- Lesson 5: Newspaper Research: Beyond Obituaries
  http://www.graonline.com/cgi-bin/gra/getlesson?-
  1+0+English+C4L5P1+graheader+gratrailer
- Lesson 6: Double the Immigration: Canadian Research
  http://www.graonline.com/cgi-bin/gra/getlesson?-
  1+0+English+C4L6P1+graheader+gratrailer

o Tracing Immigrant Origins - Course 5: Pre-1820 Immigration: Tracing Colonial Immigrant Origins
  http://www.graonline.com/cgi-bin/gra/getlesson?-
  1+0+English+education5+graheader+gratrailer

- Lesson 1: Published Lists of early Immigrants
  http://www.graonline.com/cgi-bin/gra/getlesson?-
  1+0+English+C5L1P1+graheader+gratrailer
- Lesson 2: Compiled Records
  http://www.graonline.com/cgi-bin/gra/getlesson?-
  1+0+English+C5L2P1+graheader+gratrailer
- Lesson 3: Early American Church Records
  http://www.graonline.com/cgi-bin/gra/getlesson?-
  1+0+English+C5L3P1+graheader+gratrailer

- Lesson 4: Court, Land and Other Civil Records
  http://www.graonline.com/cgi-bin/gra/getlesson?-
  1+0+English+C5L4P1+graheader+gratrailer
- Lesson 5: Hidden Clues in Periodicals
  http://www.graonline.com/cgi-bin/gra/getlesson?-
  1+0+English+C5L5P1+graheader+gratrailer
- Lesson 6: Probate Records
  http://www.graonline.com/cgi-bin/gra/getlesson?-
  1+0+English+C5L6P1+graheader+gratrailer
- Lesson 7: Lineage Societies
  http://www.graonline.com/cgi-bin/gra/getlesson?-
  1+0+English+C5L7P1+graheader+gratrailer

o Tracing Immigrant Origins - Course 6: European Sources
  http://www.graonline.com/cgi-bin/gra/getlesson?-
  1+0+English+education6+graheader+gratrailer

- Lesson 1: Tactics for Using Foreign Sources
  http://www.graonline.com/cgi-bin/gra/getlesson?-
  1+0+English+C6L1P1+graheader+gratrailer
- Lesson 2: Family Histories and Periodicals
  http://www.graonline.com/cgi-bin/gra/getlesson?-
  1+0+English+C6L2P1+graheader+gratrailer
- Lesson 3: Original Records
  http://www.graonline.com/cgi-bin/gra/getlesson?-
  1+0+English+C6L3P1+graheader+gratrailer
- Lesson 4: Departure Lists
  http://www.graonline.com/cgi-bin/gra/getlesson?-
  1+0+English+C6L4P1+graheader+gratrailer
- Lesson 5: Emigration Lists
  http://www.graonline.com/cgi-bin/gra/getlesson?-
  1+0+English+C6L5P1+graheader+gratrailer
- Lesson 6: Government Records
  http://www.graonline.com/cgi-bin/gra/getlesson?-
  1+0+English+C6L6P1+graheader+gratrailer
- Lesson 7: Networking
  http://www.graonline.com/cgi-bin/gra/getlesson?-
  1+0+English+C6L7P1+graheader+gratrailer

◆ Heritage Quest - Genealogy: Help Guide for Beginners

- Heritage Quest - Genealogy: Help Guide for Beginners
  http://www.heritagequest.com/genealogy/help/
  A Beginners Guide to Genealogy in Seven Basic Steps.

  o Introduction: What Do You Know?
    http://www.heritagequest.com/genealogy/help/html/
    introduction.html
  o Step One: Organizing Home and Family Sources
    http://www.heritagequest.com/genealogy/help/html/
    step_1.html
  o Step Two: Contacting Relatives
    http://www.heritagequest.com/genealogy/help/html/
    step_2.html
  o Step Three: Write for Death Records
    http://www.heritagequest.com/genealogy/help/html/
    step_3.html

- o Step Four: Follow Up Death Records
  http://www.heritagequest.com/genealogy/help/html/step_4.html
- o Step Five: Federal Census Search
  http://www.heritagequest.com/genealogy/help/html/step_5.html
- o Step Six: LDS Library Search
  http://www.heritagequest.com/genealogy/help/html/step_6.html
- o Step Seven: State and County Search
  http://www.heritagequest.com/genealogy/help/html/step_7.html
- o Additional Resources: Beyond Seven Steps
  http://www.heritagequest.com/genealogy/help/html/resources.html

◆ RootsWeb's Guide to Tracing Family Trees

- • RootsWeb's Guide to Tracing Family Trees
  http://rwguide.rootsweb.com/
  - o Lesson 1: Where to begin?
    http://www.rootsweb.com/~rwguide/lesson1.htm
  - o Lesson 2: What's in a name?
    http://www.rootsweb.com/~rwguide/lesson2.htm
  - o Lesson 3: Using technology to dig up roots
    http://www.rootsweb.com/~rwguide/lesson3.htm
  - o Lesson 4: Vital Records: Death, Tombstones and Cemeteries
    http://www.rootsweb.com/~rwguide/lesson4.htm
  - o Lesson 5: Vital Records: Marriage Records and Evidence
    http://www.rootsweb.com/~rwguide/lesson5.htm
  - o Lesson 6: Vital Records: Birth Records
    http://www.rootsweb.com/~rwguide/lesson6.htm
  - o Lesson 7: What is the question?
    http://www.rootsweb.com/~rwguide/lesson7.htm
  - o Lesson 8: Spelling of Names
    http://www.rootsweb.com/~rwguide/lesson8.htm
  - o Lesson 9: Census Records: Soundex, Indexes and Finding Aids
    http://www.rootsweb.com/~rwguide/lesson9.htm
  - o Lesson 10: Social Security Death Index
    http://www.rootsweb.com/~rwguide/lesson10.htm
  - o Lesson 11: Taxing Tales
    http://www.rootsweb.com/~rwguide/lesson11.htm
- o Lesson 12: Creating Worthwhile Genealogies: Evidence, Sources, Documentation, and Citation
  http://www.rootsweb.com/~rwguide/lesson12.htm
- o Lesson 13: Military Records (Worldwide)
  http://www.rootsweb.com/~rwguide/lesson13.htm
- o Lesson 14: Military Records (United States)
  http://www.rootsweb.com/~rwguide/lesson14.htm
- o Lesson 15: Tracing Immigrant Ancestors
  http://www.rootsweb.com/~rwguide/lesson15.htm
- o Lesson 16: Naturalization Records
  http://www.rootsweb.com/~rwguide/lesson16.htm
- o Lesson 17: Church Records
  http://www.rootsweb.com/~rwguide/lesson17.htm
- o Lesson 18: Fraternal Organizations
  http://www.rootsweb.com/~rwguide/lesson18.htm
- o Lesson 19: Heraldry for Genealogists
  http://www.rootsweb.com/~rwguide/lesson19.htm
- o Lesson 20: City Directories and Newspapers
  http://www.rootsweb.com/~rwguide/lesson20.htm
- o Lesson 21: Tracing Irish, Scotch-Irish and Scottish Ancestors
  http://www.rootsweb.com/~rwguide/lesson21.htm
- o Lesson 22: Italian Roots & Hispanic Heritage
  http://www.rootsweb.com/~rwguide/lesson22.htm
- o Lesson 23: Scandinavian Roots
  http://www.rootsweb.com/~rwguide/lesson23.htm
- o Lesson 24: Oh, Canada!
  http://www.rootsweb.com/~rwguide/lesson24.htm
- o Lesson 25: Ethnic Roots
  http://www.rootsweb.com/~rwguide/lesson25.htm
- o Lesson 26: Germanic Ancestors
  http://www.rootsweb.com/~rwguide/lesson26.htm
  (Plus: Austrians, Dutch, Belgians, Swiss, Luxembourgers, and Liechensteiners).
- o Lesson 27: Polish, Russians, Czechs, Hungarians, Croatians, Slovakians, etc.
  http://www.rootsweb.com/~rwguide/lesson27.htm
- o Lesson 28: English, Welsh, Australian, New Zealand, South Africa, India, South Pacific Islands
  http://www.rootsweb.com/~rwguide/lesson28.htm
- o Lesson 29: American Land Records
  http://www.rootsweb.com/~rwguide/lesson29.htm
- o Lesson 30: Court Records
  http://www.rootsweb.com/~rwguide/lesson30.htm
- o Lesson 31: Adoption and Orphans Research
  http://www.rootsweb.com/~rwguide/lesson31.htm

HUGUENOT
http://www.cyndislist.com/huguenot.htm

Category Index:

◆ General Resource Sites
◆ Libraries, Archives & Museums
◆ Locality Specific
◆ People & Families

◆ Publications, Software & Supplies
◆ Records: Census, Cemeteries, Land, Obituaries, Personal, Taxes and Vital
◆ Societies & Groups

◆ General Resource Sites

● Experiences of the French Huguenots in America
http://pages.prodigy.net/royjnagy/ressegui.htm
This document was written in about 1908 and contains information on persecutions of the French Huguenots and their flight to America. It contains information on several of the earliest French Huguenot immigrants including Alexander Resseguie and Sarah Bontecou. It also contains a journal of one of their descendants, Timothy Resseguie, a British soldier in the American Revolution.

● Huguenot & Protestant Reformed Chronology
http://www.kopower.com/~jimchstn/timeline.htm
From the Pierre Chastain Family Association.

● The Huguenot Cross
http://www.geocities.com/Heartland/Valley/8140/x-eng.htm

● Huguenot History
http://history.cc.ukans.edu/heritage/cousin/huguenot.html

● Huguenot History
http://www.home.aone.net.au/mclark/huguenot_history.htm

● Huguenot History
http://www.larocheind.com/HUGUENT.HTM
Provides brief historical details and links to other sites regarding the Huguenots.

● Huguenot Mailing List
http://www.rootsweb.com/~jfuller/gen_mail_religions.html #Huguenot

● Huguenot Resources - Olive Tree Genealogy
http://www.rootsweb.com/~ote/hugres.htm

● Huguenot Ring
http://www.geocities.com/Heartland/Valley/8140/webring.htm
The Huguenot Ring is a free program that allows Internet surfers to travel from one Huguenot related homepage to another.

● Huguenot Source List - Olive Tree Genealogy
http://www.rootsweb.com/~ote/hugsour.htm

● Huguenot Sources
http://www.kopower.com/~jimchstn/hugsrcs2.htm
From the Pierre Chastain Family Association.

● Huguenot Surnames Index - from Australian Family Tree Connections Magazine
http://www.aftc.com.au/huguenot.html

● Huguenots
http://www.geocities.com/SoHo/3809/Huguen.htm

● HUGUENOTS-WALLOONS-EUROPE Mailing List
http://www.rootsweb.com/~jfuller/gen_mail_country-fra.html #HUGUENOTS-WALLOONS-EUROPE
For anyone with a genealogical interest in the research of Huguenots and/or Walloons in Europe. For the purposes of this list, Europe includes all of continental Europe as well as the United Kingdom and Ireland.

● L'édit de Nantes
http://palissy.humana.univ-nantes.fr/CETE/TXT/EDN/ index.html
Includes the French text of the Edict of Nantes and a graphic image of the document.

● Olive Tree Genealogy - Huguenots & Walloons
http://olivetreegenealogy.com/hug/index.shtml

● Our Huguenot Ancestors
http://pages.infinit.net/barbeaum/huga/index.htm
Online slide show with notes for a conference conducted by the author.

● Revocation of the Edict of Nantes (Oct. 22, 1685)
http://history.hanover.edu/early/nonantes.htm
English translation of the Revocation.

● Traits and Stories of the Huguenots
http://lang.nagoya-u.ac.jp/~matsuoka/EG-Traits.html
By Elizabeth Gaskell - 1853.

● The Wars of Religion
http://www.lepg.org/wars.htm

● Who were the Huguenots?
http://www.geocities.com/Heartland/Valley/8140/hist-hug.htm

◆ Libraries, Archives & Museums

● Huguenot Library
http://www.ucl.ac.uk/UCL-Info/Divisions/Library/huguenot.htm
At the University College London.

- o eUCLid - the University College London Online Library Catalog
  http://library.ucl.ac.uk:4505/ALEPH
- The Huguenot Memorial Museum
  http://www.museum.co.za/index.htm
  Museum in South Africa focusing on the Huguenots of the Cape Settlements.

◆ Locality Specific

- Bristol Huguenots
  http://dspace.dial.pipex.com/pericles/french/huguenot.htm
- Devon Huguenots
  http://millennium.fortunecity.com/falmouth/566/devhugs1.htm
- French Huguenots Are Alive and Well in Texas
  http://www.virtualtexan.com/writers/kellow/rt061799.htm
  Online article by Brenda Kellow.
- French Huguenots in the Hudson Valley
  http://www.marist.edu/summerscholars/97/huge.htm
  French pilgrims influenced the culture of the Hudson Valley. Faced with religious persecution, the Huguenots left France to find a peaceful homeland.
- The French Protestant Church of London
  http://ihr.sas.ac.uk/ihr/associnstits/huguenots.mnu.html
- Huguenot Cemetery ~ St. John's County, Florida
  http://www.geocities.com/Heartland/Hills/8299/cemetery/hug_cem.htm
- Huguenot Emigrants on the James River
  http://www.geocities.com/Heartland/Bluffs/4579/huguenot.html
- The Huguenot Heritage
  http://www.orange-street-church.org/text/huguenot.htm
  From the Orange Street Congregational Church, Leicester Square, London. Founded by Huguenots in 1686.
- Huguenot Refugees in the Cape Colony of South Africa
  http://www.rootsweb.com/~ote/hugsa.htm
- Huguenots to England
  http://www.rootsweb.com/~ote/hugeng.htm
- The Huguenot Legacy - English Silver 1680 to 1760
  http://www.si.edu/ndm/exhib/silver/7.htm
  London silversmiths.

◆ People & Families

- BOESHORE (BESHORE) Family History
  http://www.enerspace.com/beshore.htm
- The Charles Jeffrey Morrissette, Sr. Family Home Page
  http://www.ghg.net/hankflagg/genealogy/
  In 1700 Pierre Morriset, a French Huguenot, arrived in James City, Virginia aboard the ship "Mary and Ann". The Huguenots on board had left France to escape religious persecution and to find new land.

- The DEYO Family in America
  http://www.deyo.org/deyo.htm
- DuVAL Family Association
  http://www.geocities.com/Heartland/Ridge/7508/
  Descendants of Daniel DuVal and his wife Philadelphia DuBois who were French Huguenots.
- The FUQUA Family Foundation
  http://www.concentric.net/~fuqua/
  Guillaume Fouquet, b. 1667, came to Virginia from France.
- Genealogy Resources: Steps in Time
  http://www.geocities.com/Heartland/Meadows/4399/
  VILLEPONTEAUX.
- GOURDIN-GOURDINE Family Association
  http://www.blackcamisards.com/gourdin/
  A French-African-American Family from South Carolina.
- The GUION Family
  http://home.t-online.de/home/weebers/guion.htm
- HEWLETT BEUZEVILLE ROUSSEL Family Home Page
  http://www.home.aone.net.au/mclark/
- Huguenot Ancestry
  http://www.uftree.com/UFT/WebPages/huguenot/default/index.htm
  BILLIOU, DU BOIS, LARZALERE, RAMBOUT.
- Huguenot Emigrants on the James River (MARTIN Family)
  http://www.geocities.com/Heartland/Bluffs/4579/huguenot.html
  Early Huguenot families at Manakintowne, VA, including MARTIN, RAPINE, TRABUE, GUERRANT, CHASTAIN.
- The Huguenot Families UZIELE and CASIER
  http://www.rootsweb.com/~ote/casuz.htm
- The Huguenots
  http://www.freeyellow.com/members5/huguenot/
  Huguenots in Denmark. Descendants of Pierre DEVANTIER born 1637 in France.
- LaRUE & Allied Families
  http://web.nstar.net/~dwat6911/myheart.htm
- Life's Short; Plunge In.
  http://members.aol.com/Nlalabungu/index.html
  BURN, WILMOT, DUPREE, VENZKE.
- Pierre CHASTAIN Family Association
  http://www.kopower.com/~jimchstn/
- The SEITZ Site
  http://home.earthlink.net/~kseitz/gene.html
  The genealogical content of this site includes biographical sketches of the known immigrant ancestors including Huguenots & Quakers.
- VALLEAU Family Association
  http://www.geocities.com/Heartland/Prairie/1181/
- VILJOEN Family Homepage
  http://www.geocities.com/Heartland/Acres/4040/index.html
  Villion, Campenaar.

◆ Publications, Software & Supplies

- Amazon.com Genealogy Bookstore - Huguenot
  http://www.amazon.com/exec/obidos/external-search/
  ?keyword=huguenot&tag=markcyndisgenealA/

- AudioTapes.com - Genealogical Lectures on Cassette
  Tapes - Huguenot
  http://www.audiotapes.com/search2.asp?Search=Huguenot

- Huguenots
  http://www.lostintime.com/catalog/books/booktop/
  bo09000.htm
  Books for sale from Lost In Time online book seller.

- Huguenot Settlers in North America and Europe,
  1600s-1900s
  http://www.bannerblue.com/600facd.html
  CD-ROM database for sale.

◆ Records: Census, Cemeteries, Land, Obituaries, Personal, Taxes and Vital

- Huguenot Cemetery ~ St. John's County, Florida
  http://www.geocities.com/Heartland/Hills/8299/cemetery/
  hug_cem.htm

- Huguenot Refugees
  http://www.rootsweb.com/~ote/hugship.htm
  *On the ship "Mary and Ann," August 12, 1700, Virginia, James City
  and on the ship "Peter and Anthony" from London to James River in
  Virginia, 20th of Sept. 1700.*

- Huguenot Ships
  http://www.mweb.co.za/roux/Huguenots/ships.htm
  *Names and dates of vessels bearing Huguenots to the Cape
  Settlements in South Africa.*

◆ Societies & Groups

- Huguenot Historical Society ~ New Paltz, New York
  http://www.hhs-newpaltz.org/

- Huguenot Historical Society ~ New Paltz, New York
  http://home.earthlink.net/~rctwig/hhs1.htm

- The Huguenot Society of California
  http://www.huguenot.netnation.com/states/california/
  index.html

- The Huguenot Society of Great Britain and Ireland
  http://www.local.ie/content/27567.shtml
  Online article from Irish Roots Magazine.

- Huguenot Society of South Africa
  http://www.geocities.com/Heartland/Valley/8140/

- The Huguenot Society of Texas of the National
  Huguenot Society
  http://www.startext.net/homes/huguenot/

- Huguenot Society of Wisconsin
  http://www.execpc.com/~drg/wihs.html

- Pierre CHASTAIN Family Association
  http://www.kopower.com/~jimchstn/

- The National Huguenot Society
  http://huguenot.netnation.com/
  *The National Huguenot Society is an organization devoted to: 1.
  Coordinating activities of member societies, and promoting and
  supporting fulfillment of their common purposes which include: a.
  perpetuating the memory and promoting the principles and virtues
  of the Huguenots; b. commemorating the great events of Huguenot
  history; c. collecting and preserving historical data and relics
  illustrative of Huguenot life, manners, and customs; 2. To give
  expression to the Huguenot tenets of faith and liberty, and to
  promote their understanding for the good of the United States; 3. To
  encourage and foster the organization of new member Societies
  within states, territories of the United States, and the District of
  Columbia where none currently exist.*

HUMOR & PROSE

http://www.cyndislist.com/humor.htm

- Alien Spaceship Theory of Genealogy
  http://homepages.rootsweb.com/~lovitt/spaceship2.html

- Amazon.com Genealogy Bookstore - Humor
  http://www.amazon.com/exec/obidos/external-search/
  ?keyword=genealogy+humor&tag=markcyndisgenealA/

- Are You a Genealogist?
  ftp://ftp.rootsweb.com/pub/roots-l/genealog/genealog.gposter
  An ASCII art poster.

- Are you a Genealogist?
  http://www.geocities.com/Heartland/Plains/3634/
  Genealogist.htm

- Barbie Doll's Family Tree
  http://www.barbiecollectibles.com/about/familyTree.asp
  For the doll-lover in all of us.

- Carl Barks's Duck Family Tree
  http://stp.ling.uu.se/~starback/dcml/chars/cb-tree.html
  Donald Duck's pedigree!

- Carol's Genealogy Taglines
  http://www.rootsweb.com/~genepool/taglines.htm

- Chester County Chuckles
  http://www.rootsweb.com/~pacheste/chester.htm
  Located on the Chester County page of the Pennsylvania GenWeb project.

- Christmas Humor
  http://homepages.rootsweb.com/~bridgett/chhumor.htm

- The Correct Spelling of the Word GENEALOGY
  http://www.oz.net/~markhow/writing/spelling.htm

- David's Genealogy Taglines
  http://www.agate.net/~davids/_genea/taglines.htm

- A "Dear Abby" Entry on Genealogy
  http://www.netfunny.com/rhf/jokes/90q1/12.html

- Diagnosis: Geneaholic
  http://members.tripod.com/~bayoujac/dg.html

- The Elusive Ancestor by Merrell Kenworthy
  http://www.angelfire.com/fl/Sumter/elusive.html

- The Even Lighter Side of Genealogy
  http://www.rootsweb.com/~autwgw/agstag.htm

- A Genealogical Menagerie: Glebe Terrier - Breed Standard Definition
  http://www.oz.net/~markhow/glebe.htm
  Humorous definition of Glebe Terriers.

- Genealogical Taglines for Your Use
  http://homepages.rootsweb.com/~bridgett/taglines.htm

- Genealogists Psalm
  http://www.geocities.com/Heartland/Plains/6431/Psalm.html

- A Genealogist's Christmas Eve
  http://home.vicnet.net.au/~dpsoc/xmas.htm

- GenealogyBookShop.com - Humor
  http://www.genealogybookshop.com/genealogybookshop/
  files/General,Humor/index.html
  The online store of Genealogical Publishing Co., Inc. & Clearfield Company.

- Genealogy Chuckles
  http://www.geocities.com/Heartland/Plains/6431/
  Chuckles.html

- Genealogy Epitaphs, Quotes, Poems
  http://showcase.netins.net/web/kadinger/anthology.htm

- Genealogy Humor
  http://www.chrysalis.org/sanford/cgn/humor.htm

- Genealogy Humor
  http://www.wgbc.org/genhumor.htm

- Genealogy Humor and Quotation Collection
  http://genealogy.about.com/hobbies/genealogy/library/humor/
  bltopicindex.htm?terms=Genealogy+Laughs
  Epitaphs, Jokes, Poetry, Quotes, Songs & Limericks, Taglines, Miscellaneous.

- Genealogy Poem by Sandy Coleman
  http://www.angelfire.com/fl/Sumter/poem.html

- Genealogy Poetry and Prose
  http://genweb.net/~gen-cds/poems.html

- Genealogy Pox
  http://www.geocities.com/Heartland/Plains/6431/Pox.htm

- Genealogy Prayer
  http://www.geocities.com/Heartland/Plains/6431/Geney
  Prayer.html

- Genealogy Songs & Movies
  http://www.cis.net/~cmmeyer/Songs.html

- Geneverse - A Collection Of Original Verse By Genealogists Inspired By Genealogy
  http://www.geocities.com/Athens/1491/

- Geneitis: The Genealogist's Disease
  http://www.GeoCities.com/Heartland/Plains/5137/geneitis.htm

- GenHumor Mailing List
  http://www.rootsweb.com/~jfuller/gen_mail_general.html
  #GenHumor
  For the exchange of genealogy and family humor including poems and jokes.

- GEN-TRIVIA-UNIVERSAL Mailing List
  http://www.rootsweb.com/~jfuller/gen_mail_general.html
  #GEN-TRIVIA-UNIVERSAL
  For genealogy trivia collected from any country. This is an offshoot of the GEN-TRIVIA-ENG list where one can share ancestral recipes, poems, rhymes, ditties, slang words, sayings, etc.

- A Glow in the Forest
  http://www.mach3ww.com/~pafways/glow/glow.htm
  A collection of taglines from Pafways in Iowa.

- GRO (Scotland) - Genealogical Gems
  http://www.gro-scotland.gov.uk/grosweb/grosweb.nsf/
  pages/gems
  Humorous selections from the Old Parish Registers.

- Humor
  http://ram.ramlink.net/~cbarker/humor.htm

- Humorous Reading
  http://homepages.rootsweb.com/~bridgett/humor.htm
  Some computer humor as well as genealogical humor here.

- "If..." - A Poem for Genealogists
  http://www.geocities.com/Heartland/Plains/5137/ifgene.htm

- I Heard It At The Library
  http://www.audiotapes.com/product.asp?ProductCode=
  'DEN98T96'
  Presentation by Craig Roberts Scott, available for sale on audio tape.

- The Inevitable Laws of Genealogy
  http://www.micronet.net/users/~searcy/laws.htm

- JEFFCO Genealogy Stories - Humorous
  http://users.ticnet.com/jeffco/stories.html-ssi

- John's Genealogy Junction - The Family Loop
  http://www.wf.net/~jyates/grandpa.htm

- Kentuckiana Genealogy - The Elusive Ancestor
  http://www.kentuckianagenealogy.org/guide/fun/elusive.html

- Kentuckiana Genealogy - Family Tree
  http://www.kentuckianagenealogy.org/guide/fun/famtree.html

- Kentuckiana Genealogy - Genealogy Pox
  http://www.kentuckianagenealogy.org/guide/fun/genpox.html

- Kentuckiana Genealogy - You know you're an addict when.......
  http://www.kentuckianagenealogy.org/guide/fun/addict.html

- Laws Of Genealogy
  ftp://ftp.rootsweb.com/pub/roots-l/genealog/
  genealog.genelaws

- The Lighter Side of Genealogy
  http://goldrush.com/~manley/gentoon.html
  Genealogy cartoons from Ray and Diane's Family Tree.

- Mary Daily's Genealogy - Poem
  http://www.geocities.com/Heartland/Meadows/1096/
  poem.html

- Our Ancestors Poem
  http://www.geocities.com/Heartland/Meadows/8965/
  ancestors.html

- The Outhouse - Genealogy & Family Humor
  http://lest-we-forget.com/The_Outhouse/index.htm

- Skywalker Family Tree
  http://home.att.net/~wee-monster/skywalker/
  For those Star Wars fans.

- The Spam Family Tree
  http://www.spam.com/sp.htm
  For lunchmeat lovers everywhere.

- Twas The Day Before Yesterday
  http://pw1.netcom.com/~eapii/genealogy/stuff.html#p3
  by Linnie Vanderford Poyneer.

- UFO-ROOTS Mailing List
  http://www.rootsweb.com/~jfuller/gen_mail_general.html
  #UFO-ROOTS
  For those whose ancestors arrived from outer space to make connections with others sharing this problem, discuss their ancestry and provide advice on possible avenues for further research.

- What the Internet Has Done To Me
  http://www.audiotapes.com/product.asp?ProductCode=
  'FWM-00-L1'
  Presentation by Cyndi Howells, available for sale on audio tape.

- Who Says We Are Not Relatives?
  http://members.aol.com/rprost/relatives.html

- Ye Olde English Sayings
  http://www.rootsweb.com/~genepool/sayings.htm

- You Know You're An Addicted Genealogist. . .
  http://www.micronet.net/users/~searcy/addicted.htm

IMMIGRATION & NATURALIZATION

http://www.cyndislist.com/immigrat.htm

Category Index:

- ◆ General Resource Sites
- ◆ Home Children
- ◆ Libraries, Archives & Museums
- ◆ Mailing Lists, Newsgroups & Chat

- ◆ Ports of Entry
- ◆ Publications, Microfilm & Microfiche
- ◆ Records

◆ General Resource Sites

- 17th Century Immigrants to New York Registry
  http://www.rootsweb.com/~ote/dnybook.htm

- Atlas of American Immigration
  http://www.albany.edu/~rws32/gog240/atlas.html
  Includes charts on immigrant origins and maps of the distribution of select immigrant groups in the United States for certain periods.

- Danish Immigration to America: An Annotated Bibliography of Resources at the Library of Congress
  http://lcweb.loc.gov/rr/genealogy/bib_guid/danish.html

- Emigration from Koblenz, Germany
  http://www.koblenz.de/bildung/stadtarchiv/emigrat.html

- Emigration Guide ~ Australia
  http://www.standard.net.au/%7ejwilliams/migrate.htm

- Emigration Port Hamburg
  http://www.hamburg.de/Behoerden/Pressestelle/emigration/englisch/welcome.htm
  Excellent online presentation of why Hamburg was a major port of departure for immigrants, how the were treated, what they faced, and how the process of departure worked.

- Exodus - Irish Emigration
  http://www.belfasttelegraph.co.uk/emigration/
  From the PRONI and the Belfast Telegraph.

- Family History SourceGuide - Research Outline - Tracing Immigrant Origins
  http://www.familysearch.org/sg/Tracing_Immigrant_Origins.html

- Hebrew Immigrant Aid Society
  http://www.hias.org/
  Successor organization to those founded in New York City in the 1880s to assist Jewish immigrants.

- German and American Sources for German Emigration to America
  http://www.genealogy.net/gene/www/emig/emigrati.htm

- German Genealogy: Emigration from Germany to America
  http://www.genealogy.net/gene/www/emig/emigr.html

- Immigrant Arrivals: A Guide To Published Sources Bibliography from the Library of Congress
  http://lcweb.loc.gov/rr/genealogy/bib_guid/immigrant.html

- Immigration: The living Mosaic of People, Culture, and Hope
  http://library.thinkquest.org/20619/index.html
  Informative site on the history of immigration into the United States with interesting graphics.

  - Immigration: The Africans
    http://library.thinkquest.org/20619/African.html

  - Immigration: The Chinese
    http://library.thinkquest.org/20619/Chinese.html

  - Immigration: The English
    http://library.thinkquest.org/20619/English.html

  - Immigration: The Germans
    http://library.thinkquest.org/20619/German.html

  - Immigration: The Irish
    http://library.thinkquest.org/20619/Irish.html

  - Immigration: The Italians
    http://library.thinkquest.org/20619/Italian.html

  - Immigration: The Japanese
    http://library.thinkquest.org/20619/Japanese.html

  - Immigration: The Jewish
    http://library.thinkquest.org/20619/Jewish.html

- Immigration and Ships Passenger List Research Guide
  http://home.att.net/~arnielang/shipgide.html
  The goal of this Guide is to help you to use Ships Passenger Lists and other Immigration records in locating the origin of your ancestors in Europe, fill in gaps in your family history, and to lead to other avenues of genealogical research . This step by step guide is written with special consideration given for the beginner researcher. For the more experienced researcher, it includes numerous links to on-line web sites as well as illustrations of documents, examples, tips, and use of traditional resources. Also, references to on-line and off-line resources for obtaining pictures and information about your ancestor's ship is included.

- Irish Emigrants
  http://genealogy.org/~ajmorris/ireland/ireemg1.htm

- The Key to Family History Research
  http://www.sierra.com/sierrahome/familytree/hqarticles/research/
  An online article by Miriam Weiner describing how to determine an immigrant's original surname.

- Learning about Your Immigrant Ancestors
  http://www.familytreemaker.com/issue8.html
  From Family Tree Maker Online.

- Migrations in Luxembourg - A historical sketch
  http://www.igd-leo.lu/igd-leo/emigration/mighist.html

  o Luxembourg emigration in the 19th century
    http://www.igd-leo.lu/igd-leo/emigration/emigrationus.html

  o The Luxembourgers in America
    http://www.igd-leo.lu/igd-leo/ties/emi.html

- Migrations Project
  http://www.migrations.org/

- Passenger Lists and Immigration-Related Materials
  http://www.hpl.lib.tx.us/clayton/px001.html
  A Guide from the Clayton Library in Houston, Texas.

- Pioneer Sikh Asian East Indian Immigration to the Pacific Coast from Punjab
  http://www.lib.ucdavis.edu/punjab/index.html
  Includes a chronology, historical photos, and a list of research specialists.

- Primer of Emigration, Immigration, etc.
  http://www.pgsa.org/primer.htm
  An article from the Polish Genealogical Society of America.

- Q & A: Naturalization 1749
  http://www.worldroots.com/misc/bg_misc/qa6.html

- Ships & Passenger Lists
  http://www.CyndisList.com/ships.htm
  See this category on Cyndi's List for related links.

- Thirteen Reasons Why Ancestors Migrated
  http://www.ancestry.com/library/view/columns/george/1436.asp
  From "Along Those Lines..." by George Morgan.

- Tracing an ancestor who was an immigrant
  http://www.channel4.com/nextstep/geno/geno3.html
  From the UK Channel 4 TV series Extraordinary Ancestors.

  o African-Americans
    http://www.channel4.com/nextstep/geno/geno3b.html

  o Africans
    http://www.channel4.com/nextstep/geno/geno3d.html

  o Asians
    http://www.channel4.com/nextstep/geno/geno3e.html

  o West Indians
    http://www.channel4.com/nextstep/geno/geno3c.html

  o Jewish
    http://www.channel4.com/nextstep/geno/geno3a.html

◆ Home Children

- British Home Children
  http://freepages.genealogy.rootsweb.com/~britishhomechildren
  A site for listing the names of the individual British Home Children.

- British Home Children Mailing List
  http://members.aol.com/gfsjohnf/gen_mail_country-can.html#BRITISHHOMECHILDREN
  A mailing list for those interested in researching the 100,000 British Home Children who were emigrated to Canada by 50 child care organizations to work as indentured farm labourers (1870-1940).

- Home Children
  http://www.archives.ca/exec/naweb.dll?fs&020110&e&top&0
  From the National Archives of Canada. Between 1869 and the early 1930s, over 100,000 children were sent to Canada from Great Britain during the child emigration movement. Members of the British Isles Family History Society of Greater Ottawa are locating and indexing the names of these Home Children found in passenger lists in the custody of the National Archives of Canada.

  o Home Children Search
    http://www.archives.ca/exec/naweb.dll?fs&02011002&e&top&0
    A searchable online index for the years 1865 to 1919 is available online.

- Labouring Children: British Immigrant Apprentices to Canada, 1869-1924
  http://www.amazon.com/exec/obidos/ISBN=080207443X/markcyndisgenealA/
  A book by Joy Parr.

- Neither Waif Nor Stray: The Search For A Stolen Identity
  http://www.amazon.com/exec/obidos/ISBN=1581127588/markcyndisgenealA/
  A book by Perry Snow.

- Young Immigrants to Canada
  http://www.dcs.uwaterloo.ca/~marj/genealogy/homeadd.html
  When the topic of child immigrants to Canada is raised many people first think of Barnardo's. Some may know about Annie Macpherson, Maria Rye, Fegan Homes, Dr. Stephenson and the National Children's Home or even some of the Roman Catholic organizations. This web site represents research into all of the organizations which brought children and young women to Canada between 1833 and 1935.

◆ Libraries, Archives & Museums

- The Balch Institute for Ethnic Studies
  http://www.libertynet.org/~balch/
  Includes a research library with materials on immigration studies.

- Center for Migration Studies ~ New York
  http://www.cmsny.org/

- Finding Aid to Naturalization Records at the Connecticut State Library
  http://www.cslnet.ctstateu.edu/natural.htm

- Fylkesarkivet i Sogn og Fjordane - Utvandring - Emigration ~ Norway
  http://www.sffarkiv.no/sffutv.htm

- Immigration History Research Center (IHRC) at the University of Minnesota
  http://www1.umn.edu/ihrc/
  An international resource on American immigration and ethnic history.

- Immigration Museum ~ Melbourne, Australia
  http://immigration.museum.vic.gov.au/home.htm

- Immigration - Research Collections in American Immigration
  http://www.lexisnexis.com/cispubs/Catalog/research%20
  collections/american%20studies/immigration/Immigration.htm

- National Archives of New Zealand: Holdings: Immigration & Shipping Lists
  http://www.archives.govt.nz/holdings/immigration.html

- National Archives and Records Administration
  http://www.nara.gov/
  o The Genealogy Page
    http://www.nara.gov/genealogy/
    - Immigration Records
      http://www.nara.gov/genealogy/immigration/
      immigrat.html

- Sources for Emigrants
  http://www.nas.gov.uk/sources_for_emigrants.htm
  From the National Archives of Scotland.

- Norsk Utvandermuseum / The Norwegian Emigrant Museum
  http://www.hamarnett.no/emigrantmuseum/

- Research Center for German Emigrants in the USA
  http://www.uni-oldenburg.de/nausa/nausae.htm

◆ Mailing Lists, Newsgroups & Chat

- Genealogy Resources on the Internet - General Mailing Lists
  http://www.rootsweb.com/~jfuller/gen_mail_general.html
  Most of the mailing list links below point to this site, wonderfully maintained by John Fuller

- British Home Children Mailing List
  http://members.aol.com/gfsjohnf/gen_mail_country-
  can.html#BRITISHHOMECHILDREN
  A mailing list for those interested in researching the 100,000 British Home Children who were emigrated to Canada by 50 child care organizations to work as indentured farm laborers (1870-1940).

- DUST-BOWL-ROOTS Mailing List
  http://www.rootsweb.com/~jfuller/gen_mail_states-
  gen.html#DUST-BOWL-ROOTS
  For anyone with a genealogical or historical interest in the Dust Bowl migrants.

- emigration-ships Mailing List
  http://www.rootsweb.com/~jfuller/gen_mail_general.html
  #EMIGRATION-SHIPS
  A mailing list for anyone who wants to discuss the ships their ancestors arrived on or post passenger lists for any ships.

- IMMI-GRAND Mailing List
  http://www.rootsweb.com/~jfuller/gen_mail_general.html
  #IMMI-GRAND
  For those attempting to do genealogical research whose grandparents (or parents) arrived in the USA after 1875.

- MIGRATION-PATTERNS Mailing List
  http://www.rootsweb.com/~jfuller/gen_mail_states-
  gen.html#MIGRATION-PATTERNS
  For discussing the migration patterns of families and "cluster" moves of towns in the United States.

◆ Ports of Entry

Angel Island - California

- Angel Island - California's "Immigration Station"
  http://www.fortunecity.com/littleitaly/amalfi/100/angel.htm
  A book published by The Women's American Baptist Home Missionary Society, Chicago, in 1917.

- Angel Island: Immigrant Journeys of Chinese-Americans
  http://www.angel-island.com/
  An oral history of Chinese immigrant detainees.

- Angel Island Immigration Station
  http://www.angelisland.org/immigr02.html
  The "Ellis Island of the West" in San Francisco is now a National Historic Landmark

- The Angel Island Immigration Station Foundation
  http://www.a-better.com/Angel/island.htm
  The Foundation's purpose is to preservation, renovation, and development efforts of Angel Island Immigration Station, a National Historic Landmark, as an interpretive site for Pacific Rim immigration.

- Angel Island - The Pacific Gateway
  http://www.immigrationstation.com/
  Angel Island Immigration Station, San Francisco Bay, 1910 to 1940.

- HoustonChronicle.com - Angel Island: Journeys Remembered by Chinese Houstonians
  http://www.chron.com/content/chronicle/special/angelisland/
  intro.html
  Interviews online.

- Images From the History of the Public Health Service
  http://www.nlm.nih.gov/exhibition/phs_history/contents.html
  o Angel Island Arrivals
    http://www.nlm.nih.gov/exhibition/phs_history/22.html
  o Angel Island Disinfection of Clothing
    http://www.nlm.nih.gov/exhibition/phs_history/23.html
  o Angel Island Testing
    http://www.nlm.nih.gov/exhibition/phs_history/24.html

- A Panoramic View of the Angel Island Immigration Station - 1915
  http://memory.loc.gov/cgi-bin/query/r?ammem/pan:@FIELD (SUBJ+@band(+Angel+Island++San+Francisco+Bay,+ Calif.++))

- Prologue: Angel Island: "Guardian of the Western Gate"
  http://www.nara.gov/publications/prologue/angel1.html
  Online article from the NARA's Quarterly magazine "Prologue". A history of the Angel Island Immigration Station in San Francisco Bay.

- San Francisco, California - Immigrant & Passenger Arrivals - Records of the Immigration and Naturalization Service
  http://www.nara.gov/publications/microfilm/immigrant/ rg85.html#sfr
  Lists of microfilm roll numbers from the National Archives and Records Administration.

Baltimore - Maryland

- Immigrating to the Port of Baltimore
  http://www.clis.umd.edu/~mddlmddl/791/communities/html/ pob.html
  Describes what it was like to immigrate into the US via Baltimore.

Galveston - Texas

- Galveston: Ellis Island of the West
  http://www.amazon.com/exec/obidos/ISBN=0873957016/ markcyndisgenealA/
  A book by Bernard Marinbach.

- Galveston: Gateway to German Settlement in Texas
  http://www.audiotapes.com/product.asp?ProductCode= 'HT-40'
  Presentation by Wolfram M. Von-Maszewski, available for sale on audio tape.

- Galveston, Texas - Immigrant & Passenger Arrivals - Records of the Immigration and Naturalization Service
  http://www.nara.gov/publications/microfilm/immigrant/ rg85.html#gal
  Lists of microfilm roll numbers from the National Archives and Records Administration.

- Gone to Texas: Migration Patterns into the Lone Star State
  http://www.audiotapes.com/product.asp?ProductCode= 'DGS-R-4'
  Presentation by Sammie Townsend Lee, available for sale on audio tape.

- Texas Seaport Museum
  http://www.tsm-elissa.org/
  Located in the historic port of Galveston, the Texas Seaport Museum explores Texas' history of seaborne commerce and immigration.

  o Texas Seaport Museum Immigration Database
  http://www.tsm-elissa.org/immigration/imminfo.html
  Computerized database of 130,000 passengers who disembarked in Galveston from the period 1846-1948. Searchable at the Museum itself or by mail for a fee.

  o Accessing the Immigration Database
  http://www.tsm-elissa.org/immigration/idbaccess.html

  o Frequently Asked Questions
  http://www.tsm-elissa.org/immigration/questions.html

- Texas Seaport Museum's Immigration Database
  http://www.audiotapes.com/product.asp?ProductCode= 'HT-6A'
  Presentation by Olivia Meyer and Paul DeOrsay, available for sale on audio tape.

Grosse Île - Canada

- Grosse Île: The Canadian Ellis Island
  http://www.audiotapes.com/product.asp?ProductCode= 'GL-33'
  Presentation by Marianna O'Gallagher, available for sale on audio tape.

- 1847, Grosse Île: A Record of Daily Events
  http://www.amazon.com/exec/obidos/ISBN=0660168782/ markcyndisgenealA/
  A book by Andre Charbonneau.

- Grosse Île Gateway to Canada
  http://www.amazon.com/exec/obidos/ISBN=0969080530/ markcyndisgenealA/
  A book by Carraig Books.

- Grosse Île and the Irish Memorial
  http://parcscanada.risq.qc.ca/grosse_ile/
  From Parks Canada.

  o 1847: A Tragic Year at Grosse Île
  http://parcscanada.risq.qc.ca/grosse_ile/history2_e.html

  o The Changing Role of Grosse Île
  http://parcscanada.risq.qc.ca/grosse_ile/history1_e.html

  o Statistics and more statistics
  http://parcscanada.risq.qc.ca/grosse_ile/history3_e.html

- Canada's Irish National Monument - Grosse Île in Quebec
  http://homepage.eircom.net/~mcmullins/grosse-ile.htm

- Irish Visions Documentaries: Grosse Île: Gateway & Graveyard
  http://www.stpatrick.com/mall/visions/documentaries/ grosse.htm
  Video for sale.

- A Register of Deceased Persons at Sea and on Grosse Île
  http://www.amazon.com/exec/obidos/ISBN=0660168774/ markcyndisgenealA/
  A book by Andre Charbonneau.

New York

- Port of New York 1820-1957 - Immigrant & Passenger Arrivals - Records of the Immigration and Naturalization Service
  http://www.nara.gov/genealogy/immigration/newyork.html
  Lists of microfilm roll numbers from the National Archives and Records Administration.

- The Barge Office
  - o Abuses at the Barge Office
    http://www.fortunecity.com/littleitaly/amalfi/100/
    abuses00.htm
    *From an article originally published in The New York Times on
    June 3, 1900.*
  - o The Barge Office - 1898
    http://members.tripod.com/~L_Alfano/bargeoff.htm
    *Online article titled The Arrival of the Immigrant by Cromwell
    Childe in the New York Times Magazine, August 14, 1898.*

- Castle Garden
  - o Castle Clinton (Castle Garden) National
    Monument
    http://www.nps.gov/cacl/
    *From the National Park Service. Located in Battery Park on the
    southern-most tip of Manhattan, Castle Garden was the arrival
    point of some eight million immigrants who entered New York
    harbor from 1855 to 1890. It was the "Ellis Island" of its day.*
  - o Immigrant's Story - Castle Garden
    http://members.tripod.com/~Silvie/CastleGarden.html
    From the New York Times of December 23, 1866.
  - o Immigration and the Commissioners of Emigration
    of the State of New York
    http://www.amazon.com/exec/obidos/ISBN=040500530X/
    markcyndisgenealA/
    A book by Friedrich Kapp.
  - o The ShipsList - Pictures & Logos
    http://www.theshipslist.com/pictures/castlegarden.html
    - Castle Garden
      http://www.theshipslist.com/pictures/castlegarden.html
      Engravings and photographs of Castle Garden.
    - Wards Island Immigration Station
      http://www.theshipslist.com/pictures/wards.html
      Engravings of the Emigrant Hospital.

- Ellis Island
  - o The American Immigrant Wall of Honor ~ Ellis
    Island
    http://www.wallofhonor.com/
  - o AudioTapes.com - Genealogical Lectures on
    Cassette Tapes - Ellis Island
    http://www.audiotapes.com/search2.asp?Search=Ellis+
    Island
  - o Changing Immigrant Names
    http://www.ins.usdoj.gov/graphics/aboutins/history/articles/
    NAMES.htm
    *Includes a list of reasons for name changes and links to stories
    about how names were changed.*
    - American Names / Declaring Independence
      http://www.ins.usdoj.gov/graphics/aboutins/history/
      articles/NameEssay.html
      *Discusses the common misconceptions about name changes
      upon arrival in America. Particularly useful for
      understanding if your "name was changed at Ellis Island".*
  - o Ellis Island
    http://www.amazon.com/exec/obidos/ISBN=1565843185/
    markcyndisgenealA/
    A book by Georges Perec.

- o Ellis Island - 1892
  http://www.fortunecity.com/littleitaly/amalfi/100/ellis.htm
  A description of the immigrant processing center written in 1892.
- o Ellis Island and the History of Immigration to the
  United States
  http://www.davison.k12.mi.us/students/meszaros/
  immigrat.htm
- o Ellis Island and the Peopling of America: The
  Official Guide
  http://www.amazon.com/exec/obidos/ISBN=1565843649/
  markcyndisgenealA/
  A book by Virginia Yans-McLaughlin & Marjorie Lightman.
- o Ellis Island: Echoes from a Nation's Past
  http://www.amazon.com/exec/obidos/ISBN=0893813974/
  markcyndisgenealA/
  A book by Lewis Hine.
- o The Ellis Island Experience
  http://www.amazon.com/exec/obidos/ISBN=B00004TJP0/
  markcyndisgenealA/
  A CD-ROM by SouthPeak Interactive.
- o The Ellis Island Experience
  http://www.southpeak.com/titles/ellis-island/default.htm
  *Companion site to the interactive CD-ROM of the same name.
  Includes a description of the CD-ROM and disc-owner access to
  the associated web site.*
- o The Ellis Island Home Page
  http://www.ellisisland.org/
- o Ellis Island Gateway to America
  http://www.amazon.com/exec/obidos/ISBN=0916489094/
  markcyndisgenealA/
  A book by Loretto D. Szucs.
- o Ellis Island: Gateway to the American Dream
  http://www.amazon.com/exec/obidos/ISBN=0517059053/
  markcyndisgenealA/
  A book by Pamela Kilian & Pamela Reeves.
- o The Ellis Island Home Page
  http://www.ellisisland.org/
  - The American Family Immigration History
    Center
    http://www.ellisisland.org/history.html
    *Located at the Ellis Island Immigration Museum, this center is
    planned to be opened late in the year 2000. A computerized
    database will allow visitors to search over 17 million
    individual names extracted from Ships' Passenger Lists from
    the Port of New York between the years 1892 and 1924.*
- o Ellis Island Interviews
  http://www.amazon.com/exec/obidos/ISBN=0816035482/
  markcyndisgenealA/
  A book by Peter Morton Coan.
- o Ellis Island (I-Channel)
  http://www.i-channel.com/features/ellis/
- o Ellis Island : New Hope in a New Land
  http://www.amazon.com/exec/obidos/ISBN=0684191717/
  markcyndisgenealA/
  A book by William Jay Jacobs.
- o Ellis Island - Through America's Gateway
  http://www.i-channel.com/features/ellis/

o History of Ellis Island/Castle Garden
http://www.rootsweb.com/~irlwat/hist.htm

o If Your Name Was Changed at Ellis Island
http://www.amazon.com/exec/obidos/ISBN=0590438298/
markcyndisgenealA/
A book by Ellen Levine.

o The Immigration Experience
http://members.tripod.com/~L_Alfano/immig.htm
An excellent account of immigration through the port of New York. Includes contemporary news articles on Castle Garden, the Barge Office, and an account of the "new" Ellis Island.

o Journey to Ellis Island
http://www.amazon.com/exec/obidos/ISBN=0786803770/
markcyndisgenealA/
A book by Carol Bierman & Laurie McGaw.

o Liberty State Park
http://www.libertystatepark.com

  • Ellis Island
  http://www.libertystatepark.com/ellis.htm

  • History Channel Exhibits: Ellis Island
  http://www.historychannel.com/exhibits/ellisisle/

  • History of Ellis Island
  http://www.libertystatepark.com/history1.htm

  • Images From the History of the Public Health Service
  http://www.nlm.nih.gov/exhibition/phs_history/
  contents.html

  • Ellis Island Trachoma Inspections
  http://www.nlm.nih.gov/exhibition/phs_history/20.html

  • Ellis Island Quarantine
  http://www.nlm.nih.gov/exhibition/phs_history/21.html

  • The Immigrant Journey
  http://www.libertystatepark.com/immigran.htm
  A description of the immigrant experience centering around Ellis Island.

o Immigration: Ellis Island History
http://library.thinkquest.org/20619/Eihist.html

o Immigration: Ellis Island Virtual Tour
http://library.thinkquest.org/20619/Eivirt.html

o New Jersey Governor's Advisory Committee on the Preservation and Use of Ellis Island
http://www.ellisislandnj.org/
From the State of New Jersey. Plans regarding New Jersey's efforts to preserve and enhance Ellis Island.

o New Jersey wins suit over Ellis Island
http://www.usatoday.com/news/court/nscot787.htm
From USA Today. The US Supreme Court determines that most of Ellis Island belongs to New Jersey, not New York.

o New York, NY, Ellis Island -- Immigration: 1900-1920
http://cmp1.ucr.edu/exhibitions/immigration_id.html
University of California, Riverside, Keystone-Mast Collection, California Museum of Photography. Photographs of immigrants, ships & Ellis Island.

o Statue of Liberty National Monument and Ellis Island
http://www.nps.gov/stli/

• Ellis Island (part of the Statue of Liberty National Monument)
http://www.nps.gov/stli/serv02.htm
From the National Park Service. From 1892 to 1954, over 12 million immigrants arrived in the United States through Ellis Island in New York harbor. The official NPS web site regarding the history and current preservation of Ellis Island. Includes visitor information.

o Selected Images of Ellis Island and Immigration, ca. 1880-1920
http://lcweb.loc.gov/rr/print/070_immi.html
From the Collections of the Library of Congress.

o A Virtual Tour of Ellis Island
http://articles.citysearch.com/New_York/virtualtour/ellis/
Series of photographs of the Ellis Island buildings, both interior and exterior.

• Pier 21 - Canada

o Pier 21
http://www.pier21.ns.ca/
Between 1928-1971, at Pier 21 on the Halifax waterfront, 1.5 million immigrants first set foot on Canadian soil. During World War II, 3,000 British evacuee children, 50,000 war brides and their 22,000 children, over 100,000 refugees and 368,000 Canadian troops bound for Europe passed through Pier 21.

  • Parks Canada Backgrounder - Pier 21 Halifax
  http://parkscanada.pch.gc.ca/library/background/
  51_e.htm

  • Parks Canada News Release - Pier 21 Recognized as a National Historic Site
  http://parkscanada.pch.gc.ca/library/newsreleases/
  english/nr38%5Fe.htm

  • Pier 21: The Gateway That Changed Canada
  http://www.amazon.com/exec/obidos/ISBN=
  0889994064/markcyndisgenealA/
  A book by J.P. Leblanc.

◆ Publications, Microfilm & Microfiche

• Amazon.com Genealogy Bookstore – Immigration
http://www.amazon.com/exec/obidos/external-search/?
keyword=immigration+genealogy&tag=markcyndisgenealA/
And Naturalization
http://www.amazon.com/exec/obidos/external-search/?
keyword=naturalization+genealogy&tag=markcyndisgenealA/

• AudioTapes.com - Genealogical Lectures on Cassette Tapes – Immigration
http://www.audiotapes.com/search2.asp?Search=Immigration
Naturalization
http://www.audiotapes.com/search2.asp?Search=
Naturalization
And Immigrant
http://www.audiotapes.com/search2.asp?Search=immigrant

• Frontier Press Bookstore - Immigration
http://www.frontierpress.com/frontier.cgi?category=imm

- GenealogyBookShop.com - Guide to Naturalization Records of the United States
  http://www.genealogybookshop.com/genealogybookshop/files/General,Immigration_Passenger_Lists_Naturalizations/5177.html
  A book by Christina K. Schaefer.

- GenealogyBookShop.com - Immigration/Passenger Lists/Naturalizations
  http://www.genealogybookshop.com/genealogybookshop/files/General,Immigration_Passenger_Lists_Naturalizations/index.html
  The online store of Genealogical Publishing Co., Inc. & Clearfield Company.

- How to Find Your Immigrant Ancestor - Passenger and Immigration Lists Index
  http://www.rader.org/how_to.htm
  Tips on using these volumes by Filby.

- Immigrant and Passenger Arrivals
  http://www.nara.gov/publications/microfilm/immigrant/immpass.html
  A select catalog of National Archives microfilm.

- Long Journey for Sevenpence - Assisted Immigration to New Zealand from the United Kingdom 1947-1975
  http://www.nzhistory.net.nz/Gallery/immigration/Index.htm
  A book available from the Victoria University Press.

- Mormon Immigration Index
  http://www.ldscatalog.com/cgi-bin/ncommerce3/ProductDisplay?prrfnbr=1916588&prmenbr=1402&CGRY_NUM=1440462&RowStart=1&LocCode=FH
  CD-ROM for sale from the LDS church. Database of approximately 93,000 immigrants who traveled from various international ports to the United States between the years 1840 and 1890. Information in this database includes the age, country of origin, ports of departure and arrival, the company leader assigned to each voyage, and general voyage information.

- Mormon Immigration Index Press Kit
  http://www.lds.org/library/display/0,4945,232-1-209-1,FF.html
  Includes sample journal entries, photographs, and information on the database.

- Naturalization and Citizenship Indexes in the Canada Gazette 1915-1951
  http://mypage.direct.ca/d/dobee/nat.html
  Describes a book for sale which indexes the publication of naturalizing Canadian citizens from 1815 to 1951.

◆ Records

- Baden, Germany Emigration Index, 1866-1911
  http://www.ancestry.com/search/rectype/inddbs/4610.htm
  Pay-for-use database containing the names of over 28,000 persons who left Baden between 1866 and 1911. Each entry includes the emigrant's name, residence or place of birth, and the year of departure.

- The Belfast Newsletter Index, 1737-1800
  http://www.ucs.usl.edu/bnl/Main.html
  Online searchable database of over 20,000 transcribed pages from the newspaper including personal names, place names, and ship names.

- Brandenburg, Prussia Emigration Records
  http://www.ancestry.com/search/rectype/inddbs/4121.htm
  Pay-for-use database containing 17,500 names of emigrants leaving Brandenburg. Each record provides the emigrant's name, age, occupation, residence, destination and year of emigration.

- Finding Historical Information
  http://www.cdphe.state.co.us/hs/genealogy.html
  A guide for genealogists and historians to assist in their research of Colorado vital records.

- Colorado State Archives Naturalization Records
  http://www.archives.state.co.us/natural.html
  Excellent site providing information on the naturalization process in general complete with scanned documents as examples. Gives an inventory of the naturalization records held by the Archives on a county-by-county basis.

  o Background History of the United States Naturalization Process
    http://www.archives.state.co.us/natinfo.htm

- Finding Immigration Records - U.S.
  http://www.history.rochester.edu/jssn/page2.htm
  Including a scanned image example.

- Howard County Indiana Naturalization Records
  http://www.kokomo.lib.in.us/genealogy/natural.html
  Found in various order books of the local courts prior to 1907.

- How Do I Use Naturalization Records to Trace My Ancestors?
  http://www.shsw.wisc.edu/genealogy/natlzn/index.html
  From the State Historical Society of Wisconsin. This is an outstanding web site about Naturalization in general and Wisconsin records in particular.

- How to Get Your Ancestor's Papers from the Immigration and Naturalization Service
  http://www.italgen.com/immigrat.htm

- Immigrant and Passenger Arrivals
  http://www.nara.gov/publications/microfilm/immigrant/immpass.html
  A select catalog of National Archives microfilm.

- Immigration Records
  http://www.nara.gov/genealogy/immigration/immigrat.html
  From National Archives and Records Administration (NARA).

- Immigrants Recruited by the Launceston Aid Immigration Society ~ Tasmania, Australia
  http://www.vision.net.au/~tashistory/immig/title.htm

- Immigration to Canada in the Nineteenth Century - Ships - Emigration Reports - Emigration Handbooks
  http://www.ist.uwaterloo.ca/~marj/genealogy/thevoyage.html
  Contains pointers to many other ships lists and sources.

- Immigration to Victoria. British Ports 1852-1879
  http://www.cohsoft.com.au/cgi-bin/db/ship.pl
  Public Record Office of Victoria, Australia has indexed the Arrivals to Victorian Ports from British Ports 1852 - 1879.

- Index of the Petitions for Naturalization at the Osage County Courthouse
  http://skyways.lib.ks.us/towns/Lyndon/genealogy/nat index1.htm
  From the Osage County Genealogical Society. ~ Lyndon, Kansas

- Indiana Naturalizations - Naturalization Databases
  http://www.state.in.us/icpr/webfile/natural/homepage.html
  Dubois, Elkhart, Hancock, Jefferson and Monroe counties.

- inGeneas Canadian Genealogy
  http://www.inGeneas.com/
  Professional genealogists specializing in Canadian immigration records. Searchable databases containing 50,000+ Canadian passenger and immigration records (c1750 to 1900) including the only electronic version of the free National Archives of Canada Miscellaneous Immigration Index

- Irish Famine Migration To New Brunswick, 1845 – 1852
  http://gov.nb.ca/archives/ols/pr/if/index.htm
  Searchable database from the Provincial Archives of New Brunswick.

- Madison County (Indiana) Naturalization Records Index
  http://apl.acsc.net/natu.htm

- McLean County, IL, Immigration Records
  http://www.mclean.gov/cc/imgrecs/imgrecs.html

- National Archives of Canada - Immigration Records
  http://www.archives.ca/exec/naweb.dll?fs&02020204&e&top&0
  - Immigration Records (1925-1935)
    http://www.archives.ca/exec/naweb.dll?fs&020118&e&top&0
    Searchable online database provides the volumes and page numbers on which the names of Canadian immigrants appear in the passenger lists.

- Naturalization Records
  http://www.gnofn.org/~nopl/info/louinfo/louinfo4.htm
  From the New Orleans Public Library. The Louisiana Division has the original naturalization records from the Civil Courts of New Orleans, 1827-1906.

- Naturalization Records
  http://www.uwm.edu/Dept/Library/arch/citizen.htm
  From the University of Wisconsin-Milwaukie. A good brief description of the naturalization process, the records which it generated, and Wisconsin-specific record location information.

- Naturalization Records
  http://www.nara.gov/genealogy/natural.html
  From the U.S. National Archives and Records Administration.

- Naturalization Records
  http://www.albanycounty.com/departments/records/online/Naturalizations/index.htm
  Online searchable database of index information for naturalizations in Albany from 1821 to 1906.

- Naturalization Records - U.S.
  http://www.history.rochester.edu/jssn/page3.htm
  Including a scanned image example.

- Naturalizations: Researching Philadelphia Records
  http://www.phila.gov/phils/Docs/Inventor/natz.htm

- New York Emigrant Savings Bank Project
  http://www.genexchange.org/esb/index.cfm
  Searchable database of the records for the Emigrant Savings Bank in New York City. Opened in 1850 and run by Irish immigrants for Irish immigrants, the ESB records for emigrants from various countries settling in many states.
  - Emigrant Savings Bank Records
    http://www.nycgenweb.com/emigrant%20savings%20bank%20records.htm
    The first 500 account numbers with account owner names and dates.
  - The New York Emigrant Savings Bank
    http://www.everton.com/FHN/27may99.htm
    Brief article from Everton's regarding the genealogical value of these Bank records.
  - A User's Guide to the Emigrant Bank Records
    http://www.nypl.org/research/chss/spe/rbk/faids/emigrant.html
    Opened in 1850 and run by Irish immigrants for Irish immigrants, the Emigrant Savings Bank records for immigrants from various countries settling in many states. This is a finding aid and description of these records from the New York Public Library's Manuscripts & Archives Division.

- Naturalization & Related Records
  http://www.archives.nysed.gov/holding/fact/natur-fa.htm
  New York State Archives Information Leaflet #6. A good general introduction to the Naturalization process during American history.

- North Dakota Naturalization Records Index
  http://www.lib.ndsu.nodak.edu/database/naturalrec.html

- Prologue: Women & Naturalization Records
  http://www.nara.gov/publications/prologue/natural1.html
  Online article from the NARA's Quarterly magazine "Prologue". Summer 1998's "Genealogy Notes" examines why women are not represented in early naturalization records.

- Public Record Office - Finding Aids - A-Z Index of All Leaflets ~ U.K.
  http://www.pro.gov.uk/leaflets/riindex.htm
  - Emigrants - Domestic Records Information 107
    http://www.pro.gov.uk/leaflets/ri2272.htm
  - Emigrants to North America After 1776
    http://www.pro.gov.uk/leaflets/ri2107.htm
  - Immigrants - Domestic Records Information 50
    http://www.pro.gov.uk/leaflets/ri2157.htm
  - Passport Records - Domestic Records Information 60
    http://www.pro.gov.uk/leaflets/ri2167.htm

- Research Guide - Chinese Immigrants and Chinese-Australians in New South Wales
  http://www.naa.gov.au/PUBLICAT/GUIDES/chinese/guide.htm
  From the National Archives of Australia.

- Research Guide - Good British Stock - Child & Youth Migration to Australia
  http://www.naa.gov.au/PUBLICAT/GUIDES/childmig/guide.htm
  From the National Archives of Australia.

- Requesting Your Ancestor's Naturalization Records from the INS
  http://www.arduini.net/tools/insreque.htm
  A guide by Dennis Piccirillo.

- State Historical Society of Wisconsin - How Do I...? - Naturalization Records
  http://www.shsw.wisc.edu/genealogy/natlzn/

  o Naturalization Records - Frequently Asked Questions
    http://www.shsw.wisc.edu/genealogy/natlzn/nat-faq.htm
    Excellent basic information on naturalization records in FAQ format.

  o Naturalization Records - Holdings at SHSW and Elsewhere
    http://www.shsw.wisc.edu/genealogy/natlzn/natlist.htm
    Describes the types, dates covered and location of naturalization records in Wisconsin.

  o Naturalization Records - The Process
    http://www.shsw.wisc.edu/genealogy/natlzn/process.htm
    An excellent short description of the various laws effecting the US naturalization process over time.

  o Naturalization Records - The Records
    http://www.shsw.wisc.edu/genealogy/natlzn/records.htm
    Describes in detail the types of documents generated by the naturalization process. Includes scanned images of examples of these documents.

- U.S. Immigration and Naturalization Service (INS)
  http://www.ins.usdoj.gov/graphics/index.htm

  o INS Forms Available for Download
    http://www.ins.usdoj.gov/graphics/formsfee/forms/
    Download forms such as G-639, Freedom of Information / Privacy Act

  o INS History, Genealogy, and Education
    http://www.ins.usdoj.gov/graphics/aboutins/history/index.htm

- Changing Immigrant Names
  http://www.ins.usdoj.gov/graphics/aboutins/history/articles/NAMES.htm
  Includes a list of reasons for name changes and links to stories about how names were changed.

- Frequently Asked Questions
  http://www.ins.usdoj.gov/graphics/aboutins/history/histq.html

- Historical Reference Library
  http://www.ins.usdoj.gov/graphics/aboutins/history/library.htm

- Historical Research Tools
  http://www.ins.usdoj.gov/graphics/aboutins/history/Tools.html

- Immigration and Emigration by Decade, 1901-1990
  http://www.ins.usdoj.gov/graphics/aboutins/statistics/300.htm

- Immigration and Naturalization Legislature from the Statistical Yearbook
  http://www.ins.usdoj.gov/graphics/aboutins/statistics/legishist/index.htm
  Compilation of federal immigration and naturalization statutes in the United States provides an overview of the legislative history of immigration to the United States. 1790-1996.

- Immigration Arrival Records
  http://www.ins.usdoj.gov/graphics/aboutins/history/ImmRecs/ImmRec.htm

- Naturalization Records
  http://www.ins.usdoj.gov/graphics/aboutins/history/NatzRec/NATREC.htm

- Ports of Entry and Their Records
  http://www.ins.usdoj.gov/graphics/aboutins/history/POELIST/POE.htm

- Utah Naturalization and Citizenship Records
  http://www.archives.state.ut.us/referenc/natural.htm
  From the Utah State Archives.

- Wuerttemberg Emigration Index
  http://www.ancestry.com/search/rectype/inddbs/3141a.htm
  Pay-for-use database contains the names of approximately 60,000 persons who made application to emigrate at Wuerttemberg from the late eighteenth century to 1900. The information supplied on each person includes: name, date and place of birth, residence at time of application and application date, and microfilm number.

ITALY / ITALIA
http://www.cyndislist.com/italy.htm

Category Index:

- General Resource Sites
- History & Culture
- How To
- Language, Handwriting & Script
- Libraries, Archives & Museums
- Locality Specific
- Mailing Lists, Newsgroups & Chat
- Maps, Gazetteers & Geographical Information

- People & Families
- Professional Researchers, Volunteers & Other Research Services
- Publications, Software & Supplies
- Queries, Message Boards & Surname Lists
- Records: Census, Cemeteries, Land, Obituaries, Personal, Taxes and Vital
- Societies & Groups

◆ General Resource Sites

- Arduini & Pizzo - An Italian-American Family History
  http://www.arduini.net/
  Many resources for Italian genealogical research.

- The Italian Genealogy Home Page
  http://www.italgen.com/

- Italian Genealogy Pages Web Ring
  http://freeweb.aspide.it/personali/SBertini/WebRing/join-webring.htm

- Italian Genealogy? Start Here!
  http://www.daddezio.com/index.html
  The D'ADDEZIO surname, articles and other helpful tools for Italian research.

- Italian Immigration to Maryland
  http://www.clis.umd.edu/~mddlmddl/791/communities/html/index.html#italian
  A scholarly review of immigration into Maryland from the very first colonists to modern immigrants.

- The Italo-Albanian Heritage Pages
  http://members.aol.com/itaalb1/web/arberesh.htm

- Italy Telephone & Address Listings
  http://www.ancestry.com/search/rectype/inddbs/4065.htm

- Italy WorldGenWeb
  http://www.rootsweb.com/~itawgw/index.html

- Immigration: The Italians
  http://library.thinkquest.org/20619/Italian.html
  A brief history of Italian immigration to the United States.

- Joe's Italian Genealogy Page
  http://www.caropepe.com/italy/

- Lou ALFANO's GeoCities Web Site
  http://www.geocities.com/Athens/Acropolis/1709/index.html
  Dedicated to Italian Genealogy, History & Culture.

- Nostro Albero
  http://www.geocities.com/SiliconValley/Park/3063/nostrow.htm
  With a searchable database of 5,300 Italian surnames.

- PIE - Pursuing Our Italian Names Together In E-mail
  http://www.cimorelli.com/pie/
  Italian Genealogy, Heritage, Culture & Databases on the WWW.

- Radici - The Italian Genealogy Webclub
  http://www.initaly.com/gene/
  Lets you build your own Online Family Bible, share the results of your research and network with other Italian descendants all over the world.

- Surnames in Italy / L'Italia dei cognomi
  http://gens.labo.net/en/cognomi/
  By entering a surname and pressing the red arrow, a distribution map of Italy is generated showing the concentrations of that particular surname in Italy.

- Yahoo!...Italy...Genealogy
  http://dir.yahoo.com/Regional/Countries/Italy/Arts_and_Humanities/Humanities/History/Genealogy/

◆ History & Culture

- De Imperatoribus Romanis - Index of Imperial Stemmata of the Roman Emporers
  http://www.salve.edu/~romanemp/stemm.htm

- The Italian American Web Site of New York
  http://italian-american.com/main.htm
  This site contains information pertaining to Italian genealogy, organizations, discrimination, travel, literature, college, sports, women and much more.

- StudyWeb: History: Country History Index: Europe Index: Italy
  http://www.studyweb.com/links/146.html

- Torrione Castle - an unusual example of a Museum for History
  http://www.gvo.it/VdSF/torrione1.html
  From Italy. Be sure to check out their Vialardi di Sandigliano lineage library.

- The Trentino Site - Genealogy, Culture, History
  http://members.aol.com/sromano937/index.htm
  A Little About the Province of Trento, especially Val di Non.

- Waldensians and Waldensian Church
  http://services.csi.it/~valdese/english.htm
  Historical information about the Waldensian church.

- Yahoo!...Italy...History
  http://dir.yahoo.com/Regional/Countries/Italy/Arts_and_Humanities/Humanities/History/

◆ How To

- How to Research Your Italian Ancestry?
  http://members.aol.com/geneaita/indexen.html

- Italy Church Record Christenings
  http://www.familysearch.org/rg/guide/IT_BT3_-_Churchrecordchristening1500-1874.ASP
  From FamilySearch.org.

- Italian Genealogy How-To Guide
  http://www.familytreemaker.com/00000375.html

- Italian Research Outline
  http://www.familysearch.org/rg/guide/Italy.ASP
  Excellent "How To" guide from FamilySearch.org.

◆ Language, Handwriting & Script

- AltaVista Translation Service
  http://babelfish.altavista.digital.com/cgi-bin/translate?
  Input a URL for a web site or a block of plain text and this site will translate for you from Italian to English or from English to Italian.

- Italian Genealogical Word List
  http://www.familysearch.org/rg/guide/WLItalia.ASP

- Italian Letter Writing Guide
  http://www.familysearch.org/rg/guide/LGItalian.ASP
  For genealogical inqueries from FamilySearch.org.

◆ Libraries, Archives & Museums

- Archivio della Provincia di Bolzano
  http://www.provinz.bz.it/sla/i/index_i.htm
  South Tyrol Archive.

- Archivi: Sistema Archivistico Nazionale
  http://www.archivi.beniculturali.it/
  National archives system of Italy.

- Family History Library Catalog
  http://www.familysearch.org/Search/searchcatalog.asp
  From the FamilySearch web site, an online catalog to the holdings of the LDS Church in Salt Lake City, Utah. Also search for other localities by place name.
  http://www.familysearch.org/fhlc/supermainframeset.asp?display=localitysearch&columns=*,180,0

- o Italy
  http://www.familysearch.org/fhlc/supermainframeset.asp?display=localitydetails&subject=98&subject_disp=Italy&columns=*,180,0

- Family History SourceGuide - Family History Centers - Europe and Scandinavia
  http://www.familysearch.org/sg/Europe_and_Scandinavia_FHC.html
  Austria, Belgium, Denmark, Finland, France, Germany, Hungary, Iceland, Italy, Netherlands, Norway, Portugal, Spain, Sweden, and Switzerland.

- Ministero per i Beni e le Attività Culturali / Ministry for the Cultural Assets and Activities
  http://www.beniculturali.it/index.asp

- Repositories of Primary Sources - Europe - Italy
  http://www.uidaho.edu/special-collections/euro1.html#it
  A list of links to online resources from the Univ. of Idaho Library, Special Collections and Archives.

- Südtiroler Landesarchiv / South Tyrol Archive
  http://www.provinz.bz.it/sla/d/index_d.htm
  Former Austrian possession now part of Italy.

◆ Locality Specific

- Calitrian Connections
  http://www.eastsidetrail.com/calitrian/
  Italian Genealogy on the town of Calitri, province of Avellino.

- Isola delle Femmine - Capaci Connection
  http://members.aol.com/femmine/isola.html
  For descendants of the families of Isola delle Femmine and Capaci, Sicily who immigrated to the United States beginning about 1890.

◆ Mailing Lists, Newsgroups & Chat

- Genealogy Resources on the Internet - Italy Mailing Lists
  http://www.rootsweb.com/~jfuller/gen_mail_country-ita.html
  Most of the mailing list links below point to this site, wonderfully maintained by John Fuller

- Amici Mailing List
  http://www.rootsweb.com/~jfuller/gen_mail_country-ita.html#Amici
  For anyone with a genealogical interest in the island of Sicily, Italy.

- ARIA Mailing List
  http://www.rootsweb.com/~jfuller/gen_mail_country-ita.html#ARIA-L
  For Australians and New Zealanders who are researching their Italian Heritage, Culture and Ancestry.

- AUSTRIA Mailing List
  http://www.rootsweb.com/~jfuller/gen_mail_country-ita.html#AUSTRIA
  For anyone with a genealogical or historical interest in Austria including the German speaking lands annexed to Italy at the end of World War I.

- BariItaly Mailing List
  http://www.rootsweb.com/~jfuller/gen_mail_country-ita.html#BariItaly
  For anyone with a genealogical interest in the province.

- CALITRI Mailing List
  http://www.rootsweb.com/~jfuller/gen_mail_country-ita.html#CALITRI
  A mailing list for those who are interested in their Calitrani (people from Calitri, Italy) heritage. Towns of interest include Calitri, Andretta, Bisaccia, Pescopagano, Ruvo, Santangelo Lombardi, and other surrounding towns.

- CHE-TICINO Mailing List
  http://www.rootsweb.com/~jfuller/gen_mail_country-swi.html#CHE-TICINO
  For anyone with a genealogical interest in the Ticino, the Italian-speaking canton of Switzerland.

- COMUNES_OF_ITALY Mailing List
  http://www.rootsweb.com/~jfuller/gen_mail_country-ita.html#COMUNES_OF_ITALY
  For those who are interested in Italian genealogy, culture and all things Italian.

- GEN-ITALIAN Mailing List
  http://www.rootsweb.com/~jfuller/gen_mail_country-ita.html#GEN-ITALIAN
  Gatewayed with the soc.genealogy.italian newsgroup.
  news:soc.genealogy.italian

- ICC - The Il Circolo Calabrese Mailing List
  http://www.rootsweb.com/~jfuller/gen_mail_country-ita.html#ICC
  For anyone with a genealogical interest in the Calabria region of Italy (the southernmost region of the Italian peninsula, the 'toe' of the boot).

- ITA-CUGGIONO Mailing List
  http://www.rootsweb.com/~jfuller/gen_mail_country-ita.html#ITA-CUGGIONO
  For anyone with a genealogical interest in Cuggiono or Milan, Italy, area.

- ITA-FROSINONE
  http://www.rootsweb.com/~jfuller/gen_mail_country-ita.html#ITA-FROSINONE
  For anyone with a genealogical interest in immigrants from Frosinone, Lazio, Italy.

- ITALIADOPTION Mailing List
  http://www.rootsweb.com/~jfuller/gen_mail_adoption.html#ITALIADOPTION
  For individuals who were born in Italy and adopted by families in the United States or Canada to seek help in locating birthparents, siblings, or other family members.

- ITA-LUCCA Mailing List
  http://www.rootsweb.com/~jfuller/gen_mail_country-ita.html#ITA-LUCCA
  For the discussion and sharing of information regarding the activities of the Lucca genealogy users group located in Lucca Province, Tuscany, Italy, and genealogical resources available in the Lucca Province area.

- ITALY Mailing List
  http://www.rootsweb.com/~jfuller/gen_mail_country-ita.html#ITALY
  For anyone with a genealogical interest in Italy.

- italy-gene Mailing List
  http://www.rootsweb.com/~jfuller/gen_mail_country-ita.html#italy-gene

- ItalyNW Mailing List
  http://www.rootsweb.com/~jfuller/gen_mail_country-ita.html#ItalyNW
  Dedicated to family history research in northern Italy.

- ITA-MENFI Mailing List
  http://www.rootsweb.com/~jfuller/gen_mail_country-ita.html#ITA-MENFI
  For anyone with a genealogical interest in Menfi or Santa Margherita di Belice, Sicily, Italy.

- ITA-PIEDMONT Mailing List
  http://www.rootsweb.com/~jfuller/gen_mail_country-ita.html#ITA-PIEDMONT
  For anyone with a genealogical interest in the Piedmont District of Italy.

- ITA-SICILY Mailing List
  http://www.rootsweb.com/~jfuller/gen_mail_country-ita.html#ITA-SICILY
  For anyone with a genealogical interest in the island of Sicily, Italy.

- ITA-SICILY-BARCELLONA-MESSINA Mailing List
  http://www.rootsweb.com/~jfuller/gen_mail_country-ita.html#ITA-SICILY-BARCELLONA-MESSINA
  For anyone with a genealogical interest in Barcellona, Pozzo di Gotto, Province of Messina, Sicily, Italy.

- PIE Mailing List
  http://www.rootsweb.com/~jfuller/gen_mail_country-ita.html#PIE
  For Italian genealogical research.

- SARDINIA Mailing List
  http://www.rootsweb.com/~jfuller/gen_mail_country-sar.html#SARDINIA

- VALLEDOLMO Mailing List
  http://www.rootsweb.com/~jfuller/gen_mail_country-ita.html#VALLEDOLMO
  For the discussion and sharing of information regarding the village of Valledolmo in the province of Palermo, Sicily, Italy.

- VATICAN-CITY Mailing List
  http://www.rootsweb.com/~jfuller/gen_mail_country-vat.html#VATICAN-CITY
  For anyone with a genealogical interest in the City/State of Vatican City located in Rome, Italy.

◆ Maps, Gazetteers & Geographical Information

- Italy Maps - The Perry-Castañeda Library Map Collection
  http://www.lib.utexas.edu/Libs/PCL/Map_collection/italy.html
  From the University of Texas at Austin.

- Map of San Marino
  http://www.lib.utexas.edu/Libs/PCL/Map_collection/europe/SanMarino.jpg
  From the Perry-Castañeda Library at the Univ. of Texas at Austin.

- Map of Vatican City
  http://www.lib.utexas.edu/Libs/PCL/Map_collection/europe/
  Vaticancity.jpg
  From the Perry-Castañeda Library at the Univ. of Texas at Austin.

- Surnames in Italy / L'Italia dei cognomi
  http://gens.labo.net/en/cognomi/
  By entering a surname and pressing the red arrow, a distribution map of Italy is generated showing the concentrations of that particular surname in Italy.

◆ People & Families

- Angelo GRIFASI ~ Milan
  http://joshua.micronet.it/utenti/mgrifasi/home.html
  Sicily, Pics, Sicilian Cooking, Names curiosities, Palermo, Milano, Ravanusa.

- FISCHETTI / SORVILLO Family Genealogy
  http://members.aol.com/rich353/index.htm
  FISCHETTI, DIGIUSEPPE, BORGIA, SORVILLO, GRAZIANO, VISCARDO, COPPOLA, GRILLO, OLIVERI.

- Giorgio ALESSANDRI's Home Page
  http://www.agora.stm.it/G.Alessandri/home.htm
  Including a case study on a recent genealogical research project and an article on church records over time.

- Joseph and Joyce ANELLO
  http://www.geocities.com/Heartland/Plains/6917/
  The ANELLO, PUSATERI, LETO and VENTURA families from Caccamo and Termini, Sicily.

- MAZZOLINI's Genealogic Page - Home Page
  Genealogica di Roberto Iannarelli MAZZOLINI
  http://www.geocities.com/Heartland/Ranch/7572
  Genealogical and historical researches other the word on Mazzolini's and Iannarelli's Italian surnames.

- Our Calabrian Heritage
  http://members.aol.com/GLilli/index.html
  A study of the Village of Oriolo, Cosenza, in the Italian Region of Calabria, its History, People and Culture.

- Royal Family of Syracuse
  http://www.mcs.drexel.edu/~crorres/Archimedes/Family/
  FamilyIntro.html
  The house of Hiero - third century B.C.

- Spence Sacco BURTON's Homepage
  http://members.home.net/sfburton
  SACCO, SANTANGELO, INDELICATO, DILORENZO, (DI) SILVESTRO, TODARO, GAIMO, BURTON, SPENCE. Sicilian genealogy, culture etc. Italian language pages available.

- The Vasto Page - La Pagina Vastese
  http://www.geocities.com/Athens/Acropolis/1709/Vasto
  Pag.htm
  Comune of Vasto, Province of Chieti, Region of Abruzzo.

◆ Professional Researchers, Volunteers & Other Research Services

- Emilio - Escort of SICILY
  http://www.mediatel.it/public/emilio/
  Professional Italian researcher and tour guide.

- European Focus
  http://www.eurofocus.com/
  Photographic portfolios of ancestral towns in Europe created for Genealogy enthusiasts in Belgium, Denmark, Eastern Europe, England, France, Germany, Great Britain, Italy, Netherlands, Norway, Poland, Sweden, Switzerland and more.

- Family Tree Genealogical and Probate Research Bureau Ltd.
  http://www.familytree.hu/
  Professional research service covering the area of what was formerly the Austro - Hungarian Empire, including: Hungary, Slovakia, Czech Republic, Austria, Italy, Transylvania, Croatia, Slovenia, former Yugoslavia (Banat), and the Ukraine (Sub-Carpathian).

- Genealogy Helplist - Italy
  http://helplist.org/ita/index.shtml

- Genealogy Research in Abruzzo, Italy
  http://abruzzo2000.com/genealogy/index.html
  Free resources and professional services for research in Abruzzo, Italy, from an Abruzzo-based group.

- Italian Research
  http://www.gentracer.com/italy.html
  Professional genealogical research in the microfilmed records at the Family History Library in Salt Lake City and on-site in Sicily.

- genealogyPro - Professional Genealogists for Italy
  http://genealogyPro.com/directories/Italy.html

- Italian Ancestral Research
  http://www.italianancestralresearch.ofutah.com/
  Carolyn B. Ugolini, Accredited Genealogist.

- New Jersey and Italian Genealogical Research Services
  http://www.italgen.com/sponsors/piccirillo/index.htm

- Pallante Center for Italian Research
  http://www.geocities.com/TheTropics/Shores/2641/
  Pallante.htm
  A virtual research center for Italian research (in-person visits available by appointment for those local to upstate New York). A growing collection of Italian related resources, including an archival collection and Italian family surname files. Professional Italian genealogy research services and other historical research relating to Italy or Italian immigrants worldwide, as well as help with dual citizenship (US/Italian), finding educational Italian resources for schools, etc.

- Southern Italian Genealogical Research
  http://expage.com/page/sitalgen
  Luke Tomson conducts genealogy for southern Italy using Napoleonic Civil records. He is fluent in Italian, and is familiar with Latin, Italian dialects, and paleography. Professional services and low rates.

◆ Publications, Software & Supplies

- Amazon.com Genealogy Bookstore - Italy
  http://www.amazon.com/exec/obidos/external-search/?
  keyword=italy+genealogy&tag=markcyndisgenealA/

- Ancestor's Attic Discount Genealogy Books - Italian Genealogy Books
  http://members.tripod.com/~ancestorsattic/index.html#secIT

- AudioTapes.com - Genealogical Lectures on Cassette Tapes – Italy
  http://www.audiotapes.com/search2.asp?Search=italian
  And Italian
  http://www.audiotapes.com/search2.asp?Search=Italy

- Frontier Press Bookstore - Italy
  http://www.frontierpress.com/frontier.cgi?category=ital

- Genealogia
  http://volftp.mondadori.com/italiani/boscolo/genealog.htm
  The first Italian software for genealogists and historians. Il primo programma italiano per studi genealogici e storici.

- GenealogyBookShop.com - Italy/Italian
  http://www.genealogybookshop.com/genealogybookshop/files/The_World,Italy_Italian/index.html
  The online store of Genealogical Publishing Co., Inc. & Clearfield Company.

- GENTREE 99
  http://perso.wanadoo.fr/gentree/
  Genealogy shareware for Windows9x. French, English, German, Italian, Catalan versions.

◆ Queries, Message Boards & Surname Lists

- Lineages' Free On-line Queries - Italy
  http://www.lineages.com/queries/Search.asp?Country=&Place=

◆ Records: Census, Cemeteries, Land, Obituaries, Personal, Taxes and Vital (Born, Married, Died & Buried)

- Italian Australian Records Project
  http://www.vu.edu.au/iarp/

- Samples of Italian Birth Certificates
  http://www.cimorelli.com/pie/document/nascita.htm

◆ Societies & Groups

- The Buffalo & Western New York Italian Genealogy Society
  http://bawnyigs.homepage.com/

- Il Circolo Calabrese
  http://www.girimonti.com/icc/

- Il Circolo Filippo Mazzei - The Washington D.C. Metropolitan Area Italian Genealogical Society
  http://www.geocities.com/Athens/Acropolis/1709/Mazzei.htm

- Italian Genealogical Society of America ~ Cranston, Rhode Island
  http://users.loa.com/~del2jdcd/igsa.html

- The Italian Genealogical Group
  http://www.italiangen.org/

- Italian Historical Society of America ~ Brooklyn, New York
  http://www.italianhistorical.org/

JEWISH
http://www.cyndislist.com/jewish.htm

Category Index:

- General Resource Sites
- History & Culture
- Libraries, Archives & Museums
- Locality Specific
- Mailing Lists, Newsgroups & Chat
- Military
- People & Families

- Professional Researchers, Volunteers & Other Research Services
- Publications, Software & Supplies
- Queries, Message Boards & Surname Lists
- Records: Census, Cemeteries, Land, Obituaries, Personal, Taxes and Vital
- Societies & Groups

◆ General Resource Sites

- Avotaynu, Inc. Home Page
  http://www.avotaynu.com/
  Products and information for Jewish genealogy.

- Calendar Conversions
  http://www.genealogy.org/~scottlee/calconvert.cgi
  Scott Lee's free on-line service for converting to/from dates in Gregorian, Julian, French republican and Jewish calendars.

- Cross-Index to HomePages of Jewish Genealogy - from FEEFHS
  http://feefhs.org/indexjew.html

- Dictionary of Jewish Surnames in Russian Empire
  http://www.ancestry.com/search/rectype/inddbs/3173.htm
  Searchable online database.

- Eastern European Jewish Immigration to Maryland
  http://www.clis.umd.edu/~mddlmddl/791/communities/html/index.html#jewish
  A scholarly review of immigration into Maryland from the very first colonists to modern immigrants. .

- Immigration: The Jewish
  http://library.thinkquest.org/20619/Jewish.html
  A brief history of Jewish immigration to the United States.

- Jamaican Jewish Genealogy
  http://www6.pair.com/silvera/jamgen/index.html

- Jewish Family & Life: Jewish Genealogy on the Web
  http://www.jewishfamily.com/Features/996/genealogy.htm
  An article by Yaffa Klugerman.

- JewishGen Family Finder (JGFF) -- ONLINE
  http://www.jewishgen.org/jgff/

- JewishGen FAQ - Frequently Asked Questions
  http://www.jewishgen.org/infofiles/faq.html

- JewishGen: The Official Home of Jewish Genealogy
  http://www.jewishgen.org/

- Jewish/Israel History: Genealogy, Archeology, Diaspora, Israel History...
  http://ucsu.colorado.edu/~jsu/history.html

- Jewish Names
  http://www.biu.ac.il/Spokesman/scholar/names.html

- Jewish Records Indexing - Poland
  http://www.jewishgen.org/jri-pl/

- Jewish Roots Ring
  http://pw1.netcom.com/~barrison/jewgenwebring.html
  A web ring for Jewish genealogy sites.

- JGL: Jewish Genealogy Links
  http://jewish.genealogy.org
  A list of several hundred Jewish Genealogy Links, cross-indexed by subject.

- JGSR Jewish Genealogy Page
  http://jgsr.net/jgsr/

- Judaism 101: Jewish Calendar
  http://www.jewfaq.org/calendar.htm

- Resources for Sephardic Genealogy
  http://www.geocities.com/Heartland/Valley/2177/resource.htm
  Sephardic genealogical research begins with the search for your ancestor's country of origin. It could be almost any country where Sephardim lived - Bulgaria, Curacao, Gibraltar, Morocco, Greece, Romania, Tunisia, Turkey, Yugoslavia, any Middle Eastern country, even Germany, Holland, Italy or Malta. Small numbers of Sephardim even lived in Poland and Russia and had names like Levine, Rangel and Calahora.

- Sephardic Genealogy Sources
  http://www.orthohelp.com/geneal/sefardim.htm

- Sephardim.com
  http://www.sephardim.com/
  A research tool for Sephardic / Jewish genealogy. This site serves as a research tool for Sephardic genealogists world-wide. Sephardim are Spanish and Portuguese Jews exiled to Iberia by the Romans. Many of these Serphardim would later disperse to the four corners of the world in 1492.

- Tracing Ancestors who were Immigrants - Jewish
  http://www.channel4.com/nextstep/geno/geno3a.html
  From the UK Channel 4 television program Extraordinary Ancestors.

- Yahrzeit Calendar
  http://www.jfda.org/news.html
  Converts Gregorian to Hebrew dates and vice versa. Gives Yizkor dates through 2012.

◆ History & Culture

- Hebrew Alphabet
  http://www.feduja.org/commserv/heschel/children/hebrew.stm

- Internet Jewish History Sourcebook
  http://www.fordham.edu/halsall/jewish/jewishsbook.html

- Jewish-American History on the Web
  http://www.jewish-history.com/Default.htm

- Judaism 101: Hebrew Alphabet
  http://www.jewfaq.org/alephbet.htm

- Sephardim and Crypto-Judaism: Definition of Terms and Brief History
  http://www.du.edu/~sward/sephardim.html

- Western Jewish History
  http://rochlin-roots-west.com/welcome.htm

- Yahoo!...Judaism...History
  http://dir.yahoo.com/Society_and_Culture/Religion_and_Spirituality/Faiths_and_Practices/Judaism/History/

◆ Libraries, Archives & Museums

- The American Jewish Archives ~ Cincinnati, Ohio
  http://huc.edu/aja/

- The Balch Institute for Ethnic Studies
  http://www.libertynet.org/~balch/
  Home of the Philadelphia Jewish Archives Center.

- Beth Hatefutsoth Museum of the Jewish People
  http://www.bh.org.il/
  The Nahum Goldmann Museum of the Jewish Diaspora

  o Beth Hatefutsoth Family Names Database
    http://www.bh.org.il/Names/index.htm

  o The Douglas E. Goldman Jewish Genealogy Center
    http://www.bh.org.il/Geneology/index.htm

- Bloom Southwest Jewish Archives ~ Arizona
  http://dizzy.library.arizona.edu/images/swja/swjalist.html

- Center for Iranian Jewish Oral History
  http://www.cijoh.org/

- Center for Jewish History
  http://www.centerforjewishhistory.com/

- The Central Archives for the History of the Jewish People ~ Israel
  http://sites.huji.ac.il/archives/

Founded in 1938 as the Jewish Historical General Archives. Their aim is the reconstruction of an unbroken chain of historical documentation, reflecting the collective past of the Jewish people.

  o Genealogy
    http://sites.huji.ac.il/archives/page7.htm

- Central Zionist Archives ~ Israel
  http://www.wzo.org.il/cza/index.html
  The Central Zionist Archives is the official historical archives of the World Zionist Organization, the Jewish Agency, the Jewish National Fund, Keren Hayesod and the World Jewish Congress. It also holds the personal papers of individuals involved in the Zionist movement or active in Palestine/Israel.

- Family History Library Catalog
  http://www.familysearch.org/Search/searchcatalog.asp
  From the FamilySearch web site, an online catalog to the holdings of the LDS Church in Salt Lake City, Utah. Also search for other localities by place name.
  http://www.familysearch.org/fhlc/supermainframeset.asp?display=localitysearch&columns=*,180,0

  o Israel
    http://www.familysearch.org/fhlc/supermainframeset.asp?display=localitydetails&subject=202&subject_disp=Israel&columns=*,180,0

- Jewish Women's Archive
  http://www.jwa.org/
  The mission of the Jewish Women's Archive is to uncover, chronicle and transmit the rich legacy of Jewish women and their contributions to our families and communities, to our people and our world.

- National Museum of American Jewish History
  http://www.nmajh.org/

- The Susser Archive
  http://www.eclipse.co.uk/exeshul/susser/
  The documents and papers of the late Rabbi Dr. Bernard Susser, historian of the Jews of South West England.

- United States Holocaust Memorial Museum
  http://www.ushmm.org/

- YIVO Institute for Jewish Research
  http://www.yivoinstitute.org/

◆ Locality Specific

- An Introduction to Jewish Genealogy in Manitoba
  http://www.concentric.net/~Lkessler/genbegin.shtml

- Belarus SIG
  http://www.jewishgen.org/belarus/
  Provides research data for Jewish genealogist with roots in the country known as Belarus, formerly Byelorussia or White Russia.

- Dutch Jewish Genealogy Homepage
  http://web.inter.nl.net/users/DJGH/

- Humenne, Slovakia Shtetlinks Website
  http://www.jewishgen.org/shtetlinks/humenne/humenne.htm

- The Jewish Genealogical Exploration Guide for Manitoba and Saskatchewan (J-GEMS)
  http://www.concentric.net/~Lkessler/jgems.shtml

- Jewish Genealogy in Australia
  http://www.zeta.org.au/~feraltek/genealogy/index.html

- Jewish Records Indexing - Poland
  http://www.jewishgen.org/JRI-PL/

- The Jews of Greece
  http://www.bsz.org/agreekjew.htm
  Jews have left their imprint in Greece in many cities and towns over the 2,000 years of the community's history. The current centers of Greek Jewry are Athens (3,000) and Salonika (1,000), although the latter is only a remnant of the huge community that thrived in the city for some 500 years. Jews are also present in Corfu, Chalkis, Joannina, Larissa, Rhodes, Trikala, and Volos.

- The Jews of Ireland Genealogy Page
  http://homepage.tinet.ie/~researchers/
  Outline of the history of the Irish Jewish community from the earliest times to the 20th century.

- JewishGen Shtetlinks Web Page for Krakes Lithuania
  http://www.jewishgen.org/litvak/krakes
  Information gathered from a variety of sources on the town of Krakes in Lithuania and it's former Jewish inhabitants.

- Lida District (Uezd)
  http://www.geocities.com/Vienna/Opera/7858/lida-site/lida-dist.htm
  Research in the former Lida uezd. Formerly in Vilna guberniya, Lithuania; Grodno guberniya, Russia; and Nowogrodskie woj., Poland. The site's primary interest is Jewish family research.

- The Middle East
  http://www.CyndisList.com/mideast.htm
  See this category on Cyndi's List for related links.

- PolishRoots: The Polish Genealogy Source
  http://www.polishroots.org/

- Researching Jewish Genealogies in South Africa - Part A
  http://www.jewishgen.org/infofiles/za-infoa.txt

- Researching Jewish Genealogies in South Africa - Part B
  http://www.jewishgen.org/infofiles/za-infob.txt

- Zabludow
  http://www.tiac.net/users/bartman/zabludow/zabintro.htm
  Memorial to Jewish Zabludow, Poland. Includes town history, family history, details of holocaust in Zabludow including an English translation of holocaust related documents. Rare photos of 17th century synagogue.

◆ Mailing Lists, Newsgroups & Chat

- Genealogy Resources on the Internet - Jewish Mailing Lists
  http://www.rootsweb.com/~jfuller/gen_mail_jewish.html
  Most of the mailing list links below point to this site, wonderfully maintained by John Fuller

- AUSTRIA-HOLOCAUST Mailing List
  http://www.rootsweb.com/~jfuller/gen_mail_jewish.html#AUSTRIA-HOLOCAUST
  For anyone with a genealogical interest in the Austrians who were interned in the German Holocaust camps.

- BELARUS Mailing List
  http://www.rootsweb.com/~jfuller/gen_mail_jewish.html#BELARUS
  A regional special interest group (SIG) mailing list for researchers with Jewish family roots in the country now known as Belarus and more specifically from the former Russian Gubernii (provinces) of Minsk, Mogilev, and Vitebsk.

- BERDICHEV Mailing List
  http://www.rootsweb.com/~jfuller/gen_mail_jewish.html#BERDICHEV
  For anyone with a genealogical interest in Berdichev, Ukraine, Russia with a focus on Jewish genealogy.

- BEREZA Mailing List
  http://www.rootsweb.com/~jfuller/gen_mail_jewish.html#BEREZA
  For the discussion for the discussion and sharing of information regarding Jewish genealogical questions, family research and existing information about the past Jewish residents of the shtetl of Bereza (aka Kartuz Bereza), Russia (now Belarus). Also included are the nearby shtetls (within a 25 mile radius) such as Antopol, Drogichin, Kobrin and Pruz'hany.

- BOBRUISK Mailing List
  http://www.rootsweb.com/~jfuller/gen_mail_jewish.html#BOBRUISK
  Devoted to sharing research data, history, and lore of Bobruisk, Minsk Guberniya, Belarus.

- CIECHANOW Mailing List
  http://www.rootsweb.com/~jfuller/gen_mail_jewish.html#CIECHANOW
  Serves as an information-gathering vehicle and clearinghouse for Jewish genealogical and historical information relating to the Jewish community in and around Ciechanow, Poland.

- COURLAND Mailing List
  http://www.rootsweb.com/~jfuller/gen_mail_jewish.html#COURLAND
  For the discussion and sharing of information regarding the acquisition, study, transcription, and creation of scanned images and computer database of census documents that contain information about Courland (within Latvia) Jews (e.g., property owners' lists, business owners' lists, house lists, census lists, tax records).

- EURO-JEWISH Mailing List
  http://www.rootsweb.com/~jfuller/gen_mail_jewish.html#EURO-JEWISH
  For anyone with a genealogical interest in the Migration, History, Culture, Heritage and Surname search of the Jewish people from Europe to the United States and their descendants in the United States.

- GALICIA Mailing List
  http://www.rootsweb.com/~jfuller/gen_mail_jewish.html#GALICIA
  For those interested in researching their Jewish roots in the former Austrian province of Galacia.

- **GERSIG Mailing List**
  http://www.rootsweb.com/~jfuller/gen_mail_jewish.html
  #GERSIG
  Focuses on Jewish genealogy in German-speaking regions (e.g., Germany, Austria, parts of Switzerland, Alsace, Lorraine, Bohemia, Moravia).

- **GRODNO Mailing List**
  http://www.rootsweb.com/~jfuller/gen_mail_jewish.html
  #GRODNO
  For anyone with a genealogical interest in Grodno Gubernia, a division of the Russian Empire.

- **H-SIG Mailing List**
  http://www.rootsweb.com/~jfuller/gen_mail_jewish.html
  #H-SIG
  For those with Jewish roots in the area known as "greater Hungary" or pre-Trianon Hungary and includes areas that at one time were predominantly Hungarian speaking.

- **IsraelGenWeb Mailing List**
  http://www.rootsweb.com/~jfuller/gen_mail_country-isr.html#IsraelGenWeb

- **JEWISHGEN Mailing List**
  http://www.rootsweb.com/~jfuller/gen_mail_jewish.html
  #JEWISHGEN
  Gatewayed with the soc.genealogy.jewish newsgroup
  news:soc.genealogy.jewish

- **Jewish Museum of Belgium**
  http://www.rootsweb.com/~jfuller/gen_mail_jewish.html
  #JEWBEL
  For anyone who is interested in Jewish genealogy; in Belgian or English.

- **JEWISH-ROOTS Mailing List**
  http://www.rootsweb.com/~jfuller/gen_mail_jewish.htm
  #JEWISH-ROOTS

- **JRI-PL Mailing List**
  http://www.rootsweb.com/~jfuller/gen_mail_jewish.html
  #JRI-PL
  The Jewish Records Indexing Poland project is designed to create a searchable database of indexes to all available Jewish vital records of Poland.

- **KEIDAN Mailing List**
  http://www.rootsweb.com/~jfuller/gen_mail_jewish.html
  #KEIDAN
  For anyone with roots or interest in Keidan and its history as a Jewish community to share information and discuss its past and present and the region that surrounds it in Lithuania.

- **KULANU-L Mailing List**
  http://www.rootsweb.com/~jfuller/gen_mail_jewish.html
  #KULANU-L
  Kulanu ("all of us") is an organization of individuals of varied backgrounds and practices dedicated to finding lost and dispersed remnants of the Jewish people.

- **LATAMSIG Mailing List**
  http://www.rootsweb.com/~jfuller/gen_mail_jewish.html
  #LATAMSIG
  For researchers with Jewish family roots in all countries of Latin America.

- **LATVIA Mailing List**
  http://www.rootsweb.com/~jfuller/gen_mail_jewish.html
  #LATVIA
  For researchers of Jewish families of Latvian descent.

- **LITVAKSIG Mailing List**
  http://www.rootsweb.com/~jfuller/gen_mail_jewish.html
  #LITVAKSIG
  For those who are interested in the preservation and computerization of primary sources of genealogical data for the descendants of the Lithuanian Jewish community.

- **LODZ Mailing List**
  http://www.rootsweb.com/~jfuller/gen_mail_country-pol.html
  #LODZ
  A mailing list in support of the Lodz Area Research Group (LARG) which aims to provide researchers with a forum, clearinghouse and resource for the collection and dissemination of genealogical and historical information relating to the Jewish communities of Lodz, Poland.

- **NESVIZH Mailing List**
  http://www.rootsweb.com/~jfuller/gen_mail_jewish.html
  #NESVIZH
  For discussions of topics of genealogical interest related to Nesvizh, Minsk Guberniya, Belarus.

- **ODESSA Mailing List**
  http://www.rootsweb.com/~jfuller/gen_mail_jewish.html
  #ODESSA
  For the discussion and sharing of information regarding Jewish genealogical questions, family research and existing information about the past Jewish communities of the city of Odessa, Russia (now Ukraine).

- **SAFRICA Mailing List**
  http://www.rootsweb.com/~jfuller/gen_mail_jewish.html
  #SAFRICA
  To discuss the genealogy and family history of Jewish communities of South Africa, Lesotho, Botswana, Zimbabwe and Zambia (Rhodesia), Swaziland, Mozambique, and the former Belgian Congo.

- **SEFARD Mailing List**
  http://www.rootsweb.com/~jfuller/gen_mail_jewish.html
  #SEFARD
  For Sephardic genealogy research (Jews who are descendants of the former Jews of Spain and Portugal).

- **SHTETLINKS Mailing List**
  http://www.rootsweb.com/~jfuller/gen_mail_jewish.html
  #SHTETLINKS
  For participants in the SHTETLINKS Project where individuals create genealogy web pages devoted to a Jewish community (shtetl) and then upload it to the JewishGen web site.

- **Turkish_Jews Mailing List**
  http://www.rootsweb.com/~jfuller/gen_mail_jewish.html
  #Turkish_Jews
  For Sephardic Jewish genealogists with roots in the former Turkish Ottoman Empire including Turkey, Serbia, Greece, and Yugoslavia.

- **VOLHYNIA Mailing List**
  http://www.rootsweb.com/~jfuller/gen_mail_jewish.html
  #VOLHYNIA
  To share information and bring together descendents of Volhynians and others with an interest in Volhynia Gubernia (Ukraine).

- YIZKOR Mailing List
  http://www.rootsweb.com/~jfuller/gen_mail_jewish.html
  #YIZKOR
  *Yizkor (Memorial) Books, published by groups of former residents
  as a tribute to their old homes and the people who were murdered
  during the Holocaust, are some of the best sources for learning
  about Jewish communities in Eastern and Central Europe.*

- Zdunska-Wola Mailing List
  http://www.rootsweb.com/~jfuller/gen_mail_jewish.html
  #Zdunska-Wola
  *Dedicated to genealogy and to the preservation of the Jewish
  heritage in Zdunska-Wola, Poland and its neighboring towns.*

◆ Military

- Jewish Soldiers in the Civil War Index
  http://jgsr.net/jgsr/database/civilwar.cgi

- National Museum of American Jewish Military
  History
  http://www.penfed.org/jwv/museum.htm

- Jews in the Civil War
  http://www.jewish-history.com/civilwar.htm

◆ People & Families

- GROSS-STEINBERG Family Tree
  http://www.geocities.com/Heartland/6721/
  Surnames from Austria, Lithuania, and Poland.

- Jasienica Patronymic Records
  http://www.jewishgen.org/JRI-PL/patronym/jasienica_
  data.htm
  From Jewish Records Indexing - Poland.

- LOEB Family Tree
  http://www.labri.u-bordeaux.fr/Equipe/CombAlg/membre/
  loeb/tree/index.html
  French and Jewish research.

◆ Professional Researchers, Volunteers & Other Research Services

- European Focus
  http://www.eurofocus.com/
  *Photographic portfolios of ancestral towns in Europe created for
  Genealogy enthusiasts in Belgium, Denmark, Eastern Europe,
  England, France, Germany, Great Britain, Italy, Netherlands,
  Norway, Poland, Sweden, Switzerland and more.*

- Gary Mokotoff, Genealogical Lecturer
  http://www.avotaynu.com/gmokotoff.html
  *One of the foremost lecturers and authors on Jewish and Eastern
  European genealogical research.*

- genealogyPro - Professional Researchers Specializing
  in Jewish Genealogy
  http://genealogyPro.com/directories/Jewish.html

- Milt Botwinick Professional Genealogist
  http://members.aol.com/botwinick/
  Pennsylvania, New Jersey and Jewish research.

- Routes to Roots
  http://www.routestoroots.com/
  Tracing Jewish Roots in Poland, Ukraine, Moldova and Belarus.

- Ted Gostin, Professional Genealogist
  http://www.generationspress.com/research.html
  *Specializing in Jewish genealogy and Southern California
  resources.*

◆ Publications, Software & Supplies

- Amazon.com Genealogy Bookstore - Jewish
  http://www.amazon.com/exec/obidos/external-search/?
  keyword=jewish+genealogy&tag=markcyndisgenealA/

- Ancestor's Attic Discount Genealogy Books - Jewish
  Genealogy Books
  http://members.tripod.com/~ancestorsattic/index.html#secJW

- AudioTapes.com - Genealogical Lectures on Cassette
  Tapes - Jewish
  http://www.audiotapes.com/search2.asp?Search=Jewish

- Avotaynu, Inc. Home Page
  http://www.avotaynu.com/
  Products and information for Jewish genealogy.

- DoroTree - Jewish Genealogy Software
  http://www.dorotree.com/
  *A multi-language software program for Jewish genealogy with user
  interfaces in English, French, Spanish, Portuguese and Hebrew. The
  only software on the market that enables the user to enter
  information in both Latin and Hebrew (Yiddish) characters, without
  a need for Hebrew Windows. Automatic name conversion from
  English to Hebrew/Yiddish, advanced Hebrew calendar, Bar/Bat
  Mitsva calculator, built-in links to Jewish genealogy sites, printing
  trees in both Latin and Hebrew characters etc.*

- Frontier Press Bookstore - Jewish Research
  http://www.frontierpress.com/frontier.cgi?category=jewish

- Heritage Books - Jewish
  http://www.heritagebooks.com/jewish.htm

- ILANOT -Software for Jewish Genealogy
  http://www.bh.org.il/Geneology/index.htm#ilanot

- Jewish Roots in Poland - Pages from the Past and
  Archival Inventories
  http://www.rtrfoundation.org/html/jacket.html
  A new book by Miriam Weiner.

- STAMMBAUM: The Journal of German-Jewish
  Genealogical Research
  http://www.jewishgen.org/stammbaum/

- Willow Bend Bookstore - Jewish Genealogy
  http://www.willowbend.net/default.asp

◆ Queries, Message Boards & Surname Lists

- Jewish Genealogy Discussion Forum at Query One
  Online
  http://www.queryone.com/topical/1029.shtml

- Missing Identity Project
  http://www.jewishgen.org/missing-identity/
  Holocaust survivor children still searching for their true identity and threads to their past.

- The SephardiConnection Discussion Forums - Jewish Genealogy
  http://sephardiconnect.com/webx/webx.cgi?sephard-13@^38693@.ee6b2b9

◆ Records: Census, Cemeteries, Land, Obituaries, Personal, Taxes and Vital (Born, Married, Died & Buried)

- American Jewish Year Book Obituary Index
  http://www.jewishgen.org/databases/ajybweb.htm

- Anglo-Jewish Miscellanies
  http://www.jeffreymaynard.com/
  Historical and genealogical information about the Jewish Community of England including online databases.

- The Boston Jewish Advocate Obituary Database
  http://www.jewishgen.org/databases/advocate.htm

- Cleveland Jewish News Obituary Database
  http://www.jewishgen.org/databases/cleveweb.htm

- Commission for the Preservation of Pioneer Jewish Cemeteries and Landmarks
  http://www.jfed.org/magnes/cemecom.htm
  Northern California.

- Concentration Camp Records May Fill in Gaps on Family Tree
  http://www.sierra.com/sierrahome/familytree/hqarticles/concencamps/
  Online article by Miriam Weiner about these records, the information they contain, and how to access them.

- Index to: Religious Personnel in Russia 1853-1854
  http://jgsr.net/jgsr/database/deych.cgi

- International Jewish Cemetery Project
  http://www.jewishgen.org/cemetery/index.htm

- Jewish Cemeteries ~ Hamburg, Germany
  http://www.rrz.uni-hamburg.de/rz3a035/jew_cem.html

- Jewish Cemeteries in Hungary
  http://www.geocities.com/winter_peter_4
  Information about Jewish cemeteries in Hungary. Cemetery surveys, descriptions, addresses of local interests, photo database of gravestones, transcription, translation.

- Jewish Cemeteries in the New York City Area
  http://www.geocities.com/Heartland/Woods/4900/JewishCemeteries.htm

- Jewish Cemetery in Košice / Old Jewish Cemetery at Kosice, Slovakia
  http://www.kosice.sk/history/zidovsky/jevish0.htm
  History of the cemetery, database of 5,517 names of buried persons.

- Jewish Cemetery of Rhodes
  http://www.rhodesjewishmuseum.org/cemetery.htm
  A listing of the 1,167 tombstones in the Jewish cemetery of Rhodes. Includes some photographs and translations of inscriptions.

- Jewish Orphanages in the United States
  http://www.scruz.net/~elias/hnoh/

- JewishGen Hotline: Jewish Cemeteries in New York City
  http://www.jewishgen.org/mentprog/m_nycem.htm

- Jewish Record Indexing - Poland
  http://www.jewishgen.org/JRI-PL/index.htm

- Jüdische Matriken Wien/Jewish Records of Vienna
  http://ihff.nwy.at/wj.htm
  From the Institute for Historical Family Research.

- The Ketubah in History
  http://www.ketubahworkshop.com/html/history.html
  Background history of the traditional Jewish wedding contract.

- London Jews Database
  http://www.jewishgen.org/databases/londweb.htm

- The Poor Jews' Temporary Shelter Database
  http://www.its.uct.ac.za/shelter/shelter.htm
  Searchable database of over 45,000 register entries of those who arrived at the Shelter in Leman Street, London from 1896 to 1914.

- Research Guide - Safe Haven - Records of the Jewish Experience in Australia
  http://www.naa.gov.au/PUBLICAT/GUIDES/haven/guide.htm
  From the National Archives of Australia.

◆ Societies & Groups

- American Jewish Historical Society ~ Waltham, MA
  http://www.ajhs.org/

- Asociación de Genealogía Judía de Argentina
  http://www.marben.com.ar/agja/
  Página Oficial de la Asociacion de Genealogia Judia de Argentina. Jewish Genealogical Society of Argentina (Official Site).

- Association of Jewish Genealogical Societies (AJGS)
  http://www.jewishgen.org/ajgs/index.html

- Australian Jewish Genealogical Society (Victoria) Inc.
  http://www.melbourne.net/csaky/Mainpage%20AJGS.htm

- Australian Jewish Historical Society
  http://www.zeta.org.au/~feraltek/genealogy/ajhs/index.html

- Columbus Jewish Historical Society ~ Ohio
  http://www.gcis.net/cjhs/

- Dallas Jewish Historical Society ~ Texas
  http://www.dvjc.org/history/

- Dallas Virtual Jewish Community - Jewish Genealogy Home Page
  http://www.dvjc.org/history/genealogy.shtml

- EugeneGen - Eugene Jewish Genealogy Study Group ~ Oregon
  http://www.users.uswest.net/~cfleishman/eugenegen.html

- European Sephardic Institute
  http://www.sefarad.org/english.html

- GenDex = / Groups and Societies
  http://www.netins.net/showcase/pafways/groups.htm #GROUPS

- The Genealogical Institute of the Jewish Historical Society of Western Canada
  http://www.concentric.net/~lkessler/geninst.shtml
  Winnipeg, Manitoba, Canada.

- Hebrew Immigrant Aid Society
  http://www.hias.org/
  Successor organization to those founded in New York City in the 1880s to assist Jewish immigrants.

- Historical Society of Jews From Egypt
  http://www.hsje.org/

- Illiana Jewish Genealogical Society
  http://www.lincolnnet.net/ijgs/
  A Jewish genealogical society covering Chicago's southern suburbs and northwest Indiana.

- The Israel Genealogical Society
  http://www.isragen.org.il/

- Jewish Cemetery Association of Massachusetts, Inc.
  http://www.jcam.org/

- Jewish Genealogical Society, Inc. ~ New York
  http://www.jgsny.org/
  The Jewish Genealogical Society (JGS) is a nonprofit organization founded in New York in 1977 and dedicated to collecting, preserving and disseminating knowledge about Jewish genealogy.

- Jewish Genealogical Society, Los Angeles (JGSLA)
  http://www.jewishgen.org/jgsla/

- Jewish Genealogical Society of Argentina
  http://www.jewishgen.org/infofiles/ar-jgs.txt

- Jewish Genealogical Society of Bergen County, New Jersey
  http://home.att.net/~erosenbaum/jgsbc.htm

- Jewish Genealogical Society of Georgia ~ United States
  http://www.jewishgen.org/ajgs/jgsg/

- Jewish Genealogical Society of Great Britain
  http://www.ort.org/jgsgb/index.htm

- Jewish Genealogical Society of Greater Boston
  http://www.jewishgen.org/boston/

- Jewish Genealogical Society of Michigan
  http://www.jgsmi.org/
  Featuring the Society's activity calendar, membership information, top Michigan resources, hyperlinks to the best resources for Jewish genealogy, and links to personal web pages.

- Jewish Genealogical Society of Montreal
  http://www.gtrdata.com/jgs-montreal/

- Jewish Genealogical Society of Oregon
  http://www.rootsweb.com/~orjgs/

- Jewish Genealogical Society of Philadelphia
  http://www.jewishgen.org/jgsp/

- Jewish Genealogical Society of Rochester ~ New York
  http://jgsr.net/jgsr/

- Jewish Genealogical Society of Sacramento ~ California
  http://www.jewishgen.org/ajgs/jgs-sacramento/

- Jewish Genealogical Society of St. Louis
  http://www.stlcyberjew.com/jgs-stl/

- Jewish Genealogical Society of St. Louis, Computer SIG
  http://www.stlcyberjew.com/jgs-stl/SIGhome.htm

- Jewish Genealogical Society (S. Alberta)
  http://www.geocities.com/Heartland/Village/9200/

- Jewish Genealogical Society of Washington State ~ Mercer Island, Washington
  http://members.tripod.com/~JGSWS/

- The Jewish Genealogy Society of Greater Washington, D.C.
  http://www.jewishgen.org/jgsgw/

- The Jewish Genealogy Society of Long Island ~ New York
  http://www.jewishgen.org/jgsli/

- Jewish Genealogy Society Southern Nevada-West
  http://www.familyhistory.com/societyhall/viewmember.asp?societyid=53655

- The Jewish Historical Society of Central Jersey
  http://www.jewishgen.org/jhscj/

- The Jewish Historical Society of England
  http://www.users.dircon.co.uk/~jhse/
  The Society was founded in 1893 by leading Anglo-Jewish scholars and communal leaders. It was created to promote research, study and publishing on the history of Jews of Britain and of countries from which British Jewry came.

- Jewish Historical Society of Greater New Haven, Inc. ~ Connecticut
  http://pages.cthome.net/hirsch/

- Jewish Historical Society of Maryland
  http://www.jhsm.org/

- JewishGen Hungarian Special Interest Group (H-SIG)
  http://www.jewishgen.org/Hungary/
  Information for people with Jewish roots in the area known as "greater Hungary" or pre-Trianon Hungary.

- Kielce-Radom SIG
  http://www.jewishgen.org/krsig/
  Jewish genealogy special interest group researching the southern Russian Polish regions of the Kielce and Radom gubernias.

- LitvakSIG (Lithuanian Special Interest Group)
  http://www.jewishgen.org/litvak/
  For researchers of Lithuanian-Jewish genealogy worldwide.

- Nederlandse Kring voor Joodse Genealogie / Netherlands Society for Jewish Genealogy
  http://www.nljewgen.org/

- San Francisco Bay Area Jewish Genealogical Society (SFBA JGS)
  http://www.jewishgen.org/sfbajgs/

- Southern Jewish Historical Society
  http://www.jewishsouth.org/

KIDS & TEENS
http://www.cyndislist.com/kids.htm

Category Index:

◆ General Resource Sites

◆ Mailing Lists, Newsgroups & Chat

◆ Publications, Software & Supplies

◆ General Resource Sites

- Ancestors: The First Series - Teacher's Guide
  http://www.pbs.org/kbyu/ancestors/firstseries/teachersguide/
  From the first television program on PBS, a teacher's guide for starting a family history project.

- AskERIC InfoGuide - Family History for Middle Schools
  http://ericir.syr.edu/plweb-cgi/fastweb?getdoc+infoguides+infoguides+104+0+wAAA+Family%26History%26for%26Middle%26Schools

- CGW for Kids
  http://www.rootsweb.com/~cangwkid/
  From the CanadaGenWeb Project.

- The COKids GenWeb Project
  http://www.rootsweb.com/~cogenweb/cokids/
  A genealogy page for kids and teens in Colorado.

- Family History Education Associates
  http://www.execpc.com/~fhea/
  Specializing in methods and materials for the teaching of family history at all grade levels.

- Family History in the Classroom
  http://www.genealogy.com/74_taylor.html
  Online Article by Maureen Taylor.

- Genealogy for Children
  http://home.iSTAR.ca/~ljbritt/

- Genealogy for Kids Room
  http://www.geocities.com/EnchantedForest/5283/genekids.htm

- Genealogy Instruction Beginners, Teenagers, and Kids
  http://home.earthlink.net/~howardorjeff/instruct.htm

- Genealogy Merit Badge
  http://usscouts.org/mb/mb056.html
  Criteria from the Boy Scouts of America.

- The Genealogy Merit Badge of the Boy Scouts of America
  http://www.oz.net/~markhow/BSA/meritbdg.htm

- Genealogy - Part of the History/Social Studies Web Site for K-12 Teachers
  http://www.execpc.com/~dboals/geneo.html

- Genealogy Unit Lesson
  http://www.geocities.com/Heartland/Plains/3729/LESSON.HTM

- Genealogy WebQuest
  http://www.ultranet.com/~olmckey/quest.htm

- Genealogy Word Search For Kids!
  http://www.genexchange.com/kidspuzzles.cfm

- In the Classroom
  http://www.myhistory.org/teaching/index.html
  From My History is America's History. Use these activities and lesson plans to make family history part of every child's learning experience.
  - All Grades
    http://www.myhistory.org/teaching/allgrades.html
  - Preschool
    http://www.myhistory.org/teaching/preschool.html
  - Elementary School
    http://www.myhistory.org/teaching/elementary.html
  - Middle School
    http://www.myhistory.org/teaching/middleschool.html
  - High School
    http://www.myhistory.org/teaching/highschool.html

- KIDPROJ Family History Projects 1997
  http://www.kidlink.org/KIDPROJ/FamHistory/links.html

- KidsClick! Worlds of Web Searching
  http://www.worldsofsearching.org/

- Kids' Corner
  http://www.myhistory.org/kids/index.html
  From My History is America's History. Use these activities and links to make history an exciting adventure for the whole family.
  - Family Projects
    http://www.myhistory.org/guidebook/family_projects.html
    - Our Family Quilt
      http://www.myhistory.org/guidebook/family_quilt.html
    - Family History Museum
      http://www.myhistory.org/guidebook/family_museum.html
    - Millennium Family Portraits
      http://www.myhistory.org/guidebook/family_portraits.html
    - Family Web Album
      http://www.myhistory.org/guidebook/family_web_album.html

- Our Family Cookbook
  http://www.myhistory.org/guidebook/family_
  cookbook.html

- Learning Curve - Schools Exhibits
  http://learningcurve.pro.gov.uk/schools.htm
  *Interactive educational topics for youngsters highlighting the
  holdings of the Public Records Office in the UK. Includes teachers'
  notes.*

  o Census Returns 1841-1891
    http://learningcurve.pro.gov.uk/millennium/DDB/domesday/
    Census/censfs.asp

  o Focus on...The Domesday Book.
    http://learningcurve.pro.gov.uk/domesday/default.htm

  o Snapshots
    http://learningcurve.pro.gov.uk/snapshots/default.htm
    *Educational Features and Activities based on Visual Sources
    from the Public Records Office in the UK.*

- More Genealogy for Kids
  http://www.ancestry.com/dailynews/08_10_99.htm#3
  By Michael John Neill for the Ancestry.com Daily News.

- National Genealogical Society - Rubincam Youth
  Award
  http://www.ngsgenealogy.org/about/content/committees/
  rubincam.html

- National Genealogical Society - Youth Resources
  Committee
  http://www.ngsgenealogy.org/about/content/committees/
  youth.html

  o Children's Books and Activities
    http://www.ngsgenealogy.org/about/content/committees/
    youth_chbk.html

  o Teaching Materials
    http://www.ngsgenealogy.org/about/content/committees/
    youth_k-12.html

  o Articles on Genealogy in the Classroom
    http://www.ngsgenealogy.org/about/content/committees/
    youth_article.html

  o Web Sites and Lesson Plans
    http://www.ngsgenealogy.org/about/content/committees/
    youth_web.html

- Oral histories for kids
  http://www.myhistory.org/guidebook/interview/histories_
  kids.html
  From My History is America's History.

- Teaching History Through Genealogy Online
  http://members.aol.com/Genhistry/class.htm
  Free online class for ages 8-14 and parent. Lasts 8 weeks.

- The Tigger Movie - Family Tree
  http://disney.go.com/disneyvideos/animatedfilms/tiggermovie/
  familytree.html
  Three family tree charts to print and fill in, from Disney.

- To Pass it On: Bringing Genealogy to the Younger
  Set
  http://www.ancestry.com/dailynews/11_23_98.htm
  By Michael John Neill for the Ancestry.com Daily News.

- U.S. Immigration and Naturalization Service - Kids
  Corner
  http://www.ins.usdoj.gov/graphics/aboutins/history/kids.htm

- U.S. Immigration and Naturalization Service -
  Teacher Resources
  http://www.ins.usdoj.gov/graphics/aboutins/history/
  teacher.htm

- USGenWeb Kidz Project
  http://www.rootsweb.com/~usgwkidz/

- WorldGenWeb For Kids
  http://www.rootsweb.com/~wgwkids/

◆ Mailing Lists, Newsgroups & Chat

- GEN-NEWBIE-L Mailing List
  http://www.rootsweb.com/~jfuller/gen_mail_info.html
  #GEN-NEWBIE-L
  *A mailing list where people who are new to computers and
  genealogy may interact using a computer's e-mail program.*

- GENTEEN-L Mailing List
  http://www.rootsweb.com/~jfuller/gen_mail_general.html
  #GENTEEN-L
  *For teenagers and young adults who are interested in genealogical
  research or others who have ideas for young genealogists.*

- MOMS_N_ME-ROOTS Mailing List
  http://www.rootsweb.com/~jfuller/gen_mail_general.html
  #MOMS_N_ME-ROOTS
  *To aid moms of all ages, but especially those with young children, in
  researching their family. Also welcome are any ideas for helping
  mothers teach their children about their heritage and the
  importance of family research.*

◆ Publications, Software & Supplies

- Amazon.com Genealogy Bookstore - Kids
  http://www.amazon.com/exec/obidos/external-search/?
  keyword=kids+genealogy&tag=markcyndisgenealA/

- AudioTapes.com - Genealogical Lectures on Cassette
  Tapes - Young People
  http://www.audiotapes.com/search2.asp?Search=young+
  people

- Family Saplings
  http://www.familysaplings.com/
  *A mail-order bookstore specializing in quality books, games,
  journals and charts for young, budding genealogists and for the
  adults who nurture and educate them.*

- Frontier Press Bookstore - Children's Guides to
  Research
  http://www.frontierpress.com/frontier.cgi?category=children

- Genealogy Books for Kids & Teaching
  http://member.aol.com/TMCorner/book_kid.htm

- Hearthstone Bookshop-Genealogy for Young People
  http://www.hearthstonebooks.com/cgi-bin/webc.cgi/
  st_main.html?catid=12&sid=2Qp5fy81a

- Storbeck's Genealogy Books for Kids
  http://www.storbecks.com/kids.htm

LAND RECORDS, DEEDS, HOMESTEADS, ETC.

http://www.cyndislist.com/land.htm

Category Index:

◆ General Resource Sites

◆ Locality Specific

◆ Publications, Software & Supplies

◆ General Resource Sites

- Analyzing Deeds for Useful Clues
  http://www.bcgcertification.org/skbld951.html
  From the Board for Certification of Genealogists - Skill Building - January 1995.

- The Bureau of Land Management - - Eastern States, General Land Office
  http://www.glorecords.blm.gov/
  The Official Land Patent Records Site. This site has a searchable database of more than two million Federal land title records for Eastern Public Land States, issued between 1820 and 1908, including scanned images of those records. The Eastern Public Land States covered in this database are: Alabama, Arkansas, Florida, Illinois, Indiana, Louisiana, Michigan, Minnesota, Mississippi, Missouri, Ohio, Wisconsin. Images of Serial patents, issued between 1908 and the mid-1960's are currently being added to this web site.

  o Frequently Asked Questions
    http://www.glorecords.blm.gov/visitor/faq.asp

  o GLO Terms and Field Definitions
    http://www.glorecords.blm.gov/help/glossary.asp

  o Land Descriptions
    http://www.glorecords.blm.gov/visitor/land_desc.asp

  o The Serial Land Patent Phase of Record Automation
    http://www.glorecords.blm.gov/visitor/statetime.asp

  o Visitor's Center
    http://www.glorecords.blm.gov/visitor/default.asp

- The Electronic Reading Room
  http://www.blm.gov/nhp/efoia/
  Bureau of Land Management Headquarters Office and Field Facilities.

- Genealogical Riches in the American State Papers
  http://www.lineages.com/reading/statepapers.asp

- Ghostseekers - Understanding Legal Land Descriptions
  http://hometown.aol.com/vikkigray/landtutorial.htm

- Graphical Display of the Federal Township and Range System ~ U.S.
  http://www.outfitters.com/genealogy/land/twprangemap.html
  Explains the division of townships and sections.

- History & Use of Land Records
  http://main.nc.us/OBCGS/searchland-rec.htm
  By Linda Haas Davenport.

- HM Land Registry ~ United Kingdom
  http://www.landreg.gov.uk/

- The Homestead Act of 1862
  http://www.apics253.com/~deeds/homestead.htm
  By Richard Pence.

- The Homestead Act May 20, 1862
  http://www.pbs.org/weta/thewest/wpages/wpgs650/homestd.htm

- Homesteaders Left Marks on Land and Paper
  http://www.ancestry.com/columns/myra/Shaking_Family_Tree07-24-97.htm
  From Shaking Your Family Tree by Myra Vanderpool Gormley, C.G.

- Homestead Papers Copied by Faith Libelo
  mailto:fsl.genie.research@erols.com
  She can visit the National Archives for you and copy the files. E-mail Faith at fsl.genie.research@erols.com for details.

- How to Search Deeds
  http://www.dohistory.org/on_your_own/toolkit/deeds.html
  From DoHistory.

  o Form for Deed Research Notes
    http://www.dohistory.org/on_your_own/toolkit/deeds_form.html

- Land Ownership Maps in the Library of Congress
  http://www.kinquest.com/genealogy/resources/lom.html
  A list by state, county and year, of the maps available in the collection held at the Library of Congress.

- Land Record Reference
  http://www.ultranet.com/~deeds/landref.htm

- Land Record Research Directory
  http://www.ultranet.com/~deeds/research.htm
  List of other researchers and the areas they are researching in.

- Land Records: History of and How to Use Them
  http://homepages.rootsweb.com/~haas/learningcenter/landinfo.html
  By Linda Haas Davenport.

- Legal Land Descriptions in the USA
  http://www.outfitters.com/genealogy/land/land.html

o Legal Land Descriptions in Federal Township and Range System
http://www.outfitters.com/genealogy/land/twprange.html

o Legal Land Descriptions in Indiscriminate Metes and Bounds
http://www.outfitters.com/genealogy/land/metesbounds.html

- Lesson 29: American Land Records
http://www.rootsweb.com/~rwguide/lesson29.htm
From RootsWeb's Guide to Tracing Family Trees.

- Public Record Office - Finding Aids - A-Z Index of All Leaflets ~ U.K.
http://www.pro.gov.uk/leaflets/riindex.htm

o Common Lands (#95)
http://www.pro.gov.uk/leaflets/ri2181.htm

o Crown and Royalist Lands, 1642-1660: Confiscations, Sales and Restorations (#88)
http://www.pro.gov.uk/leaflets/ri2175.htm

o Land Grants In America and American Loyalists' Claims (#34)
http://www.pro.gov.uk/leaflets/ri2089.htm

o Valuation Office Records Created Under The Finance (1909-1910) Act (#68)
http://www.pro.gov.uk/leaflets/ri2153.htm

- Shaking Your Family Tree: Secrets in Old Deed Books
http://www.uftree.com/bin/fg_auth?/GenealogyNewsstand/ShakingTree/Court/930325.html
By Myra Vanderpool Gormley, C.G.

- Surveying Units and Terms
http://www.lest-we-forget.com/RootsLady/universal/survey1.htm

- US Land & Property Research
http://users.arn.net/~billco/uslpr.htm
By Bill Utterback for the IIGS University.

- US Public Land Survey Methods
http://www.rootsweb.com/~mistclai/landsurv.htm

- U.S. Public Lands - Public Domain System
http://www.apics253.com/~deeds/public.htm

- Where to Obtain Land Patents/Warrants
http://homepages.rootsweb.com/~haas/learningcenter/patentlocations.html

◆ Locality Specific

- Arkansas Land Records -- Interactive Search
http://searches.rootsweb.com/cgi-bin/arkland/arkland.pl

- The Bureau of Land Management - Idaho
http://www.id.blm.gov/

- Deed Data Pool
http://www.ultranet.com/~deeds/pool.htm
Downloadable deed files for Kentucky, New York, Pennsylvania, Virginia & West Virginia.

- Deeds, Homestead Records and Store Accounts in Georgia
http://www.rootsweb.com/~gagenweb/records/dhrsa.htm

- Early Land Entries - Orange County, Indiana
http://www.usgennet.org/usa/in/county/orange/preland.htm

- The Essex County Registry of Deeds ~ Salem, Massachusetts
http://207.244.88.10/

- Federal Land Records for Arkansas
http://www.rootsweb.com/~usgenweb/ar/fedland.htm

- Federal Tract Books of Oklahoma Territory
http://www.sirinet.net/~lgarris/swogs/tract.html

- Frederick Co., Maryland Descents - Court Records from 1794 - 1837
http://members.aol.com/DorindaMD/descents.html

- GDAH Land Records
http://www.sos.state.ga.us/archives/rs/land.htm
Georgia Department of Archives and History.

- Georgia Land Lotteries
http://www.georgianetweb.com/bulloch/georgia_land_lotteries.htm
Discusses land lotteries in 1805, 1807, 1820, 1821, 1827, 1832.

- GLO / BLM Land Patent Records, California
http://www.ca.blm.gov/landpatents/
The Bureau of Land Management (BLM), established by Congress in 1946, inherited the functions and records of the General Land Office. Information presented here was derived from BLM land records (the Status database), and is a record of patents (deeds) issued by the United States in the State of California between 1856 and 1995. Because these records have been edited from the original they are not "Official Government Records." However, every effort has been made to ensure they accurately represent the original.

- Hoosier Homestead Award
http://www.state.in.us/icpr/webfile/homestead/homepage.html
Database of Indiana farms which have been in the same family for over 100 years. Over 3,000 farms are listed, the oldest dating from 1797

- Homesteading Records - Tracking Your Ancestors in South Dakota
http://members.aol.com/~gkrell/homestead/

- Illinois Public Domain Land Tract Sales
http://www.sos.state.il.us/depts/archives/data_lan.html

- An Introduction to the History of Tennessee's Confusing Land Laws
http://web.utk.edu/~kizzer/genehist/research/landlaws.htm
By Billie R. McNamara.

- Indiana Land Records Search by CompuGen Systems
http://members.aol.com/CGSystems/LRSearch.html

- INGALLS Homestead File
  http://www.nara.gov/nara/EXTRA/ingalls.html
  Scanned images of 24 original documents pertaining to the DeSmet, South Dakota homestead of the family of Laura Ingalls Wilder. A terrific example from the National Archives and Records Administration.

- In Search of Your Canadian Past: The Canadian County Atlas Digital Project
  http://imago.library.mcgill.ca/countyatlas/default.asp
  From McGill University's Rare Books and Special Collections Division. A searchable database derived from published county atlases between 1874 & 1881. Searchable by property owners' names or by location. Township maps, portraits and properties have been scanned, with links from the property owners' names in the database.

- Irish Ancestors: Land Records
  http://scripts.ireland.com/ancestor/browse/records/land/index.htm

- Kansas Land Records
  http://pixel.cs.vt.edu/library/land/kansas/

- Kentucky Secretary of State Land Office
  http://www.sos.state.ky.us/ADMIN/LANDOFFI/landoff.htm
  Describes the land office process and includes historical images of the records involved.

- Land Claim Record Books, 1871-1894
  http://www.archives.state.ut.us/referenc/xml/series/3934.html
  From the Utah State Libraries.

- Land Office Patents and Grants Collection Index
  http://image.vtls.com/collections/LO.html
  Electronic Card Indexes, Digital Collections Home Page, The Library of Virginia.

- Land Office Records
  http://www.iowahistory.org/archives/research_collections/state_gov_records/land_office_records/land_office_records.html
  From the State Historical Society of Iowa.

- Land Office Records at the Indiana State Archives
  http://www.state.in.us/icpr/webfile/land/land_off.html
  - Fort Wayne, Indiana Land Office Database Search Page
    http://www.state.in.us/icpr/webfile/land/srch_fw.html
  - The Indianapolis Donation
    http://www.state.in.us/icpr/webfile/donation/donindex.html
  - Laporte/Winamac, Indiana Land Office Database Search Page
    http://www.state.in.us/icpr/webfile/land/search.html

- Land Records - Becker County, Minnesota GenWeb
  http://www.rootsweb.com/~mnbecker/land.htm

- Land Records in Ontario
  http://wwnet.com/~treesrch/ontland.html

- Land Survey on the Great Plains
  http://www.ukans.edu/carrie/kancoll/articles/survey/
  With a simple explanation of terms, by Dick Taylor.

- Louisiana Land Records -- Interactive Search
  http://searches.rootsweb.com/cgi-bin/laland/laland.pl
  Pre-1908 Homestead and Cash Entry Patents from the Bureau of Land Management's General Land Office (GLO) Automated Records Project.

- Manitoba Homestead Records
  http://www.geocities.com/Yosemite/7431/homestead.htm
  Details on how to order these records.

- Massachusetts Registries of Deeds
  http://www.browntech.com/ma_cnty.html
  Click on map to obtain address and homepage for Registry of Deeds for your county.

- Military Tract in Cayuga Co., NY
  http://www.rootsweb.com/~nycayuga/land/mtractac.html
  Alphabetical listing of surnames including first name, township, and lot information.

- Morgan County Public Library - GenAssist - The Genealogy Assistant
  http://www.scican.net/~morglib/genasist/genasist.html
  - Morgan County Indiana Original Land Sales From U.S. Government - Sorted by Location
    http://www.scican.net/~morglib/genasist/landsal2.html
  - Morgan County Indiana Original Land Sales From U.S. Government - Sorted by Name
    http://www.scican.net/~morglib/genasist/landsal1.html

- Name Index to the Military Bounty and Donation Land Grants of Texas
  http://www.mindspring.com/~dmaxey/rep_b&d.htm

- Milestone Historic Documents - The Northwest Ordinance
  http://earlyamerica.com/earlyamerica/milestones/ordinance/index.html
  An Ordinance for the Government of the Territory of the United States, North-West of the River Ohio. As it appears in the Supplement to the First Volume of the Columbian Magazine, Philadelphia, 1787. Explains the Northwest Ordinance and its significance, with the full text and a scanned copy of the original document online.

- National Archives of Canada - Dominion Land Grants
  http://www.archives.ca/exec/naweb.dll?fs&020111&e&top&0
  Database of grants issued in Manitoba, Saskatchewan, Alberta and the railway belt of British Columbia, c. 1870-1930.

- National Land Survey of Finland
  http://www.nls.fi/index_e.html

- New York Indorsed Land Papers, 1643-1676
  http://www.tlc-gen.com/newyork.htm

- North Dakota Land Records
  http://pixel.cs.vt.edu/library/land/nodak/

- Northwest Ordinance of 1787
  http://www.statelib.lib.in.us/WWW/ihb/nword.html

- Ohio County Info: Land Auction 1819
  http://homepages.rootsweb.com/~maggieoh/land_act.html

- Ohio County Info: Ohio Lands - A Short History
  http://www.history.rootsweb.com/~ohio-lands/ohlands.html

- The Old 300 Genealogical Database ~ Texas
  http://www.bchm.org/Gene/gene.html
  "The 'Old 300' database actually includes a core listing of all settlers who had received land grants in Austin's Colony by the eve of the war for independence from Mexico".

- Original Lot Holders, Buffalo, New York
  http://www.rootsweb.com/~nyerie/buffalo/lots.htm

- PANB/UNB Cadastral Database - Searching the Grantbook Database
  http://degaulle.hil.unb.ca/library/data/panb/panbweb.html
  Records of land settlement in New Brunswick,1765-1800.

- Pennsylvania Original Land Records
  http://www.innernet.net/hively/
  Series for York County.

- Registers of Scotland Executive Agency
  http://193.32.28.22/
  Guide to Land, Sasine, Personal and Other Registers.

- Registry of Deeds - Nova Scotia
  http://nsgna.ednet.ns.ca/ndeed.html

- Retracing the Trails of Your Ancestors Using Deed Records
  http://www.ultranet.com/~deeds/deeds.htm
  By William Dollarhide, from the Genealogy Bulletin, Issue No. 25, Jan-Feb 1995.

- San Francisco Title Abstract Index
  http://pages.prodigy.net/greentrucking/GenPage/sfindex.htm
  1850 to 1918.

- SDGenWeb County Land Records
  http://www.rootsweb.com/~sdpotter/Land/home.htm

- South Dakota Land Records
  http://pixel.cs.vt.edu/library/land/sodak/

- Texas General Land Office - Archives and Records
  http://www.glo.state.tx.us/archives/

- Texas General Land Office - Finding Aids: Spanish and Mexican Land Resources
  http://www.glo.state.tx.us/archives/find_spanmex.html

- Texas General Land Office - Map Collection
  http://www.glo.state.tx.us/central/archives/mapscol.html

- Texas General Land Office - Texas Land Grants
  http://www.glo.state.tx.us/archives/info.html

- Tithe Applotment Books and Primary (Griffith) Valuation
  http://www.nationalarchives.ie/titheapplprimvalu.html
  From the National Archives of Ireland.

- Wisconsin Land Records -- Interactive Search
  http://searches.rootsweb.com/cgi-bin/wisconsin/wisconsin.pl
  Pre-1908 Homestead and Cash Entry Patents from the BLM.

◆ Publications, Software & Supplies

- Amazon.com Genealogy Bookstore – Land
  http://www.amazon.com/exec/obidos/external-search/?keyword=land+genealogy&tag=markcyndisgenealA/
  And Deeds
  http://www.amazon.com/exec/obidos/external-search/?keyword=deeds+genealogy&tag=markcyndisgenealA/

- AudioTapes.com - Genealogical Lectures on Cassette Tapes - Deeds
  http://www.audiotapes.com/search2.asp?Search=Deeds

- Computer Programs for Drawing Plat Maps
  http://www.outfitters.com/genealogy/land/compmaps.html

- Deed Mapper Software
  http://www.ultranet.com/~deeds/

- Frontier Press Bookstore - Land in America
  http://www.frontierpress.com/frontier.cgi?category=land

- GenealogyBookShop.com - Land Records
  http://www.genealogybookshop.com/genealogybookshop/files/General,Land_Records/index.html
  The online store of Genealogical Publishing Co., Inc. & Clearfield Company.

- General Land Office Records CD-ROMs For Sale
  http://www.access.gpo.gov/su_docs/sale/sale300.html
  Scroll down to "General Land Office Records" under "G".

LANGUAGES & TRANSLATIONS
http://www.cyndislist.com/language.htm

Category Index:
◆ Alphabets
◆ Foreign Language Translations ~ Genealogy
◆ Foreign Language Translations ~ General
◆ Form Letters

◆ Alphabets

- **About Arabic**
  http://www.people.virginia.edu/~amh2x/aso/language.htm

- **Alphabets & Scripts**
  http://www.asklang.co.uk/publish/alphabet.html
  Albanian, Arabic, Bengali, Bulgarian, Catalan, Chinese, Croatian, Czech, Danish, Dutch, English, Estonian, Farsi, Finnish, French, German, Greek, Gujarati, Hebrew, Hindi, Hungarian, Icelandic, Italian, Japanese, Korean, Latvian, Lithuanian, Norwegian, Polish, Portuguese, Punjabi, Russian, Serbian, Slovak, Spanish, Swedish, Thai, Turkish, Ukrainian, Urdu, Vietnamese, Welsh.

- **Alphabet Street - Transliterations and Special Characters**
  http://www.geocities.com/Athens/Parthenon/9860/street.html
  Accents, special characters, diacritic signs and transliteration systems.

- **Arabic alphabet**
  http://www.montefiore.ulg.ac.be/~salloum/abjd/alpha.html

- **Arabic2000.com - The Arabic Alphabet**
  http://www.arabic2000.com/arabic/alphabet.html

- **Belarusian Alphabet**
  http://www.library.utoronto.ca/pjrc/fonts/by-alpha.htm

- **A Brief Review of Some Historical Alternatives to the Latin Alphabet**
  http://web.idirect.com/~nfhome/change.htm

- **Bulgarian Alphabet**
  http://www.library.utoronto.ca/pjrc/fonts/bg-alpha.htm
  Includes old (pre-1945) alphabet.

- **Bulgarian Alphabet and Orthography**
  http://www.geocities.com/Athens/Academy/6490/language/alphabet.html

- **The Cherokee Alphabet and Pronunciation Guide**
  http://joyce.eng.yale.edu/~joant/CherTabl.html

- **Comparitive Hebrew Alphabets**
  http://pages.cthome.net/hirsch/heb-alph.htm

- **Creation of Slav Script**
  http://www.bulgaria.com:8080/BG/welkya/kritika/slave.html
  From Welkya - Web Magazine for Bulgarian Art and Literature.

- **Croatian Alphabet**
  http://www.library.utoronto.ca/pjrc/fonts/hr-alpha.htm

- **Croatian Cyrillic Script**
  http://www.hr/darko/etf/et04.html

- **Croatian Glagolitic Script**
  http://www.hr/darko/etf/et03.html

- **Cyrillic Alphabet**
  http://www.pbs.org/weta/faceofrussia/reference/cyrillic.html

- **The Cyrillic Alphabet**
  http://www.friends-partners.org/oldfriends/language/russian-alphabet.html
  A written & audio guide to pronouncing the letters of the Russian alphabet.

- **Czech Alphabet**
  http://www.library.utoronto.ca/pjrc/fonts/cz-alpha.htm

- **Das A B C Alphabet in Old Gothic German Script**
  http://www.lib.ndsu.nodak.edu/gerrus/books/dasabc.html
  Poster for sale from the Germans from Russia Heritage Collection. Includes an online sample.

- **Deseret Alphabet**
  http://www.mormons.org/daily/history/1844_1877/deseret_alphabet_eom.htm

- **Deseret Alphabet Frequently Asked Questions**
  http://people.delphi.com/deseret/home/alphfaq.htm

- **Estonian Alphabet**
  http://www.library.utoronto.ca/pjrc/fonts/ee-alpha.htm

- **Face of Russia: Cyrillic Alphabet**
  http://www.pbs.org/weta/faceofrussia/reference/cyrillic.html

- **Finnish Alphabet**
  http://www.library.utoronto.ca/pjrc/fonts/fi-alpha.htm

- **German Script Alphabet**
  http://www.mun.ca/rels/morav/pics/tutor/mscript2.html

- **Hebrew Alphabet**
  http://www.feduja.org/commserv/heschel/children/hebrew.stm

- **Hungarian Alphabet**
  http://www.library.utoronto.ca/pjrc/fonts/hu-alpha.htm

- **The Icelandic Alphabet**
  http://www.itn.is/~gunnsi/misc/alph.htm

- **Indo-European Scripts**
  http://www.ropnet.ru/cyryllo/script/scr.html
  From the Cyril Babaev Linguistic Studies.

- Introduction to the Russian Alphabet
  http://catcode.com/rintro/index.htm

- Judaism 101: Hebrew Alphabet
  http://www.jewfaq.org/alephbet.htm

- Ka Pi'äpä Hawai'i
  http://www.coralreefs.hawaii.edu/ReefNetwork/hawaiian.htm
  The Hawaiian Alphabet.

- Latvian Alphabet
  http://www.library.utoronto.ca/pjrc/fonts/lv-alpha.htm

- Lithuanian Alphabet
  http://www.library.utoronto.ca/pjrc/fonts/lt-alpha.htm

- Luxemburger Gazette Typeface
  http://www.eskimo.com/~lisanne/bletter.htm
  The Luxemburger Gazette was published by Nicholas Gonner, and later his son, in Dubuque, Iowa from 1871-1918. In addition to news of Luxembourg, it featured news of Luxembourgers and Luxembourg communities throughout the United States.

- Macedonian Alphabet
  http://www.library.utoronto.ca/pjrc/fonts/mk-alpha.htm

- Moldovan Alphabet
  http://www.library.utoronto.ca/pjrc/fonts/md-alpha.htm
  Pre-1989.

- Moravia Translations - The Czech Alphabet
  http://www.mtranslations.cz/40/en/Dictionary/alphabet_index.html

- Old Church Slavonic Alphabet
  http://www.library.utoronto.ca/pjrc/fonts/oc-alpha.htm
  Pre-1711.

- Polish Alphabet
  http://www.library.utoronto.ca/pjrc/fonts/pl-alpha.htm

- Romanian Alphabet
  http://www.library.utoronto.ca/pjrc/fonts/ro-alpha.htm

- Russian Alphabet
  http://www.library.utoronto.ca/pjrc/fonts/ru-alpha.htm
  Both new and pre-1918.

- Serbian Alphabet
  http://www.library.utoronto.ca/pjrc/fonts/yu-alpha.htm

- Slovak Alphabet
  http://www.library.utoronto.ca/pjrc/fonts/sk-alpha.htm

- Slovene Alphabet
  http://www.ijs.si/slo-chset.html

- Slovenian Alphabet
  http://www.library.utoronto.ca/pjrc/fonts/si-alpha.htm

- Talking Leaves and the Cherokee Phoenix
  http://www.ngeorgia.com/history/alphabet.html
  Brief history of the Cherokee alphabet.

- Transliteration of the Macedonian Cyrillic Alphabet
  http://www.erc.msstate.edu/~vkire/faq/language/alphabet.html

- Ukrainian Alphabet
  http://www.library.utoronto.ca/pjrc/fonts/ua-alpha.htm

◆ Foreign Language Translations ~ Genealogy

- Danish-English Genealogy Dictionary
  http://ourworld.compuserve.com/homepages/NormanMadsen/danish.htm

- A Glossary of German Words Used in Official Documents
  gopher://Gopher.UToledo.edu:70/00GOPHER_ROOT%3A%5BRESEARCH-RESOURCES.GENEALOGY.GERMAN-GENEALOGY%5DA-GLOSSARY-OF-GERMAN-WORDS.USED-IN-OFFICIAL-DOCUMENTS

- Family History SourceGuide
  http://www.familysearch.org/sg/index_s.html
  Genealogical word lists from the FamilySearch Internet Genealogy Service of the LDS Church.

  o Danish
    http://www.familysearch.org/sg/WLDanish.html

  o Dutch
    http://www.familysearch.org/sg/WLDutch.html

  o Finnish
    http://www.familysearch.org/sg/WLFinnis.html

  o French
    http://www.familysearch.org/sg/WLFrench.html

  o German
    http://www.familysearch.org/sg/WLGerman.html

  o Italian
    http://www.familysearch.org/sg/WLItalia.html

  o Latin
    http://www.familysearch.org/sg/WLLatin.html

  o Norwegian
    http://www.familysearch.org/sg/WLNorway.html

  o Polish
    http://www.familysearch.org/sg/WLPolish.html

  o Danish
    http://www.familysearch.org/sg/WLDanish.html

  o Portuguese
    http://www.familysearch.org/sg/WLPortug.html

  o Spanish
    http://www.familysearch.org/sg/WLSpanis.html

  o Swedish
    http://www.familysearch.org/sg/WLSweden.html

- Genealogy Exchange & Surname Registry - Translation Volunteers
  http://www.genexchange.com/tSearch.CFM

- genealogyPro - Translation Services
  http://www.genealogypro.com/directories/translators.html

- Genealogy: Terms for Document Translation (Lith) ~ Lithuania
  http://lark.cc.ukans.edu/~raistlin/genealogy/terms.html

- German-English Genealogical Dictionary
  http://www.amazon.com/exec/obidos/ISBN=0806313420/
  markcyndisgenealA/
  A book by Ernest Thode.

- German-English Letter Translation Specialists
  http://www.win.bright.net/~deichsa/welcome.html

- German Genealogy: Translation Service
  http://www.genealogy.net/gene/www/abt/translation.html

- German Study Group / German Words
  http://205.216.138.19/~websites/lynnd/vuword.html

- German Translation Service
  http://www.asherwin.com/
  Specializations: German genealogy, Fraktur and German script, legal documents.

- Latin Genealogical Word List
  http://www.familysearch.org/sg/WLLatin.html
  From the Family History SourceGuide.

- A Partial List of Latin Genealogy Terms and Their English Equivalents
  http://www.arduini.net/tools/latin.htm

- Polish Genealogical Translations
  http://adela49.freeyellow.com/index.html
  Native Polish translator/interpreter will assist you in finding your Polish roots by translating your Polish genealogical records. Twenty years of experience.

- Portuguese Lexique of Genealogy
  http://fn2.freenet.edmonton.ab.ca/~fcandido/lexique.html
  Portuguese-English translations of genealogy terms.

- Translation Service only for genealogy related material
  http://www.genealogy.net/gene/misc/translation.html
  Volunteer translators can provide you with translations between Czech, English, Dutch, French, German, & Polish. This service is provided via e-mail. Exact request syntax and length rules must be followed in order to expedite processing.

- Translation Services - PolishLessons-L
  http://www.toledolink.com/pl/translations.html
  A free genealogical translation service (maintained and coordinated by Arthur Teschler at the University of Giessen in Germany).

- UK Genealogy - Common Acronyms & Jargon
  http://www.oz.net/~markhow/acronym-uk.htm

◆ Foreign Language Translations ~ General

- AltaVista Translation Service
  http://babelfish.altavista.digital.com/cgi-bin/translate?
  Input a URL for a web site or a block of plain text and this site will translate for you to/from the following languages: English, French, German, Italian, Portuguese, and Spanish.

- Amazon.com Genealogy Bookstore - Foreign Language
  http://www.amazon.com/exec/obidos/external-search/?
  keyword=foreign+language&tag=markcyndisgenealA/

- The Cyrillic Alphabet
  http://www.friends-partners.org/oldfriends/language/russian-alphabet.html
  A written & audio guide to pronouncing the letters of the Russian alphabet.

- Deutsch Englisches Wörterbuch
  http://www.tu-chemnitz.de/urz/netz/forms/dict.html

- Dictionaries and Other Useful Sources
  http://www.cis.hut.fi/~peura/dictionaries.html

- Dictionary.com / Translate
  http://www.dictionary.com/translate/
  Translate web pages or text between these languages: English, French, German, Italian, Portuguese, Spanish.

- English - Czech Dictionary
  http://ww2.fce.vutbr.cz/bin/ecd

- English-Finnish Dictionary
  http://www.mofile.fi/-db.htm

- English-Hungarian Dictionary
  http://www.sztaki.hu/services/engdict/index.jhtml

- Foreign Language Dictionaries
  http://www.travlang.com/languages/

- FreeTranslation.com
  http://www.freetranslation.com/
  Free Translation of Web and Text for Spanish, French, German, Italian, Portuguese to and from English.

- German-English On-line Dictionary
  http://dictionaries.travlang.com/GermanEnglish/

- GLOBALINK
  http://www.globalink.com/
  Free Translation Service.

- GO Translator
  http://translator.go.com/
  Translate web pages or text between these languages: English, French, German, Italian, Portuguese, Spanish.

- Kypros - Lexicon: Greek-English-Greek Dictionary
  http://www.kypros.org/cgi-bin/lexicon

- Languages and translation
  http://www.iol.ie/~mazzoldi/lang/
  A collection of useful links and resources for translators.

- Lexin Svensk-Engelskt Lexikon / Lexin Swedish-English Dictionary
  http://www-lexikon.nada.kth.se/skolverket/sve-eng.html

- The Linguist List: Dictionaries, Etc.
  http://www.emich.edu/~linguist/dictionaries.html

- Mo'o and Lolo's Cyber Hawaiian Dictionary Online
  http://www.hisurf.com/hawaiian/dictionary.html
  5,000 English-Hawaiian words translated.

- Online Language Dictionaries and Translators
  http://rivendel.com:80/~ric/resources/dictionary.html

- Research It!
  http://www.iTools.com/research-it/research-it.html
  Has a foreign language universal translator.

- Slovak Translation Services by Jana Cupková Holmes
  http://www.dholmes.com/janatran.html

- SYSTRANET Translation Online
  http://www.systranet.com/

- Tolken99
  http://www.algonet.se/~hagsten/engindex.htm
  Word processor and English to Swedish translation software.

- The Translator's Home Companion - On-line Dictionaries and Glossaries
  http://www.rahul.net/lai/glossaries.html

- travlang's Translating Dictionaries
  http://dictionaries.travlang.com/
  Including: English, German, Dutch, French, Spanish, Danish, Portuguese, Afrikaans, Esperanto.

- Voila Translate
  http://www.voila.com/Services/Translate/
  Translate web pages or text between these languages: English, French, German, Italian, Portuguese, Spanish.

- A Web of On-Line Dictionaries
  http://www.facstaff.bucknell.edu/rbeard/diction.html
  A huge index of a variety of available dictionaries, including foreign translation sites.

◆ Form Letters

- FamilySearch Internet Genealogy Service - Research Helps
  http://www.familysearch.org/Eng/Search/rg/frameset_rhelps.asp

  o Finnish Letter-Writing Guide
    http://www.familysearch.org/Eng/Search/rg/frameset_rg.asp?Dest=G1&Aid=&Gid=&Lid=&Sid=&Did=&Juris1=&Event=&Year=&Gloss=&Sub=&Tab=&Entry=&Guide=LWGFinland.ASP

  o French Letter-Writing Guide
    http://www.familysearch.org/Eng/Search/rg/frameset_rg.asp?Dest=G1&Aid=&Gid=&Lid=&Sid=&Did=&Juris1=&Event=&Year=&Gloss=&Sub=&Tab=&Entry=&Guide=LGFrench.ASP

  o German Letter-Writing Guide
    http://www.familysearch.org/Eng/Search/rg/frameset_rg.asp?Dest=G1&Aid=&Gid=&Lid=&Sid=&Did=&Juris1=&Event=&Year=&Gloss=&Sub=&Tab=&Entry=&Guide=LGGerman.ASP

  o Italian Letter-Writing Guide
    http://www.familysearch.org/Eng/Search/rg/frameset_rg.asp?Dest=G1&Aid=&Gid=&Lid=&Sid=&Did=&Juris1=&Event=&Year=&Gloss=&Sub=&Tab=&Entry=&Guide=LGItalian.ASP

  o Polish Letter-Writing Guide
    http://www.familysearch.org/Eng/Search/rg/frameset_rg.asp?Dest=G1&Aid=&Gid=&Lid=&Sid=&Did=&Juris1=&Event=&Year=&Gloss=&Sub=&Tab=&Entry=&Guide=LWGPolish.ASP

  o Portuguese Letter-Writing Guide
    http://www.familysearch.org/Eng/Search/rg/frameset_rg.asp?Dest=G1&Aid=&Gid=&Lid=&Sid=&Did=&Juris1=&Event=&Year=&Gloss=&Sub=&Tab=&Entry=&Guide=LWGPortuguese.ASP

  o Spanish Letter-Writing Guide
    http://www.familysearch.org/Eng/Search/rg/frameset_rg.asp?Dest=G1&Aid=&Gid=&Lid=&Sid=&Did=&Juris1=&Event=&Year=&Gloss=&Sub=&Tab=&Entry=&Guide=LWGSpanish.ASP

- Family Tree Maker Online Genealogy How-To - Form Letters and Other Aids
  http://www.familytreemaker.com/00000023.html

  o Form Letters in English
    http://www.familytreemaker.com/ltr_english.html

  o Form Letters in French
    http://www.familytreemaker.com/ltr_french.html

  o Form Letters in German
    http://www.familytreemaker.com/ltr_german.html

  o Form Letters in Italian
    http://www.familytreemaker.com/ltr_italian.html

  o Form Letters in Spanish
    http://www.familytreemaker.com/ltr_spanish.html

- Form Letters for German Genealogy
  http://www.genealogy.net/gene/www/ghlp/muster.html

- Sample Letters in German to Obtain Genealogical Information
  gopher://Gopher.UToledo.edu:70/00GOPHER_ROOT%3A%5BRESEARCH-RESOURCES.GENEALOGY.GERMAN-GENEALOGY%5DGERMAN-SAMPLE-LETTER.FOR-INFORMATION-REQUESTS

LDS & FAMILY HISTORY CENTERS

The Church of Jesus Christ of Latter-day Saints
http://www.cyndislist.com/lds.htm

Category Index:

- ◆ FamilySearch Internet Genealogy Service
- ◆ Ancestral File
- ◆ Family History Centers ~ General Information
- ◆ Family History Centers ~ Locations
- ◆ The Family History Library & Salt Lake City
- ◆ Family History Library Catalog
- ◆ History of the LDS Church
- ◆ IGI - International Genealogical Index

- ◆ Mailing Lists, Newsgroups & Chat
- ◆ Microfilm & Microfiche
- ◆ Miscellaneous LDS Church & Genealogy Resources
- ◆ Pedigree Resource File
- ◆ Professional Researchers, Volunteers & Other Research Services
- ◆ Publications, Software & Supplies

◆ FamilySearch Internet Genealogy Service

- FamilySearch Internet Genealogy Service
  http://www.familysearch.org/
  THE genealogy web site of the LDS Church. Includes the ability to search the IGI, the Ancestral File, the Family History Library Catalog, and web site submissions. Also has user mailing lists, online ordering of FHL research materials and allows you to preserve your own research online.
  - o Family History Library
    http://www.familysearch.org/Eng/Library/FHL/frameset_library.asp
    - Family History Centers
      http://www.familysearch.org/Eng/Library/FHC/frameset_fhc.asp
    - Family History Library Catalog
      http://www.familysearch.org/Eng/Library/FHLC/frameset_fhlc.asp
  - o Family Search Online Distribution Center
    http://www.ldscatalog.com/cgi-bin/ncommerce3/CategoryDisplay?cgmenbr=1402&cgrfnbr=1678&RowStart=1&LocCode=FH
    Download and order software and research materials.
  - o Frequently Asked Questions
    http://www.familysearch.org/Eng/Home/FAQ/frameset_faq.asp
  - o Search for Ancestors
    http://www.familysearch.org/Eng/Search/frameset_search.asp
    - All Resources
      http://www.familysearch.org/Eng/Search/frameset_search.asp?PAGE=search_all1.asp
    - Ancestral File
      http://www.familysearch.org/Eng/Search/frameset_search.asp?PAGE=af/search_AF.asp

- International Genealogical Index
  http://www.familysearch.org/Eng/Search/frameset_search.asp?PAGE=igi/search_IGI.asp
- Pedigree Resource File
  http://www.familysearch.org/Eng/Search/frameset_search.asp?PAGE=prf/search_PRF.asp
- Web Sites
  http://www.familysearch.org/Eng/Search/frameset_search.asp?PAGE=websites/search_websites_advanced.asp
  - o Share
    http://www.familysearch.org/Eng/Share/Collaborate/frameset_share.asp
  - o What's New on FamilySearch
    http://www.familysearch.org/Eng/Home/News/frameset_news.asp

◆ Ancestral File

- The Ancestral File--Questions and Answers
  http://www.utw.com/~tornado/ancfile.html

- FamilySearch Internet Genealogy Service
  http://www.familysearch.org/
  THE genealogy web site of the LDS Church. Includes the ability to search the IGI, the Ancestral File, the Family History Library Catalog, and web site submissions. Also has user mailing lists, online ordering of FHL research materials and allows you to preserve your own research online.
  - o Ancestral File™
    http://www.familysearch.org/Eng/Search/frameset_search.asp?PAGE=af/search_AF.asp
    Search the Ancestral File from the LDS' FamilySearch website. Over 35 million names organized into families and pedigrees.
  - o Ancestral File - Tips on How to Search the Ancestral File
    http://www.familysearch.org/eng/Search/af/searchaf_hints.asp

◆ Family History Centers ~ General Information

- AudioTapes.com - Genealogical Lectures on Cassette Tapes – FHC
  http://www.audiotapes.com/search2.asp?Search=FHC
  And Center
  http://www.audiotapes.com/search2.asp?Search=center

- The Directors' Nest
  http://homepages.rootsweb.com/~fhcnet/
  Resources for directors of LDS Family History Centers.

- Family History Centers
  http://www.genhomepage.com/FHC/
  The Genealogy Home Page is collecting addresses & info regarding your local FHC.

- FamilySearch Internet Genealogy Service
  http://www.familysearch.org/
  THE genealogy web site of the LDS Church. Includes the ability to search the IGI, the Ancestral File, the Family History Library Catalog, and web site submissions. Also has user mailing lists, online ordering of FHL research materials and allows you to preserve your own research online.

  o About Family History Centers
    http://www.familysearch.org/eng/Library/FHC/frameset_fhc.asp?PAGE=library_fhc_about.asp

  o Family History Centers - Find a Family History Center Near You
    http://www.familysearch.org/eng/Library/FHC/frameset_fhc.asp

  o Frequently Asked Questions
    http://www.familysearch.org/eng/Library/FHC/frameset_fhc.asp?PAGE=faq_fhc.asp

- LDS Family History Centers
  http://www.jewishgen.org/infofiles/ldscntr.txt
  A JewishGen InfoFile.

- LDS Family History Centers - The Largest Collection In The World!
  http://www.firstct.com/fv/lds1.html
  A tutorial from the Treasure Maps site.

- ROOTS-L Resources: Family History Centers and Library
  http://www.rootsweb.com/roots-l/fhc.html

- Welcome To The Family History Center™
  http://www.lds.org/library/display/0,4945,35-1-19-1,FF.html
  An online brochure from the official LDS Church web site.

- What Is a Family History Center™?
  http://www.lds.org/library/display/0,4945,34-1-18-4,FF.html
  From the official LDS Church web site.

◆ Family History Centers ~ Locations

- Annandale Family History Center ~ Virginia
  http://www.genweb.net/AFHC/

- Atlanta Area Family History Centers in Georgia
  http://www.prairiebluff.com/resources/fhc-atl.htm

- Byrd Springs Family History Center ~ Huntsville, Alabama
  http://members.aol.com/r3morgan/byrd.htm

- Central California Family History Centers
  http://home.pacbell.net/lodifhc/cafhcenters.htm
  From the Lodi Family History Center. Includes addresses and phone numbers.

- Les centres de généalogie
  http://www.alternative.cci-brest.fr/SDJ/centres.htm
  Provides contact information for 54 LDS Family History Centers in France.

- Les Centres Généalogiques SDJ / LDS Family History Centers
  http://www.ldsmissions.net/fpm/genealogie.html
  France, Belgique, Suisse, Canada.

- Chesapeake, Virginia Family History Center
  http://sites.communitylink.org/cpl/famhistory.html

- Columbia Missouri Family History Center
  http://www.bocomo.org/LDSFHC.HTM

- Colorado Springs North Family History Center ~ Colorado
  http://www.geocities.com/Heartland/Shores/8169/

- Concord/Walnut Creek California Family History Center
  http://feefhs.org/lds/fhc/frg-fhcc.html

- Danville California Stake - Family History Center
  http://www.danvillestake.org/dsfhc_home.html

- Dartmouth Nova Scotia Family History Centre
  http://nsgna.ednet.ns.ca/fhc/index.html

- Deer Valley Stake Family History Center ~ Phoenix, Arizona
  http://members.tripod.com/dvsfhc/

- Everton's On-Line Search: Family History Centers of the U.S. or of the World
  http://emh.everton.com/fhc.htm

- Family History Center ~ Rockville, Illinois
  http://www.rootsweb.com/~ilwinneb/famhistc.htm

- Family History Center ~ Traverse City, Michigan
  http://members.aol.com/vwilson577/fhc.html

- The Family History Center
  http://www.siteone.com/clubs/mgs/neighbor/FHC_Mobile.htm
  From the Mobile Genealogical Society, Mobile, Alabama.

- Family History Center in Plainview ~ New York
  http://members.macconnect.com/users/v/vitev/genesocli/fhc.html

- Family History Center of Mission Viejo, CA ~ California
  http://www.genweb.net/Family_History_Center/

- Family History Center - The Colony, Texas
  http://genweb.net/The-Colony-fhc/

- Family History Center - Washington D.C. Temple
  http://www.mindspring.com/~giammo/FHC/

- Family History Centres in Canada
  http://www.shelburne.nscc.ns.ca/nsgna/fhc/cdnfhc.htm

- Family History Centers in Germany, Austria and Switzerland
  http://www.genealogy.net/gene/faqs/LDS.de

- Family History Centers in North Alabama
  http://members.aol.com/terryann/other.htm

- Family History Centres in Ontario
  http://www.archives.gov.on.ca/english/geneal/fmlyhist.htm

- Genealogie Forschungsstelle Dortmund ~ Germany
  http://home.t-online.de/home/GFS.Dortmund/

- Geneva Heights Family History Center ~ Orem, Utah
  http://users.sisna.com/ileenj/
  Helps for family history center workers and patrons, ward and stake family history consultants, and beginning researchers with helpful Internet links.

- Hong Kong Saints Web site - Hong Kong Family History Center
  http://www.mosiah.net/hkfhc/

- Howell Family History Center ~ Michigan
  http://www.LivGenMI.com/howfhc.htm

- The Jersey Family History Centre of the L.D.S. Church ~ Channel Islands
  http://user.itl.net/~glen/ldsci.html

- LDS Family History Center, Ann Arbor Branch ~ Michigan
  http://www.hvcn.org/info/gswc/library/libldsaa.htm
  Information from the Genealogical Society of Washtenaw County.

- The LDS Family History Center in Huntsville, Alabama
  http://members.aol.com/terryann2/fhcinal.htm

- LDS Family History Centres in the British Isles, including Ireland and Scotland
  http://www.genuki.org.uk/big/LDS/centres.txt

- Leesburg Family History Center ~ Florida
  http://www.angelfire.com/fl/Sumter/genealogy.html

- Lethbridge Family History Center ~ Alberta, Canada
  http://www.leth.net/fhc/

- The Lexington Kentucky Family History Center
  http://www.uky.edu/StudentOrgs/LDSSA/FHCpage.html

- Lodi Family History Center ~ California
  http://home.pacbell.net/lodifhc/

- Lompoc Family History Center ~ California
  http://www.geocities.com/Heartland/Ranch/5715/LFHC.html

- Los Angeles Family History Center
  http://www.rootsweb.com/~bifhsusa/fhcwhere.html
  From the British Isles Family History Society - U.S.A. web site.

- Los Angeles Family History Center ~ California
  http://www.lafhc.org/
  - Before You Visit the L.A. FHC
    http://www.lafhc.org/visit.htm
  - Los Angeles Family History Center - General Holdings and Collections
    http://www.lafhc.org/collect.htm
  - Los Angeles FHC Monthly Class Schedule
    http://www.lafhc.org/class.htm

- Madison Alabama Family History Center
  http://members.aol.com/terryann/madison.htm

- Meridian South Stake Family History Center ~ Meridian, Idaho
  http://www.homestead.com/mssfhc/files/index.htm

- Okotoks Family History Center ~ Alberta, Canada
  http://www.cadvision.com/Home_Pages/accounts/okfhc/

- Orchard Park FHC, Erie County, New York
  http://www.rootsweb.com/~nyerie/orchard_park/opfhc.htm

- Parkersburg, WV Family History Center ~ West Virginia
  http://www.rootsweb.com/~wvwood/wdfhc.htm

- Pensacola, Florida Family History Center
  http://freepages.genealogy.rootsweb.com/~familyhistory centerpensacolafl/

- Phoenix Arizona West Stake Family History Center
  http://azonline.com/~kallen/fhc.htm

- Roseburg Oregon Stake Family History Center
  http://www.geocities.com/Heartland/Acres/7892/

- San Diego Family History Centers
  http://www.cgssd.org/centers.html

- Santa Clara Family History Center ~ California
  http://reality.sgi.com/csp/scfhc/

- St. Paul Family History Center ~ Minnesota
  http://www.angelfire.com/mn/stpaulfhc/

- Sweetwater Family History Center ~ Bonita, California
  http://members.home.net/ajboyd/swfhcn.htm

- The Unofficial Home Page of the Princeton Family History Center
  http://members.aol.com/dssaari/prifhc.htm

- Utah Valley Regional Family History Center
  http://www.lib.byu.edu/dept/uvrfhc/
  On the fourth floor of the Harold B. Lee Library on the campus of Brigham Young University.

- Valley Forge, PA Family History Center ~ Pennsylvania
  http://valleyforgefhc.org/

- Williamsville Family History Center, Erie County, New York
  http://www.rootsweb.com/~nyerie/amherst/wmfhc.htm

- Winston-Salem First Ward Family History Center ~ North Carolina
  http://www.ldschurch.net/s/ws/first/genealogy.htm

◆ The Family History Library & Salt Lake City

- The Church of Jesus Christ of Latter-day Saints and the Family History Library
  http://www.genhomepage.com/LDS.html
  From the Genealogy Home Page.

- FamilySearch Internet Genealogy Service
  http://www.familysearch.org/
  THE genealogy web site of the LDS Church. Includes the ability to search the IGI, the Ancestral File, the Family History Library Catalog, and web site submissions. Also has user mailing lists, online ordering of FHL research materials and allows you to preserve your own research online.

  o About the Family History Library
    http://www.familysearch.org/Eng/Library/FHL/frameset_library.asp

    • Preparing to Visit the Library
      http://www.familysearch.org/Eng/Library/FHL/frameset_library.asp?PAGE=library_preparing.asp

- Genealogical Society of Utah
  http://www.mormons.org/daily/family_history/genealogical_society_eom.htm
  Description from All About Mormons.

- Genealogical Society of Utah
  http://www.itd.nps.gov/cwss/partners_gsu.htm
  Description from the National Park Service, Civil War Soldiers and Sailors System web site.

- The Genealogist - The Family History Library
  http://www.xcelco.on.ca/~genealog/famhilib.htm

- Going to Salt Lake City to Do Family History Research
  http://www.amazon.com/exec/obidos/ISBN=0934153140/markcyndisgenealA/
  A JewishGen InfoFile.

- Guide To LDS Family History Library, Salt Lake City, Utah
  http://www.jewishgen.org/infofiles/lds-slc.txt

- LDS Family History Library, Salt Lake City, Utah
  http://www.everton.com/genealog/genealog.ldsfhlib
  Description, maps, etc.

- New at the Family History Library
  http://www.progenealogists.com/new_fhl.htm
  Courtesy of Cottrill & Hefti, Professional Genealogists.

- News of the Family History Library in Salt Lake City
  http://members.aol.com/terryann2/lib_news.htm

- ROOTS-L Resources: Family History Centers and Library
  http://www.rootsweb.com/roots-l/fhc.html

- Salt Lake City, Family History Library Information
  http://www.aros.net/~drwaff/slcfhl.htm

- Salt Lake City Here We Come!
  http://www.rootsweb.com/~genepool/slc.htm

- Utah Valley PAF Users Group - The Salt Lake Family History Library
  http://www.genealogy.org/~uvpafug/fhlslc.html

◆ Family History Library Catalog

- The Family History Library Catalog
  http://www.utw.com/~tornado/fhlibcat.html
  A description of the FHL Catalog, from a personal web site.

- Family History Library Catalog (FHLC)™
  http://reled.byu.edu/famhist/handouts/FHLChand.htm
  From the Family History Lab at BYU. Detailed instructions on how to use the Family History Library Catalog.

- Family History Library Catalog Description
  http://www.genuki.org.uk/big/LDS/catorg.txt
  A description of the FHL Catalog, from the GENUKI project.

- Family History Library Catalog Topics
  http://www.genuki.org.uk/big/LDS/topics.txt
  Listed & cross-referenced for use in England, that allow for differences in American and English usage.

- Family Search: The Family History Library Catalog (FHLC)
  http://www.firstct.com/fv/fhlc.html
  A description of the FHL Catalog, from a personal web site.

- FamilySearch Internet Genealogy Service
  http://www.familysearch.org/
  THE genealogy web site of the LDS Church. Includes the ability to search the IGI, the Ancestral File, the Family History Library Catalog, and web site submissions. Also has user mailing lists, online ordering of FHL research materials and allows you to preserve your own research online.

  o Family History Library Catalog
    http://www.familysearch.org/eng/Library/FHLC/frameset_fhlc.asp
    Search this online version of the catalog for the LDS collection in Salt Lake City.

    • Place Search
      http://www.familysearch.org/Eng/Library/fhlc/supermain frameset.asp?display=localitysearch&columns=*,180,0

    • Surname Search
      http://www.familysearch.org/Eng/Library/fhlc/supermain frameset.asp?display=surnamesearch&columns=*,180,0

- Author Search
  http://www.familysearch.org/Eng/Library/fhlc/supermain
  frameset.asp?display=generalauthorsearch&columns=*,
  180,0

- Call Number Search
  http://www.familysearch.org/Eng/Library/fhlc/supermain
  frameset.asp?display=generalcallnosearch&columns=*,
  180,0

- Film/Fiche Search
  http://www.familysearch.org/Eng/Library/fhlc/supermain
  frameset.asp?display=generalcallnosearch&columns=*,
  180,0

  o Family History Library Catalog on CD
  http://www.ldscatalog.com/cgi-bin/ncommerce3/Product
  Display?prrfnbr=1632783&prmenbr=1402&CGRY_NUM=14
  40462&RowStart=1&LocCode=FH
  *Available for sale from the Family Search Online Distribution
  Center.*

◆ History of the LDS Church

- Deseret Alphabet
  http://www.mormons.org/daily/history/1844_1877/deseret_
  alphabet_eom.htm

- Deseret Alphabet Frequently Asked Questions
  http://people.delphi.com/deseret/home/alphfaq.htm

- The Gathering of Zion: The Story of the Mormon
  Trail
  http://www.amazon.com/exec/obidos/ISBN=0803292139/
  markcyndisgenealA/
  A book by Wallace Earle Stegner.

- Handcart Companies
  http://eddy.media.utah.edu/medsol/UCME/h/HANDCART.html

- Handcarts to Zion: The Story of a Unique Western
  Migration, 1856-1860 : With Contemporary Journals,
  Accounts, Reports; And Rosters of Members of the
  Handcart Brigades
  http://www.amazon.com/exec/obidos/ISBN=0803272553/
  markcyndisgenealA/
  A book by Leroy Reuben Hafen.

- Journals of Early Members of the Church of Jesus
  Christ of Latter-day Saints
  http://www.math.byu.edu/~smithw/Lds/LDS/Early-Saints/
  *Journals, diaries, biographies and autobiographies of some early
  Mormons and others who knew Joseph Smith, Jr.*

- Max Bertola's - The Mormon Pioneer Story
  http://www.uvol.com/pioneer/homepage.html

- Mormon Batallion
  http://people.delphi.com/deseret/home/homebatt.htm

- The Mormon Batallion (1846-1847) Roster
  http://www.cc.utah.edu/~joseph/MBatallion.html

- Mormon History - A Research Guide
  http://www.nypl.org/research/chss/grd/resguides/
  mormon.html

- Mormon History Association
  http://www.mhahome.org/

- Mormon History Resource Page
  http://www.indirect.com:80/www/crockett/history.html

  o Mormon Diaries/Journals and Biographies
  http://www.indirect.com:80/www/crockett/bios.html

  o Mormon History Resource Page - Pioneer Period
  http://www.indirect.com:80/www/crockett/pioneer.html

- Mormon Immigration Index
  http://www.ldscatalog.com/cgi-bin/ncommerce3/Product
  Display?prrfnbr=1916588&prmenbr=1402&CGRY_NUM=
  1440462&RowStart=1&LocCode=FH
  *CD-ROM for sale from the LDS church. Database of approximately
  93,000 immigrants who traveled from various international ports to
  the United States between the years 1840 and 1890. Information in
  this database includes the age, country of origin, ports of departure
  and arrival, the company leader assigned to each voyage, and
  general voyage information.*

- Mormon Immigration Index Press Kit
  http://www.lds.org/library/display/0,4945,232-1-209-1,FF.html
  *Includes sample journal entries, photographs, and information on
  the database.*

- The Mormon Pioneer Trail
  http://www.americanwest.com/trails/pages/mormtrl.htm
  From the American West Home Page.

- The Mormon Pioneer Trail
  http://www.omaha.org/trails/main.htm
  From the Douglas-Sarpy Counties Mormon Trails Association.

- The Mormon Trail
  http://www.esu3.k12.ne.us:80/districts/elkhorn/ms/curriculum/
  Mormon1.html

- MormonTrail.com - The Pioneer Experience
  http://www.mormontrail.com/
  *The Official Web Site for Stories, Facts, and Ship Logs on the
  Mormon Trail Pioneers.*

- Tracing Mormon Pioneers
  http://www.xmission.com/~nelsonb/pioneer.htm

  o Mormon Emigrant Ships (1840-1868)
  http://www.xmission.com/~nelsonb/pioneer.htm#ships

  o South African Emigration 1853-1865
  http://www.xmission.com/~nelsonb/safrica.htm

  o Tracing Scandinavian Latter-day Saints
  http://www.xmission.com/~nelsonb/scand.htm
  *For researching members of the LDS church from the
  Scandinavian Mission in the time period of 1852-1868.*

  o U.S. Mormon Batallion, Inc.
  http://www.mormonbattalion.com/

◆ IGI - International Genealogical Index

- FamilySearch Internet Genealogy Service
  http://www.familysearch.org/
  *THE genealogy web site of the LDS Church. Includes the ability to
  search the IGI, the Ancestral File, the Family History Library
  Catalog, and web site submissions. Also has user mailing lists,
  online ordering of FHL research materials and allows you to
  preserve your own research online.*

o International Genealogical Index
http://www.familysearch.org/Eng/Search/frameset_
search.asp?PAGE=igi/search_IGI.asp
*Search part of the International Genealogical Index from the
LDS' FamilySearch website. Over 360 million names extracted
from vital records and contributed by church members.*

o Tips on How to Search the International
Genealogical Index
http://www.familysearch.org/Eng/Search/igi/searchigi_
hints.asp

- The Global Gazette - English & Welsh Roots The
LDS FamilySearch© Website: Using Batch
Numbers
http://globalgenealogy.com/gazfd36.htm

- IGI Batch Number Instructions
http://users.deltanet.com/~lrawlins/igi.html

- IGI Batch Numbers - (Tracing Your English Roots)
http://www.geocities.com/Heartland/Trail/8333/index4.html
*Searchable database providing the IGI batch numbers submitted by
contributors for each county in the United Kingdom.*

- International Genealogical Index (IGI) "Batch
Numbers"
http://home.clear.net.nz/pages/nzsoghamilton/igi.htm

- IGI and Patronymics
http://www.johngareth.freeserve.co.uk/HelpPage~pearls.html
#IGIpatro

- LDS (IGI Info)
ftp://ftp.rootsweb.com/pub/roots-l/genealog/genealog.ldsigi1

- United Kingdom Batch Numbers
http://home.clear.net.nz/pages/nzsoghamilton/batch
numbers.htm
*From the Hamilton Branch of the New Zealand Society of
Genealogists.*

- Using the IGI for Wales and Monmouthshire
http://www.genuki.org.uk/big/wal/WalesIGI.html

- What is the I.G.I.? - aka The International
Genealogical Index
http://www.livgenmi.com/fhcigi.htm
A definition help page by Helen S. Ullmann, C.G.

◆ Mailing Lists, Newsgroups & Chat

- ELIJAH-L Mailing List
http://www.rootsweb.com/~jfuller/gen_mail_religions.html
#ELIJAH-L
*For believing members of the Church of Jesus Christ of Latter-day
Saints to discuss their ideas and experiences relating with genealogy
in the LDS Church.*

- FAMILYSEARCH Mailing List
http://www.rootsweb.com/~jfuller/gen_mail_computing.html
#FAMILYSEARCH
*Designed to assist anyone with questions regarding use of the
Internet for searching Family History. The Familysearch internet
site and others are discussed for genealogical research such as
searching, downloading, contributing, cross-referencing and*

*microfilm numbers, and basic "getting started" questions are also
discussed and welcomed. Surname specific research is not discussed
and you must be a subscriber to post messages to the list.*

- FHCNET Mailing List
http://www.rootsweb.com/~jfuller/gen_mail_general.html
#FHCNET
*For directors and others closely associated with the operation of
Latter-day Saint family history centers (FHCs). Topics for
discussion include staff training, microfilm circulation, collection
development, FamilySearch, equipment maintenance, and patron
services.*

- GEN-ROOTERS Mailing List
http://www.rootsweb.com/~jfuller/gen_mail_religions.html
#GEN-ROOTERS
*For members of the Church of Jesus Christ of Latter-day Saints to
share ideas and helpful hints on the "how-to's" of genealogy.*

- GHFHC-NEWS Mailing List
http://www.rootsweb.com/~jfuller/gen_mail_states-ut.html
#GHFHC-NEWS
*For dissemination of the newsletter for the Geneva Heights Family
History Center, Orem, Utah.*

- HANDCART Mailing List
http://www.rootsweb.com/~jfuller/gen_mail_religions.html
#HANDCART
*For anyone who has an interest in the genealogy, journals, and
stories of the Pioneers of the Church of Jesus Christ of Latter-day
Saints who settled in the Salt Lake Valley from 1847 to 1860.*

- LDSFHCConsultants Mailing List
http://www.rootsweb.com/~jfuller/gen_mail_general.html#LDS
FHCConsultants
*Solely for LDS Family History Center consultants to exchange
information and ideas, discuss programs and workshops, ask
questions, etc.*

- LDS-GENEALOGY Mailing List
http://www.rootsweb.com/~jfuller/gen_mail_general.html#LDS
-GENEALOGY
*For those who use the Latter-day Saints Family History Centers,
Library, and Family Search Internet Genealogy Service web site for
their genealogy research efforts to discuss the available resources
and their application.*

- LDS-Genealogy Mailing List FAQ and Subscription
Info
http://members.tripod.com/~Genealogy_Infocenter/ldsgen-
list.html

- LDS-WARD-CONSULTANT Mailing List
http://www.rootsweb.com/~jfuller/gen_mail_general.html#LDS
-WARD-CONSULTANT
*For the use of ward and stake genealogy consultants and specialists
of the Latter-day Saints (LDS) Church to exchange suggestions,
guidelines, data, etc. related to their duties.*

- MORMON-INDEX Mailing List
http://www.rootsweb.com/~jfuller/gen_mail_religions.html
#MORMON-INDEX
*Provides a weekly newsletter containing queries about Mormon
Internet Resources, responses to those queries, announcements of
Mormon Internet Resources, and compilations of resources by
subject.*

- PAF Mailing List
  http://www.rootsweb.com/~jfuller/gen_mail_software.html
  #PAF
  For discussions relating to the Personal Ancestral File program put out by the LDS.

- PAF-2.31-USERS Mailing List
  http://www.rootsweb.com/~jfuller/gen_mail_software.html
  #PAF-2.31-USERS

- PAF-3-USERS Mailing List
  http://www.rootsweb.com/~jfuller/gen_mail_software.html
  #PAF-3-USERS

- PAF-4-USERS Mailing List
  http://www.rootsweb.com/~jfuller/gen_mail_software.html
  #PAF-4-USERS
  For users of Version 4 of the Personal Ancestral File (PAF) genealogy software program to interact with other users, seek help in using the program, and exchange ideas and solutions regarding problem areas.

- PAF-TEMPLES Mailing List
  http://www.rootsweb.com/~jfuller/gen_mail_software.html
  #PAF-TEMPLES
  Specifically designed to be a discussion list for help in getting your data from the PAF computer program stage into the temple itself.

◆ Microfilm & Microfiche

- Halifax County, Nova Scotia LDS/PANS Film Numbers
  http://www.rootsweb.com/~nshalifa/Films.htm

- LDS Film Numbers for Ontario Birth Registrations
  http://www.geocities.com/Heartland/9332/lds-b.htm

- LDS Film Numbers for Ontario Death Registrations
  http://www.geocities.com/Heartland/9332/lds-d.htm

- LDS Film Numbers for Ontario Marriage Registrations
  http://www.geocities.com/Heartland/9332/lds-m.htm

- LDS Microfilm for Loudoun Co., VA
  http://www.rootsweb.com/~valoudou/film.htm

- LDS Microfilms and Microfiche for Coshocton Co., Ohio
  http://www.pe.net/~sharyn/lds.html

- LDS Polish Jewish LDS Microfilms ~ JewishGen
  http://www.jewishgen.org/jri-pl/jri-lds.htm

- Microfilm of Connecticut Records at LDS Family History Centers
  http://www.cslnet.ctstateu.edu/ldsmicro.htm

- Scottish Reference Information
  http://www.ktb.net/~dwills/13300-scottishreference.htm
  An extensive list of parish numbers and microfilm numbers to aid in doing Scottish research at an LDS Family History Center.

◆ Miscellaneous LDS Church & Genealogy Resources

- All About Mormons
  http://www.mormons.org/
  - Family History
    http://www.mormons.org/daily/family_history/index.htm

- Brigham Young University Libraries
  http://www.byu.edu/libraries/
  - Utah Valley Regional Family History Center
    http://www.lib.byu.edu/dept/uvrfhc/
    On the fourth floor of the Harold B. Lee Library on the campus of Brigham Young University

- Church of Jesus Christ of Latter-day Saints
  http://www.lds.org/

- Family History / Genealogy from the Unofficial Homepage for Austria of The Church of Jesus Christ of Latter-day Saints
  http://www.ettl.co.at/mormon/english/gen_gy.htm

- JSB Family History Lab
  http://reled.byu.edu/famhist/

- The Mormon Connection - The LDS Church and Genealogy
  http://www.leisterpro.com/doc/Articles/MormConn.html

- Submitting Names for Temple Ordinances
  http://www.pcola.gulf.net/~llscott/templery.htm

- The WWW L.D.S. Visitors Center
  http://www.mich.com/~romulans/lds.html

◆ Pedigree Resource File

- FamilySearch Internet Genealogy Service
  http://www.familysearch.org/
  THE genealogy web site of the LDS Church. Includes the ability to search the IGI, the Ancestral File, the Family History Library Catalog, and web site submissions. Also has user mailing lists, online ordering of FHL research materials and allows you to preserve your own research online.

  - Family Search Online Distribution Center - Software Products
    http://www.ldscatalog.com/cgi-bin/ncommerce3/Category Display?cgrfnbr=1804&cgmenbr=1402&CGRY_NUM=1678 &RowStart=1&LocCode=FH
    Inexpensive, quality CD-ROM databases available from the Church of Jesus Christ of Latter-day Saints.

  - Pedigree Resource File
    http://www.familysearch.org/Eng/Search/frameset_search. asp?PAGE=prf/search_PRF.asp
    Family history records submitted by individuals through the FamilySearch Internet Genealogy Service.

  - Tips on How to Search the Pedigree Resource File
    http://www.familysearch.org/Eng/Search/prf/searchprf_ hints.asp

◆ Professional Researchers, Volunteers & Other Research Services

People Specializing in Research or Resources at the Family History Library in Salt Lake City

- Ancestors Lost and Found ~ Salt Lake City, Utah
  http://www.ancestorsfound.com/

- The Basque Genealogy Homepage Research Services
  http://www.primenet.com/~fybarra/Research.html
  Specializing in Basque records from the province of Vizcaya. These records are on microfilm at the Salt Lake Family History Library, but do not get circulated.

- Genealogy Ancestors Search
  http://www.wasatch.com/~lance/
  By Family Ties Research, Sandy, Utah.

- Genie Genealogy Research
  http://genealogy.hypermart.net
  Genie Genealogy provides professional genealogy research services to help you find your ancestors. Whether you're a novice or expert, discover your family tree now - quickly and affordably. Genie also offers web page design, picture scanning, report printing, data entry, and LDS-specific genealogy services.

- GSS - Genealogical Search Services
  http://www.itsnet.com/~gss/
  Research at the Family History Library in Salt Lake City, Utah.

- Heirlines Family History and Genealogy Research Services
  http://www.heirlines.com

- Heritage Consulting and Services ~ Salt Lake City, Utah
  http://www.heritageconsulting.com/

- Natalie Cottrill Genealogical Research
  http://www.nataliesnet.com/
  United States research at the Salt Lake City, Utah Family History Library.

- The Official Iowa Counties Professional Genealogist and Researcher's Registry for LDS - Salt Lake City, Utah, USA
  http://www.iowa-counties.com/gene/lds.htm

- Professional Genealogist - Cottrill and Hefti, Salt Lake City
  http://www.progenealogists.com/
  Document retrieval and ancestry research, Salt Lake City, Utah.

- Quik-Search - A Document Retrieval Service for Genealogists and Historians
  http://www.inconnect.com/~gjnixon/
  Document retrieval from the Family History Library Collections in Salt Lake City, Utah.

- Salt Lake Chapter - Association of Professional Genealogists
  http://www.lofthouse.com/slcapg/slcapg.htm

- SAMPUBCO
  http://www.wasatch.com/~dsam/sampubco/index.htm
  Will Testators Indexes, Naturalization Records Indexes and Census Indexes online. You can order copies of the original source documents for a small fee. This service pertains only to entries found in the indexes on this web site.

◆ Publications, Software & Supplies

- Audacious Women: Early British Mormon Immigrants
  http://www.amazon.com/exec/obidos/ISBN=1560850663/markcyndisgenealA/
  A book by Rebecca Bartholomew.

- AudioTapes.com - Genealogical Lectures on Cassette Tapes - Salt Lake
  http://www.audiotapes.com/search2.asp?Search=Salt+Lake
  And Ancestral File
  http://www.audiotapes.com/search2.asp?Search=ancestral+file

- Family Search Online Distribution Center - Software Products
  http://www.ldscatalog.com/cgi-bin/ncommerce3/CategoryDisplay?cgrfnbr=1804&cgmenbr=1402&CGRY_NUM=1678&RowStart=1&LocCode=FH
  Inexpensive, quality CD-ROM databases available from the Church of Jesus Christ of Latter-day Saints.

- Hearts Turned to the Fathers: A History of the Genealogical Society of Utah, 1894-1994
  http://www.amazon.com/exec/obidos/ISBN=0842523278/markcyndisgenealA/
  A book by James B. Allen.

- LDS Booksellers Association
  http://www.ldsba.com/

- PAF 4.0 User's Guide
  http://help.surnameweb.org/genprograms/paf40.htm
  From the SurnameWeb site.

- PAF Help-Guide
  http://www.HeritageQuest.com/genealogy/books/html/paf.html
  Book for sale from Heritage Quest.

- PAF Review - Home Page
  http://www.saintclair.org/paf/
  an electronic newsletter containing information for genealogists who use the PAF ("Personal Ancestral File") genealogy software program.

- TempleReady
  http://reled.byu.edu/famhist/handouts/templeready.htm
  From the Family History Lab at BYU. Detailed instructions on how to make temple submissions.

LIBRARIES, ARCHIVES & MUSEUMS – GENERAL
http://www.cyndislist.com/lib-gen.htm

Category Index:
◆ General Library Resources

◆ Telnet

◆ General Library Resources

● Amazon.com Genealogy Bookstore - Library
http://www.amazon.com/exec/obidos/external-search/?
keyword=library+genealogy&tag=markcyndisgenealA/

● ALA - Links to Library Web Resources
http://www.ala.org/library/weblinks.html

● AudioTapes.com - Genealogical Lectures on Cassette
Tapes – Library
http://www.audiotapes.com/search2.asp?Search=library
And Libraries
http://www.audiotapes.com/search2.asp?Search=libraries

● Australian Libraries Gateway (ALG)
http://www.nla.gov.au/libraries/

● The Canadian Library Index
http://www.lights.com/canlib/

● The Care and Feeding of Genealogical Librarians
http://www.ancestry.com/columns/george/01-23-98.htm
From "Along Those Lines..." by George G. Morgan.

● CURL - The Consortium of University Research
Libraries ~ British Isles
http://www.curl.ac.uk/

● CyberTree Genealogy Database - Dewey Decimal
System Other Helpful Codes
http://www.kuhnslagoon.net/cybertree/howto/dew-othr.html

● CyberTree Genealogy Database - Dewey Decimal
System United States
http://www.kuhnslagoon.net/cybertree/howto/dew-stat.html

● Directory of Virginia Libraries - Library of Virginia
http://www.lva.lib.va.us/ldnd/dir/index.htm

● EARL: The Consortium for Public Library
Networking ~ U.K.
http://www.earl.org.uk/

● Find Libraries Online
gopher://libgopher.cis.yale.edu:70/11/

● Gabriel - Gateway to Europe's National Libraries
http://portico.bl.uk/gabriel/en/welcome.html

● Genealogical Library Master Catalog
http://www.onelibrary.com/
A CD-ROM directory of over 300,000 Family Histories, Local
Histories and Genealogical Sources at eighteen libraries.

● Genealogy Libraries in the U.S.
http://www.greenheart.com/rdietz/gen_libs.htm

● HYTELNET on the World Wide Web
http://www.lights.com/hytelnet/
An index of library catalogs online, with links to the telnet addresses
and complete logon instructions. For Telnet, you must have Telnet
software to access. Make note of logon and password when you
begin. Read more about Telnet on the "Libraries, Archives &
Museums - General" category page on Cyndi's List.
http://www.CyndisList.com/lib-gen.htm#Telnet

● International Federation of Library Associations and
Institutions
http://www.ifla.org/

● IPL - Internet Public Library
http://www.ipl.org/

● Librarian's Guide to Helping Patrons with
Genealogical Research
http://home.tampabay.rr.com/centans/genguide.html
Genealogy tutorial for librarians so they can be better prepared to
help their patrons with research. Also includes information on
building genealogy collections and forming genealogy societies at
your library.

● Librarians Serving Genealogists: Genealogy
Libraries on the WWW
http://www.genealogy.org/~holdiman/LSG/libraries.html

● The Library of Congress - State Library Web Listing
http://lcweb.loc.gov/global/library/statelib.html

● Library Resource List
http://www.dpi.state.wi.us/dpi/dlcl/pld/lib_res.html
From the State of Wisconsin, a list of over 500 Internet resources
that will be of interest to the library community.

● LIBRIS - Nationellt Bibliotekssystem - Svenska
Bibliotek I Samverkan / Union Catalogue of Swedish
Libraries
http://www.libris.kb.se/

● Libweb - Library Servers via WWW
http://sunsite.berkeley.edu/Libweb/

● Map Libraries on the World Wide Web
http://www-map.lib.umn.edu/map_libraries.html

● New England Genealogy Collections Outside of New
England
http://home.att.net/~SGTAYLOR1/NECollections.html
A list of outstanding New England genealogy collections (societies,

libraries, archives, etc.) not in New England. Arranged in state alpha order with links to the "collections" and library search engines.

- OCLC Online Computer Library Center Home Page
  http://www.oclc.org/oclc/menu/home1.htm
- Public Libraries of Europe
  http://dspace.dial.pipex.com/town/square/ac940/eurolib.html
- Public Libraries with Internet Services
  http://www.halcyon.com/treasure/virtual/library.html
- Ready, 'Net, Go! Archival Internet Resources
  http://www.tulane.edu/~lmiller/ArchivesResources.html
- SJCPL's List of Public Libraries with WWW Services
  http://sjcpl.lib.in.us/homepage/PublicLibraries/PubLibSrvs GpherWWW.html
- SJCPL's List of Public Libraries with Telnet Services
  http://sjcpl.lib.in.us/homepage/PublicLibraries/PubLibSrvs Telnet.html
- Standards for Using Records Repositories and Libraries
  http://www.ngsgenealogy.org/about/content/committees/ gene_stan.html
  Recommended by the National Genealogical Society.
- State Library Web Sites
  http://www.dpi.state.wi.us/dltcl/pld/statelib.html
- The UK Public Libraries Page
  http://dspace.dial.pipex.com/town/square/ac940/ukpublib.html
- United States Depository Libraries
  http://www.facsnet.org/report_tools/findem_fast/ appendix.html
  "A list of federal regional depository libraries, so-called super libraries".
- U.S. Public Libraries with Websites
  http://www.capecod.net/epl/public.libraries.html
- What Are Archives?
  http://americanhistory.si.edu/archives/a-1.htm
  From the Archives Center of the National Museum of American History.
- The World Wide Web Library Directory
  http://www.webpan.com/msauers/libdir/index.html
  Over 6,600 libraries in 117 countries.
- Yahoo!...History...Archives
  http://dir.yahoo.com/Arts/Humanities/History/Archives/
- Yahoo!...Reference...Libraries
  http://dir.yahoo.com/Reference/Libraries/
  - Yahoo!...Reference...Academic Libraries
    http://dir.yahoo.com/Reference/Libraries/Academic_ Libraries/
  - Yahoo!...Reference...Digital Libraries
    http://dir.yahoo.com/Reference/Libraries/Digital_Libraries/

- Yahoo!...Reference...Public Libraries
  http://dir.yahoo.com/Reference/Libraries/Public_Libraries/
- Yahoo!...Reference...School Libraries
  http://dir.yahoo.com/Reference/Libraries/School_Libraries/
- Yahoo!...Reference...Special Collections
  http://dir.yahoo.com/Reference/Libraries/Special_ Collections/
- Yahoo!...Reference...U.S. State Libraries
  http://dir.yahoo.com/Reference/Libraries/U_S__State_ Libraries/
- Yahoo!...Science...Maps...Libraries
  http://dir.yahoo.com/Science/Geography/Cartography/Maps/ Libraries/

◆ Telnet

Many libraries have their card catalogs available online via Telnet. Telnet allows you to access a computer in another location via your Internet connection, and interact with that computer as if you were sitting right in front of it. For instance, using Telnet, you can search Quest, the Seattle Public Library's catalog. In order to access a catalog via Telnet, you will need to be sure that you have Telnet access through your Internet Service Provider and you will also need to have Telnet software installed on your computer. You can download a shareware version of Telnet software from any of these shareware sites:

- NONAGS - Shareware & Freeware
  http://www.nonags.com/
- Stroud's Consummate Winsock Applications
  http://cws.internet.com/
- TUCOWS, The Worlds Best Collection of Internet Software
  http://www.tucows.com

You can use the Telnet software after dialing up your Internet connection or you can configure your web browser to launch your Telnet software program each time you click on a Telnet link on a web site. In Netscape, go to: Options, General Preferences, Apps. In the Telnet Application box, fill in the complete path, directory and file name for your Telnet software program. For example, on my computer I have: C:\Internet Stuff\Tera Term Telnet\ttermpro.exe You will find several Telnet links throughout the list of libraries on Cyndi's List. Once you've accessed a Telnet site be sure to make a note of the logon and password in case you are asked for it again during your Telnet session. See Telnet Tips for some basic instructions and help in using Telnet.
http://www.galaxy.com/hytelnet/TELNET.html

- SJCPL's List of Public Libraries with Telnet Services
  http://sjcpl.lib.in.us/homepage/PublicLibraries/PubLibSrvs Telnet.html
- Telnet Tips
  http://www.galaxy.com/hytelnet/TELNET.html

LOOKUPS & FREE SEARCHES BY VOLUNTEERS
http://www.cyndislist.com/lookups.htm

- Ancestral Findings
http://www.ancestralfindings.com/
This site will provide one FREE search per day of a wide range of genealogy historical records, including birth, marriage, census, land, military indexes, and state records.

- Books We Own List
http://www.rootsweb.com/~bwo/index.html
A list of resources owned by others who are willing to do lookups in them.

- Free4U, Genealogy Look-Ups
http://www.genealogy4u.co.uk/
Genealogy Look-Ups in the North East Lincolnshire area of England.

- Free Genealogy Lookups
http://www.ih2000.net/genealogy/sites/lookups.htm
From a variety of CDs and books listed on this page.

- Genealogy Helplist
http://helplist.org/
List of volunteers willing to help others in specific areas.

- Genealogical CDs
http://seidata.com/~genealogy/cdlist.html
Specialized free lookups from people who own genealogy CDs.

- Genealogy Look Up Forum
http://www.expage.com/page/genealogylookup

- The Genealogy Researcher's Trading Post
http://www.geocities.com/Heartland/7748/
Trade research work with other genealogists in distant locations.

- Genealogy Resources--Look-Ups
http://www.concentric.net/~Cande/lookups.shtml

- GenSwap - Free Online Genealogy Data and More
http://www.genswap.com/
GenSwap is a site where you can post to swap genealogy data you have, or for data that you want. You can also find professional genealogists, people willing to do free lookups, and links to sites with online genealogy data.

- GMW Helpers
http://www.citynet.net/mostwanted/ra/assist.htm
A list of research volunteers from Genealogy's Most Wanted.

- The Look-up Exchange
http://www.geocities.com/Heartland/Plains/8555/lookup.html
A county-by-county list of resources covering England, Scotland, Wales and the Isle of Man, made available by volunteers for free look-ups.

- Lookups from Privately Owned Publications
http://genealogyfix.tripod.com/private.html
People volunteering to do lookups in their own personal library.

- Nova's Genealogy Page
http://www.buffnet.net/~nova/
Nova will search her Social Security Death Index CD-ROM for you.

- Random Acts of Genealogical Kindness
http://raogk.rootsweb.com/
"The volunteers of this movement are agreeing once per month to either videotape cemeteries, etc., or to visit county courthouses in the county (or area of a country) they live. The cost to you would be reimbursement of costs incurred in granting your request (video tape, copy fees, etc.)".

- Resources with a Wide Array of Genealogical Interest
http://jungclas.com/common/resource.htm

- World Family Tree Genealogical CDs
http://seidata.com/~genealogy/cdwftlist.html
Specialized free lookups from people who own World Family Tree CDs.

LOST & FOUND

http://www.cyndislist.com/lost.htm

- Adopt-A-Photo - Penny Duncan's Photos for Distribution
  http://freepages.genealogy.rootsweb.com/~adoptaphoto/
  Many have residents of Mason and Logan Counties, Illinois.

- Ancestral Photos
  http://pw1.netcom.com/~cityslic/photos.htm
  Pictures found at auctions and in antique stores.

- Echoes of the Past Archive
  http://www.echoesarchive.com/
  A facility for the storage, restoration and preservation of original historic and genealogical materials and to make them available to the public for research and documentation.

- Family Papers
  http://www.teleport.com/~jimren/
  A service that helps family historians locate and own original documents pertaining to their ancestors.

- Ford and Nagle
  http://users.erinet.com/31363/fordand.htm
  Historians, Genealogists, and Collectors of Antique Family Photos, Family Bibles, and Family Documents

- Antique Family Photos - A-C
  http://users.erinet.com/31363/photos.htm
  D-G
  http://users.erinet.com/31363/photod-g.htm
  H-Q
  http://users.erinet.com/31363/photos2.htm
  R-Z
  http://users.erinet.com/31363/photo3.htm
  Family Bibles
  http://users.erinet.com/31363/family.htm
  Family Documents
  http://users.erinet.com/31363/docs1.htm

- Granny's Lost & Found
  http://www.geocities.com/~grannys_attic/lostfoun.html
  Lost: out of print books and films. Found: old photos, journals, documents, and letters.

- IAGenWeb Lost & Found
  http://www.rootsweb.com/~iaphotos/

- ILGenWeb Orphan Treasures Project
  http://www.rootsweb.com/~ilphotos/

- Lost Leaves Photos
  http://www.lostleavesphotos.com/pages/main.html

- Michigan's Orphan Artifacts
  http://www.rootsweb.com/~migenweb/artifact.htm

- Minnesota USGenWeb Family Photos, Autobiographies & Other Treasures
  http://www.rootsweb.com/~mngenweb/photos.html

- NEGenWeb Ancestors' Lost & Found
  http://www.rootsweb.com/~neresour/ancestors/index.html
  Dedicated to reuniting families with the Nebraska memorabilia their ancestors left behind: photos, family Bibles, etc.

- Old Photos Seeking New Homes - Linnie (Vanderford) Poyneer
  http://www.geocities.com/linniev2/album/index.html
  Austin, Baker, Boyce/Bayce, Bunce, Butterfield, Carr, Ford, Hall, Hart, Hobbs, Holmsberg, Keadle, Keadle, Lillie, Loske, Ludwig, Martin, Milton, Payne, Port, Pierce, Sinclair, Skinner, Swartout, Starke, Weller, Wise.

- PhotoFind Searchable Database
  http://www.everton.com/photofind/phfind.html

- Somebody's Links - Found treasures seeking family connections
  http://cgi.rootsweb.com/~genbbs/genbbs.cgi/SomebodysLinks

- Where Are Your Family Photographs?
  http://genealogyphotos.com/
  A company dedicated to reuniting people interested in their genealogy with previously unknown or lost family photographs.

- Your Family Heirlooms
  http://www.yourantiques.com/

- Your Past Connections, Inc.
  http://www.pastconnect.com/
  Helps you find original items from your family's past. Items such as: cards, letters, certificates, books, etc.

LOYALISTS

http://www.cyndislist.com/loyalist.htm

Category Index:

- ◆ General Resource Sites
- ◆ Locality or Regiment Specific
- ◆ Mailing Lists, Newsgroups & Chat

- ◆ People & Families
- ◆ Publications, Software & Supplies
- ◆ Societies & Groups

◆ General Resource Sites

- A Loyalist Bibliography
  http://www.magma.ca/~ekipp/loybib.htm

- Loyalist Institute Home Page
  http://www.royalprovincial.com/
  While the material contained herein is for use by anyone interested in this aspect of the American Revolution, it is primarily intended for those with a working background in Loyalist studies.

- Loyalist Units
  http://www.brigade.org/loy.html
  From the Brigade of the American Revolution Home Page.
  http://www.brigade.org/welcome.html

- The Olive Tree Genealogy: Loyalist Section
  http://olivetreegenealogy.com/loy/index.shtml

- On the Trail of Our Ancestors / Loyalist Muster Roll Index
  http://www.ristenbatt.com/genealogy/loyalind.htm

- Paul Bunnell will search your Loyalist ancestors - Send e-mail to Paul for details
  mailto:benjamin@capecod.net

- United Empire Loyalist
  http://geocities.com/Heartland/1146/loyalist.html
  A personal web site with many UEL links as well.

◆ Libraries, Archives & Museums

- Loyalist Collection - Harriet Irving Library
  http://www.lib.unb.ca/Collections/Loyalist/
  University of New Brunswick.

- New York State Library - Loyalist Records
  http://unix2.nysed.gov/genealogy/loyalist.htm

◆ Locality or Regiment Specific

- British Headquarters Papers, New York City 1774-1783 The Carleton Papers
  http://www2.magmacom.com/~ekipp/kingname.htm
  The King's Name Project.

- Butler's Rangers
  http://iaw.on.ca/~awoolley/brang/brang.html

- Georgia Loyalists
  http://www.rootsweb.com/~gagenweb/records/loyalist.htm
  A list of 225 Georgia Loyalists published in a 1783 issue of the Georgia Gazette. The list is part of Virginia Crilley's Georgia Military History web page.

- The King's Men: Loyalist Units in New York and North America
  http://www.geocities.com/Athens/Delphi/4171/kingsmen.htm

- The Loyal American Regiment 1777-1783
  http://users.erols.com/candidus/lar.htm
  New York Loyalists from lower Dutchess and Westchester Counties.

- The Loyalists
  http://www.rootsweb.com/~canwgw/ns/digby/perm2/loyalist.htm
  From the Digby County, Nova Scotia GenWeb site.

- Loyalists of Digby, Nova Scotia
  http://www.rootsweb.com/~canwgw/ns/digby/perm2/article2.htm
  And Black Loyalists of Digby, Nova Scotia
  http://www.rootsweb.com/~canwgw/ns/digby/perm2/article1.htm

- Maine Loyalists
  http://www.rootsweb.com/~usgenweb/me/washington/loyalist.htm

- Maryland Loyalism and the American Revolution
  http://users.erols.com/candidus/index.htm
  Recommended by the History Channel and the Discovery Channel. Contains regimental history, a muster roll, pictures and extensive links.

- The Maryland Loyalist Battalion Home Page
  http://users.erols.com/grippo/

- Muster Roll at Gulliver's Hole, St. Mary's Bay and Sissiboo ~ Digby, Nova Scotia, Canada
  http://www.rootsweb.com/~canwgw/ns/digby/perm2/muster1.htm

- The United Empire Loyalists' Association of Canada ~ Toronto, Ontario, Canada
  http://people.becon.org/~uela/uela1.htm

◆ Mailing Lists, Newsgroups & Chat

- AMERICAN-REVOLUTION Mailing List
  http://www.rootsweb.com/~jfuller/gen_mail_wars.html
  #AMERICAN-REVOLUTION
  For the discussion of events during the American Revolution and genealogical matters related to the American Revolution. The French-Indian Wars and the War of 1812 are also suitable topics for discussion.

- loyalists-in-canada Mailing List
  http://www.rootsweb.com/~jfuller/gen_mail_country-can.html
  #LOYALIST
  For those with loyalist ancestors to help one another research their loyalist history and to post any facts on the subject that they desire. Loyalists are defined as those who left the United States for Canada after the American Revolution for a number of reasons.

- UNITED-EMPIRE-LOYALIST Mailing List
  http://www.rootsweb.com/~jfuller/gen_mail_country-can.html
  #UNITED-EMPIRE-LOYALIST
  For anyone with a genealogical, cultural or historical interest in the United Empire loyalists who came to Canada from the United States during and after the American Revolution.

◆ People & Families

- Ancestors of Julia and Tim RICE
  http://www.familytreemaker.com/users/r/i/c/Craig--Rice/index.html

- Edward KIPP: Family History, KIP/KIPP Genealogy, Loyalist Genealogy, Princeton, Ontario, Alumni Western, HTML Basics
  http://www2.magmacom.com/~ekipp/index.html

- William OSTERHOUT, United Empire Loyalist
  http://citd.scar.utoronto.ca/ANTC28/Osterhout.html

◆ Publications, Software & Supplies

- Amazon.com Genealogy Bookstore - Loyalist
  http://www.amazon.com/exec/obidos/external-search/?keyword=loyalist+genealogy&tag=markcyndisgenealA/

- AudioTapes.com - Genealogical Lectures on Cassette Tapes - Loyalist
  http://www.audiotapes.com/search2.asp?Search=Loyalist

- Frontier Press Bookstore - Loyalists
  http://www.frontierpress.com/frontier.cgi?category=loyal

- GenealogyBookShop.com - Loyalists
  http://www.genealogybookshop.com/genealogybookshop/files/General,Loyalists/index.html
  The online store of Genealogical Publishing Co., Inc. & Clearfield Company.

- Global Genealogy - Books - The Loyalists
  http://www.globalgenealogy.com/loyalist.htm

- Heritage Books, Inc. - Loyalist
  http://www.heritagebooks.com/loyal.htm

- Loyalist Books, Documents and Related Materials
  http://www.shelburne.nscc.ns.ca/nsgna/sg/sg_loy.htm

LUTHERAN

http://www.cyndislist.com/lutheran.htm

Category Index:

◆ General Resource Sites

◆ Libraries, Archives & Museums

◆ Locality Specific

◆ Mailing Lists, Newsgroups & Chat

◆ Publications, Software & Supplies

◆ Societies & Groups

◆ General Resource Sites

● Evangelical Lutheran Church in America
http://www.elca.org/index.html

● The Hall of Church History - The Reformers
http://www.gty.org/~phil/rformers.htm
An interesting site with definitions, descriptions and links to a variety of resources for each religious group it highlights.

● The "Lutheran Roots" Genealogy Exchange
http://www.aal.org/LutheransOnline/Gene_Ex/
A family registry and message board for those researching surnames or specific individuals with Lutheran connections (German, Norwegian, Scandinavian, etc.).

● Martin Luther Genealogy
http://luther.hmcom.com
Over 8,000 names in alphabetical order all connected to Martin Luther.

◆ Libraries, Archives & Museums

● Catalog of the Lutheran records in the Archdiocesan Archive in Poznan ~ Poland
http://www.wsdsc.poznan.pl/arch/catallu.htm

● Concordia Historical Institute
http://chi.lcms.org/
The Department of Archives and History of the Lutheran Church-- Missouri Synod. From its beginning in 1847, the Synod has provided for its archives, first entrusting the responsibility for maintaining the church's records to the synodical secretary. In 1927 the Institute was incorporated by interested individuals in the church to provide for the preservation of its records. In 1959 the Synod designated the Institute as its official repository.

  o Family History
  http://chi.lcms.org/famhist.asp

  o Holdings & Collections
  http://chi.lcms.org/collections/index.html

● Evangelical Lutheran Church in America Archives
http://www.elca.org/os/archives/intro.html

  o ELCA Regional/Synodical Archives
  http://www.elca.org/os/archives/regsyn.html

  o Genealogy Help from ELCA Archives
  http://www.elca.org/os/archives/geneal.html

● Lutheran Archives Center at Philadelphia
http://www.ltsp.edu/krauth/archives.html
From the Lutheran Theological Seminary at Philadelphia.

● Lutheran Church of Australia - Lutheran Archives
http://www.lca.org.au/resources/archives.html

● Lutheran Electronic Archive - Project Wittenberg
http://www.ctsfw.edu/etext/
Dedicated to posting on the internet a cross-section of classic and historic texts written by Lutherans.

● North Carolina Synod Archives
http://www.nclutheran.org/resources/archives.html
From the Evangelical Lutheran Church in America.

● Pacific Lutheran University - Robert A. L. Mortvedt Library ~ Tacoma, Washington
http://www.plu.edu/~libr/

  o Archives and Special Collections
  http://www.plu.edu/~archives/home.html

    ● ELCA Region I Archives (Alaska, Southwest and Northwest Washington, Eastern Washington/Idaho and Oregon)
    http://www.plu.edu/~archives/elca/nwlhs_index.html

    ● Scandinavian Immigrant Experience Collection
    http://www.plu.edu/~archives/sie/sieindex.html
    A depository of historical materials relating to immigrants to the Pacific Northwest from Denmark, Finland, Iceland, Norway and Sweden. Closely tied to the Regional Archives of the Evangelical Lutheran Church of America.

    ● University Archives
    http://www.plu.edu/~archives/ua/uarch.html

● SGGEE Lutheran Church Archives Page
http://www.sggee.org/PolishLutheranArchives.html
From the Society for German Genealogy in Eastern Europe.

● Swenson Swedish Immigration Center
http://www.augustana.edu/administration/swenson/index.htm
Located at Augustana College. This is a national archives and research institute for the study of Swedish immigration to North America. Holdings are extensive, including materials from all sectors of the Swedish immigrant community in the USA and Canada, including immigration studies, settlement histories, immigrant literature and arts, Swedish-American biography and genealogy, as well as Swedish-American church life and social organizations.

◆ Locality Specific

- Friedens Lutheran Church Family History & Genealogy Research Page
  http://freepages.genealogy.rootsweb.com/~bruckner/friedens.htm
  Genealogical/historical records of Friedens Evangelical Lutheran Church, founded in 1745 Orange/Guilford County, N.C.

- Genealogy - Church History - St. Nicholas German Lutheran Church - Franklin County Indiana, Salt Creek Township, Peppertown
  http://members.aol.com/sycophant4/ChurPast.htm

- Georgia Lutheran Records
  http://www.sos.state.ga.us/Archives/rs/lutherans.htm
  From the Georgia Department of Archives & History.

- History of the Evangelical Lutheran Tennessee Synod
  http://freepages.genealogy.rootsweb.com/~janelle/lutherans.htm
  Excerpts from the History of the Evangelical Lutheran Tennessee Synod by Socrates Henkel, published in 1890.

- Lutheran Churches of Brooklyn Before 1900
  http://www.geocities.com/Heartland/Fields/5171/lutheran_churches.html

- Lutheran Records of New York City in The NYG&B Library
  http://www.nygbs.org/info/articles/Lutheran_Records.html
  From the New York Genealogical and Biographical Society.

- Records of St. Michael's and St. Martin's Lutheran Church - Iredell County ~ North Carolina
  http://www.iredell.com/i_church.htm

- St. John's Evangelical Lutheran Church Records ~ Yates County, New York
  http://www.linkny.com/~history/StJohn.htm

- St. John's Lutheran Church ~ Charleston, South Carolina
  http://www.stjohns-lutheran.org/
  Established in 1742. Their web page includes instructions for genealogical inquiries.

- St. Nicholas German Lutheran Church Book
  http://members.aol.com/sycophant4/ChurRec.htm
  From Peppertown, Salt Creek Township, Franklin County, Indiana.

- St. Peter's Lutheran Church Records ~ Heidelburg, Ontario
  http://members.home.net/fahidy/church.htm

- Volhynia - St. Petersburg Records Database for Lutherans from Volhynia
  http://pixel.cs.vt.edu/library/stpete/volhynia/
  Extraction project for Lutheran parishes in 19th century Volhynia.

- Zion Lutheran Church of Helotes - Archives
  http://lonestar.texas.net/~gdalum/archives.html
  Records for the Zion Lutheran Church of Helotes located in northwestern San Antonio, Bexar, Texas.

◆ Mailing Lists, Newsgroups & Chat

- Genealogy Resources on the Internet - Religions / Churches Mailing Lists
  http://www.rootsweb.com/~jfuller/gen_mail_religions.html
  Most of the mailing list links below point to this site, wonderfully maintained by John Fuller

- BIBLICAL-GENEALOGY Mailing List
  http://www.rootsweb.com/~jfuller/gen_mail_religions.html#BIBLICAL-GENEALOGY
  For the discussion and sharing of information regarding genealogy in biblical times.

- LUTHERAN-ROOTS Mailing List
  http://www.rootsweb.com/~jfuller/gen_mail_religions.html#LUTHERAN-ROOTS
  And the Lutheran Roots Mailing List Page
  http://homepages.rootsweb.com/~mdtaffet/lutheran-roots_list.htm
  For anyone with a genealogical interest in the Lutheran Church, both Evangelical and Reformed.

◆ Publications, Software & Supplies

- Amazon.com Genealogy Bookstore - Lutheran
  http://www.amazon.com/exec/obidos/external-search/?keyword=lutheran+genealogy&tag=markcyndisgenealA/

- AudioTapes.com - Genealogical Lectures on Cassette Tapes - Lutheran
  http://www.audiotapes.com/search2.asp?Search=Lutheran

◆ Societies & Groups

- Lutheran Historical Conference
  http://www.luthhist.org/index.html
  Lutheran archivists, librarians, historians and other interested individuals and institutions are invited to become members of the Lutheran Historical Conference, an interdisciplinary organization founded in 1962.

- Lutheran Historical Society ~ Gettysburg, Pennsylvania
  http://www.abs.net/~lhs/

MAGAZINES, JOURNALS, COLUMNS & NEWSLETTERS

Print & Electronic Publications for Genealogy
http://www.cyndislist.com/magazine.htm

Category Index:

◆ Columns & Columnists
◆ E-mail Newsletters

◆ E-zines ~ Electronic Magazines & Newsletters
◆ Print Magazines, Journals & Newsletters

◆ Columns & Columnists

• ComputerCredible Magazine: Index of Computer Genealogy Articles
http://www.credible.com/geneallist.html
By Alan Mann.

• Family Search by Sharon Burns
http://connections.oklahoman.net/familysearch/home.html
From the Oklahoman Online newspaper.

• Genealogical Thoughts by Gary Boyd Roberts
http://www.newenglandancestors.org/whatsnewsection/whats
new_notable_relations.asp
A weekly web site column from the NEHGS Senior Research Scholar.

• Genealogy & Technology Articles by Mark Howells
http://www.oz.net/~markhow/writing/

• Genealogy Bulletin's Weekly Feature Article by Acclaimed Author and Genealogist, William Dollarhide
http://www.GenealogyBulletin.com/HTML/current.html

   o Dollarhide's Rules for Genealogy
   http://www.GenealogyBulletin.com/HTML/rules.html

   o Genealogy Bulletin Archives
   http://www.genealogybulletin.com/archives/

• Genealogy by Ken Thomas
http://www.accessatlanta.com/living/family/genealogy/
Columnist for The Atlanta Journal-Constitution in Georgia.

• Genealogy Etc. by Donna Potter Phillips
http://www.GenealogyBulletin.com/HTML/etc.html
From Genealogy Bulletin, featuring news, notes and tips for genealogists.

• International Society of Family History Writers and Editors, Inc. (ISFHWE)
http://www.rootsweb.com/~cgc/index.htm
Formerly known as the Council of Genealogy Columnists.

• Lineage Links - My Heritage Quest Column
http://www.CyndisList.com/hqllinks.htm
A list of links featured in Cyndi's column for Heritage Quest Magazine, a bi-monthly publication.

• Mic Barnette's Columns, Genealogy & History
http://www.geocities.com/BourbonStreet/Delta/7552/
From The Houston Chronicle.

• Mobile Genealogical Society: The News Stand
http://www.siteone.com/clubs/mgs/newstand.htm
Links to genealogical columns that appear in newspapers and accept announcements and/or queries.

• rootdig.com - Ancestry Daily News Articles-alphabetical listing
http://www.rootdig.com/ancestryabc.html
From Michael Neill's Genealogy Web Site.

• Ruby M. Cusack - Genealogy & Queries
http://personal.nbnet.nb.ca/rmcusack/
Genealogical and Queries Columns in the Good Life edition of the Saint John Times Globe, Saint John, New Brunswick, Canada.

• Shaking Your Family Tree
http://www.rootsweb.com/~rwguide/syft/
A weekly newspaper column by Myra Vanderpool Gormley for the LA Times Syndicate. Hosted by RootsWeb.com. Archived columns are categorized on this page as well.

• Shaking Your Family Tree
http://www.uftree.com/bin/fg_auth?/GenealogyNewsstand/
ShakingTree/shakingtree.html
By Myra Vanderpool Gormley, alternate copies of the same column above, hosted by Ultimate Family Tree.

• Shaking Your Family Tree
http://www.ancestry.com/columns/myra/index.htm
By Myra Vanderpool Gormley, alternate copies of the same column above, hosted by Ancestry.com.

• Tri-City Herald Genealogy Online
http://www.tri-cityherald.com/genealogy/
Dozens of helpful columns written by Terry Day and Donna Potter Phillips.

• The Virtual Texan
http://www.virtualtexan.com/roots.htm
Column by Brenda Burns Kellow, featured in the Plano Star Courier, Plano, Texas.

• Winn Parish Newspaper Column - Family History by Annette Womack ~ Louisiana
http://homepages.rootsweb.com/~acwomack/news.htm

◆ E-mail Newsletters

• Ancestry Daily News
http://www.ancestry.com/library/view/news/articles/daily
news.asp

- The CyndisList Mailing List
  http://www.CyndisList.com/maillist.htm
  An announcements-only list for information regarding daily updates to the Cyndi's List web site.

- Eastman's Online Genealogy Newsletter
  http://www.rootscomputing.com/

- EMAZING - Genealogy Tip of the Day
  http://www.emazing.com/genealogy.htm
  By George Morgan, available Monday through Friday on this web site or via e-mail subscription.

- Family History News
  http://www.galethompson.freeserve.co.uk/familyhistory|news.htm
  A weekly e-mail newsletter covering the world of genealogy in the United Kingdom and beyond.

- Family Tree Finders
  http://www.sodamail.com/site/ftf.shtml
  A Monday through Friday newsletter that provides interesting and useful information for tracing your family tree. It's geared to beginners and experienced family tree trackers of any age! Written by well known genealogist, Rhonda R. McClure.

- Family Tree Magazine's Free Weekly Email Update
  http://www.familytreemagazine.com/newsletter.asp
  Brief but helpful research, organization and preservation tips free to genealogists and family historians on our electronic mailing list. Plus, pointers to new information and articles on the Family Tree Magazine web site and information on new issues of Family Tree Magazine and on genealogy books from Betterway Books.

- Genealogy Today Newsletter
  http://www.enoch.com/genealogy/newslet.htm

- Generations Heritage Quest Newsletter
  http://www.sierra.com/sierrahome/newsletter/familytree/
  Genealogy talk and tips, as well as product offers and information from SierraHome.

  o Generations Heritage Quest Newsletter Archive
    http://www.sierra.com/sierrahome/newsletter/familytree/archive/

- Joe's Genealogy E-mail Newsletter
  http://www.zen.co.uk/home/page/joe.houghton/NEWSLTR.HTM

- Legends and Legacies Free Newsletter "Hot Chocolate"
  http://www.legends.ca/newsletter/newsletter.html
  Published twice annually in May and November.

- MISSING LINKS: A Weekly Newsletter for Genealogists
  http://www.rootsweb.com/~mlnews/
  And the archive of back-issues
  ftp://ftp.rootsweb.com/pub/mlnews/
  Homepage of Missing Links, weekly genealogy E-Zine with a sample issue, plus its archives dating back to August 1996. To subscribe, send a NEW e-mail message to MISSING-LINKS-L-request@rootsweb.com and in the body of the message enter only one word: subscribe.
  By Julia M. Case and Myra Vanderpool Gormley.

- Paper Roots, A Weekly Round-Up of Genealogy in the News
  http://people.ne.mediaone.net/ehwoodward/paperroots.html
  By Hobson Woodward.

- RootsWeb Review: Genealogical Data Cooperative Weekly News
  http://www.rootsweb.com/~review/
  And the archive of back-issues
  ftp://ftp.rootsweb.com/pub/review/
  Homepage of RootsWeb Review, a weekly E-zine, pertaining to the news of RootsWeb Data Cooperative and of matters of interest to online genealogists worldwide. To subscribe, send a NEW e-mail message to ROOTSWEB-REVIEW-L-request@rootsweb.com and in the body of the message enter only one word: subscribe.

- Treasure Map's Free Monthly E-mail Newsletter
  http://www.amberskyline.com/treasuremaps/sub.html

◆ E-zines ~ Electronic Magazines & Newsletters

- Ancestry.com Columnists - Ancestry Family History Columns
  http://www.ancestry.com/learn/library/columnists/main.htm

  o Ancestry Daily News
    http://www.ancestry.com/library/view/news/articles/dailynews.asp
    Daily by Juliana Smith.

    - Ancestry Daily News Archive
      http://www.ancestry.com/library/view/news/articles/d_p_1_archive.asp

  o The Family History Compass
    http://www.ancestry.com/library/view/columns/compass/compass.asp
    New each Monday by Juliana Smith.

    - The Family History Compass Archive
      http://www.ancestry.com/library/view/columns/compass/d_p_1_archive.asp

  o Kip's Tips
    http://www.ancestry.com/library/view/columns/tips/tips.asp
    Alternating on Tuesdays, by Kip Sperry.

    - Kip's Tips Archive
      http://www.ancestry.com/library/view/columns/tips/d_p_1_archive.asp

  o Digital Genealogy
    http://www.ancestry.com/library/view/columns/digital/digital.asp
    Alternating on Tuesdays, by Drew Smith.

    - Digital Genealogy Archive
      http://www.ancestry.com/library/view/columns/digital/d_p_1_archive.asp

  o For the Record
    http://www.ancestry.com/library/view/columns/record/record.asp
    Alternating on Tuesdays, by various authors.

    - For the Record Archive
      http://www.ancestry.com/library/view/columns/record/d_p_1_archive.asp

o Dick Eastman Online
http://www.ancestry.com/library/view/columns/eastman/
d_p_1_archive.asp
New each Wednesday by Dick Eastman.

• Dick Eastman Online Archive
http://www.ancestry.com/library/view/columns/eastman/
archive.asp

o Get it Together
http://www.ancestry.com/library/view/columns/together/
together.asp
New each Thursday by Elizabeth Kelley Kerstens, CGRS.

• Get it Together Archive
http://www.ancestry.com/library/view/columns/together/
d_p_1_archive.asp

o "Along Those Lines..."
http://www.ancestry.com/library/view/columns/george/
george.asp
New each Friday by George G. Morgan.

• "Along Those Lines..." Archive
http://www.ancestry.com/library/view/columns/george/
d_p_1_archive.asp

• The Cemetery Column - Cemeteries & Genealogy
http://www.interment.net/column/index.htm
An electronic journal on everything associated with cemeteries, including news about cemeteries worldwide, reviews of other websites & books, the art of cemetery sculptures & architecture, and genealogical research.

• EMAZING - Genealogy Tip of the Day
http://www.emazing.com/genealogy.htm
By George Morgan, available Monday through Friday on this web site or via e-mail subscription.

• The Family Tree Online
http://www.teleport.com/~binder/famtree.shtml

• The Genealogy Bulletin
http://www.GenealogyBulletin.com/
Everything for the Genealogist & Family Researcher! A Heritage Quest publication.

• GenealogyNews.com - Covering the News Important to Your Research
http://www.genealogynews.com/

• Generations Heritage Quest Newsletter
http://www.sierra.com/sierrahome/newsletter/familytree/
Genealogy talk and tips, as well as product offers and information from SierraHome.

o Generations Heritage Quest Newsletter Archive
http://www.sierra.com/sierrahome/newsletter/familytree/
archive/

• Journal of Online Genealogy
http://www.onlinegenealogy.com/
Promoting the use of computers and the Internet in family history research.

• A Time for Sharing - Native American SIG Newsletter
http://members.aol.com/kathyehyde/news/index.htm

◆ Print Magazines, Journals & Newsletters

• Alabama Heritage Magazine
http://www.as.ua.edu/heritage/

• The American Genealogist [TAG]
http://www.alltel.net/~amgen/
Founded 1922 by Donald Lines Jacobus. An independent quarterly journal, dedicated to the elevation of genealogical scholarship through carefully documented analyses of genealogical problems and through short compiled genealogies.

• American Genealogy Magazine
http://store.yahoo.com/datatrace/

• Ancestry Magazine
http://www.ancestry.com/learn/publications/ancmag.htm

• Australian Family Tree Connections Magazine
http://www.aftc.com.au/

• The Computer Genealogist
http://www.nehgs.org/publications/necg.htm
A newsletter from the New England Historic Genealogical Society.

• Computers in Genealogy
http://www.sog.org.uk/cig/
A Quarterly Publication of the Society of Genealogists, U.K.

• The Dorchester County, Maryland Genealogical Magazine
http://members.tripod.com/~dcgm/dcgmindex.html
Records provided: tombstone, church, probate, newspaper, marriage, death certificates, military, queries.

• Everton's Genealogical Helper
http://www.everton.com/
Since 1947 - the largest genealogical magazine in the world.

• Family Chronicle Magazine
http://www.familychronicle.com/

• Family History News
http://www.globalserve.net/~parrspub/
Canadian genealogical publication.

• Family Puzzlers, The Next Generation
http://www.avana.net/~amymws/heritage.htm

• Family Tree Magazine ~ England
http://www.family-tree.co.uk/
The outstanding postal-delivery periodical for UK genealogical research. Each monthly issue includes in-depth articles by internationally-recognized genealogists on the unique aspects of researching ancestors from the United Kingdom. Regular features include "Questions & Answers", "Pitfalls & Possibilities", "News from the SoG" and "View from the Public Record Office". Hundreds of reader's surname interests are included in each issue along with a computer interest section. Family Tree Magazine's postal book service is outstanding for getting useful reference books on UK genealogy.

• Family Tree Magazine
http://www.familytreemagazine.com/

- Genealogical Computing
  http://www.ancestry.com/learn/publications/gencomp.htm

- Genealogical Journal
  http://www.infouga.org/journal.htm
  From the Utah Genealogical Association.

- The Genealogists Magazine: Indexes
  http://www.sog.org.uk/genmag/
  The quarterly publication of the Society of Genealogists, UK.

- Genealogy & Local History in Greater London - London Ancestor
  http://www.users.globalnet.co.uk/~longen/
  A Journal of source data for the study of genealogy and local history in Greater London, England, mostly pre 1880, and where possible pre 1837.

- Genealogy and Tennessee - GENEALOGY FRIENDS:Partyline News
  http://users.aol.com/genny1/done.html
  FREE Queries, mail or e-mail.

- GEN-EDITOR Mailing List
  http://www.rootsweb.com/~jfuller/gen_mail_general.html#GEN-EDITOR
  For editors/publishers of genealogical, surname and family newsletters to have a place to discuss and share ideas and tips.

- Generations Newsletter
  http://www.rupert.net/~lkool/page13.html
  A genealogy newsletter published 6 times per year (to be increased to 12 very soon), which contains articles of interest to anyone researching their family history in South Africa.

- GEN-MAT-REQUEST Mailing List
  http://www.rootsweb.com/~jfuller/gen_mail_material.html#GEN-MAT
  For anyone who has an interest in the buying or selling of new or used genealogical materials (e.g., books, newsletters, CDs, magazines).

- GEN-MAT-15 Mailing List
  http://www.rootsweb.com/~jfuller/gen_mail_material.html#GEN-MAT-15
  For anyone who desires to post the availability of new or used genealogical materials (e.g., books, newsletters, CDs, magazines) or services for sale at a price of $15 or less.

- Greene Genes: A Genealogical Quarterly About Greene County, New York
  mailto:mailto:PMorrowJ@cs.com
  For details send e-mail to Patricia Morrow at PMorrowJ@cs.com.

- Heritage Quest Magazine
  http://www.HeritageQuest.com/

- History Magazine
  http://www.history-magazine.com/
  From the publishers of Family Chronicle Magazine.

- The Indiaman Magazine
  http://www.indiaman.freeserve.co.uk/index.html
  Genealogical magazine dedicated to people researching their ancestry of British and European origin in India and southern Asia from 1600 to the 20th century.

- Irish Roots Magazine HomePage
  http://www.iol.ie/~irishrts/

- Isle of Man Family History Society Journal
  http://www.ee.surrey.ac.uk/Contrib/manx/famhist/fhsjidx.htm
  Volume i 1979 to Volume xii 1990, articles scanned and online!

- Journals & Newsletters covering Genealogy in South Africa
  http://www.geocities.com/Heartland/8256/others.html

- Kansas Historical Quarterly Index, 1931-1977
  http://history.cc.ukans.edu/carrie/kancoll/kbibl/khquart.html

- Kentucky Explorer Magazine
  http://www.kentuckyexplorer.com/
  Kentucky's Most Unique History & Genealogy Publication.

- Local History Magazine ~ United Kingdom
  http://www.local-history.co.uk/

- Manx Methodist Historical Society Newsletter
  http://www.ee.surrey.ac.uk/Contrib/manx/methdism/mhist/index.htm
  Index to Newsletters 1-24.

- Mennonite Family History Magazine
  http://www.masthof.com/pages/mfh.html

- Minnesota Genealogical Journal
  http://www.parkbooks.com/Html/mgjbroch.html

- The New England Historical and Genealogical Register
  http://www.nehgs.org/publications/register.htm
  Quarterly published by the New England Historic Genealogical Society.

- NGS/CIG Digest
  http://www.ngsgenealogy.org/about/content/publications/cig_digest.html
  From the Computer Interest Group, from the National Genealogical Society in the U.S. This is bound within each issue of the NGS Newsletter.

- NGS Newsletter
  http://www.ngsgenealogy.org/about/content/publications/newslet.html
  Bi-monthly, from the National Genealogical Society in the U.S.

- NGS Quarterly - A Journal for Today's Family Historian
  http://www.ngsgenealogy.org/about/content/publications/quarterly.html
  From the National Genealogical Society in the U.S.

- Northwest Ohio Quarterly
  http://www.history.utoledo.edu/NWOQ.HTML
  A joint publication of the History Department of the University of Toledo, the Maumee Valley Historical Society and the Toledo-Lucas County Public Library.

- Old Huntsville Magazine ~ Alabama
  http://oldhuntsville.com/

- O Progresso - The Quarterly Newsletter of the Portuguese Historical & Cultural Society (PHCS)
http://www.dholmes.com/o-prog.html

- Preservings ~ Steinbach, Manitoba, Canada
http://www.hshs.mb.ca/
The magazine/journal of the Hanover Steinbach Historical Society, Inc. The Hanover and Steinbach area, originally known as the "East Reserve". The magazine's emphasis is on the period 1874-1910. Back issues are available for download.

- Prologue: Quarterly of the National Archives and Records Administration
http://www.nara.gov/publications/prologue/prologue.html
  - Current Table of Contents
  http://www.nara.gov/publications/prologue/current.html
  - Genealogy Notes
  http://www.nara.gov/publications/prologue/artlist.html#genea
  - Selected Prologue Articles
  http://www.nara.gov/publications/prologue/artlist.html

- Reunions Magazine Homepage
http://www.execpc.com/~reunions/
Family reunions, class reunions etc.

- Slovak Heritage Live
http://www.iarelative.com/bc_live.htm
A quarterly publication of the Slovak Heritage and Cultural Society of British Columbia.

- Southern Queries Genealogy Magazine
http://www.mindspring.com/~freedom1/sq/sq.htm

- STAMMBAUM: The Journal of German-Jewish Genealogical Research
http://www.jewishgen.org/stammbaum/index.html

- Tidewater Virginia Families
http://users.erols.com/tvf/
"A Magazine of History and Genealogy." An independent quarterly journal.

- Wandering Volhynians
http://pixel.cs.vt.edu/pub/sources/wv.txt
Or Wandering Volhynians - German-Volhynian Newsletter
http://feefhs.org/ca/frg-wv.html
A Magazine for the Descendants of Germans From Volhynia and Poland.

- Western Kentucky Journal
http://pw1.netcom.com/~cpalmer/wkj/wkj.htm

- The Wind-Mill: A Periodical of Frisian/Germanic Heritage
http://members.aol.com/gowindmill/index.html

- W.K.R.P. (Washington/Charlotte Kounty Records Preservation) Newsletter
mailto:shwkrp@aol.com
A quarterly newsletter concerning research being done in Washington Co., Maine and Charlotte County, New Brunswick. For details e-mail Sharon at: shwkrp@aol.com.

- Yahoo!...Genealogy...Magazines
http://dir.yahoo.com/Arts/Humanities/History/Genealogy/Magazines/

MAILING LISTS
http://www.cyndislist.com/mailing.htm

Category Index:
- Briefly Defined
- The Complete Resource for Genealogy Mailing Lists
- General Resource Sites
- General Mailing Lists
- Internet Resources
- Mailing List Archives

- Military
- Miscellaneous
- Newbies
- Newsletters (Read-only Mailing Lists)
- Queries & Surnames
- Vendors: Buy, Sell or Trade

◆ Briefly Defined

- Mailing lists are similar to newsgroups, but there are thousands of mailing lists for genealogy, making them a more popular forum.
  - Mailing lists are free to subscribe to and you participate in specific genealogical or historical discussions via e-mail.
  - There are specific mailing lists for a variety of genealogical and historical topics.
  - Some mailing lists are "gatewayed" or "mirrored" with newsgroups. This means that the same messages appear on both forums.
  - To participate in a mailing list you send e-mail commands to a computer software program (i.e. Listserv, Smartlist, etc.) in order to be automatically subscribed to the list. You send e-mail messages to a different address for that mailing list in order to communicate with the other subscribers.
  - Commonly used mailing list and newsgroup terms defined by NetLingo:
    http://www.netlingo.com/
    - Deja News Research Service
      http://www.netlingo.com/lookup.cfm?term=Deja%20News%20Research%20Service
    - FAQ (Frequently Asked Questions)
      http://www.netlingo.com/lookup.cfm?term=FAQ
    - Gateway
      http://www.netlingo.com/lookup.cfm?term=gateway%20
    - LISTSERV
      http://www.netlingo.com/lookup.cfm?term=listserv
    - Mailing List
      http://www.netlingo.com/lookup.cfm?term=mailing%20list

    - Majordomo
      http://www.netlingo.com/lookup.cfm?term=Majordomo
    - Moderated Mailing List
      http://www.netlingo.com/lookup.cfm?term=moderated%20mailing%20list
    - Netiquette
      http://www.netlingo.com/lookup.cfm?term=netiquette
    - Newsgroups
      http://www.netlingo.com/lookup.cfm?term=newsgroups
    - Signature File or Sig File
      http://www.netlingo.com/lookup.cfm?term=signature%20file
    - Spam
      http://www.netlingo.com/lookup.cfm?term=spam
    - Subscribe
      http://www.netlingo.com/lookup.cfm?term=subscribe
    - Thread
      http://www.netlingo.com/lookup.cfm?term=thread
    - USENET
      http://www.netlingo.com/lookup.cfm?term=USENET

◆ The Complete Resource for Genealogy Mailing Lists

- From Genealogy Resources On the Internet by John Fuller & Chris Gaunt:
  http://www.rootsweb.com/~jfuller/internet.html
  Start here for a complete listing of all the currently available mailing lists - including details for subscribing and descriptions of the topics covered. Mailing lists for various topics are linked on appropriate category pages all throughout Cyndi's List. Surname mailing lists are listed individually on each of the Surname category pages on Cyndi's List as well.
  http://www.CyndisList.com/surnames.htm

- Genealogy Resources: Mailing Lists
  http://www.rootsweb.com/~jfuller/gen_mail.html
  - Adoption
    http://www.rootsweb.com/~jfuller/gen_mail_adoption.html
  - African-Ancestored
    http://www.rootsweb.com/~jfuller/gen_mail_african.html

o Cemeteries/Monuments/Obituaries
http://www.rootsweb.com/~jfuller/gen_mail_cemetery.html

o Computing/Internet Resources
http://www.rootsweb.com/~jfuller/gen_mail_computing.html

o Countries other than USA
http://www.rootsweb.com/~jfuller/gen_mail.html#NON-USA
See the list, arranged by country, on the main index page.

o Genealogical Material/Services
http://www.rootsweb.com/~jfuller/gen_mail_material.html

o General Information/Discussion
http://www.rootsweb.com/~jfuller/gen_mail_info.html

o Jewish
http://www.rootsweb.com/~jfuller/gen_mail_jewish.html

o Native American
http://www.rootsweb.com/~jfuller/gen_mail_natam.html

o Religions/Churches (other than Jewish)
http://www.rootsweb.com/~jfuller/gen_mail_religions.html

o Software
http://www.rootsweb.com/~jfuller/gen_mail_software.html

o Surnames
http://www.rootsweb.com/~jfuller/gen_mail.html#SURNAMES
See the alphabetical table at the bottom of the main index page

- Surnames Found in Mailing Lists Entries
http://www-personal.umich.edu/~cgaunt/surnames/surnames-lists.html
Alphabetized links to the surname mailing list details on John's site, with cross-referenced links for all variant spellings.

o Uncategorized (some great lists)
http://www.rootsweb.com/~jfuller/gen_mail_general.html

o USA
http://www.rootsweb.com/~jfuller/gen_mail.html#USA
See the list, arranged by state, on the main index page.

o Wars/Military
http://www.rootsweb.com/~jfuller/gen_mail_wars.html

◆ General Resource Sites

- AOL NetFind | Newsgroup Etiquette
http://www.aol.com/netfind/scoop/newsgroup_etiquette.html

- AOL NetFind | Newsgroup Scoop Glossary
http://www.aol.com/netfind/scoop/newsgroup_glossary.html

- Basic newsgroup and mailing list "Netiquette"
http://www.woodgate.org/FAQs/netiquette.html

- FamilySearch - Collaboration E-Mail Lists
http://www.familysearch.org/Eng/Share/Collaborate/frameset_share.asp
Create your own genealogy mailing list easily with this service from the LDS church. Browse the list of current mailing lists and subscribe to lists in an instant.

- Genealogy Resources on the Internet: Mailing Lists
http://www.rootsweb.com/~jfuller/gen_mail.html

- Interlinks - E-Mail Discussion Groups
http://alabanza.com/kabacoff/Inter-Links/listserv.html

- Larry Stephens Genealogy Page - E-mail Lists I Own
http://php.indiana.edu/~stephenl/ownlists.htm

- ListServe.com Internet Power Tool - Publicly Accessible Mailing Lists
http://www.neosoft.com/internet/paml/

- LISTSERV Help - Larry Stephens Genealogy Page
http://php.indiana.edu/~stephenl/listhelp.htm

- LISTSERV – The Mailing List Management Classic
http://www.lsoft.com/listserv.stm
Software program that runs many mailing lists.

- Liszt: Searchable Directory of e-Mail Discussion Groups
http://www.liszt.com/

- Mailing Lists Are Fun!
http://www.ancestry.com/columns/george/03-13-98.htm
From "Along Those Lines..." by George Morgan.

- Maiser Help
http://itc.fgg.uni-lj.si/maiser.htm

- The Net: User Guidelines and Netiquette
http://www.fau.edu/netiquette/net/dis.html
For Listservs/Mailing Lists/ Discussion Groups, by Arlene Rinaldi.

- ONElist E-mail Communities
http://www.onelist.com/

- Researching with Friends, Cousins and Experts on Genealogy Mailing Lists
http://www.audiotapes.com/product.asp?ProductCode='FGS00-F-129'
Presentation by Cyndi Howells, available for sale on audio tape.

- RootsWeb.com
http://www.rootsweb.com/

o Genealogy Mailing Lists at RootsWeb
http://lists.rootsweb.com/
A categorized list of the mailing lists currently hosted on the RootsWeb servers.

- New or Adoptable Mailing Lists
http://resources.rootsweb.com/adopt/

o RootsWeb: FAQ: Mailing Lists - What Are They?
http://helpdesk.rootsweb.com/help/mail1.html

o RootsWeb: FAQ: Mailing Lists - Subscribing / Unsubscribing
http://helpdesk.rootsweb.com/help/mail2.html

o RootsWeb: FAQ: Mailing Lists - Subscriber Questions
http://helpdesk.rootsweb.com/help/mail3.html

o RootsWeb: FAQ: Mailing Lists - List Administrator Questions
http://helpdesk.rootsweb.com/help/mail4.html

o RootsWeb: FAQ: Mailing Lists - RootsWeb Questions
http://helpdesk.rootsweb.com/help/mail5.html

o RootsWeb: FAQ: Mailing Lists - Temporary List Administrators-Index of Volunteers
http://helpdesk.rootsweb.com/help/mail6.html

- Search the List of Lists
http://catalog.com/vivian/interest-group-search.html

- Vicki's Home Page - Genealogy Listservers, Newsgroups & Special Homepages
http://www.eskimo.com/~chance/lists.html
Great alphabetical list of Newsgroups and Mailing Lists with subscription details.

- Yahoo!...Mailing Lists
http://dir.yahoo.com/Computers_and_Internet/Internet/Mailing_Lists/

◆ General Mailing Lists

- Genealogy Resources on the Internet - General Information / Discussion Mailing Lists
http://www.rootsweb.com/~jfuller/gen_mail_info.html
Most of the mailing list links below point to this site, wonderfully maintained by John Fuller

- agenealogychat Mailing List
http://www.rootsweb.com/~jfuller/gen_mail_info.html
#agenealogychat
For chatting about genealogy including why we love it; how it feels when you find yet another ancestor; what do you do now and how do you do it; requests for lookups; new lists, resources, and URLs; and most anything else related to genealogy.

- ALT-GENEALOGY Mailing List
http://www.rootsweb.com/~jfuller/gen_mail_info.html
#ALT-GENEALOGY
Gatewayed with the alt.genealogy newsgroup. For general genealogical discussions.
news:alt.genealogy

- GenChat Mailing List
http://www.rootsweb.com/~jfuller/gen_mail_general.html
#GenChat
For discussions of anything having to do with genealogy.

- gene-helpline Mailing List
http://www.rootsweb.com/~jfuller/gen_mail_info.html
#gene-helpline

- Genexchange-L Mailing List
http://www.rootsweb.com/~jfuller/gen_mail_info.html
#Genexchange-L

- GenHelpNetwork Mailing List
http://www.rootsweb.com/~jfuller/gen_mail_info.html
#GenHelpNetwork
For genealogy help and anything else related to genealogy.

- GENMSC Mailing List
http://www.rootsweb.com/~jfuller/gen_mail_info.html
#GENMSC-L
Gatewayed with the soc.genealogy.misc newsgroup for general genealogical discussions that don't fit within one of the other soc.genealogy. newsgroups.*
new:soc.genealogy.misc

- GENMTD Mailing List
http://www.rootsweb.com/~jfuller/gen_mail_info.html
#GENMTD-L
Gatewayed with the soc.genealogy.methods newsgroup for the discussion of genealogy research techniques and resources.
news:soc.genealogy.methods

- GEN-ROOTERS Mailing List
http://www.rootsweb.com/~jfuller/gen_mail_religions.html
#GEN-ROOTERS
For members of the Church of Jesus Christ of Latter-day Saints to share ideas and helpful hints on the "how-to's" of genealogy.

- GEN-SHARE Mailing List
http://www.rootsweb.com/~jfuller/gen_mail_info.html
#GEN-SHARE
For "seasoned" genealogy researchers to share sources and get help with tough problems. This list is not for the posting of queries addressing searches for specific ancestors and is not recommended for those new to genealogy.

- GenTips Mailing List
http://www.rootsweb.com/~jfuller/gen_mail_general.html
#GenTips-L
For anyone who has an interest in genealogy. This list hopes to provide tips about obtaining genealogy records and is useful for both beginning genealogists and experts.

- H-Net Discussion Networks
http://www2.h-net.msu.edu/lists/
Dozens of mailing lists for history and social studies.

- Internet_Genealogy Mailing List
http://www.rootsweb.com/~jfuller/gen_mail_computing.html
#Internet_Genealogy
For students of Marthe Arends' Practical Internet Genealogy series of courses at Virtual University.

- RESEARCH-HOWTO Mailing List
http://www.rootsweb.com/~jfuller/gen_mail_general.html
#RESEARCH-HOWTO
For those who are just getting started in genealogy research and those who are not novices but need information on where to go when "dead ends" are encountered.

- ROOTS-L Mailing List
http://www.rootsweb.com/~jfuller/gen_mail_general.html
#ROOTS-L
Broad-based genealogy topics - over 10,000 subscribers.

◆ Internet Resources

- Genealogy Resources on the Internet - Computing / Internet Resources Mailing Lists
http://www.rootsweb.com/~jfuller/gen_mail_computing.html
Most of the mailing list links below point to this site, wonderfully maintained by John Fuller

- The CyndisList Mailing List
http://www.CyndisList.com/maillist.htm
An announcements-only list for information regarding daily updates to the Cyndi's List web site.

- FAMILYSEARCH Mailing List
http://www.rootsweb.com/~jfuller/gen_mail_computing.html
#FAMILYSEARCH
Designed to assist anyone with questions regarding use of the Internet for searching Family History. The FamilySearch internet

site and others are discussed for genealogical research such as searching, downloading, contributing, cross-referencing and microfilm numbers, and basic "getting started" questions are also discussed and welcomed. Surname specific research is not discussed and you must be a subscriber to post messages to the list.

- GENCMP Mailing List
  http://www.rootsweb.com/~jfuller/gen_mail_computing.html#GENCMP-L
  Gatewayed with the soc.genealogy.computing newsgroup for the discussion of genealogical computing and net resources.
  news:soc.genealogy.computing

- GEN-IRC Mailing List
  http://www.rootsweb.com/~jfuller/gen_mail_computing.html#GEN-IRC
  For anyone who has an interest in genealogy and is using or would like to use Internet Relay Chat (IRC) to communicate with other genealogists.

- GEN-SITE-SWAP Mailing List
  http://www.rootsweb.com/~jfuller/gen_mail_computing.html#GEN-SITE-SWAP
  For the swapping of good genealogy URLs.

- GEN-WEB-DESIGN Mailing List
  http://www.rootsweb.com/~jfuller/gen_mail_computing.html#GEN-WEB-DESIGN
  For the discussion and sharing of information regarding the design of genealogy web pages and associated databases.

- HTMLHELP Mailing List
  http://www.rootsweb.com/~jfuller/gen_mail_computing.html#HTMLHELP
  For helping genealogists who would like to place their web pages on the internet. This is the place to learn programming and to discuss uploading and design elements.

- NEW-GENLIST Mailing List
  http://www.rootsweb.com/~jfuller/gen_mail_computing.htm#NEW-GENLIST
  For announcing new genealogy mailing lists.

- NEW-GEN-URL Mailing List
  http://www.rootsweb.com/~jfuller/gen_mail_computing.html#NEW-GEN-URL
  For announcing new or updated genealogy-related web sites.

- RootsWeb Review: Genealogical Data Cooperative Weekly News
  http://www.rootsweb.com/~review/
  And the archive of back-issues
  ftp://ftp.rootsweb.com/pub/review/
  Homepage of RootsWeb Review, a weekly E-zine, pertaining to the news of RootsWeb Data Cooperative and of matters of interest to online genealogists worldwide. To subscribe, send a NEW e-mail message to ROOTSWEB-REVIEW-L-request@rootsweb.com and in the body of the message enter only one word: subscribe.

- WEB-NEWBIE Mailing List
  http://www.rootsweb.com/~jfuller/gen_mail_computing.html#WEB-NEWBIE
  For beginners who have questions on the Internet, Internet methods, genealogy on the Internet, and how to build a web page.

◆ Mailing List Archives

- List archives at LISTSERV.INDIANA.EDU
  http://listserv.indiana.edu/archives/index.html
  Browse through the online archives for several genealogy mailing lists run by Larry Stephens.

- ROOTS-L Mailing List
  http://www.rootsweb.com/roots-l/roots-l.html
  The Internet's First Genealogy Mailing List

  o ROOTS-L Archive - Text Messages via FTP
    ftp://ftp.rootsweb.com/pub/roots-l/messages/
    Browse through this index of messages from August 1996 through the present.

  o ROOTS-L Daily Index of Mailing List Messages
    http://www.rootsweb.com/roots-l/index/

  o ROOTS-L Search Page
    http://searches.rootsweb.com/roots-l.html
    A searchable form for all messages from 1987 through the present.

- Rootsweb List Archive Searches Using CNIDR's ISearch
  http://www.shelby.net/shelby/jr/robertsn/rwsearch.htm
  An unofficial set of recommendations on how to construct search queries on the Rootsweb archives that use the CNIDR search software - from John Robertson.

- RootsWeb Mailing Lists -- Interactive Search
  http://searches.rootsweb.com/cgi-bin/listsearch.pl

- RootsWeb Threaded Mailing List Archives
  http://archiver.rootsweb.com/

- Search Features for a RootsWeb Mailing List
  http://www.rootsweb.com/rootsweb/members/archives.html
  Search messages for the last 2-4 weeks via e-mail command.

◆ Military

- Also see these category pages on Cyndi's List for related mailing list links:
  Canada – Military
  http://www.CyndisList.com/milcan.htm
  Military Resources Worldwide
  http://www.CyndisList.com/milres.htm
  U.K. – Military
  http://www.CyndisList.com/miluk.htm
  U.S. Civil War
  http://www.CyndisList.com/cw.htm
  U.S. Military
  http://www.CyndisList.com/military.htm

- Genealogy Resources on the Internet - Wars / Military Mailing Lists
  http://www.rootsweb.com/~jfuller/gen_mail_wars.html
  Most of the mailing list links below point to this site, wonderfully maintained by John Fuller

- AMERICAN-REVOLUTION Mailing List
http://www.rootsweb.com/~jfuller/gen_mail_wars.html
#AMERICAN-REVOLUTION
For the discussion of events during the American Revolution and genealogical matters related to the American Revolution. The French-Indian Wars and the War of 1812 are also suitable topics for discussion.

- AMREV-HESSIANS Mailing List
http://www.rootsweb.com/~jfuller/gen_mail_wars.html
#AMREV-HESSIANS
For anyone with a genealogical interest in the Hessian soldiers (German auxiliary troops employed by King George III of England) who remained in America after the American Revolution.

- The Anglo Boer War Discussion Page
http://www.icon.co.za/~dup42/talk.htm
This mailing list is for the discussion of the Anglo Boer War and other military related topics pre-1900.

- BLACKWARHEROS Mailing List
http://www.rootsweb.com/~jfuller/gen_mail_wars.html#BLACK
WARHEROS
For anyone with a genealogical or historical interest in Black Americans who were "heros" during any war.

- FOB-LIST - Friends of the Boers - E-mail List
http://www.webcom.com/perspekt/eng/mlist/fob.html
The primary topic of this mailing list is the centenary commemoration of the 2nd Anglo Boer War (1899-1902).

- FRENCH-INDIAN Mailing List
http://www.rootsweb.com/~jfuller/gen_mail_wars.html
#FRENCH-INDIAN

- SEMINOLE-WARS Mailing List
http://www.rootsweb.com/~jfuller/gen_mail_wars.html
#SEMINOLE-WARS

- UNITED-EMPIRE-LOYALIST Mailing List
http://www.rootsweb.com/~jfuller/gen_mail_wars.html
#UNITED-EMPIRE-LOYALIST
For anyone with a genealogical, cultural or historical interest in the United Empire loyalists who came to Canada from the United States during and after the American Revolution.

- USWARS Mailing List
http://www.rootsweb.com/~jfuller/gen_mail_wars.html
#USWARS
For anyone with a genealogical interest in the wars and military actions in which the United States fought that is not directed toward a specific war or military action.

- USWARS-1800S Mailing List
http://www.rootsweb.com/~jfuller/gen_mail_wars.html
#USWARS-1800S
For anyone with a genealogical interest in the "little" wars fought by the United States during the 1800s (e.g., Mexican War, Spanish-American War, Indian wars).

- WARBRIDES Mailing List
http://www.rootsweb.com/~jfuller/gen_mail_wars.html
#WARBRIDES
For putting WWII war brides and their children in touch with others to share reminiscences.

- WARof1812 Mailing List
http://www.rootsweb.com/~jfuller/gen_mail_wars.html
#WARof1812

- WW20-ROOTS-L Mailing List
http://www.rootsweb.com/~jfuller/gen_mail_wars.html
#WW20-ROOTS-L
For the discussion of genealogy in all 20th century wars.

◆ Miscellaneous

- ADOPTEES Mailing List
http://www.rootsweb.com/~jfuller/gen_mail_general.html
#ADOPTEES
For legal adoptees and "adoptee-lites" (people who were raised without one or both birth parents, but who were never legally adopted) to seek advice in conducting a search.

- ADOPT-FR Mailing List
http://www.rootsweb.com/~jfuller/gen_mail_general.html
#ADOPT-FR

- adopt-gene Mailing List
http://www.rootsweb.com/~jfuller/gen_mail_general.html
#adopt-gene
For the discussion of problems related to adoption.

- ADOPTING Mailing List
http://www.rootsweb.com/~jfuller/gen_mail_general.html
#ADOPTING
For anyone touched by adoption. This list offers search help, support, and tips on research related to adoption.

- ADOPTION Mailing List
http://www.rootsweb.com/~jfuller/gen_mail_general.html
#ADOPTION
Discussions of anything and everything connected with adoption.

- BlackSheep Mailing List
http://www.rootsweb.com/~jfuller/gen_mail_general.html
#BlackSheep
And the official web page
http://homepages.rootsweb.com/~blksheep/
For the International Black Sheep Society of Genealogists (IBSSG) which includes all those who have a dastardly, infamous individual of public knowledge and ill-repute somewhere in their family ... preferably in their direct lines. This individual must have been publicly pilloried in disgrace for acts of a significantly anti-social nature.

- emigration-ships Mailing List
http://www.rootsweb.com/~jfuller/gen_mail_general.html
#EMIGRATION-SHIPS
A mailing list for anyone who wants to discuss the ships their ancestors arrived on or post passenger lists for any ships.

- Families Touched by Adoption Mailing List
http://genweb.net/~famad/
For anyone personally touched by adoption and wishing to trace/share their heritage, genealogists seeking biological/adoptive family information to include an adoptee on their family tree, and for sharing guidelines for searching public records.

- Family_Bible Mailing List
http://www.rootsweb.com/~jfuller/gen_mail_general.html
#Family_Bibles
For the entry ONLY of information on any and all family bibles.

- **FOLKLORE Mailing List**
  http://www.rootsweb.com/~jfuller/gen_mail_general.html
  #FOLKLORE
  A mailing list for the exchange of folklore - folk medicine and recipes.

- **GENEALIB Mailing List**
  http://www.rootsweb.com/~jfuller/gen_mail_general.html
  #GENEALIB
  For librarians who specialize in genealogy.

- **GEN-EDITOR Mailing List**
  http://www.rootsweb.com/~jfuller/gen_mail_general.html
  #GEN-EDITOR
  For editors/publishers of genealogical, surname and family newsletters to have a place to discuss and share ideas and tips.

- **GenHumor Mailing List**
  http://www.rootsweb.com/~jfuller/gen_mail_general.html
  #GenHumor
  For the exchange of genealogy and family humor including poems and jokes.

- **GEN-MEDIEVAL Mailing List**
  http://www.rootsweb.com/~jfuller/gen_mail_general.html
  #GEN-MEDIEVAL
  Gatewayed with the soc.genealogy.medieval newsgroup for genealogy and family history discussion among people researching individuals living during medieval times.
  news:soc.genealogy.medieval

- **GEN-ROYAL Mailing List**
  http://www.rootsweb.com/~jfuller/gen_mail_general.html
  #GEN-ROYAL

- **GEN_SOCIETIES Mailing List**
  http://www.rootsweb.com/~jfuller/gen_mail_general.html
  #GEN_SOCIETIES
  For persons involved with establishing a local genealogical society in order to share program ideas, discuss means of promoting growth within a group, discuss how to work with libraries, and other related topics.

- **GenToday Mailing List**
  http://www.rootsweb.com/~jfuller/gen_mail_general.html
  #GenToday
  For the online newsletter, Genealogy Today, for the discussion and sharing of information among subscribers for genealogy in any place and at any time.
  http://www.enoch.com/genealogy/newslet.htm

- **GEN-TRIVIA-UNIVERSAL Mailing List**
  http://www.rootsweb.com/~jfuller/gen_mail_general.html
  #GEN-TRIVIA-UNIVERSAL
  For genealogy trivia collected from any country. This is an offshoot of the GEN-TRIVIA-ENG list where one can share ancestral recipes, poems, rhymes, ditties, slang words, sayings, etc.

- **GEN-UNSOLVED-MYSTERIES Mailing List**
  http://www.rootsweb.com/~jfuller/gen_mail_general.html
  #GEN-UNSOLVED-MYSTERIES
  For people whose family genealogies include "unsolved mysteries." Postings should include only mysterious disappearances or appearances, unsolved murders, questionable incarcerations, and other mysterious or unsolved events in an ancestor's life. Postings should not include "brick walls" since these would be repetitive of the content of other lists.

- **GLSHIPS Mailing List**
  http://www.rootsweb.com/~jfuller/gen_mail_states-gen.html
  #GLSHIPS
  For anyone who is researching ancestors who participated in the shipping industry on the Great Lakes of the northeastern United States.

- **HOMESPUN Mailing List**
  http://www.rootsweb.com/~jfuller/gen_mail_general.html
  #HOMESPUN
  For those who want to have a bit of fun reminiscing. Subscribers are welcome to share memories, traditions, poems, humor, stories, recipes, folklore and home remedies.

- **IIGS-UNIVERSITY Mailing List**
  http://www.rootsweb.com/~jfuller/gen_mail_general.html
  #IIGS-UNIVERSITY
  For volunteers who are working on the International Internet Genealogical Society (IIGS) University project.

- **IIGS-UNIVERSITY-LIBRARY Mailing List**
  http://www.rootsweb.com/~jfuller/gen_mail_general.html
  #IIGS-UNIVERSITY-LIBRARY
  For volunteers who are working on the International Internet Genealogical Society (IIGS) University Library project.

- **itinerantroots Mailing List**
  http://www.onelist.com/subscribe.cgi/itinerantroots
  For genealogy resources relating to itinerant professions: circus, theatre, music hall, vaudeville, fairs, showmen, portable theatres, etc.

- **Mariners Mailing List**
  http://www.rootsweb.com/~jfuller/gen_mail_general.html
  #Mariners
  For anyone who is researching their seafaring ancestors.

- **METISGEN Mailing List**
  http://www.rootsweb.com/~jfuller/gen_mail_general.html
  #METISGEN
  For the discussion and sharing of information regarding the Metis and their descendants. The Metis are North America's Fur Trading Children ... the new nation of individuals born within North America from the first unions of natives and whites.

- **MOMS_N_ME-ROOTS Mailing List**
  http://www.rootsweb.com/~jfuller/gen_mail_general.html
  #MOMS_N_ME-ROOTS
  To aid moms of all ages, but especially those with young children, in researching their family. Also welcome are any ideas for helping mothers teach their children about their heritage and the importance of family research.

- **NOTABLE-WOMEN-ANCESTORS Mailing List**
  http://www.rootsweb.com/~jfuller/gen_mail_general.html
  #NOTABLE-WOMEN-ANCESTORS
  For the discussion of female ancestors (famous and not-so-famous) and methods of researching women in conjunction with the NWA web site
  http://www.rootsweb.com/~nwa
  And the NWA Newsletter "Notable Women Ancestors: The Journal of Women's Genealogy and History".
  http://www.rootsweb.com/~nwa/news.html

- **Photo Generations - Home of the PhotoGen Mailing List Page**
  http://www.city-gallery.com/photogen/
  The Photography and Genealogy Mailing List.

- ProResearchers Mailing List
  http://www.rootsweb.com/~jfuller/gen_mail_general.html
  #ProResearchers
  Just for Professional Researchers to discuss their industry.

- RESEARCH-TRIP Mailing List
  http://www.rootsweb.com/~jfuller/gen_mail_general.html
  #RESEARCH-TRIP
  For anyone who is planning a research trip to share tips and discuss all aspects of logistics, resources, and accommodations.

- SALEM-WITCH Mailing List
  http://www.rootsweb.com/~jfuller/gen_mail_states-ma.html
  #SALEM-WITCH
  And the associated web page
  http://www.ogram.org/17thc/salem-witch-list.shtml
  A genealogy and history mailing list for descendants of the people involved in the Salem Witchcraft Trials of 1692 -- the accusers and the accused, the afflicted and the executed, as well as the magistrates, clergy, jurors, and anyone affected by the proceedings.

- TheShipsList Mailing List
  http://www.rootsweb.com/~jfuller/gen_mail_general.html
  #TheShipsList
  For anyone interested in the ships our ancestors migrated on. Subjects include emigration/immigration, ports of entry, ports of departure, ship descriptions and history, passenger lists and other related information.

- UFO-ROOTS Mailing List
  http://www.rootsweb.com/~jfuller/gen_mail_general.html
  #UFO-ROOTS
  For those whose ancestors arrived from outer space to make connections with others sharing this problem, discuss their ancestry, and provide advice on possible avenues for further research.

- WORDS Mailing List
  http://www.rootsweb.com/~jfuller/gen_mail_general.html
  #WORDS
  And the associated web page
  http://www.rootsweb.com/~genepool/amerispeak.htm
  A light-hearted discussion of English-English/American-English phrases and how they might have originated.

◆ Newbies

- GEN-NEWBIE-L Mailing List
  http://www.rootsweb.com/~jfuller/gen_mail_info.html
  #GEN-NEWBIE-L
  A mailing list where people who are new to computers and genealogy may interact using a computer's e-mail program.

  o GEN-NEWBIE-L Home Page
    http://www.rootsweb.com/~newbie/

- GENTEEN Mailing List
  http://www.rootsweb.com/~jfuller/gen_mail_info.html
  #GENTEEN-L
  For teenagers and young adults who are interested in genealogical research or others who have suggestions or ideas for young genealogists.

- Lost_Newbies Mailing List
  http://www.rootsweb.com/~jfuller/gen_mail_info.html
  #Lost_Newbies
  For people who are new to genealogy and/or the use of the Internet in genealogical research.

- NEWGEN Mailing List
  http://www.rootsweb.com/~jfuller/gen_mail_info.html
  #NEWGEN
  Created to assist those who are quite new to genealogy.

- ROOTS-L Mailing List
  http://www.rootsweb.com/~jfuller/gen_mail_info.html
  #ROOTS-L
  Broad-based genealogy topics - over 10,000 subscribers.

- WEB-NEWBIE Mailing List
  http://www.rootsweb.com/~jfuller/gen_mail_computing.html
  #WEB-NEWBIE
  For beginners who have questions on the Internet, Internet methods, genealogy on the Internet, and how to build a web page.

◆ Newsletters (Read-only Mailing Lists)

- Ancestry Daily News
  http://www.ancestry.com/dailynews/dailynews.htm

- The CyndisList Mailing List
  http://www.CyndisList.com/maillist.htm
  An announcements-only list for information regarding daily updates to the Cyndi's List web site.

- Eastman's Online Genealogy Newsletter
  http://www.rootscomputing.com/

- Family Tree Finders
  http://www.sodamail.com/site/ftf.shtml
  A Monday through Friday newsletter that provides interesting and useful information for tracing your family tree. It's geared to beginners and experienced family tree trackers of any age! Written by well known genealogist, Rhonda R. McClure.

- Family Tree Magazine's Free Weekly Email Update
  http://www.familytreemagazine.com/newsletter.asp
  Brief but helpful research, organization and preservation tips free to genealogists and family historians on our electronic mailing list. Plus, pointers to new information and articles on the Family Tree Magazine web site and information on new issues of Family Tree Magazine and on genealogy books from Betterway Books.

- Genealogy Today Newsletter
  http://www.enoch.com/genealogy/newslet.htm

- Generations Family Heritage Newsletter
  http://www.sierra.com/sierrahome/newsletter/familytree/
  From SierraHome Family Tree.

- Heritage Quest eNewsLETTER
  http://www.HeritageQuest.com

- Joe's Genealogy E-mail Newsletter
  http://www.zen.co.uk/home/page/joe.houghton/
  NEWSLTR.HTM

- MISSING LINKS: A Weekly Newsletter for Genealogists
  http://www.rootsweb.com/~mlnews/
  And the archive of back-issues
  ftp://ftp.rootsweb.com/pub/mlnews/
  Homepage of Missing Links, weekly genealogy E-Zine with a sample issue, plus its archives dating back to August 1996. To subscribe, send a NEW e-mail message to MISSING-LINKS-L-

request@rootsweb.com *and in the body of the message enter only* one word: subscribe
By Julia M. Case and Myra Vanderpool Gormley.

- Paper Roots, A Weekly Round-Up of Genealogy in the News
  http://people.ne.mediaone.net/ehwoodward/paperroots.html
  By Hobson Woodward.

- RootsWeb Review: Genealogical Data Cooperative Weekly News
  http://www.rootsweb.com/~review/
  And the archive of back-issues
  ftp://ftp.rootsweb.com/pub/review/
  Homepage of RootsWeb Review, a weekly E-zine, pertaining to the news of RootsWeb Data Cooperative and of matters of interest to online genealogists worldwide. To subscribe, send a NEW e-mail message toROOTSWEB-REVIEW-L-request@rootsweb.com and in the body of the message enter only one word: subscribe.

- Treasure Maps's Monthly E-mail Newsletter
  http://www.firstct.com/fv/sub.html

◆ Queries & Surnames

- Genealogy Resources on the Internet - "General" Surname Mailing Lists
  http://www.rootsweb.com/~jfuller/gen_mail_surnames-gen.html
  Most of the mailing list links below point to this site, wonderfully maintained by John Fuller

- GOONS-L Mailing List
  http://www.rootsweb.com/~jfuller/gen_mail_general.html#GOONS-L
  For members of the Guild of One-Name Studies (GOONS) to promote discussion of matters concerned with One-Name Studies and the Guild.

- ROLL-CALL Mailing List
  http://www.rootsweb.com/~jfuller/gen_mail_surnames-gen.html#ROLL-CALL
  For the posting of "roll calls" (lists) of the surnames you are researching so that others can determine if there is a common interest.

- RSL-UPDATE Mailing List
  http://www.rootsweb.com/~jfuller/gen_mail_surnames-gen.html#RSL-UPDATE
  The RootsWeb Surname List database monthly update of new surnames.

- soc.genealogy.surnames.* newsgroups and SURNAMES-* mailing lists
  http://www.rootsweb.com/~surnames/

- Surname Mailing Lists - Genealogy Resources on the Internet
  http://www.rootsweb.com/~jfuller/gen_mail.html
  See the alphabetical listing at the bottom of the main index.

- SURNAME-ORIGINS Mailing List
  http://www.rootsweb.com/~jfuller/gen_mail_surnames-gen.html#SURNAME-ORIGINS
  For the discussion of the etymology (word origin) of surnames, as well as the geographic origins of surnames.

- SURNAME-QUERY Mailing List
  http://www.rootsweb.com/~jfuller/gen_mail_surnames-gen.html#SURNAME-QUERY
  For users to send queries on specific surname searches.

- SURNAMES Mailing List
  http://www.rootsweb.com/~jfuller/gen_mail_surnames-gen.html#SURNAMES
  Gatewayed with the soc.genealogy.surnames.global newsgroup. Surname queries central database.
  news:soc.genealogy.surnames.global

- SURNAMES-BRITAIN Mailing List
  http://www.rootsweb.com/~jfuller/gen_mail_country-unk.html#SURNAMES-BRITAIN
  Gatewayed with the soc.genealogy.surnames.britain newsgroup. For surname queries related to Great Britain.
  news:soc.genealogy.surnames.britain

- SURNAMES-CANADA Mailing List
  http://www.rootsweb.com/~jfuller/gen_mail_surnames-gen.html#SURNAMES-CANADA
  Gatewayed with the soc.genealogy.surnames.canada newsgroup. For surname queries related to Canada.
  news:soc.genealogy.surnames.canada

- SURNAMES-GERMAN Mailing List
  http://www.rootsweb.com/~jfuller/gen_mail_surnames-gen.html#SURNAMES-GERMAN
  Gatewayed with the soc.genealogy.surnames.german newsgroup. For surname queries related to German speaking countries.
  news:soc.genealogy.surnames.german

- SURNAMES-IRELAND Mailing List
  http://www.rootsweb.com/~jfuller/gen_mail_country-unk.html#SURNAMES-IRELAND
  Gatewayed with the soc.genealogy.surnames.ireland newsgroup. For surname queries related to Ireland and Northern Ireland.
  news:soc.genealogy.surnames.ireland

- SURNAMES-MISC Mailing List
  http://www.rootsweb.com/~jfuller/gen_mail_surnames-gen.html#SURNAMES-MISC
  Gatewayed with the soc.genealogy.surnames.misc newsgroup. For surname queries for regions not addressed elsewhere in the soc.genealogy.surnames. hierarchy.*
  news:soc.genealogy.surnames.misc

- SURNAMES-USA Mailing List
  http://www.rootsweb.com/~jfuller/gen_mail_surnames-gen.html#SURNAMES-USA
  Gatewayed with the soc.genealogy.surnames.usa newsgroup. For surname queries related to the United States.
  news:soc.genealogy.surnames.usa

- WGW-SURNAMES-SCOTLAND Mailing List
  http://www.rootsweb.com/~jfuller/gen_mail_surnames-gen.html#WGW-SURNAMES-SCOTLAND
  For the discussion and sharing of information regarding surnames originating in Scotland.

◆ Vendors: Buy, Sell or Trade

- AGLL Genealogical Services Mailing List
  http://www.rootsweb.com/~jfuller/gen_mail_software.html#AGLL
  For announcements of new genealogical products and sales promotions from AGLL.

- Ancestry Daily News
  http://www.ancestry.com/library/view/news/articles/daily
  news.asp
  Daily by Juliana Smith.

- Appleton's Mailing List
  http://www.rootsweb.com/~jfuller/gen_mail_material.html
  #Appleton
  A read-only list with information on new genealogy software, CD-ROMs, books, and more from Appleton's Books and Genealogy.

- BBANNOUNCE-L Mailing List
  http://www.rootsweb.com/~jfuller/gen_mail_software.html
  #BBANNOUNCE-L
  Maintained by the Banner Blue Division of Broderbund Software for product announcements (10-15 postings a year).

- GEN-BOOKS Mailing List
  http://www.rootsweb.com/~jfuller/gen_mail_material.html
  #GEN-BOOKS
  For anyone with an interest in the buying or selling of new or used genealogy books and CDs made from these books.

- GEN-BOOKS Mailing List
  http://www.rootsweb.com/~jfuller/gen_mail_material.html
  #GEN-BOOKS1
  For announcements of genealogy or history books, maps, post cards, etc. which are available for sale, trade or on-line auction, as well as "want lists" of books or items.

- Generations Family Heritage Newsletter
  http://www.sierra.com/sierrahome/newsletter/familytree/
  From SierraHome Family Tree, makers of Generations Family Tree Software.

- GEN-MARKET Mailing List
  http://www.rootsweb.com/~jfuller/gen_mail_material.html
  #GEN-MARKET
  Gatewayed with the soc.genealogy.marketplace newsgroup for commercial postings of unique interest to genealogists.
  news:soc.genealogy.marketplace

- GEN-MAT Mailing List
  http://www.rootsweb.com/~jfuller/gen_mail_material.html
  #GEN-MAT
  This is a mailing list for anyone who has an interest in the buying or selling of new or used genealogical materials (e.g., books, newsletters, CDs, magazines).

- GEN-MAT-15 Mailing List
  http://www.rootsweb.com/~jfuller/gen_mail_material.html
  #GEN-MAT-15
  For anyone who desires to post the availability of new or used genealogical materials (e.g., books, newsletters, CDs, magazines) or services for sale at a price of $15 or less.

- GEN-MAT-HX Mailing List
  http://www.rootsweb.com/~jfuller/gen_mail_material.html
  #GEN-MAT-HX
  For anyone who has an interest in the buying or selling of new or used biographies and history books. Publishers of such books are welcome, as are resellers (businesses or individuals cleaning bookshelves).

- GenSwap Mailing List
  http://www.rootsweb.com/~jfuller/gen_mail_general.html
  #GenSwap
  For exchanging research time and swapping records for records with others (e.g., researching in your area for someone else in exchange for like efforts on their part).

- LegacyNews Mailing List
  http://www.rootsweb.com/~jfuller/gen_mail_software.html
  #LegacyNews
  A read-only mailing list maintained by Millennia Corporation for announcements of interest to users of the Legacy Family Tree genealogy software program.

MAPS, GAZETTEERS & GEOGRAPHICAL INFORMATION

http://www.cyndislist.com/maps.htm

Category Index:

- Fire Insurance Maps
- General Resource Sites
- Historical Maps, Atlases & Gazetteers
- Interactive Online Map Creation
- Libraries, Archives & Museums

- Local Boundary Resources
- National Geographic Information
- Software
- Vendors

◆ Fire Insurance Maps

- Birds-Eye Views and Fire Insurance Maps: A Powerful Combination for Urban Research
  http://www.audiotapes.com/product.asp?ProductCode='FSLC-39'
  Presentation by Brian E. Michaels, available for sale on audio tape.

- Chadwyck-Healey - Manufacturers Mutual Fire Insurance Site Maps, 1894û1954
  http://www.chadwyck.com/products/viewproduct.asp?key=539
  Microfiche for sale.

- Checklist of Sanborn Fire Insurance Maps in Branner Library
  http://www-sul.stanford.edu/depts/branner/sanborn.html
  List of holdings for California, Nevada, and British Columbia. Branner Earth Sciences Library and Map Collections, Stanford University Libraries/Academic Information Resources.

- Environmental Data Resources, Inc.
  http://www.edrnet.com/reports/historical.html
  EDR owns the Sanborn Map Company which owns the rights to the highly detailed fire insurance so helpful for genealogy and for house histories. Digital images of the Sanborn fire insurance maps may be ordered and delivered electronically for a fee.

- Fire Insurance Maps of Chicago
  http://www.uic.edu/depts/ahaa/imagebase/firemaps/

- Fire Insurance Maps of Cities & Towns
  http://www.iowahistory.org/archives/research_collections/special_collections/fire_maps.html
  From the State Historical Society of Iowa.

- Fire Insurance Maps, Their History and Applications
  http://www.angelfire.com/biz/lacewing/fireinsurancemaps.html
  A book by Diane Oswald. Good information about this under-utilized source.

- Fire Insurance Plans held by the University of Waterloo Library ~ Ontario
  http://www.lib.uwaterloo.ca/locations/umd/cart/fire insurance.html

- Fire Insurance Plans in York Libraries
  http://www.info.library.yorku.ca/depts/map/guidesgoads1.htm
  Canadian fire insurance plans housed in the libraries at York University, Toronto, Ontario, Canada.

- Sanborn Fire Insurance and Bird's Eye View Maps: Reconstructing Your Ancestor's Community
  http://www.audiotapes.com/product.asp?ProductCode='SD-112'
  Presentation by Marcia K. Wyett, available for sale on audio tape.

- Sanborn Fire Insurance Map Collections
  http://lcweb.loc.gov/spcoll/215.html
  Insurance maps of U.S. cities, from the late nineteenth and twentieth centuries, in the Library of Congress Special Collections.

- Sanborn and Other Fire Insurance Maps
  http://www.lib.berkeley.edu/EART/sanborn.html
  From the University of California, Berkeley, Earth Sciences & Map Library's Home Page.

- Sanborn Fire Insurance Maps
  http://www.lib.berkeley.edu/EART/snb-intr.html
  Extracted from Fire Insurance Maps in the Library of Congress.

- Sanborn Maps in Special Collections
  http://toltec.lib.utk.edu/~cic/sanborn.htm
  At the University of Tennessee, Knoxville Libraries.

- Trent University Archives- Coboconk, Ontario: Fire Insurance Plan
  http://www.trentu.ca/library/archives/76-024.htm

◆ General Resource Sites

- Amazon.com Genealogy Bookstore - Maps
  http://www.amazon.com/exec/obidos/external-search/?keyword=maps+genealogy&tag=markcyndisgenealA/
  And Atlases
  http://www.amazon.com/exec/obidos/external-search/?keyword=atlas+genealogy&tag=markcyndisgenealA/

- Ancestry.com - Reference - Map Center
  http://www.ancestry.com/search/rectype/reference/maps/main.asp

- Ancestry.com - Using Maps & Gazetteers in Genealogy
  http://www.ancestry.com/learn/reference/usingmaps.htm

- Ancestry Groups in the United States
  http://www.lmic.state.mn.us/dnet/maplib/ancestry/usancest.htm
  Maps which show how many people in each county of the United States identify with certain ancestry groups.

- Atlas of American Immigration
  http://www.albany.edu/~rws32/gog240/atlas.html
  Includes charts on immigrant origins and maps of the distribution of select immigrant groups in the United States for certain periods.

- AudioTapes.com - Genealogical Lectures on Cassette Tapes – Maps
  http://www.audiotapes.com/search2.asp?Search=maps
  Gazetteers
  http://www.audiotapes.com/search2.asp?Search=gazetteers
  Geography
  http://www.audiotapes.com/search2.asp?Search=geography

- Books We Own - Atlases and Gazetteers
  http://www.rootsweb.com/~bwo/atlas.html
  Find a book from which you would like a lookup and click on the submitter's code at the end of the entry. Once you find the contact information for the submitter, write them a polite request for a lookup.

- Cartography Resources
  http://geog.gmu.edu/projects/maps/cartogrefs.html

- CGRER Netsurfing: Maps and References
  http://www.cgrer.uiowa.edu/servers/servers_references.html
  Huge compilation of links from the University of Iowa.

- Geographic Information Systems - Resources on the Web
  http://www-map.lib.umn.edu/gis.html
  List from the John R. Borchert Map Library, Univ. of Minnesota.

- Getty Thesaurus of Geographic Names
  http://shiva.pub.getty.edu/tgn_browser/

- John Robertson's Genealogy & Maps
  http://www.shelby.net/shelby/jr/
  Historical county lines; genealogy atlas "how-to" and more.

- Locations - Finding United States Locations Using On-Line Aerial Photos and Topographical Maps
  http://www.cswnet.com/~sbooks/genealogy/Locations/locations.htm

- Map Related Web Sites
  http://www.lib.utexas.edu/Libs/PCL/Map_collection/map_sites/map_sites.html

- Maps Can Help You Trace Your Family Tree
  http://info.er.usgs.gov/fact-sheets/genealogy/index.html

- Map Societies Around the World
  http://www.csuohio.edu/CUT/MapSoc/index.html
  From the Cleveland State University Library. A meta index of links to societies with a focus on cartography around the globe. Includes areas of interest for each society and contact information.

- Oddens's Bookmarks - The Fascinating World of Maps and Mapping
  http://kartoserver.geog.uu.nl/html/staff/oddens/oddens.htm

- PlaceNames.com - Worldwide Index of Place Names
  http://www.placenames.com/

- Using Maps in Genealogy
  http://mapping.usgs.gov/mac/isb/pubs/booklets/genealogy/genealogy.html
  From the USGS Mapping Applications Center.

◆ Historical Maps, Atlases & Gazetteers

- 1853 Wisconsin Gazetteer On-Line
  http://moa.umdl.umich.edu/cgi/sgml/moa-idx?notisid=AFK4346
  From the University of Michigan. Scanned images of the original book.

- 1872 County Map of Colorado, Dakota, Indian Nations, Kansas, Montana, Nebraska & Wyoming
  http://www.ismi.net/chnegw/1872title.htm

- The 1891 Grain Dealers and Shippers Gazetteer
  http://www.livgenmi.com/1891shippersgaz.htm
  Another terrific map project from Pam Rietsch.

- 1895 World Atlas - U.S.
  http://www.LivGenMI.com/1895.htm

- American Memory Railroad Maps 1828-1900
  http://memory.loc.gov/ammem/gmdhtml/rrhtml/rrhome.html
  From the Geography and Map Division, Library of Congress.

- Andreas' Historical Atlas of Dakota ~ 1884
  http://www.rootsweb.com/~usgenweb/sd/andreas/

- Atlas of American Migration
  http://www.amazon.com/exec/obidos/ISBN=0816031584/markcyndisgenealA/
  A book by Stephen A. Flanders.

- Atlas des Deutschen Reichs
  http://www.library.wisc.edu/etext/ravenstein/
  This 1883 atlas of the German empire includes maps of the bordering portions of present-day Austria, Belgium, the Czech Republic, Denmark, France, Hungary, Lithuania, Luxembourg, the Netherlands, Poland, the Russian Federation, Slovakia, and Switzerland. Maps are large scale (1:850,000). Includes a thorough gazetteer of place-names. Requires the free Adobe Acrobat reader for viewing.

- Cartographic Images - Ancient, Medieval & Renaissance Maps
  http://www.iag.net/~jsiebold/carto.html

- Counties Gazetteer
  http://www.old-maps.co.uk/
  Organized by the counties of England, Scotland, and Wales, this site contains scanned images of historic maps dating from 1846 to 1899. They are at 1:10,560 scale. Over 40,000 places are indexed with links to where they appear on the maps.

- Details of the original Mason-Dixon Line Map
  http://www.mdarchives.state.md.us/msa/speccol/sc2200/
  sc2221/000017/000013/html/0000.html
  From the Maryland State Archives.

- Le Dictionnaire des communes
  http://www.es-conseil.fr/pramona/p1gen.htm#dico
  *If you are searching for a place name in France, or Algeria,
  Philippe RAMONA will do a lookup for you in this book:
  "Dictionnaire des Communes de la France, de l'Algòrie et des
  autres colonies Franôaises" (Paris 1866).*

- FEEFHS Map Room - Background and Map Index
  http://feefhs.org/maps/indexmap.html

- Greenwood's Map of London 1827
  http://www.bathspa.ac.uk/greenwood/home.html

- Highlights of the Map Collection
  http://www.nls.ac.uk/digitallibrary/map/frame_map.htm
  From National Library of Scotland.

- Historical Atlas of Canada Data Dissemination
  Project
  http://geog.utoronto.ca/hacddp/hacpage.html

- Historic Maps of the Netherlands
  http://grid.let.rug.nl/~welling/maps/maps.html

- Historic USGS Maps of New England
  http://docs.unh.edu/nhtopos/nhtopos.htm
  *UNH Dimond Library Documents Department & Data Center.
  Includes New Hampshire, Connecticut, Maine, Massachusetts,
  Rhode Island, Vermont.*
  - About the Collection
    http://docs.unh.edu/nhtopos/aboutmaps.htm
  - Alphabetic Quadrangle Listing
    http://docs.unh.edu/nhtopos/NewEnglandList.htm

- Historical Map Web Sites
  http://www.lib.utexas.edu/Libs/PCL/Map_collection/
  map_sites/hist_sites.html
  *A list by the Perry-Castañeda Library Map Collection, The
  University of Texas at Austin.*

- Historical Maps
  http://www.lib.utexas.edu:80/Libs/PCL/Map_collection/
  historical/history_main.html
  *From The Perry-Castañeda Library Map Collection, The University
  of Texas at Austin.*

- In Search of Your Canadian Past: The Canadian
  County Atlas Digital Project
  http://imago.library.mcgill.ca/countyatlas/default.asp
  *From McGill University's Rare Books and Special Collections
  Division. A searchable database derived from published county
  atlases between 1874 & 1881. Searchable by property owners'
  names or by location. Township maps, portraits and properties have
  been scanned, with links from the property owners' names in the
  database.*

- Luxembourg gazetteer of villages and towns
  http://www.igd-leo.lu/igd-leo/onomastics/villages/villages.html

- Map 1797 - Plan of Great Yarmouth, Norfolk by
  William Faden ~ England
  http://www.gtyarmouth.co.uk/html/map_1797.htm

- Map Guide to the U.S. Federal Censuses, 1790-1920
  http://www.amazon.com/exec/obidos/ISBN=0806311886/
  markcyndisgenealA/
  A book by William Thorndale and William Dollarhide.

- Map of John Snow's London in 1859
  http://www.ph.ucla.edu/epi/snow/1859map/map1859.html

- Map List
  http://www.rootsweb.com/~wggerman/map/index.htm
  For Germany from WorldGenWeb.

- Maps of National Historic & Military Parks,
  Memorials, and Battlefields ~ United States
  http://www.lib.utexas.edu/Libs/PCL/Map_collection/National_
  parks/historic_parks.html#military

- Maps & Plans
  http://www.nas.gov.uk/plans_collection_of_the_national.htm
  From the National Archives of Scotland.

- Meyers Orts- und Verkehrs-Lexikon des Deutschen
  Reichs
  http://www.amazon.com/exec/obidos/ISBN=0806316314/
  markcyndisgenealA/
  A book by Raymond Wright III.

- New York State Historical Maps
  http://www.sunysb.edu/libmap/nymaps.htm

- Old Maps of the Channel Islands
  http://user.itl.net/~glen/maps.html

- OSSHE Historical & Cultural Atlas Resource
  http://darkwing.uoregon.edu/~atlas/

- Osztrák-Magyar Monarchia (1910) / Austria-
  Hungary (1910)
  http://lazarus.elte.hu/hun/maps/1910/1910ind.htm
  Variously scaled maps of the Empire as it was in 1910.

- Panoramic Maps Collection
  http://lcweb2.loc.gov/ammem/pmhtml/panhome.html
  From the Geography and Map Division, Library of Congress.

- Pioneer Trails from U.S. Land Surveys
  http://history.cc.ukans.edu/heritage/werner/werner.html

- Sanborn Fire Insurance Maps
  http://www.lib.berkeley.edu/EART/snb-intr.html
  *A description from the Earth Sciences and Map Library at the
  University of California at Berkeley.*

- Texas General Land Office Archives - Map
  Collection
  http://www.glo.state.tx.us/central/archives/mapscol.html

- Texas Historic Sites Atlas
  http://atlas.thc.state.tx.us/

- Tithe Maps of Wales
  http://www.llgc.org.uk/dm/dm0030.htm
  From the National Library of Wales. An excellent description of the Tithe Maps and why they are of use to researchers. Includes information on how to use the Tithe Map holdings of the Library.

- U.S. Territorial Maps 1775-1920
  http://xroads.virginia.edu/~MAP/terr_hp.html

- United States Digital Map Library
  http://www.rootsweb.com/~usgenweb/maps/
  A project of the USGenWeb Archives.

  o Indian Land Cessions in the United States
    http://www.rootsweb.com/~usgenweb/maps/cessions/
    This site contains all sixty-seven maps from the 1899 paper, "Indian Land Cessions in the United States" by Charles C. Royce.

  o National Maps
    http://www.rootsweb.com/~usgenweb/maps/usa/

  o State and County Maps
    http://www.rootsweb.com/~usgenweb/maps/table2.html

- Wisconsin County Maps, 1901
  http://www.kinquest.com/genealogy/resources/1901atlas.html

◆ Interactive Online Map Creation

- Etakguide
  http://www.etakguide.com/

- Falk Online
  http://www.falk-online.de/
  Online maps of major German cities, trip planning, and atlas.

- MapBlast!
  http://www.mapblast.com/
  Create detailed street maps.

- MapQuest!
  http://www.mapquest.com/
  Interactive atlas for U.S. streets and more.

- Microsoft Expedia Maps
  http://maps.expedia.com/OverView.asp

- Multi Media Mapping
  http://uk5.multimap.com/map/piaces.cgi
  An interactive atlas of Great Britain. Enter the name of a British city, town or village to get a clickable, zoomable, detailed map.

- National Atlas of the United States of America
  http://www-atlas.usgs.gov/
  From the U.S. Geological Survey.

- Surnames in Italy / L'Italia dei cognomi
  http://gens.labo.net/en/cognomi/
  By entering a surname and pressing the red arrow, a distribution map of Italy is generated showing the concentrations of that particular surname in Italy.

- U.S. Surname Distribution Maps
  http://www.hamrick.com/names/index.html

◆ Libraries, Archives & Museums

- Association of Canadian Map Libraries and Archives
  http://www.sscl.uwo.ca/assoc/acml/acmla.html

- The Bodleian Library Map Room
  http://www.rsl.ox.ac.uk/nnj/

- Harvard Map Collection
  http://icg.harvard.edu/~maps/

- Heritage Map Museum Home Page
  http://www.carto.com/
  Antique maps from 15th to 19th century.

- MAGIC - Map and Geographic Information Center - University of Connecticut
  http://magic.lib.uconn.edu/

  o Scanned Historical Maps
    http://magic.lib.uconn.edu/cgi-bin/MAGIC_HistList.pl
    Primarily Connecticut and southern New England.

- The Map Collection at the University of Stony Brook, New York
  http://www.sunysb.edu/library/ldmaps.htm

- Map Libraries on the World Wide Web - List from the John R. Borchert Map Library, Univ. of Minnesota
  http://www-map.lib.umn.edu/map_libraries.html

- Maps
  http://commerce.state.wy.us/cr/archives/databases/database.htm
  Held by the Wyoming State Archives.

- Osher Map Library and Smith Center for Cartographic Education
  http://www.usm.maine.edu/~maps/
  University of Southern Maine, Portland.

- Perry-Castañeda Library Map Collection
  http://www.lib.utexas.edu/Libs/PCL/Map_collection/Map_collection.html
  The General Libraries, The University of Texas at Austin.

- Rare Map Collection at the Hargrett Library, University of Georgia
  http://www.libs.uga.edu/darchive/hargrett/maps/maps.html

- University of Texas at Arlington - Map Collections
  http://libraries.uta.edu/SpecColl/mapcoll.html

- UVa Library Geographic Information Center
  http://viva.lib.virginia.edu/gic/

  o Digital Resources Catalog
    http://viva.lib.virginia.edu/gic/catalog/

  o Maps Collection
    http://viva.lib.virginia.edu/gic/services/services_maps.html

  o Virginia Digital Map Library
    http://viva.lib.virginia.edu/gic/maps/maps_va.html

  o Virginia Locator Service
    http://viva.lib.virginia.edu/gic/va_locator/locator.html

- Western Association of Map Libraries
  http://gort.ucsd.edu/mw/waml/waml.html

- Yahoo!...Science...Maps...Libraries
  http://dir.yahoo.com/Science/Geography/Cartography/Maps/
  Libraries/

◆ Local Boundary Resources

- Administrative Regions of the British Isles
  http://www.genuki.org.uk/big/Regions/
  From GENUKI.

- Boundaries of the United States and the Several
  States
  http://www.ac.wwu.edu/~stephan/48states.gif
  With an animated GIF map of the Settlement of the
  United States
  http://www.ac.wwu.edu/~stephan/48states.html

- Counties of England, Scotland and Wales Prior to the
  1974 Boundary Changes
  http://www.genuki.org.uk/big/Britain.html

- County Map of Scotland
  http://www.genuki.org.uk/big/sct/sct_cmap.html
  From the GENUKI web site for Scotland.

- Evolution of United States County Boundaries
  http://www.ac.wwu.edu/~stephan/Animation/us.gif
  And an animated GIF showing county boundaries for
  1650, 1700, 1750, and census years from 1790
  onward
  http://www.ac.wwu.edu/~stephan/Animation/us.html

- Graphical Display of the Federal Township and
  Range System ~ U.S.
  http://www.outfitters.com/genealogy/land/twprangemap.html
  Explains the division of townships and sections.

- Historical County Lines
  http://www.shelby.net/shelby/jr/maps.htm#top

- Land Ownership Maps in the Library of Congress
  http://www.kinquest.com/genealogy/resources/lom.html
  *A list by state, county and year, of the maps available in the
  collection held at the Library of Congress.*

- Leitrim-Roscommon Map Collection ~ Ireland
  http://www.leitrim-roscommon.com/LR_maps.html
  *Maps that display the Parishes, Baronies and Poor Law Unions for
  these two counties.*

- A List of Counties of the United States
  http://www.genealogy.org/~st-clair/counties/welcome.html
  #countyix

◆ National Geographic Information

- AUSLIG on the Web - Australian Surveying & Land
  Information Group
  http://www.auslig.gov.au/

- Association of Canadian Map Libraries and Archives
  / Association des Cartotheques et Archives
  http://www.sscl.uwo.ca/assoc/acml/acmla.html
  ACMLA actively serves as the representative professional group for

*Canadian map librarians, cartographic archivists and others
interested in geographic information in all formats. The site
includes a page with books about Canadian maps.*

- Australian Gazetteer
  http://www.ke.com.au/cgi-bin/texhtml?form=AustGaz
  Online demo version of a software program.

- Australian Geographic Place Names (Gazetteer)
  http://www.erin.gov.au/database/gaze_ack.html

- BC Geographical Names Information System ~
  Canada
  http://www.gdbc.gov.bc.ca/bcnames/
  Searchable database.

- British Geological Survey Maps
  http://www.bgs.ac.uk/products/UK-Maps/UK-Maps-index.htm

- Canada National Atlas Information Service (NAIS)
  http://www-nais.ccm.emr.ca/

- Canadian Geographical Names / Les noms
  géographiques du Canada
  http://GeoNames.NRCan.gc.ca/

  o Canadian Geographical Names - Publications
    http://GeoNames.NRCan.gc.ca/english/publications.html
    *List of available publications on geographical names including
    policy documents and manuals, gazetteers, glossaries,
    newsletters and brochures.*

  o Origins of Canada's Geographical Names
    http://GeoNames.NRCan.gc.ca/english/schoolnet/
    origin.html

  o Places and Names of Canada
    http://www.placesandnames.on.ca/index.html
    How places in Canada received their names.

  o Querying Canadian Geographical Names:

    • Query by Geographical Name
      http://Geonames.NRCan.gc.ca/english/cgndb.html

      Or Current Names Selected by Coordinates
      http://Geonames.NRCan.gc.ca/english/cgndb_
      coord.html
      *Search this database of over 500,000 geographical names by
      name, feature type, region and by province*

- Color Landform Atlas of the United States
  http://fermi.jhuapl.edu/states/states.html

- The Data Wales Maps Page
  http://www.data-wales.co.uk/walesmap.htm

- Gazetteer for Scotland
  http://www.geo.ed.ac.uk/scotgaz/
  *Under development at the Department of Geography at the
  University of Edinburgh.*

- Geographic Names Database
  ftp://ftp.eecs.umich.edu/pub/eecs/geo/

  o Format of the Geographic Names Database
    ftp://ftp.eecs.umich.edu/pub/eecs/geo/README

- Geographic Name Server
  http://www.mit.edu:8001/geo
  Find location, county name and zip code.

- Geographic Name Server
  gopher://riceinfo.rice.edu:1103/1geo
  Look up US place names by city or zip code.

- Geographic Server by State
  gopher://george.peabody.yale.edu:71/1

- GEOserv - A German Town Locator
  http://www2.genealogy.net/gene/www/abt/geoserv.html

- Government Documents and Map Department ~ U.S.
  http://govdoc.ucdavis.edu/
  At the University of California, Davis.

- History of Australian Places Index
  http://www.zades.com.au/ozindex/ozindex.html

- Home Page of Hungarian Cartography
  http://lazarus.elte.hu/gb/hunkarta/kezdo.htm

- Instituto Português de Cartografia e Cadastro / The National Geodetic, Mapping and Cadastre Agency of Portugal
  http://www.ipcc.pt/

- Large Map of Wales
  ftp://sunsite.unc.edu/pub/academic/languages/welsh/wales.gif

- LINZ - The New Zealand Geographic Place-Names Database
  http://www.linz.govt.nz/databases/geographic/geoname.html

- Map of New Zealand - Guide to Cities & Towns
  http://www.atonz.com/genealogy/nza2.gif

- Maps to the ancient kingdoms & new counties of Wales
  http://www.britannia.com/wales/wmap1.html

- Maps of Croatia and Bosnia-Herzegovina
  http://www.applicom.com/maps/

- Ordnance Survey Home Page
  http://www.ordsvy.gov.uk/
  National Mapping Agency of Great Britain. In today's ever-changing world, Ordnance Survey's Historical Mapping reveals the history of every town and village throughout the country, giving a snapshot through time. Ordnance Survey holds an extensive archive of Historical Mapping, dating from the early nineteenth century and offers a full range of scales, from Victorian Town Plans at 1:500, 1:528 and 1:1056 (Some Town Plans even show the divisions in buildings and the names on church pews). Large scale maps at 1:1250, 1:2500, 1:10560 and 1:10 000. Small Scale Maps at 1:25 000, 1:50 000 and the very popular 1" Series. From this archive, individual black and white copies can be produced on high-quality chart paper that is ideal for framing, or film, depending on what you require.

- National Imagery and Mapping Agency - GEOnet Names Server
  http://164.214.2.59/gns/html/index.html
  United States NIMA GNPS Query Form for searching a database of foreign geographic feature names.

- National Library of Australia Map Collection
  http://www.nla.gov.au/map/mapcoll.html

- Natural Resources Canada
  http://www.NRCan.gc.ca/

- Ordnance Survey Ireland - Ireland's national mapping agency.
  http://www.irlgov.ie/osi/
  Ordnance Survey Ireland's mandate is to provide three main map services in the State. These are detailed large scale maps at 1:1000 scale in urban areas and 1:2500 and 1:5000 scale in rural areas; and the Discovery Series of tourist mapping at 1:50000 scale. These map series are created from base data, which also support a number of derivative products, including atlases and guides, and other products and services tailored to the needs of customers.

- Tiger Mapping Service Home Page (US Census Bureau)
  http://tiger.census.gov/

- UK Sensitive Map to Universities
  http://scitsc.wlv.ac.uk/ukinfo/uk.map.html

- United States Board on Geographic Names
  http://mapping.usgs.gov/www/gnis/bgn.html
  A description from the USGS Mapping Information web site.

- U.S. Gazetteer - From the U.S. Census Bureau
  http://www.census.gov/cgi-bin/gazetteer

- USGS National Mapping Information
  http://mapping.usgs.gov/
  o USGS Mapping Information: Foreign Geographic Names Gazetteers
    http://mapping.usgs.gov/www/gnis/foreign.html
  o USGS Mapping Information: Geographic Names Information System
    http://mapping.usgs.gov/www/gnis/
  o USGS Mapping Information: GNIS Data Base Query Form
    http://mapping.usgs.gov/www/gnis/gnisform.html
  o USGS Mapping Information: The National Gazetteer
    http://mapping.usgs.gov/www/gnis/pppdgn.html#1-D
  o USGS National Mapping Division Reference Collection Library and Historical Map Archives
    http://mapping.usgs.gov/html/2library.html
  o USGS NSDI Clearinghouse - Geographic Names Information System (GNIS)
    http://nsdi.usgs.gov/products/gnis.html

- Yale Peabody Museum: Geographic Names Information System (GNIS)
  http://www.peabody.yale.edu/other/gnis/
  Search the USGS Geographic Names Database. You can limit the search to a specific county in this state and search for any of the following features: airport arch area arroyo bar basin bay beach bench bend bridge building canal cape cemetery channel church cliff crater crossing dam falls flat forest gap geyser glacier gut harbor hospital island isthmus lake lava levee locale mine oilfield

other park pillar plain ppl range rapids reserve reservoir ridge school sea slope spring stream summit swamp tower trail tunnel valley well woods.

◆ Software

- CensusCD+Maps
  http://www.censuscd.com/cdmaps/censuscd_maps.htm

- Computer Programs for Drawing Plat Maps
  http://www.outfitters.com/genealogy/land/compmaps.html

- Deed Mapper Software
  http://www.ultranet.com/~deeds/

- Gold Bug
  http://www.goldbug.com/
  Historical map reproductions & county mapping software.

- Stephen Archer's Genealogical Software Home Page
  http://ourworld.compuserve.com/homepages/steve_archer/
  GenMap UK, a Windows mapping program designed mainly for UK genealogical and historical mapping.

◆ Vendors

- Aquarian Gallery Antique Prints and Maps
  http://pre1900prints.com/

- Baldwin's Old Prints, Maps & Charts
  http://commercial.visi.net/baldwins/

- The David Morgan Home Page
  http://www.davidmorgan.com/
  Has British Ordnance Survey maps for sale.

- Frontier Press Bookstore - Atlases
  http://www.frontierpress.com/frontier.cgi?category=atlas

- Frontier Press Bookstore - Maps (Finding and Making Use of Maps)
  http://www.frontierpress.com/frontier.cgi?category=map

- GenealogyBookShop.com - Atlases/Gazetteers/Place Names
  http://www.genealogybookshop.com/genealogybookshop/files/General,Atlases_Gazetteers_Place_Names/index.html
  The online store of Genealogical Publishing Co., Inc. & Clearfield Company.

- Genealogy Unlimited - Maps and Atlases from Europe
  http://www.genealogyunlimited.com/
  Maps and atlases from Poland, Prussia, and Germany.

- Generations Press - City and Town Plan Reproductions for Genealogy
  http://www.generationspress.com/citymaps.html

- Gleason's Old Maps Etc.
  http://members.aol.com/oldmapsetc/index.html
  Photocopies of Old Maps, Old Prints, and Old Articles of Interest to Genealogists and Historians Pertaining to Indiana, Illinois, Ohio, New Jersey, Pennsylvania, and more to come.

- Global Genealogy - Historical & Contemporary Maps & Atlases
  http://www.globalgenealogy.com/mapsmain.htm

- The Henry H. Schryver Collection
  http://www.bigwave.ca/~avanhald/
  A collection of historical maps and books on the geography of North America.

- Index: Old Ordnance Survey Maps - The Godfrey Edition
  http://www.alangodfreymaps.co.uk/
  List of UK and Belgium maps available at large scale in the period of about 1890 to 1915.

- Interlink Bookshop Genealogical Services ~ Victoria, B.C., Canada
  http://www.interlinkbookshop.com/

- International Map Trade Association (IMTA)
  http://www.maptrade.org/

- K.B. Slocum Books and Maps
  http://www.treasurenet.com/kbslocum/welcome.html
  A huge selection of old U.S. state and city maps.

- Macbeth Genealogical Services
  http://www.macbeth.com.au/
  Books, fiche, maps, and CD-ROMs. Australia.

- MapWorks
  http://www.mapworks.com.au/
  Map shop in Melbourne, Australia specializing in old and current editions of large scale maps for the United Kingdom, Ireland, Germany and more.

- The Memorabilia Corner
  http://members.aol.com/TMCorner/index.html
  Forms, flags, maps, software, CDs, tapes, microfilm & microfiche, books, periodicals, photographic conservation & archival materials.

- Old Maps of New England & New York - Villages, Towns & Cities & Other Items of Historical Interest
  http://members.aol.com/oldmapsne/index.html

- Old Ordnance Survey Maps - The Godfrey Edition
  http://www.alangodfreymaps.co.uk/index.htm
  These maps are invaluable for historians and genealogists. More than a thousand titles have been issued in this major series of reprints of Old Ordnance Survey Maps of towns throughout Britain and Ireland. The Maps are highly detailed, taken from the 1/2500 plans and reprinted at about 14 inches to the mile. They cover towns in great detail, showing individual houses, railway tracks, factories, churches, mills, canals, tramways and even minutiae such as dockside cranes, fountains, signal posts, pathways, sheds, wells, etc. Each map includes historical notes on the area concerned. Many also include extracts from contemporary directories. The maps are neatly folded, often with an early photograph on the cover. The maps are ideal for local historians, transport historians, and family historians, or simply those with an interest in the town they live in or have visited.

- Pacific Shore Maps
  http://www.electriciti.com/psmaps/index.html
  Antique maps and charts from around the world.

- Patton Maps - Alfred B. Patton, Inc.
  http://www.pattonmaps.com/

- Quintin Publications - Maps ~ Canada
  http://www.quintinpublications.com/maps.html

- Rallymaps of West Wellow
  http://www.rallymap.demon.co.uk/
  Genealogy books and maps for research in England, Ireland, Scotland and Wales. War Grave Commission and trench maps for Flanders.

- Reproductions of Old Town Maps in New England
  http://www.biddeford.com/~lkane/

- Roots and Branches
  http://members.aol.com/RebelSher1/index.html
  Used books, forms, maps and the Civil War info.

- Scharlau Prints and Maps
  http://www.scharlau.co.uk/
  Etchings, antiquarian engravings, maps and prints of Scotland.

- Stepping Stones
  http://www.stepping-stones.co.uk/
  Vendor of postcards of churches, including lists of recipients names and addresses, CDs available of English directories (e.g. Pigot's Trade, Kelly's Scarborough 1902 and Bulmers) and Ordnance Survey maps circa 1890s.

- Storbeck's Genealogy Books Maps CD-ROM
  http://www.storbecks.com/

- Travel Genie - Detailed Maps for Genealogy
  http://www.netins.net/showcase/travelgenie

- The Willow Bend Books - Maps
  http://www.willowbend.net/search.asp?stringfield=s_Title&stringleft=3&stringsearch=MAP

- Ye Olde Genealogie Shoppe © - Forms, Charts, Maps & Goodies
  http://www.yogs.com/

MARRIAGES
http://www.cyndislist.com/marriage.htm

Category Index:
- ◆ Ethnic Specific
- ◆ Gretna Green & Scottish Border Marriages
- ◆ How To

- ◆ Locality Specific
- ◆ Professional Researchers, Volunteers & Other Research Services

---

◆ Ethnic Specific

- Forbidden Relatives: The American Myth of Cousin Marriage
  http://www.amazon.com/exec/obidos/ISBN=0252065409/markcyndisgenealA/
  A book by Martin Ottenheimer.

- Man and Wife in America: A History
  http://www.amazon.com/exec/obidos/ISBN=0674002628/markcyndisgenealA/
  A book by Hendrik Hartog.

- The Ketubah in History
  http://www.ketubahworkshop.com/html/history.html
  Background history of the traditional Jewish wedding contract.

- Ketubbah: Jewish Marriage Contracts of the Hebrew Union College Skirball Museum and Klau Library
  http://www.amazon.com/exec/obidos/ISBN=0827603614/markcyndisgenealA/
  A book by the Hebrew Union College Skirball Museum.

- Ketubbot: Marriage Contracts from the Jewish Museum
  http://www.amazon.com/exec/obidos/ISBN=0764906186/markcyndisgenealA/
  A book by the Jewish Museum.

◆ Gretna Green & Scottish Border Marriages

- Dumfries & Galloway Family History Society - Publication Information
  http://www.nevisuk.net/dgfhs/books1.html
  Including books on irregular marriages in the shire.

- Elopement to Gretna Green
  http://www.teasdale47.freeserve.co.uk/page4.html
  One couple's story.

- Gretna Green
  http://www.gretna-green.albatross.co.uk/home.html
  Book for sale.

- The Gretna Green Story
  http://www.gretnagreen.com/gretna_story.html
  - o Famous Elopements, Scandals and Romances
    http://www.gretnagreen.com/elopements.html

- o Gretna Green's Anvil Priests
  http://www.gretnagreen.com/anvil_priests.html

- o Why Gretna Green?
  http://www.gretnagreen.com/why_gretna.html

- Irregular Border and Scottish Runaway Marriages
  http://www.gro-scotland.gov.uk/grosweb/grosweb.nsf/pages/runmar
  From the General Register Office for Scotland. A list of custodians and owners of all the known existing records of Scottish regular and runaway marriages including contact information, places, dates, and officiators.

- Lamberton Toll Marriages 1804-1816 & 1849-1855
  http://www.original-indexes.demon.co.uk/intros/SCT-002.htm
  Microfiche for sale.

- Scotch Marriages
  http://www.indiana.edu/~letrs/vwwp/bodichon/brieflaw.html#bodichon-note16
  From the Victorian Women Writers Project.

- Thousands tie the knot in tradition-bound Scottish village
  http://www.its.ilstu.edu/vidette/00/10.13/features/X008_W4.CIT.html

◆ How To

- Amazon.com Genealogy Bookstore - Marriage Records
  http://www.amazon.com/exec/obidos/external-search/?keyword=marriage+records&tag=markcyndisgenealA/

- AudioTapes.com - Genealogical Lectures on Cassette Tapes - Marriage
  http://www.audiotapes.com/search2.asp?Search=marriage

- BIGAMY Mailing List
  http://www.rootsweb.com/~jfuller/gen_mail_general.html#BIGAMY
  For the discussion of bigamy and illegitimacy including how they affect genealogy research, how to effectively research their occurrences, and how to record them.

- Finding a Marriage Date
  http://www.genealogy.com/genealogy/11_mrgdt.html
  by Karen Clifford, A.G.

- Finding Marriage Places with Bible Records
  http://www.familytreemaker.com/00000506.html

- Finding the Minimum Information for Bible Records - Marriage Dates
  http://www.familytreemaker.com/00000490.html

- Finding the Minimum Information for Bible Records - Divorce or Subsequent Marriage
  http://www.familytreemaker.com/00000576.html

- Researching Your Family's Marriages
  http://www.familytreemaker.com/issue11.html

- Terms of Confusement: Dowry and Dower
  http://www.ancestry.com/columns/myra/Shaking_Family_Tree
  10-02-97.htm
  From Shaking Your Family Tree by Myra Vanderpool Gormley, C.G.

◆ Locality Specific

- 1880-1920 Otago Daily Times Births Deaths Marriages, Anniversaries Index, Dunedin, New Zealand
  http://www.es.co.nz/~treeves/geneal.htm
  See the details near the end of this page.

- Al POTTS' Marion County, Ohio Page
  http://idt.net/~allenp19/
  Marion County, Ohio Marriages Volume I 1824-1835 and Volume II 1835-1839; Meeker Union Cemetery Records, Meeker Ohio pictures and more.

- Alabama Marriages Indexed by Grooms Name Mobile and Wilcox Cos.
  http://members.tripod.com/~mallen4896/Marriages-Alabama/
  Marriages.html

- Alblasserwaard Genealogie Page
  http://www.geocities.com/Paris/4744/ALBWRDGEN
  PAGE.HTM
  Several marriage indexes here for the early 1800's.

- Andover Marriages Index
  http://members.aol.com/andoverme/marrindex.html
  Marriages between 1805 and 1944.

- Australasia Births, Deaths and Marriages Exchange
  http://www.geocities.com/Athens/Forum/3709/exchange/
  The aim of the Australasia Births, Deaths and Marriages Exchange is to provide to genealogists a free resource, to share information about details contained on birth, death and marriage registrations registered in Australia, New Zealand and Papua New Guinea.

- Australian Registrars of Births Deaths & Marriages
  http://www.users.on.net/proformat/regs.html

- Baker County Marriages, 1877-1930 ~ Florida
  http://www.rootsweb.com/~flbaker/mgs.html

- Birth, Marriage, Death Indexes for Ontario, Canada
  http://www.geocities.com/Heartland/9332/bmd.htm

- Births, Deaths and Marriages Reported in Calgary, Alberta Newspapers, 1883-1899 ~ Canada
  http://www.calcna.ab.ca/afhs/news.html

- British Columbia Marriage Event
  http://www.hlth.gov.bc.ca/vs/marriage/

- Buncombe County, NC Marriage Records
  http://main.nc.us/OBCGS/wedindx.htm

- Caldwell County, Texas Marriages, 1848-1886
  ftp://ftp.rootsweb.com/pub/usgenweb/tx/caldwell/marriage/
  1848.txt

- Candlish Church, Free Presbyterian, Barney's River, Pictou County, Nova Scotia Marriages - 1812-1883
  http://www.rootsweb.com/~pictou/marchr.htm

- Carter County, Missouri Marriages - Book 1 1860 - 1881
  ftp://ftp.rootsweb.com/pub/usgenweb/mo/carter/marriage/
  1860-81a.txt

- Carter County Missouri Marriages - Book "A" 1881 - 1890
  ftp://ftp.rootsweb.com/pub/usgenweb/mo/carter/marriage/
  1881-90a.txt

- Carter County Missouri Marriage Book "B" 1890-1898
  ftp://ftp.rootsweb.com/pub/usgenweb/mo/carter/marriage/
  1890-98b.txt

- Carter County Missouri Marriage Book C 1898 - 1905
  http://www.rootsweb.com/~mocarter/bookc.htm

- Carter County Marriage Book D 1906 - 1915 ~ Missouri
  http://www.rootsweb.com/~mocarter/bookd.htm

- Carter County Marriages Book E ~ Missouri
  http://www.rootsweb.com/~mocarter/booke.htm

- Castine Marriages 1892-1960 ~ Maine
  http://www.kalama.com/~mariner/casmarry.htm

- Clark County, Nevada Government and Services
  http://www.co.clark.nv.us/

  o Marriage Inquiry System
    http://www.co.clark.nv.us/recorder/mar_srch.htm
    A searchable index of marriages from 1984 through the present

- Clinton County, Indiana Marriages
  http://www.rootsweb.com/~inclinto/marriages.html

- The Cochin Churchbook
  http://www.telebyte.nl/~dessa/cochin.htm
  Baptism & marriages from the Dutch Church in Cochin, India (1754-1804).

- Colorado Marriages and Divorces Search
  http://www.quickinfo.net/madi/comadi.html
  Search on all marriages from 1975 to December 1999 and divorces from 1975 to April 2000 in the state of Colorado.

- Covehead Tracadie Marriages 1887-1900
  http://homepages.rootsweb.com/~mvreid/pei/34mar.html
  For Covehead, Corran Ban, Tracadie in Queens County, Prince Edward Island, Canada.

- Crawford County Marriages 1877-1887 ~ Arkansas
  http://www.rootsweb.com/~arcrawfo/marriage.htm

- Database to an Index of Indiana Marriages Through 1850
  http://www.statelib.lib.in.us/www/indiana/genealogy/mirr.html
  Indiana State Library, Genealogy Division.

- Desoto Co Marriages, June 28, 1887 thru March 24, 1892 ~ Florida
  http://www.rootsweb.com/~fldesoto/marriages.htm

- Early Alpena County Marriages 1871 ~ Michigan
  http://www.rootsweb.com/~mialpena/early.htm

- Early Marriages By Albertus C. Van Raalte
  http://www.macatawa.org/~devries/Earlym.htm
  From Southern Ottawa County Michigan, and Northern Allegan County Michigan.

- Early Marriages of Newaygo County ~ Michigan
  http://www.usgennet.org/usa/mi/county/newaygo/marriag.html

- Early Marriages and Deaths of Village Residents ~ Grand Rapids, Michigan
  http://www.iserv.net/~bryant/grmarr.txt

- Early Marshall County Marriages ~ Alabama
  http://www.neonramp.com/pepper/marshall/marsh_marriages.html

- Erin Township, Wellington Co., Ontario Records ~ Canada
  http://www.chelmsford.com/home/priestner/Wellington.htm
  Various marriage records from 1831 through 1908.

- Every Name Index to Town Marriage Records in Tisbury, MA 1850 - 1875
  http://www.vineyard.net/vineyard/history/tmindex.htm

  o Index to Marriages in Tisbury by Bride's Name 1844-1940
    http://www.vineyard.net/vineyard/history/bridesi.htm
    Index to marriages in Tisbury, Mass. by bride's name, for the period 1844-1940. Prepared by the staff of the Tisbury Town Clerk's office.

  o Index to Marriages in Tisbury by Groom's Name 1844-1940
    http://www.vineyard.net/vineyard/history/groomsi.htm
    Index to marriages in Tisbury, Mass. by groom's name, for the period 1844-1940. Prepared by the staff of the Tisbury Town Clerk's office.

- Faculty Office Marriage License Index
  http://ourworld.compuserve.com/homepages/David_Squire/faculty.htm
  Index of marriage licenses issued by the Master of Faculties of the Archbishop of Canterbury for the period 1714 to 1850.

- Freedman's Bureau, Marriages in Arkansas 1861-1869
  http://www.freedmensbureau.com/arkansas/arkansas marriages.htm

- Freedman's Bureau, Marriages in Jacksonville, Florida 1861-1869
  http://www.freedmensbureau.com/florida/florida.htm

- Freedman's Bureau, Marriages in Mississippi 1863-1865
  http://www.freedmensbureau.com/mississippi/mississippi marriages.htm

- Freedman's Bureau, Marriages in Tennessee 1865-1869
  http://www.freedmensbureau.com/tennessee/marriages/tennesseemarriages.htm

- Freedman's Bureau, Marriages in Washington, D.C. 1861-1869, Part 1
  http://www.freedmensbureau.com/washingtondc/dc marriages1.htm
  And Part 2
  http://www.freedmensbureau.com/washingtondc/dc marriages2.htm

- Freedmen's Bureau Register of Marriages in Gloucester, Virginia 1861-1869
  http://www.freedmensbureau.com/virginia/gloucester.htm

- Greene County, AL Marriages 1823-1860
  http://www.rootsweb.com/~alpicken/greene/marriage.html

- Hillsborough County, Florida Marriage Records - Index
  http://www.lib.usf.edu/spccoll/guide/m/ml/guide.html
  Records online from January 1878 through December 1887, including a scanned photo of the original document.

- Hillsborough County Marriage Records
  http://www.lib.usf.edu/spccoll/marriage.html
  List of the special collections at University of South Florida Tampa Campus Library.

- Hood County Texas Genealogical Society Index of Records
  http://www.genealogy.org/~granbury/index.htm
  Including Birth, Marriage, Tax, & many other online records.

- Illinois Statewide Marriage Index, 1763–1900
  http://www.sos.state.il.us/depts/archives/marriage.html
  An ongoing project of the Illinois State Archives and the Illinois State Genealogical Society. Not all counties are complete. The sources for this index include original county clerk's marriage records such as marriage registers and licenses as well as publications of county genealogical societies and private individuals.

- Indexes of Marriages in St. Joseph County 1832 through 1887 ~ Michigan
  http://members.tripod.com/~tfred/marrind.html

- Index of Marriages and Deaths in New York Weekly Museum, 1788-1817
  http://users.itsnet.com/~pauld/newyork/

- Index to Death & Marriage Notices in the Vineyard Gazette 1884-1939 A – K
  http://www.vineyard.net/vineyard/history/vgind1.htm
  And L - Z
  http://www.vineyard.net/vineyard/history/vgind2.htm

- Index to Marriage Notices in the Vineyard Gazette, 1850-1863
  http://www.vineyard.net/vineyard/history/gazmar63.htm
  Index to marriage notices in the Vineyard Gazette by bride and groom - mainly covers marriages on Martha's Vineyard and Dukes County, Mass. Covers years 1850-1863. Includes names, residences, date and place of marriage, and newspaper issue.

- Index to Whitley County Marriage Applications Book 1 1905-1907 ~ Indiana
  http://home.whitleynet.org/genealogy/gswc_i1.htm

- Ionia County, Michigan - Early Marriage Records - Indexed by Groom
  http://www.usgennet.org/~ahmiioni/more.txt

- Jean's Maine Genealogy Page
  http://www.mnopltd.com/jean/
  Index of deaths and marriages as published in the Ellsworth Herald its successor, the Ellsworth American October 24, 1851 through December 29, 1865.

- Jo Daviess Co., Il Marriage Records
  http://members.tripod.com/~Chemingway/Mrg.html
  Volume B: 1855-1865, Volume E, 1870-1885.

- The Joiner Marriage Index
  http://website.lineone.net/~pjoiner/mindex/mindex.html
  A Marriage Database for County Durham, and the North Riding of Yorkshire in England.

- Kentucky Residents Married in Shawneetown, IL
  http://www.rootsweb.com/~kyhender/Henderson/ill.htm

- Kentucky Vital Records Index
  http://ukcc.uky.edu/~vitalrec/
  Marriage / Divorce / Death.

- Lafleur Archives
  http://www.lafleur.org/
  Provides birth, death and marriage records from authentic Bible records. There are scanned images of Bibles when possible.

- Lawrence County Marriages ~ Alabama
  http://members.aol.com/rpennin975/marriage.htm

- LDS Film Numbers for Ontario Marriage Registrations
  http://www.geocities.com/Heartland/9332/lds-m.htm

- Leon County Clerk of Courts - Marriage Records ~ Florida
  http://www.clerk.leon.fl.us/marriage/

- Lenawee County Marriage Records
  http://www.rootsweb.com/~usgenweb/mi/lenawee/4601marr.htm

- Lincoln County, Oklahoma Early Marriages
  http://www.skypoint.com/~jkm/oklincoln/marriage.html

- Lincoln County, TN, Marriages -- Interactive Search
  http://www.rootsweb.com/cgi-bin/tnlincoln/tnlincoln.pl

- Llanelli Marriages 1833-1837 St Elli Parish Church, South Wales, UK
  ftp://ftp.rootsweb.com/pub/wggenweb/southwales/vitals/llanelli.txt
  Also Llanelli Marriages 1864-1867 Taken from Llanelli Guardian Births, Deaths & Marriages.

- A Little Bit of Ireland
  http://home.att.net/~labaths/
  From Cathy Joynt Labath, contains many transcribed records: birth, marriage, cemeteries, deeds, directories, etc.

- Louisiana Weddings
  http://www.angelfire.com/tx/1850censusrecords/laweddings.html

- Madison County, Iowa Marriages 1850 - 1880
  http://searches.rootsweb.com/cgi-bin/Genea/iowa

- Marriage Bonds of Ontario, 1803-1834
  http://www.amazon.com/exec/obidos/ISBN=0912606266/markcyndisgenealA/
  A book by Thomas B. Wilson.

- Marriage History Search Form
  http://thor.ddp.state.me.us/archives/plsql/archdev.Marriage_Archive.search_form
  Index to Maine Marriages 1892-1966.

- Marriage Notices from the Houston Morning Star Newspaper, April, 1839-1844: ~ Texas
  http://www.geocities.com/Vienna/1516/houmarr.html

- Marriage Records of Knott County, Kentucky
  http://www.rootsweb.com/~kyknott/marriages.html

- Marriage Records of Monroe County, Michigan (Volume 1)
  http://www.amazon.com/exec/obidos/ISBN=0940696185/markcyndisgenealA/
  A book by The Genealogical Society of Monroe County.

- Marriages in Tisbury, 1850 - 1853
  http://www.vineyard.net/vineyard/history/tmar1b.htm
  Transcript of the town marriage register for the town of Tisbury, Mass., covering the years 1850-1853.

- Marriages in Tisbury, 1853 - 1875
  http://www.vineyard.net/vineyard/history/tmar2.htm
  Transcript of town marriage register for the town of Tisbury, Mass. for the years 1853-1875.

- Marriage Witness Indexes for United Kingdom, Australia, and New Zealand
  http://www.genuki.org.uk/mwi/

- Marriages and Deaths, A-D ~ Pennsylvania
  http://www.geocities.com/Heartland/Plains/3558/admarrig.htm
  1810-1818. Many from Luzerne, Bradford, & Susquehanna Counties.

- Marriages and Deaths, E-G ~ Pennsylvania
  http://www.geocities.com/Heartland/Plains/3558/egmarrig.htm
  1810-1818. Many from Luzerne, Bradford, & Susquehanna Counties.

- Marriages from the Sherburn Hospital Registers (1695-1837)
  http://www.cs.ncl.ac.uk/genuki/Transcriptions/DUR/SHO.html
  Northumberland and Durham, England.

- Marriages from the Texas Telegraph, 1841-50 ~ Houston, Texas
  http://www.geocities.com/Vienna/1516/houmart.html

- Marriages in Kalkaska County, Michigan 1871-1875
  http://members.aol.com/kingsley/kas-mar.html

- Marriages in Parishes in Castlebar-Westport Area ~ Ireland
  http://people.delphi.com/patdeese/MARR.HTML

- Marriages in Pictou County by Rev. James McGregor ~ Nova Scotia, Canada
  http://www.rootsweb.com/~pictou/hitches.htm

- Marriages in Plauschwarren, East Prussia 1778-1802
  http://www.mmhs.org/prussia/plauschm.htm

- Marriages in Rankin County, Mississippi
  http://www.vanished.com/pages/free_lib/rankin_co.html

- Marriages of Norfolk County, Virginia, 1851-1865
  mailto:ehanbury@pilot.infi.net
  This book, compiled and published by Elizabeth B. Hanbury, lists the 1300+ marriages and all pertinent information for each given in the county marriage register for that period. Arranged alphabetically by grooms' last names; brides' names are indexed. For details send e-mail to Elizabeth at:ehanbury@pilot.infi.net.

- Maryland State Archives Marriage Records in MD
  http://www.mdarchives.state.md.us/msa/refserv/html/comarria.html

- Massachusetts Genealogy: Marriages 1841-1850
  http://www.angelfire.com/ma2/massmarriages/index.html

- Miami Valley Genealogical Index
  http://www.pcdl.lib.oh.us/miami/miami.htm
  Surname index of census, tax, marriage & wills records for these counties: Butler, Champaign, Clark, Darke, Greene, Hamilton, Mercer, Miami, Montgomery, Preble, Shelby, Warren.

- Middlesex England Parish Records
  http://www.enol.com/~infobase/gen/parish/
  Database of records between 1563 and 1895, listed alphabetically by groom's last name.

- Migranet
  http://migranet.geneactes.org/
  A database of 45,000 French marriages in which one of the a people is a "migrant" (married in another department or country other than that of their birth).

- Mt. View Research Page County, Virginia Marriages 1831 - 1939
  http://www.rootsweb.com/~vapage/apagemarr.htm

- Mt. View Research Marriages 1851-1915 - A Shenandoah Co., VA.
  http://www.rootsweb.com/~vapage/shenmarriages/shenmarr-a.htm

- Nashville Local History Indexes
  http://wendy.nashv.lib.tn.us:82/
  Includes marriages 1864-1905, searchable by bride or groom; obituaries from the Nashville Banner and the Tennessean, from 1977 through present.

- New Orleans Marriage Index Daily Picayune 1837-1857
  http://nutrias.org/~nopl/info/louinfo/newsmarr/newsmarr.htm

- New South Wales Registry of Births, Deaths and Marriages
  http://www.agd.nsw.gov.au/bdm/

- New Zealand Births, Deaths & Marriages Office
  http://www.bdm.govt.nz/diawebsite.nsf/c3649e22547ea840cc25681e0008b39b/c26afa900922c388cc25683e007b9a3f?OpenDocument

- Ontario Vital Statistics Bulletin
  http://www.gov.on.ca/MCZCR/archives/english/geneal/vtlstats.htm
  Researching Birth, Death and Marriage Records in Ontario from the Archives of Ontario.

- Parksville Qualicum Marriages, 1948-1994 ~ Mid-Vancouver Island, BC, Canada
  http://macn.bc.ca/~d69hist/marriage.html

- Pickens County, AL Marriages 1881-1898
  http://www.rootsweb.com/~alpicken/pickco/marriage.html

- Pinellas Genealogy Society, Inc.
  http://www.geocities.com/Heartland/Plains/8283/
  Includes a database of 1970 - 1974 Pinellas County Marriages and Engagements.

- Pipestone County Museum Marriage Records ~ MN
  http://www.pipestone.mn.us/Museum/MALEMAR.HTM

- Porter County Marriages 1836-1850 ~ Indiana
  http://members.aol.com/kjtcet2/wedd.htm

- The POYNTZ Family in India
  http://www.hal-pc.org/~poyntz/india.html
  Selected Extracts from the India Presidencies of Bengal, Bombay and Madras Ecclesiastical Returns of Baptisms, Marriages and Burials 1713-1948.

- Prince Edward Island Data Pages - Index to PEI Database Reports
  http://homepages.rootsweb.com/~mvreid/pei/peidbidx.html
  A wonderful collection of resources from Marge Reid, including probate records, surname indexes for marriage and burial records and much more.

- Quaker Marriages
  http://www.rootsweb.com/~quakers/quakmarr.htm

- Record of Marriages and Deaths 1826-1836 ~ PA
  http://www.geocities.com/Heartland/Plains/3558/voliv.htm
  Found in "Proceedings and Collections of the Wyoming Historical & Geological Society", Vol. IV.

- Records of the Reformed Dutch Church in New York - Marriages, 1639-1699
  http://www.rootsweb.com/~ote/rdcmarr.htm

- Registrar of Births, Deaths and Marriages, Dundee ~ Scotland
  http://www.dundeecity.gov.uk/dcchtml/sservices/rbdm.html

- Revolutionary War Period Bible, Family & Marriage Records
  http://www.dhc.net/~revwar/
  Index to microfilm volumes of abstracts from pension files.

- Reynolds County Marriage Records 1870-1891
  http://www.rootsweb.com/~moreynol/reymarge.htm

- Ripley County Missouri Marriage Records {1833-1860}
  http://members.tripod.com/~tmsnyder/Ripley.htm_

- Rumford Marriage Intentions, 1801-1869
  http://www.rootsweb.com/~meoxford/rumintro.htm
  Oxford County, Maine. As recorded in William B. Lapham's History of Rumford, Maine.

- San Francisco County Ancestors' Marriage Notices ~ California
  http://www.sfo.com/~timandpamwolf/sfmar.htm

- Search Idaho Marriage Record Index
  http://abish.ricks.edu/fhc/gbsearch.asp
  Search engine for marriages in Arizona, Idaho, Nevada, Oregon, Utah 1850 - 1951.

- Search Weil im Schoenbuch Marriages ~ WŠrttemberg, Germany
  http://www.kinquest.com/genealogy/databases/marriages.html

- Selected Marriages of Trigg County ~ Kentucky
  http://www.kyseeker.com/trigg/marriages.html

- Sheridan County Marriages
  http://www.rootsweb.com/~wysherid/marriages1.htm
  The Sheridan (WY) Genealogical Society compiled this index from original records, Books 1-9, at the Sheridan County, Wyoming Courthouse.

- The Skaneateles Historical Society
  http://www.skaneateles.com/historical/
  New York. They have vital statistics records online, including marriage records and death records. A database of over 15,000 records compiled from the old newspaper records from 1831 through 1899.

- The Source: A Guidebook of American Genealogy - Chapter 4: Research in Marriage and Divorce Records
  http://www.ancestry.com/home/source/src70.htm
  A full, online version of this book, published by Ancestry, edited by Loretto Dennis Szucs and Sandra Hargreaves Luebking.

- The St. Catherine's Marriage Index
  http://www.cs.ncl.ac.uk/genuki/StCathsTranscriptions/

- Sumter County, AL Marriages 1833-1850
  http://www.rootsweb.com/~alpicken/sumter/marriage.html

- Sussex County Marriages ~ New Jersey
  http://www.gate.net/~pascalfl/marrndx.html

- Tattnall County, Georgia Marriage Records 1805-1845
  http://www.teesee.com/marriage/tattnall/marriage1.htm

- Town Marriage Records in Tisbury, 1850 -1875: An Index of Recorded Names
  http://www.vineyard.net/vineyard/history/tmindex.htm

- Tulare County Marriages - 1852 to June 1893 ~ CA
  http://cpl.cagenweb.com/tulare/tckcm.htm

- Tulare County Marriages - July 1, 1893 to Dec. 31, 1909 ~ California
  http://cpl.cagenweb.com/tulare/tcm.htm

- Tuscaloosa County, AL Marriages 1821-1860
  http://www.rootsweb.com/~aljeffer/tuscal/marriage.html

- UK Marriage Related Information
  http://members.aol.com/aisling13/ixukwit.htm

- Vital Events Indexes - BC Archives
  http://www.bcarchives.gov.bc.ca/textual/governmt/vstats/v_events.htm
  - Marriage Registration Index Search Gateway, 1872 to 1923
    http://www2.bcarchives.gov.bc.ca/cgi-bin/www2vsm

- Vital Records Extracted From "The Life, Travels, and Ministry of Milton M. Everly"
  http://www.lava.net/~tabor/jan/milton.html
  September 1901-September 1903. Extractions of records for marriages, some baptisms, and funerals.

- Vital Statistics ~ Manitoba, Canada
  http://www.gov.mb.ca/cca/vital.html
  From the Manitoba Consumer and Corporate Affairs, information on how to obtain birth, marriage and death certificates from Manitoba, Canada.

- Walpole History Vital Records to 1850 ~ MA
  http://www.walpole.ma.us/hhisdocvitalrecords.htm

- Wedding Bells From Colonial Thru 1899
  http://www.angelfire.com/tx/1850censusrecords/colonialwedbells.html
  Post marriages that took place prior to 1900.

◆ Professional Researchers, Volunteers & Other Research Services

- Anne's UK Certificates for Australians
  http://freespace.virgin.net/mark.wainwright6/uk_certificates/
  An Australian living in London who can obtain copies of English, Scottish & Welsh Birth, Marriage and Death Certificates in exchange for payment in Australian dollars.

- Marbract Services - NSW Birth, Death & Marriage Certificate Transcription Service ~ Australia
  http://www.marbract.com.au/
  NSW Births 1788-1905, NSW Deaths and Marriages 1788-1918.

MEDICAL, MEDICINE, GENETICS

http://www.cyndislist.com/medical.htm

Category Index:

- ◆ Diseases & Medical Terms
- ◆ Doctors, Nurses and Hospitals
- ◆ General Resource Sites
- ◆ Genetics, DNA & Family Health

- ◆ History
- ◆ Publications, Software & Supplies
- ◆ U.S. Civil War Medicine & Hospitals

◆ Diseases & Medical Terms

- Archaic Medical Terms for Genealogists
  http://www.gpiag-asthma.org/drpsmith/amt1.htm

- Colonial Diseases & Cures
  http://homepages.rootsweb.com/~sam/disease.html

- Disease & Definition
  http://www.rootsweb.com/~njmorris/disease.htm

- German Illness Translations
  http://pixel.cs.vt.edu/library/articles/link/illness.txt

- Glossary of Diseases
  http://www.rootsweb.com/~ote/disease.htm

- Kentuckiana Genealogy - Disease Chart
  http://www.kentuckianagenealogy.org/guide/help/
  disease.html

- A Medical Miscellany for Genealogists
  http://www.amazon.com/exec/obidos/ISBN=0788403753/
  markcyndisgenealA/
  A book by Jeanette Jerger.

- Modern Names or Definitions of Illnesses of Our
  Ancestors, A-K
  http://www.genrecords.com/library/disease.htm
  And L-Z
  http://www.genrecords.com/library/diseases2.htm
  From the Genealogy Record Service Library.

- Old Disease Names & Their Modern Definitions
  http://www3.nb.sympatico.ca/pebbles2/tools.html#disease

- Old Medical Terminology
  http://members.aol.com/AdamCo9991/medicalterminolgy.html

- Outdated Medical Terminology
  http://www.familytreemaker.com/00000014.html

- SFS Outdated Medical Terms
  http://www.demon.co.uk/sfs/diseases.htm

- Forgotten Medical Cures
  http://www.geocities.com/Heartland/Hills/8929/cures.html
  *From the "Yucky Stuff" thread on the Roots-L mailing list, October
  1998.*

◆ Doctors, Nurses and Hospitals

- Biographical Information: Doctors and Other
  Professions
  http://library.bma.org.uk/html/biographx.html
  *From the British Medical Association. Provides links and a
  bibliography for historic and biographical research for the UK
  medical professions.*

- The Civil Hospital Renkioi
  http://www.melcombe.freeserve.co.uk/source/renkioilist.htm
  *An Alphabetical list of staff who worked at the Civil Hospital
  Renkioi in Turkey during the Crimean War.*

- Deceased American Physicians' Records
  http://www.ngsgenealogy.org/library/content/ama_info.html
  *A research service available from the National Genealogical
  Society.*

- The Florence Nightingale Nurses
  http://www.melcombe.freeserve.co.uk/source/nurselist.htm
  An alphabetical list of nurses sent to military hospitals in the east.

- Medical Practitioners Database
  http://www.mdarchives.state.md.us/msa/speccol/sc4800/
  sc4800/html/0002.html
  *Medical Care in the City of Baltimore, 1752-1919. Surnames of
  practitioners arranged alphabetically.*

- Medical Profession Last Names A-L
  http://rontay.digiweb.com/visit/occupy/physa.htm
  And M-Z
  http://rontay.digiweb.com/visit/occupy/physm.htm
  *From the Occupations Census Indexes, Ron Taylor's UK Census
  Finding Aids and Indexes.*

- In Memoriam - Doctors of Hawaii
  http://hml.org/WWW/mdindex/mdindex.html
  *In Memoriam - Doctors of Hawaii is a set of seven volumes
  containing the biographical sketches of more than 600 doctors from
  the early 1800s up to 1985 who practiced medicine in Hawaii and
  are now deceased. Many of the biographies also have a photo
  available. This Index to In Memoriam - Doctors of Hawaii is an
  alphabetical list of the physicians, their dates as known, and an
  indication if a photograph and oral history is available.*

- Records of Hospitals in the Corporation of London
  Records Office
  http://www.cityoflondon.gov.uk/archives/clro/hospital.htm

- Royal College of Physicians of Edinburgh - Library
  http://www.rcpe.ac.uk/library/index.html

- The Royal College of Surgeons of Edinburgh -
  College Library
  http://www.rcsed.ac.uk/geninfo/library/Default.asp

- Tennessee Confederate Physicians : An Introduction
  http://www.state.tn.us/sos/statelib/pubsvs/docintro.htm
  *From the Tennessee State Library and Archives - Historical and
  Genealogical Information.*

- Texas Physicians Historical Biographical Database
  http://www3.utsouthwestern.edu/library/doctors/doctors.htm
  *Searchable database of citations to biographical information related
  to early Texas physicians from the Texas State Journal of Medicine
  for 1905-1966 and additional sources.*

- Victorian Nurses in the Boer War
  http://users.netconnect.com.au/~ianmac/nurses.html

- Was Your Ancestor a Doctor?
  http://user.itl.net/~glen/doctors.html

◆ General Resource Sites

- Deaths In the Melbourne Hospital, 1867-1880
  http://home.coffeeonline.com.au/~tfoen/meldeath.html
  *An index of foreign born residents of Melbourne who passed away
  at the Melbourne Hospital between 1867 and 1880.*

- FOLKLORE Mailing List
  http://www.rootsweb.com/~jfuller/gen_mail_general.html
  #FOLKLORE
  *A mailing list for the exchange of folklore - folk medicine and
  recipes.*

- Hospital Records Database
  http://hospitalrecords.pro.gov.uk/
  *Provides information on the existence and location of the records of
  the hospitals in the U.K. Currently over 2,800 entries can be found
  by searching the database using the following simple enquiry
  screen.*

- Medical Care in the City of Baltimore, 1752-1919
  http://www.mdarchives.state.md.us/msa/speccol/sc4800/
  sc4800/html/index.html
  An electronic archive from the Maryland State Archives.

- MEDICAL-GENEALOGY Mailing List
  http://www.rootsweb.com/~jfuller/gen_mail_general.html
  #MEDICAL-GENEALOGY
  *For the discussion and sharing of information regarding our
  ancestors' medical histories, old diseases, the practice of medicine
  in the past, etc.*

- U.S. National Library of Medicine (NLM) - History
  of Medicine Division
  http://www.nlm.nih.gov/hmd/hmd.html
  o Does HMD have sources for genealogical
    research?
    http://www.nlm.nih.gov/hmd/faq-hmd.html#genealogy

- The Wellcome Institute Collections
  http://www.wellcome.ac.uk/wellcomegraphic/a2/w1.dhtml
  *Books and journals, manuscripts, archives and pictures relating to
  the history of medicine.*

◆ Genetics, DNA & Family Health

- ABCNEWS.com: Geneticist: All Europeans
  Descended From Seven Matriarchal Clans
  http://abcnews.go.com/sections/science/DailyNews/daughters
  00042 0.html

- "All in the Family"
  http://www.healthgate.com/choice/uhs/cons/healthy/woman/
  1999/familyhx/index.shtml
  Article by Howard Bell.

- American Journal of Medical Genetics
  http://www.interscience.wiley.com/jpages/0148-7299/

- AudioTapes.com - Genealogical Lectures on Cassette
  Tapes - DNA
  http://www.audiotapes.com/search2.asp?Search=DNA
  And Genetic
  http://www.audiotapes.com/search2.asp?Search=genetic

- Compiling your family medical history - How
  important is it?
  http://www.mayohealth.org/mayo/9612/htm/family.htm
  o Creating a family medical history
    http://www.mayohealth.org/mayo/9612/htm/fami_1sb.htm

- Cyrillic 3
  http://www.cyrillicsoftware.com/
  Pedigree drawing software for genetic research. For Windows.

- DNA Identification Systems -- Home Collection and
  Storage Kit
  http://www.dnaidsys.com/
  *The kit can be used to collect and store family members for the
  purpose of proving or disproving lineage. Examples of this type of
  use are the genetic tracing of Thomas Jefferson and Anastasia.*

- DOS/Windows Pedigree Drawing Programs
  http://www.sfbr.org/sfbr/public/software/pedraw/
  dos_peddrw.html
  *Contact information for pedigree drawing software programs used
  for genetic research.*

- Double Helix Genealogy
  http://www.oz.net/~markhow/writing/helix.htm
  By Mark Howells.

- Ethical Issues Surround DNA Research
  http://newsnet.byu.edu/show_story.cfm?number=8701&year=
  current
  An article from NewsNet@BYU.

- Family Diseases : Are You at Risk
  http://www.amazon.com/exec/obidos/ISBN=0806312548/
  markcyndisgenealA/
  A book by Myra Vanderpool Gormley.

- GENEALOGY-DNA Mailing List
  http://www.rootsweb.com/~jfuller/gen_mail_general.html
  #GENEALOGY-DNA
  *For discussing methods and share results of DNA testing as applied
  to genealogical research.*

- Genealogy and Genetics
  http://www.geocities.com/Heartland/Pointe/1439/
  Genealogy with a special reason: Stanley Diamond's Beta-Thalassemia genetic trait research project.

- Generational Health
  http://www.generationalhealth.com/
  Family health history from Pfizer.

- Genes, Peoples and Languages
  http://www.amazon.com/exec/obidos/ISBN=0865475296/
  markcyndisgenealA/
  A book by Luigi Luca Cavalli-Sforza.

- Genetic Disorders, Databases, and Genealogy
  http://habitant.org/genetics.htm

- GeneDraw
  http://www.inviweb.com/genedraw/
  A family-tree software with a graphic interface particularly useful for the drawing of family-trees or gene maps. MacOS version available.

- Genetics of the Acadian People
  http://www.genweb.net/acadian-cajun/genetics.htm
  Describes a conference held regarding the unique genetic history of the Acadian people.

- Genetics and Genealogy: Y Polymorphism and mtDNA Analyses
  http://www.duerinck.com/genetic.html
  Discusses in detail the genealogical impacts of current genetic science.

- Germans from Russia: Volga Germans:
  - Alzheimer's Disease: New Complexities and Some Insight from Molecular Genetic Investigations
    http://www.asri.edu/genetics/brochure/agh/news/jan96/
    alz.html
  - Can You Inherit Alzheimer's Disease?
    http://www.alznsw.asn.au/library/inherit.htm
  - New Alzheimer's Candidate Gene
    http://www.accessexcellence.org/WN/SUA06/alz895.html
  - New Alzheimer's Gene Discovered On Chromosome 1
    http://www.chiroscience.com/company_information/press_
    releases/chiroscience_archive/pr950818.html
  - The Presenilin Genes and Their Role in Early-Onset Familial Alzheimer's Disease
    http://www.coa.uky.edu/ADReview/Tanzi/Tanzi.htm
  - Presenilins: a new gene family involved in Alzheimer's Disease Pathology
    http://www2.hu-berlin.de/strahlenklinik/english/editor.htm

- The Great Human Diasporas: The History of Diversity and Evolution
  http://www.amazon.com/exec/obidos/ISBN=0201442310/
  markcyndisgenealA/
  A book by Luigi Luca Cavalli-Sforza.

- Healthwatch - Family Medical History
  http://www.methodisthealth.com/health/family/fmedhstry.html

- Hemings and Jefferson: A Genealogical Enigma
  http://www.rootsweb.com/~rwguide/notable/sally.htm
  From RootsWeb's Guide to Tracing Family Trees.

- Íslensk erfðagreining / deCODE genetics
  http://www.decode.is/
  Based in Reykjavik, Iceland, deCODE genetics is a population-based genomics company conducting research into the inherited causes of common diseases. Being situated in Iceland has certain advantages for the company. The Icelandic population, with its relative genetic homogeneity, extensive genealogical records and high-quality healthcare system, provides the resources to identify genes associated with a multitude of diseases.
  - Iceland: The Case of a National Human Genome Project
    http://www.decode.is/greinar/anthro.htm
    Online article from Antropology Today discussion various social implications of the deCODE project.
  - Íslendingabók deCODE's Genealogy Database
    http://www.decode.is/ppt/genea/
    Online slide show demostration of deCODE's database software using deCODE's CEO, Kári Stefánsson, as an example. The demo traces his ancestors back to Egill Skallagrímsson, poet and viking of the 9th century AD.

- The Jefferson Scandals: A Rebuttal
  http://www.amazon.com/exec/obidos/ISBN=0819178217/
  markcyndisgenealA/
  A book by Virginius Dabney.

- JewishGen - Genealogy by Genetics
  http://www.jewishgen.org/dna/

- Joslin's Dr. Shuldiner Works with Amish on Diabetes and Genetics Studies
  http://www.joslin.org/news/shuldiner_amish.html
  Online article regarding the Amish community in Lancaster County, Pennsylvania and studies of the genetic origins of diabetes.

- Lifelinks International
  http://www.lifelinks.mb.ca/
  A family medical history and personal record keeping program.

- Mapping the Icelandic Genome
  http://sunsite.berkeley.edu/biotech/iceland/
  An anthropology of the scientific, political, economic, religious, and ethical issues surrounding the deCode Project and its global implications. Iceland has a series of distinctive characteristics, which make it suitable for such mapping. Its population is relatively small (today 275,000 but as low as 50,000 in the recent past). There exist an unusually complete set of family records in Iceland (over 80% of all Icelandic people who ever lived can be placed genealogically on a computerized database).

- The Melungeon Health Education and Support Network
  http://www.melungeonhealth.org/
  Information about inherited Mediterranean illnesses being found among Melungeon descendants.

- Molecular Genealogy
  http://molecular-genealogy.byu.edu/
  Researchers at Brigham Young University are conducting a study using DNA to reconstruct worldwide genealogies Participants for the study are being sought.

- Molecular Genealogy - Is DNA the Answer to Lost Family Records?
  http://genealogy.about.com/hobbies/genealogy/library/weekly/aa102400a.htm
  From the About.com genealogy section.

- Monticello Jefferson-Hemings Report
  http://www.monticello.org/plantation/hemings_report.html
  Report of the Research Committee on Thomas Jefferson and Sally Hemings from the Thomas Jefferson Memorial Foundation.

- National Genealogical Society - Family Health History
  http://www.ngsgenealogy.org/about/content/committees/famhealth.html

- OMIM - Online Mendelian Inheritance in Man
  http://www3.ncbi.nlm.nih.gov/Omim/searchomim.html
  Searchable database of genetic diseases.

- Oxford Ancestors
  http://www.oxfordancestors.com
  Offers DNA-based services in genealogy. MatriLine™ uses mitochondrial DNA to place a person in an evolutionary framework going back 150,000 years. MatriLine™ interprets your maternal ancestry, linking you - if your roots are in Europe - to one of seven "foremothers". MyMap™ maps out the current geographical distribution of any surname. MaleMatch™ compares Y-chromosomes to establish, or disprove, a paternal link between individuals.

- Past Imperfect: How Tracing Your Family Medical History Can Save Your Life
  http://www.amazon.com/exec/obidos/ISBN=1891661035/markcyndisgenealA/
  A book by Carol Daus.

- Pedigree/Draw
  http://www.sfbr.org/sfbr/public/software/pedraw/peddrw.html
  Pedigree drawing software for genetic research. Macintosh only.

- Sally Hemings
  http://www.amazon.com/exec/obidos/ISBN=0312247044/markcyndisgenealA/
  A book by Barbara Chase-Riboud.

- Sally Hemings and Thomas Jefferson: History, Memory, and Civic Culture
  http://www.amazon.com/exec/obidos/ISBN=0813919193/markcyndisgenealA/
  A book by Jan Lewis.

- Scientific American: Feature Article: The Puzzle of Hypertension in African-Americans: February 1999
  http://www.sciam.com/1999/0299issue/0299cooper.html
  Genes are often invoked to account for why high blood pressure is so common among African-Americans. Yet the rates are low in Africans. This discrepancy demonstrates how genes and the environment interact.

- Slave Children of Thomas Jefferson
  http://www.amazon.com/exec/obidos/ISBN=4906574009/markcyndisgenealA/
  A book by Samuel H. Sloan.

- Thomas Jefferson and Sally Hemings: An American Controversy
  http://www.amazon.com/exec/obidos/ISBN=0813918332/markcyndisgenealA/
  A book by Annette Gordon-Reed .

- Your Family's Health History
  http://www.familytreemaker.com/issue6.html
  From the Family Tree Maker site.

- Your Medical Heritage
  http://www.pbs.org/kbyu/ancestors/firstseries/viewersguide/episode-eight.html
  From Ancestors: The First Series television program on PBS.

◆ History

- The American Experience - Influenza, 1918
  http://www.pbs.org/wgbh/amex/influenza/
  Companion web site to the PBS documentary.

- Armies of Pestilence : The Effects of Pandemics on History
  http://www.amazon.com/exec/obidos/ISBN=0718829492/markcyndisgenealA/
  A book by R. S.Bray.

- Bring Out Your Dead: The Great Plague of Yellow Fever in Philadelphia in 1793
  http://www.amazon.com/exec/obidos/ISBN=0812214234/markcyndisgenealA/
  A book by J. H. Powell.

- Chicago Historical Information - 1849-1855, 1866-1867: Early Cholera Epidemics ~ Illinois
  http://www.chipublib.org/004chicago/disasters/early_cholera.html
  From the Chicago Public Library.

- The Cholera Epidemic of 1873
  http://www.uab.edu/reynolds/cholera.html
  Historic narrative of the epidemic in Birmingham, Alabama including an early map of the city showing areas of the disease.

- The Cholera Epidemic of 1873 in Birmingham Alabama
  http://www.dpo.uab.edu/~bishopdt/oindex.htm
  Online article by David Bishop.

- The Cholera Years: The United States in 1832, 1849, and 1866
  http://www.amazon.com/exec/obidos/ISBN=0226726770/markcyndisgenealA/
  A book by Charles E. Rosenberg.

- Encyclopedia of Plague and Pestilence
  http://www.amazon.com/exec/obidos/ISBN=0816027587/markcyndisgenealA/
  A book by George C. Kohn (hardback).

- Epidemics
  http://homepages.rootsweb.com/~maggieoh/epd.html

- Epidemics
  http://main.nc.us/OBCGS/epidemics.htm

- Epidemics and Military Battles
  http://www.ento.vt.edu/IHS/militaryEpidemics.html

- Epidemics in U.S. - 1657 - 1918
  http://members.aol.com/AdamCo9991/epidemics.html

- Epidemics in US 1628-1918
  http://www.geocities.com/Heartland/Acres/7241/
  epidemic.html

- Epidemics in the USA 1657 - 1819
  http://www.teesee.com/EmanuelCo/resources/epidemic.htm

- From Quackery to Bacteriology: The Emergence of
  Modern Medicine in 19th Century America
  http://www.cl.utoledo.edu/canaday/quackery/quack-
  index.html

- Genealogy Quest: Genealogical Research Assistance
  - American Epidemics
  http://www.genealogy-quest.com/glossaries/epidemics.html

- A General Study of the Plague in England 1539-1640
  With a Specific Reference to Loughborough
  http://www.gmtnet.co.uk/plague/
  *Includes information on the cessation of parochial registration at
  the height of the plague.*

- Health and Hygiene in the Nineteenth Century
  http://landow.stg.brown.edu/victorian/health/health10.html

- Historical Epidemics
  http://www.geocities.com:0080/Heartland/Prairie/9166/
  epidemics.htm

- History of Epidemics and Plagues
  http://uhavax.hartford.edu/~bugl/histepi.htm
  *This site focuses on the medical causes and transmission mechanics
  of epidemics but does give some interesting historical background.*

- History of the Health Sciences World Wide Web
  Links
  http://www2.mc.duke.edu/misc/MLA/HHSS/histlink.htm

- Major US Epidemics
  http://www.infoplease.com/ipa/A0001460.html

- Man and Microbes : Disease and Plagues in History
  and Modern Times
  http://www.amazon.com/exec/obidos/ISBN=0684822709/
  markcyndisgenealA/
  A book by Arno Karlen.

- Martha Ballard's Diary Online
  http://www.dohistory.org/diary/index.html
  *The source for the book and film "A Midwife's Tale", Martha
  Ballard wrote in her diary nearly every day from January 1, 1785 to
  May 12, 1812 (27 years) for a total of almost 10,000 entries. Her
  diary is an unparalleled document in early American history.*

- The Mississippi Valley's Great Yellow Fever
  Epidemic of 1878
  http://www.amazon.com/exec/obidos/ISBN=0807118249/
  markcyndisgenealA/
  A book by Khaled J. Bloom.

- National Library of Medicine: Exhibitions in the
  History of Medicine
  http://www.nlm.nih.gov/exhibition/exhibition.html

- New Jersey Hot Zones! : Viruses, Diseases, &
  Epidemics in Our State's History
  http://www.amazon.com/exec/obidos/ISBN=0793389194/
  markcyndisgenealA/
  A book by Carole Marsh.

- Plagues & Epidemics
  http://www.theplumber.com/plague.html
  *From a history of plumbing, this site focuses on this history of
  water-borne diseases.*

- Plagues and Epidemics in Eastern Europe
  http://members.xoom.com/Shmutzy/plagues.html

- Plagues and Peoples
  http://www.amazon.com/exec/obidos/ISBN=0385121229/
  markcyndisgenealA/
  A book by William H. McNeill.

- Poisons of the Past : Molds, Epidemics, and History
  http://www.amazon.com/exec/obidos/ISBN=0300051212/
  markcyndisgenealA/
  A book by Mary Kilbourne Matossian.

- Public Record Office | Finding Aids | Leaflets |
  Nineteenth Century Public Health and Epidemics:
  Some PRO Sources
  http://www.pro.gov.uk/leaflets/ri2180.htm

- Quarantine! : East European Jewish Immigrants and
  the New York City Epidemics of 1892
  http://www.amazon.com/exec/obidos/ISBN=0801861802/
  markcyndisgenealA/
  A book by Howard Markel.

- Reported Outbreaks of Infectious Disease, Maryland
  1731-1870
  http://www.mdarchives.state.md.us/msa/speccol/sc4800/
  sc4800/html/0005.html
  *From Medical Care in the City of Baltimore, 1752-1919. Arranged
  by year.*

- Resources for Medical History Papers
  http://www.usuhs.mil/meh/histres.html

- Some Historically Significant Epidemics
  http://www.botany.duke.edu/microbe/chrono.htm

- Viruses, Plagues, and History
  http://www.amazon.com/exec/obidos/ISBN=0195117239/
  markcyndisgenealA/
  A book by Michael B. A. Oldstone.

- The Wordsworth Encyclopedia of Plague and
  Pestilence
  http://www.amazon.co.uk/exec/obidos/ASIN/1853267538/
  markandcyndisgen
  A book by George C. Kohn (paperback).

◆ Publications, Software & Supplies

- Amazon.com Genealogy Bookstore - Medical
  http://www.amazon.com/exec/obidos/external-search/?
  keyword=medical+genealogy&tag=markcyndisgenealA/

- AudioTapes.com - Genealogical Lectures on Cassette Tapes - Medical
  http://www.audiotapes.com/search2.asp?Search=Medical

- Cyrillic 3
  http://www.cyrillicsoftware.com/
  Pedigree drawing software for genetic research. For Windows.

- Frontier Press Bookstore - Genetics and Genealogy
  http://www.frontierpress.com/frontier.cgi?category=genetics

- Frontier Press Bookstore - Medical History
  http://www.frontierpress.com/frontier.cgi?category=medical

- Pedigree/Draw
  http://www.sfbr.org/sfbr/public/software/pedraw/peddrw.html
  Pedigree drawing software for genetic research. Macintosh only.

◆ U.S. Civil War Medicine & Hospitals

- Camp Letterman Preservation Project
  http://members.aol.com/Camp%20Letterman/main.html
  Dedicated to the preservation of Camp Letterman located just outside of Gettysburg. It was the largest Civil War hospital ever established in North America.

- Civil War and 19th Century Medical Terminology
  http://members.aol.com/jweaver300/grayson/medterm.htm

- Civil War Medicine
  http://www.powerweb.net/bbock/war/

- Civil War Medicine Vocabulary
  http://cee.indiana.edu/gopher/Turner_Adventure_Learning/
  Gettysburg_Archive/Other_Resources/Medicine_
  Vocabulary.txt

- Medical Staff Press
  http://www.iserv.net/~civilmed/

- National Museum of Civil War Medicine
  http://www.civilwarmed.org/

- Resources in Civil War Medicine
  http://www.collphyphil.org/FIND_AID/histcvwr.htm
  At The Library of the College of Physicians of Philadelphia.

- Virginia's Confederate Military Hospitals
  http://members.aol.com/jweaver300/grayson/hospital.htm

MEDIEVAL

http://www.cyndislist.com/medieval.htm

- Amazon.com Genealogy Bookstore - Medieval
  http://www.amazon.com/exec/obidos/external-search/?
  keyword=medieval+genealogy&tag=markcyndisgenealA/

- AudioTapes.com - Genealogical Lectures on Cassette
  Tapes - Medieval
  http://www.audiotapes.com/search2.asp?Search=medieval

- Cartographic Images - Ancient, Medieval &
  Renaissance Maps
  http://www.iag.net/~jsiebold/carto.html

- Domesday Book
  http://www.pro.gov.uk/leaflets/ri2108.htm
  Information leaflet from the Public Records Office.

- Focus on...The Domesday Book
  http://learningcurve.pro.gov.uk/domesday/default.htm
  Online Exhibition from the Public Records Office.

- The Domesday Book Online
  http://www.domesdaybook.co.uk/index.html
  - Berkshire
    http://www.domesdaybook.co.uk/berkshire.html
  - Essex
    http://www.domesdaybook.co.uk/essex.html
  - Hampshire
    http://www.domesdaybook.co.uk/hampshire.html
  - Herefordshire
    http://www.domesdaybook.co.uk/herefordshire.html
  - Hertfordshire
    http://www.domesdaybook.co.uk/hertfordshire.html
  - Oxfordshire
    http://www.domesdaybook.co.uk/oxfordshire.html
  - Suffolk
    http://www.domesdaybook.co.uk/suffolk.html
  - Surrey
    http://www.domesdaybook.co.uk/surrey.html
  - Warwickshire
    http://www.domesdaybook.co.uk/warwickshire.html
  - Yorkshire - East Riding
    http://www.domesdaybook.co.uk/eastriding.html

- Dominion & Domination of the Gentle Sex: The
  Lives of Medieval Women
  http://library.thinkquest.org/12834/

- Frequently Asked Questions (FAQs) for
  soc.genealogy.medieval
  http://www.rand.org/personal/Genea/faqmed.html

- Frontier Press Bookstore - Medieval/Renaissance
  Studies
  http://www.frontierpress.com/frontier.cgi?category=medieval

- GEN-MEDIEVAL Mailing List
  http://www.rootsweb.com/~jfuller/gen_mail_general.html
  #GEN-MEDIEVAL

- Glossary of Medieval Terms
  http://cal.bemidji.msus.edu/History/mcmanus/ma_gloss.html

- Guide to Medieval Terms
  http://orb.rhodes.edu/Medieval_Terms.html

- History of Europe in Medieval Times, Anglo-Saxons
  http://www.worldroots.com/brigitte/royal/royal7.htm
  *Historic and genealogical information about royal and nobility
  family lines.*

- Home Erenfried
  http://sites.netscape.net/erenfried/homepage
  *Information relating to the German and imperial aristocracy of the
  tenth and eleventh centuries.*

- Images Of Medieval Art And Architecture - Maps Of
  Great Britain
  http://www1.pitt.edu/~medart/menuengl/mainmaps.html

- Internet Medieval Sourcebook
  http://www.fordham.edu/halsall/sbook.html

- Medieval England 1066-1399 - Bibliography
  http://www.history.bangor.ac.uk/H3H03/h3h03bib.htm
  *From a course at the School of History and Welsh History / Adran
  Hanes a Hanes Cymru, University of Wales, Bangor.*

- Medieval English Towns
  http://www.trytel.com/~tristan/towns/towns.html
  *An outstanding online source for medieval urban history in
  England.*

- Medieval Genealogy - An Introduction
  http://www.audiotapes.com/product.asp?ProductCode
  ='HT-14'
  Presentation by James L. Hansen, available for sale on audio tape.

- Medieval Genealogy - from Everton's
  http://www.everton.com/oe1-15/gen-med.htm

- Medieval Names Archive
  http://www.panix.com/~mittle/names/

- Medieval Paleography
  http://orb.rhodes.edu/textbooks/palindex.html
  An introductory online course to medieval handwriting.

- Medieval Studies
  http://www.georgetown.edu/labyrinth/Virtual_Library/
  Medieval_Studies.html

- Names and Naming in Republican and Imperial
  Rome
  http://www.oz.net/~bockmad/ares/naming.html

- NetSERF - The Internet Connection for Medieval Resources
  http://netserf.cua.edu/

- ORB: The Online Reference Book for Medieval Studies
  http://orb.rhodes.edu/

- The Shaping of the Medieval World - Medieval Web Links
  http://www.fordham.edu/halsall/med/medweb.html

- Some notes on medieval English genealogy
  http://www.cgp100.dabsol.co.uk/
  Much more than just "some notes" - this site provides excellent content and links for the serious medieval researcher.

  o A brief guide to medieval English genealogy
    http://www.cgp100.dabsol.co.uk/gui/guide.htm
    Discusses record types, their uses, and locations.

- Torrione Castle - an unusual example of a Museum for History
  http://www.gvo.it/VdSF/torrione1.html
  From Italy. Be sure to check out their Vialardi di Sandigliano lineage library.

- The Unit for Prosopographical Research
  http://www.linacre.ox.ac.uk/research/prosop/home.stm
  From Linacre College, Oxford, England. Promotes the study of medieval prosopography - the social science using genealogy, onomastics and demography to study the past.

- Usenet Newsgroup soc.genealogy.medieval
  news:soc.genealogy.medieval
  Gatewayed with Mailing List GEN-MEDIEVAL.

MENNONITE
http://www.cyndislist.com/menno.htm

Category Index:
- ◆ The Amish
- ◆ General Resource Sites
- ◆ Libraries, Archives & Museums
- ◆ Locality Specific
- ◆ Mailing Lists, Newsgroups & Chat

- ◆ People & Families
- ◆ Publications, Software & Supplies
- ◆ Records: Census, Cemeteries, Land, Obituaries, Personal, Taxes and Vital
- ◆ Societies & Groups

◆ The Amish

- Amish and Mennonite Links
  http://members.aol.com/rhin0/Amish.html

- The Amish In Northern Indiana
  http://www.goshen.edu/~lonhs/SamYoder.html

- Amish Mennonite Surnames
  http://www.rootsweb.com/~pasomers/amsurs.htm

- The Amish, the Mennonites, and the Plain People of the Pennsylvania Dutch Country
  http://www.800padutch.com/amish.html

- Ask The Amish!
  http://www.800padutch.com/askamish.html

- The Illinois Amish Interpretive Center
  http://www.amishcenter.com/index.html
  The first museum in Illinois dedicated to the Amish culture. It traces the history of the Amish religion and provides a glimpse into the lives of Illinois Amish.

- Joslin's Dr. Shuldiner Works with Amish on Diabetes and Genetics Studies
  http://www.joslin.org/news/shuldiner_amish.html
  Online article regarding the Amish community in Lancaster County, Pennsylvania and studies of the genetic origins of diabetes.

◆ General Resource Sites

- The Amish, the Mennonites, and the Plain People of the Pennsylvania Dutch Country
  http://www.800padutch.com/amish.html

- Anabaptist-Mennonite History
  http://www.bibleviews.com/history-index.html

- Genealogical Resources for the Low German Mennonite Researcher
  http://www.pacinter.net/users/janzen/intro.htm
  An extensive, categorized bibliography of resources from the web site of Tim Janzen. Includes references for Canada, United States, Russia, Prussia, Netherlands, Internet, General, Software and more.

- MennoLink Mennonite Information Center
  http://www.mennolink.org/mic/menno.html

- Mennonite Connections on the WWW
  http://www-personal.umich.edu/~bpl/menno.html

- Mennonite Cross-Index - from FEEFHS
  http://feefhs.org/men/indexmen.html

- Mennonite Research Corner
  http://www.ristenbatt.com/genealogy/mennonit.htm

- Olive Tree Genealogy
  http://www.rootsweb.com/~ote/
  Huguenots & Walloons, Ontario Loyalists, Mohawk, Mennonite, Palatines and Dutch Research.

◆ Libraries, Archives & Museums

- Archives of the Mennonite Church
  http://www.goshen.edu/mcarchives/
  The Historical Committee and Archives holds the official records of the program boards and agencies of the Mennonite Church, whose headquarters are in Elkhart, Indiana. The Mennonite Church as an organization dates back to 1898 when it began holding biennial conferences. The Archives also holds personal papers from individuals and records from some inter-Mennonite organizations, such as the Mennonite Central Committee.

- A Bibliography of Anabaptist - Mennonite Works at the Mennonite Historical Library, Canadian Mennonite Bible College
  http://www.mbnet.mb.ca/~mhc/biblio.htm

- The Center for Mennonite Brethren Studies ~ Fresno, California
  http://www.fresno.edu/affiliation/cmbs/

- Centre for Mennonite Brethren Studies ~ Winnipeg, Manitoba
  http://www.mbconf.ca/mbstudies/

- The Illinois Amish Interpretive Center
  http://www.amishcenter.com/index.html
  The first museum in Illinois dedicated to the Amish culture. It traces the history of the Amish religion and provides a glimpse into the lives of Illinois Amish.

- Menno Simons Historical Library
  http://www.emu.edu/library/histlib.html

- Mennonite Archives of Ontario
  http://grebel.uwaterloo.ca/mao/

- Mennonite Heritage Centre ~ Winnipeg, Manitoba, Canada
  http://www.mbnet.mb.ca/~mhc/

- The Mennonite Historians of Eastern Pennsylvania
  http://www.mhep.org/welcome.html

- Mennonite Library and Archives
  http://www.bethelks.edu/services/mla/
  Bethel College North Newton, Kansas.

- UBA - Library: Church History: Mennonite
  http://www.uba.uva.nl/en/libraries/church.html
  From the Universiteitsbibliotheek Amsterdam. Holds the collection of the Verenigde Doopsgezinde Gemeente Amsterdam (the United Mennonite Congregation of Amsterdam). It also houses the Mennonite Documention Centre from 1800 to the present.

◆ Locality Specific

- Canadian Conference of Mennonite Brethren Churches
  http://www.mbconf.ca/

- The Mennonites of Manitoba
  http://www.prairiepublic.org/features/mennonites/index.htm

- Prussian-Russian-Canadian Mennonite Genealogical Resources
  http://www.mmhs.org/mmhsgen.htm

- Rosenort History
  http://www.rosenort.com/history
  Detailed history of Rosenort and Rosenhoff Manitoba Canada Mennonite communities. Includes the 1881, 1891, 1901 census; cemetery index for 8 graveyards. Profile of early pioneers with names such as BRANDT, EIDSE, LOEWEN, FRIESEN, DUECK, HARMS, KLASSEN, KROEKER, CORNELSEN, SIEMENS.

◆ Mailing Lists, Newsgroups & Chat

- Genealogy Resources on the Internet - Religions / Churches Mailing Lists
  http://www.rootsweb.com/~jfuller/gen_mail_religions.html
  Most of the mailing list links below point to this site, wonderfully maintained by John Fuller

- MENNO.REC.ROOTS Mailing List
  http://www.rootsweb.com/~jfuller/gen_mail_religions.html
  #MENNO.REC.ROOTS
  A Mennonite genealogy and family research interest group.

- MENNO-ROOTS Mailing List
  http://www.rootsweb.com/~jfuller/gen_mail_religions.html
  #MENNO-ROOTS

- VOLHYNIAN-MENNONITES Mailing List
  http://www.rootsweb.com/~jfuller/gen_mail_country-rus.html
  #VOLHYNIAN-MENNONITES
  For anyone with a genealogical interest in the Mennonites from the Volhynia and surrounding areas of old Polish Russia, now known as the Ukraine.

◆ People & Families

- Early Russian Mennonite History - Part One
  http://members.aol.com/jktsn/mennohis.htm
  And The Thiessen Family and The Mennonite Diaspora - Part Two
  http://members.aol.com/jktsn/mennodia.htm

- The ERB Family from Lancaster to Ontario
  http://www.my-ged.com/erb
  Traces descendants of Swiss Mennonite Nicholas Erb 1680 from 1700s Lancaster Co., PA and 1800s Waterloo Co., Ontario. Allied families include: Bomberger, Bricker, Brubaker, Eby, Landis, Schaeffer, Shrantz, Shirk, and Snyder.

- Russian Mennonite Genealogy
  http://www.geocities.com/Yosemite/7431/menno.htm
  REIMER, WALL, GIESBRECHT, LOEPPKY/LEPPKE, and more. This site also had links to other related information on Prussian/Russian/Canadian Mennonites.

- Sources used by James C. Hostetler
  http://www.wgbc.org/jch.htm
  Amish, Amish-Mennonite, and Mennonite family history books and other reference material being used by Jim Hostetler in his data base. Includes many Mennonite and Brethren family names.

- WENGER Home Page
  http://www.wengersundial.com/wengerfamily/
  A database of over 78,000 names of individuals, mostly descended from 18th century Mennonites, River Brethren (Brethren in Christ) and German Baptist Brethren who settled in Lancaster, Lebanon and Franklin Counties of Pennsylvania, in Ontario, Canada and in Washington Co., Maryland and Botetourt Co., Virginia.

◆ Publications, Software & Supplies

- Amazon.com Genealogy Bookstore - Mennonite
  http://www.amazon.com/exec/obidos/external-search/?keyword=Mennonite+genealogy&tag=markcyndisgenealA/

- AudioTapes.com - Genealogical Lectures on Cassette Tapes - Mennonite
  http://www.audiotapes.com/search2.asp?Search=Mennonite

- CMHS: GRANDMA CD-ROM Project
  http://www.fresno.edu/cmhs/gpc/home.htm
  Database from the California Mennonite Historical Society.

- JR Solutions - Mennonite Genealogical Research Publications
  http://www.jrsolutions.net/publishmennonite.htm

- Masthof Bookstore and Press
  http://www.masthof.com/
  Genealogical and historical books, including many for Mennonite, Amish and Brethren research.

- Mennonite Brethren Herald
  http://www.mbherald.com/39-03/
  Be sure to see their online editions & current obituaries section.

- Mennonite Family History Magazine
  http://www.masthof.com/pages/mfh.html

- Mennonite Historian Magazine
  http://www.mbnet.mb.ca/~mhc/menhist.htm

- Mennonite Weekly Review
  http://www.mennoweekly.org/
  Internet edition of this newspaper.

◆ Records: Census, Cemeteries, Land, Obituaries, Personal, Taxes and Vital (Born, Married, Died & Buried)

- Composite Index of Early Manitoba Mennonite
  Church Registers
  http://www.mmhs.org/canada/super/super.htm
  Bergthaler (Russia) 1843, Chortitzer (Manitoba) 1878, Chortitzer (Manitoba) 1887, Chortitzer (Manitoba) 1907.

- Mennobits - Amish and Mennonite Obituaries
  http://freepages.genealogy.rootsweb.com/~mennobit/

- Mennonite Historical Society of Saskatchewan Inc. -
  Saskatchewan Mennonite Cemetery Finding Aid
  http://freepages.genealogy.rootsweb.com/~skmhss/

- O.M.I.I. Genealogical Project
  http://www.wgbc.org/hindex.htm
  A Swiss Mennonite & German Amish genealogy project.

- Unruh's South Russian Mennonite Census, 1795-
  1814
  http://pixel.cs.vt.edu/library/census/link/bhu.txt

◆ Societies & Groups

- The California Mennonite Historical Society
  http://www.fresno.edu/cmhs/

- Lancaster Mennonite Historical Society ~
  Pennsylvania
  http://lanclio.org/lmhs.htm

- Manitoba Mennonite Historical Society ~ Canada
  http://www.mmhs.org/

- Mennonite Historical Society of Alberta
  http://members.home.net/rempel/mhsa/
  The MHSA is a new society developed to support those who are interested in basic Mennonite history, those doing Mennonite genealogy/family history research, and those who are interested in the preservation and display of Mennonite historical documents and cultural artifacts.

- Mennonite Historical Society of British Columbia
  http://www.rapidnet.bc.ca/~mennohis/

- Mennonites in Canada
  http://www.mhsc.ca/
  The web site for the Mennonite Historical Society of Canada.

METHODIST

http://www.cyndislist.com/methodis.htm

Category Index:

- General Resource Sites
- Libraries, Archives & Museums
- Locality Specific

- Mailing Lists, Newsgroups & Chat
- Publications, Software & Supplies

◆ General Resource Sites

- **Calvinistic Methodists**
  http://fly.hiwaay.net/~bsrich/calvinistic.htm

- **Methodist History Research aids for Kansas, United States and United Kingdom research**
  http://history.cc.ukans.edu/heritage/um/research~1.html
  List of books, articles, archives, and other web sites of use in Methodist research.

- **United Methodist History**
  http://gbgm-umc.org/UMhistory/

◆ Libraries, Archives & Museums

- **College Archives and Holston Conference Archives**
  http://www.library.ehc.edu/web/misc/archive.html
  From Emory & Henry College. The Holston Conference Archives encompasses the records relating to the history of the United Methodist Church and its activities in the region. The Holston Conference comprises the geographic area surrounding the Holston River, and includes southwest Virginia; eastern Tennessee as far west as Oak Ridge; and a small portion of northeastern Georgia. The Conference Archives includes biographical information on the ministers who served in the region, individual church histories and records, and district and conference records, as well as the personal papers of ministers who served the Holston Conference. The collections date from the 1820s, with the bulk of the holdings dating from the late 1800s to the present.

- **DePauw University - Archives of DePauw University and Indiana United Methodism**
  http://www.depauw.edu/library/archives/archiveshome.htm
  The archives documents the development and growth of DePauw University and the United Methodist Church in Indiana.

- **General Commission on Archives and History; The United Methodist Church**
  http://www.gcah.org/
  - o Archival Holdings
    http://www.gcah.org/arch_hol.htm
  - o Directory for Local and Regional United Methodist Archives
    http://www.gcah.org/Conference/umcdirectory.htm
  - o Ministerial Genealogical Research Information
    http://www.gcah.org/minister.htm

  - o Museum Exhibit
    http://www.gcah.org/museum.htm
  - o Researching Your United Methodist Ancestors: A Brief Guide
    http://www.gcah.org/Searching.htm

- **Methodist Archives and Research Centre**
  http://rylibweb.man.ac.uk/data1/dg/text/method.html
  at the John Rylands University Library in Manchester, UK. See the link for Researching your Family History on this site.

- **Methodist Collection**
  http://www.rmc.edu/academic/library/methodis.htm
  METHODIST COLLECTION From Randolph-Macon College. The research collection is devoted to the history of the Virginia Conference of the United Methodist Church. Historic materials contained in the collection date back to 1773 and mainly include official records of the church such as the Journal and the Discipline. Also available are 19th century issues of the Richmond Christian Advocate (with an index to obituaries of ordained Methodist Ministers), other 19th century journal holdings, and a few Virginia church histories (both published and unpublished).

- **Methodist Heritage in the UK**
  http://www.forsaith-oxon.demon.co.uk/methodist-heritage/
  Methodist Heritage provides a guide to the main locations in Britain with buildings or sites of particular Methodist historic interest. Includes libraries and other research centers with Methodist holdings.

  - o Methodist Heritage - Research Libraries
    http://www.forsaith-oxon.demon.co.uk/methodist-heritage/libraries.html
    Select list of libraries and archives in Great Britain with Methodist holdings.

- **Missouri United Methodist Archives**
  http://www.cmc.edu/library/archives/ARCHIVES.html
  At the Smiley Library, Central Methodist College, Fayette, Missouri.

- **United Church of Canada / Victoria University Archives**
  http://vicu.utoronto.ca/archives/archives.htm
  Located in Ontario, the holdings in the archives include records for the Presbyterian Church in Canada; the Methodist Church (Canada); the Congregational Union of Canada; Local Union Churches; and the Evangelical United Brethren Church. There are also personal papers, biographical files and photographs.

- West Ohio Conference United Methodist Archives Center
  http://cc.owu.edu/~librweb/spuma.htm
  The West Ohio Conference United Methodist Archives Center is a collection of books, manuscripts, pamphlets, periodicals, and artifacts organized to encourage the study of the history of Methodism in Ohio. The Collection is housed at Ohio Wesleyan University and is jointly sponsored and supported by the University and the West Ohio Conference of the United Methodist Church. As part of it's mission, the Archives assists those pursuing genealogical studies of families whose ancestors include Methodist clergy serving in Ohio.

◆ Locality Specific

- The Methodist Church of Great Britain
  http://www.methodist.org.uk/
  The official web site of the Methodist Church of Great Britain.

- Records of the Cayuga and Fosterville United Methodist Churches Cayuga County, New York
  http://www.rootsweb.com/~nycayuga/caymeth.htm

◆ Mailing Lists, Newsgroups & Chat

- Genealogy Resources on the Internet - Religions / Churches Mailing Lists
  http://www.rootsweb.com/~jfuller/gen_mail_religions.html
  Most of the mailing list links below point to this site, wonderfully maintained by John Fuller

- BIBLICAL-GENEALOGY Mailing List
  http://www.rootsweb.com/~jfuller/gen_mail_religions.html #BIBLICAL-GENEALOGY
  For the discussion and sharing of information regarding genealogy in biblical times.

- METHODIST Mailing List
  http://www.rootsweb.com/~jfuller/gen_mail_religions.html #METHODIST

◆ Publications, Software & Supplies

- Amazon.com Genealogy Bookstore - Methodist
  http://www.amazon.com/exec/obidos/external-search/? keyword=methodist+genealogy&tag=markcyndisgenealA/

- AudioTapes.com - Genealogical Lectures on Cassette Tapes - Methodist
  http://www.audiotapes.com/search2.asp?Search=Methodist

- Manx Methodist Historical Society Newsletter
  http://www.ee.surrey.ac.uk/Contrib/manx/methdism/mhist/ index.htm
  Index to Newsletters 1-23.

- My Ancestors Were Methodists: How Can I Find Out More About Them?
  http://www.sog.org.uk/acatalog/SoG_Bookshop_Online_My_ Ancestors_Series_135.html#a1023
  Publication for sale from the UK's Society of Genealogists.

MICROFILM & MICROFICHE
http://www.cyndislist.com/micro.htm

Category Index:

◆ Film/Fiche Numbers

◆ National Archives

◆ Vendors

◆ Film/Fiche Numbers

- 1901 Census of Canada - Film Numbers
  http://www.tbaytel.net/bmartin/census.htm

- Genealogy Records on Microfiche - MCPL
  http://www.mcpl.lib.mo.us/ge/microfiche.htm
  At the Mid-Continent Public Library, Missouri.

- Halifax County, Nova Scotia LDS/PANS Film
  Numbers
  http://www.rootsweb.com/~nshalifa/Films.htm

- Hamburg Passenger Lists, 1850-1934
  http://www.genealogy.net/gene/www/emig/ham_pass.html
  List of microfilm numbers for the LDS Family History Library.

- LDS Film Numbers for Ontario Birth Registrations
  http://www.geocities.com/Heartland/9332/lds-b.htm

- LDS Film Numbers for Ontario Death Registrations
  http://www.geocities.com/Heartland/9332/lds-d.htm

- LDS Film Numbers for Ontario Marriage
  Registrations
  http://www.geocities.com/Heartland/9332/lds-m.htm

- LDS Microfilm for Loudoun Co., VA
  http://www.rootsweb.com/~valoudou/film.htm

- LDS Microfilms and Microfiche for Coshocton Co.,
  Ohio
  http://www.pe.net/~sharyn/lds.html

- LDS Polish Jewish LDS Microfilms ~ JewishGen
  http://www.jewishgen.org/jri-pl/jri-lds.htm

- Microfilm of Connecticut Records at LDS Family
  History Centers
  http://www.cslnet.ctstateu.edu/ldsmicro.htm

- Microfilms of Rosters for LDS voyages 1840-1868
  Sorted by Ship, Year
  http://www.xmission.com/~nelsonb/ship_film_name.htm

- Microfilms of Ship Rosters for LDS voyages 1840-
  1868 Sorted by Year, Ship
  http://www.xmission.com/~nelsonb/ship_film_year.htm

- Nova Scotia Census on Microfilm
  http://nsgna.ednet.ns.ca/ncensus.html

- Passenger Lists - Hamburg 1850-1934 - Film List for
  the LDS FHC
  http://www.genealogy.net/gene/www/emig/ham_pass.html

- Scottish Reference Information
  http://www.ktb.net/~dwills/13300-scottishreference.htm
  *An extensive list of parish numbers and microfilm numbers to aid in
  doing Scottish research at an LDS Family History Center.*

- Wilmington Diocese Catholic Parish Registers
  http://delgensoc.org/dioceswm.html
  *A list of microfilm numbers for parish registers available through
  the LDS Family History Library and Family History Centers.
  Records included on the microfilm begin in 1790 for baptisms
  through 1920, marriage and other registers through 1960 (35
  Rolls).*

◆ National Archives

- National Archives and Records Administration ~
  United States
  http://www.nara.gov/

  The Federal Population Censuses - Catalogs of
  NARA Microfilm
  http://www.nara.gov/publications/microfilm/census/
  census.html

  - 1790-1890 Federal Population Censuses -
    Catalog of NARA Microfilm
    http://www.nara.gov/publications/microfilm/census/
    1790-1890/17901890.html

  - 1900 Federal Population Census - Catalog of
    NARA Microfilm
    http://www.nara.gov/publications/microfilm/census/
    1900/1900.html

  - 1910 Federal Population Censuses - Catalog of
    NARA Microfilm
    http://www.nara.gov/publications/microfilm/census/
    1910/1910.html

  - 1920 Federal Population Census - Catalog of
    NARA Microfilm
    http://www.nara.gov/publications/microfilm/census/
    1920/1920.html

  How to Use NARA's Census Microfilm Catalogs
  http://www.nara.gov/genealogy/microcen.html

National Archives Microfilm Catalogs Online

- **American Indians - A Select Catalog of NARA Microfilm Publications**
  http://www.nara.gov/publications/microfilm/amerindians/indians.html

- **Black Studies - A Select Catalog of NARA Microfilm Publications**
  http://www.nara.gov/publications/microfilm/blackstudies/blackstd.html

- **Federal Court Records - A Select Catalog of NARA Microfilm Publications**
  http://www.nara.gov/publications/microfilm/courts/fedcourt.html

- **Genealogical and Biographical Research - A Select Catalog of NARA Microfilm Publications**
  http://www.nara.gov/publications/microfilm/biographical/genbio.html

- **Immigrant and Passenger Arrivals - A Select Catalog of NARA Microfilm Publications**
  http://www.nara.gov/publications/microfilm/immigrant/immpass.html

- **Microfilm of Connecticut Records at LDS Family History Centers**
  http://www.cslnet.ctstateu.edu/ldsmicro.htm

- **Microfilm Resources for Research - A Comprehensive Catalog**
  http://www.nara.gov/publications/microfilm/comprehensive/compcat.html

- **Military Service Records - A Select Catalog of NARA Microfilm Publications**
  http://www.nara.gov/publications/microfilm/military/service.html

National Archives Microfilm Collection in Seattle
http://www.rootsweb.com/~watpcgs/narafilm.htm
A list of 549 microfilm publications available at the Pacific Alaska Region branch of NARA.

National Archives Microfilm Rental Program
http://www.nara.gov/publications/microfilm/micrent.html

◆ Vendors

- **Amazon.com Genealogy Bookstore - Microfilm**
  http://www.amazon.com/exec/obidos/external-search/?keyword=microfilm+history&tag=markcyndisgenealA/

- **AncestorSpy - CDs and Microfiche**
  http://www.ancestorspy.com

- **Avotaynu Microfiche**
  http://www.avotaynu.com/microf.html
  Products and information for Jewish genealogy.

- **Durham and Northumberland Family History Microfiche ~ England**
  http://www.jwillans.freeserve.co.uk/default.html

- **Heritage Quest's Resources on Microfilm and Fiche**
  http://www.HeritageQuest.com/genealogy/microfilm/

  Micrographic Equipment at Everyday Low Prices
  http://www.HeritageQuest.com/genealogy/micrographics/

- **Heritage Quest - US Federal Census Schedules Available on CD-ROM and Microfilm**
  http://www.heritagequest.com/ProdFind2/census.htm
  Digitized images of the entire U.S. Federal Census from 1790 to 1920. Each of the 12,555 rolls of census microfilm are now available on CD-ROM for use on your home computer.

- **Interlink Bookshop Genealogical Services - Microfiche ~ Victoria, B.C., Canada**
  http://www.interlinkbookshop.com/fiche.htm

- **The Memorabilia Corner**
  http://members.aol.com/TMCorner/index.html
  Forms, flags, maps, software, CDs, tapes, microfilm & microfiche, books, periodicals, photographic conservation & archival materials.

- **The Microfilm Shop**
  http://www.microfilm.com/
  Commercial retailer of microfilm readers, supplies, and other equipment, located in the U.K., France, Germany, Ireland, Holland and Belgium.

- **New Zealand Society of Genealogists - Microfiche Publications**
  http://homepages.ihug.co.nz/~nzsg/Publications/fiche_main.html

THE MIDDLE EAST

http://www.cyndislist.com/mideast.htm

- Amazon.com Genealogy Bookstore - Middle East
  http://www.amazon.com/exec/obidos/external-search/?
  keyword=middle+east+genealogy&tag=markcyndisgenealA/

- ARAB-AMERICAN Mailing List
  http://www.rootsweb.com/~jfuller/gen_mail_general.html
  #ARAB-AMER
  A moderated list geared towards fostering and building community amongst North Americans of Arabic descent.

- ARMENIA Mailing List
  http://www.rootsweb.com/~jfuller/gen_mail_country-arm.html
  #ARMENIA
  For anyone with a genealogical interest in Armenia.

- The Balch Institute for Ethnic Studies
  http://www.libertynet.org/~balch/
  Includes a research library with materials on immigration studies.

  - A Guide To Manuscript And Microfilm Collections Of The Research Library Of The Balch Institute For Ethnic Studies
    http://www.balchinstitute.org/online_resources_12/html/
    contents.html
    - Armenian
      http://www.balchinstitute.org/online_resources_12/html/
      body_armenian.html
    - Lebanese
      http://www.balchinstitute.org/online_resources_12/html/
      body_lebanese.html

- Center for Iranian Jewish Oral History
  http://www.cijoh.org/

- Central Zionist Archives ~ Israel
  http://www.wzo.org.il/cza/index.html
  The Central Zionist Archives is the official historical archives of the World Zionist Organization, the Jewish Agency, the Jewish National Fund, Keren Hayesod and the World Jewish Congress. It also holds the personal papers of individuals involved in the Zionist movement or active in Palestine/Israel.

- Commonwealth War Graves Commission
  http://www.cwgc.org/
  They can provide invaluable information to genealogists on the location, condition, and other information regarding the Commonwealth soldiers' graves in their care. Please include International Reply Coupons when writing to them from outside Britain.

- Cornell University Middle East & Islamic Studies Collection
  http://www.library.cornell.edu/colldev/mideast/

- Family History Library Catalog
  http://www.familysearch.org/Search/searchcatalog.asp
  From the FamilySearch web site, an online catalog to the holdings

of the LDS Church in Salt Lake City, Utah. Also search for other localities by place name.
http://www.familysearch.org/eng/Library/fhlc/supermainframe
set.asp?display=localitysearch&columns=*,180,0

  - Armenia
    http://www.familysearch.org/eng/Library/fhlc/supermain
    frameset.asp?display=localitydetails&subject=130&subject
    _disp=Armenia&columns=*,180,0

  - Azerbaijan
    http://www.familysearch.org/eng/Library/fhlc/supermain
    frameset.asp?display=localitydetails&subject=129&subject
    _disp=Azerbaijan&columns=*,180,0

  - Bahrain
    http://www.familysearch.org/eng/Library/fhlc/supermain
    frameset.asp?display=localitydetails&subject=184&subject
    _disp=Bahrain&columns=*,180,0

  - Cyprus
    http://www.familysearch.org/eng/Library/fhlc/supermain
    frameset.asp?display=localitydetails&subject=197&subject
    _disp=Cyprus&columns=*,180,0

  - Egypt
    http://www.familysearch.org/eng/Library/fhlc/supermain
    frameset.asp?display=localitydetails&subject=223&subject
    _disp=Egypt&columns=*,180,0

  - Georgia
    http://www.familysearch.org/eng/Library/fhlc/supermain
    frameset.asp?display=localitydetails&subject=131&subject
    disp=Georgia(Republic)&columns=*,180,0

  - Iran
    http://www.familysearch.org/eng/Library/fhlc/supermain
    frameset.asp?display=localitydetails&subject=194&subject
    _disp=Iran&columns=*,180,0

  - Iraq
    http://www.familysearch.org/eng/Library/fhlc/supermain
    frameset.asp?display=localitydetails&subject=198&subject
    _disp=Iraq&columns=*,180,0

  - Israel
    http://www.familysearch.org/eng/Library/fhlc/supermain
    frameset.asp?display=localitydetails&subject=202&subject
    _disp=Israel&columns=*,180,0

  - Jordan
    http://www.familysearch.org/eng/Library/fhlc/supermain
    frameset.asp?display=localitydetails&subject=203&subject
    _disp=Jordan&columns=*,180,0

  - Kuwait
    http://www.familysearch.org/eng/Library/fhlc/supermain
    frameset.asp?display=localitydetails&subject=185&subject
    disp=Kuwait(State)&columns=*,180,0

  - Lebanon
    http://www.familysearch.org/eng/Library/fhlc/supermain
    frameset.asp?display=localitydetails&subject=200&subject
    _disp=Lebanon&columns=*,180,0

- o Oman
  http://www.familysearch.org/eng/Library/fhlc/supermain
  frameset.asp?display=localitydetails&subject=181&subject
  _disp=Oman&columns=*,180,0

- o Palestine
  http://www.familysearch.org/eng/Library/fhlc/supermain
  frameset.asp?display=localitydetails&subject=201&subject
  _disp=Palestine&columns=*,180,0

- o Qatar
  http://www.familysearch.org/eng/Library/fhlc/supermain
  frameset.asp?display=localitydetails&subject=183&subject
  _disp=Qatar&columns=*,180,0

- o Saudi Arabia
  http://www.familysearch.org/eng/Library/fhlc/supermain
  frameset.asp?display=localitydetails&subject=186&subject
  _disp=Saudi_Arabia&columns=*,180,0

- o Syria
  http://www.familysearch.org/eng/Library/fhlc/supermain
  frameset.asp?display=localitydetails&subject=199&subject
  _disp=Syria&columns=*,180,0

- o Turkey
  http://www.familysearch.org/eng/Library/fhlc/supermain
  frameset.asp?display=localitydetails&subject=196&subject
  _disp=Turkey&columns=*,180,0

- o United Arab Emirates
  http://www.familysearch.org/eng/Library/fhlc/supermain
  frameset.asp?display=localitydetails&subject=182&subject
  _disp=United_Arab_Emirates&columns=*,180,0

- o Yemen Arab Republic
  http://www.familysearch.org/eng/Library/fhlc/supermain
  frameset.asp?display=localitydetails&subject=179&subject
  _disp=Yemen_Arab_Republic&columns=*,180,0

- o Yemen People's Republic
  http://www.familysearch.org/eng/Library/fhlc/supermain
  frameset.asp?display=localitydetails&subject=180&subject
  _disp=Yemen_People_s_Republic&columns=*,180,0

- FHW Projects: Genealogy Project
  http://www.fhw.org/fhw/en/projects/genealogy.html
  From the Foundation of the Hellenic World. The Genealogy Project aims at reconstructing the family trees of the Asia Minor refugees, Greek-Orthodox inhabitants of Asia Minor and Pontos (the Black Sea region) who were expelled from their homeland after the Asia Minor disaster in 1922, and took refuge in Greece. The family data to be collected will begin with the grandparents of each Asia Minor refugee, and follow into their posterity.

- Genealogy Resources on the Internet - Armenia
  Mailing Lists
  http://www.rootsweb.com/~jfuller/gen_mail_country-arm.html

- Genealogy Resources on the Internet - Israel Mailing
  Lists
  http://www.rootsweb.com/~jfuller/gen_mail_country-isr.html

- Genealogy Resources on the Internet - Morocco
  Mailing Lists
  http://www.rootsweb.com/~jfuller/gen_mail_country-mor.html

- Genealogy Resources on the Internet - Saudi Arabia
  Mailing Lists
  http://www.rootsweb.com/~jfuller/gen_mail_country-sau.html

- Genealogy Resources on the Internet - Sudan Mailing
  Lists
  http://www.rootsweb.com/~jfuller/gen_mail_country-sud.html

- Genealogy Resources on the Internet - Turkey
  Mailing Lists
  http://www.rootsweb.com/~jfuller/gen_mail_country-tur.html

- The Hashemites: Jordan's Royal Family
  http://www.kinghussein.gov.jo/hashemites.html

  - o The Hashemite Family Tree
    http://www.kinghussein.gov.jo/rfamily_hashemites.html

- Historical Society of Jews From Egypt
  http://www.hsje.org/

- Immigration History Research Center (IHRC) at the
  University of Minnesota
  http://www1.umn.edu/ihrc/
  An international resource on American immigration and ethnic history.

  - o Archival and Library Research Collections
    http://www1.umn.edu/ihrc/research.htm#top

    - Family History Sources at IHRC
      http://www1.umn.edu/ihrc/genealog.htm#top

    - IHRC Guide to Collections
      http://www1.umn.edu/ihrc/profiles.htm

    - Armenian American Collection
      http://www1.umn.edu/ihrc/armenian.htm#top

- Iraq, History
  http://www.achilles.net/~sal/iraq_history.html

- Israel Archives Association
  http://spinoza.tau.ac.il/iaa/index.html
  Israeli archives contain data related to the development of the Jewish and Arab communities in the land of Israel, as well as the history of the Jewish people in the Diaspora.

- The Israel Genealogical Society
  http://www.isragen.org.il/

- Jewish/Israel History: Genealogy, Archeology,
  Diaspora, Israel History...
  http://ucsu.colorado.edu/~jsu/history.html

- Middle East Library, University of Utah
  http://www.lib.utah.edu/spc/mid/spcmid.html

- MidEastGenWeb
  http://www.rootsweb.com/~mdeastgw/index.html

  - o The Kingdom of Saudi Arabia GenWeb
    http://www.angelfire.com/tn/BattlePride/Saudi.html

  - o Lebanon GenWeb
    http://www.rootsweb.com/~lbnwgw/

  - o Syria GenWeb
    http://www.rootsweb.com/~syrwgw/

  - o TurkeyGenWeb
    http://www.rootsweb.com/~turwgw/

- Perry-Castañeda Library Map Collection
  http://www.lib.utexas.edu/Libs/PCL/Map_collection/
  Map_collection.html
  At the University of Texas at Austin

  o Maps of the Middle East
    http://www.lib.utexas.edu/Libs/PCL/Map_collection/
    middle_east.html

    - CIA Atlas of the Middle East
      http://www.lib.utexas.edu/Libs/PCL/Map_collection/
      Atlas_middle_east/Atlas_middle_east.html

    - Historical Maps of the Middle East
      http://www.lib.utexas.edu/Libs/PCL/Map_collection/
      historical/history_middle_east.html

- med-gene Mailing List
  http://www.rootsweb.com/~jfuller/gen_mail_country-gen.html
  #med-gene
  For anyone with a genealogical interest in the Mediterranean area.

- MidEastGenWeb Mailing List
  http://www.rootsweb.com/~jfuller/gen_mail_country-gen.html
  #MidEastGenWeb
  For anyone with a genealogical interest in the Middle East.

- Repositories of Primary Sources - Africa & the Near East - Israel
  http://www.uidaho.edu/special-collections/africa.html#il
  A list of links to online resources from the Univ. of Idaho Library, Special Collections and Archives.

- SaudiArabia Mailing List
  http://www.rootsweb.com/~jfuller/gen_mail_country-sau.html
  #SaudiArabia
  For anyone with a genealogical interest in Saudi Arabia.

- Saudi Royal Family Database
  http://www.saudiroyals.com/
  Comprehensive source for biographic and genealogical information on the Saudi Arabian Royal family.

- StudyWeb: History: Middle East
  http://www.studyweb.com/History/tocme.htm

- Turkish Archives
  http://www.archimac.marun.edu.tr/index.spml

- Turkish_Jews Mailing List
  http://www.rootsweb.com/~jfuller/gen_mail_country-ser.html
  #Turkish_Jews
  For Sephardic Jewish genealogists with roots in the former Turkish Ottoman Empire including Turkey, Serbia, Greece, and Yugoslavia.

- University of Texas - Middle East Network Information Center (MENIC)
  http://menic.utexas.edu/menic.html

- Yahoo!...Iran...History
  http://dir.yahoo.com/Regional/Countries/Iran/Arts_and_
  Humanities/Humanities/History/

- Yahoo!...Israel...History
  http://dir.yahoo.com/Regional/Countries/Israel/Arts_and_
  Humanities/Humanities/History/

- Yahoo!...Lebanon...History
  http://dir.yahoo.com/Regional/Countries/Lebanon/Arts_and_
  Humanities/Humanities/History/

- Yahoo!...Turkey...History
  http://dir.yahoo.com/Regional/Countries/Turkey/Arts_and_
  Humanities/Humanities/History/

MILITARY RESOURCES WORLDWIDE

http://www.cyndislist.com/milres.htm

Category Index:

- ◆ General Resource Sites
- ◆ Libraries, Archives & Museums
- ◆ Mailing Lists, Newsgroups & Chat
- ◆ Medals, Awards & Tributes

- ◆ Professional Researchers, Volunteers & Other Research Services
- ◆ Publications, Software & Supplies
- ◆ Records: Military, Pension, Burial
- ◆ Societies & Groups

◆ General Resource Sites

- 460 Squadron RAAF
  http://home.st.net.au/~dunn/460sqdn.htm
  Australians serving in WWII.

- Alex Chirnside's Military History Page
  http://www.geocities.com/Broadway/Alley/5443/

- Australian Genealogy Researching Armed Services Personnel
  http://www.pcug.org.au/~mjsparke/mj_page1.html

- Battling Bastards of Bataan
  http://home.pacbell.net/fbaldie/Battling_Bastards_of_
  Bataan.html
  "Our purpose as an organization is quite simple. We wish to perpetuate the story of Bataan and to leave to our descendants the truth as we knew it. We wish to correct the myths and outright lies concerning the events of Bataan in 1941-1942. We want to provide information on the Battle for Bataan and it's subsequent fall on April 9, 1942."

- The British Empire & Commonwealth Land Forces
  http://www.du.edu/~tomills/military/empire.htm

- The Buffalo Soldiers on the Western Frontier
  http://www.imh.org/imh/buf/buftoc.html
  From the International Museum of the Horse.

- Documents in Military History
  http://www.hillsdale.edu/academics/history/Documents/War/
  From Hillsdale College's collection of primary sources for military history.

- "G" for George
  http://home.st.net.au/~dunn/g4george.htm
  The Avro Lancaster B1 on display in the Aeroplane Hall at the Australian War Memorial in Canberra, ACT, Australia.

- Hellfire Corner - The Great War - 1914 - 1918
  http://www.fylde.demon.co.uk/welcome.htm

- The Mexican-American War Memorial Homepage
  http://sunsite.unam.mx/revistas/1847/

- Military History
  http://www.cfcsc.dnd.ca/links/milhist/index.html
  From the War, Peace and Security Guide, Canadian Forces College.

- The Military History Page
  http://www.du.edu/~tomills/military/index.html

  o Land Forces of Britain, the Empire and Commonwealth
    http://www.du.edu/~tomills/military/empire.htm

- Military Railways - A Potted History
  http://homepages.tesco.net/~martyn.witt/milrly/mil_rly_hist_
  contents.htm

- Military Search Bulletin Board
  http://www.geocities.com/Pentagon/Bunker/3965/search.html

- New Zealand Defence Forces, 1860 - 1883
  http://www.atonz.com/genealogy/nzdefence.html

- The Queensland Defence Force
  http://www.ozemail.com.au/~adjutant/moreton/qdf.html

- Rongstad's Worldwide Military Links
  http://members.aol.com/rhrongstad/private/milinksr.htm

- Soldiers Whom the World Have Forgotten
  http://www.geocities.com/Athens/Acropolis/9460/index.html
  Dedicated to the memory of soldiers & their families who died in and around Bangalore, India.

- War Chart
  http://www.genrecords.com/library/war.htm
  From the Genealogy Record Service.

- World War I, Links to Other Resources
  http://raven.cc.ukans.edu/~kansite/ww_one/links.html

- World War I - Trenches on the Web
  http://www.worldwar1.com/

- World War II on the Web
  http://www.geocities.com/Athens/Oracle/2691/welcome.htm

◆ Libraries, Archives & Museums

- Genealogie: Sudetenland, Böhmen/Bohemia, Mähren/Moravia - Militärarchive und militärische Personalunterlagen / Military Archives and Records
http://www2.genealogy.net/gene/reg/SUD/sudet_miarch.html

- Military Archives in Germany
http://www.bawue.de/~hanacek/info/earchive.htm#CC

- Royal Museum of the Army and Military History / Koninklijk Museum van het Leger en de krijgsgeschiedenis / Musée royal de l'armée et d'histoire militaire ~ Belgium
http://www.klm-mra.be/

- Le Musée de l'Armée - Hôtel national des Invalides ~ Paris
http://www.invalides.org/
The French Army Museum.

- The South African War Virtual Library
http://www.uq.net.au/~zzrwotto/

- The World War I Document Archive
http://www.lib.byu.edu/~rdh/wwi/
Assembled by volunteers of the World War I Military History List (WWI-L).

◆ Mailing Lists, Newsgroups & Chat

- Genealogy Resources on the Internet - Wars/Military Mailing Lists
http://www.rootsweb.com/~jfuller/gen_mail_wars.html
Most of the mailing list links below point to this site, wonderfully maintained by John Fuller

- AMERICAN-REVOLUTION Mailing List
http://www.rootsweb.com/~jfuller/gen_mail_wars.html #AMERICAN-REVOLUTION
For the discussion of events during the American Revolution and genealogical matters related to the American Revolution. The French-Indian Wars and the War of 1812 are also suitable topics for discussion.

- The Anglo Boer War Discussion Page
http://www.icon.co.za/~dup42/talk.htm
This mailing list is for the discussion of the Anglo Boer War and other military related topics pre-1900.

- AUS-MILITARY Mailing List
http://www.rootsweb.com/~jfuller/gen_mail_country-aus.html #AUS-MILITARY
For the discussion and sharing of information on Australian military history and the research of Australian military ancestors from 1788 to the present.

- BOER-WAR Mailing List
http://www.rootsweb.com/~jfuller/gen_mail_wars.html #BOER-WAR
For anyone with a genealogical or historical interest in the Boer War.

- FOB-LIST - Friends of the Boers - E-mail List
http://www.webcom.com/perspekt/eng/mlist/fob.html
The primary topic of this mailing list is the centenary commemoration of the 2nd Anglo Boer War (1899-1902).

- FRENCH-INDIAN Mailing List
http://www.rootsweb.com/~jfuller/gen_mail_wars.html #FRENCH-INDIAN
For anyone with a genealogical or historical interest in the French and Indian war.

- WW20-ROOTS-L Mailing List
http://www.rootsweb.com/~jfuller/gen_mail_wars.html #WW20-ROOTS-L
For the discussion of genealogy in all 20th century wars.

◆ Medals, Awards & Tributes

- Association des médaillés de Sainte Hélène - 1857
http://stehelene.geneactes.org/
A database of more than 80,000 soldiers of Napoleon who received the Ste. Hélène's medal in 1857. French, English, Italian and Dutch versions available.

- Australian War Medals
http://www.ozemail.com.au/~qphoto/index.html
Provides background information on campaign & gallantry awards given to Australian forces. Includes some medal rolls listing individual recipients of medals. Also has a research resource page for researching Australian servicemen.

- It's An Honour - The Australian Honours System
http://www.itsanhonour.gov.au/
  - Search It's An Honour
http://203.37.24.196/fs_search_start.html
Searchable awards database from 1901 to 1998.

- The Order of the Virtuti Militari and its Cavaliers 1792-1992
http://www.virtuti.com/order
The site contains a search engine, which will show the names of 26,500 recipients of Poland's highest military decoration for valor from 1792. It is the only such list available in the world.

- Polish Military History Books
http://www.wwdir.com/polishbk.html
Polish Orders, Medals, Badges, and Insignia. Military and Civilian Decorations, 1705 to 1985.

◆ Professional Researchers, Volunteers & Other Research Services

- Bob's Public Records Office Searches - Kew, London, England
http://www.users.dircon.co.uk/~searcher/
Including these records: Military, Royal Navy, Merchant Navy, Convict, Railway, West Indies, Passenger Lists, History Projects.

- NZEF Research Service
http://www.medal.net/nzef/
Research Service covering New Zealanders who served in the New Zealand Expeditionary Forces (NZEF) during World War 1 (1914-18).

◆ Publications, Software & Supplies

- Amazon.com Genealogy Bookstore - Military
  http://www.amazon.com/exec/obidos/external-search/?
  keyword=military+genealogy&tag=markcyndisgenealA/

- The Naval & Military Press Web Page
  http://www.naval-military-press.co.uk/
  A large selection of military books, many of interest to the genealogist.

- The Order of the Virtuti Militari and its Cavaliers 1792-1992
  http://www.wwdir.com/order/
  This book has 26,506 names of persons and military organizations. It is presented in English and Polish.

- Polish Military History Books
  http://www.wwdir.com/polishbk.html
  Polish Orders, Medals, Badges, and Insignia. Military and Civilian Decorations, 1705 to 1985.

- Tracing Military Ancestors in New France
  http://www.audiotapes.com/product.asp?ProductCode
  ='SL-116'
  Presentation by John P. Dulong, available for sale on audio tape.

- Use of German Military Records
  http://www.audiotapes.com/product.asp?ProductCode
  ='FSLC-86'
  Presentation by Martin Diestler, available for sale on audio tape.

◆ Records: Military, Pension, Burial

- British Military Records
  http://www.genuki.org.uk/big/BritMilRecs.html

- Commonwealth War Graves Commission
  http://www.cwgc.org/
  Details of 1.7 million members of UK and Commonwealth forces who died in the 1st and 2nd World Wars and other wars, and 60,000 civilian casualties of WWII. Gives details of grave site, date of death, age, usually parents/widow's address.

- HAGSOC: Australian War Graves in South Africa 1899-1902
  http://www.hagsoc.org.au/sagraves/index.html
  This project, by the Heraldry & Genealogy Society of Canberra, aims to publish the database of burial and memorial locations of Australians who died during the second South African Anglo-Boer War of 1899 - 1902. Also included are biographies, researched by the Society, of selected soldiers from each of the Australian States.

- Research Guide - The Boer War - Australians and the War in South Africa 1899-1902
  http://www.naa.gov.au/PUBLICAT/GUIDES/boerwar/
  guide.htm
  From the National Archives of Australia.

- The Trafalgar Roll
  http://www.genuki.org.uk/big/eng/Trafalgar/
  A list of 1640 officers and men who fought at the Battle of Trafalgar.

- Volksbund Deutsche Kriegsgräberfürsorge e.V.
  http://www.volksbund.de/homepage.htm
  The German Military Grave Registration Service. Maintains 2 million war graves in over 640 cemeteries. Assists in grave identification and restoration. Provides assistance in determining the fate of German war dead.

  o Vermissten und Toten Datenbank
    http://www.volksbund.de/VuTDB/vut_suche.asp
    The Missing and Dead Database. Online searchable database of over 2 million interments.

◆ Societies & Groups

- American Defenders of Bataan & Corregidor, Inc.
  http://harrison.simplenet.com/adbc/
  "Lest we forget...and will repeat a dark time in history."

- Crimean War Research Society ~ U.K.
  http://homepages.ihug.co.nz/~phil/crimean.htm

- Descendants of Mexican War Veterans
  http://www.dmwv.org/

- DISPATCH - Scottish Military Historical Society
  http://subnet.virtual-pc.com/~mc546367/journal.htm

- League of Researchers of South African Historical Battlefields
  http://www.icon.co.za/~dup42/Welcome.html

- The Military Historical Society of Australia
  http://www.pcug.org.au/~astaunto/mhsa.htm

- Scottish Military Historical Society
  http://subnet.virtual-pc.com/~mc546367/journal.htm

- The South African Military History Society / Die Suid-Afrikaanse Krygshistoriese Vereeniging
  http://rapidttp.com/milhist/

- The Western Front Association - Remembering 1914-1918
  http://www.westernfront.co.uk/

MONEY

http://www.cyndislist.com/money.htm

- British Coins 1816-2000
  http://www.genuki.org.uk/big/Coins.html

- Coins of the UK
  http://www.tclayton.demon.co.uk/coins.html
  Gives a good deal of history of the coinage of the United Kingdom by regnal years.

- Colonial Currency
  http://www.coins.nd.edu/ColCurrency/index.html

- Current Value of Old Money
  http://www.ex.ac.uk/~RDavies/arian/current/howmuch.html

- Federal Reserve Statistical Release H.10 - Historical Data
  http://www.bog.frb.fed.us/releases/H10/hist/
  Foreign Exchange Rates, 1990 to Present.

- Frontier Press Bookstore - Monetary History in America
  http://www.frontierpress.com/frontier.cgi?category=money

- Gamle norske måleenheter
  http://www.agderweb.no/org/nff/N_M_E.htm#Mynt
  From Norsk Forlishistorisk Forening. Information on old Norwegian coinage from ancient to modern times.

- Historic British Coinage
  http://www.colbybos.demon.co.uk/measures/coinage.html
  Describes the pre-decimal coinage of England.

- Historical Value of Money in the UK
  http://www.headley1.demon.co.uk/histdate/moneyval.htm

- Historical Value of the U.S. Dollar
  http://www.users.mis.net/~chesnut/pages/value.htm

- History of Money from Ancient Times to the Present Day by Glyn Davies
  http://www.ex.ac.uk/~RDavies/arian/llyfr.html

- The Inflation Calculator
  http://www.westegg.com/inflation/

- Inflation Conversion Factors for Dollars 1800 to Estimated 2010
  http://www.orst.edu/dept/pol_sci/fac/sahr/sahr.htm

- Inflation: the Value of the Pound 1750-1998
  http://www.parliament.uk/commons/lib/research/rp99/rp99-020.pdf
  Parliamentary research paper on the changing value of the Pound Sterling from 1750-1998. Requires the free Adobe Acrobat Reader to view.
  http://www.adobe.com/support/downloads/acrwin.htm

- The Leslie Brock Center for the Study of Colonial Currency
  http://www.virginia.edu/~econ/brock.html
  Original articles and essays and information on colonial currency, prices, and exchange rates.

- Major Henrick's Money in the 1860's
  http://homes.acmecity.com/babylon5/earth/95/

- Maryland State Archives - Money
  http://www.mdarchives.state.md.us/msa/refserv/html/money.html

- Money and coins
  http://home.clara.net/brianp/money.html
  Discusses the "L.S.D." pre-decimal system of coinage in the United Kingdom.

- Money in North American History
  http://www.ex.ac.uk/~RDavies/arian/northamerica.html
  From Wampum to Electronic Funds Transfer.

- Money of the Republic of Texas
  http://www.lsjunction.com/facts/tx_money.htm
  Financing the public debt and implementing a stable currency system were among the many challenges facing the government of the Republic of Texas.

- The North Carolina Collection's Currency Holdings
  http://www.lib.unc.edu/ncc/gallery/currency.html

- Ruesch International, Inc. - Global Payments Services
  http://www.ruesch.com/
  Affordable payment options for sending money to other countries.

- The Universal Currency Converter
  http://www.xe.net/ucc/classic.shtml
  And the Interactive Currency Table
  http://www.xe.net/ict/

- Washington College - The American Civil War - Money
  http://www.janke.washcoll.edu/civilwar/money.htm

- Weights, Money and Other Measures Used by Our Ancestors
  http://www.amazon.com/exec/obidos/ISBN=0806315016/markcyndisgenealA/
  A book by Colin R. Chapman.

- What is the best way to send payments to the United Kingdom from abroad?
  http://www.oz.net/~markhow/genuki/NFK/norffaq.htm#Payments
  From the Norfolk-L Genealogy Mailing List Frequently Asked Questions web pages.

MYTHS, HOAXES & SCAMS

http://www.cyndislist.com/myths.htm

Category Index:

◆ Common Genealogical Myths

◆ Consumer Protection

◆ Other Myths, Hoaxes & Scams

◆ Quality Research Methods

◆ Common Genealogical Myths

● Myth #1:
You can find your completed family history on the Internet.

● Myth #2:
Everything you find on the Internet is accurate and reliable.

- o Analyzing and Reviewing Published Sources
  http://www.bcgcertification.org/skbld975.html
  By Elizabeth Shown Mills, CG, CGL. From the Board for Certification of Genealogists - Skill Building - May 1997.

- o Beyond the Keyboard
  http://www.genealogy.com/genealogy/39_kathy.html
  By Kathleen W. Hinckley, CGRS. "Learn 5 important ways to make the best use of information you find on the Internet.".

- o Genealogical Research in the Modern Library
  http://www.ancestry.com/columns/george/10-16-98.htm
  From "Along Those Lines..." by George G. Morgan.

- o Guidelines For Publishing Web Pages On The Internet
  http://www.ngsgenealogy.org/about/content/committees/gene5_stan.html
  Recommended by the National Genealogical Society.

- o It's in Print or on the Internet--It Must Be True!
  http://www.nauvoo.com/family/chamblee/ncnash/begin.html#Print
  From the Nash County NCGenWeb. WARNING: What you Read May Hurt You.

- o Standards For Sharing Information With Others
  http://www.ngsgenealogy.org/about/content/committees/gene4_stan.html
  Recommended by the National Genealogical Society.

- o Standards for Sound Genealogical Research
  http://www.ngsgenealogy.org/about/content/committees/gene1_stan.html
  Recommended by the National Genealogical Society.

- o Standards for Use of Technology in Genealogical Research
  http://www.ngsgenealogy.org/about/content/committees/gene3_stan.html
  Recommended by the National Genealogical Society.

- o Standards for Using Records Repositories and Libraries
  http://www.ngsgenealogy.org/about/content/committees/gene2_stan.html
  Recommended by the National Genealogical Society.

- o Using Other People's Research
  http://www.ancestry.com/columns/george/01-08-99.htm
  From "Along Those Lines..." by George G. Morgan

● Myth #3:
You can find your completed family history in the files at the LDS Family History Centers (aka, the Mormon Church).

- o Welcome To The Family History Center™
  http://www.lds.org/fam_his/wel_to_the/00-Welcome_to_the_FHC.html
  An online brochure from the official LDS Church web site.

- o LDS & Family History Centers
  http://www.CyndisList.com/lds.htm
  See this category on Cyndi's List for more helpful links that will explain the LDS resources for genealogical research

● Myth #4:
Everything you find in books, in computer databases and on CDs is accurate and reliable.

- o Analyzing and Reviewing Published Sources
  http://www.bcgcertification.org/skbld975.html
  By Elizabeth Shown Mills, CG, CGL. From the Board for Certification of Genealogists - Skill Building - May 1997.

- o Genealogical Research in the Modern Library
  http://www.ancestry.com/columns/george/10-16-98.htm
  From "Along Those Lines..." by George G. Morgan.

- o Guidelines For Publishing Web Pages On The Internet
  http://www.ngsgenealogy.org/about/content/committees/gene5_stan.html
  Recommended by the National Genealogical Society.

- o Standards For Sharing Information With Others
  http://www.ngsgenealogy.org/about/content/committees/gene4_stan.html
  Recommended by the National Genealogical Society.

- o Standards for Sound Genealogical Research
  http://www.ngsgenealogy.org/about/content/committees/gene1_stan.html
  Recommended by the National Genealogical Society.

o Standards for Use of Technology in Genealogical Research
http://www.ngsgenealogy.org/about/content/committees/gene3_stan.html
Recommended by the National Genealogical Society.

o Standards for Using Records Repositories and Libraries
http://www.ngsgenealogy.org/about/content/committees/gene2_stan.html
Recommended by the National Genealogical Society.

o Using Other People's Research
http://www.ancestry.com/columns/george/01-08-99.htm
From "Along Those Lines..." by George G. Morgan

o Which Books Are Reliable? 19th Century Classic Genealogies vs. Modern Scholarship
http://www.audiotapes.com/product.asp?ProductCode='VA-79'
Presentation by Gary Boyd Roberts, available for sale on audio tape.

- Myth #5:
You can learn all about your surname in mail-order books.

o National Genealogical Society Consumer Protection Committee
http://www.ngsgenealogy.org/about/content/committees/consumer.html

  • PSST! Wanna Buy Your Name?
  http://www.ngsgenealogy.org/about/content/committees/PSST.html

o A Visit to Bath, Ohio
http://www.ancestry.com/columns/eastman/eastAug31-98.htm#bath
From Eastman's Online Genealogy Newsletter, August 31, 1998.

- Myth #6:
It MUST be true because Great Aunt Matilda told me so!

o Black Sheep and Kissing Cousins: How Our Family Stories Shape Us
http://www.amazon.com/exec/obidos/ISBN=0140119779/markcyndisgenealA/
A book by Elizabeth Stone.

o Family Legends
http://www.main.nc.us/OBCGS/famlegend.htm

o Family Legends - Can they be trusted?
http://www.hinet.net.au/~linswad/FamHist/legends.htm

o Family Legends, True or False. And How Do I Solve Them?
http://fp.sedona.net/genealogy/past4.htm
Summary of a discussion from the Sedona Genealogy Club.

o Family Traditions: How to Separate Fact From Fiction in Genealogical Research
http://www.audiotapes.com/product.asp?ProductCode='MGCS199'
Presentation by Henry (Hank) Z. Jones Jr. available for sale on audio tape.

o Rumors, Gossip, and Little White Lies
HTTP://www.ancestry.com/library/view/ancmag/88.asp
Approaching family legends with an open mind.

o Shaking Your Family Tree: Q&As: Sorting Out Those Family Legends
http://www.rootsweb.com/~rwguide/syft/misc/syftmg0093.htm
By Myra Vanderpool Gormley, C.G.

- Myth #7:
Our name was changed at Ellis Island.

o Changing Immigrant Names
http://www.ins.usdoj.gov/graphics/aboutins/history/articles/NAMES.htm
Includes a list of reasons for name changes and links to stories about how names were changed.

  • American Names / Declaring Independence
  http://www.ins.usdoj.gov/graphics/aboutins/history/articles/NameEssay.html
  Discusses the common misconception about name changes upon arrival in America.

o The Key to Family History Research
http://www.sierra.com/sierrahome/familytree/hqarticles/research/
An online article by Miriam Weiner describing how to determine an immigrant's original surname.

- Myth #8:
The courthouse burned and ALL the records were destroyed

o The Battle of the Burned Courthouse
http://www.msstate.edu/listarchives/afrigeneas/199810/msg00838.html

o The Battle of the Burned Courthouse
http://www.audiotapes.com/product.asp?ProductCode='SPM-90'
Presentation by Marsha Hoffman Rising, available for sale on audio tape.

o The Battle of the Burned Courthouse: How to Find Your Family Even if John Wayne did Burn the County Records!
http://www.audiotapes.com/product.asp?ProductCode='DEN98F171'
Presentation by Elizabeth Shown Mills, available for sale on audio tape.

o Battling the Burned Courthouse: Genealogy's Infernal Problem
http://www.audiotapes.com/product.asp?ProductCode='VA-81'
Presentation by Elizabeth Shown Mills, available for sale on audio tape.

o Burned Down, Blown Up, and Washed Away: Courthouse Destruction and Record Loss in West Virginia
http://www.audiotapes.com/product.asp?ProductCode='VA-146'
Presentation by James K. Jeffrey, available for sale on audio tape.

o "The Records Were Burned... Were They?"
http://www.genservices.com/documents/TheRecords
Burned.html
By Sue Powell Morgan.

o What to do if the courthouse burned
http://www.gregathcompany.com/burns.html

o What to Do When the Courthouse Burns
http://www.audiotapes.com/product.asp?ProductCode
='SLC-153'
Presentation by Marsha Hoffman Rising, available for sale on audio tape.

o What to Do When the Courthouse Has Burned and You are All Out of Marshmallows!
http://www.geocities.com/Heartland/Acres/9347/
burned.html

o Where to Look if the Courthouse Burned
http://www.uftree.com/bin/fg_auth?/GenealogyNewsstand/
ShakingTree/Court/880331.html
From Shaking Your Family Tree by Myra Vanderpool Gormley, C.G.

◆ Consumer Protection

• The Better Business Bureau
http://www.bbb.org/

• Consumer World: Consumer Agencies
http://www.consumerworld.org/pages/agencies.htm
List of links to consumer protection agencies worldwide.

• Contact Numbers for State, County and Local Consumer Protection Agencies
http://www.justiceonline.org/consumer/state_cons_prot.html

• The National Fraud Information Center
http://www.fraud.org/welcome.htm
From the National Consumers' League.

• State and Federal Consumer Protection Links
http://www.justiceonline.org/consumer/govt_con_links.html

• The U.S. Federal Trade Commission - Consumer Protection
http://www.ftc.gov/ftc/consumer.htm

◆ Other Myths, Hoaxes & Scams

• 1960 Census Myths and Facts--Explained
http://sul-server-2.stanford.edu/byform/mailing-lists/exlibris/
1996/04/msg00087.html

• BAKER Hoax
http://members.tripod.com/~Crystal_J/Baker-2.html

• Baronage Caveat Emptor: "Name Histories" and "Family Crests"
http://www.baronage.co.uk/bphtm-01/caveat02.html

• The Buchanan Estate Scam
http://www.vantek.net/pages/pattyh/scam.htm

• Caveat Emptor - Buy a Noble Title and Become a Lord
http://www.baronage.co.uk/bphtm-01/caveat03.html

• Errors to Beware in Burke's Peerage
http://www.baronage.co.uk/bphtm-01/essay-7.html

• Fake Seminoles in the Confederate Army (1864)
http://www.geocities.com/CollegePark/Stadium/1528/
9808.html

• False and Faked Mayflower Genealogy
http://members.aol.com/calebj/hoaxes.html

• Falsified Birth Certificates
http://members.aol.com/skiptrak23/3adofals.htm

• faq.scams from the Roots-L Library
http://ftp.cac.psu.edu/pub/genealogy/roots-l/faq/faq.scams

• Genealogy Frauds
http://www.linkline.com/personal/xymox/fraud/fraud.htm

o Fraudulent Lineages
http://www.linkline.com/personal/xymox/fraud/
fraud223.htm
Originally titled We Wuz Robbed! and published in the Genealogical Journal of the Utah Genealogical Association.

• Genealogy Scams
http://www.siscom.net/~rdrunner/HTML/Scams.html
Buyer beware.

• Genealogy Scams
http://www.powerup.com.au/~plucas/scams.htm

• Irish Genealogical Society, Int'l (IGSI) - The "Three Brothers" Paradigm
http://www.rootsweb.com/~irish/old_site/brothers.htm
An article by Richard Pence.

• The Myth of the Black Irish
http://www.darkfiber.com/blackirish/

• National Personnel Records Center, St. Louis, MO
http://www.nara.gov/regional/stlouis.html

o Military Personal Records - The 1973 Fire at NPRC(MPR)
http://www.nara.gov/regional/mprfire.html
Discusses the records, which were lost in this disastrous fire and those which survived.

• Pennsylvania Dutch are of German Heritage, Not Dutch
http://www.kerchner.com/padutch.htm

• Pitter's Cherokee Trails - So you were told you were Black Dutch or Black Irish
http://www.rosecity.net/cherokee/blackdutch.html

• Plimoth-on-Web - Pilgrim Myths and Realities
http://www.plimoth.org/Library/pilmyth.htm

• Society of Genealogists Information Leaflet No. 15 - The Right to Arms
http://www.sog.org.uk/leaflets/arms.html

• So Your Grandmother Was a Cherokee Princess?
http://www.powersource.com/cherokee/gene.html

- United States Postal Inspection Service - The Phony Inheritance Scam
  http://www.usps.gov/websites/depart/inspect/inherit.htm

◆ Quality Research Methods

- The Board for Certification of Genealogists' Genealogical Standards Manual
  http://www.amazon.com/exec/obidos/ISBN=0916489922/markcyndisgenealA/
  A book by the BCG.

- Board for Certification of Genealogists - Skillbuilding, Index of Available Columns
  http://www.bcgcertification.org/skbldidx.html

- Citing Sources
  http://www.CyndisList.com/citing.htm
  See this category on Cyndi's List for related links.

- Examining Evidence to Prove a Pedigree
  http://www.ancestry.com/columns/myra/Shaking_Family_Tree08-07-97.htm
  From Shaking Your Family Tree, by Myra Vanderpool Gormley, C.G.

- Genealogical Standards
  http://www.ngsgenealogy.org/about/content/committees/gene_stan.html
  Recommended by the National Genealogical Society.

  - Guidelines For Publishing Web Pages On The Internet
    http://www.ngsgenealogy.org/about/content/committees/gene5_stan.html

  - Standards For Sharing Information With Others
    http://www.ngsgenealogy.org/about/content/committees/gene4_stan.html

  - Standards for Sound Genealogical Research
    http://www.ngsgenealogy.org/about/content/committees/gene1_stan.html

  - Standards for Use of Technology in Genealogical Research
    http://www.ngsgenealogy.org/about/content/committees/gene3_stan.html

  - Standards for Using Records Repositories and Libraries
    http://www.ngsgenealogy.org/about/content/committees/gene2_stan.html

- Genealogical Websites Watchdog
  http://www.ancestordetective.com/watchdog.htm
  As a public service to the genealogical community, Ancestor Detective® will list Web sites which provide misleading or inaccurate genealogical information.

- How To
  http://www.CyndisList.com/howto.htm
  See this category on Cyndi's List for related links.

- Internet Genealogists for Quality
  http://www.ralls.net/igfq/

- Pitfalls in Genealogical Research
  http://www.amazon.com/exec/obidos/ISBN=0916489280/markcyndisgenealA/
  A book by Milton Rubincam, FASG. From one of the giants of genealogy, this little book is a fun read and is full of excellent advice and warnings about common errors in genealogical research.

- Producing Quality Research Notes
  http://www.bcgcertification.org/skbld971.html
  By Elizabeth Shown Mills, CG, CGL. From the Board for Certification of Genealogists - Skill Building - January 1997.

- Weighing the Evidence
  http://www.ancestry.com/columns/george/02-12-99.htm
  From "Along Those Lines..." by George G. Morgan.

- Why Bother? The Value of Documentation in Family History Research
  http://www.genealogy.com/genealogy/19_kory.html
  By Kory Meyerink, MLS, AG.

NAMES
http://www.cyndislist.com/names.htm

Category Index:
- General Resource Sites
- Locality Specific
- Mailing Lists, Newsgroups & Chat
- Patronymics
- Publications, Software & Supplies
- Surnames

◆ General Resource Sites

- By Any Other Name...
  http://www.w-link.net/~maegwin/menagerie/name.htm
  Discover the meaning of your name.

- Changing Immigrant Names
  http://www.ins.usdoj.gov/graphics/aboutins/history/articles/NAMES.htm
  From the U. S. Immigration and Naturalization Service (INS). Includes a list of reasons for name changes and links to stories about how names were changed.

- Family Naming Traditions
  http://www.rootsweb.com/~genepool/naming.htm

- First Name Basis
  http://www.hypervigilance.com/genlog/firstname.html
  To aid you in researching when all you know is the first name of a person. Focuses on unusual first names and women's first names when maiden names are unknown.

- Given Name Index
  http://www.geocities.com/Heartland/Hills/1739/givennames.html

- A Listing of Some 18th and 19th Century American Nicknames
  http://www.cslnet.ctstateu.edu/nickname.htm

- Names and Family Naming Resources
  http://www.rootsource.com/names.htm
  Some Naming Patterns Common Before 1800 from the New River Company's Genealogy and History Research Site.

- Nicknames and Naming Traditions
  http://www.tngenweb.org/franklin/frannick.htm

- Nom de Guerre - The Real People's Real Name Resource of Pseudonyms & Aliases
  http://www.walshnet.com/walshnet/punster/realname.htm

- Our Ancestor's Nicknames
  http://www.uftree.com/UFT/HowTos/SettingOut/nickname1.html

- The USGenWeb Project - Info for Researchers - Names
  http://www.usgenweb.org/researchers/names.html

- What's in a Name? OR: People Who Live in Glasshouses Should Not Throw Stones
  http://www.rootsweb.com/~irish/igsi_published/norahi01.htm

◆ Locality Specific

- 18th Century PA German Name Spelling Idiosyncrasies
  http://www.kerchner.com/spelling.htm

- 18th Century PA German Naming Customs
  http://www.kerchner.com/germname.htm

- 18th Century PA German Nicknames
  http://www.kerchner.com/nickname.htm

- British Surnames: First-names, Localities, Occupations, Nicknames
  http://www.familychronicle.com/british.htm

- Colonial Naming Customs
  http://www.intersurf.com/~rcollins/names.html

- A Dictionary of Period Russian Names
  http://www.sca.org/heraldry/paul/index.html

- An Irishman and His Name
  http://www.rootsweb.com/~irish/igsi_published/bmitch1.htm

- Maryland State Archives Junior and Senior
  http://www.mdarchives.state.md.us/msa/refserv/html/jrsr.html

- Maryland State Archives Naming Children
  http://www.mdarchives.state.md.us/msa/refserv/html/names.html

- Medieval Names Archive
  http://www.panix.com/~mittle/names/

- Names and Naming in Republican and Imperial Rome
  http://www.oz.net/~bockmad/ares/naming.html

- Naming Children in early New England
  http://www.lonestar.texas.net/~mseifert/puritan14.html
  Scholarly work on the naming patterns used by early Puritans.

- Naming Customs found in Poland
  http://rootsweb.com/~polwgw/naming.html

- Surnames in Italy / L'Italia dei cognomi
  http://gens.labo.net/en/cognomi/
  By entering a surname and pressing the red arrow, a distribution map of Italy is generated showing the concentrations of that particular surname in Italy.

- Welsh Patronymics
  http://www.melcombe.freeserve.co.uk/helps/patronym.htm
  From Helen's Genealogy Advice Pages.

◆ Mailing Lists, Newsgroups & Chat

- ALIAS-AKA Mailing List
  http://www.rootsweb.com/~jfuller/gen_mail_general.html
  #ALIAS-AKA
  For the discussion and sharing of information regarding given names or surnames that have been changed, primarily without leaving any legal record.

- SURNAME-ORIGINS Mailing List
  http://www.rootsweb.com/~jfuller/gen_mail_surnames-gen.html#SURNAME-ORIGINS
  For the discussion of the etymology (word origin) of surnames, as well as the geographic origins of surnames.

◆ Patronymics

- Constructing 16th Century Welsh Names
  http://www.sca.org/heraldry/laurel/welsh16.html

- Diana's Genealogy Pages: Patronymics
  http://dgmweb.net/Common/Patronymics.htm

- Donna Speer Ristenbatt Genealogy / Surnames From Patronymics
  http://www.ristenbatt.com/genealogy/dutch_sn.htm

- Dutch Patronymics of the 1600s
  http://olivetreegenealogy.com/nn/pat.shtml

- Forming Finnish Patronymic Names
  http://www.engr.uvic.ca/~syli/geneo/patronymic.html

- Gareth's Help Page (Technical Words) - Patronymic
  http://www.johngareth.freeserve.co.uk/hicks3.html
  #Patronymic

- IGI and Patronymics
  http://www.johngareth.freeserve.co.uk/HelpPage~pearls.html
  #IGIpatro

- Jasienica Patronymic Records
  http://www.jewishgen.org/JRI-PL/patronym/jasienica_data.htm
  From Jewish Records Indexing - Poland.

- Patronymics
  http://www.deltatango.freeserve.co.uk/patron.html
  Fixed surnames were not adopted in Netherlands until 1811-1812.

- Patronymics - Generational Family Name Changes in 18th Century Germany
  http://home.earthlink.net/~ricklefsr/rrpatro.htm
  By Ron Ricklefs, part of the Ricklefs Family Center on the Net.

- Patronymics - Ostfriesland-Patronymics
  http://www.asc.csc.cc.il.us/~mneill/html/patronymics.html
  By Michael John Neill.

- Some Common Welsh Surnames & Patronymics
  http://www.korrnet.org/welsh/surnames.html

- Welsh Names and Surnames
  http://www.korrnet.org/welsh/files/jbdavies.html

- Welsh Patronymics
  http://www.melcombe.freeserve.co.uk/helps/patronym.htm
  From Helen's Genealogy Advice Pages.

- Welsh Surnames
  http://www.data-wales.co.uk/names.htm

- Welsh Surnames
  http://www.nlw.org.uk/lc/gg02.htm#surnames
  From the National Library of Wales.

◆ Publications, Software & Supplies

- Amazon.com Genealogy Bookstore - Names
  http://www.amazon.com/exec/obidos/external-search/?keyword=genealogy+names&tag=markcyndisgenealA/

- AudioTapes.com - Genealogical Lectures on Cassette Tapes - Names
  http://www.audiotapes.com/search2.asp?Search=names
  And Naming
  http://www.audiotapes.com/search2.asp?Search=naming

◆ Surnames

- The Relevance of Surnames in Genealogy
  http://www.sog.org.uk/leaflets/surnames.html
  Society of Genealogists Information Leaflet No. 7.

- Surname Origins Index
  http://www.sonic.net/~csawyer/surnames.html

- Surnames: What's in a Name? * Name Origins & Meanings * Broken Arrow Publishing
  http://clanhuston.com/name/name.htm
  o Brief History of Surnames
    http://clanhuston.com/name/namehist.htm
  o Surnames A-D
    http://clanhuston.com/name/namea-d.htm
  o Surnames E-H
    http://clanhuston.com/name/namee-h.htm
  o Surnames I-O
    http://clanhuston.com/name/namei-o.htm
  o Surnames P-S
    http://clanhuston.com/name/namep-s.htm
  o Surnames T-Z
    http://clanhuston.com/name/namet-z.htm

NATIVE AMERICAN
http://www.cyndislist.com/native.htm

Category Index:

- ◆ General Resource Sites
- ◆ History & Culture
- ◆ Libraries, Archives & Museums
- ◆ Mailing Lists, Newsgroups & Chat
- ◆ Maps, Gazetteers & Geographical Information
- ◆ Native American Conflicts and Wars
- ◆ People & Families

- ◆ Professional Researchers, Volunteers & Other Research Services
- ◆ Publications, Software & Supplies
- ◆ Records: Census, Cemeteries, Land, Obituaries, Personal, Taxes and Vital
- ◆ Societies & Groups
- ◆ Specific Tribal or Nation Resources
- ◆ USGenWeb Project ~ Native Americans

◆ General Resource Sites

- The African - Native Genealogy Homepage
  http://hometown.aol.com/angelaw859/index.html
  Celebrating the Estelusti ~ The Freedmen Oklahoma's Black Indians of the Cherokee, Chickasaw, Choctaw, Creek, and Seminole Nations.

- AISES Gopher Site
  gopher://bioc02.uthscsa.edu/11/AISESnet%20Gopher

- American Indian Studies
  http://www.csulb.edu/~aisstudy/

- American Indian Tribal Directory
  http://www.indians.org./Resource/FedTribes99/fedtribes99.html

- First Nations in Canada
  http://www.inac.gc.ca/pubs/fnic/index.html

- Genealogy of Quebec's Native People and Francophone Metis
  http://www.cam.org/~beaur/gen/amerin-e.html

- How To Guide for Native Americans
  http://members.aol.com/bbbenge/page12.html
  By Paul R. Sarrett, Jr.

- Links to Aboriginal Resources
  http://www.bloorstreet.com/300block/aborl.htm

- Native American Genealogy
  http://members.aol.com/bbbenge/front.html

- Native American Genealogy
  http://www.system.missouri.edu/shs/nativeam.html
  A guide from the State Historical Society Of Missouri.

- Native American Genealogy in Alabama
  http://www.archives.state.al.us/referenc/notat.html#Native
  From the Alabama Dept. of Archives and History.

- Native American Gopher Entry at Berkeley
  gopher://garnet.berkeley.edu:1250/11/.race/.native

- Native American Indian Genealogy Webring
  http://members.tripod.com/~kjunkutie/natvrng.htm

- Native American Research in Michigan
  http://members.aol.com/roundsky/introduction.html
  Using the Ottawa, Chippewa and Potawatomi tribes as examples.

- Native American Research in Wisconsin
  http://members.aol.com/RoundSky/Wis-intro.html

- Native American Research Page
  http://maple.lemoyne.edu/~bucko/indian.html

- Native American Sites
  http://www.pitt.edu/~lmitten/indians.html

- National Archives Resources - Native American "Rolls"
  http://members.aol.com/bbbenge/page13.html
  By Paul R. Sarrett, Jr.

- Native American Resources
  http://members.aol.com/bbbenge/page14.html
  By Paul R. Sarrett, Jr.

- Native Ancestry Hunting
  http://www.cyberus.ca/~mfdunn/metis/AboGene/Gene.html

- NativeWeb
  http://www.nativeweb.org/

- OTA's Native American Resource Page
  http://bilbo.isu.edu/ota/nativea.html

- Tribes, States and Government Agency
  http://members.aol.com/bbbenge/newlinks.html

- Unique Peoples
  http://www.CyndisList.com/peoples.htm
  See this category on Cyndi's List for related links.

- Yahoo!...Native American...Genealogy
  http://dir.yahoo.com/Society_and_Culture/Cultures_and_Groups/Cultures/American__United_States_/Native_American/History/Genealogy/

◆ History & Culture

- Native American History and Culture
  http://www.etsu-tn.edu/cas/history/natam.htm

◆ Libraries, Archives & Museums

- The Balch Institute for Ethnic Studies
  http://www.libertynet.org/~balch/
  Includes a research library with materials on immigration studies.

  o A Guide to Manuscript and Microfilm Collections of the Research Library of the Balch Institute for Ethnic Studies
    http://www.balchinstitute.org/online_resources_12/html/contents.html

    • Native American
      http://www.balchinstitute.org/online_resources_12/html/body_native_american.html

- California Indian Library Collections
  http://www.mip.berkeley.edu/cilc/brochure/brochure.html

- Native American Genealogy
  http://www.archives.state.al.us/referenc/notat.html#indians
  Guide for holdings at the Alabama Department of Archives & History.

- Native American Research from the Library of Michigan
  http://www.libofmich.lib.mi.us/genealogy/nativeamerican.html

- Tennessee State Library and Archives
  http://www.state.tn.us/sos/statelib/pubsvs/cherokee.htm
  Historical and Genealogical Information - Suggestions for Native American Research (Cherokee).

◆ Mailing Lists, Newsgroups & Chat

- Genealogy Resources on the Internet - Native American Mailing Lists
  http://www.rootsweb.com/~jfuller/gen_mail_natam.html
  Most of the mailing list links below point to this site, wonderfully maintained by John Fuller

- AMERIND-US-SE Mailing List
  http://www.rootsweb.com/~jfuller/gen_mail_natam.html
  #AMERIND-US-SE
  Or those with a genealogical, historical, or cultural interest in the lost Indian tribes of the southeastern United States in order to help the descendants of these scattered tribes to learn about their ancestors.

- BoatFolks Mailing List
  http://www.rootsweb.com/~jfuller/gen_mail_natam.html
  #BoatFolks
  For the discussion and sharing of information regarding the ancestors and descendents of immigrants arriving in the United States prior to 1700. While the list will initially focus on the Mayflower families, all researchers whose ancestors arrived prior to 1700 are welcome. In addition, those who trace their Native American roots back to that time period are welcome.

- Chat Genealogy
  http://genealogy.about.com/hobbies/genealogy/mpchat.htm
  From the About.com genealogy section. Scheduled weekly chats for the following topics: Native American, Genealogy How-To, US Southern States, Genealogy Social, British Isles, French, Canadian.

- CHEROKEE Mailing List
  http://www.rootsweb.com/~jfuller/gen_mail_natam.html
  #CHEROKEE

- CherokeeGene Mailing List
  http://www.rootsweb.com/~jfuller/gen_mail_natam.html
  #CherokeeGene

- CHICKASAW Mailing List
  http://www.rootsweb.com/~jfuller/gen_mail_natam.html
  #CHICKASAW
  For anyone researching their Chickasaw ancestry or having a genealogical interest in the Chickasaw Nation.

- Choctaw Mailing List
  http://www.rootsweb.com/~jfuller/gen_mail_natam.html
  #Choctaw

- CHOCTAW Mailing List
  http://www.rootsweb.com/~jfuller/gen_mail_natam.html
  #CHOCTAW1
  For anyone with a genealogical interest in the Choctaw Indian tribe in Oklahoma (McCurtain County and neighboring counties).

- CHOCTAW-SOUTHEAST Mailing List
  http://www.rootsweb.com/~jfuller/gen_mail_natam.html
  #CHOCTAW-SOUTHEAST
  For anyone with a genealogical interest in the Choctaw Tribe of Native Americans. While the list will emphasize those who lived in the South-Eastern United States, especially Mississippi, all Choctaw researchers are welcome.

- CREEK-SOUTHEAST Mailing List
  http://www.rootsweb.com/~jfuller/gen_mail_natam.html
  #CREEK-SOUTHEAST
  For anyone interested in the genealogy and history of the Creek Indians of the Southeastern United States, and those living among the Creeks.

- FIVECIVILTRIB Mailing List
  http://www.rootsweb.com/~jfuller/gen_mail_natam.html
  #FIVECIVILTRIB
  For anyone who is researching the Five "Civilized" Tribes (i.e., Cherokee, Choctaw, Chickasaw, Seminole, Creek).

- FRENCH-INDIAN Mailing List
  http://www.rootsweb.com/~jfuller/gen_mail_natam.html
  #FRENCH-INDIAN
  For anyone with a genealogical or historical interest in the French and Indian war.

- GRANNYS-NA-PANTRY Mailing List
  http://www.rootsweb.com/~jfuller/gen_mail_natam.html
  #GRANNYS-NA-PANTRY
  A mailing list where Native American people can share recipes, remedies, memories, and stories of what their grannys taught and contributed to their families.

- Genealogy-Native
  http://nctc.com/~cheyanne/index.html
  #Genealogy-Native Channel on AfterNET.

- **INDIAN-CAPTIVES Mailing List**
  http://www.rootsweb.com/~jfuller/gen_mail_natam.html
  #INDIAN-CAPTIVES
  For anyone with a genealogical interest in the American pioneers that were captured by the Indians.

- **INDIAN-ROOTS-L Mailing List**
  http://www.rootsweb.com/~jfuller/gen_mail_natam.html
  #INDIAN-ROOTS

- **Indian-Territory-Roots Mailing List**
  http://www.rootsweb.com/~jfuller/gen_mail_natam.html
  #Indian-Territory-Roots
  For anyone with a genealogical interest in Indian Territory - an area that in 1907 became the eastern and south/south-eastern part of Oklahoma.

- **ITCHEROK Mailing List**
  http://www.rootsweb.com/~jfuller/gen_mail_states-ok.html
  #ITCHEROK
  For anyone with a genealogical interest in the Cherokee Nation Indian Territory in what is now Oklahoma.

- **ITCHOCTA Mailing List**
  http://www.rootsweb.com/~jfuller/gen_mail_states-ok.html
  #ITCHOCTA
  For anyone with a genealogical interest in the Choctaw Nation, Indian Territory, prior to Oklahoma statehood.

- **ITCREEKN Mailing List**
  http://www.rootsweb.com/~jfuller/gen_mail_natam.html
  #ITCREEKN
  For anyone with a genealogical interest in the Creek Nation, Indian Territory.

- **ITUNASSI Mailing List**
  http://www.rootsweb.com/~jfuller/gen_mail_natam.html
  #ITUNASSI
  For anyone with a genealogical interest in the Unassigned Lands of the Indian Territory, encompassing all or part of the present Oklahoma counties of Canadian, Cleveland, Kingfisher, Logan, Oklahoma, and Payne.

- **KEEWETIN Mailing List**
  http://www.rootsweb.com/~jfuller/gen_mail_country-can.html
  #KEEWETIN
  For anyone researching Cree fur trade family histories in Canada.

- **Melungeon Mailing List**
  http://www.rootsweb.com/~jfuller/gen_mail_states-gen.html
  #MELUNGEO
  For people conducting Melungeon and/or Appalachian research including Native American, Portuguese, Turkish, Black Dutch, and other unverifiable mixed statements of ancestry or unexplained rumors, with ancestors in TN, KY, VA, NC, SC, GA, AL, WV, and possibly other places.

- **METIS Mailing List**
  http://www.rootsweb.com/~jfuller/gen_mail_natam.html
  #METIS
  For Metis descendants, those who have mixed Native American and European (principally French) ancestry.

- **METISGEN Mailing List**
  http://www.rootsweb.com/~jfuller/gen_mail_natam.html
  #METISGEN
  For the discussion and sharing of information regarding the Metis and their descendants. The Metis are North America's Fur Trading

Children the new nation of individuals born within North America from the first unions of natives and whites.

- **MEXICAN-INDIANS**
  http://www.rootsweb.com/~jfuller/gen_mail_country-mex.html
  #MEXICAN-INDIANS
  For anyone with a genealogical, historical, or cultural interest in the native peoples of Mexico.

- **MichiganNativeAm Mailing List**
  http://www.rootsweb.com/~jfuller/gen_mail_natam.html
  #MichiganNativeAm
  For anyone who is researching their Native American ancestry in the Michigan area.

- **Mitsawokett Mailing List**
  http://www.rootsweb.com/~jfuller/gen_mail_natam.html
  #Mitsawokett
  For anyone who is researching the genealogy and history of the Indian families that originated in the territory of Mitsawokett, now known as Kent County, Delaware.

- **MIXED-BLOODS Mailing List**
  http://www.rootsweb.com/~jfuller/gen_mail_natam.html
  #MIXED-BLOODS
  For those interested in the Indigenous/Mixed-Blood ancestry in what is now known as the United States Of America.

- **MIXED-MARRIAGES Mailing List**
  http://www.rootsweb.com/~jfuller/gen_mail_natam.html
  #MIXED-MARRIAGES
  For those interested in Native American and African American, Inter-Marriages, and the hidden culture/ancestry which so many of us didn't realize existed and still currently exists in today's society.

- **NA-FAMILY-LEGENDS Mailing List**
  http://www.rootsweb.com/~jfuller/gen_mail_natam.html
  #NA-FAMILY-LEGENDS
  For anyone who is researching families with legends of Native American ancestry.

- **NA-FORUM-L Mailing List**
  http://www.rootsweb.com/~jfuller/gen_mail_natam.html
  #NA-FORUM
  For anyone with an interest in North American Indian history and/or their Indian family history.

- **NAOTTAWA Mailing List**
  http://www.rootsweb.com/~jfuller/gen_mail_natam.html
  #NAOTTAWA
  For anyone with a genealogical interest in the Ottawa Indian Nation.

- **natam-gene Mailing List**
  http://www.rootsweb.com/~jfuller/gen_mail_natam.html
  #natam-gene
  For anyone with a genealogical interest in Native Americans.

- **NATIVEAMERICAN-DELMARVA Mailing List**
  http://www.rootsweb.com/~jfuller/gen_mail_natam.html
  #NATIVEAMERICAN-DELMARVA
  For anyone researching their Native American ancestry in Delaware, Maryland, and Virginia.

- **NCQUALLA Mailing List**
  http://www.rootsweb.com/~jfuller/gen_mail_states-nc.html
  #NCQUALLA
  For anyone with a genealogical interest in Qualla Boundary, North Carolina (Cherokee Reservation).

- NEW-ENG-NATAM Mailing List
  http://www.rootsweb.com/~jfuller/gen_mail_natam.html
  #NEW-ENG-NATAM
  For anyone with a genealogical or historical interest in Native Americans in the New England and New York areas.

- NISHNAWBE Mailing List
  http://www.rootsweb.com/~jfuller/gen_mail_natam.html
  #NISHNAWBE
  For anyone researching Native Americans in Michigan and Wisconsin, and the fur traders connected with them.

- OKChoctaw Mailing List
  http://www.rootsweb.com/~jfuller/gen_mail_states-ok.html
  #OKChoctaw
  For anyone researching their Native American Choctaw ancestors who were removed from Mississippi to Oklahoma.

- OKTERR-NA Mailing List
  http://www.rootsweb.com/~jfuller/gen_mail_states-ok.html
  #OKTERR-NA
  For anyone with a genealogical interest in members of the Nations/Tribes of the Oklahoma Territory.

- POCAHONTAS Mailing List
  http://www.rootsweb.com/~jfuller/gen_mail_natam.html
  #POCAHONTAS
  A mailing list dedicated to the genealogy and history of Pocahontas (c1595-1617), daughter of Powhatan.

- POWHATAN-INDIANS Mailing List
  http://www.rootsweb.com/~jfuller/gen_mail_natam.html
  #POWHATAN-INDIANS
  For anyone with a genealogical interest in the Powhatan and Wicocomico Indians.

- PQ-Native-Gen Mailing List
  http://www.rootsweb.com/~jfuller/gen_mail_country-can.html
  #PQ-Native-Gen
  For anyone interested in Native American or Metis genealogy in the province of Quebec, Canada.

- SEMINOLE-WARS Mailing List
  http://www.rootsweb.com/~jfuller/gen_mail_natam.html
  #SEMINOLE-WARS

- SOUTHERN-METIS Mailing List
  http://www.rootsweb.com/~jfuller/gen_mail_natam.html
  #SOUTHERN-METIS
  For anyone with a genealogical interest in their Metis ancestry - those with a mix of the indigenous peoples of the Western Hemisphere and Europeans or those with mixed Native American and African ancestry.

- threefiresgenealogy Mailing List
  http://www.rootsweb.com/~jfuller/gen_mail_natam.html
  #threefiresgenealogy
  For anyone with a genealogical interest in the Ottawa, Chippewa, and Potawatomi tribes.

- Tuckahoe Mailing List
  http://www.rootsweb.com/~jfuller/gen_mail_natam.html
  #Tuckahoe
  For anyone with a genealogical interest in the Tuckahoe Indians, part of the Cherokee tribe. The Tuckahoe Indians may have been Old Settlers in Arkansas.

- WICOCOMICO-NATION Mailing List
  http://www.rootsweb.com/~jfuller/gen_mail_natam.html
  #WICOCOMICO-NATION
  For the research of the Wicocomico Indian Nation for the descendents of the Nation.

- WYWINDRI Mailing List
  http://www.rootsweb.com/~jfuller/gen_mail_states-wy.html
  #WYWINDRI
  For the discussion of genealogical and related topics associated with the Wind River Indian Reservation located in northwestern Wyoming.

◆ Maps, Gazetteers & Geographical Information

- USGenWeb Archives, United States Digital Map Library - Indian Land Cessions
  http://www.rootsweb.com/~usgenweb/maps/cessions/
  This site contains all sixty-seven maps from the 1899 paper, "Indian Land Cessions in the United States" by Charles C. Royce.

◆ Native American Conflicts and Wars

- Indian Wars
  http://www.gbso.net/skyhawk/indianwa.htm
  A brief history.

- The Indian Wars
  http://www.geocities.com/Heartland/Hills/1094/indian.htm
  From the colonial period.

- Indian Wars in the Northwest Territory
  http://users.anderson.edu/~roebuck/war.html
  Conflicts in the old Northwest.

- Journal of the Indian Wars
  http://www.savaspublishing.com/JIW.html
  Print publication regarding the conflicts.

- Order of the Indian Wars
  http://lbha.org/oiw.html
  Present-day society for the study of these conflicts.

- Order of the Indian Wars of the United States
  http://members.tripod.com/~Historic_Trust/indian.htm
  Fraternal society of ex-servicemen who served in these conflicts.

◆ People & Families

- Coats Family Blueprints - Descendants of Moytoy
  http://www.rootsquest.com/~coatsfar/wardnancd.html
  Supreme Chief of the Cherokee 1730 - 1760.

- Descendants of Nancy WARD
  http://www.nancyward.com/

- Heart of Two Nations: African Native Americans
  http://hometown.aol.com/homalosa/index.html
  Overview of the shared history of Native Americans and African Americans that includes bibliography of research and genealogical resources.

- Metis Families
  http://www.televar.com/~gmorin/

- MOYTOY - Descendants of Moytoy
  http://www.rootsquest.com/~coatsfar/wardnancd.html
  Supreme Chief of the Cherokee 1730 -- 1760.

- Pocahontas Descendants
  http://www.rootscomputing.com/howto/pocahn/pocahn.htm
  Descendants of Powhatan (Father of Pocahontas).

◆ Professional Researchers, Volunteers & Other Research Services

- Board for Certification of Genealogists - Roster of Those Certified - Specializing in Native American Genealogy
  http://www.bcgcertification.org/rosts_@n.html

- Genealogy Central Lineage Service
  http://www.geocities.com/Heartland/Woods/6036/research/index.html
  Specializes in Native American, New England and Colonial American research.

- Past Tracker ~ Coos Bay, Oregon
  http://www.harborside.com/~rice/index.html
  Native American and New England specialty searches.

◆ Publications, Software & Supplies

- African-American Ancestors Among the Five Civilized Tribes
  http://www.coax.net/people/lwf/blkind.htm
  Description of book for sale.

- Amazon.com Genealogy Bookstore - Native American
  http://www.amazon.com/exec/obidos/external-search/?keyword=native+american+genealogy&tag=mark cyndisgenealA/

- Ancestor's Attic Discount Genealogy Books - Native American Genealogy Books
  http://members.tripod.com/~ancestorsattic/index.html#secNA

- AudioTapes.com - Genealogical Lectures on Cassette Tapes - Native American
  http://www.audiotapes.com/search2.asp?Search=Native+American
  And American Indian
  http://www.audiotapes.com/search2.asp?Search=+American+Indian

- A Creek Indian Bibliography
  http://www.rhus.com/Creeks.html
  Creek Indians: Sources for History, Biography and Genealogy; Print and Internet Links.

- Frontier Press Bookstore - Native American History / Research
  http://www.frontierpress.com/frontier.cgi?category=ind

- GenealogyBookShop.com - Native American/Indian
  http://www.genealogybookshop.com/genealogybookshop/files/General,Native_American_Indian/index.html
  The online store of Genealogical Publishing Co., Inc. & Clearfield Company.

- Heritage Books - Indian
  http://www.heritagebooks.com/indian.htm

- Indian Blood
  http://indianbl.digigo.com/

- The Memorabilia Corner
  http://members.aol.com/TMCorner/index.html
  Located in Oklahoma with many Native American resources. Forms, flags, maps, software, CDs, tapes, microfilm & microfiche, books, periodicals, photographic conservation & archival materials.

- Michigan's Native Americans - A Selective Bibliography
  http://www.libofmich.lib.mi.us/genealogy/minatamerbib.html

- Native Press
  http://www.ndnscout.com/
  Specialize in American Indian genealogical source material, how-to books for American Indian genealogy, and American Indian Language renewal materials.

- S.E.N.A. South Eastern Native American Exchange
  http://www.angelfire.com/al/senaexchange
  A quarterly publication of Native American research and genealogy. Designed to make hard to find information accessible. Tribes: Creek, Choctaw, Geronimo, Creek Census.

- A Time for Sharing - Native American SIG Newsletter
  http://members.aol.com/kathyehyde/news/index.htm

◆ Records: Census, Cemeteries, Land, Obituaries, Personal, Taxes and Vital (Born, Married, Died & Buried)

- 1851 Census of Cherokee's East of the Mississippi - The Siler Rolls
  http://members.aol.com/lredtail/siler.html

- American Indians - A select catalog of National Archives microfilm.
  http://www.nara.gov/publications/microfilm/amerindians/indians.html

- Heritage Quest - US Federal Census Schedules Available on CD-ROM
  http://www.heritagequest.com/genealogy/CD-ROM/
  Digitized images of the complete US Census from 1790 to 1920 on CD-ROM. Available for sale from Heritage Quest.
  Census Schedules for Indian Territory:

  o 1900
    http://www.heritagequest.com/cgi-bin/nspage26.cpg?catalog=ProdFind2&file=cresults.htm&@where.TL1@comp.Listing@eq=MF&&@where.LL1@comp.Listing@eq=U&&@where.TL2@comp.Listing@eq=FC&&@where.TL3@comp.Listing@eq=1900&&@where.LL2@comp.Listing@eq=ITER

- Indian Captives of Early American Pioneers
  http://www.rootsweb.com/~indian/index.htm

- Indian Graves and Cemeteries
  http://history.cc.ukans.edu/heritage/werner/indigrav.html

- Illinois Database of Servitude and Emancipation
  Records 1722-1863
  http://www.sos.state.il.us/depts/archives/servant.html
  This database includes more than 2000 transactions found in governmental records involving the servitude and emancipation of Africans and, occasionally, Indians in the French and English eras of colonial Illinois (1722-1790) and African-Americans in the American period of Illinois (1790-1863).

- Intruders and Non-Citizens in the Creek Nation 1875-1895
  http://www.rootsweb.com/~itcreek/records2.htm

- Nominal Census Homepage
  http://royal.okanagan.bc.ca/census/index.html
  Data for the southern interior of the Province of British Columbia, Canada

  o Canada Census, 1881 - Yale District
    http://royal.okanagan.bc.ca/census/yale1881.html

  o Canada Census, 1891 - Yale District
    http://royal.okanagan.bc.ca/census/yale1891.html

  o Indian Census Rolls, 1885-1940
    http://www.kshs.org/ms/indian1.htm
    Indian census rolls at the Kansas State Historical Society. These are the annual censuses taken by agents or superintendents in charge of Indian reservations. Information gathered varies by year and jurisdiction, but usually includes English and/or Indian name, tribal roll number, age or date of birth, sex, and relationship to head of household. Beginning in 1930, the censuses also show degree of Indian blood, marital status, place of residence, and other information. The original censuses are in the National Archives, and the Kansas State Historical Society has only selected rolls, primarily those pertaining to tribes with a Kansas connection. These are available for interlibrary loan.

  o The IRC Census, 1877
    http://royal.okanagan.bc.ca/census/ind1877.html
    Indian Reserve Commission.

  o The OMI Census, 1877
    http://royal.okanagan.bc.ca/census/omi1877.html
    A nominal census of Native peoples taken by the Catholic missionary order, Oblates of Mary Immaculate (OMI)

- Selected Index of Intruders and Non-Citizens in the Creek Nation (1876-1897)
  http://www.rootsweb.com/~itcreek/records1.htm

◆ Societies & Groups

- The Cherokee National Historical Society
  http://www.Powersource.com/heritage/

- Lenni Lenape Historical Society and Museum of Indian Culture
  http://www.lenape.org/
  Allentown, Pennsylvania.

◆ Specific Tribal or Nation Resources

- The Ani-Stohini/Unami Nation
  http://www.ani-stohini-unami.com/
  An Algonquian language group speaking Native American tribe located in the rural Appalachian Mountain Counties of Washington, Smyth, Grayson, Wythe, Carroll, Patrick, and Floyd in the Commonwealth of Virginia and in Surry County, North Carolina.

- Ani-Stohini/Unami Nation Historical Page
  http://www.myfreeoffice.com/tribe
  Brief historical perspective of one of the oldest continuously existing tribes in the Americas.

- The Black Seminoles
  http://www.ccny.cuny.edu/library/News/seminoles2.html

- Cherokee Research

  o 1851 Census of Cherokee's East of the Mississippi - The Siler Rolls
    http://members.aol.com/lredtail/siler.html

  o Bibliography for Cherokee History (in Appalachia)
    http://www.melungeons.org/cherokee.htm

  o The Cherokee Alphabet and Pronunciation Guide
    http://joyce.eng.yale.edu/~joant/CherTabl.html

  o Cherokee by Blood
    http://www.tngennet.org/cherokee_by_blood/
    From the TNGenWeb Project.

  o Cherokee Cousins - Cherokee Genealogy, Language, Culture
    http://www.powerscurce.com/cousins/
    Research service.

  o Cherokee Genealogy - A Selected Resource List on the Cherokee Indians
    http://www.kirch.net/personal/melodie.html

  o The Cherokee Genealogy Page
    http://www.io.com/~crberry/CherokeeGenealogy/

  o Cherokee Legion - "Georgia State Guards"
    http://www.axs2k.net/fatcat/cl_index.htm

  o Cherokee Messenger
    http://www.powersource.com/cherokee/default.html

  o The Cherokee Page
    http://members.aol.com/bbbenge/page10.html

  o Cherokee Archival Project
    http://www.rootsweb.com/~cherokee/

  o A Guide to Cherokee Confederate Military Units, 1861 - 1865
    http://www.yvwiiusdinvnohii.net/history/CherConfed.htm

  o A Guide To Discovering Your Cherokee Ancestors
    http://www.public.usit.net/jerercox/guide.html

  o History of the Cherokee -- White Indian's Homepage
    http://pages.tca.net/martikw/

o The Official Homepage of the Cherokee Indian Reservation
http://www.cherokee-nc.com/

o So Your Grandmother Was a Cherokee Princess?
http://www.powersource.com/cherokee/gene.html

o The Trail of Tears Lawrence County Arkansas
http://147.97.31.30/lawrence/trail1.htm

o Talking Leaves and the Cherokee Phoenix
http://www.ngeorgia.com/history/alphabet.html
Brief history of the Cherokee alphabet.

o Yansudi's Cherokee Heritage Page
http://www.public.usit.net/jerercox/index.html

- Cheyenne Genealogy Research
http://www.mcn.net/~hmscook/roots/cheyenne.html

- The Chickasaw and Their Cessions ~ Tennessee
http://www.tngenweb.org/tnfirst/chicksaw/

- Chickasaw Historical Research Page
http://home.flash.net/~kma/

- The Choctaw Nation
http://members.aol.com/bbbenge/page5.html

- Confederated Tribes of the Chehalis ~ Washington
http://coopext.cahe.wsu.edu/~chehalis/

- First Nations Histories
http://www.dickshovel.com/Compacts.html

- FLGenWeb Project - Native American Information and Links ~ Florida
http://www.rootsweb.com/~flgenweb/links/tribes.html

- A Guide to the Great Sioux Nation
http://www.state.sd.us/state/executive/tourism/sioux/sioux.htm

- Indian People of the Edisto River
http://www.pride-net.com/native_indians/edisto.html

- Lakota Page - The Great Sioux Nation
http://members.aol.com/bbbenge/page6.html

- Lakota Wowapi Oti Kin - Lakota Information Home Page
http://maple.lemoyne.edu/~bucko/lakota.html

- The History and Genealogy of the Native American Isolate Communities of Kent County, Delaware, and Surrounding Areas on the Delmarva Peninsula and Southern New Jersey
http://www.Mitsawokett.com/

- The Mohawk Nation of Akwesasne
http://www.peacetree.com/akwesasne/home.htm

- The Naragansetts
http://members.aol.com/bbbenge/page21.htm

- Native Genealogy
http://www.edwards1.com/rose/genealogy/native-gen/native-gen.htm

For the People of the three fires, the Ojibwa, Ottawa and Potawatomi.

- Ojibwe Language and Culture, by Nancy Vogt
http://hanksville.phast.umass.edu/misc/ojibwe/index.html

- Oneida Indian Nation of NY
http://www.oneida-nation.net/

- The Osage
http://members.aol.com/bbbenge/page16.html

- The Plains and Emigrant Tribes of Kansas
http://history.cc.ukans.edu/heritage/old_west/indian.html

- Pueblo Cultural Center
http://hanksville.phast.umass.edu/defs/independent/PCC/PCC.html

- Seminole Nation of Oklahoma - Historic Preservation Office
http://www.cowboy.net/native/seminole/historic.html

- The Seminole Tribe of Florida
http://www.seminoletribe.com/

- Suquamish Tribe ~ Washington
http://www.suquamish.nsn.us/

- The Taino Genealogy Project
http://www.hartford-hwp.com/taino/docs/proj-6.html

- The Taino Inter-Tribal Council
http://www.hartford-hwp.com/taino/index.html

- Viki's Little Corner of the Web
http://www.novia.net/~vikia/
ROARK, COLBERT, LOVE, KEMP, FRAZIER, McKINNEY & Chickasaw Native American History and Genealogy

- Wampanoag History ~ Massachusetts
http://www.dickshovel.com/wampa.html

◆ USGenWeb Project ~ Native Americans

- Idaho Indian Reservations - USGenWeb Project
http://www.rootsweb.com/~idreserv/

- NC Cherokee Reservation Genealogy
http://www.rootsweb.com/~ncqualla/index.htm

- Twin Territories - Oklahoma/Indian Territory Project
http://www.rootsweb.com/~itgenweb/index.htm

- South Dakota Native American Genealogy
http://www.geocities.com/Heartland/Plains/8430/

- Washington Indian Reservation Orders
http://www.rootsweb.com/~usgenweb/wa/indians/resorder.htm

- Washington Indian Treaties
http://www.rootsweb.com/~usgenweb/wa/indians/treaties.htm

- Washington Tribes
http://www.travel-in-wa.com/DISTINCTLY/tribes.html
List of addresses for tribes in the state.

NETHERLANDS / NEDERLAND

http://www.cyndislist.com/nether.htm

Category Index:

- General Resource Sites
- History & Culture
- Libraries, Archives & Museums
- Locality Specific & Migration
- Mailing Lists, Newsgroups & Chat
- Maps, Gazetteers & Geographical Information
- People & Families

- Professional Researchers, Volunteers & Other Research Services
- Publications, Software & Supplies
- Records: Census, Cemeteries, Land, Obituaries, Personal, Taxes and Vital
- Societies & Groups

◆ General Resource Sites

- **Ancestors from the former Dutch East Indies**
  http://ourworld.compuserve.com/homepages/paulvanV/eastindi.htm

- **Arie Jan Stasse's Home Page**
  http://www.geocities.com/Paris/4744/

- **Digital Resources Netherlands and Belgium**
  http://geneaknowhow.net/digi/resources.html
  A list of resources for the Internet, bulletin board systems (bbs) and diskette/CD-Rom.

- **Donna Speer Ristenbatt Genealogy / Surnames From Patronymics**
  http://www.ristenbatt.com/genealogy/dutch_sn.htm

- **Dutch Antilles**
  http://ourworld.compuserve.com/homepages/paulvanV/nedantil.htm

- **Dutch East-Indies Informationpoint**
  http://home.wxs.nl/~vdbroeke/
  A "guide" for everybody who is interested in Eurasian culture in the Netherlands.

- **Dutch Patronymics of the 1600s**
  http://www.rootsweb.com/~ote/dtchnam.htm#patronymics

- **Dutch Research Corner**
  http://www.ristenbatt.com/genealogy/dutch_rc.htm

- **Dutch Genealogical Word List**
  http://www.familysearch.org/Eng/Search/RG/frameset_rg.asp?Dest=G1&Aid=&Gid=&Lid=&Sid=&Did=&Juris1=&Event=&Year=&Gloss=&Sub=&Tab=&Entry=&Guide=WLDutch.ASP

- **Genealogica Brabantica - Noord-Brabant**
  http://www.xs4all.nl/~defonte/brabant.htm

- **Genealogie en archieven in Nederland (Molema-Smitshoek)**
  http://www.medewerker.hro.nl/W_T_Molema-Smitshoek/

- **Genealogische Links - Genealogy Links in The Netherlands / Wortels naar het Verleden**
  http://members.tripod.com/~westland/index.htm

- **Genealogy Benelux Home Page**
  http://www.ufsia.ac.be/genealogy/

- **Genealogy Benelux Web Ring**
  http://www.geocities.com/Heartland/Plains/5521/benelux.htm
  Belgium Genealogy, Netherlands & Dutch Genealogy, Luxembourg Genealogy.

- **Het Centraal Bureau voor Genealogie / The Central Bureau for Genealogy**
  http://www.cbg.nl/

- **Holland Page**
  http://ourworld.compuserve.com/homepages/paulvanv/

- **International Civic Arms**
  http://www.bng.nl/ngw/indexgb.htm
  Over 9,500 arms of towns, states and countries.

- **Links naar databestanden met gegevens uit primaire bronnen**
  http://home.wxs.nl/~hjdewit/links.html

- **NedGen Dutch Genealogy Searchengine Nederlandse Genealogie Zoekmachine stamboom**
  http://genealogie.thewebconnection.nl/
  The first Dutch Genealogy Search Engine. Indexes Dutch genealogical homepages exclusively.

- **Netherlands Church Record Christenings**
  http://www.familysearch.org/Eng/Search/RG/frameset_rg.asp?Dest=G1&Aid=&Gid=&Lid=&Sid=&Did=&Juris1=&Event=&Year=&Gloss=&Sub=&Tab=&Entry=&Guide=NL_BT3_-_Churchrecordchristening1500-1874.ASP
  Information on how to access and use these records from FamilySearch.org.

- **The Netherlands Research Outline**
  http://www.familysearch.org/Eng/Search/RG/frameset_rg.asp1?Dest=G1&Aid=&Gid=&Lid=&Sid=&Did=&Juris1=&Event=&Year=&Gloss=&Sub=&Tab=&Entry=&Guide=Netherlands.ASP
  Excellent "How To" guide from FamilySearch.org.

- Netherlands Telephone & Address Listings
  http://www.ancestry.com/search/rectype/inddbs/4067.htm

- Patronymics
  http://www.deltatango.freeserve.co.uk/patron.html
  Fixed surnames were not adopted in Netherlands until 1811-1812.

- Research Guidance - Netherlands Events and Time
  Periods
  http://www.familysearch.org/Eng/Search/RG/frameset_rg.asp
  ?Dest=E&Juris1=143
  From FamilySearch.org.

- STORME's Genealogy Page
  http://www.ufsia.ac.be/~estorme/genealogy.html
  *Many great Benelux resource links. STORME, van WAESBERGHE,
  de LAUSNAY, BLOCK, SCHEERDERS, van SCHOUBROEK, de
  SCHRYVER, BOSTEELS.*

- Translation Service only for genealogy related
  material
  http://www.genealogy.net/gene/misc/translation.html
  *Volunteer translators can provide you with translations between
  Czech, English, Dutch, French, German, & Polish. This service is
  provided via e-mail. Exact request syntax and length rules must be
  followed in order to expedite processing.*

- Webwijzer Genealogie
  http://home.multiweb.net/~don_arnoldus/glinks_nl.htm
  *Web-wijzer Genealogie (Dutch). A linking system to websites which
  will be of interest to genealogic researchers.*

- Yahoo!...Netherlands...Genealogy
  http://dir.yahoo.com/Regional/Countries/Netherlands/Arts_
  and_Humanities/Humanities/History/Genealogy/

- Yvette's Dutch Genealogy Homepage
  http://www.twente.nl/~genealogy/

◆ History & Culture

- Koninklijk huis / The Dutch Royal House
  http://www.koninklijkhuis.nl

- Netherlands Historical Background
  http://www.familysearch.org/Eng/Search/RG/frameset_rg.asp
  ?Dest=G1&Aid=&Gid=&Lid=&Sid=&Did=&Juris1=&Event=&
  Year=&Gloss=&Sub=&Tab=&Entry=&Guide=NL_T3_Historical
  Back.ASP
  From FamilySearch.org.

- Yahoo!...Netherlands...History
  http://dir.yahoo.com/Regional/Countries/Netherlands/Arts_
  and_Humanities/Humanities/History/

◆ Libraries, Archives & Museums

- Archiefdiensten In Nederland
  http://www.ufsia.ac.be/genealogy/pages/geninfo/archi_nl.txt

- Archives in the Netherlands / Archieven in
  Nederland
  http://www.medewerker.hro.nl/SmiWT/archief.htm

- The Balch Institute for Ethnic Studies
  http://www.libertynet.org/~balch/
  Includes a research library with materials on immigration studies.

- o A Guide to Manuscript and Microfilm Collections
  of the Research Library of the Balch Institute for
  Ethnic Studies
  http://www.balchinstitute.org/online_resources_12/html/
  contents.html
  - Dutch
    http://www.balchinstitute.org/online_resources_12/html/
    body_dutch.html

- The Dutch Archives
  http://ourworld.compuserve.com/homepages/paulvanv/
  dutcharc.htm
  *Detailed information in English about the various archives in the
  Netherlands with links describing their collections & how to use
  them.*

- Family History Library Catalog
  http://www.familysearch.org/Search/searchcatalog.asp
  *From the FamilySearch web site, an online catalog to the holdings
  of the LDS Church in Salt Lake City, Utah. Also search for other
  localities by place name.*
  http://www.familysearch.org/eng/Library/fhlc/supermainframe
  set.asp?display=localitysearch&columns=*,180,0
  - o Netherlands
    http://www.familysearch.org/eng/Library/fhlc/supermain
    frameset.asp?display=localitydetails&subject=143&subject
    _disp=Netherlands&columns=*,180,0

- Family History Centers in the Netherlands
  http://www.familysearch.org/Eng/Library/FHC/FHC_
  Results.asp?FHCCountry=Netherlands&FHCStateProv=
  &FHCCounty=&FHCCity=&submit=Search

- Gemeentebibliotheek Utrecht / Municipal Public
  Library Utrecht (Netherlands)
  http://www.gbu.nl/

- Koninklijke Bibliotheek / The National Library of the
  Netherlands
  http://www.konbib.nl/

- Municipal Archives of Zwolle
  http://www.obd.nl/instel/gemarchzw/gemareng.htm

- NBD - Nederlandse Bibliotheek Dienst / Netherlands
  Library Service
  http://www.nbd.nl/www/owa/page

- Netherlands Historical Data Archive
  http://oasis.leidenuniv.nl/nhda/nhda-welcome-uk.html

- Repositories of Primary Sources - Europe -
  Netherlands
  http://www.uidaho.edu/special-collections/euro2.html#nl
  *A list of links to online resources from the Univ. of Idaho Library,
  Special Collections and Archives.*

- De Rijksarchiefdienst / State Archives Service
  http://www.archief.nl/rad/
  - o GenLias
    http://www-lias.rad.archief.nl/genlias/ara/logon?cid=-1
    *Searchable online database of genealogical records from the
    State Archives Service.*

- Stadsbibliotheek Maastricht / City Library of Maastricht
  http://www.sbm.nl/

- Stadsbibliotheek Vlaardingen / City Library of Vlaardingen
  http://www.dsv.nl/DSV/kijken-en-kopen/lezen/bibliotheek/bibindex.htm

- State Archives in the province of Overijssel
  http://www.obd.nl/instel/arch/rkarchen.htm

- Stichting Vrienden West Zeeuws-Vlaamse Archieven
  http://www.cyber.nl/zeeuw_archief/welcome.html
  Archive site in Dutch.

- UBA - Library: Church History: Mennonite
  http://www.uba.uva.nl/en/libraries/church.html
  From the Universiteitsbibliotheek Amsterdam. Holds the collection of the Verenigde Doopsgezinde Gemeente Amsterdam (the United Mennonite Congregation of Amsterdam). It also houses the Mennonite Documention Centre from 1800 to the present.

◆ Locality Specific & Migration

- Gelderland Page - Genealogie uit Gelderland
  http://www.geocities.com/Heartland/Pointe/2863/

- Genealogie in het Hageland, Brabant, Vlaanderen
  http://www.actagena.org/index.htm
  Belgium, Flanders, the Hageland. Records between 1574 and 1900 of the parishes in the area between Leuven, Aarschot, Diest and Tienen.

- Genealogy Drenthe
  http://www.medewerker.hro.nl/w_t_molema/drweb.htm
  A lot of links to familynames in the province Drenthe (Holland), historical pages.

- Genealogy Groningen (Holland)
  http://www.medewerker.hro.nl/w_t_molema/grweb.htm
  A lot of links to sites with family names in the province Groningen (Holland) and to historical pages.

- Genealogie in Limburg
  http://genealogie-limburg.net/
  Links to family pages in the province of Limburg (Netherlands, Belgium). Also available in English.

- Genealogy Hoeksche Waard (Zuid Holland - Holland)
  http://www.medewerker.hro.nl/w_t_molema/hwweb.htm
  Genealogy page with lot of information about the region Hoeksche Waard and the museum in the province Zuid Holland in Holland.

- Genealogy Zeeland
  http://www.medewerker.hro.nl/w_t_molema/zeweb.htm
  A lot of links to family names in the province Zeeland of Holland, also a mailing list.

- Hoeksche Waard - Martine's Historical Homepage
  http://stad.dsl.nl/~martine/zoehwe.htm

- Immigrant Ships
  http://www.macatawa.org/~devries/Shipindex.htm
  Immigrant ships of the Dutch Colonists of the 19th century to West Michigan and Iowa. Over 50 Lists!

- Project Ahnentafels in Limburg / Project Limburgse Kwartierstaten
  http://gallery.uunet.be/PRO-GEN.GG.LIMBURG/Ahnen.html

- stamboom Terschellinger / Vlielander / Schiermonnikooger families
  http://home-2.consunet.nl/~cb000446/stamboom.htm
  Dutch Surnames all over the world who come from the island of Terschelling and went abroad

◆ Mailing Lists, Newsgroups & Chat

- Genealogy Resources on the Internet - Netherlands Mailing Lists
  http://www.rootsweb.com/~jfuller/gen_mail_country-net.html
  Most of the mailing list links below point to this site, wonderfully maintained by John Fuller

- DUTCH-MIDWEST Mailing List
  http://www.rootsweb.com/~jfuller/gen_mail_country-net.html#DUTCH-MIDWEST
  For anyone with a genealogical interest in the ancestors and descendants of the Dutch immigrants (ca.1850 to WWI) who settled in the Chicago (Roseland) and South Holland, Illinois area and other Dutch 'colonies' in the surrounding states.

- Friesland-genealogy Mailing List
  http://www.rootsweb.com/~jfuller/gen_mail_country-net.html#Friesland-genealogy
  For anyone with a genealogical interest in the Dutch province of Friesland.

- GEN-BENELUX Mailing List
  http://www.rootsweb.com/~jfuller/gen_mail_country-net.html#GEN-BENELUX
  Gatewayed with the Usenet Newsgroup soc.genealogy.benelux
  news:soc.genealogy.benelux
  For research in the Benelux region (Belgium, the Netherlands, and Luxembourg).

- GENBNL-L Mailing List
  http://www.rootsweb.com/~jfuller/gen_mail_country-blg.html#DUTCH
  Gatewayed with the Usenet Newsgroup soc.genealogy.benelux
  news:soc.genealogy.benelux
  For research in the Benelux region (Belgium, the Netherlands, and Luxembourg).

- NETHERLANDS Mailing List
  http://www.rootsweb.com/~jfuller/gen_mail_country-net.html#NETHERLANDS
  For anyone with a genealogical interest in the Netherlands (sometimes known as Holland).

- NL-NOORD-HOLLAND Mailing List
  http://www.rootsweb.com/~jfuller/gen_mail_country-net.html#NL-NOORD-HOLLAND
  For anyone with a genealogical interest in the province of Noord-Holland, Netherlands.

- Texel Mailing List
http://www.rootsweb.com/~jfuller/gen_mail_country-net.html
#Texel
For anyone with a genealogical interest in the island of Texel, Netherlands.

- westerwolde Mailing List
http://www.rootsweb.com/~jfuller/gen_mail_country-net.html
#westerwolde
For anyone with a genealogical interest in Westerwolde, part of the province of Groningen in the northeastern part of the Netherlands.

- Wortels-nl Mailing List
http://www.rootsweb.com/~jfuller/gen_mail_country-net.html
#Wortels-nl
An unmoderated discussion list on how to search for descendants and ancestors in the old country. Emphasis will be the Netherlands and former colonies.

- Zeeland-genealogy Mailing List
http://www.rootsweb.com/~jfuller/gen_mail_country-net.html
#Zeeland-genealogy
For anyone with a genealogical interest in the Dutch province of Zeeland.

◆ Maps, Gazetteers & Geographical Information

- Historic Maps of the Netherlands
http://grid.let.rug.nl/~welling/maps/maps.html

- How to Use the Netherlands Gazetteer
http://www.familysearch.org/Eng/Search/RG/frameset_rg.asp
?Dest=G1&Aid=&Gid=&Lid=&Sid=&Did=&Juris1=&Event=&
Year=&Gloss=&Sub=&Tab=&Entry=&Guide=NL_T4_-_1640
HowToUseATopographicalDictionaryofNetherlands.ASP
Help for using Van Goor's aardrijkskundig woordenboek van Nederland from FamilySearch.org.

- Map of Amsterdam
http://www.generationspress.com/samples/amstrdam2.jpg

- Map of The Netherlands
http://www.lib.utexas.edu/Libs/PCL/Map_collection/europe/
Netherlands.jpg
From the Perry-Castañeda Library at the Univ. of Texas at Austin.

- Map of the Netherlands
http://www.familysearch.org/Eng/Search/RG/frameset_
rg.asp?Dest=G1&Aid=&Gid=&Lid=&Sid=&Did=&Juris1=&
Event=&Year=&Gloss=&Sub=&Tab=&Entry=&Guide=
MNetherlands.ASP

◆ People & Families

Individual personal home pages previously listed here can now be found alphabetically under the Personal Home Pages category:
http://www.CyndisList.com/personal.htm
or under the Surnames category:
http://www.CyndisList.com/surnames.htm

- Dutch Home Pages by Familyname ~ Index
http://members.tripod.com/~Don_Arnoldus/index.html

- Dutch Jewish Genealogy Homepage
http://web.inter.nl.net/users/DJGH/

- Genealogy of the Royal Family of The Netherlands
http://www.xs4all.nl/~kvenjb/gennl.htm
See this category on Cyndi's List for related links.

- Huguenot
http://www.CyndisList.com/huguenot.htm

- NedGen Genealogy Searchengine
http://genealogie.thewebconnection.nl/
Dutch, Belgian, German, Danish or Norwegian genealogy web sites.

- SIFA: Stichting Indisch Familie Archief
http://www.xs4all.nl/~polleke/
A private collection of family documentation from the Dutch-East Indies period

- SWINX® Zoeklijst Nederlandse Familienamen ~ Netherlands
http://www.swinx.net/
SWINX = Surname Website INdeX

◆ Professional Researchers, Volunteers & Other Research Services

- European Focus
http://www.eurofocus.com/
Photographic portfolios of ancestral towns in Europe created for Genealogy enthusiasts in Belgium, Denmark, Eastern Europe, England, France, Germany, Great Britain, Italy, Netherlands, Norway, Poland, Sweden, Switzerland and more.

- Family Affairs
http://www.familyaffairs.nl/
Genealogical research services mainly in the northern provinces of Drenthe, Friesland, Groningen, and Overijssel. Also research in other provinces and translation of documents.

- Genealogy Helplist - Netherlands
http://www.cybercomm.net/~freddie/helplist/nethlnd.htm

- Holland Family History
http://www.hfh.nl/

- Holland Page Helpdesk
http://ourworld.compuserve.com/homepages/paulvanv/
helpdesk.htm

- Mark Windover's Web Page - Quality Professional Genealogical Research ~ Williamstown, Massachusetts
http://www.windover.com/
United States, Canada (including French), England, Scotland, Ireland, Wales, Iceland, Germany, Switzerland, Norway, Sweden, Denmark, France, Belgium, and The Netherlands.

- Tracing your Netherlands ancestors
http://www.gironet.nl/home/mahaman/
I offer my services as a researcher. My pedigrees: FRANSSEN, VAN DE PUTTE, DE KLERCK. Classical Dutch recipes. Testimonial. Map of the Netherlands.

◆ Publications, Software & Supplies

- Amazon.com Genealogy Bookstore - Dutch
http://www.amazon.com/exec/obidos/external-search/?
keyword=dutch+genealogy&tag=markcyndisgenealA/

- AudioTapes.com - Genealogical Lectures on Cassette Tapes - The Netherlands
  http://www.audiotapes.com/search2.asp?Search=Netherlands And Dutch
  http://www.audiotapes.com/search2.asp?Search=dutch

- Books We Own - Netherlands
  http://www.rootsweb.com/~bwo/nether.html
  Find a book from which you would like a lookup and click on the submitter's code at the end of the entry. Once you find the contact information for the submitter, write them a polite request for a lookup.

- Brother's Keeper Software
  http://ourworld.compuserve.com/homepages/Brothers_Keeper/
  Downloadable shareware program for Windows. The latest version contains English, French, Norwegian, Danish, Swedish, German, Dutch, Polish, Icelandic, Russian, Slovak, Afrikaans, Czech.

- Frontier Press Bookstore - Dutch
  http://www.frontierpress.com/frontier.cgi?category=dutch

- GenealogyBookShop.com - Netherlands/Dutch
  http://www.genealogybookshop.com/genealogybookshop/files/The_World,Netherlands_Dutch/index.html
  The online store of Genealogical Publishing Co., Inc. & Clearfield Company.

- GeneWeb ~ Unix and Windows 95/98/NT
  http://pauillac.inria.fr/~ddr/GeneWeb/
  In French, Dutch, Swedish and English versions.

- GensData voor Windows
  http://web.inter.nl.net/hcc/F.Berkhof/gd-win.htm
  Dutch genealogy program for Windows 3.1 or Windows 95.

- Haza-Data Website
  http://www.hazadata.com
  Dutch genealogy software program. Also versions in English, German, Swedish, Norwegian, Polish.

- Heritage Books - Dutch
  http://www.heritagebooks.com/dutch.htm

- Heritage Quest Books and Microfiche
  http://www.heritagequest.com/

- Oedipus II Voor Windows
  http://web.inter.nl.net/hcc/L.G.Lamain/odp95.htm
  Only in Dutch.

- PRO-GEN Genealogie à la Carte
  http://www.pro-gen.nl/
  Dutch genealogy program capable of outputs in Dutch, English, French, Frisian and German.

- Winkwast en Genkwa
  http://home.worldonline.nl/~ac10561/programma/downloads.html
  Genealogy software.

◆ Records: Census, Cemeteries, Land, Obituaries, Personal, Taxes and Vital (Born, Married, Died & Buried)

- Alblasserwaard Genealogie Page
  http://www.geocities.com/Paris/4744/ALBWRDGENPAGE.HTM
  Several marriage indexes here for the early 1800's.

- The Cochin Churchbook
  http://www.telebyte.nl/~dessa/cochin.htm
  Baptism & marriages from the Dutch Church in Cochin, India (1754-1804).

- Digital Resources Netherlands and Belgium
  http://home.wxs.nl/~hjdewit/links_en.html
  Digital resources available on the internet, bulletin board systems and on diskette/CD-ROM.

- Dutch Immigrant Ships to Canada 1947-1960
  http://www.magma.ca/~louievb/immigration/ships.html
  Immigrant ships leaving The Netherlands transported the majority of Dutch emigrants to Canada. This covers the Volendam, Groote Beer, Waterman, Zuiderkruis, Sibajak, Johan van Oldenbarnevelt.

- Gemeentearchief Tilburg / Tilburg City Archival Service
  http://gemeentearchief.tilburg.nl/index.htm
  Index on 50,000 Devotional pictures. 90,000 surnames in the ten-year tables of nine towns.

- Records of the Reformed Dutch Church of Albany, New York, 1683-1809
  http://aleph0.clarku.edu/~djoyce/gen/albany/refchurch.html
  Marriage and baptismal register starting in 1683.

◆ Societies & Groups

- Afdeling Computergenealogie Van De Nederlandse Genealogische Vereniging - Gens Data
  http://www.gensdata.demon.nl/

- Genealogische Vereniging Prometheus / Genealogical Society Prometheus ~ Delft, Netherlands
  http://duttcbs.tn.tudelft.nl/genealogie/hg1.html

- Indische Genealogische Vereniging [Dutch Indies Genealogical Association]
  http://www.igv.nl/

- Nederlandse Genealogische Vereniging
  http://www.ngv.nl/

- Nederlandse Kring voor Joodse Genealogie / Netherlands Society for Jewish Genealogy
  http://www.nljewgen.org/

- Vereniging Veluwse Geslachten
  http://ourworld.compuserve.com/homepages/paulvanv/veluwges.htm
  Society with 1,000 members, just for a small area in the province Gelderland Nederland.

NEWSGROUPS
http://www.cyndislist.com/newsgrps.htm

Category Index:
◆ Briefly Defined
◆ General Resource Sites
◆ Localities & Ethnic Groups
◆ Military

◆ Miscellaneous
◆ Queries & Surnames
◆ Software & Computers

◆ Briefly Defined

Newsgroups, similar to e-mail mailing lists, have their roots early in the history of the Internet.

• Newsgroups are free to subscribe to and participate in.

• There are specific newsgroups for a variety of genealogical and historical topics.

• Some newsgroups are "gatewayed" or "mirrored" with mailing lists. This means that the same messages appear on both forums.

• To participate in a newsgroup you need to have newsreader software, such as Free Agent
http://www.forteinc.com/agent/freagent.htm
News Rover
http://www.newsrover.com/
Or the newsreader program that is already resident in many web browsers:

o AOL members use keyword: Newsgroups
http://www.aol.com/nethelp/news/newsusing.html

o How to Configure Internet Explorer to Read Newsgroups ~ Win95
http://support.microsoft.com/support/kb/articles/Q152/6/80.asp?LNG=ENG&SA=PER

o How to Configure Outlook Express for Internet News
http://support.microsoft.com/support/kb/articles/Q171/1/64.ASP

o Setting up Netscape Navigator to read news
http://help.netscape.com/kb/consumer/19960627-3.html

• NetLingo:
Commonly used mailing list and newsgroup terms defined by http://www.netlingo.com/

o Deja News Research Service
http://www.netlingo.com/lookup.cfm?term=Deja%20News%20Research%20Service

o FAQ (Frequently Asked Questions)
http://www.netlingo.com/lookup.cfm?term=FAQ

o Gateway
http://www.netlingo.com/lookup.cfm?term=gateway%20

o Kill File
http://www.netlingo.com/lookup.cfm?term=kill%20file

o Mailing List
http://www.netlingo.com/lookup.cfm?term=mailing%20list

o Moderated Mailing List
http://www.netlingo.com/lookup.cfm?term=moderated%20mailing%20list

o Netiquette
http://www.netlingo.com/lookup.cfm?term=netiquette

o Newsgroups
http://www.netlingo.com/lookup.cfm?term=newsgroups

o Newsreader
http://www.netlingo.com/lookup.cfm?term=newsreader

o NNTP (Network News Transfer Protocol)
http://www.netlingo.com/lookup.cfm?term=NNTP

o Signature File or Sig File
http://www.netlingo.com/lookup.cfm?term=signature%20file

o Spam
http://www.netlingo.com/lookup.cfm?term=spam

o Thread
http://www.netlingo.com/lookup.cfm?term=thread

o USENET
http://www.netlingo.com/lookup.cfm?term=USENET

◆ General Resource Sites

• Amazon.com Genealogy Bookstore - Newsgroups
http://www.amazon.com/exec/obidos/external-search/?keyword=internet+newsgroups&tag=markcyndisgenealA/

• AOL NetFind | Newsgroup Etiquette
http://www.aol.com/netfind/scoop/newsgroup_etiquette.html

• AOL NetFind | Newsgroup Scoop Glossary
http://www.aol.com/netfind/scoop/newsgroup_glossary.html

• AOL NetFind | Search Newsgroups
http://www.aol.com/netfind/newsgroups.html

• Basic newsgroup and mailing list "Netiquette"
http://www.otterbein.edu/contstud/atechpod/netiquet.HTM

- Deja.com - General Usenet Information
  http://www.deja.com/info/usenet_faq.shtml

- Deja.com
  http://www.deja.com/
  Search the newsgroups for a specific topic or keyword and read the archived messages.

- Deja.com - What are Internet Discussion Groups?
  http://www.deja.com/info/idg.shtml

- Free Agent News Reader
  http://www.forteinc.com/agent/freagent.htm

- Genealogy Usenet Newsgroups Finder/Discussions Page
  http://members.tripod.com/~Genealogy_Infocenter/genealogy-discussions.html

- Genealogy Resources on the Internet - Usenet Newsgroups
  http://www.rootsweb.com/~jfuller/gen_use.html

- How To Write a Good Newgroup Message
  http://www.gweep.bc.ca/~edmonds/usenet/good-newgroup.html
  By Brian Edmonds.

- The Net: User Guidelines and Netiquette
  http://www.fau.edu/netiquette/net/dis.html
  For Listservs/Mailing Lists/ Discussion Groups, by Arlene Rinaldi.

- Newsgroup Participation and Citizenship: Some Basic Information
  http://homepages.rootsweb.com/~socgen/jogart.htm
  By Margaret Olson.

- News Rover -- Scans, downloads and decodes Usenet newsgroup messages
  http://www.NewsRover.com
  Usenet search agent that scans Usenet genealogy newsgroups and downloads messages that are of interest to your research.

- Soc.genealogy.* Newsgroups
  http://homepages.rootsweb.com/~socgen/
  Genealogy Newsgroups - The Soc.Genealogy Hierarchy. A comprehensive and definitive site by Margaret Olson, the maven of genealogy newsgroups. Includes descriptions and details on the history and purposes of all known genealogy newsgroups.

  - Genealogy Newsgroups - About Newsgroups
    http://homepages.rootsweb.com/~socgen/Abtnews.htm

  - Genealogy Newsgroups - About the Gateway Mailing lists
    http://homepages.rootsweb.com/~socgen/Abtmail.htm

  - Genealogy Newsgroups - Archives
    http://homepages.rootsweb.com/~socgen/Archives.htm

  - Genealogy Newsgroups - One Person's Historical View
    http://homepages.rootsweb.com/~socgen/Newshist.htm

- Yahoo!...Usenet
  http://dir.yahoo.com/Computers_and_Internet/Internet/Usenet/

◆ Localities & Ethnic Groups

- alt.scottish.clans
  news:alt.scottish.clans

- dk.historie.genealogi ~ Denmark
  news:dk.historie.genealogi

- fido.eur.genealogy ~ Europe
  news:fido.ger.genealogy

- fido.ger.genealogy ~ Germany
  news:fido.ger.genealogy

- fr.comp.applications.genealogie
  news:fr.comp.applications.genealogie
  For the discussion of genealogy software used by French genealogists.
  Gateway Mailing List: GEN-FF-LOG Mailing List

- fr.rec.genealogie
  news:fr.rec.genealogie
  For the discussion of Francophone genealogy -- the genealogy of French-speaking people (traffic probably mainly in French).
  Gateway Mailing List: GEN-FF Mailing List
  http://www.rootsweb.com/~jfuller/gen_mail_country-fra.html#GEN-FF-L

- no.frittid.slektsforsking.diverse
  news:no.frittid.slektsforsking.diverse
  Norwegian genealogy conference covering any topic in genealogy except computer programs for genealogical use and searches for lost relatives and ancestors. The conference is conducted in Norwegian.

- no.fritid.slektsforsking.etterlysing
  news:no.fritid.slektsforsking.etterlysing
  Norwegian genealogy conference for searching relatives and ancestors in Norway and eventual discussions of such searches if there are dubious links published. The conference is conducted in Norwegian.

- no.fritid.slektsforsking.it
  news:no.fritid.slektsforsking.it
  Norwegian genealogy conference for discussion of computer programs and other computer-related questions as they relate to genealogy. The conference is conducted in Norwegian.

- soc.culture.basque
  news:soc.culture.basque
  A "moderated" newsgroup, that provides Basques the world over with a virtual place to discuss social, political, cultural or any other issues related to Basques, or to request information and discuss matters related to the Basque people and/or their culture. Genealogy queries are an acceptable topic.
  Gateway Mailing List: BASQUE Mailing List
  http://www.rootsweb.com/~jfuller/gen_mail_country-fra.html#BASQUE

- soc.genealogy.african
  news:soc.genealogy.african
  For the discussion of African genealogy.
  Soc.genealogy.african FAQ
  http://members.aol.com/memery/faq/

Gateway Mailing List: GEN-AFRICAN Mailing List
http://www.rootsweb.com/~jfuller/gen_mail_country-
gen.html#GEN-AFRICAN
GEN-AFRICAN-L Search Page
http://searches.rootsweb.com/sgafrican.html

- soc.genealogy.australia+nz
  news:soc.genealogy.australia+nz
  Australia & New Zealand.
  Archive
  http://www.rootsweb.com/~billingh/genanz-l.htm#Archives
  Guidelines (FAQ)
  http://www.rootsweb.com/~billingh/genanz-l.htm
  Web Site
  http://www.rootsweb.com/~billingh/
  Gateway Mailing List: GENANZ Mailing List
  http://www.rootsweb.com/~jfuller/gen_mail_country-
  aus.html#GENANZ-L

- soc.genealogy.benelux
  news:soc.genealogy.benelux
  For research in the Benelux region (Belgium, the Netherlands, and Luxembourg).
  Gateway Mailing List: GENBNL-L Mailing List
  http://www.rootsweb.com/~jfuller/gen_mail_country-
  blg.html#DUTCH

- soc.genealogy.britain
  news:soc.genealogy.britain
  Gateway Mailing List: GENBRIT Mailing List
  http://www.rootsweb.com/~jfuller/gen_mail_country-
  unk.html#GENBRIT

- soc.genealogy.french
  news:soc.genealogy.french
  For the discussion of Francophone genealogy -- the genealogy of French-speaking people.
  Gateway Mailing List: GEN-FR Mailing List
  http://www.rootsweb.com/~jfuller/gen_mail_country-
  fra.html#GEN-FR-L

- soc.genealogy.german
  news:soc.genealogy.german
  soc.genealogy.german Frequently Asked Questions List
  http://www.genealogy.net/gene/faqs/sgg.html
  Gateway Mailing List: GEN-DE Mailing List
  http://www.rootsweb.com/~jfuller/gen_mail_country-
  ger.html#GEN-DE-L

- soc.genealogy.hispanic
  news:soc.genealogy.hispanic
  For the discussion of Hispanic genealogy.
  Gateway Mailing List: GEN-HISPANIC Mailing List
  http://www.rootsweb.com/~jfuller/gen_mail_country-
  gen.html#GEN-HISPANIC

- soc.genealogy.ireland
  news:soc.genealogy.ireland
  Gateway Mailing List: GENIRE Mailing List
  http://www.rootsweb.com/~jfuller/gen_mail_country-
  unk.html#GENIRE

- soc.genealogy.italian
  news:soc.genealogy.italian
  Gateway Mailing List: GEN-ITALIAN Mailing List
  http://www.rootsweb.com/~jfuller/gen_mail_country-
  ita.html#GEN-ITALIAN

- soc.genealogy.jewish
  new:soc.genealogy.jewish
  The JewishGen Conference. Discussions of Jewish genealogy.
  JewishGen Discussion Group
  http://www.jewishgen.org/JewishGen/DiscussionGroup.htm
  Gateway Mailing List: JEWISHGEN Mailing List
  http://www.rootsweb.com/~jfuller/gen_mail_general.html
  #JEWISHGEN

- soc.genealogy.nordic
  news:soc.genealogy.nordic
  For the discussion of genealogy in the Scandinavian countries, including: Denmark, Finland, Greenland, Iceland, Norway and Sweden.
  Gateway Mailing List: GEN-NORDIC Mailing List
  http://www.rootsweb.com/~jfuller/gen_mail_country-
  den.html#GEN-NORDIC

- soc.genealogy.slavic
  news:soc.genealogy.slavic
  Gateway Mailing List: GEN-SLAVIC Mailing List
  http://www.rootsweb.com/~jfuller/gen_mail_country-
  pol.html#GEN-SLAVIC

- soc.genealogy.west-indies
  news:soc.genealogy.west-indies

- Search Soc.genealogy.west-indies Posts
  http://searches.rootsweb.com/sgwest-indies.html
  Gateway Mailing List: CARIBBEAN Mailing List
  http://www.rootsweb.com/~jfuller/gen_mail_country-
  gen.html#CARIBBEAN

- swnet.sci.genealogi
  news:swnet.sci.genealogi
  Swedish newsgroup.

- wales.genealogy.general
  news:wales.genealogy.general

◆ Military

- alt.war.civil.usa
  news:alt.war.civil.usa

- soc.history.moderated
  news:soc.history.moderated

- soc.history.war.us-civil-war
  news:soc.history.war.us-civil-war
  soc.history.war.us-civil-war Web Page
  http://www.geocities.com/BourbonStreet/Delta/7002/
  index.html

- soc.history.war.us-revolution
  news:soc.history.war.us-revolution

- soc.history.war.vietnam
  news:soc.history.war.vietnam

- soc.history.war.world-war-ii
  news:soc.history.war.world-war-ii

◆ Miscellaneous

- alt.adoption
  news:alt.adoption
  For adoptees, birthparents, adoptive parents

- alt.genealogy
  news:alt.genealogy
  General discussion.
  Gateway Mailing List: ALT-GENEALOGY Mailing List
  http://www.rootsweb.com/~jfuller/gen_mail_general.html #ALT-GENEALOGY

- alt.obituaries
  news:alt.obituaries

- rec.heraldry
  news:rec.heraldry

- soc.adoption.adoptees
  news:soc.adoption.adoptees
  The Adoptees Newsgroup
  http://www.geocities.com/Heartland/Acres/8126/

- soc.genealogy.marketplace
  news:soc.genealogy.marketplace
  FAQ soc.genealogy.marketplace
  http://www.prairienet.org/~mjolson/market.html
  Gateway Mailing List: GEN-MARKET Mailing List
  http://www.rootsweb.com/~jfuller/gen_mail_general.html #GEN-MARKET

- soc.genealogy.medieval
  news:soc.genealogy.medieval
  For genealogy and family history discussion among people researching individuals living during medieval times.
  Frequently Asked Questions for soc.genealogy.medieval
  http://users.erols.com/wrei/faqs/medieval.html
  Gateway Mailing List: GEN-MEDIEVAL Mailing List
  http://www.rootsweb.com/~jfuller/gen_mail_general.html #GEN-MEDIEVAL

- soc.genealogy.methods
  news:soc.genealogy.methods
  For the discussion of genealogy research techniques and resources.
  Gateway Mailing List: GENMTD Mailing List
  http://www.rootsweb.com/~jfuller/gen_mail_general.html #GENMTD-L
  The GENMTD-L (soc.genealogy.methods) Home Page
  http://www.rootsweb.com/~aet/
  GENMTD-L Search Page
  http://searches.rootsweb.com/sgmethods.html

- soc.genealogy.misc
  news:soc.genealogy.misc
  General genealogical discussions.
  Frequently Asked Questions For soc.genealogy.misc
  http://www.herald.co.uk/local_info/genuki/socgmisc.html
  Gateway Mailing List: GENMSC Mailing List
  http://www.rootsweb.com/~jfuller/gen_mail_info.html #GENMSC-L

◆ Queries & Surnames

- soc.genealogy.surnames.* newsgroups and SURNAMES-* mailing lists
  http://www.rootsweb.com/~surnames/

- soc.genealogy.surnames.global
  news:soc.genealogy.surnames.global
  Surname queries central database.
  Gateway Mailing List: SURNAMES Mailing List
  http://www.rootsweb.com/~jfuller/gen_mail_surnames-gen.html#SURNAMES

- soc.genealogy.surnames.britain
  news:soc.genealogy.surnames.britain
  For surname queries related to Great Britain.
  Gateway Mailing List: SURNAMES-BRITAIN Mailing List
  http://www.rootsweb.com/~jfuller/gen_mail_country-unk.html#SURNAMES-BRITAIN

- soc.genealogy.surnames.canada
  news:soc.genealogy.surnames.canada
  For surname queries related to Canada.
  Gateway Mailing List: SURNAMES-CANADA Mailing List
  http://www.rootsweb.com/~jfuller/gen_mail_surnames-gen.html#SURNAMES-CANADA

- soc.genealogy.surnames.german
  news:soc.genealogy.surnames.german
  For surname queries related to German speaking countries.
  Gateway Mailing List: SURNAMES-GERMAN Mailing List
  http://www.rootsweb.com/~jfuller/gen_mail_surnames-gen.html#SURNAMES-GERMAN

- soc.genealogy.surnames.ireland
  news:soc.genealogy.surnames.ireland
  For surname queries related to Ireland and Northern Ireland.
  Gateway Mailing List: SURNAMES-IRELAND Mailing List
  http://www.rootsweb.com/~jfuller/gen_mail_country-unk.html#SURNAMES-IRELAND

- soc.genealogy.surnames.misc
  news:soc.genealogy.surnames.misc
  For surname queries for regions not addressed elsewhere in the soc.genealogy.surnames. hierarchy.*
  Gateway Mailing List: SURNAMES-MISC Mailing List
  http://www.rootsweb.com/~jfuller/gen_mail_surnames-gen.html#SURNAMES-MISC

- soc.genealogy.surnames.usa
  news:soc.genealogy.surnames.usa
  For surname queries related to the United States.
  Gateway Mailing List: SURNAMES-USA Mailing List
  http://www.rootsweb.com/~jfuller/gen_mail_surnames-gen.html#SURNAMES-USA

◆ Software & Computers

- soc.genealogy.computing
  news:soc.genealogy.computing
  For the discussion of genealogical computing and net resources.
  Gateway Mailing List: GENCMP Mailing List
  http://www.rootsweb.com/~jfuller/gen_mail_general.html#GENCMP-L

- no.fritid.slektsforsking.it
  news:no.fritid.slektsforsking.it
  Norwegian genealogy conference for discussion of computer programs and other computer-related questions as they relate to genealogy. The conference is conducted in Norwegian.

NEWSPAPERS

http://www.cyndislist.com/newspapr.htm

Category Index:

◆ Genealogy Columns & Columnists

◆ General Resources

◆ Alphabetical Listing

◆ Genealogy Columns & Columnists

• Genealogy by Ken Thomas
http://www.accessatlanta.com/community/genealogy/
Columnist for The Atlanta Journal-Constitution in Georgia.

• International Society of Family History Writers and Editors, Inc. (ISFHWE)
http://www.rootsweb.com/~cgc/index.htm
Formerly known as the Council of Genealogy Columnists.

• Mic Barnette's Columns, Genealogy & History
http://www.geocities.com/BourbonStreet/Delta/7552/
From The Houston Chronicle.

• Mobile Genealogical Society: The News Stand
http://www.siteone.com/clubs/mgs/newstand.htm
Links to genealogical columns that appear in newspapers and accept announcements and/or queries.

• Ruby M. Cusack - Genealogy & Queries
http://personal.nbnet.nb.ca/rmcusack/
Genealogical and Queries Columns in the Good Life edition of the Saint John Times Globe, Saint John, New Brunswick, Canada.

• Shaking Your Family Tree
http://www.uftree.com/bin/fg_auth?/GenealogyNewsstand/
ShakingTree/shakingtree.html
A weekly newspaper column by Myra Vanderpool Gormley for the LA Times Syndicate, hosted online by Ultimate Family Tree.

• Shaking Your Family Tree
http://www.ancestry.com/columns/myra/index.htm
By Myra Vanderpool Gormley, alternate copies of the same column above.

• Tracing Our Roots
http://www.harrisburg.com/root.html
Column by Schuyler Brossman, featured in The Press And Journal Extra, Middletown, Pennsylvania.

• Tri-City Herald Genealogy Online
http://www.tri-cityherald.com/genealogy/
Dozens of helpful columns written by Terry Day and Donna Potter Phillips.

• The Virtual Texan
http://www.virtualtexan.com/comm/virtual/roots.htm
Column by Brenda Burns Kellow, featured in the Plano Star Courier, Plano, Texas.

• Winn Parish Newspaper Column - Family History by Annette Womack ~ Louisiana
http://homepages.rootsweb.com/~acwomack/news.htm

◆ General Resources

• AJR NewsLink Newspaper Index
http://ajr.newslink.org/news.html
American Journalism Review.

• Amazon.com Genealogy Bookstore - Newspapers
http://www.amazon.com/exec/obidos/external-search/?
keyword=genealogy+newspapers&tag=markcyndisgenealA/

• AudioTapes.com - Genealogical Lectures on Cassette Tapes - Newspapers
http://www.audiotapes.com/search2.asp?Search=Newspapers

• Editor & Publisher Interactive Online Newspaper Database
http://www.mediainfo.com/ephome/npaper/nphtm/online.htm

• Frontier Press Bookstore - Newspapers
http://www.frontierpress.com/frontier.cgi?category=news

• Historic Newspaper Archives
http://www.historicnewspaper.com/
Actual historic newspapers to give as gifts. Dating from 1880's to present.

• History Buff's Home Page
http://www.historybuff.com
Produced by The Newspaper Collectors Society of America

   o Primer on Collecting Old & Historic Newspapers
http://www.historybuff.com/primer.html

• How Newspapers Can Help You With Your Research
http://www.everton.com/oe3-18/papers.htm
From Everton's Genealogical Helper Online.

• Kidon Media-Link
http://www.kidon.com/media-link/index.shtml
Listings for Europe, USA, Americas, Asia, Africa and Oceania.

• Library of Congress Newspaper and Current Periodical Reading Room
http://lcweb.loc.gov/rr/news/ncp.html
Newspapers
http://lcweb.loc.gov/rr/news/lcnewsp.html
Periodicals
http://lcweb.loc.gov/rr/news/lcper.html

o 17th & 18th Century Foreign Newspapers
http://lcweb.loc.gov/rr/news/17th/178th.html

o Full-Text Journals Available in the Newspaper and Current Periodical Reading Room
http://lcweb.loc.gov/rr/news/full.html

o How To Find A Newspaper In This Reading Room
http://lcweb.loc.gov/rr/news/ncp-fact.html

o Internet Resources Outside the Library of Congress
http://lcweb.loc.gov/rr/news/othint.html

o Lists of Newspaper & Periodical Resources on the Internet
http://lcweb.loc.gov/rr/news/lists.html

o Online Newspaper Indexes Available in the Newspaper and Current Periodical Reading Room
http://lcweb.loc.gov/rr/news/npindex2.html

- My Virtual Newspaper
http://www.refdesk.com/paper.html
List of great newspaper links by country & by state.

- NewsDirectory.com: Newspapers: Newspapers ~ Worldwide
http://www.newsdirectory.com/news/press/

- Newspaper Abstracts
http://www.newspaperabstracts.com/
Newspaper abstracts and extracts published in United States and Canadian newspapers prior to 1923.

- Newspaper Association of America - Hotlinks
http://www.naa.org/hotlinks/index.html

- New York State Newspaper Project - For Newspaper Collectors
http://unix2.nysed.gov/nysnp/buysell.htm
A list of dealers of collectible newspapers.

- OnlineNewspapers.com
http://www.onlinenewspapers.com/

- Using Newspapers for Genealogical Research
http://www.system.missouri.edu/shs/newspap.html
From the State Historical Society of Missouri.

- Yahoo!...News and Media...Newspapers
http://dir.yahoo.com/News_and_Media/Newspapers/

◆ "A"

- Aftenposten Interaktiv ~ Oslo, Norway
http://www.aftenposten.no/

- An Phoblacht / Republican News ~ Belfast & Dublin
http://www.irlnet.com/aprn/index.html

- The Anchorage Daily News ~ Alaska
http://www.adn.com/

- The Ann Arbor News - Michigan Live
http://aa.mlive.com/

- The Anniston Star Online ~ Alabama
http://www.annistonstar.com/

- Arizona Central: Arizona Republic Archives
http://www.azcentral.com/archive/

- The Arizona Daily Star
http://www.azstarnet.com/public/pubstar/dstar.cgi

- The Arizona Newspaper Project
http://www.lib.az.us/anp/

- The Atlanta Journal-Constitution ~ Georgia
http://www.accessatlanta.com/partners/ajc/

- The Augusta Chronicle Online
http://augustachronicle.com/
"The South's Oldest Newspaper" serving Georgia and South Carolina.

- Austin 360: News: Austin American-Statesman ~ Texas
http://www.Austin360.com/news/

- Australian Newspapers on the Internet
http://www.nla.gov.au/oz/npapers.html
A list from the National Library of Australia

◆ "B"

- Bangor Daily News Interactive ~ Maine
http://www.bangornews.com/

- The Belfast Newsletter Index, 1737-1800 ~ Northern Ireland
http://www.ucs.usl.edu/bnl/Main.html
Online searchable database of over 20,000 transcribed pages from the newspaper including personal names, place names, and ship names.

- The Berkshire Eagle ~ Massachusetts
http://www.newschoice.com/newspapers/newengland/eagle/

- Billings Gazette On Line
http://www.billingsgazette.com/
Includes "Vitals" section.

- The Bismarck Tribune ~ North Dakota
http://www.ndonline.com/

- Boulder News ~ Colorado
http://www.bouldernews.com/

- The Brainerd Daily Dispatch Online ~ Minnesota
http://www.brainerddispatch.com/

◆ "C"

- Carson Appeal Newspaper Index, 1865-66, 1879-80, 1881, 1885-86
http://dmla.clan.lib.nv.us/docs/nsla/archives/appeal/appeal.htm

- Catholic Newspapers in Microform: A Directory of Works at Notre Dame ~ Indiana
http://www.nd.edu/~archives/cathnews/

- The Chicago Sun-Times Online
  http://www.suntimes.com/index/

- Chicago Tribune ~ Illinois
  http://chicagotribune.com/

- Cleveland Daily Banner
  http://www.clevelandbanner.com/
  Bradley County, Tennessee. Access daily obituaries.

- The Connaught Telegraph, Co Mayo, West of Ireland
  http://www.mayo-ireland.ie/Connaught.htm

- Connecticut Newspaper Project
  http://www.cslnet.ctstateu.edu/cnp.htm

◆ "D"

- The Daily Journal ~ Kankakee, Illinois
  http://www.daily-journal.com/

- The Daily ME ~ Maine
  http://www.thedailyme.com/

- The Daily News Online
  http://www.tdn.com/
  Longview-Kelso, Washington.

- The Daily News Worldwide ~ Halifax, Nova Scotia, Canada
  http://www.hfxnews.southam.ca/

- The Dallas Morning News ~ Texas
  http://www.dallasnews.com/

- Danish Pioneer - Den Danske Pioneer - Oldest Danish-American Newspaper in USA ~ Illinois
  http://www.dendanskepioneer.com/english/index.html

- Decatur Daily Democrat ~ Indiana
  http://www.decaturnet.com/paper/

- The Denver Post Online
  http://www.denverpost.com/

- TheDepot.com Piedmont Triad ~ North Carolina
  http://www.thedepot.com/index.htm

- The Detroit Free Press - The Freep ~ Michigan
  http://www.freep.com/index.htm

- The Detroit News ~ Michigan
  http://www.detnews.com/

- Digital City Hampton Roads
  http://www.hamptonroads.digitalcity.com
  Hampton Roads area of Eastern Virginia including York County, Gloucester County, James City County, Mathews County, and the Cities of Hampton, Newport News, and Williamsburg.

- Duluth News-Tribune ~ Minnesota
  http://www.duluthnews.com/

◆ "E"

- Eastern Counties Network ~ England
  http://www.ecn.co.uk/index.htm
  East Anglian Daily Times, Eastern Daily Press, Evening News, Evening Star.

- Echo Press Online ~ Alexandria, Minnesota
  http://www.echopress.com/

- ESCN Database Reports
  http://ourworld.compuserve.com/homepages/escn_database_reports/
  Quick Reference Indexes to the Early South Carolina Newspapers.

- Excerpts From Old Newspapers
  http://www.ida.net/users/dhanco/news.htm

◆ "F"

- The First Newspapers on Canada's West Coast: 1858-1863
  http://members.tripod.com/~Hughdoherty/index.htm

- The Florida Times-Union Online, Jacksonville, Florida
  http://www.times-union.com/

- Fredericksburg.com
  http://fredericksburg.com/
  The Internet service of The Free Lance-Star, Fredericksburg Virginia.

◆ "G"

- Galway Advertiser ~ Ireland
  http://ireland.iol.ie/resource/ga/

- The Gate
  http://www.sfgate.com/
  From the San Francisco Chronicle & the San Francisco Examiner.

- Gebbie Press - Daily Newspapers on the Web
  http://www.gebbieinc.com/dailyint.htm

- Guernsey Press On-Line ~ Channel Islands, U.K.
  http://www.guernsey-press.com/

◆ "H"

- The Halifax Herald ~ Nova Scotia, Canada
  http://www.herald.ns.ca/

- The Hamilton Spectator ~ Ontario, Canada
  http://www.hamiltonspectator.com/

- The Heritage Newspapers ~ Michigan
  http://www.heritagenews.com/

- Historical Directory of Newfoundland and Labrador Newspapers, 1806-1996
  http://www.mun.ca/library/cat/newspapers/papers.htm

- Historical Newspaper Index - FCPL
  http://www.co.fairfax.va.us/library/virginia/varoom/newsindx/
  default.htm
  *This site provides an index to eight different Fairfax County and
  northern Virginia newspapers from 1785 to 1973. Users may
  request copies of articles they would like to see. It is a complete
  subject index that includes advertisements, legal notices and general
  news items.*

- Historical Text Archive - Old Gazettes &
  Newspapers
  http://www.msstate.edu:80/Archives/History/USA/gazette.html

- Home Town News
  http://www.hometownnews.com/
  Directory of links to daily and weekly U.S. Newspapers.

- HomeTown Online
  http://www.htnews.com/
  Newspapers for Howell, Michigan.

- Honolulu Star-Bulletin ~ Hawaii
  http://www.starbulletin.com/

- Houston Chronicle Interactive ~ Texas
  http://www.chron.com/

◆ "I"

- In-Forum ~ Fargo, North Dakota
  http://www.in-forum.com/

- The Independent
  http://www.indenews.com/
  Serving the Hudson Berkshire Corridor, New York.

- Indiana Newspaper Search by CompuGen Systems
  http://members.aol.com/CGSystems/NXSearch.html

- The Irish News ~ Belfast
  http://www.irishnews.com/

- The Irish People - The Voice of Irish Republicanism
  in America
  http://inac.org/IrishPeople/top/08_21_99/082199tour.html

- The Irish Times on the Web ~ Dublin
  http://www.ireland.com/

- The Irish Voice Online ~ New York
  http://www.irishvoice.com/

- The Issaquah Press ~ Washington
  http://www.isspress.com/
  Includes historic articles.

◆ "J"

- The Joplin Globe ~ Missouri
  http://www.joplinglobe.com/

◆ "K"

- The Kingston Whig-Standard ~ Ontario, Canada
  http://www.kingstonwhigstandard.com/

- Kitchener Waterloo Record Online ~ Ontario,
  Canada
  http://www.therecord.com/

- The Knoxville Gazette
  http://www.ultranet.com/~smack/news.htm
  *Transcribed historical articles related to genealogy, from
  November 5, 1791 thru January 14, 1792. More transcriptions
  to come in this ongoing project from Tennessee*

◆ "L"

- The Landmark Newspaper
  http://www.thelandmark.com/
  *Serving the Wachusett Region: Holden, Paxton, Princeton, Rutland,
  Sterling, Massachusetts.*

- Leader-Post Online ~ Regina, Saskatchewan, Canada
  http://www.leaderpost.com/cgi-bin/Livelque.acgi$sch=
  frontpage?frontpage

- The Limerick Post Newspaper ~ Ireland
  http://www.limerickpost.ie/

- The London Gazette
  http://www.history.rochester.edu/London_Gazette/
  *Selected online editions for 1674, 1675, 1676, 1678 and 1692 from
  Electronic Historical Publications.*

- Los Angeles Times
  http://www.latimes.com/

- Lubbock Online ~ Texas
  http://www.lubbockonline.com/

- Luxemburger Gazette
  http://www.eskimo.com/~lisanne/gazette.htm
  *The Luxemburger Gazette was published by Nicholas Gonner, and
  later his son, in Dubuque, Iowa from 1871-1918. In addition to news
  of Luxembourg, it featured news of Luxembourgers and Luxembourg
  communities throughout the United States.*

◆ "M"

- Maryland State Archives Guide to Maryland
  Newspapers
  http://www.mdarchives.state.md.us/msa/speccol/html/
  0003.html

- Mennonite Brethren Herald
  http://www.mbherald.com/39-03/
  Be sure to see their online editions & current obituaries section.

- The Minnesota Daily Online ~ Minneapolis-St. Paul
  http://www.mndaily.com/

- Missoulian Online ~ Montana
  http://www.missoulian.com/

- The Monroe Evening News ~ Michigan
  http://www.MONROENEWS.COM/index.html

- The Morning Journal ~ Columbiana County, Ohio
  http://www.morningjournalnews.com/

- Mountain Democrat Online
  http://www.mtdemocrat.com/
  California's Oldest Newspaper, Placerville, California

◆ **"N"**

- NC-NEWSPAPER Mailing List
  http://www.rootsweb.com/~jfuller/gen_mail_states-nc.html
  #NC-NEWSPAPER
  To discuss genealogical information found in North Carolina newspapers.

- N.C. Newspaper Project ~ North Carolina
  http://statelibrary.dcr.state.nc.us/tss/newspape.htm

- Nevada Newspaper Indexes
  http://dmla.clan.lib.nv.us/docs/nsla/newsind.htm
  Nevada State Library and Archives and Records.

- New England Old Newspaper Index Project of Maine®
  http://www.geocities.com/Heartland/Hills/1460/

- Newspaper and Current Periodical Room - Library of Congress
  http://lcweb.loc.gov/global/ncp/ncp.html

- Newspaper Clippings - Kansas City Public Library ~ Missouri
  http://www.kcpl.lib.mo.us/sc/clips/newsclips.htm
  In the Special Collections Department. Some are online.

- Newspaper Collection
  http://www.slv.vic.gov.au/slv/newspapers/
  At the State Library of Victoria, Australia.

- Newspapers
  http://commerce.state.wy.us/cr/archives/databases/news.htm
  Held by the Wyoming State Archives.

- Newspapers of Pickens County, SC
  http://www.rootsweb.com/~scpicken/picnew.html
  Complete listing of all the newspapers, past and present, from Pickens County, South Carolina.

- Newspapers at the National Library of Canada
  http://www.nlc-bnc.ca/services/enews.htm

- Newspapers in Missouri - Newspaper Genealogy Research
  http://members.xoom.com/mellis/monewspaper.htm
  From the American Local History Network - Missouri.

- Newspapers in North Wales
  http://www.nwn.co.uk/NWNInternetpages/newspapers.html
  Links to newspaper web sites in the north of Wales.

- Newspaper Section: Online Newspapers
  http://www.statelib.lib.in.us/WWW/INDIANA/NEWSPAPER/NEWSMENU.HTML
  Listing of Indiana online newspapers from the Indiana State Library.

- Newspaper Titles Online
  http://lcweb.loc.gov/global/ncp/oltitles.html
  From the Library of Congress Internet Resource Page.

- New York State Newspaper Project
  http://www.nysl.nysed.gov/nysnp/

- The New York Times on the Web
  http://www.nytimes.com/

- North East Newspapers
  http://www.onlincam.freeserve.co.uk/planning/news.htm
  #E_Link

- Northern News Services Limited ~ Yellowknife, NW Territories, Canada
  http://www.nnsl.com/
  Serving communities in Canada's Arctic Northwest Territories and Nunavut.

- Northscape News: The Grand Forks Herald Online
  http://www.northscape.com/

- Nova Scotian Newspapers
  http://nsgna.ednet.ns.ca/nnewsp.html

- NSLA - Library Services - Newspaper Holdings List
  http://dmla.clan.lib.nv.us/docs/nsla/services/news/news.htm
  Nevada State Library and Archives and Records.

- Nunatsiaq News ~ NW Territories, Canada
  http://www.nunanet.com/~nunat/

◆ **"O"**

- Observer-Reporter Online ~ Washington, Pennsylvania
  http://www.observer-reporter.com/

- October 1881 East Coast Gale
  http://www.richard-white.freeserve.co.uk/storm/1881gale.html
  On the night of 14th October 1881, there was a tremendous westerly storm, which affected most of the east coast of Britain. The loss of life, particularly among the fishing fleets, was tremendous. Scanned images of newspaper articles about the storm plus surname, deaths, fishing vessel, and sinkings indexes are provided to the articles.

- Oklahoma Newspaper Project
  http://www.keytech.com:80/~frizzell/
  A project to preserver newspapers on microfilm.

- The Oklahoman Online
  http://www.oklahoman.com/

- OnlineNewspapers.com
  http://www.onlinenewspapers.com/

- Ottawa Citizen Online ~ Ontario, Canada
  http://www.ottawacitizen.com/

◆ **"P"**

- Pilot Online - The Virginian-Pilot ~ Hampton Roads
  http://www.pilotonline.com/

- Pioneer Planet ~ St. Paul, Minnesota
  http://www.pioneerplanet.com/

- Portland Press Herald Online ~ Maine
  http://www.portland.com/

- The Press of Connecticut
  http://www.sots.state.ct.us/RegisterManual/SectionX/Misc3.htm

- Prince Albert Daily Herald Online Edition ~ Saskatchewan, Canada
  http://www.paherald.sk.ca/home.html

- The Providence Journal-Bulletin ~ Rhode Island
  http://www.projo.com/

◆ "R"

- Recorder Online ~ Amsterdam, New York
  http://www.recordernews.com/

- The Record Online ~ Hackensack, New Jersey
  http://www.bergen.com/

- The Register-Herald, Preble County, Ohio
  http://www.registerherald.com/

- The Richmond Times-Dispatch ~ Virginia
  http://www.gateway-va.com/pages/tdmain.htm

- The Roanoke Times Online ~ Virginia
  http://www.roanoke.com/roatimes/index.html

- Rockford Register Star ~ Illinois
  http://www.rrstar.com/

◆ "S"

- Sacramento Bee ~ California
  http://www.sacbee.com/

- Saint John Times Globe
  http://www.timesglobe.com/main.htm
  Saint John, New Brunswick, Canada. Contact information and history regarding this newspaper.

- The Salt Lake Tribune ~ Utah
  http://www.sltrib.com/

- San Antonio Express-News ~ Texas
  http://www.expressnews.com

- San Francisco Bay Guardian
  http://www.sfbayguardian.com/

- The Seattle Times ~ Washington
  http://seattletimes.nwsource.com/cgi-bin/WebObjects/SeattleTimes.woa/wa/

- The Shelbyville News Online ~ Indiana
  http://www.shelbynews.com/

- Sioux City Journal Online ~ Iowa
  http://www.siouxcityjournal.com/

- Slave River Journal Interactive ~ NW Territories, Canada
  http://www.srji.com/homepage.ASP

- Southwest Virginia Enterprise ~ Wytheville, Virginia
  http://www.zwire.com/news/newslist.cfm?brd=1481

- SPAN - Serials, Periodicals, and Newspapers
  http://span.mlc.lib.mi.us:9000/
  A database of over 201,000 journals, magazines and newspapers found in Michigan's libraries.

- Star Beacon Online ~ Ashtabula County, Ohio
  http://www.starbeacon.com/

- The Star - Kansas City ~ Missouri
  http://www.kcstar.com/

- StarLine On Line: The Morning Star ~ Wilmington, North Carolina
  http://starnews.wilmington.net/

- StarNet - The Arizona Daily Star
  http://www.azstarnet.com/

- The StarPhoenix Online ~ Saskatoon, Saskatchewan Canada
  http://www.saskstar.sk.ca/

- Star Tribune Online ~ Minneapolis-St. Paul, Minnesota
  http://www.startribune.com/

- Stephen A. Goldman Historical Newspapers
  http://www.historybuff.com/mall/goldman/index.html

- Svenska Dagbladet - Nyheter ~ Sweden
  http://www.svd.se/svd/ettan/dagens/index.html

◆ T

- The Tampa Tribune on the Web ~ Florida
  http://www.tampatrib.com/

- Tango! - Worcester Telegram & Gazette Online ~ Worcester, Massachusetts
  http://www.telegram.com/

- Telegraph Journal Online ~ New Brunswick, Canada
  http://www.telegraphjournal.com/main.htm

- This is South Wales
  http://www.thisissouthwales.co.uk/
  Online site of the South Wales Evening Post & the Carmarthen Journal.

- Timothy Hughes Rare & Early Newspapers
  http://www.rarenewspapers.com/

- The Toledo Blade Online
  http://www.toledoblade.com/
  The Toledo Blade Newspaper, Toledo, Ohio.

- Trib-Net - The News Tribune ~ Tacoma, Washington
  http://www.tribnet.com/

- Tri-City Herald Online
  http://www.tri-cityherald.com/
  Kennewick, Pasco and Richland, Washington

◆ "U"

- The United States Newspaper Program Participants
  http://www.neh.gov/preservation/usnp.html

- U.S. News Archives on the Web
  http://metalab.unc.edu/slanews/internet/archives.html

- UW Suzzallo Library Microform and Newspaper
  Collections
  http://www.lib.washington.edu/Mcnews/
  University of Washington in Seattle

◆ "V"

- Valley of the Shadow Newspapers
  http://jefferson.village.Virginia.EDU/vshadow2/
  newspapers.html
  From the Civil War project at the University of Virginia.

- The Virginia Newspaper Project
  http://vsla.edu/vnp/home.html

◆ "W"

- Washington Newspaper Publishers Association
  http://www.wnpa.com/

- The Washington Post
  http://www.washingtonpost.com/

- The Washington Times National Weekly Edition
  http://www.americasnewspaper.com/

- The Wenatchee World ~ Washington
  http://www.wenworld.com/

- West Central Tribune ~ Willmar, Minnesota
  http://www.wctrib.com/

- Westchester County Newspaper Collections ~ New
  York
  http://pages.prodigy.com/HFBK19A/wcgsrs10.htm

- Western Oklahoma Newspaper Research
  http://members.tripod.com/~smcb/research.html

- Western People ~ Mayo, Ireland
  http://www.mayo-ireland.ie/WPeople.htm

- Whitehorse Star Daily ~ Yukon, Canada
  http://www.whitehorsestar.com/

- Wichita Online - A Service of the Wichita Eagle
  http://www.wichitaeagle.com/

- The Windsor Star ~ Ontario, Canada
  http://www.southam.com/windsorstar/

- The Wire - News from The Associated Press
  http://wire.ap.org/

◆ "Y"

- Yukon News Online
  http://www.yukon-news.com/

NOVELTIES

http://www.cyndislist.com/novelty.htm

- Ancestore Detective Original Apparel
  http://www.ancestordetective.com/Merchant2/merchant.mv?
  Screen=SFNT&Store_Code=A
  T-Shirts, Sweatshirts, Tote Bags and more from Ancestor Detective.

- Celebrity Birth Certificates
  http://www.online-homesales.co.uk/index.htm
  Birth and marriage certificates for celebrities born in the United Kingdom.

- Family History - A Genealogy Card Game
  http://www.webspawner.com/users/familyhistorygame/
  Totally new card game - win when you fill your family tree. Fun for all ages.

- Family Tree Genealogy Ornaments
  http://www.metalpictures.com/genealogy/
  A permanent metallic copy of YOUR PHOTO is made and placed on a 24K gold plated snowflake ornament complete with ancestor's name, date of birth and death. A FREE catalog and sample metal photo are sent upon request.

- Family Tree Printer: Genealogy Charts Beautifully Printed
  http://familytreeprinter.com/
  Specializing in printing family trees on poster-size paper.

- Genealogy Fan Chart Project
  http://www.marthabymail.com/mbm/product.asp?pfam_id=617
  &dept_id=71&main_dept=8&mscssid=HF0GM1CVMVSH2L39
  00AKH28UWKPQ3GUC
  From Martha Stewart's "Martha by Mail".

- Genealogy Trees Holiday Project
  http://marthastewart.com/television/holidays/segments/hol_
  genealogy.asp
  From Martha Stewart's Holiday Special.

- Generations
  http://www.genealogy4fun.com/
  Use this game of deductive reasoning to solve the mystery of (make-believe) family history: U.S. birthplaces, careers and lifestyles. Tell stories about who they were and where they lived. Quality, creative, fun for friends and family - high in play value.

- Genographica
  http://www.genographica.com/
  Large format genealogical tree print from GEDCOM on antique map. Most of the background images offered are XVIth century geographical maps.

- Gravestone Rubbing Kit
  http://gravestoneartwear.com/rubbingkit.html
  From Gravestone Artwear.

- Hattie's Clothesline
  http://www.hattiesclothesline.com/
  "Creative clothing for Family Historians".

- Heraldry Cross Stitch
  http://www.hometown.aol.com/mcknit1775/paint/arms.htm
  Cross stitch pattern of your family coat of arms.

- Hikada Family Emblems
  http://www.st.rim.or.jp/%7Ezhidaka/index.html
  A company which sells Japanese family emblems historically associated with Japanese surnames.

- How Psychic Roots Became an "Unsolved Mystery"
  http://www.audiotapes.com/product.asp?ProductCode
  ='WPGS99S27'
  Presentation by Henry Z. Jones Jr., available for sale on audio tape.

- I Don't Chase Dead Germans...They Chase Me!
  http://www.audiotapes.com/product.asp?ProductCode
  ='HT-130'
  Presentation by Henry Z. Jones Jr., available for sale on audio tape.

- KinShips: The Passenger Vessels of Your Immigrant Ancestors
  http://www.KinShipsPrints.com/
  Art prints, most in color, of passenger ships, primarily those sailing the North Atlantic routes between 1890 and 1940.

- Memorial Family Finder from HobbsHouse
  http://www.hobbshouse.com/
  Find extended family members with Memorial Family Finder, a product that transforms a cemetery headstone or grave marker into a communication tool. Memorial Family Finder is an attractive, unobtrusive container that affixes to a headstone or marker. The unit comes with pre-printed cards on which you can write your contact information, alerting others that you are searching for family information.

- Memorial Video Tributes
  http://www.mlvp.com/memory7.htm
  Our Video Production Company produces Video Memorializations or Memorial Tributes on Video for the clients of Funeral Homes and individuals. We use family photos, slides, film, video, and other memorabilia. We transfer these items to video and produce a video tape with music, that the family will value forever.

- Metallic Reflections
  http://www.metalpictures.com
  Family tree genealogy ornaments.

- Petersen Reproductions
  http://www.PetersenPrints.com/
  Wonderful things for the genealogist! T-shirts, mugs, mouse pads, software, family tree charts, baptismal & marriage certificates, family registers and much more.

- Photographic Family Trees by DooleyNoted Enterprises
  http://members.aol.com/Timdooley/index.html
  Your favorite family photos scanned, enhanced and put into your family tree ancestor chart. T-shirts, wall hangings, pillows make great gifts for family reunions, birthdays and anniversaries!.

- Photo Saver - Personal Screensaver
  http://www.photosaver.com/
  Turn your favorite photos into a personal screensaver.

- PrintMyFamily.com: Printing Genealogy Pedigree
  Wall Charts with Pictures & Photos
  http://www.printmyfamily.com/genealogy_home.html
  Personalized, full-color, large, wall-sized genealogy charts.

- Psychic Roots: Serendipity & Intuition in Genealogy
  http://www.amazon.com/exec/obidos/ISBN=0806313889/
  markcyndisgenealA/
  And More Psychic Roots: Further Adventures in
  Serendipity & Intuition in Genealogy
  http://www.amazon.com/exec/obidos/ISBN=0806315245/
  markcyndisgenealA/
  Two wonderful books by Hank Jones.

- Remembering A Loved One With Mourning Jewelry
  http://www.hairwork.com/remember.htm
  From the Victorian Hairwork Society. Explains the Victorian custom of creating jewelry, pictures, and other mementos of a loved one from their hair.

- Reunion T-Shirts
  http://www.bowplus.com/t-shirts/
  Personalized family t-shirts.

- ROOTSTAMPS
  http://www.whitemtns.com/~roots/
  Rubber stamp collection for genealogists.

- Twig Family Tree Project
  http://www.marthabymail.com/mbm/product.asp?pfam_id=616
  &dept_id=71&main_dept=8&mscssid=HF0GM1CVMVSH2L39
  00AKH28UWKPQ3GUC
  From Martha Stewart's Living magazine.

OBITUARIES

http://www.cyndislist.com/obits.htm

Category Index:

◆ General Resource Sites

◆ Locality or Topic Specific

◆ Mailing Lists, Newsgroups & Chat

◆ General Resource Sites

- 4Obituaries -- A Guide to Obituaries from 4anything.com
  http://4obituaries.4anything.com/

- Amazon.com Genealogy Bookstore - Obituaries
  http://www.amazon.com/exec/obidos/external-search/?keyword=genealogy+obituaries&tag=markcyndisgenealA/

- Arrangements.com
  http://www.arrangements.com/
  For posting obituaries and funeral details.

- Cemetery Junction: Obituaries in the United States
  http://www.daddezio.com/cemetery/obits/index.html

- Death Notices
  http://www.funeral.net/death_notices.htm
  Online forum to post your notices. Maintained by Armstrong Funeral Home and Funeral.Net.

- Death Records, Obituaries, and Probate Files: What the Dead Can Tell You
  http://www.audiotapes.com/product.asp?ProductCode='FGSSLT44'
  Presentation by Sheila Benedict, available for sale on audio tape.

- Family Workings Obituary Listings Index Page
  http://www.familyworkings.com/obits/obitindex.htm

- Free Obituaries On-Line
  http://www.king.igs.net/~bdmlhm/obit_links.html

- Funeral Programs, USA sponsored by LFC of MD
  http://www.angelfire.com/md/FUNERALPROGRAMSUSA/
  LFC of MARYLAND in it's ongoing attempt to assist, aid and abet the African American Researcher/Historian in their never ending quest for information and documentation, has created and maintains this page of Funeral Programs from across the country.

- Genealogy Resources on the Internet: Obituary Resources
  http://www-personal.umich.edu/~cgaunt/obits.html

- Generations - Memorials That Live On
  http://www.generations.on.ca/index.html
  Obituaries, funeral information, and a Canadian Funeral Home Directory.

- GoodBye! The Journal of Contemporary Obituaries
  http://www.panix.com/~scmiller/goodbye/index.htm

- Internet Memorials - Obituary Listing
  http://www.memorial-site.com/obit.htm

- Internet Obituary Network
  http://www.obits.com/

- Legacy.com: ObitFinder
  http://64.37.219.178/LegacySubPage1.asp?Page=ObitFinder
  Recent obituaries from more than 1,000 newspapers.

- Locating Obituaries for African Americans
  http://www.audiotapes.com/product.asp?ProductCode='DEN98T101'
  Presentation by Tony Burroughs, available for sale on audio tape.

- Memoriam.org: Where Loved Ones Are Remembered
  http://www.memoriam.org/

- ObitDetails
  http://www.obitdetails.com/
  Online obituaries, death notices and memorials.

- The Obituary Archive Search Engine
  http://www.obitcentral.com/obitsearch/

- Obituary Coding
  http://www.obituarycoding.com/
  About the PGCS or Publisher's Genealogical Coding System.

- Obituary Daily Times
  http://www.rootsweb.com/~obituary/

- The Obituary Link Page
  http://www.geocities.com/Heartland/Bluffs/7748/obit/obituary.htm
  Links to newspaper sites, state by state.

- Obituary Notice Index
  http://www.geocities.com/Heartland/Woods/7760/obit-index1.html

- The Obituary Page
  http://catless.ncl.ac.uk/Obituary/

- passedaway.com
  http://www.online-obituaries.com/

- Sirdick's Obits (An Online Obituary Service)
  http://www.sirdick.com/obits.htm

- Usenet Newsgroup - alt.obituaries
  news:alt.obituaries

- Wulkan's Online Obituaries/Eulogies
  http://www.wulkan.net/ObitIntr.html

- Yahoo!...Obituaries
  http://dir.yahoo.com/Society_and_Culture/Death_and_Dying/
  End_of_Life_Issues/Obituaries/

- You're Outta Here!
  http://www.cjnetworks.com/~roryb/outta.html
  Recent celebrity obituaries.

◆ Locality or Topic Specific

- Allen County, Indiana Searchable Data Files
  http://www.acpl.lib.in.us/genealogy/genealogy.html
  Including Fort Wayne & Allen County Obituaries, 1841-1900.

- American Jewish Year Book Obituary Index
  http://www.jewishgen.org/databases/ajybweb.htm

- Ancestor Obituaries of Coshocton ~ Coshocton
  County, Ohio
  http://www.coshocton.org/sharyn/obits.html

- The Anniston Star Online - Obituaries ~ Alabama
  http://www.annistonstar.com/obituaries/

- The Berkshire Eagle ~ Massachusetts
  http://www.BerkshireEagle.com/
  Click on the link to Obituaries on the left side of the page.

- BPL's Obituary Database ~ Massachusetts
  http://www.bpl.org/WWW/Obits.html

- The Boston Jewish Advocate Obituary Database
  http://www.jewishgen.org/databases/advocate.htm

- Bradford Era Obituary Index ~ Pennsylvania
  http://www.bradfordlandmark.org/obits/obit.html

- Bristol Herald Courier Obituaries Calendar ~ VA
  http://www.bristolnews.com/obituaries/obitcal.html

- Browning Genealogy: Evansville Area Obituary
  Search
  http://browning.evcpl.lib.in.us/
  *Extractions of obituaries from Vanderburgh County and
  surrounding southwestern Indiana, taken from the Evansville
  Courier, The Evansville Press, and The Evansville Courier and
  Press. From 1990 through present.*

- Butler County Obituaries ~ Ohio
  http://freepages.genealogy.rootsweb.com/~hamilton/
  obitindex.html

- Butler County, OH Older Obituaries
  http://www.rootsweb.com/~ohbutler/obit.htm

- Campbell County, South Dakota, Obitbook --
  Interactive Search
  http://www.rootsweb.com/cgi-bin/sdcampbell/obitbook.pl

- Canadian Genealogy and History Links - Cemetery -
  Obituary
  http://www.islandnet.com/~jveinot/cghl/cemetery.html

- Cemeteries - Wakulla County, FL
  http://mailer.fsu.edu/~rthompso/cemetery.html

- Chattanooga Times & Free Press Obituaries ~ TN
  http://www.timesfreepress.com/obits/obits.html

- Cher's Mid Michigan Obituary Pages
  http://www.geocities.com/Paris/6220/index.html
  *Obituaries of recent deaths, of people, in and around
  Mid_Michigan.*

- Clark County Obituaries ~ Ohio
  http://www.ccpl.lib.oh.us/obits/

- Cleveland Jewish News Obituary Database
  http://www.jewishgen.org/databases/cleveweb.htm

- Cleveland News Index - Search on the word
  "Obituaries"
  http://www-catalog.cpl.org/CLENIX
  Database from 1976 to present.

- Community Information: Index to Local Obituaries
  http://www.lib.chattanooga.gov/communit.htm
  *Index to Chattanooga Tennessee Obituaries 1897-present. From the
  Chattanooga-Hamilton County Bicentennial Library.*

- A compilation of obituaries listed in the Maryville
  Enterprise from 1906-1960 ~ Tennessee
  http://www.tngenweb.org/blount/newspr/menterp.htm

- CTnow - Obituaries from the Hartford Courant ~
  Connecticut
  http://courant.ctnow.com/obits/

- Cumberlink Obituaries
  http://www.cumberlink.com/obits/archive.html
  From the Sentinel, Carlisle, Pennsylvania.

- Death Notices from Saratoga Whig Newspaper,
  1840-1842 ~ New York
  http://freenet.buffalo.edu/~ae487/awhig.html

- Death Notices from the Christian Guardian, 1836-
  1850 ~ Ontario
  http://www.amazon.com/exec/obidos/ISBN=091260610X/
  markcyndisgenealA/
  A book by Donald A. McKenzie.

- Death Notices from the Christian Guardian, 1851-
  1860 ~ Ontario
  http://www.amazon.com/exec/obidos/ISBN=0912606258/
  markcyndisgenealA/
  A book by Donald A. McKenzie.

- Death Notices of Some Early Pictou County Settlers
  ~ Nova Scotia, Canada
  http://www.rootsweb.com/~pictou/obits.htm

- Deaths and Memoriams Extracted from the `New
  Zealand Herald' 1993
  http://www.geocities.com/Heartland/6123/dth_names.html
  *From New Zealand. Find a surname of interest then e-mail the
  owner of the page for details.*

- Deaths from Kerwin's 1888 Saratoga Springs City Directory ~ New York
  http://freenet.buffalo.edu/~ae487/1888.html

- Decatur Illinois Herald & Review - Central IL Index
  http://www.herald-review.com/newsidx.html#obit
  Birth and death notices since 1997.

- Detroit Free Press - Death Notices ~ Michigan
  http://www.freep.com/death_notices/index.htm

- Detroit Free Press - Obituaries ~ Michigan
  http://www.freep.com/index/obituaries.htm

- The Detroit News - Obituaries & Death Notices
  http://www.detnews.com/
  Scroll through the index on this page and click on the link to Obituaries.

- Dziennik Chicagoski Obituaries ~ Chicago, Illinois
  http://www.pgsa.org/dziennik.htm

- ECPL Obituary Listing Main Page ~ Erie County, Pennsylvania
  http://www.ecls.lib.pa.us/obits.html

- Fargo Forum Obituary Index
  http://www.lib.ndsu.nodak.edu/ndirs/bio&genealogy/forum obits.html
  Eastern North Dakota or Northwestern Minnesota. 40,000 names for obituaries posted from 1985 through 1995 and approx. 2,000 obituaries from earlier years.

- The Florida Times-Union Online Obituaries ~ Jacksonville, Florida
  http://www.times-union.com/tu-online/obituaries/

- Fort Worth Star-Telegram - Obituaries ~ Texas
  http://www.star-telegram.com/system/obits/index.htm

- Funeral Notices - The Arizona Daily Star
  http://www.azstarnet.com/public/electrifieds/0002.htm

- Gospel Advocate Obituary Index
  http://www.ag.uiuc.edu/~mcmillan/Restlit/Database/ gaobit.html
  Compiled by members of the Lehman Avenue church of Christ in Bowling Green, Kentucky.

- Highland Park Obituary Index 1874-1950, 1993-1998 ~ Illinois
  http://www.highlandpark.org/obits/

- Hopkins County Obituaries - Kentucky
  http://cgi.rootsweb.com/~genbbs/genbbs.cgi/USA/Ky/Hopkins Obits

- Horry County Historical Society Obituary Database ~ South Carolina
  http://www.hchsonline.org/search/obit.cgi

- Index to Mentone Area Obits and Death Notices 1885-1995 ~ Indiana
  http://www.rootsweb.com/~inkosciu/mentndx.htm

- Index to Obituaries Taken From The Southern Democrat, Blount County, Alabama 1915 - 1940
  http://members.aol.com/blountal/Obit.html

- Joplin Area Deaths - The Joplin Globe ~ Missouri
  http://www.joplinglobe.com/
  See the link to obituaries on this web page.

- Kansas City Star Obituaries
  http://www.kcstar.com/cgi-bin/class?template=clq-obit.htm& category=0&database=daily

- KnoxNews.com - News - Obituaries ~ Tennessee
  http://www.knoxnews.com/news/obituaries/
  Knoxville News-Sentinel Online.

- Lexington Herald-Leader On-Line Obituaries ~ KY
  http://www.kentuckyconnect.com/heraldleader/obituaries/

- Mennobits - Amish and Mennonite Obituaries
  http://freepages.genealogy.rootsweb.com/~mennobit/

- Mennonite Brethren Herald
  http://www.mbherald.com/39-03/
  Be sure to see their online editions & current obituaries section.

- Michigan Live: Obituaries
  http://www.mlive.com/obits/

- Monroe Evening News Obituaries ~ Michigan
  http://www.monroenews.com/obits/

- Nashville Local History Indexes
  http://wendy.nashv.lib.tn.us:82/
  Includes marriages 1864-1905, searchable by bride or groom; obituaries from the Nashville Banner and the Tennesseean, from 1977 through present.

- News & Record: Obituaries ~ Piedmont Triad, NC
  http://www.news-record.com/news/obits/main.shtml

- Newspaper Obituaries from The Hamilton Advocate, Hamilton, Missouri, 1991- 1995 and The Braymer Bee, Braymer, Missouri, 1991-1995
  http://www.yourlaunchpad.com/terry/caldwell/obt91-95.htm

- Newspaper Obituary Index (1862-March 15, 1962) - Beaufort County ~ South Carolina
  http://www.co.beaufort.sc.us/library/Beaufort/obit.htm

- Norfolk Obituaries
  http://hometown.aol.com/otterleigh/page2aa.htm
  Selected obituaries from early Norfolk/Portsmouth, Virginia newspapers.

- North Iowa Area Electronic Newspaper Obituaries
  http://www.mach3ww.com/~pafways/obituaries/obitone.htm

- Obituaries from the Goldthwaite Eagle-Mills County Texas
  http://www.geocities.com/Heartland/Flats/5643/Eagle/ eagle.html

- Obituaries from News-Star, Monroe, LA
  http://www.bayou.com/~suelynn/obits.html

- Obituaries from Ontario's Christian Guardian, 1861-1870
  http://www.amazon.com/exec/obidos/ISBN=0912606339/markcyndisgenealA/
  A book by Donald McKenzie.

- Obituaries from the Baton Rouge Louisiana Newspapers
  http://freepages.genealogy.rootsweb.com/~lwrr/
  1952-1959 and 1980-1991.

- Obituaries from the Houston Morning Star, Texas – 1839
  http://www.geocities.com/Vienna/1516/houobi.html
  1840
  http://www.geocities.com/Vienna/1516/houobi40.html
  1841
  http://www.geocities.com/Vienna/1516/houobi41.html
  1842
  http://www.geocities.com/Vienna/1516/houobi42.html
  1843
  http://www.geocities.com/Vienna/1516/houobi43.html
  1844
  http://www.geocities.com/Vienna/1516/houobi44.html

- Obituaries from the Texas Telegraph [Houston], 1841-44
  http://www.geocities.com/Vienna/1516/houobit.html
  1845
  http://www.geocities.com/Vienna/1516/houobi45.html
  1846
  http://www.geocities.com/Vienna/1516/houobi46.html
  1847
  http://www.geocities.com/Vienna/1516/houobi47.html
  1848
  http://www.geocities.com/Vienna/1516/houobi48.html
  1849-50
  http://www.geocities.com/Vienna/1516/houobi50.html

- Obituaries - Gibson County, Indiana
  http://www.comsource.net/~tnolcox/obituaries.htm

- Obituaries of Eastern Kentucky
  http://freepages.genealogy.rootsweb.com/~kyroots/

- Obituaries - The Beacon News - Aurora ~ Illinois
  http://www.copleynewspapers.com/BeaconNews/obits/

- Obituaries, The Citizens' Voice Newspaper, Wilkes-Barre, PA
  http://citizensvoice.com/obituaries.html

- Obituaries, Garfield County Genealogists, Inc., Enid, OK
  http://www.harvestcomm.net/org/garfield_genealogy/obits.htm

- Obituaries - Washington Times-Herald ~ Indiana
  http://washtimesherald.com/obits/obits.html
  Obituary listings since February 1998.

- Obituary Index
  http://dbase1.lapl.org/pages/rip.htm

From the Los Angeles Public Library. Provides indexes to newspaper and periodical articles of obituary information on noted actors, authors, journalists, and librarians.

- Obituary Index Search for Michigan City - Michigan City Public Library
  http://www.mclib.org/obituary.htm
  A searchable database of approximately 75,000 obituaries. The file is incomplete, but covers 1887 to present.

- Obituary Index to the Alexandria Gazette, 1916-1919
  http://www.alexandria.lib.va.us/obits/obits.htm

- Observer-Reporter Obituary Archive ~ Pennsylvania
  http://www.chartiers.com/worobits/index.html
  Obituaries for Washington and Greene counties from August 1997 through present.

- OKbits - 1883 - 1997 Obits & Tidbits
  http://www.rootsweb.com/~okbits/index.htm

- Online Obituaries for New England
  http://people.ne.mediaone.net/godbout/obits.htm

- Philadelphia Daily News: Deaths ~ Pennsylvania
  http://www.phillynews.com/content/daily_news/99/12/17/deaths/

- Philadelphia Inquirer: Obituaries ~ Pennsylvania
  http://www.phillynews.com/inquirer/2000/Mar/15/obituaries/

- PJStar Matter of Record - Peoria, IL
  http://www.pjstar.com/frontpage/records.html

- Preble County Obituary Index ~ Ohio
  http://www.pcdl.lib.oh.us/Getobit1.htm
  More than 10,500 obituaries reported in the Register-Herald for 1980-1995.

- PRHGS Obituary Index - Cuba
  http://www.rootsweb.com/~prhgs/obits_cuba_01.htm#Cuba
  Obituary Index of Hispanic people born in the Cuba from the Puerto Rican Hispanic Genealogical Society.

- PRHGS Obituary Index - Mexico
  http://www.rootsweb.com/~prhgs/obits_mexico_01.htm
  Obituary Index of Hispanic people born in Mexico from the Puerto Rican Hispanic Genealogical Society.

- PRHGS Obituary Index - USA
  http://www.rootsweb.com/~prhgs/obits_usa_01.htm
  Obituary Index of Hispanic people born in the United States from the Puerto Rican Hispanic Genealogical Society.

- Providence Journal Obituaries ~ Rhode Island
  http://projo.com/obituaries/

- Public Libraries of Saginaw Obituary Index
  http://www.tricitynet.com/pls/obit.nsf

- Pueblo Library Search - Search Obituaries - DRA Web2 ~ Colorado
  http://www.pueblolibrary.org/web2/tramp2.exe/log_in?SETTING_KEY=English&servers=obituary&guest=guest&screen=obitadvancedsearch.html
  Death records published in The Pueblo Chieftain, 1925-1997.

- The Quincy Herald-Whig: Death Notices ~ Illinois
  http://www.whig.com/deaths.shtml

- Record Herald 1911-1930 Obituary Index   ~ Fayette
  County, Ohio
  http://www.washington-ch.lib.oh.us/herald_search_
  records.html

- Richland County Obituary Index ~ Ohio
  http://members.aol.com/AEADesigns/RCOI-Index.htm

- Roanoke Times Online Obituaries ~ Virginia
  http://www.roanoke.com/roatimes/obits.html

- Rock Island County Obituaries ~ Illinois
  http://www.rootsweb.com/~ilrockis/obit/obits.htm

- St. Louis Obituary Index ~ Missouri
  http://www.slpl.lib.mo.us/libsrc/obit.htm
  *Index of names from both the Death Notice and Burial Permits
  listing, as well as Obituary Articles, found in the St. Louis Post
  Dispatch. 1900-1909, 1918-1919, 1942-1945, 1992-1999.*

- The Salt Lake Tribune - Utah Section
  http://www.sltrib.com/
  *Go to the Utah section and find the links for Utah Births and Utah
  Deaths.*

- San Francisco County Genealogy - Ancestors'
  Obituaries and Death Notices ~ California
  http://www.sfo.com/~timandpamwolf/sfranobi.htm

- Search Obituaries found in Dayton Newspaper 1985-
  97
  http://www.dayton.lib.oh.us/htbin/obit

- Search the Rochester Post Bulletin Obituary
  Database ~ Minnesota
  http://catalog.selco.lib.mn.us/data/ochs/rpbobits.cfm

- Search the Skokie Obituary Index ~ Illinois
  http://www.skokie.lib.il.us/special/skoknews/searchob.html

- Sellers' Western Kentucky Obituaries
  http://cgi.rootsweb.com/~genbbs/genbbs.cgi/USA/Ky/Sellers
  Obits

- Seventh-day Adventist Periodical Index
  http://143.207.5.3:82/search/
  Has a searchable obituary index.

- Sioux City Journal Online - Daily Obituaries ~ Iowa
  http://www.siouxcityjournal.com/editorial/obit.html

- Siskiyou County Library Obituary Search Engine
  http://www.snowcrest.net/cgi-bin/miva?~siskiyoulibrary/
  categoro.mv
  Searchable database in Siskiyou County newspapers for 1854-1990.

- SJCPL's Necrology File Online
  http://sjcpl.lib.in.us/Databases/Necrology.html
  *The Necrology File database for the South Bend Tribune for people
  who died in St. Joseph County, South Bend, Indiana.*

- Some Howard County, Indiana Deaths 1922-1935
  http://www.kokomo.lib.in.us/genealogy/Obits1922-1935.html
  Extracted from Kokomo, Indiana Newspapers.

- SouthEast Texas Obituaries
  http://www.lest-we-forget.com/RootsLady/universal/
  obituari.htm

- Southwest Virginia Enterprise - Obituaries
  http://www.wythenews.com/obit.htm
  *Obituaries from the latest edition of this newspaper in Wythe
  County, Virginia. Also see their archives for past editions from
  previous dates which also include obituaries.*
  http://www.wythenews.com/archive.htm

- Spartanburg Herald and Herald-Journal Death Index
  http://www.spt.lib.sc.us/obits/index.html
  *A listing of obituaries, created by staff of the Spartanburg County
  Public Library. 1907, 1944-1999.*

- Stephens County Obituary Diary of Guy Rangeley
  1940's
  http://members.tripod.com/davis_genealogy/OBITS.html

- Stevens Point Area Obituary Index ~ Wisconsin
  http://library.uwsp.edu/obits/
  From 1872; more than 96,000 names.

- Tacoma Obituary Database ~ Washington state
  http://www.tpl.lib.wa.us/v2/nwroom/Obit.htm

- Tampa Tribune News Obituaries ~ Florida
  http://tampatrib.com/News/obituaries.htm

- Telegram & Gazette Online -Obituaries ~ Worcester
  Massachusetts
  http://www.telegram.com/news/obits/

- Tennessee Newspaper Obituary Indexes In Public
  Libraries
  http://www.state.tn.us/sos/statelib/pubsvs/tn-obits.htm
  From the Tennessee State Library and Archives.

- Times-Dispatch Obituaries - Richmond, Virginia
  http://www.gateway-va.com/pages/tdstory/obtindex.htm

- The Times Herald Online Obituaries
  http://www.th-record.com/obits/
  New York and Pennsylvania newspaper.

- Times-Mail Online
  http://www.tmnews.com/obits/
  Obituaries online since October 1996. ~ Bedford, Illinois

- Times Online Obituaries
  http://www.timesonline.com/obitp.htm
  *Daily obituaries from the Beaver County Times, Beaver County,
  Pennsylvania.*

- The Times Record Obituary Page ~ Brunswick, ME
  http://www.timesrecord.com/obituaries

- Tulare County Obituary Index ~ California
  http://cpl.cagenweb.com/tulare/tcobit.htm

- Umatilla County, Oregon - USGenWeb Archives
  http://www.rootsweb.com/~usgenweb/or/umfiles.htm
  Includes Abstracts of obituaries from Hermiston newspapers.

- Villa Park Argus Obituary Index -- Villa Park Public Library
  http://www.villapark.lib.il.us/local/obits/index.htm
  Index of Villa Park, Illinois obituaries published since the 1931.

- Wabash Valley Obituary Index
  http://vax1.vigo.lib.in.us/~obits/index.htm
  Indiana - Vigo, Vermillion, Parke, Putnam, Clay, Owen, Sullivan and Greene Counties; Illinois - Crawford, Clark and Edgar Counties. From the Vigo County Public Library.

- WashingtonPost.com: Obituaries
  http://washingtonpost.com/wp-dyn/metro/obituaries/

- Webster County Kentucky Obituaries
  http://www.rootsweb.com/~kywebste/obits/obits.htm

- Wood County Public Library Obituary Index ~ Ohio
  http://129.1.162.211/obits.htm
  Approximately 60,000 names, covers 1870 to present.

- Zion Lutheran Church of Helotes - Member's Obituaries
  http://lonestar.texas.net/~gdalum/obits.html
  Obituaries of some members of the Zion Lutheran Church of Helotes located in northwestern San Antonio, Bexar, Texas.

◆ Mailing Lists, Newsgroups & Chat

- Genealogy Resources on the Internet - Cemeteries / Monuments / Obituaries Mailing Lists
  http://www.rootsweb.com/~jfuller/gen_mail_cemetery.html
  Most of the mailing list links below point to this site, wonderfully maintained by John Fuller

- AnnesOBITS Mailing List
  http://www.rootsweb.com/~jfuller/gen_mail_cemetery.html#AnnesOBITS
  Daily obituaries in the United States and beyond.

- CA-DEATH-INDEX Mailing List
  http://www.rootsweb.com/~jfuller/gen_mail_states-ca.html#CA-DEATH-INDEX
  For anyone who desires lookups in the California Death Index (July 1905 to 1995) or who has access to the index and can do lookups for other subscribers.

- CAN-ALB-OBITS
  http://www.rootsweb.com/~jfuller/gen_mail_country-can.html#CAN-ALB-OBITS
  For the posting of daily obituaries from the Province of Alberta, Canada.

- CAN-ONT-OBITS Mailing List
  http://www.rootsweb.com/~jfuller/gen_mail_country-can.html#CAN-ONT-OBITS
  For posting of daily obituaries for the province of Ontario, Canada.

- GEN-OBIT Mailing List
  http://www.rootsweb.com/~jfuller/gen_mail_cemetery.html#GEN-OBIT
  For obituaries

- IRISH-AMERCIAN-OBITUARIES Mailing List
  http://www.rootsweb.com/~jfuller/gen_mail_country-ire.html#IRISH-AMERICAN-OBITUARIES
  For the posting of obituaries of Irish-born Irish-Americans.

- Obitlinkspage Mailing List
  http://www.rootsweb.com/~jfuller/gen_mail_cemetery.html#Obitlinkspage
  For the announcement of the new links and other developmental updates on The Obituary Links Page.
  http://www.geocities.com/cribbswh/obit/

- OBIT-LOOKUPS Mailing List
  http://www.rootsweb.com/~jfuller/gen_mail_cemetery.html#OBIT-LOOKUPS
  And the associated web site
  http://freepages.genealogy.rootsweb.com/~obitl/
  For the discussion and sharing of information regarding the availability of lookup services for obituaries and for subscriber requests for obituaries.

- OK-OBITS Mailing List
  http://www.rootsweb.com/~jfuller/gen_mail_cemetery.html#OK-OBITS
  For the posting of obituaries and other tidbits from Oklahoma newspagers that will help others in their genealogical research in Oklahoma.

- ontario-daily-obituaries Mailing List
  http://www.rootsweb.com/~jfuller/gen_mail_country-can.html#ontario-daily-obituaries
  For volunteers to post their daily obituaries, for look-up requests of obituaries new and old, and for general questions pertaining to obituaries in the Province of Ontario, Canada.

- PA-OBITS Mailing List
  http://www.rootsweb.com/~jfuller/gen_mail_cemetery.html#PA-OBITS
  For anyone who wants to share obituaries or request obituary lookups of Pennsylvania natives or former residents.

- PA-SW-OBITS Mailing List
  http://www.rootsweb.com/~jfuller/gen_mail_cemetery.html#PA-SW-OBITS
  For anyone interested in sharing obituaries from southwest Pennsylvania. This may include, but is not limited to, the counties of Greene, Washington, Fayette, Allegheny, and Westmoreland.

- TXHUNT-OBITS Mailing List
  http://www.rootsweb.com/~jfuller/gen_mail_cemetery.html#TXHUNT-OBITS
  For the posting and discussion of obituaries pertaining to Hunt County, Texas and ancestors and descendants of those who have resided in Hunt County.

- US-OBITS Mailing List
  http://www.rootsweb.com/~jfuller/gen_mail_cemetery.html#US-OBITS
  For the sharing of obituaries from any state in the United States.

- WORLD-OBITS Mailing List
  http://www.rootsweb.com/~jfuller/gen_mail_cemetery.html#WORLD-OBITS
  A mailing list covering all countries of the world, where individuals and volunteers can submit or request obituary information on anyone, anywhere.

OCCUPATIONS
http://www.cyndislist.com/occupatn.htm

Category Index:
- ◆ General Resource Sites
- ◆ Libraries, Archives & Museums
- ◆ Mailing Lists, Newsgroups & Chat
- ◆ Specific Occupations
  - • Fishermen & Mariners

- • Medicine
- • Mining
- • Railroad
- • Miscellaneous

◆ General Resource Sites

- • Belgium-Roots Project - Genealogy : Occupations
  http://belgium.rootsweb.com/sci/genealogy/
  occupations_00.html

- • Colonial Occupations
  http://www.rootsweb.com/~rigenweb/ocupaton.html

- • Colonial Occupations
  http://www.rootsweb.com/~genepool/jobs.htm

- • Colonial Occupations
  http://www.hoosierlines.cqc.com/#Occupations

- • Colonial Occupations
  http://homepages.rootsweb.com/~sam/occupation.html

- • English Occupational Records: The Forgotten Tool
  http://www.audiotapes.com/product.asp?ProductCode=
  'BTB82'
  Presentation by Hazel Tibbetts, available for sale on audio tape.

- • Kentuckiana Genealogy - Occupation Chart
  http://www.kentuckianagenealogy.org/guide/help/
  occupations.html

- • Lacinskie Nazwy Zawodow = Latin Names of Occupations
  http://hum.amu.edu.pl/~rafalp/GEN/zawody.htm
  Latin to Polish translations.

- • A List of Occupations
  http://cpcug.org/user/jlacombe/terms.html

- • Obsolete Occupations
  http://olivetreegenealogy.com/misc/occupations.shtml
  Some Medieval and Obsolete English Trade and Professional Terms Used From 1086-1400. From The Olive Tree.

- • Occupation & Apprentice Records: England, Wales and Ireland
  http://www.audiotapes.com/product.asp?ProductCode='SLC-
  149-IR'
  Presentation by Raymond W. Madsen, available for sale on audio tape.

- • Occupations Census Indexes
  http://rontay.digiweb.com/visit/occupy/
  From Ron Taylor's UK Census Finding Aids and Indexes.

- • Occupations in Colonial India
  http://www.ozemail.com.au/~clday/occupations.htm

  - o Jute in India
    http://www.ozemail.com.au/~clday/jute.htm

- • Occupations and their Descriptions
  http://www.onthenet.com.au/~tonylang/Occupa.htm
  From the Langham Genealogy Page.

- • Occupations of Yesteryear
  http://www.noelm.com/williamson/occupations.html

- • Old German Professions and Occupations
  http://worldroots.clicktron.com/brigitte/occupat.htm

- • Old Time Jobs
  http://genweb.net/~gen-cds/jobdesc.html

- • Public Record Office - Finding Aids - A-Z Index of All Leaflets ~ U.K.
  http://www.pro.gov.uk/leaflets/riindex.htm

- • Society of Genealogists Bookshop - British Research Occupations
  http://www.sog.org.uk/acatalog/SoG_Bookshop_Online_
  Occupations_89.html

◆ Libraries, Archives & Museums

- • A. Philip Randolph/Pullman Porter Museum Gallery
  http://www.wimall.com/pullportermu/
  Celebrating this leader in the African American labor movement and the African American Railroad Attendant.

- • American Vaudeville Museum
  http://vaudeville.org/page12.html
  Has a place to post questions about vaudeville performers.

- • The Archives of the Worshipful Company of Upholders
  http://www.upholders.co.uk/archives.htm
  Includes some scanned images of original records and contact information regarding Company members.

- The Australian National University: Noel Butlin Archives Centre
http://anulib.anu.edu.au/nbac/
Collection of primary source material relating to business and labour. The NBAC holds archives of industrial organisations, businesses, professional associations, industry bodies and the labour movement.

- BT Archives
http://www.bt.com/archives/index.htm
From British Telecommunications.

- Business Archives Council
http://www.archives.gla.ac.uk/bac/
The BAC's aims are to encourage the preservation of British business records, to advise on the administration and management of archives and current records, and to promote the use of business records. Hosted by the University of Glasgow, the Business Archives Council may be of assistance to the genealogist searching for business and employment records for their ancestors.

- Centre des archives du monde du travail ~ France
http://www.archivesnationales.culture.gouv.fr/camt/

- Directory of Corporate Archives in the United States and Canada
http://www.hunterinformation.com/corporat.htm
From the Society of American Archivists Business Archives Section. Alphabetical listing of known corporate archives including contact information and terms of use. An excellent resource for finding employment records for large companies.

- HM Customs & Excise National Museum
http://www.nmgm.org.uk/customs/index.html
The museum at Merseyside, England has an associated library which includes resources of interest to the family historian researching their excise officer or customs official ancestors.

- The Library and Collection of the Worshipful Company of Clockmakers
http://www.clockmakers.org/link2.htm
The Clockmakers' Library was founded in 1813. It holds the ancient manuscript records of the Company and clockmaker's work books and related documents.

- The Library of the Goldsmiths' Company
http://www.thegoldsmiths.co.uk/Library/TheLibrary.htm
The collection of archives dates from the 14th century.

- The Mercer's Company Archives
http://www.mercers.co.uk/mainsite/pages/c_archives.html
Hold the historic records of the Mercers' Company from 1348 to the present.

- Modern Records Centre
http://cal.csv.warwick.ac.uk/services/library/mrc/mrc.html
The Centre's holdings focus on UK trade union records. It also holds the records of some interest groups and political organisations (including West Midlands), of individuals and business (particularly the motor industry. Hosted by the University of Warwick Library, the MRC holds records of interest to the genealogist regarding trades union membership amongst other topics.

- National Gas Archive
http://www.bg-group.com/archive/
The company archive of BG plc, which holds the historical records of the UK gas industry dating from the early 19th century.

- Records of the Brotherhood of Sleeping Car Porters
http://www.lexis-nexis.com/cispubs/guides/african_american/bscp/bscp3.htm
Description of the microfilmed holdings of the Chicago Historical Society and the Newberry Library.

- Records of Trades & Crafts
http://www.nas.gov.uk/records_of_trades_and_crafts.htm
From the National Archives of Scotland.

- Royal Bank of Scotland - Research Room
http://www.rbs.co.uk/about_us/memorybank/research_room/Study/default.htm
  - Research Room: Archive Guide
http://www.rbs.co.uk/about_us/memorybank/research_room/Study/default.htm

◆ Mailing Lists, Newsgroups & Chat

- CA-GOLDRUSH Mailing List
http://www.rootsweb.com/~jfuller/gen_mail_states-ca.html
#CA-GOLDRUSH
For anyone who is interested in early California miners and settlers, especially in northern California, 1848-1880.

- CANAL-PEOPLE Mailing List
http://www.rootsweb.com/~jfuller/gen_mail_general.html
#CANAL-PEOPLE
For anyone with a genealogical interest in canal workers and barge owners.

- COALMINERS Mailing List
http://www.rootsweb.com/~jfuller/gen_mail_country-unk.htm
#COALMINERS
For anyone whose ancestors were coalminers in the United Kingdom or the United States.

- FURTRAPPERS-MOUNTAINMEN Mailing List
http://www.rootsweb.com/~jfuller/gen_mail_general.html
#FURTRAPPERS-MOUNTAINMEN
For anyone with a genealogical interest in fur trappers and mountain men.

- itinerantroots Mailing List
http://www.onelist.com/subscribe.cgi/itinerantroots
For genealogy resources relating to itinerant professions: circus, theatre, music hall, vaudeville, fairs, showmen, portable theatres, etc.

- Mariners Mailing List
http://www.rootsweb.com/~jfuller/gen_mail_general.html
#Mariners
For anyone who is researching their seafaring ancestors.

- METISGEN Mailing List
http://www.rootsweb.com/~jfuller/gen_mail_general.html
#METISGEN
For the discussion and sharing of information regarding the Metis and their descendants. The Metis are North America's Fur Trading Children ... the new nation of individuals born within North America from the first unions of natives and whites.

- OCCUPATIONS Mailing List
  http://www.rootsweb.com/~jfuller/gen_mail_general.html
  #OCCUPATIONS
  For the discussion and sharing of information regarding occupations from a genealogical standpoint.

- PAPER-MILLS-MAKERS Mailing List
  http://www.rootsweb.com/~jfuller/gen_mail_general.html
  #PAPER-MILLS-MAKERS
  For anyone with a genealogical interest in paper mills and paper makers.

- RiverRats Mailing List
  http://www.rootsweb.com/~jfuller/gen_mail_states-gen.html
  #RiverRats
  For discussions of the Mississippi River "people" living on, working on, and involved in life on the "river." Any family living in any county bordering the Mississippi River, or living "on" the river, is welcome.

- THEATRICAL-ANCESTORS Mailing List
  http://www.rootsweb.com/~jfuller/gen_mail_general.html
  #THEATRICAL-ANCESTORS
  For anyone who is researching ancestors who participated in any type of theatrical or film work.

◆ Specific Occupations

Fishermen & Mariners

- CANAL-PEOPLE Mailing List
  http://www.rootsweb.com/~jfuller/gen_mail_general.html
  #CANAL-PEOPLE
  For anyone with a genealogical interest in canal workers and barge owners.

- Canals, Rivers & Waterways
  http://www.CyndisList.com/canals.htm
  See this category on Cyndi's List for related links.

- The Divers Index
  http://www.thehds.com/divers/divers.htm
  An Index of Historical Divers and Their Work.

- Down to the Sea in Ships
  http://www.star.net/misuraca/down2c.htm
  A list of men fishing out of Gloucester, Massachusetts who were lost at sea.

- Fishing? - It was "A WAY OF LIFE"
  http://www.geocities.com/Heartland/Prairie/7527/
  Devoted to and dedicated to the fishermen, mariners, their families and survivors in Nova Scotia. Has memorials, lists of lost fisherman, photographs, newspaper and book extracts, and much more.

- The Historical Diving Society ~ U.K.
  http://www.thehds.com/index.htm

- Mariners Mailing List
  http://www.rootsweb.com/~jfuller/gen_mail_general.htm
  #Mariners
  For anyone who is researching their seafaring ancestors.

- Research Guides from The National Maritime Museum ~ United Kingdom
  http://www.port.nmm.ac.uk/research/research.html
  A listing of the National Maritime Museum's online research guides to their library and collections and to other related maritime sources.

  - Research Guide No. A3 - Tracing Family History from Maritime Records
    http://www.port.nmm.ac.uk/research/a3.html
    A brief introduction to maritime records you can use to discover more about your ancestors, family history or famous people. It is intended to help you get started on your research, using the National Maritime Museum's library and archives and other resources outside the museum.

  - Research Guides - The Merchant Navy
    http://www.port.nmm.ac.uk/research/research.html#3
    Links to twelve of the National Maritime Museum's research guides regarding Britain's merchant shipping.

  - Research Guide No. F1 - Shipping Companies: Records held by the National Maritime Museum
    http://www.port.nmm.ac.uk/research/f1.html
    This guide lists the shipping companies whose records, or part-records, are held by the National Maritime Collection. These are mainly business records and do not cover operations, voyages or passenger lists.

- Records of the Registrar General of Shipping and Seamen (#5) ~ U.K.
  http://www.pro.gov.uk/leaflets/ri005.htm

- RiverRats Mailing List
  http://www.rootsweb.com/~jfuller/gen_mail_states-gen.html
  #RiverRats
  For discussions of the Mississippi River "people" living on, working on, and involved in life on the "river." Any family living in any county bordering the Mississippi River, or living "on" the river, is welcome.

Medicine

- Civilian Nurses and Nursing Services (#79) ~ U.K.
  http://www.pro.gov.uk/leaflets/ri2186.htm

- Deceased American Physicians' Records
  http://www.ngsgenealogy.org/library/content/ama_info.html
  A research service available from the National Genealogical Society.

- The Florence Nightingale Nurses
  http://www.melcombe.freeserve.co.uk/source/nurselist.htm
  An alphabetical list of nurses sent to military hospitals in the east.

- Tennessee Confederate Physicians : An Introduction
  http://www.state.tn.us/sos/statelib/pubsvs/docintro.htm
  From the Tennessee State Library and Archives - Historical and Genealogical Information.

- Texas Physicians Historical Biographical Database
  http://www3.utsouthwestern.edu/library/doctors/doctors.htm
  Searchable database of citations to biographical information related to early Texas physicians from the Texas State Journal of Medicine for 1905-1966 and additional sources.

- Was Your Ancestor a Doctor?
  http://user.itl.net/~glen/doctors.html

Mining

- CA-GOLDRUSH Mailing List
  http://www.rootsweb.com/~jfuller/gen_mail_states-ca.html
  #CA-GOLDRUSH
  For anyone who is interested in early California miners and settlers, especially in northern California, 1848-1880.

- COALMINERS Mailing List
  http://www.rootsweb.com/~jfuller/gen_mail_country-unk.html
  #COALMINERS
  For anyone whose ancestors were coalminers in the United Kingdom or the United States.

- Coal Mining History Resource Centre
  http://www.cmhrc.pwp.blueyonder.co.uk/
  Links to information on UK coal mining including coal mining accident databases.

- Coal Mining Records in the PRO (#35) ~ U.K.
  http://www.pro.gov.uk/leaflets/ri2142.htm

- Ghosts of the Klondike Gold Rush
  http://www.gold-rush.org/
  Check out the "Pan for Gold Database".

- GOLD 150 - Celebrating 150 Years of Australian Gold-Rush History
  http://www.ballarat.edu.au/sovhill/gold150//sovhill.htm

- Gold Prospectors of Colorado
  http://www.gpoc.com/

- History of Coal Mining in Nova Scotia - The Louis Frost Notes 1685 to 1962
  http://eagle.uccb.ns.ca/mining/

- List of Coal-Mining Links
  http://www.coolguitars.com/coalinks.html

- Mining History Association
  http://www.lib.mtu.edu/mha/mha.htm

- Mining History Network
  http://info.ex.ac.uk/~RBurt/MinHistNet/welcome.html

- Valdez Gold Rush Centennial
  http://www.alaska.net/~vldzmuse/goldrush1.htm

  o Valdez Museum & Historical Archive - Rush Participants Database
    http://www.alaska.net/~vldzmuse/valdez.htm
    Valdez Gold Rush 1898-1899, Names Database

- West Virginia Coal Mines
  http://www.rootsweb.com/~wvcoal/

- WYMINING Mailing List
  http://www.rootsweb.com/~jfuller/gen_mail_states-wy.html
  #WYMINING
  For anyone with a genealogical interest in miners and the mining industry in Wyoming.

Railroad

- The Life of the Pullman Porter
  http://www.scsra.org/library/porter.html
  Online article by Stewart H. Holbrook.

- Railroads
  http://www.CyndisList.com/railroad.htm
  See this category on Cyndi's List for related links.

- Records of the Brotherhood of Sleeping Car Porters
  http://www.lexis-nexis.com/cispubs/guides/african_american/bscp/bscp3.htm
  Description of the microfilmed holdings of the Chicago Historical Society and the Newberry Library.

Miscellaneous

- The Brewery History Society
  http://www.breworld.co.uk/organisations/bhs.html
  Dedicated to the promotion of research into the history of the brewing industry in the British Isles.

- Brickmakers Index
  http://ourworld.compuserve.com/homepages/david_cufley/Brkindx.htm
  Index of brickfield workers and owners gathered from census, local histories and directories in England, mainly from southeast England.

- Canals, Rivers & Waterways
  http://www.CyndisList.com/canals.htm
  See this category on Cyndi's List for related links.

- The Circus, Theatre & Music Hall Families Page
  http://www.users.globalnet.co.uk/~paulln/circus.htm

- The Drapers Company of London
  http://www.combs-families.org/~combs/records/en-drapers-hist.htm
  Its history, function and usefulness to genealogical researchers.

- Dressmakers in Brooklyn 1895
  http://www.rootsweb.com/~nygglshp/Brooklyn-Dressmakers.html
  Lain's Brooklyn & LI Business Directory of 1895.

- The Goldsmiths Company
  http://www.thegoldsmiths.co.uk/
  One of the twelve great livery companies of the City of London.

  o The Library of the Goldsmiths' Company
    http://www.thegoldsmiths.co.uk/Library/TheLibrary.htm
    The collection of archives dates from the 14th century.

- History of Guernsey Butchers ~ Channel Islands
  http://freespace.virgin.net/sg.foote/butchershome.htm
  Was your ancestor a butcher in Guernsey in the late 18th / early 19th Century?

- Index to "Paupers in Workhouses 1861" (10% sample)
  http://www.genuki.org.uk/big/eng/Paupers/
  This lists adult paupers in workhouses in England and Wales.

- Internet Movie Database
  http://us.imdb.com/search/
  Online searchable database including a cast and crew name search for people working in the film industry as early as 1890. Provides basic biographical details.

- Is That a Postmaster in Your Family Tree?
  http://www.ancestry.com/columns/george/02-06-98.htm
  From "Along Those Lines..." by George G. Morgan.

- Law Enforcement Memorial Links
  http://www.policememorial.com/memoriallinks.htm
  Links to many sites regarding law enforcement officials who died in the line of duty. Some have historic lists of names.

- The Mercer's Company Website
  http://www.mercers.co.uk/mainsite/pages/default.html
  The premier livery company of the City of London.

  o The Mercer's Company Archives
    http://www.mercers.co.uk/mainsite/pages/c_archives.html
    Hold the historic records of the Mercers' Company from 1348 to the present.

- Mountain Men and the Fur Trade
  http://www.xmission.com/~drudy/amm.html
  Sources of the History of the Fur Trade in the Rocky Mountain West.

- My Ancestor was a Clergyman of the Church of England
  http://www.lambethpalacelibrary.org/holdings/Guides/clergyman.html
  Online research guide from the Lambeth Palace Library.

- North Dakota Morticians
  http://www.rootsweb.com/~ndpembin/funeral.txt
  Lists over 100 morticians in North Dakota.

- Occupations in the Pottery Industry in Stafford, England
  http://www.rootsweb.com/~engsts/potters1.html

- Our Firemen - A History of the New York Fire Departments
  http://members.aol.com/dcbreton2/FDNY/FDNY_Notes.html
  Includes an every-name index.

- Postmasters & Post Offices of Texas, 1846-1930, by Jim Wheat
  http://www.rootsweb.com/~txpost/postmasters.html
  Listings of all postmasters in Texas, 1846-1930, with dates of appointment; listings of all post offices in Texas, 1846-1930, with dates of establishment and discontinuance.

- Post Office Records
  http://www.nara.gov/genealogy/postal.html
  From the National Archives and Records Administration.

- Public Record Office - Finding Aids - A-Z Index of All Leaflets ~ U.K.
  http://www.pro.gov.uk/leaflets/riindex.htm

  o Apprenticeship Records as Sources for Genealogy (#44)
    http://www.pro.gov.uk/leaflets/ri044.htm

  o Civilian Nurses and Nursing Services (#79)
    http://www.pro.gov.uk/leaflets/ri2186.htm

  o Coal Mining Records in the PRO (#35)
    http://www.pro.gov.uk/leaflets/ri2142.htm

  o Dockyard Employees: Documents (#15)
    http://www.pro.gov.uk/leaflets/ri015.htm

  o Metropolitan Police Records of Service (#53)
    http://www.pro.gov.uk/leaflets/ri053.htm

  o Records of Attorneys and Solicitors (#36)
    http://www.pro.gov.uk/leaflets/ri2143.htm

  o Records of the Ministry of Labour (#102)
    http://www.pro.gov.uk/leaflets/ri2266.htm

  o Records of the Registrar General of Shipping and Seamen (#5)
    http://www.pro.gov.uk/leaflets/ri005.htm

  o Records of the Royal Irish Constabulary (#11)
    http://www.pro.gov.uk/leaflets/ri011.htm

- Researching Immigrant Working Women: Case Studies of Irish Maids
  http://www.audiotapes.com/product.asp?ProductCode='DEN98F157'
  Presentation by Marie E. Daly, available for sale on audio tape.

- The Royal Bank of Scotland Memory Bank ~ U.K.
  http://www.natwestgroup.com/aboutus/memorybank/

  o Research Room: Archive Guide
    http://www.rbs.co.uk/about_us/memorybank/research_room/Study/default.htm

- Schoolmarms on the Frontier
  http://www.ancestry.com/columns/myra/Shaking_Family_Tree06-04-98.htm
  From Shaking Your Family Tree by Myra Vanderpool Gormley, C.G.

- The Society of Brushmakers' Descendants ~ Essex, England
  http://www.brushmakers.com/

- The Steam Engine Makers Database
  http://www.geog.qmw.ac.uk/lifeline/sem_db/sem_db_home.html

- The Telegrapher Web Page
  http://www.mindspring.com/~tjepsen/Teleg.html
  Research resources for the history of telegraphy and the work of women in the telegraph industry.

- Transcript of the Entry of "Professions and Trades" for Grinton in Baine's Directory of 1823 ~ England
  http://www.genuki.org.uk/big/eng/YKS/NRY/Grinton/Grinton23.html

- Western Union Collection
  http://www.si.edu/lemelson/dig/westernunion.html
  Inventory & description of the Western Union Telegraph Company Collection(1848-1963) held at the National Museum of American History.

- What Is A Cordwainer And What Is Their Background?
  http://www.thehcc.org/backgrnd.htm

- The Worshipful Company of Clockmakers
  http://www.clockmakers.org/
  One of the livery companies of the City of London.

o **The Library and Collection of the Worshipful Company of Clockmakers**
http://www.clockmakers.org/link2.htm
The Clockmakers' Library was founded in 1813. It holds the ancient manuscript records of the Company and clockmaker's workbooks and related documents.

- **The Worshipful Company of Upholders**
http://www.upholders.co.uk/pageindex.htm
One of the ancient livery companies of the City of London founded in 1360. Upholder is an archaic word for an upholsterer.

o **The Archives of the Worshipful Company of Upholders**
http://www.upholders.co.uk/archives.htm
Includes some scanned images of original records and contact information regarding Company members.

ODDS & ENDS
Interesting & Unusual Genealogy Sites That Don't Fit in Other Categories
http://www.cyndislist.com/odds.htm

Category Index:
◆ Genealogy Web Site Awards

◆ Stories, Tall Tales & Legends

◆ This & That

◆ Genealogy Web Site Awards

- 1998 Genealogical Inspirational Award
  http://home.earthlink.net/~howardorjeff/award3.htm

- The Ancestral Quest Award
  http://freepages.genealogy.rootsweb.com/~geneal/quest.html
  #Award

- Ancestry Connections Genealogy Award
  http://www.geocities.com/Heartland/Flats/4076/review
  form.html

- BaiCon Award
  http://www.geocities.com/Heartland/4714/award.html

- Charlotte's Webpage Genealogy Award of
  Excellence
  http://members.tripod.com/~rcjack/winaward.html

- Cool Site of the Month for Genealogists
  http://www.cogensoc.org/cgs/cgs-cool.htm
  From the Colorado Genealogical Society.

- DeWanna's Plant Your Family Tree Award
  http://www.geocities.com/Heartland/Hills/4693/plantree.html

- Family Chronicle - Top Ten Genealogy Websites
  Nominees
  http://www.familychronicle.com/webpicks.htm

- Gail's Genealogy Wonderland
  http://members.aol.com/gailn8058/nominees.htm

- Gathering Leaves Award
  http://www.geocities.com/Heartland/Estates/7131/gathering_
  leaves.html

- Genealogical Excellence Award
  http://www.kiva.net/~markh/award.html

- Genealogical Journeys in Time
  http://ourworld.compuserve.com/homepages/Strawn/
  topsite.htm

- Genealogy Forum Best Site Pick Award
  http://www.genealogyforum.com/gfaol/bsp.htm

- Genealogy Home Page Award of Excellence
  http://www.geocities.com/Heartland/Plains/7906/award.html

- Genealogy's Most Wanted Featured Site of the
  Month
  http://www.citynet.net/mostwanted/featured.html

- The Genie Bug Award for Genealogy Excellence
  http://www.geocities.com/Heartland/Valley/8506/award.html

- The Gierhart Family Inn's Genealogy's Helping Hand
  Award
  http://www.geocities.com/Heartland/Plains/5409/awards.html

- Gracie's World
  http://www.graciesworld.com/award.html

- Honoring Our Ancestors Award
  http://www.kichline.com/carrie/Award_page.htm

- Our Ancestry Excellence in Genealogy Award
  http://www.ourancestry.com/nominate.html

- Relatively Speaking
  http://www.geocities.com/Heartland/Meadows/1147/
  relate.htm

- Robert Bickham Family Genealogy Monthly Site
  Award
  http://www.a1webdesign.com/rebick/site.html

- Sam's Spectacular Genealogy Homepage Award
  http://homepages.rootsweb.com/~sam/specaward.html

- Sharon Herrington's Awards Page
  http://www.geocities.com/Heartland/Hills/8563/awards.htm

- Shawna's Southern Pride Genealogy Award
  http://www.concentric.net/~Shahall/git.html

- The Siggy Award
  http://www.usigs.org/registry/registry.htm
  USIGS "Access Free Records Online for Genealogy".

- Suffolk List's Award
  http://www.visualcreations.com/pers/leeann/suffolk/
  awards.html

- Tree Search Award of Excellence
  http://www.geocities.com/Heartland/Village/2706/award
  page.html

- Wood World Award of Excellence
  http://www.dlcwest.com/~mgwood/award.html

◆ Stories, Tall Tales & Legends

- Biographies
  http://www.CyndisList.com/biograph.htm
  See this category on Cyndi's List for related links.

- Excerpts from Old Newspapers
  http://www.ida.net/users/dhanco/news.htm

- Myths, Hoaxes & Scams
  http://www.CyndisList.com/myths.htm
  See this category on Cyndi's List for related links.

- Oral History & Interviews
  http://www.CyndisList.com/oral.htm
  See this category on Cyndi's List for related links.

- Serendipity.....Genealogical Discoveries with a Little Help from Above
  http://www.rootsweb.com/~genepool/serendipity/index.html
  Submit your personal story & read amazing stories from other genealogists!

- Ye Olde Wive's Tales
  http://www.ida.net/users/dhanco/tales.htm

◆ This & That

- AmeriSpeak: Expressions of Our Ancestors
  http://www.rootsweb.com/~genepool/amerispeak.htm
  A place to record those phrases that have been passed down through the generations in your family.

- The Circus, Theatre & Music Hall Families Page
  http://www.users.globalnet.co.uk/~paulln/circus.htm

- Climbing the Family Tree
  http://www.americandemographics.com/publications/ad/95_ad/9512_ad/ad845.htm
  Article in American Demographics magazine from December 1995 discussing the popularity of genealogy.

- The Correct Spelling of the Word GENEALOGY
  http://www.oz.net/~markhow/writing/spelling.htm

- Cyndi's Genealogy Home Page Construction Kit
  http://www.CyndisList.com/construc.htm

- "Dear Friend Robert Merry": Letters from Nineteenth-Century American Children
  http://members.tripod.com/~merrycoz/MUSEUM/MERY COZ.HTM
  From a collection of letters written by subscribers to Robert Merry's Museum, including an index of information gathered on many of the children who wrote the letters.

- A Genealogical Tool Kit
  http://www.cslnet.ctstateu.edu/toolkit.htm
  A complete list of the items you need to take with you when you visit cemeteries, archives, libraries, and town halls.

- Genealogy in Fiction
  http://ourworld.compuserve.com/homepages/JulieKidd/fiction.htm
  A list of books which include genealogy in the story.

- The Genealogy Merit Badge of the Boy Scouts of America
  http://www.oz.net/~markhow/BSA/meritbdg.htm
  This is where it all started for my husband, Mark!.

- Genealogy Business Takes Root
  http://www.maritz.com/mmri/apoll/release.asp?rc=92&p=2&T=P
  Summary of a Maritz Poll from March, 1996. Reports on the popularity of genealogy.

- Generations - Find Your Roots
  http://www.sierra.com/sierrahome/familytree/webcast/
  A new, interactive multimedia Internet radio/chat program for genealogy.

- Gifts from Our Forefathers - From the Gene Pool
  http://www.rootsweb.com/~genepool/gifts.htm

- Halbert's Under Cease and Desist Order
  http://www.ngsgenealogy.org/about/content/committees/halberts.html

- International Black Sheep Society of Genealogists (IBSSG)
  http://homepages.rootsweb.com/~blksheep/
  And the associated mailing list
  http://www.rootsweb.com/~jfuller/gen_mail_general.html #BlackSheep
  For those who have a dastardly, infamous individual of public knowledge and ill-repute in their family...within 1 degree of consanguinity of their direct lines. This individual must have been pilloried in disgrace for acts of a significantly anti-social nature.

- Post Office Project 2000
  http://members.aol.com/rsmall9293/pomain.htm
  My project is to provide a web page to list and provide updates to current books on Post Offices and Postmasters.

- Sixty Percent of American Intrigued by their Family Roots
  http://www.maritz.com/mmri/apoll/release.asp?rc=195&p=2&T=P
  Summary of a Maritz Poll from May, 2000. Reports an increase in interest in genealogy.

- A Study of Genealogists & Family Historians
  http://watarts.uwaterloo.ca/~rdlamber/genstudy.htm

- Who Says We Are Not Relatives?
  http://members.aol.com/rprost/relatives.html

- Ye Olde English Sayings
  http://www.rootsweb.com/~genepool/sayings.htm

ORAL HISTORY & INTERVIEWS
http://www.cyndislist.com/oral.htm

Category Index:

- General Resource Sites
- Libraries, Archives & Museums

- Publications, Software & Supplies
- Societies & Groups

◆ General Resource Sites

- The Art of the Oral Historian
  http://www.library.ucsb.edu/speccoll/oralhlec.html

- Capturing the Past: How to Prepare & Conduct and Oral History Interview
  http://www.kbyu.org/capturingpast/

- Clio Whispers About Oral History
  http://home.earthlink.net/~raulb/Clio-2.html

- Doing Oral History
  http://www.gcah.org/oral.html
  From The General Commission on Archives and History - The United Methodist Church, Archival Leaflet Series.

- Family Legends
  http://www.main.nc.us/OBCGS/famlegend.htm

- Family Legends - Can they be trusted?
  http://www.hinet.net.au/~linswad/FamHist/legends.htm

- Family Legends, True or False. And How Do I Solve Them?
  http://fp.sedona.net/genealogy/past4.htm
  Summary of a discussion from the Sedona Genealogy Club.

- Family Tree Maker's Genealogy Site: Back Issue: Oral Histories
  http://www.familytreemaker.com/issue2.html

- Family Tree Maker's Genealogy Site: Suggested Topics and Questions for Oral Histories
  http://www.familytreemaker.com/00000030.html

- Guide for Interviewing Family Members
  ftp://ftp.cac.psu.edu/genealogy/roots-l/genealog/genealog.intrview
  Abstracted from Virginia Allee's "A Family History Questionnaire" in October 1978 Family Heritage Magazine.

- Guidelines for Doing Oral History
  http://www.cms.ccsd.k12.co.us/ss/SONY/orbeta1/orlguide.htm
  Using the American Memory, Library of Congress web site.

- H-Oralhist
  http://www2.h-net.msu.edu/~oralhist/
  A member of the H-Net, Humanities & Social Sciences On-Line initiative.

- How to Do an Interview
  http://www.myhistory.org/guidebook/interview.html
  From My History is America's History.

  ○ Before the interview
    http://www.myhistory.org/guidebook/interview/before.html

  ○ The questions
    http://www.myhistory.org/guidebook/interview/questions.html

  ○ The interview
    http://www.myhistory.org/guidebook/interview/interview.html

  ○ After the interview
    http://www.myhistory.org/guidebook/interview/after.html

  ○ The last word
    http://www.myhistory.org/guidebook/interview/last_word.html

  ○ Sample questions
    http://www.myhistory.org/guidebook/interview/sample_questions.html

  ○ Oral histories for kids
    http://www.myhistory.org/guidebook/interview/histories_kids.html

- Interview Absolutely Everyone!
  http://www.ancestry.com/columns/george/04-03-98.htm
  From "Along Those Lines..." by George Morgan.

- Journal Jar Ideas
  http://www.omnicron.com/~fluzby/sister-share/journal.htm

- Legal Issues for Oral Histories
  http://primarysources.msu.edu/curricula/intro/upsthree/howto/legal.html

- Lineages' Genealogy Site: First Steps - Interview Family Members
  http://www.lineages.com/FirstSteps/Interview.asp

- One-Minute Guide to Oral Histories
  http://library.berkeley.edu/BANC/ROHO/1minute.html
  From the University of California, Berkeley.

- Oral Histories
  http://www.everton.com/GENEALOG/GENEALOG.ORALHIST
  by Patricia Jocius, from the Everton Publishers web site.

- Oral History Interview, Questions and Topics
  http://www.jewishgen.org/infofiles/quest.txt

- Oral History Interviews, Why, How, Help with Oral Family History
  http://www.marple.com/whyoral.html

- Oral History Questions - The Gene Pool
  http://www.rootsweb.com/~genepool/oralhist.htm

- An Oral History Primer
  http://bob.ucsc.edu/library/reg-hist/ohprimer.html

- Oral History Support Materials
  http://www.mov.vic.gov.au/Hidden_Histories/classroom_materials/oral.html
  From the Museum Victoria and the Department of Education in Australia.

- Oral History Techniques - How to Organize and Conduct Oral History Interviews
  http://www.indiana.edu/~ohrc/pamph1.htm

- Oral History Techniques and Procedures
  http://www.army.mil/cmh-pg/books/oral.htm
  By Stephen E. Everett for the Center of Military History.

- PIE Interview Guide - Family Folklore Interviewing Guide and Questionnaire
  http://www.cimorelli.com/pie/library/intrview.htm

- PIE - The Art of Interviewing Relatives and Getting Answers to Your Questions
  http://www.cimorelli.com/pie/library/intr_art.htm

- Preserving Community / Cuentos del Varrio
  http://web.nmsu.edu/~publhist/ohindex.html
  An Oral History Instruction Manual.

- Preserving Family Stories
  http://www.ancestry.com/columns/myra/Shaking_Family_Tree02-19-98.htm
  From Shaking Your Family Tree by Myra Vanderpool Gormley, C.G.

- Rumors, Gossip, and Little White Lies
  HTTP://www.ancestry.com/library/view/ancmag/88.asp
  Approaching family legends with an open mind.

- Set the Record Straight!
  http://users.deltanet.com/~lrawlins/set/set.html
  "An Internet Guide on Preserving and Sharing Personal & Family Histories." Advice on oral histories, publishing your work, and finding family treasures.

- Shaking Your Family Tree: Q&As: Sorting Out Those Family Legends
  http://www.rootsweb.com/~rwguide/syft/misc/syftmg0093.htm
  By Myra Vanderpool Gormley, C.G.

- Southern Oral History Program - How To
  http://www.unc.edu/depts/sohp/info.html

- Step-by-Step Guide to Oral History
  http://www.dohistory.org/on_your_own/toolkit/oralHistory.html
  From DoHistory.

  o Form for Interview Tracking
    http://www.dohistory.org/on_your_own/toolkit/oralHistory_form.html

- The Third Degree: Tips for a Successful Interview
  http://www.ancestry.aol.com/magazine/articles/interview.htm
  From Ancestry Magazine, Jan/Feb 1998, Volume 16, Number 1 by George Thurston.

- Tips for Interviewers
  http://library.berkeley.edu/BANC/ROHO/rohotips.html
  From the University of California, Berkeley.

- Tools for Oral History
  http://www.fortlewis.edu/acad-aff/swcenter/tools.htm#Tools for Oral History:
  From the Fort Lewis College Center of Southwest Studies in Colorado.

- USU Oral History Program - How to Collect Oral Histories
  http://www.usu.edu/~oralhist/oh_howto.html
  From Utah State University.

- Virginia Folklife Program Oral History Workshop: A Basic Guide to the Concepts, Techniques and Strategies of Oral History Research
  http://minerva.acc.virginia.edu/vfh/vfp/oh2.html

- Yahoo!...Oral History
  http://dir.yahoo.com/Arts/Humanities/History/Oral_History/

◆ Libraries, Archives & Museums

- Baylor University Institute for Oral History: Oral History Workshop on the Web
  http://www.baylor.edu/~Oral_History/Workshop_welcome.html

- California State Archives - California State Government Oral Histories
  http://www.ss.ca.gov/archives/level3_ohguide1.html

- CIMS Oral History Page
  http://coombs.anu.edu.au/~cims/oralhist.html
  An extensive list of links to oral history repositories from the Centre for Immigration and Multicultural Studies, Australian National University.

- Center for Iranian Jewish Oral History
  http://www.cijoh.org/

- Ellis Island Oral History Project
  http://www.i-channel.com/features/ellis/oralhist.html

- Navy Oral History Collection
  http://hometown.aol.com/famjustin/usnoentry.html
  A Collection of Veterans and Families Stories Biographies Documents and Photographs.

- Oral History and Folklore of the Miami Valley, Ohio
  http://www.muohio.edu/~oralhxcwis/index.htmlx
  From the Miami Valley Cultural Heritage Project.

- Oral History Collections at the Reuther Library
  http://www.reuther.wayne.edu/ohistory.html
  Wayne State University, Detroit, Michigan.

- The Oral History Program, University of Alaska Fairbanks
  http://www.uaf.edu/library/oralhist/home.html
- Oral History Research Center at Indiana University
  http://www.indiana.edu/~ohrc/
- Regional Oral History Office
  http://www.lib.berkeley.edu/BANC/ROHO/
  - o Tips for Interviewers
    http://www.lib.berkeley.edu/BANC/ROHO/
  - o One-Minute Guide to Oral History
    http://www.lib.berkeley.edu/BANC/ROHO/1minute.html
- The Southern Oral History Project
  http://www.unc.edu/depts/sohp/
  - o "How To" Interview Tips
    http://www.unc.edu/depts/sohp/howto/howto.htm
  - o Interview Guidelines
    http://www.unc.edu/depts/sohp/howto/guidelin.htm
- UCLA Oral History Program
  http://www2.library.ucla.edu/libraries/special/ohp/ohp index.htm
  - o Introduction to Oral History
    http://www2.library.ucla.edu/libraries/special/ohp/ohpintro.htm
  - o Planning and Conducting an Oral History Interview
    http://www2.library.ucla.edu/libraries/special/ohp/ohpdocs.htm
    Includes sample legal agreements.
- University of Kentucky Oral History Program
  http://www.uky.edu/Libraries/Special/oral_history/
- Utah State University Oral History Program
  http://www.usu.edu/~oralhist/oh.html
  - o The Significance of Oral History
    http://www.usu.edu/~oralhist/ohsignif.html
  - o How to Collect Oral Histories
    http://www.usu.edu/~oralhist/oh_howto.html
  - o Telling Effective Life Stories
    http://www.usu.edu/~oralhist/tels.html
  - o Telling Stories from our Lives
    http://www.usu.edu/~oralhist/tsfol.html
- The Western Cape Oral History Project
  http://www.uct.ac.za/depts/history/ohp1.htm

◆ Publications, Software & Supplies

- Amazon.com Genealogy Bookstore - Oral History
  http://www.amazon.com/exec/obidos/external-search/?keyword=oral+history&tag=markcyndisgenealA/
- AudioTapes.com - Genealogical Lectures on Cassette Tapes - Interviews
  http://www.audiotapes.com/search2.asp?Search=interview
- Family Stories Video Family History
  http://members.aol.com/quickbyte/familystories.html
  Professionally produced, PBS-style documentary of a parent, grandparent, or other family member telling their life story and communicating with generations across time and space, visually and orally, in their own words.
- Yourfamily.com - Videos, Albums, and Taped Oral Histories
  http://yourfamily.com/histories.shtml

◆ Societies & Groups

- Association of Personal Historians
  http://www.personalhistorians.org/
- Canadian Oral History Association
  http://www.ncf.carleton.ca/oral-history/
- International Oral History Association
  http://www.bcn.es/tjussana/ioha/
- Michigan Oral History Association
  http://www.h-net.msu.edu/~moha/
- New England Association of Oral History
  http://www.ucc.uconn.edu/~cohadm01/neaoh.html
- Oral History Association
  http://www.baylor.edu/~OHA/
  Includes an extensive list of links to oral history repositories.
- Oral History Society
  http://www.essex.ac.uk/sociology/oralhis.htm
- Oral History Association of Dickinson College ~ Pennsylvania
  http://omega.dickinson.edu/organizations/oha/
- Southwest Oral History Association
  http://www.unm.edu/~libfunds/develop/soha.html
- Texas Oral History Association
  http://www.baylor.edu/~TOHA/

ORGANIZING YOUR RESEARCH

http://www.cyndislist.com/organize.htm

Category Index:

◆ General Resource Sites

◆ Online Charts & Forms to Print or Download

◆ Publications, Software & Supplies

◆ General Resource Sites

- Get it Together
  http://www.ancestry.com/library/view/columns/together/
  together.asp
  New each Thursday by Elizabeth Kelley Kerstens, CGRS.

  o Get it Together Archive
    http://www.ancestry.com/library/view/columns/together/d_
    p_1_archive.asp

- Ancestry.com - Organizing Data
  http://www.ancestry.com/learn/start/surveying.htm

- Beginner's Guide to Family History Research -
  Organizing Your Family Records
  http://www.arkansasresearch.com/g-organ.html
  By Desmond Walls Allen and Carolyn Earle Billingsley.

- Elements of a Research Plan
  http://www.micronet.net/users/~searcy/researchplan.htm

- Genealogy Bulletin – Descendancy Numbering
  Systems
  http://www.genealogybulletin.com/archives/HTML/
  current13.html
  By William Dollarhide.

- Genealogy Bulletin - The Henry System: Assigning
  ID Numbers to Descendants
  http://www.genealogybulletin.com/archives/HTML/
  current14.html
  By William Dollarhide.

- Genealogy Bulletin - Ahnentafels and Collaterals by
  the Numbers
  http://www.genealogybulletin.com/archives/HTML/
  current11.html
  And More on ID Numbers for Collaterals
  http://www.genealogybulletin.com/archives/HTML/
  current12.html
  By William Dollarhide.

- How Do I Keep All This Stuff Straight?
  http://www.ancestry.com/columns/george/04-24-98.htm
  From "Along Those Lines..." by George Morgan.

- Numbering Systems in Genealogy
  http://www.saintclair.org/numbers/
  By Richard A. Pence.

- Organization of Genealogical Materials
  http://www.rootsweb.com/~ote/organize.htm

- Organizing Your Family History
  http://www.micronet.net/users/~searcy/organizing.htm

- Organizing Your Genealogy Using Computers
  http://www.familysearch.org/Eng/Search/RG/frameset_rg.asp
  ?Dest=G1&Aid=&Gid=&Lid=&Sid=&Did=&Juris1=&Event=&
  Year=&Gloss=&Sub=&Tab=&Entry=&Guide=ALL_RefDoc_-
  _Organizing_with_Computers.ASP
  From FamilySearch.org.

- Organizing Your Paper Files
  http://www.familysearch.org/Eng/Search/RG/frameset_rg.asp
  ?Dest=G1&Aid=&Gid=&Lid=&Sid=&Did=&Juris1=&Event=&
  Year=&Gloss=&Sub=&Tab=&Entry=&Guide=ALL_REF_DOC_
  -_Basic_Paper_Filing.ASP
  From FamilySearch.org.

- Organizing Your Paper Files Using Binders
  (Notebooks)
  http://www.familysearch.org/Eng/Search/RG/frameset_rg.asp
  ?Dest=G1&Aid=&Gid=&Lid=&Sid=&Did=&Juris1=&Event=&
  Year=&Gloss=&Sub=&Tab=&Entry=&Guide=ALL_RefDoc_-
  _Organizing_with_Binders.ASP
  From FamilySearch.org.

- Organizing Your Paper Files Using File Folders
  http://www.familysearch.org/Eng/Search/RG/frameset_rg.asp
  ?Dest=G1&Aid=&Gid=&Lid=&Sid=&Did=&Juris1=&Event=&
  Year=&Gloss=&Sub=&Tab=&Entry=&Guide=ALL_REF_DOC_
  -_Organizing_Paper_Files.ASP
  From FamilySearch.org.

- Organizing Your Research: Research Records
  http://www.parkbooks.com/Html/res_org.html
  A research guide from Park Genealogical Books.

- Producing Quality Research Notes
  http://www.bcgcertification.org/skbld971.html
  *From the Board for Certification of Genealogists - Skill Building -
  January 1997.*

- Shaking Your Family Tree: Organizing That
  Genealogy Clutter
  http://www.uftree.com/bin/fg_auth?/GenealogyNewsstand/
  ShakingTree/Beginner/921015.html
  By Myra Vanderpool Gormley, C.G.

◆ Online Charts & Forms to Print or Download

- Ancestor Detective Freebies
  http://www.ancestordetective.com/freebies.htm
  *Free downloadable Research Calendar Template for WordPerfect
  7.0 and 8.0 and Research Calendar Template for Word 97.*

- Ancestry.com - Correspondence Record
  http://www.ancestry.com/save/charts/correcord.htm

- Ancestry.com - Research Calendar
  http://www.ancestry.com/save/charts/researchcal.htm

- Ancestry.com - Research Extract
  http://www.ancestry.com/save/charts/researchext.htm

- Ancestry.com - Source Summary
  http://www.ancestry.com/save/charts/sourcesum.htm

- Family Tree Magazine - Download Forms
  http://www.familytreemagazine.com/forms/download.html
  A variety of research forms available in self-extracting files. Forms can be opened and used with Word Perfect and Microsoft Word97 or 2000.

- Genealogy Research Associates - Research Forms
  http://www.graonline.com/forms/main.asp

  o Documentation Guidelines--General Notes
    http://www.graonline.com/forms/generalnotes.htm

  o Documentation Guidelines--Source Entries
    http://www.graonline.com/forms/sourcenotes.htm

- Lineages' First Steps - Get Organized
  http://www.lineages.com/FirstSteps/Basic.asp
  Download a free tool kit of genealogical forms.

- Research Log
  http://www.familysearch.org/Eng/Search/RG/frameset_rg.asp?Dest=G1&Aid=&Gid=&Lid=&Sid=&Did=&Juris1=&Event=&Year=&Gloss=&Sub=&Tab=&Entry=&Guide=ResLog.ASP

- Research Log
  http://www.lds.org/images/howdoibeg/Research_Log.html
  From the LDS church.

- Rory's Genealogy Pages - Research Log
  http://users.erols.com/emcrcc/Res_Log.htm

- Rory's Genealogy Pages - Resources Checklist
  http://users.erols.com/emcrcc/Resources_Checklist.htm

◆ Publications, Software & Supplies

- Amazon.com Genealogy Bookstore - Organizing
  http://www.amazon.com/exec/obidos/external-search/?keyword=genealogy+organizing&tag=markcyndisgenealA/

- AudioTapes.com - Genealogical Lectures on Cassette Tapes - Organization
  http://www.audiotapes.com/search2.asp?Search=organiz

- Bygones Home Page: Genealogical Research Note-Keeping System ~ Windows and Macintosh
  http://home.utah-inter.net/bygones/index.htm
  A freeware software program designed primarily to keep genealogical research notes on a laptop computer. However, it also has databases that genealogists without laptops may find useful.

- Clooz
  http://www.clooz.com/
  An electronic filing cabinet and database for systematically storing all of the clues to your ancestry that you have been collecting. Requires Microsoft Windows 95. Clooz contains templates for all U.S. federal censuses, 1841-1891 U.K. censuses, 1852-1901 Canadian censuses, and 1901 and 1911 Irish censuses, as well as generic templates for censuses not included, such as state censuses.

  o Clooz Mailing List
    http://www.rootsweb.com/~jfuller/gen_mail_software.html#Clooz
    For users of the Clooz genealogy utility software program.

  o Clooz Newsletter
    http://www.clooz.com/issues.htm
    Newsletter for users of the software program Clooz--the electronic filing cabinet for genealogical records. Also available by e-mail subscription; to subscribe, send an empty message to clooz-subscribe@makelist.com.

- Custodian II for Family Historians
  http://members.aol.com/pandssmith/Custodian.htm
  Custodian is not a family tree program, but a series of databases with pre-defined forms, specially designed to store genealogical information. Includes more than 80 data entry forms for most UK sources.

- Genealogy Research Organizer
  http://go.to/gro
  Program to store your genealogy data using a drop-line style chart. Holds source citations, too.

- Organizational Aids: Homemade, Commercial, Computer Generated
  http://fp.sedona.net/genealogy/past11.htm
  Summary of a discussion from the Sedona Genealogy Club.

PHOTOGRAPHS & MEMORIES
Preserving Your Family's Heirlooms, Treasures & Genealogical Research
http://www.cyndislist.com/photos.htm

Category Index:

- Lost & Found
- Photo Archives, Collections and Libraries
- Photo Restoration & Care
- Photos - Miscellaneous

- Preservation & Conservation
- Scanners & Electronic Preservation
- Scrapbooks
- Vendors

◆ Lost & Found

- Adopt-A-Photo - Penny Duncan's Photos for Distribution
  http://freepages.genealogy.rootsweb.com/~adoptaphoto/
  Many have residents of Mason and Logan Counties, Illinois.

- Ancestors' Lost & Found
  http://www.rootsweb.com/~neresour/ancestors/index.html
  Dedicated to reuniting families with the memorabilia their ancestors left behind: photos, family Bibles, etc.

- Ancestral Photos
  http://pw1.netcom.com/~cityslic/photos.htm
  Pictures found at auctions and in antique stores.

- AncesTree
  http://www.ancestree.com/
  "The Family Tree with Photographs".

- Lost Leaves Photos
  http://www.lostleavesphotos.com/pages/main.html

- Ford and Nagle
  http://users.erinet.com/31363/fordand.htm
  Historians, Genealogists, and Collectors of Antique Family Photos, Family Bibles, and Family Documents

  - Antique Family Photos - A-C
    http://users.erinet.com/31363/photos.htm
    D-G
    http://users.erinet.com/31363/photod-g.htm
    H-Q
    http://users.erinet.com/31363/photos2.htm
    R-Z
    http://users.erinet.com/31363/photo3.htm
  - Family Bibles
    http://users.erinet.com/31363/family.htm
  - Family Documents
    http://users.erinet.com/31363/docs1.htm

- Family Papers
  http://www.teleport.com/~jimren/
  A service that helps family historians locate and own original documents pertaining to their ancestors.

- Granny's Lost & Found
  http://www.geocities.com/~grannys_attic/lostfoun.html
  Lost: out of print books and films. Found: old photos, journals, documents, and letters.

- Lenore Frost's Dating Family Photos Homepage
  http://www.alphalink.com.au/~lfrost/Homepage/
  A book to help date old photographs, and a project to reunite photos and families, mostly Australian, some British.

- Old Photos Seeking New Homes - Linnie (Vanderford) Poyneer
  http://www.geocities.com/linniev2/album/index.html
  Austin, Baker, Boyce/Bayce, Bunce, Butterfield, Carr, Ford, Hall, Hart, Hobbs, Holmsberg, Keadle, Keadle, Lillie, Loske, Ludwig, Martin, Milton, Payne, Port, Pierce, Sinclair, Skinner, Swartout, Starke, Weller, Wise.

- PhotoFind Searchable Database
  http://www.everton.com/photofind/phfind.html

- Where Are Your Family Photographs?
  http://genealogyphotos.com/
  A company dedicated to reuniting people interested in their genealogy with previously unknown or lost family photographs.

- Your Past Connections, Inc.
  http://www.pastconnect.com/
  Helps you find original items from your family's past. Items such as: cards, letters, certificates, books, etc.

◆ Photo Archives, Collections and Libraries

- America's First Look into the Camera - Daugerreotype Portraits and Views 1839-1864
  http://memory.loc.gov/ammem/daghtml/daghome.html
  Prints and Photographs Division, Library of Congress.

- Chicago Imagebase
  http://www.uic.edu/depts/ahaa/imagebase/
  Find a wealth of information at this site from before the Great Fire of 1871 to the present including the Fire Insurance Maps of Chicago, Robinson Atlases of Downtown Chicago (ca. 1886), Sanborn Atlas Maps, Rand McNally's Bird's-Eye Views and Guide to Chicago (ca. 1893), Historical View Books, and much more! Browse the imagebase collection by artist/architect, building and era. Find information on Using Historical Maps and Dating Buildings by Stylistic Analysis. View contemporary aerial views (ca. 1986) and photographs 1970-1990's of Chicago.

- Civil War Family Photographs
  http://members.tripod.com/~cwphotos/

- The Daguerreian Society
  http://www.daguerre.org/
  Dedicated to the history, science, and art of the daguerreotype.

- Daguerreotypes 1842-1862
  http://lcweb2.loc.gov/ammem/daghtml/daghome.html
  From the Library of Congress, American Memory collection.

- The Francis Frith Collection.
  http://www.francisfrith.com/
  Access to 330,000 photographs depicting 7,000 British towns and villages. Taken between 1860 and 1970 by the photographers of F. Frith & Co. this archive is the foremost topographical photographic record of Britain.

- Introduction to Imaging: Issues in Constructing an Image Database
  http://www.getty.edu/gri/standard/introimages/index.html

- Lost Memory - Libraries and Archives Destroyed in the Twentieth Century
  http://www.unesco.org/webworld/mdm/administ/en/detruit.html

- National Monuments Record at the RCHME
  http://www.rchme.gov.uk/nmr.html
  UK national archive of old photographs, plans, aerial photographs.

- Photo Adventures - Museum of History and Industry ~ Seattle, Washington
  http://www.seattlehistory.org/PhotoAdventures/photo_ad.htm
  A collection of historical photographs from the Pacific Northwest and Alaska.

- Photo Antiquities
  http://www.photoantiquities.com/
  Museum of Photographic History, Images and Equipment in Pittsburgh, Pennsylvania.

  o Museum preserves history in 19th-century photography
    http://www.post-gazette.com/magazine/20000503photoant2.asp
    Article on Photo Antiquities.

- Repositories of Primary Sources
  http://www.uidaho.edu/special-collections/Other.Repositories.html
  A listing of over 3000 websites describing holdings of manuscripts, archives, rare books, historical photographs, and other primary sources for the research scholar.

- Touring Turn-of-the-Century America: Photographs from the Detroit Publishing Company, 1880-1920
  http://lcweb2.loc.gov/detroit/dethome.html
  From American Memory, Library of Congress.

◆ Photo Restoration & Care

- A-1 Digiflux Photo Restoration
  http://www.htcomp.net/tfunk/photorestoration.html
  Digital Photo Restoration for torn, scratched, water damaged, faded, abused photos. Colorize your old B&W pictures! Personalized service.

- Ab Initio Books & Vintage Image Services
  http://www.abinitiobooks.com
  Ab Initio Books is a publisher of quality family histories. We also restore old images for publication or as a photographic print.

- AudioTapes.com - Genealogical Lectures on Cassette Tapes - Photographs
  http://www.audiotapes.com/search2.asp?Search=photographs

- Care and Preservation of Photographs
  http://www.gcah.org/care.html
  From The General Commission on Archives and History - The United Methodist Church

- Care and Identification of 19th-Century Photographic Prints
  http://www.amazon.com/exec/obidos/ISBN=0879853654/markcyndisgenealA/
  A book by James M. Reilly.

- Caring for Your Family Photos
  http://www.familytreemaker.com/issue10.html
  From Family Tree Maker Online.

- Castle Photographic - Photo Restoration
  http://home.earthlink.net/~castlefoto/restore.htm

- Classy Image
  http://www.classyimage.com/
  Restoration and alteration of old & new photographs; photography, web page design & graphics design.

- Computer Imaging & Genealogy
  http://www.terraworld.net/users/r/rbrook/
  Scanning and photograph restoration services.

- Conservation of Photographs
  http://www.amazon.com/exec/obidos/ISBN=0879853522/markcyndisgenealA/
  A book by George Eaton.

- Gardner Graphics Photo Restoration
  http://www.halcyon.com/dianne/index.htm

- Guidelines For Preserving Your Photographic Heritage
  http://www.geocities.com/Heartland/6662/photopre.htm

- Horn Graphics ~ Tacoma, Washington
  http://www.horngraphics.com/
  Photograph restoration and digital imaging.

- Human Touch Restorations
  http://www.localaccess.com/DAVEH/

- Just Black & White's Tips for Preserving Your Photographs and Documents
  http://www.maine.com/photos/tip.htm

- Nilsson Imaging - Photo Restoration
  http://www.nilsson.olm.net/PhotoRes/index.htm
  Restore your photographs to their original splendor. Don't let the adverse effects of time rob you of your precious memories.

- Northern States Conservation Center: Care by Type - Photographs
  http://www.collectioncare.org/cci/ccicph.html

- An Ounce of Preservation: A Guide to the Care of Papers and Photographs
  http://www.amazon.com/exec/obidos/ISBN=1568250215/markcyndisgenealA/
  A book by Craig A. Tuttle.

- Photographic Storage Tips
  http://www.lib.virginia.edu/acqpres/pres/photostore.html
  From the University of Virginia Library's Preservation Department.

- PhotoGraphics Copy & Restoration Service
  http://www.fixpix.com/
  Restoration of damaged and faded photos and documents. Photos and documents to CD and PowerPoint slides.

- Photographs: General Care and Tips
  http://www.lib.virginia.edu/acqpres/pres/phototip.html
  From the University of Virginia Library's Preservation Department.

- Photo Restoration by The Photo Medic
  http://www.photo-medic.com
  Photo-Medic repairs and restores old and damaged photos. If an old photo has faded or darkened over the decades, Photo-Medic can enhance the image to better see the people long since gone.

- PhotoRevival
  http://www.photorevival.com/

- Photos Restored by SCL - Shawnee Color Lab
  http://www.shawneecolorlab.com
  "Photos Torn, Scratched, or Faded? We can restore them for you...SATISFACTION GUARANTEED!"

- Preserving Family Albums
  http://www.eastman.org/4_educ/4_prsrv.html
  From the George Eastman House.

- Protecting Family Memories from Time
  http://www.genealogy.com/10_prsrv.html

- Re-Image
  http://www.re-image.com/
  Photographic restoration.

- Restoring Damaged Photographs
  http://www.genealogy.com/10_restr.html

- Roots 'n Shoots
  http://www.wwonline.com/~pbatek/
  Photo restoration.

- Salvaging a Faded Original
  http://www.hsdesign.com/scanning/salvaging/salvaging.html

- VINTAGE-PHOTOS Mailing List
  http://www.rootsweb.com/~jfuller/gen_mail_general.html#VINTAGE-PHOTOS
  For the discussion and sharing of information regarding vintage photos including, but not restricted to, proper storage, preservation, restoration, ageing and dating, restoration software, photo types and materials used, restoration assistance, and scanning options.

◆ Photos - Miscellaneous

- 19th Century Photography for Genealogists
  http://www.genealogy.org/~ajmorris/photo/photo.htm
  by A.J. Morris.

  - Dating 19th Century Card Mounted Portraits
    http://www.genealogy.org/~ajmorris/photo/dates.htm

  - History of Photography - A Thumbnail Sketch
    http://www.genealogy.org/~ajmorris/photo/history.htm

  - Photography and Genealogy
    http://www.genealogy.org/~ajmorris/photo/pg.htm

  - Types of Photographs
    http://www.genealogy.org/~ajmorris/photo/types.htm

- The American Tintype
  http://www.amazon.com/exec/obidos/ISBN=0814208061/markcyndisgenealA/
  A book by Floyd Rinhart.

- American Victorian Costume in Early Photographs
  http://www.amazon.com/exec/obidos/ISBN=0486265331/markcyndisgenealA/
  A book by Priscilla Harris Dalrymple.

- Ancestors: Family Records- Photographs
  http://www.kbyu.org/ancestors/records/family/intro2.html
  From the second television series.

  - Ancestors: Family Records- Photographs Guide
    http://www.kbyu.org/ancestors/records/family/table2.html

- Collector's Guide to Early Photographs
  http://www.amazon.com/exec/obidos/ISBN=0873417208/markcyndisgenealA/
  A book by O. Henry Mace.

- Dressed for the Photographer: Ordinary Americans and Fashion, 1840-1900
  http://www.amazon.com/exec/obidos/ISBN=0873385128/markcyndisgenealA/
  A book by Joan L. Severa.

- Everything You Ever Wanted to Know About Your Family Photographs But Didn't Know Who To Ask
  http://genealogy.about.com/hobbies/genealogy/library/authors/ucmishkin1a.htm
  From the About.com genealogy section.

- Guide to Victorian Studio Photographs
  http://www.bbc.co.uk/history/programmes/blood/victor_photo_1.shtml
  Information on dating photographs from the BBC's "Bloodties" series.

- Identifying Family Photographs
  http://www.ancestry.com/columns/george/08-07-98.htm
  From "Along Those Lines..." by George Morgan.

- International Guide to Nineteenth Century Photographers and Their Works: Based on Catalogues of Auction Houses and Dealers
  http://www.amazon.com/exec/obidos/ISBN=0816189382/markcyndisgenealA/
  A book by Gary Edwards.

- Ohio Photographers 1839-1900
  http://www.amazon.com/exec/obidos/ISBN=1887694072/
  markcyndisgenealA/
  A book by Diane Vanskiver Gagel.

- Photographic Biography: A Guide to Research
  http://wally.rit.edu/pubs/guides/photobio.html
  Bibliography for researching historic photographers.

- Photographs of the Villages of Poland Project
  http://www.bright.net/~dunn/

- Photography as a Tool in Genealogy
  http://freepages.genealogy.rootsweb.com/~fgriffin/photos.txt
  An article w/definitions & descriptions of types of photographs.

- Uncovering Your Ancestry Through Family
  Photographs
  http://www.amazon.com/exec/obidos/ISBN=1558705279/
  markcyndisgenealA/
  A book by Maureen A. Taylor.

- The UnWritten: Saving Your Photo Stories For The
  Future
  http://library.thinkquest.org/C001313/
  Working with one photo at a time, this quest will show you how to research, write, and save your photo-stories.

- Using Photos in Your Research
  http://www.genealogy.com/10_phtus.html

- Victorian and Edwardian Fashion: A Photographic
  Survey
  http://www.amazon.com/exec/obidos/ISBN=0486242056/
  markcyndisgenealA/
  A book by Alison Gernsheim.

◆ Preservation & Conservation

- AIC Caring for Your Treasures
  http://aic.stanford.edu/treasure/
  From the American Institute for Conservation of Historic & Artistic Works.

- Amazon.com Genealogy Bookstore - Photographic
  Preservation
  http://www.amazon.com/exec/obidos/external-search/?
  keyword=photograph+preservation&tag=markcyndisgenealA/

- Ancestors: Records at Risk- Safe Storage Places
  http://www.kbyu.org/ancestors/records/risk/extra.html#safe
  From the second television series.

- Archival Mist
  http://www.ptlp.com/a_index.html
  A non-aerosol spray product that neutralizes the acids in paper.

- Archival Products Newsletter
  http://www.archival.com/newsletter.html

  o Helpful Tips For Preserving Your Precious
    Documents And Memorabilia
    http://www.archival.com/NA13.html
    Tips on Creating an Archival Scrapbook or Photo Album by Nancy Kraft for the Iowa Conservation and Preservation Consortium.

  o Technical Tips - Care of Books, Documents and
    Photographs
    http://www.archival.com/NA16.html

- ASLAPR -- Archives Division - Preserving Personal
  Papers and Photographs
  http://www.dlapr.lib.az.us/archives/preserve.htm
  From the Arizona State Library, Archives and Public Records.

- British Association of Paper Historians
  http://www.baph.freeserve.co.uk/

- Caring for Your Artifacts: Preservation Fact Sheets
  http://www.hfmgv.org/histories/cis/pfs.html

- Clarke Historical Library Preservation - Preserving
  Memories: Caring for Your Heritage
  http://www.lib.cmich.edu/clarke/pres.htm
  Useful information about preserving family keepsakes including photographs, birth certificates, old newspaper articles etc.

- Conservation By Design Limited
  http://www.conservation-by-design.co.uk/
  United Kingdom-based vendor which provides materials and equipment for conservation and preservation.

- Conservation For Your Private Collections: Notes for
  the Household Conservator
  http://www.slv.vic.gov.au/slv/conservation/conserve.htm

- CoOL - Conservation OnLine - Resources for
  Conservation Professionals
  http://palimpsest.stanford.edu/

- Document and Photo Preservation FAQ
  http://genweb.net/~gen-cds/faq.html

- Don't Throw It Away! - Documenting and Preserving
  Organizational History
  http://www.uic.edu/UI-Service/programs/UIC248.html

- How to Preserve Genealogical Records Entrusted to
  You
  http://www.sierra.com/sierrahome/familytree/hqarticles/
  preserve/
  Online article by Dewayne J. Lenner which explains common threats to your own genealogical records and what you can do to minimize them.

- How To Save Your Stuff From a Disaster
  http://home.earthlink.net/~artdoc/
  A book by Fine Art Conservator Scott M. Haskins with complete instructions on how to protect and save your family history, heirlooms and collectables.

- The Library of Congress - Preservation
  http://lcweb.loc.gov/preserv/

  o Collections Care and Conservation
    http://lcweb.loc.gov/preserv/pubscare.html

  o Handouts from the 2nd Annual Preservation
    Awareness Workshop
    http://lcweb.loc.gov/preserv/aware2.html

o How to Donate Published Genealogies to the Library of Congress
http://lcweb.loc.gov/rr/genealogy/gifts.html

o Library of Congress Frequently Asked Questions: Preservation
http://lcweb.loc.gov/preserv/presfaq.html

● Memory of the World: A Guide to Standards, Recommended Practices and Reference Literature Related to the Preservation of Documents of All Kinds
http://www.unesco.org/webworld/mdm/administ/en/guide/guidetoc.htm

● National Archives and Records Administration: Archives and Preservation Resources
http://www.nara.gov/arch/

● NCPTT: National Center for Preservation Technology and Training
http://www.ncptt.nps.gov/pir/
A searchable database of Internet resources for heritage conservation, historic preservation and archaeology.

● Northeast Document Conservation Center
http://www.nedcc.org/

o Northeast Document Conservation Center - NEDCC Technical Leaflets
http://www.nedcc.org/leaf.htm

● Northern States Conservation Center: Collection Care
http://www.collectioncare.org/cci/cci.html

o Northern States Conservation Center: Care by Type
http://www.collectioncare.org/cci/ccic.html

● Archives
http://www.collectioncare.org/cci/ccica.html

● Books
http://www.collectioncare.org/cci/ccicboo.html

● Electronic Data
http://www.collectioncare.org/cci/ccice.html

● Newspapers
http://www.collectioncare.org/cci/ccicne.html

● Paper
http://www.collectioncare.org/cci/ccicpa.html

● Photographs
http://www.collectioncare.org/cci/ccicph.html

● Sound Recordings
http://www.collectioncare.org/cci/ccicso.html

● Textiles
http://www.collectioncare.org/cci/ccict.html

● Preservation Equipment, Ltd.
http://www.preservationequipment.com/
United Kingdom-based vendor which provides materials and equipment for conservation and preservation.

● Preservation Tips
http://www.lib.virginia.edu/acqpres/pres/tips.html
From the University of Virginia Library's Preservation Department.

● Preserving Personal Papers and Photographs: General Guidelines
http://www.lib.az.us/archives/preserve.htm
From the Arizona State Archives.

● Preserving Photographs for Photographers and Family Historians
http://members.aol.com/ARKivist/photos.htm
Learn to build a lasting family photo heritage through a low cost, information packed, four-week e-mail format class.

● Preserving Your Research
http://www.genealogy.com/67_donna.html

● Public Record Office - Preservation
http://www.pro.gov.uk/preservation/default.htm

o An Introduction to 19th and Early 20th Century Photographic Processes
http://www.pro.gov.uk/preservation/photos.htm

o An Introduction to English Paper
http://www.pro.gov.uk/preservation/paper.htm

o An Introduction to Parchment
http://www.pro.gov.uk/preservation/parchment.htm

● Saving Your Family Treasures
http://www.myhistory.org/saving/index.html
From My History Is America's History.

o Simple steps to preserving your treasures
http://www.myhistory.org/saving/simple_steps.html

o Good chemistry
http://www.myhistory.org/saving/good_chemistry.html

o Books
http://www.myhistory.org/saving/books.html

o Ceramics, glass, and stone
http://www.myhistory.org/saving/ceramics.html

o Fabrics
http://www.myhistory.org/saving/fabrics.html

o Precious paper
http://www.myhistory.org/saving/precious_paper.html

o Furniture
http://www.myhistory.org/saving/furniture.html

o Paintings
http://www.myhistory.org/saving/paintings.html

o Photographs and slides
http://www.myhistory.org/saving/photographs.html

o Scrapbooks and albums
http://www.myhistory.org/saving/scrapbooks.html

o Silver and other metals
http://www.myhistory.org/saving/silver.html

o Leather and other organic materials
http://www.myhistory.org/saving/leather.html

o Videotapes and audiotapes
http://www.myhistory.org/saving/video.html

- o Matting, mounting, and framing
  http://www.myhistory.org/saving/matting.html
- o For more information
  http://www.myhistory.org/saving/more_info.html
- A Simple Book Repair Manual
  http://www.dartmouth.edu/~preserve/tofc.html
- Tips for the Care of Water-Damaged Family Heirlooms and Other Valuables
  http://aic.stanford.edu/disaster/tentip.html
- Tips for the Care of Water-Damaged Family Heirlooms and Other Valuables
  http://americanhistory.si.edu/archives/a-3.htm
  From the Archives Center of the National Museum of American History.

◆ Scanners & Electronic Preservation

- Amazon.com Genealogy Bookstore - Electronic Scanning
  http://www.amazon.com/exec/obidos/redirect?tag=markcyndisgeneal&path=ts/browse-books/4159
- The Complete Guide to Scanning
  http://www.ulead.com/new/scanner.htm
- CompuDimension
  http://www.ao.net/~compudimension/
  Scanning services.
- Computer Imaging & Genealogy
  http://www.terraworld.net/users/r/rbrook/
  Scanning and photograph restoration services.
- Dennis Transfer to CD-ROM
  http://members.tripod.com/~crosley1/
  Specializing in transferring old 35mm film and VCR tapes to CD-ROMs.
- Digital Treasures
  http://www.digitaltreasures.com/
  Memories CDs and home film to video transfers.
- Digitizing Your Research - Bit by Bit
  http://www.oz.net/~markhow/writing/digit.htm
  By Mark Howells.
- Family History Video
  http://www.familyhistoryvideo.com/
  A service which uses old photographs, slides, and home movies to produce video documentary of your family.
- Family Tree Digital Video
  http://familytreevideo.com/
  Custom Producing Family Histories into Heartwarming Music Videos, CD or DVD.
- A Few Scanning Tips: Scanner Basics 101
  http://www.scantips.com/
- Horn Graphics ~ Tacoma, Washington
  http://www.horngraphics.com/
  Photograph restoration and digital imaging.

- Memorial Video Tributes
  http://www.mlvp.com/memory7.htm
  Our Video Production Company produces Video Memorializations or Memorial Tributes on Video for the clients of Funeral Homes and individuals. We use the families Photos, Slides, Film, Video, and other memorabilia. We transfer these items to video and produce a video tape with music, that the family will value forever.
- Northern States Conservation Center: Care by Type - Electronic Data
  http://www.collectioncare.org/cci/ccice.html
- PixScan
  http://pixscan.itool.com
  PixScan will scan photos, slides and 35mm negatives for a very modest fee.
- Plum Video Productions
  http://www.plumvideo.com/
  Family History Video Album. Transfer photos, slides, old movies into a beautifully produced video program with titles, music and special effects. Also on DVD or CD.
- The Scanning FAQ
  http://www.infomedia.net/scan/
- Sullivan's Scanning Tips Online
  http://www.hsdesign.com/scanning/tipswelcome.html
- Family History Video Photo Albums
  http://memorialvideos.com/memorialvideos/familyhis.html
  The Story of Your Lineage Preserved Forever on Video Tape.

◆ Scrapbooks

- Amazon.com Genealogy Bookstore - Scrapbooking
  http://www.amazon.com/exec/obidos/external-search/?keyword=scrapbook&tag=markcyndisgenealA/
- Crazy for Scrappin'
  http://alysta.com/scrapbooking/
- Creative Photo Albums Deluxe
  http://www.dogbyte.com/products/cpad.htm
  Scrapbooking software.
- Fiskars Photo Memories Shop
  http://www.crafts.fiskars.com/memories/
  Supplies for photo enhancement, preservation, and scrapbooking.
- Jangle.com
  http://www.jangle.com/
  For scrapbookers, stampers & crafters.
- Memory Makers Magazine
  http://www.memorymakersmagazine.com/
- Scrapbooking.com
  http://scrapbooking.com/
  A monthly scrapbooking magazine.
- The Scrapbooking Library
  http://articles.scrapbooking.com/
- Scraplink.com
  http://www.scraplink.com/

- Using Technology to Frame the Past - Electronic Scrapbooking
  http://www.oz.net/~markhow/writing/scrap.htm
  By Mark Howells.

◆ Vendors

- Antiquarian Books & Bindery ~ Atlanta, Georgia
  http://205.206.160.250/home/kaolink/
  Specializing in Bible restoration. Also a selection of rare books for sale.

- The Book Craftsman
  http://www.bookcraftsman.com/
  Restoration of Books, Custom binding.

- Creative Memories
  http://www.creative-memories.com/index.asp

- Custom Family Trees & Charts by Olsongraphics
  http://www.olsonetc.com/

- European Focus
  http://www.eurofocus.com/
  Photographic portfolios of ancestral towns in Europe created for Genealogy enthusiasts in Belgium, Denmark, Eastern Europe, England, France, Germany, Great Britain, Italy, Netherlands, Norway, Poland, Sweden, Switzerland and more.

- Family History Network
  http://www.familyhistorynetwork.com/
  We help families create scrapbooks of photos, souvenirs, and stories. We consult by phone and e-mail, and provide scanning, custom design, and production services.

- Family Photo Album for Windows
  http://www.cf-software.com/fpa.htm

- Family Trees, Family History and Genealogy
  http://dspace.dial.pipex.com/georgethomson/CALLGEN.HTM
  Charts by a professional calligrapher.

- Frontier Press Bookstore - Photography and Genealogy
  http://www.frontierpress.com/frontier.cgi?category=photo

- Frontier Press Bookstore - Preservation
  http://www.frontierpress.com/frontier.cgi?category=preserv

- GeneagraphX Wall Charts
  http://ipxnet.com/home/perry/
  Photo preservation, CD-ROMs, etc.

- Genealogy Unlimited, Inc. - Archival Supplies
  http://www.itsnet.com/~genun/archival.html

- geneamedia
  http://homepage.tinet.ie/~geneamedia/
  Photography and film services for genealogists with Irish roots.

- The Memorabilia Corner
  http://members.aol.com/TMCorner/index.html
  Forms, flags, maps, software, CDs, tapes, microfilm & microfiche, books, periodicals, photographic conservation & archival materials.

- Native Soil
  http://www.nativesoil.com/
  Point to point marketing of historical documents with special emphasis on property deeds.

- Novelties
  http://www.CyndisList.com/novelty.htm
  See this category on Cyndi's List for related links.

- Olsongraphics Custom Genealogy Family Trees
  http://www.olsonetc.com/

- Petersen Reproductions
  http://www.PetersenPrints.com/
  Reproductions of antique prints and family tree charts.

- PhotoBritain - Photos of Your Ancestors Past
  http://www.photobritain.ndirect.co.uk/
  A service to provide photographs of your British ancestors' past life. You provide the details of your ancestors' place of work, workplace or church and PhotoBritain can provide you with a photographic record to treasure.

- Plum Video Productions
  http://www.plumvideo.com/
  All sorts of video products, film transfers, slides, photos, etc. Including a Family History Video Album.

- PhotoWorks.com
  http://www.filmworks.com/main.asp
  Digital image processing - download your pictures from the Internet!

- Storytellers
  http://www.storytellers.net/
  Publishers of books & CDs to preserve your family stories.

- Supplies, Charts, Forms, Etc.
  http://www.CyndisList.com/supplies.htm
  See this category on Cyndi's List for related links.

- Suppliers - Sources of Conservation Supplies
  http://palimpsest.stanford.edu/bytopic/suppliers/

- Ye Olde Genealogy Charts, Ltd.
  http://www.webcom.com/charts/

POLAND / POLSKA
http://www.cyndislist.com/poland.htm

Category Index:

- General Resource Sites
- History & Culture
- Language, Handwriting & Script
- Libraries, Archives & Museums
- Locality Specific
- Mailing Lists, Newsgroups & Chat
- Maps, Gazetteers & Geographical Information
- Military
- People & Families

- Professional Researchers, Volunteers & Other Research Services
- Publications, Software & Supplies
- Queries, Message Boards & Surname Lists
- Records: Census, Cemeteries, Land, Obituaries, Personal, Taxes and Vital
- Religion & Churches
- Societies & Groups

◆ General Resource Sites

- Archiwum G³ówne Akt Dawnych w Warszawie - Genealogia / Roots in Eastern Poland
  http://members.nbci.com/agadadm/gene.html

- Bibliography of Polish Genealogy and Heraldry
  http://hum.amu.edu.pl/~rafalp/GEN/bibl-eng.html

- Federation of East European Family History Societies - FEEFHS
  http://feefhs.org/

- Galicia - (Galizien) Cross-Index ~ FEEFHS
  http://feefhs.org/gal/indexgal.html

- Genealogy & Poland - A Guide
  http://www.polishroots.com/genpoland/index.htm
  Online beginner's guide to Polish genealogical research.

- German-Prussian Genealogy Links
  http://www.geocities.com/SiliconValley/Haven/1538/germanpg.html

- Institute for Historical Family Research
  http://ihff.nwy.at/index.htm/
  Austria, Czech & Slovak Republics, Hungary, Slovenian Republic, Croatia, Galicia & Bukovina.

- Internet Genealogy - VU University Project Page
  http://www.geocities.com/SiliconValley/Haven/1538/index2.html
  Many helpful sites for Polish, Irish, German, German-Prussian, German-Russian, & Prussian backgrounds.

- Jewish Records Indexing - Poland
  http://www.jewishgen.org/jri-pl/

- KAJMORIAL - Kaj Malachowski's Polish Web Armorial
  http://www.geocities.com/Heartland/Plains/2739/herbarz.html
  Links to other web pages that contain Polish heraldry and coats-of-arms for Polish families.

- Naming Customs found in Poland
  http://rootsweb.com/~polwgw/naming.html

- The Order of the Virtuti Militari and its Cavaliers 1792-1992
  http://www.wwdir.com/order/
  This book has 26,506 names of persons and military organizations. It is presented in English and Polish.

- PolandGenWeb
  http://www.rootsweb.com/~polwgw/polandgen.html
  Part of the WorldGenWeb project.

- The Polish Genealogy Home Page
  http://hum.amu.edu.pl/~rafalp/GEN/plgenhp.htm

- Polish Genealogy Links
  http://www.geocities.com/SiliconValley/Haven/1538/Polishpg.html

- The Polish Genealogy Project
  http://polishproject.hypermart.net
  A comprehensive Polish genealogical research site.

- Polish Listings Cross Index - from FEEFHS
  http://feefhs.org/pol/indexpol.html

- Polish Research - Sites to Assist You in Your Polish Research
  http://maxpages.com/poland/Polish_Research

- PolishRoots: The Polish Genealogy Source
  http://www.polishroots.org/

- The Pomeranian Page
  http://www.execpc.com/~kap/pommern1.html

- Prussian Genealogy Links
  http://www.geocities.com/SiliconValley/Haven/1538/prussia.html

- Resources for Sepharadic Genealogy
  http://www.geocities.com/Heartland/Valley/2177/resource.htm
  Sephardic genealogical research begins with the search for your ancestor's country of origin. It could be almost any country where Sephardim lived - Bulgaria, Curacao, Gibraltar, Morocco, Greece, Romania, Tunisia, Turkey, Yugoslavia, any Middle Eastern country, even Germany, Holland, Italy or Malta. Small numbers of Sephardim even lived in Poland and Russia and had names like Levine, Rangel and Calahora.

- Tracing Your Roots In Poland - by Leonard Markowitz
  http://www.jewishgen.org/infofiles/pl-trav.txt

- Yahoo!...Poland...Genealogy
  http://dir.yahoo.com/Regional/Countries/Poland/Arts_and_Humanities/Humanities/History/Genealogy/

◆ History & Culture

- History of Europe, Slavic States
  http://www.worldroots.com/brigitte/royal/royal4.htm
  Historic and genealogical information about royal and nobility family lines.

- The History of Poland
  http://www.kasprzyk.demon.co.uk/www/HistoryPolska.html

- Photographs of the Villages of Poland Project
  http://www.bright.net/~dunn/

- StudyWeb: History: Country History Index: Europe Index: Poland
  http://www.studyweb.com/links/152.html

◆ Language, Handwriting & Script

- Lacinskie nazwy zawodow = Latin names of occupations
  http://hum.amu.edu.pl/~rafalp/GEN/zawody.htm
  Latin to Polish translations.

- PolishExpress, Inc. Family History Research Service in Polish Archives
  http://www.polishexpress.com/
  Devoted to finding, copying, and translating family history documents from Polish archives.

- Polish Genealogical Word List
  http://www.familysearch.org/Eng/Search/RG/frameset_rg.asp?Dest=G1&Aid=&Gid=&Lid=&Sid=&Did=&Juris1=&Event=&Year=&Gloss=&Sub=&Tab=&Entry=&Guide=WLPolish.ASP

- Polish Letter-Writing Guide
  http://www.familysearch.org/Eng/Search/RG/frameset_rg.asp?Dest=G1&Aid=&Gid=&Lid=&Sid=&Did=&Juris1=&Event=&Year=&Gloss=&Sub=&Tab=&Entry=&Guide=LWGPolish.ASP
  From FamilySearch.org.

- Translation Guide to Nineteenth Century Polish Language Civil Registration Documents (Birth, Marriage & Death Records)
  http://www.amazon.com/exec/obidos/ISBN=0961351217/markcyndisgenealA/
  A book by the Jewish Genealogical Society.

- Translation Service only for genealogy related material
  http://www.genealogy.net/gene/misc/translation.html
  Volunteer translators can provide you with translations between Czech, English, Dutch, French, German, & Polish. This service is provided via e-mail. Exact request syntax and length rules must be followed in order to expedite processing.

- Translation Services - PolishLessons-L
  http://www.toledolink.com/pl/translations.html
  A free genealogical translation service (maintained and coordinated by Arthur Teschler at the University of Giessen in Germany).

◆ Libraries, Archives & Museums

- Archidiecezja Pozna–ska
  http://www.archpoznan.org.pl/default.htm
  The Catholic Archdiocese of Poznan Poland has significant information for genealogists. Although most of it is in Polish, it is easy to make out some parts of it. Under "Archiwum Archidiecezjalno" find the address, phone and email for the Archdiocesan Archives which lists all the Catholic churches for which it has baptism, marriage and death records with years included. At bottom of the Archives Homepage find a British map for an English version. Under "Dekanatow i parafii A.P." find a map of the Archdiocese divided into deaconates with the names of all the present Catholic churches listed by the towns where they are located.

- Archiwa Panstwowe / State Archives
  http://ciuw.warman.net.pl/alf/archiwa/index.eng.html

- Archiwum Archidiecezjalne w Poznaniu / Archdiocesan Archive in Poznan
  http://www.wsdsc.poznan.pl/arch/

- The Archives of Maryland Polonia
  http://www.ubalt.edu/archives/amp/introduction.html
  Holdings in the Archives of the University of Baltimore. The Archives of Maryland Polonia was founded in 1982 to preserve, document and make available to reseachers the history of Polish immigrants and people of Polish heritage in the State of Maryland.

- The Balch Institute for Ethnic Studies
  http://www.libertynet.org/~balch/
  Includes a research library with materials on immigration studies.

  o A Guide To Manuscript And Microfilm Collections Of The Research Library Of The Balch Institute For Ethnic Studies
    http://www.balchinstitute.org/online_resources_12/html/contents.html

    - Polish
      http://www.balchinstitute.org/online_resources_12/html/body_polish.html

- Connecticut Polish American Archive
  http://wilson.ctstateu.edu/lib/archives/polish/

- Family History Library Catalog
  http://www.familysearch.org/Search/searchcatalog.asp
  From the FamilySearch web site, an online catalog to the holdings of the LDS Church in Salt Lake City, Utah. Also search for other localities by place name.
  http://www.familysearch.org/eng/Library/fhlc/supermainframeset.asp?display=localitysearch&columns=*,180,0

- o Poland
  http://www.familysearch.org/eng/Library/fhlc/supermain
  frameset.asp?display=localitydetails&subject=92&subject_
  disp=Poland&columns=*,180,0

- Herder-Institut Marberg: About the Institute
  http://www.uni-marburg.de/herder-institut/english/allgemein/
  info.html
  *According to its statutes, the Herder-Institute supports "with its
  collections and as a forum for academic discussion the research on
  the countries and peoples of East Central Europe in their European
  context, with special regard to the history of the historical German
  territories and areas of settlement in East Central Europe. In order
  to fulfill these tasks, the institute conducts its own research." The
  core subject of its work is the area of the present-day states of
  Poland, the Czech Republic, Slovakia, Estonia, Latvia and
  Lithuania.*

- Home Pages of Polish Libraries
  http://www.uidaho.edu/~majanko/ankieta/libraries.html

- Immigration History Research Center (IHRC) at the
  University of Minnesota
  http://www1.umn.edu/ihrc/
  *An international resource on American immigration and ethnic
  history.*

  - o Archival and Library Research Collections
    http://www1.umn.edu/ihrc/research.htm#top

    - Family History Sources at IHRC
      http://www1.umn.edu/ihrc/genealog.htm#top

    - IHRC Guide to Collections
      http://www1.umn.edu/ihrc/profiles.htm

    - Polish American Collection
      http://www1.umn.edu/ihrc/polish.htm#top

- Public Libraries of Europe
  http://dspace.dial.pipex.com/town/square/ac940/eurolib.html

- Repositories of Primary Sources - Europe - Poland
  http://www.uidaho.edu/special-collections/euro2.html#pl
  *A list of links to online resources from the Univ. of Idaho Library,
  Special Collections and Archives.*

◆ Locality Specific

- City of Hamtramck ~ Michigan
  http://www.cityofhamtramck.net/
  *Many Polish and other eastern European immigrants settled in
  Hamtramck and it is still one of the largest Polish enclaves
  anywhere outside Poland.*

- The Dobra Szlachecka Society
  http://www.dobra.org/
  *Devoted to the village Dobra Szlachecka, Poland. DEMKOWICZ,
  NIESIEWICZ, UHRYN, HNATUSKO, BIALAS, HRYCKIEWICZ,
  HYNKO, STALONY, GBUR, CZAJKOWSKI.*

- Genealogy: Zary, Poland
  http://www.HeritageQuest.com/genealogy/europe/html/
  zary.html
  *Photos and information about Zary from a genealogical perspective,
  from Heritage Quest Magazine and European Focus.*

- Lida District (Uezd)
  http://www.geocities.com/Vienna/Opera/7858/lida-site/
  lida-dist.htm
  *Research in the former Lida uezd. Formerly in Vilna guberniya,
  Lithuania; Grodno guberniya, Russia; and Nowogrodskie woj.,
  Poland. The site's primary interest is Jewish family research.*

- Zabludow
  http://www.tiac.net/users/bartman/zabludow/zabintro.htm
  *Memorial to Jewish Zabludow, Poland. Includes town history,
  family history, details of holocaust in Zabludow including an
  English translation of holocaust related documents. Rare photos of
  17th century synagogue.*

◆ Mailing Lists, Newsgroups & Chat

- Genealogy Resources on the Internet - Poland
  Mailing Lists
  http://www.rootsweb.com/~jfuller/gen_mail_country-pol.html
  *Most of the mailing list links below point to this site, wonderfully
  maintained by John Fuller*

- CIECHANOW Mailing List
  http://www.rootsweb.com/~jfuller/gen_mail_country-pol.html
  #CIECHANOW
  *Serves as an information-gathering vehicle and clearinghouse for
  Jewish genealogical and historical information relating to the
  Jewish community in and around Ciechanow, Poland.*

- ELBING Mailing List
  http://www.rootsweb.com/~jfuller/gen_mail_country-pol.html
  #ELBING
  *For the discussion of history and genealogy concerning the former
  German and West Prussian city of Elbing, today's Elblag in Poland.*

- Exulanten-L Mailing List
  http://www.rootsweb.com/~autwgw/agsfrx.htm
  *Exulanten is the name given to the Protestants that were forced out
  Austria (estimated as many as 100,000) during 16th to 18th century.
  The largest wave of about 22,000 left the Salzburg area in1731/32.
  Most went to East Prussia (Germany - Poland, Lithuania and
  Latvia) but some went to Siebenbürgen and Banat (today's
  Romania), Hungary and to parts of today's Slovakia.*

- GENPOL Mailing List
  http://www.rootsweb.com/~jfuller/gen_mail_country-pol.html
  #GENPOL

- GEN-SLAVIC Mailing List
  http://www.rootsweb.com/~jfuller/gen_mail_country-pol.html
  #GEN-SLAVIC
  Gatewayed with the soc.genealogy.slavic newsgroup
  news:soc.genealogy.slavic newsgroup

- HERBARZ Mailing List
  http://www.rootsweb.com/~jfuller/gen_mail_country-pol.html
  #HERBARZ
  *For the discussion of Polish and Lithuanian heraldry, the history of
  the armorial clans, and the genealogy of noble families.*

- Hrubieszow Mailing List
  http://www.rootsweb.com/~jfuller/gen_mail_country-pol.html
  #Hrubieszow
  *Dedicated to the town of Hrubieszow, Poland. List members will
  discuss issues concerning family genealogy, history, and Holocaust
  occurrences in accordance with the history of this small Polish
  town.*

- **JRI-PL Mailing List**
  http://www.rootsweb.com/~jfuller/gen_mail_country-pol.html
  #JRI-PL
  The Jewish Records Indexing Poland project is designed to create a searchable database of indexes to all available Jewish vital records of Poland. Subscribers to this mailing list will receive periodic updates on the status of the database and interrelated matters, and will be able to post their own queries related to the project.

- **LODZ Mailing List**
  http://www.rootsweb.com/~jfuller/gen_mail_country-pol.html
  #LODZ
  A mailing list in support of the Lodz Area Research Group (LARG) which aims to provide researchers with a forum, clearinghouse and resource for the collection and dissemination of genealogical and historical information relating to the Jewish communities of Lodz, Poland.

- **PGST Mailing List**
  http://www.rootsweb.com/~jfuller/gen_mail_country-pol.html
  #PGST
  For the discussion and sharing of information regarding the activities of the Polish Genealogical Society of Texas (PGST) and resources available for researching Polish ancestry.

- **PolandBorderSurnames Mailing List**
  http://www.rootsweb.com/~jfuller/gen_mail_country-pol.html
  #PolandBorderSurnames
  For anyone researching genealogy in the former historical borders of Poland including Estonia, Latvia, Lithuania, Belarus, Ukraine, Moldova, Slovakia, Czech Republic, Moravia, Hungary, Russia, the Balkans, and East Prussia.

- **Poland Border Surnames - Genealogy**
  http://maxpages.com/poland
  Companion web site for the mailing list above.

- **POLAND-ROOTS Mailing List**
  http://www.rootsweb.com/~jfuller/gen_mail_country-pol.html
  #POLAND-ROOTS

- **PolishLessons Mailing List**
  http://www.rootsweb.com/~jfuller/gen_mail_country-pol.html
  #PolishLessons
  To assist Poland researchers in translating Polish documents and to further their research while visiting/researching in Poland.

- **POL-LUBUSKIE Mailing List**
  http://www.rootsweb.com/~jfuller/gen_mail_country-pol.html
  #POL-LUBUSKIE
  For anyone with a genealogical or historical interest in the province of Lubuskie, Poland.

- **POMMERN-L Mailing List**
  http://www.rootsweb.com/~jfuller/gen_mail_country-pol.html
  #POMMERN-L
  For those interested in sharing and exchanging information on genealogy and history which has a connection to Pommerania, both the current Polish part and remaining German parts of the former Prussian province.

- **PRUSSIA-ROOTS Mailing List**
  http://www.rootsweb.com/~jfuller/gen_mail_country-ger.html
  #PRUSSIA-ROOTS
  For anyone with a genealogical interest in Brandenburg, Hannover (or Hanover), Ostpreussen (East Prussia), Pommern (Pomerania), Posen, Provinz Sachsen (Province of Saxony - northern Saxony), Schleswig-Holstein, Schlesien (Silesia), Westpreussen (West Prussia), Lubeck, Hamburg, and Bremen.

- **SCHLESIEN-L Mailing List**
  http://www.rootsweb.com/~jfuller/gen_mail_country-pol.html
  #SCHLESIEN-L
  For those with a genealogical interest in the former Prussian province of Schlesien (Silesia), which is now mostly in Poland.

- **Tarnobrzeg-Gen Mailing List**
  http://www.rootsweb.com/~jfuller/gen_mail_country-pol.html
  #Tarnobrzeg-Gen
  For anyone with a genealogical interest in the Tarnobrzeg area of South Eastern Poland.

- **TX-POLISH Mailing List**
  http://www.rootsweb.com/~jfuller/gen_mail_country-pol.html
  #TX-POLISH
  For anyone with a genealogical interest in the immigrants from Poland to Texas in the 1840-1930 timeframe.

- **Zdunska-Wola Mailing List**
  http://www.rootsweb.com/~jfuller/gen_mail_jewish.html
  #Zdunska-Wola
  Dedicated to genealogy and to the preservation of the Jewish heritage in Zdunska-Wola, Poland and its neighboring towns.

◆ Maps, Gazetteers & Geographical Information

- **FEEFHS East European Map Room - Map Index**
  http://feefhs.org/maps/indexmap.html

- **Genealogy Unlimited - Maps and Atlases from Europe**
  http://www.genealogyunlimited.com/
  Maps and atlases from Poland, Prussia, and Germany.

- **Map of Ethnic Groups of Eastern Europe**
  http://www.lib.utexas.edu/Libs/PCL/Map_collection/europe/EEurope_Ethnic_95.jpg
  From the Perry-Castañeda Library at the Univ. of Texas at Austin.

- **Map of Poland**
  http://www.lib.utexas.edu/Libs/PCL/Map_collection/europe/Poland.jpg
  From the Perry-Castañeda Library at the Univ. of Texas at Austin.

◆ Military

- **The Order of the Virtuti Militari and its Cavaliers 1792-1992**
  http://www.virtuti.com/order
  The site contains a search engine which will show the names of 26,500 recipients of Poland's highest military decoration for valor from 1792. It is the only such list available in the world.

- **Polish Military History Books**
  http://www.wwdir.com/polishbk.html
  Polish Orders, Medals, Badges, and Insignia. Military and Civilian Decorations, 1705 to 1985.

◆ People & Families

- The Family LOKUCIEWSKI
  http://www.btinternet.com/~hydro.lek/lokuhome.htm
  From 1560, in Eastern Poland now part of Belarus/Lithuania/Poland.

- Jasienica Patronymic Records
  http://www.jewishgen.org/JRI-PL/patronym/jasienica_data.htm
  From Jewish Records Indexing - Poland.

- Rafal T. Prinke Home Page
  http://hum.amu.edu.pl/~rafalp/

- The Titled Families of the Polish-Lithuanian Commonwealth
  http://www.pgsa.org/polelith.htm

◆ Professional Researchers, Volunteers & Other Research Services

- Busia's Roots - Professional Genealogy for Poland and Germany
  http://www.genealogypro.com/busias-roots.html
  Professional genealogy research, specializing in U.S. urban, Polish and German research.

- Discover Your Roots Society Poznan
  http://adenine.ibch.poznan.pl/~lukasz/roots.htm
  Travel service specializing in genealogical trips to Poland, especially the Poznan region. Professional tour guidance and genealogical assistance.

- European Focus
  http://www.eurofocus.com/
  Photographic portfolios of ancestral towns in Europe created for Genealogy enthusiasts in Belgium, Denmark, Eastern Europe, England, France, Germany, Great Britain, Italy, Netherlands, Norway, Poland, Sweden, Switzerland and more.

- Genealogy in Poland - Watta Research Service
  http://www.watta.pdi.net/
  A Poland based research service, with access to non-microfilmed documents in local parishes.

- Institute for Historical Family Research
  http://www.netway.at/ihff/index.htm/
  Austria, Czech & Slovak Republics, Hungary, Slovenian Republic, Croatia, Galicia & Bukovina.

- PolishExpress, Inc. Family History Research Service in Polish Archives
  http://www.polishexpress.com/
  Devoted to finding, copying, and translating family history documents from Polish archives.

- Polish Genealogical Translations
  http://adela49.freeyellow.com/index.html
  Native Polish translator/interpreter will assist you in finding your Polish roots by translating your Polish genealogical records. Twenty years of experience.

- Routes to Roots
  http://www.routestoroots.com/
  Tracing Jewish Roots in Poland, Ukraine, Moldova and Belarus.

- Translation Services - PolishLessons-L
  http://www.toledolink.com/pl/translations.html
  A free genealogical translation service (maintained and coordinated by Arthur Teschler at the University of Giessen in Germany).

◆ Publications, Software & Supplies

- Amazon.com Genealogy Bookstore - Poland
  http://www.amazon.com/exec/obidos/external-search/?keyword=poland+genealogy&tag=markcyndisgenealA/

- Ancestor's Attic Discount Genealogy Books - Polish Genealogy Books
  http://members.tripod.com/~ancestorsattic/index.html#secPO

- AudioTapes.com - Genealogical Lectures on Cassette Tapes – Poland
  http://www.audiotapes.com/search2.asp?Search=Poland
  And Polish
  http://www.audiotapes.com/search2.asp?Search=Polish

- Brother's Keeper Software
  http://ourworld.compuserve.com/homepages/Brothers_Keeper/
  Downloadable shareware program for Windows. The latest version contains English, French, Norwegian, Danish, Swedish, German, Dutch, Polish, Icelandic, Russian, Slovak, Afrikaans, Czech.

- Frontier Press Bookstore - European Research
  http://www.frontierpress.com/frontier.cgi?category=europe

- Frontier Press Bookstore - Poland
  http://www.frontierpress.com/frontier.cgi?category=polish

- GenealogyBookShop.com - Poland/Polish
  http://www.genealogybookshop.com/genealogybookshop/files/The_World,Poland_Polish/index.html
  The online store of Genealogical Publishing Co., Inc. & Clearfield Company.

- Genealogy Unlimited - Home Page
  http://www.itsnet.com:80/home/genun/public_html/
  Maps, books & supplies for sale.

- Interlink Bookshop Genealogical Services ~ Victoria, B.C., Canada
  http://www.interlinkbookshop.com/

- Jewish Roots in Poland - Pages from the Past and Archival Inventories
  http://www.rtrfoundation.org/
  A new book by Miriam Weiner.

- Polish Military History Books
  http://www.wwdir.com/polishbk.html
  Polish Orders, Medals, Badges, and Insignia. Military and Civilian Decorations, 1705 to 1985.

- Wandering Volhynians
  http://pixel.cs.vt.edu/pub/sources/wv.txt
  A Magazine for the Descendants of Germans From Volhynia and Poland.

◆ Queries, Message Boards & Surname Lists

- The Carpatho-Rusyn Surname Project
  http://www.carpatho-rusyn.org/surnames.htm

- Lineages' Free On-line Queries - Poland
  http://www.lineages.com/queries/Search.asp?Country=&
  Place=

- Rafal T. Prinke - Surname List (English)
  http://hum.amu.edu.pl/~rafalp/GEN/wykaz-eng.html

- Rafal T. Prinke - Surname List / Lista Nazwisk (Polish)
  http://hum.amu.edu.pl/~rafalp/GEN/wykaz.html

- RootsWeb Surname List - RSL Poland
  http://rsl.rootsweb.com/cgi-bin/rslsql.cgi
  The RSL and this form concept & design are courtesy of Karen Isaacson

- Silesian / Schlesien Research List - SILRL
  http://feefhs.org/de/sil/silrl/silrl.html

◆ Records: Census, Cemeteries, Land, Obituaries, Personal, Taxes and Vital (Born, Married, Died & Buried)

- Dziennik Chicagoski Obituaries ~ Chicago, Illinois
  http://www.pgsa.org/dziennik.htm

- LDS Polish Jewish LDS Microfilms ~ JewishGen
  http://www.jewishgen.org/jri-pl/jri-lds.htm

- Jewish Record Indexing - Poland
  http://www.jewishgen.org/JRI-PL/index.htm

- Marriages in Plauschwarren, East Prussia 1778-1802
  http://www.mmhs.org/prussia/plauschm.htm

- Obtaining Polish Records
  http://www.rootsweb.com/~polwgw/Research.html
  A how-to article from PolandGenWeb.

- Search Rzeszów Vital Records
  http://www.mikeburger.com/rzeszow.html
  Transcribed vital records for the area near the Tarnow/Rzeszow border of Poland featuring approximately 10 parishes near present day Mielec.

◆ Religion & Churches

- POLHOME - Polish Catholic Parishes in USA
  http://www.polhome.com/church-p.html

- Roman Catholic Church in Poland
  http://www.ipipan.waw.pl/~klopotek/church/rcc_in_p.htm

- Synagogues
  http://www.mznet.org/chamber/pics/synagog.htm
  Pictures of Polish synagogues and former Polish territories now part of Ukraine, Belarus, Lithuania.

◆ Societies & Groups

- The Dobra Szlachecka Society
  http://www.dobra.org/

- Federation of East European Family History Societies - FEEFHS
  http://feefhs.org/

- Kielce-Radom SIG
  http://www.jewishgen.org/krsig/
  Jewish genealogy special interest group researching the southern Russian Polish regions of the Kielce and Radom gubernias.

- Polish Genealogical Society of America ~ Chicago, Illinois
  http://www.pgsa.org/

- Polish Genealogical Society of California - PGSCA
  http://feefhs.org/pol/pgsca/frgpgsca.html

- Polish Genealogical Society of Connecticut and the Northeast
  http://members.aol.com/pgsne2/

- Polish Genealogical Society of Massachusetts
  http://feefhs.org/pol/frgpgsma.html

- Polish Genealogical Society of Michigan
  http://www.pgsm.org/

- Polish Genealogical Society of Minnesota
  http://www.mtn.org/mgs/branches/polish.html

- Polish Genealogical Society of New York State
  http://www.pgsnys.org/

- Polish Genealogical Society of Texas
  http://www.pgst.org
  Organized in 1982 to promote genealogical research among individuals of Polish heritage.

  o PGST Mailing List
    http://www.rootsweb.com/~jfuller/gen_mail_states-tx.html
    #PGST
    For the discussion and sharing of information regarding the activities of the Polish Genealogical Society of Texas and resources available for researching Polish ancestry.

- The Polish Nobility Association
  http://www.geocities.com/Athens/Atrium/9615/table.html

- Polska Liga Monarchistyczna / The Polish Monarchist League
  http://priv2.onet.pl/ka/monarchia/english.html
  Established in Warsaw in 1996 to organize and represent the noble estate, to defend its interests, and to promote and conserve the culture heritage, of Polish chivalry both material and spiritual.

- Zwiazek Szlachty Polskiej/Confederation of the Polish Nobility
  http://www.szlachta.org/
  Official site of Confederation of the Polish Nobility (Zwiazek Szlachty Polskiej). We are the only one association organizing Polish Nobility in Poland. We also publish "Verbum Nobile" - only one Polish magazine about noblemen's traditions, history and present matters.

POORHOUSES & POVERTY

http://www.cyndislist.com/poor.htm

Category Index:

◆ General Resource Sites

◆ Publications, Software & Supplies

◆ General Resource Sites

- Bawnboy Workhouse ~ Ireland
  http://www.cavannet.ie/history/archeo/sites/work-hse.htm

- Bedfordshire and Luton Archives and Record Service: Bedfordshire: Poor Law Union Records ~ U.K.
  http://www.pro.gov.uk/a2a/PODS/data/p004-pu.htm

- Charles Booth and Poverty Mapping in Late Nineteenth Century London
  http://mubs.mdx.ac.uk/Staff/Personal_pages/Ifan1/Booth/

- Charles Booth's 1889 Descriptive Map of London Poverty
  http://www.umich.edu/~risotto/home.html

- History of the Workhouse
  http://www.workhouses.org.uk/
  Excellent site full of information on the UK workhouse system. Includes information on the Poor Laws, maps of the Poor Law Unions, scans of original records on diet, instruction, and rules, and more.

- Index to "Paupers in Workhouses 1861" (10% sample)
  http://www.genuki.org.uk/big/eng/Paupers/
  This lists adult paupers in workhouses in England and Wales.

- Jo Daviess County Poor House
  http://www.rootsweb.com/~iljodavi/PoorHouse.htm

- Leitrim Poor Law Union Map ~ Ireland
  http://www.leitrim-roscommon.com/MAPS/let_plu.html

- Marion Ohio Poorhouse
  http://www.genealogy.org/~smoore/marion/poorhous.htm
  A list of admissions from 1856 through 1888.

- Museum of the Yorkshire Poor Law
  http://www.ripon.co.uk/workhouse/index.html

- The National Trust - The Workhouse, Southwell
  http://www.nationaltrust.org.uk/workhouse/
  The Workhouse was built in 1824 by the Reverend John Becher of Southwell, in Nottinghamshire. For over 150 years it housed the local poor, dominating the local landscape. But by 1997 this nationally important building was under threat of being turned into residential flats. Within a matter of weeks the National Trust stepped in to buy it with emergency funds, and started working to secure its long-term future as a monument to the Poor Laws and the poor. The Workhouse is expected to open to the public in 2002.

- Norfolk Record Office (UK) - Records of the Poor
  http://www.norfolk.gov.uk/council/departments/nro/nropoor.htm

- Norfolk Rural Life Museum, Gressenhall
  http://www.norfolk.gov.uk/tourism/museums/nrlm.htm
  Gressenhall occupies the former Mitford and Launditch Union Workhouse, built in 1776.

- The Poorhouse Story
  http://www.poorhousestory.com
  A clearinghouse for information about 19th Century American Poorhouses for history buffs, genealogists, teachers/students, and others with a similar interest. This is an ongoing project which continually updates information regarding the history and records available about the county poorhouses which dotted the American landscape from the early 1800s through the early 1900s.

  o History of 19th Century American Poorhouses
    http://www.poorhousestory.com/history.htm

  o Records - Poorhouse Records by State
    http://www.poorhousestory.com/records.htm

  o Cemetery List
    http://www.poorhousestory.com/cemetery.htm

  o 19th Century American Poorhouses Message Board
    http://pub25.bravenet.com/forum/show.asp?usernum=2115840809

- The Poor Jews' Temporary Shelter Database
  http://www.its.uct.ac.za/shelter/shelter.htm
  Searchable database of over 45,000 register entries of those who arrived at the Shelter in Leman Street, London from 1896 to 1914.

- The Poor Law
  http://dialspace.dial.pipex.com/town/terrace/adw03/peel/pltopic.htm
  From the Peel Web.

- Poor Law: Board of Guardians
  http://archives.powys.gov.uk/hold/poor.html
  From the Powys County Archives Office in Wales.

- Poor Law Records ~ UK
  http://www.btinternet.com/~p.w.w/guide/poor_law.htm

- Poor Law Union Records
  http://www.somerset.gov.uk/archives/poorlaw.htm
  From the Somerset Archive and Record Service.

- Poor Law Unions/Registration Districts
  http://www.staffs.ac.uk/schools/humanities_and_soc_sciences/census/unions.htm

- Poor Records - Shows a New York Certificate of Removal from 1836
  http://www.newyorkstateresearch.com/page16.html
- Poverty and Welfare in Industrializing England
  http://humanities.uwe.ac.uk/corehistorians/social/cores/kingcore.htm
- Public Record Office | Education | Snapshots | The 1832 Poor Law ~ UK
  http://learningcurve.pro.gov.uk/snapshots/snapshot08/snapshot8.htm
- Public Record Office | Finding Aids | Leaflets | Research Information Leaflets ~ UK
  http://www.pro.gov.uk/leaflets/default.htm
  - Court of Requests, 1485-1642: a Court for the 'Poor'
    http://www.pro.gov.uk/leaflets/ri2222.htm
  - The Poor and the Poor Laws
    http://www.pro.gov.uk/leaflets/ri2267.htm
  - Poor Law Records, 1834-1871
    http://www.pro.gov.uk/leaflets/ri2178.htm
- Public Record Office of Northern Ireland - Poor Law Records
  http://proni.nics.gov.uk/records/poor_law.htm
- Ron Taylor's UK Census Finding Aids and Indexes
  http://rontay.digiweb.com/
  Mainly from the 1851 Census
  - Institutionalized Census Indexes
    http://rontay.digiweb.com/institute/
    Including Paupers, Inmates, Convicts, Prisoners and Prostitutes.

- Roscommon Poor Law Union Map ~ Ireland
  http://www.leitrim-roscommon.com/MAPS/ros_plu.html
- Settlement Examinations - "Voices of the Poor"
  http://www.genfair.com/greenpages/settlemt.htm
  Most of our UK ancestors who face poverty appear at some stage during their lives - and often repeatedly - in the records connected with poor law administration.
- Some Washington County Poor House Records ~ New York
  http://bfn.org/~ae487/wscoalms.html
- The Union Workhouse
  http://www.judandk.force9.co.uk/workhouse.html
- Warning Out: New England Towns Less Than Hospitable!
  http://www.mayflowerfamilies.com/enquirer/warning_outs.htm
- The Workhouse Homepage
  http://www.workhouses.co.uk/
  Information on workhouses, asylums, hospitals, and more. Includes a developing directory of workhouses by county in the UK.

◆ Publications, Software & Supplies

- Amazon.com Genealogy Bookstore - Poor Law
  http://www.amazon.com/exec/obidos/external-search/?keyword=poor+law&tag=markcyndisgenealA/
- AudioTapes.com - Genealogical Lectures on Cassette Tapes
  http://www.audiotapes.com/index_conf.asp?topic=1
- Society of Genealogists (UK) Bookshop - Records of the Poor
  http://www.sog.org.uk/acatalog/SoG_Bookshop_Online_Records_of_the_Poor_93.html

PRESBYTERIAN

http://www.cyndislist.com/presbyterian.htm

Category Index:

- General Resource Sites
- Libraries, Archives & Museums
- Locality Specific

- Mailing Lists, Newsgroups & Chat
- Publications, Software & Supplies
- Societies & Groups

◆ General Resource Sites

- National Directory of Congregations of the Presbyterian Church (U.S.A.)
  http://www.pff.net/pc-list.html

- History of the Early American Presbyterian Church
  http://sdsspc1.physics.lsa.umich.edu/amckay/presintr.htm

◆ Libraries, Archives & Museums

- Historical Foundation of the Cumberland Presbyterian Church and the Cumberland Presbyterian Church in America ~ Memphis, Tennessee
  http://www.cumberland.org/hfcpc/

  o Historical Library and Archives
    http://www.cumberland.org/hfcpc/hla.htm

- Presbyterian Church Archives of Aotearoa New Zealand
  http://pcanz.freeyellow.com/index.htm
  Links & helpful suggestions & guidelines for genealogists searching for New Zealand Presbyterian Church records.

- The Presbyterian Church in Canada - The Archives and Record Office
  http://www.presbyterian.ca/archives/

  o Genealogy Resource Page
    http://www.presbyterian.ca/archives/geneal.html

- Presbyterian College Library ~ South Carolina
  http://library.presby.edu/screens/libhome.html

  o Archives and Special Collections
    http://library.presby.edu/screens/deptarchmain.html

    • Genealogical Research
      http://library.presby.edu/screens/deptarchgene.html

- St. David's Presbyterian Church Archives ~ St. John's, Newfoundland, Canada
  http://www.chebucto.ns.ca/Heritage/NGB/Research/st_david.html

- United Church of Canada / Victoria University Archives
  http://vicu.utoronto.ca/archives/archives.htm

Located in Ontario, the holdings in the archives include records for the Presbyterian Church in Canada; the Methodist Church (Canada); the Congregational Union of Canada; Local Union Churches; and the Evangelical United Brethren Church. There are also personal papers, biographical files and photographs.

◆ Locality Specific

- Alaska Presbyterian Church USA : Presbytery of the Yukon
  http://www.yukonpresbytery.com/

- Church of Scotland
  http://www.churchofscotland.org.uk/

- Cumberland Presbyterian Links
  http://members.aol.com/srobin7056/cplinks.html

- The Free Church of Scotland
  http://www.freechurch.org/

- Free Presbyterian Church of Scotland
  http://www.fpchurch.org.uk/

- The Historical Foundation of the Cumberland Presbyterian Church and the Cumberland Presbyterian Church in America ~ Memphis, Tennessee
  http://www.cumberland.org/hfcpc/

- The Presbyterian Church in Canada
  http://www.presbyterian.ca/

- The Presbyterian Church in Ireland
  http://www.presbyterianireland.org/

- Presbyterian Church (U.S.A.)
  http://www.pcusa.org/

- Presbytery of Orkney, Church of Scotland
  http://members.aol.com/OrkneyPrsb/

- The Presbytery of the Yukon ~ Eagle, Alaska
  http://www.yukonpresbytery.com/

- United Church Congregations and Pastoral Charges in Halifax Presbytery ~ Nova Scotia, Canada
  http://www.chebucto.ns.ca/Religion/UCCPresbytery/_Charges.html

- United Free Church of Scotland
  http://www.fpchurch.org.uk/

- United Presbyterian Church of Lyndon Records, 1893-1961 ~ Kansas
  http://www.kshs.org/ms/mc5009.htm

◆ Mailing Lists, Newsgroups & Chat

- Genealogy Resources on the Internet - Religions / Churches Mailing Lists
  http://www.rootsweb.com/~jfuller/gen_mail_religions.html
  Most of the mailing list links below point to this site, wonderfully maintained by John Fuller

- BIBLICAL-GENEALOGY Mailing List
  http://www.rootsweb.com/~jfuller/gen_mail_religions.html#BIBLICAL-GENEALOGY
  For the discussion and sharing of information regarding genealogy in biblical times.

- PRESBYTERIAN Mailing List
  http://www.rootsweb.com/~jfuller/gen_mail_religions.html#PRESBYTERIAN
  For anyone with a genealogical or historical interest in the Presbyterian church including all Presbyterian Denominations (e.g., A.R.P., U.S.A., P.C.A., etc.).

◆ Publications, Software & Supplies

- Amazon.com Genealogy Bookstore - Presbyterian
  http://www.amazon.com/exec/obidos/external-search/?keyword=presbyterian+genealogy&tag=markcyndisgenealA/

- AudioTapes.com - Genealogical Lectures on Cassette Tapes - Presbyterian
  http://www.audiotapes.com/search2.asp?Search=Presbyterian

- My Ancestors Were English Presbyterians/Unitarians: How Can I Find Out More About Them?
  http://www.sog.org.uk/acatalog/SoG_Bookshop_Online_My_Ancestors_Series_135.html#a1042s
  Publication for sale from the UK's Society of Genealogists.

◆ Societies & Groups

- Historical Foundation of the Cumberland Presbyterian Church and the Cumberland Presbyterian Church in America ~ Memphis, Tennessee
  http://www.cumberland.org/hfcpc/

- The Presbyterian Historical Society ~ Philadelphia, Pennsylvania
  http://history.pcusa.org/

  o The Presbyterian Historical Society
    http://www.ushistory.org/tour/tour_phs.htm
    An overview of the society from the USHistory.org web site.

PRIMARY SOURCES

http://www.cyndislist.com/primary.htm

Category Index:

- ◆ How To Locate or Order Military Records
- ◆ How To Locate or Order Miscellaneous Records
- ◆ How To Locate or Order Vital Records
- ◆ Online Primary Sources
- ◆ U.S. Census

◆ How To Locate or Order Military Records

- How to Obtain Military Pension Files from the Department of Veterans Affairs
  http://www.kinquest.com/genealogy/resources/va.html

- National Personnel Records Center
  http://www.nara.gov/regional/mpr.html
  Military Personnel Records NPRC (MPR).

- Soldiers of the First World War — Canadian Expeditionary Force
  http://www.archives.ca/exec/naweb.dll?fs&020106&e&top&0
  An index to the personnel files of over 600,000 soldiers that enlisted during the First World War. Copies of over 50,000 pages of Attestation papers have been scanned and are available online here.

- U.S. Civil War Pension & Military Records
  - o Arkansas History Commission - Request Form For Photocopies of Arkansas Confederate Pensions
    http://www.state.ar.us/ahc/form4.txt

  - o Arkansas History Commission - Request Form For Photocopies of Arkansas Military Service Records
    http://www.state.ar.us/ahc/form3.txt

  - o Civil War Records
    http://www.nara.gov/genealogy/civilwar.html
    An article from the National Archives.

  - o Civil War Records - An Introduction and Invitation
    http://www.nara.gov/publications/prologue/musick.html
    An article by Michael P. Musick from the National Archives web site.

  - o Civil War Veterans: Copies of military & pension records
    mailto:inquire@arch2.nara.gov
    Send e-mail to order form NATF 80, Veteran's Records (before WWI only). You will need to give them your postal mailing address.

  - o Confederate Ancestor Research Guide
    http://www.scv.org/genealogy/scvgen02.htm

  - o Confederate Military Records at the Archives ~ South Carolina
    http://scdah.sc.edu/confedrc.htm

  - o Confederate Military Records - Civil War Military Records in the U.S. National Archives
    http://www.misscivilwar.org/resources/bib-comp.html
    A how-to guide by Howard Beckman.

  - o Confederate Pension Records
    http://www.nara.gov/genealogy/confed.html
    An article from the National Archives.

  - o Confederate Pension Rolls, Veterans and Widows
    http://image.vtls.com/collections/CW.html
    From the Library of Virginia Digital Collections.

  - o Florida Confederate Pension Application Files
    http://www.dos.state.fl.us/dlis/barm/Pension Introduction.htm
    Search this online index then follow the instructions for ordering a copy of the pension file.

  - o Georgia Confederate Pension Applications - State of Georgia Department of Archives & History
    http://docuweb.gsu.edu/htbin/collection/colid=15|77
    "The purpose of this community service project is to digitize the microfilm associated with the pension applications of Georgia's Confederate soldiers and their widows.".

  - o How to Order Military & Pension Records for Union Civil War Veterans from the National Archives
    http://www.oz.net/~cyndihow/pensions.htm
    by Cyndi Howells.

  - o How to Request Michigan Civil War Ancestor's Military Records from the National Archives
    http://www.centuryinter.net/suvcw.mi/gr-recwv.html

  - o Index to Confederate Pension Applications ~ Texas
    http://www.tsl.state.tx.us/lobby/cpi/introcpi.htm

  - o United States Civil War Service and Pension Records
    http://www.history.rochester.edu/jssn/page5.htm
    Scanned image examples.

  - o Virtual Victoria: Confederate Pension Applicant Index
    http://www.viptx.net/victoria/history/pensions/index.html
    An index to all of the applicants from Victoria County, Texas

◆ How To Locate or Order Miscellaneous Records

● AudioTapes.com - Genealogical Lectures on Cassette Tapes - Primary
http://www.audiotapes.com/search2.asp?Search=primary

● Requesting Your Ancestor's Naturalization Records
http://www.arduini.net/tools/insreque.htm
A guide by Dennis Piccirillo.

◆ How To Locate or Order Vital Records

● Where to Write for Vital Records
http://www.cdc.gov/nchs/howto/w2w/w2welcom.htm

● Parish and Vital Records List
http://www.familysearch.org/Eng/Search/RG/frameset_rg.asp?Dest=G1&Aid=&Gid=&Lid=&Sid=&Did=&Juris1=&Event=&Year=&Gloss=&Sub=&Tab=&Entry=&Guide=PARISH.ASP
A list of indexed church and vital records available from the LDS Family History Library.

● Scots Origins
http://www.origins.net/GRO/
Scots Origins is an online "pay-per-view" database of indexes from the genealogical records of the General Register Office for Scotland - the GRO(S). The Scots Origins database contains fully searchable indexes of the Old Parish Registers of births/baptisms and banns/marriages dating from 1553 to 1854, indexes to the Statutory Registers of births, deaths and marriages from 1855 to 1898, and the index to census records for 1891. Extracts of the original entries in the GRO(S) records can be ordered directly from the database. Extract orders are processed by GRO(S) and sent via ordinary mail as paper documents.

   ○ About Scots Origins
     http://www.origins.net/GRO/about.html

   ○ Information for Family History Searching on the Scots Origins web site of the General Register Office for Scotland
     http://www.gro-scotland.gov.uk/grosweb/grosweb.nsf/pages/searchin
     From the FAQ on the web site for the General Register Office for Scotland.

   ○ Scots Origins - Discussion Group Information
     http://www.origins.net/GRO/egroups/einfo.html
     A mailing list at egroups.com, for users of the Scots Origins web site.

   ○ Scots Origins FAQ
     http://www.origins.net/GRO/faq.html

● VitalChek
http://www.vitalchek.com
Certified copies of birth certificates, death certificates, marriage certificates and other vital records.

● Vital Events Indexes - BC Archives ~ Canada
http://www.bcarchives.gov.bc.ca/textual/governmt/vstats/v_events.htm

   ○ Birth Registration Index Search Gateway, 1872 to 1898
     http://www2.bcarchives.gov.bc.ca/cgi-bin/www2vsb

   ○ Marriage Registration Index Search Gateway, 1872 to 1923
     http://www2.bcarchives.gov.bc.ca/cgi-bin/www2vsm

   ○ Death Registration Index, 1872 to 1978
     http://www2.bcarchives.gov.bc.ca/cgi-bin/www2vsd

● Vital Records Information - State Index
http://vitalrec.com/index.html
Information about where to obtain vital records (such as birth, death & marriage certificates and divorce decrees) from each state, territory and county of the United States.

● Where to Write for Vital Records
http://www.cdc.gov/nchswww/howto/w2w/w2welcom.htm
From the National Center for Health Statistics, United States

◆ Online Primary Sources

The links below represent the small number of actual scanned images of records that we have online today. It is important to remember that the majority of what you find on the Internet should only be considered research tools which point you to actual records offline. Again, the following are the exception to that rule.

● Archive of Primary Sources at DoHistory
http://www.dohistory.org/archive/index.html
Graphic images of primary source material focusing on early American history. Transcriptions for some of the sources are also provided.

● The Bureau of Land Management - - Eastern States, General Land Office
http://www.glorecords.blm.gov/
The Official Land Patent Records Site. This site has a searchable database of over two million pre-1908 Federal land title records, including scanned images of those records. The Eastern Public Land States covered in this database are: Alabama, Arkansas, Florida, Illinois, Indiana, Louisiana, Michigan, Minnesota, Mississippi, Missouri, Ohio, Wisconsin.

● Hillsborough County, Florida Marriage Records - Index
http://www.lib.usf.edu/spccoll/guide/m/ml/guide.html
Records online from January 1878 through December 1887, including a scanned photo of the original document.

● INGALLS Homestead File
http://www.nara.gov/nara/EXTRA/ingalls.html
Scanned images of 24 original documents pertaining to the DeSmet, South Dakota homestead of the family of Laura Ingalls Wilder. A terrific example from the National Archives and Records Administration.

● Lafleur Archives
http://www.lafleur.org/
Provides birth, death and marriage records from authentic Bible records. There are scanned images of Bibles when possible.

● The Library of Virginia
http://www.lva.lib.va.us/

o Archives Research and Library Reference
http://www.lva.lib.va.us/pubserv/ais.htm

o Digital Library Program
http://www.lva.lib.va.us/dlp/index.htm

• Electronic Card Indexes
http://image.vtls.com/collections/

o Genealogical Research (Family History)
http://www.lva.lib.va.us/pubserv/genie.htm

o Search Our Catalogs
http://www.lva.lib.va.us/sb/catalogs/index.htm

o Research Guides and Finding Aids at the Library
of Virginia
http://www.lva.lib.va.us/pubserv/archives/findaids.htm

• NARA Archival Information Locator
http://www.nara.gov/nara/EXTRA/nail2.html
*A pilot database of selected holdings with digital copies of selected
textual documents, photographs, maps, and sound recordings.*

• Soldiers of the First World War — Canadian
Expeditionary Force
http://www.archives.ca/exec/naweb.dll?fs&020106&e&top&0
*An index to the personnel files of over 600,000 soldiers that enlisted
during the First World War. Copies of over 50,000 pages of
Attestation papers have been scanned and are available online here.*

• United States Civil War Service and Pension
Records
http://www.history.rochester.edu/jssn/page5.htm
Scanned image examples.

◆ U.S. Census

• Heritage Quest - US Federal Census Schedules
Available on CD-ROM and Microfilm
http://www.heritagequest.com/ProdFind2/census.htm
*Digitized images of the entire U.S. Federal Census from 1790 to
1920. Each of the 12,555 rolls of census microfilm are now
available on CD-ROM for use on your home computer.*

• The USGenWeb Archives Census Project
http://www.rootsweb.com/~usgenweb/census/

o The USGenWeb Archives Census Project - Census
Images
http://www.rootsweb.com/~usgenweb/cen_img.htm
Scanned images of the U.S. Federal Census.

• Alabama
http://www.rootsweb.com/~usgenweb/cen_a.htm#AL

• Arkansas
http://www.rootsweb.com/~usgenweb/cen_a.htm#AR

• California
http://www.rootsweb.com/~usgenweb/cen_c.htm#CA

• Colorado
http://www.rootsweb.com/~usgenweb/cen_c.htm#CO

• Georgia
http://www.rootsweb.com/~usgenweb/cen_g.htm

• Illinois
http://www.rootsweb.com/~usgenweb/cen_i.htm#IL

• Indiana
http://www.rootsweb.com/~usgenweb/cen_i.htm#IN

• Iowa
http://www.rootsweb.com/~usgenweb/cen_i.htm#IA

• Kansas
http://www.rootsweb.com/~usgenweb/cen_k.htm#KS

• Kentucky
http://www.rootsweb.com/~usgenweb/cen_k.htm#KY

• Louisiana
http://www.rootsweb.com/~usgenweb/cen_l.htm#LA

• Massachusetts
http://www.rootsweb.com/~usgenweb/cen_m.htm#MA

• Michigan
http://www.rootsweb.com/~usgenweb/cen_m.htm#MI

• Minnesota
http://www.rootsweb.com/~usgenweb/cen_m.htm#MN

• Mississippi
http://www.rootsweb.com/~usgenweb/cen_m.htm#MS

• Missouri
http://www.rootsweb.com/~usgenweb/cen_m.htm#MO

• Nebraska
http://www.rootsweb.com/~usgenweb/cen_n.htm#NE

• New Jersey
http://www.rootsweb.com/~usgenweb/cen_n.htm#NJ

• New Mexico
http://www.rootsweb.com/~usgenweb/cen_n.htm#NM

• North Carolina
http://www.rootsweb.com/~usgenweb/cen_n.htm#NC

• North Dakota
http://www.rootsweb.com/~usgenweb/cen_nd.htm

• Ohio
http://www.rootsweb.com/~usgenweb/cen_o.htm#OH

• Oklahoma
http://www.rootsweb.com/~usgenweb/cen_o.htm#OK

• Pennsylvania
http://www.rootsweb.com/~usgenweb/cen_p.htm

• Rhode Island
http://www.rootsweb.com/~usgenweb/cen_r.htm

• South Carolina
http://www.rootsweb.com/~usgenweb/cen_s.htm#SC

• South Dakota
http://www.rootsweb.com/~usgenweb/cen_s.htm#SD

• Tennessee
http://www.rootsweb.com/~usgenweb/cen_t.htm#TN

• Texas
http://www.rootsweb.com/~usgenweb/cen_t.htm#TX

• Virginia
http://www.rootsweb.com/~usgenweb/cen_v.htm#VA

• West Virginia
http://www.rootsweb.com/~usgenweb/cen_w.htm#WV

• Wisconsin
http://www.rootsweb.com/~usgenweb/cen_w.htm#WI

PRISONS, PRISONERS & OUTLAWS

http://www.cyndislist.com/prisons.htm

Category Index:

◆ Convicts to Australia

◆ General Resource Sites

◆ Historic Prisons & Penitentiaries

◆ Notorious Characters

◆ Pirates, Privateers & Buccaneers

◆ U.S. Civil War Prisons & Prisoners

◆ The Wild West

◆ Convicts to Australia

● AUS-CONVICTS Mailing List
http://www.rootsweb.com/~jfuller/gen_mail_country-aus.html
#AUS-CONVICTS
*For anyone with a genealogical interest in the convicts that were
transported to Australia.*

● Australia Convicts Message Board
http://www.insidetheweb.com/messageboard/mbs.cgi/
mb80720

● Australian Shipping Arrivals and Departures 1788 to
1967 - Convictions
http://www.blaxland.com/ozships/

● Australia's First Fleet
http://www.pcug.org.au/~pdownes/dps/1stflt.htm
Convicts transported from England in 1788.

● Australia's Second Fleet
http://www.pcug.org.au/~pdownes/dps/2ndflt.htm
Convicts transported from England in 1790.

● Australia's Third Fleet
http://www.pcug.org.au/~pdownes/dps/3rdflt.txt
Convicts transported from England in 1791.

● convicts-australia Mailing List
http://www.rootsweb.com/~jfuller/gen_mail_country-aus.html
#convicts-australia
*For the discussion and sharing of information on Australia and the
convicts that were transported there.*

● Convict Gangs in 1821
http://carmen.murdoch.edu.au/community/dps/convicts/
victlist.htm
*Alphabetical list of names for 3,217 men, women and children who
were issued with rations in Sydney on Saturday September 8, 1821.*

● Convict Indexes for NSW Australia
http://www.powerup.com.au/~plucas/
Book for sale.

● Convicts, Characters & Cads - The Ancestors of
Scott and Fiona Brown
http://www.uq.net.au/~zzsbrown/family/
*Surnames including BROWN, SMITH, CALLOW, PHILLIPS,
MORTON, MOUGHTIN. The site also includes an Australian
Genealogy Bulletin Board.*

● Convicts to Australia - A Guide To Researching
Your Convict Ancestors
http://carmen.murdoch.edu.au/community/dps/convicts/
index.html
*In depth information and lists of convicts, ships, a timeline and
convict's stories.*

● Daniel BLACKWELL : Tasmanian Genealogy and
Convict History
http://www.ozemail.com.au/~kemoon/Danielb.html
*Grandfather's Grandfather - The story of Daniel BLACKWELL and
his Descendants.*

● Descendants of Convicts Group Inc.
http://home.vicnet.net.au/~dcginc/welcome.htm
*A special interest group formed by members of the Genealogical
Society of Victoria, Australia.*

● Lincolnshire Archives Index of Convict Records
1787 - 1840
http://www.demon.co.uk/lincs-archives/convicts.htm

● National Archives of Ireland: Transportation
Records
http://www.nationalarchives.ie/search01.html
Convicts from Ireland to Australia, 1788 to 1868.

● South Australian Transported Convicts
http://www.users.on.net/proformat/convicts.html

● Strahan, Sarah Island Convict Site, South West
Tasmania
http://www.ozemail.com.au/~kemoon/Strahan.html

● System of Transportation
http://www.nationalarchives.ie/transportation.html
*From the National Archives of Ireland. Very brief outline of
transportation of convicts from Ireland to Australia in the 19th
century.*

● Transportation of Irish convicts to Australia (1791-
1853)
http://www.nationalarchives.ie/transp1.html
*From the National Archives of Ireland. Detailed review of the
sources available for convict research held at the Archives.
Includes links to specific descriptions of record types and their
reference class numbers.*

- The Wellington Valley Convicts, 1823-31
  http://www.newcastle.edu.au/department/hi/roberts/
  convicts.htm
  A database of more than 1,000 convicts.

◆ General Resource Sites

- An Abstract of the Civil Law and Statute Law Now
  in Force, in Relation to Pyracy (1726)
  http://www2.prestel.co.uk/orton/family/pyracy.html

- AudioTapes.com - Genealogical Lectures on Cassette
  Tapes – Prison
  http://www.audiotapes.com/search2.asp?Search=prison
  Convict
  http://www.audiotapes.com/search2.asp?Search=convict

- Civilian Internees of the Japanese in Singapore
  during WWII
  http://user.itl.net/~glen/CivilianInternees.html
  As well as messages regarding that site
  http://user.itl.net/~glen/CivilianInternees2.html
  From Alex Glendinning's Asian Pages.

- Criminal Ancestors : A Guide to Historical Criminal
  Records in England and Wales
  http://www.amazon.com/exec/obidos/ISBN=0750910844/
  markcyndisgenealA/
  A book by David T. Hawkings.

- Executions in England from 1606
  http://www.fred.net/jefalvey/execute.html

- The Family History System - Executions in England
  from 1606
  http://www.fhsystem.demon.co.uk/fhsytem5.htm

- genealogyPro - Criminal - Arrest Researchers
  http://genealogyPro.com/directories/criminal-arrest.html

- GEN-UNSOLVED-MYSTERIES Mailing List
  http://www.rootsweb.com/~jfuller/gen_mail_general.html
  #GEN-UNSOLVED-MYSTERIES
  *For people whose family genealogies include "unsolved mysteries."
  Postings should include only mysterious disappearances or
  appearances, unsolved murders, questionable incarcerations, and
  other mysterious or unsolved events in an ancestor's life. Postings
  should not include "brick walls" since these would be repetitive of
  the content of other lists.*

- Inmates Of The Tennessee State Penitentiary 1831 -
  1850
  http://www.state.tn.us/sos/statelib/pubsvs/inmate1.htm
  From the Tennessee State Library and Archives.

- International Black Sheep Society of Genealogists
  (IBSSG)
  http://homepages.rootsweb.com/~blksheep/
  *For those who have a dastardly, infamous individual of public
  knowledge and ill-repute in their family...within 1 degree of
  consanguinity of their direct lines. This individual must have been
  pilloried in disgrace for acts of a significantly anti-social nature.*

- Internment of Ukrainians in Canada 1914-1920
  http://www.infoukes.com/history/internment/

- Ohio State Penitentiary
  http://www.genealogy.org/~smoore/marion/badguys.htm
  From admission records for 1834-1875.

- OKLAHOMBRES Online!
  http://www.oklahombres.org/
  *Oklahombres is an association for the preservation of lawman and
  outlaw history in Oklahoma. Has a searchable archive of past issues
  of our quarterly publication and a message board where
  researchers can exchange information.*

- State of Illinois Corrections Inmate Search
  http://www.idoc.state.il.us/inmates/search.htm
  *Searchable database of current and some former inmates of Illinois
  prisons.*

- Transported Felons Hang on Family Trees
  http://www.ancestry.com/columns/myra/Shaking_Family_Tree
  12-18-97.htm
  *From Shaking Your Family Tree by Myra Vanderpool Gormley,
  C.G.*

◆ Historic Prisons & Penitentiaries

- Anamosa State Penitentiary ~ Iowa
  http://www.geocities.com/Heartland/2201/index.html

- Beveren-Waas, Prisons 1857 ~ Belgium
  http://pucky.uia.ac.be/~janssen/genealogy/bev-gev.html

- Colorado State Archives Penitentiary and
  Reformatory Records
  http://www.state.co.us/gov_dir/gss/archives/prison.html
  ○ Colorado State Penitentiary Index 1871 - 1973
    http://www.archives.state.co.us/pen/index.htm

- Eastern State Penitentiary ~ Pennsylvania
  http://www.libertynet.org/e-state/

- History of the Maine State Prison
  http://www.midcoast.com/~tomshell/prison.html

- Inmates of the Ohio State Penitentiary
  http://www.genealogy.org/~smoore/marion/badguys.htm
  *For every inmate of the Ohio State Penitentiary (Columbus) with a
  Marion County connection, admissions for the years 1834-1875.*

- Inmates of the Virginia State Penitentiary in 1850
  http://www.rootsource.com/vapen.htm
  *From the New River Company's Genealogy and History Research
  Site.*

- Newgate - Newgate Prison ~ England
  http://www.fred.net/jefalvey/newgate.html
  A list of inmates, victims and those associated with the prison.

- Old Idaho Penitentiary
  http://www.state.id.us/ishs/Sites.html#anchor1254440

◆ Notorious Characters

- Evolution of an Outlaw Band: The Making of the
  Barker-Karpis Gang - Part 1
  http://www.oklahombres.org/barker1.htm
  And Part 2
  http://www.oklahombres.org/barker2.htm

- The John Dillinger File
  http://www.geocities.com/~jdillinger/

- Notorious Ancestors
  http://www.geocities.com/Heartland/Acres/8310/
  notorious.html
  Or mirror site
  http://www.geocities.com/~gensearcher/notorious.html

- Yahoo!...Outlaws
  http://dir.yahoo.com/Society_and_Culture/Crime/Outlaws/

- Your FBI - History - Famous Cases
  http://www.fbi.gov/yourfbi/history/famcases/famcases.htm

◆ Pirates, Privateers & Buccaneers

- Anne Bonny's Home Page
  http://www.geocities.com/CollegePark/4704/annebonny.html
  "The most notorious female pirate that ever lived."

- Beej's Pirate Image Archive
  http://www.ecst.csuchico.edu/~beej/pirates/

- Blackbeard the Pirate
  http://www.blackbeardthepirate.com/blackbeard1.htm

- Grace O'Malley, 1530-1603
  http://members.tripod.com/cathreese/DefiantWomen/pirates/
  granuaile.html

- Hawkins Scurvy Crew
  http://www.geocities.com/Heartland/Pointe/8616/pirates.html
  Dedicated to pirates, their lifestyle, their music, and the history they created.

- Piracy
  http://huizen.nhkanaal.nl/~wastrel/

- Pirate Roster
  http://www.geocities.com/Athens/Aegean/3111/pirate_
  roster.html

- Pirates Homepage
  http://www.powerup.com.au~glen/pirate.htm

- Pirates of the Caribbean
  http://www.geocities.com/Heartland/3973/Pirates.html

- Pirates of the Caribbean
  http://www.dlp-guidebook.de/Lands/Adventureland/
  Attractions/PiratesOfTheCaribbean.htm

- Pirates, Privateers, Buccaneers
  http://www.columbia.edu/~tg66/piratepage.htm

- Sir Henry Morgan - A Welsh Buccaneer
  http://www.data-wales.co.uk/morgan.htm

- Web Index of Piracy
  http://www.geocities.com/Athens/Parthenon/1500/piracy.html

- Yahoo!...Piracy
  http://dir.yahoo.com/Arts/Humanities/History/By_Subject/
  Maritime_History/Piracy/

◆ U.S. Civil War Prisons & Prisoners

- 36th Iowa Infantry POWs at Camp Ford, Tyler, TX
  http://www.usgennet.org/~iaappano/cw/pow.html

- Alton in the Civil War - Alton Prison ~ Illinois
  http://www.altonweb.com/history/civilwar/confed/index.html

- ANDERSONVILLE Mailing List
  http://www.rootsweb.com/~jfuller/gen_mail_wars.html
  #ANDERSONVILLE
  For the descendants and interested historians of Andersonville, the Civil War's most notorious prison camp, to swap knowledge and research the lives of Union prisoners before, during, and after their time in Andersonville.

- Andersonville National Historic Site
  http://www.nps.gov/ande/
  from the National Park Service.

- Cahaba Federal Prison, located near Selma, Alabama
  http://www.ionet.net/~cousin/dale5.html

- Camp Douglas, Illinois
  http://www.outfitters.com/illinois/history/civil/camp
  douglas.html
  Prison camp and training camp.

- Civil War Prison Elmira
  http://mars.spaceports.com/~court52/elmiran.htm

- Civil War Prison Point Lookout
  http://mars.spaceports.com/~court52/lookoutn.htm

- Confederate Prisoners of War Who Died at Rock Island, IL
  http://pw1.netcom.com/~jeansmal/rockislpow.html

- CW-POW Mailing List
  http://www.rootsweb.com/~jfuller/gen_mail_states-gen.html
  #CW-POW
  For the discussion and sharing of information regarding the Civil War prisoner of war camps and prisoners of war, both Union and Confederate.

- Elmira Prison Camp (Civil War) History
  http://www.rootsweb.com/~nychemun/prison.htm
  History of the Elmira Prison Camp (Civil War) and burials of those who died there.

- Friends of the Florence Stockade ~ Florence, South Carolina
  http://home.att.net/~florencestockade/friends.htm

- Kansas Prisoners of War at Camp Ford, Texas 1863-1865
  http://history.cc.ukans.edu/heritage/research/campford.html

- MA Ryan, Co B 14th Miss Vol Inf CSA
  http://www.izzy.net/~michaelg/ma-ryan.htm
  Experience of a Confederate Soldier in Camp and Prison in The Civil War 1861-1865.

- Ohio Prisoner of War Camp Sources
  http://my.ohio.voyager.net/~lstevens/a/prison.html

- Point Lookout, Md., Prison Camp
  http://www.clements.umich.edu/Webguides/Schoff/NP/
  Point.html
  *A prison camp for Confederate prisoners of war was built at Point
  Lookout, Md., on the tip of the peninsula where the Potomac River
  joins Chesapeake Bay. In all, over 50,000 men, both military and
  civilian, were held prisoner there.*

- Point Lookout POW Descendants Organization
  http://www.members.tripod.com/~PLPOW/plpow.htm
  *Point Lookout Prison Camp for Confederates in the state of
  Maryland, 1863 to 1865.*

- Unlikely Allies : Fort Delaware's Prison Community
  in the Civil War
  http://www.amazon.com/exec/obidos/ISBN=0811718239/
  markcyndisgenealA/
  A book by Dale Fetzer.

- Xerxes Knox, Private, Co. G, 3rd Iowa Cavalry in the
  Civil War
  http://www.oz.net/~cyndihow/xerxes.htm
  *Cyndi's 3rd great-grandfather and a prisoner at Camp Ford in
  Tyler, Texas.*

- A Yankee Prisoner in Texas
  http://www.greeceny.com/ol/herb.htm
  *William Ryan, of the 160th New York Volunteers, a prisoner in
  Camp Ford.*

◆ The Wild West

- Billy the Kid Outlaw Gang
  http://www.nmia.com/~btkog/index.html

- Cattle Brands
  http://www.tsha.utexas.edu/handbook/online/articles/view/
  CC/auc1.html
  From the Handbook of Texas.

- Cattle Brands: Heraldry of the West
  http://www.audiotapes.com/product.asp?ProductCode=
  'DCA-26'
  *Presentation by Kathleen W. Hinckley, available for sale on audio
  tape.*

- Chronology of Jesse JAMES
  http://www.sptddog.com/sotp/jesse.html
  *Detailed information on activities of the James gang, including
  several excellent images of Jesse and Frank James.*

- History of Cattle Brands
  http://www.barbwiremuseum.com/cattlebrandhistory.htm

- Jesse and Frank James: The Family History
  http://www.amazon.com/exec/obidos/ISBN=0882896539/
  markcyndisgenealA/
  A book by Phillip W. Steele.

- JESSE-JAMES Mailing List
  http://www.rootsweb.com/~jfuller/gen_mail_general.html
  #JESSE-JAMES
  *For the discussion and sharing of information regarding the friends
  and family of the outlaw Jesse James.*

- Kansas Gunfighters
  http://history.cc.ukans.edu/heritage/research/gunfighters.html

- Marshals, Lawmen, Rangers: Historical Characters
  on the Family Tree
  http://www.ancestry.com/columns/myra/Shaking_Family_Tree
  11-20-97.htm
  *From Shaking Your Family Tree by Myra Vanderpool Gormley,
  C.G.*

- OK-LAWMEN-OUTLAW Mailing List
  http://www.rootsweb.com/~jfuller/gen_mail_states-ok.html
  #OK-LAWMEN-OUTLAW
  *For the discussion and sharing of information regarding ancestors
  who were lawmen or outlaws in the Oklahoma or Indian Territories.*

- Outlaws and Lawmen of the Old West
  http://www.sky.net/~fogel/oldwest.htm

- The Outlaws - Bud and Donnie Pence
  http://www.pipeline.com/~richardpence/outlaws.htm
  They rode with the James gang.

- Scribe's Tribute to Billy the Kid
  http://www.geocities.com/SouthBeach/Marina/2057/Billy_the_
  Kid.html

- Scribe's Tribute to Jesse James
  http://www.geocities.com/SouthBeach/Marina/2057/Jesse_
  James.html

- Western Outlaw Lawman History Association
  http://home.flash.net/~pggreen/WOLA/enter.htm

- The Wild West - Outlaws
  http://get.to/wildwest

- Wild West Personalities Produce Bang-Up Pedigree
  http://www.uftree.com/UFT/FamousFamilyTrees/Earp/
  index.html
  By Myra Vanderpool Gormley, CG.

- The Wild Wild West
  http://www.gunslinger.com/west.html

PROFESSIONAL RESEARCHERS, VOLUNTEERS & OTHER RESEARCH SERVICES

http://www.cyndislist.com/profess.htm

Category Index:

- General Resources
- Speakers & Authors

- Alphabetical Listing

◆ General Resources

- **Are You Ready to Become a Professional?**
  http://www.apgen.org/ready.html
  From the Association of Professional Genealogists web site.

- **Association of Genealogists and Record Agents**
  http://www.agra.org.uk
  Professional researchers available in the United Kingdom. Membership of AGRA is limited to those who have demonstrated a high level of competence and expertise. A Code of Practice and a Complaints Procedure are in place.

- **Association of Professional Genealogists ~ Denver, Colorado**
  http://www.apgen.org/
  - APG Mailing List
    http://www.rootsweb.com/~jfuller/gen_mail_general.html#APG
  - Louisiana Chapter of Association of Professional Genealogist
    http://homepages.rootsweb.com/~acwomack/apg2.htm
  - The National Capital Area Chapter of the Association of Professional Genealogists ~ Washington, DC
    http://www.apgen.org/ncac.html
  - New York Metro Chapter of the Association of Professional Genealogists
    http://www.apgen.org/nymc.html
  - Ontario Chapter of the Association of Professional Genealogists ~ Canada
    http://members.aol.com/OntarioAPG/
  - Salt Lake Chapter Association of Professional Genealogists ~ Utah
    http://www.lofthouse.com/slcapg/slcapg.htm
  - Southern California Chapter Association of Professional Genealogists
    http://www.compuology.com/sccapg/

- **Association of Professional Genealogists in Ireland**
  http://indigo.ie/~apgi

- **AudioTapes.com - Genealogical Lectures on Cassette Tapes - Professional**
  http://www.audiotapes.com/search2.asp?Search=professional

- **Board for Certification of Genealogists ~ Washington, D.C.**
  http://www.bcgcertification.org/
  - Board for Certification of Genealogists - Roster of Those Certified - State/Country Index
    http://www.bcgcertification.org/rost_ix.html

- **Becoming an Accredited Genealogist : Plus 100 Tips to Ensure Your Success**
  http://www.amazon.com/exec/obidos/ISBN=0916489817/markcyndisgenealA/
  A book by Karen Clifford.

- **The Board for Certification of Genealogists' Genealogical Standards Manual**
  http://www.amazon.com/exec/obidos/ISBN=0916489922/markcyndisgenealA/
  A book by the BCG.

- **Certification of Genealogists - Why Should a Professional Genealogist be Certified and What is Involved in that Process?**
  http://www.rootscomputing.com/howto/certify/certify.htm
  By Gale Williams Bamman.

- **CGC Mailing List**
  http://www.rootsweb.com/~jfuller/gen_mail_general.html#CGC
  For the members of Council of Genealogy Columnists (CGC) in order to keep in touch and plan and discuss various CGC events and functions.

- **Council of Genealogy Columnists**
  http://www.rootsweb.com/~cgc/index.htm

- **Determining When You Need a Professional Genealogist**
  http://www.genealogy.com/20_myra.html
  By Myra Vanderpool Gormley, CG.

- **Hiring a Professional Genealogist**
  http://www.familysearch.org/Eng/Search/RG/frameset_rg.asp?Dest=G1&Aid=&Gid=&Lid=&Sid=&Did=&Juris1=&Event=&Year=&Gloss=&Sub=&Tab=&Entry=&Guide=HIRING.ASP

From the FamilySearch.org. Hiring a professional genealogist can be an excellent way to discover your family roots. If you lack the time and skills for research or if you encounter a very challenging research problem, you may need the assistance of an experienced professional. These guidelines will help you find and employ a competent genealogist.

- Hiring a Professional Genealogist
  http://www.jewishgen.org/infofiles/profgen.txt
  A JewishGen InfoFile.

- How to Become a Professional Genealogist
  http://www.genealogy.com/genealogy/20_hnkly.html
  By Kathleen Hinckley, CGRS.

- On the Trail of a Credentialed Genealogist
  http://www.genealogy.com/genealogy/20_trail.html
  Finding the Ancestry of Etna Briggs, by Karen Clifford, AG.

- ProResearchers Mailing List
  http://www.rootsweb.com/~jfuller/gen_mail_general.html
  #ProResearchers
  Just for Professional Researchers to discuss their industry.

- Research Services: A code of practice for family historians
  http://www.ffhs.org.uk/leaflets/research.htm
  From the Federation of Family History Societies. This online brochure gives advice on how best to formulate a research request.

- So You're Going to Hire a Professional Genealogist
  http://www.apgen.org/hire.htm

- What You Should Know Before Hiring a Professional Genealogist
  http://www.genservices.com/documents/HiringAPro.html

◆ Speakers & Authors

- Alan Mann
  http://www.alanmann.com/

- Ancestor Detective Speakers Bureau
  http://www.ancestordetective.com/bureau.htm
  The speakers bureau for professional genealogical speakers and program planners. Web brochures highlight speakers' qualifications and experience.

- AzGAB Speakers ~ Arizona
  http://www.azgab.org/speakers/speakers.html

- Barbara Renick's Lecture Schedule
  http://www.zroots.com/Schedule.htm

- Birdie Monk Holsclaw, FUGA
  http://www.henge.com/~holsclaw/bmh/index.htm
  Genealogical Lecturer, Writer, Editor, Researcher, Indexer.

- Brenda Kellow, CG, CGI
  http://www.ancestordetective.com/speakers/kellow.htm

- Charles S. "Chuck" Mason Jr., CGRS
  http://genealogypro.com/cmason.html

- Colorado Council of Genealogical Societies - Speakers Bureau Directory
  http://www.rootsweb.com/~coccgs/speak-bureau.html

- Cyndi's Speaking Schedule & Calendar
  http://www.CyndisList.com/speaking.htm

- Eileen M. O'Duill, CGRS
  http://www.ancestordetective.com/speakers/oduill.htm

- Elizabeth Kelley Kerstens, CGRS
  http://www.ancestordetective.com/speakers/kerstens.htm

- Family Detective - Kathleen W. Hinckley, CGRS
  http://www.familydetective.com
  Author, Lecturer, Researcher

- FEEFHS Database of Professional Authors and Lecturers
  http://feefhs.org/frg/frg-a&l.html
  Specializing in Central and East European Genealogy.

- Gary Mokotoff, Genealogical Lecturer
  http://www.avotaynu.com/gmokotoff.html
  One of the foremost lecturers and authors on Jewish and Eastern European genealogical research.

- GenieSpeak - Genealogy Speakers Bureau
  http://www.geniespeak.com
  Created to promote and increase contacts between societies and speakers (at all levels), and to list upcoming events and workshop resources.

- Genealogical Speaker's Guild
  http://www.genspeakguild.org/

- George G. Morgan - Genealogist, Author, Columnist and Speaker
  http://ahaseminars.com/atl/

- Georgia Genealogical Society Speakers Directory
  http://www.america.net/~ggs/speakers.htm

- Henry Z ("Hank") Jones Jr., FASG - Genealogical Author and Lecturer
  http://www.HankJones.com/
  Hank has been a professional genealogist since 1965. Hank is an entertaining genealogical lecturer, an accomplished writer and a respected Fellow of the American Society of Genealogists. He is best known for his extensive work with Palatine genealogy and for his popular book, Psychic Roots.

- Heritage Quest Genealogy Road Show
  http://www.HeritageQuest.com/genealogy/roadshow/

- Indiana Genealogical Society - Speakers Bureau
  http://www.IndGenSoc.org/speabure.htm

- John Philip Colletta, Ph.D.
  http://www.genealogyjohn.com/index.html

- John Wylie Consulting - Presentations
  http://www.johnwylie.com/lectures.html

- Kip Sperry, Brigham Young University
  http://reled.byu.edu/chist/sperryk/sperryk.htm
  Author of Reading Early American Handwriting and Genealogical Research in Ohio.

- Linda Woodward Geiger, CGRS, CGL
  http://www.ancestordetective.com/speakers/geiger.htm

- Marie Martin Murphy, CGRS
  http://www.ancestordetective.com/speakers/murphy.htm

- Marie Varrelman Melchiori, CGRS, CGL
  http://www.ancestordetective.com/speakers/melchiori.htm

- Michael Neill's Lectures
  http://www.rootdig.com/lectures.html

- Nancy J. Emmert, C.G. - Genealogist
  http://www.execpc.com/~emmert/
  Genealogy Research, Lecturer, and Instructor.

- Out of the Past Programs
  http://www.outofthepast.com/
  Professional genealogist, Richard L. Hooverson, offering over 70 topics of interest to local societies, available at any time subject to scheduling.

- Paul Milner
  http://www.ancestordetective.com/speakers/milner.htm

- Repeat Performance - Audio/Video Recording Services
  http://www.repeatperformance.com/
  Tapes of classes and presentations at several genealogy conferences and seminars for the last 18 years.

- Sandra MacLean Clunies, CG
  http://www.ancestordetective.com/speakers/clunies.htm

- Shaking Family Trees by Myra Vanderpool Gormley, CG
  http://homepages.rootsweb.com/~gormleym/speak.htm

- Sheila Benedict, CGRS
  http://www.ancestordetective.com/speakers/benedict.htm

- Sherry Irvine, CGRS, FSA(Scot)
  http://www.ancestordetective.com/speakers/irvine.htm

- Zroots - Barbara Renick's Home Page
  http://www.zroots.com/

◆ "A"

- A.A. Genealogy
  http://www.lisp.com.au/~coffey/index.htm
  Family Tree research in Australia and overseas.

- A&H Associates Genealogy Document Research.
  http://www.aha.ndirect.co.uk
  Search and supply certified copies of birth, death and marriage certificates from England and Wales.

- AAG International Research - Professional Genealogists and Family Historians
  http://www.intl-research.com/
  Accredited genealogists & family historians specializing in family history research, development & publication. Accredited by the Family History Library in Salt Lake City, the world's largest genealogical library. Tax deductions for LDS research.

- Accelerated Genealogy Research
  http://www.acceleratedgenealogy.com/
  Specializing in research of New York and Pennsylvania, and access to original records of all other U.S. states and counties. Offer full-scale LDS, immigrant, & pioneer research, as well as single searches of census, church, vital, land, probate, tax, military, and other records. Free HTML pedigree charts and family group sheets, and free, 30-lesson genealogy course.

- Accredited Genealogist in Salt Lake City, Southern States
  http://www.inconnect.com/~jdrmsonn/
  Professional researcher specializing in the Southern United States, researching at the Family History Library in Salt Lake City, Utah.

- Adelaide proformat ~ Australia
  http://www.users.on.net/proformat/jaunay.html

- Adopted We Search - Assets and Family Research Consultants ~ Toronto, Ontario, Canada
  http://www.adopted-we-search.com/
  Researcher with 15 years experience, specializing in adoption-related searches.

- Adoptees Miracle Search Network
  http://www.miraclesearch.com
  Professional who finds adoptees and their birth parents

- AID Kinresearch - Slfktservice Hemsida / AID Kinresearch Swedish Genealogy
  http://hem.passagen.se/aidkin/

- A.I.R. - Ancestor and Immigrant Research ~ Owensboro, Kentucky
  http://sites.netscape.net/marg7usa/index.html

- Allendale Ancestry Research
  http://www.vweb.co.uk/ajmacleod/
  Family history research in Scotland, by Alan J.L. MacLeod.

- American Ancestral Associates ~ Cranston, Rhode Island
  http://members.aol.com/aaagen/

- American Records Research Services
  http://www.records.org
  An affordable genealogy research service providing federal census records, passenger arrival information, Revolutionary War pension records, California vital records and Sutro Library research.

- American Research Bureau - Intl Probate Research Since 1935
  http://www.heirfinder.com/

- Amy Johnson Crow, CG
  http://www.amyjohnsoncrow.com
  Genealogical research in Ohio and Ohioans in the Civil War.

- Ancestor Detective Speakers Bureau
  http://www.ancestordetective.com/bureau.htm
  The speakers bureau for professional genealogical speakers and program planners. Web brochures highlight speakers' qualifications and experience.

- Ancestor in English
  http://www.algonet.se/~kenlar/english.htm
  Genealogic help in Sweden.

- Ancestor Gallery
  http://www.ancestorgallery.com
  Our specialty is finding your ancestors and living relatives. Research conducted at the Family History Library in Salt Lake City, UT.

- Ancestor Research Service
  http://home.att.net/~kvaars/index.htm
  Kathleen Van Ausdal, specializing in United States, British Isles, Denmark, Germany.

- Ancestors in the Attic ~ Oregon
  http://ladyecloud.hypermart.net/Ancestors.htm

- Ancestors Lost and Found ~ Salt Lake City, Utah
  http://www.ancestorsfound.com/

- Ancestors Unlimited Genealogy Research
  http://www.unlimited16.freeserve.co.uk/
  UK research specializing in the counties of Dorset and Hampshire.

- Ancestral Investigations
  http://www.ancestralinvestigation.com/
  "Offers a variety of research services at a reasonable rate, including internet research, US Archive research, CD and book searches, and organization of family information."

- Ancestral Findings
  http://www.ancestralfindings.com/
  This site will provide one FREE search per day of a wide range of genealogy historical records, including birth, marriage, census, land, military indexes, and state records.

- Ancestral Locations
  http://www.ancestorsuk.com/
  Professional genealogical research service to help you discover your family's history and find out more about how, and where, your ancestors lived in England, Wales or Scotland. Unique photographic albums give you a treasured view of your ancestor's home town or village.

- Ancestral Research in Ulster
  http://homepages.tesco.net/~Petticrew/
  Genealogy research service specializing in the nine counties of Ulster, Northern Ireland.

- Ancestral Roots
  mailto:AncestralRoots@annescales.freeserve.co.uk
  Genealogical Research in SE Wales: Glamorgan and Monmouthshire/Gwent. For details please send e-mail to: Anne Scales MSc BA, AncestralRoots@annescales.freeserve.co.uk.

- AncestryFinders
  http://www.ancestryfinders.com/

- Ancient History ~ Yamhill County, Oregon
  http://www.spessart.com/users/ggraham/anchist1.htm

- Annette Womack, Experienced Genealogy Researcher ~ Winnfield, Louisiana
  http://homepages.rootsweb.com/~acwomack/gservices.htm

- Ann McRoden Mensch, Professional Genealogist
  http://home.att.net/~mensch-family/Resume.htm
  Researching at the Allen County Public Library.

- Antecedents ...ancestors are antecedents...
  http://www.antecedents.com/
  Genealogical and Family History Research by Donald W. Moore, CGRS, in the southeast Virginia cities of: Chesapeake, Norfolk, Virginia Beach and counties of Lower Norfolk (1637-1691), Norfolk (1691-1963), Princess Anne (1691-1963).

- Armidale Family & Local History Research ~ New South Wales, Australia
  http://www.angelfire.com/ct/Armidale/index.html

- Army Ancestral Searches
  http://www.jbmartin.demon.co.uk/
  "We specialize exclusively in Records of the British Army Personnel English, Scottish, Irish and Welsh Regular Army and Home Based Militias together with those raised in North America, Germany and India."

- Arno Schmitt, Journalist from San Diego, California
  mailto:reporter@adnc.com
  He can help to find relatives, links or sources regarding ancestors by placing articles in German, Austrian and/or Swiss newspapers. For details, e-mail Arno at: reporter@adnc.com.

- Ar Turas - Independent Research on Scotland and the Scots
  http://www.ar-turas.co.uk
  Ar Turas provide a full genealogical service for tracing your Scottish ancestors.

- AskQuailind@ - Document Delivery Service for Genealogists and Family Historians ~ San Mateo, California
  http://www.AskQuailind.com/

- Association of Professional Genealogists ~ Denver, Colorado
  http://www.apgen.org/

- Association of Professional Genealogists in Ireland
  http://indigo.ie/~apgi

- Association of Scottish Genealogists and Record Agents
  http://www.asgra.co.uk/
  - ASGRA Professional Researchers
    http://www.asgra.co.uk/resrch.htm

- The Australasian Association of Genealogists And Record Agents
  http://home.vicnet.net.au/~aagra/

◆ "B"

- Back To Roots - Family History Service ~ From the United Kingdom
  http://www.wwide.co.uk/backtoroots/

- Back Tracks Genealogy Service ~ Abingdon, Virginia
  http://www.naxs.com/abingdon/backtrak/default.htm

- Barbara Jean Mathews, CG
  http://www.gis.net/~bmathews/
  Professional genealogical research in Connecticut and eastern Massachusetts.

- Barbara Smallwood Stock -- Genealogical Research in Georgia
  http://www.angelfire.com/biz2/garesearch/

- The Basque Genealogy Homepage Research Services
  http://www.primenet.com/~fybarra/Research.html
  Specializing in Basque records from the province of Vizcaya. These records are on microfilm at the Salt Lake Family History Library, but do not get circulated.

- Belaugh Research Services - Trace your family history in England
  http://www.silverlf.com/belaugh/belaugh.html
  Belaugh Research Services can help you trace your family history in England. We can undertake a small one-time research project, or trace back your family several generations.

- Beth's Genealogy Research and Consulting
  http://www.kvi.net/~bethw/
  Professional genealogy research in the Mid-Michigan area.

- BFB Research - Genealogical and Historical Research
  http://www.bfbresearch.com
  Professional researcher offering services for general US research. Specializes in New England research and Arizona. Also has family pages for BOYCE, COOK, FARROW, DAMON, FARNHAM, MORRIS, ODETTE and others.

- Bill Madon - New York State Genealogy Research Services
  http://www.treesearch.com/treesearch.html

- Bill Utterback, CGRS
  http://users.arn.net/~billco/ProGen.html
  Research in the Jackson Purchase area of Kentucky.

- Birmingham Public Libraries Genealogical Research ~ England
  http://lirn.viscount.org.uk/earl/members/birmingham/gene.htm

- Blanche McMillan and Associates
  http://web.one.net.au/~rowell/
  A professional service specializing in the location of missing persons with regard to adoption, lost relatives, friends, loved ones, school and family reunions, missing heirs with regard to deceased estates, providing an Australian information service for researchers to contact living relatives in Australia by using our data bases, researching genealogy, a certificate service to obtain Birth, Death and Marriage certificates from New Zealand.

- Board for Certification of Genealogists ~ Washington, D.C.
  http://www.bcgcertification.org/

- Bob's Public Records Office Searches - Kew, London, England
  http://www.users.dircon.co.uk/~searcher/
  Including these records: Military, Royal Navy, Merchant Navy, Convict, Railway, West Indies, Passenger Lists, History Projects.

- Books We Own List
  http://www.rootsweb.com/~bwo/index.html
  A list of resources owned by others who are willing to do lookups in them.

- Bowers Genealogy Services
  http://www.interlog.com/~kbowers/bgs2.htm
  England, Scotland, Canada.

- Brickwall Genealogy Services
  http://www.angelfire.com/biz/brickwallgenealogy/index.html
  Genealogy Lookups at all Washington D.C. area archives, libraries, DAR, Library of Congress, Suburban Maryland and Virginia.

- British Ancestral Research
  http://www.brit-a-r.demon.co.uk/

- British and Canadian Army Service Record Research Service
  http://members.tripod.com/~JamesHubbert/index-html
  Locating Army service records in Britain and Canada.

- British Columbia Genealogy Copy Service
  http://members.home.net:80/crawf/
  A service for those needing information and certificates from British Columbia, Canada.

- British Military Research
  http://www.btinternet.com/~lawrence.woodcock/
  Public Record Searches for Your Ancestors in the British Army, Royal Navy, RAF, Met Police, Merchant Navy, Royal Irish Constabulary and more.

- Bruce Murduck - Historical, Geographical and Genealogical Research Services
  http://www.ikweb.com/murduck/genealogy/research/
  Researcher in Ontario, Canada

- Busia's Roots - Professional Genealogy for Poland and Germany
  http://www.genealogypro.com/busias-roots.html
  Professional genealogy research, specializing in U.S. urban, Polish and German research.

◆ "C"

- California Adoption Research - Nationwide Adoption Searches
  http://members.aol.com/DGray92237/

- CamSearch ~ England
  http://www.camsearch.freeserve.co.uk
  Genealogical and related research in Cambridgeshire & the adjoining villages of Suffolk.

- California Genealogical Research
  http://home.pacbell.net/inglis/

- Canadian Metis Genealogy
  http://genweb.net/Metis/

- Carroll County Arkansas Genealogy Research Services
  http://www.rootsweb.com/~arcchs/research.html
  Professional genealogy research in original records at the county level and special collections at local genealogical libraries. References available on request. Carroll County Arkansas and other Northwest Arkansas counties a specialty.

- Catherine NOTH - Genealogical Consulting & Research in Alsace and Palatinate
  http://perso.club-internet.fr/noth/
  Conseil et recherches généalogiques en Alsace et au Palatinat - Genealogical Consulting & Researches in Alsace and Palatinate - Paris (F) - Strasbourg (F) - Speyer (D).

- The Cavalier Research Group ~ Central Virginia
  http://www.cavaliergroup.org/

- CBL Research
  http://users.erinet.com/36353/pages/Default.htm
  Professional genealogical researcher. Will research anywhere, especially Ohio, Indiana, Kentucky. Types of research include family history, missing heirs, court work and background work for documentaries and authors.

- Celtic Origins ~ Dublin, Ireland
  http://www.genealogy.ie/

- Cemetery Searches, Sydney Australia
  http://homepages.tig.com.au/~tezz/netscape.htm
  This service will locate your ancestors' graves and take photos if required.

- The Census Giver
  http://www.censusgiver.com/
  A no-frills, quick turn-around search and retrieval of US Federal Census records from the National Archives.

- Census Searches
  http://www.census-searches.co.uk/
  Census Searches provides a service to the legal profession by obtaining copies of UK birth, marriage and death certificates. Also by obtaining copies of wills, grants of probate and letters of administration.

- Center For Genealogical Research / Cabinet d'Etudes Généalogiques ~ U.S. & Switzerland
  http://genrsch.com/
  Genealogical research, heraldry and other products throughout Europe.

- Centre Departemental D'histoire Des Familles ~ France
  http://cdhf.telmat-net.fr/

- Charles Herbert Crookston - Family History Research
  mailto:charleshc@sfo.com
  Specializing pre-1906 San Francisco Earthquake and Fire Research and Northern California research. Send e-mail to: charleshc@sfo.com.

- Cherokee Cousins - Cherokee Genealogy, Language, Culture
  http://www.powerscurce.com/cousins/

- Chicago Genealogy and Family History Research Services
  http://members.aol.com/ChiSearch
  Professional research done in Chicago and Cook Co., Illinois. Special research projects for Italian Family History and Medical Genealogy.

- Civil War Pensions, Revolutionary War Records and Homestead Papers Copied by Faith Libelo
  mailto:fsl.genie.research@erols.com
  She can visit the National Archives for you and copy the files. E-mail Faith at fsl.genie.research@erols.com for details.

- Civil War Research Services
  http://home.att.net/~t.j.manson/index.html
  Thomas J. Manson of Frederick, Maryland.

- Clifford L. Stott & Associates, Genealogical Research
  http://www.envisionyoursite.com/stott/
  A certified genealogist, accredited genealogist, and a fellow of the American Society of Genealogists, with more than 30 years of research experience in U.S. and British records. Specializing in MA, ME, CT, VT, NY, NH, RI.

- Clippings - Genealogical Material & Research Services
  http://members.aol.com/FamilyTwig/clippings.htm
  Source for current Richland Co., OH obituaries.

- Colin Davison Research Services
  http://www.cbcs.co.uk/colindavison/
  Family and Local History Research in Bedfordshire, Huntingdonshire, Hertfordshire and Buckinghamshire counties of England. Also, full record transcription or calendar service for those difficult to read documents.

- Commissioning a Genealogical Search ~ Ireland
  http://www.bess.tcd.ie/irlgen/commiss.htm

- CompuGen Systems Home Page
  http://members.aol.com/CGSystems/index.html
  Newspaper and land records index searches for Indiana.

- Connecticut Heritage Services
  http://hometown.aol.com/donnasiem/myhomepage/index.html

- Connie Lenzen - Certified Genealogical Research Specialist
  http://www.orednet.org/~clenzen/
  Research in Oregon and southwest Washington.

- Council of Genealogy Columnists
  http://www.rootsweb.com/~cgc/index.htm

- Czechoslovak Genealogical Society Int'l - Professional Genealogical Researchers for Czech and Slovak Republics
  http://members.aol.com/cgsi/research.htm

◆ "D"

● DC Research
http://www.impactvr.com/DCResearch/
Research in the U. S. National Archives, Washington, DC. and Civil War research.

● Detroit Search ~ Michigan
http://pages.prodigy.net/kdall/yourpage.html

● Diane's Michigan Genealogy Page
http://dianesgenealogy.com/
Professional Genealogist serving Southeastern Michigan, Southwestern Ontario, Northwestern Ohio.

● Diane Tofte Kropp - United States Professional Research Services ~ Pearland, Texas
http://www.lonestargenealogy.com/kropp/index.html
United States research at one of the top genealogical libraries.

● Dickenson Research & Photo-Video Evidence
http://www.dickensonresearch.com/
Huntsville, Texas. Specializing in Locating Missing Heirs in Estate Cases and General Genealogical Research.

● Digital Family History
http://www.digitalfamilyhistory.freeserve.co.uk
A family living in Sussex, England who will visit places in the area and photograph them for Genealogists/Family Historians. Also will conduct limited local research.

● Discover Your Roots Society Poznan
http://adenine.ibch.poznan.pl/~lukasz/roots.htm
Travel service specializing in genealogical trips to Poland, especially the Poznan region. Professional tour guidance and genealogical assistance.

● Dodge County Wisconsin Genealogy Research
http://www.powerweb.net/ldorn/
Genealogy research with a personal touch for Dodge County Wisconsin, and the surrounding counties of Washington and Fond du Lac.

● Doherty Enterprises Professional Genealogical Research ~ Delaware
http://www.magpage.com/~tdoherty/tpdserve.html

● DonoD - Genealogist
http://www.donod.com/

◆ "E"

● East & Middle Tennessee Genealogical Research
http://ourworld.compuserve.com/homepages/zorsch
Research in Morgan, Knox, Roane, Anderson, Fentress Campbell Scott, Putnam counties.

● East Anglian Village Research
http://www.btinternet.com/~p.w.w/eavr.htm
Essex, Suffolk, Cambridgeshire and Norfolk.

● Eastern Townships of Quebec Genealogy
http://www.virtuel.qc.ca/simmons/
Marlene Simmons has indexed 490,000 church, census, newspaper, cemetery, some Vermont vital records, and other miscellaneous records.

● Ed's Ancestral Research Services
http://www3.sympatico.ca/patpamed/
Specializing in research for Ontario, Canada, but capable of global research.

● Eldefors Swedish Genealogy Service
http://eldefors.hypermart.net/
Professional genealogical research in all areas of Sweden.

● Elephant's Nest Genealogy Site - Audrey Collins BA, Genealogist
http://www.kenaud.dircon.co.uk
Research in England, specializing in Family Records Centre, Census, London/Middlesex, Newspapers. Talks and lectures given. Small selection of family history books for sale.

● Emilio - Escort of SICILY
http://www.mediatel.it/public/emilio/
Professional Italian researcher and tour guide.

● Eneclann: Irish Genealogical Research Services
http://www.eneclann.tcd.ie/genealogy.htm

● European Focus
http://www.eurofocus.com/
Photographic portfolios of ancestral towns in Europe created for Genealogy enthusiasts in Belgium, Denmark, Eastern Europe, England, France, Germany, Great Britain, Italy, Netherlands, Norway, Poland, Sweden, Switzerland and more.

◆ "F"

● Family Affairs ~ Netherlands
http://www.familyaffairs.nl/
Genealogical research services mainly in the northern provinces of Drenthe, Friesland, Groningen, and Overijssel. Also research in other provinces and translation of documents.

● The Family Business
http://www.hollinet.com/~suebdoo/linda.htm
Family history research, sixteen years specializing in San Benito County, California.

● Family Detective
http://www.familydetective.com
Family Detective finds people such as lost family and friends, former classmates, military buddies, unknown or missing heirs, adoptees, and cousins. Kathleen W. Hinckley combines her skills as a professional genealogist and private investigator, utilizing the Internet, public records, and genealogical sources to locate living persons.

● Family Flavors
http://home.earthlink.net/~cmccombs/index.htm
Genealogy & Record Lookups & Obituary Searches in West Virginia.

● Family Footprints
http://www.familyfootprints.com/
Colorado and Wyoming.

● Family History Land ~ Tucson, Arizona
http://www.familyhistoryland.com/

- Family History Research
  http://www.mharper36.demon.co.uk/
  U.K. sources, particularly in London.

- Family History Research
  http://members.aol.com/dheald5252/
  Family History Research specializing in Chester County, Pennsylvania research abroad for England and Wales.

- Family Ivy Research
  http://freepages.genealogy.rootsweb.com/~mumford/familyivy.html
  Professional genealogy research offering a comprehensive range of genealogical research services, but specializing in Metis genealogy and genealogy in Clay County, Minnesota and Alberta, Canada.

- Family Line Research from TPCGS
  http://www.rootsweb.com/~watpcgs/famline.htm
  For the Tacoma-Pierce County, Washington area.

- The Family Search Organization
  http://www.genealogy-search.co.uk/
  Traces ancestors in the UK counties of Sussex and Hampshire. A fast, inexpensive service by professionals.

- Family Tree Genealogical and Probate Research Bureau Ltd.
  http://www.familytree.hu/
  Professional research service covering the area of what was formerly the Austro - Hungarian Empire, including: Hungary, Slovakia, Czech Republic, Austria, Italy, Transylvania, Croatia, Slovenia, former Yugoslavia (Banat), and the Ukraine (Sub-Carpathian).

- Family Tree Research in the Outer Hebrides of Scotland
  http://www.hebrides.com/busi/coleis/
  A professional research service based in Taobh Tuath (Norton).

- FamilyNet - Genealogical Research in England and Scotland
  http://www.familynet.co.uk/index.htm
  FamilyNet, Ltd. provides a comprehensive range of professional genealogical research services in England or Scotland. Their Web site includes three databases of requests for information submitted by family historians around the world.

- The Family Tree Genealogical Consulting Company of Edmonton, Alberta
  http://www.telusplanet.net/public/hiball
  Specializing in research, workshops and lectures in Edmonton and surrounding Alberta area.

- Fawn Associates
  http://www.wizvax.net/fawn/
  Estate Genealogy, Heir Identification, Unclaimed Funds Recovery.

- FEEFHS Database of Professional Genealogists Specializing in East European Genealogy
  http://feefhs.org/frg/frg-pg.html

- 1st Roots - Scottish Genealogy Research
  http://website.lineone.net/~glauder-frost/index.htm

- Forebears Research & Associates ~ London, Ontario, Canada
  http://www3.sympatico.ca/bill.forebears/

- Forebears Research U.K.
  http://homepages.enterprise.net/forebears00000/
  Genealogical research for England, Wales and Scotland undertaken by 25 year veteran of genealogy.

- Forrest Research - Military and Library Research Service ~ U.K.
  http://www.forrestdale.dial.pipex.com/

- Free Genealogy Lookups
  http://www.ih2000.net/genealogy/sites/lookups.htm
  From a variety of CDs and books listed on this page

◆ "G"

- Gail Graham, Independent Genealogist & Research Specialist
  http://www.spessart.com/users/ggraham/gailg.htm
  Specializing in Yamhill County, Oregon; and Oregon in General.

- Garrison Communications - Family History Research Services
  http://www.garrisonau.com/
  Specializing in Queensland, Australia, with expertise in English, Scottish, Welsh and Irish records

- Gary Mokotoff, Genealogical Lecturer
  http://www.avotaynu.com/gmokotoff.html
  One of the foremost lecturers and authors on Jewish and Eastern European genealogical research.

- GEG - Gabinete de Estudos GenealÖgicos ~ Portugal
  http://paginas.teleweb.pt/~moncada/
  Web site in Portuguese, English and French.

- GenBritz Down Under
  http://ourworld.compuserve.com/homepages/vivparker/genbritz.htm
  A Genealogical Research Service for those living outside the UK but researching in England, Wales, Scotland, Ireland and the Channel Islands. Research within New Zealand also undertaken.

- GenCentral
  http://www.gencentral.com/
  GenCentral provides affordable family history services for the beginner or the experienced researcher. Consult on-line with an expert researcher, order an instant record search from the Family History Library, or hire a professional researcher.

- Genealogia e Heráldica Portuguesas - Gabinete de Genealogia e Heráldica
  http://planeta.clix.pt/holstein/
  Professional research in genealogy and heraldry in Portugal.

- Genealogical CDs
  http://seidata.com/~genealogy/cdlist.html
  People who own genealogy CDs and are willing to do lookups for others.

- Genealogical Enterprises
  http://www.geneent.com/
  Specializes in: collecting and searching records for professional genealogists; cataloguing and indexing genealogical records for librarians, societies, and genealogists.

- Genealogical Journeys in Time Biographies
  http://ourworld.compuserve.com/homepages/Strawn/
  An index of individual biographies and a service that will photocopy the biographies for you from the books in their local library.

- Genealogical Journeys in Time (Research Services)
  http://ourworld.compuserve.com/homepages/Strawn/referenc.htm

- Genealogical Research in England - English Village Research
  http://www.btinternet.com/~p.w.w/evr.htm

- Genealogical Research in Scotland
  http://website.lineone.net/~gary.young/
  Gary Young, Dunbartonshire, Scotland.

- The Genealogical Research Library ~ Toronto, Ontario, Canada
  http://www.grl.com/grl/index.shtml

- Genealogical Research Services in Ontario Canada - Suzanne Schaller
  http://www.cyberus.ca/~suzannes/research.html
  Professional researcher based in Ottawa, Ontario, Canada.

- Genealogical Services & The Genealogy Store
  http://www.genservices.com/

- Genealogist and Record Agent Ireland
  http://indigo.ie/~records/
  Hilda McGauley, M.Sc. provides a genealogical research service based in Dublin, Ireland.

- Genealogists at VU Look-ups
  http://www.concentric.net/~Cande/lookups.shtml

- Genealogy Ancestors Search
  http://www.wasatch.com/~lance/
  By Family Ties Research, Sandy, Utah.

- Genealogy and History in France
  http://www.gefrance.com/

- Genealogy Central Lineage Service
  http://www.geocities.com/Heartland/Woods/6036/research/index.html
  Specializes in Native American, New England and Colonial American research.

- Genealogy Document Searches ~ Bowie, Maryland
  http://members.aol.com/RalphK/DocumentSearch.html

- Genealogy Family History - family search - UK
  http://www.familysearch.uk.com/
  Family history research services. Several directories of professional family historians providing genealogy research in the UK and Ireland.

- Genealogy Helplist
  http://helplist.org/
  List of volunteers willing to help others in specific areas.

- Genealogy in Northumberland
  http://www.fortunecity.co.uk/picnicpark/ironbridge/76
  Research undertaken in Northumberland, England.

- Genealogy in Poland - Watta Research Service
  http://www.watta.pdi.net/
  A Poland based research service, with access to non-microfilmed documents in local parishes.

- genealogyPro - Directory of Professional Genealogists
  http://genealogyPro.com/
  An advertising and marketing directory for professional genealogists, adoption researchers, historians and translators.

- Genealogy Quest ~ Washington, D.C.
  http://www.genealogy-quest.com/

- Genealogy Record Service
  http://www.genrecords.com/

- Genealogy Research & Free Resources (Formerly known as Clippings)
  http://members.aol.com/familytwig/clippings.htm
  Virginia and Ohio.

- Genealogy Research Associates ~ Salt Lake City, Utah
  http://www.graonline.com/
  Professional research and record look-up services. Salt Lake City, UT, Washington, D.C., California.

- Genealogy Research in Abruzzo, Italy
  http://abruzzo2000.com/genealogy/index.html
  Free resources and professional services for research in Abruzzo, Italy, from an Abruzzo-based group.

- Genealogy Research Services ~ California
  http://home.pacbell.net/cageni/

- Genealogy Research Services
  http://users.erols.com/wendsoft/gene.htm
  Pay only for results! We provide a genealogy research service to help you find your family roots in the United States.

- Genealogy Research UK Worcestershire - Worcestershire Family History Research
  http://www.genealogy-worcester.co.uk/
  All types of ancestral research within the county of Worcestershire. For those wishing to locate missing friends/relatives, etc. anywhere in the UK, then the 1998/1999 UK Electoral Registers service may be of interest.

- Genealogy Search
  http://www.genealogysearch.com/

- Genealogy Services, Malta
  http://sites.waldonet.net.mt/sultan/gene.htm

- Genealogy Wizard
  http://www.genealogywizard.com/

- Genealogy Works - Ruby Coleman ~ Valentine, Nebraska
  http://incolor.inetnebr.com/rcoleman/

- Generation Link - UK Based Genealogy and Family History Research Service
  http://www.generationlink.co.uk/
  A friendly and professional genealogy and family history research company. All enquiries for UK ancestors are welcome, one name or a whole family tree.

- Genesearch : Professional Genealogy & Family History Research
  http://www.genesearch.com/
  Joe Beine of Denver, Colorado. Specializes in USA and Germany.

- Genfindit - English, Scottish & Irish Vital Records Ordering Service
  http://www.genfindit.com/index.html

- Gen-Find Research Associates
  http://www.gen-find.com/
  Specialists in Genealogy Research for Ontario & Western Canada, Scotland, Ireland, Forensic Genealogy & 20th Century Research.

- Genie Genealogy Research
  http://genealogy.hypermart.net
  Genie Genealogy provides professional genealogy research services to help you find your ancestors. Whether you're a novice or expert, discover your family tree now - quickly and affordably. Genie also offers web page design, picture scanning, report printing, data entry, and LDS-specific genealogy services.

- GenSwap - Free Online Genealogy Data and More
  http://www.genswap.com/
  GenSwap is a site where you can post to swap genealogy data you have, or for data that you want. You can also find professional genealogists, people willing to do free lookups, and links to sites with online genealogy data.

- GenSwap Mailing List
  http://www.rootsweb.com/~jfuller/gen_mail_general.html#GenSwap
  For exchanging research time and swapping records for records with others (e.g., researching in your area for someone else in exchange for like efforts on their part).

- GenTracer English Research
  http://www.gentracer.com/england.html
  Professional genealogical research in the microfilmed records at the Family History Library in Salt Lake City.

- Georgia Genealogical Society - Independent Researchers for Hire
  http://www.gagensociety.org/members.htm

- Georgia Genealogy Research Services
  http://LeeGenealogy.ofamerica.com/garesh.htm

- German Genealogical Research Service
  http://www.ggrs.com/
  Professional genealogical research in Germany, especially in South Germany (Bayern, Baden, Württemberg, Hessen). Emigration and surname databases that will be built up regularly.

- (GISA) Genealogiese Instituut van Suid-Afrika / Genealogical Institute of South Africa
  http://www.sun.ac.za/gisa/

- Glasgow Photography
  http://www.jennow.freeserve.co.uk
  Glasgow Photography provides photographs of any address or area in the Glasgow area of Scotland on digital format or hard copy.

- Glenn King - Genealogy Research, Canadian and U.K. records ~ Ontario, Canada
  mailto:kingdav@limestone.kosone.com
  For details send e-mail to Glenn at: e-mail kingdav@limestone.kosone.com.

- GMW Helpers
  http://www.citynet.net/mostwanted/ra/assist.htm
  A list of research volunteers from Genealogy's Most Wanted.

- Golden West Marketing
  http://www.greenheart.com/rdietz/
  Surname exchange, limited free searches of database, book list, professional researchers.

- Goodwin Research Associates
  http://goodwinresearch.com/index.html
  Specializes in Maine genealogy and historical research.

- Greene Genealogy
  http://www.dianegreene.com/
  Professional research at the Family History Library in Salt Lake City, National Archives and Daughters of the American Revolution Library in Washington, D.C. FREE brochure.

- GSS - Genealogical Search Services
  http://www.itsnet.com/~gss/
  Research at the Family History Library in Salt Lake City, Utah

- Guernsey Origins ~ U.K.
  http://www.thermrgroup.ca/GuernseyOrigins.html
  Professional research service specializing in Guernsey ancestry.

- Guthrigg Genealogy - Faye Guthrie's Home Page
  http://web.solutions.net.au/~guthrigg/index.htm
  Professional research services and genealogical information on Australian shipping resources, Australian Wills and Inquests, Convict ships.

◆ "H"

- Haines Research Services ~ Rural Hall, North Carolina
  http://ourworld-top.cs.com/HainesJeff/index.htm

- Headstone Hunter
  http://www.headstonehunter.com/
  A network of volunteers who will visit graveyards in their area.

- Headstones in Yorkshire
  http://www.honey23.freeserve.co.uk/Headstones/index.html
  Professional service for finding and recording headstones in Yorkshire, England.

- Heartland Genealogical Services
  http://web.shawneelink.com/~rtallen/
  Rick T. Allen C.G.R.S., Golconda, Illinois.

- Heirlines Family History and Genealogy Research Services ~ Salt Lake City, Utah
  http://www.heirlines.com

- Henry Z ("Hank") Jones Jr., FASG - Genealogical Author and Lecturer
http://www.HankJones.com/
Hank has been a professional genealogist since 1965. Hank is an entertaining genealogical lecturer, an accomplished writer and a respected Fellow of the American Society of Genealogists. He is best known for his extensive work with Palatine genealogy and for his popular book, Psychic Roots.

- Herefordshire Family History Research
http://homepages.which.net/~eleanor.harris/
Family history research in the English county of Herefordshire.

- Heritage Associates
http://www.granniesworld.com/heritage/
New England Research, specializing in pre-1850 north coast Massachusetts.

- Heritage Consulting and Services ~ Salt Lake City, Utah
http://www.heritageconsulting.com/

- Heritage Hunters of Georgia: Professional Genealogy and Family History Researchers
http://heritagehuntersofga.com/
Specializing in historical and genealogical research in North Georgia.

- HeritageLink Genealogy Research Group
http://www.heritagelink.com/
U. S., Canadian, Colonial, American Indian Adoption and Missing Persons Searches (Confidential Intermediary & Accredited Genealogist). Genealogy Books & Charts. 25 years experience.

- Hidden Heritage - United Kingdom Genealogy Research
http://www.gloster.demon.co.uk/
Specializing in and around Gloucestershire, England, including Bristol, Herefordshire, and Worcestershire.

- Higgins Family History and Other Services
http://www.concentric.net/~Higginsj/
Family history typing & publishing, document scanning for documentation, research Dallas/Fort Worth available resources including government archives.

- Highland Family Heritage
http://www.highland-family-heritage.co.uk/
Professional genealogical search services and guided historical tours throughout Scotland and the Highlands in particular.

- The Historical Detective
http://detective.ourfamily.com
Professional research services with concentration on colonial New England, Civil War soldiers, and Northern Virginia.

- Historical Matters: Historical & Genealogical Research in Kansas
http://www.historical-matters.com/
Mary Clement Douglass, Certified Genealogical Record Specialist.

- Holland Family History ~ Netherlands
http://www.hfh.nl/

- Holland Page Helpdesk
http://ourworld.compuserve.com/homepages/paulvanv/helpdesk.htm

- Holly Heinsohn Texas Genealogy
http://www.hrkropp.com/wizzf.html

- Hoopers International Probate Genealogists
http://www.hoopers.co.uk/
Established in the UK in 1923. Specializing in locating missing beneficiaries.

- HTHolly Research Services ~ Croydon, Utah
http://www.ancestryresearch.com/

- HungaroGens Genealogisches Büro / HungaroGens Genealogical Bureau
http://www.genealogy.net/hungarogens/
Genealogical research in Hungary, Austria, Slovakia, Rumania, Slovenia, Jugoslavia

◆ "I"

- I Dream of Genealogy
http://www.idreamof.com/
Professional genealogy and family history research services, free online databases, family tree evaluations and celebrity genealogies.

- Independent British Naval Researcher and Historical Investigator
http://www.btinternet.com/~samband.bretlands/
Research service for those seeking to find the service records of officers (1660 - 1923) and men (1853 - 1923) who served in the British Royal Navy. Search includes personnel records, information on the ships of the Royal Navy and any actions in which they were involved from earliest times to c. 1970, including World War 1 and World War 2.

- Independent Researchers at the PRO ~ United Kingdom
http://www.open.gov.uk/pro/independ.htm
This site provides instructions on how you can receive the UK Public Record Office's official listing of independent researchers by e-mail. Listings of specialists in various record categories held by the PRO are available.

- Infosearch Cornwall
http://www.infosearch-cornwall.co.uk/index.html
Cornwall family and local history research services.

- inGeneas Canadian Genealogical Research Services ~ Ottawa, Ontario, Canada
http://www.ingeneas.com/
Searchable databases containing 50,000+ Canadian passenger and immigration records (c1750 to 1900) including the only electronic version of the free National Archives of Canada Miscellaneous Immigration Index.

- Institute for Historical Family Research
http://ihff.nwy.at/index.htm/
Austria, Czech & Slovak Republics, Hungary, Slovenian Republic, Croatia, Galicia & Bukovina.

- International Genealogical Search
http://www.heirsearch.com/

- Investigaciones Genealogicas
  http://lanzadera.com/rozas
  Estamos especializados en el Pa's Vasco y Cantabria, Espaŝa. Genealogical research in the Basque Country & Cantabria, Spain.

- Iowa Genealogical Research
  http://sites.netscape.net/dlcooper8432coop/homepage
  Iowa-based professional genealogical researcher with expertise in researching Iowa records.

- Irish Adoptees Search Ireland
  http://hometown.aol.com/odea97/irishadoptees.html
  Irish Adoptees searching for their birth families in Ireland can find advice, suggestions and resources here.

- Irish Ancestral Research Genealogy
  http://www.irish-Ancestry.com
  Free assessment for all persons who fill in the ancestor details form.

- Irish Family History Foundation
  http://www.irishroots.net/

- Irish Professional Genealogists
  http://www.iol.ie/~irishrts/Professionals.html

- IRLGEN - Commissioning a Genealogical Search
  http://www.bess.tcd.ie/irlgen/commiss.htm

- Isle of Man - Manx Family History Search
  http://www.oz.net/~ccaine/djd/
  Donna Douglass can help you with your research.

- Italian Ancestral Research
  http://www.italianancestralresearch.ofutah.com/
  Carolyn B. Ugolini, Accredited Genealogist.

- Italian Genealogical and Heraldic Institute
  http://www.italgen.com/sponsors/ighi/index.htm

- Italian Research
  http://www.gentracer.com/italy.html
  Professional genealogical research in the microfilmed records at the Family History Library in Salt Lake City and on-site in Sicily.

- It's All Relative
  http://home.att.net/~relative2u/index.html
  Professional genealogical research in Ohio.

◆ "J"

- James F. Justin Family Tree Research Services
  http://members.aol.com/jkjustin/gensrch.html
  Genealogy Research Service for New Jersey marriage records, birth records, death certificates, census returns, wills, court records and deeds also Philadelphia National Archives.

- Janet Reakes Family History Services ~ Australia
  http://www.familytreeresearch.net/

- Janna's Genealogy Services ~ Scottsdale, Arizona
  http://www.dcfinc.com/genealogy/gensvcs.html

- Jeff Stewart Genealogical Services -- Specializing in Ontario Research
  http://members.aol.com/OntarioGen/
  Based in Toronto, the home of Ontario's major repositories.

- Jennie's Family History Services
  http://www.users.nascr.net/~madoc/
  A research service for the 1891 census of Cardiff, a burial research service, a Polaroid photograph service.

- John Wylie Consulting ~ Grand Prairie, Texas
  http://www.johnwylie.com/
  Full time professional genealogists who perform research, lecture, conduct seminars, and tutor clients.

◆ "K"

- Karen S. Smith Professional Genealogist
  http://www.greenapple.com/~ksmith
  Conducting professional research in Fairfield, Hocking, Licking, Pickaway, or Perry County, Ohio.

- KBA Research. Ancestral Research Services in the U.K
  http://members.aol.com/kbaresch
  Locate your ancestors, by using KBA Research, a professional, reliable and cost-effective service.

- Kennedy Research - Australian Family History Research Service
  http://www.marque.com.au/kenres/

- Kenneth G. Aitken & Associates FHS
  http://familyhistory.cjb.net/
  Professional local and family history services, specializing in Western Canadian and English research. Available for seminars, lectures, or private research work.

- Kentucky Genealogical and Historical Research
  http://members.aol.com/ShelbyW534/index.html

- Kentucky Research Services
  mailto:kyroots@qx.net
  Dr. Roseann Hogan has been doing research for twenty years and is the author of Kentucky Ancestry. For details, send e-mail to: kyroots@qx.net.

- Kinfolk's Korner Genealogy Services
  http://www.kinfolkskorner.com/
  Champaign Co Illinois & surrounding counties (McLean, Piatt, Douglass, Edgar and Vermilion).

- KinHelp
  http://www.web-ecosse.com/genes/genes2.htm
  A Scottish oriented genealogical service by Gordon Johnson.

- Know Your Heritage Organization ~ Salt Lake City, Utah
  http://www.knowyourheritage.org/

◆ "L"

- Lancs Research - Lancashire Family Research ~ England
  http://ds.dial.pipex.com/i3d/LancsResearch/

- Land Record Research Directory
  http://www.ultranet.com/~deeds/research.htm
  Shows you other researchers who are doing LAND RECORD work in various parts of the country.

- Larry S. Mitchell - Professional Genealogy Research
  & Services
  http://www.rootsdog.com/
  *Professional genealogical research for Michigan, Ontario, Eastern
  U.S. Resources include internet, census, vital stats, libraries, etc.
  Able to produce professional looking family history books and
  albums.*

- Lassen & Lassen: Certified Genealogical Records
  Specialists
  mailto:slassen@infoave.net
  *Work in Ashe, Wilkes, Watauga, and Alleghany Cos., NC and in
  Grayson Co., VA. Additional nearby counties by special
  arrangement. Specialties are research, reportage, and on-site
  photography. For details e-mail slassen@infoave.net.*

- Legends & Legacies Writing Services
  http://www.legends.ca

- LIFELINES Genealogical Research
  http://www.webspawner.com/users/DonDixonGRSC/
  *Don Dixon, GRS(C), LIFELINES Genealogical Research/
  Genealogical and family history research for New Brunswick,
  Canada.*

- Lineage Search Associates ~ Mechanicsville,
  Virginia
  http://www.mindspring.com/~mpollock/

- Lineages, Inc.: In-Depth Research
  http://www.lineages.com/store/InDepth.asp

- Line Search ~ Kaysville, Utah
  http://www.linesearch.com/

- Linhagens - Genealogical Research in Portugal /
  Investigação Genealógica em Portugal
  http://linages.cjb.net/

- Lists of Independent Researchers
  http://www.pro.gov.uk/readers/independent.htm
  *How to Retrieve a List of Independent Researchers by E-mail from
  the PRO.*

- The Look-up Exchange
  http://www.geocities.com/Heartland/Plains/8555/lookup.html
  *A county-by-county list of resources covering England, Scotland,
  Wales and the Isle of Man, made available by volunteers for free
  look-ups.*

- Lookups from Privately Owned Publications
  http://genealogyfix.tripod.com/private.html
  People volunteering to do lookups in their own personal library.

- Los Angeles City Directory 1930
  mailto:billcapp@ix.netcom.com
  *E-mail Bill Cappello and he will do a reasonable number of specific
  lookups for you. Allow two weeks for a reply.*

- Lynne Fiddick's Family History Research Home
  Page ~ New South Wales, Australia
  http://www.users.bigpond.com/Lynnette_Fiddick/

◆ "M"

- Maine Genealogical Researchers for Hire
  http://www.geocities.com/Heartland/Ranch/4962/resrch.html

- Manx Ancestral Tours
  http://www.advsys.co.uk/m-a-tours
  *Service offering to trace ancestors and giving a guided tour around
  the related venues on the Isle of Man.*

- Marbract Services - NSW Birth, Death & Marriage
  Certificate Transcription Service ~ Australia
  http://www.marbract.com.au/
  *NSW Births 1788-1905, NSW Marriages 1788-1918 & NSW Deaths
  1788-1945.*

- Mark Windover's Web Page - Quality Professional
  Genealogical Research ~ Williamstown,
  Massachusetts
  http://www.windover.com/
  *United States, Canada (including French), England, Scotland,
  Ireland, Wales, Iceland, Germany, Switzerland, Norway, Sweden,
  Denmark, France, Belgium, and The Netherlands.*

- Marsaudon Office of Historical Research &
  Genealogical Study ~ Avignon, France
  http://perso.wanadoo.fr/cabinet.marsaudon/
  *Olivier Marsaudon, professional genealogist in Avignon, is a
  member of the APG and France's CGP.*

- Massachusetts and New York Genealogy and History
  Research
  http://www.rbinforesearch.com/
  *Specializing in Capital District area; German, Dutch, Irish
  research. Worcester County, Massachusetts, greater Boston area
  and some New York. Specialist in searching church records*

- Michigan Genealogist for Michigan - Karen Olszeski
  http://genealogypro.com/kolszeski.html

- Middle Tennessee Genealogical Society List of
  Genealogists
  http://www.mtgs.org/mtgslist.htm

- Milt Botwinick Professional Genealogist
  http://members.aol.com/botwinick/
  Pennsylvania, New Jersey and Jewish research.

- Minnesota GenSearch
  http://www.users.uswest.net/~ottino/mngensrc.htm

- Molander's Genealogy Service
  http://www.algonet.se/~family/
  For Sweden and Norway

- Monmouth Genealogy Research Services &
  Aberdeen Matawan Cemetery List
  http://www.netlabs.net/hp/gjoynson/
  *Professional experienced researcher available for help with
  genealogy research in Monmouth County, NJ.*

- Morrigan Research Services
  http://www.morrigan.com/
  *A professional genealogical research service based in Dublin
  Ireland.*

- My Sixteen - Robert W. Marlin - Professional Genealogical Research ~ Maitland, Florida
  http://members.aol.com/MYSIXTEEN/

◆ "N"

- Nancy J. Emmert, C.G. - Genealogist
  http://www.execpc.com/~emmert/
  Genealogy Research, Lecturer, and Instructor.

- Nancy Waterhouse - Genealogical Research
  http://www.genhelp.bigstep.com/
  Located near the Family History Library in Salt Lake City, Utah. Services primarily include searches of census records, vital records, and city directories although other types of records may also be accessed upon client request.

- Natalie Cottrill Genealogical Research
  http://www.nataliesnet.com/
  United States research at the Salt Lake City, Utah Family History Library.

- The National Archives of Ireland: Genealogical and Historical Researchers
  http://www.nationalarchives.ie/gen_researchers.html
  Postal addresses of professional researchers in Ireland.

- The National Capital Area Chapter of the Association of Professional Genealogists ~ Washington, DC
  http://www.apgen.org/ncac.html

- NC Gen -- NC Professional Genealogical Research
  http://ncgen.mms.net/
  Professional genealogical research in North Carolina and nearby states.

- New Jersey and Italian Genealogical Research Services
  http://www.italgen.com/sponsors/piccirillo/index.htm

- New Jersey Genealogical Research Service
  http://www.njgrs.com/

- New Life Enterprises
  http://www.webbergroup.com/newlife/
  Offers Genealogy, Heraldry and Web Site Design services.

- The New River Company's Genealogy and History Research Site - RootSource
  http://www.rootsource.com/

- New Zealand Research
  http://home.st.net.au/~ailsa/
  Ailsa Corlett, professional researcher.

- Nicholas J. Davey, Researcher for Glamorgan and Monmouthshire, Wales
  mailto:ndavey@baynet.co.uk
  E-mail Nicholas Davey for details at: ndavey@baynet.co.uk.

- North Carolina's Professional Genealogists' Network (PGN)
  http://www.ncprogen.org/

- Northeast Professional Genealogy ~ Middlebury, Connecticut
  http://www.FamilyTreeDoctor.com/

- Nova's Genealogy Page
  http://www.buffnet.net/~nova/
  Nova will search her Social Security Death Index CD-ROM for you.

- NZEF Research Service
  http://www.medal.net/nzef/
  Research Service covering New Zealanders who served in the New Zealand Expeditionary Forces (NZEF) during World War 1 (1914-18).

◆ "O"

- The Official Iowa Counties Genealogy - Professional Genealogical Researchers
  http://www.iowa-counties.com/gene/
  This site has a page where you can post complaints and opinions regarding professional researchers that you feel haven't treated you right.

- Ohio Census Search
  http://www.witsend.org/gen/ohiocen.htm

- Oklahoma and Arkansas Research by Monroe Davis
  http://www.geocities.com/Eureka/Park/5315/research.htm

- Oklahoma Genealogical Research Enterprise ~ Oklahoma City, Oklahoma
  http://homestead.juno.com/moose128/index.html

- The Ortenburger and Hackstock Family Home Page
  http://home.earthlink.net/~rortenburger/index.htm
  German and United States family history research performed by Rick Ortenburger.

- Oxford Ancestors
  http://www.oxfordancestors.com
  Offers DNA-based services in genealogy. MatriLine™ uses mitochondrial DNA to place a person in an evolutionary framework going back 150,000 years. MatriLine™ interprets your maternal ancestry, linking you - if your roots are in Europe - to one of seven "foremothers". MyMap™ maps out the current geographical distribution of any surname. MaleMatch™ compares Y-chromosomes to establish, or disprove, a paternal link between individuals.

- Oxfordshire County Council Cultural Services - Centre for Oxfordshire Studies - Oxfordshire Genealogical Researchers ~ England
  http://www.oxfordshire.gov.uk/oxgenres.htm

◆ "P"

- The PA1776 Researchers List
  http://www.pa1776.com/PAGENE/rsr01.htm
  For help with Pennsylvania genealogical research.

- Palatine & Pennsylvania-Dutch Genealogy Personally Owned Genealogy Resources
  http://www.geocities.com/Heartland/3955/resources.htm

● **Pallante Center for Italian Research**
http://www.geocities.com/TheTropics/Shores/2641/Pallante.htm
A virtual research center for Italian research (in-person visits available by appointment for those local to upstate New York). A growing collection of Italian related resources, including an archival collection and Italian family surname files. Professional Italian genealogy research services and other historical research relating to Italy or Italian immigrants worldwide, as well as help with dual citizenship (US/Italian), finding educational Italian resources for schools, etc.

● **Past Tracker ~ Coos Bay, Oregon**
http://www.harborside.com/~rice/index.html
Native American and New England specialty searches.

● **P.A.T.H. Finders - Personal Ancestral Tours & History**
http://www.abilnet.com/pathfinders/
Specializing in Family History and Travel in the Czech and Slovak Republics.

● **Patricia Joan Ozman Horsey ~ Chestertown, Maryland**
http://chesapeake-bay.com/mrsh/genealogy.htm

● **Paul Bunnell will search your Loyalist ancestors - Send e-mail to Paul for details**
mailto:benjamin@capecod.net

● **Peck-J Genealogy Research**
http://www.trilobyte.net/peckjgen/2RESCH.htm
Do research for clients in such areas as New England, Eastern States, England, Native Americans, African Americans and Utah. Only 35 miles from Salt Lake City LDS Family History Library.

● **Peggy M. Winston, Certified Genealogical Records Specialist**
http://peggy-winston.tripod.com/
Specializing in Washington and Oregon Research.

● **Per Search**
http://users.aol.com/vcassoc/

● **Philadelphia Family Finder ~ Pennsylvania**
http://hometown.aol.com/ladybrvhrt/private/index.html

● **Photoroots: Scotland**
http://www.photoroots.co.uk/
Professional service providing by-request photographs of Scottish ancestral homes and villages and provide via e-mail.

● **Pioneer Information Services ~ Texas**
http://pioneerinfo.com/Pioneer.html
Specializing in records for north and east Texas, as well as using computers in your genealogical research.

● **PolishExpress, Inc. Family History Research Service in Polish Archives**
http://www.polishexpress.com/
Devoted to finding, copying, and translating family history documents from Polish archives.

● **Polish Genealogical Translations**
http://adela49.freeyellow.com/index.html
Native Polish translator/interpreter will assist you in finding your Polish roots by translating your Polish genealogical records. Twenty years of experience.

● **Portuguese Genealogy by Doug da Rocha Holmes**
http://www.dholmes.com/rocha1.html
Professional researcher specializing in Azorean genealogy and Portuguese translation.

● **Powell Genealogical Services ~ Wexford, Pennsylvania**
http://powellgenealogy.com/

● **Professional & Amateur Louisiana Genealogists**
http://www.rootsweb.com/~lagenweb/laprofes.htm

● **Professional Family History Services ~ California**
http://pages.prodigy.net/john_flora/pfhs.htm

● **Professional Genealogical Research in Queensland ~ Australia**
http://www.judywebster.gil.com.au/prof.html
Judy Webster.

● **Professional Genealogist - Cottrill and Hefti, Salt Lake City**
http://www.progenealogists.com/
Paul Hefti and Natalie Cottrill are professional genealogists conducting affordable United States, Canadian and European genealogy research at the Family History Library in Salt Lake City, Utah.

● **Professional Genealogist - Elizabeth K. Parkes - New Zealand**
http://genealogynz.co.nz/

● **Professional Genealogist for Georgia - Shannon Wilson**
http://genealogypro.com/swilson.html
Georgia and United States research.

● **Professional Genealogist for Michigan Counties of Ionia and Montcalm - Beth Wills**
http://genealogypro.com/bwills.html
Genealogy research and consulting in the Mid-Michigan area, particularly Ionia and Montcalm counties. Medical Research and consulting a specialty.

● **Professional Genealogist for New Jersey, Washington and Virginia - Charles S. "Chuck" Mason, Jr.**
http://genealogypro.com/cmason.html

● **Professional Genealogist for North Carolina and Virginia - N. C. Moore**
http://genealogyPro.com/nfcarter.html
North Carolina and Virginia genealogy, real estate and property research.

● **Professional Genealogist for Western Kentucky - Bill Utterback**
http://genealogypro.com/b-utterback.html
Bill Utterback, CGRS - Research in the Jackson Purchase Counties of Western Kentucky.

- Professional Genealogist in New York - Nancy Coleman
  http://www.genealogyPro.com/ncoleman.html
  Long Island and NYC (Kings, Queens, & NY Counties) Research Services.

- Professional Genealogist in New Zealand for the UK and Ireland - Tony Fitzgerald
  http://genealogypro.com/tfitzgerald.html

- Professional Genealogist in Scotland
  http://www.truffles.freeserve.co.uk/
  Scots Pine Research Services, Anne Cruickshank.

- Professional Genealogist Services for Newfoundland and Labrador - Barbara A. McGrath
  http://genealogyPro.com/bmcgrath.html

- Professional Genealogists Familiar With Connecticut State Library Collections
  http://www.cslnet.ctstateu.edu/list.htm

- Professional Genealogists of Arkansas, Inc.
  http://www.familyhistory.com/societyhall/viewmember.asp?societyid=164

- Professional Welsh Genealogist - Richard Meredith, Wales
  http://genealogypro.com/mayfair-research.html
  Experienced professional historian & genealogist for the U.K., with a specialty in central and south Wales. Expert on the Meredith surname.

- ProGenealogist.com
  http://www.progenealogist.com/
  Full-time Philadelphia, Pennsylvania area professional genealogist, Michael S. Ramage, J.D. Genealogy research & consulting in Philadelphia and Montgomery Counties, Pennsylvania and the Mid-Atlantic (NARA) Region.

- ProResearchers Mailing List
  http://www.rootsweb.com/~jfuller/gen_mail_general.html#ProResearchers
  Just for Professional Researcher to discuss their industry.

- Public Record Office Searches by Roger E. Nixon
  http://ourworld.compuserve.com/homepages/rogerenixon/
  All military, naval, seamen, naturalizations, migrants, police, convicts, FO, HO, CO searched. Wide range of subjects. Check my list first.

- Public Record Searches ~ U.K.
  http://www.users.dircon.co.uk/~searcher/index.htm
  R.W. O'Hara in Kew, Richmond

◆ "Q"

- Quik-Search - A Document Retrieval Service for Genealogists and Historians
  http://www.inconnect.com/~gjnixon/
  Document retrieval from the Family History Library Collections in Salt Lake City, Utah

◆ "R"

- Radix / Services
  http://www.bogardi.com/gen/gx001.htm
  Research services in Hungary.

- Railway Links Research ~ London & Southeast England
  http://www.bcity.com/railway_links

- Random Acts of Genealogical Kindness
  http://raogk.rootsweb.com/
  "The volunteers of this movement are agreeing once per month to either videotape cemeteries, etc., or to visit county courthouses in the county (or area of a country) they live. The cost to you would be reimbursement of costs incurred in granting your request (video tape, copy fees, etc.)".

- Rasch Research - Genealogy Research in Wisconsin
  http://www.execpc.com/~rasch/
  Services in Waukesha and Milwaukee Counties, Wisconsin.

- RECORDS.ORG -- American Records Research Services ~ San Francisco, California
  http://www.records.org/

- Research Associates of Idaho
  http://www.researchassoc-id.com
  Genealogical research, consultation, record searches, and family history publishing. Idaho, continental U.S. and Canadian research.

- The Research Resource
  http://www.toolcity.net/~vadkins/gen/resndx.html

- Research Service - Karen Chappell's Census Research Service
  http://www.angelfire.com/tn2/Fitch/
  A census research service which provides professional, economical, service with a quick turn around time for busy researchers. Specializing in the South, and East, including the state of Illinois.

- Research UK
  http://www.research-uk.com/

- Research Undertaken at the Leicestershire Record Office ~ England
  http://ourworld.compuserve.com/homepages/bwmconsultants/Research.htm

- Resources with a Wide Array of Genealogical Interest
  http://jungclas.com/common/resource.htm
  Lists a variety of volunteer services.

- Rhode Island Families Association - Genealogical Publications and Research
  http://www.erols.com/rigr/
  Research for Rhode Island, New England, Probate, and DAR including membership.

- Rhonda R. McClure Genealogical Services
  http://www.thegenealogist.com/
  A professional genealogist specializing in New England research and computerized genealogy.

- Richard M. Pope, Certified Genealogist
  http://w3.nai.net/~absuax/
  Specializing in Connecticut, Massachusetts, New York City, Germany.

- Richard W. Price & Associates Genealogy Services ~ Salt Lake City, Utah
  http://www.xmission.com/~families/

- R.J. Duprel Research Page
  http://members.theglobe.com/rduprel/index.html
  Luxembourg consulting and research.

- Robert M. Wilbanks IV, Genealogist & Historian
  http://www.robertwilbanks.com/

- Roberts Research Services: Genealogy, Historical Maps
  http://www.compusmart.ab.ca/rrs/index.html
  Current and historical maps and books for researchers of Great Britain and Ireland.

- Rootbound Genealogy's Research Services
  http://www.angelfire.com/il/Rootbound/research.html

- Roots & Branches Genealogy - Becki Hagood
  mailto:Roots4Gen@aol.com
  North Carolina statewide professional researcher. For details send e-mail to Becky at: Roots4Gen@aol.com.

- Roots Cape Breton Genealogy & Family History Centre
  http://eagle.uccb.ns.ca/mining/iona/roots.html
  A computer-assisted research service, Nova Scotia, Canada.

- Rose Research Services - Family History and Genealogical Services
  http://www.roseresearch.co.uk/
  UK genealogy and family history research services, with examples of research, historical context and family trees. Based in London.

- Routes to Roots
  http://www.routestoroots.com/
  Tracing Jewish Roots in Poland, Ukraine, Moldova and Belarus.

- Rural New York State Family Research
  http://www.newyorkstateresearch.com/
  Genealogical Services for Central, Western, and Northern New York

◆ "S"

- SAMPUBCO
  http://www.sampubco.com/
  Will Testators Indexes, Naturalization Records Indexes and Census Indexes online. You can order copies of the original source documents for a small fee.

- Sandy Allen Genealogy Searches
  http://www.superior.net/~sandal/
  Professional genealogist researching off-line sites and sources in Upstate New York. Specializing in the Mohawk Valley, Montgomery and Fulton Counties.

- Sandy Moon Publishing and Family Research Group
  http://www.oz.net/~sandymn/

- Saratoga Research Services
  http://home.att.net/~chadd/index.html
  Specializes in research in the State of New York and Saratoga County New York.

- Schröeder & Fülling GbR, German Genealogy Research Firm
  http://ourworld.compuserve.com/homepages/German_ Genealogy/homepage.htm

- Scot Roots - Scottish ancestor service
  http://www.scotroots.com
  Scot Roots is a Scottish ancestor search service which enlivens family trees with historical maps and photographs from around Scotland.

- Scots Ancestry Research Society
  http://www.royalmile.com/scotsancestry/

- Scotseek Genealogy Research
  http://www.scotseek.co.uk
  Professional research service using photography and detailed research.

- Scots Heritage Genealogy Web site / Scots Heritage of Auchterarder
  http://www.scots-heritage.co.uk/
  Professional research in all Scottish records. Particular areas of interest are Perthshire, all Lanarkshire including the Glasgow area, Lothians, Fife, Angus, Stirlingshire and neighbouring areas, Dunbartonshire and Renfrewshire.

- Scottish Ancestors - Professional Genealogist - Edinburgh, Scotland
  http://www.scottishancestors.com/

- Scottish Ancestry Research
  http://www.genealogypro.com/clcowe.html
  Charlotte L. Cowe, Professional Genealogist and Record Agent.

- Scottish Ancestry Research (Graham Maxwell)
  http://website.lineone.net/~family.history/

- Scottish Family History and Military Research
  http://www.scottishancestors.co.uk/
  Specializes in researching the deaths of British servicemen while in action.

- Scottish Family Research
  http://www.linnet.co.uk/linnet/tour/67015.htm

- Scottish Family Search
  http://www.demon.co.uk/sfs/sfshome.htm

- Scottish Forebears - Genealogists to Discerning Scots Everywhere
  http://www.scottish-forebears.co.uk
  Miss Thomasina Ross and Miss Agnes MacPherson, veteran researchers and experts on human nature can help you find your Scottish ancestors.

- Scottish Roots - Ancestral Research Services
  http://www.scottish-roots.co.uk/

- Searchline - Reuniting Adoptees and Birth Parents
  http://www.search-line.co.uk/
  A UK-based professional researcher, specializing in finding and reuniting adoptees and their birth families.

- The Service Area
  http://www.toolcity.net/~vadkins/gen/svc.html
  From The Grannies' Genealogy Helper Menu.

- Sharyn's Secretarial Services - Brisbane Cemetery Photographs ~ Australia
  http://www.ozemail.com.au/~sharynmark/page6.html
  5x7 photos or digital camera photos.

- Shirley M. De Boer, CG
  http://www.rootsweb.com/~mikent/researchers/deboer.html
  Grand Rapids, Michigan professional researcher specializing in migrations from New England, through New York to Michigan and the Midwest.

- SK Publications
  http://www.skpub.com/genie/
  Genealogy research consultants & census books for sale.

- SMG Research
  http://www.smgenterprise.com/research.html
  Complete Genealogical Research for Southern Wisconsin and Northern Illinois.

- The Snoop Sisters Family History Researchers ~ Nanaimo, B.C. Canada
  http://www.snoopsisters.net/
  England & Wales, Scotland, Ireland & N., Ireland, Eastern Europe, Canada & U.S.

- So Many Branches
  http://www.angelfire.com/biz/SoManyBranches/
  Western New York, Northern Pennsylvania, Michigan and Northern Ohio Genealogical Research.

- South & West Wales Genealogical Index
  http://members.aol.com/swalesidx
  Research in Carmarthenshire, West Glamorgan, National Library of Wales, Public Record Office and the Society of Genealogists undertaken.

- Southern California Chapter Association of Professional Genealogists
  http://www.compuology.com/sccapg/

- Southern Counties Ancestry
  http://www.sammyd.demon.co.uk
  Professional researchers throughout the UK. Access to all the main repositories & collections. Reasonable rates. Location photography and printed pedigrees.

- Southern Italian Genealogical Research
  http://expage.com/page/sitalgen
  Luke Tomson conducts genealogy for southern Italy using Napoleonic Civil records. He is fluent in Italian, and is familiar with Latin, Italian dialects, and paleography. Professional services and low rates.

- Southern Maryland Ancestry
  http://southernmarylandancestry.bizland.com/
  Specializing in genealogy for the Southern Maryland Counties of Calvert, Charles, and St. Mary's.

- Specialist Historical and Genealogical Researcher: Ireland
  http://gofree.indigo.ie/~pmcotter/
  Irish surname and clan research, genealogical research, especially pre-1800 AD work throughout Ireland.

- Stacey: Professional Genealogist
  http://members.aol.com/sbenson625/family/index.htm
  Midwestern and eastern United States - Iowa, Ohio, Missouri, Pennsylvania, Illinois and New Jersey - research services available with the original microfilmed records located at the Family History Library in Salt Lake City.

- stlouisgenealogy.com - Missouri Roots
  http://www.stlouisgenealogy.com/
  Pamela Boyer Porter,CGRS, Specializing in: southeast Missouri, St. Louis Missouri, and Missouri migration paths. Patricia Walls Stamm,CGRS, Specializing in: St. Louis, Missouri, St. Louis Catholic church records and Missouri research.

- Stonesearcher and Associates, Research Specialists in Venango County, Pennsylvania
  http://www.stonesearcher.com/

- Studio Galloway - Genealogy, Heraldry, Paintings, Illustrations ~ Switzerland
  http://www.firmnet.ch/galloway/index_e.html

- Surnames.com
  http://www.surnames.com/default.htm

- Susan Bryant
  mailto:sbry@dowco.com
  Has a Pro-CD Canadian Home Phone CD. E-mail Susan with specific details and she will do a quick lookup for you.

- Swedish Genealogy Company
  http://welcome.to/swedgenco
  Professional genealogy researcher in Sweden, specializing in American-Swedish genealogy.

◆ "T"

- TCI - Threshold Concepts, Inc. Genealogy Research Services Group
  http://www.xmission.com/~tconcept/
  Professional Research Services, Photo/Document Services, Family History Publication Services.

- Ted Gostin, Professional Genealogist
  http://www.generationspress.com/research.html
  Specializing in Jewish genealogy and Southern California resources.

- Thistle Roots Research
  http://www.geocities.com/Heartland/Plains/3735/
  George Cormack's Scottish genealogical resource based in Edinburgh.

- Time Machine: Ancestral Research ~ Alabama
  mailto:LaLynn@aol.com
  Laura Flanagan, member of the Limestone County Historical Society, SPGS, NGS with 7 years experience, working toward certification. For details send e-mail to Laura at: LaLynn@aol.com

- TimeTrackers
  http://www.timetrackers.com.au/
  Professional research and practical guidance for 'do-it-yourself' family history. Based in Perth, Western Australia. Specializes in UK and Australian family history.

- Traces From Your Past
  http://www.cadvision.com/traces/
  Genealogical Publications, Services and Resources to assist the Family Historian researching in Canada and the United Kingdom.

- Tracing your Netherlands ancestors
  http://www.gironet.nl/home/mahaman/
  I offer my services as a researcher. My pedigrees: FRANSSEN, VAN DE PUTTE, DE KLERCK. Classical Dutch recipes. Testimonial. Map of the Netherlands.

- Translation Services - PolishLessons-L
  http://www.toledolink.com/pl/translations.html
  A free genealogical translation service (maintained and coordinated by Arthur Teschler at the University of Giessen in Germany).

- The Tree Searcher - Our Reseacher
  http://www.tencorp.net/thesearcher/tts_ourres.html
  Diann L. Wells, AG.

- TRESEARCH
  http://www.tigerpaw.com/bhammond/tresearch/
  I will do research in Edgar, Clark and Coles counties in Illinois and Vermillion and Park counties in Indiana.

◆ "U"

- The Urban Genealogist
  http://www.pipeline.com/~trob/urban.htm
  Professional house historian and researcher.

- UK Family History Research
  http://web.ukonline.co.uk/gordonh/index.html
  United Kingdom Family History Research, throughout England but London and Somerset and West Wales specialized.

◆ "V"

- Vamp Volunteers Help in Southeast Georgia
  mailto:vamp@gnatnet.net
  Send her an e-mail with details.

- The Vanished Mall - History, Genealogy and Family History Mall
  http://www.vanished.com/
  Newspaper and city directory research service as well as other resources.

- Victorian London Research
  http://www.gendocs.demon.co.uk/victorian.html#HOME
  Victorian era London information on churches, *cemeteries, census information, street indices, lodgings, police divisions etc. etc.*

- Virginia Family Research
  http://www.virginiafamilyresearch.com/
  Virginia genealogy, Virginia Confederate records, Revolutionary records.

◆ "W"

- Welsh Genealogy Photography Requests
  http://www.genealogyphotographs.com
  Professional service providing by-request digital photographs of local churches, gravestones, houses, farms or buildings.

- What You Should Know Before Hiring a Professional Genealogist
  http://www.genservices.com/documents/HiringAPro.html

- Will Search Ireland Co. Ltd
  http://indigo.ie/~willsrch/

- Wisconsin Genealogical Searches Genealogy Wisconsin
  http://www.execpc.com/~prucha/
  Professional searches concentrating on, but not limited to, Western Wisconsin.

- WiSearch
  http://www.wisearch.net/
  Professional research into your Wisconsin roots, specializing in the 1820-1920 time period. Census, vital records, land records, naturalization and much more. Offering on-site photography too!.

- World Family Tree Submitter List
  http://www.inlink.com/~nomi/wftlist/index.html
  Contact info for submitters to Broderbunds WFT CDs

◆ "Y"

- Yahoo!...Genealogy...Researchers
  http://dir.yahoo.com/Business_and_Economy/Shopping_and_Services/History/Genealogy/Research/

- Yorkshire Genealogical Research ~ England
  http://website.lineone.net/~jksdelver/

- Your Family Connection ~ Yorba Linda, California
  http://www.yourfamilyconnection.com/
  Specialty areas include Danish research, lineage research and application preparation, and family health history compilation.

- Your Scottish Kin
  http://www.scotkin.u-net.com/
  Small and friendly family research service, based in the Kingdom of Fife.

- Yukon Historic Research ~ Canada
  http://www.yukonweb.com/business/yhr/

◆ "Z"

- Zorsch Genealogy Research
  http://ourworld.compuserve.com/homepages/zorsch/
  East & middle Tennessee genealogy research by Jody Humpert Zorsch.

- Zroots - Barbara Renick's Home Page
  http://www.zroots.com/

QUAKER
http://www.cyndislist.com/quaker.htm

Category Index:

- General Resource Sites
- History
- Libraries, Archives & Museums
- Locality Specific
- Mailing Lists, Newsgroups & Chat

- People & Families
- Publications, Software & Supplies
- Records: Census, Cemeteries, Land, Obituaries, Personal, Taxes and Vital
- Societies & Groups

◆ General Resource Sites

- Finding Your Quaker Roots
  http://www.rootsweb.com/~quakers/quakfind.htm

- Glossary of Quaker Terms
  http://www.rootsweb.com/~quakers/quakdefs.htm

- Meeting Organization of the Society of Friends (Quakers)
  http://www.rootsweb.com/~quakers/quakmtg2.htm

- Old Style & New Style Dates for the Quaker Calendar
  http://www.everton.com/usa/GENEALOG/
  GENEALOG.QUAKERC1

- Quaker Abbreviations
  http://www.everton.com/GENEALOG/GENEALOG.QUAKER

- Quaker Corner
  http://www.rootsweb.com/~quakers/index.htm

- Quaker Customs & Beliefs
  http://www.rootsweb.com/~quakers/quakinfo.htm

- Quaker Dates
  http://www.illuminatrix.com/andria/quaker.html

- Quaker Electronic Archive
  http://www.qis.net/~daruma/
  Has Quaker writings, meeting minutes, resource guides and a message board.

- Quaker Monthly Meetings
  http://www.rootsweb.com/~quakers/quakmtg.htm
  Searchable database.

- Quaker Queries
  http://www.localaccess.com/rubym/QuakerQu.htm
  Submit your queries for free to this publication. Search the online index to one of the recent issues.

- Quaker Queries & Archives
  http://www.rootsweb.com/~quakers/queries.htm

- Quaker Silhouettes
  http://www.rootsweb.com/~quakers/quaksilo.htm

- The Quaker Yeoman Online
  http://www.aracnet.com/~pslamb/quaker.htm

- The Religious Society of Friends
  http://www.quaker.org/

- Religious Society of Friends - by Kirby Urner
  http://www.teleport.com/~pdx4d/quakes.html

- Research Resources for Quaker Genealogy
  http://www.rootsweb.com/~quakers/resource.htm

◆ History

- Quaker History
  http://www.quaker.org/#7

- Quaker History Archives
  http://harrisroxas.com/qha/

◆ Libraries, Archives & Museums

- Friends Collection at the Earlham College Libraries
  http://www.earlham.edu/~libr/quaker/index.htm
  The Arthur and Kathleen Postle Archives and Friends Collection is one of the four or five largest in the world, with more than 12,000 books and nearly as many pamphlets, some going back to the 17th Century when the Society of Friends was founded. These works are supplemented with an extensive collection of Quaker genealogical materials. Personal diaries, letters, and detailed records of monthly and yearly meetings reveal the lives of thousands of Quaker men and women. The Friends Collection draws hundreds of scholars and genealogists to Lilly Library annually. In addition to assisting these visitors, College Archivist and Curator, Thomas D. Hamm, answers nearly 400 inquiring letters each year.

- Guilford College Friends Historical Collection ~ Greensboro, North Carolina
  http://www.guilford.edu/LibraryArt/fhc.htm

- The Quaker Room/Archives in the Edmund Stanley Library ~ Wichita, Kansas
  http://www.friends.edu/Library/Collections/Quaker/

- Tripod
  http://tripod.brynmawr.edu/
  *The library system of Bryn Mawr, Haverford and Swarthmore College Libraries. These libraries house the Quaker Collection -
  Haverford College Special Collections*
  http://www.haverford.edu/library/sc/qcoll.html
  Friends Historical Library at Swarthmore College
  http://www.swarthmore.edu/Library/friends/
  Read a Guide to Searching Tripod
  http://www.brynmawr.edu/Library/Docs/tripod_guide.html
  Then connect to the Tripod program directly using your telnet software and access capabilities.
  telnet://tripod.brynmawr.edu
  You must have Telnet software to access. Make note of logon and password when you begin. Read more about Telnet on the "Libraries, Archives & Museums - General" category page on Cyndi's List.
  http://www.CyndisList.com/lib-gen.htm#Telnet

◆ Locality Specific

- Quakers in Britain - The Religious Society of Friends - Britain Yearly Meeting
  http://www.quaker.org.uk/
  - o An Introduction to the Library
    http://www.quaker.org.uk/library.html
    - • Genealogical Sources
      http://www.quaker.org.uk/geneal.html

- Quakers [Society of Friends] in Illinois
  http://www.outfitters.com/illinois/history/family/quakers/
  quakers1.html

- The Society of Friends in Fulton County, Illinois
  http://www.outfitters.com/illinois/history/family/quakers/
  quakers.html

- Southern Quaker Genealogy
  http://www.geocities.com/Heartland/Plains/2064/squaker.htm
  A resource guide to Southern Quaker genealogy organized by state and Monthly Meeting.

  - o Wrightsboro: a Georgia Quaker Colony
    http://www.geocities.com/Heartland/Plains/2064/
    wrights.htm
    Many Ohio Quakers moved North from the short-lived Quaker colony in Wrightsboro, GA. Page gives the original charter granted to colonists, with names of grantees and acreage received, also surname links to pages and other information on Wrightsboro.

◆ Mailing Lists, Newsgroups & Chat

- Genealogy Resources on the Internet - Religions / Churches Mailing Lists
  http://www.rootsweb.com/~jfuller/gen_mail_religions.html
  Most of the mailing list links below point to this site, wonderfully maintained by John Fuller.

- PA-QUAKERS Mailing List
  http://www.rootsweb.com/~jfuller/gen_mail_religions.html
  #PA-QUAKERS
  For anyone with a genealogical interest in the Quaker families that settled and lived in Pennsylvania.

- QUAKER-L Mailing List
  http://www.rootsweb.com/~jfuller/gen_mail_religions.html
  #QUAKER-L

- QUAKER-ROOTS Mailing list
  http://www.rootsweb.com/~jfuller/gen_mail_religions.html
  #QUAKER-ROOTS
  And the QUAKER-ROOTS Discussion Group
  http://www.rootsweb.com/~quakers/quaker-r.htm

◆ People & Families

- HINSHAW Family Association
  http://www.blueneptune.com/~hinshaw/

- MENDENHALL Family Association
  http://mendenhall.org/mfa/

- The Quaker Collection
  http://home.sprynet.com/~jrichmon/qkrcoll.htm
  "A collection of Family Group Sheets, originally published on FidoNet, of a number of early, significant Quaker families".

◆ Publications, Software & Supplies

- Amazon.com Genealogy Bookstore - Quakers
  http://www.amazon.com/exec/obidos/external-search/?
  keyword=quaker+genealogy&tag=markcyndisgenealA/

- AudioTapes.com - Genealogical Lectures on Cassette Tapes - Quaker
  http://www.audiotapes.com/search2.asp?Search=Quaker

- Family Tree Maker's Genealogy Site: Quaker Records on CD-ROM
  http://www.bannerblue.com/38_marthe.html
  Marthe Arends reviews: Genealogical Records: The Encyclopedia of Quaker Genealogy, 1750-1930.

- Frontier Press Bookstore - Quaker History
  http://www.frontierpress.com/frontier.cgi?category=quaker

- Genealogical Records: The Encyclopedia of Quaker Genealogy, 1740-1930, CD 192
  http://www.bannerblue.com/192facd.html
  A CD-ROM for sale.

- Heritage Books - Quaker
  http://www.heritagebooks.com/quaker.htm

- My Ancestors Were Quakers: How Can I Find Out More About Them?
  http://www.sog.org.uk/acatalog/SoG_Bookshop_Online_My_
  Ancestors_Series_135.html#a1024s
  Publication for sale from the UK's Society of Genealogists.

- Society of Genealogists Bookshop - Quakers
  http://www.sog.org.uk/acatalog/SoG_Bookshop_Online_
  Quakers_300.html
  A source for books of interest to the family historian researching UK ancestors who were Friends.

- Where Did Hinshaw Put Those Quaker Records?
  http://www.rootsweb.com/~quakers/hinshaw.htm
  From the Quaker Corner: A simplified index to the 6-Volumes of "The Encyclopedia of American Quaker Genealogy".

- Willow Bend Bookstore - Quaker Genealogy
  http://www.willowbend.net/default.asp

◆ Records: Census, Cemeteries, Land, Obituaries, Personal, Taxes and Vital

- Barber Corners Quaker Cemetery
  http://www.rootsweb.com/~nycayuga/cem/cem86.htm
  Town of Ledyard, New York.

- Chester County Cemeteries Online - Quaker Cemeteries
  http://199.72.15.191/Sites/Gen/Chet2/scripts/ListCem.asp?denom=Quaker

- Dutchess County, New York Births
  http://www.usgennet.org/usa/ny/county/dutchess/dutchbirths.htm
  Quaker Births.

- Quaker Burying Ground Morris, New York, Surnames A-M
  http://www.rootsweb.com/~nyotsego/cemetery/morbga.htm
  And Surnames N-Z.
  http://www.rootsweb.com/~nyotsego/cemetery/morbgb.htm

- Quaker Cemetery, Knoxville, Tioga County PA
  http://www.rootsweb.com/~patioga/cemetery/quaker.htm

- Quaker Deaths, Dutchess, NY, ALHN
  http://www.usgennet.org/usa/ny/county/dutchess/quakerdeaths.htm
  Quaker Deaths from the Oblong Monthly Meeting.

- Quaker Marriages
  http://www.rootsweb.com/~quakers/quakmarr.htm

- Quaker Removals Dutchess, NY, ALHN
  http://www.usgennet.org/~ahnydutc/removalindex.htm
  Quaker Removals from the Nine Partners Monthly Meeting.

- Rahway & Plainfield Monthly Meeting
  http://members.tripod.com/~PlainfieldFriends/
  Includes Register of Births - 1705 - 1890, Register of Deaths - 1705 - 1892, Plainfield Burial Ground.

◆ Societies & Groups

- Canadian Friends Historical Association
  http://home.interhop.net/~aschrauwe/

- Evangelical Friends International
  http://www.evangelical-friends.org/

- Friends General Conference
  http://www.fgcquaker.org/

- Friends Historical Association ~ Philadelphia, Pennsylvania
  http://www.haverford.edu/library/fha/fha.html

- Friends United Meeting
  http://www.fum.org/

- National Society Descendants of Early Quakers
  http://www.terraworld.net/mlwinton/
  To promote appreciation and recognition of the accurate and extensive family records kept by the Society of Friends.

- Quaker Family History Society ~ England
  http://www.qfhs.mcmail.com/

QUERIES & MESSAGE BOARDS

http://www.cyndislist.com/queries.htm

Category Index:

◆ General Queries
◆ How To

◆ Locality Specific

◆ General Queries

- C. More Bones' Query Page - From the Skeleton Closet
  http://members.aol.com/cmorebones/queries.htm

- Family Workings
  http://www.familyworkings.com/

- Folks Online: Folks Family Message Tree
  http://www.folksonline.com/bbs3/

- GenConnect at RootsWeb
  http://cgi.rootsweb.com/~genbbs/
  A system for USGenWeb & WorldGenWeb queries, biographies and obituaries

  o Family Associations
    http://cgi.rootsweb.com/~genbbs/indx/FamAssoc.html

  o Global Surname Search
    http://cgi.rootsweb.com/~genbbs/genbbs.cgi?search

    • Search Help
      http://cgi.rootsweb.com/~genbbs/helpsrch.html

  o Special Collections
    http://cgi.rootsweb.com/~genbbs/indx/Special.html

  o USA Visitor Center
    http://cgi.rootsweb.com/~genbbs/usaindex.html

  o Visitor Center Hints and Tips
    http://cgi.rootsweb.com/~genbbs/HINTS/index.html

  o World Visitor Center
    http://cgi.rootsweb.com/~genbbs/qindex.html

- Genealogical Journeys in Time Queries Page
  http://ourworld.compuserve.com/homepages/Strawn/allqueri.htm

- Genealogical Journeys in Time Researchers Surname Page
  http://ourworld.compuserve.com/homepages/Strawn/allsurna.htm

- Genealogy Exchange and Surname Registry
  http://www.genexchange.com/index.cfm

- Genealogy Friends - Genealogy Queries
  http://members.xoom.com/rebelj/gf/index.html

- Genealogical Services - Genealogy Discussions
  http://www.genservices.com/cgi-bin/bbs/bbs_forum.cgi?forum=discussion

- GenealogyOutfitters.com - Message Boards
  http://www.genealogyoutfitters.com/messages/index.cgi

- Genealogy's Most Wanted
  http://www.citynet.net/mostwanted/

- GRD - The Genealogical Research Directory
  http://www.ozemail.com.au/~grdxxx/
  The world's largest listing of surname queries published annually in bookform, now on CD-ROM.

- Helm's Genealogy Toolbox - Query Central
  http://genealogy.tbox.com/query/index.html

- Heritage Quest - QueriesCenter
  http://www.heritagequest.com/genealogy/queriescenter/

- IIGS - International Internet Genealogical Society Queries
  http://www.iigs.org/queries/

- Irene's Genealogy Post Forum
  http://www.thecore.com/~hand/genealogy/post/

- Lineages' Free On-line Queries
  http://www.lineages.com/queries/default.asp

- Lutherans Online Genealogy Message Board
  http://www.aal.org/LutheransOnline/mboard/mboard.phtml?b=genealogy

- NGS News & Events: Queries
  http://www.ngsgenealogy.org/news/content/queries.html
  From the National Genealogical Society in the U.S.

- Parsons Genealogy Registry
  http://www.parsonstech.com/genealogy/registry.html

- Quaker Queries
  http://www.localaccess.com/rubym/QuakerQu.htm
  Submit your queries for free to this publication. Search the online index to one of the recent issues.

- The Query Corner
  http://www.toolcity.net/~vadkins/gen/querymen.html
  Contact these writers to place a query in their newspaper columns or newsletters.

- Query One Online Genealogical Resource Center
  http://www.queryone.com/index.shtml
  2000 plus genealogy related surname, topical and regional discussion forums, and 44 surname database centers.

- Sierra Home - Family Tree Message Boards
  http://forums.sierra.com/forums/familytreetopic/
  From the makers of the best-selling Generations genealogy software program.

- SURNAME-QUERY Mailing List
  http://www.rootsweb.com/~jfuller/gen_mail_surnames-gen.html#SURNAME-QUERY
  For users to send queries on specific surname searches.

◆ How To

- Internet Genealogy Lesson 2: Creating Effective Queries
  http://www.genealogy.com/201/lesson2/course2_01.html
  From an online course by Marthe Arends.

- Lineages' First Steps - Write Successful Genealogy Queries
  http://www.lineages.com/FirstSteps/WriteQueries.asp

- St. Clair County Michigan Sample Queries
  http://www.rootsweb.com/~mistclai/sample-queries.html
  A humorous and instructive guide to how NOT to write a query. Provides excellent advice on how to compose an effective query. Applicable for all queries in any locality.

- 6 Steps to Writing a Successful Genealogy Query
  http://www.firstct.com/fv/query.html

◆ Locality Specific

- Australian Family Tree Connections Missing Ancestors
  http://www.aftc.com.au/missanc.html

- Australian Genealogy Bulletin Board
  http://www.InsideTheWeb.com/messageboard/mbs.cgi/mb5856

- Bedfordshire Family History Society - Member's Interests
  http://www.kbnet.co.uk/brianp/interests.html
  A list of surnames being researched by the members.

- Chinese Surname Queries
  http://www.ziplink.net/~rey/ch/queries/

- Dallas County, Texas QueryBase
  http://www.geocities.com/TheTropics/1926/dallasquery.html
  Postings thru present date.

- Free Queries for New Brunswick, Canada
  mailto:devlin7@attglobal.net
  Rooters searching in Gloucester, Westmorland, Albert, Kings, Kent and Northumberland counties of New Brunswick, Canada can post a free query to Missing Links, a weekly genealogy newspaper column written and managed by Sandra Devlin. Queries should be to a maximum of 35 words PLUS forwarding address. Don't forget your snail mail (mandatory), and optional fax or voice mail, e-mail addresses. Send queries to: devlin7@attglobal.net.

- Gibson County Queries ~ Indiana
  http://members.sigecom.net/tnolcox/queries.htm

- HGSNY'S Query Boards
  http://www.hispanicgenealogy.com/queries/message boards.htm
  Hispanic Query Boards from the Hispanic Genealogical Society of New York.

- Irish Family History Foundation - Bulletin Boards
  http://mail.mayo-ireland.ie/WebX?14@^1320@.ee6b2a8
  Organized with folders for each county.

- The Italian Genealogy Web Forum
  http://www.italgen.com/wwwboard/wwwboard.shtml

- JEFFCO - New York Genealogical Posts
  http://users.ticnet.com/jeffco/nyposts/nyposts.html

- Kentuckiana Genealogy - Registered Message Boards Users and Their Surnames ~ Kentucky & Indiana
  http://www.kentuckianagenealogy.org/userindexa-f.html

- Lanark County Genealogical Society Members' Queries ~ Ontario, Canada
  http://www.globalgenealogy.com/LCGS/LCGSQURY.HTM

- Litchfield County, Connecticut QueryBase
  http://www.geocities.com/TheTropics/1926/litchquery.html
  Postings thru present date.

- Lonestar Genealogy - Texas Surnames
  http://www.lonestargenealogy.com/surnames/txqueries.html

- Manx Genealogy Bulletin Board
  http://www.isle-of-man.com/interests/genealogy/bulletin/

- Monroe County NY. Query Forum
  http://cgi.rootsweb.com/~genbbs/genbbs.cgi/USA/NY/Monroe

- New Brunswick Queries ~ Canada
  http://cgi.rootsweb.com/~genbbs/genbbs.cgi/Canada/New Brunswick/General

- New Haven County, Connecticut QueryBase
  http://www.geocities.com/TheTropics/1926/nhquery.html
  - Postings thru present date.

- Pennsylvania Dutch Genealogy...Surname Query Boards
  http://midatlantic.rootsweb.com/padutch/genonly/query boards.html

- Queries on The Coshocton Page - Ohio
  http://www.cu.soltec.com/~photo/coshocton.html

- Scanian Genealogy Homepage Efterlysningar 1997 / Queries 1997
  http://cgi.algonet.se/htbin/cgiwrap?user=anderzb&script=query.cgi
  Queries from the Swedish province of Scania.

- Search Genealogy Queries at German Migration Resource Center
  http://www.germanmigration.com/queries/searchgerman.asp
  Search more than 42,000 names, which refer to German migration throughout the world, any time period. Search Queries by surname, ship name, immigration year, places of origin or destination.

- South African Genealogy Queries and Surnames
  http://www.rupert.net/~lkool/page3.html

- Stark County Ohio Genealogy - Queries
  http://www.rootsweb.com/~ohstark/q.htm

- Tacoma-Pierce County Genealogical Society Queries
  Index ~ Washington
  http://www.rootsweb.com/~watpcgs/queries.htm
  Queries from 1994 to present.

- Virginia Genealogical Society Queries
  http://www.vgs.org/queries.htm

- WGS Queries - The Wichita Genealogical Society ~
  Wichita, Kansas
  http://history.cc.ukans.edu/kansas/wgs/query.html

RAILROADS
http://www.cyndislist.com/railroad.htm

Category Index:

- General Resource Sites
- History & Culture
- Libraries, Archives & Museums
- Locality Specific
- Maps, Gazetteers & Geographical Information
- More Railway Links Lists

- Official Railroad Web Sites
- Orphan Trains
- Publications, Software & Supplies
- Records: Administrative, Employment and Pensions
- Societies & Groups

◆ General Resource Sites

- 445 Railroad Definitions
  http://pavel.physics.sunysb.edu/RR/RailroadDefinitions.html

- Railroad Research Resources
  http://hera.csus.edu/students/team/rsrch.html
  Written for railroad history hobbyists, but has good information for the genealogist as well.

- Railway Links Research
  http://www.bcity.com/railway_links
  Professional research in London & Southeast England.

- Yahoo!...Trains and Railroads
  http://dir.yahoo.com/Business_and_Economy/Transportation/Trains_and_Railroads/

◆ History & Culture

- American Railroad Women Research Project
  http://railroad-women-historysite.org/
  Historic and biographical information about women in the US rail industry.

- Deadhead: A Pullman Porter Steps Out of Character
  http://newdeal.feri.org/opp/opp35242.htm
  From Opportunity, the Journal of Negro Life by the National Urban League, August, 1935.

- Instructions to Porters, Attendants and Bus Boys
  http://www.scsra.org/library/rulebook.html

- The Life of the Pullman Porter
  http://www.scsra.org/library/porter.html
  Online article by Stewart H. Holbrook.

- Military Railways - A Potted History
  http://homepages.tesco.net/~martyn.witt/milrly/mil_rly_hist_contents.htm

- Pullman Porter John Johnson
  http://www.chattanooga.net/baylor/academic/english/studentwork/watkins/russell.html
  Russell, Joy, Baylor Senior Research Paper on the story of her grandfather, a Pullman Porter.

- The Pullman Porters Win
  http://newdeal.feri.org/nation/na35217.htm
  Berman, Edward. The Nation, August 21, 1935.

- Railway Women in Wartime
  http://business.virgin.net/artemis.agency/railway/
  The history of women railway workers in the United Kingdom.

- Yahoo!...Trains and Railroads...History
  http://dir.yahoo.com/Business_and_Economy/Transportation/Trains_and_Railroads/History/

◆ Libraries, Archives & Museums

- A. Philip Randolph/Pullman Porter Museum Gallery
  http://www.wimall.com/pullportermu/
  Celebrating this leader in the African American labor movement and the African American Railroad Attendant.

- Age of Steam Railroad Museum - Dallas Texas
  http://www.startext.net/homes/railroad
  An overview and virtual tour of our Railroad Museum, which is located at historic Fair Park in Dallas Texas.

- The B&O Railroad Museum ~ Baltimore, Maryland
  http://www.borail.org/

- BC Rail Ltd. Historical Archives
  http://www.bcrail.com/bcr/archives.htm
  Formerly the Pacific Great Eastern Railway, British Columbia, Canada.

- California State Railroad Museum Library
  http://www.csrmf.org/library
  Holds records for: Atchison, Topeka & Santa Fe Railway, Western Pacific Railroad, Central Pacific, Southern Pacific Railroads.

- Center for Railroad Photography and Art
  http://www.railphoto-art.org

- Central Pacific Railroad Photographic History Museum - Transcontinental Railroad
  http://CPRR.org
  Photographs, engravings, maps, and documents illustrating the history of the first transcontinental railroad.

- The Directory of North American Railroads, Associations, Societies, Archives, Libraries, Museums and Their Collections
  http://www.ancestryresearch.com/BookLook/HotPress.htm
  A book by Holly T. Hansen, B.A.

- Erie Lackawanna Railroad Inventory
  http://www.uakron.edu/archival/ErieLack/erie1.htm
  University of Akron Archival Services.

- Guide to Railroad Archives at the Thomas J. Dodd Research Center
  http://www.lib.uconn.edu/DoddCenter/ASC/raillist.htm
  University of Connecticut.

- Guide to the New York, New Haven and Hartford Railroad Archives
  http://www.lib.uconn.edu/DoddCenter/ASC/nhtrains.htm
  University of Connecticut, Thomas J. Dodd Research Center.

- Manuscript Sources for Railroad History Research at the Special Collections Department of the University Libraries at Virginia Tech
  http://scholar2.lib.vt.edu/spec/railroad/rrintro.htm

- Modern Records Centre
  http://cal.csv.warwick.ac.uk/services/library/mrc/mrc.html
  The Centre's holdings focus on UK trade union records.

  o Genealogy at the Modern Records Centre
    http://www.warwick.ac.uk/services/library/mrc/mrcgene.shtml
    List of occupations covered by the archives for which genealogical guides are available:

    - Railwaymen
      http://www.warwick.ac.uk/services/library/mrc/rail.shtml

- The National Railway Museum, York ~ England
  http://www.nmsi.ac.uk/nrm/

- North American Railroad Museums
  http://www.uprr.com/uprr/ffh/history/narr-mus.shtml
  A list of addresses and phone numbers from the Union Pacific Railroad web site.

- Orange Empire Railway Museum
  http://www.oerm.mus.ca.us/
  OERM's purpose is to preserve and display rail transportation equipment used in Southern California, including street car equipment.

- Peters Railroad Museum ~ Wallingford, Connecticut
  http://pages.cthome.net/petersrrmuseum/

- Reading Railroad Museum ~ Pennsylvania
  http://www.readingrailroad.org/

- South Suburban Genealogical and Historical Society - Pullman Collection
  http://www.rootsweb.com/~ssghs/pullman.htm
  SSGHS staff will search employee records of the Pullman Car Works (circa 1900-1949).

- State Archives of Michigan - Circular No. 13, Railroad Records
  http://www.sos.state.mi.us/history/archive/circular/c13.html

- University of Nevada, Reno - Railroad Manuscript Collections
  http://www.library.unr.edu/~specoll/railroad.html

- University of Tennessee, Knoxville, Hoskins Library: Herbert E. Copeland Railroadiana Collection
  http://toltec.lib.utk.edu/~spec_coll/manuscripts/a0847

- University of Tennessee, Knoxville, Hoskins Library: Knoxville Railway and Light Company
  http://toltec.lib.utk.edu/~spec_coll/manuscripts/a1502

- University of Tennessee, Knoxville, Hoskins Library: Railroad Records Collection
  http://toltec.lib.utk.edu/~spec_coll/manuscripts/a1108

- University of Tennessee, Knoxville, Hoskins Library: Smoky Mountain Railroad Collection
  http://toltec.lib.utk.edu/~spec_coll/manuscripts/a0424

- University of Tennessee, Knoxville, Hoskins Library: Tennessee Central Railroad Company Collection
  http://toltec.lib.utk.edu/~spec_coll/manuscripts/a1702

- Wyoming State Archives
  http://commerce.state.wy.us/cr/Archives/
  Has records for the Union Pacific railroad.

- Yahoo!...Trains and Railroads....Museums
  http://dir.yahoo.com/Business_and_Economy/Transportation/Trains_and_Railroads/Museums/

◆ Locality Specific

- The Auburn Branch of the New York & Oswego Midland Railroad
  http://NYOW.Railfan.net/nyow/auburn/
  This branch, which ran from Norwich to Scipio NY, was later operated by the Utica, Ithaca & Elmira, then the Elmira, Cortland & Northern, and finally by the Lehigh Valley.

- Chicago & Illinois Midland Railfan Pages
  http://www.drgw.net/cim/

- The Chicago Tunnel Company Railroad
  http://www.ameritech.net/users/chicagotunnel/tunnel1.html
  Learn all about a 60-mile underground railroad that operated with 146 locomotives and 3000 freight cars 40 feet below the streets of downtown Chicago.

- The Duluth, South Shore, and Atlantic Railway Home Page
  http://habitant.org/dssa/

- Existing Railroad Stations in New York State
  http://www.spectra.net/~woolever/depot/index2.html

- Idaho Historical Railroads
  http://members.aol.com/idahorail/ihr_main.htm

- Iron Roads - Making Tracks Across Nebraska
  http://www.rootsweb.com/~nerailrd/ironroad.html

- Massachusetts Bay Railroad Enthusiasts
  http://www.massbayrre.org
  Mass Bay RRE is a non-profit organization that promotes the enjoyment of Railroads.

- Minnesota by Rail
  http://www.parkbooks.com/Html/res_rail.html
  Research Notes from Park Genealogical Books.

- Owosso Michigan Railroad Train Page
  http://www.angelfire.com/or/owosso/
  All about the rails of Shiawassee County and the engines that plied them. History and photos of Ann Arbor and Grand Trunk railroad steam locomotive and depots around Shiawassee County. M.U.T. Interurban and street cars histories and photos. Also info on the Tuscola and Saginaw Bay Railway.

- Pennsylvania Railroads
  http://members.nbci.com/amrail/webdoc4.htm

- Railroads in Kansas
  http://history.cc.ukans.edu/heritage/research/rr/railroads.html

- Utah Railway
  http://www.lofthouse.com/USA/Utah/carbon/railroad.html
  The Short Line Built by a Photo, written by C.A. Hamaker.

◆ Maps, Gazetteers & Geographical Information

- The 1891 Grain Dealers and Shippers Gazetteer
  http://www.livgenmi.com/1891shippersgaz.htm
  Another terrific map project from Pam Rietsch.

- American Memory Railroad Maps 1828-1900
  http://memory.loc.gov/ammem/gmdhtml/rrhtml/rrhome.html
  From the Geography and Map Division, Library of Congress.

- The American Railroad System - 1870
  http://www.bchm.org/wrr/recon/p1rec47.jpg

◆ More Railway Links Lists

- Becketts Depot - Becketts + 2000 Railroad Links
  http://thebecketts.com/beckettsdepot/index1.html

- The Information Train Station
  http://railroads.dm.net/linkmain.html

- Interesting Railroad Related Resources
  http://locomotive.raildreams.com/links.html

- Just Railroads
  http://www.geocities.com/Vienna/Choir/6820/a.html

- Links for Railfans to Explore
  http://web1.tusco.net/rail/railfan.html

- Railpace Interlocking
  http://www.railpace.com/interlocking/

- Railroad Information Online
  http://krypton.mankato.msus.edu/~schumann/www/rr/railfan.html

- RailServe - Historical Societies & Preservation
  http://www.railserve.com/Historical/

- Side Tracked
  http://www.railroad.net/side_track/

◆ Official Railroad Web Sites

- BC Rail, Inc. ~ British Columbia, Canada
  http://www.bcrail.com/bcr/index.htm

- Canadian National Railway Company / Canadien National
  http://www.cn.ca/cnwebsite/cnwebsite.nsf/public/splashC

- Canadian Pacific Railway
  http://www.cpr.ca/INTERNET/PlayIntroOnce.htm

- The Union Pacific Railroad
  http://www.uprr.com/
  - The Union Pacific Collection at the Western Heritage Museum ~ Omaha, Nebraska
    http://www.uprr.com/uprr/ffh/history/museum.shtml
  - Union Pacific Railroad History
    http://www.uprr.com/uprr/ffh/history/

- White Pass & Yukon Route
  http://www.whitepassrailroad.com/

◆ Orphan Trains

- Iowa Orphan Train Project
  http://www.maquoketa.k12.ia.us/orphan_train.html

- Orphans to Iowa
  ftp://ftp.rootsweb.com/pub/usgenweb/ia/various/orphans.txt

- Orphan Train Heritage Society of America, Inc.
  http://pda.republic.net/othsa/

- Orphan Train Resources
  http://www.maquoketa.k12.ia.us/ot%20resource.html

- Orphan Train Riders History
  http://www.hamilton.net/subscribers/hurd/index.html

- Orphan Trains
  http://www.outfitters.com/~melissa/ot/ot.html

- The Orphan Trains
  http://www.pbs.org/wgbh/amex/orphan/index.html
  A PBS American Experience television show regarding this unusual immigrant experience.

- Orphan Trains of Kansas
  http://kuhttp.cc.ukans.edu/carrie/kancoll/articles/orphans/index.html
  - A History of the Orphan Trains
    http://raven.cc.ukans.edu/carrie/kancoll/articles/orphans/or_hist.htm
  - Index of Children Who Rode the Orphan Trains to Kansas
    http://raven.cc.ukans.edu/carrie/kancoll/articles/orphans/or_child.htm
  - Kansas Orphan Train "Time-Line"
    http://raven.cc.ukans.edu/carrie/kancoll/articles/orphans/or_timel.htm

o Orphan Train Bibliographies
http://www.ukans.edu/carrie/kancoll/articles/orphans/
or_bibli.htm

o A Partial List of Institutions That Orphan Train
Children Came From
http://raven.cc.ukans.edu/carrie/kancoll/articles/orphans/
or_homes.htm

o A Partial List of Kansas Orphan Train Arrivals
http://raven.cc.ukans.edu/carrie/kancoll/articles/orphans/
or_arriv.htm

o Riders on an Orphan Train to Kansas - 1911
http://raven.cc.ukans.edu/carrie/kancoll/articles/orphan_
train_1911.html

- Orphan Trains of Nebraska
http://www.rootsweb.com/~neadoptn/Orphan.htm

- The Orphan Trains: Placing Out in America
http://shop.myfamily.com/ancestrycatalog/product.asp?pf%5
Fid=17646&dept%5Fid=10103002
A book by Marilyn Irvin Holt, for sale from Ancestry.

- Orphan Trains to Missouri
http://www.system.missouri.edu/upress/spring1997/
patrick.htm
Information about a book from the University of Missouri Press.

- They Rode the Orphan Trains
http://www.rootsweb.com/~mogrundy/orphans.html

◆ Publications, Software & Supplies

- AudioTapes.com - Genealogical Lectures on Cassette
Tapes - Railroad
http://www.audiotapes.com/search2.asp?Search=Railroad

- Canadian railway records: a guide for genealogists
http://www.amazon.com/exec/obidos/ISBN=1551169320/
markcyndisgenealA/
A book by Althea Douglas.

- Cathedral of Steel
http://www.burlingtonroute.com/cos_book/cos.html
*A book that affords an intimate look inside the Burlington Railroad's
roundhouses and shop facilities at Galesburg, Illinois.*

- The Directory of North American Railroads,
Associations, Societies, Archives, Libraries,
Museums and Their Collections
http://www.ancestryresearch.com/BookLook/HotPress.htm
A book by Holly T. Hansen, B.A.

- Frontier Press Bookstore - Railroad History
http://www.frontierpress.com/frontier.cgi?category=railroad

- The Ontario Genealogical Society's Publications List
http://www.ogs.on.ca/publications/pub_soc.htm
*See their book titled "Canadian Railway Records: A Guide for
Genealogists".*

- Society of Genealogists Bookshop - Railways
http://www.sog.org.uk/acatalog/SoG_Bookshop_Online_Rail
ways_166.html
This is for U.K. railwaymen only.

- Was your grandfather a railwayman?
http://www.amazon.com/exec/obidos/ISBN=0907099807/
markcyndisgenealA/
A book by Tom Richards.

◆ Records: Administrative, Employment and Pensions

- Great Northern Railway Company & Northern
Pacific Railway Company Papers
http://www.lexisnexis.com/cispubs/Catalog/research%20
collections/Social%20Sciences%20and%20the%20
Humanities/Business%20&%20Economics/Great%20Northern
%20Railway%20Co.%20Papers%20&%20Northern%20Pacific
%20Railway%20Co.%20Papers.htm

- Public Record Office | Finding Aids | Leaflets |
Railways: Staff Records ~ United Kingdom
http://www.pro.gov.uk/leaflets/ri2189.htm

- Public Record Office | Finding Aids | Leaflets |
Railways: Administrative and Other Records ~
United Kingdom
http://www.pro.gov.uk/leaflets/ri2188.htm

- Records of the Brotherhood of Sleeping Car Porters
http://www.lexis-nexis.com/cispubs/guides/african_
american/bscp/bscp3.htm
*Description of the microfilmed holdings of the Chicago Historical
Society and the Newberry Library.*

- Railroad Retirement Board Records
http://www.ancestry.com/library/view/columns/george/
897.asp
Online article by George G. Morgan.

- Riding the Rails Up Paper Mountain: Researching
Railroad Records in the National Archives
http://www.nara.gov/publications/prologue/railrd1.html
*By David A. Pfeiffer for Prologue, the quarterly of the National
Archives and Records Administration.*

- United States Railroad Retirement Board
http://www.rrb.gov/

o Abbreviations, Trade Names and Nicknames of
Railroads
http://www.rrb.gov/funfacts2.html

o Railroad Records and Genealogical Information
Before 1937
http://www.rrb.gov/geneal2.html

o The U.S. Railroad Retirement Board and
Genealogical Information After 1936
http://www.rrb.gov/geneal.html

o U.S. Railroad Retirement Board - Railroad
Industry & Railroad Union Home Pages
http://www.rrb.gov/rrlinks.html

◆ Societies & Groups

- Amtrak Historical Society
http://www.trainweb.com/ahs/

- Anthracite Railroads Historical Society
  http://arhs.railfan.net/
  Central Railroad of New Jersey, Delaware Lackawanna & Western Railroad, Lehigh Valley Railroad, Reading Company, Lehigh and New England, Lehigh and Hudson River Railroad.

- ARHS/nsw - Australian Railway Historical Society, New South Wales Division
  http://www.accsoft.com.au/~arhsnsw/

- Australian Railway Historical Society (ARHS) - (Victorian Division Inc.)
  http://home.vicnet.net.au/~arhsvic/

- Australia Railway Historical Society - Queensland Division
  http://www.arhs-qld.org.au/

- The Bridge Line Historical Society ~ Albany, New York
  http://www.tfs.net/~jashaw/rhs/blhs.html#homepage
  Historical Society of the Delaware & Hudson Railroad.

- Burlington Route Historical Society (BRHS)
  http://www.burlingtonroute.com/

- Canadian Railroad Historical Association - Association canadienne d'histoire ferroviaire
  http://www.exporail.org/association/
  The CRHA aims are the preservation and dissemination of information concerning railway heritage in Canada.

- The Chesapeake & Ohio Historical Society
  http://www.cohs.org/

- The Chicago & Eastern Illinois Railroad Historical Society
  http://www2.justnet.com/cei/

- Chicago & North Western Historical Society ~ Illinois
  http://www.cnwhs.org/

- Collis P. Huntington Railroad Historical Society ~ West Virginia
  http://www.serve.com/cphrrhs/

- Fort Wayne Railroad Historical Society ~ Indiana
  http://www.steamloco765.org/

- Grand Trunk Western Historical Society ~ Michigan
  http://www.rrhistorical.com/gtwhs/index.html

- The Great Northern Railway Historical Society
  http://www.gnrhs.org/

- Historical Model Railway Society ~ U.K.
  http://www.hmrs.org.uk/

- The Louisville & Nashville Railroad Historical Society ~ Kentucky
  http://www.rrhistorical.com/lnhs/index.html

- The Maryland and Pennsylvania Railroad Preservation and Historical Society ~ Spring Grove, Pennsylvania
  http://www.arrowweb.com/Ma&Pa/

- Milwaukee Road Historical Association ~ Antioch, Illinois
  http://www.mrha.com/
  Chicago, Milwaukee, St. Paul, and Pacific Railroad. This link is for Uncle Reggie!

- National Model Railroad Association (NMRA) Directory: Historical Societies: Individual Railroads
  http://www.ribbonrail.com/nmra/histrr.html
  And Historical Societies: NRHS/RLHS
  http://www.ribbonrail.com/nmra/histnrhs.html

- National Railway Historical Society ~ Philadelphia, Pennsylvania
  http://www.nrhs.com/

- National Railway Historical Society, UK Chapter
  http://www.siam.co.uk/nrhsuk/

- New Haven Railroad Historical and Technical Association, Inc.
  http://www.nhrhta.org

- New Jersey Midland Railroad Historical Society
  http://ourworld.compuserve.com/homepages/njmidland/

- New York Railroad Enthusiasts
  http://www.nyrre.org/

- New York, Susquehanna & Western Technical & Historical Society, Inc. ~ New Jersey
  http://www.nyswths.org/

- The Northern Pacific Railway Historical Association
  http://pw2.netcom.com/~whstlpnk/np.html

- Ontario & Western Railway Historical Society ~ New York
  http://www.nyow.org/
  The historical society for the New York, Ontario & Western Ry (1880-1957) which operated in NY, PA, and NJ. The NYO&W was originally called the New York & Oswego Midland.

- Oregon Electric Railway Historical Society
  http://www.reed.edu/~reyn/oerhs.html

- Pacific Coast Chapter - Railway & Locomotive Historical Society ~ Folsom, California
  http://www.mp1.com/

- The Pacific Northwest Chapter of the National Railway Historical Society ~ Portland, Oregon
  http://www.easystreet.com/pnwc/

- Pennsylvania Railroad Technical & Historical Society
  http://www.prrths.com/

- Railroad Historical Societies
  http://all-railroads.com/histsoc.html

- Railway Ancestors Family History Society ~ U.K.
  http://www.railwayancestors.demon.co.uk/

- San Bernardino Railroad Historical Society ~ California
  http://www.sbrhs.org/

- Santa Clara River Valley Railroad Historical Society Inc. ~ California
  http://www.fishnet.net/~johngart/

- Santa Fe Railway Historical & Modeling Society
  http://www.atsfrr.com/Society/

- Seattle, Portland & Spokane (SP&S) Railway Historical Society ~ Vancouver, Washington
  http://www.teleport.com/~amacha/spsrhs.htm

- Shore Line Historical Society ~ Chicago, Illinois
  http://www.getnet.com/~dickg/nmra/sigs/ShoreLine/ShoreLine.html
  For anyone with an interest in the Chicago North Shore and Milwaukee, the Chicago South Shore and South Bend, and/or the Chicago Aurora and Elgin railroads, including: Chicago Rapid Transit, Chicago Surface Lines, Chicago and West Towns Railways, Evanston Railway, Hammond Whiting and East Chicago Railway, and The Milwaukee Electric Railway and Light Company.

- Soo Line Historical and Technical Society ~ Wisconsin
  http://www.rrhistorical.com/sooline/index.html

- Union Pacific Historical Society ~ Cheyenne, Wyoming
  http://www.uphs.org/

- Wabash Railroad Historical Society
  http://users.aol.com/wabashrr/wabash.html

- The Washington State Railroads Historical Society ~ Pasco, Washington
  http://home1.gte.net/jimbowe/WSRHS1.htm

- Yahoo!...Trains and Railroads....Historical Societies
  http://dir.yahoo.com/Business_and_Economy/Transportation/Trains_and_Railroads/Museums/Historical_Societies/

RECIPES, COOKBOOKS & FAMILY TRADITIONS

http://www.cyndislist.com/recipes.htm

- Amazon.com Genealogy Bookstore - Heritage Cooking
  http://www.amazon.com/exec/obidos/external-search/?keyword=heritage+cooking&tag=markcyndisgenealA/

- Barnette's Family Tree Books - Cookbooks
  http://www.barnettesbooks.com/cookbks.htm

- Bent's Cookie Factory
  http://www.bentscookiefactory.com/
  Still making hardtack crackers in Milton, Massachusetts since 1801.

- Breaking Bread: A Cookbook Family History Preserved By Seven Sisters
  http://members.xoom.com/_XMCM/BreakBread/index.html
  "The seven Rossi sisters document their Polish and Italian family's favorite recipes, stories, traditions, photographs, and their genealogy in this hardbound book 463-page edition titled Baking Bread".

- The Columbian Recipes Methodist Cookbook
  http://home.att.net/~ltrifonoff/
  Contains scanned images of all the advertisements from a cookbook published in Akron, Ohio in 1893 and an index of all names found in the cookbook.

- Family Reunion Recipes
  http://www.bhglive.com/food/cookhelpers/reunion/recipes.html
  From Better Homes and Gardens magazine.

- Favorite Family Recipes - From the Gene Pool
  http://www.rootsweb.com/~genepool/recipes.htm

- FOLKLORE Mailing List
  http://www.rootsweb.com/~jfuller/gen_mail_general.html #FOLKLORE
  A mailing list for the exchange of folklore - folk medicine and recipes.

- Frontier Press Bookstore - Food/Cooking History
  http://www.frontierpress.com/frontier.cgi?category=food

- GEN-TRIVIA-UNIVERSAL Mailing List
  http://www.rootsweb.com/~jfuller/gen_mail_general.html #GEN-TRIVIA-UNIVERSAL
  For genealogy trivia collected from any country. This is an offshoot of the GEN-TRIVIA-ENG list where one can share ancestral recipes, poems, rhymes, ditties, slang words, sayings, etc.

- Grandma's Kitchen - Recipes That Span Generations
  http://www.geocities.com/Heartland/Valley/9094/recipes.html

- GRANNYS-NA-PANTRY Mailing List
  http://www.rootsweb.com/~jfuller/gen_mail_natam.html #GRANNYS-NA-PANTRY
  A mailing list where Native American people can share recipes, remedies, memories, and stories of what their grannys taught and contributed to their families.

- Homespun-Country Kitchen
  http://homepages.rootsweb.com/~homespun/index.htm
  Companion web site to the Homespun Mailing List.

- HOMESPUN Mailing List
  http://www.rootsweb.com/~jfuller/gen_mail_general.html #HOMESPUN
  For those who want to have a bit of fun reminiscing. Subscribers are welcome to share memories, traditions, poems, humor, stories, recipes, folklore and home remedies.

- Internet message led to reviving recipe, learning about author's grandmother
  http://search.tribnet.com/archive/jan%2Dmay/0510f81.html

- More Bits 'N Pieces - Recipes, Cures and More
  http://www.ida.net/users/dhanco/misc.htm

- Old & Treasured Recipes
  http://www.firstct.com/fv/famrecip.html
  From the Treasure Maps site.

- Once Upon A Thyme
  http://www.geocities.com/Heartland/Farm/3182/story.html
  Family History Stories, Heirloom Recipes, Obituaries, and a collection of old letters. Surnames: Abrahams, Eldridge, Norton, Thomas.

- Our Family Cookbook
  http://www.myhistory.org/guidebook/family_cookbook.html
  Project for kids from My History is America's History.

- Patricia B. Mitchell's Inkling Series
  http://www.foodhistory.com/inklings/books/
  Books on American food history.

- Recipes & Foodways - Germans from Russia Heritage Collection
  http://www.lib.ndsu.nodak.edu/gerrus/recipes.html

- Slovak Heritage Live - Christmas Food and Drink
  http://www.iarelative.com/xmas/bc_food.htm

RELIGION & CHURCHES

http://www.cyndislist.com/religion.htm

Category Index:

- General Resource Sites
- Libraries, Archives & Museums
- Locality Specific
- Mailing Lists, Newsgroups & Chat
- People & Families

- Publications, Software & Supplies
- Records: Census, Cemeteries, Land, Obituaries, Personal, Taxes and Vital
- Societies & Groups

◆ General Resource Sites

- Anabaptists
  http://www.anabaptists.org/

- Church Net UK - UK Churches
  http://www.churchnet.org.uk/ukchurches/

- Church of the Brethren
  http://www.brethren.org/

- Church of the Brethren Network
  http://www.cob-net.org/
  - Brethren Groups
    http://www.cob-net.org/docs/groups.htm
  - Brethren Life: Migrations
    http://www.cob-net.org/docs/brethrenlife_migrations.htm
  - Brethren History & Genealogy
    http://www.cob-net.org/genhis.htm
    - Church Genealogy Records
      http://www.cob-net.org/genchurch.htm
    - Miscellaneous Genealogy Lists
      http://www.cob-net.org/genmisc.htm
    - Genealogy Libraries
      http://www.cob-net.org/genlibrary.htm
    - Genealogy Web Sites
      http://www.cob-net.org/genlinks.htm
  - Meet the Brethren
    http://www.cob-net.org/folder.htm
    - The European Origin of the Church of the Brethren
      http://www.cob-net.org/europe.htm
    - The Migration and Expansion of the Brethren in America
      http://www.cob-net.org/america.htm
  - Fellowship of Brethren Genealogists
    http://www.cob-net.org/fobg/
    - Brethren Historical Library and Archives (BHLA)
      http://www.cob-net.org/fobg/library.htm

- Connexions - The Countess of Huntingdon's Connexion
  http://www.cofhconnexion.org.uk/

- Doukhobor Home Page
  http://www.dlcwest.com/~r.androsoff/index.htm
  A group of Russian peasants that split from the Russian Orthodox Church. Large groups of Doukhobors emigrated to Canada and homesteaded in Saskatchewan and British Columbia.

- The Doukhobors in Canada: a select bibliography
  http://library.usask.ca/SPCOL/doukhobor.html

- Ecumenical Patriarchate of Constantinople
  http://www.patriarchate.org/
  The Ecumenical Patriarchate of Constantinople is the Mother Church of all the local autocephalous or autonomous Orthodox Churches who follow Orthodox faith and canonical order.

- ExLIBRIS: English Dissenters
  http://www.exlibris.org/nonconform/engdis/index.html
  Excellent definitions and short summaries of the major Dissenter movements during the English civil war and Interregnum periods.

- Greek Orthodox Archdiocese of America
  http://www.goarch.org/

- The Hall of Church History
  http://www.gty.org/~phil/hall.htm
  An interesting site with definitions, descriptions and links to a variety of resources for each religious group it highlights.
  - The Anabaptists
    http://www.gty.org/~phil/anabapt.htm
  - The Arminians
    http://www.gty.org/~phil/arminian.htm
  - The Puritans
    http://www.gty.org/~phil/puritans.htm
  - The Reformers
    http://www.gty.org/~phil/rformers.htm
  - The Eastern Orthodox
    http://www.gty.org/~phil/orthodox.htm
  - The Medieval Churchmen
    http://www.gty.org/~phil/medieval.htm

- Hutterite Genealogy Cross-Index
  http://feefhs.org/hut/indexhut.html

- Hutterite Genealogy HomePage
  http://feefhs.org/hut/frg-hut.html

- Hutterite Society
  http://www.press.jhu.edu/press/books/titles/s97/s97hohu.htm
  A book by John A. Hostetler, for sale from the Johns Hopkins University Press.

- Moravian Church Genealogy Links
  http://www.enter.net/~smschlack/

- The Moravian Church Home Page
  http://www.moravian.org/

- NetChurch Church Directory - United States
  http://www.netchurch.com/churchlist_active_US.asp

- Olive Tree Genealogy
  http://www.rootsweb.com/~ote/
  Huguenots & Walloons, Ontario Loyalists, Mohawk, Mennonite, Palatines and Dutch Research.

- Orthodox Church in America
  http://www.oca.org/

- Restoration Movement
  http://www.mun.ca/rels/restmov/index.html
  This site features historical texts, pictures, resources for historical research and links to other relevant pages dealing with the Restoration Movement.

- The Salvation Army - How can I trace information about my Salvationist ancestors?
  http://www.salvationarmy.org/safaq.nsf/(all)/662283DCD2EC2E00802568F90052FC49
  Explains what records are available and where to write for them.

- Seventh-day Adventist Church
  http://www.adventist.org/

- Shaker Manuscripts On-Line - Prophecies, Revelations and World Outreach from the Early Shaker
  http://www.passtheword.org/SHAKER-MANUSCRIPTS/

- The Wars of Religion
  http://www.lepg.org/wars.htm

- Yahoo!...Religious...Genealogy
  http://dir.yahoo.com/Arts/Humanities/History/Genealogy/Regional_and_Ethnic_Resources/Religious/

◆ Libraries, Archives & Museums

- Archives - Anglican Diocese of Ottawa
  http://ottawa.anglican.ca/archives.html

- The Archives of the Episcopal Church USA
  http://episcopalarchives.org/
  The Archives of the Episcopal Church is responsible for the collection, management, and preservation of the records and archives of the national Episcopal Church. The national Church includes the General Convention and the Domestic and Foreign Missionary Society.

- Archives of the General Conference of Seventh-day Adventists
  http://www.adventist.org/ast/Archives.htm
  The archives houses records covering the entire period of the church's history. Patrons are able to trace the development of the church through these records, which include legal instruments, minutes, reference files, reports, correspondence, publications, recordings, films, video and audio tapes, and photographs.

- Archiwum Archidiecezjalne w Poznaniu / Archdiocesan Archive in Poznan ~ Poland
  http://www.wsdsc.poznan.pl/arch/

- Church of England Records Centre ~ London
  http://www.blackburn.anglican.org/yellow_pages/a0337.htm

- The Congregational Library & Archives
  http://www.14beacon.org/
  The archives collects material that documents the Congregational, Congregational Christian, Christian and United Church of Christ tradition throughout the world. There are approximately 900 separate archival and manuscript collections totaling 1200 linear feet.

- Covenant Archives and Historical Library
  http://www.npcts.edu/library/Archives/Covenant_Archives/index.html
  From North Park University. This collection exists for the sole purpose of preserving and making available to researchers the historical records of the Evangelical Covenant Church. Founded in 1885 by Swedish immigrants, the Covenant values its rich heritage of churches, pastors, and lay people who have given the denomination its identity and who have carried out its mission. The collection includes books and serials, microfilmed newspapers and church records, files of local churches, pastors, missionaries, educators, and administrators.

- Diocese of London Archives ~ England
  http://www.london.anglican.org/AtoZ/Archive.htm

- The Diocese of New Westminster - Anglican Church of Canada - Diocesan Archives
  http://www.vancouver.anglican.ca/Diocese/archives.htm
  The Archives of the Diocese of New Westminster are located at the Vancouver School of Theology, together with the Archives of the Ecclesiastical Province of British Columbia, Vancouver School of Theology, and the B.C. Conference of the United Church of Canada. Established in 1980, the Archives holds documents from the 1860's to the present, including textual records, photographs, architectural records and maps. The holdings document the activities of the diocesan administration, including the Bishops, officers of Synod and various boards and committees, as well as the activities of related organizations, deaneries, parishes and some individuals.

- Disciples of Christ Historical Society
  http://members.aol.com/dishistsoc/
  The three groups of the Stone-Campbell Movement are the Christian Church (Disciples of Christ), the Christian Churches/Churches of Christ and the a cappella Churches of Christ. Our Society houses 35,000 volumes, 50,000 files plus personal and institutional archival collections from across the 200 years of the Stone-Campbell Movement. Includes listings of congregational files, periodical indexes, and other records in their holdings.

- Evangelical United Brethren Collection
  http://www.su.edu/library/eub.htm
  The Smith Library at Shenandoah University maintains an archive of historical materials relating to Virginia Conference of the Evangelical United Brethren Church prior to the merger with the Methodist Church in 1968.

- Evangelisches Zentral-Archiv in Berlin ~ Germany
  http://www.ezab.de/
  Archiv der Evangelischen Kirche in Deutschland und der Evangelischen Kirche der Union.

  o Practical Information and Addresses for Genealogical Research
    http://www.ezab.de/eza10e.html

- Kirchliche Archive im Internet / Church Archives on the Internet ~ Germany
  http://www.uni-marburg.de/archivschule/deuarch3.html

- Maryland State Archives Church Records
  http://www.mdarchives.state.md.us/msa/speccol/html/0002.html

- Nazarene Archives
  http://www.nazarene.org/hoo/archintro.html
  The archives maintains approximately 1700 cubic feet of materials dating from the 1870's to the present. The collection documents the rise and development of the Church of the Nazarene through correspondence, periodicals, official minutes, sermons, personal papers, photograph collections, flyers, audio recordings, and video media.

- North Park University ~ Chicago, Illinois
  http://www.northpark.edu/

  o Library, Media Services and Archives
    http://www.campus.northpark.edu/library/Default.htm

    • Archives and Special Collections
      http://www.campus.northpark.edu/library/archives/
      Including information for the Swedish-American Archives of Greater Chicago, the Covenant Archives and Historical Library, and the Archives of the Society for the Advancement of Scandinavian Study

- Reformed Church Archives
  http://www.rca.org/resource/archives/
  From the Reformed Church of America.

  o Guide to Local Church Records in the Archives of the RCA and Other Repositories
    http://www.rca.org/images/resource/archives/papers/churchrecords.pdf
    Requires the free Adobe Acrobat Reader Plugin.
    http://www.adobe.com/products/acrobat/readstep.html

- The Schwenkfelder Library
  http://www.rpc.ox.ac.uk/rpc/sfld/s_guide.htm
  The Schwenkfelder Library is located in Pennsburg, Pa., about 40 miles north of Philadelphia, and houses some 30,000 rare books and manuscripts, the majority of which are directly related to the history of the Schwenkfelders in Europe and America. Supplementary collections treat the local history of south-eastern Pennsylvania, and the Library Board has, as well, direct responsibility for a large museum collection of artifacts, primarily related to Pennsylvania, Pennsylvania-German, and Schwenkfelder culture.

- Shaker Museum at South Union, Kentucky - Links to Other Shaker Information
  http://www.logantele.com/~shakmus/othersites.htm

- United Brethren Historical Center at Huntington College ~ Huntington, Indiana
  http://www.huntington.edu/library/ubhc.html

  o Genealogical Information
    http://www.huntington.edu/library/ubhcgen.html

- United Church of Canada Archives Network
  http://www.uccan.org/archives/home.htm

- United Church of Canada / Victoria University Archives
  http://vicu.utoronto.ca/archives/archives.htm
  Located in Ontario, the holdings in the archives include records for the Presbyterian Church in Canada; the Methodist Church (Canada); the Congregational Union of Canada; Local Union Churches; and the Evangelical United Brethren Church. There are also personal papers, biographical files and photographs.

◆ Locality Specific

- The Anglican Diocese of Nova Scotia
  http://fox.nstn.ca/~diocese/
  For Nova Scotia and Prince Edward Island, Canada.

- The Charter of the Second Reformed Protestant Dutch Church of Warren, New York
  http://www.rootsweb.com/~nyherkim/wchurch.html

- The Church of England
  http://www.cofe.anglican.org/

- The Church of Scotland
  http://www.churchofscotland.org.uk/

- Churches in Elgin County ~ Ontario, Canada
  http://www.eversweb.on.ca/Churches-Elgin/

- Churches of London
  http://www.steeljam.free-online.co.uk/londonchurchlocation.htm
  Information, history and pictures covering the churches in and around the City of London including a map showing the location of the churches.

- Connexions - The Countess of Huntingdon's Connexion ~ United Kingdom
  http://www.cofhconnexion.org.uk/

- The Free Church of Scotland
  http://www.freechurch.org/

- Genline - Svenska Kyrkböcker Online / Swedish Church Records On-line
  http://www.genline.se/

- A Historical Sketch of the Brethren in Christ Church
  http://www.easynet.ca/~johnb/tunkers/index.html
  "Known as Tunkers in Canada," by George Cober, Gormley, Ontario.

- The Hungarian Reformed Church in Paris 1938
  http://user.itl.net/~glen/HungariansinParis.html
  A Parisi Magyar Reformatus Egyhaz Presbiteriuma.

- Moravian Settlers in North Carolina
  http://users.erols.com/fmoran/morav.html
  From the Jarvis Family Home Page.

- My Ancestor was a Clergyman of the Church of England
  http://www.lambethpalacelibrary.org/holdings/Guides/clergyman.html
  Online research guide from the Lambeth Palace Library.

- Old Swedes Church ~ Wilmington, Delaware
  http://www.oldswedes.org/
  Old Swedes Church, built in 1698, is the oldest church in America still standing as originally built and open for services. Churchyard dates to 1638. Hendrickson House Museum is a 1690 Swedish farmhouse and a small Swedish gift shop.

- Richard's Church Albums
  http://www.soft.net.uk/thirdman/index.html
  A collection of over 450 photographs of English West country Churches with histories and descriptions.

- Suffolk Church Pictures ~ England
  http://www.geocities.com/Heartland/Acres/1231/

- Sumner County Churches ~ Tennessee
  http://www.rootsweb.com/~tnsumner/sumnchur.htm

◆ Mailing Lists, Newsgroups & Chat

- Genealogy Resources on the Internet - Religions / Churches Mailing Lists
  http://www.rootsweb.com/~jfuller/gen_mail_religions.html
  Most of the mailing list links below point to this site, wonderfully maintained by John Fuller

- BIBLICAL-GENEALOGY Mailing List
  http://www.rootsweb.com/~jfuller/gen_mail_religions.html
  #BIBLICAL-GENEALOGY
  For the discussion and sharing of information regarding genealogy in biblical times.

- Brethren History & Genealogy List Server Mailing List
  http://www.cob-net.org/listbhg.htm

- BRETHREN Mailing List
  http://www.rootsweb.com/~jfuller/gen_mail_religions.html
  #BRETHREN
  Dedicated to genealogy and welcomes anyone who wants to exchange information and search for Brethren Roots (i.e., ancestors and families that are or were members the Church Group founded in 1708 near Swarzenau Germany). The movement came to America mainly in two groups, one in 1719 and the other in 1729. This includes such church groups as Tunkers/Dunkers, Church Of The Brethren, and German Baptists.

- BrickChurchNC Mailing List
  http://www.rootsweb.com/~jfuller/gen_mail_religions.html
  #BrickChurchNC
  For anyone with a genealogical or historical interest in the founders and members of The Brick Church that was founded 250 years ago in what is now Guilford County, North Carolina.

- DE-OLDSWEDES Mailing List
  http://www.rootsweb.com/~jfuller/gen_mail_religions.html
  #DE-OLDSWEDES
  For anyone interested in the genealogy of families associated with the Old Swedes (Holy Trinity) Church in Wilmington, Delaware.

- EARLY-NAZARENE-CHURCH Mailing List
  http://www.rootsweb.com/~jfuller/gen_mail_religions.html
  #EARLY-NAZARENE-CHURCH

- Exulanten-L Mailing List
  http://www.rootsweb.com/~autwgw/agsfrx.htm
  Exulanten is the name given to the Protestants that were forced out Austria (estimated as many as100,000) during 16th to 18th century. The largest wave of about 22,000 left the Salzburg area in1731/32. Most went to East Prussia (Germany - Poland, Lithuania and Latvia) but some went toSiebenbürgen and Banat (today's Romania), Hungary and to parts of today's Slovakia.

- MORAVIANCHURCH Mailing List
  http://www.rootsweb.com/~jfuller/gen_mail_religions.htm
  #MORAVIANCHURCH
  For the world-wide Moravian Church, the oldest Protestant denomination. This list is for an exchange of Moravian records, genealogies, references, and historical information; especially in Europe and Colonial America.

- SDB Mailing List
  http://www.rootsweb.com/~jfuller/gen_mail_religions.html
  #SDB
  For anyone researching ancestors affiliated with the Seventh Day Baptist church.

◆ People & Families

- Descendants of * of the Ark NOAH
  http://www.parsonstech.com/genealogy/trees/dmalec/burkhamm.htm

- The Genealogies of the Bible: A Neglected Subject
  http://www.custance.org/geneal.html

- Genealogy of Christ According to Matthew
  http://php.indiana.edu/~sanford/christ.html

- Genealogy of Mankind from Adam to Japheth, Shem and Ham
  http://www.geocities.com/Tokyo/4241/geneadm2.html

- Papal Genealogy: The Families and Descendants of the Popes
  http://www.amazon.com/exec/obidos/ISBN=0786403152/markcyndisgenealA/
  A book by George L. Williams.

- Tracing lineage back to Adam not realistic goal
  http://www.tri-cityherald.com/genealogy/DAY/day6.html
  From The Family Tree by Terence L. Day.

◆ Publications, Software & Supplies

- Amazon.com Genealogy Bookstore - Churches
  http://www.amazon.com/exec/obidos/external-search/?keyword=church+genealogy&tag=markcyndisgenealA/

- Books We Own - US - Religious Groups
  http://www.rootsweb.com/~bwo/us_religious.html
  Find a book from which you would like a lookup and click on the submitter's code at the end of the entry. Once you find the contact information for the submitter, write them a polite request for a lookup.

- Early Church Records: Identifying Problems and Solutions
  http://www.audiotapes.com/product.asp?ProductCode='WPGS99S18'
  Presentation by John T. Humphrey, available for sale on audio tape.

- Frontier Press Bookstore - Religions
  http://www.frontierpress.com/frontier.cgi?category=religion

- The Genealogists Handbook for Baptismal Records and Practices
  http://www.audiotapes.com/product.asp?ProductCode='DEN98T77'
  Presentation by John T. Humphrey, available for sale on audio tape.

- GenealogyBookShop.com - Religions
  http://www.genealogybookshop.com/genealogybookshop/files/General,Religions/index.html
  The online store of Genealogical Publishing Co., Inc. & Clearfield Company.

- Picton Press - Churches
  http://www.pictonpress.com/cgi-bin/oc/picton/index.html?M4gzEpF4;parent_id=14;76

- Sabbath Keepers in History
  http://www.ozemail.com.au/~sdbbris/books/new/index2.htm
  From the Time of Christ to the 19th Century. Reprints from "Seventh Day Baptists in Europe and America" Volume 1 (pp 11 - 115), American Sabbath Tract Society, Plainfield, New Jersey. 1910.

- The Source: A Guidebook of American Genealogy - Chapter 6: Research In Church Records
  http://www.ancestry.com/home/source/src124.htm
  A full, online version of this book, published by Ancestry, edited by Loretto Dennis Szucs and Sandra Hargreaves Luebking.

◆ Records: Census, Cemeteries, Land, Obituaries, Personal, Taxes and Vital (Born, Married, Died & Buried)

- Church Records in Onondaga County ~ New York
  http://www.rootsweb.com/~nyononda/CHURCH/CHURCH.HTM

- Church Records for Ireland
  http://scripts.ireland.com/ancestor/browse/records/church/index.htm

- The Cochin Churchbook
  http://www.telebyte.nl/~dessa/cochin.htm
  Baptism & marriages from the Dutch Church in Cochin, India (1754-1804).

- Diocese of Durham - Diocesan Records ~ England
  http://www.durham.anglican.org/groups/dxgrecs.htm

- Early Virginia Religious Petitions
  http://lcweb2.loc.gov/ammem/repehtml/repehome.html
  From the American Memory project at the Library of Congress.

- Lehigh County Historical Society Church Records Collection ~ Pennsylvania
  http://www.geocities.com/Heartland/3955/lehchurches.htm

- Name Index to Barton W. Stone's Christian Messenger
  http://www.mun.ca/rels/restmov/texts/resources/index/index.html
  Names and dates from as early as 1827; transcribed by Ruth E. Browning.

- Records of Egypt Reformed Church Lehigh County, Pennsylvania 1734-1834
  http://www.geocities.com/Heartland/3955/lehegypt.htm
  From Pennsylvania Archives, Sixth Series, Volume 6.

- Records of the Reformed Dutch Church of Albany, New York, 1683-1809
  http://aleph0.clarku.edu/~djoyce/gen/albany/refchurch.html
  Marriage and baptismal register starting in 1683.

- Researching with Church Records
  http://www.familytreemaker.com/issue5.html
  From Family Tree Maker Online.

- Seventh-day Adventist Periodical Index
  http://143.207.5.3:82/search/
  Has a searchable obituary index and more.

◆ Societies & Groups

- The Evangelical & Reformed Historical Society ~ Lancaster, Pennsylvania
  http://www.lts.org/ERHS/erhs.htm?32,12
  From the Philip Schaff Library at Lancaster Theological Seminary.

- Fellowship of Brethren Genealogists
  http://www.cob-net.org/fobg/

- Shaker Heritage Society ~ Albany, New York
  http://www.crisny.org/not-for-profit/shakerwv/

REUNIONS
http://www.cyndislist.com/reunions.htm

Category Index:
- General Resource Sites
- Online Group Meeting Places
- Reunion Planning

- Reunions ~ Family Specific
- Reunions ~ Locality Specific

◆ General Resource Sites

- Amazon.com Genealogy Bookstore - Family Reunions
  http://www.amazon.com/exec/obidos/external-search/?keyword=family+reunion&tag=markcyndisgenealA/

- AudioTapes.com - Genealogical Lectures on Cassette Tapes - Reunion
  http://www.audiotapes.com/search2.asp?Search=Reunion

- ClassMates Online
  http://www.classmates.com/index.tf
  Helps high school alumni friends find each other.

- Family Reunion List
  http://www.reunionindex.com/list.html
  This site is a listing of as many prospective and ongoing family reunions as can be found on the WWW. It also offers a free webpage for a family reunion notice.

- FamilyReunion.com
  http://www.familyreunion.com/
  Use the Reunion Calendar or the searchable Reunion Resource Guide to find ideas, suggestions, information, products and services.

- Frontier Press Bookstore - Reunions
  http://www.frontierpress.com/frontier.cgi?category=reunion

- Gradfinder
  http://www.gradfinder.com/

- Hearthstone Bookshop - Family Reunions
  http://www.hearthstonebooks.com/cgi-bin/webc.cgi/st_main.html?catid=8&sid=2Qp5fy81a

- High School Alumni- A Web Site For Alumni of US High Schools
  http://www.highschoolalumni.com/
  Register your name, address and graduation date from any high school in the US.

- Military Brats Network
  http://www.military-brats.com/

- Military - Buddies, Pals, Shipmates, Families, and Friends
  http://www.shipmates.com/shipmates/

- Overseas Brats
  http://www.overseasbrats.com/

- Planet Alumni
  http://www.planetalumni.com/

- Reunion Center - The Genealogy Forum on AOL
  http://www.genealogyforum.com/gfaol/reunions.html

- Reunion Hall
  http://www.nowandthen.com/lasso.acgi?-response=/reunion/index.lasso&-nothing

- ReunionNet
  http://www.reunited.com/

- Reunion Planner
  http://www.reunionplanner.com/
  Reunion planning, products, books software for class, military, family reunions.

- Reunions Magazine
  http://www.reunionsmag.com/

- Seekers of the Lost International Reunion Registry
  http://www.seeklost.com/

- World Alumni Net
  http://www.alumni.net/

◆ Online Group Meeting Places

- eCircles.com
  http://wwwld-05-18-ec.ecircles.com/magic/products/gate/login.cgi?DebugMSG=NoAuth&nextURL=/magic/products/circles/all.cgi%3Fdont=cache

- eGroups.com
  http://www.eGroups.com/

- FamilyBuzz.com
  http://www.familybuzz.com

- MyFamily.com
  http://www.myfamily.com/

- Yahoo! Clubs...Families
  http://clubs.yahoo.com/Family___Home/Families/

◆ Reunion Planning

- Family-Reunion.com
  http://family-reunion.com
  Plan the perfect family reunion with ideas, activities, games, resources, newsletter, registry and more.

- Family Reunion Organizer ~ Windows 95/98/NT
  http://family-reunion.com/organizer/
  Planning software from Family-Reunion.com.

- Family Reunion Planning
  http://www.kfc.com/Promos/FamReunion/FR_default.htm
  Guide and tools from Kentucky Fried Chicken.

- Family Reunion Recipes
  http://www.bhglive.com/food/cookhelpers/reunion/
  recipes.html
  From Better Homes and Gardens magazine.

- Harness the Internet for Reunion Planning - Family
  Reunions The Living Legacy
  http://www.jcrogers.com/reunions/reunion.htm

- Holding a Family Reunion
  http://home.vicnet.net.au/~dpsoc/reunion.htm
  *Notes by Leone Fabre and the Dead Persons Society, Melbourne,
  Australia.*

- Pat's Reunion Help and More!
  http://home.pacifier.com/~patbauer/

- Planning a Successful Family Reunion
  http://www.bhglive.com/food/cookhelpers/reunion/
  reunion.html
  From Better Homes and Gardens magazine.

- Reunion Planner
  http://www.reunionplanner.com/
  *Reunion planning, products, books software for class, military,
  family reunions.*

- ReunionTips.com
  http://www.reuniontips.com/

- Sharing our Links to the Past
  http://www.geocities.com/~wallyg/reunions.htm

- Thinking About a Reunion?
  http://www.genealogy.com/genealogy/32_reunion.html

- What Should We Do at the Reunion?
  http://www.genealogy.com/genealogy/34_reunion.html

◆ Reunions ~ Family Specific

- BOND Family Reunion
  mailto:receiver@visioncom.net
  *Every Labor Day Sunday in Wiggins, Mississippi. E-mail A.M. Bond
  at receiver@visioncom.net for more details.*

- COGSWELL Family Association Reunion 2000
  http://www.cogswell.org/Reunion_2000.htm
  *Cogswell Family Association annual reunion, September 15-17,
  2000 at Henry Cogswell College, Everett, Washington.*

- CORNING Family Reunion
  http://bold.coba.unr.edu/corning/reunion/1fam.html
  *Corning Family Reunion, Yarmouth, Nova Scotia, Canada, July 22
  to 25, 1999.*

- MUMMEY Family Reunion Website
  http://ecicnet.org/~uboat977/
  *Mummey/Mummy family genealogy, with Hammond and Smith
  allied lines, information on annual Mummey reunion.*

- TANNAHILL Family Reunion
  http://home.att.net/~Tannahill/
  April 3, 1999, Fort Worth, Texas, USA.

◆ Reunions ~ Locality Specific

- Family Reunion Page for the Central Texas Area
  http://www.aisi.net/GenWeb/mclennanco/mainreun.htm

- The Island Register's Reunions and Events Page
  http://www.islandregister.com/reunions.html
  *Reunion announcements for the descendants of Prince Edward
  Island Families.*

- Kentucky Reunions
  http://cgi.rootsweb.com/~genbbs/genbbs.cgi/USA/Ky/Reunion

- Ohio Family Reunions
  http://www.rootsweb.com/~ohreunio/index.html

- Suffolk Family Reunions
  http://www.dbitstech.com/leeann/suffolk/reunions.html
  Upcoming Suffolk Family Reunions.

ROOTS-L & ROOTSWEB
http://www.cyndislist.com/rootsl.htm

Category Index:
- ◆ ROOTS-L Mailing List
- ◆ ROOTS-L Library, Archives and Files
- ◆ Roots Databases
- ◆ RootsWeb

◆ ROOTS-L Mailing List
ROOTS-L is the original genealogy mailing list, established in 1987, it now has more than 10,000 subscribers.

- To subscribe to the ROOTS-L mailing list send an e-mail message to: ROOTS-L-request@rootsweb.com
  mailto:ROOTS-L-request@rootsweb.com
  In the body of the message type only this one word: subscribe
  Be sure not to use a signature file with this message. Save a copy of the welcome message that you receive for future reference.

- ROOTS-L Home Page
  http://www.rootsweb.com/roots-l/roots-l.html
  - ○ Getting Started with ROOTS-L:
    - • ROOTS-L Resources: Info and Tips for Using ROOTS-L
      http://www.rootsweb.com/roots-l/rootshelp.html
    - • Welcome: Getting Started with ROOTS-L
      ftp://ftp.rootsweb.com/pub/roots-l/roots-l.welcome
    - • Welcome 1: ROOTS-L: How it Works #1
      ftp://ftp.rootsweb.com/pub/roots-l/roots-l.welcome1
    - • Welcome 2: ROOTS-L: How it Works #2
      ftp://ftp.rootsweb.com/pub/roots-l/roots-l.welcome2
    - • Welcome 3: ROOTS-L Frequently Asked Questions (FAQ)
      ftp://ftp.rootsweb.com/pub/roots-l/roots-l.welcome3
  - ○ Search Past ROOTS-L Messages:
    - • ROOTS-L Archive - Text Messages via FTP
      ftp://ftp.rootsweb.com/pub/roots-l/messages/
      Browse through this index of messages from August 1996 through the present.
    - • ROOTS-L Daily Index of Mailing List Messages
      http://www.rootsweb.com/roots-l/index/
    - • ROOTS-L Search Page
      http://searches.rootsweb.com/roots-l.html
      A searchable form for all messages from 1987 through the present.

◆ ROOTS-L Library, Archives and Files
A collection of files gathered and archived since ROOTS-L was first created.

- ROOTS-L Archives
  ftp://ftp.rootsweb.com/pub/roots-l/

- ROOTS-L File Catalog
  ftp://ftp.rootsweb.com/pub/roots-l/roots-l.catalog

- ROOTS-L Helpfile
  ftp://ftp.rootsweb.com/pub/roots-l/roots-l.helpfile

- ROOTS-L Index of FAQ Files
  ftp://ftp.rootsweb.com/pub/roots-l/faq/faq.index

- ROOTS-L: Internet Resources for Genealogy
  http://www.rootsweb.com/roots-l/intergen.html

- ROOTS-L Library
  http://www.rootsweb.com/roots-l/filelist.html
  An amazing collection of articles and links for you to explore.

◆ ROOTS Databases
The following two projects had their start on the ROOTS-L mailing list.

- Roots Location List Name Finder
  http://searches.rootsweb.com/cgi-bin/Genea/rll
  - ○ Roots Location List - Entries for North America
    ftp://ftp.rootsweb.com/pub/roots-l/family/family.locnamer
  - ○ Roots Location List - Entries for the Rest of the World
    ftp://ftp.rootsweb.com/pub/roots-l/family/family.locworld
  - ○ Roots Location List - Addresses of Submitters
    ftp://ftp.rootsweb.com/pub/roots-l/family/family.locaddr

- RootsWeb Surname List -- Interactive Search
  http://rsl.rootsweb.com/cgi-bin/rslsql.cgi
  An easily searchable database maintained by volunteer Karen Isaacson. The RSL contains more than 915,000 surnames, submitted by nearly 203,000 genealogists.
  - ○ Overview of the RootsWeb Surname List (RSL)
    http://www.rootsweb.com/roots-l/family.readme.html
  - ○ RootsWeb Surname List: Index to Files
    http://www.rootsweb.com/roots-l/rsl-index.html
    RSL entries as of May 1997.
  - ○ RootsWeb Surname List - Interactive Data Edit/Submission Form
    http://rsl.rootsweb.com/cgi-bin/rsledit.cgi
    - • RootsWeb Surname List Country Abbreviations ~ Listed by Country
      http://helpdesk.rootsweb.com/help/abbrev1.html

- Abbreviations from the RootsWeb Surname List ~ Listed by Abbreviation
  http://helpdesk.rootsweb.com/help/abbrev2.html
  o RSL: PROBLEM SOLVING: Common Questions about the RSL and the RSL-Edit Form
  http://helpdesk.rootsweb.com/help/solution.html
  o RSL Search Program - Alternate
  http://gen.roc.wayne.edu/fsl.html
  o RSL-UPDATE Mailing List
  http://www.rootsweb.com/~jfuller/gen_mail_surnames-gen.html#RSL-UPDATE
  The RootsWeb Surname List database monthly update of new surnames

◆ RootsWeb.com

- RootsWeb.com Home Page
  http://www.rootsweb.com/
  o Classifieds at RootsWeb
  http://cgi.rootsweb.com/~classifieds/
  o Communities at RootsWeb
  http://communities.rootsweb.com/
  o GenConnect at RootsWeb - Connecting Families Thru Genealogy
  http://cgi.rootsweb.com/~genbbs/
  o Genealogy Mailing Lists at RootsWeb
  http://lists.rootsweb.com/
  A categorized list of the mailing lists currently hosted on the RootsWeb servers.
  - New or Adoptable Mailing Lists
    http://resources.rootsweb.com/adopt/
  o GenSeeker - RootsWeb Site Search
  http://seeker.rootsweb.com/search.html
  o How to Subscribe to RootsWeb
  http://www.rootsweb.com/rootsweb/how-to-subscribe.html
  - Contributor Services
    http://www.rootsweb.com/rootsweb/members/
  o More About RootsWeb
  http://www.rootsweb.com/rootsweb/more-about-rootsweb/
  o Resources at RootsWeb
  http://resources.rootsweb.com/
  - Surname Resources at RootsWeb
    http://resources.rootsweb.com/surnames/
  - US County Resources at RootsWeb
    http://resources.rootsweb.com/USA/
  - US State Resources at RootsWeb
    http://resources.rootsweb.com/USA/stateindex.html

- World Resources at RootsWeb
  http://resources.rootsweb.com/world/
  o RootsWeb Genealogy Web Ring
  http://homepages.rootsweb.com/~kenbowen/rootsring/join.htm
  o RootsWeb HelpDesk: Frequently Asked Questions - FAQ
  http://helpdesk.rootsweb.com/
  o RootsWeb Mailing Lists -- Interactive Search
  http://searches.rootsweb.com/cgi-bin/listsearch.pl
  o RootsWeb Review - A Weekly E-Zine of RootsWeb.com, Inc.
  http://www.rootsweb.com/~review/
  - Archives of Past Issues
    ftp://ftp.rootsweb.com/pub/review/
  o RootsWeb's Genealogy Journal – Missing Links
  http://www.rootsweb.com/~mlnews/
  - Archives of Past Issues
    ftp://ftp.rootsweb.com/pub/mlnews
  o RootsWeb's WorldConnect Project
  http://worldconnect.genealogy.rootsweb.com/
  o RootsWeb Threaded Mailing List Archives
  http://archiver.rootsweb.com/
  o Search Engines
  http://www.rootsweb.com/rootsweb/searches/
  o Social Security Death Index Interactive Search
  http://ssdi.genealogy.rootsweb.com/cgi-bin/ssdi.cgi
  o Webpages at Freepages
  http://freepages.rootsweb.com/
  o Websites at RootsWeb
  http://www.rootsweb.com/~websites/
  - Historical and Genealogical Society Pages Hosted by RootsWeb
    http://www.rootsweb.com/~websites/gensoc.htm
  - International Pages at RootsWeb
    http://www.rootsweb.com/~websites/international.htm
  - Miscellaneous Pages Hosted by RootsWeb
    http://www.rootsweb.com/~websites/misc.html
  - United States Genealogical and Historical Resources at RootsWeb
    http://www.rootsweb.com/~websites/uspages.html
  o What's New at RootsWeb
  http://www.rootsweb.com/~whatsnew/

ROYALTY & NOBILITY
http://www.cyndislist.com/royalty.htm

Category Index:
- General Resource Sites
- Locality Specific
- Mailing Lists, Newsgroups & Chat
- People & Families
- Publications, Software & Supplies

◆ General Resource Sites

- **Almanach de Bruxelles**
  http://www.almanach.be/central.html
  Information on present and former sovereign families of non-European countries.

- **Almanach de Gotha**
  http://www.almanachdegotha.com/
  A royal genealogical reference book, published continuously from 1763-1944 and again in 1998.

- **Almanach de la Cour**
  http://www.ChivalricOrders.org/
  A compendium of articles on a variety of subjects, mostly connected with Orders of Chivalry, European Royal Houses, and the European Nobility.

- **Chivalric Research 2000**
  http://www.geocities.com/Paris/Cathedral/4800/link.html
  A site for all things heraldic, chivalric, genealogical, noble, royal or pertaining to knightly orders.

- **The Courtly Lives of Royals, Peerage, Saints, and Their Genealogy**
  http://pages.hotbot.com/family/grieve0/table.html
  Links to Royalty (Malcolm III, Edward I), Peerage (Cavendish, HRH Diana Spencer's genealogy), landed gentry (Dickerson), Saints who were royal (St Margaret, etc), and Knights (Hugh de Payens, Sinclair), and genealogy relating to all.

- **ES-SENCE - Kaj Malachowski's guide to Europaische Stammtafeln**
  http://www.geocities.com/Heartland/Plains/2739/es-sence.html
  A web guide to a series of books with genealogy of European noble and royal families with links to surname lists, libraries, abbreviations and symbols, bibliographic data, etc.

- **Europäische Stammtafeln Notes**
  http://habitant.org/tools/esnotes.htm
  Notes and translation of abbreviations and symbols for using the Europäische Stammtafeln. This book is a key tool for studying European royal and noble families.

- **European Royalty during World War II**
  http://www.tcnj.edu/~gsteinbe/royalty.html
  The site will, upon completion, comprise a list of all members of European royal houses alive during the war (with genealogical information for each).

- **Family Tree Genealogical and Probate Research Bureau Ltd.**
  http://www.familytree.hu/
  Professional research service covering the area of what was formerly the Austro-Hungarian Empire, including: Hungary, Slovakia, Czech Republic, Austria, Italy, Transylvania, Croatia, Slovenia, former Yugoslavia (Banat), and the Ukraine (Sub-Carpathian).

- **Hein's Royal Genealogy Page**
  http://www.angelfire.com/in/heinbruins/
  Lists of descendants of several European monarchs.

- **Hoelseth's Royal Corner**
  http://www.geocities.com/Athens/Crete/2122/royalty.html
  Information on the royal and princely families of the world.

- **International Royal Genealogy**
  http://www.geocities.com/Athens/Aegean/7545/genealogy.html
  Royal genealogy resources, including books and web sites.

- **Joan's Royal Favourites & Links Page**
  http://www.xs4all.nl/~kvenjb/favour.htm

- **Kings & Queens of Europe**
  http://www.camelotintl.com/royal/europe.html

- **LFM van de Pas Genealogics**
  http://members.iinet.net.au/~leovdpas/genealogics.html
  Over 300,000 entries in this database contain Royalty, Landed Gentry and all other levels of society.

- **Mark Humphrys' Family History Page**
  http://www.compapp.dcu.ie/~humphrys/FamTree/index.html
  - **Royal Descents of Famous People**
    http://www.compapp.dcu.ie/~humphrys/FamTree/Royal/famous.descents.html

- **Monarchy Links**
  http://www.users.wineasy.se/dg/mlinks.htm

- **Regalis**
  http://www.regalis.com/intro.htm
  Medieval history, royalty, heraldry, nobility, aristocracy and knighthood around the world.

- **Regnal Chronologies**
  http://web.raex.com/~obsidian/regindex.html
  A calendar of worldwide royal reigns, arranged geographically.

- Rongstad's 1999 Worldwide Royalty Links
  http://members.aol.com/rhrongstad/royalrww/royalrww.html
- Royal and Noble Genealogical Data on the Web
  http://www.dcs.hull.ac.uk/public/genealogy/GEDCOM.html
  - o Directory of Royal Genealogical Data
    http://www.dcs.hull.ac.uk/public/genealogy/royal/
    And an alternate site
    http://www.tardis.ed.ac.uk/~bct/public/genealogy/royal/
    - Master Index to Royal Genealogical Data -
      Ordered by Lastname
      http://www.dcs.hull.ac.uk/public/genealogy/royal/
      gedx.html
- Paul Theroff's Royal Genealogy Site
  http://pages.prodigy.net/ptheroff/gotha/
  - o An Online Gotha
    http://pages.prodigy.net/ptheroff/gotha/gotha.htm
- Royal Genealogies -- Menu
  http://ftp.cac.psu.edu/~saw/royal/royalgen.html
- The Royalist Society
  http://www.geocities.com/CapitolHill/3115/
  *Monarchist website dedicated to helping Monarchists from around
  the world.*
- The Royalty in History Site
  http://www.xs4all.nl/~kvenjb/kings.htm
- The Unit for Prosopographical Research
  http://www.linacre.ox.ac.uk/research/prosop/home.stm
  *From Linacre College, Oxford, England. Promotes the study of
  medieval prosopography - the social science using genealogy,
  onomastics and demography to study the past.*
- The WorldRoots Royal Pages
  http://worldroots.clicktron.com/
  - o Brigitte's Pages - European Royalty and Nobility
    http://worldroots.com/brigitte/royal/royal00.htm
    *From Brigitte Ingeborg Gastel. Historic and genealogical
    information about royal and nobility family lines*
    - Europe from A to Z and more...
      http://worldroots.clicktron.com/brigitte/b9_index.html
    - My Family Research Pages on Descendants of
      Royal Historical Figures
      http://worldroots.clicktron.com/brigitte/royal/royal17.htm
    - Private Nobility / Royal Sites, Links
      http://worldroots.com/brigitte/royal/royal9.htm
    - Royal Genealogical Data Research Books used
      by Brian C. Tompsett
      http://worldroots.com/brigitte/roybooks.htm
  - o Direct access to Royal and Nobility Genealogy
    Databases
    http://worldroots.clicktron.com/brigitte/royal/direct
    access.html
  - o Site Map and General Index
    http://worldroots.com/brigitte/royal/sitemap2.htm

- WW-Person
  http://www8.informatik.uni-erlangen.de/html/ww-person.html
  A data base of the higher nobility in Europe.

◆ Locality Specific

- The 700 Years of Grimaldi
  http://www.monaco.mc/monaco/700ans/index.html
  History of Monaco's Grimaldi dynasty.
- Ancestors of King Edward III of England and
  Philippa of Hainault
  http://www.crossmyt.com/hc/gen/edw3chrt.html
- Ancestors of H.M. King Harald 5th of Norway
  http://w1.2628.telia.com/~u262800030/harald/index1.htm
- Association of the Belarusian Nobility - Zhurtavannie
  Belaruskaj Sliachty
  http://feefhs.org/by/frg-zbs.html
  *Belarus, nobility, Grand Duchy of Lithuanian, genealogy of Belarus,
  heraldry of Belarus, history of Belarus, Polish-Lithuanian
  Commonwealth.*
- Belgium's Royal Family
  http://www.geocities.com/Heartland/Plains/5209/
- The British Monarchy - The Official Web Site
  http://www.royal.gov.uk/
  - o Family Trees of Royal Houses
    http://www.royal.gov.uk/history/trees.htm
- Bulgarian Royal Family
  http://www.b-info.com/places/Bulgaria/Royal/
- Cambodian Royal Family Tree
  http://www.cambodia.org/facts/kroygene.gif
- Casa de Su Majestad el Rey de España
  http://www.casareal.es/casareal/
  Royal family of Spain.
- De Imperatoribus Romanis - Index of Imperial
  Stemmata of the Roman Emporers
  http://www.salve.edu/~romanemp/stemm.htm
- Encyclopedia Mythica: Genealogy tables
  http://www.pantheon.org/mythica/genealogy/
- English Monarchs - from the Conquest
  http://www.headley1.demon.co.uk/histdate/monarchs.htm
  - o Rhyme to Remember them by
    http://www.headley1.demon.co.uk/histdate/monarchs.htm
    #rhyme
- Family Tree of the British Monarchy
  http://chaos1.hypermart.net/ftbm/
- Family Tree of Greek Mythology
  http://chaos1.hypermart.net/myth/ftgm.html
- Genealogical Gleanings - Royal & Noble Lineages of
  Tonga, Fiji, Hawaii, Burma and Cambodia
  http://www.uq.net.au/~zzhsoszy/index.html

- Généalogie des rois de France / Genealogy of the kings of France
  http://ourworld.compuserve.com/homepages/egosuum/

- Genealogy of the House of Bonaparte
  http://www.napoleon.org/us/us_mu/dossiers/genealogie/
  genea-principal.html

- Genealogy of the Royal House of Denmark
  http://www.chivalricorders.org/royalty/gotha/denmkgen.htm

- A Genealogy of the Rulers of the Ancient Hellenic Kingdom and Allied Families
  http://www.pipeline.com.au/users/edpa/geneanc/geneanc.htm

- Genealogy of the Royal Family of The Netherlands
  http://www.xs4all.nl/~kvenjb/gennl.htm

- The Greek Royal Page
  http://www.xs4all.nl/~ckersten/royal/greece.html

- Habsburg
  http://membres.tripod.fr/clovis/
  Genealogy of Imperial family of Austria.

- Haile Sellassie Family Web
  http://www.angelfire.com/ak/sellassie/
  Past and present of the last Imperial family of Ethiopia, the site maintained by emperor's great-grand daughter.

- The Hashemites: Jordan's Royal Family
  http://www.kinghussein.gov.jo/hashemites.html
  - The Hashemite Family Tree
    http://www.kinghussein.gov.jo/rfamily_hashemites.html

- The Historic Regality of Scandinavia
  http://home.ringnett.no/bjornstad/royals/index.html
  - British
    http://home.ringnett.no/bjornstad/royals/brittain.html
  - Danish
    http://home.ringnett.no/bjornstad/royals/Denmark.html
  - Norwegian
    http://home.ringnett.no/bjornstad/royals/Norway.html
  - Scottish
    http://home.ringnett.no/bjornstad/royals/Scotland.html
  - Swedish
    http://home.ringnett.no/bjornstad/royals/Sweden.html

- History of the Greek Royal Family
  http://www.xs4all.nl/~ckersten/royal/greece/history.html

- Home Erenfried
  http://sites.netscape.net/erenfried/homepage
  Information relating to the German and imperial aristocracy of the tenth and eleventh centuries.

- The Imperial Family of Japan
  http://www.geocities.com/Tokyo/Temple/3953/
  Biographies and information for the emperors and their families since 1850.

- The Imperial House of Russia, House of Romanoff
  http://www.romanovfamilyandfund.org/decendants.html

- Kings of Belgium
  http://members.xoom.com/ivodb/kings/index.htm

- Knightly Orders and International Nobility
  http://www.knightlyorders.org/
  Royal and noble heraldry and genealogy, dynastic history, houses of Savoy, Grimaldi, Two Sicilies.

- Kongehuset
  http://www.kongehuset.dk/
  The Danish Royal House.

- Kungl. Hovstaterna / The Royal Court in Sweden
  http://www.royalcourt.se/

- The Lineage of the Royal Princes of England
  http://www.geocities.com/CapitolHill/4793/

- Kongeraekken
  http://www.kongehuset.dk/kongeraekken/kongeraekke.html
  Danish royal line.

- Manorial Society of Great Britain
  http://www.msgb.co.uk/msgb/index.html

- Monarchs of England
  http://www.britannia.com/history/monarchs/mondex.html

- Nobleza titulada del Reino de España / Titled Nobility of the Kingdom of España
  http://www.angelfire.com/de/NOBLEZA/index.html

- The Polish Nobility Association
  http://www.geocities.com/Athens/Atrium/9615/table.html
  Dedicated to helping Poles living outside of Poland to find their families, and learn about their heraldry and genealogy.

- Polska Liga Monarchistyczna / The Polish Monarchist League
  http://priv2.onet.pl/ka/monarchia/english.html
  Established in Warsaw in 1996 to organize and represent the noble estate, to defend its interests, and to promote and conserve the culture heritage, of Polish chivalry both material and spiritual.

- Principe de Sayd et Bibino Magno - The Imperial House of Paleologos
  http://www.fast.net.au/tancarville/paleo.htm

- Queen Victoria's Census Return, 1851
  http://learningcurve.pro.gov.uk/virtualmuseum/gallery1/
  victoria/k_victoria.htm
  One of the many records held in the UK's Public Record Office.

- Romanov Genealogy
  http://www.icon.fi/~timhaapa/

- Royal Families of Wales
  http://www.britannia.com/wales/fam1.html
  Brief history of the various princely families of Wales.

- Royal Family of Hawaii
  http://www.geocities.com/Athens/Aegean/7545/Hawaii.html

- Royal Family of Syracuse
  http://www.mcs.drexel.edu/~crorres/Archimedes/Family/
  FamilyIntro.html
  The house of Hiero - third century B.C.

- The Royal House of Bourbon (Spain)
  http://www.geocities.com/Heartland/Hills/1150/

- Saudi Royal Family Database
  http://www.saudiroyals.com/
  Comprehensive source for biographic and genealogical information on the Saudi Arabian Royal family.

- The Scottish Monarchy
  http://www.highlanderweb.co.uk/monarch1.htm

- Les Seigneurs de Bohon (The Noblemen of Bohun)
  http://www.rand.org/personal/Genea/bohon.html

- Siamese Royalty
  http://www.geocities.com/three-b.geo/
  Profiles of members of the Thai Royal Family, past and present.

- The Titled Families of the Polish-Lithuanian Commonwealth
  http://www.pgsa.org/polelith.htm

- Titled Nobility of Russia - Genealogy
  http://www.geocities.com/~tfboettger/russian/

- Zwiazek Szlachty Polskiej/Confederation of the Polish Nobility
  http://www.szlachta.org/
  Official site of Confederation of the Polish Nobility (Zwiazek Szlachty Polskiej). We are the only one association organizing Polish Nobility in Poland. We also publish "Verbum Nobile" - only one Polish magazine about noblemen's traditions, history and present matters.

◆ Mailing Lists, Newsgroups & Chat

- CHARLEMAGNE Mailing List
  http://www.rootsweb.com/~jfuller/gen_mail_country-ger.html
  #CHARLEMAGNE
  For anyone researching the genealogy of Charlemagne, also called Charles the Great (742-814), and the history of that time period.

- eGroups: Royauté
  http://www.egroups.com/group/royaute
  A French mailing list for royal genealogies, history, heraldry and news.

- GEN-ROYAL Mailing List
  http://www.rootsweb.com/~jfuller/gen_mail_general.html
  #GEN-ROYAL

◆ People & Families

- 1066 List of Knights: List of Those Accompanying William the Conqueror on His Invasion of England in 1066
  http://www.rootsweb.com/~ote/knight.htm

- Ancestors of Diana, princess of Wales
  http://www.serv.net/%7Emarivim/joanss.html

- Ancestry of Princess Diana
  http://www.genealogy.com/famousfolks/royal/FG/HTML/diana/

- Celebrity Birth Certificates
  http://www.online-homesales.co.uk/index.htm
  Birth and marriage certificates for celebrities born in the United Kingdom. Includes those of the British Royal family.

- The Companions of William the Conqueror
  http://www.patpnyc.com/conq/withwm.htm

- Genealogy of Mankind from Adam to Japheth, Shem, and Ham
  http://www.geocities.com/Tokyo/4241/geneadm2.html

- The House of Ptolemy: Abbreviated Genealogy -- Kings, Queens, and the Rest of the Royal Ptolemies
  http://www.houseofptolemy.org/housegen.htm

- Roman Emperors - The Imperial Index
  http://www.salve.edu/~romanemp/impindex.htm
  An Online Encyclopedia of Roman Emperors.

- Sir Roland de VELVILLE (1474-1535)
  http://www.gmilne.demon.co.uk/roland.htm
  Information about Sir Roland de Velville (also Vielleville, Veleville or, probably more correctly, Vieilleville), reputed natural son of Henry VII.

- Some Family History of Charles, Prince of Wales
  http://www.uftree.com/UFT/FamousFamilyTrees/royal/FG/HTML/CHARLES/index.htm

◆ Publications, Software & Supplies

- Amazon.com Genealogy Bookstore - Royalty
  http://www.amazon.com/exec/obidos/external-search/?keyword=royal+genealogy&tag=markcyndisgenealA/

- AudioTapes.com - Genealogical Lectures on Cassette Tapes - Royalty
  http://www.audiotapes.com/search2.asp?Search=royal
  And Nobility
  http://www.audiotapes.com/search2.asp?Search=nobility

- European Royal History Journal
  http://www.eurohistory.com/journal.html

- GenealogyBookShop.com - Royal and Noble
  http://www.genealogybookshop.com/genealogybookshop/files/General,Royal_and_Noble/index.html
  The online store of Genealogical Publishing Co., Inc. & Clearfield Company.

SCANDINAVIA & THE NORDIC COUNTRIES INDEX

◆ General Scandinavia & Nordic Sites
◆ Denmark / Danmark
◆ Finland / Suomi
◆ Iceland / Ísland
◆ Norway / Norge
◆ Sweden / Sverige

GENERAL SCANDINAVIA & NORDIC SITES

http://www.cyndislist.com/genscan.htm

Category Index:

- General Resource Sites
- History & Culture
- Libraries, Archives & Museums

- Mailing Lists, Newsgroups & Chat
- People & Families
- Publications, Software & Supplies

◆ General Resource Sites

- Electronic Resources for the Scandinavian Scholar
  http://www.montana.edu/sass/resource.htm
  From the Society for the Advancement of Scandinavian Study.

- Greenlandic Resources
  http://www.montana.edu/sass/greenlnd.htm
  From the Society for the Advancement of Scandinavian Study.

- Nordic Notes on the Net
  http://nordicnotes.com/

- Yahoo!...Scandinavia...Genealogy
  http://dir.yahoo.com/Arts/Humanities/History/Genealogy/
  Regional_and_Ethnic_Resources/Scandinavia/

◆ History & Culture

- Encyclopedia Mythica: Genealogy tables
  http://www.pantheon.org/mythica/genealogy/

  o The Principal Gods of Norse Mythology
    http://www.pantheon.org/mythica/genealogy/principal_
    norse.html

- History of Europe in Medieval Times, Scandinavia
  http://www.worldroots.com/brigitte/royal/royal1.htm
  *Historic and genealogical information about royal and nobility
  family lines.*

◆ Libraries, Archives & Museums

- The Faroese National Archives
  http://www.sleipnir.fo/natarc.htm

◆ Mailing Lists, Newsgroups & Chat

- GEN-NORDIC Mailing List
  http://www.rootsweb.com/~jfuller/gen_mail_country-den.html
  #GEN-NORDIC
  Gatewayed with the soc.genealogy.nordic newsgroup
  news:soc.genealogy.nordic
  *For the discussion of genealogy in the Scandinavian countries,
  including: Denmark, Finland, Greenland, Iceland, Norway and
  Sweden.*

◆ People & Families

- Sami Resources
  http://www.montana.edu/sass/sami.htm
  From the Society for the Advancement of Scandinavian Study.

- Tracing Scandinavian Latter-day Saints
  http://www.xmission.com/~nelsonb/scand.htm
  *From the Tracing Mormon Pioneers web site. For researching
  members of the LDS church from the Scandinavian Mission in the
  time period of 1852-1868.*

◆ Publications, Software & Supplies

- AudioTapes.com - Genealogical Lectures on Cassette
  Tapes - Scandinavia
  http://www.audiotapes.com/search2.asp?Search=Scandinavia

- Frontier Press Bookstore - Scandinavia
  http://www.frontierpress.com/frontier.cgi?category=sca

- JamoDat - Win-Family Software
  http://www.jamodat.dk/
  *Available in Danish, Swedish, Norwegian, French, German and
  English.*

- Royal Families of Medieval Scandinavia, Flanders,
  and Kiev
  http://www.amazon.com/exec/obidos/ISBN=0964126125/
  markcyndisgenealA/
  A book by Rupert Alen.

- A Student's Guide to Scandinavian American
  Genealogy
  http://www.amazon.com/exec/obidos/ISBN=0897749782/
  markcyndisgenealA/
  A book for sale.

DENMARK / DANMARK

http://www.cyndislist.com/denmark.htm

Category Index:

- General Resource Sites
- Government & Cities
- History & Culture
- Language & Names
- Libraries, Archives & Museums
- Mailing Lists, Newsgroups & Chat
- Maps, Gazetteers & Geographical Information
- Military
- Newspapers

- People & Families
- Professional Researchers, Volunteers & Other Research Services
- Publications, Software & Supplies
- Queries, Message Boards & Surname Lists
- Records: Census, Cemeteries, Land, Obituaries, Personal, Taxes and Vital
- Religion & Churches
- Societies & Groups

◆ General Resource Sites

- Danish Immigration to America: An Annotated Bibliography of Resources at the Library of Congress
  http://lcweb.loc.gov/rr/genealogy/bib_guid/danish.html

- Danish Resources
  http://www.montana.edu/sass/denmark.htm
  From the Society for the Advancement of Scandinavian Study.

- "Days" Calendar Program for Genealogists
  http://www.thygesen.suite.dk/EngDage.htm
  DAYS is a program designed to assist genealogists in finding dates of named days and generally navigate in and between the Julian and Gregorian calendars. The original program was in Danish and intended for Danish/Norwegian genealogists.

- Denmark Church Record Christenings
  http://www.familysearch.org/Eng/Search/RG/frameset_rg.asp
  ?Dest=G1&Aid=&Gid=&Lid=&Sid=&Did=&Juris1=&Event=&
  Year=&Gloss=&Sub=&Tab=&Entry=&Guide=DK_BT3_-
  _Churchrecordchristening1500-1874.ASP
  Information on how to access and use these records from FamilySearch.org.

- Denmark Research Outline
  http://www.familysearch.org/Eng/Search/RG/frameset_rg.asp
  ?Dest=G1&Aid=&Gid=&Lid=&Sid=&Did=&Juris1=&Event=&
  Year=&Gloss=&Sub=&Tab=&Entry=&Guide=Denmark.ASP
  Excellent "How To" from FamilySearch.org.

- Denmark Telephone & Address Listings
  http://www.ancestry.com/search/rectype/inddbs/4062.htm

- Facts about Genealogical Research in Denmark
  http://www.genealogi.dk/factwors.htm
  The Road to Knowledge About Your Family and Its Homestead, by Hans H. Worsoe.

- Faroese Resources
  http://www.montana.edu/sass/faroe.htm
  From the Society for the Advancement of Scandinavian Study.

- Genealogy Resource Index for Denmark, GRID
  http://fp.image.dk/fpemartin/
  A comprehensive web site with links to Danish archives, databases, personal home pages, discussion forums, research help, etc.

- Greenlandic Resources
  http://www.montana.edu/sass/greenlnd.htm
  From the Society for the Advancement of Scandinavian Study.

- Nordic Notes on the Net
  http://nordicnotes.com/

  o Danish Genealogy
    http://nordicnotes.com/Denmark/Genealogy_Denmark/
    genealogy_denmark.html

- Research Guidance - Denmark Events and Time Periods
  http://www.familysearch.org/Eng/Search/RG/frameset_rg.asp
  ?Dest=E&Juris1=137

◆ Government & Cities

- Excite: Travel: Denmark
  http://www.excite.com/travel/countries/denmark/

- Excite: Travel: Faroe Islands
  http://www.excite.com/travel/countries/faroe_islands/

- Yahoo!...Denmark: Counties
  http://dir.yahoo.com/Regional/Countries/Denmark/Counties/
  Or Cities and Towns
  http://dir.yahoo.com/Regional/Countries/Denmark/Cities_and
  _Towns/

◆ History & Culture

- Denmark Historical Background
  http://www.familysearch.org/Eng/Search/RG/frameset_rg.asp
  ?Dest=G1&Aid=&Gid=&Lid=&Sid=&Did=&Juris1=&Event=&
  Year=&Gloss=&Sub=&Tab=&Entry=&Guide=DK_T3_Historical
  Back.ASP
  From FamilySearch.org.

- Genealogy of the Royal House of Denmark
  http://www.chivalricorders.org/royalty/gotha/denmkgen.htm

- History of Europe in Medieval Times, Scandinavia
  http://www.worldroots.com/brigitte/royal/royal1.htm
  Historic and genealogical information about royal and nobility family lines.

- StudyWeb: History: Country History Index: Europe Index: Denmark
  http://www.studyweb.com/links/121.html

◆ Language & Names

- Danish-English Genealogy Dictionary
  http://ourworld.compuserve.com/homepages/NormanMadsen/danish.htm

- Danish Genealogical Word List
  http://www.familysearch.org/Eng/Search/RG/frameset_rg.asp?Dest=G1&Aid=&Gid=&Lid=&Sid=&Did=&Juris1=&Event=&Year=&Gloss=&Sub=&Tab=&Entry=&Guide=WLDanish.ASP

- Origins of Danish Names
  http://www.ida.net/users/dhanco/dnames.htm

- Show the ANDERSENs
  http://www.bear.dk/
  Danish-English Dictionary of often used genealogy words; a short guide of Danish names and their tradition; links. MORS, AARHUS, FYN, JORDAN.

◆ Libraries, Archives & Museums

- Århus Kommunes Biblioteker / The Public Libraries of Aarhus
  http://www.aakb.dk/

- The Balch Institute for Ethnic Studies
  http://www.libertynet.org/~balch/
  Includes a research library with materials on immigration studies.

  o A Guide to Manuscript and Microfilm Collections of the Research Library of the Balch Institute For Ethnic Studies
    http://www.balchinstitute.org/online_resources_12/html/contents.html

    • Danish
      http://www.balchinstitute.org/online_resources_12/html/body_danish.html

- The Danish Archives
  http://ourworld.compuserve.com/homepages/paulvanv/danishar.htm
  A description and informational site.

- Danish Emigration Archive At Aalborg
  http://feefhs.org/dk/frg-deaa.html
  FEEFHS Resource Guide Listing.

- Danish Emigration Archives
  http://www.emiarch.dk/home.php3?l=en
  Searchable database for 1869 to 1904, working on records thru 1940.

- Danish Immigrant Archive at Dana College ~ Blair, Nebraska
  http://www.dana.edu/pformo/archive.htm

- Danish State Archives - Statens Arkiver
  http://www.sa.dk/

- Family History Library Catalog
  http://www.familysearch.org/Search/searchcatalog.asp
  From the FamilySearch web site, an online catalog to the holdings of the LDS Church in Salt Lake City, Utah. Also search for other localities by place name.
  http://www.familysearch.org/eng/Library/fhlc/supermainframeset.asp?display=localitysearch&columns=*,180,0

  o Denmark
    http://www.familysearch.org/eng/Library/fhlc/supermainframeset.asp?display=localitydetails&subject=137&subject_disp=Denmark&columns=*,180,0

    • Faeroe Islands
      http://www.familysearch.org/Eng/Library/fhlc/supermainframeset.asp?display=localitydetails&subject=141&subject_disp=Faeroe_Islands&columns=*,180,0

    • Greenland
      http://www.familysearch.org/eng/Library/fhlc/supermainframeset.asp?display=localitydetails&subject=448&subject_disp=Greenland&columns=*,180,0

- Family History Centers in Denmark
  http://www.familysearch.org/Eng/Library/FHC/FHC_Results.asp?FHCCountry=Denmark&FHCStateProv=&FHCCounty=&FHCCity=&submit=Search

- The Faroese National Archives
  http://www.sleipnir.fo/natarc.htm

- Frederiksberg Bibliotek ~ Denmark
  http://www.fkb.dk/
  Public Library with online searching in the bibliographical database.

- HYTELNET - Library Catalogs: Denmark
  http://www.lights.com/hytelnet/dk0/dk000.html
  Before you use any of the Telnet links, make note of the user name, password and any other logon information.

- Landsarkivet for Fyn / The Provincial Archives of Funen Denmark
  http://www.sa.dk/lao/

- Landsarkivet for Nørrejylland Viborg, Danmark / Provincial Archives of Northern Jutland, Viborg, Denmark
  http://www.sa.dk/lav/

- Landsarkivet for Sjælland, Lolland-Falster og Bornholm
  http://www.sa.dk/lak/

- Landsarkivet for Sønderjylland
  http://www.sa.dk/laa/

- Repositories of Primary Sources - Europe - Denmark
  http://www.uidaho.edu/special-collections/euro1.html#dk
  A list of links to online resources from the Univ. of Idaho Library, Special Collections and Archives.

- Roskilde Bibliotek / Roskilde Library
  http://www.roskildebib.dk/

- The Royal Library, Copenhagen
  http://www.kb.bib.dk/

- Stubbekøbing Bibliotek
  http://www.stubbekoebingkom.dk/biblio/main.htm
  Public library with online searching in the bibliographical database.

- webCATS: Library Catalogues on the World Wide Web - Denmark
  http://www.lights.com/webcats/countries/DK.html

◆ Mailing Lists, Newsgroups & Chat

- Genealogy Resources on the Internet - Denmark Mailing Lists
  http://www.rootsweb.com/~jfuller/gen_mail_country-den.html
  Most of the mailing list links below point to this site, wonderfully maintained by John Fuller

- DENMARK Mailing List
  http://www.rootsweb.com/~jfuller/gen_mail_country-den.html#DENMARK
  For anyone with a genealogical interest in Denmark.

- dk.historie.genealogi Newsgroup
  news:dk.historie.genealogi

- GEN-NORDIC Mailing List
  http://www.rootsweb.com/~jfuller/gen_mail_country-den.html#GEN-NORDIC
  Gatewayed with the soc.genealogy.nordic newsgroup
  news:soc.genealogy.nordic
  For the discussion of genealogy in the Scandinavian countries, including: Denmark, Finland, Greenland, Iceland, Norway and Sweden.

◆ Maps, Gazetteers & Geographical Information

- Map of Denmark
  http://www.familysearch.org/rg/guide/MDenmark.ASP

- Map of Denmark
  http://www.lib.utexas.edu/Libs/PCL/Map_collection/europe/Denmark.jpg
  From the Perry-Castañeda Library at the Univ. of Texas at Austin.

◆ Military

- Den Kongelige Livgarde
  http://lg.hok.dk/
  The Danish Royal Life Guards.

◆ Newspapers

- AJR NewsLink - Denmark Newspapers
  http://ajr.newslink.org/euden.html

- AJR NewsLink - Faroe Islands Newspapers
  http://ajr.newslink.org/eufar.html

- Danish Pioneer - Den Danske Pioneer - Oldest Danish-American Newspaper in USA
  http://www.dendanskepioneer.com/english/index.html

- E&P Media Links - Newspaper Sites in Denmark
  http://emedia1.mediainfo.com/emedia/results.htm?category=newspaper&region=europe&abbreviation=denmark

- The Ultimate Collection of News Links: Denmark
  http://www.pppp.net/links/news/Denmark.html

- Yahoo!...Newspapers...Denmark
  http://dir.yahoo.com/News_and_Media/Newspapers/Browse_By_Region/Countries/Denmark/

◆ People & Families

- Bjorn's Genealogy
  http://home4.inet.tele.dk/skin_rup/
  SKINNERUP.

- Kongehuset
  http://www.kongehuset.dk/
  The Danish Royal House.

- Kongeraekken
  http://www.kongehuset.dk/kongeraekken/kongeraekke.html
  Danish royal line.

- Regal Lines in Northern Europe - The Danish Monarchy
  http://home.ringnett.no/bjornstad/royals/denmark.html

- Scandinavian Saints
  http://www.xmission.com/~nelsonb/scand.htm
  From the Tracing Mormon Pioneers web site. For researching members of the LDS church from the Scandinavian Mission in the time period of 1852-1868.

◆ Professional Researchers, Volunteers & Other Research Services

- European Focus
  http://www.eurofocus.com/
  Photographic portfolios of ancestral towns in Europe created for Genealogy enthusiasts in Belgium, Denmark, Eastern Europe, England, France, Germany, Great Britain, Italy, Netherlands, Norway, Poland, Sweden, Switzerland and more.

- Genealogy Helplist - Denmark
  http://home.worldonline.dk/~alexandr/helplist.html

- genealogyPro - Directory of Genealogists for Denmark
  http://genealogyPro.com/directories/Denmark.html

- Mark Windover's Web Page - Quality Professional Genealogical Research ~ Williamstown, MA
  http://www.windover.com/
  United States, Canada (including French), England, Scotland, Ireland, Wales, Iceland, Germany, Switzerland, Norway, Sweden, Denmark, France, Belgium, and The Netherlands.

- Your Family Connection ~ Yorba Linda, California
  http://www.yourfamilyconnection.com/
  Specialty areas include Danish research, lineage research and application preparation, and family health history compilation.

◆ Publications, Software & Supplies

- Amazon.com Genealogy Bookstore – Denmark
  http://www.amazon.com/exec/obidos/external-search/?
  keyword=denmark+genealogy&tag=markcyndisgenealA/
  And Danish
  http://www.amazon.com/exec/obidos/external-search/?
  keyword=danish+genealogy&tag=markcyndisgenealA/

- AudioTapes.com - Genealogical Lectures on Cassette Tapes – Denmark
  http://www.audiotapes.com/search2.asp?Search=denmark
  And Danish
  http://www.audiotapes.com/search2.asp?Search=danish

- Books We Own - Denmark
  http://www.rootsweb.com/~bwo/denmark.html
  Find a book from which you would like a lookup and click on the submitter's code at the end of the entry. Once you find the contact information for the submitter, write them a polite request for a lookup.

- Brother's Keeper Software
  http://ourworld.compuserve.com/homepages/Brothers_Keeper/
  Downloadable shareware program for Windows. The latest version contains English, French, Norwegian, Danish, Swedish, German, Dutch, Polish, Icelandic, Russian, Slovak, Afrikaans, Czech.

- Frontier Press Bookstore - Scandinavia
  http://www.frontierpress.com/frontier.cgi?category=sca

- Hvem Forsker Hvad / Danish Genealogical Research Guide
  http://www.hvemforskerhvad.dk
  In English & Danish, a guide to Danish research published annually.

- WinFamily - Anvend Winfamily fra Jamodat til din slektsgransking
  http://www.winfamily.com/
  Genealogy software available in Danish, Swedish, Norwegian, French, German and English.

◆ Queries, Message Boards & Surname Lists

- RootsWeb Surname List - RSL Denmark
  http://rsl.rootsweb.com/cgi-bin/rslsql.cgi
  The RSL and this form concept & design are courtesy of Karen Isaacson

◆ Records: Census, Cemeteries, Land, Obituaries, Personal, Taxes and Vital (Born, Married, Died & Buried)

- DDD Danish Demographic Database / Dansk Demografisk Database
  http://ddd.sa.dk/
  Search a partial census database for 1787-1850 and the Danish emigrant database for 1868-1900.

- Folket i midten -en regional forskningsressource
  http://www.folketimidten.dk/
  Folketællinger for Århus-området, Danmark. Census of the county of Aarhus, Denmark, 1787, 1801, 1834, 1845.

- Lokalhistorisk Samling i Århus, Danmark
  http://www.aakb.bib.dk/lokhist/
  Features local history for that area.

◆ Religion & Churches

- Christianity Online Church Locator - Churches in Denmark
  http://www.christianity.net/churchlocator/location.php?country=Denmark

- Churches of the World - Denmark
  http://www.churchsurf.com/churches/world/Denmark/
  From the ChurchSurf Christian Directory.

◆ Societies & Groups

- Danish-American Genealogical Group
  http://www.mtn.org/mgs/branches/danish.html

- Dansk Slægtsgårdsforening / Danish Society for Family Farms
  http://www.slaegtsgaardsforeningen.dk

- DIS-Danmark - Databehandling I Slægtsforskning
  http://www.dis-danmark.dk/

- DIS-Danmark Sammenslutningen af Slægtshistoriske Foreninger
  http://users.cybercity.dk/~dko6959/ssf.htm

- Roskildeegnens Selskab for Genealogi og Personalhistorie / Genealogy Society in Roskilde, Denmark
  http://home6.inet.tele.dk/jvo/rsgp/

- Ry Slægtshistoriske Forening / Ry Genealogical Society
  http://home3.inet.tele.dk/kaagaard/

- Samfundet for dansk genealogi og Personalhistorie / The Society for Danish Genealogy and Biography
  http://www.genealogi.dk

FINLAND / SUOMI

http://www.cyndislist.com/finland.htm

Category Index:

- General Resource Sites
- Government & Cities
- History & Culture
- Libraries, Archives & Museums
- Locality Specific
- Mailing Lists, Newsgroups & Chat
- Maps, Gazetteers & Geographical Information
- Military
- Newspapers

- People & Families
- Professional Researchers, Volunteers & Other Research Services
- Publications, Software & Supplies
- Queries, Message Boards & Surname Lists
- Records: Census, Cemeteries, Land, Obituaries, Personal, Taxes and Vital
- Religion & Churches
- Societies & Groups

◆ General Resource Sites

- English-Finnish Dictionary
  http://www.mofile.fi/-db.htm

- Family History Finland - World GenWeb
  http://www.open.org/~rumcd/genweb/finn.html

- Finland Letter-Writing Guide
  http://www.familysearch.org/Eng/Search/rg/frameset_rg.asp?
  Dest=G1&Aid=&Gid=&Lid=&Sid=&Did=&Juris1=&Event=&
  Year=&Gloss=&Sub=&Tab=&Entry=&Guide=LWGFinland.ASP
  Genealogical request form letters from FamilySearch.org.

- Finland Research Outline
  http://www.familysearch.org/Eng/Search/rg/frameset_rg.asp?
  Dest=G1&Aid=&Gid=&Lid=&Sid=&Did=&Juris1=&Event=&
  Year=&Gloss=&Sub=&Tab=&Entry=&Guide=Finland.ASP
  Excellent "How To" from FamilySearch.org.

- Finnish Genealogical Word List
  http://www.familysearch.org/Eng/Search/rg/frameset_rg.asp?
  Dest=G1&Aid=&Gid=&Lid=&Sid=&Did=&Juris1=&Event=&
  Year=&Gloss=&Sub=&Tab=&Entry=&Guide=WLFinnis.ASP

- Finnish Resources
  http://www.montana.edu/sass/finland.htm
  From the Society for the Advancement of Scandinavian Study.

- Forming Finnish Patronymic Names
  http://www.engr.uvic.ca/~syli/geneo/patronymic.html

- Genealogy & Family History - David S. Saari, Ph.D.
  http://members.aol.com/dssaari/index.htm
  - Beginner's Guide to Finnish Family History Research
    http://members.aol.com/dssaari/guide.htm

- Nordic Notes on the Net
  http://nordicnotes.com/
  - Finnish Genealogy
    http://nordicnotes.com/Finland/Genealogy_Finland/
    genealogy_finland.html

- Sukututkimus Suomessa - Finnish Genealogy
  http://personal.inet.fi/koti/suku/suomi.html

- Suomen Sukututkimusseura / Genealogical Society of Finland
  http://www.genealogia.fi/
  Promotes genealogical and biographical research.

◆ Government & Cities

- Excite: Travel: Finland
  http://www.excite.com/travel/countries/finland/

- Yahoo!...Finland: Cities and Towns
  http://dir.yahoo.com/Regional/Countries/Finland/Cities_and_
  Towns/

◆ History & Culture

- History of Europe in Medieval Times, Scandinavia
  http://www.worldroots.com/brigitte/royal/royal1.htm
  Historic and genealogical information about royal and nobility family lines.

- StudyWeb: History: Country History Index: Europe Index: Finland
  http://www.studyweb.com/links/125.html

◆ Libraries, Archives & Museums

- Äänekosken kaupunginkirjasto - Aanekoski City Library
  http://www.aanekoski.fi/kirjasto/

- Arkistolaitos / The Finnish National Archives
  http://www.narc.fi/

- The Balch Institute for Ethnic Studies
  http://www.libertynet.org/~balch/
  Includes a research library with materials on immigration studies.

o A Guide to Manuscript and Microfilm Collections of The Research Library of the Balch Institute For Ethnic Studies
http://www.balchinstitute.org/online_resources_12/html/contents.html

- Finnish
  http://www.balchinstitute.org/online_resources_12/html/body_finnish.html

● Family History Library Catalog
http://www.familysearch.org/Search/searchcatalog.asp
From the FamilySearch web site, an online catalog to the holdings of the LDS Church in Salt Lake City, Utah. Also search for other localities by place name.
http://www.familysearch.org/eng/Library/fhlc/supermainframeset.asp?display=localitysearch&columns=*,180,0

o Finland
http://www.familysearch.org/eng/Library/fhlc/supermainframeset.asp?display=localitydetails&subject=111&subject_disp=Finland&columns=*,180,0

● Family History Centers in Finland
http://www.familysearch.org/Eng/Library/FHC/FHC_Results.asp?FHCCountry=Finland&FHCStateProv=&FHCCounty=&FHCCity=&submit=Search

● Fredrika Biblioteken
http://www.kustnet.fi/~fredrika/

● HELKA - The Helsinki University Libraries OPAC
http://renki.helsinki.fi/gabriel/en/countries/finland-opac-en.html
Catalog of the Helsinki University Library system. It has a large collection of official publications of the former Russian Empire.

● Helsinki City Library / Helsingin Kaupunginkirjasto
http://www.lib.hel.fi/

● HYTELNET - Library Catalogs: Finland
http://www.lights.com/hytelnet/fi0/fi000.html
Before you use any of the Telnet links, make note of the user name, password and any other logon information.

● Immigration History Research Center (IHRC) at the University of Minnesota
http://www1.umn.edu/ihrc/
An international resource on American immigration and ethnic history.

o Archival and Library Research Collections
http://www1.umn.edu/ihrc/research.htm#top

- Family History Sources at IHRC
  http://www1.umn.edu/ihrc/genealog.htm#top

- IHRC Guide to Collections
  http://www1.umn.edu/ihrc/profiles.htm

- Finnish American Collection
  http://www1.umn.edu/ihrc/finnish.htm#top

● The Mariehamn Library
http://www.mhbibl.aland.fi/eng/
Library on the Åland Islands, a Swedish speaking archipelago under Finnish sovereignty.

● MUISTI Tietokanta / Databas / Data Base
http://linnea.helsinki.fi/~muisti/MUISTI.html
The joint database of digitized national material of libraries, archives, and museums.

● National Repository Library
http://www.varasto.uku.fi/

● Repositories of Primary Sources - Europe - Finland
http://www.uidaho.edu/special-collections/euro1.html#fi
A list of links to online resources from the Univ. of Idaho Library, Special Collections and Archives.

● webCATS: Library Catalogues on the World Wide Web - Finland
http://www.lights.com/webcats/countries/FI.html

◆ Locality Specific

● Rogaland Roots
http://www.geocities.com/Heartland/Ranch/2075/Norway.html
Web site devoted to genealogy in Rogaland fylke, Norway, with how-to guides, links and queries.

◆ Mailing Lists, Newsgroups & Chat

● Genealogy Resources on the Internet - Finland Mailing Lists
http://www.rootsweb.com/~jfuller/gen_mail_country-fin.html
Most of the mailing list links below point to this site, wonderfully maintained by John Fuller

● FINLAND Mailing List
http://www.rootsweb.com/~jfuller/gen_mail_country-fin.html#FINLAND

● FinlandGen Mailing List
http://www.rootsweb.com/~jfuller/gen_mail_country-fin.html#FinlandGen

● FINNGEN Mailing List
http://www.rootsweb.com/~jfuller/gen_mail_country-fin.html#FINNGEN

● GEN-NORDIC Mailing List
http://www.rootsweb.com/~jfuller/gen_mail_country-den.html#GEN-NORDIC
Gatewayed with the soc.genealogy.nordic newsgroup
news:soc.genealogy.nordic
For the discussion of genealogy in the Scandinavian countries, including: Denmark, Finland, Greenland, Iceland, Norway and Sweden.

◆ Maps, Gazetteers & Geographical Information

● Finland - Counties of 1939
http://www.familysearch.org/Eng/Search/rg/frameset_rg.asp?Dest=G1&Aid=&Gid=&Lid=&Sid=&Did=&Juris1=&Event=&Year=&Gloss=&Sub=&Tab=&Entry=&Guide=MFinland_Counties_of_1939.ASP

● Finland - Counties of 1960
http://www.familysearch.org/Eng/Search/rg/frameset_rg.asp?Dest=G1&Aid=&Gid=&Lid=&Sid=&Did=&Juris1=&Event=&Year=&Gloss=&Sub=&Tab=&Entry=&Guide=MFinland_Counties_of_1960.ASP

- Finland - Provinces
  http://www.familysearch.org/Eng/Search/rg/frameset_rg.asp?
  Dest=G1&Aid=&Gid=&Lid=&Sid=&Did=&Juris1=&Event=&
  Year=&Gloss=&Sub=&Tab=&Entry=&Guide=mfinland-
  provinces.ASP

- Map of Finland
  http://www.lib.utexas.edu/Libs/PCL/Map_collection/europe/
  Finland.jpg
  From the Perry-Castañeda Library at the Univ. of Texas at Austin.

◆ Military

- The Allotment System
  http://hem.passagen.se/mrwalker/military.htm
  *The military system in Sweden and Finland. Finland 1682-1808 and
  Sweden 1682-1910.*

◆ Newspapers

- AJR NewsLink - Finland Newspapers
  http://ajr.newslink.org/eufin.html

- E&P Media Links - Newspaper Sites in Finland
  http://emedia1.mediainfo.com/emedia/results.htm?region=
  europe&abbreviation=finland++++++++++++++++++++++
  +++++++++&category=newspaper

- The Ultimate Collection of News Links: Finland
  http://www.pppp.net/links/news/Finland.html

◆ People & Families

- MÄNTTÄRI Family Association Ltd.
  http://www.kolumbus.fi/manttari/home-pag/main.htm

- Sami Resources
  http://www.montana.edu/sass/sami.htm
  From the Society for the Advancement of Scandinavian Study.

- Tracing Scandinavian Latter-day Saints
  http://www.xmission.com/~nelsonb/scand.htm
  *For researching members of the LDS church from the Scandinavian
  Mission in the time period of 1852-1868.*

◆ Professional Researchers, Volunteers & Other Research Services

- Genealogy Helplist - Finland
  http://jocke.twistercom.fi/suku.html

- genealogyPro - Professional Genealogists for
  Finland
  http://genealogyPro.com/directories/Finland.html

◆ Publications, Software & Supplies

- Amazon.com Genealogy Bookstore – Finland
  http://www.amazon.com/exec/obidos/external-search/?
  keyword=finland+genealogy&tag=markcyndisgenealA/
  And Finnish
  http://www.amazon.com/exec/obidos/external-search/?
  keyword=finnish+genealogy&tag=markcyndisgenealA/

- AudioTapes.com - Genealogical Lectures on Cassette
  Tapes – Finland
  http://www.audiotapes.com/search2.asp?Search=Finland
  And Finnish
  http://www.audiotapes.com/search2.asp?Search=Finnish

- Books We Own - Finland
  http://www.rootsweb.com/~bwo/finland.html
  *Find a book from which you would like a lookup and click on the
  submitter's code at the end of the entry. Once you find the contact
  information for the submitter, write them a polite request for a
  lookup.*

- Frontier Press Bookstore - Scandinavia
  http://www.frontierpress.com/frontier.cgi?category=sca

- JamoDat - Win-Family Software
  http://www.jamodat.dk/
  *Available in Danish, Swedish, Norwegian, French, German and
  English.*

◆ Queries, Message Boards & Surname Lists

- Addresses to family researchers - Index of
  Researched Surnames
  http://www.genealogia.fi/sukututk/frames.php?type=
  1&kieli=en
  From the Suomen Sukututkimusseura web site.

- RootsWeb Surname List - RSL Finland
  http://rsl.rootsweb.com/cgi-bin/rslsql.cgi
  *The RSL and this form concept & design are courtesy of Karen
  Isaacson*

◆ Records: Census, Cemeteries, Land, Obituaries, Personal, Taxes and Vital (Born, Married, Died & Buried)

- National Land Survey of Finland
  http://www.nls.fi/index_e.html

◆ Religion & Churches

- Evangelical Lutheran Church of Finland
  http://www.evl.fi/english/index.html

- HisKi project - Parish List
  http://www.genealogia.fi/hiski/eaqaol?en
  Finnish church parish records online.

◆ Societies & Groups

- Cokato Finnish-American Historical Society ~
  Cokato, Minnesota
  http://cokato.mn.us/org/fahs.html

- Finnish American Heritage Society of CT ~
  Connecticut
  http://www.fahs-ct.org/

- Finnish-American Historical Society of the West ~ Portland, OR
  http://www.teleport.com/~finamhsw/

- Genealogical Society of Finland
  http://www.genealogia.fi/indexe.htm

- Sukututkimusyhdistyksiä - Genealogical Societies
  http://www.genealogia.fi/stutkyh/

- Swedish Finn Historical Society ~ Seattle, WA
  http://home1.gte.net/SFHS/index.htm

ICELAND / ÍSLAND

http://www.cyndislist.com/iceland.htm

Category Index:

- ◆ General Resource Sites
- ◆ Government & Cities
- ◆ History & Culture
- ◆ Language & Names
- ◆ Libraries, Archives & Museums
- ◆ Mailing Lists, Newsgroups & Chat
- ◆ Maps, Gazetteers & Geographical Information
- ◆ Military
- ◆ Newspapers

- ◆ People & Families
- ◆ Professional Researchers, Volunteers & Other Research Services
- ◆ Publications, Software & Supplies
- ◆ Queries, Message Boards & Surname Lists
- ◆ Records: Census, Cemeteries, Land, Obituaries, Personal, Taxes and Vital
- ◆ Societies & Groups

◆ General Resource Sites

- Iceland on the Web
  http://www.vefur.is/iceland/
  Hundreds of categorized links to Iceland resources, with descriptions.

- Icelandic GenWeb
  http://nyherji.is/~halfdan/aett/aettvef.htm

- Icelandic Resources
  http://www.montana.edu/sass/iceland.htm
  From the Society for the Advancement of Scandinavian Study.

- Íslensk erfðagreining / deCODE genetics
  http://www.decode.is/
  Based in Reykjavik, Iceland, deCODE genetics is a population-based genomics company conducting research into the inherited causes of common diseases. Being situated in Iceland has certain advantages for the company. The Icelandic population, with its relative genetic homogeneity, extensive genealogical records and high-quality healthcare system, provides the resources to identify genes associated with a multitude of diseases.

  - Iceland: The Case of a National Human Genome Project
    http://www.decode.is/greinar/anthro.htm
    Online article from Antropology Today discussion various social implications of the deCODE project.

  - Íslendingabók deCODE's Genealogy Database
    http://www.decode.is/ppt/genea/
    Online slide show demonstration of deCODE's database software using deCODE's CEO, Kári Stefánsson, as an example. The demo traces his ancestors back to Egill Skallagrimsson, poet and viking of the 9th century AD.

- Mapping the Icelandic Genome
  http://sunsite.berkeley.edu/biotech/iceland/
  An anthropology of the scientific, political, economic, religious, and ethical issues surrounding the deCode Project and its global implications. Iceland has a series of distinctive characteristics

which make it suitable for such mapping. Its population is relatively small (today 275,000 but as low as 50,000 in the recent past). There exist an unusually complete set of family records in Iceland (over 80% of all Icelandic people who ever lived can be placed genealogically on a computerized database).

- NORDGUIDE
  http://otatrip.hut.fi/nordinfo/nordguide/
  A directory of databases in the Nordic Countries.

- Nordic Notes on the Net
  http://nordicnotes.com/

  - Icelandic Genealogy
    http://nordicnotes.com/Iceland/Genealogy_Iceland/genealogy_iceland.html

- South Iceland - so much to discover!
  http://www.south.is/
  Complete guide to Internet resources in the region, also general information about Iceland and useful tips for travelers.

◆ Government & Cities

- Excite: Travel: Iceland
  http://www.excite.com/travel/countries/iceland/

- Yahoo!...Iceland: Cities and Towns
  http://dir.yahoo.com/Regional/Countries/Iceland/Cities_and_Towns/

◆ History & Culture

- The Emigration from Iceland to America
  http://nyherji.is/~halfdan/westward/vestur.htm

- History of Europe in Medieval Times, Scandinavia
  http://www.worldroots.com/brigitte/royal/royal1.htm
  Historic and genealogical information about royal and nobility family lines.

- History of Iceland
  http://www.arctic.is/islandia/history/

- StudyWeb: History: Country History Index: Europe Index: Iceland
  http://www.studyweb.com/links/144.html

◆ Language & Names

- The Icelandic Alphabet
  http://www.itn.is/~gunnsi/misc/alph.htm

- Icelandic Genealogical Word List
  http://www.familysearch.org/Eng/Search/rg/frameset_rg.asp?
  Dest=G1&Aid=&Gid=&Lid=&Sid=&Did=&Juris1=&Event=&
  Year=&Gloss=&Sub=&Tab=&Entry=&Guide=WLIcelandic.ASP

- Icelandic Last Names
  http://www.cs.umd.edu/~bthj/bthj/nofn.html

- Icelandic Names
  http://www.itn.is/~gunnsi/family.htm

◆ Libraries, Archives & Museums

- The Balch Institute for Ethnic Studies
  http://www.libertynet.org/~balch/
  Includes a research library with materials on immigration studies.

  o A Guide To Manuscript And Microfilm Collections Of The Research Library Of The Balch Institute For Ethnic Studies
    http://www.balchinstitute.org/online_resources_12/html/
    contents.html

    ▪ Icelanders
      http://www.balchinstitute.org/online_resources_12/html/
      body_icelandic.html

- Family History Library Catalog
  http://www.familysearch.org/Search/searchcatalog.asp
  From the FamilySearch web site, an online catalog to the holdings of the LDS Church in Salt Lake City, Utah. Also search for other localities by place name.
  http://www.familysearch.org/eng/Library/fhlc/supermainframe
  set.asp?display=localitysearch&columns=*,180,0

  o Iceland
    http://www.familysearch.org/eng/Library/fhlc/supermain
    frameset.asp?display=localitydetails&subject=139&subject
    _disp=Iceland&columns=*,180,0

- Family History Centers in Iceland
  http://www.familysearch.org/Eng/Library/FHC/FHC_
  Results.asp?FHCCountry=Iceland&FHCStateProv=&
  FHCCounty=&FHCCity=&submit=Search

- HYTELNET - Library Catalogs: Iceland
  http://www.lights.com/hytelnet/is0/is000.html
  Before you use any of the Telnet links, make note of the user name, password and any other logon information.

- Landsbókasafn Íslands - Háskólabókasafn / National and University Library of Iceland
  http://www.bok.hi.is/

- Þjóðskjalasafns Íslands / The National Archives of Iceland
  http://www.archives.is/main.html

The National Archives was established in 1882. Its oldest records are from the Middle Ages, the oldest one from the church in Reykholt dating back to the year 1185.

- Repositories of Primary Sources - Europe - Iceland
  http://www.uidaho.edu/special-collections/europe.html#is
  A list of links to online resources from the Univ. of Idaho Library, Special Collections and Archives.

◆ Mailing Lists, Newsgroups & Chat

- Genealogy Resources on the Internet - Iceland Mailing Lists
  http://www.rootsweb.com/~jfuller/gen_mail_country-ice.html
  Most of the mailing list links below point to this site, wonderfully maintained by John Fuller

- ICELAND Mailing List
  http://www.rootsweb.com/~jfuller/gen_mail_country-ice.html
  #ICELAND

- GEN-NORDIC Mailing List
  http://www.rootsweb.com/~jfuller/gen_mail_country-ice.html
  #GEN-NORDIC
  Gatewayed with the soc.genealogy.nordic newsgroup
  news:soc.genealogy.nordic
  For the discussion of genealogy in the Scandinavian countries, including: Denmark, Finland, Greenland, Iceland, Norway and Sweden.

◆ Maps, Gazetteers & Geographical Information

- Lonely Planet - Iceland Map
  http://www.lonelyplanet.com/dest/eur/graphics/map-ice.htm

- Map of Iceland
  http://www.lib.utexas.edu/Libs/PCL/Map_collection/europe/
  Iceland.gif
  From the Perry-Castañeda Library at the Univ. of Texas at Austin.

◆ Military

- Iceland: The Icelandic Coast Guard
  http://www.randburg.com/is/general/general_15.html

◆ Newspapers

- AJR NewsLink - Iceland Newspapers
  http://ajr.newslink.org/euice.html

- E&P Media Links - Newspaper Sites in Iceland
  http://emedia1.mediainfo.com/emedia/results.htm?region=
  europe&abbreviation=iceland++++++++++++++++++++++
  ++++++++++&category=newspaper

- The Ultimate Collection of News Links: Iceland
  http://www.pppp.net/links/news/Iceland.html

◆ People & Families

- Tracing Scandinavian Latter-day Saints
  http://www.xmission.com/~nelsonb/scand.htm
  From the Tracing Mormon Pioneers web site. For researching members of the LDS church from the Scandinavian Mission in the time period of 1852-1868.

◆ Professional Researchers, Volunteers & Other Research Services

- Genealogy Helplist - Iceland
  http://helplist.org/isl/index.shtml

- Mark Windover's Web Page - Quality Professional Genealogical Research ~ Williamstown, Massachusetts
  http://www.windover.com/
  United States, Canada (including French), England, Scotland, Ireland, Wales, Iceland, Germany, Switzerland, Norway, Sweden, Denmark, France, Belgium, and The Netherlands.

◆ Publications, Software & Supplies

- Brother's Keeper Software
  http://ourworld.compuserve.com/homepages/Brothers_Keeper/
  Downloadable shareware program for Windows. The latest version contains English, French, Norwegian, Danish, Swedish, German, Dutch, Polish, Icelandic, Russian, Slovak, Afrikaans, Czech.

- Frontier Press Bookstore - Scandinavia
  http://www.frontierpress.com/frontier.cgi?category=sca

- JamoDat - Win-Family Software
  http://www.jamodat.dk/
  Available in Danish, Swedish, Norwegian, French, German and English.

- Tracing your Icelandic Family Tree
  http://www.amazon.com/exec/obidos/ISBN=092037400X/markcyndisgenealA/
  A book by Eric Jonasson.

◆ Queries, Message Boards & Surname Lists

- RootsWeb Surname List - RSL Iceland
  http://rsl.rootsweb.com/cgi-bin/rslsql.cgi
  The RSL and this form concept & design are courtesy of Karen Isaacson

◆ Records: Census, Cemeteries, Land, Obituaries, Personal, Taxes and Vital (Born, Married, Died & Buried)

- The National Registry
  http://www.statice.is/depart/natreg.htm
  A register of all those who have been domiciled in Iceland since 1952.

◆ Societies & Groups

- Icelandic Genealogy Society - Aðalsíða Íslensk ~ Reykjavik, Iceland
  http://www.vortex.is/aett/

NORWAY / NORGE
http://www.cyndislist.com/norway.htm

Category Index:

- General Resource Sites
- Government & Cities
- History & Culture
- How To
- Language & Names
- Libraries, Archives & Museums
- Mailing Lists, Newsgroups & Chat
- Maps, Gazetteers & Geographical Information
- Newspapers

- People & Families
- Professional Researchers, Volunteers & Other Research Services
- Publications, Software & Supplies
- Queries, Message Boards & Surname Lists
- Records: Census, Cemeteries, Land, Obituaries, Personal, Taxes and Vital
- Religion & Churches
- Societies & Groups

◆ General Resource Sites

- Ancestors from Norway
  http://homepages.rootsweb.com/~norway/index.html
  Research guide for Norwegian-American genealogy.

- Arne Moen's Home Page from Norway
  http://home.sol.no/~amoen/genealogi.html
  In Norwegian with many links to Scandinavian genealogy sites.

- Bamble Genealogiske Side / Bamble Genealogical Page
  http://home.sol.no/~sorter/
  Including probate records from Bamble & Langesund.

- "Days" Calendar Program for Genealogists
  http://www.thygesen.suite.dk/EngDage.htm
  DAYS is a program designed to assist genealogists in finding dates of named days and generally navigate in and between the Julian and Gregorian calendars. The original program was in Danish and intended for Danish/Norwegian genealogists.

- Kragerø Genealogical Page. By Per Stian Bjørnø Kjendal
  http://home.sol.no/~kjendal/engelsk.html
  Many Norwegian resources, especially for the Kragerø area, including maps, records sources and an index of those who emigrated during 1843-1899.

- Medieval Scandinavia
  http://home.ringnett.no/bjornstad/
  Previously The Bjørnstad History and Genealogy Web Site of Norway. Information for Hemsedal, Hallingdal, Ringerike and Hole of Buskerud County.

- Nordic Notes on the Net
  http://nordicnotes.com/
  o Norwegian Genealogy
    http://nordicnotes.com/Norway/Genealogy_Norway/genealogy_norway.html

- Norway Genealogy - World GenWeb
  http://www.rootsweb.com/~wgnorway/

- Norway Roots - Norske Røtter og Slektsgransking
  http://www.geocities.com/Heartland/3856/

- Norwegian American Homepage -- Genealogy
  http://www.lawzone.com/half-nor/ROOTS.HTM
  Genealogy links of relevance to Norwegian Americans.

- Norwegian Genealogy Ring - Slektsforskning
  http://steinmoen.com/slekt/

- Norwegian Resources
  http://www.montana.edu/sass/norway.htm
  From the Society for the Advancement of Scandinavian Study.

- A Select Bibliography of Works: Norwegian-American Immigration and Local History
  http://lcweb.loc.gov/rr/genealogy/bib_guid/norway.html
  Bibliography from the Library of Congress.

- Slektshistoriske Kilder 1500 - 1900
  http://home.sol.no/~asjonass/kilder/index.htm
  Provides access by locations in Norway to census, church, land, and other records available through the Internet.

- Skien Genealogiske Side / Skien Genealogical Page
  http://www.slekt.org/
  Including tax lists, probate records, cemeteries, etc for Gjerpen and Skien.

- Stein Norem WISTED's Genealogy pages
  http://www.sorco.no/~snw/sokn-eng.htm
  Includes pages on Sokndal parish in Rogaland, Norway.

◆ Government & Cities

- Excite: Travel: Norway
  http://www.excite.com/travel/countries/norway/

- Luster Kommune
  http://fjordinfo.vestdata.no/offentleg/kommunar/lusterkomm/
  luster.htm

- Yahoo!...Norway: Counties
  http://dir.yahoo.com/Regional/Countries/Norway/Counties/
  Or Cities and Towns
  http://dir.yahoo.com/Regional/Countries/Norway/Cities_and_
  Towns/

◆ History & Culture

- Gamle norske måleenheter
  http://www.agderweb.no/org/nff/N_M_E.htm#Mynt
  *From Norsk Forlishistorisk Forening. Information on old
  Norwegian coinage from ancient to modern times.*

- History of Europe in Medieval Times, Scandinavia
  http://www.worldroots.com/brigitte/royal/royal1.htm
  *Historic and genealogical information about royal and nobility
  family lines.*

- The History of Norway - from ODIN
  http://odin.dep.no/html/nofovalt/depter/ud/nornytt/
  uda-286.html

- Medieval Scandinavia
  http://home.ringnett.no/bjornstad/
  *Previously the The Bjørnstad History and Genealogy Web Site of
  Norway. Information for Hemsedal, Hallingdal, Ringerike and Hole
  of Buskerud County.*

- Norway Historical Background
  http://www.familysearch.org/Eng/Search/rg/frameset_rg.asp
  ?Dest=G1&Aid=&Gid=&Lid=&Sid=&Did=&Juris1=&Event=&
  Year=&Gloss=&Sub=&Tab=&Entry=&Guide=NOR_T3_
  HistoricalBack.ASP
  From FamilySearch.org.

- Norwegian Online Information Service - Culture &
  History
  http://www.norway.org/

- Research Guidance - Norway Events and Time
  Periods
  http://www.familysearch.org/Eng/Search/RG/events/133.asp
  From FamilySearch.org.

- StudyWeb: History: Country History Index: Europe
  Index: Norway
  http://www.studyweb.com/links/151.html

- Scandinavian History - The Viking Attacks on
  Europe
  http://home.ringnett.no/bjornstad/vikings/index.html

- Yahoo!...Norway...History
  http://dir.yahoo.com/Regional/Countries/Norway/Arts_and_
  Humanities/Humanities/History/

◆ How To

- Ancestors from Norway
  http://homepages.rootsweb.com/~norway/index.html
  Research guide for Norwegian-American genealogy

- o Ancestors from Norway - Getting Started
  http://homepages.rootsweb.com/~norway/na15.html

- o Hvordan Finner Jeg Etterkommere Av De Som
  Utvandret Til USA? / How Do I Find Descendants
  of a Norwegian Immigrant to the USA?
  http://homepages.rootsweb.com/~norway/na14.html
  *In Norwegian; for Norwegians who are tracing descendants of a
  Norwegian immigrant to the USA*

- How To Trace Your Ancestors In Norway
  http://odin.dep.no/html/nofovalt/depter/ud/publ/96/ancestors/
  index.html

- How to Trace Your Ancestors in Norway - From
  ODIN
  http://odin.dep.no/html/nofovalt/depter/ud/publ/96/ancestors/
  prep.html

- Norway Research Outline
  http://www.familysearch.org/Eng/Search/RG/frameset_rg.asp
  ?Dest=G1&Aid=&Gid=&Lid=&Sid=&Did=&Juris1=&Event=&
  Year=&Gloss=&Sub=&Tab=&Entry=&Guide=Norway.ASP
  Excellent "How To" from FamilySearch.org.

- Norwegian Genealogy How To Guide
  http://www.familytreemaker.com/00000378.html
  from Family Tree Maker.

◆ Language & Names

- Gotisk Skrift -- The Gothic Script
  http://www.netutah.com/akre/gothalf.htm
  *Two alphabets of gothic script handwriting from Norway about
  1875.*

- Norwegian Genealogical Word List
  http://www.familysearch.org/Eng/Search/RG/frameset_rg.asp
  ?Dest=G1&Aid=&Gid=&Lid=&Sid=&Did=&Juris1=&Event=&
  Year=&Gloss=&Sub=&Tab=&Entry=&Guide=WLNorway.ASP

- Norwegian Naming Practices
  http://www.uib.no/hi/nameprac.htm

◆ Libraries, Archives & Museums

- The Balch Institute for Ethnic Studies
  http://www.libertynet.org/~balch/
  Includes a research library with materials on immigration studies.

- o A Guide To Manuscript And Microfilm
  Collections Of The Research Library Of The Balch
  Institute For Ethnic Studies
  http://www.balchinstitute.org/online_resources_12/html/
  contents.html

  - Norwegian
    http://www.balchinstitute.org/online_resources_12/html/
    body_norwegian.html

- Digitalarkivet - Arkivverket
  http://www.hist.uib.no/arkivverket/
  *Digitalarkivet (The Digital Archive) is a joint project between the
  National Archives of Norway, the regional Archive of Bergen and
  the Department of History, University of Bergen.*

- Family History Library Catalog
  http://www.familysearch.org/Search/searchcatalog.asp
  From the FamilySearch web site, an online catalog to the holdings of the LDS Church in Salt Lake City, Utah. Also search for other localities by place name.
  http://www.familysearch.org/eng/Library/fhlc/supermainframe set.asp?display=localitysearch&columns=*,180,0

  o Norway
    http://www.familysearch.org/fhlc/eng/Library/supermain frameset.asp?display=localitydetails&subject=133&subject _disp=Norway&columns=*,180,0

- Family History Centers in Norway
  http://www.familysearch.org/Eng/Library/FHC/FHC_Results. asp?FHCCountry=Norway&FHCStateProv=&FHCCounty=& FHCCity=&submit=Search

- Fylkesarkivet i Sogn og Fjordane - Utvandring - Emigration ~ Norway
  http://www.sffarkiv.no/sffutv.htm

- HYTELNET - Library Catalogs: Norway
  http://www.lights.com/hytelnet/no0/no000.html
  Before you use any of the Telnet links, make note of the user name, password and any other logon information.

- Nasjonalbiblioteket / National Library of Norway
  http://teleslekt.nbr.no/

- The Norwegian Emigration Center ~ Stavanger
  http://www.utvandrersenteret.no/index.htm

- The Norwegian Emigrant Museum
  http://www.hamarnett.no/emigrantmuseum/

- Registreringssentral for Historiske Data (RHD) / Norwegian Historical Data Centre (NHDC)
  http://www.isv.uit.no/seksjon/rhd/

- Repositories of Primary Sources - Europe - Norway
  http://www.uidaho.edu/special-collections/euro2.html#no
  A list of links to online resources from the Univ. of Idaho Library, Special Collections and Archives.

- Universitetsbiblioteket i Oslo - UBO / University of Oslo Library (UBO) ~ Norway
  http://www.ub.uio.no/

- University of Minnesota Libraries
  http://www.lib.umn.edu/

  o Genealogy Resources Available at the University of Minnesota Libraries
    http://www.lib.umn.edu/subject/genealogy.html

    • Finding Norwegian Bygdebøker Held at the University of Minnesota Libraries
      http://wilson.lib.umn.edu/reference/bygdebkr-subj.html

    • Libraries and Resource Centers for Norwegian Historical and Genealogical Research in the Upper Midwest
      http://wilson.lib.umn.edu/reference/nor-centers.html

    • Norwegian Bygdebøker or Local Histories Held at the University of Minnesota Libraries
      http://wilson.lib.umn.edu/reference/bygdebkr.html

- Norwegian Geographical and Administrative Divisions
  http://wilson.lib.umn.edu/reference/nor-geog.html

- Vesterheim Genealogical Center and Naeseth Library ~ Madison, Wisconsin
  http://www.vesterheim.org/genealogy/

- webCATS: Library Catalogues on the World Wide Web - Norway
  http://www.lights.com/webcats/countries/NO.html

◆ Mailing Lists, Newsgroups & Chat

- Genealogy Resources on the Internet - Norway Mailing Lists
  http://www.rootsweb.com/~jfuller/gen_mail_country-nor.html
  Most of the mailing list links below point to this site, wonderfully maintained by John Fuller

- FAMILIE_OG_SLEKT Mailing List
  http://www.rootsweb.com/~jfuller/gen_mail_software.html #FAMILIE_OG_SLEKT
  For discussions of the "Familie og Slekt" Norwegian genealogy software program.

- GEN-NORDIC Mailing List
  http://www.rootsweb.com/~jfuller/gen_mail_country-nor.html #GEN-NORDIC
  Gatewayed with the soc.genealogy.nordic newsgroup
  news:soc.genealogy.nordic
  For the discussion of genealogy in the Scandinavian countries, including: Denmark, Finland, Greenland, Iceland, Norway and Sweden.

- NORWAY Mailing List
  http://www.rootsweb.com/~jfuller/gen_mail_country-nor.html #NORWAY

- NorwegianGenealogy Mailing List
  http://www.rootsweb.com/~jfuller/gen_mail_country-nor.html #NorwegianGenealogy
  For anyone with a genealogical interest in Norway.

- VALDRES Mailing List
  http://www.rootsweb.com/~jfuller/gen_mail_country-nor.html #VALDRES
  For the discussion and sharing of information regarding the Valdres region of Norway and immigrants from that region.

◆ Maps, Gazetteers & Geographical Information

- How to Use the Norwegian Gazetteer
  http://www.familysearch.org/Eng/Search/rg/frameset_rg.asp? Dest=G1&Aid=&Gid=&Lid=&Sid=&Did=&Juris1=&Event=& Year=&Gloss=&Sub=&Tab=&Entry=&Guide=NOR_T4-_ _How_to_use_the_Norwegian_Gazetteer.ASP
  Instructions on the use of the 1901 Norsk Stedførtegnelse from FamilySearch.org.

- Map of Norway
  http://www.familysearch.org/Eng/Search/rg/frameset_rg.asp? Dest=G1&Aid=&Gid=&Lid=&Sid=&Did=&Juris1=&Event=& Year=&Gloss=&Sub=&Tab=&Entry=&Guide=MNorway.ASP

- Norway Maps - The Perry-Castañeda Library Map Collection
  http://www.lib.utexas.edu/Libs/PCL/Map_collection/norway.html
  From the University of Texas at Austin.

◆ Newspapers

- Aftenposten Interaktiv ~ Oslo, Norway
  http://www.aftenposten.no/

- AJR NewsLink - Norway Newspapers
  http://ajr.newslink.org/eunor.html

- E&P Media Links - Newspaper Sites in Norway
  http://emedia1.mediainfo.com/emedia/results.htm?region=europe&abbreviation=norway++++++++++++++++++++++++++++++++++++&category=newspaper

- The Ultimate Collection of News Links: Norway
  http://www.pppp.net/links/news/Norway.html

- Yahoo!...Newspapers...Norway
  http://dir.yahoo.com/Regional/Countries/Norway/News_and_Media/Newspapers/

◆ People & Families

- Ancestors of H.M. King Harald 5th of Norway
  http://w1.2628.telia.com/~u262800030/harald/index1.htm

- The Royal History Homepage
  http://home.ringnett.no/bjornstad/royals/

  o The Monarchs & Regents of Norway for Near 1150 Years
    http://home.ringnett.no/bjornstad/royals/Norway.html

- Sami Resources
  http://www.montana.edu/sass/sami.htm
  From the Society for the Advancement of Scandinavian Study. Links to sites about the "Sami" a.k.a. Lapplanders.

- Tracing Scandinavian Latter-day Saints
  http://www.xmission.com/~nelsonb/scand.htm
  From the Tracing Mormon Pioneers web site. For researching members of the LDS church from the Scandinavian Mission in the time period of 1852-1868.

- Valdres Samband - The Oldest Bygdelag in America - 1899
  http://www.geocities.com/Heartland/Meadows/4842/
  This is the web site of the Valdres Samband Lag - a group of emigrant descendants from the Valdres Valley of Norway. This site serves to provide resources for those who are interested in their Valdres heritage.

◆ Professional Researchers, Volunteers & Other Research Services

- European Focus
  http://www.eurofocus.com/
  Photographic portfolios of ancestral towns in Europe created for Genealogy enthusiasts in Belgium, Denmark, Eastern Europe, England, France, Germany, Great Britain, Italy, Netherlands, Norway, Poland, Sweden, Switzerland and more.

- Genealogy Helplist - Norway
  http://helplist.org/nor/index.shtml

- genealogyPro - Professional Genealogists for Norway
  http://genealogyPro.com/directories/Norway.html

- Mark Windover's Web Page - Quality Professional Genealogical Research ~ Williamstown, Massachusetts
  http://www.windover.com/
  United States, Canada (including French), England, Scotland, Ireland, Wales, Iceland, Germany, Switzerland, Norway, Sweden, Denmark, France, Belgium, and The Netherlands.

- Molander's Genealogy Service
  http://www.algonet.se/~family/
  Professional researchers for Sweden and Norway.

◆ Publications, Software & Supplies

- Amazon.com Genealogy Bookstore – Norway
  http://www.amazon.com/exec/obidos/external-search/?keyword=Norway+genealogy&tag=markcyndisgenealA/
  And Norwegian
  http://www.amazon.com/exec/obidos/external-search/?keyword=Norwegian+genealogy&tag=markcyndisgenealA/

- AudioTapes.com - Genealogical Lectures on Cassette Tapes – Norway
  http://www.audiotapes.com/search2.asp?Search=way
  And Norwegian
  http://www.audiotapes.com/search2.asp?Search=weg

- Books We Own - Norway
  http://www.rootsweb.com/~bwo/norway.html
  Find a book from which you would like a lookup and click on the submitter's code at the end of the entry. Once you find the contact information for the submitter, write them a polite request for a lookup.

- Brother's Keeper Software
  http://ourworld.compuserve.com/homepages/Brothers_Keeper/
  Downloadable shareware program for Windows. The latest version contains English, French, Norwegian, Danish, Swedish, German, Dutch, Polish, Icelandic, Russian, Slovak, Afrikaans, Czech.

- FAMILIE_OG_SLEKT Mailing List
  http://www.rootsweb.com/~jfuller/gen_mail_software.html#FAMILIE_OG_SLEKT
  For discussions of the "Familie og Slekt" Norwegian genealogy software program.

- Frontier Press Bookstore - Scandinavia
  http://www.frontierpress.com/frontier.cgi?category=sca

- Heritage Books - Norwegian
  http://www.heritagebooks.com/norweg.htm

- WinFamily - Anvend Winfamily fra Jamodat til din slektsgranskning
  http://www.winfamily.com/
  Genealogy software available in Danish, Swedish, Norwegian, French, German and English.

◆ Queries, Message Boards & Surname Lists

● RootsWeb Surname List - RSL Norway
http://rsl.rootsweb.com/cgi-bin/rslsql.cgi
The RSL and this form concept & design are courtesy of Karen Isaacson

◆ Records: Census, Cemeteries, Land, Obituaries, Personal, Taxes and Vital (Born, Married, Died & Buried)

● Emigration from Norway, The Solem, Swiggum & Austheim Ship Index
http://www.museumsnett.no/mka/ssa/
Index of emigrant ships leaving Norway, 1825-1925. Ship descriptions and pictures. Descriptions of voyages. Some passenger lists. Shipping companies.

● Finnmark Emigration - Emigration Site for Finnmark County, Norway
http://w1.2776.telia.com/~u277600442/
The emigration list contains names of people who emigrated from Alta and Vadsø, Finnmark, North-Norway area, via Trondheim between 1867 - 1925 to USA and Canada.

● Getting into the Norwegian Census
http://www.rhd.uit.no/nhdc/michael02.htm

● Gjerpen - Slekt
http://home.sol.no/~gstrom/
Including census & churchbook resources.

● Kulturnett Sogn og Fjordane - Databases
http://www.sffarkiv.no/sffbasar/default.asp?cookietest=on

● Norway - 1801 Census
http://www.uib.no/hi/1801page.html

● Porsgrunn Genealogiske Side / Porsgrunn Genealogical Page
http://home.sol.no/~holmjohn/
Including church books & probate records for Brevik, land records for Eidanger.

◆ Religion & Churches

● Christianity Online Church Locator - Churches in Norway
http://www.christianity.net/churchlocator/location.php?country=Norway

● Churches dot Net - Global Church Web Pages - Norway
http://www.churches.net/churches/internat.htm#nor

● Churches of the World - Norway
http://www.churchsurf.com/churches/world/Norway/
From the ChurchSurf Christian Directory.

◆ Societies & Groups

● The Bygdelag Page | Norwegian Genealogy | Norwegian-American Genealogy
http://www.hfaa.org/bygdelag/
Bygdelag are organizations made up of the descendants of emigrantts from particular areas of Norway who are now living in North America.

● Dis Nord-Trøndelag
http://www.disnorge.no/nordtrond/
Computer group in Steinkjer, Norway.

● DIS-Norges hjemmeside
http://www.disnorge.no/

● Grenland Genealogy Society
http://home.sol.no/~kjendal/grenland.html
Part of Telemark in Norway.

● Norwegian-American Historical Association
http://www.naha.stolaf.edu/

● Norwegian Emigrant Museum Genealogical Society ~ Norway
http://www.hamarnett.no/emigrantmuseum/gensocie.htm

● Norwegian Genealogy Computer Interest Group
http://www.uio.no/~achristo/genealog.html

● Sognefjordlaget in America
http://home.c2i.net/bolstad/sfjlag.htm

● Sons of Norway Home Page
http://www.sofn.com/

● Sons of Norway, NordTex Lodge 1-594, Dallas, Texas
http://web2.airmail.net/gus/nordtex.htm

● Telelaget of America - A Norwegian-American bygdelag ~ Bloomington, Minnesota
http://www.geocities.com/Heartland/Hills/1545/

SWEDEN / SVERIGE
http://www.cyndislist.com/sweden.htm

Category Index:

- General Resource Sites
- Government & Cities
- History & Culture
- How To
- Language & Names
- Libraries, Archives & Museums
- Locality Specific
- Mailing Lists, Newsgroups & Chat
- Maps, Gazetteers & Geographical Information
- Military

- Newspapers
- People & Families
- Professional Researchers, Volunteers & Other Research Services
- Publications, Software & Supplies
- Queries, Message Boards & Surname Lists
- Records: Census, Cemeteries, Land, Obituaries, Personal, Taxes and Vital
- Religion & Churches
- Societies & Groups

◆ General Resource Sites

- Anders Berg's Homepage
  http://www.algonet.se/~anderzb/
  With Swedish resources.

- DataDux Släktforskning Genealogy
  http://www.datadux.se/
  In Swedish & English.

- Europa! Sweden - Genealogy, History & More
  http://members.xoom.com/follesdal/sweden.html
  Swedish genealogy and history information, links, and books.

- European Emigration - A Review of Swedish Emigration to America
  http://www.americanwest.com/swedemigr/pages/emigra.htm

- Genealogi - Ulf Berggren
  http://www.nada.kth.se/~ulfb/genealogi.html

- Genealogy in Sweden / Släktforskning i Sverige ~ In Swedish
  http://www.abc.se/~m225/slfo.html

- Nordic Notes on the Net
  http://nordicnotes.com/

  o Swedish Genealogy
    http://nordicnotes.com/Sweden/Genealogy_Sweden/genealogy_sweden.html

- Skånsk släktforskning
  http://www.algonet.se/~anderzb/genea/skane.htm
  Swedish genealogy resources. In Swedish & some English.

- Släktforskning i Sverige / Genealogy in Sweden ~ In Swedish
  http://www.lysator.liu.se/~pober/slfo.html

- Svenska Släktforskarlänkar
  http://www.itv.se/~a1089/genealogy/gen-sv.htm

- Sweden Genealogy - World GenWeb
  http://www.rootsweb.com/~wgsweden/

- Swedish Genealogy ~ In Swedish only
  http://www.abc.se/~m6921/geneal.html

- Swedish Genealogy How To Guide
  http://www.familytreemaker.com/00000386.html

- Swedish Information Service - Internet Resources for Tracing Your Swedish Roots
  http://www.webcom.com/sis/tracing.html

- Swedish Resources
  http://www.montana.edu/sass/sweden.htm
  From the Society for the Advancement of Scandinavian Study.

◆ Government & Cities

- Excite: Travel: Sweden
  http://www.excite.com/travel/countries/sweden/

- Yahoo!...Sweden...Counties
  http://dir.yahoo.com/Regional/Countries/Sweden/Counties/
  Or Cities and Towns
  http://dir.yahoo.com/Regional/Countries/Sweden/Cities_and_Towns/

◆ History & Culture

- FamilySearch Research Guidance - Sweden Historical Background
  http://www.familysearch.org/Eng/Search/rg/frameset_rg.asp?Dest=G1&Aid=&Gid=&Lid=&Sid=&Did=&Juris1=&Event=&Year=&Gloss=&Sub=&Tab=&Entry=&Guide=SW_T3_HistoricalBack.ASP

- History of Europe in Medieval Times, Scandinavia
  http://www.worldroots.com/brigitte/royal/royal1.htm
  Historic and genealogical information about royal and nobility family lines.

- Kungl. Hovstaterna / The Royal Court in Sweden
  http://www.royalcourt.se/

- StudyWeb: History: Country History Index: Europe Index: Sweden
  http://www.studyweb.com/links/160.html

- Yahoo!...Sweden...History
  http://dir.yahoo.com/Regional/Countries/Sweden/Arts_and_
  Humanities/Humanities/History/

◆ How To

- FamilySearch Research Guidance - Sweden Church Record Christenings
  http://www.familysearch.org/Eng/Search/rg/frameset_rg.asp?
  Dest=G1&Aid=&Gid=&Lid=&Sid=&Did=&Juris1=&Event=&
  Year=&Gloss=&Sub=&Tab=&Entry=&Guide=SW_BT3_-
  _Churchrecordchristening1500-1874.ASP

- FamilySearch Research Guidance - Sweden Research Outline
  http://www.familysearch.org/Eng/Search/rg/frameset_rg.asp?
  Dest=G1&Aid=&Gid=&Lid=&Sid=&Did=&Juris1=&Event=&
  Year=&Gloss=&Sub=&Tab=&Entry=&Guide=Sweden.ASP

- Have You Found a Swedish Ancestor?
  http://www.geocities.com/Heartland/Meadows/7095/
  swede.html

◆ Language & Names

- FamilySearch Research Guidance - Swedish Genealogical Word List
  http://www.familysearch.org/Eng/Search/rg/frameset_rg.asp?
  Dest=G1&Aid=&Gid=&Lid=&Sid=&Did=&Juris1=&Event=&
  Year=&Gloss=&Sub=&Tab=&Entry=&Guide=WLSweden.ASP

- Så stavar du namnen – Släktforskarförbundets namnlista / How to Spell First Names - The Swedish Genealogical Association's Names List
  http://www.genealogi.se/namnnorm.htm
  Explanations by Håkan Skogsjö.

- Swedish Language Basics for Genealogists
  http://genweb.net/~turner/dict.html
  Links to dictionaries and other language resources. The Swedish spelling reform of 1906 and other spelling changes.

- Swedish to English
  http://fp.firstinter.net/jell/swedish_to_english.htm
  Useful terms and information for the genealogist.

- Tolken99
  http://www.algonet.se/~hagsten/engindex.htm
  Word processor and English to Swedish translation software.

◆ Libraries, Archives & Museums

- American Swedish Historical Museum ~ Philadelphia, Pennsylvania
  http://www.libertynet.org/~ashm/

- The Balch Institute for Ethnic Studies
  http://www.libertynet.org/~balch/
  Includes a research library with materials on immigration studies.

  o A Guide to Manuscript and Microfilm Collections of the Research Library of the Balch Institute for Ethnic Studies
    http://www.balchinstitute.org/online_resources_12/html/
    contents.html

    • Swedish
      http://www.balchinstitute.org/online_resources_12/html/
      body_swedish.html

- Family History Library Catalog
  http://www.familysearch.org/eng/Library/FHLC/frameset
  _fhlc.asp
  From the FamilySearch web site, an online catalog to the holdings of the LDS Church in Salt Lake City, Utah. Also search for other localities by place name.
  http://www.familysearch.org/eng/Library/fhlc/supermainframe
  set.asp?display=localitysearch&columns=*,180,0

  o Sweden
    http://www.familysearch.org/eng/Library/fhlc/supermain
    frameset.asp?display=localitydetails&subject=135&subject
    _disp=Sweden&columns=*,180,0

- HYTELNET - Library Catalogs: Sweden
  http://www.lights.com/hytelnet/se0/se000.html
  Before you use any of the Telnet links, make note of the user name, password and any other logon information.

- Kungl. Biblioteket, Sveriges Nationalbibliotek / The Royal Library, National Library of Sweden
  http://www.kb.se/

- LIBRIS - Nationellt Bibliotekssystem - Svenska Bibliotek I Samverkan / Union Catalogue of Swedish Libraries
  http://www.libris.kb.se/

- Malmö Stadsbibliotek / Malmö City Library
  http://www.msb.malmo.se/

- Mölndals Stadsbibliotek / Mölndal Public Library
  http://www.molndal.se/bibl/uk.htm

- North Park University's Library, Archives and Instructional Media ~ Chicago, Illinois
  http://www.northpark.edu/library/

  o Archival Research Collections at North Park College
    http://www.northpark.edu/library/Archives/
    Including information for the Swedish-American Archives of Greater Chicago, the Covenant Archives and Historical Library, and the Archives of the Society for the Advancement of Scandinavian Study

- Repositories of Primary Sources - Europe - Sweden
  http://www.uidaho.edu/special-collections/euro2.html#se
  A list of links to online resources from the Univ. of Idaho Library, Special Collections and Archives.

- Swenson Swedish Immigration Research Center ~ Illinois
  http://www.augustana.edu/administration/swenson/

- webCATS: Library Catalogues on the World Wide Web - Sweden
  http://www.lights.com/webcats/countries/SE.html

◆ Locality Specific

- Håkan Asmundsson's Websida
  http://home1.swipnet.se/~w-14440/
  JÖNSSON, SAMUELSSON, ANDERSSON, LARSSON. Information for Swedish provinces of: Östergötland, Småland, Skåne.

- Jens Genealogy Pages
  http://www.algonet.se/~arvid/jens/gen/genealogy.html
  Presentation of research in Halland, Sweden. Links to other genealogy pages, mainly in Sweden.

- Släktforskarnas hus i Leksand / The House of Genealogy in Leksand
  http://www.genhouse-sweden.com/index.htm

- Tabergs Bergslag
  http://hem.passagen.se/rudu/taberg/
  Månsarp, Barnarp and Sandseryd, together called the mining district of Taberg - Tabergs Bergslag, in Smaland of Sweden.

◆ Mailing Lists, Newsgroups & Chat

- Genealogy Resources on the Internet - Sweden Mailing Lists
  http://www.rootsweb.com/~jfuller/gen_mail_country-swe.html
  Most of the mailing list links below point to this site, wonderfully maintained by John Fuller

- genealogica_gothorum Mailing List
  http://www.rootsweb.com/~jfuller/gen_mail_country-swe.html
  #genealogica_gothorum
  For anyone with a genealogical interest in the Swedish Provinces of Småland, Västergötland and Öland.

- GEN-NORDIC Mailing List
  http://www.rootsweb.com/~jfuller/gen_mail_country-swe.html
  #GEN-NORDIC
  Gatewayed with the soc.genealogy.nordic newsgroup
  news:soc.genealogy.nordic
  For the discussion of genealogy in the Scandinavian countries, including: Denmark, Finland, Greenland, Iceland, Norway and Sweden.

- SCANGEN Mailing List
  http://www.rootsweb.com/~jfuller/gen_mail_country-swe.html
  #SCANGEN
  For anyone with a genealogical interest in the Swedish province of Skåne (Scania) in the very south of the country.

- Swedegen Mailing List
  http://www.rootsweb.com/~jfuller/gen_mail_country-swe.html
  #Swedegen
  For discussing genealogical research in Sweden.

- SWEDE-L Mailing List
  http://www.rootsweb.com/~jfuller/gen_mail_country-swe.html
  #SWEDE-L
  For Swedish people, people related to Sweden, or people with an interest in Sweden for one reason or another.

- SWEDEN Mailing List
  http://www.rootsweb.com/~jfuller/gen_mail_country-swe.html
  #SWEDEN

- SWEDES Mailing List
  http://www.rootsweb.com/~jfuller/gen_mail_country-swe.html
  #SWEDES

- swnet.sci.genealogi Newsgroup
  news:swnet.sci.genealogi

◆ Maps, Gazetteers & Geographical Information

- FamilySearch Research Guidance - Sweden Map
  http://www.familysearch.org/Eng/Search/rg/frameset_rg.asp?
  Dest=G1&Aid=&Gid=&Lid=&Sid=&Did=&Juris1=&Event=&
  Year=&Gloss=&Sub=&Tab=&Entry=&Guide=MSweden.ASP

- Sweden Maps - The Perry-Castañeda Library Map Collection
  http://www.lib.utexas.edu/Libs/PCL/Map_collection/
  sweden.html
  From the University of Texas at Austin.

◆ Military

- Rolf Ströms Homesite, The Alottment System
  http://hem.passagen.se/mrwalker/military.htm
  A brief description of the old Swedish military system, called "The Alottment System."

◆ Newspapers

- AJR NewsLink - Sweden Newspapers
  http://ajr.newslink.org/euswed.html

- E&P Media Links - Newspaper Sites in Sweden
  http://emedia1.mediainfo.com/emedia/results.htm?region=
  europe&abbreviation=sweden++++++++++++++++++++++
  ++++++++++&category=newspaper

- Svenska Dagbladet - Nyheter
  http://www.svd.se/svd/ettan/dagens/index.html

- The Ultimate Collection of News Links: Sweden
  http://www.pppp.net/links/news/Sweden.html

- Yahoo!...Newspapers...Sweden
  http://dir.yahoo.com/Regional/Countries/Sweden/News_and_
  Media/Newspapers/

◆ People & Families

Individual personal home pages previously listed here can now be found alphabetically under the Personal Home Pages category:
http://www.CyndisList.com/personal.htm
or under the Surnames category:
http://www.CyndisList.com/surnames.htm

- Sami Resources
  http://www.montana.edu/sass/sami.htm
  From the Society for the Advancement of Scandinavian Study.

- The Swedish Monarchy for Near 1000 Years
  http://home.ringnett.no/bjornstad/royals/sweden.html

- Tracing Scandinavian Latter-day Saints
  http://www.xmission.com/~nelsonb/scand.htm
  From the Tracing Mormon Pioneers web site. For researching members of the LDS church from the Scandinavian Mission in the time period of 1852-1868.

◆ Professional Researchers, Volunteers & Other Research Services

- AID Kinresearch- Släktservice Hemsida / AID Kinresearch Swedish Genealogy
  http://hem.passagen.se/aidkin/

- Ancestor in English
  http://www.algonet.se/~kenlar/english.htm

- Eldefors Swedish Genealogy Service
  http://eldefors.hypermart.net/
  Professional genealogical research in all areas of Sweden.

- European Focus
  http://www.eurofocus.com/
  Photographic portfolios of ancestral towns in Europe created for Genealogy enthusiasts in Belgium, Denmark, Eastern Europe, England, France, Germany, Great Britain, Italy, Netherlands, Norway, Poland, Sweden, Switzerland and more.

- Genealogy Helplist - Sweden
  http://helplist.org/swe/index.shtml

- genealogyPro - Professional Genealogists for Sweden
  http://genealogyPro.com/directories/Sweden.html

- Mark Windover's Web Page - Quality Professional Genealogical Research ~ Williamstown, Massachusetts
  http://www.windover.com/
  United States, Canada (including French), England, Scotland, Ireland, Wales, Iceland, Germany, Switzerland, Norway, Sweden, Denmark, France, Belgium, and The Netherlands.

- Molander's Genealogy Service
  http://www.algonet.se/~family/
  Professional researchers for Sweden and Norway.

- Swedish Genealogy Company
  http://welcome.to/swedgenco
  Professional genealogy researcher in Sweden, specializing in American-Swedish genealogy.

◆ Publications, Software & Supplies

- Amazon.com Genealogy Bookstore – Sweden
  http://www.amazon.com/exec/obidos/external-search/?keyword=Sweden+genealogy&tag=markcyndisgenealA/
  And Swedish
  http://www.amazon.com/exec/obidos/external-search/?keyword=Swedish+genealogy&tag=markcyndisgenealA/

- Andata - Dataprogram för Släktforskare
  http://home1.swipnet.se/~w-10898/
  A Swedish genealogy software program for Windows.

- Association of Professional Genealogists in Ireland
  http://indigo.ie/~apgi

- AudioTapes.com - Genealogical Lectures on Cassette Tapes – Sweden
  http://www.audiotapes.com/search2.asp?Search=sweden
  And Swedish
  http://www.audiotapes.com/search2.asp?Search=swedish

- Brother's Keeper Software in Swedish
  http://www.torget.se/users/b/bertun/bk.html
  Or in English
  http://ourworld.compuserve.com/homepages/Brothers_Keeper/
  Downloadable shareware program for Windows. The latest version contains English, French, Norwegian, Danish, Swedish, German, Dutch, Polish, Icelandic, Russian, Slovak, Afrikaans, Czech.

- DataDux - Genealogy
  http://www.algonet.se/~datadux/
  Research in Sweden and Anarkiv Windows Genealogy software.

- Frontier Press Bookstore - Scandinavia
  http://www.frontierpress.com/frontier.cgi?category=sca

- GenealogyBookShop.com - Sweden/Swedish
  http://www.genealogybookshop.com/genealogybookshop/files/The_World,Sweden_Swedish/index.html
  The online store of Genealogical Publishing Co., Inc. & Clearfield Company.

- GeneWeb ~ Unix and Windows 95/98/NT
  http://pauillac.inria.fr/~ddr/GeneWeb/
  In French, Dutch, Swedish and English versions.

- Genius Family Tree Program
  http://www.gensol.com.au/genius.htm
  An easy to use Windows based Family Tree record keeper.

- Nättidningen RÖTTER - för dig som släktforskar
  http://www.genealogi.se/index.htm
  An e-zine from the Swedish Federation of Genealogical Societies.

- Swedish Passenger Arrivals in New York 1820-1850
  http://www.amazon.com/exec/obidos/ISBN=9995149516/markcyndisgenealA/
  A book by Nils William Olsson.

- WinFamily - Anvend Winfamily fra Jamodat til din slektsgransking
  http://www.winfamily.com/
  Genealogy software available in Danish, Swedish, Norwegian, French, German and English.

◆ Queries, Message Boards & Surname Lists

- RootsWeb Surname List - RSL Sweden
  http://rsl.rootsweb.com/cgi-bin/rslsql.cgi
  The RSL and this form concept & design are courtesy of Karen Isaacson

- Scanian Genealogy Homepage Efterlysningar 1997 / Queries 1997
  http://cgi.algonet.se/htbin/cgiwrap?user=anderzb&script=query.cgi

◆ Records: Census, Cemeteries, Land, Obituaries, Personal, Taxes and Vital (Born, Married, Died & Buried)

- Släktdata - Föreningen
  http://www.slaktdata.org/
  Searchable parish registers in Sweden.

◆ Religion & Churches

- Christianity Online Church Locator - Churches in Sweden
  http://www.christianity.net/churchlocator/location.php?country=Sweden

- Churches dot Net - Global Church Web Pages - Sweden
  http://www.churches.net/churches/internat.htm#swe

- Churches of the World - Sweden
  http://www.churchsurf.com/churches/world/Sweden/
  From the ChurchSurf Christian Directory.

- Genline - Svenska Kyrkböcker Online / Swedish Church Records On-line
  http://www.genline.se/

- Släktdatas registerarkiv/ Searchable parish registers
  http://sd.datatorget.educ.goteborg.se/cdata/reginfo.php3?lang=english#english

◆ Societies & Groups

- Computer Genealogy Society of Sweden / Föreningen för datorhjälp i släktforskningen
  http://www.dis.se/

- Eslöv's Genealogical and Folk-life Society / Eslövsbygdens Släkt- och Folklivsforskare
  http://home.swipnet.se/~w-79766/eng/
  Headquarters in the city of Eslöv, which is located in the southern part of Sweden.

- Falbygden Genealogical Society ~ Falköping, Västergötland, Sweden
  http://welcome.to/falbygdengenealogy

- Föreningar i riksförbundet Länk- och adresslista / Member Societies of The Federation of Swedish Genealogical Societies
  http://www.genealogi.se/links3.htm
  Local and regional genealogical societies in Sweden.

- Hemsida för Marks Härads Släktforskarförening
  http://hem.passagen.se/stenb/
  Home page for the Genealogical Research Society of Mark County in Sweden.

- Heraldiska Samfundet
  http://www.users.wineasy.se/elias/hersamf.htm
  A Swedish association for heraldry and related subjects, based in Stockholm, Sweden.

- Kronobergs Genealogiska Förening / The Genealogical Society of Kronoberg ~ Småland, Sweden
  http://home1.swipnet.se/~w-10898/kgf.html
  Includes contact information for searches by postal mail of a database of Birth, Marriage and Death Registers from the Parishes of the County Kronoberg.

- Sällskapet Vallonättlingar - Society The Descendents of the Walloons of Sweden
  http://www.vallon.a.se/
  A society for the descendants of Belgian emigrants to Sweden in the early seventeenth century. Genealogical research in Sweden, Finland, USA and Belgium.

- Sveriges Släktforskarförbund / The Swedish Federation of Genealogical Societies
  http://www.genealogi.se/forbund.htm

- Swedish Ancestry Research Association (SARA) ~ Worcester, Massachusetts
  http://www.members.tripod.com/~SARAssociation/sara/SARA_Home_Page.htm

- The Swedish Colonial Society ~ Philadelphia, Pennsylvania
  http://www.colonialswedes.org/index.html#anchor1104877

- Swedish Finn Historical Society ~ Seattle, Washington
  http://home1.gte.net/SFHS/index.htm

- Swedish Genealogy Group ~ Minnesota
  http://www.mtn.org/mgs/branches/swedish.html

- The Vasa Order of America
  http://www.vasaorder.com/index.htm

SCHOOLS

http://www.cyndislist.com/schools.htm

Category Index:

◆ Alumni Organizations & Resources

◆ Histories & Records

◆ Web Directories ~ General

◆ Web Directories ~ Locality Specific

◆ Yearbooks

◆ Alumni Organizations & Resources

- ClassMates Online
  http://www.classmates.com/index.tf
  Helps high school alumni friends find each other.

- Gradfinder
  http://www.gradfinder.com/

- High School Alumni- A Web Site For Alumni of US High Schools
  http://www.highschoolalumni.com/
  Register your name, address and graduation date from any high school in the US.

- Planet Alumni
  http://www.planetalumni.com/

- World Alumni Net
  http://www.alumni.net/

◆ Histories & Records

- 1925 Weisbach School Students
  http://www.rootsweb.com/~inmartin/weisbach.htm
  Weisbach School District No. 7, Halbert Twp, Martin County, Indiana, 1925.

- Amherst College Biographical Record (1821-1921)
  http://www.amherst.edu/~rjyanco/genealogy/acbiorecord/
  Biographies of 9,110 graduates and non-graduates of Amherst (Massachusetts) College, from its first hundred years.

- Berlin, Wisconsin Public Schools 1882-1883
  http://www.geocities.com/Heartland/Cabin/4857/berlin school.html
  Lists the teachers and staff and pupils from the school year 1882-1883. Lists former graduates of classes from 1865 thru 1882 and where they were in 1882-1883. There is also a photo of the Berlin High School.

- Blackwell History of Education Research Museum
  http://www.niu.edu/acad/leps/blackw1.html
  Northern Illinois University, DeKalb, Illinois.

- The Branch County Schools Page ~ Michigan
  http://www.geocities.com/TheTropics/1050/Schools.html

- Centerville School, Prospect Township, Marion County, Ohio
  http://www.genealogy.org/~smoore/marion/school.htm
  For seven school terms from 1889 to 1892.

- Changes in Pierce County School Districts Since their Inception ~ Washington
  http://www.rootsweb.com/~watpcgs/pcschool.htm
  A terrific index, by Janet Baccus, that shows the original school name, the district number, information on the consolidation, the date of the consolidation and the new school name and new district number.

- Colorado State Government Archives School Records
  http://www.state.co.us/gov_dir/gss/archives/school.html

- The Country Schoolhouse
  http://www.rootsweb.com/~neresour/schoolhouse.html
  Stories from Nebraska.

- The Early Days - Pioneer and Early Public Schools of California and Los Angeles
  http://www.lausd.k12.ca.us/lausd/history/eyr2.html
  From the Treasures of LAUSD, Children of Los Angeles Unified School District.

- Education in Gage County ~ Nebraska
  http://www.rootsweb.com/~negage/classes/index.htm

- English Educational Sources of Interest to the Family Historian
  http://www.audiotapes.com/product.asp?ProductCode= 'SD-170'
  Presentation by William B. Stephens, available for sale on audio tape.

- Era of Peace, Part 19, Schools of Kansas
  http://raven.cc.ukans.edu/~hisite/kancoll/books/cutler/eraop/ era-of-peace-p19.html#SCHOOLS OF KANSAS.
  From William G. Cutler's History of the State of Kansas.

- Establishing a School Archives
  http://www.nara.gov/education/teaching/archives/school.html

- Girl's Polytechnic School Portland, Oregon 1928
  http://freepages.genealogy.rootsweb.com/~cchouk/poly/

- Graduates of Union City High School - The First Ninety Years ~ Randolph County, Indiana
  http://php.ucs.indiana.edu/~jetorres/uchs/grads.html

- Graduating Classes of Catholic Central High School
  http://www.geocities.com/Heartland/1261/cchs.html
  Steubenville, Ohio, 1931-1938.

- High School Class Lists
  http://www.rootsweb.com/~iladams/ahighsch.htm
  Quincy High School, Illinois, Class of 1918, 1920, 1923.

- A History of Amherst College (1894), by William S.
  Tyler 1830
  http://www.amherst.edu/~rjyanco/amherst/history/1894
  tyler-ws/
  *Written in 1894, a comprehensive history of Amherst
  (Massachusetts) College, during the administrations of its first five
  presidents.*

- History of Education Site ~ Netherlands
  http://www.socsci.kun.nl/ped/whp/histeduc/

- History of Rockingham County Public Schools ~
  Virginia
  http://www.rockingham.k12.va.us/rcps_history/rcps
  history.html

- The Homeroom - British Columbia's History of
  Education Homeroom
  http://www.mala.bc.ca/homeroom/

- Index of Graduating Classes ~ Pennsylvania
  http://www.granniesworld.com/cvahs/grads/index.html
  Graduates of Conneautville High School, 1875-1910.

- Jackson High School Graduates 1910-1958 ~
  Randolph County, Indiana
  http://php.ucs.indiana.edu/~jetorres/JacksonHS.html

- Kansas One Room School House Project
  http://history.cc.ukans.edu/heritage/orsh/orsh_main.html

- List of Wood County Teachers (1904) With Post
  Office Addresses ~ Wisconsin
  http://www.scls.lib.wi.us/mcm/history/Teachers1904.html

- Martin County Schools ~ Indiana
  http://www.rootsweb.com/~inmartin/schools.htm
  Some of the earliest school superintendents.

- Minot High School History ~ North Dakota
  http://www.minot.k12.nd.us/mps/cc/history/school.html

- Museum of the City of San Francisco - Early History
  of California Public Schools
  http://www.sfmuseum.org/hist3/schools.html

- National Archives of Ireland - National School
  Records
  http://www.nationalarchives.ie/natschs.html

- The Ohio Reform School
  http://www.genealogy.org/~smoore/marion/badboys.htm

- The One-Room School Homepage
  http://www.msc.cornell.edu/~weeds/SchoolPages/
  welcome.html
  *Perspective on life in a one-room school. Commemorating the
  Caldwell School in Pennsylvania.*

- Phillips County Schools - Past and Present ~
  Montana
  http://www.rootsweb.com/~mtphilli/schools.htm

- Plaza Public School History ~ North Dakota
  http://www.plaza.k12.nd.us/history.html

- Princeton Regional Schools - School Histories ~
  New Jersey
  http://www.prs.k12.nj.us/History/Schools/

- Pupils of the Colorado School for the Deaf and the
  Blind, 1874-1883
  http://www.henge.com/~holsclaw/deafblind/csdbproj.htm
  By Birdie Monk Holsclaw.

- School Records in the Corporation of London
  Records Office
  http://www.cityoflondon.gov.uk/archives/clro/schools.htm

- Rio Grand County Teacher Certificates 1874 - 1893
  ~ Colorado
  http://www.archives.state.co.us/rio.htm

- Salem School 1907, Shelly, Pennsylvania
  http://members.tripod.com/LittlePunky/

- Schoolmarms on the Frontier
  http://www.ancestry.com/columns/myra/Shaking_Family_Tree
  06-04-98.htm
  *From Shaking Your Family Tree by Myra Vanderpool Gormley,
  C.G.*

- School Marms - Pioneer Prairie Teachers ~
  Manitoba, Canada
  http://www.norflicks.com/ph/school2.htm

- School Records as a Genealogical Resource
  http://www.parkbooks.com/Html/res_schs.html
  Research Notes from Park Genealogical Books in Minnesota.

- Seattle Public Schools Archives and Records
  Management Center ~ Washington
  http://www.seattleschools.org/district/archives/welcome.htm

- Stoney Creek High School Graduates ~ Randolph
  County, Indiana
  http://users.rootsweb.com/~inrandol/stoneycreek.htm

- The Three Rs: Reading, 'Riting and Researching
  Your Ancestors' School Records
  http://www.audiotapes.com/product.asp?ProductCode=
  'FGSSLT52'
  *Presentation by Paula Stuart Warren, available for sale on audio
  tape.*

- Victoria County School Records ~ Texas
  http://www.viptx.net/vcgs/schoolrc.html

- The Victorian Schoolroom
  http://www.amazon.com/exec/obidos/ISBN=0747802432/mark
  cyndisgenealA/
  A book by Trevor May.

◆ Web Directories ~ General

- American School Directory
  http://www.asd.com/

- National Public School and School District Locator
  http://nces.ed.gov/ccdweb/school/index.asp

- Web66: International School Web Site Registry
  http://web66.coled.umn.edu/schools.html

- Yahoo!...Canada...Schools
  http://dir.yahoo.com/Regional/Countries/Canada/Education/
  Primary_and_Secondary/Schools/

- Yahoo!...Education...Countries
  http://dir.yahoo.com/Education/Browse_by_Region/Countries/

- Yahoo!...Education...Regions
  http://dir.yahoo.com/Education/Browse_by_Region/Regions/

- Yahoo!...Education...U.S. States
  http://dir.yahoo.com/Education/Browse_by_Region/U_S__
  States/

- Yahoo!...United Kingdom...Schools
  http://dir.yahoo.com/Regional/Countries/United_Kingdom/
  Education/Primary_and_Secondary/Schools/

◆ Web Directories ~ Locality Specific

- Access Washington - Education
  http://access.wa.gov/education/awk12.asp
  Alphabetical Index of Schools in Washington state.

- King County WA High Schools & School Districts
  http://www.rootsweb.com/~waking/highscho.htm

◆ Yearbooks

- Darilee's Yearbook - The Attic
  http://www.geocities.com/Heartland/2236/yearbookindex.html
  A collection of more than 3,200 yearbooks.

- Linn County Yearbooks and Newspaper Information ~ Oregon
  http://www.rootsweb.com/~orlinn/yearnews.html

- San Francisco County Genealogy Lookup Help, School Yearbooks ~ California
  http://www.sfo.com/~timandpamwolf/sfyear.htm

- San José Public Library: California Room Yearbooks
  http://www.sjpl.lib.ca.us/Adults/CaliforniaRoom/
  yearbooks.htm

SHIPS & PASSENGER LISTS

http://www.cyndislist.com/ships.htm

Category Index:

- Famous & Historical Ships
- General Resource Sites
- Libraries, Archives & Museums
- Mailing Lists, Newsgroups & Chat
- Professional Researchers, Volunteers & Other Research Services

- Publications, Microfilm & Microfiche
- Ship, Passenger & Crew Lists
- Shipwrecks
- Societies & Groups

◆ Famous & Historical Ships

- Amistad America, Inc. - Building the Freedom Schooner
  http://www.amistadamerica.org/main/welcome.html

- Amistad - "Give Us Free"
  http://news.courant.com/special/amistad/

- Amistad Links
  http://www.amistad.org/

- Exploring Amistad: Race and the Boundaries of Freedom in Antebellum Maritime America
  http://amistad.mysticseaport.org/

- HMS Bounty Genealogies
  http://www.lareau.org/bounty6.html

- List of Officers and Sailors in the First Voyage of Columbus in 1492
  http://www.rootsweb.com/~ote/colship.htm
  Nina, Pinta, Santa Maria.

- Magellan's Voyages from The Discovery of America by John Fiske published in 1892
  http://www.rootsweb.com/~ote/magship.htm
  The Victoria and the Trinidad.

- The Mayflower
  - AudioTapes.com - Genealogical Lectures on Cassette Tapes - Mayflower
    http://www.audiotapes.com/search2.asp?Search=mayflower
  - The General Society of Mayflower Descendants
    http://www.mayflower.org/
  - MAYFLOWER Mailing List
    http://www.rootsweb.com/~jfuller/gen_mail_states-gen.html#MAYFLOWER
    A mailing list for the discussion and sharing of information regarding the descendants of the Mayflower passengers in any place and at any time.

  - Mayflower Passenger List
    http://members.aol.com/calebj/passenger.html
  - Mayflower Passengers
    http://www.ida.net/users/dhanco/mayflr.htm
  - A Mayflower Study
    http://www.maddoxinteractive.com/mayflower/
  - Mayflower Web Page
    http://members.aol.com/calebj/mayflower.html
  - Search & ReSearch Publishing Corp.
    http://www.searchresearchpub.com/
    Supplier of historical databases on CD-ROM including "Mayflower Descendant Legacy".

- The Sultana: Death on the Dark River (1865)
  http://www.rootsweb.com/~genepool/sultana.htm

- The Titanic
  - Encyclopedia Titanica
    http://www.encyclopedia-titanica.org/
  - In Memoriam: RMS Titanic
    http://miso.wwa.com/~dsp//titanic/
  - The Original Titanic Home Page
    http://www.home.gil.com.au/~dalgarry/
  - Titanic and Other White Star Ships
    http://members.aol.com/MNichol/Titanic.index.html
  - Titanic Passenger List
    http://www.lva.lib.va.us/pubserv/vnp/titanic/p2.htm
  - Titanic ~ The Unsinkable Ship and Halifax
    http://titanic.gov.ns.ca/
    A site from Halifax, Nova Scotia, Canada, including a list of those buried in cemeteries in Halifax.
  - Yahoo!...Maritime History...Titanic
    http://dir.yahoo.com/Arts/Humanities/History/By_Subject/Maritime_History/Ships/Titanic/

- Yahoo!...Mutiny on the Bounty
  http://dir.yahoo.com/Arts/Humanities/History/By_Time_Period/18th_Century/Mutiny_on_the_Bounty/

◆ General Resource Sites

- AudioTapes.com - Genealogical Lectures on Cassette Tapes - Passenger
  http://www.audiotapes.com/search2.asp?Search=passenger
  Online searchable database of over 20,000 transcribed pages from the newspaper including personal names, place names, and ship names.

- The Belfast Newsletter Index, 1737-1800
  http://www.ucs.usl.edu/bnl/Main.html

- The Divers Index
  http://www.thehds.com/divers/divers.htm
  An Index of Historical Divers and Their Work.

- Downward Bound - Great Lakes Shipping Genealogy Index
  http://www.rootsweb.com/~migls/

- Early Types of Sailing Ships
  http://www.rootsweb.com/~ote/defship.htm

- Emigration / Ship Lists and Resources
  http://www.geocities.com/Heartland/5978/Emigration.html
  From Addie's Genealogy Home Page.

- Finding Passenger Lists 1820-c.1940
  http://home.att.net/~wee-monster/passengers.html
  A basic tutorial for German Americans by Joe Beine, German Roots Webmaster.

- Genealogy Resources on the Internet: Passenger Lists; Ships; Ship Museums
  http://www-personal.umich.edu/~cgaunt/pass.html

- German and American Sources for German Emigration to America
  http://www.genealogy.net/gene/misc/emig/emigrati.html

- German Genealogy: Emigration from Germany to America
  http://www2.genealogy.net/gene/misc/emig/

- Immigration and Ships Passenger Lists Research Guide
  http://home.att.net/~arnielang/shipgide.html

- KinShips: The Passenger Vessels of Your Immigrant Ancestors
  http://www.KinShipsPrints.com/
  Art prints, most in color, of passenger ships, primarily those sailing the North Atlantic routes between 1890 and 1940.

- Links: Ships
  http://pc-78-120.udac.se:8001/www/nautica/Pointers/Ships.html
  From the Maritime History Virtual Archives.

- Locating Ship Passenger Lists
  http://www.genealogy.com/genealogy/8_mgpal.html
  by Myra Vanderpool Gormley, C.G.

- Maritime History Research on the Internet
  http://ruby.ils.unc.edu/maritime/home.shtml

- o Researching Ships
  http://ruby.ils.unc.edu/maritime/shiprsrch.shtml

- Mark Rosenstein's Sailing Page
  http://www.apparent-wind.com/sailing-page.html

- Ocean Liner Passenger Lists Catalog
  http://www.oceanliner.com/passlist.htm
  From New Steamship Consultants.

- Passenger Lists General Info from the JewishGen FAQ
  http://www.jewishgen.org/faqinfo.html#Passenger

- Passenger Lists and Immigration-Related Materials
  http://www.hpl.lib.tx.us/clayton/px001.html
  A Guide from the Clayton Library in Houston, Texas.

- Public Record Office - Finding Aids - A-Z Index of All Leaflets ~ U.K.
  http://www.pro.gov.uk/leaflets/riindex.htm

  - o The Coastguard - Military Records Information 44
    http://www.pro.gov.uk/leaflets/ri2044.htm

  - o Emigrants - Domestic Records Information 107
    http://www.pro.gov.uk/leaflets/ri2272.htm

  - o Emigrants to North America After 1776
    http://www.pro.gov.uk/leaflets/ri2107.htm

  - o Immigrants - Domestic Records Information 50
    http://www.pro.gov.uk/leaflets/ri2157.htm

  - o Passport Records - Domestic Records Information 60
    http://www.pro.gov.uk/leaflets/ri2167.htm

  - o Merchant Seamen: Medals and Honours
    http://www.pro.gov.uk/leaflets/ri2202.htm

  - o Merchant Seamen: Officers' Service Records 1845-1921
    http://www.pro.gov.uk/leaflets/ri2200.htm

  - o Merchant Seamen: Registers of Service, 1835-1857
    http://www.pro.gov.uk/leaflets/ri2196.htm

  - o Merchant Seamen: Registers of Service 1913-1941
    http://www.pro.gov.uk/leaflets/ri2197.htm

  - o Merchant Shipping: Crew Lists and Agreements, 1747-1860
    http://www.pro.gov.uk/leaflets/ri2199.htm

  - o Merchant Shipping: Crew Lists and Agreements After 1861
    http://www.pro.gov.uk/leaflets/ri2198.htm

  - o Merchant Shipping: Registration of Ships, 1786-1994
    http://www.pro.gov.uk/leaflets/ri2201.htm

  - o Navy, Royal Air Force and Merchant Navy Pension Records
    http://www.pro.gov.uk/leaflets/ri2265.htm

o Records of the Registrar General of Shipping and Seamen
http://www.pro.gov.uk/leaflets/ri005.htm

o Records Relating to RMS Titanic - Domestic Records Information 34
http://www.pro.gov.uk/leaflets/ri2141.htm

o Researching Passenger Arrival in the United States
http://www.infoukes.com/genealogy/primer/arrival.html

o Ships' Passenger Lists, 1878-1960
http://www.pro.gov.uk/leaflets/ri2163.htm

o Ships Wrecked or Sunk - Military Records Information 43
http://www.pro.gov.uk/leaflets/ri2043.htm

• Registers of Vessels Arriving at the Port of New York from Foreign Ports 1789 – 1919
http://www.slcl.lib.mo.us/slcl/sc/sc-m1066.htm
Finding aid from the Saint Louis County Public Library.

• Shipping Terminology
http://www.islandregister.com/terms.html
With a Prince Edward Island Slant.

• TheShipsList Home Page
http://www.TheShipsList.com/
TheShipsList mailing list was established to assist those seeking information on the vessels, which brought their ancestors to their new home, be that the United States, Canada, Australia, or another part of the world. Some ships passenger lists, schedules, wreck data, and other information, which is not readily available, has been collected, along with links to other sites of interest.

• Yahoo!...Maritime History...Ships
http://dir.yahoo.com/Arts/Humanities/History/By_Subject/Maritime_History/Ships/

◆ Libraries, Archives & Museums

• The Balch Institute for Ethnic Studies
http://www.libertynet.org/~balch/
Includes a research library with materials on immigration studies.

• Fylkesarkivet i Sogn og Fjordane - Utvandring - Emigration ~ Norway
http://www.sffarkiv.no/sffutv.htm

• Geelong Maritime Museum ~ Australia
http://www.zades.com.au/geelong/maritime.html

• Hampton Roads Naval Museum ~ Norfolk, Virginia
http://naval-station.norfolk.va.us/INFO/ABOUT_US/HISTORY/MUSEUM/museum.html

• The Mariners' Museum - Newport News, Virginia
http://www.mariner.org/
Archives, manuscripts, manifests & research services available.

• Maritime History Archive at Memorial University of Newfoundland
http://www.mun.ca/mha/

• The Maritime History Virtual Archives
http://pc-78-120.udac.se:8001/WWW/Nautica/Nautica.html

• Marine Museum of the Great Lakes at Kingston ~ Ontario, Canada
http://www.marmus.ca/

• Maritime Museums - Smith's Master Index to World Wide Maritime Museum Internet Resources
http://www.bobhudson.com/Smiths/
Links with descriptions to an alphabetically arranged listing of maritime museums.

• Mystic Seaport Museum ~ Mystic, Connecticut
http://www.mysticseaport.org/welcome.html

o Conducting Vessel Research
http://www.mysticseaport.org/library/infobulletins/ib674.html
Online brochure explaining general vessel research procedures.

o The Rosenfeld Collection
http://www.mysticseaport.org/public/collections/rosenfeld.html
The largest single collection of commercial and recreational maritime photographs in the United States.

• National Archives of Ireland: Transportation Records
http://www.nationalarchives.ie/search01.html
Convicts from Ireland to Australia, 1788 to 1868.

• National Maritime Museum ~ England
http://www.nmm.ac.uk/

o Centre for Maritime Research
http://www.nmm.ac.uk/cmr/index.html

• The Caird Library
http://www.nmm.ac.uk/cmr/library.html
The Caird Library is the largest and most significant reference Library of its kind in the world. The collections cover every aspect of maritime affairs, containing important and unique materials which are freely available for consultation.

• Manuscripts Guide
http://www.nmm.ac.uk/cmr/library.html

• NMM Library Catalogue
http://www.nmm.ac.uk/cgi-bin/empower?DB=library_index

• Naval Historical Center
http://www.history.navy.mil/
U.S. Navy History, Department of the Navy.

• Passenger Lists - Hamburg 1850-1934 - Film List for the LDS FHC
http://www.genealogy.net/gene/misc/emig/ham_pass.html

• Peabody Essex Museum ~ Salem, Massachusetts
http://www.pem.org/

o The Phillips Library
http://www.pem.org/phillips.html
Formerly known as the Essex Institute. A large maritime history collection including 19th- and 20th-century images of ships.

• South Street Seaport Museum ~ New York City
http://www.SouthStSeaport.org/index.htm

- Steamship Historical Society of America Collection
  http://www.ubalt.edu/archives/ship/ship.htm
  Holdings at the Archives of the University of Baltimore.

  o Online Catalog of Transatlantic Passenger Ship Photos
  http://www.ubalt.edu/archives/ship/TransAtlantic%20 Passenger%20Vessels.htm
  Lists ship photos in the collection by name, date built, and shipping line. Provides postal mail ordering instructions to obtain photos.

- Wisconsin Maritime Museum
  http://www.artcom.com/museums/nv/sz/54220-68.htm

◆ Mailing Lists, Newsgroups & Chat

- Genealogy Resources on the Internet - General Mailing Lists
  http://www.rootsweb.com/~jfuller/gen_mail_general.html
  Most of the mailing list links below point to this site, wonderfully maintained by John Fuller

- emigration-ships Mailing List
  http://www.rootsweb.com/~jfuller/gen_mail_general.html #EMIGRATION-SHIPS
  A mailing list for anyone who wants to discuss the ships their ancestors arrived on or post passenger lists for any ships.

- GLSHIPS Mailing List
  http://www.rootsweb.com/~jfuller/gen_mail_states-gen.html#GLSHIPS
  For anyone who is researching ancestors who participated in the shipping industry on the Great Lakes of the northeastern United States.

- IMMI-GRAND Mailing List
  http://www.rootsweb.com/~jfuller/gen_mail_general.html #IMMI-GRAND
  For those attempting to do genealogical research whose grandparents (or parents) arrived in the USA after 1875.

- Mariners Mailing List
  http://www.rootsweb.com/~jfuller/gen_mail_general.html #Mariners
  For anyone who is researching their seafaring ancestors.

- MAYFLOWER Mailing List
  http://www.rootsweb.com/~jfuller/gen_mail_states-gen.html#MAYFLOWER
  A mailing list for the discussion and sharing of information regarding the descendants of the Mayflower passengers in any place and at any time.

- TheShipsList Mailing List
  http://www.rootsweb.com/~jfuller/gen_mail_general.html #TheShipsList
  For anyone interested in the ships our ancestors migrated on. Subjects include emigration/immigration, ports of entry, ports of departure, ship descriptions and history, passenger lists and other related information.

  o TheShipsList Home Page
  http://www.TheShipsList.com/
  TheShipsList mailing list was established to assist those seeking information on the vessels, which brought their ancestors to their

new home, be that the United States, Canada, Australia, or another part of the world. Some ships passenger lists, schedules, wreck data, and other information, which is not readily available, has been collected, along with links to other sites of interest.

- SULTANA Mailing List
  http://www.rootsweb.com/~jfuller/gen_mail_states-gen.html#SULTANA
  For anyone who is researching the 2,000+ soldiers aboard the ill-fated steamship Sultana which exploded in 1865.

◆ Professional Researchers, Volunteers & Other Research Services

- Australian Emigrant Ship Service
  http://freespace.virgin.net/donald.hazeldine/austral.htm
  A site aimed at genealogists in Australia and New Zealand, providing the history and a photograph of emigrant ships 1875-2000.

- Independent British Naval Researcher and Historical Investigator
  http://www.btinternet.com/~samband.bretlands/
  Research service for those seeking to find the service records of officers (1660 - 1923) and men (1853 - 1923) who served in the British Royal Navy. Search includes personnel records, information on the ships of the Royal Navy and any actions in which they were involved from earliest times to c. 1970, including World War 1 and World War 2.

- inGeneas Canadian Genealogy
  http://www.inGeneas.com/
  Professional genealogists specializing in Canadian immigration records. Searchable databases containing 50,000+ Canadian passenger and immigration records (c1750 to 1900) including the only electronic version of the free National Archives of Canada Miscellaneous Immigration Index

- Passenger Ships History Service
  http://freespace.virgin.net/donald.hazeldine/history.htm
  A site offering the history, photograph, technical details, routes and dates of a specific passenger ship from 1860 onwards.

- Ships Picture Research Service
  http://www.vinehall.com.au/main.html
  Australian-based research service for helping genealogists and historians worldwide locate pictures of ships of many rigs, periods and nationalities.

◆ Publications, Microfilm & Microfiche

- Amazon.com Genealogy Bookstore - Ships
  http://www.amazon.com/exec/obidos/external-search/ ?keyword=ship+genealogy&tag=markcyndisgenealA/

- The Best Books on German Passenger Liners
  http://www.worldroots.com/brigitte/ships.htm

- The Compendium of the World's Passenger Ships
  http://freespace.virgin.net/donald.hazeldine/homepage.htm
  Offers a CD that contains details of more than 1530 passenger and cruise ships over 10000 tons (1854-2000), including color photographs.

- Frontier Press Bookstore - Maritime history (inland and seafaring)
  http://www.frontierpress.com/frontier.cgi?category=maritime

- GenealogyBookShop.com - Immigration/Passenger Lists/Naturalizations
  http://www.genealogybookshop.com/genealogybookshop/
  files/General,Immigration_Passenger_Lists_Naturalizations/
  index.html
  The online store of Genealogical Publishing Co., Inc. & Clearfield Company.

- Germans to America: Lists of Passengers Arriving at U.S. Ports 1850-1893
  http://www.genealogy.net/gene/www/emig/GermansTo
  America.html
  A description of the books by Ira A. Glazier and P. William Filby, along with a breakdown of the volume numbers and which years are covered in each volume.

- Hamburg Passenger Lists, 1850-1934
  http://www.genealogy.net/gene/misc/emig/ham_pass.html
  List of microfilm numbers for the LDS Family History Library.

- How to Find Your Immigrant Ancestor - Passenger and Immigration Lists Index
  http://www.rader.org/how_to.htm
  Tips on using these volumes by Filby.

- Immigrant and Passenger Arrivals
  http://www.nara.gov/publications/microfilm/immigrant/
  immpass.html
  A select catalog of National Archives microfilm.

- KinShips: The Passenger Vessels of Your Immigrant Ancestors
  http://www.Kin-Ships.com/
  Art prints, most in color, of passenger ships, primarily those sailing the North Atlantic routes between 1890 and 1940.

- LDS Passenger Manifests - A Guide to Using the Passenger Lists at Your Local Family History Center
  http://www.arduini.net/tools/ldsmanif.htm

- Microfilms of Rosters for LDS voyages 1840-1868 Sorted by Ship, Year
  http://www.xmission.com/~nelsonb/ship_film_name.htm

- Microfilms of Ship Rosters for LDS voyages 1840-1868 Sorted by Year, Ship
  http://www.xmission.com/~nelsonb/ship_film_year.htm

- Search & ReSearch Publishing Corp.
  http://www.searchresearchpub.com/
  Supplier of historical databases on CD-ROM including "Mayflower Descendant Legacy".

- Steamboat Press
  http://home.pacifier.com/~history/
  A mail-order publishing house which specializes in publications about the men, women and boats to whom the rivers of America were homes and livelihood.

- The Trans-Atlantic Slave Trade - A Database on CD-ROM
  http://www.cup.org/ObjectBuilder/ObjectBuilder.iwx?Process
  Name=ProductPage&Merchant_Id=1&product_id=0-521-
  62910-1&origin=search&searchField=TITLE&searchString=
  slave%20trade
  Contains the records of 27,233 transatlantic slave ship voyages made between 1595 and 1866 from all over Europe.

◆ Ship, Passenger & Crew Lists

General Lists of Links

- American Plantations and Colonies - Ship Index
  http://www.primenet.com/~langford/ships/shiplist.htm

- CIMO - Cimorelli Immigration Manifests Online
  http://www.cimorelli.com/safe/shipmenu.htm
  An online collection of databases comprised of the Morton Allan Directory, M1066 Microfilm series from NARA, various newspaper articles, Internet sources, and personal contribution.

- Discovering Family Histories Research Resources - Passengers and Ships
  http://members.xoom.com/Northing/RRpassengers_
  ships.html

- Emigration / Ship Lists and Resources
  http://www.geocities.com/Heartland/5978/Emigration.html
  From Addie's Genealogy Home Page.

- Genealogy Resources on the Internet: Passenger Lists; Ships; Ship Museums
  http://www-personal.umich.edu/~cgaunt/pass.html

- GenSwap - Online Immigration Genealogy Data
  http://www.genswap.com/immigrate.html

- Hamburg Link To Your Roots
  http://www.hamburg.de/LinkToYourRoots/english/start.htm
  Searchable database extracted from the Hamburg Passenger Lists for selected years.

  o Emigration Port Hamburg
    http://www.hamburg.de/Behoerden/Pressestelle/
    emigration/englisch/welcome.htm
    Excellent online presentation of why Hamburg was a major port of departure for immigrants, how the were treated, what they faced, and how the process of departure worked.

- Immigrant Ship Information
  http://www.fortunecity.com/littleitaly/amalfi/13/ships.htm
  An alphabetical list of ships, with details on each ship as submitted to various Internet mailing lists.

- ISTG - Immigrant Ships Transcribers Guild
  http://istg.rootsweb.com/
  We are a group of volunteers dedicated to making the search for our ancestors easier. We grew out of a need to find ships' passenger lists right here, on-line. New entries added on a daily basis and now over 3,000 ships transcribed and growing daily.

- Magellan - The Ships Navigator
  http://208.249.158.172/magellan/
  Approximately 15,000 ship biographies, pictures, and voyages.

- The Olive Tree Genealogy: Index to Ships' Passenger Lists
  http://olivetreegenealogy.com/ships/index.shtml
  - 1400-1500
    http://olivetreegenealogy.com/ships/14-15.shtml
  - 1500-1600
    http://olivetreegenealogy.com/ships/15-16.shtml
  - 1600-1700
    http://olivetreegenealogy.com/ships/16-17p01.shtml
  - 1700-1800
    http://olivetreegenealogy.com/ships/17-18p01.shtml
  - 1800-1900
    http://olivetreegenealogy.com/ships/18-19p01a.shtml
  - 1900-present
    http://olivetreegenealogy.com/ships/19-20p01.shtml
  - Index of Ships from Ireland
    http://olivetreegenealogy.com/ships/irish_index.shtml
  - Index to Huguenot Ships
    http://olivetreegenealogy.com/ships/hug_index.shtml
  - List of Ships to Philadelphia
    http://olivetreegenealogy.com/ships/palship_list.shtml
  - Ships to Australia & New Zealand 1700-1800
    http://olivetreegenealogy.com/ships/toausp01.shtml
  - Ships to Canada 1400 to 1800
    http://olivetreegenealogy.com/ships/tocanp01.shtml
  - Ships to New Netherland
    http://olivetreegenealogy.com/nn/ships/index.shtml
  - Ships to South Africa 1680-1690
    http://olivetreegenealogy.com/ships/tosafp01.shtml
  - Ships to South America
    http://olivetreegenealogy.com/ships/tosamp01.shtml
  - Ships to United Kingdom
    http://olivetreegenealogy.com/ships/toukp01.shtml
  - Ships to U.S.A. 1400 to 1600
    http://olivetreegenealogy.com/ships/tousap01.shtml
- On the Trail of Our Ancestors - Index to Ships' Passenger Lists
  http://www.ristenbatt.com/genealogy/shipind1.htm
  by Donna Speer Ristenbatt.
- Passenger Lists on the Internet
  http://members.aol.com/rprost/passenger.html
- The Ship Information Database / La Base de donnúes d'information sur les navires
  http://www.chin.gc.ca/ship
  From the Canadian Heritage Information Network.
- TheShipsList Home Page
  http://www.TheShipsList.com/
  TheShipsList mailing list was established to assist those seeking information on the vessels, which brought their ancestors to their new home, be that the United States, Canada, Australia, or another part of the world. Some ships passenger lists, schedules, wreck data, and other information, which is not readily available, has been collected, along with links to other sites of interest.

- Ship's Passenger Lists
  http://users.erols.com/fmoran/ships.html
- Start Here! Directory of Passenger Ship Arrivals
  http://www.daddezio.com/genealogy/ships/index.html
  More than 1,200 ship passenger Lists.
- Una's Genealogy Stuff
  http://idt.net/~unatg/
  Has transcriptions of several passenger lists from Liverpool to NYC.
- The Unofficial Holland America Line Home Page
  http://unofficial.net/hal/index.html
  - Passenger Lists
    http://unofficial.net/hal/passlist.html
  - Ship Index
    http://unofficial.net/hal/shpndxfr.html
  - Yahoo!...Ships
    http://dir.yahoo.com/Arts/Humanities/History/By_Subject/Maritime_History/Ships/

Specific Ships, Localities or Topics

- 1749 Phoenix Passenger List
  http://www.execpc.com/~trarbach/Patience/1749Phoenix.html
- 1768 Ship Arrivals, Charleston, SC
  ftp://ftp.rootsweb.com/pub/usgenweb/sc/ships/1768ship.txt
- AHSGR Ship and Immigration Records
  http://pixel.cs.vt.edu/library/ships/
  American Historical Society of Germans from Russia.
- American Plantations and Colonies - Ships to America Index
  http://www.primenet.com/~langford/ships/shiplist.htm
- The American Slave Brig Creole - The Creole Research Center
  http://www.kirklands.org/Creole1.htm
  Details about the slave revolt on board the American brig Creole.
- AUSNZ Passenger Lists
  http://www.users.on.net/proformat/auspass.html
- Australian Shipping, 1788-1899
  http://www.blaxland.com/ozships/
  Shipping arrivals in Australia, listing passenger ships mainly for NSW, Queensland and some entries for Victoria and Tasmania.
- Australian Shipping Arrivals and Departures 1788 to 1967 - Convictions
  http://www.blaxland.com/ozships/
- Australia's First Fleet
  http://www.pcug.org.au/~pdownes/dps/1stflt.htm
  Convicts transported from England in 1788.
- Australia's Second Fleet
  http://www.pcug.org.au/~pdownes/dps/2ndflt.htm
  Convicts transported from England in 1790.
- Australia's Third Fleet
  http://www.pcug.org.au/~pdownes/dps/3rdflt.txt
  Convicts transported from England in 1791.

- Bark "Charlotte Harrison" - July 1850 Passenger List
  http://www.execpc.com/~haroldr/hrsnlist.htm

- British Barque "Tay" - August 1840 Passenger List
  http://www.execpc.com/~haroldr/taylist.htm

- The Canary Islanders' Migration to Louisiana 1778-1783
  http://www.rootsweb.com/~lastbern/passenger.htm
  Aboard: SS Sacremento, San Ignacio de Loyola, La Victoria, Sanuan Nepomuceno, La Santa Faz, El Sagrada Corazon de Jeses, Fragata Llamada Margarita, SS Trinidad.

- Canterbury Association Passenger Manifests ~ Arrivals in Canterbury, New Zealand
  http://www2.symet.net/whitehouse/nzbound/cbyassoc.htm

- Channel Islands Maritime Miscellany
  http://freespace.virgin.net/sg.foote/maritime/index.htm
  Guernsey Crew Lists, ship index, letters of marque, etc. Some lists for 1845 through 1891.

- Chester County Ships' Lists
  http://199.72.15.191/Sites/Gen/Chet2/scripts/ListShips.asp
  Located on the Chester County page of the Pennsylvania GenWeb project.

- Clarence, Port of Galway, 19 May 1846
  http://www.rootsweb.com/~irish/igsi_published/passlist/46claren.htm

- Conqueror, Liverpool, 11 June 1850
  http://www.rootsweb.com/~irish/igsi_published/passlist/50conque.htm

- Convict Gangs in 1821
  http://carmen.murdoch.edu.au/community/dps/convicts/victlist.htm
  Alphabetical list of names for 3,217 men, women and children who were issued with rations in Sydney on Saturday September 8, 1821.

- Convicts to Australia - A Guide To Researching Your Convict Ancestors
  http://carmen.murdoch.edu.au/community/dps/convicts/index.html
  In depth information and lists of convicts, ships, a timeline and convict's stories.

- Cushla Machree - Galway - New York - 1 March 1849
  http://www.rootsweb.com/~irish/igsi_published/passlist/49cushla.htm

- Doukhobor Ship Passenger Lists
  http://www.cableregina.com/users/doukhobor.genealogy/Shiplists.htm
  With few exceptions, the Doukhobors arrived in Canada in four distinct waves in: (i) 1898 - 1899; (ii) 1904 - 1905; (iii) 1910 - 1912; and (iv) 1926 - 1928. This web site contains an index of known ship passenger lists for each of these periods.

- Dove Passenger List - 1801
  http://www.rootsweb.com/~pictou/dove1.htm
  Arriving in Pictou County, Nova Scotia, Canada.

- Down to the Sea in Ships
  http://www.star.net/misuraca/down2c.htm
  A list of men fishing out of Gloucester, Massachusetts who were lost at sea.

- Dutch Immigrant Ships to Canada 1947-1960
  http://www.magma.ca/~louievb/immigration/ships.html
  Immigrant ships leaving The Netherlands transported the majority of Dutch emigrants to Canada. This covers the Volendam, Groote Beer, Waterman, Zuiderkruis, Sibajak, Johan van Oldenbarnevelt.

- The Emigrants from the Waasland (Flanders, Belgium) to the United States and Canada 1830 - 1950
  http://www.ping.be/picavet/
  - Transatlantic Passenger Ships 1830 - 1859
    http://www.ping.be/picavet/Waas_America_Travel01.shtml
  - Transatlantic Passenger Ships 1860 - 1899
    http://www.ping.be/picavet/Waas_America_Travel02.shtml
  - Transatlantic Passenger Ships 1900 - 1913
    http://www.ping.be/picavet/Waas_America_Travel03.shtml
  - Transatlantic Passenger Ships 1919 - 1921
    http://www.ping.be/picavet/Waas_America_Travel04.shtml
  - Transatlantic Passenger Ships 1921 - 1950
    http://www.ping.be/picavet/Waas_America_Travel05.shtml

- Emigration from Norway, The Solem, Swiggum & Austheim Ship Index
  http://www.museumsnett.no/mka/ssa/
  Index of emigrant ships leaving Norway, 1825-1925. Ship descriptions and pictures. Descriptions of voyages. Some passenger lists. Shipping companies.

- Encrease, Youghal, Cork, 1679
  http://www.rootsweb.com/~irish/igsi_published/passlist/1679encr.htm

- Fifty Years in Queensland: - Living Pioneer Colonists
  http://192.148.225.23/bruce/qldpio.html
  A supplement article to "The Queenslander" Jubilee Issue:- 7 August 1909, which lists names, ages and year of arrival and the ship's name.

- Fishing? - It was "A WAY OF LIFE" and Lost At Sea
  http://www.geocities.com/Heartland/Prairie/7527/
  Dedicated to Atlantic Canada fishermen and mariners lost at sea, their families and survivors. And to all those from other countries who were lost at sea.

- "Franklin" - From Liverpool to New York, June 22, 1827
  ftp://ftp.rootsweb.com/pub/usgenweb/ny/passengerlists/ship0002.txt

- "Friedrich der Grosse" Ship Passenger List, Germany to America
  http://pw2.netcom.com/~steventw/passlist.html
  An original ship passenger list of the March 19, 1898 sailing of the Friedrich der Grosse from Bremen, Germany, to New York.

- Galveston, Texas Passenger Lists | Tips on How to Locate Them
  http://home.att.net/~wee-monster/galveston.html
  Compiled by Joe Beine, German Roots Webmaster.

- The Germanic - Partial List of Passengers from Ireland to NY in June, 1903
  http://genealogy.org/~ajmorris/ireland/ireemg3.htm

- "Gildart" Passenger List
  ftp://ftp.rootsweb.com/pub/usgenweb/md/ships/gildart.txt
  Scottish rebels from Liverpool 5 May 1747 to Port North, Potomack, Maryland: 5 August 1747.

- Grand River West and the Queen of Greenock
  http://www.islandregister.com/stpatricks.html

- Guernsey Crew Lists Index ~ Channel Islands
  http://freespace.virgin.net/sg.foote/crewindex.htm
  Some lists for 1845 through 1891.

- Hamburg Passenger Lists, 1850-1934
  http://www.genealogy.net/gene/misc/emig/ham_pass.html
  An index of the microfilm numbers for the 486 reels at the Family History Library in Salt Lake City. The original lists are held at Hamburg State Archive/Staatsarchiv, Bestand Auswandereramt.

- Hector Passenger List
  http://www.rootsweb.com/~pictou/hector1.htm
  Voyage to Pictou, Nova Scotia in 1773.

- Huguenot Ships
  http://www.mweb.co.za/roux/Huguenots/ships.htm
  Names and dates of vessels bearing Huguenots to the Cape Settlements in South Africa.

- Humphreys Passenger List --- 1806
  http://www.rootsweb.com/~pictou/hmphreys.htm

- Immigrant Ships
  http://www.macatawa.org/~devries/Shipindex.htm
  Immigrant ships of the Dutch Colonists of the 19th century to West Michigan and Iowa. Over 50 Lists!

- Immigrant Ships to New Zealand
  http://www.geocities.com/Heartland/Forest/2925/shipstonz.htm
  The ships in this index were mostly used to transport immigrants to New Zealand during the period 1835 to 1910.

- Immigration to Canada in the Nineteenth Century - Ships - Emigration Reports - Emigration Handbooks
  http://www.ist.uwaterloo.ca/~marj/genealogy/thevoyage.html
  Ships lists, passenger lists, government reports, emigration reports, emigration handbooks.

- Immigration to Victoria. British Ports 1852-1879
  http://shipping.cohsoft.com.au/db/britship.html
  Public Record Office of Victoria, Australia has indexed the Arrivals to Victorian Ports from British Ports 1852 - 1879.

- Immigrants to Canada in Nineteenth Century - Ships - Emigration Reports - Emigration Handbooks
  http://www.ist.uwaterloo.ca/~marj/genealogy/thevoyage.html
  Ships lists, passenger lists, government reports, emigration reports, emigration handbooks.

- Immigrant Ships Carrying Some of the First Colonists to the West Michigan Area
  http://www.macatawa.org/~devries/Shipindex.htm

- Index to Inward Overseas Passengers from Foreign Ports 1852 - 1859
  http://home.vicnet.net.au/~provic/185259/5259indx.htm
  From the PRO Victoria, Australia.

- Information on Records of Passenger Arrivals at the Port of New Orleans
  http://www.gnofn.org/~nopl/info/louinfo/louinfo3.htm
  From the New Orleans Public Library.

- Irish Passenger Lists
  http://freespace.virgin.net/alan.tupman/sites/irish.htm

- Irish Passenger Lists
  http://members.tripod.com/~Data_Mate/irish/Irish.htm

- "Isabellabath"
  http://www.macatawa.org/~devries/isabath.html
  From the Netherlands to New York on December 19, 1846.

- The Island Register Shipping Stories, Info, and Folklore
  http://www.islandregister.com/ships.html
  Prince Edward Island, Canada.

- "Johnson" Passenger List
  ftp://ftp.rootsweb.com/pub/usgenweb/md/ships/johnson.txt
  Prisoners, shipped on 5 May 1747 Port Oxford, Maryland 17 July 1747.

- Lammershagen - Additional Research Notes and Press Cuttings
  http://www.holum.net/holum/gen/lammershagen.htm#hagen

- Liners of the Golden Age
  http://www.powerscourt.com/liners/index.htm

- Lista de Passageiros do veleiro Elizabeth Marie - 1819 -1820 Porto do Rio de Janeiro - Brasil
  http://www.geocities.com/rogerioabreu/elizabeth.htm
  Ship's passenger list and letter to King Joao VI,1819 - Elizabeth Marie from Amsterdam to Rio de Janeiro Swiss colons to Nova Friburgo- Brazil.

- List of Ships to Philadelphia
  http://www.genealogy.org/~palam/ships.htm

- List or Manifest of Alien Passengers for the United States Immigration Officer at Port of Arrival - San Francisco, California - September 4th, 1930
  http://members.aol.com/jktsn/shiplst2.htm

- Lovely Nelly Passenger Lists, 1774 & 1775
  http://www.rootsweb.com/~pictou/lnell1.htm
  From Galloway, Scotland to Prince Edward Island.

- Lunenburg County, NSGenWeb- Passenger Lists
  http://www.rootsweb.com/~canns/lunenburg/shiplists.html

  o Cornwallis Ships to Halifax - 1749
    http://www.rootsweb.com/~canns/cornwallis.html

o Passenger List of the "SS Abyssinia"
http://www.melcombe.freeserve.co.uk/source/
abyssinia.htm
*From Liverpool and Queenstown to New York, NY, USA on 8
October 1885.*

o Passenger Lists for Ships Carrying the "Foreign
Protestants" to Nova Scotia
http://www.rootsweb.com/~canns/lunenburg/shiplist2.html
59 Families 16 May 1752 "SPEEDWELL".

o Passenger Lists for Ships Carrying the "Foreign
Protestants" to Nova Scotia
http://www.rootsweb.com/~canns/lunenburg/shiplist3.html
59 Families 30 May 1752 "BETTY".

o Passenger Lists for Ships Carrying the "Foreign
Protestants" to Nova Scotia
http://www.rootsweb.com/~canns/lunenburg/shiplist11.html
73 Families 18 May 1751 "SPEEDWELL".

o Passenger Lists for Ships Carrying the "Foreign
Protestants" to Nova Scotia
http://www.rootsweb.com/~canns/lunenburg/shiplist4.html
85 Families 2 Jul 1751 "PEARL".

o Passenger Lists for Ships Carrying the "Foreign
Protestants" to Nova Scotia
http://www.rootsweb.com/~canns/lunenburg/shiplist5.html
85 Families 5 Jun 1752 "GALE".

o Passenger Lists for Ships Carrying the "Foreign
Protestants" to Nova Scotia
http://www.rootsweb.com/~canns/lunenburg/shiplist6.html
85 Families 6 Jun 1752 "PEARL".

o Passenger Lists for Ships Carrying the "Foreign
Protestants" to Nova Scotia
http://www.rootsweb.com/~canns/lunenburg/shiplist9.html
99 Families 29 Jun 1750 "ANN".

o Passenger Lists for Ships Carrying the "Foreign
Protestants" to Nova Scotia
http://www.rootsweb.com/~canns/lunenburg/shiplist1.html
100 Families of German Protestants 25 Jun 1751 "MURDOCH".

o Passenger Lists for Ships Carrying the "Foreign
Protestants" to Nova Scotia
http://www.rootsweb.com/~canns/lunenburg/shiplist7.html
119 Families 30 May 1752 "SALLY".

o Passenger Lists for Ships Carrying the "Foreign
Protestants" to Nova Scotia
http://www.rootsweb.com/~canns/lunenburg/shiplist8.html
*Foreign Names of Those Arriving with Cornwallis, 1749 and
Others Of Interest Arriving in 1749.*

o Passenger Lists for Ships Carrying the "Foreign
Protestants" to Nova Scotia
http://www.rootsweb.com/~canns/lunenburg/shiplist12.html
*Settlers Who Are Presumed to Have Arrived on the
"ALDERNEY" or the "NANCY" in August and September 1750*

• LusaWeb Portuguese Immigrant Ship Lists
http://www.lusaweb.com/shiplist.cfm

• Marine Museum of the Great Lakes at Kingston -
Mills Ship List ~ Canada and the Great Lakes
http://130.15.161.15/mills.htm

• Marine Museum of the Great Lakes at Kingston -
Wallace Ship List ~ Canada and the Great Lakes
http://130.15.161.15/wallace.htm

• Mariners and Ships in Australian Waters
http://sites.archivenet.gov.au/Mariners/
*Indexes transcribed from the Australian Archive Office Reels of the
Shipping Master's Office, Inwards Passengers Lists commencing in
January 1873. The lists include crew, passengers, deserters,
births/deaths, stowaways, etc.*

• The Maritime Heritage Project
http://www.maritimeheritage.org/
*Stories and lists of ships, captains, passengers arriving in San
Francisco during the Gold Rush through the turn of the century.*

• Mary & John Clearing House
http://www.maryandjohn1630.com/

• Mary and John Passenger Lists
http://members.aol.com/MREgleston/MnJ.html
Left England March 1630, arrived in Boston May 30, 1630.

• Molly Passenger List - October 16, 1741
http://www.placercoe.k12.ca.us/kgissy/molly.htm
Rotterdam, Holland - Deal, England - Philadelphia, PA.

• Montcalm Passenger List
http://mypage.direct.ca/d/dobee/pilgrim.html
*From Montreal on July 16, 1936 to Antwerp and London. This was
one of several steamships that sailed from Canada to Europe in the
summer of 1936, carrying Great War veterans and their families to
ceremonies regarding the war.*

• Mormon Emigrant Ships (1840-1868)
http://www.xmission.com/~nelsonb/pioneer.htm#ships

• National Archives of Canada - Immigration Records
http://www.archives.ca/exec/naweb.dll?fs&02020204&e&
top&0

o Immigration Records (1925-1935)
http://www.archives.ca/exec/naweb.dll?fs&020118&e&
top&0
*Searchable online database provides the volumes and page
numbers on which the names of Canadian immigrants appear in
the passenger lists.*

• Nova Scotia Bound
http://www.geocities.com/Heartland/Meadows/8429/
index.html
A partial list of ships bound for Nova Scotia between 1750 and 1862

o The Albion Ship List, Surnames A-L
http://www.geocities.com/Heartland/Meadows/8429/
albal.html
And M-Z
http://www.geocities.com/Heartland/Meadows/8429/
albmz.html
*Arrived in Halifax, Nova Scotia, Canada on May 6, 1774 from
Hull, Yorkshire, England.*

o The British Queen Passenger List
http://www.geocities.com/Heartland/Meadows/8429/britqn.html
Sailed for Nova Scotia from Liverpool, England on April 1st, 1862.

o The Duke of York Passenger List
http://www.geocities.com/Heartland/Meadows/8429/dyork.html
Arrived in Halifax, Nova Scotia from Liverpool, England on May 1, 1772.

o Elisabeth and Ann Passenger List
http://www.geocities.com/Heartland/Meadows/8429/elisann.html
Sailed for Nova Scotia from Thurso, North Britain on November 8th, 1806.

o The Frank Flint Passenger List
http://www.geocities.com/Heartland/Meadows/8429/flint.html
Sailed for Halifax, Nova Scotia from Liverpool, England on May 28th, 1862.

o The Humphreys Passenger List
http://www.geocities.com/Heartland/Meadows/8429/hmphry.html
Sailed for Nova Scotia from Tobermory, North Britain on July 14th, 1806.

o The Jenny Ship List
http://www.geocities.com/Heartland/Meadows/8429/jenny.html
To Halifax, Nova Scotia, Canada from Hull, Yorkshire, England in April of 1775.

o The Providence Passenger List
http://www.geocities.com/Heartland/Meadows/8429/prvdnc.html
Arrived in Halifax on June 1, 1774 from Newcastle Northumberland.

o The Rambler Passenger List
http://www.geocities.com/Heartland/Meadows/8429/rambler.html
Sailed for Nova Scotia from Thurso, North Britain on November 8th, 1806.

o The Thomas and William or the Prince George Passenger List
http://www.geocities.com/Heartland/Meadows/8429/tmwlad.html
Arrived at Halifax from Scarborough, Yorkshire on May 14/16, 1774.

o The Two Friends Ship List
http://www.geocities.com/Heartland/Meadows/8429/2friends.html
Arrived in Halifax, Nova Scotia on May 9, 1774 from Hull, Yorkshire

• Nova Scotia Passenger Lists - The Speedwell and the Ann
http://www.rootsweb.com/~ote/nsship.htm

• On-line Sourcing of Australasian Passenger Lists
http://www.users.on.net/proformat/auspass2.html
Queries submitted for ships of interest.

• Oughton Passenger List---1804
http://www.rootsweb.com/~pictou/oughton.htm

• Palatine Immigrant Ship Patience Home Page
http://www.execpc.com/~trarbach/Patience/patience_home.html

• "Parsee" - Passenger List - Moreton Bay - 11 January 1853
http://192.148.225.23/bruce/plink.html

• Passage to America, 1851-1869 : The Records of Richard Elliott, Passenger Agent, Detroit, Michigan
http://www.amazon.com/exec/obidos/ISBN=0943112222/markcyndisgenealA/
A book by Richard Elliott & Mary L. Duncan.

• Passenger and Emigrant Lists
http://scripts.ireland.com/ancestor/browse/links/index.htm

• Passenger arrivals at Port Chalmers, New Zealand, March 1848 - January 1851
http://www.actrix.gen.nz/users/ngaiopress/drhocken.htm

• Passenger List: Angel Gabriel
http://members.aol.com/dcurtin1/gene/gabriel.htm
Wrecked off Pemaquid Pt., Maine on August 15, 1635.

• Passenger List for "Daylight" 1875
http://homepage.mac.com/warrenj/OtherGenealogy/DaylightPassengers1875.html
The emigrant ship Daylight departed London, England on Thursday 27 May 1875 and arrived in Fremantle, Western Australia on 28 August 1875.

• Passenger List for the 'Palestine'
http://www.benet.net.au/~brandis/gendata/palestine.html
From Plymouth, England, 29 November 1852 to Perth, Western Australia, 28 April 1853.

• Passenger List: Lyon 1632
http://members.aol.com/dcurtin1/gene/lyon.htm

• Passenger List of Ship Ben Nevis
http://home.sprynet.com/~harrisfarm/bennevis.htm
Ship Register Wendish Colonists of Texas, 1854, from Liverpool, England to Queenstown, Ireland to Galveston, Texas.

• The Passenger List of the "Alexander," and the Glenaladale Settlers
http://www.islandregister.com/alexandr.html
1772 - 1997, Prince Edward Island, Canada.

• Passenger List of the Brig "Fanny"
http://www.islandregister.com/fanny.html
From Charlottetown to California Nov 12 1849.

• Passenger List of the "British Queen," 1790
http://www.islandregister.com/british_queen.html

• Passenger List of the "Clarendon" - 1808 from Oban, N. Britain
http://www.islandregister.com/clarendon.html

• Passenger List of the "Elizabeth and Ann" - 1806 from Thurso, N. Britain
http://www.islandregister.com/liz_ann.html

- Passenger List of the "Falmouth" - 1770 from Greenock
  http://www.islandregister.com/falmouth.html

- Passenger List of the "Jane"
  http://www.islandregister.com/jane.html
  From Drimindarach, Scotland to Prince Edward Island, 12 July 1790.

- Passenger List of the "Lively" - 1775 from Britain
  http://www.islandregister.com/lively.html

- Passenger List of the "Lucy"
  http://www.islandregister.com/lucy.html
  Sailed in the company of the "Jane," from Drimindarach, Scotland to Prince Edward Island, 12 July 1790.

- Passenger List of the Pakeha
  http://www.islandregister.com/pakeha.html
  From Prince Edward Island to New Zealand, December 23, 1863.

- Passenger List of the "Rambler" - 1806 from Tobermory, N. Britain
  http://www.islandregister.com/rambler.html

- Passenger List of the Schooner Jeannette
  http://home.hiwaay.net/~guillory/genealogy/personal/jeannette.html

- Passenger List, Ship Anne, 1623
  http://members.aol.com/calebj/anne.html

- Passenger List, Ship Fortune, 1621
  http://members.aol.com/calebj/fortune.html

- Passenger List: Planter 1635
  http://members.aol.com/dcurtin1/gene/planter.htm

- Passenger Lists from Ireland - 1803
  http://www.ida.net/users/dhanco/passlst.htm

- Passenger Lists from Ireland #2 - 1803
  http://www.ida.net/users/dhanco/passlst2.htm

- Passenger lists of 1855 Migration
  http://www.geocities.com/Heartland/Prairie/3974/plists.html
  From Bählertal, Baden, Germany.

- Passenger Lists Published in the New York Daily Times
  http://www.pt5dome.com/PassHome.html
  New York City to California via Central America, 1851 - 1856.

- Passenger Ship Records - PA Archives
  http://www.rootsweb.com/~usgenweb/pa/1pa/ship.htm

- Passenger Ships at Bluff Before 1900
  http://www.angelfire.com/ok2/cbluff/passengerships.html
  Passenger lists for ships that arrived at the Port of Bluff, New Zealand before the year 1900.

- Passenger Ships' Lists, Pennsylvania
  http://www.ristenbatt.com/genealogy/shipind.htm
  Between 1728 and 1772.

- Passengerlist Lammershagen
  http://home.sol.no/holum/passengerlist.htm

- Passengers Aboard the Ship Bowditch (of Boston)
  http://genealogy.org/~ajmorris/ireland/ireemg2.htm
  From Liverpool, arrived at New York May 27, 1839.

- Passengers of the Brig Emile and Helene July 21, 1835
  http://www.geocities.com/Heartland/Hills/5042/EMILIE.HTML

- Passengers of the "Henry and Francis," 1685
  ftp://ftp.rootsweb.com/pub/usgenweb/nj/ships/1685nj.txt

- "Passengers of the Prince Edward"
  http://www.islandregister.com/pedward.html
  To New Zealand from Charlottetown Harbour, 1859.

- Passengers on the Emigrant Ship "Emigrant"
  http://www.swinhope.demon.co.uk/genuki/Transcriptions/Emigrant.html
  Sailed from Sunderland 10 September 1852; arrived Melbourne 3 January 1853.

- Passengers on the Emigrant Ship "Guy Mannering"
  http://www.swinhope.demon.co.uk/genuki/Transcriptions/GuyMannering.html
  Sailed from Liverpool on May 22nd 1849; arrived New York, June 28th.

- Passengers on the Emigrant Ship "Lizzie Webber"
  http://www.swinhope.demon.co.uk/genuki/Transcriptions/LizzieWebber.html
  Sailed from Sunderland 31 July 1852; arrived Melbourne 4 December 1852.

- Passengers on the Emigrant Ship "Lord Delaval"
  http://www.swinhope.demon.co.uk/genuki/Transcriptions/LordDelaval.html
  Sailed from Berwick-upon-Tweed on September 13th 1852 for London and on to Port St Philip, Victoria, Australia.

- Passengers on the Emigrant Ship "Saldanha"
  http://www.swinhope.demon.co.uk/genuki/Transcriptions/Saldanha.html
  Sailed from Liverpool in the summer of 1856 for Victoria, Australia.

- The Patience 1751
  http://www.execpc.com/~trarbach/Patience/patience_home.html

- Peter Hodge's Home Page
  http://www.pcug.org.au/~phodge/
  Information regarding the brig "Indian" from Falmouth in mid-1843 bound for Launceston, Tasmania; the "Emigrant" sailed from Plymouth on 9 August 1850 bound for Moreton Bay; and more on emigration, etc.

- Portuguese Passenger Ship Master List
  http://www.dholmes.com/ships.html

- Prince of Wales - June 28 1813 from Stromness, Orkney, Scotland
  http://members.tripod.com/~tmsnyder/PW_LIST.htm

- "Queen of the Colonies" Web Site
  http://www.garrison.gil.com.au/queen.html

- Reconstructed Passenger List of the German Ship Lammershagen
  http://www.holum.net/holum/gen/germanship.htm

- Sailing Ship the INDIA Lost at Sea 1841
  http://www.home.gil.com.au/~bbiggar/india.htm
  Sailed from Greenock Scotland on 4 June 1841 bound for the Australian colony of Port Phillip.

- Saint Andrew Galley
  http://www.enter.net/~stenlake/list.html
  September 26, 1737, Palatinates from Rotterdam and Cowes.

- Samuel - The English Immigrant Ship
  http://members.aol.com/groffh/samuel.htm
  It brought many immigrants from the Palatinate, Germany, and Switzerland to Philadelphia.

- The Sarah -- 1801
  http://www.rootsweb.com/~pictou/sarah1.htm
  To Pictou, Nova Scotia.

- Sarah Hyde Passenger List, 1854 from Antwerp to New York
  http://genweb.net/~gen-cds/hyde.html

- Ship Bowditch Passenger List
  http://www.rootsweb.com/~ote/iriship1.htm
  From The Olive Tree.

- The Ship Defence, 1635
  http://www.citynet.net/personal/gunn/defence.html

- Ship Diligent - Passenger List and General Info
  http://www.geocities.com/Heartland/Ranch/4750/LassShip.html

- Ship Edinburgh Passenger Lists
  http://www.execpc.com/~haroldr/edbrglst.htm
  From Campbeltown, Scotland to Cape Fear, North Carolina in 1770 and to Island of St. Johns (Prince Edward Island) in 1771.

- Ship *Griffin* Passenger List 1749
  http://www.worldroots.com/misc/bg_misc/ship02.html

- The Ship Marianne
  http://members.aol.com/lhchristen/marianne.htm
  Voyage from Bremen to Baltimore, Departing August 11, 1843, and Arriving September 25, 1843.

- Ship Mortonhouse
  ftp://ftp.rootsweb.com/pub/usgenweb/pa/1pa/ships/1729mrtn.txt
  Sailed from Rotterdam to Philadelphia August 17, 1729.

- Ship Samuel
  http://member.aol.com/ShipSamuel/

- Ship WILMINGTON Passenger List
  http://www.execpc.com/~haroldr/wlmtnlst.htm
  From Belfast to New York, 9 July 1803.

- Ship's List for Agostine 1841
  http://www.users.bigpond.com/Tall_Trees/shipping/agostina.htm
  Full list of Passenger Names.

- Ships & Captains...1874 Publication
  http://genweb.net/~gen-cds/ships.html
  A list of ships and their masters, and emigrants, transcribed from a book edited by John Camden Hotten and published by Chatto and Windus, London 1874.

- Ships of our Ancestors
  http://www.worldroots.com/misc/bg_misc/ship01.html

- Ships to Western Australia 1829 - 1849
  http://www.benet.net.au/~brandis/gendata/1829_49.html

- Ships to Western Australia 1899
  http://www.benet.net.au/~brandis/gendata/1899ship.html

- Ships to Western Australia 1900
  http://www.benet.net.au/~brandis/gendata/1900ship.html

- Ships to Western Australia January and February 1901
  http://www.benet.net.au/~brandis/gendata/1901ship.html

- Skandinavien-Amerika Linien
  http://liners.members.easyspace.com/skandina.htm
  A description (in Danish) with photos of ships in the Scandanavian-America line. Links to specific ships and to material on other lines from Scandanavia.

- South Australian Passenger Lists 1836-1840
  http://www.users.on.net/proformat/ships36.html

- South Australian Passenger Lists 1841-1846
  http://www.users.on.net/proformat/ships41.html

- South Australian Passenger Lists 1847-1886
  http://www.users.on.net/proformat/ships47.html

- Spencer Passenger List---1806
  http://www.rootsweb.com/~pictou/spencer.htm

- SS Lucania Partial Passenger List, Ire to NY 1898
  ftp://ftp.rootsweb.com/pub/usgenweb/ny/passengerlists/ship0001.txt

- S.S. Yukon - Ship Passenger List
  http://www.usgennet.org/~usgwakus/yukon.htm

- Steam Ship Seneca, Hobocken, NJ, 1879
  http://members.tripod.com/~tmsnyder/SS.htm

- St. George - Liverpool - New York - 08 April 1847
  http://www.rootsweb.com/~irish/igsi_published/passlist/47stgeo.htm

- St. George - London - Waterford - Maryland - Oct 7, 1677
  http://www.rootsweb.com/~irish/igsi_published/passlist/1677stgeo.htm

- St. George Partial Passenger List, Liverpool to NY 1847
  ftp://ftp.rootsweb.com/pub/usgenweb/ny/passengerlists/ship0003.txt

- Tacoma Public Library, Northwest Room - Ships and Shipping Database
  http://www.tpl.lib.wa.us/v2/NWROOM/Ships.htm

- Tantivy! - Homestead of Mindful Works - Fireside Hypothesis
  http://www.angelfire.com/on2/tantivy/
  A complete listing of assisted immigrants arriving in Sydney aboard the Tantivy in 1853 and a list of persons with the surname Ford whom arrived in Australia aboard individual ships.

- Two Lists of Intending Passengers to the New World, 1770 and 1771
  http://www.execpc.com/~haroldr/edbrglst.htm
  Ship "Edinburgh" voyage from Campbeltown, Scotland to Cape Fear, North Carolina in 1770 and to Island of St. Johns (Prince Edward Island) in 1771.

- Van Diemens Land Company's Indentured Servants Home Page
  http://www.tassie.net.au/~aduniam/
  Servants engaged to establish a land grant in Tasmania from 1826. Departure and arrival dates of the ships Tranmere, Caroline, Thomas Lawrie, Emu, Forth and others, and passenger list of those aboard.

- Various Passenger Lists Data
  http://members.aol.com/ascaife/main2.htm
  A variety of passenger list transcriptions dating from 1716 through 1929.

- The Winthrop Fleet of 1630
  http://members.aol.com/dcurtin1/gene/winthrop.htm

- Women and Female Children of the Royal Admiral 1792
  http://www.shoalhaven.net.au/~cathyd/raladies.html

◆ Shipwrecks

- California Shipwrecks
  http://shipwrecks.slc.ca.gov/
  California State Lands Commission.

- English East India Company Ships
  http://www.ships.clara.net/
  Data for all ships of the East India Company, including shipping Losses in the Mercantile Service 1600-1834 (includes Shipwrecks, Captures & Missing Vessels).

- ISRG Message Board: Specific Shipwrecks
  http://www.njscuba.com/ISRG/wreck-info/index.html
  Message board of Internet Ship Research Group sponsored by NJ Scuba.

- Lost Boats
  http://www.subnet.com/MEMORIAL/lostboat.htm
  A list of US submarines, the crew and the passengers that were lost since 1915.

- Out of Gloucester
  http://www.downtosea.com/
  Fishermen's memorial and more.

- Passenger List: Angel Gabriel
  http://members.aol.com/dcurtin1/gene/gabriel.htm
  Wrecked off Pemaquid Pt. Maine on Aug. 15, 1635.

- Records Relating to Shipwrecks (#65) ~ U.K.
  http://www.pro.gov.uk/leaflets/ri065.htm

- Research Sources and Technique with Special Emphasis on the Great Lakes Region
  http://home.xnet.com/~acpinc/research.html

- Sandusky Shipwrecks
  http://pilot.msu.edu/user/hancockp/index.htm

- Shipwreck!
  http://www.cascobay.com/history/shipwrek/shipwrek.htm
  History of 1861 shipwreck of the Bohemian from Cape Elizabeth, with links. Written by Tess Nacelewicz.

- Shipwrecks in the Atlantic
  http://www.cimorelli.com/vbclient/shipwrecks.htm
  Database of shipwrecks in the North Atlantic from 1841 - 1978.

- Spanish Shipwrecks Resources Inc.
  http://republika.pl/shipwrecksresources/
  Documents related to Spanish shipwrecks for sale.

- Yahoo!...Shipwrecks
  http://dir.yahoo.com/Social_Science/Anthropology_and_ Archaeology/Archaeology/Marine_Archaeology/Shipwrecks/

◆ Societies & Groups

- Association for Great Lakes Maritime History
  http://www.aglmh.org/

- Eastland Disaster Historical Society
  http://www.eastlanddisaster.org/
  Historical overview of a Chicago and Great Lakes Steamliner Shipwreck - Chicago's greatest maritime disaster.

- The Great Lakes Shipwreck Historical Society ~ Michigan
  http://www.lssu.edu/shipwreck/

- The Historical Diving Society ~ U.K.
  http://www.thehds.com/index.htm

- Marine Historical Society of Detroit
  http://www.oakland.edu/~ncschult/mhsd/

- Nautical Research Guild, Inc.
  http://www.Naut-Res-Guild.org/index.html
  Ship models and nautical history

  o Maritime Institution Survey
    http://www.Naut-Res-Guild.org/museum.html

- Puget Sound Maritime Historical Society ~ Seattle, Washington
  http://www.pugetmaritime.org/
  The Puget Sound Maritime Historical Society's purpose is to collect, preserve and display maritime historical objects, relics and data with particular emphasis on the Pacific Northwest. Their Puget Sound Maritime Research Library is an outstanding resource for maritime research and holds the extensive Williamson Collection of ship photographs.

- The Saginaw River Marine Historical Society
  http://www.oakland.edu/boatnerd/museums/srmhs/

- Steamship Historical Society of America
  http://www.sshsa.org/

- Titanic Historical Society
  http://www.titanic1.org/

- U S Life-Saving Service Heritage Association
  http://www.uslife-savingservice.org/

- Wisconsin Marine Historical Society
  http://www.wisconsinwebdesign.com/wmhs/homeport.htm

SOCIETIES & GROUPS – GENERAL

http://www.cyndislist.com/soc-gen.htm

Category Index:

◆ Ethnic Organizations
◆ General Resource Sites
◆ Lineage Societies
◆ Military Societies
◆ National Societies
◆ Religious Organizations

◆ *See also the complete alphabetical listing of societies on the* Cyndi's List *web site at http://www. CyndisList.com/society.htm*

NOTE: Family associations and societies can be found under *Surnames, Family Associations & Family Newsletters* (http://www.CyndisList.com/surnames.htm)

◆ Ethnic Organizations

● Ancient Order of Hibernians in America - National Web Page
http://www.aoh.com/
   o National History
   http://www.aoh.com/history/Default.htm

● The American Hellenic Educational Progressive Association
http://www.ahepa.org/info/index.html
Ethnic organization for Greek immigrants.

● Association of Jewish Genealogical Societies (AJGS)
http://www.jewishgen.org/ajgs/index.html

● B'nai B'rith
http://www.bnaibrith.org/

● CSA Fraternal Life
http://www.csafraternallife.org/
A fraternal benefits society originally for Czech immigrants.
   o The Czechoslovak Heritage Museum ~ Illinois
   http://www.csafraternallife.org/museum.htm
   Holds the records of the CSA and merged organizations.

● First Catholic Slovak Union of the United States and Canada
http://www.fcsu.com/
Slovak fraternal organization.

● Grand Orange Lodge of Canada
http://www.orange.ca/
Web site for the Loyal Orange Association of Canada, a national fraternal organization.

● The Grand Orange Lodge of Ireland
http://www.grandorange.org.uk/

● Immigration History Research Center (IHRC) at the University of Minnesota
http://www1.umn.edu/ihrc/
An international resource on American immigration and ethnic history.

   o Archival and Library Research Collections
   http://www1.umn.edu/ihrc/research.htm#top
      ● Family History Sources at IHRC
      http://www1.umn.edu/ihrc/genealog.htm#top
      Fraternal Society Material
      http://www1.umn.edu/ihrc/genealog.htm#frat
      Records of fraternal organizations contain a wealth of personal information in the form of membership application and death benefit claim forms. The membership applications generally include dates and place of birth, names of parents and siblings, religion, profession, place of residence (at time of application), and medical information. Among the fraternal organizations represented at the IHRC are the National Slovak Society, the First Catholic Slovak Union, the Slovenian National Benefit Society, the Order of AHEPA (Greek), and the Order Sons of Italy in America.

● Italian Sons and Daughters of America
http://www.orderisda.org/
A fraternal benefits association.
   o History and Benefits of the ISDA
   http://www.orderisda.org/history.htm

● National Japanese American Historical Society
http://www.nikkeiheritage.org/

● National Slovak Society
http://www.nssusa.org/
Slovak fraternal organization.

● One Stop Italian American: OSIA.org
http://www.osia.org/
The Order Sons of Italy in America.

● The Order of the Sons of Hermann in the State of TX
http://www.texashermannsons.org/
Fraternal benefits society originally for German immigrants.
   o Our History
   http://www.texashermannsons.org/hs_hist.htm

● Polish Falcons
http://www.polishfalcons.org/
A fraternal benefits society.
   o Historical Overview
   http://www.polishfalcons.org/history.html

- Polish Genealogical Society of America
  http://www.pgsa.org/

- Slovene National Benefit Society
  http://www.snpj.com/

- Society of Acadian Descendants
  http://www.acadian.org/sad.html

- The Society of Hispanic Historical and Ancestral Research (SHHAR)
  http://members.aol.com/shhar/index.html

- Sons of Hermann ~ Texas
  http://lonestar.utsa.edu/rhudson/Hermann1.html
  Fraternal benefits society originally for German immigrants.

  o A Brief History
    http://lonestar.utsa.edu/rhudson/Hermann2.html

- Sons of Norway Home Page
  http://www.sofn.com/

- União Portuguesa do Estado da California
  http://www.upec.org/
  A fraternal benefits society originally serving Portuguese immigrants to California.

  o A Short History of Our Society
    http://www.upec.org/html/body_uphist.html

- William Penn Association
  http://ourworld-top.cs.com/WPAIns/index.htm
  A fraternal benefits society originally for Hungarian immigrants to the United States.

  o History
    http://ourworld-top.cs.com/WPAIns/id3_history_wpa.htm

◆ Fraternal Organizations

- Cyndi's List - Fraternal Organizations
  soc-frat.htm
  The links in this section have been moved to their own page. Please update your bookmarks.

◆ General Resource Sites

- American Association for State and Local History
  http://www.aaslh.org

- Associations Généalogiques sur le Net
  http://www.multimania.com/numa/assgensurnet.html
  Les associations, cercles et unions généalogiques sur internet. Classement par départements.

- Association for Gravestone Studies Home Page
  http://www.berkshire.net/ags/

- AudioTapes.com - Genealogical Lectures on Cassette Tapes - Society
  http://www.audiotapes.com/search2.asp?Search=society
  And Societies
  http://www.audiotapes.com/search2.asp?Search=societies

- GEN-EDITOR Mailing List
  http://www.rootsweb.com/~jfuller/gen_mail_general.html
  #GEN-EDITOR

For editors/publishers of genealogical, surname and family newsletters to have a place to discuss and share ideas and tips.

- GEN_SOCIETIES Mailing List
  http://www.rootsweb.com/~jfuller/gen_mail_general.html
  #GEN_SOCIETIES
  For persons involved with establishing a local genealogical society in order to share program ideas, discuss means of promoting growth within a group, discuss how to work with libraries, and other related topics.

- Guild of One-Name Studies ~ United Kingdom
  http://www.one-name.org/

- Historical Societies - Society Hill Directory
  http://www.daddezio.com/society/

- Railroad Historical Societies
  http://all-railroads.com/histsoc.html

- Why Should a Genealogy Society Give Records Away?
  http://www.anet-chi.com/~jeffb/bockcomm.htm
  An article by Jeffrey A. Bockman, Naperville, IL, originally published in the FGS Forum, Winter 1997, page 25.

◆ Lineage Societies

- Associated Daughters of Early American Witches
  http://www.adeaw.org/
  National society for daughters with proven descent from someone who was accused, tried or executed for witchcraft in American colonies prior to 31 December 1699.

- AudioTapes.com - Genealogical Lectures on Cassette Tapes – Lineage
  http://www.audiotapes.com/search2.asp?Search=lineage
  DAR
  http://www.audiotapes.com/search2.asp?Search=DAR
  And Mayflower
  http://www.audiotapes.com/search2.asp?Search=mayflower

- Baronial Order of Magna Charta
  http://www.magnacharta.com/

- Board for Certification of Genealogists - Roster of Those Certified - Specializing in Lineage Societies
  http://www.bcgcertification.org/rosts_@l.html

- Continental Society Sons of Indian Wars
  http://members.tripod.com/~CSSIW/

- Daughters of Union Veterans of the Civil War 1861-1865
  http://www.starweb2000.com/duvcw/index.html

- Descendants of the Signers of the Declaration of Independence
  http://www.dsdi1776.org/default.htm
  Stories of the signers, books reviewed, how to apply to this lineage society, information about its scholarship program.

- First Families of Tennessee
  http://www.east-tennessee-history.org/firstfam.htm
  A heritage program sponsored by the East Tennessee Historical Society, honoring descendants of the first settlers of Tennessee.

- First Fleet Fellowship
  http://home.vicnet.net.au/~firstff/
  A historical society for people who have ancestors who arrived in Australia in 1788 aboard one of the ships of the First Fleet.

- GenealogyBookShop.com - Lineage Records/Hereditary Societies
  http://www.genealogybookshop.com/genealogybookshop/files/General,Lineage_Records_Hereditary_Societies/index.html
  The online store of Genealogical Publishing Co., Inc. & Clearfield Company.

- The General Society of Mayflower Descendants
  http://www.mayflower.org/

- Holland Society of New York
  http://members.aol.com/hollsoc/
  Descendants in the direct male line from those who lived in the colonies under Dutch rule in America before or during 1675.

- Jamestowne Society
  http://www.jamestowne.org/
  For descendants of the Virginia settlers in the first permanent English settlement in America.

- National Society Daughters of the American Colonists ~ Washington, D.C.
  http://www.nsdac.org/

- National Society Daughters of the British Empire in the United States of America
  http://www.mindspring.com/~dbesociety/

- National Society Magna Charta Dames and Barons
  http://www.magnacharta.org/
  The page provides information about the Society, a national organization with over 16,000 members, meeting throughout the United States. Meetings normally feature talks by historians, legislators, judges concerning the Magna Charta. The site also includes detailed information about the 25 Surety Barons as well as initial information about 56 immigrant ancestors descended from one or more of the Barons. Additional immigrant ancestors will be added in the future.

- National Society of the Daughters of the American Revolution Home Page
  http://www.dar.org/

- National Society Sons and Daughters of the Pilgrims
  http://www.nssdp.org
  The NSSDP is a national lineage society whose members have proven lineal descent from any immigrant to the American Colonies prior to 1700.

- National Society of the Sons of the American Revolution ~ Louisville, Kentucky
  http://www.sar.org/
  - 1999 SAR Patriot Index
    http://www.amazon.com/exec/obidos/ISBN=1896716121/markcyndisgenealA/
    A CD-ROM by the National Society of the Sons of the American Revolution.

- National Society United States Daughters of 1812
  http://www.geocities.com/Heartland/Pointe/1740/
  The society requires lineal descent from an ancestor who rendered military, naval or civil service between the close of the American Revolutionary War in 1783 and the close of the War of 1812 in 1815, Military service may be in any one of sixteen recognized engagements between those dates.

- Order of Descendants of Ancient Planters
  http://tyner.simplenet.com/PLANTERS.HTM
  People who arrived in Virginia before 1616, remained for a period of three years, paid their passage, and survived the massacre of 1622.

- The Order of the Founders and Patriots of America
  http://www.mindspring.com/~wxman2/gp/

- Society of California Pioneers
  http://www.wenet.net/~pioneers/

- Society of Mayflower Descendants in the Commonwealth of Pennsylvania
  http://www.sail1620.org/

- The Sons & Daughters of the Province and Republic of West Florida 1763 - 1810
  http://usersa.usunwired.net/mmoore/lghs/sonsdau.htm

- Sons of Confederate Veterans Home Page
  http://www.scv.org/
  - Sons of Confederate Veterans Genealogy Network
    http://www.scv.org/scvgen00.htm
  - Confederate Ancestor Research Guide
    http://www.scv.org/genealogy/scvgen02.htm

- Sons of Union Veterans of the Civil War
  http://suvcw.org/

- United Daughters of the Confederacy
  http://www.hqudc.org/

- The United Empire Loyalists' Association of Canada ~ Toronto, Ontario, Canada
  http://people.becon.org/~uela/uela1.htm

◆ Military Societies

- The American Legion National Headquarters
  http://www.legion.org

- Army Alumni Organizations
  http://www.army.mil/vetinfo/vetloc.htm

- The Army Home Page Organizations Index
  http://www.army.mil/public/organization.htm
  Alphabetical index of a numerous variety of organizations within the Army or related to the Army.

- The Aztec Club of 1847
  http://www.walika.com/aztec.htm
  Military society of the Mexican War.

- Canadian Peacekeeping Veterans Association
  http://www.islandnet.com/~duke/cpva.htm

- Confederate Memorial Association
  http://www.confederate.org/

- Continental Society Sons of Indian Wars
  http://members.tripod.com/~CSSIW/

- Crimean War Research Society ~ U.K.
  http://homepages.ihug.co.nz/~phil/crimean.htm

- Dames of the Loyal Legion of the U.S.A.
  http://www.usmo.com/~momollus/DOLLUS.HTM

- Daughters of Union Veterans of the Civil War 1861-1865
  http://www.starweb2000.com/duvcw/index.html

- Descendants of Mexican War Veterans
  http://www.dmwv.org/

- DISPATCH - Scottish Military Historical Society
  http://subnet.virtual-pc.com/~mc546367/journal.htm

- General Society of Colonial Wars
  http://www.ubalt.edu/gscw/

- General Society of the War of 1812
  http://www.societyofthewarof1812.org/

- Grand Army of the Republic (GAR)
  http://pages.prodigy.com/CGBD86A/garhp.htm

- Grand Army of the Republic in Illinois
  http://www.illinoiscivilwar.org/gar.html
  Lists GAR posts in Illinois.

- The Grand Army of the Republic in Michigan
  http://www.centuryinter.net/suvcw.mi/garmi.html

- Grand Army of the Republic (GAR) in Oklahoma
  http://www.ionet.net/~cousin/dale14.html
  Lists GAR records available from the Oklahoma Historical Society.

- Grand Army of the Republic Posts in Wisconsin
  http://badger.state.wi.us/agencies/dva/museum/hist/garlist.html
  From the Wisconsin Veterans Museum.

- John H. Chipman, Jr. Post #89 G.A.R. Hall
  http://members.tripod.com/GARpost89MA/
  A memorial site to the more than 500 late members of this Grand Army of the Republic Massachusetts Post. History of G.A.R. Post #89, member photos, and service records. Historical & Genealogical research material of greater Beverly, MA area men who fought in the American Civil War.

- League of Researchers of South African Historical Battlefields
  http://www.icon.co.za/~dup42/Welcome.html

- Legion Ville - First Training Camp of the United States Army, 1792
  http://tristate.pgh.net/~bsilver/legion.htm
  The Legion Ville Historical Society, Inc., The Anthony Wayne Historical Society, Inc. Includes transcriptions of West Point Orderly Books, 1792-1796.

- Maryland Society Sons of the American Revolution
  http://www.sar.org/mdssar/

- The Military Historical Society of Australia
  http://www.pcug.org.au/~astaunto/mhsa.htm

- Military Order of the Loyal Legion of the U.S.A.
  http://suvcw.org/mollus.htm

- National Civil War Association
  http://ncwa.org/index.html

- National Society Daughters of the Union 1861-1865
  http://personal.sdf.bellsouth.net/sdf/c/s/cseales/home.htm
  Hereditary Society for women descendants (lineal and collateral) of Civil War Union ancestors.

- National Society of the Daughters of the American Revolution Home Page
  http://www.dar.org/

- National Society of the Sons of the American Revolution ~ Louisville, Kentucky
  http://www.sar.org/

- National Society United States Daughters of 1812
  http://www.geocities.com/Heartland/Pointe/1740/

- Order of Indian Wars of the United States
  http://members.tripod.com/~Historic_Trust/indian.htm

- The Orders and Medals Research Society
  http://www.omrs.org.uk/
  Members of this society research the military careers of the individuals whose names are found inscribed on medals.

- Sons of Confederate Veterans Home Page
  http://www.scv.org/
  - Sons of Confederate Veterans Genealogy Network
    http://www.scv.org/scvgen00.htm
  - Confederate Ancestor Research Guide
    http://www.scv.org/scvgen02.htm

- Sons of Union Veterans of the Civil War
  http://suvcw.org/

- United Daughters of the Confederacy
  http://www.hqudc.org/

- Veterans of Foreign Wars
  http://www.vfw.org/

- Veterans of Future Wars
  http://mondrian.princeton.edu/CampusWWW/Companion/veterams_future_wars.html
  A satirical college society founded in 1936.

- The Western Front Association - Remembering 1914-1918
  http://ourworld.compuserve.com/homepages/cf_baker/

- Women in Military Service for America Memorial Foundation, Inc.
  http://www.wimsa.org/

◆ National Societies

- The American Historical Association
  http://www.theaha.org/

- Association of Professional Genealogists ~ Denver, Colorado
  http://www.apgen.org/

- Australasian Federation of Family History Organizations Inc.
  http://carmen.murdoch.edu.au/~affho/

- Canada's National History Society
  http://www.historysociety.ca/

- Dead Persons Society ~ Australia
  http://pcm.pcmedia.com.au/tags/docs/dps.html

- The Federation of Family History Societies ~ U.K.
  http://www.ffhs.org.uk/

- Federation of Genealogical Societies ~ U.S.
  http://www.fgs.org/

- The Institute of Heraldic and Genealogical Studies ~ U.K.
  http://www.cs.ncl.ac.uk/genuki/IHGS/

- National Genealogical Society ~ Arlington, Virginia
  http://www.ngsgenealogy.org/

- National Railway Historical Society
  http://www.rrhistorical.com/nrhs/

- National Trust for Historic Preservation ~ U.S.
  http://www.nthp.org/

- Nederlandse Genealogische Vereniging
  http://www.ngv.nl/

- Society of Australian Genealogists
  http://www.sag.org.au/

- Society of Genealogists, UK
  http://www.sog.org.uk/

- Sveriges Släktforskarförbund / The Swedish Federation of Genealogical Societies
  http://www.genealogi.se/forbund.htm

◆ Religious Organizations

- Association of Jewish Genealogical Societies (AJGS)
  http://www.jewishgen.org/ajgs/index.html

- Catholic Family History Society of London, England
  http://feefhs.org/uk/frg-cfhs.html

- The Catholic Knights of America
  http://www.ckoa.com/
  A fraternal benefits society.

  o History of the Catholic Knights of America
    http://www.ckoa.com/history.htm

  o The Uniform Rank
    http://www.ckoa.com/urhist.htm

- Fellowship of Brethren Genealogists
  http://www.cob-net.org/fobg/

- Knights of Columbus
  http://www.kofc.org/

  o History of the Knights
    http://www.kofc.org/knights/history/history.cfm

- Knights of Columbus - Emblems of the Order
  http://www.stjoesmendham.org/kcemblem.html
  From St. Joseph's Council No. 6462. Includes photographs of officer jewels.

- Knights of Columbus Robes and Jewels of Council Officers
  http://www.srv.net/~hlyrsry/knightsofcolumbus/information.html#Robes and Jewels
  From Holy Rosary Church Knights of Columbus Council 11841. Clip art pictures of Council Officer Jewels.

- Knights of Columbus - Structure of the Order
  http://www.stjoesmendham.org/kcstructure.html
  From St. Joseph's Council No. 6462.

- The National Huguenot Society
  http://huguenot.netnation.com/
  The National Huguenot Society is an organization devoted to: 1. Coordinating activities of member societies, and promoting and supporting fulfillment of their common purposes which include: a. perpetuating the memory and promoting the principles and virtues of the Huguenots; b. commemorating the great events of Huguenot history; c. collecting and preserving historical data and relics illustrative of Huguenot life, manners, and customs; 2. To give expression to the Huguenot tenets of faith and liberty, and to promote their understanding for the good of the United States; 3. To encourage and foster the organization of new member Societies within states, territories of the United States, and the District of Columbia where none currently exist.

- National Catholic Society of Foresters
  http://www.ncsf.com/
  A fraternal benefits society.

  o Our History
    http://www.ncsf.com/history.htm

- The Presbyterian Historical Society ~ Philadelphia, Pennsylvania
  http://www.libertynet.org/pacscl/phs/

- The United States Catholic Historical Society
  http://www.catholic.org/uschs/

- Woman's Christian Temperance Union
  http://www.wctu.org/
  Many of our foremothers were members.

  o Contact Us!
    http://www.wctu.org/contacts/default.htm
    See especially "How can I get information about a relative who was a member of the WCTU?"

SOCIETIES & GROUPS – FRATERNAL ORGANIZATIONS

http://www.cyndislist.com/soc-frat.htm

Category Index:

- ◆ General Resource Sites
- ◆ How To
- ◆ Libraries, Archives & Museums
- ◆ Locality Specific
- ◆ Publications, Software & Supplies

- ◆ Societies & Groups

NOTE: Family associations and societies can be found under *Surnames, Family Associations & Family Newsletters* (http://www.CyndisList.com/surnames.htm)

◆ General Resource Sites

- Acronyms
  http://blacksheep.rootsweb.com/acronym.html
  Links to Fraternal Societies from the International Black Sheep Society Of Genealogists.

- the e-m@son website
  http://www.freemasonry.org/
  A Masonic starting point for the Freemason, e-mason & non-Mason.

- Fraternal Organizations
  http://www.usgennet.org/topic/folklore/fraterna/fraterna.html
  From the American Local History Network.

- Many Fraternal Groups Grew From Masonic Seed (Part 1 -- 1730-1860)
  http://www.linshaw.com/vol4no11.html
  Online article by Barbara Franco.

- Many Fraternal Groups Grew From Masonic Seed (Part 2 -- 1860-1920)
  http://www.linshaw.com/vol4no12.html
  Online article by Barbara Franco.

- Masonic Resources on the Internet
  http://www.flash.net/~mason/links.html

- Non-Masonic Fraternal Organizations
  http://bessel.org/fratorgs.htm
  With links to their web sites.

◆ How To

- Fraternal Order Initials, Abbreviations & "Also Known As"
  http://www.gwgantiques.com/ffaq.htm

- Fraternalism in America (1860 - 1920)
  http://www.phoenixmasonry.org/masonicmuseum/fraternalism_in_america.htm
  Online article by Bart P. Snarf from the Phoenixmasonry Masonic Museum. Includes a brief history of the organization plus images of fraternal jewelry as an aid to identification.

- o Ancient Order of United Workmen
  http://www.phoenixmasonry.org/masonicmuseum/ancient_order_of_united_workmen_.htm

- o Ancient Order Knights of the Mystic Chain
  http://www.phoenixmasonry.org/masonicmuseum/ancient_order_knights_of_the_mys.htm

- o Benevolent Protective Order Of Elks
  http://www.phoenixmasonry.org/masonicmuseum/benevolent_protective_order_of_e.htm

- o Civil War Orders (GAR, etc.)
  http://www.phoenixmasonry.org/masonicmuseum/civil_war_orders.htm

- o Daughters of the American Revolution
  http://www.phoenixmasonry.org/masonicmuseum/daughters_of_the_american_revolu.htm

- o Foresters Group
  http://www.phoenixmasonry.org/masonicmuseum/intl_order_of_foresters.htm

- o Fraternal Order of Eagles
  http://www.phoenixmasonry.org/masonicmuseum/fraternal_order_of_eagles.htm

- o Improved Order of Redmen
  http://www.phoenixmasonry.org/masonicmuseum/iorm_improved_order_of_red_men.htm

- o The International Association of Rebekah Assemblies
  http://www.phoenixmasonry.org/masonicmuseum/ioof_rebekah_jewels.htm

- o Knights and Ladies of the Golden Eagle
  http://www.phoenixmasonry.org/masonicmuseum/knights_of_the_golden_eagle_kge.htm

- o The Knights of Pythias
  http://www.phoenixmasonry.org/masonicmuseum/knights_of_pythias.htm

- o Loyal Order of Moose
  http://www.phoenixmasonry.org/masonicmuseum/loyal_order_of_moose_loom.htm

- o Maccabees
  http://www.phoenixmasonry.org/masonicmuseum/maccabees.htm

o Nativist Orders (Order of United American Mechanics, Junior OUAM/Daughters of America, Patriotic Order Sons of America)
http://www.phoenixmasonry.org/masonicmuseum/nativist_orders_aoum_jr_aoum.htm

o New England Order Of Protection
http://www.phoenixmasonry.org/masonicmuseum/new_england_order_of_protection.htm

o Odd Fellows Service Jewels
http://www.phoenixmasonry.org/masonicmuseum/ioof_jewels.htm

o Odd Fellows - Rebekah Past (Noble) Grand
http://www.phoenixmasonry.org/masonicmuseum/rebekah_grand_noble_ioof_jewels.htm

o Oriental Order of Humility and Perfection & Ancient Mystic Order of Samaritans
http://www.phoenixmasonry.org/masonicmuseum/oreintal_order_of_humility_and_p.htm

o Patrons of Husbandry (The Grange)
http://www.phoenixmasonry.org/masonicmuseum/grange_patrons_of_husbandry.htm

o Railroad Orders
http://www.phoenixmasonry.org/masonicmuseum/railroad_orders.htm

o Supreme Council of the Royal Arcanum
http://www.phoenixmasonry.org/masonicmuseum/royal_arcanum.htm

o Townsend Clubs
http://www.phoenixmasonry.org/masonicmuseum/townsends_clubs.htm

o Woodmen of the World
http://www.phoenixmasonry.org/masonicmuseum/woodmen_of_the_world.htm

- GEN-FRATERNAL Mailing List
http://www.rootsweb.com/~jfuller/gen_mail_general.html#GEN-FRATERNAL
For family historians using fraternal or benevolent society resources in their research. This includes identifying grave marker symbols as well as organizational regalia in photographs, jewelry, and other sources to establish an ancestor's membership in an organization. From organization identification, the list will also be a forum for questions, help and direction on where and how to access the extant records of these organizations.

- Headstone Abbreviations
http://www.geocities.com/Heartland/Estates/6587/Abb.html

- Known Fraternal organizations and secret societies with abbreviations
http://www.exonumia.com/society.htm

- Lachances - Grave Marker Initials
http://www.lachances.net/links01/cemetery_markers.htm

- Lesson 18: Fraternal Organizations
http://www.rootsweb.com/~rwguide/lesson18.htm
From RootsWeb's Guide to Tracing Family Trees.

- Markers XI (1994)
http://www.gravestonestudies.org/markers.htm#11
The American Gravestone Studies Journal copies for sale. The 1994 issue contains an article entitled "Ritual, Regalia, and Remembrance: Fraternal Symbolism and Gravestones".

- Masonic Genealogy Questions
http://bessel.org/genealgy.htm
Brief instructions on how to begin researching a Masonic ancestor.

- Society Emblems
http://www.pre1900prints.com/Miscellaneous/societyemblems1896.htm
Lithograph from 1896.

- Sword Collectors Information Page - Society Swords
http://www.ruble-enterprises.com/society_marks.htm
Includes pictures of some examples of Knights of Columbus, Grand Army of the Republic, and K of C Uniform Rank sword hilts.

- Woodmen of the World: On the Search of Graves
http://www.interment.net/column/feature/jimd/index.htm
Online article from The Cemetery Column.

◆ Libraries, Archives & Museums

- All Masonic Libraries & Museums in the World
http://bessel.org/maslibs.htm
Includes contact information.

- Crawfordsville District Public Library ~ Indiana
http://www.cdpl.lib.in.us/

  o Local History
http://www.cdpl.lib.in.us/localh.html
Holds the records of the Supreme Tribe of Ben Hur, a fraternal insurance association.

  o Ben-Hur Museum
http://www.ben-hur.com/page7.htm
Sells a history of the Supreme Tribe of Ben Hur.

- Masonic Library & Museum Association
http://bessel.org/mlma.htm
With links to Association member libraries.

- The Museum of Our National Heritage ~ Lexington, Massachusetts
http://www.mnh.org/
An American history museum founded and supported by 32° Scottish Rite Freemasons.

  o The Van Gorden-Williams Library
http://www.mnh.org/library/content.htm
Holds one of the most comprehensive collections on American Masonry in the world. The library also collects material on other fraternal organizations whose development paralleled or was influenced by Masonry

- Western Historical Manuscript Collection - Columbia
http://www.system.missouri.edu/whmc/
At the University of Missouri in Columbia, Missouri.

  o Family History Research at WHMC-C
http://www.system.missouri.edu/whmc/gene/exhibit.htm

o   Social and Fraternal Organizations
    http://www.system.missouri.edu/whmc/socfrat.htm
    *Records of social and civic service organizations and fraternal
    groups, such as Kiwanis, Lions, Rotary clubs, and Masonic
    lodges.*

◆ Locality Specific

- Andreas' History of the State of Nebraska - Douglas
  Co. - Omaha - Societies
  http://www.ukans.edu/carrie/kancoll/andreas_ne/douglas/
  douglas-p20.html
  *Masonic, I.O.O.F., Knights of Pythias, Ancient Order United
  Workmen.*

- Grandview Cemetery Woodmen of the World
  Burials ~ Fort Collins, Colorado
  http://www.interment.net/data/us/co/larimer/grandview/
  grandview_wow.htm
  *Interesting photographic examples of Woodmen grave markers from
  Cemetery Records Online.*

◆ Publications, Software & Supplies

- American Orders And Societies And Their
  Decorations
  http://www.naval-military-press.co.uk/details.dbm?Code=
  3159
  Book for sale from the Naval & Military Press.
  http://www.naval-military-press.co.uk/

- American Society Medals: An Identification Guide
  http://www.amazon.com/exec/obidos/ISBN=0965333809/
  markcyndisgenealA/
  A book by Lee E. Bishop.

- AudioTapes.com - Genealogical Lectures on Cassette
  Tapes - Fraternal
  http://www.audiotapes.com/search2.asp?Search=fraternal

- Fraternal Organizations
  http://www.amazon.com/exec/obidos/ISBN=0313214360/
  markcyndisgenealA/
  A book by Alvin J. Schmidt.

- Fraternally Yours: A Decade of Collecting
  http://www.amazon.com/exec/obidos/ISBN=0802600247/
  markcyndisgenealA/
  A book by Barbara Franco.

- The International Encyclopedia of Secret Societies
  and Fraternal Orders
  http://www.amazon.com/exec/obidos/ISBN=0816038716/
  markcyndisgenealA/
  A book by Alan Axelrod.

- My Ancestor Was A Freemason
  http://www.sog.org.uk/acatalog/SoG_Bookshop_Online_My_
  Ancestors_Series_135.html#a1112s
  *Book for sale from the UK's Society of Genealogists regarding
  British Freemasonry.*

◆ Societies & Groups

- Artisans Order of Mutual Protection
  http://www.artisansaomp.org/

- BPO Elks Online
  http://www.elks.org

  o   Our History
      http://www.elks.org/history/default.cfm

  o   Once An Elk, Eternally An Elk
      http://www.elks.org/history/hs_cemetery.cfm
      *Describes and gives some locations for "Elk Rests" - BPO Elks
      cemeteries.*

- General Military Council - IOOF
  http://www.gmc-ialapm.org/
  *The Patriarchs Militant of the Independent Order of Odd Fellows -
  the Odd Fellow's uniformed branch.*

  o   History of the Patriarchs Militant
      http://www.gmc-ialapm.org/history.html

  o   1890s Uniforms, Regalia and Flags
      http://www.angelfire.com/wa2/pmioof/antique.html
      From the Department of Washington, P.M.

  o   Decorations of Chivalry
      http://www.angelfire.com/wa2/pmioof/antique2.html

  o   Medals & Badges
      http://www.angelfire.com/wa2/pmioof/antique3.html

- The Grand Lodge of Ancient, Free and Accepted
  Masons
  http://www.GrandLodgeScotland.com/
  The web site of the main Masonic movement in Scotland.

- The Grange Connection
  http://www.grange.org/
  "America's Family Fraternity."

- Fraternal Order of Eagles
  http://www.foegrandaerie.org/

  o   Eagle History
      http://www.foegrandaerie.org/History.htm

  o   The Grand Auxiliary
      http://www.foegrandaerie.org/GrandAux.htm

- The Improved Order of Red Men
  http://members.nbci.com/redmen/

- Independent Order of Foresters
  http://www.iof.org/

  o   IOF History
      http://www.iof.org/History.htm

- Independent Order of Odd Fellows and Rebekahs
  http://norm28.hsc.usc.edu/IOOF.shtml

  o   Family History Research
      http://norm28.hsc.usc.edu/IOOF/FamilyResearch.html
      Instructions and details from I.O.O.F.

  o   IOOF Jewels
      http://norm28.hsc.usc.edu/ioof/IOOF/IOOF/Jewels/
      Jewels.html
      A guide to identification of Odd Fellows' and Rebekahs' insignia

  o   Links to IOOF History
      http://norm28.hsc.usc.edu/ioof/IOOF/IOOF/IOOF
      History.html

- JOUAM - Junior Order United American Mechanics
  http://bessel.org/jouam.htm
  Basic history of the organization.

- Knights of Columbus
  http://www.kofc.org/

- Lions International
  http://www.lions.org/

- Modern Woodmen of America
  http://www.modern-woodmen.org/

  o Modern Woodmen of America - A Few Words On History
    http://www.modern-woodmen.org/PubRel/AboutUs/AFew
    WordsOnHistory.htm

- Moose International - The Family Fraternity
  http://www.mooseintl.org/

- National Fraternal Congress of America
  http://www.nfcanet.org/
  The Association for America's Fraternal Benefits Societies.

  o Member Societies
    http://www.nfcanet.org/public/articles/index.cfm?cat=11

  o Society Name Changes & Mergers
    http://www.nfcanet.org/public/articles/details.cfm?id=14

- Neighbors of Woodcraft
  http://www.nowfbs.com/index.htm
  A fraternal benefits society.

  o History of Woodcraft
    http://www.nowfbs.com/history.htm

- The Order of Knights of Pythias
  http://www.pythias.org/
  An international, non-sectarian fraternal order, founded in 1864.

- Royal Arcanum
  http://www.royalarcanum.com/
  A fraternal benefits society.

  o History
    http://www.royalarcanum.com/history.html

- Prince Hall Freemasonry
  http://www.connecti.com/~joelbee/phall.htm

- The Shrine and Shriners Hospital
  http://shrinershq.org/

- The United Grand Lodge of England
  http://www.grand-lodge.org/
  The web site of the main Masonic movement in the UK.

- Woodmen of the World
  http://www.woodmen.com/

  o History of Woodmen
    http://www.woodmen.com/history.htm

  o Grave Markers
    http://www.woodmen.com/abograve.htm

SOFTWARE & COMPUTERS
http://www.cyndislist.com/software.htm

Category Index:

- ◆ Articles & Reviews
- ◆ CD-ROMs: Books, Databases & Indexes
- ◆ GEDCOM: GEnealogical Data COMmunications
- ◆ Genealogy Software Programs
- ◆ Genealogy Tools & Utilities
- ◆ Genealogy Web Page/Site Generators
- ◆ Handhelds, Palmtops and PDAs
- ◆ Macintosh Resources

- ◆ Mailing Lists, Newsgroups & Chat
- ◆ Miscellaneous Software
- ◆ PAF ~ Personal Ancestral File
- ◆ Privacy Issues
- ◆ Publications, Magazines & Newsletters
- ◆ Societies & Groups
- ◆ Vendors

◆ Articles & Reviews

- ● Dick Eastman Online
  http://www.ancestry.com/library/view/columns/eastman/
  eastman.asp
  New each Wednesday by Dick Eastman.

  - o Dick Eastman Online Archive
    http://www.ancestry.com/library/view/columns/eastman/
    d_p_1_archive.asp

- ● Genealogy Software - Freeware/Shareware
  http://www.geocities.com/Heartland/Plains/3959/Generev.htm
  List of links and brief reviews from Chuck Roberts.

- ● Genealogy Software Guide
  http://www.amazon.com/exec/obidos/ISBN=0806315814/
  markcyndisgenealA/
  A book by Marthe Arends.

- ● Genealogy Software Springboard
  http://www.gensoftsb.com/
  *Descriptions, specs, contact info, pros & cons, links, developer info
  and much more on Windows, Mac, Unix and DOS platforms.*

- ● Louis Kessler's Genealogical Program Links
  http://www.lkessler.com/gplinks.shtml

- ● Reviews of Genealogical Macintosh Software
  http://utopia.knoware.nl/users/evim/software.html

◆ CD-ROMs: Books, Databases & Indexes

- ● 1999 SAR Patriot Index
  http://www.amazon.com/exec/obidos/ISBN=1896716121/
  markcyndisgenealA/
  *A CD-ROM by the National Society of the Sons of the American
  Revolution.*

- ● Acadian-Cajun Family Trees
  http://www.amazon.com/exec/obidos/ISBN=1896716105/
  markcyndisgenealA/
  A CD-ROM by Yvon Cyr.

- ● ALT Publisher Co. - Family Histories on CD Rom
  http://www.altpubs.com
  *Gates, White, Cox, and Adams family histories on CD ROM. Books
  are scanned images, indexed, able to be printed, all easy to use
  software is included on CD. CD's vary in length from 350 pages to
  over 3000 pages.*

- ● American Heritage Imaging, Inc.
  http://www.a-h-i-inc.com/

- ● Appleton's Fine Used Bookseller and Genealogy -
  Genealogy CD-ROMs and Diskettes
  http://www.appletons.com/genealogy/genemcdr.html
  *Hundreds of genealogy CD-ROMs (including Family Tree Maker)
  and genealogy software programs for sale. Free demos available to
  download.*

- ● The Archive CD Books Project
  http://www.fweb.org.uk/pub/books/index.htm
  *Makes CD-ROMs of old and rare books from the United Kingdom
  available to genealogists and historians at a reasonable price. It is a
  user-supported project.*

- ● ArchivesOnDemand.com
  http://www.archivesondemand.com
  *ArchivesOnDemand.com provides images of actual rare books and
  documents online not just indexes to data but the real thing.*

- ● CensusCD
  http://www.censuscd.com/cd/censuscd.htm

- ● CensusCD+Maps
  http://www.censuscd.com/cdmaps/censuscd_maps.htm

- ● Census View - Actual Census on CD-ROM
  http://www.galstar.com/~censusvu/

- ● Cheap and Easy CD-ROMs
  http://www.oz.net/~markhow/writing/cheap.htm
  *Written by Mark Howells for one of several different genealogical
  publications.*

- ● CMHS: GRANDMA CD-ROM Project
  http://www.fresno.edu/cmhs/gpc/home.htm
  Database from the California Mennonite Historical Society.

- Cornish Roots!
  http://www.cornwall-net.co.uk/multimed/roots.htm
  A CD-ROM being produced in Cornwall, England.

- Databases for the Study of Afro-Louisiana History
  and Genealogy, 1699-1860: Computerized
  Information from Original Manuscript Sources
  http://www.amazon.com/exec/obidos/ISBN=0807124826/
  markcyndisgenealA/
  A CD-ROM by Gwendolyn Midlo Hall.

- Databases for the Study of Afro-Louisiana History
  and Genealogy, 1699-1860
  http://lsumvs.sncc.lsu.edu/lsupress/catalog/Backlist/fall99/
  99fall_book/hall.html
  *CD-ROM containing over 100,000 records of African-Americans in
  Louisiana. Includes Louisiana Slave Database 1719-1820,
  Louisiana Free Database 1720-1820, a compilation of Louisiana
  censuses from 1699 through 1860, and various New Orleans,
  Pensacola, and Mobile censuses from 1784 to 1850.*

- Easy As Pulling Teeth Extracting Dentists from the
  1881 Census CD-ROMs
  http://www.oz.net/~markhow/writing/drilling.htm
  *By Mark Howells. Explains the use of Folio Views 4.2 for drilling
  into data the LDS won't let you search for on the CD-ROMs.*

- The Ellis Island Experience
  http://www.amazon.com/exec/obidos/ISBN=B00004TJP0/
  markcyndisgenealA/
  A CD-ROM by SouthPeak Interactive.

- The Ellis Island Experience
  http://www.southpeak.com/titles/ellis-island/default.htm
  *Companion site to the interactive CD-ROM of the same name.
  Includes a description of the CD-ROM and disc-owner access to the
  associated web site.*

- Eneclann: CD-ROM Index of Irish Wills 1484-1858
  http://www.eneclann.ie/cd1.htm
  *CD-ROM includes over 70,000 records that have never published
  before, containing over 100,000 names.*

- Family Archive CD Spotlight
  http://www.familytreemaker.com/issue22.html
  From Family Tree Maker Online.

- Family Archive Viewer, Version 4.0
  http://www.familytreemaker.com/abtffiv.html
  *Software from Broderbund which allows you to read their CD-ROM
  products.*

- Family Forest
  http://www.FamilyForest.com/
  CD-ROM indexes.

- Family Search Online Distribution Center -
  Software/Databases
  http://www.ldscatalog.com/cgi-bin/ncommerce3/Category
  Display?cgrfnbr=1804&cgmenbr=1402&CGRY_NUM=1678
  &RowStart=1&LocCode=FH
  *Inexpensive, quality CD-ROM databases available from the Church
  of Jesus Christ of Latter-day Saints.*

- o 1851 British Census
  http://www.ldscatalog.com/cgi-bin/ncommerce3/Product
  Display?prrfnbr=2483&prmenbr=1402&CGRY_NUM=1804
  &RowStart=1&LocCode=FH
  For the counties of Norfolk, Devon, and Warwick only.

- o 1881 British Census and National Index
  http://www.ldscatalog.com/cgi-bin/ncommerce3/Product
  Display?prrfnbr=61322&prmenbr=1402&CGRY_NUM=1804
  &RowStart=1&LocCode=FH
  *An automated index that contains information for over 30 million
  individuals from England, Wales, and Scotland.*

- o Australian Vital Records Index
  http://www.ldscatalog.com/cgi-bin/ncommerce3/Product
  Display?prrfnbr=2482&prmenbr=1402&CGRY_NUM=1804
  &RowStart=1&LocCode=FH
  *An indexed collection of references to 4.8 million birth,
  christening, marriage, and death records. This index covers only
  New South Wales (1788--1888), Tasmania (1803--1899), Victoria
  (1837--1888), and Western Australia (1841--1905).*

- o British Vital Records Index
  http://www.ldscatalog.com/cgi-bin/ncommerce3/Product
  Display?prrfnbr=11905&prmenbr=1402&CGRY_NUM=1804
  &RowStart=1&LocCode=FH

- o Family History SourceGuide
  http://www.ldscatalog.com/cgi-bin/ncommerce3/Product
  Display?prrfnbr=2486&prmenbr=1402&CGRY_NUM=1804
  &RowStart=1&LocCode=FH
  *A reference library that contains more than 150 research
  outlines, historical maps, letter-writing guides, word lists, forms,
  and addresses for Family History Centers worldwide.*

- o North American Vital Records Index
  http://www.ldscatalog.com/cgi-bin/ncommerce3/Product
  Display?prrfnbr=2471&prmenbr=1402&CGRY_NUM=1804
  &RowStart=1&LocCode=FH
  *More than 4.6 million christenings, births, and marriages that
  occurred in the United States and Canada from about 1700 to
  1888.*

- o Pedigree Resource File - Disc 1
  http://www.ldscatalog.com/cgi-bin/ncommerce3/Product
  Display?prrfnbr=479289&prmenbr=1402&CGRY_NUM=
  1804&RowStart=436688&LocCode=FH
  Disc 2
  http://www.ldscatalog.com/cgi-bin/ncommerce3/Product
  Display?prrfnbr=367303&prmenbr=1402&CGRY_NUM=
  1804&RowStart=61322&LocCode=FH
  Disc 3
  http://www.ldscatalog.com/cgi-bin/ncommerce3/Product
  Display?prrfnbr=353627&prmenbr=1402&CGRY_NUM=
  1804&RowStart=61322&LocCode=FH
  Disc 4
  http://www.ldscatalog.com/cgi-bin/ncommerce3/Product
  Display?prrfnbr=479340&prmenbr=1402&CGRY_NUM=
  1804&RowStart=436688&LocCode=FH
  Disc 5
  http://www.ldscatalog.com/cgi-bin/ncommerce3/Product
  Display?prrfnbr=529169&prmenbr=1402&CGRY_NUM=
  1804&RowStart=436688&LocCode=FH
  *Family history records submitted by individuals through the
  FamilySearch™ Internet Genealogy Service.*

- Family Tree Maker's Family Archive CDs
  http://www.familytreemaker.com/facds.html

- Free Genealogy Lookups
  http://www.ih2000.net/genealogy/sites/lookups.htm
  From a variety of CDs and books listed on this page.

- Frontier Press Bookstore
  http://www.frontierpress.com/frontier.cgi

- Genealogical Library Master Catalog
  http://www.onelibrary.com/
  A CD-ROM directory of over 300,000 Family Histories, Local Histories and Genealogical Sources at eighteen libraries.

- GenealogyBookShop.com - CD-ROM Publications
  http://www.genealogybookshop.com/genealogybookshop/files/General,CD-ROM_Publications/index.html
  The online store of Genealogical Publishing Co., Inc. & Clearfield Company.

- Genealogy Software- CDs and Diskettes
  http://www.gencd.com/txtidx.htm

- Getting More From the 1881 British Census on CD-ROM
  http://www.oz.net/~markhow/writing/more.htm
  By Mark Howells. A shorter version of the "dentist" article above, using different occupation examples and showing how to search by address with Folio Views 4.2 on the 1881 Census CD-ROM.

- GRD - The Genealogical Research Directory
  http://www.ozemail.com.au/~grdxxx/
  The world's largest listing of surname queries published annually in bookform, now on CD-ROM.

- Guild Press of Indiana - Civil War CD-ROMs
  http://www.guildpress.com/cdroms.htm#civilwar

- Heritage Books, Inc.
  http://www.heritagebooks.com/
  CD-ROMs available.

- Heritage Quest - US Federal Census Schedules Available on CD-ROM and Microfilm
  http://www.heritagequest.com/ProdFind2/census.htm
  Digitized images of the entire U.S. Federal Census from 1790 to 1920. Each of the 12,555 rolls of census microfilm are now available on CD-ROM for use on your home computer.

  - o Setting the Standard for Data Extraction and Delivery
    http://www.heritagequest.com/genealogy/CD-ROM/html/indexes.html

- Irish Vital Records 1400s-1800s
  http://www.gencd.com/sx010022.htm
  Ships Passenger List; Irish Wills 1400's-1800's, 1659 Census, Irish of Liverpool 1851.

- Lookups from Genealogical CDs
  http://seidata.com/~genealogy/cdlist.html
  People who own genealogy CDs and are willing to do lookups for others.

- Lost in Time
  http://www.lostintime.com/
  Books, CDs, software, maps, and accessories.

- Macbeth Genealogical Services
  http://www.macbeth.com.au/
  Books, fiche, maps, and CDROMs. Australia.

- The Memorabilia Corner
  http://members.aol.com/TMCorner/index.html
  Forms, flags, maps, software, CDs, tapes, microfilm & microfiche, books, periodicals, photographic conservation & archival materials.

- Portage Technologies - L'Acadie CD-ROM
  http://www.portageinc.com/

- Quintin Publications
  http://www.quintinpublications.com/
  Materials relating to Canada.

- RMIT Publishing Genealogy
  http://www.rmitpublishing.com.au/
  Australian databases on CD. Includes: Family History On Disc, New South Wales Between the Wars 1919-1945, New South Wales Pioneer Index - Pioneers Series 1788-1888, New South Wales Pioneer Index - Federation Series 1889-1918, Tasmanian Pioneers Index 1803-1899, Victorian Pioneers Index 1837-1888, Western Australian Pioneers Index 1841-1905.

- S&N Genealogy Supplies
  http://www.genealogy.demon.co.uk/
  Publishers of UK parish records, census, poll books and directories on CD-ROM. Plus a wide range of genealogical supplies.

- Search & ReSearch Publishing Corp.
  http://www.searchresearchpub.com/
  Supplier of historical databases on CD-ROM including "The Early Vital Records of Massachusetts" and "Mayflower Descendant Legacy".

- Storbeck's Genealogy Books Maps CD-ROM
  http://www.storbecks.com/

- The Trans-Atlantic Slave Trade - A Database on CD-ROM
  http://www.cup.org/ObjectBuilder/ObjectBuilder.iwx?ProcessName=ProductPage&Merchant_Id=1&product_id=0-521-62910-1&origin=search&searchField=TITLE&searchString=slave%20trade
  Contains the records of 27,233 transatlantic slave ship voyages made between 1595 and 1866 from all over Europe.

- World Family Tree Submitter Information Service
  http://www.familytreemaker.com/cgi-bin/subinfo.cgi
  Use the information from your WFT CD to look up the submitter information in this database.

- World Family Tree Submitter List
  http://www.inlink.com/~nomi/wftlist/index.html
  Names, addresses and e-mail addresses for various submitters to the WFT CD-ROMs.

◆ GEDCOM: GEnealogical Data COMmunications

- FixSex 1.0
  http://mail.pratt.lib.md.us/~bharding/rippleeffect/FixSex/FixSex.html
  A utility to help you fix the sex codes in a GEDCOM file.

- GED2GO (GEDCOMs to go)
  http://www.geocities.com/Yosemite/Trails/4849/evb/
  For MS-DOS, runs under Windows also. A utility program which automatically finds and removes living persons from GEDCOM files.

- GED2HTML: A GEDCOM to HTML Translator
  http://www.gendex.com/ged2html/
  Use this software to put your GEDCOM on your web page.

- Ged2Web
  http://www.oramwt.demon.co.uk/GED2WEB/ged2web.htm

- GED2WWW
  http://www.lesandchris.com/ged2www/
  Free software to convert GEDCOM files to HTML web pages. Emphasis on producing a minimal amount of HTML.

- Ged4Web GEDCOM to HTML Genealogy Webpage Software ~ Windows
  http://www.ged4web.com/
  Converts GEDCOM to HTML family sheets, pedigree charts, surnames lists and more.

- GED Browser
  http://www.misbach.org/
  Creates a pedigree chart of your entire database. Shows descendants & ancestors in one easy to view chart. Free!.

- GEDClean Home Page
  http://www.raynorshyn.com/gedclean/
  For Windows. A utility used to "clean" info about living individuals out of a GEDCOM file in order to maintain privacy.

- GEDCOM-L Mailing List
  http://www.rootsweb.com/~jfuller/gen_mail_software.html
  #GEDCOM-L
  A technical mailing list to discuss the GEDCOM specifications.

- The GEDCOM Standard Release 5.5
  http://www.tiac.net/users/pmcbride/gedcom/55gctoc.htm

- GEDCOM to HTML service on RootsWeb.com
  http://www.rootsweb.com/~nozell/gedcom-service.html
  A demo by Marc Nozell.

- GEDCOM Utilities
  http://www.rootsweb.com/~gumby/ged.html
  Includes: addnote, gedcaps, gedliving.

- GEDCOM Viewer
  http://www.northnet.com.au/~generic/gedcom/

- GedHTree
  http://www.gedhtree.com/gedhtree.htm
  A program for Windows 95/98 that processes GEDCOM files to generate ancestor tree pages, family group pages, index pages, note pages, source pages and photo links in HTML format.

- GEDitCOM Genealogy Software Home Page ~ Macintosh
  http://www.geditcom.com/
  GEDitCOM is the customizable genealogy application for Power Macintoshes. It can view and edit GECDCOM files and supports all of GEDCOM's features. GEDitCOM is free as a GEDCOM file browser and shareware to edit files as well.

- Gedpage
  http://www.frontiernet.net/~rjacob/gedpage.htm
  A program that will convert your GEDCOM file to web pages using a family group sheet format.

- GEDPrivy
  http://members.aol.com/gedprivy/index.html
  For Windows. A program to create privacy for data in genealogy files (GEDCOMs).

- The GedX GEDCOM Genealogy Site
  http://www.GedX.com/gedx/default.html
  The GEDCOM file information web site and home page for GEDCOM Explorer, a shareware program for viewing, editing, and converting GEDCOM files to handle the idiosyncrasies between various genealogical software products. A wealth of features make this the ultimate GEDCOM utility.

- GenBrowser 1.0
  http://mail.pratt.lib.md.us/~bharding/rippleeffect/GenBrowser/GenBrowser.html
  HTML2GED for downloading GEDCOM information from the Internet. Automated searching of genealogy indexes and web search engines.

- Indexed GEDCOM Method for Genweb Authoring
  http://www.rootsweb.com/~gumby/igm.html

- JavaGED Genealogical Display System
  http://www.sc3.net/JavaGEDHome.html
  A Java applet shareware program designed to display your GEDCOM file using the interactive capabilities of the Java programming language.

- Res Privata
  http://www.ozemail.com.au/~naibor/rpriv.html
  For Windows. An easy to use application for filtering private data from genealogy database (GEDCOM or GED) files. It can filter birth, death, marriage, adoption, notes, source and other details.

- RootsView
  http://home.earthlink.net/~naturalsoft/rootsview.htm
  Both a GEDCOM file viewer and a Web page generator.

- Sparrowhawk
  http://www.bradandkathy.com/genealogy/sparrowhawk.html
  A GEDCOM-to-HTML conversion program for the Macintosh.

- Stardust Family Tree Publisher 99
  http://www.sdust.com/familytree/index.htm
  Easy to use wizard guides you step-by-step through the process of transforming your GEDCOM file into a web site.

- Transforming Your GEDCOM Files Into Web Pages
  http://www.oz.net/~markhow/writing/gedcom.htm
  By Mark Howells.

- webGED: Progenitor
  http://www.mindspring.com/~giammo/webged/
  Produces a complete set of files for a self-contained, searchable WWW site from a GEDCOM file, using Java.

- Webified Genealogy - WebGen
  http://www.atticmemories.com/webgene/index.html
  GEDCOM viewer.

◆ Genealogy Software Programs

- Ancestors and Descendants¨
  http://www.AIA-AnD.com/
  For IBM-compatible PCs, regardless of operating system.

- ANCESTRA - Logiciel de généalogie
  http://ancestra.virtualave.net/
  From France, for Windows 3.1 & 95.

- Ancestral Quest
  http://www.ancquest.com/
  For Windows, downloadable demos available.

- Andata - Dataprogram fšr Släktforskare
  http://home1.swipnet.se/~w-10898/
  A Swedish genealogy software program for Windows.

- Behold - The Genealogist's Companion and Research Tool
  http://www.concentric.net/~Lkessler/behold.shtml
  Shareware for Windows 95 and 3.1.

- BirdsEye TreeView
  http://members.aol.com/btvinfo
  Software provides an overview of genealogical databases.

- Brother's Keeper Software
  http://ourworld.compuserve.com/homepages/Brothers_Keeper/
  Downloadable shareware program for Windows. The latest version contains English, French, Norwegian, Danish, Swedish, German, Dutch, Polish, Icelandic, Russian, Slovak, Afrikaans, Czech.

- Computer Programs for Drawing Plat Maps
  http://www.outfitters.com/genealogy/land/compmaps.html

- Cumberland Family Software
  http://www.cf-software.com/
  Shareware program for Windows.

- DataDux - Genealogy
  http://www.algonet.se/~datadux/
  Research in Sweden and Anarkiv Windows Genealogy software.

- DoroTree - Jewish Genealogy Software
  http://www.dorotree.com/
  A multi-language software program for Jewish genealogy with user interfaces in English, French, Spanish, Portuguese and Hebrew. The only software on the market that enables the user to enter information in both Latin and Hebrew (Yiddish) characters, without a need for Hebrew Windows. Automatic name conversion from English to Hebrew/Yiddish, advanced Hebrew calendar, Bar/Bat Mitsva calculator, built-in links to Jewish genealogy sites, printing trees in both Latin and Hebrew characters etc.

- Drake Software Genealogy Programs and Information
  http://www.tdrake.demon.co.uk/genindex.htm
  BIRDIE (British Isles Regional Display of IGI Extracts) for Windows, Buckinghamshire Posse Comitatus (1798), British Date Calculator and more.

- DYNAS-TREE ~ Win95 or NT
  http://www.dynas-tree.de/
  German or English.

- Eastman's Online Genealogy Newsletter - Genealogy Programs for the Blind
  http://www.ancestry.com/columns/eastman/east Nov23-98.htm#blind
  Brian Mumme offers side-by-side comparisons of Windows software adaptable for the visually impaired.

- EZITREE Family History Program
  http://www.ram.net.au/users/ezitree/
  DOS program from Australia.

- Family History Composer for the Macintosh
  http://home.att.net/~paulrswan/cygsoft/
  A genealogical utility, which creates a family history document in a new, elegantly designed format focused on your direct ancestors.

- The Family History System
  http://fhs.tallahassee.net/
  A set of programs for creating and maintaining files of family information, including relationships, and for printing charts and reports presenting information in those files.

- Family Matters¨ Genealogy Software - From MatterWare
  http://members.aol.com/matterware/index.html
  Shareware for Windows.

- Family Origins Genealogy Software
  http://formalsoft.com/
  For Windows.

- Family Scrapbook Genealogy Software by Chris Long
  http://www.pcug.org.au/~chowell/fsbf.htm
  For DOS.

- Family Search Online Distribution Center - Software/Databases
  http://www.ldscatalog.com/cgi-bin/ncommerce3/Category Display?cgrfnbr=1804&cgmenbr=1402&CGRY_NUM=1678 &RowStart=1&LocCode=FH

  o Personal Ancestral File® Companion 2.0 on 3.5 disk
    http://www.ldscatalog.com/cgi-bin/ncommerce3/Product Display?prrfnbr=1683&prmenbr=1402&CGRY_NUM=1804 &RowStart=1&LocCode=FH
    PAF add-on program for printing a variety of reports and charts.

  o Personal Ancestral File® Companion 2.0 on compact disc
    http://www.ldscatalog.com/cgi-bin/ncommerce3/Product Display?prrfnbr=2472&prmenbr=1402&CGRY_NUM=1804 &RowStart=1&LocCode=FH
    PAF add-on program for printing a variety of reports and charts.

- Family Search Online Distribution Center - Software Downloads - Free
  http://www.ldscatalog.com/cgi-bin/ncommerce3/Category Display?cgrfnbr=373032&cgmenbr=1402&CGRY_NUM=1678 &RowStart=1&LocCode=FH

  o PAF 4.0.4 - Personal Ancestral File® 4.0.4 ~ Windows
    http://www.ldscatalog.com/cgi-bin/ncommerce3/Product Display?prrfnbr=369179&prmenbr=1402&CGRY_NUM=373 032&RowStart=1&LocCode=FH

o Personal Ancestral File® Companion 2.1 Upgrade
http://www.ldscatalog.com/cgi-bin/ncommerce3/Product
Display?prrfnbr=369206&prmenbr=1402&CGRY_NUM=373
032&RowStart=1&LocCode=FH

o Personal Ancestral File® 3.01M Upgrade
http://www.ldscatalog.com/cgi-bin/ncommerce3/Product
Display?prrfnbr=369180&prmenbr=1402&CGRY_NUM=373
032&RowStart=1&LocCode=FH

- Family Treasures from Family Technologies
http://www.famtech.com/FamilyTres.htm
For Windows 3.1 or higher. Additional databases available that work with this program.

- Family Tree Journal
http://www.cherrytreesoftware.com/

- Family Tree Maker
http://www.familytreemaker.com
For Windows and Macintosh.

- Famtree - Easy to Use Family Tree Genealogy Software for Windows
http://www.famtree.co.uk/

- Fzip Family Tree ~ Windows
http://www.ozemail.com.au/~acroft/

- GEDitCOM Genealogy Software Home Page ~ Macintosh
http://www.geditcom.com/
GEDitCOM is the customizable genealogy application for Power Macintoshes. It can view and edit GECDCOM files and supports all of GEDCOM's features. GEDitCOM is free as a GEDCOM file browser and shareware to edit files as well.

- GenDesigner - The Graphical Family Tree Builder
http://www.gendesigner.com/

- GENEAL
http://www.geneal.com
French genealogy software for Windows 98/NT.

- Genealogia
http://volftp.mondadori.com/italiani/boscolo/genealog.htm
The first Italian software for genealogists and historians. Il primo programma italiano per studi genealogici e storici.

- The Genealogical Companion v2.2a
http://www.geocities.com/SiliconValley/2399/tgc.htm
A freeware Windows program which compliments the Family Origins¨ standard set of reports.

- Genealogy Research Organizer
http://go.to/gro
Program to store your genealogy data using a drop-line style chart. Holds source citations, too.

- Genealogy Software Guide
http://www.amazon.com/exec/obidos/ISBN-0806315814/
markcyndisgenealA/
A book by Marthe Arends.

- Généatique pour windows / Geneatique for Windows
http://www.cdip.com/
French software

- Genelines - Companion Software for Genealogy
http://www.progenysoftware.com/genelines.html
*A charting companion for Family Tree Maker 4.x * and PAF 3.0.*

- Gene Macintosh Genealogy Software
http://www.ics.uci.edu/~eppstein/gene/

- Generations Grande Suite 8.0 (from Amazon.com)
http://www.amazon.com/exec/obidos/ASIN/B000035YA7/
markcyndisgenealA/
Genealogy software by Sierra Online. Includes 15 CDs with more than 350 million names and references, 3 individual software programs, and a copy of Netting Your Ancestors.

- Generations Family Tree 8.0 Beginners Edition (from Amazon.com)
http://www.amazon.com/exec/obidos/ASIN/B00002SUFR/
markcyndisgenealA/
Genealogy software by Sierra Online.

- Generations Millennium Collection (from Amazon.com)
http://www.amazon.com/exec/obidos/ASIN/B00004KD65/
markcyndisgenealA/
Genealogy software by Sierra Online.

- Generations Family Tree 6.0 Deluxe Edition (from Amazon.com)
http://www.amazon.com/exec/obidos/ASIN/B00001N2ME/
markcyndisgenealA/
Genealogy software by Sierra Online.

- Generations - SierraHome Family Tree
http://www.sierra.com/sierrahome/familytree/
Previously Reunion for Windows.

  o Database Research Center
  http://www.sierra.com/sierrahome/familytree/records/
  Visit regularly to check out the free, monthly database.

  o Family Tree Products
  http://www.sierra.com/sierrahome/familytree/titles/

    - Generations Grande Suite 8.0
    http://www.sierra.com/sierrahome/software/catalog/
    familytree/ggs8/

    - Generations Beginners Edition 8.0
    http://www.sierra.com/sierrahome/software/catalog/
    familytree/gbegin/

    - Generations Millennium Collection
    http://www.sierra.com/sierrahome/software/catalog/
    familytree/gen2000/

    - Generations Heritage Edition
    http://www.sierra.com/sierrahome/software/catalog/
    familytree/heritage/

    - Generations Easy Family Tree
    http://www.sierra.com/sierrahome/familytree/titles/eft/

  o Genealogist's Corner
  http://www.sierra.com/sierrahome/familytree/gencorner/

  o Generations Tips & Tricks
  http://www.sierra.com/sierrahome/familytree/prodsupport/
  tips/
  By Mike Hobart, an avid genealogist and Generations user.

o Insider's Guide
http://www.sierra.com/sierrahome/familytree/gencorner/guide/
Expert tips from Generations guru Mike Hobart.

o Product Comparison Chart
http://www.sierra.com/sierrahome/familytree/titles/compare/

o Resources for Generations Users
http://www.sierra.com/sierrahome/familytree/prodsupport/resources/

o Sierra Home - Family Tree Message Boards
http://forums.sierra.com/forums/familytreetopic/
From the makers of the best-selling Generations genealogy software program.

● GeneWeb ~ Unix and Windows 95/98/NT
http://pauillac.inria.fr/~ddr/GeneWeb/
In French, Dutch, Swedish and English versions.

● Genius Family Tree ~ Windows
http://www.gensol.com.au/
"The easy genealogy program".

● GenMVD - A Genealogical Browser for the Psion 3a, 3c, 3mx and Siena
http://www-theory.dcs.st-and.ac.uk/~mnd/export/genmvd/

● GensData voor Windows
http://web.inter.nl.net/hcc/F.Berkhof/gd-win.htm
Dutch genealogy program for Windows 3.1 or Windows 95.

● GENTREE 99
http://perso.wanadoo.fr/gentree/
Genealogy shareware for Windows9x. French, English, German, Italian, Catalan versions.

● Getting the Most Out of Family Origins
http://www.amazon.com/exec/obidos/ISBN=0966171322/markcyndisgenealA/
A book by Getting the Most Out of Family Origins.

● GIM Home Page - Genealogical Information Manager
http://www.mindspring.com/~dblaine/gimhome.html
Shareware for DOS.

● Grenham's Irish Recordfinder
http://indigo.ie/~rfinder/
A software system designed to help you determine relevant resources for your specific Irish genealogical research.

● Haza-Data Website
http://www.hazadata.com
Dutch genealogy software program. Also versions in English, German, Swedish, Norwegian, Polish.

● Heredis
http://www.heredis.com/
French genealogy software program for Macintosh or Windows.

● Heritage Genealogy Software
http://www.eskimo.com/~grandine/heritage.html
Ver. 3.01 for Mac.

● ILANOT -Software for Jewish Genealogy
http://www.bh.org.il/Genealogy/index.htm#ilanot

● Kin Ware Family History Software for Windows 95 and NT
http://www.kinware.com/
Family Explorer.

● Legacy Family Tree ~ Windows
http://www.legacyfamilytree.com/

● LifeLines - Genealogy Software for UNIX
http://www.genealogy.org/~ttw/lines/lines.html

● LifeLines - Genealogy Software for UNIX
http://www1.shore.net/~ttw/lines/lines.html
Alternate site.

● LifeLines - Genealogy Software
http://www.bartonstreet.com/software/lines/
For Unix. Alternate site.

● The Master Genealogist
http://www.WhollyGenes.com/
For Windows or DOS.

● My Family History
http://www.ozemail.com.au/~pkortge/MFH.html
For Windows WFW & Windows 95, from Australia.

● Oedipus II Voor Windows
http://web.inter.nl.net/hcc/L.G.Lamain/odp95.htm
Only in Dutch.

● PAF 4.0 User's Guide
http://help.surnameweb.org/genprograms/paf40.htm
From the SurnameWeb site.

● PAF Help-Guide
http://www.HeritageQuest.com/genealogy/books/html/paf.html
Book for sale from Heritage Quest.

● Parents 4.6 Genealogy Software for Windows
http://ourworld.compuserve.com/homepages/NickleWare/

● Parsons Technology Creative Studio
http://www.parsonstech.com/genealogy/index.html
Windows software: Family Origins, Family Atlas & Family Images Software.

● Pedigree Family History System
http://ourworld.compuserve.com/homepages/pedigree software/
For MSDOS and also runs under Windows. A full Windows 3.1 and Win95 version is expected in Spring 1999.

● Prima's Official Companion to Family Tree Maker Version 5
http://www.amazon.com/exec/obidos/ISBN=0761516778/markcyndisgenealA/
A book by Myra Vanderpool Gormley, C.G.

● PRO-GEN Genealogie à la Carte
http://www.pro-gen.nl/
Dutch genealogy program capable of outputs in Dutch, English, French, Frisian and German.

● Quinsept's Family Roots "Orphans"
http://www.ogram.org/familyroots/index.shtml
Information page for users of the Family Roots program by Quinsept, a company that closed in August 1997.

- Relations 2.3
  http://members.home.net/msdsoft/relations2.html
  A genealogy shareware program for Newton devices.

- Relatively Yours
  http://www.relativelyyours.com
  Genealogy software package for Windows 95/98 with trial download and selective list of web mapping sites.

- Reunion Home Page
  http://www.leisterpro.com/
  Software for Macintosh.

- SpanSoft Genealogy Software
  http://ourworld.compuserve.com/homepages/SpanSoft/
  "Kith and Kin" - shareware for Windows 3.1 and "TreeDraw" for Windows.

- Stammbaum 4.0 in Stichworten
  http://www3.pair.com/hblanken/stb.htm
  From Germany, for Windows.

- Stephen Archer's Genealogical Software Home Page
  http://ourworld.compuserve.com/homepages/steve_archer/
  IGIREAD, a file conversion utility (DOS) for the IGI on CD-ROM and GenMap UK, a Windows mapping program designed mainly for UK genealogical and historical mapping.

- Visual Généalogie
  http://visugene.free.fr/
  French genealogy software program for Windows.

- WinFamily - Anvend Winfamily fra Jamodat til din slektsgransking
  http://www.winfamily.com/
  Genealogy software available in Danish, Swedish, Norwegian, French, German and English.

- WinGenea
  http://freespace.virgin.net/dave.risley/index.htm
  WinGenea is a Windows shareware program that enables you to draw standard English dropline chart. Allows details of family and individuals to be stored; dates, places, photos, etc. Individuals can be moved on the chart using drag and drop.

- Winkwast en Genkwa ~ Netherlands
  http://home-1.worldonline.nl/~ac10561/programma/
  downloads.html

◆ Genealogy Tools & Utilities

- Aspen 2000 Windows (Cemetery, Funeral Home & Obituary Records
  http://www.dhc.net/~design/aspen.htm
  For indexing, publishing or storing these all important records. Complete publishing features including .rtf, .doc and more. Picture or image attachments are also a feature of this genealogy package.

- Brian Harneys WebPages, Software Corner
  http://members.aol.com/bdharney2/software.htm
  2 GEDCOM programs including R3GED2FT which aids in transferring Roots III data to Family Tree Maker for Windows.

- Bygones Home Page: Genealogical Research Note-Keeping System ~ Windows and Macintosh
  http://home.utah-inter.net/bygones/index.htm
  A freeware software program designed primarily to keep genealogical research notes on a laptop computer. However, it also has databases that genealogists without laptops may find useful.

- Clooz
  http://www.clooz.com/
  An electronic filing cabinet and database for systematically storing all of the clues to your ancestry that you have been collecting. Requires Microsoft Windows 95. Clooz contains templates for all U.S. federal censuses, 1841-1891 U.K. censuses, 1852-1901 Canadian censuses, and 1901 and 1911 Irish censuses, as well as generic templates for censuses not included, such as state censuses.

  - Clooz Mailing List
    http://www.rootsweb.com/~jfuller/gen_mail_software.html
    #Clooz
    For users of the Clooz genealogy utility software program.

  - Clooz Newsletter
    http://www.clooz.com/issues.htm
    Newsletter for users of the software program Clooz--the electronic filing cabinet for genealogical records. Also available by e-mail subscription; to subscribe, send an empty message to clooz-subscribe@makelist.com.

- Custodian II for Family Historians
  http://members.aol.com/pandssmith/Custodian.htm
  Custodian is not a family tree program, but a series of databases with pre-defined forms, specially designed to store genealogical information. Includes more than 80 data entry forms for most UK sources.

- Cyrillic 3
  http://www.cyrillicsoftware.com/
  Pedigree drawing software for genetic research. For Windows.

- DAYS Calendar Program For Genealogists
  http://octhygesen.homepage.dk/
  Designed to assist genealogists in finding dates of named days and generally navigate in and between the Julian and Gregorian calendars. The original program was in Danish and intended for Danish/Norwegian genealogists.

- Deed Mapper Software
  http://www.ultranet.com/~deeds/
  For IBM PC compatibles running DOS 3.3 or higher.

- DOS/Windows Pedigree Drawing Programs
  http://www.sfbr.org/sfbr/public/software/pedraw/
  dos_peddrw.html
  Contact information for pedigree drawing software programs used for genetic research.

- Family History System
  http://fhs.tallahassee.net/
  Family History System, a set of programs for creating and maintaining files of family information, including relationships, and for printing charts and reports presenting information in those files.

- FixSex 1.0
  http://mail.pratt.lib.md.us/~bharding/rippleeffect/FixSex/Fix
  Sex.html
  A utility to help you fix the sex codes in a GEDCOM file.

- GEN-BOOK Home Page
  http://www.foothill.net/~genbook/
  GENerate a GENealogy BOOK from GEDCOM / PAF2.31 / PAF3.0 to WordPerfect or MS Word.

- GENBOX Version 2.02 for DOS
  http://www.thoughtfulcreations.com/genbox/
  Genealogy box charts.

- The Genealogy Timeline
  http://pweb.netcom.com/~mpparker/index.html
  Genealogical-Historical Timeline and Research Organizer. Software that merges historical events and personal events of ancestors.

- Genie Helper Soundex Code Conversion Software for PC
  http://www.geocities.com/wcraigjnb/index.html

- GenIndex Main Page
  http://www.staubassociates.com/genindex/genindex.htm
  Windows software for creating "everyname" or "back of the book" indexes.

- GenRef On the Web - Data Tools and Services (DTS)
  http://www.itsnet.com/home/genref/
  Vital Records Assistant (Windows).

- IXM, Software for creating "Back of the Book Indexes"
  http://members.aol.com/bdharney2/ixm/bh6.htm

- KINWRITE Plus
  http://www2.dtc.net/~ldbond/
  Converts a PAF file into a book.

- PAF Bookmaker
  http://www.geocities.com/bluebunnysoftware/
  PAF Bookmaker turns your PAF 3.x and 4.x files into a book, complete with chapters, footnotes, and an index. Very easy to use, and lots of configuration options to get the output you want.

- Pedigree/Draw
  http://www.sfbr.org/sfbr/public/software/pedraw/peddrw.html
  Pedigree drawing software for genetic research. Macintosh only.

- Progeny Software - Companion Software for Quality Charts and Reports
  http://www.progenysoftware.com/
  *Download demos of PAF*Mate and GED*Mate.*

- SKY Software
  http://www.sky-software.com/
  End of book indexing software.

◆ Genealogy Web Page/Site Generators

See also: Privacy Issues below.
See also: Cyndi's Genealogy Home Page Construction Kit
http://www.CyndisList.com/construc.htm

- Ancestral Quest
  http://www.ancquest.com/
  For Windows, downloadable demos available.

- Familia - Web Publishing of Family Tree and Photo Album
  http://www.dralex.com/
  Free genealogical software for creating web site with family photo album and family tree; supports group pictures.

- Family Origins
  http://formalsoft.com/

- Family Tree Maker
  http://www.familytreemaker.com/

- Free HTML Pedigree Chart & Family Group Sheet - from Elaine Johnson
  http://www.ida.net/users/elaine/pedigre2.HTM

- GED2HTML: A GEDCOM to HTML Translator
  http://www.gendex.com/ged2html/
  Use this software to put your GEDCOM on your web page.

- Ged2Web
  http://www.oramwt.demon.co.uk/GED2WEB/ged2web.htm

- GED2WWW
  http://www.lesandchris.com/ged2www/
  Free software to convert GEDCOM files to HTML web pages. Emphasis on producing a minimal amount of HTML.

- Ged4Web GEDCOM to HTML Genealogy Webpage Software ~ Windows
  http://www.ged4web.com/
  Converts GEDCOM to HTML family sheets, pedigree charts, surnames lists and more.

- GEDCOM to HTML service on RootsWeb.com
  http://www.rootsweb.com/~nozell/gedcom-service.html
  A demo by Marc Nozell.

- GedHTree
  http://www.gedhtree.com/gedhtree.htm
  A program for Windows 95/98 that processes GEDCOM files to generate ancestor tree pages, family group pages, index pages, note pages, source pages and photo links in HTML format.

- Gedpage
  http://www.frontiernet.net/~rjacob/gedpage.htm
  A program that will convert your GEDCOM file to web pages using a family group sheet format.

- GenBrowser
  http://mail.pratt.lib.md.us/~bharding/rippleeffect/GenBrowser/GenBrowser.html
  HTML2GED for downloading GEDCOM information from the Internet. Automated searching of genealogy indexes and web search engines.

- Genealogy Site Builder
  http://www.bargeron.com/software/gsb/index.htm
  Creates web (HTML) pages from your GEDCOM file. This program creates the standard Family Group Sheet format with marriage and burial records. Formats facts, sources and notes in a manner to facilitate printing.

- Generations Grande Suite 6.0
  http://www.sierra.com/sierrahome/familytree/titles/gengs/

- GeneWeb ~ Unix and Windows 95/98/NT
  http://pauillac.inria.fr/~ddr/GeneWeb/
  In French, Dutch, Swedish and English versions.

- Indexed GEDCOM Method for Genweb Authoring
  http://www.rootsweb.com/~gumby/igm.html

- JavaGED Genealogical Display System
  http://www.sc3.net/JavaGEDHome.html
  A Java applet shareware program designed to display your GEDCOM file using the interactive capabilities of the Java programming language.

- Kinship Archivist
  http://www.kinshiparchivist.com/
  Shareware program that will create web pages.

- Legacy Family Tree ~ Windows
  http://www.legacyfamilytree.com/

- The Master Genealogist
  http://www.WhollyGenes.com/

- Misbach.org - GED Browser
  http://www.misbach.org/gedbrowser/index.html

- PAF 4.0.4 - Personal Ancestral File® 4.0.4 ~ Windows
  http://www.ldscatalog.com/cgi-bin/ncommerce3/Product Display?prrfnbr=369179&prmenbr=1402&CGRY_NUM=373032&RowStart=1&LocCode=FH

- "Relatives" Genealogical Software
  http://mypage.direct.ca/v/vdouglas/RelIntro.html
  Completely graphical software to chart your family tree and publish it on the Internet.

- Reunion 5 for Macintosh
  http://www.leisterpro.com/

- RootsView
  http://home.earthlink.net/~naturalsoft/rootsview.htm
  Both a GEDCOM file viewer and a Web page generator.

- Sparrowhawk
  http://www.bradandkathy.com/genealogy/sparrowhawk.html
  A GEDCOM-to-HTML conversion program for the Macintosh.

- Stardust Family Tree Publisher 99
  http://www.sdust.com/familytree/index.htm
  Easy to use wizard guides you step-by-step through the process of transforming your GEDCOM file into a web site.

- Transforming Your GEDCOM Files Into Web Pages
  http://www.oz.net/~markhow/writing/gedcom.htm
  By Mark Howells.

- uFTi 1.5 for Windows 95 and NT
  http://www.ufti.demon.co.uk/homepage.htm
  For creating HTML web pages.

- Ultimate Family Tree
  http://www.uftree.com/
  From Palladium Interactive.

- webGED: Progenitor
  http://www.mindspring.com/~giammo/webged/

Produces a complete set of files for a self-contained, searchable WWW site from a GEDCOM file, using Java.

◆ Handhelds, Palmtops and PDAs

Definitions from NetLingo:
http://www.netlingo.com/
Palm Pilot
http://www.netlingo.com/lookup.cfm?term=Palm%20Pilot
PDA (Personal Digital Assistant)
http://www.netlingo.com/lookup.cfm?term=PDA

- The Cemetery Column - A Tombstone in Your Palm
  http://www.interment.net/column/records/palmpilot/index.htm
  An article by Steve Paul Johnson about using your Palm Pilot to record tombstone details in a database.

- GedPalm - Genealogy Browser for Your Palm Pilot
  http://www.ghcssoftware.com/
  Shareware for the Palm Pilot operating system, which allows the user to download GEDCOMs into the Palm Pilot for viewing. Does not support data entry - the product is designed as a "viewer" only.

- GenPalm Mailing List
  http://www.rootsweb.com/~jfuller/gen_mail_software.html#GenPalm
  For the discussion and sharing of information regarding the use of genealogical software for Handheld or Palm devices.

- My Roots
  http://sites.netscape.net/tapperware/MyRoots/
  Shareware for the Palm Pilot operating system. Supports importing GEDCOMs into your Palm Pilot, note taking, and exporting new GEDCOMs back to your PC.

- MyRoots Mailing List
  http://www.rootsweb.com/~jfuller/gen_mail_software.html#myroots
  For the discussion and sharing of information regarding the "My Roots" genealogy software program for the Palm Computing Platform.

- PalmGear H.Q. Software Search Results - Genealogy Software
  http://www.palmgear.com/software/answer.cfm?sid=20832220000519091513&quicksearch2=genealogy

- PalmGear H.Q. Software Search Results - Soundex Converters
  http://www.palmgear.com/software/answer.cfm?sid=20832220000519091513&quicksearch2=soundex

- PALM-GEN Mailing List
  http://www.rootsweb.com/~jfuller/gen_mail_software.html#PALM-GEN
  For the discussion and sharing of information regarding the use of Palm PDA's in genealogical research.

- Palmtop Genealogy (Gen/PT)
  http://www.world4you.com/genealogy/palmtop/
  About using palmtop computers using Windows CE.

- Palm Tree
  http://www.southernx.com.au/palmtree.html
  A small family history program designed to run on handheld devices powered by the Palm Operating System.

- Pocket Family Researcher
  http://www.dwalker.demon.co.uk/pocketfamilyresearcher.htm
  Pocket Family Researcher is a Microsoft Windows CE program for viewing and editing standard GEDCOM files.

- Pocket Pedigree
  http://members.tripod.com/%7Epbhanney/pocket_ pedigree.html
  A beta version of a genealogy program for the Windows CE operating system for Handheld PCs.

- Relations 2.3
  http://members.home.net/msdsoft/relations2.html
  A genealogy shareware program for Newton devices.

- Trev's Home Page - Genealogy - Freeware for the Palm Pilot
  http://members.aol.com/TJLivett/#PRC
  Available for free download, this program is designed to use quick fill in forms that cover Births, Deaths and Marriages. There is a user defined popup list for easy viewing from the main screen, and built in help page.

◆ Macintosh Resources

- Family History Composer for the Macintosh
  http://home.att.net/~paulrswan/cygsoft/
  A genealogical utility which creates a family history document in a new, elegantly designed format focused on your direct ancestors.

- Family Tree Maker
  http://www.familytreemaker.com/macinfo.html

- GEDitCOM Genealogy Software Home Page ~ Macintosh
  http://www.geditcom.com/
  GEDitCOM is the customizable genealogy application for Power Macintoshes. It can view and edit GECDCOM files and supports all of GEDCOM's features. GEDitCOM is free as a GEDCOM file browser and shareware to edit files as well.

- GeneDraw
  http://www.inviweb.com/genedraw/
  A family-tree software with a graphic interface particularly useful for the drawing of family-trees or gene maps. MacOS version available.

- Gene Macintosh Genealogy Software
  http://www.ics.uci.edu/~eppstein/gene/

- Heredis
  http://www.heredis.com/
  French genealogy software program for Macintosh or Windows.

- Heritage Genealogy Software
  http://www.eskimo.com/~grandine/heritage.html
  Ver. 3.01 for Mac.

- Macintosh Genealogy Software FAQ
  http://members.home.net/gsteiner1/macgsfaq/

- Nexial Systems - MacPAF Report Utility (MPRU)
  http://members.aol.com/nexialist/

- Pedigree/Draw
  http://www.sfbr.org/sfbr/public/software/pedraw/peddrw.html
  Pedigree drawing software for genetic research. Macintosh only.

- Resources for Macintosh Users
  http://www.rootsweb.com/~mac/

- Reunion Home Page
  http://www.leisterpro.com/

- ReunionTalk Mailing List
  http://www.leisterpro.com/doc/RT/RT.html

- Reviews of Genealogical Macintosh Software
  http://utopia.knoware.nl/users/evim/software.html

- Sparrowhawk
  http://www.bradandkathy.com/genealogy/sparrowhawk.html
  A GEDCOM-to-HTML conversion program for the Macintosh.

- Your Roots are Showing
  http://macworld.zdnet.com/1995/06/opinion/899.html
  Mac genealogy software review.

◆ Mailing Lists, Newsgroups & Chat

- Genealogy Resources on the Internet - Computing/Internet Resources Mailing Lists
  http://www.rootsweb.com/~jfuller/gen_mail_computing.html

- Genealogy Resources on the Internet - Software Mailing Lists
  http://www.rootsweb.com/~jfuller/gen_mail_software.html
  Most of the mailing list links below point to this site, wonderfully maintained by John Fuller

- AGLL Genealogical Services Mailing List
  http://www.rootsweb.com/~jfuller/gen_mail_software.html #AGLL
  For announcements of new genealogical products and sales promotions from AGLL.

- Ancestral Quest Mailing List
  http://www.rootsweb.com/~jfuller/gen_mail_software.html #Ancestral-quest

- AZ-AGCIG Mailing List
  http://www.rootsweb.com/~jfuller/gen_mail_states-az.html #AZ-AGCIG
  For the discussion and sharing of information regarding the activities of the Arizona Genealogical Computer Interest Group.

- BARUG Mailing List
  http://www.rootsweb.com/~jfuller/gen_mail_software.html #BARUG
  Sponsored by the Bay Area (San Francisco) Roots Users Group to share information about the Ultimate Family Tree genealogy software program and related topics.

- BBANNOUNCE-L Mailing List
  http://www.rootsweb.com/~jfuller/gen_mail_software.html #BBANNOUNCE-L
  Maintained by the Banner Blue Division of Broderbund Software for product announcements (10-15 postings a year).

- BK5forum Mailing List
  http://www.rootsweb.com/~jfuller/gen_mail_software.html #BK5forum
  For the discussion of the Brother's Keeper genealogy program. The list is for the Scandinavian countries so please note that the language for this list is Norwegian, Danish and Swedish.

- BK Mailing List
  http://www.rootsweb.com/~jfuller/gen_mail_software.html
  #BK-L
  For the discussion of the Brother's Keeper genealogy program.

- BYGONES-USERS Mailing List
  http://www.rootsweb.com/~jfuller/gen_mail_software.html
  #BYGONES-USERS
  For anyone who is using the Bygones freeware genealogical notekeeping program for laptops to discuss program functions, operation, and problems.

- CA-CVGS-CIG Mailing List
  http://www.rootsweb.com/~jfuller/gen_mail_states-ca.html
  #CA-CVGS-CIG
  For the discussion and sharing of information about the ways to use computers as an aid for researching and recording data about the ancestors and descendents of members of the Conejo Valley Genealogical Society.

- CFT-WIN Mailing List
  http://www.rootsweb.com/~jfuller/gen_mail_software.html
  #CFT-WIN
  Discussion and support for Cumberland Family Software products.

- Clooz Mailing List
  http://www.rootsweb.com/~jfuller/gen_mail_software.html
  #Clooz
  For users of the Clooz genealogy utility software program.

- CPAFUG Mailing List
  http://www.rootsweb.com/~jfuller/gen_mail_computing.html
  #CPAFUG
  Restricted to the members of the Capital PAF Users Group (Washington, DC metro area), to discuss all aspects of genealogical computing techniques.

- CUSTODIAN Mailing List
  http://www.rootsweb.com/~jfuller/gen_mail_software.html
  #CUSTODIAN
  For the discussion and sharing of information regarding the Custodian genealogy software program.

- CyndisList Mailing List
  http://www.rootsweb.com/~jfuller/gen_mail_computing.html
  #CyndisList
  A read-only list to provide users of the Cyndi's List web site with daily site updates, number of new/updated links, names of updated categories, answers to frequently asked questions, and descriptions of new features or improvements.

- FAMILIE_OG_SLEKT Mailing List
  http://www.rootsweb.com/~jfuller/gen_mail_software.html
  #FAMILIE_OG_SLEKT
  For discussions of the "Familie og Slekt" Norwegian genealogy software program.

- FAMILY-ORIGINS-USERS Mailing List
  http://www.rootsweb.com/~jfuller/gen_mail_software.html
  #FAMILY-ORIGINS-USERS

- FAMILYROOTS Mailing List
  http://www.rootsweb.com/~jfuller/gen_mail_software.html
  #FAMILYROOTS

- And the Quinsept's Family Roots "Orphans" Web Page
  http://www.ogram.org/familyroots/familyroots-list.shtml
  For DOS and Macintosh users of Quinsept's Family Roots genealogy software who were "orphaned" when Steve Vorenberg closed the Quinsept company in August 1997.

- FAMILYSEARCH Mailing List
  http://www.rootsweb.com/~jfuller/gen_mail_computing.html
  #FAMILYSEARCH
  Designed to assist anyone with questions regarding use of the Internet for searching Family History. The Familysearch internet site and others are discussed for genealogical research such as searching, downloading, contributing, cross-referencing and microfilm numbers, and basic "getting started" questions are also discussed and welcomed.

- FAMILY-TREASURES Mailing List
  http://www.rootsweb.com/~jfuller/gen_mail_software.html
  #FAMILY-TREASURES
  For anyone using the Family Treasures genealogy software program.

- FO-etc Mailing List
  http://www.rootsweb.com/~jfuller/gen_mail_software.html
  #FO-etc
  For Family Origins software users to exchange ideas and discuss their assorted genealogy projects. Expands beyond software-specific questions and issues to include assorted topics as they are associated with users' various projects and/or methodologies.

- fr.comp.applications.genealogie Newsgroup
  news:fr.comp.applications.genealogie
  Gatewayed with the GEN-FF-LOG mailing list for the discussion of genealogy software used by French genealogists.

- FT2TMG Mailing List
  http://www.rootsweb.com/~jfuller/gen_mail_software.html
  #FR2TMG
  For those who have questions and comments relating to importing (DOS) Family Roots (FR) data into The Master Genealogist (TMG) (Windows).

- FTMTECH-L Mailing List
  http://www.rootsweb.com/~jfuller/gen_mail_software.html
  #FTMTECH-L
  Maintained by the Banner Blue Division of Broderbund Software for the discussion of technical issues regarding the Family Tree Maker genealogy program.

- GEDCOM-L Mailing List
  http://www.rootsweb.com/~jfuller/gen_mail_software.html
  #GEDCOM-L
  A technical mailing list to discuss the GEDCOM specifications.

- GENCMP Mailing List
  http://www.rootsweb.com/~jfuller/gen_mail_computing.html
  #GENCMP-L
  Gatewayed with the soc.genealogy.computing newsgroup for the discussion of genealogical computing and net resources.

- Generations Mailing List
  http://www.sierra.com/sierrahome/familytree/community/discussion/

- Generations-update Mailing List
  http://www.rootsweb.com/~jfuller/gen_mail_software.html
  #Generations-update
  The Generations Family Heritage Update list is a read-only list that provides a monthly update about the Generations genealogy product line, the Generations team, family heritage, and happenings in the genealogy community.

- GEN-FF-LOG Mailing List
  http://www.rootsweb.com/~jfuller/gen_mail_software.html
  #GEN-FF-LOG
  Gatewayed with the fr.comp.applications.genealogie newsgroup, for the discussion of genealogy software used by French genealogists.

- GEN-IRC Mailing List
  http://www.rootsweb.com/~jfuller/gen_mail_computing.html
  #GEN-IRC
  For anyone who has an interest in genealogy and is using or would like to use Internet Relay Chat (IRC) to communicate with other genealogists.

- GEN-MAT-REQUEST Mailing List
  http://www.rootsweb.com/~jfuller/gen_mail_material.html
  #GEN-MAT
  For anyone who has an interest in the buying or selling of new or used genealogical materials (e.g., books, newsletters, CDs, magazines).

- GEN-MAT-15-REQUEST Mailing List
  http://www.rootsweb.com/~jfuller/gen_mail_material.html
  #GEN-MAT-15
  For anyone who desires to post the availability of new or used genealogical materials (e.g., books, newsletters, CDs, magazines) or services for sale at a price of $15 or less.

- GenPalm Mailing List
  http://www.rootsweb.com/~jfuller/gen_mail_software.html
  #GenPalm
  For the discussion and sharing of information regarding the use of genealogical software for Handheld or Palm devices.

- GEN-SITE-SWAP Mailing List
  http://www.rootsweb.com/~jfuller/gen_mail_computing.html
  #GEN-SITE-SWAP
  For the swapping of good genealogy URLs.

- GENSOFT Mailing List
  http://www.rootsweb.com/~jfuller/gen_mail_software.html
  #GENSOFT
  For anyone interested in genealogy software (e.g., users, developers, technical support personnel), to discuss any genealogy-related product including specific genealogy applications, general applications adapted to genealogy (e.g., word-processing templates for reports), and applicable database programs. Topics include how to get programs to work, what programs to buy, where particular features can be found, and product information about new releases.

- GEN-WEB-DESIGN Mailing List
  http://www.rootsweb.com/~jfuller/gen_mail_computing.html
  #GEN-WEB-DESIGN
  For the discussion and sharing of information regarding the design of genealogy web pages and associated databases.

- HTMLHELP Mailing List
  http://www.rootsweb.com/~jfuller/gen_mail_computing.html
  #HTMLHELP
  For helping genealogists who would like to place their web pages on the internet.

- Internet_Genealogy Mailing List
  http://www.rootsweb.com/~jfuller/gen_mail_computing.html
  #Internet_Genealogy
  For students of Marthe Arends' Practical Internet Genealogy series of courses at Virtual University.

- Legacy Mailing List
  http://www.rootsweb.com/~jfuller/gen_mail_software.html
  #LEGACY
  For the discussion and sharing of information regarding the Legacy Family Tree genealogy software program.

- LegacyNews Mailing List
  http://www.rootsweb.com/~jfuller/gen_mail_software.html
  #LegacyNews
  A read-only mailing list maintained by Millennia Corporation for announcements of interest to users of the Legacy Family Tree genealogy software program.

- LegacyUserGroup Mailing List
  http://www.rootsweb.com/~jfuller/gen_mail_software.html
  #LegacyUserGroup
  For users of the Legacy Family Tree genealogy software program to share ideas with other Legacy users.

- LINES-L Mailing List
  http://www.rootsweb.com/~jfuller/gen_mail_software.html
  #LINES-L
  Serves as a vehicle for topics related to the enhancement of "LifeLines Genealogical Database and Report Generator" (an experimental, second-generation genealogical system).

- MyRoots Mailing List
  http://www.rootsweb.com/~jfuller/gen_mail_software.html
  #myroots
  A mailing list for the discussion and sharing of information regarding the "My Roots" genealogy software program for the Palm Computing Platform.

- NEW-GENLIST Mailing List
  http://www.rootsweb.com/~jfuller/gen_mail_computing.html
  #NEW-GENLIST
  For announcing new genealogy mailing lists.

- NEW-GEN-URL Mailing List
  http://www.rootsweb.com/~jfuller/gen_mail_computing.html
  #NEW-GEN-URL
  For the posting of information on genealogy-related web sites in order to save researchers time in locating new web sites and determining the location of significant web resources.

- PAF Mailing List
  http://www.rootsweb.com/~jfuller/gen_mail_software.html
  #PAF
  For discussion and help regarding the use of all versions of the Personal Ancestral File genealogy program.

- PAF-2.31-USERS Mailing List
  http://www.rootsweb.com/~jfuller/gen_mail_software.html
  #PAF-2.31-USERS

- PAF-3-USERS Mailing List
  http://www.rootsweb.com/~jfuller/gen_mail_software.html
  #PAF-3-USERS

- PAF-4-USERS Mailing List
  http://www.rootsweb.com/~jfuller/gen_mail_software.html
  #PAF-4-USERS

- PAF-TEMPLES Mailing List
  http://www.rootsweb.com/~jfuller/gen_mail_software.html
  #PAF-TEMPLES
  For the discussion and sharing of information regarding the Personal Ancestral File (PAF) genealogy program. Postings may also include related topics on Temple work in the Latter-Day Saints Church.

- PALM-GEN Mailing List
  http://www.rootsweb.com/~jfuller/gen_mail_software.html
  #PALM-GEN
  For the discussion and sharing of information regarding the use of Palm PDA's in genealogical research.

- ReunionTalk Mailing List
  http://www.leisterpro.com/doc/RT/RT.html

- TMG-L Mailing List
  http://www.rootsweb.com/~jfuller/gen_mail_software.html
  #TMG-L
  For those interested in The Master Genealogist software program.

- TMG-NORTHTX-USERS Mailing List
  http://www.rootsweb.com/~jfuller/gen_mail_software.html
  #TMG-NORTHTX-USERS
  For the discussion and sharing of information regarding The Master Genealogist (TMG) software program that has been presented at the North Texas TMG Users Group Meeting.

- TMG-PAZ Mailing List
  http://www.rootsweb.com/~jfuller/gen_mail_software.html
  #TMG-PAZ
  For the members of the Sun Country (Phoenix, Arizona) TMG Users Group to discuss all aspects of The Master Genealogist genealogy software program.

- UFT Mailing List
  http://www.rootsweb.com/~jfuller/gen_mail_software.html
  #UFT
  For the exchange of ideas, tips, and suggestions for using Palladium genealogy software including Ultimate Family Tree.

- Usenet Newsgroup soc.genealogy.computing
  news:soc.genealogy.computing
  Genealogical computing & net resources. Gatewayed with the GENCMP-L mailing list.
  http://www.rootsweb.com/~jfuller/gen_mail_general.html#GENCMP-L

- UT-PAF-NOTICES Mailing List
  http://www.rootsweb.com/~jfuller/gen_mail_software.html
  #UT-PAF-NOTICES
  A read-only mailing list, sponsored by the Utah Valley PAF Users Group, for notifications of meetings and other items of Group interest.

- WEB-NEWBIE Mailing List
  http://www.rootsweb.com/~jfuller/gen_mail_computing.html
  #WEB-NEWBIE
  For beginners who have questions on the Internet, Internet methods, genealogy on the Internet, and how to build a web page.

- Y2K Mailing List
  http://www.rootsweb.com/~jfuller/gen_mail_general.html#Y2K
  For the discussion of Year 2000 issues as they relate to genealogy.

◆ Miscellaneous Software

- About Achievement of Arms (tm)
  http://members.aol.com/grammarman/grammarstuff/about achieve.html
  Software for designing shields, crests, etc.

- Blazon and Blazon95 Software
  http://www.platypus.clara.co.uk/blazon.htm

- Family Photo Album for Windows
  http://www.cf-software.com/fpa.htm

- Family Reunion Organizer ~ Windows 95/98/NT
  http://family-reunion.com/organizer/
  Planning software from Family-Reunion.com.

- Genealogy Clip Art
  http://www.wf.net/~jyates/genart.html

- Heraldry Software
  http://digiserve.com/heraldry/hersoft.htm

- Life.com - My Life Software
  http://www.life.com/
  Personal history software that lets you tell your life's story in text, family photos, audio and video.

- My Life
  http://www.amazon.com/exec/obidos/ISBN=B00003OPEC/ markcyndisgenealA/
  Software by Life.com.

- MyStory - The Complete Autobiography Writing System!
  http://www.mystorywriter.com/

- Universal Calendar Calculator
  http://www.cf-software.com/ucc.htm
  The Universal Calendar Calculator can display and convert between 10 different calendars: Julian Day Number, Gregorian (New Style), Julian (Old Style), Roman-Julian, French Revolution, Hebrew, Islamic, Chinese, Chinese/Gregorian, and Thai Suriyakati Calendar. The Universal Calendar Calculator also contains: * Dates of holidays for the United States, Christian (Nicean Rule and Modern), Islamic, Jewish, and Chinese. * Regional date of conversion from the Old Style (Julian) to the New Style (Gregorian) for more than 100 localities. * Almost 100 Medieval European Regional Day Name Calendars. These calendars allow you to easily identify the specific Julian Calendar day of many Latin day names given in Medieval documents.

- Walden Font
  http://www.waldenfont.com/
  Several different fonts for sale, including: The Gutenberg Press German Fraktur Fonts, The Civil War Press, Old State House, German Script, US Presidents.

◆ PAF ~ Personal Ancestral File

- Family Search Online Distribution Center - Software/Databases
  http://www.ldscatalog.com/cgi-bin/ncommerce3/Category Display?cgrfnbr=1804&cgmenbr=1402&CGRY_NUM=1678 &RowStart=1&LocCode=FH

o Personal Ancestral File® Companion 2.0 on 3.5 disk
http://www.ldscatalog.com/cgi-bin/ncommerce3/Product
Display?prrfnbr=1683&prmenbr=1402&CGRY_NUM=1804
&RowStart=1&LocCode=FH
PAF add-on program for printing a variety of reports and charts.

o Personal Ancestral File® Companion 2.0 on compact disc
http://www.ldscatalog.com/cgi-bin/ncommerce3/Product
Display?prrfnbr=2472&prmenbr=1402&CGRY_NUM=1804
&RowStart=1&LocCode=FH
PAF add-on program for printing a variety of reports and charts.

• Family Search Online Distribution Center - Software Downloads - Free
http://www.ldscatalog.com/cgi-bin/ncommerce3/Category
Display?cgrfnbr=373032&cgmenbr=1402&CGRY_NUM=1678
&RowStart=1&LocCode=FH

o PAF 4.0.4 - Personal Ancestral File® 4.0.4 ~ Windows
http://www.ldscatalog.com/cgi-bin/ncommerce3/Product
Display?prrfnbr=369179&prmenbr=1402&CGRY_NUM=373
032&RowStart=1&LocCode=FH

o Personal Ancestral File® Companion 2.1 Upgrade
http://www.ldscatalog.com/cgi-bin/ncommerce3/Product
Display?prrfnbr=369206&prmenbr=1402&CGRY_NUM=373
032&RowStart=1&LocCode=FH

o Personal Ancestral File® 3.01M Upgrade
http://www.ldscatalog.com/cgi-bin/ncommerce3/Product
Display?prrfnbr=369180&prmenbr=1402&CGRY_NUM=373
032&RowStart=1&LocCode=FH

• Genealogy Training Video Using Personal Ancestral File paf4 Software from The Church of Jesus Christ of Latter-Day Saints
http://www.pafvideo.com/
Self paced video for PAF 4.0.

• Genelines - Companion Software for Genealogy
http://www.progenysoftware.com/genelines.html
*A charting companion for Family Tree Maker 4.x * and PAF 3.0.*

• KINWRITE Plus
http://www2.dtc.net/~ldbond/
Converts a PAF file into a book.

• Nexial Systems - MacPAF Report Utility (MPRU)
http://members.aol.com/nexialist/

• PAF-2.31-USERS Mailing List
http://www.rootsweb.com/~jfuller/gen_mail_software.html
#PAF-2.31-USERS

• PAF-3-USERS Mailing List
http://www.rootsweb.com/~jfuller/gen_mail_software.html
#PAF-3-USERS

• PAF 3.0 Hotkeys
http://reled.byu.edu/famhist/handouts/PAFHotkeys.htm
From the Family History Lab at BYU. Listing of PAF hotkeys.

• PAF-4-USERS Mailing List
http://www.rootsweb.com/~jfuller/gen_mail_software.html
#PAF-4-USERS

• PAF 4.0 User's Guide
http://help.surnameweb.org/genprograms/paf40.htm
From the SurnameWeb site.

• Personal Ancestral File® 4.0.4
http://reled.byu.edu/famhist/handouts/paf4.htm
From the Family History Lab at BYU. Information on using PAF 4.0.4.

• PAF Bookmaker
http://www.geocities.com/bluebunnysoftware/
PAF Bookmaker turns your PAF 3.x and 4.x files into a book, complete with chapters, footnotes, and an index. Very easy to use, and lots of configuration options to get the output you want.

• PAF Help-Guide
http://www.HeritageQuest.com/genealogy/books/html/paf.html
Book for sale from Heritage Quest.

• PAF Mailing List
http://www.rootsweb.com/~jfuller/gen_mail_software.html
#PAF
For discussion and help regarding the use of all versions of the Personal Ancestral File genealogy program.

• PAF Review - Home Page
http://www.saintclair.org/paf/
An electronic newsletter containing information for genealogists who use the PAF ("Personal Ancestral File") genealogy software program.

• PAF-TEMPLES-L Mailing List
http://www.rootsweb.com/~jfuller/gen_mail_software.html
#PAF-TEMPLES-L
For the discussion of any version of PAF (Personal Ancestral File) genealogy software including Temple Ready issues related to PAF, taking floppy disks to the temple, LDS online internet databases such as Ancestral File, and just about any PAF or LDS related temple issue.

• PafWeb Genealogy Program
http://rmeservy.byu.edu/
Family Histories and Genealogies over the Internet: - What is now available.

◆ Privacy Issues

Thinking of putting a genealogy web site online? Do you post family information on mailing lists or newsgroups? Are you considering publishing your family history research? Please remember your family members and their right to privacy before you publish any personal information or place it online. Use some of the software utilities below to remove any information about living individuals from your GEDCOM file before generating reports and web pages. Read the articles below for advice and current opinions on this topic.

Articles and other online privacy resources:

• Adventures in Cyberspace
http://www.ancestry.com/columns/myra/Shaking_Family_Tree
07-09-98.htm
From Shaking Your Family Tree by Myra Vanderpool Gormley, C.G.

- Exposing Our Families to the Internet
  http://www.ancestry.com/columns/myra/Shaking_Family_Tree
  06-19-97.htm
  From Shaking Your Family Tree by Myra Vanderpool Gormley,
  C.G.

- Privacy and Genealogy - GEN100 Logo
  http://www.frumble.freeserve.co.uk/gen100.htm

- Privacy and Genealogy on the Internet
  http://home.sprynet.com/~harrisfarm/warning.htm

- Privacy Rights Clearinghouse
  http://www.privacyrights.org/

- USNews: Home-page snoops
  http://www.usnews.com/usnews/issue/980511/11mone.htm
  An article by Margaret Mannix.

- USNews: Stolen identity - It can ruin your credit.
  And that's just the beginning
  http://www.usnews.com/usnews/issue/980601/1thef.htm
  An article by Margaret Mannix.

- Wanted: Dead Only!
  http://homepages.rootsweb.com/~cregan/privacy.htm
  From the Cregan Ancestry Privacy Issues web page, graphics for
  you to use on your web site to show that you respect the privacy of
  your living family members

Software:

- GED2GO (GEDCOMs to go)
  http://www.geocities.com/yosemite/trails/4849/evb/
  For MS-DOS, runs under Windows also. A utility program which
  automatically finds and removes living persons from GEDCOM
  files.

- GEDClean Home Page
  http://www.raynorshyn.com/gedclean/
  For Windows. A utility used to "clean" info about living individuals
  out of a GEDCOM file in order to maintain privacy.

- gedliving
  http://www.rootsweb.com/~gumby/ged.html
  For Windows. Software that privatizes a GEDCOM file.

- GEDPrivy
  http://hometown.aol.com/gedprivy/index.html
  For Windows. A program to create privacy for data in genealogy
  files (GEDCOMs).

- Res Privata
  http://www.ozemail.com.au/~naibor/rpriv.html
  For Windows. An easy to use application for filtering private data
  from genealogy database (GEDCOM or GED) files. It can filter
  birth, death, marriage, adoption, notes, source and other details.

◆ Publications, Magazines & Newsletters

- Amazon.com Genealogy Bookstore - Software
  http://www.amazon.com/exec/obidos/external-search/?
  keyword=software+genealogy&tag=markcyndisgenealA/

- The Computer Genealogist
  mailto:nehgs@nehgs.org
  A newsletter from the New England Historic Genealogical Society.
  For a free sample send e-mail to: nehgs@nehgs.org.

- ComputerCredible Magazine: Index of Computer
  Genealogy Articles
  http://www.credible.com/geneallist.html

- Computers in Genealogy
  http://www.sog.org.uk/cig/
  A quarterly publication of the Society of Genealogists, U.K.

- Dick Eastman Online
  http://www.ancestry.com/library/view/columns/eastman/
  eastman.asp
  New each Wednesday by Dick Eastman.

  o Dick Eastman Online Archive
    http://www.ancestry.com/library/view/columns/eastman/
    archive.asp

- Frontier Press Bookstore - Computers and
  Genealogy
  http://www.frontierpress.com/frontier.cgi?category=com

- Genealogical Computing Magazine
  http://www.ancestry.com/learn/publications/gencomp.htm

- GenealogyBookShop.com - Computers
  http://www.genealogybookshop.com/genealogybookshop/
  files/General,Computers/index.html
  The online store of Genealogical Publishing Co., Inc. & Clearfield
  Company.

- Journal of Online Genealogy
  http://www.onlinegenealogy.com/
  Promoting the use of computers and the Internet in family history
  research.

- Publishing Your Family History on the Internet
  http://www.compuology.com/book2.htm
  By Richard S. Wilson.

◆ Societies & Groups

- Afdeling Computergenealogie Van De Nederlandse
  Genealogische Vereniging - Gens Data ~
  Netherlands
  http://www.gensdata.demon.nl/

- Amateur Computer Group of New Jersey -
  Genealogy Special Interest Group
  http://www.castle.net/~kb4cyc/gensig.html

- APAFUG - Auburn PAF User Group Home Page ~
  California
  http://www.apafug.com/

- Arizona Genealogy Computer Interest Group
  http://www.agcig.org/

- BARUG - Bay Area Roots User's Group ~ California
  http://homepages.rootsweb.com/~barug/
  For learning about the ROOTS (now called Ultimate Family Tree or
  UFT) genealogy software program.

- Blue Mountain PAF Users Group
  http://www.eoni.com/~paf/
  Eastern Oregon & Southeast Washington.

- CAGG-NI - Northern Illinois, USA
  http://www.rootsweb.com/~ilcaggni/
  Computer Assisted Genealogy Group.

- Central Florida Computer Society
  http://www.cfcs.org/

- Central Texas PC Users' Group, Austin - Genealogy SIG
  http://www.ctpcug.org/SIGDetail.asp?tSIGID=7

- Computer Genealogy Society of Long Island ~ New York
  http://members.macconnect.com/users/v/vitev/genesocli/

- The Computer Genealogy Society of San Diego (CGSSD) ~ California
  http://www.cgssd.org/

- Computer Genealogy Society of Sweden / Föreningen för datorhjälp i släktforskningen
  http://www.dis.se/

- DIS-Danmark - Databehandling I Slægtsforskning
  http://www.dis-danmark.dk/

- Dis Nord-Trøndelag
  http://www.disnorge.no/nordtrond/
  Computer group in Steinkjer, Norway.

- DIS-Norges hjemmeside
  http://www.disnorge.no/
  Computer interest group in Norway.

- Elkhart PC Users Group Genealogy SIG ~ Indiana
  http://www.skyenet.net/~stevens/gensig1.htm

- GCSGA - Genealogical Computer Society of GA ~ Atlanta, Georgia
  http://members.xoom.com/gcsga/

- GENCAP: Genealogical Computing Association of Pennsylvania
  http://www.libertynet.org/~gencap/

- GenCom PC Users Group of Shreveport, Louisiana
  http://www.softdisk.com/comp/gencom/

- Genealogical Computer Society of Georgia
  http://www.mindspring.com/~noahsark/gcsga.html

- Genealogical Society of South Africa - Computer Interest Group
  http://www.geocities.com/Athens/7783/

- Genealogy SIG
  http://www.lmug.org/sigs/genealogy.html
  Lancaster Microcomputer Users Group in central Pennsylvania including Lancaster, York, Dauphin, Lebanon, and Berks counties.

- Genealogy SIG
  http://www.net-gate.com/pcugsj/sigs/genealogy_sig.htm
  PC Users Group of South Jersey based in Cherry Hill, New Jersey serving southern & central New Jersey and Philadelphia.

- Genealogy SIG - Rolla Area Computer Users Group ~ Rolla, Missouri
  http://www.fidnet.com/~racug/page13.html

- GENTECH Information
  http://www.gentech.org/
  "GENTECH, Inc. is an independent, non-profit organization chartered in the state of Texas to educate genealogists in the use of technology for gathering, storing, sharing and evaluating their research."

- HAL-PC Genealogy SIG Home Page ~ Houston, Texas
  http://www.hal-pc.org/~lwpost/gene.shtml

- Manasota PAF Users Group ~ Bradenton, Florida
  http://members.xoom.com/manasotapaf/

- Melbourne PAF Users Group ~ Australia
  http://www.cohsoft.com.au/afhc/melbpaf.html

- Milwaukee PAF Users Group Home Page
  http://www.execpc.com/~bheck/mpafug.html

- Mother Lode PAF User Group ~ Nevada City, California
  http://www.jps.net/pjrowell/paf_index.htm

- North East Ohio-Computer Aided Genealogy - NEO-CAG
  http://members.harborcom.net/~kliotj/neocag/

- Norwegian Genealogy Computer Interest Group
  http://www.uio.no/~achristo/genealog.html

- Olympia Microcomputers Users Group - Genealogy Special Interest Group ~ Washington
  http://www.olymug.org/level2_sigs/genealogy.htm

- PAF-WAYS, A Genealogy/Computer Users Group ~ North-Central Iowa
  http://www.mach3ww.com/~pafways/

- Pikes Peak Computer Genealogists ~ Colorado
  http://home.rmi.net/~mid/pcgweb.htm

- PRO-GEN gebruikersgroep LIMBURG / PRO-GEN users' group LIMBURG ~ Belgium
  http://gallery.uunet.be/PRO-GEN.GG.LIMBURG/index.html

- Roots Users Group of Arlington, Virginia
  http://www.rootsusers.org/

- Roots Users Group of Portland Oregon
  http://members.tripod.com/rug1/

- Southern Oregon PAF Users Group (SO-PAF-UG)
  http://www.webtrail.com/sopafug/index.html

- SV-PAF-UG Homepage ~ San Jose, California
  http://www.svpafug.org/sys-tmpl/door/
  Silicon Valley PAF Users Group.

- Tampa Bay Computer Society - Genealogy SIG ~ Florida
  http://www.tampa-bay.net/sigs.htm#Gen

- TMG Users Groups
  http://www.WhollyGenes.com/html/ugroups.htm
  The Master Genealogist.

- Utah Valley PAF Users Group
  http://www.uvpafug.org/

- Victorian GUM (Genealogists Using Microcomputers) Inc. ~ Australia
  http://www.vicgum.asn.au/

◆ Vendors

- Ancestor Trails
  http://www.ancestor.com/

- Ancestor's Attic Discount Genealogy Books - Software & Computer Genealogy Books
  http://members.tripod.com/~ancestorsattic/index.html#COMP

- Ancestry
  http://www.ancestry.com/
  Books, Computers, Maps, Miscellaneous, Services.

- Appleton's Fine Used Bookseller and Genealogy ~ Charlotte, North Carolina
  http://www.appletons.com/genealogy/homepage.html
  Genealogy books, software, CD-ROMs, and more. Free genealogy catalog and e-mail list.

- Digital Antiquities
  http://www.digital-antiquities.com/
  CD-ROMs for sale. A user supported digital library of genealogical research materials.

- Everton's Genealogy Supply Store
  http://www.everton.com/webcart/ep-store.htm
  Store with CD-ROM, books, archival quality sheets, binders, magazines and software.

- FamilyStoreHouse.com
  http://www.familystorehouse.com/fshstore/index.htm
  The store has a complete line of products from all genealogical vendors. In addition to genealogy, FSH offers a wide range products for today's family with ready-to-ship food storage, healthy living nutritionals, educational material, books, computer hardware and software as well as unique gifts from around the world. In addition, FSH offers a lucrative affiliate program for web site owners to receive commission on customers originating from their site.

- Genealogical Services & The Genealogy Store
  http://www.genservices.com/

- Genealogy Research Source
  http://Perry-family.org/books
  Genealogy books, software, trip planning, sale or exchange of genealogy books and more.

- Genealogystore
  http://go.to/genealogystore
  Genealogy software and books.

- GLOBAL Genealogical Supply
  http://www.globalgenealogy.com/

- Gould Books - Family & Local History Specialist
  http://www.gould.com.au/Computer.htm
  Computer software catalogue from Australia. Also books, maps, charts, microfiche, video & audio.

- Hearthstone Bookshop
  http://www.hearthstonebooks.com/
  Alexandria, Virginia.

- Joe's Genealogy - Genealogy Software Links
  http://www.zen.co.uk/home/page/joe.houghton/SOFTWARE.HTM

- Lark Enterprises Software & Hardware Store - Genealogy
  http://www.netsales.net/pk.wcgi/lark/cat/1099

- Lineages' Genealogy Site: Online Store - Software
  http://www.lineages.com/store/Software.asp

- Lofthouse Publishing - Genealogy Software
  http://www.Lofthouse.com/

- Lost In Time
  http://www.lostintime.com/
  Books, CDs, software, maps, and accessories.

- The Memorabilia Corner
  http://members.aol.com/TMCorner/index.html
  Forms, flags, maps, software, CDs, tapes, microfilm & microfiche, books, periodicals, photographic conservation & archival materials

- Petersen Reproductions
  http://www.petersenprints.com/
  Wonderful things for the genealogist! T-shirts, mugs, mouse pads, software, family tree charts, baptismal & marriage certificates, family registers and much more.

- RootsBooks: A Genealogy and Local History Bookstore!
  http://www.readthemovie.com/rootsbooks/index.html
  An online genealogy bookstore featuring books on local and family histories, how-tos and techniques, ethnic and military research, immigration, software and more.

- S & N Genealogy Supplies
  http://ourworld.compuserve.com/homepages/Genealogy_Supplies/
  And their mirror site
  http://www.genealogy.demon.co.uk/
  Genealogy software & hardware store in the United Kingdom. Has reviews of genealogy programs and lots of useful advice and can supply a wide range of programs, utilities and data CD-ROMs containing historical records for many parts of the country.

- Tanner Computer Services - Genealogy Services
  http://www.xroads.com/~tcs/genealogy/genealogy.html
  Their Genealogy Software Registry has lists of vendors with addresses, phone numbers, prices, etc. They also have computer-related genealogy books.

- TWR Computing ~ U.K.
  http://www.twrcomputing.co.uk/
  Computers and software for family historians and genealogists.

- **Willow Bend Books**
  http://www.willowbend.net/

- **Win-Family**
  http://www.zipworld.com.au/~wls/
  Australian reseller of Win-Family Genealogy Software.

- **Yahoo!...Genealogy...Software**
  http://dir.yahoo.com/Business_and_Economy/Companies/
  Information/Genealogy/Software/

- **Your Family Legacy**
  http://www.webyfl.com/
  Everything for the family history researcher. Genealogy supplies books, forms, software, and archival supplies. Special items for beginners.

SOUTH AFRICA / SUID-AFRIKA

http://www.cyndislist.com/soafrica.htm

Category Index:

- General Resource Sites
- History & Culture
- Libraries, Archives & Museums
- Mailing Lists, Newsgroups & Chat
- Military
- People & Families

- Professional Researchers, Volunteers & Other Research Services
- Publications, Software & Supplies
- Queries, Message Boards & Surname Lists
- Records: Census, Cemeteries, Land, Obituaries, Personal, Taxes and Vital
- Societies & Groups

◆ General Resource Sites

- Advice on How to Conduct South African Research
  mailto:mercon@global.co.za
  Send e-mail to Mr. Conrad Mercer at mercon@global.co.za and he will share his knowledge of family history research in South Africa. However he DOES NOT provide research services. See also the link below to his web site: South African Genealogy.

- GENEALOGIESE NAVORSING: Kielie-kielie, so soek jy jou familie!
  http://expage.com/page/mielie
  In the Afrikaans language: a humorous and informative guide on searching for your ancestors in South Africa.

- Genealogy Bulletin Board Systems for South Africa
  http://www.geocities.com/Athens/7783/bbs1.htm#sabbs

- German Genealogy in South Africa
  http://www.geocities.com/Heartland/Meadows/7589/genea_en.html
  Genealogy and History of German immigrants to South Africa over the last 150 years.

- (GISA) Genealogiese Instituut van Suid-Afrika / Genealogical Institute of South Africa
  http://www.sun.ac.za/gisa/index.html

- LEHMKUHL Family Home Page
  http://www.rupert.net/~lkool/

- South African Genealogy
  http://home.global.co.za/~mercon/index.htm
  From Conrod Mercer, past president of the Genealogical Society of South Africa.

- South African Time Line: Whit's End
  http://home.pix.za/dw/dw000002/TL.HTM
  A chronological list of mainly South African historic events.

◆ History & Culture

- StudyWeb: History: Country History Index: Africa Index: South Africa
  http://www.studyweb.com/links/522.html

- Yahoo!...South Africa...History
  http://dir.yahoo.com/Regional/Countries/South_Africa/Arts_and_Humanities/Humanities/History/

◆ Libraries, Archives & Museums

- Albany Museum Ancestry Research - Genealogy
  http://www.ru.ac.za/departments/am/geneal.html

- Anglo-Boer War Museum ~ Bloemfontein, South Africa
  http://www.anglo-boer.co.za/

- Family History Library Catalog
  http://www.familysearch.org/eng/Library/FHLC/frameset_fhlc.asp
  From the FamilySearch web site, an online catalog to the holdings of the LDS Church in Salt Lake City, Utah. Also search for other localities by place name.
  http://www.familysearch.org/eng/Library/fhlc/supermainframeset.asp?display=localitysearch&columns=*,180,0

  o South Africa
    http://www.familysearch.org/eng/Library/fhlc/supermainframeset.asp?display=localitydetails&subject=280&subject_disp=South_Africa&columns=*,180,0

- The Huguenot Memorial Museum
  http://www.museum.co.za/index.htm
  Museum in South Africa focusing on the Huguenots of the Cape Settlements.

- Repositories of Primary Sources - Africa & the Near East - South Africa
  http://www.uidaho.edu/special-collections/africa.html#za
  A list of links to online resources from the Univ. of Idaho Library, Special Collections and Archives.

- Rhodes University Library: Cory Library for Historical Research
  http://www.rhodes.ac.za/library/cory/
  Genealogical services within a Southern African historical research library and archive centre.

- The South African War Virtual Library
  http://www.uq.net.au/~zzrwotto/

- The Western Cape Oral History Project
  http://www.uct.ac.za/depts/history/ohp1.htm

◆ Mailing Lists, Newsgroups & Chat

- Genealogy Resources on the Internet - South Africa
  Mailing Lists
  http://www.rootsweb.com/~jfuller/gen_mail_country-soa.html
  *Most of the mailing list links below point to this site, wonderfully
  maintained by John Fuller*

- The Anglo Boer War Discussion Page
  http://www.icon.co.za/~dup42/talk.htm
  *This mailing list is for the discussion of the Anglo Boer War and
  other military related topics pre-1900.*

- BOER-WAR Mailing List
  http://www.rootsweb.com/~jfuller/gen_mail_wars.html
  #BOER-WAR
  *For anyone with a genealogical or historical interest in the Boer
  War.*

- FOB-LIST - Friends of the Boers - E-mail List
  http://home.ease.lsoft.com/archives/fob-list.html
  *The primary topic of this mailing list is the centenary
  commemoration of the 2nd Anglo Boer War (1899-1902).*

- SAFRICA Mailing List
  http://www.rootsweb.com/~jfuller/gen_mail_jewish.html
  #SAFRICA
  *To discuss the genealogy and family history of Jewish communities
  of South Africa, Lesotho, Botswana, Zimbabwe and Zambia
  (Rhodesia), Swaziland, Mozambique, and the former Belgian
  Congo.*

- SA-HISTORY Mailing List
  http://www.rootsweb.com/~jfuller/gen_mail_country-
  soa.html#SA-HISTORY
  *For anyone interested in South African genealogy to discuss and
  share information that will help to provide a historical context to
  their research efforts.*

- SOUTH-AFRICA Mailing List
  http://www.rootsweb.com/~jfuller/gen_mail_country-
  soa.html#SOUTH-AFRICA

- SOUTH-AFRICA-SOURCES Mailing List
  http://www.rootsweb.com/~jfuller/gen_mail_country-
  soa.html#SOUTH-AFRICA-SOURCES
  *For the members of the Genealogical Forum of South Africa
  (G.F.S.A.) and anyone else interested in the preservation of
  genealogical sources in South Africa.*

◆ Military

- The Anglo Boer War Discussion Page
  http://www.icon.co.za/~dup42/talk.htm
  *This mailing list is for the discussion of the Anglo Boer War and
  other military related topics pre-1900.*

- The Boer War - South Africa, 1899-1902
  http://www.geocities.com/Athens/Acropolis/8141/
  boerwar.html

- Commonwealth War Graves Commission
  http://www.cwgc.org/
  *They can provide invaluable information to genealogists on the
  location, condition, and other information regarding the
  Commonwealth soldiers' graves in their care. Please include
  International Reply Coupons when writing to them from outside
  Britain.*

- Fatal Casualties In Canadian Contingents of the Boer
  War
  http://www.islandnet.com/~duke/boercas.htm

- FOB-LIST - Friends of the Boers - E-mail List
  http://www.webcom.com/perspekt/eng/mlist/fob.html
  *The primary topic of this mailing list is the centenary
  commemoration of the 2nd Anglo Boer War (1899-1902).*

- League of Researchers of South African Historical
  Battlefields
  http://www.icon.co.za/~dup42/Welcome.html

- The South African War Virtual Library
  http://www.uq.net.au/~zzrwotto/

◆ People & Families

- BOSMAN Family Genealogy
  http://home.intekom.com/entrepreneur/bosmanfg.htm
  Descendants of Hermanus Lambertus Bosman in South Africa.

- The ELLIS Family and Relations
  http://users.iafrica.com/e/el/ellis/
  *Genealogical database of one branch of the Ellis family in South
  Africa, including: HAVINGA, KENNEDY, CRAUSE, VAN WYK.*

- Huguenot Refugees in the Cape Colony of South
  Africa
  http://www.rootsweb.com/~ote/hugsa.htm

- LEHMKUHL Family Home Page
  http://www.rupert.net/~lkool/

- The MERCER Family
  http://www.geocities.com/Heartland/Acres/6302/
  A chronicle of the antecedents of a South African Mercer.

- The POTGIETER Genealogy Pages
  http://www.geocities.com/Heartland/Park/7152/
  *If you are interested to trace your Potgieter family roots in South
  Africa, then this is the place for you to start. This site hosts
  genealogy information, a mailing list, a discussion forum,
  biographies and history. .*

- Researching Jewish Genealogies in South Africa -
  Part A
  http://www.jewishgen.org/infofiles/za-infoa.txt

- Researching Jewish Genealogies in South Africa -
  Part B
  http://www.jewishgen.org/infofiles/za-infob.txt

- Ron SMIT's South African Family Pages
  http://home.intekom.com/ron/
  *SMIT, SCHIEFNER, MOLLENDORF, ISAAC, ZEEMAN,
  DUVENHAGE / DUVENAGE / Du VINAGE.*

- South African Descendants of John POWER
  http://www.geocities.com/Heartland/Pines/5384/Genealogy/
  Descendants of John POWER and Mary NASH who emigrated to South Africa sometime in 1870.

- Tracing Mormon Pioneers
  http://www.xmission.com/~nelsonb/pioneer.htm

  o South African Emigration 1853-1865
    http://www.xmission.com/~nelsonb/safrica.htm

- VILJOEN Family Homepage
  http://www.geocities.com/Heartland/Acres/4040/index.html
  Villion, Campenaar.

- Whit's End: WHITLOCK / WHITFIELD Genealogy
  http://home.pix.za/dw/dw000002/index.htm
  The genealogy of the Whitlock and Whitfield families in England and South Africa over a period of about 800 years and 26 generations.

◆ Professional Researchers, Volunteers & Other Research Services

- Genealogy Helplist - South Africa
  http://helplist.org/zaf/index.shtml

- (GISA) Genealogiese Instituut van Suid-Afrika / Genealogical Institute of South Africa
  http://www.sun.ac.za/gisa/

◆ Publications, Software & Supplies

- Amazon.com Genealogy Bookstore - South Africa
  http://www.amazon.com/exec/obidos/external-search/?keyword=south+africa+genealogy&tag=markcyndisgenealA/

- AudioTapes.com - Genealogical Lectures on Cassette Tapes - South Africa
  http://www.audiotapes.com/search2.asp?Search=South+Africa

- Brother's Keeper Software
  http://ourworld.compuserve.com/homepages/Brothers_Keeper/
  Downloadable shareware program for Windows. The latest version contains English, French, Norwegian, Danish, Swedish, German, Dutch, Polish, Icelandic, Russian, Slovak, Afrikaans, Czech.

- Generations Newsletter
  http://www.rupert.net/~lkool/page13.html
  A genealogy newsletter published 6 times per year (to be increased to 12 very soon), which contains articles of interest to anyone researching their family history in South Africa.

- Journals & Newsletters Covering Genealogy in South Africa
  http://www.geocities.com/Heartland/8256/others.html

◆ Queries, Message Boards & Surname Lists

- South African Genealogy Queries and Surnames
  http://www.rupert.net/~lkool/page3.html

◆ Records: Census, Cemeteries, Land, Obituaries, Personal, Taxes and Vital (Born, Married, Died & Buried)

- Commonwealth War Graves Commission
  http://www.cwgc.org/
  They can provide invaluable information to genealogists on the location, condition, and other information regarding the Commonwealth soldiers' graves in their care. Please include International Reply Coupons when writing to them from outside Britain.

- Fatal Casualties in Canadian Contingents of the Boer War
  http://www.islandnet.com/~duke/boercas.htm

- HAGSOC: Australian War Graves in South Africa 1899-1902
  http://www.hagsoc.org.au/sagraves/index.html
  This project, by the Heraldry & Genealogy Society of Canberra, aims to publish the database of burial and memorial locations of Australians who died during the second South African Anglo-Boer War of 1899 - 1902. Also included are biographies, researched by the Society, of selected soldiers from each of the Australian States.

◆ Societies & Groups

- The Genealogical Research Group Port Elizabeth
  http://www.cs.upe.ac.za/staff/csagdk/GNGPE/

- The Genealogical Society of South Africa
  http://www.rootsweb.com/~zafgssa/Eng/

  o Durban and Coastal Branch
    http://www.rootsweb.com/~zafgssa/Eng/DurbanC.htm

  o East Cape Branch
    http://www.rootsweb.com/~zafgssa/Eng/ECape.htm

  o East Gauteng Branch
    http://www.rootsweb.com/~zafgssa/Eng/EGauteng.htm

  o Free State Branch
    http://www.rootsweb.com/~zafgssa/Eng/FState.htm

  o Johannesburg Branch
    http://www.rootsweb.com/~zafgssa/Eng/Johannesburg.htm

  o Natal Midlands Branch
    http://www.rootsweb.com/~zafgssa/Eng/NatalM.htm

  o Northern Transvaal Branch
    http://www.rootsweb.com/~zafgssa/Eng/NTvl.htm

  o Vaal Triangle Branch
    http://www.rootsweb.com/~zafgssa/Eng/Vaaltriangle.htm

  o Western Cape Branch
    http://www.rootsweb.com/~zafgssa/Eng/WCape.htm

- Genealogical Society of South Africa - Computer Interest Group
  http://www.geocities.com/Athens/7783/

- Huguenot Society of South Africa
  http://www.geocities.com/Heartland/Valley/8140/

- League of Researchers of South African Historical Battlefields
  http://www.icon.co.za/~dup42/Welcome.html

- The South African Military History Society / Die Suid-Afrikaanse Krygshistoriese Vereeniging
  http://rapidttp.com/milhist/

- The South East Witwatersrand Family History Society ~ Gauteng, Republic of South Africa
  http://www.geocities.com/Heartland/8256/

- UPEGIS
  http://www.cs.upe.ac.za/staff/csagdk/GisRes/UPEGIS/
  The University of Port Elizabeth Genealogical Information System

SPAIN, PORTUGAL & THE BASQUE COUNTRY / ESPAÑA, PORTUGAL Y EL PAÍS VASCO

http://www.cyndislist.com/spain.htm

Category Index:

- General Resource Sites
- History & Culture
- Language, Handwriting & Script
- Libraries, Archives & Museums
- Mailing Lists, Newsgroups & Chat
- Maps, Gazetteers & Geographical Information
- People & Families

- Professional Researchers, Volunteers & Other Research Services
- Publications, Software & Supplies
- Queries, Message Boards & Surname Lists
- Records: Census, Cemeteries, Land, Obituaries, Personal, Taxes and Vital
- Societies & Groups
- WorldGenWeb Project

◆ General Resource Sites

- Anillo de Genealogía Hispana (Hispanic Genealogy Ring)
  http://www.elanillo.com/
  Paginas de Genealogía Hispana en Español. Hispanic Genealogy pages in Spanish. Lots of great resources for those searching their roots in Spain or Latin American countries.

- Archivos de Genealogía Española / Spanish Genealogy
  http://www.geocities.com/CapitolHill/Senate/4593/geneal.html
  Collection of resources for Spanish genealogy, in Spanish.

- Azores: Source of Immigration to the Americas
  http://www.lusaweb.com/azores/

- Basque Genealogy Homepage
  http://www.primenet.com/~fybarra/
  From Susan Yvarra. YBARRA, ARESTI, AYO, URIGUEN, ARISTEGUI, MENDICOTE, MIRAGAYA and SESUMAGA.

- Blasón Virtual, Heráldica en la Red
  http://www.ctv.es/blason/

- Buber's Basque Page
  http://students.washington.edu/buber/Basque/
  *Euskaldunen Diaspora Eta Genealogia * The Basque Diaspora and Genealogy * La Diaspora Y Genealogia Vascas * La Disaspora Et Genealogie Basque.*

- Buber's Basque Page: Genealogical Tips
  http://students.washington.edu/buber/Basque/Diaspora/search.html
  Tips for doing genealogical research, tailored for researchers of the Basque Country.

- Centre Généalogique des Pyrénées-Atlantiques (Béarn et Pays Basque)
  http://www.world-address.com/cgpa/

- Centro De Estudios Heraldicos
  http://www.net64.es/heraldica/

- Centro de Patrimonio Documental de Euskadi - IRARGI - Presentación
  http://www.irargi.org
  The official web of the Basque Gouvernement's Service on Archives and Documental Heritage. With many links of different services and a search into many public and private archives in the Basque Country. For the moment, there are 130,000 archival references, with a focus on tracing ancestors. In Basque, Spanish, English and French.

- Genealogy in Portugal
  http://www.everton.com/resources/world/portugal.htm
  Links from Everton Publishers.

- Fernando CANDIDO's Portuguese Genealogy Home Page
  http://fn2.freenet.edmonton.ab.ca/~fcandido/

- Heráldica y genealogía hispana, escudos de armas de apellidos de origen español
  http://www.ctv.es/artes/
  Heraldry for surnames of Spanish origin, coats of arms, genealogy.

- Hispanic, Central & South America, and the West Indies
  http://www.CyndisList.com/hispanic.htm
  Including Mexico, Latin America and the Caribbean. See this category on Cyndi's List for related links.

- Hispanic Genealogy Address Book - Portugal
  http://users.aol.com/mrosado007/portugal.htm

- Islenos - Canary Islands
  http://www.intersurf.com/~rcollins/ilenos.html

- LusaWeb - Azores: Source of Immigration to the Americas
  http://www.lusaweb.com/azores/

- LusaWeb Portuguese Family Roots Database
  http://www.lusaweb.com/genealogy/gendata/portroots/

- LusaWeb - Portuguese Genealogy Resources
  http://www.lusaweb.com/html/genea.cfm

- Madeira: Sharing and Searching
  http://www.geocities.com/Heartland/Plains/9462/

- PortugueseAncestry.com
  http://www.portugueseancestry.com/
  Portuguese Genealogist Master Database.

- Portuguese Genealogy Information Page from Doug da Rocha Holmes
  http://www.dholmes.com/rocha2.html

- Portuguese Genealogy Lexique
  http://fn2.freenet.edmonton.ab.ca/~fcandido/lexique.html
  Portuguese-English translations of genealogy terms.

- Portuguese Genealogy Workshop
  http://www.dholmes.com/99workshop.html
  November 21, 1999 in Sacramento, California.

- Portuguese Resources on the Web
  http://www.maui.net/~makule/port.html

- Reynolds Hunter Y Puebla Heráldica Y Blasones - Heraldries
  http://www.audinex.es/~hunter/

- Spain Genealogy Address Book
  http://user.aol.com/mrosado007/spain.htm

- Spanish Yellow Pages - Páginas Amarillas Multimedia
  http://www.paginas-amarillas.es/

- Western Europe
  http://www.CyndisList.com/westeuro.htm
  See this category on Cyndi's List for related links.

◆ History & Culture

- Heráldica Española
  http://members.xoom.com/chema/
  Heráldica de apellidos de origen español. Heráldica oficial de localidades de España.

- LusaWeb: Portuguese-American Communities on the World Wide Web
  http://www.LusaWeb.com/

- Spanish Shipwrecks Resources Inc.
  http://republika.pl/shipwrecksresources/
  Documents related to Spanish shipwrecks for sale.

- StudyWeb: History: Country History Index: Europe Index: Portugal
  http://www.studyweb.com/links/4031.html

- StudyWeb: History: Country History Index: Europe Index: Spain
  http://www.studyweb.com/links/159.html

- Yahoo!...Portugal...History
  http://dir.yahoo.com/Regional/Countries/Portugal/Arts_and_Humanities/Humanities/History/

- Yahoo!...Spain...History
  http://dir.yahoo.com/Regional/Countries/Spain/Arts_and_Humanities/Humanities/History/

◆ Language, Handwriting & Script

- AltaVista Translation Service
  http://babelfish.altavista.digital.com/cgi-bin/translate?
  Input a URL for a web site or a block of plain text and this site will translate for you from Spanish or Portuguese to English or from English to Spanish or Portuguese.

- FamilySearch Research Guidance - Portuguese Genealogical Word List
  http://www.familysearch.org/Eng/Search/rg/frameset_rg.asp?Dest=G1&Aid=&Gid=&Lid=&Sid=&Did=&Juris1=&Event=&Year=&Gloss=&Sub=&Tab=&Entry=&Guide=WLPortug.ASP

- FamilySearch Research Guidance - Portuguese Letter Writing Guide
  http://www.familysearch.org/Eng/Search/rg/frameset_rg.asp?Dest=G1&Aid=&Gid=&Lid=&Sid=&Did=&Juris1=&Event=&Year=&Gloss=&Sub=&Tab=&Entry=&Guide=LWGPortuguese.ASP
  For genealogical inquiries from FamilySearch.org.

- FamilySearch Research Guidance - Spanish Genealogical Word List
  http://www.familysearch.org/Eng/Search/rg/frameset_rg.asp?Dest=G1&Aid=&Gid=&Lid=&Sid=&Did=&Juris1=&Event=&Year=&Gloss=&Sub=&Tab=&Entry=&Guide=WLSpanis.ASP

- FamilySearch Research Guidance - Spanish Letter Writing Guide
  http://www.familysearch.org/Eng/Search/rg/frameset_rg.asp?Dest=G1&Aid=&Gid=&Lid=&Sid=&Did=&Juris1=&Event=&Year=&Gloss=&Sub=&Tab=&Entry=&Guide=LWGSpanish.ASP

◆ Libraries, Archives & Museums

- Arquivo da Universidade de Coimbra ~ Portugal
  http://www.ci.uc.pt/auc/

- Arquivo Distrital de Beja (Portugal)
  http://www.cidadevirtual.pt/arq-dist-beja/

- Arquivos Distrital do Porto / Porto Distrital Archive
  http://www.ncc.up.pt/adp/

- Biblioteca Nacional / Portuguese National Library ~ Portugal
  http://www.biblioteca-nacional.pt/

- Biblioteca Nacional de España / National Library of Spain
  http://www.bne.es/

- Biblioteca Pública e Arquivo de Angra do Heroísmo ~ Portugal
  http://www.gzcah.pt//arede/entid/bpaah.htm

- Center for Basque Studies ~ Reno, Nevada
  http://basque.unr.edu/

- Family History Library Catalog
  http://www.familysearch.org/eng/Library/FHLC/frameset_fhlc.asp
  From the FamilySearch web site, an online catalog to the holdings of the LDS Church in Salt Lake City, Utah. Also search for other localities by place name.
  http://www.familysearch.org/eng/Library/fhlc/supermainframeset.asp?display=localitysearch&columns=*,180,0

  o Portugal
    http://www.familysearch.org/eng/Library/fhlc/supermainframeset.asp?display=localitydetails&subject=108&subject_disp=Portugal&columns=*,180,0

  o Spain
    http://www.familysearch.org/eng/Library/fhlc/supermainframeset.asp?display=localitydetails&subject=104&subject_disp=Spain&columns=*,180,0

- FamilySearch - Family History Centers
  http://www.familysearch.org/eng/Library/FHC/frameset_fhc.asp

  o Family History Centers in Portugal
    http://www.familysearch.org/eng/Library/FHC/FHC_Results.asp?FHCCountry=Portugal&FHCStateProv=&FHCCounty=&FHCCity=&submit=Search

  o Family History Centers in Spain
    http://www.familysearch.org/eng/Library/FHC/FHC_Results.asp?FHCCountry=Spain&FHCStateProv=&FHCCounty=&FHCCity=&submit=Search

- Instituto dos Arquivos Nacionais / Torre do Tombo
  http://www.iantt.pt/

- Instituto Portugues de Museus / Institute of Portuguese Museums
  http://www.ipmuseus.pt/

- Portuguese Libraries, Archives and Documentation Services on the Internet
  http://www.sdum.uminho.pt/bad/bibpte.htm

- Repositories of Primary Sources - Europe - Portugal
  http://www.uidaho.edu/special-collections/euro2.html#pt
  A list of links to online resources from the Univ. of Idaho Library, Special Collections and Archives.

- Repositories of Primary Sources - Europe - Spain
  http://www.uidaho.edu/special-collections/euro2.html#es
  A list of links to online resources from the Univ. of Idaho Library, Special Collections and Archives.

◆ Mailing Lists, Newsgroups & Chat

- Genealogy Resources on the Internet - Portugal Mailing Lists
  http://www.rootsweb.com/~jfuller/gen_mail_country-por.html
  Most of the mailing list links below point to this site, wonderfully maintained by John Fuller

- Genealogy Resources on the Internet - Spain Mailing Lists
  http://www.rootsweb.com/~jfuller/gen_mail_country-spa.html
  Most of the mailing list links below point to this site, wonderfully maintained by John Fuller.

- AZORES Mailing List
  http://www.rootsweb.com/~jfuller/gen_mail_country-por.html#AZORES

- BASQUE Mailing List
  http://www.rootsweb.com/~jfuller/gen_mail_country-fra.html#BASQUE
  A "moderated" mailing list, gatewayed with the soc.culture.basque "moderated" newsgroup, that provides Basques the world over with a virtual place to discuss social, political, cultural or any other issues related to Basques, or to request information and discuss matters related to the Basque people and/or their culture. Genealogy queries are an acceptable topic for the list.

- BASQUE-L Mailing List
  http://www.rootsweb.com/~jfuller/gen_mail_country-fra.html#BASQUE-L
  A forum for the dissemination and exchange of information on Basque culture. Genealogy-related issues are often discussed on the list though the main topics of discussion are socio-political current affairs, gastronomy, Basque music, poetry, anthropology (e.g., origin of Basques), etc.

- MadeiraExiles Mailing List
  http://www.rootsweb.com/~jfuller/gen_mail_states-il.html#MadeiraExiles
  Devoted to the research of Dr. Robert Reid Kalley's Portuguese Presbyterian exiles from Madeira, Portugal who emigrated to Trinidad and then to Illinois (ca 1846-1854).

- MA-MVPGP Mailing List
  http://www.rootsweb.com/~jfuller/gen_mail_country-por.html#MA-MVPGP
  For anyone with a genealogical interest in the Portuguese immigrants who settled in Martha's Vineyard, Massachusetts.

- PORTUGAL Mailing List
  http://www.rootsweb.com/~jfuller/gen_mail_country-por.html#PORTUGAL

- PORTUGUESE-WESTINDIES Mailing List
  http://www.rootsweb.com/~jfuller/gen_mail_country-wes.html#PORTUGUESE-WESTINDIES
  For anyone with a genealogical interest in the Portuguese immigrants to the West Indies.

- SEFARD Mailing List
  http://www.rootsweb.com/~jfuller/gen_mail_jewish.html#SEFARD
  For Sephardic genealogy research (Jews who are descendants of the former Jews of Spain and Portugal).

- SPAIN-ISLAS-CANARIAS Mailing List
  http://www.rootsweb.com/~jfuller/gen_mail_country-spa.html#SPAIN-ISLAS-CANARIAS
  For anyone with a genealogical interest in the Canary Islands, Spain.

- SPAIN Mailing List
  http://www.rootsweb.com/~jfuller/gen_mail_country-spa.html#SPAIN

◆ Maps, Gazetteers & Geographical Information

- Basque Homeland
  http://www.ee.ed.ac.uk/~ja/Images/mapa.jpg

- Instituto Português de Cartografia e Cadastro / The National Geodetic, Mapping and Cadastre Agency of Portugal
  http://www.ipcc.pt/

- Map of Portugal
  http://www.lib.utexas.edu/Libs/PCL/Map_collection/europe/Portugal.jpg
  From the Perry-Castañeda Library at the Univ. of Texas at Austin.

- Map of Spain
  http://www.lib.utexas.edu/Libs/PCL/Map_collection/europe/Spain.jpg
  From the Perry-Castañeda Library at the Univ. of Texas at Austin.

- Topographic Maps of the Azores Islands
  http://www.dholmes.com/az-maps.html
  Maps for sale for each of the islands.

◆ People & Families

- ABARCA. Genealogía y Heráldica del apellido
  http://www.ctv.es/USERS/abarca/
  de Aragón (España).

- El apellido ALFARO / The Surname ALFARO
  http://members.tripod.com/~Antonioalfaro/
  Spain, Portugal, Italy, Chile, Argentina, Brazil, Peru, Ecuador, Costa Rica, Panama, Puerto Rico, Mexico, the United States.

- Basque Genealogy Homepage
  http://www.primenet.com/~fybarra/
  From Susan Yvarra. YBARRA, ARESTI, AYO, URIGUEN, ARISTEGUI, MENDICOTE, MIRAGAYA and SESUMAGA.

- Casa de Su Majestad el Rey de España
  http://www.casareal.es/casareal/

- The COBRA Family Genealogy Home Page
  http://www.geocities.com/Athens/Acropolis/3515/
  History and genealogy of the Cobra Family in Portugal and its modern branches in Canada, Brazil, and the U.S.A.

- The (Do) ESPIRITO SANTO Family Club / Clube Das Famílias "Do ESPíRITO SANTO"
  http://members.tripod.com/~EspiritoSanto/

- Dosis sola facit venenum (Paracelso)
  http://www.arrakis.es/~toffana/pagina/home.htm
  Surname PICABEA. History, heraldry and information. Genealogy links.

- A Família Lima Verde ~ In Portuguese
  http://www.geocities.com/Heartland/2177/lv.htm

- Genealogía de Imanol M. Pagola SALAZAR
  http://www.geocities.com/Heartland/Hills/7393/

- Genealogia e Heráldica Portuguesa - Portuguese Genealogy and Heraldry
  http://www.geocities.com/Heartland/Hills/1008/
  álvaro HOLSTEIN Home Page.

- Genealogia Imanol M. Pagola SALAZAR
  http://www.geocities.com/Heartland/7399/

- The MEDEIROS Web - Heraldry and Genealogy
  http://www.maui.net/~makule/medgene.html

- Nelson SILVA Genealogy - Genealogia
  http://www.magnac.com/nsilva/genealogy.html
  With categorized links for Genealogy in Portugal - Genealogia em Portugal.

- Nobleza titulada del Reino de España / Titled Nobility of the Kingdom of España
  http://www.angelfire.com/de/NOBLEZA/index.html

- Papagaia's Journey of Discovery
  http://www.geocities.com/Heartland/Hills/1065/

- Portuguese Family Histories Home Page
  http://www.dholmes.com/fam-hist.html

- Portuguese Genealogy Home Pages
  http://www.geocities.com/CapitolHill/6506/Genealogy.html

- The Royal House of Bourbon (Spain)
  http://www.geocities.com/Heartland/Hills/1150/

◆ Professional Researchers, Volunteers & Other Research Services

- The Basque Genealogy Homepage Research Services
  http://www.primenet.com/~fybarra/Research.html
  Specializing in Basque records from the province of Vizcaya. These records are on microfilm at the Salt Lake Family History Library, but do not get circulated.

- GEG - Gabinete de Estudos Genealógicos ~ Portugal
  http://paginas.teleweb.pt/~moncada/
  Web site in Portuguese, English and French.

- Genealogia e Heráldica Portuguesas - Gabinete de Genealogia e Heráldica
  http://planeta.clix.pt/holstein/
  Professional research in genealogy and heraldry in Portugal.

- genealogyPro - Professional Genealogists for Spain and Basque Country
  http://genealogyPro.com/directories/Spain.html

- Investigaciones Genealogicas
  http://lanzadera.com/rozas
  Estamos especializados en el País Vasco y Cantabria, España. Genealogical research in the Basque Country & Cantabria, Spain.

- Linhagens - Genealogical Research in Portugal / Investigação Genealógica em Portugal
  http://linages.cjb.net/

- Portuguese Genealogy by Doug da Rocha Holmes
  http://www.dholmes.com/rocha1.html
  Professional researcher specializing in Azorean genealogy and Portuguese translation.

◆ Publications, Software & Supplies

- Amazon.com Genealogy Bookstore - Hispanic
  http://www.amazon.com/exec/obidos/external-search/?keyword=hispanic+genealogy&tag=markcyndisgenealA/

- AudioTapes.com - Genealogical Lectures on Cassette Tapes - Spain
  http://www.audiotapes.com/search2.asp?Search=Spain

- Borderlands Bookstore
  http://www.borderlandsbooks.com/
  Historical and genealogical books about Texas, Mexico, Spain, and Portugal.

- GenealogyBookShop.com - Spain/Spanish/Hispanic
  http://www.genealogybookshop.com/genealogybookshop/files/The_World,Spain_Spanish_Hispanic/index.html
  The online store of Genealogical Publishing Co., Inc. & Clearfield Company.

- O Progresso - The Quarterly Newsletter of the Portuguese Historical & Cultural Society (PHCS)
  http://www.dholmes.com/o-prog.html

- Portuguese Gift Shop
  http://www.dholmes.com/portgift.html
  Books, documents, maps, and more.

- Portuguese Pioneers of the Sacramento Valley
  http://www.dholmes.com/new-book.html
  A new book project.

◆ Queries, Message Boards & Surname Lists

- Basque Surname Research
  http://students.washington.edu/buber/Basque/Surname/surlist.html

- Lineages' Free On-line Queries - Portugal & Spain
  http://www.lineages.com/queries/Search.asp?Country=&Place=

- Portuguese Genealogist Master List
  http://www.dholmes.com/master-l.html
  - o Angola
    http://www.dholmes.com/angola.html
  - o Azores
    http://www.dholmes.com/azores.html
    - • Corvo
      http://www.dholmes.com/corvo.html

- • Faial
  http://www.dholmes.com/faial.html
- • Flores
  http://www.dholmes.com/flores.html
- • Graciosa
  http://www.dholmes.com/graciosa.html
- o Brasil
  http://www.dholmes.com/brasil.html
- o Cabo Verde (Cape Verde)
  http://www.dholmes.com/caboverd.html
- o Madeira
  http://www.dholmes.com/madeira.html

◆ Records: Census, Cemeteries, Land, Obituaries, Personal, Taxes and Vital (Born, Married, Died & Buried)

- LusaWeb Portuguese Immigrant Ship Lists
  http://www.lusaweb.com/shiplist.cfm

- Portuguese Passenger Ship Master List
  http://www.dholmes.com/ships.html

- Portuguese Voters of 1872 in California
  http://www.dholmes.com/voters.html

◆ Societies & Groups

- Portuguese Genealogical Society of Hawaii
  http://www.lusaweb.com/genealogy/html/phgs.cfm

- Portuguese Historical & Cultural Society (PHCS) ~ Sacramento, California
  http://www.dholmes.com/calendar.html

◆ WorldGenWeb Project

- WorldGenWeb
  http://www.worldgenweb.org/
  - o MediterraneanGenWeb
    http://www.mediterraneangenweb.org/
    - • Azores GenWeb
      http://home.pacifier.com/~kcardoz/azoresindex.html
    - • España GenWeb
      http://www.rootsweb.com/~espwgw/index.htm
    - • La Genealogía de Las Islas Canarias / The Genealogy of The Canary Islands
      http://www.rootsweb.com/~espcanar/index.html
    - • Portugal GenWeb
      http://mediterraneangenweb.org/portugal/

SUPPLIES, CHARTS, FORMS, ETC.
http://www.cyndislist.com/supplies.htm

Category Index:
- General Resource Sites
- Mailing Lists, Newsgroups & Chat
- Online Charts & Forms to Print or Download
- Vendors

◆ General Resource Sites

- Charts, Forms and Logs
  http://www.redrival.com/cstern/explain.html

- The Forms Needed to Order Records from the National Archives
  http://www.ancestry.com/columns/george/05-15-98.htm
  From "Along Those Lines..." by George G. Morgan.

- Free Genealogy Products
  http://www.genfree.com/
  A selection of free products and services that will help both the new and experienced genealogical researcher to complete family roots projects in a cost efficient manner.

- Genealogy Charts and Forms
  http://members.tripod.com/~wnyroots/index-forms.html

- National Genealogical Society - NGS Beginner's Kit
  http://www.ngsgenealogy.org/education/content/beginkit.html

- National Genealogical Society - Genealogical Forms and Research Aids
  http://www.ngsgenealogy.org/education/content/gen_forms.html

- The SGGS "German Card"
  http://feefhs.org/sggs/sggs-gc.html

- Universal Family Group Sheet
  http://www.geocities.com/Heartland/Meadows/7970/vfgs.html
  An online form which allows you to enter your data and e-mail it to another researcher.

◆ Mailing Lists, Newsgroups & Chat

- GEN-MARKET Mailing List
  http://www.rootsweb.com/~jfuller/gen_mail_general.html
  #GEN-MARKET
  Gatewayed with the soc.genealogy.marketplace newsgroup for commercial postings of unique interest to genealogists.
  news:soc.genealogy.marketplace

- GEN-MAT-REQUEST Mailing List
  http://www.rootsweb.com/~jfuller/gen_mail_general.html
  #GEN-MAT
  This is a mailing list for anyone who has an interest in the buying or selling of new or used genealogical materials (e.g., books, newsletters, CDs, magazines).

- GEN-MAT-15-REQUEST Mailing List
  http://www.rootsweb.com/~jfuller/gen_mail_general.html
  #GEN-MAT-15
  For anyone who desires to post the availability of new or used genealogical materials (e.g., books, newsletters, CDs, magazines) or services for sale at a price of $15 or less.

◆ Online Charts & Forms to Print or Download

- Abstract Printable Forms for Census Records ~ U.S.
  http://www.familytreemaker.com/00000061.html
  - 1790
    http://www.familytreemaker.com/00000062.html
  - 1800
    http://www.familytreemaker.com/00000063.html
  - 1810
    http://www.familytreemaker.com/00000064.html
  - 1820 – 1
    http://www.familytreemaker.com/00000065.html
  - 1820 – 2
    http://www.familytreemaker.com/00000066.html
  - 1830 – 1
    http://www.familytreemaker.com/00000067.html
  - 1830 – 2
    http://www.familytreemaker.com/00000068.html
  - 1840 – 1
    http://www.familytreemaker.com/00000069.html
  - 1840 – 2
    http://www.familytreemaker.com/00000070.html
  - 1850
    http://www.familytreemaker.com/00000071.html
  - 1860
    http://www.familytreemaker.com/00000072.html
  - 1870 – 1
    http://www.familytreemaker.com/00000073.html
  - 1870 – 2
    http://www.familytreemaker.com/00000074.html
  - 1880 – 1
    http://www.familytreemaker.com/00000075.html
  - 1880 – 2
    http://www.familytreemaker.com/00000076.html
  - 1890 – 1
    http://www.familytreemaker.com/00000077.html

o 1890 – 2
http://www.familytreemaker.com/00000078.html

o 1900 – 1
http://www.familytreemaker.com/00000079.html

o 1900 – 2
http://www.familytreemaker.com/00000080.html

o 1910 – 1
http://www.familytreemaker.com/00000081.html

o 1910 – 2
http://www.familytreemaker.com/00000082.html

o 1910 – 3
http://www.familytreemaker.com/00000083.html

o 1920 – 1
http://www.familytreemaker.com/00000084.html

o 1920 – 2
http://www.familytreemaker.com/00000085.html

o 1920 – 3
http://www.familytreemaker.com/00000086.html

- **AHSGR Genealogical Forms**
http://www.ahsgr.org/ahsgrfrm.html
Forms for members of the American Historical Society of Germans from Russia.

- **Ancestor Detective Freebies**
http://www.ancestordetective.com/freebies.htm
Free downloadable Research Calendar Template for WordPerfect 7.0 and 8.0 and Research Calendar Template for Word 97.

- **Ancestors: The First Series - Charts and Records**
http://www.pbs.org/kbyu/ancestors/firstseries/teachersguide/charts-records.html
From the television program on PBS. Includes a Pedigree Chart, Family Group Record, 2nd Page Family Group Record, Timeline Page, Research Log, Family and Home Information Sources Checklist, and Child's Pedigree Chart.

- **Ancestry.com - Ancestral Chart**
http://www.ancestry.com/save/charts/ancchart.htm

- **Ancestry.com - Correspondence Record**
http://www.ancestry.com/save/charts/correcord.htm

- **Ancestry.com - Family Group Sheet**
http://www.ancestry.com/save/charts/familysheet.htm

- **Ancestry.com - Research Calendar**
http://www.ancestry.com/save/charts/researchcal.htm

- **Ancestry.com - Research Extract**
http://www.ancestry.com/save/charts/researchext.htm

- **Ancestry.com - Source Summary**
http://www.ancestry.com/save/charts/sourcesum.htm

- **Ancestry Corner Reference Library - FREE Forms**
http://www.ancestrycorner.com/Pages/forms.shtml
Requires the free Adobe Acrobat Reader Plugin.
http://www.adobe.com/products/acrobat/readstep.html
Includes Four Generation Ancestor Chart, Research Log, Four Generation Chart w/Tree, Blank Soundex Cards, Four Generation Vertical Chart, Vertical Family Group Sheet, Cousin Finder Chart, Cemetery Abstract Chart, Marriage Abstract Chart, Abstract for Soundex Research, Census History Form for Individuals.

- **Checklist of Home Sources**
http://www.rootscomputing.com/howto/checkl/checkl.htm

- **Easy Genealogy Forms**
http://www.io.com/~jhaller/forms/forms.html
Pedigree charts and family group sheets to download and print from your word processor or spreadsheet programs. Available in Macintosh or PC formats.

- **Everton's Free Forms**
http://www.everton.com/charts/freeform.html
Pedigree Chart and Family Group Sheet.

- **FamilySearch Research Guidance - Document Types**
http://www.familysearch.org/Eng/Search/rg/frameset_rhelps.asp
Free forms to print from the FamilySearch Internet Genealogy Service. The following forms are best printed in PDF format, which requires the free Adobe Acrobat Reader Plugin.
http://www.adobe.com/products/acrobat/readstep.html

  o U.S. Census

  - 1790
http://www.familysearch.org/Eng/Search/rg/frameset_rg.asp?Dest=G1&Aid=&Gid=&Lid=&Sid=&Did=&Juris1=&Event=&Year=&Gloss=&Sub=&Tab=&Entry=&Guide=FUS1790.ASP

  - 1800/1810
http://www.familysearch.org/Eng/Search/rg/frameset_rg.asp?Dest=G1&Aid=&Gid=&Lid=&Sid=&Did=&Juris1=&Event=&Year=&Gloss=&Sub=&Tab=&Entry=&Guide=Fus1800.ASP

  - 1820
http://www.familysearch.org/Eng/Search/rg/frameset_rg.asp?Dest=G1&Aid=&Gid=&Lid=&Sid=&Did=&Juris1=&Event=&Year=&Gloss=&Sub=&Tab=&Entry=&Guide=Fus1820.ASP

  - 1830/1840
http://www.familysearch.org/Eng/Search/rg/frameset_rg.asp?Dest=G1&Aid=&Gid=&Lid=&Sid=&Did=&Juris1=&Event=&Year=&Gloss=&Sub=&Tab=&Entry=&Guide=Fus183.ASP

  - 1850
http://www.familysearch.org/Eng/Search/rg/frameset_rg.asp?Dest=G1&Aid=&Gid=&Lid=&Sid=&Did=&Juris1=&Event=&Year=&Gloss=&Sub=&Tab=&Entry=&Guide=Fus1850.ASP

  - 1860
http://www.familysearch.org/Eng/Search/rg/frameset_rg.asp?Dest=G1&Aid=&Gid=&Lid=&Sid=&Did=&Juris1=&Event=&Year=&Gloss=&Sub=&Tab=&Entry=&Guide=Fus1860.ASP

  - 1870
http://www.familysearch.org/Eng/Search/rg/frameset_rg.asp?Dest=G1&Aid=&Gid=&Lid=&Sid=&Did=&Juris1=&Event=&Year=&Gloss=&Sub=&Tab=&Entry=&Guide=Fus1870.ASP

  - 1880
http://www.familysearch.org/Eng/Search/rg/frameset_rg.asp?Dest=G1&Aid=&Gid=&Lid=&Sid=&Did=&Juris1=&Event=&Year=&Gloss=&Sub=&Tab=&Entry=&Guide=Fus1880.ASP

- 1900
  http://www.familysearch.org/Eng/Search/rg/frameset_
  rg.asp?Dest=G1&Aid=&Gid=&Lid=&Sid=&Did=&Juris1=
  &Event=&Year=&Gloss=&Sub=&Tab=&Entry=&Guide=
  Fus1900.ASP

- 1910
  http://www.familysearch.org/Eng/Search/rg/frameset_
  rg.asp?Dest=G1&Aid=&Gid=&Lid=&Sid=&Did=&Juris1=
  &Event=&Year=&Gloss=&Sub=&Tab=&Entry=&Guide=
  Fus1910.ASP

- 1920
  http://www.familysearch.org/Eng/Search/rg/frameset_
  rg.asp?Dest=G1&Aid=&Gid=&Lid=&Sid=&Did=&Juris1=
  &Event=&Year=&Gloss=&Sub=&Tab=&Entry=&Guide=
  Fus1920.ASP

o Canada Census

- 1851
  http://www.familysearch.org/Eng/Search/rg/frameset_
  rg.asp?Dest=G1&Aid=&Gid=&Lid=&Sid=&Did=&Juris1=
  &Event=&Year=&Gloss=&Sub=&Tab=&Entry=&Guide=
  FCan1851.ASP

- 1861
  http://www.familysearch.org/Eng/Search/rg/frameset_
  rg.asp?Dest=G1&Aid=&Gid=&Lid=&Sid=&Did=&Juris1=
  &Event=&Year=&Gloss=&Sub=&Tab=&Entry=&Guide=
  FCan1861.ASP

- 1871/1881
  http://www.familysearch.org/Eng/Search/rg/frameset_
  rg.asp?Dest=G1&Aid=&Gid=&Lid=&Sid=&Did=&Juris1=
  &Event=&Year=&Gloss=&Sub=&Tab=&Entry=&Guide=
  FCan1871.ASP

- 1891
  http://www.familysearch.org/Eng/Search/rg/frameset_
  rg.asp?Dest=G1&Aid=&Gid=&Lid=&Sid=&Did=&Juris1=
  &Event=&Year=&Gloss=&Sub=&Tab=&Entry=&Guide=
  FCan1891.ASP

- 1901
  http://www.familysearch.org/Eng/Search/rg/frameset_
  rg.asp?Dest=G1&Aid=&Gid=&Lid=&Sid=&Did=&Juris1=
  &Event=&Year=&Gloss=&Sub=&Tab=&Entry=&Guide=
  FCan1901.ASP

o Other Forms

- British Census Worksheet
  http://www.familysearch.org/Eng/Search/rg/frameset_
  rg.asp?Dest=G1&Aid=&Gid=&Lid=&Sid=&Did=&Juris1=
  &Event=&Year=&Gloss=&Sub=&Tab=&Entry=&Guide=
  FBritish.ASP

- Family Group Record
  http://www.familysearch.org/Eng/Search/rg/frameset_
  rg.asp?Dest=G1&Aid=&Gid=&Lid=&Sid=&Did=&Juris1=
  &Event=&Year=&Gloss=&Sub=&Tab=&Entry=&Guide=
  FamGrpRe.ASP

- Ireland 1901/1911
  http://www.familysearch.org/Eng/Search/rg/frameset_
  rg.asp?Dest=G1&Aid=&Gid=&Lid=&Sid=&Did=&Juris1=
  &Event=&Year=&Gloss=&Sub=&Tab=&Entry=&Guide=
  FIreland.ASP

- Pedigree Chart
  http://www.familysearch.org/Eng/Search/rg/frameset_
  rg.asp?Dest=G1&Aid=&Gid=&Lid=&Sid=&Did=&Juris1=
  &Event=&Year=&Gloss=&Sub=&Tab=&Entry=&Guide=
  PedChart.ASP

- Research Log
  http://www.familysearch.org/Eng/Search/rg/frameset_
  rg.asp?Dest=G1&Aid=&Gid=&Lid=&Sid=&Did=&Juris1=
  &Event=&Year=&Gloss=&Sub=&Tab=&Entry=&Guide=
  ResLog.ASP

- FamilyTree Genealogy Book Store - Free Forms to
  Download
  http://genealogy.theshoppe.com/bk_freebies.htm

- Family Tree Magazine - Download Forms
  http://www.familytreemagazine.com/forms/download.html
  *A variety of research forms available in self-extracting files. Forms
  can be opened and used with Word Perfect and Microsoft Word97
  or 2000.*

- Form for Deed Research Notes
  http://www.dohistory.org/on_your_own/toolkit/deeds_
  form.html

- Form for Interview Tracking
  http://www.dohistory.org/on_your_own/toolkit/oralHistory_
  form.html
  From DoHistory.

- Genealogy Chart
  http://www.gcpl.lib.oh.us/services/gcr/gen_resources/
  gtree.htm

- Genealogy Research Notebook
  http://sites.netscape.net/skyebrght/notebook
  *Printable Scottish census forms for the years 1841, 1851, 1881,
  1891. Also research notebook for sale.*

  o 1841 Scottish Census Form
    http://sites.netscape.net/skyebrght/1841Scotcensus.gif

  o 1851 Scottish Census Form
    http://sites.netscape.net/skyebrght/1851Scotcensus.gif

  o 1881 Scottish Census Form
    http://sites.netscape.net/skyebrght/1881Scotcensus.gif

  o 1891 Scottish Census Form
    http://sites.netscape.net/skyebrght/1891Scotcensus.gif

- Greene County Room Genealogy Resources
  Genealogy Tree
  http://www.gcpl.lib.oh.us/services/gcr/gen_resources/
  gtree.htm

- Lineages' First Steps - Get Organized
  http://www.lineages.com/FirstSteps/Basic.asp
  Download a free tool kit of genealogical forms.

- The Pedigree Chart
  http://www.HeritageQuest.com/genealogy/help/html/
  pedigree.html
  From Heritage Quest.

- Pedigree Chart - From the LDS Church
  http://www.lds.org/fam_his/how_do_i_beg/Pedigree_
  Chart.html

- Research Log
  http://www.lds.org/images/howdoibeg/Research_Log.html
  From the LDS church.

- ROOTS-L Resources: Printable Forms
  http://www.rootsweb.com/roots-l/forms.html
  Postscript forms to print.
- Rory's Genealogy Pages - Family Record Sheet
  http://users.erols.com/emcrcc/Family_Record.htm
- Rory's Genealogy Pages - Four Generation Pedigree Chart
  http://users.erols.com/emcrcc/pedigree.htm
- Rory's Genealogy Pages - Research Log
  http://users.erols.com/emcrcc/Res_Log.htm
- Rory's Genealogy Pages - Resources Checklist
  http://users.erols.com/emcrcc/Resources_Checklist.htm
- The Tigger Movie - Family Tree
  http://disney.go.com/disneyvideos/animatedfilms/tiggermovie/familytree.html
  Three family tree charts to print and fill in, from Disney.

◆ Vendors

- Appleton's Fine Used Bookseller and Genealogy
  http://www.appletons.com/genealogy/homepage.html
- Barnette's Family Tree Book Company - Genealogy Charts
  http://www.barnettesbooks.com/charts.htm
  And Genealogy Forms
  http://www.barnettesbooks.com/forms.htm
- Chartform
  http://www.chartform.com/
  Family tree wallcharts.
- Conservation By Design Limited
  http://www.conservation-by-design.co.uk/
  United Kingdom-based vendor which provides materials and equipment for conservation and preservation.
- Custom Family Trees & Charts by Olsongraphics
  http://www.olsonetc.com/
- Dacrid's Genealogy Prints
  http://www.dacrid.com/playit/genealgy.htm
- Design Software - Genealogy Charts & Forms
  http://www.dhc.net/~design/desig1-5.htm
- Everton's Genealogy Supply Store
  http://www.everton.com/webcart/ep-store.htm
  Store with CD-ROM, books, archival quality sheets, binders, magazines and software.
- Family Tree Printer: Genealogy Charts Beautifully Printed
  http://familytreeprinter.com/
  Specializing in printing family trees on poster-size paper.
- Genealogical Services & The Genealogy Store
  http://www.genservices.com/
- Genealogy Charts and Reports
  http://www.concentric.net/~ekkm/Charts.html

- Genealogy Unlimited - Home Page
  http://www.itsnet.com/~genun/
- Genographica
  http://www.genographica.com/
  Large format genealogical tree print from GEDCOM on antique map. Most of the background images offered are XVIth century geographical maps.
- GLOBAL Genealogical Supply
  http://www.globalgenealogy.com/
- Grant Misbach's Genealogy Charts
  http://www.misbach.org/charts/index.html
  "The best selling and most popular pedigree chart in the world.".
- GRL Genealogy Supplies
  http://www.grl.com/grl/supplies.shtml
  Charts, albums and software from the Genealogical Research Library.
- Hearthstone Bookshop ~ Alexandria, Virginia
  http://www.hearthstonebooks.com/
- Keeping Memories Alive - Scrapbook Supplies
  http://www.scrapbooks.com/
- Kleerub Paper Company
  http://www.kleerub.com
  Vendor of quality rubbing paper for taking duplicate rubbings. Kleerub Paper Company is a family owned business that has served many monument companies, cemeteries and genealogical associations since 1949.
- Legacy Printing - Large Format Printing
  http://www.metalworkingsystems.com/legacy.htm
  Your Ancestor and Descendant Trees printed on a single sheet of paper up to 36" by 45". These black and white laser printed Trees are high quality for framing and gifts for your relatives yet affordable enough to use as working charts. The charts can be printed from any GEDCOM or Family Tree Maker files in PC format. Files can be sent by email or on a disk.
- The Memorabilia Corner
  http://members.aol.com/TMCorner/index.html
  Forms, flags, maps, software, CDs, tapes, microfilm & microfiche, books, periodicals, conservation & archival materials.
- Olsongraphics Custom Genealogy Family Trees
  http://www.olsonetc.com/
- Origins' Catalog and Online Ordering
  http://origins.safeshopper.com/
  Original forms, charts and genealogical supplies.
- Petersen Reproductions
  http://www.petersenprints.com/
  Wonderful things for the genealogist! T-shirts, mugs, mouse pads, software, family tree charts, baptismal & marriage certificates, family registers and much more.
- Preservation Equipment, Ltd.
  http://www.preservationequipment.com/
  United Kingdom-based vendor which provides materials and equipment for conservation and preservation.

- PrintMyFamily.com: Printing Genealogy Pedigree Wall Charts with Pictures & Photos
  http://www.printmyfamily.com/genealogy_home.html
  Personalized, full-color, large, wall-sized genealogy charts.

- Quintin Publications
  http://www.quintinpublications.com/
  Materials relating to Canada.

- Roots and Branches
  http://members.aol.com/RebelSher1/index.html
  Used books, forms, maps and the Civil War info.

- Suppliers - Sources of Conservation Supplies
  http://palimpsest.stanford.edu/bytopic/suppliers/

- Ye Olde Genealogie Shoppe © - Forms, Charts, Maps & Goodies
  http://www.yogs.com/

- Ye Olde Genealogy Charts, Ltd.
  http://www.webcom.com/charts/

- Your Family Legacy
  http://www.webyfl.com/
  Everything for the family history researcher. Genealogy supplies books, forms, software, and archival supplies. Special items for beginners.

SURNAMES, FAMILY ASSOCIATIONS & FAMILY NEWSLETTERS – GENERAL SURNAME SITES

http://www.cyndislist.com/surn-gen.htm

Category Index:

◆ General Surname Sites

◆ Mailing Lists, Newsgroups & Chat

◆ Publications, Software & Supplies

◆ General Surname Sites

● Acadian/French-Canadian SURNAME Researchers
http://www.acadian.org/resrch.html
From the Acadian Genealogy Homepage.

● Acadian Genealogy Homepage - List of Surnames on the Acadian CD
http://www.acadian.org/surnames.html

● Advice from the Experts: Running a Family Association
http://www.genealogy.com/26_runfm.html

● All Irish Clans And Names
http://www.clansandnames.org
Find out about Clans dealing with your Irish Surname.

● Changing Immigrant Names
http://www.ins.usdoj.gov/graphics/aboutins/history/articles/NAMES.htm
From the U. S. Immigration and Naturalization Service (INS). Includes a list of reasons for name changes and links to stories about how names were changed.

● Chinese Surnames
http://www.geocities.com/Tokyo/3919/

● Common Threads
http://www.gensource.com/common/
A searchable database with e-mail addresses for submitters

● Connect with Surnames Genealogy Directory
http://www.geocities.com/Heartland/Bluffs/7708/

● Council of Scottish Clans and Associations' (COSCA)
http://www.tartans.com/cosca/

● Dutch Home Pages by Familyname
http://members.tripod.com/~Don_Arnoldus/

● Family Associations 101
http://www.familytreemaker.com/26_famas.html

● Family Chronicle - Surname Origin List
http://www.familychronicle.com/surname.htm

● Family History Research Register
http://symbiosis.uk.com/fhistory/
Register your surnames here and search the list for entries by others

● Family Workings Links by Surname
http://www.familyworkings.com/links/surdir.htm

● Family History Library Catalog
http://www.familysearch.org/eng/Library/FHLC/frameset_fhlc.asp
Search this online version of the catalog for the LDS collection in Salt Lake City.

  ○ Surname Search
http://www.familysearch.org/Eng/Library/fhlc/supermainframeset.asp?display=surnamesearch&columns=*,180,0

● GenConnect Surname Boards
http://genconnect.rootsweb.com/indx/FamAssoc.html
Message boards sponsored by RootsWeb. Each surname message board set is divided into the following topics: Queries, Bibles, Biographies, Deeds, Obituaries, Pensions, Wills.

● GENDEX Database
http://www.gendex.com/
A searchable index of over 1 million names

● Genealogy Surnames - Genealogy Search Engine - Add Your URL On Genlink Genealogy Index
http://www.genlink.org/
Genlink is a genealogy search engine, capable of indexing all the surnames on your genealogy surnames page in one go if you are using Ged2www, Gedpage, Ged2HTML, Gedbrowser or Ged4Web.

● Genealogy Exchange and Surname Registry
http://www.genexchange.com/

● Genealogy Resources on the Internet - Surnames on the Web
http://www-personal.umich.edu/~cgaunt/surnames.html

● Genealogy's Most Wanted Surname Links Page
http://www.citynet.net/mostwanted/surlinks/surnames.htm

● GeneaNet - Genealogical Database Network
http://www.geneanet.org/
A surname database with web site or e-mail references for more than 10 million surnames. French or English versions available.

● GENUKI Surname Lists
http://www.genuki.org.uk/indexes/SurnamesLists.html
Lists for each county in the United Kingdom and Ireland

● Global Genealogy - Family Histories & Genealogies
http://www.globalgenealogy.com/famhist.htm

- Google Web Directory .... Genealogy>Surnames
  http://directory.google.com/Top/Society/Genealogy/Surnames/
- Guild of One-Name Studies ~ United Kingdom
  http://www.one-name.org/
- H-GIG Surname Registry
  http://www.ucr.edu/h-gig/surdata/nameform.html
- The Key to Family History Research
  http://www.sierra.com/sierrahome/familytree/hqarticles/research/
  An online article by Miriam Weiner describing how to determine an immigrant's original surname.
- Kinseeker Publications Surname Newsletters
  http://www.angelfire.com/biz/Kinseeker/newsletters.html
- The most frequent Hungarian surnames
  http://www.bogardi.com/gen/g022.htm
- Open Directory - Society: Genealogy: Surnames
  http://www.dmoz.org/Society/Genealogy/Surnames/
- The Origins of Family Names
  http://www.rootscomputing.com/howto/names/names.htm
- The relevance of surnames in genealogy
  http://www.sog.org.uk/leaflets/surnames.html
  From the Society of Genealogists (UK). Explains the history behind the taking of surnames and the difficulty of reliance on surnames in modern genealogy.
- RootsWeb Surname List -- Interactive Search
  http://rsl.rootsweb.com/cgi-bin/rslsql.cgi
  An easily searchable database maintained by volunteer Karen Isaacson. The RSL contains more than 750,000 surnames, submitted by nearly 75,000 genealogists.
  - Overview of the RootsWeb Surname List (RSL)
    http://www.rootsweb.com/roots-l/family.readme.html
  - RootsWeb Surname List: Index to Files
    http://www.rootsweb.com/roots-l/rsl-index.html
    RSL entries as of May 1997.
  - RootsWeb Surname List - Interactive Data Edit/Submission Form
    http://rsl.rootsweb.com/cgi-bin/rsledit.cgi
    - RootsWeb Surname List Country Abbreviations ~ Listed by Country
      http://www.rootsweb.com/roots-l/cabbrev1.html
    - Abbreviations from the RootsWeb Surname List ~ Listed by Abbreviation
      http://www.rootsweb.com/roots-l/cabbrev2.html
- Surname Interests Registry
  http://surnamesite.com/surnames.htm
  View surnames being researched and post your surnames to connect with others researching your line.
- The Surname Mine
  http://members.spree.com/1ofthefamily/surname/index.html
- Surname Resources at RootsWeb
  http://resources.rootsweb.com/surnames/

- Surnames: What's in a Name? * Name Origins & Meanings * Broken Arrow Publishing
  http://clanhuston.com/name/name.htm
  - Brief History of Surnames
    http://clanhuston.com/name/namehist.htm
  - Surnames A-D
    http://clanhuston.com/name/namea-d.htm
  - Surnames E-H
    http://clanhuston.com/name/namee-h.htm
  - Surnames I-O
    http://clanhuston.com/name/namei-o.htm
  - Surnames P-S
    http://clanhuston.com/name/namep-s.htm
  - Surnames T-Z
    http://clanhuston.com/name/namet-z.htm
- Stone Soup for Genealogists (Publishing a One-family Periodical)
  http://www.genealogy.com/26_wylie1.html
- Surname Database Cross-Index
  http://feefhs.org/index/indexsur.html
  FEEFHS Cross Index of 27 Surname databases.
- Surname Helper Search for a Surname
  http://surhelp.rootsweb.com/srchall.html
- Surnames in Italy / L'Italia dei cognomi
  http://gens.labo.net/en/cognomi/
  By entering a surname and pressing the red arrow, a distribution map of Italy is generated showing the concentrations of that particular surname in Italy.
- Surname Springboard
  http://www.geocities.com/~alacy/spring.htm
  Dedicated to internet researchers who have indexed their GEDCOM data & converted it to HTML pages
- The SurnameWeb
  http://www.surnameweb.org/
  The Surname Genealogy Web Project
- Top 50 Surnames in the United States
  http://www.genrecords.com/library/usnames.htm
- SWINX ® Zoeklijst Nederlandse Familienamen ~ Netherlands
  http://www.swinx.net/
  SWINX = Surname Website INdeX
- U.S. Surname Distribution Maps
  http://www.hamrick.com/names/index.html
  - Local Names in Each State
    http://www.hamrick.com/names/localnam.txt
  - Top 100 Names in the State of....
    http://www.hamrick.com/names/top100.txt
- USGenWeb Lineage Researcher Pages
  http://www.rootsweb.com/~lineage/
- What's in a Surname?
  http://www.familytreemaker.com/issue18.html
  From Family Tree Maker Online

◆ Mailing Lists, Newsgroups & Chat

- **AUS-NSW-SURNAMES Mailing List**
  http://www.rootsweb.com/~jfuller/gen_mail_surnames-gen.html#AUS-NSW-SURNAMES
  Provides a connection point for people researching specific surnames in New South Wales, Australia.

- **BRIT-SURNAMES Mailing List**
  http://www.rootsweb.com/~jfuller/gen_mail_surnames-gen.html#BRIT-SURNAMES
  For anyone researching British surnames.

- **GEN-EDITOR Mailing List**
  http://users.aol.com/johnf14246/gen_mail_general.html#GEN-EDITOR
  For editors/publishers of genealogical, surname and family newsletters to have a place to discuss and share ideas and tips

- **GOONS-L Mailing List**
  http://users.aol.com/johnf14246/gen_mail_general.html#GOONS-L
  For members of the Guild of One-Name Studies (GOONS) to promote discussion of matters concerned with One-Name Studies and the Guild

- **ROLL-CALL Mailing List**
  http://www.rootsweb.com/~jfuller/gen_mail_surnames-gen.html#ROLL-CALL
  For the posting of "roll calls" (lists) of the surnames you are researching so that others can determine if there is a common interest

- **RSL-UPDATE Mailing List**
  http://www.rootsweb.com/~jfuller/gen_mail_surnames-gen.html#RSL-UPDATE
  The Roots Surname List database monthly update of new surnames

- **soc.genealogy.surnames.* / SURNAMES-* FAQ files**
  http://www.rootsweb.com/~surnames/

- **Surname Mailing Lists - Genealogy Resources on the Internet**
  http://users.aol.com/johnf14246/gen_mail.html
  See the alphabetical listing at the bottom of the main index

- **SURNAME-ORIGINS Mailing List**
  http://www.rootsweb.com/~jfuller/gen_mail_surnames-gen.html#SURNAME-ORIGINS
  For the discussion of the etymology (word origin) of surnames, as well as the geographic origins of surnames.

- **SURNAME-QUERY Mailing List**
  http://www.rootsweb.com/~jfuller/gen_mail_surnames-gen.html#SURNAME-QUERY
  For users to send queries on specific surname searches

- **SURNAMES Mailing List**
  http://www.rootsweb.com/~jfuller/gen_mail_surnames-gen.html#SURNAMES
  Gatewayed with the soc.genealogy.surnames.global newsgroup
  news:soc.genealogy.surnames.global
  Surname queries central database

- **SURNAMES-BRITAIN Mailing List**
  http://www.rootsweb.com/~jfuller/gen_mail_surnames-gen.html#SURNAMES-BRITAIN
  Gatewayed with the soc.genealogy.surnames.britain newsgroup
  news:soc.genealogy.surnames.britain
  For surname queries related to Great Britain

- **SURNAMES-CANADA Mailing List**
  http://www.rootsweb.com/~jfuller/gen_mail_surnames-gen.html#SURNAMES-CANADA
  Gatewayed with the soc.genealogy.surnames.canada newsgroup
  news:soc.genealogy.surnames.canada
  For surname queries related to Canada

- **SURNAMES-GERMAN Mailing List**
  http://www.rootsweb.com/~jfuller/gen_mail_surnames-gen.html#SURNAMES-GERMAN
  Gatewayed with the soc.genealogy.surnames.german newsgroup
  news:soc.genealogy.surnames.german
  For surname queries related to German speaking countries

- **SURNAMES-IRELAND Mailing List**
  http://www.rootsweb.com/~jfuller/gen_mail_surnames-gen.html#SURNAMES-IRELAND
  Gatewayed with the soc.genealogy.surnames.ireland newsgroup
  news:soc.genealogy.surnames.ireland
  For surname queries related to Ireland and Northern Ireland

- **SURNAMES-MISC Mailing List**
  http://www.rootsweb.com/~jfuller/gen_mail_surnames-gen.html#SURNAMES-MISC
  Gatewayed with the soc.genealogy.surnames.misc newsgroup
  news:soc.genealogy.surnames.misc
  For surname queries for regions not addressed elsewhere in the soc.genealogy.surnames. hierarchy*

- **SURNAMES-USA Mailing List**
  http://www.rootsweb.com/~jfuller/gen_mail_surnames-gen.html#SURNAMES-USA
  Gatewayed with the soc.genealogy.surnames.usa newsgroup
  news:soc.genealogy.surnames.usa
  For surname queries related to the United States

- **WGW-SURNAMES-SCOTLAND Mailing List**
  http://www.rootsweb.com/~jfuller/gen_mail_surnames-gen.html#WGW-SURNAMES-SCOTLAND
  For the discussion and sharing of information regarding surnames originating in Scotland. A companion to the SCOTLAND-GENWEB list.

◆ Publications, Software & Supplies

- Amazon.com Genealogy Bookstore - Surnames
  http://www.amazon.com/exec/obidos/external-search/?keyword=genealogy+surnames&tag=markcyndisgenealA/

- Ancestor Publishers Microfiche - Family Histories
  http://www.firstct.com/fv/surnames.html

- AudioTapes.com - Genealogical Lectures on Cassette Tapes – Surnames
  http://www.audiotapes.com/search2.asp?Search=surname
  Association
  http://www.audiotapes.com/search2.asp?Search=association
  Newsletter
  http://www.audiotapes.com/search2.asp?Search=newsletter

- Books We Own - Family History by Surname
  http://www.rootsweb.com/~bwo/surindex.html
  Find a book from which you would like a lookup and click on the submitter's code at the end of the entry. Once you find the contact information for the submitter, write them a polite request for a lookup.

- Boyd Publishing Company - Family Histories
  http://www.hom.net/~gac/family.htm

- Heritage Books - Genealogies
  http://www.heritagebooks.com/geneal.htm

- Higginson Book Company - Surname Books A to Z
  http://www.higginsonbooks.com/surnameb.htm

- Surname distribution maps in England, Northern Ireland, Scotland and Wales
  http://www.surnamemaps.co.uk
  Presentation packages for sale of maps showing the distribution and concentration of surnames in England, Northern Ireland, Scotland and Wales.

- Willow Bend Bookstore - Families, Genealogies or Surnames
  http://www.willowbend.net/default.asp

- Yahoo!...Genealogy: Publications: Individual Family Histories
  http://dir.yahoo.com/Business_and_Economy/Shopping_and_Services/History/Genealogy/Publications/Individual_Family_Histories/

SURNAMES, FAMILY ASSOCIATIONS & FAMILY NEWSLETTERS – "A"

Resources Dedicated to One Surname
http://www.cyndislist.com/surn-a.htm

Category Index:

- ◆ General Surname Sites and Resources
- ◆ Surname Specific Sites and Resources
- ◆ Surname Mailing Lists

◆ General Surname Sites and Resources

- 'A' Surnames at RootsWeb
  http://resources.rootsweb.com/surnames/a.html

- Connect with Surnames - A
  http://www.geocities.com/Heartland/Bluffs/7708/a.html

- Dutch Home Pages by Familyname ~ Letter A
  http://members.tripod.com/~Don_Arnoldus/a.htm

- FamilyHistory.com - Message Boards - Surname - A
  http://www.familyhistory.com/messages/list.asp?prefix=AA

- Family Tree Maker Online User Home Pages - A
  http://www.familytreemaker.com/users/a/index.html

- Family Workings A Surname Links
  http://www.familyworkings.com/links/sura.htm

- GenConnect Surname Index - "A"
  http://genconnect.rootsweb.com/indx/surnames/A.html
  Message boards sponsored by RootsWeb. Each surname message board set is divided into the following topics: Queries, Bibles, Biographies, Deeds, Obituaries, Pensions, Wills.

- Genealogy Resources on the Internet - "AA-AH" Surname Mailing Lists
  http://www.rootsweb.com/~jfuller/gen_mail_surnames-aa.html
  "AI-AL"
  http://www.rootsweb.com/~jfuller/gen_mail_surnames-ai.html
  "AM-AN"
  http://www.rootsweb.com/~jfuller/gen_mail_surnames-am.html
  "AO-AT"
  http://www.rootsweb.com/~jfuller/gen_mail_surnames-ao.html
  "AU-AZ"
  http://www.rootsweb.com/~jfuller/gen_mail_surnames-au.html
  Search the index of surname mailing lists below: Surname Mailing Lists.

  o Genealogy Resources on the Internet - Surnames Included in Mailing Lists - "A"
    http://www-personal.umich.edu/~cgaunt/surnames/a.names.html

This is a computer generated list of the surnames, and all variant spellings for those names, that are found in the surname mailing lists detailed on the pages shown above.

- Genealogy Resources on the Internet - Surname Web Sites for "A" Surnames
  http://www-personal.umich.edu/~cgaunt/surnames/a.html

- Genealogy's Most Wanted - Surnames Beginning with "A"
  http://www.citynet.net/mostwanted/a.htm

- Google Web Directory .... Genealogy>Surnames>A
  http://directory.google.com/Top/Society/Genealogy/Surnames/A/

- Heartland Genealogy Society Membership List - A
  http://www.geocities.com/Heartland/Ranch/2416/hgs-mlist-a.html

- H-GIG Surname Registry - Surnames Beginning A
  http://www.ucr.edu/h-gig/surdata/surname1.html

- Higginson Book Company - Surnames Beginning with A
  http://www.higginsonbooks.com/a.htm

- inGeneas Table of Common Surname Variations and Surname Misspellings - A-B
  http://www.ingeneas.com/A2B.html

- The Obituary Link Page - Family Obituary Archives Online - A
  http://www.geocities.com/~cribbswh/obit/a.htm

- Open Directory - Society: Genealogy: Surnames: A
  http://www.dmoz.org/Society/Genealogy/Surnames/A/

- Surname Springboard Index - A
  http://www.geocities.com/~alacy/spring_i.htm

- SurnameWeb Surname Registry - A Index
  http://www.surnameweb.org/registry/a.htm

- SWINX Zoeklijst Nederlandse Familienamen / SWINX Searchlist Dutch Surnames - A
  http://www.swinx.net/swinx/swinx_aa_nl.htm

- Websites at RootsWeb: A Surnames
  http://www.rootsweb.com/~websites/surnames/a.html

◆ Surname Specific Sites and Resources

- Homepage of the ABEE Reunion
  http://www.trellis.net/steel/abee/
  ABEE, AEBI, EBY, family which settled in Lancaster County, Pennsylvania in the early 1700's.

- ABERCROMBIE Family Association
  http://members.surfsouth.com/~ka4wujga/

- Descendants of George ABERNETHY De Barrie
  http://www.parsonstech.com/genealogy/trees/babernat/Abernath.htm

- ABLETT Genealogy
  http://www.webspawner.com/users/liverpoolablett/
  ABLETT from the Liverpool, England.

- Centralized ABNEY Archives
  http://www.geocities.com/Heartland/Park/2300/

- ABREU Genealogy Website Homepage
  http://members.aol.com/abreugenea/index.htm
  A site dedicated to the Abreu family of Cuba, with family surnames, surname descriptions, brief histories of Spain and Cuba, and the Abreu Family Tree.

- The AGES- Acheson GEnealogical Society
  http://www.gwi.net/ages/
  For anyone researching the surname "Acheson", or any of the other varied spellings of this Clanns surname, i.e., Atcheson, Atkinson, Etchison, Aitchison, etc.

- ACKER Family - A Legacy of Survival
  http://hometown.aol.com/jaacker/index.htm
  ACKER family from South Carolina. Key Surnames: CLEMENT, HAGOOD, IVESTOR, MATTISON, MCCULLOUGH, ROWE, STARR, TARRENT, WEBB.

- Ancestors of George Russell ACKERMANN
  http://home.mpinet.net/ala/ackerman/index.htm
  Clemens Ackermann was born in Bavaria, Germany c1838, died 11 Mar 1896 in Wheeling, Ohio, WV. Clemens emigrated circa 2 Jun 1870, possibly arriving NY, whereupon he set out to find his future in the American "west." After a short period of working in the coal mines of PA, he made his way to Wheeling, WV, found work in his field as a blacksmith, and married Barbara Heil in Wheeling, Ohio, WV, 2 Jun 1870. Barbara was born 16 Jul 1842 in Wheeling, Ohio, WV, the daughter of Andrew Heil and Elizabeth Hohmann (both of Hesse, Germany), and died 27 Jun 1922 in Wheeling, Ohio, WV. Clemens and Barbara raised a large family. On 6 Sep 1880, he petitioned to become an American citizen and was naturalized. My husband is a great-grandson of Clemens and we are hoping to discover the identity of his parents, etc. We welcome any information that would assist us in this endeavor.

- David ACKERMAN Descendants
  http://ackerman-1662.rootsweb.com
  David Ackerman, born in the Dutch Republic who, with his wife Elizabeth BELLIER, came to New Amsterdam in 1662 with their 7 children.

- ACKLEY Family Genealogy
  http://www.geocities.com/heartland/prairie/4437
  Descendants of Nicholas Ackley, Zebulon Ackley and Scoby Ackley.

- ACUFF-ECOFF Family Archives Website
  http://www.acuff.org/
  ACUFF, ECOFF, ECKOFF, EICKHOFF, and their spelling variants.

- Hot on the Trail: ADAIR
  http://homepages.rootsweb.com/~jclaytn/adair.html
  Adair Surname (GA>LA>MS>TX).

- ADAMS Addenda II
  http://www.qpt.com/~ad-ad/index.html

- ADAMS' Family Home Page
  http://www.sevastopol.k12.wi.us/hs/adams.html
  Descendants of Robert Adams (1602-1682) of Newbury, Mass and of Uriah Mason Adams (1832-1900) and Jane Woods (McKain) Adams (1847-1913).

- ADAMS Family in Georgia
  http://www.angelfire.com/ga2/adams
  Descendants of Elijah ADAMS in Gwinnett Co., GA from about 1837.

- ADAMS Family Page
  http://www.bconnex.net/~dcadams/
  Descendants of Robert ADAMS who first came to Ipswich in 1635; believed to have come from Devonshire and to have been a son of Robert and Elizabeth SHARLON ADAMS and a cousin of Henry of Braintree, the ancestor of Presidents, John and John Quincy ADAMS, U.S. Presidents.

- The ADAMS Family Tree
  http://www.geocities.com/adamsfamilytree/
  Descendants of Thomas ADAMS, Sr. (1782 - 1865) and Isabella McBride (1787 - 1871), from county Monaghan, Ireland, migrating to Haldimand Township, Northumberland County, Ontario, Canada

- The ADGATE Family in America
  http://homepages.rootsweb.com/~hal
  The descendants of Thomas ADGATE, of Saybrook and Norwich, CT.

- ADKINS Family Information
  http://fly.hiwaay.net/~jjadkins/genealogy/adkinsinfo.html

- In AEBNIT - ABNET, ATNIP, ATNIPP, INABENET, INABNIT, INABNITT
  http://members.tripod.com/~ajobebrown/Atnip.html

- The AHERN Family
  http://world.std.com/~ahern/aherns.html
  A website for genealogists researching Ahern, Ahearn, O'Hern, and O'Hearn worldwide. Ahern(e), Ahearn(e), Hearn(e), O'Hearn(e), [2] Heachthigheirn, [2] Heachthigherna, [2] Heichthigheirn, [2] Heachthighearna, [2] Heachiairn.

- AKEHURSTER World
  http://www.akehursters.co.uk/
  A(c)(k)(e)hurst family research worldwide.

- **AKIN Ancestry**
  http://cgserver.cgtelco.net/~jimini/akin.htm
  Descendants of John EAKIN & Mary McQUIGG, especially James AIKEN & Hannah FORSYTHE.

- **Clan AKINS & The Clan AKINS Society**
  http://www.angelfire.com/al2/akinsclanwebsite/index.html
  Scottish Clan Akins history, crest badge, motto, tartan, and membership information for the Clan Akins Society. A few surname spellings include Akins, Akin, Aikin, Aiken, Aken, Aitken, Akyne, Akine, Eakin, Eakins.

- **Our Southern AKINS**
  http://homepages.rootsweb.com/~catinjax/akins/
  Southern AKINS, all spellings, in PA, VA, MD, SC, NC, GA, TN, KY, AR, MO, TX and AL.

- **ALABASTER One Name Study**
  http://ourworld.compuserve.com/homepages/Laraine_Hake/

- **ALABASTER Society**
  http://www.alabaster.org.uk
  Family originating from the counties of Suffolk/Norfolk, UK.

- **ALBAUGH Researched Information Home Page**
  http://members.tripod.com/~albaughtn/index.html
  Albaugh, Ahlbach.

- **Everything ALBAUGH**
  http://albaugh.ourfamily.com
  Data collected on the Albaugh surname and variations: Ahlbach, Albach, Albaugh, Allbaugh, Aulabaugh, Alpaugh.

- **The ALBERT Family Tree**
  http://AlbertTree.genealogy.org
  The Albert Family Tree: Representing the German Albert line and Related Families who emigrated to America in the pre-Revolutionary war period.

- **ALBERT Genealogy**
  http://www.joe2557.com
  Four different ALBERT lines who settled in Canada.

- **ALDEN House Museum and ALDEN Kindred of America**
  http://www.alden.org/
  Descendants of John Alden and Priscilla Mullins, passengers on the Mayflower.

- **David's Place - ALDERSON Genealogy**
  http://www.slip.net/~dgf/

- **The ALDINGER Family Homepage**
  http://www.aldinger.com/family/

- **The National ALDRICH Family Association**
  http://www.geocities.com/SouthBeach/Marina/2343/

- **ALDRIDGE / ARLEDGE Family Homepage**
  http://www.tx3.com/~arledge/
  For Aldridge, Aldrich, Arledge, Aldred, Allred.

- **ALEFOUNDER Ancestors**
  http://www.fortunecity.com/victorian/cloisters/116/Alefounder.html
  Everything relating to the ALEFOUNDER surname. Site includes family trees, indexes to marriages and people mentioned in wills, information on the origin of the name and heraldry.

- **El Apellido ALFARO / The Surname ALFARO**
  http://members.tripod.com/~Antonioalfaro/
  Spain, Portugal, Italy, Chile, Argentina, Brazil, Peru, Ecuador, Costa Rica, Panama, Puerto Rico, Mexico, the United States.

- **ALFORD American Family Association**
  http://www.alford.com/alford/aafa/homepage.html

- **ALGEO Family Newsletter**
  mailto:kepler@oro.net
  For details e-mail Marianne Keplet at kepler@oro.net.

- **ALLARD Family Page**
  http://www.angelfire.com/az/JMSHomepage/ALLARD.html

- **ALLCHURCH / HALLCHURCH and Related Families**
  http://ourworld.compuserve.com/homepages/tim_hallchurch/genstart1.htm

- **The ALLEE Families**
  http://www.directcon.net/tomas/
  Includes ALLIE, ALLEY, ALYEA, ELYEA, ELYA, etc.

- **ALLEN Family Tree**
  http://www.fm.mcmail.com/
  Record of every Allen baptised, married or buried at Wye, Kent, England.

- **The ALLEN Family Project**
  http://www.vineyard.net/vineyard/history/allen/allenhp.htm
  Fifteen generations of the descendants of George Allen of Sandwich 1637.

- **ALLEN Family of Person County, NC**
  http://home.att.net/~artiz/home.htm

- **ALLISON Genealogy**
  http://pages.prodigy.com/Allison/

- **The Gathering of the ALLISON Clan**
  http://www.allisonclan.org/

- **The ALLPHIN Family Home Page**
  http://www.allphin.org
  The Israel Dodge Allphin family has developed a data base for all known Allphin, Alphin families in the U.

- **The ALLRED Family Organization, Inc.**
  http://www.allredfamily.org/

- **The ALLRED Family Roster**
  http://www.allredroster.com/
  Every Name Index of over 127,000 Allred family members + histories & obituaries.

- **ALLYN Family History**
  http://www2.whidbey.net/ballyn
  Descendants of Thomas and Matthew Allyn, two brothers who immigrated to Barnstable, Massachusetts in 1637.

- **ALTON-ALLTON-AULTON Association**
  http://members.aol.com/altonnews/aaaafn.htm

- **Jeff ALVEY Genealogy History**
  http://www.fred.net/jefalvey/jeffmain.html
  Jeff's index of Alveys from 1500 to present.

- The ALWOOD Family Tree
  http://home.att.net/~j.hanna/
  Alwood, Allwood, Alward. Descendants of William Allwood.

- The AMASON * AMERSON FAMILY Website
  http://freepages.genealogy.rootsweb.com/~amasonamerson/index.html
  *A website devoted to the research of the AMASON and AMERSON families, including alternate spellings of Amoson, Amosson, Amison, Amisson etc. Transcribed data from various Amason and Amerson records and updated information on our nationwide AMASON * AMERSON HOMECOMING & HERITAGE QUEST events.*

- la page de gilles AMIEL
  http://gilles.amiel.free.fr/
  Ma page de genealogie personnelle du lauragais, de l'auvergne et de la belgique. Ainsi que des pages consacrÉes au patronyme AMIEL.

- AMONETT, AMMONET, AMMONETTE, Roots, Branches and Twigs
  http://members.aol.com/barbhutch1/Amonett.index.html

- Les Familles D'AMOURS d'Amerique
  http://www.genealogie.org/famille/damours/damours.htm
  D'AMOURS in medieval time and in North America.

- ANDERSON Genealogy - PA in 1700's to ON in 1800
  http://freepages.genealogy.rootsweb.com/~jima/
  Descendants of John ANDERSON born about 1774-80, Pennsylvania, and wife Susannah, emigrated 1800 Pennsylvania to Ontario, Canada. Genereux, Smith, Gordon, Pettit, Trembley, Roy, Glendenning, Hoggett, Mciver.

- Everett ANDERSON Memorial Collection of Colonial Virginia ANDERSON Families
  http://homepages.rootsweb.com/~anderson/virginia.html

- ANDERSON Genealogy
  http://members.aol.com/ArletaHowe/Anderson.html
  Descendants of James ANDERSON b. ca 1698 Charles City Co.,VA, (grandson of Reynard ANDERSON & Elizabeth SKIFFEN) and Elizabeth LIGON b. 1701.

- The ANDREWS Family Collection
  http://members.aol.com/gandr22/andrews.htm
  100 & growing distinct families of: Andrews, Anderson, Anders, Andrus, Andros.

- ANDREWS Surname Query Board
  http://hometown.aol.com/gandrews777/andrews.htm

- The Descendants of Francis ANDRUS
  http://www5.pair.com/vtandrew/andrews/andrews.htm

- Descendants of Joannes ANGENENDT
  http://www.parsonstech.com/genealogy/trees/cangenen/angenent.htm
  Plus 8 more branches available in Dutch.

- ANNABLE / ANABLE Family Genealogical Mailing List
  http://members.tripod.com/~pannable/list.html
  Linking ANNABLE/ANABLE family genealogist through a free subscription mailing list. Send queries, share information, meet your cousins on this mailing list.

- Charles Cormac ANNIS Family in the United States and Canada
  http://www.angelfire.com/mi/annisall/index.html
  A genealogical history of the descendants of Charles "Cormac" Annis (1638-1717) of Enniskillen, Ireland and Newbury, MA and other early Annis lineages in the United States.

- ANSLEY Family Homepage
  http://ansley-family-assn.org
  Includes ANNESLEY, AINSLEY, AINSLIE, ENSLEY, etc. Covering ALL time periods and locations.

- APGAR Family Association, Inc.
  http://www.apgarfamily.com
  Descendants of Johannes Peter Apgar who settled in Hunterdon Co., NJ in the mid-18th century.

- APPLEBY Heritage Association
  http://appleby.rootsweb.com
  Genealogy, articles from APPLEBY newsletters, pictures, family charts.

- APPLEGATE Genealogy Home Page
  http://www2.vcn.com/~applegatej/

- APPLESEED Alley
  http://www.geocities.com/Heartland/Fields/9587/
  A site devoted to Johnny Appleseed and his family, through his half-brother Nathaniel. Surnames: Chapman, Bell, Kelly, Frazee.

- An APPLETON Family
  http://community.webtv.net/AppletonRF/THEAPPLETON FAMILY
  From 1300 in England.

- ARBON Family History Organization
  http://www.arbonfamily.org/

- ARBUTHNOTT Family Association
  http://www.arbuthnot.freeserve.co.uk/
  Arbuthnott, Arbuthnot.

- ARD Genealogy
  http://www.ard.net/Ardalert/ardalert.html

- ARDISnet
  http://www.ardisnet.com/
  ARDIS, ALLERDICE, including the present-day spellings of ALARDYCE, ALDERDICE, ALDERDYCE, ALERDYCE, ALLARDICE, ALLARDYCE, ALLERDICE, ARDES, ARDIS, and ARDYCE and the historical/possibly obsolete spellings of ALARDUS, ALDARDICE, ALDARDYCE, ALDIRDICE, ALERDASH, ALERDES, ALERDICE, ALERDISE, ALERDYSE, ALIRDASSE, ALIRDES, ALLARDES, ALLARDIS, ALLARDISE, ALLARDYSE, ALLDERDICE, ALLDERDYCE, ALLERDAIS, ALLERDAS, ALLERDASH, ALLERDASHE, ALLERDES, ALLERDYCE, ALLIRDAS, ALLIRDASSE, ALLIRDES, ALLYRDAS, ALLYRDES, ALREDEIS, ALRETHES, ALYRDES, ARDICE.

- The ARENDER Family Roots
  http://www.angelfire.com/on/ArenderFamilyRoots/index.html
  Traces the ARENDER family origin to the Nordic Region of Sweden and Finland in 1772.

- **ARMSTRONG Genealogy**
  http://www.geocities.com/Heartland/Acres/2172/
  Descendants of Lt. Col John Armstrong of Armstrong's Ford, NC 1750 to 1800. Abstracts from colonial and state records including census, marriage, wills, probate, birth, ship passenger lists, and more.

- **ARMSTRONG Genealogy and History Center**
  http://www.gendex.com/~guest/martin/enigma/index.htm

- **ARNOLD Ancestry Home Page - ARNOLD Ancestry Newsletter**
  http://members.aol.com/kinseeker6/arnold.html

- **ARNOLDs of Southern Illinois & Related Families**
  http://www.mcs.net/~desoto/

- **ARNOTT Family Web Page: The Descendants of Henry ARNOT Sr.**
  http://hometown.aol.com/djarnott/myhomepage/index.html
  ARNOTT descendants from Orange Co. NY, Monroe Co. WV, Roane Co. WV, and Meigs Co. OHIO. Other descendants include PHILLIPS, TRUESDALE, LOWE, LOVE and ROUSH.

- **The ARSENAULT / ARSENEAU / ARSENEAULT / ARCENEAUX Genealogy Web Site**
  http://personal.nbnet.nb.ca/djsavard/Arseno/arseno.htm

- **ARTHUR's Courtyard**
  http://homepages.rootsweb.com/~arthur/
  A research site for the surname ARTHUR, ARTHER, ARTHOR, ARTER.

- **The ARTHUR Family Register**
  http://ourworld.compuserve.com/homepages/David_Ramsdale/homepage.htm
  From the parochs of Abercorn, Bathgate, Borrowstouness, Carriden, Dalmeny, Ecclesmachen, Kirkliston, Linlithgow, Livingston, South Queensferry, Torphichen and Whitburn in the county of West Lothian, Scotland.

- **EARTHY and ARTHY Family History**
  http://www.earthy.net/

- **Genealogie van de familie ARTS - AERTS**
  http://www.huizen.dds.nl/~aamarts/stamboom.htm
  Family of Venray, Venlo (Holland).

- **The ASBILL Family**
  http://arapaho.nsuok.edu/~asbill/asbillpg.htm
  Some more common variant spellings of the name: Asbill, Asbell, Azbel(L), Asbyll and Azbill.

- **The ASBURY Family Homepage**
  http://members.fortunecity.com/jeasbury/index.html
  Descendants of Henry Asbury, abt 1650-1707, from England to Westmoreland County, Virginia.

- **ASCOLANI Family Home Page**
  http://www.geocities.com/Heartland/2999/ascolani.htm

- **ASHBURN Homepage.**
  http://www.geocities.com/Heartland/Park/3741/Ashburn/Ash hompg1.html

- **Descendants of Anthony ASHER I**
  http://www.ovis.net/~lathorn/asher.htm
  Asher family of Washington County, PA, Monongalia County, WV, and Tyler County, WV.

- **ASHLEY Family Genealogy**
  http://members.aol.com/blackcover/ashley/ashley.html
  ASHLEY family of St. Lawerence City, New York.

- **ASHWORTH Genealogy Resource Center**
  http://freepages.genealogy.rootsweb.com/~brentspage/ashworthgrc/

- **Familia ASSIS BRASIL**
  http://assisbrasil.org/
  This site presents the families ASSIS BRASIL and BRASILIENSE. His first representative was PEDRO LUIZ DE SOUZA (Ilha Terceira, Azores), also called PEDRO LUIZ DO BRASIL, that came to Brazil arriving in Laguna, State of Santa Catarina.

- **The ATKINSON Family Tree**
  http://www.pfwsystems.com/atkinson/
  ATKINSONs of Botany, Howard Township, Kent County, Province of Ontario, Canada. Descendants of William ATKINSON of Buckden, the West Riding of Yorkshire, England.

- **AUBÉ, AUBER et AUBERT - Hommages à Claude AUBER**
  http://pages.infinit.net/slowgo/
  AUBE, AUBER and AUBERT of North America. Descendants of Claude Auber and his wife, Jacqueline Lucas.

- **AUGER Surname Family Center**
  http://my.voyager.net/hamp/auger/
  Augur, Aunger, Audger, Augier, Augar, Anger.

- **AUMACK in New York, Michigan and Canada**
  http://www.cadvision.com/millerj/familytree/aumack.htm
  A report of Abraham AUMACK (b. 1757)and descendants. Name variations include AUMOCK, AUMACH, AUMICK, AMAK.

- **The AUSTILL / AUSTELL Family Genealogy Page**
  http://members.aol.com/elzyaust/index.htm

- **AUSTIN Families Association of America (AFAOA)**
  http://www.rahul.net/afaoa/index.html

- **AUSTINs of America Genealogical Society**
  http://www.AOAGS.org/
  The Austins of America Genealogical Society is the largest group of Austin family researchers in the U.S. devoted to helping people determine their Austin roots and to publishing their research to preserve it for posterity.

- **AUTRY Genealogy Page**
  http://homepages.rootsweb.com/~autry/
  Autry, Autrey, Autery, Awtry, Awtrey, Awtray, d'Autry, D'Autry, Dautry, Outry, Otray, Aughtry, Auttry, Autri, Alterius.

- **Henry Clay & Sarah (SPENCER) AVENT**
  http://www.crosswinds.net/~sirert/family/avent/wc_toc.htm
  Descendants of Henry Clay AVENT (1820-1897) and Sarah C. SPENCER (1825-1887) of Webster County, Mississippi. A few of the surnames found this line are ALDRIDGE, CROWLEY, GRIFFIN, GRIFFITH, HENLEY, LAMB, QUINN and MILLER.

- Jeduthan AVERETT Family Association
  http://www.aros.net/~everett
  Averett, Averitt, Averyt, Avery, Everett descendants of Jeduthan AVERETT whose will was probated February 1798 in Nash County, North Carolina. Earliest proven ancestor of the Averett/Avery/Everett families who trace their lineage through Perry County, Alabama.

- AUVENSHINE Family Tree
  http://home.flash.net/~genie/

- AVIS Family Resource Center
  http://www.geocities.com/avis_center/index.html
  AVES, AVICE.

- AXSOM Association of America
  http://users.southeast.net/~leaxsom/

- AXTELL Family Organization
  http://www.sover.net/~daxtell/axtell/
  Axtell, Axtel, Axtelle.

- AYERS / AYRES Sightings Florida: 1850 and Before
  http://lehto.rootsweb.com/AyersAyres.html

- Capt. John AYERS of Ipswich, MA
  http://home.mpinet.net/ala/ayer/index.htm

- AYRAUD Family Tree
  http://hometown.aol.com/paulayraud/PaulsStuff/index.htm
  Lists the descendents of Jean Ayraud (Eyraud) who originated in France. The family immigrated to Louisiana around the time of the American Revolution.

◆ Surname Mailing Lists

- "AA-AH" Surname Mailing Lists
  http://www.rootsweb.com/~jfuller/gen_mail_surnames-aa.html
  AAMOT (includes Aamodt, Amot), AARON (includes Arnn, Aron, Arun, Aarons), ABBEY, ABBOT, ABBOTT (includes Abbot, Abot, Abott), ABBOTT, ABDALLA (includes Abdallah, Abdel, Abdelal, Abdelaziz, Abdeldayen, Abdelhamid, Abdella, Abdelmuti, Abdelrahman,, Abdelwahed, Abdul, Abdula, Abdulaziz, Abdulkarim, Abdulla, Abdullah, Abdullai, Abdulmateen, Abdulmuniem, Abed,, Abedelah, Abedi), ABEL, ABEL (includes Abell, Able, Ables), ABELL, ABER, ABERCROMBIE (includes Abbercrombie, Abbercrumby), ABERNATHY (includes Abernethy), ABERNETHY, ABLE, ABLES, ABNER, ABNET (includes Abinet, Abnetin, Abnett, Abnick, Abnieck, Abniet, Abriet, Adnet, Ebinet, Ebnet, Ebnit, Enabnett,, Enabnit, Enapnit, Enepnit, Inabnit), ABNEY (includes Abner, Albini, Aubigney, Aubignú, d'Abney, d'Albini, d'Aubigney, d'Aubignú, de Saint-Sauveur), ABNEY, ABRAHAM, ABRAHAMSON, ABRAMS, ABRELL (includes Abrelle), ABSHIRE (includes Ahsear, Absear, Abshere, Ipsher, Abcher, Abscher, Absher, Abshair, Absheer, Absheir, Abshir,, Abshier, Abshur, Apshire, Abshear, Apshear, Aleshire, Abshaw, Habisch, Habischer, Apsher, Alesher, Apshier, Ipsher,, Abshar, Upsher, Upshaw, Upshire), ABSTON, ACHESON, ACHORD, ACKER, ACKERMAN (includes Ackermann, Aukerman, Ackeman, Akerman, Acerman, Ockerman), ACKERMANN, ACKERSON, ACKLES (includes Accles), ACKLEY, ACKLIN, ACORD, ACOYA, ACREE, ACRES, ACTON, ACUFF (includes Ecoff, Eickhoff, Ayscough, Eckhoff, Achuff, Acoff), ADAIR, ADAM, ADAMEK, ADAMS (includes McAdams, Addams), ADAMSKI (includes Adamsky), ADAMSON, ADAY (includes Ady, Addy, Adie, Edie, Eadie, Eddy), ADCOCK,

ADCOCK, ADDINGTON, ADDIS, ADDISON, ADDY, ADE, ADIX (includes Addicks, Adicks, Addix, Addecks, Adecks), ADKINS (includes Adkinson, Atkins, Atkinson), ADKINSON, ADLER, ADMIRE (includes Admyer), ADNEY, ADRIAN (includes Adrion, Adrain, Adrianse), ADSHEAD (includes Adshade, Adshede), ADSIT, AEBERSOLD (includes Aebersole, Aebersol, Abersold, Abersol, Ebersold, Ebersohl, Ebersole), AFFLECK (includes Afflick, Auchenleck), AGAN, AGAR, AGASSIZ, AGEE, AGER, AGNER (includes Agnor, Aigner, Agender, Egner, Egnor, Eygner, Eigner), AGNEW, AGOSTON, AGUERO, AGUILER (includes Aguila, Aguilera), AGYAR, AHAUS, AHEARN, AHERN, AHLF, AHRENS.

- "AI-AL" Surname Mailing Lists
  http://www.rootsweb.com/~jfuller/gen_mail_surnames-ai.html
  AIELLO, AIKEN, AIKENS, AIKIN, AIKMAN, AILSTOCK (includes Aylstock, Alestock), AINSLEY, AINSLIE, AINSWORTH, AIRD, AIROV, AITCHISON, AITKEN, AKEHURST (includes Ackhurst, Ackehurst, Akhurst, Akurst), AKENHEAD, AKENS, AKER, AKERS (includes Ackers, Acree, Akerman, McAkers, Eckers), AKIN, AKINS, ALARCON, ALBAN, ALBAUGH, ALBAUGH, ALBEE (includes Albe, Allbee, Alby, Albie, Aulby), ALBERS, ALBERT (includes Aulbert, Alburt, Alberts), ALBERTSON, ALBIN, ALBRECHT (includes Aubrecht, Ahubrecht, Ahlbrecht, Albright), ALBRECHT, ALBRIDGE, ALBRIGHT, ALBRITTON, ALBRO, ALCOCK, ALCORN (includes Alcon, Allcorn), ALCORN, ALDEN (includes Aldin), ALDER, ALDERMAN, ALDERSON (includes Aldersen, Aldersan), ALDRED, ALDRICH (includes Aldridge), ALDRICH, ALDRIDGE, ALDY, ALESCI, ALESHIRE, ALEXANDER (includes McAlexander, Elaxander, Alexein), ALEXANDRATOS, ALEXANDRE, ALFORD (includes Alfred, Allford, Halford, Hallford, Holford, Olford, Ollford), ALFRED, ALGAR, ALGEO (includes Ajo, Aldgeo, Aldioye, Aldjeo, Aldjo, Aldjoe, Aldjoy, Algar, Algee, Algeo, Alger, Algie, Algoe, Algo,, Algow, Aljeo, Aljho, Aljo, Aljoy, Allgeo, Allgoe, Alljo, Aljoe, Alljoy, Auldje, Auldjo, Auldjoy, Awldioy, Ciojo, Hallio,, Ouldjo), ALGER, ALISON, ALKIRE, ALL, ALL, ALLAN, ALLARD, ALLBRIGHT, ALLEE (includes D'Ailly, Alyee, Alyie, Alyea, Allie), ALLEMAN, ALLEN (includes Allan, Allyn), ALLEN, ALLEN (includes Allun, Allin), ALLEN, ALLENDER, ALLER, ALLERTON, ALLEY, ALLGAR, ALLGOOD, ALLIN, ALLING, ALLINGHAM (includes Alligam), ALLIS, ALLISON (includes Alison, Ellison, Elison), ALLMAN, ALLOWAY, ALLPHIN, ALLPORT, ALLRED, ALLSHOUSE, ALLUM, ALLYN, ALMAND, ALMAS (includes Almis, Almos, Almost, Almus), ALMOND (includes Almon, Alman, Almand), ALMY, ALSOP, ALSPACH, ALSTON, ALSUP, ALT, ALTER, ALTHOUSE (includes Althaus), ALTIG (includes Altic, Altice, Altick, Altis, Altus), ALTMAN (includes Aultman, Altmann), ALTON, ALVERSON (includes Alvison, Alberson, Olverson), ALVEY, ALVIS, ALWINE (includes Allwein, Allwine, Alwin), ALWOOD.

- "AM-AN" Surname Mailing Lists
  http://www.rootsweb.com/~jfuller/gen_mail_surnames-am.html
  AMARAL, AMBLER, AMBROSE, AMBURGEY, AMEND, AMERSON, AMERSON, AMES, AMES, AMEY, AMICK (includes Amey, Amock, Amack, Emick, Emig, Emigh, Emich), AMIDON, AMIS, AMMERMAN, AMMON, AMMONS, AMONETT (includes Amonette, Ammonet, Ammonette, Amonet), AMOS, AMPHLETT, AMPLEFORD, AMPOLSK (includes Yampolsk, Yampolski), AMSBURY (includes Amesbury, Amsberry), AMSDEN, AMSEL (includes Amzel), AMY, ANDERLINI, ANDERS, ANDERSDOTTER, ANDERSEN, ANDERSON, ANDERSON, ANDERSON, ANDERSON, ANDERSSON, ANDERT, ANDERTON, ANDIS (includes Andes), ANDRADE, ANDRE, ANDREAS, ANDREAS (includes Andress, Endress, Andrews, Andres, Anders), ANDRES,

ANDRESEN, ANDREW, ANDREWARTHA (includes Andrawartha), ANDREWS (includes Anderson, Andrus, Anders, Andres, Andrew, Andrewsen, Anderssen, Andress, McAndrews), ANDRUS, ANGEL, ANGELL, ANGEVINE, ANGLE, ANGLESEY, ANGLIN, ANIBA, ANNABLE (includes Anable, Anible), ANNABLE, ANNING (includes Annynge, Anneng, Anneg, Annyg, Anninger, Anningson), ANNIS, ANNOOT, ANSELL, ANSELMO, ANSLEY (includes Annesley, Ainsley, Ainslie, Aynsley, Ausley, Antley, Angley, Endsley, Ensley), ANSON, ANSPACH (includes Anspaugh, Aunspach), ANSTEY, ANSTINE (includes Einstein, Anstein), ANTHONY, ANTHONY, ANTLE, ANTRICAN (includes Antriken, Antrikin, Antreken, Antrekin, Anterkin, Anterken, Antercan, Enterkin, Enterken,, Entriken, Entrekin, Entreken, Entrikin), ANTRIM, ANTROBUS, ANWAY.

- **"AO-AT" Surname Mailing Lists**
  http://www.rootsweb.com/~jfuller/gen_mail_surnames-ao.html
  APGAR, APODACA, APPEL, APPENZELLER, APPINO, APPLE, APPLEBY, APPLEGATE, APPLEGATE (includes Appelgate, Applegarth, Applegath), APPLEMAN, APPLETON, APPLEWHITE, APPLING, APPS, ARAGON, ARANT (includes Arrant), ARANT, ARBING, ARBOGAST, ARBUCKLE, ARCHAMBAULT, ARCHBOLD, ARCHER, ARCHIBALD, ARD, ARENDS, ARENS, AREY, ARGUE, ARIS (includes Ayres, Eyres, Ariss, Eyores), ARKWRIGHT, ARLEDGE (includes Aldridge, Allred), ARMACOST (includes Armacost, Arbegast, Erbegast), ARMBRUSTER, ARMENTOR, ARMENTROUT, ARMES, ARMISTEAD, ARMITSTEAD, ARMITAGE, ARMOUR, ARMS, ARMSTEAD, ARMSTED, ARMSTRONG (includes Armstrang, Fortenbra, Fortebraccio), ARNDT, ARNER, ARNESON, ARNET, ARNETT, ARNEY (includes Ernigh, Erneigh, Erney), ARNEY, ARNOLD, ARNOT, ARNOTT, ARON (includes Aaron), ARRANTS, ARRASMITH, ARRENDELL (includes Arendell, Arendall, Arandal, Arundle), ARRINGTON, ARROWOOD, ARROWSMITH, ARTHUR (includes Arther, Arter), ARTZ, ARUNDEL, ARUNDELL, ARVIN, ARWOOD (includes Arrowood, Earwood, Garrowood, Harrowood,

Yearwood), ASBERRY, ASBURY, ASDELL (includes Asdel, Azdell, Azdel, Asdale, Esdale, Esdell), ASH, ASHBAUGH, ASHBROOK, ASHBURN, ASHBY, ASHCRAFT, ASHE, ASHER, ASHER (includes Ashert, Ashearst, Ayrshire), ASHFIELD, ASHFORD, ASHLEY, ASHLOCK, ASHMAN, ASHMORE, ASHTON, ASHWELL, ASHWILL (includes Ashwell, Ashwil, Ashwel), ASHWORTH, ASKEW, ASKEY, ASKINS, ASTLE, ASTON, ATCHINSON, ATCHISON, ATCHLEY, ATEN, ATHA, ATHERTON, ATHEY (includes Athy, Athon, Athan, Athen, Athons, Athens, Athans), ATKEY, ATKIN, ATKINS, ATKINSON (includes Adkinson, Atkisson, Adkisson), ATNIP (includes Allnip, Allnipp, Alniss, Amminet, Apnip, Arnit, Atnipe, Atnip In, Atnipp, Atnips, Atniss, Inabnit), ATTAKULLAKULLA, ATTAWAY, ATTEBERRY, ATTERBERRY, ATTERBURY, ATTEY, ATTWOOD, ATWATER, ATWELL, ATWOOD (includes Attwood, Atewood, Attewood, Atwod, Atte Wode), ATYEO (includes Atyoe, Atteyo).

- **"AU-AZ" Surname Mailing Lists**
  http://www.rootsweb.com/~jfuller/gen_mail_surnames-au.html
  AUBERT, AUBIN, AUBREY, AUBRY, AUCOIN, AUDLEY, AUDSLEY, AUER, AUERBACH, AUFDERHEIDE, AUGER (includes Augur, Augir, Audger, Aunger, Agar, Odger, Angier, Augier, Anger, Elger, Alger), AUGHE (includes Ache, Aughey, Aughee, Achey), AUGUST, AUGUSTIN, AUGUSTINE, AULD, AULT, AULTMAN, AUMILLER (includes Ommiler, O'miller), AURAND (includes Aurandt, Arand, Arandt, Ayrand), AUSMUS, AUSMUS (includes Aussmus, Osmus), AUSTEN, AUSTIN, AUTEN (includes Anton, Auton, Autin, Awten, Awton, Otten, Aten, Atten), AUTREY, AUTREY, AUTRY (includes Autrey, Autery, Awtry, Awtrey, Awtray, d'Autry, D'Autry, Dautry, Outry, Otray, Aughtry, Auttry,, Autri, Alterius), AUVIL, AUXIER, AVANT, AVARA (includes Avera), AVEN, AVERILL, AVERY, AVEY, AVILA, AWTREY, AXFORD, AXTELL, AYARS, AYCOCK, AYER, AYERS, AYERS (includes Ayres), AYLOR (includes Alor, Ehler, Ahler, Ohler, McEller), AYNSLEY, AYNSLIE, AYOTTE (includes Hayot), AYRES (includes Ayers), AYRIS, AYTES (includes Aites, Ates).

SURNAMES, FAMILY ASSOCIATIONS & FAMILY NEWSLETTERS – "B"

Resources Dedicated to One Surname
http://www.cyndislist.com/surn-b.htm

Category Index:

◆ General Surname Sites and Resources

◆ Surname Specific Sites and Resources

◆ Surname Mailing Lists

◆ General Surname Sites and Resources

- 'B' Surnames at RootsWeb
  http://resources.rootsweb.com/surnames/b.html

- Connect with Surnames - B
  http://www.geocities.com/Heartland/Bluffs/7708/b.html

- Dutch Home Pages by Familyname ~ Letter B
  http://members.tripod.com/~Don_Arnoldus/ba.htm

- FamilyHistory.com - Message Boards - Surname - B
  http://www.familyhistory.com/messages/list.asp?prefix=BA

- Family Tree Maker Online User Home Pages - B
  http://www.familytreemaker.com/users/b/index.html

- Family Workings B Surname Links
  http://www.familyworkings.com/links/surb.htm

- GenConnect Surname Index - "B"
  http://genconnect.rootsweb.com/indx/surnames/B.html
  Message boards sponsored by RootsWeb. Each surname message board set is divided into the following topics: Queries, Bibles, Biographies, Deeds, Obituaries, Pensions, Wills.

- Genealogy Resources on the Internet - "BAA-BAD" Surname Mailing Lists
  http://www.rootsweb.com/~jfuller/gen_mail_surnames-baa.html
  "BAE-BAH"
  http://www.rootsweb.com/~jfuller/gen_mail_surnames-bae.html
  "BAI-BAN"
  http://www.rootsweb.com/~jfuller/gen_mail_surnames-bai.html
  "BAO-BAR"
  http://www.rootsweb.com/~jfuller/gen_mail_surnames-bao.html
  "BAS-BAT"
  http://www.rootsweb.com/~jfuller/gen_mail_surnames-bas.html
  "BAU-BD"
  http://www.rootsweb.com/~jfuller/gen_mail_surnames-bau.html

  "BEA-BED"
  http://www.rootsweb.com/~jfuller/gen_mail_surnames-bea.html
  "BEE-BEH"
  http://www.rootsweb.com/~jfuller/gen_mail_surnames-bee.html
  "BEI-BEN"
  http://www.rootsweb.com/~jfuller/gen_mail_surnames-bei.html
  "BEO-BET"
  http://www.rootsweb.com/~jfuller/gen_mail_surnames-beo.html
  "BEU-BH"
  http://www.rootsweb.com/~jfuller/gen_mail_surnames-beu.html
  "BI-BK"
  http://www.rootsweb.com/~jfuller/gen_mail_surnames-bi.html
  "BL-BN"
  http://www.rootsweb.com/~jfuller/gen_mail_surnames-bl.html
  "BOA-BOD"
  http://www.rootsweb.com/~jfuller/gen_mail_surnames-boa.html
  "BOE-BOH"
  http://www.rootsweb.com/~jfuller/gen_mail_surnames-boe.html
  "BOI-BON"
  http://www.rootsweb.com/~jfuller/gen_mail_surnames-boi.html
  "BOO-BOT"
  http://www.rootsweb.com/~jfuller/gen_mail_surnames-boo.html
  "BOU-BQ"
  http://www.rootsweb.com/~jfuller/gen_mail_surnames-bou.html
  "BRA-BRD"
  http://www.rootsweb.com/~jfuller/gen_mail_surnames-bra.html
  "BRE-BRH"
  http://www.rootsweb.com/~jfuller/gen_mail_surnames-bre.html
  "BRI-BRN"
  http://www.rootsweb.com/~jfuller/gen_mail_surnames-bri.html
  "BRO-BRT"
  http://www.rootsweb.com/~jfuller/gen_mail_surnames-bro.html

"BRU-BT"
http://www.rootsweb.com/~jfuller/gen_mail_surnames-bru.html

"BUA-BUH"
http://www.rootsweb.com/~jfuller/gen_mail_surnames-bua.html

"BUI-BUQ"
http://www.rootsweb.com/~jfuller/gen_mail_surnames-bui.html

"BUR-BUR"
http://www.rootsweb.com/~jfuller/gen_mail_surnames-bur.html

"BUS-BZ"
http://www.rootsweb.com/~jfuller/gen_mail_surnames-bus.html

Search the index of surname mailing lists below: Surname Mailing Lists.

- o Genealogy Resources on the Internet - Surnames Included in Mailing Lists - "B"
  http://www-personal.umich.edu/~cgaunt/surnames/b.names.html
  This is a computer generated list of the surnames, and all variant spellings for those names, that are found in the surname mailing lists detailed on the pages shown above.

- Genealogy Resources on the Internet - Surname Web Sites for "B" Surnames
  http://www-personal.umich.edu/~cgaunt/surnames/b.html

- Genealogy's Most Wanted - Surnames Beginning with "B"
  http://www.citynet.net/mostwanted/b.htm

- Google Web Directory .... Genealogy>Surnames>B
  http://directory.google.com/Top/Society/Genealogy/Surnames/B/

- Heartland Genealogy Society Membership List - B
  http://www.geocities.com/Heartland/Ranch/2416/hgs-mlist-b.html

- H-GIG Surname Registry - Surnames Beginning B
  http://www.ucr.edu/h-gig/surdata/surname2.html

- Higginson Book Company - Surnames Beginning with B
  http://www.higginsonbooks.com/b.htm

- inGeneas Table of Common Surname Variations and Surname Misspellings - A-B
  http://www.ingeneas.com/A2B.html

- The Obituary Link Page - Family Obituary Archives Online - B
  http://www.geocities.com/~cribbswh/obit/b.htm

- Open Directory - Society: Genealogy: Surnames: B
  http://www.dmoz.org/Society/Genealogy/Surnames/B/

- Surname Springboard Index - B
  http://www.geocities.com/~alacy/spring_b.htm

- SurnameWeb Surname Registry - B Index
  http://www.surnameweb.org/registry/b.htm

- SWINX Zoeklijst Nederlandse Familienamen / SWINX Searchlist Dutch Surnames - B
  http://www.swinx.net/swinx/swinx_ba_nl.htm

- Websites at RootsWeb: B Surnames
  http://www.rootsweb.com/~websites/surnames/b.html

◆ Surname Specific Sites and Resources

- BABBITT Family Association
  http://www.babbitt.org/
  Descendents of Edward BOBET of Taunton, Massachusetts.

- BACHMAN / BAUGHMAN Genealogy
  http://members.aol.com/ewbaugh/index.htm
  Descendants of Ulrich Bachmann (1610) of Lauperswil, Signau District, Canton Berne, Switzerland.

- BACON Genealogy - Michael Bacon of Dedham, 1640 and His Descendants
  http://www.flinthills.com/~bacon/Bacon/Preface.html

- BAGNALL Genealogy
  http://www.ukmail.org/~stuartb
  Site dedicated to the history of the surname BAGNALL and the place of that name in Staffordshire, UK.

- BAGUST Family History
  http://www.jbagust.freeserve.co.uk/
  BAGUST worldwide.

- BAILEY/BAYLEY, BAILY, Etc.
  http://www.angelfire.com/mo/BaileyInfo
  Information on all BAILEYs all spellings and all areas, descendant charts, births, marriages, deaths, books, periodicals.

- BAILEY/BAYLEY, etc. Family Research & Home of the Bailey Database
  http://www.geocities.com/Heartland/Ridge/9537/index.htm
  Database for all BAILEY/BAYLEY, etc. anywhere/anyplace.

- BAILEY Brood Genealogy Book
  http://members.nbci.com/baileybrood/

- BAILEY Family Forum
  http://members.boardhost.com/bailey/

- BAILEY Periodicals and Publications
  http://www.rootsweb.com/~sueskay/misc/bailey.htm

- Catherine BAILLON Royal Connection Research Association
  http://habitant.org/baillon/

- The BAIRD Family
  http://www.angelfire.com/nf/baird/index.html
  BAIRD family in MO, MA, PA, OH & more.

- The BAISDEN, BASDEN, BASDON, BASEDANE Family Homepage
  http://homepages.rootsweb.com/~dwb1/baisden.htm

- BAKER Genealogy
  http://members.aol.com/PowellGen/BAKERGenealogy.html
  Excerpts from the 1979 Dorothy Merrifield book entitled "A Genealogical Record of the Moses BAKER Family" which includes family history stories.

- BAKERs of Edgmont
  http://www.springhillfarm.com/baker/index.html
  Genealogy of the BAKER family which emigrated from Edgmond, Shropshire, England in 1684 and settled in Edgmont Township, Chester (now Delaware) County, Pennsylvania.

- The BAKERs of England, Pennsylvania, Illinois and Texas
  http://members.xoom.com/bakertree/

- BAKER Surname
  http://homepages.rootsweb.com/~jclaytn/baker.html
  BAKER surname: (MA>NC>KT>TX).

- Martin and Hannah Ann CLARK BAKER of Halifax Co., VA and Garrard Co., KY and their Descendants
  http://www.wiu.edu/users/mfeak/
  This site focuses on this one BAKER family and their more than 1,400 descendants.

- The BALCH House Associates
  http://members.tripod.com/~BALCHNews/
  BALCH Family Association, including online newsletter, photo gallery of "1636 BALCH House," genealogical links, and Massachusetts vital record lookup service for 175 towns.

- BALDWIN Family Home Page - Genealogy
  http://members.home.net/baldwinfamily/

- BALLARD Family Tree
  http://www.users.globalnet.co.uk/~kenelks/ballard.htm
  Daisy Ellen Ballard and her ancestors.

- BALL, EDWARD Surname Mailing List
  http://www.rootsweb.com/~jfuller/gen_mail_surnames-bai.html#EDBALL
  Edward Ball and other Newark, NJ founding families.

- BALL(S) Family History
  http://www.geocities.com/aballfamily/
  Includes Henry BALLS (1806), Turvey in Bedfordshire, Henry John BALLS (1836), South End Green London and Maynard BALL, Walsall West Midlands (1889).

- The BALL Room: Descendants of Edward Ball (1640-1724) of NJ
  http://www.rootsweb.com/~genepool/edballnj.htm
  Or Descendants of Edward BALL of New Jersey - GEDCOM Repository Site
  http://www.altlaw.com/edball/

- BALLEW Association
  http://www.ballewassn.org/

- BALTZEGAR Family News
  http://www.orbiter.com/baltzega/INDEX.HTM
  Researching BALTZEGAR family history, including Baltzigar, Baltezagar, Baltzagler & Balltzglier.

- BANCROFTs from Yorkshire
  http://freepages.genealogy.rootsweb.com/~bancroftsfrom yorkshire/

- BANDY Family Website
  http://www.Bandy.co.uk

- BANFIELD Families
  http://clubs.yahoo.com/clubs/banfieldandbanfieldfamilies

- BANGS and Allied Families
  http://www.buffnet.net/~jcole/
  For descendants of Edward Bangs, the Pilgrim, who arrived at Plymouth, Massachusetts on the Anne in July of 1623.

- BANKS / BANKES Families (U.S.)
  http://members.aol.com/rayhbanks/title.html

- The BANNER Family of North Carolina
  http://juliemorrison.com/gen/banner/
  Henry BANNER, born about 1727, came to Rowan County, North Carolina about 1751.

- BANTHER Family History from 1618 to 1996
  http://www.banther.com
  Also BENDER, PANTHER, PAINTER, PANTER, NANNEY.

- The BARBEE Place
  http://www.geocities.com/Heartland/Oaks/5200
  A place for all relatives and friends to visit and learn about the BARBEE family.

- BARBER Family History
  http://www.wco.com/~barber/family/
  Descendants of Samuel BARBER, born around 1785 in Maryland.

- BARBER Family
  http://members.tripod.com/~Stonestepper/b/frame302.htm
  Ancestors and descendants of Samuel B. BARBER and Elizabeth (Betsy) BARROW. Also WILLIAMS, MALEY, HATCHER, and many others.

- BARBER Home Page
  http://hometown.aol.com/~barbrfam/index.html
  Genealogies for about 75 different families most of which are not related.

- BARCLAY One-Name Study
  http://www.clanbarclay.com/genealogy.htm

- The BARD Family Web Page
  http://members.localnet.com/~cbard/Bard_Gen_Page/bard_family.html

- BARDSLEY One-Name Study
  http://www.bardsley.mcmail.com/

- BARE Family Notes Huntington Co., Indiana
  http://members.tripod.com/Dr.G/bare.htm
  Descendants of Jacob & Mary BARE who emigrated to Huntington Co., Indiana.

- Index of the BARG Family Web Site
  http://www.geocities.com/Paris/Musee/7075/index.html
  Dedicated to the genealogy and history of the BARG, BERG, BARK & BARCK Jewish Families and the Barg one-name study.

- BARGER Family History Society
  http://members.tripod.com/~suzid/index.html

- BARKER Mailing List Home Page
  http://www.rootsweb.com/~scwhite/barker/index.html

- BARKLOW Family Web Page
  http://www.fortunecity.com/millenium/cslewis/3/index.html
  Also Barklow, Bartlow, Barkelow, Barkeloo.

- BARLOW Clearinghouse
  http://freepages.genealogy.rootsweb.com/~barlow/
  To aid any and all researchers of the BARLOW surname.

- Irene's Family Web Page - BARNARD & BUTTLE
  http://www.geocities.com/Athens/6896/

- Pages in Memory of Adam BARNER of Liverpool, PA
  http://www.monumental.com/wbarner/
  Dedicated to his descendants.

- BARNES Genealogy
  http://www.martygrant.com/gen/barnes-sc.htm
  BARNES Genealogy of Marion Co, SC.

- BARNETT Family Page
  http://www.geocities.com/Heartland/Prairie/2089/
  Descendants of Joseph BARNETT (1754-1838) of Port Barnett PA and related families in Wisconsin, including CLIFFORD, HENEY, SCHUBERT, FLECKENSTEIN, KALTENBACH, CALLIS.

- The BARNEY Family Historical Association
  http://www.barneyfamily.org/

- BARNEY Family History Association
  http://www.rootsweb.com/~daisy/1bfha.htm

- BARNHOUSE Branches - A Surname Resource Center
  http://www.nataliesnet.com/barnhouse
  Surname genealogy research for all U.S. Barnhouse branches.

- The History & Genealogy of John S. BARNS
  http://www.geocities.com/Heartland/3958/

- BARNUM Family Genealogy
  http://www.barnum.org/
  A research database for those researching the Barnum, Barnham, Barnam surname in England and North America. Contains 5,400 individuals.

- BARNWELL Family GenealogyIndex
  http://members.tripod.com/~Dave_Barnwell/barnwell_index.html

- BARR Family Tree Trackers
  http://hometown.aol.com/MGBARR/INDEX.HTML

- BARRACLOUGH Surname Study
  http://users.net2000.com.au/~football/index.html
  Including all variants of the surname: BARACLOUGH, BARROWCLOUGH, BARACLIFFE, BARRACLIFFE, BARROWCLIFFE, BARACLIFF, BARRACLIFF, BARROWCLIFF.

- The BARRELL Home Page
  http://www2.fwi.com/~mjbarrell/
  An ever-growing database of the BARRELL family that originated in the Norfolk and Sussex England area and came to the US in 1854. Key names include BUFFHAM, PRIME, CHILD, OLMSTEAD, PIERCE. Includes image files of historic documents and photos.

- BARROW Family Association of America
  http://www.geocities.com/Heartland/Flats/9562/
  The purpose of the Barrow Family Association is to encourage the collection and publication of genealogical records of those Barrow men and women who were early colonists in Virginia and North Carolina and their descendants. However, all Barrow descendants are invited to link to this site with the hope that this will encourage additional research and cross-referencing.

- The BARTHOLOMEW Family
  http://www.geocities.com/Heartland/Estates/4456/table.html

- BARTLETT Family Research
  http://homepages.rootsweb.com/~cst/bartlett/
  Surname Resource Center to assist others in researching the BARTLETT surname and its variations. Also the homepage for the BARTLETT-L genealogy discussion group, and contains lineages, a query page and links to other resources.

- The BARTLETT Family - BARTLETTs of Pendomer
  http://www.bartlett.to/
  Ancestors and descendants of Robert Hamilton BARTLETT, who was born in Australia in 1878 and subsequently moved back to the United Kingdom, where he lived his life until dying at the age of 90 in Hove, Sussex.

- BARTOLD / BERTHOLD Surname Resource Center
  http://www.bartold.com/genealogy/
  History of its origin in Southern Europe before the end of the first millennia.

- BARTLETT Genealogy Foundation
  http://www.bartlettgenealogy.org/

- The Official BASEGGIO Family Website
  http://www.baseggio.net
  Including: de Baseggio, Basegio and Bazeggio.

- The BASFORD Family Genealogy
  http://www.basford.org/genealogy/index.html
  Includes a database with the descendants of Jacob BASFORD of Hampton, NH, and a database of extracted census data.

- The BASKERVILLE Families of the World
  http://www.moonrakers.com/genealogy/baskerville/index.html

- BASTIN Family Website
  http://www.geocities.com/Heartland/Prairie/9714/
  Descendants of Thomas & Hannah Bastin (1745-1834) of Caswell Co, North Carolina.

- BATCHELDER / BATCHELLER Family Origins
  http://www.mindspring.com/~jogt/surnames/batcheld.htm
  Excerpts from: Batchelder, Batcheller Genealogy, by F. C. Pierce, 1898.

- BATCHELOR / BACHELDER Marriages
  http://members.aol.com/gma529/B-Marriages.htm

- The BATES Family of Old Virginia
  http://www.bfoov.org/
  Dedicated to a reverence of Virginia history and assembling and publishing documented information on Virginia Bates.

- Descendants of Carey Dexter BATES
  http://users.eoni.com/~jbates/

- The BATHURST Home Page
  http://www.geocities.com/Heartland/Acres/5783/

- Battlist
  http://www.onelist.com/subscribe.cgi/battlist
  Battlist is an unmoderated mailing list devoted to the Batt, Bott, and Bath Surnames worldwide but with a particular emphasis on Batt/Bott's from the GER-RUS colonies on the Volga River.

- The BATTERSON Page
  http://www.geocities.com/Heartland/Flats/7628/batterson.htm
  Focuses on the BATTERSON family of Connecticut, New York, New Jersey, Ohio, Pennsylvania, Iowa, etc.

- Clubs BAUMGARTNER BUMGARDNER BUMGARNER
  http://clubs.yahoo.com/clubs/baumgartnerbumgardner bumgarner

- BAUR Genealogy
  http://www.thebaur.com

- BAYLES Families
  http://www.geocities.com/Heartland/Stream/4113/
  Also BAYLESS, BAYLIS, BAYLISS, BAILIFF, BOYLES, BAILIS, BAILES and other related spellings.

- The BAYLESS Page
  http://www.geocities.com/Heartland/Ranch/5456/baypage.html
  Bayles/Bayless families, descendants of John Bayles of Long Island, NY. Link to the Bayless Families of OH. Census, burials, wills, etc.

- The BEACH Family Journal
  http://members.aol.com/eugeneb/home.htm
  Home page of the Beach Family Journal; a genealogical newsletter devoted to Beach/Beech family history. For descendants of Richard, John and Thomas Beach, of New Haven, Connecticut, together with all other Beach or Beech families in America.

- Descendants of Richard, John and Thomas BEACH of Connecticut
  http://www5.pair.com/vtandrew/beach/beach.htm

- The BEALL HomePage
  http://www.geocities.com/Athens/5568/beallstuff.html

- BEAMAN Genealogy Page
  http://members.aol.com/caroltapp/beaman.html

- Uriah BEAN / BANE Descendants
  http://Members.iquest.net/~dbane
  Descendants of Uriah Bean/Bane of Wythe, Bland and Tazewell County, VA. This family migrated to Wayne County, IN beginning about 1901.

- BEARD / BAIRD Genealogy
  http://www.outfitters.com/~chelle/

- BEATTY Project 2000
  http://www.digroots.com/Beatty.htm
  Beaty / Beatty Families.

- The BEATTY Project 2000
  http://members.aol.com/jacob59/bty/bty_info.html
  An association of more than 250 BEATTY (all spellings) descendants and researchers organized to promote research and documentation on BEATTY family history.

- Charlene Beaty Bailey's BEATY-SNOWDON Genealogy Page
  http://www.digroots.com/beatsnow.htm
  Descendants of John Jesse BEATY (b. 1821) and Mary Frances SNOWDON (b. 1823).

- The House of BEAUPREZ
  http://members.iex.net/~bopray/default.html

- Famille BEAUSOLEIL Association Inc. / BROUSSARD Family Reunion
  http://www.vrml.k12.la.us/vermilion/famille/

- The BEAVINGTON Papers - 502 Years of BEAVINGTON Genealogy
  http://www.silk.net/personal/gordonb/
  England, 1495-1997. Beventon, Bevington.

- BEAVIS Society - BEAVIS Genealogy
  http://www.beavis.co.uk/births.htm

- BECNEL Genealogy
  http://members.aol.com/DSchnatz/dbsindex.html
  Descendants of Thomas BECNEL and Catherine BROU who married in Louisiana in 1742.

- The Home Page Dedicated to BEDINGFIELD Family Research
  http://members.aol.com/TPaplanus/tpaplanus.html

- Mary's Place - Your BEEBE Connection
  http://www.bright.net/~bbe/

- The BEESON Family Homepage
  http://www.geocities.com/Heartland/Prairie/1643/beeson.html
  Descendants of Edward and Rachel (PENNINGTON) BEESON, a prominent Quaker family who lived in PA then spread throughout the US.

- Rick BEGEMAN's Home Page
  http://www.best.com/~rickb794/be02000.html

- BEGENT Family Genealogy & Contact Forum
  http://www.begent.freeserve.co.uk/begent.htm

- Jim's Irish Family Surnames - BEGLEY
  http://www.cris.com/~Maguire/Begley.html

- BEHN Family Genealogical Database
  http://www.angelfire.com/ma2/behn/index.html
  A database of BEHNs compiled from submissions and extractions from the Internet. Original source and contact for the information is given in its' entirety.

- BEHYMER Genealogy Group
  http://www.geocities.com/Heartland/Hills/3927/
  And all variant spellings.

- The BEIDELMAN Genealogy Researchers List
  http://members.aol.com/KarenBeid/beidlist.htm

- **The BELANGER Family Home Page**
  http://www.geocities.com/heartland/canyon/4107
  Researching BELANGER family members and their spouses, beginning with Nicolas and Francois BELANGER.

- **BelbinMania**
  http://www.homeusers.prestel.co.uk/belbinmania/
  A web site for anyone with BELBIN ancestors or current Belbin connections. Information about all worldwide Belbins sought and exchanged. Some important variants are Belben, Bellbein, Bellbin and Balbyn.

- **The BELKNAP / BELNAP Homepage**
  http://www.belknap.net/011596a.htm

- **Clan BELL - BELL Family Association of the United States**
  http://www.clanbell.org/

- **RootsWeb's WorldConnect Project: Descendants of Hardy H. BELL**
  http://worldconnect.genealogy.rootsweb.com/cgi-bin/igm.cgi?db=bjbarnhill
  Bell, Canady, Revels, Hammons/Hammonds, Burnett/Burnette, Locklear, Lowery, Hardin, Smith, Carter.

- **Yahoo! Clubs - Bell Surname**
  http://clubs.yahoo.com/clubs/bellsurname
  Or people in search of the BELL surname. It is a place to post your messages and even chat if you would like with other BELL searchers.

- **BELLOWS Family Genealogy Page**
  http://www.gis.net/~bkinmonth/bellows.html

- **BEMIS Landing**
  http://members.xoom.com/bemis
  BEMIS family from Dedham, Essex, England. Joseph and Sarah BEMIS moved to Watertown, Massachusetts in 1641. Children: Sarah, Mary, Joseph, Ephraim, Martha, Joseph III, Rebecca, Ephraim II and John.

- **Colin BENDALL - The BENDALLs of Gloucestershire**
  http://www.bendall.org/
  BENDALL, BENDAL, BENDELL, BENDEL, BENDLE, etc., originating from Gloucestershire, England.

- **Persons in BENDING Genealogy**
  http://www.jbending.demon.co.uk/
  Index of names from Bending genealogy research, with links to personal histories, family trees and sources.

- **BENEDICT Family History News**
  http://members.aol.com/benedictnz/BenedictNews/home.htm
  Information and indexes to a quarterly newsletter for all interested in the surname BENEDICT and its variations. The newsletter was founded in 1993.

- **BENGE Research Network**
  http://www.users.mis.net/~chesnut/pages/benge.htm
  Bange, Bench, Bengay, Bengey, Benjay, Benjey, Binch, Bing, Binge, Bunch, Byng, Bynge.

- **BENNINGTON Family Homepage (and BENINGTON and BINNINGTON)**
  http://www.dcfinc.com/genealogy/benningt.html
  Index to "Bennington Bulletin" newsletter. Early history of the surname. Author has database with over 10,000 connected names and sources.

- **The BENOY Page**
  http://www.benoy.com/family/index.htm

- **BENSON Families Newsletter - E-mail Alan Benson for details at: alanbenson@delphi.com**
  mailto:alanbenson@delphi.com
  Quarterly newsletter for Benson and other related surnames (Bensen, Bentsen, Bensingh, Bennison, Bjornson, etc.).

- **BENNETT - B530 Mail List**
  http://primusweb.com/genealogy/B530/
  Benet, Bennet, Bennett ... Families.

- **BENNINGTON Family Homepage**
  http://www.dcfinc.com/genealogy/benningt.html
  Benington and Binnington.

- **BERESFORD Family Society**
  http://www.beresfordfamilysociety.freeserve.co.uk/

- **BERRY Family Genealogy - Descendants of John BERRY born 1749 in Lancashire, England**
  http://ourworld.compuserve.com/homepages/JOHNBERRY/homepage.htm

- **BERRY Resource Center**
  http://home.flash.net/~skaspar/resberry.htm

- **Sergio BERTINI's Homepage**
  http://www.freeweb.org/personali/SBertini/
  Genealogical information about surname Bertini in Italy and the world.

- **BERTONE Family of Molise**
  http://www38.pair.com/kbertone
  History and genealogy of the BERTONE family of the villages of Santa Angelo in Grotte and Santa Maria del Molise in the region of Molise, Italy.

- **Famille BESNER d'origine française**
  http://www.besner.org
  Most all BESNERs in North America are related as descendants of Jean BESNER.

- **BETHEL / BETHELL Genealogy**
  http://pages.prodigy.com/DDHW32A/
  A book for sale titled, The Early Bethells and Their Descendants 1635-1994.

- **Descendants of John BETHUNE Surname List**
  http://bethune.ourfamily.com/jbethune/surnames.htm

- **The BETHUREM Family Homepage**
  http://www.bethurem.com/
  Dedicated to anyone and anything related to the BETHUREM Family. Armitage, Bethurem, Blanshan, Bridgford, Falk, Legros, Melotte, Reschlein, Tubbs, Russell.

- **BETTERTON Families of the World Web Site**
  http://www.geocities.com/Heartland/Prairie/2570/betterto.htm

- The Descendants of Philip BETTINGER, Soldier of the Revolution
  http://www.bettinger.org/
  A short overview of the 200+ year genealogical history being compiled by a descendant of a founding central New York family, including surnames of Bettinger, Lower/Lauer, Shoemaker, Harter, Woolever, Kenyon, and Deuel, among others.

- BEVERLY Family Newsletter
  http://ourworld.compuserve.com/homepages/rbeverly/bfamnews.htm
  And the BEVERLY Query Page
  http://ourworld.compuserve.com/homepages/rbeverly/bevquery.htm

- BEVIER - ELTING Family Association
  http://members.aol.com/Edie143/elt7_web.html
  Including a page with information and a photograph of the Bevier-Elting House on Huguenot Street in New Paltz, New York.

- The BEVINS Genealogy Pages
  http://www.btsinc.net/famtree/
  To post personal histories, articles, writings, stories, photos etc. of BEVINS family members and related surnames.

- BEVIS & COFFEE Descendants
  http://www.digroots.com/bevicoff.htm
  Descendants of John A. Bevis and John M. Coffey.

- BIBBINS Genealogy Website
  http://www.rootsweb.com/~tlmorris/bibbins/index.html
  Bibben(s), Bibbon(s), Bevin(s), Bevan(s), soundex code B152.

- The Family BIBLE
  http://www.geocities.com/Heartland/2252/
  Or the The BIBLE Family
  http://www.rootsweb.com/~bible/

- BICKHAM Family Home Page
  http://www.bickham.org/

- On Beacon Hill
  http://www.bicknell.net
  The complete reference for BICKNELL & BECKNELL family, over 6,000 entries, coats of arms, origins, message forum - much more!.

- BIDDLECOMBE Family Page
  http://www.biddlecombe.demon.co.uk/bidhome.html
  Biddlecombe, Biddlecomb, Biddlecome, Biddlecom, Biddlescombe and Biddlescomb.

- BIDEWELL One Name Study
  http://www.familytreemaker.com/users/b/i/d/William-H-Bidewell/

- BIFFLE Researchers Newsletter
  mailto:j-rose@tc.umn.edu
  Send e-mail to Janet Roseen at j-rose@tc.umn.edu for details.

- BIEBER History and Genealogy
  http://home.att.net/~long.hair/bieber/
  BIEBER/ BEAVER family who emigrated from Alsace to Pennsylvania in the mid-18th century.

- BIGALK Surname Resource Center
  http://genweb.net/~ltupy/bigalkmain.htm
  The purpose of this page is to unite, in one location, all forms of the name BIGALK including Bigalke, Begalke and Begalka in the hopes of finding "lost" branches of our trees.

- The BIGELOW Society
  http://www.slic.com/bigelow/bigsoc1.htm

- BILODEAU 2000
  http://bilodeau.iquebec.com/bilodeau
  Website dedicated to the genealogy and history of the surnames Bilodeau and Billeaudeaux. Site de l'Association des Bilodeau, descendants de Jacques Billaudeau arrivé à Québec en 1652. Bienvenue aussi aux descendants de Michel Billeaudeaux arrivé en Louisianne vers 1791.

- BILODEAU Family Tree Home Page
  http://www.bilodeau.org/

- The BINGHAM Genealogy Project
  http://ourworld.compuserve.com/homepages/dkbingham/GENPROJ.htm

- BIRKHOLZ Family History Search
  http://www.geocities.com/Athens/8020/birkholz.html
  Birkholz, Berkholz, Burkholz, etc.

- BIRNEY Family Tree
  http://www3.sympatico.ca/ken.birney/

- BIRTCHER Surname
  http://freepages.genealogy.rootsweb.com/~mariahswind/birtcher/birtcher.html

- The BISCHOFF Family Archives
  http://www.geocities.com/~bischoff-page
  Information on the BISCHOFF family of Illingen, Wurttemberg, Germany.

- BISHOP Genealogy - Discovering Your BISHOP Ancestors
  http://www.bishopgenealogy.org/

- BISSETT Family
  http://www.mindspring.com/~giammo/Bissett/
  Descendants of Jacques BISSETT & Anne Catherine METTHEY, who emigrated to Nova Scotia in 1752.

- BISSETT Family Home Page
  http://www.barney.org/bissett.html
  Bissett, Bisset, Basok, Beceit, Besack, Besat, Besate, Besek, Beset, Bessat, Bis, Biscet, Biset, Biseth, Bisey, Bissait, Bissaite, Bissart, Bissat, Bissate, Bissed, Bisseth, Bissit, Bissott, Bizat, Bize, Bizet, Bizett, Bizitt, Bizzet, Bizzett, Buset, Buseit, Bysat, Byset, Byseth, Byssate and Byssot.

- BITTING Family History
  http://homepages.rootsweb.com/~bitting/
  Bitting Family in America. Descendants of Henrich and Ann Catherina Bitting who immigrated to Pennsylvania in 1723.

- BLACK Family Cemetery Easley, S.C.
  http://www.angelfire.com/sc/blackcemetary/
  BLACK, LONG, HAMMETT.

- BLACK Family Page
  http://www.angelfire.com/az/JMSHomepage/BLACK.html

- **BLACKBURN Family Association, Inc.**
  http://www.blackburn-tree.org/
  The descendants of John BLACKBURN Sr. b. 17__ Ireland & Mary COURTNEY b. 1701 Ireland (1st wife) & Rachel MORTON b. 1694 Ireland (2nd wife).

- **Lemuel and Mary BLACKFORD's Descendants**
  http://www.bright.net/~wesley/black.html

- **BLACKMAN / BLACKMON Genealogy - Emphasis on Marion County, South Carolina and Area**
  http://www.martygrant.com/gen/blackman.htm

- **BLACKMORE Site**
  http://www.geocities.com/Heartland/Lane/1109/index.html
  An index to on and off line reference material on the surname BLACKMORE.

- **The BLACKSHEAR Connection**
  http://members.tripod.com/~KickStartJoe/index.html
  BLACKSHEAR, BLACKSHIRE, BLACKSHARE, BLACKSHERE, BLACKSHER.

- **BLACKWELL Genealogy Study Group Notebook**
  http://oasys.drc.com/~blackwell/

- **The BLACKWELL Researchers Newsletter**
  http://www.angelfire.com/mo/howdy2u/blawell.html

- **Descendants of James BLACKWOOD Revolutionary War Soldier and Settler of Dennysville, Maine**
  http://home.mpinet.net/ala/blackwood/index.htm
  According to family tradition, James was born c1741/2 in Belfast, Ireland, came to America in May or June 1777 (he was 35 in Spring of 1777). He was an officer of the British Army and served with Burgoyne at Saratoga; captured at Stillwater in 1777, and, when released, joined the American forces. After his discharge, James was employed by/friends with Col. Benjamin Lincoln, a Hingham, MA farmer. Early in the season of 1786, an expedition comprised of Hingham farmers "set sail from Massachusetts Bay to take possession of a new purchase in Maine." James Blackwood settled on a farm at Young's Cove (now Pembroke, ME), and he and his wife are buried somewhere on this lot, although the graves are not easy to discern and/or identify.

- **The Australian BLAIR Family**
  http://www.pcug.org.au/~kenblair/

- **BLAIRs of the World**
  http://home.sprynet.com/~srblair/

- **BLAIRs of Vermont and New Hampshire**
  http://people.ne.mediaone.net/jablair/index.html

- **BLAIR Society for Genealogical Research**
  http://blairsociety.org/

- **Clan BLAIR Society**
  http://www.clanblair.org/

- **Guide to BLAIR Genealogy**
  http://members.home.net/jcblair/blair.htm
  A complete source for all your Blair genealogy needs.

- **The Thomas BLAIR Family**
  http://www.familytreemaker.com/users/t/i/l/Susan-G-Tillman/
  Of Pennsylvania and Maryland.

- **The BLAISDELL Family National Association**
  http://www.gwi.net/~blaisdel

- **The BLAKE Files**
  http://www.geocities.com/Heartland/Acres/9900/
  Genealogy of the Blake Families of Ohio & New England with roots in Somerset, England. Descendants of William Blake who sailed from Plymouth, England on March 20, 1630 aboard the "Mary and John" and arrived in Nastasket, Massachusetts on May 30, 1630.

- **Joel BLAKESLEE Home Page**
  http://members.aol.com/joelb2/joel.htm
  Information on Joel BLAKESLEE and descendants of Samuel BLAKESLEE, including family tree.

- **BLAKESLEE Log Cabin**
  http://www.ashtabula.net/blakeslee/
  Descendants of Samuel Blakeslee, pioneer Sala Blakeslee's genealogy, life and history are documented. His original log cabin is now listed in the National Register of Historic Places.

- **A BLALOCK Genealogy Page**
  http://www.familytreemaker.com/users/b/l/a/Jessie--Blalock/

- **My BLALOCK Genealogy Page**
  http://freepages.genealogy.rootsweb.com/~grizzard/blalock1.htm
  Blalock, Blaylock.

- **The BLAKE Files**
  http://www.geocities.com/Heartland/Acres/9900/
  William BLAKE sailed from England to America in 1630. This site is devoted to his descendants.

- **BLANCHARD Home page**
  http://www.geocities.com/Athens/Academy/3569/
  BLANCHARD families who originated from Prince Edward Island.

- **BLANKENSHIP**
  http://members.aol.com/AunteeChel/blankenship.html
  A website devoted to the lineage of Ralph BLANKENSHIP (1662-1714) of Henrico Co., VA presented in family group sheet format with links to history, graphics, sources, other BLANKENSHIP researchers, plus more. Contributions welcomed!.

- **BLATHERWICK Surname**
  http://www.judandk.force9.co.uk/blather.htm
  BLATHERWICK family, a rare Nottinghamshire name (UK) which has spread to USA, Australia, etc.

- **Association of BLAUVELT Descendants**
  http://www.blauvelt.org
  Bringing together the descendants of Gerrit Hendrickszen (BLAUVELT) de blau boer, who arrived in America from Deventer, Province of Overijssel in the Netherlands in 1638.

- **BLAYLOCKs of Middle Tennessee**
  http://homepages.rootsweb.com/~blalock/
  Blalock, Blaylock, Blacklock.

- **BLEACH Genealogy**
  http://www.bleach.net/genealogy/
  Family of Jacob Joseph Bleach.

- **Jim Boulden's BLEECKER Genealogy Home Page**
  http://ourworld.compuserve.com:80/homepages/JBoulden/

- BLEECKER Genealogy Homepage
  http://ourworld.compuserve.com/homepages/JBoulden/
  Descendants of Jan Jansen Bleecker (1641-1732) the progenitor of the name in America.

- Familie BLEIJS
  http://www.bleijs.net
  Also BLEYS, BLIJS, BLEIS.

- BLENCOWE Families Association
  http://www.geocities.com/Heartland/5088/
  Blenco, Blencoe, Blencow, Blencowe, Blenko, Blinco, Blincow, Blinchko, Blinko.

- BLETHEN Family Tree
  http://www.pilgreen.com/blethen/

- BLEVINS Research Page
  http://www.hooked.net/users/rkinnie/listblev.html

- BLICK Surname Home Page
  http://www.geocities.com/Heartland/Farm/6311
  Descendants of Hans Jakob Blickensderfer - surnames covered include: Blick, Blickenderfer, Blickensderfer, Blickenstaff.

- The BLIMLING Family Homepage: Descendents of Casper BLIMLING & Anna YECK
  http://homepage.davesworld.net/~klokdok/blimling.htm

- BLISH Genealogy
  http://www.blish.org
  Information, photos, treeviews and timelines for BLISH family members and kin. Tens of thousands of interlinkages, submission forms for new entries and much more. Early 1600's through present.

- BLOCKLEY of Leicestershire
  http://www.blockleys.ic24.net

- BLODGETT Ancestors in England & America
  http://www.rootsweb.com/~genepool/blodgett2.htm
  Descendants of Thomas BLOWGATE (abt 1490-1560).

- BLONDIA and family
  http://members.aol.com/rblondia/genealogy/index.htm
  A Belgian family.

- BLOOR Family Web Site
  http://www.bloor.demon.co.uk/

- BLOW Family Newsletter
  http://members.aol.com/BloStnd/
  For the descendants of George & Katharine Blow.

- The National BLUE Family Association
  http://www.glasscity.net/users/sbitter/BlueF1.htm

- BOARD Family Tree
  http://www.SouthBaltimore.com/Board/index.html
  BOARD, HENDERSON, PEAKE, LONG, MEAD.

- The BOBO Family Association
  http://www.familybobo.com/

- The BOCKWINKEL Family History
  http://www.bockwinkel.com
  ALSO BUCKWINKEL. BOWINKEL.

- The BOEN Researcher
  http://www.theboenresearcher.com/
  BOENs and various spellings at any time and any place.

- The BOHM Family
  http://www.bohm.org/
  The official Internet site for the entire BOHM clan of the world. Including information on the LANGLOTZ family of Ruhla, East Germany.

- BOHNSACK Bonds Newsletter
  mailto:dhoffgr@sensible-net.com
  An exchange of Bohnsack surnames. Will also include other variations of BOHNSACK: Bohn, Bohnenen, etc. For details e-mail Donna Hoff-Grambau at dhoffgr@sensible-net.com or Alice J. Bohnsack at ajbohnsack@aol.com.

- BOISSEAU Family Website
  http://home.att.net/~suntanr2/kind.html
  Rev. James BOISSEAU of France who came to America in 1689 and his descendants.

- BOLCH Genealogy
  http://www.geocities.com/Heartland/Plains/2953/
  Descendants of Johan Adam Bolch and his wife Anna Christina, who landed in Philadephia on 24 September 1753 on the ship Neptune from Rotterdam. Balch, Balich, Boalich, Bohlich, Bohlig, Bolch, Boleck, Boley, Bolich, Bolick, Boliek, Bolig, Boligh, Bolih, Bolish, Bollich, Bollick, Bollig, Bolligh, Bolock, Bolsch.

- BOLEYs of Virginia
  http://Boleys.homepage.com
  Research on BOLEYs from early 1600's in Northumberland Co. VA through migration through other VA counties and then west throughout US.

- BOLICK Family Page
  http://members.home.net/teylu/bolick/

- The BOLLING Family Association
  http://www.bolling.net/

- BOLT Surname Genealogy Research Site
  http://millennium.fortunecity.com/ruthven/123/ target=

- BOMMER Genealogy
  http://homepages.rootsweb.com/~imrie/bommer.html

- The B(U)ONAPARTE family
  http://home.t-online.de/home/weebers/buonap.htm
  The genealogy of the BONAPARTE/BUONAPARTE family of Corsica, ancestors of Napoleon.

- BOND Family Reunion
  mailto:receiver@visioncom.net
  Every Labor Day Sunday in Wiggins, Mississippi. E-mail A.M. Bond at receiver@visioncom.net for more details.

- BONE Family History
  http://community.webtv.net/geniefriend/BONEFAMILY HISTORY
  BONE family in the U.S.A., England, and Canada.

- BONJOUR Family Genealogy
  http://www.geocities.com/Heartland/2700/index.html

- Descendants of Jean BONNEAU of La Rochelle, France
  http://www.mindspring.com/~jtfleming/bonneau.htm

- The BOOKOUT Web
  http://www.rootsweb.com/~daisy/bookout.htm
  BOOKOUT family, including Boeckhout, Bouchout, Buckhout, Bookhout or any other related spelling.

- Ancestors and Descendants of the BOONE Family
  http://personal.bhm.bellsouth.net/bhm/s/h/sharrah/boone.html
  Including information on the famous Daniel BOONE.

- My BOONE Ancestors
  http://members.aol.com/HKees/Webpages/Boone.htm
  Starting with Nicholas BOON b.1615 England and over 3600 descendants.

- The BOONE Family
  http://www.rootsweb.com/~kygenweb/sources/fam/boone.html

- The BOONE Society, Inc.
  http://booneinfo.com/society/

- BOOTH Family History
  http://members.tripod.com/~kbush/index.htm
  Descendants of William BOOTH, Sr. born 3 Oct 1786 in Virginia.

- BOOTHBY Genealogy Page
  http://www.geocities.com/~mimi_tabby/boothby.html
  One-name surname page for BOOTHBYs from all over, containing census material, history of the family, heraldry information.

- The BOQUIN Family
  http://www.quinnquinn.com/boquin.html
  The history of the BOQUIN family in Honduras dates from colonial times to the present.

- National Genealogy Database for BORING, BOREN
  http://users.penn.com/~tshu/

- The BOþECKER Family History Web Site
  http://www.mindspring.com/~sbosecker/
  Bosecker/Boseker.

- BOSHART Genealogy - 1750 to Present
  http://home.sprintmail.com/~debflanagan/boshart.html
  Descendants of John Boshart and many other Mennonite families from Waterloo, Ontario, Iowa, Indiana, Nebraska, and Oregon. BOSHART, JANTZI, ROTH.

- BOSMAN Family Genealogy
  http://home.intekom.com/entrepreneur/bosmanfg.htm
  Descendants of Hermanus Lambertus Bosman in South Africa. The BOSMAN Family Genealogy Site aims to contact all BOSMANS in South Africa to partake in compilation of an updated BOSMAN Family History.

- BOSS Family Home Page
  http://home.swbell.net/kayarm
  Clearinghouse for Boss family, including Baker, Fulk, Goss, Hamilton, Jack, Speidell, Strain, Wayman, Wilison and Wininger.

- The BOSSCHAERTS-PERSYN Genealogical Homepage
  http://www.geocities.com/ResearchTriangle/Thinktank/9487/index.html

- *Dutch genealogy (de) BOSSCHAERT-BOSSCHAERTS-BOSSCHAART-BOSSAERT etc. Also Genealogy of Rudi BOSSCHAERTS-Ilse PERSYN.*

- BOSTICK Newsletter Online
  http://www.geocities.com/Heartland/Plains/6598/BostickOnline.htm
  For Bostick / Bostic / Bostwick families of America.

- The BOTHWELL Family History and Surname Resource Center
  http://www.bothwell.cx
  This is a central site where all researchers of the BOTHWELL surname (and variant spellings) can share information, ask questions, or submit to the master database of BOTHWELL ancestors.

- BOTT-BATH-BATT-PATT Family Page
  http://www.geocities.com/Heartland/Oaks/4764/
  Descendents of Johann George BATH, family reunion, photos, short stories, recipes, lots of family histories from those researching those surnames.

- The BOTTOM(S) Genealogical Archives
  http://www.bottoms.org/
  BOTTOM, BOTTOMS, CARPENTER, CASEY, DANFORD, HARTSFIELD, HICKS, JORDAN, LEAPTROT, MILLS.

- The World-Wide BOULDIN Page
  http://www.bouldin.org/
  Bouldin, Boulden.

- The BOULDING BOULDEN BOLLYNG Family of East Kent
  http://www.geocities.com/Heartland/Estates/4205/

- BOULTBEE Family History
  http://www.boultbee.freeserve.co.uk/bfh/frontpg.htm

- The BOURCIER / BOURSIER Genealogy Page
  http://www.magma.ca/~rbour/
  A list of about 400 marriages in the Bourcier family, 1673-1980. This is a French-Canadian family.

- BOURNE Descendants
  http://www.geocities.com/Heartland/Prairie/6694/bourne.html
  Descendants of George Edward BOURNE from the early 1800's.

- L'Association des BOUTIN d'AmÈrique Inc. / Boutin Association of America
  http://www.genealogie.org/famille/boutin/boutin.html

- BOWDEN Genealogy and Queries
  http://members.aol.com/joesears/bowden.html

- BOWEN Depository
  http://homepages.rootsweb.com/~kenbowen/
  A site for the genealogy study of all Bowen lines.

- BOWER Family Homestead
  http://bowercommunity.com/homestead/
  A global clearinghouse for Bower[s], Bauer and their 81+ variant spellings. Adoption and birthparents helps available for these surnames.

- BOWER(s) Genealogy in PA
  http://www.geocities.com/Heartland/Cliffs/5410
  BOWERS(s)/BAUERS(s); part of the BOWER Cottage Continuum.

- BOWLES Genealogy - Emphasis on Surry County, North Carolina
  http://www.martygrant.com/gen/bowles.shtml

- BOWLEY Family Register
  mailto:tom@therecordworks.com
  Collecting data and researching all BOWLEY families that immigrated from England to Canada at any time. Currently information on 41 different families spanning from 1789 to 1971. Please contact Thomas Ryerson at tom@therecordworks.com.

- The BOWLING Beat
  http://home.att.net/~dgbowling
  Bolling / Bowling family database with over 1,200 entries.

- Index of BOWYERS
  http://home.earthlink.net/~lenker/Tree/bowyer
  This site records known descendants of William Bowyer, b. ca. 1803.

- The BOYD Family Pages
  http://www.pasadero.com/boyd/
  Two families of Boyds, one in Canada, the other in the United States, both descendants of a common ancestor, James Bucky Boyd, son of James (Sr.), born in Ireland around 1798.

- Clan BOYD International
  http://homepages.rootsweb.com/~clanboyd/index.htm

- The Association of American BOYERs
  http://www.hooked.net/users/rkinnie/assoc.html

- BOYER Research List
  http://www.hooked.net/users/rkinnie/listboye.html

- Family BOYLE
  http://family.boyle.net/
  BOYLE family genealogy and history, emphasizing Michael Boyle family of Iowa. Boyle, Howe, Reddin.

- The BOYLE Family Genealogy Home Page
  http://www.geocities.com/Heartland/Hills/9507/
  This page is intended to provide access to resources for people interested in the Boyle family name.

- BOYNTON Genealogy
  http://www.pluvoy.com/boynton.html

- BRADBURN Family Genealogy
  http://www.vvm.com/~bradburn

- The BRADFORDs of Charles City County, Virginia and Some of Their Descendants
  http://members.home.net/kylawyer/
  Full text version (searchable!) of book published in 1994 telling the story of eleven generations of the BRADFORD family, beginning with Richard BRADFORD who emigrated into VA in about 1652. Other families include: BARKER, BISHOP, CARLISLE, ENGLISH, FULLER, HIGGS, HUDSPETH, MANN, NENNINGER, TAYLOR, TUDOR, WELCH, WIERWILLE, WORLAND and others. Excellent historical information about Charles City County, VA, Granville County NC, Nelson County, KY and Mississippi and Scott County, MO.

- The BRADLEE Genealogy and Historical Database
  http://www.bradlee.org/default.html

- The Olive Tree Genealogy: The Norwegian BRADT Family
  http://www.rootsweb.com/~ote/albradt.htm
  Albert Andriessen De NOORMAN aka BRADT and his first wife, Annetie Barents (Van) ROTTMERS, was one of the earliest settlers in New Netherland. He sailed, accompanied by his wife, Annetje Barents of "Rolmers," and two children, on October 8, 1636, on the "Rensselaerswyck," which arrived at New Amsterdam March 4, 1637.

- BRADY Family
  http://www.wf.net/~billk/Brady.html
  Descendants of William Wallace BRADY and Harriett Rebecca BRYAN.

- BRADY Family Heritage Association
  http://www.bradyheritage.org/
  Hugh BRADY and wife Hannah and their seven sons, their wives and children. Announcing the discovery of the 254-year old two story homestead. Also a proposed reincarnation of a BRADY Family Heritage Association and newsletter.

- BRAINERD/ BRAINARD Genealogy
  http://www.geocities.com/Heartland/Park/7294/

- BRAINERD / BRAINARD Genealogy
  http://freepages.genealogy.rootsweb.com/~brainerd/
  One line of Brainerds from 1641-1935. Descendants of Daniel BRAINERD who arrived in Hartford, Connecticut in or about the year 1649. Brainerd, Spencer, Arnold, Bushnell, Austin, Cone, Bailey, Clark, Wheeler, Morse.

- BRAKE Family History
  http://www.eg.bucknell.edu/~hyde/brake/
  The purpose of this web site is to encourage research and exchange of genealogical information on - as well as preserve - the family history of the Virginia/West Virginia BRAKE families descending from Johan Jacob and Mary Margaret BRAKE of Germany.

- The BRAMBLETT / BRAMLETT Information Center
  http://www.bramblett.com/
  A site dedicated to collecting and disseminating information on descendants (and ancestors!) of the original American Bramlett -- William Bramlett, Sr. who was in VA by no later than 1715. Surnames Bramblett, Bramlett, Bramlitt, and all variations.

- BRAMMER Branches Newsletter
  mailto:brammer@access.mountain.net
  A quarterly newsletter for descendants of BRAMMER pioneers of colonial Virginia. For details e-mail Charles Brammer at brammer@access.mountain.net.

- BRAMMER Family and Its Branches
  http://hometown.aol.com/ohroots/index.htm
  For BRAMMER descendants of Colonial Virginia. Contains over 200 searchable family group sheets, that are indexed, linked and cross linked, to make your search easier.

- The BRAND Family Home Page
  http://www.brand-dd.freeserve.co.uk/
  300 years of the Brand family in Fife, Scotland.

- The BRANDT Family Tree of NE Missouri, La Grange (Lewis County) including Iowa, Illinois, VA, PA. Quincy
  http://home1.gte.net/jbrandt/brandt/
  Descendants of Benjamin & Elizabeth BRANDT.

- BRANHAM - BRANNAN Family of Roane Co.
  http://www.roanetn.com/brannan.htm

- BRANIFF-L Mailing List
  http://www.osg.net/suzette.estacaille/BRANIFF-L.htm

- Clan BRANIFF Family History
  http://members.tripod.com/braniffcentre/index.html
  An index of resources both on-line and off-line regarding the surname Braniff and similar surnames. Branniff, Brannif, Braniffe, Breniff, Branoff.

- BRANSCOMBE Home Page
  http://www.geocities.com/Athens/2155/home.html
  Branscombes, Branscomes, Branscombs, Branscums & Brownscombes.

- BRANSOM / BRANSON Information Center
  http://members.aol.com/ImaBR/page2/index.htm
  A site for ALL known data for the BRANSOM / BRANSON surname, including, births, burials, census, deaths, land records, wills, etc.

- BRANSON Surname Mailing List
  http://www.sonic.net/~yvonne/branson.html
  Includes Bransen, Bransan.

- BRANTLEY Association of America
  http://members.tripod.com/BrantleyAssociation/
  Some other surnames include: Applewhite, Bridges, Bass, Barlow, Blake, Boatright, Braswell, Brooks, Phillips, Lewis, Young.

- Genealogy BRASCAMP, BRASKAMP, KLEIN BRASKAMP
  http://home.wxs.nl/~brascamp/title.html

- BRASWELL Branches Newsletter
  http://www.rof.com/gene/brasnews.htm

- The BRASWELL Family
  http://www.braswell.org/

- BRASSINGTON Genealogy
  http://homepages.rootsweb.com/~imrie/Brassington.htm

- BRATCHER Family History
  http://www.geocities.com/~dbratcher/
  A collection of BRATCHER source data, including census records, wills, land records, marriages and military records.

- BRATTON Worldwide Clan
  http://grampa.GenDex.COM/~guest/69751/BrattonHomePage/

- BRAUSCH Family History
  http://www.brausch.net/

- John BRAY Genealogy Home Page
  http://www.geocities.com/Heartland/Park/6471
  Ancestors & descendants of John Bray, Sr. (b. 1787 Delaware d. 30 April 1868 Swan Twp, Vinton Co, Ohio).

- BRAYSHAW One Name Study
  http://hometown.aol.com/carolmilla/myhomepage/heritage.html
  Brayshaw and variant spellings, one name study.

- BREADMORE One-Name Study
  http://www.tylehurst.demon.co.uk/breadmore/

- BREAZEALE Kinfolk
  http://millennium.fortunecity.com/rollingacres/427/
  BREAZEALE, BRAZEALE, BRAZEAL.

- BRENDEL Forum Home Page
  http://freepages.genealogy.rootsweb.com/~brendelforum/
  Researching the surname BRENDEL, BRENDLE, BRINDEL, BRINDLE and related surnames.

- Descendants of Jakob BRENN
  http://www.parsonstech.com/genealogy/trees/sbrenn12/jbrenn.htm
  Born before 1685 and married to Maria HOEFFLIN before 1701.

- Schuylkill County BRENNANs
  http://geocities.com/schuylkillcountybrennans/
  A website for researchers of the BRENNAN surname in Schuylkill County, Pennsylvania. Contains BMD information, BRENNAN census listings, and information on researchers individual lines.

- BRENNANs of Kilkenny
  http://clubs.yahoo.com/clubs/brennansofkilkenny

- BREW Surname Genealogy Site
  http://www.sigment.com/brew/
  Brew One Name Study Genealogy Site with searchable databases.

- The BRICE Family Genealogy Homepage
  http://www.mindspring.com/~dbn/Brice.html
  Devoted to descendants of Edward BRICE who settled County Antrim, Ireland and eventually Fairfield County, SC. Includes additional information on surnames: SIMONTON, BURTON, MILLER, MOORE, WADE, GASTON, and McEWEN.

- BRICK Family Tree
  http://www.angelfire.com/ne/onebrickshort/brickfam.html
  BRICK, provides family tree info on the Brick line from Wales to the United States.

- The BRICKHOUSE Family Association
  http://www.voicenet.com/~gbrick/

- BRIDGE Family Website
  http://www.tier.net/bridgefamily/
  For and by the descendents of John Bridge, Puritan.

- The BRIDGES-L Census Project
  http://members.aol.com/webowhizo/bridges/index.htm
  Compilation of BRIDGES/BRIDGER census records 1790-1910.

- The BRIERLEY Family History Society
  http://www.geocities.com/~bfhsociety/
  Brierl(e)y, Brerel(e)y, Bryerl(e)y, Brearl(e)y, Brerelegh, Byerl(e)y, Brayl(e)y, Birl(e)y, Burl(e)y, Briarl(e)y.

- Just another BRIGGS in the Wall
  http://www.geocities.com/Heartland/Pointe/1891/

- BRILEY and Allied Families
  http://www.pipeline.com/~margomc/

- The BRILEY Family Homepage
  http://elu_ancs.tripod.com/
  BRIERLY, BRIARLY, BRYLEY, BRILY, BRALEY.

- The BRINGIER Family Home Page and BRINGIER Tomb Association
  http://www.connecti.com/~bringie/

- BRINK Genealogical Page
  http://www.connexusinc.com/~Ron_Gines/brink/index.htm
  The Brink family from Westphalia, Prussen, German to Washington County, Illinois.

- The BRISTOL Family Association
  http://freepages.genealogy.rootsweb.com/~bristolfamily association/
  This is a genealogy site for families named BRISTOL and not a geography site for places named Bristol.

- The BROCKLEHURST Revival Society
  http://www.fbrocko.demon.co.uk/brs.html

- The BROLSMA Family Home Page
  http://www.pronouncement.com/brolsma/
  Dedicated to the Frisian (Dutch) family, BROLSMA, worldwide.

- BRONSON, BROWNSON, BRUNSON
  http://www.geocities.com/Heartland/Ridge/2509/brownson.html

- The BRONSON, BROWNSON, BRUNSONs of Earl's Colne Essex and Connecticut
  http://www.nwlink.com/~pbronson/intro.htm

- The BROOKS Historian
  http://home.fda.net/bbrooks/public_html/brooks.htm
  This web site was established 1-22-99 as a meeting point for the active and inactive members of the BROOKS Historical Society and anyone else who has an interest in BROOKS genealogy or the related surnames, descendants and ancestors of the BROOKS surname. This site is maintained by Bill Brooks, the former editor of the BROOKS Historian. The Brooks Historical Library is dedicated to the preservation of genealogical and historical information relating to the Brook, Brooke, Brooks, Brookes, and all other variations of the 'BROOKS' surname and their related family lines. The website has a query section, links, and back issues of the Brooks Family Bulletin, Brooks Family Query Exchange, and The Brooks Historian spanning from 1973 to 1998 (currently in work).

- BROOMHALL Genealogy
  http://www.springhillfarm.com/broomhall
  BROOMHALL, including BROOMALL and BROOMELL. While most of our research has been in Pennsylvania USA, we have some in OH and other states. This family is found in the UK, USA, Canada, Australia and New Zealand.

- The BROUGHTON Family Tree
  http://www.geocities.com/Heartland/Woods/7917
  It's not just a pedigree chart! True tales of BROUGHTONS in AL, TX, LA & AR (1800's-now) Pictures, maps, a Research Resource Center w/links, inquiry page, even a castle! & Much More!

- The BROWER Family
  http://www.angelfire.com/mo/brower
  Chronicles the family from Smith BROWER and Ella J. CLOCK till present including lost family members.

- BROWNBILL Genealogy Page
  http://www.cix.co.uk/~tbrownbill/brownbill.html
  Site for promoting research and providing information on the surname, BROWNBILL.

- BROWN(E) Family History Page
  http://home.earthlink.net/~schleper/index.html
  Family line from James BROWN and Catherine MILLER of Hunterdon Co., NJ.

- BROWN Family Genealogical Society
  http://www.brownfamily.org/

- Descendants of Andrew BROWN, Sr., Settler of Black Point, Maine
  http://www.geocities.com/Heartland/Plains/1208/Brown/index.htm
  Andrew, who had "been bred a merchant from his youth upwards," came to this country in c1643. His son Andrew lived in Scarborough, but removed to York, where he resided in 1699. Andrew bought land at Winter Harbor in 1717, and lived there a short time, but removed to Arundel before 1719. He owned mills on "Brown's mill river," where he resided. He must have been a very aged man at the time of his removal into this town; and he lived but a few years after that period.

- Descendants of Peter BROWNE (of ancient Windsor, Connecticut)
  http://members.aol.com/ptrbrwn
  Born ca. 1632 at Plymouth (Duxbury), Massachusetts, died 9 March 1691/92 in Windsor, Hartford County, Connecticut.

- BROWNLEE Lineages
  http://hometown.aol.com/Brudo2/

- BROYLES/BRILES Family History
  http://homepages.rootsweb.com/~george/index.shtml
  Produced and maintained for the tens of thousands of descendants of the immigrant Johannes BREYHEL (or John BROYLES, Johannes BREUEL and other variations of the name). Broyles, Briles, Bryles, Brile, Briel, Broil, Broiles, Bryoll, BreØhel, BrŸl, Breuel, Brohl, Bruel, Breiel, Brouel, Bruile, Broyhill.

- BRUCE International
  http://www.brucefamily.com/
  Bruce International, U.S.A. Branch is a non-profit organization established to create and promote kinship amongst its family members and to encourage interest in the family of BRUCE and its history.

- BRUCHER Genealogy
  http://www.geocities.com/televisioncity/7783/Brucher.html

- Welcome to TIBN - The International BRUHNS Network
  http://www.bruhns.dk/tibn/

- BRUMBAUGH Family History
  http://www.cnw.com/~kennlee/brumbaugh
  10 Generations of BRUMBAUGHs in America.

- BRUNTLETT Home Page
  http://homepages.tesco.net/~richard.parker/pubpage.htm
  Point of contact for Bruntlett family members and those interested in the name which originates from Lincolnshire England. Family members settled in US in 1850s Iowa.

- **BRYANT Family Home Page**
  http://members.xoom.com/ronbryant/index.html
  This web site contains several databases including BRYANT genealogy, hundreds of obits, and a growing collection of gravestone photos.

- **BRYSON Genealogy**
  http://www.martygrant.com/gen/bryson.htm
  Bryson in PA, NC, SC, TN, GA and other states.

- **Clan BRYSON Home Page**
  http://www.brysonclan.net

- **BUCHANAN**
  http://www.vantek.net/pages/pattyh/buchanan.htm
  Study of the Clan Buchanan and septs.

- **BUCHANAN Family Genealogy**
  http://www15.pair.com/buchanan/genes/index.htm

- **The Clan BUCHANAN**
  http://www.tartans.com/clans/Buchanan/buchanan.html

- **The Descendants of Thomas BUCK**
  http://www.parsonstech.com/genealogy/trees/gbuck/thobuck.htm
  BUCK Family in Virginia.

- **BUCKELL & BUCKLE (and some variations)**
  http://www.soft.net.uk/buckell/
  Lists all births and some marriages of the surname Buckell and variations in England and Wales.

- **BUCKLEY - One Name Study**
  http://ourworld.compuserve.com/homepages/colin_wood/BUCKLEY1.htm

- **Joseph BUCKLIN Society**
  http://www.bucklinsociety.net/
  Bucklin Family Genealogy; American Revolution History; Gaspee history; Joseph Bucklin Society welcomes descendants of William Bucklin (c. 1609).

- **The BUCKNER Page**
  http://enws347.eas.asu.edu/~buckner/buckner.html

- **BUDELIER Family**
  http://members.aol.com/cjb761/family.html
  Descendants of Fidelis BUDELIER of Baden, Germany.

- **BUELL Family Research Project**
  http://www.geocities.com/Heartland/Pointe/3237/FAMILY.HTM

- **BUIE Surname Resource Center**
  http://freepages.genealogy.rootsweb.com/~geneal/src/BuieSRC.html

- **BULL Research Pages**
  http://www.artback.com/IsaacBull/
  Data regarding Isaac BULL, son of Edward BULL of Donnington, Gloucester, England.

- **BULLOCK Family Association**
  http://homepages.rootsweb.com/~scismfam/bullock/
  A central reference site associated in support of the Bullock-L@rootsweb.com, and the asssociated GenConnect suite.

- **The BULLOCK Home Page**
  http://www.geocities.com/CapitolHill/6596/

- **BULMER - The Bulmer Family**
  http://www.bulmer.org/
  Surnames - BULMER, KLUWE, DIEHL, WRIGHT.

- **BUMBLIS Bulletin**
  http://www.bignet.net/~peterson/

- **BUMP Family Association**
  http://medgen.iupui.edu/~rebecca/bump.html
  Bump, Bumpas, Bumpass, Bumps, Bumpus, etc.

- **BUMPUS Brother's Web Site - Stephen D. and Paul S.**
  http://home.ici.net/customers/dexlex/dexlex.html
  Genealogical database including most derivations of Bump, Bumpas, Bumpass, Bumpus et al. Descendants of Edouad Bompasse.

- **BUNCH.Org**
  http://www.bunch.org/
  For the surname BUNCH, with focus on origins in the Southeastern Kentucky area.

- **Descendants Of Charles BUNCH**
  http://members.xoom.com/donpayne/bunchfamtree.html
  Also Payne, Boles, Nall, Phillips, Bay, Christensen-Bay, Ramsey, McClung.

- **BUNKERS Family**
  http://krypton.mankato.msus.edu/~susanna/bunkers.htm
  Research on the Buenker/Bunker/Bunkers surname. They came to the U.S. from Germany in the 1840s.

- **BUNKER Family Association**
  http://www.BunkerFamilyAssn.org/index.html

- **BUNN Family of North Carolina**
  http://sites.netscape.net/tombunnusa/homepage

- **BUNN Family Page**
  http://www.geocities.com/Heartland/Hills/6858/

- **The BUNTYN Family Page**
  http://users.ev1.net/~sbuntyn/gen/buntyn/buntyn.html
  Descendants of Joseph/Geraldus BUNTYN (??-1826). Includes Bunten, Buntin, Buntine, Bunting, Bunton, Buntyne.

- **BURBURY Family History Web Page**
  http://www.vision.net.au/~dburbury/burbury.htm

- **BURCH Connection U.S.A.**
  http://www.janics.com/doug/
  Genealogical gathering place for the research of the surname Burch, Burtch, Birch.

- **BURDICKs on the Web!**
  http://ra.nilenet.com/~hburdick/botw.html
  The Descendants of Robert BURDICK of Rhode Island, arriving from England in 1651.

- **BURGESS Family of Virginia**
  http://www.surnames.com/burgess/burges.html

- **The BURGETT Family in America**
  http://www.geocities.com/Heartland/Acres/3309/

- BURGUM Family History Society
  http://freepages.genealogy.rootsweb.com/~bfhs/
  BURGUM and BURGHAM. The society has over one hundred members in the UK, Australia, Brazil and the USA.

- The BURKE Museum
  http://members.tripod.com/~temec/burke.html
  Created for members of the Burke Family of Clinton, Iowa to share vintage photos, family history and genealogy, family heirlooms, stories and memories. In addition to pictures of the ancestors who migrated to Clinton in the mid-1800's, there are also historical pictures of the Clinton area. Surnames include QUINLAN, FORQUER, BLESSINGTON, TUCKING, RYAN, MEIGHAN, COSTELLO, MURHPY.

- BURKS Research Page
  http://members.tripod.com/~bjcasey/index.html
  Dedicated to the Burks/Burk families of Virginia, especially information on early Burk, Burks, of Goochland, Albemarle, Amherst and surrounding counties.

- BURLING Family History
  http://usrwww.mpx.com.au/~burlingr/index.html
  Descendants of Allan and Mary BURLING (nee PEACHEY) in Australia.

- BURNESS One-Name Study
  http://www3.sympatico.ca/jburness/burness.html
  Study of the surname BURNESS which originated in Kincardineshire Scotland.

- BURNETT Family
  http://www.geocities.com/Heartland/3348/burnettsurname.htm

- BURNETT Family Ancestry
  http://hp1.switchboard.com/FetchPage/7688/default.htm

- The House of BURNETT
  http://home.pacbell.net/roothub/
  Burnett, Burnet, Burnette, Bernat, Burnat, Bernet, Burnap, Burnard, Barnard, Barnett, Barnette, Barnet, Bornet, Bornat, Mac Burnet.

- The BURNHAM Page
  http://freepages.genealogy.rootsweb.com/~burnhamfamilys/

- BURR Family
  http://www2.tpg.com.au/users/bruss/
  BURR, SEITNER, DAVIDSON, MAGOR, ROY, WINGATE, MAHONEY, BARROWCLIFFE, LEIGH.

- BURRELL / BURRILL Family Association
  mailto:Barbara_L_Burrill@compuserve.com
  A quarterly newsletter for research on the names Burrell, Burrill, Burwell. E-mail Barbara Burrill for details at: Barbara_L_Burrill@compuserve.com.

- BURT Family Genealogy
  http://www.rootsweb.com/~burtsou/
  The genealogy of the BURT family of the southeastern United States.

- BUSBEE / BUSBY Family Homepage
  http://home.cdsnet.net/~nashoba/index.htm

- BUS'D'KER Family Genealogy
  http://members.dencity.com/royb/directry.htm
  Includes Busdiecker, Busdieker, Busdeker, Bushdiecker, Bussdieker, Buszdieker, Busdicker, Busdecker, Busdeicker.

- BUSH Family Genealogy
  http://www.geocities.com/Heartland/Plains/9130/
  Descendants of Philip Bush and Mary Bryan, circa 1732, Orange County, Virginia.

- BUSHFIELD Family History
  http://www.angelfire.com/in/bushfield/index.html

- BUSS Surname Web Site
  http://www.ameritech.net/users/leebuss/index.htm

- BUSSELL'S Fallen Leaves
  http://www.angelfire.com/ks/fallenleaves/
  Bussell, Busselle, Bustle, Busle, Busell.

- BUSTARD Genealogy Home Page
  http://www.infc.ulst.ac.uk/~dave/Bustard/

- BUSTER Central
  http://millennium.fortunecity.com/ellerburn/536/index.htm

- Genealogija Rodbine BUTINA iz Kostela, Slovenija, Vasje Butina
  http://www.creativ.si/genealog/
  The BUTINA'S Family Genealogy from Kostel, Slovenia by Vasja Butina. Butina, Batinica, Golik, Kajfez, Mihelcic, Rebolj, Sumi, Zdravic, Zidar, Zupancic.

- BUTKUS, a One Name Study (with Variations)
  http://www.geocities.com/Heartland/Estates/2204
  A central place for BUTKUS research including many variations on the spelling and derivation.

- BUTLER Family Name Study
  http://website.lineone.net/~john.d.butler/index.htm

- BUTLER Families in 19th Century Alabama
  http://www.geocities.com/texian1846/family/alabuts.htm

- BUTLERs in Jackson County, Tennesee
  http://www2.aros.net/~cbutler//index.htm
  Early Butlers in Jackson County, TN and their descendants. Butler, Montgomery, Kindall, Kirkpatrick, Tinsely, Davis, Ussery, Plumlee, Sergent.

- The BUTLER Society
  http://www.butler-soc.org/

- BUTT, BUTTE, BUTTS and BUTZ Family Genealogy
  http://steveandcamella.com
  Butt, Butte, Butz, Butts Families who may be descendants of Richard Butt who died in Prince George's County, Maryland in 1715.

- BUTTON Genealogy Page
  http://members.harborcom.net/~cpr/Button.html

- BUTTON - Genealogy of the Family from Cornwall
  http://www.cia.com.au/jabutton/index.htm
  Descendants of Jacobi Button 1740, including Adams, Weblet, Wear, Shannon, and many more.

- BUTTRAM Family Association
  http://www.buttramfamily.com/
  The Descendants of William Buttram I & Margaret of Rowan County, North Carolina.

- HOELSCHER-BUXKEMPER Family Heritage Association
  http://www.hostville.com/hoelscher/
- BYAM-BYHAM Family Home Page
  http://www.familytreemaker.com/users/b/y/h/Edgar-K-Byham/
  A partial list of descendants of George BYAM, who died 1680 in Chelmsford, Massachusetts.
- BYBEE Homesite
  http://www.cybcon.com/~toad/genealogy/bybee.htm
  Website is sponsored by the BYBEE Northwest Pioneer Project and dedicated to the BYBEE family pioneers of Oregon and Washington.
- Clan O'BYRNE - USA Division of the BYRNE Clann
  http://www.byrneclanusa.com/
  History, activities in USA, Australia, South Africa and France, genealogy and heraldry, membership and contact information, news of rallies and gatherings.

◆ Surname Mailing Lists

- "BAA-BAD" Surname Mailing Lists
  http://www.rootsweb.com/~jfuller/gen_mail_surnames-baa.html
  BAADE (includes Bade), BAALHAM, BAAS, BABB, BABBITT, BABBITT (includes Babit, Babbot, Bobet), BABCOCK, BABER, BABOCK, BABY (includes Babie, Baubie, Baybee, Bayby, Baybye), BACA, BACCUS, BACH, BACHER, BACHER, BACHILER, BACHMAN (includes Bachmann, Backman), BACHMANN, BACHSCHMIDT (includes Bachschmit, Bachsmith), BACK, BACKER, BACKER (includes Baker), BACKMAN, BACKSTER, BACKUS, BACON, BACSTER, BADER, BADGER, BADGER, BADGEROW (includes Badgro, Badgero, Badgrow, Badjero), BADGET, BADGLEY.

- "BAE-BAH" Surname Mailing Lists
  http://www.rootsweb.com/~jfuller/gen_mail_surnames-bae.html
  BAEHR, BAER, BAER, BAGBY, BAGG, BAGGARLY (includes Beggarly, Beggerly), BAGGETT, BAGGS, BAGLEY (includes Bagby, Bagsby, Bigsby, Baxley, McBagly), BAGNALL, BAGSHAW (includes Bagshawe), BAGWELL, BAHLINGER, BAHR.

- "BAI-BAN" Surname Mailing Lists
  http://www.rootsweb.com/~jfuller/gen_mail_surnames-bai.html
  BAIER, BAILEY (includes Bailee, Baley, Boehle), BAILIFF, BAILLIE, BAILY, BAIN, BAINBRIDGE, BAINES, BAIR, BAIRD (includes Beard), BAIRD (includes Beard), BAISDEN (includes Basden, Baseden, Basdon), BAITY, BAJWA, BAKER (includes Baxter, Becker, Baxley, Backster, Packer), BAKER, BAKER, BAKER (includes Bolin, Bolen, Bowlin, Bolling, Bowling), BAKKE (includes Backe), BAKKER, BALA, BALCH (includes Bolch), BALCOM, BALDINGER, BALDOCK, BALDRIDGE, BALDWIN, BALE, BALES (includes Bailes, Beals, Bayles), BALES, BALFOUR, BALL, BALL, BALLANTYNE, BALLARD, BALLEAU (includes Balleaux, Ballew), BALLENBERGER (includes Berger), BALLENGER, BALLENTINE, BALLERSTEDT (includes Ballenstedt, Ballerstadt, Ballenstadt, Ballersteadt), BALLEW (includes Blue, Beleu, Balew), BALLIET, BALLIET, BALLINGER (includes Ballenger, Ballanger, Bollinger, Bellinger), BALLOU, BALLS, BALMAIN (includes Ballmain, Balmen), BALMER, BALSEN (includes Balzen, Baltzer, Baltzen), BALSLEY, BALWEARIE, BALZER, BAMFORD, BAMMEL, BANCROFT,

BANDY, BANE, BANEY, BANFIELD, BANGERT, BANGS, BANISTER, BANKER, BANKHEAD, BANKS (includes Bancks), BANKSTON (includes Bankson, Bankstone, Bengtsson), BANNERMAN, BANNING, BANNISTER, BANNON, BANTA, BANTA (includes Bonta).

- "BAO-BAR" Surname Mailing Lists
  http://www.rootsweb.com/~jfuller/gen_mail_surnames-bao.html
  BARBEE, BARBER, BARBER, BARBIER, BARBOUR, BARCLAY, BARCLAY, BARCROFT, BARD (includes Beard), BARD, BARDEN (includes Bardin, Bardon), BARDIN, BARE, BAREFOOT, BARFIELD, BARFIELD, BARGELT (includes Bergelt, Borgelt, Baurgeldt), BARGER (includes Bargar, Barrier, Berger), BARHAM, BARIL, BARING, BARKER, BARKLEY, BARKMAN, BARKSDALE, BARLAGE (includes Barlow), BARLETT (includes Barlet), BARLEY (includes Barlee, Barely, Barleigh), BARLITT (includes Barlit, Barlet, Barlett), BARLOW, BARMORE, BARNABY, BARNARD, BARNES (includes Barnet, Barns, Barney, Bjairnes, Bournes, Byrnes, Parnes, Barnett, Burnes), BARNET, BARNETT, BARNETTE, BARNEY, BARNEY, BARNFATHER, BARNHARDT, BARNHART (includes Barnhardt), BARNHILL, BARNHOUSE, BARNS, BARNTHOUSE, BARNUM (includes Barnam, Barnham), BARNWELL, BARON, BARONE, BARR, BARRACLOUGH (includes Barrowclough, Barracluff), BARRATT, BARRE, BARRESCAL, BARRESDALE, BARRET, BARRETT (includes Barrott, Barrette, Barritt), BARRICK, BARRIE, BARRIENTOS, BARRINGER (includes Baringer, Berringer), BARRINGTON, BARRISKILL, BARRON, BARRON, BARROW, BARROWS, BARRUS, BARRY, BARSTOW, BARTEE, BARTEL, BARTELS, BARTER, BARTH (includes Barthel), BARTHEL, BARTHOLOMEW, BARTLE, BARTLETT, BARTLETT, BARTLETT, BARTLEY, BARTO, BARTON (includes Barten, Bartin), BARTON, BARTOSH, BARTRAM, BARTZ, BARWICK, BARWIS (includes Barwyse, Berwis).

- "BAS-BAT" Surname Mailing Lists
  http://www.rootsweb.com/~jfuller/gen_mail_surnames-bas.html
  BASCOM, BASFORD (includes Bassford), BASH, BASHAM (includes Bassham), BASHFORD, BASINGER, BASKETT, BASKIN, BASISTA (includes Bashista), BASS, BASSET, BASSETT (includes Basset, Bassette), BASSFORD, BASTABLE (includes Bastabel, Bastabell, Bastabl, Bastables, Bastaple, Bastible, Beastable, Bestable, Bostable,, Bustable, Barnstaple, Barnstable), BASTIAN, BASTIN (includes Bastyn, Baston, Basten, Bastjn, Beisstin, Bashteen, Bastian), BATCHELDER, BATCHELOR, BATCHELOR (includes Bachelor, Batchelder, Bachiler), BATDORF, BATE, BATEMAN (includes Batemon, Batman), BATES, BATESON, BATH, BATHRICK (includes Batrick, Batherick, Buttrick), BATMAN, BATSON, BATT, BATTAIN, BATT, BATTE, BATTEN, BATTERSHELL, BATTERSON, BATTERTON, BATTIN, BATTLE, BATTLES, BATTS, BATTY, BATY, BATZ.

- "BAU-BD" Surname Mailing Lists
  http://www.rootsweb.com/~jfuller/gen_mail_surnames-bau.html
  BAUCOM (includes Baucum, Bawcom, Baughcom, Balcombe, Balcom, Balkcom, Van Baucom), BAUDREAU (includes Baudreau dit Graveline, Baudrou, Budrow, Budreau, Baudrow, Baudro, Budro), BAUER, BAUGH, BAUGH (includes Baughman, Baughn, Bough, Baw), BAUGHEN (includes Baughan, Baugham, Baughn, Bauffin, Baffin, Boffin, Boughan, Boughn, Bohon, Bangham,, Banghan), BAUGHER, BAUGHMAN, BAUGHN, BAUM, BAUMAN, BAUMANN, BAUMBACH, BAUMES (includes Baumis, Bomus), BAUMGARDNER, BAUMGARTNER, BAUR, BAVIDGE,

BAWDEN, BAXLEY, BAXTER, BAXTER, BAXTER, BAY *(includes Bays, Bais)*, BAYER, BAYES *(includes Bays, Bayse)*, BAYLES, BAYLESS, BAYLEY, BAYLIS, BAYLISS, BAYLY, BAYNE *(includes Bane, Baine, Bain, Bean, Beane)*, BAYNES, BAYS, BAYSINGER *(includes Basinger, Bessinger, Pessinger, Beisinger)*.

- **"BEA-BED" Surname Mailing Lists**
  http://www.rootsweb.com/~jfuller/gen_mail_surnames-bea.html
  BEACH *(includes Beech)*, BEACHAM *(includes Beachim, Beachum, Beachem, Beauchamp, Beecham, Beechem)*, BEADLE, BEADLES, BEAGLE, BEAIRD, BEAL, BEALE, BEALL *(includes Bell, Beal, Bealle)*, BEALS *(includes Bales)*, BEAM *(includes Beem, Boehm)*, BEAMAN, BEAMER, BEAN *(includes Been, Beene, MacBean)*, BEANE, BEANBLOSSOM *(includes Bohnenblust, Beenblossom)*, BEAR *(includes Bar, Bare, Bair, Bahr, Behr)*, BEARD, BEARD, BEARDEN *(includes Beardon)*, BEARDON, BEARDSLEY, BEARSE *(includes Bearce, Bearss, Barss, Bierce)*, BEASLEY *(includes Beaszly, Beesley)*, BEASON, BEASTON, BEATON, BEATTIE, BEATTY, BEATTY, BEATY, BEAUCHAMP *(includes Beecham, Beauchamps)*, BEAUDOIN, BEAUDOIN, BEAUDRY *(includes Baudry)*, BEAUFORT, BEAULIEU, BEAUMONT, BEAUREGARD *(includes Beauregard dit Jarret, Beauregard dit Vincent, Beauregard dit Davignon, Beauregard, Toutant)*, BEAUVAIS *(includes Bauvais, Bova, St. Gemme, St. Gem, St. James, Vanesse dit Beauvais, Coderre dit Beauvais,, Beauvet, Bauvet)*, BEAVER, BEAVERS, BEAVERSON, BEAZLEY, BEBB, BECHLEM, BECHTEL *(includes Bechdol, Bachtel, Bechtold, Bechthold, Beachtel, Bachtell, Bechtell, Buchtel, Beghtol, Bechtolt,, Bechtol, Baechtold, Bechdolt, Becktal, Bechtal, Bechtle, Bectal, Beghtel, Beghtol, Beightol, Bachtold, Backtell, Bechtl,, Becktel, Becthel, Bucktel, Buechtel)*, BECHTOLD, BECK, BECKER, BECKETT *(includes Becket, Beckit, Beckitt)*, BECKHAM *(includes Beckum, Bekum)*, BECKLEY, BECKMAN, BECKMANN, BECKNER, BECKWITH, BECKWORTH, BECRAFT, BECTON, BEDARD, BEDELL, BEDELL, BEDFORD, BEDSOLE *(includes Bedsaul, Bedsol)*, BEDWELL.

- **"BEE-BEH" Surname Mailing Lists**
  http://www.rootsweb.com/~jfuller/gen_mail_surnames-bee.html
  BEE, BEEBE, BEECH, BEECHAM, BEECHER, BEEDE *(includes Bede, Beedee, Beedy)*, BEEKMAN, BEELER *(includes Bealer, Biller, Buhler, Beiler, Byler)*, BEEM, BEEMAN, BEEMER, BEENE, BEER, BEERS, BEERY, BEESLEY, BEESON, BEETHAM *(includes Betham, De Betham, Beethom, Bethome, Beethome, Bethume)*, BEEZLEY, BEGG, BEGG, BEGGS, BEGLEY, BEHELER, BEHLER, BEHLING, BEHM, BEHME, BEHNE *(includes Bene)*, BEHNKE, BEHR, BEHREND, BEHRENS, BEHYMER *(includes Becklehimer, Picklesimer)*.

- **"BEI-BEN" Surname Mailing Lists**
  http://www.rootsweb.com/~jfuller/gen_mail_surnames-bei.html
  BEIDELMAN *(includes Beutelman, Biddleman, Beitelman, Beidelmann, Beidleman)*, BEIER, BEIERS *(includes Byers, Boyer, Byar)*, BEIMS *(includes Beimes)*, BEIN, BEITER *(includes Beither, Beitter, Beytter, Baither, Biter, Beuter)*, BEKAERT, BEKETOWIC, BELAND, BELANGER, BELCHAMBER *(includes Bellchamber)*, BELCHER, BELDEN *(includes Belding, Baildon)*, BELDING, BELEW, BELFORD, BELK, BELKNAP, BELL, BELLAH, BELLAMY, BELLAR, BELLER, BELLES, BELLFLOWER, BELLINGER, BELLIS, BELLISTON, BELLOWS, BELSHAM, BELT, BELTON, BEMIS *(includes Bemiss)*, BENAVIDES *(includes Benavidez, Venavides)*, BENCE, BENDA, BENDALL, BENDER *(includes Binder)*, BENDZALA *(includes Bendzale, Bendzalla)*, BENEDICT, BENEFIELD, BENES, BENFIELD, BENGE *(includes*

Bange, Bench, Bengay, Bengey, Benjay, Benjey, Binch, Bing, Binge, Bunch, Byng, Bynge)*, BENGTSSON, BENHAM, BENJAFIELD, BENJAMIN, BENJEY, BENN, BENNER, BENNET, BENNETT *(includes Bennet)*, BENNETT, BENNETT *(includes Bennet, Bennitt, Benet)*, BENNIE, BENNINGFIELD, BENNINGTON, BENNISON, BENOIT, BENSLEY *(includes Benslay, Bensle)*, BENSON *(includes Bensen, Bentsen, Bensingh, Bennison)*, BENT, BENTHAMER, BENTLEY *(includes Bently)*, BENTON, BENTZ, BENZ.

- **"BEO-BET" Surname Mailing Lists**
  http://www.rootsweb.com/~jfuller/gen_mail_surnames-beo.html
  BERARD, BERENDS, BERESFORD, BEREZOWSKY *(includes Berezofsky, Beresowsky, Beresofsky)*, BERG, BERGANDINE, BERGEN, BERGER *(includes Burger)*, BERGERON, BERGERON, BERGERSON, BERGESON *(includes Bergesen)*, BERGEY *(includes Berkey, Berge, Berky)*, BERGHUIS, BERGIN, BERGMAN, BERGMANN, BERGSTROM, BERINGER, BERKELEY, BERKEY, BERKHEIMER *(includes Barkhimer, Berkhimer, Barkhimer, Berkhamer, Barkhamer, Barkhamer)*, BERLETT *(includes Berlet)*, BERLIN, BERNA, BERNARD, BERNER, BERNET, BERNHARD *(includes Bernhart, Burnhard, Burnhart, Barnhart, Barnhard, Bernard, Burham)*, BERNHARDT, BERNIER, BERNSTEIN, BERRER, BERRICK *(includes Barrick)*, BERRIER, BERRIMAN, BERRY *(includes Barry, Barrie)*, BERRY *(includes Barry, Bery, Berrey)*, BERRYHILL, BERRYMAN, BERTRAM, BERTRAND, BERTSCH, BESHEAR, BESHEARS, BESS, BESSANT, BESSE, BESSEY *(includes Besse)*, BEST, BETHEA, BETHEL, BETHELL, BETHUNE, BETHUREM *(includes Bethurum)*, BETTERLEY, BETTIN, BETTIS, BETTS *(includes Betz)*, BETZ.

- **"BEU-BH" Surname Mailing Lists**
  http://www.rootsweb.com/~jfuller/gen_mail_surnames-beu.html
  BEURLE, BEUTEL, BEVAN, BEVANS, BEVELHEIMER, BEVELHIMER, BEVELHYMER, BEVERIDGE, BEVERLY, BEVILL *(includes Beville)*, BEVINGTON, BEVYS, BEWLEY, BEYER, BEYERS, BEYETTE *(includes Biguet, Billet, Beyett, Biette, Byett, Peyette, Peyett, Piette, Pyette)*, BEZANSON *(includes Bescanson)*, BEZER, BEZONA *(includes Bazonian, Bezoni, Bisoglio, Bisoni, Benzoni, Bezonis, Bezonia, Bezolio, Bezolia, Begolio, Begolia)*, BEZONA *(includes Bazonian, Bezoni, Bisoglio, Bisoni, Benzoni, Bezonis, Bezonia)*, BEZY.

- **"BI-BK" Surname Mailing Lists**
  http://www.rootsweb.com/~jfuller/gen_mail_surnames-bi.html
  BIALIK, BIAM *(includes Piam)*, BIAS *(includes Byas, Byus, Byars)*, BIBB, BIBBINS *(includes Bevan, Bevans, Bevin, Bevins, Bivin, Bivins, Blevin, Blevins)*, BIBBY, BIBLE, BIBLER, BICE, BICKEL, BICKER *(includes Bickers)*, BICKERDYKE, BICKFORD *(includes Beckford)*, BICKFORD, BICKHAM, BICKHART *(includes Beckhart, Piccard)*, BICKLE, BICKLEY, BICKMORE *(includes*

Bigmore, Biggmore, Beckmore)*, BICKNELL, BIDDIX *(includes Bittick, Bitticks, Biddick, Biddicks)*, BIDDLE, BIDDY, BIDGOOD, BIDWELL *(includes Bedwell)*, BIEBER, BIEDENBACK *(includes Biedenbach)*, BIELA, BIENEMANN *(includes Bieneman, Beneman)*, BIER, BIERBAUER, BIERMAN, BIFFLE *(includes Buffel)*, BIGALK *(includes Bigalke, Begalke, Begalka)*, BIGBEE, BIGELOW, BIGGE, BIGGER *(includes Biggers, Biggor, Biggors, Biggar, Biggars, Bieger, Biegers)*, BIGGERS, BIGGERSTAFF *(includes Bickerstaff)*, BIGGS, BIGHAM *(includes Bigum, Biggum)*, BIGLER, BIGLEY, BIGOD, BILBO, BILBREY *(includes Billberry)*, BILDERBACK, BILES, BILGER, BILL, BILLER, BILL *(includes Bills)*, BILLING, BILLINGS *(includes Billing)*, BILLINGSLEY, BILLINGTON, BILLS, BILLUPS, BILODEAU, BILOTTA, BILTCLIFFE *(includes Biltcliff, Billcliffe)*, BILYEU *(includes Billiou, Balew, Ballou, Belieu, Belew,*

Boileau), BINDER, BINFORD, BING (*includes Byng*), BINGAMAN, BINGER, BINGHAM, BINKLEY, BINNEY, BINNICKER, BINNIE, BINNING, BINNS (*includes Binn, Benn, Benns*), BINSKIN, BINYON (*includes Binion, Benyon, Bingham*), BIRCH, BIRCHARD, BIRCHFIELD, BIRD (*includes Byrd, Burd*), BIRDSALL, BIRDSEY, BIRDSEYE, BIRDSONG, BIRDWELL, BIRGE, BIRKHOLZ (*includes Berkholz, Burkholz, Birkholtz*), BIRMINGHAM (*includes Burmingham*), BIRNEY, BIRNIE, BIRONG (*includes Berong, Berrong*), BIRRELL, BIRT, BIRTCHER, BISBEE, BISCHOFF, BISE (*includes Bice*), BISER (*includes Bizer*), BISH (*includes Bisch*), BISHOP, BISHOP (*includes Bishopp, Bischoff, Lévesque*), BISHOP, BISLER, BISSELL, BISSETT, BISSON, BITLER, BITNER, BITTINGER, BITTNER, BITZ (*includes Bits, Bitts, Pitz*), BITZELL, BITZER, BIVENS, BIXBY, BIXBY, BIXLER, BJERKE, BJORK.

- **"BL-BN" Surname Mailing Lists**
  http://www.rootsweb.com/~jfuller/gen_mail_surnames-bl.html
  BLACK, BLACK, BLACKADAR (*includes Blackadder, Blackader, Blackater, Blacater, Blacketer*), BLACKALL, BLACKARD, BLACKBURN, BLACKER, BLACKERBY, BLACKFORD, BLACKHAM, BLACKIE, BLACKKETTER, BLACKLOCK, BLACKMAN, BLACKMAN, BLACKMER, BLACKMON, BLACKMORE, BLACKSHAW, BLACKSHEAR, BLACKSTOCK, BLACKSTONE, BLACKWELL, BLACKWOOD, BLADES, BLAGDON (*includes Blagden, Blackden*), BLAGG, BLAGG, BLAHA, BLAHNIK, BLAIN, BLAIN (*includes Blaine*), BLAINE, BLAIR (*includes Blare, van Blaricom, van Blare*), BLAIR, BLAIR, BLAKE, BLAKE, BLAKELEY, BLAKELY (*includes Blackly, Blakeney*), BLAKEMAN, BLAKEMORE, BLAKENEY, BLAKER (*includes Blakers, Blaccar, Blakker, de Blakker, Blayker, Blecor, Blacer, Blacker, Blackar, Blacher, Blakey,, Blaaker, Bleaker, Bleeker, Bleecker, Blaikhir, Blackear, Blaquir, de Blaquier, Blaquire, Blaquiere, Blacquiere*), BLAKESLEE (*includes Blakesley*), BLAKESLEY, BLAKEY, BLAKLEY, BLALOCK (*includes Blaylock*), BLANCE, BLANCH, BLANCHARD (*includes Blancher, Blanchar*), BLAND, BLANDFORD, BLANDING (*includes Bland, Blandin, Blanton*), BLANEY, BLANK (*includes Blanck, Planck*), BLANK (*includes Blanke, Blanc, Blancke*), BLANKENBAKER, BLANKENSHIP, BLANKLEY (*includes Blankly*), BLANKS, BLANN, BLANSETT (*includes Blancet, Blancett, Blanset, Blanscett, Blansit*), BLANSHAN (*includes Blanchan*), BLANTON (*includes Blantons, Blantan, Blantans, Blanten, Blantens, Blantin, Blantins*), BLASSINGAME, BLATCHFORD, BLATCHLEY, BLATTENBERGER (*includes Blottenberger, Blattenberg, Plattenberger, Plattenburg*), BLAUVELT, BLAXALL (*includes Blaxill, Blaxell, Blaxcell, Blaxhall*), BLAYLOCK, BLAZER, BLEASE, BLEDSOE, BLEE, BLENDAN (*includes Blendon, Blenden*), BLESSING, BLEVINS (*includes Blevin, Blivins*), BLEWETT, BLICKENSTAFF (*includes Blickensderfer, Pleichendefer*), BLIGHT, BLIGHTON (*includes Blyton, Bliton, Brighton, Blighten*), BLINDAUER, BLISS, BLIVEN, BLIZZARD, BLOCH, BLOCHER (*includes Blocker, Blokker, Plocher, Ploucher*), BLOCK, BLOCKER, BLOCKLEY, BLODGETT, BLOEDAU (*includes Bloedow, Bladou, Bloedoe, Bloedeau, Bladau*), BLOM, BLOOD, BLOODWORTH, BLOOM, BLOOMER, BLOOMFIELD, BLOSS (*includes Blose*), BLOSSER, BLOSSOM, BLOUNT (*includes Blunt, Blund, Blound*), BLOW, BLOWERS (*includes Bloor, Bloors, Blowes, Blower*), BLOWES, BLOXHAM, BLOYD (*includes Bloid, Bloyed, Bloyth*), BLUE, BLUHM, BLUM, BLUME, BLUMENTHAL, BLUNDELL, BLUNDELL, BLUNK, BLUNT, BLURTON (*includes Blerton, Blirton*), BLY, BLYTH, BLYTHE (*includes Blyth, Blithe*).

- **"BOA-BOD" Surname Mailing Lists**
  http://www.rootsweb.com/~jfuller/gen_mail_surnames-boa.html
  BOAKES, BOAL, BOALES, BOARD, BOARDMAN, BOATH, BOATMAN, BOATRIGHT (*includes Boatwright*), BOATWRIGHT, BOAZ, BOBB, BOBBITT, BOBO, BOBROFF, BOCHAT (*includes Bochert, Boshay*), BOCK, BODDIE (*includes Bodie, Boddy, Body, Boddye*), BODE, BODEN, BODENNER, BODEWIN, BODINE, BODKIN (*includes Botkin*), BODOH.

- **"BOE-BOH" Surname Mailing Lists**
  http://www.rootsweb.com/~jfuller/gen_mail_surnames-boe.html
  BOE, BOEHM, BOEHME, BOEN, BOESCH, BOESE, BOETTCHER, BOGAN, BOGARD, BOGARDUS, BOGART, BOGDONOFF (*includes Bogdanoff, Bogdonov*), BOGEL, BOGER, BOGERS, BOGERT, BOGGAN, BOGGESS (*includes Bagguss, Baugus, Boggas, Bogiss, Bougus*), BOGGS, BOGLE, BOGUE, BOHANNAN, BOHANNON (*includes Bohanon, Bohannan, Bohanan, Buchanan, Buchannan, Bucannan*), BOHANON, BOHLEN, BOHM, BOHM, BOHMBACH (*includes Bohnenberg, Bombach, Bohmback*), BOHN (*includes Bahn*), BOHRER.

- **"BOI-BON" Surname Mailing Lists**
  http://www.rootsweb.com/~jfuller/gen_mail_surnames-boi.html
  BOICE, BOISSEAU, BOISVERT, BOJSEN (*includes Bøjsen, Boisen, Boyson*), BOKERS, BOLAM (*includes Bolan, Bolum, Bollum*), BOLAND, BOLANDER, BOLAR (*includes Bollar, Boller, Baller*), BOLCH (*includes Balch, Balich, Boalich, Bohlich, Bohlig, Bolch, Boleck, Boley, Bolich, Bolick, Boliek, Bolig, Boligh,, Bolih, Bolish, Bollich, Bollick, Bollig, Bolligh, Bolock, Bolsch*), BOLDEN, BOLDING, BOLDT, BOLDWYN (*includes Baldwin*), BOLEN, BOLENDER, BOLES, BOLEY (*includes Bowley, Bolley*), BOLHUIS, BOLICK, BOLIN, BOLING, BOLINGER, BOLISON, BOLLEN, BOLLERMAN, BOLLES, BOLLIER, BOLLING, BOLLINGER (*includes Bolinger, Bullinger, Ballinger*), BOLLINGER (*includes Bolinger*), BOLSTER (*includes Balster, Boldster, Bowlster, Bollster, Boldsteerman*), BOLT, BOLTE, BOLTON, BOLTZ, BOMAN (*includes Bowman*), BOMAR, BOMMER, BOMZE (*includes Bomzer, Bomser*), BONAR, BOND (*includes Bonds, Bonde, Bondes, Bone, Bondi*), BONDS, BONDURANT, BONE (*includes Boane, Boon*), BONHAM (*includes Benham, Bonnum, Bonnem*), BONIFACE, BONIFAY, BONIN (*includes Bonen*), BONINE (*includes Bownene, Bownine, Banine*), BONNELL, BONNER (*includes Banner, Boner, Benner*), BONNET, BONNETT, BONNETTE (*includes Bonet, Bonnet, Bonnett, Bont, Bonte, Bontea, Bonadeau, Bonnedau*), BONNEVILLE (*includes Bonwell, Bonewell, Bonniwell, Bonnaville*), BONNEY, BONSAL, BONSALL (*includes Bonsal, Bonsale, Bonsell*), BONSER.

- **"BOO-BOT" Surname Mailing Lists**
  http://www.rootsweb.com/~jfuller/gen_mail_surnames-boo.html
  BOOCO (*includes Boucau, Bucco*), BOOHER, BOOK, BOOKER, BOOKOUT, BOOMHOUR (*includes Baumhouer, Boomhower, Bumhower*), BOON, BOONE (*includes Boon, Bohun*), BOOT, BOOTH, BOOTH, BOOTHE, BOOTS, BOOZER, BOPP, BORA (*includes Borah, Barre*), BORDAS, BORDEAUX, BORDEN, BORDEN, BORDERS, BORDEWICH, BORDNER (*includes Bortner, Burtner*), BOREMAN (*includes Boarman*), BOREN (*includes Bowen*), BORGER, BORGESON, BORING, BORIS, BORKOWSKI, BORLAND, BORMAN, BORN, BOROWSKI, BORST, BORSTLAP, BORTON (*includes Bourton*), BORTZ, BORUFF, BOS,

BOSANKO (includes Besanko, Bosanco), BOSCH, BOSCHEE, BOSKET, BOSKILL, BOSLEY, BOSMAN, BOSS, BOSSERMAN (includes Bassermann), BOSSERT, BOSSUOT (includes Bossuet), BOST (includes Bast), BOSTIC, BOSTICK, BOSTOCK, BOSTON, BOSTWICK, BOSTWICK, BOSWELL (includes Boswill, Baswell), BOSWORTH, BOTELER, BOTHWELL, BOTHWELL (includes Boutwell, Botwell, Bathwell, Boswell, Buthwell), BOTSFORD, BOTT, BOTTEMILLER, BOTTENUS, BOTTOM (includes Bottoms), BOTTOMLEY, BOTTOMS, BOTTORFF (includes Batdorf, Putoff), BOTTS, BOTWINICK.

- **"BOU-BQ" Surname Mailing Lists**
  http://www.rootsweb.com/~jfuller/gen_mail_surnames-bou.html
  BOUCHARD, BOUCHER (includes Butcher, Bowcher, Bouch, Baugher, Bougher), BOUDE, BOUDREAU (includes Budrot, Boudreaux, Boudreault), BOUDREAU, BOUDREAUX, BOUDRIA (includes Boudrias), BOUDROT, BOUGH (includes Booh, Boo, Buhe, Boughner, Bougher, Baugh), BOUGHNER, BOUGHTON, BOUKNIGHT, BOULDEN, BOULDIN, BOULINEAU (includes Bouleneau, Bolineau, Beaulineau), BOULTER, BOULTINGHOUSE, BOULTON, BOULTON, BOULWARE (includes Bowler, Boler, Bouler), BOUNDS, BOURDEAU, BOURG, BOURGEOIS, BOURGUIGNON, BOURKE, BOURLAND, BOURN, BOURNE, BOUSE, BOUSQUET, BOUTCHER, BOUTILIER, BOUTON (includes Boughton), BOUTTE, BOUTWELL, BOUVIER, BOVARD, BOVEE (includes Bovie, Bovy, Beaufils, Bovier, Bouvier), BOWARDR, BOWATER, BOWDEN (includes Baudon, Baudouin, Boden, Boudoin, Bowdoin, Bowdin, Bowdon, Bowdown), BOWDER, BOWE, BOWELL, BOWEN (includes Bowin), BOWEN, BOWER (includes Bowers, Bauer, Bauers), BOWERMAN, BOWERS, BOWES, BOWIE, BOWKER, BOWLER, BOWLES, BOWLEY, BOWLIN, BOWLING (includes Bowlin, Bolen, Bolin, Bolling, Boling), BOWLS, BOWMAN, BOWN, BOWNE, BOWRA, BOWRING, BOWRON (includes Boldron, Bowran), BOWSER (includes Bausser), BOWYER, BOX, BOXDORFER, BOYCE (includes Boice, Boise, Boys), BOYD (includes Boid, Boide, Boit, Boyde, O'Boyd, McBoyd), BOYD, BOYDEN, BOYER, BOYES, BOYETT (includes Boyt, Boyet, Boyte, Boyette), BOYKIN, BOYLAN, BOYLE (includes Boil, Boile, Bole), BOYLES, BOYNTON (includes Boyington), BOYS, BOYSE, BOYSEN, BOZARD (includes Bossart), BOZEMAN (includes Bozman, Bosman), BOZILE.

- **"BRA-BRD" Surname Mailing Lists**
  http://www.rootsweb.com/~jfuller/gen_mail_surnames-bra.html
  BRABANT, BRABAZON, BRACE, BRACEWELL, BRACEY (includes Bracy, Bressie, Brassey), BRACHER, BRACKEN, BRACKENBURY, BRACKETT, BRACKHONGE, BRADBERRY, BRADBURN, BRADBURY, BRADBURY (includes Bradberry), BRADDOCK, BRADDOM, BRADDY, BRADEN, BRADFIELD, BRADFORD (includes Brafford, Bradforthe), BRADING, BRADISH, BRADLEY (includes Bradlee, Bradely, Bradleigh, Bratley, Badley), BRADSHAW (includes Bratshaw), BRADSTREET, BRADT, BRADY (includes Braddy, Bradi, Bradie), BRAGDON, BRAGG (includes Brag), BRAIN, BRAINARD, BRAINERD (includes Brainard), BRAITHWAITE, BRAKE, BRALEY, BRAMAN, BRAMBLETT, BRAME, BRAMHALL, BRAMLETT, BRAMLEY, BRAMMER, BRANCH, BRAND, BRANDENBERG, BRANDENBURG, BRANDL, BRANDON, BRANDT, BRANHAM (includes Bramham, Branam, Branum, Branin, Branen, Brannon), BRANIFF (includes Breniff), BRANN, BRANNAN, BRANNEN, BRANNIGAN, BRANNING, BRANNON (includes Brannin, Brannan, Brannen), BRANNON, BRANSFIELD, BRANSON (includes Bransen, Bransan), BRANT, BRANTLEY, BRANTON, BRASHEAR. BRASHEARS. BRASHER. BRASINGTON.

BRASSINGTON, BRASWELL (includes Bracewell), BRASWELL (includes Bracewell), BRATCHER (includes Brashear, Brassiear, Brasher, Brazier, Brasier, Bradsher, Bradshaw, Bratshaw), BRATT, BRATT (includes Bradt, Brat, Brad, Brodt, Brott), BRATTON, BRATVOLD, BRAUER, BRAUKER, BRAUN, BRAUND, BRAWLEY (includes Braley, Braly, O'Brawley), BRAWNER, BRAY (includes Brady, Pray, Brie, Brill, Brilly, McBrey), BRAY, BRAZDA, BRAZEAL, BRAZELTON, BRAZIER, BRAZZIL (includes Brazzill, Brazzell, Brazil, Brazel, Brazzel, Brazill, Brazell).

- **"BRE-BRH" Surname Mailing Lists**
  http://www.rootsweb.com/~jfuller/gen_mail_surnames-bre.html
  BREADON, BREAZEALE, BREAZEALE (includes Brazeal, Brazil, Bras), BRECHT, BRECKENRIDGE, BREECH, BREED (includes Brede, Bread), BREEDEN, BREEDING, BREEDLOVE (includes Breadlove, Bradlove), BREEN, BREES, BREESE (includes Brees), BREEZE, BREHAUT (includes Burhoes, Brehaux, Brehaults), BREITENBUCHER (includes Broadbooks, Breitenbuecher, Breitenberg), BREITENSTEIN (includes Breidenstein), BREITHAUPT, BRELAND, BRELSFORD, BREMER, BREMNER, BREMNER, BREMSINGER (includes Brimsinger, Bremsenger, Brimsenger, Bramsinger, Bramsenger), BRENNAN, BRENNEMAN (includes Branneman, Breneman), BRENNENSTUHL (includes Brininstool, Brenenstahl), BRENNER, BRENT, BRENTON, BRERETON, BRESHEARS (includes Breashears, Brashears, Brasher, Brashier, Brazier, Broshers, Bratcher, Brucher, Bezer,, Brasseur, Bradshawe, Bashaw, Basham), BRESHIRES (includes Boshears, Boshers, Brashears, Bratcher), BRESLIN, BRESNER, BRETHERTON, BRETT, BRETZ, BREVARD, BREW, BREWER, BREWSTER (includes Bryce, Bruster), BREWSTER, BREWTON.

- **"BRI-BRN" Surname Mailing Lists**
  http://www.rootsweb.com/~jfuller/gen_mail_surnames-bri.html
  BRIANT, BRICE (includes Bryce, Bruce), BRICK, BRICKELL (includes Brickel, Brickle), BRICKENDEN, BRICKER (includes Brunker), BRICKEY, BRICKLAND, BRICKMAN, BRIDDELL (includes Bridell, Bredell, Briddle), BRIDENSTINE, BRIDGE, BRIDGEMAN, BRIDGER, BRIDGES (includes Bridger), BRIDGEWATER, BRIDGFORD (includes Bridgeford), BRIDGMAN (includes Bridgeman), BRIDLE, BRIDWELL, BRIEN, BRIERLEY, BRIGANCE, BRIGGS (includes Brygge, Brigge, Bryggs), BRIGGS, BRIGHAM, BRIGHT (includes Brecht, Bryte), BRIGHTBILL (includes Brechbill, Brechtbill, Brechbeil, Brackbill), BRIGHTMAN, BRIGHTWELL, BRIGMAN, BRIGUGLIO (includes Briguglia, Brigugleo, Briguglea), BRILES (includes Broyles, Breyhel, Brehel, Brile, Bryle, Bryles, Broil, Broils, Broiles, Bruel, Bruhl, Brühl, Breuel, Brohl,, Debruel, Debrule), BRILEY, BRILL (includes Brile), BRILL, BRIM, BRIMER, BRIMM (includes Brim, Brimn, Bream), BRIMMER, BRINCKERHOFF (includes Brinkerhoff, Brinckerhoffe, Brinkerhoff, Brink), BRINDLE, BRINDLEY, BRINEGAR, BRINK, BRINKER, BRINKERHOFF (includes Blinkerhoff), BRINKLEY (includes Binkley, Brinkly), BRINKMAN, BRINSON (includes Brunson, Brimson), BRINTON, BRION (includes Breon), BRISBIN, BRISCOE, BRISKEY, BRISTOL, BRISTOW, BRITT, BRITTAIN, BRITTEN, BRITTINGHAM, BRITTON, BRIX, BRIXEY (includes Bricksey).

- **"BRO-BRT" Surname Mailing Lists**
  http://www.rootsweb.com/~jfuller/gen_mail_surnames-bro.html
  BROACH, BROACH (includes Brooch, Broatch, Broch, Broche), BROAD, BROADAWAY (includes Broadway), BROADBENT, BROADDUS, BROADFOOT (includes Bradford, Bredfort, Proudfoot), BROADHEAD, BROADHURST (includes Broaddus), BROADUS, BROADWATER (includes Broadwaters), BROADWAY,

BROADWELL, BROBST (includes Probst), BROCK, BROCKBANK (includes Brocklebank, Brooksbank), BROCKETT, BROCKLEBANK, BROCKLEY, BROCKMAN, BROCKWAY, BROCKWAY, BROCKWELL, BRODBECK (includes Broatbeck, Brobeck, Broderick), BRODERICK, BRODES (includes Brodis, Brodus, Brodust, Broadus, Broaddus, Broadhurst), BRODESS (includes Broddis, Brodis, Broadis, Brodus, Brodas, Broaduss, Bradus, Bradish, Broadas), BRODIE, BRODY, BROGAN, BROGDEN, BROGDON, BROKAW, BROMFIELD, BROMLEY, BRONSON, BRONTE (includes Brunty, Prunty), BROOK, BROOKE, BROOKER, BROOKES, BROOKMAN, BROOKS (includes Brookes), BROOKS, BROOKS (includes Bruks, Brucke, Brookes, Brouckes, Brucks, Brook, Brooke), BROOKS (includes Brook, Brookes), BROOKSHIRE, BROOM, BROOM (includes Broome), BROOM, BROOME (includes Broom), BROOMFIELD, BROOMHALL (includes Broomall, Broomell), BROPHY, BROSCH, BROSIUS, BROSSEAU, BROTHERS, BROTHERTON, BROTT, BROTZMAN (includes Brutzman, Prutzman, Prottsman), BROUGH, BROUGHER, BROUGHTON, BROUHARD (includes Broughard, Brohard, Brougherd, Brouherd, Broherd), BROUSSARD, BROUWER, BROWDER, BROWER, BROWN, BROWN, BROWN, BROWN, BROWN (includes Braun), BROWNE, BROWNE, BROWNELL, BROWNFIELD, BROWNING, BROWNLEE (includes Brownlie), BROWNLOW, BROWNSON, BROYLES (includes Breyhel, Brehel, Briles, Brile, Bryle, Bryles, Broil, Broils, Broiles, Bruel, Bruhl, Brühl, Breuel,, Brohl, Debruel, Debrule).

- **"BRU-BT" Surname Mailing Lists**
  http://www.rootsweb.com/~jfuller/gen_mail_surnames-bru.html
  BRUBAKER (includes Brubacher, Brubacker, Brewbaker), BRUBAKER (includes Brewbaker, Brubacher, Brubacker), BRUCE (includes Brus, Bruse, Brusse, de Brus, de Bruse, de Brusse), BRUCE, BRUCH, BRUCK, BRUDER, BRUENING, BRUFFEY (includes Bruffy), BRUGH, BRUHN, BRUIN, BRUMBAUGH, BRUMBELOW, BRUMFIELD (includes Broomfield, Bromfield), BRUMLEY, BRUMMEL, BRUMMETT, BRUMMETTE, BRUN, BRUNDAGE, BRUNER, BRUNET, BRUNK, BRUNNER (includes Bruner), BRUNNING, BRUNO, BRUNS, BRUNSKILL (includes Brunskil, Brunskel, Brumshall), BRUNSON, BRUNT, BRUNTON, BRUSH, BRUTON, BRYAN, BRYANT (includes Bryan, Briant, O'Briant), BRYANT (includes Briand, Bryan, Brian, Briant, Brion, Briont, Briond), BRYCE, BRYDEN, BRYSON.

- **"BUA-BUH" Surname Mailing Lists**
  http://www.rootsweb.com/~jfuller/gen_mail_surnames-bua.html
  BUCCLEUCH (includes Buckalew, Buckelew, Bucklew), BUCE (includes Buse), BUCH, BUCHAN, BUCHANAN, BUCHER, BUCHHEIT, BUCHHEIT (includes Buckheit, Buheit, Buchite, Buckite, Buhite, Buchhardt), BUCHHOLZ, BUCHMAN (includes Buchmann, Buckman, Buckmann), BUCHMANN, BUCHNER, BUCK, BUCKALEW (includes Buccleuch, Buckelew, Bucklew), BUCKEY, BUCKINGHAM, BUCKLAND (includes Bucklen, Bucklin), BUCKLE, BUCKLER, BUCKLES, BUCKLEW, BUCKLEY, BUCKLIN, BUCKMAN, BUCKMASTER, BUCKNAM, BUCKNER, BUCKNER, BUCKOVICH (includes Bucks), BUCY, BUDD, BUDDE, BUDGE, BUEHLER, BUEHLER, BUELL, BUETTNER, BUFFINGTON, BUFORD, BUGBEE, BUGG, BUHMANN.

- **"BUI-BUQ" Surname Mailing Lists**
  http://www.rootsweb.com/~jfuller/gen_mail_surnames-bui.html
  BUIE, BUIJS, BUIST, BUKER, BUKOVE, BULCH, BULGER, BULGRIN (includes Bulgren), BULKELEY, BULL, BULLARD, BULLARD, BULLAS (includes Bullass, Bulless, Bullace, Bullus,

Bullous, Bullouse, Bullos, Bullose, Bulhouse, Bullhouse), BULLEN, BULLER, BULLINGTON, BULLIVANT, BULLOCH, BULLOCK (includes Bulloch, Bollock, Bullick, Boughloch), BULLOCK, BULMAN, BULMER, BUMGARDNER, BUMGARNER, BUMP (includes Bumpas, Bumpass, Bumpers, Bumps, Bumpus), BUMSTEAD (includes Bumpstead, Bumsted), BUNCE, BUNCH, BUNDICK (includes Bundack, Bundok), BUNDRANT, BUNDY, BUNG (includes Bong), BUNGARD, BUNKER, BUNN, BUNNELL, BUNT (includes Bont), BUNTIN, BUNTING, BUNTON, BUNYARD.

- **"BUR-BUR" Surname Mailing Lists**
  http://www.rootsweb.com/~jfuller/gen_mail_surnames-bur.html
  BURBAGE (includes Burbidge, Burbridge, Burbadge), BURBAGE, BURBANK, BURBEY (includes Berube, Berrube, Berubay), BURBIDGE (includes Burbage, Burbridge, Burridge), BURBRIDGE, BURBURY (includes Burbery, Burberry, Burbeary), BURCH (includes Birch, Burtch), BURCHAM, BURCHARD, BURCHER (includes Bircher), BURCHETT (includes Burchitt), BURCHFIELD, BURD, BURDEN, BURDETT, BURDETTE (includes Burdett, Burdete, Burdet), BURDICK, BURDINE, BURDITT, BURDUE (includes Bardue, Bardeau), BURFORD (includes Burfoot, Burfort, Burfotte), BURG, BURGAJL, BURGAN, BURGE, BURGER, BURGES, BURGESS (includes Burges, Burgis, Burgiss), BURGETT (includes Burget, Burgette, Burgert), BURGHARDT, BURGIN, BURGOYNE, BURHANS, BURK (includes Burks, Burke, Burkes, Berk, Berks, Birk, Birks), BURKE, BURKE, BURKET, BURKETT, BURKEY, BURKHALTER, BURKHAMMER (includes Berkheimer, Pirckheimer, Barkhammer, Berkhammer), BURKHARDT, BURKHART, BURKHISER (includes Berkiser, Berkhiser, Burkiser, Burkizer, Berkizer), BURKHOLDER, BURKLOW (includes Burkelow, Burkalow, Burcleo, Burklo, Van Burklow, Van Burkelow, Van Burkalow, Van, Burcleo, Van Burklo), BURKS, BURLEIGH, BURLESON, BURLEY (includes Burleigh, Berley), BURLING, BURLINGAME (includes Burlingham, Burlingam, Burlinham), BURN, BURNELL, BURNER, BURNES, BURNET, BURNET, BURNETT (includes Burnet), BURNETT, BURNETTE, BURNEY, BURNHAM (includes Burnam, Bernham, Barnham), BURNLEY, BURNS, BURNSIDE, BURR, BURRELL, BURRELL, BURRESS (includes Burriss, Burrus), BURRIDGE, BURRILL, BURRIS, BURROUGHS, BURROW, BURROWS, BURSEY (includes Burcey, Burcy), BURSON, BURT, BURT, BURTCH, BURTCHER, BURTCHER, BURTLE, BURTON, BURTON, BURWELL, BURZYCKI, BURZYNSKI.

- **"BUS-BZ" Surname Mailing Lists**
  http://www.rootsweb.com/~jfuller/gen_mail_surnames-bus.html
  BUSBY (includes Busbye, Bushby, Bushbye, Busbee, Buzbee, Buzby, Busbie, Busbey), BUSBY (includes Busbye, Bushby, Bushbye, Busbee, Buzbee, Buzby, Busbie, Busbey), BUSCH, BUSH, BUSHELL, BUSHEY, BUSHFIELD, BUSHMAN, BUSHNELL, BUSHONG, BUSING (includes Bussing, Busig), BUSKE (includes Buskie, Buskey), BUSKIRK, BUSS, BUSSA, BUSSARD, BUSSE, BUSSELL (includes Busselle, Bustle, Busell, Beisell, Buzzell, Buswell), BUSSEY, BUSSEY, BUSTER, BUSWELL, BUTCHER (includes Bücher), BUTLER, BUTMAN, BUTNER, BUTT (includes Butts, Butte, Butz), BUTTER, BUTTERCASE (includes Buttars, Buttarcase, Butercase, Butars), BUTTERFIELD, BUTTERWORTH, BUTTON, BUTTRAM, BUTTS, BUTZ, BUVIA, BUXTON, BUYS (includes Buis, Buijs, Bice, Boice, Buyce), BUYS, BUZZARD, BUZZELL, BYARD, BYARS, BYBEE (includes Biby, Bibbey, Byby), BYE, BYER, BYERLY, BYERS, BYLER (includes Beiler, Boiler, Beyeler), BYNUM, BYRAM, BYRD, BYRNE, BYRNES, BYRUM.

SURNAMES, FAMILY ASSOCIATIONS & FAMILY NEWSLETTERS – "C"

Resources Dedicated to One Surname
http://www.cyndislist.com/surn-c.htm

Category Index:

◆ General Surname Sites and Resources
◆ Surname Specific Sites and Resources

◆ Surname Mailing Lists

◆ General Surname Sites and Resources

- Connect with Surnames - C
  http://www.geocities.com/Heartland/Bluffs/7708/c.html

- 'C' Surnames at RootsWeb
  http://resources.rootsweb.com/surnames/c.html

- Dutch Home Pages by Familyname ~ Letter C
  http://members.tripod.com/~Don_Arnoldus/c.htm

- FamilyHistory.com - Message Boards - Surname - C
  http://www.familyhistory.com/messages/list.asp?prefix=CA

- Family Tree Maker Online User Home Pages - C
  http://www.familytreemaker.com/users/c/index.html

- Family Workings C Surname Links
  http://www.familyworkings.com/links/surc.htm

- GenConnect Surname Index - "C"
  http://genconnect.rootsweb.com/indx/surnames/C.html
  Message boards sponsored by RootsWeb. Each surname message board set is divided into the following topics: Queries, Bibles, Biographies, Deeds, Obituaries, Pensions, Wills.

- Genealogy Resources on the Internet - "CAA-CAH" Surname Mailing Lists
  http://www.rootsweb.com/~jfuller/gen_mail_surnames-caa.html
  "CAI-CAN"
  http://www.rootsweb.com/~jfuller/gen_mail_surnames-cai.html
  "CAO-CAR"
  http://www.rootsweb.com/~jfuller/gen_mail_surnames-cao.html
  "CAS-CAT"
  http://www.rootsweb.com/~jfuller/gen_mail_surnames-cas.html
  "CAU-CD"
  http://www.rootsweb.com/~jfuller/gen_mail_surnames-cau.html
  "CE-CG"
  http://www.rootsweb.com/~jfuller/gen_mail_surnames-ce.html
  "CHA-CHD"
  http://www.rootsweb.com/~jfuller/gen_mail_surnames-cha.html

  "CHE-CHN"
  http://www.rootsweb.com/~jfuller/gen_mail_surnames-che.html
  "CHO-CHZ"
  http://www.rootsweb.com/~jfuller/gen_mail_surnames-cho.html
  "CI-CN"
  http://www.rootsweb.com/~jfuller/gen_mail_surnames-ci.html
  "COA-COD"
  http://www.rootsweb.com/~jfuller/gen_mail_surnames-coa.html
  "COE-COH"
  http://www.rootsweb.com/~jfuller/gen_mail_surnames-coe.html
  "COI-CON"
  http://www.rootsweb.com/~jfuller/gen_mail_surnames-coi.html
  "COO-COT"
  http://www.rootsweb.com/~jfuller/gen_mail_surnames-coo.html
  "COU-CQ"
  http://www.rootsweb.com/~jfuller/gen_mail_surnames-cou.html
  "CRA-CRD"
  http://www.rootsweb.com/~jfuller/gen_mail_surnames-cra.html
  "CRE-CRN"
  http://www.rootsweb.com/~jfuller/gen_mail_surnames-cre.html
  "CRO-CT"
  http://www.rootsweb.com/~jfuller/gen_mail_surnames-cro.html
  "CU-CZ"
  http://www.rootsweb.com/~jfuller/gen_mail_surnames-cu.html
  Search the index of surname mailing lists below: Surname Mailing Lists.

  o Genealogy Resources on the Internet - Surnames Included in Mailing Lists - "C"
    http://www-personal.umich.edu/~cgaunt/surnames/c.names.html
    This is a computer generated list of the surnames, and all variant spellings for those names, that are found in the surname mailing lists detailed on the pages shown above.

- Genealogy Resources on the Internet - Surname Web Sites for "C" Surnames
  http://www-personal.umich.edu/~cgaunt/surnames/c.html

- Genealogy's Most Wanted - Surnames Beginning with "C"
  http://www.citynet.net/mostwanted/c.htm

- Google Web Directory .... Genealogy>Surnames>C
  http://directory.google.com/Top/Society/Genealogy/Surnames/C/

- Heartland Genealogy Society Membership List - C
  http://www.geocities.com/Heartland/Ranch/2416/hgs-mlist-c.html

- H-GIG Surname Registry - Surnames Beginning C
  http://www.ucr.edu/h-gig/surdata/surname3.html

- Higginson Book Company - Surnames Beginning with C
  http://www.higginsonbooks.com/c.htm

- inGeneas Table of Common Surname Variations and Surname Misspellings - C
  http://www.ingeneas.com/C.html

- The Obituary Link Page - Family Obituary Archives Online - C
  http://www.geocities.com/~cribbswh/obit/c.htm

- Open Directory - Society: Genealogy: Surnames: C
  http://www.dmoz.org/Society/Genealogy/Surnames/C/

- Surname Springboard Index - C
  http://www.geocities.com/~alacy/spring_c.htm

- SurnameWeb Surname Registry - C Index
  http://www.surnameweb.org/registry/c.htm

- SWINX Zoeklijst Nederlandse Familienamen / SWINX Searchlist Dutch Surnames - C
  http://www.swinx.net/swinx/swinx_ca_nl.htm

- Websites at RootsWeb: C Surnames
  http://www.rootsweb.com/~websites/surnames/c.html

◆ Surname Specific Sites and Resources

- The CABELL Foundation, Inc.
  http://foundation.cabell.org/
  Dedicated to the descendents of Dr. William CABELL of Virginia.

- CAHILL Family Ancestors
  http://pages.prodigy.net/cahill_ancestors/
  Cahill, Cohill, Cahall, etc. Free comparisons of your earliest known Cahill ancestors with over 400 different lines in the database. Recent self-verified match rate of over 1 in 5. The newsletter is being discontinued after 14 years, but the old issues may be added to this site later.

- The CAISSY Family of Acadia
  http://www.caissy.com/
  Caissy, Caissie, Quessy, Casey, Roger, Rogers, also Caissy dit Roger. Family branches in Canada, US (mostly Louisiana) and Australia.

- CADWELL Central
  http://www.wilkinsons.com/Cadwell/
  A website devoted to the surname CADWELL including a genealogical database, query page, and more.

- CALDERON Ancestry
  http://clubs.yahoo.com/clubs/calderonancestry

- CALDWELL Genealogy
  http://www.geocities.com/Heartland/Estates/6455/

- CALIANNO Home Page
  http://members.xoom.com/Calianno/index.htm
  CALIANNO family here in the US and Italy

- CALLAHANs WWW Home Page Introduction
  http://userweb.interactive.net/~mailman/intro.html
  Callahan, Callaghan, O'Callaghan.

- CALLAWAY Family Association
  http://www.lgc.peachnet.edu/callaway/cfa1.htm

- CALMES Notes Newsletter
  mailto:genecox@bluebon.net
  "Calmes Notes," a newsletter, is published four times each year, for descendants of Marquis de la Calmes, the Huguenot, who came to America in the late 1600s. The descendants are organized in the Genealogical Society of Versailles, named in honor of his grandson, Marquis Calmes, IV, who served as a captain in the Revolutionary War and later as a brigadier general with Kentucky troops in the War of 1812. General Calmes founded and laid out the town of Versailles, Kentucky, which he named in honor of his friend and associate, General Lafayette. The general and his wife, the former Priscilla Heale, are buried in a mausoleum in what is now a horse farm pastured about midway between Versailles and Lexington. The society named in his honor maintains the mausoleum. "Calmes Notes" covers information of interest about the early Calmes' families and their descendants. For details, send e-mail to Eugene Cox at genecox@bluebon.net.

- Descendants of Lord Baltimore CALVERT
  http://www.familytreemaker.com/users/s/p/e/Vicki-K-Spencer/

- The CAMPBELL Database
  http://www.csihq.com/campbell/
  With CAMPBELL marriage records and census records.

- Norman & Sarah CAMPBELL and Their Descendants
  http://home.att.net/~hbridges/camptree.htm
  CAMPBELLs from Richmond County, NC.

- CAMBERG Connections
  http://www.angelfire.com/or/treeresearch/camberg.html
  CAMBERG, KAMBERG, CAMBER, KAMBER research homepage.

- CANNAFAX Archives Page
  http://www.geocities.com/Heartland/Forest/7377

- CANNON Family Home Page
  http://www.rootsweb.com/~auntjean/cannon/index.htm
  Cannon / Kennon.

- CANUPnet Genealogy
  http://www.hal-pc.org/~canupnet/geno.html
  *Canup. Cannup, Canupp, Cannupp, Cunnup, Canups, Cannups, Canupps, Caneup, Cunnop, Canop, Kanup, Kannup, Kanupp, Kanups, also some *Knup, and Knupp*.*

- CAPLES Surname Mailing List
  http://homepages.rootsweb.com/~lcompton/caples/maillist.html
  Includes Cables, Kapels, Chapels.

- CAPLICE Family Records
  http://home.st.net.au/~dunn/caplice/caplice.htm

- The CAPSHAW Family History
  http://home.cfl.rr.com/capshaw/

- CAREY Family History Home Page
  http://homepages.ihug.co.nz/~Smckelvey/Carey/index.html
  A resource page for the Carey Family, one of the earliest settlers in Otago, New Zealand (1840).

- The CARY/CAREY Family Homepage
  http://www.advsolutions.com/carey
  Descendants of John CARY, b. 1610 and Elizabeth GODFREY.

- The CAREY Family of Guernsey
  http://www.careyroots.com/
  Comprehensive history of the CAREY Family of Guernsey from A.D.1393 - 2000.

- The CAR(E)Y Family Research Page
  http://home.earthlink.net/~howardorjeff/cary/

- CAREY Genealogy Hub
  http://www3.ewebcity.com/aceweb/carey/
  Searchable database of Carey ancestors and genealogy requests, plus a brief history of the origins of the Carey/Cary name.

- CARHART Genealogy
  http://freepages.genealogy.rootsweb.com/~carhart/

- CARLTON (Clafee) & MASON Descendants
  http://www.digroots.com/carlmaso.htm
  William Branch Carlton (or Clafee) b. 1856 m. Ethel Mason.

- CARMAN Family History
  http://home.att.net/~rcarman/

- CARMAN Genealogy
  http://www.carman.net/
  Descendants of John and Florence CARMAN from their arrival to New England in 1631 and principally their descendants on Long Island.

- CARMICHAEL Descendants of Comrie, Perthshire, Scotland
  http://members.aol.com/tch6535/carmichael/carmichael.htm
  For the descendants of the CARMICHAEL families originating from Comrie, Perthshire, Scotland. Includes Carmichael, Comrie, Drummond, Morrison, Robertson, Steven, Heddrick, McLaren, McGregor, Anderson.

- CARMICHAEL Family
  http://www.teleport.com/~mattc
  Resource for all Carmichael researchers, especially Scotland to Canada and U.S.

- Clan CARMICHAEL USA Genealogy
  http://ourworld.compuserve.com/homepages/dkerner/

- CARMICHAEL Worldwide Genealogy
  http://www.mersinet.co.uk/~jimmy/
  CARMICHAEL worldwide database of CARMICHAEL's and allied families.

- Donald CARMICHAEL and his Descendants
  http://members.aol.com/tch6535/donald.htm
  ANDERSON, CARMICHAEL, DRUMMOND. Descendants of Comrie, Perthshire, Scotland that migrated to New South Wales, Queensland and Victoria, Australia.

- CARNRIKE Family Association
  http://www.geocities.com/Heartland/Estates/8751/
  More than 3,500 names related to Carnrike, Canright, Carnright, Carnrick, Carnwright.

- CAROTHERS Genealogy
  http://members.home.net/dcarothers/carothers.html

- CARPER Ancestry Web Site
  http://geneavillage.com/cecjr/start.htm
  From the book by Janice M. CARPER and Lois C. MARBERT 'The CARPERs of Carper Valley' an area near Winchester, VA.

- The CARRIKER Family Homepage
  http://pages.prodigy.com/CARRIKER/

- CARROLL Home Page - CARROLL Cables Newsletter
  http://members.aol.com/kinseeker6/carroll.html

- CARSTARPHEN Family Homepage
  http://www.edwards1.com/rose/genealogy/carstar/carstar.html
  And many variant spellings.

- CARTER Census On-Line
  http://members.tripod.com/~texson/

- CARTER, Thomas James & Descendants
  http://www.parsonstech.com/genealogy/trees/tcarter/tjc.htm
  Adams, Harvey, Jeffus, Johnson, Kearby, Meador, Moseley, Riddling, Turner, Wood.

- CARTWRIGHT Research Center
  http://www.fortunecity.com/millenium/sherwood/163/index.html
  A one name study center for the Cartwright surname, any place, any time including any variation of spelling: Cartright, Cutright, and others.

- The CARY / CAREY Family Home Page - 10,800 Descendants
  http://www.familytreemaker.com/users/l/a/r/Lisa-A-Larchevesque/
  Descendents of John CARY, born 1610, and Elizabeth GODFREY.

- CASE Genealogy
  http://www.maggiesworld.com/case.htm
  Descendants of Ephriam Alpha CASE, born around Albany, New York in 1823.

- The CASEY Family Association
  http://home.swbell.net/cfa/

CASTEEL Family History
http://freepages.genealogy.rootsweb.com/~dstrong155/
casteelindex.htm
Also CASTEAL or CASTILE.

Apellido CASTILLA
http://usuarios.iponet.es/fcastilla/ppalapel.html

CASTLEBERRY Genealogy
http://www.clubs.yahoo.com/clubs/castleberry

The CASTLES Page - CASTLES of Ireland
http://www.geocities.com/Heartland/Flats/7628/
Descendants of the children of John and Letitia CASTLES of Northern Ireland.

CASTOR Association of America (CAOA)
http://users.cwnet.com/maverik/castor/index.htm
A non-profit organization dedicated to the discovery and preservation of family history for the surname of CASTOR and all of the variations of it. Kuster, Koster, Custer, Kusterd, Kuester, Kester, Custard, Kustard, Kistard, Kister, Gerster, Caster, Castor, Kaster, Kastor, Kiester, Koester, Keister.

CASSIDY Clan Web Site
http://www.cassidyclan.org/

CASSITY / CASSIDY Family Association
http://www.gendex.com/users/LC49/ccfa/
This is the offical website of the Cassity/Cassidy Family Association, featuring our database, research updates, history, queries, etc. concerning the genealogy of the CASSITYs and CASSIDYs of Kentucky and their allied surnames.

The CASTOR Association of America
http://members.tripod.com/~EbneterG/index-9.html
Caster, Custer, Kester and other variants.

The CASWELL Homepage
http://www.moonrakers.com/genealogy/caswell/
Carswell, Casswell, Caswill, Caswall, Karswell, Coswell, Cassill, etc.

The CATLEY Desk
http://thecatleydesk.webjump.com/
A one name study of the CATLEY surname and its variants: Cattley, Catly, Cateley and Katley.

The CATO Homepage
http://www.webkeeper.com/cato/c.html
Cato & Catoe, many Cater, Cator, Caytor, Cayter, Cayto, Cate, Kayto, Caton and numerous other spellings.

CAVE's Cove
http://members.aol.com/CavesCove/CavesCove.htm
CAVE worldwide.

CAVEYs' Family World Wide Society
http://www.geocities.com/~jlcavey/cavey/main.htm

CAY Family History
http://www.cayco.com/cayhist

CEASE's Web Page
http://www.geocities.com/cease5_1999

The CHACHULA Family Page
http://members.tripod.com/~jedimom/index.htm
Family history and photos of six generations of a Polish-American immigrant family from Turobin to Newark, NJ and beyond. Surname oriented.

CHADDOCK Genealogy
http://www.gather.com/chaddock/

CHADY homepage
http://www.cs.stedwards.edu/~chady/

CHALMERS Family, Cork
http://homepage.tinet.ie/~decfam
Genealogy of the Chalmers family and related branches from 1640 in Banffshire, Scotland to present day in Ireland.

CHAMBERLAIN Chain
http://www.cet.com/~weidnerc/

The World CHAMBERLAIN Genealogical Society
http://www.livingonline.com/~welmar/wcs.html

The CHAMBERS Family
http://www.concentric.net/~norrisc/chambers.shtml

CHAMBLEE & CHAMLEE Family Genealogy Network
http://www.nauvoo.com/family/chamblee/

The Association of CHARRON and DUCHARME, Inc
mailto:dmiale@exis.net
For details e-mail Dick Miale at dmiale@exis.net or in French e-mail Pierre Ducharme at: duchap00libertel.montreal.qc.ca.

Pierre CHASTAIN Family Association
http://www.kopower.com/~jimchstn/

CHCIUK Family Source Site
http://www.teleport.com/~flyheart/chciuk.htm
Descendants of Jan CHCIUK and his son Michal KCIUK, born about 1798, died March 9th, 1851 in Majdan Zbydniowski, a small village in southeastern Poland.

CHEESBROUGH One Name Study Home Page
http://www.users.globalnet.co.uk/~gdl/cheesbro.htm

CHENOWETH Family
http://www.accessone.com/~jegge/chenweth.htm
Descendants of John CHENOWETH & Mary CALVERT.

CHERDRON / SHETRONE Home Page
http://www.gentree.com/cherdron/
CHARDRON, CHERDRON, CHAUDRON, CHARDON, SHEDRON, SHETRON, SHETRONE and related families.

CHESNUT / CHESTNUT Research Network
http://www.users.mis.net/~chesnut/pages/chessurn.htm
Chastain, Chesnai, Chesnau, Chesnet, Chesney, Chesnutt, Chestnut, Chestnutt, McChesney.

The CHEVAL dit St-Jacques Resource Center
http://www.geocities.com/Heartland/Shores/2693/index.htm

CHEVIET & Vincent Gènèalogie de la Famille
http://www.chez.com/cheviet/
Ascendance d'Antoine et Mathilde CHEVIET.

- CHEYNE Home Page
  http://www.rootsweb.com/~cheyne/

- CHICKEN Family Histories
  http://ourworld.compuserve.com/homepages/Chicken_
  Matthews/

- The CHIDGEY Family Tree Home Page
  http://www.geocities.com/Heartland/Garden/9600/
  *Chidgey and all variants including Chedgey, Chedzey, Chedsey,
  Chedzoy, Chedsoy, Chedzy, Chedsy, Chidsey, Chidzey. Records at
  present are back to 1600 in Watchet, Somerset, UK.*

- CHILD Genealogy Web Site: CHILD, CHILDE,
  CHILDS, CHYLDE
  http://www.childgenealogy.org

- CHILTON
  http://www.geocities.com/Heartland/Acres/2234/chilton/
  chilton.html
  *Coming to Virginia in the 1660's, this page deals mostly with the
  Tennessee and Missouri branches of the family.*

- The CHOISSER Family
  http://www.choisser.com/family/

- The CHOQUET-CHOQUETTE Genealogy
  http://jchoquette.org/english
  Genealogy of the Choquet and Choquette families of North America.

- Genealogy CHRISTIAANSE
  http://www.geocities.com/Heartland/Valley/2729/
  Surname found mainly in the Netherlands.

- The CHRISTLIEB-CHRISLIP-CRISLIP Family
  Association
  http://pages.prodigy.net/jeffchristlieb/ccc.html

- CHRISTOPHER Family Website
  http://www.geocities.com/Heartland/Estates/8863

- CHRISTOPHER Family
  http://homepages.tesco.net/~christopherfamilyhistory/
  index.htm#

- CHURCH Family Chronicles
  http://members.aol.com/kinseeker6/church.html

- CHURCHMAN Genealogy Website
  http://www.churchman.com/family
  *Descendants chart and biography pages for more than 6,000
  CHURCHMANs, dating from 1682 when John CHURCHMAN came
  to Pennsylvania from England with William PENN.*

- CISCO / SISCO Genealogy Data
  http://www-epi.soph.uab.edu/cisco/htm/
  *Descendants of Moses SISCO, b. 28 Sep 1799 in Newark, New
  Jersey.*

- The CLAMPETT Family Centre
  http://www.clampett.net
  *Meeting palce for the Clampett family, with a discussion forum,
  Email and web site addresses, and a genealogy section.*

- CLARDY Family Genealogy
  http://www.huscarl.com/clardy/index.htm
  *A clearinghouse for information on the Clardy family and their
  associations.*

- CLARK Family Home Page
  http://www3.teleplex.net/gclark/homepage/clarkstart.html
  *Dedicated to the descendants of John B. Clark of Rowan/Davie
  County, NC, and to all the Clark Family Researchers that choose to
  contribute, download, or add to our database.*

- CLARK Genealogical Society
  http://www.the-clarks.com/genealogy/index.htm

- The Descendants of James CLARK of Vermont
  http://members.aol.com/MShermanL/clark.html
  Born 1601 probably in England, died probably in Vermont.

- CLASPER One-Name Study worldwide.
  http://freespace.virgin.net/rod.clayburn/clasper/clasper.htm

- Moses CLAWSON Family Organization
  http://www.mosesclawson.com/

- CLAYBURN One-Name Study worldwide.
  http://freespace.virgin.net/rod.clayburn/clayburn/clayburn.htm

- CLAYCOMB Family Home Page
  http://www.familytreemaker.com/users/a/d/n/Mary-A-Adney/
  *Descendants of the 11 children of Johann Conrad CLAYCOMB and
  his two wives.*

- CLAYTON Surname
  http://homepages.rootsweb.com/~jclaytn/clayton.html
  Clayton Surname: (DE>GA>AL>TX).

- CLEARY - Resource Index
  http://www.thinktech.demon.co.uk/genealogy/surnames/
  cleary/resource.htm
  *One name resources for the CLEARY surname, including variants
  CLERY and O'CLERY.*

- Patrick CLEBURNE Society
  http://www.patrickcleburne.com/
  *Dedicated to the study of the life and military career of Maj. Gen.
  Patrick Cleburne.*

- Clan CLELAND Web Site
  http://www.clan-cleland.org

- CLEMENT Cuzins
  http://www.geocities.com/Heartland/Valley/9263
  Clement, Clements, Clemens surname and its derivatives.

- CLEMETT Family History
  http://mysite.xtra.co.nz/~clemett/page1.html
  *"all known present day bearers of the name CLEMETT, descend
  from a single Devon family".*

- The CLEREY Family
  http://www.clerey.net/
  *The first recorded instance is documented as being Ann Clare
  Clerey, born in 1551 in Dedham, Essex, England and married to
  Edmund Sherman on 11 September 1594.*

- CLEVELAND Family Chronicles
  http://www.angelfire.com/il/ClevelandFamilyChron/index.html

- The CLIFTON Family Home Page
  http://www.rootsweb.com/~clifton/clifton/

- CLIFTONs of Cornwall
  http://www.clifton.com/clifton.html

- CLINE, KLEINE, KLEIN Heavenly Web Pages
  http://members.aol.com/clineroots/main.html
  The #1 Site for KLEIN, KLEINE, DEKLEINE, DEKLEIN, KLINE, CLINE, CLYNE.

- The Descendants of John CLINE
  http://members.tripod.com/~jlschneider/index.htm

- CLOPTON Family Genealogical Society and CLOPTON Family Archives
  http://homepages.rootsweb.com/~clopton/
  Dedicated to the preservation and sharing of accurate information relating to the ancestors and descendants of Sir Thomas CLOPTON, and his wife, Dame Katherine MYLDE.

- CLOPTON Family Homepage
  http://www.seanet.com/~clopton/

- CLOUGH-L Home Page
  http://genweb.net/~clough/
  Descendants of John Clough (1613-1691).

- The CLOUTIER - CLUTCHEY Family - A Genealogical History
  http://www.naples.net/~clutchey/
  Zacharie CLOUTIER, to Canada in 1634.

- CLOVER Family Page from the CLOVER Family Exchange Newsletter
  http://members.aol.com/junebyr/index.html

- CLUGSTON Family History & Genealogy
  http://www.cstone.net/~clugston/

- COATES, COATE, COATS Family Digital Archive
  http://www.rootsquest.com/~coatsfar/

- COATES-L Surname Mailing List
  http://members.aa.net/~jdcoates/list/coates-l.htm
  Includes Coats, Coate.

- COATNEY Surname List Home Page
  http://COATNEY.listbot.com
  A list for the discussion of the COATNEY Surname - any place, any time.

- COBBAN Family Tree
  http://www.magma.ca/~jcobban/FamilyTree/cobban.html
  Descendants of John (Earnest) COBBAN (1758-1813). Includes: Brodie, Wilton, Collins, Forsyth, Campbell.

- The COBBETT One Name Study Group
  http://members.tripod.co.uk/Cobbett/index.htm

- The COBBETT Study Group
  http://members.aol.com/cobbettsg/
  The Cobbett one name Study Group, aims to link all Cobbett's and Cobbett descendants past and present, for Cobbett family history, and conversation.

- COBERNUS, KOBERNUS, KOBERNUSS, KOBERNUSZ Family Home Page
  http://members.aol.com/gkobernus/index.html

- COBLEY Family History
  http://www.cobley-history.co.uk/
  A brief history of the Cobley family in Cheshire and their origins in Leicestershire, including the families Gamble, Berry, Neale, Rowe, Mountford, Parker, Povey, Redfern.

- The COBRA Family Genealogy Home Page
  http://www.geocities.com/Athens/Acropolis/3515/
  History and genealogy of the Cobra Family in Portugal and its modern branches in Canada, Brazil, and the U.S.A.

- Clan COCHRANE in North America
  http://www.jps.net/guyrc/cochrane.htm

- COCKITT Family History
  http://www.geocities.com/Heartland/Garden/9217/
  A brief histry of the Cockitt family of Cheshire including potted biographies of some of its more interesting characters.

- COCKRELL Collections
  http://www.surnames.com/burgess/cockweb.html
  All Cockrell, Cockrill, Cockerill families in America.

- COFFEY Cousins' Clearinghouse
  http://www.geocities.com/Heartland/Plains/6233/coffey cousins.html

- COFFEY Clues Online
  http://www.geocities.com/Heartland/Estates/7040
  Coffe, Coffee, Caughey, Coughey.

- COFFIN Quest
  http://www.geocities.com/Heartland/Woods/5540/coffin/ coffin.html
  Surname recource center for those researching COFFIN, COFFYN, COFFEN, COFFAN.

- COGSWELL Family Association
  http://www.cogswell.org
  The Cogswell Family Association lists info on their Board of Directors, Membership, Meetings and Books about Cogswell history.

- John Waite COGSWELL and his Descendants
  http://www.celticweb.com/users/katiesanders
  Genealogy of John Waite Cogswell, descendant of John Cogswell originally from Westbury, England.

- COIL/KILE/KYLE Family
  http://freepages.genealogy.rootsweb.com/~firebird/
  Descendants of Valentine GEIL of VA.

- COKER Forum
  http://www.geocities.com/Heartland/Park/8848/index.html
  The online meeting place for discussion and sharing of information regarding the surname COKER, related variations, and closely allied families, in any place and at any time.

- Descendants of Abraham COLBY
  http://www.geocities.com/solongago.geo/kin/gen70021.htm
  Includes descendants of Lieut. Thomas COLBY (1756-1848) and wife Susanna COLBY (1748-1832) of Amesbury, Mass. and Dunbarton and Bow, N.H.

- A COLE Dictionary
  http://home.earthlink.net/~zem1
  COLEs from Plymouth Rock through the American Revolution; from Aaron to Zephanea.

- The FONDREN and COLE Families
  http://members.aol.com/jogt/fondren.htm
  Of North Carolina and South Carolina.

- COLEHOUR / COLEHOWER / COLHOUER / COLHOUR Family
  http://www.ultimatefamilytree.com/UFT/WebPages/william
  colehour/INDEX/index.htm
  All descendants of two brothers, Henry and John Kohlhauer, who came to America in 1804 from Germany. Includes all females lines that are known.

- The COLEMAN Family of Mobjack Bay, Virginia
  http://home1.gte.net/ndcfl/index.htm
  Family history based on the immigrant ancestor, Robert Coleman, who came to VA from England as a headright in 1638.

- COLEMAN Surname Mailing List
  http://homepages.rootsweb.com/~lcompton/coleman/

- The COLERIDGE Family Genealogy
  http://www.geocities.com/Athens/4017/
  Including the poet, Samuel Taylor Coleridge.

- The COLLING System BBS
  http://www.pi.se/collings-system/

- The COLLINS Family
  http://www.mbayweb.com/~mbigelow/collins/collinsintro.htm
  James and Ann COLLINS 1749 to Elizabeth Anne COLLINS 1966. Blakey, Buckingham, Churchill, Collins, Eddins, George, Hughes, Kimes, Rex, Wyatt.

- COLLINS Mess or Mess of COLLINS
  http://pages.prodigy.com/YWMZ46A/collinsm.htm
  And the COLLINS Bulletin Board
  http://pages.prodigy.com/YWMZ46A/CBB.htm

- The COLVIN Family History Page
  http://www.rootsweb.com/~mcolvin/colvinfh/

- COLYER Genealogy
  http://users.midamer.net/colyer55/
  Colier, Collier, Collyer, Colyar, Colyear, Colyer.

- The COMBS-COOMBS &c. Research Group, Inc.
  http://www.combs-families.org/
  Includes Com, Comb, Combe, Combes, Combs, Come, Comes, Coom, Coomb, Coombe, Coombes, Coombs, Coome, Coomes, Coumbes, Cowmbe, Cumbe, Cumbes, Cumbs, Kom, Kome, Komes, &c.

- L'Association des COMEAU D'AmÈrique
  http://home.istar.ca/~acomeau/aca/bonjour.htm

- COMPTON Ancestory
  http://members.xoom.com/desotojohn/
  Information for COMPTONs of all lines. Archives of queries from COMPTON Mailing List. Emphasis on Larkin COMPTON of NC and his descendents in IN and elsewhere.

- COMPTON Family Genealogy
  http://home.gci.net/~mcompton/
  Ancestors and descendants of Eugene "Gene" Duane Compton and Mary "Genny" Genevieve Stimson, who originated in Minnesota and homestead in the prairies of Saskatchewan, North Dakota and Montana at the turn of the 1900's.

- COMPTON Home Site
  http://www.geocities.com/Heartland/Acres/4730/compton/compton.html

- The COMSTOCK Project
  http://hammer.prohosting.com/~comfam/

- CONDER Family
  http://www.duke.edu/web/chlamy/conder.html
  Descendants of Lewis Conder and Elizabeth Muller or Miller.

- CONE Genealogy
  http://home.rose.net/~edcone/
  Descendants of William Cone and Keziah Barber.

- CONE Research Site Home Page
  http://www.geocities.com/conereseach

- One-Name Genealogical Study
  http://www.conibere.freeserve.co.uk/
  Coneybeer, Conybeer, Conibeer, Conibeere, Conibeare, Connebear, Connibeere, Coniber, Coneybeare, Connabeer, Conybear, Connibeer, Conibear, Conybeare, Conibere, Conibeer, Conabeer.

- CONKLIN-L Surname Mailing List
  http://www.rootsweb.com/~nozell/CONKLIN-L/

- CONLEY Family Forum
  http://members.boardhost.com/conley/

- The CONMY Chronicles: A Genealogical Tour
  http://www.surfsouth.com/~tippie
  A genealogical study of Bartholomew John CONMY I, Castleconnor Parish, Stokane, Co. Sligo, Ireland, and his descendants.

- CONNICK Genealogy Search Web Site
  http://www.Connicks.com/

- CONNOLLY Genealogy Forum
  http://www.connollyweb.com/geneology/

- CONOVER Family Genealogy
  http://www.conovergenealogy.com/
  Descendants of Wolpert Gerretse Van Kouwenhoven.

- The CONROY Home Page
  http://www.conroyhome.net/

- COOGAN Family of County Monaghan
  http://members.aol.com/moncoog/index.htm
  Story of COOGAN family descended from Patrick COOGAN of County Monaghan, Ireland (born c.1800).

- COOK COOKE KOCH
  http://members.aol.com/CookCooke
  Over 600 Family charts of Cook's from members of the Cook Discussion Goup at Rootsweb.

- COOK Families of Kentucky and Tennessee with Census Data
  http://www.geocities.com/Heartland/Estates/4375/cookmain.html

- The COON Families of East Central Indiana
  http://homepages.rootsweb.com/~coonweb/
  COON, KOON and KUHN who originally migrated from what is now West Virginia and settled in Hancock and Henry Counties, Indiana. Unrelated families with this surname also covered.

- COOPER Home Page - COOPER Collections Newsletter
  http://members.aol.com/kinseeker6/cooper.html

- The COOTER Family History Web Site
  http://www.30snelling.freeserve.co.uk/

- The COPAGES & COPPAGES of Warwickshire
  http://copage.virtualave.net
  Families orginating from the UK village of Tanworth in Warwickshire and the surrounding area and possible origins of this surname.

- COPELAND Cuzzins Newsletter
  mailto:CarlCindy2@aol.com
  For details send e-mail to Lucinda (Cindy) Olsen, editor and publisher, at CarlCindy2@aol.com.

- SStapor's COPELAND Home Page
  http://members.aol.com/SStapor/Copeland.html
  The descendants of Joel Copeland 1734-1814 of Overton Co., TN. He was the g-g-grandson of John Copeland (b 1616) the immigrant.

- COPINGER Home Page
  http://www.copinger.org.uk
  COPINGER & COPPINGER originating in Ireland & England, and all variants, throughout the world with a copy of the family history published in 1884.

- COPSON Home Page
  http://www.copson.org

- CORAM Family of Benevolence, GA
  http://hometown.aol.com/motmaroc/index.html
  Family tree of Thomas Jefferson CORAM in pictures.

- The CORBETT Study Group
  http://website.lineone.net/~corbett_group

- CORCORRAN Clan Home Page
  http://www.corcorran.com/
  A Site for all CORCORRANs, CORCORANs, O'CORCORANs, COCHRANs, COCHRANEs and any other descendants of the MacCORCRAINs.

- eGroups : CORDER
  http://www.onelist.com/subscribe/CORDER/
  Mailing list for the discussion and research of the Corder surname, anywhere, anytime.

- The CORDER Surname Project
  http://www.geocities.com/Heartland/Flats/2701/index.html

- CORLEY World Wide Reunion
  http://members.tripod.com/~ClFR/index.html
  All of my CORLEY Genealogical Info plus other info that I've found and that's been shared with me. Links to other CORLEY-related web sites.

- CORFMAN Family Web Site
  http://www.corfman.com/
  Also KORFFMANN.

- CORMIER Family - Send e-mail to Robin Finley
  mailto:moxie40@vivanet.com

- CORNEs Family History Society
  http://www.geocities.com/Heartland/Bluffs/3832
  Also Corne, Corn, Corns, Cornes, and Corness worldwide.

- CORNELL Family Genealogy Home Page
  http://www.netusa1.net/~tvcornel/gene.html
  Includes Cornell, Cornwell and Cornwall in Canada and US.

- CORNWELLGenealogy
  http://members.tripod.com/eastbourne

- CORNES Family History Society
  http://www.geocities.com/Heartland/Bluffs/3832/
  CORNE, CORN, CORNS, CORNES, CORNESS.

- CORNING Connections
  http://mrmac-jr.scs.unr.edu/corning/corning.html

- CORNING Family Reunion
  http://bold.coba.unr.edu/corning/reunion/1fam.html
  Corning Family Reunion, Yarmouth, Nova Scotia, Canada, July 22 to 25, 1999.

- CORSON / COLSON Family History Association
  http://homepages.rootsweb.com/~ccfha/index.htm/

- CORYs Of America
  http://members.aol.com/albcory/index.htm

- COSSITT Family Association, Ltd.
  http://www.cossitt.org/

- COTTEW
  http://www.geocities.com/Heartland/Ridge/9572/Cottew.html
  For any one interested in the COTTEW surname or its variant spellings of CUTTEW and COTTEAU.

- COUCH Genealogy
  http://www.couchgenweb.com/

- The COULSON Family Tree
  http://millennium.fortunecity.com/teletubby/630/
  American descendants of the COULSON line originating in Derbyshire, England.

- The COULTER / COALTER Family - Genealogy
  http://www.internet-partners.com/mcdonald/index.htm

- COUNTISS Connections Home Page
  http://members.home.net/famhist/countiss.htm

- COURTENAY History and Genealogy
  http://www.webcom.com/scourt/
  The Courtenay Society is based at Powderham Castle in Devon, England. Significant branches of the family are located today in England, Ireland, Canada, the United States, New Zealand, and Australia.

- COURTNEY Chronicle On-Line Family Magazine
  http://www.geocities.com/RainForest/3608/

- The COUSINS Family Tree Project
  http://cftp.cjb.net/
  To unite the 12000 'Cousins' families around the world. Some of the names include Cousins, Kirwan, Mahoney, Hoey, Guswell, Murnane and many more!

- COUSINS/COZENS/COUZENS Family Genealogy
  http://web2.airmail.net/lwi941/
  From Virginia since 1694.

- John's COUTANT Family Tree
  http://thorn.pair.com/thorn/coutant/coutant1.htm

- Association des Familles COUTON, COUTHON, COUSTON et alliÈes
  http://members.aol.com/coutonstef/afccc/index.htm
  Etude des familles au niveau mondial portant ces patronymes ainsi que les patronymes CO(T)ON, allies aux COUTON.

- COVINGTON
  http://members.aol.com/covingtonw/home.htm
  Descendants of Terrel Covington, born in Richmond County, NC.

- COVINGTON History
  http://www.covingtonhistory.co.uk

- COWAN Clan United
  http://www.sure.net/~rcowan/index.html

- COWAN Clues Genealogy Newsletter
  http://www.angelfire.com/ar/cowanclues/index.html

- The COWAN List
  http://members.tripod.com/~TMock/cowan.htm
  Cowan, Cowen.

- The COWART Family
  http://home.att.net/~dpdklong/Cowart.htm
  The Cowart family of Central Alabama. Descendants of Isham Cowart.

- COWHERD Genealogy
  http://www.geocities.com/Heartland/Prairie/4917/
  Descendants of James COWARD, immigrant who came to Virginia from England in 1688.

- The COWLEY Space
  http://www.users.uswest.net/~scowley/cowley.html
  Descendants of Charles and Ann COWLEY of Kirk Michael, Isle of Man. The site contains genealogical information for WALL, SHAW and GOTTFREDSON family lines.

- COX Connection
  http://www.geocities.com/Heartland/Estates/4913/
  A listing of all the COX's that can be found anywhere in the world.

- COX Coop Library
  http://www.wisecomp.com/ccl/coxcoop.html
  Data and links for researchers of the COX surname and its variations.

- COX Family of Ohio Genealogy
  http://www.jacksonville.net/~bjcox/
  Benjamin J COX (1773-1846) et al. Links to more COX family resources, etc.

- The John COX Family
  http://www.telusplanet.net/public/cfdun/coxnav.htm
  From King's County, Ireland to Manchester, England to Canada.

- Welcome to The COXON Name
  http://freespace.virgin.net/harry.coxon
  History of the name, census, snippets, connections.

- COYAN Genealogy Homepage
  http://www.zoomnet.net/~acoyan/
  Descendants of Hugh and Elizabeth Coyan of Allegheny County, Pennsylvania and southern Ohio.

- COYTE Family History
  http://www.coyte.com/

- The CRABBE Family Page
  http://www.geocities.com/Heartland/Ranch/7299/
  World-Wide One-Name Study of CRABBE families.

- CRABTREE Family Roots Homepage
  http://php.indiana.edu/~crabtre
  World's Largest Online Repository of Crabtree Genealogy.

- CRAGG the name
  http://www.ozemail.com.au/~woolwash/cragg/engcragg1.htm
  CRAGG - Cumberland County, England
  http://www.ozemail.com.au/~woolwash/cragg/engcragg2.htm
  CRAGG - Keswick, Cumberland County, England
  http://www.ozemail.com.au/~woolwash/cragg/engcragg3.htm
  CRAGG - Workington, Cumberland County, England
  http://www.ozemail.com.au/~woolwash/cragg/engcragg4.htm

- CRAGO Famiy Quest
  http://home.switchboard.com/mcrago
  Crago, Cragoe, Cragow, Craigo, Crego, Cregoe, Cruggoe, Cruggow. Overview of CRAGO history in England and the migration to America, 1548 to 1850.

- CRAIG Genealogy
  http://www.qni.com/~geo/craig.htm
  Descendants of Samuel Craig, born 1760 in York County, Pennsylvania.

- CRAIG Genealogy Homepage
  http://www.geocities.com/Heartland/Meadows/9791
  CRAIG and its variant spellings around the world.

- CRAIGMYLE Genealogy
  http://members.aol.com/Rdkfour/craigmyle.html

- CRAMP(E) One Name Association
  http://www.geocities.com/Heartland/Flats/7866/

- Some CRANDALL, CRAIN, COWAN, & CLARY Genealogy
  http://www.geocities.com/MotorCity/1949/

- CRANDALL Family Association
  http://www.geocities.com/~wyatt1599/cfa/contents.html

- CRANE Family Message Board
  http://www.rootsweb.com/~genepool/crane/index.html

- CRANKSHAW Family History
  http://www.angelfire.com/ga/Crankshaw/

- The Peter CRAPO Clan
  http://cc.usu.edu/~fath6/PCClan.html
  All currently known descendants of Peter CRAPO who arrived in Massachussets about 1695.

COLQUITT, COLSELL (includes Colsill, Colsil, Coleshill, Coshill), COLSON (includes Coleson, Coulson, Colston), COLT (includes Coult), COLTON, COLVER, COLVILLE (includes Carville, Colvil), COLVIN (includes Calvin, Colven), COLWELL, COLYER, COMBS, COMEAU, COMEAUX, COMER, COMERFORD, COMFORT, COMLEY, COMPER (includes Cumper), COMPTON (includes Cumpton, Comton, Crumpton, Campton), COMSTOCK, COMSTOCK, CONANT, CONATSER, CONATY (includes Connachtaighs, Connerty), CONAWAY (includes Conway), CONBOY, CONCANNON, CONDER, CONDIE, CONDIT, CONDON, CONDREN, CONDRON, CONDRON (includes Condren, Condran, Condrin), CONE, CONERLY, CONES, CONEY, CONFER, CONGDON, CONGER, CONGLETON, CONIBEAR, CONINE (includes Conyn, Konyn, Canine, Cornine), CONKLE, CONKLIN, CONKLING, CONKRIGHT (includes Conkwright), CONLAN, CONLEY, CONLEY, CONLIN, CONLISK, CONLON (includes O'Conlon, O'Conlan, Conlan, O'Conlin, Conlin, O'Conlen, Conlen), CONN (includes Con), CONNALLY, CONNAWAY, CONNELL, CONNELL (includes O'Connell), CONNELLY (includes Conley, Connally, Connolly), CONNER, CONNERS, CONNERY, CONNETT, Connolly (includes Conly, Conely, Connelly, Conley), CONNOLLY, CONNOR, CONNORS, CONOVER (includes Coavenhoven, Coenhoven, Cofenhofen, Coneover, Connoven, Connower, Connoyer,, Conoven, Conver, Couen Houen, Couenhouen, Coughvenhoven, Counoven, Counover, Couvenhoven,, Couwehowen, Couwenhove, Couwenhoven, Couwenhowen, Couwenoven, Coven Hoven, Covenhove, Covenhoven,, Covenhover, Cowerhoven, Cownnover, Cownouer, Cownover, Cownovr, Coyenhoven, Crownover, Koienhoven,, Koienoven, Konover, Korenoven, Kouenhoven, Kouveoven, Kouwenhove, Kouwenhoven, Kouwenove,, Kouwenoven, Kovenhoven, Kowenhoven, Kownoven, Koyenhoven, Van Couwenhoven, Van Covenhoven, Van, Cowenhoven, Van Kouwenhoven), CONPROPST (includes Cornpropst), CONRAD (includes Coonradt), CONROY, CONSIDINE, CONSTABLE, CONSTANCE, CONSTANT, CONVERSE (includes Conyerse), CONVERY, CONVEY, CONWAY, CONWELL, CONWELL (includes Cornwell, Cornwall), CONYERS.

- **"COO-COT" Surname Mailing Lists**
  http://www.rootsweb.com/~jfuller/gen_mail_surnames-coo.html
  COODY, COOK (includes Cooke, Kuch, Koch), COOKE, COOKSEY, COOKSLEY, COOKSON, COOL, COOLEY, COOLIDGE, COOMBE, COOMBER (includes Comber, Cumber), COOMBS (includes Com, Comb, Combe, Combes, Combs, Come, Comes, Coom, Coomb, Coombe, Coombes,, Coome, Coomes, Coumbes, Cowmbe, Cumbe, Cumbes, Cumbs, Kom, Kome, Komes), COOMES, COON (includes Coons, Koon, Koons, Kuhn, Kuhns, Maccoone, McCune), COONEY, COONROD, COONS, COOPER (includes Kooper, Koeper, Kupfer, Kuyper, Coopers, Cooperman, Coper, Coober, Coopey, Copper), COPE, COPELAND (includes Coplen, Coplan, Copelan, Coupland), COPENHAVER, COPEN (includes Copin), COPES, COPLEY, COPP, COPPER, COPPERSMITH (includes Kupferschmidt, Kuppersmith, Cuppersmith, Coopersmith), COPPESS (includes Coppes, Copes), COPPIN, COPPING, COPPLE, COPPOCK (includes Koppic, Kopec, Coppick, Cuppack, Coppage, McCobic), COPSEY (includes Copsy), CORADINE, CORAM, CORBET, CORBETT (includes Corbet, Corbitt, Corbit), CORBIN (includes Corbett), CORBITT, CORBLY, CORBY, CORCORAN, CORDELL, CORDER, CORDER, CORDES, CORDRAY, CORE, COREY (includes Cory), CORIALE, CORKUM, CORL, CORLETT, CORLEY (includes Cawley, Cauley), CORLISS, CORMACK, CORMIER, CORN (includes Corns, Cornn, Corne, Cornes, Cornns), CORNELIS, CORNELISON, CORNELIUS (includes Corneliusen, Kornelius, Corder, Cornelli), CORNELL (includes Cornwell, Cornwall, Cornewell), CORNER (includes

Corners), CORNETT (includes Cornet, Canute), CORNETT, CORNEY, CORNFORTH (includes Cornfurth, Cornfurthe, Cornforthe, Comforth), CORNICK, CORNISH, CORNMAN (includes Kornman, Corman, Corneman), CORNS, CORNWALL, CORNWELL, CORRELL (includes Currell, Corell), CORRIGAN (includes O'Corrigain, O'Corrigan, O'Carrigan, O'Corrican, O'Kerrigan, Carrigan, Corrican, Kerrigan), CORRY, CORSAUT (includes Cossart, Casad, Cashow, Cassairt, Cassart, Cassat, Cassatt, Cassou, Cazort, Coesart,, Corzatt, Cosad, Cosart, Cosat, Coshow, Cossaart, Cossaer, Cossaert, Cossairt, Cossat, Cossatt, Cozad, Cozar,, Cozart, Cozat, Cozatt, Cozzart, Crozatt, Kershaw, Kershow, Kossart), CORSON (includes Colson, Courson, DeCoursey, Courssen, Coarson, Corzine, Carsten), CORT, CORUM, CORWIN, CORY, CORYELL, CORZINE, COSBY, COSENTINO, COSGROVE, COSHOW (includes Cashew, Cusho, Kershaw), COSLEY (includes Costly, Costley, Casley, Coussoule), COSLOW, COSPER (includes Gasper), COSS, COSSEY, COSTA, COSTELLO, COSTER, COSTIGAN, COSTILLO, COSTILOW, COSTIN, COSTLEY, COSTNER, COSTON, COTA, COTE, COTNER (includes Gortner, Goertner, Curtner, Carther, Cortner, Kartner), COTTAM, COTTEN, COTTER, COTTEW (includes Cotteau, Cuttew), COTTINGHAM, COTTLE, COTTON, COTTRELL (includes Cottrill, Cotterell, Cotteral), COTTRILL.

- **"COU-CQ" Surname Mailing Lists**
  http://www.rootsweb.com/~jfuller/gen_mail_surnames-cou.html
  COUCH (includes Crouch, Kouch), COUGHLAN, COUGHLIN, COUILLARD (includes Coulliard, Couliard, Coulard, Coullard, Couilyard, Coulyard, Coolyard, Colyard), COULBECK (includes Colbeck, Colebeck, Cowlbeck), COULEHAN, COULING (includes Cowling), COULL, COULOMBE (includes Coulome, Colombe, Colomb), COULSON, COULTER, COULTHARD, COUNCIL, COUNTISS, COUNTRYMAN (includes Gunterman, Gunderman, Gonterman, Kunderman, Kunterman, Cunderman, Contreman,, Counterman, Gautherman), COUNTS (includes Countz, Koontz), COUPLAND (includes Copeland, Copland), COURSEY, COURSON, COURT, COURTENAY, COURTER, COURTNEY, COURTOIS, COURTRIGHT (includes Cortrecht, Cortregt, Cortright, Cortwright, Kortrecht, Kortregt, Kortright, Kortryk,, Kortwright, Van Kortright, Van Kortryjk), COURVILLE, COUSINEAU, COUSINS, COUTON (includes Couston, Couthon, Coutton, Coaston, Cowstonne), COUTS (includes Kutz, Kouts, Coots, Cootts, Coutts, Koutz), COUTTS, COUTURE, COVALT, COVELL, COVENEY, COVENHOVEN, COVENTRY (includes Covingtry), COVER, COVERDALE (includes Coverdell, Coverdill), COVERDILL, COVERT (includes Coevert, Coovert, Coever), COVERT (includes Coevert, Coovert, Couvert, Coever, Covet), COVEY, COVINGTON, COWAN (includes Cowen, Cown, McCowan), COWARD, COWARD, COWART, COWDEN, COWDREY, COWELL, COWEN (includes Cowing), COWFER (includes Cougher, Cowher), COWGER, COWGILL, COWIN, COWING, COWLES, COWLEY (includes Cooley), COWPER, COWSERT (includes Cousar, Cousart, Couser, Cousert, Cowsar, Cowser), COX, COXON, COY (includes Coye), COYLE, COYNE, COZAD, COZART (includes Cossart, Cozad, Cassart, Kosart, Kozad), COZBY (includes Cosby), COZINE.

- **"CRA-CRD" Surname Mailing Lists**
  http://www.rootsweb.com/~jfuller/gen_mail_surnames-cra.html
  CRABB, CRABBE (includes Crabb, Craib), CRABTREE, CRADDOCK, CRADDUCK, CRAFT (includes Kraft), CRAFTON, CRAGG, CRAGO (includes Craigo), CRAIG, CRAIN (includes Crane, Craine), CRALL, CRAM, CRAMBLETT, CRAMER, CRAMPTON, CRANDALL (includes Crandell, Crandle, Crandol),

CRANDLEMERE (includes Crandlemier, Crandlemeir), CRANE, CRANFIELD, CRANFORD, CRANGLE, CRANMER, CRANSTON (includes Cranstoun, Cranson), CRANSWICK (includes Cranswicke), CRATE, CRATE (includes Krate), CRATON (includes Crayton, Creighton), CRATTY, CRAUN (includes Krahne, Krahn, Kraun, Krawn, Kron, Krohne, Crawn, Crahn, Cron, Crowne), CRAVEN, CRAVENS, CRAVER, CRAVEY, CRAVEY (includes McCravey), CRAW, CRAWFORD (includes Craford, Crafford, Crowfoot), CRAWLEY, CRAYCRAFT (includes Craycroft, Cracraft, Cracroft, Creacroft), CRAYTON, CRAZY.

- **"CRE-CRN" Surname Mailing Lists**
  http://www.rootsweb.com/~jfuller/gen_mail_surnames-cre.html
  CREAGER (includes Krieger, Kruger, Cregar, Creger, Crugar, Creggar, Krueger), CREAGER, CREAM (includes Creamer), CREAMER, CREASEY, CREASON (includes Creeson), CREASY, CRECELIUS, CREE (includes Cre, Crie, Crea, Crey), CREECH (includes Creach, Screech, Screach, Cruch), CREECY, CREED (includes Creede, Creedon), CREEK, CREEKMORE, CREEL (includes Creal), CREESON, CREGAN, CREIGHTON, CREMEANS, CRENSHAW (includes Crinshaw, Cranshaw, Crashaw), CRENSHAW, CRESAP, CRESS, CRESSWELL, CRESSY (includes Cressey, Crecey, Crecy, Cresse), CRESWELL, CRETORS (includes Creators, Creater), CREVIER (includes Creviere), CREVLIN, CREW, CREWE, CREWS (includes Cruise, Cruse, Crewse), CRIBBS, CRICHTON, CRIDDLE, CRIDER, CRILLEY (includes Crilly), CRIM, CRINER (includes Creiner, Greiner, Kreiner, Kriner, Crider), CRIPE, CRIPPEN (includes Crippin, Grippen), CRIPPEN (includes Crippin, Grippen, Grippin), CRIPPS, CRISMAN, CRISP (includes Chrisp, Crispe), CRISPIN, CRIST (includes Christ, Criss), CRISWELL, CRITCHFIELD, CRITCHLOW, CRITES, CRITTEN, CRITTENDEN.

- **"CRO-CT" Surname Mailing Lists**
  http://www.rootsweb.com/~jfuller/gen_mail_surnames-cro.html
  CROASDALE, CROCKER, CROCKET, CROCKETT, CROCKFORD, CROESEN (includes Cruise, Cruser, Crusen, Cruzen, Kroesen, Krewson, Krusen, Kruser), CROFOOT (includes Crowfoot, Crofut, Crofutt, Croffut), CROFT, CROKER (includes Croaker, Crocker), CROLEY (includes Crowley, Cralle, Crawley), CROLL, CROMB, CROMER, CROMPTON, CROMWELL, CRON, CRONE, CRONIN, CRONK (includes Craunk, Kronk, Kraunk, Cronkhite, Krank), CRONWOVEN, CROOK (includes Crooks), CROOKS, CROPPER, CROSBIE, CROSBY, CROSHAW, CROSIER, CROSLEY, CROSS, CROSS, CROSSLAND, CROSSLEY, CROSSMAN, CROSSON, CROSTHWAITE (includes Crosthwait,

Crosswaite, Crosswait, Crosswhite), CROTHERS, CROTTY, CROTZER, CROUCH, CROUSE (includes Krouse, Krause), CROW, CROWDER, CROWE, CROWELL, CROWL, CROWLEY, CROWN, CROWNOVER, CROWSON, CROWTHER, CROXTON, CROY, CROYLE, CROZIER, CROZIER, CRUCE, CRUEY (includes Crewey), CRUICKSHANK, CRUIKSHANK, CRUISE, CRULL, CRUM, CRUME, CRUMLEY (includes Crumly), CRUMMEL (includes Krummel, Cromell, Crumel, Crumal, Crummell, Croommel), CRUMP, CRUMPLER, CRUMPLER, CRUMPTON, CRUMRINE, CRUNK, CRUNKLETON, CRUSE, CRUSENBERRY, CRUSER (includes Kruser, Crusa, Croesen), CRUTCHER, CRUTCHFIELD, CRYAN (includes O'cryan, O'crean, Crean, Crehan, O'cregan, O'croidheain), CRYER, CRYSTAL.

- **"CU-CZ" Surname Mailing Lists**
  http://www.rootsweb.com/~jfuller/gen_mail_surnames-cu.html
  CUBBAGE (includes Cubage), CUDDEBACK (includes Caudebec, Codebec, Cudaback, Kodebec, Codeback, Cotteback, Cudeback), CUDDY, CUENI, CUFFE, CULBERT (includes Cuthbert, Culpert), CULBERTSON, CULBREATH, CULL, CULLEN, CULLER, CULLEY, CULLINAN (includes Cullen, Cullinane, Quillinane, O'Cullinan, O'Cullinane), CULLOP (includes Kohlhep, Köhlhep, Kohlhop, Köhlhop, Culop), CULLUM, CULLY, CULP, CULPEPER, CULPEPPER (includes Culpeper, Colepeper), CULVER, CULVERHOUSE (includes Culberhouse, Culverhause), CUMBEE, CUMBERLAND, CUMMIN, CUMMING, CUMMINGS, CUMMINS (includes Cummons, Commons, Commins), CUNDIFF (includes Condiff, Conduff), CUNHA, CUNLIFFE, CUNNINGHAM (includes Cunnyngham, Konningham, Koenigam, Cummings), CUPP (includes Kopp, Kop, Cop, Cope, Cup, Cap), CUPPLES, CUPPY, CURBELO (includes Curbello, Corbello, Courvelle, Courville), CURCIE, CURD, CURL, CURLEE, CURLEY, CURNUTT (includes Curnutte, Carnutt, Cornutt, Kurnutt), CURNUTT, CURNUTTE, CURRAN (includes Coran, Currin, Curan, Currann, Currans, Curreen, Curren, O'Curran), CURRAN, CURRELL, CURRENCE (includes Currance, Currens, Currans), CURRIE, CURRIER, CURRY, CURTIN, CURTIS (includes Curtiss), CURTISS, CUSACK CUSENBARY (includes Cushenbary, Cushenberry, Crusenbary), CUSHING, CUSHMAN, CUSICK, CUSSON, CUSTARD, CUSTER, CUTBIRTH, CUTHBERT, CUTHBERTSON, CUTHRELL (includes Cuthriell, Cutrell), CUTLER, CUTLER (includes Cuttler), CUTLIP (includes Cutlipp, Cutliff, Cutliffe, Cudlip, Cudlipp, Cutlett), CUTRESS, CUTRIGHT (includes Cartright, Curtright, Curtrite, Cutrite, Cartrite, Carwright, Courtright), CUTTER, CUTTING, CUTTLE, CUTTS, CUTWAY, CUYPERS (includes Cooper, Kuyper, Kuipers), CYGANOWSKI, CYPHER, CYPLES, CYR, CYRUS.

SURNAMES, FAMILY ASSOCIATIONS & FAMILY NEWSLETTERS – "D"

Resources Dedicated to One Surname
http://www.cyndislist.com/surn-d.htm

Category Index:

◆ General Surname Sites and Resources
Surname Specific Sites and Resources

◆ Surname Mailing Lists

◆ General Surname Sites and Resources

• Connect with Surnames - D
http://www.geocities.com/Heartland/Bluffs/7708/d.html

• 'D' Surnames at RootsWeb
http://resources.rootsweb.com/surnames/d.html

• Dutch Home Pages by Familyname ~ Letter D
http://members.tripod.com/~Don_Arnoldus/d.htm

• FamilyHistory.com - Message Boards - Surname - D
http://www.familyhistory.com/messages/list.asp?prefix=DA

• Family Tree Maker Online User Home Pages - D
http://www.familytreemaker.com/users/d/index.html

• Family Workings D Surname Links
http://www.familyworkings.com/links/surd.htm

GenConnect Surname Index - "D"
http://genconnect.rootsweb.com/indx/surnames/D.html
Message boards sponsored by RootsWeb. Each surname message board set is divided into the following topics: Queries, Bibles, Biographies, Deeds, Obituaries, Pensions, Wills.

Genealogy Resources on the Internet - "DA-DD" Surname Mailing Lists
http://www.rootsweb.com/~jfuller/gen_mail_surnames-da.html
"DEA-DED"
http://www.rootsweb.com/~jfuller/gen_mail_surnames-dea.html
"DEE-DEH"
http://www.rootsweb.com/~jfuller/gen_mail_surnames-dee.html
"DEI-DEN"
http://www.rootsweb.com/~jfuller/gen_mail_surnames-dei.html
"DEO-DET"
http://www.rootsweb.com/~jfuller/gen_mail_surnames-deo.html
"DEU-DH"
http://www.rootsweb.com/~jfuller/gen_mail_surnames-deu.html
"DI-DN"
http://www.rootsweb.com/~jfuller/gen_mail_surnames-di.html
"DO-DQ"
http://www.rootsweb.com/~jfuller/gen_mail_surnames-do.html

"DR-DT"
http://www.rootsweb.com/~jfuller/gen_mail_surnames-dr.html
"DU-DZ"
http://www.rootsweb.com/~jfuller/gen_mail_surnames-du.html
Search the index of surname mailing lists below: Surname Mailing Lists.

o Genealogy Resources on the Internet - Surnames Included in Mailing Lists - "D"
http://www-personal.umich.edu/~cgaunt/surnames/d.names.html
This is a computer generated list of the surnames, and all variant spellings for those names, that are found in the surname mailing lists detailed on the pages shown above.

• Genealogy Resources on the Internet - Surname Web Sites for "D" Surnames
http://www-personal.umich.edu/~cgaunt/surnames/d.html

• Genealogy's Most Wanted - Surnames Beginning with "D"
http://www.citynet.net/mostwanted/d.htm

• Google Web Directory .... Genealogy>Surnames>D
http://directory.google.com/Top/Society/Genealogy/Surnames/D/

• Heartland Genealogy Society Membership List - D
http://www.geocities.com/Heartland/Ranch/2416/hgs-mlist-d.html

• H-GIG Surname Registry - Surnames Beginning D
http://www.ucr.edu/h-gig/surdata/surname4.html

• Higginson Book Company - Surnames Beginning with D
http://www.higginsonbooks.com/d.htm

• inGeneas Table of Common Surname Variations and Surname Misspellings - D-E
http://www.ingeneas.com/D2E.html

• The Obituary Link Page - Family Obituary Archives Online - D
http://www.geocities.com/~cribbswh/obit/d.htm

• Open Directory - Society: Genealogy: Surnames: D
http://www.dmoz.org/Society/Genealogy/Surnames/D/

- Surname Springboard Index - D
  http://www.geocities.com/~alacy/spring_d.htm

- SurnameWeb Surname Registry - D Index
  http://www.surnameweb.org/registry/d.htm

- SWINX Zoeklijst Nederlandse Familienamen /
  SWINX Searchlist Dutch Surnames - D
  http://www.swinx.net/swinx/swinx_da_nl.htm

- Websites at RootsWeb: D Surnames
  http://www.rootsweb.com/~websites/surnames/d.html

◆ Surname Specific Sites and Resources

- Descendants of Valentin DAHLEM
  http://www.netropolis.net/jpounds/dahlem/dahlem.htm
  Gathered from a family tree created in Germany by Direktor Hermann Dahlem. Appended with descendants of Freidrich Wilhelm Dahlem.

- DAHLSTEDT Family Roots
  http://sony.inergy.com/DahlstedtRoots/
  Descendants of Nils DAHLSTEDT, born in 1749, died in M–nsterÅs, May 20, 1817.

- Association des descendants d'Olivier DAIGRE
  http://www.multimania.com/adod/introduction.html
  Site officiel de l'Association des descendants d'Olivier Daigre du Québec.

- DALLING Heritage Site
  http://www.geocities.com/NapaValley/Vineyard/1252/

- The DALRYMPLEs of Nova Scotia and Stair
  http://home.mem.net/~dalrympl/
  Descendants of James Dalrymple (b.1761) of Nova Scotia and descendants of James Dalrymple, First Viscount of Stair.

- DALTON Genealogical Society
  http://members.aol.com/DaltonGene/index.html

- The Descendants of Crohan DALY in America
  http://people.ne.mediaone.net/pford/index.htm
  Their emigration from Ireland to America in 1863.

- The DALTON Genealogical Society
  http://members.aol.com/Daltongene/index.html

- Descendants of (Laurence) Simon DALY of Waratah NSW Australia
  http://www.users.bigpond.com/rjdaly/
  Includes DOHERTY, ARNOLD, LUCERNE, OGRADY.

- The Olive Tree Genealogy: The DAMEN Family of New York
  http://www.rootsweb.com/~ote/damen.htm
  Descendants of Jan Cornelise Damen, from Bunnik, a village on the Ryn in Utrecht, and his wife Fytie/Sophia Martens. Jan and Sophia were in Long Island by 1650.

- The DAMERON-DAMRON Family Association
  http://www.mindspring.com/~ccchaney/ddfa/ddfa.html

- DAMETZA Genealogy
  http://www.geocities.com/Heartland/Woods/5540/dametz/dametz.html
  Surname Resource Center for those researching these surnames: DAMETZ, DEMETZ, DAMITZ, DEMITZ, DAMETTS, DEMETTS and other variations.

- Gènèalogie de la Famille D'AOUST Genealogy Web Page
  http://members.xoom.com/daoust/
  Descendants of Guillaume D'Aoust. D'Aout, Daoust, Dault, Deault, Doe, Daot, Dauld, Dahult.

- Coteau de France - DASPIT de Saint-Amand
  http://www.concentric.net/~Jpdaspit/history1.htm
  "The name derives from the part of Louisiana where Pierre Daspit de Saint Amand's land grant was located."

- DARRINGTON Genealogy
  http://members.aol.com/drngton/darrind.htm
  Genealogy of the DARRINGTON surname and variants (DERRINGTON, DORRINGTON, etc.), including surname origins, data, chronologies, genealogies, queries, links, and much more.

- DASSONVILLE Net
  http://www.dassonville.net
  Website of the family DASSONVILLE, worldwide.

- DAUDELIN
  http://www.geocities.com/Heartland/Flats/6626
  Genealogy of all the DAUDELIN in Canada and USA Daudelin, Deaudelin, Daudlin, Dodelin, Audelin, Dudley, Dolan, Carmel.

- DaVAR Individuals
  http://www.macatawa.org/~brianter/davar.htm

- Diggin' for DAVISes Newsletter
  http://www.greenheart.com/rdietz/diggin1.htm
  Available on the GoldenWest Marketing page.

- The DAVIS Family History Pages#160;
  http://ferry.polymer.uakron.edu/genealogy/

- DAVIS Genealogy - Descendants - 1800, WAR, ENG
  http://www.itmagic.demon.co.uk/genealogy/davis.htm
  Descendants of William DAVIS & Sarah.

- DAVISON / DAVIDSON Genealogy
  http://web.wt.net/~wdavison/index.htm
  Devoted to the Davison / Davidson Family of Amelia and Prince Edward Counties, VA, Fayette County, KY, Anson and Montgomery Co. NC, Maury County, TN, Orleans Parish, LA and Polk, Dallas and Newton Counties, MO.

- DAWSON Family History Project
  http://ntfp.globalserve.net/dawson/

- The World of DAYs
  http://www.day-family.freeserve.co.uk/
  Worldwide One Name Study for the surname DAY and it's variants DAYE, DEY and DEYE.

- **DAY Genealogy**
  http://www.angelfire.com/pa/DayFamilies/
  Line of Robert DAY of Hartford CT. Many links to sites containing information and lines on various DAY families, DAY Family Message Board.

- **DEASON Resource Center**
  http://www.rddeason.com/deason.htm
  Covers the entire United States as well as foreign countries.

- **DEATON Family in America**
  http://www.deaton.com/
  DEATON family in Montgomery County, NC and related families. McQueen, Jordan, Allen, Maness, Smith, Cornelison, Leach.

- **DeBORD (Debord DeBord DeBoard) Surname** Raleigh P. DeBORD has a wealth of information dating back to 1703. For details e-mail him at: Rdebord@aol.com.
  mailto:Rdebord@aol.com

- **Descendants of Count Denis De COURSEY**
  http://www.ovis.net/~lathorn/racer.htm
  Racer family from France and Washington County, Ohio.

- **Patrick DEE Family Web Page - Patrick DEE and Hanora POWERS**
  http://members.tripod.com/~graceyline/Deeindex-2.html
  Patrick was born about March 1829, married to Hanora in Michigan.

- **DEEDS World**
  http://www.iowa-counties.com/genealogy/

- **DEER Family Links**
  http://members.tripod.com/MSgent/MSgent/index.html
  Genealogy for these families: DEER, DEERE, DEAR, DEARE.

- **The DeFRANCE Family Home Page**
  http://www.helenet.com/~larry/fam_home.html

- **DeHART Family Genealogy Page**
  http://homepages.rootsweb.com/~am1/dehart.html

- **Genealogie of the family (DE) JERPHANION Haute Loire France**
  http://members.tripod.lycos.nl/AMJerph/index.htm
  Jerphanion, de Jerphanion, Gerphanion, Gerphagnon, Jarphanion, Jarphagnon, Gerphaignon, Gerfaignon.

- **DEKLE Net**
  http://www.dekle.net/
  John Leanord DEKLE and his descendants. DEKLE, DEAKLE, HORN, DURDEN, and 61 other families.

- **DELASHAW - DILLASHAW - DILLESHAW - DELACHAUX -DELLECHAUX HOME PAGE**
  http://www.familytreemaker.com/users/w/a/r/Sandra-Delashaw-Warden/
  Archive of this surname, anywhere in the world.

- **DELISA Family History**
  http://www.mindspring.com/~delisa/delisa.html
  Genealogy and family history information about DELISA families with origins in South Central Italy, including the towns of Sassano and Roccavivara. Includes: DeLisa, D'Elisa, DiLisa and DiLissio.

- **DeLOACH, John R. and Descendants**
  http://www.parsonstech.com/genealogy/trees/tcarter2/jrd.htm
  Fendley, Hamilton, Holland, Holt, Lowrance, McCade, Owens, Reeder, Shaw, Worley.

- **DELVEE Family Association**
  http://genweb.net/Delvee/
  Delvee, Delva, Delvy family and all descendants

- **DEMETER Surname Resource Center**
  http://www.geocities.com/Heartland/Canyon/8775/

- **DEMLING Family Genealogy**
  http://www.personal.isat.com/fdemling/demling/demling.htm
  Demling lineage and history starting with the earliest known ancestor - Barbara Demling of Bavaria. Other surnames include: DEBOARD, GRIFFITH, NORRIS, WOODCOCK.

- **DENG Clan Genealogy**
  http://www.geocities.com/Tokyo/3998/deng.htm

- **The DENISON Society**
  http://www.mv.com/ipusers/pcsrus/Denison/denison_society.htm
  Has a description of the Society, an application form, and a genealogy book of one of the Denison lines.

- **DENKE Genealogy / DENKE Surname Home Page**
  http://www.denke.org

- **DENT Family Research Center**
  http://www.rootsweb.com/~auntjean/dent/

- **The DENVER Family**
  http://www.vegaswebworld.com/roots/denver/
  Includes spellings of Denvers and Denvir.

- **DE ROOIJ - Family tree**
  http://ourworld.cs.com/rderooij
  Family tree 'DE ROOIJ' the Netherlands 1742 - now.

- **DERRYBERRYs in the United States**
  http://www.artvilla.com/ndfa
  Activities of the National Derryberry Family Association, particularly the annual reunion. Derryberry Newsletter and family photos as they are available.

- **The Peter DERSLEY Family Home Page**
  http://www.familytreemaker.com/users/d/e/r/Peter-G-Dersley/
  Researching DERSLEY everywhere.

- **Descendants of Toussaint Hunault Dit DESCHAMPS**
  http://www.familytreemaker.com/users/l/a/c/Frances-J-Lachance/index.html
  Compiling a descendancy for Toussaint Hunault dit Deschamps. Over 23,000 direct descendants and 13,000 marriages. Deschamps, Hunault, Quevillon, Joly, Charpentier, Phaneuf (Farnsworth) and many more.

- **Généalogie des DESCLAUX, DESCLOS et DUCLOS**
  http://www3.sympatico.ca/d.duclos/
  Also HANDARAGUE. First 3 generations of the descendants of Antoine DESCLAUX/Marguerite GUAY and Jean DESCLAUX/Madeleine Huarddit DÉSILETS, both from Bayonne (France).

- DESHAZO Ancestors
  http://www.geocities.com/Heartland/Valley/3220
  A website containing compiled list (sources listed) of individuals with the surname of DESHAZO (and various variants of the name). It dates from 1704 to 1910. Many census listings are included.

- The DESMOND Family History Page
  http://www.mindspring.com/~wdesmond/
  Desmond family history from the Earls of Desmond to present-day Desmonds, many history links and genealogical records.

- DETWEILER-DETWILER Family History (1793-1991)
  http://home.earthlink.net/~maryharris/WC_TOC.HTM
  Family History beginning with Samuel Detweiler of Swiss extraction (Mennonite), the father of Henry W. Detweiler born in Bucks County, Pennsylvania 1793.

- The DEVEAU Family of Chéticamp, NS ~ Nova Scotia, Canada
  http://www.geocities.com/Heartland/Pointe/6654/deveau.html

- DEVIN Family Timber
  http://freepages.genealogy.rootsweb.com/~devin/
  Home page for the descendants of William DEVIN and Sarah SMITH (m. 1750) of Pittsylvania County, Virginia.

- DeVORE/DEVORE/deVORE/DEVOOR/DuFOUR Genealogy Page
  http://www.geocities.com/Heartland/3946/

- Genealogy of DE VUYST (roots in Herzele, Belgium)
  http://www.my-ged.com/devuyst/
  Descendants from Franciscus DE VUYST x Barbara VVAN SNICK (born +/- 1720 in Sint-Antelinks, Herzele, Belgium). De Vuyst, Dierickx, De Roover, De Pril, Van Iseghem, De Prez.

- DEWEES - DEWEESE Family Home Page
  http://home.earthlink.net/~tdewees/
  Dewees - Deweese - Dewese - Dewease.

- The DeWITT Collaboration Project
  http://freepages.genealogy.rootsweb.com/~geneal/src/DeWitt/
  DeWITT, DeWIT, de WITT, and variations.

- DeWITT Family Lines of North America
  http://pages.prodigy.com/DeWitt/

- DEYO Family Association
  http://members.aol.com/bethrn3ca/deyoindex.html

- The DEYO Family in America
  http://www.deyo.org/deyo.htm

- DIBBLE History
  http://www.borg.com/~troybuil/history.htm
  DIBBLEs descended from Jonathan/Jonathon DIBBLE (b. 1711) Stamford, Hartford, CT, and some related families. Surnames include: HALDEN, MORUD, ORZECHOWSKI, FLAKIEWICZ, JOHNSON, SEARCEY, KOWITZ, COPLAN, JESSUP.

- What The DICKENS?
  http://ladyecloud.hypermart.net/Dickens.htm
  Dicken(s) and Dickin(s).

- DICKSON's Family History Home Page
  http://hometown.aol.com/md750/dicksontree.htm
  David DICKSON (1754), who came from Scotland to America, his family and forefathers.

- DIEBOLD Genealogical Database
  http://genweb.net/gedcom/Diebold/Diebold.html
  Diebold family, pre-1700, originating in Jungingen, Hohenzollern, Baden-Wurttemburg, several of whom emigrated to USA, in 1850's, ultimately settling in Louisville, Kentucky.

- DIERSING Family Genealogy Page
  http://users.sunline.net/cbdj/

- DIGBY - List of 1,200 marriages into the Digby line, 1200-1900 in England.
  mailto:adigger@ghplus.infi.net
  E-mail Joe at adigger@ghplus.infi.net for details.

- The William DIGGS Family
  http://www.aracnet.com/~pslamb/diggs.htm
  Descendants of William Degge and Judith Haley, Louisa Co., Virginia & Anson Co., North Carolina.

- DILDAY Researchers and Their Families
  http://hometown.aol.com/sldilday/index.html

- Descendants of Zenas DILLINGHAM of Frog Alley, Tisbury, Dukes Co., Mass.
  http://www.vineyard.net/vineyard/history/dillingham.htm
  Includes the families of DILLINGHAM, LINTON, WEST, SMITH, and others on Martha's Vineyard.

- Descendants of Henry and Elinor DILLON
  http://www.parsonstech.com/genealogy/trees/ddillon/dillon.htm
  From Franklin Co., Virginia., Monroe Co., Virginia and Raleigh Co., West Virginia.

- DILLOW Family Genealogy
  http://www.familytreemaker.com/users/d/i/l/Eric-D-Dillow/
  Descendants of Robert DILLOW from Northeast Kentucky and Southeast Ohio.

- DINGMAN Genealogy Info Site
  http://www.geocities.com/Heartland/Plains/4858/
  For descendants of Adam DINGMAN (to North America in about 1650) and other DINGMAN researchers.

- The DINWOODIEs of Scotland
  http://members.aol.com/jwarr87480/index.html
  A one name study of all Dinwoodies (and surname variant) in the British Isles. These names have been correlated and gathered into families wherever possible.

- DIPLEY Family
  http://www.homestead.com/dipley
  Descendants of John DIPLEY with emphasis on the family of Walter Scott DIPLEY.

- Homepage of the DISBESCHL / DESSBESELL / DESPESELLE / DESPEZELLE Family
  http://www.geocities.com/disbeschl/
  The surname is found in France, Germany, Belgium, Brazil and the Netherlands.

- DISMORE Family Genealogy
  http://www.markadavis.com/dismorefamily.htm

- DISTLER Family Genealogy
  http://www.ancestryweb.com/distler/
  Distler, Diestler, Dishler and other variant spellings.

- DITTMAR Net
  http://www.dittmar.net/
  DITTMAR, CANNING, CARTER, ELLIS, HELM, MORGAN, BURTON, DUGAN, SIMPSON, RICHARDSON.

- DITTUS Family Home Page
  http://members.aol.com/psdb/dittus/index.htm
  A Gathering Place for all Dittus Family Lines.

- DIX Heritage
  http://www.geocities.com/Heartland/Woods/4822/
  A history of the Dix family in South Australia and their English heritage, including extensive research on the families of Clynton, Higgins, Oxley and Malpas.

- The DIXONs
  http://thedixons.net/dixon/

- The DOAK / DOKE Junction
  http://members.aol.com/blueeyesdd/family/index2.htm

- The DOANE Family Association, Inc.
  http://www.doane.edu/dfa/dfa2.htm

- Charles DOBIE's Genealogy Home Page
  http://freepages.genealogy.rootsweb.com/~cdobie/index.htm
  Documents and photographs relating to the Dobie and Dobbie families, mainly in Canada, but also world-wide.

- DOCKERY Family Association, Inc.
  http://www.tib.com/dfai/
  A group of 350 members working together to find their ancestors. Major surnames: Allen, Dockery, Lunsford, Lonsford and Woody. Assoc. projects: (1) Replacing and restoration of old tombstones, and (2) Restoring old photographs of our older ancestors.

- DOCTEUR Genealogy
  http://www.frontiernet.net/~docteur/pages/index.htm

- The DODGE Family Association
  http://www.dodgefamily.org/

- The Dogs of Menteith - The Family History of DOG, DOEG, DOIGE, and DOIG
  http://www.psnw.com/~kendoig/Doig_Genealogy.htm
  The family of DOG from 1263 in Kilmadock, Perthshire, Scotland. The name became spelled Doig, Doeg, Dogg, Doige, Doigg. Early marriages to Nory or Norrie, Hamilton, Stewart, Cunnyghame or Cunningham, Graham, Gourlay, Buchannan, and Dow.

- DOGGETTs and Other Cousins
  http://www.doggettfam.org/index.htm
  Devoted to the study of the family history of the Rev. Benjamin Doggett of Lancaster County, Virginia.

- La Famille DOIRON
  http://www.doiron.org
  The Acadian surname DOIRON found in France, Canada, and Louisiana.

- The DOLLARD Family Genealogy Page
  http://members.primary.net/~dollard/

- DOMKE Ancestors
  http://domke.wustl.edu/DomkeAncestors.html
  Domke-surnamed ancestor lists.

- The John D. DONALDSON of Melbourne, Australia, Home Page
  http://www.familytreemaker.com/users/d/o/n/John-D-Donaldson/
  Donaldson, Marris, Seyler, Hollywood, Helmrich, Butler, Cornell. Includes a DONALDSON one name study.

- Clan DONALD-USA
  http://www.clan-donald-usa.org/

- Die Familie DONATH / The DONATH Family
  http://mitglied.tripod.de/froboesefamily/donath-3.html
  The DONATHs in Brandenburg/Prussia.

- The DONKERSLOOT Web Site
  http://www.multiweb.nl/~h.dsloot
  Genealogy of the Donkersloot Family in Dutch and English Seeking Donkersloots all over the world.

- DONLON Family History, Ireland
  http://www.hylit.com/info/Genealogy/Donlon.html
  A genealogy of the Donlon family, recently of Westmeath, Ireland, and originally of Galway. The Galway genealogy starts as far back as 1400.

- The DONLEY Family - Genealogy
  http://www.internet-partners.com/donley/index.htm

- The DONNAN Home Page
  http://www.clis.com/donnan/

- The DONOGH Family Tree
  http://www.donogh.com/family/family.html
  DONOGH in Canada and U.S.

- The DONOVAN Family Center
  http://www.crosswinds.net/~hallisey/Donovan/index.html
  Donovan, Donavan, Dunavan, O'Donovan.

- DONSHEA DUNSHEA DUNSHEE Genealogy Page
  http://www.angelfire.com/ny/earthstar/index.html
  Scots-Irish ancestors.

- DORLING Family History and Genealogy Worldwide
  http://www.dorl.freeserve.co.uk/
  Research from one name study of the Dorling surname, in process of publishing information collected from civil, parish, census and living Dorlings.

- Genealogy of the family van DORT
  http://www.geocities.com/Paris/6547/index.htm
  Netherlands, Sri Lanka, Malaysia, Belgium, U.S., Canada, Australia.

- The DOSS Family Association
  http://members.xoom.com/janicekmc/dossasc.htm

- Genealogy for DOTTERER / DUDDERAR / DUDDRA / DUTRO / DUDDERA / DOTTER / DUTTERER / DUTROW / DUTTEROW / DUTTER
  http://www.angelfire.com/az/rdutter/

- DOUD(E) / DOWD Family Association
  http://www.angelfire.com/ny/doudsearcher/index.html
  Researching the descendants of Henry Doude who settled in Guilford, CT in 1639 from England.

- Clan DOUGLAS Society
  http://www.hom.net/~jdarbyd/

- DOUTT Family Web Home
  http://www.bigfoot.com/~doutt/
  Genealogy of the descendants of John DOUTT/DAUT and the families related to them.

- The DOWBIGGIN Family History Society
  http://www.netmagic.net/~taz/dfhs.html

- The DOWDY Xchange
  http://geocities.com/Heartland/Oaks/3719/DowdyX.html
  An exchange of family lines and research for the Dowdy surname in North Carolina, Tennessee, Kentucky and Missouri.

- DOWLING Family History
  http://fp.dowling.f9.co.uk/
  One name research and history on Dowlings and variations: Doolan, Doolin, Dooley, Dooly, Dooling, etc.

- DOWNING Family Times
  http://expage.com/page/downingfamilytimes
  DOWNING Family Historical Society of America's quarterly newsletter and information on how to join!

- Home Page of Ray DOWNING - DOWNING Family of Downingtown, PA
  http://hometown.aol.com/RDown3657/index.html
  Descendants of Thomas Downing (1691-1771), founder of Downingtown, Pennsylvania. ALSPAUGH, DOWELL, DOWNING, EDGE, GHEEN, REDFIELD, STOREY, TRIMBLE, VALENTINE, WOODWARD.

- The DOYLE Page
  http://www.doyle.com.au/
  The Clann O Dubhghaill / Clan Doyle: Doyle, Doyel, O'Doyle, Dowel, McDowell, McDowall, Dowell, Dowall, Duggal, McDuggal or their relatives.

- DRAGOO Family Web Page
  http://members.aol.com/DragooFA/homepage.htm
  Dragoo Family Association Web Page. Researching Dragoo, Draggoo, Dragaux, Dragault, Dragaud, etc. Includes information on the Association's Newsletter and Family History.

- DRAKE Family Genealogy WorldWide
  http://www.users.bigpond.com/lrandrew/drake/drakepage.htm

- DRESSER Family Genealogy Page
  http://plainfield.bypass.com/~jdresser/index.html

- DREWRY Family History in America
  http://www.anniebees.com/Drewry/Drewry.htm
  The Ancestors and Descendants of Harry Moss Drewry 1886 - 1970.

- Looking for DREW's? Look no further!
  http://members.stratos.net/mikeandcindy/drew.htm

- DRINKARD Family Genealogy
  http://members.aol.com/Elaine64/DrinkardGenealogy.html
  Quotes from the book "The Drinkards in the United States - Their History and Genealogy" written in 1946 by Charles Arthur Drinkard.

- DRIVER Family Historical Society
  http://tdcweb.com/tdfhs/

- The DRUCKER's
  http://www.druckers.com/
  The DRUCKER's website has photos dating back to the late 1800s, trees, genealogical links, voices from the past and tons more to keep the family connected.

- DRUMM News
  http://hometown.aol.com/drummnews/DrummNews.html
  A web site and newsletter for anyone researching the Drum and/or Drumm surname.

- Clan DRUMMOND Society of North America
  http://www.angelfire.com/al/metaphysicsgalore/Drummond.html

- DRUMMOND Family
  http://www.sensible-net.com/dhoffgr/Drummond.wbg
  Enumeration of the descendants of Samuel Drummond and Nancy Clugston of Franklin/Cumberland County, Pennsylvania.

- Descendants of Chretien duBOIS
  http://members.aol.com/DuBoisJon/FamTree.htm
  DuBOIS, ULRICH, TYRREL, WEIFENBACH, EDWARDS, LEYBOLD

- DuBOIS Family Association
  http://members.aol.com/DuBoisDBFA/index.html

- DUBOSE Forum
  http://members.tripod.com/~DuBose_Forum/index.html
  Or mirror site
  http://www.geocities.com/Heartland/Ridge/9480/index.html
  The online meeting place for sharing and discussion regarding the surname DUBOSE, related variations (DUBOIS, DUBOISE, DU BOSC, DEBOSE, etc.), and closely allied families, in any place and at any time.

- DuBOURDIEU of Newfoundland
  http://www.familytreemaker.com/users/d/u/b/Cyril-G-Dubourdieu/index.html

- The Association of CHARRON and DUCHARME, Inc
  mailto:dmiale@exis.net
  For details e-mail Dick Miale at dmiale@exis.net or in French e-mail Pierre Ducharme at: duchap00libertel.montreal.qc.ca.

- DUDLEY Homepage and Database
  http://www.geocities.com/Heartland/Hills/8388/

- DUEY History
  http://dueyhistory.org/

- The DUFFIELD Family
  http://access.mountain.net/~braxton/duffield.html
  Dufield/Duffields.

DUFFUS - Sept of Clan Sutherland - 1000 Years of History
http://www.duffus.com
Genealogy and history of Duffus for last 1000 years.

DUGGER Genealogy
http://www.martygrant.com/gen/dugger.htm
Emphasis on Virginia, Tennessee and North Carolina.

DUHIGG Resource Website and Family Tree
http://www.duhigg.org/

DUKESHIRE Lines
http://www.mdc.net/~wmduke/
A family association, publications and a database including the surnames Dukeshire, Rawding, Beeler, Feindell, Ringer, Freeman.

The DULONG Family
http://habitant.org/dulong/

The DUMENIL Family Home Page
http://www.angelfire.com/az/dumenilarchives/index.html
The Descendants of Jean François DUMENIL (1777-1814) and Marie Anne MARCHAL (1765-1843).

DUNAVANT Genealogy
http://members.aol.com/CrysDH/index.html

DUNCAN Genealogy
http://www.geocities.com/Heartland/Forest/7113/Pages/homepage.html
History and descendants of George and Elizabeth (PRIMROSE) DUNCAN.

DUNCAN Surname Association
http://www.networksplus.net/wad/dsa/dsa.htm

DUNDON and Related Families in Great Britain
http://www.familytreemaker.com/users/d/u/n/Paul-Scott-Dundon/

DUNGAN and Related Families
http://www.mindspring.com/~jogt/surnames/dungan.htm
Descendants of Thomas Dungan, son of William Dungan, a perfumer, from London, England, born about 1606.

History of the DUNHAM-DONHAM Family in America
http://www.rootsquest.com/~sirjames/dunham/
Descendants of Deacon John DUNHAM, born about 1589, died 2 March 1668/69 in Plymouth, Massachusetts.

DUNKS' Family Genealogical Society
http://dunks.org/
Dedicated to the preservation of Dunks family genealogy and history. The goals of the Dunks Family Genealogical Society are to stimulate and promote the exchange of genealogical information relating to the surname Dunks (and its associated spellings Dunk, Donk, Donks, Donck, Doncks, Dunch, Donchs, Dunches, Doncyx).

DUNLOP / DUNLAP Clan Page
http://www.angelfire.com/fl/ClanDunlop/

The DUNN Family of Castle Bay and Dominion, Cape Breton Island ~ Nova Scotia, Canada
http://www.geocities.com/~dunnfamily/

- William DUNN from Little Bray, Devon, England
  http://home.st.net.au/~dunn/wdunn.htm

- The DUNTON Homesite
  http://www.dunton.org/
  Dunton, Dunten, Dutton.

- The DUPUIS Family - Les DUPUIS Troujours
  http://www.lawebworks.com/dupuis/

- The DUQUET(TE) Family Forest
  http://www.DUQUETTE.org
  French-Canadian DUQUET(TE)s, DUCAT(TE)s, DUKET(TE)s.

- DURAND Heritage Foundation
  http://www.durandfoundation.com/

- DURBIN Genealogy
  http://www.usmo.com/~madurby/pages/durbpages.html

- The Thomas DURFEE Family Tree
  http://members.aol.com/MShermanL/durfee.html
  Descendants of Thomas Durfee, born 1643 in England, died July 1712 in Portsmouth, Rhode Island.

- The DURHAM Family Home Page
  http://www.familytreemaker.com/users/s/t/o/Terri-L-Stone/
  Descendants of Robert DURHAM, born 1811 and Elizabeth Riggs, born 1825.

- The Society of Genealogy of DURKEE
  http://www2.andrews.edu/~calkins/durkeefa.html

- The DURNFORD Family
  http://members.home.com/cdurnford/default.htm

- DUTCHER Family
  http://www.genealogy.org/~smoore/dutchers/

- DuVAL Family Association
  http://www.geocities.com/Heartland/Ridge/7508/
  Descendants of Daniel DuVal and his wife Philadelphia DuBois who were French Huguenots.

- DuVAL Family Descendants
  http://www.geocities.com/Heartland/Flats/6149/duval/index.htm
  Ten generations of descendants of Daniel DuVal and his wife, Philadelphia DuBois DuVal.

- Patriot's Page
  http://www.pabko.com/PK/patriotspage.htm
  You will find some of the proud generations of descendants of Huguenot Daniel DUVAL who have proudly served in our countries Armed Forces.

- DUXBURY Family History
  http://home.att.net/~jtduxbury/duxbury.htm
  Descendants of Ralph DUXBURY, Lancashire, England to Rhode Island, Wisconsin and beyond, 1696 to Present. Colne/Waterside Line.

- DUXBURY Family Website
  http://www.bigfoot.com/~duxbury

- The Family of Hans Laurentszen DUYTS
  http://www.uh.edu/~jbutler/gean/dyeshome.html
  DUYTS. DEY

- DYCHE Families of American Home Page Dyche Book
  http://members.aol.com/dychebook/index.htm
  Includes other spelling such as Dyke, Dike, Deck and Dyches.

- DYE Data - The Family of Hans Laurentszen Duyts, 1644 - 1708
  http://www.uh.edu/~jbutler/gean/dyes.html

- The DYE Genealogical Index
  http://www.vvm.com/~ataylor

- The New England DYER Connection
  http://www.geocities.com/Heartland/Plains/4663/
  Genealogies of five different DYER families in New England from the 17th century. Also a reference to "Genealogies of the Families of Braintree, Ma" by Sprague.

- DYESS Family
  http://www.geocities.com/Heartland/5438/

- DYSART Genealogy
  http://members.aol.com/caroltapp/dysart.html

◆ Surname Mailing Lists

- "DA-DD" Surname Mailing Lists
  http://www.rootsweb.com/~jfuller/gen_mail_surnames-da.html
  DABBADIE (includes d'Abbadie, d'Abadie, Dabadie, Dabady, Abbadie, Abadie, Labadie, Labady, LaBaddie), DABBS, DABNEY (includes de Aubigne, de Aubigny, Daubinge), DACAMARA (includes DeCamara), DADY, DAELLENBACH (includes Dallenbach, Dallenbaugh, Dallenbough, Delabaugh, Delebaugh, Delenbaugh, Delinbaugh,, Dellabaugh, Dellanbaugh, Dellebaugh, Dellenbach, Dellenback, Dellenbaug, Dellenbaugh, Dellenbough, Dilenbaugh,, Dillabough, Dillebachin, Dillenbachin, Dillenbaugh, Dillonbough, Dollenbough, Dullenbaugh), DAFFORN (includes Daffern, Daffarn, Daffurn, Dafforne, Daffin, Daffon, Daffen), DAFOE, DAFT, DAGGETT (includes Dagget, Dagett, Doggett, Dogett), DAGGY, DAGLEY, DAGNAN, DAHL, DAHLE, DAHLEM (includes Dahlen, Dalem, Dallem), DAHLING, DAHLINGHAUS (includes Dalinghaus, Darlinghaus), DAHLSTROM, DAIGLE, DAILEY, DAILY, DAINS (includes Daynes, Daines, Deens), DAKE (includes Deake), DAKIN, DALBY (includes Dolby, Dalbey, Dalbie, Dalbee, Dolbie, Dolbey), DALBY (includes Dalbey, Dolby, Dolbey, Dolbie, Dalbie), DALDRY (includes Daldy, Dardy, Dardry), DALE, DALEMBERTE (includes D'Alemberte, d'Alembert), DALES, DALEY, DALLAS, DALLY, DALPE, DALRYMPLE, DALRYMPLE, DALTON (includes Daulton, Dolton, Dolten), DALY (includes O'Daly, Daley, Daily), DALY, DALZELL (includes Delzell, Dalziel, Dalzel, Dazell, Delzel), DAME, DAMERON, DAMEWOOD (includes Damwood), DAMM, DAMMANN, DAMON, DAMPIER (includes Dampear, Dampierre, Damphear, Damphere), DAMRELL, DAMRON, DANA, DANCE, DANCER (includes Danser, Dantzer, Tanzer), DANCY, DANDRIDGE, DANE, DANEKE, DANENHOWER (includes Danenhour, Dannenhower, Dannehower), DANFORD (includes Deneford, Denford, Derneford, Dernford), DANFORTH (includes Danforthe, Danford, Danforde, Daneford, Darnford, Darneforde, Dampford, Dampforde,, Dernford, Dernforth, Derneforthe), DANGERFIELD, DANIEL, DANIELEY (includes Daniely, Danielee), DANIELL, DANIELS, DANIELSON, DANIS, DANKER, DANKS, DANN (includes Dan), DANNAR (includes Danner), DANNEMANN, DANNER, DANNER, DAOUST, DARBY (includes Derby, Darbyshire), DARCY, DARDEN, DARE, DARLAND (includes Darlan, Darlandt, Dorland,

Dorlandt, Durland, Durlandt, Durlin, Durling), DARLAND (includes Darlandt, Dorland, Dorlandt, Dorlant, Durland, Durlandt), DARLING, DARLINGTON, DARMODY (includes Dermody), DARNALL, DARNELL, DARNEY, DARPEL, DARR, DARRAH (includes Durrah, Darragh), DARRAUGH, DARROCH, DARROW, DARSEY, DARST, DART, DARWIN, DARWIN, DASH, DASHER, DASHER, DASHNER (includes Dashny, Dagenais, Daganais, Daschner), DATES, DAUB, DAUBERT (includes Dauber), DAUGHERTY, DAUGHTERY, DAUGHTRY, DAUM, DAUPHIN (includes Daffin), DAVAULT, DAVENPORT, DAVERN (includes Davoren, Daverin), DAVES, DAVEY, DAVID (includes Davis), DAVIDOW, DAVIDS, DAVIDSON (includes Davison), DAVIE, DAVIES, DAVIS (includes Davies, Dave, Daves, Davey, Daveys, Davison, Davisson), DAVIS, DAVIS (includes Davies, Dave, Daves, Davey, Daveys, Davison, Davisson), DAVIS, DAVIS, DAVISON, DAVISSON, DAVY, DAW, DAWE, DAWES, DAWKINS, DAWLEY, DAWSON, DAWSON, DAY (includes Dey), DAY, DAY (includes Dey, Tag), DAYHOFF (includes Dehoff), DAYMUDE (includes Dammed, Demude), DAYTON.

- "DEA-DED" Surname Mailing Lists
  http://www.rootsweb.com/~jfuller/gen_mail_surnames-dea.html
  DEACON, DEAKE, DEAL (includes Deel, Diehl, Dial), DEAN, DEAN, DEAN, DEANE, DEANS, DEARBORN (includes Dearborne), DEARDEN, DEARDORFF (includes Diedorff), DEARING, DEARING1 (includes Deering, Dearinger, Derring), DEARMAN (includes Durman, Durmon, Dorman, Dearmon, Derman, Dermon, D'arman, Darman, De Arman,, De'arman, D'armand, De Arman), DEARMOND, DEAS, DEASON, DEATH, DEATHERAGE, DEATON (includes Deyton, DeAton), DEAVER (includes Dever, Deavers, Devore, Devier), DEBELL (includes Dobell), DEBERRY, DEBOARD, DEBOLT (includes DeBolt, Debolt, Diebold, Dieboldt), DEBORD, DE BRACY (includes Bracy DEBUSK, DECAMP (includes D'Camp, Van Camp, Van Campen), DECK (includes Dech, Dick, Dach, Dack, Dych), DECKARD, DECKER, DECLARE, DECOSTE (includes Coste), DECUIR (includes Decuir, Decuire, Decuyre, deCuir), DEDMON (includes Deadman, Dedman, Deadmon, Dedmond).

- "DEE-DEH" Surname Mailing Lists
  http://www.rootsweb.com/~jfuller/gen_mail_surnames-dee.html
  DEE, DEEDS, DEEGAN, DEEL (includes Diehl, Deihl), DEEM, DEEMER, DEEN, DEER, DEERING, DEES, DEESE, DEETER (includes Teeter, Deeder, Dieter), DEETS, DEFFENBAUGH (includes Davenbaugh, Deifenbaugh), DEFLEY, DEFOE, DEFOO (includes DeFir, DeFur), DEFOOR, DEFORD, DEFORE (includes DeFoor, Defoe, Defir, DeForest), DEFOREST, DEFRANCE, DEFREITAS, DEGAN (includes Deegan, Diggin, Degnan), DEGARMO, DEGENHARDT (includes Degenhard, Degenhart, Dagenhardt, Degenhard, Dagenhart, Degener), DEGNAN, DEGRAFF, DEGRAFFENREID, DEGRANGE (includes Des Granges, De La Grange), DEGROOT, DEGRUCHY (includes Gruchy), DEHAAS (includes Haas, Hass, Haff), DEHART, DEHART, DEHAVEN (includes Den Hoffen, Ten Hauven, Inhoff).

- "DEI-DEN" Surname Mailing Lists
  http://www.rootsweb.com/~jfuller/gen_mail_surnames-dei.html
  DEIGHTON, DEIHL, DEITZ, DEJARNETTE, DEJONG, DEKING, DEKLE, DELAGE, DELAHUNTY (includes Delahanty, Delehanty, Delahunt), DELAITTRE, DELAMARRE (includes Delamar, Delamer), DELAMATER, DELANEY, DELANO, DELANY, DELAP, DELASHMUTT (includes Delahsmut, de la Chamotte), DELAUDE (includes Delatter, Delatrre, Delawter, Delater, De Lattre, Delator,

DELCHER, DELISLE, DELK, DELL, DELLINGER (includes Dillinger), DELLINGER (includes Dillinger), DELOACH (includes DeLoache, DeLoatch, DeLoch, D'Loatche), DELONG, DELOREY (includes DeLory, DesLauriers), DELORME, DELOZIER, DELP, DELPH, DELUNG (includes DeLunge, Deelung, DaLung, DaLunge, DeaLung), DELZELL (includes Dalzell, Dalziel, Dalzel, Dazell, Delzel), DEMARAY, DEMAREST (includes DesMarest, DeMaree, DeMoree), DEMARS, DEMASTUS (includes Demasters, Demastis, Demastes), DEMENT, DEMERS, DEMING, DEMOSS, DEMOTT, DEMPSEY, DEMPSTER, DEMUTH (includes Damuth, Demuth, DeMuth), DENBOW (includes Denbo, Denboe, Denbowe), DENBY, DENCKER, DENDY (includes Dandy, Dandie, Denday), DENGLER, DENHAM, DENIS, DENISON, DENISSEN, DENMAN, DENMARK, DENNEHY, DENNERLL (includes Denerlle), DENNETT, DENNEY (includes Denny), DENNING, DENNIS, DENNISON (includes Tennison, Dannygston, Donohosen, Danielston), DENNISTON, DENNY, DENSMORE, DENSON, DENT, DENT, DENTON (includes Dent).

- **"DEO-DET" Surname Mailing Lists**
  http://www.rootsweb.com/~jfuller/gen_mail_surnames-deo.html
  DEONIER, DEPEW, DEPPEN, DEPRIEST, DEPUTAT, DEPUY (includes DePui, DePue, Depue, DuPue, Dupue, DePuis, Depuis, DePew, Depew, Dupee, DePoe, Dupree,, DePu, Duppery), DEQUASIE, DERBY, DERHAM (includes Durham), DERIDDER (includes De Ridder, De Ritter, Deritter), DERKACZ, DERMODY, DERR (includes Duerr, Durr, Dir, Doerr), DERRICK, DERRICOTT, DERRY, DERRYBERRY, DERSCHOW (includes Derschau, Von Derschau, Dershow, Dierschow, Derschaw), DERVAN (includes Dervin), DESBOUILLON, DESCHAMPS, DESENTIS (includes Sentis), DESHAZO, DESKINS (includes Diskins), DESMARAIS (includes Demarais, de Marrais), DESMOND, DESPAIN, DESROSIERS, DETER, DETERMAN (includes Dettermann, Determann, Detterman), DETHLEFSEN (includes Detlefsen), DETLING (includes Dettling), DETRICK, DETWEILER, DETWILER.

- **"DEU-DH" Surname Mailing Lists**
  http://www.rootsweb.com/~jfuller/gen_mail_surnames-deu.html
  DEUEL, DEUTSCH, DEVANEY, DEVASIER (includes DeVasher, Devasure, Devazier, Devazur), DEVAUGHN, DEVAULT, DEVER (includes DaVar, Daver, Davers, Davor, Deaver, Deavers, Devar, Devers, Devor, Devore, Devere, Devers,, Dover), DEVER, DEVEREAUX, DEVEREUX, DEVERS, DEVIN, DEVINE, DEVITT, DEVLEN, DEVLIN, DEVOE, DEVOL, DEVORE, DEVOS, DEVRIES, DEW (includes Dewe, Dews, Dewes, Due, Dhu, Deu, Deugh), DEWALD, DEWALT, DEWAR, DEWBERRY, DEWBERRY (includes Deberry, Dubery), DEWEES, DEWEESE (includes Dewees, Dewese, Dewease, Duese, Duest), DEWEY, DEWHURST (includes Dewhirst, du Hurst, d'Hurst), DEWITT, DEWOLF (includes Dewolff, Dolph, Deaolph, D'Olf), DEWOLFE, DEXTER, DEY, DEYO, DEYOUNG.

- **"DI-DN" Surname Mailing Lists**
  http://www.rootsweb.com/~jfuller/gen_mail_surnames-di.html
  DIAL, DIAMOND, DIAZ, DIBBLE, DICAIRE (includes Decare, Decaire), DICE, DICK, DICKEN, DICKENS, DICKENSON, DICKER, DICKERMAN, DICKERSON (includes Dickson), DICKERT, DICKEY, DICKIE, DICKINS, DICKINSON, DICKINSON, DICKMAN, DICKS, DICKSON, DICUS, DIDIER, DIECKMEYER, DIEDRICH, DIEGEL (includes Deigel, Deigle, Deagle), DIEHL, DIEL, DIEPOLDER, DIERDORFF, DIETER, DIETERICH, DIETERLE, DIETRICH, DIETRICK, DIETZ, DIEZ, DIFFEE, DIGBY, DIGGENS (includes Diggins), DIGGS, DI

GIOVANNA, DIGMAN, DIJKGRAAF (includes Dijckgraaf, Dijkgraaff, van den Dijkgraaf, Dykgraaf, Dijkgraeff, Dijkgreave), DIKE, DIKES, DILAMATA (includes Delimater), DILDINE, DILL, DILLARD (includes Dilliard, Dillards, Dilyard), DILLER, DILLEY (includes Dille, Dilly, Dillie, Dilli, Dilla), DILLINGER, DILLINGHAM, DILLION, DILLMAN, DILLON (includes Dillion, Dillen, Dillin, Dellow, Delon, Delone, Dillian, Dillieon, Dillow, Dillyan, Dillyon, Dilon, Dilow,, Dulon), DILTS, DILWORTH, DIMICK, DIMLERS, DIMMICK, DIMMITT, DIMOCK, DINEEN, DINES, DINGES, DINGLE, DINGLER (includes Dengler, Dingle), DINGMAN, DINGWALL, DINKIN (includes Dinkins), DINKINS, DINSMORE, DINSMORE (includes Dinsmoor), DINWIDDIE, DION, DIONNE, DISBROW, DISHAROON (includes Dishroon, Disheroon), DISHER, DISHMAN, DISHONG (includes Deshong, Deshon, Dischong), DISMUKES (includes Dysmokes, Demeux, Demaux, Demeausse, Disquemue, Dixmund, Disimieu), DISNEY, DISSLER (includes Ditzler, Dizler, Disler), DISTAD, DITTMAN, DITTMAR, DITTMER, DITTO, DIVELEY, DIVENS, DIVINE, DIX, DIXON (includes Dixson, Dickson), DIXSON.

- **"DO-DQ" Surname Mailing Lists**
  http://www.rootsweb.com/~jfuller/gen_mail_surnames-do.html
  DOAK, DOAN (includes Doane), DOANE, DOBBIE (includes Dobie), DOBBIN, DOBBINS, DOBBS (includes Daubs, Dabbs), DOBLE, DOBSON, DOCHERTY, DOCKENDORFF (includes Dockendorf), DOCKERY, DOCKSTADER (includes Docksteader, Doxtoder, Doxteader), DOCWRA (includes Dockwra, Dockwray, Dockray, Dockrey, Dockerill, Dockerell, Docura, Dockera, Docra, Docray), DODD, DODDS, DODGE (includes Doidge, Dogge), DODSON (includes Dotson), DOE, DOEGE (includes Döge), DOEGE (includes Döge), DOERING, DOERR, DOGGETT, DOHENY, DOHERTY, DOHERTY, DOHME, DOHRMANN, DOIRON, DOLAN, DOLBY, DOLE, DOLL, DOLLAHITE, DOLLAR, DOLLEY (includes Dolly, Doly), DOLLIVER, DOLLY, DOLPHIN, DOMAGALA, DOMBROWSKI, DOMENY, DOMER, DOMINGO, DOMINGUEZ, DON, DONACHY (includes Donachie), DONAGHY (includes Doneghy, MacDonagh, O'Donaghy, McDonough), DONAHOE, DONAHUE, DONALD, DONALDSON (includes Donalson, Donelson), DONALSON, DONAVAN, DONEGAN, DONELSON, DONER, DONIER, DONLEY, DONN, DONNELL, DONNELLAN (includes Donelan, Donilon, Donlan, Donlin, Donlon, Donnelan), DONNELLY (includes Donneley, Donelly, Donnley, Doneley, Donely), DONNER, DONNEWALD, DONNICI, DONOHO, DONOHOE, DONOHUE, DONOVAN (includes O'Donovan, Donavan, Dunavan), DOODY, DOOL, DOOLEY (includes Dooly, Dula, Dooling, Dowling, Duley), DOOLIN, DOOLITTLE, DOOLITTLE (includes Dowlittell, Dowlittle), DOORS, DOPP, DOPSON, DOPSON, DORAN, DORE, DOREMUS, DORGAN, DORGAN (includes Dargan, Dorgin, Dargin, Dargon, Darrigan, Dorrigan, Durgin), DORLAND, DORLAND, DORMAN (includes Durman, Durmon, Dearman, Dearmon, Derman, Dermon, D'arman, Darman, De Arman, De'arman, D'armand, De Arman), DORMER, DORN, DORNER (includes Doerner), DORR, DORRIS, DORRIS, DORSCHER, DORSET (includes Dorsett, Doorset), DORSETT, DORSEY, DORSHER, DORWEILER, DOSS, DOSSETT, DOSTER, DOTSON, DOTSON (includes Dodson), DOTY, DOUB, DOUCET, DOUCETTE, DOUD, DOUGAN, DOUGHERTY (includes Daughardy, Daugherty, Daughetee, Daughetry, Daughettee, Daughhetee, Daughhettee,, Daughtery, Daughtrey, Daughtry, Doughertey, Doughrety, Doughterty), DOUGHTY, DOUGLAS (includes Douglass), DOUGLASS, DOUSHARM, DOUSMAN (includes Dausman, Dousmann, Dausmann), DOUTHIT, DOUTHIT, DOVE, DOVER, DOVYDAITIS (includes Dovidaitis), DOW, DOWBIGGIN (includes Dowbiggen, Daubigin, Dowbikin, Dawbikin, Dowbekin, Dowkin, Dowberkin, Dawbigin,,

Dowbekerkin, Dowfbyging, Dalbikin), DOWD, DOWDA (includes Dowdy), DOWDALL, DOWDELL, DOWDEN, DOWDLE (includes Doudle, Dowdall, Dowdell, Dodil, Dowdale), DOWDY, DOWDY, DOWELL, DOWER, DOWIE, DOWIS, DOWLING, DOWN, DOWNARD, DOWNER, DOWNES, DOWNEY, DOWNHAM, DOWNHILL, DOWNING, DOWNS, DOWNS (includes Downes), DOWRICK (includes Dowrack, Dowrich, Dowerick, Dowerack, Dowerich, Dourick, Dourack, Dourich, Daurick,, Daurack, Daurich), DOWSETT, DOXSIE (includes Doxie, Doxey, Doxsee, Doxy, Dox, Docksey, Doxee), DOYEL, DOYLE, DOZIER.

- **"DR-DT" Surname Mailing Lists**
  http://www.rootsweb.com/~jfuller/gen_mail_surnames-dr.html
  DRABING, DRAEGER, DRAFFEN (includes Draffin, Draffan), DRAGER, DRAGONETTE (includes Dragonnette), DRAIN (includes Drane), DRAKE (includes Dratz, Drak, Drakes), DRAKE, DRANE, DRAPER, DRAUGHON, DREBENSTEDT, DREES, DREESE (includes Dries, Dreis, Drease, Tries, Treis, Trease, Treece, Treese), DREGER, DREHER, DREHMER (includes Dramer, Dremer, Dreamer), DREIDOPPEL, DREISBACH, DRENNAN, DRENNON (includes Drennan, Drennen), DRESCHER, DRESSBACK, DRESSER, DRESSLER, DREW, DREWRY, DREWS, DREYER, DRIGGERS (includes Dreggers, Dreggors, Drigger, Dregger, Dreggor, Duggar, Dugger), DRINKARD, DRINKWATER (includes Drinkwalter), DRISCOLL, DRISCOLL, DRISKELL, DRISKILL, DRIVER (includes Drivers, Dryver, Drive, Dreve), DROEGE (includes Dröge), DROLLINGER, DROST, DROWN, DRUEDING (includes Druding), DRUIN (includes Druen), DRUM, DRUMHELLER, DRUMM (includes Trumm, Tromm), DRUMMOND, DRURY, DRY, DRYDEN (includes Driden, Dreiden, Dreden), DRYER (includes Dreyer, Drier, VanDryer), DRYMAN (includes Drymon, Driman, Drimon, Dreyman, Dreiman), DRYSDALE.

- **"DU-DZ" Surname Mailing Lists**
  http://www.rootsweb.com/~jfuller/gen_mail_surnames-du.html
  DUANE (includes Devine), DUBBELD, DUBE, DUBEAU, DUBINSKY, DUBOIS (includes Du Bois), DUBOSE, DUBOSE (includes DuBois, du Bosc), DUBREUIL (includes Dubbray, Dubrey), DUBREUIL, DUCHAM (includes Duchamp), DUCHARME, DUCK, DUCKETT, DUCKWORTH, DUCLOS, DUDECK, DUDEK, DUDGEON, DUDLEY (includes Dudly, Duley, Duly), DUE, DUENNERMANN (includes Dunnermann), DUESING, DUFF. DUFFIELD. DUFFIN. DUFFY. DUFOUR, DUFRESNE,

DUGAN, DUGGAN, DUGGER (includes Duger, Duggar, Dugar), DUGGER, DUGGINS, DUGUAY, DUGUID, DUHAIME (includes Duhaine), DUIGNAN, DUIMSTRA, DUKE (includes Dukes), DUKES, DULANEY, DULEY, DULEY (includes Duly), DULIN, DULL, DUMAS, DUMBLETON, DUMOND, DUMONT, DUNAGAN, DUNAVAN, DUNAWAY, DUNAWAY, DUNBAR, DUNCAN (includes Dinkins, Dockin, Dunkan, Dunkin, Denkens), DUNCAN (includes Dunkin, Dancun, Dockan, Dankan, Durkin, Denkens), DUNCAN, DUNCANSON, DUNCOMBE, DUNDAS (includes Dundass), DUNFORD, DUNGAN, DUNHAM, DUNHAM (includes Donham), DUNK, DUNKEL, DUNKERTON, DUNKIN, DUNKLE, DUNKLEY, DUNKS, DUNLAP, DUNLAP, DUNLEVY (includes Dunleavy), DUNLOP, DUNMIRE (includes Dornmeyer, Dornmier), DUNN, DUNNAWAY, DUNNE, DUNNIGAN, DUNNING, DUNNINGTON, DUNPHY, DUNSMOOR (includes Dunsmore, Dinsmoor, Dinsmore, Densmore), DUNSTAN, DUNSTER, DUNSTON, DUNTON (includes Dunten, Dutton), DUPES, DUPLESSIS (includes Dupplessis, Duplesis, Dupplesis, Duplesis), DUPONT, DUPRE, DUPREE, DUPUIS, DUPUY, DURAN, DURAND, DURANT, DURBIN, DURDEN, DUREN, DURFEE (includes Durfey, Durfy), DURHAM (includes Durhan, Duran, Duren, Daram), DURIE (includes Duree, Duryea, Duryee), DURKAN (includes Durkin, MacDurkin, MacDurkan, MacDurcan, MacDurkain, MacCurkan, Durcan, Gurkin, Gurken,, Zurkin), DURKEE, DURKIEWICZ, DURKIN, DURLING, DURMAN (includes Durmon, Dorman, Dearman, Dearmon, Derman, Dermon, D'arman, Darman, D'armand, De, Arman), DUROCHER, DUROSE, DURR, DURRANCE (includes Durrence, Durance), DURRANT, DURRENCE (includes Durrance), DURRETT, DURST, DURYEA, DUSCH, DUSENBERRY (includes Dusenbury), DUSING (includes Duesing), DUSTON, DUTCH (includes Duch, Duche), DUTCHER (includes Ducher, Duyster, De Duyster, De Duytser, De Duytscher), DUTTON, DUTTON, DUTTON, DUTY (includes Doty, Deuty, Dewty), DUVAL, DUVALL (includes DeVall, DeVeault, DeVolld, Deuel, Devault, Devol, Dewell, Divell, Divil, Divoll, Dowell, DuVal,, DuVall, Duvol, Duwault, Duel, Formy-Duvall), DUXFORD, DVORAK, DWELLY, DWIGHT, DWINELL (includes Dunnel, Donnel), DWY, DWYER (includes O'Dwyer, Dwire, Dwyre, Dwyar, Dwier), DYAS, DYE, DYER, DYESS (includes Dyess, Dyes, Dice, Dias, Diaz, Diez, Dyas), DYKE (includes Dike, Dyche), DYKES, DYKOWSKI (includes Dekowski, Dykowsky, Dekowsky, Dykovski, Dykofski, Dykofsky), DYMOCK, DYMOND, DYSART (includes Dysert, Diesert, Disart), DYSON.

SURNAMES, FAMILY ASSOCIATIONS & FAMILY NEWSLETTERS – "E"

Resources Dedicated to One Surname
http://www.cyndislist.com/surn-e.htm

Category Index:

◆ General Surname Sites and Resources

◆ Surname Specific Sites and Resources

◆ Surname Mailing Lists

◆ General Surname Sites and Resources

- Connect with Surnames - E
  http://www.geocities.com/Heartland/Bluffs/7708/e.html

- Dutch Home Pages by Familyname ~ Letter E
  http://members.tripod.com/~Don_Arnoldus/e.htm

- 'E' Surnames at RootsWeb
  http://resources.rootsweb.com/surnames/e.html

- FamilyHistory.com - Message Boards - Surname - E
  http://www.familyhistory.com/messages/list.asp?prefix=EA

- Family Tree Maker Online User Home Pages - E
  http://www.familytreemaker.com/users/e/index.html

- Family Workings E Surname Links
  http://www.familyworkings.com/links/sure.htm

- GenConnect Surname Index - "E"
  http://genconnect.rootsweb.com/indx/surnames/E.html
  Message boards sponsored by RootsWeb. Each surname message board set is divided into the following topics: Queries, Bibles, Biographies, Deeds, Obituaries, Pensions, Wills.

- Genealogy Resources on the Internet - "EA-ED" Surname Mailing Lists
  http://www.rootsweb.com/~jfuller/gen_mail_surnames-ea.html
  "EE-EH"
  http://www.rootsweb.com/~jfuller/gen_mail_surnames-ee.html
  "EI-EN"
  http://www.rootsweb.com/~jfuller/gen_mail_surnames-ei.html
  "EO-ET"
  http://www.rootsweb.com/~jfuller/gen_mail_surnames-eo.html
  "EU-EZ"
  http://www.rootsweb.com/~jfuller/gen_mail_surnames-eu.html
  Search the index of Surname Mailing Lists below: Surname Mailing Lists.

  o Genealogy Resources on the Internet - Surnames Included in Mailing Lists - "E"
    http://www-personal.umich.edu/~cgaunt/surnames/e.names.html
    This is a computer generated list of the surnames, and all variant spellings for those names, that are found in the surname mailing lists detailed on the pages shown above.

- Genealogy Resources on the Internet - Surname Web Sites for "E" Surnames
  http://www-personal.umich.edu/~cgaunt/surnames/e.html

- Genealogy's Most Wanted - Surnames Beginning with "E"
  http://www.citynet.net/mostwanted/e.htm

- Google Web Directory .... Genealogy>Surnames>E
  http://directory.google.com/Top/Society/Genealogy/Surnames/E/

- Heartland Genealogy Society Membership List - E
  http://www.geocities.com/Heartland/Ranch/2416/hgs-mlist-e.html

- H-GIG Surname Registry - Surnames Beginning E
  http://www.ucr.edu/h-gig/surdata/surname5.html

- Higginson Book Company - Surnames Beginning E
  http://www.higginsonbooks.com/e.htm

- inGeneas Table of Common Surname Variations and Surname Misspellings - D-E
  http://www.ingeneas.com/D2E.html

- The Obituary Link Page - Family Obituary Archives Online - E
  http://www.geocities.com/~cribbswh/obit/e.htm

- Open Directory - Society: Genealogy: Surnames: E
  http://www.dmoz.org/Society/Genealogy/Surnames/E/

- Surname Springboard Index - E
  http://www.geocities.com/~alacy/spring_e.htm

- SurnameWeb Surname Registry - E Index
  http://www.surnameweb.org/registry/e.htm

- SWINX Zoeklijst Nederlandse Familienamen / SWINX Searchlist Dutch Surnames - E
  http://www.swinx.net/swinx/swinx_eb_nl.htm

- Websites at RootsWeb: E Surnames
  http://www.rootsweb.com/~websites/surnames/e.html

◆ Surname Specific Sites and Resources

- **EARTHY and ARTHY Family History**
  http://www.earthy.net/

- **The EARWOOD Genealogical Society**
  http://members.xoom.com/earwood/index.html
  Serves as a meeting place and a database for the mystical and mysterious Earwood surname.

- **EASTMAN Genealogy and History**
  http://home.netcom.com/~seven007/index.html
  Descendants of Roger EASTMAN, born 1610, immigrated to America about 1638 on the ship "Confidence" to the Massachusetts Bay Colony.

- **EASTON**
  http://www.jps.net/easton
  Easton genealogy; homepage of the Easton-L mail-list.

- **EASTRIDGE Genealogy**
  http://www.geocities.com/Heartland/Woods/5540/eastridge/
  eastridge.html
  Surname Resource Center uniting those researching these families: EASTRIDGE, ESTRIDGE, EASTRIGE, ESTRIGE, EASTERIDGE and various other spellings.

- **Descendants of the EAST WOOD**
  mailto:AllysonMT@aol.com
  For details send e-mail to Allyson Tilton at AllysonMT@aol.com. Allyson Monroe Tilton, 148 Belglen Lane, Los Gatos, CA 95032.

- **EATOCK / EATOUGH History Page**
  http://www.skyfamily.com/eatock
  Surnames of Lancashire, England.

- **EBY Family Home Page (AEBI, EBI, EBEY, EABY etc.)**
  http://www.familytreemaker.com/users/q/u/a/B-D-Quast/
  The descendants of Theodorus Aebi(1), as well as those of David Davis Ebi(3?), and Andreas Eby(2) who may well be the nephew of Theodorus.

- **ECK Family Directory**
  http://www.geocities.com/EnchantedForest/Creek/4968/
  Dir.html

- **EDDLEMAN Database Home Page**
  http://www.netusa1.net/~eddleman/eddleman.htm

- **EDDLEMAN Family Home Pages**
  http://www.tisd.net/~eddlemsg/index.htm
  Dedicated to the descendants of David EDDLEMAN born in 1810 in Licolnton N.C. Eddleman, Edelman, Edelmann, Woolard, Sanders, Parker, Hull, Cline, Meyer, Shuford.

- **The EDDLEMAN Genealogy Library**
  http://www.disknet.com/indiana_biolab/eg.htm
  "The Largest International Online Collection of Authentic Edelmann - Eddleman Genealogy Data."

- **The EDDY Family Association**
  http://www.eddyfamily.com/
  Association formed to preserve the history of those who have the

EDDY surname. Primarily the descendents of William EDDYE, Vicar of the Cranbrook Church in England during the late 1500's and early 1600's.

- **The EDDY Family of Martha's Vineyard**
  http://www.vineyard.net/vineyard/history/eddy.htm
  Biographical and genealogical information of John EDDY (b. 1637) and Hepzibah DAGGETT of Tisbury, Dukes Co., MA.

- **EDELMAN(N) Genealogy Project**
  http://www.edelman-rp.com
  Edelman(n) and derivative spellings. Also related surnames, i.e. Bulmer, Christy, Jackson, Jarrell, etc.

- **EDENFIELD Genealogical Society**
  http://edenfield.org/
  A searchable database of over 20,000 Edenfield descendants, as well as background information on the Edenfield surname and place-name, a village in Lancashire, England.

- **EDICK Family ~ EDIC Family ~ EDEE Family ~ ITTIG Family ~ 300 Years in America**
  http://members.delphi.com/edic/index.html
  Early background information on the family names Edick, Edic, and Edee, all derived from the German Ittig.

- **The EDMONDS Page**
  http://www.geocities.com/Heartland/Hills/3839/
  genealogy.html
  Site cover the EDMONDS genealogy mostly from the Northwest portion of Georgia around Stephens, Habersham, and Franklin Counties. Period covers 1846-1910 currently.

- **The EDSON Genealogical Association**
  http://members.aol.com/genee76689/

- **Descendants of Abel EDWARDS and Polly POTTS**
  http://geocities.com/johnny6_28_66/
  Family came from Virginia and Tennessee.

- **John G. EDWARDS Family - Harrison Co., KY**
  http://www.rootsweb.com/~kyharris/edwards_harco.htm
  Other early KY EDWARDS families also.

- **Descendants of John (1) EDWARDS**
  http://members.mint.net/laton/
  EDWARDS, KNOWLTON, CROCKETT, McLELLAN.

- **EELLS/ELLS Families of North America**
  http://www.angelfire.com/tx/EellsNet

- **The Unofficial Page of the Clan EGAN Association - Australian Branch**
  http://users.globec.com.au/~egan/egan.htm
  Gaelic: MACAODHAGAIN. MacEgan, Egan, Eagan, Eagen, Keegan, Hagen.

- **World Wide EGGLESTON Family Roots**
  http://hometown.aol.com/MREgleston/index.html

- **EGGLESTONs of Corinth, NY**
  http://members.xoom.com/eggy77/main.htm
  Starting from Bygod EGGLESTON to recent.

- **EICHELBERGER Genealogy Home Page**
  http://freepages.genealogy.rootsweb.com/~jodiem/
  Ecenbarger, Echelbarger, Eckelbarger, Eckelberry, Eikelberger, Eichenberger, Ekelbarger and others.

- The EISELMAN / EISELMAN Home Page
  http://www.geocities.com/Heartland/Acres/9843/
  One-name study. Includes variant spellings: EISELE, EISEMAN, EISENMAN, and others.

- EISEN Family Tree
  http://home.att.net/~cdlevi/Geneology.html
  600 people linked through 9 generations of the EISEN family, tracing back to Jonah in Russia, c. 1780. Also significant is EDELMAN.

- The ELAM Family Research Page
  http://homepages.rootsweb.com/~celam/

- The ELAM Page
  http://www.webpak.net/~kyblue/elam/index.htm

- ELDER Family Newsletter
  http://www.intrepid.net/~fanfare/EFN.html

- ELGIN Net
  http://www.geocities.com/~elginsite/

- ELKINS Surname
  mailto:oldbooks@olypen.com
  E-mail Steve Elkins at oldbooks@olypen.com for more details on his research.

- ELKINS Genealogy Data
  http://homepages.rootsweb.com/~darburns/elkins/index.html
  For all ELKINS researchers; ELKINS data anytime, anywhere, anyplace. Elkins, Elkuns, Elkens, Alkins, Alkuns, Aklens, Alking, Alkung, Alkeng, Elkings, Elkengs, Elkungs.

- ELKS Family Tree
  http://www.users.globalnet.co.uk/~kenelks/elks.htm
  Details of Albert Edward Elks and his ancestors.

- ELL Family Heritage Page
  http://mars.ark.com/~rbell/html/ellfam.htm

- ELLER Family Association
  http://www.geocities.com/Heartland/Acres/2724/
  Eller Chronicles newsletter and Eller info.

- The Dabner Wansley ELLIOTT Family Home Page
  http://www.familytreemaker.com/users/e/l/l/John-C-Elliott/index.html
  Lumpkin Co., Hall Co, Dawson Co., and Forsyth Co., Georgia.

- ELLIOTT Genealogical Repository
  http://members.tripod.com/~cheeseheadnate/
  Elliot, Elliott and variants.

- Gateway The ELLIOT Clan Society
  http://members.home.com/ecs-webmaster/
  The official homepage for the ELLIOT Clan Society. For all Elliots, Elliotts, Eliots, and all other spellings.

- ELLIS Cousins Newsletter
  http://www.wtrt.net/~case/
  Quarterly publication for all ELLIS families in U.S. and Canada. Published for 20 years. All back issues available at $4 each.

- The ELRICKs - ELRICK Genealogy Research Page
  http://www.elricks.com/

- ELSEY Family Association & the ELSEY Echoes Newsletter
  mailto:Ellzeyj@msn.com
  Elsey, Ellzey, Elzey, Ellzea, Elsea, Ellsea, Elzie, Elsy. For details send e-mail to Joan Ellzey at: Ellzeyj@msn.com.

- BEVIER / ELTING Family Association
  http://home.earthlink.net/~rctwig/bevier.htm

- BEVIER - ELTING Family Association
  http://members.aol.com/Edie143/elt7_web.html
  Including a page with information and a photograph of the Bevier-Elting House on Huguenot Street in New Paltz, New York.

- ELWOOD Echoes
  http://ladyecloud.hypermart.net/Elwood.htm
  Elwood, Ellwood.

- EMANS Genealogy Homepage
  http://php.iupui.edu/~jalash/
  Descendants of Jan Emans, Sr. of Gravesend, New York married to Sarah Jansen in about 1660 and to Engeltie in about 1680.

- Descendants of Thomas EMERSON
  http://www.parsonstech.com/genealogy/trees/lemerson/temerson.htm
  Descendants of Thomas EMERSON, born in England, settled in Ipswich, Massachusetts in 1636.

- EMMERICH EMERICH EMERICK EMRICK EMRICH
  http://genweb.net/~dlemrick/

- The EMPSON Family Page
  http://www.angelfire.com/de/empson/family.html

- EMRY / EMERY Family Genealogy
  http://www.lanset.com/memry/emrygen.html

- ENDICOTT Genealogy Webpage
  http://www.angelfire.com/ky/Endicott
  ENDICOTT, ENDECOTT, & ENDACOTT, any time, any place.

- ENGELBACH Home Page
  http://soli.inav.net/~jme240
  Engelbach, Englebach, Engleback. This site is devoted to the world-wide surname of Engelbach and the families, past and present. A world-wide Engelbach Gathering Place.

- Descendants of John Marcus ENGELHORN II
  http://www.wenet.net/~jschremp/eng1782.html
  Born December 11, 1782, died October 25, 1869.

- ENGLE News Letter
  mailto:THZQ38A@prodigy.com
  Includes any spelling of the name Engel, Ingall, Engall, etc. For details send e-mal to Lisa Herdahl at: THZQ38A@prodigy.com.

- An Overview of the ENNEVER, ENEVER, ENEFER Family, 500 Years of History
  http://website.lineone.net/~ennever/
  An index of references to the family Ennever including all variations in spelling dating from as early as the 15th century. Enever, Enefer, Inever, Juniver, Eniver, Enivere, Enyver.

- The ENRIGHT Family Home Page
  http://www.familytreemaker.com/users/w/e/b/Bruce-J-Webster-Jr/

- The ERB Family from Lancaster to Ontario
  http://www.my-ged.com/erb
  Traces descendants of Swiss Mennonite Nicholas Erb 1680 from 1700s Lancaster Co., PA and 1800s Waterloo Co., Ontario. Allied families include: Bomberger, Bricker, Brubaker, Eby, Landis, Schaeffer, Shrantz, Shirk, and Snyder.

- ERDAHL (ERDAL) Family History
  http://home.att.net/~jtduxbury/erdahl.htm
  Descendents of Jokum Kristenson ERDAL ca. 1560, Norway to Minnesota.

- ERSKINE-L Home Page
  http://www.spirallight.com/erskine/

- History of the ESICK/ESSICK Family
  http://www.axs2k.net/mandm/

- ESKEW Family
  http://home.fuse.net/jdeskew
  ESKEW family.

- ESPEY Family History
  http://freepages.genealogy.rootsweb.com/~espey/
  Descendants of Hugh ESPEY and Mary STEWART.

- The (Do) ESPIRITO SANTO Family Club / Clube Das Famìlias "Do ESPÕRITO SANTO"
  http://members.tripod.com/~EspiritoSanto/

- ESSERY Genealogy & Family History
  http://www.essery.demon.co.uk/history.htm

- The ESSIG / ESSICK Family
  http://www.axs2k.net/mandm/
  Descendants of Rudolph Essig and sons, Georg Abraham and Hans Michael. Arrived in Philadelphia from Wurtenburg, Germany, on the "Princes Agusta" on September 16, 1736.

- ESTEP Connections
  http://www.homestead.com/estepconnections/
  Website for Eastep - Esteb - Estep - Estepp researchers.

- ESTEP Generations
  http://estepgen.homestead.com
  Dedicated to finding the Estep Roots with families dating back to the 1600's. The site has a searchable index and easy to read family charts. You can also submit your own part of the Estep Family tree.

- Descendants of Josef ESTERAK
  http://home.att.net/~thebarriers/esrkmain.htm
  An outline of the Texan descendents of Joseph Esterak, born circa 1800 in Vsetin, Moravia, Czechoslovakia. ADAMCIK, CHERNOSKY, EDWARDS, GALLOWAY, JIRASEK, LANGMAIER, LESHIKAR, MAREK, MIKESKA, THOMPSON.

- ETCHETO Basque Family Genealogy Home Page
  http://reno.quik.com/detcheto/
  ETCHETO, ECHETO, ETCHETTO, D'ETCHETO, ECHETOA, ETXETO.

- ETTIE Family History
  http://www.geocities.com/CapeCanaveral/9895/
  Ettie, Kniffen, Bashford, Bowlby, Dell, Ette, Eytte, Ettie, Farlonger, Furlonger, Groombridge, Hall, Kniffen, Kniffin, Lemon, McAteer, Ryerse, Simpson, Warner, Wride.

- HETU, ETU, ESTU, ITCHUE : Gènèalogie
  http://home.ican.net/~rhetu/
  Family genealogy: Searchable database of the descendants of Georges Estu dit Lafleur.

- ETZEL Genealogy
  http://homepages.rootsweb.com/~imrie/Etzel.html

- EUBANK Family Genealogy Home Page
  http://www.geocities.com/Athens/Styx/7031/genealogy1.html

- EUSTACE Family History Homepage
  http://dspace.dial.pipex.com/town/square/ga40/index.htm

- EVANS Ancestors
  http://skyport.com/spirit/evansl/evhtml.htm
  GEDCOM files collected from the Evans Surname Mailing List.

- The EVANS Genealogy Harbour
  http://members.aol.com/levans3352/public/index.html
  Descendants of John William Evans.

- The EVERALL Home Page
  http://hometown.aol.com/egrdn/page/index.htm

- EVERETT Database
  http://everettdatabase.8m.com

- EVERETT Families of the South
  http://www.azstarnet.com/~everett/
  EVERETT, EVERITT families originating in the southern states. Other surnames included = ROGERS, NELSON, HARRIS, BARKSDALE.

- EVERSOLE / EBERSOLE Research
  http://homepages.rootsweb.com/~eversole/
  Genealogy information on almost 5000 individuals with surnames of EVERSOLE or EBERSOLE, however spelled. Includes "E162news" newsletter periodically. Ebersol, Eversull, Ebersohl, Ebersoll.

- EVERSOLE / EBERSOHL Research Network
  http://www.users.mis.net/~chesnut/pages/eversole.htm
  Includes Abersold, Abersole, Aebersold, Aebersole, Ebersold, Ebersole, Eibersold, Eibersolt, Eversold, Eversole, Eversoll.

- Clan EWING in America
  http://members.xoom.com/ClanEwing/ClanEwing.htm
  This is the official site for Clan Ewing in America, a nation-wide organization devoted to research of the Ewing families descended from 33 immigrant Ewings who came to America prior to 1776.

- EWING Family History
  http://www.sandcastles.net/
  Descendants of Thomas Ewing Sr.(1695-1748) and Mary Maskell (1701-1784) Surnames include: Latimer, Caruthers, Sherman, Clark, Patterson, Rhea, Morgan, Harris, and Hunt.

- EWING Home Page - EWING Exchange Newsletter
  http://members.aol.com/Kinseeker6/ewing.html

- EYREs Family Album
  http://eyres.home.texas.net/
  Album for the EYREs that came to North America from Ireland in the 1800s.

- EYRE Home Page
  http://mail.standard.net.au/~daneyre/

- Genealogy of the EYMANN Family
  http://www.iig.uni-freiburg.de/~eymann/genealog.htm
  Germany, Switzerland and the U.S.

◆ Surname Mailing Lists

- "EA-ED" Surname Mailing Lists
  http://www.rootsweb.com/~jfuller/gen_mail_surnames-ea.html
  EADES, EADIE, EADS (includes Eades, Edes, Edds), EADY, EAGAN, EAGER, EAGLE (includes Eigle, Igel, Igle), EAGLEN (includes Eaglin), EAGLES, EAKER, EAKIN, EAKINS, EALY (includes Ealee, Ealey), EAMES, EARHART, EARL, EARLE, EARLES, EARLEY, EARLY, EARNEST, EARNSHAW, EARP (includes Earpe, Earps, Arp, Arpe, Arps, Irp, Irpe, Irps, Urp, Urpe, Urps), EARWAKER (includes Earwicker), EASLEY (includes Easly, Easle), EASON, EAST, EASTER, EASTERDAY, EASTERLING, EASTERLY, EASTERWOOD, EASTHAM, EASTMAN, EASTON (includes Easten, Eastin, Eston, Eastom), EASTRIDGE (includes Estridge, Eastrige, Estrige, Eastridger, Estridger, Easteridge), EASTWOOD, EATON, EAVES (includes Eves), EBANKS, EBELING, EBERHARD, EBERHARDT, EBERHART, EBERLE (includes Eberly, Everly, Everley), EBERLY, EBERSOLD, EBERSOLE (includes Abersold, Abersol, Aebersold, Aebersole, Ebersold, Eibersold, Eibersolt, Eversold, Eversole,, Eversolh, Eversoll), EBERT, EBERTING, EBINGER, EBLE, EBNER, EBY (includes Ebi, Ebey, Eaby, Aebi, Evy, Ewy), ECCLES, ECHOLS (includes Eckols, Ecles, Eccles, Eckels, Eckles, Eckels, Ecles), ECK, ECKEL, ECKENBACH, ECKENRODE, ECKER, ECKEROTE (includes Eckercote), ECKERSON, ECKERT, ECKHARDT, ECKHART, ECKHOFF, ECKOLDT, ECKSTEIN, ECROYD, EDDIE, EDDINGS, EDDINS, EDDLEMAN (includes Edelman, Edleman, Eddlemann, Adelman), EDDY, EDDY, EDE, EDELMANN, EDEN, EDENFIELD, EDENS (includes Eden, Eddins, Eadens, Eddens), EDENS (includes Eden, Eddins, Eadens, Eddens), EDGAR, EDGE, EDGELL (includes Edgel, Edgill, Edgil, Edgin), EDGERTON, EDGEWORTH, EDGINGTON, EDGMON (includes Edgemon, Edgmond, Edgemond, Edgman, Edgeman), EDGMON (includes Edgemon, Edgemond, Edgmond, Egmond, van Egmont), EDICK, EDIE, EDINGTON (includes Eddington, Edgington), EDISBURY, EDMENSON, EDMISTON, EDMOND, EDMONDS (includes Edmond, Edmund, Edmunds, Edmans, Edminston, Edmonston), EDMONDSON (includes Edmonson, Edmiston, Edmunson), EDMONSON, EDMUNDS, EDMUNDSON, EDNEY, EDRINGTON, EDRIS (includes Ader, Eder, Etter, Etters, Etris, Eteris, Eders, Ateris, Ater, Oether, Otter), EDSON, EDWARD, EDWARDS, EDWARDS.

- "EE-EH" Surname Mailing Lists
  http://www.rootsweb.com/~jfuller/gen_mail_surnames-ee.html
  EFFERT (includes Effort), EGAN, EGBERT, EGE, EGGER, EGGERS, EGGERT, EGGLESTON, EGNER (includes Egnor, Agner, Agnor, Eigner, Eignor, Aigner, Aignor, Egender, Igender, Aegender, Aginder), EGOLF, EHINGERR, EHLERS (includes Eilers, Elers, Alers), EHLERS, EHMER, EHR, EHRHARDT.

- "EI-EN" Surname Mailing Lists
  http://www.rootsweb.com/~jfuller/gen_mail_surnames-ei.html
  EICHELBERGER, EICHER, EICHLER, EIDE, EIDSON, EIERMANN (includes Eierman, Eyerman, Eyermann), EIKEL, EIKENBERRY (includes Ikenberry), EIKLOR (includes Agler, Eickler, Eckler, Aigler, Eichler, Ekelaer, Eigler, Eggler, Eagler, Egler, Eklor), EILER, EISE, EISELE, EISENLORD, EISENMAN, EISENMANN, EKIS (includes Ekie, Ike, Eke, Ekiss, Ickes, Eckes, Eacus, Eachus), EKSTROM, EKAUT (includes Eckeaut), ELAM (includes Ellam, Ealam, Ellim), ELDER, ELDER, ELDERKIN, ELDRED, ELDREDGE, ELDRIDGE (includes Eldred, Eldbridge, Aldridge, Aldrich, McEldred, Eldrith, Elredge, Eldrith, Ellige, Eldredge, Eldith,, Erldrith, Eldrige, Elddreg, Elrage, Eldrig), ELEY (includes Eli, Ely), ELGIN, ELGIN, ELHOFF, ELIAS, ELIOT, ELKIN, ELKINS (includes Alkins, Alkens, Elkens, Elkons, Elkuns, Alkons, Alkuns), ELL (includes Elle, Ehle, Elles, Ells), ELLARD, ELLEDGE (includes Elige, Ellage), ELLENBURG, ELLER (includes Ellers, Oehler), ELLET, ELLIFFE (includes Ellisse), ELLINGER, ELLINGHAM, ELLINGTON, ELLIOT, ELLIOTT, ELLIOTT, ELLIS, ELLIS (includes Elis, Elys, Ellise, Ellyse, Allis), ELLISON, ELLISTON, ELLSWORTH, ELLYSON, ELLZEY, ELMES, ELMORE (includes Elmo, Almore, Ulmo, Olmeer, Elmer, McElmo, StElmo), ELMS, ELRINGTON, ELROD, ELS, ELSBERRY, ELSEY, ELSOM, ELSON, ELSTON, ELSWICK, ELTON, ELVIN, ELWARDT (includes Elwart, Elwert), ELWELL, ELWOOD, ELWOOD (includes Elwoods, Ellwood, Ellwoods, Elwod, Elwaud, Elewoud, Elywood, Aylwood, Elward, Elwald,, Aylward, Ailward, Ellyard, Eilert, Eliard, Eliert, Eliet, Eliot, Elliot, Ailiet, Elle, Eli, Elood, Woodel, Allwood, Aluuoldus,, Aluuolt, Alfuuold, Aluoldi, Aelfweald), ELY, ELZINGA, EMANUEL, EMBREE, EMBREY, EMBRY, EMCH, EMERICK, EMERSON, EMERT, EMERY (includes Emry, Emory, Embry), EMERY (includes Embry), EMIGH, EMLEN, EMMERSON, EMMERT, EMMES (includes Emms, Emes, Ems), EMMETT, EMMONS, EMMONS, EMOND, EMORY, EMPEY (includes Empy, Empie), EMPSON, ENGBERG, ENDERS (includes Endres, Ender, Endress, Endris, Endries), ENDICOTT (includes Endecott), ENDICOTT, ENDRES, ENDRESS, ENDSLEY, ENDSLEY, ENFIELD, ENGBROCK, ENGEBRETSON, ENGEL (includes Engle), ENGELBRECHT (includes Englebrecht, Engelbreck, Engelbright), ENGELHARDT, ENGELKEN, ENGELMAN, ENGELMANN, ENGLAND, ENGLE (includes Engel, Engler), ENGLEMAN, ENGLEMAN (includes Engelman, Engelmann), ENGLER, ENGLISH (includes Ingliss), ENGLUND, ENJOERT (includes Engard, Engart, Enger, Enjard, Enjart, Enjert, Enuard, Enyard, Enyardt, Enyart, Enyeart, Ingard,, Iniart, Inniard, Injaart, Injard, Inyard, Inyart, Inyerd, Inyord, Yoreard, Yoriear), ENLOW, ENNEVER (includes Enever, Enefer), ENNIS, ENNIS, ENO (includes Enos, Enno, Henno, Hennot), ENO, ENOCH, ENOCHS, ENOS, ENRIGHT, ENSIGN, ENSLEY, ENSLOW, ENSMINGER, ENSOR, ENTREKIN (includes Entrican, Entrikin, Entriken), ENTWISTLE, ENYARD (includes Engard, Engart, Enger, Enjard, Enjart, Enjert, Enjoert, Enuard, Enyardt, Enyart, Enyeart, Ingard,, Iniart, Inniard, Injaart, Injard, Inyard, Inyart, Inyerd, Inyord, Yoreard, Yoriear), ENYART (includes Engard, Engart, Enger, Enjard, Enjart, Enjert, Enuard, Enyard, Enyardt, Enyeart, Ingard,, Iniart,, Inniard, Injaart, Injard, Inyard, Inyart, Inyerd, Inyord, Yoreard, Yoriear), ENYEART (includes Engard, Engart, Enger, Enjard, Enjart, Enjert, Enjoert, Enuard, Enyard, Enyardt, Enyart, Ingard,, Iniart, Inniard, Injaart, Injard, Inyard, Inyart, Inyerd, Inyord, Yoreard, Yoriear).

- **"EO-ET" Surname Mailing Lists**
  http://www.rootsweb.com/~jfuller/gen_mail_surnames-eo.html
  EOFF, EPLER, EPLEY, EPPERSON (includes Apperson), EPPES, EPPES, EPPING, EPPLER, EPPS, EPSTEIN, EPSTEIN, ERB, ERCOLANI, ERDBRUGER (includes Erdbruegger, Erdbrueger), ERDMAN, ERDMANN, ERHARD, ERICKSON (includes Ericcson, Ericsson, Ericson, Erikson), ERMLER, ERNEST, ERNST, ERRINGTON, ERSKINE, ERVIN (includes Erwin, Irvin), ERVINE, ERWIN, ESCH, ESHLEMAN, ESKEW (includes Askew), ESPIEG, ESPOSITO, ESSEX, ESSEX, ESSIG, ESSLEMONT (includes Esselmont, Esslement), ESTELLE (includes Estell, Estill, Estil, Estle, Estal, Estile), ESTEP (includes Eastep, Esstep, Esttep, Estepp), ESTES (includes Estis, Estive, Estep, Eastus), ESTILL, ESTRADA, ESTY, ETCHESON (includes Etchison, Etchenson), ETCHIESON, ETCHINSON, ETCHISON, ETHEL (includes Ethell, Ethall, Etholl, Athol, Atholl), ETHERIDGE (includes Ethridge, Etheredge), ETHERINGTON, ETHRIDGE, ETIER, ETTER, ETZEL, ETZLER (includes Etsler, Aetsler, Utsler).

- **"EU-EZ" Surname Mailing Lists**
  http://www.rootsweb.com/~jfuller/gen_mail_surnames-eu.html
  EUBANK, EUBANKS, EUBANKS, EUDY, EUSTACE, EUTSLER (includes Eutzler, Utzler, Utsler, Hutzler, Hutzlern, Utesler, Eutseller, Utseller, Yutzler, Jutzler), EVANS, EVANS, EVANS, EVANS, EVANS, EVARTS, EVELAND (includes Iffland, Ifflandt, Iffelandt), EVENSON, EVERALL (includes Everal, Everel, Everell), EVERARD, EVERETT, EVERHART, EVERINGHAM (includes Everham, Evernham, Evringham), EVERITT, EVERITT, EVERLY, EVERS, EVERSOLE, EVERSON, EVERSON, EVERTON, EVERTS, EVES, EVITTS, EWALT (includes Evalt, Ewald), EWART, EWELL, EWEN, EWERS, EWING (includes Ewen, Ewin, MacEwen, MacEwin), EWOLDT, EXLINE (includes Öchslen, Oechslen, Axline), EXMAN (includes Essman), EXTON, EYE (includes Iye, Iee), EYER, EYLER, EYRE, EYRE, EYRES, EZELL.

SURNAMES, FAMILY ASSOCIATIONS & FAMILY NEWSLETTERS – "F"

Resources Dedicated to One Surname
http://www.cyndislist.com/surn-f.htm

Category Index:

◆ General Surname Sites and Resources
◆ Surname Specific Sites and Resources

◆ Surname Mailing Lists

◆ General Surname Sites and Resources

- Connect with Surnames - F
  http://www.geocities.com/Heartland/Bluffs/7708/f.html

- Dutch Home Pages by Familyname ~ Letter F
  http://members.tripod.com/~Don_Arnoldus/f.htm

- FamilyHistory.com - Message Boards - Surname - F
  http://www.familyhistory.com/messages/list.asp?prefix=FA

- Family Tree Maker Online User Home Pages - F
  http://www.familytreemaker.com/users/f/index.html

- Family Workings F Surname Links
  http://www.familyworkings.com/links/surf.htm

- 'F' Surnames at RootsWeb
  http://resources.rootsweb.com/surnames/f.html

- GenConnect Surname Index - "F"
  http://genconnect.rootsweb.com/indx/surnames/F.html
  Message boards sponsored by RootsWeb. Each surname message board set is divided into the following topics: Queries, Bibles, Biographies, Deeds, Obituaries, Pensions, Wills.

- Genealogy Resources on the Internet - "FA-FD" Surname Mailing Lists
  http://www.rootsweb.com/~jfuller/gen_mail_surnames-fa.html
  "FE-FH"
  http://www.rootsweb.com/~jfuller/gen_mail_surnames-fe.html
  "FI-FN"
  http://www.rootsweb.com/~jfuller/gen_mail_surnames-fi.html
  "FO-FQ"
  http://www.rootsweb.com/~jfuller/gen_mail_surnames-fo.html
  "FR-FT"
  http://www.rootsweb.com/~jfuller/gen_mail_surnames-fr.html
  "FU-FZ"
  http://www.rootsweb.com/~jfuller/gen_mail_surnames-fu.html
  Search the index of Surname Mailing Lists below: Surname Mailing Lists.

  o Genealogy Resources on the Internet - Surnames Included in Mailing Lists - "F"
    http://www-personal.umich.edu/~cgaunt/surnames/f.names.html

This is a computer generated list of the surnames, and all variant spellings for those names, that are found in the surname mailing lists detailed on the pages shown above.

- Genealogy Resources on the Internet - Surname Web Sites for "F" Surnames
  http://www-personal.umich.edu/~cgaunt/surnames/f.html

- Genealogy's Most Wanted - Surnames Beginning with "F"
  http://www.citynet.net/mostwanted/f.htm

- Google Web Directory .... Genealogy>Surnames>F
  http://directory.google.com/Top/Society/Genealogy/Surnames/F/

- Heartland Genealogy Society Membership List - F
  http://www.geocities.com/Heartland/Ranch/2416/hgs-mlist-f.html

- H-GIG Surname Registry - Surnames Beginning F
  http://www.ucr.edu/h-gig/surdata/surname6.html

- Higginson Book Company - Surnames Beginning with F
  http://www.higginsonbooks.com/f.htm

- inGeneas Table of Common Surname Variations and Surname Misspellings - F-G
  http://www.ingeneas.com/F2G.html

- The Obituary Link Page - Family Obituary Archives Online - F
  http://www.geocities.com/~cribbswh/obit/f.htm

- Open Directory - Society: Genealogy: Surnames: F
  http://www.dmoz.org/Society/Genealogy/Surnames/F/

- Surname Springboard Index - F
  http://www.geocities.com/~alacy/spring_f.htm

- SurnameWeb Surname Registry - F Index
  http://www.surnameweb.org/registry/f.htm

- SWINX Zoeklijst Nederlandse Familienamen / SWINX Searchlist Dutch Surnames - F
  http://www.swinx.net/swinx/swinx_fe_nl.htm

- Websites at RootsWeb: F Surnames
  http://www.rootsweb.com/~websites/surnames/f.html

◆ Surname Specific Sites and Resources

- The FACCETTI Family Tree
  http://www.geocities.com/Heartland/Park/9789/
  Genealogy of Fachetti/Faccetti by Richard B. Fachetti (1930-1997).

- My Neck of the Woods
  http://members.home.net/lyle.woods/
  Fair, Fleming.

- Descendants of William FAIRBANKS
  http://www.parsonstech.com/genealogy/trees/lkeester/
  fairbank.htm
  Descendants of William FAIRBANKS b.Yorkshire, England. Linked through Jonathon Fairbanks of Dedham, Mass. 1000+ families and over 5000 individuals, mostly between 1600 and 1897. Jonathon is generally accepted as the common ancestor of all Fairbanks & related surnames in the US.

- FAIRCLOTH Genealogy
  http://personal.lig.bellsouth.net/lig/s/t/starfair/STARFAIR.html

- FAIRHEAD Family Fellowship
  http://www.fairhead.ic24.net/
  Aims to provide an online resource for all those interested in the history of this great East Anglian family.

- Genealogy FAIRRAR, FARRER
  http://members.tripod.co.uk/Gentree
  A list of Birth, Marriage, Death, Wills etc. from 1600 to 1998 for the names. Fairer, Farrar, Farrer, Farrow, Fayrer and their variant names.

- The FAITHFULL Page
  http://www.isn.net/~dfaith/front_page.html

- FALK Family Page
  http://homepages.rootsweb.com/~falkfmly/
  For the Descendants of Franz F. FALK and Augustine C. PETERMAN. Surnames include BURNS, ENGEL, and RESCHLEIN.

- FANCHER Family Genealogy
  http://members.tripod.com/~KandyF/index.html

- FANKHAUSER Genealogy
  http://www.geocities.com/Hollywood/Hills/1416/
  The Swiss Family in the 1300s. Also FUNKHOUSER.

- FANNING Family Newsletter
  http://members.aol.com/bsmith1311/fanning.htm
  Online version of the Fanning Family Newsletter, a family history and family genealogy newsletter for the descendants of Bill and Ellie Fanning of Fayetteville, Tennessee.

- FANTHORPE Family History
  http://www.geocities.com/SunsetStrip/Stage/5429/northwill/
  famhistory.html
  Incomplete information relating to members of the FANTHORPE family who emigrated to Australia in the nineteenth century.

- Descendants of Charles FANTLE
  http://parsonstech.com/genealogy/trees/sfantle/fantle.htm
  Cree, Widlon, Eiseman, Levinger.

- FARNI-FARNEY-FORNEY Family
  http://www.nwlink.com/~nichols
  A genealogical website devoted to all variations of the Farni-Farney-Forney surname.

- FARNSWORTH and PHANEUF
  http://www.microtec.net/aphane/english.htm

- The FARR Compendium
  http://www.winslow.farr.org/
  The Winslow FARR Sr. Family Organization.

- Cherry Stone Creek - Official Home of the FARTHING Family in America
  http://www.geocities.com/Heartland/Plains/9515/

- FAUGHNAN Genealogy Home Page
  http://members.aol.com/faughnan1/Faughnan/faugh.htm

- FAULCONER Family
  http://www.mindspring.com/~jogt/surnames/faulcon.htm
  Virginia and Kentucky.

- FAULKNER Researchers Page
  http://www.geocities.com/Heartland/Prairie/3597/
  Falconar, Falconer, Falkiner, Falkner, Faulknor, Forkner, Fortner.

- The FAY Family
  http://www.fayfamily.org
  FAY worldwide.

- The FEATHERSTONE Society
  http://www.geocities.com/~pfeatherstone/

- FEAZEL FEAZELL FEASEL FEAZLE FEEZEL Genealogy Family History
  http://www.shadow.net/~feazel/index.html
  Feisel, Feazel, Fezel, Feezell.

- FEHR's Famous Family
  http://www3.bc.sympatico.ca/donfehr/fehr.htm
  The family of Benjamin Fehr and his wife, Elisabeth, in Manitoba and Saskatchewan, Canada.

- The FIG Tree News - FENTON International Genealogy
  http://draco.cwru.edu/homes/figtree/

- The FERDERER (FÖRDERER, FOERDERER) Family Home Page
  http://www.familytreemaker.com/users/f/e/r/Robert-L-Ferderer/
  From Germany in the early 1800's to Russia and from Russia in the early 1900's to America.

- FERGUSON Home Page - FERGUSON Files Newsletter
  http://members.aol.com/Kinseeker6/ferguson.html

- FERGUSONs of Ireland
  http://freepages.genealogy.rootsweb.com/~colin/Fergusons
  OfIreland/
  *Extracted parish, census and other records plus collated queries all
  concerning the surname FERGUSON in Ireland.*

- Clan FERGUSSON Society of North America
  http://www.CFSNA.org/

- FERMOR Family History
  http://ourworld.compuserve.com/homepages/SheilaFClarkson

- The FERNALD Genealogy Page
  http://members.aol.com/Drumn8/RFernald.html
  *Descendants of Renald FERNALD of Bristol, England and
  Portsmouth, New Hampshire.*

- The Descendants of Jeffery FERRIS of England
  http://members.aol.com/MShermanL/ferris.html
  *Born 1610 in England; died May 31, 1666 in Greenwich,
  Connecticut.*

- FETTERLY Forum
  http://clubs.yahoo.com/clubs/fetterlyforum
  Fetterly, Vetterlie, Vatterlie, and other related surnames.

- The FEULING Family Genealogy
  http://www.star.net/People/~mga60/feulhome.htm

- All things FEWSTER
  http://www.fewster.com
  *FEWSTER research and contacts throughout the world, with a focus
  on Yorkshire in England. Other names include STRICK,
  NORWOOD, PASHBY, and COLBECK.*

- The FICKEISEN Family History Genealogy
  Website
  http://www.albany.net/~go/fickeisen/
  Also Fickies - Fickeis.

- FICKLIN-FICKLEN-FICKLING Family
  http://www.ficklin-fickling.org

- The FIEGEL Surname Genealogy Project
  http://www.fiegelnet.org/

- From a Distant FIELD - The Living Edition on the
  Internet
  http://acsys.anu.edu.au/FromADistantField/
  *Descendants of the New South Wales (Australia) pioneers,
  EDWARD and ELIZABETH FIELD.*

- The FIFIELD One-Name Study
  http://homepages.rootsweb.com/~fifield/index.html

- The FIGGITT Family
  http://www.btinternet.com/~trevor.figgitt/

- FIGHT/FIGHTMASTER Family
  http://members.aol.com/jogt/fightfam.htm

- FIGNER Family Research
  http://members.delphi.com/tfigner/index.html
  Figners in the U.S. from the 1700s, 1800s, etc.

- FIGUEROA Home Page
  http://www.freeyellow.com/members8/figueroa/main.html
  *This site is dedicated to the study of the Figueroa surname. Este
  sitio se dedica al estudio del apellido Figueroa.*

- FINCANNON Family Tree
  http://members.tripod.com/~drbobl/fincannonfamilytree.html
  *Genealogy of William FINCANNON (1755-1831) emphasizing
  family of John Alexander FINCANNON (1894-1945).*

- FINGER Family Genealogy
  http://www.fingerfamily.com/
  *Includes many AUSTIN, FINGAR, HULL, LAZORIK / LAZUREK,
  MUNSON and ROWLAND ancestors.*

- FINLEY Family History
  http://opac.sonoma.edu/finley

- FINNEY UK
  http://freepages.genealogy.rootsweb.com/~finney/
  One name study for the FINNEY surname from the UK.

- FIRESTONE Surname Website Newsletter
  http://homepages.rootsweb.com/~preston/FirestoneRoot/
  Firestone_Surname.html
  *Includes all variants: FEUERSTEIN, FEYERSTEIN, FIRSTINE,
  FERSTONE, etc., anywhere, any time.*

- FISHBURN Genealogy
  http://members.aol.com/clineroots/FISHBURN.main.html
  *Fishburn, Fishbourne, Fishborn, Fishburne, and any other spelling
  of the name.*

- A History of the FISKE Family in England
  http://www.fiske.clara.net/
  *A history and genealogy of the FISK/FISKE surname, concentrating
  on the English side of the family, and including background articles
  and photographs.*

- FISTE/FOIST/FOYST Family Reunion
  http://foist.tripp.org
  *Descendants of John FOIST (1774) and Eleanor FARTHING (1779)
  who lived in MD, VA and OH.*

- The FITE Family
  http://www.1fite.com/
  The Johannes branch of the Fite family from 1749 - 1950.

- Origins of the FITZMAURICE Families
  http://www.fitzmaurice.ie/origins/
  *The site is intended to list every person in the direct titled male line
  from recent peers back more than a thousand years to Tuscany.*

- Descendants of Jeremiah FITZPATRICK
  http://www.uftree.com/UFT/WebPages/chrisbarttels/HTML/
  index.htm
  *6 Generations of Jeremiah Fitzpatrick descendants. Jeremiah came
  into Ohio about 1802. He settled into Fox Township before the 1820
  census and about 1836 went to Jackson Co, OH. He probably died
  in Jackson County about 1847-48.*

- FITZPATRICKS of New Orleans, Louisiana
  http://members.tripod.com/FitzpatrickNO
  Includes a Message Board for Fitzpatricks.

- The Thomas A. FITZPATRICK Family Home Page
  http://www.familytreemaker.com/users/s/m/i/Donn-M-Smith/

- FITZSIMMONS Family Web Page
  http://www.geocities.com/Heartland/Valley/1410/fitzsimmons/
  index.html
  Fitzsimmons, Fitsimmons, Fitzimmons.

- The FLANDERS Family of Martha's Vineyard
  http://www.vineyard.net/vineyard/history/flanders.htm
  *Descendants of John Flanders and Sarah Hillman of Chilmark,
  Martha's Vineyard, Dukes Co., Mass.*

- FLANNERY Clan / Clann FHLANNABHRA
  http://members.xoom.com/flanneryclan/index.htm
  To preserve the heritage of Flannerys and Flannellys world-wide.

- FLANNERY Family Genealogy
  http://www.FlanneryGenealogy.com/
  *Descendants of William Riley FLANNERY and Nancy A.
  DAVIDSON,and connecting families, Skeens, Kegley, Conn, Rabb,
  Butcher, Dancy, Wingler.*

- FLATT Footings
  http://www.halcyondays.com/Flatt/flatt_footings.htm
  Quarterly newsletter dedicated to the Flatt surname.

- FLEET Family Tree
  http://freepages.genealogy.rootsweb.com/~fleet/fleet.htm
  *Fleete, Flete, Flett, Flet, de Flet, ate Flete, de Fleta, le Fleet, del
  Flete, de Floeta, Fleota, le Fleota, Fleotig, Flot, le Floto, Flotto, de
  Flotto, and de la Flotte.*

- FLELLO - A One Name Study
  http://www.frumble.freeserve.co.uk/flello.htm

- From FLENNIKEN to FLANNIGAN
  http://www.geocities.com/Heartland/Valley/2967/

- FLESHMAN/FLEISCHMANN Family History &
  Databases
  http://homepages.rootsweb.com/~george/flesh.html

- FLETCHER Family Research Bulletin
  http://www.cswnet.com/~fletcher/

- FLEUETTE Family Association
  http://www.kersur.net/~fleuette/
  Fluet, Fluette and Fleuette.

- FLINDERS Genealogy
  http://homepages.ihug.co.nz/~flinders
  Worldwide study of the surname FLINDERS.

- FLIPPIN Files
  http://www.homestead.com/flippinfiles/
  Flippen, Flippin, Flipping, Phippen.

- FLOORE Family History
  http://www.geocities.com/Heartland/Meadows/5110
  *Searching for the ancestors and descendants of Samuel FLOORE
  who settled around Louisville, Kentucky between 1795 and 1800.*

- The FLOURNOY Family
  http://www.mindspring.com/~bigo/flournoy.htm
  Descendants of Nicholas FLEURNOIR.

- FLOWERS Family Historical Society
  http://www.geocities.com/Heartland/Ridge/7524
  *Traces the heritage of the Flowers Family and connected surnames,
  1600 to present.*

- FLOYD Folks
  http://www.halcyondays.com/Floyd/FloydFolks.htm
  *Quarterly newsletter dedicated to research on the Floyd family
  name.*

- Stephen FLUHARTY Descendants
  http://www.ovis.net/~billcham/sfluh/
  *Descendants of Stephen Fluharty, born 1746 and died 1825 in West
  Virginia.*

- FLYNN Clan of America
  http://pages.prodigy.com/GPGJ41A/flynn.htm

- FLYNT Family History & Genealogy Online
  http://members.tripod.com/flyntgenealogy
  *FLYNT/FLINT family history, wills, bibles, census, database,
  biographies, photo album, queries, marriages, cemetery records,
  reunions. Family origins in Scotland migrating to America in
  1600's.*

- FOALE Family
  http://www.tecumseh.esu6.k12.ne.us/family_genealogy/
  index.htm
  Descendants of Peter FOALE of Nebraska.

- The FOCHT Family
  http://www.phillipsplace.net/genealogy/surnames/focht.html
  *History of the Adam Focht family, which came from Pennsylvania to
  Union Township, Auglaize County, Ohio about 1836.*

- FOLKER One-Name Study
  http://www.geocities.com/Heartland/Woods/7208/

- FOLSOM Family Association of America
  http://home.flash.net/~miamibig/folsom/

- The FONDREN and COLE Families
  http://members.aol.com/jogt/fondren.htm
  Of North Carolina and South Carolina.

- FONES (FOWNES) Family Genealogy
  http://www.fones.org/

- FONNESBECK / Deerstream
  http://www.fortunecity.com/millenium/castleton/262/
  Excellent Interests Fonnesbeck Genealogy Page.

- Canadian FONTAINE Genealogy Association
  http://www.geocities.com/heartland/farm/5233
  Fontaine, Fountain, LaFontaine, LaFountain.

- FOOR Family Genealogy (FOOR, FOORE, FUHR,
  FUHRER)
  http://www.geocities.com/~shellyinoh/
  Single surname study.

- FOORD One Name Study
  mailto:lfoord@saturn.execulink.com
  *Including FOORD, FOORDE, FORDE but not FORD unless the
  variant has a direct link. Database includes both submitted family
  trees and historical information. Contributors and queries very
  welcome. Not online, only via e-mail: lfoord@saturn.execulink.com.*

- FOOTE Family Association of America
  http://www.footefamily.org/
  *This is the reorganization of the original Association of FOOTE
  descendants who trace their roots back to the early 1500's in
  England.*

- The FORBES Families of North Carolina
  http://www.geocities.com/Heartland/Pointe/2430/index.html

- The William FORD Society
  http://users.erinet.com/31363/fordfam.htm
  Descendants of William Ford who was born in 1722 in Charles County, Maryland and died in 1821 in what is now Taylor County, West Virginia.

- FORDYCE Family Archives
  http://www.fordyce.org/genealogy
  Extensive archive of records - birth, death, marriage, cemetery records, obituaries, biographies, etc.

- FOREHAND Surname Genealogy
  http://members.xoom.com/Kathleen1/forehand.htm

- FORREST Family Home Page
  http://members.aol.com/harley1369/forrest.html
  Forrest-Forrester-Forist-Forest-Forraster, and other variant spellings.

- Clan FORRESTER Society, Inc.
  http://members.aol.com/forroots/index1.html

- FORRET.org: The Web Home for FORRETs Worldwide
  http://www.forret.org/

- Clan FORSYTH Society of Canada
  http://members.home.net/syl.penner/clan_forsyth.html

- Clan FORSYTH Society U.S.A.
  http://www.xmission.com/~forsyth/

- Généalogie de la famille FORTIER
  http://www.dsuper.net/~efortier/
  Descendants of Antoine FORTIER & Madeleine CADIEU.

- The FORTIN Genealogy Page
  http://www.gaudreau.org/arthur/genealogy/fortin.sht

- FORTIN's Web Site, Home Page
  http://www3.sympatico.ca/denis.fortin20/fortin/a-index.htm
  Fortin, Fortain, Forthin, Fourtin, Furtin, Furtaw, etc.

- The FORTINEUX Family Home Page
  http://www.public.usit.net/davegoff/fortineux.htm
  The Fortineux family lived in the Palatinate in the 17th century and descendants include persons living in North America today with the surnames Fortney, Fortna, Furtney, and Fordney.

- FOSBROOKE Surname, England
  mailto:richardj@converting.co.uk
  E-mail Richard Jones at richardj@converting.co.uk and he will check his extensive database.

- History of the FOSTER Family
  http://member.aol.com/eleom/genealogy/foster_history.html
  History of the FOSTER family, written by D.I. FOSTER in 1902. Duvall, Figard, Fluke, Foster, Horton, Johnston, Lewis, Negley, Penn, Wright.

- FOSTERing
  http://www.geocities.com/Heartland/Acres/9561/ring.html
  A webring for personal genealogical homepages pertaining to research of the Foster surname.

- The FOTHERGILL Family In America
  http://www.angelfire.com/co2/fothergill/index.html
  FOTHERGILLs of Kane and DeKalb Counties, Illinois. With a page for submissions of other FOTHERGILL Families in America. Also Ward, Winans, Ballard, Torry, Moore, Johnnine, Nelson, Buzzell.

- The FOUNTAIN Family Outline
  http://www.mosquitonet.com/~luht/fount.htm

- The FOUST/FAUST Family
  http://members.aol.com/jogt/foustfam.htm
  Of North Carolina and Tennessee.

- FOUST / FAUST Genealogy Resource Page
  http://w2.parkland.cc.il.us/~jfoust/Foust/f_foust.htm

- FOWLER Family
  http://hometown.aol.com/wtgmike/genealogy/Fowler.html
  Ancestors and Descendants of William FOWLER, the magistrate b. 1606 d. 1660.

- John W. FOWLER b. 11/7/1846
  http://www.uftree.com/UFT/WebPages/JanetRowan/FOWLER98/index.htm
  Also RUNNING, HAIR, McCONNEL, DURHAM, ROWAN, SILKS, SWARTZ.

- FOY Family History
  http://www.tcarden.com/tree/foy/index.htm
  The Foys of Craven, Jones, & Onslow Counties, North Carolina, and their descendants.

- The FRAME Family
  http://www.phillipsplace.net/genealogy/surnames/frame.html
  Descendants of James Frame, who died 1754 in Augusta, moved steadily westward through Kentucky, Ohio, Indiana, and even on to Oregon. An emphasis in this family history is Jeremiah Frame and his descendants in Porter County, Indiana.

- FRANCEY Family Directory
  http://www.workerscomp.com/franceys/

- Descendants of John and Jane FRANCIS
  http://www.geocities.com/Heartland/Plains/4268/
  Including the FRANCIS/FRANCE Family Newsletter.

- The FRANCISCO Researcher
  mailto:rdsmyrna@aol.com
  E-mail Rick at rdsmyrna@aol.com for details on this newsletter.

- "The House of FRANCISCUS"
  mailto:jj@amug.org
  Book with over 7,200 descendants of Christophel Franciscus. E-mail Jan Johnson at jj@amug.org for lookups in this book - Francisco or Franciscus.

- Genealogy & Heraldry of the FRANCOM Family
  http://users.aol.com/mefrancom/genealogy/index.html

- FRANCKE Genealogie te Walcheren, Zeeland
  http://home.hccnet.nl/s.j.francke
  Familie Francke komt uit Zeeland, Pietr is de eerst bekende, hij woonde nabij Middelburg, omstreeks 1600.

- FRANKLIN Cousins Unite!
  http://www.geocities.com/Athens/Rhodes/3818/Franklincousins.htm

- FRANKLIN Family Researchers United
  http://freepages.genealogy.rootsweb.com/~ffru/
  Includes back issues of the newsletter, links to other FRANKLIN sites, registry of researchers and a queries page.

- FraserUK
  http://www.egroups.com/group/FraserUK
  A mailing list for people researching the surnames Fraser, Frazer, Frazier and other derivations in the U.K.

- FRAZER Family
  http://www.kenora.net/frazer
  Frazers living in Manitoba Canada, starting with Richard Patterson Frazer born 1818.

- Les Descendants des FRÉCHETTE, Inc.
  http://www.angelfire.com/ca/frechette/

- The FREDERICK Genealogy Home Page
  http://www.greatnorthern.net/~terryf/Frederick.html
  Descendants of John Frederick, born 12 Sept. 1787 and Mary Ann Easterday.

- Descendants of Franklin FREEMAN
  http://members.cftnet.com/stevew/freeman.htm
  Born 1815, died 1892 in Burlington, Vermont.

- The FREEMAN Repository and Research Center
  http://genweb.net/freeman/

- Descendants of John FREEMAN, Sr. of Bladen Co., NC b c 1775
  http://www.geocities.com/markfreemn/freemanj.html

- Gabriel and Lucy FREEMAN's Descendants
  http://www.wintektx.com/freeman/
  Gabriel born about 1770 in VA?, died Jan.31,1834 in GA?.

- FREER Family Genealogy Research
  http://home.cc.umanitoba.ca/~sfreer/

- Solomon FREER Family Association
  mailto:jfrog@hop-uky.campus.mci.net
  For details send e-mail to John H. Freer at jfrog@hop-uky.campus.mci.net.

- FREER / LOW Family Association
  http://members.aol.com/BethRN3CA/freerindex.html

- FREEZE & FRIES Family History
  http://www.geocities.com/Heartland/1134/
  From New Jersey in the early 1700s to everywhere in the present time.

- FRESHWATER Family Website
  http://www.freshwaters.co.uk
  FRESHWATER around the world.

- Heinrich FREY Family Association
  http://freepages.genealogy.rootsweb.com/~twiggins/

- The FRICANO Family
  http://www.fricano.com/
  The one and only Internet site for all Fricano's around the world.

- FRIEND Family Association of America
  http://pages.prodigy.com/MChipman/

- The FRIGGIERI Family Home Page
  http://www.familytreemaker.com/users/f/r/i/Vince-Friggieri
  Also be spelled as Frigeri, Frigieri or Friggeri.

- The FRIGGIERI Family Newsletter
  http://www.friggieri.com/index.html
  Published quarterly by Vince Friggieri.

- FRISTOE Genealogy
  http://www.mindspring.com/~fristoe/
  Fristo, Fristow, Fristowe, Frestow, Friston, etc.

- Die Geschichte der Familie FROBESE/FROBOSE / The History of the FROBESE/FROBOSE Family
  http://mitglied.tripod.de/froboesefamily/index.html

- The FROMM Family
  http://www.phillipsplace.net/genealogy/surnames/fromm.html
  History of the descendants of Frederick Fromm, who immigrated in 1737 and settled in Bern Township, Berks County, Pennsylvania.

- FRY, FRYE, FREY
  http://freepages.genealogy.rootsweb.com/~jtfmwm
  Descendants of Philip Martin FREY.

- FULBRIGHT Family Association
  http://www.concentric.net/~Mcclaran/fulbright.htm
  VOLLBRECHT - FULBRIGHT.

- FULKERSON Family History and Genealogy
  http://main.wavecom.net/~fulker/
  Researching the Fulkersons from colonial days to 1900, linking more than 80 Fulkerson cousins and assisting Unattached Branches.

- FULKERSON Surname Resource Center
  http://freepages.genealogy.rootsweb.com/~geneal/src/FulkSRC.html
  FULKERSON, VOLCKERTZSEN, VOLCKERTSEN, FOLKERTS, VOLKERTS and variations.

- Descendants of Cornelius FULLER of Upper Smithfield Twp., Northampton Co., Pa.
  http://www.uftree.com/UFT/WebPages/PaschkeP/FULLER2/index.htm
  His three sons Eli FULLER, Ira FULLER and Johiel FULLER migrated to Sussex Co, N.J. in the early 1800s. Descendant surnames include FULLER, COLE, LANNING, GUNN, COURTRIGHT.

- FULLER Family Tree - Descendants of Thomas FULLER
  http://homepages.ihug.co.nz/~jfuller/
  Ten generations of Fullers from East Kent England.

- The FULLER Society
  http://redrock.sedona.net/fullersociety
  Genealogy Society pertaining to Mayflower Pilgrims, Edward FULLER and his brother Dr. Samuel FULLER.

- Edward FULLER (Mayflower Passenger) Genealogy
  http://pages.prodigy.net/dave_lossos/cooper.htm

- FULTON Genealogy
  http://www.frontiernet.net/~elisa96/hirth/fulton.htm
  Genealogy of James FULTON b. 7 August 1739 in Dalkeith/Musselburgh, Scotland; died the 23 November 1824 in the Fulton Settlement, Bethel, Sullivan County, New York. Also includes general background information on the Fulton surname.

- The FULTZ Family Genealogy
  http://www.geocities.com/Heartland/1415/fultz.html
  Fultz, Fults, Fulce, Fulks, etc. In honor of the descendants of Obadiah Fults/z or see also the following site:

- Descendants of Obadiah FULKS-FULTZ 1765-1845--Home Page
  http://www.familytreemaker.com/users/f/u/l/Patrick-M-Fultz/index.html

- FUNNELL - One Name Study
  http://members.aol.com/funnellons/index.html

- The FUQUA Family Foundation
  http://www.concentric.net/~fuqua/

- FURBISH Family History
  http://users.abac.com/elfurb/

- FURR Family Web Page
  http://members.aol.com/bfurr1/index.html
  With over 5,000 descendants of Heinrich Furrer (Furr), mostly from North Carolina and Mississippi.

- The FURR Surname
  http://www.geocities.com/Heartland/Estates/5554
  This page contains the results of my many years of research of the descendants of Heinrich Furrer of Cabarrus County, North Carolina, including the Mississippi Furrs. Additions or corrections are welcomed. I have also collected some information on other Furr families, particularly the Virginia Furrs. I believe, but cannot prove, that there is a connection between the North Carolina and Virginia Furrs. I and other Furr researchers are also continuing our quest for the ancestors of Heinrich Furrer. There are two likey candidates, but so far no definitive, primary-source material to "prove" which one is correct.

- FUTCH Family Roots
  http://www.icsi.net/~gfutch/html/history.html
  Descendants of Jacob Futch, from Germany to North Carolina in 1709.

◆ Surname Mailing Lists

- "FA-FD" Surname Mailing Lists
  http://www.rootsweb.com/~jfuller/gen_mail_surnames-fa.html
  FAAS, FABER, FABIAN, FACEMIRE (includes Facemyer, Facemeyer, Fasemyer, Fasemeyer), FACKLER, FACKRELL, FAFFORD, FAGAN, FAHEY, FAILE (includes Fail, Fails), FAIN (includes Fayne, Fane, Fann, Fine, Few), FAIR (includes Fehr), FAIRBAIRN, FAIRBANKS, FAIRBANKS, FAIRBANKS, FAIRCHILD, FAIRCLOTH, FAIRCLOUGH, FAIRES, FAIRFAX, FAIRFEILD, FAIRFIELD, FAIRHURST, FAIRLEY, FAIRMAN, FAIRWEATHER (includes Fayrweather, Fayerweather), FAITH (includes Fate, Fait), FALCONER, FALES, FALIN (includes Fallin), FALK (includes Faulk, Falck), FALKNER, FALLA, FALLAVOLLITA, FALLER, FALLIS, FALLON, FALLS, FALVEY, FAMBRO (includes Fambrough), FAMOUS (includes Famos), FANCHER, FANN, FANNIN, FANNING, FANTOM (includes

Fantham, Fanton), FARBER, FARGESON, FARGO, FARIS, FARISH, FARLEY (includes Farler), FARLOW, FARMER, FARMER, FARMERIE (includes Farmarie, Firmery, Formery), FARNAM, FARNAN, FARNEY, FARNHAM, FARNI (includes Farney, Forney), FARNSWORTH (includes Fanef, Faneuf, Farneth, Farnworth, Phaneuf, Farneworth, Farnom, Farnot, Fearneworth,, Fearnoth, Fernworth), FARNSWORTH, FARNUM, FARQUHAR (includes Farquharson), FARR (includes Pharr, Far), FARRAND, FARRAR, FARRELL, FARRELLY, FARREN, FARRER, FARRINGTON, FARRIS (includes Faris, Faries, Pharris, Phares, Pharis), FARRIS, FARROW, FARTHING, FARWELL, FASNACHT (includes Fassnacht, Fosnacht, Fosnocht), FAST, FATULA, FAUBION (includes Fabion, Fawbian, Fabian), FAUGHN, FAULCONER, FAULK, FAULKENBERRY (includes Fortenberry), FAULKNER (includes Falconar, Falconer, Falkiner, Falkner, Faulconer, Faulknor, Folkner, Forkner, Fortner), FAUNCE, FAUNTLEROY, FAURE, FAUROT (includes Faurote, Ferote, Ferot, Fouratt), FAUST (includes Foust), FAVATA, FAWCETT (includes Faucett, Faucette), FAXON, FAY.

- "FE-FH" Surname Mailing Lists
  http://www.rootsweb.com/~jfuller/gen_mail_surnames-fe.html
  FEAGIN (includes Feagan, Fagin, Fagan), FEAKE, FEARN, FEARNE, FEARNOW, FEASTER, FEATHERS (includes Feather, Fetter, Fetters, Fether, Vetter), FEATHERSTONE (includes Featherston, Featherstonehaugh, Featherstonhaugh, Fetherstone, Fetherston,, Fetherstonehaugh, Fetherstonhaugh), FEE, FEELEY (includes Feely, Feeheley, Feehely, Feheley, Feehley, Feehily, Fehily, Fehely, Fehilly, Field), FEENEY, FEES, FEG, FEGAN, FEGLEY (includes Fagley, Figley, Voegeli), FEHR, FEIST, FELCH, FELDER, FELDMAN, FELDMANN, FELIX, FELIZ, FELKER, FELL, FELLER, FELLERS (includes G' Fellers, Gefellers, G. Fellers), FELLOWS, FELMINGHAM (includes Fellingham), FELPS, FELSBURG, FELSHAW, FELT, FELTER, FELTHAM, FELTNER, FELTON (includes Felten), FELTS, FELTY, FENDER, FENIX, FENN, FENNELL, FENNER, FENNIMORE (includes Fenimore), FENSTERMACHER, FENTON, FENTON, FENWICK, FERBER, FEREBEE, FERGERSON, FERGUS, FERGUSON (includes Fergesen, Fergerson, Furgusun, Fergersen), FERGUSON, FERGUSON (includes Farguson), FERGUSSON (includes Ferguson), FERLAND, FERMANIS, FERMOR, FERN, FERNALD (includes Furnald), FERNANDES, FERNANDEZ, FERNOR, FERRARA, FERRARI, FERREE (includes Fehree, Ferry, Fery, Fairy, Forry, Furry, Firry), FERREIRA, FERRELL, FERRIER, FERRIN (includes Farron, Farren, Fearrin), FERRIS, FERRY, FESSLER, FETTER, FETTERS, FETZER, FEW, FEWELL, FEY, FEYOCK.

- "FI-FN" Surname Mailing Lists
  http://www.rootsweb.com/~jfuller/gen_mail_surnames-fi.html
  FICHNER (includes Finchner), FICK, FICKE, FICKEISEN (includes Fickies, Fickeissen, Fickiesen, Fickerson), FICKLE (includes Fickel), FICKLIN, FICKLING (includes Ficklin, Ficklen), FIDDES, FIDDIE, FIDDLER (includes Fidler), FIDLER, FIEDLER, FIELD, FIELDER, FIELDING, FIELDS (includes Field), FIES (includes Fees, Fiess, Fiese, Feis, Feise, Feese), FIFE, FIFE, FIFIELD, FIGGERS (includes Figures, Figers, Figuars, Figge, Fegins, Fegans, Fegens, Feagans, Feagins, Feugers, Figgerst), FIGHTMASTER (includes Fight, Fite), FIKE (includes Fyke, Fykes), FILDES (includes Filds), FILER, FILES, FILKINS, FILLINGHAM, FILLMORE (includes Phillmore, Fillmour, Fillimore), FILLOON (includes O'Fallon, Fallon, Falloon), FILON, FILSON, FINCH (includes Fink, Feench, Funk, Wench, Venigs, Fenwick, McFince), FINCHER, FINCHNER, FINCK, FINDLAY, FINDLEY, FINE (includes Fein, Fyn, Vine, Fines), FINERTY,

FINGER, FINGERSON, FINK, FINKBEINER (includes Finkenbiner, Finkenbender), FINKBEINER, FINKE, FINKELSTEIN, FINKILL, FINKLE, FINLAY, FINLAYSON, FINLEY, FINN, FINNEGAN, FINNELL, FINNERTY (includes Finerty, Finarty, Finnarty, Fenerty, Fennerty, Fenarty, Fenaughty), FINNESETH, FINNEY (includes Finnie, Finny, Phinnie), FINNIE, FINNIGAN, FINNIS, FINSON, FIRESTONE, FIRTH, FISCHBACH, FISCHER, FISCUS, FISH, FISHBURN, FISHENDEN (includes Fessenden, Fisenden, Fissenden, Vyshenden), FISHER (includes Fischer), FISHER, FISK, FISKE (includes Fisk), FITCH (includes Fitche, Fytche, de Montifitchet), FITCHETT (includes Fitchet), FITE, FITTS, FITZ, FITZ-RANDOLPH (includes Fitz Ralph, Fitz Ranulf), FITZALAN, FITZER, FITZGERALD (includes Fitzgearld, Fitz-Gerald), FITZHUGH (includes Fitchew), FITZMAURICE, FITZPATRICK, FITZRANDOLPH, FITZSIMMONS, FITZWATER, FITZWILLIAM, FIVEASH (includes Fiveashe, Fivash, Fireash, Viveash), FIVEASH (includes Fiveashe, Fivash, Fireash, Viveash), FIX, FLACK, FLAGG (includes Flegg), FLAHERTY, FLAKE, FLANAGAN, FLANARY, FLANDERS, FLANIGAN, FLANNERY, FLANNIGAN, FLATER (includes Flatter, Flitter, Fletter, Flutter), FLATT, FLAVEL (includes Flavell, Favill, Flamville, Flannel, Flamwell), FLAX (includes Flacks, Flaks), FLEAGLE (includes Flagle, Fliegel, Fluegel), FLECK, FLEENOR, FLEET, FLEETWOOD, FLEISCHER, FLEISCHMANN, FLEISHER, FLEMING, FLEMMING, FLESCHER, FLESHER (includes Flescher, Fleisher, Fleischer), FLESHMAN, FLETCHER, FLETT, FLEURY, FLEWELLING, FLEWWELLING (includes Flewellen, Flewellyn, Fluallen), FLICK, FLICKINGER, FLIGHT, FLINCHUM (includes Flincham, Flinchem, Finchem, Finchum, Fincham), FLINK, FLINN (includes Flin, Fline, Flyn, Fling), FLINT (includes Flynt, Flinte, Flintt), FLINT, FLIPPO, FLOCK (includes Floch, Flach), FLOHR (includes Floor, Flor), FLOOD, FLOOK (includes Fluck, Fluke), FLORA (includes Flory, Fleury, Florin, Flori, Floray, Flury, Florea, Florey), FLORENCE, FLORES, FLORITY, FLORY, FLORY (includes Flora, Fleury), FLOURNOY, FLOWER, FLOWERS, FLOYD, FLUHR (includes Fluehr, Flur, Fluer), FLY, FLYNN (includes Flinn, O'Flynn, Flin), FLYNT.

- **"FO-FQ" Surname Mailing Lists**
  http://www.rootsweb.com/~jfuller/gen_mail_surnames-fo.html
  FOALE, FOARD, FOCHT, FODEN, FODNESS, FOERSTER, FOGARTY, FOGEL, FOGG, FOGLE, FOISSET (includes Foisett, Foissett, Foissette, Foisette, Foisete, Fuset, Fusset), FOLAND (includes Folland, Folant, Wohland, Yoland, Volland), FOLEY, FOLGER, FOLK, FOLLANSBEE, FOLLETT, FOLLOWELL, FOLSOM (includes Fulsom, Folsum, Folsome, Folson, Foulsham, Folsham), FOLTZ, FOLWELL (includes Follwell, Fulwell, Fowel, Fowle), FONDA, FONDREN, FONES, FONTAINE, FONTENOT, FONTENOT (includes Fonteneau), FONVILLE (includes Fonvielle), FOOKS, FOORD, FOOSE, FOOT, FOOTE (includes Foot), FORAN, FORBES, FORBIIS, FORBIS, FORCE (includes Forse, Fors, Vorce, La Force, De La Force), FORD, FORDE, FORDHAM, FORDYCE (includes Fordice, Fordise), FORDYCE, FORE, FOREHAND, FOREMAN, FOREPAUGH (includes Forbach, Vorbach), FOREST, FORESTER, FOREY (includes Forry, Forrey, Foray), FORGEY, FORMAN, FORNEY, FORQUER (includes Forker), FORQUERANN, FORREN, FORREST (includes Forrester, Forest, Forist, Foraster, Faust, Corstorphine), FORRESTER, FORSBERG, FORSHEE, FORSTER, FORSYTH, FORSYTHE (includes Forsyth, Forsithe), FORT, FORTENBERRY, FORTENBERRY, FORTIER, FORTIER, FORTIN, FORTNER.

FORTNEY, FORTSON, FORTUNE (includes LaFortune), FORWOOD, FOSDICK, FOSHEE, FOSS, FOSTER (includes Forster), FOSTER, FOTHERGILL, FOTHERGILL (includes Forthergil), FOTHERINGHAM (includes Fothringham, Fotherham), FOUGHTY (includes Fouty, Foutty), FOULK, FOUNTAIN, FOUNTAINE (includes de la Fountaine, Fountain, Fontain), FOURDRAINE, FOURNIER, FOUST, FOUTCH (includes Fouch, Fouche), FOUTS, FOUTZ, FOWERS, FOWLE, FOWLER (includes Fouller), FOWLES, FOX (includes Fuchs), FOX, FOX, FOXHALL (includes Foxall), FOXWELL, FOY.

- **"FR-FT" Surname Mailing Lists**
  http://www.rootsweb.com/~jfuller/gen_mail_surnames-fr.html
  FRAILEY, FRAIN, FRAKER, FRAKES, FRALEY, FRAME, FRAMPTON, FRANCE, FRANCIOSI, FRANCIS, FRANCIS, FRANCISCO, FRANCK, FRANCO, FRANCOEUR, FRANCOIS, FRANK, FRANKE, FRANKENFIELD (includes Frankenfeld), FRANKENSTEIN, FRANKLIN, FRANKS (includes Frank, Francks), FRANKSEN, FRANKUM, FRANTZ (includes Frantzin), FRANTZ, FRANZ, FRANZEN, FRAPPIER (includes Frappie, Frapier), FRARY, FRASER, FRASIER, FRATER, FRAY, FRAZEE, FRAZER, FRAZIER (includes Frasier, Frazer, Fraser), FREAS, FRECHETTE, FRED, FREDERICK, FREDERICKS, FREE, FREEBODY, FREEBURN, FREEBURY, FREED, FREEDMAN, FREELAND, FREELS, FREEMAN, FREENY (includes Fryney), FREER, FREESE, FREESTONE, FREEZE, FREGOE, FREILING (includes Freyling, Fruhling, Fruyling, Veryling, Freeling), FREITAG, FRENCH, FRERICHS (includes Frereks, Frerick, Frerich), FRERICKS, FRESHOUR, FRETWELL, FRETZ, FREUND, FREW, FREY, FRIBERG, FRICK, FRICK, FRICKE, FRICKER, FRIDAY, FRIED, FRIEDBERG (includes Frieberg, Freeberg, Frieburg), FRIEDLANDER, FRIEDMAN (includes Friedmann, Freeman, Freedman), FRIEDRICH, FRIEL, FRIELINGHAUS, FRIEND, FRIER, FRIES, FRINK, FRISBIE, FRISBY, FRISCH, FRITH, FRITSCH, FRITTS, FRITZ, FRIZZELL (includes Frizzel, Frizell, Frizel, Frizzle, Frizle), FRKOVICH (includes Frkovic), FROCK (includes Frack, Fruck), FROELICH, FROESCHLE, FROGGE, FROMAN (includes Frohman), FROMKE, FROMMHERZ (includes Fromherz, Fromhercz, Fromhart, Fromhartz), FROSHOUR, FROSIG (includes Frøsig, Frysig), FROST, FRUGAR, FRUGE (includes Ferger, Fruget, Fruger), FRUIT, FRY (includes Frei, Frye, Frey), FRYAR (includes Fryer, Friar, Frier), FRYBERGER, FRYE, FRYER, FRYMAN.

- **"FU-FZ" Surname Mailing Lists**
  http://www.rootsweb.com/~jfuller/gen_mail_surnames-fu.html
  FUCHS, FUCICH, FUDGE (includes Futch), FUERST, FUGATE, FUHRMAN, FUHRMANN, FULBRIGHT (includes Fullbright, Fulbrite, Fulbrecht), FULCHER, FULFORD, FULGHAM, FULK, FULKERSON, FULKS, FULLER, FULLER, FULLERTON, FULLMER (includes Fulmer, Follmer, Vollmer), FULLUCK (includes Fullock), FULMER (includes Fullmer, Folmer, Follmer, Vollmer), FULTON, FULTON, FULTS, FULTZ, FUNDERBURK, FUNK, FUNKHOUSER, FUNKIE, FUQUA, FURBUSH, FURBY (includes Ferriby, Ferrabee, Firby, Furiby), FURCHES (includes Furchess), FUREY, FURGERSON, FURLONG, FURMAN, FURNESS, FURNESS, FURR, FURR, FURRY, FURST, FUSON, FUSSELL, FUTCH, FUTRELL, FUTRILL (includes Futrille, Futral, Futrell, Fewtral), FYFE, FYFE (includes Fyff, Fife, Phyfe, Fyffe), FYKE.

SURNAMES, FAMILY ASSOCIATIONS & FAMILY NEWSLETTERS – "G"

Resources Dedicated to One Surname
http://www.cyndislist.com/surn-g.htm

Category Index:
◆ General Surname Sites and Resources
◆ Surname Specific Sites and Resources
◆ Surname Mailing Lists

◆ General Surname Sites and Resources

● Connect with Surnames - G
http://www.geocities.com/Heartland/Bluffs/7708/g.html

● Dutch Home Pages by Familyname ~ Letter G
http://members.tripod.com/~Don_Arnoldus/g.htm

● FamilyHistory.com - Message Boards - Surname - G
http://www.familyhistory.com/messages/list.asp?prefix=GA

● Family Tree Maker Online User Home Pages - G
http://www.familytreemaker.com/users/g/index.html

● Family Workings G Surname Links
http://www.familyworkings.com/links/surg.htm

● GenConnect Surname Index - "G"
http://genconnect.rootsweb.com/indx/surnames/G.html
Message boards sponsored by RootsWeb. Each surname message board set is divided into the following topics: Queries, Bibles, Biographies, Deeds, Obituaries, Pensions, Wills.

● Genealogy Resources on the Internet - "GA-GD" Surname Mailing Lists
http://www.rootsweb.com/~jfuller/gen_mail_surnames-ga.html
"GE-GH"
http://www.rootsweb.com/~jfuller/gen_mail_surnames-ge.html
"GI-GN"
http://www.rootsweb.com/~jfuller/gen_mail_surnames-gi.html
"GO-GQ"
http://www.rootsweb.com/~jfuller/gen_mail_surnames-go.html"GRA-GRD"
http://www.rootsweb.com/~jfuller/gen_mail_surnames-gra.html
"GRE-GRH"
http://www.rootsweb.com/~jfuller/gen_mail_surnames-gre.html
"GRI-GRN"
http://www.rootsweb.com/~jfuller/gen_mail_surnames-gri.html
"GRO-GRT"
http://www.rootsweb.com/~jfuller/gen_mail_surnames-gro.html
"GRU-GT"
http://www.rootsweb.com/~jfuller/gen_mail_surnames-gru.html

"GU-GZ"
http://www.rootsweb.com/~jfuller/gen_mail_surnames-gu.html
Search the index of Surname Mailing Lists below: Surname Mailing Lists.

○ Genealogy Resources on the Internet - Surnames Included in Mailing Lists - "G"
http://www-personal.umich.edu/~cgaunt/surnames/g.names.html
This is a computer generated list of the surnames, and all variant spellings for those names, that are found in the surname mailing lists detailed on the pages shown above.

● Genealogy Resources on the Internet - Surname Web Sites for "G" Surnames
http://www-personal.umich.edu/~cgaunt/surnames/g.html

● Genealogy's Most Wanted - Surnames Beginning with "G"
http://www.citynet.net/mostwanted/g.htm

● Google Web Directory .... Genealogy>Surnames>G
http://directory.google.com/Top/Society/Genealogy/Surnames/G/

● 'G' Surnames at RootsWeb
http://resources.rootsweb.com/surnames/g.html

● Heartland Genealogy Society Membership List - G
http://www.geocities.com/Heartland/Ranch/2416/hgs-mlist-g.html

● H-GIG Surname Registry - Surnames Beginning G
http://www.ucr.edu/h-gig/surdata/surname7.html

● Higginson Book Company - Surnames Beginning with G
http://www.higginsonbooks.com/g.htm

● inGeneas Table of Common Surname Variations and Surname Misspellings - F-G
http://www.ingeneas.com/F2G.html

● The Obituary Link Page - Family Obituary Archives Online - G
http://www.geocities.com/~cribbswh/obit/g.htm

● Open Directory - Society: Genealogy: Surnames: G
http://www.dmoz.org/Society/Genealogy/Surnames/G/

- Surname Springboard Index - G
  http://www.geocities.com/~alacy/spring_g.htm

- SurnameWeb Surname Registry - G Index
  http://www.surnameweb.org/registry/g.htm

- SWINX Zoeklijst Nederlandse Familienamen /
  SWINX Searchlist Dutch Surnames - G
  http://www.swinx.net/swinx/swinx_ga_nl.htm

- Websites at RootsWeb: G Surnames
  http://www.rootsweb.com/~websites/surnames/g.html

◆ Surname Specific Sites and Resources

- Genealogische Website van Johan GAAL
  http://www.geocities.com/Heartland/Flats/6768/
  Genealogie en kwartierstaat GAAL en aanverwanten.

- GABLE Family of the South
  http://www.familytreemaker.com/users/g/a/b/Carl-I-Gable/index.html
  Descendants of John Henry GABLE, who immigrated to Saxe-Gotha Township, SC, in 1747.

- GAGE Genealogies
  http://www.geocities.com/Heartland/Meadows/8824/
  Descendants of William GAGE of Freetown, MA.

- Rev. John F. GAGNIER
  http://home.eznet.net/~jgagnier/
  GAGNIER, GAGNE.

- The GAINES Place
  http://www.geocities.com/Heartland/Plains/7221/

- The GAINFORTH Name in Ireland, Ontario, and Michigan
  http://members.aol.com/sherryew/Gainforth/gain.html
  Ancestry and descendants of Thomas and Margaret (Hatchell) Gainforth of Wexford, Ireland. Son Thomas emigrated to Ontario in 1815. Related names: Adlam. Bull, VanHorn, Bell, Dennis, Currey, Butler.

- GAIR Genealogy - Descendants - 1800, MDX, ENG
  http://www.itmagic.demon.co.uk/genealogy/gair.htm
  Descendants of William GAIR (1836-?) and Hannah JOHNSON.

- All GAITHER's in America
  http://home.inreach.com/calcoca/family.htm

- The Clan GALBRAITH
  http://www.tartans.com/clans/Galbraith/galbraith.html
  Calbreath, Colbreath, Culbreath, Galbreath, Gilbreath, Gilreath, Kilbreath, Kulbeth and other variant spellings.

- Clann O'GALLCHOBHAIR (GALLAGHER) World-Wide
  http://home.rmci.net/ogollaher/
  The "virtual Tir Chonnaill" of the ancient Irish clann O'GLLCHOBHAIR, including GALLAGHER, GALLAHER, GOLLAHER, GOLLIHER, GALLAHUE, etc.

- The GALLIHUGH Family
  http://www.geocities.com/~gallihugh/
  Descendents of Sarah (SARY) GALLOHUGH, through her GALLIHUGH sons, from Michigan and Virginia.

- GAMBLE Family Surname UK Research
  http://www.gambles.org.uk/
  Information on the origin of the Gamble surname and links to reference sites in England, Wales, Scotland, Ireland and across the world.

- GAMBLE / GAMBILL Research Group Home Page
  http://www.vabch.com/kyarberr/GRGhome.html
  Genealogy Home Page of GAMBILL Research Group including researchers investing the Gamble, Gambill, Gambrel, Gambrell, Gamel, Gambol families including variations.

- The GANDER One-Name Study
  http://www.gander.cjb.net/
  One-Name Study of the GANDER surname, mostly of British or British origin and includes much GANDAR information; includes Births, Marriages and Deaths Registrations for England and Wales for GANDER/GANDAR 1837-1900; also descriptions of Hoop Bender and Carmen occupations; also Des Gander's TILL and BURT families.

- GANDY Gathering Genealogy
  http://www.geocities.com/Heartland/Pointe/1462/

- GANTTREES Newsletter
  mailto:bengantt@hal-pc.org
  E-mail Ben GANTT at bengantt@hal-pc.org for subscription details. Covers the Gant(t), Gent, Gaun(t) families in the U.S.

- Gènèalogie des GARCEAU Genealogy
  http://www.firstcontact.com/garceau/
  Association des Descendants de Jean Garceau dit Tranchemontagne (ADJG-T), who arrived in French Acadia in 1698.

- GARDNER-GARDINER Family
  http://members.theglobe.com/Lauralerner/GARDNERS.HTM
  Family genealogy in Massachusetts, Rhode Island and England. Includes photos of land and gravesites, cemetery records, some Shaker Census Information (1790-1870).

- Les Familles GAREAU
  http://www.genealogie.org/famille/gareau/gareau.htm
  An association of GAREAUs, descendants of the 5 main stocks, aimed on genealogy and history of the GAREAUs. (FranÁais - English).

- GARREN Goodies Online
  http://www.brinet.com/~garren/
  Descendants of Garren families from colonial Rowan (now Davidson and Randolph) County, North Carolina.

- GARRETT World Wide Genealogy
  http://clubs.yahoo.com/clubs/garrettsworldwidegenealogy

- GARSTFamily.com - GARST Genealogy and Family Research Center
  http://www.geocities.com/Heartland/Bluffs/8855/
  Extensive GARST/GERST genealogy files and pictures for download, Y2K reunion information.

- GARTMAN GIRTMAN Family Resource Page
  http://homepages.rootsweb.com/~rickman/index.htm

- GASKILL Genealogy
http://clubs.yahoo.com/clubs/gaskillgenealogy
Also related surnames (e.g. GASCOYNE).

- GASSIOT Family Genealogy Site
http://members.nbci.com/gassiots/Chuck.html
Gassiot, Gassiott, Gasiot.

- GASTON Crier Homepage
http://mvn.net/genealogy/GastonCrier.htm
GASTON Crier homepage is for anyone researching the GASTON surname.

- GASTON Family Main Site Information Netpage
http://mvn.net/genealogy/Gaston.htm
GASTON Archive is for anyone researching the GASTON surname.

- GASTWIRTH, GASWIRTH, GASWORTH Website
http://www.gastwirth.com/

- The GATENBYs of Yorkshire
http://www.gatenby.freeserve.co.uk
Includes MIDGLEY, ROBINSON, BARKER.

- GATLIN Surname Resource Center
http://freepages.genealogy.rootsweb.com/~geneal/src/Gatlin SRC.html

- The GAUDREAU Genealogy Page
http://www.gaudreau.org/arthur/genealogy/gaudreau.sht
Gaudreau, Gaudreault, Gautras, Gautreau, Geaudreau, Godereau, Godrault, Godreau, Godreault, Gotereau, Gotreau, Gottrau, Gottreau, Goudreau.

- GAUER Family Home Page
http://users.uniserve.com/~morbeus
The Gauer surname is very unusual. Gauer folks are related in some way. This is a collection of everything I have been able to find about people with the Gauer surname. Gauers started in Germany but can now be found all over the world. If you have a Gauer anywhere in your family history this is the place to look.

- GAUNT / GAUNTT / GANT / GANTT Families Page
http://www-personal.umich.edu/~cgaunt/Gaunt/gaunt.html

- Association de Genealogie des Familles GAUTHIER / GAUTHIER Family Genealogical Association
http://www.iquebec.com/gauthierfam/

- Association familles GAUTHIER
http://association.gauthier.est-ici.org/
Worldwide association for genealogical research of the patronym Gautheir, Gautier, Gaultier.

- GAUTHIER Family Tree
http://members.tripod.com/~cheysmom/gauthier.html
The Gauthier Family tree is full of Gauthier Surname history. Learn what the coat of arms looks like, its description and how it became. Learn about the history behind our surname. View my family line, other Gauthier researchers query's, post your query and more.

- GAWTHROP Families of America
http://www.gawthrop.org/

- The GDULA Genealogy
http://members.tripod.com/gdula

- GEDDIE World, The Worldwide Geddie Family Page
http://www.booksphere.com/gedworld/

- GEEnealogy - Genealogy of the GEE Family
http://www2.arkansas.net/~mgee/genealo.html

- GEESEY Family Tree
http://www.uftree.com/UFT/WebPages/BAGeesey/GEESEY/index.htm
Descendants of Peter GYSI (b. 1565, Switzerland) and especially Conradt GIESE (b. 1718), immigrant to York Co., PA in 1741. Surnames: GEESEY, GIESE, GYSI, KEESEY.

- Firstborn Sons of the GEHLING Family
http://www.geocities.com/Heartland/Bluffs/8479
Biographies and descendants of six firstborn sons of this midwestern family. Connecting links to the Timp, Schirck, Wernimont, Reiling, Reinart and Garciat families.

- GEHREN (or GERHEN, GHEREN, GHERREN, GUEHREN, GHUERREN)
http://www.geocities.com/Heartland/Bluffs/2945/
This is the home-page of GEHREN family in Brazil. Its objective is: to set up the lineage of Stephan GEHREN and Ana Maria GORGES, to show Stephan GEHREN ascendancy, to tell the history of this couple of emigrants that left Germany in the century XIX, to explain the reason of the large variety of graphs of this surname, a large integration of the family.

- GEIGER Genealogical Site
http://home.hetnet.nl/~tomirene/index.html
Dutch family.

- The GEISWEID Family Archives
http://www.geocities.com/ResearchTriangle/1155/
Research to family members world wide since 1976. May spellings exist, such as Geijsweijt, Geistweit, Geistwhite, Guisewite, Gisewhite, Guiswite, Guistwhite, Geisewite, Geiswite many others. Also, genealogies and biographies of related families are kept in the Archive.

- GENUNG / GANONG / GANUNG / GANOUNG Home Page
http://www.familytreemaker.com/users/g/e/n/Norman-B-Genung/index.html
Descendants of Jean Guenon (1640-1714), a French Huguenot.

- GEORGE Family Webpage
http://geocities.com/Heartland/Ridge/9153
GEORGE in Allegheny, PA and East Liverpool, OH areas back to the eighteenth century. Other names: Shellaby, Gill, Cochran.

- Descendants of Reuben and Ann (Handley) GEORGE
http://www.rootsweb.com/~moandrew/george/reub-1.html
Married in 1797, Greenbrier Co, WV; lived in Monroe Co, WV; moved to Butler Co, OH about 1810.

- GERAGHTY World Genealogy
mailto:williamm@4dcomm.com
For details on this group, send e-mail to williamm@4dcomm.com.

- The MUMBY - GERAGHTY Family History Project
  http://www.ionline.net/~djm/
  Conducting personal genealogy research and a one name study of Mumby, (Lincolnshire, England), and Geraghty, (Ireland), including the origins of the names.

- GERGEL / GURGEL / GARGEL / GERGLE / GURGLE / GORGEL / GERGAL
  http://homepages.go.com/~gergelfamilytree/gergel familytree.html

- GERHARDSTEIN Home Page
  http://gerhardstein.org/

- GEROW Family Association
  http://members.xoom.com/Gerow.1/

- GERRANS Kin FHS
  http://www.geocities.com/Athens/4725/

- GERSTENBERGER Genealogy Home Page - The GERSTENBERGER Immigrants and Their Descendants in America
  http://members.aol.com/gerstdf/
  A Compendium of Vital Statistics by Duane Francis Gerstenberger, M.D., MPH, and Ruthelma Millie Vedder Gerstenberger.

- The Descendants of Antoine GEVAUDAN
  http://www.zoomnet.net/~cdmiller/gevaudan
  History of the French Huguenot, Antoine GEVAUDAN, Manakintowne, VA starting in 1700. Also Jividen, Gividen, Gevedon, Gevaudan.

- The GEYER Family: Germans from Russia
  http://www.angelfire.com/ny/earthstar/geyer.html
  Descendants of Frederick W. C. Geyer, born about 1808 and his wife Margaret, born about 1813.

- Thomas GIBBS Association
  mailto:ctjesters@aol.com
  For all descendants of Thomas Gibbs (ca 1615-1693) of Sandwich, Massachusetts. Contact Stephanie Allen by e-mail at ctjesters@aol.com.

- GIBNEY One-Name Study Homepage
  http://www.geocities.com/heartland/cottage/1358
  One name study of GIBNEY surname and variant spellings, Gibboney, Giboney, Gibny, McGibney, etc. Has searchable database with memos, sources, endnotes and bibliography.

- The GIBSON Family from New York State's Hudson River Valley
  http://members.aol.com/GibbJ/index.html

- The GIBSON Family Tree
  http://www.geocities.com/Heartland/Meadows/6579/
  Descendants of William Gibson, born ca. 1700.

- GIBSON Home Page - Gathering GIBSONs Newsletter
  http://members.aol.com/Kinseeker6/gibson.html

- GIDEON's Trumpet - The GIDEON Genealogy Home Page
  http://members.tripod.com/~rootbound/index.html

- GIERING Family Trees
  http://www.giering-family-trees.org/
  A site identifying GIERINGs (spelling variants include GUEHRING and GĐHRING) around the world, including medical history information.

- GILBERTHORPE One-Name-Study
  http://www.geocities.com/Heartland/Oaks/7033

- Alexander GILCREASE, GILCHRIST, GILCHREST, KILCREASE
  http://freepages.genealogy.rootsweb.com/~gilcrease

- GILINSKY
  http://www.aldrington.freeserve.co.uk/
  This family originated in Eastern Europe. Galanski, Galansky, Galinski, Galinsky, Gilinski, Gilinsky, Glinski, Glinsky.

- GILLETTE, GILLETT, GILLET, GILET, GILETT
  http://members.tripod.com/~RobertGillette/GILLETTE_FOR_GILLETTES.htm

- GILLIGANs in New England
  http://www.angelfire.com/ma2/Gilligan

- GILTRAP Family History Pages
  http://www.giltrap.junglelink.co.uk/
  Descendants of Henry GILTRAP and more.

- GINDLESPERGER Family History Association
  http://homepages.rootsweb.com/~gfha/
  Descendants of Ulrich Gindlesperger who came to America September 15, 1749.

- The GIRDLER Family
  http://www.girdler.com/

- GIRLING Family Search
  http://members.tripod.co.uk/JGirling/girling.html
  Most Girlings originate in the English counties of Norfolk, Essex and Suffolk.

- The GIROUARD Family Tree
  http://www.girouard.org/

- The GIROUX Surname Resource Center
  http://www.crosswinds.net/~tagiroux/girouxsrc/girouxsrc.htm

- GITTINS Genealogy
  http://dspace.dial.pipex.com/gittins/ancestry/index.htm
  Gittins, Gittens, Gittings, Gettings, Gettens, Gitton, Gittons, Gethin, Gyttyn, Guttine.

- Searching GIVNEY Names
  http://www.geocities.com/Heartland/Estates/4121/

- GLADNEY Home Page
  http://members.aol.com/retteacher/gladney.html
  In South Carolina, descendants of Richard GLADNEY, b. ca. 1670 Res. Kinbally, Skerry Parish, Antrim, IRELAND.

- The Origins of the GLENDINNINGs
  http://user.itl.net/~glen/glendinningorigins.html

- GLENISTER Family History and Worldwide One Name Study
  http://www.glenister.demon.co.uk/

- **GLIDEWELL Genealogy Page**
  http://www.micro.com/~sfitzg/index.html
  GLIDEWELL of Virginia, Indiana, Missouri, other places. Judd, Earles, Sayre, Fitzgibbons, Gibbons, Stewart, Harrison, Hubbard, Goode.

- **The GLINES Family**
  http://www.usgenealogy.com/glines/
  The GLINES family came to America from the United Kingdom, some in the 17th century. These pages are the results of research by many people, mostly descendants of the earliest Glines in America.

- **GLOVER Genealogy**
  http://members.aol.com/diannegl33/GloverPages/Glover1.html
  Wills, land, Bible, marriage, military, census & immigration records, family trees, researchers and connections.

- **The GLOWACKI Family Tree - (GLOW, GLOWASKI, GRANT)**
  http://www.geocities.com/glowackifamilytree/
  Descendants of Antonius Glowacki and Katarzyna Pylypyc.

- **GOAD Genealogy Site**
  http://www.rootsweb.com/~mikegoad/goad.htm
  GOAD surname and variations: GOADE, GOARD, GOARDE, GORD (primarily North America).

- **The Unofficial GOBER Home Pages**
  http://www.goberfamily.org/Goberxxx/
  For general and specific genealogical data on the descendants of William Gober 1718 - 1794.

- **GOBLE Genealogy Homepage**
  http://members.aol.com/goblenews/homepage/index.htm
  A one name study sponsored by Goble Family Association, which includes English, German, Irish and unconnected Goble, Gobel, Gable, Gobble, Gobbell, Goeble and variations.

- **GOCHENOUR Genealogy**
  http://web2.airmail.net/wagoch/gene.htm
  From the editor of the "The Trail Seekers" newsletter for Gochenour/Coughenour/Gochnauer.

- **Descendants of Thomas J. GODARD**
  http://www2.arkansas.net/~jgoddard/
  Thomas was born in Tennessee about 1824.Tennessee > DeKalb County, Alabama > Craighead County, Arkansas > Scott County, Missouri.

- **The GODBOUT Genealogy**
  http://people.ne.mediaone.net/godbout/index.html
  Godbouts, Goodbouts, Godebouts, Gaudbouts.

- **The GODDARD Association's Homepage**
  http://www.eese.qut.edu.au/~mgoddard/gae_gaa1.htm

- **GODWIN Research**
  http://clubs.yahoo.com/clubs/godwinresearch

- **GODWIN Genealogy, Family History and Surname Research**
  http://homepages.rootsweb.com/~godwin/surname/
  Includes Godwyn, Godwine, Godin, Gadwin.

- **The GOFF/GOUGH Family Page**
  http://www.inmind.com/people/dcooper/

- **GOLDER / GOULDER / GOLDEN Family Genealogy Listings**
  http://www.facstaff.bucknell.edu/goldcoop/geneal.html
  Descendants of William Golder, born 1613 in Ireland, died 1680, Long Island, NY.

- **The All GOLDFARB Site**
  http://www.mrbig.com/goldhome2.html

- **GOMERY / GOMMERY / GOMRY and GUMERY / GUMMERY / GUMRY Genealogy**
  http://freepages.genealogy.rootsweb.com/~gomery/
  GOMARY, GOMBERY, GOMBERRY, GOMBREY, GOMBRY, GOMBURY, GOMEREY, GOMEROY, GOMMERY, GOMREY, GOMRY, GOOMBERY, GOOMBURY, GUMARY, GUMBARY, GUMBERY, GUMBERRY, GUMBREY, GUMBRY, GUMBUREY, GUMBURY, GUMEREY, GUMERY, GUMMARY, GUMMERY, GUMREY, GUMRY.

- **The Descendents of Isaac GOOD, Sr.**
  http://www.angelfire.com/in/isaacgood
  Isaac GOOD, Sr. (1800-1900) of Rochester, Fulton County, Indiana and his descendants.

- **The GOOD Family**
  http://www.phillipsplace.net/genealogy/surnames/good.html
  History of Jacob Good and Eve Mosser of York and Washington Counties, Pennsylvania as well as Tuscarawas County, Ohio.

- **The GOODCHAP Family Home Page**
  http://www.familytreemaker.com/users/g/o/o/Frederick-G-Goodchap/
  Researching GOODCHAP worldwide.

- **Fran's Genealogy Adventure - The GOODENOW's**
  http://www.geocities.com/~deskin/
  Goodenow, Goodnow, Goodno, Goodenough, Goodnough.

- **The GOODMAN Family**
  http://www.bcpl.net/~dmg/goodman.html
  With a clearinghouse for all people researching GOODMAN.

- **GOODSON Family History Site**
  http://www.goodson-family.com

- **GOOTEE Genealogy**
  http://www.ecosinc.com/gootee/

- **The Descendants of Arne Henriksen GOPLEN**
  http://www.familytreemaker.com/users/g/o/p/Lawrence-M-Goplen/

- **The GORBY Family History and Genealogy**
  http://w3.one.net/~thegorb/index.htm
  The US Descendants of Samuel GORBY born ca1700 in England. The Canadian & Irish Descendants of Joseph GORBY born ca1800 in Ireland.

- **The GORDON Family Tree**
  http://www.angelfire.com/tn/gordongenealogy
  Genealogy of Alexander GORDON born King William Co., SC about 1755, died 1831, married Sarah LEE, fought in Rev. War His descendants migrated to Kentucky, Arkansas, Texas and Tennessee. Surnames: Lee, King, Morgan, Walton, Chambers, Armstrong, McPherson.

- House of GORDON, Clan GORDON USA
  http://www.HouseOfGordon.com/

- House of GORDON, Georgia
  http://www.geocities.com/Heartland/5917/HOG.htm

- The GORE Family Connection
  http://www.yucca.net/jglocke/

- GORSHA Family Homepage (Slovenian surname
  GORSE ad variants like GORSHA, GORSHE)
  http://www.angelfire.com/wa/gorsha/
  *1920 Census transcriptions and index for Gilbert, Minnesota (in
  progress, currently 350 individuals). Surname indices for articles on
  history of Cleveland, Ohio and Maple Heights, Ohio.*

- GORSLINE Family Surname Genealogy
  http://members.aol.com/lyngperry/gorsline
  Also GORSSLINE, GORSALINE, GOSLINE, GOSLIN, GOSSELIN.

- GOSE Descendants Page
  http://members.tripod.com/~GoseDescendants/index.html
  Descendants of Stephan GOSE (GOOS) 1719 to Present.

- GOSSETT/GOSSET Genealogy
  http://members.surfsouth.com/~fgossett/

- GOTCHER Family Home Page
  http://www.wsu.edu:8080/~giles/gotcher/gotcher.htm
  *Variations: Goacher, Goatcher, Gochar, Gocher, Gotcher,
  Goucher.*

- GOTTSCH Family History
  http://www.angelfire.com/ne/gottschfamily/
  A history of the Gottsch family 1800 to present day.

- GOTTSEGEN Family Home Page
  http://www.ccil.org/~jcg/home.html

- The Alfred W. GOUCHER Home Page
  http://homestead.juno.com/algouch/goucher.html
  *Descendants of George W. Goucher born 30 Aug. 1840 in Green
  Brier, Indiana.*

- The GOULD Family in America
  http://www.orbitworld.net/blgould/genealog.html
  Gold, Goold, Goolde, Goole, Gould, Gowle.

- Jan GOULEVITCH, DFC
  http://home.st.net.au/~dunn/goolie.htm
  *Born 21 Feb 1919 in Blagoveshschensk in Siberia, died 24 Dec
  1994 in Townsville, Australia.*

- GOURDIN-GOURDINE Family Association
  http://www.blackcamisards.com/gourdin/index.html
  A French-African-American Family from South Carolina.

- The GOVERNALE Family
  http://www.governalefamily.com/
  *Governale, Governali, Governoli, Governole or Governal. Also
  looking for Grasso, Setticase, Stabile, Castro and more.*

- GOWEN Research Foundation
  http://www.llano.net/gowen/
  *Gowen, Gowen, Gowan, Gowans, Gowing, Goin, Going, Goins,
  Goings, Gooing, Goan, Goan, Goen, Goens, Gowin, Gowins,
  Goyne, Goynes, Guyne, Guynes.*

- The GRACEY Family webpage
  http://members.tripod.com/~graceyline/
  *Descendants of William GRACEY and Agness CRAIG of Northern
  Ireland.*

- The Clan GRAHAM Society
  http://www.clan-graham-society.org/

- The GRAHAM Family Page
  http://www.spessart.com/users/ggraham/graham1.htm

- GRAHAM Home Page - GRAHAM Group
  Newsletter
  http://members.aol.com/Kinseeker6/graham.html

- GRANFORS, origin ~ Sweden
  http://www.algonet.se/~arneg/k100e/granfors/k1granfo.htm

- GRANOVSKY's `R Us
  http://pages.prodigy.com/JeffersonGraham/gran.htm
  *A site for members of the Granovsky family, originally from the
  Ukraine, circa 1800s.*

- The GRANT Family in Ireland - a History
  http://www.grantonline.com/history.htm
  *Detailed history of the GRANT family, which went to Ireland as part
  of the original Norman conquest in 1169. The history tracks them
  over the next 800 years in Ireland, and follows a number of the
  GRANT families who emigrated to North America and Australia.*

- GRANT Genealogy
  http://www.martygrant.com/gen/grant.shtml
  Emphasis on North Carolina, Tennessee and Virginia.

- The Edward GRANTHAM Family
  http://www.familytreemaker.com/users/g/r/a/Christopher-P-
  Grantham/index.html
  *Descendants of Edward Grantham, born 1643 and died September
  1704 in Grantham's Reeds, Surry Co., VA.*

- The GRANTHAM Gazette
  mailto:rjohnson@graham.main.nc.us
  *A quarterly newsletter devoted to the Grantham surname. For
  details send e-mail to Ron Johnson and Lori Grantham at:
  rjohnson@graham.main.nc.us.*

- GRŸPER Homepage en Genealogie
  http://odur.let.rug.nl/~graeper/
  *A search for the GRAEPERS / GRŸPERS from Moorfleet
  (Hamburg)in Germany and Amsterdam in The Netherlands.*

- The GRAVES Family Association
  http://www.gravesfa.org/

- GRAVITT Gathering - GRAVITT Surname
  Resource Center
  http://www.geocities.com/Heartland/Prairie/2435/
  *Includes Gravit, Gravat, Gravatt, Gravatte, Gravet, Gravett,
  Gravette.*

- The GRAY Family
  http://www.phillipsplace.net/genealogy/surnames/gray.html
  *History of the John Edward Gray family, who immigrated from
  London, England to Victoria, British Columbia, Canada about
  1907.*

- **GREATHOUSE Point**
  http://www.geocities.com/Heartland/Pointe/6094/
  A surname resource center for researchers of the GREATHOUSE surname and family and online home of the GREATHOUSE Cousin Network.

- **The Samuel Thomas GREENE Genealogical Page**
  http://www.cgocable.net/~ccarbin/greene.html
  The first deaf teacher of deaf students in the Canadian province of Ontario, October 1870.

- **GREENLEE Genealogical Clearing House**
  http://angelfire.com/mi2/theteach/family.html
  A hub of other sites connected with the surname GREENLEE.

- **GREENLEE Genealogy**
  http://home.att.net/~margreenlee/
  Descendants of Edward GREENLEE (of Mason County, West Virginia).

- **GREENSHIELDS Family Tree**
  http://freespace.virgin.net/wendy.greenshields/greenshi.htm
  A one name study of GREENSHIELDS.

- **GREENWOOD Genealogies, 1154-1914**
  http://www.rootsweb.com/~genepool/grnwdind.htm

- **GREERS West - The webpage for the Nathaniel Hunt GREER Family Organization**
  http://members.aol.com/GreersWest/index.html
  For the descendants of Nathaniel Hunt GREER and Nancy Ann Terry ROBERTS.

- **GREGG Family**
  http://www.geocities.com/Heartland/Ridge/5850/
  Also PAXTON, HUNTER, HARTONG, ROTHROCK, MOORE.

- **GREGG Family Documents and History**
  http://pw1.netcom.com/~jog1/greggndex.html
  GREGG / GRIGGS / GREGGS.

- **GRIBBLE One Name Site**
  http://www.users.bigpond.com/jgribble/

- **GRICE Family Home Page**
  http://ourworld.compuserve.com/homepages/ra_grice/grice.htm

- **GRIERSON World Project**
  http://www.geocities.com/Heartland/Park/7403/
  Grierson World Project is a ten year research effort to document (in One Name Study Format) the surname variations of the name Grierson, to include, but not limited to: Grierson, Grearson, Greirson, Greerson, Grier, Greir, Greer, Grear, Greear.

- **GRIERSON World Project & Information Exchange**
  http://www.tqci.net/~dagrierson/
  GRIERSON is a sept of Clan MACGREGOR or GREGOR Clan.

- **GRIFFIN Family**
  http://www.isu.edu/~grifpaul
  Annotated bibliography of the Griffin/Griffin family, plus descendants (7 generations) of Edward Griffin, born 1602 in Wales.

- **GRIFFITTS Family History and Genealogy**
  http://homepages.rootsweb.com/~laura/
  This web site explores the ancestry of Isaac Yokum Griffitts and Thomas Box Griffitts. Brunk, Jackson, Brower, Burgess, Box.

- **GRIGGS Mailing List**
  http://www.onelist.com/subscribe.cgi/griggs
  Devoted to researching the Griggs family, especially the descendants/ancestors of Michael and/or Jeremiah Michael Griggs of early Virginia.

- **National GRIGSBY Family Society**
  http://www.grigsby.org/

- **GRIM / GRIMM Genealogy**
  http://freepages.genealogy.rootsweb.com/~heywood/grimm/index.html
  From Fayette and Ross Counties in Ohio from 1800 to present.

- **The Official GRIM - GRIMM Family Home Page**
  http://fvl.k12.mi.us/~grimm/index.html

- **GRINNELL Family Association**
  http://www.gate.net/~grinnell/

- **The GRISWOLD Family Association**
  http://www.griswoldfamily.org/

- **GRIVEL Website**
  http://egrivel.tripod.com/

- **The Canadian GROBE's**
  http://www.ionline.net/%7egrobee/tree/index.html
  Descendants of Johann GROBE and Sophia KULOW.

- **The GROGAN's Home Page**
  http://users.lewiston.com/grogan

- **GRONINGER Family Record Newsletter**
  mailto:jonk59@interaccess.com
  E-mail Jon Kroninger at jonk59@interaccess.com for details. Name variations are: Groninger, Greninger, Croninger, Chroninger, Kroninger.

- **GROOMS**
  http://www.rio.com/~shoch/grooms.html
  Descendants of Abraham GROOMS, born 1740 in Gunpowder Falls, Maryland and Margaret SATTERFIELD.

- **The GROOMS Family Page**
  http://www.angelfire.com/mo/groomsfamilypage/index.html

- **GROOVER Genealogy Homepage**
  http://members.aol.com/shawngroov/groover.html
  I am looking for any descendants of Peter GRUBER.

- **GROSBOEL Family**
  http://grosboll.homepage.dk/
  Grosboll, Grosböl, Grosboel, Grosbøl, Graasbøll, Graasbøl, Graasbol.

- **GROSS Genealogy Home Page**
  http://hometown.aol.com/anniv2776/page2/index.htm
  GROSS and related families in Virginia and surrounding states.

- **The GROTON Family Trees**
  http://www.grotonresearch.org/html2/index2.html
  The Groton Family Trees, researching all branches of the Groton, Grotton, Graton, Groten, Grotten and Gratten families in North America. Research dates back to Thomas Groton circa 1650, in Massachusetts and William Groton circa 1650, in Virginia. Inquiries are welcome.

- The Ernest Alma GROVER Family Association
http://freepages.genealogy.rootsweb.com/~ellieb/grover.htm
*Dedicated to the research of the following surnames: Grover,
Garner, Cole, Jenkins, Field. All families were early LDS, and
crossed on the Mormon Trail to Utah between 1847 and 1856. Later
generations settled in Idaho.*

- GRUBE Genealogie
http://www.grube.de/_gene/
*Genealogy of various GRUBE lines as well as Tucholski, Schwarz,
Riesenfeld and many others.*

- GRUWELL Gatherings Site Index
http://members.aol.com/rngruwell/

- The GUARNIERI Home Web Page
http://www.Guarnieri.com/

- GUBBINS
http://www.avnet.co.uk/home/briangubbins
*Over 5,300 records in the world-wide database for the surname
GUBBINS. Nominee for GUBBINS in the UK's Guild of One-Name
Studies.*

- GUEINZIUS Genealogy
http://www.gueinzius.de
*All 353 members of the GUEINZIUS family are registered and over
15 generations.*

- GUENTHER Genealogy - Passionate Possessions of
Faith
http://home1.gte.net/kanetani/guenther/index.htm
*A book for sale about The Jacob Guenther Family 1725-present,
including Goertzen, Duerksen, Peters, Warkentin, Adrian, Loewen,
Petkau, Isaac, Fadenrecht, Thiessen and others.*

- GUILD Genealogy
http://www.geocities.com/Heartland/Pines/5838/
*Genealogy of the descendancy of John Guild, a Proprietor in
Dedham, MA in 1640, from the work of Charles Burleigh, 1887 -
The Genealogy and History of the Guild, Guile, and Gile Family.*

- GUILE - GILE - GUILES Genealogy
http://homepages.rootsweb.com/~guile164/Default.htm
Guile, Gile, Guiles, Guild, Guilde, Gilde, Gyle, Clough

- The GUILLIATT Family Home Page
http://www.crabtree.demon.co.uk/

- Dave and Janice GUINAN's Page
http://members.xoom.com/djguinan/index.htm
*A brief history of the GUINAN surname, and the known descendants
of Thomas and Mary (BUTLER) GUINAN who emigrated to North
America from Ireland.*

- Descendants of Luke GUIRE
http://i.am/guyre/
*This is a page dedicated to the descendants of Luke Guire of
Fairfield County, Connecticut. These descendants have been
documented in Illinois, Indiana, Iowa, Ohio, New Jersey and
Delaware County, New York under the names of Guire, Guyre and
Guyer.*

- Clan GUNN Society of North America
http://www.nsynch.com/~clangunn/

- The GURKIN Family History Site
http://members.aol.com/jlgurkin/gurkin-research/
*Contains most of the early Gurkin land records, wills, deeds, census
records, births, marriages and deaths, for Beaufort, Hyde, Martin
and Washington counties in North Carolina, (births and deaths for
Beaufort County only). Included is a detailed history of the early
Gurkins, and, in another section, their descendant printouts.*

- GUSHUE, of the West Coast of Newfoundland
http://www.members.home.net/sandratree/gushue/index.html

- GUSTIN Family Forum
http://www.harborside.com/~p2241/Gustin.html
*GUSTIN/GUSTINE family research and documentation, with a list
of researchers and their ancestors.*

- GUTH / GOOD Researchers
http://www.lakeside.net/goodgenes/ggresearchers.html

- The GUTHRIE Family Web Page
http://www.nstep.net/dorgon/guthrie.htm

- The GUYs of Bottesford, Leicestershire &
Associated Families
http://freespace.virgin.net/guy.etchells/
*GUY of Bottesford, Leicestershire, England. Online Transcripts of
Parish Records, Bottesford Families & much more.*

- The GYLLENHAAL Family Tree Project
http://www.voicenet.com/~egyllenh/Html/treepage.html

◆ Surname Mailing Lists

- "GA-GD" Surname Mailing Lists
http://www.rootsweb.com/~jfuller/gen_mail_surnames-ga.html
*GABAY, GABBARD (includes Gabbert, Gebert, Gebhard,
Gebhardt), GABBERT, GABEL, GABLE, GABRIEL, GABY,
GADBERRY, GADD, GADDIS, GADDY (includes Gaddie, Gady,
Gadde), GAEDE, GAERTE (includes Gartey, Gerty, Gaerty, Garty),
GAFFNEY, GAGE, GAGERN (includes Von Gagern, De Gavere,
Gavre, Gawarn, Gawerne, Gawern, Ghaweren, Gaweren), GAGNE,
GAGNON, GAHAGAN, GAILEY, GAILLARD, GAINER, GAINES,
GAINEY, GAITHER, GALATI, GALBRAITH (includes Galbreath,
Gilbreath, Gilreath, Gilbreth, Kilbreath, Kulbeth, Colbreath),
GALBREATH (includes Galbreth, Galbraith, Gilbreath, Gilbraith),
GALE (includes Gales, Gayle, Gail), GALEANO, GALES, GALL,
GALLACHER (includes þGallchobhair, Gallagher, Gallchoir),
GALLAGHER (includes Gallacher, Gallaugher, Golliher),
GALLAGHER, GALLAHER (includes Gallagher, Gollaher,
Golliher, Galliher, O'Gallaher), GALLANT, GALLAWAY, GALLE,
GALLEGOS, GALLIGAN, GALLIMORE (includes Gallamore,
Gallemore, Galmore, Moore), GALLION (includes Galyon, Galyen,
Galyean), GALLIVAN (includes Galvin, Gallavan), GALLO,
GALLOP, GALLOWAY, GALLUP, GALPIN, GALT, GALVIN,
GAMAGE, GAMBILL (includes Gambil, Gambel, Gambell),
GAMBLE (includes Gambol), GAMBLIN, GAMBRELL, GAMEL
(includes Gammel, Gammell, Gamell, Gamill, Gammil, Gammill),
GAMMON, GANDY, GANN, GANNAWAY, GANNON (includes
Ganon, Gann, Gammon, Gamon), GANOE, GANT (includes Gantt,
Gaunt, Gauntt, Gent, Ghent), GANTLEY (includes Gantly),
GANTNER (includes Gaentner, Gentner), GANTT, GANTZ,
GANUS, GANZER, GAPES, GAPPA, GARBER (includes Gerber,
Garver, Carver), GARBUTT, GARCIA, GARD, GARDENER,
GARDINER, GARDNER, GAREMYN, GARFIELD, GARIS,
GARLAND, GARLICK, GARLOCK, GARMAN, GARMANY,
GARMON, GARNAND (includes Gernand, Gernandt, Gernannt),*

GARNER, GARNETT (includes Garnet), GARNIER, GAROUTTE (includes Garrott, Garrot, Garott, Gariot, Garrett, Garriott, Gerratt, Gariott, Garriot), GARRABRANT, GARRARD, GARREN, GARRET, GARRETSON, GARRETT (includes Garratt, Garret, Garot), GARRIGAN, GARRIOTT, GARRIS, GARRISON (includes Garretson), GARRITY, GARST (includes Gerst, Gharst), GARTMAN, GARTNER, GARTON, GARVER, GARVEY, GARVIE (includes Garvey, Jarvie), GARVIN (includes Garven, Garvan, Garvey, McGarvin, O'Garvin, O'Garvey), GARWOOD, GARY (includes Garry, Geary, McGary), GARZA, GASCOIGNE, GASH, GASKELL, GASKILL (includes Gasgoyne, Gasgoigne), GASKIN, GASKINS, GASPAR (includes Gasper), GASPER, GASS, GASSAWAY (includes Gasaway, Gazaway), GAST, GASTON, GASTWIRTH, GATCHELL, GATES, GATEWOOD, GATLIN, GATT, GATTON, GAUDET, GAUGHAN, GAUKROGER (includes Gaukrodger), GAUL, GAULDING (includes Gauldin, Goulding, Gouldin), GAULT, GAUNT, GAUSE, GAUSS (includes Gaus, Goss, Gause, Goos), GAUTHIER, GAUTHIER, GAUTIER, GAUW (includes Gaw, de Gauw, van Gauw, van der Gauw, von Gauw, von der Gauw, zur Gauw, von zur Gauw, Gouw), GAVIN, GAVITT, GAWTHORPE (includes Gawthorp), GAY (includes Gayre, Guy), GAYLE (includes Gale, Gail), GAYLOR, GAYLORD, GAYNOR, GAZAWAY (includes Gasway, Gasaway, Gassaway, Gazway, Gazzaway, Gazoway, Gazeway).

- **"GE-GH" Surname Mailing Lists**
  http://www.rootsweb.com/~jfuller/gen_mail_surnames-ge.html
  GEARHART (includes Gerhardt, Gearhardt, Gierhart, Gearheart), GEARY, GEBERT, GEBHARD, GEBHARDT, GEBHART, GEDDES, GEDNEY (includes Gednee, Gedeney, Gidney), GEE, GEER (includes Gere, Gear, Gehr), GEERS, GEESEMAN (includes Geesaman, Geesman, Geezeman, Gieseman, Giessaman, Giesseman, Giesserman, Guesman,, Guseman, Gusseman), GEFFEN, GEHRING, GEHRKE, GEIBEL (includes Geible), GEIER, GEIGER (includes Kiger, Kyger, Keiger, Gyger, Giger, Gieger), GEISHEIMER, GEISINGER (includes Geissinger, Guysinger, Gissinger), GEISLER, GEIST, GELLER, GELNETT (includes Gilnett, Goelnitz, Gelnitz), GELSTON, GEMMELL, GEMMILL, GENDRON, GENIK (includes Genyk, Gennick), GENSMER (includes Genzmer, Gensemer), GENT, GENTLE, GENTNER (includes Genther, Gantner), GENTRY, GENZ, GEORGE, GERAGHTY, GERALD (includes Gerrald, Garrell, Garrall), GERARD (includes Gerrard, Garrard), GERBER, GERBIG, GERDAU, GERE, GERHARDSTEIN (includes Gerhartzstein, Geroldstein, Gerolstein, Gerholstein, Girardstein), GERHARDT, GERISCHER, GERLACH, GERMAIN, GERMAN, GERMANY (includes German), GEROW, GERRARD, GERREN, GERSTER, GERVAIS, GESBECK (includes Gesback, Gesbock, Gesbech, Gesbach, Gesbecksen, Gesbeckson, Gesbecksan, Gesbechson,, Gesbechsan, Gesbechsen), GESCHWIND, GESELL (includes Gazelle, Gezell), GESS, GESSERONDITBRULOTTE, GETCHALL, GETCHELL, GETHINGS, GETMAN (includes Gettman), GETTEMY (includes Gettamy), GETTER (includes Goetter), GETTLE (includes Godel, Gettel, Geotel, Goetle), GETTY, GETZ, GETZ, GEYER (includes Geier, Gyer, Gayer, Guyer, Geer, Geere, Gear, Gier, Gehr, Coyer), GHEE, GHEEN, GHOLSON.

- **"GI-GN" Surname Mailing Lists**
  http://www.rootsweb.com/~jfuller/gen_mail_surnames-gi.html
  GIACOMETTI, GIBB, GIBBINS, GIBBON, GIBBONS (includes Gibbins, Gibens), GIBBS (includes Gibb, Gibbes, Gibbses, Gybbys), GIBBS, GIBBS (includes Gybes, Gebbes), GIBLER, GIBLIN, GIBSON, GICKER, GIDDENS, GIDDINGS (includes Giddins, Giddens, Gideon), GIDEON, GIDLEY, GIESE, GIESEMAN (includes Geesaman, Geeseman, Geesman, Geezeman, Giessaman, Giesseman, Giesserman, Guesman,, Guseman, Gusseman),

GIESLER, GIESSEMAN (includes Geesaman, Geeseman, Geesman, Geezeman, Gieseman, Giessaman, Giesserman, Guesman,, Guseman, Gusseman), GIESSERMAN (includes Geesaman, Geesman, Geeseman, Geezeman, Gieseman, Giessaman, Giesseman, Giesserman,, Guesman, Guseman, Gusseman), GIESWEIN, GIFFARD, GIFFIN, GIFFORD (includes Gafford), GIGLER, GILBERT, GILBERTSON, GILBREATH, GILCHRIST (includes Gilcrease, Gilcrist, Gilchrest, MacGilchrist), GILDEA, GILDER, GILDERSLEEVE, GILE (includes Guile, Gyle, Guyle, Guiles, Guyles), GILES, GILHAM, GILKEY, GILL, GILLAM (includes Gillim, Gillem, Gilham, Gilliam, Gillham, Gillum), GILLAN, GILLARD, GILLASPIE, GILLEN, GILLENTINE, GILLENWATER, GILLES, GILLESPIE (includes Gillaspy), GILLESPIE, GILLESPIE, GILLET, GILLETT, GILLETTE, GILLEY, GILLHAM, GILLIAM, GILLIES, GILLIGAN, GILLIHAN (includes Gillahan, Gillehan, $G(a,e,i)ll(a,e,i)h(a,e,i)(m,n)$), GILLILAND (includes Gilland, Gilleland, Gillyland), GILLINGHAM, GILLIS, GILLISPIE, GILLMAN, GILLMORE, GILLOCK, GILLUM, GILMAN (includes Gillman), GILMARTIN (includes Gillmartin, Guilmartin, Kilmartin, Martin), GILMER, GILMORE (includes Gilmour, Gilmoore, Gilmer), GILMOUR, GILPIN, GILPIN, GILREATH, GILROY, GILRUTH, GILSON, GILSTRAP, GINGRICH, GINN, GINSBURG (includes Ginsberg, Ginzburg, Ginzberg, Gintzburg, Gintzberg), GINTER, GIORDANO, GIORGIO, GILPATRIC, GIPPLE (includes Kipple), GIPSON, GIQUEL, GIRARD, GIRDLER, GIRLING (includes Gurling), GIROUX, GIRTON, GISH, GIST (includes Guest, Guess, Giss, Gass, Gess), GITTINGS, GIUFFRE (includes Guiffre), GIVEN, GIVENS, GIVIDON (includes Jividen), GLADDEN, GLADNEY, GLANTON, GLANVILLE, GLASBY, GLASCOCK, GLASER, GLASGOW, GLASS (includes Glas, Glasse), GLASSCOCK, GLASSON, GLATFELTER, GLATTFELDER (includes Glotfelty, Glatfelder, Gladfelter, Clodfelter, Glotfelter, Clotfelter), GLAUM, GLAZE, GLAZEBROOK, GLAZENER, GLAZIER, GLEASON, GLEESON, GLEGHORN (includes Gleghorne, Cleghorn, Cleghorne), GLEICH, GLEISBERG (includes Glesberg, Glezberg), GLEN, GLENDAY (includes Glendey, Glendy, Glandee, Glendei, Glenny), GLENDENING, GLENDENNING, GLENN (includes Glen, Glynn), GLENNON, GLENROY, GLICK, GLIDDEN, GLIDEWELL, GLINES, GLITHERO, GLOD, GLOMB, GLOVER, GLYNN.

- **"GO-GQ" Surname Mailing Lists**
  http://www.rootsweb.com/~jfuller/gen_mail_surnames-go.html
  GOAD, GOBER (includes Gobee, Gobe), GOBLE (includes Gobel, Gable, Gobble, Gobell), GODARD, GODBOLD, GODBOUT (includes Goodbout, Godebout), GODBY (includes Godbey), GODDARD (includes Godard), GODDEN, GODFREY, GODIN, GODOWN (includes Godon, Godoun, Goedowne, Godowne, Goodown, Godowns), GODSEY, GODSHALK (includes Godschall, Godschalk, Godshall, Godtschalk, Gotschall, Gottschalk, Gottshall, Gottshalk), GODWIN (includes Godwyn, Godwynne, Godwine, Godwinne, Godin, Gadwin), GOEBEL, GOEGLEIN (includes Goegline), GOELLER, GOEREN, GOERING (includes Goring, Gorring, Gohering), GOESER, GOETZ, GOETZ (includes Getz, Goetsche, Gates, Kitts, Gotz), GOFF, GOFORTH, GOGGIN, GOHR (includes Gohre, Gohrke, Gohring, Gohrs, Gohres, Gohrban), GOIN, GOINES, GOING (includes Goings, Goin, Goins, Ganey, Gainey), GOINGS, GOINS, GOLCHERT, GOLD, GOLDBERG, GOLDBERG, GOLDEN, GOLDER, GOLDIE, GOLDING, GOLDMAN (includes Goldmann), GOLDSBERRY, GOLDSBOROUGH, GOLDSMITH, GOLDSTEIN, GOLDSWORTHY, GOLEMAN (includes Golemon), GOLLA, GOLLAHER (includes Golliher, Golleher, Gallaher, O'Gallaher), GOLLAHER (includes Gallagher, Gallchobhair, Golliher, Galliher, Gallaher, Golleher), GOLLWITZER, GOMAN (includes Gomar, Goeman, Gowan), GOMBERT, GOMBOS (includes Gombus,

Gombas), GOMEZ, GOMILLION (includes Gremillion),
GONSALUS, GONTAR, GONZALES, GONZALES, GONZALEZ,
GOOCH, GOOD, GOODALE, GOODALL, GOODBREAD
(includes Gutbrodt), GOODE (includes Good), GOODELL,
GOODEN, GOODENOUGH, GOODENOW (includes Goodenowe,
Goodenough, Goodno, Goodnow, Goodinowe, Goodyknow,
Goodynow,, Goodenough, Goodnough), GOODFELLOW,
GOODGAME, GOODGION, GOODHIND, GOODIN, GOODING,
GOODLETT, GOODMAN, GOODNIGHT, GOODPASTURE
(includes Goodpaster, Goodpastor), GOODREDS, GOODRICH,
GOODRUM, GOODSELL, GOODSON, GOODSON,
GOODSPEED, GOODWILL, GOODWIN, GOODYEAR,
GOOLSBY, GOOSIC (includes Goosick), GORBET, GORDEN,
GORDON, GORDON, GORDON (includes Gorden, Gordan),
GORDY, GORDY (includes Gorden, Gordie, Gordey, Gorday,
Gawdy), GORE (includes Goar, Goare, Goore, Gohr), GORHAM,
GORIN, GORIN, GORMAN (includes O'Gorman, MacGorman),
GORMLEY, GORRELL (includes Gorel, Goril, Gorrill, Garrell,
Garil, Garel), GORRINGE, GORSUCH, GORTON, GOSCHE,
GOSE (includes Goos, Goss, Gost, Ghost, Gase, Gore), GOSHE
(includes Gosche), GOSLEE, GOSLING, GOSNELL, GOSS,
GOSSAGE, GOSSELIN, GOSSETT, GOSSMAN, GOTCHER
(includes Boren), GOTHARD, GOTSHALL (includes Gotschalk),
GOTT, GOTTFRIED, GOTTLIEB, GOTTSCHALL, GOUCHER,
GOUDELOCK (includes Gowdylock, Guldilok, Gowenlok),
GOUDIE, GOUGE, GOUGH, GOUGH (includes Goff), GOULD
(includes Gold), GOULDEN, GOULDING, GOULET, GOURLEY,
GOVE, GOVER, GOW, GOWDY (includes Goudy), GOWDY,
GOWEN (includes Gowan, Goyne, Goins), GOWER,
GOYCOECHEA, GOYETTE.

- **"GRA-GRD" Surname Mailing Lists**
  http://www.rootsweb.com/~jfuller/gen_mail_surnames-gra.html
  GRAAF, GRABANSKI (includes Grabinski), GRABENSTEIN,
  GRABER, GRABILL, GRACE, GRACEY, GRADY, GRAESSLE,
  GRAF (includes Graff, Graph), GRAFF, GRAFTON, GRAGG,
  GRAHAM, GRAINGER, GRALEY (includes Grayley, Graille),
  GRAMMAR (includes Grahmar), GRAMMER, GRAMMICH,
  GRANBERRY, GRANDE, GRANDSTAFF (includes Granstaff,
  Grindstaff, Grinstaff, Granstoff, Crantzdorf, Cranzdorf), GRANDY,
  GRANGE, GRANGER (includes Grainger), GRANLUND,
  GRANSTRAND (includes Grandstrand), GRANT, GRANTHAM
  (includes Granttham, Granthum), GRANTLAND, GRANTLAND
  (includes Grantlin), GRANTZ, GRAPER, GRASBY, GRATON,
  GRATTAN, GRATTIDGE (includes Gratwick, Gratwich,
  Greatorex), GRATTON, GRAU, GRAUPNER (includes Graubner),
  GRAVELY, GRAVENOR, GRAVES (includes Graff), GRAVES
  (includes Greaves), GRAVIS, GRAY (includes Grey), GRAY
  (includes Grey), GRAYBEAL (includes Graybill, Grable),
  GRAYBILL, GRAYSON.

- **"GRE-GRH" Surname Mailing Lists**
  http://www.rootsweb.com/~jfuller/gen_mail_surnames-gre.html
  GREAR, GREATHOUSE (includes Groethausen, Grothouss,
  Grothausen, Grothauss, Grothausze, Grosshaus, Grothaus,,
  Gratehouse, Greatehouse, Grotehouse, Graytower, Greethouse,
  Grotehose, Gratchouse), GREATON, GREAVES, GRECO,
  GREELEY, GREEN (includes Greene), GREEN, GREENAN
  (includes Greenhan, Greenen), GREENAWAY, GREENBERG,
  GREENE (includes Green), GREENFIELD, GREENHALGH,
  GREENHAW, GREENHILL, GREENING, GREENLAND,
  GREENLAW, GREENLEAF, GREENLEE, GREENLEES,
  GREENMAN, GREENO, GREENSLADE, GREENSLIT (includes
  Greenslet), GREENSTREET (includes Greenstret, Greenstrait),

GREENUP, GREENWALD, GREENWALT, GREENWAY,
GREENWELL, GREENWOOD, GREER, GREESON, GREGER,
GREGG (includes Mac Gregor, Greig), GREGOIRE, GREGOR,
GREGORY, GREGORY (includes Grigory, Gregery, Gregary,
Gregor), GREGORY, GREGSON, GREIG, GREINER, GREIWE
(includes Grieve, Greve, Grewe), GRENFELL, GRENIER,
GRESENS, GRESHAM, GRESSER, GREY.

- **"GRI-GRN" Surname Mailing Lists**
  http://www.rootsweb.com/~jfuller/gen_mail_surnames-gri.html
  GRIBBLE, GRICE, GRIDER, GRIDLEY, GRIEBLING, GRIER,
  GRIERSON (includes Greirson, Greerson, Greirson, Grier, Griere,
  Greer, Greere, Greir, Greire, Grear, Greear, McGreer,, McGrier,
  O'Greer), GRIESER, GRIESHABER (includes Griesshaber,
  Grießhaber), GRIEST (includes Greist, Grist, Ghrist), GRIEVE,
  GRIFF (includes Griffith, Griffiths, Griffeth, Griffeths, Griffin,
  Griffins), GRIFFEE (includes Griffie, Griffey, Griffy), GRIFFEN,
  GRIFFIN, GRIFFIN, GRIFFIS, GRIFFITH, GRIFFITHS,
  GRIFFITTS (includes Griffitt, Griffit, Grifit), GRIGG, GRIGGS
  (includes Grigg), GRIGGS, GRIGNON, GRIGSBY, GRILL, GRIM,
  GRIMES, GRIMES (includes Grime, Grymes, Gream, Greim,
  O'Greidhm, Mac Grime, Gormley, Grehan, Graham), GRIMM
  (includes Grim), GRIMMER, GRIMMETT (includes Grimmette,
  Grimit, Grimmit, Grimmitt, Grimmitte), GRIMSHAW, GRIMSLEY
  (includes Grimslee, Grimsly), GRINDLE (includes Grendel,
  Grindel, Grendil), GRINDSTAFF, GRINER, GRINNELL,
  GRINSTEAD, GRISHAM (includes Gresham, Grissom), GRISSO
  (includes Gresso), GRISSOM (includes Grisham, Grishem, Grissam,
  Grissum, Grisum), GRIST, GRISWOLD, GRIZZARD (includes
  Grissard), GRIZZLE (includes Grizzel, Grizzell).

- **"GRO-GRT" Surname Mailing Lists**
  http://www.rootsweb.com/~jfuller/gen_mail_surnames-gro.html
  GROAT, GROB, GROCE, GROEN, GROENDYK (includes
  Groenendyk, Groenendijk, Groendyke, Groendick, Grondick,
  Grundick), GROFF, GROGAN (includes Croghan), GROGAN,
  GROH, GROOM (includes Grooms), GROOMS, GROOT,
  GROOVER, GROOVER (includes Gruber), GROSE, GROSECLOSE
  (includes Groseklose, Grousclose, Grousclous, Grossclose),
  GROSS, GROSSART (includes Grossarth, Grozarth, Großarth),
  GROSSER (includes Groser), GROSSMAN (includes Grosman,
  Grossmann, Groceman), GROSVENOR, GROTE (includes Groot,
  Groat, DeGroote, DeGroat, DeGrote), GROTH, GROUND,
  GROUNDS, GROUT, GROVE, GROVER, GROVES, GROW.

- **"GRU-GT" Surname Mailing Lists**
  http://www.rootsweb.com/~jfuller/gen_mail_surnames-gru.html
  GRUBB, GRUBBS, GRUBE, GRUBEN, GRUBER, GRUBER,
  GRUEBNER, GRUGETT, GRUND, GRUNDLER, GRUNDY,
  GRUNEWALD (includes Greenawalt, Greenwald, Gruenewald).

- **"GU-GZ" Surname Mailing Lists**
  http://www.rootsweb.com/~jfuller/gen_mail_surnames-gu.html
  GUARD, GUARDIAN (includes Gard, Garde, Guard), GUARRAIA,
  GUDGEON, GUDGEON, GUDGER (includes Gudyer),
  GUENTENSPERGER (includes Güntensperger, Gutensperger,
  Guentensberger, Gutenberger, Guttenberg), GUENTHER,
  GUEREQUE (includes de Guereque, Guerequi, Huereque),
  GUERIN, GUERIN, GUERRANT, GUERRERO, GUERTIN,
  GUESMAN (includes Guseman), GUESS, GUEST, GUETZKOW,
  GUFFEY, GUFFY, GUGLIERI, GUICE, GUIDRY (includes
  Guidrey, Guedry, Gaidry, Guildry, Gaitry), GUILD (includes
  Guilds), GUILLORY, GUINAN, GUINN, GUINSLER, GUION,
  GULDEN, GULICK, GULLAND (includes Gullend, Guland),
  GULLEDGE. GULLETT. GULLEY. GULLICKSON. GULLIFER

(includes Gulliver, Guliford), GULLINE, GULLION, GUM, GUMP, GUNDERSON, GUNN, GUNNING, GUNTER, GUNTHER, GURDEN, GURLEY, GURNEY, GURRY (includes Gury, Gurrie), GURTLER (includes Guertler, Gürtler, Girtler, Gïrtler, Gertler, Gërtler, Gortler, Görtler), GURULE (includes Grole, Grolet, Grollet, Garole, Garule, Burule), GURULE, GUSHLOW, GUSTAFSON, GUSTAFSSON, GUSTIN (includes Gustine),

GUTERL (includes Gutehrle, Gutoehrlein), GUTH, GUTHRIDGE (includes Gutridge), GUTHRIE (includes Guthree, Guttrie, Lahiff), GUTIERREZ, GUY, GUYER, GUYETTE, GUYON, GUYTON, GUZIK (includes Guzick), GWALTNEY, GWIN (includes Gwinn, Guin, Gwynn), GWINN, GWINNER, GWINNUTT, GWYNN, GWYNNE, GYE.

SURNAMES, FAMILY ASSOCIATIONS & FAMILY NEWSLETTERS – "H"

Resources Dedicated to One Surname
http://www.cyndislist.com/surn-h.htm

Category Index:

◆ General Surname Sites and Resources

◆ Surname Specific Sites and Resources

◆ Surname Mailing Lists

◆ General Surname Sites and Resources

- Connect with Surnames - H
  http://www.geocities.com/Heartland/Bluffs/7708/h.html

- Dutch Home Pages by Familyname ~ Letter H
  http://members.tripod.com/~Don_Arnoldus/ha.htm

- FamilyHistory.com - Message Boards - Surname - H
  http://www.familyhistory.com/messages/list.asp?prefix=HA

- Family Tree Maker Online User Home Pages - H
  http://www.familytreemaker.com/users/h/index.html

- Family Workings H Surname Links
  http://www.familyworkings.com/links/surh.htm

- GenConnect Surname Index - "H"
  http://genconnect.rootsweb.com/indx/surnames/H.html
  Message boards sponsored by RootsWeb. Each surname message board set is divided into the following topics: Queries, Bibles, Biographies, Deeds, Obituaries, Pensions, Wills.

- Genealogy Resources on the Internet - "HAA-HAD" Surname Mailing Lists
  http://www.rootsweb.com/~jfuller/gen_mail_surnames-haa.html
  "HAE-HAH"
  http://www.rootsweb.com/~jfuller/gen_mail_surnames-hae.html
  "HAI-HAN"
  http://www.rootsweb.com/~jfuller/gen_mail_surnames-hai.html
  "HAO-HAR"
  http://www.rootsweb.com/~jfuller/gen_mail_surnames-hao.html
  "HAS-HAT"
  http://www.rootsweb.com/~jfuller/gen_mail_surnames-has.html
  "HAU-HD"
  http://www.rootsweb.com/~jfuller/gen_mail_surnames-hau.html
  "HEA-HED"
  http://www.rootsweb.com/~jfuller/gen_mail_surnames-hea.html

  "HEE-HEH"
  http://www.rootsweb.com/~jfuller/gen_mail_surnames-hee.html
  "HEI-HEN"
  http://www.rootsweb.com/~jfuller/gen_mail_surnames-hei.html
  "HEO-HET"
  http://www.rootsweb.com/~jfuller/gen_mail_surnames-heo.html
  "HEU-HH"
  http://www.rootsweb.com/~jfuller/gen_mail_surnames-heu.html
  "HI-HN"
  http://www.rootsweb.com/~jfuller/gen_mail_surnames-hi.html
  "HOA-HOD"
  http://www.rootsweb.com/~jfuller/gen_mail_surnames-hoa.html
  "HOE-HOH"
  http://www.rootsweb.com/~jfuller/gen_mail_surnames-hoe.html
  "HOI-HON"
  http://www.rootsweb.com/~jfuller/gen_mail_surnames-hoi.html
  "HOO-HOT"
  http://www.rootsweb.com/~jfuller/gen_mail_surnames-hoo.html
  "HOU-HT"
  http://www.rootsweb.com/~jfuller/gen_mail_surnames-hou.html
  "HU-HZ"
  http://www.rootsweb.com/~jfuller/gen_mail_surnames-hu.html
  Search the index of surname mailing lists below: Surname Mailing Lists.

  o Genealogy Resources on the Internet - Surnames Included in Mailing Lists - "H"
    http://www-personal.umich.edu/~cgaunt/surnames/h.names.html
    This is a computer generated list of the surnames, and all variant spellings for those names, that are found in the surname mailing lists detailed on the pages shown above.

- Genealogy Resources on the Internet - Surname Web Sites for "H" Surnames
  http://www-personal.umich.edu/~cgaunt/surnames/h.html

- Genealogy's Most Wanted - Surnames Beginning with "H"
  http://www.citynet.net/mostwanted/h.htm

- Google Web Directory .... Genealogy>Surnames>H
  http://directory.google.com/Top/Society/Genealogy/Surnames/H/

- Heartland Genealogy Society Membership List - H
  http://www.geocities.com/Heartland/Ranch/2416/hgs-mlist-h.html

- H-GIG Surname Registry - Surnames Beginning H
  http://www.ucr.edu/h-gig/surdata/surname8.html

- Higginson Book Company - Surnames Beginning with H
  http://www.higginsonbooks.com/h.htm

- 'H' Surnames at RootsWeb
  http://resources.rootsweb.com/surnames/h.html

- inGeneas Table of Common Surname Variations and Surname Misspellings - H-J
  http://www.ingeneas.com/H2J.html

- The Obituary Link Page - Family Obituary Archives Online - H
  http://www.geocities.com/~cribbswh/obit/h.htm

- Open Directory - Society: Genealogy: Surnames: H
  http://www.dmoz.org/Society/Genealogy/Surnames/H/

- Surname Springboard Index - H
  http://www.geocities.com/~alacy/spring_h.htm

- SurnameWeb Surname Registry - H Index
  http://www.surnameweb.org/registry/h.htm

- SWINX Zoeklijst Nederlandse Familienamen / SWINX Searchlist Dutch Surnames - H
  http://www.swinx.net/swinx/swinx_ha_nl.htm

- Websites at RootsWeb: H Surnames
  http://www.rootsweb.com/~websites/surnames/h.html

◆ Surname Specific Sites and Resources

- The HABERSTROH Genealogy Page
  http://www.haberstroh.org
  HABERSTROHs who emigrated to the US from either Diefenbach in Wuerttemberg or Duerrn in Baden around the middle of the last century.

- Descendants of George HACHENBERGER (1755-1830) and Anna Maria HOLLINGER (1763-1836)
  http://www.henge.com/~holsclaw/hackenbe/index.htm

- HADLEY - The Family of George HADLEY of Ipswich, Massachusetts, 16xx-1686
  http://hadley.webjump.com/

- HAEFNER Family Tree Outline
  http://www.sky.net/~shaefner/famtree.htm
  Descendants of William and Frank ?? HAEFNER.

- The Descendants of Hans Jacob HAGEY
  http://alpha.nornet.on.ca/~hlhagey/
  Largely a genealogical history of Daniel HAGEY and his wife Elizabeth BERGEY who emigrated to Canada in 1822.

- Johannes HAHN Family History
  http://users.twave.net/lhsetzer/hahn.html
  Descendants of Johannes Hahn, born 1712 in Frechenfeld, Germany, died 1793 in Lincoln, Catawba, NC.

- HAILEY Families Home page
  http://www.geocities.com/Heartland/Ranch/8581/
  Searching for; HAILEYS, BARNS, PICKARD, SPURGEON, HANTLA, DAVIS, BLAYLOCK, RUMSEY and WHINNEY.

- HALE Family History Web Site
  http://www.argonet.co.uk/users/ghale
  Genealogical research of HALE in Gloucestershire, Bristol & Somerset and Monmouthshire, UK.

- HALE Genealogy
  http://www.qni.com/~geo/jhale.htm
  Descendants of John Hale, Revolutionary War soldier, born 1753.

- HALE Roots Home Page
  http://members.aol.com/haleroots/index.html
  Single surname study for the surname HALE. Various spellings include, HALE, HAIL, HAILE, HEALE, HALES, HAYLE. Origin of the surname, marriage, birth and death records, famous Hale's in history, queries, lineages, wills, chat room, picture album, message board, search engine, reunions and much more.

- HALEY Surname Discussion List
  http://www.iqthost.com/velocity/

- The HALL Families of Wilkes County, NC
  http://aesir.damerica.net/~dhardy/Notes/hall.htm

- The HALL Family Genealogy Site
  http://members.home.com/clanhall

- The HALLs and HENNINGs of Ireland
  http://members.aol.com/Rdkone/HallMain.html
  Descendants of Samuel HALL and Robert HENNING.

- HALL Genealogy
  http://hometown.aol.com/jhall46646/Index.html
  Direct line of Edward Hall born 1611, Henbury, Gloucestershire, England who came to Plymouth, Massachusetts in 1636 and died in Rehoboth, Massachusetts, 27 November 1670.

- HALL Surname Page
  http://bethg.shutdown.com/hall/index.html
  This page is dedicated to those researching the surname HALL, in all locations. Over 200 researchers are listed.

- HALLAM Family Genealogy
  http://www.geocities.com/Heartland/Oaks/5005
  The origin, meaning, and evolution of the Hallam family name. The location of the lost village of Hallam, Hallam heraldry, and the real Hallam coat of arms.

- ALLCHURCH / HALLCHURCH and Related Families
  http://ourworld.compuserve.com/homepages/tim_hallchurch/genstart1.htm

- The HALLISEY Spot
  http://hometown.aol.com/silkladyf/myhomepage/index.html

- The HALSETH Family
  http://www.edb-hjelp.no/Halseth/

- HALSEY Family Resource Page
  http://freepages.family.rootsweb.com/~families/halsey/
  index.html

- The Virginia HALSTEADs
  http://freepages.genealogy.rootsweb.com/~halstead/
  *The Virginia Halstead line that began with Henry HALSTEAD who
  arrived In 1651 and his descendants.*

- HALTERMAN Hollow
  http://www.scioto.org/Halterman/index.html
  Halterman, Halderman, Haltiman, Haldeman.

- HAM Country
  http://www.oeonline.com/~odon/HamCountry/HAM
  Country.html
  *HAM Surname in France prior to 1700. HAM Surname in England
  1150 to 1720. HAM Surname in Virginia (USA) 1621 to 1830. HAM
  Surname in AL, KY, NC, SC, TN prior to 1850.*

- Koiviston HÄMÄLÄISET / HÄMÄLÄINEN from
  Koivisto ~ Finland
  http://www.megabaud.fi/profilink/hama.htm
  *HAMALAINEN, HÄMÄLÄINEN, KURKI, HAMLIN, SEPPINEN,
  PULLI, KAUKIAINEN, PELTONEN, KAIPIAINEN, MANNONEN.*

- Descendants of HAMBLEN or HAMBLIN or
  HAMLIN
  http://www.qni.com/~anderson/HamblenTOC.html

- HAMBROOK Family History Society
  http://www.hambrook.net/

- HAMBYs on the Web
  http://www.hambytree.com/index.html
  *Over 20,000 Hambys, links to other Hambys on the web, Hamby
  researchers, Hamby Message Board, stories and photographs*

- Will of Stephen HAMM
  http://members.aol.com/jogt/hammwl.htm

- Clan HAMILTON Society
  http://members.sysconn.com/hamilton/welcome.htm

- HAMILTON Historical Newsletter
  mailto:IMAKSICKAR@aol.com
  E-mail Ann Kirkpatrick Hull at IMAKSICKAR@aol.com for details.

- HAMILTON National Genealogical Society, Inc.
  http://www.hamiltongensociety.org/
  *A non-profit organization devoted to assembling and preserving
  genealogical and historical materials pertaining to the Hamilton
  (ALL spellings: Hamelton, Hameleton, Hambleton, Hambelton)and
  Allied families. Membership is open to all persons interested in
  genealogical research and preservation of records. We publish a
  Monthly Newsletter "The Connector."*

- HAMLEY, HAMBLY & HAMLYN Family History
  Society
  http://freespace.virgin.net/ham.famis/

- HAMMAN Surname Research Center
  http://homepages.rootsweb.com/~andert/hamman/
  hamfam.htm
  Includes Descendants of Jacob Hamman.

- The HAMMETT Family of Martha's Vineyard
  http://www.vineyard.net/vineyard/history/hammett.htm
  *The Descendants of Edward Hammett (c. 1680 - 1745) and
  Experience Bowles of Tisbury, Dukes Co., MA.*

- The North American HAMMILL Family Forum
  http://www.webcom.com/hammill/
  *Hammill, Hammil, Hamill, Hamil, Hammel, Hammell, Hamel,
  Hamell.*

- HAMMOND Genealogy
  http://www.arq.net/~ljacobs/hamm1.htm
  *Descendants of William Hammond who died in Swansea, MA in
  1675.*

- HAMMONS Genealogy Page
  http://genweb.net/Hammons
  A data base for all spellings of Hammonds including Ammons.

- HAMP Surname Hunters Index
  http://members.xoom.com/plhamp/hamp_mead/hamp
  index.html
  *The Descendants of Hans HAMPP, born ca 1520 in Buoch,
  Wurttemberg. Families represented include MEAD, SCHREYJACK,
  and WALKER and cover many, many others spread across the USA
  and Australia.*

- HAMRICK HAMBRICK
  http://homepages.rootsweb.com/~hamrick/

- The HANCOCK Family History Page
  http://www.geocities.com/Heartland/Meadows/9255/
  index.html

- The HANDLEY Genealogy Index Page
  http://members.aol.com/Sftrail/handley/

- HANDSAKER Home Page
  http://www3.bc.sympatico.ca/Handsakers_Homepage
  *This is a study of the Handsaker family from various parts of the
  world.*

- HANDSPIKER / HANSELPACKER Genealogy
  http://www.jedh.com/genealogy/hpiker.htm
  *Also variations: HENSELBEKKER, HANDLESPIKER,
  HENSILPACKER, HANDELSPIKER, etc. Most entries are from
  those now or once residing in Digby County, NS, Canada.*

- HANDWERK Family Research in Germany
  http://people.we.mediaone.net/richardz/index.html
  Hantwerck; Handwercker; Handtwerck; Handwerk and Handwerg.

- HANKEL Genealogy
  http://people.mn.mediaone.net/jgoepfert/hankel_
  genealogy.htm
  *Descendants of Herman HANKEL, b. 1817, Germany. His family
  immigrated to the U.S. between 1855 and 1863.*

- HANKS Family Homestead
  http://www.homestead.com/hanksforthememories/hanksfamily
  homestead.html

- HANKS Family of Virginia and Westward
  http://www.homestead.com/hanksfamilyofvawestward/hanks
  familyofvirginiawestward.html
  *HANKS Family of Virginia and Westward by Adin Baber is being
  reprinted in 1999 by his daughter Nancy Baber McNeill. Valuable
  HANKS family reference book.*

- Biography of John HANNA of Barton, NY
  http://pages.prodigy.com/RFQN34A/jhanna.htm
  *Born in Scotland, was one of the earliest settlers of Tioga Co., NY.
  Also include a large list of descendants.*

- The GRAHAM-HANNA Family Genealogy
  http://www.geocities.com/Heartland/5149/ghindex.html
  *Descendants of Robert Hanna, Sr. 1755-1837. Surnames: Hanna,
  Graham, Whalen, Hammers, Wilborn, Norris, Probasco, Ogden,
  Hamilton, Norris, Ogden.*

- The HANNA Surname Resource Center
  http://members.theglobe.com/slhanna/hanna.html
  *The site is for the study of the Hanna, Hannah, Hannay, Hanner
  surnames and variations. Its purpose is to link to relevant sites, to
  collect information and to present this information on the web so
  that it can be freely accessed.*

- Clan HANNAY Welcomes You
  http://ourworld.compuserve.com/homepages/James_Hannay/

- HARBERT Family Home Page
  http://pages.prodigy.net/dharbert/
  *This home page is to provide information on the genealogy of
  HARBERT and related West Virginia families and to promote an
  exchange of information to expand the known descendants of
  Thomas Harbert, born 1734.*

- HARBOUR Light Newsletter
  http://www.halcyondays.com/harbour/HarbourLight.htm
  *Quarterly newsletter dedicated to the Harbour/Harber and other
  variation surnames.*

- HARBOUR's USA Genealogy Mailing List
  http://www.egroups.com/list/harboursusa/
  Primarily for the descendents of Thomas and Sara-Witt HARBOUR.

- HARDESTY Hangout
  http://www.geocities.com/Heartland/Prairie/1215/

- The HARDICK Page
  http://www.hardick.org/
  Hardick, Hardiek, Hardieck, Haardiek, Haardick & Haardieck.

- The HARDIN Family Compendium
  http://www.flex.net/~hardin/

- The HARDEN-IN-ING Newsletter
  http://members.aol.com/workaide/hfa/
  *This is the on-line Newsletter of the Harden-Hardin-Harding Family
  Association. The association has 1200 members (500 active, dues-
  paying members) who share genealogical information about these
  three spellings of the family name..*

- HARDING Family Genealogy
  http://ourworld.compuserve.com/homepages/jwmuse/
  harding.htm
  *Some descendants of Abraham HARDING (1619-1654)of
  Massachusetts.*

- HARDWICK Hunters
  http://www.s-hornbeck.com/hardhunt.htm
  A clearinghouse for HARDWICK Hunters, queries.

- HARDWICK Hunting Newsletter
  http://www.s-hornbeck.com/hardwick.htm

- HARGETT Database Home Page
  http://www.netusa1.net/~eddleman/hargett.htm

- The HARLAN Family in America
  http://www.harlanfamily.org/

- HARMER Family Association (U.K.)
  http://www.harmer12.freeserve.co.uk/

- HARMER Family Association (U.S.)
  http://www.angelfire.com/wa/harmer1/index.html

- My Canadian HARMER Family History Pages
  http://www.angelfire.com/hi2/harmer/

- HARMON Genealogical Society
  http://www.geocities.com/Heartland/Valley/4236/

- The HARNEDs of North America
  http://homepages.rootsweb.com/~harned/
  *Site for the Harned family of North America, descendants of Edward
  Harnett, at Salem by 1637, including Harnet, Harnett, Horned.*

- HARNETT Genealogy
  http://freepages.genealogy.rootsweb.com/~harnett/index.htm
  *Harnett, Harned, Harnet, Horned, Hornett family from
  Pennsylvania, Ohio, Kentucky, Indiana and Illinois to present-day.*

- HARNEY Family Research
  http://freepages.genealogy.rootsweb.com/~harney2/
  Includes 20 years of research on the Harney families worldwide.

- HARRIGAN That's Me!
  http://personal.nbnet.nb.ca/wbharrig/homepage.html
  *Includes an index of all individuals born (or adopted) with the
  Harrigan surname, especially those who emigrated from County
  Cork, Ireland, to New Brunswick, Canada.*

- HARRINGTON Genealogy Association
  http://www.genealogy.org/~bryce/harrgene.html

- HARRINGTON'S Family Newsletter - The Round
  Robin News
  http://www.geocities.com/Heartland/Hills/8776/index.html
  *Family newsletter the round robin news is a newsletter that helps
  keep our family informed and to make hopefully easier to connect
  our genealogy with others.*

- Southern HARRINGTON Genealogical Research
  Website
  http://www.harringtons.org/southern/index.htm

- HARRIS-HUNTERS Website
  http://millennium.fortunecity.com/newchurch/11/

- HARRIS Surname Webring Homepage
  http://www.geocities.com/Heartland/Bluffs/7708/familytree/
  harris.html
  *Harris Surname Webring links genealogy pages that have research
  on the surname Harris.*

- The HARRISON Genealogy Repository
  http://moon.ouhsc.edu/rbonner/harintro.htm

- My HARRISON Line
  http://harrison.simplenet.com/
  Descendants of Richard HARRISON, born about 1663, Leeds, Yorkshire, England.

- HARROD / HERROD Family
  http://members.tripod.com/ebastin/index.html
  Database of 11961 individuals mainly in KY and TN with Harrod Orange Descendants and Ancestors.

- The HARROD Family Page
  http://www.hypervigilance.com/genlog/harrod.html
  Descendants of James (abt. 1668) and Maria (Kent) Harrod, from Bedfordshire, England in about 1720-1722.

- HARROLD and Related Roots On-Line Database
  http://www.harrold.org/
  Harrold, Rees, Turner, Hilliard, Kelley, McFarland, Smart, Brayton genealogy w/phototree & histories and links to other Harrold sites.

- The Descendants of Stephen HART
  http://www.ultranet.com/~harts/family/harts/
  Dea. Stephen Hart, who arrived in Plymouth, Massachusetts in 1632.

- HART Family Association
  http://www.opcweb.com/hart/hfa.htm
  Including Hart, Heart, O'Hart, Harte, and Hartt.

- HARTLEY & CHANDLER & OGDEN Genealogy
  http://members.aol.com/darlajov/page/index.htm
  Descendants of Zimri HARTLEY and Sarah Ann CHANDLER, married August 24, 1843 in Platte County, Missouri.

- HARTMAN Genealogy
  http://www.java-connect.com/hartman/
  Descendants of John HARTMAN and Margaret SCHADEL. The HARTMAN families on these pages originated in the 1890's in Southside, Pittsburgh, PA.

- HARTWELLs of America
  http://www.hartwell.org/

- The HARVEY Genealogist / The HARVEY Resource
  http://www.geocities.com/Heartland/6575/
  A surname association that includes Harvy, Harvie, Hervey, Hervy and Hervie.

- HARVEY/HERVEY Genealogy
  http://www.geocities.com/Heartland/Trail/2767/
  Descendants of HARVEYs of Northumberland Co., VA; Halifax Co., NC, and the South. Much original source material; information on other Harvey/Hervey families of PA, NY, TN, OH, TX, and other states. Some families tied back to England.

- HASBROUCK Family Association
  http://thorn.pair.com/hasbrouck/index.html

- HASCALL Home Page
  http://www.familytreemaker.com/users/h/a/s/Richard-K-Hascall/index.html
  HASCALL, HASKELL. Researching the descendants of John HASCALL and Mary SQUIRE.

- HASTINGS Memorial website
  http://www.geocities.com/Heartland/Pointe/5841/Hastings Mem.htm
  A site primarily focused on the ancestry and descendants of Thomas HASTINGS (c1605-1685) of England and Watertown, MA. Also discusses related families of BLISS, COOLIDGE, FISKE, FLAGG, GODDARD, PERSON, RICE, STONE, WOODWARD.

- Jacob HATCH (1786-1876) His Ancestors and Descendants includes the Scituate, MA HATCH Family
  http://www.users.uswest.net/~kaeh/
  Dedicated to the descendants of Thomas and William Hatch of Scituate, Massachusetts. Also includes descendants of John Wild and Thomas Thayer of Braintree and Williamsburg, Massachusetts and Garlick/Garlock/Gerlach, Mohawk Valley, New York State.

- The Orin and Maria Thompson HATCH Family
  http://freepages.genealogy.rootsweb.com/~hatch/
  Descendants of Orin (1830 - 1906) and Maria (1838 - 1911).

- The HATCHELL page
  http://www.hostville.com/hatchellpage/

- The HATCLIFFE Family
  http://freepages.genealogy.rootsweb.com/~lisid/
  *Ide Haddeclive * de Hatclyf * Attlyf * Hatteclyf * Hatlyff * Hatley * Hatclyffe * Hatlefe * Hatlif * Hatchcliffe * Hatliff * Hatcliff.*

- William HATFIELD Descendants
  http://members.aol.com/Elaine64/WilliamHatfield Genealogy.html
  Also search for DeWitt Clinton Hatfield and Fry, Jefferies, Butcher.

- HATFIELD Family History Introduction / Genealogy Trees
  http://www.ghat.com/hatfintr.htm
  HATFIELD surname study and personal homepage.

- HATFIELD Genealogy Homepage
  http://members.aol.com/HatwellE/genealogy.html

- HATHAWAY One-Name Study
  http://www.hathaway51.freeserve.co.uk/
  HATHAWAY, HATHWAY, HATHERWAY.

- HATTs Page
  http://members.xoom.com/hatts

- HAUGHT Family
  http://www.geocities.com/heartland/cliffs/5848

- HAUPT Family Origins
  http://www.geocities.com:80/Heartland/Lake/3234/Haupt.html
  Haupt family history from 1600's through to the colonial period in US history. Haup, Haupe, Hawpe, Houp, Houpe, Houpt.

- HAVEKOST Genealogy
  http://www.tdi.net/havekost/

- The HAVEMANN Family History Center
  http://www.havemann.com/
  HAVEMANNs worldwide: queries, photos, wills, deeds, census records, etc. Other surnames include BAUER, BERESFORD, BROWN, CONKLIN, FRAME, HARTUNG, HEAD, MUSTERER, WETZEL, WILLOCK and WINGENDORFF.

- HAVENS Harbor (HH)
  http://www.dfn.com/~johavens/harbor.htm
  A quarterly newsletter for HAVEN, Havens (all variants).

- HAWES HAWS Genealogy
  http://members.aol.com/JimHawes/Hawes.html
  This page is dedicated to persons researching one of the oldest names in American history: HAWES, HAWS, HOUSE, HAUS, HAUSE, HAWSE, HOWES.

- The HAWORTH Association of America
  http://www.haworthassociation.org

- Clan HAY
  http://www.dch-design.com/CLAN_HAY/

- HAYDEN Family History
  http://www.pastracks.com/hayden/

- HAYDEN Family History
  http://www.hayden.org/
  Heydon, Haydon, Haden, Hadden, Hyden, Headen, Haddon and others. Sponsored by some of The Descendants of Joseph Thompson Hayden.

- HAYNES Family Genealogy
  http://members.aol.com/chrishayne/index.html
  Genealogy of Bartholomew, David and James Haynes.

- HEABERLIN Family Genealogy Online
  http://www.pulpgen.com/gen/heaberlin/
  Descendants of Andrew Heaberlin, a weaver, who emigrated from Germany to Maryland around the time of the American Revolution.

- HEAD Family Genealogy
  http://members.home.net/khead1/intro.htm
  Eleven generations of the HEAD family, originating in Wymondham, Norfolk, England in 1663, to the present day.

- HEALD Surname Resource Center
  http://freepages.genealogy.rootsweb.com/~geneal/src/Heald SRC.html
  HEALD, HALE and variations.

- HEALY/HEALEY - Homeland of Kerry
  http://www.angelfire.com/ma/healytree/index.html
  Healy, Healey, Murphy, Devine, O'Sullivan, O'Leary, Moran, Shea, Riordan, and other of Co. Kerry, Ireland. Tarrant/Breen of Co. Cork. Trying to gather all Healys together at this website as a communication network for Healys.

- HEARNE History Home
  http://members.xoom.com/cragun/hearne/history/index.html
  An on-line searchable web version of "Brief History and Genealogy of the HEARNE Family" by William T. HEARNE, which is now out of print; 759 pages of HEARNE family information.

- HEARNE Surname Resource Center
  http://freepages.genealogy.rootsweb.com/~geneal/src/Hearne SRC.html
  Also HEARN, HERNE, HERRON, etc.

- HEASLEY Genealogy HomePage
  http://www.geocities.com/Heartland/Pointe/5096/
  HEASLEY Genealogy beginning with HAUSSLI, the original spelling for HEASLEY.

- HEATHFamily.org - The Official HEATH Family Website
  http://www.heathfamily.org/

- HEATH Family History - Introduction
  http://freepages.genealogy.rootsweb.com/~wgheath/index.htm
  One line of the family of Cheshire, England, from 1685 to present day, including branches in USA and Australia.

- HEAVISIDE Family Home Page
  http://www.gcheaviside.freeserve.co.uk/index.htm
  Interest in establishing connection between de Heviside / Heuside and close variations of this name from the 13th century in the Kelso area and the small hamlet of Heavyside south of Kelso, Roxburghshire, Scotland with large numbers of families with similar names - Heaviside, Heavyside, Heaveside, originating in County Durham, England from at least mid-16th century.

- HEBERT Family Genealogy
  http://www.genweb.net/acadian-cajun//hebert.htm

- The HEBERT Genealogy Page
  http://www.gaudreau.org/arthur/genealogy/hebert.sht

- HECKENBACH Family History
  http://users.sisna.com/jheckenbach

- HEDGES Family History Website
  http://ourworld.compuserve.com/homepages/PHedges/

- HEDGES Website
  http://www.eden.com/~denhed/
  This site is dedicated to the Hedges family of Kentucky.

- HEDRICK Surname Mailing List
  http://lists.rootsweb.com/index/surname/h/hedrick.html
  Includes Headrick.

- HEIMBACH.org, the Heimbachs' home on the Web
  http://www.heimbach.org/

- HEINRICH Family History
  http://www.geocities.com/~gdheinrich/
  The Heinrich Family and many German Moravian, Moravian, German Bohemian, Bohemian, German Russian, German, & Czech Families.

- HEISSERER Genealogy
  http://members.tripod.com/~Hollie_7/Heisserer.html
  Descendants of Jean Georges Heisserer (Heusserer), from Alsace-Lorraine and in U.S.

- HELMAN Family Home Page
  http://homepages.rootsweb.com/~helman/

- HELMS: North Carolina
  http://freepages.genealogy.rootsweb.com/~helmsnc
  Results of HELMS research to find the parents of George, Tilman and Jonathan who appeared in NC about 1750.

- Family Pedigree of the HELSBY Family
  http://www.geocities.com/Hollywood/1880/Famtree.html
  A Norman-French Pedigree by Thomas Helsby, Esq., of Lincoln's Inn.

- HEMINGWAY / HEMENWAY Genealogy
  http://www.hemingway.net/

- HENDERSHOT Family Genealogy
  http://www.mindspring.com/~noahsark/family.html

- Clan HENDERSON Society of the United States and Canada
  http://www.msu.edu/~hende117/

- HENDON Family Chronicles
  http://www.geocities.com/ewhendon/
  Dedicated to the Henden/Hendon family who migrated from England to the Gunpowder River region of Maryland early in the 18th century. Some moved to the Carolinas and Georgia by 1800, then westward to Alabama, Arkansas, Louisiana, Mississippi, Missouri, Tennessee, and Texas by 1900.

- HENDRIX / HENDRICKS Family Archives
  http://www.geocities.com/Athens/9640/index.html

- HENLEY Family Genealogy
  http://www.vii.com/~jensenet/henley/
  Henley/Henly/Hensley/Hensly/Hendly/Hendley. Origins in Virginia branched out to North and South Carolinas then the normal migration route of Alabama, Mississippi, etc.

- HENNEBERRY Family Genealogy
  http://www.henneberry.org/
  Henneberry / Henebry / Hennebery Family Genealogy: Counties Cork, Limerick, Kilkenny, Tipperary in Ireland.

- HENNEKES Genealogy Page
  http://www.hennekes.com/cadwolf/
  HENNEKES family from Dordrecht, Holland, descended from Laurens HEIJNEKEN (baptized as Laurentz HEINEKEN) in Bremen, Germany.

- The Peter Henrich HENNING Family League
  http://www.henning.org/
  Register of all Hennings in South Africa.

- HENRY and Related Families of Harrison County, Kentucky
  http://www.mindspring.com/~jogt/surnames/henry2.htm

- The HENRY Herald
  http://ladyecloud.hypermart.net/Henry.htm
  Henri(e), Henery, Henry.

- HENSLEY Genealogy
  http://www.martygrant.com/gen/hensley.shtlm
  Emphasis on North Carolina, Tennessee and Virginia.

- HENSON Genealogy#160;
  http://www.rootsweb.com/~kyharris/henson.htm
  Early Virginia and Kentucky family.

- HERALD Surname Resource Center
  http://members.home.com/jimherald/
  Or alternate site
  http://herald-surname-genealogy.8m.com/

- HERMISTON / HERMESTON / HARMISTON Genealogy
  http://www.uwindsor.ca:7000/hk/hermiston/hermy

- The HERNDON Family Research & Genealogy Links Page
  http://www.geocities.com/Heartland/Meadows/2010/
  A site mainly pertaining to the HERNDON name. This site includes a chat room and message board.

- HERNDON Genealogy Clearinghouse
  http://members.xoom.com/HerndonPage/
  Descendants of William and Catherine Digges Herndon. Over 14,000 descendants.

- The HERNLEY Family
  http://hernly.geology.iupui.edu/
  Hoernle, Hoernli, H–rnle, H–rnli, Hernley, Hernly, Harnly, Harnley, Hearnly.

- The HEROUX Family in the USA
  http://members1.visualcities.com/heroux/
  The site is primarily for recording Heroux immigrants from Quebec, Canada and their descendants.

- The HERSEY Family
  http://gwis2.circ.gwu.edu/~shersey/index5.html
  Tracing the Descendants of William HERSEY of Hingham, MA (1635-1998).

- Genealogy of the HERSHEY's
  http://www.raccoon.com/~hershey/

- Roots and Branches of the HERVEY & HARVEY Families
  http://freepages.genealogy.rootsweb.com/~hervey/
  Primarily descendants & relations of Onesiphorus HARVEY of Lancaster & Northumberland Counties, VA, but includes info on other HERVEY, HARVEY families including newsletter.

- HESS Family Tree
  http://members.tripod.com/~KSKarr6/HessFamilyindex-2.html
  Family history of Joseph HESS, founder of Hessville Indiana.

- HEWETT Genealogy
  http://www.cs.utexas.edu/users/hewett/genealogy/
  Extensive Hewett genealogy archives plus links to other sites and general genealogy information.

- HEWSTONE Family Trees
  http://easyweb.easynet.co.uk/~hewstone/hewstonefamily trees.htm#familytreetop

- The HEYWOOD Family
  http://www.phillipsplace.net/genealogy/surnames/heywood.html
  Story of Sophia Heywood, who was born in Liverpool, England in 1789.

- The HIBBARD Family
  http://www.hibbardfamily.com
  HIBBARD worldwide.

- Descendants of Robert HIBBARD of Salem, Mass
  http://www.c-com.net/~psh/
  Hibbard, Hebard, Hebbard, Hebberd, Heberd, Hibberd, Hibbert, Hibberts, Hiberd, Hibert.

- The HUMPHREYS Society
  http://www.dcsi.net/~hohin/humphreys/main.html
  Humphrey, Humphreys, Humphries, umphreys, umphrey or any other spelling.

- HUMPHRIES Family
  http://www3.sympatico.ca/opanon/humphries/
  Descendants of Edward HUMPHRIES (1824-1877) and Sarah TAYLOR (1825-1904), of Redditch, England. HOLLIS, HARDING, BILLETT, KNIGHT, MOGG.

- HUNSUCKER Family Genealogy
  http://www.geocities.com/Heartland/Ranch/8679/
  Hunsucker, Hunsicker, Huntzicker, Huntzinger, Hunsinger, Honaker, Hunsaker and all name variations.

- The HUNT Family Genealogy Page
  http://community.webtv.net/hayes211/THEHUNTFAMILY
  Family of Ralph HUNT of Long Island, NJ.

- The HUNT Line Online
  http://www.genweb.net/~hunt/index.html

- HUNTList Website
  http://www.genweb.net/~hunt/list/index.html

- HUNTING / HUNTTING Genealogy
  http://www.cs.cornell.edu/dean/hunting.htm
  Descendants of John HUNTING or HUNTTING (1597-1690) who immigrated from England to Dedham, MA in 1638. Also includes information on later HUNTING immigrants.

- HUNTINGTON Family Association
  http://www.huntington.tierranet.com/

- HUNTOON Family HomePage
  http://www.geocities.com/Heartland/Pines/3164
  Descendants of George Washington and Lucinda HUNTOON. Includes the following surnames: McDANIEL, SHUMAN, WELLER, WHALEN, STEARNS, CRYDERMAN, BURTON, SHAKESPEARE, COLVIN, THOMPSON.

- HURLBUT - HURLBURT Genealogy
  http://www.idsonline.com/userweb/hurlburt/
  The descendants of Thomas Hurlbut who came to America about the year 1630.

- Brian HURST Family Page
  http://www.familytreemaker.com/users/h/u/r/Brian-R-Hurst/index.html
  500 years of the HURST family originating from the counties of Oxfordshire and Buckinghamshire in England.

- The HURST Family
  http://www.phillipsplace.net/genealogy/surnames/hurst.html
  Story of the Hurst family from James Hurst who immigrated from Manchester, England to Campbell County, Kentucky to his daughter, Mary Hurst McMurray, who removed to Auglaize County, Ohio.

- HURST Heritage Newsletter
  http://www.theboydfamily.com/hurstheritage.htm

- The Genealogical History of the HURST family.
  http://www.geocities.com/tracy-1/genealogy/hurst/index.html

- The HURT Family Genealogy Site
  http://www.hurt.org
  The best resource for researchers of the HURT surname.

- HUSTED Family Lines
  http://www.geocities.com/Heartland/Meadows/5363/
  HUSTED family from Dorset County, England to Massachusetts, Connecticut, New Jersey, Ohio.

- HUTCH Hunters
  http://members.aol.com/hutchroots/FREESAMPLENEWSLETTERindex.html
  Hutcheson, Hutcherson, Hutchenson, Hutchison, Hutchinson, Hutchingson, Hutchins, Hutchens. Lots of queries, with a link to lots of other Hutch( )son related family material.

- Wills of John and Mary HUTCHERSON - Harrison Co., KY
  http://members.aol.com/jogt/hutch.htm
  Formerly of Spotsylvania Co., Virginia.

- HUTCHISON Genealogy Web Page - Alexander HUTCHISON
  http://members.tripod.com/graceyline/hutchisonindex-2.html

- HUTCH(__)SON Family Tree Genealogy Newsletter
  http://members.aol.com/HutchRoots/Gen-Newsletter-index.html
  This site is for ALL researchers of the names of Hutcheson, Hutcherson, Hutchenson, Hutchison, Hutchinson, Hutchingson, Hutchins, and any other variations of the name HUTCHINSON.

- HUTSON World Wide Genealogy
  http://clubs.yahoo.com/clubs/hutsonworldwidegenealogy

- HUXTABLE Family Research
  http://home.st.net.au/~dunn/huxtable.htm
  Huxtable, Hokestaple, Hosestaple, Hucstapull, Hukestabull, Hucstapyll. Huxtable = "a spur of land with a post."

- The HYDE Registry
  http://genweb.net/The-Hyde-Registry/
  A genealogical records depository for HIDE, HYDE and variations thereof.

- HYLAND Family, Cork/Tipperary, Ireland
  http://www.hylit.com/info/Genealogy/Hyland.html
  A genealogy of the Hyland family of North Cork, Ireland. Other variants of the Hyland name: O'Faolain, Whelan, Phelan.

◆ Surname Mailing Lists

- "HAA-HAD" Surname Mailing Lists
  http://www.rootsweb.com/~jfuller/gen_mail_surnames-haa.html
  HAACK, HAAG, HAAKE, HAAS, HAASE, HACKBARTH, HACKBARTH, HACKER, HACKETT (includes Hacket), HACKIT, HACKLER (includes Hechler), HACKLEY, HACKMAN, HACKNEY, HACKWORTH (includes Hackworthe, Hack), HADATH, HADAWAY, HADDEN, HADDIX, HADDOCK, HADDON, HADDOW, HADEN, HADENFELDT, HADFIELD, HADLEY, HADLOCK.

- **"HAE-HAH" Surname Mailing Lists**
http://www.rootsweb.com/~jfuller/gen_mail_surnames-hae.html
HAFER, HAFFEY (includes Haffy), HAFFTEN, HAFLEY, HAGA (includes Haaga, Haiga, Hayga, Heyga), HAGAMAN (includes Hageman, Hagerman, Hegeman), HAGAN, HAGAR, HAGEDORN (includes Van Hagedorn, Van Hagedoorn, Hagedoorn), HAGELIN, HAGEMAN, HAGEN, HAGENBUCH, HAGER, HAGERMAN, HAGERTY (includes Haggerty, Hegarty, Heagerty, Heaggarty, O'Heagarty, O'Hagerty, O'Haggerty), HAGEY, HAGGARD, HAGGART, HAGGERTY, HAGLER (includes Haigler, Hegler), HAGMANN, HAGOOD (includes Haygood, Haigwood, Heygood), HAGUE (includes Haigh), HAGUEWOOD, HAGY (includes Hage, Hagey), HAHN.

- **"HAI-HAN" Surname Mailing Lists**
http://www.rootsweb.com/~jfuller/gen_mail_surnames-hai.html
HAIG, HAIGHT, HAIL, HAILE, HAILEY, HAIN, HAINER, HAINES, HAIR, HAIRE (includes Hair, O'Hair, O'Haegher), HAIRSTON, HAKE, HAKE, HALAMA, HALBACH (includes Halback, Hallbach, Hallback), HALBERT, HALCROW, HALDEMAN, HALE (includes Haile, Heale), HALES, HALEY (includes Hailey, Haly), HALFACRE (includes Halfaker, Huffaker), HALFORD, HALKETT, HALL, HALL, HALL, HALL, HALL, HALL, HALLADAY, HALLAM, HALLDAVID, HALLENBECK, HALLER, HALLETT, HALLEY, HALLFORD (includes Halford), HALLIDAY, HALLIGAN, HALLISEY (includes Hallissey, Hallissy, Hallacy, Halsey), HALLIWELL, HALLMAN (includes Heilman, Heilmann), HALLMARK, HALLOCK, HALLORAN (includes O'Halloran, Holloran), HALLOWELL, HALLUM, HALPEN, HALSELL, HALSEY, HALSEY, HALSTEAD, HALSTED, HALTER, HALTERMAN (includes Halderman, Haltiman), HALVERSON, HAM, HAMAKER (includes Hamacher, Haymaker), HAMANN, HAMBLEN, HAMBLETON (includes Hambleden), HAMBLIN, HAMBLY, HAMBRICK, HAMBY, HAMEL, HAMELIN, HAMER (includes Hamor), HAMERLY, HAMES, HAMIL, HAMILL, HAMILTON, HAMLET, HAMLETT, HAMLIN (includes Hamblin), HAMLYN, HAMM, HAMMACK (includes Hammock, Hamack), HAMMAKER, HAMMAN (includes Hammon, Hammond, Hammen, Hammin), HAMMEL, HAMMER, HAMMERSON, HAMMETT, HAMMOCK, HAMMON, HAMMOND, HAMMOND, HAMMONDS, HAMMONS, HAMMONTREE, HAMNER (includes Hanmer), HAMPSHIRE, HAMPSON, HAMPTON, HAMRICK (includes Hambrick, Hemric), HANCE, HANCHARD, HANCHETT, HANCOCK (includes Handcock), HANCOCK, HAND (includes Hann), HANDCOCK, HANDLEY (includes Handly, Hanley, Hanly), HANDLON, HANDS, HANDY, HANES, HANEY (includes Hany, Heany, Heaney, Heny), HANFORD, HANGS, HANGSTORFER (includes Hangstafer, Hangstaufer, Hangstdoerfer, Hangsdorfer, Hangstoerfer, Hangstaffer,, Hangsterfer), HANKE, HANKINS, HANKS (includes Hank, Hanke, Hankey, Hancks, Hanckes, Henks, Henke, Henkins), HANLEY, HANLON (includes O'Hanlon), HANN, HANNA (includes Hannah, Hannay), HANNAFORD, HANNAH, HANNAN, HANNEKEN (includes Haneken), HANNEMAN, HANNEMANN, HANNIBAL, HANNIGAN (includes Hannigen, Hanigan, Hanegan), HANNON, HANNUM, HANRAHAN, HANRATTY (includes Hanretty), HANS, HANSEL, HANSELL, HANSEN, HANSFORD, HANSON, HANSSON.

- **"HAO-HAR" Surname Mailing Lists**
http://www.rootsweb.com/~jfuller/gen_mail_surnames-hao.html
HAPEMAN, HAPGOOD, HAPPE, HAPPE, HARADON, HARALSON, HARBAUGH, HARBERT (includes Herbert),

HARBIN, HARBISON (includes Harbinson, Harbeson, Harvison, Harveson, Harberson), HARBOUR, HARBUCK, HARCOURT (includes d'Harcourt), HARD, HARDCASTLE, HARDEMAN (includes Hardyman, Hardiman), HARDEMAN, HARDEN (includes Hardin, Hardan), HARDENBERGH, HARDER, HARDESTY (includes Hardisty, Hardiesty, Hardestie, Hardister, Hardester), HARDIE, HARDIN (includes Harden, Harding), HARDING, HARDINGER (includes Hartinger), HARDISON, HARDISTER (includes Hardester, Hardster), HARDMAN (includes Hardeman, Hardiman, Hardyman), HARDMAN (includes Hardeman, Hardiman, Hardyman), HARDWICK, HARDWICK, HARDY (includes Hardee, Hardie), HARDY (includes Hardie), HARE, HARFORD, HARGER, HARGETT (includes Hargratt, Hargate), HARGIS (includes Hargas, Harges, Hargiss, Hargus), HARGRAVE, HARGRAVES, HARGREAVES (includes Hargreave, Hargrave, Hargraves, Hargrove, Hargroves), HARGREAVES, HARGROVE, HARING, HARKER, HARKEY (includes Herch, Herche, Herche Der Junge), HARKIN, HARKINS, HARKNESS, HARLAN, HARLAND, HARLESS, HARLESS (includes Harles, Harlos, Herlass), HARLEY, HARLING, HARLOW (includes Harlowe, Harlough), HARMAN (includes Harmon), HARMER, HARMISON, HARMON, HARMS, HARNDEN, HARNED (includes Harnett, Horned), HARNER, HARNESS, HARNETT, HARNEY, HARNISH, HARNSBERGER (includes Hansberger, Hansborgow, Harrensparger, Heerensperger), HAROLD, HARP, HARP, HARPER (includes Herber), HARPOLD (includes Harpool, Harpole, Herboldt), HARPOLE, HARR, HARRADEN (includes Harreden), HARRAH (includes Harrow, O'Harrow, Harra), HARRELL (includes Harrill, Haral, Harral, Harold, Harrold), HARRELSON, HARRIES, HARRIGAN, HARRIMAN, HARRINGTON (includes Herrington, Harington), HARRINGTON, HARRIS, HARRIS, HARRIS, HARRISON (includes Harison, Harrisson, Harreston, Herrison), HARROD, HARROLD, HARROP (includes Harrap, Harrup, Haroppe), HARRY, HARSH, HARSHBARGER, HARSHMAN, HART (includes Hartt, Heart), HARTER, HARTFORD, HARTIGAN, HARTILL (includes Harthill), HARTLE, HARTLEB, HARTLESS, HARTLEY, HARTLOFF, HARTMAN (includes Hartmann), HARTMANN, HARTNESS, HARTNETT, HARTRUM, HARTSELL (includes Hartzell, Hartsel, Hartzel), HARTSHORN (includes Hartshorne, Hartson), HARTSOCK, HARTSOOK (includes Herzog, Hartsock, Heartsock, Hartog, Hartough, Hartsough), HARTUNG, HARTWELL, HARTWICK, HARTWIG, HARTY, HARTZELL, HARTZOG, HARVELL, HARVES, HARVEY (includes Harvie), HARVICK, HARVIE, HARVILLE, HARVIN, HARWELL, HARWOOD (includes Harrod, Harewood, Horwood).

- **"HAS-HAT" Surname Mailing Lists**
http://www.rootsweb.com/~jfuller/gen_mail_surnames-has.html
HASBROUCK (includes Hasbrock, Hasbrook), HASEMAN (includes Hasseman, Hasemann), HASH (includes Hashe, Hache), HASHBERGER (includes Harshberger, Hirchberger), HASKELL, HASKET, HASKIN, HASKINS, HASLAM, HASLETT, HASS, HASSELDIECK (includes Hasseldick, Hazeldick, Hazeldeck, Hasseldeck, Haseldick, Hasildick), HASSELL, HASSETT, HASSINGER, HASSLER, HASSON, HASTEN (includes Hastings, Hasting, Hastin, Haston), HASTIE, HASTINGS, HASTY, HASWELL (includes Hasswell), HATAWAY, HATCH (includes Hacche, Hach), HATCHELL, HATCHER, HATCHETT, HATFIELD, HATHAWAY (includes Haddaway, Hataway), HATHCOCK, HATLEY, HATT, HATTAWAY, HATTEN, HATTON, HATTRUP (includes Hattrupp, Hatrupp, Hartrup, Hartrupp, Harttrupp).

- **"HAU-HD" Surname Mailing Lists**
  http://www.rootsweb.com/~jfuller/gen_mail_surnames-hau.html
  HAUCK, HAUER, HAUG, HAUGEN, HAUGH, HAUGHN (includes Hahn), HAUGHT, HAUGHTON, HAUK, HAULK, HAUN, HAUN, HAUPT, HAUS, HAUSE, HAUSER, HAVARD, HAVEN, HAVENS, HAVERFIELD, HAVILAND, HAVINS (includes Havens), HAWES, HAWES (includes Haws), HAWK (includes Hawkes, Hawks, Hauk), HAWK, HAWKE, HAWKEN, HAWKER, HAWKES, HAWKINS (includes Hawkyns, Hawking), HAWKS, HAWLEY, HAWMAN, HAWORTH, HAWS, HAWTHORN, HAWTHORNE, HAWVER, HAY, HAYCOCK, HAYDEN (includes Heydon, Haydon, Hadden, Haden, Hyden), HAYDON, HAYES (includes Hays, Hayse, Haze), HAYGOOD, HAYHURST, HAYLINGS, HAYMAKER, HAYMAN, HAYMOND, HAYNE, HAYNEN (includes Heenan, Heanen, Henning), HAYNES (includes Hanes, Haines), HAYNIE, HAYS, HAYS, HAYSLIP, HAYTER, HAYTON, HAYWARD, HAYWOOD, HAZARD (includes Hasard, Hazzard, Hassard), HAZEL, HAZEL (includes Hazell, Hassell), HAZELL, HAZELRIGG (includes Heselridge), HAZELTINE, HAZELTON, HAZELWOOD, HAZEN, HAZLETT (includes Haslett, Haislett, Haslit, Haslitt, Hayslett, Heaslett, Hazlitt), HAZLEWOOD.

- **"HEA-HED" Surname Mailing Lists**
  http://www.rootsweb.com/~jfuller/gen_mail_surnames-hea.html
  HEACKER (includes Hecker, Hacker, Hüecker), HEAD (includes Headlee, Headley, Headly), HEADEN, HEADLEY, HEADRICK, HEADY, HEALD, HEALEY (includes Healy), HEALY, HEANEY, HEAP, HEARD, HEARN, HEARNE (includes Hearn, Hern, Herrin, Herron, Heron), HEARST, HEASLEY, HEATH (includes Heathcock, Heathcote, Heather, Heatherington), HEATHCOCK, HEATHCOTE, HEATHERINGTON, HEATLEY, HEATON, HEAVEN, HEAVER, HEBERLIG, HEBERLING, HEBERT, HEBERT (includes Abear, Abert, Abair), HECHLER, HECHT, HECK, HECKEL, HECKER, HECKERT, HECKMAN (includes Heckaman, Hickman), HECTOR (includes Hecter, Hecktor, Heckter, Hektor, Hekter), HECTORNE, HEDDEN (includes Headen, Heden, Heddan, Heddin, Heddins, Hadden, Haddon, Heady, Heddy), HEDGE, HEDGEPETH (includes Hedgpeth), HEDGER, HEDGES (includes Hedge), HEDLEY, HEDRICK (includes Headrick), HEDRINGTON.

- **"HEE-HEH" Surname Mailing Lists**
  http://www.rootsweb.com/~jfuller/gen_mail_surnames-hee.html
  HEFFERNAN, HEFFLEY, HEFFNER, HEFFRON (includes Heffernan), HEFLIN (includes Hefflin, Heflen, Heffernon), HEFNER, HEGARTY, HEGGIE, HEGLE (includes Hiigle, Higley, Hegley, Heigley, Hagle).

- **"HEI-HEN" Surname Mailing Lists**
  http://www.rootsweb.com/~jfuller/gen_mail_surnames-hei.html
  HEIDEMANN, HEIDEN, HEIDENREICH, HEIDER, HEIDL, HEIFNER, HEIL, HEILMAN, HEILMANN, HEIM, HEIMBACH, HEIN, HEINBAUGH, HEINE, HEINEMANN, HEINITZ, HEINKLE, HEINLEIN (includes Heulein, Hainline), HEINONEN, HEINRICH, HEINTZ, HEINZ, HEINZE (includes Heinz), HEISE, HEISER, HEISLER, HEITMANN, HEITZ, HELD, HELFERICH (includes Helfrich), HELL, HELLER, HELLUMS, HELM (includes Helms, Hellums, Elam, Ellams, Hallam, Kellums, Nelms, Halm, Helmig, Helmoldus, Chelm, Cellums,, Shelem, Shalem, Gelm, Hellmann, Helmstedter, Helmreich, Hjelm, Helmont, Helmbold, Swethelm, Helmsley,, McHelm, Helmers, Elmo, Helmes, Holmes), HELMAN (includes Hellman, Hellmann, Heilman, Heylman), HELMANDOLLAR (includes Helmanduller, Helmundollar,

- *Helmundoller), HELMER, HELMICK, HELMS, HELSEL, HELTON, HELTON, HELVEY (includes Helvie, Helvy, Helwig), HELWIG, HEMBREE, HEMENWAY, HEMING (includes Hemming), HEMINGWAY, HEMINGWAY (includes Hemmingway, Hemenway, Heminwaye), HEMMING, HEMOND (includes Hemon, Hemont, Haimond, Emond, Emon, Emont, Aymond, Aymong, Aymon, Aumont,, Aumond), HEMP, HEMPHILL, HEMPHILL, HEMSLEY, HENAULT, HENCH, HENDERSHOT, HENDERSON, HENDERSON, HENDERSON, HENDERSON, HENDLEY, HENDON, HENDREN, HENDRICK, HENDRICKS, HENDRICKSON, HENDRICKS (includes Hendrix, Hendrickson), HENDRIX, HENDRY, HENEAGE, HENEAULT, HENES, HENKE, HENKEL, HENLEY, HENLY (includes Henley, Hendly, Hendley), HENN, HENNEBERRY, HENNELLY, HENNESSEE, HENNESSEY, HENNESSY, HENNING (includes Hening), HENNING, HENNINGER, HENNION (includes Henion, Henyon, Henyan), HENRY (includes Henri, Henery, McHenry), HENSCHEL, HENSEL, HENSHAW, HENSLEY (includes Hindsley, Henslee, Handsley), HENSON, HENTHORN, HENTHORN (includes Henthorne, Hinthorn, Hinthorne, Hanthorn), HENTON, HENWOOD.*

- **"HEO-HET" Surname Mailing Lists**
  http://www.rootsweb.com/~jfuller/gen_mail_surnames-heo.html
  HEPBURN, HEPLER (includes Heppler, Hoppler), HEPP, HERALD, HERAMB (includes Heram), HERBAGE, HERBERGER, HERBERT, HERBST, HERD (includes Heard, Hird, Hurd), HEREFORD (includes Herryford, Herriford, Heryford), HERGERT, HERION (includes Herron), HERLIHY (includes Herelehy, Herelihy, Herely, Herihily, Heriley, Herily, Herlahy, Herlehay, Herleher, Herlehey,, Herlehy, Herleihy, Herley, Herlighy, Herlihan, Herlihen, Herlihey, Herling, Herly, Hierlehy, Hierley, O'Heirlihy,, O'Herlihy), HERMAN (includes Hermann, Herrman, Herrmann), HERMANN, HERMES, HERNANDEZ, HERNDON, HEROLD, HERON, HERR, HERREN, HERRICK, HERRIDGE, HERRIDGE (includes Herriage, Herrage), HERRIMAN, HERRIN, HERRING (includes Herrin, Herron), HERRINGSHAW, HERRINGTON, HERRMAN, HERRMANN, HERROD, HERRON, HERSEY, HERSH, HERSHBERGER, HERSHELMAN (includes Herschelman, Herschelmann, Hirschelmann, Hesselman, Hoerschelmann), HERSHEY, HERSUM (includes Hersom, Hershum, Horsam, Horsom, Horsum), HERTEL, HERVEY, HERZ, HERZOG, HESCH, HESLAR, HESLER (includes Hessler, Heslar, Hesslar, Hosler, Hossler), HESLIN, HESLOP, HESS, HESSE, HESSEK (includes Hesek, Hezek, Heszek), HESSION, HESSLER, HESTER, HESTERLY (includes Hesterlee, Hesterle, Hesterley, Hestle), HESTON, HETHERINGTON, HETRICK, HETT, HETTINGER, HETZEL (includes Hezel, Heltzel), HETZEL.

- **"HEU-HH" Surname Mailing Lists**
  http://www.rootsweb.com/~jfuller/gen_mail_surnames-heu.html
  HEUS, HEUTON, HEWER, HEWES, HEWETT, HEWIT, HEWITT, HEWITT-COLEMAN, HEWLETT, HEWSON, HEYDEL (includes Dzieduszycki), HEYDON, HEYL, HEYMAN, HEYWARD, HEYWOOD.

- **"HI-HN" Surname Mailing Lists**
  http://www.rootsweb.com/~jfuller/gen_mail_surnames-hi.html
  HIATT (includes Hyatt, Hiett, Hyett), HIBBARD, HIBBERT, HIBBERT (includes Hibberd, Hibbard), HIBBINS (includes Hybbens, Hibon, Hibons, Hibbin, Hibben, Hibbens), HIBBS, HIBBS, HIBDON (includes Hibden, Hebden), HIBEL (includes Hebel, Hübel, Huebel, Heubel, Hubal), HICKAM (includes Hickem, Hickham, Hickhem), HICKENLOOPER, HICKERSON, HICKEY

(includes Hicke, Hicki, Hickie, Hicky), HICKMAN, HICKOCK, HICKOK, HICKOX, HICKS, HICKSON, HIEBER (includes Heber, Heiber, Heaber), HIERS, HIESTAND, HIESTER, HIETT, HIGBEE, HIGBIE (includes Higbee, Higby), HIGDON, HIGGASON, HIGGENSON, HIGGINBOTHAM (includes Higgingbottom, Hickingbottom, Hickenbottom, Hickingbotham), HIGGINS (includes Higgie, O'Higgins, Higgens, O'Higgeen, O'hUigin), HIGGINS, HIGGINSON, HIGGS, HIGH, HIGHLAND, HIGHMORE (includes Highmoor), HIGHSMITH, HIGHT, HIGHTOWER, HIGLEY, HILARIDES (includes Hylarides, Hijlarides), HILBERT, HILDEBRAND, HILDEBRANDT, HILDRETH, HILE, HILER, HILES (includes Hyles), HILL (includes Hills, Hille), HILLENBURG, HILLER, HILLERY (includes Hilleary, Hillary, Hilliary), HILLEY, HILLHOUSE, HILLIARD, HILLIER (includes Hillierd, Hilliar, Hilliard, Hillyer), HILLIKER (includes Hillaker, Hillicker), HILLIS, HILLMAN, HILLOCK, HILLS, HILLYARD, HILLYER, HILT, HILTON (includes Hylton), HILTS, HILTZ, HILYARD, HIMES, HIMMELBERG, HIMMELBERGER, HINCH, HINCHEE (includes Hinchey, Hinchy), HINCHLIFFE (includes Hinchcliffe, Hinchcliff, Hinchecliffe, Inchcliffe, Hinchliffe, Hinchliff, Hinchsliffe, Hinchsliff,, Hinsliffe, Hinsliff, Hincliffe, Hinckliefff, Hinchley, Inchley, Henchcliffe, Henchcliff, Henchle), HINCHMAN, HINCHMAN, HINCKLEY, HIND, HINDLE, HINDMAN, HINDS, HINDS (includes Hind, Hines), HINE, HINER, HINES, HINK, HINKEL, HINKLE, HINKLEY, HINKSON (includes Hinkston), HINMAN, HINOJOSA (includes Hino, Hionjos, Hinojoza), HINSDALE, HINSHAW (includes Henshaw, Henshall), HINSON (includes Henson), HINTON, HINTZ, HINZMAN, HIPP (includes Hepp, Hip, Hipps, Hepps), HIPPARD, HIPPLE, HIRASUNA (includes Hirasago, Hirasako), HIRD, HIRSCH, HIRST, HIRT, HISCOCK, HISE (includes Heiss, Heise, Heis, Hys, Hice, Van Hise, Voorheis), HISER, HISSOM (includes Hisson, Hissun, Hesson, Hession, O'Hession, Oh'Oission), HISSONG, HITCH, HITCHCOCK, HITCHMAN, HITE, HITT, HITTLE (includes Hittel, Hyttel), HIVELY, HIX, HIXON, HIXON, HIXSON.

- **"HOA-HOD" Surname Mailing Lists**
  http://www.rootsweb.com/~jfuller/gen_mail_surnames-hoa.html
  HOADLEY, HOAG, HOAGLAND, HOAR, HOARD, HOARE, HOBACK, HOBAN (includes Hoben, Hobin, Hooban, Howbane, Huban, Hubane), HOBARD, HOBART, HOBART (includes Hubbard), HOBBS, HOBBY, HOBDAY, HOBGOOD, HOBSON (includes Hopson), HOCH, HOCHARD, HOCHINTRAVANUG (includes Hockintaganing), HOCK, HOCKADAY (includes Hockday, Hoccaday, Hochaday, Hoccadie, Hockerdy), HOCKENBERRY (includes Hockenbery, Hackenberry, Hawkenbury, Hachenberg), HOCKER, HOCKETT, HOCKING, HOCUTT (includes Hoket, Howcott, Hocot), HODDY, HODGE, HODGES (includes Hodge, Hedge), HODGES, HODGINS, HODGKINS, HODGKINSON, HODGSON, HODNETT, HODO (includes Hodoe, Hodos, Hoda), HODSON.

- **"HOE-HOH" Surname Mailing Lists**
  http://www.rootsweb.com/~jfuller/gen_mail_surnames-hoe.html
  HOEFLER, HOEHN, HOEY (includes Hoy, Haughey), HOFBAUER (includes Hoffbauer), HOFER, HOFF (includes Huff, Hough), HOFFECKER, HOFFER, HOFFMAN (includes Hofman, Hoffmann, Hofmann, Huffman, Hufman), HOFFMANN, HOFFPAUIR (includes Hoffpauer, Huffpower), HOFMANN, HOGAN, HOGAN, HOGE, HOGENCAMP (includes Hogancamp, Hovencamp, Hovenkamp), HOGG (includes Hoge, Hogue, Hague), HOGGARD, HOGGE, HOGGETT (includes Hoggatt), HOGLE (includes Hogel), HOGSHEAD, HOGUE, HOHMANN, HOHN, HOHNBAUM.

- **"HOI-HON" Surname Mailing Lists**
  http://www.rootsweb.com/~jfuller/gen_mail_surnames-hoi.html
  HOISINGTON (includes Hossington, Hosington, Hassington, Hissington, Hossenton, Hyselton, Hesselton), HOKE, HOLBEN, HOLBERT (includes Halbert, Hulbert), HOLBERT (includes Halbert, Haubert, Hurlburt, Howbert), HOLBROOK, HOLCOMB, HOLCOMBE, HOLD, HOLDEMAN, HOLDEN, HOLDEN (includes Holding, Holdin, Holder), HOLDENGRABER (includes von Holdengraber, von Holdengraeber, Holdengraeber, Holden), HOLDER (includes Holdour, Holdor), HOLDERNESS (includes Houlderness, Holdernes, Houldernesse, Holdernesse), HOLDING, HOLDRIDGE, HOLDSWORTH, HOLE, HOLEHOUSE, HOLEMAN, HOLFORD, HOLGATE, HOLIDAY, HOLIFIELD (includes Hollifield, Hollyfield, Holyfield, Holderfield), HOLL, HOLLADAY, HOLLAND, HOLLAND, HOLLAND (includes Hollands, Holand, Oland), HOLLANDER, HOLLARS, HOLLENBECK, HOLLER (includes Hollar, Haller), HOLLETT, HOLLEY, HOLLIDAY (includes Halliday, Halladay, Holladay, Halladie), HOLLIMAN, HOLLINGER (includes Hullinger), HOLLINGSHEAD, HOLLINGSHEAD, HOLLINGSWORTH, HOLLINGWORTH, HOLLINS, HOLLIS, HOLLISTER, HOLLISTER, HOLLOMAN (includes Hollyman), HOLLOPETER (includes Hollipeter, Hollopter, Hallopeter, Hollopetre, Hullopeter, Holopeter, Hollopater), HOLLOWAY, HOLLOWELL (includes Hallowell, Holliwell, Halliwell, Hollewell, Hallewell), HOLLY, HOLLYMAN (includes Holliman, Holleman, Holloman), HOLM, HOLMAN (includes Hollman, Hallman), HOLMBERG, HOLMBO, HOLMEN, HOLMES (includes Hohmes, Holemes, Holms, Hom, Home, Homes, Hooms), HOLMWOOD (includes Homewood), HOLSAPPLE (includes Holsopple, Holtzapfel), HOLSEY, HOLST, HOLSTEIN, HOLSTON, HOLSTROM, HOLT (includes Holte), HOLTEN, HOLTHUSEN (includes Holdhusen, Holthousen), HOLTON, HOLTRY, HOLTZ, HOLTZCLAW (includes Holtsclaw, Holsclaw, Holseclaw), HOLYFIELD, HOLYOKE, HOLZ, HOMAN, HOMER, HOMEWOOD, HOMME, HOMMEL (includes Hommell, Homel, Hummel, Humel, Humble), HOMOKI, HONAKER, HONE, HONEA (includes Honey, Honay), HONEY, HONEYCUTT (includes Honneycutt, Honeycut, Honneycut, Huneycutt, Hunneycutt, Huneycut, Hunneycut, Honicutt,, Honnicutt, Honicut, Honnicut, Hunicutt, Hunnicutt, Hunicut, Hunnicut), HONEYMAN, HONIG, HONKANEN, HONNOLL (includes Hunnell), HONTZ (includes Hons, Haunce, Honts, Hants), HONYCHURCH (includes Honeychurch).

- **"HOO-HOT" Surname Mailing Lists**
  http://www.rootsweb.com/~jfuller/gen_mail_surnames-hoo.html
  HOOD, HOOFNAGEL (includes Hoofnagle, Hofeneghel, Hoofenagel, Hofnagle, Hufnagel, Hufnagle, Huffnagle), HOOK, HOOKER, HOOKS (includes Hook), HOOLEY, HOOPER, HOOPER, HOOPER, HOOPES, HOOPINGARNER, HOOTEN, HOOTER, HOOTON, HOOTS, HOOVER, HOPE (includes Hoppe), HOPEWELL (includes Hopwell), HOPKINS, HOPKINSON, HOPP, HOPPE, HOPPENRATH, HOPPER (includes Hooper, Hoppe, Hoppen), HOPPES, HOPSON, HOPWOOD, HORALEK, HORAN, HORAN, HORD, HORINE, HORLER (includes Horlor, Harler, Horley), HORN, HORNADAY, HORNBEAK, HORNBECK (includes Hornback), HORNBECK, HORNBERGER, HORNBUCKLE, HORNBUCKLE, HORNBY, HORNE (includes Horn), HORNER, HORNEY, HORNING, HORNSBY (includes Hornby), HORNUNG, HOROWITZ, HORRELL, HORRIDGE, HORRIGAN (includes Horgan, Hourigan), HORROCKS, HORSEMAN, HORSEPOOL, HORSLEY, HORST, HORTENBURY (includes Hortenberrry, Whortenbury, Whortenberry, Hortenburg, Whortenbburg), HORTON (includes Horten, Orton), HORTON, HORTON,

HORVATH, HOSBACH, HOSEY (includes Hossey, Hosea, Hozey, Hosse, Hose), HOSFORD, HOSIER, HOSKEN (includes Hoskin, Hoskins, Hosking, Hoskyn), HOSKING, HOSKINS, HOSKINSON, HOSMAN, HOSMER, HOSS, HOSTETLER, HOSTETTER, HOSTRUP, HOTCHKISS, HOTCHKISS, HOTRUM, HOTTEL, HOTZ.

- ## "HOU-HT" Surname Mailing Lists
  http://www.rootsweb.com/~jfuller/gen_mail_surnames-hou.html
  HOUCHENS (includes Houchins, Houchen, Houchin), HOUCHIN, HOUCHINS, HOUCK (includes Houk, Hauck, Hauk), HOUGH, HOUGHTALING, HOUGHTON (includes Haughton), HOUK, HOULE, HOULIHAN, HOUNSELL, HOUSDEN (includes Housdan, Housdon, Howsden, Howsdon, Howson), HOUSE, HOUSEHOLDER (includes Housholder, Hausholter, Haushalter), HOUSEL, HOUSEMAN, HOUSER, HOUSH, HOUSTON (includes Huston), HOUT (includes Haudt, Haut, Haute, Houte), HOUX, HOVATTER, HOVER (includes Huber, Hoover), HOVEY, HOVIS, HOW, HOWARD, HOWARD (includes Hayward, Howarth), HOWARTH, HOWDER (includes Houder, Houter, Hauder, Hauter), HOWE (includes How), HOWELL, HOWELL, HOWELLS, HOWER, HOWERTON, HOWERY (includes Hauri, Haury, Hourie, Howrey, Howrie, Howry), HOWES, HOWETH, HOWEY, HOWIE, HOWINGTON, HOWLAND, HOWLE, HOWLETT, HOWLEY, HOWREN (includes Howran), HOWSE, HOXIE, HOXTER, HOY, HOYER, HOYLAND, HOYLE (includes Hoile), HOYT (includes Haight), HOYT (includes Haight).

- ## "HU-HZ" Surname Mailing Lists
  http://www.rootsweb.com/~jfuller/gen_mail_surnames-hu.html
  HUBAND (includes Hubolt), HUBBARD (includes Hobart, Hubert, Hibbard, Hubbel, Halbert, O'Hubbard), HUBBELL (includes Hubble, Hubbel, Hubel, Hubball), HUBBERT, HUBBLE, HUBBS, HUBER, HUBERT, HUBLER, HUBLEY (includes Hubely, Hubele), HUCK, HUCKABEE (includes Huccoby, Huckaby), HUCKABY (includes Huccoby, Huckabee), HUCKBODY, HUCKS (includes Hux), HUCKSTEP, HUDDLESTON (includes Hudelson), HUDGENS, HUDGINS, HUDNALL, HUDON, HUDSON, HUDSON (includes Hutson, Hutsen, Husten, Cudson, Huttson),

HUDSPETH, HUEBNER, HUESMAN (includes Husmann, Huseman, Hussman, Huisman), HUETT (includes Huitt), HUEY, HUFFINES (includes Huff, Hoffheintz), HUFF, HUFFAKER, HUFFMAN (includes Hufman, Hofman, Hoffman), HUFFORD (includes Hoffarth, Hoffart, Hoffort, Hoffert, Huffert, Hufferd), HUFSTEDLER, HUG, HUGG, HUGGINS (includes Hudgins), HUGHES (includes McHugh, McCue, Huge, Hough, Hews, Hughs, Hughey), HUGHES, HUGHES, HUGHEY (includes Hughie, Huey), HUGHEY, HUGHS, HUGHSON, HUHN, HUIE (includes Hui, Houy, Houay, Huet, Howie, Howey, Huey), HUKILL, HULBERT, HULEN, HULET, HULETT, HULING, HULL, HULLENDER, HULME (includes de Hulme), HULSE, HULSE (includes Hulce, Huls, Hults, Hultz, Holsaert, Hulsart, Hulseheart), HULSEY, HULTENIUS, HUMAN (includes Humann, Hueman, Hughman, Hewman), HUMBER, HUMBERT, HUMBLE (includes Umble), HUME, HUMES, HUMFLEET (includes Umfleet), HUMMEL, HUMMER, HUMPHREY, HUMPHREYS (includes Humphries, Humphrey, Umphrey), HUMPHRIES, HUND, HUNDLEY, HUNGERFORD, HUNN, HUNNICUTT, HUNSAKER, HUNSBERGER, HUNSICKER, HUNSUCKER (includes Hunsicker, Hunsinger, Honsooker, Huntsucker, Hunsecker, Huntsicker), HUNT, HUNTER, HUNTING, HUNTING (includes Huntting), HUNTINGTON, HUNTLEY, HUNTOON (includes Hunton, Hanton, Henton, Hinton, Honton, Hynton), HUNTSMAN, HUNTZICKER, HUPP, HURD, HURDLE (includes Hurdel, Hurdell), HURFORD, HURLBURT, HURLBUT, HURLBUTT, HURLESS, HURLEY, HURLOCK, HURREN, HURST, HURST, HURST, HURSTER, HURT, HURT (includes Hurtt), HURT, HURTFIELD, HURTT, HURTUBISE, HUSBAND (includes Husbands, Husbend, Husbends, Husbind, Husbinds), HUSER, HUSK, HUSKEY (includes Husky), HUSKIE, HUSON, HUSS, HUSSEY (includes Huse, Husse, Hussy), HUSSIN, HUSTED (includes Huested, Hustead), HUSTON, HUTCHCRAFT, HUTCHENS, HUTCHESON, HUTCHINGS, HUTCHINS, HUTCHINSON (includes Hudgins, Houghton, Hodgeson, Huggins, Hutcheson), HUTCHISON (includes Hutchinson, Hutcheson, Hutcherson, Hutchins), HUTH, HUTSON, HUTT, HUTTO, HUTTON, HUTTY (includes Utty, Uttey, Huttie, Futty), HUXTABLE, HYATT, HYDE, HYDEN (includes Hiden), HYDER, HYLAND, HYLTON, HYMAN, HYMER, HYNE, HYNES, HYRE.

SURNAMES, FAMILY ASSOCIATIONS & FAMILY NEWSLETTERS – "I"

Resources Dedicated to One Surname
http://www.cyndislist.com/surn-i.htm

Category Index:

◆ General Surname Sites and Resources

◆ Surname Specific Sites and Resources

◆ Surname Mailing Lists

◆ General Surname Sites and Resources

● Connect with Surnames - I
http://www.geocities.com/Heartland/Bluffs/7708/i.html

● Dutch Home Pages by Familyname ~ Letter I
http://members.tripod.com/~Don_Arnoldus/i.htm

● FamilyHistory.com - Message Boards - Surname - I
http://www.familyhistory.com/messages/list.asp?prefix=IA

● Family Tree Maker Online User Home Pages - I
http://www.familytreemaker.com/users/i/index.html

● Family Workings I Surname Links
http://www.familyworkings.com/links/suri.htm

● GenConnect Surname Index - "I"
http://genconnect.rootsweb.com/indx/surnames/I.html
Message boards sponsored by RootsWeb. Each surname message board set is divided into the following topics: Queries, Bibles, Biographies, Deeds, Obituaries, Pensions, Wills.

● Genealogy Resources on the Internet - "I" Surname Mailing Lists
http://www.rootsweb.com/~jfuller/gen_mail_surnames-i.html
Search the index of surname mailing lists below: Surname Mailing Lists.

  ○ Genealogy Resources on the Internet - Surnames Included in Mailing Lists - "I"
  http://www-personal.umich.edu/~cgaunt/surnames/i.names.html
  This is a computer generated list of the surnames, and all variant spellings for those names, that are found in the surname mailing lists detailed on the pages shown above.

● Genealogy Resources on the Internet - Surname Web Sites for "I,J" Surnames
http://www-personal.umich.edu/~cgaunt/surnames/ij.html

● Genealogy's Most Wanted - Surnames Beginning with "I"
http://www.citynet.net/mostwanted/i.htm

● Google Web Directory .... Genealogy>Surnames>I
http://directory.google.com/Top/Society/Genealogy/Surnames/I/

● Heartland Genealogy Society Membership List - I
http://www.geocities.com/Heartland/Ranch/2416/hgs-mlist-i.html

● H-GIG Surname Registry - Surnames Beginning I
http://www.ucr.edu/h-gig/surdata/surname9.html

● Higginson Book Company - Surnames Beginning with I
http://www.higginsonbooks.com/i.htm

● inGeneas Table of Common Surname Variations and Surname Misspellings - H-J
http://www.ingeneas.com/H2J.html

● 'I' Surnames at RootsWeb
http://resources.rootsweb.com/surnames/i.html

● The Obituary Link Page - Family Obituary Archives Online - I-J
http://www.geocities.com/~cribbswh/obit/i-j.htm

● Open Directory - Society: Genealogy: Surnames: I
http://www.dmoz.org/Society/Genealogy/Surnames/I/

● Surname Springboard Index - I
http://www.geocities.com/~alacy/spring_i.htm

● SurnameWeb Surname Registry - I Index
http://www.surnameweb.org/registry/i.htm

● SWINX Zoeklijst Nederlandse Familienamen / SWINX Searchlist Dutch Surnames - I
http://www.swinx.net/swinx/swinx_i_nl.htm

● Websites at RootsWeb: I Surnames
http://www.rootsweb.com/~websites/surnames/i.html

◆ Surname Specific Sites and Resources

● The IBACH Family Archives
http://homepages.rootsweb.com/~ibach/index.htm
A surname repository for IBACH, EBACH, EBOCH, EBAUGH, EIBACH, EPOCH, JBACH.

- **ICENOGLE Genealogy**
  http://homepages.rootsweb.com/~icenogle/
  A web site for Isnogle, Icenoggle, Eisnaugle, Icenagle, Eissenagel, Icnogle, Isenogle, Isanogel, Eyesnogle, Icenogle genealogy.

- **deYgolvyndenne - a.k.a The Most Misspelled Name in History**
  http://freepages.genealogy.rootsweb.com/~iggulden/iggs.htm
  Iggulden, Iggleden, Igglesden, Eggleden, Egglesden, Higglesden.

- **IMRIE**
  http://homepages.rootsweb.com/~imrie/imrie.html

- **Descendants of William IMUS**
  http://www.parsonstech.com/genealogy/trees/rdwyer/imus%20fam.htm
  Lineage of the Imus family in America.

- **INGERSOLL Family Genealogy Research**
  http://www.ingersoll.net/

- **Jonathan INGLEE Descendants Home**
  http://www.asan.com/users/shypuppy/inglee0.html
  Descendants of Jonathan INGLEE of Middleboro + Taunton, MA, c1705-c1748, including the families of Ebenezer BABBITT, Ralph PHILLIPS, and Ichabod LINCOLN. Inglee, Ingell, Ingles, Ingley, Engley.

- **The INMAN Compendium**
  http://inman.surnameweb.org/index.htm
  Inman, Inmon.

- **The INMAN Compendium Genealogical Database**
  http://inman.surnameweb.org/genweb/Inman/Inman.htm
  A database that contains 1,001 names.

- **Descendants of Andrew and Anna IRION**
  http://members.aol.com/sherryew/Irion/Fam00072.html
  Ancestry and descendants of Andrew J. and Anna K. (ZELLER) IRION of Brittheim, Wurtemburg, Germany. Surnames include: Wagner, Wurm, Otto, Schmidt.

- **Genealogy of the IRVINE Clan - IRVINE Genealogy**
  http://www.irvineclan.com/
  The Irvine Clan stemming from Enniskillen, Northern Ireland, Ulster Province, County Fermanagh. Coming to America and branching off to Pennsylvania, St. Louis, Missouri, Mobile, Alabama, Washington DC, and many more.

- **IRVINE Family History**
  http://www.islandnet.com/~wji/reunion.html
  Irvines in Victoria, BC since 1851, formerly of Orkney County, Scotland, formerly of Drum Castle and Clan Irwin in 1369.

- **The ISELI Family Web Site**
  http://iseli.simplenet.com/
  Eseli, Esely, Esley, Isaly, Iseli, Isely, Isley, & Islie in America. Isel, Izel, Yselle, Yseli, & Yssel in South Africa.

- **ISMAY One Name Study**
  http://www.geocities.com/Athens/Crete/2737/
  The goal of the Ismay One Name Study (ONS) is to trace all occurrences of the name Ismay and variants, develop family trees and histories, publish the results and deposit the findings in international and national libraries for the benefit of other family historians both in the present and future. An added secondary benefit is providing a forum for family historians to discover more about their own personal ancestors, their characters, hopes, dreams and have a lot of fun doing it. The Ismay ONS is registered with the Guild of One Name Studies in London, England.

◆ Surname Mailing Lists

- **"I" Surname Mailing Lists**
  http://www.rootsweb.com/~jfuller/gen_mail_surnames-i.html
  IACOVELLI (includes Icovelli), IBBETSON, ICE, ICENOGLE (includes Eisennagel, Eisnaugle, Icenoggle, Isnogle, Isenogle, Isanogel, Icenagle, Eyesnogle), ICKES, IDDENDEN (includes Idenden, Iddenton, Iggenden, Eddenden, Edenden, Illenden), IDE, IDELL, IFFT (includes Ift, Eft, Yft), IGO, IJAMS (includes Iiams, Iams), ILES, ILLINGWORTH, IMBODY (includes Inbody, Imboden), IMIG (includes Immich), IMLER, IMMEL (includes Imel, Emil, Emmil, Emmel), IMMING (includes Immig, Immink, Imminck, Immingk, Immynck, Emming), IMPSON (includes Imson, Emson, Empson), IMRIE, IMRIE, IMUS, INABNIT (includes Abnet, Atnip, Ebinet, Enabnett, Enabnit, Enapnit, Enepnit, Hinderpint, Imäbnit, Im Äbnit, Im Aebnit,, Inabenent, Inabenet, Inabenett, Inabenint, Inabent, Inabet, Inabinet, Inabinett, Inabnet, Inabnett, Inabnip, In Äbnit,, Inabnitt, Inaebinet, In Aebnath, Inaebnit, In Aebnit, In Aebnith, Inapnit, Inatnip, Inbind, Inchnar, Indbnit, Indinet, Inebenet,, Inebinet, In Ebnet, Inebnit, InEnet, Inenet, Inent, Innabnit, Innapinit, Innepnet), INCE, INFINGER (includes Enfinger, Emfinger, Empfinger), INGALLS (includes Engolls, Ingolls, Ingals), INGE, INGERSOLL (includes Ingerson, Ingersole, Ingersol), INGHAM, INGHRAM, INGLE, INGLIS, INGRAHAM, INGRAM (includes Ingraham, Ingrahame, Ingrams), INMAN (includes Innman, Inmann, Hinman), INNERARITY (includes Inverarity), INNES, INSALL (includes Incel, Incil, Insalle, Insol), INSKEEP (includes Inskip), INSLEY, INYARD (includes Engard, Engart, Enger, Enjard, Enjart, Enjert, Enjoert, Enuard, Enyard, Enyardt, Enyart, Enyeart,, Ingard, Iniart, Inniard, Injaart, Injard, Inyart, Inyerd, Inyord, Yoreard, Yoriear), INYART (includes Engard, Engart, Enger, Enjard, Enjart, Enjert, Enjoert, Enuard, Enyard, Enyardt, Enyart, Enyeart,, Ingard, Iniart, Inniard, Injaart, Injard, Inyard, Inyerd, Inyord, Yoreard, Yoriear), IRBY, IRELAN (includes Ireland), IRELAND, IRION, IRISH, IRIZARRY (includes Irizarri, Yrizarri), IRONS, IRVIN (includes Irvine, Irving), IRVINE, IRVING, IRWIN, ISAAC, ISAACS (includes Isacks, Isaacks), ISAACSON, ISBELL (includes Isbel, Isabell), ISBISTER, ISENBERG (includes Eisenberg), ISHAM, ISHERWOOD, ISHMAEL, ISINGHOOD, ISLEY (includes Iseley, Iseli, Sele, Icely), ISNER (includes Iesner, Isnur, Isneur, Eyesner, Eysner), ISOM, ISON, ISRAEL, ITTER, ITTERMANN (includes Itterman), IVERS, IVERSON, IVES, IVESTER (includes Isbister), IVIE (includes Ivey, Ivy), IVORY, IVY, IWANIW (includes Evanue, Iwanow, Iwannow), IZATT (includes Isatt, Iset, Izet).

SURNAMES, FAMILY ASSOCIATIONS & FAMILY NEWSLETTERS – "J"

Resources Dedicated to One Surname
http://www.cyndislist.com/surn-j.htm

Category Index:

◆ General Surname Sites and Resources
◆ Surname Specific Sites and Resources

◆ Surname Mailing Lists

◆ General Surname Sites and Resources

- Connect with Surnames - J
  http://www.geocities.com/Heartland/Bluffs/7708/j.html

- Dutch Home Pages by Familyname ~ Letter J
  http://members.tripod.com/~Don_Arnoldus/j.htm

- FamilyHistory.com - Message Boards - Surname - J
  http://www.familyhistory.com/messages/list.asp?prefix=JA

- Family Tree Maker Online User Home Pages - J
  http://www.familytreemaker.com/users/j/index.html

- Family Workings J Surname Links
  http://www.familyworkings.com/links/surj.htm

- GenConnect Surname Index - "J"
  http://genconnect.rootsweb.com/indx/surnames/J.html
  Message boards sponsored by RootsWeb. Each surname message board set is divided into the following topics: Queries, Bibles, Biographies, Deeds, Obituaries, Pensions, Wills.

- Genealogy Resources on the Internet - "JA-JD" Surname Mailing Lists
  http://www.rootsweb.com/~jfuller/gen_mail_surnames-ja.html
  "JE-JH"
  http://www.rootsweb.com/~jfuller/gen_mail_surnames-je.html
  "JI-JZ"
  http://www.rootsweb.com/~jfuller/gen_mail_surnames-ji.html
  Search the index of surname mailing lists below: Surname Mailing Lists.

  o Genealogy Resources on the Internet - Surnames Included in Mailing Lists - "J"
    http://www-personal.umich.edu/~cgaunt/surnames/j.names.html
    This is a computer generated list of the surnames, and all variant spellings for those names, that are found in the surname mailing lists detailed on the pages shown above.

- Genealogy Resources on the Internet - Surname Web Sites for "I, J" Surnames
  http://www-personal.umich.edu/~cgaunt/surnames/ij.html

- Genealogy's Most Wanted - Surnames Beginning with "J"
  http://www.citynet.net/mostwanted/j.htm

- H-GIG Surname Registry - Surnames Beginning J
  http://www.ucr.edu/h-gig/surdata/surname10.html

- Google Web Directory .... Genealogy>Surnames>J
  http://directory.google.com/Top/Society/Genealogy/Surnames/J/

- Heartland Genealogy Society Membership List - J
  http://www.geocities.com/Heartland/Ranch/2416/hgs-mlist-j.html

- Higginson Book Company - Surnames Beginning with J
  http://www.higginsonbooks.com/j.htm

- inGeneas Table of Common Surname Variations and Surname Misspellings - H-J
  http://www.ingeneas.com/H2J.html

- 'J' Surnames at RootsWeb
  http://resources.rootsweb.com/surnames/j.html

- The Obituary Link Page - Family Obituary Archives Online - I-J
  http://www.geocities.com/~cribbswh/obit/i-j.htm

- Open Directory - Society: Genealogy: Surnames: J
  http://www.dmoz.org/Society/Genealogy/Surnames/J/

- Surname Springboard Index - J
  http://www.geocities.com/~alacy/spring_j.htm

- SurnameWeb Surname Registry - J Index
  http://www.surnameweb.org/registry/j.htm

- SWINX Zoeklijst Nederlandse Familienamen / SWINX Searchlist Dutch Surnames - J
  http://www.swinx.net/swinx/swinx_ja_nl.htm

- Websites at RootsWeb: J Surnames
  http://www.rootsweb.com/~websites/surnames/j.html

◆ Surname Specific Sites and Resources

- **JACKSON Brigade Association, Inc.**
  http://www.eg.bucknell.edu/~hyde/jackson/
  Genealogical Association for Descendants of John JACKSON (1715 - 1801). The purpose of the Jackson Brigade Association, Inc. is to research, preserve and exchange genealogical information about the family in the United States who are descendants of John and Elizabeth (Cummins) Jackson; and to strengthen family ties.

- **JACOY, JECOY, JOCOY Page**
  http://members.tripod.com/debyns/jecoy.html

- **JAMES Family in America**
  http://www.ericjames.net
  The largest JAMES surname database on the net. Includes the outlaws, Jesse & Frank JAMES. Free queries to Jesse JAMES historian, Phil Stewart.

- **The JAMES Family Web Site - JAMES Surname Web**
  http://www.rootsweb.com/~daisy/jameskin.htm

- **The JAMESON Perspective**
  http://geocities.com/Heartland/Cottage/8016/index.html
  JAMESONs of all spellings from around the world.

- **Descendants of Jonas and Stina JANSSON**
  http://www.ndepot.com/jansson/
  Jonas born May 6, 1820 in Syltebacka, Brålanda Sweden and Stina born November 23, 1823 in adjacent Kjelleberg, Brålanda Sweden. They emigrated to the US (ultimately Nicollet County, MN) in 1865.

- **JARMAN Genealogy & Family History**
  http://www.inct.net/~german/
  Jarman, Jarmon, German, Gearman, Jerman families of North Carolina, Tennessee or the lower South.

- **The JAYCOCK Family Tree**
  http://members.home.net/mpjaycock/tree.html
  Research for the name Jaycock in Canada and the UK. Also Jeacock.

- **JAYNES Family History**
  http://members.aol.com/~rtalbot105/
  The JAYNES/JANES from Pendelton Co. VA/WVA in the 1700's to Northwest MO by the 1840's. Many related names: CALDWELL, FLESHER, TOMLINSON, WAY, SNYDER, BROOKS.

- **JEANERETTE & JENERETTE & JENRETTE**
  http://members.aol.com/vandoniii/
  Family history from about 1600 - French/Swiss Protestants.

- **The JELBERT Society**
  http://www.boswarva.demon.co.uk/jelbsoc.html

- **JENKINS Genealogy Homepage**
  http://hometown.aol.com/GJenk32888/Jenkhom/index.htm

- **JENKINS of North Carolina**
  http://www.personal.isat.com/fdemling/jenkins/jenkins.htm
  Descendants of Lewis B. JENKINS.

- **JENKS Genealogy Center**
  http://www.users.uswest.net/~acme/jenks.html
  Jenks, Jenkes, Jenckes, Jenques, Gynkes, Jinks, Janks, Jankes.

- **The JENKS of Ohio - A Family Genealogy**
  http://www.jenksohio.ourfamily.com
  A branch of Ohio Jenks, descendent from Joseph Jenks Sr., tracing our line back to Shropshire, Clun, England.

- **Anders JENSEN from Aalborg, Denmark**
  http://home.st.net.au/~dunn/jensen.htm

- **JEPSON Surname Mailing List**
  http://www.eskimo.com/~chance/j.html#JEPSON

- **JERNIGAN Family Home Page**
  http://members.aol.com/jernigan01/homepg1.htm
  Some of the spellings include Jarnagan, Jarnegan, Jannikin, Janagen, Jernagan, Jonikan, Johnikin, Jonikin, Journagan, Jernegan, Jermegan, Jonerkin, Jernican, Jurnigan, Gernigan, Jerningham, Jarningham, and so on.

- **Genealogie of the family (DE) JERPHANION Haute Loire France**
  http://members.tripod.lycos.nl/AMJerph/index.htm
  Jerphanion, De Jerphanion, Gerphanion, Gerphagnon, Jarphanion, Jarphagnon, Gerphaignon, Gerfaignon.

- **History and Family Tree of John JEWELL**
  http://www.dcscomp.com.au/jewell/family-history/
  His Ancestors in Cornwall and his Descendants in Australia 1567 - 1996.

- **JICKLING Connection**
  http://members.aol.com/famhistbuf/jickling.htm
  Jickling and variant spellings, any time and any place. Family newsletter (by e-mail or snail) and family directory.

- **JOBE, JOB, JOBES, JOBS - Links to Great Information**
  http://members.tripod.com/~ajobebrown/Jobe.html

- **Genealogie JOGHEMS, JOCHEMS**
  http://web.inter.nl.net/users/Joghems
  This genealogy describes the descendants of Severinus JOCHEMS baptised in Reijkevorsel (Belgium) 31 December 1714. He moves to Vianen a town in the center of the Netherlands to marry Dirkje Boogaard 19 April 1754. His descendants currently live in the Netherlands, the USA and Argentina and carry either the name JOCHEMS or JOGHEMS.

- **The Acadian JOHNSON Association / Association Des JOHNSON D'acadie**
  http://www.geocities.com/BourbonStreet/5102/index.html

- **The A.D. JOHNSON Family Association**
  http://users.penn.com/~rbt/index.html

- **Descendants of William JOHNSON Sr.**
  http://www.netins.net/showcase/vbciowa/genie/Johnson/Johnson.htm
  Born Dec. 17, 1789 in Dauphin Co., PA. Died Sept. 23, 1845 in Van Buren Co., IA.

- **Pioneer JOHNSONs of Wayne County, KY**
  http://www.enetis.net/~ejohnson/
  Johnsons of Wayne & Pulaski County, Kentucky, pioneer families arriving in Wayne County before 1830.

- Descendants of Eli JOHNSTON
  http://www.nextek.net/djohnson/swartz.htm
  The Johnston Genealogy in Ohio beginning with Eli Johnston who died in 1841 in Butler County, Ohio. The Johnston surname was changed to Johnson in the mid 1850s. Surnames: Johnston, Johnson, Terry, Mercer, Hanby.

- JOHNSTON Clan History & Scottish Links
  http://members.aol.com/ntgen/taylor/jnstnhistory.html

- Clan JOHNSTON/E Association of Australia
  http://www.felglow.com.au/webpgs/valdes/index.htm
  Society for all, JOHNSTON, JOHNSTONE, and JOHNSTOUNE in Australia and New Zealand. Has genealogical officer and maintains a one-name database.

- The Clan JOHNSTONE Heritage Page
  http://home.eznet.net/~jeff/clan.html

- JOINER / JOYNER One Name Study
  http://website.lineone.net/~jjoiner/joiner/

- JOLLETT Hollar
  http://www.geocities.com/Heartland/Valley/3048/
  This site records the JOLLETT family genealogy in Virginia. Shiflett (all spellings), Breeden, Meadows.

- The International JONAS Family Genealogy Homepage
  http://www.on-vacation.com/Jonas
  Containing over 2,500 listings of people with the Jonas Surname these homepages have been created to foster cooperation in researching the Jonas surname.

- JONES Country Homepage
  http://mvn.net/genealogy/jnscntry.htm
  For researchers of the JONES surname.

- JONES Family Main Site Information Netpage
  http://mvn.net/genealogy/Jones.htm
  This site is for anyone researching the JONES surname.

- JONES Genealogy Webring
  http://nav.webring.org/cgi-bin/navcgi?ring=jones genealogy;list

- Keeping up with the JONES's...
  http://ourworld.compuserve.com/homepages/jones/
  Database of "Sought" JONES ancestors worldwide.

- JORON Family Reunion and Family Tree Information
  http://www.nt.net/~gofor/Joron.htm

- JORDANs From SC To TX
  http://www.familytreemaker.com/users/k/e/n/Lois-Faye-Kennedy/index.html
  This database covers the partial listing of the John Jordan Family and the family of Radford Jourdan/Jordan.

- JOSEPH Family of Augusta County, Virginia
  http://www.familytreemaker.com/users/d/i/m/Barbara-L-Dimunno
  Descendants of Daniel Joseph, born about 1760, died about 1797.

- JOWETT Variations One Name Study
  http://www.jowitt1.org.uk/
  Jauet, Jawet, Jawett, Jawit, Jawitt, Jewet, Jewett, Jewette, Jewit, Jewitt, Joet, Joett, Joiet, Joiett, Jooet, Jooett, Jouet, Jouett, Jouiet, Jouiett, Jowat, Jowatt, Jowet, Jowete, Jowets, Jowett, Jowette, Jowit, Jowitt, Jowt, Jowwat, Jowyit, Jowytt, Juett, Juit, Juitt. Contains histories, wills, parish record indexes, biographies and many other features.

- The JOYCE Connection
  http://www.familytreemaker.com/users/j/o/y/Thomas-Joyce/index.html
  JOYCEs of North Carolina, specifically descendants and relatives of Thomas and Alexander JOYCE in Rockingham Co., NC.

- The JUDKINS Family Association
  http://users.aol.com/judkinsfa/judkins.htm

- The JUDKINS Family Association
  http://www.geocities.com/Heartland/Oaks/1781/
  JUDKINS Family Association, history, covering Job of Boston, MA & Samuel of Surry, VA, Union & Confed. pension lists.

- The JUDSON Connection
  http://www.geocities.com/TheTropics/1926/judson.html

- JUETT / JOUETT / JEWETT Family
  http://www.mindspring.com/~jogt/surnames/juett.htm

- Joseph JUNKIN Family Tree
  http://www.iwaynet.net/~lsci/junkin/family/tree.htm
  This Scotch-Irish family of Covenanters (Reformed Presbyterians) first immigrated to the Colonies in 1735/6. Joseph settled on the Pennsylvania frontier near Carlisle in 1747. The Junkin family included many Reformed Presbyterian ministers. The most famous was Dr. George Junkin (1790-1868). His daughter Eleanor was the first wife of Thomas "Stonewall" Jackson.

- JUNOD Généalogie - Lignières - Neuchâtel - Suisse
  http://www.junod.ch/
  Genealogy and history of the JUNOD from Neuchâtel, Switzerland since the 15th century, including emigration to the USA.

◆ Surname Mailing Lists

- "JA-JD" Surname Mailing Lists
  http://www.rootsweb.com/~jfuller/gen_mail_surnames-ja.html
  JABLONOWSKI, JACK, JACKMAN, JACKS, JACKSON, JACKSON, JACKWITZ, JACO, JACOB, JACOBI, JACOBS, JACOBSEN, JACOBSON, JACOBUS, JACOBY, JACOMB (includes Jacombe, Jacombes, Jacombs, Jacom, Jacum), JACQUES, JAECOOKES (includes Jaecocks), JAEGER, JAEHNE, JAGER, JAGGARD (includes Jagger, Jagard), JAGGER, JAGGERS, JAGO, JAHN, JAHNKE, JAKES, JAKWAY, JAMES (includes Jamison, Jimeson, Jameson, Jamieson, Hymeson, Jomes, Jame, Jamie, Chameson, Hameson, Iameson,, Gunn, Games, Chames, Jacobs, Gemison), JAMES, JAMES, JAMESON (includes Jamieson, Jamison, Jamerson, Jemmison, Jemmerson, Jimerson), JAMIESON, JAMISON, JANES (includes Jaynes), JANKE, JANKEL, JANKOWSKI, JANNEY, JANNING (includes Jannin), JANS, JANSE, JANSEN, JANSON, JANSSEN, JANSSON, JANTZ (includes Jantzen), JANUARY (includes Janvier), JANZEN, JAQUES, JARBOE (includes Jarbo, Jerbo), JARDINE, JARESH (includes Jares), JARMAN (includes Jermyn, Jarmon, German, Gearman), JAROSH, JARREL, JARRELL, JARRELL (includes Garrell, Jerrell, Jarriel), JARRETT (includes Jerrett, Jarret, Jaret), JARVIS,

JASINSKI, JASPER, JASTER, JAUDON, JAY, JAYCOCK (includes Jeacock, Jeacox, Jeacocks, Jacocks, Jacox), JAYNE, JAYNES, JAYROE.

- "JE-JH" Surname Mailing Lists

  http://www.rootsweb.com/~jfuller/gen_mail_surnames-je.html
  JEAN, JEANS, JEANS, JEFFCO, JEFFCOAT, JEFFERIES, JEFFERS (includes Jeffres, Jefferis, Jeffords), JEFFERSON, JEFFERSON, JEFFERY, JEFFRES (includes Jeffries, Jefferies, Jeffreys, Jefferis, Jeffris, Jeffrie, Jefferey, Jeffereys), JEFFREY (includes Jeffery), JEFFREYS, JEFFRIES, JEFFRIES (includes Jeffreys, Jeffrys), JEFFRIS (includes Jeffries, Jefferies, Jeffreys, Jefferis, Jeffres, Jeffrie, Jefferey, Jeffereys), JELLISON, JEMISON, JENCKES, JENKIN, JENKINS, JENKINS (includes Jenkyn, Jinkins), JENKINSON, JENKS, JENNER, JENNINGS, JENSEN, JENT, JEPHSON (includes Jepson), JEPSEN, JEPSON, JEREMIAH, JERKINS (includes Jurkins, Judkins, Jirkins, Gerkins), JERNIGAN (includes Journagen, Jarnigan, Churnigan, Kernican, Gernikan), JEROME, JERRETT, JERVIS, JESMORE (includes Jessmore, Jesmear, Jesmere), JESS, JESSE, JESSEE (includes Jesse, Jessie, Jessy), JESSOP, JESSUP, JESTER (includes Chester, Gester), JETER, JETT, JETTON (includes Jeton, Gitton), JEWELL (includes Jule, Juell), JEWELL, JEWELL, JEWETT, JEWSBURY.

- "JI-JZ" Surname Mailing Lists

  http://www.rootsweb.com/~jfuller/gen_mail_surnames-ji.html
  JIMMERSON, JINES, JOB, JOBE (includes Job, Jobes), JOBSON, JOBUSCH (includes Jobush), JOGHS, JOHANNES, JOHANNSEN, JOHANSDOTTER, JOHANSEN, JOHANSON, JOHANSSON, JOHN (includes Johns), JOHNCRESS, JOHNS, JOHNSON (includes Johnston, Jonson, Jonsen, Johanson), JOHNSON, JOHNSON, JOHNSON, JOHNSON, JOHNSON (includes Johnston, Johnstone), JOHNSTON, JOHNSTONE, JOINER (includes Joyner), JOLLEY, JOLLIFFE, JOLLY, JONAS, JONES, JONES, JONSDOTTER, JONSON, JONSSON, JOPLIN (includes Jopling), JOPLING, JORDAN (includes Jardon, Jerden, Jerdon, Jorden, Jordon, Jourdan, Jourden, Jourdon, Jourdain), JORDON, JORGENSEN, JOSE, JOSEPH, JOSEPHSON, JOSEY, JOSLIN, JOST, JOUBERT, JOURDAIN, JOURDAN, JOWERS, JOY, JOY, JOYAL, JOYCE, JOYCE, JOYNER, JOYNT, JUCH, JUDD, JUDGE, JUDGWYN, JUDKINS, JUDSON, JUDY, JUHL (includes Juul, Jul, Jewell), JULIAN, JULIAN, JULIEN, JUMP, JUMPER, JUNG, JUNGCK (includes Jungk, Jung, Youngck, Yungck, Young), JUNGE, JUNKER, JUNO (includes Jouno, Juneau, Juneaux), JUNOR, JURGENS, JURIN, JURY, JUST, JUSTICE (includes Justis, Justus, Justiss, Gustafsson), JUSTUS.

SURNAMES, FAMILY ASSOCIATIONS & FAMILY NEWSLETTERS – "K"

Resources Dedicated to One Surname
http://www.cyndislist.com/surn-k.htm

Category Index:

◆ General Surname Sites and Resources

◆ Surname Specific Sites and Resources

◆ Surname Mailing Lists

◆ General Surname Sites and Resources

- Connect with Surnames - K
  http://www.geocities.com/Heartland/Bluffs/7708/k.html

- Dutch Home Pages by Familyname ~ Letter K
  http://members.tripod.com/~Don_Arnoldus/k.htm

- FamilyHistory.com - Message Boards - Surname - K
  http://www.familyhistory.com/messages/list.asp?prefix=KA

- Family Tree Maker Online User Home Pages - K
  http://www.familytreemaker.com/users/k/index.html

- Family Workings K Surname Links
  http://www.familyworkings.com/links/surk.htm

- GenConnect Surname Index - "K"
  http://genconnect.rootsweb.com/indx/surnames/K.html
  Message boards sponsored by RootsWeb. Each surname message board set is divided into the following topics: Queries, Bibles, Biographies, Deeds, Obituaries, Pensions, Wills.

- Genealogy Resources on the Internet - "KA-KD" Surname Mailing Lists
  http://www.rootsweb.com/~jfuller/gen_mail_surnames-ka.html
  "KEA-KEH"
  http://www.rootsweb.com/~jfuller/gen_mail_surnames-kea.html
  "KEI-KEN"
  http://www.rootsweb.com/~jfuller/gen_mail_surnames-kei.html
  "KEO-KH"
  http://www.rootsweb.com/~jfuller/gen_mail_surnames-keo.html
  "KI-KK"
  http://www.rootsweb.com/~jfuller/gen_mail_surnames-ki.html
  "KL-KM"
  http://www.rootsweb.com/~jfuller/gen_mail_surnames-kl.html
  "KN-KN"
  http://www.rootsweb.com/~jfuller/gen_mail_surnames-kn.html
  "KO-KT"
  http://www.rootsweb.com/~jfuller/gen_mail_surnames-ko.html

"KU-KZ"
http://www.rootsweb.com/~jfuller/gen_mail_surnames-ku.html
Search the index of surname mailing lists below: Surname Mailing Lists.

  - Genealogy Resources on the Internet - Surnames Included in Mailing Lists - "K"
    http://www-personal.umich.edu/~cgaunt/surnames/k.names.html
    This is a computer generated list of the surnames, and all variant spellings for those names, that are found in the surname mailing lists detailed on the pages shown above.

- Genealogy Resources on the Internet - Surname Web Sites for "K" Surnames
  http://www-personal.umich.edu/~cgaunt/surnames/k.html

- Genealogy's Most Wanted - Surnames Beginning with "K"
  http://www.citynet.net/mostwanted/k.htm

- Google Web Directory .... Genealogy>Surnames>K
  http://directory.google.com/Top/Society/Genealogy/Surnames/K/

- Heartland Genealogy Society Membership List - K
  http://www.geocities.com/Heartland/Ranch/2416/hgs-mlist-k.html

- H-GIG Surname Registry - Surnames Beginning K
  http://www.ucr.edu/h-gig/surdata/surname11.html

- Higginson Book Company - Surnames Beginning with K
  http://www.higginsonbooks.com/k.htm

- inGeneas Table of Common Surname Variations and Surname Misspellings - K-L
  http://www.ingeneas.com/K2L.html

- 'K' Surnames at RootsWeb
  http://resources.rootsweb.com/surnames/k.html

- The Obituary Link Page - Family Obituary Archives Online - K
  http://www.geocities.com/~cribbswh/obit/k.htm

- Open Directory - Society: Genealogy: Surnames: K
  http://www.dmoz.org/Society/Genealogy/Surnames/K/

- Surname Springboard Index - K
  http://www.geocities.com/~alacy/spring_k.htm

- SurnameWeb Surname Registry - K Index
  http://www.surnameweb.org/registry/k.htm

- SWINX Zoeklijst Nederlandse Familienamen /
  SWINX Searchlist Dutch Surnames - K
  http://www.swinx.net/swinx/swinx_ka_nl.htm

- Websites at RootsWeb: K Surnames
  http://www.rootsweb.com/~websites/surnames/k.html

◆ Surname Specific Sites and Resources

- KAELIN Ancestry Page
  http://hometown.aol.com/Kalin14683/Index.html
  KAELIN, KALIN from Einsiedeln, Switzerland.

- The KAMPEL Family / Stiftelse KAMPEL
  http://kampel.com
  Kampel, Campel, Kampela, Kampelmacher, Hodick, Ochakofsky, Lenson .

- KANALEY's Web Page
  http://members.xoom.com/kanaley/ireland.htm

- KANE Family
  http://members.juara.com/kane/index.html

- Seeking the KARANT Family
  http://www.visi.com/~jnunn/Karant.html

- The KARBOWSKI(Y) Family Home Page
  http://www.rootsweb.com/~clifton/karbowsk/

- KASIAH Genealogy
  http://www.maxpages.com/kasiah

- KASSELL Connections!
  http://www.geocities.com/Heartland/Estates/4375/kassell.html
  Information about CASSELL / KASSELL families of the greater St. Louis and Chicago area from mid-1800's to present.

- Calvary Cemetery St. Louis, Mo KASSEL Surnames ~ Missouri
  http://www.alltel.net/~ps53630/kassellcalvary.html
  Interments: Cassell / Kassel / Kassell surnames.

- KASSELL Connections
  http://www.geocities.com/Heartland/Estates/4375/kassell.html
  St Louis, MO Area Kassell, Cassell, Kissell, Kissell families.

- The KATOOZIAN's Website
  http://anexa.com/thekatoozianswebsite
  This site, originally made to reunite the KATOOZIAN family via the web, also has wonderful bookmarks/links, photo album, chatrooms, etc.

- Clan K/CAVANAUGH
  http://incolor.inetnebr.com/aris3301/clan.htm
  Many variant spellings.

- KAVANAGH Family
  http://www.kavanaghfamily.com/
  The origins and early history of the Kavanagh Family / Clan.

- KAYE Ancestry and the Region of Brabant, Belgium
  http://ourworld.compuserve.com/homepages/michael_kaye/
  KAYE family tree, originating in Brabant, Belgium, Kaye, Capiaux, Gillard, Gerard, Harboort, Dewit, Kohlmay, Otto.

- The KAYE Files -- Genealogy Archives
  http://homepages.rootsweb.com/~kayefile/index.html
  An archive site for records pertaining to KAYE, KAY, and KAYS families.

- KAYEsite.com
  http://KAYEsite.com
  Family originating in Hamme-Mille, Brabant, Belgium: KAYE, GILLIARD, VERKIST, CAPIAUX, HARBOORT, KNAP, GERARD.

- The KEAREY Clans
  http://www.ctv.es/USERS/kearey/

- KEATHLEY / KEITHLEY Genealogy
  http://www.keathleywebs.com/keathley/
  Keathley, Keithley, Kethley or any other variant.

- The KEEFE Homepage
  http://www.keefe.org/

- KEELAN Clan Homepage
  http://www.keelan.com
  With links to Irish and Celtic resources.

- Highland Rim KEEN and Kin Family Newsletter
  mailto:ejkeen@juno.com
  Keen, Keene, Kean, Keane. The owner maintains a 75,000 name database, with the main areas of interest being in Virginia, North Carolina, Tennessee, Kentucky, Illinois, Indiana, Missouri and Arkansas. For details e-mail Edward Keen at ejkeen@juno.com.

- KEENAN Surname Forum
  http://www.delphi.com/Keenansurname/
  This is a forum for those people world wide who researching the KEENAN surname. Information includes name origins and several KEENAN family trees.

- The KEENER Family Tree
  http://www.geocities.com/heartland/hollow/4015
  History of Keener Family in WV.

- KEENEY Genealogy
  http://www.keeney.net/

- KEESEE-KISSEE National Family Reunion
  http://www.geocities.com/kissee_2000
  Keesee, Kissee, Kozee, Kazee and Kezee National Family Reunion will be held in Danville, Virginia on June 1-3, 2000.

- KEESLING Genealogy
  http://www.geocities.com/Heartland/Plains/3299/kegen.htm
  Kißling / Kisling / Kissling / Keesling.

- Descendants of George KEIFFER
  http://www.flash.net/~dkeiffer
  Includes Armentrout, Garfield, Meadows, Mullins, Scarborough, Tew.

- KEITH Family in Virginia
  http://www.geocities.com/Heartland/Pointe/7430/
  KEITH, RING, BAKER.

- Clan KEITH Society, USA
  http://hometown.aol.com/clankeith1/keith2.html

- The KEITH Genealogy Book Project
  http://pages.prodigy.com/KeithName/

- KEITHLEY Surname Mailing List
  http://www.rootsweb.com/~karen/keithley/
  Includes Keithly, Keathley, Keathly.

- KEITH Clan
  http://www.keithclan.com/
  Keith, Keeth, Keath, Kieth, Keyth, etc., including genealogies in North America, the family's general history and clan notables in Scotland.

- KELLEY Heritage Quest
  http://members.aol.com/famlyfndr/kelley.htm
  KELLEY / KELLY Research Homepage.

- KELLEY Family Homepage
  http://www.geocities.com/PicketFence/Garden/5624/
  index.html
  KELLEY, KELLY database from Louisiana, Texas, Alabama, Tennessee, Virginia, including military, marriage, Native American information

- KELLEY / KELLY Family History
  http://www.geocities.com/Heartland/Estates/7201/
  Descendants of Moses Kelley/Kelly born 1754 in Maryland and served in the Revolutionary War.

- KELLOGG and Allied Families' Footsteps
  http://worldconnect.genealogy.rootsweb.com/cgi-bin/igm.cgi?
  op=GET&db=granma-nona&id=I1
  Descendants of Jonathan KELLOGG, b. 16 June 1780, CT, and allied families. Surnames: WOOD, THEBO, PORTER, BORST, BROWN, FUNK, WEST, BEST, MITCHELL (MICHELL).

- KELLOGGs Out West
  http://www.geocities.com/NapaValley/Vineyard/8830/
  index.html
  Tracing our KELLOGG family history from England to Mass. in the 1600's and on to California in 1846.

- KELLY-CLAN of County Armagh, Northern Ireland
  http://www.kelly-clan.com
  A KELLY-CLAN web site to help all Kelly's / Kelley's of the world research their family line.

- KELLY/KELLEY NY Research Page
  http://members.tripod.com/~Reneewr/Index-2.html

- KELSALL Genealogy
  http://kelsall.home.mindspring.com/

- KELSO Genealogy Resource
  http://members.tripod.com/~joe_kelso/index.html

- KELTON Family HomePage
  http://rampages.onramp.net/~ekelton/index.html
  A repository of information about the KELTON family, covering the three major branches in the United States, the family links to Scotland, and noteworthy KELTONs.

- KEMP Family Association
  http://www.geocities.com/TheTropics/1926/

- KEMP Family Chronicles
  http://www.angelfire.com/in/genman/index.html
  Descendants of Nathaniel L. (Nathan) Kemp born ca. 1774 in North Carolina.

- KEMPSTER Genealogy
  http://mypage.goplay.com/KempsterName

- KENDALL Families in New South Wales, Australia
  http://www.northnet.com.au/~kendalli/index.html
  Web pages for all KENDALL families who lived in New South Wales, Australia, from 1788 until 1888. Information has been extracted from the IGI, convicts records and the Blue Books of the colony 1788 - 1824. Much of the information is incomplete and requires additional work. Assistance greatly appreciated.

- Descendants of Anthony KENNEDY
  http://users.sisna.com/kennedy/
  Descendants of Anthony Kennedy from County Mayo, Ireland and Cork Settlement, New Brunswick, Canada. Includes Kennedy, Coughlin, O'leary, Murphy, Houston, Noonan, Danforth.

- KENNEDY Family of Garrard County, KY - David Son of David
  http://freepages.genealogy.rootsweb.com/~josephkennedy/
  Default.htm
  David, Son of David traces my paternal heritage through eight generations (1735 to present) of men named David KENNEDY. Includes related families (MATTINGLY, FAULKNER, POINTER, WHITE, BRYANT, HENDERSON, MULLINS, CAIN, VAUGHN, STEWART, STUART, DAVIS) from various counties in Virginia, North Carolina, Tennessee, Kentucky and Georgia.

- KENNEDY Homepage
  http://www.moonrakers.com/genealogy/kennedy/index.html

- The KENNEDY Society Genealogy Group
  http://Kennedysociety.KennedyWeb.com/

- KENNEDY & YOUNG Information Pages
  http://millennium.fortunecity.com/sherwood/553/
  General genealogy information on KENNEDY and allied families including a list of researchers.

- KENNERLY Family Research
  http://autorepairreferral.com./kennerly/kenerly2.htm
  Kennerly, Kenerly, Kennerley, Kenerley and related Families.

- KENT Family Genealogy
  http://www.athens.net/~ethelind/genealogy/kent/kent.html
  Descendants of Thomas (1749-1835) and Ann(e) (Ralston) Kent of Ireland and Pennsylvania.

- The KENTON Kin Association
  http://www.rootsweb.com/~daisy/kenton.htm

- KENYON One-Name Study worldwide.
  http://freespace.virgin.net/rod.clayburn/kenyon/kenyon.htm

- The KERCHEVAL Genealogy Homepage
  http://kercheval.simplenet.com/
  Descendants of Samuel KERCHEVAL, Jr., born ca. 1720, of Virginia.

- KERCHNER Genealogy Home Page
  http://www.kerchner.com/kerchner.htm

- The KERN Genealogy Homepage
  http://www.enter.net/~stenlake/kern.html

- KERLIN Family - Online Genealogy Community
  http://kerlinfamily.org
  Some related surnames are Nance, Barrett, Thomas, Warren, Kennebrew, Cook, Travis and Bishop.

- The Clan KERR Society
  http://www.tartans.com/clans/Kerr/society/society.html

- The East Tennessee KERR Project
  http://web.infoave.net/~sheppard/kerr.htm
  Descendants of Jesse KERR of Blount Co., TN. Includes two KERR lines found in East TN.

- KERSEY Family Research Links
  http://www.halcyon.com/millerm/html/kerseylinks.htm

- The KERSEY Page
  http://www.artwells.com/kersey/
  For the descendants of James KERSEY (1867-1960) and Sarah Jane LEIGH Kersey (1873-1936).

- KESER / KISER Genealogy Page
  http://www.geocities.com/Heartland/Valley/9926/
  Keser Line in America, Kiser line in Switzerland. Descendants of Johann Melchior Kiser, born in 1790, married to Anna-Marie Fanger, born in 1765.

- Genealogy of the KETTLE Family
  http://www.kettlenet.demon.co.uk/kettle/
  One name study of Kettle, Kittell and many other variants including Kiddle, Cattle, Kidel.

- The KETTWIG Family Center
  http://kfc.jlkettwig.de/
  The purpose of this site is to collect and present information regarding the Kettwig family and surname in all known variants (e.g. Kettwich). Kettwig; Kettwich; Poscher; Knamm; Liebelt; Heiser.

- The KEZAR Network
  http://www.kezar.net/

- KIDD Konnections
  http://www.geocities.com/Heartland/Meadows/9710/

- KIDWELL Genealogy
  http://www.familytreemaker.com/users/k/i/d/Marilyn-A-Kidwell/
  KIDWELL Genealogy has an index of over 11,000 Kidwells - the largest on the internet.

- Descendants of Johann Fredrich Ferdinand KIECKBUSCH
  http://www.parsonstech.com/genealogy/trees/kickbush/kickbush.htm

- KIELLOR Family Tree
  http://www.geocities.com/Heartland/Lane/8397
  One-name study for KIELLOR and also RAWDEN.

- KIFF net Home Page
  http://www.kiff.net/
  One name study, newsletter and more.

- KIGER Kounter Newsletter
  mailto:JYoung6180@AOL.COM
  For the surnames Kiger, Kyger, Kiker, and Geiger. E-mail Joan Young for details at JYoung6180@AOL.COM.

- KILBOURNE Genealogy Home Page
  http://freepages.genealogy.rootsweb.com/~csanders/Kilborn/rr_toc.htm
  Descendants of Richard Kylborn. Particularly the Michigan and Pennsylvania branches.

- Pages for List for Genealogy of KILIANs, KILLIANs, KILLIONs, ...
  http://www.genealogy.org/~green/Killian.html

- The KILLION / KILLIAN Genealogy Page
  http://www.mcs.net/~shs/killion.html
  Focusing on Irish descent.

- KIMBALL Family Genealogy
  http://www.geocities.com/Eureka/Office/6826/
  Dedicated to the Kimball family history. Specifically, descendants of William Lewis Kimball & Della Elizabeth (Williams) Kimball.

- KIMBALL Genealogy Online
  http://www.kimbell.org/
  Kimball, Kimbell, Kimbrell, Kimbriel, Kimble, and Kemble.

- The KIMBER Genealogy Index
  http://www.kimber.co.uk/
  Steven & Sarah KIMBER's ancestors. Kimber, Denton, Robinson, Cooper, Manson, Mcnee, Sowden, Hartley, Miller.

- KIMBROUGH & Allied Families
  http://home.earthlink.net/~sks6/
  For research of the KIMBROUGH surname and allied families through daughters' lines. Includes research, transcriptions of some original documents, downloadable copies of newsletters and other writings by KIMBROUGH descendants.

- The KIMMEL Family Record
  http://www2.fwi.com/~tkimmel/
  For Kimmel, Kimmell, Kimel, Kimmal, Kummel, Keehmle surname variations.

- History of the KIMMERLING Family
  http://kimmerling.history.itgo.com/

- KIMMERLY Genealogy
  http://www.geocities.com//Broadway/Orchestra/2447/index.html
  Descendants of Andrew Kimmerly, born in Stone Arabia, New York in 1765. During the Revolutionary War, he was a Loyalist serving in the Kings Royal Regiment of New York. He settled in Richmond Twp., Lennox & Addington Co., Ontario. Other names included are SAGER, FRETZ, BOWEN, BOWER, SMITH, ROBLIN, SOLMES, FOOTE.

- The KINCAID Researcher
  http://www.alphalink.com.au/~kincaidr/
  For Kincaid, Kincade, Kinkade, Kinkead, Kinket, etc.

- Thomas KING's Home Page
  http://www3.sympatico.ca/sue.king/Home.htm
  Descendants of Thomas KING and Hannah DARLOW, of Lincolnshire, England. Thomas King was born in Holbeach, St.Johns, Lincolnshire, England in 1866. Came to Canada around the mid-1880s.

- KINNAIRD Worldwide
  http://www.kinnaird.net/
  A site with the goal of understanding the history of the name and connecting families with the names of KINNAIRD, KINNARD, KINARD and other name variations.

- KINNEY Family Genealogy Page
  http://www.greggkinney.com/

- KINNEY Genealogy Odds and Ends
  http://www.geocities.com/Heartland/Meadows/5699/kinney.html

- The KINNICK Project
  http://cadvantage.com/~vision2a/kinnick.html

- KINSEY Family One Name Study
  http://www.geocities.com/yesnikrp/index.html
  Focusing on the KINSEY family in Cheshire and Lancashire, England.

- Descendants of Henry J.C. KIRCHHOFF
  http://www.uftree.com/UFT/WebPages/michaelkirchhoff/KIRCHH/index.htm
  From 1846 to the present. Includes FRANZEN, MARTENS, KORTHAUER, SCHULE, SHEDDIN, SCOFFERN, TIEDEMANN, HEINE, KATERBAU.

- The Association of the Descendants of John and Tabitha KIRK
  http://www.cleverlink.com/kirk/

- KIRK Family
  http://www.crosswinds.net/~mkirk
  Descendants of Michael KIRK and his wife Margaret who emigrated from Connaught, Ireland and settled in Ste. Sophie, Quebec, Canada.

- KIRK Society
  http://www.kirksoc.co.uk/kirksoc.htm

- The House of KIRKPATRICK International Association
  http://members.tripod.com/~PPPat/index.html

- KIRKPATRICK Genealogy Web Page
  http://www.geocities.com/Heartland/6540/
  And related families of Kilpatrick and Gilpatrick.

- KIRKPATRICK Historical Newsletter
  mailto:IMAKSICKAR@aol.com
  E-mail Ann Kirkpatrick Hull at IMAKSICKAR@aol.com for details.

- KIRK Society Web Site
  http://www.kirksoc.co.uk/kirksoc.htm
  Including variant spellings: Kirk, Kirke, Kyrke, Kircke, Kyrcke, Cirk, Cirke, Cyrke, Kircke, Kyrcke.

- KIRTON Genealogy
  http://homepages.rootsweb.com/~kirton/

- KISER Family - Descendants of Charles "Carl" Keyser
  http://www2.dgsys.com/~october/main.htm

- KISER, KAYSER, KEYSER Genealogy
  http://www.geocities.com/Heartland/Village/4612/index.html
  Charles Kiser was born in Rohraeker, Wurttemberg, Germany 1702 near Stuttgart. Charles died 1777/1778 (an estimate based on the date of the will) in Shenandoah Co., Va.

- Michael & Mary KISER of Virginia
  http://www.geocities.com/Heartland/Hills/6359/kiser/kiser.html
  They and their ten children came to the Shenandoah Valley of Virginia in about 1783.

- KISCADDEN Family Page
  http://www.iw1.net/kiscaddens/
  Kiscadden, Kiscaden, Kiscaddin, Kiskadden, Kiskaden, Kiskaddon.

- KITNEY, KIDNEY Family Home Page
  http://users.netlink.com.au/~gkitney/

- KITTERMAN Genealogy Place
  http://soli.inav.net/~shepherd/kitt/kitt.html
  Dedicated to finishing the search begun by Oscar Avery Kitterman for the proven birthright of his father, Reverend Bird Kitterman.

- KIVETT Family Genealogy
  http://www.angelfire.com/nc2/nance/kivett.html
  Descendants of Peter Kivett/Peiter Kieviet (1726-1794).

- Will of Peter KIVETT
  http://members.aol.com/jogt/kivettwl.htm

- KLAGES Surname Mailing List
  http://www.rootsweb.com/~jfuller/gen_mail_surnames-ki.html#KLAGES

- The KLAMERT Family Ties
  http://www.inspiringwebs.com/klamert/
  Finding KLAMERTs all around the world. Klamert, Richards, Sturdivant, Moss, and Kindl.

- KLEINECKE Family
  http://www.wf.net/~billk/Kleinecke.html
  Descendants of Charles Fritz KLEINECKE and Mary Henrietta HOENIS.

- The KLEINKAUF Family
  http://www.geocities.com/Heartland/Acres/6656/
  A one name study of the Kleinkauf's any place any time.

- Genealogy for KLEINS - KLINES - CLINES
  http://www.genealogy.org/~yoderj/

- KLERCK
  http://home.worldonline.co.za/~klerck/klerck/
  A whimsical look at the history of the Klercks in the Netherlands and also in South Africa; lots of interesting accurate information and pics.

- KLIPPEL Genealogy Home Page
  http://www.suresite.com/ny/k/klippel/
  This site is dedicated to the genealogical history of the old and distinguished KLIPPEL family name.

- **Descendants of Jacob KNAPP and Martha BENSON**
  http://grnet.com/knappgen/INDEX.HTM
  Besides the KNAPP surname, many allied families are represented including: Foust, Benson, Meek, and Benedict.

- **The KNAPP Database**
  http://www.members.zoom.com/knappdb/
  Site totally dedicated to Knapp research, including GEDCOM's, links to other Knapp pages, and e-mail addresses to other Knapp researchers.

- **KNEE One-Name Study**
  http://homepages.nildram.co.uk/~kneearch/HomeHTM.html
  Including some instances of Nee, Kne, Kney, Ney.

- **KNEELAND Home**
  http://www.kneeland.ourfamily.com
  The KNEELAND families of New England, originating from Scotland. Descendants of Philip and Edward KNELAND/KNEELAND of Topsfield and Ispwich, MA, USA.

- **K/NIBB/S One Name Study**
  http://freepages.genealogy.rootsweb.com/~knibbetc/
  A database of 12,000+ individuals worldwide with the surnames Knibb, Knibbs, Nibb, Nibbs, etc.

- **KNICKERBOCKER Family Home Page**
  http://www.knic.com/

- **KNOTTS Untangled**
  http://www.geocities.com/Heartland/Cottage/1808/

- **KNOWLES Family File Home Page**
  http://homepages.rootsweb.com/~knowles/

- **KNOWLTON Genealogy Home Page**
  http://www.benetech.com/knowlton/
  A collaborative effort of the members of the mailing list.

- **COBERNUS, KOBERNUS, KOBERNUSS, KOBERNUSZ Family Home Page**
  http://members.aol.com/gkobernus/index.html

- **KoehnFamily.com**
  http://www.koehnfamily.com/index2.html

- **Dit is de homepage van Marcel KOEK**
  http://home.westbrabant.net/~mkoek/marcel.htm
  Surname Koek from Scheveningen, The Netherlands.

- **The KOLODNY Family World Page**
  http://www.geocities.com/~kolodny/

- **KONVALINKA Home Page**
  http://ourworld.compuserve.com/homepages/jkonvalinka/
  Allied families: BENNETT, CONWAY, SANDERS, SWEENEY.

- **Descendants of Georg and Theresia KORNELY**
  http://home.att.net/~jjanssens/
  Left Gau-Algesheim, Germany for America in September 1853, arriving in Manitowoc, Wisconsin.

- **The John KORTING Family Web Pages**
  http://www.kortingfamily.org/
  Genealogy of Korting, Kotting, Kortink and Körting from 1650 to 1950 in Germany, Netherlands, USA, Australia, Great Britain, South Africa and Canada.

- **KORVER Genealogy**
  http://homepages.rootsweb.com/~imrie/korver.html

- **Genealogy.com: KOSTRUBALA**
  http://www.familytreemaker.com/users/k/o/s/E-c-Kostrubala/index.html
  All KOSTRUBALAs living in the USA are descended from these folks.

- **KOWALSKI Genealogy**
  http://www6.50megs.com/john6/
  Family history from mid nineteenth century Poland to present day Canada.

- **KRAEJÕNWINKILA Project 2000**
  http://perso.club-internet.fr/pjcdjc
  Multilingual site for research into the various families whose name is derived from the archetype surname KRAEJÕNWINKILA, such as C/KRAEINKEL type variations.

- **KRAMER Genealogy Page**
  http://www.sentex.net/~kramer/genealogy/
  Krämer - Kramer - Krammer - Kraemer - Kremer - Kremmer - Crämer - Cramer - Crammer - Craemer - Cremer - Cremmer.

- **Genealogical Data and Genealogy of the KRAUTWURST Family**
  http://home.eznet.net/~larryn/
  Descendants of Martin Krautwurst of Groß-Breitenbach in Thuringia, Germany, 1515.

- **KREINBERG Genealogy**
  http://members.xoom.com/kreinberg
  KREINBERG.

- **KRUIT from Westfriesland**
  http://spidernet.nl/~kees_kruit/
  Searching for descendants of Dirck Pietersz CRUIJT, present in Winkel Westfriesland since 1611. Surnames: CRUIJT, KRUIJT and KRUIT.

- **The KUCHARIK Connection**
  http://pages.prodigy.com/kucharik/

- **KUEHL / KÜHL Connections**
  http://www.rootsweb.com/~wiwood/MAK-roots/Kuehl/s-kuehl.htm

- **KUHN Kuzns**
  http://ladyecloud.hypermart.net/Kuhn.htm
  Coon, Cune, Koon, Kuehn, Kunz, Koonse, Koontz, Kuntz and other variations.

- **The KUHRING Family's Homepage**
  http://ourworld.compuserve.com/homepages/annette_c_jost/
  Kuring, Kuhrick, Churing.

- **KUNSTEL Family Website**
  http://www.teleport.com/~dkunstel/
  Descendents of Robert KUNSTEL family who emigrated from Austria to the U.S. in 1900.

- **KUNZE Family Home Page**
  http://www.ghgcorp.com/smutchler/genek.html
  The KUNZE family is of New York City, and Brooklyn areas.

- **KUTCH Family**
  http://www.geocities.com:80/Heartland/Village/8086/
  The Descendants of Dedrick and Susannah Kutch.

- **The KUYKENDALL Genealogy Page**
  http://w3.gorge.net/forest/
  Coykendall, Kirkendall, Keykendall, Kikendall, Cuykendall, Kuykindolph, Kirkendol, Curkendall, Kuyrkendall, Kuykendal.

- **Homepage Genealogie Familie KUZEE**
  http://members.tripod.lycos.nl/~kusee/index.htm
  Also Kusee, Cusee.

◆ Surname Mailing Lists

- **"KA-KD" Surname Mailing Lists**
  http://www.rootsweb.com/~jfuller/gen_mail_surnames-ka.html
  KABLE, KACZMAREK, KADEL (includes Kadell, KaDell, Kaidel), KAEDING, KAEHN, KAELBER, KAELIN (includes Kälin), KAFKA, KAGAN (includes Kaganov, Kaganovich), KAHL, KAHLE, KAHLER, KAHLEY (includes Kaley), KAHN, KAHNE, KAIL, KAIPER (includes Kaper), KAISER, KALBACH (includes Kalboch, Kolbach, Kolboch, Kalback, Kalbock, Kolback, Kolbock, Kolbaugh, Kolbough,, Kalbaugh, Kalbough, Kahlbach, Kahlbaugh, Kallbach, Kallbough, Kaulbach, Koelback, Kohlback), KALER (includes Kalor, Kaylor, Kayler), KALL (includes Kahl, Kael, Kehl, Cahl, Cael, Cehl), KALTENBACH, KAMINSKI (includes Kaminsky, Kamenski, Kamensky), KAMM, KAMMER, KAMMERER, KAMP, KANALEY (includes Kanalley, Canalley, Kineally, Keneally, Kinailly), KANALLAKAN, KANE, KANENBLEY (includes Kenenbley, Canenbley), KANGAS, KANGAS, KANNALY, KANOUSE, KANTNER, KANTOR (includes Kanter, Cantor, Canter), KAPLAN, KAPP, KAPPLER, KARAS, KARBOWSKI (includes Karbowsky, Karboski, Karbosky, Carboski), KARCHER, KARDA, KARDOLUS (includes Kardolis, Cardollis, Cordollis, Cardols), KARG, KARL, KARLSSON, KARNES, KARNS, KARP (includes Carp, Karpinski, Karpelenko), KARR, KARRER (includes Karrar, Karer, Karar), KARRICK, KARWALD, KASPER, KASSEL, KASTEN, KASTER, KASTNER (includes Castner, Cassner, Kassner, Cosner, Cossner, Costner), KASTOR, KATZ, KAUFFMAN, KAUFMAN, KAUFMANN, KAUTZ, KAVANAGH, KAVANAUGH, KAY, KAYE (includes Kay), KAYLOR, KAYS, KAYSER.

- **"KEA-KEH" Surname Mailing Lists**
  http://www.rootsweb.com/~jfuller/gen_mail_surnames-kea.html
  KEACH, KEADLE, KEALEY (includes Kealy), KEALY, KEAN, KEANE, KEAR, KEARNEY, KEARNS, KEATH, KEATING (includes Keaton, Keeting), KEATLEY (includes Keetly, Keatlee), KEATON, KECK, KEECH (includes Keach, Ketch), KEEFE, KEEFER, KEEFFE, KEEGAN, KEEL, KEELE, KEELER, KEELEY, KEELIN, KEELING, KEELING, KEELY, KEEN, KEENAN, KEENE, KEENER (includes Canor, Keehner, Keinar, Keiner, Kienar, Kiener, Kuehner, Kyhner, Kyner), KEENEY, KEES, KEESE, KEESEE, KEESEE (includes Kesee, Kezee, Keese, Keezee, Kissee), KEETER (includes Keiter), KEETON, KEETON (includes Keaton, Keighton, Keyton), KEEVER (includes Keefer), KEFFER (includes Kieffer), KEGLEY, KEGREISS (includes Kegereiss, Kegriss, Kegeris, Kegreitz, Kegerice), KEHL, KEHOE, KEHR, KEHRWECKER (includes Kehrwicker, Kehrweicker, Kerwicker, Kerrwicker, Kerwecker, Kerrwecker, Carwicker, Carwecker, Carricker).

- **"KEI-KEN" Surname Mailing Lists**
  http://www.rootsweb.com/~jfuller/gen_mail_surnames-kei.html
  KEIL, KEIM (includes Kime, Kimes, Koyme, Kymes, Kaim, Keym, Kiehm, Kimery), KEINADT, KEINADT (includes Keinath, Koiner, Koyner, Coiner, Coyner, Kyner, Kiner, Kinard, Keinert, Keinerd, Keiner), KEIPER, KEIRNES, KEISER, KEISLING, KEISTER, KEITH, KEITH, KEITHLEY (includes Keithly, Keathley, Keathly), KELCH (includes Keltch, Koelsch), KELCHNER, KELL, KELLAM (includes Killam, Kilham, Kellum), KELLAR (includes Keller), KELLAS, KELLEHER (includes Keleher, Keliher), KELLER, KELLERMAN, KELLETT (includes Kellet, Kellitt), KELLETT, KELLEY (includes Kelly, O'Kelly), KELLIHER, KELLINGTON, KELLOGG, KELLUM (includes Kellam), KELLY, KELSAY, KELSEY (includes Kelso, Kelsy, Kelly, Kelley), KELSO, KELTNER, KELTS (includes Kilts, Kitts), KEMBLE, KEMLO (includes Kemloe, Kemley, Kemly, Kemlay, Kemblo, Kembloe, Comlow, Kemlow, Kenmow, Gemlo, Gamlo,, Kenmo, Gemlow, Kemblie, Kemle, Kemla), KEMMERER (includes Kammerer, Cammerer), KEMNITZ, KEMP, KEMPE, KEMPER, KEMPERS (includes Camper), KEMPF, KEMPLE, KEMPTHORNE (includes Kempthorn), KEMPTON, KENDALL (includes Kindel, Kindell, Kindal, Kindall, Kindle), KENDERDINE (includes Kinderdine), KENDIG, KENDRICK (includes Kindrick, Kynric), KENNAMER (includes Kennemer, Kenimer, Kennemur), KENNARD, KENNEDY, KENNEDY (includes Cannady, Kennedie, O'Kennedy, MacKennedy Kenedy, Canady), KENNEDY (includes Cannady, Kennedie, O'Kennedy, MacKennedy, Kenedy, Canady), KENNEDY, KENNEFIC, KENNELLY (includes Kenealy, Kennealy), KENNER, KENNERLY, KENNEY, KENNISON, KENNON (includes Cannon), KENNY, KENT (includes Kente, Cant, Cante, Kind, Kindt, Kint, Keent), KENT, KENTNER, KENTON, KENWORTHY, KENYON (includes Kinyon, Kenion, Kinion, Kennon).

- **"KEO-KH" Surname Mailing Lists**
  http://www.rootsweb.com/~jfuller/gen_mail_surnames-keo.html
  KEOGH, KEOUGH (includes Keogh, Kehoe), KEOWN, KEPHART, KEPLER, KEPLEY, KEPLINGER, KERBOW (includes Kirbo, Kirbow, Kerbo, Kerbow, Curbo, Curbow, Cerbeaux, Carbaugh), KERBY, KERLEY, KERLEY (includes Kirley, Curley, Carley), KERLIN, KERN (includes Kerns, Kearn, Kearns, Karn, Karns), KERNAN, KERNER, KERNOHAN (includes Kernahan, Kernaghan), KERNS, KERR (includes Ker, Carr), KERRIGAN, KERSCHEN, KERSCHNER (includes Kershner, Kirschner), KERSEL (includes Kersell, Kerswell, Kersall, Karsell), KERSEY (includes Keirsey, Kiersey), KERSEY, KERSHAW, KERSHNER, KERWIN, KESLER, KESSEL, KESSINGER, KESSLER (includes Kesler, Kepler), KESSLER, KESTER, KESTERSON, KETCHAM, KETCHUM, KETNER, KETTLE, KETTNER (includes Ketner, Kaettner, Koetner), KETTWIG (includes Kettwich), KEVERN (includes Keverne), KEY, KEYES, KEYS, KEYSER.

- **"KI-KK" Surname Mailing Lists**
  http://www.rootsweb.com/~jfuller/gen_mail_surnames-ki.html
  KIBBE, KIBLER, KILBY (includes Kilbey, Killbee), KIDD, KIDDER, KIDNEY, KIDWELL, KIEFER, KIEFFER, KIEL, KIELY, KIERCE (includes Kierse, Keirse, Keirce, Kerce, Kearse, Kearce), KIERLEY, KIERNAN, KIERSTEAD (includes Keirstead, Kierstede), KIERSTEAD, KIERSTEDE, KIESTER, KIFER (includes Käufer, Keefer, Keifer, Kiffer), KIFFER (includes Kifer), KIGER, KIGHT, KIKER (includes Keicher, Kiger, Kyker, Cyger), KILBORN, KILBOURN, KILBOURNE, KILBURN, KILDAY, KILE (includes Keil), KILEY, KILGORE, KILGORE (includes Kilgour), KILGOUR (includes Kilgore, Killgore), KILIAN, KILLAM, KILLEBREW

(includes Kilabrew, Kilabrue, Killabru, Killibrew, Kilibrew, Kilebrew, Kilebrue, Killabrue), KILLEEN, KILLEN, KILLIAN *(includes Kilian, Killion),* KILLINGSWORTH, KILLION, KILLOUGH, KILMER, KILPATRICK, KILROY, KIMBALL *(includes Kimbell, Kimbrell, Kimble, Kemble, Kembold),* KIMBER, KIMBERLIN *(includes Kummerling, Kimberling),* KIMBERLIN, KIMBERLY, KIMBLE, KIMBRELL, KIMBRO, KIMBROUGH, KIME, KIMES, KIMMEL *(includes Komel, Kummel),* KIMMEY, KIMMONS, KIMSEY, KINARD, KINCAID *(includes Kincade, Kincaide, Kinkade, Kinkaid, Kinkead, Kinket),* KINCAID, KINCH, KINCHELOE *(includes Kinslo, Kinslow),* KINCHEN, KINDER, KINDIG, KINDLE, KINDRED, KINDT, KING *(includes Koenig),* KING, KING, KINGDON, KINGERY, KINGHAM, KINGHORN, KINGMAN, KINGS, KINGSBURY, KINGSLAND, KINGSLEY *(includes Kinsley, Kingseley),* KINGSMILL, KINGSTON, KINKADE, KINKEAD, KINKLE, KINMAN, KINNAN, KINNARD, KINNE, KINNEAR, KINNEAR, KINNEY *(includes Keene, Keeney, Kenny, Kenney, Kinne, Kinnie, McKinney, Kinnear),* KINNICK *(includes Kennick),* KINNISON, KINSELLA, KINSER, KINSEY, KINSINGER, KINSMAN, KINSTLEY *(includes Kinsley),* KINTER, KINZER *(includes Kintzer, Kinser, Kenser, Kincer, Kuntzer, Ginter),* KIP, KIPP *(includes Kip, Kyp, de Kype, DeKype),* KIPPAX *(includes Kippas, Kippis, Kippus),* KIRBY *(includes Kerby),* KIRCHER, KIRCHNER, KIRK, KIRKENDALL, KIRKHAM, KIRKHAM, KIRKHAM, KIRKLAND, KIRKLAND, KIRKLEY, KIRKMAN *(includes Kirchman),* KIRKMAN, KIRKPATRICK *(includes Kilpatrick),* KIRKSEY, KIRKUP, KIRKWOOD, KIRSCH, KIRSCHNER, KIRSTEIN, KIRTLEY *(includes Kertly, Kertley, Kirtlett, Kirtly),* KIRTON *(includes Kerton, Kirkton, de Kirketon, Kirktoune, Kierton),* KIRWAN, KIRWIN *(includes Kirwan, Kerwin, Kerwan, Curwen, Carawan, Curwin),* KISER *(includes Keyser),* KISSINGER, KISTARD, KISTER, KISTLER, KISTNER, KITCH *(includes Kitsch, Kitszch, Kech, Kich),* KITCHELL, KITCHEN, KITCHENS, KITCHING, KITE, KITLEY, KITNEY *(includes Kidney, Kytney),* KITSON, KITTERMAN, KITTLE, KITTRELL, KITTS, KITZMILLER, KIVETT, KIZER.

- **"KL-KM" Surname Mailing Lists**
  http://www.rootsweb.com/~jfuller/gen_mail_surnames-kl.html
  KLAASSEN, KLAGES, KLASSEN, KLATT, KLAUK *(includes Klauck, Klauke),* KLAUS, KLEBACK *(includes Clebak, Hlyebak, Chlebak),* KLECKNER, KLEIN, KLEINE, KLEINHENN, KLEINSCHMIDT, KLEMANN, KLEMME, KLINCKE *(includes Klimcke, Klinke, Klinkey, Clinky),* KLINE, KLING, KLINGENSMITH, KLINGENSMITH, KLINGER, KLINGLER, KLINGNER, KLINK, KLINKHAMMER, KLIPFEL, KLIPSTEIN, KLOCK, KLOPP *(includes Klop, Clopp, Clop, Glopp, Glupp, Klupp),* KLOSS, KLOTZ, KLOUCHECK *(includes Kloucek),* KLUG, KLUSMEYER *(includes Klusmeire, Klusmeijer).*

- **"KN-KN" Surname Mailing Lists**
  http://www.rootsweb.com/~jfuller/gen_mail_surnames-kn.html
  KNAGGS, KNAPP *(includes Knap, Knopp),* KNAPPEN *(includes Knapen, Knapping, Knaping),* KNARR, KNAUER, KNAUSS, KNEBEL *(includes Knoebel, Knabel),* KNECHT, KNEEBONE, KNEESHAW, KNELL, KNELLER *(includes Neller, Nellar, Knellar),* KNEPPER, KNEVITT *(includes Knevett, Knyvett),* KNIBB *(includes Knibbs, Nibbs),* KNICKERBOCKER, KNIGHT, KNIGHT *(includes Night, Knecht, Kniht),* KNIGHTEN, KNIGHTON, KNIGHTS, KNIPP, KNIPSCHEER, KNISLEY *(includes Kneisley, Kniesley, Nisley, Nicley, Nissley),* KNOBLAUCH, KNOBLOCK *(includes Knobloch, Knoblauch),* KNOCK, KNOCKWOOD, KNOLL, KNOLLER, KNOPF, KNOPP, KNORR, KNOTT, KNOTT, KNOTTS *(includes Knott, Nott, Notts, Nutt),* KNOWLES *(includes Knolls,*

Knoales, Nowells, Noales), KNOWLTON, KNOWLTON, KNOX *(includes Knocke),* KNUCKLES, KNUDSEN, KNUDSON, KNUPP, KNUTH, KNUTSON.

- **"KO-KT" Surname Mailing Lists**
  http://www.rootsweb.com/~jfuller/gen_mail_surnames-ko.html
  KOBEL *(includes Coble),* KOBER, KOBERNUSS *(includes Cobernuss, Kubbernuss),* KOBERSTEIN *(includes Coverstone),* KOCH, KOCHER, KOCK, KOEHL, KOEHLER *(includes Kohler, Köhler, Keller, Kahler, Culler, Kuehler, Kohlar, Koller, Von K"hler, Koellar, Caler,, k"hler, Kähler, Callar, Kellar, Caller, Kellar, Calor, Kroehler, Caylor, Kailer, Kaler, Collar, Kalor, Kayler, Kaylor,, Kohl, Kohle),* KOEHN *(includes Kahn, Kaehn, Kohn),* KOELLE *(includes Kölle),* KOELLING, KOEN, KOENIG *(includes Konig),* KOEPKE, KOEPPEN, KOERNER, KOESTER, KOHL, KOHLER, KOHLMANN, KOHN, KOHOUT, KOHR *(includes Core, Kore),* KOJAN, KOK, KOLB, KOLBERG, KOLESAR, KOLLER, KOLLOCK, KOLTERMAN *(includes Koltermann),* KOMONCZI, KOOGLER *(includes Kugler, Coogler),* KOOL, KOON, KOONS, KOONTZ, KOPACZ, KOPECKY, KOPP *(includes Kob),* KOPPE, KORDYBAN *(includes Kordiban, Kurdyban, Kurdiban, Korduba),* KORN, KORNEGAY *(includes Cornegay, Carnagee),* KORNGIEBEL, KORTE, KORVER *(includes Courver, De Korver, Coerver, De Corver),* KOS, KOSHAREK *(includes Kasharek),* KOST, KOSTER, KOUWENHOVEN *(includes Van Kouwenhoven, Covenhoven, Crownover, Cronwoven, Conover),* KOVACS, KOVACH *(includes Kovak),* KOWALD, KOWALSKI, KRABAL *(includes Kral, Krebal, Krabel, Kreybill, Kreyball, Kraybal, Krabell),* KRAEMER, KRAFFT, KRAFT, KRAHENBUHL, KRALING, KRALMAN *(includes Krallman, Kralmann, Krallmann, Krahlmann),* KRAMER *(includes Cramer, Krammer, Crammer, Kraemer, Craemer, Creamer, Kreamer, Kremer),* KRANTZ, KRANZ, KRATZ, KRATZER, KRAUS, KRAUSE, KRAUSS, KREBS, KREIDER, KREITZER, KREJCI, KRELL, KREMER, KREMMEL, KRESIEN, KRESS, KRETCHMER *(includes Kretschmer, Kretschmar, Kretchmar),* KREUL, KRICK, KRIEG, KRIEGER, KRIJGSMAN *(includes Krijgsma, Krygsman),* KROEGER, KROENING *(includes Kraning, Kroning, Croning),* KROGMAN, KROHN, KROL, KROLL, KROMER, KRONHEIM, KROPF, KROUPA, KRUCK, KRUEGER *(includes Kruger, Krieger),* KRUG, KRUGER, KRUGH, KRUM, KRUMM, KRUPP, KRUSE, KRUTSINGER *(includes Cutsinger, Curtsinger, Krutzinger, Katsinger).*

- **"KU-KZ" Surname Mailing Lists**
  http://www.rootsweb.com/~jfuller/gen_mail_surnames-ku.html
  KUCERA *(includes Kuchera),* KUCK *(includes Kuk),* KUEBER *(includes Küber),* KUEFNER, KUEHL *(includes Kühl),* KUEHN, KUES, KUESTER, KUESTERS, KUGLER, KUHL, KUHLMAN, KUHN, KUHNS, KUHRING, KUIPER, KUJAWA, KULHANEK, KULL, KUMMLER *(includes Kumler, Komler, Coomler, Cumbler),* KUNEY, KUNKEL *(includes Conkle, Gunkel, Kunkle, Kunckel, Gunckel, Konkel, Konkle, Kunkler, Kunkelmann, Kinkel,, Conkel),* KUNKLE, KUNTZ, KUNZ, KUNZA, KUPCAK *(includes Kupcek),* KURFESS, KURLAND *(includes Courland, Curland, Kourland),* KURRAT, KURTH, KURTZ, KURZ, KUSHNER *(includes Kushnir, Kushnar, Kushnur, Kushnure, Kushnire, Kushnare, Kushnere, Cushner, Cushnir,, Cushnar, Cushnur, Cushnere, Cushnire, Cushnare, Cushnure, Kush, Cush),* KUSTARD, KUSTER, KUSTERD, KUTA, KUTZ, KUYKENDALL *(includes Van Kuykendaal, Kikendall, Kirkendall, Coykendall, Cuykendall),* KUZMINSKI, KWAPIL *(includes Kvapil),* KWIATKOWSKI, KYGER, KYLE, KYLER, KYLER, KYSER.

SURNAMES, FAMILY ASSOCIATIONS & FAMILY NEWSLETTERS – "L"

Resources Dedicated to One Surname
http://www.cyndislist.com/surn-l.htm

Category Index:

◆ General Surname Sites and Resources

◆ Surname Specific Sites and Resources

◆ Surname Mailing Lists

◆ General Surname Sites and Resources

- Connect with Surnames - L
  http://www.geocities.com/Heartland/Bluffs/7708/l.html

- Dutch Home Pages by Familyname ~ Letter L
  http://members.tripod.com/~Don_Arnoldus/l.htm

- FamilyHistory.com - Message Boards - Surname - L
  http://www.familyhistory.com/messages/list.asp?prefix=LA

- Family Tree Maker Online User Home Pages - L
  http://www.familytreemaker.com/users/l/index.html

- Family Workings L Surname Links
  http://www.familyworkings.com/links/surl.htm

- GenConnect Surname Index - "L"
  http://genconnect.rootsweb.com/indx/surnames/L.html
  Message boards sponsored by RootsWeb. Each surname message board set is divided into the following topics: Queries, Bibles, Biographies, Deeds, Obituaries, Pensions, Wills.

- Genealogy Resources on the Internet - "LAA-LAD" Surname Mailing Lists
  http://www.rootsweb.com/jfuller/gen_mail_surnames-laa.html
  "LAE-LAH"
  http://www.rootsweb.com/jfuller/gen_mail_surnames-lae.html
  "LAI-LAN"
  http://www.rootsweb.com/jfuller/gen_mail_surnames-lai.html
  "LAO-LAT"
  http://www.rootsweb.com/jfuller/gen_mail_surnames-lao.html
  "LAU-LD"
  http://www.rootsweb.com/jfuller/gen_mail_surnames-lau.html
  "LEA-LED"
  http://www.rootsweb.com/jfuller/gen_mail_surnames-lea.html
  "LEE-LEH"
  http://www.rootsweb.com/jfuller/gen_mail_surnames-lee.html
  "LEI-LEN"
  http://www.rootsweb.com/jfuller/gen_mail_surnames-lei.html
  "LEO-LET"
  http://www.rootsweb.com/jfuller/gen_mail_surnames-leo.html
  "LEU-LH"
  http://www.rootsweb.com/jfuller/gen_mail_surnames-leu.html
  "LI-LN"
  http://www.rootsweb.com/jfuller/gen_mail_surnames-li.html
  "LO-LT"
  http://www.rootsweb.com/jfuller/gen_mail_surnames-lo.html
  "LU-LZ"
  http://www.rootsweb.com/jfuller/gen_mail_surnames-lu.html
  Search the index of surname mailing lists below: Surname Mailing Lists.

  o Genealogy Resources on the Internet - Surnames Included in Mailing Lists - "L"
    http://www-personal.umich.edu/~cgaunt/surnames/l.names.html
    This is a computer generated list of the surnames, and all variant spellings for those names, that are found in the surname mailing lists detailed on the pages shown above.

- Genealogy Resources on the Internet - Surname Web Sites for "L" Surnames
  http://www-personal.umich.edu/~cgaunt/surnames/l.html

- Genealogy's Most Wanted - Surnames Beginning with "L"
  http://www.citynet.net/mostwanted/l.htm

- Google Web Directory .... Genealogy>Surnames>L
  http://directory.google.com/Top/Society/Genealogy/Surnames/L/

- Heartland Genealogy Society Membership List - L
  http://www.geocities.com/Heartland/Ranch/2416/hgs-mlist-l.html

- H-GIG Surname Registry - Surnames Beginning L
  http://www.ucr.edu/h-gig/surdata/surname12.html

- Higginson Book Company - Surnames Beginning with L
  http://www.higginsonbooks.com/l.htm

- inGeneas Table of Common Surname Variations and Surname Misspellings - K-L
  http://www.ingeneas.com/K2L.html

- 'L' Surnames at RootsWeb
  http://resources.rootsweb.com/surnames/l.html

- The Obituary Link Page - Family Obituary Archives Online - L
  http://www.geocities.com/~cribbswh/obit/l.htm

- Open Directory - Society: Genealogy: Surnames: L
  http://www.dmoz.org/Society/Genealogy/Surnames/L/

- Surname Springboard Index - L
  http://www.geocities.com/~alacy/spring_l.htm

- SurnameWeb Surname Registry - L Index
  http://www.surnameweb.org/registry/l.htm

- SWINX Zoeklijst Nederlandse Familienamen / SWINX Searchlist Dutch Surnames - L
  http://www.swinx.net/swinx/swinx_la_nl.htm

- Websites at RootsWeb: L Surnames
  http://www.rootsweb.com/~websites/surnames/l.html

◆ Surname Specific Sites and Resources

- LABADIE Family Reunion
  http://members.aol.com/redwing386/labadie.html
  May 4th, 1997, Kalamazoo, Michigan.

- The LABERGE-LABARGE Genealogy Homepage
  http://ourworld.compuserve.com/homepages/LaBarge_C/laberge.htm
  Most persons bearing the Laberge or LaBarge name in North America are descended from Robert de la BERGE who left France in 1658 and settled in the area which would become L'Ange Gardien, Quebec.

- LaBRUE Family Home Page
  http://freepages.genealogy.rootsweb.com/~labrue/
  LABRUE family, and its origins back through LEBREUX (in Canada) and BREUX (in France).

- Les familles LABROSSE et Raymond
  http://www3.sympatico.ca/rlabrosse/

- Elton & Bonnie LACEY's Family Homepage
  http://homepages.rootsweb.com/~elacey/

- The LACHARITŠ Genealogy Project
  http://home.sprynet.com/~rllachar/
  The LacharitÈ Genealogy Project is committed to searching out and recording the genealogical history of the Lampron, LacharitÈ and DesfossÈs families with emphasis on the LacharitÈ name.

- The LACOMBE Page
  http://cpcug.org/user/jlacombe/index.html

- LADD Digging Ground
  http://homepages.rootsweb.com/~ladd/

- LADUKE Genealogy Homepage
  http://www.geocities.com/Heartland/Garden/2760/
  History of the LADUKE (LEDUC) family.

- LaFEVRE Family Association
  http://home.earthlink.net/~rctwig/lafever.htm

- The LAGAN Genealogical Database
  http://www.geocities.com/Athens/Crete/4571/index.htm
  A comprehensive search of genealogical records in Ireland pertaining to the surname Lagan, Logan, Legan and other variations.

- The LAIDLERs Genealogy Web Page
  http://www.laidler.com

- LAIDMAN One Name Study
  http://www.mharper36.demon.co.uk/laidmen.html

- LAIRD Family, Carrick-on-Shannon, Leitrim, Ireland
  http://www.hylit.com/info/Genealogy/Laird.html
  A genealogy of the Laird family of Killukin, Roscommon (near Carrick-on-Shannon, Co. Leitrim, Ireland), starting around 1730.

- LAKE and LEAKE Family Home Page
  http://www.dcfinc.com/genealogy/lakeleak.html

- The LAMBERT Family Archive and Home Pages
  http://www.motor-software.co.uk/home/

- The LAMBERT Family of Martha's Vineyard
  http://www.vineyard.net/vineyard/history/lambert.htm
  Descendants of Jonathan Lambert (1657-1738) and Elizabeth Eddy of Martha's Vineyard, Dukes Co., MA. The History of Martha's Vineyard by Dr. Charles Banks: Volume III Family Genealogies: pp. 228 - 233.

- The LAMBERTUS Family Homepage
  http://www.familytreemaker.com/users/l/a/m/Brian-M-Lambertus/index.html
  Genealogy of the Lambertus family, who came to Canada in 1835, from the southern regions of Germany.

- LAMBRECHT Genealogy
  http://homepages.rootsweb.com/~imrie/lambrecht.html

- LAMBRECHTSEN Online ~ Netherlands
  http://utopia.knoware.nl/users/evim/index.html
  Joos Lambrechtsen, born November 9, 1597 in Petegem near Deinze in East-Flanders.

- Clan LAMONT Society of North America
  http://www.jps.net/ogdenj/lamont/lamont.htm
  Information on the Scottish clan Lamont, its septs, and its modern clan societies in the U.S., Canada, Australia, and Scotland.

- LAMPERT Home Page
  http://www.lamperts.com/
  Descendants of Jacob R. Lampert, immigrated from Flasch, Switzerland in the 1800's.

- Genealogical Office LAMPING Family
  http://www.lamping.demon.nl/genea/
  Descendants of Lamping, Lampink and Lambing. German & Dutch roots.

- LAMPRECHT Genealogy
  http://clubs.yahoo.com/clubs/lamprechtgenealogy

- LAMPSON WITMUS Family Organization
  http://freepages.genealogy.rootsweb.com/~lampson/lampwit.html
  For descendants of William LAMPSON, born 1761 in Boston, Mass. and Wilhelm WITTMUETZ born 1799 in Ruegen Island, Germany.

- LAMSHED / LAMBSHEAD Genealogy
  http://www.lamshed.org

- LANDER Genealogy
  http://homepages.rootsweb.com/~imrie/Lander.html

- L'Association Des Familles LANDRY D'AmÈrique Inc.
  http://www3.nbnet.nb.ca/landryp/landry.htm

- The LANDRY Family Website
  http://www.landryfamily.com

- LANE Descendants
  http://homepages.rootsweb.com/~bowers/lane/

- LANEs In Indiana
  http://www.spingola.com/genealogy/Lane.htm
  LANE families who settled in Indiana who came from Tennessee, Virginia, Maryland, North Carolina or Kentucky.

- Descendants of # 1 Pieter LANGEDIJK
  http://www.parsonstech.com/genealogy/trees/jlangedi/LANGEDIJ.htm

- LANGILLE Home Page
  http://www.geocities.com/Heartland/Farm/8262
  Langille genealogy from Montbeliard (now France) to Nova Scotia and across N. America. One name study.

- LANGMACHER Surname Project
  http://members.xoom.com/tsterkel/surname_projects/langmach.htm

- LANGSTON Ancestry Home Page
  http://www.geocities.com/Heartland/Estates/2932/
  LANGSTON family in the early history of South Carolina.

- LANGSTON Main Page - In Search of Pre-1900 LANGSTON Histories
  http://homepages.rootsweb.com/~tugaloo/

- LANIGAN Family History, Waterford, Cork, Ireland
  http://www.hylit.com/info/Genealogy/Lanigan.html
  A genealogy of the Lanigan family of Waterford and then of Cork, Ireland.

- LANNING Page
  http://members.xoom.com/bbolden
  Records and references to LANNINGs in England, 1510-1914 and links to other LANNING sites.

- LANTY Genealogy and Literature
  http://members.tripod.com/~lanty/index.html
  Research into the Lanty name in genealogy, literature, geography, and race horse names.

- The LANTZ Family
  http://hometown.aol.com/blantzjr/page/index.htm
  The descendants of John LANTZ of Juanita County, Pennsylvania.

- LAPORTE ST-GEORGES Family Association
  http://www.genealogie.org/famille/laporte/

- LAPORTE
  http://members.nbci.com/efortier/
  The descendants of Jacques de LAPORTE & Nicole DUCHESNE. French & English versions.

- LAPP Family Tree
  http://users.snip.net/~jlapp/
  LAPP worldwide.

- LAQUE Genealogy Home Page
  http://www.familytreemaker.com/users/r/o/b/Linda-G-Robin/index.html

- LARBALESTIER Family Home Page ~ Channel Islands
  http://www.angelfire.com/fl/larbalestier/index.html

- LAREAU Family Online
  http://freepages.genealogy.rootsweb.com/~lampson/lampwit.html

- LARKIN of Galway
  http://www.patrick.larkin.org
  Family of County Galway, Ireland and their descendants worldwide.

- The LARKMAN Page
  http://www.btinternet.com/~richard.larkman/larkman.htm

- Le Grand-Livre Des Familles LAROCQUE Family History Book
  http://www.easynet.ca/~larocque/
  Descendants of Philibert Couillaud de La Roque de Roquebrune who came to Canada in 1665 with the regiment of Carignan, from France. Larocque, LaRocque, LaRoque, Roquebrune, Rocbrune, LaRock, Rock, Rochbrune, Rockburn, Roburn.

- LASATER Lineages Newsletter
  mailto:CarlCindy2@aol.com
  For details send e-mail to Lucinda (Cindy) Olsen, editor and publisher, at CarlCindy2@aol.com.

- LASHBROOK Genealogy
  http://www.dreamwater.com/mlashbrook/
  Lashbrook, Lashbrooke, Lashbrooks.

- The LATHAM Genealogy Homepage
  http://members.aol.com/Jonnialogy/Homepage.html
  Descendants of Carye LATHAM of New London, CT, and Robert LATHAM of Bridgewater, MA.

- LATHAN Family Connections
  http://www.Lathan.org/
  Bringing the descendants of Curtis LATHAN (b. 1800) of New York and associated families together.

- The Descendants of Rev. John LATHROP
  http://www.nstep.net/dorgon/lathrop.html

- LA TOURETTE Genealogy Resource Center
  http://freepages.genealogy.rootsweb.com/~brentspage/latourettegrc/

- Historic Latta Plantation, A Living History Farm, Huntersville, NC
  http://www.lattaplantation.org/
  Built in 1800 by James LATTA and Jane KNOX LATTA.

- The LATTA Genealogy Newsletter
  http://www.latta.org/

- The LATTIN Notebook
  http://pages.prodigy.com/military/lattin.htm

- LAUBACH Family Association
  http://members.xoom.com/Laubachs/

- LAUDENSLAGER Genealogy Home Page
  http://www.kerchner.com/laudslgr.htm

- Association des Familles LAUZON d'AmÈrique
  http://www.geocities.com/Heartland/7967/

- Acadian Families
  http://people.ne.mediaone.net/tlavash/index.html
  LaVACHE.

- LAVINDER / LAVENDER
  http://www.geocities.com/Heartland/Valley/4502/Jim.html
  LAVENDER family of Kanawha County, W.VA.

- LAWHORN Family In America
  http://www.library.eku.edu/direct/couture/lawhorn1.htm
  Mostly in Kentucky, but also surrounding states.

- The LAWRENCE One-Name Study
  http://home.earthlink.net/~lawren05/

- LAWSON One Name Study Home Page
  http://www.users.globalnet.co.uk/~gdl/lawson.htm

- LAWTON Branches - Your Source for Lawton Information
  http://millennium.fortunecity.com/safari/166

- The LAY Family Genealogical Association
  http://www.geocities.com/Heartland/Acres/8896
  Non-profit organization formed to encourage research on all Lay, Ley, Loy, Leigh, Laye, etc. surnames.

- LAY Family Genealogy, Descendents of John LAY Sr.
  http://www.geocities.com/Heartland/Ranch/6661/
  This site is about one line starting with John LAY Sr. b. abt 1610 in Eng. Settled in Old Saybrook, Ct. abt 1637 and was one of the founding Fathers of Old Lyme, Ct. Covers LAY, Demings, Sutherland, Crandall, and more.

- John LAZELL / LASSELL of Hingham, Massachusetts abt. 1619 - 1700
  http://www.geocities.com/Heartland/Ranch/4750/

- LEACH Resource Center
  http://www.surnameweb.org/leach/
  The starting point for your research into the LEACH surname, and variations e.g., LEACHE, LEECH, and LEITCH.

- The Descendants of Christopher LEAMING
  http://home.att.net/~flba/0001.htm

- LEAS Surname Resource Center
  http://www.treecity.com/dleas/leassurn.html

- LEATHLEY Genealogy
  http://www.leathley.com/index.htm
  Lelay, Ledalai, Lellay, Lathley, Letheley, Lethlaye, Leathlaye, Lethlay, Leathlay, Leathly, Lethely, Leythely, Lethley.

- LAKE and LEAKE Family Home Page
  http://www.dcfinc.com/genealogy/lakeleak.html
  Index to "Lake/Leake Newsletter". Projects in progress: Lake/Leake/Leek database. 1850 census extraction.

- LEATHLEY Genealogy
  http://www.leathley.com/index.htm

- The National Association of LEAVITT Families, Inc.
  http://pw2.netcom.com/~bayouboy/Entrance.html

- Association des Familles LEBLOND, Inc.
  http://www.genealogie.org/famille/leblond/home.html

- The 'Le COCQ' family of Alderney - Channel Islands
  http://www.genealogy.guernsey.net/LeCocq/RR_TOC.htm

- The Samuel B. LEDFORD Home Page
  http://www.familytreemaker.com/users/l/e/d/Mary-E-Ledford/index.html
  Ledford, Basham, Crabb, Browning, Green

- Association des Familles LEDUC
  http://www.geocities.com/Heartland/5063/index.html

- LEE Genealogy - of English Descent
  http://www.geocities.com/Heartland/7748/

- The LEE Family
  http://members.xoom.com/wunble/
  The LEE Clan from Taishan originated from Nan Hung via Wunbo.

- Ye Olde LEE Genealogy
  http://www.crosswinds.net/~leegenealogy/

- La Gènèalogie des LEFEBVRE dit BOULANGER
  http://boulan.citeweb.net/

- La Gènèalogie de Sylvain LEFEBVRE et la Descendance de Pierre LEFEBVRE
  http://www.genieaudio.com/lefebvre/

- LEFTWICH Historical Association
  http://www.leftwich.org/

- Descendants of Alexander LEGGE
  http://www.familytreemaker.com/users/d/r/u/Christina-C-Drushal/ODT3-0001.html
  Legge, Sharman, Fraser, Tegt, Boydston.

- The LEHNHERR Genealogy
  http://www.lehnherr.com/genealogy/

- The LEIBENGUTH/LIVENGOOD Surname Resource Center
  http://www.geocities.com/leibenguthsurname/

- LEIST - Resource Index
  http://www.thinktech.demon.co.uk/genealogy/surnames/leist/resource.htm
  One name resources for LEAST and LEIST.

- The LELAND Family Name
  http://homepages.rootsweb.com/~leland/
  LELAND, LAYLAND, LEALAND, LEYLAND, LALANDE.

- LE NEUF Family Research Project
  http://habitant.org/leneuf/

- LENHART Family Web Site
http://www.lenhartfamily.org/
History of the Lenhart family, from Germany in 1748 and eventually settling Lenhartsville, Pennsylvania. Includes HOLLIS, LANEHART, LEONHART, LENHARD, LUZIER, CHILDS, AUGHENBAUGH, DAUB, MARGARETHA, GRAHAM, MAINES, DE LOZIER, NYDEN, MCBRIDE, VON, SMITH, WADE, CROW, MILLER, HERMAN, PARTYKA, LONG, STEWART.

- LENNON Surname Resource Center
http://freepages.genealogy.rootsweb.com/~geneal/src/LennonSRC.html
LENNON, LENNAN and variations.

- LENZ, LENTZ - Brickwalls, Most Wanted Ancestors
http://www.geocities.com/Heartland/Bluffs/3264/lenzlist.htm
This is a gathering of information submitted by LENZ/LENTZ and variants researchers.

- Famille LESCHOT, L□CHOT et LACHOT d'Orvin
http://www.home.ch/~spaw2902/index.html
The history and genealogy of the Family LESCHOT, L□CHOT and LACHOT from Orvin and the history of the village are presented on these pages of this personal site.

- LESLIE Family History Resources
http://www.io.com/~rlsd/leslie.htm
Includes Scottish origins, description and contact information on the Clan LESLIE Society, annotated bibliography of published works and Internet resources, with links to other researchers and locations signficant in LESLIE family history in North America, Ireland, and Scotland.

- LESSARD Genealogy Home Page
http://pages.prodigy.com/CUGF40A/
Descendants of Louis (Paul) LESSARD Family from Chambois in lower Normandy, France.

- LESSLEY Family Records Web Site
http://www.mindspring.com/~samlessley/
LESSLIE, LESLEY, LESLIE. Descendants of Samuel LESSLEY and Sarah HUTCHINSON of the Carolina Waxhaws.

- LETHER / LEETHER Family Genealogical Society ~ Netherlands
http://www.presstige.nl/Genealogy/

- LETSON Family Discussion List
http://yogi.nmmi.cc.nm.us/~nancy/letson/

- 10 Generations of/de LÉVESQUE - Descendants of Robert LÉVESQUE
http://www.geocities.com/Eureka/Plaza/4458/index2.html

- Association LÉVESQUE Inc. - Les Lévesque d'ici et d'ailleurs
http://www.genealogie.org/famille/levesque/levesque.htm

- LEWIS Family Genealogical Resource
http://www.lewisgenealogy.com/
Any Lewis research, particularly for descendants of John Lewis, Pioneer b. 1678 d. 1762.

- Most Wanted LEWIS Ancestors
http://user.dcci.com/herpich/lewismw/lewis1.html
Queries submitted by those searching for their elusive LEWIS ancestors.

- The LEWIS Family Newsletter
http://pages.prodigy.com/jimlewis/

- L'HEUREUX Genealogy
http://www.happyones.com/genealogy/lheureux/index.html
L'HÈrault, L'Heros, Lurix.

- The John LIBBY Family Association
http://www.libbyfamily.org/
John LIBBY (1602-1682) settled in New England.

- LIESCH/LEISCH/LESCH Genealogy
http://home.netcom.com/~rristow/liesch/liesch.html
Liesch, Leisch, Lesch families that immigrated to Wisconsin from Luxembourg, Germany and Switzerland.

- LIGNOWSKI
http://homepages.rootsweb.com/~lignowsk/
LIGNOWSKI surname and all variants (Lignoski, Lignosky, Lingnowski, Lingnofski, Lichnovsky).

- North Carolina LILLY Families
http://www.angelfire.com/nc/lillyfamily

- LILWALL One Name Study
http://users.bigpond.com/lilwall/index.html

- Family LIMPERT
http://www.geocities.com/Athens/7765/family/4.html

- LINDER Family Association
mailto:rumples949@aol.com
For details, send e-mail to Bonnie Dailey at rumples949@aol.com

- Daniel LINDER Family
http://www.intercom.net/local/richardson/Linder.html
Review of the Swiss LINDERS who originated in Switzerland with VAN METER connections.

- LINDNER / LINTNER
http://members.aol.com/DsnCA/LINDNER.html

- LINDNER-LINTNER Memorabilia
http://freepages.genealogy.rootsweb.com/~oldphoto/index.html

- Clan LINDSAY Association, USA, Inc.
http://www.clanlindsayusa.org/

- LINDSAY Family Newsletter
mailto:BMReid92@aol.com
For details e-mail Barbee Reid at BMReid92@aol.com.

- Descendants of Samuel S. LINDSAY
http://showcase.netins.net/web/vbciowa/genie/Lindsay/lindsay.htm
Born in 1760, died in 1819 in South Carolina.

- Our LINDSAY Family
http://freepages.genealogy.rootsweb.com/~treeofme/
Descendants of John LINDSAY (immigrated 1748?) and Polly PARKER.

- LINDSLEY Families
  http://www.geocities.com/Heartland/Woods/5540/src.html
  Also Coffin, DaMetz, Eastridge, Horn, McIlvain, Rice, York.

- The LINFORD Family Centre
  http://www.geocities.com/Heartland/Woods/6475/src/template.htm

- The LINK Family of Newport, Virginia
  http://freepages.genealogy.rootsweb.com/~plowscrew/index.htm
  Focuses on the descendants of Gasper LINK who lived in the Newport area of Giles Co., Virginia.

- LINNEN
  http://www.vantek.net/pages/pattyh/linnen.htm
  One name study of the surname Linnen (Linen).

- LISTON - Worldwide One-Name Study
  http://liston.ourfamily.com/

- George LITTLE Family Association
  http://www.execpc.com/~budtamms/glfa.htm
  A tailor on Unicorn Street (near London Bridge), came to America in 1640 and was one of the first settlers in Newbury, Massachusetts.

- LITTLE Family History and Genealogy
  http://genweb.net/~little
  Descendants of Patrick S. LITTLE who settled in Fulton County, Illinois in 1833.

- The LITTLEFIELD Family Research Page
  http://www.eden.com/~gregandi/lfd.html
  The descendants of Edmund Littlefield of Wells, Maine.

- The LITTLEFIELD Genealogy Pages
  http://www3.fast.co.za/~alittle/genealog.htm
  The descendants of Francis Littlefield and his son James Littlefield of Titchfield, Hampshire, UK.

- LIVINGSTON Family History
  http://www.geocities.com/Heartland/Estates/7131/
  Descendants of Henry Reed E. Livingston, born October 10, 1818 in Somerset County, Pennsylvania.

- The LOAR Families
  http://www.iinet.com/users/menace/genealogy.htm
  Descendant information for Abraham, George, Jacob, and Peter LOAR Families. Surnames: FRECHMAN, HERRMANN, NOLTEMEYER, OSBORN, PHALEN, SCHIESER, and TYLER.

- LOCKE Family Association
  http://people.ne.mediaone.net/ddhayes/index.html

- LOCKE Family Genealogy
  http://members.aol.com/LOCKEroots/index.html
  Descendants of George Sims LOCKE b. 1849. Links to other Lock(e) Family web sites and online Census Records.

- LOCKE Genealogy
  http://kingsley.locke.net/
  William Locke of Woburn, MA, 1628-1720.

- The LOCKHART Limb of Toni's Tree
  http://www.geocities.com/Heartland/Estates/6909/index.html
  A line that descends from the Lockhart family of Lee & Carnwath, Lanarkshire, Scotland., focusing on those descendants who settled in Anson. Richmond and other North Carolina counties.

- Genealogy: LOCKWOOD Family Tree, Introduction
  http://home.att.net/~jg245/lkwd.htm
  Descendants of EDMUND LOCKWOOD, Sr., baptized September 9, 1594 in Combs, Sussex, England.

- LOFGREN, LOFGREEN, LOVGREN, LOVGREEN
  http://www.ped.umu.se/~kenlo/ancestry.shtml

- LOFTUS Family Registry
  http://www.loftusweb.com/

- The LOGAN Letter
  http://pages.prodigy.com/TheLOGANLETTER/
  A newsletter based on Andrew LOGAN and his descendants.

- LOGHRY Ledger
  http://members.xoom.com/Loghry_unite/

- The LOGUE Family
  http://www.geocities.com/Heartland/Pines/7607/Logueintro.html
  Descendants of Amandus LOGUE, an Irish immigrant who came to America in 1860 and settled in Allentown, Lehigh Co., PA.

- LOITERTON Family Homepage
  http://www.hinet.net.au/~jblstat/loitsearch.html

- The LOKRIG Family Association
  http://www.geocities.com/Heartland/Hills/8593/
  Genealogy research and exchange for all spellings of surnames sounding like Lokrig (Lockridge, Lochridge, Laughridge, Loughridge, Loughrige, Laughrige, Loachridge, Lorthridge, Lothridge, Lottridge, Lotridge, and any other variant).

- The Family LOKUCIEWSKI
  http://www.btinternet.com/~hydro.lek/lokuhome.htm
  From 1560, in Eastern Poland now part of Belarus/Lithuania/Poland.

- LONDON Family Genealogy
  http://freepages.genealogy.rootsweb.com/~london/
  The Descendants of John LONDON of Little Egg Harbor, NJ.

- Descendants of Henry LONGCRIER Sr.
  http://www.geocities.com/Heartland/Ranch/7402/

- David Uhrey's LONGFELLOW Connection
  http://www.geocities.com/heartland/ridge/6281
  Descendants of William Longfellow born 1679.

- The LONGSTREET Society
  http://www.longstreet.org/
  Dedicated to the celebration of the life of Lieutenant General James Longstreet, C.S.A., 1821-1904.

- LONGWELL, LONGWILL, LANGWELL, LANGRALL and Related Families
  http://www.familytreemaker.com/users/l/o/n/Laurie-M-Longwell/index.html

- Some Descendants of Stephen and Mary (MILLER) LOOMER
  http://members.xoom.com/olivierlynn/

- Family Group Record of William Spencer LORDS
  http://www.lordsfamily.org/research/wslords/index.html
  Born 13 October 1820 at Alton, Penobscot, Maine.

- LOROW Family Home Page
  http://www.geocities.com/Heartland/Woods/1546/
  Home page of the LOROW family descended from John and Mary Thomas LOROW, born about 1807 in Pennsylvania.

- LOSOS Genealogy
  http://pages.prodigy.net/dave_lossos/losos.htm

- LOTHROPP Family Foundation
  http://www.lothropp.org/home/index.shtml
  Descendants of Rev. John Lothropp and Mark Lothrop. Some variations in surname spelling include: Lathrop, Lothorp, Lothrop, Lothrope, Lowthrop, Lowthorppe, Lowthrup, Lowthruppe, Lowthrope, Lowthroppe.

- LOTT's of West Virginia
  http://www.harley-lott.com/
  Descendants of John Lott born February 11, 1781.

- The LOUGHREY Family of America
  http://www.loughrey.org
  Home page for the LOUGHREY Family Association of America, which includes surnames Loughrey, Loughry, Loughery, Laughery, Laughrey, Loghrey and Loghrey.

- LOUGHNEY Web Page, with other allied Wisconsin Families
  http://home.att.net/~alter.idem
  Irish and Swiss ancestors who settled in Sauk and St. Croix Counties, Wisconsin, some branches having first stopped in Simcoe County, Ontario, Canada, Connecticut and Pennsylvania. Primary surnames are Fable/Furger, Hawkins, and McLaughlin.

- LOVEGROVE Information Centre
  http://www.lovegrove.org.uk/
  Data from the author's LOVEGROVE One-Name Study (registered with the Guild of One-Name Studies), statistics, links, personal pages, queries, etc.

- LOVELAND Family History
  http://www.tmcl.demon.co.uk/loveland/index.htm

- LOVETT & LOVITT Genealogy
  http://www.lovitt-genealogy.com/~lovitt/
  LOVETT/LOVITT (all areas, all lines), James, Richardson, McDonald, McDaniel. Includes census and other records for the Lovett surname.

- FREER / LOW Family Association
  http://home.earthlink.net/~rctwig/freer.htm

- LOWARY Home Page
  http://www.lowary.org/
  Dedicated to the Lowary, Lowery, Lowrey, Lowry, Loughry names and any other spelling variations.

- LOWBRIDGE Surname Research Center
  http://www.geocities.com/Heartland/Cottage/3625/

- Keeping A LOWE Profile
  http://www.geocities.com/Heartland/Plains/2684/
  A genealogy newsletter for the LOWE surname including these variant spellings: Lowe, Low, Lough, Loe, Louw & Lau.

- LOWE Surname Boards
  http://showcase.netins.net/web/vbciowa/lowe/
  Lowe Surname Boards including Low, Loe, Lau, Lough & Louw for Queries, Obits., Bible Records, Wills, Deeds, etc.

- Georgia LOWREY Families
  http://lowreys.net/georgialowreys
  LOWREY, LOWERY and LOWRY families who lived in Georgia in the late 1700's and the 1800's.

- The Official LOWTHIAN Webpage
  http://www.lowthian.com/Ed/

- LUBY Family
  http://members.aol.com/CMElaine/LUBYFamily.html
  A story of Peter Luby, resident of St. Louis, Missouri from the late 1800s and lists descendants of Peter Luby down through three generations.

- LUCEY and LUCY Family History
  http://www.rickmansworthherts.freeserve.co.uk/

- LUCIUSNet Genealogical Forum - Forum der Familien LUCIUS
  http://www.luciusnet.de/
  Worldwide forum for all LUCIUS families: genealogy, history, heraldics.

- The LUCKY Tree
  http://www.rootsweb.com/~daisy/lucky.htm
  Descendants of William LUCKY and Nancy Ann PREWITT.

- LUCRAFT One-Name Study
  http://www.lucraft.demon.co.uk/
  Variants: Luckraft, Luccraft, Luckarift, Lowcrofte, Locraft.

- StÈphane LUCE`s Homepage
  http://www.multi-medias.ca/luce/
  The immigration of Phillippe LUCE from Jersey to Canada (1861).

- LUCEY and LUCY Family History Page
  http://www.rickmansworthherts.freeserve.co.uk/
  Family History published by Norman Lucey. Database of individuals and background history dating back to 1066, in particular Lucey, Lucy, De Lucy, Sigournay, Sigourney and many others.

- LUCEY and LUCY Genealogy in Australia
  http://sites.archivenet.gov.au/allluceys/

- The Official LUFFMAN Family Home Page
  http://homepages.rootsweb.com/~luffman/luffmanhome.html

- LUM / LUMM Family
  http://www.geocities.com/Heartland/Cottage/6977/Lumm_Family.html
  Records of Lumm and Lumm families in the U.S., with emphasis on the 19th-century Midwest (for now).

- LUMMIS Family Genealogy
  http://www.btinternet.com/~lummis
  LUMMIS family database in England with links to Australia.

- House of LUMSDEN Association
  http://www.alumsden.freeserve.co.uk/

- LUNNY News Home Page
  http://homepage.dave-world.net/~lunny/

Good Ol' Mountain News
http://members.aol.com/bonessgt/GOMN.htm
Dedicated to The LUNSFORD (and variants) All-Time, World-Wide Family Tree. Lunsford, Luncford, Lundsford and Lunceford.

LUTHER Surname Mailing List
http://home.att.net/~dreer/luther-lines.html
Includes Luter, Louther.

LYLES Surname Resource Center
http://www.geocities.com/Heartland/Pointe/2152/index.html
Genealogical research of the surnames Lyles, Lyle, Liles, Lile, and other variations.

LYNCH Genealogy
http://www.qni.com/~geo/lynch.htm
Descendants of Joshua W. Lynch, born 1790 in Maryland.

The Patrick LYNCH Family
http://www.telusplanet.net/public/cfdun/lynchnav.htm
Descendants of Patrick LYNCH and his wife, Ellen GRAHAM, emigrants from Ireland to Puslinch Township, Wellington County.

The LYNEM Family Home Page
http://www.geocities.com/Heartland/Woods/8620/
Descendants of Sheely Lynem, born circa 1818, Fayette County, Kentucky and Sarah (Sally) Ayers, born circa 1820, of Harrison County Kentucky. Linum, Lynum, Lynem.

LYNESS Index
http://ourworld.compuserve.com/homepages/raybowyer/lyness.htm
North American descendants of William LINAS of Yorkshire, England of the early eighteenth century.

LYNN/LINN Lineage Quarterly
http://www.lynn-linn-lineage-quarterly.com

LYNNs of Prince William Co., Virginia
http://members.aol.com/lynnpwco/index.htm
LYNN surname in Prince William Co., Virginia.

The LYNSKEY Homepage
http://www.lynskey.com
LYNSKEYs worldwide. Also information on Linsky, Lynsky, Lynch and other variations.

John LYONS Genealogy
http://members.home.net/davidl2/geneal/files/lyons_main.htm
John Lyons, born circa 1750; died circa 1834, St. Landry Parish, LA.

The LYON(S) Families Association of America
http://users.neca.com/bclyon/lyon(s).htm

LYTLE Families of America
http://www.geocities.com/~lytle/lytlefam/intro.html
Numerous searchable databases related to Lytle families of the United States, with some in Canada and beyond.

WDC GenWeb - LYTTON Study Group
http://www.primenet.com/~dlytton/wdc/lytton.html
Lytton, Litton, Letton, Letten, Leyton, Litten, etc.

◆ Surname Mailing Lists

"LAA-LAD" Surname Mailing Lists
http://www.rootsweb.com/~jfuller/gen_mail_surnames-laa.html
LABAR, LABARR, LABELLE, LABERGE, LABONTE, LABORDE, LABOYTEAUX (includes LaBerteaux, Laboyteau, Labertew, LeBoiteaux, Le Boyteulx, Boiteau, Boiteaux, Petue), LABRECQUE, LACEY (includes Lacy), LACH, LACHANCE, LACHAPELLE, LACHS (includes Lax, Lacks, Lacs), LACHS (includes Lax, Lacksz, Lacks, Laks), LACKEY, LACOUR, LACQUEMENT (includes Lockman), LACROIX, LACY (includes Lacey, De Lacy), LADD, LADE, LADEMANN, LADNER.

"LAE-LAH" Surname Mailing Lists
http://www.rootsweb.com/~jfuller/gen_mail_surnames-lae.html
LAFAYETTE (includes Lafeuillade, Lafevillade), LAFFER (includes Lafer, Laffar, Lafar), LAFFERTY (includes Laferty, Laverty), LAFFOON, LAFLAMME, LAFLEUR, LAFOLLETTE (includes LaFarlett, LaFarlette), LAFON, LAFONTAINE (includes Lariou dit Lafontaine), LAFORCE, LAFORGE (includes LeForge, Leforge, Lefurge, LeForgey), LAGRANGE (includes La Grange, De La Grange, De Grange), LAGRONE, LAGRONE (includes Legrone, La Grone, Lacrone, Lecrone, Legron, LeCrown, LeGrand, LeGronne, Leckrone,, Lakrone), LAHEY, LAHR, LAHUE.

"LAI-LAN" Surname Mailing Lists
http://www.rootsweb.com/~jfuller/gen_mail_surnames-lai.html
LAIB (includes Laible, Laibach), LAIDLAW, LAIN, LAINE, LAING, LAIR, LAIR, LAIRD (includes Lard, Leard), LAISHLEY, LAKE, LAKE, LAKEMAN, LAKEY, LAKIN, LALIBERTE, LALLY, LALONDE (includes De Lalonde, D'aoust), LAMAISTRE, LAMAR, LAMARCHE, LAMB, LAMB, LAMBARD, LAMBERT (includes Lambeth), LAMBERT (includes Lamberth, Lambeth, Lambuth), LAMBERTON, LAMBOURNE, LAMBRECHT, LAMBRIGHT, LAMENDOLA, LAMEY, LAMKIN, LAMM, LAMMERS, LAMOND, LAMONT (includes Lamond), LAMOREAUX (includes Lamoreux), LAMOS (includes Lomax, Lammas, Lomas, Loomis), LAMOUREUX, LAMP, LAMPE, LAMPHERE, LAMPHIER, LAMPKIN (includes Lamkin), LAMPLEY (includes Lamplugh, Lamplay, Lamphey, Lamphrey, Lambeley, Lambley), LAMPMAN (includes Lampmann), LAMPRO (includes Lamproe), LAMPRO (includes Lampra, Lampropoulos), LAMSON, LANCASTER, LANCASTER, LANCE, LANCON, LAND, LAND, LANDAU, LANDER, LANDES, LANDIS, LANDKAMMER, LANDON (includes Landen, Langden, Langdon), LANDRESS, LANDRETH, LANDRINE, LANDRUM, LANDRY, LANDWEHR, LANE, LANEHART (includes Laneheart, Lainhart, Lainheart), LANEY, LANG, LANGAN, LANGDON, LANGDON, LANGE, LANGEN, LANGER, LANGEVIN, LANGFORD, LANGHAM, LANGHORN (includes Langhorne), LANGILLE (includes Langel, Langile, Languilles), LANGLANDS, LANGLEY (includes Langly), LANGLOIS, LANGMAID, LANGSTON (includes Langstone, Lankston), LANGTON, LANGWORTHY, LANHAM, LANIER, LANIGAN, LANIUS, LANKFORD, LANNING (includes Laning), LANPHEAR (includes Lanphere, Lamphear, Lamphere), LANPHERE, LANSDOWNE (includes Lansdown), LANSFORD, LANSING, LANTHRUM, LANTRIP (includes Lanthrip, Lanthrop, Landtroop), LANTZ, LANYON.

"LAO-LAT" Surname Mailing Lists
http://www.rootsweb.com/~jfuller/gen_mail_surnames-lao.html
LAPEER, LAPHAM, LAPIERRE, LAPLANTE, LAPORTE, LAPP, LAPP. LAPRADE. LAPSLEY. LARGE. LARGENT. LARIMER

(includes Larmore, Lorimer, Larimore, Larmer), LARIMORE, LARIVIERRE, LARK, LARKE (includes Lark), LARKIN, LARKINS, LARMER, LARMOUR, LARN (includes Larne, Lawn, Laugharne, Lorne), LARNED (includes Larnerd, Learnerd), LAROCHE, LAROCQUE, LAROS (includes Larash, Laroch, Larosh, Laroche, Larocque, Larose, Loras, Loris, Lorash, Lorach), LAROSE, LARR, LARRABEE (includes Laribee, Larabee, Laraby, Larobouy), LARRISON, LARSDOTTER, LARSEN, LARSON, LARSSON, LARUE, LARZELERE (includes Larzalere, Larzeilier), LASATER, LASCOLA, LASCOMB (includes Lascum, Laskum, Lascombe), LASH (includes Lesh, Lasch), LASHER, LASHLEY (includes Lasley, Lassley), LASLEY (includes Lassley, Lashley), LASSETER, LASSITER (includes Laciter, Lasater, Lasseter, Lasster, Lester, Leister, Laycestre, Lyster, Luster), LASSLEY (includes Lasley, Lashley), LASTER, LASWELL, LATENDRESSE, LATEY, LATHAM (includes Lathem, Lathim, Lathom, Lathum, Laytham, Leatham, Leathem, Leathim, Leathom, Leathum,, Letham, Leytham, Lapham), LATHAN, LATHROP (includes Lothrop, Lothropp), LATIMER (includes Lattimer, Latimore, Latimar), LATOURETTE (includes La Tourette, LaTourette, Laturett), LATSHAW, LATSON (includes Latsen, Letsen, Letson), LATTA (includes Latty, Latto, Lattea), LATTIMORE, LATTIN.

- **"LAU-LD" Surname Mailing Lists**
  http://www.rootsweb.com/~jfuller/gen_mail_surnames-lau.html
  LAU, LAUBACH, LAUCHU (includes Lau-Chu), LAUDER, LAUDERDALE, LAUER, LAUFENBERG, LAUFFER, LAUGHLIN (includes O'Laughlin, MacLaughlin, Loughlin), LAUGHLIN, LAUGHTON (includes Lawton), LAUHARN, LAUMAN, LAURENCE, LAURENSON, LAURENT, LAURIE, LAUTZENHISER (includes Loutzenhiser, Latzenhiser, Lautzenheiser, Loutzenheiser), LAUX, LAVALLEE, LAVALLEY (includes Lavalle, Lavallee, La Valley), LAVELLE, LAVENDER, LAVERTY, LAVERY, LAVIN, LAW, LAWFORD, LAWHORN (includes Lawhorne, Lowhorn, Lawhern, Lawhon, Laugherne, Lahon, Lahorn), LAWLER (includes O'Lalor, Lawlor, Lollar), LAWLESS, LAWLESS (includes Lawlis, Lallis, Lagles, Lealos, Laighleis, De Laighleis), LAWLEY, LAWLOR, LAWRENCE, LAWRENZ, LAWREY, LAWRIE, LAWS (includes Law, Lawes), LAWS (includes Law, Lawe, Lawes, Laws, Lawse, McLaw, McLaws), LAWSHAE, LAWSON, LAWSON, LAWTON, LAXTON, LAY, LAYCOCK, LAYCOCK (includes Lacock), LAYMAN, LAYNE, LAYTON, LAYZELL (includes Lazell, Lazsell, Layzsell, Laszelle, Laselle, Lascelles), LAZARUS, LAZENBY, LAZNA.

- **"LEA-LED" Surname Mailing Lists**
  http://www.rootsweb.com/~jfuller/gen_mail_surnames-lea.html
  LEA, LEACH (includes Leech, Leitch), LEADBETTER, LEADER, LEAHEY, LEAHY, LEAK, LEAKE, LEAMON, LEAN, LEAP, LEAR, LEARN, LEARNED, LEARY, LEAS, LEASE, LEASK, LEASURE, LEATH (includes Leith, Leeth), LEATHERMAN (includes Lederman), LEATHERS, LEATHERWOOD, LEAVENWORTH, LEAVITT, LEAVY, LEBEAU, LEBEDA, LEBER, LEBLANC, LEBO, LEBREAUX, LECHNER, LECKIE, LECLAIR, LECLERC, LECLERC, LECOMPTE, LECROY, LEDBETTER (includes Leedbetter, Leadbetter), LEDDY, LEDEBUR, LEDERACH, LEDERER, LEDFORD (includes Lydford, Leadford), LEDGERWOOD, LEDLOW (includes Ledlowe, Ledloe, Ledlo, Leadlow, Letlow, Letlowe, Letloe, Letlo, Ludlow, Ludloe, Ludlo), LEDOUX, LEDUC.

- **"LEE-LEH" Surname Mailing Lists**
  http://www.rootsweb.com/~jfuller/gen_mail_surnames-lee.html
  LEE (includes Lea, O'Leahy, Leigh, Levy, Leay, Schlee, Ley), LEE, LEE, LEECH, LEECH, LEEDS, LEEK, LEEL, LEEMING, LEENET, LEEPER (includes Lieper, Leiper, Leaper), LEES, LEESON, LEETE (includes Leet), LEFAUCHEUR, LEFEBVRE, LEFEVER, LEFEVRE, LEFFLER, LEFFORGE (includes Leforge, Laforge, Leforgee), LEFLER, LEFLORE (includes Lefleur, Leflo, Lafleur, Leflow), LEFTWICH (includes Leftwycke), LEGALLAIS (includes LeGalley, LeGallee), LEGATE, LEGER, LEGG (includes Legge), LEGGATT, LEGGE, LEGGETT (includes Legat, Legate, Legatt, Legett, LeGett, LeGette, Legget, Leggette, Leggit, Leggitt, Liggett), LEGRAND, LEGROS (includes LeGros, Le Gros, Legros), LEHENY (includes Lehany, Leheany, Lehane), LEHMAN (includes Lehmann, Layman, Lahman, Lemons, Lemmons, Lemon, Lemmon), LEHMANN, LEHMANN (includes Lehman, Layman, Laymon, Leeman), LEHMKUHL, LEHN, LEHNHERR, LEHR, LEHRMANN (includes Lehrman).

- **"LEI-LEN" Surname Mailing Lists**
  http://www.rootsweb.com/~jfuller/gen_mail_surnames-lei.html
  LEIB, LEIBOVITZ (includes Lebovitz, Leibowitz, Lebowitz, Liebowitz, Leibovich, Liebovich, Leibovici), LEIBOWITZ (includes Leibovitz, Lebowitz, Lebovitz, Lebovits, Leibovitz), LEIDY, LEIGH, LEIGHTON, LEIMEISTER, LEIN, LEININGER, LEINPINSEL, LEISHMAN (includes Lishman, Leechman, Leesman), LEIST, LEISURE, LEITCH, LEITH, LEITNER, LEITZELL (includes Leitzel), LEJEUNE, LELAND, LEMAIRE, LEMASTER, LEMASTERS (includes Lemaster, Lamaster, Lamasters, Lemaitre), LEMAY, LEMEN (includes Laman, Lamon, Lamond, Lamont, Leman, Lehman, Lemin, Leming, Lemins, Lemings, Lemmin,, Lemming, Lemmins, Lemmings, Lemon, Lemond, Lemons, Lemonds, Lemmon, Lemmond, Lemmons, Lemmonds,, Les Moine, Limon, Lyman), LEMERY, LEMIEUX, LEMIRE, LEMKE, LEMKE, LEMLEY, LEMMON, LEMMONS, LEMOINE, LEMON, LEMOND, LEMONS, LENDERMAN, LENHARDT, LENHART, LENNEVILLE, LENNON, LENNOX, LENOIR, LENOX, LENT (includes van Lent, Lint, Lynt), LENTZ (includes Lence, Lance, Lantz), LENTZ, LENZ.

- **"LEO-LET" Surname Mailing Lists**
  http://www.rootsweb.com/~jfuller/gen_mail_surnames-leo.html
  LEOFGREN, LEONARD (includes Lowenart, Loweryd, Learned, Lernert, Lenhardt), LEONE, LEONHARDT, LEOPARD, LEOPOLD, LEPINE, LEPP (includes Loepp, Lopp, Lapp, Lipp), LEQUYER, LERAY, LERCH, LERNER, LEROUX, LEROY, LERVOLD, LESAGE (includes LeSage, Le'Sage, Lesage', LaSage, Lasage, La'Sage, Lasage'), LESEBERG (includes Leseburg, Lesberg), LESHER, LESLEY, LESLIE (includes Lesley, Lessley), LESTER, LETHER, LETSON (includes Litson, Ledson, Lidson), LETT, LETVINCHUK.

- **"LEU-LH" Surname Mailing Lists**
  http://www.rootsweb.com/~jfuller/gen_mail_surnames-leu.html
  LEU, LEUCK, LEUZE, LEVALLEY, LEVAN, LEVASSEUR, LEVEL (includes Leavell, Levell), LEVER, LEVERETT, LEVERICH (includes Leveridge), LEVERING, LEVESQUE, LEVETT, LEVI, LEVIN, LEVINE, LEVINER (includes Leeviner, Levener, Leiviner), LEVINESS (includes LaViness, LaVigne, LeVines, Levines, Levine, LeVigne), LEVINESS, LEVIS, LEVY, LEWALLEN (includes Lewellen, Lieuallen, Llewellyn, Luallen), LEWANDOWSKI, LEWELLEN, LEWIN, LEWINS, LEWIS, LEWIS, LEY, LEYDEN, LHEUREUX (includes Lereau, L'Hereault, L'Herault, L'Heros, Lurix, Happy).

- **"LI-LN" Surname Mailing Lists**
  http://www.rootsweb.com/~jfuller/gen_mail_surnames-li.html
  LIABEL, LIBBY, LIBERTY, LICAUSI (includes Causi), LICHTER, LIDDELL, LIDDIARD, LIDDLE, LIDE, LIEBERMAN, LIEBICH, LIEN, LIENHARD, LIERLE, LIGGETT, LIGHT, LIGHTBODY, LIGHTBOWN (includes Lightboun, Lightbowne, Lightboune, Lightbourn, Lightburn, Lightbound, Lightbrown), LIGHTFOOT, LIGHTKEP (includes Lightcap, Leightkep, Leightcap), LIGHTNER, LIGNOWSKI (includes Lignoski, Lignowsky, Lingnowski, Lingnofski, Lichnovsky), LIGON, LIHOU (includes Leehoo, Lihow, Lihan), LILE (includes Lyle, Liles, Lyles), LILES, LILLARD, LILLEY, LILLIE, LILLIG, LILLIS, LILLY (includes Lily, Lilie, Lylie), LIMOGES (includes Lamarge, Lamudge, Lamugh, Lemoge, Lemoges, Lemogne), LIMPUS (includes Lympus, Lympas, Lympais), LINCK, LINCOLN, LIND, LINDBERG, LINDELL, LINDEMAN, LINDEMANN, LINDEN, LINDER, LINDERMAN, LINDGREN, LINDHOLM, LINDHORST, LINDLEY, LINDNER, LINDQUIST, LINDSAY (includes Lindsey, Linsey), LINDSEY, LINDSLEY, LINDSTROM, LINE, LINEBACK (includes Leinbach), LINEHAN, LINES (includes Line, Lyne, Lynes), LING, LINGARD, LINGENFELTER, LINGER, LINGNER, LINGO, LINK, LINKE, LINKENHOKER, LINKOUS (includes Linkuss, Leinkous, Leinkuss, Leankous, Leankuss), LINN, LINNELL (includes Linel, Linnel, Linell), LINNEY (includes Linny), LINSAY, LINT, LINTHICUM, LINTNER (includes Lindner, Lindtner), LINTON, LINVILLE, LINZY, LIPE (includes Leib, Leipp, Lype), LIPP, LIPPERTS, LIPPINCOTT (includes Lippencott), LIPPOLDT, LIPPS, LIPSCOMB, LIPSEY, LISENBY, LISK, LISLE (includes Lyle, Lysle), LISTEN (includes Liston), LISTER, LISTON (includes Listen), LITCHFIELD (includes Lechfeild, Lechfeld, Lechfield, Leechfield, Lichfeild, Lichfield, Litchfeald, Litchfeeld,, Litchfeild, Litchfelde, Litchfild), LITHGOW, LITSEY, LITTLE (includes Littell, Littel, Litel, Lytel, Lytell, Lyttelle, Littelle, Lytle, Lyttle), LITTLECHILD, LITTLEFIELD, LITTLEFORD, LITTLEJOHN, LITTLEPAGE, LITTLEPAGE, LITTLETON, LITTON, LITTRELL (includes Litteral, Literal, Luttrell), LIVELY, LIVENGOOD, LIVERMORE, LIVERSAGE (includes Liversedge, Liverstitch), LIVESAY, LIVINGSTON (includes Livingstone, Levingston), LIVINGSTONE, LIZER (includes Leiser, Lieser, Leisure), LLEWELLYN, LLOYD.

- **"LO-LT" Surname Mailing Lists**
  http://www.rootsweb.com/~jfuller/gen_mail_surnames-lo.html
  LOADER, LOBB, LOBDELL, LOCH, LOCHHEAD, LOCK, LOCKABY, LOCKARD, LOCKE (includes Lock), LOCKER (includes Locher), LOCKETT, LOCKEY, LOCKHART, LOCKLEAR, LOCKLIN, LOCKWOOD (includes De Lockwood), LODEN, LODGE, LOE, LOEB, LOEFFLER, LOEHR, LOESCH, LOEW (includes Loewenstein, Loeb), LOEWE, LOEWEN, LOFTHOUSE, LOFTIN, LOFTIS, LOFTON, LOFTUS, LOGAN, LOGGINS, LOGHRY, LOGSDON, LOGSTON (includes Logsdon), LOGUE, LOHMANN, LOHR, LOHSE, LOKER, LOKKEN, LOKRIG (includes Laughridge, Loachridge, Lochridge, Lockridge, Lorthridge, Lothridge, Lotridge, Lottridge,, Loughridge, Loughrige), LOKRIG (includes Laughridge, Loachridge, Lochridge, Lockridge, Lorthridge, Lothridge, Lotridge, Lottridge,, Loughridge, Loughrige), LOLLAR, LOMAN, LOMAX, LOMBARD, LOMBARDI, LOMBARDO, LOMMASON (includes Lambertson, Lammason, Lamerson, Lammerson, Lammison, Lomeson, Lomerson,, Lommasson, Lomison), LONERGAN, LONES, LONEY, LONG, LONGACRE, LONGCOR, LONGCORE (includes Longcor, Longcoure, Langhaar), LONGFELLOW, LONGLEY, LONGMAN, LONGSHORE, LONGSTAFF, LONGSTREET (includes Langestraet, Langstraat), LONGWELL (includes Longwill, Langwell, Langwall), LONGWORTH, LONSDALE, LOOFBOURROW (includes Loofborrow, Loufborrow,

Loughbourough, Loveberry), LOOK, LOOKINGBILL (includes Luckenbell, Lukenbell, Luckenbill, Lookabell, Luckenbaugh), LOOMER (includes Lumer, Loamer, Lomer), LOOMIS (includes Lummys, Lummuys, Lummyus, Lomax), LOOMIS, LOONEY (includes Luna, Lunney, Leeney, O'Looney), LOOP, LOOPER, LOOS, LOPER, LOPEZ, LOPP, LOPP, LORANCE (includes Lowrance), LORBER, LORD, LORDS, LORENTZ, LORENZ, LORENZEN, LORIMER, LORING, LORT, LOSEE, LOSEY, LOSH (includes Loesch, Losch), LOSS, LOSSING (includes Lassen, Lassing, Lassingh), LOTHROP, LOTSPEICH (includes Lotspiech), LOTT (includes Lot, Lotte, Lote), LOTT, LOTZ, LOUCKS, LOUCKS, LOUDENSLAGER, LOUDERBACK, LOUDON, LOUGH, LOUGHARY, LOUGHREY, LOUNSBERRY, LOUNSBURY (includes Lounsbery, Lounsberry, Lounsbury, Lownsbury), LOURAMORE (includes Loramore, Laurimore, Lauremore, Larimer, Larimore), LOVE, LOVEALL (includes Lovell, Lovall, Loval, Lovel), LOVEDAY, LOVEGROVE, LOVEJOY, LOVEJOY, LOVELACE (includes Loveless, Lovlis, Lovlys, Lovlace), LOVELACE, LOVELADY, LOVELAND, LOVELESS, LOVELL, LOVELOCK (includes Loveluck, Lieflock, Lovelocke, Lovflok, Lovlock), LOVELY, LOVERSIDGE (includes Leversedge), LOVETT (includes Lovette, Lovet), LOVETTE (includes Lovett, Lovet), LOVICK (includes Lovicke), LOVING (includes Lovin), LOVVORN, LOW, LOWDEN (includes Loudoun, Louden, Lowdoun), LOWDER (includes Louder, Loudder, Lauder, Loder), LOWE (includes Low, Lo, Lough), LOWELL, LOWENKAMP, LOWENSTEIN, LOWER, LOWERY, LOWMAN, LOWMASTER (includes Lawmaster, Laumaster, Laumeister, Loumaster), LOWNDES (includes Lownds, Lounds), LOWRANCE (includes Lorentz, Lorance), LOWREY, LOWRY (includes Lowery, Lowrey), LOWTHER, LOXTON (includes Luxton, Lockstone), LOY, LOYD (includes Lloyd).

- **"LU-LZ" Surname Mailing Lists**
  http://www.rootsweb.com/~jfuller/gen_mail_surnames-lu.html
  LUCADA (includes Luckadoo, Luckadu), LUCAS, LUCE, LUCENTE, LUCERO, LUCK, LUCKABAUGH, LUCKETT, LUCKY (includes Luckey, McLuckey, McLucky), LUCY (includes Luce, Lucey, Lossee), LUCZYNSKI, LUDDINGTON (includes Ludington), LUDDY (includes Liddy, Leddy, Loody), LUDLAM (includes Ludlum), LUDLOW, LUDWICK, LUDWIG, LUECK, LUEDTKE, LUENGEN (includes Lüngen), LUERSEN, LUFBORROW, LUFFMAN (includes Lufman), LUFSEY (includes Leavcy, Leivsay, Leivsey, Leofsiege, Leofsy, Levacy, Levesee, Levisee, Levsay, Lievsay, Lifsay,, Lifsey, Lipsey, Litsey, Livasy, Livcey, Livecy, Livesa, Livesaly, Livesay, Livese, Liveseay, Liveseley, Livesey, Livesie,, Livesley, Livesly, Livesy, Livessay, Livesy, Livezay, Liveszey, Livey, Liveze, Livezely, Livezey, Livezley, Livezly,, Livezy, Lovcey, Lovci, Lovecey, Lovesay, Lovesee, Lovesey, Lovesy, Lufcy, Luffsey, Lufsey, Lyffsey), LUGAR (includes Luger), LUKE, LUKEN, LUKER, LULL, LUM, LUMAN, LUMBLEY (includes Lumley, Lumbey, Lumly, Lumby), LUMLEY, LUMLEY, LUMPKIN, LUMSDEN, LUNA, LUNCEFORD, LUNCEFORDS, LUND (includes Lunn, Lunde), LUNDBERG, LUNDGREN, LUNDQUIST, LUNDSTROM, LUNDY, LUNG, LUNGER, LUNGREN (includes Lungreen), LUNSFORD (includes Lunceford, Lonsford, Lansford, Luntsford), LUNT, LUPTON, LURVEY, LUSBY, LUSCOMBE, LUSH (includes Lushe), LUSK (includes Loosk), LUSSIER, LUST, LUSTER, LUTES, LUTHER (includes Luter, Louther), LUTTRELL, LUTWIN, LUTZ, LUTZINGER (includes Ledsinger, Litsinger, Schlessinger, Letsinger), LUX, LYALL, LYBRAND, LYDON, LYGON, LYKE (includes Leick, Like, Leich), LYKINS, LYLE, LYLES, LYMAN (includes Liman, Layman), LYNCH (includes Linch), LYNCH (includes Lench, De Lench, Linch, Linche), LYNDE, LYNE, LYNGAR (includes Lingar, Linguar), LYNN, LYNSKEY (includes Lynsky, Linskey, Linsky), LYON, LYONS (includes Lyon), LYONS, LYTLE, LYTTON (includes Litton, Litten, Letton).

SURNAMES, FAMILY ASSOCIATIONS & FAMILY NEWSLETTERS – "M"

Resources Dedicated to One Surname
http://www.cyndislist.com/surn-m.htm

Category Index:

◆ General Surname Sites and Resources

◆ Surname Specific Sites and Resources

◆ Surname Mailing Lists

◆ General Surname Sites and Resources

- Connect with Surnames - M
  http://www.geocities.com/Heartland/Bluffs/7708/m.html

- Dutch Home Pages by Familyname ~ Letter M
  http://members.tripod.com/~Don_Arnoldus/m.htm

- FamilyHistory.com - Message Boards - Surname - M
  http://www.familyhistory.com/messages/list.asp?prefix=MA

- Family Tree Maker Online User Home Pages - M
  http://www.familytreemaker.com/users/m/index.html

- Family Workings M Surname Links
  http://www.familyworkings.com/links/surm.htm

- Family Workings Mac Surname Links
  http://www.familyworkings.com/links/surmac.htm

- Family Workings Mc Surname Links
  http://www.familyworkings.com/links/surmc.htm

- GenConnect Surname Index - "M"
  http://genconnect.rootsweb.com/indx/surnames/M.html
  Message boards sponsored by RootsWeb. Each surname message board set is divided into the following topics: Queries, Bibles, Biographies, Deeds, Obituaries, Pensions, Wills.

- Genealogy Resources on the Internet - "MAA-MAD"
  Surname Mailing Lists
  http://www.rootsweb.com/~jfuller/gen_mail_surnames-maa.html
  "MAE-MAH"
  http://www.rootsweb.com/~jfuller/gen_mail_surnames-mae.html
  "MAI-MAN"
  http://www.rootsweb.com/~jfuller/gen_mail_surnames-mai.html
  "MAO-MAR"
  http://www.rootsweb.com/~jfuller/gen_mail_surnames-mao.html
  "MAS-MAT"
  http://www.rootsweb.com/~jfuller/gen_mail_surnames-mas.html

"MAU-MB"
http://www.rootsweb.com/~jfuller/gen_mail_surnames-mau.html
"MCA-MCB"
http://www.rootsweb.com/~jfuller/gen_mail_surnames-mca.html
"MCC-MCC"
http://www.rootsweb.com/~jfuller/gen_mail_surnames-mcc.html
"MCD-MCD"
http://www.rootsweb.com/~jfuller/gen_mail_surnames-mcd.html
"MCE-MCH"
http://www.rootsweb.com/~jfuller/gen_mail_surnames-mce.html
"MCI-MCN"
http://www.rootsweb.com/~jfuller/gen_mail_surnames-mci.html
"MCO-MCT"
http://www.rootsweb.com/~jfuller/gen_mail_surnames-mco.html
"MCU-MD"
http://www.rootsweb.com/~jfuller/gen_mail_surnames-mcu.html
"ME-MH"
http://www.rootsweb.com/~jfuller/gen_mail_surnames-me.html
"MI-MN"
http://www.rootsweb.com/~jfuller/gen_mail_surnames-mi.html
"MOA-MOH"
http://www.rootsweb.com/~jfuller/gen_mail_surnames-moa.html
"MOI-MON"
http://www.rootsweb.com/~jfuller/gen_mail_surnames-moi.html
"MOO-MOT"
http://www.rootsweb.com/~jfuller/gen_mail_surnames-moo.html
"MOU-MT"
http://www.rootsweb.com/~jfuller/gen_mail_surnames-mou.html
"MU-MZ"
http://www.rootsweb.com/~jfuller/gen_mail_surnames-mu.html
Search the index of surname mailing lists below: Surname Mailing Lists.

o Genealogy Resources on the Internet - Surnames Included in Mailing Lists - "M"
http://www-personal.umich.edu/~cgaunt/surnames/m.names.html
This is a computer generated list of the surnames, and all variant spellings for those names, that are found in the surname mailing lists detailed on the pages shown above.

- Genealogy Resources on the Internet - Surname Web Sites for "M" Surnames
http://www-personal.umich.edu/~cgaunt/surnames/m.html

- Genealogy's Most Wanted - Surnames Beginning with "M"
http://www.citynet.net/mostwanted/m.htm

- Genealogy's Most Wanted - Surnames Beginning with "Mc"
http://www.citynet.net/mostwanted/mc.htm

- Google Web Directory .... Genealogy>Surnames>M
http://directory.google.com/Top/Society/Genealogy/Surnames/M/

- Heartland Genealogy Society Membership List - M
http://www.geocities.com/Heartland/Ranch/2416/hgs-mlist-m.html

- H-GIG Surname Registry - Surnames Beginning M
http://www.ucr.edu/h-gig/surdata/surname13.html

- Higginson Book Company - Surnames Beginning with M
http://www.higginsonbooks.com/m.htm

- inGeneas Table of Common Surname Variations and Surname Misspellings - M
http://www.ingeneas.com/M.html

- 'M' Surnames at RootsWeb
http://resources.rootsweb.com/surnames/m.html

- The Obituary Link Page - Family Obituary Archives Online - M
http://www.geocities.com/~cribbswh/obit/m.htm

- Open Directory - Society: Genealogy: Surnames: M
http://www.dmoz.org/Society/Genealogy/Surnames/M/

- Surname Springboard Index - M
http://www.geocities.com/~alacy/spring_m.htm

- SurnameWeb Surname Registry - M Index
http://www.surnameweb.org/registry/m.htm

- SWINX Zoeklijst Nederlandse Familienamen / SWINX Searchlist Dutch Surnames - M
http://www.swinx.net/swinx/swinx_ma_nl.htm

- Websites at RootsWeb: M Surnames
http://www.rootsweb.com/~websites/surnames/m.html

◆ Surname Specific Sites and Resources

- Descendants of John McAFEE, Sr.
http://www.halcyon.com/jennyrt/Register/RR_TOC.HTML
Descendants of John McAFEE Sr. of Scotland and Co. Armagh, Ireland who settled in Mercer Co., Kentucky in the latter 1700s.

- Clan McALISTER of America
http://www.mcallister.com/cma.html
A nonprofit genealogy organization operated exclusively by volunteering clan cousins of the McAlister, McAllister, McCalister, McCallister, McCollister family in America. Publish a 50-page journal to all members quarterly. Over 50,000 descendants in our database.

- McANINCH Family History Newsletter
mailto:FrankMac@worldnet.att.net
E-mail Frank McANINCH at FrankMac@worldnet.att.net for subscription & database details. For the surnames McAninch / McIninch /McNinch and variations.

- The McATEE Surname Family Center
http://pages.ivillage.com/ps/mcatee99/mcatee.html
Queries, message board, archives and records, meaning and origins of the McATEE name, researchers, downloadable GEDCOM files, online database, and McATEE genealogy links.

- McBRAIR Genealogy
http://www.geocities.com/heartland/woods/4676/index.html
McBrair and McBrayer families (and variants).

- The Descendants of Patrick and Jane Greene McCAHAN
http://www.adeptweb.com/mccahan/
Patrick born March 14, 1766, about twenty miles north of Dublin, Ireland.

- West Virginia McCALLISTER Genealogy
http://millennium.fortunecity.com/donald/547/menu.htm
Specializes in (but is not limited to) West Virginia McCallister genealogy lines. McCallister is generic for the various spellings such as McAlister, McAllister, McCalister, McCollister, McCallester, McCallaster, McCalaster, McAllaster, etc.

- The McCARLEY Genealogy Station
http://members.aol.com/PipL7x3/index.html

- McCARTEN.com
http://www.mccarten.com/
Vital records, family pictures, ancestor trees, and more.

- McCARTY Clan Page
http://members.tripod.com/Windrider/McCartyClan.html
Genealogy and history pages for McCARTY/MacCARTHY researchers.

- McCARTY Family History
http://members.aol.com/texastag/mccarty.html
Descendants of Jacob McCarty (1765-1841) and Mary MORROW as compiled of ten generations. Other surnames include Roberts, Hollis, Richardson, Walker, Penry, and others.

- **McCHRYSTAL, McCRYSTAL, McCRISTALL Surnames and All Variants**
  mailto:John.Hollis@london-research.gov.uk
  E-mail John Hollis at John.Hollis@london-research.gov.uk and he will search his database for you.

- **McCHRYSTAL And All Variants**
  http://members.aol.com/amcchrysta

- **The McCLANAHAN Society**
  http://hometown.aol.com/joemac1938/home.htm

- **McCLANAHAN Time Online**
  http://www.geocities.com/Heartland/Prairie/3895/

- **McCLATCHY Family Genealogy Center**
  http://www.angelfire.com/md/mcclatchy/index.html
  Resource center for researchers of the McClatchy surname, in its various spellings, around the world. Including, history of the name, heraldry associated with the name, queries, links to sites of interest to MCCLATCHY researchers, and online records, such as cemetery records, etc.

- **The McCLEAVE Line of Nantucket**
  http://worldconnect.genealogy.rootsweb.com/cgi-bin/igm.cgi?db=nathan1942
  Nine generations of the MCCLEAVE Family. Other surnames: SHERMAN, APPLETON, BACKUS, BARNARD, DAYTON, LAKE, WILCOX, CHASE, & FISHER (FISH).

- **McCLELLAN Family Home Page**
  http://www-personal.umich.edu/~ebeeman/genealogy/mcclellan/mcclellan.htm

- **McCLENDONs and McLENDONs - Genealogy: McCLENDONs and McLENDONs on the Internet**
  http://mcclendon.rootsweb.com/
  McClendon (McLendon), Graves, Hathorne, Lott, Knight, Britt, Cooper, Pounds, Keller.

- **McCLOSKEY International Family**
  http://www.pbq.com.au/home/mccloskey/macnet.htm

- **McCONNELL Genealogy**
  http://www.baynet.net/users/tmcconnell/main.htm

- **The McCORD Family Association**
  http://www.mccordfamilyassn.com/

- **The McCOURT Family Website**
  http://www.zyworld.com/jmccourt/home.htm
  Descendants of Joshua and Elizabeth Cave McCourt of Armagh, Ireland and Richmond, Quebec.

- **McCOYs Online**
  http://userwww.service.emory.edu/~dmcco01/McCoy/
  Genealogy, full-text articles and current news regarding MCCOYs.

- **The McCRACKEN Families of South Carolina**
  http://www.familytreemaker.com/users/m/c/c/Ken-O-Mccracken/
  Specializing in the Horry County area from the 1700's to the present.

- **Hugh McCRARY Family History**
  http://home.att.net/~lamccrary
  Family research and information exchange homepage for descendants of Hugh McCrary of Chester Co., PA and Rowan Co., NC.

- **Perry G. McCRARY Homepage**
  http://www.geocities.com/Heartland/Valley/3367/index.html

- **MCCRIMMON and MACCRIMMON Family Registry**
  http://www.geocities.com/Heartland/Lane/2230/

- **McCULLAR Genealogy Page**
  http://members.self-serv.net/rocker/gene/mccullar.htm
  McCullar, McCullars, McCuller, McCullers, McCullough.

- **The Unofficial McCULLOUGH Family Genealogy Page**
  http://members.aol.com/mcjill/index.html

- **McCULLY - McCULLEY - McCULLIE**
  http://mysite.xtra.co.nz/~mccullymcculley/
  One name study. Also transcripts service for any BDM in Scotland on and after 1885.

- **Genealogy of McCUMSEY And Related Families.**
  http://members.delphi.com/mccumsey/index.html
  McCumsey, McComsey, McCompsey, McComsy.

- **McCUMSEY, Robert**
  http://members.xoom.com/FellowFaith/
  The genealogy of Robert MCCUMSEY (b. 1756) and his descendants.

- **The McCUTCHAN Family Tree**
  http://www.mccutchan.org/

- **McCUTCHEN Family Tree**
  http://members.aol.com/kimcha/index.html
  Information from several McCutchen researchers with pages for Virginia and South Carolina. Also information on the family of John Ames McCutchen, including these surnames: Riddle Phemister Kennamer McCutcheon.

- **McDANIEL Family of Maryland and Kentucky**
  http://members.aol.com/jogt/mcdaniel.htm

- **The McDARIS Mall**
  http://www.mcdaris.com/
  McDaris, Medaris, Medearis, Davis, McPhetters, Buckner, Chambers, Roberts, Sizemore, Harron.

- **McDAVITT Family Historical Page**
  http://www.dallasadmall.com/McDavitt/
  Descendants of Levi McDAVITT, born June 4, 1800 in Virginia and Susannah Hott, born January 7, 1804.

- **The McDONALD Family - Genealogy**
  http://www.internet-partners.com/mcdonald/index.htm

- **Silas McDOWELL and Southern Apples**
  http://www.rabun.net/~phillips
  A biography of Silas McDowell with some information on his ancestry and children.

- **McELHONE Page**
  http://freepages.genealogy.rootsweb.com/~rogertpages/
  mcelhone.html
  Worldwide search for the McElhone family starts here.

- **eGroups: McELROY**
  http://www.eGroups.com/list/mcelroy
  For those interested in researching McElroy families, primarily in North America, especially descendants of James and Nancy A. (Smith) McElroy of Delaware and Southeastern Ohio. All McElroy researchers are welcome to post their queries and archival material.

- **The McEVILLY Web Site**
  http://www.mcevilly.org.uk/

- **McFANN Family History**
  http://students.washington.edu/mcfann/FamilyHistory/
  McFann/index.htm

- **McFARLAND Clan Homepage**
  http://www.geocities.com/Heartland/Bluffs/9826/
  McFarland family link to the McFarland Family e-mail discussion site.

- **McGEE Surname Researchers**
  http://www.geocities.com/Heartland/Prairie/3570/
  McGee, MacGee, Magee, McGhee, McGhie, McGahey, McGhee, MaGeeHee, McGeehan, McGahan and others.

- **McGILL / MAGILL Genealogy Web Ring**
  http://www.webring.org/cgi-bin/webring?ring=magillring;list

- **Clan McGINNIS Home Page**
  http://users.why.net/wejr/Publish/
  Descendants of William Erasmus McGINNIS and Cora Pauline ENGLISH, 1865-1942.

- **McGINNIS Genealogy**
  http://ddi.digital.net/~hmcginni/McHome.html

- **McGINNIS Genealogy Home Page**
  http://members.tripod.com/~cheysmom/index.html
  Dedicated to descendants of William McGinnis and his wife Mary Micheltree and other McGinnis'.

- **The McGIVNEY Homepage**
  http://www.geocities.com/heartland/lane/6153
  McGIVNEY genealogy site across the world.

- **McGUIRT Genealogy Homepage**
  http://cust.iamerica.net/aircom/mcguirt.html

- **McINTIRE Genealogy**
  http://www2.coastalnet.com/~s6r3s3dc/
  Books published on the Descendants of William McINTYRE, Micum McINTIRE, Philip McINTIRE and Robert and Helen McINTIRE.

- **Clan McINTOSH**
  http://www.mcintoshweb.com/clanmcintosh/main.asp

- **McINTOSH Family Newsletter**
  http://members.aol.com/tamers
  James Caleb McIntosh b. 1811 married Margaret Scott b. 1823. Surnames include Scott, Bell, Evans, Horn(e), Howard, McPherson, Vaughn, Ward and Zuinkman. Family migrated from Scotland to Ontario, Canada 1840-1900. Michigan, Minnesota, Montana, Washington and Utah 1900-present.

- **McKANE One Name Study**
  http://www.mckane.waterloo.on.ca/geneal/igm/McKaneOne/
  McKaneOne.htm

- **North American Descendants of Archibald McKAUGHAN**
  http://genweb.net/~mckaughan
  Descendants of Archibald McKAUGHAN who, with his family, immigrated to America from Antrim County, Ireland in 1747.

- **McKEE Family Surname**
  http://www.angelfire.com/on/mckee

- **McKERCHER's Index**
  http://www.geocities.com/mckerchers/

- **McKINLEY's One and All**
  http://members.tripod.com/~McKinley783/index.html

- **McKINNEY Genealogy**
  http://www.mckinneys.org/

- **McKINNEY / McKENNEY Family Miscellaneous Documents and Data**
  http://www.mindspring.com/~jogt/surnames/mckendoc.htm

- **A Clan McLEAN Connection**
  http://geocities.com/heartland/canyon/6387/
  A genealogical study of two McLEAN families who migrated from Scotland to Australia in the mid 1800s and eventually united in marriage in the 1900s.

- **Descendants of Alexander McLEAN circa 1765**
  http://doug-mclean.tripod.com/index-5.html
  Alexander McLean who was born in Amulree, Perthshire, Scotland circa 1765.

- **Descendants of John McMAHAN, Jr.**
  http://www.halcyon.com/jmashmun/mcmahan/index.html
  Born 23 May 1741 in County Cavan, Ireland.

- **McMAHAN Surname Mail List Home Page**
  http://freepages.genealogy.rootsweb.com/~mahanweb/
  mcmahan/home.htm

- **McMONEGAL of Westchester County and the Bronx, New York**
  http://members.aol.com/popmick/mcmon.htm
  Descendants of John McMONEGAL, then Dominick McMONEGAL of Ireland.

- **McMORRAN One Name Study**
  http://www.ozemail.com.au/~msafier/McMorran/
  mcmorran.html
  MacMorran, McMoran, McMorren, McMorine, McMorrine, McMorrin, McMurran, McMurrain, McMurrian, McMurrin, McMurren.

- **McNABBs of Tennessee Genealogy**
  http://hometown.aol.com/jkinzalow/myhomepage/news.html
  The McNABB family from 1700 Scotland to Virginia to North Carolina to E. Tennessee. Includes immigrant William MacNab & his descendants.

- McNAMER Families of Virginia and West Virginia
  http://members.tripod.com/~oldtree/McNamerFH.html
  *McNamar, McNemar, McNemer, McNamarrow, McNamarrah and
  other spellings. (Formerly McNamer Family History, Reorganized
  To Help Weed Out The Truth!).*

- McNEESE / McNEES / McNIECE Family
  Genealogical Research
  http://www.mcneese.com/

- Clan MacNEIL in Canada Genealogy Page
  http://www.clanmacneil.ca/genealogy.htm

- McNELIS Genealogy Home Page
  http://www.personal.psu.edu/faculty/j/w/jwd6/mcnelis.htm
  *McNellis, McNealas, McNeilis, McNeelis, McNail, McNaylis,
  McNealie, Mcneilly, McNealis, McNeil, McNeilis, McNelis,
  McNelus, McNolos.*

- McNERNEY Family
  http://www.mcnerney.org/mcnerney.htm
  *An attempt by various McNerneys to pool our resources. Variations
  on the name McNerney are McNerney, McInerney, McInerey,
  McNerny, McEnery*

- The Descendants of Paul McPHERSON 1734-1828
  of The King's 17th Foot Regiment
  http://www.geocities.com/Heartland/Prairie/8367/

- McQUAID Home Page
  http://www.angelfire.com/on2/mcquaid/index.html

- McQUEEN - CREWS Homepage - A Gathering
  Place for Descendants of John McQUEEN and
  Nancy CREWS
  http://www.geocities.com/dmporter_2/

- McQUEEN Surname Resource Center
  http://www.mdnetfactory.com/gen/mcqueen.htm
  *Including: McQuin, MacQuin, McQuinn, MacQuinn, McQuean,
  MacQuean and Queen.*

- McQUEEN Genealogy
  http://homepages.rootsweb.com/~imrie/mcqueen
  macqueen.html

- McRAE Family Tree
  http://members.xoom.com/lynneslocker/mcraefamilytree.html
  *About Charles McRae 1837 - 1925, from Skye, who settled in
  Victoria, Australia and his descendants.*

- McSWAN Home Page
  http://www.durham.igs.net/~lmcswan
  *Origins and lineage of the McSwan and MacSwans of Australia,
  Canada, England, Scotland and the United States.*

- McTAGUE Genealogy
  http://members.xoom.com/WWWPD/
  From Ireland to New Zealand.

- The Name McTURK or MacTURK
  http://home.clara.net/iainkerr/kerr/McTurk.htm

- McWH*RTER Genealogy
  http://homepages.rootsweb.com/~mcwgen/
  *McWhorter, McWhirter, McWherter, McWorter, Mewhorter,
  McQuirter, McQuarter, Mawhorter, Mewhirter, Mewherter,
  McQuerter, McWharter, Mawhirter, etc.*

- MABRY Page
  http://homepages.rootsweb.com/~mabry/
  For names: Mabery, Maberry, Mabray, Mabrey, Mabry, Mayberry.

- Genealogy: Don MABRY's Relatives Plus Some
  Other Sources
  http://mabry.argentinacity.com/family/genlgy.html

- Clann MAC AODHAGAIN
  http://www.geocities.com/Heartland/Bluffs/5500/
  *Centralized site for researching the name Mac Aodhagain, Egan,
  Eagan, Keegan, Mac Egan and other variations.*

- The MacARTHUR Family Tree Project
  http://web.netactive.co.za/~donmac/

- Clan MacCALLUM / MALCOLM Society
  http://clan-maccallum-malcolm.3acres.org/

- MacDERMOT Clan Association Homepage
  http://aoife.indigo.ie/~mcdermot/

- MacDONOUGH Homepage
  http://www.geocities.com/Athens/Crete/3816/INDEX.html
  *MacDonoughs of Co. Sligo, IRL. Includes McDonagh; McDonough;
  Mullin; (O')Rourke; Wilson; MacKechnie.*

- Clan MacDOUGALL Society of North America
  http://www.macdougall.org/

- Clan MacDUFF Society of America
  http://www.tartans.com/official/MacDuff/usa/

- MacDUFFEE Family Tree
  http://www.macduffee.homepage.com/index.html
  *The MacDUFFEE and McDUFFEE families from Binghamton to
  Palmyra, NY and of Bradford County, PA.*

- The Douglas E. MACE Family Page
  http://www.familytreemaker.com/users/m/a/c/Douglas-E-
  Mace/index.html

- MacEACHAIN McCAUGHAN McKAUGHAN
  McCOIN Genealogy
  http://members.tripod.com/~McCoin_Geneology/index-
  18.html
  *MacEachain genealogy from 247 AD forward over 600 pages 30
  variations of name.*

- Clan MacFARLANE - The Official Homepage of the
  Clan MacFARLANE Society, Inc.
  http://www.macfarlane.org/

- THORBURN-MACFIE Family Society
  http://home1.swipnet.se/~w-10723/thormac1.htm
  *Descendants of William Thorburn and his wife Jessy (nÈe Macfie)
  who in July 1823 removed to Sweden from Leith in Scotland.*

- MACIEJEWSKI / MAJESKI Family
  http://www.familytreemaker.com/users/m/a/j/Dick-Majeski/

- Clan MacINTYRE Society
  http://www.clanmacintyre.org/

- McINTYRE of Blackavon Genealogy Homepage
  http://www.grassroots.ns.ca/~makowiec/McIntyre/

- Clan MacKAY
  http://www.geocities.com/Heartland/Park/8030

- The MACK / MOCK List
  http://home.gzinc.com/tmock/list.htm

- Clan MacKENZIE Society in the Americas
  mailto:gwmckenz@freenet.mb.ca
  E-mail address for the society.

- MACKISON's World
  http://www.geocities.com/Heartland/Bluffs/7732/
  A place for Mackisons of the world to come together to find common ancestors.

- MacKNEW / McNEW
  http://www.geocities.com/Heartland/Ranch/1984/
  Descendants of Jeremiah MacKNEW I who emigrated in 1668 to Charles County, MD.

- Clan MacLACHLAN Association of North America, Inc.
  http://www.shirenet.com/MacLachlan

- The Descendants of James MacLACHLAN
  http://www5.pair.com/vtandrew/mcglauf/mcglauf.htm

- Clan MacLEAN / MacLAINE History Server
  http://www.gillean.com/

- Clan MacLELLAN
  http://www.clanmaclellan.org/

- Clan MacLEOD Society
  http://www.clan-macleod.com/

- MACNAMARA Clan Association
  http://www.macnamara.org

- Clan MacNICOL Federation
  http://www.cnsnet.net/user/bnicol/nicol.htm

- The MACOMBER Project
  http://www.macomberproject.com

- Clan MACPHERSON Association
  http://www.clan-macpherson.org/

- The Clan MacRAE Home Page
  http://www.geocities.com/Heartland/Plains/6803/
  Crae, Cree, Macara, Macarra, Maccra, MacCrach, MacCrae, MacCraith, MacCraw, MacCray, MacCrea, MacCreath, MacCree, MacCrie, MacCrow, MacCroy, MacGrath, MacGraw, Machray, Macra, MacRach, MacRaith, MacRath, MacRaw, MacRay, McRay, MacRie, McCraw, McCray, McCrea, McRae, Rae, Raith, Ray, Rea, Reath.

- Clan MACRAE Online
  http://www.clanmacrae.org/

- Clan MacSPORRAN Association
  http://start.at/macsporran
  All variants of McSparran, McSparren, McSparrin, McSparron, McSporran, McSpurren and even Purcell.

- Descendants of James MacTAGGART and Nancy COOLEY
  http://home.t-online.de/home/mckenzie/mctag.htm
  Ontario family.

- The Official Clan MacTAVISH Homepage
  http://www.tartans.com/official/MacTavish/mactavish.htm

- MADDOCK-L Surname Mailing List
  http://www.ikweb.com/murduck/genealogy/maddock-l/intro.htm
  Includes Maddix, Maddock, Maddocks, Maddox, Maddux, Mattix, Mattock, Mattocks, Mattox, Muddock, Muddox. Muttock, Muttox.

- The MADDOX Family
  http://www.tfs.net/~gbyron/kin/maddox.html
  History to 500 a.d., 6000 names with photos and history of Maddox, Madoc, Maddux, Mattox, Maddock.

- MADDUXCousins
  http://homepages.rootsweb.com/~madcuzns/Index.htm
  Descendants of Alexander Maddox, born 1613, arrived in Virginia 1635, died 1660. Variant spellings: Madawg, Madoc, Madog, Madox, Maddeaux, Maddocks, Maddox, Maddux, Mattix, Mattocks, Mattox.

- David MADER Family History
  http://www.jmts.com/mader/
  History of the David Mader Family in America.

- MAGNER Family Genealogy
  http://www.magner.org/
  Fifty families in three countries sharing information. 4,500 name database.

- MAGNY Family Association
  http://hometown.aol.com/kbschoony/myhomepage/index.html

- Jim's Irish Family Surnames - MAGUIRE - Myth & History
  http://www.cris.com/~Maguire/Maguire2.html

- MAGUIRE Clan
  http://www.csn.ul.ie/~ger/maguire/main.html

- MAHADY One Name Study Resource Center
  http://www.geocities.com/Heartland/Bluffs/4447/
  For all variations of the surname Mahady including Mahaddy, Mahadey, Mahardy, Mahedy, Maheady, Maheddy, Maherdy, Mahide, Mahidy, Mahody.

- MAHAN Surname Mail List Home Page
  http://freepages.genealogy.rootsweb.com/~mahanweb/mahan/homepage.htm

- MAHER (MEAGHER / MAHAR) Surname
  http://homepages.rootsweb.com/~maher/
  Information for those researching the Maher, Meagher, Mahar (and variants) surname.

- Some Descendants of Ezekiel MAINE
  http://users.exis.net/~nancn/main/index.htm
  Descendants of Ezekiel MAINE, born 1641, York, Maine, died June 1714 in Stonington, Connecticut and Mary HATCH born 03 Oct 1652 in Stonington.

- MALEY Family Web Site
  http://www.maley.org/

- The MALLANDAINE Family History Page
  http://pages.hotbot.com/gene/mallandaine
  Family history from 1670. Spelling variations of surname include MALANDAIN, MALLANDAIN, MALLINDINE, MALLANDINE.

- MALLETT Family History
  http://www.ott.igs.net/~rhmallett/index.htm
  MALET, MALLET, MALLETT and related families in (primarily) "West Country" England, Canada, USA, and Australia, from 1066 until now.

- MALLOY
  http://www.geocities.com/Heartland/Fields/7103/
  A family history of the MALLOYs, since they moved here from Ireland over one hundred years ago.

- Descendents of Richard MALONE
  http://genweb.net/~rmalone
  Descendents of Richard MALONE born 1735 died 1801 in Centre County Pennsylvania.

- MALOWNEY
  http://www.irishgenealogy.com/MALOWNEY.htm
  Malonek, Maloney, Malowany, Malowny, Malowney, Mallowney, Moloney, Mullowney.

- Andrew MANAR where are you???
  http://www.familytreemaker.com/users/h/i/a/Nora-Ann-Hiatt-WA/

- The Mandeville Newsletter
  mailto:shhhharon@primary.net
  A quarterly newsletter devoted to the Mandeville family lines, all branches, any spelling variations (Mandeville, Manvil, Mandevil, D'Mandewijl, Manderville, Mandeviel, De Mandeville, Manterville, etc.). For details send e-mail to Sharon West at shhhharon@primary.net.

- The MANGUM Family
  http://fly.hiwaay.net/~lparham/
  Mangham, Mangrum, Mangram, Mangun, Mangam, etc.

- The MANN Family
  http://mannmanns.homestead.com/
  MANN / MANNS family of Breathitt County, Kentucky.

- MANNING's of Elmira, NY
  http://www.familytreemaker.com/users/m/a/n/James-L-Manning
  Descendants of James and Hannah (NOONAN) MANNING. Hannah Noonan was born in Ireland, 1858, to Daniel and Mary Noonan.

- The MANSKER Chronicles
  http://www.mansker.org/
  Descendants of Ludwig M"intzger, from Germany to Philadelphia in September of 1749. Mansker, Minsker, Mintsker, Mansco, Mesker, Meinzer, and all of the other variations on the family name.

- MÝNTTÝRI Family Association Ltd. ~ Finland
  http://www.kolumbus.fi/manttari/home-pag/main.htm

- The Genealogical History of the MAPLES family.
  http://www.geocities.com/tracy-1/genealogy/maples/index.html

- MARBLE Family Genealogy Homepage
  http://www.ameritech.net/users/lrmarble/Main.htm
  Includes Marble surname index, corresponding spouse surname index, and descendant family pages for more than 9,000 Marble surname individuals. Includes surname variants: Marble, Marable, Marvel, Marvell, Marvelle, Marbel, Marbell, Marbelle.

- MARIS Genealogy Home Page
  http://www.gendex.com/users/RayMaris/maris/maris.htm
  Descendants of George (1632-1705) and Alice Willsmith/Wellsmith (-1699) MARIS, who immigrated to Pennsylvania from England in 1683. Maris, Newlin, Mendenhall, Hadley, Lindley, Harvey, Packer Paxson, Hunter, Taylor.

- MARKLEY Central
  http://www.nevans.freeserve.co.uk
  Markeley, Markilie, Markilley, Markillie, Marklew, Markley, Marquillier, Merkle, Mickley, Muckley.

- Marks Family Association
  http://www.geocities.com/Heartland/5622/MarksHome Page.html
  Marks - Merck - Murks.

- Peter van MARKUS Homepage
  http://www.casema.net/~markuspv/
  From the Netherlands. Descendants of Pieter Louissen van Markus, married 1718 Catharina van Wijck.

- MARPLES Family History
  http://www.users.globalnet.co.uk/~rmarpl/index.html
  Personal introduction, MARPLES' coats of arms, earliest refrenecs to the name, Derbyshire connections.

- MARR Family
  http://www.wf.net/~billk/Marr.html
  Descendants of Martha Maria TAYLOR and Nathaniel Hancock MARR.

- MARRINON "Family Tree" and all associated Families, Worldwide
  http://users.bigpond.com/davemarrinon/
  Descendants of John Hargrove MARRINON and Emily JOHNSTON who arrived in Australia in the mid-19th century.

- The MARSDEN Page
  http://ourworld.compuserve.com/homepages/johnmarsden/mars-1.htm

- MARSH Genealogy
  http://homepages.rootsweb.com/~halmar48
  A collection of data, links, photos, census information, etc. pertaining to the surname MARSH and its various spellings.

- MARSHALL Genealogy - Aaron
  http://pages.about.com/marshall4418/site1.index.html
  Descendants of Aaron MARSHALL and Sarah SNOWDEN.

- **Descendants of Randall MARSHALL**
  http://www.geocities.com/Athens/Pantheon/4136/
  Randall Marshall (1714-1780) and Hannah Chew of Blackwood, New Jersey.

- **The MARSHALLs of East Texas**
  http://www.dallas.net/~vrnews/
  The Jesse & Catherine MARSHALL Family of Upshur County, Texas.

- **The (MARSHALL) Family Tree**
  http://hometown.aol.com/dmarsh1041/famtree.htm
  Descendants of Martin MARSHALL and his siblings of Calvert County, Md. Also BADGETT, JOYCE, SPARGER, TALBOTT, WRAY.

- **MARSLAND Family**
  http://catalog.com/beanies/marsland/
  MARSLAND, A site for registering information re: surname MARSLAND, by and for MARSLANDs, for the purposes of researching Family Genealogy.

- **MARSTELLER Family Research Association**
  http://www.marsteller.org/
  Masteller, Mosteller, Mausteller, Mostellar, Mostoller, Marstella, Mostiller, Marstallar, Mosteller, Marstiller, Moshteller, Marstaller.

- **Henry MARTIN of Cumberland County, VA (d. 1752)**
  http://bladerunner.dartmouth.edu/~emily/H.Martin.html

- **The MARTIN's**
  http://www.angelfire.com/tx/lineage/index.html
  Documented history of William Martin VA>NC>SC>TN>MS.

- **The UK Family History Society of MARTIN**
  http://fhsofmartin.org/
  A charitable society dedicated to furthering knowledge of the surname MARTIN and all its variants.

- **The MASHBURN Genealogical Archives**
  http://www.avana.net/~mashburn/mashburn/index2.htm
  Descendants of Edward Mashburn, born 1676 in London, England who became a schoolmaster in NC in 1712.

- **MASON Family History Center**
  http://members.tripod.com/mayfield1652/

- **MASSEY Family Genealogy**
  http://clubs.yahoo.com/clubs/masseyfamilygenealogy
  MASSEY research worldwide and for any given time period.

- **Greg Harper's MASSINGHAM Genealogy WWW Page**
  http://home.x-stream.co.uk/~gregharper/index.htm
  MESSINGHAM, MISSINGHAM.

- **The MASTENS of Sullivan Co., NY**
  http://gloversville.freeyellow.com/index.html

- **The MASTERS Family Association**
  http://www.geocities.com/Heartland/Prairie/4153/

- **MASTIN Family Genealogy - Pennsylvania, Ohio, Illinois, Missouri, Iowa and beyond**
  http://members.xoom.com/mdm812/
  Mastin. Masten. Maston.

- **MATHERS Genealogy**
  http://www.geocities.com/Heartland/Vista/3910/

- **Dan MATNEY and Allied Families**
  http://www.angelfire.com/or/matney/

- **MATHIS Genealogy Page**
  http://genealogy.mathis.net
  Famille MATHIS de Ribeauvillé, Alsace, France (Database Online).

- **MATTESON Historical Congress of America, Inc.**
  http://www.angelfire.com/pe/rcmatteson/congress.html

- **MATTHEWS Genealogical Research Foundation**
  http://users.viawest.net/cone/~butchmat/MathewFam Page99.html
  Mathew, Mathews, Matthews, etc. surname research in Wales and all the British Isles.

- **MATTHEWSa Surname Resource Center**
  http://freepages.genealogy.rootsweb.com/~geneal/src/MatthSRC.html
  MATTHEWS, MATHEWS and variations.

- **MATTICE Family Tree**
  http://www.fortunecity.com/millenium/greendale/152/findex2.htm

- **MAULE Genealogy Homepage**
  http://vls.law.vill.edu/prof/maule/home/famhist/maulehpg.htm

- **MAUPIN Family**
  http://www.geocities.com/Heartland/Bluffs/6987/
  Descendants of Gabriel Maupin and His Wife Marie Hersent of Gargeau, France; Amsterdam, Netherlands and Williamsburg, Virginia & Their Son Daniel Maupin and His Wife Margaret Via of Albemarle County, Virginia.

- **MAUPIN Family Reunion**
  http://geocities.com/Heartland/9723/reunion.htm

- **MAWHINNEY**
  http://homepages.rootsweb.com/~imrie/mawhinney.html

- **MAXFIELD Genealogy**
  http://www.users.fast.net/~max
  Genealogy information for all Maxfields, with a focus on the descendants of William MAXFIELD of Windham, Maine.

- **MAXFIELDS Of The World**
  http://www.maxfield.org

- **MAXSTED Genealogy**
  http://home.connexus.net.au/~mem1

- **The MAYEUX Genealogy Project**
  http://public.surfree.com/bbotzong/mayeux.htm
  Information on the Mayeux family of Louisiana, descendants of Pierre Mayeux.

- **MAYFIELD Family Genealogy Home Page**
  http://members.xoom.com/philnorf/

- **MAYFIELD Home Page**
  http://freepages.genealogy.rootsweb.com/~mingledmayfields/home.html

- MAYFIELD Manor
  http://members.xoom.com/DonnaCHamm/MayfieldHome.htm
  The official web site for the Rootsweb Mayfield mailing list. It is a work in progress focused on providing as much Mayfield surname related information as possible in a single site.

- MAYHEAD Family
  http://www.alan-rosie.demon.co.uk/
  Mayhead and variants, one name study - Mayhead, Mayhood, Madhead.

- MAYNARD Project
  http://www.wizard.net/~aldonna/maynard.htm
  Descendants of John Maynard of Sudbury, Massachusetts.

- MAYNE FAMILY.COM - The MAYNE Family (From the Devon Area of England)
  http://www.maynefamily.com/
  Dedicated to those who search for MAYNES from the Devon area of England (Mayne, Mendenhall, Mullins, Whipple, Zylka).

- M*CH*M*RE One-Name Study
  http://www.picknowl.com.au/homepages/bobm/
  Michelmore, Mitchamore, Mitchelmore, Mouchemore, Muchamore, Muchemore, Muchmore.

- M(E)AT(T)YE(A)R One Name Study
  http://home.clara.net/dchilds/mtyr/mtyr-ons.html
  Matcher, Matear/eer, Mathiar, Matier, Mattear, Mattia, Matye(a)r, Mea(t)cher, Meatchier, Meatye(a)r, Me(s/t)tayer or Le Metayer, Metiar/er/or, Met(t)ye(a)r.

- The MEDEIROS Home Page
  http://www.maui.net/~makule/medhome.html

- MEDERNACH
  http://gallery.uunet.lu/M.Brouwer/
  The village Medernach or the name Medernach from Luxembourg.

- The MEDLYCOTT-MEDLICOTT Family Tree
  http://www.chariot.net.au/~bluebird

- MEDLEY Surname Mailing List
  http://www.jas.net/~sueowens/meddir.htm

- MEIGS Family History Page
  http://www.meigs.org/history.htm

- The MELANSON / MELANCON / MALONSON / MALANSON Family Project
  http://www.geocities.com/Heartland/Meadows/7961/

- MELLOR One Name Study
  http://ourworld.compuserve.com/homepages/mike_mellor_coventry/

- MELTON Surname Resource Center
  http://meltons.8m.com
  MELTON and variants, e.g., MILTON, MELTEN, MELTAN, MELTIN, etc.

- MENARY Resource Center
  http://homepages.rootsweb.com/~menary/index.htm
  MANAREY, MANARY, MENARAIS, MENARRY, MENARY, MENERAY, MENERET, MENEREY, MENURET, MINARY.

- MENDENHALL Family Association
  http://www.mendenhall.org/

- The MENEFEE Family - Harrison Co., HY and VA#160;
  http://www.rootsweb.com/~kyharris/menefee.htm

- Genealogy of the MENSO family / Genealogy van familie MENSO
  http://w1.302.telia.com/~u30202898/
  The MENSO family comes from Holland and can be traced to the 16th century.

- The MERIAN Family Home Page
  http://homepages.infoseek.com/~kmerian/index.html
  Descendants of Jean Merian who emigrated from Oberentzen, Alsace to Texas in 1847.

- The MERIWETHER Society, Inc.
  http://members.aol.com/tmsimc/index.html
  Established by descendants of Nicholas Meriwether I (1631-1678).

- The MERRILL Newsletter
  http://merrill.olm.net/TMN/

- MERRILLs of Franklin County, MA
  http://www.bearhaven.com/merrills.htm

- Number of MERRILLs in the United States, 1850-1990
  http://www.bearhaven.com/family/merrill/p1850-1990.html

- MERRIMAN Family Information Page
  http://www2.memlane.com/merriman/genealogy.html

- Miles MERWIN Association
  http://www.merwin.org

- MESCHEDE Genealogy Homepage
  http://members.aol.com/familygeo/mesch/index.htm
  Also Von MESCHEDE.

- MESSERVY Home Page
  http://www.meserve.org/
  Meserve, Meservey, Messervy, Meservy.

- Messerville
  http://www.hci.net/~windsong/
  For the Messer surname, including the descendants of Captain "Robert" Messer.

- MESSINGER Family History: Immigrants in 1732 to Pennsylvania
  http://www.wyoming.com/~Carol/Messinger.shl
  Includes 8 generations of the descendants of Johannes and Elisabeth Messinger in PA, OH, IL and OR.

- The METCALFE Society
  http://www.metcalfe.org.uk/
  Home Page of the METCALFE Society devoted to researching the name Metcalfe and all its variants, including Medcalf, Metcoff and the like. Society was founded in the UK in 1980 and has more than 450 active members worldwide.

- METHENY Pages - Online Newsletter
  http://www.geocities.com/~methenyd/newsltr.html
  A Family Newsletter for METHENY, MATHENY, MATHENA Families.

- METHVIN / METHVEN Around the World
  http://www.scottsboro.org/~piercedc/default.htm
  From Scotland to the New World.

- MEYRICK Family Homepage
  http://www.knighton.freeserve.co.uk/homepage/homepage.htm
  Meyrick, Meurig, Merret, Merrick.

- Association des Familles MICHAUD, Inc.
  http://www.genealogie.org/famille/michaud/
  This site describes Michaud Families'Association, explain their Coat of Arms, gives highlights of ancestor Pierre Micheau's life in New France.

- The MIDDLEMISS Family, 1769 -- 1996, From Berwick-on-Tweed to New Zealand
  http://home.clear.net.nz/pages/middlemiss/
  Descendants of Andrew MIDDLEMIST, born 1769 in Berwick On Tweed.

- MIDDLETON Home Page
  http://members.aol.com/donmid1/families/middletn.htm
  Descendants of James Middleton born 1750 died 1798 in Broadcreek Hundred, Sussex County, Delaware.

- The Other MIDDLETON Home Page
  http://members.aol.com/srwings/middleton/index.htm
  Descendants & ancestors of John Andrew MIDDLETON born about 1833 in Virginia.

- The MIDDOUR Family History
  http://members.aol.com/pmiddour/genealgy/index.htm
  Middour, Mittauer, Mittower.

- The MIDGLEY Page
  http://home.earthlink.net/~petegm/index.html

- MIKESELL Genealogy Home Page
  http://www.novagate.com/~mikesell/genealogy.html

- The MILAM Family History
  http://www.robertwilbanks.com/milam.htm

- The MILAM Family History and Genealogy Archives
  http://www.Steelpenny.net
  The largest online Milam Family database in the world. Dedicated to finding and sharing ALL available information on the World-wide Milam family.

- MILLER Genealogy
  http://www.qni.com/~geo/miller.htm
  For the descendants of Reason Miller, born January 7, 1817.

- MILLER Genealogy Page
  http://www.unf.edu/~fmille/miller.htm
  MILLERs of Adams and Cumberland Counties, PA.

- MILLESON Genealogy Home Page
  http://ourworld.compuserve.com/homepages/milleson/

- The MILLINGTON Archive
  http://public.logica.com/~millington
  Central contact point for those interested in the Millington surname.

- MILLS Ancestry
  http://www.geocities.com/Heartland/8496/
  Descendants, ancestors and allied families of the Mills of colonial New York and New England, as well as throughout the US and Canada to the present time.

- MILLS Musings
  http://ladyecloud.hypermart.net/Mills.htm

- MILSOMs of Bath
  http://www.milsom.org
  Surnames include, POPE, COLLINS, HOPPES, PEARCE, RISELEY, BUTLER, MANN, FOX AND TYLER.

- The MILTON / MELTON Pot
  http://www.geocities.com/Heartland/Flats/5596/

- MINNEY and MINNELL One Name Family History Study
  http://freespace.virgin.net/b.minney/index.htm

- MINNICH Ancestry
  http://members.xoom.com/wattsnew/
  Descendants of Peter Daniel Minnich b.1794 of PA, including biographical sketches of family members.

- From the Isle of Thanet to the Rest of the World - MIRAMS: A One Name Study
  http://home.cfl.rr.com/mirams/

- MIRAMS Genealogy
  http://www.purplenet.net/~ziggy/
  A one name study of the surname MIRAMS.

- MISTLER Genealogy
  http://hometown.aol.com/cdmistler/myhomepage/heritage.html
  Descendants of Henry MISTLER (Misler, Missler, Mishler) and Margaret Mary E. WHITE. Other surnames are Hunt, Rector, Vaught, Frey, Lawson, Shillinger, Tyree, Birdsong, Devore. Locations include Alsace-Lorraine, PA, KY, OH, MO, and OK.

- The MIXON / MIXSON Family Web Site
  http://www.lakelanier.com/mixons/index.htm

- MOBLEY Surname Home Page
  http://www.genealogy.org/~mobley/

- MOCK Family
  http://home.gzinc.com/tmock/jmock.htm
  Descendants of Johannes MACK (John MOCK). Also CLINARD, COPPESS, HINKLE, FOLTZA, RAPER, SICELOFF, SINK.

- The MOCK Family Historian
  http://mock.rootsweb.com/
  A family organization related to all variant spellings of the Germanic surnames Mock, Mack, Mauck, Mauk, Moak, Maag, Moch, Moght, Mag, Mog, Mak, Muck and others in America and thoroughly the world.

- MOCK-GEN-L Surname Mailing List
  http://home.ease.lsoft.com/archives/mock-gen-l.html
  Includes Mauk, Mauck, Mack, Macht, Mauch, Maught.

- Descendants of Gerhardt MOELLENBROCK - MOELLENBROCK Family Genealogy
  http://www.geocities.com/rebel29108/
  This family's ancestors immigrated to the US during the mid 1800's from Hannover, Germany.

- MOFF Family Genealogy Page
  http://homepages.rootsweb.com/~moff

- MOFFITT Surname Mailing List
  http://www.sonic.net/~yvonne/moffitt.html
  Includes Moffett.

- The Clan MOHAN
  http://mik23.tripod.com/mohanindex.html
  Dedicated to all Irish MOHANs. Message board available.

- MOHER Family History and Genealogical Web Site
  http://www.geocities.com/Heartland/Ridge/2876/

- The MOHLER Family Tree
  http://pw2.netcom.com/~mohlerl/lances.htm
  History of the Mohler family in the U.S., starting with Lancaster County, Pennsylvania.

- The Gathering of the MOHRs
  http://www.whitesite.com/mohr/
  Mohr, Moore, Maurer & Mowrer Genealogy.

- MOLLICA Genealogy
  http://www.mollica.net/genealog.htm
  Worldwide genealogy resource for the MOLLICA family, which originated in Sicily and Italy.

- The MONAGHAN Clan
  http://www.geocities.com/Heartland/Park/6748/clan.html
  For the Monaghan surname. An opportunity to join, network and brainstorm with other Monaghan researchers.

- Clan MONCREIFFE U.S.A.
  http://www.geocities.com/Augusta/1452/
  MONCREIFFE, MONCREIFF, MUNCRIEF, MONCRIEF, MONTCREEF world-wide.

- MONKMAN Family Tree
  http://boco.net/monkman/
  One name study of the surname MONKMAN. 3000 listings & growing.

- MONLUX In America
  http://nwrain.com/~monlux/MonluxInAmerica.html
  Includes information on published family records and a descendants list of family patriarch William M. Monlux 1750-1837.

- MONROE Genealogy of Cumberland, Moore and Robeson County, NC.
  http://www.monroegen.org/
  Several lines of the surname MUNROE/MONROE from the upper Cape Fear valley of central North Carolina and later Georgia, Alabama, Louisiana and Texas.

- The Clan MONTGOMERY Society International
  http://www.geocities.com/Heartland/Acres/6070/index.htm

- The MONTGOMERY Family Home Page
  http://www3.sk.sympatico.ca/monta/

- The MOODY Family
  http://www.zekes.com/~mmoody/
  Records of the descendants of Mr. John MOODY of Hartford Connecticut 1636. Collected and Compiled by the Rev. Plinius Moody, AM 1856.

- MOODY Surname Home Page
  http://home.pacbell.net/mbare
  Also MOODYE and MOODIE.

- MOON Genealogy Page
  http://members.aol.com/acmoon01/moon1.html

- MOON Family Pages
  http://junior.apk.net/~moondog
  Searchable database. Links and photos. Bucks Co., PA and OH MOON sites.

- MOORE Genealogy
  http://homepages.rootsweb.com/~moorel/
  Companion website to the Moore-L and the Moore-research-L discussion lists.

- MOORE-L Web Page
  http://www.rootsweb.com/~nozell/MOORE-L/

- MOORE News - A Weekly E-mail Newsletter
  mailto:JBrown7169@aol.com
  Send e-mail to Joyce Browning at Jbrown7169@aol.com for details.

- MOORE-POLING Web Page
  http://www.zoomnet.net/~sllewis/moore/index.html
  Descendants of Daniel Moore, born abt 1760 and Deborah Poling, born 1774 in Virginia.

- MOQUINs of North America
  http://www.geocities.com/Heartland/Oaks/9567
  Brief history of the Moquin,s of North America and a list of descendants of Mathurin Moquin.

- MORAAL Family History
  http://come.to/moraal
  Tales and family trees from the Moraal family.

- MORDEN's Web Page
  http://morden.evisionfamily.com/
  MORDEN family from England to the US to Canada and back to the US.

- MOREL & Co. / La page personnelle de la famille MOREL
  http://home.nordnet.fr/~jlmorel/
  Gènèalogie des familles Morel et BricePicardie, Pas-de-Calais, nordmètiers anciens, cartes postales anciennes.

- MORFORD Family History
  http://www.netins.net/showcase/iagenealogy/index.htm

- The MORGAN Society
  http://www.gn.apc.org/clmorgan/society/

- MORGAN / SHIRLEY Lines
  http://www.geocities.com/Heartland/River/1744/Morgan.html
  Descendants of Mary SHIRLEY b. 1809 VA and Edward MORGAN; married in Hamilton Co., OH, 1828; lived in Preble Co., OH till 1843.

- Descendants Of Andre MORIN and Marguerite MOREAU
  http://www.newnorth.net/~kind/morin.html
  Settled in Quebec around 1665 and married in 1670.

- Association des Familles MORISSETTE Inc. ~ Quebec
  http://www.genealogie.org/famille/morissette/morissette.htm

- The Charles Jeffrey MORRISSETTE, Sr. Family Home Page
  http://www.ghg.net/hankflagg/genealogy/
  In 1700 Pierre Morriset, a French Huguenot, arrived in James City, Virginia aboard the ship "Mary and Ann". The Huguenots on board had left France to escape religious persecution and to find new land.

- MORRIS Family Association
  http://genweb.net/~morris/

- MORRIS Genealogy Web Site
  http://www.geocities.com/Heartland/Hills/1914/genealogy.htm
  Coffey, Conley, Green, Herring, Miller, Pennell, Phillips, Teachey, Yates.

- MORRIS Home Page - MORRIS Members Newsletter
  http://members.aol.com/Kinseeker6/morris.html

- The MORRISON Resource Center
  http://homepages.rootsweb.com/~crystal/morrison/

- Clan MORRISON Society of North America, Mid-Atlantic Region
  http://patriot.net/~morrison/

- Untold MORRISON Story
  http://www2.coastalnet.com/~g7d3j4nb
  MORRISON, DAVIDSON, ALEXANDER, CHISHOLM, KIMBRO, SHEPPARD, DIAZ, MCKEE and associated families.

- The MORSE Society
  http://morssweb.com/morse/index.htm
  American and Canadian Descendants of Samuel Morse, Anthony Morse, William Morse, Joseph Morse, John Moss.

- The MORT Family Homepage
  http://www.execpc.com/~drg/mort.html
  Genealogy & Research on all American Mort Families.

- The MORT Family Page
  http://www.geocities.com/Heartland/Valley/1031/mort.htm

- MORTIBOYS Family History
  http://www.mortiboy.freeserve.co.uk/fh.htm
  Mortiboys, Mortiboy, Morteboy.

- MORTIMER Surname in Scotland
  http://www.users.globalnet.co.uk/~mortimer
  MORTIMER in Scotland, between 1126 and 1700.

- The MOSEY Family
  http://www.geocities.com:80/Heartland/2148/mosey.html
  Sign up for the Mosey Surname List for Mosey information world-wide.

- The MOSS Family Genealogy
  http://www.pathway.net/lcampbell/
  Moss Families from Virginia and West Virginia. Includes these collateral surnames: Gibson, Herron, Kuhl, Reaser, Rhoades, Wilfong, Wright.

- The MOSTERT Page
  http://huizen2.dds.nl/~mosterts/

- MOTT Family Genealogy
  http://homepages.rootsweb.com/~mottgene/
  Descendants of the MOTT Family from Long Island, NY who removed to Alburg, VT about 1789

- MOULD Family History
  http://freepages.genealogy.rootsweb.com/~mould/index.htm
  Family lines include: Ann MOULD of St. Leonard on Sea, Sussex; Ezekiel MOULD and Joane EDES, Cornwall; Edward B MOULD of New York. Also the MOULD Family Research Group (Australia) Newsletters and Links.

- MOWER Family History Association
  http://www.xmission.com/~mower/

- The MUCHMORE Families
  http://www.muchmore.org/
  Muchmore, Muchemore, Mutchmore, Mutchmor, Michelmore, Garard, Bruen, Lum, Kitchel plus "muchmore." A Genealogy of the Descendants of John & Hannah Muchmore John & Anne Muchemore and All Allied Families.

- MUDERSBACH's Family Genealogy: Interactive Site
  http://mudersbach.virtualave.net/

- The MULBERRY Family of Idaho
  http://www.netcom.com/~jog1/mulberry/ofidaho.html

- The MULBERRY Family of Kentucky
  http://www.netcom.com/~jog1/mulberry/jacob.html

- "MULL" - Family/Surname Forum
  http://www.geocities.com/Heartland/Meadows/9473/mull2.html

- Our MULLEN Family Line
  http://members.aol.com/christ922/genealgy/index.htm
  William Scott Mullen to present.

- The MUMBY - GERAGHTY Family History Project
  http://www.ionline.net/~djm/
  Conducting personal genealogy research and a one name study of Mumby, (Lincolnshire, England), and Geraghty, (Ireland), including the origins of the names.

- MUMFORD
  http://www.cadvision.com/mumford/index.html

- The MUMMA-MOOMAW Family Page
  http://www.mumma.org/mumma.html
  Mewmaw, Moomau, Moomaw, Muma, Mumau, Mumaugh, Mumaw, Mumma, Mummah, Mummau and Mummaw.

- MUMMEY Family Reunion Website
  http://ecicnet.org/~uboat977/
  Mummey/Mummy family genealogy, with Hammond and Smith allied lines, information on annual Mummey reunion.

- MUNDY / MONDAY / MONDY
  http://freepages.genealogy.rootsweb.com/~ellieb/
  Researching the family and descendants of Henry MUNDY of NC and IN.

- Thomas MUNSON Foundation
  http://www.thomas-munson.org/

- MURDISON Family History Site
  http://www.interlog.com/~opanon/murdison/
  Database listing all known descendants of Andrew MURDISON of Peebles, Scotland in the 1700's. Other surnames include Watson, Spears Or Speirs, Reynolds, Marselis or Marsales, Reeder or Reader.

- MURDUCK-L Surname Mailing List
  http://www.ikweb.com/murduck/genealogy/murduck-l/intro.htm
  Includes Murdock, Murdoch, Murdocke, Murducke, Mardock, Merdock, Moorduck, Midduck.

- MURNANEs of Tipperary, Cork and Limerick
  http://www.murnane.org/

- MURPHY Home Page - MURPHY Mates Newsletter
  http://members.aol.com/Kinseeker6/murphy.html

- The MURRAY Clan Society of Queensland
  http://www.globec.com.au/~egan/
  For anyone bearing the surname of: Murray, MacMurray, Moray, Murrie, Morrow or the Clan's affiliated septs : Balneaves, Dinsmore, Dunsmore, Fleming, Geraghty, Ginsmore, Harrington, Macmorrow, Neaves, Piper, Pyper, Small, Smail, Smeal, Spaulding, Thomas or Tomas.

- MURRAY Family Web
  http://www.murrayfamily.org/
  Descendants of Patrick Murray who married circa 1795 and resided on the Townland of Curragh, Clondulane, Fermoy, Co. Cork, Ireland.

- MURRAY Matters Home Page
  http://www.telusplanet.net/public/baines7/murraym.html
  Genealogy of the family of Angus MURRAY and Elizabeth McDONALD who came to Pictou County, Nova Scotia from Sutherland, Scotland about 1831.

- Descendants of Hieronymus MURRI
  http://members.xoom.com/cragun/murri/hmurri/index.htm
  Hieronymus Murri was born in Switzerland. His descendants settled in Midway, Utah.

- MUSE Family Genealogy
  http://ourworld.compuserve.com/homepages/jwmuse/musefam.htm
  Some descendants of John MUSE of Virginia.

- MUSETTI Surname Resource Center
  http://www.geocities.com/Heartland/Valley/2702/musetti.htm
  A place for MUSETTI's around the world to gather and share

genealogical information. Site includes: Family Crest, Origin of Surname, Addresses, Passenger Arrivals, Military Records, Social Security Records, etc.

- MUSICK Family Geneology
  http://www.musickfamily.com/

- MUSMACHER Family Genealogy Page
  http://members.xoom.com/ronniem1/
  Musmacher, Musmacker, Drexler, Cummings, Grossarth, Cavanaugh, Lewis, Leahy, O'keefe, Corke, Thorthon.

- MUTCHLER Family Home Page
  http://www.ghgcorp.com/smutchler/genem.html
  From W–rth, Alsace Lorriane area of France and Germany around the early 1600s.

- The MUTIMER Family Home Page ~ Australia
  http://www.lzs.com.au/~lmutimer

- MYERS Genealogy Ring
  http://www.geocities.com/Heartland/Bluffs/5062/myersgenring.html

- MYERS Genealogy & Tina's Link_List
  http://www.geocities.com/Heartland/Bluffs/5062/
  MYERS genealogy links and discussion lists. Gurney, Bowers, Haney, Hanii, Lawson, Robinette, Murphy.

- MYERS GenLog Genealogy Database
  http://home1.gte.net/casper01/myers/myers.htm
  Searchable database specifically designed for researchers of the MYERS name.

◆ Surname Mailing Lists

- "MAA-MAD" Surname Mailing Lists
  http://www.rootsweb.com/~jfuller/gen_mail_surnames-maa.html
  MAAS, MAASS, MABE (includes Maib, Mayaab), MABIE, MABRY (includes Mayberry, Marbury, Mabrie), MACALEESE, MACALUSO, MACARTHUR, MACAULAY, MACAULAY, MACCOISE, MACCURRY, MACDANIEL, MACDONALD, MACDONNELL, MACDOUGALL (includes McDougall, MacDougal, McDougal, McDowell, McDowal), MACDOWALL (includes Mcdowall, Macdowell, Mcdowell), MACDUFF, MACE (includes Mayse, Mase, Mays), MACFARLAND, MACFARLANE, MACFERGUS, MACGREGOR, MACIEJEWSKI, MACINTOSH, MACK, MACKAY, MACKENROTH (includes McKinroth), MACKENZIE, MACKENZIE (includes McKenzie, McKinzie, McKensie), MACKEY, MACKIE, MACKIN, MACKIN (includes Macken, McKin, McClain, McCann), MACKINNON, MACLAINE, MACLAREN, MACLAUGHLIN, MACLEAN, MACLEISH, MACLEOD, MACMILLAN, MACNAB, MACOMBER, MACON, MACPHERSON, MACQUEEN (includes McQueen), MACRAE (includes Ra, Rae, Rea, MacRa, MacRea, McRae, McRa, McRea, M'Rae, M'Ra, M'Rea, Ray, Reey,, Reay), MACRAE, MACY, MADAWG, MADDEAUX, MADDEN, MADDOCK (includes Maddix, Maddock, Maddocks, Maddox, Maddux, Mattix, Mattock, Mattocks, Mattox,, Muddock, Muddox, Muttock, Muttox), MADDOCK, MADDOCKS, MADDOX, MADDUX, MADDUX (includes Maddox, Maddeaux, Maddocks, Mattocks, Madawg, Madog), MADERAS (includes Madaris, Medearis, Medaris, McDarris), MADERE (includes Mader, Madern, Matern, Materne), MADIGAN, MADILL (includes Mac Dougall), MADISON, MADOG. MADSEN.

- **"MAE-MAH" Surname Mailing Lists**
http://www.rootsweb.com/~jfuller/gen_mail_surnames-mae.html
MAES, MAGEE, MAGELLAN (includes Magalhães, Magallanes), MAGER, MAGGARD (includes Maegert, Magot, Maggot, Maggott, Mackert), MAGILL (includes McGill), MAGNER, MAGNESS, MAGOON (includes MacGoon, McGoon), MAGOON (includes Magoun, McGoon), MAGRUDER, MAGUIRE, MAGUIRE, MAGYAR, MAHAFFEY, MAHAN, MAHAR, MAHER, MAHLBERG, MAHLER, MAHON, MAHONEY, MAHONY, MAHORNEY, MAHR.

- **"MAI-MAN" Surname Mailing Lists**
http://www.rootsweb.com/~jfuller/gen_mail_surnames-mai.html
MAICH, MAIDEN, MAIDENS, MAIER, MAILANDER (includes Mailänder, Maylander, Mayländer), MAILLET, MAIN, MAINE, MAINWARING, MAIR, MAITLAND, MAIZE, MAJOR, MAJORS (includes Major, Magers), MAKAL, MAKEMIE, MAKEPEACE, MAKIEJ (includes Maciej), MAKIN, MAKING, MAKINSON, MALCOLM, MALCOM, MALDONADO, MALE, MALET, MALEY (includes Malley, Maly, Mayley, Mealey, Mealy, Mailey), MALIK, MALIN, MALISH (includes Mehlish, Mehlisch, Malisch), MALKIN, MALKIN, MALLABAR, MALLARD (includes Mellard), MALLET, MALLETT, MALLEY, MALLINSON, MALLON, MALLORY, MALLOY, MALONE (includes Maloney, Mahoney, Mallory, O'Malley, Molone), MALONEY, MALOTT, MALOWNEY (includes Maloney, Mullowney, Moloney, Mallowney, Malowny, Malowany), MALOY, MALTBY, MAME, MANCEY, MANCHESTER, MANCILL, MANCUSO, MANDER, MANDERSON, MANDEVILLE, MANES, MANESS, MANGAN, MANGOLD, MANGUM, MANION, MANIRE (includes Manier), MANIS (includes Manes, Mannis, Manous, Manious, Mannis, Minus, Maines, Manas, Menis, Mannix, Manice,, Mannice, Maniss, Manus, Magnus, McNamee, McName, Mennis, Maners, Manners), MANKINS (includes Manchan, Mankin), MANLEY (includes Manly, Mannley), MANLOVE, MANN (includes Man, Munn, Monn, Mahon), MANN, MANNIG, MANNING, MANNION, MANRY (includes Manary, Manery), MANSELL, MANSER, MANSFIELD, MANSON, MANSSON, MANTLE, MANUEL, MANVILLE, MANWARING.

- **"MAO-MAR" Surname Mailing Lists**
http://www.rootsweb.com/~jfuller/gen_mail_surnames-mao.html
MAPES, MAPLE, MAPLES, MARBLE, MARBURY, MARCELL, MARCELLINO, MARCH, MARCHAND, MARCHANT, MARCHE, MARCHMAN, MARCHMENT (includes Marshment), MARCONI, MARCOUX, MARCUE, MARCUM, MARCUS, MARCY, MARDELL (includes Mardle, Mardall, Mardoll, Mardley), MARDEN, MARDORF, MAREK, MARGASON, MARGESON, MARGISON (includes Margeson, Margisun, Margesun, Morgeson, Murgeson), MARIE, MARINARO, MARINER, MARING, MARINO, MARION (includes Marien, Marrion, Marrien, Maryion), MARIS, MARJORIBANKS (includes Marchbank, Marchbanks, Marshbanks, Banks), MARK, MARKEL, MARKER (includes Maercker, Merker), MARKEY, MARKHAM (includes Marcum, Marcom, Markram, Markam), MARKLAND, MARKLE, MARKLEY (includes Markillie, Merkle, Merckle, Mickley, Muckley, Marklew, Michelot, Michelet), MARKS, MARKUM, MARKWARD, MARKWELL, MARLATT (includes Malott, Mellott, Marlett, Merlette, Melott, Melot), MARLER, MARLEY, MARLEY, MARLIN, MARLOW (includes Marlowe), MARLOWE, MARONEY (includes Moroney, Mulrooney, Murrowney, Marooney, Maroni, Murroney, O'Moroney), MARPLE, MARQUARDT, MARQUESS (includes Marquis, Marques), MARQUETTE, MARQUIS, MARR, MARRIAN (includes Marrion,

Marian), MARRIOTT, MARROW, MARRS, MARS, MARSDEN, MARSEE (includes Marsie, Marsey, Marcie, Massa, Massey, Massy, Marcee, Marcey), MARSH (includes March, Mash, Marsch), MARSHALL, MARSLAND, MARSTELLER (includes Mostoller, Marstiller, Masteller, Mosteller, Marstella), MARSTON, MARTEL, MARTELL, MARTELL, MARTEN, MARTENEY (includes Marteny, Marteeney, Marteeny, Martini, Mastery), MARTENS, MARTI, MARTIN (includes Martyne, Maryte, Martyn, Martye, Martel, Morton, Martinez), MARTIN, MARTIN, MARTIN, MARTINDALE, MARTINEAU, MARTINEZ, MARTINO, MARTINS, MARTINSON, MARTYN, MARTZ, MARULLI, MARVILL, MARVIN, MARWOOD, MARX, MARY.

- **"MAS-MAT" Surname Mailing Lists**
http://www.rootsweb.com/~jfuller/gen_mail_surnames-mas.html
MASHBURN, MASK, MASON, MASONER (includes Masner, Masnor), MASSE, MASSENGALE, MASSENGILL (includes Massengale), MASSEY (includes Massy), MASSICOT (includes Mexicote, Massicott, Massicotte), MASSIE, MASSINGHAM, MASSON, MAST, MASTEN, MASTENBROOK, MASTERS (includes Master, Meschter, Meister, Maaster, Maestre), MASTERSON, MASTIN (includes Masten, Maston), MATATTEDONA, MATCHETT, MATEU, MATHENA (includes Methena, Matheny, Metheny, Mathenie, Mathenee), MATHENY, MATHER, MATHERS, MATHES, MATHESON (includes Mathieson, Mathison, Matheison, Mathewson), MATHEW, MATHEWS (includes Matthews), MATHEWSON, MATHIAS, MATHIESEN (includes Matthiessen, Mathiasen, Matthysen, Mathesen), MATHIESON, MATHIS (includes Mathes, Mathias, Matis, Mathys, Matthias), MATHISON (includes Matheson, Mathieson, Matherson, Mathewson), MATLOCK (includes Medlock, Matlack, Matloch), MATLOSZ, MATNEY (includes Mattingley, Matinglee, Matenle, Matinlee, Matinglee, Matingley, Matenler, Matteny, Mateney), MATON, MATSON, MATTER, MATTERN, MATTESON, MATTHES, MATTHEW, MATTHEWS (includes Mathissen, Mathes, Matherson, Mathias, Marthaws), MATTHEWS, MATTHIAS, MATTHYS (includes Matthijs, Mattheys, Mattijs, Mattys), MATTICE, MATTILA, MATTINGER (includes Mottinger), MATTINGLY (includes Mattenlee, Matteey, Matley, Matney), MATTISON, MATTIX (includes Mattox, Maddox, Maddock), MATTOCKS, MATTOX, MATTSON, MATUSZAK (includes Matuszek, Matuczak, Matuzak), MATZ (includes Motts, Motz).

- **"MAU-MB" Surname Mailing Lists**
http://www.rootsweb.com/~jfuller/gen_mail_surnames-mau.html
MAUCK, MAUDSLEY, MAUDSLEY, MAUGHAN, MAUK, MAUL, MAULDIN (includes Mauldon, Maldin, Malden, Moldin, Molding, Maulding, Maulden, Mulden, Modlin, Madlin), MAULE, MAULLER, MAUNDER (includes Mander, Manders, Maunders), MAUPIN, MAURER (includes Maurers, Mauer, Mower, Mowers), MAURICE, MAUS, MAUZEY, MAVOR (includes Maver, Mavir), MAWHINNEY, MAXEY, MAXFIELD, MAXON, MAXSON, MAXSTED (includes Maxted, Maxstead), MAXWELL, MAY (includes Maye, Mays, Mayes, Mayhew, Mayhue, Mayberry, Mayflower), MAYBERRY, MAYCHELL (includes Machell), MAYCOCK (includes Maicock, Maicocque, Mycock, Macock, Maycott, Maycote, Meacock, Mecock), MAYER (includes Maier, Maher), MAYERS, MAYES, MAYFIELD (includes Mayfeldt), MAYHEW, MAYHUGH, MAYNARD (includes Mainard, Mainord, Manard), MAYNE, MAYNEZ, MAYO, MAYRAND (includes Merand, Merrand), MAYS, MAZE, MAZUR, MAZZA, MAZZANTI, MAZZEO (includes Mazzio).

- **"MCA-MCB" Surname Mailing Lists**
  http://www.rootsweb.com/~jfuller/gen_mail_surnames-mca.html
  McADAM, McADAMS, McADOO, McADOO (includes McAdow), McAFEE, McAFEE, McAFEE, McALEER, McALEXANDER, McALINDEN (includes McLinden, Maclinden), McALISTER, McALLISTER (includes MacAlester, McAlister, Allister, Alester), McALLISTER, McALPIN, McALPINE, McANALLY, McANDREW, McANDREWS, McARDLE, McARTER, McARTHUR, McATEE, McAULEY, McAULIFFE, McAVOY, McBAIN, McBATH, McBEATH, McBEE (includes MacBee, Magby), McBETH, McBRAYER, McBRIDE, McBRIEN (includes MacBrien, McBrine, MacBrine, McBryan, MacBryan, McBrian, MacBrian, McBryen,, MacBryen, McBrain, MacBrain, McBreen, MacBreen, Bryan, Brien), McBROOM, McBURNEY.

- **"MCC-MCC" Surname Mailing Lists**
  http://www.rootsweb.com/~jfuller/gen_mail_surnames-mcc.html
  McCABE, McCAFFERTY, McCAFFERY, McCAFFREY, McCAIG, McCAIN, McCALEB, McCALIP, McCALL, McCALLIE, McCALLISTER, McCALLMON, McCALLUM (includes Malcolm, McCallum, McCollum, Collum), McCALLUM, McCALMAN (includes McCalmont, McCamant, McCammon, McCommon), McCAMISH (includes McCammish, McCommish, McComish, Mcamis, MacHamish, MacCamish), McCAMMON, McCAMMOND, McCAMPBELL, McCAN, McCANDLESS (includes McCandlish, McCanles, McCanless, McCandliss, McCandlass, Chandless, Candish,, M'Caunles, McCanlies, Quinlish, Quinlisk, O'Quinlish, Quinless), McCANDLESS (includes McCanless, McCanles, McCandles, McAnlis), McCANDLISH, McCANN, McCARD, McCARDLE, McCARLEY, McCARROLL, McCARRON, McCART, McCARTER, McCARTHY, McCARTNEY, McCARTT (includes McCart, McKart), McCARTY (includes McArty, McCarthy), McCASKILL, McCASLAND, McCASLIN, McCAULEY, McCAUSLAND (includes McCaustland, McCasland, McCaslin, McCauslin, McCashland, McCashlan, Macaselin,, MacAshland, McAsland, McCoslin, McAusland, McAslin, McAuslan, McAusland, McAuslin, McCachin,, McCarsland, McCarstland, McCash, McCashin, McCashing, McCashlan, McCashlen, McCashlin), McCAY, McCHESNEY, McCHRISTIAN, McCLAIN (includes McCain, McCane), McCLANAHAN (includes McClenahan, McClenaghan), McCLARY, McCLAUGHRY, McCLEAN, McCLEARY, McCLEERY, McCLELLAN, McCLELLAN (includes Clelland, M'Kilikin, MacKilligan, McGillolane, MacGillolane, MacClelland, M'Kilican,, MacKillican, McGillelane, MacGillphaolain, Gillefillian, M'Kelican, Guilliland, McGillalane, MacGillelane, Gilfillian,, M'Gulican, Gilleland, McGilelan, MacClelland, Gillphillan, M'Culiken, Gilland, McClellane, M'Lolane, Gilphillan,, M'Culican, Gilelin, McClellan, M'Lellane, Gillephillane, M'Killican, Gillilan, McClelan, M'Lelen, Gillefillane,, McGillican, Guileland, McCleilane, M'Lelann, Gilfillane, McGilligain, Guliland, Maklolayn, M'Lelane, Gilfulain,, M'Giligan, Guililand, Maklellane, M'llleland, Gilfulan, MacGilligan, Gulliland, Maklellan, M'lleolan, Gillefolan,, MacKilligin, Gilliland, Makellane, M'llelan, Gilfolan, McKilligane, McLolane, MacLelland, M'Gillelan, Gillifelan,, McKillichane, McLolan, MacLellan, M'Cleallane, Gilfayln, McKillicane, McLellane, MacLelane, Kneland, Gilfelan,, M'Culikan, McLellan, MacLeland, Cliland, Gillefayln, M'Culigin, McLelane, MacLelan, Clenel, Gilfillan,, M'Culigan,, McLelan, MacLallan, Clellane, M'Killigin, McKelecan, McLallen, MacLalland, Clelland, McKillican, McKelegan,, McLalan, Macknellan, Clelend, Makulikin, MacGilligin, McKlellane, Macklellane, Cleland, M'Kulikan, MacKillicane,, McKlellan, Macklellan, Cleiland), McCLELLAND, McCLENAHAN,

McCLENNEN (includes McLennan, McClennan), McCLESKEY (includes McCluskey, McCloskey), McCLINTOCK (includes McClintoch, McLintock, McClintick, McClintic, McLintick), McCLOSKEY, McCLOSKY (includes Mikolayczak), McCLOUD, McCLUNG (includes McClun, McClurg), McCLURE (includes McLure, McClurg, Clary, McCleary, McClaran, MacLarry), McCLURG, McCLURKIN, McCLUSKEY, McCLUSKEY, McCOACH, McCOLL, McCOLLEY, McCOLLISTER, McCOLLUM (includes McCallum, MacCollum, McCollom), McCOMAS, McCOMB, McCOMBS (includes McComb, Macomb, McCoombs, Macoombs, McCombe, McCombes, Macomber,, McComber, McCombie, McComas, Coombs), McCONKEY, McCONLOUGH, McCONNEL, McCONNELL, McCONVILLE, McCOOK, McCOOL, McCOOL (includes McCoole, MacCool), McCORD (includes Corder, McCardell, Cardin, McGarr, McKord), McCORKLE, McCORMACK, McCORMICK (includes McCormack), McCOSH, McCOUCH, McCOUN, McCOURT, McCOWAN, McCOWEN, McCOWN, McCOWN (includes McCowan, McCowen, McCowin, McCoun, McKown), McCOY (includes McKoy, McCoig, McKay), McCRACKEN (includes McCrackin), McCRADY, McCRAE, McCRANEY, McCRANIE, McCRARY, McCRAW (includes McGraw), McCRAY (includes McRay, MacCray, MacRay), McCREA, McCREADY, McCREARY, McCREERY, McCRORY, McCUBBIN, McCUBBINS (includes MacCubbin, MacCubein, MakCubyn, MakCumbyn), McCUE, McCUEN, McCULLEY (includes McCully, McCaulley), McCULLOCH, McCULLOUGH, McCULLY, McCUNE, McCURDY (includes Macurdy, McKirdy, MacKirdy, MacCurdy), McCURLEY, McCURRY, McCUTCHEN, McCUTCHEON.

- **"MCD-MCD" Surname Mailing Lists**
  http://www.rootsweb.com/~jfuller/gen_mail_surnames-mcd.html
  McDADE, McDANIEL, McDANIEL, McDANIEL, McDERMITT (includes McDermott), McDERMOTT, McDEVITT, McDILL, McDONALD, McDONALD (includes MacDonald), McDONELL, McDONNELL, McDONOUGH, McDORMAN, McDOUGAL, McDOUGALD, McDOUGALL, McDOW, McDOWELL (includes MacDowell, McDowel), McDOWELL, McDUFFIE.

- **"MCE-MCH" Surname Mailing Lists**
  http://www.rootsweb.com/~jfuller/gen_mail_surnames-mce.html
  McEACHERN, McEACHIN (includes McEachain, McEachen), McELHANEY, McELHONE (includes McElhoney, McIlhone), McELLIGOTT, McELREAVY (includes McElravy, McElravey, McElraevy, McElrevey, McElrevy, McIlravie, McIlreavy, McIlrevy,, McElvery, McLravy), McELROY, McELROY (includes McIlroy), McELROYS, McELWAIN, McELWEE (includes McElway, McIlwee, McIlway), McELYEA, McENTEE (includes McAtee, McIntee, MacAtee, MacIntee, MacEntee, MacEtye), McENTIRE, McENTURFF (includes Mcinturff), McENTYRE (includes MacIntyre, McIntyre, McIntire, McIntire, McEntire, MacAtee, Matear, Mateer, Matier,, Matire, McAtear, McAteer, McAtier, McAtee, McTear, McTeer, McTier, Meteer, Metteer, Tyre), McERVALE, McEVER (includes McEvers, McEaver, McEavers, McIver, McIvers, McKeever, McKeevers, McCever,, McCevers, McKeaver, McKeavers), McEVILLY (includes MacEvilly, McEvily, McEvilla), McEVOY, McEWAN, McEWEN (includes MacEwen, McEwan, McEwin), McFADDEN, McFADDIN (includes McFadden), McFALL, McFARLAND, McFARLANE, McFAUL (includes McFall), McFEATERS (includes McFeeters, McPheeters), McFEATERS (includes McFeeters, McPheeters, McFeatters), McGANN, McGARRY, McGARRY, McGARTY, McGARVEY, McGARY, McGAUGHEY, McGEE (includes Mc Gee, MacGee, Mac

Gee), McGEHEE (includes McGhee, Magee, Megee, Megehee), McGEORGE, McGEOUGH, McGHEE, McGILL, McGILLIS, McGILLIVARY, McGILLIVRAY, McGIMPSEY (includes McJimsey, McJimpsey, McGimsey), McGING (includes McGinn, Maginn, Ging), McGINLEY, McGINN, McGINNESS, McGINNIS, McGINNIS, McGINTY, McGIRR (includes MacGirr, McGhir, McGurr, McGerr), McGIVERN (includes McGiverin, McGiveren, McGivirin), McGLAUGHLIN, McGLAUGHON (includes McGlaun, McGlaughn), McGLONE, McGLOTHLIN, McGLYNN, McGOEY, McGOLDRICK, McGOUGH, McGOVERN, McGOVNEY (includes McGoveney, McGivney), McGOWAN (includes Magowan, MacGowan, McGowen, McGown, McGoune, O'Gowan, Smith, Smythe), McGOWEN, McGRADY, McGRAIL, McGRATH, McGRAW, McGREGOR, McGREGOR (includes MacGregor), McGREW, McGUCKIN, McGUFFEY, McGUFFIN, McGUIGAN, McGUINESS, McGUIRE (includes Maguire, MacGuire, McQuire, MacQuire), McGUIRK, McGURK, McGURN (includes Magurn, McGourne, McGurrin), McHALE, McHARG (includes Maharg, Meharg, McIlhagga, McHargue), McHARGUE, McHENRY, McHONE (includes Mahone), McHUGH (includes McCue, MacHugh, MacCue, McKew, McQue).

- **"MCI-MCN" Surname Mailing Lists**
  http://www.rootsweb.com/~jfuller/gen_mail_surnames-mci.html
  McILVAINE (includes McIlvain, McElvain, McElvaine, McElwain, McElwaine, McIlwain, McIlwaine, Macelvaine,, Mcelvany, Malven, Malvern, Malvin, McIlvane), McILVEEN, McINERNEY, McINNES, McINNIS, McINTIRE, McINTOSH, McINTYRE (includes MacIntyre, McEntyre, MacIntire, McIntire, McEntire, MacAtee, Matear, Mateer, Matier,, Matire, McAtear, McAteer, McAtier, McAtee, McTear, McTeer, McTier, Meteer, Metteer, Tyre), McISAAC, McIVER, McJUNKIN (includes McJenkin, McJunkins, Junkin, Junkins), McKAGUE, McKAMEY, McKANE, McKAY, McKAY, McKEAN, McKEE, McKEEL, McKEEMAN, McKEEN, McKEEVER, McKELLAR, McKELVEY, McKELVY, McKENDREE, McKENNA, McKENNEY, McKENZIE, McKEON (includes McKeown, McKeone), McKEOWN, McKERCHER, McKERN (includes McCarn), McKEY (includes McKay, McKee, McKie), McKIBBEN, MCKIBBIN (includes McKibben, McKibbon), McKIE, McKIERNAN, McKILLOP, McKIM, McKINLEY, McKINNEY, McKINNON, McKINSTRY, McKINZIE, McKISSICK, McKNELLY, McKNIGHT (includes MacKnight, McKnitt, McKnit), McKOWN (includes McKeown), McLACHLAN, McLAIN, McLAMB, McLANE, McLAREN, McLARTY, McLAUGHLIN, McLEAN, McLEES (includes MacAleese, MacLeish), McLEISH, McLELLAN, McLEMORE, McLENDON (includes McClendon), McLENNAN, McLEOD, McLINDEN, McLOHON, McLURE, McMACKIN, McMAHAN, McMAHILL (includes McMayhill, Mayhill, McMahale, McMahell, McMahil, McMehill, MacMahill, McMohil,, McMahall, McMahil, McMahie, McMahel, McMehill, McMickel, McMichel, McMihel, McMihil, McMihill,, McMichell, McMichle, McMehel, McMehill, McMickel, McMickle), McMAHON (includes McMahan, McMahen, McMachen, Mahon, Mahan), McMAINS (includes McMain, MacMain, McManis), McMANAMAN (includes McManamon), McMANAMON, McMANNESS, McMANUS, McMASTER (includes McMasters, MacMaster, MacMasters), McMASTERS, McMATH, McMECHAN, McMEEN (includes McMean, McMin), McMENAMIN, McMENEMY (includes McMenamy, McMenamin, McMenemie, McManamy), McMICHAEL, McMILLAN, McMILLEN (includes MacMillen, McMillan, MacMillan, McMillon, MacMillon, McMullen, MacMullen, McMullan,, MacMullan, McMullon, MacMullon, McMillian, MacMillian, McMellon, MacMellon), McMILLIAN, McMILLON, McMINN, McMONAGLE, McMORROW, McMULLAN (includes McMullen), McMULLEN, McMULLIN, McMURDY

(includes MacMurdy), McMURRAY, McMURRY (includes McMurray, McMury, McMuray, McMurey), McMURTRY, McNAB, McNABB (includes McKnab), McNAIR, McNALLY, McNAMARA, McNAMEE, McNANEY (includes McAney, McenNanny, McNanny), McNARY, McNATT, McNAUGHTON, McNEAL, McNEAR, McNEEL, McNEELEY, McNEELY, McNEER, McNEESE, McNEIL, McNEILL, McNEILLY (includes McNeely, McNeily, McNeilley, McNeeley), McNEW (includes McKnew, MacNew, MacKnew), McNICHOL, McNICHOLS, McNULTY, McNUTT.

- **"MCO-MCT" Surname Mailing Lists**
  http://www.rootsweb.com/~jfuller/gen_mail_surnames-mco.html
  McPHAIL (includes McPhall, McFall, McFail), McPHEE, McPHERSON, McQUAID, McQUARY (includes McQuarry), McQUEEN, McQUESTION, McQUHAE, McQUILKIN (includes McQuilken, MacQuilken, MacQuilken, McWilkin, McWilken, MacWilkin, MacWilken), McQUILLAN, McQUISTON, McQUOWN, McRAE, McREE, McREYNOLDS (includes McRannalds, McRannels, McRunnels), McROBERTS (includes McRobert, MacRobert, MacRoberts), McSHANE, McSPADDEN, McSWAIN, McSWEENEY, McTAGGART, McTAGGART, McTAVISH, McTEER, McTEER (includes Mateer, McTear, McTier, Matear, McIntyre, McIntire, McTire, Minter, McTyre), McTURK (includes MacTurk).

- **"MCU-MD" Surname Mailing Lists**
  http://www.rootsweb.com/~jfuller/gen_mail_surnames-mcu.html
  McVAY, McVEAN, McVEY (includes McVay, McVeigh), McVICKER, McVOY (includes McAvoy, McEvoy, McAboy), McWHIRTER, McWHORTER (includes McWhirter, McWherter, MacWhorter), McWILLIAMS (includes Micwilliams, Macwilliams, Mickwilliams, Mackwilliams).

- **"ME-MH" Surname Mailing Lists**
  http://www.rootsweb.com/~jfuller/gen_mail_surnames-me.html
  MEACHAM (includes Meecham, Meechum, Mecham, Mitchum, Mitcham), MEACHEM, MEAD (includes Meade, Mede), MEADE, MEADOR (includes Meadors), MEADORS, MEADOWS, MEAGHER, MEALS, MEANES (includes Means, Meannes, Meanns, Miens, Meins, Mienes, Meines, Meens, Meenes), MEANS, MEARS, MEASE, MECHEN (includes Mechan), MEDBURY (includes Medbery, Medberry), MEDEIROS, MEDFORD, MEDIN, MEDINA, MEDLEY, MEDLEY, MEDLICOTT (includes Medlycott), MEDLIN, MEDLOCK, MEE, MEEHAN (includes Mehan, Meighan, Meighen), MEEK, MEEKER, MEEKER, MEEKINS, MEEKS, MEESE, MEFFORD, MEGER, MEIER, MEIGS, MEIJER, MEIKLE, MEININGER, MEISENHEIMER (includes Misenheimer, Misenhimer), MEISER, MEISNER, MEISSNER (includes Meisner, Meixner), MEISTER, MELDRUM, MELINE, MELLEN, MELLINGER, MELLON, MELLOR, MELLOTT, MELLOWS, MELOON, MELROSE (includes Mellrose, Milrose, Millrose, Malross), MELSON, MELTON, MELTON (includes Meltin, Melten, Meltan, Milton), MELTON, MELVILLE, MELVIN, MELYN, MEMBERY, MEMELINK, MENADUE, MENAPACE, MENARD, MENARY (includes Manary, Menarey, Manerey, Menerey), MENDEL (includes Mendell, Mindel), MENDENHALL, MENDENHALL, MENDEZ, MENDOZA, MENEFEE, MENGEL, MENKE, MENNINGER, MENSEN, MENTZER, MENZIES, MERCER (includes Mercier, Messer), MERCHANT, MERCIER, MERCK, MERCURIO, MEREDITH (includes Meredydd, Morgetiud, Merrilth), MERIWETHER (includes Merriweather, Merriwether, Meriweather), MERKEL, MERKLE, MERKLEIN, MERKLEY, MERLINA, MERREDEW, MERRELL, MERRETT, MERRIAM, MERRICK, MERRICK, MERRIFIELD, MERRIHEW, MERRILL (includes Merrell, Merils), MERRIMAN, MERRION

(includes Merion, Meryon, Maryon, Marion, Marrion, Merian, Merrian, Marian, Marrian), MERRITT *(includes Merrit, Mariett, Merritts, Meritt, Merit, Marit, Marriot, Marrat, Marritt, Mariott, Merrett,, Meratt, Muritte, Maret, Marett, Marite, Marrot, Marrit, Marrett)*, MERRY, MERRYMAN, MERSEREAU *(includes Mercereau, Mercerean, Meisereau)*, MERSHON, MERTEN, MERTENS, MERTZ, MERZ *(includes Mertz)*, MESERVE, MESLER, MESSENCOP, MESSENGER, MESSER, MESSICK, MESSIER, MESSINGER, MESSINO, MESSNER, METCALF, METCALFE, METHENY *(includes Methany, Methene, Methenee, Methane)*, METHVIN *(includes Methven)*, METRAS, METTLER, METZ *(includes Mets, Metts)*, METZGER, METZLER, MEULLER *(includes Muller, Mueller)*, MEYER, MEYERS, MEZICK.

● **"MI-MN" Surname Mailing Lists**
http://www.rootsweb.com/~jfuller/gen_mail_surnames-mi.html
MICHAEL *(includes Mikel, Michaels)*, MICHAELS, MICHALSKI, MICHAUD, MICHAUX, MICHEL, MICHELS *(includes Michaels)*, MICHIE, MICHUM, MICK, MICKEY, MICKLE, MICKLEBERRY *(includes Mickelborough)*, MICKLETHWAITE *(includes Micklethwait, Micklewaite)*, MIDDAGH, MIDDAUGH, MIDDLEBROOK, MIDDLEBROOKS, MIDDLEMASS *(includes Middlemas, Middlemast, Middlemess, Middlemis, Middlemiss, Middlemist, Middlemoss,, Middlemost, Middlemus)*, MIDDLETON, MIDDLETON, MIDGLEY *(includes Midgely, Midgeley)*, MIDKIFF, MIELKE, MIER *(includes Mier-Bonafe)*, MIERS, MIESS *(includes Mease, Meece, Mehs, Musse)*, MIGHILL *(includes McGill, MacGill)*, MIGLIACCIO, MIKELL, MIKESELL, MILAM *(includes Mileham, Milem, Mylem)*, MILAM, MILAM, MILAM, MILBURN *(includes Milbourn, Milbern, Millborne)*, MILES *(includes Myles)*, MILEY, MILHOLLAND, MILK, MILL, MILLAN *(includes Million, Millon, Milan)*, MILLAR, MILLARD, MILLER *(includes Milner, Milnik, Muller, Hagermiller, Reimiller, Muiller, Mueller)*, MILLER, MILLER, MILLER, MILLET, MILLETS, MILLETT, MILLHOUSE, MILLICAN, MILLIE, MILLIGAN, MILLIGAN, MILLIKAN, MILLIKEN, MILLINGTON, MILLION, MILLS, MILLS, MILLSAP *(includes Millsaps)*, MILLWARD, MILLWOOD *(includes Milwood, Milwoody, Milwee, Millwee, Millward)*, MILNAMOW, MILNE, MILNER, MILOSIERNY, MILSTEAD, MILTON, MIMS *(includes Mymmes, Mymms, Mimms, Minns)*, MINARD, MINCEY *(includes Mincy, Mincie, Minshew, Minchew)*, MINCHEW, MINDER, MINEAR, MINER, MINESINGER *(includes Meinsinger, Meinzinger)*, MINEYKO *(includes Minejko, Miniat, Mineikos)*, MINGUS *(includes Manges, Mangus, Menges, Mengus, Minges)*, MINIER *(includes Manier, Minegar, Mynhier, Minear, Minniear, Minnir, Mineer, Menear, Mynheer, Menier)*, MININGER *(includes Menninger, Meinninger, Munchinger)*, MINK, MINNER, MINNICH, MINNICK, MINNINGER, MINNIS, MINOR *(includes Miner, Meinhert, Maynor, Minar, Minnear, Minherr)*, MINSHALL, MINTER, MINTON *(includes Mintor, Mintern, Minthorn, Mintin, Minten, Mineton)*, MINTON, MINTZ, MINYARD, MION, MIRACLE, MIRANDA, MIRON *(includes Magneron, Migneron, Mayrand, Meran, Mero, Meron, Myron, Mireau)*, MISENER, MISHLER, MISNER *(includes Misener, Mizner, Mizener, Mizenar, Meisner)*, MISNER, MITCHEL, MITCHELL *(includes Michell, Mischel)*, MITCHELL, MITCHELL *(includes Mischell, Michell, Mitchel)*, MITCHENER *(includes Michener, Mitchiner, Michiner)*, MITER *(includes Mitter, Mitre)*, MITTELSTAEDT, MITTELSTET *(includes Mittelstaedt)*, MITTON, MITTS, MIVILLE, MIX, MIXON, MIZE *(includes Mise, Myze, Myse, Mies)*, MIZELL.

● **"MOA-MOH" Surname Mailing Lists**
http://www.rootsweb.com/~jfuller/gen_mail_surnames-moa.html
MOAK, MOATS, MOBERLEY, MOBLEY, MOBLEY, MOCK *(includes Mauk, Mauck, Mack, Macht, Mauch, Maught)*, MOCK,

MOCZYGEMBA, MODGLIN, MODLIN *(includes Maudlin, Maudlen)*, MOE *(includes Mow, LeMoe, Lemoux)*, MOELLER, MOEN, MOFF *(includes Muff, Mofs)*, MOFFAT, MOFFATT, MOFFETT, MOFFITT *(includes Moffett)*, MOGAR, MOGDAN *(includes Mogden)*, MOGDEN, MOHAN, MOHLER, MOHR.

● **"MOI-MON" Surname Mailing Lists**
http://www.rootsweb.com/~jfuller/gen_mail_surnames-moi.html
MOIR, MOLDER, MOLDT *(includes Molt)*, MOLINAR, MOLL, MOLLER, MOLLETT *(includes Mullett, Mollette)*, MOLLETT, MOLLISON, MOLLOY, MOLONEY, MOLSBERRY *(includes Malsbury)*, MOLYNEUX *(includes Mullinax, Mulnix, Mullenneaux, Molineux, Moliner, Molynes)*, MONACO, MONAGHAN, MONAHAN, MONCRIEF, MONCUR, MONCUS *(includes Munkus, Monkus, Munkres, Muncus)*, MONDAY, MONET, MONEY *(includes Monnett, Mooney)*, MONFORT, MONINGTON *(includes Mannington, Monnington)*, MONK, MONKS, MONLEY, MONROE, MONROE *(includes Munroe)*, MONS *(includes Moens, Monts)*, MONSON, MONTAGUE, MONTANO, MONTEITH, MONTGOMERY *(includes Montgolfier, Montague, McGomry)*, MONTOYA.

● **"MOO-MOT" Surname Mailing Lists**
http://www.rootsweb.com/~jfuller/gen_mail_surnames-moo.html
MOODIE, MOODY *(includes Mooty)*, MOOERS, MOOERS *(includes Moores, Moors)*, MOON *(includes Moone, Mohun)*, MOONEY *(includes Mainey, Meeny, Moony, O'Mooney)*, MOOR, MOORE *(includes Moor, More, Moores, Mohr)*, MOORE, MOORE, MOORE, MOOREHOUSE, MOORES, MOORHEAD *(includes Muirhead, Moorehead, Morehead, Morhead)*, MOORMAN, MOOSE, MORA, MORACA *(includes Muraca)*, MORALES, MORAN, MORCK *(includes Morick)*, MORDEN, MORE, MOREAU *(includes Merau, Maureau, Maure, Moro, Moreaux, Moreault)*, MOREFIELD *(includes Moorefield, Mofield)*, MOREFIELD *(includes Moorefield, Mofield, Mourfield, Morfield)*, MOREHEAD, MOREHOUSE *(includes Morhouse, Moorhouse)*, MOREL, MORELAND, MORELL, MORELOCK, MORENO, MORETON, MOREY, MORFORD, MORGAN *(includes Morgain, Ap Morgan, Rhys Morgan, Rose Morgan)*, MORGAN, MORGAN, MORGAN, MORIARITY, MORIARTY, MORIN, MORING *(includes Mooring, Morring)*, MORISON, MORITZ, MORLEY, MORLOCK, MORNINGSTAR, MORONEY, MORR, MORRELL, MORRILL, MORRIS, MORRIS, MORRISEY, MORRISH, MORRISON, MORRISON, MORRISS, MORRISSETTE, MORRISSEY, MORROW, MORROW, MORSE, MORTENSEN, MORTIMER, MORTON, MOSBY, MOSCROP *(includes Mosscrop, Moscropp, Mosscrip, Moscrip)*, MOSELEY, MOSELEY *(includes Mosely, Mosley)*, MOSELEY, MOSELY, MOSER, MOSES *(includes Moser, Mosses)*, MOSEY, MOSHER *(includes Mosier)*, MOSIER, MOSKAL, MOSKOWITZ, MOSLEY, MOSS, MOSSER, MOST, MOSTERT *(includes Mostaert, Mosterd)*, MOTE, MOTE, MOTES, MOTHERSHED *(includes Mottershed, Mottershead)*, MOTLEY, MOTT, MOTTER, MOTTRAM, MOTZ.

● **"MOU-MT" Surname Mailing Lists**
http://www.rootsweb.com/~jfuller/gen_mail_surnames-mou.html
MOUDY, MOULD, MOULDEN, MOULTON, MOUNCE, MOUNT *(includes Mounts)*, MOUNTAIN, MOUNTCASTLE, MOUNTJOY, MOUNTS, MOUSALL, MOUSER, MOUSSEAU, MOUTRAY, MOWAT, MOWBRAY, MOWBRAY *(includes Mowbrey, Moubray, Mowberry)*, MOWERY *(includes Mowry)*, MOWRY, MOXLEY, MOYE *(includes Moy)*, MOYER, MOYERS, MOYLAN, MOYLE, MOYNIHAN, MOZINGO, MOZINGO *(includes Mazingo, Monzingo, Musingo)*.

- ## "MU-MZ" Surname Mailing Lists
http://www.rootsweb.com/~jfuller/gen_mail_surnames-mu.html
MUCKEY (includes Mucky), MUCKLEROY (includes Muckelroy), MUDD (includes Mud, Modh), MUDGE, MUELLER, MUENCH, MUETZ (includes Müetz, Mutz), MUGAN (includes Mogan, Moogan), MUGG, MUIC, MUIR, MUIRHEAD, MULCAHY, MULCASTER (includes Muncaster), MULDER, MULDOON, MULFORD, MULHERIN, MULHERN, MULHOLLAND, MULKEY, MULL, MULLALLY (includes MallAlly, Mullaley, Mullolley), MULLAN, MULLANEY, MULLEE (includes Malley, Molloy, Mulloy, Maillee, O'Mailaooha), MULLEN, MULLEN, MULLENS, MULLER, MULLICA, MULLICAN, MULLIGAN, MULLIKIN (includes Mullligan, Mulliken), MULLIN, MULLINAHONE (includes Mullally, O'Mullally), MULLINAX, MULLINEUX, MULLINIX, MULLINS (includes Mullen, Mullens, Mullin, Mullinnex, Mullineaux), MULLIS, MULVANEY, MULVIHILL, MUMFORD (includes Munford, Monfort, Momphard), MUMMERT, MUNCEY, MUNCH, MUNCRIEF, MUNCY, MUNDAY, MUNDELL, MUNDT, MUNDY, MUNGARY, MUNGER, MUNK (includes Muennink, Munik, Munick, Münk, Münke, Münnich, Münik, Mönnich, Mönich, Mönch,, Moennich), MUNN, MUNNS.

MUNRO, MUNROE, MUNSELL, MUNSON, MURCH, MURCHISON, MURDOCH, MURDOCK, MURDUCK (includes Murdock, Murdoch, Murdocke, Murducke, Mardock, Merdock, Moorduck, Midduck), MURFIN, MURIE, MURNANE (includes Marnane), MURNEY, MURPHEY, MURPHREE, MURPHREY, MURPHY (includes O'Muracha, O'Murphy, Murchoe, Morphy, MacMurrough, MacMurrough Kavanagh,, MacMurrow, Morrowson, Murrough, Morrough, Morrogh, Murrow, Morrow, MacMurchy, Murchison), MURPHY (includes Murphrey), MURR, MURRAY (includes Moray, Murrey, Murry, Murrie, Merry, Murrihy, MacMurry, MacMorry, MacMorray,, MacMurray, McMurray, MacMorrow, Morrow, Currie, Curry, MacKilmurray, Kilmurry, Kilmary, Kilmore,, Gilmore), MURRAY (includes Murrey, Murry), MURRELL, MURROW, MURRY, MURTAUGH, MUSE (includes Mewes, Mews, Muis), MUSGRAVE, MUSGROVE (includes Musgrave, Mosgrove), MUSICK, MUSSELMAN, MUSSELWHITE, MUSSER, MUSSON, MUSTAIN, MUTCHLER (includes Mutschler, Mutchlar, Muchler, Muchlar), MUTH, MUTZ, MYATT (includes Miot, Miatt), MYER, MYERS (includes Myer, Meyers, Meyer, Meier), MYERS, MYHRE (includes Myre), MYLES, MYRES, MYRICK.

SURNAMES, FAMILY ASSOCIATIONS & FAMILY NEWSLETTERS – "N"

Resources Dedicated to One Surname
http://www.cyndislist.com/surn-n.htm

Category Index:

◆ General Surname Sites and Resources
◆ Surname Specific Sites and Resources

◆ Surname Mailing Lists

◆ General Surname Sites and Resources

- Connect with Surnames - N
  http://www.geocities.com/Heartland/Bluffs/7708/n.html

- Dutch Home Pages by Familyname ~ Letter N
  http://members.tripod.com/~Don_Arnoldus/n.htm

- FamilyHistory.com - Message Boards - Surname - N
  http://www.familyhistory.com/messages/list.asp?prefix=NA

- Family Tree Maker Online User Home Pages - N
  http://www.familytreemaker.com/users/n/index.html

- Family Workings N Surname Links
  http://www.familyworkings.com/links/surn.htm

- GenConnect Surname Index - "N"
  http://genconnect.rootsweb.com/indx/surnames/N.html
  Message boards sponsored by RootsWeb. Each surname message board set is divided into the following topics: Queries, Bibles, Biographies, Deeds, Obituaries, Pensions, Wills.

- Genealogy Resources on the Internet - "NA-ND" Surname Mailing Lists
  http://www.rootsweb.com/~jfuller/gen_mail_surnames-na.html
  "NE-NH"
  http://www.rootsweb.com/~jfuller/gen_mail_surnames-ne.html
  "NI-NN"
  http://www.rootsweb.com/~jfuller/gen_mail_surnames-ni.html
  "NO-NT"
  http://www.rootsweb.com/~jfuller/gen_mail_surnames-no.html
  "NU-NZ"
  http://www.rootsweb.com/~jfuller/gen_mail_surnames-nu.html
  Search the index of surname mailing lists below: Surname Mailing Lists.

  o Genealogy Resources on the Internet - Surnames Included in Mailing Lists - "N"
    http://www-personal.umich.edu/~cgaunt/surnames/n.names.html
    This is a computer generated list of the surnames, and all variant spellings for those names, that are found in the surname mailing lists detailed on the pages shown above.

- Genealogy Resources on the Internet - Surname Web Sites for "N" Surnames
  http://www-personal.umich.edu/~cgaunt/surnames/n.html

- Genealogy's Most Wanted - Surnames Beginning with "N"
  http://www.citynet.net/mostwanted/n.htm

- Google Web Directory .... Genealogy>Surnames>N
  http://directory.google.com/Top/Society/Genealogy/Surnames/N/

- Heartland Genealogy Society Membership List - N
  http://www.geocities.com/Heartland/Ranch/2416/hgs-mlist-n.html

- H-GIG Surname Registry - Surnames Beginning N
  http://www.ucr.edu/h-gig/surdata/surname14.html

- Higginson Book Company - Surnames Beginning with N
  http://www.higginsonbooks.com/n.htm

- inGeneas Table of Common Surname Variations and Surname Misspellings - N-Q
  http://www.ingeneas.com/N2Q.html

- 'N' Surnames at RootsWeb
  http://resources.rootsweb.com/surnames/n.html

- The Obituary Link Page - Family Obituary Archives Online - N
  http://www.geocities.com/~cribbswh/obit/n.htm

- Open Directory - Society: Genealogy: Surnames: N
  http://www.dmoz.org/Society/Genealogy/Surnames/N/

- Surname Springboard Index - N
  http://www.geocities.com/~alacy/spring_n.htm

- SurnameWeb Surname Registry - N Index
  http://www.surnameweb.org/registry/n.htm

- SWINX Zoeklijst Nederlandse Familienamen / SWINX Searchlist Dutch Surnames - N
  http://www.swinx.net/swinx/swinx_na_nl.htm

- Websites at RootsWeb: N Surnames
  http://www.rootsweb.com/~websites/surnames/n.html

◆ Surname Specific Sites and Resources

- **NAAS Genealogy**
  http://www.geocities.com/novas100/index.htm
  A Genealogy site of a 24 year old German farmer, who became the patriarch of the NAAS, NASS, NAUSS, NASSEE families of Canada.

- **NABERING Family Page**
  http://members.tripod.com/~NABRING/index.html
  NACHBARINK Family Since 1556, NABERING, NABERINGHS, NABERINK, NABRING, NABRINK, NEIGHBORING from R–dinghausen, Deutschland.

- **The NAFZGER Genealogy Home Page**
  http://sailfish.exis.net/~tjnoff/
  NAFZGER / NOFFSINGER.

- **The NALE Family Page**
  http://www.nidlink.com/~rsnale/

- **NANCE Family History Web Page**
  http://cust.iamerica.net/tnance/history.htm

- **NANGLE Family's Genealogy Homepage**
  http://www.geocities.com/Heartland/Cliffs/4019

- **The NARRAMORE Files**
  http://www.geocities.com/Heartland/Fields/3015/welcome.html
  History of the Narramore family in North America, 1664 - 1900.

- **NASCHOLD Homepage**
  http://home.t-online.de/home/M.NASCHOLD/naschold.htm
  NASCHOLD, NASHOLD, NASHOLDS, NASHOLT, NASHOLTS and other spelling variations.

- **NASH Project**
  http://www.hevanet.com/drothery/
  Descendants of Thomas and Margery (Baker) Nash of New Haven, Connecticut, 1640.

- **NATT Family History**
  http://www.nattfamily.org/
  Personal Accounts and family history; one family's story of the Holocaust.

- **NAUGHTON Genealogy Page**
  http://miso.wwa.com/~naughton/genealogy.html

- **NAYLOR Family Home Page**
  http://bally.fortunecity.com/navan/99
  The NAYLOR surname and any if its variations, covering births, marriages, deaths, taxes, etc. We invite you view our page and contribute your information!

- **The Descendants of George NAYLOR of Bradford England**
  http://www5.pair.com/vtandrew/naylor/joenaylr.htm

- **The NEAVILLE Family Archives**
  http://www.prairienet.org/neaville/
  Site with genealogical info on the families NEAVILLE, NEAVILL, and NEAVEILL.

- **NEEDHAM Family & Friends**
  http://members.xoom.com/DNeedham/friends.htm
  Descendants of George W. NEEDHAM. Additionally, all Needham info is posted.

- **NEEL Descendants Home Page**
  http://www.jps.net/mmcknight/
  Descendants of Thomas NEEL (born 1770) and Jane NEEL (born 1775) who raised their family at Dry Fork, Sumner county, Tennessee.

- **The Official NEELEY'S Web Site - The NEELEY'S From Whence They Came**
  http://www.genweb.net/~neeley
  The NEELEY'S [all spelling variations] Neely/Neelly/Nealy/Neley, etc. of Europe?, Pennsylvania, Indiana, North Carolina, Tennessee, Oklahoma, California. Descendants of William NEELEY & Eleanor?

- **Descendants of Joseph NEELY**
  http://www.wizard.net/~aldonna/jndesc.htm
  Joseph was born 25 Oct 1758, died 26 Oct 1811 in Gibson County, Indiana.

- **Family History - Genealogy of the NEEP / KNAPP Family**
  http://www.neep.demon.co.uk/fhist/neep-knapp.htm

- **NEFF Genealogy**
  http://ourworld.compuserve.com/homepages/neff_genealogy/
  For the Exchange of NAEF, NAF, NAFF, NAVE, NEAVE, NEEF, NEFF, etc.

- **The Descendants of Alexander NEIBAUR**
  http://www.neibaur.org/alex.html

- **NEISINGH Family History**
  http://freepages.genealogy.rootsweb.com/~neisingh/
  Descendants of Wiebe NEISINGH and Dieurke FOL.

- **NELMS / NELMES / ELMS - Family History**
  http://members.tripod.com/~Peter_Nelms/Family_History.html
  Nelms family history in England and Australia including details of immigration in 1873.

- **NELSON Cousins**
  http://members.aol.com/nacanut/nelson/WC_TOC.htm
  Descendants of James F. NELSON, b. 1805 in VA, lived in GA and LA.

- **NESBITT / NISBET Society (UK Branch)**
  http://www.angelfire.com/ne/nesbitt/index.html
  And the NESBITT / NISBET Society (US Branch)
  http://www.ibydeit.com/

- **NESBITT / NISBET Links Crossroads**
  http://www.nesbitt.demon.co.uk/nesbitt/ target=

- **NEU Family Genealogy**
  http://members.nbci.com/Neu_Family_Genealogy
  Descendants of Philip NEU (1845) of St. Louis, and a lot of other NEU family members, listing over 250 NEU family members and another 600 of their relations.

- **NEVILLE Heritage Society**
  http://www.prairienet.org/neville/homepage.html

- NEWBERRY / NEWBERY / NEWBURY Surname Researchers & Lineages
  http://www.geocities.com/Heartland/Estates/8415/

- NEWCOMB or NEWCOMBE Genealogy Page
  http://www.geocities.com/Heartland/Acres/2957/index.html
  In the USA the name is invariably spelled NEWCOMB. In Canada, the common spelling is NEWCOMBE. Additional variant spellings: Newcom, Newcomen, Neucomen, Neucome, Newcome, Neucum, Neucom, Nucum, Nucumb, Neukomb, Newkomb, Neucombe, Neucomb, Newcum, and Newkombe.

- Hugo le NEWCOMEN
  http://www.ziplink.net/~joelinda/hugo.htm
  Lord of the Manor of Saltfleetby in Lincolnshire, England.

- Augusta NEWMAN
  http://csc.techcenter.org/~mneill/augusta.html

- NEWMAN Name Society
  http://www.peninsula.starway.net.au/~pbeckett/newman.htm
  The Worldwide One Name Study for the name of NEWMAN.

- K/NIBB/S One Name Study
  http://freepages.genealogy.rootsweb.com/~knibbetc/
  A database of 12,000+ individuals worldwide with the surnames KNIBB, KNIBBS, NIBB, NIBBS, etc.

- Our NICHOLS Family Ties
  http://home.att.net/~jamesdelmer/
  William NICHOLS family from VA to NC, SC, TN and to Marion Co. AL.

- The NICKENS Family Resource Page
  http://homepages.rootsweb.com/~nickens/

- NICKERSON Family Association
  http://www.capecod.net/nfaoncape
  NICKERSON the founder of Chatham MA on Cape Cod and descendants throughout North America especially those Planters and Loyalists that went to NS and NB Canada.

- NICOL Family Homepage
  http://members.aol.com/jne26/
  NICOL family who immigrated from Carluke, Scotland about 1820 to Hammond, New York. Includes the surnames MITCHELL, BRONLEE, POLLACK, BLACKER, MARTINSON, GANNON, FLETCHER.

- NIDEROST Family History
  http://www.niderost.com
  A history and genealogy of the NIDEROST Family from Switzerland from the 14th century with photos, stories, links.

- NIEDERMEYER History Research Project
  http://www.niedermeyers.net/
  The Project, proposed in March of 1997, encompasses all variant spellings of the surname, such as Niedermeier and Niedermaier, as well as collateral lines up to four generations.

- NIPPGEN Familienseite
  http://w1.855.telia.com/~u85500290/
  The Nippgen / Nipgen family in Europe and the United States.

- NISWONGER's Nest
  http://members.xoom.com/Niswonger/

- Une Généalogique Alsacienne La Famille NITHART
  http://www.philippe.nithart.com

- NIX Family Web Site
  http://www.cei.net/~cnix/

- NOBEL Family of the Netherlands
  http://www.poboxes.com/jnobel

- Of NOBLE Lineage
  http://ourworld.compuserve.com/homepages/noble/

- NONNAMAKER Genealogy
  http://www.nonnamaker.com/
  Descendants of Andrew NONNAMAKER (Andreas NONNENMACHER).

- NORDMEYER Homepage
  http://www.nordmeyer.com
  Nordmeyer Family homepage for 4+ generations (and growing!). Descendants of Heinrict (F. G.) Nordmeyer (1821-1882).

- NORMAN Family Genealogy
  http://normangenealogy.rootsweb.com/page0001.htm

- John NORTON of Kentucky
  http://www.nortonfamily.net/
  The Nortons of Kentucky 1784, Bourbon, Pendleton, Grant.

- The NORWOOD Family Page
  http://www.geocities.com/Heartland/Estates/4805/index.html
  The Massachusetts and Maine Lines, Descendants of Francis Norwood.

- The NOTHNAGLE Family Center
  http://www.geocities.com/CollegePark/Lab/9914/nothnagle.htm
  Reference site for the Surname NOTHNAGLE.

- NUCKOLLS Kindred Worldwide
  http://www.nuckolls.org/

- NUCKOLLS Worldwide Kindred Society
  http://members.aol.com/nuck141/Nuckolls.html
  NUCKOLLS / NUCKOLS / NUCHOLS / NUCKLES / KNUCKLES and others include: DUKE, SWIFT, BAGBY, BARBER, DABNEY, HALE, SHELTON, TRIMBLE, THORNTON, WALTON.

- NUETZELs on the Web
  http://www.nuetzel.com/family/

- NUGENT Family Genealogy
  http://www.geocities.com/Heartland/Flats/4401/
  A gathering spot for all NUGENT family members and researchers. Online trees, resources, information and more!

- NUGENT Family History
  http://www.eatough.net/history/nugent/index.htm
  Descendants of William NUGENT (1792-1901) of the Little Egg Harbor area of New Jersey.

- NUTTALL Genealogy Site
  http://members.xoom.com/a_barrett/index.htm
  Dedicated to the name Nuttall of Lancashire England.

- The NUTTER Family Bulletin Board
  http://members.aol.com/NutterWV/index.htm
  *Descendants of Christopher NUTTER, born abt 1638-1642 and
  Mary DORMAN.*

- The NYE Family Home Page
  http://www.crosslink.net/~bobnye/nyehome.htm

◆ Surname Mailing Lists

- "NA-ND" Surname Mailing Lists
  http://www.rootsweb.com/~jfuller/gen_mail_surnames-na.html
  *NABORS, NACE (includes Nase, Nehs, Nees, Ness), NADEAU,
  NADING, NADLER, NAFF (includes Naf, Naef, Nave, Naeve,
  Neave, Neuve, Neef, Neve, Neff, Knaff, Knaf, Knap, Knapp, Knafe,,
  Knefe, Knof, Knoff), NAGEL, NAGLE (includes Nagel, Naugle),
  NAGY, NAIL, NAIRN, NALL, NALLY, NANCARROW, NANCE,
  NANKERVIS (includes Nekervis, Nekerwis, Ankervis, Ankerwis),
  NANKEVILLE, NANNA (includes Nanny, Nannau, Nanney,
  Nannah), NANNINGA, NAPIER (includes Napeir, Nepair, Nepeir,
  Neper, Napare, Naper, Naipper), NAPOLITANO, NARDI,
  NARRAMORE (includes Naramore), NASH, NASON, NATCHER
  (includes Knatcher), NATHAN, NATION, NATIONS, NAU,
  NAUGHTON, NAUMANN, NAVARRE, NAVE, NAVICKAS,
  NAYLOR, NAYLOR (includes Nailor, Nailer).*

- "NE-NH" Surname Mailing Lists
  http://www.rootsweb.com/~jfuller/gen_mail_surnames-ne.html
  *NEAGLE, NEAL, NEAL, NEALE, NEALON, NEALY, NEAR,
  NEARY (includes Nary, Narry), NEASE (includes Nehs, Nees,
  Neace, Niece), NEASHAM (includes Neisham, Neesham, Nesham),
  NEAVE, NECESSARY (includes Necessury, Nesussary, Nesussury),
  NECKLEIN, NEDROW (includes Netherow, Nethero, Neiderauer,
  Nitterauer), NEECE, NEED, NEEDHAM, NEEL, NEELEY (includes
  Neely, Nealy, Neley, Neelly, Nely), NEELY, NEEP (includes Knipe,
  Heap, Sneap), NEESE, NEFDT, NEFDT (includes Nedft, Neft,
  Neftd), NEFF, NEGRYCH (includes Negrich), NEHS, NEIBAUR
  (includes Neubauer), NEIFERGOLD, NEIGHBORS, NEIGHBOURS
  (includes Nabors), NEIKIRK (includes Nikirk, Newkirk, Neukirch,
  Neukrich, Nykirk), NEIL, NEILAN, NEILL, NEILSEN, NEILSON,
  NEIMAN, NEISES, NEISLER (includes Niesler, Neuschler, Niceler,
  Neislar, Nieslar), NELDER, NELL, NELLIGAN, NELLIS (includes
  Nelles), NELMS, NELSON, NEMETH, NERNES (includes Nerness,
  Nernaes), NERNES (includes Nerness), NESBIT, NESBITT (includes
  Nesbit), NESMITH, NESS, NESTER, NESTLE (includes Nestel,
  Nessel, Nestell), NETHAWAY, NETHERTON, NETTERVILLE,
  NETTLES, NETTLETON, NETTROUR, NEU, NEUBAUER,
  NEUENSCHWANDER, NEUFELD, NEUHART (includes Newhart,
  Neyhart, Nihart), NEUMAN, NEUMANN, NEUN, NEUSTADTER
  (includes Neustetter, Neustaedter, Neystatter), NEUTZE, NEVE,
  NEVES, NEVEU (includes Nephew, Nevue, Nauvau, Naview),
  NEVILLE (includes Nevill, Nevills, Neavill, Neaveill, Nevel, Nevell,
  Nevels, Nevils, Neufville), NEVILLE (includes Nevill, Nevills,
  Neavill, Neaveill, Nevel, Nevell, Nevels, Nevils, Neufville), NEVIN,
  NEVIN, NEVINS, NEVISON (includes Nevinson, Navison,
  Neverson), NEVITT (includes Knevitt), NEW (includes Neu),
  NEWBERRY (includes Newbery, Newbury), NEWBOLD,
  NEWBURY, NEWBY, NEWCOMB (includes Newcombe,
  Newcomber), NEWCOMBE, NEWCOMER, NEWELL, NEWFIELD
  (includes Newfelt, Neufieldt), NEWHALL, NEWHAM (includes*

*Neuham, Newnham, Newingham), NEWHOUSE, NEWITT,
NEWKIRK, NEWLAND, NEWLIN, NEWLON, NEWMAN (includes
Newsome, Newmon, Newmen, Newsame, Newsam, Newsom),
NEWPORT, NEWSOM (includes Newsome, Nusom), NEWSOME,
NEWSTEAD, NEWTON, NEY, NEYLAND (includes Neeland,
Neylans, Kneeland).*

- "NI-NN" Surname Mailing Lists
  http://www.rootsweb.com/~jfuller/gen_mail_surnames-ni.html
  *NIBLACK, NICE, NICELY, NICHOL, NICHOLAS, NICHOLL
  (includes Nichol, Nicol, Nickle, Nickel, Nikill, Nicholls, Nichols),
  NICHOLLS, NICHOLS (includes Nickels, Nickles, Nuckolls, Nicol),
  NICHOLSON, NICHOLSON, NICKEL, NICKELL, NICKELS,
  NICKENS, NICKERSON, NICKLES, NICOL (includes Nicoll,
  MacNicol), NICOLAS, NICOLL, NICOLSON, NIEBRUGGE
  (includes Niebrügge, Niebruegge), NIEDERHOFFER,
  NIEFERGOLD, NIEHAUS, NIELSEN, NIELSON, NIEMAN,
  NIEMANN, NIEMCZYK, NIEMEYER, NIENHAUS (includes
  Neuhaus), NIERNSEE, NIGHTINGALE, NIGHTWINE, NILAN,
  NILES, NILSDOTTER, NILSEN, NILSSON, NIMMO, NIMROD,
  NIMS, NININGER, NIPER, NIPPER, NIPPER, NIPPLE (includes
  Knipple, Nipel, Nippel, Nippell, Nopfle, Niles), NISBET, NISTLER,
  NISWENDER, NISWONGER, NIX (includes Nicks), NIXON.*

- "NO-NT" Surname Mailing Lists
  http://www.rootsweb.com/~jfuller/gen_mail_surnames-no.html
  *NOACH (includes Noak), NOAH, NOAKES, NOBLE (includes
  Nobel), NOBLES, NOBLETT, NOBLIN, NOCITA (includes Nucita,
  Nocida, Nucida, Noccita, Nuccita, Noccida, Nuccida, Nochita,
  Nochida, Nuchita,, Nuchida), NODEN, NODINE (includes Naudin,
  Naudain), NOE, NOEL, NOFFSINGER, NOGGLE, NOGGLE,
  NOLAN, NOLAND, NOLD, NOLEN, NOLES, NOLF (includes
  Nulph, Nolff, Nulf), NOLF (includes Nulf, Nolph, Nulph), NOLL,
  NOLTE, NOON, NOONKESTER, NOONAN, NOONE, NORBY
  (includes Norrby, Norbey, Nordby, Nordbye), NORCROSS,
  NORDSTROM, NOREJKO, NORFLEET (includes Northfleete),
  NORGROVE, NORMAN, NORRIS (includes Noreys, Norreys,
  Norrice, Norriss), NORSTEDT, NORSWORTHY, NORTH (includes
  Northend, Northern), NORTHCOTT, NORTHCUTT (includes
  Northcut, Northcott, Northcot), NORTHERN, NORTHEY,
  NORTHINGTON, NORTHROP, NORTHRUP, NORTHUP,
  NORTHUP (includes Northrup), NORTHWAY (includes
  Northaway), NORTON (includes Naughton), NORVAL (includes
  Norvall, Norvel, Norvell, Narval, Narvall, Narvel, Narvell, Norrval,
  Norrvall), NORVELL, NORWOOD (includes Northwoode), NOSS,
  NOTHESTINE, NOTHNAGLE (includes Nothnagel), NOTT,
  NOTTINGHAM, NOVAK, NOWAK, NOWELL, NOWELS, NOWLIN
  (includes Nolan, Nolen, Knowlan, Knowland, Nowland, Noland,
  Nowlan, Nowlen, O'Nawlin), NOYCE, NOYES.*

- "NU-NZ" Surname Mailing Lists
  http://www.rootsweb.com/~jfuller/gen_mail_surnames-nu.html
  *NUCKOLLS, NUCKOLS, NUDD, NUGENT, NULL, NUNALLY,
  NUNEMAKER (includes Nonemaker, Nonnemacher), NUNER
  (includes Nooner), NUNEZ, NUNLEY, NUNN, NUNNALLY,
  NUNNELLEY (includes Nunely, Nunley), NURSE, NUSBAUM,
  NUSS (includes Nufs, Nusz, Nuse, News), NUSSBAUM, NUTBEAM
  (includes Nutbeem, Nutbean, Nutbeen), NUTHALL, NUTT,
  NUTTALL, NUTTER, NUTTING, NYE.*

SURNAMES, FAMILY ASSOCIATIONS & FAMILY NEWSLETTERS – "O"

Resources Dedicated to One Surname
http://www.cyndislist.com/surn-o.htm

Category Index:

◆ General Surname Sites and Resources
◆ Surname Specific Sites and Resources

◆ Surname Mailing Lists

◆ General Surname Sites and Resources

- Connect with Surnames - O
  http://www.geocities.com/Heartland/Bluffs/7708/o.html

- Dutch Home Pages by Familyname ~ Letter O
  http://members.tripod.com/~Don_Arnoldus/o.htm

- FamilyHistory.com - Message Boards - Surname - O
  http://www.familyhistory.com/messages/list.asp?prefix=OA

- Family Tree Maker Online User Home Pages - O
  http://www.familytreemaker.com/users/o/index.html

- Family Workings O Surname Links
  http://www.familyworkings.com/links/suro.htm

- GenConnect Surname Index - "O"
  http://genconnect.rootsweb.com/indx/surnames/O.html
  Message boards sponsored by RootsWeb. Each surname message board set is divided into the following topics: Queries, Bibles, Biographies, Deeds, Obituaries, Pensions, Wills.

- Genealogy Resources on the Internet - "OA-OD" Surname Mailing Lists
  http://www.rootsweb.com/~jfuller/gen_mail_surnames-oa.html
  "OE-OH"
  http://www.rootsweb.com/~jfuller/gen_mail_surnames-oe.html
  "OI-ON"
  http://www.rootsweb.com/~jfuller/gen_mail_surnames-oi.html
  "OO-OT"
  http://www.rootsweb.com/~jfuller/gen_mail_surnames-oo.html
  "OU-OZ"
  http://www.rootsweb.com/~jfuller/gen_mail_surnames-ou.html
  Search the index of surname mailing lists below: Surname Mailing Lists.

  o Genealogy Resources on the Internet - Surnames Included in Mailing Lists - "O"
    http://www-personal.umich.edu/~cgaunt/surnames/o.names.html
    This is a computer generated list of the surnames, and all variant spellings for those names, that are found in the surname mailing lists detailed on the pages shown above.

- Genealogy Resources on the Internet - Surname Web Sites for "O" Surnames
  http://www-personal.umich.edu/~cgaunt/surnames/o.html

- Genealogy's Most Wanted - Surnames Beginning with "O"
  http://www.citynet.net/mostwanted/o.htm

- Google Web Directory .... Genealogy>Surnames>O
  http://directory.google.com/Top/Society/Genealogy/Surnames/O/

- Heartland Genealogy Society Membership List - O
  http://www.geocities.com/Heartland/Ranch/2416/hgs-mlist-o.html

- H-GIG Surname Registry - Surnames Beginning O
  http://www.ucr.edu/h-gig/surdata/surname15.html

- Higginson Book Company - Surnames Beginning with O
  http://www.higginsonbooks.com/o.htm

- inGeneas Table of Common Surname Variations and Surname Misspellings - N-Q
  http://www.ingeneas.com/N2Q.html

- The Obituary Link Page - Family Obituary Archives Online - O
  http://www.geocities.com/~cribbswh/obit/o.htm

- Open Directory - Society: Genealogy: Surnames: O
  http://www.dmoz.org/Society/Genealogy/Surnames/O/

- 'O' Surnames at RootsWeb
  http://resources.rootsweb.com/surnames/o.html

- Surname Springboard Index - O
  http://www.geocities.com/~alacy/spring_o.htm

- SurnameWeb Surname Registry - O Index
  http://www.surnameweb.org/registry/o.htm

- SWINX Zoeklijst Nederlandse Familienamen / SWINX Searchlist Dutch Surnames - O
  http://www.swinx.net/swinx/swinx_od_nl.htm

- Websites at RootsWeb: O Surnames
  http://www.rootsweb.com/~websites/surnames/o.html

◆ Surname Specific Sites and Resources

- **The O'BRIEN Clan**
  http://www.obrienclan.com/
  O'Brien family genealogy including O'BRIEN, WILLIAMSON. Hundreds of links and lots of Irish and O'Brien information.

- **O'BRIEN Genealogy (Bandon, Cork, Ireland)**
  http://www.hylit.com/info/Genealogy/OBrien.html
  A genealogy of the O'Brien family of West Cork.

- **O'BRIEN's Genealogy Homepage**
  http://www.netwiz.net/~obrienm/index.htm

- **O'COBHTHAIGH HomePage**
  http://www.genealogy.com/genealogy/users/c/o/h/Debra-P-Cohig-Colorado/index.html
  COUHIG, COHIG, COWHIG, COHICK, COWHICK, COUIG, COWHAGG, COHEIG, COUIC and other spellings of the Irish O'COBHTHAIGH name.

- **Dingle O'CONNOR Ancestors**
  http://members.aol.com/waterlilys/Ancestors.html

- **O'CONNOR Family Website**
  http://www.geocities.com/Heartland/Prairie/1473
  Information about Peter O'CONNOR and his descendants from Ireland to Canada.

- **O'DEA Online**
  http://homepage.tinet.ie/~odeaclan/
  Home Page of the Dysert O'Dea Clan Association (Clan Ua DÈaghaid) for those with surnames O'Dea, O'Day, Dee, or Day. Includes a short clan history, application for Clan Association membership, a genealogical exchange, and details on the Fourth International O'Dea Clan Gathering in July 1999.

- **ODEA home page**
  http://www.clan.odea.net/
  Home Page of Clan UA DŠAGHAIDH for all those with surnames O'Dea, O'Day, Dee, or Day.

- **ODELL/ODLE Family**
  http://freepages.genealogy.rootsweb.com/~jacmac/odell.htm
  Descendants of THOMAS ODELL and SARAH (RIDGELY) BREWER of Maryland, Ohio, and Indiana.

- **ODELLs: Lost & Found**
  http://members.tripod.com/~mygenerations/odellslostandfound.html
  Odell, O'Dell, Odle.

- **ODELLs - The World's Greatest**
  http://family.odell.net
  ODELL and its variants - O'Dell, Oaddle, Odle, Oadle, Odill, Wodle, Wodhull, Wodell, Woodell.

- **The Chronicles of the O'DEMPSEY Family**
  http://www.webspawner.com/users/thechronicles/odempseychronicles.html
  The O'Dempsey family From Rathcannon, County Tipperary, Ireland to Upper Freestone, Queensland, Australia.

- **Genealogy ODIJK, VAN ODIJCK, VAN OIJCK**
  http://home.wxs.nl/~odijk002/
  Odijk, Franken, Oostrum, Van Der Kooij, Swanenburg, Benthem, Korpershoek, Van Geland, Vriens, Mackdaniel.

- **OFFICER Surname Census Extracts**
  http://freepages.genealogy.rootsweb.com/~officer/
  Attempts to transcribe ALL occurrences of the OFFICER surname in the US and state census records.

- **Official Website of the O'DOCHARTAIGH (DOHERTY) Family Research Centre and Inishowen Genealogy**
  http://www.islandnet.com/~doherty/clann/
  Darity, Daugherty, Docherty, Dogherty, Doherty, Dority, Dougherty.

- **ODOM Genealogy, Greenville Co., S.C.**
  http://members.aol.com/melo0909/index.html
  Related families in Greenville Co., S.C. Odom, Odam, Cannada, Taylor, Brown, Loftis, Roberts, Martin, Dill, Moon, Howell and many more.

- **OFFRINGA Familytree with more than 3,000 Offringa's**
  http://home.wxs.nl/~offringa/indexeng.htm
  From Dick OFFRINGA in Emmeloord, Netherlands.

- **Clann O'GALLCHOBHAIR (GALLAGHER) World-Wide**
  http://home.rmci.net/ogollaher/
  The "virtual Tir Chonnaill" of the ancient Irish clann O'GLLCHOBHAIR, including GALLAGHER, GALLAHER, GOLLAHER, GOLLIHER, GALLAHUE, etc.

- **OGASAWARA Clan Genealogy**
  http://members.aol.com/uchuujin/oga.html
  Genealogical information of the descendants of Ogasawara Jiro Nagakiyo (1163- 1242) who descended from the 56th Japanese emperor, Emperor Seiwa (849 - 880).

- **OGBOURNE Chronicles**
  http://www.oginet.com/Chronicles/
  Historical & Genealogical Information relating to the names of Ogbourne, Ogborne, Ogborn, Ogburn.

- **The African American OGBURNs And The House of OGBURNs**
  http://www.oginet.com/Chronicles/hoogbrn.htm

- **The OGLE / OGLES Family Association**
  http://www.ogles.org
  This not-for-profit organization is dedicated to the preservation of the history and genealogy of the Ogle and Ogles families in North America.

- **The O'HARA Family Genealogy Page**
  http://www.geocities.com/Heartland/Ridge/5346/
  Darby, Dittman/N, Kleiman, Leonard, Menchen, Miller, O'Hara, Rigney, Speaker, Sullivan.

- **OHLINGER / OLINGER Family**
  http://members.tripod.com/olinger

- OHNMEISS Family Genealogy
  http://members.aol.com/madisonfpe/ohnmeiss.html
  Ohnmeis, Ohmneis, Ohmnies, Ohmeis.

- O'KEEFFE Home Page
  http://www.usinternet.com/users/jokeefe/home.htm

- OLDHAM Genealogical Database
  http://www.rootsweb.com/~gumby/genweb/Oldham/
  Oldham.html
  A database that contains 16,578 names.

- OLIN Family Society
  http://www.mindspring.com/~trolin/ofs/index.html
  Descendants of John OLIN and Susannah SPENCER.

- OLIVER Surname Mailing List
  http://www.sonic.net/~yvonne/oliver.html

- OLLIFFE One Name Study
  http://www.colliffe.freeserve.co.uk/

- The Boston OLLIS Family Home Page
  http://www.familytreemaker.com/users/o/l/l/Prentis-L-
  Ollis/index.html
  *For descendants of Boston Ollis, born abt. 1743 in Wales, died
  March 9, 1835, buried in Morgan County, TN.*

- OLLIS - OLLIS Genealogy
  http://freepages.genealogy.rootsweb.com/~ollis/

- OLLIVETTE, OLIVET, OLLIVETTE,
  deOLLIVETT
  http://www.geocities.com/allollivetts

- The O'MAHONY Society
  http://cat.spindata.com/mahony/

- O'MALLEY Family in Australia - The Descendants
  of John MALAY
  http://www.users.bigpond.com/omalley/
  *Malay, Maley, Malley, O'Malley family of Westbury Tasmania,
  Australia.*

- The Official Website of the O'MALLEY Clan
  Association
  http://www.omalley-clan.org

- O'MARY Genealogy Homepage
  http://www.syspac.com/~somary/gene.html

- The OMASTA Pages
  http://come.to/omasta
  Pages dedicated to the Omasta family worldwide.

- O'NEILL Clan Homepage
  http://www.clansandnames.org/oneill.shtml

- OP DEN GRAEF / UPDEGRAFF Family
  http://www.siscom.net/~rdrunner/HTML/Updegraff.html

- The Descendants of William OPENSHAW
  http://www5.pair.com/vtandrew/openshaw/openshaw.htm

- OPP Genealogy
  http://pages.prodigy.net/dave_lossos/opp.htm

- The ORANGES Family - California
  http://www.webspawner.com/users/theorangesfamily/
  *"With the advent of The Internet we have been in contact with many
  Oranges from all over the world. Dino Oranges, Sr. & family from
  New York, Alfredo Oranges from Panama, & a group from Sao
  Paulo, Brazil. As additional information comes in we will keep you
  posted! "*

- ORAVECZ Families Web Site
  http://www.oravecz.org
  *General site for all Oravecz families. Currently includes
  descendants of George Oravecz, Sr. and Miller and Partsch
  ancestors of Miriam Jane Partsch Oravecz. Hosting: Oravecz,
  Oravec, Oravetz, Oravets, Oravez, Oravis, and Orawetz.*

- The ORBAN's
  http://www.geocities.com/CapeCanaveral/7473/orban.html
  Belgium, Hungary.

- ORGAN Family Research and Genealogy Site
  http://freepages.genealogy.rootsweb.com/~organ/

- ORMAN Surname Resource Site
  http://members.tripod.com/dunderwood/ormanindex.html
  *Online documents, message board and links to aid all researchers
  for Orman surname.*

- O'ROURKE Families and Connections
  http://clubs.yahoo.com/clubs/orourkefamiliesandconnection

- O'ROURKE Family Genealogy Home Page
  http://www.geocities.com/Heartland/Plains/3552/orourke.htm
  *Dedicated to the research and discussion of genealogy on the
  O'Rourke, Rourke, O'Rorke, Roark, O'Roarke family lines.*

- OROZCO Family
  http://members.home.net/salvus

- ORRELL Family Association
  http://www.orrellfamily.com/
  Orrell, Orrill, Orrel, Orel, Orell, Orrels, Orill, etc.

- ORTON Family History Society
  http://www2.prestel.co.uk/orton/fhs/index.html

- OSBORNE Family of Tennessee
  http://www.homestead.com/DOsborneFamilyTree/index.html
  *The Tennessee connection includes the Counties of Madison,
  Gibson, & Maury.*

- OSBORNE Origins
  http://home.att.net/~osborne_origins/

- OSBURN Connection
  http://www.freeyellow.com/members3/osburns

- O'SHIELDS / O'SHEILDS Family History
  http://home.texoma.net/~mmcmullen/o/oshield.htm

- The OSTRANDER Family Association (OFA)
  http://home.earthlink.net/~ostrander/index.html
  Ostranders in America Since 1660.

- OSTRANDER KELLEY Family Page
  http://www.familytreemaker.com/users/k/e/l/terence--
  kelley/index.html
  *Descendants of Pieter OSTRANDER who married Rebecca
  Traphagen in 1679 in New Amsterdam.*

- Clan O'TOOLE Web Site
  http://clanotoole.org/index.html

- O*T*RIDGE Genealogy
  http://homepages.rootsweb.com/~otridge
  *Website for a One-name Study of the O*T*RIDGE family, including OTRIDGE, OATRIDGE, OTTRIDGE and related variations (but not OUTRIDGE).*

- OTTworld
  http://people.a2000.nl/jott

- Dr. Bodo OTTO Association
  http://www.geocities.com/Heartland/Prairie/8833/

- Le HOUYMET Internet - Home on the Internet of Les Descendants de Jean OUIMET, Inc.
  http://www.geocities.com/~couimet/lehouymet.html
  Ouimet, Houymet, Vilmet, Wemet, Wemett, Wuillemette, Wilmot and numerous other spelling variations.

- The OULTON Project
  http://www.cct.infi.net/~funbooks/html/index/oulton.htm
  An attempt to trace the Oultons back to the Irish-Norse Vikings who settled in Cheshire England. Also includes most all Oulton genealogy in America.

- OUTTEN Family History
  http://members.aol.com/outtengene/Outten.htm

- OWEN/OWINGS SAGA
  http://www.angelfire.com/wa2/Gsows

- OWENS / OWEN Family Genealogical Database
  http://www.geocities.com/Heartland/Farm/3150

- OWSLEY Family Historical Society
  http://home.dwave.net/~skeeter/owsley.html

- The OWSLEY Tidepool
  http://www.owsley.org/
  Ousley, Owsley, Howsley, Housley, Oisle.

- OXFORDs of America
  http://www.geocities.com/Heartland/Acres/3974/

- OXFORDs of the World
  http://freepages.genealogy.rootsweb.com/~oxford/

◆ Surname Mailing Lists

- "OA-OD" Surname Mailing Lists
  http://www.rootsweb.com/~jfuller/gen_mail_surnames-oa.html
  OAK, OAKES, OAKLEY, OAKLEY, OAKS, OATES, OATMAN (includes Outman, Oudtman, Van Oudtman), OATS, OATSVALL, OBANNON (includes O'Banion, O'Bannion, O'Banyan), OBER, OBERG, OBERHOLTZER, OBERLIN, OBOYLE, OBRE, OBRIAN, OBRIANT, OBRIEN (includes Byrom, Bynum, Byran, Biron, Brian), OBRYAN, OBRYANT, OBYRNE, OCALLAGHAN, OCHS, OCONNELL, OCONNER, OCONNOR (includes O'Conner, Connor, Conner, O'Conor), OCONNOR, OCONNOR (includes O'Connor, Connors, Conner, Connor), ODAM, ODAY, ODDING, ODDY, ODEA, ODELL (includes Odel, Odle, O'Dell, O'Del), ODELL (includes O'Dell), ODELL (includes O'Dell, Odle, Oadell), ODEN, ODEN, ODENBAUGH (includes Odenbach, Offenbach, Adenbach, Adenbaugh, Von Adenbach), ODER, ODLE, ODOM, ODONNELL

(includes Odonell, O'Donnel), ODONOGHUE, ODONOVAN, ODOR (includes Oder), ODOWD, ODUM, ODWYER.

- "OE-OH" Surname Mailing Lists
  http://www.rootsweb.com/~jfuller/gen_mail_surnames-oe.html
  OERTLING, OESTERREICH, OESTREICH, OFFICER, OFFLEY, OFFUTT, OFLAHERTY, OGAN, OGBURN, OGDEN, OGG, OGILVIE, OGLE, OGLENCKI (includes Oglinsky), OGLESBY, OGLETHORPE, OGLETREE, OGRADY, OHALLORAN, OHANLON, OHARA (includes O'Hara), OHARA, OHARE, OHAVER, OHEARN, OHL.

- "OI-ON" Surname Mailing Lists
  http://www.rootsweb.com/~jfuller/gen_mail_surnames-oi.html
  OKEEFE, OKEEFFE, OKELLEY, OKELLY, OKEY, OLD, OLDAKER, OLDALE (includes Oldall, Oldehall), OLDEN, OLDFIELD, OLDHAM, OLDHAM, OLDS (includes Old, Auld, Aulds), OLEARY (includes Leary, O'leary), OLEFORD, OLESON, OLINGER, OLIPHANT, OLIVE, OLIVEIRA, OLIVER, OLIVERIO (includes Aliverio, Ahliverio, Ohliverio, Olahverio), OLIVIER, OLLER, OLLERTON, OLLIS, OLMSTEAD, OLMSTED (includes Almstead, Umstedt), OLNEY, OLOUGHLIN, OLSDOTTER, OLSEN (includes Olson), OLSEN, OLSON, OLSSON, OLSZEWSKI, OMALLEY, OMAN, OMARA, OMEARA (includes O'mara, Mara, Meara), OMEARA, ONEAL, ONEALL (includes O'Neill, O'Neal, O'Neil, Neal, Neale), ONEIL, ONEILL, ONEY, ONKEN, ONSTINE, ONLY.

- "OO-OT" Surname Mailing Lists
  http://www.rootsweb.com/~jfuller/gen_mail_surnames-oo.html
  OOTEN (includes Euten, Ooton), OPDENGRAEFF (includes UpdeGrave, OpDeGraff, UpdeGrove), OPDYCK (includes Updike, Op den Dyck, Opdycke), OPENSHAW, OPIE (includes Oppy, Oppey, Opee, Oppe), OPP, ORAM, ORANGE, ORBAN (includes Orbin, Orbant, Orbaneja, Orbanic), ORBAN, ORCHARD, ORCUTT, ORDWAY, OREAR (includes O'Rear, ORear, Orrear, Orea), OREGAN, OREILLY, OREM (includes Oram, Orum), ORFORD, ORGAN, ORIANS (includes Oreans, Arians, Arrians), ORMAN, ORME, ORMISTON, ORMOND, ORMSBY, ORMSTON (includes Ormiston, Ormsby), ORNDORFF, OROURKE, ORPHEY, ORPWOOD (includes Arpwood, Arpod), ORR, ORRICK, ORRISON, ORSER, ORTH, ORTIZ, ORTON, OSBORN (includes Osborne, Ozburn, Ozbirn, Osbourne), OSBORNE, OSBOURNE, OSBURN, OSGOOD, OSHAUGHNESSY, OSHEA, OSMOND, OSMOND (includes Osmund), OSMUN (includes Osman, Osmin, Osmond, Ozmun), OSTEEN, OSTENDARP, OSTER, OSTERBERG (includes Osterburg, Ostberg), OSTHEIMER, OSTRANDER (includes Oostrander, Hostrander, Van Ostrander, Van Nostrunt, Vanostran, Ostervanter, Ostrancer,, Ostronden, Ostrandt, Osslander, Osatrander, Noortstrande), OSTROM (includes Ostrum, Oosteroom), OSTROWSKI, OSULLIVAN, OSWALD, OSWALT, OTEY (includes Otee, Otie), OTIS, OTOOLE, OTOSKI, OTT, OTTEN, OTTERY, OTTO, OTWELL.

- "OU-OZ" Surname Mailing Lists
  http://www.rootsweb.com/~jfuller/gen_mail_surnames-ou.html
  OUDERKIRK, OUELLETTE, OUSLEY (includes Owsley), OUTLAND, OUTLAW, OUZTS, OVERACKER (includes Overocker, Overacre, Oberacher), OVERALL (includes Overhall), OVERBAUGH (includes Oberbach), OVERBY, OVERHOLT, OVERLOCK, OVERLOCK (includes Overlook, Oberlock, Oberloch, Overlack, Oberlack, Ueberloch), OVERMAN, OVERSTREET, OVERTON, OVIATT (includes Ovitt), OVIATT, OWEN (includes Owens, Oen, Owing), OWENS, OWINGS, OWNBY, OWSLEY, OXFORD, OXFORD, OXLEY, OYLER, OZIER, OZMENT (includes Osment).

SURNAMES, FAMILY ASSOCIATIONS & FAMILY NEWSLETTERS – "P"

Resources Dedicated to One Surname
http://www.cyndislist.com/surn-p.htm

Category Index:

◆ General Surname Sites and Resources

◆ Surname Specific Sites and Resources

◆ Surname Mailing Lists

◆ General Surname Sites and Resources

● Connect with Surnames - P
http://www.geocities.com/Heartland/Bluffs/7708/p.html

● Dutch Home Pages by Familyname ~ Letter P
http://members.tripod.com/~Don_Arnoldus/p.htm

● FamilyHistory.com - Message Boards - Surname - P
http://www.familyhistory.com/messages/list.asp?prefix=PA

● Family Tree Maker Online User Home Pages - P
http://www.familytreemaker.com/users/p/index.html

● Family Workings P Surname Links
http://www.familyworkings.com/links/surp.htm

● GenConnect Surname Index - "P"
http://genconnect.rootsweb.com/indx/surnames/P.html
Message boards sponsored by RootsWeb. Each surname message board set is divided into the following topics: Queries, Bibles, Biographies, Deeds, Obituaries, Pensions, Wills.

● Genealogy Resources on the Internet - "PAA-PAQ" Surname Mailing Lists
http://www.rootsweb.com/~jfuller/gen_mail_surnames-paa.html
"PAR-PAR"
http://www.rootsweb.com/~jfuller/gen_mail_surnames-par.html
"PAS-PD"
http://www.rootsweb.com/~jfuller/gen_mail_surnames-pas.html
"PEA-PED"
http://www.rootsweb.com/~jfuller/gen_mail_surnames-pea.html
"PEE-PEH"
http://www.rootsweb.com/~jfuller/gen_mail_surnames-pee.html
"PEI-PEN"
http://www.rootsweb.com/~jfuller/gen_mail_surnames-pei.html
"PEO-PEZ"
http://www.rootsweb.com/~jfuller/gen_mail_surnames-peo.html
"PF-PH"
http://www.rootsweb.com/~jfuller/gen_mail_surnames-pf.html

"PI-PN"
http://www.rootsweb.com/~jfuller/gen_mail_surnames-pi.html
"PO-PQ"
http://www.rootsweb.com/~jfuller/gen_mail_surnames-po.html
"PR-PT"
http://www.rootsweb.com/~jfuller/gen_mail_surnames-pr.html
"PU-PZ"
http://www.rootsweb.com/~jfuller/gen_mail_surnames-pu.html
Search the index of surname mailing lists below: Surname Mailing Lists.

○ Genealogy Resources on the Internet - Surnames Included in Mailing Lists - "P"
http://www-personal.umich.edu/~cgaunt/surnames/p.names.html
This is a computer generated list of the surnames, and all variant spellings for those names, that are found in the surname mailing lists detailed on the pages shown above.

● Genealogy Resources on the Internet - Surname Web Sites for "P" Surnames
http://www-personal.umich.edu/~cgaunt/surnames/p.html

● Genealogy's Most Wanted - Surnames Beginning with "P"
http://www.citynet.net/mostwanted/p.htm

● Google Web Directory .... Genealogy>Surnames>P
http://directory.google.com/Top/Society/Genealogy/Surnames/P/

● Heartland Genealogy Society Membership List - P
http://www.geocities.com/Heartland/Ranch/2416/hgs-mlist-p.html

● H-GIG Surname Registry - Surnames Beginning P
http://www.ucr.edu/h-gig/surdata/surname16.html

● Higginson Book Company - Surnames Beginning with P
http://www.higginsonbooks.com/p.htm

● inGeneas Table of Common Surname Variations and Surname Misspellings - N-Q
http://www.ingeneas.com/N2Q.html

● The Obituary Link Page - Family Obituary Archives Online - P
http://www.geocities.com/~cribbswh/obit/p.htm

- Open Directory - Society: Genealogy: Surnames: P
  http://www.dmoz.org/Society/Genealogy/Surnames/P/

- 'P' Surnames at RootsWeb
  http://resources.rootsweb.com/surnames/p.html

- Surname Springboard Index - P
  http://www.geocities.com/~alacy/spring_p.htm

- SurnameWeb Surname Registry - P Index
  http://www.surnameweb.org/registry/p.htm

- SWINX Zoeklijst Nederlandse Familienamen /
  SWINX Searchlist Dutch Surnames - P
  http://www.swinx.net/swinx/swinx_pa_nl.htm

- Websites at RootsWeb: P Surnames
  http://www.rootsweb.com/~websites/surnames/p.html

◆ Surname Specific Sites and Resources

- Genealogie PAANS
  http://users.telekabel.nl/jahengel/Paans.html

- PAAR Genealogy Research Project
  http://www.pub.nxs.net/jpaar/genealogy/paar/paar.asp?
  MenuItem=9

- PACE
  http://www.phc.igs.net/~gordpace/
  Also ARCH, LESTER, SQUIRE, EMERY, HAYNES, DODSWORTH, WILDIG, WEBBER.

- The PACE Network
  http://freepages.genealogy.rootsweb.com/~pace/

- PACE Society of America Inc.
  http://freepages.genealogy.rootsweb.com/~psapages/

- PACKARD Family History Web site
  http://members.aol.com/azpack/family/index.htm
  Descendants of Noah PACKARD and Sophia BUNDY.

- PACKER One Name Study
  http://www.packer-ons.org
  Devoted to all references to the surname PACKER world-wide.

- PADILLA Genealogy
  http://www.mindspring.com/~padilla/
  Padilla Genealogy from Albanchez, Almeria, Andalucia, Spain. Descendants of Francisco Padilla Gonzalez, born 1836, Albanchez Spain.

- PAGEOT-PAGEAU-PAJOT Genealogy Home Page
  http://www.novagate.com/~rpaggeot/

- PAIGE/PAGE Family Ancestry
  http://worldconnect.genealogy.rootsweb.com/cgi-bin/igm.cgi?
  db=uncle_bud
  This site caters to any PAIGE or PAGE family researcher who may be descended from John PAGE and Mary MARSH of Hingham & Haverhill, MA abt. 1635.

- Descendants of Ralph PAIN
  http://freepages.genealogy.rootsweb.com/~gungazo/
  Descendants of Ralph and Dorithea PAIN of Freetown, Bristol Co., MA. Other surnames: Payne, Paine, Stewart, Briggs, Slocum, Wetherell, Chase.

- Those Prolific PAINs
  http://members.tripod.com/~ProlificPains/index.html
  Payn, Payne, Pane, Paine and Pain.

- PAINCHAUD Family
  http://home.att.net/~stephen.painchaud
  Painchaud family genealogy in Quebec and USA.

- My PAINE/PAYNE Family
  http://members.tripod.com/~Silvie/Payne.html

- PAIR Place
  http://members.aol.com/epg51/genealgy/index.htm
  A resource center for Pair, Pare, Pear, Par, Parr, Paire, and similar surnames containing compiled family histories and original resources.

- PALGRAVE Society, One-Name Study, Genealogy, Heraldry & Biography
  http://www.ffhs.org.uk/members/palgrave.htm
  Palgrave, Pelgrave, Polgrave, Pagrave, Pedgriff, Pedgrift, etc. Mainly East Anglia, England, but also anywhere in the world.

- PALLISER Family Home Page
  http://www.palliser-genealogy.mcmail.com/
  For anyone with an interest in the Palliser surname, or its variants, such as Pallister, Pallyser, etc.

- Walter PALMER Society
  http://www.walterpalmer.com/
  For descendants of Walter Palmer who arrived in Salem, Massachusetts in June 1629.

- The PAMPLIN Family & Connections Home Page
  http://www.pamplin.net/pamplin.htm

- The PANCAKE Pages
  http://members.xoom.com/pankake/index.htm
  Pancake, Pankake, Pannenkuchen, etc. family data.

- PARKE, PARK, PARKS, Genealogy Page
  http://www.mcn.org/h/parke_roots/
  Descendants of Roger Parke, born 1648 in Cumberland England.

- The PARK/E/S Family Research Page
  http://home.earthlink.net/~howardorjeff/park/

- The PARKE Society, Inc.
  http://ourworld.compuserve.com/homepages/Tad_Parks/
  Clearinghouse for research on all Park/e/s immigrants from the British Isles.

- PARLE / PEARL Family Association
  http://www.geocities.com/Athens/Acropolis/4933/parle.html
  A gathering point for information concerning the surname Parle and all possible variations including Pearl.

- The PARMELEE Family Home Page
  http://www.geocities.com/mrjimwalters/
  The PARMELEE family in all its spellings: Parmely, Parmley, Parmly, Palmerlee, Parmele, Parmaly, Parmale, Parmalee Parmeley, etc.

- The Pioneering PARMENTERs of America
  http://www.parmenter-fam-assn.org/
  The Parmenter Family Association. Palmenter, Palmentor, Palmerter, Palmeter, Palmiter, Palmster, Palmuter, Pamarter, Pamener, Pamenter, Pamerter, Pamerton, Pameter, Parmanter, Parmater, Parmentr, Parmentar, Parmente, Parmento, Parmentor, Parmentr, Parmerter, Parmeter, Parmether, Parmetor, Parmetr, Parmetur, Parminter, Parmiter, Parmitter, Parmorter, Parmortr, Parmntr, Parmter, Parnenter, Pearmnter, Pelmater, Pelmeter, Pemerton, Pemertor, Pemetor, Permenter, Permento, Permertor, Permeter, Perminter, Permiter, Permitter, Prmentr.

- PARNELL Genealogy
  http://angelfire.com/ky/johnparnell/
  Research on the PARNELL family in Kentucky and Illinois with submited information on other PARNELLs, along with collateral lines of Mays, Kemp, Coffey, Linton, Rogers, Coomer, Hurtt, Fyfe.

- Descendants of James PARRISH 1690-1754 Brunswick Co., VA.
  http://Planetall.homestead.com/posiesroots/index.html

- La famille PARROT du Canada
  http://www.parrot.ca/parrot.asp
  Histoire de la famille PARROT, venue de Audincourt, France.

- PARSONS Family Association
  mailto:KATHYR@prodigy.net
  The Parsons Family of the South Branch of the Potomac and Cheat River VA/WV. For details send e-mail to Katherine Ray at KATHYR@prodigy.net.

- PARSONS Family Genealogy Web Site
  http://www.howdycousin.com/parsons.html
  PARSONS of South Carolina, Arkansas, Mississippi, and Arkansas. Census, Wills, Probate Records, Photos.

- The PARTEE Pages
  http://pages.prodigy.com/Goodtrader/partee.htm
  For the PARTEE surname in North Carolina and Georgia.

- PARTIN Genealogy Gateway
  http://www.ronpartin.com/genealogy/genealogy.html
  National clearinghouse for PARTIN family of SE Kentucky.

- The PARTRIDGE Family Nest
  http://www.partridgenest.com/

- PASCHALL Roots & Branches
  http://victorian.fortunecity.com/tiffany/469/

- Descendants of Quinton PATCH
  http://members.cftnet.com/stevew/partch.htm
  Born 1727 in England, died February 9, 1818 in Danbury, Connecticut. PATCH, PARTCH.

- PATCH Families of Australia
  http://www2.one.net.au/~archnex/Patch.html

- PATENAUDE Families of North America
  http://meltingpot.fortunecity.com/virginia/670/
  Descendants of Nicolas Patenostre ou Patenaude. Includes Patenaude, Pattenaude, Patnaude, Patnode, Patenoe, Patnaud, Patnod, Patno, Patnoe, Patnude, Patenude, Pattenotre, Patenot, Pedno.

- The PATE-PAIT Historical Society
  http://www.geocities.com/Heartland/Park/4923/

- Descendants of James PATERSON
  http://www.parsonstech.com/genealogy/trees/apaterso/paterson.htm

- PATTERSON Home Page - PATTERSON People Newsletter
  http://members.aol.com/Kinseeker6/patterson.html

- The PATTON Exchange
  http://members.aol.com/M55442/index.html

- PAUL Family Association
  http://Mainetoday.koz.com/maine/paul
  Dedicated to the preservation, promotion and dissemination of information pertaining to the history and genealogy of the descendants of Daniel PAUL. Surnames include; Paul, Fernald, Shapleigh, Bragdon, Staples, Hammond, Remick, Tobey, Main, Weare.

- PAVEL Families - Early Bohemian Settlers in Butler County, Nebraska
  http://members.aol.com//busybusy96/pavel.html
  Ancestors and descendants of John PAVEL, Sr. who settled in Nebraska in 1869.

- PAWSEY Genealogy
  http://members.tripod.co.uk/Pawsey/genindex.htm

- Cissie P's PAYNE Genealogy Web Site
  http://www.cissiep.com/
  Payne / Paine / Pain.

- The Joseph and Phoebe PAYNE Family of Bedford County Virginia
  http://w3.one.net/~evaughan/vaughan/wilson.htm

- The Joseph PAYNE Family of Virginia, Tennessee and Mississippi
  http://members.aol.com/jogt/payne.htm

- The PAYNEs of Virginia
  http://www.icon.net/~sdcaller/payne.htm
  Descendants of John Payne, born ca 1615 in England.

- PEABODY Family Home Pages
  http://www.pbdy.com
  Velton Peabody's compilation of ALL Peabodys in the U.S.

- PEACH Family Tree
  http://www.users.globalnet.co.uk/~kenelks/peach.htm
  William Peach, born 10 October 1878 at Somercotes, Derbyshire, and his ancestors.

- PEACOCK Family Association of the South
  http://www.peacockfamily.org/

- Stephen PEARCE's Web Page - Family History - Genealogy
  http://www.interlog.com/~spearce/
  Descendants of William PEARCE of Nova Scotia, Henry PEARCE of New Brunswick and Other Families. Henry and William Pearce were brothers who came to Nova Scotia in the 1780's. Records of Henry show that he was with the Westchester Refugees in New York

before he came and was in their early land grants. William lived in Kings County N.S. and Henry moved to Kings County New Brunswick. This is the record of their descent. Some branches of GATES and SPINNEY and other Nova Scotia families are recorded at some length.

- **A PEARMAN Family Home Page**
  http://home.att.net/~cgpiere/
  Dedicated to documenting Pearman family history in early Virginia. It contains Pearman historical references, documents and family charts.

- **PEARSALLs Corner**
  http://www.geocities.com/Heartland/Acres/5417/
  PEARSALL family from 1645 to the present. BEDELL, CARMAN, HAWKINS, MOTT AND KAVANAUGH.

- **PEARSON Genealogy**
  http://members.tripod.co.uk/pears1/index.html
  PEARSON genealogy from Ireland to Canada.

- **PEARSON of Kilconquhar**
  http://roderickcraig.ourfamily.com/pearson/index.htm
  Descendants of Alexander PEARSON and Christian KENNEDY, married in 1786.

- **Missing PEARSONs**
  http://www.freeyellow.com/members8/missingpearson/index.html
  Photos, family trees, search function and message board.

- **The PEASLEE Puzzle**
  http://home.earthlink.net/~melindaroo/peaslee.html
  PEASLEE (PEASLEY) families of Michigan and Ontario, their descendants and their New England ancestors. Surnames: CRAWFORD, BARNES, HILLIKER, BANKER, BRADLEY, SHAW, FULLER.

- **Descendancy Narrative of Ira PECK**
  http://www.geocities.com/Heartland/Ranch/1520/page2.html
  Descendants of Ira Peck, Dean, Dunham, Leguee, Steffen, Bruce, Nixon.

- **PEDEN, William - Descendants**
  http://www.uftree.com/UFT/WebPages/ClarePedenMidgley/PEDEN/
  Son of George PEDEN, born in Londonderry, Ireland circa 1796. Died 13 Mar 1875 in Johnstown, Cambria, Pennsylvania.

- **PEDRON Home Page**
  http://PEDRON.listbot.com
  A e-mail discussion list for the surname PEDRON and various other spellings.

- **The PEELE Family Association**
  http://www.txdirect.net/~hpeele/
  Peelle, Peele, Peel and Peal. Horace PEELE's Genealogy, Etc. - The First PEELLE Family in America.

- **PEERY Family History Home Page**
  http://www.cc.utah.edu/~pdp7277/

- **PEFFLEY Family Association**
  http://homepages.rootsweb.com/~scismfam/peffley/
  A comprehensive focal point for Peffley and Pefley family research, connected to Gen Connect query boards, resources, and the Peffley-L@rootsweb.com.

- **PEGELOW Post**
  http://pegelowpost.freeyellow.com/index.html
  Pegelow family in America and Germany.

- **The PEGGIE Homepage**
  http://www.users.globalnet.co.uk/~peggie/
  A history of one branch of the Peggie family in Falkland, Fife, Scotland from the 1760s to the current day.

- **PEGRAM Family Album**
  http://www.patch.net/
  Descendants of Daniel Pegram (c1720-1776) of Williamsburg, VA and Warren County, NC.

- **PELICH World Pages**
  http://www.geocities.com/Athens/Thebes/8126/

- **PELLAND Family Genealogy**
  http://www.cyberbeach.net/~jrpellan/pellan2.htm
  Pelland, Pellan, Pellant, Penlan.

- **Association des Familles PELLETIER**
  http://www.quebectel.com/pelletier/

- **PELLETIER Genealogy**
  http://www.genealogy.org/~gapellet/

- **PENDERGRAFT and PENDERGRASS Family Web Page**
  http://members.home.net/lpenderg/pendergr.htm
  Descendants of James Pendergrass (Prendergast), who was born about 1640 in Ireland and came to Virginia in about 1668.

- **PENDROY Surname History Information**
  http://home.att.net/~pendroy

- **PENHARLOW Family**
  http://users2.50megs.com/penhallow/
  Also PENHALLOW, PENHOLLOW. Worldwide to 1300 England. Extensive historical family data.

- **PENNEBAKER History**
  http://www.communique.net/~pepbaker/pennebkr.htm
  Pannebakker, Pannebecker, Pfannebecker.

- **PENNINGTON Research Association Homepage**
  http://penningtonresearch.org/
  The Pennington Research Association (PRA) was founded for the sole purpose of the collection, preservation, maintenance, and dissemination of materials relating to the genealogical structure of the Pennington Family. We strive to be the most comprehensive source of accurate genealogical information, material and events concerning the Pennington Family. We will strive to utilize Internet technology as an informative and educational tool for our members and all other genealogy researchers.

- **The PENNOCKS of Primitive Hall**
  http://homepages.infoseek.com/~pennock/index.html
  Descendants of Christopher PENNOCK of Chester Co., PA. Other surnames: MENDENHALL, COATES, MARIS, LUKENS, LEVIS, CONNELL.

- **The PENNY / PENNEY Home Page**
  http://www.inch.com/~penney/gene/

- **PENROSE Home Page**
  http://www.cliftonpenrose.co.uk
  PENROSE family of Cornwall, London, Yorkshire, England and Ireland.

- **PENTECOST Genealogy Homepage**
  http://www.pentecost.org/
  Pentecost, Penticost, Pentacost.

- **PENWELL Papers**
  http://clubs.yahoo.com/clubs/penwellpapers
  PENWELLs worldwide.

- **L'Association des Familles PEPIN**
  http://pages.infinit.net/afp

- **The Northwest Twig of the PEPPAN / PEPIN Family Tree**
  http://www.escargot.com/lisap
  The descendants of Louis Seymour Peppan and his wife, Emma Sarah Peppan nee Houston.

- **PERKINS Family History**
  http://www.eclipse.co.uk/perkins.family.tree/
  Family history of PERKIN/PERKINS, Devonshire, Monmouthshire, Warwickshire and Austraila.

- **Genéalogie de la Famille PERREAUX**
  http://www3.sk.sympatico.ca/perrex

- **Association Des Familles PERRON D'AmÈrique**
  http://www.oricom.ca/pperron/

- **Granny Peach's PERRY Page**
  http://members.tripod.com/~GrannyPeach/
  Search for the origins of Burrell PERRY and his wives, Mary Ann RAINWATER and Jane BATTS. They lived in NC, TN, GA, MS, LA and TX. Also contains the history and possible lineage of the seven PERRY brothers of NC and VA.

- **PESCE Family Web Page**
  http://www.geocities.com/Heartland/Valley/1410/pesce_index.html

- **PETERMAN Resource Center**
  http://member.aol.com/asheneberg/Peterman/index.htm

- **The PETTIGROVE Genealogy Page**
  http://www.personal.psu.edu/faculty/j/w/jwd6/pettigro.htm

- **PETTY Family**
  http://www.fortunecity.com/millenium/galaxyway/409
  U.S. family, includes variant spellings. About 8,000 individuals are in this database.

- **PETTYPIECE Family Genealogy**
  http://www.csd.uwo.ca/~pettypi/tree/
  Descendants of John PETTYPIECE of County Sligo, Ireland.

- **PFANNEBECKER Family Association**
  http://www.sover.net/~rutins/
  Pannebakker, Pfannebecker, Pannebecker, Pennebaker, Pennybacker, Pennypacker.

- **PFEIFFER Family**
  http://www.nstep.net/dorgon/pfeifer.htm
  The descendancy of Joseph Pfeifer 1759.

- **Home Pages of Richard PFOUTS**
  http://home.earthlink.net/~pfoutsr/
  Pfautz, Pfoutz, Fouts, Foutz.

- **PFRIMMER Family**
  http://www.asatek.com/pfrimmer/index.html
  History of PFRIMMER Family, addresses of researchers, online newsletters.

- **PHEBUS Genealogy Index**
  http://www.phebus.com/
  Phoebus, Pheobus, Phebues, Febus, etc.

- **PHELPS Connections**
  http://www.phelps-connections.org/

- **PHIFER Surname Research**
  http://homepages.rootsweb.com/~lcompton/phifer/

- **The PHILIPP/PHILLIPS Family from Alsace to Ohio**
  http://www.geocities.com/Heartland/Acres/4585
  Read about the Phillips family from Fairfield County, Ohio and their Philipp ancestors from Friesen, Alsace, France. Related names include Buechler, Kilburger, Krile, Messbarger, Piper, Rauch, Saum, Steck and Winter.

- **PHILLIPS Family 1593-1997**
  http://members.aol.com/PSulzer/Phillips.html
  This line originated in County Norfolk, UK before 1593 with Christopher Phillips.

- **The PHILLIPS Family of North Carolina, Georgia, and Beyond**
  http://www.familytreemaker.com/users/p/h/i/Robert-V-Phillips/index.html
  Descendants of Solomon PHILLIPS of Edgecombe County, North Carolina. Includes McCALL, HARRIS, WILLIAMS, PEARSON, JOHNSON, LANE, RICKETSON, BLANCHARD, SECKINGER.

- **PHILLIPS Genealogy**
  http://www.gnt.net/~vawr/
  Family of Andrew Phillips Sr. of Charlestown, Massachusetts, circa 1640.

- **The Association of the PICHE Families**
  http://www.abacom.com/~dgdupre/#The association of the Piche families

- **The PHOENIX's of County Down, Ireland**
  http://www.geocities.com/Heartland/Fields/2484/

- **The PICARD Surname Homepage**
  http://freepages.genealogy.rootsweb.com/~picard/Index.html
  A combination of research and the work of others for PICARD, DESTROISMAISONS, "dit" PICARD as well as PECOR, PECORE, PICAR, and THREEHOUSE and many others variants. Primarily in Quebec and United States.

- **PICKELSIMER and PICKLESIMER Ancestry**
  http://members.aol.com/manypikls/index.html

- **PICKENS Place**
  http://www.PickensPlace.com
  A treasure chest of information for researchers of PICKENS, dedicated to preserving the history, traditions, and memories of Pickens families everywhere.

- PICKLES Genealogy Home Page
  http://freepages.genealogy.rootsweb.com/~csanders/Pickles/RR_TOC.HTM
  Descendants of John PICKLES and Hannah WHITNEY, principally of England and Michigan.

- PICOT Home Page / Page Web PICOT
  http://Fox.nstn.ca:80/~nstn1528/index.html

- PIERCE Family in Mississippi
  http://geocities.com/heartland/cabin/5385
  Descendants of Randall PIERCE (1769-1853) and his wife Mary/Nancy WHATLEY from NC to GA down to Lawrence Co., MS in 1814.

- PIERCE Surname Genealogy SC>GA>TX>
  http://members.nbci.com/ldpierce/
  PIERCE, WILBANKS, ABERCROMBIE, SCOTT, FINLEY, LOTT, FAUS.

- The Descendants of Richard PIERCE
  http://www5.pair.com/vtandrew/pierce/pierce.htm

- Descendants of Arent PIETERS
  http://www.geocities.com/acorpa_nl/
  Paap, Jaane, Jane, Koper, Koning in Zandvoort in the province of Noord-Holland, Netherlands.

- PILCHER Family Roots
  http://www.geocities.com/Heartland/Hills/7046/

- PILGRIM's Landing
  http://www.cyberus.ca/~pmarchan/pilgrim.html

- The PILLERS/PILLARS Family Page
  http://www.gac.edu/~dobler/pillers/
  Information about the surnames PILLERS and PILLARS.

- The PILLOT Family
  http://www.pielou55.freeserve.co.uk
  An old French Huguenot family, its descendants in Ireland and elsewhere bearing the names Pilot, Pielou, Peilow, Pielow .

- PILLOW And Associated Families
  http://www.webspawner.com/users/pillowfamilies/
  Genealogical research of the French Huguenot surname, PILLOW.

- PINE / PYNE Family Connections
  http://pages.tca.net/billpine/index.html
  Descendants of Robert PINE (1765-1849) and his American Posterity. Also Cammack/Cammock, Cottle.

- The PINNEY Surname Resource
  http://www.sunflower.org/~kpinney

- PINSON Chronicles
  http://home1.gte.net/dpinson/PINSON.HTM
  PINSON families world-wide.

- PIPKIN Family Association
  http://www.u.arizona.edu/~freitas/pipkin.html

- PIROWSKI Family History Since Year 1520
  http://perso.club-internet.fr/jadwiga/pirowski

- www.PITCHFORD.org
  http://www.pitchford.org/
  Articles and images related to the history, genealogy, and interests of the world wide PITCHFORD family.

- PITRE Trail
  http://www.m3consortium.co.uk/genealogy/pitre
  PITRE-only descendants of Jean PITRE/Marie PESSELEY; includes early Acadia, rest of Canada, France, Louisiana, Michigan and other areas.

- The PITSENBARGER Family of America
  http://www.calweb.com/~wally/darke/w-pits1.htm

- The PITTELKAU Family Page
  http://www.users.uswest.net/~hpittelkau/
  Pittelkau, Pettelkau, Pittelkow and Peddelkau family - genealogy and geographical history of an old Prussian family.

- PITTMAN Genealogy
  http://members.aol.com/ArletaHowe/Page4.htm
  Descendants of William PITTMAN (1810 Richmond Co., VA) and Mary Ann JOHNSON (1826 Cape Girardeau Co., MO).

- PIXLEY Family Online
  http://www.wavefront.com/~pjlareau/pixleyfo.html

- PLAIN Family Tree
  http://www3.bc.sympatico.ca/PlainFamilyTree/index.html/
  History of the PLAIN family from earliest European roots to their migration to North America and the rest of the world.

- Ancĺtre de tous les PLAMONDON en AmÈrique du nord
  http://www.qbc.clic.net/~mrplam/plamgenf.html

- Association des familles PLANTE inc.
  http://pages.infinit.net/plante/

- PLANTZ Family
  http://www.sensible-net.com/dhoffgr/Plantz.wbg
  Descendants of Johannes Mathies Plantz Family originally of Albany Bush, Montgomery/Fulton County, New York.

- The PLATT Page
  http://users.aol.com/CPlatt1/platt.html

- Généalogie des familles PLOUFFE et PLOOF / Genealogy of the PLOUFFE and PLOOF families
  http://members.xoom.com/jpplouffe/index.html
  Descendants de Jean Blouf, ancêtre des familles PLOUFFE et PLOOF (Descendants of Jean Blouf, ancestor of the PLOUFFE and PLOOF families).

- Descendants of the Rev. William PLOWMAN
  http://homepage.ntlworld.com/stephen.plowman/plowman.htm
  Descendants of the Rev. Plowman of Dorset, England, born c.1647, died 1712.

- The PLUCKROSE Name
  http://www.geocities.com/pluckroses/

- The PLUNKETT Family Genealogy Network. Plunkett History, Plunkett Ancestry, Plunkett Genealogy
  http://www.plunkett.net/

- The POHL Page
  http://members.aol.com/pohlpage
  Descendants of Christian F. Pohl.

- POINDEXTER Descendants Association
  http://www.geocities.com/~poingdestre/
  American descendants of the Poingdestre Family, Isle of Jersey, Channel Islands. George Poingdestre, arrived in the Colony of Virginia in 1657.

- POLLARD Family of VA and KY
  http://members.aol.com/jogt/pollard.htm

- POLLEY Genealogy - Welcome to the World of POLLEY!
  http://members.home.net/rcrandt/polley.htm
  Subtitle: Have you seen my wife's great-great-great-grandfather lately? Descendants of David POLLEY. Family surname site devoted to POLLEY and spelling variants. Reports on contents of former Polley Pointers newsletter available at some libraries.

- Clan POLLOCK
  http://www.tartans.com/clans/Pollock/pollock.html

- POLSTON / POSTON Family
  http://www.geocities.com/Heartland/Valley/2778/
  Database of 11961 individuals mainly of Kentucky. Civil War Records, Family Groups, Family History Journals, Wills, Cemetery Records, and Photos.

- PONTO Family Treehouse
  http://darkwing.uoregon.edu/~rponto/ponto/
  Dedicated to the collection and dissemination of genealogical information about families with the surname of PONTO (PONTOW, PONTOU). Most of these families are of Germanic origin and we are interested in linking as many of them as we possibly can.

- POOCHIGIAN Archives - Family History & Genealogy
  http://www.geocities.com/Heartland/Ridge/6925
  Family history of the Poochigian family who began their migration to America from Peri, Kharpert, Armenia in the 1800's. Includes photo gallery, family tree, feature articles, links and more!

- POPE Family Genealogy Home Page
  http://members.tripod.com/~PopeFamily/index.html
  Census, marriage, land, and other records. Researchers registry, queries, and links to home pages.

- POPIEL / POPEL / POPIL / POPEIL
  http://members.tripod.com/kingpopiel/
  The history of the Clan since 1380 in English and Polish.

- POPLIN Genealogy
  http://www.awod.com/gallery/rwav/lpoplin/

- POPP Family Genealogy Web Page
  http://popp-family.rootsweb.com/

- The POPWELL Family
  http://home.att.net/~dpdklong/Popwell.htm
  The Popwell family, descended from Ruben Poppleweil, first arriving in Alabama in 1828. With links to a four-generation family tree and other related families.

- Pieter AndrÈ de la PORTE Family Home Page
  http://www.adlp.nl/stichting/index.html

- The PORTER Research Site
  http://freepages.genealogy.rootsweb.com/~porters/

- The Olive Tree Genealogy: The New Jersey POST Family
  http://www.rootsweb.com/~ote/post.htm
  Descendants of Adriaen Crijnen POST & Clara (Claartje) MOOCKERS. Adriaen and Clara settled on Staten Island in 1655. By 1665 he was living in Bergen New Jersey and is the ancestor of most NJ POSTs.

- POST Notes
  http://www.halcyondays.com/Post/PostNotes.htm
  Quarterly newsletter dedicated to research on the Post family surname.

- The POTGIETER Genealogy Pages
  http://www.geocities.com/Heartland/Park/7152/
  If you are interested to trace your Potgieter family roots in South Africa, then this is the place for you to start. This site hosts genealogy information, a mailing list, a discussion forum, biographies and history.

- The POTTEN Pages
  http://www.vaugrat.demon.co.uk/

- POTTER Profiles
  http://www.geocities.com/potterfamilyhistory/

- South African Descendants of John POWER
  http://www.geocities.com/Heartland/Pines/5384/Genealogy/
  Descendants of John POWER and Mary NASH who emigrated to South Africa sometime in 1870.

- POWLING Family History
  http://www.geocities.com/TheTropics/Resort/4536/
  A Powling One-Name Study.

- POWNALL / POWNELL Surname Resource Center
  http://www.geocities.com/Heartland/Farm/2182/index.html

- POYNTER Genealogy Network / PGN
  http://www.angelfire.com/in/poynternetwork/

- The POYNTZ Family in India
  http://www.hal-pc.org/~poyntz/india.html
  Selected Extracts from the India Presidencies of Bengal, Bombay and Madras Ecclesiastical Returns of Baptisms, Marriages and Burials 1713-1948.

- Dennis PRANGNELL's Home Page
  http://www.pragndr.demon.co.uk/index.htm
  Prangell, Pragnell.

- PRATER.org
  http://www.prater.org/

- PRATHER Family History Mailing List
  http://www.angelfire.com/in/prather/index.html

- PRATHER / PRATER Genealogy
  http://home1.gte.net/hmartinp/

- **The Ascott Martyrs**
  http://www.geocities.com/Heartland/Plains/6081/
  An Historical Link to the Pratly, Pratley and Prattley Families of New Zealand.

- **The Descendants of Thomas PRATT**
  http://members.aol.com/MShermanL/pratt.html
  Born Abt 1615 London, England, died 1705-1706 Watertown, Massachusetts.

- **PREAS Family Genealogy**
  http://home1.gte.net/jrpreas
  Also PREAST.

- **PREECE Family History - Home Page**
  http://www.preece67.fsnet.co.uk
  PREECE and variants; offers off-line access to large database of PREECE records.

- **PRENTICENet**
  http://www.prenticenet.com/
  Prentiss, Prentis, Prentys, and other variations.

- **PRESLEY-PRESSLEY History Site**
  http://www.presley-pressley.com
  Presley and Pressley families, and all obvious spelling variants (Pressly, Prestly, Presler etc.)

- **PRESTON Genealogy**
  http://cust2.iamerica.net/fpreston/prestong.htm
  Mostly on Prestons of Southwest Virginia but also some in New England, England and Ireland.

- **Eastern Kentucky PRESTONs**
  http://www.freeyellow.com/members6/crosspicker
  Includes DILLS, FAIRCHILDS, CANTELLS and others.

- **The PRETORIUS Website**
  http://members.xoom.com/pretoriusweb/
  Dedicated to the PRETORIUS family. Although the original family-father is from Germany/The Netherlands, PRAETORIUS, any person with the surname PRETORIUS has his/her origin in South Africa.

- **PRETTYMAN.ourfamily.com**
  http://prettyman.ourfamily.com/

- **PREVATT(E) Historical Society**
  http://www.prevatthistory.org/
  Descendants of Pierre PREVATTE of Manakintowne, Virginia and his son Petre PREVATT of New Bern, NC.

- **Descendants and Ancestors of Frank PRIBYL**
  http://members.aol.com//busybusy96/pribdesc.html
  Family came from Moravia and settled in Butler County, Nebraska in 1879.

- **PRICE Information Page**
  http://millennium.fortunecity.com/sherwood/553/price/price.html

- **The PRICE Family Archives**
  http://www2.tscnet.com/pages/lprice/
  Including information on Thomas Price of Wales to Welsh Hills, Ohio 1821 and his family descendants.

- **Zacharia PRICE and Emily WORKMAN PRICE**
  http://freepages.genealogy.rootsweb.com/~jeanne/
  Zacharia born 05-20-1845, Emily born 08-23-1846, married 12-18-1868 Bald Knob, Boone County, West Virginia.

- **PRIDGEN Family Genealogy - PRIDGEN Pages of the Past**
  http://www.geocities.com/Heartland/Meadows/6297
  Site for Pridgen Family trees, Bibles, military info and address for Pridgen Family mailing list on the Internet. This is for the Pridgen Family anywhere, anytime.

- **PRIEST Family Research**
  http://members.aol.com/famlyfndr/priest1.htm

- **PRIESTNALL Family Genealogy**
  http://www.priestnall.org.uk/
  A genealogical study of the Priestnall family (and variations of the surname) in the UK, with emphasis on data collected, including transcripts of parish records, census returns and wills etc.

- **PRIME Time 1275 - 1997 - The PRIME Family History Centre**
  http://www.taunton.demon.co.uk/
  A national and global one name study of the name PRIME.

- **PRIOR Family History Society**
  http://www.vicnet.net.au/~priorfhs/

- **PRISK Genealogy Worldwide**
  http://www.prisk.org/

- **PRISK Worldwide Genealogy**
  http://start.at/prisk

- **PROELL's from Minneapolis, Mn.**
  http://www.familytreemaker.com/users/e/n/f/Lynn-M-Enfield/
  Franz (Frank) Proell, emigrated from Germany about 1885. Also spelled Pral, Prall, Pröll and Porell.

- **Provenzano.org**
  http://www.provenzano.org/
  A website entirely devoted to helping users tracing genealogy concerning the PROVENZANO surname.

- **Descendants of Claude PRUNIER of Malzeville, Meurthe-et-Mozelle, France**
  http://www.geocities.com/Heartland/Plains/1208/Prunier/index.htm
  My great-grandfather, Joseph Peter Prunier (Preney), a descendant of Claude Prunier, left Quebec, Canada sometime between 1862 and 1865 and emigrated to Bath, ME, where he married my great-grandmother and raised a very large family.

- **PUMMILL / PUMMELL Genealogy Web Page**
  http://members.aol.com/tropster/

- **PURCELL Family History Society**
  http://home.iprimus.com.au/nicholaspurcell/pfhs.htm

- **PURCELL Family of America**
  http://www.snowgoosegallery.com/pfa.htm

- PURCHASE Family Genealogies
  http://www.purchase-family.co.uk/
  Genealogical information relating to the surname PURCHASE and its many variants (PURCHES, PURCHASS, etc). Home of the PURCHASE one-name study.

- PURCHASE / PURCHES - Resource Index
  http://www.thinktech.demon.co.uk/genealogy/surnames/purchase/resource.htm
  One name study including these spelling variations: Pirchis, Purchas, Purchase, Purchass, Purches, Purchese, Purchess, Purchis and Purchiss.

- PUTTOCK & PUTTICK one-name study
  http://www.puttockfamily.fsnet.co.uk/

- The PYATT History Homepage
  http://home.istar.ca/~tamman/
  Descendants of James Pyatt - to Canada in the 1860's.

- The PYMAN Family
  http://www.pyman-family.freeserve.co.uk/
  PYMANs everywhere. Links to Australian PYMAN site.

◆ Surname Mailing Lists

- "PAA-PAQ" Surname Mailing Lists
  http://www.rootsweb.com/~jfuller/gen_mail_surnames-paa.html
  PABST, PACE (includes Pacy, Pais, Pase, Pashe), PACELLI, PACK, PACK (includes Packe), PACKARD, PACKER, PACKHAM, PACKWOOD, PACKWOOD, PADDACK, PADDOCK (includes Paddack, Paddick, Padduck, Padock, Padack, Padick, Paduck), PADEN, PADGET, PADGETT, PAGAN, PAGE, PAGEL, PAIGE, PAINE, PIANTANIDA, PAINTER, PAISLEY, PALADINO, PALERMO, PALIN, PALLARDY (includes Palardy, Palardie, Pallardie), PALM, PALMER, PALMERTREE (includes Parmertree, Parmyntree), PALUMBO, PANCOAST, PANGBURN, PANKEY, PANKRATZ, PANNEBECKER (includes Pennybacker, Pennybaker, Pennebaker, Pfannebakker, Pennypacker, Pannebaker,, Panebaker, Panebecker, Pannabecker, Pannebecker), PANNELL, PANTOZZI (includes Pannozzo, Pannozzi, Fantozzi), PAOLINO, PAPE, PAPINEAU (includes Testard, Tetard, Testard de Follville, Fortville, Forville, Testard de Folleville dit Papineau,, Popenoe), PAPKE, PAQUETTE, PAQUIN.

- "PAR-PAR" Surname Mailing Lists
  http://www.rootsweb.com/~jfuller/gen_mail_surnames-par.html
  PARADIS, PARAMORE, PARCHER, PARDEE, PARDO, PARDUE (includes Perdue), PARDY, PARE, PAREDES (includes Paredez), PARENT, PARENTE, PARENTEAU, PARHAM (includes Paaram), PARIS, PARISH (includes Parrish, Paris, Parys, Pary), PARK, PARKE, PARKE, PARKER, PARKER, PARKERSON (includes Parkinson, Parkison), PARKES, PARKHURST, PARKIN, PARKINS, PARKINSON, PARKMAN, PARKS (includes Park, Parke, Parkes), PARKS (includes Parke), PARLE (includes Pearl, Parrill, Perrell), PARLIER, PARMAN (includes Parmin, Parmon, Perman, Permon, Permin), PARMELEE, PARMENTER, PARMENTIER, PARMER, PARNELL, PARR (includes Paar), PARRACK (includes Parrick, Parrock, Parack, Parick, Parock), PARRENT (includes Parent), PARRETT, PARRIOTT (includes Parriot, Pariot, Parrot), PARRIS, PARRISH, PARRISH, PARROTT, PARRY, PARSHALL, PARSHALL, PARSLEY, PARSLOW, PARSON, PARSONAGE (includes Personage, Parsonidge, Parsnidge), PARSONS, PARTAIN,

PARTEE (includes Pardee), PARTEN, PARTIN, PARTLOW, PARTON, PARTRIDGE.

- "PAS-PD" Surname Mailing Lists
  http://www.rootsweb.com/~jfuller/gen_mail_surnames-pas.html
  PASCH, PASCHAL, PASCOE, PASHLEY, PASLEY, PASS (includes Pas, Passe, Pace), PASSAGE, PASSAILAIGUE (includes Passailaique, Passailaigne), PASSER, PASSMORE, PASTEUR (includes Pfarrer), PASZKIEWICZ, PATCH, PATE (includes Pait, Payte, Pates), PATENAUDE (includes Patnode, Patnoe, Paternostre, Patno), PATERSON, PATNODE, PATON, PATRICK (includes Patrik, Patric, Patricks), PATTON (includes Patten, Payton), PATTEN, PATTERSON (includes Peterson, Patrickson, Paterson, Batterson), PATTERSON, PATTILLO, PATTISON, PATTULLO (includes Pattillo), PATTY, PATZER, PATZKOWSKI (includes Pasckowski, Paszkowski, Patzkowsky, Paczkoswki, Pacskowski), PAUBEL (includes Poubel, Pobel), PAUGH, PAUL (includes Paull, Paule), PAULEY (includes Pawley, Polly), PAULEY, PAULIN, PAULK, PAULL, PAULLIN, PAULSEN, PAULSON, PAULUS, PAVEY, PAVY, PAWLEY, PAWLOWSKI, PAXSON, PAXTON, PAXTON, PAYANT (includes Payan), PAYNE (includes Paine, Payn), PAYNE (includes Paine), PAYNE (includes Paine, Payn, Pain, Payen, Paien, Pagan, Pyne, Paynell), PAYNTER, PAYTON, PAZICS (includes Pazich, Pazicks).

- "PEA-PED" Surname Mailing Lists
  http://www.rootsweb.com/~jfuller/gen_mail_surnames-pea.html
  PEABODY, PEACE, PEACH, PEACH (includes Peachy, Peachey, Peck, Peckham), PEACHEY, PEACOCK, PEAK, PEAKE, PEALE (includes Peal), PEARCE (includes Piers, Pierce, Peirce, Peers), PEARL, PEARMAN, PEARS, PEARSALL (includes Parshall, Peirsol), PEARSE, PEARSON, PEARSON (includes Peeresonne), PEARSON, PEART, PEASE, PEASLEY, PEAVEY, PEAVLER (includes Peveler, Peevler, Peavley, Peevley, Pevley), PEAVY, PEAY, PEBSWORTH (includes Pebworth), PECH, PECK, PECKHAM, PEDDICORD (includes Peddycoard, Petticoat, Peddycort), PEDEN (includes Paden, Peeden), PEDERSEN, PEDERSON, PEDIGO (includes Peregoy, Perrigo, Perigo, Petigo, Petticoat), PEDLEY (includes Pedly), PEDNEAU (includes Pedno, Pednio, Pednow, Pednaw, Pedneaw), PEDRON.

- "PEE-PEH" Surname Mailing Lists
  http://www.rootsweb.com/~jfuller/gen_mail_surnames-pee.html
  PEEBLES, PEEK, PEEL, PEEL, PEELE (includes Peelle, Peel, Peal), PEELER, PEEPLES, PEER (includes LaPeer, Peers), PEERY, PEERY, PEET, PEFFLEY (includes Peffly, Peffle, Pefley, Pefly), PEGG, PEGLEY.

- "PEI-PEN" Surname Mailing Lists
  http://www.rootsweb.com/~jfuller/gen_mail_surnames-pei.html
  PEIFFER, PEIL, PEILL, PEIRCE, PEKAR, PELC (includes Peltz), PELHAM, PELKEY, PELL, PELL, PELLEGRINI, PELLERIN, PELLETIER, PELS (includes Pel, Pelles, Pells, Pelz, Pelzz, Pultz), PELTIER, PELTON, PEMBERTON, PENCE (includes Pentz, Pense, Bentz), PENDARVIS, PENDER, PENDERGAST, PENDERGRASS, PENDEXTER, PENDLETON, PENDLEY, PENDRY, PENIX (includes Pennock, Penick, Pinnex, Pinex, Phenix), PENLAND (includes Penlan, Penlin, Pendland, Pendlum), PENLEY, PENMAN, PENN, PENNELL, PENNEY, PENNEY, PENNIMAN, PENNINGTON (includes Peninton, Penitone, Pennton, Piniton, Penistone, Peddington, Penninton), PENNINGTON, PENNOCK, PENNOYER (includes Penoyer,

Pennoire), PENNY *(includes Penney, Pennay)*, PENROD, PENROSE, PENTECOST.

● **"PEO-PEZ" Surname Mailing Lists**
http://www.rootsweb.com/-jfuller/gen_mail_surnames-peo.html
PEOPLES, PEPIN, PEPPER, PERAZZO, PERCIABOSCO, PERCIFIELD, PERCIVAL, PERCY, PERDUE, PEREIRA, PEREZ, PERFECT, PERHAMUS, PERILLOUX (includes Perioux, Periou, Perrilloux, Perriloux, Perrillioux), PERKEY, PERKINS, PERKINSON, PERL, PERLEY (includes Pearley, Pearly, Perly, Parly, Parley, Pearlee), PERRAULT, PERRIGO, PERRIN, PERRINE, PERRY (includes Parrie), PERRYMAN (includes Periman, Perriman), PERSING, PERSINGER, PERSINGER, PERSON, PERSONS, PERSSON, PETEFISH (includes Biedefisch, Bütefisch, Peterfish), PETER, PETERMAN, PETERS (includes Peter, Peterson), PETERSEN, PETERSON, PETERSON, PETERSSEN (includes Peterzen), PETERSSON, PETIT, PETREE, PETREY (includes Petry, Pettry, Petrie, Pettrie, Petre, Pettre, Petree, Pettrey), PETRI, PETRIE, PETRIE (includes Pettrie, Petry), PETRO, PETRY, PETTENGILL (includes Pettingell, Pettingill, Pettengall, Pettengale), PETTETT, PETTEY, PETTIBONE, PETTIGREW (includes Peticru, Petticrew, Bettigrew), PETTIS, PETTIT, PETTIT, PETTUS (includes Pettis), PETTUS, PETTY, PETTYJOHN (includes Pettijohn), PETTYPOOL, PETZ, PETZOLT (includes Petzold, Petzoldt, Paetzolt, Paetzold, Paetzoldt, von Petzolt), PEUGH, PEVEHOUSE (includes Peaveyhouse, Peveyhouse, Peveehouse), PEW, PEYER, PEYTON.

● **"PF-PH" Surname Mailing Lists**
http://www.rootsweb.com/~jfuller/gen_mail_surnames-pf.html
PFAFF, PFAU, PFAUTZ, PFEFFER, PFEIFER (includes Pfeiffer), PFEIFFER, PFEIFLE (includes Pfiefle, Peffly, Peffley, Pefley, Piffle, Pfafle, Paffele), PFISTER (includes Pfisterer), PFLIEGER, PFOUTS (includes Pfautz, Pfoutz, Fouts, Foutz), PHALEN, PHARES, PHARR, PHAY, PHELAN (includes Phalen, Phalon, Pheland, Felan), PHELPS, PHELPS, PHENIX (includes Fenix, Feeneys, Phoenix, Penninck, Fenwick, Pfennigs, Fenex), PHIFER (includes Fifer, Fiffer, Phiffer, Pfeiffer, Pfeifer), PHILBIN, PHILBRICK (includes Philbricke, Philbreck, Philbrook, Fillbrick, Felbrigg, Fylbrigg), PHILIPPI, PHILIPS, PHILLIPPI, PHILLIPS (includes Philips, Philipps), PHILLIPS (includes Philips), PHILPOT, PHILPOTT (includes Philpot), PHILPOTT, PHINNEY, PHIPPEN, PHIPPS (includes Phips, Fipps), PHOENIX.

● **"PI-PN" Surname Mailing Lists**
http://www.rootsweb.com/~jfuller/gen_mail_surnames-pi.html
PIATT (includes Pyeatt, Pyott, Piat, Pyatt), PIBWORTH (includes Pebworth, Pepworth), PICARD (includes Piccard, Pickard, Destroismaisons dit Picard), PICHELOUP, PICKARD, PICKEL, PICKENPAUGH, PICKENS, PICKERILL, PICKERIN, PICKERING, PICKETT, PICKLE, PICKLES, PICKRELL, PICKREN, PICKUP, PICOU, PIDGEON, PIECHOROWSKI (includes Piechurowski), PIEPER, PIERCE (includes Pearse, Pearce, Peirce, Pers, Percy), PIERCY, PIERPONT, PIERSON (includes Pearson, Peirson), PIERZCHALSKI (includes Pierz), PIETERS, PIFER, PIGG, PIGGIN, PIGGOTT, PIGOTT (includes Piggott, Pygott, Pigate), PIGRAM, PIKE, PILCH, PILCHER, PILE, PILES, PILETTE, PILGER, PILGRIM (includes Pillgrim, Pilgram, Pilgrem, Pilgrum), PILKINGTON, PILLOT, PILLSBURY, PIMENTEL, PINARD, PINCKNEY, PINDER, PINE, PINE, PINEGAR, PINER, PING, PINION, PINKERTON, PINKHAM, PINKLEY, PINKMAN, PINKNEY, PINKSTON, PINNECKER (includes Peanecker, Pinager, Penicah, Pinacker), PINNELL, PINNEY, PINSON (includes Penson), PINT (includes Pinte, Pihnt), PINTER (includes Pintr), PIPE, PIPER, PIPES, PIPKIN, PIPPEN,

PIPPIN (includes Pippen, Pepin, Papin, Pappin), PIRIE, PIRKLE (includes Birkel, Berkel, Pirtle), PIRRONE, PIRTLE, PIRZ, PISCOPO, PITCHER, PITCHFORD, PITCOCK (includes Pidcock, Pitcox, Pittcock), PITKIN, PITMAN, PITRE, PITRE (includes Peter, Peters, Peets), PITSENBARGER (includes Pitzenberger), PITT, PITTELKOW, PITTENGER, PITTMAN (includes Pitman, Pitmon, Pyttman, Pickman, Pyteman, Peatman, Putman, Pettman), PITTROFF (includes Pitroff), PITTS, PITTSLEY (includes Pixley, Pitts, Pigsley), PITZEN, PITZER, PIXLER, PIXLER (includes Bixler), PIXLEY, PLACE (includes Plaise, Pleas, de la Place), PLANK, PLANT, PLANTAGENET, PLANTE, PLANTENER, PLANTZ (includes Plant, Plants), PLASTER (includes Plasters, Plasterer), PLATA, PLATE, PLATT, PLATT, PLATZ, PLAXTON, PLAYER, PLAZIER, PLEASANT, PLEASANTS, PLEBUCH, PLEDGER, PLESS, PLETCHER, PLETSCH (includes Pletch), PLIMPTON (includes Plymptom, Plimton), PLOTNER, PLOTT, PLOUF, PLOWMAN (includes Ploughman), PLOWS, PLUHATOR, PLUMB (includes Plume, Plumbe), PLUMLEE, PLUMMER (includes Plumer), PLUMPTON (includes Plumton), PLUMRIDGE, PLUNK, PLUNKETT, PLY.

● **"PO-PQ" Surname Mailing Lists**
http://www.rootsweb.com/~jfuller/gen_mail_surnames-po.html
POAGE, POARCH (includes Porch), POBJOY (includes Popjoy, Popejoy, Pobje, Popinjay), POCOCK, PODESTA, PODMORE, POE, POFF, POGUE, POHL, POIDEVIN, POINDEXTER, POINER, POINSETT, POINTER, POIRIER, POLAND, POLE, POLEN, POLHEMUS, POLHEMUS (includes Polhemius, Polhamus, Paulhamus, Pulhamus, Perhamus, Hamous), POLING (includes Poland, Polen), POLK (includes Pogue, Pollack, Pollock), POLL, POLLARD, POLLEY (includes Polly), POLLEY, POLLITT, POLLOCK, POLLY, POLSON, POLSTON (includes Poulson, Polson, Poston), POMEROY, POMRANING (includes Pommeraning), PONCY, POND, PONDER (includes Pounder, Pounders, Pinder, Pender, Pynder), PONIATOWSKI, PONTIUS, PONTO, PONTON, PONTUS, POOL, POOLE (includes Pool, Pettypool, Pettypoole, Van Pool, Van Poole), POOLEY, POOR, POORE, POORMAN, POPE, POPEJOY, POPHAM, POPLIN, POPP, POPWELL (includes Poppleweil, Popplewell), PORCH, PORTALES, PORTEOUS, PORTER, PORTERFIELD (includes Potterfield, Porteous, Borderfield, Porter), PORTWINE (includes Potvin), PORTWOOD, POSEY, POSS, POST, POSTON, POTEET, POTTEIGER (includes Pottergher), POTTER, POTTS (includes Philpott, MacKillop, Pott, Pot, Potter, Botts, Bott, Bot), POTVIN, POULIN, POULSEN, POULSON, POULTER, POULTON, POUNCEY, POUND, POUND, POUNDS, POVEY, POWE, POWELL, POWELL, POWELL, POWER, POWERS (includes Power, Bowers, Poors, Poore, Bauers), POWNALL (includes Pownell), POWNELL (includes Pownall), POWSON (includes Pouson, Powsons, Powsonne, Powsson, Pousson, Poucin, Pousin, Poussin), POYNER, POYNTER, POYNTZ (includes Poynts, Points, Poynes), POYTHRESS.

● **"PR-PT" Surname Mailing Lists**
http://www.rootsweb.com/~jfuller/gen_mail_surnames-pr.html
PRAA, PRAGER, PRAGER, PRATER, PRATHER (includes Prater, Prayter, Praytor, Prator), PRATT, PRAY, PREADMORE (includes Predmore, Pridemore, Pridmore, Prigmore), PREBLE, PRECIADO, PREECE, PREIZEL, PRENCE, PRENDERGAST, PRENTICE, PRENTISS, PRESBURY (includes Presbry, Presby, Presson, Preston), PRESCOTT, PRESLAR, PRESLEY (includes Pressley, Pressler, Preslar), PRESLEY (includes Pressley), PRESNELL, PRESS, PRESSGROVE (includes Presgrove, Presgrave, Pressgrave, Presgraves), PRESSLER, PRESSLEY, PRESTON, PRESTRIDGE (includes Prestage), PREVO (includes Privo), PREVOST, PREWITT, PRIBBLE, PRIBIL, PRICE (includes Pryce),

PRICHARD (includes Pritchard), PRICKETT, PRIDDY, PRIDE, PRIDE, PRIDEAUX, PRIDEMORE, PRIDGEN, PRIDGEON, PRIDMORE, PRIEBE, PRIEST, PRIESTLEY, PRIFOGLE (includes Pryfogle, Pryfogel, Prifogel, Breyfogle, Breyvogel), PRIGGE (includes Prich), PRIKRYL, PRIME, PRIMM, PRINCE (includes Printz, Prinns), PRINCIOTTA, PRINDLE, PRINE, PRINGLE, PRINS, PRIOR, PRISOCK, PRITCHARD, PRITCHETT, PRIVETT, PROBASCO, PROBST, PROCHNOW, PROCK, PROCTER, PROCTOR (includes Procter, Prochtor, Prochter), PROFAZI, PROFFITT (includes Proffit, Profitt, Profit, Prophet), PROFITT, PRONDZINSKI, PROOS, PROPER, PROPST, PROSSER, PROTIVINSKY, PROUDFOOT, PROUDLOCK, PROULX, PROUT, PROUTY, PROVENCHER, PROVOST, PROWSE (includes Prouz, Prose, Prouse, Prouze), PRUDDEN, PRUETT, PRUITT (includes Prewitt, Prewet, Pruit, Prout, Pratt), PRYE, PRYOR (includes Prior, Prier, Pryer, Pryar), PRYOR.

- "PU-PZ" Surname Mailing Lists
  http://www.rootsweb.com/~jfuller/gen_mail_surnames-pu.html
  PUCEL, PUCKERIDGE, PUCKETT, PUFFER, PUGH, PUGH, PUJOL (includes Pujola), PULIS, PULLEN (includes Pullin, Pullan, Pullein), PULLEY, PULLIAM, PULLIG, PULLIN, PULVER, PUMPHREY, PUPULIN, PURCELL, PURCHASE, PURDOM, PURDON, PURDUE, PURDY (includes Purdey, Purdee, Purdon, Purdie), PURFURST (includes Purfuerst, Purfeerst, Purfürst), PURGET (includes Purgit, Purgitt, Purgat), PURINTUN, PURKEY, PURNELL, PURPLE, PURPLE (includes Purpill, Purplel), PURSELL, PURSLEY (includes Presley, Purcell, Pursell, Purselley), PURVES, PURVIANCE (includes Perviance, Pervines, Purvines, Purveance), PURVIS, PURYEAR, PUSEY, PUSHEE (includes Pushie, Poucie), PUTMAN, PUTNAM, PUTT, PUTZ (includes Puc), PYATT, PYE, PYLE (includes Pyles, Pile, Piles, Pihl, Pials), PYLES, PYNE, PYRON (includes Peron, Peronne, Perron, Piran, Pirent, Pierent, Pryon, Pyrain, Pyram, Pyrant, Pyrom, Pyront,, Pyrum, Pyrun).

SURNAMES, FAMILY ASSOCIATIONS & FAMILY NEWSLETTERS – "Q"

Resources Dedicated to One Surname
http://www.cyndislist.com/surn-q.htm

Category Index:

◆ General Surname Sites and Resources

◆ Surname Specific Sites and Resources

◆ Surname Mailing Lists

◆ General Surname Sites and Resources

- Connect with Surnames - Q
  http://www.geocities.com/Heartland/Bluffs/7708/q.html

- Dutch Home Pages by Familyname ~ Letter Q
  http://members.tripod.com/~Don_Arnoldus/q.htm

- FamilyHistory.com - Message Boards - Surname - Q
  http://www.familyhistory.com/messages/list.asp?prefix=QA

- Family Tree Maker Online User Home Pages - Q
  http://www.familytreemaker.com/users/q/index.html

- Family Workings Q Surname Links
  http://www.familyworkings.com/links/surq.htm

- GenConnect Surname Index - "Q"
  http://genconnect.rootsweb.com/indx/surnames/Q.html
  Message boards sponsored by RootsWeb. Each surname message board set is divided into the following topics: Queries, Bibles, Biographies, Deeds, Obituaries, Pensions, Wills.

- Genealogy Resources on the Internet - "Q" Surname Mailing Lists
  http://www.rootsweb.com/~jfuller/gen_mail_surnames-q.html
  Search the index of surname mailing lists below: Surname Mailing Lists.

  o Genealogy Resources on the Internet - Surnames Included in Mailing Lists - "Q"
    http://www-personal.umich.edu/~cgaunt/surnames/q.names.html
    This is a computer generated list of the surnames, and all variant spellings for those names, that are found in the surname mailing lists detailed on the pages shown above.

- Genealogy Resources on the Internet - Surname Web Sites for "Q,R" Surnames
  http://www-personal.umich.edu/~cgaunt/surnames/qr.html

- Genealogy's Most Wanted - Surnames Beginning with "Q"
  http://www.citynet.net/mostwanted/q.htm

- Google Web Directory .... Genealogy>Surnames>Q
  http://directory.google.com/Top/Society/Genealogy/Surnames/Q/

- Heartland Genealogy Society Membership List - Q
  http://www.geocities.com/Heartland/Ranch/2416/hgs-mlist-q.html

- H-GIG Surname Registry - Surnames Beginning Q
  http://www.ucr.edu/h-gig/surdata/surname17.html

- Higginson Book Company - Surnames Beginning with Q
  http://www.higginsonbooks.com/q.htm

- inGeneas Table of Common Surname Variations and Surname Misspellings - N-Q
  http://www.ingeneas.com/N2Q.html

- The Obituary Link Page - Family Obituary Archives Online - Q-R
  http://www.geocities.com/~cribbswh/obit/q-r.htm

- Open Directory - Society: Genealogy: Surnames: Q
  http://www.dmoz.org/Society/Genealogy/Surnames/Q/

- 'Q' Surnames at RootsWeb
  http://resources.rootsweb.com/surnames/q.html

- Surname Springboard Index - Q
  http://www.geocities.com/~alacy/spring_q.htm

- SurnameWeb Surname Registry - Q Index
  http://www.surnameweb.org/registry/q.htm

- SWINX Zoeklijst Nederlandse Familienamen / SWINX Searchlist Dutch Surnames - Q
  http://www.swinx.net/swinx/swinx_q_nl.htm

- Websites at RootsWeb: Q Surnames
  http://www.rootsweb.com/~websites/surnames/q.html

◆ Surname Specific Sites and Resources

- QUAID Families Clearing House
  http://www.pclink.com/kg0ay/quaidclr.htm

- QUAITE Family Association - Clan Farquharson
  http://clanhuston.com/quaite.htm

- QUANTRILL or QUANTRELL Family
  http://www.homesuitehomes.com/hobbies/genes/quantrill.htm

- QUARLES Genealogical Site
  http://members.tripod.com/~melissawells/quarleshome.htm
  Site for the Surname QUALLS/QUARLES.

- QUARTERMAN Family History Project
  http://www.quarterman.org/

- QUEBEDEAUX Quest
  http://members.tripod.com/~quebquest/index.html
  QUEBEDEAUX, QUEBEDEAU, QUIBODEAUX, KIBODEAUX.

- QUEEN Family Genealogy
  http://www.geocities.com/Heartland/Bluffs/5932/queen.html
  This site is dedicated to the QUEEN surname including links to QUEEN GenConnect boards, QUEEN Mailing List (Rootsweb) and our family.

- QUENNEVILLE Family History
  http://www.geocities.com/Paris/LeftBank/4595/
  Quenneville, Quenville, Quinville, Kenville.

- QUICKSALL Family Genealogy Home Page
  http://www.effingham.net/quicksall/genealogy/main.htm
  Official web site for the Quicksall Family at-large. This growing site has the eventual goal of linking all Quicksalls in the USA into one family tree.

- QUINANE Genealogy Home Page
  http://www.tip.net.au/~ivecm/hist.htm
  Home Page of the Quinane's from Tipperary, Ireland who emigrated to Australia between 1850 and 1880.

- QUINN QUARTERLY Newsletter
  http://www.users.uswest.net/~ottino/newslett.htm

- Homepage der Stammlinienforschung QUIRING
  http://members.tripod.de/jpquiring/
  QUIRING, QUERING in West- and East-Prussia, Russia, Ukraine and their Mennonite ancestors; katholic QUIRING in Banat and Batschka.

- QUISENBERRY Chat
  http://forums.delphi.com/preview/main.asp?sigdir=Quisenberry
  Quisenberry, Quesenberry, Quiesenberry, Cushingberry.

- QUISTORF Family Name
  http://www.angelfire.com/wa2/quistorf/
  History, origins and links to the surname Quistorf / Quistorff / von Quistorp and variations. Including lineage of Werhner von Braun, NASA Rocket Scientist.

- QUITTENTON Genealogy Page
  http://website.lineone.net/~heathq/Ft/Quittenton.htm
  Including the descendants of James QUITTENTON.

◆ Surname Mailing Lists

- "Q" Surname Mailing Lists
  http://www.rootsweb.com/~jfuller/gen_mail_surnames-q.html
  QUACKENBUSH (includes Quackenbos, Quackenbosch, Quackenbusch, Quocumbos), QUAIN (includes Kwain, Kwane, Qwain, Qwane), QUALLS (includes Quarles), QUARLES, QUARTERMAN (includes Quartermaine), QUARVE (includes Kuarv, Kuarve,Qwarv, Qwarve), QUAST, QUATTELBAUM, QUATTLEBAUM, QUATTRONE (includes Quatrone), QUAYLE, QUEBEDEAU, QUEBEDEAUX (includes Quebedeau, Quevedo), QUEEN, QUESENBERRY, QUESTED (includes Questead, Questid), QUETON (includes Kweton, Kweeton, Qweton, Qwueton), QUICK, QUICKEL, QUIGG (includes Kwig, Kwigg, Qwig, Qwigg), QUIGGLE, QUIGLEY, QUILLEN, QUILLIAN (includes Quilliam, Quillan, Quillen, Quillin, MacQuillian, McQuillen, McQuillin, McQuillan), QUILLIN, QUIMBY, QUINET (includes Quinnett, Quinnet, Quinett, Quinne), QUINLAN, QUINLEY (includes Quinlee), QUINN (includes O'Quinn), QUINONES (includes Qonones, Quononess, Quononest, Qwonones, Qwononis), QUINTIER (includes Quinteir), QUINTON, QUINTRELL, QUIRAM (includes Quirandt, Quirant, Quirin, Quiring, Queram, Kwiram, Kweram, Kwirandt, Kwirant, Chwiram), QUIRK, QUISENBERRY, QUIZENBEURY (includes Quizenberry, Quizenbuery).

SURNAMES, FAMILY ASSOCIATIONS & FAMILY NEWSLETTERS – "R"

Resources Dedicated to One Surname
http://www.cyndislist.com/surn-r.htm

Category Index:

◆ General Surname Sites and Resources
◆ Surname Specific Sites and Resources

◆ Surname Mailing Lists

◆ General Surname Sites and Resources

- Connect with Surnames - R
  http://www.geocities.com/Heartland/Bluffs/7708/r.html

- Dutch Home Pages by Familyname ~ Letter R
  http://members.tripod.com/~Don_Arnoldus/r.htm

- FamilyHistory.com - Message Boards - Surname - R
  http://www.familyhistory.com/messages/list.asp?prefix=RA

- Family Tree Maker Online User Home Pages - R
  http://www.familytreemaker.com/users/r/index.html

- Family Workings R Surname Links
  http://www.familyworkings.com/links/surr.htm

- GenConnect Surname Index - "R"
  http://genconnect.rootsweb.com/indx/surnames/R.html
  Message boards sponsored by RootsWeb. Each surname message board set is divided into the following topics: Queries, Bibles, Biographies, Deeds, Obituaries, Pensions, Wills.

- Genealogy Resources on the Internet - "RA-RD" Surname Mailing Lists
  http://www.rootsweb.com/~jfuller/gen_mail_surnames-ra.html
  "REA-REH"
  http://www.rootsweb.com/~jfuller/gen_mail_surnames-rea.html
  "REI-REO"
  http://www.rootsweb.com/~jfuller/gen_mail_surnames-rei.html
  "REP-RH"
  http://www.rootsweb.com/~jfuller/gen_mail_surnames-rep.html
  "RI-RN"
  http://www.rootsweb.com/~jfuller/gen_mail_surnames-ri.html
  "ROA-ROD"
  http://www.rootsweb.com/~jfuller/gen_mail_surnames-roa.html
  "ROE-ROH"
  http://www.rootsweb.com/~jfuller/gen_mail_surnames-roe.html
  "ROI-RON"
  http://www.rootsweb.com/~jfuller/gen_mail_surnames-roi.html
  "ROO-ROT"
  http://www.rootsweb.com/~jfuller/gen_mail_surnames-roo.html
  "ROU-RT"
  http://www.rootsweb.com/~jfuller/gen_mail_surnames-rou.html
  "RU-RZ"
  http://www.rootsweb.com/~jfuller/gen_mail_surnames-ru.html
  Search the index of surname mailing lists below: Surname Mailing Lists.

  o Genealogy Resources on the Internet - Surnames Included in Mailing Lists - "R"
    http://www-personal.umich.edu/~cgaunt/surnames/r.names.html
    This is a computer generated list of the surnames, and all variant spellings for those names, that are found in the surname mailing lists detailed on the pages shown above.

- Genealogy Resources on the Internet - Surname Web Sites for "Q,R" Surnames
  http://www-personal.umich.edu/~cgaunt/surnames/qr.html

- Genealogy's Most Wanted - Surnames Beginning with "R"
  http://www.citynet.net/mostwanted/r.htm

- Google Web Directory .... Genealogy>Surnames>R
  http://directory.google.com/Top/Society/Genealogy/Surnames/R/

- Heartland Genealogy Society Membership List - R
  http://www.geocities.com/Heartland/Ranch/2416/hgs-mlist-r.html

- H-GIG Surname Registry - Surnames Beginning R
  http://www.ucr.edu/h-gig/surdata/surname18.html

- Higginson Book Company - Surnames Beginning with R
  http://www.higginsonbooks.com/r.htm

- inGeneas Table of Common Surname Variations and Surname Misspellings - R-S
  http://www.ingeneas.com/R2S.html

- The Obituary Link Page - Family Obituary Archives Online - Q-R
  http://www.geocities.com/~cribbswh/obit/q-r.htm

- Open Directory - Society: Genealogy: Surnames: R
  http://www.dmoz.org/Society/Genealogy/Surnames/R/

- 'R' Surnames at RootsWeb
  http://resources.rootsweb.com/surnames/r.html

- Surname Springboard Index - R
  http://www.geocities.com/~alacy/spring_r.htm

- SurnameWeb Surname Registry - R Index
  http://www.surnameweb.org/registry/r.htm

- SWINX Zoeklijst Nederlandse Familienamen /
  SWINX Searchlist Dutch Surnames - R
  http://www.swinx.net/swinx/swinx_ra_nl.htm

- Websites at RootsWeb: R Surnames
  http://www.rootsweb.com/~websites/surnames/r.html

◆ Surname Specific Sites and Resources

- Genealogy: RABE & RAABE Family History
  http://pages.hotbot.com/family/dcarls02/rabe.html

- RADCLIFF Homepage
  http://www.geocities.com/heartland/village/8251
  *Other family surnames featured are HUGHES, CARTWRIGHT,
  ROBINSON. Countries involved are Quebec, Canada, New York
  State, USA, Staffordshire and Warwickshire, England, and County
  Down, Ireland.*

- RADER Genealogy Home Page
  http://www.rader.org
  Rader, Reader, Raeder, Roder, Roeder, Rotter.

- RADFORD Genealogy Homepage
  http://www.ozemail.com.au/~rampant/
  RADFORD Surname Resource Center.

- RADLOFFs in CyberSpace
  http://www.loudoun-net.com/rad/default.htm

- RAGSDALE Genealogy
  http://members.aol.com/ArletaHowe/Page6.htm
  *Descendants of Obediah RAGSDALE (ca 1768 Pittsylvania Co., VA,
  grandson of Benjamin RAGSDALE, Sr. and Martha JONES) and
  Elizabeth ANDERSON, daughter of Charles & Lucy (STOKES)
  ANDERSON.*

- RAINBOW
  http://www.geocities.com/RainForest/Andes/9897/index.html

- RAINEY Times
  http://www2.1starnet.com/mbryant/rainey.htm
  *Surname publication with records on family spellings including
  RANEY, RAINY, REANEY, RENNIE, RANNY, RANY, etc.*

- RAMBIN Family: Colonial Louisiana Pioneers
  http://www.angelfire.com/or/rambin

- The RAMBO Family Tree
  http://members.aol.com/rsbeatty/rambo.htm
  *Includes surnames: BANKSTON, MATTSON, NORTH and dozens of
  other lines.*

- Descendants of James RAMPLEY
  http://csc.techcenter.org/~mneill/jamesramp.html

- RAMSDALE Family Register
  http://www.ramsdale.org/2homepag.htm
  Ramsdall, Ramsdal, Ramsdell, Ramsdill and Ramsdaille.

- RAMSDELL Genealogical Archive
  http://www5.pair.com/vtandrew/ramsdell/archive.htm
  *Ramsdell, Ramsdale, Ramsden, Ramsdall, Ramsdill, Ramsdal and
  Ramsdel.*

- RAMSEY Researchers
  http://www.geocities.com/Heartland/Plains/1717/ram.htm

- The RANGER Family History Home Page
  http://www.familytreemaker.com/users/r/a/n/R-D-
  Ranger/index.html
  Descendants of Amos Ranger, born April 1766.

- RANGNOW Family Tree
  http://members.tripod.com/~rangnow_familytree/
  *The RANGNOWs were a family with thirteen children who came to
  the US From Prussia in the late 1800's. All present RANGNOWs in
  the US are descendants of that original family.*

- RANSOM Family Genealogy
  http://www.peak.org/~mransom/ransom.html
  Ransom / Ransome and Ranson / Ransone resources.

- RANDLE Family Genealogy Homepage
  http://members.aol.com/eleanorcol/Homepage.html
  *Descendants of James and Roseanna GRAVES RANDLE. Related
  families are Graves, Coffee, McGehee, Lamar, Jordan, Bayne.*

- RANKE Family Genealogy Site
  http://users.vvi.net/charles8/index.html
  *Descendants of Charles RANKE, Jr. and Barbara Catherine
  SCHNEIDER, from Germany to Hamilton, Ohio.*

- RAPER-RAPIER Family Home Page
  http://www.cdepot.net/raper/
  *RAPER/RAPIER surname clearinghouse with emphasis on
  descendants of William RAPER born 1725 in England, died 1795 in
  North Carolina.*

- RARDIN Family Info Center
  http://freepages.genealogy.rootsweb.com/~rardin
  *Descendents of John RARDIN/REARDON, an Irish immigrant who
  settled on the western Pennsylvania frontier. His seven known
  children are Thomas, John, William, Timothy, Moses, Jacob and
  Nellie.*

- The RATCLIFF Family Tree
  http://don.ratcliff.net/tree/
  Ratcliff, Ratliff, Radcliff.

- The RATHBONE Register
  http://www.stanford.edu/~dorcas/Rathbone.html
  *The largest one-name study of the surname RATHBONE and its
  variations, Including - Rathborn(e), Rathbourn(e), Rathburn(e),
  Rabon(e) Rathbond, Rathban(d) etc.*

- RATHBUN - RATHBONE - RATHBURN Family
  Historian
  http://hometown.aol.com/rathcrest/RATHBUN/index.html
  *Descendants of John and Margaret (Acres) Rathbone of County
  Lancashire, England and Block Island, Rhode Island Settled in USA
  about 1654 to Block Island in 1661.*

- **RAWLS.net**
  http://www.rawls.net/
  RAWLS History Descendents of Johannes RALL of Lexington, SC. Also: Ralls, Rhal, Price, Gartman, Bernhard, Sims, Gamadanis.

- **RAWSON Family Association History and Genealogy**
  http://www.rawsonfamily.org/

- **RAYMENT Family History**
  http://members.tripod.com/~Peter_Nelms/Rayment.html
  RAYMENT in England and Australia.

- **Andrew Marion RAY**
  http://members.aol.com/gaatlanta/
  Descendants of Andrew Marion RAY of Hart County, GA. JONES, BERRYMAN, THOMPSON, MOORE.

- **REAVIS Family of Vance County, NC**
  http://www.angelfire.com/nc/yourday/reavis.html
  Descendants of Samuel REAVUS who relocated in Vance County, NC, and a special tribute to REAVIS Confederate soldiers.

- **REBBECK One Name Study, Newsletter**
  mailto:RayjudyW@aol.com
  For details send e-mail to Judy Rebbeck Watten at RayjudyW@aol.com.

- **REBER Genealogy**
  http://family.reber.org/

- **RECORD One Name Study**
  http://www7.50megs.com/fairfax/

- **REED (READ) Family Genealogy**
  http://ourworld.compuserve.com/homepages/jwmuse/reed.htm
  Traces some descendants of 3 immigrants to America.

- **The REEDER / READER Family Web Site**
  http://creeder.taylordata.com/TheReeders/

- **REEDS BDM Extractions**
  http://www.angelfire.com/folk/reedsonly
  Extractions of all REEDS from the English GRO BDM Indexes.

- **REEL Surname Resource Center**
  http://freepages.genealogy.rootsweb.com/~geneal/src/ReelSRC.html

- **The Official REESE Family Website**
  http://reeseweb.virtualave.net
  REESE (RHYS, REIS, REES, etc.) surname.

- **The REESOR Family in Canada**
  http://www.reesorfamily.on.ca
  REESOR, REIFF, RIESER, RISSER. The Reesor Family in Canada Genealogical & Historical Society Inc. preserves and fosters its Canadian, American and European roots and heritage through historical conservation, research, publication of a genealogical record, family contacts and regular reunions. For a complete list of surnames, see our Reesor Index on the web site.

- **Paul REEVES Home Page**
  http://members.aol.com/rreeves204/reeves.html

- **The REEVES Registry**
  http://www.vantek.net/reevesregistry.com/
  Reave, Reaves, Reavis, Reeve, Reeves, Reive, Reives, Reve, Reves, Rieve, Rieves, Rive, Rives, Ryve, Ryves.

- **REGAS .About the name**
  http://msnhomepages.talkcity.com/BoomerSt/regas/index.html
  About the name REGAS. Is it Greek or Catalan?

- **REGNIER Family Genealogy**
  http://ourworld.compuserve.com/homepages/jwmuse/regnier.htm
  Descendants of Henri REGNIER, who immigrated from La Rochelle, France to Canada.

- **A gathering of REIDYs**
  http://www.geocities.com/Athens/Parthenon/6108/reidy.htm

- **REINHART Genealogy and Niedernberg, Germany**
  http://ourworld.compuserve.com/homepages/niedernberg/niedernberg.html

- **REISDORF, Peter - Descendants**
  http://www.uftree.com/UFT/WebPages/ClarePedenMidgley/REISDORF/
  Peter REISDORF born before 1726, died 9 Aug 1741 in Zusch, Nonnweiler, Pr. Rheinland.

- **REISWIG Roots**
  http://www.geocities.com/Heartland/Forest/1589/
  A one name study of the surname REUSSWIG and it's variations Reiswig, Risewick, Reiswick, Reuswig, Ricewick. REUSSWIG's have lived in Niedermittlau, Neunhasslau, Hasselroth (and surrounding villages) in Hesse, Germany since the late 1500's. Locations include Germany, Russia, USA, and Canada.

- **International RELF Society Local & Family History of RELF REALF RELPH**
  http://www.relfsociety.org/
  Interests and membership details of the International Relf Society; Focusing on the family names of RELF, REALF, RELPH, RELFE, RIULF in Kent,Sussex, Brightling, Winterborne Zelston, UK.

- **REM Family and REM Genealogy**
  http://rem.genealogy.org/

- **REMMICK Home Site**
  http://members.aol.com/remmick1/Remmick.Home.Site.index.html/
  German-Russian heritage connected to Edenkoben, Palatinate migration to Worms/Odessa, S. Russia then Streeter, ND, USA. Remmick, Roemmich, Remick, Remich, Roemigius, Roemig.

- **REMPEL - Mennonite (Russian) Family History**
  http://members.home.net/rempel/
  Mennonite family history/genealogy, especially in Tsarist Russia.

- **The RENDALL Network**
  http://rendall.net/

- **RENNERs of Frederick Co., Maryland**
  http://pages.prodigy.net/theresek/renner.txt
  Descendants of Abraham Renner & Elizabeth Overholtz.

- The RENOWDEN Family One Name Study
  http://freepages.genealogy.rootsweb.com/~renowden/
  The online database of the GOONS registered One Name Study for the RENOWDEN family including spelling variations Renoden, Trenowden and Trenorden.

- REPASS Family Homepage
  http://www.repass.net/
  Descendants of Hans Jacob RIPPAS and Anna GERBER, natives of Ziefen, Switzerland (Basel Canton). Immigrated to America in 1768.

- REPLOGLE-REPROGLE Genealogy: The Family History of a Surname
  http://homepages.rootsweb.com/~preplogl/
  Concerned with all descendants of the immigrants to America with the surname Replogle or Reprogle (or Reblogel in the German), both male and female.

- The RETTIG Genealogy Home Page
  http://members.aol.com/JWR184/rettig.html

- REYNOLDS Home Page - REYNOLDS Records Newsletter
  http://members.aol.com/Kinseeker6/reynolds.html

- REX Family Research
  http://web.shockware.com/users/srex/index.html

- RHOADES / RHODES / RHOADS Family Researchers
  http://members.AOL.com/BUDI/Rhoades.htm

- RHYMES Family Genealogy
  http://wymple.gs.net/~longstrt/rhymes.html
  Descendants of John Rhyne, born 1745 in North Carolina.

- Le Groupe RHYNO
  http://www.geocities.com/Heartland/2194/rhyno.html
  Other possible spellings are Reynaud, Renaud, Reneau, Reno, Ryno, Rino, Rhino and more.

- Deacon Edmund RICE (1638) Association
  http://web2.airmail.net/drrice/

- The Edmund RICE (1638) Association, Inc.
  http://www.edmund-rice.org
  Descendants of Edmund RICE who arrived in the Massachusetts Bay Colony about 1638 and settled in Sudbury.

- The RICE Family: "End-of-the-Century Publishing Project"
  http://heaven.gofast.net/~rosemary/

- RICE Family History
  http://www.users.bigpond.com/munsie
  The History of the RICE Family migrating to South Australia, starting in the early 1600's.

- The RICH Family Association
  http://www.richfamilyassociation.org/
  The purpose and objectives of this Association shall be to discover, procure, and preserve whatever may relate to the Rich Family in America; to procure and maintain collections of photographs, records, heirlooms, etc., relating to the Rich Family; to encourage study and research relating to the Rich Family; and to disseminate

information thereon. The Rich Family Association accepts membership from anyone with a connection to an ancestor with the surname "Rich." or variations such as Ricci, Richie, Riche, Reich, etc.

- Samuel Whitney RICHARDS - His Wives, Children and Descendants
  http://www.n1.net/~mcward/swr.htm
  Born 9 August 1824 in Richmond, Berkshire, Massachusetts.

- RICHARDSON Genealogy
  http://homepages.rootsweb.com/~imrie/Richardson.htm

- RICHARDSON & Related Families
  http://www.parsonstech.com/genealogy/trees/rchrdsn/rchrdsn.htm
  Descendents of George RICHARDSON and Sarah Wallace GRIFFIN; Illinois & Oregon ancestry.

- Descendants of Robert RICHARDSON (c1637 - 1682)
  http://www.intercom.net/local/richardson/
  Owned a 2000 acre plantation, land grant dated November 9, 1666, in Somerset County, later Worcester County Maryland.

- The RICHARDSONS of Harrison Co., Kentucky
  http://www.rootsweb.com/~kyharris/har_richardson.htm
  Includes RITCHERSON, RICHESON, etc.

- RICHBOURG Surname
  http://homepages.rootsweb.com/~jclaytn/richbourg.html
  Richbourg Surname: France>SC>AL>MS>TX.

- RICHFORD One-Name Study
  http://ourworld.compuserve.com/homepages/Kevin_H_Jennings/

- RICHINS Surname Association
  http://www.paonline.com/trichins/RSA/

- RICHMOND Family Genealogy
  http://www.geocities.com/Heartland/Ridge/7927/
  RICHMOND Family Genealogy, ancestors and descendants of John RICHMOND of Taunton, Massachusetts. Information of Early RICHMOND Family and Richmond Castle Yorkshire, England. Other surnames include, Antheil, Alles, Broadwell, Rogers, Skellenger, Warner, and Zuckuhr.

- RICKEY Family Association
  mailto:rickeyroot@aol.com
  For details send e-mail to Stanton M. Rickey at rickeyroot@aol.com.

- The Descendants of Jonas RICKS and Other RICKS Families in America
  http://www.geocities.com/Heartland/Plains/1948/index.html
  Mainly for Jonas Ricks, who was in Rowan County, North Carolina, in 1768, died in Guilford County 1821.

- RICKLEFS Family Center
  http://home.earthlink.net/~ricklefsr/
  Ricklefs, Ricklef, Rickles, Rickel, Rickels, Ricklefsen plus other derivations.

- RIDER Family Chronicles
  http://www.geocities.com/Heartland/Hills/5650/

- **RIDGWAY - RIDGEWAY Surname Study**
  http://www.geocities.com/Heartland/Meadows/4826/ridgeway_toc.html

- **RIEGEL / RIGGLE Freundschaft Association**
  http://members.xoom.com/riegeld/newsletter.htm

- **RIEPE Roots**
  http://freepages.genealogy.rootsweb.com/~ariepe/
  RIEPE families in the U.S.

- **RIFFE - R100 Mailing List**
  http://www.cdc.net/~primus/genealogy/R100/R100.htm
  Reiff, Reif, Rief, Riffe, Rife ... Families.

- **RIGG Family Website**
  http://members.xoom.com/riggfamily/
  RIGG family in Kansas, Illinois, and Virginia.

- **RIGGS Surname Study**
  http://homepages.rootsweb.com/~riggs/

- **RIGSBY Genealogy**
  http://hometown.aol.com/mkrigsby/page/index.htm
  RIGSBY genealogy from 1066 to present.

- **RILEY Family Genealogy**
  http://members.aol.com/PowellGen/RILEYFamilyGenealogy.html
  History of the Ninian Riley Sr. (a Revolutionary War Patriot) and his family with a listing of three generations of his descendants.

- **RILEY Genealogy Home Page**
  http://freepages.genealogy.rootsweb.com/~csanders/Riley/RR_TOC.HTM
  Descendants of Barnabas O'REILLY and Anna Marie FERREE of south central Pennsylvania.

- **The RING Family Tree Homepage**
  http://www.angelfire.com/md/ringtree/index.html
  Descendants of Dennis Ring, emigrated from Cork, Ireland to New York via Liverpool in 1839.

- **RINGER Connection**
  http://www.netins.net/showcase/ringers
  Multiple RINGER researchers together on one site.

- **RINTOUL Home Page**
  http://www3.sympatico.ca/david.rintoul

- **RIORDAN Family Homepage**
  http://www.geocities.com/Heartland/Park/6886/index.html
  Tony & Elaine Riordan share their family research and provide and excellent Noteboard for all Riordan/Reardon researchers.

- **Association Perche-AmÈrique**
  http://www.geocities.com/Heartland/Flats/1865/index.htm
  This site chronicles the RIVARD family from 1571 in Perche, France through 300 years in North America, including Loranger, Dufresne, Lacoursiere, Lanouette, Laglanderie, Bellefeuille, Giasson, Feuilleverte, Montendre, Preville.

- **ROACH * ROACHE * ROCHE Genealogy Research**
  http://www.geocities.com/Heartland/Acres/5725/

- **The ROAN Irish Surname Page**
  http://www.geocities.com/Athens/Delphi/4658/Roan.01.html
  Roan, Rohan, Roughan, Rowan.

- **ROARK Surname Research "Texas Clan" Home Page**
  http://www.phaenom.com.roark
  Roark in Texas - One-Name research for all surnames Roark, Roarke, Rourk, Rourke, O'Roark, O'Roarke, O'Rourk, & O'Rourke in Texas since the Repulic was settled.

- **Levi ROBBINS Family of Overton County, Tennessee**
  http://www.inct.net/~german/robbins.htm
  Descendants of Levi Robbins (c1806-c1856) and James Robbins of Overton Co., TN.

- **The ROBBINS Families of Southern Indiana**
  http://members.aol.com/robinnews/
  Online edition of "The Round Robin" a newsletter for the ROBBINS Families of Southern Indiana. Includes genealogy information for Robbins, Robins, Hartwell, Curran, Davidson and others.

- **ROBBINS Genealogy**
  http://users.bigpond.net.au/robbins/genealogy/
  Promote new genealogical contacts with ROBBINS (ROBINS) relations (known to have lived in England, Scotland, Australia, New Zealand, America) originating from Hanslope/Hartwell region of England in the 1700's.

- **ROBERSHOTTE Descendants Homepage**
  http://www.angelfire.com/tx/robershotte/
  ROBERSHOTTE family history from Swiss immigrant to today with family photos and opportunities to help complete our story!

- **HOLCOMB and ROBERSON/ROBINSON**
  http://members.aol.com/jogt/holcomms.htm

- **ROBERTS Genealogy Online**
  http://www.geocities.com/Heartland/1963/
  A page for Roberts researchers with queries indexed by first name of ancestor.

- **Cornelius ROBERTS Descendants**
  http://home.flash.net/~bharris5/Roberts.html

- **Chuck ROBERTS Genealogy Page**
  http://www.geocities.com/Heartland/Plains/3959/
  Index of over 1,300+ ROBERTS.

- **REID-ROBERTSON of Straloch**
  http://www.saunalahti.fi/martinas/peregrina/docs/reid.html
  A history of the Reid Barons of Straloch written in 1727 by James Robertson and printed in 1887.

- **ROBERTSON Families of the World**
  http://www.shelby.net/shelby/jr/robertsn/

- **ROBEY / ROBIE / ROBY Family Association**
  http://www.geocities.com/Heartland/Hollow/2507/
  The family history from early England to America.

- **ROBICHAUD Genealogy Exchange**
  http://www.genweb.net/~robichaud
  Robichaud, Robichaux, Robicheau, Robicheaux, Robich. 29,000+ names.

- ROBINETT Family Association
  http://hometown.aol.com/robinettfa

- ROBINETTE Family Genealogy
  http://www.geocities.com/~robinette/
  Genealogy research of the Robinette family including Conley, Damron and Adkins.

- ROBLEE Genealogy
  http://www.greencity.org/roblee/index.htm
  A site to satisfy researchers of the ROBLEE surname (which is sometimes spelled as Robblee or Rublee and includes other variations such as Robley, Rublier, Rublyer, and Rubleyer.

- ROCK Family
  http://www.pipcom.com/~cjrock
  Information about the Rock family in Ontario and the U.K. and some info on other surnames associated with the Rocks.

- Descendants of Goddard ROCKENFELLER
  http://showcase.netins.net/web/vbciowa/genie/Rockefellow/rock.htm
  Born in 1590 in Fahr, Germany.

- The ROCKNE/ROKNE Family Tree
  http://home.sol.no/~birgerro/slekttre.htm
  The ancestors of Martha A. KVITNO and Knut K. ROKNE.

- ROCKWELL Family Foundation
  http://www.rockwell-family.org/

- The RODRIGUE Families
  http://www.er.uqam.ca/nobel/g17176/rodrigue/engindex.html
  Quebec and Ontario in Canada, Louisiana and New England in the U.S.

- ROGERS Hunters Home Page
  http://jax.gulfnet.com/user_pages/ecornell/rogershp.htm

- Some Descendants of Adam ROGERS of New London, Connecticut
  http://hometown.aol.com/jimmerjam/myhomepage/index.html

- Thomas ROGERS Society
  http://www.thomasrogerssociety.com
  Thomas ROGERS of the Mayflower

- ROHRBOUGH Surname Genealogy, History, Study and Research
  http://www.geocities.com/Heartland/Bluffs/2916/src/rohrindex.html

- ROLFE Family Genealogy Webring
  http://members.tripod.com/~AlanCheshire/rolfering.html

- Genealogy of the family ROLLENHAGEN
  http://www.rollenhagen.de/
  Devoted to collecting data on all Rollenhagens worldwide.

- Paul ROMAINE Genealogy Interests
  http://homepages.rootsweb.com/~promaine/romaine/index.html
  Descendants of John ROMAINE (1798-1852) of New York City and Westchester County, NY.

- ROMINE Family Group Genealogy
  http://www.geocities.com/Heartland/Plains/8574/
  Includes Romeyn, Romain, Romaine, Romines, Romeyns, Romains Romaines, Remine, etc.

- ROMMELs Genealogy
  http://www.angelfire.com/bc/Rommel
  ROMMELs back to 1610 in both English and German. Helping to find both German and American tree branches. Surnames include: Rommel, Wooten, Swhitrow, Zinn, Dileta, Kohn, Desjardins, Douglas, Meling, Propp and more.

- Family History
  http://www.brid43.freeserve.co.uk/
  One name study for WHINCUP (Wincup, Whincop, Winkup, etc.) and RONDEAU.

- ROSE Family Association Nationwide
  http://ourworld-top.cs.com/Christine4Rose/index.htm
  Rose family records nationwide; hundreds of thousands of Rose records.

- ROSE Family Society Home Page
  http://www.vaxxine.com/rosefamilysociety
  A Society for the world-wide collection and dissemination of ROSE surname information. Includes recognized variants.

- ROSHONG / ROSHON Genealogy
  http://www.geocities.com/Heartland/Forest/3533
  Descendants of Pierre RO(U)CHON, the beginning of most ROSHONGs/ROSHONs in America.

- The ROSS Genealogy Database
  http://www.dementedmind.com/genealogy/Ross/

- ROSSON Genealogy Page
  http://www.xau.net/rosson/

- ROTHENHÖFER (ROTHENHOEFER) Lineages
  http://www.azstarnet.com/~bkcntry/rotnhofr/
  Rothenhöfer Lineages explores this surname and its derivational forms. The site is principally directed at identifying the pre-1750 lineages throughout modern southwest Germany.

- The ROTHUIZEN / RODENHOUSE Family Web Site
  http://www.sigma.net/etymes/
  Eleven generations (with about 500 names) of the family of Anton and Wilhelmina Rothuizen (who changed the family name to Rodenhouse in 1919), originally from Osterbeek, Gelderland, Netherlands. The site makes a case for the theory that all those named "Rothuizen" or "Rotshuizen" might be related.

- ROUNSEFELL One-Name Study
  http://homepages.rootsweb.com/~rounsfel/

- ROUSH (RAUSCH) & Allied Families Association of America, Inc.
  http://www.roush.org/index.htm

- Les ROUSSEL en AmÈrique du Nord / ROUSSEL Families in North America
  http://www.cam.org/~mauricel

- ROWAN
  http://www.uftree.com/UFT/WebPages/Jan_Rowan/ROWAN/index.htm
  Jan ROWAN family from Alabama and related families: ROAN, RWILLIAMSON, McMILLION, STARNES, MINNIX, FOWLER, HAIR, GRACE and SILKS.

- ROWBERRY One-Name Study
  http://www.newbury.net/rowberry/index.html
  Rubery, Rowbury, Ruberry, Rewbury, Robery, Roebury, Rovery, Rowbery, Rowbory, Rowbree, Rowbrey, Rowburrey, Rubbery, Rubbra, Rubrey, Rubra, Rubury.

- ROWBOTHAM Genealogy Website UK
  http://home.freeuk.net/mrowbotham/
  One name study for ROWBOTHAM and variants including Robottom, Rowbottom, Robothom, Robotham, Rowbothom, Rowbothame, Roobottom, Roobottam, Rubottom.

- ROWE Family Tree Branches
  http://georgerowe.webprovider.com/first.html
  Southern ROWE families.

- ROYER Family in America
  http://freepages.genealogy.rootsweb.com/~royer/

- Descendants of Isaac RUCKER of Amerhert County, Virginia
  http://csc.techcenter.org/~mneill/ruckerisaac.html

- Wills of Peter RUCKER & John RUCKER
  http://members.aol.com/jogt/ruckerwl.htm

- The Peter RUCKER, Immigrant, Home Page
  http://www.familytreemaker.com/users/e/d/w/Mary-D-Edwards/index.html
  Genealogical Research of descendants of Peter RUCKER, Immigrant.

- The RĐCKER Family Society
  http://www.mindspring.com/~jogt/surnames/ruckerfs.htm

- The RUDGE Family Page
  http://kanga.cc.wmich.edu/~rudged/gen/rudgefp.html
  A site devoted to the genealogy of the Rudge family in England and the U.S.

- RUDISILL Family Association Page
  http://www.geocities.com/Heartland/Estates/6698/

- The RUE Family in the U.S.A.
  http://www.catskill.net/rue/family/rue/

- RUGGLES Family
  http://gator1.brazosport.cc.tx.us/~truggles/rug.htm

- Ira A. RUNYAN Genealogy
  http://WWW.MEMBERS.TRIPOD.COM/RUNYAN2/
  The Kentucky RUNYON/RUNYAN FAMILY.

- RUSHING Family Surname and Genealogy Information
  http://www.rushings.com/info.html

- The RUSSELL Family - Genealogy
  http://www.internet-partners.com/russell/index.htm

- RUSSELL Family Genealogy
  http://russellfamily.webjump.com
  Descendants of Samuel Russell and Sarah Hatcher of Loudoun Co., VA.

- RUTHERFORD Family
  http://rutherford.webjump.com
  RUTHERFORDS from Scotland 1853 to Victoria and South Australia and 1870 on to New Zealand.

- The RUTLEDGE Family Association
  http://www.rootsweb.com/~rutledge/

- RUTTLEDGE History and Genealogy
  http://www.geocities.com/MadisonAvenue/3333/ruttledge.html
  A history of ROUTLEDGES (Rutledges, Ruttledges) a Reiving family from the Border region UK and their subsequent exodus to Ireland and the new world.

- The RYAN Clan Association, U.S. Sept
  http://www.ryans.org

- RYCKMAN Genealogy
  http://www.geocities.com/jackylar/ryckman.html

- Ryerse-Ryerson Family Association
  mailto:phyllis@webnet.com
  Or alternate address
  mailto:tom@therecordworks.com
  Looking for descendants of either spelling of this family name. Hardcover book published on Canadian branch. Newsletter, published 3 times a year has family stories and genealogy. For more information contact Phyllis Ryerse in the USA at phyllis@webnet.com and Thomas Ryerson in Canada at tom@therecordworks.com.

- RYKER-RIKER Historical Society, Inc.
  http://homepages.rootsweb.com/~ryker2/
  A pictorial/textual presentation of RYKER-RIKER family genealogy. This Dutch family traces its roots in America to 1638, when Abraham RYCKEN emigrated from Holland and settled in New Amsterdam (present-day New York City) with his wife, Grietie HARMENSEN.

◆ Surname Mailing Lists

- "RA-RD" Surname Mailing Lists
  http://www.rootsweb.com/~jfuller/gen_mail_surnames-ra.html
  RAAB, RAABE, RAAFF (includes Raaf), RABB (includes Rab, Raab), RABBITT, RABE, RABENSTEIN (includes Rabenstine, Raubenstine), RABORN, RABURN (includes Rayburn, Raborn, Rayborn, Raiburn, Raiborn, Raybourne), RABY, RABY, RABY (includes Rabey, Rabe), RACE, RACHMANN, RACKHAM, RACKLEY, RADABAUGH, RADCLIFF, RADCLIFFE, RADDATZ, RADER (includes Reader, Raeder, Roder, Roeder, Rotter), RADER (includes Raider), RADFORD, RADFORD, RADKE, RADLE, RADLEY (includes Radly), RADLOFF, RADNEDGE, RADTKE, RAE, RAFFERTY, RAGAN (includes Reagan, Regan), RAGER, RAGLAND (includes Raglin), RAGSDALE (includes Bragsdale, Ridgedale, Ragsdall, Regisdale, Racksdale), RAHN, RAIFORD, RAIL, RAILLARD, RAINBOLT, RAINE, RAINES, RAINEY (includes Rainy), RAINFORD, RAINS (includes Raines, Ranes, Reynes, Raynes), RAINS, RAINWATER (includes Rainwaters), RAKESTRAW (includes Rickstrew, Rexstraw, Bakestraw, Rakestran), RALEIGH, RALEY, RALLS, RALPH, RALSTON, RAMAGE, RAMBO, RAMBONNET, RAMER, RAMEY (includes Remy, Rhamy, Ramie),

RAMIREZ, RAMONAT, RAMOS, RAMSAY, RAMSAY (includes Ramsay, Ramsey, Dalhousie, Maule, Brecheen), RAMSBOTTOM, RAMSBURG, RAMSDELL, RAMSDEN, RAMSEY (includes Ramsay, Ramseur), RAND, RANDALL (includes Randal, Randel), RANDALL, RANDAZZO, RANDEL, RANDLE, RANDLES (includes Randalls, Randals, Randle), RANDOLPH, RANEY (includes Riney), RANGE, RANGER, RANKIN (includes Ranken), RANSOM, RANSON, RAPALJE, RAPE (includes Reap, Reph), RAPER, RAPIER, RAPP, RAPPOLD, RAPSKE, RARICK, RASBERRY (includes Raspberry), RASCHKE, RASEY (includes Racey, Raisee, Raisey, Raisy, Rasy, Razee, Razey, Razy, Reasey), RASH, RASMUSSEN, RASNER, RASNICK (includes Rasnyck, Rasneck), RASURE (includes Razor, Rasor), RATCLIFF, RATCLIFFE, RATERMAN, RATH, RATHBONE, RATHBUN, RATHKE, RATLIFF (includes Ratcliff, Ratliffe, Radcliff, Rattle), RATTRAY, RATZ, RATZLAFF, RAU, RAUB, RAUCH, RAUSCH, RAUSCHER, RAVEN, RAVENCRAFT, RAVENSCRAFT (includes Ravencraft, Ravenscroft, Ravencroft), RAWLEY, RAWLINGS, RAWLINS, RAWLINSON, RAWLS, RAWORTH (includes Rayworth), RAWSON, RAWSTHORNE, RAY (includes Wray), RAYBURN, RAYER, RAYFIELD, RAYL, RAYMOND, RAYNER, RAYNES (includes Raines), RAYNOR, RAYNSFORD.

- **"REA-REH" Surname Mailing Lists**
  http://www.rootsweb.com/~jfuller/gen_mail_surnames-re.html
  REA, READ (includes Reade, Reed, Reid), READE, READER, READING, READY, REAGAN, REAL, REAM, REAMS, REARDON, REASE, REASONER, REAVES, REAVIS (includes Reaves, Revis, Rivis, Reeves, Rives), REBBECK (includes Ribbeck, Rebbick, Ribbick), REBER, RECKINGER, RECKMANN (includes Reckman), RECTOR (includes Richter, Recter, Rektor), REDD, REDD, REDDEN, REDDICK (includes Riddick, Redick, Redrick, Rhedick), REDDIN, REDDING, REDDISH, REDERICK, REDFEARN, REDFERN, REDFIELD (includes Redfin, Redfen, Redfyn, Redfyne), REDFORD, REDGRAVE, REDGROVE, REDMAN, REDMON, REDMOND, REDNER, REDPATH, REDUS (includes Readus, Reedis, Redish), REDWINE (includes Reitweil, Riedweyl, Redwile, Riethweil, Reedwile), REEB, REECE, REECK (includes Rieck), REED, REED, REEDER, REEDER (includes Reader), REEDY, REEDY (includes Riedy, Riedi), REEL (includes Reele, Real, Reale), REEP, REES, REESE (includes Rees), REETZ, REEVE, REEVES (includes Reaves, Rieves, Reeve), REEVES, REEVES (includes Rive, Ryve, Reeve), REGAN, REGISTER (includes Regester), REGNER, REHG (includes Regh, Reh), REHM, REHMET.

- **"REI-REO" Surname Mailing Lists**
  http://www.rootsweb.com/~jfuller/gen_mail_surnames-re.html
  REICH, REICHARD, REICHEL, REICHERT (includes Reichart), REICHTER, REID, REID (includes Reed, Read), REIDY, REIFF (includes Reif, Rieff, Reif, Rife, Riffe, Riffey), REIFSNYDER (includes Raifsnider, Reiffschneider), REIJNGOUD (includes Reijngoudt, Reyngoudt, Ringold), REILLY (includes O'Reilly), REIMANN, REIMER, REIMERS, REIML, REINACHER (includes Reinaker, Reinacker), REINBOLD, REINDERS (includes Rinders, Reynders, Rynders, Reinners, Reiners, Reinerts, Reijnders, Rhijnders), REINECKE, REINEKER, REINER, REINERT, REINHARD, REINHARDT, REINHART, REINHOLD, REINKE, REIS, REISDORF (includes Reischdorff), REISER (includes Reisser, Rieser), REISINGER (includes Risinger), REISS, REISWIG (includes Risewick, Ricewick, Reiswick, Reiswich, Reisswick, Reisswich, Reisswig, Reiszwig, Reuswig,, Reusswig), REITER, REITH, REITZ, REITZEL (includes Reitzle), REMALEY (includes Ramaley, Remeley, Remly), REMBERT (includes Rambert), REMICK, REMINGTON (includes Remmington), REMPEL (includes Remple), REMY, REN, RENAUD, RENDALL, RENDER, RENEAU, RENFRO, RENFROE, RENICK (includes Rennick,

Rennix), RENKES, RENNER (includes Runner), RENNIE (includes Raynie), RENNINGER, RENNO, RENO (includes Reynaud, Reneau), RENSHAW, RENTON, RENTON, RENTZ, RENWICK, RENZ, RENZA.

- **"REP-RH" Surname Mailing Lists**
  http://www.rootsweb.com/~jfuller/gen_mail_surnames-re.html
  REPASS, REPKING (includes Rebbekinck, Rebbeking, Rebbekings, Rebbekink), REPLOGLE, REPPERT, REPROGLE, RESCH, RESCHKE (includes Raschke), RESEIGH, RESTER, RETAN (includes Rettan, Rutan, Ruttan), RETTIG (includes Rettich), REUSS, REUTER, REVEL, REVELL, REVETTE (includes Revett), REX, REXROAD, REXRODE, REY, REYES, REYNARD (includes Rinard, Renert, Reinard. Raynart, Raynard,Reinart, Reynord), REYNARD (includes Rinard, Renart), REYNIERSEN (includes Reynerson, Rynearson, Rinearson, Rhynearson, Rynerson), REYNIERSON, REYNOLDS, REYNOLDSON, REZEAU, REZNY (includes Resny, Reszny), RHAMES, RHEA (includes Rea, Wray, Rae, Ray), RHINEHART, RHOADES, RHOADS, RHODEN, RHODES (includes Rodes, Rhoades), RHONE (includes Rohn, Rahn), RHORER, RHYMES (includes Rimes, Rhimes, Rymes), RHYNER, RHYNO (includes Rhino, Rino, Reneau, Ryno).

- **"RI-RN" Surname Mailing Lists**
  http://www.rootsweb.com/~jfuller/gen_mail_surnames-ri.html
  RIACH (includes Riabhach, Reoch, Raich, Rioch, Reiach), RIBBECK (includes Ribbecke), RIBBLE, RICCI, RICE, RICE, RICE (includes Rhys, Ries), RICH (includes Ritch, Ryche, Riche), RICHARD, RICHARDS, RICHARDSON (includes Richards), RICHARDSON, RICHBOURG (includes Richebourg, Richburg, Richbourgh), RICHEY, RICHIE, RICHINGS (includes Richins, Richens), RICHMAN, RICHMOND, RICHTER (includes Reighter, Richster), RICK, RICKABAUGH (includes Rickaback, Rickenbaugh. Rickabough), RICKARD, RICKER (includes Ricard, Riccar, Recore), RICKERT, RICKETSON, RICKETT, RICKETTS, RICKEY, RICKMAN, RICKS, RIDDELL, RIDDICK, RIDDLE (includes Riddles, Riddell, Ridle, Reidle, Ritle, Ruddle, Rydale, Rydel), RIDEN, RIDENOUR, RIDEOUT, RIDER (includes Ryder), RIDGE, RIDGELL, RIDGELY, RIDGEWAY, RIDGWAY (includes Ridgwaie, Ridgeway, Rugewaye, Rudgwy, Rydeware, Rydgeway, Wrydgway), RIDINGER, RIDINGS, RIDLEY, RIDOUT, RIDSDALE (includes Rudsdale, Ridsdall), RIEBE, RIEBOLDT (includes Riebolt, Riebold, Reiboldt, Reibolt, Reibold, Rybolt, Ryboldt, Rybold), RIEDEL, RIEDINGER, RIEDL, RIEGEL (includes Reagle, Riggle), RIEGER, RIEHLE (includes Rheile), RIEL, RIEL, RIENSTRA, RIES, RIESE (includes Reese, Ries, Rees, Reece), RIETH, RIFE, RIFFE, RIFFLE, RIGBY, RIGDON, RIGG, RIGGINS, RIGGS, RIGNEY, RIGSBY, RIKER (includes Ryker, Rycke, Rycken), RILEY, RILEY, RIMA, RIMELL (includes Rymel, Rimmell), RIMMER, RINCK (includes Rink), RINE, RINEARSON, RINEBOLD, RINEHART, RINELLA, RINER, RINEY, RING, RINGER, RINKER, RIORDAN, RIPLEY, RIPPEE (includes Rippy, Rippie), RIPPETOE (includes Rippeto, Rippeteau), RIPPLE, RIPPY, RISEBOROUGH, RISENHOOVER, RISER, RISING, RISINGER, RISK, RISLEY, RISNER, RISTAU, RITCHEY (includes Richey, Richy, Ritchie), RITCHIE, RITCHIE, RITTENHOUSE (includes Rettinghousen, Rittinghuysen), RITTER (includes Writter), RITTINGER (includes Rettenger, Rettinger), RITZ, RITZMAN, RIVARD, RIVENBURG (includes Rivenberg, Rivenbark, Rifenburgh, Reiffenberg), RIVERA, RIVERS, RIVES, RIVIERE, RIX, RIZZO.

- **"ROA-ROD" Surname Mailing Lists**
  http://www.rootsweb.com/~jfuller/gen_mail_surnames-re.html
  ROACH, ROACH (includes Roche), ROACHE (includes Roche, Roach, Roch), ROADY, ROAN, ROARK (includes Ruark, Rork, O'Rork, Rourick, Rowark), ROBARDS, ROBB, ROBBINS,

ROBERDS, ROBERGE, ROBERSON, ROBERT, ROBERTS, ROBERTS, ROBERTSON, ROBERTSON, ROBESON, ROBEY *(includes Roby)*, ROBIE, ROBILLER *(includes Robillier)*, ROBIN, ROBINETT *(includes Robinet, Robinette, Robnet)*, ROBINETTE, ROBINETTE, ROBINS, ROBINSON *(includes Robertson, Robison, Robeson, Roberson, Robbins, Robins)*, ROBISON, ROBLEE *(includes Robblee, Rublee, Robleyer, Rublier, Robley)*, ROBLIN, ROBSON, ROBY, ROCHE, ROCHESTER, ROCHFORD, ROCK, ROCKETT, ROCKHOLD, ROCKWELL, RODDA, RODDEN *(includes Roden, Rowden, Routen, Routon, Rowdon, Rauten)*, RODDIN, RODDY *(includes Rhody, Roddey, Roddye)*, RODDY, RODE, RODEBAUGH *(includes Rodenbaugh)*, RODEN, RODENHIZER, RODER, RODERICK, RODGER, RODGERS, RODGERS, RODMAN *(includes Redmond, Rodham, Redman, Broadman, Rothmann, Hrothmann, Roadman, Hrodman,, Rathman, Rutman, Redmon, Rothman, Rideman, Brodman)*, RODNEY, RODRIGUES, RODRIGUEZ.

- "ROE-ROH" Surname Mailing Lists
  http://www.rootsweb.com/~jfuller/gen_mail_surnames-re.html
  ROE, ROEBUCK, ROECKER *(includes Roeker, Raker)*, ROEDER, ROEHRIG, ROEMER, ROEMHILDT *(includes Rhoemhildt, Roemhild)*, ROESCH, ROESLER, ROFFEY, ROGAN, ROGASCH *(includes Rogash, Roggosch)*, ROGER, ROGERS *(includes Rodgers)*, ROGERS, ROGERSON, ROGGE, ROHAN, ROHR, ROHRBACH, ROHRBOUGH *(includes Rohrbaugh, Rohrbach, Rohrabaugh, Rohrabacher, Rorapaugh)*, ROHRER *(includes Rhorer, Rorer, Rorrer, Roher)*, ROHWER *(includes Roher, Rohr, Rower, Rorer, Rohwedder)*.

- "ROI-RON" Surname Mailing Lists
  http://www.rootsweb.com/~jfuller/gen_mail_surnames-re.html
  ROI, ROJAS, ROLAND *(includes Rowland, Rawlings, Rawlin, Rollens, Rollings, Rollins, Rolin)*, ROLF, ROLFE, ROLL *(includes Raal, Rall, Ral, Rol, Rool, Rools, Mengalrol, Mangles)*, ROLLASON *(includes Rolason, Rollinson)*, ROLLER, ROLLINGS, ROLLINS, ROLLO, ROLOFF *(includes Rolloff, Rohloff)*, ROLSTON, ROMAN, ROMANO, ROMANS, ROME, ROMERO, ROMIG, ROMINE *(includes Romeyn, Romain, Romaine, Romines, Romeyns, Romains, Romaines, Remine)*, ROMMEL, ROMOLO, ROMSPERT, RONDEAU, RONEY.

- "ROO-ROT" Surname Mailing Lists
  http://www.rootsweb.com/~jfuller/gen_mail_surnames-re.html
  ROOD, ROOF, ROOK *(includes Rooke, Rooks)*, ROOKER, ROOKS, ROOME, ROONEY, ROOP, ROOS, ROOSA, ROOSE, ROOT *(includes Roote)*, ROPER, ROQUEMORE, ROSA, ROSAMOND, ROSCOE, ROSE *(includes Roosa, Rosa, Rutsen, Ruzen)*, ROSE, ROSE, ROSEBERRY, ROSEBOOM *(includes Rooseboom)*, ROSEBOROUGH *(includes Rosebrough, Rosbrough, Roseboro)*, ROSECRANS, ROSEN, ROSENBAUM, ROSENBERG, ROSENBERGER *(includes Rosenberg)*, ROSENBLATT, ROSENBLUM, ROSENER *(includes Rosner, Roesener)*, ROSENFELD, ROSENTHAL, ROSEVEAR, ROSIER, ROSS, ROSSER, ROSSI, ROSSITER *(includes Rossitter, Rosseter)*, ROSSITER, ROSSON, ROSSOW, ROSZELL *(includes Roszel, Roszelle, Roszele, Rosel, Rossel, Rossele, Rosell, Rossell, Rosele, Roselle, Rosselle,, Rozel, Rozzel, Rozzele, Rozell, Rozzell, Rozele, Rozelle, Rozzelle, Roessell)*, ROTE, ROTH *(includes Rothe, Wroth)*,

ROTHENBERGER, ROTHENFLUCH, ROTHON, ROTHROCK, ROTHWELL, ROTTON *(includes Roton, Wroton, Roughton, Raughton, Rauton, Wrauton)*, ROTZLER.

- "ROU-RT" Surname Mailing Lists
  http://www.rootsweb.com/~jfuller/gen_mail_surnames-re.html
  ROUGH, ROUGHLEY *(includes Ruffley, Ruffly)*, ROUGHSEDGE *(includes Roughsage, Roughsich, Roughsuch, Rousedge, Roughseich)*, ROULLIER, ROULSTON, ROUM, ROUND, ROUNDS, ROUNDTREE, ROUNDY, ROUNSEVELL, ROUNTREE, ROURKE, ROUSE *(includes Roush, Rausch)*, ROUSEY *(includes Rowzee, Rowzie)*, ROUSH, ROUSSEAU, ROUSSEL, ROUTH *(includes Ruth)*, ROUTLEDGE, ROUTT, ROUX, ROVER *(includes Ruffer, Rouffer, Rovier, Rouvier, Rouviere, De Rover)*, ROW, ROWAN, ROWBERRY *(includes Rubery, Rowbury, Ruberry, Rewbury, Robery, Roebury, Rovery, Rowbery, Rowbory,, Rowbree, Rowbrey, Rowburrey, Rubbery, Rubbra, Rubrey, Rubra, Rubury)*, ROWDEN, ROWE *(includes Row)*, ROWELL *(includes Rowel, Rowley)*, ROWLAND, ROWLES, ROWLETT *(includes Rawlett, Rowlette, Roulet)*, ROWLETT *(includes Rawlett, Rowlette, Rowlet, Roulet)*, ROWLEY, ROWLEY, ROWND *(includes Round, Rownds, Rounds)*, ROWNEY, ROWZEE *(includes Rousey, Rowzie)*, ROWZIE *(includes Rousey, Rowzee)*, ROY *(includes Roye)*, ROYAL *(includes Royall)*, ROYALL, ROYALTY, ROYCE *(includes Royse, Roys, Rice)*, ROYER, ROYLE, ROYSDON, ROYSTON *(includes Roystone)*, ROZSA, ROZON.

- "RU-RZ" Surname Mailing Lists
  http://www.rootsweb.com/~jfuller/gen_mail_surnames-ru.html
  RUARK, RUBERG, RUBERT *(includes Ruberts, Rheubart, Rubart, Rubarts, Reuber, Ruber, Reubart, Reubert, Ruebart)*, RUBIN, RUBLE, RUBOTTOM, RUBY, RUCH, RUCINSKI, RUCK, RUCKEL *(includes Rockel, Ruckle, Ruttle)*, RUCKER *(includes Rücker)*, RUCKMAN, RUDACILLE *(includes Rudisill, Rudisilla, Rudaciller)*, RUDD *(includes Rud)*, RUDDELL *(includes Ruddel, Rudel, Ruddle, Rudle)*, RUDDICK, RUDDLE, RUDE, RUDISILL, RUDMAN, RUDNICK *(includes Rudnik)*, RUDOLPH, RUDOW, RUDY, RUE *(includes LaRue, Rew)*, RUE, RUFF, RUFF, RUFFIN, RUFFING *(includes Rufing, Ruffingh, Rufingh)*, RUFFNER, RUGG, RUGG, RUGGIERS *(includes Ruggiero, Ruggers)*, RUGGLES *(includes Ruggle, deRuggle, deRuggele)*, RUHL, RULAND, RULE, RULES *(includes Ruyles)*, RUMBAUGH, RUMBERG *(includes Rumburg)*, RUMMEL *(includes Rumel, Rummell, Romel, Rommel)*, RUMMELT, RUMPEL, RUMSEY, RUNDELL, RUNDLE, RUNGE, RUNION, RUNKEL, RUNKLE, RUNNALLS, RUNNELS, RUNNELS, RUNNER *(includes Ranner, Ronner)*, RUNYAN, RUNYON *(includes Runyan, Runion)*, RUPE, RUPERT, RUPLE, RUPP *(includes Rupo, Rüpp)*, RUPPERT, RUPPIN, RUSCH, RUSH *(includes Rushe)*, RUSHING, RUSHTON, RUSK, RUSS, RUSSEL, RUSSELL, RUSSELL, RUSSO, RUST *(includes Russ)*, RUTAN, RUTH, RUTHERFORD, RUTLAND, RUTLEDGE *(includes Rutlidge, Rutlege, Rutlige, Rutlage)*, RUTTER, RUTZ, RUYLE, RUZICKA, RYALS, RYAN *(includes Rian, Mulryans, Mhaolrians)*, RYAN, RYAN, RYAN, RYDER, RYE, RYERSON *(includes Reijer, Reijerson, Reijerszen, Ryers, Ryerse, Ryersse, Ryason, Ryer, Ryers, Rayerson, Reyrse,, Rierson, Rerjersz, Ryierson, Rayson, Rawson, Adriance, Martense)*, RYLAND *(includes Riland, Rylands)*, RYLE, RYMES.

SURNAMES, FAMILY ASSOCIATIONS & FAMILY NEWSLETTERS – "S"

Resources Dedicated to One Surname
http://www.cyndislist.com/surn-s.htm

Category Index:

- ◆ General Surname Sites and Resources
- ◆ Surname Specific Sites and Resources
- ◆ Surname Mailing Lists

◆ General Surname Sites and Resources

- Connect with Surnames - S
  http://www.geocities.com/Heartland/Bluffs/7708/s.html

- Dutch Home Pages by Familyname ~ Letter S
  http://members.tripod.com/~Don_Arnoldus/sa.htm

- FamilyHistory.com - Message Boards - Surname - S
  http://www.familyhistory.com/messages/list.asp?prefix=SA

- Family Tree Maker Online User Home Pages - S
  http://www.familytreemaker.com/users/s/index.html

- Family Workings S Surname Links
  http://www.familyworkings.com/links/surs.htm

- GenConnect Surname Index - "S"
  http://genconnect.rootsweb.com/indx/surnames/S.html
  Message boards sponsored by RootsWeb. Each surname message board set is divided into the following topics: Queries, Bibles, Biographies, Deeds, Obituaries, Pensions, Wills.

- Genealogy Resources on the Internet - "SA-SB" Surname Mailing Lists
  http://www.rootsweb.com/~jfuller/gen_mail_surnames-sa.html
  "SCA-SCG"
  http://www.rootsweb.com/~jfuller/gen_mail_surnames-sca.html
  "SCH-SCH"
  http://www.rootsweb.com/~jfuller/gen_mail_surnames-sch.html
  "SCI-SD"
  http://www.rootsweb.com/~jfuller/gen_mail_surnames-sci.html
  "SE-SG"
  http://www.rootsweb.com/~jfuller/gen_mail_surnames-se.html
  "SHA-SHD"
  http://www.rootsweb.com/~jfuller/gen_mail_surnames-sha.html
  "SHE-SHH"
  http://www.rootsweb.com/~jfuller/gen_mail_surnames-she.html
  "SHI-SHN"
  http://www.rootsweb.com/~jfuller/gen_mail_surnames-shi.html
  "SHO-SHT"
  http://www.rootsweb.com/~jfuller/gen_mail_surnames-sho.html
  "SHU-SHZ"
  http://www.rootsweb.com/~jfuller/gen_mail_surnames-shu.html
  "SI-SJ"
  http://www.rootsweb.com/~jfuller/gen_mail_surnames-si.html
  "SK-SL"
  http://www.rootsweb.com/~jfuller/gen_mail_surnames-sk.html
  "SM-SN"
  http://www.rootsweb.com/~jfuller/gen_mail_surnames-sm.html
  "SO-SO"
  http://www.rootsweb.com/~jfuller/gen_mail_surnames-so.html
  "SP-SS"
  http://www.rootsweb.com/~jfuller/gen_mail_surnames-sp.html
  "STA-STD"
  http://www.rootsweb.com/~jfuller/gen_mail_surnames-sta.html
  "STE-STH"
  http://www.rootsweb.com/~jfuller/gen_mail_surnames-ste.html
  "STI-STN"
  http://www.rootsweb.com/~jfuller/gen_mail_surnames-sti.html
  "STO-STQ"
  http://www.rootsweb.com/~jfuller/gen_mail_surnames-sto.html
  "STR-STT"
  http://www.rootsweb.com/~jfuller/gen_mail_surnames-str.html
  "STU-STZ"
  http://www.rootsweb.com/~jfuller/gen_mail_surnames-stu.html
  "SU-SZ"
  http://www.rootsweb.com/~jfuller/gen_mail_surnames-su.html
  Search the index of surname mailing lists below: Surname Mailing Lists.

  - ○ Genealogy Resources on the Internet - Surnames Included in Mailing Lists - "S"
    http://www-personal.umich.edu/~cgaunt/surnames/s.names.html
    This is a computer generated list of the surnames, and all variant spellings for those names, that are found in the surname mailing lists detailed on the pages shown above.

- Genealogy Resources on the Internet - Surname Web Sites for "S" Surnames
  http://www-personal.umich.edu/~cgaunt/surnames/s.html

- Genealogy's Most Wanted - Surnames Beginning with "S"
  http://www.citynet.net/mostwanted/s.htm

- Google Web Directory .... Genealogy>Surnames>S
  http://directory.google.com/Top/Society/Genealogy/Surnames/S/

- Heartland Genealogy Society Membership List - S
  http://www.geocities.com/Heartland/Ranch/2416/hgs-mlist-s.html

- H-GIG Surname Registry - Surnames Beginning S
  http://www.ucr.edu/h-gig/surdata/surname19.html

- Higginson Book Company - Surnames Beginning with S
  http://www.higginsonbooks.com/s.htm

- inGeneas Table of Common Surname Variations and Surname Misspellings - R-S
  http://www.ingeneas.com/R2S.html

- The Obituary Link Page - Family Obituary Archives Online - S
  http://www.geocities.com/~cribbswh/obit/s.htm

- Open Directory - Society: Genealogy: Surnames: S
  http://www.dmoz.org/Society/Genealogy/Surnames/S/

- 'S' Surnames at RootsWeb
  http://resources.rootsweb.com/surnames/s.html

- Surname Springboard Index - S
  http://www.geocities.com/~alacy/spring_s.htm

- SurnameWeb Surname Registry - S Index
  http://www.surnameweb.org/registry/s.htm

- SWINX Zoeklijst Nederlandse Familienamen / SWINX Searchlist Dutch Surnames - S
  http://www.swinx.net/swinx/swinx_sa_nl.htm

- Websites at RootsWeb: S Surnames
  http://www.rootsweb.com/~websites/surnames/s.html

◆ Surname Specific Sites and Resources

- SACKETT Surname Mailing List
  http://www.nmmi.cc.nm.us/~nancy/sackett/
  Includes Sacket, Seckett, Secket, Sachet, Sacket, Sackette, Sackitt, Sackat, Sackatt, Sackutt, Sackville, Saccavilla.

- SADOWSKI / SANDUSKY Family Home Page
  http://members.aol.com/anderson73/sandusky.html
  Descendants of Antoni SADOWSKI of Pennsylvania and others researching the SANDUSKY or SADOWSKI name.

- SALISBURY Genealogy Site
  http://members.aol.com/dalesman/
  SALISBURY surname and deriviants UK, USA, Canadian and Australian data from various sources.

- SAMSON Family Home Page
  http://www.familytreemaker.com/users/s/a/m/Charles-A-Samson
  The Samson Family Homepage traces the descendants of the first Samson immigrants to New France (Quebec) in 1665.

- SANDERS Family Association of the South
  http://www.geocities.com/~rewoodham/sanders.html

- SANDHAUS World HomePage
  http://members.aol.com/Sandhaus/Index.html
  All things SANDHAUS, including genealogical information.

- The SANKEY One Name Study
  http://www.sankey.demon.co.uk/genindex.html

- SANT Family Name
  http://www.gwbrown.freeuk.com/
  For the SANT surname, particularly in the U.K. and the U.S.

- SAPP Family History, Genealogy
  http://members.aol.com/Sapps/SFH.html

- SARGENT Family Page
  http://www.angelfire.com/az/JMSHomepage/SARGENT.html

- The SASSO Meeting Place
  http://members.aol.com/combit3/index.html
  A simple webpage for anyone researching the surname of Sasso especially, but not limited to those with roots in New York.

- The SAULNIER Genealogy HomePage
  http://www.geocities.com/Heartland/Acres/6946/
  Descendants of Louis Saulnier and Louise Bastinaud dit Pelletier, who arrived in Acadia (now Nova Scotia) c.1685.

- The SAUM Family Album
  http://www.softcom.net/users/lfiedler/saum/default.htm
  Other surnames are Roe, Stahl, Carver, Feasel, Shaver, Helmick, Miller, and Brubaker.

- SAUNDERS (SANDERS) Family Genealogy - From Colonial Virginia to Pioneers Out West
  http://home.att.net/~eesaunders/tp.html
  Phillip Saunders, William Saunders, James & Sarah Gunnel Saunders.

- SAUVE Family History Pages
  http://sauvefamilyhistory.homepage.com

- The SAVAGE Family
  http://home.att.net/~dpdklong/Savage.htm
  The SAVAGE family of central Alabama, with stories of their origin and an unusual Civil War story.

- SAVAGE Surname Resource Center
  http://freepages.genealogy.rootsweb.com/~geneal/src/SavageSRC.html

- Les SAVARD d'Amérique / SAVARDs of America
  http://www.bigfoot.com/~csavard/

- David SAYRE & Elizabeth WELLS
  http://pweb.netcom.com/~sayre/

- SCADDING, SCADDAN, SCADDEN, SCADDENG Genealogy
  http://www.scadding.demon.co.uk/gene1.htm
  Genealogical homepage for all those interested in the Scadd* families and their Devon, Dorset and Cornish origins.

- SCAIFE Study Group (Family History Society)
  http://www.chesh12.freeserve.co.uk/index.htm
  One name study dedicated to researching the SCAIFE surname and its variants.

- SCAMP - The Genealogy of a Gypsy Family
  http://ourworld.compuserve.com/homepages/rogerbaker/

- The SCASBROOK Study
  http://www.geocities.com/scasbrook/
  SCASBROOK or a variant (e.g., SCARSBROOK, SCARISBRICK, SCAISBRICK, SKASEBROOK).

- SCHAEFFER Genealogy
  http://www.geocities.com/Heartland/Prairie/5275
  Schaeffer surname list, Schaeffer Photographs, Pennsylvania Deutsch, early settlers of Ohio and Illinois.

- The SCHAEFFERs of the Tulpehocken Settlement
  http://www.familytreemaker.com/users/s/c/h/David-L-Schaeffer/
  SCHAEFFER, SCHAEFER, SCHAFER, SHAEFFER, SHAEFER, SHAFFER, SCHAVER, SHAVER, SHEFFER.

- SCHAAF-Homepage
  http://www.stud.uni-saarland.de/~stsca/schaafe.htm
  Schaaf, Schaaff, Schaff, Schoaf in Germany, France, America and the whole world.

- The SCHAKES of La Charette 1855 - 1996
  http://www.rootsweb.com/~mowarren/schake/intro.html
  From Humfeld, Lippe (Germany) of the Teutoburger Forest to Charette Township, Warren County, Missouri.

- The SCHAPPELL Family Genealogy Page
  http://www.jgilbert.org/chapell.html
  History of the SCHAPPELL Family in Berks County, Pennsylvania.

- The official SCHMIDERER Web site
  http://www.schmiderer.de

- Die Genealogie der Familie SCHIMMELPFENNIG / The Genealogy of the SCHIMMELPFENNIG Family
  http://www.schimmelpfennigweb.de/
  Branches in USA and Netherlands from 1300 to today. The most important surnames are: Schimmelpfennig, Schimelpfenig, Schimmelpenninck, Schimmelpfeng, Von Schimmelpfennig, Schimmelfennig Von Der Oye.

- SCHMUTZ Roots
  http://www.schmutzroots.org/
  Genealogy and history of Hans Schmutz (1554) and descendants from Vechigen, canton Bern.

- SCHNARE Family Reunion
  http://freepages.genealogy.rootsweb.com/~schnare
  Gathering all descendants of George SCHNARE and Desire Ann NICKERSON of Sambro, Nova Scotia, Canada.

- SCHNATZ Family
  http://members.aol.com/DSchnatz/index.html
  Descendants of Adam Schnatz, born 1791 in Germany, died April 1871 in New York.

- SCHNELLER Genealogy
  http://pages.prodigy.net/dave_lossos/schnel.htm

- SCHOENEBERGER Resource Center
  http://members.aol.com/asheneberg/Schoen/
  Includes Sheneberger, Shenberger, Schoenberger, Schoeneberger, Schoenenberger, Shoenberger, Sheanaberger, Shanaberger, Shenneberger, Shaneberger, Shoneberger, Schoneberger, Schineberger, Shineberger, Shinebarger, Shinaberger, Shenenberger, Shenenberg.

- SCHOLDERER-SHOLDER Family Genealogy Home Page
  http://www.siscom.net/~rdrunner/index.htm
  Family from Stuttgart, Germany who settled in Pennsylvania in 1832. Other related families, Lycoming County, PA: UPDEGRAFF, HEIM, STABLER, KIESS, WALTZ, ULMER, GOEDEKING, REMMERT.

- SCHOOLER Family
  http://www.geocities.com/Heartland/Farm/6582/
  I Descendants of William Schooler b. abt 1640 in England who came to Virginia.

- SCHOONMAKER Family Association
  http://members.aol.com/BethRN3CA/schoonmaker.html

- Eli and Magdalena (Wenger) SCHROCK Family History
  http://www.bibleviews.com/schrock.html
  Brief history of the Mennonite family of Eli and Magdalena (WENGER) SCHROCK of Waterloo County, Ontario, Canada and Elkhart Co., Indiana, starting in 1816. The name SCHROCK was also spelled SHRUCK in the Waterloo County records; SCHRAG on his tombstone; and SCHROG in Ezra Eby's book. Also includes data on Shirk, Eby, Good, Berkey, Stauffer.

- The SCHRYVER Page
  http://www.schryver.org/
  Schryver, Schryver, Schriber, Schriver, de Schryver, De Schryver.

- SCHULER Family Genealogy
  http://ourworld.compuserve.com/homepages/RSchuler/schulerf.htm
  Descendants of Gabriel Schuler of Skippack, Montgomery County, Pennsylvania (c.1672-1779).

- SCHUMAN SCHUMANN Surname Project
  http://members.xoom.com/tsterkel/surname_projects/schuman.htm

- Genealogie Familie SCHUTTE(N)
  http://leden.tref.nl/hschutte
  Ik zoek alles betreffende de naam "Schutte" en specifiek uit de Achterhoek en Zuid-Holland.

- **SCHWANGER Family Association**
  http://homepages.rootsweb.com/~swanger/Schwanger/index.htm
  Descendants of Jacob SCHWANGER who landed in Philadelphia and signed an Oath of Allegiance to the Province of Philadelphia on October 20, 1747.

- **SCHWEISSGUT Historical Society**
  http://www.sns-access.com/~lamackey/swise.html
  Schwainsgute, Schweisgut, Schweisgood, Schweisgute, Schweisguth, Schweissgut, Schweissguth, Schweiszguth, Swaisgood, Sweisgood, Swicegood, Sweisguth, Swysgood, Weisgut.

- **SCHWEITZER, SWISHER, SWITZER Website**
  http://members.aol.com/TNash74528/Index.html

- **SCHWENKNet**
  http://www.cyberhighway.net/~gordons/
  Dedicated primarily to those living descendants of Conrad Schwenk (1601-1686), weaver, of Laichingen, Baden-Wuerttemberg in So. Germany.

- **SCISM Family Association**
  http://homepages.rootsweb.com/~scismfam/
  Includes Scissom, Scisson, Sissom, Sisson, Chisholm, Chism, Cissom, Cism, Scizm.

- **SCISSONS Surname Research Project**
  http://www.scissons.com/genealogy
  Information and research on the SCISSONS surname.

- **Scotney.org**
  http://www.scotney.org
  Devoted to the SCOTNEY family worldwide.

- **Clan SCOTT Society**
  http://www.clanscott.org/

- **SCOVILLE List**
  http://www.onelist.com/subscribe.cgi/Scoville
  For those interested in the surname SCOVILLE. Helping people to connect with one another, share data & knowledge.

- **SCUDDER Family Resource Center**
  http://www.geocities.com/Heartland/Ridge/1381/scudder/scudder.htm
  Descendants and Ancestors of Thomas SCUDDER of Salem, MA. Includes some descendants of John and his sister, Elizabeth, SCUDDER of Barnstable, MA.

- **The SEALE Family**
  http://www.dallas.net/~seale/

- **Seale.html**
  http://freepages.genealogy.rootsweb.com/~rpeld/seale.html
  The St. Helena Seale family data base. Seale, Bagley, Funge, Greentree, Higham, Janisch, Knipe, Phillips, Pledger, Worrall.

- **Descendants of Capt. John SEAMAN, Hempstead, Long Island, NY**
  http://www.familytreemaker.com/users/r/u/b/James-David-Rubins-CA/index.html

- **SEARLES in Westchester County, New York**
  http://members.aol.com/jl3bluhm/sarles.htm
  Sarles, Sarlls, Sarls, Serls, Sirls, and Surles.

- **SEARS Family Association**
  http://www.genealogy.org/~lrsears

- **SEDGWICK Genealogy**
  http://www.sedgwick.org/genealogy/

- **SEDORIS Family Tree**
  http://sedoris.homepage.com/Sedoris_Family.html

- **SEE Family Web Page**
  http://www.geocities.com/Heartland/Valley/1410/see/index.html
  Jean Sy from Calais France was the father of Isaac See, who went to NY and began a huge family in the US. SEE family starts in Holland and came to New York and Virginia.

- **SEEs of New York**
  http://pages.preferred.com/~dsee/genie.html
  This site concentrates on descendants of Isaac SY who came from Picardy, France to Tarrytown, NY via the English ship Diamond in 1674. Related surnames include Devoe, Conklin, Dutcher, Gardenier, Foseur, Ackerman, and Van Wert. The site includes a growing list of 1850 census entries for SEEs in the U.S.

- **SEIJKENS Genealogy**
  http://millennium.fortunecity.com/quarrybank/36/
  Seijkens, Seykens, Seikens, Sijkes, Sijkens, Zeijkens (1007 names & 327 families) connected through marriage.

- **SELF Family Addendum**
  http://expage.com/page/selfadd

- **SELF Family Newsletter**
  http://www.self-family.com/
  SELF, SELFE, SELPH.

- **SELF Portraits: The SELF Family NetLetter**
  http://www.inland.net/~tim/

- **Genealogy: SELLECK**
  http://home.att.net/~jg245/selleck.htm
  Descendants of David Selleck, born in England, died 1654 in Virginia.

- **SELLERS Family Genealogy**
  http://showcase.netins.net/web/sellerfamily/
  Sellers, Sollars, Cellars, Zellers.

- **The SENSEBACH Family Research Association Home Page**
  http://www.geocities.com/Heartland/Meadows/4596/
  Sensabaugh, Sensebaugh, Sensibaugh, Sencabaugh, Sencebaugh, Sencibaugh, Sensiboy, Sinsabaugh, Sinsapaugh, Sincebaugh, Cencebaugh, Sencenbaugh, Sensenbaugh, Sensanbaugh, Sincerbeaux, Cincebeaux, Cincebox, Sinsebox, Sincerbox, Sencerbox, Sencaboy.

- **The SERNAs of New Mexico Newsletter**
  http://www.geocities.com/Heartland/Pointe/4410
  SERNAs in New Mexico and Spain. Also newsletter.

- **SEWELL Family History ~1760-1997~**
  http://www.edm.net/~Pjsewell/
  Descendants of English Abraham SEWELL and Mary CARPENTER.

- **SEXTON Genealogy Research Page**
  http://www.genealogy.org/~sexton/
  Sexton. Sexten. Saxon. Saxton. Saxe.

- Descendants of Johann Georg SHADE
  http://members.xoom.com/washade/Shade/shade.htm
  From Germany, George settled in Warrington Township, York County, Pennsylvania and died there in 1775. His descendants spread through PA, OH, KS and other places.

- SHADE Families - PA / OH / IL / MO / Etc.
  http://www.familytreemaker.com/users/s/h/a/Forrest-D-Shade/index.html
  Descendants of Andreas Shade who emigrated from Germany and settled in Pennsylvania in 1750. Descendants of eight Shade men and their spouses. Most of these men came from Germany and settled in Pennsylvania in the mid 1700's.

- The SHANKLAND One-Name Group
  http://ourworld.compuserve.com/homepages/shankland/

- SHANKLE Family Genealogy
  http://homepages.rootsweb.com/~wshankle
  Information related to various SHANKLE family groups in North America (Canada and United States). It includes the following surname variations: Shankles, Schenkel, Shinkle, Shenkel.

- SHANNON Genealogy & History
  http://www.geocities.com/Heartland/Hills/5600/

- SHANNON Genealogy & History Message board
  http://www.InsideTheWeb.com/messageboard/mbs.cgi/mb11299
  SHANNON, SHANAHAN.

- SHANNON Searchers Newsletter
  mailto:JSBRIDG@aol.com
  For details send e-mail to Joyce Shannon Bridges at JSBRIDG@aol.com.

- The SHAPLEIGH Family Association
  http://mainetoday.koz.com/maine/shapleigh
  Descendants of Alexander Shapleigh the Immigrant, one of the founders of Kittery, Maine.

- SHARMAN Family History
  http://home.eznet.net/~rsharman/
  SHARMAN family members from 1794 to 1998, from England to Scotland to America.

- Descendants of George Washington SHATTLES ~ 1772
  http://www.my-ged.com/shattles/

- John SHAVER & Mary BLACKWELDER of North Carolina, Tennessee, and Arkansas
  http://www.geocities.com/Heartland/Hills/6359/shaver/shaver.html

- SHEA Genealogy Links
  http://www.geocities.com/Heartland/Valley/1410/shea_index.html
  Shea, Shay.

- The SHEALTIEL Family Worldwide
  http://www.shealtiel.org/
  Saltiel, Shaltiel, Shaaltiel, Sealtiîl, Chaltiel, Chartiel and Schaltiel.

- Descendants of John SHEARIN
  http://www.parsonstech.com/genealogy/trees/gshearin/SHEARIN.htm
  Born about 1626 in England. Includes Shearin, Shearon, Sherron and many more.

- The SHEATHERS - Our Australian Heritage
  http://www.wts.com.au/~pwsheather/phil/australi.html

- The SHELBY Exchange
  http://www.familytreemaker.com/users/t/r/o/Judith-A-Trolinger/
  Home page and quarterly newsletter.

- SHELDON Family Association
  http://www.sheldonfamily.org/

- My SHELTON Family
  http://www.mindspring.com/~jogt/surnames/sheltfam.htm
  One Branch from Virginia.

- Ralph SHELTON, Sr., Genealogy Notes
  http://members.xoom.com/janicekmc/ralphsr.htm
  Shelton, Crisp/Crispin/Crispen.

- SHEPPARD Family Association
  http://www.geocities.com/sheppardfamilyassociation/
  Association of those interested in the surnames Sheppard, Shepard, Shepherd, Shephard and other variants; site of One-Name Study.

- SHERESHEVSKY Home Page
  http://www.teleport.com/~arl/Shereshevsky.html

- SHERIDAN Sentinel
  http://members.xoom.com/revjsheridan/
  Descendants of John Sheridan Sr. Ireland-Virginia-Kentucky.

- My SHERMAN Family Page
  http://members.aol.com/MALUTZ/tips.html

- The SHERMANs of Yaxley Home Page
  http://members.aol.com/macpinhead/sherman.html
  The group is name for Tom Sherman (1422-1493) of Yaxley, Suffolk, England, one of the earliest proven ancestors.

- SHERMANs of Yaxley
  http://www.geocities.com/Heartland/Ranch/3064/sherman.htm
  This site contains wills transcribed from "Some of the Descendants of Philip Sherman, First Secretary of Rhode Island" by Roy V. Sherman.

- The SHERRILL/SHERRELL Family Assn.
  http://www.abraxis.com/tuckahoe/shersher/shersher.html

- SHERWOOD Home Page
  http://www.sherwood.org.uk/

- The SHIELDS Family Web Page
  http://www.neibaur.org/shields.html
  Descendants of James Shields 1777.

- SHIFFER Genealogy Page
  http://home.att.net/~jsgehrig/index.html
  Home page for the name SHIFFER. Lists the descendants of Edward Shiffer, born 1828 in Pennsylvania.

- SHIFLETT Family Genealogy
  http://www.geocities.com/Heartland/Hills/4575/
  Shiflet, Shifflett, Shiplet, Shiplett, Shifflet.

- The SHILLABEER Connection
  http://members.aol.com/cshillabee
  One-Name Genealogical Study on the surname Shillabeer and variants which include Shillibeer, Shellabear(e), Shillaber and Shillibier.

- SHIPPEE, SHIPPEY, SHIPPY Genealogy
  http://www.geocities.com/Heartland/Plains/4799/shippee.html

- SHIRAH Genealogy Project
  http://www.geocities.com/heartland/lane/8468/shirahmain.html

- Journeys of a Mennonite - "The SHIRK Family"
  http://www.encode.com/user/shirk/
  This site provides a listing of ships that SHERK / SHIRK / SCHURCH and the other 60 plus spellings of the name may have traveled on from Switzerland in the 1600's to 1800's from Europe. Additional pages identifies books published by Schurch authors about their genealogy and a list of current family historians. A link is provided to access the Schurch Family Association of North Americas information web site that should provide updated information regarding the Association and upcoming Family Reunions.

- The SHIRLEY Association
  http://www.shirleyassociation.com/

- The SHIVERS Family Newsletter
  mailto:glydie@alaska.net
  E-mail Glydie Nelson for details at: glydie@alaska.net.

- Richard SHOCKLEY and Ann BOYDEN Descendants
  http://www.patpnyc.com/shock1de.htm#

- SHOEMAKE Family History Page
  http://www.tlxnet.net/~bradjudy/

- Maiden's Choice: The Website for the Descendents of Lawrence SHOOK and Other SHOOK, SHOCK, SHUCK, SCHOCH, SCHUCK, etc. Families
  http://www.omegatower.com/shook/
  Concentrates on Lawrence SHOOK (1733-c.1820) and Herman SHOOK (c.1718-1789) of West Virginia. Also offers a huge collection of genealogies for similar surnames, like Shock, Shuck, Schuck, and links to many researchers and resources.

- Russ SHOPBELL's Web page
  http://www.bright.net/~rshop

- SHOUN Family Association - SHOUN Branches
  http://shoun.occgs.com/welcome.html
  Shoun, Shawn, Shown.

- SHUCK Family Home Page
  http://homepage.interaccess.com/~nealu/shuck.htm
  Information exchange for researchers of the Shuck surname including the spelling variants Shook, Shock, Shoc, Shoch, Schuck, Schook, Schock, Schoc, Schoch, Schuh, Shue and Schug.

- SHULLEY Genealogy Home Page
  http://freepages.genealogy.rootsweb.com/~csanders/Shulley/RR_TOC.HTM
  Descendants of Frederick Shulley of south central Pennsylvania.

- SHULL Family Genealogy
  http://www.geocities.com/Heartland/Ranch/8593/
  Shull genealogy from Jonathan Shull and Abraham Shull.

- SHUMAN Genealogy
  http://homepages.rootsweb.com/~shuman/welcome.html
  A clearinghouse for all those who are researching the surname SHUMAN in its numerous spellings, including but not limited to Schuman, Schumann, Scheman, Sewman, Sheman, Shewman, Shoeman, Shueman, Shöman, and Suman.

- The SHUMWAY Root Cellar
  http://www.shumway.org/

- SIBILLE Family Narratives and Genealogy
  http://www.rootsquest.com/~fifolet
  Joseph SIBILLE and Penelope Burleigh and descendents from 1814 to the present.

- SIDES Lines
  http://www.halcyondays.com/famnames/sides/side_lines.htm
  A quarterly newsletter dedicated to the Sides/Seitz/Sites family surname.

- The SIDNEY Internet Directory
  http://www.i-way.co.uk/~sid/sidney.html
  The World Wide Web site of all things Sidney. Includes the surname Sydney.

- SIDWELL Genealogy and Family History
  http://homepages.rootsweb.com/~raydon65/sidwell.htm
  Hugh SIDWELL I and Elizabeth GOLDING Genealogy.

- The SIKES / SYKES Families Association
  http://www.sikes-sykesfamilies.org
  Information about the family association for anyone with an interest in the surnames of SIKES or SYKES and allied family names.

- SILKS
  http://www.uftree.com/UFT/WebPages/JanRowan/SILKS98/index.htm
  Descendants of David SILKS born April 16, 1751. SILKS, DETRICK, GRACE, HAIR, CASNER, JENNINGS.

- The SIMARD Genealogy Page
  http://www.gaudreau.org/arthur/genealogy/simard.sht

- SIMISTER Family Association
  http://www.simister.org/

- The SIMMONS Home Page
  http://www.genesis.net.au/~simmons/

- SIMONEAU - Histoire et genealogie de familles Simoneau
  http://www.securenet.net/members/psimonea/
  Histoire et gÈnÈalogie de familles SIMONEAU du QuÈbec, Canada, Etats-Unis, Louisiane, USA, de France et d'ailleurs.

- SIMPSON Surname Centre
  http://members.tripod.com/SimpsonGenes/index.html

- The SIMS et al. GEDCOM Project
  http://www.world.std.com/~lsimms/simms2.html
  A centralized collection of over 2,000 Sims surnames and variant spellings: Sims, Simms, Syms, Symms, Symes, Symmes, Sim, Simm, Sime, Simmes, Syme, Symme, Sym, Symm, Sems, Semms, Semes, Semmes, Symns, Symmns et al.

- SINCLAIR Genealogy#160;
  http://www.rootsweb.com/~kyscott/sinclair.htm
  Early VA and KY family. Includes: SINCLOR, SINCLEAR, ST. CLAIR or SINKLER.

- SINEX Family Newsletter
  mailto:waughtel@oz.net
  Send e-mail to Antoinette Waughtel Sorensen at waughtel@oz.net for details.

- SINGLETON Descendants of Colonial North Carolina
  http://www.geocities.com/~ncsingletons/
  From Colonial North Carolina to Tennessee, Arkansas, Missouri, Mississippi, Illinois, Texas, Indiana.

- Genealogie SJOLLEMA ~ Netherlands
  http://www.rendo.dekooi.nl/~sjollema/genealogie.htm
  De naam Sjollema en honderden andere namen geparenteerd aan de Sjollema's.

- SKILES - SKYLES Website
  http://homepages.rootsweb.com/~skifri/Index.htm
  SKILES - SKYLES anywhere in the United States.

- Descendants of Thomas and Deborah (?) SKILLINGS of Cumberland Co, Maine
  http://www.geocities.com/Heartland/Plains/1208/Skillings/index.htm
  Thomas Skillings was from Salem and was among the early settlers of Gloucester, MA. His land was near the ancient burying ground. As early as 1651, he had moved to Falmouth (Portland), but had returned and was living in Gloucester in 1658, and that year came back to Falmouth and died there in 1667. In 1658, he purchased the farm at Back Cove from George Cleeves, which he occupied until his death and which was held in the family for many years.

- SKINNER Family Association
  http://www.geocities.com/Paris/1051/SkinnerFamAssc.htm

- SKIPWORTH Family Homepage
  http://members.aol.com/bartology/bartology/SkipworthHome.html

- The SKRINE Resource - A Study of the Surname
  http://www.skrine.fsbusiness.co.uk/default.htm
  Includes variants such as SCRINE, SCREEN, SKRYNE, SCRENE etc.

- Revealing Family Ancestry - SLAGG Family History
  http://www.hal-pc.org/~jsb/page36.html

- SLÄKTEN STÅLNACKE - STÅLNACKEN suku The Family STÅLNACKE
  http://angelfire.com/ri/stolnacke/index.html
  Sweden, Finland and Norway.

- Descendants of Thomas SLEDD
  http://csc.techcenter.org/~mneill/thomassledd.html

- The SLEE One-Name Society
  http://www.homeusers.prestel.co.uk/naylor/sons/slee.htm

- Descendants of John SLOAN / SLONE 1700-1999
  http://msnhomepages.talkcity.com/PicnicPl/tami_99/

- SLOUGH Depository
  http://www.geocities.com/~kjbowen/slough2.htm

- SMALL Genealogy Web Pages
  http://www.geocities.com/Heartland/Hills/1760/sgwp.html
  Genealogy and history of the SMALL surname and its variants, Smalle, Smalley, Scmalz, etc. 1600's to present.

- SMALL, George Descendants
  http://www.theparrs.com/genealogy/small/
  George SMALL (1765-1852) who settled in Montgomery Co., KY. His descendants spread to Tipton, Howard and Hamilton Counties, IN; IL, MN and beyond.

- SMALTZ Genealogy-Part 1
  http://pages.prodigy.com/MD/xnra99a/xnra99a3.html
  With links to Part 2 and other surnames.

- SMART Memorial Preservation Society
  http://www.geocities.com/Heartland/Meadows/7602/
  Descendants of Reverend James SMART, born October 13, 1714 in Prince George Co., Virginia and his wife Elizabeth LEDBETTER.

- SMELSER / SMELTZER Descendants Genealogy Group
  http://members.tripod.com/~tracers/
  Smelser/Smeltzer family in America and possibly Germany.

- SMERDON Family Genealogy and Contact Forum
  http://www.begent.freeserve.co.uk/smertree.htm

- SMILEY Families of Philadelphia
  http://www.geocities.com/heartland/grove/8895

- Descendants of John B. SMILEY
  http://www.creativealternatives.net/geneal/smiley/
  Born May 18, 1763 in Donegal, Ireland; came to New Jersey with his family; fought with the Continental Army; lived in Orange Co., NY, Ulster Co., NY, Tompkins Co., NY and Chautauqua Co., NY.

- SMITH Families of England and New England Newsletter
  mailto:CarlCindy2@aol.com
  For details send e-mail to Lucinda (Cindy) Olsen, editor and publisher, at CarlCindy2@aol.com.

- The SMITH Family Homepage
  http://members.aol.com/redwing386/smith.html
  SMITH Family in Delaware and Franklin county, Ohio, along with local history and photos.

- SMITH Genealogy
  http://members.aol.com/ImaBR/index.html
  Descendants of Freeman R. SMITH, b. 25 Oct. 1814 in North Carolina.

- SMITH Name Registry
  http://www.geocities.com/Heartland/Plains/3264/ASmith.html
  Register your Smith names for inclusion in this growing database.

- Some Descendants of James SMITH of Weymouth, Massachusetts
  http://www.prenticenet.com/home/vandy/smith.htm

- SMITHIN / SMITHSEND Family Genealogy
  http://dspace.dial.pipex.com/town/drive/acs34/

- The SMITHSON Association
  http://members.aol.com/Rickishay/shp.html/
  The Smithson Family Exchange Newsletter, mailing list, photo archive and more.

- The SMITTER Family Tree
  http://users.netonecom.net/~pwn/smitter/index.html
  Descendants of Wobbes SMITTER, born in the 1700's, died in 1823.

- SMOOT Ancestry
  http://www.familytreemaker.com/users/s/m/o/Steve-L-Smoot/
  Devoted to the descendants of William SMUTE, born 1596.

- The SMOTHERMAN / SMOTHERMON / SMITHERMAN Family Homepage
  http://www.geocities.com/Heartland/7581/
  Dedicated to genealogy research into the Smotherman and Smothermon surnames, with special emphasis on Middle Tennessee and West Kentucky. Because the names Smotherman and Smothermon evolved from the name Smitherman, the Smitherman surname is also included.

- SMUIN Genealogy pages
  http://www.smuin.demon.co.uk/pages/geneo1.htm
  Smuin, Smewing, Smewin, etc.

- SNELGROVE Family History Page
  http://members.home.net/snelgrov

- Descendants of John SNELLGROVE
  http://www.parsonstech.com/genealogy/trees/psnellgr/charlie.htm
  Snellgrove, Shealy, Amick, Oxner, Palmer.

- The SNELSON DataBase & Index
  http://www.southernx.com.au/snelson/

- SNIPES Family History, Person County, North Carolina
  http://www.geocities.com/Heartland/Estates/3882/Snipes.html
  Descendants of Richard SNAPE, born in Oxford Co., England.

- SNIPES Family of America Home Page
  http://www.familytreemaker.com/users/s/n/i/Robert-T-Snipes/

- SNODGRASS Family Genealogy Page
  http://www.communinet.org/QA/Snodgrass/index.html
  Descendants of Benjamin Snodgrass (b. 1761) and Agnes "Nancy" McClung (b. 1763).

- The SNOWDON Family Record
  http://www.glinx.com/~snowdon/
  Descendants of Pickering Snowdon (1750-1830) a native of Yorkshire and Dorcas Easterbrooks (1753-1827) a native of Rhode Island Pioneers settlers in Sackville, New Brunswick.

- SNYDER Surnames Search
  http://www.angelfire.com/fl/SNYDER/index.html

- SODEN Family Researchers
  http://member.aol.com/basii/basii.htm
  Origin of Soden, Sodon, Sowden, Sowdan surname from Germany, England and Ireland. Traces earliest Soden ancestors in North America. Spouses Applegate, Hillyer.

- The SOLE Society
  http://www.solesociety.freeserve.co.uk/sole.htm
  A British Family History Society researching Sole, Saul, Sewell, Solley and their variants.

- SOLON Surname Registry and Family History
  http://www.geocities.com/Heartland/Plains/8270/solon/
  Researching all occurrences of the SOLON or SOLAN surname.

- SORRELL Genealogy
  http://www.webpak.net/~kyblue/sorrell/index.htm

- The SORTORE Family
  http://www.mcn.net/~hmscook/jsortore/sortore.html
  Also SORTOR and SORTER.

- SOUTHARD Genealogy Research Center
  http://www.paradoxdesigns.com/southard

- SOUTHER Family Association
  http://www.geocities.com/Heartland/Estates/9785/SoutherHomePage.html
  Descendants of Joseph (SOWTHER) SOUTHER of Boston, Massachusetts. Immigrated from England in the early 1600s. The Souther family long resided in the towns of Hingham & Cohasset, MA. Other important families: Lincoln; Pineo; Sprague; Stowell; Tower & Valli.

- The SOUTHERN Family in North Carolina
  http://www.mindspring.com/~msouthern/
  A history of William and Magdalen SOUTHERN of Stokes County, N.C., and the first generations of their descendants.

- SOUTHON One-Name Study
  http://home.clara.net/iainkerr/kerr/southon.htm
  Sotheran, Sothern, Sotheron, Southan, Southin, Southen, Southon, Southerin, Southern, Sowtan, Sowten, Sowton, Sudran, Sudrenn, Sudron, Sutherin, Suthern, Sutherns, Suthren, Suthryn.

- The SOUTHWORTH Home Page
  http://members.aol.com/sforg/index.html

- Descendants of Constant SOUTHWORTH
  http://users.ev1.net/~hmltn/southworthbook/title.htm
  This is the place to find the book, "Descendants of Constant Southworth..." by Samuel Webber published in 1905.

- SOWDER / SOUDER Collections
  http://www.geocities.com/~jdanielson/sowder.htm

- The SOWDER Genealogical & Historical Society
  http://www.familytreemaker.com/users/s/o/w/DALE-E-SOWDER/

- The SPANGLER / SPENGLER Family Genealogy Page
  http://www.txdirect.net/~spangler/

- The SPANN Family Genealogy Home Page
  http://pweb.netcom.com/~spann/
  A meeting place for researchers of the SPANN family and related families.

- The SPEARRITT Genealogy One-Name Study Group
  http://www.radices.freeserve.co.uk/
  SPURRETT, SPEARIETT, SPIRIT, SPERET, SPORET.

- SPEELMAN Family Tree
  http://www.speelman.net/speelman/
  Descendants of Jacob Speelman - Speelman (Speelmon), Castleberry, Thompson, McManus.

- The SPELTZ Web
  http://www.speltz.com

- SPENCELEY Family Names
  http://www.marton.demon.co.uk/spengene.htm

- Descendents of Henry G. SPENCER
  http://www.parsonstech.com/genealogy/trees/gspencer/hspencer.htm
  Includes WHITBREAD, HILLS.

- Descendants of Henry G. SPENCER
  http://freepages.genealogy.rootsweb.com/~george

- SPENCER Historical and Genealogical Society, Inc.
  http://www.spectrumdata.com/shgs/

- SPERRY Genealogy - The Family Seedling
  http://members.tripod.com/earlylight/sperry.html
  Seeking SPERRY connections from Illinois and Missouri, descendants of Manley Peck SPERRY.

- SPICKERMAN Family Database
  http://spickerman.cjb.net
  Database of all Spickermans residing in the United States.

- The SPIKER / SPEICHER / SPYKER Family National Registry
  http://users.intercomm.com/spike/

- SPINNEY Family Genealogy
  http://www.geocities.com/Heartland/Meadows/2069/
  Spiney, Sinneye, Spinneys.

- SPLAWN Family Search
  http://www.hal-pc.org/~splawn/

- The International SPRACKLEN Home Page
  http://www.phaenom.com/spracklen
  Spracklen, Spracklin, Sprackling, Sprackland, Spradlin, Spradling, Sparklin etc. in England, Canada, South Africa and the US.

- SPRAGUE Database
  http://www.sprague-database.org/
  (The Composite Sprague Data Base) Compiled by Richard E. (Dick) Weber, over 110,000 individuals.

- Descendants of Dennis SPRINGER and Ann PRICKETT
  http://www.geocities.com/Heartland/Prairie/8794
  Web page for the family research group which publishes a newsletter and is preparing a book for publication on the over 13,000 descendants of this couple.

- SPRINKLE - Sprenckel - SPRANKLE Family Homepage
  http://www.familytreemaker.com/users/e/d/e/Kristy-Edenfield/index.html
  The hard work of over 60 researchers is available here regarding the SPRINKLE surname and it's many spelling variations.

- SPROUSE Family History
  http://homepages.rootsweb.com/~sprouse/
  Researching the name SPROUSE, SPROUCE mainly from the Virginia line of Vincent and Mary Sprouse from early 1700's and movement of this and other families throughout the US. Includes researcher database for all known Sprouse lines.

- Descendants of Dr. Godfrey SPRUILL
  http://www.rootsweb.com/~takelley/spruill/godfrey.htm
  Born about 1650 in Scotland and died about 1719 in North Carolina.

- The SPURLOCK Family Association
  http://www.geocities.com/Heartland/Hills/4411/

- SPEYRER Family Association
  http://www.geocities.com/Vienna/6980/
  For descendants of Balthasar SPEYRER from Doerrenbach in the RheinlandPfalz, Germany. A reference point for members of the SPEYRER Family Association in the United States and abroad.

- The STACEY/STACY Chatline
  http://www.InsideTheWeb.com/mbs.cgi/mb130299
  Tales, recipes, folklore, and details about Stacey, Stacy, Stacie, Stace, Statia, Delastacia, Eustace, Estacia, etc. families which are in many cases related by ancestry. Also Wray, Westover, and Parks.

- The STACY Journal
  http://lightning.prohosting.com/~stacy/Journal/

- STAERKEL, STOERKEL, STŸRKEL, STÖRKEL, STARKEL, STERKEL Surname Project
  http://members.xoom.com/tsterkel/surname_projects/sterkel.htm

- The STAFFORD Families
  http://www.johnstafford.org
  Also BRUNT, EATON, HARDIMAN, BLACK, GILES, BRATTON, JOHNSTON, HETHERINGTON, WESLEY.

- STAGG Family Genealogy Page
  http://www.geocities.com/Heartland/Estates/3470/
  Researching the name Stagg, Stag, Staggs, Steg, Stegg, Stegge, Steegh and Stage descended from a Thomas STAGG (STEGGE) b. 1645 who settled in Hackensack Meadows, southeast of the present day Rutherford, New Jersey.

- STAGOLL Family History
  http://www-personal.monash.edu.au/~tim/Stagoll.html

- The STAMPER Family
  http://home.att.net/~BoKay1/index.html

- STAMPER Family Project
  http://www.stampers.org/
  Stamper and connecting family names. Stampers migrated from NC to KY and on to other states.

- The STAMPS Family History
  http://members.aol.com/hollwd/
  The history of our family from Etamps, France to England and on to Virginia aboard the Plaine Joan in 1635.

- STANDERFER, etc. Research Site
  http://www.carolyar.com/
  Standerfer, Standifer, Standefer, Standiford, Standforth, Sanderford, Sandefur, Sandefer, Standford, Sanford.

- The STANFIELD Family
  http://home.sprynet.com/~jrichmon/stfdfaml.htm
  Also Stanfill, Stansfield lines.

- National STANLEY Family Association
  http://www.stanleyfamily.org/
  An emphasis on the descendants of Thomas Stanley of Hanover County, Virginia, the progenitor of most Quaker Stanleys.

- A History of the STAPLETON Family in America
  http://stapletongenealogy.com/
  Research of STAPLETON family in VA MD NC KY TN MO and other locations of migration from the 1600's.

- The Official STARKWEATHER Genealogy Website
  http://dansabo.com/starkweather-genealogy.html

- STARLING Family Tree
  http://homepages.rootsweb.com/~starling/

- STARNES / STARNS Triennial Association
  http://www.trellis.net/steel/sta/
  From the Rhineland Palatinate in Germany, the STARING family immigrated to the Mohawk Valley in New York. Site features the descendants of Frederick Starnes who migrated to the New River Valley in Southwest Virginia in 1745.

- Descendants of Thomas STARR
  http://www.parsonstech.com/genealogy/trees/rrooy1/starr.htm
  Born about 1540 in New Romney, Kent, England.

- STAUFFER Genealogy Welcome
  http://www.angelfire.com/mo/stauffer3/index.html
  Also MARTIN, MINIER.

- STAVELEY Family Genealogy - The Staveleys of Aysgarth, Yorkshire
  http://www2.ucsc.edu/~possum/staveley.htm
  Ancestors and descendants of George Staveley and Dorothy Wray (m. 1806) of Aysgarth. Includes Staveleys of East Witton, Thoralby, Aysgarth, and Manchester.

- The STEAD/STEED One-Name Study
  http://www.stead-steedons.freeserve.co.uk/frames.htm
  Collecting all possible information on the Stead, Steed, Sted, Steade, Stade, Stede, Steede, Steds, Steeds, Stid, Stidd and Stide surnames.

- The W.T. STEAD Page
  http://members.iinet.net.au/~sharpen/stead.html
  Dedicated to William Thomas Stead (1849 - 1912).

- STEATHAM Genealogy
  http://www.steatham-wright.demon.co.uk/genealogy/steatham/steatham.html
  The complete site for the origins of the Steatham surname.

- The STEBBINS Ancestral Society
  http://www.sover.net/~neills/Stebbins.html
  For all descendants of the surname Stebbins. Presently there are three major lines represented in the database of 49,000 individuals: Rowland Stebbins, Edward Stebbins and John Stebbins.

- STEBBINS National Bank
  http://www.stebbins.com/

- Families of STEEL(E)
  http://www.geocities.com/Heartland/Ridge/6203

- The Descendants of Ninian STEELE b. 1669
  http://freepages.genealogy.rootsweb.com/~mariahswind

- The STEELE Family: The Descendants of Thomas STEELE (born 1837, Birmingham, England)
  http://members.aol.com/SteeleGenealogy/
  Descendants of Thomas and George STEELE, the orphaned sons of Thomas Steele (born 1837), who left England for Canada as part of England's child labor emigration program.

- STEELE National Repository of the STEELE Family
  http://www.metronet.com/~steele/snr/

- STEELE Quarterly News
  mailto:Tlsteeled@aol.com
  For details send e-mail to Tammy Steele at: Tlsteeled@aol.com.

- STEELMAN Family Homepage
  http://www.trellis.net/steel/steelman/
  STEELMAN, family beginning with Hans MANSSON, and Ella STILLE, immigrants from Sweden in 1641, and featuring the family of Matthias Steelman who migrated from Kent County, Delaware to Surry County, North Carolina in the early 1770's.

- The STEEN Place
  http://steenplace.com/
  One name study for STEEN.

- STEHLE Worldwide
  http://homer.span.ch/~spaw1529/genealog/

- STEILEN Homepage
  http://members.aol.com/msteilen/index.html

- The STELLJES Genealogy Project
  http://www.geocities.com/ResearchTriangle/1794/Stelljes.html
  STELJES, STELLJIS.

- STENFELT Family Genealogy
  http://www.ndepot.com/stenfelt/
  Traces primarily the STENFELT lineage including the variations STONEFELT, STONEFIELD and STENFELDT, from George STENFELT to the known current living descendants. Also partial royal (Sweden) lineages of Vasa.

- STENHOUSE
  http://www.geocities.com/sharon_hawkins_2000/stenhous.htm
  STENHOUSE families in Southern Scotland.

- The STENLAKE Genealogy Homepage
  http://www.enter.net/~stenlake/stenlake.html

- STEPHENS.Hunters
  http://www.webspawner.com/users/stephenshunters/
  From Alexander STEPHENS, the immigrant to all southern states.

- The STEPHENSON Family Homepage
  http://www.flash.net/~sparks12/family.html
  A comprehensive outline of the descendants of Joseph STEPHENSON, with current emphasis on the tribe of Joseph's son, William M. STEPHENSON of NC/TN.

- The STEPIEN's
  http://www.geocities.com/Heartland/Prairie/8473/stepien.html

- STEPP's Along The Way
  http://members.home.net/hstepp/

- Welcome to the STEPP/STAPP Families Chronicles
  http://www.ydg.com/stepp/

- Clan STIRLING-STERLING Online
  http://www.clanstirling.org/

- STERRY Worldwide
  http://www.zip.com.au/~rsterry/gen/

- STEVENSON Family History from the Eastern
  Shore of Maryland, Worcester Co, MD to Woodford
  Co, KY to Putnam Co, IN by Margaretta Stevenson
  1968.
  ftp://ftp.rootsweb.com/pub/STEVBOOK.EXE
  *This is an executable file that you can download via FTP by clicking
  on the link above. It is an 877KB file, including a viewer and a
  scanned copy of this book. This book lists STEVENSON's in
  Worcester Co, Maryland from about 1700-1790, Woodford Co, KY
  1790-1824, and then Indiana from early 1800's. Other surnames
  mentioned are Cropper, Cox, Littleton, Whittington, Fassitt,
  Campbell, Nelson. If you have any questions, contact George
  Stevenson by e-mail at: george@psychoed.com.*

- The ~ STEVENSON ~ Genealogy Page
  http://freepages.genealogy.rootsweb.com/~druryfamily/
  stevenson.htm

- STEVICK Family Tree Index
  http://bhs.broo.k12.wv.us/homepage/alumni/dstevick/tree/
  index.htm

- Clan STEWART Society in America (CSSA)
  http://www.tartans.com/clans/Stewart/society/

- STEWART Kin
  http://www.Stewartkin.com/
  *Descendants of Joseph STEWART and Sarah GILBERT of Overton
  Co., Tennessee; Also Descendants of Elijah AVERETT(1810); and
  Abel LAMB (1801)*

- STEWART Clan Newsletter
  http://members.aol.com/jlcooke/gscn.htm
  For Stewart, Steward, and Stuart.

- The Timen STIDDEM Society
  http://members.aol.com/RLSteadham/TimenWeb.index.html
  *A family association for the descendants of Timen Stiddem, the
  immigrant from Sweden to "New Sweden" (now Wilmington,
  Delaware) in the 17th century. Includes the various spellings of the
  surname including: Stidham, Stedham, Steadham, Steddom, and
  others.*

- STICE Web
  http://homepages.rootsweb.com/~stice/
  *All known STICE descendants, linked into a single tree. Also an
  invitation to join the STICE mailing list.*

- The STICKLANDs or STRICKLANDs of Cornwall
  Homepage
  http://sites.netscape.net/sticklandstrick/home

- STILES Family of America & Affiliated Families,
  Inc.
  http://www.psci.net/~rstiles/

- STIRK One-Name Study
  http://www.stirkons.force9.co.uk/

- STITT Family Genealogy Page
  http://www.ctaz.com/~shadgraf/stitt.htm

- STITT Surname Mailing List
  http://www.ctaz.com/~shadgraf/stitt-l.htm

- STIVER Family Home Page
  http://members.aol.com/flstiver/stiver.html
  *Descendants of Dietrich STÖVER and wife Magdalena EBERWEIN
  of Frankenberg, Germany. Stöver, Stoever, Staver, Stiver.*

- The STOCKDILL Family History Society
  http://ourworld.compuserve.com/homepages/roystock/

- The STOCKMAN Family Newsletter
  http://www.zianet.com/stockman_allen/
  *History and genealogy of the STOCKMAN/STUCKMAN family in
  the United States.*

- STONECLIFFE Genealogy
  http://people.ne.mediaone.net/j-tcarroll/home.htm

- STONE Quarry...The Descendants of James STONE
  http://freepages.genealogy.rootsweb.com/~hendon/
  *Records, photos, and census of the STONE family. STONE,
  BURCHAM, GUEST, STINNETT, SANDERS, HILL, LEE,
  RATLIFF, WELCH, RUSSELL.*

- STONEROCK Family in Oklahoma
  http://www.geocities.com/Petsburgh/Zoo/9571/index.html
  STONEROCKs who have migrated from Ohio.

- Origins of the STONEROCK Family
  http://www.geocities.com/Heartland/Village/6581
  *Contains valuable vital information for STONEROCKs who lived in
  Pickaway, Ross and Darke Countys of Ohio ca 1805. A list of
  STONEROCK veterans from the civil war to WWII is provided.*

- "The Family STOREY" On-Line
  http://members.tripod.com/TFamStor/
  *Extensive compilation of South Carolina branch of STOREY /
  STORY surname, all descended from George STOREY (1725-1805).
  On-Line version of "The Family Storey," a 140 page publication by
  William M. Storey in 1955.*

- STORM / STURM (S365) Genealogy
  http://members.aol.com/chiefstorm/gen/oth-s365.htm
  Collected Storm / Storms / Sturm information and queries.

- STORY Genealogy Research Library
  http://members.xoom.com/storygen/
  *On-line assistance for researchers of the Story, Storey or Storie
  surnames.*

- STOTZER and STOTSER Family Home Page
  http://freepages.genealogy.rootsweb.com/~stotzer/
  allstotz.html
  *List of most Stotzer families in the USA that emigrated from Buren
  an dr Aare, Switzerland in the 1800s and 1900s.*

- My STOUT Family Ancestral Line
  http://dizzy.library.arizona.edu/users/mount/stout.html

- STOUT Genealogy
  http://www.geocities.com:0080/Heartland/7096/stout.html
  Descended from Richard and Priscilla (Kent) Van Princen (sp?) STOUT of New Jersey.

- STOUT Seekers
  http://www.stout.org/

- My STOVALL Family - Of England and America
  http://members.aol.com/imabr/stovall.htm
  Descendants of George STOVALL, born ca. 1555, probably in Surrey, England.

- STOVALL Family Association
  http://www.geocities.com/Heartland/Falls/1591/sfa/sfa.html?

- Bucks and Montgomery County Pa STOVER's
  http://stover.ancestry.gen-next.com/
  STOVER, STAUFFER family in Pennsylvania.

- STOVER / STOBER Genealogy Page
  http://www.geocities.com/Heartland/Hills/8220/
  Ancestors and Descendants of Johan Valentin Stober/Stover (1692-1741) with emphasis on the Stover families of Centre County, PA.

- Trekking STOVER Cousins Webpage
  http://www.geocities.com/Heartland/Meadows/1043/
  Descendants of Jacob Stover and Sarah Boone. Jacob Stover came to America from Switzerland in 1710.

- STRAHAN Family Page: My Family Then and Now
  http://www.gnt.net/~anne/strahan.html

- STRAWBRIDGE Family History
  http://www.erols.com/aswhite
  Family history information for descendants and other relatives of John STRAWBRIGE, born northern Ireland ca. 1715, died Cecil County, Maryland, 1768, including photographs, articles, letters, and family tree. Surnames include Maffitt, Ledyard, Welsh, Sailer, Van Sise, Gilpin, Stokes, Lowber, West.

- Genealogical Journeys in Time - STRAWN Surname & others
  http://ourworld.compuserve.com/homepages/Strawn/

- STREEPERS in America
  http://www.n1.net/~mcward/sia.htm
  Descendants of Wilhelm/Willem STREYPERS and Mary/Mercken WILLEMSEN LUCKEN.

- STREVEL Genealogy Website
  http://members.aol.com/bstr2/index.htm
  Dedicated to Johannes Striebel and his descendants.

- Jim STRICKLAND's Family Tree
  http://members.home.net/jimstr/
  Information about the Strickland surname in general and specific data about Jim Strickland's ancestors.

- STROCK Family, Genealogy, and Reunion, STRACK Family
  http://freepages.family.rootsweb.com/~strockfamily/

- STROMQUIST Genealogical Society
  http://www.angelfire.com/mo/stromquistgenealogy/index.html
  Descendants of Johannes Jonsson Stromquist & Christina Jonsdotter Anderson Stromquist. Collateral lines: GEIS, GRANT, LAUBACH, LINDSTROM, LORENZ, PAULSEEN, WILLMAN.

- SFAA Homepage - STRONG Family Association of America
  http://www.geocities.com/Heartland/Prairie/4715/

- STRONG Family Genealogy Page
  http://freepages.genealogy.rootsweb.com/~dstrong155/strong index.htm
  Families of the Upper Cumberland Valley of VA.

- STRONG Genealogy Network
  http://www.geocities.com/Heartland/Meadows/5744/
  Strong, Stronge, Strang, Strange, L'Estrange, etc.

- The STRONG Quest
  http://home.hiwaay.net/~rts2/
  Research on the surname Strong(e), anywhere, anytime, including any phonetic, graphic, or etymologic equivalents, such as Strang(e) and Straughan, Strawn, etc. Home Page on the WWW of the Strong Mail List.

- STRONG Roots Database
  http://fly.hiwaay.net/~jgilbert/main/srd-toc.htm

- STRUTTON Family Connections
  http://www.STRUTTON.org
  A resource center for all STRUTTON / STRATTON family researchers. Other main lines include Bass, Cantrell, Farmer, Luttrell, Stone, Womack.

- STUBBLEFIELD Family Home Page
  http://www.geocities.com/Heartland/Lake/9074/index.html

- STUDEBAKER Family National Association
  http://www.studebakerfamily.org/
  Studebaker, Studabaker, Studybaker, Studenbaker, Studenbecker.

- STUDER History
  http://www.studerhistory.org
  STUDERs' from the 1500's to current, from Europe to the United States, featuring descendants of the Masevaux valley STUDERs' from the region of Alsace, France. Also data on "Other Studer Families."

- The STURGILL Genealogical Society
  http://shadybanks.net/sturgill/

- STRUDWICK Family History Website
  http://www.sunstruck.clara.net/strudwick.htm

- STUKES Family Genealogy Page
  http://members.tripod.com/~Big_S_Ranch/genpage.html
  Nearly 400 years of Stukes from Cambridge, England, to South Carolina.

- STURTEVANT Surname Page
  http://freepages.genealogy.rootsweb.com/~julie/sturtevant.html

- The STYLLEMAN STYLEMAN STELLMAN STILEMAN STYLMAN STEELMAN STILMAN STILLMAN STELMAN Family Genealogy
  http://www.stillman.org/

- Chicago SUCHOMSKI Ancestry Website
  http://ourworld.compuserve.com/homepages/jdsummers_chgo
  Ancestry of John SUCHOMSKI (1852-1933) of Poland and Chicago, IL, and his family. Also articles that relate to other SUCHOMSKI families.

- The SUDBURY Home Place
  http://home.att.net/~asudberry/index.html
  Sudbury, Sudberry, Sutberry, Sedberry, and other spellings of the Sudbury name.

- SUITE-SUIT-GENEALOGY
  http://www.onelist.com/subscribe/SUITE-SUIT-GENEALOGY
  Also Suitt, Suits, Sute, Suet and related lines.

- The SULFRIDGE Family
  http://www.geocities.com/Heartland/Hills/4221/index.htm
  Includes variations (SELFRIDGE, SUFFRAGE etc). First known ancestor is John SULFRIDGE born 1784. Allied families include Mullins, Cook, Beeler, Taylor, Ausmus, Bollinger, Sharp and Hunter. Site also contains misc. excerpts from the earliest Claiborne Co., TN newspapers (1872-1888).

- Synopsis of SULLENS / SULLINS Genealogy
  http://www.theColeFamily.com/hobby/sullins.htm
  Early generations of SULLENS and SULLINS in the U.S.A.

- SULLENS and SULLINS Census Records
  http://freepages.genealogy.rootsweb.com/~sullins/census/
  It is a depository of ~all~ known U.S. census records for the SULLENS/SULLINS clan. Thousands of records.

- Richard SULLINS' Descendants
  http://freepages.genealogy.rootsweb.com/~sullins/sulli00t.htm

- SULLIVAN Stories
  http://www.clanstories.com/

- SULOUFF or SULOFF, We're One Family
  http://www.geocities.com/Heartland/Ranch/8094/
  Descendants of Johannes ZULAUF, arrived from Germany at Staten Island on 15 August 1776.

- SULSER Family Page
  http://sulser.rootsweb.com/
  A clearinghouse for all variations of the SULSER surname: SULSAR, SULCER, SULTZER, SULSOR, SULTSER, etc.

- SURGENER Genealogy Research Sources
  http://home.rmci.net/adamewa
  Research records collection for the Surgener name and its many variations: Surginer, Surginor, Sojourner, etc.

- SUTTON Archives / Genealogy of Forrest S. SUTTON
  http://forrestsutton.com

- Milo SUTTON Home Page
  http://www.geocities.com/Heartland/5248/
  Links to many Sutton resources including a newsletter and mailing list.

- SUTTON Place
  http://www.homestead.com/suttonplace/index.html
  All the known descendants of Thomas SUTTON, who was living in Mississippi in 1835 and owned a sawmill and grist mill. His descendants tended to name their sons Thomas, John, Seneca, Stephen, Charles, George Washington, and George Cecil.

- The SUTTON Searchers Newsletter Genealogy Homepage
  http://sutton.org/

- SVARE Genealogy
  http://www.inconnect.com/~jsvare/slekt/slekt.html
  Descendants of Hans Hansen SVARE (1819-1891) and Else HANSDATTER TEIGEN (1821-1899) of VÂGÂ, Oppland County, Norway.

- Seining SWAIMs
  http://www.geocities.com/Heartland/Ridge/9157/
  Descendants of William A. Swaim, North Carolina.

- SWAIN Searching
  http://www.fortunecity.com/millenium/abbeydale/408/
  All SWAINS, including descendants of Richard SWAYNE/SWAIN. SWAIN query board.

- The SWANCOTT Family Name
  http://www.pearson43.freeserve.co.uk/swancott/
  SWANCOTT, SWANCUTT, SWANCOAT, SWANCOTE, SWANSCOT, SWANCOT.

- SWANSON's Landing, Texas - The "Original" 1860 Store Ledger
  http://members.aol.com/ASRogers4/Swanson.index.html
  From the Historic Steamboat Landing on Caddo Lake, Harrison County, Texas founded by Peter Swanson.

- The SWATEK / SVATEK Genealogy Page
  http://www.swatek.com/genealogy.htm
  Descendants of Frank A. Swatek/Svatek and Josephine Richter.

- SWARTHOUT Family Homepage
  http://home.earthlink.net/~scentralpark/index.html
  SWARTHOUT, SWARTOUT, SWARTWOUT family in America. Information on the upcoming and past reunions.

- SWARTZ Genealogy Page
  http://www.angelfire.com/id/swartzriblet/
  Contains info on SWARTZ families in Bedford Co., PA, Wayne Co., OH, Medina Co., OH, Ashland Co., OH.

- Richard SWEPSON of Mecklenburg, Virginia & His Descendants
  http://www.rootsweb.com/~txstonew/swepson.htm
  Some information about Richard Swepson, the names of all children listed in his will and the names of most of their spouses, with references.

- SWIHART Genealogy Mailing List
  http://swihart.listbot.com/
  Swihart. Schweinhardt. Swinehart.

- The SWINBURN(E) Family History Site
  http://www.geocities.com/Athens/Atlantis/8805
  All references and genealogies of the Swinburn(e) family originating from Swinburn, Northumberland, England.

- SWINDLEY Family History Page
  http://www.swindley.demon.co.uk/famhist/swindleys.html

- SWINSCOE Home Page
  http://www.users.bigpond.com/waugh/frames.htm
  Swinscoe, Swinscow, Swainscoe.

- Jacob Rivers SWISHER Descendants
  http://members.delphi.com/floa/index.html

- SYERS Seeker's Nest
  http://members.aol.com/SyerSeeker/index.html
  Syers, Sires, Siers, Syas, Syrus, Syars, Syres, Seyers, Swyers, Sias, Syras, Cyrus, Sayers, Swyres, Syerson, Syears.

- SYLCOX Family
  http://www.sylcox.com
  The search for SYLCOX, SILCOCK, SILCOX.

- SYME Surname
  http://hometown.aol.com/RSy2717/syme.html

- SYMINGTON Genealogy
  http://homepages.infoseek.com/~iansymington/index.html
  Home page for the Symington Family History Society.

- The SYMONS Family Home Page
  http://www.geocities.com/Heartland/Park/1041/
  This site is dedicated to the descendants of Arthur and Kate SYMONS, married in the year 1900.

- Genealogical Research Center for the CYRENNE or SYRENNE Families in Canada
  http://www3.sympatico.ca/gpfern/EHOME.HTM

◆ Surname Mailing Lists

- "SA-SB" Surname Mailing Lists
  http://www.rootsweb.com/~jfuller/gen_mail_surnames-sa.html
  S425, SAATHOFF, SABAN, SABEL, SABERS, SABIN, SACHS, SACKETT (includes Sacket, Seckett, Secket, Sachet, Sacket, Sackette, Sackitt, Sackat, Sackatt, Sackutt), SADDLER, SADDLER, SADLER, SAFFELL (includes Saffle, Saffel, Saffels), SAFFOLD, SAFFORD, SAFLEY (includes Saftley, Safly, Saphley, Sapley, Saufley, Sofley, Softly), SAGAR, SAGE, SAGEN, SAGER (includes Seger), SAGLE, SAGRAVES, SAHLSTROM (includes Salstrom, Sahlström), SAHR (includes Sahre, Saar), SAILOR, SAINSBURY, SAINT (includes Sant), SALA, SALAMON (includes Salomon, Solomon), SALAZAR, SALE, SALES, SALING, SALISBURY (includes Sailsberry, Sailsbery, Salesbury, Salisburie, Salsberry, Salsbery, Salsburie, Salsburry,, Salsbury, Salsibury, Salusbury, Saulisbury, Saulsberry, Saulsbury), SALLEE (includes Sallé, Salle', Salle, Salee, Sally, Salley, Saley, Saly, Sallée, Sallie, Sailey, Salla, Sallings), SALLEY, SALLIS, SALLOWS, SALLS (includes Sarles, Searles, Serls), SALMON, SALO, SALOME (includes Solome, Slome), SALTER, SALTSMAN, SALYER, SALYERS, SAMMONS, SAMPLE, SAMPLES (includes Sample, Semple, Sempel), SAMPLES (includes Sample, Semple), SAMPLEY, SAMPSON (includes Samson), SAMPSON, SAMS (includes Sames, Samms, Semmes, Salms, Sahms), SAMSON, SAMUEL, SAMUELS, SAMUELSON, SANBORN, SANCHEZ, SAND, SANDELL, SANDER, SANDERS (includes Sander, Saunders, Sounder, Souder), SANDERS (includes

Saunders, Anderson), SANDERSON (includes Sandersen), SANDFORD, SANDIDGE (includes Sandage, Sandige, Sandridge, Sandredge, Sandwich), SANDIFER, SANDLIN (includes Sanland, Sandland, Sandiland), SANDOVAL, SANDS, SANDTNER, SANDUSKY, SANDY, SANFORD (includes Sandford, Samford), SANFT, SANGER, SANGSTER, SANJOSE, SANKEY, SANSOM, SANSONETTI, SANSTROM, SANT, SANTEE (includes Santea, Santey, Santeay), SANTI, SANTIAGO, SAPP, SAPPINGTON, SAPPINGTON, SARANILLIO, SARDESON, SARGEANT, SARGENT (includes Sargeant, Sergent), SARLLS, SARTAIN, SARTIN (includes Sartain, Sertain, Certain, Certing, Sarton), SARTOR, SARVER, SARVIS, SASS, SASSER, SASSMANNSHAUSEN (includes Sassaman, Sassman, Sossaman), SATARIANO, SATCHELL, SATTERFIELD, SATTERLEE, SATTERTHWAITE, SATTERWHITE, SATTLER, SAUBLE (includes Saubel, Sawbel, Sawbell), SAUCEDA (includes Saucedo, Sauseda, Sausedo), SAUCIER, SAUER (includes Sauers, Sower, Sowers), SAUL, SAULSBURY, SAUMENIG (includes Saumanig), SAUNDERS, SAUNDERSON, SAUTER, SAUVAGE, SAUVAGEAU, SAUVE, SAVAGE, SAVELL, SAVERCOOL, SAVIDGE (includes Savedge, Savige, Savage), SAVILLE (includes Savil, Savill, Sayvell, Civil), SAVOIE, SAVORY, SAWEY (includes Sawye, Sawyer, Sawyers, Soe, Soye, Soy, Saye, Sahe, Seay), SAWHILL, SAWYER, SAWYERS, SAXBURY (includes Saxberry), SAXE, SAXMAN (includes Soxman), SAXON, SAXTON, SAY, SAYER, SAYERS, SAYLES, SAYLOR, SAYRE, SAYRES (includes Sayers, Sayer, Sears).

- "SCA-SCG" Surname Mailing Lists
  http://www.rootsweb.com/~jfuller/gen_mail_surnames-sca.html
  SCAFF, SCAGGS, SCAIFE, SCALES, SCAMMAHORN, SCAMMELL (includes Scammel, Scamell, Scamel), SCANLAN, SCANLON, SCANNELL, SCARBOROUGH (includes Scarboro, Scarbrough, Scarborrow, Scarbro), SCARBROUGH, SCARLET, SCARLETT, SCATES.

- "SCH-SCH" Surname Mailing Lists
  http://www.rootsweb.com/~jfuller/gen_mail_surnames-sch.html
  SCHAAF, SCHADE, SCHADT, SCHAEFER, SCHAEFFER, SCHAFER, SCHAFFER, SCHAFFNER, SCHAGEL (includes Scadgel, Scegel, Schadgel), SCHAKE (includes Schacke), SCHALL, SCHALLER, SCHAMBACH (includes Shambo, Shambaugh, Shambough), SCHANBECK, SCHANEY (includes Schanie, Schany, Scheine, Schini, Schoeni, Schoni, Schonie, Schoene, Shaney, Shoney,, Shoeny), SCHANTZ, SCHAREK, SCHARF, SCHARFF, SCHARPING, SCHATZ, SCHAUB (includes Schawb, Schaup, Schauble, Schaible, Scheuble, Schüblin, Schaab, Shobe, Schoup), SCHAUER (includes Shauer, Shower), SCHECK, SCHEEL, SCHEER, SCHEIBER (includes Schieber), SCHEIG, SCHELL (includes Shell, Shull, Shaul, Shoul, Schelle), SCHELLER, SCHELLIN, SCHENCK, SCHENK, SCHENKEL, SCHERER, SCHERMERHORN, SCHICK, SCHIEFELBEIN, SCHIEVELBEIN, SCHILD, SCHILL, SCHILLER, SCHILLING, SCHILLINGER, SCHIMMEL, SCHIMPF, SCHINDLER, SCHIRMER, SCHIRPKE (includes Tschirpka), SCHISSLER (includes Schiesler, Schisler, Schoessler, Schuessler, Shisler, Schizler), SCHITTKOWSKI (includes Shittkowsk, Schitkowski, Schellkowski, Scheuttkowske, Schetkowski, Schettkowski,, Schipkowski, Schütkowski, Schillkowski, Schettouska, Schell), SCHLACK, SCHLAGER, SCHLEICHER, SCHLEIERMACHER, SCHLEKAU, SCHLEMMER (includes Schlemer, Schlimmer, Slimmer), SCHLERETH, SCHLOSS, SCHLOSSER, SCHLOTMAN (includes Schlottmann, Schlotmann, Schlottman, Schlatman, Schlattmann, Schlatmann, Schlattman), SCHLOTTE (includes von Schlotte), SCHLUETER, SCHMAKEIT, SCHMAL, SCHMATJEN, SCHMELZER, SCHMID, SCHMIDT

(includes Schmitt, Schmite, Schmide, Schmid), SCHMIDTKE, SCHMIEDER, SCHMIT, SCHMITT, SCHMITZ, SCHMOLL, SCHMOYER *(includes Schmeyer, Smoyer),* SCHMUTZ, SCHNEBELE *(includes Snavely, Snively),* SCHNECK, SCHNEEWEIS, SCHNEIDER, SCHNELL, SCHNORF, SCHOCH, SCHOCK, SCHOELLHAMMER *(includes Schollhammer, Schollhamer, Shollhammer, Shollhamer, Schöllhammer, Schöllhamer,, Schellhammer, Schellhamer, Schelhammer, Schelhamer),* SCHOEN, SCHOENEBERGER *(includes Sheneberger, Shenberger, Shoneberger, Shaneberger),* SCHOENFELD, SCHOENMAKER *(includes Shumaker, Shoemaker, Schoemaker),* SCHOFIELD, SCHOLES, SCHOLL *(includes Sholl, Shull),* SCHOLZ, SCHONE *(includes Schoon, Schön, Schöne, Schönen, Schoone, Schoene, Schoen),* SCHOOLCRAFT, SCHOOLEY, SCHOONMAKER, SCHOONOVER, SCHOTT, SCHRADER, SCHRAM, SCHRAMEL *(includes Schrammel),* SCHRAMM, SCHRANK, SCHRANZ *(includes Schranze, Schrantz, Schrance),* SCHRECK *(includes Schrack, Schraack),* SCHREIBER *(includes Schriever, Shriver, Schreibman, Schreber),* SCHREINER, SCHRIEBER, SCHROCK, SCHRODER, SCHROEDER *(includes Schroder, Schrader),* SCHUBERT, SCHUCK, SCHUESSLER, SCHUETTE, SCHUETZ, SCHUH, SCHUHMACHER, SCHULER, SCHULTE, SCHULTE, SCHULTHEIS, SCHULTHEISS, SCHULTZ *(includes Shultz, Schulz, Schulze, Shults),* SCHULTZE, SCHULZ, SCHULZE, SCHUMACHER, SCHUMAKER, SCHUMANN, SCHUPP, SCHURTER, SCHUSTER, SCHUTT, SCHUTTE *(includes Schuette, Schuett, Schutt, Schuetze, Schuetz),* SCHUTZ, SCHUYLER, SCHWAB, SCHWAN, SCHWARTZ, SCHWARZ, SCHWECHTEN, SCHWEDE, SCHWEIGERT, SCHWEISSGUTH *(includes Swicegood, Swisegood, Swaisgood),* SCHWEISSGUTH *(includes Schweisgut, Schweissgut, Schweisguth, Schweissguth, Swaisgood, Sweisgood,, Sweisguth, Swicegood, Swisegood, Swysgood, Weisguth),* SCHWEITZER, SCHWENK, SCHWEPPENHEISER, SCHWIESOW *(includes Schwieso, Schwisow),* SCHWYHART *(includes Schyhart, Shwyhart).*

- **"SCI-SD" Surname Mailing Lists**
  http://www.rootsweb.com/~jfuller/gen_mail_surnames-sci.html
  SCISM *(includes Scissom, Scisson, Sissom, Sisson, Scizm, Chisholm, Chism, Cissom, Cism, Cisme, Cissum, Cisson),* SCITES, SCOBEE, SCOFIELD *(includes Schofield),* SCOGGIN, SCOGGINS, SCOGIN *(includes Scoggin, Scoggins, Scroggin, Scroggins, Scogen, Scoggen),* SCOLES, SCOTHERN *(includes Scothorn, Scotthorn),* SCOTT, SCOTT, SCOTT, SCOULDING, SCOURFIELD, SCOVILLE *(includes Scovill, Schovel, Scovell),* SCOVILLE, SCRANTON, SCRIBNER, SCRIPTURE, SCRIVEN, SCROGGINS, SCRUGGS, SCUDDER *(includes Scuder),* SCULL, SCULLY.

- **"SE-SG" Surname Mailing Lists**
  http://www.rootsweb.com/~jfuller/gen_mail_surnames-se.html
  SEABOLT, SEABORN, SEABROOK, SEAGER, SEAGO, SEAGRAVE, SEAL *(includes Seals, Seale, Seales),* SEALE, SEALEY, SEALOCK, SEALS, SEAMAN, SEAMANS, SEARCY, SEARL, SEARLE, SEARLES, SEARS, SEARS, SEASHOLTZ *(includes Seazholtz, Siesholtz, Seisholz, Sussholtz, Seaholz, Seeholz, Susholz),* SEAT, SEATH, SEATON, SEATS, SEAVER, SEAVEY, SEAVEY *(includes Seavy, Sevy, Zevie),* SEAY, SEBASTIAN, SEBELIST *(includes Seibelist, Siebelist, Siebenlist, Sieblist),* SEBRING, SECCOMB *(includes Seccombe, Secombe, Secomb, Seacomb, Seacombe),* SECHRIST, SECOR *(includes Sicard, Seacord, Secord),* SECORD, SECREST, SEDDON, SEDGEWICK, SEDGWICK, SEDGWICK *(includes Sedwick),* SEDRICK, SEE *(includes Sie, Sea, Zea, Zie, Zeh, Cie),* SEEBACHER *(includes Sebacher, Seebach),* SEEDEN, SEEFELDT, SEEGER, SEELEY, SEELY *(includes Sealy, Selly, Seligh, Salee, Sallee, Saley, Salley),* SEGAR, SEGER,

SEGGIE *(includes Seggy),* SEGUIN, SEIBEL, SEIBER, SEIBERT, SEIDEL, SEIDERMAN, SEIDL *(includes Seidel, Siedel, Siedl),* SEIELSTAD *(includes Seilstad, Segelstad),* SEIFERT, SEIGHMAN *(includes Seigmann),* SEILER, SEIP, SEITER, SEITHER, SEITZ *(includes Sides, Sitz, Sites, Sights),* SELBY *(includes Selbey),* SELCER, SELCH, SELDEN, SELDON, SELF *(includes Selph, Selfe),* SELF *(includes Selph, Selfe),* SELF *(includes Selph, Selfe),* SELF *(includes Selph, Selfe),* SELF *(includes Selph, Selfe),* SELKA, SELL, SELLARDS, SELLARS, SELLE, SELLERS *(includes Sellars, Cellers, Sollars, Zellers),* SELLON *(includes Sellen),* SELLS *(includes Cells, Cell),* SELMAN, SELVAGE, SEMAINE, SEMIAO, SEMPLE, SEMPLE *(includes Sempill, Sempel),* SENEY, SENGER, SENIOR, SENN, SENSENBACH, SENTELL, SENTER, SENTMAN, SEPULVEDA, SEPULVEDA, SEQUIN, SERGEANT, SERRES, SERVOS *(includes Servoss, Servis, Serviss, Service),* SESMA, SESSIONS, SETTLE, SETTLES, SETZER, SETZLER, SEVCIK, SEVENOAK, SEVERANCE, SEVERNS, SEVERO, SEVERS, SEVIER *(includes Severe, Xavier),* SEWARD, SEWARD *(includes Seaward),* SEWELL *(includes Seawell, Sowell, Showell),* SEXSON *(includes Sexton, Saxon),* SEXTON *(includes Saxton, Saxon, Sesten, Saxe),* SEYBERT, SEYBOLD, SEYLER, SEYMORE, SEYMOUR.

- **"SHA-SHD" Surname Mailing Lists**
  http://www.rootsweb.com/~jfuller/gen_mail_surnames-sha.html
  SHACKELFORD *(includes Shackford, Shackleford, Shakford),* SHACKLEFORD, SHACKLETON, SHACKLETT *(includes Shacklette, Shacklet, Jacquelot),* SHADDOCK, SHADE, SHADLE, SHADWICK, SHAEFFER, SHAFER, SHAFFER *(includes Shafer, Shaeffer, Schaeffer, Schaefer, Schaffer, Schafer),* SHAHAN, SHAIN, SHALLA *(includes Schalla, Challa),* SHAMRAY, SHANAHAN, SHANDS, SHANE, SHANER *(includes Schaner, Schoener, Shiner, Shoner, O'Shaner, Shane, O'Shane),* SHANK, SHANKLE *(includes Schenkel, Shankel, Shankles),* SHANKLES, SHANKLIN, SHANKS, SHANKS *(includes Shank, Schanks, Scanks, Schenk, Shenk),* SHANLEY, SHANNON *(includes Shannahan),* SHANTZ, SHAPLEIGH *(includes Shapley, Shappley),* SHAPTON, SHARKEY, SHARMAN, SHARP, SHARPE, SHARPLES, SHARPLESS, SHARPLEY, SHARRETT, SHARROCK, SHATSWELL, SHATTO *(includes Chateau, Schatteau, Schaddeau, Shaddeau, Shatow, Shedo, Scheddo, Schedo, Shattoe, Shado,, Shadow, Shadel, Shadell, Shadle, Shaddle, Shaddo, Schatto, Schaddo, Shatts, Shotta, Shattow, Shattoo, Shato),* SHATTUCK, SHAUGHNESSY, SHAVER, SHAW, SHAW, SHAWHAN *(includes Shawn, Shahan, Shehane, Sheehane, Shehawn, Shehawne, Shehauon, Shehorn, Shahorn,, Sheehaan, Sheahorn, Shehan, Shaughen, Sheohan, Shaan, Shehen),* SHAWLEY *(includes Schally, Schalley, Shalley, Sholly, Schaulay, Chalet, Sholley),* SHAY.

- **"SHE-SHH" Surname Mailing Lists**
  http://www.rootsweb.com/~jfuller/gen_mail_surnames-she.html
  SHEA *(includes O'Shea),* SHEAR, SHEARD, SHEARER, SHEARIN, SHEARMAN, SHEARS, SHEATHER, SHEATS, SHEDDEN, SHEDDRICK, SHEEHAN, SHEEHY, SHEELY *(includes Sheeley, Shealy, Schiel, Schiele, Schiehl, Schiell),* SHEETS *(includes Sheetz, Scheets, Scheetz),* SHEFFER, SHEFFIELD *(includes Shuffield, Sherfield, Scofield, Schufield, Shiffield),* SHEHORN *(includes Shahan, Sehorn, Shehorne, Shehane, Shehan),* SHEKELL *(includes Sheckell, Shekel, Shakle, Shekells, Sheckells, Shekels, Shekelle),* SHELBY, SHELDON, SHELDRICK *(includes Shildrick, Sheldrack, Sheldrake, Shildrake),* SHELL, SHELLEY, SHELLNUT, SHELLY, SHELTON, SHENK *(includes Schenk, Schenck, Shanks, Shank),* SHENKEL, SHEPARD, SHEPHARD, SHEPHERD, SHEPHERD *(includes Sheppard),* SHEPHERDSON, SHEPLER *(includes Sheplar),* SHEPLEY, SHEPPARD, SHEPPERD, SHERBONDY

(includes Sherbundy, Shobundy, Shorbundy, Shorbondy), SHERBORNE, SHERBURNE, SHERD, SHERER, SHERESHEVSKY, SHERIDAN, SHERIFF, SHERLOCK, SHERMAN (includes Shearman), SHERMER, SHERRELL, SHERRILL, SHERROD, SHERRY, SHERWIN, SHERWOOD, SHETTLES (includes Shuttles, Shuttlesworth), SHEW, SHEWAN (includes Shuan).

- **"SHI-SHN" Surname Mailing Lists**
  http://www.rootsweb.com/~jfuller/gen_mail_surnames-shi.html
  SHIABLE (includes Schiable, Shable, Schable), SHICK, SHIEL, SHIELDS (includes Shiels, Shield, Shiel, O'Shields, O'Shield), SHIELDS, SHIFFLETT, SHIFLET, SHIFLETT, SHIFLETT, SHILLING, SHILTZ (includes Shilts, Shieltz), SHIMP, SHINE, SHINGLETON, SHINKLE, SHINN, SHINNICK (includes Shennick, Schenick, Schinnick, Shinick, Shinnock), SHIPLEY, SHIPMAN, SHIPP, SHIPPEE (includes Shippy, Scheppe, Shippey), SHIPPEN (includes Shippin), SHIPPEY, SHIPTON, SHIREMAN (includes Shierman, Scheurman, Scheurmann, Scheuerman, Shewerman, Scherman, Schermann,, Scharman, Scheyerman, Shearman, Shereman), SHIRER, SHIREY, SHIRK (includes Schurch, Sherk, Shoerg, Schrock, Sherrick), SHIRKEY, SHIRLEY (includes Sheale, Shurley), SHIRLEY, SHIVELY, SHIVER, SHIVERS, SHIVERS.

- **"SHO-SHT" Surname Mailing Lists**
  http://www.rootsweb.com/~jfuller/gen_mail_surnames-sho.html
  SHOAF, SHOCK, SHOCKEY (includes Schacke), SHOCKLEY, SHOECRAFT, SHOEMAKE, SHOEMAKER (includes Shumaker, Schumacher), SHOENFELT, SHOESMITH (includes Shoosmith), SHOFNER, SHOLAR (includes Sholer, Sholars, Scholer, Scholar), SHOOK, SHOOP, SHOPE, SHORB (includes Schorb, Schorben, Sherb, Sherbs, Shorp, Shurp), SHORE, SHORES, SHORT, SHORTER, SHORTRIDGE, SHORTT, SHOTTS, SHOTWELL (includes Shadwell, Shotwill, Shotto), SHOUGH, SHOUN (includes Shown, Shawn), SHOUP, SHOVER, SHOWALTER, SHOWERS, SHOWS (includes Shouse, Schaus, Schauss, Schauß), SHRADER, SHREVE, SHREVE (includes Shreeve, Shreves, Sherrif, Sheriff), SHREWSBERRY (includes Shrewsbeiry, Shrewsbiery), SHREWSBURY (includes Shrewsberry), SHRICKER (includes Schricker), SHRIGLEY, SHRIMPLIN, SHRIVER, SHROLL, SHROPSHIRE, SHRUM (includes Schramm), SHRYOCK (includes Schreyack, Shyrock, Van Schrieck, Schreijack).

- **"SHU-SHZ" Surname Mailing Lists**
  http://www.rootsweb.com/~jfuller/gen_mail_surnames-shu.html
  SHUCK, SHUEY, SHUFF (includes Schoff, Schoffe, Schuff), SHUFFETT (includes Shuffet, Shoffit, Shuffit, Shuffitt), SHUFORD, SHUGART, SHULER, SHULL, SHULTIS, SHULTS, SHULTZ, SHUMAKER, SHUMAN (includes Schuman, Schumann, Scheman, Sewman, Sheman, Shewman, Shoeman, Shueman, Suman), SHUMARD (includes Shumar, Chumard, Chumar), SHUMATE, SHUMWAY (includes Shamway, Chamois), SHUPE, SHURTLEFF, SHURTLIFF, SHURTZ, SHUSTER, SHUTE, SHUTT, SHUTTLEWORTH.

- **"SI-SJ" Surname Mailing Lists**
  http://www.rootsweb.com/~jfuller/gen_mail_surnames-si.html
  SIAS, SIBBACH, SIBLEY, SIBOLE, SIBRELL, SICARD, SICKLES (includes Sickels, Seckel, Sickals), SIDDENS, SIDDLE (includes Siddel, Siddall), SIDDON, SIDEBOTTOM, SIDELINGER, SIDERS (includes Sider, Seiders, Seider, Syders, Syder, Sydars, Sydar, Seiders, Seider, Ciders, Cider, Cydrus,, Cyders, Cyder, Zeiders, Zeider, Zeitter, Zeitters, Sidders, Sitters, Siter, Siters), SIDES (includes Sites, Zeits), SIDEY, SIDWELL, SIEBERT, SIEGEL,

SIEGERT, SIEGFRIED, SIEGLER, SIEVERS, SIEVERT, SIEWER SIFFORD (includes Siefert, Seaferd, Siffard), SIGLER, SIGLIN, SIGMAN, SIGNAL, SIGSBEE, SIGSBEY, SIHRER, SIKES (include Sykes), SIKORA, SILAR (includes Seiler), SILCOCK, SILCOX, SILER, SILHAVY, SILK, SILKWORTH, SILL (includes Soell, Sell, Celle), SILLS, SILVA, SILVER, SILVERNAIL, SILVERNAIL, SILVERS, SILVERTOOTH, SILVESTER, SILVEY, SILVIUS (includes Silfies, Selfoos, Silfoos, Silfouse, Silfrese, Silfues, Silfus, Silfuse, Silfuss, Silicus, Silveius, Silveous,, Silvers, Silveus, Silvey, Silvious, Silvis, Silvuse, Silfies, Silfoose, Syeephus, Syefuse), SIM, SIMARRO, SIMCOCK (includes Simcox, Symcock), SIMCOX, SIMKINS, SIMMERS, SIMMONDS, SIMMONS, SIMMONS, SIMMS, SIMON, SIMON (includes Simeaux, Simoneaux, Sieman, Zieman), SIMONDS (includes Simons, Symonds, Symons, Simon, Symons, Simmonds, Simmons), SIMONS, SIMONSEN, SIMONSON, SIMONTON, SIMPKINS, SIMPSON (includes Simson), SIMPSON, SIMS, SINCLAIR, SINCLAIR (includes St. Clair, Sinkler), SINCLAIR (includes St. Clair, Sinkler, Sinclear), SINDELAR, SINE, SING, SINGER, SINGLETARY, SINGLETON, SINGLEY, SINKS, SINNOTT, SINTES, SINTON, SIPE, SIPES, SIRES (includes Siers, Syers, Sias, Cyrus), SIRMAN (includes Sirmans, Sirmon, Sirmons, Sermon, Sermons, Surman, Surmans, Surmon, Surmons), SIROIS, SISCO (includes Francisco, Cisco), SISEMORE, SISK, SISLER, SISNEY (includes Sisna, Cisna, Cisne, Sisne, Cissna), SISSOM, SISSON (includes Sissom, Sissons), SITES, SITLINGTON (includes Sitlinton, Sittlington, Sidlington), SIX, SIXBERRY (includes Saxbury, Sigsbee), SIZEMORE, SIZEMORE, SIZEMORE, SIZER.

- **"SK-SL" Surname Mailing Lists**
  http://www.rootsweb.com/~jfuller/gen_mail_surnames-sk.html
  SKAFTE, SKAGGS (includes Scaggs, Skeggs, Sceggs), SKALA (includes Skaler), SKEEN, SKEENS, SKELLY, SKELTON, SKENE (includes Skeen, Skeens, Skeans), SKIDMORE, SKIFF, SKILES (includes Skyles), SKILLMAN, SKINNER, SKIPPER, SKIPWITH, SKIPWORTH (includes Skipper, Skipwith), SKIRVEN, SKOV (includes Skow), SLACK, SLADE, SLAFTER, SLAGHT, SLAGLE (includes Slagel), SLANEY, SLATE, SLATER, SLATER, SLATON (includes Slaten, Slatton), SLATON (includes Slaten), SLATTERY, SLAUGHTER, SLAUGHTER (includes Slauter), SLAUTER (includes Slaughter), SLAVEN (includes Slavey, Slavin, Slavens, Slavy), SLAVENS, SLAVEY, SLAVIN, SLAWSON, SLAYDEN, SLAYMAKER, SLAYMAKER, SLAYTON, SLECHT, SLEDD, SLEDGE (includes Slech), SLEEKING (includes Sleking, Schleking, Schleeking), SLEETH, SLEMP, SLIDER, SLIGER (includes Sligo, Sluggo, Schleicher, Slaker), SLOAN (includes Slone), SLOANE, SLOAT (includes Sloot, Slote, Slot, Slott, Slute, Sluet, Slaught, Van der Sloot, Sloet), SLOCUM, SLONAKER (includes Sloneker, Sloniker, Slonneger, Schlunneger, Schluneger, Schloneker), SLONE SLOOP, SLOUGH, SLUDER, SLUSHER, SLUSSER, SLY (includes Slye, Sligh), SLYE, SLYGH (includes Sligh, Slie, Sly).

- **"SM-SN" Surname Mailing Lists**
  http://www.rootsweb.com/~jfuller/gen_mail_surnames-sm.html
  SMALL, SMALL (includes Smalls, Smales), SMALLEY, SMALLWOOD, SMART (includes Smartt), SMASHEY (includes Smashea, Smacky, Smashia, Smushe, Smash, Smack, Smashe), SMAW, SMEATON, SMEDLEY, SMELLIE, SMELSER, SMELSER (includes Smelzer), SMELSER (includes Smeltzer, Smelcer, Schmeltzer), SMELTZER, SMILEY, SMITH, SMITH (includes Smyth), SMITH, SMITH, SMITH (includes Smythe, Smyth), SMITH, SMITH, SMITHERMAN, SMITHERS, SMITHEY (includes Smithe, Smitha), SMITHSON, SMITHWICK, SMITS (includes Smitz, Smitts, Smittz), SMOCK, SMOOT (includes Smoote, Smootes, Smote, Smoudt, Smout, Smoute, Smute), SMOTHERMAN (includes Smitherman), SMOTHERS, SMOUSE, SMOUT, SMUIN (includes

Smeuin, Smewin, Smuinz, Smewings), SMYTH, SMYTHE, SNAITH, SNAPP, SNARE (includes Snair, Schnerr), SNAVELY, SNEAD, SNEATH, SNEDDON, SNEED, SNELL, SNELLGROVE, SNELLING, SNELSON (includes Snelston, Senellestone, Senelestune), SNEYD, SNIATKOWSKI, SNIDER, SNIPES, SNIPES (includes Snape), SNODDY, SNODGRASS, SNOOK, SNOOTS, SNOW (includes Snaw, Show, Schnee, Snowman), SNOWBERGER, SNOWDEN, SNOWDON (includes Snowden), SNUFFIN, SNYDER (includes Snider, Schneider).

- **"SO-SO" Surname Mailing Lists**
  http://www.rootsweb.com/~jfuller/gen_mail_surnames-so.html
  SOCKWELL, SODEN, SOESBE, SOLBERG, SOLES, SOLESBURY (includes Soulesbury, Soulsbury, Soulesbury, Solesberry), SOLIS (includes Soliz), SOLLEE, SOLLINGER, SOLOMON, SOLON, SOLTES, SOMERS, SOMERVILLE (includes Sommerville, Sumervell, Summerville), SOMES, SOMMER, SOMMERS, SOMMERVILLE, SONGER, SONNENBERG, SONNTAG, SONS (includes Son), SOOK, SOPER, SORENSEN, SORENSON, SORRELL (includes Sorrells, Sorrelle, Sorrel, Sorell, Sorel), SORRELLS, SORRELS, SORTORE (includes Sortor, Sorter), SOTERIOU, SOTO, SOUCY (includes Souci, Soucie, Soucis, Soucisse, Sucese), SOUDER, SOUDERS, SOUFFRONT, SOULE (includes Sowle, Sole), SOULSBY, SOUNDY (includes Sowndey, Soundie), SOUTER, SOUTH, SOUTH, SOUTHALL, SOUTHARD, SOUTHARD, SOUTHCOTT, SOUTHER, SOUTHERLAND, SOUTHERN, SOUTHEY (includes Sothey, Southay, Southee, Southtye, Southy, Soutie, Sowthey, Sowtheye, Sowthie, Sowthy,, Suthey, Suthie), SOUTHGATE (includes Sowgate), SOUTHON (includes Southen, Sowton, Souton), SOUTHWARD, SOUTHWELL, SOUTHWICK, SOUTHWORTH, SOUTTER, SOUZA, SOWA, SOWDER (includes Souder, Sowders, Souders), SOWELL, SOWERBY, SOWERS.

- **"SP-SS" Surname Mailing Lists**
  http://www.rootsweb.com/~jfuller/gen_mail_surnames-sp.html
  SPACE, SPADE, SPAFFORD, SPAINHOUR, SPALDING (includes Spaulding), SPAN, SPANGLER, SPANN, SPARKES, SPARKMAN, SPARKS (includes Spark, Sparkes), SPARLING, SPARROW, SPATH, SPAULDING, SPAWTON, SPEAKMAN, SPEAR, SPEARMAN, SPEARS (includes Spear, Speer, Speers, Speir, Speirs), SPECHT, SPECK, SPEED, SPEELMAN, SPEER, SPEERS, SPEESE (includes Spees, Spies, Speece), SPEIDEL (includes Spidell, Spidle, Spydel), SPEIGHT, SPEIR, SPELL, SPELLER, SPELLMAN, SPELMAN, SPENCE (includes Spens), SPENCER (includes Spenser, Spincer, Spinser), SPERLING, SPERO, SPERRY, SPETNAGEL (includes Spetnagle), SPICER, SPICER, SPICKARD (includes Spicard, Spickert, Spicker, Speakhard), SPIEGEL, SPIER, SPIERS, SPIES, SPIKER (includes Speicher, Spyker, Spicker), SPILCKER, SPILLER, SPILMAN (includes Spillman, Spelman, Spellman, Spielman, Espielman), SPINA, SPINDLER, SPINK, SPINKS (includes Spink, Spincks, Spynks, Spyncks), SPINNEY, SPIRES, SPITLER, SPITTLEHOUSE, SPIVEY (includes Spiva), SPOERL, SPOFFORD, SPOHN, SPOKES, SPONBERG (includes Sponeburgh, Sponburg), SPOON, SPOONER, SPORE, SPORES (includes Spore, Spoor, Spoors, Spur, Spurr, Spahr, Spohr, Sparr, Spoar), SPOTSWOOD (includes Spottswood, Spottiswoode), SPOTTS, SPRADLEY, SPRADLIN, SPRADLING, SPRAGG, SPRAGUE, SPRATLING, SPRATT, SPRAY, SPRECHER, SPRENGER, SPRIGG, SPRIGGS (includes Sprig, Sprague), SPRING, SPRINGER, SPRINGETT, SPRINGFIELD, SPRINGMAN (includes Springmann), SPRINGSTEEN, SPRINKLE (includes Sprankle, Sprenckel), SPRINT (includes Sprindt), SPROAT, SPROUL, SPROUSE (includes Sprouce), SPROUT, SPRUILL (includes Sprueil, Sprule, Sprewel, Spruell, Sproul), SPRY (includes Sprey, Spray, Sprie, Spree, Sprye), SPURGEON, SPURGIN

(includes Spurgeon), SPURLIN, SPURLIN, SPURLING, SPURLOCK, SPURR, SPURRELL, SPURRIER, SPURVEY, SPURWAY, SQUIBB (includes Squib), SQUIER, SQUIRE, SQUIRES.

- **"STA-STD" Surname Mailing Lists**
  http://www.rootsweb.com/~jfuller/gen_mail_surnames-sta.html
  STAAB, STAATA, ST-ARNAUD (includes St. Arnou, St. Arnould, St. Arnoud, St. Arnaux, St. Arnault), STAATS (includes Statts, Stadts, States, Stats, Staat, Staet), STABLER, STACEY, STACEY (includes Stacy), STACK, STACKHOUSE, STACY (includes Stacey), STADLER, STAFFORD, STAFFORD, STAFFORD, STAGG (includes Stage, Stag, Staggs, Steg, Stegg, Stegge, Stegges, Du Stage), STAGGS, STAGNER (includes Stagnor, Stegner, Steigner), STAHL, STAIB, STAINER, STAINER, STALCUP, STALEY, STALKER (includes Stoliker, Stocker, Stolker), STALL, STALLARD, STALLINGS (includes Stalings, Stallons, Stalins, Stallins, Stalions, Stallions, Stillings, Stilings), STALLWORTH, STALNAKER, STALTER, STAMBAUGH, STAMM, STAMP, STAMPER, STAMPLEY (includes Stampfeli), STAMPS, STANALAND (includes Stanland, Stanalan, Stanlan), STANCIL, STANDERFER (includes Standifer), STANDIFER, STANDIFORD, STANDISH, STANDLEY, STANDRIDGE, STANFIELD, STANFORD, STANGE, STANGER (includes Stenger), STANHOPE, STANLEY (includes Standley, Standly, Stanly), STANNARD, STANSBERRY, STANSBOROUGH (includes Stanborough), STANSBURY, STANSFIELD, STANTON, STANWOOD, STAPLEFORD, STAPLES (includes Steeples, Staple), STAPLETON (includes Stapelton, Stableton, Stebleton, Stapylton, Stepleton, Steveldon, Stapulton, Stapilton,, Stapledon, Staplton, Stebelton, Steppleton, Stapledown), STAPP (includes Stepp, Stapf), STARBUCK, STARK (includes Starke, Starks), STARKE, STARKEY, STARKOVICH (includes Starcevic, Starcevich), STARKS, STARKWEATHER, STARLING (includes Starlin, Starlyn, Starlyng, Starlynge), STARNER, STARNER, STARNES, STARNS, STARR (includes Star), STARRETT, STARRHRY, STARRITT (includes Sterrett, Stirrat, Stirret, Stirrit, Starrat, Stirrat), STARRY, START, STASCZAK, STATEN (includes Staton), STATHAM, STATLER (includes Stadler, Stetler, Stotler), STATON, STATZER, STAUB, STAUCH (includes Stough, Stouch), STAUFFACHER, STAUFFER, STAUNTON, STAUSS, STAVELY, STCLAIR.

- **"STE-STH" Surname Mailing Lists**
  http://www.rootsweb.com/~jfuller/gen_mail_surnames-ste.html
  STEAD, STEADMAN, STEARMAN, STEARNS (includes Starnes, Stearne, Sterne, Sterns, Stearnes), STEBBINS (includes Stebbings), STECK, STECKEL (includes Stoeckel, Stoeckli, Stickle), STEDMAN (includes Steadman, Steedman), STEDNER, STEED, STEEDMAN, STEEL, STEELE (includes Steel, Stahl, McSteely, Sterling, Stoele), STEELMAN, STEELS, STEELY, STEEN, STEER, STEERS, STEFFEN, STEFFENS, STEFFES, STEFFEY, STEFFY, STEGALL (includes Stigall, Steggles, Steagall), STEGALL (includes Stratton), STEGER, STEICHEN (includes Stechen), STEIGER, STEIN, STEINBACH, STEINBERG, STEINBRECHER, STEINEBACH (includes Steinbach), STEINER, STEINKAMP, STEINKE, STEINMAN, STEINMETZ, STEINROCK, STELCK, STELL, STELTING (includes Stolting, Stoelting, von Stolten), STEMBRIDGE (includes Stanbridge, Stonebridge), STEMBRIDGE, STEMWEDEL (includes Stemmwedel, Stemwedle, Sternwedel), STENABAUGH, STENGEL, STENGER, STENHOUSE (includes Stanners, Stennis, Stanhous, Stanhouse, Stanhus, Stanus, Stanis, Stainehous, Stenos,, Stannouse, Stenhous, Stennous), STENNETT, STENON, STENSON (includes Steenson, Stinson, Stevenson, Stephenson), STENTAFORD, STEPHAN, STEPHEN, STEPHENS (includes Stevens, Stephenson), STEPHENS, STEPHENSON,

STEPP, STEPTOE, STERLING, STERN, STERN, STERNBERG, STERNE (includes Sternes), STERNER, STERNES, STERRETT, STETLER, STETSON, STETTLER, STEVEN, STEVENS, STEVENSON, STEWARD, STEWARDSON, STEWART (includes Stuart, Steuart, Steward), STGEORGE.

- **"STI-STN" Surname Mailing Lists**
  http://www.rootsweb.com/~jfuller/gen_mail_surnames-sti.html
  STIBBS, STICE, STICKLAND, STICKLAND, STICKLE, STICKLER, STICKLEY, STICKNEY, STICKNEY, STIDHAM (includes Stiddem, Steadman, Stedman), STIEMLY (includes Steimly, Stimley, Steinle), STIFF, STIFFLER, STIGALL, STIGERS (includes Staggers), STILES, STILL, STILLEY, STILLMAN, STILLWAGON (includes Stillwaggon, Stelvegen), STILLWELL (includes Stilwell), STILSON, STILTNER (includes Stilton), STILWELL, STIMPSON, STIMSON, STINCHCOMB, STINCHFIELD, STINE, STINGER, STINNETT (includes Stennett, Stinet, Stinit), STINSON, STIPAK, STIRLING, STITES, STITH, STITT, STIVER, STIVERS, STJOHN, STLOUIS.

- **"STO-STQ" Surname Mailing Lists**
  http://www.rootsweb.com/~jfuller/gen_mail_surnames-sto.html
  STOBER, STOCK, STOCKBRIDGE, STOCKDALE, STOCKER (includes Stucker, Stooker), STOCKFORD, STOCKHAM, STOCKING, STOCKINGER, STOCKMAN, STOCKS (includes Stock, Stox, Stacks), STOCKSLAGER (includes Stocksleger), STOCKSTILL, STOCKTON, STOCKWELL, STODDARD, STODDART, STOEHR, STOEVER, STOFER, STOGNER, STOGSDILL, STOKELY, STOKER, STOKES, STOKES, STOKES, STOKESBURY (includes Stotesbury), STOKKA, STOLL, STOLTZ, STOLZ (includes Stoltz, Stultz, Stults), STONE, STONE, STONEBRAKER, STONEBURNER, STONECIPHER, STONEKING, STONEMAN, STONER, STONEROCK, ST. ONGE (includes Saintonge), STOOPS, STOPPS, STORCH, STORCKE (includes Stork, Storckman, Storch, Storke, Storckwitz, Storc, Storck), STORER, STOREY, STORIE, STORIER (includes Storrier), STORK, STORKSON, STORM (includes Storms, Sturm), STORMS, STORRS, STORY (includes Storie, Storey, Stori), STOTT, STOTTER, STOTTS, STOUDT, STOUFFER, STOUGHTON, STOUT, STOUTJESDIJK (includes Stoutjesdyk), STOVALL, STOVER, STOW, STOWE, STOWELL (includes Stowel, Stoel, Stawell), STOWERS.

- **"STR-STT" Surname Mailing Lists**
  http://www.rootsweb.com/~jfuller/gen_mail_surnames-str.html
  STRACENER (includes Strasner, Strayaner, Straysoner, Strszner, Stracner, Strasser, Strayanor, Strazner, Straisner,, Strassner, Strayson, Strissner, Strasson, Stracer, Straighter, Strossoner), STRACHAN, STRACK, STRADER, STRADTMAN (includes Strattman, Stradmann, Strathman), STRAHAN, STRAHLE, STRAIGHT (includes Strait, Streit), STRAIN, STRAIT, STRALEY, STRANAHAN, STRAND, STRANG, STRANGE, STRASSER (includes Strawser, Strauser, Strausser, Strazer, Strauzer), STRATFORD, STRATTON, STRATTON, STRAUB (includes Straube, Stroub, Stroube, Stroup, Stroupe, Stroubel, Strouble, Strube), STRAUGHN, STRAUSBAUGH (includes Strasbach, Stasbach, Trasbart, Drrasbart, Strasbaugh, Strassbach, Strawsbaugh,, Strosback, Stratsbaugh), STRAUSS, STRAW, STRAWN, STRAYER, STRAYHORN, STREATFIELD, STREET, STREETER (includes Streater), STREETMAN, STREETY (includes Streaty, Streetie, Streete, Streetee, Streetey, Strutty), STREIGHT, STREIT, STRIBLING (includes Stripling, Striplan, Stribland, Stribln, Striplin), STRICKER, STRICKLAND (includes Stricklin), STRICKLANDNC, STRICKLER (includes Stickler), STRICKLIN, STRICKLING, STRINGER, STRINGER, STRINGFELLOW, STRINGHAM, STRIPLIN, STROBEL, STROCK (includes Strack), STRODE, STROH, STROHM, STROHSCHNEIDER, STROM,

STROMAN, STROMBERG (includes Stramburg, Stramberg, Stromburg), STRONG (includes Stronge, Strongman, Straughan, Straughn, Strang, Strange, Strangeman, Strachan, Strawn), STROSNIDER, STROTHER, STROUD (includes McStroud, Straub, Staub, Strauss, Stroupe, Strode), STROUP, STROUSE, STROUT, STRUBE, STRUNK, STRUTHERS, STRUTT, STRUVE (includes Strube, Struven, Strueve), STRYKER.

- **"STU-STZ" Surname Mailing Lists**
  http://www.rootsweb.com/~jfuller/gen_mail_surnames-stu.html
  STUART, STUBBLEFIELD, STUBBS, STUCK, STUCKER, STUCKEY, STUCKLEY (includes Stuckey), STUCKMAN, STUDDARD (includes Studard, Stoddard), STUDEBAKER (includes Studybaker, Studabaker), STUDER, STUDLEY (includes Studly, Studlay, Studely, Stodley, Stoodley, Stoodely, Studelay), STUDSTILL, STUFFLES, STULCE, STULL, STULTS, STULTZ, STULTZ, STUMBLES, STUMP (includes Stomp), STUMPF, STUMPH (includes Stump, Stumpf), STUPP, STURDEVANT, STURDIVANT, STURGEON, STURGES, STURGESS, STURGILL, STURGIS (includes Sturges, Turges, Turgis), STURM, STURMAN, STURT, STURTEVANT, STUTZMAN, STUYVESANT (includes Stivenson, Stiverson), STYERS, STYLES.

- **"SU-SZ" Surname Mailing Lists**
  http://www.rootsweb.com/~jfuller/gen_mail_surnames-su.html
  SUAREZ, SUBLETT (includes Sublet, Sublete, Sublette, Sublit, Soblet), SUCH, SUCKLING (includes Sucklyn, Sucklin, Sucklyng), SUDBURY (includes Sudberry, Sedberry, Sutberry), SUDDARTH (includes Sudderth, Suddoth, Sudduth, Suddith, Suddata, Suddreth), SUDEK, SUDSBERRY, SUGG, SUGGS (includes Sugg), SUITE (includes Suit, Suits, Suitt, Sute, Soot, Soots), SUITE (includes Suit), SULFRIDGE (includes Selfridge, Suffrage, Sulfrage, Suffridge), SULGROVE, SULLENGER, SULLICK (includes Zullick, Szolak, Sulek), SULLINS (includes Sullens, Sullen, Sullin), SULLIVAN (includes Sullavan, Sullivant, Sullavant, O'Sullivan, O'Sullavan, O'Sullivant, McSullivan, McSullavan,, McSullivant), SULLIVANT, SULSER (includes Sulcer, Sulsar), SUMMA, SUMMER, SUMMERFIELD, SUMMERLIN, SUMMEROUR, SUMMERS, SUMMERVILLE, SUMNER (includes Somner, Summoner, Somnier, Sumners), SUMNERS, SUMNEY, SUMPTER (includes Sumter), SUMRALL, SUNDAY, SUNDERLAND, SURBER (includes Sorber, Serber, Sarver, Server, Surbaugh), SURFACE, SURGENER (includes Surginer, Surginor, Sojourner), SURRATT (includes Sarratt, Sarrett), SUSSEX, SUTCLIFFE, SUTER, SUTFIN (includes Sutphen, Sutphin, Zutphen), SUTHERLAND, SUTHERLIN, SUTPHEN, SUTPHIN, SUTTER, SUTTIE, SUTTLE, SUTTLES, SUTTON, SUYDAM, SVENDSEN (includes Swenson), SVENSDOTTER, SVENSON, SVENSSON, SVOBODA, SWACKHAMMER, SWAFFORD (includes Swaffard, Swoffard, Swoford), SWAIM, SWAIN (includes Swaine, Swayne, Swaim, Swaime, Swayme, Swem), SWALLOW (includes Swallows), SWAN, SWANBOROUGH (includes Swansborough), SWANGER, SWANGO (includes Schwangau), SWANK, SWANLUND (includes Svanlund, Swanland), SWANN, SWANSON, SWARBRICK, SWART, SWARTOUT, SWARTWOUT, SWARTZ, SWARTZBAUGH (includes Schwartzbach), SWAYNE, SWAYZE (includes Swezey, Swayzie, Sweazy, Swasey, Sweezey), SWAYZE, SWEARINGEN, SWEAT, SWEATMAN, SWEATT, SWEEDEN (includes Sweeten), SWEENEY (includes Sweeny, Swiney), SWEENY, SWEET (includes Sweat, Sweatt, Sweatte), SWEETING, SWEETLAND, SWEETMAN, SWEETSER, SWEITZER, SWENSON, SWEPSON (includes Sweptson, Swepston, Swepstone, Swepton, Sweepson, Sweepston, Sweepstone, Sweepton,, Sivepson), SWETT, SWEZEY, SWICK, SWIFT, SWIGART (includes Schwigart), SWILLEY, SWIM (includes Swimm, Swym, Swymm), SWINDELL, SWINDLE, SWINDLER,

SWINEHART (includes Swanhart), SWINFORD, SWINGLE, SWINK, SWINNEY, SWINSON, SWINTON, SWISHER, SWISHER (includes Sweitzer), SWITZER, SWOPE (includes Schwab, Swoope), SWORD, SWORDS (includes Soards, Sowards, Sword), SYDNOR, SYKES, SYLVESTER, SYME, SYMES, SYMMES, SYMONDS, SYMONS, SZABO, SZARNICKI, SZATKOWSKI (includes Szadkowski, Shatkowski, Shadkowski, Shakowski, Shadowski), SZCZDROWSKI (includes Szczodrowski, Szodroski, Szodrowski, Schodrowski, Schodroski, Schodrovski,, Shodroske), SZENDREI (includes Szendrey), SZILVASI, SZTERN (includes Stern, Stein), SZYMANSKI.

SURNAMES, FAMILY ASSOCIATIONS & FAMILY NEWSLETTERS – "T"

Resources Dedicated to One Surname
http://www.cyndislist.com/surn-t.htm

Category Index:

◆ General Surname Sites and Resources
◆ Surname Specific Sites and Resources

◆ Surname Mailing Lists

◆ General Surname Sites and Resources

- Connect with Surnames - T
  http://www.geocities.com/Heartland/Bluffs/7708/t.html

- Dutch Home Pages by Familyname ~ Letter T
  http://members.tripod.com/~Don_Arnoldus/t.htm

- FamilyHistory.com - Message Boards - Surname - T
  http://www.familyhistory.com/messages/list.asp?prefix=TA

- Family Tree Maker Online User Home Pages - T
  http://www.familytreemaker.com/users/t/index.html

- Family Workings T Surname Links
  http://www.familyworkings.com/links/surt.htm

- GenConnect Surname Index - "T"
  http://genconnect.rootsweb.com/indx/surnames/T.html
  Message boards sponsored by RootsWeb. Each surname message board set is divided into the following topics: Queries, Bibles, Biographies, Deeds, Obituaries, Pensions, Wills.

- Genealogy Resources on the Internet - "TA-TD" Surname Mailing Lists
  http://www.rootsweb.com/~jfuller/gen_mail_surnames-ta.html
  "TE-TH"
  http://www.rootsweb.com/~jfuller/gen_mail_surnames-te.html
  "TI-TN"
  http://www.rootsweb.com/~jfuller/gen_mail_surnames-ti.html
  "TO-TQ"
  http://www.rootsweb.com/~jfuller/gen_mail_surnames-to.html
  "TR-TT"
  http://www.rootsweb.com/~jfuller/gen_mail_surnames-tr.html
  "TU-TZ"
  http://www.rootsweb.com/~jfuller/gen_mail_surnames-tu.html
  Search the index of surname mailing lists below: Surname Mailing Lists.

  - Genealogy Resources on the Internet - Surnames Included in Mailing Lists - "T"
    http://www-personal.umich.edu/~cgaunt/surnames/t.names.html
    This is a computer generated list of the surnames, and all variant spellings for those names, that are found in the surname mailing lists detailed on the pages shown above.

- Genealogy Resources on the Internet - Surname Web Sites for "T" Surnames
  http://www-personal.umich.edu/~cgaunt/surnames/t.html

- Genealogy's Most Wanted - Surnames Beginning with "T"
  http://www.citynet.net/mostwanted/t.htm

- Google Web Directory .... Genealogy>Surnames>T
  http://directory.google.com/Top/Society/Genealogy/Surnames/T/

- Heartland Genealogy Society Membership List - T
  http://www.geocities.com/Heartland/Ranch/2416/hgs-mlist-t.html

- H-GIG Surname Registry - Surnames Beginning T
  http://www.ucr.edu/h-gig/surdata/surname20.html

- Higginson Book Company - Surnames Beginning with T
  http://www.higginsonbooks.com/t.htm

- inGeneas Table of Common Surname Variations and Surname Misspellings - T-Z
  http://www.ingeneas.com/T2Z.html

- The Obituary Link Page - Family Obituary Archives Online - T
  http://www.geocities.com/~cribbswh/obit/t.htm

- Open Directory - Society: Genealogy: Surnames: T
  http://www.dmoz.org/Society/Genealogy/Surnames/T/

- Surname Springboard Index - T
  http://www.geocities.com/~alacy/spring_t.htm

- SurnameWeb Surname Registry - T Index
  http://www.surnameweb.org/registry/t.htm

- SWINX Zoeklijst Nederlandse Familienamen / SWINX Searchlist Dutch Surnames - T
  http://www.swinx.net/swinx/swinx_ta_nl.htm

- 'T' Surnames at RootsWeb
  http://resources.rootsweb.com/surnames/t.html

- Websites at RootsWeb: T Surnames
  http://www.rootsweb.com/~websites/surnames/t.html

◆ Surname Specific Sites and Resources

- TABBITT Genealogy - Descendants of William TABBITT
  http://www.tabbitt.fsbusiness.co.uk

- The TACKETT Family Association
  http://www.jps.net/jtackitt/index.html

- The TAFT Family Association Home Page
  http://members.aol.com/sbroker12/taft/index.html

- TAGGART Surname Resource Center
  http://www.geocities.com/ResearchTriangle/Forum/9942/

- The TAIT and TATE Families of America
  http://www.geocities.com/Heartland/Farm/4806/
  TAIT/TATE families who lived in the state of GA and other Southern States.

- TALIAFERRO
  http://www.gensouth.com/taliaferro/

- TALIAFERRO Family History
  http://www.homestead.com/taliaferro/TALIAFERRO.html
  The Taliaferro Family - Three Centuries In America, a new reference book written after 47 years of research.

- www.TALIAFERRO.net
  http://taliaferro.net
  Offering a virtual cornucopia of family information, genealogy, historical vignettes, news, and some interesting links.

- TALIAFERRO Genealogy
  http://assentweb.com/taliaferro/
  Research into the lineage of the Taliaferro, Toliver, Tolliver, Tagliaferro families. From Italy to England to America, this historic Virginia family represents 12 generations in the United States.

- TALIAFERRO Times
  http://www.spingola.com/TaliaferroTimes/TT.htm
  This site contains 50 back issues of the Taliaferro Times, a now defunct e-mail newsletter of interest to persons researching the surname Taliaferro. Lots of great information.

- Genealogy of the TANKERSLEY Family in the United States
  http://members.aol.com/gkobernus/tankfamhp/tankindx.html
  Descended from an old English family of that name in Tankersley Parish, Yorkshire, England.

- TANNAHILL Family Reunion
  http://home.att.net/~Tannahill/
  April 3, 1999, Fort Worth, Texas USA.

- TANNEHILL - TANNAHILL Surname Resource Center
  http://freepages.genealogy.rootsweb.com/~geneal/src/Tann SRC.html
  Also TANNYHILL, TANNEYHILL, TANIHILL, and variations.

- TAPP Genealogy
  http://members.aol.com/caroltapp/tapp.html

- TARKINGTON Family History
  http://www.tarkington.com/
  Home of TARKINGTON / TARKENTON/ TARKINTON Genealogy.

- TARLING Family History
  http://www.tarling.net
  Family history site, searching for TARLING worldwide, ancestors, genealogy and links on the web.

- The TARPEY Home Page
  http://web.bham.ac.uk/C.M.Tarpey/tarpeys/

- TARVIN Family Association
  http://tarvin.genweb.org/

- TASSET Tree Trunks Family Association & Newsletter
  http://www.familytreemaker.com/users/k/o/e/Laura-L-Koehn

- TATE Surnames
  http://www.infocom.com/~dtate/tate-web.htm

- The TATUM Archives
  http://www.rootsquest.com/~ranlewis/
  A collection of information, links and researchers of the Tatum family of the United States.

- TATUM Genealogy
  http://www.geocities.com/Heartland/Ridge/1732
  Research of Tatum descendants of Edward Tatum d. 1744 in Brunswick County Virginia, Guilford County North Carolina, Stokes County North Carolina.

- TAYLOR Family Association
  http://www.taylorassociation.com/
  Descendants of Joseph Sr. and Nancy Taylor of North Carolina, ca 1728-1808. Descendants of Richard Taylor and Thomas Taylor of North Carolina, 1730-. Genealogists interested in early Virginia to North Carolina Taylor migration. Includes LDS Pioneer descendants of William Taylor & Elizabeth Patrick.

- TAYLOR Family History
  http://taylorgenealogy.homepage.com/taylor1.htm

- TAYLOR Family History
  http://pionet.net/~glinden/HISTORY.htm
  Genealogy of William TAYLOR & Elizabeth WELLS of Lincolnshire England, then immigrated to Cincinnati; descendants in Iowa, Kansas, Indiana & Colorado.

- TAYLOR Genealogy Webring
  http://www.geocities.com/Heartland/Bluffs/6953/

- Descendants of Henry TEACHOUT (1781 - 1852) of Chittenden Co, Vermont
  http://www.teachout.org/gen/index.html

- The Teal's of Fewston, Yorkshire Family History Web Site
  http://www.tealfamily.cwc.net/
  Descendants of Thomas Teal 1705 - 1771 of the Parish of Fewston in the Washburn Valley.

- TEASDALE Newsletter
  http://www.teasdale47.freeserve.co.uk/
  Teasdale, Teasdaile, Teasdal, Teasdalle, Teasdell, Teasdall, Teasedill, Teasdayle, Teasdil, Teasdill, Teasdle, Teasdaill, Teasedell, Teasedale, Teasdele, Teesdale, Teesdell, Tesdall, Tesdale, Tesdal, Tesdil, Teisdaill, Teysdall, Teisdalle, Tesdail, Teysdell, Teesedayl, Tisdale, Tisdell, Tisdall, Tiesdale, Tysdall.

- TEATHER (TETHER) Genealogy Web Site
  http://www3.sympatico.ca/andrew.teather/tgen.htm

- TEECE Family History
  http://www.teece.greatxscape.net
  A one-name study on TEECE and TEESE.

- Our TEELGenealogy
  http://www.teelfamily.com/genealogy/
  A homepage with one TEEL family's namesake line.

- TEFFT Family Association
  http://www.geocities.com/tefft_family/
  Dedicated to researching the ancestry of John Tefft of Rhode Island and William Tefft of Massachusetts. The surname TEFFT includes variations such as Teft, Tifft, Tift, Teffe, Teff, and is linked with many families, including Gardiner, Barber, Bradford, Crandall.

- The TEFFT Genealogy Site
  http://www.gwi.net/~troutfly/tefthome.html
  Desecndants of John TEFFT of Rhode Island. Also Kenyon, Barber, Gardiner, and other RI surnames.

- The TEGART Treeclimbers
  http://www.tegart.com/gen/

- TEICHs on the Web
  http://www.alteich.com/teichweb.htm
  An evolving directory of people named TEICH on the world wide web.

- TEMPLE & Related Lines In America
  http://users.erols.com/lptemple/house.htm

- TEMPLER Family Home Page
  http://www.geocities.com/Heartland/Ridge/2072
  A web site for the descendants of James & Martha Huff Templer, about 1755 from Shelbourne Parish, Loudoun County, VA.

- Researching and Documenting the TEMPLIN Family Genealogy
  http://templin.rootsweb.com/

- TENNENT Genealogy Tree
  http://www.wolfe.net/~dtennent/Tennents.html

- TENNEY Family Association
  http://www.tenneyfamily.org/

- TENNYSON / TENNISON Family History Exchange
  http://www.insidetheweb.com/mbs.cgi/mb420132
  Also Tennessen, Tenison, Tenneson, or other spellings.

- The TERHUNE Family Home Page
  http://home.earthlink.net/~hjterhune
  TERHUNE family lore includes both French and Dutch origins and immigrant, Albert Albertse TER HUNEN and descendants

- The TERON Family Home Page
  http://home.istar.ca/~cteron/index.shtml
  TERON who emigrated from Bukovina. Also TYRON, TERRON.

- The TERPENING Family Home Page
  http://freepages.genealogy.rootsweb.com/~fgriffin/terp.html
  Variations include TERPENNING, TERPENNY, TARPENNING, TARPENING, TURPENING, and TEERPENNING.

- TERRELL Society of America, Inc.
  http://www.CairoNet.Com/TERRELL/INDEX.HTM
  Serves all who have any variation of TERRELL that can be made by substituting a,e,i,o,u,y or any combination thereof for either "E" and using 1 or 2 "R" and/or 1 or 2 "L." Taral, Tarrall, Terrell, Terrill, Tirrill, Turrell, Tyrrell, Therrell, ETC.

- Descendants of James TERRY, Sr.
  http://www.parsonstech.com/genealogy/trees/djohnso5/terry.htm

- TERRY Family
  http://www.wf.net/~billk/Terry.html
  Descendants of James Doss TERRY and Katharina FERBER.

- TERRY Family Historian
  http://www.terry-family-historian.com/
  Information from the Terry Family Historian 1982-1988, by Mike Terry editor.

- The TERWILLIGER Family Association
  http://home.earthlink.net/~rctwig/

- TERWILLIGER Surname Research Center
  http://members.tripod.com/vickielynnyoung/twigs.htm

- TEWKSBURY Tracings - A Surname Resource Center
  http://www.nataliesnet.com/tewksbury
  Tewksbury family in the U.S. Genealogy site, queries, source records, links, researchers list, descendancies, etc.

- THAYER Families Association
  http://thayer.genealogist.net

- Acadian Family of Joseph T. THERIAULT
  http://family-joseph-t.theriault.com
  THERIAULT, THERRIAULT, TERRIAU, TERRIO, TERRIOT, THERIOT, THERRIOTH. The site also includes a biography of Jehan and Perinne TERRIAU, the progenitors of THERIAULTs in North America.

- Famille THERRIEN
  http://www.genealogie.org/famille/therrien/
  Home page for the Therrien Family Association also known as "Le Ralliement des familles Jean et Pierre Therrien".

- Histoire et gènèalogie - THIBAUDEAU - THIBODEAU - History and Genealogy
  http://www.qouest.net/~jljmt/index.htm
  Pierre THIBEAUDEAU, le pionnier Acadien. Thibodaux, Thibeaudeau, Thibaudeaux, Thibodeaux, Tebedore, Tibedore, Thibodeault, Thibaudeault, Thybaudeau, Thibedeau, Tibido, Thibidaux, Thibaudau, Thibodot, Bodeau, Bodo, Thibadeau, Thebado, Tibbedeaux, Tibado, Tolado.

- THODY Family History
  http://www.cix.co.uk/~sat/Gene/Gene.html
  Personal research into THODY family history in Bedfordshire.

- THOMAS Family Archives
  http://thomasfamily.homepage.com/
  Descendants of Job Thomas b. c 1736 Virginia.

- THOMAS Family Tree
  http://homepage.dave-world.net/~davidt/Thomas.html
  *Descendants of Michael Thomas, born 1759 Fayette Co,
  Pennsylvania, died 1840 Ross Co, Ohio and Elizabeth Bennett*

- Andrew THOMPSON of Wythe and Bland Counties,
  Virginia and Descendants
  http://members.xoom.com/cragun/thompson/

- Descendants of Benjamin R. THOMPSON
  http://bakingmasters.com/power/thompsn.htm

- Descendants of William THOMPSON
  http://bakingmasters.com/power/thompson.htm

- THOMPSON Family of Eastern North Carolina
  http://www.angelfire.com/nj2/thompson
  *The Thompson family who came to the colonies in the early 1700s
  settling in VA and then moving to NC. The line begins with
  Theophilus and his 6 sons...particularly Trimigan.*

- THOMPSON One Name Study
  http://www.geocities.com/Athens/2249/

- THOMPSON/THOMSON in Christian, Todd, Trigg
  Cos., KY
  http://dgmweb.net/Thompson/ChristianToddTriggKY.htm
  *Over 250 family group sheets, complete census data and tax rolls
  for all THOMPSON/THOMSON and kin in these Kentucky counties
  through 1850.*

- THORBURN-MACFIE Family Society
  http://home1.swipnet.se/~w-10723/thormac1.htm
  *Descendants of William Thorburn and his wife Jessy (nÈe Macfie)
  who in July 1823 removed to Sweden from Leith in Scotland.*

- THORNDELL Descendants, 1599-1999
  http://members.aol.com/davethornl/thorndell/index.htm
  *Descendants of Edward Thorndell and Ann Scollock married 14 Jan
  1599 in Gloucestershire, England.*

- THORNSBERRY Genealogy
  http://www.aros.net/~deboraht/genealogy.htm
  *Thornsberry, Thornsborough, Thornsburgh, etc. and related
  families back to 1060 AD and beyond. Some related surnames are
  Hall, Bates, Mendenhall. Quakers and English royalty ancestors
  abound.*

- Descendants of Thomas THORNTON
  http://home.forbin.com/gwinslow/thor.html

- THORNTON Family List Genealogy
  http://www.geocities.com/Heartland/Hills/2496/Thornton/
  *Website for the Thornton-List@rootsweb.com. Site contains
  GEDCOM files for multiple THORNTON researchers, also has links
  to other THORNTON researchers and a query page on our "lost"
  THORNTON ancestors.*

- THORNTON Family Page
  http://www.busprod.com/basleep/thornton.htm

- THRASHER Genealogy
  http://www.eskimo.com/~greg/thrasher.html
  A mailing list, queries, cemetery information and more.

- THURLOW One Name Study
  http://www3.ns.sympatico.ca/weston/default.htm

- THURMAN's Quest
  http://freepages.genealogy.rootsweb.com/~lthurman/
  index.html
  *THURMAN and related on-line surname repository with over
  49,000 in 6 major databases.*

- TIDEMANN - Descendants of Ole Christian
  Tidemann
  http://www.geocities.com/Heartland/Prairie/8430/tidemann/
  tid-2.htm
  *Bier, Hansen, Husum, Jensdotter, Marsdotter, Nielsen, Nissen,
  Pedersdotter, Tidemann and more. The Tidemann family was from
  Gram, Haderslev, Denmark. In the 1870s and 1880s several
  members came to America and settled in Iowa and Nebraska.*

- TIGHE Genealogy Page
  http://members.aol.com/Tltighe/index.html
  *TIGHE, TIGH. Siblings immigrated from Sligo, Ireland to Canada
  and the United States.*

- The TILLOTSON Project
  http://www.tillotson.net/
  *Tillotson, Tilston, Tillerson, Tilson, Tillitson, Tilletson, Tillison,
  Tilestone, Tileston, Tillson, Tilleston.*

- TILGHMAN Genealogy
  http://www.TilghmanGen.com/
  *Descendants of Johannes Tilghman (Tillman / Tilman) from 1255 to
  present including information on allied families.*

- The TILTON Family of Martha's Vineyard (Banks
  Vol. III, pp. 471 - 482.)
  http://www.vineyard.net/vineyard/history/tilton.htm
  *The TILTON Family of Martha's Vineyard, Dukes Co., MA, as
  transcribed from Vol. III of "The History of Martha's Vineyard" by
  Dr. Charles Banks, c. 1930. Traces the descendants of Samuel
  Tilton (1637/8 - 1731) and Hannah Moulton of Lynn, MA; Hampton,
  NH, and Chilmark, MA, whose descendants reside on Martha's
  Vineyard.*

- TIMPERLEY Family History and Genealogy
  http://www.timperley.org/
  Temperley, Temperly, Timberley, Timberly, de Timperley, Timperly.

- TINDELLs of Calhoun Co., FL
  http://homepages.rootsweb.com/~catinjax/tindell/
  *Tindel/Tindal and all spelling variants throughout the southern
  USA.*

- TINNEY Surname
  http://www.geocities.com/Heartland/Ranch/5409/

- TIMPERLEY of Hintlesham
  http://homepages.strath.ac.uk/~cjis19/timp.htm
  *Timperley family of Hintlesham, Suffolk, England and connected
  families, e.g. Markham, Harington.*

- **Descendants of John TINSLEY**
  http://csc.techcenter.org/~mneill/tinsjohn.html

- **The TIPTON Family Association Of America**
  http://home.att.net/~tiptongen/tipform1.htm

- **TITHERADGE, TITHERIDDGE, TYTHERIDGE and TIDRIDGES**
  http://www.titheradge.junglelink.co.uk/

- **TITTENSOR One-Name Study Homepage**
  http://www.ftittensor.freeserve.co.uk/ons_homepage.html

- **The TITTERTON Family Web Site**
  http://www.titterton.mcmail.com
  TITTERTON families live all around the world and not just in the UK. The web site looks at the origin of the surname and the various families using the name.

- **Descendants of Silius TITUS**
  http://www.familytreemaker.com/users/p/e/t/Richard-L-Pettitt/

- **The TOADVINE Family**
  http://www.intercom.net/user/toadvine/index.html
  Nicholas TOADVINE from Guernsey Island to Maryland in approx. 1675.

- **Thomas TOBEY of Sandwich Descendants**
  http://homepages.rootsweb.com/~explor19/tobey.htm
  Also descendants of James TOBEY of Kittery.

- **TODD Family Message Board**
  http://www.rootsweb.com/~genepool/toddboard.htm

- **TOLLES in America**
  http://fairfax2.laser.net/~tolles/book.html
  A book for sale that contains about 4,500 names and more than 1,500 Tolles (and some related Toles).

- **The TOLLINGTON Home Page**
  http://www.hotstar.net/~moose/index.htm

- **TONEY Genealogy Exchange**
  http://www.toneyweb.com/exchange/

- **TOOTHAKER Genealogy, 7 Generations of TOOTHAKERs in America**
  http://ramsey.users5.50megs.com/toothakr.html
  Genealogy of family from Roger Toothaker (b1612), who came to Plymouth in 1635.

- **Descendents of Roger TOOTHAKER**
  http://www.jps.net/jcoffman
  Database containing about 6,000 of the Descendents of Roger TOOTHAKER born 1612.

- **Thomas TORCHIA Family**
  http://www.geocities.com/~mimi_tabby/torchia.htm
  Genealogy site for all people with the surname Torchia.

- **The TORMEY Family History Website**
  http://www.geocities.com/~mtormey/
  Exploring our Irish & American Roots: A repository of historical and genealogical information on the TORMEY surname.

- **Raymond dit TOULOUSE**
  http://www.cam.org/~gilray/genealogie/raymond.dit.toulouse.html
  Forum de discussion des descendants des familles Raymond dit Toulouse.

- **TOWNE Family Association, Inc.**
  http://hometown.aol.com/brbaylis/myhomepage/index.html/
  Descendants of William TOWNE and Joanna BLESSING who came to America from Great Yarmouth, England and settled in Salem, Massachusetts about 1635.

- **TOWNSEND Society of America**
  http://www.townsend-society.org/

- **The TOWNSLEY Family History Home Page**
  http://homepages.tesco.net/~townsleyb/TownsFH/history1.htm
  Archives of information related to the Townsley name, mainly in England but with some for Scotland and Ireland. Also archives for the Sheeky (Sheekey, Sheehy) and Strangeway(S) family names in England.

- **TOWSE Tree Family HomePage**
  http://members.tripod.com/~DCohig/index.html
  Towse surname worldwide.

- **The TRACEWELL Family Genealogy Site**
  http://www.bonk.com/tracewell/

- **TRACHY: People from Jersey, Channel Islands**
  http://www.familytreemaker.com/users/t/r/a/Marie-T-Trachy/
  Genealogy of the TRACHY family since 1275.

- **TRAPHAGEN Heritage**
  http://www.geocities.com/Heartland/Cottage/7239/index.htm
  A site for anyone having a Traphagen, Traphagan, Triphagen or Trapphagen in the United States or Germany. Burhans and Ostrander researchers will find they descend from Willem Jansen Traphagen through his two daughters.

- **TRAPP Family in Brazil**
  http://www.geocities.com/lgtrapp/trappbre.htm

- **TRAPP Surname Center**
  http://www.geocities.com/lgtrapp/trappsrc.htm
  Dedicated to provide resources for the TRAPP surname worldwide.

- **R.W. TRASK Family Home Page**
  http://www.geocities.com/Heartland/8860/
  With a listing of other TRASK researchers.

- **Juel TRASK's Home Page**
  http://www.geocities.com/Athens/Forum/2225/
  History - TRASK Family.

- **The TRAUTVETTERs of Hancock County, Illinois**
  http://asc.csc.cc.il.us/~mneill/trautv/trautv.htm
  Originating in and around Bad Salzungen, Thuringen, Germany.

- **TRAYLOR Family Links**
  http://www.my-ged.com/traylor/
  Traylor, Trayler, Trailor, Trailer, Traler.

- **The TREADWAY Web**
  http://members.tripod.com/~Randy_T/treadweb.html
  Bloodlines of Nathaniel, Thomas and Richard Treadway, Burial Records, Obituaries, Bible Records, Treadway Honorary Hall.

- TREASE Family Home Page
  http://www.geocities.com/Heartland/Pointe/1420
  Surname information on Trease, Treece, Treace, Triece.

- L'Association des Familles TREMBLAY /
  Association of the TREMBLAY of America
  http://www.genealogie.org/famille/tremblay/tremblay.htm
  Trombley, Trembley, Trumble.

- The TREMBLE-SAWYER Families
  http://homepages.rootsweb.com/~schwartz/Tremble/
  index.html
  *Ancestors and Descendants of Hiram TREMBLE and Sarah
  SAWYER, pioneers of Coles County, Illinois.*

- TRETHEWY Society
  http://web.triton.net/kc8jhy/
  *Trethewy, Trethewey, Trethewie and Trethteway, originating in
  Cornwall.*

- TREVATHAN & TREVETHAN - A Family from
  Cornwall
  http://www.geocities.com/BourbonStreet/7769/

- TREVITHICK Family Tree
  http://users.idcomm.com/trevithick

- The Association of Descendants of Philippe du
  TRIEUX
  http://www.apci.net/~truax/
  *A Walloon Huguenot who came to New Amsterdam in 1624.
  Descendants have the surnames Truax, Truex, Trueax, Truaxe, and
  other variants.*

- TRIGG Family Worldwide
  http://www.sohost.com/trigg/

- TRIPLETT Genealogy
  http://people.mn.mediaone.net/jgoepfert/triplett_
  genealogy.htm
  *Research of the descendants of Francis TRIPLETT, b. 1635, first
  TRIPLETT to immigrate to the U.S.*

- TRIPP Genealogical Web
  http://www.users.hockinghills.net/~bobt/discus/
  *Descendants of TRIPP families, sons and daughters lines. Mainly:
  John TRIPP of Rhode Island; Nicholas TRIPP of South Carolina;
  Sylvanus TRIPP of Maine.*

- TRITT Family Research
  http://www.tritt.org
  *Nonprofit organization dedicated to research & publication of a
  documented account of Tritt (Tritten, Dritt, Trait, Treat, Trate)
  family history from as early a period as records exist.*

- The TRIVETT Family History 1040 - 2000
  http://dspace.dial.pipex.com/town/close/gg02/

- TROOST Site
  http://E_Troost.tripod.com
  *Genealogy of people with the surname TROOST (Netherlands) or
  TROAST (USA).*

- TRUDE Family Genealogy
  http://www.intplsrv.net/tltrude/
  Trude or DeTrude in America and Canada.

- TRUMAN Family Chronology; Containing Possible
  Connections to the Family of Peter Truman the
  Loyalist
  http://members.aol.com/jatappero/truman.htm
  *Peter Truman of Alburgh, Grand Isle, Vermont. Includes Mott,
  Latham, Truman, Barnum, Brouwer, Haring, Wait and more.*

- The TRUMBLE-TRUMBULL Family History and
  Genealogy
  http://www.trumble-trumbull.com
  Everything about the Trumble/Trumbull families in America.

- TRUSLER / TRUSLOW Surname Home Page
  http://home.earthlink.net/~artcheryl/

- The Descendants of Moses TUCKER and Mary
  MASTERS
  http://www.webspawner.com/users/mosestucker
  *Moses TUCKER b. 1758 Westfield NJ, d. prob OH. Family lived in
  OH, IN, and IL. Branches include Masters, Stull, Hefner, Foster,
  Camp.*

- The TUCKER Kingdom Web Ring
  http://earth.vol.com/~ecochran/ring.html

- World TUDDENHAM Family Tree
  http://www.users.globalnet.co.uk/~jerryt/

- The TUFTY Foundation
  http://www.Tufty.com/
  *Vital information on American descendants from the TUFTE farm in
  Norway who settled in Minnesota and South Dakota.*

- TUNKS Descendants Association Incorporated
  http://go.to/Tunks
  Descendants of William TUNKS (TONKS) & Sarah LYONS.

- TUPMAN Family Data
  http://freespace.virgin.net/alan.tupman/sites/down1.htm

- The TURKEL Tribe
  http://www.geocities.com/Heartland/3511
  *Turkel, Tirkel, Turkl, Tirkl, Tuerkel, Turkle, Turkell, Tirkell, Terkel,
  Terkl.*

- TURMAN Book - 1820-1973 by Gladys Turman
  http://www.geocities.com/Heartland/Flats/5596/thome.html

- Border Clan TURNBULL
  http://www.turnbulls.org/

- TURNBULL Clan Association
  http://turnbullclan.com/

- The James TURNER Family of Amherst Co., VA,
  Sumner Co., TN and Marshall Co., MS
  http://members.aol.com/jogt/turnerja.htm

- David TURNER Mormon Pioneer
  http://www.geocities.com/Heartland/Fields/8488
  Descendants of David TURNER and Rose COLLIER.

- TURNER Archive & Historical Records Collection
  http://members.aol.com/tahrc/
  *Descendants of Jesse Porter Turner & Malinda Francis Barnhart
  Turner, Boone County, Missouri.*

- TURNER Family Genealogy
  http://members.aol.com/PSulzer/Turner.html
  Descendants of John TURNER and his son Fielding, born 1706 Northumberland Co., Virginia.

- The TURNER Genealogy Ring Home Page
  http://genweb.net/~turner/ring/home.html

- TUTT Family Home Page
  http://freespace.virgin.net/philip.rhind-tutt/family.html

- TWEEDIE or TWEEDY Genealogy and Family History
  http://www.apgate.com/fam_his/index.html
  Information regarding this family's origins in the Scottish Border Country.

- TWINER Family Genealogy
  http://www.geocities.com/Heartland/Bluffs/5932/twiner.html
  This site is dedicated to the TWINER surname including links to TWINER GenConnect boards, TWINER Mailing List (Rootsweb) and our family.

- TWISS of Hunstanton
  http://www.geocities.com/Heartland/Oaks/9803/index.html
  Photographic gallery of the TWISS family taken in and around Hunstanton Norfolk England.

- TWITCHELL Links
  http://www.geocities.com/Heartland/Cottage/7066/
  Descendants of Benjamin TWITCHELL who immigrated from Buckinghamshire, England in about 1630. Includes these spellings: Twichel, Twichell, Twitchel.

- TYLCOAT TYLECOTE TALCOTT Genealogy
  http://ourworld.compuserve.com/homepages/dave_tylcoat/

- The TYREE Name
  http://users.aol.com/rtyree/a/TyreeName.html
  Tyrie, Tiri, Tyree, etc. in Scotland.

- TYZACK Genealogy
  http://www.tyzack.net/
  Tyzack, Tysick, Tyzacks, Tysack.

◆ Surname Mailing Lists

- "TA-TD" Surname Mailing Lists
  http://www.rootsweb.com/~jfuller/gen_mail_surnames-ta.html
  TABAR (includes Taber, Tabor), TABER, TABOR (includes Taber), TACKABERRY (includes Thackaberry), TACKETT (includes Tackitt), TACON, TAFFE (includes Taffie), TAFT, TAGG (includes Tag), TAGGART (includes McTaggart, MacTaggart), TAGLIAPIETRA, TAGUE, TAIT, TAKACS (includes Tkacs, Tackach, Takach), TALBERT, TALBOT (includes Talbott, Tolbert, Talbert), TALBOTT, TALCOTT, TALIAFERRO (includes Talifero, Toliver, Talafero), TALKINGTON, TALLADAY (includes Talada, Tallady, Tallada), TALLANT, TALLENT, TALLEY (includes Tally), TALLEY (includes Tolley, Toley, Tally, Zolley, Zoley, Taly), TALLMAN (includes Tallmon, Tollman, Talman, Taleman), TALLY, TALMADGE, TAMMANY, TANDY, TANKERSLEY (includes Tankersly, Tanksley), TANNAHILL (includes Tannehill, Tannyhill), TANNER, TANQUARY (includes Tanquery, Toncray, Tonkery, Toncre, Tonkery, Tonkray, Tonchre), TANSEY, TANSLEY, TANT, TAPLEY, TAPLIN, TAPP, TAPPTICO (includes Tapp), TAPSCOTT (includes Tapscot, Tabscott), TARABOCHIA, TARASENKO (includes Tarsenko), TARASI, TARBELL, TARDIF (includes Tardiff,

Tardy, Tardieu), TARKINGTON (includes Tarkenton), TARLETON (includes Tarlton), TARLING, TARLTON, TARNO (includes Tarnow, Torno, Tarnowski, Tarnowsky, Tarnoski), TARPEY, TARPLEY, TARR, TARRANT, TARSHIS, TART (includes Tarte, Tartt), TARTER, TARVER, TARVIN, TARWATER (includes Theurwachter, Torwater, Tawater), TASKER, TASSET, TATE (includes Tait, Tatum), TATMAN (includes Tateman, Totman), TATTERSALL, TATTRIE (includes Tatteray, Tatterie), TATUM (includes Tatem, Tatom, Tatam), TATUM, TATZKE, TAUBES (includes Tobias), TAUCHEN, TAULBEE (includes Talbee, Tolby, Talby), TAUNTON (includes Tanton, Tonton), TAWES (includes Taws, Tawse), TAWNEY (includes DeTani, DeToni, De Toeni, Thaney, Taney), TAY, TAYLOR, TAYLOR, TAYLOR, TAYLOR.

- "TE-TH" Surname Mailing Lists
  http://www.rootsweb.com/~jfuller/gen_mail_surnames-te.html
  TEACHOUT (includes Tietsort, Titsworth), TEAGUE (includes Tegge), TEAL, TEAS (includes Tees, Tice, Tease), TEASDALE, TEASLEY (includes Teasler), TEBBETTS (includes Tibbetts), TEBBS, TECKEMEYER, TEDDER, TEDFORD, TEDROW (includes Tetterow, Detro, Titro), TEECE (includes Teese, Tease), TEED, TEEL (includes Teal), TEEPLE, TEER, TEES, TEESDALE, TEETER, TEETERS, TEFFT, TEGTMEIER, TEGYI, TEITKE (includes Tietke, Teidke), TELFER, TELFORD, TEMPLAIN, TEMPLE (includes Temples), TEMPLEMAN, TEMPLETON, TEMPLIN, TENEYCK, TENNANT, TENNANT, TENNEY (includes Tinney), TENNICK, TENNISON, TENNYSON, TEPOLT (includes Tipolt, Tippelt), TEPPER (includes Topper, Toeppfer), TEREAU, TERESI, TERHUNE, TERPENING (includes Teerpenning, Terpenning, Tarpanning, Tarpeny, Terbening), TERRELL, TERRIL, TERRILL, TERRY, TERWILLIGER (includes Terwilligar, Terwilleger, Terwillegar, Twilegar, Terwilegar), TERWILLIGER, TESCH, TESKE, TESKEY, TESLER (includes Tessler, Teszler, Teslyar, Tsesler, Tchesler, Dessler), TESSENEER (includes Tesseeneer, Testanier, Tasenier, Tesanier, Tessneer, Tesnier, Tasenary, Tesseueer, Tesoneer,, Tesinier), TESSIER, TESTER, TESTERMAN (includes Testermann, Testermen, Testermenn, Tistemin, Tustermun), TESTON, TETER, TETLEY (includes Tetlow, Tetlaw, Titley, Tetterley), TETRICK, TEVAULT (includes Devolt), TEVIS, TEVRUCHT, TEW, TEWKSBURY, THACKER, THACKER, THAMES (includes Timms, Tims), THARP, THATCHER (includes Thacher), THAWLEY, THAXTON (includes Thackston), THAYER, THEIS, THEISS, THEOBALD, THERIAULT, THEROUX, THERRIEN (includes Terrien, Therrian, Therrault, Terrian), THETFORD, THEURER, THIBAULT, THIBODEAU, THIBODEAUX, THIEDE, THIEL, THIELE, THIELEN, THIEM, THIERY, THIGPEN, THOM, THOMA, THOMAS (includes Tomas, Thomason), THOMAS, THOMASON (includes Thomasson, Thompson, Thomas), THOMASSON, THOMPSON (includes Thomson, Tompson), THOMPSON, THOMS, THOMSEN, THOMSON, THONE (includes Thoney, Thony), THOR (includes Tor), THORBURN, THORESON (includes Toreson), THORLEY, THORN (includes Thorne), THORNBURG (includes Thornberg, Thornburgh), THORNBERRY, THORNE, THORNHILL, THORNICROFT, THORNLEY, THORNTON, THORP, THORPE, THORSEN, THRAILKILL, THRALL, THRASH, THRASHER (includes Thresher), THRASHER, THREADGILL, THREET (includes Threat, Threatte, Thweat, Thweatte, Thwreat), THRELKELD, THRIFT, THROCKMORTON, THROWER (includes Trower), THRUSH, THUESEN (includes Thiesen, Thiessen), THUMMA (includes Thuma), THURBER, THURBER, THURGOOD, THURLOW (includes Thurloe, Thallow, Tallow, Thorlow, Thirlow, Thorley), THURMAN, THURMOND, THURSTON, THWEATT.

- **"TI-TN" Surname Mailing Lists**
  http://www.rootsweb.com/~jfuller/gen_mail_surnames-ti.html
  TIBBETT, TIBBETTS, TIBBS (includes Tebbs), TICE, TICHENOR, TICKNER, TICOSSI, TIDD, TIDD, TIDESWELL, TIDWELL (includes Tidywell, Tadwell), TIERNAN, TIERNEY, TIETZ, TIFFANY, TIFFIN, TIGHE, TIGNER, TIGNOR (includes Tigner, Tickner), TILDEN, TILL, TILLER, TILLERY, TILLETT, TILLEY, TILLINGHAST, TILLIS, TILLMAN, TILLOTSON, TILSON, TILTON, TIMBERLAKE, TIMBERMAN, TIMBRELL (includes Timbrel), TIMBRELL (includes Timbrel), TIMM, TIMMERMAN, TIMMINS, TIMMONS, TIMMS, TIMS, TINCHER, TINCKLER (includes Tinkler), TINDALE, TINDALL, TINER, TING, TINGLE, TINGLER, TINGLER, TINGLEY, TINGSTROM, TINKER (includes Tincher), TINKHAM, TINKLE, TINKLER, TINLEY (includes Tindley), TINNELL (includes Tennille, Tennell, Tennill), TINNEY, TINNIN, TINSLEY, TIPPERY, TIPPETT, TIPTON, TIPTON, TISDALE, TITSWORTH, TITTLE, TITUS, TITUS, TITZER.

- **"TO-TQ" Surname Mailing Lists**
  http://www.rootsweb.com/~jfuller/gen_mail_surnames-to.html
  TOADVINE, TOBERGTA, TOBEY, TOBIAS, TOBIN, TOCA, TODD, TODRIFF (includes Tendreff, Todderiff), TOHER, TOIVONEN, TOLAND (includes Tolland, Tolan, Tolen), TOLBERT, TOLER (includes Tolar, Tollar, Toller), TOLIVER, TOLKEN, TOLL, TOLLE, TOLLES, TOLLESON, TOLLETT, TOLLEY (includes Tolly, Tollie), TOLLIVER, TOLMAN, TOLSON, TOMAN, TOMASZEWSKI, TOMBLIN, TOMERLIN, TOMKINS, TOMLIN, TOMLINSON (includes Tomalinson, Tomlin, Tomilson, Timlinson), TOMLINSON, TOMPKINS, TOMS, TONER, TONEY, TONG, TONKIN, TONKS (includes Tunks, Tunx), TONN, TONY, TOOHEY, TOOLE, TOOLEY, TOOMBS (includes Toms, Tombs), TOOMEY, TOON, TOOTHAKER, TOOTHMAN (includes Toothmun, Toothmand, Toothmund, Tuthman, Tuthmun), TOPE, TOPHAM, TOPLEY, TOPPER (includes Tapper), TOPPING, TORBERT, TORBETT (includes Torbet, Tarbet, Tarbett, Tarbert, Torbert, Tarbitt, Torbitt, Tarbutt, Torbutt), TORGERSON, TORGESON, TORRANCE, TORRENCE, TORRES, TORREY, TORRICO, TORRY, TORSCHER, TORSDOTTAR, TOSELAND (includes Tosland, Tozeland, Tozland), TOSELEY (includes Tosley), TOSSELL (includes Tossel, Tossal), TOTEN (includes Tatan, Tatin, Taton, Tattan, Tattin, Tatton, Tatum, Tootan, Tooten, Totin, Toton, Tottan, Tottin,, Totton, Tutan, Tuten, Tutin, Tuttan, Tutten, Tutton), TOTH, TOTTEN, TOTTY (includes Tottie, Tottey, Tottye, Toddy, Toddie, Toty, Tolly, Tollie Tutte, Tutty), TOUCHETTE, TOUCHSTONE, TOUGH, TOURCHER, TOURTELLOTTE (includes Tourtillott, Tortlot, Tourtellott), TOURTELLOTTE (includes Tourtellott, Tourtellot, Tourtelott, Tourtelotte, Tourtillott, Tourtillotte, Tourtillot), TOVREA (includes Toverea, Tovera, Tovery, Toovery), TOWELL, TOWER, TOWERS, TOWLE, TOWLER, TOWLES, TOWN, TOWNE, TOWNER, TOWNLEY, TOWNS, TOWNSEND, TOWNSLEY, TOWSLEE, TOWSLEY, TOY (includes Toye, Tay), TOY, TOYE, TOZER, TOZIER.

- **"TR-TT" Surname Mailing Lists**
  http://www.rootsweb.com/~jfuller/gen_mail_surnames-tr.html
  TRABUE (includes Trabuc), TRACEY, TRACHSEL, TRACY, TRADER (includes Armitrader, Treder), TRAEGER (includes Treger), TRAHAN, TRAHERN, TRAIL, TRAILER, TRAILOR, TRAIN, TRAINER, TRAINOR, TRALER, TRAMELL, TRAMMEL, TRAMMELL, TRANSOU, TRANT, TRANTER, TRANTHAM, TRAPHAGEN (includes Traphagan, Triphagen, Trapheagen, Trophagen, Trapphagen, Troppenhagen, Traphager), TRAPP,

TRASK, TRASTER (includes Treaster, Traister), TRAUGOTT, TRAUTMAN, TRAUTNER, TRAVER, TRAVERS, TRAVIS, TRAYLER, TRAYLOR (includes Traylo, Traler, Trailer, Trayler, Trailor), TRAYNOR, TREADWAY (includes Tredway), TREADWELL (includes Tredwell), TREAT, TREEBY (includes Treby), TREECE, TREFZ, TREGUNNA (includes Tregunner, Tregonna, Tregunne, Tregenna), TREICHEL, TRELOAR (includes Trelore, Trelour, Trelowath, Treloath), TREMAIN (includes Tremaine, Tremane, Tremayne, Trumane), TREMBATH (includes Trenbarth, Trimbath), TREMBLAY, TREMBLE (includes Trembly, Trembley), TREMPER, TRENARY, TRENHAM, TRENT, TREOLO (includes Treola, Triolo), TREON (includes Trion, Treion, Trine, Drion), TREON (includes Trion, Trian, Trine), TRESCOTT, TRESIDDER, TRETT, TRETTER, TREVATHAN, TREVINO (includes Trevi), TREVORROW (includes Trevorow, Trevorro, Trevor), TREW, TREWHITT, TREXLER, TRIBBITT, TRIBBLE, TRICE, TRICE, TRICKEY, TRICO, TRIDENTE, TRIGG, TRIMBLE, TRIMBLE, TRIMMER, TRIMPEY (includes Trimpe), TRIPLETT, TRIPP, TRITT, TRITTON (includes Tritten, Tryton), TRIVETTE (includes Tribet, Trivet, Trivett), TROBAUGH, TROLLINGER, TROMBLEY, TRORBAUGH (includes Trobach, Trorbach, Trorebaugh, Trarbaugh, Trarbach, Drorbach), TROTT, TROTTER (includes Trot, Tretter), TROTTI (includes Trottie, Trotty, Trottee), TROTTIER, TROTTON (includes Trotten), TROUP, TROUSDALE, TROUT (includes Traut), TROUT, TROUTMAN, TROUTWEIN, TROUTWINE, TROW, TROWBRIDGE, TROWELL, TROWER, TROXEL (includes Troxell, Trachsel), TROXELL, TROY, TRUAX (includes Truex, Trueax, Truaxe, Du Trieux), TRUBEE (includes Truby, Trube, Trubeau), TRUBY, TRUDEAU, TRUE (includes Trew), TRUEBLOOD, TRUELOVE, TRUEMAN, TRUESDALE, TRUESDELL, TRUESDELL (includes Truesdale, Trusdell, Truesdail), TRUITT, TRUITT (includes Truett), TRUJILLO, TRULL, TRULOCK, TRUMAN, TRUMBO, TRUMP, TRURAN (includes Truren), TRUSCOTT, TRUSLOVE, TRUSTY, TRYBUS, TRYON (includes Tryan, Trion, Trial, Tryall), TSCHUDI, TSCHUMY (includes Tschumi, Tschummy).

- **"TU-TZ" Surname Mailing Lists**
  http://www.rootsweb.com/~jfuller/gen_mail_surnames-tu.html
  TUBB, TUBBS, TUCK, TUCKER (includes Tuck, Tucks), TUCKNESS (includes Tucknis, Tucknies, Tutnis), TUDOR, TUFTS, TUGGLE, TULL, TULLAR (includes Tuller), TULLIS, TULLOCH, TULLOS, TULLY, TUMA, TUMBLESON, TUMLIN, TUNE, TUNGATE (includes Tongate, Tonget, Tongett, Tunget, Tungett), TUNISON, TUNNELL (includes Tunnel), TUNSTALL, TUPMAN, TUPPER, TURBERVILLE (includes Turbeville, Troublefield, Turbervyle), TURK (includes Turck), TURLEY, TURLINGTON, TURMAN, TURNAGE, TURNBOW, TURNBULL, TURNER (includes Turney, Doerner, Durner, Tarner, Terner, Tourneau, Tirner, Torner, Tearner), TURNEY, TURNIPSEED, TURPIN, TURPIN, TURRELL, TURRENTINE, TURVEY (includes Turvy), TURZYNSKI (includes Tuszynski), TUSTISON, TUTCHER, TUTHILL, TUTT, TUTTLE, TUTWILER (includes Duttweiler), TUXHORN, TWADDLE, TWEED (includes Tweedy, Tweedie), TWEED, TWEEDIE, TWEEDY, TWEEDY, TWIDWELL, TWIGG, TWILLA, TWILLEY (includes Twilly), TWINER, TWINING, TWISS, TWITCHELL, TWITTY, TWOMEY (includes Tome, Toomay, Toomee, Toomey, Tumee, Tumey, Tuomy, Twoomy, O'Tuama), TWYMAN, TYDINGS, TYE, TYER, TYLER (includes Tighler, Tiler, Tiller, Tylor), TYLER, TYLER, TYNAN, TYNAN, TYNER, TYNES (includes Tines, Tyne), TYO (includes Taillon), TYREE, TYRRELL, TYSON, TYSVER.

SURNAMES, FAMILY ASSOCIATIONS & FAMILY NEWSLETTERS – "U"

Resources Dedicated to One Surname
http://www.cyndislist.com/surn-u.htm

Category Index:

◆ General Surname Sites and Resources
◆ Surname Specific Sites and Resources

◆ Surname Mailing Lists

◆ General Surname Sites and Resources

- Connect with Surnames - U
  http://www.geocities.com/Heartland/Bluffs/7708/u.html

- Dutch Home Pages by Familyname ~ Letter U
  http://members.tripod.com/~Don_Arnoldus/u.htm

- FamilyHistory.com - Message Boards - Surname - U
  http://www.familyhistory.com/messages/list.asp?prefix=UA

- Family Tree Maker Online User Home Pages - U
  http://www.familytreemaker.com/users/u/index.html

- Family Workings U Surname Links
  http://www.familyworkings.com/links/suru.htm

- GenConnect Surname Index - "U"
  http://genconnect.rootsweb.com/indx/surnames/U.html
  Message boards sponsored by RootsWeb. Each surname message board set is divided into the following topics: Queries, Bibles, Biographies, Deeds, Obituaries, Pensions, Wills.

- Genealogy Resources on the Internet - "U" Surname Mailing Lists
  http://www.rootsweb.com/~jfuller/gen_mail_surnames-u.html
  Search the index of surname mailing lists below: Surname Mailing Lists.

  o Genealogy Resources on the Internet - Surnames Included in Mailing Lists - "U"
    http://www-personal.umich.edu/~cgaunt/surnames/u.names.html
    This is a computer generated list of the surnames, and all variant spellings for those names, that are found in the surname mailing lists detailed on the pages shown above.

- Genealogy Resources on the Internet - Surname Web Sites for "U,V" Surnames
  http://www-personal.umich.edu/~cgaunt/surnames/uv.html

- Genealogy's Most Wanted - Surnames Beginning with "U"
  http://www.citynet.net/mostwanted/u.htm

- Google Web Directory .... Genealogy>Surnames>U
  http://directory.google.com/Top/Society/Genealogy/Surnames/U/

- Heartland Genealogy Society Membership List - U
  http://www.geocities.com/Heartland/Ranch/2416/hgs-mlist-u.html

- H-GIG Surname Registry - Surnames Beginning U
  http://www.ucr.edu/h-gig/surdata/surname21.html

- Higginson Book Company - Surnames Beginning with U
  http://www.higginsonbooks.com/u.htm

- inGeneas Table of Common Surname Variations and Surname Misspellings - T-Z
  http://www.ingeneas.com/T2Z.html

- The Obituary Link Page - Family Obituary Archives Online - U-V
  http://www.geocities.com/~cribbswh/obit/u-v.htm

- Open Directory - Society: Genealogy: Surnames: U
  http://www.dmoz.org/Society/Genealogy/Surnames/U/

- Surname Springboard Index - U
  http://www.geocities.com/~alacy/spring_u.htm

- SurnameWeb Surname Registry - U Index
  http://www.surnameweb.org/registry/u.htm

- SWINX Zoeklijst Nederlandse Familienamen / SWINX Searchlist Dutch Surnames - U
  http://www.swinx.net/swinx/swinx_u_nl.htm

- 'U' Surnames at RootsWeb
  http://resources.rootsweb.com/surnames/u.html

- Websites at RootsWeb: U Surnames
  http://www.rootsweb.com/~websites/surnames/u.html

◆ Surname Specific Sites and Resources

- The UFKES Genealogy Home Page
  http://asc.csc.cc.il.us/~mneill/ufkes/main.html
  Descendants of Hinrich Jansen UFKES (1797-1873) and his wife Trientje Eilts POST (1803-1878) of the Holtrop and Wiesens area of Ostfriesland, Germany.

- UMPLEBY of Yorkshire
  http://users.netwit.net.au/~rosem/index.html

- Descendants of Thomas UNDERWOOD
  http://www.ovis.net/~lathorn/underwood.htm
  Underwood family in Tyler and Doddridge counties in West Virginia.

- UPPER Family
  http://hometown.aol.com/CaptBilly/Uppers.html
  Descendants of George UPPER (Johann Jerj OPFER) and Anna Dorothea SCHMIDT 1734 to present.

- UPTEGROVE Archives
  http://ourworld.compuserve.com/homepages/liese/archives.htm
  Uptegrove, Op Den Graeff, Updegrove, Upthegrove, Updegrove, Horton, Genung, Youmans, Slaughter, Brewster.

- URIE Family History
  http://www.geocities.com/Heartland/Acres/6884/index.html
  A one name study of the URIE name.

- The URRY Family - URRY An Isle of Wight Family
  http://www.marcireau.fr/urry/urry.htm
  Urray, Ury, Urie, Urrie, Uri, Urri, Urey, Hurry, Orry, Orri, Horrey.

- USSERY - USERY - USRY - URSERY - ESSARY and Associated Families Genealogy
  http://www.geocities.com/~cindycasey/

- The URTON Family Tree
  http://www.familytreemaker.com/users/u/r/t/John-C-Urton/
  URTON Family name project. Over 1100 surnames.

- The UTNAGE Family Information
  http://members.home.net/utnage/
  Surnames: Utnage, Judnitz, Conlee, Tyer, Helms, Cox, Kelley, McCormick, Hodgkiss, and Morrow.

◆ Surname Mailing Lists

- "U" Surname Mailing Lists
  http://www.rootsweb.com/~jfuller/gen_mail_surnames-u.html
  UBER, UFFORD, UFFORD, UHL (includes Uhle), UHLENKOTT, ULENBERG, ULLMAN (includes Uhlman, Ullmann), ULLRICH, ULM, ULMER, ULRICH, ULTZ, UMBARGER (includes Umbargur, Umbargir, Yumbarger), UMBERGER (includes Umburger), UMSTEAD, UNANGST, UNBEHAUN, UNDERHILL, UNDERWOOD, UNGER, UNRUH, UNVERZAGT (includes Unversagt), UPCHURCH, UPDIKE, UPHAM, UPPERMAN, UPSHAW (includes Upshur, Upsher, Upcher, Upshire, ApShaw), UPSON, UPTEGROVE, UPTON, URAN (includes Urin, Urann), URBAN, UREN, URIBE, URICH (includes Yurich, Eurich, Urish, Yurish, Eurish), URIDGE (includes Euridge, Ewridge), URQUHART, USHER, USSERY (includes Usery, Usrey, Usry), UTENBOGERT (includes Utyden Bogert, Uitden Bogart, Uytden Bogard, Uyten Bogert, Uittten Bogerd, Uittenbogert,, Uit Den Boomgaart, Uitde Boomgaart, Uitden Bogert, Uit d Bogaart, Uytten Bogaert, Uytden Bogart, Outen Bogert,, Outenbogard, Bogert, Bogart, Bogard, Bogerd, Boomgaart, Bogaart, Bogaert), UTLEY (includes Uttley), UTLEY (includes Uttley, Utly), UTT, UTTER, UTTERBACK, UTZ, UTZS.

SURNAMES, FAMILY ASSOCIATIONS & FAMILY NEWSLETTERS – "V"

Resources Dedicated to One Surname
http://www.cyndislist.com/surn-v.htm

Category Index:

◆ General Surname Sites and Resources
◆ Surname Specific Sites and Resources

◆ Surname Mailing Lists

◆ General Surname Sites and Resources

- Connect with Surnames, V
  http://www.geocities.com/Heartland/Bluffs/7708/v.html

- Dutch Home Pages by Familyname ~ Letter V
  http://members.tripod.com/~Don_Arnoldus/v.htm

- FamilyHistory.com, Message Boards, Surname, V
  http://www.familyhistory.com/messages/list.asp?prefix=VA

- Family Tree Maker Online User Home Pages, V
  http://www.familytreemaker.com/users/v/index.html

- Family Workings V Surname Links
  http://www.familyworkings.com/links/surv.htm

- GenConnect Surname Index - "V"
  http://genconnect.rootsweb.com/indx/surnames/V.html
  Message boards sponsored by RootsWeb. Each surname message board set is divided into the following topics: Queries, Bibles, Biographies, Deeds, Obituaries, Pensions, Wills.

- Genealogy Resources on the Internet, "VA-VD" Surname Mailing Lists
  http://www.rootsweb.com/~jfuller/gen_mail_surnames-va.html
  "VE-VZ"
  http://www.rootsweb.com/~jfuller/gen_mail_surnames-ve.html
  Search the index of surname mailing lists below: Surname Mailing Lists.

  o Genealogy Resources on the Internet - Surnames Included in Mailing Lists - "V"
    http://www-personal.umich.edu/~cgaunt/surnames/v.names.html
    This is a computer generated list of the surnames, and all variant spellings for those names, that are found in the surname mailing lists detailed on the pages shown above.

- Genealogy Resources on the Internet - Surname Web Sites for "U,V" Surnames
  http://www-personal.umich.edu/~cgaunt/surnames/uv.html

- Genealogy's Most Wanted, Surnames Beginning with "V"
  http://www.citynet.net/mostwanted/v.htm

- Google Web Directory .... Genealogy>Surnames>V
  http://directory.google.com/Top/Society/Genealogy/Surnames/V/

- Heartland Genealogy Society Membership List, V
  http://www.geocities.com/Heartland/Ranch/2416/hgs-mlist-v.html

- H-GIG Surname Registry, Surnames Beginning V
  http://www.ucr.edu/h-gig/surdata/surname22.html

- Higginson Book Company, Surnames Beginning with V
  http://www.higginsonbooks.com/v.htm

- inGeneas Table of Common Surname Variations and Surname Misspellings, T-Z
  http://www.ingeneas.com/T2Z.html

- The Obituary Link Page, Family Obituary Archives Online, U-V
  http://www.geocities.com/~cribbswh/obit/u-v.htm

- Open Directory - Society: Genealogy: Surnames: V
  http://www.dmoz.org/Society/Genealogy/Surnames/V/

- Surname Springboard Index, V
  http://www.geocities.com/~alacy/spring_v.htm

- SurnameWeb Surname Registry, V Index
  http://www.surnameweb.org/registry/v.htm

- SWINX Zoeklijst Nederlandse Familienamen / SWINX Searchlist Dutch Surnames, V
  http://www.swinx.net/swinx/swinx_va_nl.htm

- 'V' Surnames at RootsWeb
  http://resources.rootsweb.com/surnames/v.html

- Websites at RootsWeb: V Surnames
  http://www.rootsweb.com/~websites/surnames/v.html

◆ Surname Specific Sites and Resources

- VAHEY W.O.R.D.S Photos and Poems
  http://home.integrityonline.com/vahey/

- VALLEAU Family Association
  http://www.geocities.com/Heartland/Prairie/1181/

- VALLET Web Site
  http://www.mypad49.freeserve.co.uk
  Recording data on Vallet in UK and France. Valette, Valet, Vallette.

- VALLETTES of New Orleans
  http://www.geocities.com/BourbonStreet/Bayou/3653/tree/

- Surnames Beginning with VAN, VANDER & VANDEN Newsletter
  mailto:CarlCindy2@aol.com
  For details send e-mail to Lucinda (Cindy) Olsen, editor and publisher, at CarlCindy2@aol.com.

- VAN AKEN and VAN AUKEN Genealogy
  http://wworks.com/~macbeth/

- VanAUKEN Family History & Genealogy
  http://pages.prodigy.net/vanauken1/vanauken/
  VanAuken / VanAken / VanNocker. Dutch family who settled in America as early as 1652.

- VANCE Family Association
  http://homepages.rootsweb.com/~rtr89/Vance/

- VAN CLEEF, VAN CLEVE, VAN CLEAVE Connections
  http://www.thescenicroute.com/cmterrell/van_cleef/
  With VAN COUWENHOVEN, VAN MATER, SCHENCK, RAPALJE, VAN DER BEEK(REMSEN).

- The VANDAL Family Home Page
  http://home.earthlink.net/~chield/
  Vandal, Vandall, Vandale, Vandel, Vandell, Van Del, Vandle, Wandal, Wandel, Wandell, Wandale, Wendall, Wendell.

- The VANDENBOSCH Family in America
  http://www.macatawa.org/~dobo/
  Descendants of Tamme VANDENBOSCH 1798-1874.

- VANDENBOSSCHE Family Home Page
  http://www-personal.umich.edu/~ebeeman/genealogy/vandenbossche/vbossche.html

- VANDERGRIFT Family of America
  http://members.tripod.com/vandergrift/index.htm

- Genealogy of Family VAN DER LEER
  http://members.tripod.com/~van_der_Leer/
  Originally the family-members were born near "Hendrik-Ido-Ambacht" in the Netherlands (Holland).

- Genealogie VAN DER SCHAAFF Familie
  http://vanderschaaff.virtualave.net/
  Includes VAN DER SCHAAFF and VANDER SCHAAFF families in the Netherlands and the USA.

- The VAN DER VEER Name
  http://www.buxx.com/genealogy/VanDerVeer.html

- Genealogy of the VAN DER VEUR family
  http://www.vanderveur.com

- The VAN DOMELEN Family Tree
  http://www.execpc.com/~domelen
  Arnoldus van DOMMELEN, married Hendrina CUIJPERS on June 1,1826 in Waalre Noord Brabant, Holland.

- VAN DORSSEN Genealogy
  http://www.escapenet.com.au/users/vandorssen

- VAN GORDER / VAN GODEN Genealogy
  http://www.geocities.com/Heartland/Bluffs/9638/
  A history of the Van Gorder/Van Gorden families and a story of interest to family members.

- Genealogie - VAN GRONDELLE
  http://home.wxs.nl/~wjvangrondelle/wjvangrondelle/
  Van GRONDELLE, Van GRONDEL and GRONDEL families in Holland and abroad.

- The National VAN HOOK Genealogical Database and Other Families
  http://www.geocities.com/Heartland/Flats/7746/database/easy.htm

- VAN HORN Family Page
  http://www.jerrie.vanhorn.com/
  Van Horn family descendants of Christian Barendt. Van Horn in New Jersey, Bucks County Pennsylvania, Gilmer County West Virginia and the allied families of: Rudderow, Stiles, Dircks, Sheets Boggs, Smith and Bennett.

- VAN HORN Genealogy
  http://www.angelfire.com/in/susannahome/vanhorn.html

- The Van MA(A)REN Society
  http://home.wxs.nl/~maare019/
  The geneological organisation of the Dutch families Van Maren, Van Maaren, Van Maare, Van der Mare and Van der Maren.

- The VAN NORMAN Family
  http://www.multiboard.com/~spettit/vn.html
  Descendants of Joseph & Elizabeth (Wybern) VAN NORMAN.

- The VAN NORMAN Family Association
  http://homepages.rootsweb.com/~vnfa/index.html

- VAN ORDEN Family Web Page
  http://www.nstep.net/dorgon/vanorden.htm
  A family research site for the surname VanOrden or any spelling variation.

- The VAN OTTEN Family Organization
  http://www.vanotten.org/
  Vanotten genealogy in Belgium, Netherlands and U.S.A. 8,500 persons.

- VAN RENSBURG Genealogy
  http://www.geocities.com/Athens/Atlantis/4364/
  Family research in South Africa.

- VAN RISSSEGHEM Family Genealogy Project
  http://www.homestead.com/onamia
  Lineage from Belgium to America. Descendants immigrating to Onamia, Minnesota and Zion, Illinois.

- VANSANDTs
  http://www.pacifier.com/~vansandt/
  VANZANDT, VANSANDT, VANZANT, VANSANT, etc. Mostly Bucks Co.. PA.

- The Olive Tree Genealogy: The VAN SLYKE Family
  http://www.rootsweb.com/~ote/vslyke.htm
  The descendants of Cornelise Antonissen VAN SLYKE, 1604-1676 and his Mohawk Wife Ots-Toch. Cornelis settled in Rensellaerswyck in 1634. Cornelis and his nephew Willem Pieterse VAN SLYKE aka NEEF, were the ancestors of the VAN SLYKE families in New York.

- VAN TASSEL Family History Homepage
  http://members.aol.com/RickVT/index.html
  One-name study of the Van Tassel family.

- VANTINE / VANTYNE Descendants of Carel FONTEYN and Catharine de BAILE
  http://homepages.rootsweb.com/~cyocom/
  Vantine, Vantyne, Van Tine, Van Tyne, Fonteyn.

- National Association of the VAN VALKENBURG Family
  http://haven.ios.com/~wordup/navvf/navvf.html
  Descendants of Lambert VAN VALCKENBURG of the Netherlands and Annetie JACOBS of Schleswig, Holstein, married in Amsterdam in 1642, came to North America and became colonists in New Amsterdam in 1644.

- The VAN VOORHEES Association
  http://www.vanvoorhees.org/
  Includes Van Voorhees, Van Voorhies, Van Vorhies, Van Voris, Van Vorous, Van Voorhis, Van Vource, Van Voorus, Van Vorys, and Van Vories.

- The VAN ZANDT Society
  http://www.user1.netcarrier.com/~muriel/VanZandtSociety/
  International society for research of Van Zandt, and other spellings, including Van Sant, Vanzant, Vinzant, Van Zant, van de Sandt, and others.

- VARN BUHLER/VAN BUHLER Genealogy Home Page
  http://www.volcano.net/~varnbuhler

- VARNEDOE Family Web Page
  http://www.Varnedoe.com

- VARNUM Genealogy
  http://www.geocities.com/Heartland/Plains/7945/

- VASCONCELOS
  http://www.geocities.com/Vienna/Opera/1110/
  Family of Vila do Conde, Portugal.

- Whispers from the past....
  http://www.ronrichardson.com/
  The genealogical study of the VASTOLA family departing Poggiomarino (Naples) Italy in 1896 and making a new home in Buffalo, New York.

- VAUGHAN VAUGHN Resource Page
  http://www.geocities.com/Heartland/Meadows/1849/vaudgr.htm
  Hundreds of marriage records, biographies, wills, census, land patent records and many more. Research for all countries and all spelling variations.

- The VAUGHT Connection
  http://homepages.rootsweb.com/~mvyoung1/

- The VEALE Family Tree
  http://roswell.fortunecity.com/silbury/423/
  The dynasty of James Carr VEALE through eight generations 1750-2000 and the descendants of William H. VEALE 1870-2000.

- VEBLEN Family Home Page
  http://vader.castles.com/jeffm
  The VEBLEN Family in America and relatives of noted economist Thorstein VEBLEN (1857-1929).

- Sir Roland de VELVILLE (1474-1535)
  http://www.gmilne.demon.co.uk/roland.htm
  Information about Sir Roland de Velville (also Vielleville, Veleville or, probably more correctly, Vieilleville), reputed natural son of Henry VII.

- Genealogie VERBEEK
  http://users.telekabel.nl/jahengel/verbeek.html
  Genealogy of Gerrit VERBEEK who married Maria VAN VLIEDT abt 1750.

- Marc VERMEIRSSEN's Homepage
  http://bewoner.dma.be/mvermeir/
  Vermeirssen, Vermeerssen, Vermeirsschen, Vermeirssch, Vermeerren.

- VERMILYEA Family Association
  http://members.aol.com/vfa95/vfa.htm
  Vermilya, Vermilye, Vermilyea, Vermilyer.

- VERRALLS Family Homepage
  http://www.glink.net.hk/~verralls/
  Research into family name VERRALLS.

- VERTS / VERTZ / VIRTS / VIRTZ / WERTS / WERTZ Family History
  http://members.aol.com/loudounva/virts.html
  Searching for descendants of Wilhelm Wurtz. Family names of Verts Vertz, Virts, Virtz, Werts, Wertz.

- VEST Genealogy
  http://www.geocities.com/Heartland/Estates/8081/vest.html
  Collection point for information regarding branches of the VEST family.

- VEYTIA World
  http://www.veytia.com

- VIAU / VIEAU / VIEUX
  http://www.geocities.com/Heartland/Acres/1636/
  Descendants of Michel Viau of France, b. 1655.

- The VIENNEAU Genealogy
  http://www3.nbnet.nb.ca/davienn/Testpage2ang.htm
  And a French Version
  http://www3.nbnet.nb.ca/davienn/Testpage2.htm
  Descendants of Michel VIENNEAU and Thérèse Baude, including these surnames: Vienneau, Huard, Cormier, Richard, Thèriault, Lagacè, Pitre, Couture. All from Atlantic region in Canada.

- VIERLING Genealogy
  http://homepages.rootsweb.com/~imrie/vierling/html

- VILES Family Genealogy Book is Ready!
  http://members.aol.com/judymckinn/vilesbook.html
  VILES, William (born 1797-died 1870) married Martha Banta in 1820 in Switzerland, Co., IN. This is a 600 page, 1200 photograph book I have prepared of their descendants.

- VILLAREAL Genealogy
  http://members.aol.com/daniel5822/villarrealindex.html
  Family from before 1490 in Spain through Conquest of Mexico and into South Texas.

- The VILLNEFF / VILNEFF Family Pages
  http://www.geocities.com/Heartland/Village/2489/

- My VINCENT Ancestors
  http://members.aol.com/Brud123/Vincent.html
  John VINCENT, born 24 Aug 1750 in Kensington, Middlesex, England; Hampshire Co. Virginia; died 26 May 1837 in Franklin Co. Indiana.

- VINCENT Family Genealogy
  http://www.servtech.com/~vincent/
  Queries and other information of interest to those researching the surname VINCENT.

- VINDEN and VINDIN Family History
  http://website.lineone.net/~mcgoa/vinden.html

- VINING Genealogy Exchange
  http://www.geocities.com/Heartland/Plains/3863/

- The VOELL Family Website
  http://www.voell.com/
  Interactive news, calendars, and picture archives.

- VOGLER Family of Nova Scotia
  http://www.glinx.com/~philv/vogler.htm
  The history of the Vogler family in Nova Scotia, Canada from 1752 to modern day.

- VOILs to VOYLES, A Journey in Time
  http://sites.netscape.net/kateira/journey
  Descendants of Jacob Voils and his four sons, William, Thomas, James and John, from Wales.

- von BEHREN & BEHRENT Genealogy
  http://members.aol.com/SvonBehren/index.html
  National site for surnames von Behren and Behrent.

- VOSSELLER Home Page
  http://members.tripod.com/~jvhc/
  Vosseller, Fusler, Vosler, Vossler, Vusler.

◆ Surname Mailing Lists

- "VA-VD" Surname Mailing Lists
  http://www.rootsweb.com/~jfuller/gen_mail_surnames-va.html
  VACIK, VADEN, VAIL, VAILLANCOURT, VAISEY (includes Vacey, Vasy, Vesey), VALADE, VALE, VALENTE, VALENTINE, VALKENBURG (includes Valkenburgh, Valckenburg, Valckenburgh, Van Valkenburg, Van Valckenburgh, Falkenburg,, Falckenburgh), VALLANCE, VALLIERE, VAN, VANAKEN, VANAKIN, VANALSTYNE, VANANTWERP, VANARSDALE (includes van Aersdalen, Van Artsdalen, Van Ausdoll, Vannorsdall, Van Arsdale, Vannorsdoll,, Vanasdalan, Vanorsdale, VanArsdalen, Van Orsdale, Vanosdoll, Vanausdoll, Van Osdol), VANBARKELO (includes Barkelo, Barkaloo, Barkulo, Borckelloo, Van Barkeloo, Van Burkleo), VANBENSCHOTEN (includes Van Benschoten, Benscoter, Van Scoten, Van Scoter), VANBIBBER (includes Van Bebber, Van Beber, Vanbibber, Vanbebber, Bebber), VANBLARCOM (includes Van Blarkum, Van Blarcum, Van Blarkem, Van Blerkum, Van Blerkom, Van Blerkem), VAN BOESCHOTEN, VANBROCKLIN, VANBUREN, VANBUSKIRK, VANCAMP, VANCAMPEN, VANCE (includes Vanss, Vans, Vaux, Wauss, Waus, Vass, Vauss, Vaus), VANCIL, VANCLEAVE (includes Van Cleef, Van Cleve), VANCLEEF, VANDAMME, VANDEGRIFT, VANDENBERGHE (includes Vandenberge, Vandenberg), VANDENBRANDT, VANDERBEEK, VANDERBILT, VANDERBURG (includes Vanderburgh, Vanderberg, Vanderburgt), VANDEREN, VANDERFORD, VANDERGRIFT (includes Vandegrift, Vandagriff, Vandigriff, Vandegriff, Vandergriffe), VANDERHALL, VANDERHOFF (includes Vanderhough, Vanderhauf, Vanderhuff), VANDERHOFF, VANDERHOOF, VANDERPOOL (includes Van De Poel), VANDERSLICE, VANDERVOORT (includes Vandivort, Vandeford, Vandervort), VANDEVENTER, VANDIVER, VANDOESBURG, VANDOVER (includes Vandaver, Vandever, Vandiver, Vandivier, Vandiviere), VANDRESSER, VANDUSEN (includes Vandusen, Van Deusen, Van Deursen, Van Duzee, Van Duzer, Van Duzen), VANDYKE, VANERT (includes Van Ert), VAN EVERY (includes Van Avery, Van Evera, Van Iveren, Vanevery), VANFLEET (includes VanFleet, VanVliet), VANGIESEN (includes Van Geisen, Van Giesan), VANGILDER (includes VanGuilder, VanGelder, VanGalder), VANGUNDY, VANHAARLEM, VANHALDER, VANHOOK (includes VanHoeck, VanHoek), VANHOOSE (includes VanHooser, VanHoos, VanHusum, VanHussum, VanHoesen, VanHouse), VANHORN, VANHORNE (includes Van Horn, Van Hoorn), VANKEUREN (includes Van Curen), VANKIRK, VANKLEECK (includes Van Kleeck, VanKleeck, Van Kleek), VANLANDINGHAM (includes Vallandingham), VANMARTER, VANMETER, VANN, VANN (includes Vaughn), VANNESS, VANNEST, VANNORMAN (includes VanAernam, VanArlem, VanArnam, VanArnem, VanArnhem, VanArnon, VanOrman), VANNOSTRAND (includes Van Noordstraandt, Van Nostrandt), VANNOY, VANORDEN (includes Van Naarden), VANORDER (includes Van Order, VanOrder, Vanorder, VanOrden, Vanorden, Van Orden, VanNorden, Vannorden,, Van Norden, VanOrde, Vanorde, Van Orde), VANOVER, VANPELT, VANRIPER (includes Van Ryper, Van Rype, Van Rypen), VANROOIJ, VANROSSUMJ, VANSANT, VANSCHOONHOVEN, VANSCOY (includes Van Scoy, Van Sky, Van Scoyoc, Van Schaick, Vernooy), VANSICKLE, VANSLYKE, VANSTONE, VANTASSEL, VANTHOFF, VANTINE, VANVALKENBURG (includes VanVolkenburg, VanVolkenbourgh, Van Voulkenburgh), VANVLIET, VANVOORHEES (includes Voorhees, Voorhies), VANWERT, VANWINKLE, VANWOGGELUM (includes Van Waggelen, Van Woggelum, Van Woglom, Van Wouglim, Waggelen, Wakely,, Wogelom, Woggelom, Woggelum, Woglin, Woglom, Woglum, Wolghem, Wooglam, Wooglum, Wuggelum, Gamacjekyck,, Gemackylick, Gemakelyck, Mackelick, Mackelyck, Macklick, Makkelie, Soo Gemackelyck, Soogemackelyck,, Soogemakelyck), VANWYE, VAN_WYE (includes Van Wye, Van Wey, Van Wy, Van Y, Van Wei, Van Wie, Van Wien, Van Wein, Van Weye,, Van Weyen, Van Weij, Van Weik, Van Wiek, Van Way, Van Why, Van Whye, Van Whyen), VANZANDT, VANZANT, VARDAMAN, VARDY (includes Vardey), VARGA, VARGAS, VARLEY, VARNADO (includes Varnedo, Varnydo, Varnadoe, Varnedeau), VARNAM, VARNER (includes Verner, Werner, Warner, Ferner, Vernor, Venable), VARNER, VARNEY, VARNUM, VASKO, VASQUEZ, VASS, VASSER, VATCHER, VAUGHAN (includes Vaughn), VAUGHN, VAUGHT, VAUSE, VAUTRIN, VAVRA, VAWTER.

● "VE-VZ" Surname Mailing Lists

http://www.rootsweb.com/~jfuller/gen_mail_surnames-ve.html

VEACH (includes Veatch, Veitch, Veech), VEAL (includes Veale), VEALE, VEASEY, VEATCH (includes Veach, Veitch, Veech), VEAZEY, VEDDER (includes Veeder), VEECH (includes Veitch, Veatch, Veach), VEITCH (includes Veach, Veatch, Veech), VEJVODA (includes Weiwoda, Vevoda, Weyvoda), VELASQUEZ, VENABLE, VENCATO, VENCILL, VENEGONI, VENENGA, VENTURA, VENUS, VEREGGE, VERHOFF, VERMILLION, VERNABLE, VERNER, VERNON, VERRALL, VERVOREN, VERWEY (includes Verway, Ver Wey), VESEY, VESSEY, VEST, VESTAL (includes Vastal, Vestall, Vestol, Vastel), VETTER (includes Vetters, Fetter, Fetters, Feather, Feathers), VEZOLLES, VIA (includes Viah, Viar, Vier, Viet), VIAR, VIATOR (includes Villatoro), VIBBERT, VICE (includes Vise), VICK, VICKER (includes Wicker, Vickery, Vickers, Weicher, Weigert, Wica, Whicker), VICKERS, VICKERY, VICKROY (includes Vicroy, Vickory, Vicory), VICTOR, VIDAL, VIDEAU (includes Videaul, Videaux), VIEAU (includes Viau, Vieaux, Vieu, Vieo), VIENS (includes Vien, Vient, Come, Cumm, Cummings), VIERECK, VIEREGGE (includes Veregge, Vieregg, Von Vieregge, Viereck),

VIERLING, VIFQUAIN (includes Vifquin), VIGGERS, VILES, VILLENEUVE, VILLINES (includes Verlaines, Valins, Villins), VILLINES, VINAL, VINCENT, VINCENT, VINE, VINER, VINES (includes Vine), VINEYARD, VINING (includes Vinen, Venning), VINKIE, VINSON, VINTINNER, VINTON, VIRES, VIRGIN, VIRTUE, VIRTUE, VISSER, VITALE, VITTY, VIVIAN, VIVRETT, VLEREBOME, VOELKER, VOGEL, VOGT (includes Voght), VOIGHT, VOIGT, VOLK, VOLLE, VOLLICK (includes Follick), VOLLMER, VOLLWEILER (includes Vollwiler, Volwiler, Fullwiler, Fulwiler, Follwiler, Folwiler), VOLPE, VOLZ, VONASCHWEGE (includes vonAschwede), VONBEHREN, VONDEREHE, VON FREYMANN, VON SCHULMANN (includes von Schulman, Shulman, Scholman, Sholman), VOORHEES (includes VanVoorhees, Voorhies), VOORHIES (includes VanVoorhees, Voorhees), VORE, VOS, VOSBURGH, VOSE, VOSS (includes Vause), VOSSINAS, VOTAW (includes Votau, Vatau, Voteau, Votan, Vatan, Vatow, Votow, Vataw, Votaugh, Vataugh, Vatough, Voutow,, Voutaw, Vawten, Vater, Votar, Votare), VOUGHT, VOWEL (includes Vowell), VOYLES, VREDENBURGH (includes Fredenburg, Fredenburgh, Van Vredenburgh), VREELAND, VROOMAN. VUCASOVICH.

SURNAMES, FAMILY ASSOCIATIONS & FAMILY NEWSLETTERS – "W"

Resources Dedicated to One Surname
http://www.cyndislist.com/surn-w.htm

Category Index:

◆ General Surname Sites and Resources

◆ Surname Specific Sites and Resources

◆ Surname Mailing Lists

◆ General Surname Sites and Resources

- Connect with Surnames - W
  http://www.geocities.com/Heartland/Bluffs/7708/w.html

- Dutch Home Pages by Familyname ~ Letter W
  http://members.tripod.com/~Don_Arnoldus/w.htm

- FamilyHistory.com - Message Boards - Surname-W
  http://www.familyhistory.com/messages/list.asp?prefix=WA

- Family Tree Maker Online User Home Pages - W
  http://www.familytreemaker.com/users/w/index.html

- Family Workings W Surname Links
  http://www.familyworkings.com/links/surw.htm

- GenConnect Surname Index - "W"
  http://genconnect.rootsweb.com/indx/surnames/W.html
  Message boards sponsored by RootsWeb. Each surname message board set is divided into the following topics: Queries, Bibles, Biographies, Deeds, Obituaries, Pensions, Wills.

- Genealogy Resources on the Internet - "WAA-WAK" Surname Mailing Lists
  http://www.rootsweb.com/~jfuller/gen_mail_surnames-waa.html
  "WAL-WAQ"
  http://www.rootsweb.com/~jfuller/gen_mail_surnames-wal.html
  "WAR-WD"
  http://www.rootsweb.com/~jfuller/gen_mail_surnames-war.html
  "WEA-WEH"
  http://www.rootsweb.com/~jfuller/gen_mail_surnames-wea.html
  "WEI-WEQ"
  http://www.rootsweb.com/~jfuller/gen_mail_surnames-wei.html
  "WER-WG"
  http://www.rootsweb.com/~jfuller/gen_mail_surnames-wer.html
  "WH-WH"
  http://www.rootsweb.com/~jfuller/gen_mail_surnames-wh.html

"WIA-WIK"
http://www.rootsweb.com/~jfuller/gen_mail_surnames-wia.html
"WIL-WIL"
http://www.rootsweb.com/~jfuller/gen_mail_surnames-wil.html
"WIM-WIQ"
http://www.rootsweb.com/~jfuller/gen_mail_surnames-wim.html
"WIR-WN"
http://www.rootsweb.com/~jfuller/gen_mail_surnames-wir.html
"WO-WT"
http://www.rootsweb.com/~jfuller/gen_mail_surnames-wo.html
"WU-WZ"
http://www.rootsweb.com/~jfuller/gen_mail_surnames-wu.html
Search the index of surname mailing lists below: SURNAME MAILING LISTS.

- o Genealogy Resources on the Internet - Surnames Included in Mailing Lists - "W"
  http://www-personal.umich.edu/~cgaunt/surnames/w.names.html
  This is a computer generated list of the surnames, and all variant spellings for those names, that are found in the surname mailing lists detailed on the pages shown above.

- Genealogy Resources on the Internet - Surname Web Sites for "W" Surnames
  http://www-personal.umich.edu/~cgaunt/surnames/w.html

- Genealogy's Most Wanted - Surnames Beginning with "W"
  http://www.citynet.net/mostwanted/w.htm

- Google Web Directory .... Genealogy>Surnames>W
  http://directory.google.com/Top/Society/Genealogy/Surnames/W/

- Heartland Genealogy Society Membership List - W
  http://www.geocities.com/Heartland/Ranch/2416/hgs-mlist-w.html

- H-GIG Surname Registry - Surnames Beginning W
  http://www.ucr.edu/h-gig/surdata/surname23.html

- Higginson Book Company - Surnames Beginning with W
  http://www.higginsonbooks.com/w.htm

- inGeneas Table of Common Surname Variations and Surname Misspellings - T-Z
  http://www.ingeneas.com/T2Z.html

- The Obituary Link Page - Family Obituary Archives Online - W
  http://www.geocities.com/~cribbswh/obit/w.htm

- Open Directory - Society: Genealogy: Surnames: W
  http://www.dmoz.org/Society/Genealogy/Surnames/W/

- Surname Springboard Index - W
  http://www.geocities.com/~alacy/spring_w.htm

- SurnameWeb Surname Registry - W Index
  http://www.surnameweb.org/registry/w.htm

- SWINX Zoeklijst Nederlandse Familienamen / SWINX Searchlist Dutch Surnames - W
  http://www.swinx.net/swinx/swinx_wa_nl.htm

- Websites at RootsWeb: W Surnames
  http://www.rootsweb.com/~websites/surnames/w.html

- 'W' Surnames at RootsWeb
  http://resources.rootsweb.com/surnames/w.html

◆ Surname Specific Sites and Resources

- Descendants of Thomas Young WADDELL
  http://www.parsonstech.com/genealogy/trees/jwaddel1/wadle.htm
  Of Polk County, Missouri.

- WADDELOW Society Home Page
  http://www.fwaterhouse.freeserve.co.uk/
  For anyone interested in the WADDELOW and WADLOW names. Families from Cambridgeshire, Norfolk, England and USA, plus many more.

- WADE Families Page
  http://www.k-wade.freeserve.co.uk/

- WADE Family Genealogy Web Ring
  http://members.tripod.com/WadeHome/webring.htm

- Descendants of James WADE I
  http://members.aol.com/DWCJMC7249/pubpage.htm

- My WADE (WAID) Family Tree
  http://www.homestead.com/wadewaid/index.html
  Dedicated to the Wade-Waid family descendents of brothers Abraham & Calvin.

- WADFORD / WATFORD Family Homepage
  http://sites.netscape.net/fayettebill/homepage
  A site dedicated to research of the surname WADFORD, WATFORD, and phonetically close variants WARFORD, WHADFORD, WADEFORD, WAFORD.

- The WAGGONER / WAGONER / WAGNER Family Pages
  http://personal.lig.bellsouth.net/lig/c/w/cwcrash/waggon.htm

- WAHL and WALL Family Genealogy
  http://clubs.yahoo.com/clubs/wahlandwallfamilygenealogy
  WAHLs and WALLs worldwide.

- WAITE Family History
  http://members.tripod.com/~Scott_Michaud/index-3.html
  Waites of Maine. Michaud, Waite, Daigle, Boynton, McLaughlin, Smyth.

- WAITE Genealogy Research Forum
  http://www.waitegenealogy.org/
  Waite, Wait, Waitt, Wayte, Wayt.

- WAKELEE Avenue
  http://home1.gte.net/bwakeley/genealogy/
  Descendants of Henry WAKELEE (or Wakeley, Wakely, Wakelyn, Wakley, or Waklee), one of the founders of Hartford, Connecticut. Also will include information on others with the above surnames.

- Lucy Ann WALBERT Genealogy & Lineage Search Home Page
  http://www.kerchner.com/walbert.htm

- WALDROPs of America
  http://www.geocities.com/Heartland/Prairie/6572
  Lineage of James Waldrop b. ca. 1734 and his descendants. Includes several allied family sites and additional Waldrop sites. Six generations of Waldrops in America. Some family photos, time line, speculation on the earliest Waldrops in America.

- WALKER Family History Project
  http://members.tripod.co.uk/walker_familyhistory/

- John WALKER Family Organization
  http://www.walkerfamily.org/
  John is a descendant of Robert Walker and Sarah Leager, emigrants from England to Boston via the Winthrop Fleet of 1630. Born 20 June 1794 in Peacham, Caledonia, Vermont. Died 18 Oct 1869 in Farmington, Davis, Utah.

- WALKER Home Page
  http://www.communinet.org/QA/walker/
  Descendants of Lewis John Walker (b. 1877) and Irene Eva Williams (b. 1881). Also Walker Reunion information.

- WALLACEs
  http://wallaces.webjump.com
  WALLACE descendants from Ayrshire Scotland 1863 to New Zealand today.

- WALLER Family of the Netherlands
  http://home.wxs.nl/~wallerhb/familie.htm

- WALSH Family Genealogy Home Page
  http://homepages.rootsweb.com/~walsh/

- WALSH Surname Mailing List
  http://homepages.rootsweb.com/~walsh/maillist.html

- The WALTER Family History
  http://home.netcom.com/~dwwalter/walter.html
  Descendants of Simon and Wilhelm WALTER of Pennsylvania and Maryland.

- The WALTERHOUSE Family Page
  http://personal.lig.bellsouth.net/lig/w/a/walterho/
  Descendants of Philip Benjamin Walterhouse - his four families and 13 children. Information on other Walterhouse families - are they yours? [Note: Philip Benjamin Walterhouse is Cyndi's 4th great-grandfather].

- The WALTER(S) and Allied Families Genealogy Page
  http://www.familytreemaker.com/users/w/a/l/John-A-Walters/index.html
  Descendants of Thomas Walter(s), died 6 Jul 1724 in Charlestown, MA, and Hannah Gray.

- WAMPACH
  http://homepages.rootsweb.com/~imrie/Wampach.htm
  A website devoted to the study of the name WAMPACH. It appears to have originated in Luxembourg where there are several place names with WAMPACH in the name. The name itself means streamlet. Our particular branch of the name came from Luxembourg to Minnesota and eventually to Oregon.

- WAMSLEY~WEB Newsletter
  mailto:Wamsleyweb@aol.com
  For details send e-mail to Wanda Wamsley Balducci at: Wamsleyweb@aol.com.

- WANLESS Web (a one-name study of Wanless/Wandless and all spelling variations)
  http://www.hollyhockpress.com/~wanless/wanlessweb/
  Data exchange & resource center for researchers of the WANLESS, WANDLESS, WANLASS, WANLISS, etc. name, in any time period or location.

- WANNALL Family Home Page
  http://www.wannall.com
  Profiles and family links for over 150 people surnamed WANNALL.

- Descendants of Nancy WARD
  http://www.nancyward.com/

- WARDELL Genealogy
  http://www.rootsweb.com/~autwgw/gen/wardell.htm

- WARDEN - WORDEN Surname Resource Center
  http://freepages.genealogy.rootsweb.com/~geneal/src/WordenSRC.html
  WARDEN, WORDEN, WERDEN and variations.

- WARDLAW
  http://members.aol.com/LADATH/index.html
  WARDLAW from Scotland in the 1200's to America in early 1700's.

- WARKENTIN WARKENTIEN WARKENTHIEN WARCKENTIN Genealogy
  http://pages.hotbot.com/family/dcarls02/wark.html

- WARNER and BURLINGAME Descendants
  http://www.digroots.com/burlwarn.htm
  Descendants of Eliza Warner and Jeremiah Burlingame.

- WARNER - Who, When & Where Home Page
  http://members.aol.com/kinseeker6/warner.html

- WARREN Family Genealogy
  http://members.aol.com/HatwellE/WarrenGenealogy.html
  A ten generation descendant chart from Christopher Waring (Warren) down to Richard Waring who sailed from England to Boston on the ship Endeavor in 1654. Link to Arthur Alexander Warren family history.

- WARRENs of Virginia and Maryland
  http://www.familytreemaker.com/users/w/a/r/Shirley-L-Warren/
  Also of England, Europe, GA, MS, MI, MO, TN, KY, IL, IA, TX.

- Richard WARREN (Mayflower Passenger) Genealogy
  http://pages.prodigy.net/dave_lossos/warren.htm

- WASDIN / WASDEN Family Home Page
  http://www.why.net/home/waz/

- WASHBURN Family History Page
  http://home.earthlink.net/~cwashburn/history.html
  John Washburn Jr. (1621-1686) and His Descendants.

- The National Society of the WASHINGTON Family Descendants
  http://members.tripod.com/~NSWFD/
  Members are descendants of any of the ancestors of George Washington who lived in Colonial America between 1607 and 1732.

- WASSENBERG Genealogy
  http://www.wassenberg.de
  Genealogie der Familie Wassenberg aus dem Raum Duesseldorf, weitere Namen: Kurth, Martell.; Genealogy of the Wassenberg Family, other names I'm looking for: Kurth and Martell; a shop, where you can buy genealogical books and CD's of the Duesseldorf-area is "under construction".

- WASSON Connections
  http://homepages.rootsweb.com/~wassonc/HOMEPAGE.htm
  WASSON or WASON surnames.

- WATERS / WATTERS (and Sometimes WALTERS) Genealogy
  http://www.cwo.com/~genetti/

- Worldwide WATERS Research Site
  http://www.fortunecity.com/millenium/lilac/38/index.html

- WATKINS Family History Society
  http://members.iinet.net.au/~davwat/wfhs/index.html

- A WEAVER's Source Book: Uphome with Jonas and Emma
  http://www.sitematrix.com/uphome
  Information about a recent 304-page publication of stories and genealogy for the Weaver family. The book spans the 500 years since the Radical Reformation, tracing fifteen generations of one family in the Swiss-Anabaptist Waber-Weber-Weaver lineage.

- WEBB One Name Register
  http://www.wonr.org.uk/
  GOONS registered society for WEBB surname and variants.

- The Joseph WEBER Family
  http://www.angelfire.com/il/weberjb/index.html

- The WEDGWOOD Family Worldwide
  http://www.geocities.com/Heartland/3203/

- WEEDMAN Family Genealogy
  http://ourworld.compuserve.com/homepages/HNWEEDMAN/

- WEEKS Family Genealogy
  http://www2.southwind.net/~rwweeks/weeksg.html
  Descendants of George Weeks, born abt. 1603, Devonshire, England and Jane Clapp, born abt. 1604, Salcombe Regis, Devonshire, England.

- WEEKS Family Registry
  http://www.geocities.com/~weekseekers/
  A registry of the descendants of Benjamin and Mary Chase Weeks of Falmouth, Massachusetts and Carteret County, North Carolina.

- WEEMS Family History
  http://www.genealogy.org/~weems/

- WEGG Genealogy and One Name Study
  http://www.wegg.mcmail.com/

- The Genealogy of Joseph WEHRLE and WILEY Descendents
  http://www.wileytree.org
  Tracing the genealogy of Joseph Wehrle / Wiley, German Immigrant to Rosiere, NY (Jefferson County, NY) in 1834.

- WEINIG Family
  http://home.t-online.de/home/mckenzie/weinig.htm
  Weinig, Weni, Weiney, Weiny, Weinie, Winey, etc.

- WEITZ, Germans from Russia
  http://www.webbitt.com/weitz/
  The lineage is traced from Germany, to the Volga Valley in Russia and then onto the US and Canada. Includes obits, immigration records, border crossings and old photos. Scanned images of old documents include a rare parochial certificate, naturalization forms and social security applications.

- Aaron and Ruth (WIGGINS) WELLS Family Assoc.
  http://www.webpub.com/~jhagee/wells.html
  Ancestors and descendants of Aaron Wells and Ruth Wiggins, who were married 31 July 1790 in Mason Co. KY (then still Virginia). They had 15 children who mostly settled in the parts of Mason County which became Nicholas Co. and later Robertson Co.

- The WELLS & Allied Families of the Eastern Shore of Maryland & Delaware
  http://freepages.genealogy.rootsweb.com/~welles/WELLES/
  10 Generations of Wells from 1600 in Virginia through Delaware, Maryland, Pennsylvania to New York in 1995.

- WELLS Family Genealogy
  http://home.att.net/~jtwells?
  Descendants of William Wells (b. 1605) of Southold, Long Island.

- WELLS Family Genealogy Web Site
  http://www.crosswinds.net/~willflyforfood/index.htm
  Family Tree of Richard WELLS, descendent of Robert Wells b. 1746. Also BEVAN, KREUL, MEYERS, DUMKE, KOWALSKI, CARLSON, SLACK, and HUBLER.

- The WELLS Family Research Association
  http://www.rootsweb.com/~wellsfam/wfrahome.html

- WELLS Surname Mailing List
  http://www.zekes.com/~dwells/list.html

- Tunis WELLS family of Fayette Co., PA
  http://members.home.net/dave-wells/Wells.htm
  Descendants of Richard WELLS who settled in Frederick Co, VA about 1750.

- WELLS Worldwide
  http://clubs.yahoo.com/clubs/wellsworldwide
  WELLS and WELLES.

- WELNER Surname Resource Center
  http://freepages.genealogy.rootsweb.com/~geneal/src/Welner SRC.html
  Also WELLNER, WELNA and variations.

- WENGER Home Page
  http://www.wengersundial.com/wengerfamily/
  A database of over 78,000 names of individuals, mostly descended from 18th century Mennonites, River Brethren (Brethren in Christ) and German Baptist Brethren who settled in Lancaster, Lebanon and Franklin Counties of Pennsylvania, in Ontario, Canada and in Washington Co., Maryland and Botetourt Co., Virginia.

- The WENTZEL(L) Genealogy Society
  http://www.qcis.ns.ca/wentzell/

- WEST Genealogy Page and WEST Surname Search
  http://ccwf.cc.utexas.edu/~shannon1/west/
  A page about the West family, history of the surname, a page to research fellow Wests, and links to West surname mailing lists and more!

- WESTGARTH Family History - WESTGARTH Across the World Wide Web
  http://www.westgarth.org.uk/
  Westgarth family history, family trees from around the world, biography and heraldry as well as history of the names origin.

- The Descendants of John and Sarah WESTON in America
  http://members.aol.com/microfud/private/weston.html

- VisitGenealogy.htm - A Family Genealogy - WETTIGs World Wide
  http://www.Wettig.org/VisitGenealogy.htm
  Kansas, East St. Louis, Illinois, Kleinneuheusen & Sedona.

- The WEYMOUTH Home Page
  http://www.tiac.net/users/weymouth/

- WHALEY6: Roots - Branches, Twigs, & Leaves
  http://members.aol.com/Whaley6/index.htm
  Dedicated to the descendants of Elijah McAnally & Alexander WHALEY.

- Surname WHALLEY Web Site
  http://home.pacifier.com/~wwhalley/

- The family of Thomas WHARTON - 201 individuals
  http://wharton.ourfamily.com/

- The WHARTONs of Philadelphia
  http://www.wharton.freeservers.com/index.html
  Covering the descendants of Thomas WHARTON who arrived in Philadelphia 1683. Information on allied families including: Carpenter, Fitzwater, Fishbourne and Lloyds.

- WHATLING Family History - A One Name Study
  http://www.visualcreations.com/pers/leeann/whatling/index.html

- Descendants of Rev. Thomas WHEAT (1789-1860)
  http://www.familytreemaker.com/users/w/h/e/John-M-Wheat/

- WHEAT Front Page
  http://www.geocities.com/Heartland/7785/

- Francis WHEAT Genealogy
  http://www.geocities.com/Heartland/7785/FrancisWheat2.htm
  Born February 21, 1737/38 in St. John Piscataway, Prince George's, Maryland.

- Web Family Cards - The WHEELER Clan
  http://users.iafrica.com/w/wh/wheeler/WC_TOC.HTM
  WHEELERS of the Isle of Wight, County Hampshire, England 1475 to 2000. Evolving from Willier, Whillear, Willieur, Whilliar, Whelliar, Whilliar, Whillier.

- Richard WHEELER Family History Genealogy
  http://members.tripod.com/Dr.G/wheeler.htm
  The WHEELER family of Clermont County, Ohio and Lincoln, Middlesex, Norfolk, & Worcester Counties Massachusetts.

- WHEELOCK Family Genealogy
  http://www.wheelockgenealogy.com/
  A history and genealogy of the WHEELOCK Family in the United States, with an emphasis on the Charlton, MA Wheelocks.

- WHELPLEY WHELPLY Information
  http://www.geocities.com/Heartland/Meadows/1761/

- Family History
  http://www.brid43.freeserve.co.uk/
  One name study for WHINCUP (Wincup, Whincop, Winkup, etc.) and RONDEAU.

- The WHINNERY Research Network
  http://members.aol.com/janfwatson/
  Whinery, Whinnery, Whinrey.

- The WHIPPLE Web Site
  http://www.whipple.org/

- WHIPPLE Weekend '99
  http://www.whipple.org/weekend99/index.html

- WHISNANT Surname Center
  http://homepages.rootsweb.com/~whisnant/
  Whisnant, Whisenant, Whisenand, Whisonant, Whisante, Whisenhunt, Visinand.

- The WHITACRE Genealogy Center
  http://www.jps.net/creising/whitacres.html
  Also WHITAKER.

- WHITAKER Family History & Genealogical Research Homepage.
  http://www.geocities.com/Heartland/Park/3741/genhopg1.html

- Alfred WHITE Family Organization
  http://kuhnslagoon.net/awfo/
  For records pertaining to the ancestors and descendants of pioneers Alfred Talmon WHITE (1778-1853/54) and his wife, Mary PERRY (1785-1866/68).

- The WHITE Family Chronicles
  http://www.geocities.com/Heartland/Ridge/7982
  Pertains to the family of Joseph White of Amelia and Bedford Co's VA with links for the Weber/Malueg family of Wisconsin.

- The WHITE Family Trails
  http://freepages.genealogy.rootsweb.com/~blue/

- WHITE Genealogy - Descendants - 1800, SOM
  http://www.itmagic.demon.co.uk/genealogy/white.htm
  Descendants of William Thomas WHITE and Elizabeth FERRIS.

- The WHITEHORNE Family Page
  http://www.whitehorne.com/Genealogy/index.html
  Also WHITEHORN

- WHITEWAY Central
  http://ourworld.compuserve.com/homepages/whiteway
  A web meeting place for those bearing the Whiteway name, wherever they may be.

- THE WHITFILL / WHITFIELD FAMILY
  http://freepages.genealogy.rootsweb.com/~whitfill
  WHITFILL / WHITFIELD found in the Nelson County, KY area in the late 1700's and early 1800's.

- Whit's End: WHITLOCK / WHITFIELD Genealogy
  http://home.pix.za/dw/dw000002/index.htm
  The genealogy of the Whitlock and Whitfield families in England and South Africa over a period of about 800 years and 26 generations.

- WHITMER, WITMER, Genealogy
  http://sites.netscape.net/louiswhitmer/homepage
  Descendants of Peter WITMER.

- WHITNAH Family Heritage
  http://www.xmission.com/~whitnahd/
  Descendants of Henry F. WHITENAH (WHITNAH) and Margaret BURNS of West Virginia.

- The WHITNEY Family
  http://www.gentree.com/whitney/home.html

- WHITNEY Family Genealogy
  http://ourworld.compuserve.com/homepages/jwmuse/whitney.htm
  Descendants of emigrant ancestors John WHITNEY of Watertown, MA, Henry WHITNEY of Long Island and CT and Samuel WHITNEY of Bermuda.

- WHITNEY Research Group
  http://www.whitneygen.org/
  Resources for all WHITNEY families, including vital, census, probate, and military records, genealogies, queries, a bibliography famous people, and much more!

- WHITNEY Genealogical Database
  http://www.rootsweb.com/~gumby/genweb/Whitney/Whitney.html
  A database that contains 6,654 people, 6,652 names.

- **WHITNEY Research Group**
  http://www.whitneygen.org/
  Online Transcription Project for the 1895 genealogy "The Descendants of John Whitney, who came from London, England, to Watertown, Massachusetts, in 1635".

- **The Gene Pool Colorful Families: WHITON**
  http://www.rootsweb.com/~genepool/whiton.htm

- **WHITTED Family Homepage**
  http://www.geocities.com/Heartland/Meadows/5097/
  Descendants of the Anderson and Mariah Whitted family, originally of Hillsboro Township (now Hillsborough), North Carolina.

- **The WHITTLETON Family WEB Site**
  http://www.whittleton.com/

- **WHITWORTH Family Association**
  http://www.geocities.com/Heartland/Lane/3130/wfa.html

- **The WHITWORTH Family Genealogy Home Page**
  http://www.familytreemaker.com/users/w/h/i/Gwen-W-Whitworth-Jr/
  Information for the WHITWORTH Family Association. Descendants of William H. WHITWORTH, born February 22, 1841 in Franklin County, Missouri, and died October 21, 1913 in Missouri.

- **WHITWORTH Genealogy Homepage**
  http://www.rww96.demon.co.uk/

- **WIBE - A Family from Norway**
  http://www.accessone.com/~jegge/wibe.htm

- **The WHOLEY Family History Society**
  http://www.geocities.com/Heartland/Farm/1906/
  Everything you could want to know about the surname Wholey and varients: Wholley, Whooley, Whoolley, etc.

- **WIANT / WYANT Family History**
  http://home.columbus.rr.com/wiant/
  Wiant, Wyant, Weygandt, Weigandt, Wiegandt, Wiand, Weyant.

- **WICKER Family Genealogy**
  http://www.bright.net/~cwicker

- **WICKER Genealogy**
  http://members.aol.com/ArletaHowe/Wicker.html
  Twelve generations, beginning about 1502, including descendants named Booth, Simmons, Holley, Hester, Sheppard, Johnson, and Pittman.

- **WICKHAM Family**
  http://home.t-online.de/home/mckenzie/wick.htm
  Descendants of William O. WICKHAM of NY and OH.

- **WICKWARE - WICKWIRE Genealogy**
  http://www.wickware.com
  A historical look at the genealogy and origins of the following surnames: Wickware; Wickwarr; Wickwarre; Wickwire; Wyckware; Wyckwarr; Wyckwarre.

- **WIDDOWS One-Name Study**
  http://www.lamerton.demon.co.uk/wid-onst.htm

- **Genealogy of the WIEGEL family**
  http://welcome.to/wiegel
  A glass blower family, (in Dutch and English language) from about 1670 until now.

- **WIGGINS Family**
  http://www.btinternet.com/~davidwig/Web/Wiggins.htm
  WIGGINS worldwide.

- **WIGGINTON, WIGINTON, WIGINGTON, WIGGINGTON Genealogy**
  http://members.aol.com/JanGulick

- **WIGGLESWORTH**
  http://www.pipeline.com/~david_w/wiggs.htm
  Family History of David WIGGLESWORTH.

- **WIGHTMAN Newsletter**
  http://www.shianet.org/~wightman/
  Genealogy of all WIGHTMANs in the U.S. and those WHITMANs that changed their names from WIGHTMAN.

- **WIGLEY Surname Webring**
  http://www.webring.org/cgi-bin/webring?ring=wigleyring;list

- **WIGMORE**
  http://homepages.tesco.net/~lyndon.wigmore/default.htm
  Descendants of Richard Wigmore (1660-1711); Wigmores Worldwide.

- **WILAND Genealogy**
  http://wiland.home.att.net
  All WILAND surnames currently including Michael WILAND (- ca 1794), William WILAND (ca 1785-1854), and their respective descendants.

- **WILBANKS Web**
  http://homepages.rootsweb.com/~wilbanks/
  A resource for those researching the Wilbanks surname (including variants such as Willbanks or Woolbanks)

- **WILBANKS-WILLBANKS Family History**
  http://www.robertwilbanks.com/wilbanks.htm

- **Mark's Genealogy Page - WILCOX, WILLCOX, WILCOCKSE**
  http://members.tripod.com/~MARK_DAMON_SMITH/INDEX.HTM

- **WILCOX Genealogy Area**
  http://www.magnate.demon.co.uk/genealogy/
  Wilcox in England.

- **WILCOXON Family**
  http://www.wilcoxon.org/

- **Jenny WILEY Association**
  http://freepages.genealogy.rootsweb.com/~jwiley/index.htm
  Descendants of Jenny Sellards WILEY (a 1790 Indian captive) and Hezikiah SELLARDS. WILEY, SELLARDS, WILLIAMSON, NELSON, VAN HOOSE, CASTLE, DANIELS, HARMON, SKAGGS.

- **WILEY Tree.org - The Genealogy of Joseph WEHRLE and WILEY Descendents**
  http://www.wileytree.org/
  Tracing the genealogy of Joseph Wehrle / Wiley, German immigrant to Rosiere, NY (Jefferson County, NY) in 1834. Extensive family tree spanning over 600 names and 6 generations. Many photos and documents.

- **WILHELM Surname**
  http://hometown.aol.com/EWGEN/WILHELM/index.html

- WILHOIT/WILHITE Family History
  http://homepages.rootsweb.com/~george/wilhoit.html

- WILKERSON Family Tree
  http://www.cjwilkes.com/wilkerson/
  Descendants of William WILKERSON.

- The WILKEY WILKIE Book
  http://wilkey-wilkie-book.org/
  Genealogy family outlines of WILKEY, WILKIE, EISON, DAME, FRANKLIN, SISK.

- WILKINSON Connection Newsletter
  mailto:pgleich@aol.com
  For all Wilkinson, Wilkerson, Wilkenson, Wilkins, Wilkens, etc. researchers. $15.00/year, quarterly. Submit queries or info by snail mail or by e-mail: Peggy Rockwell Gleich, Editor, PO Box 8003, Janesville WI 53547-8003, pgleich@aol.com.

- WILKINSONS on the Web
  http://www.wilkinsons.com/Wilkinsons.html

- The Descendants of Enoch WILLARD
  http://www.bgwilliams.apexhosting.com/gen/willard/surnames.htm

- WILLARD Family Association Home Page
  http://www.discover.net/~rwillard/wfa.html

- www.willemssen.com
  http://www.willemssen.com/
  A factual and chronological description of the Willemssen family from 1700s to the present, which includes news and information on family trees, living and deceased relatives, maps from the USA and Europe, histories on the name and family members, profiles, albums, letters and notes, list of guests who have visited the site and a forum for to sign the guest book.

- The WILLETT's of Roane Co., Tennessee
  http://www.familytreemaker.com/users/w/i/l/Shirley-Willett/index.html
  Research of the WILLETT family from Roane Co., Tennessee.

- "WILLEYs" in the U.K.
  http://expage.com/page/fairlight
  A history of the WILLEY clan in the English midlands.

- My WILLIAMS Family Genealogy Page
  http://www.ctaz.com/~shadgraf/williams.htm
  Descendants of William WILLIAMS and Sara CHATTIN.

- Roger WILLIAMS Family Association
  http://www.mouseworks.net/rogerwilliams/index.htm
  For the descendants of Roger Williams, founder of Rhode Island. Provides biographical data and membership requirements.

- Your WILLIAMS Home Page
  http://www.williamspage.com/
  This site is for ALL Williams descendants. Searchable database by NAME or STATE. Over 6500 submissions, submit your own!

- WILLS Family History with Associated Jacobite Documents
  http://www.alan.wills.btinternet.co.uk/home.htm
  WILLS family in Scotland.

- WILSFORD Family
  http://www.mindspring.com/~jogt/surnames/wilsford.htm

- WILSON's Network
  http://members.tripod.com/~Wilson_Network/index.htm

- WILSONs From New England
  http://home.att.net/~ramosgang/KenStevens.html
  An electronic "brochure" of the book series by Ken Stevens. Ken's research has spanned nearly 40 years.

- WilsonSurname.com - WILSON Network Surname Genealogical Resource
  http://members.tripod.com/~Wilson_Network/index.html
  WILSON, WILLSON.

- Henry Bascom WILSON Family Home Page
  http://www.familytreemaker.com/users/v/a/n/Elizabeth-E-Vandenberg/
  Ancestry and descendants of Henry Bascom WILSON, of Hancock County, Indiana (1824 -1913).

- WIMBERLY Family Genealogy
  http://members.accessus.net/~twimberly/index.htm
  WIMBERLY, WIMBERLEY.

- Descendants of Alexander Jones WINANT
  http://members.cftnet.com/stevew/winant.htm
  Born June 30, 1837 in Granville, Staten Island, New York, died December 14, 1911. WINANT, FREEMAN, PATCH, PARTCH.

- WINCH Genealogical Database
  http://www.rootsweb.com/~gumby/genweb/Winch/Winch.html
  A database that contains 18,307 names.

- WINCHESTER Genealogy
  http://www.winchesters.net
  Descendents of Willoughby and Mary Wallace WINCHESTER of South Carolina.

- The WINDEMUTH Family Organization
  http://www.kern.com/maykoski/wintermute.htm

- Or The WINDEMUTH Family Organization
  http://www.jefnet.com/wintermute/
  Descendants of Johan Christoph WINDEMUTH and Mary Marguerite KLEPPLINGER
  Windemuth, Wintamute, Wintemute, Wintermote, Wintermute, Wintermuth.

- The WINEMILLER Family Inn
  http://www.winemiller.org/

- Descendants of Matthew WING
  http://www.uftree.com/UFT/WebPages/RaymondWing/WINGDESC/index.htm
  Six generations from Matthew & Mary WING of Banbury, England.

- The WINGARD Family
  http://home.att.net/~dpdklong/Wingard.htm
  The Wingards, German immigrants who made their way to Alabama in the early 19th century. Descendants of John Adam Wingard who immigrated from Wurtenburg, Germany, in 1761, and arrived in Charleston.

- WINGFIELD Family Society
  http://www.wingfield.org

- WINGO Ancestry
  http://www.geocities.com/Heartland/Park/2419/
  Descendants of John Wingo, of Virginia and Ohio.

- The WINGO Family Page
  http://www.spessart.com/users/ggraham/wingo.htm

- WINGROVEs of the Wide World
  http://members.xoom.com/mwingrove/10-10-index.htm
  The Wingrove surname appears to originate in England and the surname has evolved over the years. Wingrove and Wingrave seem to be the only two forms that have survived.

- WINKER Family Web Site
  http://winker.net/

- WINMILL Home Page
  http://members.aol.com/winmill01/
  Descendants of Richard and Elizabeth Laird WINMILL.

- Genealogy Homepage for WINN ~ WYNN ~ WYNNE & Associated Families
  http://members.aol.com/lunetta595/main.html
  Descendants of Dr. Thomas Wynne, born 1627 in Wales.

- Our House of WINNETT
  http://members.net-tech.com.au/winnett/
  Winnot, Whinnett Winet - 12 generations from France to England to Australia.

- WINSHIP One-Name Study
  http://members.aol.com/winstudy/winship.htm

- WINSTEAD Home Page
  http://www.lanset.com/gkemper/winstead.htm
  Descendants of Samuel Winstead (1701).

- Wandering WINTER(S)
  http://www.geocities.com/Heartland/Hills/8929/

- WINTER(S) Query & Newsletter
  mailto:lora@empnet.com
  Free monthly e-mail newsletter for WINTER and WINTERS.

- WINTER HICKERT Family Web Site
  http://www.mwsoftware.com/history
  Descendants of Michael WINTER and Elizabeth HICKERT.

- The WINTHROP Society
  http://members.aol.com/WinthropSQ/society.htm
  For those with proven descent from one or more passengers of the Winthrop fleet, or of others who settled in the Massachusetts Bay Colony before December 31, 1632.

- Descendants of Johannes Conrad WIRZ and Anna GOETSCHY
  http://pages.prodigy.net/reed_wurts/cpwurts/surnames.html
  Descendants of Johannes Conrad Wirz and Anna Goetschy, compiled mostly from a book by Charles Pemberton Wurts published in 1889, with additions by Reed M. W. Wurts.

- WISDOM Connectors
  http://members.tripod.com/WisdomLuker

- The WISEMAN Family Association
  http://members.tripod.com/~dwiseman/index.html

- WISHAM Family
  http://www.geocities.com/PicketFence/Garden/4188/JWISHAM.html

- The WISSINGER Genealogy Page
  http://freepages.genealogy.rootsweb.com/~bobwiss/index.htm
  A central resource for people researching the Wissinger surname. Contains surname history, surname index, pictures, coat-of-arms, list of contributors and links to other Wissinger sites. Includes Wisinger, Wysinger, Wiesinger, Wiessinger, and others.

- WITHERSPOON Family Research Home Page
  http://members.tripod.com/~witherspoon/

- LAMPSON WITMUS Family Organization
  http://freepages.genealogy.rootsweb.com/~lampson/lampwit.html
  For descendants of William LAMPSON, born 1761 in Boston, Mass. and Wilhelm WITTMUETZ born 1799 in Ruegen Island, Germany.

- WITTENBERG Family Association
  http://members.aol.com/wittnberg/index.htm
  Also Whittenburg, Whittenberg, Wittenberg, Wittenburg.

- WITT's End Newsletter - WITT / WHITT / WHIT Genealogy
  http://www.witts-end.org/

- The WLADYKA Genealogy Forum
  http://cbt.bungi.com/surnamewladyka/

- WOFFORD Family Clearinghouse Database
  http://www.angelfire.com/ok2/kristi/

- WOLDIN-SITZ Family History
  http://www.catskill.net/rue/family/woldin/

- WOLF Home Page - Wandering WOLFs Newsletter
  http://members.aol.com/Kinseeker6/wolf.html

- The John WOLFE Family
  http://www.telusplanet.net/public/cfdun/wolfenav.htm
  Descendants of famine emigrant, John WOLFE and his wife, Ann O'HEARN of Limerick County, Ireland and Wellington County, Ontario, Canada.

- WOLFENSBERGER Family Association
  http://www.icon.net/~wolfberg/
  Also: Wolfersberger, Wolfersparger, Wolfensparger, Wolfenbarger, Wolfenberger, Wolfinbarger, Sparger AND Spargur.

- The WOLTZ & WALTZ Ancestors
  http://www.geocities.com/Heartland/Pointe/6000/genealogy/
  The largest collection of genealogical data on the Woltz & Waltz Families on the World Wide Web.

- WOOLUM Genealogy
  http://freepages.genealogy.rootsweb.com/~kellygirl3398/
  Includes all spelling variations of the name, such as WOLLAM, ULM, ULLOM.

- WOLVERTON / WOOLVERTON Family Heritage Society
  http://www.ualr.edu/~mamiller1/

- WOMACK Family News
  http://members.tripod.com/~RGWomack/index.htm

- The WOMACK Genealogy Network (WGN)
  http://members.aol.com/womacknet/home.html

- WOMELSDORF Family Association
  http://gonow.to/wfa
  Womeldorf, Womeldorff, Womeldorph, Womelsdorff, Womelsdorf, Wommelsdorff, Womelsduff.

- WOOD Family
  http://members.aol.com/HatwellE/WoodFamilyHistory.html
  History of Jacob & Stephen Wood's family who settled in Greene Co., IL and their descendants, including POWELL, RILEY, BAKER families.

- The Descendants of Peter Atte WOOD of England and Henry WOOD of Plymouth Massachusetts
  http://www5.pair.com/vtandrew/wood/wood.htm

- WOOD Family
  http://members.aol.com/HatwellE/WoodFamilyHistory.html
  Jacob Wood Descendant's Family History.

- WOOD World - WOOD Family Genealogy
  http://www.dlcwest.com/~mgwood/

- The WOODARD Family Tree
  http://www.woodardfamilytree.com
  Comprehensive listing of Woodard family members, including family narratives.

- WOODCOCK Family
  http://www.cwoodcock.com/

- WOODCOCK Genealogy
  http://home.earthlink.net/~awoodc/
  Descendants of John WOODCOCK (1615) of Rehoboth, MA.

- WOODHAM Family Association
  http://www.geocities.com/~rewoodham/woodham.html

- The Descendents of Alford and Mariah WOODHAM
  http://members.aol.com/mwoodha/genealgy/index.htm
  Genealogy of the African-American family Woodham in Darlington and Lee County, South Carolina.

- The Online WOODLIEF / WOODLIFF Family Association
  http://members.home.net/teylu/woodlief/assn/

- WOODLIEF Family Page
  http://members.home.net/teylu/woodlief/

- WOODRUFF Genealogy
  http://www.geocities.com/Heartland/Acres/3792/
  For all WOODRUFF's Anytime, Anywhere.

- WOODRUFF Genealogy
  http://hometown.aol.com/mntassoc/ruffndx.htm
  Descendants of Joseph Woodruff (c 1735, England-1799, GA); Families primarily of GA, SC, AL, FL & MS; Allied families: BECKWITH, GLOVER, HERIOT, NEWMAN, O'NEAL, WASHBURNE.

- My Neck of the WOODS
  http://members.home.net/lyle.woods/
  Researching the WOODS family from the Isle of Wight. Also surnames Fair, Fleming, Olson, Quinton and Smart.

- WOODWARD-MATTSON Family Newsletter
  http://www.woodward-mattson.com/newsletter.html
  For the descendants of John Jackson Woodward (1812-1875) and his wife Hannah Mattson Woodward (1816-1894) of Kennett Township, Chester County, Pennsylvania.

- WOODWARDs WeSearch Newsletter
  http://www.studiosr.com/woodward/
  Provides access to the subject index to the quarterly publication (beginning October 1992) of the WOODWARDs WeSearch Newsletter embracing all Woodwards (including spelling variations) throughout the United States. Access is also provided for an application form and links to URL for subscribers home pages.

- Richard WOODWARD 1587-1664 immig. to Massachusetts, & his descendants
  http://www.geocities.com/Athens/Ithaca/2594/woodward/genre00t.htm
  Some descendants of Richard WOODWARD of Watertown, Mass. 356 individuals, 12 generations, mostly in MA & NH. Illustrated (in progress), citations, and fully indexed. Includes 1965 Nobel Prize winner Robert Burns Woodward.

- WOODY Gap
  http://homepages.rootsweb.com/~woodygap/
  WOODY surname, all spellings, all areas and related families.

- Wo*l*m Genealogy
  http://www.geocities.com/Heartland/Plains/2316/
  Genealogy of Woolam, Woolem, Woolum, Ulm, Ullum, Wollam, Woollam, Woollum Families.

- WOOLMAN Central
  http://msnhomepages.talkcity.com/HobbyCt/woolmans/index.html
  Dedicated to the documentation of the Woolman family and to educating about John Woolman and the John Woolman Memorial Association, Mount Holly, N.J.

- The WOOLWORTH Family
  http://www.thewoolworths.com/
  The Descendants of Richard WOOLERY/WOOLWORTH (1648-1696).

- The WORCESTER Family in America
  http://www.worcesterfamily.com/
  Descendants of Rev. William WORCESTER, first pastor of the church of Salisbury, Massachusetts, 1638.

- WORK Family Genealogy
  http://www.redriverok.com/workfamilygene/
  WORK, WARK, WAYMIRE, and related families from the Orkneys to the USA, 1693 to present.

- WORSFOLD Genealogy
  http://members.xoom.com/edmckie/worsfold.html
  WORSFOLD throughout the world

- WORSHAM & WASHAM Family History Home Page
  http://www.geocities.com/Heartland/Valley/1360/
  Worsham, Washam, Washum, Warsham, Wisham, and Washham surnames from 1640 to present.

- WORTELBOER Genealogy
  http://www.wortel.demon.nl/

- WORSTEN Genealogical Society - Wroclaw, Poland (Surname Society)
  http://www.feefhs.org/surname/frgworst.html

- Descendants of John WORTH of Nantucket
  http://vineyard.net/vineyard/history/worthw1.htm
  WORTH, MACY, and other related families of Nantucket and Martha's Vineyard, and their descendants in America 1642 to present.

- WORTHINGTON
  http://members.aol.com/hdw3/worthington.html
  A website devoted to the lineage of Capt. John Worthington (1650-1701) of Anne Arundel Co., Md presented in family group sheet format with links to Ancestors, Sources, other Worthington researchers, plus much more! Contributions welcomed!

- WORTHINGTON Family Notes, Randolph Co NC
  http://members.tripod.com/Dr.G/worthgtn.htm
  Descendants of John WORTHINGTON who located in Randolph Co., NC from Virginia.

- The WORTMAN Exchange: a Discussion Forum on the Genealogy of Wortman, Workman, Woertman, Wortmann
  http://208.231.16.38/

- The WORTMAN Family Tree
  http://ourworld.compuserve.com/homepages/Warren_Wortman/
  Descendants of Milton Lad Wortman.

- WOTUS Family History
  http://www.familytreemaker.com/users/k/a/s/Jane-E-Kasper/
  Descendants of Frank Wotus.

- WOUDSMA Online: Alles Over De Familienaam WOUDSMA / Everything About The Surname WOUDSMA
  http://home-1.worldonline.nl/~rwoudsma/index.html
  Woudsma, Spaander, Hiddema, Volger, Damsma, Huizinga.

- The WRIGHT Areas
  http://pw1.netcom.com/~jjordan2/ritearea.html

- Descendants of Richard WRIGHT, Sr. of Rowan County, North Carolina
  http://freepages.genealogy.rootsweb.com/~herbarkin
  Includes Colglazier, Cooley, Gilstrap, Goss, Morgan, Mullenix, Parrish, Purlee, Wright, Zink.

- WRIGHT Families of Georgia
  http://www.mindspring.com/~wwfredatlcom.net/

- WRIGHT Researchers
  http://www.athens.net/~ethelind/genealogy/wright/wright.html

- The WRIGHT Tidbits
  http://www.geocities.com/Heartland/5917/Tidbits.htm

- World WYKES Web
  http://www.wykes.org/

- WYMAN Family
  http://www.wyman.org/
  More than 16,000 descendants and relatives of Francis Wyman of Westmill, England.

- WYNKOOP Family Research Library
  http://members.tripod.com/~wynkoop/index.htm

- WYNN Family and Kinsman Association, Est.1971
  http://www.ausaweb.com/drwynn
  WYNNE including variant spellings: Wynne Winne Wynn Winn Gwynne Gwynn Gwyn Win Winnie Gwynn Gwyn Gwyne.

- Genealogie der Familie WYSTRACH aus Obershlesien / Genealogy of the WYSTRACH Family from Upper Silesia
  http://www.wystrach.de

◆ Surname Mailing Lists

- "WAA-WAK" Surname Mailing Lists
  http://www.rootsweb.com/~jfuller/gen_mail_surnames-waa.html
  WACH, WACHTEL, WACHTER, WACKER, WACTOR (includes Wachter, Waechter, Waktor, Wacter, Wackter, Wakter, Wyghter), WADDELL, WADDINGTON, WADDLE, WADE (includes Wayde, Waid, Wayd, Waddel), WADKINS, WADLE, WADLEY, WADLINGTON, WADSWORTH, WAECHTER, WAFFORD (includes Warford, Wofford, Walford), WAGAMAN, WAGENER, WAGER, WAGES, WAGGONER, WAGGONER (includes Wagoner, Wagner), WAGHALTER, WAGLEY, WAGNER, WAGNON, WAGONER (includes Wagonner, Waggoner), WAGSTAFF, WAHL, WAINSCOTT, WAINWRIGHT, WAIT, WAITE, WAITS, WAKE, WAKEFIELD, WAKEHAM, WAKELAND, WAKELEY (includes Waklee, Wakley), WAKEMAN.

- "WAL-WAQ" Surname Mailing Lists
  http://www.rootsweb.com/~jfuller/gen_mail_surnames-wal.html
  WALBORN, WALBRIDGE, WALCH, WALD, WALDEN (includes Waldan, Waldin, Waldon, Waldun), WALDER, WALDO, WALDON, WALDREP, WALDRIP, WALDRON, WALDROP, WALDSCHMIDT, WALES, WALFORD, WALK, WALKER, WALKER, WALKER, WALKER, WALKER, WALKER, WALKUP, WALL (includes Walls), WALLACE (includes Wallis, Wallas), WALLEN, WALLER (includes De Waller), WALLES, WALLEY, WALLICK, WALLICK, WALLING, WALLING (includes Wallen, Wallin), WALLING, WALLINGFORD (includes Wallingsford, Warringsford, Warrensford), WALLIS, WALLS, WALMSLEY, WALOCH (includes Walloch), WALRATH (includes Wallrath, Walradt, Walreth, Wolreth), WALRAVEN (includes Wallraven, Waldraven), WALSH, WALSTON, WALSTROM, WALTER, WALTERS, WALTES, WALTHALL, WALTHER, WALTMAN, WALTON, WALTZ, WALZ, WAMPACH, WAMPLER, WAMSLEY, WANLESS, WANN, WANNER, WANTZ.

- "WAR-WD" Surname Mailing Lists
  http://www.rootsweb.com/~jfuller/gen_mail_surnames-war.html
  WARBURTON, WARD, WARD (includes Warde), WARD, WARD, WARDELL, WARDEN, WARDER, WARDLAW, WARDLE, WARDLOW (includes Wardlaw), WARDROP, WARDWELL, WARE (includes Wear, Wair, Warr), WAREHEIM (includes Wareheim, Warehime), WARFIELD, WARFORD, WARING, WARLICK, WARMAN, WARMOTH (includes Warmouth, Warmath, Wormoth, Wormeth, Wurmuth), WARNE, WARNER, WARNOCK, WARNOX (includes Warnock), WARR (includes Warre), WARREN, WARRENER,

WARRICK, WARRICK, WARRINER, WARRINGTON, WARRINOR, WARWICK, WASDEN, WASH, WASHBROOK (includes Washbrooke), WASHBURN, WASIELEWSKI (includes Wasilewski), WASLEY, WASS, WASSON (includes Wason), WATERBURY, WATERFIELD, WATERHOUSE, WATERMAN, WATERS (includes Watters, Watrous), WATERS, WATERSTRAAT, WATERWORTH, WATES, WATFORD (includes Wadford), WATHAN (includes Wathen), WATHEN (includes Wathan), WATKIN, WATKINS, WATKINS (includes Wadkens, Wadkins), WATKINS, WATROUS, WATSON, WATT, WATTENBARGER, WATTERS, WATTERSON, WATTS, WATTS, WAUGH, WAXHAM (includes Waxam, Waxhann, Waxsom, Waxsome, Waxson), WAY, WAYLAND, WAYMAN, WAYMARK (includes Weymark, Whymark, Wimark, Wimarc, Wymark, Wymarc, Vymark, Wiuhmarch, Whimark,, Whimarc), WAYNE (includes Wain, O'Wayne, McWayne, Weign, Weyne, Wynne).

- **"WEA-WEH" Surname Mailing Lists**
  http://www.rootsweb.com/~jfuller/gen_mail_surnames-wea.html
  WEAKLEY, WEAR, WEARDEN, WEARE, WEATHERFORD, WEATHERFORD, WEATHERHEAD, WEATHERILL (includes Weatherall, Weatherell, Wetherill), WEATHERLY (includes Wetherly, Wetherleigh, Withersby), WEATHERS (includes Withers, Wethers, Whethers), WEATHERSBEE, WEAVER (includes Wever, Weber), WEAVIL (includes Weavel), WEBB, WEBB, WEBBER, WEBER (includes Webber), WEBORG, WEBSTER, WEDDELL (includes Wedel, Weddle), WEDDINGTON (includes Waddington), WEDDLE, WEDDLE, WEDEL, WEDERELL, WEDGE, WEDGWOOD (includes Wedgewood), WEED, WEEDEN, WEEKES, WEEKHOUT (includes Weekholt, Weekhold, Weekhoud), WEEKLEY (includes Weekly, Weakley, Weakly), WEEKS, WEEMS, WEESE, WEGER (includes Wayger, Wager, Weager), WEGGEMANS, WEGMANN (includes Wiegman, Wiegmann, Weigman, Weigmann, Wedman), WEGNER, WEHN, WEHRLE.

- **"WEI-WEQ" Surname Mailing Lists**
  http://www.rootsweb.com/~jfuller/gen_mail_surnames-wei.html
  WEIDEMANN, WEIDMAN, WEIDNER, WEIDOW (includes Weida), WEIGAND, WEIGART, WEIGEL, WEIGHT, WEIKERT, WEIKLE (includes Wical, Wykle, Wikle, Weigle, Michael), WEIL, WEILAND, WEILER, WEIMER, WEINBERG, WEINER, WEINGARTNER, WEINHOLD, WEINRICH, WEINSTEIN, WEIR, WEIS, WEISE, WEISEL (includes Weissel, Weisell), WEISENAUER, WEISENSEL, WEISER (includes Wiser, Wisser), WEISHAUPT, WEISS, WEITZ, WEITZEL, WEKKING, WELBAUM (includes Wellbaum), WELBORN, WELCH, WELCH, WELCHEL, WELCHER, WELD, WELDAY (includes Weldy), WELDON, WELFELT (includes Wellfelt, Welfeldt, Wefelt, Welfeld, Wilfelt), WELKER, WELLBORN, WELLER, WELLES, WELLING, WELLINGTON, WELLMAN, WELLNER (includes Welner, Welnor), WELLS, WELLS, WELLS, WELLS, WELLS, WELLS, WELLS, WELSH, WELTER, WELTON, WELTY (includes Weldy, Welday, Velty, Felty), WEMYSS (includes Weems, Weemes, Weames, Wiems, Wims, Whims), WENDEL, WENDELL, WENDEN (includes Wendon, Wendin, Wending), WENDLING, WENDT, WENGER, WENNER, WENNING, WENRICH (includes Weinrich, Wenrick, Venrick), WENSLEY (includes Whensly, Wednesley, Wansley, Winsley), WENSTROM, WENT (includes Wendt), WENTWORTH, WENTZ, WENTZEL, WENZ (includes Wenzousky, Wenzowsky, Wezowski, Wiezowski, Wiazowski), WENZEL, WEPKING.

- **"WER-WG" Surname Mailing Lists**
  http://www.rootsweb.com/~jfuller/gen_mail_surnames-wer.html
  WERK (includes Werque), WERKING (includes Working, Werkinger, Workinger), WERLE, WERNER, WERT, WERTH, WERTHEIMER, WERTS, WERTZ (includes Wert, Werts, Wirtz, Wuertz, Wurtz, Wurz, Wurts), WESCOTT, WESLEY, WESNER (includes Weisner, Westner, Wessner, Wisener), WESOLOWSKI, WESSEL, WESSELS (includes Wessells, Wesselse, Wesselsen), WESSLING (includes Wesling, Wesseling), WESSON, WEST, WEST, WEST, WESTALL, WESTBROOK (includes Westbroke, Westbrok), WESTBROOK (includes Westbrooke, Wesbroek, Westbrooks), WESTCOTT, WESTENDORF, WESTER, WESTER, WESTERFIELD, WESTERLING, WESTERMAN, WESTERVELT, WESTFALL, WESTGATE, WESTLAKE, WESTMORELAND, WESTON, WESTON, WESTOVER, WESTPHAL, WESTRA, WESTWOOD, WETHERELL (includes Witherell), WETHERINGTON (includes Witherington, Widdrington), WETHINGTON (includes Withington, Witherton, Whittington), WETMORE (includes Whitmore), WETZEL, WETZEL, WETZELL (includes Wetzel).

- **"WH-WH" Surname Mailing Lists**
  http://www.rootsweb.com/~jfuller/gen_mail_surnames-wh.html
  WHALEN, WHALEY (includes Whalley, Whally, Whalen), WHARTON, WHATLEY (includes Watley, Whately, Wheatley, Wheatly, Whitley, Whitely), WHATLING (includes Watling, Watlyng, Watlynge, Wattling, Wattlyng), WHATTON (includes Whatten, Watton, Wathone, Waton, Watone), WHEAT, WHEATLEY (includes Wheatly), WHEATLEY (includes Wheatly, Wheetly, Whatley, Whiteley), WHEATON, WHEELER, WHEELOCK, WHEELOCK, WHELAN, WHELCHEL, WHELDON, WHELESS, WHETSEL, WHETSTONE, WHIDDEN (includes Whitten, Whyddon Whiddon, Witten, Wheadon), WHIDDEN, WHIDDON, WHIGHAM (includes Wigham, Whiggam, Wiggam), WHIFFEN (includes Whiffin, Wiffin, Wiffen, Whiffing), WHILLANS (includes Wealands, Wealans, Wealens, Wealleans, Weallens, Wheelans, Wheeleans, Whelans,, Whelens, Whellens, Whillace, Whillance, Whillas, Wholans, Willance, Willands), WHIPKEY (includes Whipya, Whipka, Hipge), WHIPPLE, WHISENANT, WHISLER (includes Whislor, Whistler, Wisler, Wissler), WHISMAN, WHISNANT (includes Wissenandt, Visanand, Whisenhunt, Whisenant, Whisonant), WHITACRE, WHITACRE (includes Whitaker, Whittaker, Whiteacer, Whitecar), WHITAKER (includes Whittaker, Whitacre), WHITBREAD, WHITBY, WHITCHER (includes Witcher), WHITCOMB, WHITCOME, WHITE (includes Whyte, Whiet), WHITE, WHITE, WHITECOTTON, WHITED, WHITEFIELD, WHITEFORD, WHITEHAIR, WHITEHEAD, WHITEHORN, WHITEHOUSE, WHITEHURST, WHITELAW, WHITELEY, WHITELOCK, WHITEMAN, WHITENACK, WHITENER, WHITESELL, WHITESIDE (includes Whitesides), WHITFIELD, WHITFILL, WHITFORD, WHITING, WHITING, WHITLEY, WHITLOCK, WHITLOW (includes Whytlow), WHITMAN, WHITMARSH, WHITMER (includes Whitmore, Witmore, Vitmer), WHITMIRE, WHITMORE, WHITNEY, WHITNEY, WHITNEY, WHITRIGHT, WHITSETT, WHITSON, WHITSON, WHITT, WHITTAKER, WHITTEMORE, WHITTEN, WHITTENBERG (includes Whittenberger, Wittenberg, Wittenberger, Whittenburg, Whittenburger, Wittenburg,, Wittenburger, Wurtemberg, Wurtemberger, Wattenberg, Wattenberger, Wattenburg, Wattenburger), WHITTIER, WHITTINGHAM, WHITTINGTON, WHITTLE, WHITTLESEY, WHITTON. WHITWELL. WHITWORTH. WHORTON. WHYTE.

- **"WIA-WIK" Surname Mailing Lists**
  http://www.rootsweb.com/~jfuller/gen_mail_surnames-wia.html
  WIANT, WIBERT (includes Wibirt, Wybert), WIBLE (includes Weible, Wibel), WICHMANN, WICHTERMAN (includes Wichtermann), WICK (includes Wicks, Week, Weeks), WICKENDEN, WICKER, WICKERSHAM, WICKHAM, WICKIZER, WICKMAN, WICKS, WIDDOWS (includes Widows, Widdoes, Widders), WIDDRINGTON (includes Witherington, Wetherington), WIDEMAN (includes Weideman), WIDENER (includes Weidner, Widner), WIDMANN, WIDMER, WIEDENFELD, WIEDERMAN (includes Weiderman, Wiedermann), WIEGAND, WIELAND (includes Wienand, Wiejant), WIER (includes Weir, Wehr), WIESE, WIGDERSON, WIGGINS (includes Wiggens, Wiggs), WIGGINTON, WIGGINTON, WIGGLESWORTH (includes Wiglesworth, Wigelsworth), WIGGLESWORTH, WIGHT (includes Whight, Wycht), WIGHTMAN, WIGLEY.

- **"WIL-WIL" Surname Mailing Lists**
  http://www.rootsweb.com/~jfuller/gen_mail_surnames-wil.html
  WILAND (includes Wyland, Wayland, Weiland, Wieland, Weyland), WILBANKS (includes Willbanks, Woolbanks), WILBER, WILBORN, WILBOURN, WILBUR, WILBURN (includes Wilborn, Wilbourn, Wilbourne), WILCOX (includes Willcox, Willcoxson), WILCOXSON, WILD, WILDBLOOD, WILDE (includes Wild, Wilder, Wyld, Wylde, Wilds), WILDER, WILDER (includes Wylder), WILDER (includes Wylder), WILDING, WILDMAN, WILDS, WILES, WILES, WILEY (includes Wylie, Wylly), WILEY, WILFORD, WILHELM, WILHELM, WILHITE (includes Wilhoit, Wilheit, Willert, Wilert, Willheit, Willhoit, Willhite), WILHOIT (includes Wilhite, Wilheit, Willert, Wilert, Willheit, Willhoit, Willhite, Wilhoite, Willhoite), WILK, WILKE, WILKEN, WILKENS, WILKERSON, WILKES (includes Wilks, Welkes, Walkes, Wolkes, Volkes, Wellkes, McWilk), WILKIE (includes Wilke), WILKIN (includes Wilkins), WILKINS, WILKINSON (includes McQuilkin, McQuilken, McQuilkan, MacQuilkin, MacQuilken, MacQuilkan), WILKINSON (includes Wilkenson, Wilkerson, Wilkins, Wilkerson), WILKS, WILL, WILLARD, WILLCOX, WILLCUTT (includes Willcut, Wilcutt, Wilcut), WILLE, WILLEMETE (includes Willimete), WILLEMS, WILLEMSSEN (includes Willms, Willems), WILLENER (includes Willner, Williner), WILLENS (includes Wilensky, Wilenski), WILLER, WILLETT, WILLEY, WILLIAM, WILLIAMS (includes McWilliams, Willis, Wilkinson, Williamson, O'Williams), WILLIAMS, WILLIAMS, WILLIAMSON, WILLIAMSON, WILLIAMSON, WILLIFORD, WILLINGHAM, WILLIS, WILLISON, WILLMAN, WILLMON (includes Wildman, Wileman, Willimon), WILLOUGHBY (includes Wilobe, Willabe, Willowbe), WILLOVER, WILLOW, WILLS, WILLSON, WILLSTROP (includes Wilstrop, Wylestrope, Wilstrope, Vilstrup, Wilstrup), WILMAN, WILMORE, WILMOT (includes Wilmarth, Willmuth, Wilmottsen, Willmouth, Walmarth, Wilmoth), WILMOTH (includes Wilmot, Wilmoarth, Wilmuth, Wilmouth, Wilmount, Wilmath), WILSEY, WILSFORD (includes Willeford, Wilford, Willesford, Williford), WILSON (includes Willson), WILSON, WILSON, WILSON, WILSON, WILT (includes Willt), WILTON, WILTSHIRE.

- **"WIM-WIQ" Surname Mailing Lists**
  http://www.rootsweb.com/~jfuller/gen_mail_surnames-wim.html
  WIMBERLEY, WIMBERLY, WIMER, WIMMER, WINANS, WINANS, WINBORNE (includes Winburn, Winburne, Winborn), WINCH, WINCHCOMB (includes Winchcombe, Wynchcomb, Wynchcombe, Wenscom, Wenchcom, Winchcom), WINCHELL (includes Wincall), WINCHELL, WINCHESTER, WINDER (includes Winders, Winter, Winters), WINDHAM (includes

Wyndham, Windom, Windam), WINDLE, WINDROW, WINDSOR (includes Winsor), WINE, WINE, WINEGARDNER (includes Winegartner, Weingartner, Winegarden, Winegarten, Weingarden, Weingarten,, Winegardener, Winegart, Weingart, Wingart, Wingert), WINELAND (includes Weinland), WINEMAN (includes Weinman, Wyneman, Wiman, Wyman), WINEMILLER, WINES, WINFIELD, WINFREY, WING (includes Winge, Wyng, Wynge), WINGARD, WINGATE, WINGER, WINGERT, WINGET, WINGET (includes Wingate, Wyngate, Wingett), WINGFIELD (includes Winfield), WINGLER, WINGO, WINGO, WININGER, WINK, WINKELER (includes Winkler, Winckler), WINKELMAN, WINKLE (includes Winkel), WINKLER, WINKOWSKI, WINN (includes Wynne, Wynn, Winne), WINN (includes Wynne, Wynn, Winne), WINNE, WINNER, WINNINGHAM (includes Winingham, Willingham, Winham, Wingham), WINOGRAD, WINSHIP, WINSLOW, WINSOR, WINSTEAD, WINSTON, WINTER, WINTERBOTTOM, WINTERBURN, WINTERS (includes Winter, Winder, Winders), WINTHROP, WINTON (includes Wynton).

- **"WIR-WN" Surname Mailing Lists**
  http://www.rootsweb.com/~jfuller/gen_mail_surnames-wir.html
  WIRE, WIRTH, WIRTZ, WISDOM, WISE (includes Wees, Weese, Weis, Weise, Weiss, Weisse, Weisz, Wice, Wiece, Wiese, Wiess, Wyse, Wyss), WISECUP, WISELY, WISELY, WISEMAN, WISER, WISHART, WISHON, WISLER, WISNER, WISNIEWSKI, WISNIEWSKI, WISTAR, WISWALL, WISWEH, WITCHER, WITHAM, WITHERINGTON (includes Wetherington, Weatherington, Widdrington), WITHERS, WITHERSPOON (includes Weatherspoon, Wotherspoon), WITHEY, WITHINGTON, WITHROW, WITKOWSKI, WITMER, WITT, WITT, WITTE, WITTEKIND (includes Wedeking), WITTEN, WITTER, WITTIG, WITTMANN, WITTMER, WITULSKI, WITZ, WIXON (includes Wixson, Wixom, Wixam).

- **"WO-WT" Surname Mailing Lists**
  http://www.rootsweb.com/~jfuller/gen_mail_surnames-wo.html
  WOFFORD, WOFFORD, WOHLEBEN (includes Woleben, Wolleben, Wohlleben, Woliver, Woolever, Welliver, Willever, Livewell, Nebelow), WOJCIEHOWSKI, WOJCIK, WOJTOWYCZ, WOJTYNA, WOLBERS (includes Wolber, Walbers), WOLCOTT, WOLD (includes Wuld, Woold, Vold, Vuld), WOLETZ, WOLF, WOLF (includes Wolfe, Woolf), WOLFE (includes Wolf, Wolff, Woolf, Wulf, Wulff, Rolfe, Rolph), WOLFENSBARGER, WOLFENSBERGER (includes Wolfensperger, Wolfersberger, Wolfersperger, Wolfenbarger, Wolfenberger,, Wolfinbarger, Sparger, Spargur), WOLFF, WOLFGANG, WOLFGANG (includes Wolfgong), WOLFGRAM, WOLFORD, WOLFORT, WOLFSHAUT (includes Wolfsont, Wolfsout, Wolfshout, Wolfshant, Wolfsant), WOLFSKILL (includes Wolfskhel, Wolfkill), WOLGAMOTT (includes Wohlgamuth, Vulgamott, Vulgamore), WOLLAM, WOLLARD, WOLLASTON, WOLSKI, WOLSTENCROFT, WOLTER, WOLTZ (includes Waltz, Wolz, Walz, Waltzer, Waltser), WOLVERTON (includes Woolverton, Wolberton, Wolferton, Wulferton, Wolferstan, Wulferstan, Wolvington,, Wolverstone), WOMACK, WOMBLE, WOOD, WOODALL, WOODALL, WOODARD (includes Woodward), WOODBRIDGE, WOODBURN, WOODBURY, WOODCOCK, WOODEN, WOODFIN, WOODFORD, WOODGATE, WOODHAM, WOODHOUSE (includes Wodehouse, Woodhousem, Woodhouser), WOODHULL, WOODIN, WOODLAND, WOODLEY, WOODLIEF (includes Woodliff), WOODLING, WOODMAN, WOODMANSEE, WOODMORE, WOODRING, WOODROW, WOODRUFF (includes Woodroof, Woodrough, Woodruffe), WOODRUM, WOODS (includes Wood), WOODSIDE, WOODSON, WOODWARD,

WOODWARD, WOODWORTH, WOODY (includes Woodie, DeWoody), WOOLBRIGHT, WOOLDRIDGE, WOOLERY, WOOLEY, WOOLF, WOOLFOLK, WOOLFORD, WOOLFORD, WOOLGAR (includes Woolger), WOOLLEY, WOOLMAN, WOOLRIDGE, WOOLSEY (includes Wolsey, Wulci), WOOLUM (includes Woollam, Woolums, Ullom, Ulm, Wolm), WOOLUMS, WOOLVERTON, WOOLWINE (includes Wohlwein), WOOLWORTH, WOON, WOOSLEY (includes Wooseley, Ousley, Owsley), WOOSTER, WOOTEN (includes Wooton, Wootton), WOOTON, WOOTTEN, WOOTTON, WORBINGTON, WORCESTER, WORD, WORDEN, WORK, WORKMAN (includes Wortman), WORKS, WORLEY (includes Warley, Werly, deWerly, Wherley, Whorley, Wirley, Wyrley), WORMAN, WORMSER, WORRALL, WORRELL, WORSFOLD (includes Wirsfold, Worsfield, Worsford, Worsfould, Worsfull), WORSHAM, WORSLEY, WORTH, WORTHAM, WORTHEN, WORTHEY (includes Worthy, Foxworthy, Fox Worthy), WORTHINGTON (includes Werthington, Wirthington), WORTHY, WORTLEY (includes Worthley), WORTMAN, WORWAG (includes Wörwag, Woerwag, Werenwag),

WOTRING, WOZNIAK, WRATHALL (includes Wrathall-Bull), WRAY (includes Ray), WREFORD (includes Wraford, Wrayford), WREN, WRENCH, WRENN (includes Wren), WRENS, WRIGHT, WRIGHT (includes Right, Rite, Write, Wryte), WRIGLEY.

- **"WU-WZ" Surname Mailing Lists**
  http://www.rootsweb.com/~jfuller/gen_mail_surnames-wu.html
  WUEST, WULF, WUNDER, WUNDERLICH, WUNSCH, WURSTER, WURTZ, WYATT (includes Wiatt, Wiat, Wyatte, Wyat), WYCHE, WYCKOFF, WYETH, WYGOLD, WYKOFF, WYLES, WYLIE, WYLLIE, WYMAN, WYMER, WYMORE (includes Weimer, Wimer, Wigmore, Wimmer, Weimmer, Wighmore, Wimore, Wymoore, Wimour,, Wayman, Wyman), WYNES (includes Wines), WYNKOOP, WYNKOOP (includes Wijnkoop, Wyncoop, Wijncoop, Winkoop, Wincoop, Wienkoop, Wienkopp, van, Wynkoop, van Wijnkoop, van Wyncoop, van Wijncoop, van Winkoop, van Wincoop van Wienkoop, van, Wienkopp), WYNN, WYNNE, WYRE, WYRICK (includes Weirich, Wirick, Wirich), WYSOCKI, WYSONG.

SURNAMES, FAMILY ASSOCIATIONS & FAMILY NEWSLETTERS – "X"

Resources Dedicated to One Surname
http://www.cyndislist.com/surn-x.htm

Category Index:

◆ General Surname Sites and Resources

◆ General Surname Sites and Resources

- Dutch Home Pages by Familyname ~ Letter X
  http://members.tripod.com/~Don_Arnoldus/x.htm

- FamilyHistory.com - Message Boards - Surname - X
  http://www.familyhistory.com/messages/list.asp?prefix=XA

- Family Tree Maker Online User Home Pages - X
  http://www.familytreemaker.com/users/x/index.html

- GenConnect Surname Index - "X"
  http://genconnect.rootsweb.com/indx/surnames/X.html
  Message boards sponsored by RootsWeb. Each surname message board set is divided into the following topics: Queries, Bibles, Biographies, Deeds, Obituaries, Pensions, Wills.

- Genealogy's Most Wanted - Surnames Beginning with "X"
  http://www.citynet.net/mostwanted/x.htm

- Google Web Directory .... Genealogy>Surnames>X
  http://directory.google.com/Top/Society/Genealogy/Surnames/X/

- Heartland Genealogy Society Membership List - X
  http://www.geocities.com/Heartland/Ranch/2416/hgs-mlist-x.html

- H-GIG Surname Registry - Surnames Beginning X-Z
  http://www.ucr.edu/h-gig/surdata/surname24.html

- Higginson Book Company - Surnames Beginning with X
  http://www.higginsonbooks.com/x.htm

- inGeneas Table of Common Surname Variations and Surname Misspellings - T-Z
  http://www.ingeneas.com/T2Z.html

- The Obituary Link Page - Family Obituary Archives Online - X-Y-Z
  http://www.geocities.com/~cribbswh/obit/x-y-z.htm

- Open Directory - Society: Genealogy: Surnames: X
  http://www.dmoz.org/Society/Genealogy/Surnames/X/

- Surname Springboard Index - X
  http://www.geocities.com/~alacy/spring_x.htm

- SurnameWeb Surname Registry - X Index
  http://www.surnameweb.org/registry/x.htm

- Websites at RootsWeb: X Surnames
  http://www.rootsweb.com/~websites/surnames/x.html

SURNAMES, FAMILY ASSOCIATIONS & FAMILY NEWSLETTERS – "Y"

Resources Dedicated to One Surname
http://www.cyndislist.com/surn-y.htm

Category Index:
◆ General Surname Sites and Resources
◆ Surname Specific Sites and Resources

◆ Surname Mailing Lists

◆ General Surname Sites and Resources

● Connect with Surnames - Y
http://www.geocities.com/Heartland/Bluffs/7708/y.html

● Dutch Home Pages by Familyname ~ Letter Y
http://members.tripod.com/~Don_Arnoldus/y.htm

● FamilyHistory.com - Message Boards - Surname - Y
http://www.familyhistory.com/messages/list.asp?prefix=YA

● Family Tree Maker Online User Home Pages - Y
http://www.familytreemaker.com/users/y/index.html

● Family Workings Y Surname Links
http://www.familyworkings.com/links/sury.htm

● GenConnect Surname Index - "Y"
http://genconnect.rootsweb.com/indx/surnames/Y.html
Message boards sponsored by RootsWeb. Each surname message board set is divided into the following topics: Queries, Bibles, Biographies, Deeds, Obituaries, Pensions, Wills.

● Genealogy Resources on the Internet - "X,Y,Z" Surname Mailing Lists
http://www.rootsweb.com/~jfuller/gen_mail_surnames-xyz.html
Search the index of surname mailing lists below: Surname Mailing Lists.

  ○ Genealogy Resources on the Internet - Surnames Included in Mailing Lists - "Y"
  http://www-personal.umich.edu/~cgaunt/surnames/y.names.html
  This is a computer generated list of the surnames, and all variant spellings for those names, that are found in the surname mailing lists detailed on the pages shown above.

● Genealogy Resources on the Internet - Surname Web Sites for "X,Y,Z" Surnames
http://www-personal.umich.edu/~cgaunt/surnames/xyz.html

● Genealogy's Most Wanted - Surnames Beginning with "Y"
http://www.citynet.net/mostwanted/y.htm

● Google Web Directory .... Genealogy>Surnames>Y
http://directory.google.com/Top/Society/Genealogy/Surnames/Y/

● Heartland Genealogy Society Membership List - Y
http://www.geocities.com/Heartland/Ranch/2416/hgs-mlist-y.html

● H-GIG Surname Registry - Surnames Beginning X-Z
http://www.ucr.edu/h-gig/surdata/surname24.html

● Higginson Book Company - Surnames Beginning with Y
http://www.higginsonbooks.com/y.htm

● inGeneas Table of Common Surname Variations and Surname Misspellings - T-Z
http://www.ingeneas.com/T2Z.html

● The Obituary Link Page - Family Obituary Archives Online - X-Y-Z
http://www.geocities.com/~cribbswh/obit/x-y-z.htm

● Open Directory - Society: Genealogy: Surnames: Y
http://www.dmoz.org/Society/Genealogy/Surnames/Y/

● Surname Springboard Index - Y
http://www.geocities.com/~alacy/spring_y.htm

● SurnameWeb Surname Registry - Y Index
http://www.surnameweb.org/registry/y.htm

● SWINX Zoeklijst Nederlandse Familienamen / SWINX Searchlist Dutch Surnames - Y
http://www.swinx.net/swinx/swinx_y_nl.htm

● Websites at RootsWeb: Y Surnames
http://www.rootsweb.com/~websites/surnames/y.html

● 'Y' Surnames at RootsWeb
http://resources.rootsweb.com/surnames/y.html

◆ Surname Specific Sites and Resources

● YABSLEY and YEABSLEY Family History
http://people.clemson.edu/~myabsle/yabsley.htm

- **YANCEY Cousins United**
  http://www.lest-we-forget.com/Yancey/
  Yancy, Yance, Yonce, Yoncy, Yaney, Yanney, Nanny, Nanney.

- **The YARBERRY Family Tree**
  http://www.vabch.com/kyarberr/yarberry.html
  Yarberry / Yarbrough / Yarborough family and closely associated families.

- **YARNALL - YARNELL Home Page**
  http://members.xoom.com/yarnall_ell/yarnall_ell/YARN PAGE.htm
  Yarnall, Yarnell, Yarnal, Yarnel, Yarnill, Yarnold, etc.

- **YEARY Clearinghouse**
  http://user.icx.net/~booboo/yeary.html
  Study of the YEARY surname and variations including Youree, Yourie, Urie, Eure, Jury.

- **My YEARY Line**
  http://user.icx.net/~booboo/paternal.html
  Descendants of Henry YEARY, Sr., born 1730 in Virginia and Elizabeth CROXSTALL, born 1729 in Maryland.

- **Descendants of Johannes YEATER**
  http://www.parsonstech.com/genealogy/trees/bwaller2/Yeater.htm

- **The YELTON Family**
  http://homepages.rootsweb.com/~yelton/
  Descendants of James Yelton & Isabel Hinson of Stafford County, VA. Other surnames are Davis, Ellis, Garland, Gosney, Graham, Griffing, Taylor.

- **Official Home Page of the YELVERTON / YELVINGTON / ELVINGTON Families of America**
  http://www.execpc.com/~kvcw/
  The search for the descendants of John Yelverton (1680-1750) of NC. Names include Yelverton, Yelvington, Elvington.

- **The YEO Family in North America**
  http://www.ncf.carleton.ca/~ai369/yeo/
  Descendants of James Yeo, born 1765 Kilkhampton, Cornwall, England. Most emigrated to Prince Edward Island, Canada.

- **YODER Family Information Archives Online**
  http://www.yodernewsletter.org/

- **YONTS, YOUNT, YONCE, YANTA, YOUT, JANSS Genealogy**
  http://www.nii.net/~yonts
  We are a non-profit site dedicated to ALL spellings and variations of the YONTS surname, including: Jans, Jansson, Jants, Johntz, Jundt, Yand. and Yontz.

- **YORK Family Genealogy (The URL of YORK)**
  http://freepages.genealogy.rootsweb.com/~allyorks

- **Our YOUNG Genealogy**
  http://members.aol.com/WILLIGE/index.html
  Young families from NY and PA including Moyer, Moe, Kesner, Priest, Lerch, Bish, Weckerly, Barth, and others.

- **The YOUNGER Family Home Page**
  http://www.familytreemaker.com/users/y/o/u/Clifford-D-Younger-sr/index.html
  Descendants of Charles Henry YOUNGER, Sr., born about 1803 in Germany. His birth name was Karl Heinrich JUNGER.

- **YOUNKIN Family News Bulletin**
  http://www.intrepid.net/genealogy/junghen/

- **YULE YOOL YUILLE ZUIL Connection**
  http://members.aol.com/eyulepryor/GOLD.HTM
  The surname can be found in Scotland as Yule, Yool and Yuille, England as Youl aand Yull, Sweden as Oel, Denmark as Juul and Norway as Jullvatter. Zuil and Zuille is the Latin form of the surname.

◆ Surname Mailing Lists

- **"Y" Surname Mailing Lists**
  http://www.rootsweb.com/~jfuller/gen_mail_surnames-xyz.html
  YADON (includes Yaden, Yeadon), YAEGER, YAGER, YALE, YANCEY (includes Yancy), YANCY, YANDELL, YANKOWSKI, YARBOROUGH, YARBROUGH (includes Yarbro, Yarber), YARBROUGH, YARD, YARDLEY, YARISH (includes Yarrish, Yerish, Yerrish), YARNELL, YARNES, YATES (includes Yeats, Yeates), YAUDES (includes Youdis, Jaudes), YAWN (includes Yaun, Yon, Yonn), YEAGER (includes Yager, Yaeger), YEAKEL (includes Yeakle, Jackel, Jäckel, Jæckel, Yeagle), YEAROUT, YEARY (includes Yerry, Yarry, Eare, Urie, Jury), YEARY, YEATES, YEATON, YEAZEL (includes Yazel, Yeasle, Yeazle, Yazell), YELTON, YELVERTON, YEO, YEOMAN, YEOMANS, YERBY, YERKES, YETTER, YINGLING (includes Yungling, Juengling, England, Yinglin), YOCKEY, YOCUM (includes Yoakum, Yokum, Yocom, Jochem, Joachim), YODER (includes Joder, Jotter, Yeater, Yetter, Yoders, Yoter, Yother, Yotter, Youter, Youther, Yuter, Yutter), YOHE, YOHO, YOKUM, YONKER, YOPP (includes Iopp, Yop), YORK, YORK, YORK, YORKE, YORSTON, YOST (includes Jost), YOTSLER (includes Yutsler, Youtsler, Youstler), YOUMANS (includes Yeomans), YOUNG, YOUNG, YOUNGBLOOD (includes Jungblut, Jungbluth, Jongblud), YOUNGER, YOUNGLOVE, YOUNGS, YOUNKER (includes Yonker, Yunker), YOUNKIN (includes Youngkin, Youngken, Yonkin, Junghen), YOUNT, YOUST, YOWELL, YULE.

SURNAMES, FAMILY ASSOCIATIONS & FAMILY NEWSLETTERS – "Z"

Resources Dedicated to One Surname
http://www.cyndislist.com/surn-z.htm

Category Index:

- General Surname Sites and Resources
- Surname Specific Sites and Resources

- Surname Mailing Lists

◆ General Surname Sites and Resources

- Connect with Surnames - Z
  http://www.geocities.com/Heartland/Bluffs/7708/z.html

- Dutch Home Pages by Familyname ~ Letter Z
  http://members.tripod.com/~Don_Arnoldus/z.htm

- FamilyHistory.com - Message Boards - Surname - Z
  http://www.familyhistory.com/messages/list.asp?prefix=ZA

- Family Tree Maker Online User Home Pages - Z
  http://www.familytreemaker.com/users/z/index.html

- Family Workings Z Surname Links
  http://www.familyworkings.com/links/surz.htm

- GenConnect Surname Index - "Z"
  http://genconnect.rootsweb.com/indx/surnames/Z.html
  Message boards sponsored by RootsWeb. Each surname message board set is divided into the following topics: Queries, Bibles, Biographies, Deeds, Obituaries, Pensions, Wills.

- Genealogy Resources on the Internet - "X,Y,Z" Surname Mailing Lists
  http://www.rootsweb.com/~jfuller/gen_mail_surnames-xyz.html
  Search the index of surname mailing lists below: Surname Mailing Lists.

  ° Genealogy Resources on the Internet - Surnames Included in Mailing Lists - "Z"
    http://www-personal.umich.edu/~cgaunt/surnames/z.names.html
    This is a computer generated list of the surnames, and all variant spellings for those names, that are found in the surname mailing lists detailed on the pages shown above.

- Genealogy Resources on the Internet - Surname Web Sites for "X,Y,Z" Surnames
  http://www-personal.umich.edu/~cgaunt/surnames/xyz.html

- Genealogy's Most Wanted - Surnames Beginning with "Z"
  http://www.citynet.net/mostwanted/z.htm

- Google Web Directory .... Genealogy>Surnames>Z
  http://directory.google.com/Top/Society/Genealogy/Surnames/Z/

- Heartland Genealogy Society Membership List - Z
  http://www.geocities.com/Heartland/Ranch/2416/hgs-mlist-z.html

- H-GIG Surname Registry - Surnames Beginning X-Z
  http://www.ucr.edu/h-gig/surdata/surname24.html

- Higginson Book Company - Surnames Beginning with Z
  http://www.higginsonbooks.com/z.htm

- inGeneas Table of Common Surname Variations and Surname Misspellings - T-Z
  http://www.ingeneas.com/T2Z.html

- The Obituary Link Page - Family Obituary Archives Online - X-Y-Z
  http://www.geocities.com/~cribbswh/obit/x-y-z.htm

- Open Directory - Society: Genealogy: Surnames: Z
  http://www.dmoz.org/Society/Genealogy/Surnames/Z/

- Surname Springboard Index - Z
  http://www.geocities.com/~alacy/spring_z.htm

- SurnameWeb Surname Registry - Z Index
  http://www.surnameweb.org/registry/z.htm

- SWINX Zoeklijst Nederlandse Familienamen / SWINX Searchlist Dutch Surnames - Z
  http://www.swinx.net/swinx/swinx_za_nl.htm

- Websites at RootsWeb: Z Surnames
  http://www.rootsweb.com/~websites/surnames/z.html

- 'Z' Surnames at RootsWeb
  http://resources.rootsweb.com/surnames/z.html

◆ Surname Specific Sites and Resources

- ZACHER Family
  http://freepages.genealogy.rootsweb.com/~zacher/
  Casper Zacher, born 1806 Prussia and Fredericka born 1802 Prussia.

- ZACHER Family Tree
  http://freepages.genealogy.rootsweb.com/~zacherfamily/
  Descendants of Johann (John) ZACHER and Catherine BAEDER.

- ZAERA
  http://personal.redestb.es/ivan-zaera/

- The ZALEWSKI Surname Resource Center
  http://freepages.genealogy.rootsweb.com/~zalewski/

- ZAMARRIPA Genealogy
  http://www.Zamarripa.com

- ZAMMIT Connection
  http://www.searchmalta.com/surnames/zammit/index.shtml

- The ZAPPE Surname Page
  http://freepages.genealogy.rootsweb.com/~zappe/

- ZAVESKY Family Homepage
  http://members.aol.com/busybusy99/opinions3

- ZECH Family History
  http://www.concentric.net/~Lzech/zech/
  From Jacob Zech, 1600s to present.

- ZELLNER Genealogy
  http://freepages.genealogy.rootsweb.com/~zellner/
  Zellner, Zoellner, Zollner, Zelner, Zillner, Sellner, Selner.

- ZEMAITIS Homepage
  http://www.webmart.net/~zemaitis/zemaitis.htm
  Origin of Zemaitis surname and Lithuanian heritage.

- ZETTERBERG's Genealogy Page
  http://members.aol.com/lynnzr/life1/index.htm
  Searching for information in Sweden on a Carl Albin F. Zetterberg born between 1840-1850.

- Michael M. ZIEFLE - The Family ZIEFLE
  http://ourworld.compuserve.com/Homepages/M_Ziefle/ziefle_e.htm

- Family ZIHLER
  http://www.zihler.com
  This is the official international Homepage of the family ZIHLER. Das ist die offizielleund internationale Homepage von der Familie ZIHLER. H

- ZIMMERMAN & ZIMMERMANN Surnames in Wisconsin
  http://homepages.rootsweb.com/~zimzip/zim/zim.htm
  Surname database listed alphabetically by first name, includes time period and place/s lived in Wisconsin, and when available name of parents, birth and death dates & locations, name of spouse, and name of contact person.

- Descendants of George ZINN 1742 - 1826 Genealogy Page
  http://members.aol.com/jdgenealog/ZinnPage.html
  The ZINN family in America from 1742.

- The ZWIEBACK Family Name
  http://home1.gte.net/ezwiebac

◆ Surname Mailing Lists

- "Z" Surname Mailing Lists
  http://www.rootsweb.com/~jfuller/gen_mail_surnames-xyz.html
  ZABEL, ZABOWSKI, ZABRISKIE (includes Zaborisko, Zabowrisko, Zabrisky, Zaborowskij, Cawbrisco, Jabriskie, Labrisky, Sabriskie,, Sabrowiski, Zebriskie), ZACHARIAS, ZACHARY, ZACHMAN, ZACHMANN, ZAHM, ZAHN, ZAJAC, ZAK, ZALLAR (includes Zalar), ZANDER, ZAPPE, ZAPPONE, ZARLEY (includes Sarley), ZASTROW, ZATOVICH, ZAVELSKY, ZAWACKI, ZDZIARSKI (includes Zdiarski, Zdarske, Zdarstic), ZEELEY, ZEHNER (includes Zahner), ZEIGLER, ZEIS, ZEISER, ZEISLER, ZELL (includes Zeller, von Zell), ZELLER, ZELLERS, ZELLNER (includes Zillner, Zoellner), ZEMAN, ZENTZ, ZENZ, ZEPP, ZERBE, ZERKEY (includes Zerke, Zerkee, Zerky, Xerke, Xerkee, Xerkey, Zurkee, Zurkey), ZETTLER, ZICKEFOOSE (includes Zicafoose, Zickafoose), ZIEMBA, ZIEGLER (includes Zeigler, Zaigler), ZIELINSKI, ZIELINSKI, ZIELKE, ZIEMER, ZILLGITT, ZIMBELMAN, ZIMBLE (includes Zimbal, Zimball, Zimbul), ZIMMER, ZIMMERMAN, ZIMMERMANN, ZIMPEL (includes Zimple), ZIMPLE, ZINK, ZINN, ZIRKLE (includes Zircle, Zerkle, Zerkel, Circle, Sircle), ZIV, ZOELLER, ZOELLERS, ZOLLER, ZOLNOWSKI (includes Zenowski), ZOOK, ZOPF (includes Zoph, Zooph, Sopff, Zaap, Saph), ZORN, ZORNES, ZOUCHE, ZOTZKY, ZUBER, ZUCCHERO, ZUEHLKE (includes Zuhlke, Zulke, Zuelke, Zuehlcke, Zuhlcke, Zühlke), ZUENDEL, ZUG (includes Zook, Zuck, Zaug), ZUMBACH, ZUMWALT, ZURAWICZ (includes Zurawic, Zurawik, Zurawitz), ZURBRIGGEN, ZURCHER, ZUREK, ZUTZ, ZVANIGA. ZVENIGORODSKY.